Jazz on Record
The First Sixty Years

by Scott Yanow

Backbeat
Books
San Francisco

Published by Backbeat Books
600 Harrison Street, San Francisco, CA 94107
www.backbeatbooks.com
email: books@musicplayer.com

An imprint of the Music Player Network
Publishers of *Guitar Player*, *Bass Player*, *Keyboard*, and other magazines

United Entertainment Media, Inc.
A CMP Information company

CMP
United Business Media

Distributed to the book trade in the US and Canada by
Publishers Group West, 1700 Fourth Street, Berkeley, CA 94710

Distributed to the music trade in the US and Canada by
Hal Leonard Publishing, P.O. Box 13819, Milwaukee, WI 53213

Text Design and Composition by Happenstance Type-O-Rama
Cover Design by Damien Castaneda

Library of Congress Cataloging-in-Publication Data

Yanow, Scott
    Jazz on record : the first sixty years / by Scott Yanow
       p. cm.
    Includes index.
    ISBN 0-87930-755-2 (alk. paper)
    1. Jazz—Discography. 2. Jazz—History and criticism. I. Title.

    ML156.4.J3Y36 2003
    781.65'0266—dc22
    2003062780

Printed in the United States of America

03 04 05 06 07   5 4 3 2 1

Contents

Contents

There are few greater joys in the world than watching a creative jazz band perform. Unlike in classical music where the musicians recreate note for note the work of a composer, or in pop music where the performers often do their best to play their hits in concert in a similar fashion to how they sound on record, jazz is about spontaneity, constant invention, and self-expression.

Even when performing a popular song with a set melody, chord changes, and a general framework, jazz musicians are constantly taking chances on stage. When a musician solos, he uses his accumulated knowledge of his instrument, of the piece he is performing, and of his own musical history to create something new. The artist may make mistakes and occasionally stumble (the danger is part of the excitement), but quite often wrong turns lead to fresh directions. The very best jazz artists are constantly creating new ideas before audiences, performing a high-wire act without a net, often on a nightly basis.

Only a small percentage of jazz performances make it on to records where they are saved forever. Whether performed in recording studios or taken from concerts or club appearances, these snapshots form the recorded history of jazz and allow today's listener to hear music from the past just as it was played at the time, even if it was 80 years ago. We cannot hear what Mozart or Liszt sounded like improvising on piano, but King Oliver and Jelly Roll Morton are very much alive today due to their good fortune in being recorded.

The availability of recordings has also indirectly affected jazz history. Avant-garde bandleader Sun Ra reportedly shifted his repertoire toward swing (although played in an eccentric way) in the 1970s after listening closely to the Fletcher Henderson four-LP set **A Study in Frustration**. The large number of reissue programs that proliferated in the 1970s, making classic hard bop and bebop performances available to a younger generation, indirectly resulted in the Young Lions movement of the 1980s, where skilled musicians in their twenties (including trumpeter Wynton Marsalis) sought to find their voices in hard bop rather than fusion or the avant-garde. Charlie Parker spent one summer woodshedding to some Count Basie records that featured Lester Young. And many musicians in later years were able to master their horns more quickly by jamming to Charlie Parker records.

It is now almost impossible to interview any musicians who were active in the 1920s (Benny Carter, Artie Shaw, and the still-active violinist Claude Williams are among the very few who are still with us as of this writing), and only a handful of performers are left from the 1930s. However, today's listeners can experience the music of the 1920s and '30s at least secondhand through the many surviving records, and it is for the recordings that the late early greats of jazz will be remembered.

One of the faults of many jazz history books is that they tend to focus almost exclusively on the cutting edge innovations of a certain period. Simplifying jazz's evolution has resulted in it often being said that a newer style was an "improvement" on the older one, as if the latter no longer existed after it was "replaced." Swing begat bebop begat cool jazz begat hard bop begat free jazz begat fusion, etc. Despite all of the begatting, none of the older styles ceased to exist. One may think of the second half of the 1940s as being the bebop era, but in reality Dixieland was also going through a prime period at the same time. The 1950s may have seemed to be dominated by cool jazz and hard bop, but mainstream swing (played by veterans of an era that was considered dominant only a decade earlier) was enjoying a revival. There was a lot of bebop being played during the so-called avant-garde 1960s, and one of the main events of the mid-1970s when fusion was having its greatest impact, was the rise of such young swing-oriented players as Scott Hamilton and Warren Vache. One should not forget that Benny Goodman and Count Basie were still playing swing long after Charlie Parker and John Coltrane were no longer alive. Things have only become more confused and crowded in the years since. In addition, using a simplified "great man" theory skips over the hundreds (if not thousands) of important interpreters and original voices in favor of just emphasizing ten or fifteen top musicians.

Jazz on Record: The First Sixty Years, while covering the most groundbreaking events of jazz's first 60 years of recordings, also discusses the various mainstream and revival jazz movements and never makes the judgment that new styles are superior to the older ones. The best jazz is timeless and never becomes dated or "old school." Nor are musicians who play creatively in older styles deserving of being overlooked.

I have divided the years of 1895–1976 (covering the 22 years that preceded the first jazz recording in the 1895–1920 chapter) into ten time periods, with each chapter essentially being an independent book that sticks to that particular era. Not every single recording by every single artist is discussed (this book would be many times larger), nor is there a complete listing of personnel. That is the work of other books, such as the *All Music Guide to Jazz*. But what is here is a sampling of the most important available recordings by virtually all of the significant jazz musicians and singers of each time period.

Each chapter has subsections dealing with a specific topic relevant to the period. Sprinkled throughout each chapter are Timelines that not only summarize the events already covered, but add a great deal of additional information and give listeners a sampling of the jazz events that took place in each individual year. "Voices of the Future" sections have the birth dates and places of the musicians and singers born in that period. This is usually the first mention of these significant performers in the book. Conversely, the "Passings" sections, which list the performers' death dates and places, serve as a farewell to these irreplaceable heroes. The emphasis throughout is on CDs even though compact discs did not replace LPs until the late 1980s, so nearly every CD referred to is actually a reissue unless it was a long-lost session issued for the first time in a later period. If a cited recording is an LP, it says so; otherwise it is a CD. If it is an essential release, there is a ◉ before the recording's title, and it is also listed at the end of the chapter (unless already covered earlier in the book). The reviews are in most cases purposely very brief, so as many recordings are covered as possible. I have also concentrated on the most significant reissues (either complete compilations or superior samplers) because much of this material, particularly from the swing era, has been repackaged a countless number of times.

Why does this book stop after 1976? While some of the nay-sayers seem to think that jazz's evolution, and therefore its relevance, stopped after the mid-1970s, I have always felt the opposite. In reality, there have been so many record releases since that time that there was simply not enough room in this book to adequately cover the past quarter-century. That may very well be the subject of another book in the future. As the sole author of *Jazz on Record: The First Sixty Years*, I am solely responsible for any errors that might have crept in. If there is a breathless feel to this survey, it is because there has been an enormous amount of high-quality jazz recordings released through the years. I hope that my enthusiasm and love for the music always comes through.

Many people helped cheer me on during this ambitious project, giving me moral support and encouragement, and I am grateful to all of them. In addition, I want to personally thank Matt Kelsey and Richard Johnston of Backbeat Books for trusting me and believing in this important project; Brian Ashley, who got me started in the jazz writing business back in 1976 when he formed *Record Review*; and the much-maligned but invaluable jazz publicists (including Ann Braithwaite, Lynda Bramble, Lori Hehr, Terri Hinte, and Don Lucoff) who make life much easier for jazz journalists. Greatly deserving of gratitude for their patience, support, and putting up with my 16-hours-a-day listening schedule are my wife, Kathy, and daughter, Melody.

Chapter One

1895–1920:
The Lost Beginnings

In 1895, the word "jazz" was unknown. The music did not exist except in the South (where it was in its most rudimentary form), and the music world in general was dominated by classical music, sentimental ballads, spirituals, and the decades-old songs of Stephen Foster. By 1920, jazz was considered an exciting new phenomenon that was being introduced not only to New York but to Europe, record labels were going out of their way to document imitators of the Original Dixieland Jazz Band, and a blues craze was just getting underway. The world changed drastically during this 25-year period, but jazz actually evolved quite slowly after its initial formation. If reports by survivors made decades after the fact are accurate, there was not all that much difference between jazz in 1900 and the way it sounded in 1915 and even 1920, despite changes in names and the passing of years. This was largely due to there being no jazz on records prior to 1917. Progress was slow since the only way to hear the music was in person. But by 1920, jazz was in the process of becoming a potent force worldwide, and records were fueling its popularity and growth.

A Few Basic Questions

The most typical questions asked about the beginnings of jazz are "What exactly is jazz?" "When did it start?" and "Where did it come from?" Despite thousands of books on the subject of jazz, none of these three questions has been definitively answered.

Since at least the 1930s, scholars, musicians, and fans have tried their best to define jazz. The problem is that jazz is a constantly evolving music. Although one can define what has thus far taken place, any rules set up today will surely be violated a few years from now by creative innovators. While the great majority of jazz musicians are interpreters (doing their best to find their own voice and be creative within the mainstream of the music), jazz has always been populated by some very original individuals who blazed their own paths and were rule breakers by nature. How can you be an innovator by merely following the guidelines and restrictions of the past? If jazz had been stuck in a little restrictive box, forced to follow specific rules, the music would have gone stale many years ago, not surviving the Depression except perhaps as regional folk music.

As far as a definition goes, and ignoring Louis Armstrong's (or was it Fats Waller's?) quip that "If you don't know what it is, don't mess with it," the closest I have been able to come is saying that jazz is a type of music that emphasizes improvisation and always has the feeling of the blues. Improvisation (creating solos and sometimes ensembles spontaneously) and the blues feeling seem to be the only specific qualities that classic jazz, swing, and bebop have in common with the avant-garde, fusion, and modern jazz. The "feeling of the blues" does not refer to actually playing a 12-bar blues, but to occasionally bending notes and always putting one's soul into the music. There are no bent notes in classical music!

I realize that this definition of jazz is a bit too open since some other styles (including improvised rock, gospel, and the blues itself) could be included despite only being relatives of jazz. But it seems clear that, even in future decades, jazz will always feature a generous amount of improvising and individuality; otherwise it would cease to exist except as a museum piece.

When did jazz become jazz? Because of the lack of recordings and the fact that it was not documented in print at the time (contemporary newspapers took little interest in the creativity of African-Americans), there is not one obvious moment in history that can be considered the birth of jazz. Cornetist Buddy Bolden was the first famous jazz musician, and he formed his earliest band in

---

BIRTH DATES OF THE EARLY JAZZ AND RAGTIME PIONEERS

Vess Ossman (banjo), Aug. 21, 1868, Hudson, NY

Scott Joplin (composer, piano), Nov. 24, 1868, Texarkana, TX

W.C. Handy (composer, cornet), Nov. 16, 1873, Florence, AL

Tony Jackson (piano, composer), June 5, 1876, New Orleans, LA

Buddy Bolden (cornet), Sept. 6, 1877, New Orleans, LA

Fred Van Eps (banjo), Dec. 30, 1878, Somerville, NJ

James Reese Europe (leader), Feb. 22, 1881, Mobile, AL

Eubie Blake (piano, composer), Feb. 7, 1883, Baltimore, MD

Mamie Smith (vocals), May 26, 1883, Cincinnati, OH

James Scott (composer, piano), Feb. 21, 1885, Neosho, MI

King Oliver (cornet, leader), May 11, 1885, Abend, LA

Jelly Roll Morton (piano, composer, leader, vocals), Sept. 20, 1885, Gulfport, LA

Chris Kelly (cornet), Oct. 18, 1885, Plaquemine Parish, LA

Kid Ory (trombone, leader), Dec. 25, 1886, La Pace, LA

Joseph Lamb (composer, piano), Dec. 6, 1887, Montclair, NJ

Nick LaRocca (cornet, leader), Apr. 11, 1889, New Orleans, LA

Noble Sissle (vocals, composer), July 10, 1889, Indianapolis, IN

Freddie Keppard (cornet), Feb. 27, 1890, New Orleans, LA

Paul Whiteman (leader), Mar. 28, 1890, Denver, CO

Henry Ragas (piano), 1891, New Orleans, LA

Eddie Edwards (trombone), May 22, 1891, New Orleans, LA

Johnny Dodds (clarinet), Apr. 12, 1892, New Orleans, LA

J. Russell Robinson (piano, composer), July 8, 1892, Indianapolis, IN

Larry Shields (clarinet), Sept. 13, 1893, New Orleans, LA

Buddy Petit (cornet), 1897, White Castle, LA

Sidney Bechet (soprano, clarinet), May 14, 1897, New Orleans, LA

Tony Sbarbaro (drums), June 27, 1897, New Orleans, LA

Baby Dodds (drums), Dec. 24, 1898, New Orleans, LA

1895, so that event can be symbolically used to date the birth of jazz. But since it is not known exactly what his group sounded like, and since jazz probably existed in its most primitive forms earlier on (what would one call the music played by honky tonk pianists who played in bars in the Wild West?), jazz's birth can never be accurately pinpointed.

Where did jazz come from? While simplified jazz history books sometimes say that first came the blues, then ragtime, then Dixieland , with the jazz pioneers going up the Mississippi River from New Orleans to Chicago (never mind that the Mississippi does not actually reach Chicago), the truth is much more complicated. In reality, jazz was a contemporary of both blues and ragtime; in fact, Buddy Bolden formed his first group four years before Scott Joplin's "Maple Leaf Rag" ushered in the ragtime age.

One of jazz's main strengths has been its ability to borrow from other styles of music, adapt the features that best fit the music, and make it its own. Jazz at its beginnings took aspects of many different styles of often dissimilar music. African rhythms from up to 200 years before had been brought (reluctantly) from overseas by slaves and passed down through generations. They were combined with marches to create infectious syncopations. Black spirituals from churches, along with work songs sung in the fields by physical laborers, contributed to the format of expressive blues and jazz. Classical music contributed intonation, technique, and self-discipline. Improvising pianists playing in bars as one-man bands helped develop both ragtime and stride piano. And jazz's early repertoire included popular melodies of the 1890s, Stephen Foster tunes, simplified classical themes, and sentimental ballads along with blues-based originals and adaptations of marches.

When asked when jazz was born (as if it were a specific moment), I entertain the theory that it began when brass band musicians in New Orleans, who often played lengthy versions of songs while marching, began to improvise a bit, infusing their music with blue notes, melodic variations, and new ideas. But we will never know for sure.

Major Events of 1895–1920

It is almost unimaginable to think about what the Southern United States was like in 1895. Not only was this era before television and the movies, it preceded radio, airplanes, and automobiles, and was a period when the newest inventions (the electric light bulb and the telephone) were not available to most citizens, particularly not poor blacks. It was just 30 years after the end of the Civil War, and, although slavery was illegal, most blacks were struggling in poverty, often working unrewarding jobs in the fields for extremely low wages. Racism was not only prevalent, it was the accepted way of life, even in the North, which remained largely segregated for decades. Very few blacks had the opportunity to vote in the 1896 election in which William McKinley defeated William Jennings Bryan. National politics were largely irrelevant to African-Americans anyway, as neither the Republican nor Democratic parties were the slightest bit interested in promoting civil rights or the right of minority citizens to vote.

Many events took place during the next 25 years. The Spanish-American War of 1899 gave the United States its first opportunity to act like an international power, even though the fight with the declining Spanish empire did not have much suspense. The automobile became common during 1900–10, making the horse and buggy a relic of the 19th century. After William McKinley's assassination in 1901, the Teddy Roosevelt era (1901–08) found the United States mostly feeling very good about itself as the economy was booming, although those at the bottom did not reap its rewards. It was a great time to be white and rich since there was no income tax; conversely, it was a particularly harsh era to be poor and part of a minority. Laissez-faire government meant that it was up to every citizen to fight for him- or herself; there was no protection for the weak, oppressed, unemployed, or handicapped.

In 1912, the Democratic party (which had been dominated by racist Southerners and right-wingers) and the Republicans (ruled by big business) began to switch places. The decision of Teddy Roosevelt to challenge his former protégé William Howard Taft (Roosevelt's successor in the White House) in the 1912 election split apart the GOP, with Roosevelt's moderate wing (which became the short-lived Bull Moose Party) essentially throwing the election to Woodrow Wilson and the Democrats. Although the Southern segregationists would mostly remain Democrats into the 1960s, from this point on the GOP (Abe Lincoln's party) began shifting to the right, while the Northern Democrats gradually moved toward fighting for civil rights. Still, it would be another 36 years (1948) before a firm stance was taken that African-Americans deserved equal treatment under the law, and that was only the beginning of a long struggle.

World War I broke out in 1914, and although Wilson won re-election as president in 1916 partly by promising to stay out of the European conflict, during 1917–18 the United States was an active participant, winning the war for the Allies, even as Russia became the communist Soviet Union.

A disastrous influenza epidemic made life increasingly dangerous during 1918–19, resulting in many deaths, including the Original Dixieland Jazz Band's pianist Henry Ragas. The passing of the Volstead Act, which began the Prohibition era in 1919, was a depressing event to millions of Americans who were surprised to find that drinking liquor was suddenly illegal; organized crime quickly stepped in to fill the void. Women had the right to vote for the first time in 1920, but the American public preferred more of a figurehead (Warren Harding) than an activist as president, and the government mostly functioned as an observer of events rather than as a participant in social reform.

While the world changed drastically between 1895 and 1920, jazz's evolution was much slower.

Jazz's First Star

Jazz would not appear on records until 1917 and the name "jazz" was not applied to music until around 1915–16, but it existed in its earliest form in the mid-1890s. New Orleans is often cited as its birthplace, and although it was not the only area where jazz developed (stride piano was first played on the East Coast, while ragtime solidified in Missouri), New Orleans was an important center for music. Being a major port, New Orleans had many overlapping musical cultures, from Africa, France, Spain, Cuba, and Latin America. A very cultured area in the 1890s where classical music and opera were showcased, New Orleans was one of the few American cities where music was a major part of day-to-day life. One of the city's most attractive features was its brass bands, which seemed to be everywhere. Brass bands worked steadily, whenever there was an excuse for a parade or a celebration, including at parties, dances, funerals, picnics, and a variety of social functions. New Orleans brass bands gave steady work to many musicians (both black and white), many of whom also had regular day jobs.

Buddy Bolden   The subject of many legends that have since been disproved (Bolden was never a barber nor did he publish a scandal sheet), Buddy Bolden was a larger than life figure. Unfortunately he was also jazz's first casualty. In 1906, he began to suffer from mental illness that was so severe that the following year he was committed to Jackson Mental Institution for the remainder of his life, passing away completely forgotten 24 years later. Although rumors have persisted that he recorded a cylinder in 1897 or '98, no recording of Bolden has ever been found, so one can only speculate what this early founder of jazz really sounded like.

Ragtime

While jazz in New Orleans and the South was in its early stages, for the first time an African-American art form swept the country. During its peak years (1899–1914), ragtime was the most popular music in the United States. Although sometimes mistakenly thought of as a style of jazz, ragtime is in actuality "America's classical music."

Ragtime differs from jazz in that in its classic form all of the music is written down (rather than improvised), and there is an absence of blues feeling. During ragtime's prime era, most rags featured four related themes performed in the format of A-A-B-B-A-C-C-D-D. Its syncopated rhythms were influenced by marches and (to a lesser extent) classical music, serving as an influence itself on early jazz. In fact, before the word "jazz" caught on, some New Orleans–style groups called themselves ragtime bands, a practice that continued for decades.

The first known rag was Tom Turpin's "Harlem Rag" from 1892 although it was not published until 1897. Scott Joplin, who would become known as "The King of Ragtime," published his first two songs in 1895, really hitting it big in 1899 when his "Maple Leaf Rag" was published, launching the ragtime era. Ragtime was largely thought of as solo piano music (although orchestras also performed the pieces), and it coincided with the peak in popularity of the piano itself, an era when many families used the piano for their main entertainment. In those days, when the recording industry was in its infancy and no blacks other than a few spiritual groups were recorded, the success of new songs was judged by their sheet music sales. "Maple Leaf Rag" sold more than 75,000 copies of sheet music during its first year alone (it would eventually top one million), sparking the ragtime craze.

Scott Joplin Soft-spoken and distinguished, Scott Joplin was an unusual choice to be the first black musical superstar. Born in Texarkana, Texas, Joplin lived in St. Louis during 1885–93, where he played piano in local clubs and bars, developing his songwriting abilities. After appearing at the 1894 Chicago World's Fair with a band, and working with the Texas Medley Quartet in vaudeville, Joplin moved to Sedalia, Missouri, in 1895. Joplin formed a musical partnership with publisher John Stark that resulted in a large number of his rags and songs being published during the next 20 years. "Maple Leaf Rag" made Joplin into a household name.

Although easily the best known of all ragtime composers, Joplin was far from the only one active during the 1900–15 period. Two musicians very much inspired by Joplin, James Scott and Joseph Lamb, were considered the other members of "the big three." Tom Turpin published a few more of his rags, the young Eubie Blake had his "Charleston Rag" published shortly after "Maple Leaf Rag" began to catch on and Euday Bowman came out with "12th Street Rag" in 1914. Other important ragtime composers include Louis Chauvin, Ben Harney, Charles Hunter, Charles Johnson, Tony Jackson (although best known for his pop hit "Pretty Baby"), Arthur Marshall, Artie Matthews, Charley Straight, Charles Thompson, and Percy Wenrich.

Ragtime became so popular that the 1904 St. Louis World's Fair held a ragtime contest. John Philip Sousa included orchestrated versions of rags in his repertoire, banjo recording stars Vess Ossman and Fred Van Eps transferred the piano parts from rags to their instruments, and James Reese Europe arranged ragtime pieces for his orchestra to perform with the famous dance team of Vernon and Irene Castle.

But, as inevitably happens with any new music that catches on big, it began to turn into a fad, much to the chagrin of Scott Joplin. Joplin's goal was to take ragtime far beyond its roots and establish it as Americans' main music. He staged a ballet ("The Ragtime Dance") and wrote two ragtime operas ("The Guest of Honor" and "Treemonisha"), but was unable to gain financial backing for the latter, which became the major frustration of his life.

Ill with syphilis, Joplin (who wrote his final two rags in 1914) lived to see a major backlash against ragtime. So-called reformers and religious leaders considered ragtime primitive and indecent, due to both its catchy rhythms and the fact that many of the top composers were black. There was also a trivializing of the music that Joplin had lovingly created. By 1912, songs having nothing to do with ragtime (most notably Irving Berlin's "Alexander's Ragtime Band") were being written to take advantage of the popularity of rags, resulting in confusion in the public's perception of ragtime. Even now, some less knowledgeable historians refer to "Alexander's Ragtime Band" (a pop song) as a rag. While early jazz, swing, bebop, and bossa novas would in later years be strong enough to survive being turned into fads by the mass media, ragtime did not stand a chance. By 1915, the charming if fragile music had pretty well gone as far as it could within its limitations, and it was gradually being replaced by 32-bar pop songs (including those written by Berlin and Jerome Kern) and early jazz.

Scott Joplin's death on April 1, 1917, in New York City (61 days after the first recordings by the Original Dixieland Jazz Band) officially ended the ragtime era.

The Start of the Record Industry

In 1877, Thomas Edison invented sound recording, registering a patent for a machine that played round tubes (cylinders). Since Edison was involved in other projects at the time (including inventing the electric light bulb), nothing much was done initially with his recording machine other than documenting the voices of some contemporaries. In 1887, Emile Berliner patented a disc phonograph (known as a gramophone) that played flat round 78s. Both cylinders and 78s usually clocked in between two to four minutes, with 78s eventually including a second song on the flip side of the record. Cylinders, although common in the 1890s, would gradually decline in popularity until they were no longer being made after the late 1920s. Since Edison, a genius in so many areas, had a tin ear when it came to music (not an unusual feature for record company executives!), only a little bit of jazz appeared on his Edison label; most surviving Edison cylinders are of lesser interest musically today. Edison's company would in time also make 78s, but although his discs were advanced with superior sound and often contained over four minutes of music, the label ceased operations altogether in 1929.

While cylinders eventually became extinct, 78s were the recording industry standard up until the development of the LP during the late 1940s. The earliest instrumental recording that I know of is "Electric Light Quadrille" by Issler's Orchestra Band from 1889. The dance music, which has a narrator yelling out the dance steps, is interrupted part of the way through with an important announcement, telling how the electric light bulb is going to be demonstrated for the first time the following day! Obviously the makers of that cylinder, which has been reissued as part of the three-LP set **First Commercially Successful Recordings** (Murray Hill 60092), did not think that the performance was going to survive very long.

As the 1890s progressed, the number of recordings increased (both on 78s and cylinders). Unfortunately, the quality of the performances was usually pretty low technically and today's reissues feature mostly very scratchy reproductions. Many of the recordings are "comedy" sketches (which in those early days tended to be quite racist), semiclassical works, or novelties. There is no jazz to be heard and only a few ragtime-influenced pieces were recorded in the late 1890s. Best are the performances by the concert orchestras—particularly John Philip Sousa—and the occasional virtuoso soloists. The latter included saxophonist Jean Moeremans, who in 1898 on "Carnival of Venice," reissued on the LP **Original Sounds of the 1890s** (Westwood 501), performed variations, which are so complex and passionate that they sound in spots like John Coltrane!

Although no jazz appeared on records during 1900–16, there were some interesting recordings along the way. The two main labels of the era were Victor (which was formed as the Victor Talking Machine Co. in 1901 and associated with Berliner) and Columbia. Strangely enough, ragtime was very rarely recorded as a solo piano piece. The only ragtime-influenced pianists of the time (such as Felix Arndt, who composed the hit "Nola," and Mike Bernard) tended to be powerful players who infused classical melodies with syncopations in novel ways.

Scott Joplin never recorded (nor did James Scott, while Joseph Lamb was not captured on records until the late 1950s), but he did cut some piano rolls, including a few versions of "Maple Leaf Rag." Piano rolls were at best mechanical reproductions of what a pianist played, and they could be altered afterward by punching additional holes in the rolls. Rhythmically they tend to sound inflexible, but they do preserve the styles of a few otherwise undocumented pianists, including Joplin and Scott. Such 1920s giants as James P. Johnson, Fats Waller, Jelly Roll Morton, and George Gershwin managed to overcome the piano roll's technical limitations to an extent, but real recordings are always preferred.

However, ragtime was documented in other ways including by top banjoists (most notably Vess Ossman and Fred Van Eps), orchestras (such as the ensembles led by John Philip Sousa and Arthur Pryor), and even as vocal pieces. Today's listeners cannot help but be impressed by the virtuoso semiclassical solos of trombonist Pryor and cornetist Herbert L. Clarke, even if they were completely worked out in advance.

Prejazz Recordings

John Philip Sousa, "The March King," is justly famous for having composed "The Stars and Stripes Forever." He led one of the top bands in the world during 1892–1932, an outfit with impeccable musicianship that performed a diverse repertoire that included his marches, waltzes, some ragtime, semiclassical works, and vocal pieces. ◉ **Sousa Marches** (Crystal 461-3), a three-CD set, has every one of Sousa's recordings of his marches (including four of "The Stars and Stripes Forever"), programmed in the order that the pieces were composed rather than by recording date, with the versions of his most famous march scattered throughout the program, including a rare 1929 radio broadcast that he verbally introduces. With any luck, someday the Sousa band's recordings of ragtime material will also be issued in as definitive a manner.

EIGHT ESSENTIAL RECORDS OF 1895–1920

John Philip Sousa, **Sousa Marches** (Crystal 461-3)

Marion Harris, **The Complete Victor Releases**
    (Archeophone 5001)

Various Artists, **Real Ragtime** (Archeophone 1001)

Various Artists, **Ragtime to Jazz 1** (Timeless 1-035)

Various Artists, **Ragtime to Jazz 3** (Timeless 1-070)

James Reese Europe, **James Reese Europe's 369th U.S. Infantry "Hell Fighters" Band**
    (Memphis Archives 7020)

Original Dixieland Jazz Band, **75th Anniversary**
    (Bluebird 61098)

Mamie Smith, **Vol. 1** (Document 5357)

Arthur Pryor, Sousa's top soloist until 1902, led a major orchestra of his own for the next 30 years. **Trombone Soloist** (Crystal 451) puts the focus on his virtuosic trombone playing, performing 26 of his features. Some of these renditions (such as "Blue Bells of Scotland") are astounding, featuring wide interval jumps (which would be difficult to negotiate on a trumpet, much less a trombone), a beautiful tone, and flawless technique, even at rapid tempos. It would be quite a few years before the jazz world produced anyone comparable to Pryor. Herbert L. Clarke's **Cornet Soloist** (Crystal 450) has 26 impressive solos from Sousa's favorite cornetist, dating from 1900–17 (with two selections from 1922) that are particularly recommended to any overconfident trumpet players.

The 1890s, Vol. 1 (Archeophone 9004) has 30 selections (a few of which are barely listenable) ranging from racist comedy and adequate vocalizing to contemporary versions of such songs as "At a Georgia Camp Meeting" sung by Dan Quinn, "My Old Kentucky Home," "The Band Played On," and "Yankee Doodle" by Vess Ossman. It gives listeners a good idea what was available on cylinder and 78s during the first decade of recordings. **1912: "Waitin' on the Levee"** (Archeophone 9003) has surprisingly good recording quality, and much of the music is excellent considering the era, with such singers as Billy Murray, Al Jolson, Ada Jones, Harry Lauder, the American Quartet, and even Enrico Caruso. In addition to forgotten period pieces, the songs include such standards as "Oh, You Beautiful Doll," "Moonlight Bay," "Waiting for the Robert E. Lee," and "Down by the Old Mill Stream." One of the major stage stars of the era and a showbiz legend who would make an unlikely comeback in the mid-1940s, Al Jolson was never a jazz singer (despite starring in the 1927 film *The Jazz Singer*) but he could swing in his own way. His first 24 recordings are on **Volume One** (Stash 564) including "You Made Me Love You," which he introduced. Jolson's way of shouting out the words is typical of the era, and those who saw him live have said that he was at his very best when performing on stage.

Marion Harris is a difficult singer to place in music history. Popular on the stage and in vaudeville, Harris (who was white) was recording as early as 1916 (when she was 20) and had a real feel for jazz even though she was not a jazz singer herself. On ◗ **The Complete Victor Releases** (Archeophone 5001), which dates from 1916–19 with two later ballads from 1928, she is particularly impressive in that her laidback delivery (much different from most of the belters of the time period) hints at the approaches of Ruth Etting and Annette Hanshaw a decade later. Marion Harris's versions of "I Ain't Got Nobody" (from 1916), "After You've Gone," "A Good Man Is Hard to Find," and "Take Me to the Land of Jazz" are some of the earliest versions of those standards, and her charm is still obvious after 85 years. Though they are not included on this CD, she also helped introduce such songs as "Tea for Two," "It Had to Be You," and "I'll See You in My Dreams."

Although there has been no rush to reissue vintage ragtime recordings, in recent times some important CDs have been released. ◗ **Real Ragtime** (Archeophone 1001) has 28 performances from the ragtime era (only three numbers are later than 1915). These range from banjoists Vess Ossman and Fred Van Eps's versions of rags and orchestra pieces to vocal numbers in which the word "rag" is tossed around (although most of those pieces are actually pop songs). The music is consistently rewarding and full of obscure gems even if Scott Joplin's music is missing altogether. Also of interest is **Cakewalks, Rags & Blues—Military Style** (Renovation 7003), which has 25 selections from 1900–15, mostly featuring military bands (including Sousa, James Reese Europe, and Prince's Orchestra) performing rags and early blues. Highlights include Sousa's "At a Georgia Camp Meeting," the U.S. Marine Band in 1909 playing the ten-year-old "Maple Leaf Rag," and Prince's Orchestra in 1914–15 helping to introduce "The Memphis Blues" and "St. Louis Blues."

◗ **Ragtime to Jazz 1** (Timeless 1-035), **Ragtime to Jazz 2** (Timeless 1-045), and ◗ **Ragtime to Jazz 3** (Timeless 1-070) also contain a great deal of valuable early material. Each disc is programmed in chronological order, crossing over into early jazz by their later selections. **Ragtime to Jazz 1** has piano solos from Roy Spangler and Mike Bernard, James Reese Europe's 1913 recordings of "Too Much Mustard" and "Down Home Blues," numbers by the Versatile Four and clarinetist Wilbur Sweatman, four selections by the Original Dixieland Jazz Band (including the first jazz recordings: "Darktown Strutters Ball" and "Indiana"), and songs from the Frisco Jass Band (including "Night-Time in Little Italy"), Earl Fuller's Famous Jazz Band (with Ted Lewis), Eubie Blake's Jazzone Orchestra, Dabney's Band, and the Louisiana Five.

TIMELINE 1895–1920

1895 Buddy Bolden forms his first band, symbolically "founding" jazz.

1896 W.C. Handy begins touring as a cornet soloist with Mahara's Minstrels.

1897 Buddy Bolden allegedly records a cylinder that has never been found.

1898 Singer Ma Rainey appears in the show *A Bunch of Blackberries* in Columbus, Georgia, at the age of 12.

1899 Scott Joplin's "Maple Leaf Rag" launches the ragtime era. • Duke Ellington is born. • Eubie Blake composes "Charleston Rag" at age 16.

1900 Twenty-eight-year-old Bill Johnson takes up the bass; he would be the first to lay down his bow and pick out notes with his fingers.

1901 Louis Armstrong is born.

1902 This is the year that Jelly Roll Morton (who was just 12 at the time) would later claim to have invented jazz. • Yellow Nunez plays clarinet in New Orleans with the Right at Em's Razz Band. • Scott Joplin writes "The Entertainer," "The Ragtime Dance," and "Elite Syncopations."

1903 Cornetist Manuel Perez becomes leader of the Onward Brass Band in New Orleans.

1904 Ed Garland plays bass with Buddy Bolden's group. • James I. Lent records the first drum solo on "The Ragtime Drummer."

1905 Eight-year-old clarinetist Sidney Bechet shocks onlookers by sitting in successfully with Freddie Keppard's band.

1906 Alberta Hunter runs away from home and starts working as a singer; she is 11 years old. • Freddie Keppard forms the Olympia Orchestra. • Buddy Bolden begins to suffer from mental illness.

1907 Eubie Blake starts an eight-year period playing solo piano at the Goldfield Hotel in Baltimore. • Pianist Fate Marable begins performing on the steamboat *J.S.* • Paul Whiteman plays violin with the Denver Symphony. • King Oliver starts his rise to fame. • Buddy Bolden is committed to Jackson Mental Institution.

1908 Richard M. Jones begins a nine-year stint playing piano at Lulu White's Mahogany Hall in Storyville. • Nick LaRocca leads his first band.

1909 Sidney Bechet (now 12) plays with Buddy Petit's Young Olympians. • Bill Johnson becomes one of the first New Orleans musicians to leave town, settling in California temporarily.

1910 Cornetist Oscar Celestin forms and leads the Tuxedo Band. • Fourteen-year-old singer Ida Cox runs away from home to tour with White and Clark's Minstrels.

1911 Scott Joplin completes "Treemonisha." • Gene Greene ("The Ragtime King") records the first scat vocal ("King of the Bungaloos"), 15 years before Louis Armstrong's "Heebies Jeebies."

1912 Trombonist Kid Ory moves to New Orleans, immediately forming one of the city's top jazz bands. • James Reese Europe's Society Orchestra accompanies Vernon and Irene Castle in the show *Watch Your Step*. • W.C. Handy composes "Memphis Blues" (originally called "Mr. Crump"). • Tony Jackson moves to Chicago. • James P. Johnson becomes a professional, playing piano on the East Coast and developing stride piano. • Twelve-year-old clarinetist Tony Parenti works with Papa Jack Laine's band in New Orleans. • Bessie Smith sings with Fats Chappelle's Rabbit Foot Minstrels. • Pianist Willie "The Lion" Smith starts appearing in clubs in New York and Atlantic City.

1913 On New Year's Eve, 11-year-old Louis Armstrong is arrested for shooting a pistol in the air in celebration; he is sent to the New Orleans Colored Waif's Home for Boys for a couple of years, where he begins to play the cornet seriously. • James Reese Europe's Orchestra makes its first recordings. • Nine-year-old Earl Hines takes up the piano. • Clarinetist Jimmie Noone joins Freddie Keppard's band. • Mamie Smith moves to New York and starts working in vaudeville.

1914 Arranger/pianist Ferde Grofe joins drummer Art Hickman's band; within the next couple of years he develops the concept of big band dance band music, becoming the first to divide ensembles into trumpet, trombone, and reed sections. • W.C. Handy composes "St. Louis Blues." • Bill Johnson sends for Freddie Keppard to join his Original Creole Orchestra in Chicago. • Jelly Roll Morton visits Chicago for the first time. • The Victor Military Band records W.C. Handy's "The Memphis Blues," which may be the first song with a blues progression to be documented on record.

TIMELINE 1895–1920 (continued)

1915 Bill Johnson's Original Creole Orchestra brings jazz to New York City, although few notice. • Chris Kelly moves from his hometown of Plaquemine Parish to New Orleans where he quickly becomes one of the city's top cornetists. • Jelly Roll Morton plays jazz in San Francisco. • Manuel Perez visits Chicago with the Arthur Sims band. • Noble Sissle and Eubie Blake meet in Baltimore and begin their musical partnership. Sissle also joins James Reese Europe's band. • Jimmy Dorsey, who is 11, switches from trumpet to alto sax and clarinet. • Cornetist Sam Morgan puts together his jazz band in New Orleans.

1916 Freddie Keppard is offered an opportunity to be the first jazz musician to record, but turns it down. • Phil Napoleon makes his recording debut, as a classical cornetist. • Johnny Stein's Jazz Band in Chicago features Nick LaRocca, Eddie Edwards, Yellow Nunez, and Henry Ragas for a few months until an argument results in the four sidemen (along with drummer Tony Sbarbaro) forming the Original Dixieland Jazz Band. • Nunez departs from the ODJB on October 31 after an argument with the fiery LaRocca, being replaced by Larry Shields. • Cornetist Paul Mares and clarinetist Leon Roppolo play in Tom Brown's band on the riverboat *Capitol*.

1917 The Original Dixieland Jazz Band relocates to New York, makes the first jazz recordings ("Darktown Strutters Ball" and "Indiana") and has a giant hit with "Livery Stable Blues." • James P. Johnson makes his first piano rolls. • Pianist Lil Hardin moves to Chicago where she works as a song demonstrator in Jones's Music Store. • Among the many other musicians moving to Chicago this year are Sidney Bechet, trumpeter Tommy Ladnier, bassist Wellman Braud, and trombonist Roy Palmer. • Clarinetist Johnny Dodds and trumpeter Mutt Carey go on tour with Mack's Merry Makers. • W.C. Handy makes his recording debut with his Memphis Orchestra. • Handy discovers cornetist Johnny Dunn and 15-year-old clarinetist Buster Bailey, both of whom join his orchestra for a time. • Phil Napoleon forms the first version of the Original Memphis Five, naming his New York–based band after W.C. Handy's "Memphis Blues." • Earl Fuller's Famous Jazz Band (with

Ted Lewis) records. • In Washington, D.C., Duke Ellington writes his first composition, "Soda Fountain Rag." • Jelly Roll Morton begins a five-year stay on the West Coast. • Buddy Petit plays in Los Angeles briefly with Morton. • Ethel Waters moves to New York where she begins performing in clubs. • Oscar Celestin and trombonist William Ridgely co-lead the Original Tuxedo Orchestra. • Fate Marable puts together his most famous group, the Kentucky Jazz Band, which includes Johnny Dodds, drummer Baby Dodds, bassist Pops Foster, banjoist Johnny St. Cyr, and Louis Armstrong. • Scott Joplin dies. • Dizzy Gillespie is born.

1918 After hearing a record by the Original Dixieland Jazz Band, Bix Beiderbecke (then 15) takes up the cornet. • Drummer Jimmy Bertrand joins Erskine Tate's Vendome Orchestra in Chicago, staying for ten years. • Freddie Keppard, pianist Jimmy Blythe, and singer Lizzie Miles move to Chicago. • Joe Sanders and Carleton Coon meet in a Kansas City music store. Two years later they form the Coon-Sanders Novelty Orchestra. • Bill Johnson's Original Creole Orchestra records one title ("Tack It Down"), but it is never released. • George Morrison's band in Denver includes Andy Kirk and Jimmie Lunceford in its personnel. • Pianist Bennie Moten puts together a trio that plays regularly in Kansas City. • Yellow Nunez records with the Louisiana Five. • Armand J. Piron forms his orchestra in New Orleans. • Tenor saxophonist Benny Waters plays with Charlie Miller's band in Philadelphia. • Pianist Arthur Schutt joins Paul Specht's Orchestra. • Paul Whiteman organizes his orchestra, playing at San Francisco's Fairmont Hotel.

1919 The ODJB equals their American success when they become the first jazz band to play in Europe, including nine months at London's Hammersmith Palais. • Sidney Bechet joins Will Marion Cook's Southern Syncopated Orchestra and causes a sensation with his solos in Europe. • Cornetists King Oliver, Paul Mares, and George Mitchell move to Chicago. • Louis Armstrong takes Oliver's place with Kid Ory's band. • Ory moves to California for his health; he lives another 54 years. • James Reese Europe's Orchestra records 24 selections and

Ragtime to Jazz 2 actually focuses on early jazz rather than ragtime (other than Fred Van Eps's "Teasing the Cat" from 1916), with selections by the Original Dixieland Jazz Band, Earl Fuller, Paul Biese's Novelty Orchestra, the Louisiana Five, Yerkes's Novelty Five, a Vincent Lopez group, the Whiteway Jazz Band, Eubie Blake, Brown and Terry Jazzola Boys, Lanin's Southern Serenaders, Mamie Smith's Jazz Hounds, Ladd's Black Aces, Husk O'Hare, Bobby Lee's Music Landers, the Syncopating Skeeters, and a couple of completely unidentified bands.

Ragtime to Jazz 3 contains a real find. It has been an oft-told legend that scat-singing (vocalizing nonsense syllables instead of words) was first recorded when Louis Armstrong dropped the music during his 1926 recording of "Heebies Jeebies" and sought to cover up his mistake. Actually, other scatting jazz performances, most notably Don Redman singing "My Papa Doesn't Two-Time" with the Fletcher Henderson Orchestra in 1924, and Cliff Edwards (aka Ukulele Ike) on several numbers as early as 1923, predated "Heebies Jeebies." However, **Ragtime to Jazz 3** features singer Gene Greene (who was popular enough in vaudeville to bill himself as "The Ragtime King") scatting on a couple choruses of "King of the Bungaloos," back in 1911! What Greene (who lived until 1931) thought of the scat singers of the late-1920s is unknown, but he seems to have been the uncredited pioneer.

Also in this enjoyable set are quite a few very early banjo and string band rag-oriented performances, Pete Hampton singing "Bill Bailey" in 1904, Roy Spangler's solo piano version of "Cannonball Rag," Conway's Band ripping through "Hungarian Rag," and early jazz performances by the Emerson Symphony Orchestra, the Frisco Jass Band, Eubie Blake (playing "Hungarian Rag" in a two-piano trio from his initial session in 1917), Ford Dabney, the Original New Orleans Jazz Band (with Jimmy Durante on piano), the Louisiana Five, James P. Johnson (his 1921 rendition of "The Harlem Strut"), and the Society Harmonizers ("Ostrich

---

TIMELINE 1895–1920 (continued)

triumphantly tours the United States before Europe is stabbed to death on May 10. • Pianist/arranger Luis Russell wins $3,000 in a lottery and uses the money to move with his mother and sister from his native Panama to New Orleans. • Cornetist Abbie Brunies forms the Halfway House Orchestra in New Orleans. • Dorsey's Novelty Six (co-led by Tommy and Jimmy Dorsey) begins playing regularly in the Baltimore area. • "Swanee," sung by Al Jolson in the show *Sinbad*, is George Gershwin's first hit. • Ferde Grofe joins the Paul Whiteman Orchestra, and becomes his chief arranger. • Ted Lewis starts his own band, using the nucleus of Earl Fuller's group. • Ben Selvin (an occasional violinist) leads his first record date. During the next 15 years he would be at the head of more than 9,000 titles. • Bessie Smith stars in her *Liberty Belles* show. • Violinist Joe Venuti and guitarist Eddie Lang work in a band in Atlantic City. • Fifteen-year-old Fats Waller is hired as the house organist for the Lincoln Theatre, playing stomping organ during silent movies. • Evangelist Billy Sunday warns that jazz has already caused the downfall of a half million girls.

1920 Mamie Smith records Perry Bradford's "Crazy Blues," leading to a major demand for female blues singers. • The ODJB returns home and has a minor hit with "Margie." • Paul Whiteman moves his home base to New York and makes "Whispering" and "Wang Wang Blues" into standards. • Lil Hardin leads a band at the Dreamland in Chicago, but is soon succeeded by King Oliver's Creole Jazz Band, which she joins along with trombonist Honore Dutrey, Johnny Dodds, and Baby Dodds. • Roy Bargy is hired as pianist and musical director of the Benson Orchestra of Chicago. • Drummer Sonny Greer first plays with Duke Ellington in Washington, D.C. • Trumpeter Dewey Jackson leads the Golden Melody Band in St. Louis. • Ed Kirkeby helps organize the California Ramblers. • George E. Lee begins leading his Singing Orchestra in Kansas City. • Jimmie Noone joins Doc Cook's Gingersnaps in Chicago. • Charlie Parker is born. • The 25th anniversary of Buddy Bolden forming his first band goes completely unmentioned. • Nearly 150 million records are sold in the United States.

Walk" à la the Original Dixieland Jazz Band but in 1923) among others.

There are still many ragtime-oriented recordings long overdue to appear on CD. The double LP **Ragtime** (French RCA 45687) consists of 32 of the most important ragtime numbers from 1900–17 plus six later performances. In addition to Sousa, Pryor, Ossman, and Van Eps, also heard from are glass xylophonist Chris Chapman (introducing "Dill Pickles"), accordionist Pietro Deidro, pianist Felix Arndt ("Desecration Rag"), James Europe's Society Orchestra, the all-saxophone Six Brown Brothers ("Bull Frog Blues"), and James I. Lent, who takes the second-ever recorded drum solo on "The Ragtime Drummer" from 1912; the first was his 1904 version. Also of strong interest is the fluent playing of the two great banjo pioneers Vess Ossman and Fred Van Eps who are featured on seven numbers apiece on **Kings of the Banjo Ragtime** (Yazoo 1044).

Early Jazz: 1900–1916

The pioneering jazz musicians in New Orleans and throughout the South were quite aware of ragtime. The structures of the music (with its multiple themes) and syncopations became influences. But jazz developed on a different path.

During Buddy Bolden's day, New Orleans jazz began to form. The music was primarily ensemble-oriented, the improvising stuck close to the melody, and the chord changes were fairly basic. Musicians were rated high in the as yet unnamed jazz community if they had a pretty tone, knew how to infuse the music with blue notes, were expressive, never lost sight of the melody, and could get audiences dancing.

In smaller combos, usually the cornetist or trumpeter was in charge of the melody, the trombonist played harmonies, and the clarinetist created countermelodies and melodic variations. The frontline was accompanied by rhythm banjo or guitar, tuba or string bass, and drums with a violin occasionally being included. Brass bands had many more horns and separate musicians playing snare bass and bass drums. Pianists, who functioned as one-man bands, were primarily independent soloists; no marching band used a piano! Some pianists, including Jelly Roll Morton, Tony Jackson, and Richard M. Jones, were employed in the bordellos of New Orleans's legal red light district, Storyville.

The music scene in New Orleans developed gradually during 1900–16, with new songs and musicians constantly revitalizing the slowly forming style. After Bolden was committed in 1907, Freddie Keppard was considered the city's top cornetist, at least until he went north in 1914. By then Joe "King" Oliver had largely succeeded him and he would be rated at the top until his departure from New Orleans in 1921. Other major names included cornetists Manuel Perez and Oscar Celestin, clarinetists Johnny Dodds, Jimmie Noone, Lorenzo Tio, and Sidney Bechet, trombonist Kid Ory (who moved to New Orleans in 1912 and immediately started leading one of the city's top bands), pianist Fate Marable (who headed notable orchestras on riverboats going to and from St. Louis), and Papa Jack Laine, who was one of the pioneer white bandleaders. Among the best-known groups in the city during this period were the Excelsior, Eureka, Onward, and Imperial Brass Bands, but there were many lesser-known ensembles too.

The most important development in jazz during 1910–15 was the gradual exodus of musicians out of New Orleans. Many African-Americans decided to move out of the racist South to the slightly more hospitable North. In the case of the musicians, some had wandering spirits and enjoyed exploring new locations, while others were searching for more lucrative work. Some left town with minstrel shows, which was not an ideal situation considering the often-wretched working conditions, dated music, and use of blackface even on dark-skinned performers. Others played in black theatres or rundown clubs where entertainment was desired, while some performed in a supportive role in traveling shows, including one led by blues singer Ma Rainey. Bassist Bill Johnson left town in 1909, introduced jazz to California, and sent for Freddie Keppard to join his Original Creole Orchestra in 1914; the following year they were among the first jazz bands to appear in New York. Jelly Roll Morton, who first visited Chicago in 1914, spent several years in California. By 1917, a strong black jazz community was forming in Chicago, which during the first half of the next decade would be the center of jazz.

W.C. Handy   Other important developments during the waning years of the ragtime era involved W.C. Handy and James Reese Europe. Handy became known as "The Father of the Blues" even though he was not much of a musician himself. A rather stiff-sounding cornetist who played with Mahara's Minstrels during 1896–1903 and led an orchestra in the South, Handy's main contributions were as a composer. He was impressed by the music he heard by solo blues performers who played in the streets. Handy wrote down some of the melodies and lyrics, added some of his own, and became the first published composer of blues, starting with 1912's "Mr. Crump" (which was originally a campaign song), eventually retitled "Memphis Blues." Handy's "St. Louis Blues" (1914) was a huge hit and was followed by "Yellow Dog Blues" (1914), "Beale Street Blues" (1916), "Ole Miss," "Hesitatin' Blues," and "Careless (or Loveless) Love" in 1921. It did not take long for these songs to be adopted by jazz musicians.

W.C. Handy's Memphis Blues Band (Memphis Archives 7006) has 16 of Handy's recordings (from 1917–23), including his ten earliest. Unfortunately, the music is disappointing. The songs (nearly all of them Handy compositions, including "St. Louis Blues," "Yellow Dog Blues," and "Muscle Shoals Blues") are excellent, but the playing by the band (consisting of Handy's cornet, a trombone, four reeds, three violinists including Darnell Howard, piano, tuba or string bass, and drums) is rhythmically wooden, and the leader's cornet is remarkably inflexible and weak. Clearly Handy's main talent was in composing, not playing music.

James Reese Europe   James Reese Europe was most significant as a pioneering African-American band-leader whose music preceded jazz. Well trained musically on the piano and violin, he worked as the assistant director of the U.S. Marine Band, moving to New York as early as 1904 where he worked as pianist and director of musical comedies and traveling shows. Europe founded and led the Clef Club Orchestra, and his Society Orchestra accompanied the world-famous dancers Vernon and Irene Castle, most notably in the show *Watch Your Step* in 1912.

In 1913, Europe's Society Orchestra became the first black nongospel group to record. His ensemble, which often consisted of trumpet, clarinet, three violins, two pianos, drums, and a five-piece banjo section, cut eight selections during 1913–14, including "Too Much Mustard," "Down Home Rag," and "Castle Walk." These performances display the influence of ragtime's rhythms although there is no significant improvising. Historical revisionists who claim that Europe's was the first jazz band

to record probably never heard these records (which have only been reissued in piecemeal fashion) or have an extremely wide definition of jazz.

However, Europe was a significant bandleader of the era, performing at Carnegie Hall, utilizing 125 musicians and singers, almost a decade before Paul Whiteman's famous Aeolian Concert of 1924. During World War I, Lieutenant James Reese Europe directed the 369th Infantry Regiment Band (which was nicknamed the Hell Fighters), touring Europe. After returning to the United States in 1919, Europe's orchestra recorded 24 titles in four record dates, showing the influence of the new jazz music although still sounding mostly restrained and tightly rehearsed rather than spontaneous. Unfortunately, Europe never had the opportunity to make an impact during the 1920s—he was stabbed to death on May 10, 1919, in Boston by his snare drummer, Herbert Wright.

◉ **James Reese Europe's 369th U.S. Infantry "Hell Fighters" Band** (Memphis Archives 7020) and **Featuring Noble Sissle** (IAJRC 1012) have exactly the same music, all of the pioneering bandleader's selections from 1919 (but not the 1913–14 selections). While the IAJRC disc has the selections in chronological order (the Memphis Archives set shuffles the songs a bit) and does a better job of identifying the personnel, the Memphis Archives release includes a 48-page booklet as opposed to IAJRC's dozen pages and therefore gets the edge. The music overall is closer to jazz than Europe's earlier sessions, with vocals by Noble Sissle, march rhythms, and some future jazz standards, rags, waltzes, and novelties. This is superior prejazz dance music that hints at early jazz and almost swings in spots.

The Original Dixieland Jazz Band   In 1916, Freddie Keppard was reportedly offered the opportunity to be the first jazz musician to record. He turned it down, fearful that other cornetists would be able to copy his solos. In retrospect, it was a major error. Although he appeared on records starting in 1923, Keppard would not get a chance to lead his own record date until 1926, by which time he was greatly overshadowed by later players, most notably Louis Armstrong. It was a mistake not repeated by the Original Dixieland Jazz Band.

In 1917, the year of the Russian Revolution, the music world had a revolution of its own. Although jazz had existed for more than 20 years by that point, it was not until the music was finally recorded that it was heard by a large audience beyond New Orleans and isolated spots. The impact of the Original Dixieland Jazz Band recordings was immediate and the music world would never be the same again.

The stage was set the previous year when, on March 1, 1916, cornetist Nick LaRocca left New Orleans to join drummer Johnny Stein's band in Chicago. The group also included clarinetist Alcide "Yellow" Nunez, trombonist Eddie Edwards, and pianist Henry Ragas. The word "jass" was just beginning to be used as a musical term (its earlier definition had been sexual), and Stein's Dixie Jass Band was a big hit at Schiller's Café, playing for large dancing crowds. After three months, LaRocca and the other musicians wanted to break the contract Stein had signed to accept a higher paying job elsewhere. Stein refused and the sidemen rebelled, forming the Original Dixieland Jazz Band with LaRocca as its leader and Tony Sbarbaro as the group's drummer, performing at the Del'Abe Cafe at the higher salaries. On October 31, Yellow Nunez lost an argument with LaRocca (their personalities had frequently clashed) and soon Larry Shields became the band's clarinetist.

In January 1917, the Original Dixieland Jazz Band decided to try New York. They became a sensation playing at Reisenweber's, gaining a great deal of notoriety and essentially launching what would be known as "the jazz age." On January 30, the ODJB made the first-ever jazz records, uninhibited versions of "Darktown Strutters Ball" and "Indiana" for the Columbia label. However, the record company executives did not know what to think of these wild sounds, and fearing hostility from a public used to melodic dance music, they decided not to release the records. So, on February 26, the ODJB went to the Victor label and recorded "Livery Stable Blues" and "Dixie Jass Band One Step." Victor came out with the record quickly and "Livery Stable Blues," a novelty number, which features the horns imitating animals, became a major hit. It was such a big seller that Columbia reversed itself and soon released the "Darktown Strutters Ball" coupling.

Comparing the ODJB's music to other contemporary bands makes one understand Columbia's fears. The freewheeling music (which actually has each of the musicians playing very specific roles) is extremely extroverted and even barbaric compared to what had previously been heard, even the James Reese Europe records. The music is exclusively ensembles (other than brief two-bar breaks)

with no solos at all, propelled by a heated rhythm provided by Tony Sbarbaro that was a major step forward from the military drum style formerly heard.

During 1917–18, the Original Dixieland Jazz Band introduced such future standards as "Darktown Strutters Ball," "Indiana," "Tiger Rag," "At the Jazz Band Ball," "Fidgety Feet," "Sensation," and "Clarinet Marmalade," switching briefly to the AV label (when Victor was having legal problems with patents) before returning to Victor. The ODJB recorded a total of 53 numbers during 1917–23, and all 23 of its RCA recordings are on ● **75th Anniversary** (Bluebird 61098), including its famous versions of "Livery Stable Blues," "Dixie Jass Band One-Step," "Tiger Rag," "Sensation Rag," and "Margie." **The Complete Original Dixieland Jazz Band** (RCA 66608) is a two-CD set that not only has the 23 RCA numbers but all of the music from the ODJB's "comeback" of 1936: six quintet remakes and the eight big band selections.

As soon as "Livery Stable Blues" caught on, many other white bands appeared on records, doing their best to emulate the ODJB, including the Original New Orleans Jazz Band (a quintet that had future showbiz star Jimmy Durante on piano), Earl Fuller's Famous Jazz Band (with the soon-to-be famous gaspipe clarinetist Ted Lewis), and Anton Lala's Louisiana Five (a trumpetless quintet with Yellow Nunez on clarinet). In addition, as the word "rag" had been used and misused by composers during 1910–15, now "jazz" begins popping up constantly in the song titles of tunes by Tin Pan Alley composers.

Jazz Invades Europe

World War I ended in 1918 and the United States emerged as a world power, although one that preferred to be isolationist. In early 1919, the Original Dixieland Jazz Band (whose reputation had preceded it) became the first American jazz group to visit Europe. By then trombonist Eddie Edwards (who had been drafted) was replaced by Emile Christian and the influenza epidemic had claimed the life of pianist Henry Ragas, who was succeeded by J. Russell Robinson. The ODJB's nine-month run at the Hammersmith Palais in London garnered major headlines and led to the jazz craze taking hold in Europe, although it would be a decade before more than a few European musicians could hold their own with the Americans. In addition, the band recorded 17 titles in London, which have been reissued on **In England** (EMI

Pathe 252716). Ranking with the group's finest work, some of these performances were originally on 12-inch (as opposed to the more standard 10-inch) 78s and two are over four minutes in length. In addition to remakes, such numbers as "My Baby's Arms," "I've Got My Captain Working for Me Now," "I'm Forever Blowing Bubbles," "Mammy O' Mine," "I've Lost My Heart in Dixieland," and a charming version of "Alice Blue Gown" are among the most memorable selections. Also on the CD are five selections from four British bands of the 1917–24 period, who are interesting, but not up to the level of the ODJB.

After their return to the United States in 1920, the Original Dixieland Jazz Band found that the jazz world had continued to evolve in their absence. With Eddie Edwards back on trombone (Emil Christian lived in Europe until World War II), the ODJB reluctantly added altoist Bennie Krueger to their recordings so as to "modernize" their sound. They had a minor hit in J. Russell Robinson's "Margie" later in 1920 and showed that they were not out of the running yet.

1917/1923 (Jazz Archives 158492) completes the ODJB story on records. It has the two historic Columbia selections ("The Darktown Strutters Ball" and "Indiana") although it inaccurately says that they are from May 31, 1917, rather than January 30, the seven cuts for the AV label in 1917 (including "At the Jass Band Ball" and "Oriental Jazz"), the band's four 1922–23 recordings, plus 11 numbers for Victor that are duplicates from the other sets.

In June 1919 (a few months after the ODJB arrived in London), Will Marion Cook's Southern Syncopated Orchestra traveled to Europe. This huge show band was most notable for featuring clarinetist Sidney Bechet, whose solos garnered great applause. Bechet, who would not record until 1923 nor buy his first soprano saxophone (which became his main instrument) until 1920, was the first major jazz soloist to be heard by a large audience. In October, Swiss conductor Ernest Ansermet wrote a remarkably perceptive review for the *Revue Romande,* which partly read: "There is with the Southern Syncopated Orchestra an extraordinary virtuoso, the first of his race, I am told, to have composed perfectly elaborated blues on his clarinet…. Here undoubtedly, was a new style, and its form was striking—abrupt and rugged, with a brusque, merciless ending, as in Bach's second Brandenburg Concerto. I want to mention the name of this genius among musicians, for, personally, I shall never forget it: Sidney Bechet…. For all we know,

this way may well be the highway where tomorrow's world traffic will stream."

1920: Mamie Smith, the Start of the Blues Craze, and Paul Whiteman

On February 14, 1920, Mamie Smith (whose musical director and chief sponsor was songwriter-singer Perry Bradford) made her recording debut, singing "That Thing Called Love" and "You Can't Keep a Good Man Down." Smith, who was 36, had been working in show business since the turn of the century, as a dancer in the Midwest with Tutt-Whitney's Smart Set company, with an otherwise white vaudeville group called the Four Mitchells, and singing in Harlem clubs. In 1920, she appeared in *Maid of Harlem* at the Lincoln Theatre. When Sophie Tucker, the show's star, bowed out of a recording session, Smith was given her big break. She was the first nongospel black singer captured on record (if one does not count actor-comedian Bert Williams, who tended to speak his words rather than sing). Her record sales were good, and on August 10 she recorded one of the songs from *Maid of Harlem,* "Crazy Blues," along with "It's Right Here for You." Within six months, that 78 sold over a million copies and began a blues craze. During the next few years, dozens of singers (mostly females, both black and white, who worked in vaudeville) were given opportunities to record in hopes of duplicating the success of "Crazy Blues."

All of Mamie Smith's recordings have been reissued by the Document label on four CDs. ❶ **Vol. 1** (Document 5357) includes "That Thing Called Love," "Crazy Blues," "It's Right Here for You," "If You Don't Want Me Blues," "Royal Garden Blues" (one of four instrumentals by her Jazz Hounds, which rank with the earliest jazz performances on record by a black band), "I Want a Jazzy Kiss," and "Sax-O-Phoney Blues." Smith was wise to always use the top musicians in New York; this disc has appearances by pianist Willie "The Lion" Smith, cornetist Johnny Dunn, and clarinetists Garvin Bushell and Buster Bailey.

Mamie Smith's "Crazy Blues" was not technically the first blues ever recorded ("Memphis Blues" was waxed back in 1914 and the ODJB's "Livery Stable Blues" was a blues), nor the first vocal blues to be recorded (Nora Bayes's "Homesickness Blues" in 1916 and Marie Cahill's "Dallas Blues" from 1917 were predecessors), but it was the first time that a black vocalist was captured singing a blues, and it was a hugely influential record. In the early 1920s, the word "blues" was part of the titles of scores of records, most of which had nothing to do with the blues, repeating the prior overuse of "rag" and "jazz." **Tin Pan Alley Blues** (Memphis Archives 7003) has some of these nonblues blues. The first half of the disc features some real rarities, such as the Nora Bayes and Marie Cahill numbers, although the inclusion of some major blues singers from later in the 1920s (such as Bessie Smith and Trixie Smith) waters down the plot of the CD, which could have been a tribute to blues-singing vaudevillians.

As early as 1920, at least on recordings (which did not reflect the entire scene), the jazz world was dividing into two. On one side was the ODJB and similar bands that played freewheeling music mostly by ear. The other faction was large orchestras they utilized arrangements and featured very little spontaneity and improvisation. Arrangers of the period were just beginning to try to include the feel of jazz in what were really dance band charts. Pianist/arranger Ferde Grofe, who worked with Art Hickman's Orchestra during 1914–19, was among the first to divide the horns into trumpet, trombone, and saxophone sections. In 1919, he joined the Paul Whiteman Orchestra, which was a three-horn, four-rhythm septet until 1921. Whiteman, who first formed his band in 1918, started off with his home base in San Francisco, shifting to Atlantic City, and, by 1920, New York. His recordings of 1920 included a major seller in "Whispering" and popular records in "Wang-Wang Blues" and "The Japanese Sandman." Trumpeter Henry Busse (a very basic player with a charming if soon-dated sound) was the group's main soloist, but the ensembles were all written down with Busse's spots being worked out in advance and rarely changing. Even at this early stage, Paul Whiteman was being touted as one of the leaders of jazz, one who smoothed down and refined the more primitive aspects of the music as introduced by the ODJB.

As 1920 ended, the successes of the ODJB, Paul Whiteman, and Mamie Smith were inspiring record labels to record more jazz. However, because very few African-Americans had appeared on record, and thus far nearly all of the recording activity had taken place in New York, one cannot gain a complete picture of the jazz world of this period purely from records. Such important names as King Oliver, Jelly Roll Morton, and Freddie Keppard were thus far undocumented. But that would change very soon.

VOICES OF THE FUTURE

Alphonse Picou (clarinet), Oct. 19, 1878, New Orleans, LA

Oscar "Papa" Celestin (trumpet, leader), Jan. 1, 1884, Napoleonville, LA

Ma Rainey (vocals), Apr. 26, 1886, Columbus, GA

Luckey Roberts (piano, composer), Aug. 7, 1887, Philadelphia, PA

Lovie Austin (piano), Sept. 19, 1887, Chattanooga, TN

Willie "The Lion" Smith (piano, composer), Nov. 25, 1887, Goshen, NY

Lonnie Johnson (guitar, vocals), Feb. 8, 1889, New Orleans, LA

Bunk Johnson (cornet), Dec. 27, 1889, New Orleans, LA

Steve Brown (bass), Jan. 13, 1890, New Orleans, LA

Johnny St. Cyr (guitar, banjo), Apr. 17, 1890, New Orleans, LA

Charlie Creath (trumpet, leader), Dec. 30, 1890, Ironton, MO

Mutt Carey (cornet), 1891, Hahnville, LA

Wellman Braud (bass), Jan. 25, 1891, St. James Parish, LA

James P. Johnson (piano, composer), Feb. 1, 1891, New Brunswick, NJ

Emile Barnes (clarinet), Feb. 18, 1892, New Orleans, LA

Pops Foster (bass), May 18, 1892, McCall, LA

Richard M. Jones (piano, composer), June 13, 1892, Donaldson, LA

Jim Robinson (trombone), Dec. 25, 1892, Deer Range, LA

Clarence Williams (piano, composer, vocals), Oct. 8, 1893, Plaquemine Parish, LA

Isham Jones (leader, composer), Jan. 31, 1894, Coalton, OH

Carleton A. Coon (drums, vocals), Feb. 5, 1894, Rochester, MN

Bessie Smith (vocals), Apr. 15, 1894, Chattanooga, TN

Punch Miller (trumpet), June 10, 1894, Raceland, LA

Joe Sanders (piano, vocals, arranger), Oct. 15, 1894, Thayer, KS

Bennie Moten (piano, leader), Nov. 13, 1894, Kansas City, MO

Lizzie Miles (vocals), Mar. 31, 1895, New Orleans, LA

VOICES OF THE FUTURE

Alberta Hunter (vocals), Apr. 1, 1895, Memphis, TN

Jimmie Noone (clarinet), Apr. 23, 1895, Cut Off, LA

Cliff Edwards (vocals, ukulele, kazoo), June 14, 1895, Montreal, Quebec, Canada

Sam Wooding (leader, piano), June 17, 1895, Philadelphia, PA

Darnell Howard (clarinet), July 25, 1895, Chicago, IL

Sonny Greer (drums), Dec. 13, 1895, Long Branch, NJ

Merritt Brunies (cornet, valve trombone), Dec. 25, 1895, New Orleans, LA

Jimmy O'Bryant (clarinet), 1896, AK

Ida Cox (vocals), Feb. 25, 1896, Cedartown, GA

Vic Berton (drums, tympani), May 7, 1896, Chicago, IL

Natty Dominique (trumpet), Aug. 2, 1896, New Orleans, LA

Bert Ambrose (leader), Sept. 15, 1896, London, England

Ethel Waters (vocals), Oct. 31, 1896, Chester, PA

Johnny Dunn (trumpet), Feb. 19, 1897, Memphis, TN

Sweet Emma Barrett (piano, vocals), Mar. 25, 1897, New Orleans, LA

Ruth Etting (vocals), Nov. 23, 1897, David City, NE

Sippie Wallace (vocals), Jan. 11, 1898, Houston, TX

Lil Hardin Armstrong (piano), Feb. 3, 1898, Memphis, TN

Jimmy Yancey (piano), Feb. 20, 1898, Chicago, IL

Leo Watson (vocals), Feb. 27, 1898, Kansas City, MO

Miff Mole (trombone), Mar. 11, 1898, Roosevelt, Long Island, NY

Zutty Singleton (drums), May 14, 1898, Bunkie, LA

Andy Kirk (leader), May 28, 1898, Newport, KY

Andrew Blakeney (trumpet), June 10, 1898, Quitman, MS

Peck Kelley (piano), Oct. 22, 1898, Houston, TX

Fletcher Henderson (leader, arranger, piano), Dec. 18, 1898, Cuthbert, GA

Charles Irvis (trombone), 1899, New York, NY

George Mitchell (cornet), Mar. 8, 1899, Louisville, KY

Jean Goldkette (leader), Mar. 18, 1899, Valenciennes, France

Duke Ellington (piano, composer, arranger, leader), Apr. 29, 1899, Washington, D.C.

Paul Barbarin (drums), May 5, 1899, New Orleans, LA

Red McKenzie (comb, vocals), Oct. 14, 1899, St. Louis, MO

Mezz Mezzrow (clarinet, tenor), Nov. 9, 1899, Chicago, IL

Hoagy Carmichael (composer, vocals, piano), Nov. 22, 1899, Bloomington, IN

Charlie Green (trombone), 1900, Omaha, NE

Wilbur DeParis (trombone, leader), Jan. 11, 1900, Crawfordsville, IN

Abbie Brunies (cornet), Jan. 19, 1900, New Orleans, LA

Juan Tizol (valve trombone, composer), Jan. 22, 1900, San Juan, Puerto Rico

Walter Page (bass), Feb. 9, 1900, Gallatin, MO

Jimmy Bertrand (drums, washboard, xylophone), Feb. 24, 1900, Biloxi, MS

Tiny Parham (piano, leader), Feb. 25, 1900, Kansas City, MO

Albert Nicholas (clarinet), May 27, 1900, New Orleans, LA

Tommy Ladnier (trumpet), May 28, 1900, Florenceville, LA

Valaida Snow (trumpet, vocals), June 2, 1900, Chattanooga, TN

Paul Mares (trumpet, leader), June 15, 1900, New Orleans, LA

Capt. John Handy (alto), June 24, 1900, Pass Christian, MS

George Lewis (clarinet), July 13, 1900, New Orleans, LA

Don Redman (arranger, composer, vocals, clarinet, alto, leader), July 29, 1900, Piedmont, WV

Tony Parenti (clarinet), Aug. 6, 1900, New Orleans, LA

Lucky Millinder (leader), Aug. 8, 1900, Anniston, AL

Elmer Snowden (banjo, guitar), Oct. 9, 1900, Baltimore, MD

Jimmy Harrison (trombone), Oct. 17, 1900, Louisville, KY

Willie Humphrey (clarinet), Dec. 29, 1900, New Orleans, LA

Jimmy Blythe (piano), May 20, 1901, Keene, KY

Edmond Hall (clarinet), May 15, 1901, New Orleans, LA

Frank Signorelli (piano, composer), May 24, 1901, New York, NY

Frankie Trumbauer (C-melody), May 30, 1901, Carbondale, IL

Louis Armstrong (trumpet, vocals), Aug. 4, 1901, New Orleans, LA

Phil Napoleon (trumpet), Sept. 2, 1901, Boston, MA

Lee Collins (trumpet), Oct. 17, 1901, New Orleans, LA

Paul "Polo" Barnes (clarinet, reeds), Nov. 22, 1901, New Orleans, LA

Danny Polo (clarinet), Dec. 22, 1901, Toluca, IL

Blanche Calloway (vocals), 1902, Rochester, NY

Benny Waters (tenor, clarinet, alto), Jan. 23, 1902, Brighton, MD

George Brunies (trombone), Feb. 6, 1902, New Orleans, LA

Chick Webb (drums), Feb. 10, 1902, Baltimore, MD

Leon Roppolo (clarinet), Mar. 16, 1902, Lutcher, LA

Albert Burbank (clarinet), Mar. 25, 1902, New Orleans, LA

VOICES OF THE FUTURE

Rosy McHargue (C-melody, clarinet), Apr. 6, 1902, Danning, IL

Sharkey Bonano (trumpet), Apr. 9, 1902, New Orleans, LA

Jimmie Lunceford (leader), June 6, 1902, Fulton, MO

Joe Smith (trumpet), June 28, 1902, Ripley, OH

Buster Bailey (clarinet), July 19, 1902, Memphis, TN

Cliff Jackson (piano), July 19, 1902, Culpepper, VA

Omer Simeon (clarinet), July 21, 1902, New Orleans, LA

Luis Russell (piano, arranger, leader), Aug. 6, 1902, Careening Cay, Panama

Garvin Bushell (clarinet, bassoon, oboe), Sept. 25, 1902, Springfield, OH

Jimmy Archey (trombone), Oct. 12, 1902, Norfolk, VA

Eddie Lang (guitar), Oct. 25, 1902, Philadelphia, PA

Julia Lee (vocals, piano), Oct. 31, 1902 Booneville, MO

Arthur Schutt (piano), Nov. 21, 1902, Reading, PA

Paul Lingle (piano), Dec. 3, 1902, Denver, CO

Bubber Miley (trumpet), Jan. 19, 1903, Aiken, SC

Bix Beiderbecke (cornet), Mar. 10, 1903, Davenport, IA

Bing Crosby (vocals), May 3, 1903, Tacoma, WA

Emmett Hardy (cornet), June 12, 1903, New Orleans, LA

Ben Pollack (drums, leader), June 22, 1903, Chicago, IL

Claude Hopkins (piano), Aug. 24, 1903, Alexandria, VA

Jimmy Rushing (vocals), Aug. 26, 1903, Oklahoma City, OK

Joe Venuti (violin), Sept. 16, 1903, Philadelphia, PA

Earl Hines (piano, composer, leader), Dec. 28, 1903, Duquesne, PA

Donald Lambert (piano), 1904, Princeton, NJ

Tricky Sam Nanton (trombone), Feb. 1, 1904, New York, NY

Wingy Manone (trumpet, vocals), Feb. 13, 1904, New Orleans, LA

De De Pierce (trumpet, vocals), Feb. 18, 1904, New Orleans, LA

Jimmy Dorsey (alto, clarinet, leader), Feb. 29, 1904, Shenandoah, PA

Glenn Miller (leader, arranger, trombone), Mar. 1, 1904, Clarinda, IA

Pete Johnson (piano), Mar. 25, 1904, Kansas City, MO

Fats Waller (piano, vocals, composer, organ), May 21, 1904, New York, NY

Otto Hardwicke (alto, C-melody), May 31, 1904, Washington, D.C.

Raymond Burke (clarinet), June 6, 1904, New Orleans, LA

Don Murray (clarinet, tenor), June 7, 1904, Joliet, IL

Pinetop Smith (piano, vocals), June 11, 1904, Troy, AL

Adrian Rollini (bass sax, vibes), June 28, 1904, New York, NY

Bill Challis (arranger), July 8, 1904, Wilkes Barre, PA

Ikey Robinson (banjo, guitar, vocals), July 28, 1904, Dublin, VA

Dick McDonough (guitar), July 30, 1904, New York, NY

Bill Coleman (trumpet), Aug. 4, 1904, Centreville, KY

Jess Stacy (piano), Aug. 11, 1904, Bird's Point, MO

Count Basie (piano, leader), Aug. 21, 1904, Red Bank, NJ

Stump Evans (C-melody), Oct. 18, 1904, Lawrence, KS

Art Hodes (piano), Nov. 14, 1904, Nikoliev, Russia

Coleman Hawkins (tenor, leader), Nov. 21, 1904, St. Joseph, MO

Horace Henderson (arranger, piano), Nov. 22, 1904, Cuthbert, GA

Eddie South (violin), Nov. 27, 1904, Louisiana, MO

Jimmy Lytell (clarinet), Dec. 1, 1904, New York, NY

Arthur Whetsol (trumpet), 1905, Punta Gorda, FL

Percy Humphrey (trumpet), Jan. 13, 1905, New Orleans, LA

Louis Metcalf (trumpet), Feb. 28, 1905, Webster Groves, MO

Bertha "Chippie" Hill (vocals), Mar. 15, 1905, Charleston, SC

Bernard Addison (guitar), Apr. 15, 1905, Annapolis, MD

Tommy Benford (drums), Apr. 19, 1905, Charleston, WV

Red Nichols (cornet, arranger, leader), May 8, 1905, Ogden, UT

Sidney DeParis (trumpet), May 30, 1905, Crawfordsville, IN

Doc Cheatham (trumpet), June 13, 1905, Nashville, TN

Teddy Grace (vocals), June 26, 1905, Arcadia, LA

Ivie Anderson (vocals), July 10, 1905, Gilroy, CA

Jack Teagarden (trombone, vocals, leader), Aug. 29, 1905, Vernon, TX

Meade Lux Lewis (piano), Sept. 4, 1905, Chicago, IL

Reuben Reeves (trumpet), Oct. 25, 1905, Evansville, IN

Eddie Condon (leader, guitar), Nov. 16, 1905, Goodland, IN

Tommy Dorsey (trombone, leader), Nov. 19, 1905, Shenandoah, PA

Wayman Carver (flute), Dec. 25, 1905, Portsmouth, VA

Frankie Newton (trumpet), Jan. 4, 1906, Emory, VA

Wild Bill Davison (cornet), Jan. 5, 1906, Defiance, OH

Bobby Stark (trumpet), Jan. 6, 1906, New York, NY

Barney Bigard (clarinet), Mar. 3, 1906, New Orleans, LA

Frank Teschemacher (clarinet, alto), Mar. 14, 1906, Kansas City, MO

Pee Wee Russell (clarinet), Mar. 27, 1906, St. Louis, MO

VOICES OF THE FUTURE

Bud Freeman (tenor), Apr. 13, 1906, Chicago, IL

Alex Hill (piano, arranger), Apr. 19, 1906, North Little Rock, AR

Ward Pinkett (trumpet), Apr. 29, 1906, Newport News, VA

J.C. Higginbotham (trombone), May 11, 1906, Social Circle, GA

Johnny Hodges (alto), July 25, 1906, Cambridge, MA

Vic Dickenson (trombone), Aug. 6, 1906, Xenia, OH

Eddie Durham (guitar, trombone, arranger), Aug. 19, 1906, San Marcos, TX

Freddy Jenkins (trumpet), Oct. 10, 1906, New York, NY

Victoria Spivey (vocals), Oct. 15, 1906, Houston, TX

Cozy Cole (drums), Oct. 17, 1906, East Orange, NJ

Joe Sullivan (piano), Nov. 5, 1906, Chicago, IL

Muggsy Spanier (cornet), Nov. 9, 1906, Chicago, IL

Pete Brown (alto), Nov. 9, 1906, Baltimore, MD

Joe Marsala (clarinet), Jan. 4, 1907, Chicago, IL

Benny Morton (trombone), Jan. 31, 1907, New York, NY

Rex Stewart (cornet), Feb. 22, 1907, Philadelphia, PA

Mildred Bailey (vocals), Feb. 27, 1907, Tekoa, WA

Jimmy McPartland (cornet), Mar. 15, 1907, Chicago, IL

Caspar Reardon (harp), Apr. 15, 1907, Little Falls, NY

Billie Pierce (piano, vocals), June 8, 1907 Marianna, FL

Gene Sedric (tenor, clarinet), June 17, 1907, St. Louis, MO

Doc Evans (cornet), June 20, 1907, Spring Valley, MN

Jimmy Mundy (arranger), June 28, 1907, Cincinnati, OH

Albert Wynn (trombone), July 29, 1907, New Orleans, LA

Lawrence Brown (trombone), Aug. 3, 1907, Lawrence, KS

Benny Carter (alto, arranger, trumpet), Aug. 8, 1907, New York, NY

Edgar Sampson (composer, arranger, alto), Aug. 31, 1907, New York, NY

Albert Ammons (piano), Sept. 23, 1907, Chicago, IL

Carl Kress (guitar), Oct. 20, 1907, Newark, NJ

Joe Turner (piano), Nov. 4, 1907, Baltimore, MD

George Wettling (drums), Nov. 28, 1907, Topeka, KS

Connie Boswell (vocals), Dec. 3, 1907, New Orleans, LA

Cab Calloway (vocals), Dec. 25, 1907, Rochester, NY

Martha Boswell (vocals, piano), 1908, New Orleans, LA

Henry "Red" Allen (trumpet), Jan. 7, 1908, Algiers, LA

Stephane Grappelli (violin), Jan. 26, 1908, Paris, France

Hot Lips Page (trumpet, vocals), Jan. 27, 1908, Dallas, TX

Claude Williams (violin, guitar), Feb. 22, 1908, Muskogee, OK

Nat Gonella (trumpet, vocals), Mar. 7, 1908, London, England

Lionel Hampton (vibes), Apr. 20, 1908, Birmingham, AL

Dave Tough (drums), Apr. 26, 1908, Oak Park, IL

Red Norvo (vibes, xylophone, leader), May 31, 1908, Beardstown, IL

Louis Jordan (vocals, alto, leader), July 8, 1908, Brinkley, AR

Russell Procope (alto, clarinet), Aug. 11, 1908, New York, NY

Willie Bryant (bandleader, vocals), Aug. 30, 1908, New Orleans, LA

Max Kaminsky (cornet), Sept. 7, 1908, Brockton, MA

Kid Sheik Colar (trumpet), Sept. 15, 1908, New Orleans, LA

Sammy Price (piano), Oct. 6, 1908, Honey Grove, TX

Herman Chittison (piano), Oct. 15, 1908, Flemingsburg, KY

Spike Hughes (bass, composer), Oct. 18, 1908, London, England

Bunny Berigan (trumpet), Nov. 2, 1908, Hilbert, WI

Clancy Hayes (banjo, vocals), Nov. 14, 1908, Caney, KS

Jabbo Smith (trumpet, vocals), Dec. 24, 1908, Pembroke, GA

John Kirby (bass, leader), Dec. 31, 1908, Baltimore, MD

Teddy Bunn (guitar), 1909, Freeport, NY

Helvetia Boswell (vocals), 1909, New Orleans, LA

Herschel Evans (tenor), 1909, Denton, TX

Tab Smith (alto), Jan. 11, 1909, Kingston, NC

Danny Barker (guitar, banjo), Jan. 13, 1909, New Orleans, LA

Quentin Jackson (trombone), Jan. 13, 1909, Springfield, OH

Gene Krupa (drums, leader), Jan. 15, 1909, Chicago, IL

Oscar Aleman (guitar), Feb. 20, 1909, Restencia, Argentina

Ben Webster (tenor), Feb. 27, 1909, Kansas City, MO

Marty Marsala (trumpet), Apr. 2, 1909, Chicago, IL

Matty Matlock (clarinet, arranger), Apr. 27, 1909, Paducah, KY

Benny Goodman (clarinet, leader), May 30, 1909, Chicago, IL

Dickie Wells (trombone), June 10, 1909, Centerville, TN

Garland Wilson (piano), June 13, 1909, Martinsburg, WV

Ray Bauduc (drums), June 18, 1909, New Orleans, LA

Joe Thomas (tenor), June 19, 1909, Uniontown, PA

Teddy Buckner (trumpet), July 16, 1909, Sherman, TX

Joe Thomas (trumpet), July 24, 1909, Webster, Groves, MO

Claude Thornhill (piano, composer, leader), Aug. 10, 1909, Terre Haute, IN

VOICES OF THE FUTURE

Stuff Smith (violin, vocals, leader), Aug. 14, 1909, Portsmouth, OH

Art Tatum (piano), Oct. 13, 1909, Toledo, OH

Johnny Mercer (composer, vocals), Nov. 18, 1909, Savannah, GA

Teddy Hill (leader, tenor), Dec. 7, 1909, Birmingham, AL

Jonah Jones (trumpet, vocals), Dec. 31, 1909, Louisville, KY

Clyde Hart (piano) 1910, Baltimore, MD

Big Sid Catlett (drums), Jan. 17, 1910, Evansville, IN

Django Reinhardt (guitar, composer), Jan. 23, 1910, Liverchies, Belgium

Al Sears (tenor), Feb. 21, 1910, Macomb, IL

Harry Carney (baritone), Apr. 1, 1910, Boston, MA

Mary Lou Williams (piano, arranger), May 8, 1910, Atlanta, GA

Jack Jenney (trombone), May 12, 1910, Mason City, IA

Artie Shaw (clarinet, leader), May 23, 1910, New York, NY

Ray McKinley (drums, vocals, leader), June 18, 1910, Fort Worth, TX

Milt Hinton (bass), June 23, 1910, Vicksburg, MS

Shad Collins (trumpet), June 27, 1910, Elizabeth, NJ

Cootie Williams (trumpet), July 24, 1910, Mobile, AL

Raymond Scott (composer, arranger, leader, piano), Sept. 10, 1910, New York, NY

Chu Berry (tenor), Sept. 13, 1910, Wheeling, WV

Annette Hanshaw (vocals), Oct. 18, 1910, New York, NY

Willie Smith (alto), Nov. 25, 1910, Charleston, SC

Armand Hug (piano), Dec. 6, 1910, New Orleans, LA

Budd Johnson (tenor, soprano, arranger), Dec. 14, 1910, Dallas, TX

John Hammond (producer), Dec. 15, 1910, New York, NY

Sy Oliver (arranger, trumpet, vocals), Dec. 17, 1910, Battle Creek, MI

Roy Eldridge (trumpet), Jan. 30, 1911, Pittsburgh, PA

Freddie Green (guitar), Mar. 31, 1911, Charleston, SC

Mario Bauza (arranger, trumpet), Apr. 28, 1911, Havana, Cuba

Yank Lawson (trumpet), May 3, 1911, Trenton, MO

Pete Daily (cornet), May 5, 1911, Portland, IN

Maxine Sullivan (vocals), May 13, 1911, Homestead, PA

Big Joe Turner (vocals), May 18, 1911, Kansas City, MO

Eddie Miller (tenor, clarinet), June 23, 1911, New Orleans, LA

Jo Jones (drums), July 10, 1911, Chicago, IL

Herb Jeffries (vocals), Sept. 24, 1911, Detroit, MI

Johnny Richards (arranger, composer), Nov. 2, 1911, Queretaro State, Mexico

Dick Wilson (tenor), Nov. 11, 1911, Mt. Vernon, IL

Buck Clayton (trumpet), Nov. 12, 1911, Parsons, KS

Ernie Caceres (baritone, clarinet), Nov. 22, 1911, Rockport, TX

Louis Prima (trumpet, vocals), Dec. 7, 1911, New Orleans, LA

Stan Kenton (leader, piano, arranger, composer), Dec. 15, 1911, Wichita, KS

Lu Watters (trumpet, leader), Dec. 19, 1911, Santa Cruz, CA

Cutty Cutshall (trombone), Dec. 29, 1911, Huntington County, PA

Trummy Young (trombone, vocals), Jan. 12, 1912, Savannah, GA

Bob Zurke (piano), Jan. 17, 1912, Detroit, MI

Paul Bascomb (tenor), Feb. 12, 1912, Birmingham, AL

Machito (leader, vocals, percussion), Feb. 16, 1912, Tampa, FL

Les Brown (leader), Mar. 14, 1912, Reinerton, PA

Gil Evans (arranger, composer, leader), May 13, 1912, Toronto, Ontario, Canada

Alix Combelle (tenor, clarinet), June 15, 1912, Paris, France

Jerry Jerome (tenor), June 19, 1912, Brooklyn, NY

Will Bradley (trombone, leader), July 12, 1912, Newton, NJ

Alvin Alcorn (trumpet), Sept. 7, 1912, New Orleans, LA

Don Byas (tenor), Oct. 21, 1912, Muskogee, OK

Franz Jackson (tenor, clarinet), Nov. 1, 1912, Rock Island, IL

Tyree Glenn (trombone, vibes), Nov. 23, 1912, Corsicana, TX

Teddy Wilson (piano), Nov. 24, 1912, Austin, TX

Marshall Royal (alto), Dec. 5, 1912, Sapulpa, OK

Irving Fazola (clarinet), Dec. 10, 1912, New Orleans, LA

Adele Girard (harp), 1913, unknown location

Barrett Deems (drums), Mar. 1, 1913, Springfield, IL

Earl Bostic (alto), Apr. 25, 1913, Tulsa, OK

Woody Herman (leader, clarinet, alto, soprano, vocals), May 16, 1913, Milwaukee, WI

Pee Wee Erwin (trumpet), May 30, 1913, Falls City, NE

Helen Humes (vocals), June 23, 1913, Louisville, KY

George Van Eps (guitar), Aug. 7, 1913, Plainfield, NJ

Bob Crosby (leader, vocals), Aug. 23, 1913, Spokane, WA

Charlie Teagarden (trumpet), Sept. 9, 1913, Vernon, TX

John Collins (guitar), Sept. 20, 1913, Montgomery, AL

Wally Rose (piano), Oct. 2, 1913, Oakland, CA

VOICES OF THE FUTURE

Charlie Barnet (tenor, leader), Oct. 26, 1913, New York, NY

Boyd Raeburn (leader), Oct. 27, 1913, Faith, SD

Blue Lu Barker (vocals), Nov. 13, 1913, New Orleans, LA

Ray Nance (cornet, violin, vocals), Dec. 10, 1913, Chicago, IL

Kenny Clarke (drums), Jan. 2, 1914, Pittsburgh, PA

Bob Haggart (bass, composer, arranger), Mar. 13, 1914, New York, NY

Sun Ra (keyboards, leader), May 22, 1914, Birmingham, AL

Shorty Baker (trumpet), May 26, 1914, St. Louis, MO

Ziggy Elman (trumpet), May 26, 1914, Philadelphia, PA

Billy Eckstine (vocals, leader), July 8, 1914, Pittsburgh, PA

Billy Kyle (piano), July 14, 1914, Philadelphia, PA

Erskine Hawkins (trumpet, leader), July 26, 1914, Birmingham, AL

Graeme Bell (piano, leader), Sept. 7, 1914, Melbourne, Australia

Leonard Feather (journalist, composer), Sept. 13, 1914, London, England

Slam Stewart (bass), Sept. 21, 1914, Englewood, NJ

Eddie Sauter (arranger, composer), Dec. 2, 1914, Brooklyn, NY

Chano Pozo (percussion), Jan. 7, 1915, Havana, Cuba

Bobby Hackett (cornet), Jan. 31, 1915, Providence, RI

Taft Jordan (trumpet), Feb. 15, 1915, Florence, SC

Buddy Tate (tenor), Feb. 22, 1915, Sherman, TX

Lee Castle (trumpet), Feb. 28, 1915, New York, NY

Flip Phillips (tenor, bass clarinet), Mar. 26, 1915, Brooklyn, NY

George Chisholm (trombone), Mar. 29, 1915, Glasgow, Scotland

Billie Holiday (vocals), Apr. 7, 1915, Baltimore, MD

Les Paul (guitar), June 9, 1915, Waukesha, WI

Milt Buckner (organ, piano), July 10, 1915, St. Louis, MO

Wynonie Harris (vocals), Aug. 24, 1915, Omaha, NE

Al Casey (guitar), Sept. 15, 1915, Louisville, KY

Lee Wiley (vocals), Oct. 9, 1915, Fort Gibson, OK

Harry "Sweets" Edison (trumpet), Oct. 10, 1915, Columbus, OH

Billy Bauer (guitar), Nov. 14, 1915, New York, NY

Billy Strayhorn (composer, arranger, piano), Nov. 29, 1915, Dayton, OH

Eddie Heywood (piano), Dec. 4, 1915, Atlanta, GA

Frank Sinatra (vocals), Dec. 12, 1915, Hoboken, NJ

Turk Murphy (trombone, leader), Dec. 16, 1915, Palermo, CA

Pete Rugolo (arranger, composer), Dec. 25, 1915, San Piero, Sicily

Slim Gaillard (guitar, vocals), Jan. 1, 1916, Santa Clara, Cuba

Jay McShann (piano, vocals), Jan. 12, 1916, Muskogee, OK

Bill Doggett (organ, piano), Feb. 6, 1916, Philadelphia, PA

Svend Asmussen (violin), Feb. 28, 1916, Copenhagen, Denmark

Red Callender (bass, tuba), Mar. 6, 1916, Haynesville, VA

Harry James (trumpet, leader), Mar. 15, 1916, Albany, GA

Ken Kersey (piano), Apr. 3, 1916, Harrow, Ontario, Canada

Burt Bales (piano), Apr. 20, 1916, Stevensville, MO

Dud Bascomb (trumpet), May 16, 1916, Birmingham, AL

Paul Quinichette (tenor), May 17, 1916, Denver, CO

Tiny Grimes (guitar), July 7, 1916, Newport News, VA

Dick Cary (piano, trumpet, alto horn), July 10, 1916, Hartford, CT

Cat Anderson (trumpet), Sept. 12, 1916, Greenville, SC

Al Killian (trumpet), Oct. 15, 1916, Birmingham, AL

Bill Harris (trombone), Oct. 28, 1916, Philadelphia, PA

Joe Bushkin (piano), Nov. 7, 1916, New York, NY

Billy May (arranger, composer), Nov. 10, 1916, Pittsburgh, PA

Don Ewell (piano), Nov. 14, 1916, Baltimore, MD

Charlie Ventura (tenor, baritone, leader), Dec. 2, 1916, Philadelphia, PA

Bob Scobey (trumpet), Dec 9, 1916, Tucumcari, NM

Oscar Moore (guitar), Dec. 25, 1916, Austin, TX

Johnny Frigo (violin, bass), Dec. 27, 1916, Chicago, IL

Freddie Webster (trumpet), 1917, Cleveland, OH

Billy Butterfield (trumpet), Jan. 14, 1917, Middletown, OH

Fred Beckett (trombone), Jan. 23, 1917, Nellerton, MS

Tadd Dameron (composer, piano, leader), Feb. 21, 1917, Cleveland, OH

Nat King Cole (piano, vocals), Mar. 17, 1917, Montgomery, AL

Johnny Guarnieri (piano), Mar. 23, 1917, New York, NY

Ella Fitzgerald (vocals), Apr. 25, 1917, Newport News, VA

Denzil Best (drums), Apr. 27, 1917, New York, NY

Jimmy Hamilton (clarinet, tenor), May 25, 1917, Dillon, SC

Dave Lambert (vocals, arranger), June 19, 1917, Boston, MA

Lena Horne (vocals), June 30, 1917, Brooklyn, NY

VOICES OF THE FUTURE

Lou McGarity (trombone), July 22, 1917, Athens, GA

Charlie Shavers (trumpet), Aug. 3, 1917, New York, NY

Laurindo Almeida (guitar), Sept. 2, 1917, Sao Paulo, Brazil

Buddy Rich (drums, leader), Sept. 30, 1917, Brooklyn, NY

J.C. Heard (drums), Oct. 8, 1917, Dayton, OH

Thelonious Monk (piano, composer, leader), Oct. 10, 1917, Rocky Mount, NC

Dizzy Gillespie (trumpet, leader, composer), Oct. 21, 1917, Cheraw, SC

Howard Rumsey (bass, leader), Nov. 7, 1917, Brawley, CA

Eddie "Cleanhead" Vinson (vocals, alto), Dec. 18, 1917, Houston, TX

Betty Roche (vocals), Jan. 9, 1918, Washington, DE

Howard McGhee (trumpet), Mar. 6, 1918, Tulsa, OK

Marian McPartland (piano), Mar. 20, 1918, Slough, England

Sir Charles Thompson (piano, organ), Mar. 21, 1918, Springfield, OH

Peanuts Hucko (clarinet), Apr. 7, 1918, Syracuse, NY

Hank Jones (piano), July 31, 1918, Vicksburg, MI

Eddie Jefferson (vocals, composer), Aug. 3, 1918, Pittsburgh, PA

Arnett Cobb (tenor), Aug. 10, 1918, Houston, TX

Ike Quebec (tenor), Aug. 17, 1918, Newark, NJ

Jimmy Rowles (piano), Aug. 19, 1918, Spokane, WA

Gerald Wilson (arranger, composer, leader, trumpet), Sept. 4, 1918, Shelby, MS

Cachao (Israel Lopez) (bass), Sept. 14, 1918, Havana, Cuba

Jimmy Blanton (bass), Oct. 5, 1918, Chattanooga, TN

Bebo Valdes (piano), Oct. 9, 1918, Quivican, Cuba

Bobby Troup (composer, vocals, piano), Oct. 18, 1918, Harrisburg, PA

Chubby Jackson (bass), Oct. 25, 1918, New York, NY

Claire Austin (vocals), Nov. 21, 1918, Yakima, WA

Wild Bill Davis (organ), Nov. 24, 1918, Glasgow, MO

Joe Williams (vocals), Dec. 12, 1918, Cordele, GA

Panama Francis (drums), Dec. 21, 1918, Miami, FL

Eddie Safranski (bass), Dec. 25, 1918, Pittsburgh, PA

Jimmy Jones (piano), Dec. 30, 1918, Memphis, TN

Al McKibbon (bass), Jan. 1, 1919, Chicago, IL

Herbie Nichols (piano, composer), Jan. 3, 1919, New York, NY

Israel Crosby (bass), Jan. 19, 1919, Chicago, IL

Snooky Young (trumpet), Feb. 3, 1919, Dayton, OH

Fred Katz (cello), Feb. 25, 1919, New York, NY

Mercer Ellington (composer), Mar. 11, 1919, Washington, D.C.

Lennie Tristano (piano, composer), Mar. 19, 1919, Chicago, IL

Benny Harris (trumpet), Apr. 23, 1919, New York, NY

Georgie Auld (tenor), May 19, 1919, Toronto, Canada

Al Viola (guitar), June 16, 1919, Brooklyn, NY

Ernie Wilkins (arranger, composer, tenor), July 20, 1919, St. Louis, MO

George Shearing (piano, leader), Aug. 13, 1919, London, England

Hal Singer (tenor), Oct. 8, 1919, Tulsa, OK

Art Blakey (drums, leader), Oct. 11, 1919, Pittsburgh, PA

Anita O'Day (vocals), Oct. 18, 1919, Chicago, IL

Babs Gonzales (vocals), Oct. 27, 1919, Newark NJ

Joe "Bebop" Carroll (vocals), Nov. 25, 1919, Philadelphia, PA

Jimmy Forrest (tenor), Jan. 24, 1920, St. Louis, MO

Abe Most (clarinet), Feb. 27, 1920, New York, NY

John La Porta (clarinet), Apr. 1, 1920, Philadelphia, PA

Carmen McRae (vocals), Apr. 8, 1920, New York, NY

Gil Fuller (arranger), Apr. 14, 1920, Los Angeles, CA

John Lewis (piano, composer, leader), May 3, 1920, La Grange, IL

Peggy Lee (vocals), May 26, 1920, Jamestown, ND

Britt Woodman (trombone), June 4, 1920, Los Angeles, CA

Shelly Manne (drums, leader), June 11, 1920, New York, NY

Thomas Jefferson (trumpet, vocals), June 20, 1920, Chicago, IL

Herbie Harper (trombone), July 2, 1920, Salina, KS

Paul Gonsalves (tenor), July 12, 1920, Boston, MA

Harry Arnold (leader), Aug. 7, 1920, Halsingborg, Sweden

Charlie Parker (alto, composer, leader), Aug. 29, 1920, Kansas City, KS

Yusef Lateef (tenor, flute, oboe, leader), Oct. 9, 1920, Chattanooga, TN

Jerome Richardson (tenor, flute, soprano, alto), Nov. 15, 1920, Sealy, TX

Dave Brubeck (piano), Dec. 6, 1920, Concord, CA

Clark Terry (flugelhorn, vocals, trumpet), Dec. 14, 1920, St. Louis, MO

Irving Ashby (guitar), Dec. 29, 1920, Sommerville, MA

PASSINGS

Scott Joplin (48), Apr. 11, 1917, New York, NY

Henry Ragas (27), Feb. 18, 1919, New York, NY

James Reese Europe (38), May 10, 1919, Boston, MA

Chapter Two

1921–1925:
Jazz Sweeps the Nation

Jazz's evolution began to speed up drastically as soon as recordings became common and made it possible for music to spread around the globe. In fact, jazz changed more during the five years covered in this chapter than it had in the previous ten or even twenty years. Musicians who sounded fresh, new, and novel in 1920 were considered stale and old hat by 1926 unless they continually modernized their styles. While the Original Dixieland Jazz Band and Mamie Smith were big news in the music world in 1920, by 1926 the ODJB was considered a relic of the past while Smith was thought of as old-fashioned. Such new names as Louis Armstrong, Bessie Smith, and James P. Johnson had taken their place and were now leading the way.

Having become a world power during the Great War, the United States was turning inward during the early 1920s, doing its best to ignore the rest of the world. Prosperous and at peace, the United States was gradually loosening its morals from the strictures of the Victorian era that had dominated since the 1890s. Although quite conservative compared to today's lifestyles, its turn to the left on a social basis was a cause for alarm by the overly religious. There was a backlash with conservative Republicans in the White House (Warren G. Harding until his mysterious death in 1923, followed by the straitlaced Calvin Coolidge), bigotry on the rise (the Ku Klux Klan was at the height of its popularity in the mid-1920s), and liquor remaining illegal, but the average citizen was optimistic about the future. Since it was believed that there would be no more major wars after "the war to end all wars," many Americans concentrated on building up their own businesses, making money (often through the booming stock market), and having a good time. The latter often included dancing to the hot music called jazz and trying out a new dance step called the Charleston.

When alcohol was outlawed in 1919, organized crime stepped in to fill the void. By the early 1920s, liquor flowed freely in speakeasies; illegal bars, nightclubs, and gambling establishments served the "needs" of thirsty citizens. Although the bootleg booze varied greatly in quality and was often overpriced, speakeasies proliferated and, for entertainment, the gangsters often hired hot jazz combos.

Jazz musicians also played in theaters and as backup or novelty groups in vaudeville, but their main purpose as far as the general public was concerned was to inspire dancers. Jazz, even as it started to proliferate and influence the popular music of the time, was considered primarily a stimulating form of entertainment. There was very little talk this early on of the music actually being an important art form, no serious writing about it appeared in print (other than reporting the comings and goings of musicians in a showbiz fashion), and only the most fanatical nonmusicians thought that the music would last more than a few more years.

The Pacesetters: 1921–1925

The typical dance orchestra on records in 1921 was touched by jazz but retained its ties to the military band and vaudeville traditions. Instruments were often treated as novelties, with trumpets making "doo wacka doo" sounds, saxophonists taking "rooty-toot" breaks, trombonists emphasizing their humorous side with an excess of sliding percussive sounds, and the overall phrasing often being staccato rather than legato. "Getting hot" usually meant utilizing repetition and increasing the volume and tempo of the music, which although initially exciting, was pretty superficial. But by 1925 and the rise of Louis Armstrong, subtlety and the use of space for dramatic effect made jazz a much more mature music.

Before electrical recording was developed in 1925 and started becoming widespread the following year, everything was recorded acoustically. Musicians were positioned around a large horn, with the louder instruments being furthest away. The results were often quite tinny, without much fidelity. Records from the period give listeners an idea what musicians and singers sounded like but would never be mistaken for a live performance. Due to problems with getting a proper balance, drummers were not able to use their full drum set (no bass drums at all), banjos were preferred over the nearly inaudible guitar, and bass instruments were considered optional at best. Some record companies had creative sound engineers, while others such as Paramount became infamous for their noisy sound quality. This is why, for today's listeners, jazz on record before 1926 is often difficult to enjoy. One has to listen very hard (it is advisable to turn up the volume) in order to really hear what was going on in the acoustic jazz recordings of the early 1920s.

It is not completely fair to judge the jazz scene of 1921 by the recordings of the year because so many major talents who were active in Chicago and New Orleans were not appearing on records yet. But the recordings of 1921–22 give listeners a hint of what the jazz world sounded like, and the documented performances of 1923–25 make it apparent that things were changing quickly.

During this period, many small groups used the instrumentation of cornet/trumpet, trombone, clarinet, possibly a second reed (usually an alto), piano, banjo,

TIMELINE 1921

King Oliver's Creole Jazz Band plays in San Francisco and Los Angeles. • Eubie Blake and Noble Sissle write and produce the music for *Shuffle Along*, the first all-black musical on Broadway. • J. Russell Robinson leaves the ODJB and is replaced by Frank Signorelli; the band just records five titles this year. • The Friar's Society Orchestra (soon renamed the New Orleans Rhythm Kings) is formed. • The California Ramblers make their first records. They would cut 618 titles (not counting alternate takes) by the end of 1931, making it the most prolific jazz-oriented band of the era. • Zez Confrey's "Kitten on the Keys" is a novelty ragtime hit. • Lucille Hegamin, the second of the classic blues singers to record, has best-selling records in "I'll Be Good but I'll Be Lonesome" and "Arkansas Blues." • Trixie Smith wins a blues contest sponsored by Black Swan Records and soon begins her recording career. • Also making their recording debuts in 1921 are Alberta Hunter, James P. Johnson, Fletcher Henderson, Ethel Waters, and Clarence Williams (who weds singer Eva Taylor, beginning a 44-year marriage). • Sidney Bechet is deported from England. • Coleman Hawkins joins Mamie Smith's Jazz Hounds for a two-year stay. • Fletcher Henderson tours with Ethel Waters. • Jack Hylton begins leading his dance band in England. • Jimmy and Tommy Dorsey play with Billy Lustig's Scranton Sirens. • Jack Teagarden works in Texas with Peck Kelley. • At the age of 12, Benny Goodman wins an amateur contest by imitating Ted Lewis. • Glenn Miller plays with Boyd Senter. • At age 14, Benny Carter buys a trumpet, but when he is unable to master it in a couple of hours, he trades it in for a C-melody sax.

and drums. Bigger bands might add a second or third trumpet, a second trombone, a third reed, and tuba.

In New Orleans, the top cornetist was usually given the title of "King," including Buddy Bolden, Freddie Keppard, Joe "King" Oliver, and Louis Armstrong. As jazz began to be recorded, cornetists and trumpeters (most cornetists in time switched to the nearly identical-sounding trumpet) were usually the lead voices in ensembles. Johnny Dunn, considered to be one of the top trumpeters in New York prior to Louis Armstrong's arrival in 1924, serves as a good example of what many trumpeters/cornetists sounded like in the early 1920s, sticking close to the melody except for occasional bluish notes, and rarely constructing a complete statement that did not include some novelty effects. While that was the dominant trend prior to 1923, the better trumpeters of the time, such as Nick LaRocca of the ODJB, Phil Napoleon, Frank Guarente, and Paul Mares, were capable of swinging melodies and leaving space in the ensembles for the other horns while using legato phrasing. Although initially an ensemble-oriented player, King Oliver in 1923 displayed an expertise with mutes and the ability to take a forceful solo. Bix Beiderbecke emerged on records in 1924 with the Wolverines, creating a beautiful tone and a relaxed lyrical style of his own that sounds much more modern than most of his contemporaries. But it was Louis Armstrong, with the Fletcher Henderson Orchestra during 1924–25, on classic sides with Clarence Williams's combos, and in his first Hot Five session, who showed what a dramatic instrument the cornet/trumpet really could be, influencing everyone that followed.

The trombone was used in New Orleans mostly as a harmony instrument that played percussive lines behind a cornetist; Kid Ory's approach was definitive. Overlooking the novelty players who used the trombone as a prop for comedy, Ory, George Brunies, Charlie Green (a skillful blues player), Charlie Irvis (a pioneer in using the plunger mute), and the up-and-coming Joe "Tricky Sam" Nanton were among the top players, with Miff Mole displaying more technique and adventurous ideas than the others.

In New Orleans, clarinetists created countermelodies behind the cornetist, having the most liberated role of the three main frontline instruments. In the early 1920s, there were two basic types of clarinet players. A "gaspipe" school that was inspired by Larry Shields's animal sounds

on the ODJB's hit record of "Livery Stable Blues" featured odd tonal distortions and a wide variety of silly and tasteless sounds, best exemplified by such vaudeville-oriented clarinetists as Ted Lewis (who was very popular in the 1920s despite his inability to play all that well), Wilbur Sweatman (said to be able to play three clarinets at once although unfortunately never on record), Boyd Senter, Fess Williams, and Wilton Crawley (a master at laughing through his horn). In contrast were the major jazz clarinetists Sidney Bechet (who would shift his main emphasis to soprano sax), Johnny Dodds, Leon Roppolo, the virtuosic Buster Bailey, and the cooler sounds of Jimmie Noone and Jimmy Lytell. Their solos were as advanced as anything documented in jazz during the time.

The saxophone was an insignificant instrument in jazz before 1920 and was still considered fairly minor in 1925 except in big bands. The first major tenor saxophonist was Coleman Hawkins, who rose to prominence with the Fletcher Henderson Orchestra starting in 1923. Hawk's early playing employed dated effects (such as slap tonguing) and his phrasing was rhythmically awkward even if he was from the start a master at understanding chords. Louis Armstrong's period with Henderson had a major effect on Hawkins, and by the time Armstrong departed in mid-1925, the young tenor was on the verge of becoming an important jazz improviser himself.

The alto sax was used as a sweetener on jazz dates starting with Benny Krueger with the ODJB in 1920–21. No major solo voices on alto emerged before 1926, but it was an important instrument in the ensemble of big bands. There were also no significant baritone saxophonists during the 1921–25 era, but three major players emerged on other saxophones. The C-melody sax (voiced between the tenor and the alto) was mastered by Frankie Trumbauer, who popped up on records by Gene Rodemich, the Mound City Blue Blowers, and the Benson Orchestra of Chicago. The bass sax has never sounded more exciting than when played by Adrian Rollini, who rose to prominence with the California Ramblers and its subsidiary groups, and Sidney Bechet's brilliance on soprano was heard on records as early as 1923.

Of all the instruments, the piano had the largest number of impressive soloists during the first half of the 1920s. James P. Johnson's stride piano style (keeping time by "striding" with his left hand back and forth between bass notes and chords that were an octave or two higher) became very influential; he utilized the piano as a miniature orchestra. Johnson, his pal Willie "The Lion" Smith, and his protégé Thomas "Fats" Waller starred at nightly rent parties and cutting contests in Harlem. Jelly Roll Morton, who arrived in Chicago in 1923, recorded a stunning series of piano solos in his own individual style. Other up-and-coming pianists included Cliff Jackson, Claude Hopkins, Frank Signorelli, Arthur Schutt, Earl Hines, and Duke Ellington; the latter two made more of an impact a few years later.

While ragtime was considered extinct by 1920 with Scott Joplin dead and the other top ragtime composers (including James Scott and Joseph Lamb) permanently in obscurity, novelty ragtime was in vogue for a few years. Ragtime was mostly designed to be played at slow-to-medium tempos and in most cases its sheet music could be interpreted by part-time pianists, but novelty ragtime featured extremely complicated pieces that were impossible to play by anyone but virtuosos. The style, as with ragtime, was outside of jazz because no real improvisation took place, but since the word "jazz" itself was applied to all types of music in the 1920s, it was often grouped with the emerging new music. Novelty

ragtime caught on in 1921 with Zez Confrey's "Kitten on the Keys." Confrey was its main star and top composer; his other songs included "Stumbling," "Dizzy Fingers," and "Nickel in the Slot," a humorous piece that features the pianist imitating a rather rapid nickelodeon. The highpoint for the novelty ragtime movement was when Confrey was given a feature spot at Paul Whiteman's Aeolian Hall concert on February 12, 1924, debuting his "Three Little Oddities." But within a few years, interest in that music had greatly lessened, and novelty ragtime largely faded away into history. Before that happened, some other pianists (including Arthur Schutt and Rube Bloom) wrote and recorded their own complex works, as did the remarkable banjoist Harry Reser.

The use of stride pianists with active, timekeeping left hands made most other rhythm instruments quite optional in small groups. Since the primitive recording equipment of the era made it difficult to hear a guitar, banjos were much more in demand due to their louder volume. Most banjoists simply played rhythmic chords, with the exception of Harry Reser, a brilliant soloist who extended the tradition of Fred Van Eps and Vess Ossman. Larger bands usually utilized a tuba for a strictly two-beat

25 ESSENTIAL RECORDS OF 1921–1925

The Original Memphis Five, **Vol. 1** (Collector's Classics 16)

New Orleans Rhythm Kings and Jelly Roll Morton, **New Orleans Rhythm Kings and Jelly Roll Morton** (Milestone 47020)

The Halfway House Orchestra, **Complete Recordings: Recorded in New Orleans, 1925–1928** (Jazz Oracle 8001)

New Orleans Owls, **The Owls' Hoot** (Frog 2)

Ethel Waters, **1925–1926** (Classics 672)

Alberta Hunter, **1924–1927** (Document 5424)

Bessie Smith, **The Complete Recordings, Vol. 1** (Columbia/Legacy 47091), 2 CDs

Bessie Smith, **The Complete Recordings, Vol. 2** (Columbia/Legacy 47471), 2 CDs

Ma Rainey, **Vol. 2** (Document 5582)

Ida Cox, **Vol. 2** (Document 5323)

King Oliver's Creole Jazz Band, **1923–1924** (Retrieval 79007), 2 CDs

Jelly Roll Morton, **Fred "Jelly Roll" Morton** (Retrieval 79002)

James P. Johnson, **Harlem Stride Piano** (Hot 'N' Sweet 151032)

Paul Whiteman, **Greatest Hits** (Collector's Choice 61)

Bix Beiderbecke, **Bix Restored, Vol. 1** (Sunbeam BXCD 1-3), 3 CDs

Louis Armstrong and Fletcher Henderson, **Louis with Fletcher Henderson 1924–1925** (Forte 38001/2/3), 3 CDs

Clarence Williams, **1921–1924** (Classics 679)

Clarence Williams, **1924–1926** (Classics 695)

Eva Taylor, **Vol. 2** (Document 5409)

The Georgians, **1922–23** (Retrieval 79003)

Isham Jones, **Isham Jones** (Timeless 067)

Various Artists, **New Orleans in the '20s** (Timeless 1-014)

Various Artists, **The Chicago Hot Bands 1924–1928** (Timeless 1-041)

Those Fabulous Gennetts, **Vol. 1 1923–1925** (Timeless 1-062)

Those Fabulous Gennetts, **Vol. 2 1922–1925** (Timeless 1-080)

accompaniment. String bassists (who, unlike tuba players, could play four beats to the bar without gasping for air) were not that common in jazz yet, but Steve Brown with the Jean Goldkette Orchestra and Bill Johnson with his own groups were exceptions. Listening to drummers of the era and trying to determine what they were playing can be frustrating, for drummers were not allowed to use their full drum set (particularly the bass drum) for fear that it would destroy the balance of the recordings. Drummers functioned primarily as quiet percussionists, hitting woodblocks, cowbells, and cymbals, with the washboard sometimes substituting for drums altogether. The top early drummers were Tony Sbarbaro (who later changed his name to Spargo) from the ODJB, Ben Pollack, and Baby Dodds.

The most listenable early jazz vocalists were the better female classic blues singers. The singing of Mamie Smith, Ethel Waters, Alberta Hunter, and particularly Bessie Smith were expressive and adaptable, and their most rewarding records still communicate well to today's listeners despite the recording quality. In contrast, few of the male singers are listenable. During that era, vocalists were prized most for their volume and ability to articulate words rather than for their tone, choice of notes, or ability to swing. Prior to Louis Armstrong's emergence in late 1925, nearly the only worthwhile male jazz singer on records was Cliff Edwards (known as Ukulele Ike), who was scatting and swinging in his own fashion as early as 1923.

Although today's listeners may have difficulty with the recording quality of records from the first half of the 1920s, there are many rewards to be found in studying this music closely. In many cases, it is analogous to hearing a story told for the first time, rather than being satisfied with a remake from a later period.

The End of the ODJB

As 1920 concluded, the Original Dixieland Jazz Band was the best known group in jazz and seemed to have a great deal of potential for the future. In addition to being the first jazz band to record, the ODJB had created sensations in Chicago, New York, and London, and in 1920 had a hit with their version of "Margie." And yet they were already in their declining years.

Two factors resulted in the ODJB's demise. The group never modernized its style, sticking exclusively to ensembles even when soloists were beginning to make an impact on jazz. And Nick LaRocca's prickly personality started to rub the other musicians the wrong way, resulting in major defections.

J. Russell Robinson, an important composer who would later write "Portrait of Jenny," was the first to depart, after cutting six recordings with the band during December 1920 to January 1921. Frank Signorelli took his place. The ODJB recorded four songs during May and June of 1921, including "Jazz Me Blues" and "Royal Garden Blues," and in December returned to the studios to cut the humorous "Bow Wow Blues (My Mama Treats Me Like a Dog)," which has a guest "barking" over the breaks. Apparently those records did not sell well because it would be nearly a year before the ODJB recorded again. By then, Larry Shields had left (a major loss), replaced at first by the teenage Jimmy Lytell and for records by the obscure Artie Seaberg. With the forgotten Henry Vanicelli on piano and soprano saxophonist Don Parker added, the band (which still had LaRocca, Eddie Edwards, and Tony Sbarbaro) cut two numbers in November 1922 and a pair of remakes ("Tiger Rag" and "Livery Stable Blues") on April 20, 1923. However, the group sounded almost prehistoric compared to King Oliver's Creole Jazz Band and had clearly slipped behind the times.

The ODJB continued playing until January 1925 when Nick LaRocca had a mental breakdown and retired from music. By then, the group had been largely forgotten, overshadowed by more advanced and innovative players.

While the ODJB was largely finished after 1921, the two most widely recorded ensembles of the 1920s were making their debuts: the Original Memphis Five, New York–based musicians who never played in Memphis, and the California Ramblers, a band originally formed in Ohio that never visited California!

The Original Memphis Five   Trumpeter Phil Napoleon first formed the Memphis Five in 1917, inspired by the ODJB and naming his band after W.C. Handy's "Memphis Blues." The initial group did not record, but, after a period of freelancing, in July 1921 Napoleon recorded "Memphis Blues" and "St. Louis Blues" with Lanin's Southern Serenaders, following it up the next month with hit versions of "Shake It and Break It" and "Aunt Hagar's Children's Blues." That particular sextet teamed Napoleon with trombonist Moe Gappell, clarinetist Doc Behrendson, altoist Loring McMurray, drummer Jack Roth, and a pianist by the name of Jimmy Durante (a year before he became a full-time comedian). The same band recorded eight titles that year as Ladd's Black Aces, some of the finest music on record in 1921.

By the spring of 1922, Napoleon and a reformed Original Memphis Five started their very busy recording career, with trombonist Miff Mole (who was replaced later that year by Charles Panelli), clarinetist Jimmy Lytell, pianist Frank Signorelli, and drummer Jack Roth. The band recorded 111 titles during 1922–23 alone and 65 more songs during 1924–25, not counting selections cut under the names of the Ambassadors, Bailey's Lucky Seven, the Broadway Syncopators, the Cotton Pickers, Jazzbo's Carolina Serenaders, the Savannah Six, the Southland Six, and the Tennessee Ten, plus additional numbers as Ladd's Black Aces, under Sam Lanin's leadership, and as the backup group for singer Leona Williams.

Brass players in New York were generally technically skilled, but much less familiar with jazz than the undocumented Chicago musicians. Very unusual for a New York–based trumpeter of 1921–23, Napoleon played melodic lines with legato (rather than staccato) phrasing, avoiding novelty effects, and swinging melodies with subtlety and swing. Extremely few trumpeters were on his level during 1921–22. Jimmy Lytell proved to be perfect in the role of clarinetist with the Original Memphis Five. A professional musician since 1916 when he was just 11, Lytell was with the Original Indiana Five (1921) and the Original Dixieland Jazz Band (Larry Shields's replacement during 1922–24) in addition to recording an enormous number of selections with the Original Memphis Five (1922–26). A fluent clarinetist, Jimmy Lytell did not become that well known in the jazz world because he began to emphasize classical music by 1925 (becoming a member of the Capitol Theatre Orchestra) and spent years working as a studio musician.

The Original Memphis Five's large recorded legacy has not been completely reissued, but three CDs have some of the highlights. ○ **The Original Memphis Five, Vol. 1** (Collector's Classics 16) has all nine selections dating from 1922 by Jazzbo's Carolina Serenaders, two from the Southland Six, and a dozen tunes by the Original Memphis Five. **Columbia's 1923–1931** (Retrieval 79026) features the 21 selections made by the Original Memphis Five for Columbia-affiliated labels

during 1923–25 plus four numbers from the final OMF date in 1931. **1922/1931** (Jazz Archives 159542) contains a few duplicates from the other CDs, but serves as a fine overview, containing a dozen numbers from 1922–23, eight from 1924–28, and two of the selections from the 1931 session.

The Cotton Pickers' name was used by the members of the Original Memphis Five for their Brunswick recordings of 1922–26. There were 36 titles in all and 24 of their first 30 recordings are on **The Cotton Pickers** (Timeless 1-029). The music is melodic, danceable, and fairly strong jazz for the era, especially the titles from 1922–23, featuring Phil Napoleon or Roy Johnson on trumpet, Miff Mole or Charles Panelli on trombone, Bennie Krueger, Jimmy Lytell or Larry Abbott on clarinet, C-melody saxophonist Frankie Trumbauer and Frank Signorelli or Rube Bloom on piano. Although the Original Memphis Five was certainly an outgrowth of the ODJB, Napoleon's solid playing and the fresh material (which usually avoided the ODJB's hits in favor of jazz versions of recent pop songs) gave the group its own personality.

The California Ramblers   When it comes to pioneering big bands, the California Ramblers tend to be overlooked, but they actually predate most of the jazz-oriented orchestras except Paul Whiteman's. Formed in Ohio by banjoist Ray Kitchenman, the band relocated to New York by November 1921 when it made its recording debut. By the end of 1925, the Ramblers had recorded nearly 300 titles under its own name, and the number would accelerate through 1931 by which time it had topped 600, a remarkable total for the era. In addition, the ensemble recorded under the pseudonyms of the Golden Gate Orchestra and Ted Wallace's Orchestra, and made a countless number of small group sides as the Little Ramblers, the Vagabonds, the Goofus Five, the Five Birmingham Babies, Bailey's Dixie Dudes, the Kentucky Blowers, the University Six, and the Varsity Eight.

The California Ramblers and their small groups exemplified the carefree happy spirit of the 1920s era, featuring concise melodic solos, period vocals, and a high-quality repertoire. Although the band started out without famous names, by the spring of 1922, the great bass saxophonist Adrian Rollini, trumpeter Bill Moore, and altoist/clarinetist Bobby Davis were key players. In 1925, cornetist Red Nichols, trombonist Tommy Dorsey, and

Jimmy Dorsey (who doubled on alto and clarinet) spent time with the band (managed by Ed Kirkeby), which for a period was based at the Ramblers Inn near New York City. The California Ramblers, who were at their prime during 1924–27, always performed the type of music that the youth of the era loved to dance to.

The Varsity Eight (Timeless 1-062), just one of the many bands that used some of the personnel from the California Ramblers, recorded 62 songs during 1923–25, 22 in 1926–27, three in 1928, and nine in 1930. Twenty-four of the first 62 titles (plus one song from 1926) are on this "best of" CD, which gives a good example of how the group sounded. The main stars are Bill Moore, Bobby Davis, Red Nichols (on five numbers), and Adrian Rollini.

The New Orleans Rhythm Kings (NORK) and Related Bands

In 1922, the New Orleans Rhythm Kings became one of the first jazz groups to break away from the model of the ensemble-oriented Original Dixieland Jazz Band and feature major soloists. Ironically, this significant band actually lasted less than two years despite its key members all being good friends, but it made a very strong impact during its brief time together.

Cornetist Paul Mares, trombonist George Brunies, and clarinetist Leon Roppolo all grew up in New Orleans and were childhood buddies. Back in 1916, Mares and Roppolo had played together in Tom Brown's band on the riverboat *Capitol*. In 1919, Mares traveled up to Chicago to join drummer Gababy Stevens's group, of which Brunies became a member the following year. In August 1921, when Mares was asked to organize a band for singer Bee Palmer at Chicago's Friar's Inn, he hired Brunies and sent for Roppolo. A few weeks later when Palmer left, Mares became the leader of the Friar's Society Orchestra, which was soon renamed the New Orleans Rhythm Kings.

The New Orleans Rhythm Kings made its recording debut during August 29–30, 1922, when it had its first two of eight record sessions. An octet at the time (with Jack Pettis on C-melody sax, pianist/arranger Elmer Schoebel, banjoist Lou Black, bassist Steve Brown, and drummer Frank Snyder), the band sounded far ahead of its competitors. Mares's mellow phrases, which were much smoother than Nick LaRocca's, and use of mutes (influenced by the as yet unrecorded King Oliver) worked well with expert ensemble player Brunies and the brilliant Roppolo, who took one of the first notable recorded horn solos on "Tiger Rag." Two sessions from March 12–13, 1923, has the NORK as a stripped-down quintet (with pianist Mel Stitzel and drummer Ben Pollack); "Tin Roof Blues" is highlighted by a famous solo from Brunies. The NORK also introduced such future Dixieland standards as "Farewell Blues," "Bugle Call Blues" (later renamed "Bugle Call Rag"), "Panama," "That's a Plenty," and "Weary Blues."

TIMELINE 1922

The New Orleans Rhythm Kings make their first recordings. • Kid Ory's band (under the name of Spike's Seven Pods of Pepper Orchestra) records "Ory's Creole Trombone" and "Society Blues." • Duke Ellington visits New York for the first time, playing briefly with Wilbur Sweatman's Orchestra. • King Oliver's Creole Jazz Band returns to Chicago, uses the Lincoln Gardens as its home base and welcomes Louis Armstrong on second cornet. • Paul Whiteman records "Hot Lips," featuring Henry Busse. • Bessie Smith stars in the *How Come* revue. • Eva Taylor becomes a pioneer radio performer. • Eddie Condon plays banjo with Hollis Peavey's Jazz Bandits. • Jimmy Lytell replaces Larry Shields with the ODJB and also records prolifically with the Original Memphis Five. • Isham Jones's Orchestra features trumpeter Louis Panico. • The Coon-Sanders Novelty Orchestra (soon the Coon-Sanders Nighthawks) makes its first radio broadcast on December 5 on WOAF in Kansas City. • Don Redman moves to New York where he plays with Billy Paige's Broadway Syncopators. • Doc Cook begins a six-year period leading his band at Harmon's Dreamland Ballroom in Chicago. • Trumpeter Frank Guarente and the Georgians record some of the hottest jazz of the era. • Sara Martin's recording of "Sugar Blues" is a hit. • Ben Bernie organizes the Hotel Roosevelt Orchestra. • Buddy Petit plays with Frankie Dusen's band in California but soon returns to New Orleans, never to record. • Red Nichols makes his recording debut with the Syncopating Five. • Fats Waller cuts his first two solo piano records. • At age 18, Adrian Rollini joins the California Ramblers, buys a bass sax, and masters it within a week.

When the job at the Friar's Inn came to an end in the spring of 1923, the NORK disbanded. Mares and Roppolo became members of Al Siegal's band in New York, while Brunies worked with Eddie Tancil's group. Two sessions from July 17–18 find the three horns having a reunion in a new version of the band, expanding to ten pieces. Pettis, Glenn Scoville, and Don Murray were on saxophones, banjoist Bob Gillette and tuba player Chink Martin joined Pollack in the rhythm section, and either Jelly Roll Morton or Kyle Pierce was on piano. Morton's important appearance on several of the numbers (including his "Mr. Jelly Lord" and "Milenburg Joys") made this one of the earliest integrated jazz sessions and serves as proof of how highly rated the NORK was by both the white and black jazz communities.

Unfortunately, the musicians soon went their separate ways. Brunies joined Ted Lewis's Orchestra for 11 years, Roppolo played briefly with Peck Kelley in Texas, and Mares returned to New Orleans. In January 1925, after turning down an offer to join the Wolverines as Bix Beiderbecke's replacement (which would have been ironic since he was one of Bix's early idols), Mares organized a final version of the NORK in New Orleans with Roppolo, trombonist Santo Pecora (Brunies was no longer available), Charlie Cordilla on tenor, and a local rhythm section, recording four titles. However Roppolo (who also recorded with the Halfway House Orchestra) was in shaky health and soon suffered a mental breakdown, resulting in his being confined to a mental institution for his final 27 years. On March 26, 1925, the New Orleans Rhythm Kings had their final record date, with Roppolo absent and Charlie Cordilla switching to clarinet, sounding fine on two songs. But that was the group's swan song. The 25-year-old Paul Mares chose to retire from music and work at his family's fur business, and the NORK slipped into history.

⊙ **New Orleans Rhythm Kings and Jelly Roll Morton** (Milestone 47020) has all of the master takes from the NORK's 1922–23 sessions, including "Farewell Blues," "Panama," "Tiger Rag," "That's a Plenty," and "Tin Roof Blues," along with the Jelly Roll Morton performances. The three alternate takes with Morton are here, but not the poorly recorded alternate takes from the other dates (which were on an earlier Milestone double-LP). The two NORK sessions from 1925 are available on **New Orleans in the '20s** (Timeless 1-014) and as part of the New Orleans Owls' CD **The Owls' Hoot** (Frog 2).

Cornetist Abbie Brunies (one of four musical Brunies brothers along with George, cornetist Merritt, and trombonist Henry) led the Halfway House Orchestra in New Orleans during the 1920s. ⊙ **Halfway House Orchestra** (Jazz Oracle 8001) has all of the band's 22 numbers, including four selections not released until the 1970s. The ill-fated Leon Roppolo (doubling on alto) is on the first two numbers and otherwise the band (which was clearly influenced by the New Orleans Rhythm Kings) has Brunies, Charlie Cordilla or Sidney Arodin on clarinet, altoist Joe Loyacano, and a four-piece rhythm section with Chink Martin on tuba or bass. There are quite a few worthwhile (if now obscure) group originals plus hot versions of "Maple Leaf Rag" and "Let Me Call You Sweetheart."

The New Orleans Owls played music in a similar vein and were even a little stronger than the Halfway House Orchestra. The group's ancestor was the Invincibles String Band of 1912–21, an ensemble consisting of violin, mandolin, guitar, banjo, ukulele, piano, bass, and drums. When the New Orleans Owls were formed in 1922, most of the musicians stayed, changing instruments to become a jazz band. The Owls cut 18 numbers during five recording sessions (1925–27). The septet (cornet, two reeds, piano, banjo, tuba, and drums) added a trombonist and a third reed in 1926, and a second cornetist in 1927, staying active until its breakup in 1929. ⊙ **The Owl's Hoot** (Frog 2) has their complete output, including such exciting numbers as "Stomp Off, Let's Go," "The Owl's Hoot," "Dynamite," "White Ghost Shivers," "The Nightmare," "Brotherly Love," and "That's a Plenty." In addition, this generous disc has two numbers and two alternate takes from John Hyman's Bayou Stompers (a septet with cornetist Hyman, who later changed his name to Johnny Wiggs, and the fluent harmonica of Alvin Gautreaux) and the final session of the New Orleans Rhythm Kings.

When the New Orleans Rhythm Kings left the Friars Inn in 1923, Merritt Brunies put together his own Friars Inn Orchestra to take its place. The group (with Henry Brunies on trombone) was based at the Friars Inn for two years and lasted until 1926. The LP **Up Jumped the Devil** (Retrieval 124) has all 15 recordings by the band plus two previously unreleased test pressings. The repertoire includes some future jazz standards (such as "Clarinet Marmalade" and "Sugar Foot Stomp"), a few originals (including "Angry" which was cowritten by Merritt and

Henry Brunies), current pop tunes, and the novelty "Masculine Women! Feminine Men!" In addition to the Brunies brothers, clarinetist Volly DeFaut is a major asset.

The Original Indiana Five (which was not from Indiana) was formed in New York in 1922. Originally consisting of leader/pianist Newman Fier, trumpeter Johnny Sylvester, trombonist Vincent Grande, clarinetist Johnny Costello, and drummer Tom Morton, in late 1923 they became a sextet with the addition of Nick Vitalo on clarinet and alto, trombonist Charles Panelli, pianist Harry Ford, and banjoist Tony Colucci. The personnel would remain the same into the fall of 1925 when Pete Pellezzi became the OIF's trombonist. The group began recording in 1923 and would cut 96 titles as the OIF through 1929, plus some other titles under different names. **Original Indiana Five, Vol. 1** (Jazz Oracle 8019) starts at the very beginning with two numbers by the Indiana Syncopators (before the band had settled on its name). In addition to the Original Indiana Five selections, it has one number in which vaudeville singer Benny Davis is backed by the group and six tunes by the same band when it recorded under Johnny Sylvester's name. Such titles as "Louisville Lou," "Staving Change," "I Wanna Jazz Some More," and "King Porter Stomp" demonstrate that the Original Indiana Five is one of the most underrated and overlooked groups of the 1920s. **Original Indiana Five, Vol. 2** (Jazz Oracle 8030) has 24 selections from 1925, including two songs recorded as a similar group called the St. Louis Rhythm Kings, and two selections backing singer Maggie Jones. Among the superior obscurities are such forgotten songs as "Indiana Stomp," "Siberia," "I'm Gonna Hang Around My Sugar," and "Everybody's Doin' the Charleston Now." The Original Indiana Five may never have become famous, but they fit into the mid-1920s mainstream quite well and were one of many groups that were touched by the innovations of the New Orleans Rhythm Kings.

The Classic Blues Singers

The surprise success of Mamie Smith's recording of "Crazy Blues" in 1920 launched a blues fad in which scores of songs, many of which had nothing to do with the blues, were written with "Blues" in their titles. Record labels rushed to take advantage of the "race" market—their term for records that were marketed to the black audience—by recording many female vocalists during 1921–25, the majority taken from vaudeville with just a select few actually being major blues artists. Many of the performers, including some talented ones, were only documented for a handful of songs and then never heard from on record again. The complete output of many of the more obscure vocalists can be heard on the intriguing 14 CDs released under the title of **Female Blues Singers** (Document 5505-5518). However, some of the singers had longer and more significant careers.

The Austrian Document label has done an invaluable job of reissuing the complete output of the great majority of pre-1945 blues artists on CDs, including all of the significant classic blues singers (other than Bessie Smith, who has been covered by Sony/Columbia). Of course, when a set is "complete," including alternate takes, the

TIMELINE 1923

Among those making their recording debuts this year are King Oliver's Creole Jazz Band (with Johnny Dodds and Louis Armstrong), Jelly Roll Morton, Freddie Keppard (with Erskine Tate's Orchestra), Sidney Bechet, Bessie Smith, Ma Rainey, Ida Cox, Earl Hines (with Lois Deppe's Pittsburgh Serenaders), Armand J. Piron's New Orleans Orchestra, Bennie Moten's Orchestra, the Original Indiana Five, and Cliff Edwards (aka Ukulele Ike). • Jelly Roll Morton moves to Chicago and records a series of stunning piano solos. • Bessie Smith has a hit with Alberta Hunter's "Downhearted Blues." • James P. Johnson writes the score for the Broadway musical *Runnin' Wild*, which includes "Old Fashioned Love" and "The Charleston," inspiring a dance craze that lasted for five years. • The Washingtonians (led by banjoist Elmer Snowden and including Duke Ellington) first work in New York. • Benny Carter starts playing professionally. • Don Redman becomes Fletcher Henderson's main arranger, and Coleman Hawkins makes his first records with Henderson. • Ted Weems's "Somebody Stole My Gal" is a hit record. • Clarence Williams begins his series of classic jazz combo recordings, featuring Sidney Bechet. • The New Orleans Rhythm Kings have four recording sessions (including one with guest Jelly Roll Morton), but break up when the job at the Friar's Inn ends. • Boogie-woogie makes its first tentative appearance on records with pianist Clay Custer's "The Rocks."

chances are that not every performance will be at the same high level. But it is rewarding to be able to listen to a singer's entire recorded legacy rather than being stuck with a "best of" sampler.

Mamie Smith   Mamie Smith recorded 91 selections in her career, all but 18 during 1920–23, and everything has been reissued on her four Document CDs. **Vol. 2** (Document 5358) has some of the best classic blues vocal performances on record in 1921, continuing into the middle of the following year. The titles include "Mama Whip, Mamma Spank," "I'm Free, Single, Disengaged, Looking for Someone to Love," "Get Hot," and "Let's Agree to Disagree." Coleman Hawkins made his recording debut with Smith on some of these numbers. **Vol. 3** (Document 5359) also includes some contributions from Hawkins (who takes a couple of solos) along with Johnny Dunn, cornetist Joe Smith, and Sidney Bechet ("Lady Luck Blues" and "Kansas City Man Blues"). Although now mostly remembered for 1920's "Crazy Blues," the undervalued Mamie Smith's voice actually became stronger as the 1920s progressed.

Lucille Hegamin   Lucille Hegamin was one of the first classic blues singers to appear on record after Mamie Smith, making her debut in November 1920. She had previously worked with Jelly Roll Morton on the West Coast and introduced Tony Jackson's "Pretty Baby." In 1921, Hegamin had hits with "I'll Be Good but I'll Be Lonesome" and "Arkansas Blues," touring with her Blue Flame Syncopators. Essentially a versatile vaudeville singer, she was one of the better vocalists of the early 1920s and her entire output is available on four Document discs. **Vol. 1** (Document 5419) includes "The Jazz Me Blues," "Arkansas Blues," "Wang Wang Blues," "Wabash Blues," and two versions of "He May Be Your Man but He Comes to See Me Sometimes," a standard that she originally popularized. On **Vol. 2** (Document 5420), Hegamin is accompanied by bands (the Blue Flame Syncopators, the Dixie Daisies, Her Bang-Up Six from Georgia, and Sam Wooding's Society Entertainers) and solo pianists (J. Russell Robinson and Cyril Fullerton). Highlights include "I've Got What It Takes but It Breaks My Heart to Give It Away," "Beale St. Mama," "Aggravatin' Papa," "Downhearted Blues," "Saint Louis Gal," and "Dina." **Vol. 3** (Document 5421) covers 1923–26 (the Dixie Daisies, J. Russell Robinson, and Clarence Williams's group help out), finishing with two

obscure numbers from 1932, her last recordings until 1960. **Alternate Takes & Remaining Titles** (Document 1011) completes this series with four songs formerly bypassed, and 18 alternate takes.

Ethel Waters   The year 1921 was notable for the start of the recording careers of both Ethel Waters and Alberta Hunter. Ethel Waters, although she started out known as a blues singer, proved over time that she could sing practically anything. After picking up experience singing in Philadelphia and Baltimore, Waters moved to New York in 1917 and was popular from the start. Her clear enunciation and solid sense of swing (more jazz-oriented than many of the other singers) were major assets. One of the stars of the Black Swan label (the first record company to be owned by African-Americans), Waters excelled both on blues and popular songs of the period. In 1925, she was signed to Columbia (which gave her a high profile) and she became an influential force, second among female singers of the era to Bessie Smith.

Ethel Waters's first recordings are on **1921–1923** (Classics 796), including five instrumentals by her backup group. The technical quality is quite primitive, even for 1921. However, at that early stage, Waters was already a highly individual singer as she shows on such tunes as "Oh Daddy," "There'll Be Some Changes Made," "Oh Joe, Play that Trombone," and "Memphis Man." Various numbers on **1923–1925** (Classics 775) include Joe Smith, Lovie Austin's Blues Serenaders, and Fats Waller, with Waters heard in her early prime on "You Can't Do What My Last Man Did," "Craving Blues," "Sweet Georgia Brown," and "Go Back Where You Stayed Last Night." Joe Smith also is a major asset on four songs included on ◉ **1925–1926** (Classics 672), most notably a joyful "I've Found a New Baby." Other highlights include the original version of "Dinah," "Maybe Not at All" (which has Waters doing close impressions of Bessie and Clara Smith), "Shake that Thing," "Sugar," and "Heebies Jeebies."

Alberta Hunter   Alberta Hunter had been performing in public ever since 1906, when she ran away from home at the age of 11. She worked for a time in Chicago, moved to New York, and proved to be a very versatile singer who (like Ethel Waters) was able to sing not only blues but jazz and pop songs as well. As with Mamie Smith, Hunter always used the best musicians she could find, and her backup groups on records included such players as Louis Armstrong, Sidney Bechet, Fats Waller,

King Oliver, Fletcher Henderson, the Original Memphis Five, Duke Ellington, and Eubie Blake.

Alberta Hunter's first 22 recordings are on **1921–1923** (Document 5422), but the erratic sound quality and often-scratchy transfers make the music difficult to listen to. However, completists will enjoy "Someday Sweetheart," "Downhearted Blues" (a year before Bessie Smith had a hit with Hunter's song), "I'm Going Away Just to Wear You Off My Mind," and one of the earliest recordings of "'Tain't Nobody's Bizness." **1923–1924** (Document 5423), which includes "Aggravatin' Papa," "Loveless Love," and "Old Fashioned Love," is of particularly strong interest for the musicians that Hunter uses, including cornetist Joe Smith, Fats Waller, and Lovie Austin's Blues Serenaders, plus a pair of very early appearances by Duke Ellington ("It's Gonna Be a Cold Cold Winter" and "Parlor Social De Luxe"). ● **1924–1927** (Document 5424) features Hunter at her early best, interacting with Perry Bradford's Mean Four, pianist Clarence Williams, and the Red Onion Babies (which has Louis Armstrong on five numbers and Sidney Bechet on three) including "Nobody Knows the Way I Feel Dis Mornin'" and "Everybody Loves My Baby." Also notable are her versions of "Your Jelly Roll Is Good," "I'm Hard to Satisfy," "Everybody Mess Around," and "Heebies Jeebies."

Trixie Smith   After winning a blues contest in 1921, Trixie Smith began her recording career for the Black Swan label. She recorded 16 songs (not counting alternate takes) for Black Swan during 1921–23, 16 for Paramount in 1924–25, and the remainder in 1926 (two versions of "Messin' Around" with Freddie Keppard), 1938 (seven numbers with Sidney Bechet and trumpeter Charlie Shavers in a sextet), and a final song in 1939 with trumpeter Henry "Red" Allen. All of her performances are on her two Document CDs. **Vol. 1** (Document 5332) includes "Trixie's Blues," "He May Be Your Man but He Comes to See Me Sometimes," "My Man Rocks Me with One Steady Roll," and "Freight Train Blues," while **Vol. 2** (Document 5333), which starts at the beginning of 1925, finds Smith performing with the Original Memphis Five ("Everybody Loves My Baby" and "How Come You Do Me Like You Do"), on two sessions with Louis Armstrong (including "The World's Jazz Crazy and So Am I"), and four songs with all-stars from the Fletcher Henderson Orchestra plus the later titles with Keppard, Bechet, and Allen. Although not quite on the

level of the top classic blues singers, Trixie Smith's recordings have many moments of interest.

Lizzie Miles and Sara Martin   Two other singers who emerged before Bessie Smith were Lizzie Miles and Sara Martin. Lizzie Miles (born Elizabeth Mary Pajaund) sang with circuses and minstrel shows during 1909–17. She was in Chicago during 1918–20, moved to New York the following year, and began recording in 1922, mostly with obscure musicians, before spending 1924–26 in Europe. Miles's recordings mostly sound good today, for her delivery was straightforward, sincere, and musical. **Vol. 1** (Document 5458) has such numbers as "Hot Lips," "The Yellow Dog Blues," and "You've Gotta Come and See Mama Every Night."

Sara Martin, one of the older classic blues singers (born in 1884), had a busy life, becoming a widow twice and a divorcée three times! After working in the South and Chicago, she was introduced to Clarence Williams in New York in 1922 and quickly had a hit with "Sugar Blues." **Vol. 1** (Document 5395) includes that song plus "I Got What It Takes," "Nobody in Town Can Bake a Sweet Jelly Roll Like Mine," and a variety of period material from 1922–23, with backing by pianist Williams, W.C. Handy's Orchestra, and pianist/composer Shelton Brooks, plus three vocal duets with Eva Taylor. **Vol. 2** (Document 5396) mostly has sparse accompaniment from Williams, pianist Porter Grainger, or guitarist Sylvester Weaver, in addition to four numbers with Clarence Williams's Blue Five (including Sidney Bechet). **Vol. 3** (Document 5397) is in the same vein (with Weaver, Williams, or pianist Lemuel Fowler), but highlighted by such jazzy blues-oriented tunes as "He's Never Gonna Throw Me Down," "Old Fashioned Sara Blues," "Eagle Rock Me, Papa," "Daddy Ease this Pain of Mine," "I'm Gonna Hoodoo You," and "I'd Rather Be Blue than Green."

Bessie Smith   While the 1920–22 period brought a rash of classic blues singers hoping to duplicate Mamie Smith's success, the discovery of the Empress of the Blues, Bessie Smith, in 1923 dwarfed everything that had occurred previously. Smith began her career as a teenager singing with the Moses Stock Company, an ensemble that starred her early inspiration, Ma Rainey. She also worked with Fats Chappelle's Rabbit Foot Minstrels and the Florida Cotton Pickers, developing a powerful and hypnotic style. By 1919, Smith was heading her own *Liberty Belles* show, and in 1922 she was the headliner of the *How Come* revue and a major attraction throughout the South.

In New York in February 1923, Bessie Smith had a major hit with her first recording, Alberta Hunter's "Downhearted Blues." Between 1923 and 1925, she made 82 of her 160 recordings. Fortunately, her entire recording career is available on five two-CD sets, with ◉ **The Complete Recordings, Vol. 1** (Columbia/Legacy 47091) and ◉ **The Complete Recordings, Vol. 2** (Columbia/Legacy 47471) having the first 75 selections. The former set includes such gems as "Downhearted Blues," "Baby, Won't You Please Come Home," "'Tain't Nobody's Bizness If I Do," and "Ticket Agent, Ease Your Window Down." The backing (often Clarence Williams or Fletcher Henderson on piano) is merely adequate, but the singer makes every performance powerful. The Complete Recordings, **Vol. 2** has Smith joined frequently by Charlie Green, Joe Smith, and Buster Bailey, all from the Fletcher Henderson Orchestra. Highlights include "Cake Walkin' Babies from Home, "The Yellow Dog

Blues," and "At the Christmas Ball." In addition, nine of the numbers (including "St. Louis Blues," "Careless Love," and "I Ain't Goin' to Play Second Fiddle") feature Louis Armstrong sharing the stage with Smith. The results are often classic as they are heard clearly inspiring and challenging each other. The recording quality may have been primitive at times and the accompaniment occasionally indifferent, but it did not hinder the singer in the slightest. The Empress of the Blues easily overcame all obstacles and created music so powerful that it still sounds fresh and relevant today. During this era, there was simply no singer on Bessie Smith's level.

Ma Rainey   In addition to Bessie Smith, 1923 also brought the recording debuts of Ma Rainey, Ida Cox, Clara Smith, and Sippie Wallace. Ma Rainey (born Gertrude Pridgett) became known in time as "The Mother of the Blues" due to her pioneering efforts and her influence on Bessie Smith. As far back as 1898, she appeared at age 12 in the show *A Bunch of Blackberries*, and performed with the Rabbit Foot Minstrels, Tolliver's Circus, and the Moses

TIMELINE 1924

On February 12, Paul Whiteman's concert at Aeolian Hall features guest Zez Confrey along with the debut of "Rhapsody in Blue" (with George Gershwin on the piano). • Disputes over money result in Johnny and Baby Dodds leaving King Oliver's group. • Louis Armstrong and Lil Hardin get married and depart from Oliver's band a few months later when Armstrong accepts Fletcher Henderson's offer to join his big band in New York. • The Fletcher Henderson Orchestra becomes the house band at Roseland Ballroom. • Bix Beiderbecke makes his recording debut with the Wolverines, meets Frank Trumbauer and is briefly with the Jean Goldkette Orchestra. • Red McKenzie's Mound City Blue Blowers (a group consisting of the leader's comb wrapped with tissue paper, Dick Slevin on kazoo, and banjoist Jack Bland) has a hit with their recording of "Arkansas Blues," which reportedly sold over a million copies. • A money dispute results in Duke Ellington taking over the Washingtonians from Elmer Snowden. They soon begin a three-year run at the Hollywood (later renamed the Kentucky) Club. • Among those making their recording debut this year are Ellington's Washingtonians (with new trumpeter Bubber Miley), Charlie Creath's Jazz-O-Maniacs, Wingy Manone (with the Arcadian Serenaders), and Muggsy Spanier (with the Bucktown Five). • Jimmy Blythe cuts "Chicago Stomp," considered the first full-length boogie-woogie recording. • Johnny Dodds puts together a band that plays at Bert Kelly's Stables on and off into 1930. • Jelly Roll Morton records two duets with King Oliver. • Fate Marable makes his only two recordings, but they are disappointments. • George Brunies joins Ted Lewis's band. • Pee Wee Russell plays with Peck Kelley's Bad Boys in Texas (making his recording debut in St. Louis with Herbert Berger). • Steve Brown becomes an influential member of the Jean Goldkette Orchestra. • Sixteen-year-old Roger Wolfe Kahn (whose father was a multimillionaire) begins his bandleading career by purchasing Arthur Lange's Orchestra. • Lovie Austin records with her Blues Serenaders. • Don Redman takes an early scat vocal on "My Papa Doesn't Two Time" with Fletcher Henderson. • Noble Sissle and Eubie Blake write and produce *Chocolate Dandies* on Broadway. • Alphonse Trent takes over Eugene Crook's Synco Six and organizes his own legendary territory band. • Violinist Clifford Hayes leads the first jug band on record (performing with Sara Martin). • Paul Howard forms the Quality Serenaders in Los Angeles. • Bennie Moten has a hit with "South."

Stock Company. Unfortunately Rainey's recordings were all cut for the Paramount label, a company with notoriously noisy pressings, which make her performances somewhat inaccessible and distant for today's listeners. The complete Ma Rainey (including all of the alternate takes) is available on five Document CDs. The surface noise can be distracting, so play her performances loud and listen closely! **Vol. 1** (Document 5581) mostly features accompaniment from Lovie Austin's Blues Serenaders (with cornetist Tommy Ladnier and clarinetist Jimmy O'Bryant), though there are also a couple of songs in which Rainey is just backed by the Pruitt Twins (siblings playing banjo and guitar). Although no major hits resulted (best known is "Ma Rainey's Mystery Record"), Paramount was inspired to keep on recording her. ◐ **Vol. 2** (Document 5582) is notable for it has Rainey's one session with Louis Armstrong, which resulted in "See See Rider" (which she introduced), "Jelly Bean Blues," and "Countin' the Blues." Other selections find Rainey joined by Fletcher Henderson sidemen, Lovie Austin's Blues Serenaders, her regularly working group the Georgia Band (with Lil Henderson on piano), or various obscure players.

Ida Cox   Ida Cox, like Ma Rainey, but unlike most of the other classic blues singers of the period, stuck exclusively to the blues. She ran away from home in 1910 when she was 14 to tour with White and Clark's Minstrels. Cox moved to Chicago in 1922 and for a few years was ranked second to Bessie Smith among blues singers. **Vol. 1** (Document 5322) has all of her 1923 recordings, including "Any Woman's Blues," "Graveyard Dream Blues," "Ida Cox's Lawdy, Lawdy Blues," "I've Got the Blues for Rampart Street," and "Bear Mash Blues." Other than on "Bear Mash," the blues singer is joined by pianist Lovie Austin, with and without her Blues Serenaders (Tommy Ladnier and Jimmy O'Bryant). ◐ **Vol. 2** (Document 5323) showcases Cox with an expanded version of the Blues Serenaders, sidemen from the Fletcher Henderson Orchestra, and (on two songs) the Pruitt Twins. Among the better songs are "Chicago Monkey Man Blues," "Blues Ain't Nothing Else But," "Wild Women Don't Have the Blues," and "Death Letter Blues." Notice that some of the lyrics on "Chicago Monkey Man Blues" shows up years later in "Goin' to Chicago."

Clara Smith   Clara Smith, one of the five unrelated Smith singers (along with Bessie, Trixie, Mamie, and the obscure Laura), was billed as "Queen of the Moaners." Her voice was fairly sweet and she was not a strong enough singer to overcome her instrumental backing if it was weak, but she held her own on three recorded duets with Bessie Smith and recorded steadily throughout the 1920s. The first half of Clara Smith's career is fully covered on the first three volumes in her Document series. **Vol. 1** (Document 5364) mostly has Smith accompanied by Fletcher Henderson's piano although there are also three small group sides and two duets ("Far Away Blues" and "I'm Going Back to My Used to Be") with Bessie Smith. Among the other better numbers are "I Got Everything a Woman Needs," "I Never Miss the Sunshine," and "I'm Gonna Tear Your Playhouse Down." **Vol. 2** (Document 5365) covers 1924 and finds Smith assisted by Henderson and some of his sidemen (including Coleman Hawkins and Don Redman) on various tracks, although the numbers with Ernest Elliott (on alto and clarinet) are hurt by Elliott's bizarre gaspipe sounds. Highlights include "Chicago Blues," "West Indies Blues," "Don't Advertise Your Man," "Back Woods Blues," and "Death Letter Blues." **Vol. 3** (Document 5366) is most notable for Smith's two dates with Louis Armstrong (best are "Nobody Knows the Way I Feel Dis Mornin'" and the two takes of "Court House Blues") plus "My Good-for-Nuthin' Man," "My Two Timing Papa," "When My Sugar Walks Down the Street" (a rare departure from the blues), and a collaboration with Bessie Smith on "My Man Blues." Although Clara Smith was not on the same level as the very best classic blues singers, her recordings are not without many moments of interest.

Sippie Wallace   Sippie Wallace was known as "The Texas Nightingale" and was part of a musical family that included pioneering boogie-woogie pianist George W. Thomas, blues pianist Hersal Thomas, and her niece, singer Hociel Thomas. After growing up in Texas and New Orleans, Wallace moved to Chicago and began recording for the Okeh label in 1923. **Vol. 1** (Document 5399), the first of two CDs that have all of Sippie Wallace's pre-1958 recordings, features the singer backed by Eddie Heywood, Sr., Hersal Thomas, Perry Bradford's Jazz Phools, King Oliver, Clarence Williams, and two of Williams's groups, including a quintet with Louis Armstrong and Sidney Bechet (for "Baby, I Can't Use You No More" and "Trouble Everywhere I Roam"). Primarily a powerful and somber blues singer, Wallace definitely gets her message across on such songs as "Up the Country Blues," "Mama's Gone, Goodbye," "Let My Man Alone Blues," and "Devil Dance Blues."

Rosa Henderson, Maggie Jones, and Monette Moore

Rosa Henderson, Maggie Jones, and Monette Moore were each fine second-level classic blues singers. Rosa Henderson, who was not related to Fletcher or Horace Henderson, recorded steadily during 1923–27, 89 titles counting alternate takes (fully reissued on four Document CDs), some originally under the pseudonyms of Flora Dale, Rosa Green, Mae Harris, Mamie Harris, Rose Henderson, Sara Johnson, Sally Ritz, Josephine Thomas, Gladys White, and Bessie Williams. **Vol. 1** (Document 5401) finds Henderson in fine form on "I Ain't No Man's Slave," "So Long to You and the Blues," "He May Be Your Dog but He's Wearing My Collar," and "Got the World in a Jug, the Stopper's in My Hand," mostly backed by Fletcher Henderson. **Vol. 2** (Document 5402) includes "I'm a Good Gal but I'm a Thousan' Miles from Home," "West Indies Blues," "My Papa Doesn't Two-Time No Time," "Strut Yo' Puddy," and "Somebody's Doing What You Wouldn't Do." **Vol. 3** (Document 5403) is the strongest of her Document CDs due partly to the backup groups (the Choo Choo Jazzers and the Kansas City Five, which sometimes include cornetists Rex Stewart, Louis Metcalf, and Bubber Miley, plus dates with pianists Cliff Jackson and Fats Waller). The most memorable selections include "Hard-Hearted Hannah," "Don't Advertise Your Man," "Nobody Knows the Way I Feel 'Dis Mornin'," "Get It Fixed," and "What's The Matter Now."

The somewhat obscure but talented Maggie Jones (born Faye Barnes) is most notable for leading two sessions that include Louis Armstrong. **Vol. 1** (Document 5348) has the first 24 of her 40 recordings, including six titles with Armstrong ("Anybody Here Want to Try My Cabbage," "Screamin' the Blues," and "Good Time Flat Blues" among them) plus such other fine songs as "You Can't Do What My Last Man Did," "Early Every Morn," and "Undertaker's Blues." Monette Moore could sing both blues and jazz quite effectively. After a period singing in obscurity, she became a top vaudeville performer late in 1925, which was ironically after most of her recordings were made. On **Vol. 1** (Document 5338), she shows off her flexibility during such numbers as "Sugar Blues," "Gulf Coast Blues," "Muddy Water Blues," and "I Wanna Jazz Some More," mostly backed by

obscure players other than two cuts with Tommy Ladnier and Jimmy O'Bryant, one with Jimmy Blythe, and a few later contributions by Rex Stewart and Bubber Miley. **Vol. 2** (Document 5339) is highlighted by "The Bye Bye Blues," "Put Me in the Alley Blues," "Undertaker's Blues," and "If You Don't Like Potatoes." Mostly from 1924–25, **Vol. 2** also has two numbers from 1926, three from 1927, and a fine performance from 1932 (a medley of "Shine on Your Shoes" and "Louisiana Hayride" with Fats Waller) that was not released for decades.

Most of these singers, who worked in theatres, tent shows, and vaudeville, started out using sparse accompaniment (often just a piano) on records. By 1925, with the rise in popularity of jazz and the gradual decline of the blues craze, they were frequently joined by small combos. Ironically, as recording techniques improved and the quality of the backup musicians became much higher by the mid-1920s, the number of classic blues recordings dropped sharply due to the general change in musical tastes. However, the major names such as Bessie Smith, Ethel Waters, and Ma Rainey still had important contributions to make way beyond 1925.

King Oliver and the Creole Jazz Band

During 1917–22, only a small portion of the important jazz musicians were recorded, and only a very tiny sampling of black performers were documented. Other than the relatively primitive recordings of James Reese Europe's Orchestra, there are hints in the playing of Mamie Smith's Jazz Hounds (which cut a few instrumentals), the primitive trumpeter Johnny Dunn, and the piano solos of James P. Johnson of what jazz sounded like during this period in the African-American community. Of strong interest are two titles ("Ory's Creole Trombone" and "Society Blues") recorded by Kid Ory's band with cornetist Mutt Carey (under the odd title of "Spike's Seven Pods of Pepper Orchestra") in Los Angeles in 1922.

But 1923 was the major breakthrough year for black performers, with Sidney Bechet, Jelly Roll Morton, Freddie Keppard, Earl Hines, and Bennie Moten's Orchestra among the many who made their recording debut, in addition to Bessie Smith, Ma Rainey, and Ida Cox. Most important were the recordings of what is thought of as the premiere classic New Orleans jazz group, King Oliver's Creole Jazz Band.

Joe "King" Oliver started originally on trombone before switching to cornet. Oliver was considered a major force on the New Orleans jazz scene by 1907 and during the next decade he worked with many top local bands, including the Melrose Brass Band, the Olympia Band, the Onward Brass Band, the Magnolia Band, the Eagle Band, the Original Superior Band, Allen's Brass Band, Richard M. Jones's Four Hot Hounds, and Kid Ory's ensemble. He grew in power and importance each year, earning the title of "King" after defeating Freddie Keppard and Manuel Perez in cornet battles. By 1915, he was considered the most significant cornetist in the city.

In March 1919, Oliver moved to Chicago where he worked with the bands of clarinetist Lawrence Duhe and Bill Johnson. By 1920, he was leading his own group at the Dreamland Café, which he called the Creole Jazz Band. Featuring such notable players as trombonist Honore Dutrey, clarinetist Johnny Dodds, pianist Lil Harden, and drummer Baby Dodds, the group spent much of 1921 on the West Coast, working in San Francisco and Los Angeles. After returning in triumph to Chicago in 1922, Oliver's Creole Jazz Band settled in at Lincoln Gardens. Soon Oliver sent to New Orleans for his protégé, Louis Armstrong.

With Armstrong playing second cornet, the Creole Jazz Band greatly impressed its audiences, which soon included impressionable white teenage musicians (informally known as the Austin High Gang) along with their black contemporaries. Oliver was particularly adept at creating tonal distortions with the help of his mutes, inspiring Paul Mares, Bubber Miley, Tommy Ladnier, and Muggsy Spanier, among others. Armstrong was already a powerful player, although he seemed content playing second fiddle to Oliver. Dutrey was expert in ensembles, and Johnny Dodds had an intense cutting sound that was quite unique. The rhythm section was solid, with Lil Hardin playing four-to-the-bar chords and Baby Dodds contributing a variety of percussive sounds, and the music was mostly ensemble-oriented other than occasional solos such as Oliver's famous three-chorus improvisation on "Dippermouth Blues." Armstrong knew Oliver's style well, and the ad-libbed harmonized breaks by the cornetists often amazed onlookers and particularly other musicians.

King Oliver's Creole Jazz Band might have only been a lost legend (as was Buddy Bolden's band) except that they were fortunate enough to record in 1923 for Gennett, Okeh, Columbia, and Paramount. ❍ **King Oliver's Creole Jazzband 1923–1924** (Retrieval 79007) is a double CD that has all 37 recordings by the classic group, music that had formerly been scattered among many releases. The recording quality is sometimes erratic and primitive, but the music (particularly when listened to closely in order to hear exactly what the four horns were doing) still communicates well and is often exciting. Highlights include "Canal Street Blues," "Chimes Blues" (which has Armstrong's first recorded solo), two versions of "Dippermouth Blues," "Froggie Moore," "Snake Rag," "Sobbin' Blues," and "Buddy's Habits." Also included on this essential two-fer are Oliver's 1924 date with the vaudeville team Butterbeans & Susie and his two duets ("King Porter Stomp" and "Tom Cat") with Jelly Roll Morton.

King Oliver's Creole Jazz Band's recordings were closely studied by other top jazz musicians at the time and have always been influential, particularly decades later during the 1940s Dixieland revival. Unfortunately, the original band did not last long. In early 1924, after a major dispute over money, Johnny and Baby Dodds left; the clarinetist was soon leading his own group at Kelly's Stables. Louis Armstrong, urged on by Lil (his new wife) who felt that he should not have to play second horn to anyone, even his idol, in the middle of the year accepted an offer to join the Fletcher Henderson Orchestra in New York. King Oliver's Creole Jazz Band continued through 1924 with substitutes (including Bob Shoffner, Lee Collins, and Tommy Ladnier in Armstrong's spot) before breaking up in the fall. King Oliver spent a few months as the main soloist with Peyton's Symphonic Syncopators and then in February 1925 formed a new band, the Dixie Syncopators, which played regularly at the Plantation Café in Chicago. Its recordings (starting in 1926) show that Oliver was doing a good job of keeping up with the current musical styles, even while his former protégé was beginning to overshadow him.

Sidney Bechet   Sidney Bechet was among the very first horn soloists to appear on records. As a child in New Orleans, Bechet was considered a prodigy on clarinet, sitting in with Freddie Keppard's band when he was only eight in 1905 and working professionally soon afterward. During 1908–14 as a teenager he played with such groups as the Silver Bells Band, Buddy Petit's Young Olympians, John Robichaux, the Olympia Band, and the Eagle Band.

In 1914, Bechet became a constant traveler, at first working throughout the South with a variety of shows.

By 1917, he had made it to Chicago where he played with King Oliver and Keppard. After becoming a member of Will Marion Cook's Southern Syncopated Orchestra, Bechet traveled with the large band to Europe where he made quite a hit throughout the continent. He bought his first soprano sax in London and that became his main instrument, although he continued playing the clarinet as a double. After working in France and England during 1920–21, Bechet was deported from Great Britain on an assault charge and returned to the United States. A fiery personality whose temperament was constantly changeable, Bechet was a passionate player whose wide vibrato was both loved and hated, and whose musicianship was impressive. Bechet insisted on playing lead, which led to some confrontations with trumpeters; he was one of the few human beings in the world who ultimately did not get along with the lovable Louis Armstrong!

Sidney Bechet made his recording debut in an impressive fashion on July 30, 1923, being showcased on "Wild Cat Blues" and "Kansas City Man Blues" with Clarence Williams's Blue Five. Those recordings, although performed in a three-horn quintet, find the emphasis solely played on Bechet's solo talents and were unprecedented at the time, a major step forward from jazz's former emphasis on ensembles.

Bechet's main recordings of the 1923–25 period were made with Williams (reissued under the pianist's name by the Classics label and discussed later in this chapter). Highlights include collaborations with the rapidly emerging Louis Armstrong from October 1924 to March 1925, including "Cake Walking Babies from Home" and Bechet's unique solo on bass sarrusophone on "Mandy Make Up Your Mind." He also recorded behind a variety of blues singers (including Alberta Hunter on "Nobody Knows the Way I Feel 'Dis Mornin'," and Sara Martin, Mamie Smith, Eva Taylor, and Sippie Wallace) plus two titles with the Get Happy Band. However, after a variety of activities (playing with Bessie Smith, spending a few months with Duke Ellington's Washingtonians in 1924, working with James P. Johnson, and running a Harlem establishment called the Club Basha), in September 1925 Bechet returned to Europe, sailing to Paris with the *Revue Negre*, a show featuring Josephine Baker. Because he would spend much of the next six years overseas, Sidney Bechet's influence as jazz's first major horn soloist on records would be much less than one would expect.

Jelly Roll Morton   One of the most colorful figures in jazz history, Jelly Roll Morton (born Ferdinand Joseph La Menthe) may not have actually invented jazz as he claimed later in life, but he was one of jazz's main pioneers, a distinctive pianist who was a major transitional figure between ragtime and classic jazz, and one of jazz's first significant composers and arrangers. Morton began on guitar and trombone before settling on piano when he was ten. He worked in Storyville during his early days and did not consider music to be his full-time profession until the early 1920s. He traveled throughout the South starting around 1910 and among his many jobs was time spent as a pool hustler, boxing promoter, tailor, gambling house manager, hotel manager, comedian in traveling shows, pimp (which may have been the most lucrative of his jobs), and occasionally pianist. Morton first visited Chicago in 1914 and San Francisco in 1915. He was mostly based in Los Angeles during 1917–22, also playing music in Alaska, Wyoming, Denver, Tijuana, Canada, and northern California.

Because he was such a braggart (a personality trait that probably helped him survive during his early period), Morton antagonized many people along the way, and for decades there was a tendency to underrate his abilities because he did not quite live up to some of his claims. Although he did not have a chance to record until 1923 and it is impossible to know how he really sounded in 1915, it now seems apparent that Morton was one of the first major jazz soloists, and that his improvising and composing abilities foreshadowed what was to come in jazz. He effectively used two- and four-bar breaks, treated the piano as if it were a miniature orchestra, and was a master of dynamics, thinking of each performance as a complete work rather than merely repeating the same ideas from chorus to chorus as the ODJB often did.

In 1923, Morton moved to Chicago and began his recording career. During 1923–24 he recorded 20 brilliant piano solos (introducing such originals as "King Porter Stomp," "Grandpa's Spells," "Kansas City Stomps," "Wolverine Blues," "Shreveport Stomp," "Jelly Roll Blues," and "The Pearls") and ten surprisingly primitive band selections. In addition, Morton recorded a session with the New Orleans Rhythm Kings, in 1924 cut two duets with King Oliver, and made two additional band numbers in 1925 and early 1926. **Jelly Roll Morton** (Milestone 47018) and ◯ **Ferd "Jelly Roll" Morton** (Retrieval

79002) are nearly the same. Both of these single CDs contain all 20 of Jelly Roll Morton's piano solos of 1923–24, some of the very best jazz on record during that era. Where they differ is that the Milestone disc has four of Morton's early band sides and his two duets with King Oliver (which are available elsewhere under Oliver's name), while the Retrieval CD has Morton's four exciting piano solos from 1926 that include superior remakes of "The Pearls" and "King Porter Stomp." In addition, Morton recorded possibly as many as 16 piano rolls in his life, mostly from 1924 with "Dead Man Blues" cut two years later. Four are lost but the other dozen are available on **Piano Rolls** (Nonesuch 79363). This fine CD does the best possible job of bringing the metronomic performances back to life. But, other than the classic piano solos, Jelly Roll Morton's most important work would start being documented in 1926.

James P. Johnson   The king of stride pianists, James P. Johnson was the definitive pianist of the 1920s and the star of a countless number of jam sessions and rent parties, often bringing along his friends Fats Waller and Willie "The Lion" Smith. Johnson took piano lessons from his mother, and starting in 1912, he played in clubs, toured in vaudeville, cut piano rolls (beginning in 1917), and worked in theatres. Johnson (along with Jelly Roll Morton) was among the first pianists to move music beyond ragtime into classic jazz. While Morton's style was very personal, Johnson's was more influential, and his phrases can be heard in the playing of many slightly younger pianists, including Duke Ellington. As if his piano talents were not enough, Johnson composed such works as "Carolina Shout" (which became the test piece for young pianists), "Keep Off the Grass," "Snowy Morning Blues," "You've Got to Be Modernistic," and "Jingles," led combo dates, recorded with a variety of classic blues singers (sounding especially inspiring with Bessie Smith and Ethel Waters), and wrote such pop tunes as "If I Could Be with You One Hour Tonight," "Old Fashioned Love," and the theme song of the 1920s, "The Charleston," which he did not get around to recording until late in life.

⊙ **Harlem Stride Piano** (Hot 'N' Sweet 151032) and **1921–1928** (Classics 658) are similar, with the Hot 'N' Sweet disc getting the edge. Both discs have James P. Johnson's 11 piano solos from 1921–27 (including "The Harlem Strut," "Keep Off the Grass," "Carolina Shout,"

and "Snowy Morning Blues"), a band version of "Carolina Shout" from 1921, and six combo selections. The Hot 'N' Sweet CD also has Johnson's piano roll version of "The Charleston," and six selections from 1929 (including two more piano solos and four band tracks). The Classics disc, which has three fewer selections, includes Johnson's two numbers with Johnny Dunn and Fats Waller ("What's the Use of Being Alone" and "Original Bugle Blues") plus a number with Perry Bradford ("Lucy Long"), music that is available elsewhere. Johnson's playing was so brilliant throughout the 1920s that he must be ranked near the top of jazz pianists of all time.

Paul Whiteman   By the mid-1920s, bandleader Paul Whiteman was often being billed as "The King of Jazz." Although he was well aware that that description was inaccurate (except to listeners who at the time were completely unaware of the music of African-Americans), Whiteman did have the most popular dance band of the 1920s, and he was a household name before most people had ever heard of Louis Armstrong.

Whiteman was the son of a well-respected music teacher, Wilberforce J. Whiteman. Starting on violin when he was seven, Paul Whiteman played with the Denver Symphony Orchestra during 1907–14. He worked with the San Francisco Symphony Orchestra, led a 40-piece band during his brief period in the navy, and in 1918 started his own dance band (which was briefly co-led by cornetist Henry Busse), playing at San Francisco's Fairmont Hotel. After performing a bit in Los Angeles and Atlantic City, Whiteman's orchestra became based in New York in 1920. His hit recordings of "Whispering," "Three o'Clock in the Morning," and "The Japanese Sandman" immediately made Paul Whiteman famous, and he followed it up with popular recordings of "Wang Wang Blues" and "Hot Lips."

Whiteman always hired technically skilled musicians, and his sidemen during 1921–25 included Busse, arranger/composer Ferde Grofe (who originally played piano with his orchestra), banjoist Mike Pingitore, clarinetist Russ Gorman, and trombonist Wilbur Hall. Ironically for "The King of Jazz," there were no major jazz soloists in his band during this period, and the rapidly growing ensemble (which sometimes included a string section and two pianos) rarely swung. Whiteman's oft-stated goal was to uplift dance music and jazz to a high level of respectability, to "make a lady out of jazz," taming and civilizing the wild music and making it accessible to a large audience. The goal was lofty, but in reality jazz was only a small part of the musical formula heard in Whiteman's 1921–25 performances, along with semiclassical works, waltzes, straight dance music, and novelties.

The highpoint for the Paul Whiteman Orchestra (which toured Europe in 1923) during this period took place on February 24, 1924, at their prestigious Aeolian Hall concert, which was billed as "An Experiment in Modern Music." In addition to looking back at jazz's history (stretching back all of seven years to the ODJB!) and featuring current hits by Zez Confrey, Whiteman looked toward what he thought would be the future, symphonic jazz, by introducing George Gershwin's "Rhapsody in Blue," with the composer improvising on piano.

Considering how much Paul Whiteman recorded in the 1920s, it is surprising that there are not more CDs available of his music. ◐ **Greatest Hits** (Collector's Choice 61) generally lives up to its title, featuring some of Whiteman's best-selling records of 1920–28, including "The Japanese Sandman," "Whispering" (a million seller in 1920), "Hot Lips," "Three o'Clock in the Morning," and the second version of "Rhapsody in Blue." The jazz content from "The King of Jazz" is light, but the dance-oriented music is enjoyable. Also well worth picking up

(if it can be found) is a two-LP set titled **An Experiment in Modern Music** (Smithsonian Collection 2-0518). Through vintage recordings by Whiteman, the Original Dixieland Jazz Band, the Great White Way Orchestra, Art Hickman, Zez Confrey (including "Kitten on the Keys" and "Nickel in the Slot"), the Broadway Dance Orchestra, Jean Goldkette, and others, Whiteman's 1924 Aeolian Hall concert is recreated, including all of the highlights and low points (a few of the somewhat pompous extended works). A special inclusion is the original version of "Rhapsody in Blue" from 1924, a performance whose primitive recording quality and atmospheric sounds from the orchestra (which includes George Gershwin on piano) is quite charming.

Bix Beiderbecke and the Wolverines   Six days before Paul Whiteman's Aeolian Hall concert helped consolidate his position in the public's mind as "The King of Jazz," a different jazz king made his recording debut. Bix Beiderbecke's life, with its rise and fall, overindulgence with bootleg liquor, brilliant and often intuitive playing, his golden tone on the cornet, and his movie star looks, would make for a perfect Hollywood movie. In addition, Bix's ability to not only play with but greatly impress the very best musicians of the era (Louis Armstrong was among his many admirers) was proof that creative jazz

TIMELINE 1925

Nick LaRocca suffers a mental breakdown, causing the breakup of the ODJB. • The New Orleans Rhythm Kings briefly come back together for a couple of recording sessions, but Leon Roppolo's shaky mental health dooms the band. • Sixteen-year-old Benny Goodman joins Ben Pollack's Orchestra. • Sam Wooding's *Chocolate Kiddies* begins its historic trailblazing tours overseas, visiting Europe for the first time. • Sidney Bechet travels to Paris with the *Revue Negre*, an ensemble that includes Josephine Baker and Claude Hopkins's Orchestra. • Kid Ory moves to Chicago to join King Oliver's Dixie Synco-pators. • Mutt Carey takes over Ory's band in Los Angeles and renames it the Liberty Syncopators. • Ben Bernie's Orchestra (with tenor saxophonist Jack Pettis) is captured on an early sound film short, playing the recently composed "Sweet Georgia Brown." • Bud Freeman, who had been playing C-melody sax for two years, switches permanently to the tenor sax. • Bix Beiderbecke spends the summer working in St. Louis with an orchestra led by Frankie Trumbauer. • Later in the year, Trumbauer becomes the musical director of the Jean Goldkette Orchestra. • Among those making their recording debut in 1925 are the Boswell Sisters (teenagers at the time), the Halfway House Orchestra, the New Orleans Owls, Hoagy Carmichael (with Hitch's Happy Harmonists), and Oscar Celestin. • Charlie Johnson's Paradise Ten begins a ten-year stint at Small's Paradise in New York. • Walter Page takes over leadership of the Blue Devils. • Jack Teagarden works with Doc Ross's Jazz Bandits. • Fess Williams forms his Royal Flush Orchestra. • On December 3, Harry Reser's Clicquot Club Eskimos debut on the radio. • Guitarist/singer/violinist Lonnie Johnson wins a talent contest sponsored by the Okeh label and launches his productive recording career. • Louis Armstrong returns to Chicago, where on November 12 he makes his first Hot Five recordings.

was never confined solely to the African-American music community.

Born in Davenport, Iowa, Leon Bix Beiderbecke grew up in a conservative middle-class family; his mother was a talented pianist. When Bix was just four, he picked out songs on his family's piano. His classical piano lessons did not last long when he showed a preference to "improve" written music by memorizing his teacher's playing and improvising rather than learning to read music. In 1918, when his older brother brought home records by the Original Dixieland Jazz Band, Bix was so intrigued by the music that he soon acquired a cornet and began practicing constantly, playing purely by ear.

Because his parents were worried about the direction that his life was taking, they sent him to Lake Forest Military Academy in 1921 in hopes that he would learn self-discipline, but the school was located just 35 miles north of Chicago, the center of jazz at the time! Beiderbecke often went to town to see the New Orleans Rhythm Kings (with whom he occasionally sat in), violating his school's curfew on a regular basis. When he was caught once too often, he was expelled from the academy, not an unhappy event for the cornetist who was now free to become a full-time musician. Bix spent much of 1922–23 freelancing in the Midwest, improving his beautiful tone and improvising skills.

In October 1923, Beiderbecke became the cornetist with a new group called the Wolverines, which at first resembled the New Orleans Rhythm Kings. The group recorded 16 songs during February–October 1924, Bix's first records. His haunting tone and cool style were a major contrast to the "hot" players of the period, making him a sort of Miles Davis to Louis Armstrong's Dizzy Gillespie. Although unknown to all but a small segment of the general public, Beiderbecke's playing was quickly noticed by other musicians; Red Nichols even copied his first solo ("Jazz Me Blues") note for note on George Olsen's recording of "You'll Never Get to Heaven with Those Eyes." In addition, Beiderbecke occasionally played piano, including taking a piano solo on the Wolverine's "Big Boy." All of Bix's recordings have been reissued on a series of four three-CD sets put out by the Sunbeam label and titled **Bix Restored**. The cornetist's 1924–25 recordings (plus dates from 1926–27) are included in ◉ **Bix Restored, Vol. 1** (Sunbeam BXCD 1–3), which is discussed in the next chapter. **And the Chicago Cornets** (Milestone 47019) has all of the recordings by the

Wolverines (including the two later songs with Jimmy McPartland in Bix's place), Beiderbecke's early dates with the Sioux City Six and the Rhythm Jugglers, and seven unrelated numbers from the Bucktown Five, a fine 1924 quintet with cornetist Muggsy Spanier and clarinetist Volly DeFaut. The Wolverine recordings (which also have tenor saxophonist George Johnson taking some impressive spots) are highlighted by "Riverboat Shuffle" (the first Hoagy Carmichael song ever recorded), "Tiger Rag," "Royal Garden Blues," and "Big Boy."

During a trip to New York in the fall of 1924, the Wolverines made a strong impression, particularly Bix, who was soon offered a job with the Jean Goldkette Orchestra. After a few final performances and working with his replacement Jimmy McPartland, Bix joined Goldkette's band. Unfortunately, despite his tone and solo abilities, Beiderbecke still barely knew how to read music and he only lasted a short time before Goldkette reluctantly let him go. The Wolverines, who recorded two songs on one record date with McPartland, faded away into obscurity after struggling for a couple of years without Bix. Bix seemed to fade away for a time too.

In 1925, Beiderbecke worked with Charlie Straight's band (although he was also fired from that job for not being able to read music well), made one record date with a pickup group called the Rhythm Jugglers (introducing his "Davenport Blues"), attended the University of Iowa for two weeks before being expelled for being in a drunken brawl, and worked in St. Louis with an orchestra led by Frankie Trumbauer. During the latter engagement, Bix Beiderbecke strongly improved his sight-reading and became poised to make a major contribution to jazz during the second half of the 1920s.

Louis Armstrong and Fletcher Henderson Louis Armstrong was the most important jazz musician of all time. He did not invent the music and was not jazz's first soloist, but his innovations and accomplishments were enormous and his influence is still very strong, more than 30 years after his death.

Born in a poor section of New Orleans on August 4, 1901 (although he believed that his birth date was on July 4, 1900, his birth certificate was discovered posthumously), Armstrong first performed music singing on the streets in a vocal group for pennies. Inspired by the city's brass bands, he began trying to play cornet when he was 11, working odd jobs to help support his mother and sister (his father had long since abandoned the family). On New Year's Eve of 1912, Armstrong in celebration shot off a pistol in the air, was arrested, and sent to live in a waif's home. This ended up being a big break for him, for while in the orphanage, Armstrong began to seriously study the cornet. When he was released two years later, he was already an impressive player. "Little Louis" befriended King Oliver (who gave him a few informal lessons) and worked with a variety of local bands while having day jobs. In 1919, when Oliver went to Chicago, he recommended Armstrong for his spot with Kid Ory's band. Louis also spent time playing on riverboats with Fate Marable's group.

In 1922, when King Oliver's Creole Jazz Band settled in at Chicago's Lincoln Gardens, Oliver sent to New Orleans for his protégé to join him on second cornet. Initially nervous, Armstrong fit right in with the classic group, playing parts behind his idol in ensembles, spontaneously harmonizing two-bar breaks with Oliver, and taking occasional short solos. During this period he gained the nickname of "Satchelmouth" (to match Oliver's "Dippermouth"); it would not be shortened to "Satchmo" until the early 1930s. Armstrong appears on all of King Oliver's Creole Jazz Band's recordings in 1923, taking his first solo on "Chimes Blues." Louis Armstrong married King Oliver's Creole Jazz Band's pianist Lil Hardin (his second of four wives) in early 1924. He continued playing with Oliver even after the Dodds brothers left due to a money dispute, but eventually he heeded Lil's advice. Knowing that her husband would never be a star if he played second cornet forever, she persuaded Louis to accept an offer by Fletcher Henderson to join his orchestra in New York. That decision would change music history.

In 1924, Fletcher Henderson was leading the top black big band, one that was competing in some ways with Paul Whiteman. Henderson (the older brother of pianist/arranger Horace Henderson) began playing piano when he was six. He earned degrees in chemistry and mathematics from Atlanta University College (which he attended during 1916–20) and came to New York in 1920 in hopes of gaining work as a chemist. He quickly found out that black chemists (even in the relatively liberal North) were not in demand. So Henderson got a job as a song demonstrator for the Pace-Handy Music Company. Although he was never better than just an adequate pianist, Henderson's distinguished and soft-spoken

manner, along with his obvious intelligence, resulted in him soon becoming the recording manager for Harry Pace's Black Swan record label. He led the backup band for Ethel Waters from the fall of 1921 through mid-1922 and then became the house pianist for several labels (particularly Paramount, which had purchased Black Swan), recording with many blues and vaudeville singers during the next few years. He also began recording as a leader in 1921, performing dance music.

In 1923, Henderson's career became busy and he formed a ten-piece orchestra, purely for recordings at first. Among his sidemen were altoist/clarinetist Don Redman (who became his chief arranger) and the young tenor saxophonist Coleman Hawkins. By the early months of 1924, the Fletcher Henderson Orchestra had become a regularly working band, playing at the Club Alabam and in the summer at the Roseland Ballroom, its home base for the next decade.

It is a pity that the most prolific period of Henderson's recording career was before Louis Armstrong showed his musicians how to swing. Five Classics CDs fully document this early stage: **1921–1923** (Classics 794), **1923** (Classics 697), **1923–1924** (Classics 683), **1924** (Classics 683), and **1924, Vol. 2** (Classics 657). **1921–1923** has the only three unaccompanied piano solos of Henderson's career, some primitive band numbers from 1921–22, and the very beginnings of his big band from the following year. The many Henderson recordings of 1923 to mid-1924 are intriguing for what they do and do not include. The musicianship of the band was very good for the time and the musicians were proud of their ability to play Redman's complicated and often-futuristic charts. But the band sounds quite stiff rhythmically, the short solos (including those of Hawkins) often emphasize effects and odd sounds rather than solid ideas, and the music (syncopated dance music rather than creative jazz) rarely ever swings. In fact, the first time the Henderson band really swung on records was on the second half of "Charley, My Boy" on July 30, 1924, the orchestra's 80th recording of the 1923–24 period!

Trombonist Charlie Green (who joined in August 1924) was the band's first important soloist, and in October, Buster Bailey joined up. But it was the arrival of Louis Armstrong that changed everything. Although the New York musicians thought that they were among the best in the world, in reality the often-undocumented

Chicagoans (especially those who had moved from New Orleans) were far ahead of them, particularly in swinging and infusing jazz and dance music with the blues. Henderson's sidemen had doubts about Armstrong when they looked at his appearance and out-of-date clothes—that is, until he blew his horn. Then their eyebrows were raised and their minds were blasted open.

Louis Armstrong's legato (rather than staccato) lines, use of space and silence to dramatic effect, beautiful tone, and wide range were obvious. Most important was his ability to tell a story in his solos, not just stringing together a series of clichés and effects. His effect on the other musicians was immediate as Redman streamlined and loosened up his arrangements, Hawkins gradually modernized his phrasing, and the other musicians began to swing. During Armstrong's year with Henderson (October 1924 to November 1925), not only did he influence his fellow sidemen but all of New York's top musicians, who could not help but be impressed by his advanced ideas, use of bent notes, and ability to improvise over chord changes while keeping the melody in mind. It literally revolutionized the music world, with jazz sounding much different in late 1925 than it had 18 months before. And by the time Armstrong left to return to Chicago, the Fletcher Henderson Orchestra was the strongest big band in jazz.

⦿ **Louis with Fletcher Henderson 1924–1925** (Forte 38001/2/3) is a three-CD set that has all 65 of Armstrong's recordings with Henderson (including 22 alternate takes). It is remarkable how far ahead of all of the other musicians Armstrong sounds on the earlier numbers, as if he were playing in a different style altogether, one filled with creative ideas and rhythmic freedom. Among the more memorable selections are "Shanghai Shuffle," "Copenhagen," "Everybody Loves My Baby," and "Sugar Foot Stomp" (a reworking of King Oliver's "Dippermouth Blues"). In contrast to that definitive set, **Fletcher Henderson and Louis Armstrong** (Timeless 1-003) is a complete mess. This single CD has ten complete performances from Armstrong's period with Henderson along with 14 excerpts, some of which add his spliced-in solos from other takes. This would be fine, except that the music is not programmed in chronological order and not all of Armstrong's solos are included, making this set rather pointless. The two Classics CDs that cover Fletcher Henderson's band during this era, **1924, Vol. 3** (Classics 647) and **1924–1925**

(Classics 633), start with the session before Armstrong joined the band and conclude with the first date after he departed. But since the alternate takes are not included, the Forte set is much preferred.

Louis Armstrong helped lead the way toward jazz quickly evolving from group improvising (à la King Oliver's Creole Jazz Band) to the music being a forum for virtuoso soloists. In addition, Armstrong was on a series of blues-oriented sessions by singers, some of which practically feature him as a costar; the dates include meetings with Bessie Smith, Alberta Hunter, Margaret Johnson, Maggie Jones, Virginia Liston, Ma Rainey, Clara Smith, Trixie Smith, Eva Taylor, Sippie Wallace, and the team of Grant & Wilson. Armstrong also appeared on a series of records by Clarence Williams's Blue Five.

Louis Armstrong returned to Chicago after leaving Henderson in November 1925. His reputation was growing quickly among musicians who were starting to realize that he was the new leader of jazz, but at this point he was little known to the general public and even to many jazz fans. He had not yet sung on records (other than a cameo on Henderson's "Everybody Loves My Baby") and had not led any of his own record sessions. However on November 12, 1925, Louis Armstrong's Hot Five (with trombonist Kid Ory, clarinetist Johnny Dodds, pianist Lil Armstrong, and banjoist Johnny St. Cyr) recorded their first three songs ("My Heart," "Yes, I'm in the Barrel," and "Gut Bucket Blues") with Armstrong verbally introducing the musicians on "Gut Bucket Blues." These near-classic New Orleans jazz performances were early steps in what would soon be a monumental career.

Clarence Williams   Like Fletcher Henderson, Clarence Williams was just an okay pianist, but an inspired talent scout. Unlike Henderson, Williams was also a skilled businessman and a real hustler. He grew up in New Orleans, played piano in Storyville and worked as an emcee, dancer, and singer. Williams began writing songs in 1913 and became very interested in music publishing after a song that he had forgotten about ("Brownskin, Who You For") was recorded by a New York band and he received a surprise check of $1,600. Williams co-ran a publishing company with Armand J. Piron before moving to Chicago in 1920, where he ran a music store for a short time and then put together a very successful publishing company.

In 1921, Clarence Williams married singer Eva Taylor (their marriage lasted until his death 44 years later) and recorded six songs as a vocalist. In 1923, Williams started developing a profitable system to promote his music. He wrote songs, published them himself, sold the sheet music, had his wife sing the tunes on the radio, and arranged to have them recorded by some of the finest jazz players of the decade. Among the future standards that Williams wrote during this period (some co-composed with the unrelated Spencer Williams) are "Baby Won't You Please Come Home," "Royal Garden Blues," "Sugar Blues," "Everybody Loves My Baby," "'Tain't Nobody's Business If I Do," and "I Ain't Gonna Give Nobody None of My Jelly Roll." Williams became a major talent scout for Okeh (a post he held until 1928) and was constantly involved in setting up record dates. During his prime years (1923–31), Williams recorded 162 selections under his own name, including piano solos, jams with fairly large bands, and many combo sides. There were 12 selections cut in 1923, seven in 1924, and 13 in 1925 with the highlights including Sidney Bechet's first recordings and 16 selections with Louis Armstrong, including nine that matched Armstrong with Bechet (their only joint recordings other than a 1940 session). In addition, Williams organized other groups that recorded under pseudonyms, accompanied many blues singers (he was partly responsible for Columbia signing Bessie Smith), and appeared on his wife's records too.

Clarence Williams's lengthy and very valuable series of recordings is available in full (other than alternate takes) on 14 CDs put out by Classics. ◗ **1921–1924** (Classics 679) starts with Williams's six rare vocals from 1921 and then includes four piano solos and his first dates with his Blue Five. Sidney Bechet is heard on his recording debut (outstanding versions of "Wild Cat Blues" and "Kansas City Man Blues"), and Louis Armstrong makes contributions on three numbers in 1924 (including "Everybody Loves My Baby"). ◗ **1924–1926** (Classics 695) is particularly rewarding, with Louis Armstrong a major factor on the first 13 songs, six of which also include Bechet. "Mandy Make Up Your Mind" has Bechet taking a unique solo on the bass sarrusophone (the only time he used that instrument) while "Cake Walking Babies from Home" finds the two masters challenging each other, with Armstrong winning this time. The later numbers, which feature such

notables as Joe Smith, Bubber Miley or Ed Allen on trumpet or cornet, trombonist Charlie Irvis, Buster Bailey, and Coleman Hawkins (who takes a rare baritone solo on "Dinah") are quite enjoyable too.

The wife of Clarence Williams, Eva Taylor (born Irene Gibbons), was a good singer with a very likable voice and an easygoing style. She performed as a child, married Williams in 1921, and in 1922 became an important early performer on radio. Taylor appeared on many records (often with Williams's groups) including 72 titles of her own during 1922–32, which have been reissued in full on three Document CDs. **Vol. 1** (Document 5408) features Taylor on such numbers as "Oh Daddy Blues," the humorous "I've Got the Yes! We Have No Banana Blues," "Baby Won't You Please Come Home," "That Da-Da Strain," "12th Street Rag," "Farewell Blues," and "Original Charleston Strut." Taylor is assisted by such musicians as her husband, cornetists Johnny Dunn and Thomas Morris, Charlie Irvis, and Sidney Bechet on clarinet. ◗ **Vol. 2** (Document 5409) has much better recording quality and similar musicians (plus trumpeter Jabbo Smith) in the backup groups. There are quite a few memorable selections on this CD, including "Jazzin' Babies Blues," "Old Fashioned Love," "Ghost of the Blues," "Senorita Mine," a definitive version of "When the Red, Red Robin Comes Bob, Bob, Bobbin' Along," "Nobody but My Baby Is Getting My Love," "Candy Lips," and "If I Could Be with You."

Johnny Dunn   Cornetist Johnny Dunn was a victim of jazz's rapid evolution in the 1920s. Thought of as one of the leading jazz players of 1921, he was considered a has-been by 1926 (when he was 29) because his style had stayed the same. Dunn attended Fisk University and had a solo act in Memphis before he was discovered by W.C. Handy in 1917. Performing with Handy's band, Dunn was one of the pioneers at creating tonal distortions and expressive effects with the plunger mute, while his double-time breaks, although repetitive and predictable, gained a lot of attention for a time. He was a member of Mamie Smith's Jazz Hounds (1920–21), recorded with singer Edith Wilson, and led 14 titles with his Original Jazz Hounds during 1921–23. Dunn worked with Will Vodery's Plantation Orchestra in 1922 and visited Europe in 1923 with the *Dover to Dixie* revue.

Johnny Dunn (Frog 33) has all of the cornetist's recordings as a leader except two selections. Dunn does sound rather exciting on his early numbers, particularly

"Jazzin' Babies Blues" and "I Promise Not to Holler, but Hey! Hey!" But the best performances are actually his last ones, five titles (counting an alternate take) with Jelly Roll Morton in 1928 and two classic numbers from the same year with both Fats Waller and James P. Johnson on pianos. Also worth mentioning are **Johnny Dunn & Edith Wilson, Vol. 1** (RST 1522) and **Johnny Dunn, Vol. 2** (RST 1523), which duplicate the Frog CD (other than the Morton alternate) while also containing the missing Dunn sides plus his 18 numbers backing singer Edith Wilson (which are of lesser interest).

The Georgians   During the swing era, many big bands featured "specialty numbers" by jazz-oriented combos taken out of the orchestra. The first time that concept was used was by the Virginians (musicians from Paul Whiteman's band). The Georgians, a particularly strong unit whose members were taken out of Paul Specht's orchestra, was second and much more jazz-oriented. Trumpeter Frank Guarente started on trumpet while living in his native Italy, moved to the United States in 1910, and lived in New Orleans in 1914. After a period in the army and freelancing, he joined Specht in 1921. Starting in the fall of 1922, Guarente headed the Georgians, a small group from Specht's large ensemble that consisted of four horns and a three-piece rhythm section (with pianist Arthur Schutt and drummer Chauncey Morehouse). Guarente and Schutt provided the arrangements, and the Georgians recorded 42 numbers during 1922–24 that rank with the most swinging performances of the era despite the fact that the group has been long forgotten. ❍ **The Georgians 1922–23** (Retrieval 79003) has the band's first 24 recordings, instrumentals that are on the same high level as those of the Original Memphis Five of the period, with melodic ensembles, concise solos (Guarente was an excellent player), and strong musicianship. The Georgians lasted until May 1924 when Guarente moved to Europe, where he led the New Georgians for a few years.

Lovie Austin   Lovie Austin (born Cora Calhoun) was well schooled, studying music at Roger Williams University (in Nashville) and Knoxville College. She worked in theatres, toured with Irving Mills's *Blue Babies*, and played in New York with the Club Alabam show. A well-respected pianist/arranger who became the house pianist for Paramount Records (accompanying such blues singers as Ma Rainey, Ida Cox, Alberta Hunter, and Ethel Waters), Austin led her Blues Serenaders on 16 recordings during 1924–26, all of which are on **1924–1926** (Classics 756). Austins provided the arrangements and frameworks, but ironically her own playing is largely inaudible. There are ten cuts with clarinetist Jimmy O'Bryant and Tommy Ladnier or Bob Shoffner on cornet ("Steppin' on the Blues," "Charleston, South Carolina," and "Rampart Street Blues" are most memorable), plus six that utilize cornetist Natty Dominique, Kid Ory, and Johnny Dodds. Austin and some members of her group are also heard accompanying singers Edmonia Henderson, Ford & Ford, and Viola Bartlette.

Jimmy O'Bryant   Clarinetist Jimmy O'Bryant had the distinction of often sounding very close tonewise to Johnny Dodds. Very little is known about O'Bryant beyond his musical career. He worked with the Tennessee Ten during 1920–21 and had brief associations with Jelly Roll Morton (1923) and King Oliver (1924). In addition to session work backing a variety of blues singers, O'Bryant is best known for his recordings with Lovie Austin (1924–25) and with his Washboard Band (28 selections during 1924–26). **Vol. 1** (RST 1518) and **Vol. 2/Vance Dixon** (RST 1519) have all of his dates as a leader. The former set has two songs apiece in which O'Bryant, Tommy Ladnier, and Lovie Austin accompany singers Julia Davis and Sodarisa Miller. Otherwise the music features the clarinetist's Famous Original Washboard Band, a trio/quartet with pianist Jimmy Blythe, Jasper Taylor on washboard, and (on six numbers) Bob Shoffner. O'Bryant's many catchy originals compensate for the primitive recording quality of the Paramount pressings. The last nine numbers by O'Bryant's band start off **Vol. 2**, which also includes virtually the entire recording career of Vance Dixon, a decent if just adequate clarinetist. Dixon is heard with Lois Deppe's Serenaders (1923's "Congaine," which was pianist Earl Hines's first recording), two numbers backing future actress Hattie McDaniel in 1929, and all 11 of his selections as a leader; duets with pianist Kline Tyndall, and combo sides.

The Coon-Sanders Nighthawks   The Coon-Sanders Nighthawks was the first band to make it big on the radio. Pianist/singer/arranger Joe Sanders, while serving as a sergeant at Camp Bowie, Texas, during World War I, led a combo called the Camp Bowie Jazz Hounds. Drummer/singer Carleton A. Coon was a captain during the war. In December 1918 when Sanders was on leave, he stopped in a Kansas City music store, picked out a few songs to play, and started singing one of the tunes. Coon happened to be there, spontaneously harmonized with Sanders, and they immediately became friends. After being discharged from the military the following year, they formed the Coon-Sanders Novelty Orchestra. The ensemble epitomized the optimistic nature of the 1920s, featuring Sanders's snappy arrangements, lots of good-natured vocal interplay from the co-leaders, and surprisingly few solos; most of their spontaneous-sounding music was actually written out. Based in the Midwest, the group recorded four numbers in 1921 (only one was released) and on December 5, 1922, made their first radio broadcast for WOAF in Kansas City. Due to the late time of the show (which aired from midnight until 2:00 A.M.), the group was renamed the Coon-Sanders Nighthawks. They were popular from the start and, after relocating to Chicago in 1924, they began recording regularly for Victor. In addition to the band's one 1921 recording ("Some Little Bird"), **Vol. 1** (The Old Masters 111) has their first 22 selections for Victor, including such infectious numbers as "Night Hawk Blues," "Red Hot Mama," "Some of These Days," "Who Wouldn't Love You," and "Flamin' Mamie."

Isham Jones   Isham Jones is best known for the many wonderful songs he composed, including "It Had to Be You," "I'll See You in My Dreams," "The One I Love Belongs to Somebody Else," "There Is No Greater Love," and "On The Alamo," but he also led significant bands for 15 years. Jones played tenor sax as a youth, first led a band in 1912 when he was 18, and after moving to Chicago in 1915, he put together a trio that by 1921 had grown to 11 pieces. During 1922–24, his jazz-influenced dance band featured trumpeter Louis Panico, a talented trumpeter who nevertheless became best known for his corny playing on Jones's hit version of "Wabash Blues."

Despite covering the same period of time, there are only three duplicates between the 23 cuts put out by Timeless on ◉ **Isham Jones** (Timeless 067) and the 18 numbers on the Memphis Archives reissue, **Swinging Down the Lane** (Memphis Archives 7014). Timeless has 17 of the better selections with Louis Panico, including "Those Longing for You Blues," "Aunt Hagar's Children Blues," "Somebody's Wrong," and "Never Again." In addition, there are six numbers from 1925–26 (including "Riverboat

Shuffle" and "Charleston") before Jones's music became much more commercial. **Swinging Down the Lane** has six Panico appearances, two cuts by the Ray Miller Orchestra (with Jones conducting), eight tunes from 1925–26, and two somewhat out-of-place selections from 1930.

Armand J. Piron   Leader of one of the most interesting bands in New Orleans, Armand J. Piron had an orchestra that fell between society music and jazz. A violinist, Piron became a professional musician by 1904 and led his first group four years later. He worked with Clarence Williams in a publishing company and was credited with writing "I Wish I Could Shimmy like My Sister Kate," which Louis Armstrong (who felt cheated and always refused to play the song) always claimed was his original. Piron formed his New Orleans Orchestra in 1918, recording 18 selections during 1923–25 (including two apiece backing singers Ester Bigeou and Lela Bolden) that were last available on the British LP **Piron's New Orleans Orchestra** (Retrieval 128), including such numbers as "Bouncing Around," "Kiss Me Sweet," and "Mama's Gone Goodbye." The music is melodic and polite yet bluesy in spots, with a charm of its own.

Clifford Hayes   The first of four Clifford Hayes CDs, **Vol. 1** (RST 1501), contains some historic recordings. A decent country-style violinist, Hayes's records overlap into jazz, blues, and very early country music. Most notable on this disc are the ten numbers from September 1924 in which Hayes leads a trio with banjoist Curtis Hayes and Earl McDonald on jug behind blues singer Sara Martin, the earliest of all jug band recordings. Hayes is also heard with the Old Southern Jug Band (the same band with cornetist Theo Boone and banjoist Cal Smith in Sara Martin's place), Clifford's Louisville Jug Band (recorded six months later with the identical lineup), and on one number ("Boodle-Am-Shake") from late 1926 with the Dixieland Jug Blowers. In addition, there are four selections from Whistler & His Jug Band, a similar quartet without Hayes.

The Mound City Blue Blowers   In his career, Red McKenzie was just an okay ballad singer, but he had no competitors on the comb, which he wrapped with tissue paper and played like a kazoo. McKenzie had early jobs as a jockey (before breaking both arms in a fall) and a bellhop. He loved jazz and in 1923 formed the Mound City Blue Blowers, a very popular novelty trio consisting of his comb, Dick Slevin on kazoo, and banjoist Jack Bland. In 1924, they had a hit recording of "Arkansas Blues" (which sold over a million copies) and later in the year they became a quartet with the addition of Eddie Lang on guitar. The Mound City Blue Blowers recorded for Brunswick and (as Red McKenzie's Candy Kids) for Vocalion during 1924–25. All of those recordings are available on **Red McKenzie Vol. I** (Sensation 15164), including two songs that have Frank Trumbauer added on C-melody sax.

Various Artists   Several notable various artists CDs emphasize music from the 1921–25 period. **Edison Diamond Disc—Fox Trots** (Diamond Cut 307) has 20 examples of early 1920s dance music, performances originally released by the Edison label. The recording quality is good and the results are quite musical even if there is little actual improvising. Bands represented include Kaplan's Melodists, the Green Brothers Novelty Bands (with the virtuosic Charles Hamilton Green on xylophone), Harry Raderman ("Make that Trombone Laugh"), and the Broadway Dance Orchestra.

● **New Orleans in the '20s** (Timeless 1-014), recorded by the Okeh label during two New Orleans field trips in 1924–25, shows that there was a lot of worthwhile music still to be heard in the city even after the mass exodus to Chicago. Although such legends as Chris Kelly, Buddy Petit, and the young Bunk Johnson escaped being documented, nine important bands are on this CD, including Johnny De Droit's New Orleans Orchestra, Fate Marable (his only session, two disappointing songs), the Original Crescent City Jazzers (with cornetist Sterling Bose), Johnny Bayersdorffer's Jazzola Novelty Orchestra, the Halfway House Orchestra (with Leon Roppolo), Tony Parenti's Famous Melody Boys, Oscar Celestin's Original Tuxedo Jazz Orchestra, John Tobin's Midnight Serenaders, and the New Orleans Rhythm Kings session from January 23, 1925.

The complete work of cornetist Johnny De Droit (nine numbers) is on **Johnny De Droit and the New Orleans Jazz Orchestra** (Retrieval 79029), with his fine septet performing happy versions of "Panama," "The Swing," and "When My Sugar Walks Down the Street." But the main reason to acquire this CD is for the 14 selections by the Original Crescent City Jazzers and the very similar Arcadian Serenaders. With either Sterling Bose (his finest recordings) or Wingy Manone on cornet, this NORK-influenced band from 1924–25 (recorded in New Orleans and St. Louis) features inventive frameworks, easy-to-take vocals, and superior material, including "Who Can Our Regular Be Blues," "Fidgety Feet," "Back Home in Illinois," "You Gotta Know How," and "Just a Little Bit Bad."

Switching geographically, ● **The Chicago Hot Bands 1924–1928** (Timeless 1-041) has a variety of mostly lesser-known Midwest bands, with 26 selections in chronological order. The hot jazz-oriented reissue is comprised of performances from the Benson Orchestra of Chicago, Lloyd Turner's Villa Venice Orchestra, Al Katz's Kittens, Al Handler's Alamo Café Orchestra, Sol Wagner, Ray Miller, the Louisiana Rhythm Kings (the Coon-Sanders Orchestra in 1928), Danny Altier (featuring Muggsy Spanier), and all six numbers by Thelma Terry's Playboys.

● **Those Fabulous Gennetts, Vol. 1 1923–1925** (Timeless 1-062) puts the focus on the very significant Gennett label. Best remembered for its classic NORK, King Oliver, Wolverines, and Jelly Roll Morton sessions, Gennett also documented many lesser-known but talented bands. This CD has dates by Howard Lanin's Arcadia Orchestra, Guy Lombardo's Royal Canadians (four jazz-oriented numbers from their debut session of March 10, 1924), the Romance of Harmony Orchestra, the Lange-McKay Orchestra, Ross Reynolds's Palais Garden Orchestra, Perley Breed's Shepard Colonial Orchestra, Richard Hitter's Blue Knights, Marion McKay ("Doo Wacka Doo" which at one time was believed to have had a cornet solo by Bix Beiderbecke), the Chubb-Steinberg Orchestra (its three numbers feature the recording debut of cornetist Wild Bill Davison), Wally Erickson's Coliseum Orchestra, and Henry Thies's Castle Farm Orchestra. ● **Those Fabulous Gennetts, Vol. 2 1922–1925** (Timeless 1-080) is on the same level with performances by Husk O'Hare's Super Orchestra of Chicago, Pete Bontsema's Hotel Tuller Orchestra, and Eddie Mitchell's Orchestra. Of greatest interest are the recordings of Hitch's Happy Harmonists (Hoagy Carmichael guests on piano for two songs) and the seven selections (plus four alternates) from the Bucktown Five, a 1924 quintet that includes cornetist Muggsy Spanier's debut and clarinetist Volly De Faut.

By 1925, there was little doubt that jazz was no longer confined to New Orleans, Chicago, or New York. It was sweeping the country, the rage among young musicians and dancers alike. The jazz age was in full swing.

VOICES OF THE FUTURE

Wardell Gray (tenor), Feb. 13, 1921, Oklahoma City, OK

Eddie "Lockjaw" Davis (tenor), Mar. 2, 1921, New York, NY

Harry Babasin (bass, cello), Mar. 19, 1921, Dallas, TX

Candido (conga, percussion), Apr. 22, 1921, San Antonio De Los Baños, Cuba

Jimmy Giuffre (tenor, clarinet, baritone, composer), Apr. 26, 1921, Dallas, TX

Humphrey Lyttelton (trumpet, clarinet, leader), May 23, 1921, Windsor, England

Tal Farlow (guitar), June 7, 1921, Greensboro, NC

Erroll Garner (piano), June 15, 1921, Pittsburgh, PA

Tony Scott (clarinet), June 17, 1921, Morristown, NJ

George Barnes (guitar), July 17, 1921, Chicago Heights, IL

Mary Osborne (guitar), July 17, 1921, Minot, MD

Billy Taylor (piano), July 24, 1921, Greenville, NC

Herb Ellis (guitar), Aug. 4, 1921, Farmersville, TX

Buddy Collette (flute, tenor), Aug. 6, 1921, Los Angeles, CA

Norris Turney (alto, flute, tenor), Sept. 8, 1921, Wilmington, OH

Jon Hendricks (vocals, composer), Sept. 16, 1921, Newark, OH

Bill De Arango (guitar), Sept. 20, 1921, Cleveland, OH

Chico Hamilton (drums), Sept. 21, 1921, Los Angeles, CA

Julius Watkins (French horn), Oct. 10, 1921, Detroit, MI

Monk Montgomery (bass), Oct. 10, 1921, Indianapolis, IN

Roy Kral (vocals, piano), Oct. 10, 1921, Chicago, IL

Chico O'Farrill (arranger, composer), Oct. 28, 1921, Havana, Cuba

John Bunch (piano), Dec. 1, 1921, Tipton, IN

Johnny Otis (leader, drums, vibes), Dec. 28, 1921, Vallejo, CA

Frank Wess (tenor, flute, alto, arranger), Jan. 4, 1922, Kansas City, MO

Ray Anthony (trumpet, bandleader), Jan. 20, 1922, Bentleyville, PA

Kay Starr (vocals), Jan. 21, 1922, Dougherty, OK

Page Cavanaugh (piano, vocals), Jan. 26, 1922, Cherokee, KS

Joe Wilder (trumpet), Feb. 22, 1922, Colwyn, PA

King Pleasure (vocals), Mar. 24, 1922, Oakdale, TN

Duke Jordan (piano), Apr. 1, 1922, New York, NY

Mongo Santamaria (congas, percussion), Apr. 7, 1922, Havana, Cuba

Mundell Lowe (guitar), Apr. 21, 1922, Laurel, MS

Charles Mingus (bass, leader, composer, arranger), Apr. 22, 1922, Nogales, AZ

Lou Stein (piano), Apr. 22, 1922, Philadelphia, PA

Toots Thielemans (harmonica, guitar, whistling), Apr. 29, 1922, Brussels, Belgium

Gerald Wiggins (piano), May 12, 1922, New York, NY

Eddie Bert (trombone), May 16, 1922, Yonkers, NY

Kai Winding (trombone), May 18, 1922, Aarhus, Denmark

Jaki Byard (piano), June 15, 1922, Worcester, MA

Manny Albam (arranger), June 24, 1922, Samana, Dominican Republic

Johnny Smith (guitar), June 25, 1922, Birmingham AL

Ralph Burns (arranger, piano), June 29, 1922, Newton, MA

Rolf Ericson (trumpet), Aug. 29, 1922, Stockholm, Sweden

Joe Newman (trumpet), Sept. 7, 1922, New Orleans, LA

Charles Brown (piano, vocals), Sept. 13, 1922, Texas City, TX

Buddy Stewart (vocals), Sept. 22, 1922, Derry, NH

Jack Costanzo (bongos, congas), Sept. 24, 1922, Chicago, IL

Oscar Pettiford (bass, cello, composer), Sept. 30, 1922, Okmulgee, OK

Von Freeman (tenor), Oct. 3, 1922, Chicago, IL

Stan Hasselgard (clarinet), Oct. 4, 1922, Bollnas, Sweden

Neal Hefti (arranger, composer), Oct. 29, 1922, Hastings, NE

Illinois Jacquet (tenor, bassoon, leader), Oct. 31, 1922, Broussard, LA

Ralph Sutton (piano), Nov. 4, 1922, Hamburg, MO

Al Hirt (trumpet), Nov. 7, 1922, New Orleans, LA

Cecil Payne (baritone), Dec. 14, 1922, Brooklyn, NY

Milt Jackson (vibes), Jan. 1, 1923, Detroit, MI

Osie Johnson (drums), Jan. 11, 1923, Washington, D.C.

Mel Powell (piano, arranger), Feb. 12, 1923, New York, NY

Buddy DeFranco (clarinet), Feb. 17, 1923, Camden, NJ

Dexter Gordon (tenor), Feb. 27, 1923, Los Angeles, CA

Thad Jones (trumpet, composer, arranger, leader), Mar. 28, 1923, Pontiac, MI

VOICES OF THE FUTURE

Ray Sherman (piano), Apr. 15, 1923, Chicago, IL

Bennie Green (trombone), Apr. 16, 1923, Chicago, IL

Percy Heath (bass), Apr. 30, 1923, Wilmington, NC

Red Garland (piano), May 13, 1923, Dallas, TX

Ellis Larkins (piano), May 15, 1923, Baltimore, MD

George Russell (composer, arranger), June 23, 1923, Cincinnati, OH

Elmo Hope (piano, composer), June 27, 1923, New York, NY

Pete Candoli (trumpet), June 28, 1923, Mishawaka, IN

Johnny Hartman (vocals), July 13, 1923, Chicago, IL

Philly Joe Jones (drums), July 15, 1923, Philadelphia, PA

Jimmy Witherspoon (vocals), Aug. 8, 1923, Gurdon, AR

Dill Jones (piano), Aug. 19, 1923, Newcastle Emlyn, Wales

Idrees Sulieman (trumpet), Aug. 27, 1923, St. Petersburg, FL

Fats Navarro (trumpet), Sept. 24, 1923, Key West, FL

Sam Rivers (tenor, soprano, flute, piano, leader), Sept. 25, 1923, Reno, OK

Barney Kessel (guitar), Oct. 17, 1923, Muskogee, OK

Willie Cook (trumpet), Nov. 11, 1923, Tangipahoa, LA

Charlie Mariano (alto), Nov. 12, 1923, Boston, MA

Serge Chaloff (baritone), Nov. 24, 1923, Boston, MA

Bob Dorough (piano, vocals, composer), Dec. 12, 1923, Cherry Hill, AR

Max Roach (drums, leader), Jan. 10, 1924, New Land, NC

J.J. Johnson (trombone, arranger, composer), Jan. 22, 1924, Indianapolis, IN

Joe Albany (piano), Jan. 24, 1924, Atlantic City, NJ

Alice Babs (vocals), Jan. 26, 1924, Kalmar, Sweden

Sonny Stitt (alto, tenor), Feb. 2, 1924, Boston, MA

Ray Crawford (guitar), Feb. 7, 1924, Pittsburgh, PA

Dick Katz (piano arranger), Mar. 13, 1924, Baltimore, MD

Brew Moore (tenor), Mar. 26, 1924, Indianola, MS

Sarah Vaughan (vocals), Mar. 27, 1924, Newark, NJ

Charlie Rouse (tenor), Apr. 6, 1924, Washington, D.C.

Dorothy Donegan (piano), Apr. 6, 1924, Chicago, IL

Shorty Rogers (trumpet, flugelhorn, arranger, composer, leader), Apr. 14, 1924, Great Barrington, MA

Teddy Edwards (tenor), Apr. 26, 1924, Jackson, MS

Marshall Allen (alto), May 25, 1924, Louisville, KY

Lucky Thompson (tenor, soprano), June 16, 1924, Columbia, SC

Louie Bellson (drums), July 6, 1924, Rock Falls, IL

Major Holley (bass), July 10, 1924, Detroit, MI

Al Haig (piano), July 22, 1924, Newark, NJ

Bill Perkins (tenor, baritone), July 22, 1924, San Francisco, CA

Corky Corcoran (tenor), July 28, 1924, Tacoma, WA

Tom Talbert (arranger, composer), Aug. 4, 1924, Minneapolis, MN

Dinah Washington (vocals), Aug. 29, 1924, Tuscaloosa, AL

Kenny Dorham (trumpet, composer), Aug. 30, 1924, Fairfield, TX

Putte Wickman (clarinet), Sept. 10, 1924, Falun, Sweden

Bud Powell (piano, composer), Sept. 27, 1924, New York, NY

John Graas (French horn), Oct. 14, 1924, Dubuque, IA

George Wallington (piano, composer), Oct. 27, 1924, Palermo, Sicily, Italy

Dick Cathcart (trumpet), Nov. 6, 1924, Michigan City, IN

Sam Jones (bass, cello), Nov. 12, 1924, Jacksonville, FL

Paul Desmond (alto), Nov. 25, 1924, San Francisco, CA

Arne Domnerus (alto, clarinet), Dec. 20, 1924, Stockholm, Sweden

Francisco Aguabella (percussionist), 1925, Matanzas, Cuba

Sam Woodyard (drums), Jan. 7, 1925, Elizabeth, NJ

Marty Paich (arranger, piano), Jan. 23, 1925, Oakland, CA

Jutta Hipp (piano), Feb. 4, 1925, Leipzig, Germany

Elliot Lawrence (arranger, piano), Feb. 14, 1925, Philadelphia, PA

Dave Pell (tenor, leader), Feb. 26, 1925, Brooklyn, NY

Wes Montgomery (guitar), Mar. 6, 1925, Indianapolis, IN

Roy Haynes (drums), Mar. 13, 1925, Roxbury, MA

James Moody (tenor, flute, alto), Mar. 26, 1925, Savannah, GA

Harold Ashby (tenor), Mar. 27, 1925, Kansas City, MO

Gene Ammons (tenor), Apr. 14, 1925, Chicago, IL

Leo Parker (baritone), Apr. 18, 1925, Washington, D.C.

Tito Puente (timbales, vibes, leader), Apr. 20, 1925, New York, NY

Sonny Berman (trumpet), Apr. 21, 1925, New Haven, CT

Al Grey (trombone), June 6, 1925, Aldie, VA

Cal Tjader (vibes, leader), July 16, 1925, St. Louis, MO

Nat Pierce (piano, arranger), July 16, 1925, Somerville, MA

VOICES OF THE FUTURE

Jimmy Scott (vocals), July 17, 1925, Cleveland, OH

Earl Coleman (vocals), Aug. 12, 1925, Port Huron, MI

Benny Bailey (trumpet), Aug. 13, 1925, Cleveland, OH

Oscar Peterson (piano, leader, composer), Aug. 15, 1925, Montreal, Quebec, Canada

Art Pepper (alto, clarinet), Sept. 1, 1925, Gardena, CA

Mel Tormé (vocals, drums, composer), Sept. 13, 1925, Chicago, IL

Charlie Byrd (guitar), Sept. 16, 1925, Chuckstuck, VA

George Wein (piano), Oct. 3, 1925, Boston, MA

Bill Dixon (trumpet), Oct. 5, 1925, Nantucket, MA

Zoot Sims (tenor, soprano), Oct. 29, 1925, Inglewood, CA

Errol Parker (piano, drums), Oct. 30, 1925, Oran, Algeria

Teo Macero (tenor, composer, producer), Oct. 30, 1925, Glens Falls, NY

Gunther Schuller (composer, French horn), Nov. 11, 1925, Jackson Heights, NY

June Christy (vocals), Nov. 20, 1925, Springfield, IL

Johnny Mandel (composer, arranger), Nov. 23, 1925, New York, NY

Al Cohn (tenor), Nov. 24, 1925, New York, NY

Gigi Gryce (alto, composer), Nov. 28, 1925, Pensacola, FL

Bob Cooper (tenor), Dec. 6, 1925, Pittsburgh, PA

Jimmy Smith (organ), Dec. 8, 1925, Norristown, PA

Dodo Marmarosa (piano), Dec. 12, 1925, Pittsburgh, PA

Sal Salvador (guitar), Dec. 21, 1925, Monson, MA

PASSINGS

Tony Jackson (44), Apr. 20, 1921, Chicago, IL

Tom Turpin (48), Aug. 13, 1922, St. Louis, MO

Vess Ossman (55), Dec. 8, 1923, Minneapolis, MN

Chapter Three

1926–1932:
From Boom to Bust

During 1926–29, the evolution of jazz shot forward quickly as dozens of major musicians, singers, and arranger/composers burst upon the scene. The most important event affecting jazz recordings was a technical one. Up until 1925, all recordings were made acoustically with the results sounding tinny and only hinting at what the music really was like live. Starting in 1925, with the development of electrical recording, which used microphones and electric amplifiers, fidelity was dramatically improved and the sounds of individual instruments were duplicated in a much more lifelike fashion. The improvement in recording quality (which was adopted by most labels by 1927 and by all record companies by 1929) indirectly led to such important events as the rise of the soloist, the replacement of the banjo with the formerly nearly inaudible guitar, full drum sets finally being recorded, and much more musical and subtle vocalists catching on. It also makes music from 1927 much more listenable to today's jazz fans than performances from 1923.

The record industry boomed during the second half of the 1920s, with 150 million records being sold in the United States alone in 1929. Such record labels as Columbia (which had almost gone bankrupt in 1923 due to the rise of radio), Victor, Brunswick, Vocalion, Okeh, Gennett, Paramount, and a variety of smaller labels all recorded significant jazz, including "race records" specifically made for the black market but also purchased by enlightened whites.

During 1926–29, an overwhelming number of major musical moments were captured on record. Just as a few examples, there were Louis Armstrong's Hot Five and Hot Seven recordings (along with his first dates with big bands), the peak of Bix Beiderbecke's career, the big bands of Fletcher Henderson and Duke Ellington, the wild, chance-taking piano of Earl Hines, Jelly Roll Morton's finest combo recordings, the beginnings for Eddie Condon and the Chicagoans, the unusual music of Red Nichols's Five Pennies, the start of Jack Teagarden's career, King Oliver's Dixie Syncopators, the team of Joe Venuti and Eddie Lang, and many singers ranging from Bessie Smith and Annette Hanshaw to Bing Crosby.

The year 1926 began with Calvin Coolidge, one year into his second term as president, presiding in a passive and quiet way over a booming peacetime economy. With the stock market hitting new heights, prosperity looked endless and the general optimism was reflected in the music of the time. So happy were Americans with the economy and the general way of life (despite some warning signals) that the Republicans retained the White House during the 1928 election, with Herbert Hoover defeating Al Smith in spite of Smith being in favor of repealing Prohibition.

However, just nine months into Hoover's term in 1929, the stock market began to collapse and the mood of the country changed immediately, putting a halt to the classic jazz era. With the unemployment rate reaching 25 percent by 1932 and no safety net in existence, Americans were really struggling, with the government acting powerless to change the situation. Soothing dance bands and ballad-oriented vocalists started to dominate pop music, while jazz (which was to many people a reminder of the carefree and somewhat irresponsible 1920s) was pushed aside for the moment. Even the defeat of Herbert Hoover by the upbeat Franklin Delano Roosevelt in the 1932 presidential election did not stop things from looking grim.

The stock market crash resulted in the collapse of the record industry (only a total of 10 million records were sold in 1933, less than 7 percent of the 1929 total) and the rise of commercial dance bands. The most technically skilled white players became studio musicians while many of their black counterparts either slipped into obscurity or became parts of big bands. The center of jazz shifted from Chicago (1920–27) to New York,

and by the early 1930s much of the most significant music was being played by black big bands in Harlem. The stage was set for the swing era by 1932 when Duke Ellington recorded "It Don't Mean a Thing If It Ain't Got that Swing." But swing as a national phenomenon was still three years away, and jazz was mostly underground, a temporary victim of the Depression.

The Pacesetters: 1926–1932

As 1926 began, the New Orleans method of group improvising was being de-emphasized, with a greater emphasis on individual solos and arranged ensembles. The improved recording quality made larger bands much more feasible to record, and since jazz was thought of as an exciting type of dance music, why have a six-piece band when one could use twelve musicians?

During 1926–27, the cornet was largely replaced by the trumpet as a dominant instrument. While the veterans Freddie Keppard (who made his best records in 1926) and King Oliver were still quite active, all eyes in the jazz world were on Louis Armstrong. His beautiful tone, impressive technique, and legato phrasing were already becoming influential in 1926, and his ability to "tell a story" in his solos, while infusing pop tunes with blues feeling, was changing the way that jazz was being improvised. Other than his very first session with his Hot Five in late 1925, Armstrong had not recorded as a leader previously, but that changed very quickly. His Hot Five recordings of 1926–27, Hot Seven sessions of 1927, and Savoy Ballroom Five dates of 1928 made Armstrong an innovative force in jazz who was years ahead of his time. When he began recording pop tunes with big bands in 1929 (turning everything he played into

---

TIMELINE 1926

Jelly Roll Morton begins recording for Victor and is heard at the height of his powers. • Louis Armstrong's Hot Five recordings include "Heebies Jeebies" and "Cornet Chop Suey." • Bix Beiderbecke joins the Jean Goldkette Orchestra. • Steve Brown's playing with Goldkette sets the standard among bassists. • Fifteen-year-old Annette Hanshaw makes her recording debut. • Trumpeter Punch Miller settles in Chicago. • Lovie Austin makes her last recordings for 34 years and becomes the musical director of the Monogram Theatre. • Fess Williams's Royal Flush Orchestra is based at New York's Savoy Ballroom. • Red Nichols's Five Pennies make their first recordings, as does the team of Joe Venuti and Eddie Lang. • Fletcher Henderson stars Coleman Hawkins on "The Stampede." • The Bennie Moten Orchestra switches to the Victor label. • Benny Goodman and Glenn Miller make their recording debuts with Ben Pollack.

creative jazz), Satch's fame began spreading far beyond the jazz world.

Louis Armstrong's influence on other trumpeters could be felt as early as 1926 (Shirley Clay was an early follower) and grew during the next few years to such an extent that most trumpeters by 1930 sounded like disciples. Certainly Satch's extroverted storytelling style can be heard in the playing of Cootie Williams, Rex Stewart, Henry "Red" Allen, and Jabbo Smith by 1929, although those four trumpeters also were developing their own sounds and approaches.

In the late 1920s, there were two other main ways to play the trumpet and/or cornet in jazz groups. Bix Beiderbecke had a cooler sound and a lyrical style, using whole-tone runs and unusual choices of notes while still playing melodically; his approach touched the styles of Red Nichols and Jimmy McPartland. Joe Smith and Arthur Whetsol also had cool tones, although they were not influenced by Beiderbecke. The other approach was distorting the tone of the trumpet/cornet with a variety of mutes that allowed brass men to create unusual sounds. Johnny Dunn and King Oliver were among the pioneers although Bubber Miley exceeded them in his ability to come up with eerie otherworldly tones. Cootie Williams, who became Miley's successor with Duke Ellington's Orchestra in 1929, took it even further in the 1930s.

Most time periods find one or two instruments being liberated from their former role. During 1926–32, it was the trombone's turn. Kid Ory's percussive style had formerly been the main way that the trombone was utilized in jazz, when it was not being cast as a humorous prop. Charlie Green (who was particularly effective on the blues), the underrated Charlie Irvis, and Tricky Sam Nanton (who was Bubber Miley's equivalent on trombone in his mastery of mutes) all made important contributions. But Miff Mole was the first trombonist to take a major step forward in freeing his horn from being just a supportive instrument, playing the trombone on the same level as a trumpet. His wide interval jumps and eccentric choice of notes (heard at its best with Red Nichols's groups) sounded somewhat futuristic. However, Mole's staccato phrasing could be a bit awkward and his influence was limited. Jimmy Harrison (one of Fletcher Henderson's stars) was a much smoother player, but he never had the opportunity to lead his own sessions. It was ultimately up to Jack Teagarden (who arrived in New York in 1927) to permanently change the role of the trombone. Not only could he play the blues at Charlie Green's level and solo with the authority of both Mole and Harrison, but his distinctive sound and impressive technique on trombone were unprecedented in jazz at the time. His likable personality and expert blues-based singing added to his appeal. Other significant trombonists who emerged during this era included the rambunctious J.C. Higginbotham, the highly expressive and humorous Dickie Wells, Tommy Dorsey, whose lovely tone was difficult to top, and Lawrence Brown.

The clarinet probably had more unique voices during the 1926–32 period than any other instrument. Johnny Dodds's cutting tone, heard with the Hot Five and Hot Seven, Jelly Roll Morton, King Oliver, and his own groups, has rarely been duplicated. Although Sidney Bechet spent much of this period overseas and was largely unknown to the general American public, he remained an important force.

While the trombone was not abused much after the mid-1920s as a novelty instrument, the "gaspipe" style of clarinet lingered on until the end of the decade. The often-silly tonal distortions indulged in by Ted Lewis (who other musicians tended to laugh at rather than with), Boyd Senter, and Fess Williams sound annoying today, although Wilton Crawley was such an extremist with his sounds that he still comes across as humorous if heard in small doses.

More significant in the long run was the rise of Jimmie Noone. Dodds and Bechet were so individual that few of their contemporaries were able to copy them. Noone, who had a smoother and more generic sound, ended up becoming the biggest clarinet influence of the time, particularly on the tone of Benny Goodman. With his Apex Club Orchestra, Noone showed that the clarinet could be a lead voice and make a trumpetless group sound quite complete. Other top clarinetists of the 1926–32 period include the up-and-coming Benny Goodman, Buster Bailey, Jimmy Dorsey, Pee Wee Russell, and Frank Teschemacher.

The trumpet/cornet, trombone, and clarinet were major instruments by 1920, but it took a bit longer for the saxophone to catch on. The tenor sax was mostly just used as a percussive ensemble instrument in the early 1920s, and even the young Coleman Hawkins filled his solos with dated effects and slap tonguing, until he heard Louis Armstrong. Hawkins learned quickly from Satch and by 1925, his solos began to become more coherent and purposeful. His 1926 recording with Fletcher Henderson, "The Stampede," had the first significant tenor solo, and Hawkins became his instrument's pacesetter. His large, thick tone, mastery of chords, and advanced ideas set the standard, even if rhythmically he was not all that smooth yet. Hawkins so dominated his instrument that both Chu Berry and Ben Webster (who emerged in the early 1930s) paid tribute to Hawk with every note. Only Bud Freeman, who had a lighter tone and a more angular style, was able to carve out an individual voice during this time.

The other saxophones all had their stars. The alto saxophone had been mostly used as a sweetener on jazz dates in the early 1920s and as the lead voice in saxophone sections. Jimmy Dorsey in 1926 emerged as the first top alto soloist. He was soon followed by Johnny Hodges, whose beautiful tone sometimes overshadowed his swinging style, and Benny Carter. The baritone sax was an obscure instrument until Harry Carney joined Duke Ellington in 1927; his tone was definitive. The soprano sax continued to be dominated by Sidney Bechet. Two other horns had their leaders: Frankie Trumbauer on the C-melody sax and bass saxophonist Adrian Rollini. But while the tenor and alto caught on, the baritone sax was used in few big bands other than Ellington's during this era, the soprano remained a rarity, the C-melody sax would become extinct after Trumbauer's period in the spotlight, and the bass sax's function was assumed by the string bass by the late 1920s.

Alberto Socarras took a few solos on flute in the 1920s, and Wayman Carver emerged in the early 1930s (recording with Spike Hughes and joining Chick Webb's orchestra). Despite that, the flute would be little more than a rare novelty in jazz until the 1950s. The violin, a part of many very early New Orleans bands, had its first major soloists starting in the mid-1920s with the rise of the brilliant Joe Venuti, Eddie South, and Stuff Smith (the latter two would make their greatest impact later in the 1930s) although there would never be more than a few great jazz violinists active at any one time in jazz history.

The most dominant instrument in the rhythm section was the piano. In fact, when the stride piano style was played with the facility of a James P. Johnson or Fats Waller, there was almost no need for any other rhythm instruments. Blues and boogie-woogie pianists (such as Pinetop Smith, Meade Lux Lewis, and Jimmy Blythe) developed an alternate tradition during the time, but the stride players dominated the scene. However, the metronomic nature of jazz pianists began to loosen up with the rise of Earl "Fatha" Hines later in the decade. Hines loved to suspend time, had the trickiest (and most unpredictable) left hand, and took startling breaks with his right hand, somehow never losing the beat. His playing pointed toward the future.

When the bands were larger or the pianist had a lighter touch, other rhythm instruments were employed. While Harry Reser (who led the popular Cliquot Club Eskimos on the radio) was a remarkable novelty ragtime banjo soloist, most other banjoists were employed primarily to play rhythmic chords in the ensembles. With the development of electric recording, by 1927 the constant clanging of the banjo began to be seen as a liability. Guitarist Eddie Lang's ability to play complex chords and single-note solos and to uplift every session rhythmically no matter what the style made him greatly in demand for record dates, with Carl Kress and Dick McDonough soon joining him in the studios. Teddy Bunn, who guested on a record date with Duke Ellington in 1929, was a versatile player specializing in single-note bluesy lines who sounded quite at home in the happy ensemble music of the Washboard Serenaders and the Spirits of Rhythm. Lonnie Johnson was the first guitarist from the blues world (where his instrument was considered much more important than in jazz) to cross over and add his solo strength to jazz dates. But other than those players and just a few others, guitarists in jazz were restricted to the background where they solidified rhythm sections while still being barely audible much of the time.

Many jazz combo sessions of the 1920s had piano, banjo, and drums as their rhythm section, with the bass or tuba considered an unnecessary frivolity. In retrospect, most groups would have swung more and been greatly strengthened if they had included bass or tuba. The tuba was louder (and favored on the acoustic recordings), but the bass could be played four notes to the bar without the musician having to gasp for air. Steve Brown (the first important bassist on records) with the Jean Goldkette Orchestra in 1924–27 showed just how flexible the bass could be, often swinging the big band during a song's final chorus. After Brown drifted into obscurity during 1928, Wellman Braud and Pops Foster were considered the top bassists. Tubas were still employed by many groups until around 1932 (Cyrus St. Clair with

Clarence Williams's bands was among the most prominent on the instrument) before becoming completely eclipsed by string bassists, which became an essential part of big bands.

Before 1927, drummers were only able to utilize part of their drum set on recordings, generally just woodblocks, cymbals, and perhaps the snare, but never the bass drum. By 1927, recording techniques had improved enough so Gene Krupa could become the first drummer to use his full set (on the classic McKenzie-Condon Chicagoans sides). While Zutty Singleton with Louis Armstrong's Savoy Ballroom Five in 1928 and Baby Dodds with the Jelly Roll Morton trio made the most out of minimalism, by 1929 drummers were finally being documented properly. Chick Webb and Dave Tough joined Krupa, Dodds, and Singleton as the most respected drummers, although it would be a few years before drummers were considered potential stars, rising above the level of just keeping time.

Most male singers who appeared on jazz records in the 1920s and the early '30s are difficult to listen to, and collectors wait impatiently for their chorus to end so the real jazz can resume. Such studio singers as Irving Kaufman, Jack Kaufman, Scrappy Lambert, Smith Ballew, Dick Robertson (who would improve in later years), Chick Bullock, and Wesley Vaughan took up too much space on far too many jazz records, and the popularity of Rudy Vallee and Russ Colombo seems bewildering today. But fortunately there were a few major exceptions.

The unjustly overlooked Cliff Edwards ("Ukulele Ike") was among the very first jazz singers on record and one of the first scat singers. But for many, male jazz singing really began with Louis Armstrong, who phrased like a horn, was subtle in improving the melody of songs, and could scat on a higher level than anyone of the era. Jack Teagarden had a similar (if lazier) approach and both Satch and Mr. T. were influences on Bing Crosby, who brought jazz phrasing into pop music. Cab Calloway combined the outlandish excesses of Al Jolson with swinging jazz and his own "Hi-De-Ho" musical personality to create a legendary character. And the Mills Brothers, who expertly imitated instruments while only being backed by a rhythm guitar, were in their own category.

While only a few male vocalists (other than musicians who occasionally sang) would be considered jazz performers, there were many more females. Bessie Smith, Alberta Hunter, and Ethel Waters proved to be the most durable of the classic blues singers. Ruth Etting was the Bing Crosby of female singers, bringing jazz into pop music. The Boswell Sisters were an innovative and exciting vocal group, and both Annette Hanshaw and Mildred Bailey emerged as major singers.

Jazz arranging came of age during 1926–32 with the work of Don Redman and Duke Ellington. Redman, whose use of clarinet trios with the Fletcher Henderson Orchestra was a trademark, took what he learned from hearing Louis Armstrong play nightly during 1924–25 and orchestrated some of those ideas for the Henderson big band, showing that arrangements could swing. By 1928, he was the creative genius behind McKinney's Cotton Pickers. Duke Ellington, who emerged during 1926–27, improved year by year and was a master at writing for individual voices and at creating unusual atmospheric pieces. Bill Challis's charts made both the Jean Goldkette and Paul Whiteman Orchestras swing, and other important writers of the time included Benny Carter, Gene Gifford (with the Casa Loma Orchestra), and Jelly Roll Morton, who did wonders with small to medium-size combos.

When one considers all of the major talent at work during this era, it is no surprise that for collectors of vintage records, the 1926–32 period is thought of as an early golden age.

Louis Armstrong   By the end of 1925, when he left the Fletcher Henderson Orchestra and moved back to Chicago, Louis Armstrong had a growing reputation among musicians, although he was largely unknown to the general public since he had been working almost exclusively as a sideman. However, by 1932, he had surpassed Paul Whiteman as the most famous performer in jazz, both in the United States and internationally.

Although Armstrong primarily worked in big bands during the 1926–28 period in Chicago (first with his wife Lil Armstrong's group and then Erskine Tate's Vendome Orchestra and the Carroll Dickerson Orchestra, taking over the latter for a time), it was his recordings with his Hot Five and Hot Seven during 1926–27 that caused the biggest impact in the jazz world. Strangely enough, the Hot Five, which sounded like an organized group, only actually appeared in public once, at a special concert held by the Okeh label.

The original Hot Five consisted of Armstrong (who switched from cornet to trumpet in 1927), clarinetist

Johnny Dodds, trombonist Kid Ory, pianist Lil Armstrong, and banjoist/guitarist Johnny St. Cyr. Because Satch was such a major soloist, he could not be confined to just a few short breaks, a chorus, or leading the ensembles. His rapid emergence as a virtuoso (his playing on "Cornet Chop Suey" was unprecedented in jazz at the time) was watched closely and emulated by his contemporaries. One could say that in these recordings (which include the Hot Seven dates of 1927 with John Thomas filling in for Ory on trombone and both drummer Baby Dodds and Pete Briggs on tuba being added), Armstrong led the way from New Orleans jazz to swing.

 ❍ **The Complete Hot Five and Hot Seven Recordings** (Columbia/Legacy 63527) is an essential four-CD set that has all 33 songs by the 1925–27 Hot Five, 11 numbers from the Hot Seven, and 19 tunes by the 1928 Savoy Ballroom Five, plus three big band selections (from Armstrong's Stompers and Carroll Dickerson) in addition to a variety of other related numbers (including songs from Lil's Hot Shots and Johnny Dodds, a few cuts originally mistakenly released as by the Hot Five, and some songs featuring blues singers that use part of the Hot Five personnel). The basic 66 numbers (without the extras) are also available as four separate CDs that trace Armstrong's development from late 1925 through 1928. **Hot Fives, Vol. 1** (Columbia/Legacy 44049) has the first 16 Hot Fives including "Gut Bucket Blues" (during which Armstrong verbally introduces the members of the band), "Come Back Sweet Papa," "Heebies Jeebies" (Satch's first real scat vocal, allegedly taken spontaneously when he dropped the music during the recording), "Cornet Chop Suey," and the original version of Kid Ory's "Muskrat Ramble." **Hot Fives and Sevens, Vol. 2** (Columbia/Legacy 42253) has numbers by both the Hot Five ("Jazz Lips," "Big Butter and Egg Man," and the strangely eerie "Skid-Dat-De-Dat" are most memorable) and Hot Seven ("Willie the Weeper," "Wild Man Blues," and "Potato Head Blues," with the latter having a superb Armstrong solo over a stop-time rhythm). During 1926–27, no other jazz soloist was on Louis Armstrong's level, and he had a strong enough technique to seemingly play every adventurous idea that popped into his head.

Although Armstrong is thought of as a symbol of New Orleans jazz, the music that he plays on **Hot Fives and Sevens, Vol. 3** (Columbia/Legacy 44422) and **Louis Armstrong and Earl Hines, Vol. 4** (Columbia/Legacy 45142) is often far beyond the confines of his

native city's music. **Vol. 3** has the final recordings of both the Hot Seven and the original Hot Five, with some remarkable playing on "Struttin' with Some Barbecue" (which has a perfect Armstrong solo, complete with beginning, middle, and end), "Got No Blues," and "Hotter Than That" (the last two featuring guitarist Lonnie Johnson as a guest). In addition, this CD has the first numbers from the Savoy Ballroom Five ("Fireworks" and "A Monday Date").

If anything, Armstrong was a more adventurous soloist in 1928 than he had been the year before. Constantly challenged by Earl Hines, with whom he had first played in big bands more than a year earlier, Satch put together a completely new group for his 1928 recordings. The Savoy Ballroom Five (which was really a sextet/septet) consisted of the duo plus drummer Zutty Singleton, whose playing was continually inspiring, trombonist Fred Robinson, clarinetist/tenorman Jimmy Strong, banjoist Mancy Cara, and occasionally altoist Don Redman. **Vol. 4** has Armstrong's three big band numbers from 1926–27 plus all of the rest of his 1928 sessions, including the original version of "Basin Street Blues" and an early rendition of "St. James Infirmary." The Armstrong-Hines duet recording of "Weatherbird" is as advanced as any jazz record of 1928, while "West End Blues" would always be the trumpeter's personal favorite recording. The latter features a remarkable opening cadenza, some impressive wordless vocalizing by Armstrong, and a dramatic closing statement. If he had only recorded this one performance, Louis Armstrong would be considered immortal.

But there were many other accomplishments by the young trumpeter/singer during this time. **Louis Armstrong and the Blues Singers** (Affinity 1018), a six-CD box, collects together all 120 selections in which Armstrong accompanies other singers, dating from 1924–30. Not all of the music is essential, but there are many gems to be heard, with the trumpeter uplifting quite a few songs and often stealing the show altogether. Among the more memorable selections are Ma Rainey's "See See Rider Blues," Virginia Liston's "Early in the Morning," Maggie Jones's "Anybody Here Want to Try My Cabbage," Alberta Hunter and Sidney Bechet on "Nobody Knows the Way I Feel 'Dis Morning," Armstrong and Bechet romping with Eva Taylor on "Cake Walking Babies from Home," Bessie Smith's "St. Louis Blues" and "Careless Love," Perry Bradford's "I Ain't

Gonna Play No Second Fiddle If I Can Play the Lead," Chippie Hill's "Trouble in Mind," Lillie Delk Christian's "Too Busy" (which has Armstrong taking an exuberant vocal), Victoria Spivey's "How Do You Do It that Way," and country singer Jimmie Rodgers's "Blue Yodel No. 9."

With the release of his combo dates, Louis Armstrong was considered the top soloist in jazz by early 1929. He was given an offer to play in New York and took it, relocating with the entire Carroll Dickerson Orchestra (which surprised his bookers who just wanted him as a single). Satch had a feature role in the show *Hot Chocolates* where he introduced Fats Waller's "Ain't Misbehavin'," and he appeared in Harlem clubs with big bands, including Dickerson's and Luis Russell's. Armstrong no longer functioned as part of an ensemble, but instead was featured as the trumpet and vocal star; his recordings of 1929–46 mostly have him backed by jazz orchestras. Rather than emphasize jazz originals, he recorded superior new pop tunes, which he turned into jazz. In addition to "Ain't Misbehavin'," Armstrong's recordings of such songs as "When You're Smiling," "Rockin' Chair," "I'm Confessin' that I Love You," "Body and Soul," "Lazy River," "Star Dust," "Sleepy Time Down South" (his permanent theme song), and even the pioneering anti-racism song "Black and Blue" made them into standards.

Although his recordings of 1929–31 were not as innovative as his earlier Hot Fives, they are generally of very high quality and helped to make Armstrong into a national star, influencing the musical generation to come. ❍ **Louis in New York, Vol. 5** (Columbia/Legacy 46148) starts with a lone jam session number, "Knockin' a Jug," which was the first time that Armstrong and Jack Teagarden recorded together, plus a few tunes in which the trumpeter backs the rather horrible singer Seger Ellis and the much better Victoria Spivey. But the reason to acquire this CD is for the classic big band performances, including "I Can't Give You Anything but Love," "Mahogany Hall Stomp," and "Ain't Misbehavin'." ❍ **St. Louis Blues, Vol. 6** (Columbia/Legacy 46996), which traces Armstrong's recordings up to the fall of 1930, is highlighted by "Song of the Islands," "Blue Turning Grey Over You," "Dear Old Southland" (a duet with pianist Buck Washington), "I'm Confessin'," "Body and Soul" (the definitive version of the era), and "I'm a Ding Dong Daddy from Dumas." The latter has some particularly exciting scat singing by Armstrong and a solo that builds and builds—one of those statements where every note

is perfect. ❍ **You're Driving Me Crazy, Vol. 7** (Columbia/Legacy 48828) covers the next year and includes such classics as "Shine," the humorous "I'll Be Glad When You're Dead, You Rascal You," and beautiful renditions of "Memories of You" and "Sweethearts on Parade." Because there was never a Vol. 8 in Columbia's Armstrong series, **1931–1932** (Classics 536) fills in the gap (other than leaving out two alternate takes). Although these recordings are not on the same level as Satch's earlier big band dates, the renditions of "Home," "The New Tiger Rag," and "Lawd, You Made the Night Too Long" are well worth acquiring.

Armstrong used Luis Russell's big band as his backup group for six months in 1930 and went out to California later in the year where he led the Les Hite Orchestra. Armstrong and drummer Vic Berton were busted for marijuana possession in 1931, but he was soon bailed out and the incident did nothing to hurt the trumpeter's rapidly growing popularity. Satch first visited Europe in July 1932 and was an immediate hit overseas, having made the improbable progression from growing up in the poorest section of New Orleans to becoming jazz's most influential musician and singer, and an international star. When an English writer fumbled on his Satchelmouth title and called him Satchmo, Louis Armstrong had a lifelong nickname. He was still just 31.

Jelly Roll Morton   Pianist/composer Jelly Roll Morton and cornetist King Oliver only recorded together once (two duets in 1924), but their careers peaked and declined during the same periods. Both were born in 1885 (Oliver was four months older), became important pioneers in New Orleans jazz, after a period out west made their recording debuts in Chicago in 1923, and eventually moved to New York where, after a burst of glory, the Great Depression cut short their recording careers either permanently (Oliver) or temporarily (Morton).

Prior to 1926, Jelly Roll Morton's most important recordings were his series of piano solos from 1923–24. However, in 1926, he recorded one classic combo side after another. His use of dynamics, surprising transitions, and both arranged and jammed ensembles (Morton was one of jazz's first major arranger/composers) resulted in his music being unpredictable and unique for the period. Separating improvised solos on his records from some that were written out is often difficult since the solos flow so naturally from the ensembles, which often featured cornetist George Mitchell (whose sound perfectly fit Morton's music), Kid Ory, and clarinetist Omer Simeon, among others. After moving to New York in February 1928, Jelly Roll at first repeated his artistic success but soon found the city much less hospitable than Chicago. Musicians not that familiar with his accomplishments tended to laugh at and ridicule Morton's constant bragging. His 1929–30 Victor recordings were sometimes overcrowded and erratic, although there were some gems along the way. But even during his peak years, Jelly Roll had difficulty keeping a regularly working band together.

⦿ Jelly Roll Morton Centennial: His Complete Victor Recordings (Bluebird 2361) is a five-CD set that has every Morton performance for the Victor label including all of the alternate takes. These 111 performances (mostly from 1926–30 with additional titles from 1939) rank with the greatest work of any jazz musician from any era. With such classics as "Black Bottom Stomp" (which has a particularly inspired arrangement that seems to change the instrumentation every half-chorus), "The Chant," "Dead Man Blues," "Grandpa's Spells," "Doctor Jazz" (highlighted by Morton's only recorded vocal of the 1920s), "The Pearls," "Wolverine Blues," "Mr. Jelly Lord" (the latter two are trio numbers with Johnny and Baby Dodds), "Kansas City Stomps," "Shreveport Stomp," "Mournful Serenade" (which has trombonist Geechie Fields's most famous solo), "Seattle Hunch," "Tank Town Bump," "Fussy Mabel," "Low Gravy," and "Strokin' Away," this is essential music. Among the personnel along the way includes cornetists/trumpeters George Mitchell, Ward Pinkett, Henry "Red" Allen, and Bubber Miley, trombonists Kid Ory, Geechie Fields, and J.C. Higginbotham, clarinetists Omer Simeon, Johnny Dodds, Albert Nicholas, and Barney Bigard, the short-lived C-melody saxophonist Stump Evans, banjoist Johnny St. Cyr, bassist John Lindsay, and drummers Andrew Hilaire, Baby Dodds, Tommy Benford, and Zutty Singleton, among others. Vintage jazz collectors have long enjoyed many of these selections. It is wonderful to have them all together in a single package so one can fully enjoy Jelly Roll Morton's musical genius.

Despite recording so many classics, when Morton's Victor contract ran out in 1930, it was not renewed. He would only appear on record once during the next eight years (on a 1934 Wingy Manone date), and having made

precious few friends, he struggled throughout the Depression in anonymity, forgotten by the jazz world.

King Oliver   Joe "King" Oliver's career reached its height in 1923 when he led his Creole Jazz Band in Chicago (with Louis Armstrong on second cornet), but he adjusted surprisingly well to later musical trends. In February 1925 he formed the Dixie Syncopators, a more modern group than his earlier band, featuring arrangements, heated solos, and such soloists as clarinetists Albert Nicholas and Omer Simeon, and Barney Bigard on tenor; Oliver and Jelly Roll Morton shared some of the same sidemen. The Dixie Syncopators recorded frequently during 1926–28. **Sugar Foot Stomp** (GRP/Decca 616) has the master takes of the Syncopators' first 22 selections (including "Too Bad," "Snag It," "Deep Henderson," "Jackass Blues," and a remake of "Dippermouth Blues" that was called "Sugar Foot Stomp"). Two CDs for the small Frog label, **⦿ Vol. 1—Sugar Foot Stomp** (Frog 34) and **⦿ Vol. 2—Farewell Blues** (Frog 35) are preferred for they contain the full story with all of the music from the Decca disc plus the alternate takes (Oliver's famous "Snag It" was actually performed four times), the cornetist's appearances on a few numbers with singers Irene Scruggs and Teddy Peters, the last six titles by the Dixie Syncopators from August to November 1928, and from 1931 the final three sessions ever released under Oliver's name.

Oliver's Dixie Syncopators toured the Midwest in 1927 and then often performed at their home base in New York's Savoy Ballroom. However, Oliver made a fatal mistake when he turned down a long-term contract with the Cotton Club because he was not happy with the amount of money offered; Duke Ellington would get the job and take full advantage of the regular radio broadcasts. A little while later, after the run at the Savoy ended, the Dixie Syncopators disbanded.

Oliver appeared on many records during the second half of 1928, accompanying a variety of classic blues singers plus being one of the stars on 21 selections with Clarence Williams. In 1929, he began recording with a new band for Victor, a superior 10–11 piece orchestra. However, his neglect of his teeth—as a youth Oliver had often consumed "sugar sandwiches"—now made playing the cornet quite painful. Oliver's solos became briefer and some dates listed as "by King Oliver's Orchestra" did not have a note played by the leader, instead using such guests as cornetists/trumpeters Louis Metcalf, Punch Miller, Henry "Red" Allen, Bubber Miley, and Oliver's nephew Dave Nelson, who wrote many of the arrangements. Sometimes Oliver was able to play a heroic solo ("Too Late" is a superb record), but his decline was steady.

King Oliver's Victor sessions of 1929–30 resulted in 35 master takes in all, with the first seven songs actually featuring Louis Metcalf and Punch Miller rather than Oliver. **The New York Sessions** (Bluebird 9903) is a confusing 22-song sampler that has one previously unreleased alternate take ("Olga") and two versions of "Nelson Stomp" while leaving out eight of Oliver's later numbers. Much better is ⚫ **King Oliver and His Orchestra** (RCA Tribune 66538), a double CD from French RCA that has 32 performances, everything but "When You're Smiling" and second versions of "Everybody Does It in Hawaii" and "Frankie and Johnny." Highlights include "Too Late," "I'm Lonesome, Sweetheart," "St. James Infirmary" (with Bubber Miley), "Edna," and "Struggle Buggy."

After April 1931, the recordings stopped for King Oliver. His teeth problems made playing the cornet a very rare event and Oliver began a steep decline, leaving New York and leading his band through obscure and low paying jobs on one disastrous tour after another. The former "king" was largely neglected by the jazz world and the Depression made conditions worse for him each year.

Jazz in New Orleans

The center of jazz moved to Chicago by 1920 and New York around 1927, with the importance of New Orleans declining after 1917, even as (ironically) a large number of former New Orleanians (most notably Louis Armstrong, King Oliver, and Jelly Roll Morton) were among the most significant leaders of jazz. However, New Orleans still had a pretty busy jazz scene throughout the 1920s.

The Unrecorded Legends

Occasional "field trips" from Okeh, Columbia, Brunswick, and Victor resulted in some record sessions being made in New Orleans. Unfortunately, a few of the legendary names never made it to the recording studios. Emmett Hardy was part of the local scene during 1917–21, playing with Papa Jack Laine, Brownlee's Orchestra, and other local groups. The cornetist spent several months in 1921 working with singer Bee Palmer and Carlisle

Evans groups in the Midwest, reportedly making a strong impression on Bix Beiderbecke. After those ventures fizzled out, Hardy spent a couple of years back in New Orleans. In early 1924, he moved to Chicago when Paul Mares and Leon Roppolo were regrouping and expanding the New Orleans Rhythm Kings to five horns, but a dispute with the local Musicians Union resulted in Hardy returning back to New Orleans. A short time after, he contracted pulmonary tuberculosis, passing away on June 16, 1926, four days after his 23rd birthday.

Three other lost legends were also cornetists. Chris Kelly (who was never even photographed) was born in Plaquemine Parish, Louisiana, moved to New Orleans in 1915, and worked steadily throughout the 1920s, becoming best known for his highly expressive version of "Careless Love" and his use of the plunger mute. But he chose to stay exclusively in New Orleans, drank excessively, and died from a heart attack on August 19, 1929.

Buddy Petit founded the Young Olympia Brass Band with Sidney Bechet in 1915, co-led a group with Jimmie Noone, and in 1917 went to Los Angeles to play with Jelly Roll Morton. However, Morton ridiculed Petit and the other sidemen for their out-of-date clothes and tendency to cook in the dressing room and eat onstage. Petit soon quit and returned to New Orleans. In 1918, bassist Bill Johnson sent for Petit to join his band in Chicago, but the cornetist refused to leave the South; King Oliver went in his place. Petit stayed in New Orleans for the remainder of his life and, like Kelly, became a heavy drinker. He died at the age of 34 in 1931 from the combination of overeating and excessive drinking at a July 4th picnic at which he had performed.

Manuel Perez would have a much longer life, but with the same undocumented results. Born in 1871, Perez was considered a "legit" player who made the transition to jazz, playing in bands as early as the 1890s. He led the Imperial Orchestra (1901–08) and the Onward Brass Band (1903–30), but, other than visits to Chicago in 1915, 1919, and 1927 (the latter with Charles Elgar's Orchestra), he stayed in New Orleans. In 1930, the 58-year-old retired from music and became a full-time cigar maker.

Recordings from the 1920s

Fortunately, some of the other top New Orleans musicians of the 1920s were recorded.

Oscar Celestin and Sam Morgan   Oscar Celestin worked in New Orleans as early as 1906, heading the Tuxedo Band (1910–13) and co-leading the Original Tuxedo Jazz Orchestra with trombonist William Ridgley during 1917–25. He renamed the latter ensemble the Tuxedo Jazz Orchestra when he took over sole leadership. Although not a major trumpeter soloist himself, Celestin was a crowd pleaser and a superior bandleader. During 1925–28, Celestin's band recorded 17 performances during five record dates organized during field trips by Okeh and Columbia. ○ **Celestin's Original Tuxedo Jazz Orchestra/Sam Morgan's Jazz Band** (Jazz Oracle 8002) has all of those selections, including "Original Tuxedo Rag," "Station Calls," "It's Jam Up," and a previously unreleased alternate take of "Station Calls." Among the key players are trumpeter Kid Shots Madison, altoist Paul Barnes, cornetist Ricard Alexis, pianist Jeannette Kimball, and (in 1928) banjoist Narvin Kimball.

Also featured on the CD is an ensemble headed by trumpeter Sam Morgan who had led bands in New Orleans during 1915–25. After suffering a minor stroke in 1925 at the age of 37, Morgan recovered and put together a new group. In 1927, his band made two record dates for Columbia, totaling eight selections and all included on the Jazz Oracle set. The ensemble-oriented band, whose best-known sideman was trombonist Jim Robinson, is particularly spirited on its versions of "Sing On," "Down by the Riverside," and "Bogalusa Strut." After the Depression started to be felt, Oscar Celestin retired from music to work in a shipyard, while Sam Morgan stayed active until a second stroke in 1932 forced his retirement.

Tony Parenti   Clarinetist Tony Parenti was playing professionally as young as 12 (with Papa Jack Laine in 1912). He started leading his own groups in 1917 and recorded during 1925–26 and 1928 with his Famous Melody Boys and his Liberty Syncopators plus a duet with pianist Vic Breidis in 1929, all of which are on **Strut Yo' Stuff** (Frog 4). The first 19 selections, from 1925–26, have Parenti also playing alto and baritone with a band that was pretty wooden rhythmically. However, there are some fine moments along the way and a few of the songs (particularly "Cabaret Echoes," "Dizzy Lizzie," "Strut Yo' Stuff," and "Up Jumped the Devil") are worth reviving. Four tunes from 1928 show a lot of improvement, but 1929's "Old Man Rhythm" (the duet

with Breidis) is the obvious highpoint. By then Parenti had left the Crescent City and was working in New York as a studio musician, and he is in brilliant form on this lone performance. While in New York in the early Depression years, Parenti was employed on the staff of CBS, recorded with Red Nichols, and occasionally subbed with Ben Pollack.

Lee Collins   Arguably the finest jazz recorded in New Orleans during the 1920s was the session by the Jones-Collins Astoria Hot Eight in 1929. Trumpeter Lee Collins, who had the knack for being in the wrong place at the wrong time (staying in New Orleans and Chicago long after their golden ages had ended), had the potential be a top trumpet star. He was working in New Orleans by 1916, organized the Young Eagles with bassist Pops Foster, and gigged with many local groups. In 1924, he went to Chicago where he was Louis Armstrong's replacement with King Oliver and recorded with Jelly Roll Morton, but moved back to New Orleans after six months. ○ **Sizzling the Blues** (Frog 5) has New Orleans recordings by Louis Dumaine's Jazzola Eight (an octet with cornetist Dumaine and trombonist Earl Humphrey) including numbers backing singers Genevieve Davis and Ann Cook, Johnnie Miller's New Orleans Frolickers, and Monk Hazel's Bienville Roof Orchestra (both of which feature trumpeter Sharkey Bonano and clarinetist Sidney Arodin). But best are the four hot titles (plus two alternate takes) by the Jones-Collins Astoria Hot Eight, an ensemble co-led by Lee Collins and tenor saxophonist David Jones. Not only was this one of the most exciting record dates of the period and the highpoint of Lee Collins's career, but the session by the Jones-Collins Astoria Hot Eight was the last significant recording cut in New Orleans until the 1940s.

For New Orleans, the important birthplace of jazz, the 1930s would be the equivalent of the musical dark ages, with little work and virtually no recordings for the local musicians who had not ventured up North. But there would be a renaissance in the future.

Early Jazz: Black and White

Jazz has long been one of the most democratic of all musical genres. Even during the days when America experienced its worst racism, once a musician got on a bandstand, it did not matter to other musicians what his or her race was but how much talent was there. However, jazz of the 1920s, '30s, and '40s (and to a lesser extent the '50s) was plagued by segregation due to the culture of the time that was practiced by the public, the media, and the government. Both blacks and whites contributed many innovators to jazz and were certainly quite aware of each other's existence, but they were stuck in parallel and largely separate musical worlds. Mixed bands on stage were unheard of in the 1920s other than in very special circumstances. Whites occasionally sat in with black groups, but blacks were often forbidden from even entering white clubs, much less playing with the house band. On recordings, integration took place much more often since the public could not always tell the race of the performers, but even here it was not that common to have mixed bands.

The stereotype, which was often (but not always) true in the 1920s, was that white musicians were better technically trained, had superior instruments, and developed more "legitimate" sounds, while blacks were more adventurous improvisers, infused their music with the blues, had more primitive (less classical-oriented) sounds, and swung more. White musicians learned from their black counterparts and had much more lucrative opportunities to make a living (many doors would be closed to African-Americans for decades), but blacks also picked up musical tips from the white musicians.

Because they were largely parallel worlds, the black and white jazz scenes in Chicago and New York are dealt with separately in this chapter.

The Black Chicago Jazz Scene

Chicago's jazz scene was at its prime during 1923–27 and was still significant up until the early 1930s despite the exodus of many of its top musicians to New York. Large black bands, often showcasing transplanted soloists from New Orleans, were featured in theatres and dance halls while combos played in smaller clubs. Louis Armstrong, Jelly Roll Morton, and King Oliver have received the most attention from the jazz history books, but this was a huge music scene, as shown by the many recordings made in the Midwest by the Chicago musicians.

Freddie Keppard   After having successfully resisted being recorded in 1916, when it might have made a big difference, veteran cornetist Freddie Keppard settled in Chicago in 1918. He worked in the city with Doc Cook's Gingersnaps and the orchestras of Erskine Tate and

Ollie Powers. Keppard finally made his first recordings in 1923, and ◉ **The Complete Freddie Keppard 1923/27** (King Jazz 111) has all 25 selections that he got around to cutting. The earliest numbers (two cuts with Erskine Tate's Vendome Orchestra in 1923 and six with Cook's Dreamland Orchestra in 1924) are primitively recorded and generally difficult to listen to. Keppard's best recordings are nine numbers from 1926 with Doc Cook (including "Messin' Around," "Spanish Mama," and two versions of "Here Comes the Hot Tamale Man"), three cuts with Jimmy Blythe's Ragamuffins (which also include trombonist Roy Palmer, Johnny Dodds, Jasper Taylor on washboard, and singer Trixie Smith), two songs from a date led by Jasper Taylor, and a pair of numbers (plus an alternate take) with Keppard's own Jazz Cardinals. The latter date has blues banjoist Papa Charlie Jackson singing the two versions of "Salty Dog" quite effectively, while Keppard is heard at his best on "Stockyard Strut." Freddie Keppard was a significant jazz musician further back in history than just about anyone who had a chance to record. In his percussive breaks, which hint at New Orleans brass bands and military groups, one can get an idea what jazz sounded like in the years before the music was ever recorded. But although Keppard was just 36 in 1927, his excessive drinking and inability to update his style resulted in him slipping away into obscurity by the beginning of the next decade.

Jimmy Blythe   A key figure in Chicago jazz recordings, but one whose life is largely a mystery, pianist Jimmy Blythe (who was particularly adept on blues) appeared on many jazz and blues dates during the classic jazz era. Born in Kentucky, Blythe moved to Chicago in 1918, made dozens of piano rolls, and started appearing on records in 1924. His "Chicago Stomp" during that year is considered to be the first full-length boogie-woogie recording. Other than his sessions with the State Street Ramblers, Lonnie Johnson, Johnny Dodds, and Buddy Burton (all of which are readily available elsewhere), **Jimmy Blythe** (RST 1510) has the complete output by the pianist. He is showcased on eight piano solos (including the historic "Chicago Stomp"), accompanies singers Viola Bartlette and Alexander Robinson, plays two-piano duets with Charles Clark, and jams good-time music with his Sinful Five, Birmingham Bluetette, the Midnight Rounders, and the Washboard Wizards.

Among the sidemen are W.E. Burton, drummer/washboardist Jimmy Bertrand, trumpeter Punch Miller, clarinetist Darnell Howard, and singer Half Pint Jaxon. Active during the first few months of 1931, Jimmy Blythe died on June 14 of that year from meningitis, less than a month after his 30th birthday.

Junie Cobb   Junius "Junie" Cobb was a highly versatile musician who played piano, banjo, clarinet, and saxophones. Cobb moved to Chicago in the early 1920s, worked as a pianist, played clarinet with Everett Robbins's Jazz Screamers (1921), and was King Oliver's banjoist during two undocumented stints (1924–25 and 1926–27). He recorded two numbers on alto and clarinet with the Pickett-Parham Apollo Syncopators (1926) and played banjo with Jimmie Noone's Apex Club Orchestra during 1928–29. ❍ **The Junie Cobb Collection 1926–29** (Collector's Classics 14) has virtually all of Junie Cobb's other recordings from the 1920s. The nine numbers that Cobb recorded as a leader (including his popular "Once or Twice") have been expanded to 13 with the inclusion of an alternate take of "Endurance Stomp" and three selections from a previously unissued session. Cobb is also featured on a couple of quartet numbers playing clarinet next to Johnny Dodds, and with his Grains of Corn (which sometimes includes

brother Jimmy Cobb on trumpet, pianist Alex Hill, and bassist Bill Johnson), the State Street Stompers (a quartet with Hill, guitarist Tampa Red, and Jimmy Bertrand), and the Windy Rhythm Kings. There are also four unrelated numbers (by the Kansas City Tin Roof Stompers and the Kansas City Stompers) that are similar in style but do not include Cobb, and two memorable jams ("Transatlantic Stomp" and "Barrelhouse Stomp") with E.C. Cobb and his Corn-Eaters; Bertrand takes an early xylophone solo on "Transatlantic Stomp." Although not on the level of Louis Armstrong's Hot Fives, these heated performances perfectly exemplify hot black Chicago jazz of the 1920s. Junie Cobb, who spent part of 1930 leading a group in Paris, chose to stay in Chicago, and although continuously active (including in later years as a solo pianist and leading a record date for Riverside in 1961), he faded away into obscurity.

Johnny Dodds   Johnny Dodds, whose sound on clarinet was unique, was quite busy during the 1920s. After leaving King Oliver in early 1924, he gigged with Honore Dutrey and Freddie Keppard before putting together a band that played at Bert Kelly's Stables off and on up to 1930. Dodds appeared on many records, backing blues singers, making notable appearances with Jelly Roll Morton, Lovie Austin's Blues Serenaders, Freddie Keppard,

TIMELINE 1927

Louis Armstrong records gem after gem with his Hot Five and Hot Seven, including "Struttin' with Some Barbecue," "Potato Head Blues," and "Hotter Than That." • Eubie Blake and Noble Sissle break up their musical partnership, but both continue successful solo careers. • Meade Lux Lewis records "Honky Tonk Train Blues." • Bix Beiderbecke and Frankie Trumbauer record "Singin' the Blues." • The Jean Goldkette Orchestra disbands. • Beiderbecke starts his Bix and His Gang series of recordings. • Bix and Tram join Paul Whiteman. • Bing Crosby and Al Rinker also join Whiteman where they are teamed up with Harry Barris as the Rhythm Boys. • Cornetist Sylvester Ahola moves to England where during the next three years he appears on over 3,000 titles. • Bert Ambrose's Orchestra begins playing regularly at London's Mayfair Hotel, becoming England's most popular big band. • Sam Wooding's Orchestra helps introduce jazz to South America. • Frank Teschemacher, Joe Sullivan, Eddie Condon, and Gene Krupa all make their recording debuts with the McKenzie-Condon Chicagoans. • Adrian Rollini, Bud Freeman, Dave Tough, and clarinetist Danny Polo are among those American jazz musicians who visit Europe. • Jimmie Lunceford records with his Chickasaw Syncopators. • Duke Ellington's Orchestra acquires a manager (Irving Mills), a bassist (Wellman Braud), a baritonist (Harry Carney), and a home base (the Cotton Club). • King Oliver moves to New York. • Mary Lou Williams makes her recording debut with the Synco Jazzers. • Don Redman leaves the Fletcher Henderson Orchestra to lead McKinney's Cotton Pickers. • At the age of 23, pianist Count Basie is stranded in Kansas City when the Gonzelle White Show breaks up. He decides to stay awhile.

Jimmy Bertrand, and bluesman Blind Blake, and being one of the key players with Louis Armstrong's Hot Five and Hot Seven. In addition, starting in 1927, Dodds began leading hot sessions of his own.

Four CDs on Classics, ● **1926** (Classics 589), **1927** (Classics 603), ● **1927–1928** (Classics 617), and **1928–1940** (Classics 635), not only have all of the clarinetist's dates as a leader (although without the alternate takes), but also his most significant sideman sides (other than his work with Morton and Armstrong). **1926** features Dodds with Jimmy Blythe, the New Orleans Wanderers, the New Orleans Bootblacks (the latter two groups are essentially the Louis Armstrong Hot Five with George Mitchell in Armstrong's place and altoist Joe Clark added), Freddie Keppard, Junie Cobb, and the Dixieland Jug Blowers. **1927** has more Dodds sideman sessions with Keppard, Blythe, and Jimmy Bertrand, plus duets with pianist Tiny Parham, trios with Lil Armstrong, and banjoist Bud Scott, and a session by Dodds's Black Bottom Stompers that has Louis Armstrong and Earl Hines (the pianist's only recording with Dodds); their version of "Melancholy" is a classic. **1927–1928** is the finest CD of the four, since it includes the exciting Chicago Footwarmers recordings ("Brush Stomp" and the various versions of "Oriental Man" have the best moments on record by the frequently erratic cornetist Natty Dominique), dates with Blythe, Jasper Taylor, and the State Street Ramblers, and two of Dodds's sessions as a leader, including one that resulted in "Come On and Stomp, Stomp, Stomp." **1928–1940** has Dodds's last four dates as a leader in the 1920s, "I'm a Mighty Tight Woman" with blues singer Sippie Wallace, titles with the Beale Street Washboard Band, and Dodds's later sessions from 1938 and 1940. Completists will also be interested in **Blue Clarinet Stomp** (Frog 3), which augments Dodds's six dates as a leader from 1928–29 with all of the alternate takes including two that were not released before. The beginning of the Depression suspended Johnny Dodds's recording career for nine years, although he would continue playing in Chicago throughout the 1930s.

Jimmie Noone   In contrast to Dodds's very distinctive sound, Jimmie Noone's smooth tone was easier to copy. Born ten miles outside of New Orleans in Cut Off, Noone started on clarinet shortly after moving to New Orleans with his family in 1910, taking lessons from Lorenzo Tio, Jr., and Sidney Bechet (who was actually four years

his junior!). Noone worked with Freddie Keppard, co-founded the Young Olympia Band with Buddy Petit, and first played in Chicago in 1917 with Keppard in the Original Creole Band. He worked on and off with Doc Cook's Gingersnaps during 1920–26 (with whom he recorded in 1924 and 1926–27) and made his recording debut with Ollie Powers in 1923. After leaving Cook, Noone led a band at the Nest (which was soon renamed the Apex Club) through the spring of 1928 when the Apex closed, and in other Chicago establishments for the next 15 years. His ensemble (called the Apex Club Orchestra) was unique in that Noone's clarinet was matched with an altoist (originally Joe Poston) whose main role was to play the melody constantly behind Noone's solos. Among the other sidemen were pianist Earl Hines in 1928, his successor (a Hines sound-a-like) Zinky Cohn, and Eddie Pollack (doubling on alto and baritone), who took Poston's place when the latter became ill.

1923–1928 (Classics 604) is unusual because none of the 23 selections were actually led by Jimmie Noone. The CD consists of the clarinetist's two titles with Ollie Powers in 1923 along with Doc Cook's entire recorded legacy, most of which is also available on Freddie Keppard's King CD; excellent jazz-oriented dance band music. ● **The Jimmie Noone Collection, Vol. 1** (Collector's Classics 6) has all of the clarinetist's dates as a leader (plus six alternate takes and a version of "I Ain't Got Nobody" with singer Stovepipe Johnson) from 1928. The selections by the Apex Club Orchestra, which generally have prominent solo space by Earl Hines, are highlighted by such classics as "I Know that You Know," "Four or Five Times," "Apex Blues," "Oh Sister, Ain't That Hot," and "Sweet Lorraine" (a song that originally became a standard because of this version). Some collectors will want to opt for **1928–1929** (Classics 611), which instead of the alternates, has Noone's first five recordings from 1929 with his band. It also fits in nicely with **1929–1930** (Classics 632) and **1930–1934** (Classics 641), which despite occasional vocals, contain very consistent music. Zinky Cohn and Eddie Pollack worked out well as replacements for Hines and Poston after 1928, and cornetist George Mitchell and singers Mildred Bailey and Georgia White make worthy appearances on some of the 1930s titles although Noone is the main star. One can hear from Jimmie Noone's smooth sound and logical solos where the future of jazz clarinet was heading.

The State Street Ramblers and Roy Palmer The State Street Ramblers name was used for four different overlapping groups organized by Jimmy Blythe that recorded in 1927, 1928, and 1931. **State Street Ramblers, Vol. 1** (RST 1512) has all of the music from the first three versions of the group plus three selections from the fourth band. There are three songs (including "There'll Come a Day") from a quartet consisting of Blythe, Natty Dominique, Johnny Dodds, and Baby Dodds on washboard. Dominique and Blythe are joined by W.E. Burton on washboard and an unknown (and somewhat amateurish) altoist for a session in 1928 that resulted in such tunes as "Oriental Man," "My Baby," and a humorously erratic "Tack It Down." The third group, also from 1928, retained Blythe and Burton (who switched to kazoo), adding Baldy McDonald on alto, clarinetist Alvin Fernandez, Bill Johnson, and drummer Clifford Jones, resulting in 11 rambunctious performances. The final 1931 sessions have Blythe, James "Bat" Robinson on kazoo, Burton on washboard, banjoist Ed Hudson, trombonist Roy Palmer, and clarinetist Darnell Howard, finishing off **Vol. 1** with "Tiger Moan," "Barrel House Stomp," and "Georgia Grind."

Roy Palmer is the main star of ❍ **State Street Ramblers, Vol. 2** (RST 1513). The trombonist had worked in New Orleans early on with Richard M. Jones (1911), Willie Hightower, the Tuxedo Brass Band, and the Onward Brass Band. After moving to Chicago in 1917, he performed locally with many groups including those of Johnny Dodds, Jelly Roll Morton, and Freddie Keppard, recording with Morton, Dodds, Ida Cox, and Richard M. Jones. A percussive player out of the Kid Ory tradition who had a strong musical background and witty personality, Palmer is heard at his very best on **Vol. 2**. The CD opens with six numbers from the fourth version of the State Street Ramblers and three romps from the rhythm quartet without Palmer and Howard. A similar group, the Memphis Nighthawks (also known as the Alabama Rascals), has all of its dozen selections reissued on this CD too. This exciting, spontaneous, and good-time music was definitely out of place for 1932, teaming Palmer and Howard with cornetist Alfred Bell, either Bob Hudson or Buddy Burton on piano, Jimmy Bertrand, and an unidentified saxophonist and banjoist. Among the more memorable tunes are "Georgia Grind," "Nancy Jane," "Stomp that Thing," and a previously unissued and very charming Palmer-Hudson duet, "The Trombone Slide." Rounding off the 26-selection disc are the four numbers cut in 1936 by the Chicago Rhythm Kings, a similar sextet with Palmer, clarinetist Arnett Nelson, and Bertrand.

Richard M. Jones Richard M. Jones, like Clarence Williams, was just an okay pianist but was quite important as a bandleader, songwriter, and talent scout. Jones played regularly at Lulu White's Mahogany Hall (a famous bordello) in New Orleans during 1908–17. He performed with Oscar Celestin in 1918 and moved to Chicago soon afterward, working in Clarence Williams's publishing company. As the manager of the "race" department of the Okeh label in the mid-1920s, Jones was in a position of power, organizing many record dates. He also was able to help make his better tunes ("Trouble in Mind," "Jazzin' Babies Blues," and "Riverside Blues") into standards.

During 1923–29, Jones was the leader on a variety of sessions that resulted in 22 songs. The great majority are included on **1923–1927** (Classics 826). Jones is heard as a solo pianist in 1923, with several versions of his Jazz Wizards (Albert Nicholas gets solo honors on the early trios, while the later quintet/sextets are erratic), and on two songs apiece with singer Lillie Delk Christian, Don Nelson's Paramount Serenaders, and cornetist Willie Hightower's Night Hawks. **1927–1944** (Classics 853) has the remainder of Richard M. Jones's recorded legacy including so-so band sides from 1927–28, a strong group from 1929 with Omer Simeon and Roy Palmer, big band titles from 1935, vocal performances of "Trouble in Mind" and "Black Rider" (with trumpeter Lee Collins helping out) from 1936, and four worthwhile numbers by a combo from 1944. Overall, Richard M. Jones's recordings have their moments, but tend to be inconsistent.

Tiny Parham After moving to Chicago, pianist Hartzell Strathdene "Tiny" Parham co-led the Pickett-Parham Apollo Syncopators with violinist Leroy Pickett (1926–27), a group that recorded two songs in December 1926. Parham soon broke away to form his own band, recording three numbers in 1927 and leading eight very productive record sessions during 1928–30 as Tiny Parham and His Musicians, performances that are full of atmospheric treasures. ❍ **1926–1929** (Classics 661) features the sides by the Pickett-Parham Apollo Syncopators and Parham's pickup group from 1927 (with blues banjoist/singer Papa Charlie Jackson and Kid Ory) before focusing on Parham's Musicians. The sextet/septet consists of either Punch Miller or Ray Hobson on cornet, the haunting violin of Elliott Washington, trombonist Charles Lawson, Charlie Johnson on clarinet and alto, banjoist Mike McKendrick, Quinn Wilson on tuba, and Ernie Marrero on drums and washboard, plus the leader's piano. The arrangements are unpredictable, clever, and haunting, particularly in their use of the violin. The repertoire is filled with such obscure and high-quality originals as "The Head-Hunter's Dream," "Jogo Rhythm," "Stompin' on Down," "Blue Melody Blues," "Blue Island Blues," and "Washboard Wiggles."

1929–1940 (Classics 691) starts off with a similar group (with Punch Miller on cornet and Dalbert Bright taking Charlie Johnson's place) for nine sometimes-eerie selections from 1929 including "Sud Buster's Dream," "Dixieland Doin's," and "Black Cat Moan." Parham's 1930 band (Hobson, trombonist John Thomas, Bright, Jimmy Hutchinson on clarinet and tenor, McKendrick, Milt Hinton making his recording debut on tuba, and drummer Jimmy McEndre) is heard on 11 titles including "Doin' the Jug Jug," "Back to the Jungle," and "Nervous Tension." One misses the violin, but the arrangements help make the music sound unique. **1929–1940** concludes with three numbers from 1940 played by a quartet with Parham doubling on organ, an anticlimactic close to Tiny Parham's career. Collectors who wish to truly get the complete Tiny Parham will want to search for the LP **Tiny Parham Vol. Four** (Swaggie 834), which has 14 intriguing alternate takes from 1928–30 that were bypassed in the Classics series.

Punch Miller   Ernest "Punch" Miller played cornet as a youth, served in World War I, and was part of the New Orleans jazz scene until his departure in 1924. He made his recording debut in January 1925 with Mack's Merrymakers, and in 1926 he moved to Chicago, where he worked with Kid Ory, trombonist Albert Wynn, Freddie Keppard, Chippie Hill, Tiny Parham, Omer Simeon, Jimmy Bertrand, Jelly Roll Morton, Erskine Tate, Frankie Franko's Louisianians (on and off during 1929–35), Zilner Randolph's W.P.A. Band, and Walter Barnes, plus his own groups at local clubs. All of his early recordings (except the dates with the Levee Serenaders and Tiny Parham) are on **1925–1930** (RST 1517). Miller is heard with the team of Billy and Mary Mack,

jamming at his best with Albert Wynn (including memorable versions of "She's Crying for Me" and "Parkway Stomp"), playing with Jimmy Wade's Dixielanders, on a good-time set with clarinetist King Mutt, with Jimmy Bertrand's Washboard Wizards, backing the jivey singer Frankie "Half Pint" Jaxon, and in 1930 starring with Frankie Franko's Louisianians in excellent versions of "Somebody Stole My Gal" and "Golden Lily Blues." He should have been able to find fame, but Punch Miller (like Lee Collins) decided to stay in Chicago during the 1930s rather than moving to New York, and as a result, he was under-recorded during the decade and remains underrated today.

Ikey Robinson   Like Punch Miller, Ikey Robinson could have been a major name. Robinson, who was primarily a talented banjoist/singer but also played guitar and occasionally clarinet and piano, fit comfortably into both the jazz and blues worlds. He started out working as a barber, but had a part-time band starting in 1918 when he was 14. Robinson played in Virginia with Harry Watkins's Orchestra (1922–24) and Bud Jenkins's Virginia Ravens (1924–26) before moving to Chicago in 1926. He worked with the Alabamians, Jelly Roll Morton, and Clarence Moore, recorded as a sideman with Sammy Stewart's Ten Knights of Syncopation (1928), Jabbo Smith (1929), and Clarence Williams, and moved to New York in 1930 for four years before returning permanently to Chicago. **"Banjo" Ikey Robinson** (RST 1508) has every selection that Ikey ever led (except for two songs featuring Half Pint Jaxon's vocals). Robinson is heard in many settings, including with a pair of good-time jazz/blues groups (the Hokum Trio and the Pods of Pepper), a quintet that includes Jabbo Smith and Omer Simeon singing the blues, accompanying singer Charlie Slocum, and leading the swing-oriented Windy City Five, playing clarinet on "Swing It." Everything works well.

Buddy Burton   The obscure and somewhat shadowy Buddy Burton was even unknown during his prime musical years. On records he played piano, organ, drums, percussion, and kazoo in addition to singing. After moving to Chicago in 1923, he recorded on drums and kazoo with Jelly Roll Morton, but did most of his recordings in 1928 other than a few selections in 1929, 1932, and 1936 before disappearing altogether. **W.E. "Buddy" Burton & Ed "Fats" Hudson** (RST 1511) has all of Burton's recordings other than his dates with Morton. Burton is heard as a soloist (singing and playing piano), dueting with Jimmy Blythe, backing blues singers Tillie Johnson and Mae Mathews, playing with the Dixie Four and the Harlem Trio, dueting with pianist Bob Hudson, and backing singer Irene Sanders in 1936. Highlights include the two-part "Ham-Fatchet Blues," "Dustin' the Keys," "Five o'Clock Stomp," and three versions of "Block and Tackle." The CD concludes with a pair of vocals by the very obscure banjoist Ed "Fats" Hudson, accompanied by Jimmy Blythe on the pianist's final recording.

Pinetop Smith Clarence "Pinetop" Smith, like Ikey Robinson, fit into both jazz and blues. Smith worked in the Pittsburgh area early in his career as a pianist, dancer, and comedian, including accompanying Butterbeans & Susie and Ma Rainey. He moved to Chicago around 1927 where he became a pioneering boogie-woogie pianist. On December 29, 1928, Smith recorded two numbers (including "Pine Top's Boogie Woogie") that were followed by two others on January 14, 1929, and four additional numbers the following day. Counting three alternate takes, Smith's entire musical legacy was 11 performances, eight of which are on the LP **Piano in Style** (MCA-1332) along with four-song piano solo sessions from Jelly Roll Morton and James P. Johnson. Tragically, two months after his third recording date, Pinetop Smith was accidentally shot to death in a Chicago dance hall fight; he was only 24. Nine years later, the Tommy Dorsey Orchestra's adaptation of "Boogie Woogie" (based closely on "Pine Top's Boogie Woogie") helped launch a boogie-woogie revival that made Pinetop Smith into a legend long after his death.

Earl Hines Up until the rise of Earl Hines, virtually all jazz pianists stated the rhythm on the beat (other than during occasional two- or four-beat breaks), with the stride piano style of James P. Johnson and his followers being dominant. Hines, however, became known as the first "modern" jazz pianist because, rather than keeping the beat with a steady stride, he broke up the rhythm with his left hand, suspending time during wild breaks, but always coming back without missing a beat. At the same time, his right hand often played octaves so as to ring clearly over ensembles; this was soon called "trumpet style."

Hines (who grew up in Pittsburgh) started out on cornet, switching to piano when he was nine. Singer Lois

Deppe discovered the teenager in the early 1920s, got him a job with Arthur Rideout's Orchestra, and used Hines with his Pittsburgh Serenaders with whom he made his recording debut in 1923, taking a piano solo on "Congaine." In 1924, Hines moved to Chicago where he worked steadily from the start, including with Sammy Stewart's Ten Knights of Syncopation, Erskine Tate's Vendome Orchestra, and Carroll Dickerson (1925–26). When Louis Armstrong took over Dickerson's group at the Sunset Café in 1927, Hines became the band's musical director. Hines and Armstrong first recorded together on a Johnny Dodds date and with Armstrong's big band ("Chicago Breakdown").

1928 was a year full of great achievements for Hines. His regular night gig was with Jimmie Noone's Apex Club Orchestra, and he was a key soloist on Noone's recordings. He matched wits with Louis Armstrong on the classic Savoy Ballroom Five recordings, including his "My Monday Date," dueting with Satch on "Weather Bird," and helping make "West End Blues" into a timeless classic. And his series of piano solos in December are remarkable. To top off the year, on his 25th birthday, he debuted with the Earl Hines Orchestra at Chicago's Grand Terrace Ballroom. ◗ **1928–1932** (Classics 545) contains essential music. Hines's dozen piano solos of 1928 are here (including "Blues in Thirds," "Chicago High Life," two versions of "My Monday Date," "Chimes in Blues," "Caution Blues," and "57 Varieties") plus his ten big band recordings of 1929 (including "Everybody Loves My Baby," "Beau-Koo Jack," and "Grand Piano Blues"), the original 1932 version of the big band's theme "Deep Forest," and a Hines piano solo on "Glad Rag Doll." The Earl Hines big band, featuring the reeds of Omer Simeon and Darnell Howard, was a success from the start. It would be one of the most significant big bands based in the Midwest during the 1930s, helping keep alive the legacy of Chicago black jazz during the swing era.

Clifford Hayes Chicago, a future blues center, was also the home for a series of record dates by violinist Clifford Hayes that fall between several musical genres, including classic jazz, blues, and early country music. Hayes teamed with banjoist Cal Smith in such groups as the Old Southern Jug Band, Clifford's Louisville Jug Band, the Dixieland Jug Blowers (1926–27), and Hayes's Louisville Stompers (1927–29). Johnny Dodds was prominent on one of the dates by the Dixieland Jug Blowers, and the sophisticated Earl Hines was on some of the selections from the rather primitive Louisville Stompers.

All of Clifford Hayes's dates as a leader, which ended in 1931, are on four RST CDs. **Vol. 2** (RST 1502) has a dozen numbers from the Dixieland Jug Blowers, including six in which clarinetist Johnny Dodds is a rather notable guest; "House Rent Rag" has a humorous monologue. The group otherwise consists of Hayes on violin, altoist Lockwood Lewis, three banjos, and the enthusiastic Earl McDonald on jug. Also on this disc are eight selections from McDonald's Original Louisville Jug Band and four titles from Whistler's Jug Band. **Vol. 3** (RST 1503) has the ten later songs by the Dixieland Jug Blowers (with trombonist Hense Grundy, two reeds, Hayes, pianist Johnny Gatewood, and Cal Smith on banjo and guitar, along with a few guest vocalists but no jug player), plus the same group (without the reeds) performing as Clifford Hayes's Louisville Stompers. Seven of the 14 Stompers numbers have pianist Earl Hines taking Gatewood's place, somehow fitting his advanced style into the good-time music. **Vol. 4** (RST 1504) consists of a lot of different sessions including three more titles from Clifford Hayes's Louisville Stompers (with Hines and a guest spot for singer Sippie Wallace), two cuts by the Kentucky Jazz Babies, eight from Phillips's Louisville Jug Band (an unusual band consisting of C-melody sax, what is called a walking-cane flute, guitar, and "jazzhorn"), four cuts by singer Kid Coley (backed by Hayes's violin), two final numbers by Whistler's Jug Band, and features for singers Jimmie Rodgers, Ben Ferguson, and John Harris in which they are accompanied by groups that include Hayes and Earl McDonald on jug. But after 1931, nothing more is known of Clifford Hayes's activities.

Reuben "River" Reeves and Jabbo Smith   In 1929, the success of Louis Armstrong's records on Okeh led to three other labels signing up potential trumpet kings. Henry "Red" Allen was recorded by Victor, Jabbo Smith by Brunswick, and Reuben "River" Reeves by Vocalion. Reeves started playing trumpet in high school. He moved to New York in February 1924 to study dentistry, but soon became a full-time musician and relocated to Chicago. He played with Erskine Tate's Vendome Orchestra during 1925–28, earned a Master's degree at the American Conservatory, taught music at a high school, and led a band at the Regal Theatre. Reeves made his

recording debut on a couple of numbers with Fess Williams's Joy Boys and then in 1929 recorded 15 selections for Vocalion, the highpoint of his career. ❍ **Reuben Reeves & Omer Simeon** (RST 1516) has all of those recordings, which are wild, exciting, and sometimes reckless. Reeves took a lot of chances in his playing, sounding a little like the Roy Eldridge of the late 1920s. The other key stars are clarinetists Omer Simeon and Darnell Howard, Blanche Calloway, and Reuben's older brother, trombonist Gerald Reeves. Highlights include "River Blues," "Papa 'Skag' Stomp," and "Bugle Call Blues." Also on the CD are the four decent but slightly disappointing selections from Reeves's 1933 big band, Omer Simeon's only dates as a leader during the era (two titles in a small group with Earl Hines), and four selections from the Dixie Rhythm Kings, a 1929 septet with Simeon, and both Shirley Clay and George Mitchell on cornets.

While Reuben Reeves made his finest recordings by his 24th birthday, Jabbo Smith's career peaked when he was just 20. Smith attended the Jenkins Orphanage in Charleston, South Carolina, from the time he was six, learning both trumpet and trombone. He played with the orphanage's band from the age of ten, but ran away from the home several times, successfully in 1925 when he was 16. After being discovered in Atlantic City by pianist Charlie Johnson, Smith was well featured with Johnson's Paradise Ten during 1925–28, recording exciting solos on "Charleston Is the Best Dance After All," "Paradise Wobble," and "You Ain't the One." Smith also recorded with Eva Taylor, Perry Bradford's Georgia Strutters, and Duke Ellington (subbing for Bubber Miley on "Black and Tan Fantasy"), but turned down a chance to join Ellington because he felt the job did not pay enough. A short time later, he was fired by Charlie Johnson due to his unreliability and excessive drinking. Smith played in the pit orchestra of *Keep Shufflin'*, recording some of the show's songs in a quartet known as the Louisiana Sugar Babes, with James P. Johnson, Fats Waller on organ, and Garvin Bushell's reeds. After the show closed in Chicago in November 1928, Smith had short stints with many local bands, including those of Carroll Dickerson, Sammy Stewart, Earl Hines, Erskine Tate, Charles Elgar, and Tiny Parham.

After Jabbo took honors on a pair of Ikey Robinson records ("Got Butter on It" and "Ready Hokum"), he was signed to Brunswick as the leader of the Rhythm Aces, a quintet with Omer Simeon or George James on reeds,

Cassino Simpson, Alex Hill, Kenneth Anderson or Earl Frazier on piano, Hayes Alvis or Lawson Buford on tuba, and Ikey Robinson. Both ● **1929–1938** (Retrieval 79013) and **1929–1938** (Classics 669) contain all 19 of Jabbo Smith's Rhythm Aces sides along with a previously unreleased "Weird and Blue." These performances are quite advanced, occasionally death-defying, and among the most exciting recordings of the period. Smith's range, speed, and creative ideas are impressive. He was a fine singer, and he even takes an effective trombone solo on "Lina Blues." "Till Times Get Better," "Jazz Battle," "Band Box Stomp," "Sweet and Low Blues," and "Decatur Street Tutti" are also memorable. The Retrieval disc has the trumpeter's two numbers with Ikey Robinson, while the Classics CD skips those cuts and instead has Smith's four selections from his 1938 session, his only other date as a leader after 1929. Unfortunately, those numbers are routine (with three Jabbo vocals and very little of his trumpet) so the edge goes to the Retrieval release, despite its inaccurate title since it actually only includes performances from 1929.

Neither Reuben Reeves nor Jabbo Smith would again reach the heights that they did in 1929. Jabbo Smith was essentially a has-been at the age of 21, for his recordings did not sell well (nor did Reeves's), and when the Depression hit, he was off records altogether. He settled in Milwaukee, and although he played locally, he fell into complete obscurity. Reeves was a member of Cab Calloway's Orchestra during 1931–32 and had a big band the following year, but stayed in Chicago and never became famous. Chicago was no longer the center of jazz. Musicians who chose to stay in that city, or in New Orleans, would find it difficult to gain much fame in the 1930s.

Other Black Chicago Jazz Bands   Three CDs from the Frog label further display the richness of the early Chicago scene. **Get Easy Blues** (Frog 9) has a variety of top bands from the 1928–30 period, including the Levee Serenaders (a Jelly Roll Morton group with Frances Hereford singing "Midnight Mama" and "Mr. Jelly Lord"), Jasper Taylor's Original Washboard Band (with Johnny Dodds), pianist Lil Hardaway's sextet, Sammy Stewart's Orchestra, Albert Wynn, Jimmy Wade's Dixielanders, Jimmy Bertrand's Washboard Wizards (a 1929 quartet with Punch Miller, Darnell Howard, and Jimmy Blythe), the Beale Street Washboard Band (Johnny Dodds, trumpeter Herb Morand, pianist Frank Melrose,

and Baby Dodds on washboard) and Frankie Franko's Louisianians. **Hot Stuff—Black Chicago Big Bands 1922–29** (Frog 28) starts off with a pair of test pressings from the completely unknown Sunset Band in late 1922, an ensemble that might have been led by Carroll Dickerson. The bulk of the CD consists of the one session by Elgar's Creole Orchestra (including a particularly haunting version of "Nightmare" and exciting work by the two cornetists on "Brotherly Love") and all ten performances by Walter Barnes's Royal Creolians during 1928–29. Also on **Hot Stuff** are the two songs that Fess Williams recorded with his Joy Boys while spending a year in Chicago, the earlier of two dates by Carroll Dickerson's Savoy Orchestra (featuring trumpeter Willie Hightower and the nucleus of Louis Armstrong's Savoy Ballroom Five on "Missouri Squabble" and "Black Maria"), and the two band sides by cornetist Oliver Cobb's Rhythm Kings. **That's My Stuff** (Frog 7), which has dates from 1929–30, shows that Chicago still had quite a bit of jazz talent even as its first golden age was ending. Included are clarinetist Omer Simeon's two recordings as a leader (accompanied by Earl Hines), Simeon leading a contingent from the Earl Hines Orchestra behind singer Helen Savage, the four numbers by the Dixie Rhythm Kings, and sessions by the overlapping bands of Alex Hill, Harry Dial, and Lloyd Smith.

The White Chicago Jazz Scene and the Austin High Gang

In the early 1920s, a group of youngsters from Austin High School (located in a suburb of Chicago) frequently got together after school at a local malt shop, the Spoon and Straw, to play 78s on the store's Victrola. The available records were usually of the top pop/dance bands, but one day a new release by the New Orleans Rhythm Kings was in the pile. The music had such an impact on the teenagers that they all decided spontaneously to become professional musicians. Some, like Jimmy McPartland and his brother, guitarist Dick McPartland, Eddie Condon, Frank Teschemacher, and Joe Sullivan were already playing music, though Dick McPartland and Teschemacher were actually learning violin at the time. The others in the loose aggregation, such as Bud Freeman, Dave Tough, Jim Lannigan, and Gene Krupa, were starting at the beginning. Soon many of the youths were going out to see the NORK and King Oliver's Creole Jazz Band as often as possible, getting ideas and inspiration from the masters. They played music constantly although with more enthusiasm than skill at this early stage. Within a few years, each of these youths was revitalizing the Chicago jazz scene.

The music that the Austin High Gang developed would be called Chicago jazz and eventually Dixieland. Essentially it was New Orleans jazz with more room set aside for individual solos, usually beginning and ending each song with one or two jammed ensembles.

Eddie Condon   One of Austin High Gang's ringleaders, Eddie Condon, started off on ukulele, worked as a banjoist (including with Hollis Peavey's Jazz Bandits in 1922), and by the mid-to-late 1920s was playing rhythm guitar. Though never a soloist, Condon worked steadily and proved masterful at organizing freewheeling bands. On December 8 and 16, 1927, he led the McKenzie-Condon Chicagoans (a group sponsored by singer/comb-player Red McKenzie) on two recording sessions that resulted in four numbers, "Sugar," "China Boy," "Nobody's Sweetheart," and "Liza." These exuberant performances were the recording debuts of Condon, Frank Teschemacher (heard on clarinet), tenor saxophonist Bud Freeman, pianist Joe Sullivan, bassist Jim Lannigan, and drummer Gene Krupa, with cornetist Jimmy McPartland (who had recorded as early as 1924) leading the ensembles.

In 1928, Condon was part of the Chicagoans' exodus from Chicago to New York. He led three record dates during 1928–29, which included two features for Teschemacher (on clarinet and alto) in a quartet, notable solos by trombonist Jack Teagarden ("I'm Gonna Stomp, Mr. Henry Lee" and "That's a Serious Thing"), some brilliant trumpet playing by Leonard Davis (on an interracial session from 1929), and spots for Jimmy McPartland and Joe Sullivan. Condon also appeared as a sideman on dates with Louis Armstrong ("Mahogany Hall Stomp"), Fats Waller, and Billy Banks (1932), toured with Red Nichols (1929), and worked with Red McKenzie's Mound City Blue Blowers (1930–31). Despite that activity, the early years of the Depression would be a struggle for him since his style of freewheeling jazz was out of vogue.

Jimmy McPartland   Most of the Chicagoans did not have opportunities to lead sessions of their own during this period but were important sidemen in both the Chicago (1924–27) and New York (1928–30) scenes.

Jimmy McPartland was the first of these players to mature, playing professionally as a 16-year-old in 1923 and becoming Bix Beiderbecke's replacement with the Wolverines in late 1924 when he was still in high school. McPartland recorded "When My Sugar Walks Down the Street" and "Prince of Wails" at the last Wolverines date, worked with Art Kassel in 1926, and became a key soloist with Ben Pollack's Orchestra (1927–29). He also recorded with the Original Wolverines (1927), the All-Star Orchestra, Benny Goodman, Irving Mills's Hotsy-Totsy Gang, the Whoopee Makers, and Jimmy McHugh's Bostonians (1928–29), in addition to Condon. Although his style was touched by his idol Bix, McPartland had his own sound and was strong enough technically to work in Broadway pit bands during the worst years of the Depression.

Frank Teschemacher   The short-lived Frank Teschemacher symbolized the carefree spirit of the Chicagoans. Born in Kansas City, Missouri, Tesch grew up in Chicago, started playing violin when he was ten (followed by mandolin and banjo), and began on alto sax at 14. After becoming part of the Austin High Gang and hearing the NORK, Teschemacher began studying clarinet. He performed with the Red Dragons, Husk O'Hare's Wolverines, Muggsy Spanier, Floyd Town, Sig Meyers, and Art Kassel. Teschemacher recorded on the famous Chicagoans sessions and moved to New York in June 1928 where he worked briefly with Ben Pollack and Red Nichols, making additional recording dates. However, he became homesick for Chicago and returned home after just three months. Although not a flawless player on clarinet or alto (reportedly he was nervous whenever he recorded and was a better soloist live than on record), Teschemacher was a spirited musician whose enthusiasm and willingness to take chances are reminiscent of early Pee Wee Russell. A member of cornetist Wild Bill Davison's promising new big band, Teschemacher was killed in an accident when Davison's car was blindsided by a taxicab on February 29, 1932. He was two weeks short of his 26th birthday.

Frank Teschemacher recorded a total of 34 selections (all but one as a sideman), and his entire output was made available in the early 1980s on a three-LP set, **Frank Teschemacher** (Time-Life 123), which also included six obscure items that he might have been on. The recordings range from sessions with Charles Pierce, the Chicago Rhythm Kings, the Jungle Kings, Wingy Manone, Miff Mole, and Elmer Schoebel to two unintentionally humorous recordings with Ted Lewis. Otherwise, Tesch's recordings are just available in scattershot form on CD.

Bud Freeman   Bud Freeman, who started on C-melody sax in 1923 and switched to tenor two years later, took quite a few years to get his playing up to the level of the other Chicagoans. Freeman worked in Chicago with the Blue Friars, Husk O'Hare's Wolverines, Charles Pierce, and Thelma Terry before moving to New York in late 1927. After playing a little with Ben Pollack, Freeman (purely on a lark) took a boat to France along with Dave Tough, spending a few months overseas in 1928. Back in the United States, he led a record date, worked with Red Nichols, and freelanced for several years in New York, including with the orchestras of Roger Wolfe Kahn and Gene Kardos. Freeman was among the very few tenor saxophonists of the late 1920s who was not heavily under the influence of Coleman Hawkins, developing a softer sound and a very angular style.

Joe Sullivan and the Other Austin High Players
Joe Sullivan became one of the first pianists to have his style touched by Earl Hines. After studying piano at the Chicago Conservatory of Music, he led a group in Indiana during the summer of 1923, worked on the vaudeville circuit, recorded with some of the Austin High players, and moved to New York in 1928. Sullivan kept quite busy during the next four years, recording dates with Eddie Condon, Louis Armstrong ("Knockin' a Jug"), Billy Banks, the Chicago Rhythm Kings, Benny Goodman, the Jungle Kings, the Louisiana Rhythm Kings, Miff Mole, Red Nichols, and Frank Teschemacher, among others, and working with Red Nichols, Roger Wolfe Kahn, and Red McKenzie's Mound City Blue Blowers (1931–32).

Other Austin High players included Jim Lannigan, Gene Krupa, and Dave Tough. Lannigan was a valuable part of the Chicago scene, doubling on bass and tuba. He differed from his friends in that he never did emigrate to New York, playing jazz in Chicago through the 1930s. Gene Krupa studied percussion, considered Baby Dodds to be one of his early inspirations, and was working professionally by 1925. When he made his recording debut with the McKenzie-Condon Chicagoans in 1927,

he became the first drummer to appear on record using a full drum set, including the previously banned bass drum. He moved to New York in 1929 where he worked with Red Nichols and a variety of commercial dance bands, riding out the Depression years. Dave Tough started his career playing drums with some of the Austin High musicians, freelanced in Chicago through 1927, and sailed to Europe with Bud Freeman. He actually made his recording debut in Germany, played with Red Nichols in New York in 1929, and then had to temporarily retire from music for a few years due to ill health, not helped by his alcoholism.

Mezz Mezzrow   Mezz Mezzrow was older than the other Chicagoans and probably saw himself as being a father figure to the Austin High Gang. An erratic but enthusiastic clarinetist and saxophonist who was at his best on the blues, Mezzrow was a New Orleans jazz purist who hated commercialism and was sometimes more of a thorn in the side of the Chicago players than an asset. He began playing saxophone while briefly in jail in 1917, freelanced in Chicago, and recorded with the Jungle Kings, Frank Teschemacher, and the Chicago Rhythm Kings. After moving to New York in 1928, he recorded with Eddie Condon and worked briefly with Ben Pollack and Red Nichols.

Muggsy Spanier   Francis "Muggsy" Spanier was a strong Chicago-based musician before the Austin High Gang emerged. Spanier began on cornet when he was 13 and was a professional within two years, working in Chicago with Elmer Schoebel (1921), Sig Meyers (1922–24), Charlie Straight, Charles Pierce, Floyd Town (1925–28), and Ray Miller. His main influences were King Oliver and Louis Armstrong, but he always had his own sound, recording with the Bucktown Five (1924), the Stomp Six, and in 1928 with Danny Altier, the Chicago Rhythm Kings, the Jungle Kings, the Louisiana Rhythm Kings, Charles Pierce, and Ray Miller. Originally a drummer, Miller started leading bands shortly after seeing the Original Dixieland Jazz Band in 1916, and he began recording in 1920. **1924–1929** (Timeless 1-066) has 24 of the Ray Miller Orchestra's best and most jazz-oriented recordings. Frankie Trumbauer, Miff Mole, and Muggsy Spanier ("That's a Plenty" and "Angry") are among the stars, with the other highlights including "Lots o' Mama," "Mama's Gone, Goodbye," "Red Hot Henry Brown," "Spanish Shawl," "Weary

Blues," and "My Honey's Lovin' Arms." Ray Miller's Orchestra also worked in New York and Cincinnati before breaking up in 1930; the leader disappeared into history at that point. Muggsy Spanier also disappeared for a time, becoming a longtime member of Ted Lewis's cornball band in 1929.

Thelma Terry   A unique bandleader of whom little is known is Thelma Terry. Very few female instrumentalists led records in the 1920s, and extremely few females recorded during the decade on any instrument but piano or violin. Female bassists were virtually unknown on records, and no other bassists (other than Bill Johnson) led their own record date during the decade. Thelma Terry recorded six numbers on two sessions in 1928 with her Playboys, playing string bass at the level of Steve Brown (her main influence) or Wellman Braud. The 9- to 10-piece piece band included trombonist Floyd O'Brien and Gene Krupa on the first four songs, and pianist Bob Zurke on the last two numbers. All of Thelma Terry's recordings are available as part of **The Chicago Hot Bands 1924–1928** (Timeless 1-041) and also on **The Obscure and Neglected Chicagoans** (IAJRC 1007). But where she gained her talent and inspiration from, and what happened to her after 1928, is not known.

In addition to the Thelma Terry recordings, ◐ **The Obscure and Neglected Chicagoans** (IAJRC 1007) has some particularly intriguing recordings. Three sessions trace the evolution of the Wolverines after Bix Beiderbecke's departure, dating from 1925–28 when the group recorded as Dud Mecum's Wolverines and the Original Wolverines. There are also 11 strong numbers by Ray Miller's Orchestra, including five with Muggsy Spanier.

Wingy Manone   Joseph "Wingy" Manone was from New Orleans, but was a part of the Chicago jazz scene in the late 1920s. He earned the lifelong name of "Wingy" after losing his right arm in a streetcar accident when he was ten. Soon afterward he began playing trumpet, becoming a professional at 17. Manone played on riverboats, was a member of the Crescent City Jazzers in Mobile in 1924, and recorded with the same group in St. Louis when they were called the Arcadian Serenaders. His trumpet playing and jivey vocalizing were influenced by Louis Armstrong, but also reflected his own good-time personality. Manone played with many

territory bands (including Peck's Bad Boys in Texas) and had associations with the orchestras of Ray Miller, Charlie Straight, and Speed Webb. ◐ **The Wingy Manone Collection Vol. 1** (Collector's Classics 3) has Manone's first dates as a leader, cut during 1927–28 in New Orleans and Chicago with such sidemen as Bud Freeman, Gene Krupa, and Frank Teschemacher. In addition, Wingy is heard on a Benny Goodman date from 1929, with the Cellar Boys, and leading an ensemble called Barbecue Joe and His Hot Dogs. Among the hotter cuts are two versions of "Up the Country Blues," "After a While," the three takes of "Barrel House Stomp," "Big Butter and Egg Man," and a song that uses riffs that would later be the basis for "In the Mood," "Tar Paper Stomp."

Ben Pollack, Benny Goodman, and Glenn Miller
One of the very best white bands to emerge from the Chicago jazz scene of the 1920s was the one headed by drummer Ben Pollack. Pollack, who was one of the better drummers of the 1920s, sought to balance his jazz instincts with commercialism but never quite gained the fame that he hoped for. He performed early on with Dick Schoenberg (1921), pianist Izzy Wagner, and the New Orleans Rhythm Kings in 1923. After freelancing in Los Angeles, Chicago, and New York, Pollack worked on the West Coast as a bandleader (1924–25), adding a 16-year-old clarinetist named Benny Goodman to his group. Moving his band to Chicago in the spring of 1926, the 22-year-old Pollack soon had an orchestra that featured as its main soloists Goodman, Jimmy McPartland, and trombonist Glenn Miller.

Benny Goodman started playing clarinet when he was ten and developed very quickly. In 1921, when he was 12, Goodman won a talent contest by imitating Ted Lewis. He joined the Musicians Union the following year and was considered an unofficial member of the Austin High Gang although he was easily the youngest of the teenagers. Goodman worked with local bands, met Bix Beiderbecke in 1923, and performed with Art Kassel during 1924–25. By the time he joined Ben Pollack's Orchestra, he was already an accomplished musician.

Glenn Miller grew up in Nebraska, Missouri, and Colorado, originally playing cornet and mandolin before switching to trombone by 1916. He worked with Boyd Senter (1921–22), attended the University of Colorado, and joined Ben Pollack in 1926, where he was for a time the trombone soloist and one of the main arrangers. He departed from Pollack's orchestra after Jack Teagarden joined. Miller realized at that early stage that his future was in writing music rather than being a jazz trombonist, although he would continue to do both for some time. He worked in New York with Paul Ash (1928) and Red Nichols (1929–30), appearing on some record dates (his finest solo was on "Hello Lola" with the Mound City Blue Blowers), working as a freelance arranger, and performing in theatre orchestras for Broadway shows.

Ben Pollack's Orchestra began recording on December 9, 1926 (the recording debuts of both Goodman and Miller). Four CDs put out by Jazz Oracle have all of the big band's sides through November 1929. Pollack's recordings, while hinting at potential greatness, were often compromised by the leader's desire to balance the jazz with commercially accessible arrangements and vocals. **Vol. 1 1926–1928** (Jazz Oracle 8015) covers a nearly two-year period and is highlighted by "He's the Last Word," "Memphis Blues," "Buy Buy for Baby (or Baby Will Bye Bye You)," and "The Whoopee Stomp," one of three numbers released as Jimmy McHugh's Bostonians. In addition to Goodman, McPartland, Miller, and trombonist Jack Teagarden (who by 1928 had replaced Miller), other key players include Fud Livingston, Larry Binyon, or Bud Freeman on tenor. Fifteen songs are joined by ten alternate takes placed at the end of the CD, and in general even the least interesting performance has a worthwhile jazz solo by one of the main voices. **Vol. 2 1928–1929** (Jazz Oracle 8016), which was recorded after Pollack relocated to New York, just covers a four-month period and finds the Pollack Orchestra being quite productive. In addition to another date as McHugh's Bostonians, they also recorded as the Louisville Rhythm Kings and a septet called Ben's Bad Boys. The vocals of Gene Austin, Dick Robertson, Irving Kaufman, Smith Ballew, Scrappy Lambert, and Pollack himself (who told him he could sing?) do not help, although Goodman, McPartland, and Teagarden (who should have been the one singing) have their spots. The better numbers include "Futuristic Rhythm," "Wang Wang Blues," "Yellow Dog Blues," a previously unreleased version of "Shirt Tail Stomp" (a satire of cornball bands), and "Louise."

The LP **Vol. 3 1929** (Jazz Oracle 8017) completes the Goodman-McPartland period of Pollack's Orchestra with such tunes as "Wait 'Til You See Ma Cherie," "My Kinda Love," and "True Blue Lou." By then Ray Baudau was on drums, and Pollack was just directing the orchestra and taking occasional insipid vocals along with Scrappy Lambert and Smith Ballew. **Vol. 4 1929–1930** (Jazz Oracle 8026) covers the period after Goodman and McPartland departed, with Jack Teagarden as the main soloist and even being heard as the leader of one date with the nucleus of the Pollack band. Once again Ballew, Lambert, and unfortunately Pollack take most of the vocals (there are no instrumentals). Teagarden's five spots, particularly his versions of "Beale Street Blues" and "If I Could Be with You" (both recorded when the group made records under altoist Gil Rodin's name), are quite worthy. However, the band's potential as a jazz group had long since taken a backseat to commercial concerns, and it no longer showed any sign of living up to its formerly great potential.

TIMELINE 1928

Louis Armstrong records with Earl Hines ("Weather Bird") and the Savoy Ballroom Five ("West End Blues," "Basin Street Blues," and "St. James Infirmary"). • Earl Hines records with Jimmie Noone's Apex Club Orchestra, makes a stunning series of piano solo records, and begins leading his new big band. • Jelly Roll Morton moves to New York. • Armand J. Piron breaks up his orchestra. • Henry Busse leaves the Paul Whiteman Orchestra and starts his own big band. • Sam Wooding's Orchestra returns to Europe where it remains a popular attraction for the next four years. • Carroll Dickerson's Orchestra makes its only recordings. • C-melody saxophonist Stump Evans and Jimmy O'Bryant die. • Ma Rainey makes her final recordings. • Alberta Hunter costars with Paul Robeson in the London production of *Showboat*. • Frank Guarente returns to the United States and studio work after leading the New Georgians in Europe for four years. • Jack Teagarden, who had arrived in New York the previous summer, joins Ben Pollack's Orchestra. • The Dorsey Brothers Orchestra makes its first recordings. • Johnny Dunn moves to Europe. • Arthur Whetsol rejoins Duke Ellington's Orchestra while Barney Bigard and Johnny Hodges become new long-term members.

The Coon-Sanders Nighthawks   One of the most popular Chicago-based bands of the classic jazz era was the Coon-Sanders Nighthawks. The ensemble had moved to Chicago in 1924, and the Blackhawk Restaurant was its home base during 1926–30. ● **Coon-Sanders Nighthawks, Vol. 2** (The Old Masters 112) finds the group at the peak of its powers during 1926–28, particularly on such classics as "My Baby Knows How," "Brainstorm," "I Ain't Got Nobody," "Roodles," "Slue Foot," and "Hallucinations." So tight are the ensembles and the joyous vocals of drummer Carleton Coon and pianist Joe Sanders (who also wrote the arrangements) that it is easy to miss the fact that there are actually very few solos. **Coon-Sanders Nighthawks, Vol. 3** (The Old Masters 113), which covers a six-month period during 1928–29, has a few departures. There are four titles from a session that the Coon-Sanders Orchestra recorded under the pseudonym of the Louisiana Rhythm Kings. Two of those songs are instrumentals, while two others have vocals by Harry Maxfield instead of Coon and Sanders. In addition, this CD has a 27-minute radio show called "The Maytag Frolic" from January 17, 1929, featuring the band playing a strong set of songs, including several that they never recorded otherwise. Of the conventional recordings, "What a Girl! What a Night," "Little Orphan Annie," and particularly "Here Comes My Ball and Chain" are highlights.

Disagreements with the Victor label resulted in the Coon-Sanders Nighthawks not making any recordings during 1930–31. However, near the end of a six-month stay in New York, the band was finally back on records with two sessions in March 1932. After returning to Chicago, the Nighthawks had begun a residency at the Hotel Sherman when Carleton Coon had surgery for an abscessed tooth. He contracted blood poisoning from the operation, and after a few weeks, he died on May 4 at the age of 38. The band struggled on for a year, but audiences missed the interplay between Coon and Sanders. The magic was gone, and the Nighthawks disbanded in April 1933.

Coon-Sanders Nighthawks, Vol. 4 (The Old Masters 114) has 13 selections from 1929 (highlighted by "Kansas City Kitty" and "After You've Gone") and the nine final numbers that the ensemble cut in 1932, plus one of two piano solos ("Improvisation") made by Joe Sanders. While serious collectors and 1920s fans will want all four of the Nighthawks' Old Masters CDs, more

general collectors who just want a solid sampling of the band's recordings will enjoy the 24 numbers included on **The Best of Coon-Sanders** (Retrieval 79019), performances, which serve as a fine tribute to this highly enjoyable band's musical legacy.

The World of Bix Beiderbecke

Cornetist Bix Beiderbecke's life and music stand apart from everyone else's in the 1920s, not fitting into the world of Chicago or New York jazz and not being overly influenced by his black counterparts. His experiences with the big bands of Jean Goldkette and Paul Whiteman, his musical partnership with Frankie Trumbauer, his accomplishments, his golden sound, and his rise-and-fall life are the stuff of legend.

Bix Beiderbecke, Frankie Trumbauer, Jean Goldkette, Hoagy Carmichael, and Paul Whiteman   As 1926 began, Bix Beiderbecke had been in obscurity ever since leaving the Wolverines in late 1924. The cornetist, whose highly individual and haunting tone was a perfect voice for his sophisticated ideas, had been freelancing in the Midwest during the previous year. He spent the summer working in St. Louis with Frankie Trumbauer's Orchestra, a period during which he had worked hard to learn how to read music. In March 1926, Jean Goldkette kept his promise and rehired Beiderbecke for his orchestra, an impressive ensemble that also featured Trumbauer on C-melody sax.

Venturing to New York, the Jean Goldkette Orchestra won a "battle of the bands" contest with Fletcher Henderson, surprising the overconfident New Yorkers with their swinging rhythm section (propelled by Steve Brown), top soloists (Beiderbecke, Trumbauer, clarinetist Don Murray, and trombonist Bill Rank), and inventive arrangements, particularly those of Bill Challis.

Unfortunately, few classic recordings resulted from the Goldkette band. Their record producer at Victor hated jazz and he saddled the group with unsuitable "guest" vocalists and inferior songs, discouraging any hot solos. Because of that interference, the Goldkette recordings tend to be disappointing, with the band only cutting loose now and then on their final choruses. Only "My Pretty Girl" and their final recording, "Clementine," really show what the band could do.

Ironically, Jean Goldkette had better luck with his recordings made both before and after the Beiderbecke period. Born in Valenciennes, France, Goldkette (who moved with his family to the United States in 1911) was trained as a concert pianist. After deciding to make his career in popular music, he became the musical director of the Benson Orchestra of Chicago, moving to Detroit in 1921 where at first he ran a second Benson Orchestra. Goldkette purchased a Chinese restaurant, transformed it into the Graystone Ballroom, and used the venue (which was soon recognized as Detroit's top nightclub) as a home base for his bands. Skilled at organizing orchestras, Goldkette at his peak controlled more than 20 bands, including two that became independent, McKinney's Cotton Pickers and the Casa Loma Orchestra.

The earliest version of the Jean Goldkette Orchestra to record was in 1924 and its personnel included trombonist Tommy Dorsey, Jimmy Dorsey on clarinet and alto, Don Murray, and Joe Venuti. Two versions of Goldkette's big band recorded in 1926, and a few months after his most famous ensemble broke up in the summer of 1927, Goldkette was back with a new orchestra that lasted until 1929, featuring at various times cornetists Andy Secrest and Sterling Bose (both of whom closely emulated Beiderbecke), trombonist Pee Wee Hunt, clarinetist Volly de Faut, and (briefly) Hoagy Carmichael on piano and vocals. A sampling of Goldkette's better recordings before and after Bix was issued on the LP **1924–1929** (The Old Masters 47), which includes swinging versions of such melodic pieces as "I Want to See My Tennessee," "Where the Lazy Daisies Grow," "Dinah," and "Here Comes the Showboat," plus a few tunes arranged by Don Redman. Jean Goldkette never recorded with his own orchestras. He appeared as a piano soloist with the Detroit Symphony Orchestra in 1930 and then largely dropped out of music despite only being 31.

The height of Bix Beiderbecke's musical life took place during 1927 when he was in peak form. While still a member of the Jean Goldkette Orchestra, he began recording as a star sideman with strong pickup groups led by Frankie Trumbauer, and started leading Dixieland bands on records under the title of Bix and His Gang. The Trumbauer recordings resulted in such classics as "Singin' the Blues" (which has Bix's most famous improvisation and a classic statement from Trumbauer, who was often known as Tram), "I'm Comin' Virginia" (a showcase for Beiderbecke who is heard in his longest recorded cornet solo), "Way Down Yonder in New Orleans," and "Ostrich Walk." The Bix and His Gang dates emphasize

freewheeling playing including hot versions of "Jazz Me Blues," "Royal Garden Blues," and "At the Jazz Band Ball," although the lack of a string bassist kept some of the ensembles from swinging as hard as they could have. In addition, Beiderbecke, who in his career composed four impressionistic piano pieces, recorded "In a Mist" as a piano solo in 1927, although he never got around to waxing "Candlelights," "Flashes," and "In the Dark." After the Goldkette Orchestra broke up in the summer, Bix and Tram played for two months with a legendary but unrecorded orchestra led by bass saxophonist Adrian Rollini. After that ensemble disbanded, Beiderbecke and Trumbauer became members of the Paul Whiteman Orchestra, a very prestigious association.

Due to his short life, and the fact that one can hear his rise and fall in his music, every recording by Bix Beiderbecke is valuable. Fortunately, the Sunbeam label has released a series of four-CD sets that include not only every recording on which Bix can be heard, but every performance that he plays on, even ones with Paul Whiteman where he is completely inaudible. ● **Bix Restored, Vol. 1** (Sunbeam BXCD 1-3) has all of the Wolverine sessions with Bix plus his dates with the Sioux City Six, Jean Goldkette (a lone solo from 1924 and the intriguing if compromised sessions of 1926–27), the Rhythm Jugglers ("Toddlin' Blues" and "Davenport Blues"), the first and best Trumbauer sessions, and Beiderbecke's solo version of "In a Mist." Wrapping up this essential release are Jess Stacy's piano solos from 1935 and 1939 of Beiderbecke's other three piano pieces.

By 1926, Paul Whiteman was widely known as "The King of Jazz" yet his orchestra was actually quite weak in the jazz department. Partly because he did not want to be embarrassed as the "King," and also because he enjoyed utilizing jazz as one of the flavors in his orchestra's menu, Whiteman started hunting for new talent. Red Nichols, Tommy Dorsey, and Jimmy Dorsey spent some time with his orchestra, and a couple of promising jazz singers, Bing Crosby and Al Rinker, were teamed by Whiteman with Harry Barris and featured as the Rhythm Boys. **Original 1927 Recordings** (Nostalgia Arts 3006) has all of the Whiteman sessions from July 13 to November 23, 1927, concluding with "Washboard Blues," which was the first appearance of Bix Beiderbecke with the band. The diverse material has Whiteman changing his focus from dance music to jazz while still featuring some semiclassical works. Highlights include

"Whiteman Stomp," "Sensation," "Shaking the Blues Away," and a remake of "Wang Wang Blues." Two other sets that do an excellent job of summing up Whiteman's career during 1920–36 (and only have a few duplicates from the Beiderbecke sets) are **King of Jazz** (ASV/Living Era 5170) and the double-LP set **Jazz à La King** (French RCA 42413).

Whiteman had been familiar with Beiderbecke's playing since the Wolverine days. In the fall of 1927, after both the Jean Goldkette Orchestra and the short-lived Adrian Rollini big band failed, he hired most of the best Goldkette alumni, including Bix, Frankie Trumbauer, Bill Rank, Min Leibrook, and Bill Challis. Combining those talents with his technically skilled sidemen resulted in Whiteman having quite a mighty orchestra during 1928–29. In addition, in 1929 Joe Venuti and Eddie Lang were hired. By then Whiteman's orchestra included four trumpeters, four trombonists, six reed players, a full string section, two pianos, banjo, guitar, bass sax, tuba, bass, drums, and up to six vocalists.

Bix became a member of the Paul Whiteman Orchestra at the busiest time in the bandleader's career. Not only was Whiteman constantly on the radio and performing at hotels and concerts, but in mid-1928 he switched from the Victor label to Columbia. Whiteman made dozens of recording dates to finish off his Victor contract, and followed that with a large number for his new label. Beiderbecke was featured in short solos on many records including "There Ain't No Sweet Man that's Worth the Salt of My Tears," "San," "Dardanella," and "You Took Advantage of Me" (which has a famous tradeoff between Bix and Tram), although he was most proud of his ability to play the difficult trumpet part in George Gershwin's "Concerto in F." In addition, Beiderbecke continued recording with Trumbauer and on his own Bix and His Gang dates.

● **Bix Restored Vol. 2** (Sunbeam BXCD 4-6) just covers five months (September 28, 1927, to February 28, 1928), while ● **Bix Restored, Vol. 3** (Sunbeam BXCD 7-9) spans less than four (February 28, 1928, to June 18, 1928), so the combined six CDs fully document a very productive nine-month period in Beiderbecke's life. **Vol. 2** has some sessions with Trumbauer, the beginning of the Bix and His Gang series, dates with the Broadway Bellhops and Willard Robison, and the start of Beiderbecke's association with Paul Whiteman, including "Changes," "Ol' Man River," "San," "Mississippi Mud,"

"There Ain't No Sweet Man," "From Monday On," and other pieces in which Bix cannot be heard (including the two-part "Grand Fantasia from Wagneriana"). **Vol. 3** has 69 selections from a 111-day period; two dates led by Trumbauer, one from Bix and His Gang, and the bulk (including "Borneo," "Louisiana," "You Took Advantage of Me," and "'Tain't So, Honey, 'Tain't So") by Paul Whiteman's Orchestra. ● **Bix Restored Vol. 4** (Sunbeam BXCD 10-12) covers Beiderbecke's other 1928–29 Whiteman recordings, his final combo dates with Trumbauer, and his last recordings from 1930. More general collectors who just want a taste of Bix at his peak will probably be satisfied with **Vol. 1: Singin' the Blues** (Columbia 45450) and **Vol. 2: At the Jazz Band Ball** (Columbia 46175), single discs that contain the best of the Trumbauer and Bix and His Gang titles.

Paul Whiteman was always very resourceful. In 1928 when his longtime cornet star Henry Busse, who was feeling neglected in many of the arrangements because Bix was getting the better solo spots, got in an argument with Whiteman and quit to form his own orchestra, a soundalike (Harry Goldfield) was immediately hired in his place. And when Bix Beiderbecke, who by 1928 was a frequently ailing alcoholic, suffered a nervous breakdown in January 1929 and had to be hospitalized, Whiteman hired Andy Secrest to take Bix's solos. Beiderbecke soon returned, but Whiteman kept both cornetists on, just in case. As it turned out, Bix could not stop drinking and continued to decline throughout 1929. His playing became erratic (he really fumbles on "Futuristic Rhythm" with Trumbauer on March 8), and he eventually suggested that Secrest take his place on Trumbauer's future recordings. A cross-country trip did not help his health, and on September 13, after taking a short solo with Whiteman on "Waiting at the End of the Road," he collapsed, was forced to leave the band, and returned home to Davenport, Iowa, to try to recover.

In early 1930, at the height of his fame, Paul Whiteman was in Hollywood with his 27-piece orchestra plus singers, filming *The King of Jazz*. Unfortunately, the movie is as overblown as some of Whiteman's music, but it does have a few great moments, including a 90-second Joe Venuti-Eddie Lang duet, the Rhythm Boys singing "Mississippi Mud," a version of "Happy Feet," and a humorous comedy routine by the virtuosic trombonist Wilbur Hall. When Whiteman returned to New York, the worsening economic situation caused by the Depression forced him to cut back to a mere 20 pieces; Venuti and Lang departed, as did the Rhythm Boys. Whiteman did remain quite famous to the American public, and his orchestra (which still included Frankie Trumbauer and Bill Rank in addition to adding Mildred Bailey) worked regularly during the Depression years.

Unfortunately, Bix Beiderbecke's decline continued after leaving Whiteman's orchestra. Beiderbecke checked into a hospital for a time, took occasional gigs, and tried to stop drinking, but he was not strong enough to beat his addiction. In 1930, he recorded three times (a session of his own and dates with Irving Mills's Hotsy-Totsy Gang and Hoagy Carmichael), but his tone had clearly deteriorated. Bix turned down an offer to rejoin Whiteman and disappointed the members of the Casa Loma Orchestra by sounding weak during a tryout. On August 6, 1931, in Queens, New York, at the age of 28, Bix Beiderbecke died from pneumonia, a frozen-in-time legend who is permanently associated with the jazz age.

Frankie Trumbauer had better luck in his life and was wise enough to mostly stay away from alcohol. Tram grew up in St. Louis where he played piano, trombone, flute, and violin before switching to C-melody sax, also learning alto and bassoon. A bandleader at 17, Trumbauer served in the navy, freelanced in St. Louis after his discharge, and in 1922 made his recording debut with Gene Rodemich, also recording with the Benson Orchestra of Chicago, Ray Miller, the Mound City Blue Blowers, and the Cotton Pickers. From the start he had impressive technique and an original style. Trumbauer was the musical director of the Jean Goldkette Orchestra during 1925–27, was part of Adrian Rollini's band, and joined Paul Whiteman at the same time as Bix.

Three CDs put out by The Old Masters label have all of Trumbauer's dates as a leader through 1934 other than the 1927–29 sessions with Bix Beiderbecke, which are readily available elsewhere. ◗ **Tram 1** (The Old Masters 107) starts out with Trumbauer's most significant solos as a sideman, featuring him with the Benson Orchestra of Chicago (1923), the Mound City Blue Blowers ("San" and "Red Hot"), the Cotton Pickers, Ray Miller, Red Nichols, Paul Whiteman (1928–29), and the Mason-Dixon Orchestra (including a classic version of "What a Day"). Also included are two previously unreleased numbers featuring Bee Palmer. She was not much of a singer, but on 1929's "Singin' the Blues," Palmer unwittingly pioneered vocalese (putting words to recorded solos), 20 years

before Eddie Jefferson and Jon Hendricks! **Tram 1** finishes off with Trumbauer's first dates as a leader (May 21–22, 1929) with Andy Secrest in Bix's place.

Secrest certainly has a strange place in jazz history, being best known as a Bix Beiderbecke fill-in and imitator. He worked in Cincinnati and the Midwest with various bands, joining the Jean Goldkette Orchestra in the fall of 1927 (the version of the band that succeeded the famous Bix-Tram outfit). By then he already sounded a lot like Beiderbecke, even if he never had Bix's creative genius. When Paul Whiteman needed someone to sub for the ailing cornetist in January 1929, he hired the 21-year-old Secrest. Decades later, record collectors would often debate over which solos were by Bix, and which by his follower, who remained a part of Whiteman's orchestra until 1932 before becoming a studio musician.

Tram 2 (The Old Masters 108) has plenty of examples of Secrest playing with Trumbauer's combos during 1929–30 plus Tram's key solos with Paul Whiteman and Joe Venuti's Blue Four; best are "Nobody's Sweetheart," "Manhattan Rag," "Runnin' Ragged," "Happy Feet," and "New Tiger Rag." **Tram 3** (The Old Masters 109) has varied titles from Trumbauer's groups of 1931–32 and 1934, including commercial sides where the ensembles are joined by a vocal group (the King's Jesters), a couple of Bing Crosby's most jazz-oriented vocals (including an exciting "Some of These Days"), and Tram's first session with Jack Teagarden. Unlike Beiderbecke, who was a happy-go-lucky alcoholic with a serious playing style, Trumbauer was a sober and reliable musician whose solos could often be whimsical. He faded in importance (as did the C-melody sax) as the 1930s evolved, but worked steadily with Paul Whiteman for nine years.

Some of the key sidemen with Trumbauer, Goldkette, and Whiteman should be mentioned although none of them led record dates during this era. Bill Rank was a solid trombonist who worked with Goldkette during 1923–27, and followed Bix and Tram to the Rollini band and the Whiteman Orchestra where he stayed for a decade. He takes solos on nearly all of the Trumbauer and Bix and His Gang selections.

Don Murray played tenor with the New Orleans Rhythm Kings in 1923, was with Goldkette (on clarinet and baritone) during 1924–27, and after working with Rollini's ensemble, chose to avoid Whiteman and instead perform with Broadway theatre orchestras. Murray (an alcoholic) was with Ted Lewis's band during 1928–29 before falling on his head against a parked car while in Los Angeles, passing away on June 2, 1929, five days short of his 25th birthday.

Joseph "Fud" Livingston was a decent clarinetist and tenor saxophonist whose strongest talents were as an arranger. He worked with Ben Pollack (1924–25), the California Ramblers, Goldkette (1925), and back with Pollack (1926–27). After moving to New York, Livingston performed with studio orchestras and was on quite a few freelance recording dates, including with Red Nichols, Miff Mole, Frankie Trumbauer, and Joe Venuti, contributing arrangements that sometimes bordered on the avant-garde. Livingston worked in England with Fred Elizalde during March–June 1929 and performed with Paul Whiteman during the summer of 1930 before largely retiring from playing to become a studio arranger.

Min Leibrook was equally talented on bass sax, tuba, and string bass. He was the tuba player with the Wolverines in 1924, recorded with the Sioux City Six, and was a member of the Paul Whiteman Orchestra during 1927–31, appearing on many records with Trumbauer and Beiderbecke. Leibrook was often thought of as the ideal substitute on bass sax for Adrian Rollini.

Chauncey Morehouse was a professional drummer as early as 1919. He worked with Paul Specht's Society Serenaders (1922–24) and recorded with the Georgians. Morehouse was with Jean Goldkette (1925–27), the Rollini Orchestra, and Don Voorhees before becoming a studio musician in 1929. Along the way he recorded with Trumbauer, Bix and His Gang, Joe Venuti, Hoagy Carmichael, Red Nichols, Miff Mole, the Dorsey Brothers, Wingy Manone, and many others.

Bill Challis was responsible for many of the arrangements for Goldkette and Whiteman that had important solo space for Bix. Self-taught on piano and C-melody sax, Challis never actually recorded on any of his instruments. His work for Goldkette during 1926–27 included "Sunday," "My Pretty Girl," and "Clementine," and among his best-known charts for Whiteman (1927–30) were "San," "Ol' Man River," "Changes," "Dardanella," "Louisiana," "'Tain't So Honey, 'Tain't So," "Because My Baby Don't Mean Maybe Now," and "Oh Miss Hannah." He also wrote for Frankie Trumbauer's small group dates with Bix Beiderbecke and helped Bix document his four piano pieces, hurriedly writing down the music as Beiderbecke improvised.

The best known of Bix Beiderbecke's associates was the famous songwriter Hoagy Carmichael, a close friend of Bix's. Howard Hoagland "Hoagy" Carmichael played piano in Indianapolis at dances and with jazz bands in the early 1920s, even while studying to be a lawyer. He met Bix early on and his "Riverboat Shuffle" was recorded by the Wolverines in 1924. Carmichael recorded with Hitch's Happy Harmonists in 1925, worked a bit for Jean Goldkette in 1927, and recorded "Washboard Blues" with Paul Whiteman. He also led some record dates during 1927–30, including one that featured Bix, Bubber Miley, Benny Goodman, and Bud Freeman. However, his main talent was not as a pianist and occasional cornetist, but as a songwriter and a personable vocalist. Some of his songs (most notably "Stardust," which was originally thought of as an uptempo stomp, "Georgia on My Mind," and "Rockin' Chair") were recorded by Louis Armstrong and were already standards by 1932. ◐ **Stardust, and Much More** (Bluebird 8333) has many of Carmichael's key recordings of 1927–34, 19 vintage numbers plus versions (both from 1960) of "Stardust" that begin and end the collection. Carmichael is heard with the Jean Goldkette Orchestra ("So Tired") and Sunny Clapp's Band o' Sunshine, as a solo pianist/vocalist (including playing "Lazybones" and a different version of "Stardust"), performing "Washboard Blues" with Whiteman, and heading all-star bands. Among the many highlights are early versions of "Rockin' Chair," "March of the Hoodlums," "Georgia on My Mind," and "Up the Lazy River." Although his work would in time lead him away from jazz, Hoagy Carmichael would always be proud of his early association with both jazz and Bix Beiderbecke.

Jazz Singing, from Bessie Smith to Bing Crosby

Prior to 1926, only a relatively few singers on jazz records were worth hearing. Best were the female classic blues singers who were showcased on their own records. But most of the time when a jazz date had a "vocal refrain," the singer was merely taking up space, wasting a chorus that would have been much better utilized by having a trumpet solo instead. The development of the microphone and of electric recordings made it possible for more subtle and musical singers to be heard, but the practice continued of employing routine studio singers (such as Scrappy Lambert, Smith Ballew, Dick Robertson,

Irving Kaufman, Chick Bullock, and Wesley Vaughan) on countless white jazz-oriented sessions. Their purpose was to satisfy song pluggers who wanted to hear the words of a song sung fairly straight, and they continued to flourish throughout the early Depression years. There were some equivalent black singers, but generally the white orchestras had less freedom (and sometimes less desire) to play more freewheeling jazz.

However, with the rise of Louis Armstrong (whose hornlike phrasing was a revelation), Jack Teagarden, and especially Bing Crosby, many singers became more jazz-oriented by the early 1930s. Often the best singing was done by musicians who knew how to improvise and scat, and no one was better than Armstrong at adding and substituting notes and syllables to improve his interpretations of songs.

Bessie Smith   While the classic blues era was at its height during 1921–25, the better singers from that time period continued to record during the second half of the 1920s. Bessie Smith, just 31 in 1926, was at the peak of her powers during the next few years. All of her recordings are available on five two-CD box sets. ● **The Complete Recordings, Vol. 3** (Columbia/Legacy 47474) goes from late 1925 until February 1928 and is highlighted by "I Want Every Bit of It," the memorable "Back Water Blues" (from Smith's first session with her perfect accompanist, James P. Johnson), "After You've Gone," "Muddy Water," "There'll Be a Hot Time in the Old Town Tonight," "Trombone Cholly" (featuring Charlie Green), "Send Me to the 'Lectric Chair," and "Mean Old Bedbug Blues." Inspired by her talented accompanists (often drawn from the Fletcher Henderson Orchestra), Bessie Smith not only had no real competition in the blues field among female singers, but she also sounded quite comfortable and swinging on jazz tunes. ● **The Complete Recordings, Vol. 4** (Columbia/Legacy 52838) traces Bessie Smith's career up to 1931 and her final two record dates, including the two-part "Empty Bed Blues," the risqué "Kitchen Man," "Moan You Moaners," and the immortal "Nobody Knows When You're Down and Out." The latter song seemed to predict the Empress of the Blues' later career when the rise of the Depression and the change in the public's musical tastes brought hard times to most of the surviving classic blues singers. And although Bessie Smith was still in prime voice during 1929–31, the collapse of the recording industry

resulted in her recordings coming to a halt after 1931 other than one final effort (organized by producer John Hammond) in 1933.

The Complete Recordings, Vol. 5 (Columbia/Legacy 57546) has Bessie's last recordings (including "Gimme a Pigfoot"), the five existing alternate takes from her career and the complete nearly 15-minute soundtrack of her 1929 short movie *St. Louis Blues*, which was Smith's only appearance in films. However, the second disc in **Vol. 5** is of much less significance for it consists of 78 minutes of taped reminiscences of Ruby Smith (Bessie's niece) as she was interviewed in the 1960s by Chris Albertson. The stories deal more with Bessie Smith's personal life and preferences than with her musical career and are only worth hearing once.

Although her recording career had stopped, Bessie Smith, who was still famous in the black community, continued to work during the next few years although with less prominence, and she had hopes of making a comeback.

Ida Cox   Ida Cox also found the environment for her brand of low-down blues changing by the late 1920s, although she made a generous number of recordings during 1925–28. **Vol. 3** (Document 5324) is mostly from April 1925 to July 1926, and in addition to Lovie Austin's Blues Serenaders, Cox is joined on various tracks by trumpeter Dave Nelson, pianist Jesse Crump, and banjoist Papa Charlie Jackson, who shares the vocal on the two-part "Mister Man." "Southern Woman's Blues," "Coffin Blues," and "'Fore Day Creep" are among the better-known numbers. Except for the final two selections (taken from the 1938 "Spirituals to Swing" concert) and two numbers from 1929 in a trio with Roy Palmer and Tiny Parham, **Vol. 4** (Document 5325) is from 1927–28. Cox is accompanied for three of the five sessions just by her husband Jesse Crump's piano, excelling in the intimate setting. But no hits resulted and her recording career stopped after 1929. Cox managed to keep working at lower level engagements during the 1930s, mostly in the South where her career had begun.

Mamie Smith   It was ironic that Mamie Smith only recorded 18 of her 91 selections after 1923, for her voice actually became stronger as the decade progressed. **Vol. 4** (Document 5360) hints at what the singer could have accomplished if she had been more fully documented later in her career. In addition to one number from 1923 and six from 1924, there are two sessions with cornetist Thomas Morris in 1926 that include "What Have You Done to Make Me Feel this Way," and the classic "Goin' Crazy with the Blues." This disc also has three previously unreleased numbers from 1929, the four songs from Smith's final recording date in 1931 (including "Don't You Advertise Your Man"), and three numbers from film soundtracks from 1929, 1940, and 1942. Mamie Smith toured with her Jazz Hounds during the 1920s, appeared in the short *Jailhouse Blues* in 1929, and led her Beale Street Boys in the 1930s, but surprisingly she was never rediscovered and brought back to the recording studio.

Ma Rainey   Ma Rainey's recording career only lasted five years (1923–28) so there was no decline in her singing during her brief period on records; unfortunately the pressings on her Paramount discs did not improve much during this era either. **Vol. 3** (Document 5583) has Rainey performing such numbers as "Slave to the Blues," "Titanic Man Blues," "Stack o'Lee Blues," "Down in the Basement," and "Trust No Man" with a few notables in the backing groups, including Joe Smith, Charlie Green, Buster Bailey, Coleman Hawkins, trombonist Albert Wynn, and Jimmy Blythe. **Vol. 4** (Document 5584) is mostly from 1927 with Rainey assisted by blues guitarist Blind Blake ("Morning Hour Blues"), Blythe, Kid Ory, and pianist Claude Hopkins among others. Highlights include "Weepin' Woman Blues," "Don't Fish in My Sea," "Blues the World Forgot," "New Bo-Weevil Blues," and "Ma Rainey's Black Bottom." Ma Rainey is heard at her best in her 1928 sessions on ● **Vol. 5** (Document 5156), making it rather unfortunate that these were her final recordings. Most of the selections match her in a relatively intimate setting with pianist Georgia Tom Dorsey and guitarist Tampa Red, and one can really hear her artistry on "Hear Me Talking to You," "Victim of the Blues," "Blame It on the Blues," and "Tough Luck Blues." Rainey's last two sessions feature her dueting with banjoist/singer Papa Charlie Jackson. Listeners who can be satisfied with a sampling of the singer's best work may want to pick up **Ma Rainey** (Milestone 47021), which contains 23 of her finest performances including her date with Louis Armstrong and some of the 1928 cuts. Unlike Bessie Smith and Ethel Waters, Rainey stuck to the blues throughout her career, even after it went out of style.

Clara Smith   At the height of her career in the mid-1920s, Clara Smith ran her own successful Theatrical Club, appeared in many revues and theatres, and recorded regularly up until 1932. On **Vol. 4** (Document 5367), Smith is accompanied either by so-so pianists or obscure players (other than two appearances by Joe Smith). She does her best to update her style with humor and creative lyrics on "Rock, Church, Rock," "Whip It to a Jelly," "Ain't Nothin' Cookin' What You're Smellin,'" "You Don't Know Who's Shakin' Your Tree," and "That's Why the Undertakers Are Busy Today." Trumpeter Freddie Jenkins, Joe Smith, and Charlie Green appear on a session apiece with Clara Smith on **Vol. 5** (Document 5368), but it is James P. Johnson (heard on four songs including "Oh! Mister Mitchell") who steals solo honors. As was often the case with the classic blues singers, Clara Smith did some of her finest work at the end of her recording career, when the recording quality had improved as had the musicianship of her backing musicians. **Vol. 6** (Document 5369), which dates from 1930–1932, wraps up her legacy with four enjoyable vocal duets with Lonnie Johnson and such numbers as "Low Land Moan," "I Want a Two-Fisted Double Jointed Man," "Unemployed Papa—Charity Working Mama," and "I'm Tired of Fattenin' Frogs for Snakes." The Depression hurt business, but Clara Smith continued working for a time, particularly in New York, Detroit, and Cleveland.

Rosa Henderson, Maggie Jones, and Gladys Bentley   Rosa Henderson hit the peak of her success in 1928 when she performed in *Showboat* in London. Unfortunately, her husband died later that year and she lost interest in show business, recording two final selections in 1931 and retiring in 1932. **Vol. 4** (Document 5404), which has her final recordings, is most notable for the six numbers in which Rosa Henderson is accompanied by James P. Johnson, including her two selections from 1931.

Maggie Jones, Vol. 2/Gladys Bentley (Document 5349) starts off with the final 16 recordings of Jones's career. The singer (assisted by some Fletcher Henderson sidemen on a few numbers) sounds good on "Cheatin' on Me," "You Ain't Gonna Feed in My Pasture Now," and "Mama Stayed Out the Whole Night Long." However, she unaccountably stopped recording after 1926. Jones worked with the Clarence Muse Vaudeville Company in

1927 and had a small part in Lew Leslie's *Blackbirds of 1928* before returning to her native Texas in the early 1930s and retiring from music. Gladys Bentley, who just recorded eight numbers as a leader, was a singer/pianist who sometimes worked as a male impersonator due to her low voice. Her recordings on this CD, four solos and four duets with Eddie Lang, are a bit primitive but have some moments of interest.

Sara Martin   Sara Martin worked often in the mid-1920s, but by 1928 her brand of old-time blues had gone out of style. She diversified by singing more pop tunes in addition to acting (including the 1927 film *Hello Bill* with Bill "Bojangles" Robinson and 1930's *Dark-Town Scandals Revue*), but her last recordings, included on **Vol. 4** (Document 5398), were in 1928. These sessions find her singing such fine jazz tunes as "Yes Sir, That's My Baby," "That Dance Called Messin' Around," "What's the Matter Now," and "Cushion Foot Stomp" along with a few final blues. But after temporarily losing her voice in the early 1930s before a stage appearance, Sara Martin became very religious and performed from then on as a gospel singer.

Lizzie Miles   Lizzie Miles spent much of 1924–26 successfully singing in Europe. She was busy on the U.S. theatre circuit for the next few years, but was knocked out of action during 1931 by a serious illness that kept her inactive for four years. **Vol. 2** (Document 5459) has eight selections from 1923 and 14 from 1927–28 after Miles returned from Europe. Most memorable are "When You Get Tired of Your New Sweetie," "Lonesome Ghost Blues," and two takes of "A Good Man Is Hard to Find." **Vol. 3** (Document 5460) has some of Lizzie Miles's most jazz-oriented recordings, including two selections with the trio of King Oliver, flutist/altoist Albert Socarras, and Clarence Williams ("You're Such a Cruel Papa to Me" and "My Dif'rent Kind of Man"), a pair of tunes with a pickup group led by Jasper Davis ("Georgia Gigolo" and "It Feels So Good"), and a date in which she is accompanied by Jelly Roll Morton ("I Hate a Man Like You" and "Don't Tell Me Nothin' 'Bout My Man"). The CD concludes with eight selections from 1939 in which Miles (still sounding in prime form) is joined by the Melrose Stompers for a variety of good-time tunes.

Sippie Wallace   Sippie Wallace, a promising young classic blues singer, became less active after her brother,

pianist Hersal Thomas, died of food poisoning in 1926. **Vol. 2** (Document 5400) has two of her dates with Louis Armstrong along with such tunes as "Murder's Gonna Be My Crime," "Suitcase Blues," "Special Delivery Blues," "A Man for Every Day in the Week," and two versions of Wallace's most famous song, "I'm a Mighty Tight Woman." After May 6, 1927, Sippie only recorded two songs in 1929 and then was not in a recording studio again until 1945 when she cut two additional songs in a quintet with Lonnie Johnson and pianist Albert Ammons; both of those dates are on this CD. After the Depression hit, Sippie Wallace retired to Detroit and spent decades confining her singing to church.

Alberta Hunter   Alberta Hunter, one of the first classic blues singers to record, always reached beyond blues in her career. She recorded some duets with Fats Waller in 1927, co-starred with Paul Robeson in the London production of *Showboat* during 1928–29, worked in Paris, and sang straight ballads and cabaret music with John Jackson's Orchestra in England, spending most of the 1930s in Europe. More would be heard from her in future decades.

Chippie Hill   Although the classic blues craze was largely over by 1925–26, there were two major discoveries during this period: Bertha "Chippie" Hill and Victoria Spivey. Hill grew up as one of 16 children. As a teenager she worked as a dancer at Leroy's in Harlem and was part of Ma Rainey's troupe as a singer and dancer. After settling in Chicago in 1925, Chippie recorded 24 selections during the next four years, all of which are on **Complete Recorded Works** (Document 5330). Louis Armstrong is in the backup group on ten songs and other sidemen include Richard M. Jones (sometimes with his group), Georgia Tom Dorsey, and Tampa Red. Among the better tunes are "Lonesome, All Alone and Blue," "Pleadin' for the Blues," "Some Cold Rainy Day," "Christmas Man Blues," and two versions of a song that Chippie Hill introduced, Richard M. Jones's "Trouble in Mind." The singer worked regularly in Chicago until 1930 when she left full-time music to raise her seven children.

Victoria Spivey   Victoria Spivey, born in 1906, was the youngest of all the early classic blues singers. She played piano at the Lincoln Theatre in Dallas when she was 12, worked throughout the South, and first recorded in St. Louis in 1926 when she was 19, having a big hit with "Black Snake Blues," which sold 150,000 copies. Spivey considered her main influence to be Ida Cox and had a more rural sound than most of her predecessors. She recorded 56 titles during 1926–31, counting seven two-sided songs, and all have been reissued on her three Document CDs. **Vol. 1** (Document 5316) starts off with "Black Snake Blues" and mostly features either John Erby or Porter Grainger on piano with some important guest appearances by Lonnie Johnson. "Hoodoo Man Blues," "Got The Blues So Bad," "Steady Grind," "The Alligator Pond Went Dry," "T-B Blues," and "Dope Head Blues" are most memorable. **Vol. 2** (Document 5317) has Spivey's two-sided double-entendre vocal duets with Lonnie Johnson ("New Black Snake Blues," "Furniture Man Blues," "Toothache Blues," and "You Done Lost Your Good Thing Now"), three numbers with Clarence Williams's Blue Five (featuring King Oliver and Eddie Lang), four tunes with trumpeter Red Allen and an octet from the Luis Russell Orchestra, and two selections ("Funny Feathers" and "How Do You Do It That Way") with Louis Armstrong in 1929. **Vol. 3** (Document 5318) has the singer on four additional songs with Allen and Russell, and matching wits on two-sided vocal duets with Porter Grainger and Howling Smith. In addition, she sings "Dreaming 'Bout My Man" with Hunter's Serenaders in 1931 and leads a swing sextet on four selections from 1936, trying her best to adjust to modern times with "Black Snake Swing." Victoria Spivey, who had a major acting role in the 1929 black film *Hallelujah* (although Nina Mae McKinney got to play the "bad girl," a jazz singer), worked steadily throughout the 1930s, doing her best to keep the classic blues style alive.

Ethel Waters   The one classic blues singer of the early 1920s to successfully make the transition to being a jazz and pop singer a decade later was Ethel Waters. Although she started out singing the usual vaudeville blues of the day on her records of 1921–23, Waters always had something special. She was as easy to understand as Bessie Smith, had a more laidback style (although she could be forceful), and displayed the ability to create winning and personal interpretations of the best songs of her day. By 1925, she was already recording for Columbia and performing such nonblues numbers as "Sweet Georgia Brown," "Go Back Where You Stayed Last Night," "I've

Found a New Baby," "Sugar," and "Dinah" (which she introduced). ● **1926–1929** (Classics 688), which has pianist James P. Johnson as a major asset on four songs, features Waters in her early prime, particularly on "I'm Coming Virginia," "Home," "Take Your Black Bottom Outside," "Someday Sweetheart," "Some of These Days," "Guess Who's in Town," "My Handy Man," "Do What You Did Last Night," and the initial classic version of "Am I Blue." Waters introduced the latter song in the underrated 1929 movie *On with the Show*, one of the very few times in the 1920–30s that a black performer was treated with some dignity on film.

On **1929–1931** (Classics 721) Waters is mostly accompanied by white studio musicians who fortunately could play jazz (including Tommy Dorsey, Jimmy Dorsey, Benny Goodman, Muggsy Spanier, and Joe Venuti). The emphasis is generally on straightforward versions of current pop songs (as it was on Louis Armstrong's records of the period). But even though "Three Little Words" is overly sentimental, there are fine versions of "True Blue Lou," "Waiting at the End of the World," "Memories of You," "You're Lucky to Me," and "Please Don't Talk About Me When I'm Gone." By 1932, Ethel Waters was the best-known black female singer in music (having surpassed Bessie Smith) and a major influence on other vocalists, including Mildred Bailey and Lee Wiley.

Annette Hanshaw   Annette Hanshaw, one of the first significant white female jazz singers, could have been a major star, but she disliked performing in public and even turned down movie roles. Hanshaw began her recording career in 1926 when she was just 15 (discovered by the A&R man for the Pathe label, her future husband Herman Rose). She was billed as "The Personality Girl" and her trademark became saying "That's all" at the end of her records; she had spontaneously ad-libbed that phrase at one of her early sessions. Her recordings of 1926–34 are mostly jazz-oriented, featuring some of the major jazz talent of the time, and her renditions of "I'm Gonna Meet My Sweetie Now," "It All Depends on You," "Get Out and Get Under the Moon," "Daddy, Won't You Please Come Home," "Lovable and Sweet," and "My Future Just Passed" are definitive. She also had the ability to write her own lyrics, adding verses to songs that did not previously have them. Some of her records find her expertly imitating the boop-boop-a-doop flapper girl Helen Kane (recording under such pseudonyms as Gay

Ellis, Patsy Young, and Dat Dere), but her most rewarding dates feature her singing in her own highly appealing style.

All of Annette Hanshaw's recordings are scheduled to be reissued by the Canadian Sensation label on ten CDs in the future. Strangely enough, Vols. 5 and 6 are the only ones out as of this writing. **Vol. 5, 1928–29** (Sensation 769 748 022) unfortunately has Frank Ferera's Hawaiian Trio (consisting of steel guitar, regular guitar, and ukulele) joining the young singer on ten of the 25 selections. Hanshaw sounds fine, but there is far too much heard from the steel guitar. The other 15 selections include four cartoonish Helen Kane imitations (best is the humorous "Is There Anything Wrong in That") and excellent versions of "I Can't Give You Anything but Love," "That's Just My Way of Forgetting You," "My Blackbirds Are Bluebirds Now," and "You're the Cream in My Coffee." ❍ **Vol. 6, 1929** (Sensation 769 748 023) can be recommended without any reservations at all. Only four Frank Ferera numbers are included and there are classic renditions of "A Precious Little Thing Called Love," "Mean to Me," "Lover Come Back to Me," "Big City Blues," "My Sin," "I Get the Blues When It Rains," "I've Got a Feeling I'm Falling," "Am I Blue," "Daddy, Won't You Please Come Home," "True Blue Lou," and "Lovable and Sweet." The backup groups on this strong CD include Jimmy Dorsey, Tommy Dorsey on trumpet, and Phil Napoleon. Although it is advisable to wait for the other

eight Sensation CDs to be released, **Lovable and Sweet** (Living Era 5220) is an excellent sampler that spans the singer's entire recording career. The 25 selections are highlighted by "Black Bottom," "Big City Blues," "Lovable and Sweet," "Little White Lies," "Fit as a Fiddle," and "Let's Fall in Love," with appearances along the way by Red Nichols, Miff Mole, the Dorsey Brothers, Benny Goodman, trumpeter Manny Klein, and Jack Teagarden.

Ruth Etting   Ruth Etting, who was born 13 years before Annette Hanshaw, also began recording in 1926 and was Hanshaw's pop equivalent. Although she did not improvise, Etting swung, had a charming delivery, and had an appealing cry in her voice. She moved to Chicago in 1915 when she was 17 and studied costume design at the Chicago Academy of Fine Arts. But Etting soon worked as a chorus girl, dancer, and eventually a singer. She married the gangster "Moe the Gimp" (Martin Snyder) in 1922 and with his help (which in time became a hindrance) began appearing on the radio with Abe Lyman's Orchestra. In reality, Etting could very well have made it on her own, for her voice and cheerful optimism perfectly fit the era. Starting in 1926, she recorded 203 songs during the next 11 years. Etting appeared in the *Ziegfeld Follies* of 1927 (where she had a hit with "Shakin' the Blues Away"), introduced "Love Me or Leave Me" in the Eddie Cantor show *Whoopee*, and in 1930's *Simple Simon* she sang "Ten Cents a Dance," a remarkable song about

TIMELINE 1929

Bix Beiderbecke's bad health forces him to leave Paul Whiteman. • Louis Armstrong relocates to New York and begins recording with big bands. • Bessie Smith records "Nobody Knows You When You're Down and Out" and stars in the short film *St. Louis Blues*. • The pioneering big budget black film *Hallelujah* has an appearance by Curtis Mosby's Dixieland Blue Blowers and a major role for Victoria Spivey. • Ethel Waters introduces "Am I Blue" in the film *On with the Show*. • Mildred Bailey joins the Paul Whiteman Orchestra. • Henry "Red" Allen becomes a member of the Luis Russell Orchestra and begins recording as a leader. • The Jones-Collins Astoria Hot Eight has its one record date. • The New Orleans Owls and the Original Indiana Five break up. • Cootie Williams replaces Bubber Miley with Duke Ellington. • Duke Ellington's Orchestra appears in the short film *Black and Tan*. • Among those making their recording debut in 1929 are Lawrence Brown and Lionel Hampton (both with Paul Howard's Quality Serenaders), Andy Kirk's Twelve Clouds of Joy, and the Casa Loma Orchestra. • Jabbo Smith and Reuben "River" Reeves make their greatest recordings. • Benny Goodman and Jimmy McPartland leave Ben Pollack's Orchestra. • Coleman Hawkins records "One Hour" and "Hello Lola" with the Mound City Blues Blowers. • Chris Kelly, Don Murray, and Pinetop Smith die. • The revue *Hot Chocolates* features Louis Armstrong, Cab Calloway, and the music of Fats Waller and Andy Razaf. • Count Basie joins the Bennie Moten Orchestra. • The stock market crashes, starting the Great Depression.

taxi dancers. She also appeared in 41 film shorts and four full-length movies (*Roman Scandals* with Eddie Cantor was most notable), in addition to starring on the radio. ● **Ten Cents a Dance** (Living Era 5008) has 20 of her best recordings from 1926–30, including the memorable title cut, "Mean to Me," "Dancing with Tears in My Eyes," "Shakin' the Blues Away," "You're the Cream in My Coffee," and "Love Me or Leave Me."

Lee Morse   A competitor of Ruth Etting and a fine cabaret singer, Lee Morse was often accompanied on records by top jazz musicians. She started singing professionally on the West Coast (usually accompanying herself on guitar), performed in vaudeville during 1920–22, appeared in several Broadway plays, was a regular on radio, and began recording in 1924. Morse had a Southern drawl, a wide range, and the ability to make her occasional (and always unexpected) yodeling seem logical. She sang in a style that fell between jazz and 1920s pop. She was often joined by her Blue Grass Boys, who sometimes included Benny Goodman, Tommy Dorsey, Harry Reser, and Eddie Lang among others. Two excellent LPs contain some of her best recordings of 1927–31: **Lee Morse and Her Blue Grass Boys** (Take Two 201) and **Lee Morse Revisited** (Take Two 213). Unfortunately, Lee Morse's excessive drinking and emotional personality caused her to miss some major opportunities along the way, including the chance to debut "Ten Cents a Dance" in the show *Simple Simon*; it became Ruth Etting's hit. She never quite had the major break that her talent deserved.

Mildred Bailey   While Annette Hanshaw, Ruth Etting, and Lee Morse are forever associated with the late 1920s, Mildred Bailey's career was just getting started at the time. Bailey went to school in Spokane, Washington, worked as a song demonstrator, and sang on the radio in Los Angeles. In 1927 when her brother, singer Al Rinker, and his friend Bing Crosby were in L.A. looking for work, Bailey persuaded Paul Whiteman to give them a listen and their careers were launched. Two years later, Bailey sang at a party that Whiteman was attending and she was quickly hired, becoming the first female vocalist to be a regular part of a big band. Inspired by Ethel Waters and Bessie Smith (and soon becoming an influence on the up-and-coming Lee Wiley), but having a little girl's voice of her own, Mildred Bailey became closely associated during her period with Whiteman with two Hoagy Carmichael

songs: "Georgia on My Mind" (which she first recorded in 1931) and "Rockin' Chair" (from 1932). In fact, she would be billed for a time as "The Rockin' Chair Lady." **Vol. One** (The Old Masters 103) has Bailey's early dates with Eddie Lang (1929's "What Kind of Man is You"), Frankie Trumbauer ("I Like to Do Things with You"), and Jimmie Noone (two songs from early 1931). In addition, the singer is backed on various tracks by the Casa Loma Orchestra, Paul Whiteman, and Matty Malneck. Among the better numbers from her early dates are "You Call It Madness," "Wrap Your Troubles in Dreams," "Home," and her earliest recording of "Georgia on My Mind."

Cliff Edwards   Cliff Edwards (best known as "Ukulele Ike") was one of the very first jazz singers on record (no significant male jazz vocalist preceded him), and he was documented scatting a couple of years before Louis Armstrong recorded "Heebies Jeebies." Edwards, who played ukulele and kazoo along with his singing, left home as a teenager to work in show business, initially performing in St. Louis–area bars. After a few years of struggling, he became successful in vaudeville and appeared in Broadway shows. Edwards, who often sang in a falsetto voice, introduced "Fascinatin' Rhythm" in the 1924 Gershwin show *Lady Be Good*. He was one of the stars of the *Ziegfeld Follies* in 1927 where he debuted "I'll See You in My Dreams," and he made "Singin' in the Rain" famous in the film *Hollywood Revue of 1929*.

Edwards first recorded in 1922 with Bailey's Lucky Seven and Ladd's Black Aces. During 1923–33 he recorded over 125 songs, often using such top jazz musicians as Adrian Rollini, Red Nichols, Miff Mole, Jimmy Dorsey, and Eddie Lang. His work has yet to appear coherently on CD, but several of his LPs are worth searching for. Best is **Cliff Edwards and His Hot Combination 1925–26** (Retrieval 203), which has Ukulele Ike singing "Remember," "Dinah," "Clap Hands Here Comes Charlie," "Sunday," and a variety of hot obscurities. Also worth acquiring are **The Vintage Recordings of Cliff Edwards** (Totem 205), which has "I'll See You in My Dreams," "It's Only a Paper Moon," "I Can't Give You Anything but Love," and "Singin' in the Rain," and **I'm a Bear in a Lady's Boudoir** (Yazoo 1047). The latter, mostly dating from 1924–30 (along with a couple of risqué party records from the mid-30s), is highlighted by "Hard Hearted Hannah," the two-part "Stack o' Lee," and "It Had to Be You." Strange to think that after such a promising start, Cliff Edwards (whose position as the first important male jazz singer is rarely acknowledged) after 1930 became addicted to both liquor and gambling and could only find work as a low-level B-movie actor.

Red McKenzie   Red McKenzie, who had had unexpected success with the Mound City Blue Blowers during 1924–25 as a comb player, made a few isolated recordings during 1927–28, led a greatly expanded Mound City Blue Blowers on a dozen selections during 1929–31, and then became a ballad singer, working with Paul Whiteman during 1932–33. **Red McKenzie Vol. II** (Sensation 24233) covers the 1927–31 period and has two numbers in which McKenzie is backed by the team of Joe Venuti and Eddie Lang, versions of "Hello Lola" and "One Hour" with Coleman Hawkins, Pee Wee Russell, and Glenn Miller, and other selections with such sidemen as Benny Goodman, Bud Freeman, and Fats Waller before concluding with eight vocal ballads. McKenzie was important behind the scenes, securing record dates along the way for the New Orleans Rhythm Kings, Bix Beiderbecke, Eddie Condon, and the Spirits of Rhythm. He proved to be a better comb soloist than a singer, but hot comb playing was apparently out of vogue by 1932.

Blanche Calloway   Due to the fame that her younger brother Cab gained, Blanche Calloway is largely forgotten. After singing in Baltimore, she worked in New York and Chicago by the mid-1920s. Calloway recorded a pair of blues in 1925 (accompanied by Louis Armstrong and Richard M. Jones) and worked in shows and revues. In 1931, she was in Philadelphia with Andy Kirk's Orchestra, recording three numbers and trying her best to lure away Kirk's sidemen, but only persuading two trumpeters to join her new orchestra. Calloway did manage to form a fine big band, one that for a time included tenor saxophonist Ben Webster, pianist Clyde Hart, and drummer Cozy Cole. **1925–1935** (Classics 783) has all of Calloway's dates as a leader except for her session with Kirk's Orchestra (which have been reissued under Kirk's name). Included are the two blues numbers from 1925, her other 1931 dates (highlighted by "Just a Crazy Song," "It's Right Here for You," "I Got What It Takes," and "Make Me Know It"), and the two last sessions from the Blanche Calloway Orchestra (eight songs from 1934–35 including two instrumentals and her trademark song "I Need Lovin' "). Throughout, Calloway sings with plenty of extroverted

spirit and sass, showing that she was in the same league with her famous brother. But there was apparently only room for one Calloway in the top echelons of the music business.

Cab Calloway   And that one member of the family was Cab Calloway. Calloway grew up in Baltimore and Chicago, studied at Crane College, and appeared in the *Plantation Days* show in 1927. After working as the relief drummer and master of ceremonies at Chicago's Sunset Café in 1928, Calloway led and sang with the Alabamians at the Savoy in New York for a time in 1929, but the band was simply not strong enough to compete in the Big Apple. Meanwhile, Cab gained his initial recognition when he was featured in the *Hot Chocolates* show, a revue that featured Fats Waller's music and Louis Armstrong. In 1930 Calloway took over the Missourians, an excellent hot jazz band that had recorded 14 numbers during the past year but was struggling for work and on the verge of breaking up.

Cab's breakthrough year was 1931. With the Missourians renamed the Cab Calloway Orchestra, Calloway's group became the house band at the Cotton Club in February; the club's radio broadcasts soon made Cab into a national star. He had begun recording in July 1930, and on March 3, 1931, cut "Minnie the Moocher," which would be his trademark song for the rest of his life. Calloway, who did not play music himself, was a talented singer, an inventive (if sometimes silly) scatter, and a charismatic performer whose dancing, conducting, and gyrations on stage caused a sensation. Although overshadowed by the leader's antics, the Cab Calloway Orchestra was always a talented big band. ◉ **1930–1931** (Classics 516) covers the first 11 months of Calloway's career on records, a period in which he went from being a complete unknown to a major star. In addition to the original version of "Minnie the Moocher," other gems include "St. Louis Blues," "St. James Infirmary," "Blues in My Heart," and "Six or Seven Times." **1931–1932** (Classics 526) is also highly recommended since it includes such selections as a famous arrangement of "Bugle Call Rag," "Trickeration," "Kickin' the Gong Around," "Corinne Corinna," "Cabin in the Cotton," "Minnie the Moocher's Wedding Day," and "Dinah." **1932** (Classics 537) is highlighted by "Old Yazoo," "Reefer Man," "Old Man of the Mountain," "I've Got the World on a String," the weird "Dixie Doorway," and "Beale Street Mama." One can perfectly understand, listening to these exciting and colorful performances, why Cab Calloway seemed born to be a star.

The Boswell Sisters   There were many sister vocal groups in the 1920s, including the Keller Sisters (who recorded with Jean Goldkette), the Brox Sisters, and the Hannah Sisters. Most, at best, featured pretty voices and little else, but the Boswell Sisters were on a different level altogether. They were simply the most jazz-oriented and creative of all the sister groups of the past century. Connie, Martha, and Helvetia (Vet) Boswell were born and raised in New Orleans one year apart from each other during 1907–09. Connie, the group's main soloist, contracted polio during infancy and was never able to walk; she always appeared in public in a well-hidden wheel chair. Each of the sisters played instruments early on, with Connie learning cello, piano, alto sax, and trombone, Vet playing violin, and Martha (the only one to actually record on her instrument) becoming a fine pianist. As teenagers, the Boswells in 1925 recorded "Nights When I'm Lonely" with Connie having a solo feature on "I'm Gonna Cry." They created a stir appearing five nights a week on radio in Los Angeles and began recording regularly in 1930.

What made the Boswell Sisters different from similar groups is that their arrangements were adventurous (with surprise tempo and key changes), they mixed together lyrics and hot scatting, they swung hard, and they built up their performances to unpredictable conclusions. The Boswells became a hit in 1931 when they appeared regularly at New York's Paramount Hotel and made several films; best is their version of "Crazy People" in *Big Broadcast of 1932*.

All of the Boswell Sisters' regular studio recordings have been reissued on five CDs from the Danish Nostalgia Arts label (available through Storyville). ● **The Boswell Sisters Collection, Vol. 1** (Nostalgia Arts 3007) chronologically reissues all of their recordings from March 1931 to April 1932, including two obscure numbers cut with Victor Young's Orchestra. The backup bands (which include the Dorsey Brothers, trumpeter Jack Purvis, Joe Venuti, Eddie Lang, trumpeter Bunny Berigan, and a host of others) are top-notch, clearly inspiring the Boswells. Among the classics are "When I Take My Sugar to Tea," "Roll On, Mississippi, Roll On," "Shout, Sister, Shout," "Heebies Jeebies," "River, Stay 'Way

from My Door," "Was That the Human Thing to Do," "Put that Sun Back in the Sky," "Everybody Loves My Baby," "There'll Be Some Changes Made," and "If It Ain't Love." **The Boswell Sisters Collection, Vol. 2** (Nostalgia Arts 3008) has the 1925 selection "Nights When I Am Lonely," the Boswell's six recordings from 1930, some rare alternate takes, guest appearances originally issued under other orchestras' names including Jackie Taylor, the Brunswick Concert Orchestra, Victor Young, Red Nichols, and Don Redman, plus a few multiartist medleys in which the sisters make an appearance. After a few additional alternate takes, ● **The Boswell Sisters Collection, Vol. 3** (Nostalgia Arts 3009) continues the Boswell Sisters' chronology up to April 11, 1933, with exciting versions of "Old Yazoo," "We Just Couldn't Say 'Goodbye'," "Down Among the Sheltering Palms," "Sentimental Gentleman from Georgia," "Crazy People," and "Forty-Second Street."

The Mills Brothers   The only vocal group that was on the same level as the Boswell Sisters in the early 1930s was the Mills Brothers. The group originally consisted of John, Herbert, Harry, and Donald Mills. The brothers (all born in Piqua, Ohio) sang in vaudeville shows locally during the late 1920s. Due to their uncanny ability to imitate instruments, taking Louis Armstrong's vocal innovations to the next level, the siblings (billed as "four boys and a guitar") often sounded as if they utilized a trumpet, trombone, and bass too. In 1931, the Mills Brothers began recording and became a hit on stage, on the radio, and eventually through their guest spots in movies.

● **Chronological, Vol. 1** (JSP 301), which has also been made available by the Nostalgia Arts label, consists of the Mills Brothers' first recordings. The group is particularly exciting on three renditions of "Tiger Rag," "Nobody's Sweetheart," "Sweet Sue," and a few numbers (including "Dinah" and "Shine") with Bing Crosby.

The Rhythm Boys and Bing Crosby   The most important singer of the era (other than Louis Armstrong) and one whose popularity dwarfed everyone was Bing Crosby. Harry Lillis "Bing" Crosby sang with his high school band in Washington State and was self-taught on drums. While reluctantly studying law at Gonzaga University in Spokane, Crosby met vocalist Al Rinker and was soon playing drums and singing with Rinker's Musicaleaders. After graduating in 1925, Crosby quickly discarded any plans to be a lawyer and instead formed a duo with Rinker. They relocated to Los Angeles and stayed with Rinker's sister, Mildred Bailey, through whom they met and were hired by Paul Whiteman. Quickly assessing the duo's strengths and weaknesses, Whiteman teamed them with singer/pianist/songwriter Harry Barris, billing them as the Rhythm Boys.

The Rhythm Boys were a popular attraction with the Paul Whiteman Orchestra during 1927–30, recording as a separate unit, while backed by Whiteman's big band and sometimes as part of a contingent of singers that also included Jack Fulton, Austin "Skin" Young, and Charles Gaylord. The good-humored vocal group's better recordings include "I'm Coming Virginia," "Mississippi Mud," "Out of Town Gal," and "Happy Feet." Their cheerful interplay, humorous scatting, and Barris's way of saying a drawn-out "pahh" at the end of their performances gave them their own musical identity. In addition, during this period Crosby had an occasional solo number, including "Muddy Water," "Mary," "Ol' Man River," "Make Believe," and "'Tain't So, Honey, 'Tain't So."

The Rhythm Boys can be seen singing "Mississippi Mud" in the 1930 Paul Whiteman film *The King of Jazz*. However, their constant carousing and Whiteman's need to cut his budget resulted in them soon departing, to join Gus Arnheim's Orchestra in Los Angeles. By 1931, Crosby's solos were receiving much more attention than the trio, and a short time after, the Rhythm Boys broke up. Al Rinker ended up working behind the scenes, while Harry Barris (who should have become a major star himself) wrote songs (including "I Surrender Dear") and had tantalizingly brief and usually unbilled cameos in quite a few films.

Crosby, one of the first singers to really master using the microphone, was a major change from the boy tenors and pompous, semi-operatic male singers who had been dominating pop music. He sounded much more natural, relaxed, and accessible, and he had the ability to take the vocal innovations of Louis Armstrong and Jack Teagarden and utilize them in pop music. Crosby had tremendous success with his series of 15-minute radio programs on CBS, and his recordings included such hits as "Just One More Chance," "I Found a Million-Dollar Baby," "Please," "Brother Can You Spare a Dime" (the quintessential Depression song), and "June in January." In 1932, Crosby was still singing a fair amount of jazz (in *The Big Broadcast* he performs

"Dinah" while backed by his regular accompanist Eddie Lang), and he would always retain a strong love for early jazz even as he moved elsewhere musically.

◉ **1926–1932** (Timeless 1-004) is a superior summation of Bing Crosby's early years, particularly his recordings of 1927–29. Crosby's best solo sides with Paul Whiteman (including "Muddy Water," "Mary," "Ol' Man River," and "Make Believe") are included along with specialties with the Rhythm Boys and other Whiteman vocalists (highlighted by "Changes," "From Monday On," "Louisiana," "You Took Advantage of Me," and "Happy Feet"). In addition, Crosby is heard with Sam Lanin, the Dorsey Brothers Orchestra, and, during 1930–32, with Gus Arnheim ("One More Time"), the Mills Brothers ("Dinah"), and Duke Ellington ("Three Little Words" with the Rhythm Boys and solo on "St. Louis Blues"). It is not a "complete" reissue series (which is long overdue), but a very good sampler of early Bing.

Bing Crosby, like Hoagy Carmichael, would retain a fondness for early jazz throughout his life, even as he became the biggest name in pop music.

1920s White New York Jazz: Hot Jazz and Dance Bands

After Louis Armstrong's brilliant playing with the Fletcher Henderson Orchestra during 1924–25 made its impact on jazz musicians in New York, the Big Apple was poised to become the center of jazz. Most of the major record labels were based in New York as were the studios and some of the most significant radio stations, while Harlem was becoming a mecca for black Americans and jazz alike. The mass exodus of top musicians from Chicago to New York during 1927–28 added to the richness of the local scene.

New York City was one of the most liberal areas in the United States, but its music scene was totally segregated except for some mixed jazz record dates, and the audience tended to be segregated too. One of the odder cases was the Cotton Club, which employed black musicians and entertainers, but with very rare exceptions only allowed white patrons to see the shows. As far as mixed bands actually appearing on stage, other than at some after-hours jam sessions, it simply was not permitted in New York.

Although the top white musicians generally preferred to play jazz with freewheeling combos, the reality of the music business was that they could make much better livings performing with dance bands and large orchestras, in addition to the studio work. When one has fairly low expectations of these dance bands, the music is much more rewarding and listenable than expected, with routine "vocal refrains" frequently followed by a hot solo chorus or two. However, if one expects such white big bands as that of Jean Goldkette, Ben Pollack, and Paul Whiteman to stick to jazz, it is easy to become disappointed. Their music and that of the other white orchestras tends to be compromised, with an eye toward satisfying the record label, song pluggers, and dancing public.

Although black and white jazz musicians influenced each other (historical revisionists aside, it was never just a one-way street of whites emulating blacks), as in Chicago, the two jazz scenes were independent of each other and will be treated that way in this chapter.

Phil Napoleon and the Original Memphis Five

Phil Napoleon, who was among the first trumpeters in New York to swing, stayed busy during the second half of the decade. The Original Memphis Five name was only used for 25 titles during 1925–29 (a major drop off from the previous years) plus four numbers from a final session in 1931, but Napoleon also appeared on jazz dates with the Charleston Chasers, the California Ramblers, the Dorsey Brothers, the Emperors, the Hot Air Men, the Hotsy-Totsy Gang, Miff Mole's Little Molers, the New Orleans Blackbirds, Boyd Senter, and Milt Shaw, with a variety of singers, and on 29 selections recorded during 1926–29 under his own name. **The Original Memphis Five/Napoleon's Emperors/ The Cotton Pickers 1928–1929** (Timeless 1-049), other than the 1931 Memphis Five date, has the final sessions of the Original Memphis Five, Napoleon's Emperors, and the Cotton Pickers. The first two groups utilize Napoleon, Tommy Dorsey, Jimmy Dorsey, and sometimes Joe Venuti, Frank Signorelli, Eddie Lang, Joe Tarto, and Stan King or Vic Berton. Half of the Cotton Pickers dates have a similar lineup, but its first two sessions feature Tommy Dorsey on trumpet and Glenn Miller along with Jimmy Dorsey. No matter the lineup, the music throughout (which includes a version of Libby Holman singing "Moanin' Low") is high-quality and fairly freewheeling 1929 jazz. Two LPs covering this era also showcase Napoleon in fine form. **Featuring the Original Memphis Five** (IAJRC 26) has six

titles from 1926–27 with Napoleon's medium-size band plus eight selections from the Original Memphis Five of 1927–29. **1929–1931** (The Old Masters 13) includes the final Original Memphis Five session from 1931 with the Dorsey Brothers along with Napoleon's dates with the Hot Air Men, one title ("You Made Me Love You") with Miff Mole's Molers, and the five-song session by Napoleon's Emperors from May 14, 1929. But despite all of this work, Phil Napoleon never became famous with the general public, and he spent the early Depression years playing anonymously with radio orchestras.

The Charleston Chasers   One of the many groups that Phil Napoleon recorded with was the Charleston Chasers. The name "the Charleston Chasers" was used for a series of recording groups during the 1925–31 period though none of the bands ever played in public. The first Charleston Chasers session featured trumpeter Leon McConville, Miff Mole, and Arthur Schutt. There were 15 songs recorded by a version of the Chasers in 1927–28 that was similar to Red Nichols's Five Pennies, with cornetist Nichols, Miff Mole, Jimmy Dorsey, or Pee Wee Russell on clarinet, and usually Schutt, Dick McDonough, Joe Tarto on tuba, and Vic Berton. In 1929, the Chasers were reborn as a Phil Napoleon–led band with Mole or Tommy Dorsey, Benny Goodman, Fud Livingston or Jimmy Dorsey, a rhythm section, and singers Eva Taylor (who is in particularly strong form during her six numbers) and Roy Evans.

The fourth and final version of the Charleston Chasers on February 9, 1931, was an 11-piece group with trumpeter Charlie Teagarden, Jack Teagarden, Glenn Miller, Benny Goodman, and Gene Krupa. Two songs had pop vocals by Paul Small, but it is the classic renditions of "Basin Street Blues" and "Beale Street Blues" (with Jack Teagarden's singing) that are the highpoints (and final acts) of this group's existence. ● **The Charleston Chasers Vol. 1** (Timeless 1-040) has all of these sessions except for four of the Napoleon numbers from 1930 and the classic 1931 date. Among the more memorable selections are "After You've Gone," two surprisingly effective numbers with singer Kate Smith, "Davenport Blues," "Delirium" (which has drummer Vic Berton playing a metallophone!), "Imagination," "Moanin' Low," "Lovable and Sweet," and "What Wouldn't I Do for that Man." The music ranges from inventive jazz to hot dance music.

The California Ramblers, the Goofus Five, and the Little Ramblers   The California Ramblers, a big band that had recorded literally hundreds of selections by 1925, continued at a prolific pace through 1931, recording as a full unit, as the Vagabonds and Ted Wallace's Orchestra, and as smaller combos called the Little Ramblers, the Goofus Five, the Five Birmingham Babies, and the Varsity Eight. The group was at its prime during 1924–27, but after its main soloists (Adrian Rollini, trumpeter Chelsea Quealey, and Bobby Davis on alto and clarinet) sailed to Europe in 1927, it evolved into a much more conventional dance band.

◉ **1925–1928** (Timeless 053) has some of the California Ramblers' strongest jazz recordings. The 25 selections are only a tiny percentage of the band's total output (not even 4 percent), but it gives listeners an excellent idea how the group sounded at its peak. Featured on various tracks are Quealey, Davis, Rollini, and trombonist Abe Lincoln; Red Nichols and the Dorsey Brothers also make appearances. The Ramblers are heard in top form on "Everything Is Hotsy Totsy Now," "The Girl Friend," "She Knows Her Onions," "Stockholm Stomp," "Vo-Do-Do-De-O Blues," "Nothin' Does-Does Like It Used to Do-Do-Do," and "Make My Cot Where the Cot-Cot-Cotton Grows."

Ed Kirkeby managed the California Ramblers and in the late 1930s he managed Fats Waller's career. He started working for Columbia Records in 1916 as a salesman and was soon promoted to assistant recording manager. Kirkeby organized and signed Earl Fuller's Jazz Band (which featured Ted Lewis) to Columbia as an early competitor to the Original Dixieland Jazz Band. In 1920, Kirkeby was hired by the California Ramblers, which he soon reorganized, gaining the band a foothold in New York and helping set up its extremely busy recording schedule. In 1926, Kirkeby first recorded as a vocalist with the band, and he took occasional vocals in their later sessions. In 1927, Kirkeby started leading dates of his own, using the pseudonym of Ted Wallace. On **Vol. One** (The Old Masters 110), Kirkeby only takes vocals on four of the 24 performances; Smith Ballew, Scrappy Lambert, and Russell Douglas actually do most of the singing during these performances from 1927–30. The earlier titles feature musicians from the California Ramblers (including Chelsea Quealey and Adrian Rollini) although within a year the style of these Kirkeby sessions evolved into dance music played by top studio musicians. The performances overall are superior, and there

are some worthwhile jazz solos along the way. Highlights include "Who-oo? You-oo, That's Who," "Zulu Wail," "There's Something Spanish in Your Eyes," "I May Be Wrong, but I Think You're Wonderful," and "Love Ain't Nothing but the Blues."

The Goofus Five was a quintet taken from the lineup of the California Ramblers. A "goofus" is the name of a miniature saxophone that sounds like a mouth organ and was occasionally played by Adrian Rollini. The band (which recorded for Okeh) originally consisted of Rollini, trumpeter Bill Moore, pianist Irving Brodsky, banjoist Tommy Felline, and Stan King. It soon grew beyond five pieces with the addition of Bobby Davis, tenor saxophonist Sam Ruby, and Abe Lincoln. In 1926, Chelsea Quealey took over on trumpet. That version of the group (with a few minor personnel changes) stayed intact into the fall of 1927. However, the later recordings by the Goofus Five (from 1928–29) are essentially the full California Ramblers under a different name. **The Goofus Five** (Timeless 1-017), which dates from 1926–27, covers the prime period of the group, containing all 24 recordings that it made with the Quealey-Rollini lineup. The emphasis is on heated melodic jazz, excellent songs (many of which became standards), and plenty of youthful spirit, the type of music that made the youth of the era want to dance.

A similar group (Bill Moore, Red Nichols, Roy Johnston or Chelsea Quealey on trumpet, Tommy Dorsey or Herb Winfield on trombone, Bobby Davis, occasional tenor players, Adrian Rollini on bass sax and goofus, pianist Irving Brodsky, banjoist Tommy Felline, and Stan King or Herb Weil on drums) recorded 26 titles during 1924–27 as the Little Ramblers. All of the group's recordings (except for the first four titles that have Rollini just on goofus) are included on **The Little Ramblers** (Timeless 1-037). The ensembles are well played, Rollini often takes solo honors, and Red Nichols is an asset on four numbers.

The Original Indiana Five   The Original Indiana Five recorded steadily from 1923 until its breakup in 1929. The band (with drummer/leader Tom Morton, trumpeter Johnny Sylvester, trombonist Pete Pellezzi, clarinetist/altoist Nick Vitalo, banjoist Tony Colucci, and pianist Harry Ford) had stable personnel during the 1926–29 period (other than Tony Tortomas taking over on trumpet in late 1926) and continued playing in a similar freewheeling style as the Original Memphis Five and the New Orleans Rhythm Kings. **Everybody Stomp** (Frog 23) has all 26 selections that the group made for the Harmony label, including three from 1929 that were issued under Tom Morton's name. The music is primarily from 1925–27, and the quintet/sextet plays their happy brand of music on such numbers as "Everybody's Doin' the Charleston Now," "So Is Your Old Lady," "I'd Leave Ten Men Like Yours to Love One Man Like Mine," and "Stockholm Stomp."

Red Nichols and Miff Mole   Ernest Loring "Red" Nichols was extremely busy in the 1920s. Born in Ogden, Utah, Nichols studied cornet with his father from the age of five, playing with his father's brass band when he was 12. In 1922, Nichols made his recording debut with the Syncopating Five. Soon he took over the band and renamed it the Royal Palms Orchestra, performing in Atlantic City and Indiana. After hooking up in New York with bandleader and contractor Sam Lanin in late 1924, Nichols was on his way to becoming one of the most recorded musicians in the world. The cornetist, who was a very skilled technician, had a sound and style that was influenced by Bix Beiderbecke although his tone was emotionally cooler and he was a less spontaneous player. Sometimes Nichols has been given a bad rap as being a lesser Beiderbecke, but he actually created fresh music of his own, being an underrated writer whose arranged ensembles and transitions were constantly full of surprises. Nichols could also add a touch of jazz to any setting as a player, so he constantly recorded with studio orchestras in addition to spending a few months with the Paul Whiteman Orchestra in 1927.

Red Nichols was most significant as a bandleader and talent scout. In 1926, he began recording as the leader of his Five Pennies, having a surprise hit in 1927 with his version of "Ida, Sweet as Apple Cider." The original Five Pennies consisted of Miff Mole, Arthur Schutt, Eddie Lang, and drummer Vic Berton (who doubled on tympani). Nichols's unique collaborations with Mole (1926–28) often utilized whole-tone runs, unusual interval jumps, and sudden outbursts of improvised Dixieland. Most of the Five Pennies recordings feature a slightly larger band than five pieces, with other key players at various times, including Dudley Fosdick (jazz's first mellophone soloist), Jimmy Dorsey, Pee Wee Russell, Benny Goodman, Leo McConville, Gene Krupa, Jack Teagarden, and Glenn Miller.

In addition to the Five Pennies dates, during 1926–32, Nichols recorded an enormous number of recordings using similar groups under such names as the Charleston Chasers, the Arkansas Travelers, the Red Heads, the Louisiana Rhythm Kings, the Wabash Orchestra, and Red & Miff's Stompers among others. Nichols also led larger bands on some records, worked as a sideman (including with Miff Mole's Molers) and headed the orchestras for the shows *Strike Up the Band* and *Girl Crazy*.

It is surprising that more of Red Nichols's 1920s recordings are not yet available on CD. Best is ◉ **Red Nichols & Miff Mole** (Retrieval 79010), which features Nichols on all of his sessions with the Original Memphis Five, the Arkansas Travelers (including "Washboard Blues," "That's No Bargain," and "Boneyard Shuffle"), and the Six Hottentots, plus four of his seven titles with the Hottentots. The personnel includes Nichols, Mole, Jimmy Lytell, Jimmy Dorsey, pianist Rube Bloom, Frank Signorelli, Arthur Schutt, Joe Tarto, and Vic Berton. **Red Nichols on Edison 1924–27** (Jazz Oracle 8007) has 18 performances, eight of which are over four minutes long; the Edison label often put out 12-inch 78s that contained additional playing time. But because nine of the selections on the CD are alternate takes (four songs are heard in three versions apiece), the set (which has numbers by the Charleston Seven, the California Ramblers, Don Voorhees, and Red & Miff's Stompers) will most be enjoyed by Nichols completists. **Radio Transcriptions 1929–30** (IAJRC 1011) has some intriguing music that Red Nichols recorded in 1927, 1929, and 1930 specifically for the radio, complete with announcements. The 1927 *Brunswick Brevity* series has versions of "Say It with Music" (used as a theme song) sandwiching such tunes as "I May Be Wrong," "They Didn't Believe Me," "On the Alamo," and "That's a Plenty." There is also a *Brunswick Brevity* from 1929 and several episodes of *The Heat* series from 1930. Among Nichols's sidemen along the way are Glenn Miller (who provided some of the arrangements), Jack Teagarden, Jimmy Dorsey, Pee Wee Russell, Benny Goodman, Adrian Rollini, Joe Sullivan, and Gene Krupa.

But most of Red Nichols's early recording legacy has yet to be reissued on CD. Many of the finest Nichols performances are on five LPs put out by the Australian Swaggie label: **Red Nichols and His Five Pennies— Vols. One–Five** (Swaggie 836, 837, 838, 839, and 840). These important albums have all of Nichols's recordings (with many intriguing alternate takes) with his Five

Pennies from December 8, 1926, to February 8, 1929, plus his selections leading the Louisiana Rhythm Kings, the Captivators, and a larger orchestra, ending with a June 11, 1929, session. All of this music, plus Nichols's other dates up to 1932, deserve to be reissued coherently on CD. Other LPs that draw from the cornetist's huge discography include **Real Rare Red** (Broadway 110), **Real Rare Red Vol. II** (Broadway 120), **With Sam Lanin's Orchestra** (Broadway 105), **Red & Miff** (Saville 146), **Red & Ben** (Broadway 103), which splits the program between Nichols's selections with the Wabash Dance Orchestra and numbers from Ben Pollack's Orchestra, **Starring Benny Goodman, 1929–31** (Sunbeam 137), and **1929–1932** (IAJRC 22).

Miff Mole was one of the most advanced trombonists of 1926–28. Mole had lessons on violin and piano before switching to trombone when he was 15. He worked with Gus Sharp's Orchestra for two years, was a member of the Original Memphis Five (1922), gigged with Abe Lyman in California, and in New York played with the orchestras of Sam Lanin, Ray Miller, Russ Gorman, and Roger Wolfe Kahn (1926–27). Mole recorded frequently with Nichols during 1926–29, and his staccato runs and wide interval jumps gave him a very unusual style while showing that the trombone could be played with as much adventure and unpredictability as a trumpet. He generally used Nichols's Five Pennies in his recordings as Miff Mole's Molers during 1927–30, all of which have been reissued on ◉ **Slippin' Around** (Frog 19) and **Slippin' Around—Again** (Frog 20). The former set has 14 numbers by the Molers of 1927–28, including four cuts in which his group backs stage singer Sophie Tucker (heard at her prime in 1927). In addition, there are four cuts with Red & Miff's Stompers, two by Nichols's Orchestra, and a pair of test pressings from a Mole session in 1930 (with Phil Napoleon). The adventurous versions of "Hurricane," "Delirium," "Davenport Blues," "Imagination" and "Feelin' No Pain" are most memorable. **Slippin' Around—Again** starts off with six alternate takes (all formerly test pressings) and has the last dates by Mole's Molers, with Phil Napoleon taking over for Nichols. Also on this CD are two numbers from a radio broadcast in 1936 that feature Mole, and a pair of selections (plus an alternate take) from Mole's only session as a leader during the swing era. By then Miff Mole (who had ended his association with Red Nichols in early 1929) was in his longtime position as a

staff musician on NBC and had lost much of his individuality in favor of sounding like Jack Teagarden.

One of the most intriguing of Red Nichols's sidemen was Dudley Fosdick, and not just because of his name! Fosdick was a master of the mellophone, a brass instrument very rarely ever used as a solo instrument in jazz. Fosdick, who worked with his brother Gene Fosdick's Hoosiers (with whom he recorded in 1922), Ted Weems (1924–25), the Melody Artists, Don Voorhees, and Roger Wolfe Kahn (1928–29), recorded frequently with Nichols, Mole, and the Louisiana Rhythm Kings during 1928–29. His solos were quite fluent and fit into the music very well. But when he rejoined Ted Weems's increasingly commercial band in 1931, Dudley Fosdick permanently left the jazz scene.

Jack Teagarden   During 1926–29, there was a pool of impressive white jazz musicians in the New York area who appeared on many record dates; many were fortunate enough to get jobs in the studios during the early Depression years. Some are forever associated with the 1920s (meaning that they dropped out of jazz after 1930) while a few of them had long careers in creative music.

Jack Teagarden fell into the latter category. Teagarden came from a very musical family; his younger brother was trumpeter Charlie Teagarden, a fine Dixieland player who started his career with stints with Ben Pollack (1929–30) and Red Nichols. In addition, Jack's younger sister was pianist Norma Teagarden, and his mother played ragtime piano. Jack, who was born in Texas, began on piano when he was five, baritone horn at seven, and trombone at ten. After moving to Chappell, Nebraska, with his family in 1918, he first worked professionally in local theatres with his mother. Teagarden picked up important experience gigging in Texas with Peck Kelley's Bad Boys (1921–23) and with a variety of territory bands, including Doc Ross's Jazz Bandits (1925–27), making his recording debut in late 1927 with Johnny Johnson's Statler Pennsylvanians. Teagarden first came to New York in February 1928 when he played with Billy Lustig's Scranton Sirens at the Roseland Ballroom. His arrival in town caused a major stir among musicians for Teagarden played trombone with the fluidity of a trumpet, creating warm legato lines full of the blues. His solos made both Kid Ory and Miff Mole sound wooden and stiff in comparison. Teagarden also proved to be a significant jazz singer, influencing Bing Crosby's style with his lazy relaxed approach and the way he made every pop song sound bluesy.

Teagarden played with Tommy Gott's group for two months and then spent nearly five years (June 1928 to May 1933) as a member of Ben Pollack's Orchestra, where his playing so overshadowed Glenn Miller that Miller de-emphasized his own trombone playing from then on. Teagarden (nicknamed "Mr. T.") was in great demand for record dates, and among the many sessions that he uplifted during 1928–32 were dates led by Roger Wolfe Kahn ("She's a Great, Great Girl"), Eddie Condon ("I'm Gonna Stomp, Mr. Henry Lee" and "That's a Serious Thing"), Louis Armstrong ("Knockin' a Jug"), Red Nichols, the Big Aces, Hoagy Carmichael, the Charleston Chasers (1931), the Dorsey Brothers Orchestra, Benny Goodman, Ted Lewis, the Louisiana Rhythm Kings, Jimmy McHugh's Bostonians, Irving Mills's Hotsy-Totsy Gang, Mills's Merry Makers, the Mound City Blue Blowers, the New Orleans Ramblers, Jack Pettis, Willard Robison, Joe Venuti, Fats Waller, and Virginia Willrich's Texas Rangers.

In addition, Teagarden led a series of sessions of his own during this time, all of which are included on **1930–1934** (Classics 698). The seven dates range from dance band music to Dixieland-oriented jams with the trombonist joined by 10–13 piece bands, often drawn from the Ben Pollack (soon to be Bob Crosby) Orchestra. Among his main sidemen are tenor saxophonist Eddie Miller, Benny Goodman, Charlie Teagarden, Pee Wee Russell, Fats Waller (who shares vocals with Teagarden on "You Rascal You" and the silly "That's What I Like About You") and Bud Freeman; a highlight is Teagarden's initial recording of the touching "A Hundred Years from Today." Two samplers cover Teagarden's work for the Victor label, dating from 1928–57. While **That's a Serious Thing** (Bluebird 9986) has 21 fine selections (including "I'm Gonna Stomp, Mr. Henry Lee," "That's a Serious Thing," "She's a Great Great Girl," three mid-1940s numbers with Louis Armstrong, and two from 1957 with Bud Freeman), ● **The Indispensable Jack Teagarden** (RCA 961 327), a double-disc from French RCA, is much better. It has 31 songs in all, including most of the songs already mentioned plus strong samplings of Teagarden's work with Ben Pollack, Paul Whiteman, and the Mound City Blue Blowers.

Pee Wee Russell   Charles "Pee Wee" Russell would develop into one of the most original and unpredictable of all clarinetists. Russell took lessons on violin, piano, and drums before switching to clarinet where he was originally inspired by Yellow Nunez. He performed in the Midwest, played on riverboats, toured with tent shows, and worked with Peck Kelley's Bad Boys in Texas in 1924. Russell made his recording debut with Herbert Berger in 1924 in St. Louis when he was 18 and spent part of 1925 in Frankie Trumbauer's band, where he was drinking buddies with Bix Beiderbecke. He was part of the Jean Goldkette Orchestra in the summer of 1926 but did not record with the band. After moving to New York in 1927, Russell worked with Red Nichols on and off during the next two years, taking a well-received solo on "Ida, Sweet as Apple Cider." At the time he sounded a bit like Frank Teschemacher, but within a couple of years Russell's style had become quite individual. He appeared on record dates with the Charleston Chasers, Miff Mole, the Red Heads, Frankie Trumbauer (in a group that included Beiderbecke), pianist Irving Brodsky, the Louisiana Rhythm Kings, the Hotsy-Totsy Gang, the Whoopee Makers, the Mound City Blue Blowers, Jack Teagarden, Jack Bland, and a heated session under Billy Banks's name that co-starred trumpeter Henry "Red" Allen in 1932. By then, Russell's eccentric style was becoming recognizable, and impossible to copy.

Archie Schutt, Frank Signorelli, and Lennie Hayton Unlike Teagarden and Russell, pianists Arthur Schutt, Frank Signorelli, and Lennie Hayton reached their creative heights in the 1920s. All three appeared on many record dates during the era. Arthur Schutt was a professional at the age of 13 (playing piano for silent movies) and was with Paul Specht's Orchestra during 1918–24, recording with both the big band and the Georgians (contributing some of the arrangements for the latter). During 1926–29, Schutt was on many of Red Nichols's records where his novelty ragtime style and interest in classical music made him stand out. In addition to appearing on a countless number of dates, Schutt led five obscure band sessions during 1929–30 and also recorded nine novelty ragtime piano solos (during 1923, 1928–29, and 1934), all but one of which are included on the LP that he shares with Rube Bloom, **Novelty Ragtime Piano Kings** (Folkways 41).

Frank Signorelli was a founding member of the Original Memphis Five in 1917 with whom he played until September 1926, appearing on their records as late as 1931. J. Russell Robinson's replacement with the Original Dixieland Jazz Band in 1921, Signorelli also worked with Adrian Rollini's New Yorker Band during September and October 1927, and appeared on many records, including with Bix and His Gang, the Charleston Chasers, the Cotton Pickers, the Dorsey Brothers Orchestra, Cliff Edwards, Annette Hanshaw, the Hotsy-Totsy Gang, Eddie Lang, Jimmy Lytell, Miff Mole, Phil Napoleon, Boyd Senter, the Tennessee Ten, Frankie Trumbauer, Joe Venuti, the Whoopee Makers, and a lone session of his own.

Lennie Hayton started playing piano when he was six and studied music extensively. He worked with Cass Hagan's Orchestra in 1927 and was second pianist with Paul Whiteman during September 1928 to May 1930. Hayton made records with Bix and His Gang, the Charleston Chasers, the Mason-Dixon Orchestra, Red Nichols's Five Pennies, Jack Pettis, Frankie Trumbauer, Joe Venuti, and Whiteman, also leading a single session in 1928.

After the classic jazz era, Arthur Schutt became a studio musician, Frank Signorelli was primarily a songwriter (including composing "I'll Never Be the Same" and "Stairway to the Stars"), and Lennie Hayton became a well-respected arranger for the studios and the musical director for his wife, singer Lena Horne.

Adrian Rollini   Adrian Rollini was generally one of the main stars on every recording in which he appeared. A child prodigy who played a Chopin concert on piano

75 ESSENTIAL RECORDS OF 1926–1932

when he was four, Rollini also led a band that same year, playing piano and xylophone. In 1922 (when he was 18), Rollini joined the California Ramblers, bought a bass sax, and on a challenge, mastered it within a week. He recorded frequently in the 1920s, not just on bass sax but on "hot fountain pen" (a miniature clarinet with a saxophone mouthpiece), the goofus (a tiny saxophone keyboard), vibes, and various miscellaneous instruments. In addition to his work with the California Ramblers and its various offshoots, Rollini was an important part of sessions led by Frankie Trumbauer, Red Nichols, and Joe Venuti. In the fall of 1927, he led an unrecorded all-star band for a few months that included Bix Beiderbecke and Frankie Trumbauer before it quickly failed. Rather than follow most of his sidemen into the Paul Whiteman Orchestra, Rollini spent December 1927 to December

1929 in Europe where he worked with Fred Elizalde and other local bands. After returning to the United States, he played with Bert Lown's Orchestra (1930–31) and became a studio musician for a few years. Surprisingly, Rollini did not lead any record dates of his own in the 1920s, but he had a strong impact (becoming baritonist Harry Carney's main early influence), even if he could not save the bass sax from becoming extinct by the mid-1930s.

Joe Venuti and Eddie Lang   Although the violin was a part of many early New Orleans jazz bands, particularly before recordings were made, in reality jazz violin began with Giuseppi "Joe" Venuti. He grew up in Philadelphia, was a childhood friend of Eddie Lang, and worked in Atlantic City with Lang as early as 1919.

75 ESSENTIAL RECORDS OF 1926–1932

Cab Calloway, **1930–1931** (Classics 516)

The Boswell Sisters, **The Boswell Sisters Collection, Vol. 1** (Nostalgia Arts 3007)

The Boswell Sisters, **The Boswell Sisters Collection, Vol. 3** (Nostalgia Arts 3009)

Mills Brothers, **Chronological, Vol. 1** (JSP 301)

Bing Crosby, **1926–1932** (Timeless 1-004)

The Charleston Chasers, **Vol. 1** (Timeless 1-040)

California Ramblers, **1925–1928** (Timeless 053)

Red Nichols and Miff Mole, **Red Nichols & Miff Mole** (Retrieval 79010)

Miff Mole, **Slippin' Around** (Frog 19)

Jack Teagarden, **The Indispensable Jack Teagarden** (RCA 961 327), 2 CDs

Joe Venuti and Eddie Lang, **The 1920s and 1930s Sides** (JSP 3402), 4 CDs

Eddie Lang, Carl Kress, and Dick McDonough, **Eddie Lang/Carl Kress/Dick McDonough** (Retrieval 79015)

Ted Weems, **The Essential Ted Weems 1923–1930** (Retrieval 79034), 2 CDs

Benny Goodman, **B.G. and Big Tea in NYC** (GRP/Decca 609)

The Dorsey Brothers Orchestra, **Vol. 1, 1928** (Jazz Oracle 8004)

James P. Johnson, **1928–1938** (Classics 671)

Fats Waller, **Turn on the Heat** (Bluebird 2482)

Clarence Williams, **1926–1927** (Classics 718)

Washboard Rhythm Kings, **Vol. 1** (Collector's Classics 17)

Lonnie Johnson, **Vol. 3** (Document 5065)

Fletcher Henderson, **A Study in Frustration** (Columbia/Legacy 57596), 3 CDs

Coleman Hawkins, **1929–1934** (Classics 587)

McKinney's Cotton Pickers, **Put It There, Vol. 1** (Frog 25)

Don Redman, **1931–1933** (Classics 543)

Luis Russell, **1926–1929** (Classics 558)

Luis Russell, **1930–1934** (Classics 606)

Henry "Red" Allen, **1929–1933** (Classics 540)

Charlie Johnson, **The Complete Charlie Johnson Sessions** (Hot 'N' Sweet 5110)

Duke Ellington, **Early Ellington** (Bluebird 6852)

Duke Ellington, **Early Ellington** (GRP/Decca 640), 3 CDs

Duke Ellington, **Okeh Ellington** (Columbia 46177), 2 CDs

Various Artists, **Jazz in Saint Louis 1924–1927** (Timeless 1-036)

Various Artists, **Richmond Rarities** (Jazz Oracle 8008)

Fred Elizalde, **The Best of Fred Elizalde and His Anglo American Band** (Retrieval 79011)

Spike Hughes, **Vols. 1 & 2** (Kings Cross 001/002), 2 CDs

Various Artists, **Hot British Dance Bands** (Timeless 1-005)

Various Artists, **What Kind of Rhythm Is That?** (Frog 31)

Andy Kirk, **1929–1931** (Classics 655)

Bennie Moten, **Vol. 1, Justrite** (Frog 29)

Bennie Moten, **Vol. 2, Kansas City Breakdown** (Frog 30)

The violinist played with Bert Estlow's quintet (1921), the Hotel Knickerbocker Orchestra, and Red Nichols. Venuti directed the Book-Cadillac Hotel Orchestra for Jean Goldkette in 1924 with whom he made his recording debut. After moving to New York in 1925, Venuti became very busy, appearing on scores of recording sessions with Goldkette, Roger Wolfe Kahn, Frankie Trumbauer, the Dorsey Brothers, Hoagy Carmichael, dance bands, singers, and studio orchestras. As a leader on records, Venuti recorded exciting violin-guitar duets with Lang starting in 1926 (including "Stringing the Blues"), freewheeling jazz dates (often with his Blue Four), and with a jazz-oriented dance band filled with top musicians. He also worked with the short-lived Adrian Rollini Big Band in 1927 and was a member of the Paul Whiteman Orchestra (May 1929 to May 1930). Whenever a hot jazz violin solo was needed by any New York–based white orchestra during the classic jazz era, Venuti was the first one to be called.

● **The 1920s and 1930s Sides** (JSP 3402), a double CD, has all 42 selections that Venuti recorded during 1926–31 as a leader of small groups. Most of these performances are classics that find Venuti and Eddie Lang making an ideal team and interacting with such guests as Arthur Schutt, Adrian Rollini, Don Murray, Frank Signorelli, Rube Bloom, Jimmy Dorsey, and Frankie Trumbauer. Highlights include "Stringing the Blues," "Wild Cat," "The Wild Dog," "Kickin' the Cat," "Beatin' the Dog," "Sensation," "Runnin' Ragged," "Raggin' the Scale," and "Little Girl" (with a vocal from composer Harold Arlen). **Fiddlesticks** (Conifer 172) perfectly complements the JSP release, for this single CD has 20 additional performances from a slightly later period. The recording date of October 22, 1931, by the Venuti-Lang All-Star Orchestra (with Benny Goodman and Jack and Charlie Teagarden) resulted in very exciting versions of "Beale Street Blues," "After You've Gone," "Farewell Blues," and "Someday Sweetheart." Also on this CD is Venuti's final recording with Lang, two orchestra features for the violinist, the last Venuti Blue Five date (from 1935 with both Adrian Rollini and his younger brother, tenor saxophonist Arthur Rollini), and the only four recordings by the Joe Venuti Big Band: the titles are "Flip," "Flop," "Something," and "Nothing."

The 32 selections on **Stringing the Blues** (Koch 7888) form an excellent sampler for this double CD (a straight reissue of a Columbia double LP), which has 17 numbers that are duplicated on the JSP set, eight features for Eddie Lang (including several guitar duets with Lonnie Johnson), and seven other numbers (including three features for Tommy Dorsey on trumpet); however, the JSP set is preferred. Joe Venuti's dates at the head of a larger dance band during 1928–33 are overdue to be reissued on CD. The music was last available on the LPs **Big Bands of Joe Venuti, Vol. 1** (JSP 1111) and **Big Bands of Joe Venuti, Vol. 2** (JSP 1112). Since there are many vocals by Scrappy Lambert, Smith Ballew, Don Elton, and Frank Luther, these recordings are not as significant as the Blue Five performances. But there are some solid solos along the way from Venuti, trumpeters Leo McConville and Manny Klein, Tommy Dorsey, Jimmy Dorsey, and Jack Teagarden, and the melodic music has its period charm.

More than any other guitarist, Eddie Lang (born Salvatore Massaro) was responsible for his instrument taking over from the banjo in bands of the mid-to-late 1920s. Lang was the first jazz guitar virtuoso. He actually started on violin when he was seven and played violin in public in 1917, but soon switched to banjo while doubling on guitar. Although he was quite capable of playing single-note lines during solos, it was Lang's sophisticated chord voicings that kept him in great demand. The guitarist worked with Charlie Kerr (1920–23), Bert Estlow, Vic D'Ipplito, Billy Lustig's Scranton Sirens (which also featured the Dorsey Brothers), and Red McKenzie's Mound City Blue Blowers (1924–25). From that point on, Lang performed constantly on radio and recordings, often teaming up with his childhood friend Joe Venuti. Among his most notable associations since 1926 were Roger Wolfe Kahn (1926–27), Jean Goldkette, Adrian Rollini's big band (1927), and Paul Whiteman (1929–30), plus recordings with (among many others) Venuti, Frankie Trumbauer (including "Singin' the Blues"), guitar duets with his blues counterpart Lonnie Johnson (Lang used the pseudonym of "Blind Willie Dunn" so as to hide the fact that these were integrated dates), and a pair of memorable duets with Carl Kress ("Pickin' My Way" and "Feelin' My Way"). Lang also recorded 20 selections as a leader during 1927–29, mostly showcases for his guitar although six songs found him at the head of combos. In 1932, he became Bing Crosby's regular accompanist. He appeared in two notable movies: a wonderful 90-second performance with Venuti in the 1930 Paul Whiteman film *The King of Jazz* and played "Dinah" with Bing Crosby in the 1932 movie *The Big Broadcast*.

Dick McDonough, Carl Kress, and Eddie Lang   Dick McDonough and Carl Kress were also very important guitarists during the era, often being called for studio work when Lang was not available. Dick McDonough started on banjo, but was doubling on guitar as early as 1926. Among his better assignments of the classic jazz era were sessions with Red Nichols, Miff Mole, the Dorsey Brothers, Cliff Edwards, Benny Goodman, Jack Pettis, Jack Teagarden, Frankie Trumbauer, and the Boswell Sisters. Carl Kress had an even more sophisticated chordal style than Lang. After starting on piano and banjo, Kress switched to guitar. He was with the Paul Whiteman Orchestra in 1926 and then became busy in the studios, recording with the Chicago Loopers (which featured Bix Beiderbecke and Frankie Trumbauer), Red Nichols, Miff Mole, the Dorsey Brothers, and many others. The high-points of his early years were his two duets with Lang in 1932, and it is a measure of how highly he was thought of that Lang consented to play single-note lines so Kress's chordal style could be prominent.

○ **Eddie Lang/Carl Kress/Dick McDonough** (Retrieval 79015) has the 14 Lang showcases. A dozen numbers feature the guitarist either unaccompanied or joined by Arthur Schutt, Frank Signorelli, or Rube Bloom on piano, with the spotlight very much on his guitar. Highlights include "Eddie's Twister," "Perfect," "Add a Little Wiggle," and "There'll Be Some Changes Made." Lang's two classic guitar duets with Carl Kress are also here; they are so perfect that they deserve to be orchestrated for a full band. In addition, the four Carl Kress–Dick McDonough duets from 1934 and 1937 (including "Chicken-a-la-Swing") and Kress's six solo recordings of 1938–39 (highlighted by "Peg Leg Shuffle," "Sutton Mutton," and the three movements of "Afterthoughts") round out this definitive set of early jazz guitar.

Joe Tarto   During this era, combo dates often did not use string bass or tuba, which in retrospect was a mistake. Certainly the Bix and His Gang sessions would have swung much more and sounded a lot more complete if Steve Brown had been utilized. When a tuba player or bassist was called for on a jazz record date in New York, Joe Tarto was often the musician who was called. Tarto started on trombone at 12 before switching to tuba. After lying about his age, he served in the army

during World War I when he was 15. After his discharge in 1919, Tarto worked with Cliff Edwards (1921–22), Paul Specht (1922–24), Sam Lanin, Vincent Lopez, and Roger Wolfe Kahn; he was also in the orchestras for several Broadway shows. Tarto appeared on many record dates, most notably with Red Nichols, Miff Mole, the Dorsey Brothers, Eddie Lang, Phil Napoleon, Bix Beiderbecke, Ethel Waters, and the Boswell Sisters, sometimes doubling on bass.

Vic Berton, Stan King, and Chauncey Morehouse   Three of the busiest drummers in the New York jazz scene of the late 1920s would fade out by the mid-1930s. Vic Berton was the most innovative because not only was he a very versatile drummer, but he was jazz's first (and nearly only) timpanist. Berton, who started on violin and piano, was playing drums in the pit orchestra at the Alhambra Theatre in Milwaukee at the age of seven. He worked in symphony orchestras as a teenager, had a spell in Sousa's band, spent the first half of the 1920s in Chicago, and worked with top local groups. Berton managed the Wolverines during 1924–25 and was the group's drummer part of the time. Moving to New York in 1926, Berton was an important part of the Five Pennies' recordings, showing how the timpani could be used in classic jazz (although no one followed his example!). He also worked with Roger Wolfe Kahn, Don Voorhees, and Paul Whiteman (1927), but mostly freelanced. With the rise of the Depression, Berton moved to Los Angeles where he became a studio musician, working for the movie studios, and as a percussionist with the L.A. Philharmonic.

Stan King worked with the California Ramblers (1922–26), Roger Wolfe Kahn, Jean Goldkette, Paul Whiteman, Bert Lown's Hotel Biltmore Orchestra (1929–31), and the Dorsey Brothers Orchestra in the show *Everybody Welcome* before becoming buried in the studios. Chauncey Morehouse shared a similar fate. While still in high school in 1919, Morehouse formed the Versatile Five. He played with Paul Specht (1922–24), recording with the Georgians. Morehouse's later jobs included Howard Lanin, Ted Weems, Jean Goldkette (1925–27), the Adrian Rollini Orchestra, and Voorhees, along with recordings with Frankie Trumbauer, Bix and His Gang, Joe Venuti, Hoagy Carmichael, Red Nichols, Miff Mole, the Dorsey Brothers, Wingy Manone, and many others.

Bill Moore Trumpeter Bill Moore was a unique figure in 1920s jazz because he was a light-skinned black man, (the son of a mixed marriage) who spent most of his life "passing" and appearing on recordings with otherwise completely white bands. Very few people knew that he was continually breaking down racial boundaries. Moore appeared on hundreds of records in the 1920s including with the California Ramblers, the Five Birmingham Babies, the Goofus Five, the Lumberjacks, Ben Bernie, Don Voorhees, Bert Lown, Jack Pettis, Irving Mills's Hotsy-Totsy Gang, the Whoopee Makers, the Mississippi Maulers, the New Orleans Blackbirds, the Vagabonds, the Varsity Eight, Bailey's Dixie Dudes, the Broadway Broadcasters, Al Goering's Collegians, the Kentucky Blowers, the Little Ramblers, Fred Rich, and the Dorsey Brothers (1930–31), all of which were white bands. This trumpeter took short and hot solos on many of the sessions, and proved to be a flexible and top-notch musician, adding a bit of jazz to many dance band dates. Whenever there was any doubt about Moore's ancestry, he billed himself as "The Hot Hawaiian," even though he had never been to Hawaii! He continued breaking down racial boundaries (though no one knew about it) after 1930 when he became a full-time studio musician, the only black musician to appear on a countless number of sessions.

Ted Lewis A style that was dated by 1926 but managed to linger on for a few more years was that of the gaspipe clarinetists. Ted Lewis was an oddity in show business. His clarinet and occasional alto sax playing were primitive at best, though he loved to play and could never understand why jazz musicians made fun of him behind his back. His overly sentimental singing about the good old days was both corny and insipid. Despite (or perhaps because of) this, Lewis was a major name throughout the 1920s and '30s. He recorded with Earl Fuller's Famous Jazz Band during 1917–18 before leaving with all of Fuller's sidemen and forming his own quintet. A vaudeville star, Lewis made "Me and My Shadow" and his theme "When My Baby Smiles at Me" famous along with the trademark phrase "Is everybody happy?" His band, which in its early days sometimes featured a laughing trombone from Harry Raderman, recorded frequently and grew to ten pieces by 1924, the year that George Brunies joined. Don Murray (1928–29), Frank Teschemacher (1929), and Muggsy Spanier (who started a long stint in 1929) gave Lewis's

music some credibility despite the leader, and such guests as pianist Fats Waller, Jack Teagarden, and Benny Goodman are heard on some of his recordings.

Ted Lewis Classic Sessions 1928–1929 (Nostalgia Arts 3021) has a strong sampling of Lewis's better jazz sides from that period, with assistance in the clarinet department from Don Murray (also heard prominently on baritone) and Frank Teschemacher. Highlights include "Oh Baby," "Clarinet Marmalade," "Roses of Picardy," "Farewell Blues," and "Wabash Blues," although Lewis's brand of corn is always close by. **Jazzworthy 1929–1933** (Challenge 79014) has more of Lewis's best jazz recordings. Teschemacher, Brunies, Spanier, Jimmy Dorsey, Goodman, and Waller all help out "the top-hatted tragedian of jazz," whose vocal on "Dip Your Brush in the Sunshine" has to be heard to be believed!

Boyd Senter Boyd Senter records tend to be frustrating because, despite the leader's obvious technical skills on clarinet and alto and some impressive sidemen, Senter never evolved past the "gaspipe" style. Senter worked in local theatres in Nebraska as a teenager, led a band in Atlantic City during 1921–22, and recorded with Jelly Roll Morton (on clarinet, kazoo, and banjo) in 1924. During 1924–30, Boyd Senter's Senterpedes recorded 67 titles, but the leader's playing never advanced beyond its roots in vaudeville. **Jazzologist Supreme** (Timeless 1-032) has the last 24 recordings of Senter's recording career (using such sidemen as Tommy Dorsey, Phil Napoleon, Jimmy Dorsey, Frank Signorelli, Carl Kress, and trumpeter Mickey Bloom), but the results generally border on corn despite a few good solos along the way. In the 1930s, Boyd Senter settled in Detroit where he led an orchestra in obscurity.

Irving Mills's Hotsy-Totsy Gang Irving Mills, who is best remembered as Duke Ellington's manager, put together many record dates during the classic jazz era that featured top white players. Mills worked initially as a song demonstrator and a singer. In 1919, he founded the publishing company Mills Music with his brother Jack Mills. In addition to being Ellington's manager during 1926–39, Mills worked as a talent scout, record producer, band manager, singer, and underrated lyricist. In addition, Mills organized record dates for the Whoopee Makers and his Hotsy-Totsy Gang. **Vol. 1** (Sensation 24) and **Vol. 2** (Sensation 25) has all of the recordings (including alternate takes) by Mills's Hotsy-Totsy Gang (except two numbers on which they are backed by the tap dancing of Bill "Bojangles" Robinson), along with selections by Mills's Merry Makers and the one title ("At the Prom") cut by Mills's Modernists. Mills himself only has a few forgettable vocals, but his groups include plenty of all-stars. **Vol. 1** features such notables as Jimmy McPartland, Dudley Fosdick, Fud Livingston, Jack Pettis, Eddie Lang, Jack Teagarden, Benny Goodman, Tommy Dorsey, Jimmy Dorsey, and Miff Mole. **Vol. 2** has many of the same musicians plus the additional bonus of hearing Hoagy Carmichael on several numbers (including "Stardust") along with a declining but still intriguing Bix Beiderbecke on the June 6, 1930, session. Recording with the Hotsy-Totsy Gang provided a few musical vacations for the all-star musicians from their usual gigs with dance bands and studio orchestras.

Ben Bernie and Jack Pettis   In addition to Whiteman, Goldkette, Pollack, and the California Ramblers, quite a few other orchestras were active in New York during this era. Ben Bernie, a personable singer and an occasional songwriter, had played violin in vaudeville. He formed the Hotel Roosevelt Orchestra in 1922 and during the next decade recorded hundreds of titles and was a regular fixture on the radio. Among his most significant sidemen were C-melody and tenor saxophonist Jack Pettis, pianist/arranger Al Goerning, Bill Moore, classical pianist/comedian/actor Oscar Levant, and altoist Dick Stabile. The LP **Ben Bernie and His Hotel Roosevelt Orchestra** (Sunbeam 11) has a strong sampling of his more jazz-oriented titles from 1924–30, including a classic rendition of "Crazy Rhythm" (with Bernie on the vocal), an early version of "Sweet Georgia Brown," "Miss Annabelle Lee," and "Cannonball Ball Rag." After the early 1930s, Ben Bernie became a radio personality and dropped the band.

Bernie's top soloist, Jack Pettis, started playing C-melody sax when he was 16. He was a member of the New Orleans Rhythm Kings during 1922–23, and after moving to New York, he was featured with Bernie during 1924–30. The double CD **◉ Jack Pettis** (Kings Cross Music 005/006) has all of Pettis's sessions as a leader (24 selections plus three alternate takes) along with his sessions with Al Goering's Collegians, the Ambassadors, the Whoopee Makers, Mills's Musical Clowns, and Irving Mills's Modernists, plus one of Ben Bernie's most jazz-oriented dates. Other than his work

with the NORK and the Hotsy-Totsy Gang, and a very elusive final session from 1937, this perfectly constructed twofer has all of Jack Pettis's most important recordings, including several versions of his three top originals, "A Bag o' Blues," "Freshman Hop," and "Sweetest Melody." Sidemen include Bill Moore, Tommy Dorsey, Jack Teagarden, Don Murray, Benny Goodman, Joe Venuti, Eddie Lang, and Dick McDonough.

Roger Wolfe Kahn   Roger Wolfe Kahn, the son of multimillionaire Otto Kahn, led high-quality, jazz-influenced dance orchestras during the second half of the 1920s when he was barely out of his teens. Although Kahn had had extensive lessons on violin, piano, woodwinds, and brass, he never soloed on records and only actually played (alto and tenor) on his very first session. At the age of 16, he purchased Arthur Lange's Orchestra and started leading his own big band, which was based at the Hotel Biltmore throughout his main musical years. He also owned a booking office and a nightclub in addition to writing several standards including "Crazy Rhythm" and "Imagination." **1925–1932** (Jazz Oracle 8013) has 25 of the Roger Wolfe Kahn Orchestra's finest recordings other than the master take of "It's a Great Great Girl" (an important early Jack Teagarden recording) although the alternate take is included; the master has been reissued several other places. Kahn's orchestra mostly performed syncopated dance music with scattered jazz solos from Miff Mole, Joe Venuti (often with backing by Eddie Lang), and lesser-known players. Most of these numbers are quite listenable (except perhaps for the purposely corny "Fit as a Fiddle") and the better performances include "Hot-Hot-Hottentot," "Jersey Walk," "Where the Wild, Wild Flowers Grow," "Crazy Rhythm," and "It Don't Mean a Thing." There are also two songs from 1930 featuring the famous torch singer Libby Holman.

Harry Reser   A remarkable banjo player, Harry Reser was a virtuoso who recorded a series of novelty ragtime features. However, Reser was best known for leading the Clicquot Club Eskimos, a very popular radio hot dance band that specialized in novelties. Reser played guitar at eight, took piano, violin, and cello lessons, and around 1916 settled on the banjo. After performing locally, in December 1920 he arrived in New York City, working for Nathan Glantz, Bennie Krueger, Sam Lanin, and Ben Selvin, debuting on records with Milo Rega's Dance

Orchestra in October 1921, and working with Paul Whiteman in 1923. Reser began recording as a leader in October 1922 (as the head of the Okeh Syncopators) and appeared on a session with Bessie Smith in 1924. On December 3, 1925, the Clicquot Club Eskimos debuted on radio. During the next five years, Reser recorded an enormous number of records as a bandleader. His group, usually consisting of either Earl Oliver or Tommy Gott on trumpet, trombonist Sammy Lewis, the reeds of Larry Abbott and Norman Yorke, pianist Bill Wirges, Jimmy Johnston on bass sax, and drummer Tom Stacks, was a major fixture on the radio, featuring the cheerfully odd vocals of Stacks along with lots of novelty effects and comedy. In addition to recording as the Cliquot Club Eskimos, the same basic unit cut sessions as the Blue Kittens, the Bostonians, the Campus Boys, the Four Minstrels, the High Hatters, the Jazz Pilots, the Parlophone Syncopators, the Plantation Players, the Rounders, the Seven Little Polar Bears, the Seven Rag Pickers, the Seven Wildmen, the Six Hayseeds, the Six Jumping Jacks, and the Victorian Syncopators! A sampling of their performances has been reissued as **The Six Jumping Jacks, Vol. 1** (The Old Masters 120) and **The Six Jumping Jacks, Vol. 2** (The Old Masters 128). Although there are hot solos on most of the cuts (which date from 1926–28), the cornball humor (some of the jokes and sound effects are so broad that one has to chuckle) and Tom Stacks's strange voice often overwhelm the music. Such titles as "The Wind Blew Through His Whiskers," "She Was Just a Sailor's Sweetheart," "Masculine Women, Feminine Men," "I'm Just Wild About Animal Crackers," and "When You Dunk a Doughnut" from **Vol. 1**, and "Cock-a-Doodle, I'm Off My Noodle," "The Coat and Pants Do All the Work," "You'll Never Get Nowhere Holding Hands" (which is quite funny), "I'm Gonna Dance Wit the Guy Wot Brung Me," and "Get 'Em in a Rumble Seat" from the second set give listeners a strong idea of the Cliquot Club Eskimos' brand of humor.

Strangely enough, Reser's often-remarkable novelty ragtime banjo showcases have not yet been reissued on CD, so one should search for **Banjo Crackerjack** (Yazoo 1048), which has 14 brilliant Reser workouts including "Lollypops," "The Cat and the Dog," "Flapperette," "Crackerjack," and Zez Confrey's "Kitten on the Keys." After the early 1930s, Harry Reser worked primarily as a studio musician and in Broadway pit bands for the remainder of his life.

Sugar Hall   A pianist and songwriter, Fred "Sugar" Hall headed an underrated series of hot dance band records during 1925–30. After working for publishing houses as a song plugger and staff composer, Hall led over 150 selections, some of which were issued as the Hometowners, the Pennsylvania Melody Syncopators, Arthur Fields and His Assassinators, and the Tin Pan Paraders. During 1926–32, Hall also teamed up with singer Arthur Fields (who is on many of the records) to cowrite songs, best known of which is "I Got a Code in By Dose." **Fred Hall & His Sugar Babies** (The Old Masters 106) has 24 of his most worthwhile numbers from 1927–30, featuring a fine ensemble most notable for including Hall on piano and occasional scat vocals, regular vocals by Arthur Fields, and a special treat in the excellent jazz harmonica of Phillip d'Arcy, who also plays violin and second piano. Novelties such as "What a Funny World this Would Be," "On the Night We Did the Boom-Boom by the Sea," "I'm Wild About Horns on Automobiles," and "She's the Sweetheart of Six Other Guys" alternate with strong jazz performances, including "'Tain't No Sin," "Harmonica Harry," and "Come On, Baby"). But when the Depression made Sugar Hall's style of happy dance music out of fashion, he dropped out of music, making his last recordings in 1932.

Jan Garber   Jan Garber became famous during the swing era for leading sickeningly sweet orchestras, which featured a remarkable excess of vibrato from his reed section, but in the 1920s his big band played high-quality dance music along with some hot jazz. Garber, who played violin in the Philadelphia Symphony Orchestra starting around 1915, switched to popular music in 1921, and with pianist Milton Davis, cofounded the Garber-Davis Orchestra. In 1924, Garber and Davis went their separate ways and the Jan Garber Orchestra was formed. **The Hot Years 1925–30** (The Old Masters 119) has melodic and swinging music (in its own fashion) with decent solos and okay vocals. Best are "Sister Kate," "Tiger Rag," "Steppin' Around" (with guest banjoist Harry Reser), "'Round Evening," "She's a Great Great Girl," "When a Woman Loves a Man," and this particular Garber group's one hit, "Baby Face." But once the Depression hit, Jan Garber began to change his group's sound and by 1933, he was having great success imitating Guy Lombardo's sweet music.

Ted Weems   Ted Weems had a solid dance band during the swing era, but his 1920s outfit was much more inspired by jazz. Weems played violin and trombone, worked with Paul Specht, and first started leading bands in 1922, having a hit record of "Somebody Stole My Gal" in 1923. With Parker Gibbs on vocals and excellent soloists in clarinetist Don Watt, trumpeter Art Weems (Ted's brother), and mellophonist Dudley Fosdick, Weems performed a variety of danceable jazz, novelties, and college songs. Released in 1929, "Piccolo Pete" was a big hit, followed by "Harmonica Harry." That year Weems relocated from New York to Chicago where he worked and broadcast regularly when not touring during the next 12 years.

The double CD ◉ **The Essential Ted Weems 1923–1930** (Retrieval 79034) does a superlative job of summing up the musical legacy of the early Weems band. The 50 selections include Weems hits (including "Somebody Stole My Gal" and "Piccolo Pete") plus such superior hot dance band performances as "She's Got 'It'," "Miss Annabelle Lee," "Come On, Baby," "What a Day," "Miss Wonderful," "The Man from the South," and "Slappin' the Bass."

Benny Goodman   Influenced by Jimmie Noone and Frank Teschemacher but already showing strong originality, clarinetist Benny Goodman led four small-group record dates during 1928–29, highlighted by a humorous satire of Ted Lewis on "Shirt-Tail Stomp" and his first trio session (with pianist Mel Stitzel and drummer Bob Conselman). After leaving Ben Pollack's Orchestra in September 1929, Goodman worked with Red Nichols for a few months and then became a very busy studio musician in New York during the early years of the Depression. He appeared on the radio constantly, made countless recordings as a mostly anonymous sideman (including with Sam Lanin, Nat Shilkret, Meyer Davis, Ben Selvin, and Johnny Green), and played in the pit bands of Broadway shows (such as *Strike Up the Band* and *Girl Crazy*). Goodman, who often doubled on alto or baritone for these commercial sessions, also occasionally recorded in jazz settings, including with Nichols, Ted Lewis (!), Eddie Lang-Joe Venuti, Adrian Rollini, the Charleston Chasers, and as a leader for a few dates in the 1920s followed by six so-so dance band sessions

from 1930–31. However, the selections on ◉ **B.G. and Big Tea in NYC** (GRP/Decca 609) are taken from some of Goodman's most rewarding early sessions as a sideman. The young clarinetist is heard on eight numbers with Red Nichols's Five Pennies (including "Indiana," "China Boy," and "The Sheik of Araby"), four selections with Irving Mills's Hotsy-Totsy Gang (a 1930 date that also has Bix Beiderbecke in the lineup), five decent tunes with Adrian Rollini from 1934, and, best of all, four exciting numbers with the Joe Venuti–Eddie Lang All-Star Orchestra, "Beale Street Blues," "After You've Gone," "Farewell Blues," and "Someday Sweetheart." Jack Teagarden (who is often the costar) is also on all 21 selections and other notables include Gene Krupa, Joe Sullivan, and Charlie Teagarden. The two-LP set **A Jazz Holiday** (MCA/Decca 4018) duplicates part of **B.G. and Big Tea in NYC**, but also has ten selections with Goodman as a leader in the 1920s including "Wolverine Blues," "Jungle Blues" (his only recording on trumpet), "Shirt-Tail Stomp," and the two cuts by the very first Benny Goodman Trio: "That's a Plenty" and "Clarinetitis."

Ben Selvin and Fred Rich   With the rise of the Depression in late 1929, the jazz content of White dance band records decreased, with the emphasis shifting toward straighter renditions of melodies and predictable vocals. However, because there were often short solos from top jazz musicians, most of these recordings (including those of Ben Selvin and Fred Rich) at least have some moments of interest. Benny Goodman, Tommy Dorsey, Jimmy Dorsey, Joe Venuti, Eddie Lang, and the up-and-coming trumpeter Bunny Berigan seemed to be playing with everyone during the 1930–32 period, often anonymously in ensembles but with occasional moments of brief glory.

Ben Selvin was the most recorded bandleader of the 1920s and possibly of all time, cutting over 9,000 recordings during 1919–34 under as many as 125 names! Selvin played violin in public as early as 1905, and during 1917–24 he led the house band at the Moulin Rouge in Manhattan. His recording of "Dardanella" sold over a million copies, and he recorded for virtually every label. In 1928, Selvin became an important recording director for Columbia, overseeing most of the sessions for Columbia and its associated labels up until the mid-1930s. Of the countless first-class dance band recordings that he cut during the 1929–32 period, 44 are on **Vol. One** (The Old Masters 102) and **Vol. Two** (The Old Masters 117). The quality of the music is consistently high even if the jazz content only pops through the arrangements now and then. Best are "You're My Everything," "Makin' Faces at the Man in the Moon," a "Hot-Cha Medley," "Happy Days Are Here Again," and "When Yuba Plays the Rumba on the Tuba" on **Vol. One**, and two versions of "The Free and Easy," "Smile, Darn Ya Smile," "'Tain't No Sin," and "Cheerful Little Earful" from the second CD.

Fred Rich was another major force during the era. Born in Poland, he settled in New York City with his family as a child, took up the piano, and by 1915 was accompanying silent pictures at a movie theatre. During 1922–28, Rich led the orchestra at the Astor Hotel, was a regular on the radio, toured Europe a few times, and began recording extensively starting in 1925. He gained the powerful post of musical director for the CBS network during 1928–38 and led record dates constantly, documenting a similar type of dance music as Ben Selvin, often using some of the same musicians. **Vol. One** (The Old Masters 101) has some of Rich's best recordings from 1929–30. The vocalists are the Rollickers, Paul Small, or Smith Ballew, and there are spots for Tommy and Jimmy Dorsey, and Venuti and Lang (featured on "I Got Rhythm") although most of the musicians are unidentified. This brand of melodic dance music was perfect for the audiences of the era and is mostly still quite listenable today.

Bert Lown   Bert Lown, who was one of the composers of "Bye Bye Blues," was never on Ben Selvin's or Fred Rich's level as a prolific bandleader, but he recorded some excellent sides during his prime. Originally a violinist, Lown began leading his orchestra in early 1929, made his first recordings on February 11, and cut 86 selections during the next four years. Miff Mole was on Lown's first two sessions, and Adrian Rollini and Stan King appeared on many of the dates during 1929–30; most of the other sidemen were pretty obscure. Lown's Orchestra was based at the Biltmore Hotel in New York during 1929–31 and broadcast regularly. **Bert Lown & His Biltmore Hotel Orchestra** (The Old Masters 105) has 23 recordings from Lown's ensemble, dating from 1929–33. Adrian Rollini, Spencer Clark (his successor on bass sax), Mole, trumpeter Frank Cush, and

trombonist Al Philburn are among the key players, with vocals by Smith Ballew, the Biltmore Rhythm Boys, Elmer Feldkamp, and Ted Holt. The performances are typical of an early Depression dance band with only the first number ("Jazz Me Blues") finding the musicians cutting loose. Other titles include "Bye Bye Blues," "Lovin' You the Way I Do," "Heartaches," and "When I Take My Sugar to Tea." But despite the commercial compromises made in his music, Bert Lown ended up being a victim of the Depression, and his orchestra broke up in 1933 when he switched careers and became a manager.

The Dorsey Brothers   Unlike most of the dance bands covered in this section, the Dorsey Brothers Orchestra and the Casa Loma Orchestra would be significant beyond the early Depression years. The early years of Jimmy Dorsey and Tommy Dorsey often overlapped since the siblings performed with many of the same groups. The Dorseys were sons of a coal miner who became a music teacher and band director. Jimmy started out playing cornet, performing with his father's band at the age of seven. Four years later he switched to alto sax and clarinet. Meanwhile Tommy was taught trombone and trumpet by the elder Dorsey. The brothers co-led Dorsey's Novelty Six and Dorsey's Wild Canaries, playing regularly in Baltimore starting in 1919. They worked together in Billy Lustig's Scranton Sirens in 1921 and moved to New York in the fall of 1924.

Jimmy Dorsey worked at first with the California Ramblers and then became very busy, performing with the orchestras of Jean Goldkette, Ray Miller, Vincent Lopez, Paul Whiteman, and Ted Lewis, appearing on countless records. Dorsey was an important player on the early recordings of Red Nichols's Five Pennies, and he is heard on Frankie Trumbauer's "Singin' the Blues." One of the first jazz virtuosos on alto sax (predating Benny Carter and Johnny Hodges), Dorsey also ranked high among clarinetists and was constantly in demand both for commercial and jazz dates. Tommy Dorsey also worked with Goldkette, Lopez, and Whiteman in addition to Roger Wolfe Kahn, Fred Rich, and other studio orchestras. TD would make his reputation on trombone with his beautiful sound and expertise on ballads, but he could also play jazz, although he felt inferior next to Jack Teagarden. During this period he also enjoyed doubling on trumpet, where he had a "dirty" and primitive sound.

Because both Dorseys were technically skilled, they had no trouble securing studio work during the Depression. And beginning in 1928, they co-led the Dorsey Brothers Orchestra, which was strictly a recording group for its first five years and mostly performed hot dance music rather than freewheeling jazz, featuring a medium-sized group, and arranged ensembles, vocals, and short solos from the co-leaders. All of the group's recordings of 1928–31 are on three Jazz Oracle CDs, including the alternate takes. ◉ **The Dorsey Brothers Orchestra, Vol. 1—1928** (Jazz Oracle 8004) includes "Mary Ann," a memorable version of "My Melancholy Baby," two numbers ("It's Right Here for You" and "Tiger Rag") that feature Tommy Dorsey jamming on trumpet with a rhythm section that includes Eddie Lang, and the overly ambitious two-part "Was It a Dream" by the Dorsey Concert Orchestra; Paul Whiteman was an obvious role model for the latter. **The Dorsey Brothers Orchestra, Vol. 2—1929–1930** (Jazz Oracle 8005) has Bing Crosby starring on three numbers from a January 26, 1929, session (including "Let's Do It" and "My Kinda Love"), Tommy Dorsey playing almost as much trumpet as trombone (being showcased on "Daddy, Change Your Mind" and "You Can't Cheat a Cheater"), and two outstanding Jimmy Dorsey showcases ("Beebe" and "Praying the Blues"). **The Dorsey Brothers Orchestra, Vol. 3—1930–1933** (Jazz Oracle 8006) consists of 15 more dance band numbers (some of which were issued under the name of the Travelers). Despite mediocre vocals by Scrappy Lambert, Wesley Vaughan, Elmer Feldkamp, and Tony Sacco, there are some strong moments along the way, particularly the trumpet solos of Bunny Berigan in 1931 and such numbers as "Sweet and Hot," "Parkin' in the Moonlight," and "Home." **Vol. 3** concludes with Jimmy Dorsey featured on two versions apiece of "Beebe" and "Oodles of Noodles" (the latter's middle section would later become his theme song, "Contrasts"), while Tommy Dorsey is showcased on three versions of the rather intriguing "Three Moods," which partly shows off his background in concert band music, and two versions of the Gershwin ballad "Maybe."

The Casa Loma Orchestra   The Casa Loma Orchestra was arguably the first white swing band and would prove to be influential on the big bands that followed, including Benny Goodman's. Originally one of Jean Goldkette's many orchestras, the ensemble was initially known as the Orange Blossom Band and based in Detroit when it was scheduled to play at the Casa Loma Hotel in Toronto, Canada. Although that gig fell through when the venue never opened, the band took its name from the hotel, became independent of Goldkette, and was reformed as a co-op that was owned by all of the founding musicians. One of its saxophonists, Glen Gray, was elected the band's president. The Casa Loma Orchestra made their recording debut in 1929. They predated the swing era with their swinging riffs (if occasionally mechanical sounding and overly hyper) and arrangements. Guitarist Gene Gifford, who had formerly played with Blue Steele and Henry Cato's Vanities Orchestra, was Casa Loma's main arranger, composing "Black Jazz," "White Jazz," "Casa Loma Stomp," and the haunting "Smoke Rings" (which became the band's theme). The key soloists during the Casa Loma Orchestra's first few years were clarinetist Clarence Hutchenrider and trombonist/singer Pee Wee Hunt, with Kenny Sargent offering ballad vocals. Unfortunately Casa Loma's recordings have not been well served by domestic releases yet. **Best of the Big Bands** (Columbia 45345) does not bother listing recording dates or personnel and looks very much thrown together. Still, there are several gems on this CD, including "Smoke Rings," "Black Jazz," "Maniac's Ball," "Casa Loma Stomp," and "Limehouse Blues." Two LPs fill in some of the gaps. **Casa Loma Stomp** (Hep 1010) has some of the big band's finest recordings of 1929–30, including "China Girl," "San Sue Strut," and "Casa Loma Stomp." **Casa Loma Orchestra 1929/1932** (Harrison N) has the original version of "Smoke Rings," a heated "Clarinet Marmalade," and a rare publicity record version of "Casa Loma Stomp." Some of this music sounds five years ahead of its time, helping to set the stage for the swing era.

Black New York Jazz: Stride Pianists, Hot Soloists, and Harlem Big Bands

While many of the top white jazz musicians in New York played regularly with dance bands at hotels or worked in the studios, their black counterparts were increasingly based in Harlem nightclubs. The better clubs, cabarets, and theatres had lavish stage shows with singers, dancers, and other performers along with a jazz band or orchestra. New York musicians had always prided themselves on their high musicianship, and after

Louis Armstrong made his impact during 1924–25 and the players eliminated their earlier rhythmic awkwardness, New York became the center of both jazz and show business. Among the many notable clubs that flourished in Harlem during this period were the Alhambra Ballroom, the Bamboo Inn, Barron's, the Capitol Palace, Connie's Inn, the Cotton Club, the Lafayette Theatre, the Lenox Club, the Nest Club, Roseland, the Savoy Ballroom, and Small's Paradise.

The Harlem Renaissance, which gave blacks a rare opportunity to express themselves artistically (whether in poetry, stories, theatre, or dancing), took place during the 1920s and early '30s, but jazz was only a small part of it. In fact, jazz was thought of as a bit of a stepchild because many in the black middle class wished to "uplift the Negro race" and tended to look down upon jazz, blues, and folk music, preferring to imitate white society, at least in its music. So it is properly ironic that jazz recordings from the period often sound fresher than the well-intentioned poetry! The four-CD set **Rhapsodies in Black—Music and Words from the Harlem Renaissance** (Rhino 79874) celebrates the Harlem Renaissance with brief poetry readings of 20 vintage pieces (read by black celebrities of today), 65 early recordings, and a very good booklet. The music (dating from 1921–35) is of a consistent high quality and includes a lot of less obvious choices such as Wilbur Sweatman's "Indianola," Cleo Brown's "Lookie, Lookie, Lookie, Here Comes Cookie," Paul Whiteman's "Charleston," pianist Fred Longshaw's "Chili Pepper," Fess Williams's "Do Shuffle," and Buck & Bubbles's "Lady Be Good."

James P. Johnson   The exodus of top musicians from Chicago (including King Oliver in 1927, Jelly Roll Morton in 1928, and Louis Armstrong in 1929) invigorated the local scene. One aspect to New York's nightlife that was not imported from Chicago or even New Orleans was stride piano. James P. Johnson, the definitive exponent of that style, had been performing nightly in New York clubs, jam sessions, and rent parties ever since the end of World War I, and his mastery grew throughout the 1920s. He continued writing songs (few dancers probably knew that he was the composer of "The Charleston") and recording piano solos, with combos, and working as a highly stimulating accompanist to many classic blues singers, most notably Bessie Smith and Ethel Waters. In July 1928, his extended work *Yamekraw* was debuted at Carnegie Hall, with Fats Waller on piano. Johnson and Fats Waller worked together in the show *Keep Shufflin'* and he directed the band in 1929 for the Bessie Smith short film *St. Louis Blues*. ⊙ **1928–1938** (Classics 671) features James P. Johnson with the Gulf Coast Seven (a Perry Bradford–led sextet in 1928 filled with Duke Ellington sidemen), in 1938 with a freewheeling Pee Wee Russell group, and on his own solos and band sides of 1929–31. Highlights include unaccompanied renditions of "What Is this Thing Called Love," "You've Got to Be Modernistic," and "Jingles," and a couple of piano duets with Clarence Williams (including the humorous "How Could I Be Blue"). But after a very busy decade, Johnson voluntarily spent most of the 1930s out of the limelight, concentrating on composing large-scale orchestral works, including "Harlem Symphony," "Jassamine," "Symphony in Brown," and a blues opera called "De Organizer."

TIMELINE 1930

The Paul Whiteman Orchestra films *The King of Jazz*. • Duke Ellington's Orchestra appears in *Check and Double Check*. • The Boswell Sisters begin to record regularly. • Honore Dutrey retires from music. • A petition drawn up by a group of British trumpeters bans foreigners (particularly Sylvester Ahola) from recording with any group in England other than one's main employer. • Cab Calloway takes over the Missourians. • Hoagy Carmichael leads a record date that features both Bix Beiderbecke and Bubber Miley. • Jelly Roll Morton records as a leader for the last time for eight years. • Ruth Etting introduces "Ten Cents a Dance." • Louis Armstrong and Lil Hardin Armstrong record "Blue Yodel No. 9" with country singer Jimmy Rodgers. • Don Azpiazu has a major hit in "The Peanut Vendor" and his Havana Casino Orchestra (which includes bongos, timbales, clave, and maracas) is the first authentic Cuban dance band to play in the United States. • Mario Bauza arrives in the United States from Cuba. • Cliff Jackson records with his Krazy Kats. • Bunny Berigan joins Hal Kemp's band.

Fats Waller For Thomas "Fats" Waller, the 1920s were the beginning of a very productive career. He began playing harmonium at the age of five and piano the following year, performing with his school orchestra. Waller's father was a very strict minister who disapproved of him playing anything but religious music, but Fats much preferred popular music and the great stride pianists. After his mother died, Waller befriended James P. Johnson, moved away from home, and became the older pianist's protégé. In 1919 at the age of 15, Waller became the Lincoln Theatre's house pipe organist, stomping off solos for silent movies and becoming jazz's first organist. He soon composed his first of many songs, "Squeeze Me," began making piano rolls (there would be 20 in all), cut his first solo records in 1922, and played at nightly rent parties with Johnson and Willie "The Lion" Smith.

In the 1920s, Fats Waller was on records backing many singers and on sessions with the Fletcher Henderson Orchestra (most notably "Henderson Stomp" and "The Chant"), Johnny Dunn, the Louisiana Sugar Babes, Nat Shilkret, James P. Johnson, McKinney's Cotton Pickers, the Little Chocolate Dandies, and the Mound City Blue Blowers. Waller also worked with lyricist Andy Razaf on the shows *Keep Shufflin'* (1928), *Hot Chocolates* (1929), and *Load of Coal*, writing such standards as "Ain't Misbehavin'," "Honeysuckle Rose," and "Black and Blue," and he appeared at Carnegie Hall in James P. Johnson's *Yamekraw*. In addition, Waller led a wide variety of record dates for the Victor label during 1924–30.

Piano Masterworks, Vol. 1 (Hot 'N' Sweet 5106) has all of Fats Waller's piano solos from the 1920s (including the many alternate takes) except for two from December 4, 1929. Many of the selections are purposely very melodic (such as the original version of "Ain't Misbehavin'") rather than being too adventurous, but there are some exceptions including the virtuosic "Handful of Keys" and "Valentine Stomp." ◉ **Turn on the Heat** (Bluebird 2482) is a two-CD set that duplicates all of the music on the **Hot 'N' Sweet** CD except for Waller's two solos from 1922 ("Muscle Shoals Blues" and "Birmingham Blues") and a third take of "I've Got a Feeling I'm Falling." However, the twofer easily compensates by also having Waller's 17 additional piano solos from his later years (going up to 1941), including "African Ripples," "Clothes Line Ballet," "Tea for Two," and "Honeysuckle Rose," along with a pair of piano duets ("St. Louis Blues"

and "After You've Gone") with Bennie Payne (Cab Calloway's regular pianist) in 1930.

With the exception of a few alternate takes, all of the pianist's small-group sessions as a leader from the 1920s are on ◉ **Fats Waller and His Buddies** (Bluebird 61005), including such exciting and hot performances as "The Minor Drag," "Harlem Fuss," "Ridin' but Walkin'," "Fats Waller Stomp," and "Red Hot Dan." The CD also has six of the seven performances by the Louisiana Sugar Babes (all but the alternate for "Willow Tree"), which has restrained playing from the quartet of Jabbo Smith, Garvin Bushell (clarinet, alto, and bassoon), James P. Johnson, and Waller on organ. In addition, Waller recorded 24 unaccompanied organ solos during 1926–29, but these have yet to be comprehensively reissued on CD. Sixteen are on the LP **Young Fats at the Organ, Vol. 1** (French RCA 741.052).

Outside of a vocal on "Red Hot Dan" during one of his sessions from 1927, Waller did not sing at all on records until 1931. He began to emerge that year as a vocalist and humorous personality on solo versions of "I'm Crazy 'Bout My Baby" and "Dragging My Heart Around," and during dates with Ted Lewis and Jack Teagarden. Waller also had an opportunity to visit France and England in 1932. It is remarkable that Fats Waller could accomplish so much, particularly since he was constantly drinking, eating, partying, and carousing excessively!

Willie "The Lion" Smith In contrast to Fats Waller, Willie "The Lion" Smith, despite being active in the New York scene, barely recorded at all in the 1920s. Smith (born William Henry Joseph Bonaparte Bertholoff) started playing piano when he was six and appeared in New York and Atlantic City clubs as early as 1912. He served in the Army in France during 1916–19 where, supposedly because of his heroics in World War I, he gave himself the title of "The Lion." With his bowler hat, an everpresent cigar in his mouth, and his bragging personality, Smith could be an imposing figure at after-hours jam sessions, but his playing was often surprisingly sensitive and lyrical. He became a strong influence on Duke Ellington, and although a braggart, he always seemed lovable rather than abrasive (unlike Jelly Roll Morton). The Lion, who was based at Pod's and Jerry's during the late 1920s and early '30s, only appeared on records in the early days with Mamie Smith (including "Crazy Blues"), two songs with the Gulf Coast Seven (1925), three with the Blue Rhythm Orchestra (1925), two with the Georgia Strutters (1927), and possibly two with the Seven Gallon Jug Band (1929).

Cliff Jackson Another major stride pianist from the era, Cliff Jackson worked in Washington, D.C., and Atlantic City before moving to New York in 1923. After working with Happy Rhone's Club Orchestra, Lionel Howard's Musical Aces, and Elmer Snowden (recording with Bob Fuller and Snowden in 1927), Jackson formed the Crazy Kats. In 1930, the band recorded 11 songs, all of which are on the LP **Cliff Jackson & His Crazy Kats** (Retrieval 119) plus an alternate version of "The Terror." Although some of the tunes are commercial, even the least interesting arrangements have some hot solo breaks, and three numbers are explosive classics: "Horse Feathers," "Torrid Rhythm," and "The Terror." After the band broke up in the early 1930s, Jackson returned to working as a soloist, occasionally backing singers.

Clarence Williams and Eva Taylor Some of the finest small group jazz recordings of the 1920s and early '30s were led by Clarence Williams. Although he had reached a height during 1923–25 when his recordings frequently featured Sidney Bechet and/or Louis Armstrong, Williams's recordings managed to stay at the same high level through 1931. He worked as a talent scout for Okeh during 1923–28 and with other labels for a few years afterward, and he always had new songs that he wanted to sell and document. Whether under his own name or using such pseudonyms as the Barrelhouse Five Orchestra, the Bluegrass Footwarmers, the Dixie Washboard Band, the Four Spades, the Jamaica Jazzers, the Lazy Levee Loungers, and the Seven Gallon Jug Band, Williams was a consistent force in the record industry during the classic jazz years.

 ◉ **1926–1927** (Classics 718), which has notable contributions from cornetists/trumpeters Bubber Miley, Louis Metcalf, Tommy Ladnier, and Ed Allen (Williams's longtime regular brassman), trombonists Tricky Sam Nanton and Jimmy Harrison, clarinetist Buster Bailey, and Coleman Hawkins, is full of gems, particularly "Jackass Blues," "Morocco Blues," "Senegalese Stomp," and a two-clarinet jam on "Candy Lips." **1927** (Classics 736) consists of 22 selections recorded in less than a seven-month period. With Ed Allen, Charlie Irvis, Buster Bailey, trumpeter Red Allen (in his recording debut), and Louis

Metcalf taking key solos, the music is often quite exciting, particularly "Cushion Foot Stomp" (heard in three different versions), "Old Folks Shuffle," Williams's vocal on the charming "When I March in April with May," and "Shooting the Pistol," which has a solo from Alberto Socarras that is probably the first ever on record by a jazz flutist.

Clarence Williams's **1927–1928** (Classics 752) has two Williams piano solos, two numbers in which his singing is backed by James P. Johnson (including the eccentric "Farm Hand Papa"), and combo performances with Ed Allen, Buster Bailey, Coleman Hawkins, King Oliver, and tenor saxophonist Benny Waters; highlights include "Jingles," "Church Street Sobbin' Blues," "Sweet Emmalina," and "Mountain City Blues." King Oliver makes some notable appearances on **1928–1929** (Classics 771), including on "Bozo" and "Bimbo." The usual players (plus Eddie Lang) uplift such tunes as "New Down Home Blues," "Organ Grinder Blues," "Have You Ever Felt that Way," and "Pane in the Glass." **1929** (Classics 791) has less variety in personnel with Ed Allen and clarinetist Arville Harris being constants, but it does include fine versions of "Steamboat Days," "Baby Won't You Please Come Home," "In Our Cottage of Love," and "Breeze." **1929–1930** (Classics 810) benefits greatly from James P. Johnson being on eight of the selections, including "You've Got to Be Modernistic," and two piano duets with Williams (the humorous "How Could I Be Blue" and "I've Found a New Baby"). Other numbers include "High Society," "Railroad Rhythm," and "Whip Me with Plenty of Love." The rise of the Depression did nothing to change Clarence Williams's music initially, as can be heard on **1930–1931** (Classics 832), which includes "You're Bound to Look Like a Monkey When You Get Old," "He Wouldn't Stop Doin' It," "Papa De-Da-Da," and four versions of "Shout Sister Shout" (each with different personnel). Among the musicians are clarinetist Cecil Scott, pianist Herman Chittison, Ikey Robinson, Ed Allen, Red Allen, and blues guitarist Lonnie Johnson. But after so much activity, Clarence Williams's importance began to wane, and he was mostly absent from records for the next two years.

Eva Taylor, Clarence Williams's wife, continued recording under her own name during 1928–29, usually using her husband's pickup bands (although she also made a few cuts with a white group called the Knickerbockers). **Vol. 3** (Document 5410) includes such numbers as "Back in Your Own Back Yard," "Have You Ever Felt That

Way," "Moanin' Low," and "When I'm Housekeeping for You," plus two cuts from 1932 that match her voice with that of Williams and Lil Armstrong.

Alberto Socarras   Socarras (who was born in Cuba) preceded the better-known Wayman Carver on records by several years. He originally played in a family band that accompanied silent movies. After emigrating to New York, Socarras (who also played alto, soprano, and clarinet) worked with a few Cuban bands and Lew Leslie's Blackbirds Orchestra (1928–33). In addition to freelance recordings on his other instruments, Socarras took pioneering flute solos on "Shooting the Pistol" and "Have You Ever Felt That Way" with Clarence Williams, "You're Such a Cruel Papa to Me" in 1928 with Lizzie Miles, and on a date with Bennett's Swamplanders (1930). But because he became a studio musician and the leader of Latin bands, Alberto Socarras never gained the recognition due him as jazz's pioneering flutist.

Cecil Scott   Cecil Scott was Clarence Williams's regular clarinetist (doubling on tenor) starting in 1930. A fluent, good-humored soloist, Scott put together a trio in 1919 while still in high school, with older brother Lloyd Scott on drums and pianist Don Frye. The group expanded to become a septet by 1922, when it was known as Scott's Symphonic Syncopators, working in the Midwest, Canada, and New York. In 1927, the ensemble (which now included trombonist Dickie Wells) recorded three titles under Lloyd Scott's name. In 1929, as Cecil Scott's Bright Boys, the band cut four songs, included on **Thumpin' and Bumpin'** (Frog 11) that are highlighted by happily eccentric versions of "Lawd Lawd" and "In a Corner." The group stayed together until Cecil Scott was hurt in a car accident in the early 1930s. Fortunately, he recovered, becoming an important part of Clarence Williams's bands for several years.

Wilton Crawley   The most colorful and outlandish of all the gaspipe clarinetists was Wilton Crawley, who was a master at slap tonguing, laughing through his horn, and creating odd tonal distortions. Crawley grew up in Philadelphia and developed a variety act for vaudeville that featured his clarinet playing, humorous singing, juggling, and his skills as a contortionist! Although he apparently found it difficult to play clarinet and not bend himself into odd angles at the same time, he managed to record 14 titles as a leader during 1927–28 and

three combo dates in 1929–30, two of which included Jelly Roll Morton. **Wilton Crawley** (Jazz Oracle 8020) has all of the clarinetist's recordings except for his final two selections from his 1930 date. The 26 numbers, which total over 79 minutes, are often quite funny if heard in small dosages. The first 17 numbers (three of which were previously unreleased) have Crawley showcased in trios and quartets with such sidemen as Eddie Lang, Lonnie Johnson, and pianist Eddie Heywood, Sr. In addition, Crawley is heard with musicians taken from Luis Russell's band (including Red Allen and Charlie Holmes) plus guitarist Teddy Bunn, and on his dates with Morton. Best are "You Oughta See My Gal," "I'm Her Papa, She's My Mama," and "Big Time Woman." Having toured Europe during 1930–32, Wilton Crawley soon faded from the scene, but his musical antics have never quite been equaled.

Johnny Dunn and Thomas Morris   The rise of Louis Armstrong resulted in older trumpet and cornet styles (particularly those using staccato phrasing and inflexible wa-wa effects) being considered passé. Johnny Dunn, once considered New York's most advanced cornetist, spent much of 1926 in Europe playing with the *Blackbirds of 1926* show and recording with the Plantation Orchestra. He led a short-lived big band in New York in 1927 and the following year made his best recordings (with Jelly Roll Morton and the team of James P. Johnson and Fats Waller). However, in 1928 when he was just 31, Dunn was considered a has-been and he moved permanently back to Europe, playing on the Continent but never recording again.

Cornetist Thomas Morris also found his style becoming rapidly out of date by 1926 even though he was only 28 at the time. Morris was on many records during 1923–27, particularly with groups associated with Clarence Williams and with a variety of classic blues singers. **1923–1927** (Classics 823) and **When a 'Gator Hollers** (Frog 1) unfortunately overlap. The Classics CD has the master takes of all of Morris's sessions as a leader (eight songs from 1923 and his ten selections with his Seven Hot Babies in 1926) plus dates with the New Orleans Blue Five, singer Margaret Johnson, and the Nashville Jazzers ("St. Louis Blues" from 1927). However, all of the music except for the eight 1923 selections and "St. Louis Blues" is on the Frog CD, which benefits from the inclusion of 11 alternate takes. Since Morris was heard at his best throughout 1926, **When a 'Gator Hollers** gets the edge. Among the better selections from these primitive but fun sessions are "Jackass Blues" (featuring trombonist Tricky Sam Nanton), "Georgia Grind," "The King of the Zulus," and "The Mess." By 1927, Morris's unchanged if charming style sounded old-fashioned, particularly on his three numbers with Charlie Johnson's Orchestra where he was overshadowed by Jabbo Smith. Sometime after making his final recordings (on December 1, 1927, with Fats Waller), Morris left music, becoming a red cap at New York's Grand Central Station.

Sidney DeParis and Leonard Davis   The careers of trumpeters Sidney DeParis and Leonard Davis went in different directions. DeParis was the younger brother of trombonist Wilbur DeParis. He started his career touring with his father's carnival band on the vaudeville circuit, moving to New York in 1924. DeParis played with Andrew Preer's Cotton Club Orchestra (making his recording debut) and was with Charlie Johnson during 1926–31, other than a year spent with his brother's group in Philadelphia. He also recorded with McKinney's Cotton Pickers in November 1929. After leaving Johnson, DeParis (who had a strong reputation as a soloist) worked with the big bands of Fletcher Henderson (1931) and Don Redman (1932–36).

Leonard Davis had a beautiful tone and a wide range, assets that ironically worked against him. He performed and recorded in St. Louis with Charlie Creath (1924–25), and after moving to New York, he played with Charlie Skeete, Edgar Hayes, Arthur Gibbs, and Charlie Johnson (1928–29). The highpoint of his career took place on February 8, 1929, when Davis took beautiful solos on "I'm Gonna Stomp Mr. Henry Lee" and particularly the blues "That's a Serious Thing" during a date with Eddie Condon's Hot Shots; they have been reissued (happily with two takes apiece) on **The Indispensable Jack Teagarden** (RCA Jazz Tribune 66606). But otherwise, he was employed as a lead trumpeter, an important post in big bands but one that involved no soloing or any real chance for fame.

Ward Pinkett   A trumpeter with a great deal of potential, Ward Pinkett was an important part of the New York jazz scene in the late 1920s/early '30s. He started playing music when he was ten, attended the New Haven Conservatory of Music, worked with the White Brothers Orchestra in Washington, D.C., and by the mid-1920s had settled in New York. Pinkett worked with a variety of groups during the next few years, including Charlie Johnson, Willie Gant, Billy Fowler, Joe Steele, Charlie Skeete, Chick Webb, and Bingie Madison. He recorded 62 songs as a sideman, including "Georgia Swing," "Kansas City Stomps," and "Shoe Shiner's Drag" with Jelly Roll Morton in 1928, and "Strokin' Away" and "Low Gravy" with Morton in 1930. In fact, Pinkett can be considered Morton's main discovery while in New York, a trumpeter who was technically skilled and not afraid to take chances during his solos. Pinkett also recorded with King Oliver's Orchestra, Joe Steele, Chick Webb's Jungle Band, Bubber Miley's Mileage Makers, Clarence Williams, Mamie Smith, and James P. Johnson. However, after 1931, the trumpeter's alcoholism began to drastically slow down his career, and he never reached his potential.

The Missourians   The Missourians have already been mentioned in this book in connection with Cab Calloway. Formed as Wilson Robinson's Syncopators in the early 1920s, in 1925 the group became the Cotton Club Orchestra, serving as the house band at the Cotton Club for the next two years and recording eight titles, including one under the name of its leader, Andrew Preer. Preer died unexpectedly in 1927, and after the ensemble toured with Ethel Waters, it was renamed the Missourians. Led by altoist/clarinetist George Scott, the Missourians played regularly at the Savoy Ballroom during 1928–29, recording a dozen exciting numbers at three recording sessions during 1929–30. **Cab Calloway and the Missourians** (JSP 328) has the band's complete output plus its first ten selections as the Cab Calloway Orchestra. The instrumentals show that this was one of the top jazz groups of the late 1920s; most impressive are the solos of trumpeters R.Q. Dickerson and Lammar Wright. The group originals include such spirited pieces as "Market Street Stomp," "400 Hop," "Swingin' Dem Cats," and "Stoppin' the Traffic." The numbers with Cab Calloway (which directly preceded "Minnie the Moocher") include a spectacular version of "St. Louis Blues," "Happy Feet," "Some of These Days," "Nobody's Sweetheart," and a classic rendition of "St. James Infirmary." Since the Missourians were on the verge of breaking up in early 1930, Cab Calloway taking over the leadership both saved the group and ended its independent existence. From then on, it would be known as the Cab Calloway Orchestra, returning to its original home at the Cotton Club.

The Savoy Bearcats   The Savoy Bearcats, an exciting ten-piece band, recorded six songs during 1926, and all of them are on **Hot Notes** (Frog 8), highlighted by a version of "Stampede" that is faster than Fletcher Henderson's, "Senegalese Stomp," and "Nightmare." Also on this intriguing CD is Evelyn Preer singing "If You Can't Hold the Man You Love" (backed by a contingent from Duke Ellington's band in early 1927), the three recordings by Lloyd Scott's band, two songs from Joe Steele, three by Leroy Smith, and the master takes from all of Charlie Johnson's recordings of 1927–29 (leaving out his first session). This disc is well worth picking up, particularly for the Savoy Bearcats numbers, except perhaps to listeners already owning the Charlie Johnson recordings. At first glance, **Don't You Leave Me Here** (Frog 12) appears to be a close rerun of **Hot Notes** since it repeats most of the same titles, but in reality nearly all of the music is alternate takes; it is strange that nothing is said about that on the disc's cover. There are four alternate takes and three previously unissued performances by the Savoy Bearcats, alternates of two of Lloyd Scott's three numbers, one by Leroy Smith, two from Bubber Miley, two by Joe Steele, and ten from Charlie Johnson's Orchestra. In addition, the master take of Russell Wooding's "That's My Desire" (with Alberto Socarras on flute) wraps up this excellent collector's disc.

The Washboard Rhythm Kings and Other Offbeat Combos   During the early 1930s, a large portion of jazz (including King Oliver and Jelly Roll Morton) mostly disappeared from records, replaced by sweet bands, commercial dance orchestras, and soothing vocalists. However, there were a few spirited exceptions. Seventeen overlapping groups recorded as the Alabama Washboard Stompers, the Washboard Rhythm Kings, the Five Rhythm Kings, the Washboard Rhythm Band, the Washboard Rhythm Boys, and the Georgia Washboard Stompers during 1930–35. What these bands offered were uninhibited good-time music, usually featuring a washboard player, two or three horns, and spirited group vocals, falling stylistically between Dixieland and swing. Among the musicians (many of whom are unidentified) in these rather spontaneous ensembles are guitarist Teddy Bunn, trumpeters Taft Jordan and Valaida Snow, singers Jake Fenderson and Leo Watson, pianist

Clarence Profit, banjoist/vocalist Steve Washington, and Ben Smith on clarinet and alto. Five CDs from the Collector's Classics label (released under the name of the Washboard Rhythm Kings) cover these bands, with the first three volumes falling into this time period. ◗ **Vol. 1** (Collector's Classics 17) has Teddy Bunn on ten of the numbers and quite a few examples of the spontaneous jam bands covering other groups' hits, including "Minnie the Moocher," "You Rascal You," "I'm Crazy 'Bout My Baby," "Star Dust," and "Georgia on My Mind." **Vol. 2** (Collector's Classics 18) consists of four complete sessions from 1932 and is highlighted by "You Can Depend on Me," "Was That the Human Thing to Do," "Tiger Rag," and "Sloppy Drunk Blues." **Vol. 3** (Collector's Classics 25) has some fine trumpet work from Valaida Snow, spirited vocals from George "Ghost" Howell, and an early vocal version of "I'm Getting Sentimental Over You." The hotter numbers include "Sentimental Gentleman from Georgia," "I Would Do Anything for You," "Blue Drag," and "Old Man Blues." **Vol. 4** (Collector's Classics 26) has three complete sessions from 1933 with spots for trumpeter Taft Jordan (who sometimes purposely copies Louis Armstrong) and pianist Clarence Porfit, while **Vol. 5** (Collector's Classics 30) gathers together music from a variety of sources (from bands called the Washboard Serenaders, the Scorpion Washboard Band, the Tramp Band, and the Five Rhythm Kings) including a 1935 London session and such songs from 1930–31 as "Kazoo Moan," "Washboards Get Together," and "Call of the Freaks"). The music may be a bit repetitive and derivative, but it is always quite fun and colorful.

Some other recordings from the era are a bit off the beaten path but are certainly of interest to early jazz listeners. **Harps, Jugs, Washboards, & Kazoos** (RST 1505) has a variety of good-time jazz/blues bands similar in style to the Washboard Rhythm Kings. The first 14 selections are all of the recordings by the Five Harmaniacs, a group consisting of harmonica, kazoo, a second kazoo player who doubles on jug, and washboard, banjo, and guitar. Among the tunes performed are exuberant versions of "Sadie Green, Vamp of New Orleans," "Coney Island Washboard," and "What Did Romie-O-Julie When He Climbed Her Balcony." Also featured on this collection are recordings by such groups as the Salty Dog Four, the Scorpion Washboard Band, and Rhythm Willie.

Blue Yodelers 1928–1936 (Retrieval 79020) shows the crossover that often took place in the early days of country music between the pioneering Western singers and jazz. This CD has eight numbers by Jimmie Rodgers (including "Blue Yodel No. 9" with Louis Armstrong), nine songs from Roy Evans (assisted along the way by James P. Johnson, the Dorsey Brothers, and Benny Goodman), and the final rare session by minstrel singer Emmett Miller from 1936. Although it can be a bit disconcerting to hear occasional yodels in these settings, the performances generally work quite well.

Lonnie Johnson   In the mid-to-late 1920s, male country blues singers and guitarists began to be documented fairly frequently. Among those giants are Blind Lemon Jefferson, Blind Blake, Blind Willie McTell, Tampa Red, and pianist Cow Cow Davenport. Their music developed on a different path from the more jazz-oriented female classic blues singers. Fans of early jazz will definitely want to explore the blues artists of the era since the roots of the music are often similar. One blues performer, Lonnie Johnson, was often utilized on jazz dates during the time although he eventually chose to stick to blues and sentimental ballads. Johnson started out his career playing both guitar and violin in New Orleans, and performing in London during 1917–19. After a period playing on riverboats with Fate Marable, Johnson spent 1922–24 in St. Louis, working in a steel foundry during the day while gigging at night on guitar, violin, and piano. In 1925, he won a talent contest sponsored by the Okeh label, leading to the beginning of his very prolific recording career, which started with him taking a vocal and playing violin on Charlie Creath's "Won't Don't Blues."

Working in Chicago and New York, Johnson's solo career was augmented by quite a few guest appearances on jazz recordings, including with Louis Armstrong's Hot Five ("I'm Not Rough," "Savoy Blues," and most notably "Hotter than That"), Duke Ellington ("Hot and Bothered" and "The Mooche"), McKinney's Cotton Pickers, the Chocolate Dandies, Victoria Spivey, Clara Smith, Clarence Williams, Blind Willie Dunn's Gin Bottle Four (a group also including Eddie Lang, King Oliver, and Hoagy Carmichael), and ten exciting guitar duets with Lang during which Johnson held his own playing single-note lines to Lang's chords.

All of Lonnie Johnson's recordings as a leader during 1925–32 are on seven Document CDs, and although many are strictly solo blues performances, there are also quite a few jazz-oriented selections, particularly the rare instrumentals. On **Vol. 1** (Document 5063), Johnson not only plays guitar but at various times violin, banjo, and harmonium; three selections (including "Johnson's Trio Stomp") are instrumentals. **Vol. 2** (Document 5064) puts the emphasis on Johnson's guitar on "To Do This, You Got to Know How," "I Done Tole You," "Steppin' on the Blues," "Four Hands Are Better than Two," and "Woke Up with the Blues in My Fingers." ◐ **Vol. 3** (Document 5065) has nine instrumentals among the 25 selections (including "6/88 Glide" and "Playing with the Strings"), and Jimmy Blythe pops up on three songs. **Vol. 4** (Document 5066) is most notable for Johnson's vocal duets with Victoria Spivey on "New Black Snake Blues," "Toothache Blues," and "Furniture Man Blues" (each of which are two-part performances), five guitar duets with Eddie Lang (including "A Handful of Riffs" and "Have to Change Keys to Play These Blues"), Johnson's date with Blind Willie Dunn's Gin Bottle Four, and a few vocal duets with Spencer Williams.

Vol. 5 (Document 5067) has the other five duets with Lang (including "Bull Frog Moan" and the accurately titled "Hot Fingers"), more vocal collaborations with Spencer Williams and Victoria Spivey ("You Done Lost Your Good Thing Now"), "Wipe It Off" (which teams Johnson with Clarence Williams and James P. Johnson), and such titles as "From Now On Make Your Whoopee at Home," "She's Making Whoopee in Hell Tonight," and "Another Woman Booked Out and Bound to Go." **Vol. 6** (Document 5068) sticks mostly to blues with appearances by Spencer Williams and Clara Smith, while **Vol. 7** (Document 5069), other than two songs that add pianist Fred Longshaw, is strictly solo blues and good-time vocal numbers. These are fine performances that show that the blues world's gain was jazz's loss.

Fletcher Henderson, His Sidemen, and Coleman Hawkins   One could argue that swing began when Louis Armstrong joined the Fletcher Henderson Orchestra in 1924. Certainly by the time Satch left the big band in the fall of 1925, Henderson had a great swing band, one that would be at the peak of its powers for the next few years. While Henderson was not much of a pianist and his arranging skills did not develop until the early 1930s (Don Redman was his main writer up to 1927), he was a masterful talent scout. During the

1926–32 period, such major players as cornetists/trumpeters Joe Smith, Tommy Ladnier, Rex Stewart, Bobby Stark, and Cootie Williams, trombonists Charlie Green, Benny Morton, Jimmy Harrison, Sandy Williams, and J.C. Higginbotham, clarinetist Buster Bailey, tenor saxophonist Coleman Hawkins, altoists Benny Carter and Russell Procope, bassist John Kirby, and drummers Kaiser Marshall and Walter Johnson were members of the all-star orchestra. **1925–1926** (Classics 610), **1926–1927** (Classics 597), and **1927** (Classics 580) features the orchestra at its prime. **1925–1926** is highlighted by "Dinah" (Hawkins plays the melody on baritone), "I've Found a New Baby," and "Jackass Blues" while **1926–1927** has such gems as "The Stampede" (which includes Hawkins's first famous tenor solo), "Henderson Stomp" with Fats Waller guesting on piano, "The Chant," a heated "Clarinet Marmalade," and "Snag It" (Tommy Ladnier at his best).

Don Redman left Henderson during **1927**, lured away by the opportunity to lead McKinney's Cotton Pickers. At first the band continued on at the same level since they had a backlog of Redman charts; **1927** includes such memorable performances as "Fidgety Feet" (which has some great Jimmy Harrison trombone as well as the distinction of being one of the first recordings to have a Dixieland drum break near its conclusion), "St. Louis Shuffle," "Variety Stomp," "Whiteman Stomp," "I'm Coming Virginia," and "Hop Off." But after 1927, the band's progress began to stall. Henderson was involved in a car accident in 1928, and after that incident, he seemed much less interested in business. Although the orchestra remained based at the Roseland Ballroom in New York, it only recorded 17 numbers during 1928–30, so a lot of potential classics went undocumented. **1927–1931** (Classics 572) does find the band in excellent form, with fine solos from Rex Stewart, Bobby Stark, Benny Carter, Buster Bailey, and Coleman Hawkins, and the highpoints including "King Porter Stomp," "Oh Baby," and "Raisin' The Roof." By the time the music on **1931** (Classics 555) was recorded (which includes a remake of "Sugar Foot Stomp," "Roll On, Mississippi, Roll On," and a version of "Singin' the Blues" that has Rex Stewart paying tribute to Bix Beiderbecke), the Fletcher Henderson Orchestra was being overshadowed by Duke Ellington's and there were several other Harlem big bands that were strong competitors. On the brighter side, Fletcher Henderson and his brother Horace were both developing into

talented arrangers and the band's solo strength remained impressive. But by the following year, represented on **1931–1932** (Classics 546), record company pressure resulted in the band often recording commercial material such as "Strangers" and two songs backing child star Rose Marie. In addition, some of the instrumentals find the band sounding similar to the Casa Loma Orchestra, sacrificing some of its individuality.

For listeners who just want the very best of Fletcher Henderson, the three-CD set ◉ **A Study in Frustration** (Columbia/Legacy 57596) will be perfect. The 64 selections (all but eight from 1923–33) quickly dispense with the early pre–Louis Armstrong period (just two numbers) and then emphasize the glory years. Among the many highpoints are "Shanghai Shuffle," two versions of "Sugar Foot Stomp," three of "King Porter Stomp," "The Stampede," "Henderson Stomp," "St. Louis Shuffle," "Oh Baby," "Clarinet Marmalade," and "Honeysuckle Rose."

Few of Fletcher Henderson's sidemen recorded under their own names during this period, but many had highly individual voices. Joe Smith gave Henderson's band a mellow and lyrical tone on the cornet, which contrasted with the hotter playing of Louis Armstrong, Tommy Ladnier, and Bobby Stark. Smith, whose brother Russell Smith played lead trumpet with Henderson for many years, worked with Ethel Waters (1922), Mamie Smith, and Billy Paige's Broadway Syncopators, recorded with many classic blues singers (he was Bessie Smith's favorite cornetist), first played with Henderson in 1921, and was a regular part of the band during 1925–28. Smith later worked with McKinney's Cotton Pickers (1929–30 and 1931–32) before his health began to fail in 1932.

Rex Stewart grew up near Washington, D.C., and played piano, violin, and alto horn before settling on cornet. In 1921, he toured with Ollie Blackwell's Jazz Clowns, and after moving to New York in 1923, he worked with Elmer Snowden (1925–26) and made a fair number of freelance recordings. He first joined the Fletcher Henderson Orchestra in 1926 when he was 19. Although he sounds fine on such recordings as "Jackass Blues" and "Static Strut," Stewart did not feel that he was up to playing in a position that a year earlier had been filled by Louis Armstrong. After eight months, he left Henderson, working instead with lesser-known groups. By 1928, he had much more confidence, rejoined Fletcher Henderson, and was one of the band's main soloists for the next two years. After a short period playing with Alex Jackson and McKinney's Cotton Pickers, he was back with Henderson a third time during 1932–33.

Tommy Ladnier's period with Fletcher Henderson was only a small part of his career. He grew up near New Orleans, took trumpet lessons with Bunk Johnson, and had stints working in Chicago (starting in 1917) and St. Louis. Ladnier recorded with Ollie Powers, Lovie Austin's Blues Serenaders, and with several classic blues singers. He worked briefly with Fate Marable and King Oliver and then spent a year in Europe touring with Sam Wooding's *Chocolate Kiddies* and in Poland with Louis Douglas's revue. As Henderson's main trumpet soloist during 1926–28, Ladnier was well featured including on such recordings as "The Chant," "Clarinet Marmalade," "Snag It," "Tozo," "I'm Coming Virginia," "St. Louis Blues," and several versions of "St. Louis Shuffle." His heated style fell stylistically between King Oliver and Louis Armstrong. Ladnier's post-Henderson years included another year in Europe with Sam Wooding, stints overseas with Benny Peyton, Harry Flemming's Blue Birds, Louis Douglas, and his own band in France, and playing in the United States in 1931 with Noble Sissle's Sizzling Syncopators. While with Sissle, he formed a friendship with Sidney Bechet, and in 1932 they starred in the short-lived but memorable New Orleans Feetwarmers.

Based on his playing with Henderson, Bobby Stark should have been famous. Starting in mid-1925, Stark worked with many local bands plus an early version of McKinney's Cotton Pickers and Chick Webb's first group (1926–27). Stark was influenced by Louis Armstrong but had a sound of his own. He was a featured soloist with the Fletcher Henderson Orchestra from November 1927 to mid-1934 (other than a short period in 1932 that he spent with Elmer Snowden), taking particularly rewarding solos on three versions of "King Porter Stomp" from 1927, 1932, and 1933.

Charlie Green was Fletcher Henderson's first main trombone soloist, a superior blues player who also fared well on more complex arrangements. He was with Henderson during 1924–27 and 1928–29, appeared on several important sessions with Bessie Smith (including "Trombone Cholly," which was named after him), and also backed some of the top classic blues singers. After leaving Henderson in 1929 (he had been overshadowed during his last year by Jimmy Harrison), Green worked with a variety of groups including Benny Carter (1929–31), Elmer Snowden, Louis Armstrong (1932),

Jimmie Noone, McKinney's Cotton Pickers, Sam Wooding, Don Redman, and Chick Webb (1932–33).

Benny Morton, who had worked with Billy Fowler's band off and on during 1923–26, had two stints with Henderson, being a key soloist during 1926–28 and 1931–32. He also had a stint with Chick Webb (1930–31) and ended the classic jazz era working with Don Redman.

While Morton was a smooth player with an appealing tone, Jimmy Harrison bordered on being a virtuoso. Harrison started playing trombone when he was 15 and living in Detroit. In 1919, he worked in Atlantic City with his own group, also performing with the orchestras of Charlie Johnson and Sam Wooding. In 1923, Harrison moved to New York where he played with Fess Williams, June Clark, Billy Fowler, briefly with Duke Ellington, and Elmer Snowden. He was with the Fletcher Henderson Orchestra during 1927–30, taking solos on many records and also being featured on occasional vocals in a talking conversational style closely based on that of Bert Williams. Harrison also recorded with the Blue Rhythm Orchestra, the Chocolate Dandies, the Georgia Strutters, the Gulf Coast Seven, Charlie Johnson, Sara Martin, Charlie Skeete, Bessie Smith, Eva Taylor, Chick Webb, and Clarence Williams. But in the summer of 1930, he became ill while on tour with Henderson and was forced to stop playing. Jimmy Harrison rejoined Henderson for a little while in 1931, but died of stomach cancer on July 23, 1931, when he was just 30. One of the first trombonists to solo with legato phrasing, Harrison's early death was a major loss, particularly to his good friend Jack Teagarden, whose music had developed along similar lines.

Horace Henderson, though a better pianist than his older brother as well as being a talented arranger, was always in Fletcher Henderson's shadow. While attending college, he formed the Wilberforce Collegians, a band that initially worked during summer vacations starting in 1924. The ensemble broke away in time and was renamed the Horace Henderson Orchestra in 1926 and the Dixie Stompers in 1928, but unfortunately it never recorded. Horace Henderson had a new orchestra during 1929–31, one that was taken over by Don Redman; Horace stayed as the band's pianist until 1933. In the early 1930s, he also worked as a freelance arranger and guested on a few of his brother's records, playing piano in 1931 with the Fletcher Henderson Orchestra on "Hot and Anxious" and "Comin' and Goin'."

Big band drumming largely began in Fletcher Henderson's band. Kaiser Marshall, who was born in Georgia but grew up in Boston, moved to New York in the early 1920s. As a member of Henderson's orchestra during 1923–30, his solid and subtle beat helped establish the art of playing drums (as opposed to percussion) for big bands. After he departed, he led his own group in 1931 (the Czars of Harmony) and then worked with McKinney's Cotton Pickers. Walter Johnson, Marshall's replacement, was an important transitional figure between early jazz and swing. He had previously worked with Freddie Johnson's Red Devils (1924), Bobby Brown, Elmer Snowden, and Billy Fowler. Johnson was Henderson's drummer during 1930–34 and, although overshadowed by flashier players, he was influential even though, like Marshall, he rarely ever took a solo.

The most famous of Fletcher Henderson's sidemen from the 1926–32 period was tenor saxophonist Coleman Hawkins. Hawkins played piano when he was five and cello two years later, starting on tenor at nine. A professional musician at 16, Hawkins had to invent his own s tyle for he had no predecessors in jazz as a tenor sax soloist. He worked in a Kansas City theatre orchestra and toured with Mamie Smith during 1921–23, making his recording debut with the classic blues singer. He began recording with Fletcher Henderson in August 1923 and became an official part of the big band the following January. Though Hawkins always had a strong tone and impressive technique, at first he used slap tonguing, staccato runs, and novelty effects in his playing, which makes his early solos sound quite dated. However, after Louis Armstrong joined Henderson, Hawkins learned quickly and modernized his playing. His improvisation on 1926's "Stampede" is considered the first great tenor sax solo, and most other tenor saxophonists of the early 1930s (including such up-and-comers as Chu Berry and Ben Webster) were heavily influenced by Hawkins's sound and style. ● **1929–1934** (Classics 587) has most of the tenor's more significant early recordings when he wasn't playing with Fletcher Henderson. Hawk is featured on six numbers with the Mound City Blue Blowers (including famous versions of "One Hour" and "Hello Lola") alongside such musicians as Pee Wee Russell, Glenn Miller, Muggsy Spanier, and Jimmy Dorsey, on three numbers with trumpeter Jack Purvis, for a full set headed by Horace Henderson that utilized the Fletcher Henderson band (highlighted by Hawk's ballad feature "I've Got to Sing a Torch Song"), and on his first six songs as a leader. Although Coleman Hawkins still had to smooth out some of the rhythmic awkwardness from his style (he sometimes tried to fit too many notes into too small a time period), he was widely recognized as the king of the tenor sax.

Don Redman and McKinney's Cotton Pickers The one person most responsible for the sound of the early Fletcher Henderson Orchestra, and arguably the most important member of the band (other than Louis Armstrong) prior to 1928, was Don Redman. Redman was a musical prodigy who began on trumpet when he was three before shifting to reed instruments. By the time he was 12, he was playing clarinet, various saxophones, and oboe. Redman graduated from Storer's College at the age of 20 and also studied at the Chicago and Boston Conservatories. He moved to New York in 1922, worked with Billy Paige's Broadway Syncopators, and joined Henderson in 1923. Despite his early instrumental abilities, Redman was a better section player than he was a soloist on clarinet and alto. However, his real talents lay in arranging. He was, along with Ferde Grofe, one of the very first to divide a big band into trumpet, trombone, and reed sections, and he was responsible for most of Henderson's charts during 1923–27. His early work was futuristic but overly ambitious and busy. After Louis Armstrong joined the big band, Redman learned fast, streamlined his writing, and concentrated on creating swinging riffs. Of his arrangements, "Sugar Foot Stomp" and "The Stampede" are classics, and Redman had the distinction of taking one of the earliest scat vocals on 1924's "My Papa Doesn't Two Time."

It was considered a major blow when Redman was persuaded to leave Henderson and lead McKinney's Cotton Pickers in June 1927. One of the top bands run by Jean Goldkette, the ensemble began as the Synco Septet in 1923. Goldkette renamed them and signed up the orchestra to work as the house band for his Greystone Ballroom in Detroit. With the hiring of Redman as the group's musical director, arranger, clarinetist, altoist, singer, and front man, the Cotton Pickers entered the big time. In its prime during 1928–31 (the period when it recorded regularly for Victor), the group featured such top musicians as John Nesbitt (who also contributed some fine arrangements), Langston Curl, Joe Smith and Rex Stewart on trumpets and cornets, trombonists Claude

Jones and Ed Cuffee, and saxophonists Milton Senior, George Thomas, Prince Robinson, and Benny Carter. Redman took good-natured philosophical vocals (which were as much spoken as sung), and the Cotton Pickers introduced such future standards as "Baby Won't You Please Come Home," "I Want a Little Girl," "Gee Baby, Ain't I Good to You," and "Cherry," the last two composed by Redman. In November 1929, when the band moved from Chicago to New York, Redman augmented the band's nucleus with several all-stars for his recordings, including Coleman Hawkins and Fats Waller.

⊙ **Put It There, Vol. 1** (Frog 25), **Cotton Picker's Scat, Vol. 2** (Frog 26), and **Shag Nasty, Vol. 3** (Frog 27) contain McKinney's Cotton Pickers' complete output. **Put It There**, which is highlighted by such tunes as "Milenburg Joys," "Cherry," "There's a Rainbow 'Round My Shoulder," "I've Found a New Baby," and "Miss Hannah," has the master takes of the band's records from 1928–29. **Cotton Picker's Scat**, which fully covers 1930, is nearly at the same level with "Honeysuckle Rose," "Baby, Won't You Please Come Home," and "I Want a Little Girl" all getting inventive treatments. **Shag Nasty** has the Cotton Pickers' four titles from 1931, the band's 17 alternate takes, and the 1928 session in which they had recorded under the name of the Chocolate Dandies. The Classics label has released all of the same music but without the many alternate takes as **1928–1929** (Classics 609), **1929–1930** (Classics 625), and **1930–1931/1939–1940** (Classics 649). The latter CD augments the final Cotton Pickers sessions with four songs recorded by Don Redman's ensemble

in 1932 under the name of vocalist Harlan Lattimore, and most of his 1939–40 recordings with his own swing era big band. Of lesser interest is **The Band that Don Redman Built** (Bluebird 2275), a single disc sampler that has 22 of McKinney's Cotton Pickers' better titles.

In the summer of 1931, Don Redman formed his own big band, and that was the beginning of the end for McKinney's Cotton Pickers. Although Benny Carter took over the Cotton Pickers for a year, they recorded only two additional selections in September and began a quick decline. Carter left in 1932 and the band broke up two years later.

Don Redman's own orchestra worked for the next nine years but never really caught on big. ⊙ **1931–1933** (Classics 543) features the band when it included such players as trumpeter Sidney DeParis, trombonists Claude Jones and Benny Morton, clarinetist Edward Inge, tenor saxophonist Robert Carroll, and (on the first two sessions) Henry "Red" Allen. Highlights include "Shakin' the African," "Nagasaki," "How'm I Doin'," a two-part version of "Doin' the New Lowdown" (with guests Cab Calloway, the Mills Brothers, and tap dancer Bill "Bojangles" Robinson), and Redman's mysterioso theme "Chant of the Weed." The band sounds quite promising, but it would never really surpass the excitement of these first recordings.

Benny Carter   Benny Carter assumed Don Redman's positions with both Fletcher Henderson and McKinney's Cotton Pickers, but had much more success with

---

TIMELINE 1931

Bix Beiderbecke dies at the age of 28. • Mamie Smith makes her final records. • Cab Calloway records "Minnie the Moocher" and his orchestra becomes the house band at the Cotton Club. • The Rhythm Boys leave Paul Whiteman to join Gus Arnheim, but soon break up as Bing Crosby starts becoming a major star. • Jimmy Blythe, Jimmy Harrison, and Buddy Petit pass away. • Blanche Calloway tries unsuccessfully to take over Andy Kirk's Orchestra. • Sam Wooding's Orchestra breaks up in Belgium. • King Oliver makes his final recordings. • Louis Armstrong and Lil Hardin Armstrong separate. • Don Redman leaves McKinney's Cotton Pickers to form his own band. • Chick Webb's orchestra starts playing regularly at the Savoy Ballroom. • Fats Waller records with Ted Lewis. • Irving Mills takes over the Coconut Grove Orchestra and renames it the Mills Blue Rhythm Band. • Claude Hopkins's Orchestra plays regularly at Roseland. • Walter Page's Blue Devils and Sam Wooding's Orchestra break up. • The Original Memphis Five makes its last recordings. • The Mills Brothers become a hit. • Ivie Anderson becomes Duke Ellington's first regular vocalist. • Buddy Bolden's death is not even noticed by the jazz world.

countless other ventures during his long career. Carter learned piano from his mother as a youth and began playing C-melody sax in 1921. He became a professional musician in 1923 and the following year switched to alto sax, playing with June Clark, Billy Paige's Broadway Syncopators, Lois Deppe, Earl Hines (on baritone), Horace Henderson's Collegians (1925–26), and briefly with Fletcher Henderson. As a member of Charlie Johnson's Orchestra during 1927–28, he made his recording debut. Carter worked with Fletcher Henderson during 1928–31 both as an altoist and as an arranger/composer; "Blues in My Heart" was his first song to become a standard. Carter joined McKinney's Cotton Pickers in 1931 and took over the band after Don Redman departed, but the band was on a downward spiral. In 1932, he formed his own big band and by then was doubling on trumpet, working as a freelance arranger, and being considered (along with Johnny Hodges and Jimmy Dorsey) the top altoist in jazz. **1929–1933** (Classics 522) actually only has five selections released under Carter's name (three of which he sings on), instead emphasizing some of his best sideman sessions of the time. Carter is featured on two songs with the Little Chocolate Dandies, five with the Chocolate Dandies, and the first 11 numbers that bassist Spike Hughes led while in the United States in 1933. This was only the beginning for Carter's rather lengthy and very productive career.

Luis Russell and Henry "Red" Allen Pianist/arranger Luis Russell led one of the best big bands of 1929–31, a group that both looked backward toward New Orleans jazz and ahead toward swing. Born in Panama, Russell studied guitar, violin, organ, and piano, settling on the latter when he accompanied silent films in 1917. Two years later Russell won $3,000 in a lottery, using the money to move with his mother and sister to New Orleans. He worked around New Orleans for five years before moving to Chicago in 1924 to play with Doc Cook. As a member of King Oliver's Dixie Syncopators during 1925–27, Russell toured, recorded, and moved to New York in 1927. He led two recording sessions in 1926 while still in Chicago, dates most notable for the superior playing of Barney Bigard (his finest recordings on tenor sax) and cornetist Bob Shoffner.

In the summer of 1927, Russell joined George Howe's band, taking over as its leader in October and working at the Nest Club for a year before moving his group's home base to the Saratoga Club. By mid-1929, Russell had a very strong band that consisted of four major

soloists (trumpeter Henry "Red" Allen, trombonist J.C. Higginbotham, clarinetist Albert Nicholas, and altoist Charlie Holmes), a pair of under-featured players (trumpeter Bill Coleman and tenor saxophonist Teddy Hill), and one of the finest rhythm sections in jazz (his piano, guitarist Will Johnson, bassist Pops Foster, and drummer Paul Barbarin). ● **1926–1929** (Classics 558) and ● **1930–1934** (Classics 606) comprise all of the band's recordings except for five alternate takes. **1926–1929** begins with the early outings by Russell's Hot Six, his Heebie Jeebie Stompers, and his Burning Eight. Also included are two numbers in which Russell and a contingent from his early band accompany singer Ada Brown, two selections by the Jungle Town Stompers (featuring Louis Metcalf and Charlie Holmes), and Victoria Spivey's October 1, 1929, session with the Russell band. Best are the seven numbers from the 1929 Luis Russell Orchestra, including "Feelin' the Spirit," "Jersey Lightning," and "Broadway Rhythm." **1930–1934** is mostly from 1930–31 (best are "Saratoga Shout," "Louisiana Swing," and "Panama") plus the two numbers from J.C. Higginbotham's Six Hicks (the same basic group) and the six numbers cut by the 1934 edition of the band. The Luis Russell Orchestra also accompanied Louis Armstrong for a few months in 1929 and recorded as a smaller combo on dates headed by Red Allen, Sweet Pease Spivey, and (without Russell) Jelly Roll Morton. However, after 1931, the Luis Russell Orchestra's fortunes declined and its top musicians were lured away by more commercially successful bands.

Luis Russell's top soloist was Henry "Red" Allen, one of the most important trumpeters to emerge during the era. Born in New Orleans, Allen was the son of a brass band leader (Henry Allen, Sr.), and he was always proud to get a chance to play and march with his father's band. He played locally in New Orleans and on the riverboats with Fate Marable. In 1927, Allen moved up to Chicago where he worked with King Oliver and made his recording debut with Clarence Williams, but soon became homesick and returned to New Orleans. However, he had quickly gained a strong reputation and in 1929 he was given two offers: to join Duke Ellington as Bubber Miley's replacement or to become a member of the Luis Russell Orchestra. He chose the latter because of the many New Orleans musicians in the band. On Russell's records, he took superior solos on "Jersey Lightning,"

"Saratoga Shout," and "Louisiana Swing," and showed a great deal of individuality and chance-taking.

Because of Louis Armstrong's great success with his recordings for the Okeh label, other record companies sought to develop get trumpet stars of their own. Jabbo Smith signed with Brunswick, Reuben "River" Reeves was snatched up by Vocalion, and Red Allen began recording as a leader for Victor on July 16, 1929. Unlike Smith and Reeves (both of whom never surpassed their work of 1929), Allen's recordings (which sometimes also had him taking a swinging if eccentric vocal) helped launch a major solo career. His first session resulted in outstanding solos on "It Should Be You" and "Biff'ly Blues," and he led five recording dates during 1929–30, mostly using musicians from Russell's Orchestra. ● **1929–1933** (Classics 540) and **The Henry Allen Collection Vol. 2** (JSP 333) have all of Henry "Red" Allen's recordings as a leader during his first four years on records. **1929–1933** includes such memorable performances as "It Should Be You," "Biff'ly Blues," "Swing Out," "Pleasin' Paul," "Sugar Hill Function," "Roamin'," and "I Wish I Could Shimmy Like My Sister Kate." This CD is rounded off with seven numbers from 1933 that costar Coleman Hawkins and draws much of its personnel from the Fletcher Henderson Orchestra. **The Henry Allen Collection Vol. 2** is quite valuable for it has 17 alternate takes from Allen's 1929–30 dates (including two additional and very different versions of "It Should Be You" and selections with vocals by Victoria and Sweet Pease Spivey), plus lesser-known numbers with Luis Russell. Red Allen, who also recorded during the period with Don Redman, Jelly Roll Morton, and Billy Banks's Rhythmakers, left Russell's band in 1932 and spent a few months with Charlie Johnson's band before joining Fletcher Henderson.

Trombonist J.C. Higginbotham proved to be such a good match with Red Allen while they were with Luis Russell that they teamed up many times over the years. Higginbotham grew up in Cincinnati where he played locally but also learned tailoring at a school and briefly worked as a mechanic for General Motors. By 1924, he had decided to become a full-time musician, performing in Cincinnati until moving to New York in 1928. Soon after arriving in town, Higginbotham sat in with Chick Webb's band at the Savoy Ballroom. Russell was in the audience and he quickly signed the trombonist for his band. A boisterous and enthusiastic player with strong technique, Higginbotham was given plenty of

solos with Russell during the next three years, and he recorded two numbers ("Give Me Your Telephone Number" and "Higginbotham Blues") as a leader in 1930. The following year he joined the Fletcher Henderson Orchestra where his playing also sounded perfectly at home.

While Red Allen and J.C. Higginbotham first gained fame with Luis Russell, clarinetist Albert Nicholas already was well known in the jazz world a few years earlier. He began playing clarinet in his native New Orleans when he was ten and worked with the who's who of New Orleans jazz (including Buddy Petit, King Oliver, and Manuel Perez). In 1924, he moved to Chicago, becoming a key member of King Oliver's Dixie Syncopators for two years, also recording with Richard M. Jones and the Chicago Hottentots. A world traveler during 1927–28, Nicholas spent a year in Shanghai, China, where he played with drummer Jack Carter's group, and he also worked in Egypt and in Paris. Nicholas joined Russell's orchestra in November 1928, staying nearly five years in addition to recording with Fats Waller and Jelly Roll Morton. He was one of the most technically skilled of the New Orleans clarinetists, and his warm sound was always immediately recognizable.

The other main soloist in Russell's band, altoist Charlie Holmes, never really lived up to his potential. Born and raised in Boston, Holmes was a childhood friend of both Johnny Hodges (an influence on his playing) and Harry Carney. He played oboe with the Boston Civic Symphony Orchestra in 1926, moved to New York in 1927, and worked with Chick Webb, Henri Saparo, Joe Steele, and George Howe. He held his own next to Allen, Higginbotham, and Nicholas while with Russell during 1929–32, but after he left to join the Mills Blue Rhythm Band in 1932, Holmes became a much less significant player despite being one of the finest altoists of the early 1930s.

While Russell was just a fine section pianist and Will Johnson played rhythm guitar, both Pops Foster and Paul Barbarin were important New Orleans players. Barbarin was part of a very musical family and developed into a superior parade drummer who specialized in the press roll. He played in Chicago during 1917–22 (including with Freddie Keppard and Jimmie Noone), was back in New Orleans during 1923–24, and then returned to Chicago where he worked with King Oliver (1925–27). His playing was flexible enough for him to be a driving force in Luis Russell's band during 1928–32. Pops Foster grew up in New Orleans where, after playing cello for three years, he became one of the city's top bassists, doubling on tuba so he could play for parades. Foster worked with Fate Marable on riverboats (1917–21), spent a couple of periods in St. Louis working with Charlie Creath and Dewey Jackson, and was in Los Angeles with Kid Ory and Mutt Carey during 1923–25. Surprisingly, he was never part of the Chicago jazz scene, moving to New York in 1928. Foster, whose slap bass playing was always colorful and percussive, ranked with Wellman Braud as the top jazz bassist during 1929–31, the period when he was part of the Luis Russell rhythm section.

Charlie Johnson's Paradise Ten   Charlie Johnson's Orchestra (originally called his Paradise Ten) was based at Small's Paradise during 1925–35. Johnson, a decent ensemble pianist who never soloed, actually started out on trombone, freelancing in the New York area starting in 1914. But within a short time he switched to piano and showed a real knack for putting together bands full of young all-stars. Johnson started leading groups in 1918, recorded four titles with classic blues singer Mary Stafford in 1921, and during 1925–29 led five notable recording dates, all of which are on ● **The Complete Charlie Johnson Sessions** (Hot 'N' Sweet 5110). The 14 titles plus ten alternate takes include such exciting numbers as "Don't You Leave Me Here," "You Ain't the One," "Charleston Is the Best Dance After All," and three versions of "Walk that Thing." Among the key players are cornetists/trumpeters Thomas Morris, Jabbo Smith, Leonard Davis, and Sidney DeParis, trombonists Charlie Irvis, Jimmy Harrison, and Benny Carter, and tenor saxophonist Benny Waters plus guest singer Monette Moore; Carter and Waters provided many of the arrangements. Jabbo Smith steals the show on a couple of occasions, but overall both the ensemble work and the solos are on a consistently high level.

The Mills Blue Rhythm Band, Claude Hopkins, and Jimmie Lunceford   Three Harlem orchestras that would make more of an impact after 1932 were the Mills Blue Rhythm Band, Claude Hopkins, and Jimmie Lunceford. The Mills Blue Rhythm Band was originally known as the Blue Rhythm Band and led by drummer Willie Lynch. After it became the Coconut Grove Orchestra, it accompanied Louis Armstrong on a few recordings in 1930 (including "Dinah" and "Tiger Rag"). Producer/manager Irving Mills took over the ensemble in early 1931, renaming it after himself and having it

work as the relief band at the Cotton Club for Cab Calloway and Duke Ellington. Because it was a fill-in group, the Mills Blue Rhythm Band never really developed its own musical personality. However, it did make some fine recordings starting in 1931, with Edgar Hayes as the musical director and main arranger. **1931** (Classics 660) has quite a few vocals by Dick Robertson, Charlie Lawman, George Morton, and Chick Bullock, arrangements by Harry White and Edgar Hayes, and some hot numbers including "Blue Rhythm," "Red Devil," and "Futuristic Jungleism." **1931–1932** (Classics 676) finds Billy Banks taking over as the vocalist (he is a big improvement on the others). The highlights include "Savage Rhythm," "Snake Hips," "Heat Waves," "The Growl," and "Jazz Cocktail," but the arrangements are generally more exciting than the soloists; only altoist Charlie Holmes was at all notable in the personnel at that point in time.

Claude Hopkins was a great stride pianist. He grew up in Washington, D.C., started playing piano at seven, and first led a band in Atlantic City in 1924. After working with Wilbur Sweatman, Hopkins sailed to Europe in 1925, leading the orchestra that accompanied Josephine Baker. Back in New York, he led a few unrecorded bands during 1926–29 and in 1930 his new orchestra was based at the Savoy Ballroom, replacing Fletcher Henderson's at Roseland in 1931. In 1932, the Claude Hopkins Orchestra had its first recording date (Jimmy Mundy's colorful arrangement of "Mush Mouth" was a highpoint) and introduced its theme song, "I Would Do Anything for You."

Jimmie Lunceford was a straitlaced bandleader who always expected strong musicianship from his players. He grew up in Denver where he took music lessons from Paul Whiteman's father, Wilberforce Whiteman. Lunceford had training on many instruments, played alto with George Morrison's Orchestra in 1922, and earned a music degree from Fisk University in 1926. He taught music at Manassas High School in Memphis and gradually formed a band with his students that he named the Chickasaw Syncopators. They recorded two selections in 1927, which have been reissued on **What Kind of Rhythm Is That** (Frog 31). The ensemble at that early stage included two future band members, bassist Moses Allen (heard on tuba) and drummer Jimmy Crawford. In 1929, the band (which now had altoist Willie Smith and pianist/arranger Edwin Wilcox) became professional, recording two more titles the following year that have been reissued on **Memphis Stomp** (Frog 24). Leaving Memphis, the Jimmie Lunceford Orchestra spent time working in Cleveland and Buffalo and was waiting for its big break as 1932 ended.

Alex Hill   If he had had better health and a longer life, chances are that Alex Hill, a very talented arranger/composer and pianist, would have led a major swing band. He became a professional musician as a teenager, worked with Alphonso Trent, and led a band in 1924. Hill worked in Los Angeles during 1927–28 with Mutt Carey's Jeffersonians and did some studio work in Hollywood. While in Chicago during 1928–29, Hill worked with Jimmy Wade, Carroll Dickerson, Jerome Pasquall, and Jimmie Noone, playing piano and contributing arrangements. His song "Beau Koo Jack" was recorded by Louis Armstrong's Savoy Ballroom Five. After moving to New York in 1929, Hill worked with Sammy Stewart and became a staff arranger for Irving Mills, contributing charts for Duke Ellington, Benny Carter, Claude Hopkins, Andy Kirk, Paul Whiteman, and many others bands. Alex Hill led five record dates during 1929–30 and 1934, all of which are on **1928–1934** (Timeless 1-050), plus his sessions with Albert Wynn's Gut Bucket Five, Jimmy Wade's Dixielanders, Jimmie Noone, Junie Cobb's Grains of Corn, Eddie Condon (1933), and the Hokum Trio. One can hear Hill's potential throughout these performances, particularly as a writer.

Duke Ellington   Even considering how many talented big bands were based in Harlem in the early 1930s, Duke Ellington's towered above all the others, even Fletcher Henderson's. One reason was that Ellington wrote arrangements specifically to feature his sidemen rather than generic charts that could be played as well by other ensembles. Another reason was that the band's leader was a genius.

Edward Kennedy "Duke" Ellington made his mark during the 1926–32 period as a composer, arranger, pianist, and bandleader. He started on piano in his native Washington, D.C., when he was seven, but for a time it appeared as if he would make his career as an artist; he was even offered an art scholarship to Brooklyn's Pratt Institute. However, his main interest was music, so he turned the scholarship down and instead hung around local dives and any place where he could hear the piano "professors" jam. Ellington (who earned the lifelong name of "Duke" due to his suave and sophisticated

nature) did his best to emulate the keyboardists, including slowing down James P. Johnson piano rolls to half-speed so he could copy the fingering. He earned a living as a sign painter, even as he developed his writing skills, composing his first song in 1917, "Soda Fountain Rag." Before he even had a regular group, Ellington wisely took out a very large ad in the local Yellow Pages about his band. By 1918 he was supplying several groups a night for parties and dances, making cameo appearances with each of the units even though he barely knew any songs himself at that point! However, Duke hurriedly worked to improve his piano technique and repertoire and was successful at putting up a good front until he could live up to his reputation.

After several years of working around town, in 1923 Ellington first went to New York, traveling with Sonny Greer and Otto Hardwicke to join Wilbur Sweatman's band. But the gig did not last long, and after a period of struggling, the trio returned home. A few months later, Elmer Snowden formed the Washingtonians, a group consisting of his banjo, Hardwicke, Greer, Arthur Whetsol, and Fats Waller. By the time the musicians arrived in New York, Waller had left town, probably to avoid being served with an arrest warrant due to his not having made alimony payments. Snowden immediately sent to Washington, D.C., for Ellington to fill the piano spot. The Washingtonians worked in New York for a few months, but in the summer of 1924 a dispute over money resulted in Snowden being ousted and Ellington becoming the band's leader.

Duke Ellington soon got a job for the Washingtonians at the Hollywood Club (which a little while later was renamed the Kentucky Club), an association that lasted for three years. When Whetsol returned to Washington, D.C., to attend medical school, Bubber Miley took his place. Formerly a sweet band, the addition of Miley (with Charles Irvis soon joining on trombone) gave the orchestra a unique "jungle" sound featuring unusual tone colors with the brass players utilizing a variety of mutes to distort their sounds. For a few months in 1924, Sidney Bechet (Ellington's favorite musician) was also in the Washingtonians although unfortunately that version of the band never recorded; Bechet and Miley must have made a very potent team. In November 1924, the Washingtonians, a sextet at the time with Fred Guy on banjo as Snowden's replacement, recorded two impressive numbers, "Choo Choo" and "Rainy Nights." As it turned out, this was a false start. The band's next four sessions (1925–26) had shifting personnel, and the eight resulting songs were erratic and surprisingly primitive, certainly not hinting at what was to come.

On November 29, 1926, with the recording of "East St. Louis Toodle-oo" (Ellington's theme song until 1941) and "Birmingham Breakdown," the Duke Ellington sound was born. The personnel of the band by then consisted of Miley, Louis Metcalf, Tricky Sam Nanton (who replaced Irvis and built upon his innovations), Hardwicke, Prince Robinson on tenor, Ellington, Guy, Bass Edwards on tuba, and Greer. **The Birth of a Band, Vol. 1** (EPM 5104) has every Duke Ellington record prior to 1927. Included is his lone piano roll ("Jig Walk"), "Choo Choo," "Rainy Nights," the eight weaker numbers by the orchestra, and dates in which Duke backs vocalist Alberta Hunter, Jo Trent, Sonny Greer (who sings on "Oh, How I Love My Darling"), Florence Bristol, Irving Mills, and Alberta Jones. The CD concludes with the Duke Ellington Orchestra finding its sound during November–December 1926 with "East St. Louis Toodle-oo," "Birmingham Breakdown," "Immigration Blues," and two takes of "The Creeper."

The year 1927 was the most important year in Ellington's career. Irving Mills became his manager, helping the band gain and maintain a very busy recording schedule with quite a few labels. Ellington's "Black and Tan Fantasy" and "Creole Love Call" debuted, with the former song borrowing from Chopin, while the latter, brought in by Rudy Jackson and adapted for the band, was (unknown to Ellington) King Oliver's "Jazzin' Babies' Blues." Adelaide Hall's singing on "Creole Love Song" is considered the first entirely wordless vocal. Harry Carney (the band's baritonist until 1974) and Wellman Braud joined and became important members of the band. Most importantly, the Duke Ellington Orchestra passed an audition at the Cotton Club and became the famous club's house band, starting on December 4, 1927, and continuing regularly into 1931. Working at the Cotton Club meant that the band gained fame on their regular radio broadcasts, and Duke had the opportunity to develop his talents as an arranger/composer, writing material for both his orchestra and a bit for the club's famous floor shows.

Most big bands hire musicians who can best play their arrangements. In Duke Ellington's case, he first hired the most distinctive musicians he could find and then wrote arrangements that would best feature them, somehow blending together all of the unique voices. Because he was an innovative arranger who didn't so much break the rules as simply overlook them, he was an expert at creating atmospheric pieces as well as more swinging works. In Ellington's band, much more than most others, the sidemen were of major importance. Their spontaneous ideas led to some of Duke's songs (many of his originals were really collaborations), yet those pieces would probably have been forgotten had Ellington not written them down, extended them, and made them highly personal works for the band.

Each of Duke Ellington's sidemen are well worth mentioning. The original Washingtonians featured drummer Sonny Greer who, although never a virtuoso or much of a soloist, added percussive effects and colors to the band. Four years older than Duke, Greer freelanced around New Jersey, first coming to Washington, D.C., in 1919 and began playing with Ellington the following year. At the Cotton Club in the late 1920s, Greer was placed high up on the stage and surrounded by an expensive setup that included a gong, tympani, skulls, vibes, and chimes in addition to his drums.

Otto "Toby" Hardwicke started on bass when he was 14, playing with Carroll's Columbia Orchestra in 1920. He soon switched to the C-melody sax and started working with Ellington in D.C. By the time he traveled with Duke on his two trips to New York, Hardwicke was also playing alto, soprano, baritone, and bass saxophones. His sweet sound on the alto (his main instrument) helped define the tone of the original group. He remained with Ellington until leaving for the first time in 1928. Hardwicke worked in Paris with Noble Sissle, played with Chick Webb in 1929, and led an orchestra in 1930 that actually beat Ellington's in a battle of the bands. In 1932, he rejoined Duke, in time to take a famous recorded solo on "Sophisticated Lady," a song he cowrote with Ellington. However, by then Johnny Hodges was the band's alto soloist, and Hardwicke would be greatly underutilized.

Trumpeter Arthur Whetsol was renowned for his lyrical style and haunting tone. He grew up in Washington, D.C., was a childhood friend of Ellington's, and started working with Duke in 1920. Whetsol was with the Washingtonians during 1923–24, but chose to return to D.C. to study medicine at Howard University. When he was finished with his studies in March 1928, he rejoined Ellington, who was now a major success at the Cotton Club. Whetsol's thoughtful style and soft tone were a contrast to the more extroverted styles of Bubber Miley, Freddie Jenkins, and later Cootie Williams, and he was particularly effective in ensembles as a first trumpeter. He took memorable spots on "Mood Indigo" and "Black Beauty," and is prominent in the 1929 Duke Ellington short film *Black and Tan*.

Trombonist Charlie Irvis made the mistake of not staying with Duke Ellington's Orchestra long enough. Irvis worked with Lucille Hegamin's Blue Flame Syncopators (1920–21) and Willie "The Lion" Smith before joining the Washingtonians in 1924. A pioneer in using the plunger mute on the trombone to create unusual tonal distortions, Irvis preceded Tricky Sam Nanton and assisted Bubber Miley in creating the original "jungle" sound. But he left Ellington in 1926, working with Charlie Johnson (1927–28), Jelly Roll Morton (1929–30), and the short-lived Bubber Miley Orchestra (1931), recording with those groups plus Fats Waller, Thomas Morris, and Clarence Williams (1924–27). His career faded out with the rise of the Depression.

The first leader of the Washingtonians, Elmer Snowden, was a fine banjoist. As a teenager in Baltimore, he worked with pianist Addie Booze (1914), Eubie Blake (1915), and Joe Rochester (1916–19). In 1920, Snowden first played with Duke Ellington in a Washington, D.C., trio. He performed with Claude Hopkins in 1921 and led a band (soon named the Washingtonians) that played in Washington, D.C., and Atlantic City before moving to New York in September 1923. The group, which briefly consisted of Snowden, Greer, Whetsol, Hardwick, and Fats Waller, soon had Ellington on piano filling the vacancy left by Waller. A few months later, Bubber Miley took over Whetsol's place and Irvis was added. But a money dispute resulted in Snowden being ousted in the summer of 1924. He worked briefly with Ford Dabney's Orchestra and then led several unrecorded bands of his own. However, as a sideman, Snowden recorded during 1924–25 with Charles Booker, the Six Black Diamonds, the Kansas City Five, and Jake Frazier, making many records with the trio of clarinetist Bob Fuller and pianist Lou Hooper in 1925–26 under the names Bob Fuller, the Pennsylvania Syncopators, the Rocky Mountain Trio, the Three Hot Eskimos, the Three Jolly Miners, and the Three Monkey Chasers. The banjoist also appeared on records with TeRoy Williams

(1927) and in 1929 with Jasper Davis, the Jungletown Stompers, and the Musical Stevedores, in addition to backing many classic blues singers.

Fred Guy was Elmer Snowden's replacement in the Washingtonians. Guy grew up in New York, worked with Joseph C. Smith's orchestra, and led his own band. After joining Ellington, Guy's rhythm banjo (and occasional guitar) were at first an important part of the group's ensemble sound although over time his significance waned.

Joining Ellington, Greer, and Guy in the rhythm section by 1927 was bassist Wellman Braud. The oldest member of the band (born in 1891), Braud early on played violin, trombone, guitar, and drums before settling on bass. He freelanced in Chicago starting in 1917 (including with the Original Creole Orchestra and Charlie Elgar), visited London in 1923 with Will Vodery's *Plantation Revue*, and worked with Wilbur Sweatman. After Ellington had Bass Edwards on tuba during 1925–27, Braud was hired on bass in the summer of 1927 and Ellington never used a tuba again. Wellman Braud ranked with Pops Foster and Steve Brown as the top bassist of the era. He always made sure that his bass could be heard on Duke's records, and his playing added a lot of drive to the band.

Duke Ellington's horn section at the time of his Cotton Club debut consisted of Bubber Miley, Louis Metcalf, Tricky Sam Nanton, Otto Hardwicke, Harry Carney, and Rudy Jackson. None was more important initially in establishing Ellington's "jungle band" sound than Miley. The cornetist grew up in New York, served in the Navy during 1918–19, and worked locally with the Carolina Five, Willie Gant, and Mamie Smith's Jazz Hounds, with whom he made his recording debut during 1921–22. After hearing King Oliver play at the Dreamland in Chicago and also being inspired by Johnny Dunn, Miley began using the plunger mute. He worked with Thomas Morris's Past Jazz Masters in 1923 and made many recordings during 1922–26 including with Perry Bradford's Georgia Strutters, the Kansas City Five, the Six Black Diamonds, Clarence Williams, various blues singers, and some unusual duets with the reed organ of Arthur Ray. He first worked with the Washingtonians in September 1923 when the band was led by Elmer Snowden, was officially hired in 1924, and was in and out of the band until becoming a "permanent" member in June 1926.

By November 1924 when he starred on Duke Elling-ton's first recordings, and particularly by 1926, Bubber Miley had become a master of the plunger mute, often used in collaboration with a straight mute. Miley was able to achieve a wide variety of haunting and memorable speechlike sounds, and his playing helped change the Washingtonians from a sweet-sounding dance band to a gutbucket blues-oriented ensemble. From November 1926 to January 1929, Miley was featured on dozens of Ellington's recordings, and he cowrote with Duke "Black and Tan Fantasy," "Doin' the Voom Voom," and the eerie "East St. Louis Toodle-oo." Miley also took memorable solos on "Jubilee Stomp," "The Mooche," "Hot and Both-ered," "Bandanna Babies," "Diga Diga Do," and "Tiger Rag." An indispensable part of the band's sound, Miley was unfortunately an alcoholic, and by January 1929 he had become unreliable. Although legend has since stated that Duke Ellington never fired anyone, he was forced to reluctantly let Miley go; Cootie Williams took his place. Miley's post-Ellington period was surprisingly busy. He visited France with Noble Sissle's Orchestra in May 1929, played in New York with Zutty Singleton and Allie Ross, and in 1930 worked with Leo Reisman's White orchestra, usually appearing with the band during those segregated times hidden behind a screen. His haunting solo on Reis-man's recording of "What Is this Thing Called Love" is a classic (despite the wretched vocal that follows), and he can also be heard on "Without Your Love." Other Miley recordings of 1930 include four songs with Jelly Roll Morton ("Fussy Mabel" is a standout), "St. James Infir-mary" with King Oliver, a Hoagy Carmichael session that includes Bix Beiderbecke (highlighted by "Rockin' Chair"), and six numbers as a leader, which are included on **Thumpin' & Bumpin'** (Frog 11); "I Lost My Gal from Memphis" and "Black Maria" are quite rewarding. In 1931, Miley accompanied dancer Roger Pryor Dodge in the *Sweet and Low* revue for several months and led a band backed by Irving Mills. But tuberculosis exacer-bated by his alcoholism struck Bubber Miley down, and he died in 1932 when he was only 29.

Bubber Miley's equivalent on trombone but a much more reliable personality, Joe "Tricky Sam" Nanton, was also a master with mutes, creating all kinds of original and otherworldly sounds. Nanton worked early on with Earl Frazier's Harmony Five (1923–25), Cliff Jackson, and Elmer Snowden, recording with Thomas Morris. Tricky Sam (Otto Hardwicke gave him his nickname)

joined Ellington in mid-1926, replacing Charlie Irvis, and he took solos on scores of records through the years. Nanton worked quite well with Miley and his successor Cootie Williams, helping the younger trumpeter learn the intricacies of working with mutes.

Harry Carney was the most loyal of sidemen, for he spent virtually his entire career as a member of Duke Ellington's Orchestra. Carney started on piano and clar-inet before switching to alto sax. He worked in Boston, took lessons from Benny Waters, and moved to New York in 1927, gigging with Fess Williams. Influenced prima-rily by Coleman Hawkins and Adrian Rollini, Carney joined Ellington in June 1927, playing alto, clarinet, and baritone sax. Within a short time he would be primarily a baritone saxophonist, among the first in jazz, and his huge sound both set the standard and helped his instru-ment become accepted as a solo instrument in jazz.

Louis Metcalf and Rudy Jackson had much more minor roles in the world of Duke Ellington. Metcalf was a fine trumpeter for the era, but never really found a role for himself in Ellington's band. He worked with Charlie Creath in St. Louis, and after moving to New York in 1923, Metcalf played with Jimmie Cooper's *Black & White Revue*, Willie "The Lion" Smith, Andrew Preer's Cotton Club Syncopators, Elmer Snowden, Sam Wood-ing, and Charlie Johnson. He appeared on many records during 1924–29 with top classic blues singers plus the Cotton Club Orchestra, Clarence Williams, James P. Johnson, the Musical Stevedores, the Jungle Town Stom-pers, Jasper Davis's Orchestra, the Gulf Coast Seven, Harry's Happy Four, the Kansas City Five, the Original Jazz Hounds, the Wabash Trio, and King Oliver. While with Ellington (from late 1926 until June 1928), Metcalf had some solos (best on "Harlem River Quiver" and "Bugle Call Rag"). But his plunger mute work was not on Miley's level, he was not as lyrical as Whetsol, and he never fulfilled the role of a "hot soloist" as well as Fred-die Jenkins would. Still, although he had many decades of playing ahead of him, he would always be known as an alumnus of Duke Ellington's band. After playing with Jelly Roll Morton, Luis Russell (the first half of 1929), Connie's Inn Revue, and Vernon Andrade's Orchestra, Louis Metcalf became quite obscure in the 1930s.

Rudy Jackson was Duke Ellington's first clarinet soloist. He grew up in Chicago, started playing locally in 1918, and worked with Carroll Dickerson, King Oliver (for a few months in 1924 as Johnny Dodds's replacement),

Billy Butler, Vaughn's Lucky Sambo Orchestra, and Oliver again in 1927. During his six months with Ellington (June–December 1927), he took solos on five record dates but angered Ellington by passing off Oliver's "Jazzin' Babies' Blues" (which Duke transformed into "Creole Love Call") as his own song. After leaving Ellington, Jackson worked with Noble Sissle during 1929–33 and then was largely forgotten, having blown his chance for musical immortality.

Adelaide Hall, a fine cabaret singer who could scat, was never a member of Duke Ellington's Orchestra, but due to her recording of "Creole Love Call," she was always identified with Duke. Hall performed in theatres and shows starting in the early 1920s, including 1921's *Shuffle Along*, in Europe with the *Chocolate Kiddies Revue* (1925), and back in New York with *Desires of 1927*. On October 26, 1927, she recorded "The Blues I Love to Sing" and "Creole Love Call" with Ellington. In the show *Blackbirds of 1928*, Hall introduced "I Can't Give You Anything but Love." She also recorded with Lew Leslie's Blackbirds Orchestra in 1928, visited England in 1931, and in 1932 brought pianist Art Tatum to New York as her regular accompanist. During that year she recorded with Ellington again, resulting in "I Must Have that Man" and "Baby."

Three new soloists joined Duke Ellington in 1928. Barney Bigard, who became Ellington's clarinetist in January 1928, actually started out his career as one of jazz's top tenor saxophonists. Born in New Orleans, Bigard came from a very musical family that included his uncle, violinist Emile Bigard, his brother, drummer Alex Bigard, and cousins Natty Dominique and Armand J. Piron. Bigard started on the clarinet when he was seven, taking lessons from Lorenzo Tio, Jr. He worked in New Orleans with local groups, including Albert Nicholas and Luis Russell. In late 1924, Bigard moved to Chicago to join King Oliver's Dixie Syncopators on tenor. He was with Oliver off and on until mid-1927, recording with Jelly Roll Morton on two occasions (in 1926 and a trio date in 1929). On November 17, 1926, Bigard had his finest recording session on tenor, cutting four titles with Luis Russell's sextet and showing that he was second on that instrument only to Coleman Hawkins at the time. However, when he joined Ellington (replacing Rudy Jackson), Bigard largely put his tenor away and worked almost exclusively as a clarinetist where his strong musicianship and New Orleans sound were major assets.

Eventually the most famous of all of Ellington's sidemen, Johnny Hodges had a tone on alto that was quite beautiful. Hodges started out on drums and piano, not switching to saxophone until he was 14. He had lessons from Sidney Bechet on soprano and was considered his protégé, worked in Boston, and after moving to New York in 1924, performed with Willie "The Lion" Smith, Bechet (at Club Basha), Chick Webb, and Luckey Roberts. Hodges joined Ellington's Orchestra on May 18, 1928 (replacing Otto Hardwicke), doubling on alto and soprano. He would soon rank at the top with Benny Carter and Jimmy Dorsey among altoists, excelling on blues and stomps yet most beloved for his work on ballads.

With Bubber Miley creating otherworldly sounds with his plunger mute and Arthur Whetsol offering a lyrical voice, it was up to Freddie Jenkins to take "hot" trumpet solos influenced by Louis Armstrong, giving Ellington three very different voices on trumpet. Jenkins (nicknamed "Posey") attended Wilberforce University and worked with Edgar Hayes's Blue Grass Buddies and Horace Henderson's Collegians (1924–28). He joined Ellington in October 1928 and had spots on many records, including "Tiger Rag" and "When You're Smiling." A colorful performer, Jenkins can be seen prominently during Duke Ellington's Orchestra's performance of "Old Man Blues" in the 1930 Amos and Andy film *Check and Double Check*.

During 1928, Duke Ellington's band became well known, soon being billed as his "Famous Orchestra." Even the loss of Bubber Miley in January 1929 did not hurt the band, for Cootie Williams very ably took his place. Williams started off playing trombone, tuba, and drums in school before teaching himself the trumpet. He worked in Alabama, toured with the Young Family Band (which included the up-and-coming Lester and Lee Young), and worked in Florida with clarinetist Eagle Eye Shields and Alonzo Ross's De Luxe Syncopators (1926–28). After moving to New York in 1928, Williams recorded with James P. Johnson, worked with Chick Webb, and spent a couple of months in the Fletcher Henderson Orchestra. After joining Ellington in February 1929, Williams at first played open horn for a couple of weeks until it dawned on him that he had been hired in Miley's spot. With the assistance of Tricky Sam Nanton, Cootie soon mastered the plunger mute and in time he surpassed his predecessor, becoming one of the top trumpeters of the 1930s.

Also joining Duke Ellington's Orchestra in 1929 was Juan Tizol, a technically skilled valve trombonist who was valuable in ensembles. Born in San Juan, Puerto Rico, Tizol came to the United States in 1920, working in New York with the Marie Lucas Orchestra, Bobby Lee's Cotton Pickers, and the White Brothers' Band. Although rarely soloing with Ellington (other than playing the straight melody) after joining in September 1929, Tizol was a fluent ensemble player who could fill in for a missing saxophonist, and in time proved to be a skilled songwriter too.

Duke Ellington and his orchestra recorded constantly during 1927–32, cutting around 280 performances including alternate takes and multiple versions of the same song (often rearranged) on different days. All of his music from this period is owned by RCA/BMG, Universal/Decca, or Sony/Columbia, and the quality of the performances, arrangements, and solos is consistently very high. The remarkable 24-CD set **The Centennial Edition** (RCA 09026-63386) has every selection that Ellington recorded for RCA Victor during 1927–73. The first seven discs cover the 1927–34 period and hopefully will someday be available as a separate set. Since that limited edition box (released in 1999) is not inexpensive, less fanatical Ellington collectors may want to pick up a couple of the single CD Bluebird sets that have been released instead: ◍ **Early Ellington** (Bluebird 6852), **Jungle Nights in Harlem** (Bluebird 2499), and **Jubilee Stomp** (Bluebird 66038). Unfortunately, those discs each overlap timewise, often splitting up a particular session between a couple of CDs. **Early Ellington**, which contains "Black and Tan Fantasy," "Creole Love Call," "Black Beauty," "Mood Indigo," and "Rockin' in Rhythm," is the best overall. **Jungle Nights in Harlem** has some offbeat material including the two-part "A Night at the Cotton Club" (narrated by Irving Mills) and a pair of three-song medleys, while **Jubilee Stomp** includes a classic version of "Bugle Call Rag," and a variety of atmospheric mood pieces.

◍ **Early Ellington** (GRP/Decca 640) is a three-CD set that has all 67 Ellington performances for labels now owned by Universal, starting with the initial version of "East St. Louis Toodle-oo" and including such tunes as "Black Beauty," "The Mooche," the two-part "Tiger Rag," "Wall Street Wail," "Cotton Club Stomp," "Mood Indigo,"

and "Creole Rhapsody." This three-fer is the perfect place to begin in collecting recordings from the first period of Duke Ellington. Almost on the same level is ◍ **Okeh Ellington** (Columbia 46177), a two-CD reissue that has the master takes (but unfortunately not the alternates) from Duke's 50 recordings for the Okeh (now Sony) label during 1927–30. Containing some of the same titles as the Victors, but often with different arrangements, highlights include "Black and Tan Fantasy," "Sweet Mama," "Doin' the New Low Down," "Saturday Night Function," "Double Check Stomp," "Old Man Blues," and "Mood Indigo." For completists who want all of the Sony material with the alternate takes and the later sessions from the classic jazz era, a search will have to be done to acquire the first five of 15 two-LP sets put out by French CBS in the 1970s: **Vol. 1 1925–1928** (CBS 67264), **Vol. 2 1928–1930** (CBS 68275), **Vol. 3 1930–1932** (CBS 88000), **Vol. 4 1932** (CBS 88035), and **Vol. 5 1932–1933** (CBS 88082).

By 1929, when Ellington made his debut on films in the short *Black and Tan* (actually playing a semi-distinguished role rather than the stereotypical part almost always given to blacks in movies), he was thought of as a cut above all the other bandleaders. His steady stream of compositions included "Double Check Stomp," "Cotton Club Stomp," "Shout 'Em, Aunt Tillie," "Mood Indigo" (cowritten with Barney Bigard), "Old Man Blues," and "Rockin' in Rhythm." The constant recordings and the radio broadcasts from the Cotton Club allowed Ellington to largely circumvent the Depression, which slowed down or short-circuited the careers of many other top black jazz musicians. In fact, Ellington continued to grow in stature. In 1929, he recorded his first extended piece, a version of "Tiger Rag" that took up two sides of a 78, totaling nearly six minutes. While that piece was largely an arranged jam, in 1931 his two-part "Creole Rhapsody" inspired a lot of discussion about jazz as an art form and "serious" music.

In 1932, Duke Ellington added an important new trombonist to his band. Lawrence Brown, the son of a minister, had a relatively somber personality, never smoking, drinking, or gambling. Early on, Brown took classes in medicine at Pasadena Junior College but also played in the school orchestra and chose to become a musician. He was active in the late 1920s Los Angeles jazz scene, working with Leon Herriford, Curtis Mosby's Blue Blowers, Paul Howard's Quality Serenaders (with whom he recorded and soloed during 1929–30), and Les

Hite's Orchestra, which recorded with Louis Armstrong in 1930. When he joined Ellington in the spring of 1932, some of Duke's fans were worried that Brown's fluency (well featured on "The Sheik of Araby") would result in the band getting far away from its "jungle" roots, but Brown ended up being a perfect contrast to the primitive sounds of Tricky Sam Nanton.

Ivie Anderson was the first vocalist to be a part of Duke Ellington's Orchestra, and arguably the best. She was classy, sophisticated, and flexible enough to sound at home with moody ballads and lowdown blues alike. Anderson worked at the Cotton Club in Los Angeles as early as 1925, toured with *Shuffle Along*, and sang with Curtis Mosby's Blue Blowers, Paul Howard's Quality Serenaders, Sonny Clay, and in Chicago with Earl Hines's big band. She joined Ellington in 1932 and her first recording was "It Don't Mean a Thing If It Ain't Got that Swing," a performance that looked toward the swing era, which was still three years in the future.

Duke Ellington had accomplished a great deal by the end of 1932 when he was still just 33, and he had over four decades of accomplishments still ahead of him!

Other Black New York Bands

A cross section of excellent New York recording groups from 1925–30 are featured on **Happy Rhythm—New York Columbia Recordings, Vol. 1** (Frog 32). The Cotton Club always had top bands so it is not surprising that the six selections from the 1925 Cotton Club Orchestra (which three years later would re-emerge as the Missourians) are quite enjoyable. Also featured on this highly recommended disc are the Get Happy Band, the Gulf Coast Seven, the Blue Ribbon Syncopators, Fowler's Favorites (led by pianist Lemuel Fowler), Leroy

Tibbs's Connie's Inn Orchestra, the Musical Stevedores, and Bennett's Swamplanders. Among the many top musicians heard from are R.Q. Dickerson, Louis Metcalf, Sidney Bechet (with the Get Happy Band), Tricky Sam Nanton, Thomas Morris, Jimmy Harrison, Buster Bailey, Charlie Holmes, and Alberto Socarras. **Go Harlem—New York Columbia Recordings, Vol. 2** (Frog 38) has eight more groups from 1927–31. Trombonist TeRoy Williams is the leader on two hot numbers ("Oh Malinda" and "Lindbergh Hop") with an octet featuring Rex Stewart, James P. Johnson heading three group dates, two songs apiece from Jasper Davis's Orchestra, Marlow Hardy's Alabamians (recorded the day of the Wall Street crash!), and Trombone Red's Blue Six, plus four tunes from Vance Dixon's Pencils and six by King Carter's Royal Orchestra (which is really the Mills Blue Rhythm Band).

A variety of intriguing New York sessions from 1929–31 are on **Thumpin' and Bumpin'** (Frog 11). James P. Johnson leads a band that includes King Oliver, Fats Waller, and an odd vocal group on "You Don't Understand" and "You've Got to Be Modernistic." Dave Nelson's two 1931 sessions with the King Oliver Orchestra are included, as are a Eubie Blake dance band session from 1931 and the three titles from Russell Wooding's Grand Central Red Caps. Of greatest importance are the four numbers from Cecil Scott's Bright Boys (including very colorful and humorous versions of "Lawd Lawd" and "In a Corner") and all six titles by Bubber Miley's Mileage Makers. Of the latter, "I Lost My Gal from Memphis" and "Black Maria" compensate for the final somewhat sappy session.

TIMELINE 1932

The Big Broadcast stars Bing Crosby and has memorable appearances by the Boswell Sisters, Cab Calloway, the Mills Brothers, and Eddie Lang. • Louis Armstrong visits Europe. • Frank Teschemacher is killed in a car crash. • Sidney Bechet and Tommy Ladnier record as the New Orleans Feetwarmers. • Benny Carter leads his first big band. • Red Allen and Pee Wee Russell record with Billy Banks's Rhythmakers. • Eddie Lang and Carl Kress record a pair of classic guitar duets. • Bubber Miley and Carleton Coon die. • Lawrence Brown joins Duke Ellington's Orchestra. • Art Tatum becomes one of Adelaide Hall's accompanists, and moves to New York. • Milton Brown and Bob Wills record together as the Fort Worth Doughboys, which is considered the earliest Western swing session. • Ellington's "It Don't Mean a Thing If It Ain't Got that Swing" and Bennie Moten's "Moten Swing" look toward the future.

Territory Bands

Although New York became the center of jazz during 1927–28, particularly after the main innovators formerly based in Chicago relocated in the Big Apple, jazz was already on its way to becoming not only a national phenomenon but an international phenomenon. Most American cities were developing their own local jazz scene, and jazz was beginning to be played by Europeans too. While it is true that many of the musicians in the territory bands (the name given to ensembles not based in New York, Chicago, or New Orleans) were primitive players and that sometimes the styles they performed were several years behind that heard in New York, there were some excellent bands based outside of the main areas, often featuring top up-and-coming players. The more fortunate groups were documented, either by the Midwest-based Gennett label, a tiny local record company, or the larger labels during their infrequent field trips.

Four-Four Rhythm (The Old Masters 130) has a sampling of recordings from some of the better white bands that were based on the East Coast, including Paul Tremaine (whose "Four-Four Rhythm" from 1929 brags about how modern its music is), Henny Hendrickson's Louisville Serenaders, Kay Kyser (years before his band caught on), Phil Baxter, Tal Henry's North Carolinians, Billy Hays, and Doc Daugherty.

St. Louis: Charlie Creath and Dewey Jackson

St. Louis, which had been an important area for ragtime, was a major stop for steamships that traveled from the South. Its local jazz scene in the 1920s was most notable for being the home of both Charlie Creath's Jazz-O-Maniacs and Dewey Jackson's Peacock Orchestra. Charlie Creath originally played alto sax before switching to trumpet as a teenager. After leading a band in Seattle, Creath moved to St. Louis in 1918. Three years later he put together his own jazz band, and during 1924–27 they recorded a dozen selections. Creath mostly played in the ensembles, having Leonard Davis or Dewey Jackson as his trumpet soloist and also featuring Lonnie Johnson, Pops Foster, and the leader's brother-in-law, drummer Zutty Singleton. Creath's Jazz-O-Maniacs was considered the best jazz band in St. Louis until illness knocked him out of action for much of 1928–30. Charlie Creath mostly played alto and accordion in later years but never regained his earlier fame.

Dewey Jackson spent virtually his entire career in the Midwest. The trumpeter started off playing with Tommy Evans (1916–17) and George Reynolds's Keystone Band, worked on riverboats regularly with Creath and Marable, and led the Golden Melody Band during 1920–23. In 1924, he put together the Peacock Orchestra, his main association during the next decade. Other than four months performing at the Cotton Club with Andrew Preer's Orchestra in 1926, Jackson just played in St. Louis or on riverboats. He was barely documented in his career. Other than possibly accompanying singers Missouri Anderson, Luella Miller, and Bert Hatton during 1926–27, there were four memorable songs cut as a leader on June 21, 1926 (including "She's Crying for Me" and "Going to Town"), two hot numbers ("Butter-Finger Blues" and "Crazy Quilt") with Charlie Creath's Jazz-O-Maniacs on May 2, 1927, and a couple of Dixieland standards made with tuba player Singleton Palmer in 1950.

◉ **Jazz in Saint Louis 1924–1927** (Timeless 1-036) has all of the recordings by Creath's Jazz-O-Maniacs and Jackson's Peacock Orchestra. In addition, there are numbers by Phil Baxter's Texas Tomies, the Palledo Orchestra of St. Louis, Benny Washington's Six Aces, Jesse Stone's Blue Serenaders, and the St. Louis Levee Band (an odd Jelly Roll Morton group that performs "Soap Suds"). It is unfortunate that so little of the St. Louis jazz scene was recorded, but lucky that this much survived or Dewey Jackson would have been totally lost to history.

Memphis: Snooks and His Memphis Stompers

Memphis, Tennessee, gained its greatest musical fame as a blues center and an early home base for W.C. Handy. However, there was a solid Memphis jazz scene in the 1920s, particularly during the second half of the decade. **Memphis Stomp** (Frog 24) has sessions recorded by Victor during its field trips to Memphis during 1927–30. Singers Sadie McKinney and Baby Moore are backed by a duet consisting of cornetist Charley Williamson and pianist James Alston, and Jimmie Lunceford's Chickasaw Syncopators performs two numbers ("In Dat Mornin'" and "Sweet Rhythm") from 1930. The bulk of the CD has the complete output of Williamson's Beale Street Frolic Orchestra (four songs and four alternates by a sextet that includes cornetist Williamson and Alston) and the Memphis Stompers (eight numbers and three alternates by a group directed by drummer Snooks Friedman).

In 1929, Friedman brought his Memphis Stompers to New York. Before then, the drummer had played with such territory bands as the Ole Miss Jesters, Meyer Davis, and Hip Bennett. Renamed Snooks and His Memphis Stompers, the band played at the Swanee Club, Roseland, the Crazy Cat Club, and in 1931 at the Paramount Hotel, where they added a string quartet. Forty-one recordings were made during 1931–32, 22 of which are included on **Snooks and His Memphis Stompers** (Parklane 100) (along with 1928's "Memphis Stomp"). None of the sidemen would become famous, but the ensembles had plenty of spirit and the hot dance music is joyous, highlighted by "Hello Beautiful," "I'm Crazy 'Bout My Baby," "One More Time," "Roll On, Mississippi, Roll On" and "Nothing to Do but Love." Snooks Friedman made the recordings just in time, for with the collapse of the record industry, he would have no further chances to record even though the Memphis Stompers stayed together until the beginning of World War II.

Texas: Peck Kelley and Jimmy Joy   In Texas, John "Peck" Kelley became as famous for his desire not to record as for his pianistic abilities. Though he finally relented and recorded some private sessions in the 1950s, there is no documentation at all of him in the 1920s when Peck's Bad Boys were playing regularly in Texas and had among its sidemen Jack Teagarden and Pee Wee Russell. Kelley, who made brief visits to St. Louis (1925), Shreveport, Louisiana (1927), and New Orleans (1934), turned down opportunities to play with Paul Whiteman, Bing Crosby, and the Dorsey Brothers, so there is no way to know how advanced a pianist he was during his early prime years.

Some other Texas musicians fared better. Clarinetist James Maloney, who led a band called the Soul Killers in 1920, renamed his group Jimmy's Joys in 1922 and five years later changed his own name legally to Jimmy Joy. Joy, who occasionally played two clarinets simultaneously (including on records), worked steadily with his group in the 1920s and '30s throughout Texas, Louisville, and the West Coast. **Jimmy's Joys** (Arcadia 2017D) is a two-LP set that has all of his band's 1923–29 recordings except alternate takes. Starting as a sextet influenced by the NORK and to a lesser extent the ODJB, the band grew to 11 pieces by 1928, but never lost its youthful spirit, as can be heard on such numbers as

"Wolverine Blues," "Riverboat Shuffle," "Everybody Stomp," "From Monday On," and "Harmonica Harry." The Jimmy Joy Orchestra (which made a final record date in 1940) lasted until the mid-1940s.

Jazz in Texas 1924–1930 (Timeless 1-033) has music by a variety of Dallas, Houston, and San Antonio bands, including Jimmy Joy's St. Anthony's Hotel Orchestra, Lloyd Finlay, Fatty Martin, Randolph McCurtain's College Ramblers, Leroy's Dallas Band, and Fred Gardner's Texas University Troubadours. While those groups are generally excellent, the main reason to acquire this disc is for "Shadowland Blues," "Dreamland Blues" (the latter two are extended two-sided performances), and "Wabash Blues," the complete recordings of Troy Floyd's Plaza Hotel Orchestra. Tenor saxophonist Herschel Evans made his recording debut on "Dreamland Blues" while trumpeter Don Albert also has a few impressive solos. **Texas & Tennessee Territory Bands** (Retrieval 79006) features five of the best southern territory bands of the 1920s: Blue Steele, Slim Lamar, Mart Britt, Sunny Clapp, and Phil Baxter. The only sidemen who became known later on were cornetist Tony Almerico, clarinetist Sidney Arodin, and pianist Terry Shand, but the musicianship is decent and the music generally swings well on this excellent territory band collection.

The Midwest   While drummer Speed Webb's legendary territory band never made it to records, Alphonso Trent's did. Trent learned piano as a child, led a band in Oklahoma in 1923, and in 1924 took over Eugene Crook's Synco Six, a group based at the time in Little Rock, Arkansas. The Alphonso Trent Orchestra played for several years at the Adolphus Hotel in Dallas and was based in the Southwest through the mid-1930s. ❿ **Richmond Rarities** (Jazz Oracle 8008) has the complete output of four major territory bands including Trent's four sessions. With trumpeter Mouse Randolph, trombonist Snub Mosley, and violinist Stuff Smith starring, the eight selections by Trent include classic versions of "After You've Gone" and "St. James Infirmary." Zach Whyte's Chocolate Brummels (with trumpeter/arranger Sy Oliver, tenor saxophonist Al Sears, and pianist Herman Chittison) also had four record dates, and Red Perkins's Dixie Ramblers sounds exciting in spots, although Alex Jackson's Plantation Orchestra's four numbers (including a memorable "Jackass Blues") often steal the show.

Los Angeles: Paul Howard, Lionel Hampton, and Curtis Mosby   Although Los Angeles had been where Kid Ory's band recorded two pioneering selections in 1922 as the Seven Pods of Pepper Orchestra, and it had a strong local scene during the classic jazz years, many of the bands never made it to records, including Mutt Carey's Liberty Syncopators. Fortunately, Paul Howard's Quality Serenaders was featured on four record dates, for it may have been L.A.'s top jazz band of the time. Howard played cornet, alto, clarinet, oboe, bassoon, flute, and piano before settling on tenor. He moved to Los Angeles in 1913, played with Wood Wilson's Syncopators (1916), Satchel McVea's Howdy Band, Harry Southard's Black and Tan Band, King Oliver, Jelly Roll Morton, and Harvey Brooks's Quality Four (with whom he recorded in 1923) before forming his own Quality Serenaders in 1924. The band was based at Sebastian's Cotton Club (1927–29) and the Kentucky Club. The octet (which grew to ten pieces by 1930) had two players who would be famous in future years: trombonist Lawrence Brown and Lionel Hampton, who at the time was a drummer.

Jazz in California 1923–1930 (Timeless 1-034) has performances by Sonny Clay's Plantation Orchestra, Vic Meyers, Henry Halstead, Reb Spike's Majors and Minors, and Tom Gerunovich's Roof Garden Orchestra, along with the complete output (13 performances) of Paul Howard's Quality Serenaders. Howard's band, playing arrangements by its altoist Charlie Lawrence, featured quite a few excellent soloists, and the ensembles manage to sound both well rehearsed and spontaneous.

While the Quality Serenaders broke up in the early 1930s, Lionel Hampton's career was just beginning. Born in Louisville, Kentucky, Hampton grew up in Alabama, Wisconsin, and Chicago. While working in Chicago as a teenager, he took xylophone lessons from his idol, Jimmy Bertrand. In 1928, Hampton moved to California where he played with the Spikes Brothers and made his recording debut with Paul Howard in 1929. Even at that early stage, his enthusiasm was infectious. Hampton also worked with Les Hite's Orchestra at Sebastian's Cotton Club in Culver City. When Louis Armstrong visited Los Angeles in 1930, he used Hite's big band as a backup group. At a recording session, Armstrong noticed a set of vibes in the studio and asked Hampton if he could play a few notes behind him. Luckily, Hamp had been practicing on vibes and his playing with Armstrong

on "Shine" and "Memories of You" rank as the first significant appearances of the vibraphone on a jazz record. Hampton worked with Les Hite for a few years, studied music at the University of Southern California, and led his own unrecorded band in Los Angeles.

Another Los Angeles band that was on the same high level as Paul Howard's Quality Serenaders was Curtis Mosby's Dixieland Blue Blowers. Mosby was leading a group as early as 1918 in Chicago. After spending time playing music in Oakland and accompanying Mamie Smith for two years, he settled in Los Angeles in 1924. Mosby's band made a two-song test pressing during 1924–25 that was not released until 75 years later. They had three recording dates during 1927–29 that show how exciting a band it was despite its lack of major names; only tenor saxophonist Bumps Myers would make a name for himself in future years. Mosby's Dixieland Blue Blowers appears prominently for a few minutes in the 1929 film *Hallelujah*, probably the first regularly working black orchestra to be heard and seen in a motion picture. **Curtis Mosby and Henry Starr** (Jazz Oracle 8003) has all of the Mosby recordings (other than the soundtrack from *Hallelujah*), including the initial release of the scratchy if historic 1924–25 test pressing. Mosby's eight selections and four alternates from 1927–29 are full of spirit and strong musicianship, with "Weary Stomp," "Whoop 'Em Up Blues," "Hardee Stomp," and the three versions of "Tiger Stomp" (which is really "Tiger Rag") all being quite heated. The pianist during the 1927 session, Henry Starr (who sings on "In My Dreams"), is featured on the second half of this disc. He plays piano on four solo numbers from 1928–29 (singing on two songs), and is teamed with singer Ivan Harold Browning and a rhythm section in London in 1935, performing vocal duets on seven infectious and rather rare performances, including "Let's Go Ballyhoo," "Lulu's Back in Town," and "Truckin'."

Other Parts of the United States   Three worthy CDs feature jazz from unexpected places. **Jazz Is Where You Find It 1924–1930** (Timeless 1-048) collects a variety of obscure but intriguing bands. Cities that are represented include Buffalo (the Blue Ribbon Syncopators and George Warmack), Richmond, Virginia (Roy Johnson's Happy Pals and the Bubbling Over Five), Asheville, North Carolina (Foor-Robinson's Carolina Club Orchestra), Indianapolis

(Charlie Davis's Orchestra), Annapolis (the U.S. Naval Academy Ten playing "Navy Girl" and "My Dream Ship"), Framingham, Massachusetts (Frank Ward), Cleveland (Emerson Gill and Harold Ortli's Ohio State Collegians), Knoxville, Tennessee (Maynard Baird performing "Postage Stomp"), Butte, Montana (Ernest Loomis), St. Paul, Minnesota (George Osborne), Seattle (Jackie Souders), and Minneapolis (Arnold Frank and his Roger's Café Orchestra). **Odds & Bits 1926–1930** (Timeless 1-055) consists of performances by Charlie Straight's Orchestra of 1926 and 1928, Husk O'Hare's Footwarmers, Cline's Collegians from Dallas, Harris Brother's Texans, the Marigold Entertainers, Slatz Randall (a Minneapolis band heard playing a memorable rendition of "Skirts"), Moe Baer's Wardman Park Orchestra, George Belshaw's KFAB Orchestra, Herman Waldman, and Henry Lange; these performances are drawn from the Brunswick/Vocalion catalog. **Gennett Rarities** (Jazz Oracle 8009) starts with selected performances from bands recorded in Birmingham, Alabama (the Triangle Harmony Boys, Eddie Miles's Florentine Orchestra, pianist George Tremer, Dunk Rendleman's Alabamians, Frank Bunch's Fuzzy Wuzzies, and the Black Birds of Paradise). All four songs that the latter group recorded are here, including an excellent "Bugahoma Blues" and a hilariously clam-filled "Tishomingo Blues." Also on this disc are the four hot numbers recorded by Syd Valentine's Patent Leather Kids (a trio with trumpeter Valentine, pianist Slick Helms, and banjoist Paul George recorded in Richmond, Indiana), and four songs in which the Patent Leather Kids accompany singer Horace Smith.

Jazz in England

In addition to spreading across the United States during the 1920s, jazz also began to be heard in Europe, particularly in England. Although thought of as American music, as early as the 1920s, there were a few significant jazz bands heard in England that were carving out their own paths.

Fred Elizalde, Jack Hylton, and Spike Hughes   England had welcomed the Original Dixieland Jazz Band as early as 1919, and although its jazz scene was mostly pretty derivative in the 1920s, there were a few worthwhile jazz bands that were struggling to survive. Probably the first musician based in England to make at least a small impression in the jazz world was Fred Elizalde. Born in the Philippines, Elizalde was a child prodigy, composing a minuet when he was four. Elizalde had extensive classical training in England, Spain, and the United States, attending Stanford University. **Fred Elizalde and the Hollywood/Sunset Bands** (Timeless 1-061) features the pianist leading a fine nonet in 1926, holding his own with the other Americans on eight performances and taking "Siam Blues" as a piano solo. Also on this disc of rarities are a variety of other obscure Los Angeles–based dance bands (most with unidentified personnel) from 1924–26 on performances that were made for the tiny Hollywood and Sunset labels.

While attending Cambridge University in England later in 1926, Elizalde became the leader of the Quinquaginta Ramblers, playing piano and arranging. After a period of freelancing, Elizalde opened at London's Savoy Hotel in 1928 with an impressive band that was comprised of both English and American musicians, including several former members of the California Ramblers. Fred Elizalde's big band recorded 39 selections in 1928 and four others in 1929, 22 of which are on ◉ **The Best of Fred Elizalde and His Anglo American Band** (Retrieval 79011). Trumpeters Chelsea Quealey and Norman Payne, Bobby Davis on clarinet and alto, Adrian Rollini (bass sax, goofus, and hot fountain pen), Fud Livingston, and tenor saxophonist Arthur Rollini (Adrian's younger brother) all have their spots, while guitarist Al Bowlly (who would become famous with Ray Noble a few years later) has three vocals. Elizalde, who has some piano solos, provided the arrangements, which are mostly quite jazz-oriented, making this the finest non-American jazz orchestra of the 1920s. But jazz (except in a watered-down form) was not considered all that acceptable in England at the time. Fred Elizalde's Orchestra did not have its contract renewed at the Savoy Hotel in September 1928. After a tour of England and Scotland, the pianist reluctantly broke up the band in 1929. Elizalde studied classical music in Spain and with Maurice Ravel in France (1930–32), made a few final jazz recordings (mostly piano solos) in England during 1932–33, and then spent the rest of his life playing and composing classical music.

While Fred Elizalde did not stay committed to jazz very long, Jack Hylton managed to balance dance music with jazz in England and led his orchestra for many years. Hylton danced and sang in shows from the age of seven. Although he had early gigs playing piano and organ, Hylton was much more significant as a bandleader, starting in 1921. By the latter part of the decade, he was considered one of England's biggest names, the country's Paul Whiteman, with his orchestra appearing in vaudeville, on stage, constantly on the radio, on records (some of which were jazz-oriented), and in tours of the European continent. The LP **Jack Hylton and His Orchestra** (GNP/Crescendo 9017), which dates from 1931–33, has a remarkable "Ellingtonia Medley," which finds the band sounding very close to Duke Ellington's on "Black and Tan Fantasy," "Mood Indigo," "It Don't Mean a Thing," and "Bugle Call Rag." Other highlights include "St. Louis Blues," "Black and Blue Rhythm," "Some of These Days," a "42nd Street Medley," and a version of "Dinah" on which the group imitates Guy Lombardo, Tommy Dorsey, Louis Armstrong, Bing Crosby, and Joe Venuti among others.

Spike Hughes was a fine British bassist who was also an advanced arranger/composer, but like Fred Elizalde, his time in jazz would be brief. Hughes played bass with the band at Cambridge University and led a series of record dates during 1930–32 (with his Decca-Dents) that utilized some of the top British jazz musicians plus Americans Sylvester Ahola and Bobby Davis. The pair of two-CD sets ◐ **Vols. 1 & 2** (Kings Cross 001/002) and **Vols. 3 & 4** (Kings Cross 003/004) have all of Hughes's British recordings. **Vols. 1 & 2** feature such interesting soloists as trumpeters Sylvester Ahola, Max Goldberg, and Norman Payne, altoist Philip Buchel, clarinetist Danny Polo, and Buddy Featherstonhaugh on tenor. In addition, Muggsy Spanier guests on one cut and Jimmy Dorsey sounds quite remarkable (particularly on "I'm Just Wild About Harry") during his session with Hughes's Three Blind Mice, a small group taken out of the orchestra. Not all of the performances are classic (some of the vocals are just adequate), but there is an awful lot of rewarding music to be heard, much of it little known. The same can be said for **Vols. 3 & 4,** which almost come up to the same level, featuring Hughes leading larger bands and has Norman Payne and Buddy Featherstonhaugh often taking solo honors. Taken as a whole, these discs contain some of the finest British jazz of the era.

Ranging from 1925–37, ◐ **Hot British Dance Bands** (Timeless 1-005) has 22 selections from 22 different British bands heard at their most torrid. Programmed in chronological order, highlights include the Kit-Cat Band (in 1925) playing "Riverboat Shuffle," the Devonshire Restaurant Dance Band's "Sugar Foot Stomp," Jack Hylton's "Tiger Rag," the Arcadians Dance Orchestra on "'Leven-Thirty

Saturday Night," Madame Tussaud's Dance Orchestra's "Rockin' in Rhythm," Harry Roy's "Milenburg Joys," and Ambrose's remarkable "Cotton Pickers' Congregation." None of these bands featured jazz on a full-time basis, but these recordings show they could hold their own with many of their American counterparts.

World Travelers

While some of the early New Orleans players left town to travel in the South, Sidney Bechet and the orchestra led by pianist Sam Wooding helped introduce jazz to many areas of Europe. Their music was considered exotic and a bit strange, but the joyful rhythms and general excitement drew many younger Europeans to the music, some of whom would later become jazz musicians themselves.

Sam Wooding and Sidney Bechet　While England had American jazz musicians visiting as early as 1919, it was up to the Sam Wooding Orchestra to introduce jazz to many other countries. Wooding worked as a pianist in Atlantic City during 1912–14. After serving in the Army during World War I, in 1919 he began leading his Society Syncopators. In May 1925, Wooding and his orchestra sailed for Europe where they accompanied the *Chocolate Kiddies* revue. During the next couple of years, Wooding's band played all over the European continent, including in Berlin, Scandinavia, Russia, Turkey, Romania, Hungary, Italy, and England. Their performances were often historic and significant in introducing jazz to many areas where the music had never been heard before. The Sam Wooding Orchestra included Tommy Ladnier, trombonist Herb Flemming, Garvin Bushell on reeds, altoist Willie Lewis, and clarinetist Gene Sedric among the key sidemen. They recorded 18 selections in Berlin during two record dates in 1925–26. Wooding and his ensemble also played in South America before returning to the United States in the summer of 1927. After appearances on the East Coast, the orchestra (with Ladnier, Lewis, Sedric, trumpeter Doc Cheatham, trombonist Albert Wynn, and pianist Freddy Johnson in the personnel) went back to Europe in June 1928, playing in Germany, Scandinavia, France, Italy, and Spain during the next three years. Wooding's band recorded 31 songs during sessions in Barcelona and Paris in 1929 and 1931.

Few of Wooding's recordings have appeared on CD. The LP **Sam Wooding's Chocolate Kiddies** (Jazz

Panorama 20) has 15 of the numbers from 1925 and 1929, and shows the sometimes uncomfortable balancing act that the band attempted between jazz, dance music, and exuberant (but quickly dated) novelty effects. However, by spending so much time overseas, the Sam Wooding Orchestra fell behind the times, particularly by 1931. It broke up in Belgium in November of that year, and although Wooding made further attempts to organize orchestras in the United States, none was successful. However, he had accomplished a great deal in spreading the message of jazz around the world.

Sidney Bechet spent many of the same years overseas too, although his style was timeless and stayed consistently inspired. He returned to Europe in September 1925, playing in Paris with the *Revue Negre*, which featured Josephine Baker (who became a huge hit) and Claude Hopkins's Orchestra. After leaving the show in February 1926, Bechet toured Russia for three months, led a band in Berlin, joined Noble Sissle's Orchestra in the summer of 1928, and worked with Benny Peyton in France. The hot-tempered Bechet was jailed in Paris for 11 months due to a shooting incident with banjoist Mike McKendrick. After his release, he played in Berlin and Amsterdam before returning to New York. Bechet rejoined Sissle in early 1931 and in 1932 co-led the New Orleans Feetwarmers with Tommy Ladnier. That explosive band (which Bechet hoped would help bring back New Orleans jazz) recorded six memorable numbers on September 15, 1932, but folded by early 1933 because its spontaneous and heated style failed to catch on during the worst period of the Depression.

Kansas City: The Beginnings of Swing

Despite Prohibition and the Depression, there was no lack of work for talented black musicians in Kansas City, Missouri. A wide-open city run by a corrupt local government, Kansas City was full of gambling joints, bootleg liquor, and nightclubs that rarely closed. The environment was perfect for musicians eager to play. Starting in the early 1920s and continuing to the late '30s, marathon jam sessions were the norm, and out of these all-night affairs came ideas that would later invigorate the swing era, particularly through the Count Basie Orchestra.

George E. Lee, Walter Page, Andy Kirk, Mary Lou Williams, and Bennie Moten   George E. Lee played baritone sax and piano in a U.S. Army band in 1917.

After his discharge, he came home to Kansas City and organized George E. Lee's Singing Orchestra, a constant fixture in local clubs during 1920–40. Lee's band recorded two numbers in 1927 and six fairly sophisticated charts (mostly by Jesse Stone) in 1929, including three songs in which they backed the vocals of Lee's sister Julia Lee. Best known among the sidemen was tenor saxophonist Budd Johnson.

Another Kansas City band that was highly rated was Walter Page's Blue Devils. Page started off playing tuba and bass drum in local brass bands, switching to string bass while in high school. He was an early member of the Bennie Moten Orchestra (1918–23, mostly on tuba and baritone sax). After touring in 1925 and getting stranded with trombonist Emir Coleman's group in Oklahoma City, Page became its leader. Walter Page's Blue Devils for six years was considered the top jazz combo in the Kansas City area, with such sidemen at various times as trumpeter Hot Lips Page, pianist Count Basie, tenor saxophonist Lester Young, and singer Jimmy Rushing. But Moten, keen to eliminate his competitors, one by one lured away each of Page's key artists, offering them better pay and steadier work. Page's Blue Devils, which only recorded two selections during its six-year existence, was a casualty of the Depression. In 1931, Walter Page gave up, left the band to trumpeter James Simpson, and joined Moten himself.

◐ What Kind of Rhythm Is That? (Frog 31) has all of the numbers by George E. Lee's Orchestra (with and without Julia Lee) and the two performances ("Blue Devil Blues" and "Squabblin'") by Walter Page's Blue Devils. In addition, this CD has all the existing performances by some other groups from different cities: Bill Brown's Brownies, the Chickasaw Syncopators (Jimmie Lunceford's debut recordings from 1927), Maynard Baird's Southern Serenaders, Hunter's Serenaders (with a guest vocal by Victoria Spivey), and Grant Moore's New Orleans Black Devils. This is a very valuable release, both historically and musically.

The one Kansas City orchestra of the late 1920s to make it into the 1940s was Andy Kirk's Twelve Clouds of Joy. Kirk played bass sax and tuba, but was not much of a musician, never soloing or writing any music. He grew up in Denver, worked with George Morrison's band starting in 1918, and in 1925 moved to Dallas where he joined Terrence Holder's Dark Clouds of Joy. A money dispute resulted in Holder departing in

January 1929, and Kirk was elected the band's leader. He switched the group's home base to Kansas City where it worked steadily during the next seven years.

Although not a member of Kirk's orchestra yet, Mary Lou Williams (born Mary Elfrieda Scruggs) was the band's solo star during its 1929–30 recordings. She grew up in Pittsburgh and attracted a great deal of attention with her brilliant piano playing. Williams was self-taught as a musician and working in public from the age of six (using the name Mary Lou Burley). She toured throughout the Midwest as a teenager and married saxophonist John Williams when she was 16. Mary Lou Williams's first recordings were made in 1927 (eight titles with the Synco Jazzers that were released under the names of either singer Jeanette James or John Williams). When her husband joined Terence Holder's Dark Clouds of Joy later in the year, Mary Lou took over leadership of the Synco Jazzers for a time. In 1929 when Andy Kirk was the new leader of the renamed Twelve Clouds of Joy, Mary Lou Williams was often present at the band's performances. She started contributing arrangements to the group and subbed on piano for their first recording sessions in November. Because she fit in so well, the record label's producers insisted that she be on piano for all of Kirk's other recordings from 1929–30. A superb stride player, Williams made her first two solo piano records ("Night Life" and "Drag 'Em") in 1930, finally becoming Kirk's regular pianist the following year.

◉ 1929–1931 (Classics 655) has all 25 recordings by Andy Kirk's early orchestra, including two numbers originally issued as being by John Williams's Memphis Stompers and three selections in which the band accompanied Blanche Calloway. With Mary Lou Williams, violinist Claude Williams, baritonist John Williams, clarinetist John Harrington, and trumpeters Gene Prince and Edgar "Puddinghead" Battle, this was one of the hottest bands in Kansas City during the era. Highlights include "Blue Clarinet Stomp," "Cloudy," "Lotta Sax Appeal," "Mary's Idea," and "Once or Twice." Surviving a takeover attempt by Blanche Calloway, the Andy Kirk Orchestra (even though it made no recordings during 1932–35) was a popular attraction in Kansas City during the worst years of the Depression.

Saving the most important Kansas City band of the time for last, the Bennie Moten Orchestra overshadowed all of its competitors. Moten played baritone horn at 12 but soon switched to piano. He led a ragtime trio (called BB & D) during 1918–21 and in 1922 expanded to a sextet that over time grew to become a big band. His orchestra first recorded in 1923, making a dozen songs for the Okeh label, including a hit record of "South." All are on **1923–1927** (Classics 549), along with Moten's first Victor recordings of 1926–27.

Although the Bennie Moten Orchestra visited New York in the fall of 1928, the big band remained based in Kansas City where it gradually lured away most of the members of its top competitor, Walter Page's Blue Devils. By October 1929, Count Basie was the band's pianist on all of its recordings, with Moten only actually playing a few numbers a night in clubs. Other key sidemen included trumpeter Ed Lewis, Eddie Durham on trombone and guitar, Harlan Leonard on reeds, baritonist Jack Washington, Hot Lips Page, Jimmy Rushing, Bennie's brother Buster Moten on occasional accordion, and Walter Page himself by 1931.

Moten and his orchestra recorded regularly for Victor during 1926–30, and these performances often approach the level of Fletcher Henderson's. **South** (Bluebird 3139) and **Basie Beginnings** (Bluebird 9768) are samplers that contain some (but not all) of the band's highpoints. Much better are ◉ **Vol. 1—Justrite** (Frog 29) and ◉ **Vol. 2— Kansas City Breakdown** (Frog 30) since those two CDs have all of the band's performances from late 1926 to late 1929, including quite a few rare and never-before-released alternate takes. Among the many memorable performances are "Kansas City Shuffle," "Sugar," "The New Tulsa Blues," "Moten Stomp," "Kansas City Breakdown," "Get Low Down Blues," a remake of "South," "Terrific Stomp," and "That Certain Motion." Two of the Classics releases, **1929–1930** (Classics 578) and **1930–1932** (Classics 591), continue where the Frog series has thus far left off. **1929–1930** (which has Count Basie taking over on piano) includes "New Goofy Dust Rag," "Band Box Shuffle," "Boot It," and "New Vine Street Blues."

The music on **1930–1932**, particularly the marathon date of December 13, 1932, leads directly to the music of the late 1930s. Hot Lips Page, tenor saxophonist Ben Webster, and Count Basie are among the key soloists on such swinging numbers as "Blue Room," "Lafayette," and the original version of "Moten Swing." One can hear, in the light rhythms, the riffing horns, and the advanced solos that the swing era was not far in the future.

VOICES OF THE FUTURE

Bucky Pizzarelli (guitar), Jan. 9, 1926, Paterson, NJ

Melba Liston (arranger, composer, trombone), Jan. 13, 1926, Kansas City, MO

Curtis Counce (bass), Jan. 23, 1926, Kansas City, MO

Bobby Jaspar (tenor, flute), Feb. 20, 1926, Liege, Belgium

Stan Levey (drums), Apr. 5, 1926, Philadelphia, PA

Randy Weston (piano, composer), Apr. 6, 1926, Brooklyn, NY

Blossom Dearie (vocals, piano, composer), Apr. 28, 1926, East Durham, NY

Jimmy Cleveland (trombone), May 3, 1926, Watrace, TN

Miles Davis (trumpet, leader), May 25, 1926, Alton, IL

Bud Shank (alto, flute), May 27, 1926, Dayton, OH

Russ Freeman (piano), May 28, 1926, Chicago, IL

Johnny Coles (trumpet), July 3, 1926, Trenton, NJ

Ray Copeland (trumpet), July 17, 1926, Norfolk, VA

Urbie Green (trombone), Aug. 8, 1926, Mobile, AL

Mal Waldron (piano, composer), Aug. 16, 1926, New York, NY

Frank Rosolino (trombone), Aug. 20, 1926, Detroit, MI

Ernie Henry (alto), Sept. 3, 1926, Brooklyn, NY

Jack McDuff (organ), Sept. 17, 1926, Champaign, IL

Bill Smith (clarinet), Sept. 22, 1926, Sacramento, CA

John Coltrane (tenor, soprano, leader), Sept. 23, 1926, Hamlet, NC

Julie London (vocals), Sept. 26, 1926, Santa Rosa, CA

Oscar Brown, Jr. (vocals, lyricist), Oct. 10, 1926, Chicago, IL

Terry Gibbs (vibes), Oct. 13, 1926, Brooklyn, NY

Ray Brown (bass), Oct. 13, 1926. Pittsburgh, PA

Don Elliott (mellophone, vibes, trumpet), Oct. 21, 1926, Somerville, NJ

Jimmy Heath (tenor, soprano, arranger, composer), Oct. 25, 1926, Philadelphia, PA

Lou Donaldson (alto), Nov. 1, 1926, Badin, NC

Billy Mitchell (tenor), Nov. 3, 1926, Kansas City, MO

George Masso (trombone), Nov. 17, 1926, Cranston, RI

Claude Williamson (piano), Nov. 18, 1926, Brattleboro, VT

Allen Eager (tenor), Jan. 10, 1927, New York, NY

J.R. Monterose (tenor), Jan. 19, 1927, Detroit, MI

Antonio Carlos Jobim (composer, piano), Jan. 25, 1927, Rio de Janeiro, Brazil

Ronnie Scott (tenor), Jan. 28, 1927, London, England

Ahmed Abdul-Malik (bass), Jan. 30, 1927, New York, NY

Stan Getz (tenor), Feb. 2, 1927, Philadelphia, PA

Don Fagerquist (trumpet), Feb. 6, 1927, Worcester, MA

Buck Hill (tenor), Feb. 13, 1927, Washington, D.C.

Dick Hyman (piano), Mar. 8, 1927, New York, NY

Ruby Braff (cornet), Mar. 16, 1927, Boston, MA

Bill Barron (tenor, soprano), Mar. 27, 1927, Philadelphia, PA

Amos Milburn (vocals, piano), Apr. 1, 1927, Houston, TX

Gerry Mulligan (baritone, arranger, composer), Apr. 6, 1927, New York, NY

Walter Bishop, Jr. (piano), Apr. 10, 1927, New York, NY

Connie Kay (drums), Apr. 27, 1927, Tuckahoe, NY

Big Jay McNeely (tenor), Apr. 29, 1927, Watts, CA

Bill Holman (arranger, composer, leader), May 21, 1927, Olive, CA

Dick Hafer (tenor), May 29, 1927, Wyomissing, PA

Red Holloway (tenor, alto), May 31, 1927, Helena, AR

Attila Zoller (guitar), June 13, 1927, Visegrad, Hungary

Doc Severinsen (trumpet), July 7, 1927, Arlington, OR

Conte Candoli (trumpet), July 12, 1927, Mishawaka, IN

Danny Moss (tenor), Aug. 16, 1927, Redhill, England

Jimmy Raney (guitar), Aug. 20, 1927, Louisville, KY

Martial Solal (piano), Aug. 23, 1927, Algiers, Algeria

Elvin Jones (drums, leader), Sept. 9, 1927, Pontiac, MI

Jackie Paris (vocals), Sept. 20, 1927, Nutley, NJ

Johnny Dankworth (alto, clarinet, leader), Sept. 20, 1927, London, England

Red Mitchell (bass, piano), Sept. 20, 1927, New York, NY

Red Rodney (trumpet), Sept. 27, 1927, Philadelphia, PA

Lee Konitz (alto), Oct. 13, 1927, Chicago, IL

Sonny Criss (alto), Oct. 23, 1927, Memphis, TN

Warne Marsh (tenor), Oct. 26, 1927, Los Angeles, CA

Cleo Laine (vocals), Oct. 28, 1927, Southall, Middlesex, England

Chris Connor (vocals), Nov. 8, 1927, Kansas City, MO

Mose Allison (vocals, piano, composer), Nov. 11, 1927, Tippo, MS

Dolo Coker (piano), Nov. 16, 1927, Hartford, CT

Charlie Palmieri (piano), Nov. 21, 1927, New York, NY

Jimmy Knepper (trombone), Nov. 22, 1927, Los Angeles, CA

Dick Wellstood (piano), Nov. 25, 1927, Greenwich, CT

Gene Quill (alto), Dec. 15, 1927, Atlantic City, NJ

Ernie Andrews (vocals), Dec. 25, 1927, Philadelphia, PA

Bill Crow (bass), Dec. 27, 1927, Othello, WA

VOICES OF THE FUTURE

Ruth Brown (vocals), Jan. 12, 1928, Portsmouth, VA

Harold Land (tenor), Feb. 18, 1928, Houston, TX

Pierre Michelot (bass), Mar. 3, 1928, St. Denis, France

Lou Levy (piano), Mar. 5, 1928, Chicago, IL

Wilbur Little (bass), Mar. 5, 1928, Parmele, NC

Bob Wilber (clarinet, soprano), Mar. 15, 1928, New York, NY

Lem Winchester (vibes), Mar. 19, 1928, Philadelphia, PA

Fraser MacPherson (tenor), Apr. 10, 1928, Winnipeg, Canada

Ken Colyer (trumpet, guitar, leader), Apr. 12, 1928, Great Yarmouth, England

Teddy Charles (vibes), Apr. 13, 1928, Chicopee Falls, MA

Tommy Turrentine (trumpet), Apr. 22, 1928, Pittsburgh, PA

Johnny Griffin (tenor), Apr. 24, 1928, Chicago, IL

Willis "Gator" Jackson (tenor), Apr. 25, 1928, Miami, FL

Lars Gullin (baritone), May 4, 1928, Visby, Sweden

Maynard Ferguson (trumpet, leader), May 4, 1928, Montreal, Quebec, Canada

Joe Gordon (trumpet), May 15, 1928, Boston, MA

Jackie Cain (vocals), May 22, 1928, Milwaukee, WI

Rosemary Clooney (vocals), May 23, 1928, Maysville, KY

Freddie Redd (piano, composer), May 29, 1928, New York, NY

Bob Gordon (baritone), June 11, 1928, St. Louis, MO

Eric Dolphy (alto, flute, bass clarinet), June 20, 1928, Los Angeles, CA

Bill Russo (arranger, composer), June 25, 1928, Chicago, IL

Don Lanphere (tenor, soprano), June 26, 1928, Wenatchee, WA

Richard Wyands (piano), July 2, 1928, Oakland, CA

Leroy Vinnegar (bass), July 13, 1928, Indianapolis, IN

Joe Harriott (alto, tenor), July 15, 1928, Kingston, Jamaica

Bola Sete (composer, guitar), July 16, 1928, Rio de Janeiro, Brazil

Joe Morello (drums), July 17, 1928, Springfield, MA

Vince Guaraldi (piano, composer), July 17, 1928, San Francisco, CA

Carl Fontana (trombone), July 18, 1928, Monroe, LA

Keeter Betts (bass), July 22, 1928, Port Chester, NY

Carl Perkins (piano), Aug. 16, 1928, Indianapolis, IN

Art Farmer (flugelhorn, trumpet), Aug. 21, 1928, Council Bluffs, IA

Peter Appleyard (vibes), Aug. 26, 1928, Cleethorpes, England

Kenny Drew (piano), Aug. 28, 1928, New York, NY

Horace Silver (piano, composer, leader), Sept. 2, 1928, Norwalk, CT

Albert Mangelsdorff (trombone), Sept. 5, 1928, Frankfurt am Main, Germany

Cannonball Adderley (alto), Sept. 15, 1928, Tampa, FL

Frank Foster (tenor, arranger, composer), Sept. 23, 1928, Cincinnati, OH

Jon Eardley (trumpet), Sept. 30, 1928, Altoona, PA

Junior Mance (piano), Oct. 10, 1928, Chicago, IL

Clare Fischer (piano, keyboards, composer, arranger), Oct. 22, 1928, Durand, MI

Herb Geller (alto), Nov. 2, 1928, Los Angeles, CA

Ernestine Anderson (vocals), Nov. 11, 1928, Houston, TX

Hampton Hawes (piano), Nov. 13, 1928, Los Angeles, CA

Etta Jones (vocals), Nov. 25, 1928, Aiken, SC

Moe Koffman (flute, tenor), Dec. 28, 1928, Toronto, Ontario, Canada

Jack Montrose (tenor, arranger), Dec. 30, 1928, Detroit, MI

Joe Pass (guitar), Jan. 13, 1929, New Brunswick, NJ

Jimmy Cobb (drums), Jan. 20, 1929, Washington, D.C.

Benny Golson (tenor, arranger, composer), Jan. 25, 1929, Philadelphia, PA

Acker Bilk (clarinet), Jan. 28, 1929, Pensford, Somerset, England

Floyd Dixon (piano, vocals), Feb. 8, 1929, Marshall, TX

Fred Anderson (tenor), Mar. 22, 1929, Monroe, LA

Buster Cooper (trombone), Apr. 4, 1929, St. Petersburg, FL

Andre Previn (piano, composer), Apr. 6, 1929, Berlin, Germany

Art Taylor (drums), Apr. 6, 1929, New York, NY

Barbara Lea (vocals), Apr. 10, 1929, Detroit, MI

Ray Barretto (conga), Apr. 29, 1929, New York, NY

Mel Lewis (drums, leader), May 10, 1929, Buffalo, NY

Larance Marable (drums), May 21, 1929, Los Angeles, CA

Clora Bryant (trumpet), May 30, 1929, Denison, TX

Lennie Niehaus (alto, arranger), June 1, 1929, St. Louis, MO

VOICES OF THE FUTURE

Jackie Coon (flugelhorn), June 21, 1929, Beatrice, NE

Alex Welsh (cornet), July 9, 1929, Edinburgh, Scotland

Alan Dawson (drums), July 14, 1929, Marietta, PA

Charlie Persip (drums), July 26, 1929, Morristown, NJ

Lorez Alexandria (vocals), Aug. 14, 1929, Chicago, IL

Bill Evans (piano), Aug. 16, 1929, Plainfield, NJ

Prince Lasha (flute), Sept. 10, 1929, Ft. Worth, TX

Charles Moffett (drums), Sept. 11, 1929, Fort Worth, TX

Joe Temperley (baritone, soprano), Sept. 20, 1929, Cowdenbeath, Scotland

John Carter (clarinet), Sept. 24, 1929, Fort Worth, TX

Howard Roberts (guitar), Oct. 2, 1929, Phoenix, AZ

Ed Blackwell (drums), Oct. 10, 1929, New Orleans, LA

Gabe Baltazar (alto), Nov. 1, 1929, Hilo, HI

Francy Boland (piano, arranger), Nov. 6, 1929, Namur, Belgium

Sheila Jordan (vocals), Nov. 18, 1929, Detroit, MI

Pat Patrick (baritone, alto), Nov. 23, 1929, East Moline, IL

Toshiko Akiyoshi (arranger, piano, leader), Dec. 12, 1929, Dairen, China

Barry Harris (piano), Dec. 15, 1929, Detroit, MI

Bob Brookmeyer (valve trombone, arranger), Dec. 19, 1929, Kansas City, MO

Chet Baker (trumpet, vocals), Dec. 23, 1929, Yale, OK

Monty Budwig (bass), Dec. 26, 1929, Pender, NE

Oscar Klein (trumpet, guitar), Jan. 5, 1930, Graz, Austria

Jack Nimitz (baritone), Jan. 11, 1930, Washington, D.C.

Johnny Varro (piano), Jan. 11, 1930, Brooklyn, NY

Kenny Wheeler (trumpet, flugelhorn), Jan. 14, 1930, Toronto, Ontario, Canada

Spike Robinson (tenor), Jan. 16, 1930, Kenosha, WI

Derek Bailey (guitar), Jan. 29, 1930, Sheffield, England

Buddy Montgomery (piano, vibes), Jan. 30, 1930, Indianapolis, IN

Joe Maini (alto), Feb. 8, 1930, Providence, RI

Marty Grosz (guitar, vocals), Feb. 28, 1930, Berlin, Germany

Ornette Coleman (alto, composer), Mar. 9, 1930, Fort Worth, TX

Blue Mitchell (trumpet) Mar. 13, 1930, Miami, FL

Tommy Flanagan (piano), Detroit, MI, Mar. 16, 1930

Grover Mitchell (trombone, leader), Mar. 17, 1930, Whatley, AL

Paul Horn (flute, alto), Mar. 17, 1930, New York, NY

Bill Henderson (vocals), Mar. 19, 1930, Chicago, IL

Ornette Coleman (alto, composer, leader), Mar. 19, 1930, Fort Worth, TX

Claude Bolling (piano, leader), Apr. 10, 1930, Cannes, France

Richard Davis (bass), Apr. 15, 1930, Chicago, IL

Herbie Mann (flute), Apr. 16, 1930, Brooklyn, NY

Sam Noto (trumpet), Apr. 17, 1930, Buffalo, NY

Chris Barber (trombone), Apr. 17, 1930, Welwyn Garden City, England

Frank Strazzeri (piano), Apr. 24, 1930, Rochester, NY

Papa Bue Jensen (trombone, leader), May 8, 1930, Copenhagen, Denmark

Betty Carter (singer), May 16, 1930, Flint, MI

Kenny Ball (trumpet), May 22, 1930, Ilford, Essex, England

Dave McKenna (piano), May 30, 1930, Woonsocket, RI

Ahmad Jamal (piano, leader), July 2, 1930, Pittsburgh, PA

Pete Fountain (clarinet), July 3, 1930, New Orleans, LA

Hank Mobley (tenor), July 7, 1930, Eastman, GA

Helen Merrill (vocals), July 21, 1930, New York, NY

Richie Kamuca (tenor), July 23, 1930, Philadelphia, PA

Annie Ross (vocals, composer), July 25, 1930, Mitcham, England

Abbey Lincoln (vocals, composer), Aug. 6, 1930, Chicago, IL

Eddie Costa (piano), Aug. 14, 1930, Atlas, PA

Sonny Rollins (tenor, composer, leader), Sept. 7, 1930, New York, NY

Bill Berry (trumpet), Sept. 14, 1930, Benton Harbor, MI

Muhal Richard Abrams (piano/composer), Sept. 19, 1930, Chicago, IL

Ray Charles (vocals, piano, leader), Sept. 23, 1930, Albany, GA

Nancy Harrow (vocals), Oct. 3, 1930, New York, NY

George Girard (trumpet, vocals), Oct. 7, 1930, New Orleans, LA

Pepper Adams (baritone), Oct. 8, 1930, Highland Park, MI

Clifford Brown (trumpet), Oct. 30, 1930, Wilmington, DE

Booker Ervin (tenor), Nov. 31, 1930, Denison, TX

Jim Hall (guitar), Dec. 4, 1930, Buffalo, NY

Sam Most (flute, tenor), Dec. 16, 1930, Atlantic City, NJ

VOICES OF THE FUTURE

Ed Thigpen (drums), Dec. 28, 1930, Chicago, IL

Walter Dickerson (vibes), 1931, Philadelphia, PA

John Jenkins (alto), Jan. 3, 1931, Chicago, IL

Dizzy Reece (trumpet), Jan. 5, 1931, Kingston, Jamaica

Horace Parlan (piano), Jan. 19, 1931, Pittsburgh, PA

John Pisano (guitar), Feb. 6, 1931, Staten Island, NY

Max Collie (trombone), Feb. 21, 1931, Melbourne,
Australia

Paul Motian (drums, leader), Mar. 25, 1931,
Philadelphia, PA

Jake Hanna (drums), Apr. 4, 1931, Roxbury, MA

Dick Twardzik (piano), Apr. 30, 1931, Danvers, MA

Ira Sullivan (trumpet, tenor, alto, soprano, flute),
May 1, 1931, Washington, D.C.

Richard "Groove" Holmes (organ), May 2, 1931,
Camden, NJ

Richard Williams (trumpet), May 4, 1931,
Galveston, TX

Dewey Redman (tenor), May 17, 1931, Ft. Worth, TX

Jackie McLean (alto), May 17, 1931, New York, NY

Louis Smith (trumpet), May 20, 1931, Memphis, TN

Joao Gilberto (vocals, guitar), June 1931,
Bahia, Brazil

Grant Green (guitar), June 6, 1931, St. Louis, MO

Plas Johnson (tenor), July 21, 1931,
Donaldsonville, LA

Sonny Clark (piano), July 21, 1931, Herminie, PA

Kenny Burrell (guitar), July 31, 1931, Detroit, MI

Derek Smith (piano), Aug. 17, 1931, London, England

Frank Capp (drums, leader), Aug. 20, 1931,
Worchester, MA

Willie Ruff (bass, French horn), Sept. 1, 1931,
Sheffield, AL

Clifford Jordan (tenor), Sept. 2, 1931, Chicago, IL

Ken McIntyre (alto, flute, oboe, bassoon, bass clarinet),
Sept. 7, 1931, Boston, MA

Freddy Cole (vocals, piano), Oct. 15, 1931, Chicago, IL

John Gilmore (tenor), Oct. 29, 1931, Summit, MS

Phil Woods (alto, leader), Nov. 2, 1931, Springfield, MA

Nat Adderley (cornet), Nov. 25, 1931, Tampa, FL

Jack Sheldon (trumpet, vocals), Nov. 30, 1931,
Jacksonville, FL

Wynton Kelly (piano), Dec. 2, 1931, Jamaica, British
West Indies

Phineas Newborn (piano), Dec. 14, 1931, Whiteville, TN

Ray Bryant (piano), Dec. 24, 1931, Philadelphia, PA

Walter Norris (piano), Dec. 27, 1931, Little Rock, AR

Grady Tate (drums, vocals), Jan. 14, 1932, Durham, NC

Irene Kral (vocals), Jan. 18, 1932, Chicago, IL

Jodie Christian (piano), Feb. 2, 1932, Chicago, IL

Sir Roland Hanna (piano), Feb. 10, 1932, Detroit, MI

Eddie Higgins (piano), Feb. 21, 1932, Cambridge, MA

Michel Legrand (composer, arranger, piano), Feb. 24,
1932, Paris, France

Leroy Jenkins (violin), Mar. 11, 1932, Chicago, IL

Mark Murphy (vocals), Mar. 14, 1932, Syracuse, NY

Slide Hampton (trombone), Apr. 4, 1932, Jeanette, PA

Andy Simpkins (bass), Apr. 29, 1932, Richmond, IN

David Izenzon (bass), May 17, 1932, Pittsburgh, PA

Bob Florence (piano, arranger, composer, leader),
May 20, 1932, Los Angeles, CA

Dakota Staton (vocals), June 3, 1932, Pittsburgh, PA

Oliver Nelson (tenor, alto, soprano, arranger, composer),
June 4, 1932, St. Louis, MO

Pete Jolly (piano), June 5, 1932, New Haven, CT

Tina Brooks (tenor), June 7, 1932, Fayetteville, NC

Lalo Schifrin (piano, arranger, composer), June 21, 1932,
Buenos Aires, Argentina

George Gruntz (piano, arranger, composer, leader),
June 24, 1932, Basel, Switzerland

Joe Zawinul (keyboards, composer), July 7, 1932, Vienna,
Austria

Dorothy Ashby (harp), Aug. 6, 1932, Detroit, MI

Duke Pearson (piano, arranger, composer), Aug. 17,
1932, Atlanta, GA

Walter Davis, Jr. (piano), Sept. 2, 1932, Richmond, VA

Wilbur Ware (bass), Sept. 8, 1932, Chicago, IL

Bengt Hallberg (piano), Sept. 13, 1932, Gothenburg,
Sweden

Lol Coxhill (soprano), Sept. 19, 1932, Portsmouth,
England

Alvin Batiste (clarinet), Nov. 7, 1932, New Orleans, LA

Paul Bley (piano), Nov. 10, 1932, Montreal, Canada

Ed Bickert (guitar), Nov. 29, 1932, Hochfield,
Manitoba, Canada

Jimmy Lyons (alto), Dec. 1, 1932, Jersey City, NJ

Donald Byrd (trumpet), Dec. 9, 1932, Detroit, MI

Bob Cranshaw (bass), Dec. 10, 1932, Evanston, IL

PASSINGS

Emmett Hardy (23), June 16, 1926, New Orleans, LA

Stump Evans (23), Aug. 29, 1928, Douglas, KS

Jimmy O'Bryant (32), June 24, 1928, Chicago, IL

Pinetop Smith (24), Mar. 15, 1929, Chicago, IL

Don Murray (24), June 2, 1929, Los Angeles, CA

Chris Kelly (43), Aug. 19, 1929, New Orleans, LA

Jimmy Blythe (30), June 21, 1931, Chicago, IL

Buddy Petit (34), July 4, 1931, New Orleans, LA

Jimmy Harrison (30), July 23, 1931, New York, NY

Bix Beiderbecke (28), Aug. 6, 1931, New York, NY

Buddy Bolden (54), Nov. 4, 1931, Jackson, LA

Frank Teschemacher (25), Feb. 29, 1932, Chicago, IL

Carleton Coon (36), May 4, 1932, Chicago, IL

Bubber Miley (29), May 24, 1932, New York, NY

Chapter Four

1933–1938:
Swing's the Thing

As 1933 began, jazz was largely underground, a victim of the Depression and of being associated with the often-irresponsible good times of the 1920s. Audiences of the period seemed to prefer straight dance music that emphasized the melody and vocalists who stuck to the lyricist's words. At least that was what the public was being constantly fed on radio (a valuable free entertainment during the Depression), on records (particularly those played by faceless studio orchestras), and in dance halls.

The plight of jazz was not the uppermost thing on most people's minds in 1933. The Depression meant that the unemployment rate was 25 percent, some Americans were close to starvation, and the future looked gloomy. However, the election of 1932 had brought Franklin D. Roosevelt into the White House, and FDR soon did away with Prohibition. Legal liquor flowed again with speakeasies being replaced by bars, nightclubs, and restaurants, and the mood of the public was not quite as bleak as it had been under the self-paralyzed Herbert Hoover administration.

During the period of 1931–34, jazz did not die; it was just well hidden, particularly from the white world. Occasionally there would be a short solo on the most commercial of records, and that eight-bar spot might be filled by an anonymous Tommy Dorsey or Bunny Berigan. The Casa Loma Orchestra showed that spirited jazz could be balanced with quiet ballads, while Bing Crosby's great success helped loosen up some of the singing in the pop world.

Jazz was more out in the open in Harlem where black big bands such as those led by Duke Ellington, Cab Calloway, Fletcher Henderson, and Chick Webb delighted dancers and often worked with elaborate shows. But although Ellington, Calloway, and Louis Armstrong were national celebrities, the 1933–34 period looked grim for many jazz musicians, and quite a few of its former followers were not too hopeful that it would continue to grow, much less thrive, in the future.

But then came Benny Goodman's rise to fame.

Benny Goodman: The King of Swing

As the Depression hit and took hold during 1929–33, Benny Goodman was both an artistic victim and a commercial beneficiary of the worsening economic situation. He had known what it was like to be poor, growing up in poverty in Chicago, but fortunately he found his purpose in life quite early, playing clarinet from the age of 11. Goodman was just 16 when he became Ben Pollack's top soloist in August 1925, and his four years with the drummer's band gave him a strong reputation in the jazz world. Settling in New York, Goodman worked with Red Nichols's Five Pennies and then became a very busy studio musician, riding out the Depression years by playing on a countless number of commercial record dates and radio programs with large orchestras. Goodman's strong technical skills kept him constantly in demand, but he felt frustrated by the dull music that he was hired to perform. Even the 20 recordings released under his own name during 1930–31 were just bland dance music. On the brighter side, the money was good, and there were occasional jazz sessions (with the Charleston Chasers in 1931, the Joe Venuti-Eddie Lang All-Star Orchestra, and Irving Mills's Hotsy-Totsy Gang). His own dates of 1933–34 were on a fairly high level, featuring Jack Teagarden, Billie Holiday (who made her recording debut with BG), Coleman Hawkins, and Mildred Bailey. All of his early recordings as a leader are on **1928–31** (Classics 693), **1931–33** (Classics 719), and **1934–35** (Classics 744).

But the clarinetist wanted to make a major change from his day-to-day life and consistently play the music he loved. In 1934, Goodman made his move by forming his first big band, playing regularly at Billy Rose's Music Hall and signing a record contract with Columbia. In November 1934, his ensemble won an audition (by one vote) to be one of the three orchestras featured on the new *Let's Dance* radio series, along with Xavier Cugat (who played Latin music) and Del Murray (commercial dance music); Goodman would provide the jazz. The regular work allowed him to stabilize his personnel, which soon included trumpeter Pee Wee Erwin, tenor saxophonist Arthur Rollini, drummer Gene Krupa (who Goodman had used on records as early as 1931), and singer Helen Ward. When it was apparent that the orchestra did not have enough new material for the series, producer John Hammond suggested that Goodman hire Fletcher Henderson to fill in his book. Henderson, whose own

orchestra was struggling and would soon break up, was grateful for the extra money, and his charts (along with BG's vision) helped form the Benny Goodman Orchestra's swinging style. A new recording contract with the Victor label in April 1935 was also a step up for the orchestra.

1935—Let's Dance Broadcasts (Circle 50) has some of the performances from the legendary *Let's Dance* broadcasts. At the time, Goodman's band was already quite recognizable, featuring vocals by Helen Ward (who wrote the liner notes for this reissue) and solos from Pee Wee Erwin, altoist Toots Mondello, and Arthur Rollini. The clarinetist is the main star throughout and some of the better numbers include "Three Little Words," "I Got Rhythm," "Japanese Sandman," "I Know that You Know," and "King Porter Stomp."

Up until the 1950s, record labels were opposed to their recordings being played on the radio, feeling that consumers would not pay for music that they could hear over the airwaves for free. To fill in airtime, musicians were usually granted permission to record radio transcriptions. These performances were made strictly for the radio and were not available for sale to the general public, at least not until decades later when they were rediscovered. In addition to regular studio recordings and on-air live performances, radio transcriptions add a great deal to the legacy of many swing orchestras and jazz combos. On June 6, 1935, the Goodman big band spent a very busy day in the studios, recording 50 songs as transcriptions. Twenty-five of the numbers have been reissued most recently on the CD **Good to Go** (Buddha 7446599624), while all 50 were last on the three LPs **Rhythm Makers Orchestra Vols. 1–3** (Sunbeam 101-103). Considering that every performance was a first take and that the band simply went through their book, playing song after song, the results are quite consistent, a testament to the discipline that Goodman imposed on his sidemen. Erwin, Mondello, Rollini, and BG are the main soloists, showing what the Goodman big band sounded like right before it hit it big.

Two historic events occurred in July. The exciting trumpet soloist Bunny Berigan had been persuaded to leave the studios and join Goodman's big band. On July 1, he took classic choruses on Goodman's recordings of "King Porter Stomp" and "Sometimes I'm Happy," both of which would become hits. And, as a break from the big band, on July 13 the Benny Goodman Trio (with Krupa and pianist Teddy Wilson) made their first recordings. But with the end of the *Let's Dance* series the previous May, the future of the Benny Goodman Orchestra was beginning to look perilous. How could the clarinetist keep his band together much longer without any regular work?

Willard Alexander, an important booking agent, set up a cross-country tour for the big band to see if the orchestra had a future. It was certainly a colorful trip, with some minor successes and dismal failures along the way, particularly when club owners insisted that the band play waltzes and tangos. It seemed as if few people had heard of Goodman, so crowds were often quite small, and the musicians' morale sunk lower the closer they came to the West Coast. The band was well received in Oakland, but by the time they reached Los Angeles for their August 21 engagement at the Palomar Ballroom, they were exhausted and close to giving up. At first Goodman played it safe before the audience, performing dance music during the early sets, but the surprisingly large crowd seemed bored and only gave polite applause. Finally, knowing that there was nothing left to lose, the clarinetist decided to cut loose and go down playing the music he believed in. The audience's reaction was explosive, and the teenagers certainly let the musicians know their appreciation. Every night from then on became a swinging joyous dance party, and the engagement had national and eventually international implications. Unknown to Goodman, the *Let's Dance* radio show had been very popular on the West Coast and, after five years of bland commercial music, the new generation of dancers and listeners was hungry for new music. Swing became the thing and the swing era was officially born.

After the Palomar engagement ended, the Benny Goodman Orchestra had a long run at Chicago's Congress Hotel that solidified their West Coast triumph. Within a short time, swinging big bands were plentiful throughout the United States and Goodman was crowned "The King of Swing."

Unlike Paul Whiteman, who never deserved the "King of Jazz" title in the 1920s, Goodman actually was the leader of swing and was largely responsible for the style dominating pop music for the next decade. In addition, he was one of the greatest clarinet players of all time and his band became quite influential. Goodman's 1935–36 orchestra was most notable for the leader's playing, Helen Ward (who was just 18 when she joined the band), the occasional hot trumpet solos of Ziggy Elman (who joined in 1936), the increasingly assertive drumming of Gene Krupa, and the impeccable ensembles. Goodman was a perfectionist, so his band was always in-tune and swinging at danceable tempos, even during the faster "killer dillers." ❍ **The Birth of Swing** (Bluebird 61038), a three-CD set, has all of the Benny Goodman Orchestra's studio recordings from April 1935 to November 1936. The 71 performances (which include some alternate takes) show why Goodman became a household name. Strong contributions are made by Berigan (who returned to the studios after the Palomar success), Elman, pianist Jess Stacy, and Helen Ward, but it is the swinging ensembles and Goodman's clarinet that really give the band its own personality. Among the better numbers are "Japanese Sandman," "Always," "Blue Skies," "Sometimes I'm Happy," "King Porter Stomp," a swinging "Jingle Bells," "When Buddha Smiles," "Stompin' at the Savoy," "Goody Goody" (Helen Ward's biggest hit), "House Hop," "Swingtime in the Rockies," "You Turned the Tables on Me," "Down South Camp Meeting," "Bugle Call Rag," and "Jam Session."

Benny Goodman's delight at playing in a less structured setting with Teddy Wilson and Gene Krupa resulted in him using the new Benny Goodman Trio as a change of pace not only in his recordings and radio appearances but also at live performances. This was considered a revolutionary step, not so much music-wise but socially because Wilson was black. Goodman, whose personal faults included being self-centered and absent-minded, was never racist—it was said in later years that he treated all musicians, no matter what their race, equally badly! With John Hammond's urging, he continued breaking down racial boundaries in the cause of creating better music at a time when mixed groups were a real rarity in public. In 1936, after Goodman, Krupa, and Wilson spontaneously jammed in Los Angeles with vibraphonist Lionel Hampton, Hamp was added to the combo to form the Benny Goodman Quartet. ❍ **The Complete Small Group Recordings** (RCA 68764), a three-CD set, has all 67 selections (20 of which are alternate takes) by Goodman's Trio, Quartet, and Quintet of 1935–39, Dave Tough, Buddy Schutz, and Hampton appearing on the later numbers in Krupa's former spot, and bassist John Kirby being added on a special occasion. The classics include "After You've Gone," "Body and Soul," "All My Life" (with Helen Ward), "Nobody's Sweetheart," "Dinah," "Tiger Rag," "Stompin' at the Savoy," "Avalon," "Bei Mir Bist Du Schon" (with singer Martha Tilton and Ziggy Elman added), and "I Cried for You."

After finishing his extended engagement at Chicago's Congress Hotel (a one-month run that became six), Benny Goodman returned to New York in triumph, creating a sensation with his run at the Paramount Ballroom. Helen Ward's decision to retire from what had become the most coveted position in swing in order to get married (she would later return to music but never regained her prominence) was a major loss, but, after a period, Goodman replaced her with the cheerful Martha Tilton. The year 1937 found his big band reaching its height with the addition of Harry James who, along with Ziggy Elman and Chris Griffin, formed a trumpet section that was considered second to none. Each of those musicians could not only play exciting solos and read their parts perfectly, but also take turns as first trumpeter.

The Harry James Years, Vol. 1 (Bluebird 66155) and **Wrappin' It Up: The Harry James Years, Vol. 2** (Bluebird 66549) have highlights from the January 1937–March 1939 period. Unfortunately, these are not complete sets, and Goodman's recordings of the era do deserve to be reissued complete and in chronological order on a domestic label. **Vol. 1** includes Harry James's "Peckin'," the studio recording of "Sing, Sing, Sing," "Roll 'Em," and two versions apiece of "Life Goes to a Party," "Don't Be that Way," and "One o'Clock Jump." **Vol. 2** features the Goodman big band after the departure of Gene Krupa, swinging such numbers as "The Blue Room," "Big John Special," "Wrappin' It Up," "Smoke House," and "Undecided," with guest appearances by tenors Lester Young and Bud Freeman (who spent a short, unhappy period in the band). Goodman's orchestra was often heard at its most exciting live, playing before an enthusiastic dancing audience. **On the Air** (Columbia/Legacy 48836) has 49 of the 1937–38 orchestra's best radio appearances, including stirring big band numbers (such as a spontaneously extended version of "St. Louis Blues" featuring Harry James) and trio/quartet romps.

Featured on the *Camel Caravan* radio series throughout much of 1937, the Benny Goodman Orchestra continued to be the most popular band in the music world. Goodman's career hit its peak on January 16, 1938, when he performed the first full-length jazz concert ever at Carnegie Hall, the classical music temple. Despite some initial nervousness, the concert was a huge success and is still considered legendary. Highlights were many, starting with Krupa's first drum break on the opening "Don't Be that Way" (which woke up the orchestra), a rousing "One o'Clock Jump," a brief "History of Jazz" medley (reaching all the way back 20 years for a quick ODJB tribute), an all-star jam session on "Honeysuckle Rose" (with Lester Young, Buck Clayton, Count Basie, Johnny Hodges, and Harry Carney along with Goodman and James), heated trio and quartet excursions, and, most of all, "Sing, Sing, Sing," a feature for Gene Krupa's excitable drumming that was partly stolen by Jess Stacy's surprising impressionistic piano solo. A dozen years later, the recordings of the concert (which were made by Albert Marx, Helen Ward's husband of the time) were discovered in Goodman's closet and released to the public, becoming a best-selling set. Its latest reissue, ● **Benny Goodman Carnegie Hall Jazz Concert** (Columbia 65167), is a two-CD set that has every surviving note from the event (including two poorly recorded songs formerly only put out by the tiny Sunbeam label) and is essential for all music collections.

Although his early bands lacked any major trombone and saxophone soloists, several key swing stars got their starts with Goodman. Gene Krupa was an early sidekick who, after making an impact on the Chicago jazz scene, moved to New York in 1929 where he met up with Goodman in the studios. In December 1934, he joined BG's new orchestra where at first he was a quiet and supportive drummer. As 1936 progressed, Krupa became more assertive in his playing and began to be noticed by the public, becoming the first superstar jazz drummer. Krupa had the image of a smiling, gum-chewing drummer who seemed to put so much effort into each drum break he took, no matter how easy it really was; the public loved it. There were certainly more musical drummers around during his prime, but Krupa became a hero because it was due to him that drummers were finally taken seriously as both potential stars and inventive instrumentalists. His nightly feature on "Sing, Sing, Sing" in 1937 led to some tension with Goodman because Krupa was getting so much applause, and the drummer began acting a bit too big for his britches. After the success of the 1938 Carnegie Hall concert, Krupa and Goodman had a personality clash with the result being that Krupa quit the band and went off to form his own orchestra.

Gene Krupa and the Other Goodman Sidemen

The famous duo soon reconciled, though the Gene Krupa Orchestra in time became a competitor to Benny

Goodman's big band. **1935–1938** (Classics 754) and **1938** (Classics 767) have all of the recordings that the drummer led prior to 1939. The former set has a session apiece from 1935 (a date with some Goodman sidemen plus Israel Crosby who takes one of the earliest significant recorded bass solos on "Blues of Israel") and 1936 (two vocal numbers by Helen Ward and a couple of explosive instrumentals, "I Hope Gabriel Likes My Music" and "Swing Is Here," with Goodman, Roy Eldridge, and Chu Berry). Otherwise, the CD consists of the first 15 numbers from the Gene Krupa Orchestra with six vocals by Irene Daye, two by Ward (who came out of retirement for this set with her old friend), and excellent instrumentals in "Prelude to a Stomp," "I Know that You Know," and "Wire Brush Stomp." **1938** documents the evolving Krupa Orchestra, with ten vocals by Daye, four by the eccentric Leo Watson (including "Nagasaki" and "Tutti Frutti"), and some solos from tenors Vido Musso and Sam Donahue. Krupa's big band did not have its own sound yet, but the drummer's popularity allowed him to keep the orchestra together until its eventual breakthrough.

Jess Stacy, who was the Benny Goodman Orchestra's regular pianist during July 1935–July 1939, would always be best known for his association with the clarinetist. Stacy had played on riverboats as early as 1921, recorded with Al Katz's Kittens in 1926, and was part of the Chicago jazz scene for quite a few years. While with Goodman, he tended to be underutilized but can be heard prominently behind the vocalists (where his playing really shone) and during his surprise solo on Carnegie Hall's "Sing, Sing, Sing."

Helen Ward could have been a major name as a singer, but she made the mistake of retiring just when she was becoming famous. Her happy voice, swinging style, and ability to uplift lyrics made her a major asset from the time she joined Goodman's *Let's Dance* radio series in late 1934 until she decided to quit two years later, at the age of 20. Among her most popular numbers were "Goody Goody," "It's Been So Long," "All My Life," "Too Good to Be True," "These Foolish Things," and "You Turned the Tables on Me." After Ward's retirement, Goodman spent a few months trying out different singers until he settled on the perky Martha Tilton who, although not quite on Ward's level, was likable and open to recording whatever she was given.

Teddy Wilson was the definitive pianist of the swing era. His touch was much lighter than that of the earlier stride players yet no less forceful, and he gave the impression that he was incapable of making a mistake or playing a distasteful note. Wilson started working professionally in 1929 when he was 16, performing with Speed Webb's legendary (but unrecorded) territory band during 1929–31 and working in Chicago with Erskine Tate, Louis Armstrong's big band (with whom he recorded in 1933), Jimmie Noone, and Benny Carter. Wilson, who also worked with the Willie Bryant Big Band (1934–35), was a favorite of producer John Hammond, who recorded him at the head of all-star swing combos during 1935–42 and teamed him regularly on records with Billie Holiday. Wilson was never a regular member of the Benny Goodman big band, but appeared on records with the BG Trio in mid-1935 and became a regular "extra added" attraction at concerts with the combo in 1936.

Lionel Hampton, who made his initial impression as a drummer with Paul Howard's Quality Serenaders during 1929–30 and briefly as a vibraphonist with Louis Armstrong, worked with Les Hite in Los Angeles during 1932–34, led his own orchestra for two years, and had an appearance in the Bing Crosby film *Pennies from Heaven* as a masked drummer in Louis Armstrong's band. He was discovered by Goodman in the summer of 1936 and became a member of the Benny Goodman Quartet that November. In addition to his vibraphone playing (which was unprecedented at the time), Hampton could sing, fill in on drums, and (perhaps most importantly) make Goodman smile with his energy and enthusiasm. While with BG in 1937, Hampton also began leading a series of all-star swing record dates (covered in the following chapter).

Moving to Goodman's trumpet section of 1937, Ziggy Elman (born Harry Finkelman) had the potential to be a star, but he never quite got to that level. Elman started out playing all of the reed instruments in addition to trumpet and trombone. He worked regularly in Atlantic City and was well featured (often on trombone) with Alex Bartha's band. Elman joined Goodman in September 1936 and was at first his main trumpet soloist, but Harry James's arrival caused him to be overshadowed. Chris Griffin was in a similar position, except that Elman overshadowed him! Griffin had worked with Charlie Barnet (off and on during 1933–35), Joe Haymes, and in the studios. He joined Goodman in May 1936, and although rarely getting to solo, he was always capable of fitting into Elman and James's shoes.

Harry James was never overshadowed by anyone. He played drums when he was seven and took trumpet lessons from his father, who conducted orchestras for circuses. James was a natural trumpeter and, by the time he was 12, he was heading his own group for the Christy Brothers Circus. James worked in territory bands in Texas for several years, joining Ben Pollack's orchestra in 1935 (with whom he made his recording debut) when he was 19. In January 1937 (when he was two months shy of 22), James became the star trumpeter of the number one swing band, the Benny Goodman Orchestra, and he was a hit from the beginning. Among his feature solos were on "St. Louis Blues," his own "Life Goes to a Party," and "Sing, Sing, Sing."

With this roster of talent, Benny Goodman was able to hold his own against competitors throughout 1938, even with the loss of Gene Krupa.

The Pacesetters: 1933–1938

The swing era, which officially began in mid-1935, was a remarkable time in which jazz overlapped with pop music; in fact, much of swing could be considered the popular music of the era. The main reason that swing caught on so big is that it was ideal dance music. It is strange to think that hundreds of big bands were working all over the United States when the Depression was raging on, but with millions of young dancers eager to hear the music (which was broadcast for free over the radio), for many their main entertainment was going out and dancing to the bands.

It is fortunate that the swing era coincided with a period when there was an unprecedented number of extremely talented songwriters. Those were the days when Hollywood was entering its artistic prime, when Broadway shows actually had songs that became standards, and when radio orchestras and swing bands were in constant need of new material. Luckily such major talents as composers Irving Berlin, George Gershwin (whose death in 1937 was a major loss), Jerome Kern, Hoagy Carmichael, Cole Porter, Harold Arlen, Richard Rodgers, Fats Waller, Harry Warren, and Duke Ellington, and such lyricists as Johnny Mercer, Ira Gershwin, Al Dubin, Andy Razaf, Mitchell Paris, Yip Harburg, Dorothy Fields, and Lorenz Hart were all quite active.

Every week brought new songs, some of which became hits, fueling the excitement of the swing era.

Swing was everywhere after 1935. Rather than jazz being played in speakeasies, jazz bands could be found in hotels, movie theatres (the stage shows alternated with the films), nightclubs, dance halls, and most importantly, on radio and records.

The typical big band of the time had three trumpets, two trombones, four reeds (counting a clarinet soloist), piano, rhythm guitar, bass, and drums, plus a vocalist or two. The success of Benny Goodman led to many other similar bands being formed during 1936–37, and also generally helped the popularity of the better surviving orchestras, including the black Harlem bands. Not all of jazz was played by big bands (although smaller groups were seen more as a contrast than as a potent force) and not all big bands were jazz-oriented, for sweet dance orchestras (such as those of Guy Lombardo, Jan Garber, and Russ Morgan) were also quite popular.

While some of the top jazz soloists of the 1920s faded from the scene, others continued to grow and evolve. Louis Armstrong remained the most beloved and influential trumpeter although his own big band (the former Luis Russell Orchestra, which Satch took over in 1935) mostly just functioned as background support for his playing and singing talents. Bunny Berigan emerged as the most impressive new trumpeter of 1933–38, Harry James was on his way to becoming a household name, and Roy Eldridge's harmonic complexity and chance-taking style were giving younger trumpeters new ideas.

Although Jack Teagarden was considered jazz's finest trombone soloist, he was tied up in a longtime contract with the Paul Whiteman Orchestra. Tommy Dorsey, the "Sentimental Gentleman of Swing," became famous for his beautiful tone, while Duke Ellington featured the three very different styles of Lawrence Brown, Tricky Sam Nanton, and Juan Tizol.

Benny Goodman was the King of Swing, but in 1938 he began to be seriously challenged among clarinetists by Artie Shaw, whose own big band was taking off. Jimmy Dorsey was technically on BG's level although his own orchestra had not made it big yet, while Woody Herman led an interesting outfit of his own. Although all were still quite active, the New Orleans trio of Johnny Dodds, Jimmie Noone, and Sidney Bechet was often unknown to swing fans of the time.

Not thought of as a major solo instrument yet, the alto sax nevertheless was the main ax of a trio of significant stylists: Johnny Hodges, Benny Carter, and Willie Smith (from Jimmie Lunceford's orchestra), not to mention Jimmy Dorsey. With Coleman Hawkins away in Europe, many tenor players were competing for his top spot, including Chu Berry (featured with Cab Calloway by 1937), the freelancing Ben Webster, Herschel Evans from Count Basie's band, Bob Crosby's Eddie Miller and veteran Bud Freeman. However, it was the cool-toned Lester Young who emerged as the most significant new voice, showing saxophonists that there was a different, lighter way to play than the heavier Hawkins approach. The soprano sax (even with Bechet and occasionally Charlie Barnet) and the baritone (with Harry Carney and Basie's Jack Washington) remained minor instruments but were flourishing compared to the C-melody sax and the bass sax, both of which became largely extinct.

While stride piano stayed quite popular (Fats Waller became famous during this time), pianists in big swing bands had a lighter approach than formerly since they did not need to function as a one-man orchestra. Teddy Wilson's de-emphasis of the "oom-pah" nature of the left hand was greatly emulated and Earl Hines's ringing octaves (if not his knack for suspending time) was also influential. With Count Basie's arrival from Kansas City, he introduced a "less is more" approach in which every note counted, space and silence became a dramatic part of solos, and the timekeeping function shifted to the string bass. Boogie-woogie was catching on in 1938, giving employment to the infectious playing of Albert Ammons, Pete Johnson, and Meade Lux Lewis. And Art Tatum amazed listeners with improvisations so advanced and incredible that he sounded as if he was from a different planet.

Although the guitar had replaced the banjo, most guitarists were only used as rhythm players, stating the chords on the beat behind soloists; the acoustic guitar was more felt than heard. The only exceptions were in a few small groups, most notably in Europe where Django Reinhardt's brilliant playing with the Quintet of the Hot Club of France was far ahead of any American players. By 1938, some players were starting to experiment with the new electric guitar, most notably Eddie Durham (featured on recordings with the Kansas City Five and Six), George Barnes, and Les Paul, but outside of Django, no guitarist was ready yet to make a major impact. The same

could be said for bassists who, having replaced the tuba, were becoming more indispensable to jazz bands. The Benny Goodman Trio and Quartet did not use a bass, but all big bands did and, with the lightening of most pianists' left hands, the great majority of jazz combos considered a bass to be a must. There were just a few bass solos of significance this early on, particularly Israel Crosby's "Blues for Israel" in 1935 (with a Gene Krupa small group) and Milt Hinton with Cab Calloway. Other top bassists included Walter Page (with Basie), Bob Haggart (with Bob Crosby), John Kirby (who in 1938 put together an important sextet), and Slam Stewart.

The most famous drummer in the world during the early swing era was Gene Krupa, his instrument's first superstar. However, there were more musical and lighter drummers around including Jo Jones, Sid Catlett, Cozy Cole, Dave Tough, Ray McKinley, Ray Bauduc, and O'Neill Spencer, while Chick Webb ruled the Savoy Ballroom nightly. Buddy Rich, who was just beginning to be heard in 1938, would in time top them all.

Joe Venuti, the top jazz violinist of the 1920s, had competition during the next decade from Stuff Smith, Stephane Grappelli, and Svend Asmussen, but the violin remained a minor instrument in jazz and was virtually ignored by the big bands. The same can be said for the flute, which, other than Wayman Carver with Webb's orchestra, was completely neglected.

Not to be overlooked are the many arrangers who emerged after Don Redman, Fletcher Henderson, and Duke Ellington. With so many big bands around, the work of Gene Gifford (Casa Loma Orchestra), Edgar Sampson (Chick Webb), Benny Carter, Horace Henderson, Jimmy Mundy, Sy Oliver, Mary Lou Williams, and Eddie Sauter, among others, was greatly in demand.

The most important male vocalists of the early 1930s, Bing Crosby, Louis Armstrong, and Jack Teagarden, were each major forces throughout the decade, as were the Mills Brothers. In general, when the swing bands employed a male vocalist who was not a musician, they used him for straight ballads, offering a contrast to the swinging jazz. An exception was the great Jimmy Rushing, who belted out blues with Count Basie. It was a different story for some of the female vocalists. The classic blues singers were mostly all retired or deceased by the late 1930s, other than Ethel Waters and Alberta Hunter, who made the transition to swinging jazz. But with such new swing singers as Ella Fitzgerald, Helen Ward, Helen

Forrest, Helen Humes, Mildred Bailey, and Ivie Anderson emerging from big bands, not to mention Billie Holiday, there was no shortage of bright new talent.

Fletcher Henderson   With the great success of Benny Goodman during the second half of 1935, suddenly big bands were everywhere. In addition to the new ensembles formed in hopes of building on Goodman's success, the big bands already in existence found that they were in greater demand and receiving much more publicity, despite the competition from Goodman and the other upstarts.

Ironically, the original Fletcher Henderson Orchestra reached the end of its line in early 1935. Henderson had developed into a major arranger in the early 1930s, but his band's progress became stalled despite the many all-stars in the personnel. **1932–34** (Classics 535) has such classic performances as "New King Porter Stomp" (highlighted by trumpeter Bobby Stark's greatest solo), "Honeysuckle Rose," "Yeah Man," "Queer Notions," a Coleman Hawkins feature on "It's the Talk of the Town," "Limehouse Blues," "Big John's Special," and "Down South Camp Meeting," showing just how strong a band Henderson had during the pre-swing era.

Coleman Hawkins, who was frustrated that Henderson's band was not receiving greater recognition, ended his ten years with the orchestra in 1934, sailing to Europe where he worked steadily and was treated as royalty for the next five years. Even with Hawkins's departure, the Fletcher Henderson Orchestra still featured Red Allen, Bobby Stark, Ben Webster (Hawkins's replacement after a brief and unsuccessful stint by the cooler-toned Lester Young), and altoist Hilton Jefferson among its many other stars. But Henderson failed to capitalize on his band's talents and there were lost opportunities. Cash was raised by selling arrangements to Benny Goodman for his *Let's Dance* broadcasts, but even with that, in early 1935 Henderson was forced to disband.

After a period on the sidelines, in 1936 Henderson put together a new orchestra and had a quick hit with "Christopher Columbus," featuring Roy Eldridge and Chu Berry. But his band did not have a follow-up and, despite Benny Goodman constantly singing his praises, Henderson's ensemble just struggled along. **1934–1937** (Classics 527) and **1937–1938** (Classics 519) have all of the studio recordings (other than alternate takes) from the Fletcher Henderson Orchestra of this period.

1934–1937 starts off with the final session from the original Henderson big band (a heated set that includes "Wild Party," "Rug Cutter's Swing," and "Hotter than 'Ell") with the rest of the CD (other than one cut from 1937) being from 1936. Eldridge, Berry, and Buster Bailey are the stars on "Christopher Columbus," "Blue Lou," "Stealin' Apples" (Henderson's theme song), "Riffin'," and "You Can Depend on Me." Unfortunately, **1937–1938** is generally not on the same level. Chuck Roberts takes dull vocals on 11 of the 18 numbers although there are fine versions of "Back in Your Own Backyard," "Chris and His Gang," and "Moten Stomp," with solos from trumpeter Emmett Berry, J.C. Higginbotham, and several different tenor saxophonists.

Horace Henderson   Fletcher Henderson's younger brother Horace, who was actually a better pianist than Fletcher and had emerged as a top arranger shortly before his sibling, was important in the background during this era. He worked often with Fletcher's big band during 1933–34, splitting the piano duties and contributing many arrangements, including "Yeah Man," "Queer Notions," and "Big John's Special." In 1933, he used the nucleus of Fletcher's band for his debut recording as a leader, which has been reissued on Coleman Hawkins's **1929–1934** (Classics 587). He kept busy during the swing era as a freelance arranger, writing for such bands as the Casa Loma Orchestra, Benny Goodman ("Japanese Sandman" and "Dear Old Southland"), Charlie Barnet, Tommy Dorsey, Jimmie Lunceford, Earl Hines, and his brother, who used 30 of his charts including "Christopher Columbus." In 1937, Horace Henderson formed his own big band, but during the next four years it failed to create much of a stir.

Don Redman   It is surprising that the Don Redman Orchestra never really caught on big. After all, Redman's arrangements had practically invented swing in the mid-1920s. But, although the leader was a genial front man, a colorful and philosophical singer (who often half-spoke his words), and a brilliant arranger, his big band remained fairly obscure. **1933–1936** (Classics 553) shows that the band's recordings of the time were surprisingly routine, with far too many vocals from Harlan Lattimore and Chick Bullock, and the emphasis on dated novelties. **1936–1939** (Classics 574) is mostly on a higher level with such swingers as "Bugle Call Rag," "Swingin' with the Fat Man," "Down Home Rag," and

"Milenburg Joys." But the Don Redman Orchestra lacked an original personality that allowed it to rise above the crowd.

Paul Whiteman   Leader of the most popular big band of the 1920s, Paul Whiteman seemed somewhat lost during the swing era. His orchestra worked steadily, but it was no longer the influential force it had been earlier and was largely directionless; Whiteman never seemed to understand swing very well. Among his sidemen during the period were Bunny Berigan for a few uneventful months in 1933, Jack Teagarden (signed to a five-year contract keeping him with Whiteman during 1934–39), trumpeter Charlie Teagarden, Miff Mole, and the reliable Frankie Trumbauer, who remained into 1936, forming his own unsuccessful orchestra in 1938. Rather than letting his ensemble break loose very often, Whiteman preferred to present extended concert works like "Cuban Overture" and "An American in Paris." During 1938–39 there were some recordings by contingents from his orchestra, including Whiteman's "Swing Wing," the "Swinging Strings," his "Bouncing Brass," and a "Sax Socette," but these remain long out of print. **Paul Whiteman and His Chesterfield Orchestra** (Mr. Music 7008) has two complete radio broadcasts from 1938. Artie Shaw is a guest on one program, playing "Flying Down to Floy Floy" with a quartet and "I Surrender Dear" with Whiteman. Cornetist Bobby Hackett, with a Dixieland septet, performs two numbers on the other broadcast. But otherwise Joan Edwards has two vocals on each date, the Modernaires vocal group is heard from a couple of times, and Jack Teagarden just gets a few solos. The Paul Whiteman Orchestra sounds pretty faceless throughout, as if it had lost its purpose and was now a relic of the past.

The Casa Loma Orchestra   The Casa Loma Orchestra, which during 1930–32 had been ahead of its time (leading the way toward Benny Goodman), remained a busy if underrated big band during the swing era. Gene Gifford was still the chief arranger of the orchestra, which featured such soloists as clarinetist Clarence Hutchenrider, trombonist/singer Pee Wee Hunt, trumpeter Sonny Dunham, and ballad singer Kenny Sargent. The band's two-part remake of "Casa Loma Stomp" (1937) and a high-note feature for Dunham on "Memories of You" were both major hits. Unfortunately, relatively few of the band's records have appeared on CD yet. **The Continental** (Hindsight 261) is a set of radio transcriptions that puts the emphasis on swing (there is only one Kenny Sargent vocal) with such standards as "Who's Sorry Now," "Blue Room," and "Chinatown, My Chinatown." However, the band's biggest sellers and trademark songs are scarce, forcing one to search for the LP **Glen Gray and the Original Casa Loma Orchestra's Greatest Hits** (Decca 75016).

The Dorsey Brothers Orchestra   A year before Benny Goodman hit it big, the Dorsey Brothers Orchestra was working steadily and hoping for a breakthrough. Trombonist Tommy Dorsey and his older brother Jimmy (who doubled on clarinet and alto sax) were often known as the "battling Dorseys" because, although they loved each other, they loved to fight almost as much. They had started co-leading the Dorsey Brothers Orchestra in 1928, but it was strictly a recording group for the next five years, frequently featuring hot trumpet solos by Bunny Berigan starting in 1931. **Mood Hollywood** (Hep 1005) and **Harlem Lullaby** (Hep 1006) document the Dorsey Brothers Orchestra in 1933, just before it became a regular band. **Mood Hollywood** starts with seven songs (plus four alternate takes) by the Dorsey Brothers (an octet) with the great swing trumpeter Bunny Berigan

TIMELINE 1933

Mildred Bailey and Red Norvo get married. • Charlie Barnet leads his first record dates. • After the death of her mother and sister, Ma Rainey retires from music. • Jimmie Lunceford's orchestra moves to New York. • Duke Ellington tours Europe while Louis Armstrong begins a two-year stay overseas. • Art Tatum records his first solo recordings. • Eddie Lang dies from a botched tonsillectomy. • Bessie Smith makes her last recordings. • Billie Holiday makes her first recordings. • Django Reinhardt and Stephane Grappelli meet and soon form the Quintet of the Hot Club of France.

often stealing the show (particularly on "Someone Stole Gabriel's Horn"). The original rendition of "I'm Getting Sentimental Over You" is also included (in two versions) with a vocal by Jean Bowes along with a concluding orchestra date arranged by Bill Challis that has vocals by Johnny Mercer, Mildred Bailey, and Jerry Cooper. On **Harlem Lullaby**, the Dorsey Brothers group (the same unit with Berigan) accompanies Bing Crosby on three numbers (including two takes of "Stay on the Right Side of the Road") and Mildred Bailey for eight songs (highlighted by "There's a Cabin in the Pines"). There are also four numbers in which the Dorsey Brothers Orchestra interacts with Ethel Waters, including the original version of "Stormy Weather."

In 1934, the brothers formed a regularly working band since they had tired of working in the studios. For a year they had some success, with Glenn Miller providing many arrangements, and vocals provided by Bob Crosby (succeeded in the spring of 1935 by Bob Eberle) and Kay Weber. They recorded around 120 titles during this period ranging from straight dance band performances to Dixieland-oriented pieces, but remarkably few have been reissued on CD yet. In May 1935, while playing at the Glen Island Casino, the battling Dorseys had an argument over the tempo of "I'll Never Say 'Never Again' Again" and Tommy stormed off the bandstand. Jimmy Dorsey became the sole leader of the band (which was promptly renamed the Jimmy Dorsey Orchestra) while Tommy Dorsey soon took over the struggling Joe Haymes Orchestra. The Dorseys would not work together again on a regular basis for 17 years.

Cab Calloway   Throughout the 1930s, Cab Calloway was a household name, leader of an exciting (if underrated) big band and the king of "Hi-De-Ho," in addition to being an influential singer and personality. All of his studio recordings from 1930–47 (except alternate takes) are available on a dozen CDs released by Classics. During the period covered in **1932–1934** (Classics 544), Cab Calloway's Orchestra was solid if not featuring any major names among the sidemen. Doc Cheatham played first trumpet, trombonist Harry White contributed some of the arrangements, Eddie Barefield was heard on clarinet, and Walter Thomas was the tenor soloist. **1932–1934** has Cab singing "Doin' the New Low-Down" on a variety number with the Don Redman Orchestra and the Mills Brothers, and such colorful tunes as "The Lady with

the Fan," "Harlem Camp Meeting," "Zaz Zuh Zah," "I Learned About Love from Her," and "'Long About Midnight." Calloway's singing is equal parts Louis Armstrong, Al Jolson, opera, and his own zany personality. **1934–1937** (Classics 554) has Ben Webster joining the band in the spring of 1936; highlights include "Keep that Hi-De-Hi in Your Soul," "Nagasaki," "I Love to Sing'a," "Copper Colored Gal," and "That Man Is Here Again." **1937–1938** (Classics 568) finds rhythm guitarist Danny Barker strengthening the rhythm section (which included pianist Bennie Payne and, since 1936, Milt Hinton), and Chu Berry replacing Webster as the band's main soloist. Among the more memorable selections are "She's Tall, She's Tan, She's Terrific," "Mama, I Wanna Make Rhythm," "Hi-De-Ho Romeo," the atmospheric "Azure," and a few instrumentals including "Queen Isabella," which is really Berry's "Christopher Columbus" under a different name. **1938–1939** (Classics 576) includes the hit "F.D.R. Jones" and such spirited numbers as "Mister Paganini, Swing for Minnie" and "Do You Wanna Jump, Children." All of these releases should greatly interest Cab Calloway fans and make it clear why he was such a popular show business personality. They also give listeners an opportunity to hear how strong Cab's band had become by the late 1930s. Although he was always the main star, Calloway was wise enough to pay and treat his musicians very well, making being a sideman in Cab Calloway's Orchestra one of the most treasured jobs for black musicians in the 1930s.

Chick Webb and Ella Fitzgerald   Chick Webb was the king of the Savoy Ballroom during 1931–39. Stricken early in life by tuberculosis of the spine, Webb became a dwarf with a hunched back. Despite that, he started playing drums as a child and developed quickly. Webb moved to New York from his native Baltimore in 1925 and led a variety of bands during the next six years, first recording in 1929. After he became settled at the Savoy, where he played for some of the country's most adventurous and enthusiastic dancers, Webb and his big band were major attractions, often sharing the bandstand with other orchestras in "battle of the bands" contests, which Webb invariably won due to his home court advantage. Edgar Sampson wrote such songs as "Stompin' at the Savoy," "Don't Be that Way," and "If Dreams Come True" for Webb in 1934 (Benny Goodman would have bigger hits with those tunes during the next couple of years), and the orchestra featured Taft Jordan and Bobby Stark on trumpets, trombonist Sandy Williams, tenor saxophonist Elmer Williams, and Sampson on alto. Webb took occasional solos but was mostly notable for driving his hard-swinging band. ◗ **1929–1934** (Classics 502) has two early tracks from 1929, a 1931 session that has one of the first versions of Benny Carter's "Blues in My Heart," and the first 20 recordings by Webb's Savoy Orchestra. Highlights include Taft Jordan's Louis Armstrong tribute on "On the Sunny Side of the Street" and the original versions of "Stompin' at the Savoy," "Don't Be that Way," "If Dreams Come True," and "Blue Lou." **1935–1938** (Classics 517) is most notable for the four numbers from Chick Webb's Little Chicks, a small group taken from Webb's orchestra that has the frontline of clarinetist Chauncey Haughton and the early jazz flutist Wayman Carver; pity that they did not record more extensively. Also on this set are "Go Harlem," "Clap Hands! Here Comes Charlie," and "Liza."

In 1935, an 18-year-old singer named Ella Fitzgerald joined Webb's big band and soon became its most important member. Although her early life was grim (including a period spent homeless), Ella always sang with a great deal of joy and perfectly in tune. In 1934, she won the amateur contest at the Apollo Theatre, singing "Judy" in the style of her main early influence Connie Boswell. Because her appearance and shoddy clothes were not too appealing, Ella was turned down for a job with Fletcher Henderson. Benny Carter (who had seen the amateur contest) helped persuade Chick Webb to give her a chance. Webb was not initially impressed, until he heard her sing and noted the audience's enthusiastic response. Although she was often given juvenile novelties to sing while with Webb, Ella proved to be quite winning on ballads and in 1938 she had a huge hit with "A-Tisket, A-Tasket." All of her early recordings (including her sessions with Webb, which were purposely skipped in Chick's two Classics CDs) are available on **1935–1937** (Classics 500), **1937–1938** (Classics 506), and **1938–1939** (Classics 518). Among the more memorable selections are "I'll Chase the Blues Away," "Goodnight My Love" (with Benny Goodman), and "Mr. Paganini, You'll Have to Swing It" from **1935–1937**, two numbers with the Mills Brothers, and "A-Tisket, A-Tasket" on **1937–1938**, and "You Can't Be Mine," "Saving Myself for You," "Wacky Dust," "F.D.R. Jones," and "Undecided" on **1938–1939**.

Because of Ella Fitzgerald's popularity, the Chick Webb Orchestra was at the height of its commercial success during 1938, but, sadly, its leader's health was starting to fail.

Claude Hopkins   The Claude Hopkins Orchestra had the misfortune of peaking before the swing era and they never caught on. Founded in 1930 and based at the Roseland Ballroom (succeeding Fletcher Henderson) during 1931–34, the band is heard at its best on the recordings included on ◗ **1932–1934** (Classics 699). Jimmy Mundy's eccentric "Honey Hush" is a highlight, as is "I Would Do Anything for You," "Three Little Words," "California Here I Come," "Honeysuckle Rose," and "Washington Squabble." Hopkins's powerful stride piano playing has several features, and his band includes trumpeter/vocalist Ovie Alston, trombonist Fernando Arbello, tenor man Bobby Sands, and a young Edmond Hall on clarinet and baritone, although its popular high-note vocalist Orlando Roberson is a bit hard to take at times. **1934–1935** (Classics 716) has 14 vocals by Roberson (including a horrendous version of "Trees") along with some fine instrumentals, including "Harlem Rhythm Dance," "Three Little Words," "In the Shade of the Old Apple Tree," and an exciting version of "King Porter Stomp." But after being dropped by the Decca label, the band was off records altogether for two important years, and its period at the Cotton Club (1935–36) did not lead to greater things. **1937–1940** (Classics 733) has the big band's final recordings (five of the six numbers from 1937 are features for singer Beverly White and new trumpeter Jabbo Smith is barely heard at all), including six cuts from 1940 and a date led by Ovie Austin with Hopkins sitting in on piano. By the end of 1940, the Claude Hopkins Orchestra was no more.

The Mills Blue Rhythm Band   The Mills Blue Rhythm Band had some glorious moments on records before it also died. Taken over by Irving Mills in 1931, who named the former Blue Rhythm Band after himself, it was used as a relief group at the Cotton Club for Cab Calloway and Duke Ellington. The early band was mostly comprised of fine ensemble players, but by 1934, Henry "Red" Allen, J.C. Higginbotham, and Buster Bailey had joined. **1933–1934** (Classics 686) has such hot numbers as "Ridin' in Rhythm," "Harlem After Midnight," "The Stuff Is Here (and It's Mellow)," "The Growl," and "Dancing Dogs." **1934–1936** (Classics 710) captures the band at its prime on "Back Beats," "Ride Red Ride," Joe Garland's "There's Rhythm in Harlem" (which hints strongly at "In the Mood" a few years before it was "composed"), "Harlem Heat," and "Truckin'." **1936-1937** (Classics 731) starts off with 14 numbers by the same group (with altoist Tab Smith and pianist Billy Kyle making the orchestra even stronger) including "St. Louis Wiggle Rhythm," "Merry-Go-Round," "Big John's Special," and "Algiers Stomp." But at the end of 1936, the personnel changed almost completely, and the final version of the Mills Blue Rhythm Band (which retained Smith and Kyle and had young trumpeters Charlie Shavers and Harry "Sweets" Edison), although fine, was not on the same level as the Red Allen group of the year before. Because the Mills Blue Rhythm Band never had a single musical vision, leader, or head arranger, it did not develop its own audience and broke up in 1938.

Jimmie Lunceford   Much more successful was Jimmie Lunceford's big band. Lunceford, a taskmaster who had been a former schoolteacher, really knew how to drill his sidemen, and his orchestra became famous for its showmanship, high musicianship, colorful stage shows, and tight ensembles. Lunceford was well trained on reeds, trombone, and guitar, but rarely played music himself in public. He earned a music degree from Fisk University and started teaching in Memphis in 1926. He put together a band with his best students the following year (the Chickasaw Syncopators) that recorded two songs. By 1929, his students formed the nucleus for his professional ensemble. They recorded two more numbers in Memphis in 1930 and spent time playing in Cleveland and Buffalo before moving to New York in 1933. The following year they started to make it big. The Jimmie Lunceford Orchestra had an unusual sound, with colorful arrangements from Sy Oliver and pianist Ed Wilcox, and many of the musicians doubling as cheerful singers. Tommy Stevenson in the early days provided high notes on the trumpet, and there were brief purposeful solos from altoist Willie Smith, tenor saxophonist Joe Thomas, Oliver on trumpet, and (starting in 1937) trombonist Trummy Young. Smith, Thomas, Oliver, and Young all took turns singing, although the band's regular (but insipid) ballad vocalist, Dan Grissom, has often accurately been called "Dan Gruesome" by some listeners.

Stomp It Off (GRP/Decca 608) and ● **For Dancers Only** (GRP/Decca 645) are excellent "best of" sets covering Jimmie Lunceford's dates during September 1934-June 1937, skipping over the inferior vocal numbers. **Stomp It Off** is highlighted by the infectious "Rhythm Is Our Business," "Dream of You," some miraculous saxophone ensemble work on "Sleepy Time Gal," and a trio of Duke Ellington songs. **For Dancers Only** has Sy Oliver arrangements on 14 of the 20 numbers and such gems as "Swanee River," "My Blue Heaven," "Organ Grinder's Swing," "The Merry-Go-Round Broke Down," and "For Dancers Only." **1937-1939** (Classics 520), which picks up where the Decca sets leave off, has the hit versions of "'Tain't What You Do" and "Margie" (with Trummy Young well featured) plus "Put on Your Old Grey Bonnet," "By the River St. Marie," and "Cheatin' on Me." Although not the greatest jazz band of the era, the Jimmie Lunceford Orchestra certainly carved out its own niche and deserved the success that it was achieving.

Duke Ellington   Duke Ellington must have looked on the success of Benny Goodman and other new big bands with a bit of amusement, for he was operating in a different world. Well established since late 1927, Ellington was gradually being recognized as one of the world's great arranger/composers and as a unique genius. He toured Europe for the first time in 1933 and that year introduced such songs as "Sophisticated Lady" and "Drop Me Off in Harlem" plus a remarkable musical recreation of a train trip called "Daybreak Express." 1934 brought "Stompy Jones" and "Solitude," 1935 resulted in "In a Sentimental Mood" and the melancholy four-part "Reminiscing in Tempo," while 1936 found Ellington writing individual features for Barney Bigard ("Clarinet Lament") and Cootie Williams ("Echoes of Harlem"). Juan Tizol's "Caravan," "Harmony in Harlem," "Diminuendo in Blue," and "Crescendo in Blue" came out of 1937, while 1938 included "I Let a Song Go Out of My Heart" (which became a hit for Benny Goodman and Martha Tilton), "Prelude to a Kiss," and Rex Stewart's showcase on "Boy Meets Horn."

Because Ellington (after Isham Jones broke up his band) was virtually the only major songwriter to be leading a swing orchestra, he was able to keep his repertoire fresh and unique. And his knack for blending together unusual voices and featuring his sidemen's strengths made his music very difficult to copy. During the 1933-38 period, he was fortunate enough to have very stable personnel. His lineup of January 1933 (Arthur

Whetsol, Freddy Jenkins, and Cootie Williams on trumpets, Tricky Sam Nanton, Lawrence Brown and Juan Tizol on trombones, Johnny Hodges on alto and soprano, baritonist Harry Carney, clarinetist Barney Bigard, guitarist Freddy Guy, bassist Wellman Braud, drummer Sonny Greer, and singer Ivie Anderson) only had four changes during the next five years. Otto Hardwicke rejoined the band on alto, Wellman Braud left in 1935 and was replaced by two bassists (Billy Taylor and Hayes Alvis) with Alvis departing in 1938, and both Freddy Jenkins and Arthur Whetsol were forced to retire.

Jenkins suffered from a serious lung ailment in 1934 when he was just 27. He made a comeback the following year, recording six numbers during his only date as a leader. He worked with Luis Russell a bit in 1936 and rejoined Ellington for a few months in 1937–38. But after going out on his own and co-leading a band with Hayes Alvis, his lung ailment returned and later in 1938 he had to permanently give up music. Rex Stewart, a master at distorting his tone by using a half-valve technique, took over the hot trumpet chair. Arthur Whetsol was struck down in 1936 with a serious brain disease and, other than a couple of brief attempts, never came back to music. His lyrical style and haunting tone have never been duplicated. His spot as first trumpeter was taken by the non-soloing Wallace Jones.

The most rewarding Duke Ellington CDs covering this period are a pair of two-CD sets ◉ **The Duke's Men: Small Groups, Vol. 1** (Columbia/Legacy 46995) and ◉ **The Duke's Men: Small Groups, Vol. 2** (Columbia/Legacy 48835). The 88 selections on the two releases feature combos from Ellington's orchestra, supposedly led by Rex Stewart, Barney Bigard, Cootie Williams, and Johnny Hodges, but really run by Ellington himself (who is usually on piano). Early versions of such tunes as "Caravan," "Stompy Jones," "Echoes of Harlem," "Jeep's Blues," "I Let a Song Go Out of My Heart," "Pyramid," "Prelude to a Kiss," and "The Jeep Is Jumpin'" are heard. Some of the songs received their debut in these combo settings before the big band tried them. The Ellington sidemen excel quite well in the relatively freewheeling settings.

As far as the Ellington big band recordings of the period go, Columbia has yet to make most of their important performances available domestically on CD. The Classics label has reissued all of the master takes on **1933** (Classics 637), **1933–1935** (Classics 646),

1935–1936 (Classics 659), **1936–1937** (Classics 666), **1937 Vol. 1** (Classics 675), **1937 Vol. 2** (Classics 687), **1938 Vol. 1** (Classics 700), and **1938 Vol. 2** (Classics 717). Unfortunately, from 1936 on, these releases also duplicate the small group dates, so the preferred acquisitions are the first three CDs. Why is the Sony label asleep on this timeless material?

Louis Armstrong and the Swing Era The most famous name in jazz, Louis Armstrong had been a hit in Europe during his tour of July 1932. Back in the United States, his recordings for Victor during 1932–33 were not at the same level as his earlier big band dates because his orchestras (which often include Teddy Wilson and tenor saxophonist Budd Johnson) were under-rehearsed and not always in tune. In a way, it did not matter that much because Satch was generally the entire show, but he did deserve to be in more simulating settings. **1932–1933** (Classics 529) picks up where **1931–1932** (Classics 536) had left off, consisting of the master takes of all the remaining Victor recordings including "I've Got the World on a String," "Hustlin' and Bustlin' for Baby," remakes of "Basin Street Blues" and "Mahogany Hall Stomp," the bizarre "Laughin' Louie," and "St. Louis Blues." The four-CD **The Complete RCA Victor Recordings** (Bluebird 68682) has all of this music plus eight intriguing alternate takes, Armstrong's meeting with country singer Jimmie Rodgers "Blue Yodel No. 9"), and two CDs from his second period with Victor (1946–47 and 1956) that will be covered in a later chapter.

In 1933, Louis Armstrong returned to Europe for an extended stay. Suffering from both management and trumpet chops trouble, he took it easy for two years, staying overseas and only making one recording session. He did appear in his first performance film, playing classic versions of "I Cover the Waterfront" and "Dinah" while in Scandinavia.

In general, little was heard from Armstrong until his return to the United States in the fall of 1935. At that point in time, he signed with Joe Glaser, who acted as his manager for the remainder of his career, making life much easier for the trumpet star and helping to make them both rich. Armstrong arrived home to find that the swing era was very much underway. Although he had inspired the whole movement, ironically he would be a minor participant in swing, a famous personality who occasionally appeared in movies (starting with Bing

Crosby's 1936 film *Pennies from Heaven*) and was a big name, but was considered as much a personality by fans as a jazz innovator. Armstrong took over the struggling Luis Russell Orchestra, using them as the nucleus of his band through 1940. Although there would be some solo space along the way for J.C. Higginbotham and Charlie Holmes, in general the orchestra did little but back Armstrong, and it gradually lost most of its personality.

Satch recorded for the Decca label during 1935–42, and his big band recordings of the era have long been considered controversial. Many fans and scholars felt that Armstrong's music was watered down during this period because it did not reach the creative heights of his Hot Five dates. Although it is true that many of his orchestra dates did not result in classics, in reality they have a charm of their own. Armstrong had simplified his playing style somewhat, but he was always capable of generating a great deal of excitement, and his vocalizing continued to grow in power and expressiveness.

While the American labels that have owned Decca through the years have been content to only come out with samplers, the European Classics label reissued all of the master takes (but no alternates) of Satch's Decca years. ◉ **1934–1936** (Classics 509) starts off with Armstrong's lone record date while in Europe, a particularly inspired session that includes "St. Louis Blues," "Tiger Rag," and the atmospheric "Song of the Vipers." Other than the final selection, the remainder of this CD features Satch leading the Luis Russell Orchestra. The musicianship of the band is excellent, and they sound enthusiastic on these recordings, particularly on memorable renditions of "You Are My Lucky Star," "La Cucaracha," "Ol' Man Mose," and "Thanks a Million." **1936–1937** (Classics 512) has a "Pennies from Heaven Medley" with Bing Crosby and actress Francis Langford,

several numbers on which Armstrong is backed by Jimmy Dorsey's Orchestra, and such tunes as "Swing that Music" (which has Satch hitting the same high note dozens of times), "The Skeleton in the Closet," four odd songs with a Hawaiian group led by Andy Iona, and Armstrong's first recordings with the Mills Brothers ("Carry Me Back to Old Virginny" and "Darling Nellie Gray"). **1937–1938** (Classics 515) includes both novelties and unexpected classics. Best are two numbers with the Mills Brothers, versions of "Once in a While" and "On the Sunny Side of the Street" with an octet taken from the Luis Russell Orchestra, "I Double Dare You," "Jubilee," a remake of "Struttin' with Some Barbecue," and Armstrong's earliest version of "When the Saints Go Marching In." **1938–1939** (Classics 523) has quite a variety of material, including another meeting with the Mills Brothers (highlighted by a touching "The Song Is Ended"), four spirituals with the Decca Mixed Chorus, a couple of strange "Elder Eatmore Sermons" (talking records that do not really come off), two Hoagy Carmichael tunes performed with the Casa Loma Orchestra, and a dozen numbers (including "Jeepers Creepers") with his regular big band. In general, Louis Armstrong's Decca recordings, while not as significant as his earlier Hot Fives or Benny Goodman's sessions of the period, are well worth checking out, for there are plenty of underrated performances to be discovered and savored.

Tommy Dorsey   The Dorsey Brothers Orchestra split into two shortly before Benny Goodman had his great success. Tommy Dorsey, after storming off the bandstand in the summer of 1935, took over the failing Joe Haymes Orchestra and whipped it into shape. Taking his cue from Paul Whiteman, Dorsey featured an eclectic

---

TIMELINE 1934

Benny Goodman's new orchestra is featured regularly on the Let's Dance radio series. • Coleman Hawkins sails to Europe. • Jack Teagarden signs a five-year contract with Paul Whiteman. • The Dorsey Brothers Orchestra becomes a regularly working band. • Chick Webb records "Stompin' at the Savoy." • Ben Pollack's Orchestra breaks up at the end of the year and is soon reorganized as the Bob Crosby Orchestra. • The Erskine Hawkins Big Band moves to New York. • Fats Waller starts to record with Fats Waller's Rhythm. • Louis Prima and Wingy Manone also begin recording extensively. • Buck Clayton leads a 14-piece orchestra that starts a two-year stint playing in Shanghai, China. • Heart trouble forces Clara Smith to retire from music. • Ella Fitzgerald wins an amateur contest at the Apollo Theatre.

variety of music, from "killer diller" swing romps and Dixieland-flavored numbers (the latter by a combo taken out of his big band called the Clambake Seven) to ballads, vocal features by his girlfriend Edythe Wright and Jack Leonard, and dance music. Dorsey was always in awe of Jack Teagarden's jazz skills so, although he could play a good jazz chorus or two, he tended to mostly feature his trombone on ballads (including his theme song "I'm Getting Sentimental Over You") where his tone was at its prettiest. In 1937, Dorsey's band moved up several notches. Bunny Berigan was in the orchestra for six weeks, and his exciting trumpet solos helped make "Marie" (which featured Jack Leonard's vocal answered by the band's glee club singing) and "Song of India" into major hits. Other sidemen along the way included Bud Freeman, clarinetist Johnny Mince, and trumpeter Pee Wee Erwin.

All of Tommy Dorsey's studio recordings from this era are available on **1928–1935** (Classics 833), **1935–36** (Classics 854), **1936** (Classics 878), **1936–1937** (Classics 916), **1937** (Classics 955), **1937 Vol. 2** (Classics 995), **1937 Vol. 3** (Classics 1035), **1937–1938** (Classics 1078), **1938** (Classics 1117), **1938 Vol. 2** (Classics 1156), and **1938–1939** (Classics 1197). Because Tommy Dorsey always recorded on a very prolific basis and much of his repertoire was outside of jazz, none of these 11 CDs is essential by itself; a "best of" jazz collection is long overdue. But listening to song after song from this era, one is struck at the high musicianship and clean ensembles that Dorsey successfully demanded of his sidemen. There are also three CDs available that have the bulk of the Clambake Seven performances. **Featuring the Clambake Seven** (Jazz Archives 3801262), **The Music Goes Round and Round** (Bluebird 3140), and **Having a Wonderful Time** (RCA 51643) have very few duplicates between them and feature such players as trumpeters Max Kaminsky, Sterling Bose, Pee Wee Erwin, Yank Lawson, and Charlie Shavers, clarinetists Joe Dixon, Johnny Mince, Buddy DeFranco, Bud Freeman, and Edythe Wright on good-humored Dixieland jams.

Jimmy Dorsey   The Jimmy Dorsey Orchestra took longer to catch on. His band had a few minor novelty hits (including "Long John Silver," "Dusk in Upper Sandusky," and "Parade of the Milk Bottle Caps") and excellent players in drummer Ray McKinley, pianist Freddie

Slack, and trumpeter Shorty Sherock along with ballad vocals by Bob Eberle. But as 1938 finished, it was still considered a minor outfit that was searching for its sound despite its leader's continuing fame. Few of its early studio recordings are available on CD. JD's band would make more of an impact in future years.

Bunny Berigan   Rowland "Bunny" Berigan was arguably the top trumpeter in jazz during 1935–38, particularly if one does not count Louis Armstrong and the up-and-coming Roy Eldridge. Berigan started out playing in local bands and college groups in the Midwest, failed his first audition with Hal Kemp's Orchestra in 1928 (his tone was considered too thin, a situation he quickly fixed) and, after much practice, in 1930 was hired by Kemp. Berigan recorded a few titles with Kemp and toured Europe. In 1931, he joined Fred Rich's CBS studio band, staying for four years except for a few disappointing months with Paul Whiteman.

Berigan had a beautiful sound, a wide range (his low notes could be as memorable as his upper register shouts), and a chance-taking style that brought excitement to every session he appeared on. Unfortunately, he was also an alcoholic and a bit reckless in his private life (he never should have tried to be a bandleader). But during the early years of the swing era, he had few competitors. Berigan appeared on many recordings as a hot jazz soloist during 1931–35, including with the Dorsey Brothers and the Boswell Sisters. In 1935, he was persuaded by Benny Goodman to join his orchestra for a few months (taking the famous solos on "King Porter Stomp" and "Sometimes I'm Happy" and being part of the band on its historic tour out West) before returning to the lucrative studio scene. In 1937, Berigan had his short stint with Tommy Dorsey's band. When he left TD, Berigan decided that it was time for him to have a big band of his own.

Bunny Berigan had already recorded quite a bit. **The ARC Years 1931–36** (IAJRC 1013) captures the trumpeter as an anonymous but important sideman, adding bits of jazz to dance band music played by studio orchestras. **1935–1936** (Classics 734) has Berigan leading small-group dates (featuring tenors Eddie Miller and Bud Freeman, altoist Edgar Sampson, Artie Shaw, and singer Chick Bullock) plus numbers done with pianist Frank Froeba and vocalist Midge Williams. Highlights include "You Took Advantage of Me," "Chicken and Waffles," and "I'm Comin' Virginia" plus Berigan's earliest recording of "I Can't Get Started." **1936–1937** (Classics 749) has some more small-group recordings (although too many Art Gentry vocals) and the first sessions by the new Bunny Berigan big band.

At first, things looked bright for the Bunny Berigan Orchestra, which had a major hit in "I Can't Get Started" that became its theme song. With a Bluebird record contract and such sidemen as the young tenor Georgie Auld (who sounded a lot like Charlie Barnet at the time) and drummer Buddy Rich (on his first major job), Berigan had a promising orchestra. **1937** (Classics 766) includes many of the most rewarding Berigan big band recordings including "Mahogany Hall Stomp," "I Can't Get Started," "The Prisoner's Song" (which contains one of Bunny's finest trumpet solos), "A Study in Brown," and "In a Little Spanish Town." **1937–1938** (Classics 785) finds the Bunny Berigan Orchestra stalling, and being stuck recording far too many "dog" tunes, including "Piano Tuner Man," "Rinka Tinka Man," "An Old Straw Hat," and "Moonshine Over Kentucky." **1938** (Classics 815) also has some dreck, but unaccountably the band's output greatly improved in November 1938, with such numbers as "Sobbin' Blues" and "Jelly Roll Blues" plus octet versions of six Bix Beiderbecke numbers, including some of the earliest versions of his piano pieces; four of the compositions are on this CD ("In a Mist," "Flashes," "Davenport Blues," and "Candlelights"). However, Berigan's constant drinking resulted in lost opportunities, and his lack of business skills certainly did not help the fortunes of his struggling band.

Two CDs of Berigan's radio transcriptions are quite rewarding: **Sing! Sing! Sing!** (Jass 627), which features Berigan leading a studio band in 1936 and his 1938 orchestra, and **1938: Devil's Holiday** (Jass 638). Those two CDs are less commercial than Berigan's later Bluebird recordings, and these sessions gave the leader quite a few opportunities to cut loose. But the one Bunny Berigan CD to acquire is the definitive sampler ◉ **The Pied Piper 1934–40** (Bluebird 66615). It not only includes "I Can't Get Started," "The Prisoner's Song," and six of the best Berigan big band numbers, but also five songs with Benny Goodman, four with Tommy Dorsey (including all the hits with those two bands), and various appearances with all-star groups. This disc features Berigan at his peak and shows why he was one of the all-time great trumpeters.

Artie Shaw While Tommy Dorsey and Bunny Berigan made major stirs in the jazz/swing world during 1937, Artie Shaw (born Arthur Arshawsky) merged in 1938 as Benny Goodman's main competitor, both as a clarinetist and as a very popular bandleader. Shaw was always an odd choice to become a jazz celebrity, for he spent most of his life running away from commercial success, yet constantly finding it despite himself. He began playing saxophone and clarinet when he was 12. Shaw developed very quickly, playing with the New Haven High School band and leading the Bellevue Ramblers. By the time he was 15 (in 1925), he was already touring with bands. Shaw played with a variety of obscure ensembles (including Irving Aaronson's Commanders), moved to New York City in 1930, and worked with such orchestras as Paul Specht, Vincent Lopez, Roger Wolfe Kahn, and Red Nichols. He became a studio musician during the worst years of the Depression, made a lucrative living, and then quit music for the first time in 1934 to live on a farm and attempt to write a novel. But Shaw ran out of money before he made much progress on his book so he returned to New York by the following year and was back in the studios.

Shaw's big break came on April 8, 1936. For a major big band concert, he was hired to lead a group for ten minutes between sets by bigger names. Rather than head an orchestra, Shaw performed "Interlude in B Flat" on clarinet with a string quartet and a rhythm section. This performance was the hit of the concert, leading to calls for him to form a band of his own. Shaw took the radical step of putting together an ensemble consisting of four horns (including Tony Pastor on tenor and trumpeter Lee Castle), a string quartet, and a four-piece rhythm section, which certainly made his band stand out from the typical swing orchestra of 1936. **The Best of the Big Bands** (Columbia/Legacy 46156) and **It Goes to Your Feet** (Columbia/Legacy 53423) have Shaw's earliest recordings as a bandleader. Although **The Best of the Big Bands** unfortunately does not bother listing personnel or recording dates, it has Shaw's first four sessions complete and in chronological order. The music is gentle and the ensemble sound quite appealing, with highlights including "The Japanese Sandman," "A Pretty Girl Is Like a Melody," "Sugar Foot Stomp," and "The Skeleton in the Closet." **It Goes to Your Feet** has the remaining 15 selections from Shaw's first band (including

"Sobbin' Blues," "Copenhagen," and "Streamline") plus the first three cuts by his second orchestra.

Despite his best efforts, Artie Shaw was not able to have a success with his initial band; it was too far ahead of its time. Frustrated by its failure, Shaw decided to form a much more conventional orchestra in 1937 and beat the other big bands at their own game. The band recorded 33 additional numbers for Columbia (not yet reissued on CD) and struggled for a year before lightning struck. For his first session for the Bluebird label (July 24, 1938), Shaw recorded a Cole Porter song called "Begin the Beguine." The recording was such a hit that overnight the Artie Shaw Orchestra was considered a sensation. Tony Pastor offered occasional Louis Armstrong–inspired vocals (including on "Indian Love Call"), Billie Holiday toured with the band for a few difficult months (her only recording with Shaw was "Any Old Time" due to her being signed to a different label), and the clarinetist played beautifully on such recordings as "Nonstop Flight," "Softly as in a Morning Sunrise," and "Nightmare" (his dark theme song). By year end, Artie Shaw was competing favorably with Benny Goodman. **Begin the Beguine** (Bluebird 6274) is an excellent sampler covering the years 1938–41, while **22 Original Big Band Recordings** (Hindsight 401) and **Radio Years Vol. 1** (Jazz Unlimited 2018) feature Shaw's increasingly popular band on radio broadcasts.

Isham Jones and Woody Herman   In addition to Tommy Dorsey taking over the failing Joe Haymes band, two other important big bands were born out of the ashes of others. The great songwriter Isham Jones led a first-class dance band during the first half of the 1930s. **The Isham Jones Centennial Album** (Viper's Nest 156) has 17 selections from a surprisingly jazz-oriented version of Jones's Orchestra from 1935, featuring a young Woody Herman on vocals and clarinet. The intriguing ensemble (which has three violins and both bass and tuba) sounds a bit like the Benny Goodman Orchestra, except that it was a few months before BG hit it big. Also on this disc are five selections from Jones's obscure band of 1937.

During the summer of 1936, Isham Jones broke up his orchestra, calling it quits for a time. Woody Herman had been a performer from the time he was a child, singing in vaudeville. He began playing alto when he was 11 and clarinet at 14, performing with territory bands as

a teenager, most notably with Tom Gerun during 1929–34. At 21 in 1934, Herman joined Isham Jones and he was just 23 when he formed his own big band out of the nucleus of Jones's ensemble. During the 1936–38 period, the majority of Herman's recordings featured him as a crooner and his orchestra searched without much success for its own personality. **1936–1937** (Classics 1042) and **1937–1938** (Classics 1090) have seven numbers featuring Herman with Isham Jones and then the first 38 recordings by the Woody Herman Orchestra, only three of which are instrumentals. These are primarily of historic interest, for the Herman big band was given the "B list" of songs to record, being considered a second-level band during this early period.

Ben Pollack and Bob Crosby   Poor Ben Pollack. Throughout his career, Pollack was continually discovering new talent that would be swiped away by better-known bandleaders. His 1927 group had had Benny Goodman, Glenn Miller, and Jimmy McPartland, and in 1929 he featured Jack Teagarden in his orchestra, but all eventually left him. During 1933–34, Pollack had a big band that included trumpeter Yank Lawson, tenor saxophonist Eddie Miller, and clarinetist Matty Matlock, but his concern for the career of his girlfriend Doris Robbins (whom he featured excessively as a singer and hoped to make into a movie star) and his reluctance to let his jazz soloists cut loose resulted in a revolt that led to the breakup of his orchestra in December 1934.

The former Pollack musicians wanted to stay together and at first approached Jack Teagarden about becoming their leader. Unfortunately, Teagarden had signed a five-year contract with Paul Whiteman and was unavailable, so the musicians next turned to Bing Crosby's younger brother, Bob Crosby. Crosby, who had sung with the Dorsey Brothers Orchestra, was not a musician or an arranger and just an okay singer, but he was considered an ideal frontman. At first the Bob Crosby Orchestra was fairly conventional, but by 1936 the band was gaining strong popularity as the first New Orleans–style big band. With such soloists as Lawson, trumpeter Billy Butterfield (who joined in 1937), clarinetist Irving Fazola (a member of the band starting in 1938), Matlock, and Miller, and a rhythm section that included pianist Bob Zurke, guitarist/singer Nappy Lamare, bassist/arranger Bob Haggart, and drummer Ray Bauduc, many of the ensembles had the feel of New

Orleans jazz. In addition, starting in November 1937, the Bob Crosby Bobcats (a four-horn octet taken from the big band) became an extra added attraction, performing Dixieland specialties in concert and on records. Among the best recordings overall by the band during 1936–38 are "Dixieland Shuffle," "Come Back, Sweet Papa," "Savoy Blues," "Gin Mill Blues," Joe Sullivan's "Little Rock Getaway," Haggart's "South Rampart Street Parade," "At the Jazz Band Ball," and "Honky Tonk Train Blues," plus from the Bobcats "Fidgety Feet," "March of the Bob Cats," "Palasteena," and "Call Me a Taxi," featuring Eddie Miller. Also, the duo of Haggart (doubling on whistling) and Bauduc had a major hit with "The Big Noise from Winnetka," while Billy Butterfield was showcased on Haggart's "I'm Free," which was soon renamed "What's New." The majority of these big band selections are currently available on ❍ **South Rampart Street Parade** (GRP/Decca 615), a definitive single-CD sampler of the orchestra, although there is nothing from the Bobcats. Also available is **1937–1938** (ABC 838 477), which has 11 tunes from the Bobcats, seven from the big band, and only four repeats from the Decca disc. Hopefully a more complete retrospective of the Bob Crosby Orchestra and Bobcats will come out eventually, for the Crosby organizations recorded quite a bit of rewarding material, even if the leader is absent from virtually all of its best performances.

As for Ben Pollack, after he gave up trying to make Doris Robbins famous, he put together a new orchestra in 1936 that featured a young trumpeter whom he discovered in Texas, Harry James. Three recording sessions later, James was playing with Benny Goodman. Pollack's 1937 band featured trumpeter Muggsy Spanier, but he became seriously ill the following year. His replacement Clyde Hurley was with Pollack until Glenn Miller nabbed him, and the final recordings by the Ben Pollack Orchestra in 1938 featured a ghost of the past, Andy Secrest, who soon became a full-time studio musician. Ben Pollack never did graduate to the big leagues.

Glenn Miller   In 1938, Glenn Miller was completely unknown to the general public. Miller, after playing and arranging for Ben Pollack during 1926–28, freelanced in the studios, worked with pit bands for shows, and was with the Dorsey Brothers Orchestra (1934–35) and Ray Noble's American Band in 1935. Miller knew that he was not a major trombone soloist and that his main talents

lay in arranging. In 1937, he put together the first Glenn Miller Orchestra, but he had not yet developed his signature sound. **Best of the Big Bands** (Columbia/Legacy 48831) has 16 of the 18 selections that Miller recorded for Columbia and Brunswick, including two numbers from 1935 (which have brief trumpet solos by Bunny Berigan) and ten selections from 1937 (including "I Got Rhythm" and "Community Swing"), which find the Miller band sounding conventional and not displaying any real personality. After breaking up the band at the beginning of 1938, Miller put together his second band a few months later. Its first session is also on this CD with singer Ray Eberle making his debut on "Don't Wake Up My Heart." The Miller sound (with a clarinet doubling the melody an octave above the sax section) was just beginning to emerge, but 1938 would be a year of struggle. Miller did sign with the Bluebird label in the fall and recorded one date, but his orchestra had not made an impression yet.

Larry Clinton   Larry Clinton, who was self-taught on trumpet and trombone, like Miller, was primarily an arranger and bandleader rather than a soloist. He contributed arrangements to a variety of bands starting in 1932, including Isham Jones, the Dorsey Brothers, Glen Gray, Louis Armstrong, Tommy Dorsey, and Bunny Berigan. For Dorsey he wrote his best-known original, "The Dipsy Doodle." After leading two sessions of his own that became surprisingly popular, a reluctant Clinton was persuaded to start a big band, one that lasted for four years (1937–41). Ironically, he was forbidden by his label (Victor) to record "The Dipsy Doodle" since it was TD's hit, but he had successes with his adaptation of classical works (particularly "My Reverie"), playing first-class dance music and featuring vocals by the underrated Bea Wain. **Shades of Hades** (Hep 1037) has all of the music from Clinton's two sessions with studio players and his first three with his new band. The stronger jazz numbers among the mixture of solid dance band music and Wain vocals are "Midnight in the Madhouse," "Abba Dabba," "The Campbells Are Swingin'," a catchy arrangement of "Oh Lady Be Good," and "Wolverine Blues." ❍ **Studies in Clinton** (Hep 1052), which dates from 1938 with five numbers from 1939–40, has Wain's hit versions of "My Reverie," "Deep Purple," and "Martha" plus six of Clinton's riff-instrumental "Studies" (which had begun with "A Study in Brown," recorded by Bunny Berigan): "A Study in Blue," "A Study in Green," "A Study in Red," "A Study in Scarlet," "A Study in Surrealism," and "A Study in Modernism." Listening to those recordings and others such as "Milenburg Joys," "Dippermouth Blues," "Zig Zag," and "Sunday," it seems obvious that Clinton had one of the most underrated jazz big bands of the era. None of his sidemen were major names, but tenor saxophonist Tony Zimmers was a fine player, many of the musicians were quite capable of taking concise solos, and though Clinton's charts may have been a bit derivative at times, they always swung. Also quite worthy is an album of radio transcriptions, **Vol. 1** (Nostalgia Arts 3016), which dates from 1937–38. The 75-minute disc opens with the only studio version of Clinton playing "The Dipsy Doodle" during the era. Bea Wain is featured on around half of the numbers and the arrangements are inventive within the context of ensemble-oriented swing.

Red Norvo and Mildred Bailey   Red Norvo (born Kenneth Norville), jazz's first and practically only xylophone soloist, started on piano and took up the xylophone while in high school. In 1925, Norvo toured the Midwest with the Collegians, a marimba band. He worked in Chicago with Paul Ash and Ben Bernie, performed in vaudeville as a solo act (which included tap dancing), led a band on radio station KSTP, and played with Victor Young. Norvo was a member of the Paul Whiteman Orchestra (1931–32) where he met Mildred Bailey. They were married in 1933, shortly after they went out on their own.

◉ **Dance of the Octopus** (Hep 1044), dating from 1933–36, has Norvo's first 26 recordings as a leader. There are numbers from his 1936 octet (an unusual group with the leader's xylophone and arranger Eddie Sauter's mellophone in prominent spots) and all-star octets of 1934–35, which include such future big bandleaders as Artie Shaw, trombonists Jack Jenney, Charlie Barnet, Teddy Wilson, and Bunny Berigan. Best of all are four chamber jazz classics from 1933. Norvo's xylophone and marimba are showcased on "Knockin' on Wood" and "Hole in the Wall" in a quartet with Jimmy Dorsey, pianist Fulton McGrath, and bassist Artie Bernstein. There are haunting versions of Bix Beiderbecke's "In a Mist" and the playful "Dance of the Octopus" with a quartet that includes Benny Goodman (mostly on bass clarinet), Bernstein, and Dick McDonough.

Meanwhile, Mildred Bailey was gaining a reputation as one of jazz's top female singers. Her high-pitched voice was unusual, as was her ability to swing virtually any song. **Vol. 2** (The Old Masters 104) has a couple of items from 1931, six numbers from 1932 (including her earliest version of "Rockin' Chair"), and such performances from 1933–34 as "Is That Religion," "Shoutin' in the Amen Corner," "Lazy Bones," "There's a Cabin in the Cotton," "Ol Pappy," and "Emaline." Bailey is often joined by the Dorsey Brothers and Bunny Berigan, with the later selections featuring Coleman Hawkins and Benny Goodman.

In 1936, Norvo and Bailey (who were known as "Mr. and Mrs. Swing") headed a small big band that grew in size during 1937–38. Most unusual was Eddie Sauter's arrangements, which allowed Norvo's xylophone to be heard over the ensembles. Mildred Bailey's limited-edition ten-CD set **The Complete Columbia Recordings** (Mosaic 10-204) has 214 selections (counting alternate takes), most of the singer's recordings from the swing era including her dates with the Norvo band, and other special sessions. Obviously, this is the best all-around Mildred Bailey reissue to get although it is not inexpensive and will go out of print quickly. Those who cannot locate or

TIMELINE 1935

Benny Goodman becomes a sensation, first at the Palomar Ballroom in Los Angeles, then throughout the nation, ushering in the swing era. • Teddy Wilson's series of small-group records (many with Billie Holiday) begins. • Ella Fitzgerald joins Chick Webb. • Fletcher Henderson's big band breaks up. • Due to a fight, Tommy and Jimmy Dorsey split up and one orchestra becomes two. • Louis Armstrong returns to the United States, takes over the Luis Russell Orchestra. • After Bennie Moten's unexpected death, Count Basie forms his own band. • Benny Carter and Bill Coleman both move to Europe. • Milt Gabler becomes the first to start reissuing records. • Les Brown forms the Duke Blue Devils while attending Duke University. • Harry James is featured with Ben Pollack's Orchestra.

afford that set may want Bailey's **1937–1938** (Classics 1114) and **1938** (Classics 1160). **1937–1938** includes such gems as "There's a Lull in My Life," "Just a Stone's Throw from Heaven," and "Lover Come Back to Me." **1938** has among its highlights "Washboard Blues," "My Melancholy Baby," "Born to Swing," and "St. Louis Blues."

Norvo's ◉ **1936–1937** (Classics 1123) features both the instrumentals and vocal numbers of Norvo's orchestra, including "I Got Rhythm," "A Porter's Love Song to a Chambermaid," "It's Love I'm After," "Smoke Dreams," "Remember," and "I Would Do Anything for You." **1937–1938** (Classics 1157), which has "Russian Lullaby," "The Weekend of a Private Secretary," and "Please Be Kind," and **1938–1939** (Classics 1192), highlighted by "Just You, Just Me," "Undecided," "Rehearsin' for a Nervous Breakdown," and a session in which Bailey and Norvo are joined by the John Kirby Sextet, are also well worth picking up and include most of the other recordings by the Red Norvo Orchestra.

Erskine Hawkins   Erskine Hawkins, who was billed as "The 20th Century Gabriel," had a colorful if bombastic style on the trumpet, and was able to hit high notes with ease. He started out playing drums when he was seven, spent a few years on trombone, and switched to trumpet as a teenager. Hawkins played with the 'Bama Street Collegians at the State Teachers College in Montgomery, Alabama, and became its leader. In 1934, the band became independent of the college, moved to New York, and became the Erskine Hawkins Orchestra. Hawkins's ensemble was expert at playing swinging tempos that dancers loved, especially when booked at the Savoy Ballroom. With Dud Bascomb taking the medium-register trumpet solos and Paul Bascomb or Julian Dash on tenor, pianist Avery Parrish, and baritonist Heywood Henry as key soloists along with the leader, this was a powerful and very jazz-oriented band. **1936–1938** (Classics 653) has the band's first recordings, including such jump tunes as "Swingin' in Harlem," "Big John's Special," "Uproar Shout," "I Found a New Baby," and "Carry Me Back to Old Virginny."

Willie Bryant   For a few years, Willie Bryant led a continually interesting big band. Although he had tried unsuccessfully to learn the trumpet as a youth, Bryant primarily worked as a dancer (in his early days), emcee, and an occasional singer in vaudeville and shows. In late 1934, he organized a big band that had five recording

sessions during 1935–36 and a final obscure effort in 1938. **1935–1936** (Classics 768) has all but the later date, with Bryant taking good-natured vocals on 14 of the 22 selections. But much more important than the leader are the contributions of his sidemen, which include Teddy Wilson, tenor saxophonist Johnny Russell, Benny Carter (on trumpet), Ben Webster, Taft Jordan, and Cozy Cole. Some of the better selections include "It's Over Because We're Through" (Bryant's theme song), "Long About Midnight," "The Sheik," "Jerry the Junker," and "Liza." However Bryant gradually lost all of his star sidemen and reluctantly broke up his orchestra in 1938.

Teddy Hill   Teddy Hill, who had played tenor with the Luis Russell Orchestra during 1928–29, formed his own band in 1932. The 1935 version had such notables in the lineup as Roy Eldridge, Bill Coleman, Chu Berry, and Dickie Wells, while trumpeters Frankie Newton, Shad Collins, and a 20-year-old Dizzy Gillespie also spent time with Hill's slightly later groups. **Dance with His NBC Orchestra** (Jazz Archives 157012) has all 26 of the Hill Big Band's recordings. Although there are a few novelty numbers and too many Bill Dillard vocals, there are also a few important early solos by Eldridge, Wells, and Berry plus Gillespie's first session (which includes his solo on "King Porter Stomp"). Among the other highlights are "Lookie, Lookie, Lookie Here Comes Cookie," "At the Rug Cutter's Ball," "A Study in Brown," and "China Boy."

Earl Hines   While nearly all of the most significant swing era big bands were based in New York at least part of the time, one stayed in Chicago and two others emerged from Kansas City. Earl Hines, a major influence on other pianists in the 1930s (including Jess Stacy, Joe Sullivan, Nat King Cole, Teddy Wilson, and Art Tatum), had been leading his own big band in Chicago since its opening on December 28, 1928 (his 25th birthday), performing regularly at the Grand Terrace Ballroom. **1932–1934** (Classics 514), which has solo piano versions of "Love Me Tonight" and "Down Among the Sheltering Palms," features the early Hines orchestra. The key soloists include Hines, trumpet/vocalist Walter Fuller, Jelly Roll Morton's favorite clarinetist Omer Simeon (also playing alto and baritone), and Trummy Young (prior to him joining Jimmie Lunceford), with Jimmy Mundy providing most of the arrangements. "Blue Drag," the original version of Hines's "Rosetta," "Cavernism," and

"Madhouse" are among the highlights. **1934–1937** (Classics 528) has Darnell Howard added to the group on clarinet, alto, and violin, and swinging versions of "That's a Plenty," "Sweet Georgia Brown," "Copenhagen," "Rock and Rye," and "Pianology" making this a worthy acquisition. While many of the musicians who chose to remain in Chicago in the 1930s slipped away into obscurity, the Earl Hines Orchestra (helped by its radio broadcasts) managed to have a strong national reputation.

Andy Kirk   Kansas City was a particularly attractive town for black musicians in the early 1930s because, despite Prohibition, it was a wide-open city where speakeasies, gambling joints, bars, restaurants, and clubs were open all the time and in need of entertainment. All-night jam sessions were regular occurrences, and in that environment, many top jazz players quickly developed their styles. By the mid-1930s, the city was beginning to decline although it still had a very strong music scene. Andy Kirk's Twelve Clouds of Joy, which had recorded during 1929–31, was signed by Decca in 1936 and brought to New York. They soon had a hit record of "Until the Real Thing Comes Along" (with a high-note vocal by Pha Terrell). However, the band was more significant for featuring the arrangements and piano solos of Mary Lou Williams, and some fine spots on tenor by Dick Wilson. Although the group's recordings from this period have been reissued in full by the Classics label on **1936–1937** (Classics 573), **1937–1938** (Classics 581), and **1938** (Classics 598), it is best to get ❍ **Mary's Idea** (GRP/Decca 622) since this is a sampler covering 1936–41 that has the orchestra's finest instrumentals (including "Walkin' and Swingin'," "Froggy Bottom," "The Lady Who Swings the Band," "Mess-a-Stomp," "Mary's Idea," and "The Count") with only one Terrell vocal.

Count Basie   The biggest news in the swing world in late 1936 was the discovery of Count Basie's Orchestra in Kansas City and its trip east. Bill Basie, born in Red Bank, New Jersey, had been encouraged early on by Fats Waller on both piano and organ. Basie played locally in New York and New Jersey and spent several years working with traveling revues in theaters. He was with the *Gonzelle White Show* during 1925–27, but when it left him stranded in Kansas City in 1927, Basie liked the local music scene and decided to stay. He first accompanied silent pictures, became a member of Walter Page's Blue Devils the following year, and in 1929 was hired by

the Bennie Moten Orchestra. So impressed was Moten by Basie's playing that the leader did not record again as a pianist and only played a few songs a night with the band, preferring to have Basie assume his spot. The Bennie Moten Orchestra began to struggle in 1933, and for a few months in 1934, Basie broke away to form his own group although he soon returned. When Bennie Moten died unexpectedly in 1935 of complications from a tonsillectomy (he was only 40), Bennie's brother Buster Moten took over the band and Basie permanently went out on his own. Basie, who was dubbed "Count" by a radio announcer, led a trio that became an ensemble (the Barons of Rhythm), which he co-led with altoist Buster Smith before becoming its sole leader. Basie's early band featured trumpeter/singer Hot Lips Page (who was soon lured away and sent east by manager Joe Glaser), singer Jimmy Rushing, trumpeter Buck Clayton, trombonists Dan Minor and Eddie Durham, the contrasting tenors of Lester Young and Herschel Evans, baritonist Jack Washington, guitarist/violinist Claude Williams, bassist Walter Page, and drummer Jo Jones.

The Basie rhythm section helped give jazz a new sound. Although always having a slight Fats Waller influence, Count Basie pared his piano style to the bare essentials, making expert use of silence, displaying perfect time, and making every note count. The space that he left was filled by the 4/4 on-the-beat rhythm of the guitar and bass. Jo Jones's light drumming (a major contrast to Gene Krupa's pounding of the bass drum with Benny Goodman) shifted the timekeeping function from the bass drum to the cymbals, giving the Basie orchestra a light sound even when playing uptempo. In addition, Lester Young's cool tone on the tenor and relaxed floating style was innovative and new, much different from Coleman Hawkins's hard tone and harmonically advanced explorations.

The Basie band broadcast regularly from Kansas City's Reno Club on station W9XBY and was heard one night by John Hammond in Chicago. Hammond, a masterful talent scout and a sympathetic (if sometimes intrusive) record producer, made the mistake of mentioning his new find to a few other people. By the time he made it to Kansas City and persuaded Basie to take his band east, Count had already signed a record contact with Decca that was not all that lucrative. However, Hammond still worked with Basie and helped guide his future. Since the Basie band was only nine pieces at the time, new musicians had to be added to the band in a hurry along with arrangements; most of the band's tunes had been played by heart. It took a few months of struggling for the orchestra to solidify and there were some flops along the way, especially a stint at the Grand Terrace Ballroom where the ensemble's weak sight-readers made it difficult for the orchestra to accompany specialty acts. Shortly after reaching New York in 1936, Lester Young made his recording debut with a quintet from the band (his "Lady Be Good" solo with Jones-Smith Incorporated is a classic), and in early 1937 the full orchestra appeared on records for the first time. Hammond persuaded Basie to make further changes in the personnel. Claude Williams was replaced by rhythm guitarist Freddie Green because Hammond did not like jazz violinists; ironically, Williams (after decades of obscurity) would have a major comeback and outlive everyone from the early Basie band.

By the end of 1937, the Count Basie Orchestra was considered one of the hottest bands in jazz, and both its theme "One o'Clock Jump" and "Jumpin' at the Woodside" were quickly becoming standards. Billie Holiday was the band's female singer for much of a year (when she left, Helen Humes took her place), and such new soloists as trumpeter Harry "Sweets" Edison and trombonists Benny Morton and Dickie Wells were major additions. ◉ **The Complete Decca Recordings** (GRP/Decca 611), a three-CD set, has all 57 of the selections that the Basie big band recorded while with Decca from January 21, 1937, through February 4, 1939, including six alternate takes. Such swing classics as "Honeysuckle Rose," "Boogie Woogie," "John's Idea," "Sent For You Yesterday and Here You Come Today," "Blue and Sentimental" (Herschel Evans's most famous solo), "Jive at Five," and the original versions of "One o'Clock Jump" and "Jumpin' at the Woodside" are among the many highpoints from this increasingly influential orchestra. Count Basie may not have preceded Benny Goodman, but his band would in time become known as the definitive swing orchestra.

Billie Holiday   Billie Holiday is still a magical name more than 40 years after her death. She was the most notable singer to emerge during the 1933–38 period; Ella Fitzgerald was still musically immature in 1938. Holiday (born Eleanora Harris and nicknamed "Lady Day" by Lester Young) did not have a large voice and her

improvising was fairly basic, but her behind-the-beat phrasing, the emotional intensity that she put into her singing, and the way she interpreted lyrics (which often described her life and her feelings) put her in a class by itself. The daughter of guitarist Clarence Holiday, who spent a period playing with Fletcher Henderson, she had a very difficult childhood. Her father abandoned her mother early on (they were never married), and Holiday grew up feeling alone and unloved, gaining a lifelong inferiority complex due to harrowing episodes in her childhood. The turning point in Holiday's life came in 1933 when she was 18. She was heard singing in a Harlem club by John Hammond, who became a major booster. He set up her first record date (two songs with Benny Goodman) and, although those performances ("Your Mother's Son-in-Law" and "Riffin' the Scotch") were not memorable, Holiday's career was on its way.

A few words should be said about John Hammond since he made such a major contribution to the swing era and was arguably the most important nonmusician involved in the early years of swing. A member of a very rich family and educated at Yale, Hammond was from the start a masterful talent scout, a fighter against racism, and a propagandist for the music that he loved. In 1933, the 22-year-old not only "discovered" Billie Holiday but arranged what would be Bessie Smith's final record date; he had previously produced a particularly strong session for Fletcher Henderson. He befriended Benny Goodman, convinced the clarinetist to acquire Henderson arrangements for the *Let's Dance* radio series, produced American jazz dates for the European market, worked with Benny Carter, and in 1936 discovered the Count Basie Orchestra (the band was only known in Kansas City at the time) while randomly scanning the radio dial. The early highpoint of his career was organizing the two famous "From Spirituals to Swing" all-star Carnegie Hall concerts that took place in December 1938 and December 1939. Hammond could be a bit dominant and overly forceful in his viewpoints, but time has found him to have been generally right and well intentioned.

Billie Holiday freelanced in 1934 and made a short film with Duke Ellington the following year. It was John Hammond's idea to team Holiday on records with all-star combos led by Teddy Wilson. These also overlapped with a similar series of recordings released under Lady Day's name (starting in 1937); both continued regularly until 1942. During this period of time, Holiday had stints with the bands of Count Basie (1937) and Artie Shaw (1938), but only one selection ("Any Old Time" with Shaw) was recorded because she was signed with a competing record label. Fortunately, though, her small-group dates resulted in many timeless classics.

The ten-CD box set **The Complete Billie Holiday on Columbia 1933–1944** (Columbia/Legacy 85470) has all of those recordings plus alternate takes and a few radio appearances. Listeners with a large budget will consider that set essential, but fortunately the master takes of the studio sessions are also available on nine individual CDs in **The Quintessential Billie Holiday** series. **The Quintessential Billie Holiday Vol. 1** (Columbia 60646) has the two numbers from 1933 with the remainder from 1935, including "What a Little Moonlight Can

Do," "Miss Brown to You," and "Twenty-Four Hours a Day." Key sidemen include Roy Eldridge, Benny Goodman, Ben Webster, Chu Berry, and of course Teddy Wilson. **The Quintessential Billie Holiday Vol. 2** (Columbia 40790) is highlighted by "These Foolish Things," "I Cried for You" (which has some wonderful playing by Johnny Hodges), "Summertime," "Billie's Blues," and "The Way You Look Tonight." Jonah Jones, Bunny Berigan, Artie Shaw, and Webster all make their presence felt.

In 1937, Billie Holiday recorded for the first time with Lester Young (whom Lady Day nicknamed Pres) and Buck Clayton, her musical soul mates. Young's lighter-than-air tone and lyrical thoughtful style perfectly gelled with Holiday, while Clayton's restrained playing had

38 ESSENTIAL RECORDS OF 1933–1938

Benny Goodman, **The Birth of Swing** (Bluebird 61038), 3 CDs

Benny Goodman, **The Complete Small Group Recordings** (RCA 68764)

Benny Goodman, **Benny Goodman Carnegie Hall Jazz Concert** (Columbia 65167), 2 CDs

Chick Webb, **1929–1934** (Classics 502)

Claude Hopkins, **1932–1934** (Classics 699)

Jimmie Lunceford, **For Dancers Only** (GRP/Decca 645)

Duke Ellington, **The Duke's Men: Small Groups, Vol. 1** (Columbia/Legacy 46995), 2 CDs

Duke Ellington, **The Duke's Men: Small Groups, Vol. 2** (Columbia/Legacy 48835), 2 CDs

Louis Armstrong, **1934–1936** (Classics 509)

Bunny Berigan, **The Pied Piper 1934–40** (Bluebird 66615)

Bob Crosby, **South Rampart Street Parade** (GRP/Decca 615)

Larry Clinton, **Studies in Clinton** (Hep 1052)

Red Norvo, **Dance of the Octopus** (Hep 1044)

Red Norvo, **1936–1937** (Classics 1123)

Andy Kirk, **Mary's Idea** (GRP/Decca 622)

Count Basie, **The Complete Decca Recordings** (GRP/Decca 611), 3 CDs

Billie Holiday, **The Quintessential, Vol. 4** (Columbia 44252)

Billie Holiday, **The Quintessential, Vol. 5** (Columbia 44423)

Teddy Grace, **Teddy Grace** (Timeless 1-016)

Maxine Sullivan, **1937–1938** (Classics 963)

Art Tatum, **Classic Early Solos** (GRP/Decca 607)

Fats Waller, **The Early Years, Part 1** (Bluebird 66618), 2 CDs

Stuff Smith, **1936–1939** (Classics 706)

Raymond Scott, **Reckless Nights and Turkish Twilights** (Columbia 53028)

Slim Gaillard, **Complete Recordings 1938–1942** (Affinity 1034), 3 CDs

Roy Eldridge, **Little Jazz** (Columbia 45275)

Lil Hardin Armstrong, **1936–1940** (Classics 564)

Spike Hughes, **1933** (Retrieval 79005)

Coleman Hawkins, **In Europe 1934/39** (Jazz Up 317/18/19), 3 CDs

Bill Coleman, **1936–1938** (Classics 764)

Django Reinhardt, **1937 Vol. 1** (Classics 748)

Svend Asmussen, **Musical Miracle** (Phontastic 9306)

Ambrose, **Swing Is in the Air** (Avid 690), 2 CDs

Nat Gonella, **Georgia on My Mind** (ASV/Living Era 5300)

Sharkey Bonano, **Sharkey Bonano** (Timeless 001)

Eddie Condon, **1928–1938** (Classics 742)

Bud Freeman, **1928–1938** (Classics 781)

Various Artists, **Jazz in the Thirties** (DRG/Swing 8457/8458), 2 CDs occasional outbursts of excitement that fit the lyrics quite well. Continuing with the Quintessential series, **Vol. 3** (Columbia 44048) contains plenty of magic on "This Year's Kisses" and "I Must Have that Man" (both with Pres and Clayton) plus "Pennies from Heaven," "I Can't Give You Anything but Love" (on which Holiday shows off the influence of Louis Armstrong), "I've Got My Love to Keep Me Warm," and "This Is My Last Affair." ◐ **Vol. 4** (Columbia 44252) has the Holiday-Young combination on classic versions of "I'll Get By," "Mean to Me," "Foolin' Myself," "Easy Living," "Let's Call the Whole Thing Off," "They Can't Take That Away from Me," and "Me, Myself And I." Also well featured are Clayton, Hodges, and Cootie Williams. ◐ **Vol. 5** (Columbia 44423) features Young and Clayton on all but four songs, with the height of their musical partnership with Holiday being heard on "Without Your Love," "Getting Some Fun Out of Life," "He's Funny that Way," "When You're Smiling," and "I Can't Believe that You're in Love with Me." Although Billie Holiday and Lester Young were apparently never romantically involved, their mutual love is quite obvious in listening to them perform together. **Vol. 6** (Columbia 45449) finishes off this period with fine versions of "You Go to My Head," "Having Myself a Time," "The Very Thought of You," and "You Can't Be Mine." This is frequently exquisite music that finds Billie Holiday (known later on for her very serious moods) sounding happy with life.

Other Vocalists

In addition to Billie Holiday, Mildred Bailey, Louis Armstrong, and Cab Calloway, as well as vocalists who primarily sang with bands (including Jimmy Rushing, Ella Fitzgerald, and Helen Ward), there were a variety of other singers who had important solo careers during this period.

Bing Crosby   The most famous male singer of the 1930s was Bing Crosby, who introduced scores of standards and whose friendly baritone voice was extremely accessible. After the Rhythm Boys broke up in 1931, Crosby sang with Gus Arnheim's Orchestra, appeared in the 1932 film *The Big Broadcast*, became a major hit on the radio, and signed with Decca where he recorded a wide variety of music. Although Crosby (whose success was phenomenal in radio, records, concerts, and movies) mostly moved away from jazz, he retained a love

for Dixieland and occasionally was heard in that format through the years. The four-CD box set **Bing—His Legendary Years 1931 to 1957** (MCA 4-10887) has many of the highlights from a 26-year period in the singer's career, including "Just One More Chance," "I'm Through with Love," "I Found a Million Dollar Baby," "It's Easy to Remember," "I'm an Old Cowhand," "Pennies from Heaven," "Don't Be that Way," and many others.

Red McKenzie   Red McKenzie, who had largely given up his comb playing in 1931 in favor of ballad singing, led sessions during 1931–37, both under his own name and as the leader of the Mound City Blue Blowers. **Red McKenzie** (Timeless 1-019) has some fine small-group swing numbers featuring Bunny Berigan (on eight cuts), Bobby Hackett, Adrian Rollini, Jonah Jones, and the team of trumpeter Eddie Farley and trombonist Mike Riley plus decent vocalizing from McKenzie. Also of interest is **Mound City Blue Blowers** (Classics 895) from 1935–36, which has contributions from Berigan, Yank Lawson, and Eddie Miller. McKenzie only takes four vocals on that disc, with the singing chores also shared by Nappy Lamare, Billy Wilson, Spooky Dickenson, and a vocal group. There are only two instrumentals, but most of the songs have a couple of strong solos, falling between Dixieland and small-group playing.

The Mills Brothers   The Mills Brothers continued to prosper during the 1930s as the top jazz-oriented male vocal group. They appeared in movies (including *The Big Broadcast*, *Twenty Million Sweethearts*, and *Broadway Gondolier*), toured Europe, and made many exciting records. The unexpected death of John Mills in 1936 was a major blow, but his place was soon taken by the Mills Brothers' father, Herbert Mills, who joined sons Herbert, Jr., Harry, and Donald. Since John had played guitar in addition to singing, from then on the Mills Brothers' guitarist came from outside of the family. They still did not utilize any other instruments, for their voices were expert at imitating trumpet, trombone, saxophone, and bass. **Chronological, Vol. 2** (JSP 302) has the vocal quartet meeting up with Duke Ellington, Cab Calloway, Don Redman, Alice Faye, and Bing Crosby (a classic version of "My Honey's Lovin' Arms"), in addition to having such memorable performances as "The Old Man of the Mountain," "Coney Island Washboard," "Smoke Rings," "Swing It Sister," and "I've Found a New Baby." **Vol. 3** (JSP 303) is highlighted by "Put on Your Old Grey Bonnet,"

"Nagasaki," "Limehouse Blues," and two songs with film star Dick Powell. **Vol. 4** (JSP 304), which dates from 1935–37, has the Mills Brothers' first joint recordings with Louis Armstrong (including "Carry Me Back to Old Virginny" and "In the Shade of the Old Apple Tree"), a couple of numbers with Ella Fitzgerald, and joyful versions of "Shoe Shine Boy," "Pennies from Heaven," and "The Love Bug Will Bite You," along with two Harry Mills solo records. **Vol. 5** (JSP 320) includes more meetings with Louis Armstrong, three earlier alternate takes, and memorable versions of "Organ Grinder's Swing" and "Caravan." **Vol. 6** (JSP 345) continues to August 1939 with two earlier alternate takes, a pair of numbers featuring Harry Mills with Andy Kirk's Orchestra, and such tunes as "You Tell Me Your Dream," "Jeepers Creepers," and "Basin Street Blues." The Mills Brothers would continued to perform remarkable music up until 1942 when, with a hit record of "Paper Doll," they gradually dropped the imitations of instruments and became a much more routine middle-of-the-road pop vocal group.

The Boswell Sisters   While the Mills Brothers would continue on for decades, the Boswell Sisters called it quits early in the swing era. The Boswells were at their prime when they appeared in the film *The Big Broadcast* (1932), performing "Crazy People." They visited Europe in 1933 and 1935 and continued making jazz-oriented records for a few years, even after signing up with the relatively conservative Decca label. Unfortunately, in 1936 the group came to a premature end when all three sisters got married and both Vet and Martha decided to retire. Connie Boswell (whom Ella Fitzgerald always cited as her main influence) continued with a solo career that included memorable recordings with Bob Crosby's Orchestra and brief appearances in a variety of movies, but she never individually reached the creative heights of the Boswell Sisters.

The Boswell Sisters Collection, Vol. 4 (Nostalgia Arts 3022) starts off with seven alternate takes and then covers the second half of 1933 and 1934. Bunny Berigan gets off a few hot solos, and even though the backup groups are a little more tightly arranged than usual on some selections, there are plenty of noteworthy performances, including "Coffee in the Morning," "Rock and Roll," "If I Had a Million Dollars," and "The Object of My Affection." **The Boswell Sisters Collection, Vol. 5** (Nostalgia Arts 3023) has two alternates, wraps up 1934,

and closes with the Sisters' last recordings, eight numbers from 1935 and four from early 1936. The later selections are a bit more predictable than earlier due to the wishes of record company executives, but there was certainly no decline in the Boswell Sisters' voices. That is not surprising since Connie, the oldest of the Boswells, was only 28 when the group broke up. It is a pity that they chose to end their singing careers just as the swing era was catching on, leaving a gap that would be filled by the less adventurous Andrews Sisters.

Fans of the Boswells who want additional CDs are advised to get **The Boswell Sisters 1930–1935** (Retrieval 79009) and **Syncopating Harmonists from New Orleans** (Take Two 406). The Retrieval CD consists of six studio records, plus three radio broadcasts from 1930 with the singers backed just by Martha Boswell's piano, and one with an orchestra in 1931. **Syncopating Harmonists from New Orleans** has nine regular studio records, but also nine numbers from 1930 radio shows plus two cuts from a 1935 Dodge show; none of the radio material had been released before and those performances are well worth hearing. But sadly enough, the Boswell Sisters' recorded legacy (other than their initial recording) only covered a six-year period, and there would be no recorded reunions.

While the Boswell Sisters were always jazz-oriented, the Andrews Sisters (Patti, Maxine, and Laverne) tended to stick to the same routines once they were worked out. The cheerful group had its first hit in 1937 with "Bei Mir Bist Du Schon," recorded many popular songs, appeared in 15 films, and ironically are much better known today than the Boswells.

Ethel Waters   Among female jazz singers of the era, Billie Holiday and Ella Fitzgerald were the main newcomers, and the top band singers included Mildred Bailey, Helen Ward, and Helen Forrest (featured in 1938 with Artie Shaw). Ethel Waters stood apart from everyone. She was the only classic blues singer (other than Alberta Hunter) to successfully make the transition to swing, she was a pioneering black actress, and she was a famous name before the swing era began. Waters spent the 1935–39 period with her own touring show, using a band run by her husband of the period, trumpeter Eddie Mallory. **1931–1934** (Classics 735) includes two tunes with the Duke Ellington Orchestra ("I Can't Give You Anything but Love" and "Porgy") and appearances by

Bunny Berigan, a Benny Goodman pickup group, and musicians from the Chick Webb Orchestra. Highlights include the original version of "Stormy Weather," "Don't Blame Me," "Heat Wave," and "A Hundred Years from Today." Strangely enough, Waters barely recorded at all during 1935–37 (just two songs), and although highly respected as a personality and actress, she operated almost independently of the swing era.

Teddy Grace   A singer who has been long forgotten, Teddy Grace deserved better. She began performing professionally in 1931, sang on the radio in the South, and worked with Al Katz, Tommy Christian, and Mal Hallett (1934–37). During 1937–40 Grace recorded a series of jazz dates (most of which were integrated) using such top sidemen as Jack Teagarden, Bud Freeman, Pee Wee Russell, Bobby Hackett, Charlie Shavers, and Buster Bailey among others. ● **Teddy Grace** (Timeless 1-016) has six complete sessions that total 22 numbers, including "Downhearted Blues," "Arkansas Blues," "Oh Daddy Blues," "You Don't Know My Mind," and "Hey Lawdy Papa." Also worth acquiring is **Turn On that Red Hot Heat** (Hep 1054), which only duplicates one song and has her singing with the Mal Hallett and Bob Crosby Orchestras. These two CDs combined have all of Grace's recordings as a leader except for five songs and show how talented and expressive a jazz and blues vocalist she was.

Lee Wiley   A smoky cabaret singer with indescribable charisma who expressed a great deal of inner heat, Lee Wiley would make her greatest impact starting in 1939.

After moving to New York in the late 1920s, she worked with Leo Reisman and then for a few years was closely tied with composer Victor Young. **The Complete Young Lee Wiley 1931–1937** (Vintage Jazz Classics 1023) features her during a period when she was being groomed as a sophisticated performer by Young and mostly singing ballads while backed by orchestras. She is joined on various cuts by Leo Reisman's orchestra, Victor Young, the Dorsey Brothers, and the Casa Loma Orchestra; best are "A Hundred Years from Today" and "Easy Come, Easy Go."

Maxine Sullivan   When it comes to gentle swinging from a singer who puts the proper warmth into lyrics, few could top Maxine Sullivan. She was discovered while singing on the radio in Pittsburgh with a group called the Red Hot Peppers. Pianist Claude Thornhill became her musical director, and at age 16, on her second record date in 1937, she had a major hit with a swinging version of the Scottish folk song "Loch Lomond." ● **1937–1938** (Classics 963) has her first 23 recordings, with accompaniment either by the early John Kirby Sextet (with Thornhill on piano) or a studio orchestra that includes cornetist Bobby Hackett. In addition to "Loch Lomond," similar treatment was given to such songs as "Annie Laurie," "The Folks Who Live on the Hill," "Darling Nellie Gray," "Moments Like This," and "Down the Old Ox Road." Maxine Sullivan's lightly swinging approach would be influential on many singers in the future, including Rosemary Clooney, Susannah McCorkle, and Rebecca Kilgore.

TIMELINE 1936

Count Basie's band heads east from Kansas City. • The Benny Goodman Quartet is formed. • Helen Ward temporarily retires. • Fletcher Henderson's new band has a hit in "Christopher Columbus." • The Bing Crosby movie *Pennies from Heaven* features a good role for Louis Armstrong. • Artie Shaw is a hit at a big swing concert, performing "Interlude in B Flat" with a string quartet. He soon forms his first orchestra. • Isham Jones breaks up his orchestra so Woody Herman uses the nucleus to form his own big band. • The Red Norvo Orchestra is formed and features Mildred Bailey. • Andy Kirk's Twelve Clouds of Joy resumes recording after five years and has a hit with "Until the Real Thing Comes Along." • The Boswell Sisters break up as Vet and Martha Boswell retire. • Stuff Smith plays at the Onyx Club with his new group. • The Original Dixieland Jazz Band makes a comeback. • Annette Hanshaw permanently retires at the age of 25. • Boogie-woogie pianist Albert Ammons makes his recording debut. • Nat King Cole appears on records for the first time, playing piano on four songs with his brother Eddie Coles's Solid Senders.

Small Swing Groups and Top Soloists

While big bands dominated jazz and popular music during 1933–38, there were still occasional small groups to be heard in little clubs and on recordings. Starting with the Benny Goodman Trio and Quartet, several of the swing era big bands featured combos out of their orchestras, including Tommy Dorsey's Clambake Seven, Chick Webb's Little Chicks, Bob Crosby's Bobcats, and several combinations of musicians from the Duke Ellington Orchestra. But beyond that, some of the more freewheeling soloists were able to work regularly with combos, perhaps not generating the headlines of a Benny Goodman but making a strong impact in the long run.

Art Tatum   It can be stated with certainty that the greatest small group of the swing era (and arguably all time) performed whenever Art Tatum sat down at the piano. Tatum's blinding speed on the piano defied belief, his chord voicings and harmonies were at least 30 years ahead of their time, and his technique was phenomenal. One listen to his 1933 solo recording of "Tiger Rag" should be enough to convince any listener that Tatum came from a different musical world altogether, and obviously had at least five hands!

Born with cataracts, Tatum was blind in one eye and only had partial vision in the other. He started playing piano quite young and by 1926 (when he was 16) was working regularly in his native Toledo. Tatum appeared on local radio on a regular basis, mostly playing solo. In 1932, he was hired as one of two pianists (the other Frances Carter) to accompany Adelaide Hall's singing, moving to New York. **1932–1934** (Classics 507) has a rare aircheck version of "Tiger Rag" from August 5, 1932, the four selections that he made accompanying Hall, plus various incredible solos from 1933–34 that are also available elsewhere. ⊙ **Classic Early Solos** (GRP/Decca 607) has Tatum's solo sessions of 1934 and 1937, including "Emaline," two versions of "After You've Gone," "The Shout," "Liza," and "The Sheik of Araby"; the pianist continually makes impossible runs seem logical and effortless.

Albert Ammons, Pete Johnson, and Meade Lux Lewis   John Hammond's "From Spirituals to Swing" concert held at Carnegie Hall in December 1938 was notable on several levels. One of its most lasting effects is that it featured three boogie-woogie pianists, Albert Ammons, Pete Johnson, and Meade Lux Lewis, along with singer Big Joe Turner. This appearance gave a

momentum to the career of those four formerly neglected performers. Boogie-woogie (playing a double-time repetitive eight-note pattern to the bar on a blues tune) had first been heard on records in the 1920s, most notably Meade Lux Lewis's "Honky Tonk Train Blues" and the few recordings by Pinetop Smith. Tommy Dorsey's big band recording of "Boogie Woogie" was directly taken from one of Smith's recordings, and boogie-woogie was on the verge of becoming a trend in 1938.

It was only right that some of its top practitioners would get a bit of attention. Albert Ammons began playing in clubs in Chicago in the late 1920s, worked with some obscure groups (including Louis Banks's Chesterfield Orchestra during 1930–34), and began leading his Rhythm Kings in 1936, making his recording debut that year. **1936–1939** (Classics 715) has his combo dates from 1936 and piano solos cut for the Jazz Piano, Vocalion, Blue Note, and Solo Art labels.

Meade Lux Lewis, despite recording "Honky Tonk Train Blues," was forced to have a day job during the early years of the Depression, working in a W.P.A. shovel gang and driving a taxi. John Hammond helped him revive his musical career, arranging for him to rerecord "Honky Tonk Train Blues" and gain work as a full-time musician again. **1927–1939** (Classics 722) has the original version of "Honky Tonk Train Blues," two other versions of the song (from 1935 and 1937), and a few numbers on which Lewis whistles ("Whistlin' Blues") or plays celeste.

Since Pete Johnson and Big Joe Turner (who had often worked together in Kansas City with Turner employed as a singing bartender) did not initially record until December 30, 1938, they will be covered in the next chapter, as will the gentler boogie-woogie pianist Jimmy Yancey.

Fats Waller   Fats Waller, who hated boogie-woogie, which he called "twelve bars of nothing," but loved Art Tatum (once making the pronouncement after spotting Tatum that "God is in the house") became a major star during 1933–38. Known formerly in jazz circles for his brilliant stride piano playing, his occasional work on organ, and his songwriting, Waller emerged in 1934 as a vocalist and a humorous personality. During 1934–42, he recorded an extensive series of performances for the Victor label with his Rhythm, a sextet which often included trumpeter Herman Autrey, Gene Sedric on tenor and clarinet, guitarist Al Casey, and drummer

Slick Jones with various bassists; there were occasional substitutions in the personnel. In addition to playing some of his own tunes and standards, Waller displayed the ability to turn trash into treasures. When faced with an inferior song, Fats often satirized the lyrics mercilessly, unless he saw some value in the tune (as in "I'm Gonna Sit Right Down and Write Myself a Letter"). Along with all of the verbal merriment (which was filled with plenty of ad-lib comments), Waller usually included a brilliant chorus of stride piano, swinging hard with his group.

Fortunately all of Fats Waller's Victor recordings have been reissued. ● **The Early Years, Part 1** (Bluebird 66618), **The Early Years, Part 2** (Bluebird 66640), and **The Early Years, Part 3** (Bluebird 66747) are each two-CD sets, tracing Waller's music (other than piano solos) from May 1934–November 1936. Although not every number is a classic, each one has its moments, and some are riotous. **Part 1** is highlighted by "A Porter's Love Song to a Chambermaid," "Serenade for a Wealthy Widow," "How Can You Face Me," "Believe It Beloved," and "You've Been Taking Lessons in Love." **Part 2** has "I'm Gonna Sit Right Down and Write Myself a Letter," "Dinah," "Somebody Stole My Gal," and "Got a Bran' New Suit," and **Part 3** includes "Christopher Columbus," "Black Raspberry Jam," "Floatin' Down to Cotton Town," and "Swingin' Them Jingle Bells." **The Middle Years, Part 1** (Bluebird 66083), a three-CD reissue covering December 1936 to the spring of 1938, has one of the few sessions from Waller's occasional big band (which he put together for special tours), plenty of dog tunes, and such memorable numbers as "I'm Sorry I Made You Cry," "Honeysuckle Rose," "Blue, Turning Grey Over You," the hit "The Joint Is Jumpin'," and "Every Day's a Holiday." Because general collectors may not need all of these sets (plus the ones in the following chapter), **The Early Years, Part 1** is recommended as a good place to start although each of the Waller reissues is a joy.

Stuff Smith   One of the key centers for small groups of the swing era was 52nd Street, an area in New York City that got going in 1935 and for the next decade (its heyday lasted until 1947) had so many clubs in such a concentrated area that it unofficially became known as "Swing Street." Violinist Stuff Smith had great success for a few years playing at the Onyx Club with his exciting quintet. Hezekiah "Stuff" Smith started on the violin

when he was seven and began working professionally in 1924. He toured and recorded with Alphono Trent's territory band (1926–30) and led groups in Buffalo for a few years. In 1936, he was playing on 52nd Street with a band that co-featured the spirited swing trumpeter Jonah Jones. ● **1936–1939** (Classics 706) has all of the band's recordings except for one session from 1940. Cozy Cole is usually on drums, and Buster Bailey is added on clarinet for one date. But it is the driving and explosive solos of Smith and Jones that make this band into one of the most memorable of the era—did any jazz violinist swing harder than Stuff Smith? This definitive CD has the group's one hit ("I'se a Muggin'") and such exciting jams as "I Hope Gabriel Likes My Music," "After You've Gone," "You'se a Viper," "Old Joe's Hittin' the Jug," and the classic "Here Comes the Man with the Jive."

Eddie South   Eddie South never had the popularity of Stuff Smith, but his violin playing (more classical-oriented and influenced by his interests in gypsy and European folk music) was on the same level. South grew up in Chicago, was a child prodigy, and could have been a major concert violinist if the door had been open to black musicians. Instead he worked in Chicago in the 1920s with Charles Elgar, Erskine Tate, Mae Brady, and Jimmy Wade's Syncopators (1924–27). South visited Europe during 1928–31 with his group, the Alabamians, led combos in Chicago during the 1930s, and spent part of 1937–38 back in Europe. **1923–1937** (Classics 707) features South in 1923 on "Someday Sweetheart" with Jimmy Wade's Moulin Rouge Orchestra, on nine numbers with his Alabamians (1927–29), and performing two songs in 1931 and six cuts from 1933 with his swing band. Some of the early music (which includes "By the Waters of Minnetonka," "Two Guitars," "Marcheta," and "Hejre Kati") is an uncomfortable mix of gypsy influences and jazz, but the 1933 group (with Milt Hinton on bass) swings well. **1923–1937** concludes with eight exciting selections recorded in Paris in 1937 with Django Reinhardt and Stephane Grappelli, which are among the highpoints of South's career. As a bonus, "Lady Be Good" features South, Grappelli, and Michel Warlop all soloing on violin.

The Raymond Scott Quintette   The Raymond Scott Quintette was one of the great novelty groups of all time. Scott (born Harold Warnow) worked at CBS as an arranger and pianist starting in 1931. In 1937, he organized his group, which, although only lasting two years, made a permanent impression. Their crazy episodic music had no improvising (every note including the solos was worked out beforehand), and amazingly enough, the complicated parts were memorized rather than written down. In time, Scott's tunes, which often had hilariously picturesque titles, became a staple of Warner Brothers cartoons. "Powerhouse," "Twilight in Turkey," and "The Toy Trumpet" were hits during the group's relatively brief existence. ◉ **Reckless Nights and Turkish Twilights** (Columbia 53028) has 20 of the Quintette's 24 recordings plus two slightly later big band selections. The three hits are joined by such offbeat material as "New Year's Eve in a Haunted House," "Dinner Music for a Pack of Hungry Cannibals," "Reckless Night on Board an Ocean Liner," "Bumpy Weather Over Newark," and "War Dance for Wooden Indians." Somehow the music fits the titles. Also worth searching for is **Vol. One: Powerhouse** (Stash 543), which unfortunately was never followed by a second disc. This CD has radio broadcasts and rehearsals plus two performances by an unrecorded early sextet from 1934–35. Such "new" numbers are added to the legacy of Raymond Scott as "Devil Drums," "Sleepwalker," "Celebration on the Planet Mars," "Serenade to a Lonesome Railroad Station," and "Confusion Among a Fleet of Taxicabs Upon Meeting with a Fare."

Slim and Slam   While the Raymond Scott Quintette often featured musical silliness, verbal jive reached a height with Slim and Slam. In the mid-1930s, Slim Gaillard had a solo act during which he played guitar while tap dancing! In 1936, he began teaming up with bassist Slam Stewart as Slim and Slam. Gaillard could play fairly basic guitar and piano, while Stewart, who had studied at Boston Conservatory, was one of the top bassists of the era. Stewart had heard Ray Perry sing along with his violin solos, and he did the same thing on bass, vocalizing witty lines an octave above his bowed solos. Gaillard had a warm and cheerful voice, and was a master at creating nonsensical dialects, with a liberal use of the words "vout" and "oreenee." The first Slim and Slam recording, on January 19, 1938, resulted in their biggest hit, "Flat Foot Floogie." ◉ **Complete Recordings 1938–1942** (Affinity 1034) is a three-CD set that contains all of their joint recordings, including 19 alternate takes among the 82 selections. Slim and Slam are heard in a variety of groups ranging from a duet up to a sextet with some

appearances by tenors Kenneth Hollon and Ben Webster, trumpeter Al Killian, pianist Jimmy Rowles, and drummer Chico Hamilton. In addition to "Flat Foot Floogie" (which was all the rage during the second half of 1938), there are such unique recordings as "Tutti Frutti," "Laughin' in Rhythm," "Buck Dance Rhythm," "Chicken Rhythm," and "Matzoh Balls."

Roy Eldridge   Roy "Little Jazz" Eldridge emerged during 1935–36 as a strong competitor to Louis Armstrong and Bunny Berigan. With his crackling sound, chance-taking style, harmonically advanced ideas, and lack of fear in aiming for high notes, Eldridge soon became an influential force, particularly on the young Dizzy Gillespie. Eldridge began playing professionally in 1927, leading his own group that he called Roy Elliott and His Palais Royal Orchestra. He worked early on with Horace Henderson, Zach Whyte, and Speed Webb. After moving to New York in November 1930, Eldridge had associations with Cecil Scott, Elmer Snowden, Charlie Johnson, Teddy Hill, and McKinney's Cotton Pickers. In 1935, he started appearing on records, including with Teddy Wilson/Billie Holiday and Hill. In 1936, Eldridge worked with Fletcher Henderson (taking a memorable solo on "Christopher Columbus") and began leading his own groups, which expanded to a big band by 1938. ◉ **Little Jazz** (Columbia 45275) has the best of early Eldridge, including "Lookie, Lookie, Lookie Here Comes Cookie" with Teddy Hill, selections with Henderson, Teddy Wilson, Billie Holiday, and Mildred Bailey, and six numbers (plus an alternate take) that comprised his first two sessions as a leader in 1937. "Wabash Stomp," "Heckler's Hop," and "After You've Gone" (which became his signature song for a time) are given classic renditions.

Henry "Red" Allen   Another one of the top trumpeters of the 1930s, Henry "Red" Allen, left Luis Russell's band (where he had found his initial fame) in 1932, and after a few months with Charlie Johnson, he was well featured with Fletcher Henderson (1933–34) and the Mills Blue Rhythm Band (1934–37). In addition, he continued leading an extensive series of small-group sides. **1933–1935** (Classics 551) has such sidemen as Coleman Hawkins (who co-leads the first date), Dickie Wells, Buster Bailey, Chu Berry, and (for the final four numbers) J.C. Higginbotham and Albert Nicholas. There are a fair number of memorable performances on this CD, including "You're

Gonna Lose Your Gal," "Pardon My Southern Accent," "Rug Cutter Swing," "Believe It Beloved," "Rosetta," and "Truckin'." **1935–1936** (Classics 575), which has similar personnel (plus altoist Tab Smith), is highlighted by "On Treasure Island," "Red Sails in the Sunset," "Lost," "Algiers Stomp" (the lone instrumental), and "On the Beach at Bali-Bali," although the material was gradually declining and Allen's so-so vocals often took up valuable space that could have been better filled by solos. **1936–1937** (Classics 590) is a bit weaker with two of the better songs ("He Ain't Got Rhythm" and "This Year's Kisses") easily being overshadowed by Billie Holiday's versions from the same period. Despite all of these recordings, Red Allen never became a big name in the swing era. In 1937, he began a three-year period playing anonymously with the Russell big band as it functioned as the backup group for Louis Armstrong.

Lil Hardin Armstrong   Although Lil Hardin Armstrong would always be associated with the 1920s and her husband Louis Armstrong's Hot Five recordings, she was actually quite active during the second half of the 1930s. Armstrong was a house pianist for the Decca label during 1936–40, and in addition to appearing as a sideman on many sessions, she recorded 26 selections as a leader herself, all of which are on ◉ **1936–1940** (Classics 564). Strangely enough, Lil does not play any piano

on the first 18 numbers, just sticking to taking vocals while backed by swing combos with such sidemen as trumpeter Joe Thomas, Buster Bailey, Chu Berry, and J.C. Higginbotham. "Brown Gal," "It's Murder," and "Just for a Thrill" (one of her best-known originals) are among the highlights. Overall, she shows more vocal talents on these recordings than she did in the 1920s, and the fine backup bands have plenty of concise solos. The final 1938 session has four more vocals (though Armstrong also plays piano) including on the spirited "Harlem on Saturday Night." This CD concludes with four numbers from 1940 with Jonah Jones and altoist Don Stovall. Overall the program shows that there was more to Lil Armstrong than her work with her husband, whom she divorced in 1938.

The Original Dixieland Jazz Band   The Original Dixieland Jazz Band made an unlikely comeback in 1936. Even with the passing of 11 years since its breakup, the musicians were not all that elderly, with Nick LaRocca being the oldest at 47. During the 1925–35 period, LaRocca had run a contracting business, Eddie Edwards performed in society orchestras, Larry Shields was retired from music, J. Russell Robinson was a successful songwriter, and only Tony Sbarbaro continued playing full time. In 1936, LaRocca was approached about getting the ODJB back together to appear in the movie *The Big*

TIMELINE 1937

Tommy Dorsey has hits with "Marie" and "Song of India." • Bunny Berigan forms his own orchestra, scoring with "I Can't Get Started." • Chu Berry becomes Cab Calloway's top soloist. • Harry James joins Benny Goodman. • Billie Holiday records for the first time with Lester Young and Buck Clayton. • Lionel Hampton begins leading a series of small-group swing dates. • George Gershwin dies. • Artie Shaw breaks up his string band, and forms a more conventional orchestra. • Bob Crosby's Bobcats make their initial recordings. • Glenn Miller leads his first big band. • The Count Basie Orchestra begins recording regularly. • Maxine Sullivan has a hit with "Loch Lomond." • Eddie South plays in Europe with Django Reinhardt and Stephane Grappelli. • The Raymond Scott Quintette is formed. • Bessie Smith dies in a car accident. • Cat Anderson records with the Carolina Cotton Pickers in Birmingham, Alabama. • Billy Butterfield joins Bob Crosby's big band. • Red Callender makes his recording debut with Louis Armstrong's Orchestra. • Chick Webb's Little Chicks record four numbers, teaming Chauncey Haughton's clarinet with Wayman Carver's pioneering jazz flute. • In Oklahoma City, 21-year-old Charlie Christian buys his first electric guitar. • Joe Marsala's group features drummer Buddy Rich and Marsala's wife, Adele Girard, on harp. • Charlie Christian buys his first electric guitar. • Bassist Jimmy Blanton works with the Jeter-Pillars Orchestra. • Eighteen-year-old Joe Williams sings in Chicago occasionally with Jimmie Noone's band. • Fifteen-year-old Kay Starr begins singing with Joe Venuti's Orchestra. • Dizzy Gillespie makes his recording debut with Teddy Hill.

Broadcast of 1937. He turned down the offer because he did not think the group could be up to speed that quickly, but he decided to try to revive the band. After a long period of practice, the ODJB appeared together on the Ed Wynn radio show, generating a lot of fan mail after playing "Tiger Rag." On an occasional basis, the band made special appearances during the next year. LaRocca also organized a 14-piece big band (which included Shields, Robinson, and Sbarbaro) that was just okay, recording in September 1936. The reborn ODJB recorded six remakes of vintage tunes, all of which are on the double CD **The Complete Original Dixieland Jazz Band** (RCA 66608). Although their music sounded way behind the times (sticking to ensembles without any solos), the musicians showed a lot of spirit in their playing. Unfortunately, LaRocca and the other players had not mellowed with age, and personality conflicts resulted in the ODJB permanently breaking up on February 1, 1938. There would be some partial reunions in the future, but LaRocca never played again.

Paul Mares   The New Orleans Rhythm Kings never had a reunion because Leon Roppolo was institutionalized for the rest of his life, never recovering from his mental illness. Paul Mares retired from music in 1925 (when he was just 25) to run his family's fur business. In 1934, he moved to Chicago, opening up a barbecue restaurant. He began to play cornet again and on January 26, 1935, recorded four songs with his Friar's Society Orchestra, still sounding fairly strong. But otherwise Mares did not record again, being content to follow the music scene from a distance.

A Bleak Time for Some 1920s Veterans

The swing era found many jazz musicians gaining employment in big bands, and such players as Louis Armstrong, Benny Goodman, and Duke Ellington becoming world famous. But some of the musicians and singers who had starred in the 1920s and survived the early years of the Depression suffered from continuing hard times for a variety of reasons, including bad health, having their music considered out of date, being in the wrong geographical area, not being flexible enough, or suffering from plain bad luck.

By the time Freddie Keppard died of tuberculosis in 1933 when he was just 43 (not helped out by a huge daily input of alcohol), the New Orleans pioneer had been long forgotten. Eddie Lang's death that year was more of a shock because it was due to a botched tonsillectomy and he had been quite active as Bing Crosby's accompanist. Bennie Moten died of the same cause in 1935, leading indirectly to the beginning of the Count Basie Orchestra.

Classic blues singing had gone out of style by the late 1920s, and one by one most of the early blues singers dropped out of the scene. Ma Rainey retired in 1933, and Clara Smith stopped singing the following year. Victoria Spivey, who did not even turn 30 until 1936, continued touring with bands, and Lizzie Miles (after a period off the scene) resumed singing that same year, but neither were considered major names of the swing era. Trixie Smith and Ida Cox returned to records late in the decade although also without regaining their former prominence. And by then the Empress of the Blues, Bessie Smith, had met a tragic end.

Bessie Smith   Bessie Smith made her final record date in 1933, performing four nonblues (including "Gimme a Pigfoot") with an integrated band that included Jack Teagarden. Still just 39 at the time, Smith was a victim of jazz's rapid evolution, but she sought to keep up with the times, gradually reinventing herself as a bluesy standards singer. In 1934, she toured in *Hot from Harlem*, played at the Apollo a few times in 1935, and substituted for Billie Holiday in one show. Smith was earning favorable reviews and was set for a major comeback. She would most likely have performed at John Hammond's "From Spirituals to Swing" concert in December 1938 and returned to records. But on September 26, 1937, she died in a car accident at the age of 43. Although well-meaning reports at the time claimed that she had been taken to a white hospital that refused to treat her, those stories ended up being false. She was so seriously injured that there was no chance of her survival.

Ruth Etting and Annette Hanshaw   Two other singers from the 1920s slipped away from the music scene under much less tragic circumstances. Ruth Etting simply retired in 1937, not singing again for a decade. In the case of Annette Hanshaw, she simply lost interest. The LP **The Personality Girl** (Sunbeam 511) has her final records from 1932–34 (including "Say It Isn't So," "Fit as a Fiddle," "Moon Song," "I Cover the Waterfront," and "Don't Blame Me"), showing that she could have easily made the transition to swing. But Hanshaw hated performing and in 1936 she called it quits, at the age of 25, spending her remaining 49 years outside of music.

Jimmie Noone   During the 1930s, New Orleans was musically silent, with no significant recordings taking place in the Crescent City. The New Orleans veterans who settled in Chicago often did not appear on records much either. Johnny Dodds, Baby Dodds, and Natty Dominique played now and then in Chicago, but they also had day jobs. Johnny Dodds made his only trip to New York in 1938 for a record date, cutting six decent titles in a small group with the young trumpeter Charlie Shavers. Jimmie Noone fared better, recording five sessions during 1933–37 and two sets in 1940. His Apex Club Orchestra (with Eddie Pollack on alto and baritone and pianist Zinky Cohn) lasted into 1935, although his later recordings had more conventional instrumentation. **1934–1940** (Classics 651) has the final six numbers from the Apex Club Orchestra, plus sessions with a freewheeling New Orleans group (featuring trumpeter Guy Kelly and trombonist Preston Jackson), an excellent outing with Charlie Shavers and altoist Pete Brown, two numbers from 1940 with an erratic Natty Dominique, and four final songs that were hurt a bit by Ed Thompson's dull vocals. Throughout, Jimmie Noone's playing is so consistently strong that one regrets he did not venture to New York and work on 52nd Street.

Kid Ory, King Oliver, and Jelly Roll Morton   Kid Ory, King Oliver, and Jelly Roll Morton all found work opportunities drying up by 1931. Ory moved back to Los Angeles (where he had first recorded in 1922), and by 1933 had left music to help his brother run a chicken farm. King Oliver stayed in music as long as possible but with no success. He had begun to lose his cornet chops in 1928 (due to bad teeth that were never fixed) and was barely able to play at all by 1931. Although he had adjusted well musically to jazz's evolution during 1924–30, Oliver was now considered a has-been, even though he kept on leading bands, touring the South and Midwest with one misfortune after another, struggling along in poverty. His pride did not allow him to accept financial help from his friends (including the world-famous Louis Armstrong) and things never improved. In 1937, he took a lowly job as a poolroom attendant in Savannah, Georgia, passing away the following year at the age of 52.

While King Oliver faded away, Jelly Roll Morton was not going to give up without a fight. After his Victor

contract ended in 1930, Morton only appeared on one record date during 1931–37, an obscure effort with Wingy Manone in 1934. His bragging and abrasive personality had burned a lot of bridges during his peak years, and now Morton scuffled, playing in pit bands for minor musical revues and in dives. During 1936–38, he worked regularly at the Jungle Club, a rundown dump in Washington, D.C. Morton's situation was particularly galling because many of his songs (particularly "King Porter Stomp") were being performed on a regular basis by swing bands on the radio, but because he was cheated by his publishers, he was receiving little or no money and just as little recognition.

In 1938, things began to look up a bit. From May to July, Morton was interviewed extensively by Alan Lomax for the Library of Congress about the early days of New Orleans. Not only did he tell stories, but he played and sang, including a demonstration of "Maple Leaf Rag," showing how that rag was transformed into jazz, and tracing the evolution of "Tiger Rag." The performances and storytelling, not released to the public until after Morton's death, were formerly available on eight LPs. Four CDs, **Kansas City Stomps** (Rounder 1091), **Animule Dance** (Rounder 1092), **The Pearls** (Rounder 1093), and **Winin' Boy Blues** (Rounder 1094), have all of the musical highlights (**Kansas City Stomps** includes the "Maple Leaf Rag" and "Tiger Rag" segments), but leave out much of Jelly Roll's talking, which deserves to be reissued in full since it is often quite fascinating. Later in the year Morton returned to New York with high hopes, although his health (due partly to being stabbed a few months before) was beginning to become troublesome.

Ward Pinkett, Reuben "River" Reeves, and Jabbo Smith   Three trumpeters whose careers looked bright in 1929 failed to live up to their potential. Ward Pinkett, who took some notable solos with Jelly Roll Morton during 1928 and 1930, became such an excessive alcoholic that his career was completely ruined by the early '30s. During 1935–36, Pinkett played a bit with Albert Nicholas at Adrian Rollini's Tap Room, and he popped up on recordings by Freddy Jenkins's Harlem Seven and the Little Ramblers. But his drinking continued, he refused to eat much, and he died in 1937 when he was just 30.

Both Reuben "River" Reeves and Jabbo Smith had long lives, but never came close again to the levels that they had achieved in their 1929 recordings. Reeves worked with Cab Calloway during 1931–32, and in 1933 led a 12-piece orchestra called the River Boys that made one record date. Otherwise he freelanced in obscurity and ended his life as a bank guard. Jabbo Smith settled in Milwaukee in the early 1930s and played locally. His few recordings later in the 1930s (including one session as a leader and with Claude Hopkins's band with whom he played during 1936–38) do not even hint at his former brilliance. Smith spent many years working at a used car dealership.

Clarence Williams   Clarence Williams, who was so important to the recording scene in the 1920s, continued making records during 1933–37 after a two-year absence. His band was more predictable than earlier, and **1933** (Classics 845) mostly features quartet numbers with Williams's piano, cornetist Ed Allen (who never should have sung), clarinetist Cecil Scott, and Floyd Casey on washboard. Clarinetist Albert Nicholas, pianists Herman Chittison and Willie "The Lion" Smith, and Eva Taylor make appearances along the way. The music was behind the times but still reasonably enjoyable. Although "Breeze" is a memorable number, none of Williams's new songs became hits or future standards. **1933–1934** (Classics 891) finds the quality of the music slipping due

to only three of the 23 numbers being instrumentals and the insipid (but always enthusiastic) Chick Bullock taking seven of them. James P. Johnson is an asset on a few songs, but most of this program is just so-so. **1934** (Classics 891) is helped out by the playing of Willie "The Lion" Smith and guitarist Ikey Robinson. "Sugar Blues," "Jerry the Junker," and "The Stuff Is Here and It's Mellow" are memorable, but it was clear that Williams was running out of ideas and fresh material. **1934–1937** (Classics 918) finds Williams gamely entering the swing era. The five sessions have some good moments from Allen, Scott, and Buster Bailey (who is on the six selections from 1937), though it does seem a little odd to hear a washboard during this period of time. There are vocals from Chick Bullock (fortunately just three), Eva Taylor, William Cooley, and Williams himself. **1937–1941** (Classics 953) wraps up the Clarence Williams story. The first 15 selections are listed as being by "Clarence Williams's Swing Band," though all but three numbers are spirituals that showcase the annoying singing of William Cooley. The potentially impressive group (Ed Allen, Buster Bailey, altoist Russell Procope, and Cecil Scott) has little to do. The CD concludes with three selections from 1938 by an organ/piano/drums trio that does not include Williams, and two songs from 1941 on which Eva Taylor and Williams are heard on vocals while

TIMELINE 1938

Benny Goodman's Carnegie Hall concert symbolizes the height of the swing era. • Gene Krupa leaves Goodman and starts his own orchestra. • Ella Fitzgerald records "A-Tisket, A-Tasket" with Chick Webb. • The Mills Blue Rhythm Band breaks up. • Artie Shaw records "Begin the Beguine" and his band challenges Goodman's in popularity. • The Glenn Miller Orchestra breaks up. Miller soon forms a second big band and tries again. • Slim and Slam have a hit with "Flat Foot Floogie." • Jelly Roll Morton records for the Library of Congress. • Hugues Panassie comes to the United States and records Tommy Ladnier, Mezz Mezzrow, and Sidney Bechet. • Milt Gabler's Commodore label debuts by recording Eddie Condon. • Louis and Lil Armstrong divorce. • Blue Lu Barker has a hit with the mildly risqué "Don't You Make Me High." • Jimmy Blanton works on riverboats with Fate Marable. • The Les Brown Orchestra is formed. • In Cuba, bassist Cachao and his brother, pianist Orestes Lopez, invent the mambo rhythm while with Arcano's Orchestra. • Blanche Calloway breaks up her orchestra. • Benny Carter ends three years in Europe, returning to the United States in May. • Fats Waller visits Europe. • The King Cole Trio records their first radio transcriptions. • Louis Jordan forms a group that develops into the Tympani Five. • Big Joe Turner and Pete Johnson make their recording debut on December 30. • Cornetist Muggsy Spanier becomes seriously ill but recovers by the following year. • John Hammond's first "From Spirituals to Swing" concert takes place at Carnegie Hall. • The John Kirby Sextet is formed. • King Oliver dies. • Trixie Smith makes her first recordings in a dozen years, cutting seven titles with Sidney Bechet and Charlie Shavers. • In December, Billy Strayhorn meets Duke Ellington for the first time.

joined by pianist James P. Johnson, two guitars, and Wellman Braud. This final date hints at Clarence Williams's earlier music when he was so significant to jazz. But unfortunately, other than appearing on a radio broadcast in 1945, he left music permanently in 1943 when he sold his catalog to Decca for $50,000.

Other 1920s Veterans

Some of the key members of the New York jazz scene of the 1920s did not have tragic lives but just faded in prominence during the 1930s. Red Nichols, who was so busy in the previous decade, led a low-level big band. Miff Mole worked in the studios for NBC, joining Paul Whiteman for a two-year stretch in 1938. Phil Napoleon played in the background with radio orchestras and had a short-lived big band in 1938. Joe Venuti, who was shocked by Eddie Lang's sudden death, toured Europe in 1935 and then put together a forgettable big band that lasted on and off into the early 1940s. Frankie Trumbauer led occasional record dates and in 1936 briefly co-led the Three T's with Jack and Charlie Teagarden, a small group that did not last long. He remained with Paul Whiteman until 1938 when Tram organized his own big band, which promptly went nowhere.

Adrian Rollini led 14 record dates during 1933–35 that ranged from mundane dance music to some worthwhile jazz (little of this music has appeared on CD) and ran the club Adrian's Tap Room during 1934–36. By then he was shifting his focus from the bass sax (which he recorded on for the last time in 1938) to the vibes. Although his only real competitor on the vibes was Lionel Hampton, Rollini failed to make much of an impression on his new instrument. His vibes/guitar/bass trio were featured on some records through the years, but Adrian Rollini was never again considered a major force in jazz.

Western Swing

Swing music was not only played in New York and the main metropolitan areas. It also had a strong influence on other styles of music played in rural areas. In the 1930s, country and western (sometimes called hillbilly) music was on the rise in popularity in the South. An interesting fusion occurred between early country music and 1920s/'30s jazz that was soon called Western swing. White country musicians in the South sometimes played jazz on their string instruments, and it was

not uncommon to hear a group consisting of fiddle, guitar, mandolin, banjo, piano, and bass, adding a couple of horns and playing jazz standards, or jazzing up Southern ballads. The main pioneers in this music were singer Milton Brown, fiddle player/vocalist Bob Wills, and their sidemen.

Milton Brown In 1932, Milton Brown and Bob Wills were part of a quartet called the Fort Worth Doughboys that recorded two numbers ("Sunbonnet Sue" and "Nancy Jane") and is considered the first Western swing record date. Born in Stephensville, Texas, in 1903, Brown had odd jobs in the 1920s and began working as a singer in 1930; he did not play an instrument. He worked with Bob Wills in the Light Crust Doughboys during much of 1930–32 before going out on his own and forming Milton Brown and His Musical Brownies, the first full-time Western swing band. They were a hit from near the start and were involved in seven marathon recording sessions during 1934–36 that resulted in over 100 titles. Featured were Derwood Brown on guitar and harmonica, Cecil Brower on fiddle, pianist Papa Calhoun, bassist Wanna Coffman, and banjoist Ocie Stockard. Ted Grantham or Cliff Bruner was added on second fiddle on some dates, and in 1935 Bob Dunn joined the band on electric steel guitar.

Tragically, on April 8, 1936, Milton Brown fell asleep at the wheel of his car and was in a car accident, passing away five days later at the age of 32. All of the recordings by his pioneering group (including the early date by the Fort Worth Doughboys and 14 later numbers cut after Brown's death) are available on the five-CD set **The Complete Recordings of the Father of Western Swing** (Texas Rose 1-5).

Bob Wills Bob Wills stepped into the vacuum created by Milton Brown's death, although he was already a close competitor. Born March 6, 1905, in Kosse, Texas, Wills learned how to play mandolin and guitar before settling on violin. He was playing professionally by the mid-1920s and in 1929 formed the Wills Fiddle Band; Milton Brown joined in 1930. Playing regularly on the radio the following year, they were known as the Light Crust Doughboys due to their sponsor. In the summer of 1933, Wills went out on his own, forming the Texas Playboys and working regularly in Tulsa. The group originally consisted of Wills on fiddle and vocals, Tommy Duncan on piano and vocals, guitarist June Whalin, banjoist

Johnnie Lee Wills, and Kermit Whalin on steel guitar and bass. Within a short time the band added steel guitarist Leon McAuliffe, pianist Al Stricklin, drummer Snokey Dacus, and a horn section, becoming extremely popular in Oklahoma and Texas.

The Texas Playboys began to record in 1935 and over time continued to expand, becoming an 18-piece big band by 1940. Although the group always played some Western ballads and pure country music, jazz was a part of its repertoire, even in later years when most of the horns were dropped. **Take Me Back to Tulsa** (Proper Box 32) is a definitive four-CD box that has most of the Texas Playboy's best recordings from 1935–50, serving as a perfect introduction to the genre-crossing music of Bob Wills.

Other Western Swing Collections

The four-CD set **Doughboys, Playboys, and Cowboys** (Proper Box 6) has 99 selections from a wide variety of Western swing bands in chronological order dating from 1932–47. These include Brown's Brownies, Wills's Texas Playboys, Bill Boyd's Cowboy Ramblers, the Tune Wranglers, Jimmie Revard's Oklahoma Playboys, Cliff Bruner's Wanderers, the Modern Mountaineers, Adolph Hofner's Texans, Hank Penny's Radio Cowboys, Spade Cooley, and many others. Also of interest are the single discs **Ragged but Right** (Bluebird 8416), which has some of the country swing bands of the 1934–38 period (including Gid Tanner's Skillet Lickers and the team of Ted Hawkins and Riley Puckett) and **Are You from Dixie** (Bluebird 8417), which is admittedly further away from jazz. The latter features country music played by brother teams during 1930–39, including the Allen Brothers (their "Jake Walk Blues" is a classic), the Lone Star Cowboys, the Monroe Brothers, and the Blue Sky Boys.

Jazz in Europe

Although it is tempting to think that all significant jazz has taken place in the United States—some would even claim that virtually everything of importance occurred in New York—jazz was performed overseas as early as 1919. Europe was seen as a mecca by some black Americans in the 1930s where they could escape most racism and (if they were a major jazz musician) be treated as an artist rather than merely as an entertainer. In addition, Europe was beginning to contribute some strong talent of its own to jazz.

Spike Hughes One of the most promising British jazz musicians was bassist/arranger/composer Spike Hughes, who led a series of fine record dates during 1930–32. In 1933, he went to New York and organized all-star black groups (using Benny Carter's big band as a nucleus) for four superb record dates, mostly playing his own advanced compositions. ◉ **1933** (Retrieval 79005) has those 14 selections plus two sessions by the Benny Carter big band. The Hughes sessions consist of nine of his originals, one traditional theme, and four jams on standards. The bands (14–15 pieces) include such major players as Henry "Red" Allen, Dickie Wells, Benny Carter, Wayman Carver (taking some of his earliest flute solos), Coleman Hawkins, and Chu Berry. Hughes's writing was a bit influenced by Duke Ellington and classical music, but also sounds quite original in spots. Unfortunately, he chose to have this highpoint be his last act in jazz. Spike Hughes (who was only 24) soon retired from playing bass, becoming a full-time music journalist who also composed classical music.

Coleman Hawkins, Benny Carter, and Bill Coleman The three top American musicians to spend a lengthy period of time in Europe in the 1930s were Coleman Hawkins, Benny Carter, and Bill Coleman. Hawkins, one of the main stars of the Fletcher Henderson Orchestra during 1923–34, became frustrated by the band's lack of progress and lost opportunities, and he wired Jack Hylton in England, saying that he was available in case the British bandleader wanted to use him. Hylton jumped at the chance, and Hawkins spent much of 1934–39 in Europe where he was treated with the respect due a great musician and artist. ◉ **In Europe 1934/39** (Jazz Up 317/18/19) is a superb three-CD set that has all of Hawkins's recordings from his five years overseas, including alternate takes. The highly influential tenor is heard with small groups, with the Dutch group the Ramblers, on duets with pianist Freddy Johnson, with Jack Hylton, and starring on a famous session with Benny Carter, Alix Combelle, and Django Reinhardt that resulted in classic versions of "Honeysuckle Rose" and "Crazy Rhythm." The same material plus some related early dates are also available (but without alternate takes) on **1929–1934** (Classics 587), **1934–1937** (Classics 602), and **1937–1939** (Classics 613).

Benny Carter led his first of several big bands during 1932–35, a fine ensemble that did not catch on despite being quite musical. Carter broke up his orchestra about the time that the swing era was just beginning, worked with Willie Bryant (mostly on trumpet) and then, following Coleman Hawkins's lead, was based in Europe during 1935–38. While overseas, he played with Willie Lewis, was the staff arranger for Henry Hall's orchestra, and led a variety of bands, really showing off his versatility as a soloist. **1933–1936** (Classics 530) has Carter as a sideman on three songs with Spike Hughes, featured on a session with the Chocolate Dandies (which also includes Chu Berry and Teddy Wilson), and leading his big band for eight selections, featuring trumpeter Irving Randolph, trombonists J.C. Higginbotham and Benny Morton, Ben Webster, and Teddy Wilson as his main sidemen. Among the better big band cuts are "Symphony in Riffs," "Blue Lou," and "Everybody Shuffle." This CD concludes with Carter's first two sessions in Europe as a leader, playing not only alto and trumpet, but also clarinet, tenor, and piano on such numbers as "Big Ben Blues" (on which he takes the vocal), "When Day Is Done," and the original version of his "Just a Mood."

1936 (Classics 541) has music recorded in London, Copenhagen, and Stockholm. Carter backs cabaret singer Elisabeth Welch on four numbers and is heard with a few big bands, a quartet, and a quintet. Most notable among these swing numbers is "Waltzing the Blues" (one of the very first jazz waltzes), "Scandal in A Flat," "Accent on Swing," "Bugle Call Rag," "Jingle Bells," and the two earliest recordings of Carter's future standard "When Lights Are Low." **1937–1939** (Classics 552) has Carter's last five European dates, recorded in London, Holland, and Paris. In three cases he is heard at the head of big bands, contributing arrangements in addition to alto, trumpet, clarinet, and tenor solos. The small group dates have spots for Coleman Hawkins, Freddy Johnson, Alix Combelle, and Django Reinhardt; highlights include "Nagasaki," "I'm in the Mood for Swing," "Skip It," "Blues in My Heart," "Mighty Like the Blues," and "I'm Coming Virginia." The CD concludes with Carter's first American date in five years, which served as the recording debut for his promising new American big band.

Bill Coleman is a perfect example of a small fish in a giant pond who decided to become a large fish in a much smaller pond. Born near Paris, Kentucky, Coleman would ironically spend a lot of time in Paris, France. A mellow-toned trumpeter who was an excellent but overshadowed soloist in the United States, Coleman worked during the second half of the 1920s with many bands, including J.C. Higginbotham, Edgar Hayes, Lloyd Scott, Cecil Scott, and Luis Russell. His period with Russell proved to be frustrating because Henry "Red" Allen received nearly all of the trumpet solos. Coleman had associations with Cecil Scott's Bright Boys, Charlie Johnson, Russell again (1931–32), Ralph Cooper's Kongo Knights, Lucky Millinder (with whom he visited Europe in 1933), Benny Carter, and Teddy Hill (1934–35), having an opportunity to record with Fats Waller. In September 1935, Coleman sailed to Europe where he worked with Freddy Taylor, recorded frequently (including as a leader), and worked with Leon Abbey's orchestra in Bombay, India (1936–37), and Willie Lewis's band in Paris (1937–38). ● **1936–1938** (Classics 764) has all of Coleman's dates as a leader prior to 1949. Coleman (who also takes an occasional vocal) is showcased in a trio with Herman Chittison, jamming with a sextet that includes Oscar Aleman, and interacting in Paris with the likes of Stephane Grappelli, Django Reinhardt, and tenor saxophonist Big Boy Goudie, playing enthusiastically at the peak of his powers.

Valaida Snow   Valaida Snow had a unique career. A fine trumpeter who also sang, she was born in Chattanooga, Tennessee, but became much better known in Europe than she was in the United States. Valaida (her sisters were named Lavaida and Alvaida) was appearing in shows as a teenager, and traveling long distances as early as 1926 when she worked with Jack Carter's band in Shanghai. In 1929, she performed in the Soviet Union, the Middle East, and Europe. Snow worked opposite Earl Hines at the Grand Terrace Café in Chicago during 1933–34 and then went back overseas, being based in London and Stockholm. **Queen of Trumpet & Song** (DRG 8455) is a two-CD set that has all 41 recordings that she led during her prime. Snow is heard with medium-size groups in London, Stockholm, and Copenhagen, singing and playing most of the trumpet solos, showing that she deserved to be a star during the swing era.

Herman Chittison   A brilliant stride pianist, Herman Chittison displayed more feeling in his playing the older he became. He started on piano when he was eight, worked professionally in 1927 with the Kentucky Derbies, and was part of Zack Whyte's territory band (1928–31). After working as an accompanist to actor Stepin Fetchit,

Adelaide Hall, and Ethel Waters (and recording with Clarence Williams), Chittison worked in Europe with Willie Lewis (1934–38) and was in Louis Armstrong's backup band during his 1934 European tour. **1933–1941** (Classics 690) mostly has Chittison performing piano solos in Paris. His earlier solos are very impressive technique-wise (on the level of an Art Tatum) even if they lack much feeling. However, Chittison improved during the decade and must be ranked high among pianists of the time. Also on this disc are two numbers in which Chittison accompanies the Cab Calloway–inspired singing of banjoist Ikey Robinson.

Garland Wilson Another American pianist, Garland Wilson, had a relatively short career but recorded some fine music in the 1930s. Wilson started playing piano at 13, studied at Howard University, moved to New York in 1929, and was a fixture in Harlem clubs for three years. In 1932, he moved to France, working at first as actress/singer Nina Mae McKinney's accompanist and playing regularly as a soloist in England and France. **1931–1938** (Classics 808) has all of Wilson's recordings as a leader. There are piano solos from 1931 (two lengthy test pressings made for producer John Hammond and not released for decades), 1932–33, 1936, and 1938, plus a pair of duets with violinist Michel Warlop and two vocals features by Nina Mae McKinney. Garland Wilson is particularly sensitive at slower tempos, so it is a pity that (except for a few numbers backing others) this is his entire recorded legacy.

Django Reinhardt and Stephane Grappelli When it comes to discussing European jazz musicians, the name Django Reinhardt immediately comes to mind. Although not the first European jazz player, Django was the first overseas innovator and one of the greatest guitarists of all time. Between the time of Eddie Lang's 1933 death and the emergence of Charlie Christian in 1939, Reinhardt had no real competitor, and some would say that he was superior to Lang and Christian.

A Belgian gypsy who was illiterate and often unreliable, Django was also a natural musician. He started on violin and was working as a banjoist in 1928 when a fire in his caravan badly burned his left hand, resulting in two of his fingers being unusable. He made a miraculous comeback, altered his style a bit to compensate for his handicap, and discovered some Louis Armstrong records, which made him want to explore jazz. In early 1933,

Django met violinist Stephane Grappelli and it was obvious from their first jam that they worked together perfectly despite their different temperaments and lifestyles. Soon the pair formed the Quintet of the Hot Club of France, an ensemble that also included two rhythm guitars and a bass. The band lasted until the outbreak of World War II, making many recordings. Grappelli, who started out on piano and was self-taught initially on violin, studied at the Paris Conservatory during 1924–28. From his first recordings with Reinhardt, it was obvious that he deserved to be mentioned in the same breath with Joe Venuti, Eddie South, and Stuff Smith. Unlike Reinhardt, Grappelli was reliable, urbane, sophisticated, and well read, but, like Django, Grappelli could swing up a storm.

Djangology (EMI 780660-780669) is a magnificent ten-CD set that contains 243 selections that Reinhardt made for labels owned by EMI. It includes the finest performances from the Quintet of the Hot Club of France, has Django's intriguing wartime recordings, his first sessions with his postwar quintet (with clarinetist Hubert Rostaing), and a reunion date with Grappelli. However, since that box is not inexpensive or easy to come by, listeners may want to explore the Classics' Django Reinhardt releases: **1934–35** (Classics 703), **1935** (Classics 772), **1935–36** (Classics 739), ◉ **1937 Vol. 1** (Classics 748), **1937 Vol. 2** (Classics 762), **1937–38** (Classics 777), and **1938–39** (Classics 793). These invaluable reissues include the performances by the Quintet plus more intimate performances recorded under the guitarist's name and some of his better sideman performances. **1937 Vol. 1**, which has three complete sessions by the Quintet, is a fine place to start in exploring this exciting and hard-swinging music. Also quite worthy is the three-CD set **Django with His American Friends** (DRG 8493), which is mostly from 1935–40 and has the guitarist's most notable recordings with American all-stars, including Coleman Hawkins, Benny Carter, Bill Coleman, Freddy Taylor, Dickie Wells, Eddie South, Rex Stewart, and harmonica king Larry Adler.

Alix Combelle, Oscar Aleman, and Svend Asmussen Alix Combelle was considered one of France's top swing tenors, and he recorded now and then with Django Reinhardt. In the 1930s, he played with Gregor (1932–33), Arthur Briggs, violinist Michel Warlop, Ray Ventura, and with his own groups, recording with Bill Coleman and on the famous "Crazy Rhythm" session with Reinhardt, Hawkins, and Carter. **1935–1940** (Classics 714), which has two numbers on which he is backed by the Quintet of the Hot Club of France, also features Combelle in a sextet with Bill Coleman, a quartet with cornetist Phillippe Brun, and with larger groups full of French all-stars. Influenced by Hawkins, Combelle could always be relied upon to contribute swinging solos.

Oscar Aleman was in the unfortunate position of being a soundalike to Django Reinhardt, although he always claimed that Django was not an influence on his guitar playing. Aleman was born in Argentina, moved to Europe in 1929 where he played in a show featuring tap dancer Harry Fleming, and settled in Paris around 1932, leading Josephine Baker's band on and off during the decade. Aleman recorded with Freddy Taylor, Danny Polo, and Bill Coleman. However, when he was offered a job with Duke Ellington's Orchestra in 1933 (during Ellington's European tour), Josephine Baker persuaded him to turn it down. Aleman did have an opportunity to lead his own band in Paris, but was overshadowed by his good friend Django Reinhardt. Aleman recorded four numbers in December 1938 (which are included in the two-CD set **Swing Guitar Masterpieces**, covered in the next chapter), including unaccompanied solo versions of "Nobody's Sweetheart" and "Whispering." Perhaps if he had taken the job with Ellington, Aleman would have escaped his eventual obscurity.

While Django Reinhardt's existence made it difficult for Oscar Aleman, Svend Asmussen never received the fame given Stephane Grappelli. Asmussen had been one of jazz's top violinists since the early 1930s. Born in Copenhagen, Denmark, he began playing violin when he was seven and was a professional by 1933 when he was 17. ⊙ **Musical Miracle** (Phontastic 9306) has a sampling of Asmussen's small-group recordings of 1935–40 and is comprised of American swing standards. Asmussen (also heard on a few vocals and playing vibes) is mostly joined by excellent if obscure local musicians (other than two numbers with Oscar Aleman) and shows that, if he had been willing to relocate to England or the United States, he might have become much more famous. Although a more complete reissue of Asmussen's early recordings would be preferred, this single CD is an excellent introduction to his music.

Bert Ambrose, Nat Gonella, and George Chisholm

Switching to England, Bert Ambrose (known professionally as Ambrose) led one of the top British dance bands of the 1920s and '30s. Born in London, Ambrose spent some time in the United States, playing violin with Emil Coleman (1916), freelancing, and directing the band at New York's Club de Vingt (1917–20). He returned to England in 1922, heading a group at the Embassy Club. Ambrose became nationally famous when he led his big band at the Mayfair Hotel in London (March 1927–July 1933), broadcasting regularly on the BBC starting in 1928. His dance band was flavored with jazz, and for a time he featured two Americans, trumpeter Sylvester Ahola and clarinetist Danny Polo. During 1933–36, his orchestra was again based at the Embassy. The double CD ⊙ **Swing Is in the Air** (Avid 690) has 52 of Ambrose's most rewarding (and usually jazz-oriented) recordings from the 1933–39 period, including the classic "Cotton Pickers' Congregation," "Limehouse Blues," "Swinganola," "Streamline Strut," "Deep Henderson," "Ambrose's Tiger Rag," and several Raymond Scott songs, showing that by the mid-1930s, even the more straitlaced British performers were willing to swing now and then.

Probably the most beloved jazz star in Great Britain during the swing era was trumpeter/singer Nat Gonella. Thought of as the "Louis Armstrong of England," Gonella's trumpet playing was influenced by Satch, while his singing looked more toward Wingy Manone. He worked in the late 1920s with various local groups and became famous when he was featured with Billy Cotton (1929–33), Roy Fox (1931–32), Ray Noble (1931–34), and Lew Stone (1932–35), having a hit record of "Georgia on My Mind." During 1934–39, he led the Georgians and was at the height of his powers. ⊙ **Georgia on My Mind** (ASV/Living Era 5300) has 25 of his best performances from the period, including a version of the title cut, and features Gonella playing music that falls between swing and New Orleans jazz.

George Chisholm, one of the top trombonists in Europe and one whose playing career continued into the 1990s, was born in Scotland in 1915. He first worked as a pianist while a teenager before switching to trombone. Inspired by Jack Teagarden, Chisholm was a fine soloist by the time he joined Teddy Joyce in 1934. He worked with the top British bands, including Ambrose, played in the studios, went on a three-month tour with Benny

Carter, and (most importantly) was always available for jazz dates. **1935–1944** (Timeless 1-044) features Chisholm with Danny Polo (1938), pianist Gerry Moore's Chicago Brethren (1937), Lew Stone's Stonecrackers (1941), and on his first three dates as a leader (from 1938 and 1944); all of the alternate takes are included too. The spirited music has such soloists as Polo, trumpeter Tommy McQuater, Benny Winestone on clarinet and tenor, and clarinetist Andy McDevitt. The earliest selection on this disc is extraordinary—a private acetate recording of "Pardon Me, Pretty Baby" cut on the very day in 1935 that Chisholm first arrived in London. The trio consists of Chisholm, Winestone on tenor, and a 21-year-old pianist named Leonard Feather!

Hints of a Revival

While swing was the dominant music in jazz of 1933–38, and even small groups often had written ensembles or used repetitive riffs, New Orleans–type jazz was underground and occasionally resurfacing in a new form. This music, soon called Dixieland (a term that some of its practitioners did not care for), tended to feature a jammed opening chorus or two, individual solos over fairly basic chord changes, and then (if there was time) a couple more ensemble choruses, sometimes climaxing with a four-bar drum break followed by four bars from the full band. Most music of the 1920s was not Dixieland, nor was it heard much in this "pure" form in New Orleans where, while the functions of each instrument were similar, the format was looser. It actually began to consolidate in the Dixieland format in the 1930s.

While Louis Armstrong, who symbolized this music, was mostly playing swing, some small groups were as close to Dixieland as to swing. Certainly Fats Waller's Rhythm dates, Tommy Dorsey's Clambake Seven, and Bob Crosby's Bobcats could be considered Dixieland. Waller's success in 1934 led to singers Putney Dandridge and Bob Howard doing their best to duplicate his formula on their series of records, imitating his vocals and using a few trad and swing horn players.

Louis Prima, Wingy Manone, and Sharkey Bonano

Louis Prima had great success because he was a fine trumpeter and his good-humored singing, while strongly influenced by Louis Armstrong, also had his own brand of Italian humor. Prima taught himself trumpet when he was 13 in 1925 and was part of the New Orleans scene

until 1932 when he moved to New York and joined Red Nichols. In 1934, he began leading his own combo at the Famous Door on 52nd Street and recording extensively. **1934–1935** (Classics 1048) has Prima at the head of combos that include George Brunies, clarinetist Sidney Arodin, Eddie Miller, and pianist Claude Thornhill, with clarinetist Pee Wee Russell on the later tracks. The music falls between swing and Dixieland, with Prima's good-natured singing and fine trumpet always fun to hear. **1935–1936** (Classics 1077) has a lot more of Russell (who would later call this one of his favorite periods), some performances with a 12-piece group, and Prima in excellent form on such numbers as "How'm I Doin'," "Lazy River," "Dinah," and the original version of a notable song that he composed, "Sing Sing Sing." **1937–1939** (Classics 1146) has further titles by Prima's New Orleans Gang, which by 1937 did not have any major names among the sidemen. Clarinetist Meyer Weinberg is a key soloist on good-time performances, which include "Danger, Love at Work," "Yes, There Ain't No Moonlight (So What)," and "Jitterbugs on Parade."

Wingy Manone was always committed to New Orleans jazz/Dixieland, with his jivey vocals sometimes being in a similar vein as Prima's. He had started recording as a leader in 1927, but as with Prima, began hitting his stride in 1934. **The Wingy Manone Collection, Vol. 2** (Collectors Classics 4) has Manone playing with a band billed as "The New Orleans Rhythm Kings," a combo playing songs associated with both the NORK (George Brunies is aboard for this project) and the ODJB in a "modern Dixieland" style. Manone is also heard jamming "Shine" with the Four Bales of Cotton, leading a group of musicians taken from Ben Pollack's Orchestra, and on a most unusual session. The latter (four songs and three alternate takes) has Manone in an all-star group with Dickie Wells, Artie Shaw (four years before he became famous), Bud Freeman, guitarist Frank Victor, John Kirby, drummer Kaiser Marshall, and either Teddy Wilson or Jelly Roll Morton on piano. Morton is heard on "Never Had No Lovin'" and "I'm Alone Without You," his only appearances on records during 1931–37.

The Wingy Manone Collection, Vol. 3 (Collector's Classics 5) and **Vol. 4** (Collector's Classics 20) reissue his music into early 1936. **Vol. 3** has Manone's biggest hit, "The Isle of Capri," welcoming such sidemen as Eddie Miller and Matty Matlock and guesting on

"Sliphorn Sam" with Russ Morgan's orchestra. **Vol. 4** consists of 25 selections by Manone's bands recorded in an eight-month period, with strong moments by Matlock, Miller, Freeman, Brunies, Joe Marsala, and (on five numbers) Jack Teagarden. Manone's music was beginning to get into a routine, particularly by the time of **1936** (Classics 849), **1936–1937** (Classics 887), and **1937–1938** (Classics 952); Manone's jivey vocals get a bit tiring if heard for too long. In fact, other than two instrumentals on **1936**, all of the music on these three CDs feature Manone's enthusiastic but limited vocals. However, the spirited trumpet work and occasional brief statements from a supporting cast that at times includes Marsala, Matlock, and Miller, are worth hearing in small doses, and Wingy's optimism and joy are difficult to resist.

Sharkey Bonano was another trumpeter who stuck to playing New Orleans jazz throughout his life. An excellent ensemble player who played hot melodic solos, Bonano was considered a bit too primitive when he unsuccessfully tried out for the Wolverines in 1924 as Bix Beiderbecke's possible successor. He did work with Jean Goldkette (1927), led the Melody Masters (1928–30), was a fixture back in his native New Orleans (1930–36), and returned to New York to briefly work with Ben Pollack. He put together his Sharks of Rhythm, playing in New York into the early 1940s. ● **Sharkey Bonano** (Timeless 001) is definitive. Bonano is heard in 1928 on two numbers with Johnnie Miller's New Orleans Frolickers and four with Monk Hazel's Bienville Roof Orchestra. Most of the rest of this CD consists of the 14 numbers recorded by Sharkey's Sharks of Rhythm during their four sessions of 1936–37. Among the players participating in these Dixieland sets are pianists Armand Hug, Clyde Hart, and Joe Bushkin, trombonists Santo Pecora and George Brunies, clarinetists Irving Fazola and Joe Marsala, drummers Ben Pollack and George Wettling, and Eddie Condon on rhythm guitar. This highly enjoyable CD closes with four numbers from Santo Pecora's Back Room Boys, which is similar in its Dixieland style to the Bonano band except that Shorty Sherock is on trumpet.

Sidney Bechet and Mezz Mezzrow

The great Sidney Bechet, who spent most of 1925–31 in Europe, returned to the United States as a member of Noble Sissle's Orchestra. In 1932, he formed the New Orleans Feetwarmers with Tommy Ladnier (who had also been with Sissle), and they recorded six mostly explosive numbers on September 15. Unfortunately, New Orleans jazz was very much out of vogue at the time, and by early 1933, the band folded. For a few months Bechet operated the Southern Tailor Shop with Ladnier in New York, but because they spent more time playing at jam sessions in the backroom than they did attending to business, that venture also failed. Bechet returned to Noble Sissle's Orchestra during 1934–38, working fairly steadily but out of the spotlight. **1923–1936** (Classics 583) has Bechet on two early blues numbers with singer Rosetta Crawford, the exciting 1932 session with the New Orleans Feetwarmers ("Shag" and "Maple Leaf Rag" are classics), and performances with Sissle's commercial but generally interesting big band ("Polka Dot Rag" is excellent). **1937–1938** (Classics 593) has its moments of excitement with Bechet featured with Sissle, with a small group out of the orchestra, in back of Trixie Smith (who was making a short-lived comeback), accompanying the vocal team of Grant & Wilson, and leading a sextet date that includes baritonist Ernie Caceres.

Hugues Panassie, an important jazz critic from France who championed New Orleans jazz over swing, came to the United States in 1938 with plans to record a few jazz sessions featuring some of his favorite musicians. Mezz Mezzrow, a limited clarinetist (best on blues) who had more enthusiasm than technique, was one of the beneficiaries of Panassie's attention, as were Tommy Ladnier and Bechet. Mezzrow's **1936–1939** (Classics 694) has the clarinetist leading swing-oriented combos in 1936–37 (with such players as trumpeter Frankie Newton, Bud Freeman, Willie "The Lion" Smith, Sy Oliver, and J.C. Higginbotham) and two of the three sessions with Ladnier. When Panassie arrived in the United States, Ladnier was nowhere to be found, not having been heard from much since 1933. As it turned out, he was still playing on a part-time basis in New Jersey, Connecticut, and upstate New York. Panassie and Mezzrow got Ladnier back in the recording studios on three occasions. One was a somewhat tumultuous date with Sidney DeParis, which found the two trumpeters not getting along musically, and the other one included on the Mezzrow CD is with a pianoless quintet that also includes Teddy Bunn, Pops Foster, and Manzie Johnson. Most successful was a matchup with Mezzrow and Bechet that resulted in four titles, including "Really the

Blues," included on Bechet's **1938–1940** (Classics 608). Although not in perfect health anymore, Ladnier still sounded pretty strong when he appeared with Bechet at John Hammond's "From Spirituals to Swing" concert in December.

Eddie Condon and Bud Freeman The most important early events in the rise of Dixieland centered around Eddie Condon and Milt Gabler. Gabler's father owned the Commodore Music Shop. In 1926, Gabler persuaded his father to turn it into one of the top record stores in New York. At a time when reissues were unheard of (when records sold out, they became unavailable), Gabler talked several labels into letting him lease vintage items for his United Hot Clubs of America label. Those releases from 1935 were the very first reissues. By 1937, the major labels were starting to realize the value of their older recordings and were doing their own reissues. So in January 1938, Gabler started recording new music for his Commodore label, emphasizing freewheeling jazz from smaller combos. The first artist who recorded for Commodore was Eddie Condon.

A natural leader who had already helped define Chicago jazz in the four McKenzie-Condon Chicagoans recordings of 1927, Condon was a rhythm guitarist who never soloed but kept a steady beat, a wisecracker who made for a colorful emcee, a skilled organizer of all-star bands, and an important propagandist for the music he loved. After struggling and freelancing throughout the Depression, in 1938 he was more than ready to start working as a leader. On January 17, 1938, Condon recorded five titles with his Windy City Seven, an octet comprised of cornetist Bobby Hackett, George Brunies, Pee Wee Russell, Bud Freeman, Jess Stacy, bassist Artie Shapiro, and drummer George Wettling, plus his own guitar; this was the real birth of the Condon sound. ❶**1928–38** (Classics 742) has the McKenzie-Condon Chicagoans numbers, six other titles that Condon led during 1928–29 (including "I'm Gonna Stomp, Mr. Henry Lee" and "That's a Serious Thing," which feature Jack Teagarden and trumpeter Leonard Davis), six numbers from 1933 (highlighted by two versions of Freeman's quirky feature "The Eel"), and the five songs from January 1938, which include a heated "Love Is Just Around the Corner" and some beautiful playing on "Ja Da." **1928–1938** concludes with two selections from a similar April 1938 session (with Teagarden in

Brunies's place), including a lyrical Bobby Hackett solo on "Embraceable You" that Miles Davis years later would say was a strong influence on his approach. The remainder of that session and two jubilant titles from November ("Sunday" and "California Here I Come") are on **1938–1940** (Classics 759), which is covered in Chapter 5.

Eddie Condon's bands, like Duke Ellington's, teamed together a variety of unlikely individualists. One of Condon's associates deserves special mention for his recordings of 1938, tenor saxophonist Bud Freeman. A member of the Austin High Gang, Freeman moved to New York in 1927 and worked with Red Nichols, Roger Wolfe Kahn, Ben Pollack, Gene Kardos, and other local groups. During the swing era he played with the orchestras of Joe Haymes, Ray Noble, Tommy Dorsey (1936–38), and briefly with Benny Goodman. Freeman's soft tone and angular style were virtually the only alternative to Coleman Hawkins's approach on tenor before Lester Young became prominent. ❶**1928–1938** (Classics 781) has two songs from his session of 1928 and a spirited 1935 sextet date that matches Bud with Bunny Berigan. Most of the CD features the inspired combination of Freeman, Jess Stacy, and George Wettling in 1938. This classic tenor/piano/drums trio romps joyfully through such numbers as "You Took Advantage of Me," "I Got Rhythm," "Keep Smiling at Trouble," and "My Honey's Loving Arms." Also on this CD are five numbers on which Freeman leads an all-star Eddie Condon–style octet, also including Bobby Hackett, Pee Wee Russell, Stacy, and Condon himself.

Although the threat of war in Europe during 1938 cast a shadow over the world, jazz was flourishing in a way that never would have been predicted at the beginning of 1933. The Depression may have still been raging on, but for jazz, the good times were back.

Various Artists Collections

There have been many "Best Of" repackagings of the music of the swing era, most of which merely recycle the same old hits over and over endlessly. However, here are eight sets that are real standouts and recommended to listeners who are not exploring the more complete Classics label. ❶ **Jazz in the Thirties** (DRG/Swing 8457/8458) is a two-CD set with 40 selections from 1933–35. Among the all-star groups are the Venuti-Lang Blue Four, a later Venuti combo with Benny Goodman, a Goodman small group with Jack Teagarden, Adrian Rollini's Orchestra, Joe Sullivan piano solos, Jess Stacy's trio, and bands headed by Bud Freeman, Gene Krupa, and Bunny Berigan. **Ridin' in Rhythm** (DRG Swing 8453/8454), also a two-fer but covering black bands rather than white ones, has notable performances from Duke Ellington, the Mills Blue Rhythm Band, and the big bands of Benny Carter, Fletcher Henderson, and Horace Henderson, plus some piano solos from Meade Lux Lewis and quite a few Coleman Hawkins performances.

More integrated are the single-CD samplers **The 1930s: The Singers** (Columbia 40847), **The 1930s: Big Bands** (Columbia 40651), and **The 1930s: The Small Combos** (Columbia 40833). Each contains 16 or 17 selections, with a different artist or group on each cut, serving as ideal introductions to the swing era.

52nd Street Swing—New York in the '30s (GRP/Decca 646) has high-quality, small-group swing from the Spirits of Rhythm, Stuff Smith, John Kirby's Sextet, Hot Lips Page, the Delta Four (a quartet with Roy Eldridge and Joe Marsala), Sammy Price (with Lester Young), and a group organized by critic Leonard Feather that features Bobby Hackett, altoist Pete Brown, and Benny Carter. **Swing Is Here—Small Band Swing 1935–1939** (Bluebird 2180) has Gene Krupa's first date as a leader (featuring Roy Eldridge, Benny Goodman and Chu Berry), Bunny Berigan starring on a session led by arranger Gene Gifford, a few numbers from Mezz Mezzrow, Frankie Newton, and James P. Johnson in exciting form on "Rosetta" and "The World Is Waiting for the Sunrise," and seven of Wingy Manone's better recordings.

Finally, there is **Saturday Night Swing Club Vols. 1 & 2** (Jazz Unlimited 2056/2057), a two-fer that reissues an exciting 90-minute radio broadcast from June 12, 1937. The cast of players is very impressive, including the Quintet of the Hot Club of France (on the first live transatlantic hookup), a Duke Ellington small group, pioneering jazz harpist Casper Reardon, the Raymond Scott Quintette, Adrian Rollini (on vibes), Bunny Berigan, the Casa Loma Orchestra, the Benny Goodman Trio and Quartet, and the guitars of Carl Kress and Dick McDonough. In addition, there is a half-hour broadcast from October 31, 1936, featuring Berigan with the house band and a special appearance by the reunited Original Dixieland Jazz Band. But beyond the music, what is most notable about this release is the youthful enthusiasm heard from the musicians, the surprisingly knowledgeable announcers, and the audience. There can be little doubt that during this time period, jazz and swing were embraced by the younger generation, and that the music made a potentially dreary world seem very hopeful.

VOICES OF THE FUTURE

Sadao Watanabe (alto), Feb. 1, 1933, Utsunomiga, Japan

John Handy (alto), Feb. 3, 1933, Dallas, TX

Nina Simone (vocals, piano), Feb. 21, 1933, Tryon, NC

David "Fathead" Newman (tenor, flute, alto), Feb. 24, 1933, Dallas, TX

Quincy Jones (arranger, composer, leader), Mar. 14, 1933, Chicago, IL

Cecil Taylor (piano, leader), Mar. 15, 1933, New York, NY

Dave Frishberg (piano, vocals, composer), Mar. 23, 1933, St. Paul, MN

Tete Montoliu (piano), Mar. 28, 1933, Barcelona, Spain

Bill Hardman (trumpet), Apr. 6, 1933, Cleveland, OH

Ian Carr (trumpet), Apr. 21, 1933, Dumfries, Scotland

Cal Collins (guitar), May 5, 1933, Medora, IN

Stu Williamson (trumpet, valve trombone), May 14, 1933, Brattleboro, VT

Michael White (violin), May 24, 1933, Houston, TX

Ben Riley (drums), July 17, 1933, Savannah, GA

Sonny Simmons (alto), Aug. 4, 1933, Sicily Island, LA

Wayne Shorter (tenor, soprano, composer), Aug. 25, 1933, Newark, NJ

Gene Harris (piano), Sept. 1, 1933, Benton Harbor, MI

Steve McCall (drums), Sept. 30, 1933, Chicago, IL

Gary McFarland (vibes, arranger), Oct. 23, 1933, Los Angeles, CA

Bob Barnard (trumpet), Nov. 24, 1933, Melbourne, Australia

Dennis Charles (drums), Dec. 4, 1933, St. Croix, VI

Borah Bergman (piano), Dec. 13, 1933, Brooklyn, NY

Leo Wright (alto, flute), Dec. 14, 1933, Wichita Falls, TX

Johnny "Hammond" Smith (organ), Dec. 16, 1933, Louisville, KY

Frank Morgan (alto), Dec. 23, 1933, Minneapolis, MN

Cedar Walton (piano, composer), Jan. 17, 1934, Dallas, TX

King Curtis (tenor), Feb. 7, 1934, Fort Worth, TX

Willie Bobo (conga, timbales), Feb. 28, 1934, New York, NY

Doug Watkins (bass, cello), Mar. 2, 1934, Detroit, MI

Jimmy Garrison (bass), Mar. 3, 1934, Miami, FL

Shirley Scott (organ, piano), Mar. 14, 1934, Philadelphia, PA

Lanny Morgan (alto), Mar. 30, 1934, Des Moines, IA

Stanley Turrentine (tenor), Apr. 5, 1934, Pittsburgh, PA

Horace Tapscott (piano, composer, leader), Apr. 6, 1934, Houston, TX

Victor Feldman (piano, vibes, drums), Apr. 7, 1934, London, England

Shirley Horn (piano, vocals), May 1, 1934, Washington, D.C.

Dave Grusin (keyboards, composer, arranger), June 26, 1934, Denver, CO

Bobby Bradford (trumpet), July 19, 1934, Cleveland, MS

Junior Cook (tenor), July 22, 1934, Pensacola, FL

Steve Lacy (soprano), July 23, 1934, New York, NY

Don Ellis (trumpet, leader), July 25, 1934, Los Angeles, CA

Oliver Jones (piano), Sept. 11, 1934, Montreal, Quebec, Canada

Abdullah Ibrahim (piano, composer, leader), Oct. 9, 1934, Capetown, South Africa

Eddie Harris (tenor, electric sax), Oct. 20, 1934, Chicago, IL

Jimmy Woods (alto), Oct. 29, 1934, St. Louis, MI

Houston Person (tenor), Nov. 10, 1934, Newberry, SC

Ellis Marsalis (piano), Nov. 13, 1934, New Orleans, LA

Gato Barbieri (tenor), Nov. 28, 1934, Rosario, Argentina

Tony Coe (tenor, clarinet), Nov. 29, 1934, Canterbury, England

Art Davis (bass), Dec. 5, 1934, Harrisburg, PA

Curtis Fuller (trombone), Dec. 15, 1934, Detroit, MI

Hank Crawford (alto), Dec. 24, 1934, Memphis, TN

Bill Chase (trumpet), 1935, Boston, MA

Kenny Davern (clarinet, soprano), Jan. 7, 1935, Huntington, NY

Tubby Hayes (tenor, vibes), Jan. 30, 1935, London, England

Rob McConnell (valve trombone, arranger, composer, leader), Feb. 14, 1935, London, Ontario, Canada

VOICES OF THE FUTURE

George Coleman (tenor), Mar. 8, 1935, Memphis, TN

Karl Berger (vibes), Mar. 30, 1935, Heidelberg, Germany

Ran Blake (piano), Apr. 20, 1935, Springfield, MA

Paul Chambers (bass), Apr. 22, 1935, Pittsburgh, PA

Gary Peacock (bass), May 12, 1935, Burley, IN

Cecil McBee (bass), May 19, 1935, Tulsa, OK

Ramsey Lewis (piano), May 27, 1935, Chicago, IL

Albert "Tootie" Heath (drums), May 31, 1935, Philadelphia, PA

Ted Curson (trumpet), June 3, 1935, Philadelphia, PA

Misha Mengelberg (piano, composer), June 5, 1935, Kiev, Soviet Union

Julian Priester (trombone), June 29, 1935, Chicago, IL

Rashied Ali (drums), July 1, 1935, Philadelphia, PA

Frank Wright (tenor), July 9, 1935, Grenada, MS

Big John Patton (organ), July 12, 1935, Kansas City, MO

Marion Brown (alto), Sept. 8, 1935, Atlanta, GA

James Clay (tenor), Sept. 8, 1935, Dallas, TX

Les McCann (piano, vocals, keyboards), Sept. 23, 1935, Lexington, KY

Henry Grimes (bass), Nov. 3, 1935, Philadelphia, PA

Roswell Rudd (trombone), Nov. 17, 1935, Sharon, CT

Lou Rawls (vocals), Dec. 1, 1935, Chicago, IL

Dannie Richmond (drums), Dec. 15, 1935, New York, NY

Bobby Timmons (piano, composer), Dec. 19, 1935, Philadelphia, PA

Sonny Greenwich (guitar), Jan. 1, 1936, Hamilton, Ontario, Canada

Hod O'Brien (piano), Jan. 19, 1936, Chicago, IL

Buell Neidlinger (bass, cello), Mar. 2, 1936, Westport, CT

Gabor Szabo (guitar), Mar. 8, 1936, Budapest, Hungary

Harold Mabern (piano), Mar. 20, 1936, Memphis, TN

Harold Vick (tenor), Apr. 3, 1936, Rocky Mount, NC

Jimmy McGriff (organ), Apr. 3, 1936, Philadelphia, PA

Scott LaFaro (bass), Apr. 3, 1936, Newark, NJ

Manfred Schoof (trumpet), Apr. 6, 1936, Magdeburg, Germany

Don Menza (tenor, arranger), Apr. 22, 1936, Buffalo, NY

John Tchicai (tenor, bass clarinet, alto), Apr. 28, 1936, Copenhagen, Denmark

Klaus Doldinger (tenor, soprano, leader), May 12, 1936, Berlin, Germany

Rufus Harley (bagpipes, reeds), May 20, 1936, Raleigh, NC

Gary Foster (alto), May 25, 1936, Leavenworth, KS

Marcus Belgrave (trumpet), June 12, 1936, Chester, PA

Lin Halliday (tenor), June 16, 1936, De Queen, AR

Albert Ayler (tenor, alto), July 13, 1936, Cleveland, OH

Nick Brignola (baritone), July 17, 1936, Troy, NY

Carmell Jones (trumpet), July 19, 1936, Kansas City, KS

Don Patterson (organ), July 22, 1936, Columbus, OH

Jim Galloway (soprano), July 28, 1936, Kilwinning, Ayrshire, Scotland

Joe Diorio (guitar), Aug. 6, 1936, Waterbury, CT

Rahsaan Roland Kirk (tenor, manzello, stritch, flute, clarinet), Aug. 7, 1936, Columbus, OH

Chuck Israels (bass), Aug. 10, 1936, New York, NY

Billy Higgins (drums), Oct. 11, 1936, Los Angeles, CA

Mel Rhyne (organ), Oct. 12, 1936, Indianapolis, IN

Sathima Bea Benjamin (vocals), Oct. 17, 1936, Cape Town, South Africa

Bertha Hope (piano), Nov. 8, 1936, Los Angeles, CA

Don Cherry (pocket trumpet), Nov. 18, 1936, Oklahoma City, OK

Bill Allred (trombone), Nov. 19, 1936, Rock Island, IL

Roy McCurdy (drums), Nov. 28, 1936, Rochester, NY

Eddie Palmieri (piano, leader), Dec. 15, 1936, East Harlem, NY

Chris McGregor (piano, leader), Dec. 24, 1936, Umtata, South Africa

Neville Dickie (piano), Jan. 1, 1937, Durham, England

Big Bill Bissonnette (trombone, producer), Feb. 5, 1937, Bridgeport, CT

Ed Polcer (cornet), Feb. 10, 1937, Paterson, NJ

Kirk Lightsey (piano), Feb. 15, 1937, Detroit, MI

Nancy Wilson (vocals), Feb. 20, 1937, Chillicothe, OH

Carol Sloane (vocals), Mar. 5, 1937, Providence, RI

Gene Bertoncini (guitar), Apr. 6, 1937, New York, NY

Joe Henderson (tenor), Apr. 24, 1937, Lima, OH

Ron Carter (bass), May 4, 1937, Ferndale, MI

VOICES OF THE FUTURE

Archie Shepp (tenor), May 24, 1937,
Ft. Lauderdale, FL

Louis Hayes (drums), May 31, 1937,
Detroit, MI

Grachan Moncur, III (trombone), June 3, 1937,
New York, NY

Reggie Workman (bass), June 26, 1937,
Philadelphia, PA

Andrew Hill (piano, composer), June 30, 1937,
Chicago, IL

Charlie Shoemake (vibes), July 27, 1937, Houston, TX

James Spaulding (alto, flute), July 30, 1937,
Indianapolis, IN

Charlie Haden (bass), Aug. 6, 1937, Shenandoah, IA

Malachi Favors (bass), Aug. 22, 1937, Chicago, IL

Alice Coltrane (piano, harp), Aug. 27, 1937,
Detroit, MI

Ellyn Rucker (piano, vocals), Aug. 29, 1937, Des
Moines, IA

Gunter Hampel (vibes, bass clarinet), Aug. 31, 1937,
Goettingen, Germany

Joseph Jarman (reeds), Sept. 14, 1937, Pine Bluff, AR

Sunny Murray (drums), Sept. 21, 1937, Idabel, OK

Guido Basso (trumpet, flugelhorn), Sept. 27, 1937,
Montreal, Canada

Leon Thomas (vocals), Oct. 4, 1937, East St. Louis, IL

Ernie Carson (trumpet), Dec. 4, 1937, Portland, OR

Don Sebesky (arranger, composer, trombone),
Dec. 10, 1937, Perth Amboy, NJ

Joe Farrell (tenor, soprano, flute), Dec. 16, 1937,
Chicago Heights, IL

Milcho Leviev (piano, keyboards), Dec. 19, 1937,
Plovdiv, Bulgaria

Julius Hemphill (alto, soprano, composer), Jan. 24,
1938, Ft. Worth, TX

Mike Wofford (piano), Feb. 25, 1938, San Antonio, TX

Charles Lloyd (tenor, flute, leader), Mar. 15, 1938,
Memphis, TN

Dave Pike (vibes), Mar. 23, 1938, Detroit, MI

Steve Kuhn (piano), Mar. 24, 1938, Brooklyn, NY

Booker Little (trumpet), Apr. 2, 1938, Memphis, TN

Alex Schlippenbach (piano, composer), Apr. 7, 1938,
Berlin, Germany

Freddie Hubbard (trumpet, flugelhorn, composer),
Apr. 7, 1938, Indianapolis, IN

Pete LaRoca (drums), Apr. 7, 1938, New York, NY

Denny Zeitlin (piano), Apr. 10, 1938, Chicago, IL

Hal Galper (piano), Apr. 18, 1938, Salem, MA

Ross Tompkins (piano), May 13, 1938, Detroit, MI

Tony Oxley (drums), June 15, 1938, Sheffield,
Yorkshire, England

Albert Dailey (piano), June 16, 1938, Baltimore, MD

Mike Mainieri (vibes), July 4, 1938, Bronx, NY

Lee Morgan (trumpet), July 10, 1938, New York, NY

Dudu Pukwana (alto), July 18, 1938, Port Elizabeth,
South Africa

Joanne Brackeen (piano), July 26, 1938, Ventura, CA

Perry Robinson (clarinet), Aug. 17, 1938,
New York, NY

Roy Brooks (drums), Sept. 3, 1938, Detroit, MI

Mark Levine (piano, trombone), Oct. 4, 1938,
Concord, NH

Carlos Garnett (tenor), Dec. 1, 1938, Red Tank,
Canal Zone

McCoy Tyner (piano, leader), Dec. 13, 1938,
Philadelphia, PA

Dick Sudhalter (trumpet), Dec. 28, 1938, Boston, MA

PASSINGS

Eddie Lang (30), Mar. 26, 1933, New York, NY
Freddie Keppard (43), July 15, 1933, Chicago, IL
Bennie Moten (40), Apr. 2, 1935, Kansas City, MO
Charlie Green (35), Feb. 1936, New York, NY
Alex Hill (30), Feb. 1, 1937, North Little Rock, AR
Ward Pinkett (30), Mar. 15, 1937, New York, NY

Johnny Dunn (40), Aug. 20, 1937, Paris, France
Bessie Smith (43), Sept. 26, 1937, Clarksdale, MS
Joe Smith (35), Dec. 2, 1937, New York, NY
King Oliver (52), Apr. 8, 1938, Savannah, GA
Dick McDonough (33), May 25, 1938, New York, NY
James Scott (53), Aug. 30, 1938, Kansas City, KS

Chapter Five

1939–1944:
The War Years

As 1939 began, swing and big bands were at the peak of their popularity. Benny Goodman, Artie Shaw, Gene Krupa, Tommy Dorsey, Duke Ellington, Count Basie, and Jimmie Lunceford were all household names. Before the year ended, Glenn Miller, Charlie Barnet, and Will Bradley had hit pay dirt, while Harry James, Jack Teagarden, Benny Carter, Teddy Wilson, and Coleman Hawkins were among those who had started new orchestras. It almost became a status symbol that someone could not be a true swing star without being at the head of his own orchestra.

The start of World War II on September 1, 1939, at first did not directly affect jazz except for those American musicians who were temporarily stuck overseas. Tours of Europe came to an end, but the American swing world continued to flourish since the United States was officially neutral in the European conflict.

By 1940–41, there were so many swing bands active that some observers complained that the music was becoming watered down. A group of younger musicians, who felt that swing had become an overly predictable music, stretched out at jam sessions (most notably at Minton's Playhouse and Monroe's Uptown House in New York City), experimenting with advanced harmonies and rhythms—the early steps of a music that would, by 1944, develop into bebop. On the other hand, vintage pre-swing jazz was beginning to make a comeback on several levels. Eddie Condon's all-star groups (some of which included musicians active in swing) were developing Dixieland, and collectors of early music were beginning to dig up and rediscover surviving New Orleans veterans, including trumpeter Bunk Johnson. In San Francisco, Lu Watters's Yerba Buena Jazz Band was reviving jazz of the early 1920s while being creative within the earlier musical boundaries.

But swing remained the dominant force in American popular music during this era, even after the Japanese attack of Pearl Harbor on December 7, 1941, forced the United States to enter the war. With many musicians being drafted and travel restrictions making it difficult for orchestras to be on the road, some of the big bands did not survive. Glenn Miller, Artie Shaw, Claude Thornhill, and Bob Crosby were among those who enlisted, and the big bands that continued on often had to utilize underage musicians or older players.

In an exercise of terrible timing, the Musicians Union (which had a dispute with radio stations over records being played for free on the air) called a recording strike that started August 1, 1942. No commercial records were made again until the Decca label signed an agreement in September 1943. Some of the other small labels (such as the new Blue Note company) made peace with the union later in 1943, but Columbia and Victor did not settle until November 1944, which meant that many of the major bands did not record for a 27-month period. Although the wiser labels had stockpiled recordings during the months before the recording ban and were able to come out with "new releases" in the interim, more current musical trends and upcoming musicians were not documented. Singers, in contrast, were not considered musicians and were free to continue recording with amateur players or in a cappella groups. This exposure was a major advantage and helped lead to their dominance in the postwar years.

For most of the established bands, the record ban hurt, but the orchestras still appeared regularly on the radio and were free to record V-discs for the government. V(ictory)-discs were records made specifically for the military, giving servicemen who were stationed overseas some much needed entertainment. Although those recordings were supposed to be destroyed at the end of the war, fortunately copies of most of the performances survived. Decades later, the V-discs and radio broadcasts that have been issued give listeners an opportunity to hear what most of the significant bands sounded like during 1942–44, although unfortunately the 1943 Earl Hines Orchestra (the first bebop big band) was one of the few to slip through the cracks and not be documented at all.

While new bands found it difficult to catch on during 1942–44 due to travel restrictions and the recording ban, the best-known swing orchestras were often able to prosper. In fact, several added full string sections. Artie Shaw was finally able to fulfill his dream of leading a successful string orchestra in 1940, and during the next few years Tommy Dorsey, Harry James, and Gene Krupa were among those who, for a time, expanded their personnel. In addition to the use of strings by the more prosperous orchestras, swing era big bands in general grew in size during the first half of the 1940s, with some ensembles adding a fourth trumpeter, a third trombone (Duke Ellington had had three since the early 1930s), and a baritone sax as their fifth saxophone.

During the swing era, the main labels were RCA (which owned Victor), Columbia (Okeh, Brunswick, and Vocalion), and Decca. However, there were some important new competitors, including Milt Gabler's Commodore label (the first company dedicated solely to jazz), Alfred Lion's Blue Note (formed in 1939), and Capitol, which was born in 1942 with lyricist Johnny Mercer as one of the original owners. When the recording strike began to end during 1943–44, many new small labels began to be involved in jazz, including Savoy and Harry Lim's Keynote.

The D-Day invasion of June 6, 1944, and the end of the recording strike resulted in a great optimism among swing fans who looked forward to the postwar years when the swing era would certainly continue at its earlier level. But the future is always impossible to predict.

Glenn Miller

Glenn Miller's orchestra was the most commercially successful of all the swing bands. Ironically, as 1939 began, Miller had thus far failed to make an impression on the public. His first big band, which lasted during most of 1937, had flopped, and his second orchestra, formed in the spring of 1938, seemed destined for a similar fate. On April 4, 1939, at the band's third record date for the Bluebird label, they recorded their romantic theme song "Moonlight Serenade." Six days later, Miller waxed "Little Brown Jug" and "Sunrise Serenade," both of which caught on. On May 17, the band opened what would be a 14-week stint at the Glen Island Casino in New Rochelle, New York, and began broadcasting regularly over two networks. It was on its way to becoming a sensation, particularly after recording "In the Mood" on August 1.

During the next three years, the Glenn Miller Orchestra had a remarkable number of hit records, easily dwarfing the sales of Benny Goodman and Artie Shaw. In addition to the tunes already mentioned, such songs as "Tuxedo Junction" (overshadowing Erskine Hawkins's earlier recording), "Pennsylvania 6-5000," "Anvil Chorus," "Song of the Volga Boatmen," "Perfidia," "Chattanooga Choo Choo," "I Know Why," "Elmer's Tune," "A String of Pearls," "Moonlight Cocktail," "Don't Sit Under the Apple Tree," "American Patrol," "I've Got a Gal in Kalamazoo," "Serenade in Blue," "At Last," and "Juke Box Saturday Night" helped form the soundtrack of the era.

Glenn Miller rarely soloed himself, instead shaping the arrangements of others while insisting on flawless ensembles and keeping a tight ship. He had developed a signature sound (with a clarinet doubling the melody above the saxophone section) and a show that included lots of repetitive riffing, ballad vocals from Ray Eberle, novelty numbers featuring singer Marian Hutton, good-natured vocalizing and tenor solos from Tex Beneke, and some swinging instrumentals. Miller knew that his band would never be as hard-swinging as Count Basie's, and he was not eager to add virtuosic soloists, being content to have reliable section players who could add a touch of jazz to their short spots. His hot trumpeter of 1939, Clyde Hurley (who can be heard soloing on "In the Mood"), did not last long because he did not care for the lack of spontaneity, and the only later soloist of note, cornetist Bobby Hackett (who took a famous chorus on "A String of Pearls"), was often content to get a steady check while playing rhythm guitar. Miller's formula worked remarkably well, and his orchestra was the most beloved by the general public not only from mid-1939 through 1942, but for many years after it faded into history. In 1942, Glenn Miller applied for and was accepted as a captain in the Army Air Force. After September 27, the Glenn Miller Orchestra (the most popular swing band in the world) was no more.

A black box, **The Complete Glenn Miller** (Bluebird 78636 10152), houses 13 CDs that contain all of the Glen Miller Orchestra's studio recordings from September 27, 1938, through July 15, 1942, with the alternate takes grouped on the final disc. All of the many hits plus quite a bit of lesser-known material is on this very comprehensive set. However, more general collectors will prefer a smaller sampling. There have been a countless number of Glenn Miller reissues, repackaging the same songs in an infinite number of combinations. ◐ **The Popular Recordings** (Bluebird 9785), a three-CD set, is pretty definitive since it has all of the band's hits, studio highpoints, and the better jazz, ballads, and dance band records. Also of strong interest is **A Legendary Performer** (Bluebird 0693), a single disc that has most of Miller's more significant radio appearances, starting off with an early number from when the band was quite unknown (the announcer sounds obviously bored). Also included is a New Year's Eve version of "In the Mood," Miller being awarded the first gold record in history for "Chattanooga Choo Choo," live and extended versions of many of his hits, and an emotional farewell after Miller announces his enlistment in the military.

When Glenn Miller broke up his orchestra and became a captain in the Army Air Force, he hoped to do his part for his country during the war. Successfully fighting conservative bureaucrats and red tape, by mid-1943 Miller had put together his greatest orchestra, the Army Air Force Band. It was his goal to use the orchestra to boost the morale of servicemen overseas. After a period based in the United States, the orchestra was shipped to England in the spring of 1944. Although no commercial recordings were made, there were V-discs, constant radio broadcasts, and numerous concerts.

The Glenn Miller Army Air Force Band, which made "St. Louis Blues March" popular, was quite a mighty orchestra with a full string section and such key players as pianist/arranger Mel Powell, drummer/vocalist Ray McKinley, clarinetist Peanuts Hucko, and trumpeters Bobby Nichols and Bernie Privin. It was stronger from a jazz standpoint than Miller's civilian orchestra, yet could also play very effective mood music featuring the strings. And Miller did not have to worry about paying salaries or having his musicians leave to join other bands!

Although none of his military band's recordings were available to civilians in the 1940s, many recordings have since been released, particularly in recent times. ◉ **Glenn Miller Army Air Force Band** (Bluebird 63852) is the perfect place to start, being a four-CD set that expands upon an early five-LP box. The 61 selections include spirited remakes of earlier Miller hits, jazz instrumentals (the teenaged trumpeter Bobby Nichols really excels on these), patriotic swing numbers, ballad vocals (from Johnny Desmond), and some of Miller's famous "Something Old, Something New, Something Borrowed, and Something Blue" medleys. **The Glenn Miller V-Disc Sessions: Vol. One** (Mr. Music 7001) and **Vol. Two** (Mr. Music 7002) have all 43 of Miller's V-discs with the second CD being a little stronger from the jazz standpoint.

RCA and the British Avid label have come out with overlapping Miller series. **The Secret Broadcasts** (RCA 75605-52500) is a well-rounded three-CD set that features the Glen Miller Orchestra in 1944 while **The Lost Recordings** (RCA 09026-68320) is a single disc consisting of six propaganda broadcasts. The latter has a female announcer speaking in German and Miller doing his best phonetically (the broadcasts were aired in Germany) along with some fine music. All of the performances on **The Secret Broadcasts** are included in the pair of two-CD sets **Vol. One: American Patrol** (Avid

556) and **Vol. Two: Keep 'Em Flying** (Avid 557) plus 19 additional selections. **Vol. Three: All's Well Mademoiselle** (Avid 558) and **Vol. Four: The Red Cavalry March** (Avid 559) are single discs and mostly feature the Army Air Force Band in 1945. **Vol. Five: The Complete Abbey Road Recordings** (Avid 560) is a two-CD set that is a more complete version of **The Lost Recordings**. **Vol. Six: Blue Champagne** (Avid 561), **Vol. Seven: S'Wonderful** (Avid 588), **Vol. Eight: Get Happy** (Avid 589), and **Vol. Nine: King Porter Stomp** (Avid 635), all single CDs, add to the rich legacy of this legendary if short-lived band, dating from 1943–45. The complete broadcasts of the Glenn Miller Army Air Force Band have yet to be reissued in chronological order, but the Avid CDs, the pair of discs from Mr. Music, and the Bluebird box (which together total 18 CDs) are a healthy and very enjoyable chunk of that orchestra's legacy.

Glenn Miller wanted to have his orchestra play on the European continent, but, as he flew over the English Channel on December 15, 1944, on his way to France to make arrangements for his band's arrival, his plane was shot down (possibly by friendly fire) and lost forever. The Army Air Force Band stayed together under Ray McKinley's leadership for an additional year before the musicians were discharged from the military.

Although Glenn Miller would certainly have progressed musically after World War II, his premature death has resulted in his music being permanently frozen in the 1939–42 period, as played by the Glenn Miller ghost orchestra and many nostalgia big bands.

The Pacesetters: 1939–1944

The basic swing solo styles were pretty well established by 1938 and did not change that drastically during the next six years although there were plenty of up-and-coming talents. Trumpeters still looked up to Louis Armstrong. Even though his big band was just a second-level outfit and the swing world seemed to pass him by, Satch remained the king among trumpeters for his phrasing, sound, and ability to uplift melodies with subtle melodic creativity. With the decline and death of Bunny Berigan, Roy Eldridge was considered the next step beyond Armstrong with his crackling sound, wide range, and harmonically advanced choice of notes. Add a stronger sense of humor and a cleaner sound and one had Charlie Shavers. Other major swing trumpet soloists included Ziggy Elman (who switched from Benny

---

TIMELINE 1939

Glenn Miller's Orchestra hits it big and is soon the most popular of the all the swing bands. • Bunny Berigan declares bankruptcy. • Jimmy Blanton joins Duke Ellington's big band. • Benny Goodman has a hit in "And the Angels Sing." • Charlie Christian joins Benny Goodman. • Sy Oliver leaves the Jimmie Lunceford Orchestra to join Tommy Dorsey. • Chick Webb dies and Ella Fitzgerald takes over his orchestra. • Billie Holiday records "Strange Fruit." • Lee Wiley begins her songbook series. • The original Quintet of the Hot Club of France breaks up. • Stephane Grappelli works in England with George Shearing. • Sidney Bechet records a hit version of "Summertime." • Artie Shaw flees to Mexico. • Muggsy Spanier records "The Great 16" with his Ragtime Band. • Herschel Evans dies and is replaced in the Count Basie Orchestra by Buddy Tate. • The Will Bradley Orchestra is formed. • Dizzy Gillespie joins Cab Calloway. • The International Sweethearts of Rhythm is organized at the Piney Woods County Life School in Mississippi. • Jan Savitt's Top Hatters have a hit with "720 in the Books." • The no-name Joe Venuti Orchestra makes its only recordings, four songs titled "Flip," "Flop," "Something," and "Nothing." • W.C. Handy records four songs on cornet with an all-star group of musicians taken from the Louis Armstrong/Luis Russell band, but his phrasing is so wooden that it is clear that he never learned how to swing. • Ida Cox and Lizzie Miles both make brief comebacks, appearing on records for the first time since the 1920s. • Tony Parenti begins a six-year stint playing with Ted Lewis's band. • Adrian Rollini, now a full-time vibraphonist, records a series of a dozen numbers (during 1939–40) with his trio for Vocalion before fading away into obscurity. • Garland Wilson returns to the United States after seven years overseas. • Fourteen-year-old pianist Oscar Peterson wins a talent show in his native Canada and soon begins starring on a weekly radio show in Montreal.

Goodman to Tommy Dorsey's band), Buck Clayton, Harry "Sweets" Edison, Bobby Hackett, Dud Bascomb (with Erskine Hawkins), the lyrical Frankie Newton, Hot Lips Page, and such Duke Ellington soloists as Cootie Williams, his successor Ray Nance, and Rex Stewart. However, the best-known trumpeter of the era was Harry James, whose warm sound, brilliant technique, and accessible style led to his band becoming the most popular in the land from the fall of 1942 (when Glenn Miller broke up his orchestra) through 1945.

Louis Armstrong was a strong influence on all of these trumpeters plus such Dixieland-oriented players as Muggsy Spanier, Wingy Manone, Henry "Red" Allen, Yank Lawson, Billy Butterfield, and Wild Bill Davison. About the only trumpeters whose styles were not touched directly by Satch's were Bunk Johnson (who had preceded Armstrong and was rediscovered in 1942) and the bebop pioneers such as Dizzy Gillespie (who was most influenced by Roy Eldridge) and Howard McGhee. The range of the trumpet continued to expand beyond what Louis Armstrong could play, with Al Killian (who had stints with Count Basie and Charlie Barnet), Paul Webster (hitting high notes with Jimmie Lunceford), and especially Cat Anderson (who joined Duke Ellington in 1944) making the stratosphere sound reachable.

Among trombonists, Jack Teagarden remained the leader. Liberated from the Paul Whiteman Orchestra, but now burdened with his own struggling big band, Teagarden's smooth Dixieland-oriented playing actually sounded best in small groups. The two trombonists with the most successful big bands, Glenn Miller and Tommy Dorsey, were in awe of Teagarden's playing to the point where Miller rarely played and TD preferred to feature his pretty tone on ballads. Other individual voices on the trombone included Ellington's Lawrence Brown and Tricky Sam Nanton, Jack Jenney (whose technique impressed his contemporaries), J.C. Higginbotham, Vic Dickenson, Lou McGarity, and the eccentric Dickie Wells. By 1944, Kid Ory was coming out of retirement and J.J. Johnson was starting to be noticed for his fluent technique and advanced ideas.

Benny Goodman continued his reign as the King of Swing during 1939–44, but he had close competition among clarinetists from the equally talented Artie Shaw. Jimmy Dorsey, although still a major player, did not sound all that creative in his orchestra, and Woody Herman was never in the same league with BG and Shaw.

Pee Wee Russell began to gain attention for his playing with Eddie Condon's freewheeling bands, while Buddy DeFranco with Tommy Dorsey was one of the leaders by 1944. Edmond Hall emerged as a very distinctive player, and Ellington was able to make up for Barney Bigard's departure by featuring Jimmy Hamilton. But the clarinet, in general, declined in importance as the 1940s progressed.

In contrast, the tenor sax, which had been a minor instrument in the 1920s, continued to grow in popularity as jazz's top horn. In addition to Coleman Hawkins (who returned from Europe in time to regain his place at the top) and Lester Young (who had emerged as Hawkins's equal), such major players as Ben Webster, Chu Berry, Bud Freeman, Eddie Miller, Don Byas, Illinois Jacquet, and Arnett Cobb each displayed their own fresh musical personalities. The alto sax had fewer major voices, although the big three of the swing era, Johnny Hodges, Benny Carter, and Willie Smith, continued in their prime. Tab Smith showed a great deal of potential, Louis Jordan made a major name for himself as a singer and personality, and Charlie Parker was beginning to impress younger forward-thinking musicians. The baritone sax continued to be owned by Harry Carney, while Sidney Bechet's mastery of the soprano sax largely chased all other competitors away from that instrument.

There was certainly no shortage of great pianists during this era. A condensed list would have to include the three giants of 1920s stride (James P. Johnson, who emerged from semi-retirement, Fats Waller, and Willie "The Lion" Smith), the incredible Art Tatum, Teddy Wilson (the definitive swing pianist), the boogie-woogie stylists Albert Ammons, Pete Johnson, and Meade Lux Lewis, and such swing-oriented players as Earl Hines, Joe Sullivan, Bob Zurke, Mary Lou Williams, Art Hodes, Nat King Cole, Mel Powell, and the sparse Count Basie. Lurking in the background was Bud Powell, whose revolutionary approach to playing piano would make many of the swing players sound, if not obsolete, a bit old-fashioned in comparison.

During the 1939–44 period, both the guitar and the bass became liberated from their earlier roles. Charlie Christian was the first major electric guitar soloist and he played with such horn-like fluency that his only competitor was Django Reinhardt in Europe. Similarly, Jimmy Blanton made most other bassists sound unimaginative and predictable in comparison. There were many similarities to the careers of Christian and Blanton, including both being closely associated with a major big band, having brief lives shortened by tuberculosis, and being more than a decade ahead of their time. After Christian's period in the spotlight, the guitar started becoming better known as a solo (rather than a rhythm) instrument, while Blanton showed that bassists could do more than merely play four notes to the bar.

Gene Krupa was still considered the number one star drummer, but he was easily topped technique-wise by the remarkable Buddy Rich, while Jo Jones often outswung both Krupa and Rich. Lionel Hampton's reign as the top vibraphonist was only moderately challenged by the more subtle Red Norvo after Norvo switched from xylophone in 1943. While Joe Venuti was playing in obscurity, Stephane Grappelli, Stuff Smith, Eddie South, Svend Asmussen, and Ray Nance continued to show that the violin could swing in jazz as much as any other instrument.

Louis Armstrong, Jimmy Rushing, and Big Joe Turner were the top male jazz vocalists, while Bing Crosby and Frank Sinatra led the way in popular music, and Jack Teagarden, Leo Watson, and Billy Eckstine offered three very different approaches to interpreting lyrics. There were many female jazz singers, including Billie Holiday, the rapidly maturing Ella Fitzgerald, Lee Wiley, Maxine Sullivan, Mildred Bailey, Helen Humes, the veteran Ethel Waters, and such newcomers as Anita O'Day, Peggy Lee, Dinah Washington, and Sarah Vaughan, not to mention the numerous band singers such as Helen Forrest, Helen O'Connell, and Bea Wain.

There may have been a major war going on and a ruinous recording strike, but there was certainly no shortage of talent during the second half of the swing era.

18 Major Big Bands

Each year during 1939–44 featured the debut of several new major orchestras. Benny Goodman, Glenn Miller, Duke Ellington, and Count Basie were at the top of the swing world but they were challenged constantly by scores of other big bands including those led by Tommy Dorsey, Artie Shaw, Harry James, Stan Kenton, Woody Herman's Herd, Charlie Barnet, Will Bradley, Erskine Hawkins, Jimmie Lunceford, and Gene Krupa. Swing was King even during World War II, and this era, now considered the golden age of American popular music, resulted in a remarkable amount of high-quality music.

Duke Ellington   Although his records did not sell on the same level as those of Glenn Miller, Duke Ellington and his orchestra were at the peak of their powers during 1939–42. Ellington, who had been a major success since 1927, really stood apart from the swing era in a variety of ways. His abilities were well known years before swing caught on, so he did not have to struggle to establish his band's musical identity. Most of his repertoire came from either the leader or from inside his band, so he was rarely in the position of being obliged to song-pluggers for new material or stuck covering other band's hits. Unlike other bands that had two or three main soloists, virtually every musician in the Duke Ellington Orchestra (other than rhythm guitarist Fred Guy, a holdover from the early days) was a potential star, and they were prized for their individuality rather than for their ability to emulate the pacesetters. Why hire a Harry James imitator when Duke could feature Cootie Williams or Rex Stewart?

The lineup of Ellington's orchestra had been quite stable for much of the 1930s. As 1939 began, it included trumpeters Cootie Williams and Wallace Jones (a potentially fine soloist in the Arthur Whetsol vein who mostly was restricted to just playing first trumpet), cornetist Rex Stewart (whose half-valve technique was being utilized in Duke's writing), and the three very different trombone styles of Tricky Sam Nanton, Lawrence Brown, and Juan Tizol. The sax section had four veterans of the 1920s in clarinetist Barney Bigard, altoist Johnny Hodges, baritonist Harry Carney, and Otto Hardwicke on second alto. The rhythm section was comprised of Ellington's piano, guitarist Fred Guy, bassist Billy Taylor (second bassist Hayes Alvis had departed the previous year), and drummer Sonny Greer. And yet, as strong as the Ellington Orchestra was, with Ivie Anderson taking occasional vocals, three additions during 1939–40 would make it even more powerful.

In late 1938, Duke Ellington met Billy Strayhorn, a promising young pianist/composer/arranger from Pittsburgh. He was impressed by Strayhorn's abilities (the teenager had already written "Lush Life"), and he hired him initially to write arrangements for the small-group dates led by his sidemen. But in reality, Strayhorn's role with Ellington was unlimited and undefined. They collaborated constantly on new compositions and arrangements, Strayhorn contributed songs of his own to the band (including "Take the 'A' Train," which became

Ellington's theme song), and he occasionally filled in on piano. Their musical relationship would result in gem after gem being written and recorded.

In the fall of 1939, Jimmy Blanton joined Ellington's orchestra. At first he played as second bassist with Billy Taylor, but within a short time Taylor recognized Blanton's superiority and voluntarily left the band. Blanton, who turned 21 on October 5, 1939, had started out as a violinist, not switching to bass until he attended Tennessee State College in 1936. He worked with Fate Marable on riverboats, moved to St. Louis, and played with the Jeter-Pillars Orchestra during 1937–39. By the time Blanton joined Ellington, he was quietly revolutionizing his instrument. Although there had been a few bassists who were struggling to get their instrument beyond being a mere timekeeper (Milt Hinton with Cab Calloway's Orchestra was fairly advanced for the time), Blanton was light years ahead of everyone else. Rather than just playing four-to-the-bar lines with notes right on the beat like every other bassist (both in ensembles and as a soloist), Blanton (who had a large tone) displayed the fluency of a guitarist, occasionally came up with double-time runs, and soloed like a saxophonist in addition to swinging the band. Ellington recognized Blanton's talent and utilized him as a soloist from the start.

The third addition took place near the beginning of 1940 when Ben Webster became Ellington's first major tenor soloist. Webster also started out on violin, but, after a period on piano, he switched to tenor, taking lessons from Budd Johnson and working with the Young Family Band in the late 1920s. He recorded with Blanche Calloway in 1931, was with the Bennie Moten Orchestra (1931–33), and was one of the stars on Moten's last record date. Webster spent time with a variety of orchestras, including Andy Kirk (1933), Fletcher Henderson (1934) where he replaced Coleman Hawkins, Benny Carter, Willie Bryant, Cab Calloway (1936–37), Roy Eldridge, and the Teddy Wilson Big Band (1939–40); he also recorded with Billie Holiday. Thought of as one of the big three of swing tenor (next to his main influence Coleman Hawkins and Lester Young), Webster had a very large sound and was capable of playing brutish and forceful solos with plenty of roars and growls on uptempo tunes, yet purring like a pussy cat on romantic ballads. By joining the Duke Ellington Orchestra, Webster gave Duke another unique voice to utilize in his arrangements.

The year 1939 was highlighted by a European tour just prior to the start of World War II and such recordings as "Portrait of the Lion" (for Ellington's main piano influence, Willie "The Lion" Smith), "I'm Checkin' Out Go'om Bye," "Tootin' Through the Roof" (which has a climatic tradeoff by Cootie Williams and Rex Stewart), and a pair of piano/bass duets that showcase Blanton's virtuosity, "Blues" and "Plucked Again." In 1940, Ellington switched from the Columbia to the Victor label and the classics began to really come out, including "Jack the Bear," "Ko-Ko," "Concerto for Cootie" (a feature for Cootie Williams that would be reborn when outfitted with lyrics as "Do Nothing Till You Hear from Me"), "Bojangles," "Cotton Tail" (featuring a famous Ben Webster solo and a wonderful chorus for the sax section), "Harlem Air Shaft," "All Too Soon" (with its colorful Webster and Lawrence Brown solos), "Sepia Panorama," four more bass/piano duets (including "Pitter Panther Patter"), the sensuous "Warm Valley," and a non-Ellington song that became the biggest hit for his new vocalist Herb Jeffries, "Flamingo."

In addition to Jeffries' joining the group, there was one other important personnel change. After 11 years with the band, Cootie Williams decided to accept an offer to join Benny Goodman. This was considered such a major move that the Raymond Scott Orchestra recorded a new song, "When Cootie Left the Duke," which unfortunately was not all that memorable. Luckily, Ellington was able to immediately obtain the services of Ray Nance. Nance, who took violin lessons for seven years and, unlike Webster and Blanton, continued playing it throughout his life, was better known as a cornetist. He led a sextet in Chicago for a few years and worked with Earl Hines (1937–38) and Horace Henderson (1939–40). After joining Ellington, he not only was a perfect successor to Cootie as a specialist with the plunger mute, but he was Duke's first violin soloist and arguably the finest male vocalist that Ellington ever had.

On February 15, 1941, Nance immediately showed his value by taking a famous solo on the initial recording of Strayhorn's "Take the 'A' Train," which became Ellington's permanent theme song (replacing "East St. Louis Toodle-oo"). Other recordings from that year included two originals from Duke's son Mercer Ellington ("Blue Serge" and "Jumpin' Punkins"), "I Got It Bad" (one of many songs written for the short-lived Los Angeles civil rights show *Jump for Joy*), "Rocks in My Bed," and "Chelsea Bridge." In November, tragedy struck as Jimmy Blanton was afflicted with tuberculosis and forced to enter a sanitarium. He never recovered and died on July 30, 1942, at the age of 23. It would not be until the 1950s and the maturation of Charles Mingus before jazz bassists would catch up and finally surpass Blanton's innovations.

Ellington continued on with Junior Raglin in Blanton's place. While Raglin fared well playing Blanton's former features, he was just a very good player rather than a visionary. Still, 1942 brought such songs as Juan Tizol's "Perdido," "C Jam Blues," Mercer Ellington's "Moon Mist," "What Am I Here For," and Strayhorn's "Johnny Come Lately." Unfortunately, the recording strike kept the band off commercial records after July 1942 until December 1944.

Shortly before the strike, Barney Bigard had tired of the road and left Ellington after a 15-year stint. His place was at first taken by Chauncey Haughton and then in 1943 by Jimmy Hamilton. While Bigard's style was born in New Orleans, Hamilton (who had previously worked with Lucky Millinder, Jimmy Mundy, and for two years with the Teddy Wilson Sextet) had a much cooler tone, was a bit influenced early on by Benny Goodman, and had an adventurous style that looked toward bebop; he was considered controversial among Ellington fans for quite a while. Other personnel changes included the soft-toned Harold "Shorty" Baker being added on fourth trumpet (where he essentially filled the role of the late Arthur Whetsol), and Ivie Anderson retiring to Los Angeles in mid-1942 due to a bad case of asthma that would result in her premature death. She was replaced by Betty Roche who was unable to make much of an impression due to the recording strike.

On January 23, 1943, Duke Ellington had his first Carnegie Hall concert. As with Benny Goodman's five years before, this was a prestigious affair, but it differed in that Ellington (in addition to performing some of his three-minute miniatures) debuted the 50-minute "Black, Brown and Beige Suite," which was subtitled "A Tone Parallel to the History of the American Negro." Although this is a brilliant work that yielded the beautiful spiritual "Come Sunday" (featuring Johnny Hodges), the reviews of the concert were quite mixed. Classical critics seemed a bit outraged that Ellington was at Carnegie Hall at all, while those from the jazz world (including John Hammond) criticized Duke for not sticking exclusively to the "jungle music" that had made him famous. Ellington was

stung by the criticism and never again performed the full-length version of "Black, Brown and Beige," instead occasionally reworking it as excerpts.

Despite that critical (but not artistic) setback, Ellington continued on, performing regularly in clubs, on the radio, and (on a yearly basis) at Carnegie Hall. Taft Jordan (formerly Chick Webb's trumpet soloist) joined the band on fifth trumpet in mid-1943, Al Hibbler replaced Herb Jeffries as the band's vocalist, and Ben Webster went out on his own with Skippy Williams temporarily taking his place. The year 1944 brought a few more changes as Shelton Hemphill replaced Wallace Jones as the nonsoloing lead trumpeter, both Shorty Baker and Juan Tizol departed (Tizol's place was taken at first by Claude Jones), Joya Sherrill and Kay Davis joined Hibbler on vocals, and the exciting tenor saxophonist Al Sears took over the role of Ben Webster. The end of the recording strike gave Ellington the opportunity to record such numbers as "I Ain't Got Nothing but the Blues," "I'm Beginning to See the Light" (which became a hit for Harry James), and "I Didn't Know About You." An important new addition to Ellington's band in December 1944 was Cat Anderson, who was arguably the greatest high-note trumpeter ever. Anderson, a fiery character who earned his lifelong "Cat" nickname due to his fighting ability, had previously played with the Carolina Cotton Pickers, Claude Hopkins, Lucky Millinder, Erskine Hawkins, and Lionel Hampton. His ability to play incredible high notes would be a delight for Duke (who often used him to climax pieces), but Anderson was also quite handy with mutes too. His addition to the band gave Ellington yet another major soloist.

1939 (Classics 765), **1939 Vol. 2** (Classics 780), and **1939–1940** (Classics 790) reissue the last Ellington recordings from Ellington's first extended period with Columbia (including small-group dates led by sidemen). ● **The Blanton-Webster Band** (Bluebird 5659), a three-CD set, has all of the master takes from Ellington's Victor recordings of 1940–42, with the 66 selections containing dozens of all-time classics. The music (whether acquired this way or in the gigantic **The Centennial Edition** box) is absolutely essential.

1939–40 (Jazz Unlimited 2022) has two radio broadcasts of the Ellington band (both before and during Blanton's period with Duke), including spirited versions of "Jazz Potpourri," "Old King Dooji," "Little Posey," and "Tootin' Through the Roof." **The Duke at Fargo 1940** (Storyville 8316/17) is a two-CD set that saves forever what would have been just a typical night in the life of the Duke Ellington Orchestra. Recorded with permission by Jack Towers and Dick Burris, these 45 selections show just how strong the ensemble was, with Ben Webster's version of "Star Dust" taking solo honors. While a few of the numbers are brief, the band stretches out beyond five minutes on 11 of the songs, including "The Mooche," Rex Stewart's famous feature on "Boy Meets Horn," "Honeysuckle Rose," and "Across the Track Blues." And by pure luck, this recording documents Ray Nance's very first night with the band.

The Complete Standard Transcriptions (Soundies 4107) is comprised of Ellington's radio transcriptions of 1941. Due to the ASCAP strike of the period, Duke's own compositions (and those of other ASCAP writers) could not be played on the radio for a few months, so most of these 29 selections are standards, composed by Billy Strayhorn or Mercer Ellington, or from other writers outside of the band. The unusual repertoire makes this set of strong interest for Ellington collectors. **The Great Ellington Units** (Bluebird 6751) has most (but not all) of the small-group dates led by Johnny Hodges, Rex Stewart, and Barney Bigard during 1940–41, including the first versions of "Day Dream," "Good Queen Bess," "Passion Flower," "C Jam Blues," and Mercer Ellington's greatest hit, "Things Ain't What They Used to Be." **Solos, Duets and Trios** (Bluebird 2178) spans a long period of time with Ellington heard taking piano solos in 1932, 1941, and 1967 and at a 1965 concert in addition to playing two trio numbers from 1945 and a pair of adventurous piano duets with Strayhorn from 1946 ("Tonk" and "Drawing Room Blues"). Most significant on this disc are Ellington's four duets with Blanton from 1940 plus five alternate takes. The bassist is the lead voice throughout, which was unprecedented in jazz at the time.

Fortunately, Duke Ellington's six Carnegie Hall concerts were recorded and have been released; all are two-CD sets. ● **The Carnegie Hall Concerts—January 1943** (Prestige 34004) is the prize of the lot because it contains the full-length "Black, Brown and Beige" along with superior interpretations of such songs as "Black and Tan Fantasy," "Jumpin' Punkins," "Portrait of Bojangles," "Johnny Come Lately," and "Cotton Tail." **Live at Carnegie Hall, December 11, 1943** (Storyville 1038341) was formerly the most elusive of the concerts until its 2002 release. Ellington, who sounds quite defensive in some of his introductions (saying that the music "is not too heavy"),

premiered "New World A-Coming," which clocked in at 14 minutes (as opposed to the 50 of "Black, Brown and Beige"), sticking mostly to briefer pieces, including fine versions of "C Jam Blues," "Ring Dem Bells," and "Rockin' in Rhythm." **The Carnegie Hall Concerts—December 1944** (Prestige 24073) debuts the "Perfume Suite," has a half-hour of excerpts from "Black, Brown and Beige," and includes "Blutopia," "Midriff," "Trumpets No End," and a wonderful feature for Tricky Sam Nanton on "Frankie and Johnny."

All of these recordings show that Duke Ellington had created his own musical world, independent of the swing era. As 1944 closed, the 45-year-old Ellington still had nearly 30 years of accomplishments ahead of him.

Benny Goodman   The King of Swing reached the height of his success at his January 1938 Carnegie Hall concert. Despite the loss of Gene Krupa and competition from Artie Shaw, Benny Goodman retained his popularity, with Dave Tough in Krupa's spot for part of 1938 and such stars as Harry James, Ziggy Elman, Bud Freeman (who played tenor with BG for several months), Jess Stacy, and (in the trio and quartet) Teddy Wilson and Lionel Hampton keeping the music swinging. 1939 began with Harry James going out on his own—he had become too big a star to be a sideman forever—and he was soon followed by Teddy Wilson. Goodman had one major hit that year, "And the Angels Sing," a feature for Martha Tilton's singing and its composer Ziggy Elman's trumpet solo. The piece had been previously recorded under Elman's name as an instrumental, "Fralich in Swing," but Johnny Mercer's words put it over the top.

Benny Goodman was a constant on the radio throughout the swing era, and many of his broadcasts have since been released on records. **Camel Caravan Broadcasts 1939 Vols. I–III** (Phontastic 8817, 8818, and 8819) feature the band during the first four months of 1939. The airchecks have Johnny Mercer as the emcee and a personable singer with occasional features for the Benny Goodman Trio and Quartet, some Martha Tilton vocals, and a few "killer dillers." **Vol. 1** is particularly interesting because Billie Holiday and Leo Watson have guest vocals on one broadcast, while Jack Teagarden (who is heard announcing the formation of his new big band) is showcased on the January 31 performance.

The 1939 Goodman big band featured Elman, Goodman's longtime trombonist Vernon Brown, tenorman

Jerry Jerome, and, by year-end, its new vocalist Helen Forrest. But of greatest interest was the clarinetist's new sextet, featuring the brilliant pioneering electric guitarist Charlie Christian.

Born in Dallas, Christian grew up in Oklahoma City and started playing acoustic guitar when he was 12. He worked with territory bands (including Alphonso Trent), played locally, and in 1937 switched to electric guitar. At that time, the electric guitar was very new. During the next year, Les Paul (who had long experimented with amplifying his sound), George Barnes, Eddie Durham (who recorded the first significant jazz electric guitar solos with the Kansas City Five and Six) and Floyd Smith (playing an amplified Hawaiian guitar with Andy Kirk) were the first jazz electric guitarists, but Christian's accomplishments would soon overshadow all of them. Playing in Oklahoma City with Leslie Sheffield's group, he was heard by Teddy Wilson and Mary Lou Williams, who were both passing through town. John Hammond was alerted, and the producer flew to Oklahoma and was amazed by Christian's playing. The guitarist, who was influenced by Lester Young and other horn players, had the ability to create riff-filled solos that never seemed to run out of ideas, playing his instrument with the drive and single-note lines of a horn. Only Django Reinhardt was on his level, and Django was still playing acoustic guitar.

Hammond flew Christian to Los Angeles where Benny Goodman was appearing. BG was at first not impressed by Christian's flashy clothes, but reluctantly gave him an audition, calling out the song "Rose Room." Forty-five minutes later, Goodman and Christian were still playing the same tune, and the King of Swing had a new guitarist. During the next two years, Christian was a regular member of Goodman's small groups (called a sextet even though it sometimes had seven musicians), initially performing next to Lionel Hampton, Fletcher Henderson (a temporary member of Goodman's band after his own big band broke up in 1939), bassist Artie Bernstein, and drummer Nick Fatool.

In the summer of 1939, Goodman switched from the Victor label, where he had been since just before his great successes of 1935, to Columbia. **1939** (Classics 1025) has the final Victor numbers plus the band swinging for Columbia on such songs as "Jumpin' at the Woodside," "Stealin' Apples," and "Spring Song." **1939, Vol. 2** (Classics 1064) has big band selections with vocals by Louise Tobin and Mildred Bailey (Martha Tilton had recently

departed), the first sextet recordings (including "Rose Room," the initial version of "Flying Home," and the heated "Seven Come Eleven"), a rare spot for Christian with the big band on "Honeysuckle Rose," and the long overdue initial studio recording of Goodman's theme song, "Let's Dance." **1939–1940** (Classic 1098) has a memorable feature for Elman ("Zaggin' with Zig"), some excellent Helen Forrest vocals, arrangements by Fletcher Henderson and Eddie Sauter, and four sextet numbers (two apiece with either guest Count Basie or Johnny Guarnieri on piano).

In July 1940, Benny Goodman had to undergo surgery due to his sciatica, so he reluctantly broke up his orchestra. When he reformed a few months later, many of his sidemen were working elsewhere. Lionel Hampton had put together his own orchestra, Ziggy Elman was playing with Tommy Dorsey, and Johnny Guarnieri was with Artie Shaw. Luckily, Goodman still was able to hire back Christian, Forrest, and Sauter, and he soon put together a superior orchestra. His biggest coup was getting Cootie Williams from Ellington's band, who became the first black musician to be featured as a regular member of Goodman's orchestra rather than as an added attraction with his small groups. Also important was the addition of Georgie Auld, formerly with Artie Shaw, who became his new tenor soloist. **1940** (Classics 1131) has the last recordings from the original Goodman big band, including two numbers featuring the singing of dancer/actor Fred Astaire. In addition, there are five numbers from the Goodman sextet with Christian and Hampton. Concluding this CD are BG's first recordings after his operation, four exciting numbers ("Wholly Cats," "Royal Garden Blues," "As Long as I Live," and "Benny's Bugle") with his new sextet with Christian, Cootie Williams, Georgie Auld, Artie Bernstein, drummer Harry Jaeger, and Count Basie. The recordings with the Cootie-Auld-Christian sextet would be among Goodman's most exciting small-group dates ever.

1940–1941 (Classics 1154) finds the orchestra (with Cootie, trombonist Lou McGarity, Auld, and BG as the big band's main soloists) still ranking near the top of its field. In addition to another sextet date, this time with Ken Kersey on piano, of particular interest are Eddie Sauter's increasingly adventurous arrangements, including (on this disc) "Benny Rides Again," "Superman," and "Moonlight on the Ganges." **1941** (Classics 1202) documents Goodman's band up to March 4, 1941, with the highlights including Sauter's writing on "Time on My Hands" and "Scarecrow," Charlie Christian's dazzling feature with the big band on "Solo Flight," some of Helen Forrest's best singing with the band, and a sextet date with Count Basie that includes "Breakfast Feud" and "On the Alamo."

Unfortunately, the Classics Benny Goodman series has not yet completed his work in the war years, and Columbia has not coherently reissued all of its important Benny Goodman recordings of 1939–46. There are a few domestic sampler CDs available that have some of the music. **Best of the Big Bands** (Columbia 45338) skips all over the place and does not bother with personnel or date listings, but does include "Taking a Chance on Love," "Shake Down the Stars," "Air Mail Special," and Peggy Lee's hit "Why Don't You Do Right." **Featuring Helen Forrest** (Columbia/Legacy 48902) has 16 of the singer's better recordings with Goodman, including "The Man I Love," "I'm Always Chasing Rainbows," "This Is New," and "Oh! Look at Me Now."

In June 1941, Charlie Christian was stricken with tuberculosis. Just like Jimmy Blanton, Christian spent a long period in a sanitarium, but never recovered, passing away on March 2, 1942, at the age of 25. Before he was cut down, he had recorded quite a bit, mostly with Benny Goodman's small groups. Christian had also appeared at the 1939 "From Spirituals to Swing" concert (with Lester Young and Buck Clayton as part of the Kansas City Six in addition to the Benny Goodman Sextet), made a few freelance recordings (including a 1939 jam session with Jerry Jerome), and stretched out at Minton's Playhouse in 1941 with Thelonious Monk and Dizzy Gillespie.

The Genius of the Electric Guitar (Columbia 40846) has "Solo Flight" and such Benny Goodman Sextet performances as "Seven Come Eleven," "Wholly Cats," "Royal Garden Blues," "Breakfast Feud," and "Air Mail Special" plus fascinating excerpts from a practice session one day when Goodman was late. **Featuring Charlie Christian** (Columbia 45144) is drawn from the same sessions and includes "Flying Home," "Stardust," "Gilly," "On the Alamo," and "A Smo-o-o-oth One," among others. Best of all is the four-CD set ◉ **The Genius of the Electric Guitar** (Columbia/Legacy 65564), which contains all of Christian's studio recordings with Goodman's sextet and big band including many alternate takes (some previously unreleased), excerpts from rehearsals, and a number from a date with the Metronome All-Stars.

On every one of these recordings, Christian's constant creativity and fresh ideas are a joy.

Solo Flight (Vintage Jazz Classics 1021) consists of 24 of Christian's best live performances (mostly taken from radio airchecks) by Goodman's sextet. The opening version of "Flying Home" predates any of the group's studio dates, and there is an alternate big band version of "Solo Flight." Of greatest interest are five numbers recorded on October 28, 1940, by a rather remarkable octet comprised of Goodman, Christian, Lester Young, Buck Clayton, Count Basie, Freddie Green, Walter Page, and Jo Jones. Other odds and ends are included on **Radioland 1939–1941** (Fuel 2001 302 061 167), including numbers backing singer Eddy Howard, a few jams at Minton's, and dates with Edmond Hall's Celeste Quartet, the Kansas City Six, Lionel Hampton, and the Jerry Jerome jam session.

It would be a quarter-century (not until the rise of fusion) before the jazz guitar developed much beyond the innovations, ideas, and sound of Charlie Christian, whose influence would be heard in later years in the playing of Tiny Grimes, Barney Kessel, Tal Farlow, Wes Montgomery, and George Benson.

As for Benny Goodman, he survived the loss of Christian as he had the defections of Gene Krupa and Harry James. He continued leading top-notch bands and featuring combos from the orchestra. **Small Groups: 1941–1945** (Columbia 44437) puts the focus on Goodman's post-Christian 1941–42 sextet (with Lou McGarity, pianist Mel Powell, and occasionally Peggy Lee) plus some numbers from 1944–45 when his quintet included Red Norvo and Teddy Wilson. When Helen Forrest left Goodman's orchestra in mid-1941 to join Harry James, her place was taken by the young unknown Peggy Lee. The two-CD set **Peggy Lee & Benny Goodman— The Complete Recordings** (Columbia/Legacy 65686) has all 35 selections that Lee recorded with BG during 1941–42, starting with a version of "Elmer's Tune" on which Lee sounds scared to death, plus three songs from a 1947 reunion session. Highlights include "I Got It Bad," "Somebody Else Is Taking My Place," "Let's Do It," "Where or When," and her big hit "Why Don't You Do Right." Lee's restrained, cool-toned singing fit well with the Goodman band during her two years with the clarinetist, launching her career while adding some fresh blood to BG's music.

Johnny Guarnieri was back with Goodman for the first half of 1941. When he departed, his place was taken by a brilliant 18-year-old pianist/arranger named Mel Powell. Powell, whose playing was a cross between Earl Hines and Teddy Wilson, wrote such memorable arrangements as "The Earl," "Mission to Moscow," "Clarinade," and a hit version of "Jersey Bounce." In time, the Classics reissue series will get to those sessions.

Even with a variety of personnel changes (Cootie Williams departed to form his own band in the fall of 1941), Goodman's big band continued its high-quality string of recordings until the recording strike began at the end of July 1942. However, World War II made things difficult even for the King, and he broke up his orchestra in late 1942, spending time making appearances in Hollywood movies. During 1943–44, he was at the head of several short-lived big bands (including one with Roy Eldridge), recording V-discs, appearing on the radio, and renewing ties with Red Norvo, Teddy Wilson, and even Gene Krupa, who was briefly in Goodman's big band in late 1943. Still just 35, Benny Goodman was ready to launch a new big band and sextet as 1945 began.

Artie Shaw   During the first half of 1939, Artie Shaw had the most popular big band in swing, having surpassed Benny Goodman the previous year, due partly to his hit record of "Begin the Beguine." An intellectual who constantly ran away from success, Shaw was an unlikely celebrity. He simply wanted to play good music and was willing to work hard at it. As a clarinetist, Shaw had developed his own sound and was nearly at Goodman's level (some musicians thought he was better). His band was well rehearsed, but loose enough to have an air of spontaneity that was not often present in the music of Glenn Miller and Jimmie Lunceford. Shaw's 1939 orchestra was bolstered by the additions of drummer Buddy Rich and tenor saxophonist Georgie Auld (both of whom left Bunny Berigan's struggling outfit) with vocals by Helen Forrest and Tony Pastor. The sampler sets discussed in Chapter 4 include some of the highlights from 1939 too. Among Shaw's better recordings during this year are "Carioca," "Alone Together," "One Night Stand," "Traffic Jam," and "Lady Be Good."

Unfortunately, the pressure of being the number one swing band began to get to Shaw. Illness knocked him out for a little while in mid-1939. He railed against "jitterbugs" (acrobatic dancers in the audience who sometimes overwhelmed the music), and in November he shocked the music world by walking off the bandstand during a performance and fleeing to Mexico. Shaw's musicians tried unsuccessfully for a few months to continue on under 20-year-old Georgie Auld's leadership before breaking up.

After a couple of months, Shaw returned to the United States. His Victor contract was still current and he needed to make some money. For a session on March 3, 1940, the clarinetist put together a 32-piece orchestra (with 13 strings and extra woodwinds). Four of the songs were quickly forgotten, but "Frenesi" became a giant hit, the second biggest of the clarinetist's career. It seemed as if he could not avoid success!

Shaw took advantage of the popularity of "Frenesi" to organize the string orchestra he had always dreamed of. By the summer he was leading a 23-piece band, which included nine strings and such fine soloists as trumpeter Billy Butterfield, trombonist Jack Jenney, Jerry Jerome on tenor, and pianist Johnny Guarnieri. For the fun of it, Shaw recorded with a sextet from the band (including Butterfield and Johnny Guarnieri on harpsichord) as the Gramercy Five. Without even trying, their "Summit Ridge Drive" became a million seller! **The Complete Gramercy Five Sessions** (Bluebird 7637) has this group's eight selections (including catchy versions of "Special Delivery Stomp," "My Blue Heaven," and "Smoke Gets in Your Eyes") plus the seven numbers from Shaw's 1945 Gramercy Five, a more conventional group with Roy Eldridge, pianist Dodo Marmarosa, and guitarist Barney Kessel.

Shaw's third orchestra, his string band, did not last that long, only into the spring of 1941, having seven recording dates. However, a high percentage of its recordings are notable, including "Temptation," a two-part "Blues" arranged by classical composer William Grant Still, "Dancing in the Dark," the extended "Concerto for Clarinet" (quite a showcase for Shaw), and what is arguably the finest recording ever of "Star Dust." From Butterfield's dramatic opening solo through Shaw's impressive improvisation and Jack Jenney's effortless (but apparently very difficult) spot on trombone, this is one of those recordings where every note is perfect; it is impossible to improve upon!

After some time off in the summer of 1941 (including leading an excellent integrated record date with Henry "Red" Allen, J.C. Higginbotham, Benny Carter, Lena Horne, and strings), Shaw organized his fourth big band. This ensemble had plenty of variety with such notables as trumpeter/singer Hot Lips Page, trumpeter Max Kaminsky, trombonist/arranger Ray Conniff, Dave Tough, a full string section, and alumni Jack Jenney, Georgie Auld, and Johnny Guarnieri in the personnel. Whether it was features for Page on "St. James Infirmary" and "Take Your Shoes Off, Baby," the ad-lib "Just Kiddin' Around" or more "serious" classical-oriented works such as "Nocturne," "Dusk," and "Suite No. 8," this was a potentially classic band. However, soon after Pearl Harbor, Artie Shaw broke up this outfit and enlisted in the navy.

The five-CD set ◉ **Self-Portrait** (Bluebird 09026-63808) has 95 selections picked by Shaw in 2001 as the most significant of his career. Other than neglecting the vocals of Helen Forrest from his 1938–39 band, the results are a well-rounded retrospective of his career, with a bit of an emphasis on Shaw's final Gramercy Five of 1954 and the inclusion of some broadcast performances. A superb introduction to Shaw's career (although in reality none of his recordings are without interest), this box has two songs by his short-lived string ensemble of 1936, 25 from the "Begin the Beguine" orchestra, 13 by the 1940–41 band, and 10 from the 1941–42 Hot Lips Page group.

Artie Shaw's fifth orchestra was completely undocumented (except for a broadcast version of "Begin the Beguine"), for it was his navy band of 1942–43, which played in often-dangerous circumstances in the Pacific war theatre. By late 1943, Shaw was seriously ill, and in February 1944 he was given a medical discharge. Fortunately, Shaw completely recovered within a few months, and by the fall his sixth orchestra debuted. The 18-piece band (no strings this time) was most notable for having Roy Eldridge, Ray Conniff, tenor saxophonist Herbie Steward, Dodo Marmarosa, and Barney Kessel in its personnel. Its one record date before year-end resulted in a fine Eldridge feature on "Lady Day."

With five big bands in five years, it is not an understatement to say that Artie Shaw created a great deal of interesting music during 1939–44.

Charlie Barnet   The year 1939 was the breakthrough year for Charlie Barnet. The tenor saxophonist (who also played alto and, very unusual for the era, soprano) had been trying to lead big bands since 1933. He had the advantage of coming from a very rich family and did not have to worry about coming up with financing

for his orchestra. His family had hoped that he would be a lawyer, but ironically Barnet ended up making more money in jazz than he would have in the law! He became a professional musician in 1929 when he was 16, moved to New York in 1932, and debuted on records the following year. However, it took Barnet six years to make it because, even though he recorded for the Banner label in 1933–34 and for Bluebird during 1935–37, with a few exceptions most of these sessions were quite commercial and his band did not have its own sound. However, in 1939 it all clicked. Barnet's theme song "Cherokee" (composed by Ray Noble and arranged by Billy May) became a hit and was soon followed by such popular instrumentals as "Pompton Turnpike," "Redskin Rhumba," "Southern Fried," and "Charleston Alley." The leader proved to be a distinctive saxophonist, his trumpet soloist Bobby Burnet was excellent, and the band was loose and spirited, reflecting Barnet's partying attitude. Inspired by both Duke Ellington (whose music he often emulated) and Count Basie, Barnet had one of the hardest swinging white big bands of the time.

All of Barnet's Bluebird recordings (dating from 1933–42) were made available in the late 1970s on six double LPs, which have not been duplicated on CD. ◉ **Clap Hands Here Comes Charlie** (Bluebird 6273) is an excellent single disc overview of the 1939–41 period. The hits are here plus "The Duke's Idea," "The Count's Idea," and "The Right Idea" (but unfortunately not Barnet's hilarious satire of sweet bands, "The Wrong Idea"). Bus Etri takes some pioneering electric guitar solos, there are two vocals by Mary Ann McCall, and Lena Horne sings "You're My Thrill." For their radio transcription session of January 27, 1941, the Barnet band was quite busy, recording 25 selections, all of which are included on **The Transcription Performances 1941** (Hep 53). The arrangements by Horace Henderson, Billy May, Billy Moore, Bud Estes, and Barnet are excellent, with the emphasis on no-nonsense swing.

In 1942, Barnet switched to the Decca label right before the recording strike. By 1944 when he returned to records, he had a particularly strong outfit, featuring trumpeter/vocalist Peanuts Holland, pianist Dodo Marmarosa, guitarist Barney Kessel, singer Kay Starr, and, as a guest on a few dates, Roy Eldridge. ◉ **Drop Me Off in Harlem** (GRP/Decca 612) has Barnet's 20 best recordings of the 44 he cut for Decca during 1942–46. "Skyliner" was a major hit, and other highlights include "The

Moose," "The Great Lie," "Gulf Coast Blues," "West End Blues," and "Andy's Boogie." Barnet's band had a few modernists in its personnel by 1944 (particularly Marmarosa and Kessel, both of whom would soon join Artie Shaw) and his orchestra was at the peak of its powers.

Will Bradley   Will Bradley (born Wilbur Schwichtenberg) was in an odd position during the swing era. A technically skilled trombonist and a busy studio musician who enjoyed playing ballads, in 1940 he found himself reluctantly at the head of a rollicking big band best known for its exuberant boogie-woogie numbers. Bradley worked in the late 1920s with Milt Shaw and Red Nichols before joining the staff of CBS. He was with Ray Noble's American band during 1935–36, but otherwise was content working in the studios. However, MCA's Willard Alexander convinced the trombonist to lead his own big band with drummer/singer Ray McKinley as his unofficial co-leader. With pianist Freddy Slack (who, like McKinley, left Jimmy Dorsey to join Bradley) as a key soloist, the Will Bradley Orchestra was a fine second-level band. In 1940, it had its first hit with the eccentric "Celery Stalks at Midnight," and then on May 21, the band recorded its biggest seller, the two-sided "Beat Me Daddy, Eight to the Bar." From then on, the Will Bradley Orchestra was associated with boogie-woogie, with such songs as "Rock-A-Bye the Boogie," "Scrub Me Mama with a Boogie Beat," "I Boogied When I Should Have Woogied," "Chicken Gumboogie," "Boogie Woogie Conga," "Bounce Me Brother with a Solid Four," "Booglie Wooglie Piggy," and "Fry Me Cookie with a Can of Lard" seeking to duplicate "Beat Me Daddy's" success. Although "Down the Road a-Piece" was popular and the band flourished in 1941, Bradley became bored with much of the music. In February 1942, he and McKinley went their separate ways, forming separate orchestras, but neither band recorded and both were history within a few months. Ray McKinley joined Glenn Miller's Army Air Force Band while Bradley permanently returned to the studios.

Hallelujah (Hep 1061) has 24 of the first 30 selections made by the Will Bradley Orchestra, tracing the band's chronology up to March 1940, two months before it recorded "Beat Me Daddy, Eight to the Bar." This CD features the Bradley band as a solid swing unit with highlights, including "The Love Nest," "Memphis Blues," "Strange Cargo," "Jimblues Blues," and "Rhumboogie." **It's**

Square, but It Rocks (Hep 1071) has four of the "missing" numbers from the early days and then includes 20 of the next 38 selections (mostly just skipping indifferent vocal numbers). Among the more memorable selections are "It's a Wonderful World," "Beat Me Daddy," "Rock-A-Bye the Boogie," "Scrub Me Mama, with a Boogie Beat," "Three Ring Ragout," and "Chicken Gum Boogie." **Swingin' Down the Lane** (Hep 1078) wraps up the Will Bradley story with 18 of the orchestra's final 36 numbers (including "In the Hall of the Mountain King," "From the Land of Sky Blue Waters," and small-group jams on "Basin Street Boogie" and "Tea for Two"). The disc concludes with seven songs that Bradley recorded during 1946–47 with fellow studio musicians, including a remake of "Celery Stalks," and the intriguing "Bop 'N' Boogie." But by then there was no demand for Will Bradley to form a new orchestra, so those recordings were quickly forgotten, unlike "Beat Me Daddy, Eight to the Bar."

Bob Crosby   One would think that with the gradual comeback of Dixieland in the early 1940s, the Bob Crosby Orchestra and Bobcats would be leading the way. Crosby's big band had been gaining a following ever since its formation in 1935, updating the New Orleans jazz tradition, and the Bobcats' recordings (starting in November 1937) were quite successful. In 1939, at first Crosby's music continued in the same vein. Both the band and the Bobcats (the hot combo taken from the orchestra) featured trumpeter Billy Butterfield, trombonist Warren Smith, clarinetist Irving Fazola, tenor saxophonist Eddie Miller, and pianist Bob Zurke as its main soloists. Among the better recordings from the year were a remake of "South Rampart Street Parade," "Hindustan," "Boogie Woogie Maxine," and "High Society." Some of the Bobcats recordings found the combo backing singers (including the Andrews Sisters and regular band singer Marion Mann), but there were still plenty of freewheeling moments, including their February 6, 1940, session, which helped make Isham Jones's "Spain" into a standard.

Unfortunately, in 1940 Crosby and Gil Rodin decided to change the band's direction toward more commercial swing, probably hoping to expand Bob Crosby's audience. As it turned out, it had the opposite effect as Crosby's music became more run-of-the-mill. The leader even began singing on some of the Bobcats performances and since Crosby was actually the weak point of his band's music, this was an obvious mistake. Jess Stacy had taken over on piano in late 1939, and after Butterfield joined Artie Shaw, Muggsy Spanier spent a half-year as the band's cornet soloist, but no hits resulted. Yank Lawson's return in the fall of 1941 was a joyful event, resulting in the Bobcats performances improving (January 29, 1942, had four hot Dixieland instrumentals), but before year-end, Bob Crosby had broken up the band.

I Remember You (Vintage Jazz Classics 1046) has radio transcriptions from 1941–42 and finds the band having an identity crisis. Despite the talent (Lawson, Matlock, Miller, Stacy, and Bob Haggart), the orchestra was featuring far too many dull vocals from Crosby, David Street, Liz Tilton, Muriel Lane, and Gloria De Haven, with only seven instrumentals among the 27 selections.

Having messed up a successful formula, Bob Crosby freelanced as a singer and performer before spending 1944–45 serving in the Marines.

Count Basie   By 1939, the Count Basie Orchestra was thought of as the definitive swing band. Although it did not have hit records on the level of Glenn Miller or Artie Shaw, Basie's ensemble was universally admired for its light and swinging sound. With such soloists as Buck Clayton, Harry "Sweets" Edison, Dickie Wells, Lester Young, and (by May 1940) altoist Tab Smith, plus singers Jimmy Rushing and Helen Humes, the Basie band was in one of its prime periods. The band suffered a major loss on February 9 with the death of Herschel Evans (who had a weak heart), but Buddy Tate proved to be a solid replacement. Basie soon switched labels to Columbia/Okeh and continued recording significant swing performances, including small-group dates with Lester Young and Dickie Wells that resulted in "Lester Leaps In" and "Dickie's Dream." Young's sudden and mysterious decision to leave the band in 1941 was a blow, but Don Byas worked out as his first replacement.

1939 (Classics 513) has the band's last Decca recordings and initial dates on Vocalion, including "Rock-A-Bye Basie" and "Taxi War Dance." **1939 Vol. 2** (Classics 533) has plenty of prime Lester Young, including "Dickie's Dream" and "Lester Leaps In." **1939–1940** (Classics 563) continues through October 1940, highlighted by "I Never Knew," "Tickle Toe," and "Easy Does It." After the first session of **1940–1941** (Classics 623), Lester Young departed—a rumor has persisted that it

was because he did not want to record on Friday the 13th). But with Byas and Tate as the band's tenors (Coleman Hawkins guests on two songs from April 10, 1941), there was no decline in the Basie band. **1941** (Classics 652) is highlighted by "Basie Boogie," and Jimmy Mundy's "Fiesta in Blue" and "Down for Double." The odd "King Joe," a tribute to boxer Joe Louis, has a vocal by Paul Robeson (his only recording in a jazz context) who sounds a bit lost rhythmically. **1942** (Classics 684) continues the reissue of all of the Basie band's recordings before the recording strike, including a remake of "One o'Clock Jump," "Basie Blues," Buck Clayton's "It's Sand Man," and a fine small-group date featuring the classic Basie rhythm section. Buck Clayton and Don Byas are added on four of the eight blues-oriented numbers.

Domestically, Sony has thus far only reissued Basie's music in piecemeal fashion on three CDs. **The Essential Count Basie Vol. 1** (Sony 40608), **Vol. 2** (Sony 40835), and **Vol. 3** (Sony 44150) contain highlights from 1939–42, but the Classics series is superior since Basie recorded few throwaways during this era. **Rock-A-Bye Basie** (Vintage Jazz Classics 1033) has live performances from the Basie band of 1938–39, mostly performed at the Famous Door where the band's music became solidified and tighter; quite a few of these selections were not otherwise recorded by the orchestra. The two-CD set **Café Society Uptown 1941** (Jazz Unlimited 2006/07) features the band during a seven-week stay at Café Society in New York. The radio broadcasts are particularly well recorded and among the more memorable performances are "There'll Be Some Changes Made," "Yes Indeed," "9:20 Special," "Jumpin' at the Woodside," and "Swinging the Blues."

Count Basie was able to keep his orchestra together during the war years, but there were some personnel changes. Walter Page and Buck Clayton were drafted, and were replaced by Rodney Richardson and Joe Newman. Lester Young returned to the Basie band in 1943, and Basie appeared on one of Young's small-group sessions, but the great tenor did not have the opportunity to record with the full Basie orchestra due to the recording strike. However, he can be heard with Basie on radio transcriptions, V-discs, and broadcasts, some of which are on **Old Manuscripts, Broadcast Transcriptions** (Music & Arts 884) and **Beaver Junction** (Vintage Jazz Classics 1018). In addition to Young (in generally exciting form), there are strong spots for Tate, Wells, Edison, Rushing, and such newcomers to the Basie band as trumpeter Joe Newman and tenors Illinois Jacquet and Lucky Thompson. In mid-1944, Young and Jo Jones were both drafted, replaced by Jacquet and Shadow Wilson. **1943–1945** (Classics 801) finds the Count Basie Orchestra successfully weathering all of these changes. This interesting disc has V-discs from 1943–44 (including a few numbers with Lester Young) and the band's return to records in December 1944, including solid versions of "Taps Miller" and "Red Bank Boogie."

During the war years, the Count Basie Orchestra was recognized as a swing institution, a band so strong that it could survive even the loss of a Lester Young without any decline in its music.

Andy Kirk   While the Count Basie Orchestra was the most famous band to emerge from Kansas City, Andy Kirk's big band was also significant for a time during the swing era. In 1939, Andy Kirk's band featured the hard-to-take but popular vocals of Pha Terrell, the tenor solos of Dick Wilson, and the swinging arrangements of pianist Mary Lou Williams. **1939–1940** (Classics 640) is most notable for "Floyd's Guitar Blues" (a feature for Floyd Smith's odd-sounding electric Hawaiian guitar that predated Charlie Christian), "Big Jim's Blues," "Scratching in the Gravel," and a few good vocals from June Richmond. **1940–1942** (Classics 681) finds the Kirk Orchestra undergoing many changes. Pha Terrell went out on his own, Dick Wilson passed away from tuberculosis just 13 days past his 30th birthday in December 1941, and the following year an underpaid and overworked Mary Lou Williams left, replaced by

Ken Kersey. **1940–1942** has a surprising number of rewarding numbers, including "Little Miss," "The Count," "Twelfth Street Rag," "Ring Dem Bells," "Boogie Woogie Cocktail," and a feature for the band's up-and-coming trumpet soloist Howard McGhee, "McGhee Special." However, the Andy Kirk Orchestra was past its prime after 1942.

Cab Calloway   Cab Calloway, one of the most famous personalities in the music world in the 1930s, continued his reign at the top throughout the first half of the '40s. In 1939, his band was at its strongest with the 22-year-old trumpeter Dizzy Gillespie joining in August. Other soloists included trombonist Tyree Glenn, altoist Hilton Jefferson, and Chu Berry (Cab's musical director) on tenor. The rhythm section consisted of pianist Bennie Payne, rhythm guitarist Danny Barker, bassist Milt Hinton, and drummer Cozy Cole. **1939–1940** (Classics 595) has individual features for Cole ("Crescendo in Drums"), Hinton ("Pluckin' the Bass"), and Gillespie ("Pickin' the Cabbage," which finds the trumpeter hinting at bebop). There are also such typically zany Calloway pieces as "The Ghost of Smoky Joe," "The Jumpin' Jive," "Jiveinformation Please," and "Chop, Chop Charlie Chan." **1940** (Classics 614) contains many solos by Gillespie, who was in the process of getting his style together and often sounds overly advanced for the setting. Berry is heard on his most famous recording, an overly sentimental version of "Ghost of a Chance." Calloway is typically jubilant on "Topsy Turvy," "Hi-De-Ho Serenade," "Fifteen Minute Intermission," "Papa's in Bed with His Britches On," and "Are You Hep to the Jive." **1940–1941** (Classics 629)

TIMELINE 1940

The King Cole Trio has a minor hit in "Sweet Lorraine." • Cootie Williams leaves Duke Ellington and is succeeded by Ray Nance. • Ben Webster joins Duke Ellington. • Due to sciatica, Benny Goodman temporarily breaks up his orchestra and a few months later returns with a new big band. • Will Bradley has a big hit with "Beat Me Daddy, Eight to the Bar." • Lester Young leaves Count Basie. • Bassist Wellman Braud opens up a pool hall, becoming a part-time player. • After a year of co-leading the Harlem Rhythmakers in Egypt, the outbreak of World War II forces Bill Coleman to return to the United States. • Artie Shaw records "Star Dust." • The orchestras of Claude Hopkins and Don Redman break up. • Machito (Frank Grillo) forms the Afro-Cubans. • Frankie Trumbauer records 17 selections with his two-year-old big band, but his orchestra breaks up before the year ends. • Frustrated with the music business, Teddy Grace stops singing. A few years later she joined the WACs, but after performing at too many strenuous bond rallies and shows, she loses her voice and was never able to sing again. • Tiny Parham makes his final records, as an organist. • The Jay McShann Orchestra with Charlie Parker arrive in New York.

continues at the same high level with Gillespie heard on "Take the 'A' Train," Jonah Jones becoming an important addition to the trumpet section (celebrated on "Jonah Joins the Cab"), altoist Hilton Jefferson showcased on "Willow Weep for Me," Benny Carter contributing the arrangement for "Lonesome Nights," and Andy Gibson writing many charts for the band. Calloway is in top form on "A Chick Ain't Nothin' but a Bird," "Are You All Reet," "Hep Cat's Love Song," "Geechy Joe," and a remake of "St. James Infirmary."

Although strongly influenced by Coleman Hawkins, Chu Berry (who was at his best on uptempo material) was growing more individual while with Calloway's orchestra. He appeared along the way as a guest on small-group recordings led by Wingy Manone, Henry "Red" Allen, and Lionel Hampton; his playing with Hamp on "Sweethearts on Parade" was a highpoint. ◐ **1937–1941** (Classics 784) has the master takes of all of Berry's five sessions as a leader. Among the other players are trumpeters Hot Lips Page, Irving "Mouse" Randolph, and Roy Eldridge plus fellow tenor Charlie Ventura. Berry's version of "Body and Soul" (made a year before Coleman Hawkins's famous rendition) is actually stolen by Eldridge who takes a memorable double-time trumpet solo. Other highlights include "Indiana," "Chuberry Jam," "Sittin' In," and "Monday at Minton's." Tragically, Chu Berry died in a car accident on October 30, 1941, at the age of 33.

Dizzy Gillespie also left Calloway in 1941. Dizzy's adventurous trumpet solos had largely annoyed Cab, but, to the singer's credit, he gave Gillespie a lot of solo space on recordings. However, Dizzy's joking on stage was an irritant and when a spitball was thrown at Calloway during a performance, he angrily confronted Dizzy offstage. A fight resulted and Gillespie was fired; years later it was revealed that Jonah Jones had actually been the culprit.

1941–1942 (Classics 682) has the last Berry and Gillespie recordings with Calloway. In addition, Jonah Jones is well featured (tenor saxophonist Ike Quebec would soon become a key soloist) and there are many arrangements by Buster Harding and Andy Gibson. Calloway uses a vocal group (the Cabaliers) on some numbers (best is "Virginia, Georgia and Caroline") and is in top form on "Blues in the Night," "I Want to Rock," "I Get the Neck of the Chicken," and his third studio version of "Minnie the Moocher." Cab Calloway was one of the

stars of the 1943 film *Stormy Weather* and his future looked limitless, but in reality he had reached the peak of his success.

Erskine Hawkins   When it came to solid swinging and exciting dancers, few ensembles were on the level of the Erskine Hawkins Orchestra. In addition to the leader (who took high-note solos), the band featured trumpeter Dud Bascomb (whose fine middle-register solos were often mistakenly credited to Hawkins), Paul Bascomb and/or Julian Dash on tenors, baritonist Heywood Henry, and pianist Avery Parrish. ◐ **The Original Tuxedo Junction** (Bluebird 9682) is a superior single-disc sampler of the Hawkins big band at its best; it includes Hawkins's three hits: "Tuxedo Junction" (recorded before Glenn Miller's rendition), "After Hours" (a showcase for Parrish's blues piano), and 1945's "Tippin' In." Other highlights are "Weary Blues," "Swing Out," "Gin Mill Special," "Cherry," and "Bear Mash Blues." But because nearly all of the recordings by the Hawkins big band are jazz-oriented and swinging, their complete output is also well worth acquiring. **1938–1939** (Classics 667), **1939–1940** (Classics 678), **1940–1941** (Classics 701), and **1941–1945** (Classics 868) each contain plenty of obscure but swinging gems. Even after the Bascomb Brothers went out on their own and Parrish departed, the Erskine Hawkins Orchestra remained one of the most swinging of all big bands, keeping the dancers happy at the Savoy Ballroom.

Jimmie Lunceford   For years Jimmie Lunceford was one of those who had what could be called a "family band," one in which the personnel rarely changed and the sidemen were quite loyal to the leader. So it was a major blow in 1939 when his top arranger, Sy Oliver, accepted a lucrative offer from Tommy Dorsey. Although never fully recovering from Oliver's defection, Lunceford partly made up for it by hiring both Snooky Young and Gerald Wilson for his trumpet section. Wilson would quickly develop into a major arranger himself, contributing "Hi Spook" and "Yard Dog Mazurka." However, it hurt even more in 1942 when Willie Smith, complaining about his abysmal salary (Lunceford's sidemen were grossly underpaid), left to join Charlie Spivak's orchestra. Due to the war, there was much more turnover during the first half of the 1940s than there had been all of the last decade, but Joe Thomas and pianist/arranger Ed Wilcox stayed, Omer Simeon was an important new addition on clarinet and alto, and the Lunceford Orchestra—which helped introduce "Blues in the Night"—remained a mighty force.

After being with the Decca label during 1934–38, Lunceford switched to Vocalion during 1939–40. The highlights of this period are on ● **Lunceford Special** (Columbia/Legacy 65647), which has 21 tracks, including "Tain't What You Do, It's the Way that You Do It" (a Sy Oliver classic sung by Trummy Young), "Ain't She Sweet," "Well Alright Then," "Uptown Blues" (which has famous solos from Willie Smith and Snooky Young), and "Lunceford Special." After 1940, Lunceford switched back to Decca. Completists may opt for **1939–1940** (Classics 565) and **1940–1941** (Classics 622) since Lunceford actually recorded 63 titles for Vocalion. The latter set also has the band's first recordings from its second period with Decca, including Gerald Wilson's "Yard Dog Mazurka" and "Hi Spook," plus the two-sided "Blues in the Night." **1941–1945** (Classics 862) covers the war years, including "I'm Gonna Move to the Outskirts of Town," "Strictly Instrumental," and "Jeep Rhythm." Since Lunceford's band had a stylized sound and did not sound all that different in 1944 from how it had in 1934, it was in danger of falling behind the times. But at least at that point, the group's showmanship and many past hits allowed it to retain its popularity.

Tommy Dorsey   For Tommy Dorsey, 1939–44 was the prime of his career. He had already been quite successful with hit records in "Marie" and "Song of India" during 1937, alternating swing romps, ballad vocals, and novelty Dixieland performances with his Clambake Seven, but TD wanted to move to a higher level. In 1939, he persuaded Sy Oliver to leave Jimmie Lunceford's orchestra and become a staff arranger with his band. With the collapse of Artie Shaw's orchestra, Dorsey was able to get drummer Buddy Rich, and he also persuaded the young Frank Sinatra to leave Harry James's struggling band. By 1940, Dorsey had Jo Stafford, Connie Haynes, and the Pied Pipers joining Sinatra as his vocalists, greatly increasing the commercial appeal of his band. In the spring, Bunny Berigan was back in his trumpet section, but unfortunately that reunion did not work out. Berigan's worsening alcoholism made him erratic and unreliable, and he was reluctantly let go by TD after four months. However, when Benny Goodman temporarily broke up his orchestra in the summer, Ziggy Elman was

free and Dorsey was able to add him to his band. Other key players passing through the Dorsey organization during 1940–42 included clarinetists Johnny Mince and Heinie Beau, and pianists Joe Bushkin (who wrote the standard "Oh Look at Me Now") and Milt Raskin. In 1942, with hit versions of "I'll Never Smile Again" and "Opus #1" in his recent past, Dorsey (who was appearing often in Hollywood films) added a string section to what was now a 26-piece orchestra. By 1944, when his new vocal group was known as the Sentimentalists and his band included clarinetist Buddy DeFranco, Dorsey's orchestra was up to 32 pieces.

● **Yes Indeed** (Bluebird 9987) has some of the highpoints of the Sy Oliver/Buddy Rich/Ziggy Elman period of Tommy Dorsey's Orchestra, with the emphasis on instrumentals (other than two Sy Oliver vocals). Highlights include "Yes Indeed," "Quiet Please," Oliver's rearrangement of "Swanee River," "Well Git It" (which has a famous trumpet tradeoff by Elman and Chuck Peterson), a guest appearance by Duke Ellington on "The Minor Goes Muggin'," and a remake of the hit "Opus #1" with strings. Frank Sinatra fans will want to get the five-CD set **The Song Is You** (RCA 66353) because it has all 110 studio selections and broadcast performances that Sinatra made with TD during 1940–42, including "I'll Be Seeing You," "Polka Dots and Moonbeams," "Fools Rush In," "East of the Sun," "I'll Never Smile Again," and "The Song Is You." The emphasis is on ballads and Sinatra shows why he would soon be the favorite among bobbysoxers, even outstripping the popularity of the Tommy Dorsey band in time.

Jimmy Dorsey   Unlike his younger brother's orchestra, Jimmy Dorsey's band had not developed its own musical personality by 1939 although it worked fairly steadily. And with drummer Ray McKinley and pianist Freddie Slack departing that year to join Will Bradley's new big band, JD's fortunes probably did not seem so promising at the time. However, he soon added an attractive young vocalist in Helen O'Connell. In early 1941, she and Bob Eberle (Dorsey's male vocalist since 1936) began recording duets together and the result was a string of popular and very appealing records, including "Amapola," "Yours," "In the Hush of the Night," "Time Was," "It Happened in Hawaii," "Any Bonds Today," "I Said No," "Not Mine," a filmed version of "Star Eyes," and hit records in "Green Eyes," "Tangerine," and "Brazil."

Much of the time Dorsey was a minor figure on his own records, taking a jazz chorus in between Eberle's ballad vocalizing and O'Connell's spirited singing.

While the more popular Eberle and O'Connell vocal numbers usually appear on Jimmy Dorsey greatest hits collections, ◉ **Contrasts** (GRP/Decca 626), which dates from 1936–43, has some of the often-overlooked instrumental highpoints of Dorsey's recordings, including "Parade of the Milk Bottle Caps," "I Got Rhythm," "Long John Silver," "Dusk in Upper Sandusky," "King Porter Stomp," and Dorsey's haunting theme "Contrasts." Also included are three O'Connell vocals, including "Tangerine," her hit with Eberle.

Gene Krupa   Gene Krupa, like Jimmy Dorsey and Harry James, was quite well known as a soloist when he formed his orchestra, but, as with the other two, it took a few years for his band to make it big. Krupa's 1939–40 orchestra was most notable for Irene Daye's pleasing vocals and the solos of trumpeter Shorty Sherock. **1939** (Classics 799), **1939–1940** (Classics 834), **1940** (Classics 859), **1940, Vol. 2** (Classics 883), and **1940, Vol. 3** (Classics 917) have all of the recordings by Krupa's band of the period, but, due to far too many mundane ballad vocals by Howard Dulaney in 1940 and not enough instrumentals, a better choice is to skip the Classics and instead acquire Krupa's **Drum Boogie** (Columbia/Legacy 53245). Dulaney is completely absent on this CD and only Daye's best vocals are here along with such fine instrumentals as the hit "Drum Boogie," "No Name Jive," "Rhumboogie," "Boog It," "Sweet Georgia Brown," and the two-part "Blue Rhythm Fantasy."

The Gene Krupa Orchestra entered its prime in 1941. Roy Eldridge joined on trumpet and Anita O'Day became Krupa's most famous vocalist. The combination of Krupa, O'Day, and Eldridge clicked and they had hits in "Let Me Off Uptown" and "Thanks for the Boogie Ride." The interplay between O'Day and Eldridge was magical, even though they really did not like each other much and Eldridge had difficulties being a black musician traveling with a white band.

There are several different ways to acquire the famous 1941–42 Gene Krupa recordings. **1941** (Classics 960) has Irene Daye's final vocals with Krupa (including "Drum Boogie"), nine appearances by Howard Dulaney (only "Green Eyes," which he shares with O'Day, is worthwhile), and Anita O'Day's first nine vocals with the band

(including "Let Me Off Uptown"). **1941, Vol. 2** (Classics 1006) is highlighted by Eldridge's features on "Rockin' Chair" and "After You're Gone," and O'Day's "Stop, the Red Light's On." **1941–1942** (Classics 1056) includes "Bolero at the Savoy," "Skylark," and "Thanks for the Boogie Ride." **1942–1945** (Classics 1096) is particularly valuable for it has the last recordings by the Krupa-O'Day-Eldridge band (including "Knock Me a Kiss," "That Drummer's Band," and "Murder, He Says"), two trio cuts from 1944 with pianist Dodo Marmarosa and clarinetist Buddy DeFranco, and selections from Krupa's promising new band in 1945.

However, everyone but completists will prefer the definitive single CD ◉ **Uptown** (Columbia 65448), which has the 20 best selections (including all of the songs mentioned in the last paragraph other than "Drum Boogie") plus four numbers from 1949 when Eldridge had a second period with Krupa's Orchestra. Many of the same songs (plus three from 1945) are repeated on Anita O'Day's **Let Me Off Uptown** (Columbia/Legacy 65625), which puts the emphasis on the singer and also includes some of her lesser-known material with Krupa.

The Gene Krupa Orchestra came to a premature end in May 1943 when the drummer was framed on a marijuana rap by narcotics agents eager to nab a star. After a short time in jail and a great deal of publicity, Krupa was cleared of the charges. He was back with Benny Goodman (who welcomed him with open arms) during September–December 1943 and spent seven months in 1944 with Tommy Dorsey's band. By August 1944, Krupa was leading a new big band, one that was dubbed "the band with strings that swings." This huge ensemble had ten strings, a vocal group (the Escorts), and even a second drummer (Joe Dale) who could play when Krupa was conducting. However, the recording strike meant that only two songs later in the year were recorded and that this particular band never caught on. But with some streamlining, 1945 would find Krupa making a full comeback.

Harry James   When Harry James left Benny Goodman at the beginning of 1939 and formed his own big band, it was predicted that he would quickly become quite successful. The prediction was correct except that it took two years longer than expected. **1937–1939** (Classics 903) starts off with three four-song sessions that were made while James was still with Goodman, two of which utilize Count Basie stars (including Herschel Evans, trombonist

Eddie Durham, Walter Page, Jo Jones, and Helen Humes); highlights include "Life Goes to a Party" and "One o'Clock Jump." The session from April 1938 also has some Goodman sidemen plus Harry Carney from Duke Ellington's band. Shortly after going out on his own, James recorded four hot blues in a quartet with either Pete Johnson or Albert Ammons contributing boogie-woogie piano, which are also on this disc. **1937–1939** concludes with the first six selections from James's new big band, including the original version of his theme song "Ciribiribin" and "Two o'Clock Jump" (which is just "One o'Clock Jump" under a different title).

James's big band lacked any major names other than the leader, but it was a fine swing outfit. **1939** (Classics 936) includes "Indiana," "King Porter Stomp," "Feet Dragging Blues," an exciting showcase for James with just his rhythm section ("Sleepy Time Gal"), two vocals for Connie Haines, and eight for the trumpeter's new vocalist, Frank Sinatra, including "All or Nothing at All," which would become a hit upon its rerelease years later. **1939–1940** (Classics 970) was recorded during a low period in James's career. His band was demoted from Columbia to the company's subsidiary Varsity because of low sales, and Frank Sinatra was lured away by Tommy Dorsey's lucrative offer. However, James's music was generally excellent and Dick Haymes proved to be a perfect replacement for Sinatra. Among the highpoints of this CD are "Flash," "Cross Country Jump," "Concerto for Trumpet," "Tuxedo Junction," "Alice Blue Gown," and a trumpet feature on "Carnival of Venice." **1940–1941** (Classics 1014) finds James's band gradually growing in popularity, returning to the Columbia label and by January 1941 adding a string quartet to the orchestra. "Music Makers" was a minor hit and among the other selections included are James's initial version of "Flight of the Bumble Bee," "Super Chief," and "Exactly Like You." **1941** (Classics 1052) brings the band up to May 1941 with "I'll Get By" (a popular feature for Haymes), "Jeffrie's Blues," "Sharp as a Tack," and several semiclassical features for James's trumpet: remakes of "The Flight of the Bumble Bee" and "The Carnival of Venice" plus the two-part "Trumpet Rhapsody."

For Harry James, the turning point of his career happened on May 20, 1941, with his instrumental recording of the old Al Jolson hit "You Made Me Love You," which had been revived by Judy Garland. The trumpeter's fairly straight rendition of the slow sentimental ballad was such a big hit that from that point forward, Harry James's band shot to the top of the swing world. While many of his earlier fans bemoaned the fact that he did not exclusively play jazz (James could sound pretty schmaltzy at times and loved to show off his classical chops), it was difficult to argue with his remarkable success. By mid-1942 when Glenn Miller went into the Army Air Force, James had the most popular big band in the world, a position he would hold into 1946. **1941** (Classics 1092) has "You Made Me Love You," ballad features for Dick Haymes, a few semiclassical features, and fine swing romps in "Jughead" and "Record Session." **1941–1942** (Classics 1132) has Helen Forrest becoming James's female vocalist and adding warmth to such numbers as "But Not for Me," "I Remember You," "Skylark," and the hit "I Don't Want to Walk Without You," a touching number recorded just four days after Pearl Harbor. Other highlights include "B-19," "The Mole," "Strictly Instrumental," and "The Clipper." In 1942, James's string section expanded to seven and his 24-piece band included a French horn. **1942** (Classics 1178), which reaches up to July 22, 1942, includes popular numbers in the somewhat maudlin "Sleepy Lagoon," the swinging "James Session," "Cherry," and three Helen Forrest vocals: "I Cried for You," "I Heard You Cried Last Night," and "I Had the Craziest Dream."

Even the recording strike did nothing to stop Harry James's rise to superstar status. In fact, he was in such a good position that he became more famous during the next two years. James appeared regularly on the radio, his records were hits on jukeboxes, he appeared in Hollywood films, and he married the glamorous movie star Betty Grable. When James was finally able to return to records on November 21, 1944, that session resulted in another hit with Duke Ellington's "I'm Beginning to See the Light," featuring Kitty Kallen on vocals. By then James's orchestra was 32-strong with 14 strings and new members in valve trombonist Juan Tizol, altoist Willie Smith, and tenor saxophonist Corky Corcoran, each of whom would be with James for years to come. **1942–1944** (Classics 1227) is a particularly intriguing set because, other than the first four numbers (from the last James Columbia date of mid-1942), all of the music is taken from V-disc performances. One gets to hear alternate versions of such songs as "Two o'Clock Jump," "I'll Walk Alone," "There Goes that Song Again," and "I'm Beginning to See the Light."

While his band was struggling to survive in 1939, by 1944 Harry James was at the top of the swing world.

Lionel Hampton   Jazz's first great vibraphonist, Lionel Hampton starred with the Benny Goodman Quartet during 1936–38 and was part of the first Benny Goodman Sextet (alongside Charlie Christian) in 1939–40. During 1937–40, Hamp led a series of frequently brilliant small-group dates for Victor, using all-star players from a variety of top swing big bands. All of the music was perfectly reissued on the six-LP set **The Complete Lionel Hampton** (RCA AXM6-5536) in the 1980s, but unfortunately RCA has only reissued some of the music in a rather haphazard fashion on **Hot Mallets, Vol. 1** (Bluebird 6458), **The Jumpin' Jive, Vol. 2** (Bluebird 2433), and **Tempo and Swing** (Bluebird 66039), sometimes splitting sessions between different discs.

It is much wiser to instead acquire the Hampton discs in the European Classics series. **1937–1938** (Classics 524) features such notables as Ziggy Elman, Cootie Williams, Johnny Hodges, Jess Stacy, and Jonah Jones, with the highlights including "Hampton Stomp," "Stompology," and Hodges's playing on "On the Sunny Side of the Street." Not only does Hampton jam on vibes, but he is heard on drums, taking vocals, and occasionally playing very fast lines with two fingers on the piano. **1938–1939** (Classics 534) has Hampton joined by Elman, Hodges, Williams, Jonah Jones, Benny Carter, Herschel Evans, Chu Berry, Rex Stewart, and Harry Carney among others. In addition to "Shoe Shiner's Drag," "Memories of You," and "Twelfth Street Rag," there is a session on which Chu Berry is the only horn; his playing on "Sweethearts on Parade" is one of the highpoints of Berry's career. **1939–1940** (Classics 562) starts out with four songs featuring a remarkable sax section comprised of Benny Carter and Coleman Hawkins, Chu Berry, and Ben Webster on tenors. The choice for the trumpet chair was unusual: Cab Calloway's 22-year-old soloist Dizzy Gillespie, who on "Hot Mallets" sounds fairly individual for one of the first times, getting away from his Roy Eldridge role model. Other sessions on this CD include spots for Red Allen, J.C. Higginbotham, Ziggy Elman, Edmond Hall, and (on the last four numbers) the King Cole Trio.

When Benny Goodman temporarily broke up his orchestra in mid-1940 due to his sciatica, Hampton formed his own big band. Except for special guest appearances (including occasional reunions with BG), the vibraphonist would always be a leader from then on. A real crowd pleaser, Hampton had no difficulty catching on although his full orchestra would not record until December 1941. **1940–1941** (Classics 624) has four additional titles in which Hampton heads the King Cole Trio, a series of small-group dates (mostly with musicians from his big band), and finally his first four titles as a big band leader. In 1942, Hampton had his breakthrough by recording a classic version of a song he had previously played with the Benny Goodman Sextet, "Flying Home." The tenor solo by Illinois Jacquet served as one of the main inspirations for rhythm and blues, the high-note trumpet blasts (by Ernie Royal) would be typical of Hampton's excitable bands, and the vibraphonist sounds quite jubilant throughout. **1942–1944** (Classics 803) has that classic performance, which ironically was Jacquet's only studio session with Hampton. The recording strike kept Hampton off records until March 1944 and by then Jacquet had departed. However, Arnett Cobb was a perfect replacement, as can be heard on "Flying Home No. 2." Most of the selections on **1942–1944** are from 1944, including a two-sided V-disc performance of "Flying Home" and the first version of Hampton's second greatest hit, "Hamp's Boogie Woogie." Dinah Washington, who made surprisingly few recordings with Hampton, was the band's vocalist and became a major attraction herself during their performances. Cat Anderson popped out high notes for Hamp until he joined Duke Ellington. Trombonists Booty Wood and Fred Beckett (the latter an early inspiration for J.J. Johnson), altoist Earl Bostic, and pianist Milt Buckner (whose block chords became influential) joined Cobb and Hampton as some of the key players in the ensemble. This was an exciting band putting on wild shows that pointed the way for swing to evolve into R&B.

Earl Hines   The Earl Hines Orchestra was based in Chicago's Grand Terrace Ballroom during 1929–40. **1937–1939** (Classics 538) has the band's last titles from 1937, seven obscure numbers from 1938 (including some that feature cornetist/singer Ray Nance two years before he joined Duke Ellington), and the beginning of its very rewarding series of recordings for Bluebird. Hines takes "The Father's Getaway" and "Reminiscing at Blue Note" as piano solos and his big band really romps on "Indiana," "Father Steps Out," and "Piano Man." With such key players as trumpeter/vocalist Walter Fuller, clarinetist Omer Simeon, and Budd Johnson on tenor, Hines had one of the most swinging bands in jazz.

In 1940, Hines temporarily broke up his orchestra and then reorganized, retaining only a few of his musicians (including Budd Johnson and his new singer Billy Eckstine), but continuing on at the same high quality. ● **Piano Man** (Bluebird 6750) is a fine sampler of Hines's 1939–42 recordings that consists of five piano solos, "Blues in Thirds" in a small group with Sidney Bechet, and 16 of his best big band recordings, including his 1940 hit "Boogie Woogie on St. Louis Blues," "Piano Man," "Jelly Jelly" (Billy Eckstine's first significant recording), and "Second Balcony Jump." More serious collectors will continue with the Classic releases, including **1939–40** (Classics 567), which has "Rosetta" from 1939 and all of Hines's orchestra's 1940 recordings before and after its breakup. **1941** (Classics 621) fully covers that year in the pianist's life with four big band sessions (including "Windy City Jive," "The Father Jumps," and "The Jitney Man") and a pair of brilliant piano solos ("On the Sunny Side of the Street" and "My Melancholy Baby").

Earl Hines only had one big band recording before the recording strike, resulting in four songs, including Billy Eckstine singing "Stormy Monday Blues." Other than an aircheck from October 1944, his big band would not be caught on records again until January 12, 1945. Amazingly enough, there are also no existing radio broadcasts from this period. It would not matter all that much except that the 1943 Earl Hines Orchestra was the first bebop big band.

With the urging of Billy Eckstine, Hines hired trumpeter Dizzy Gillespie (who debuted his "A Night in Tunisia" with Hines), altoist Charlie Parker (but on tenor where there was an opening), and singer Sarah Vaughan (who also played second piano) for his band in early 1943. But due to its complete lack of documentation, it is impossible for anyone who came of age since that time to really know what this big band sounded like, making the Earl Hines Orchestra the most significant casualty of the recording strike. By 1944, Gillespie, Parker, and Vaughan had all departed to join Billy Eckstine's new big band, and Hines (who had not altered his playing style) was back to featuring advanced swing. **1942–1945** (Classics 876) has the one session from the 1942 band (including "Second Balcony Jump"), small-group dates featuring Hines in 1944 (which include guitarist Al Casey, bassist Oscar Pettiford, Ray Nance, Johnny Hodges, and tenor saxophonist Flip Phillips), and the first orchestra date

from 1945. But one can only guess what Hines's music sounded like during the silent period.

Woody Herman   In 1939 Glenn Miller and Charlie Barnet became major names in swing, and to a lesser extent that was true for Woody Herman. After two years of struggling, Herman had a hit in the catchy blues "Woodchopper's Ball." Since he also recorded "Blues Downstairs" and "Blues Upstairs" on that same day (April 12), Herman's orchestra was soon billed as "The Band that Plays the Blues." Herman began to sing a little less and feature his band a bit more, although the orchestra lacked any major soloists (Herman on clarinet, trumpeter Cappy Lewis, and flugelhornist Joe Bishop came the closest). **1939** (Classics 1128) has the three blues numbers plus "Dallas Blues," "The Sheik of Araby," "Farewell Blues," and "East Side Kick." There are also four selections in which the Herman orchestra backs Connie Boswell (who is in good voice) and there are five Herman vocals plus two from his new female singer Mary Ann McCall. **1939–1940** (Classics 1163) unfortunately only has three instrumentals (best is "Blues on Parade") and finds the Herman band still struggling to find its own musical identity.

It would take some time. The year 1940 was most notable for the band's recording of "Blue Prelude" and for Herman's jams with his rhythm section (his Four Chips) on "Chip's Boogie Woogie" and "Chip's Blues." The Herman orchestra was thought of as a reliable but relatively insignificant band that was often used to record inferior remakes of other band's hits, including "Frenesi," and "Beat Me Daddy, Eight to the Bar." In 1941, Herman recorded "Blue Flame" and "Blues in the Night" with his big band and, on a small-group session with his Woodchoppers, "Fan It." Those three songs would remain in his repertoire, but in general, the band was just a pleasing middle-of-the-road swing orchestra. Recordings in 1942 included an advanced Dizzy Gillespie arrangement ("Down Under") that led Herman to advise the young trumpeter to stick to writing and give up playing! Gillespie did not take his advice. ● **Blues on Parade** (GRP/Decca 606) has the best early Herman recordings with all of the key instrumentals from 1937–42; even the leader's eight vocals are jazz-oriented. Not only is this a strong prelude to Woody Herman's first band, but it contains almost all of this particular orchestra's worthwhile recordings.

The war led to Herman's orchestra having a lot of turnover, but so did his increasingly adventurous spirit. When he returned to records in November 1943, Herman was featuring Dave Matthews's Duke Ellington-influenced arrangements with guest soloist Ben Webster; Johnny Hodges guests on Herman's 1944 recording of "Perdido." Most importantly, the band now included bassist Chubby Jackson, who urged Herman to hire younger and more modern musicians. During 1944, Herman's orchestra had an almost complete change of personnel, and although not well recorded yet, its radio broadcasts and concerts were starting to generate a strong buzz. **Old Gold Rehearsals 1944** (Jazz Unlimited 201 2079) shows what the excitement was about. On these rehearsals for radio shows, the Herman Orchestra is heard during August–October 1944 at a time when the personnel for what would be known as Herman's Herd was almost entirely in place. The trumpet section included lead trumpeter Pete Candoli, his teenage brother Conte Candoli (on summer vacation from school), and Neal Hefti, who was also contributing arrangements. The other soloists included the rambunctious trombonist Bill Harris and the hard-driving tenor Flip Phillips (who was especially warm on ballads), while the rhythm section consisted of arranger Ralph Burns on piano, guitarist Billy Bauer, Chubby Jackson, and drummer Dave Tough. Though most of the songs are swing-oriented and not all that different in feel from the 1942 band, the soloists are on a much higher level and there is a joyful spirit to the band that would become more exciting within the following year. In addition to such numbers as "It Must Be Jelly 'Cause Jam Don't Shake Like That," Hefti's "Jones Beachhead," and "Basie's Basement," the band looks toward the near future on "Apple Honey."

22 Other Big Bands, from A to Z

In addition to the bands at the top of the heap, there were hundreds of others that were struggling to survive during this period. The 22 in this section are of particular interest because they contain historic figures and/or were documented performing some unique music that added to the richness of the era.

Louis Armstrong In some ways, the second half of the swing era was an off period for Louis Armstrong. Although Armstrong was acknowledged as a highly influential trumpeter/singer who was a major showbiz personality, many of the younger musicians in jazz were thinking of Satch as being old hat, particularly in comparison with Roy Eldridge, Harry James, and Charlie Shavers. His big band never developed a personality of its own beyond its leader, and few of his sidemen had opportunities to star. In mid-1940, most of the alumni from the old Luis Russell Orchestra were dropped (although Russell remained), but the newer Louis Armstrong band was not all that different from how it had been, mostly functioning as a background for its leader. Yet Armstrong always put on a good show, and there were always moments when he sounded particularly inspired and showed that he still had a great deal more to offer.

1939–1940 (Classics 615) has some lesser remakes of past glories (including "West End Blues") and many novelties, including "Me and Brother Bill," "You've Got Me Voodoo'd," and "You Run Your Mouth, I'll Run My Business," but best are four numbers with the Mills Brothers, including "W.P.A.". **1940–1942** (Classics 685) is again most memorable for a small-group date, four intriguing numbers (including "Down in Honky Tonk Town") with Sidney Bechet that find the two rivals fighting for dominance; Satch wins, barely. Otherwise, there are a couple of mostly uneventful septet sessions and some decent, but not essential big band numbers, including "Cut Off My Legs and Call Me 'Shorty!'" Ironically, Armstrong's singing was at its best during this time, as heard on "Among My Souvenirs," but his abilities as a "crooner" were not displayed very often. However, his playing at the January 1944 Esquire All-American concert (where he soloed opposite such greats as Jack Teagarden, Barney Bigard, Coleman Hawkins, and Art Tatum) showed that perhaps Louis Armstrong would sound best with a small group in the future. It was a first hint at what was to come.

Georgie Auld Georgie Auld's career fell into several periods. Born in Canada, in 1929 he moved to Brooklyn with his family when he was ten, taking up the alto sax. In 1935, he switched to tenor and was playing professionally the following year. As a key soloist with Bunny Berigan's big band (1937–38), Auld usually sounded pretty close to Charlie Barnet. However, during a year with Artie Shaw (1938–39), his tone changed and he was much more influenced by Lester Young. When Shaw spontaneously fled to Mexico, Auld—just 20—was appointed leader of the band after Tony Pastor opted to go out on his own. There was little demand for the Shawless Artie Shaw alumni band and after a few months, it broke up. **Jump, Georgie, Jump** (Hep 27) starts off with eight of the ten titles recorded by the "ghost band" in 1940 and, although they form an interesting postscript to the legacy of Shaw's "Begin the Beguine" orchestra, they are not that memorable. After a short stint with Jan Savitt, Auld became an important member of the Benny Goodman Orchestra (1940–41), making a strong impression with his playing on the recordings of the Benny Goodman Sextet with Cootie Williams and Charlie Christian. He was back with Shaw during 1941–42 and, after a short stretch in the army, formed his own big band in 1943, which lasted for three years.

In addition to the 1940 sessions, **Jump, Georgie, Jump** also includes ten fine performances from a radio transcription date in 1944 (trumpeter Sonny Berman is the most impressive soloist) and four songs from a 1945 broadcast that has some rare solos from Al Porcino (usually a nonsoloing first trumpeter).

Bunny Berigan   Bunny Berigan, the top trumpeter during the first half of the swing era, quickly declined during 1939–42. Ironically, his big band's recordings of late 1938–39 were superior to most of the ones that he had recorded earlier in 1938. But despite remaining a major name, many lost opportunities and his worsening alcoholism resulted in Berigan being forced to declare bankruptcy and break up his band by the end of 1939. He rejoined Tommy Dorsey's orchestra for a few months in 1940, but was not happy being a sideman again, never stopped drinking, and was so erratic that Dorsey reluctantly fired him. In 1941, Berigan put together a final big band, but (other than drummer Jack Sperling) the young sidemen were all doomed to obscurity. Berigan's health continued to decline and on June 2, 1942, he died when he was just 33, having suffered the same basic fate as Bix Beiderbecke 11 years earlier. **1938–1942** (Classics 844) has the final recordings from Berigan's moderately successful band of 1937–39. These include two Bix Beiderbecke pieces, "In the Dark" and "Walkin' the Dog," "Jazz Me Blues," "There'll Be Some Changes Made," and "Peg O' My Heart" plus the eight rather rare recordings of 1941–42, which are unfortunately all dominated by vocals. If only Bunny Berigan

had been able to take care of himself, he could have been a competitor for Harry James. In addition, it would have been interesting to see how he would have handled bebop.

Les Brown   No jazz big band lasted longer under the same leader as Les Brown's Band of Renown. Brown was a consistent musician, never overly exciting either in his playing (clarinet and saxophones), writing, or bandleading, but very reliable. The same can be said for his orchestra, which swung consistently, but rarely stood out from the crowd. Brown, who was a section player rather than a soloist, formed a big band in 1935 while attending Duke University that was called the Duke Blue Devils. After a year, that ensemble broke up and Brown freelanced as a player and an arranger. In 1938, he formed the Les Brown Orchestra, a group that worked steadily during the swing era and was influenced initially by Benny Goodman's sound. He did not have his first real hit until 1944's "Sentimental Journey," which featured the young singer Doris Day; that tune became one of the most popular of the final year of World War II.

Three CDs have some of the highlights of Les Brown's long string of recordings, dating mostly from 1940–46 with a few later selections. **Best of the Big Bands** (Columbia 45344) has flawed packaging (no personnel listing or recording dates), but otherwise is an excellent collection of Les Brown's greatest hits, including his theme song "Leap Frog," "Sentimental Journey," "Bizet Has His Day," "I've Got My Love to Keep Me Warm" (which became a hit in 1948, two years after it was recorded), and some of his better instrumentals. **Doris Day with Les Brown** (Columbia 46244) includes selections from the singer's two stints with Brown (1940–41 and 1945–46), 16 selections, including "Aren't You Glad You're You," "We'll Be Together Again," "There's Good Blues Tonight," and "It Could Happen to You." **Les Brown and His Great Vocalists** (Legacy/Columbia 66373) consists of selections from Doris Day (three songs, including a repeat of "Sentimental Journey"), Butch Stone (his trademark number "A Good Man Is Hard to Find"), Stumpy Brown, Lucy Ann Polk, and other Brown vocalists from the 1941–50 period.

The Les Brown Orchestra would last a remarkable 62 years, until the leader's death.

Benny Carter   In 1938, Benny Carter returned to the United States after three years overseas. He worked as a freelance arranger and altoist, forming a big band in 1939 that performed regularly around New York for a few years without catching on big with the general public. Carter had the same difficulty as Teddy Wilson. They were both very professional and musical, but there were no catchy trademarks in their music, they were not extroverted showmen, and the lack of any hits resulted in them being in the second echelon of big bands (at least commercially), way behind Benny Goodman, Duke Ellington, Artie Shaw, and the other major names. **1939–1940** (Classics 579) features Carter's big band. The main soloists are Carter, trumpeter Joe Thomas, trombonist Vic Dickenson, and pianist Eddie Heywood. By 1940, the band had been reorganized with Bill Coleman and trombonist Sandy Williams among the principal players. Among the better big band selections on this disc are "Savoy Stampede," "Scandal in 'A' Flat," "Shufflebug Shuffle," "Night Hop," and "When Lights Are Low." The CD concludes with two numbers from an all-star group with Coleman Hawkins, a session that is continued on **1940–1941** (Classics 631) with a classic version of "I Can't Believe that You're in Love with Me," which has a typically thoughtful and perfectly constructed Carter alto solo. The latter CD also has an all-star date with Bill Coleman, Georgie Auld, and singer Joe Turner, but otherwise the CD also concentrates on Carter's big band. Trumpeters Jonah Jones and Sidney DeParis, trombonists Benny Morton and Jimmy Archey, and pianist Sonny White are the key players other than the leader.

In 1942, Benny Carter relocated to Los Angeles where he wrote for the movie studios (including the film *Stormy Weather*) and led another big band on a part-time basis for the next three years. **1943–1946** (Classics 923), which is also covered in the next chapter, documents Carter's West Coast orchestra. The 1943 session is most notable for having trombonist J.J. Johnson's first recorded solo ("Love for Sale"). The May 21, 1944, date, which uses a lineup that includes pianist Gerald Wiggins and drummer Max Roach, shows that Carter was looking ahead toward other modern developments while retaining his own classic style.

The Casa Loma Orchestra   Glen Gray's Casa Loma Orchestra, one of the very first swing big bands, worked steadily throughout the 1940s. In 1939, its lineup still included trumpeter Sunny Dunham, trombonist/singer Pee Wee Hunt, clarinetist Clarence Hutchinrider, and ballad singer Kenny Sargent, and in 1940 the band had a final hit in the two-sided "No Name Jive." But the recordings stopped altogether after 1942 and the Casa Lomans were unable to duplicate their earlier success. Two LPs, **1939–40** (Hindsight 104) and **1943–1946 Vol. 2** (Hindsight 120), feature excellent radio transcriptions from the band. While the earlier album has some remakes of the band's hits along with other swing standards from the period, **1943–1946** is particularly valuable for it documents the orchestra when it was no longer appearing on records and its personnel had drastically changed. Red Nichols takes particularly inventive solos on "Don't Take Your Love from Me" and "Dancing on the Ceiling" while Bobby Hackett is heard on five songs.

Larry Clinton   Larry Clinton's Orchestra had reached its peak by 1939, but it still continued recording its leader's excellent swing charts for two additional years. **Feeling Like a Dream** (Hep 1047) has some of the band's best recordings from 1940–41. Bea Wain had left to start her own solo career, but Peggy Mann was a fine replacement as Clinton's main vocalist. Butch Stone (who would soon become associated with Les Brown's band) was an asset, more as a good-humored singer than as a baritonist, and the quality of Clinton's obscure sidemen remained quite high. Among the better selections on this Hep CD are "Feeling Like a Dream," Buster Harding's "Jump Joe," "Arab Dance," and "Jazz Me Blues."

However, Larry Clinton's combination of riff-filled swing charts, adaptations of themes from classical music, and dance band numbers ran its course. At the end of 1941, he broke up his band, joining the Army Air Corps as a flight instructor.

Ella Fitzgerald and Chick Webb   Chick Webb was at the height of his popularity and fame as 1939 began, riding high due to his star attraction Ella Fitzgerald and her hit record of "A-Tisket, A-Tasket." But tragically, the drummer's health was failing rapidly. He had a few short stays in the hospital, was plagued by heart troubles and pleurisy, and on June 16, 1939, passed away at the age of 37. His last words were reportedly, "I'm sorry, but I gotta go."

What to do about his band? The 22-year-old Ella Fitzgerald was made its leader, or really, its front person since she had little to do with the band's musical direction. **Ella Fitzgerald's 1939** (Classics 525) consists of the final Ella Fitzgerald vocals with Webb (including "'Tain't What You Do" and "Don't Worry 'Bout Me") and the first session by Ella Fitzgerald's Famous Orchestra, with Bill Beason now on drums. **1939–1940** (Classics 566) has just three instrumentals among the 23 selections since the former Webb band was now secondary compared to the gradually maturing singer. Fitzgerald was still being saddled with some juvenile novelties (such as "My Wubba Dolly"), but was already superb on ballads, including "My Last Goodbye," "Moon Ray," "Sugar Blues," and "Imagination." **1940–1941** (Classics 644) is most notable for her versions of "Shake Down the Stars," "I'm the Lonesomest Gal in Town," "The One I Love," and "Can't Help Lovin' 'Dat Man."

By the summer of 1941, Ella Fitzgerald was such a big name that she no longer needed to be fronting the Webb ghost band, so the orchestra broke up.

Horace Henderson   In 1939, the Fletcher Henderson Orchestra disbanded. His younger brother Horace Henderson, after writing a great deal for Fletcher during 1936–37, formed his own Chicago-based orchestra in 1937. His band lasted four years and had five recording sessions, all of which are on **1940–1941** (Classics 648). The key players are trumpeter Emmett Berry, Ray Nance on cornet, violin, and vocals (right before he joined Duke Ellington), tenor saxophonist Elmer Williams (formerly with Chick Webb), singer Viola Jefferson, and (by August 1940) bassist Israel Crosby. The band swings well on its 21 recordings (which include "Shufflin' Joe," "Honeysuckle Rose," "Swingin' and Jumpin'," "When Dreams Come True," and "Smooth Sailing"), but it never really caught on and broke up in 1941. That same year Fletcher Henderson, attempting a comeback, had his only session with his third short-lived orchestra, which is also included on **1940–1941**.

While Fletcher Henderson finished the swing era as a freelance arranger, Horace spent 1942–43 in the army, became Lena Horne's accompanist for a time, and despite leading later bands, never emerged from his older brother's shadow.

Stan Kenton   Stan Kenton always had ambitious goals. One of his main ones was to create a concert jazz orchestra, an ensemble that played for an attentive audience rather than for dancers, and one that would not have to compromise in order to stay solvent. To a certain extent he succeeded, becoming a cult figure with a dedicated following that helped make his most adventurous plans possible if not financially prosperous.

Kenton grew up in California, began playing piano as a teenager (Earl Hines was always his main playing influence), and worked locally with a variety of groups, including Everett Hoagland (1933–34), Russ Plummer, Hal Grayson, Gus Arnheim (1936), and Vido Musso. In 1940, he put together a rehearsal band, which in the summer of 1941, worked regularly at the Rendezvous Ballroom in Balboa Beach near Los Angeles. The unique music soon picked up a devoted if regional base of fans. Kenton, who did most of the writing for his first band, loved thick-toned tenors and screaming trumpeters (being inspired by the Jimmie Lunceford Orchestra) and among his early originals was "Artistry in Rhythm," which became his theme song. The key members of his first band were Red Dorris (on tenor and vocals), trumpeter Chico Alvarez, and bassist Howard Rumsey.

Kenton can be heard on some radio transcriptions as early as July 25, 1941. He recorded nine selections for Decca during 1941–42 ("Reed Rapture" is most interesting), but none sold that well. For a short time it looked as if the Kenton Orchestra had gotten its big break when it was signed to be the house band on the Bob Hope radio show, but it was soon apparent that playing in the background for Hope and his comedy guests was not an ideal position for Kenton, and they parted ways. Les Brown would get the job in the near future and hold on to it for a half-century.

Much more significant for Kenton was signing with the new Capitol label in November 1943, an association that lasted 25 years. The Kenton Orchestra, which by then featured trumpeter Buddy Childers, altoist Art Pepper, and (in 1944) Anita O'Day, had its first hit in "Eager Beaver," waxed "Artistry in Rhythm," and O'Day made "And Her Tears Flowed Like Wine" popular. Already at this early stage, Kenton's band could be quite pompous and bombastic, carving out its own unique niche. **1940–1944** (Classics 848) has "Etude for Saxophones" (from November 1, 1940), the Decca recordings, and the first dates for Capitol. The three-CD set **Artistry in Kenton** (Jazz Unlimited 204 2081) has Kenton's first recorded piano solo ("High, Wide and

Handsome" with Gus Arnheim's Orchestra in 1937), five titles with a pickup group from 1938 that was issued under tenor saxophonist Vido Musso's name, and a variety of radio transcriptions, live concerts, and radio appearances from 1941 and 1943–46. The solo stars are Red Dorris, Chico Alvarez, Anita O'Day, altoist Boots Mussulli, singer June Christy, tenorman Vido Musso, and trombonist Kai Winding. The radio broadcasts include an odd "vocal" by actor Gary Cooper and Kenton guesting as a pianist with the Vaughan Monroe Orchestra. **Broadcast Transcriptions** (Music & Arts 883) consists of two intriguing sets of recordings, with 13 selections recorded before Kenton's initial studio dates (including "Reed Rapture" and "Harlem Folk Dance") and 17 numbers from December 1944; Anita O'Day has six vocals and the young tenor Stan Getz is heard on two numbers.

If the Stan Kenton Orchestra had broken up in 1945, it would have been only wistfully remembered as a little-known cult band. But, as it turned out, its impact would be much bigger than that.

Harlan Leonard Harlan Leonard played alto, clarinet, and baritone. He worked with George E. Lee (1923) and the Bennie Moten Orchestra (1923–31), taking many solos on the latter's records. Leonard co-led the Kansas City Skyrockets with trombonist Thamon Hayes during 1931–34, being its only leader during 1934–37. In 1938, he put together a new big band, the Kansas City Rockets, which traveled East to New York from Kansas City in 1940, following in the wake of Andy Kirk and Count Basie. While in New York and Chicago, Leonard's orchestra recorded 23 selections, all of which are included on **1940** (Classics 670). Tenor saxophonist Henry Bridges is the best soloist, although there are also spots for trombonist Fred Beckett, a short-lived player whom J.J. Johnson would later cite as his main influence. The Kansas City Rockets swing infectiously, including on seven arrangements contributed by Tadd Dameron (most notably "Rock and Ride," "À La Bridges," and "Dameron Stomp").

The group soon returned to Kansas City, working around town until 1943 when Leonard relocated to Los Angeles. In 1945, the orchestra broke up and Harlan Leonard retired from music, getting a job with the Internal Revenue Service.

Lucky Millinder Lucius "Lucky" Millinder was not a musician and was only a fair singer, but served well as a colorful frontman of a significant orchestra during 1940–52. Millinder had previously worked as a master of ceremonies in the late 1920s, led an unrecorded orchestra in 1931 and fronted the Mills Blue Rhythm Band during 1934–38.

The Lucky Millinder Orchestra in the early 1940s featured the passionate vocals and fluent guitar solos of Sister Rosetta Tharpe, tenor saxophonist Stafford Simon, altoist Tab Smith, and for a few months in 1942, trumpeter Dizzy Gillespie. **1941–1942** (Classics 712) has all of the music from Millinder's band during this period. Sister Rosetta Tharpe, an exciting performer, stars on "Trouble in Mind," "Rock Daniel," "Shout Sister Shout," "Rock Me," and "That's All." Dizzy Gillespie takes strong solos on "Mason Flyer" and "Little John Special" (the latter hints at the as-yet unwritten "Salt Peanuts"), and the other soloists include the greatly underrated Smith, Simon, Buster Bailey, and pianist Bill Doggett. Other than a few throwaways, mostly dated patriotic numbers, this is a highly enjoyable set of solid swing.

Red Nichols One of the busiest musicians during 1925–32, Red Nichols led a dance band for a few years (recording 16 titles during 1934), headed radio orchestras, and in late 1936 formed his own swing band. It seemed only right that Nichols would become a bandleader again since many of the stars of the swing era who would be leading successful big bands (including Benny Goodman, Tommy Dorsey, Jimmy Dorsey, Gene Krupa, Artie Shaw, and Glenn Miller) were alumni of Nichols's Five Pennies. The Red Nichols Orchestra recorded ten obscure titles for Varsity in 1937 and then extensively for Bluebird in 1939, with four songs for Okeh in 1940. The Bluebird and Okeh dates have been reissued in full on **Wail of the Winds** (Hep 1057), and it is quite a mixed bag. Many of the songs are saddled with Bill Darnell's vocals and some are just straight dance music rather than jazz. The only notable musicians in Nichols's outfit were pianist/arranger Billy Maxted and (in 1940) clarinetist Heinie Beau. However, there are some fine performances along the way, including Nichols's "The King Kong," "Davenport Blues," a swinging version of Henry Busse's "Hot Lips," "Poor Butterfly," "Overnight Hop," and Nichols's theme of the period, "Wail of the Winds." There is also a small-group session by the Five Pennies although only "My Melancholy Baby" is a standout. But overall, the Red Nichols Big Band was overshadowed by the many other more original jazz orchestras and it did not survive 1940.

After trying to lead another short-lived orchestra, Nichols was mostly outside of music for a few years, not returning until September 1944 when he put together a successful version of the Five Pennies, a Dixieland sextet.

Louis Prima   The good-humored trumpeter and vocalist Louis Prima had several different stages to his long career. After leading Dixieland-oriented groups during 1934–39, Prima formed a big band in late 1939 that lasted throughout the 1940s. Prima was easily the main star of his group; in fact, the personnel of his orchestra is largely unknown, other than young trumpeter Sonny Berman who played in the ensembles of the 1940–41 band. **1940–1944** (Classics 1201) has such Prima hits as "Robin Hood," "Angelina," and "Oh Marie" (all from 1944), and Lily Ann Carol does well on her vocal features. But the orchestra does not display an original personality beyond its leader, whose New Orleans trumpet playing and happy vocals (which both celebrate and poke fun at his Italian ancestry) are the main reasons to acquire this disc.

Boyd Raeburn   Like Andy Kirk, Boyd Raeburn was not much of a musician, originally playing tenor before switching to baritone and bass sax, but he led one of the most interesting big bands of the mid-1940s. Starting in the late 1930s, Raeburn first headed some commercial orchestras, the kind that were often disparagingly called "Mickey Mouse bands." In 1944, when some of the other sweet bands (including Jan Garber and Kay Kyser) were turning toward swing, Raeburn followed the trend, reorganizing his orchestra and featuring altoist Johnny Bothwell (who was heavily influenced by Johnny Hodges), Sonny Berman, tenor saxophonist Al Cohn, baritonist Serge Chaloff, drummer Shelly Manne and (on record) Roy Eldridge, Trummy Young, and bassist Oscar Pettiford at various times. The band sometimes sounded a bit like Count Basie's, featured arrangements by pianist George Handy, George Williams, and Eddie Finckel, and was among the first to have Dizzy Gillespie's "A Night in Tunisia" in its repertoire.

1944 (Circle 22) and **1944–1945** (Circle 113) consist of radio transcriptions from the early Raeburn band during its swing phase. Don Darcy and Marjorie Wood take some so-so vocals, but there are good solos along the way from Bothwell, trumpeter Benny Harris, and trombonist Earl Swope. **1944** is highlighted by "A Night in Tunisia," "Hep Boyd," "March of the Boyds," "Early Boyd," "Boyd Meets the Duke," "Little Boyd Blue," and "Boyd Meets Girl." **1944–1945** has guest appearances by Dizzy Gillespie (on "Barefoot Boy with Cheek" and a vocal version of "A Night in Tunisia") and trombonist Trummy Young (who sings "Is You Is or Is You Ain't My Baby").

Things would take a drastic turn to the left for the Boyd Raeburn Orchestra in 1945 (discussed in Chapter 6), assuring both its artistic immortality and commercial death.

Bobby Sherwood   Bobby Sherwood had more than his share of talents. He was a fine trumpeter, played steady rhythm guitar, wrote arrangements, sang now and then, and was also an appealing personality. Born to vaudevillians, he began playing music professionally as a teenager in the late 1920s, and in 1933 (at 19) he became the late Eddie Lang's replacement as Bing Crosby's accompanist. Sherwood spent three years with Crosby and then became a busy studio musician in Los Angeles (1936–42), including playing guitar on Artie Shaw's recording of "Frenesi." In 1942, he was persuaded by Johnny Mercer to form a big band and record for Capitol. Sherwood originally planned to stay in the studios, but his first session resulted in a major hit in "The Elk's Parade" and he hit the road, struggling to keep his orchestra together for several years.

The Issued Recordings 1942–1947 (Jazz Band 2143) has the great majority of the recordings of the Bobby Sherwood Orchestra. Sherwood's ensemble lacked any major names, although there are appearances by singer Kitty Kallen on "Moonlight Becomes You," trombonist Jack Jenney, and tenors Dave Pell and Herbie Haymer. The band is heard at its best on "The Elk's Parade," "Swinging at the Semloh," "Bob's Mob," "New World Jump," Bix Beiderbecke's "In the Dark," "Cotton Tail," "Bugle Call Rag," and its 1946 hit "Sherwood's Forest."

Freddie Slack   Freddie Slack originally played the drums, not switching exclusively to piano until he was 17 in 1927. He played in a variety of territory bands based in Chicago and Los Angeles before spending two years with Ben Pollack (1934–36). Slack was a valuable member of the Jimmy Dorsey Orchestra (1936–39) and gained recognition for his playing with Will Bradley (1939–41), being featured on "Beat Me Daddy, Eight to the Bar" and other boogie-woogie numbers.

In 1941, Slack formed his own big band in Los Angeles, an outfit that lasted for seven years. Unfortunately, his recordings (a session made for Decca in 1941 and dates for Capitol during 1942 and 1944–47) have yet to be reissued on CD. His biggest hit was 1942's "Cow Cow Boogie" (featuring Ella Mae Morse's singing) and he had steady sellers in "Strange Cargo," "Mister Five by Five," and "Blackout Boogie." Hopefully his 50 recordings from 1941–47 (some of which were made with a quartet) will someday be put out as a double CD, for the music is quite rewarding.

Jack Teagarden The great trombonist Jack Teagarden, who had excelled during a five-year period with Ben Pollack (1928–33), signed a five-year contract with Paul Whiteman in 1934. Mr. T. grew to regret that contract for, although he was featured liberally with the former King of Jazz, such associates as Benny Goodman and Tommy Dorsey became famous as bandleaders while Teagarden was out of the spotlight.

In January 1939, the contract ran out and Teagarden was free at last, immediately forming his own orchestra. Unfortunately, the big band field was already overcrowded and, although there was room for a few more successes (such as Glenn Miller and Harry James), Teagarden's orchestra never really stood out. It worked fairly steadily during the first half of the 1940s, but never prospered or had any hits. **1934–1939** (Classics 729) starts off with three numbers from a 1934 octet date that stars Teagarden and his brother trumpeter Charlie, Benny Goodman, Frankie Trumbauer, and Casper Reardon (the first jazz harpist), but otherwise the disc features Teagarden's 1939 big band. Charlie Spivak (who would soon be leading a sweet-oriented big band of his own) was on first trumpet, Ernie Caceres played baritone, the leader's nephew Cubby Teagarden was on drums, and Linda Keene takes a few vocals, but Jack Teagarden is the star throughout. He is in excellent form on such numbers as "Persian Rug," "The Sheik of Araby," "I Gotta Right to Sing the Blues" (which became his theme song), and "Aunt Hagar's Blues." **1939–1940** (Classics 758) has fine performances in "Peg O' My Heart," "Muddy River Blues," "Wolverine Blues," and "If I Could Be with You," but far too many vocals from Kitty Kallen. **1940–1941** (Classics 839) is mostly a disappointment due to the

excess of forgettable vocals from Kallen, Marianne Dunne, and David Allyn. Only the final two sessions are worthwhile, including four effective big band numbers with trumpeter Pokey Carrier and clarinetist Danny Polo among the soloists. One of those dates—the December 15, 1940, session—is also on **Jack Teagarden's Big Eight/Pee Wee Russell's Rhythmakers** (Original Jazz Classics 1708). On that occasion, Teagarden had a rare vacation away from his big band to lead an integrated eight-piece group that includes Ellingtonians Rex Stewart, Barney Bigard, and Ben Webster; "St. James Infirmary" and "The World Is Waiting for the Sunrise" are particularly memorable. In addition, this CD includes a spirited if unrelated Dixielandish date from 1938 featuring Pee Wee Russell, James P. Johnson, and trumpeter Max Kaminsky.

It's Time for T/Has Anybody Here Seen Jackson (Jazz Classics 5012) is a double CD that has all of the Teagarden big band's radio transcriptions. Dating from 1941–44, these performances are generally superior and more jazz-oriented than the band's studio recordings; half of the number are swinging instrumentals. **1941–1943** (Classics 874) is the most rewarding of the Teagarden big band Classics CDs due to the variety. The dozen orchestra numbers fortunately only have one occasional vocalist: Teagarden himself. "Dark Eyes," "St. James Infirmary," "A Hundred Years from Today," and "Nobody Knows the Trouble I've Seen" are best. There are also two numbers from the movie *Birth of the Blues* (with Bing Crosby and Mary Martin) and seven selections from the Capitol International Jazzmen. The latter is an all-star group from 1943 with trumpeter Billy May (who is much better-known as an arranger, but acquits himself quite well), either Jimmie Noone or Heinie Beau on clarinet, and tenor saxophonist Dave Mathews. Teagarden is in prime form on "Casanova's Lament," "I'm Sorry I Made You Cry," and "Stars Fell on Alabama."

It must have been obvious to just about everyone (except maybe Jack Teagarden) that, by 1944, his big band was pointless. He needed to be liberated again.

Claude Thornhill Claude Thornhill had one of the most unusual of the swing era big bands. Thornhill began playing piano when he was ten, studied at the Cincinnati Conservatory and the Curtis Institute, and worked with the late 1920s orchestras of Austin Wylie and Hal Kemp. After moving to New York in the early

1930s, Thornhill had stints with Don Voorhees, Freddy Martin, Paul Whiteman, Benny Goodman (1934), Leo Reisman, and Ray Noble in addition to working in the studios. He was also Maxine Sullivan's musical director at the time that she recorded "Loch Lomond."

In 1940, Thornhill formed his first big band. His orchestra emphasized ballads and vocals, but had a unique sound, utilizing very little vibrato, long floating tones, and unusual tone colors (which sometimes included six clarinets). Its music fell between sweet and swing. At first the band played the arrangements of Thornhill and Bill Borden, gaining recognition for its haunting theme song "Snowfall," adaptations of classical themes to a dance band style (including Brahms's "Hungarian Dance No. 5" and Schumann's "Traumerei"), and having a minor hit in "Where or When." Thornhill introduced the beautiful "Autumn Nocturne," "Portrait of a Guinea Farm" was certainly unusual, and Irving Fazola's clarinet was a lead voice in the ensembles. In 1942, Gil Evans joined Thornhill's arranging staff, contributing "Buster's Last Stand" and "There's a Small Hotel." The band expanded by using a vocal group (the Snowflakes) and two French horns. But before 1942 ended, Thornhill joined the navy for three years, spending part of the time playing with Artie Shaw's military band. He would not record again until his second big band began in 1946.

Fortunately, all of the Thornhill big band's recordings have been getting reissued by the Scottish Hep label. ◉ **Snowfall** (Hep 1058) has the first 25 selections, taken from a period when Fazola, trumpeter Rusty Dedrick,

tenor saxophonist Hammon Russum, and Thornhill were the main soloists. There are some decent vocals, but it is the moody instrumentals that stand out, including "Hungarian Dance No. 5," "Traumerei," "Portrait of a Guinea Farm," "Where or When," and "Snowfall." **Autumn Nocturne** (Hep 1060) has the next 24 numbers, including the title cut, "Somebody Nobody Loves," and Gil Evans's arrangement of "Somebody Else Is Taking My Place." **Buster's Last Stand** (Hep 1074) wraps up this three-CD series with some rare items plus the title cut, two versions of "Lullaby of the Rain," "There's a Small Hotel," "I Don't Know Why," and a surprisingly hot version of "Stealing Apples."

Paul Whiteman   As the swing era continued on, Paul Whiteman's importance gradually declined. He was never quite sure what to do about swing, and his classical/jazz fusion of the 1920s was considered out of date. Jack Teagarden departed in January 1939 to form his own orchestra, but Whiteman continued working for a time, appearing often on the radio. In 1939, small units out of his orchestra recorded as Paul Whiteman's Bouncing Brass (four trumpets, three trombones, two guitars, and drums), his Sax Soctette (eight woodwinds, guitar, bass, and drums), and his Swing Wing (a jazz nonet that was dominated by the Four Modernaires). Among his sidemen that year were Charlie Teagarden, Miff Mole, and George Wettling, but all of those Decca recordings are long out of print and little of any value was recorded by Whiteman during 1940–41.

TIMELINE 1941

Harry James's version of "You Made Me Love You" catapults his band to the top of the swing world. • Both Charlie Christian and Jimmy Blanton are stricken with tuberculosis. • Stan Kenton's Orchestra plays at the Rendezvous Ballroom in Balboa Beach during the summer. • Ella Fitzgerald breaks up her big band and begins her solo career. • Mario Bauza joins Machito's Afro-Cubans. • A car crash cuts short the life of Chu Berry. • British trumpet and vocal star Nat Gonella joins the army, playing in service bands for the next four years. • Jelly Roll Morton dies. • Trombonist/guitarist/arranger Eddie Durham begins a two-year period as the musical director for the all-female International Sweethearts of Rhythm. • Drummer Chico Hamilton makes his recording debut with Slim Gaillard. • The first great jazz harpist Caspar Reardon dies at the age of 33. • Pianist Donald Lambert strides his way through four classical themes (including "Anitra's Dance" and "Pilgrim's Chorus") during the only studio session of his career. • Another stride pianist, Lucky Roberts, has his song "Ripples of the Nile" changed into the Glenn Miller hit "Moonlight Cocktail." • Zutty Singleton begins a two-year stint leading the Dixieland group at Ryan's. • Eddie Safranski joins Hal McIntyre's Orchestra, soon becoming one of the top bassists in jazz. • Miles Davis at 15 begins playing with Eddie Randall's Blue Devils. • The attack on Pearl Harbor makes many big band leaders consider enlisting in the military.

The Complete Capitol Recordings (Capitol 30103) serves as a perfect end to the active career of the "King of Jazz." There are eight selections from June 1942, including some worthwhile swing (Jimmy Mundy contributed two arrangements) and guest appearances by Billie Holiday (on "Trav'lin' Light") and the vocal duo of Jack Teagarden and Johnny Mercer (for Hoagy Carmichael's "The Old Music Master"). There are also 1951 versions of "Rhapsody in Blue" and "An American in Paris" and, most intriguing, 1945 versions of "San" and "Wang Wang Blues" that are in the style of the early 1920s band. In fact, five of the seven musicians who were on the 1920 rendition of "Wang Wang Blues" reprised their original roles: trombonist Buster Johnson, clarinetist Gus Mueller, pianist Ferdie Grofe, banjoist Mike Pingitore, and drummer Harold MacDonald. Although there would be a few later celebrations, this 25th anniversary recording essentially ended the Paul Whiteman story.

Cootie Williams   When Cootie Williams left the Duke Ellington Orchestra in 1940, it was considered major news in the swing world. He had been one of Duke's most important soloists for 11 years, but decided to accept a lucrative offer to join Benny Goodman for a year. While with BG, Cootie had to suffer through the indignities of being a black player with a white band, but he was one of the stars with the orchestra and jammed next to Georgie Auld and Charlie Christian in the Benny Goodman Sextet. When his year was up, he asked Ellington for his old job back, but Duke, already having Ray Nance in Cootie's former spot, convinced him that it would make more sense for him to form his own big band. The Savoy Ballroom became the trumpeter's home base for the next five years.

1941–1944 (Classics 827) starts off with a septet set in which Cootie Williams leads a group mostly taken from the Goodman band (except for Jo Jones) through four songs. The remainder of the disc features his underrated orchestra. There are two selections from 1942, including the first version ever of Thelonious Monk's "Epistrophy." At the time, Cootie's big band included trumpeter Joe Guy, trombonist Sandy Williams, Eddie Cleanhead Vinson on alto and vocals, and pianist Ken Kersey. Jumping to 1944, Williams is heard on eight numbers with a very interesting sextet taken from his big band that includes Vinson, tenor saxophonist Eddie "Lockjaw" Davis, and (on his first recordings) pianist

Bud Powell. In addition, the big band backs the vocals of Vinson (including "Cherry Red Blues") and Pearl Bailey. Of the big band selections from later in the year, "Air Mail Special" is quite heated and Monk's "Round Midnight" receives its debut. The short spots of Powell look toward the future, as do the R&B-ish solos of tenor saxophonist Sam "The Man" Taylor. But because these recordings were made for the tiny Hit/Majestic label, they were little noticed at the time, and the Cootie Williams Big Band was only known on a regional basis.

Bob Zurke   Bob Zurke should have been a star. A very talented stride pianist, he was a child prodigy who played with Oliver Naylor's orchestra in 1925 when he was just 13. Zurke recorded with Thelma Terry's Playboys in 1928 and worked around his native Detroit for years. When Joe Sullivan was stricken with tuberculosis in 1937, Zurke took his place with the Bob Crosby Orchestra, staying for two and a half years and helping to make Sullivan's "Little Rock Getaway" famous.

In 1939, Zurke formed a big band that during a ten-month period recorded 30 selections, 28 of which (all but two vocals) are on **Honky Tonk Train Blues** (Hep 1076). Although four veterans from the 1920s were in the band (trumpeters Chelsea Quealey and Sterling Bose, tenor saxophonist Larry Binyon, and drummer Stan King), Zurke was its only significant soloist. Despite some excellent recordings (including "Southern Exposure," "Hobson Street Blues," "Honky Tonk Train Blues," "I've Found a New Baby," and a classic rendition of "Tea for Two"), the Bob Zurke Orchestra only lasted a year before breaking up. Zurke mostly worked as a solo pianist for a few years, based at times in Chicago, Detroit, and Los Angeles. He died on February 16, 1944, from a heart attack when he was only 32. Bob Zurke's early death resulted in him merely being a footnote in jazz history, an unfair fate for such a strong talent.

The "From Spirituals to Swing" Concerts

In the 1930s, John Hammond pursued several dreams. He wanted jazz to be documented properly, so he produced sessions as early as 1933. He was a fierce proponent of integration, so whenever possible he recorded integrated groups and persuaded white musicians (most notably Benny Goodman) to use blacks. And he loved creative swing, early jazz, blues, and spirituals, so he presented two major all-star concerts at Carnegie Hall, which were called "From Spirituals to Swing." The December 23, 1938, event (11 months after Benny Goodman's famous Carnegie Hall concert) featured the Count Basie Orchestra, Hot Lips Page (playing "Blues with Lips" with Basie), a small group out of the Basie band (the Kansas City Five), Helen Humes, Jimmy Rushing, Sister Rosetta Tharpe, Mitchell's Christian Singers, the New Orleans Feetwarmers (with Sidney Bechet and Tommy Ladnier), Big Bill Broonzy, Sonny Terry, and James P. Johnson. Most notable was the combination of a boogie-woogie trio of Albert Ammons, Pete Johnson, and Meade Lux Lewis with singer Big Joe Turner, all of whom suddenly had major careers due to this concert. The December 24, 1939, event featured the Golden Gate Quartet, the Benny Goodman Sextet (with Charlie Christian and Lionel Hampton), James P. Johnson, Ida Cox, Big Bill Broonzy, Sonny Terry, the Count Basie Orchestra, Charlie Christian sitting in with the Kansas City Six, and a closing jam session on "Lady Be Good." The three-CD set ❶ **From Spirituals to Swing** (Vanguard 169/71) is a greatly expanded version of the earlier two-LP set and contains all of the existing music from these significant concerts, some of which is quite unique.

Boogie-Woogie

Boogie-woogie (playing an eight-note pattern to a blues) was at the height of its popularity when John Hammond presented Albert Ammons, Pete Johnson, and Meade Lux Lewis playing together as the Boogie-Woogie Trio at the 1938 "From Spirituals to Swing" concert. During the next few years the three pianists would work steadily (often at New York's Café Society), sometimes as a trio or in various duets, but also as soloists.

The Boogie-Woogie Trio, Big Joe Turner, and Jimmy Yancey Meade Lux Lewis was initially best known of the three pianists due to his classic 1927 recording of "Honky Tonk Train Blues." Hammond had first recorded him in 1935, but Lewis's career became busier after the Carnegie Hall concert. He and Albert Ammons were recorded by Alfred Lion on the very first session for the new Blue Note label on January 6, 1939. All of that music has been reissued as **The First Day** (Blue Note 98450), consisting of seven Lewis solos, nine by Ammons, and two exciting piano duets. Lewis's **1939–1941** (Classics 743) and the previously reviewed **1927–1939** (Classics 722) also contain Lewis's portion of

that day. In addition, **1939–1941** has a variety of other Lewis solos (including "Nineteen Ways of Playing a Chorus"). **1941–1944** (Classics 841) has rarities from the Asch label along with some Blue Notes; among the highpoints are "Yancey's Pride," "Lux's Boogie," and "Chicago Flyer."

Ammons, who was arguably the most powerful of the three pianists, had been leading groups since 1936. **1936–1939** (Classics 715) includes his contributions to the debut Blue Note session along with his earlier dates. **1939–1946** (Classics 927) has other solos from 1939, 1944, and 1946, two songs from 1945 in which Ammons backs veteran blues singer Sippie Wallace (her first session since the late 1920s), and a heated small-group date for Commodore from 1944 with Hot Lips Page and Don Byas. Also of strong interest is **Boogie Woogie Stomp** (Delmark 705), a grab bag of mostly live performances from the Hotel Sherman in 1939 with nine Ammons solos, six from Lewis, two by Johnson, and a lone Ammons-Lewis duet.

Until December 1938, Pete Johnson and singer Big Joe Turner had never recorded. Johnson started his career as a drummer in his native Kansas City, working professionally during 1922–26. He did not become a full-time pianist until 1926 when he was already 22. Johnson worked steadily in Kansas City and was part of the city's legendary late night jam sessions, often teaming up with Turner, who initially worked as a singing bartender. Big Joe, who had the ability to turn everything into the blues (even some unlikely standards), had a very accessible style that made him a popular attraction first locally and eventually on an international scale.

Pete Johnson's ❶ **1938–1939** (Classics 656) is the pianist's definitive release. He is heard on two classic numbers with Turner (the original versions of "Goin' Away Blues" and "Roll 'Em Pete"), jamming with Harry James ("Boo Woo" and "Home James"), with his Boogie Woogie Boys (a sextet that includes Turner and Hot Lips Page), interacting with Albert Ammons and Meade Lux Lewis (who join Turner on "Café Society Rag"), and on a pair of trio numbers. Rarest are Johnson's ten unaccompanied piano solos, which were mostly released previously by the tiny Solo Art label. **1939–1941** (Classics 665) has Johnson leading a jamming Kansas City group on "627 Stomp," dueting with Ammons, heading a later trio date, and taking some more piano solos.

All of Big Joe Turner's early recordings (except for the two Pete Johnson numbers) are on **I've Been to Kansas**

City (MCA/Decca 42351) and **Every Day in the Week** (GRP/Decca 621). The former has dates with either Willie "The Lion" Smith or Sammy Price on piano plus a session led by Art Tatum. Highlights include "Piney Brown Blues," "Wee Baby Blues," "Corrine, Corrina," and "Nobody in Mind." **Every Day in the Week** finishes up the Deccas (with Freddie Slack, Pete Johnson, or Fred Skinner on piano), includes some alternate takes and has five later numbers from 1964 and 1967; the more memorable selections overall include "Rocks in My Bed," "Goin' to Chicago," and "Blues in the Night." For those listeners who just want Turner's dates from this period (leaving off the Tatum session, the alternates, and the later tracks), **1941–1946** (Classics 940) should suffice.

Although he did not receive the fame of Albert Ammons, Pete Johnson, and Meade Lux Lewis or record at all before 1939, Jimmy Yancey was a father figure of the boogie-woogie movement. His gentle, subtle style was heard at its best on slower tempos, although he could romp too. Yancey had the humorous habit of ending every song in E flat (no matter what key the rest of the song was in), resulting in some abrupt and occasionally hilarious endings! Born in 1894, by 1900 he was performing in vaudeville as a singer and tap dancer, and by 1915 was working professionally as a pianist. However, Yancey's day job during 1925–51 was as a groundskeeper at Comiskey Park for the Chicago White Sox. He finally made it to records in 1939, recording on eight occasions during the next 12 years. Seven of those sessions (six from 1939–40 and 1943 and a date in 1950) are on a trio of CDs. ◉ **Complete Recorded Works Vol. 1** (Document 5041) has such solos as "The Fives," "South Side Stuff," "Yancey's Getaway," "Yancey Stomp," and "State Street Special." **Vol. 2** (Document 5042) is highlighted by "Bear Trap Blues," "Death Letter Blues," "Yancey's Bugle Call," a version of "How Long Blues" that has Yancey switching to harmonium behind his wife Mama Yancey's singing, and the pianist's only four recorded vocals. **Vol. 3** (Document 5043) includes a couple more Mama Yancey vocals and such numbers as "White Sox Stomp," "Yancey Special," and two versions of "Pallet on the Floor." This CD concludes with the only four numbers that Jimmy's older brother, the more ragtime-oriented pianist Alonzo Yancey, ever recorded. Blues and early jazz pianist collectors will definitely want all three of these valuable CDs, which help show where boogie-woogie came from.

Five Major Swing Combos

While most of the most significant groups of the 1939–44 period were big bands, there were some exceptions. In fact by 1944, combos were becoming much more common due to their lower expense and the growing popularity of small jazz clubs.

The John Kirby Sextet   One of the most unusual small groups was the John Kirby Sextet. Kirby, the only bassist to be a successful bandleader during the era, originally doubled on tuba in the late 1920s. He worked with Bill Brown's Brownies (1928–30), the Fletcher Henderson Orchestra (1930–33), Chick Webb (1933–35), back with Henderson (1935–36), and the Mills Blue Rhythm Band (1936–37). A supportive player who occasionally took brief solo breaks, Kirby developed his concept for his sextet during 11 months (1937–38) when he led a group at the Onyx Club in NYC.

For a time Kirby's sextet included trumpeter Frankie Newton and altoist Pete Brown. But neither quite fit the bassist's concept, and by the time the group had its first recording session on October 28, 1938, both had been replaced. Twenty-one-year-old Charlie Shavers was the perfect choice on trumpet because he was flexible. An underrated arranger/composer (who contributed a standard in "Undecided"), Shavers was willing to play quiet muted solos even though he would in time gain a reputation for being an explosive player with very impressive technique. Shavers worked with Frankie Fairfax's band in Philadelphia (1935), Tiny Bradshaw, and the Mills Blue Rhythm Band (1937) before joining Kirby.

Clarinetist Buster Bailey, who was 36, had been a major player since at least 1924, the year that he left King Oliver's Creole Jazz Band to start the first of his three stints with Fletcher Henderson (1924–28, 1934, and 1936–37). Adding to the Kirby Sextet's unusual ensemble was altoist Russell Procope. Procope had been a journeyman for a decade, playing alto and clarinet with Jelly Roll Morton (1928), Benny Carter (1929), Chick Webb (1929–31), Fletcher Henderson (1931–34), Tiny Bradshaw (1934–35), Teddy Hill (1936–37), and Willie Bryant. As with Shavers and Bailey, Procope's technique was admirable and his tone became an indispensable part of the group's sound. Billy Kyle's light touch on the piano was also a strong asset. He had been a member of the Mills Blue Rhythm Band (1936–38). O'Neill Spencer, like Connie Kay two decades later with the Modern Jazz Quartet, was almost as much a percussionist as a drummer, adding color to the group and playing with great subtlety. As did Kirby, Shavers, and Kyle, Spencer spent time as a member of the Mills Blue Rhythm Band (1931–36).

All of the studio recordings by the John Kirby Sextet have been reissued on four Classics CDs, three of which fit this time period. ● **1938–1939** (Classics 750) shows that the band started out very strong, with such songs as "Rehearsin' for a Nervous Breakdown," "From A Flat to C," the original rendition of "Undecided," the atmospheric "Dawn on the Desert," "Anitra's Dance," "Royal Garden Blues," "Rose Room," and "Nocturne." Kirby's love for classical music is constantly displayed in the light swing versions of classical melodies. The band's distinctive sound points toward cool jazz of the 1950s. The rhythm section could swing hard when called upon, and each of the soloists sounds quite individual. The performances are tightly arranged, with solos being concise and purposeful, and the advanced voicings justify the group being billed during the period as "the biggest little band in the world." **1939–1941** (Classics 770) is as worthy as the earlier CD, highlighted by "Humoresque," "Jumpin' in the Pump Room," "Sextet from Lucia," "Zoomin' at the Zombie," and "Beethoven Riffs On."

Of related interest is Buster Bailey's **1925–1940** (Classics 904), which has all of the clarinetist's dates as a leader prior to the 1950s. There are two rather scratchy trio sides from 1925 and a pair of numbers apiece with Fletcher Henderson's sidemen in 1934 (including "Shanghai Shuffle") and singer Jerry Kruger in 1937. Otherwise, Bailey is featured with early overlapping versions of Kirby's group (some with Frankie Newton and Pete Brown) and on a couple of sessions from 1940 (four numbers with Kirby's sextet and a date with a similar lineup except, including Benny Carter). Bailey really lets loose on the demented "Man with a Horn Goes Berserk" and is heard in top form on "Dizzy Debutante," "The Blue Room," and "Pine Top's Boogie Woogie."

All of Billy Kyle's dates as a leader are on **1937–1938** (Classics 919) and **1939–1946** (Classics 941). **1937–1938** has Kyle heading a group that includes Shavers, Tab Smith, and (on two vocals apiece) the Palmer Brothers and Leon Lafeel. In addition, he is heard as part of the Spencer Trio (the only date led by O'Neill Spencer), with Timme Rosenkrantz's Barrelhouse Barons (featuring Rex Stewart and Don Byas) and backing calypso singer Jack Sneed. **1939–1946** has Kyle in 1939 playing with a couple of

organ groups (with vocals by Spencer), performing two additional numbers with Sneed, and with an augmented version of Kirby's Sextet that includes Benny Carter and British trumpeter/singer Nat Gonella. In addition, there are some later titles with a quartet, and in 1946, with an octet that includes Trummy Young and Buster Bailey.

During the period when Kirby's **1941–1943** (Classics 792) was recorded, there were some unfortunate changes in the personnel of the John Kirby Sextet. After the July 25, 1941, session, Spencer left the band due to being stricken with tuberculosis. He rejoined the group for a time during 1942–43, but had to drop out again and died in 1944 when he was just 34. His place was taken originally by Specs Powell and eventually by Bill Beason, who had earlier succeeded Chick Webb in Webb's big band after that drummer passed away. By 1943, Procope and Kyle were in the army so their places were taken by altoist George Johnson and pianist Clyde Hart. Despite that, the Kirby group's sound stayed essentially the same. **1941–1943**, which includes nine V-disc performances along with the group's regular Victor recordings, is highlighted by "Coquette," "Close Shave," "Bugler's Dilemma," "Night Whispers," and "St. Louis Blues," the latter a display of Buster Bailey's circular breathing. Kirby's excellent radio transcriptions are slated to be reissued in full on three CDs. Thus far **Vol. 1** (Jazz Unlimited 2047), which covers 1941, and **Vol. 2** (Jazz Unlimited 2052), from 1941 and 1943, are available and are up to the high standard of the regular studio sessions.

Charlie Shavers was absent (replaced at first by an unidentified trumpeter) at the time of the final selection ("Can't We Be Friends") on **1941–1943**. He left Kirby to join Raymond Scott's CBS Orchestra and he recorded frequently as a freelancer in 1944, no longer having to keep a mute on his trumpet. Shavers' **1944–1945** (Classics 944) features the trumpeter not only holding his own with such major players as Coleman Hawkins, Tab Smith, Earl Hines, Teddy Wilson, and Buddy DeFranco, but starring on virtually every selection in exciting fashion. His decision to leave Kirby's sextet doomed that band although that was not obvious to the bassist, who kept on dreaming of further success for his sextet.

The King Cole Trio While the John Kirby Sextet stood alone and was not influential (no other groups coming up chose to imitate Kirby's), Nat King Cole's band led to the popularity of other piano/guitar/bass trios.

Nat Cole (born Nathaniel Coles) was born in Montgomery, Alabama, but grew up in Chicago. At 12, Cole was playing organ and singing in church, soon switching to piano. He made his recording debut in 1936 with his brother, bassist Eddie Cole, and Eddie's band, the Solid Swingers. Nat's two other brothers, pianist Ike and pianist/singer Freddie Cole, both emerged as fine players many years later. Nat led the band for the revival of the *Shuffle Along* revue, and when it broke up in Los Angeles, he settled in that area. In September 1937, he formed the King Cole Trio with guitarist Oscar Moore and bassist Wesley Prince. In October 1938, the group first recorded the beginning of an extensive series of radio transcriptions. The four-CD set **The Complete Early Transcriptions** (Vintage Jazz Classics 1026-29) covers the years 1938–41. Cole, whose main inspiration on piano was Earl Hines (although his own percussive left hand was a bit more predictable), was on his way to being one of the most appealing swing pianists of the 1940s. The 102 performances on the Vintage Jazz Classics set have the interplay between the musicians that one associates with the King Cole Trio, but differs from their later performances in that the emphasis is much more on group singing than on Cole's solo vocals, and the group is sometimes heard backing the vocals of others, including Bonnie Lake, Juanelda Carter, Pauline Byrns, and the Dreamers. **The King Cole Trio 1938–39** (Savoy 1205) does not duplicate the Vintage Jazz Classics set at all and it has the group's earliest studio recordings, four selections apiece from January 14 and December 1939 that were originally released on the tiny Ammor and Davis & Schwegler labels. In addition, there are 12 radio transcriptions, four of which have vocals by Maxine Johnson.

On December 6, 1940, the King Cole Trio recorded the first of its 16 studio recordings for Decca. **Hit that Jive Jack** (GRP/Decca 42350) has all of those performances plus Cole's 1936 recording debut with his brother's group. "Sweet Lorraine," Nat's first solo vocal, was a minor hit and helped the trio become popular beyond Los Angeles. Other highlights are "Honeysuckle Rose," "Early Morning Blues," "This Will Make You Laugh," "I Like to Riff," and the catchy "Hit that Jive Jack."

Several other sets have been released that feature the King Cole Trio on radio transcriptions from the first half of the 1940s. **The MacGregor Years, 1941/45** (Music & Arts 911), a four-CD set, has 120 selections that form

the bulk of Cole's transcriptions from 1941 and 1944–45. Although the programming would have been improved if it was strictly in chronological order, the music is excellent. The trio is featured as a unit as an accompanying group to singers Anta Boyer (on 33 cuts), Ida James (15 songs), Anita O'Day, and the Barrie Sisters (five songs apiece for the latter two). Of particular interest are two six-song instrumental medleys that put the emphasis on Cole's piano playing. **The Nat King Cole Trio Recordings** (Laserlight 15 915) is a five-CD set, although the music could have actually fit on three discs. Some of the performances duplicate the Music & Arts reissue, but there are also six numbers from 1940 and a few songs performed on the Dorsey Brothers TV show and on Cole's own television series in 1956. **WWII Transcriptions** (Music & Arts 808) only duplicates the Laserlight set slightly and not the larger Music & Arts box at all. This single disc has 30 broadcast transcriptions by the Trio, mostly from 1944. Anita O'Day and Ida James are heard on two songs apiece and the Trio sings four songs, but otherwise the swinging material is instrumental. Fans of the King Cole Trio have plenty to choose from!

In 1943, as soon as the recording strike ended, Nat King Cole began an association with the Capitol label that would last until his death. The Mosaic label put out an incredible 18-CD set, **The Complete Capitol Trio Recordings** (Mosaic 18-138), that not only has all of the King Cole Trio's recordings for Capitol during 1943–49, but scores of previously unavailable radio transcriptions owned by Capitol plus all of Cole's post-1949 recordings that at least have the presence of the trio. Unfortunately, that box has gone out of print so one has to adopt a more piecemeal approach to acquiring the better Cole Capitol sides. Best is ● **Jumpin' at Capitol** (Rhino 71009), a definitive single-disc sampler that features the King Cole Trio, mostly from 1943–47. With Oscar Moore and Johnny Miller (who took Wesley Prince's place on bass after Prince was drafted in 1942), Cole is heard in prime form on such numbers as "Straighten Up and Fly Right," a remake of "Sweet Lorraine," "It's Only a Paper Moon," "The Frim Fram Sauce," "For Sentimental Reasons," "Come to Baby, Do," and the original version of Bobby Troup's "Route 66."

The Art Tatum Trio The remarkable Art Tatum mostly played solo piano up to 1944. Tatum can be heard creating unaccompanied explorations on **Solos** (MCA/Decca

42327), which has 15 performances (plus an alternate take) from 1940, including "Humoresque," "Get Happy," "Indiana," and a remake of "Tiger Rag." The two-CD set **The Standard Transcriptions** (Music & Arts 673) consists of 61 mostly very concise piano solos (eight performances are under two minutes in length and only three are over three minutes) with Tatum making the most of every moment; **Standards** (Black Lion 760143) has 24 of those selections on a single disc. In addition, **California Melodies** (Memphis Archives 7007) includes some rare radio appearances by Tatum from 1940.

Art Tatum was a gigantic talent, but he was not perfect. In time, Tatum was criticized in a variety of ways by writers who had initially exhausted all of their favorable adjectives on him. Some of his strengths were suddenly viewed as weaknesses. His detractors claimed that he played too many notes (never mind that no one else could come close to what he was playing), that he worked out some of his solos in advance (some of which became miraculous set pieces), and that he could not play with other musicians. The truth of the latter was actually the opposite, for musicians tended to be afraid to play with Tatum rather than the other way around. What more could other musicians add after Tatum went into one of his blindingly fast runs?

I Got Rhythm (GRP/Decca 630) actually features Tatum sounding quite comfortable playing with other musicians. In addition to three piano solos from 1939, Tatum is heard with a mostly unidentified band in 1935 playing "Take Me Back to My Boots and Saddle," leading a sextet in 1937, and jamming with trumpeter Joe Thomas and Edmond Hall on two numbers from 1940. The bulk of this CD features his 1944 trio (inspired by the King Cole Trio) with guitarist Tiny Grimes and bassist Slam Stewart, including "I Got Rhythm," "Liza," and "Honeysuckle Rose." **1944** (Classics 825) has further material by Tatum's trio (originally recorded for Dial and Asch) plus six typically remarkable piano solos. The interplay between Tatum and Grimes (who sounds a bit heroic trying to keep up with the pianist) is exciting; among the tunes that they explore is "I Know that You Know," "Flying Home," and "Dark Eyes."

The first regular band that Tatum ever led, the 1943–45 trio, was quite popular, playing regularly on 52nd Street. Unlike Cole's group, which started out with guitarist Oscar Moore being a near-equal of Cole's, Tiny

Grimes would never have been crazy enough to think of himself as Tatum's equal. Twenty-seven at the time, Grimes was one of the best of the guitarists to emerge right after Charlie Christian, his main influence. Grimes had an open-minded style (featuring Charlie Parker as a sideman on his first date as a leader) and was an advanced swing guitarist open to the new R&B music that was emerging. Slam Stewart had been with Slim Gaillard, but was free after Gaillard went in the army in 1943. His bowed solos, which he sang along with, added wit to the trio's colorful music.

Fats Waller and His Rhythm   Ever since he began his string of Victor recordings in 1934, Fats Waller was a major commercial success. As a pianist, vocalist, and personality, Waller was one of the most popular of all jazz musicians. He began 1939 leading the most famous version of His Rhythm, a sextet with trumpeter Herman Autrey, Gene Sedric on tenor and clarinet, guitarist Al Casey, bassist Cedric Wallace, and drummer Slick Jones. John Hamilton took over for Autrey starting in the summer of 1939 (Autrey returned for a bit in late 1941) and Arthur Trappier succeeded Jones near the end of 1941, but otherwise the personnel stayed mostly the same into the summer of 1942. During this period Waller continued his very busy schedule of nightclub appearances, recordings for Victor, radio shows, and nonstop partying. He visited England shortly before World War II began, composing and recording his six-part "London Suite." His recordings during this era alternated between treasures and trash. The latter includes such odd numbers as "Fat and Greasy," "Little Curly Hair in a High Chair," "You're a Square from Delaware," "Eep, Ipe, Wanna Piece of Pie," "My Mommie Sent Me to the Store," "Abercrombie Had a Zombie," "Come Down to Earth, My Angel," and other weak songs that Waller could barely save through his satire and humor. But on the brighter side are the rambunctious "Hold Tight," "Your Feet's Too Big," "Fats Waller's Original E Flat Blues," and "The Jitterbug Waltz." The latter, which was recorded in 1942, was one of the first memorable jazz waltzes.

The Complete Associated Transcription Sessions (Storyville 203 2076), a two-CD set, has Waller's radio transcriptions. The first disc has 31 selections from March 11, 1935, all of which are solos except for a couple of songs that add Rudy Powell on reeds. Waller backs his own vocals and provides commentary that introduces most of the tunes. The second disc consists of 16 numbers from August 7, 1939, with Waller's Rhythm, five piano solos, and an unissued excerpt from an organ solo cut the same day. These add to Waller's very strong musical legacy. **The Middle Years, Part 2** (Bluebird 66552), a three-CD set, has his studio recordings from April 12, 1938, through January 12, 1940, including "Hold Tight," "Your Feet's Too Big," "Two Sleepy People," "Yacht Club Swing," and "I'll Dance at Your Wedding." ❍ **The Last Years** (Bluebird 9883), also a three-CD set, consists of Waller's last Victor recordings (from April 11, 1940, to January 23, 1943), with the usual irresistible combination of gems and humorous nonsense. Although all of the Bluebird Waller sets are recommended and contain many memorable moments, **The Last Years** (which includes "The Jitterbug Waltz") is the perfect place to start in exploring Waller's joyful brand of music.

In 1943, Fats Waller appeared in the best of his three movies (*Stormy Weather*, in which he is seen in a nightclub scene playing "Ain't Misbehavin'") and wrote the music for the show *Early to Bed*. But all of the partying, excessive liquor, and overeating finally took its toll. On a train trip traveling from Los Angeles to New York, he caught pneumonia and passed away on December 14, 1943, outside of Kansas City at the age of 39. Even 60 years later, there has never been anyone quite like Fats Waller.

The Eddie Heywood Sextet   Eddie Heywood, Jr., the son of Eddie Heywood, Sr. (a fine pianist in the 1920s who had accompanied the vaudeville vocal duo Butterbeans & Susie), took piano lessons from his father when he was eight. Six years later he was playing professionally in Atlanta. After moving to New York in 1937, Heywood freelanced, working with the Benny Carter Orchestra (1939–40), Zutty Singleton's trio, Don Redman, and Billie Holiday, in addition to appearing on Coleman Hawkins's "The Man I Love" recording session in late 1943. In 1941, he started playing with his own sextet. By 1944, the Heywood group had caught on, having a hit in "Begin the Beguine." Originally the sextet had a frontline of trumpeter Doc Cheatham, trombonist Vic Dickenson, and altoist Lem Davis, featuring tightly arranged ensembles, a lightly swinging rhythm section, and its leader's distinctive piano. **1944** (Classics 947) has the band's Commodore recordings and its first selections for Decca. In addition, this CD features Heywood in a very different combo session with Ray Nance and Don Byas, and as part of a trio with Johnny Hodges and drummer Shelly Manne. In listening to the recordings of the Eddie Heywood Sextet, there are times when one wishes that the musicians would cut loose from the charts, but in general the conservative music is pleasing, and it is easy to understand why its records were popular for a time.

Other Swing Stars

In addition to all of the musicians already discussed in this chapter are quite a few others who, though occasionally leading their own bands, were most notable for their distinctive solo styles.

Teddy Wilson   Teddy Wilson, like Gene Krupa, Harry James, and Lionel Hampton, left Benny Goodman's employment to start a big band. But unlike the other three, Wilson's outfit only lasted a year and failed to make much of an impact. Wilson was too dignified a player and laidback a leader to have success in the big band world. In June 1940, he formed a sextet that lasted through 1944, working and recording steadily in New York while continuing to be the definitive swing pianist.

Wilson led all-star swing dates during 1935–42 and all have been reissued by the Classics series, but unfortunately these include his many sessions with Billie Holiday, which are duplicated in Lady Day's reissue programs. There are some piano solos, instrumentals, and sessions with other singers included on **1934–1935** (Classics 508), **1935–1936** (Classics 511), **1936–1937** (Classics 5210), **1937** (Classics 531), **1937–1938** (Classics 548), and **1938** (Classics 556), but the Holiday dates dominate, making these discs of lesser interest due to the duplication.

1939 (Classics 571) is more valuable. In addition to Holiday's last date under Wilson's leadership (resulting in a classic version of "Sugar" with Roy Eldridge and Benny Carter), there are some fine piano solos and the first dozen recordings by the Teddy Wilson Big Band. The orchestra had such fine players as Ben Webster, trumpeter Shorty Baker, and guitarist Al Casey (on leave from Fats Waller) plus singers Thelma Carpenter and Jean Eldridge. **1939–1941** (Classics 620) has the band's final eight songs, more piano trios, and combo dates by Wilson with vocals from Helen Ward and Lena Horne. For listeners who wish to have all of the studio recordings by the Wilson Orchestra on one CD, **Jumpin'**

for Joy (Hep 1064) is recommended, as it has their 20 numbers plus an octet date with Bill Coleman and Helen Ward. For additional material from the era, **Teddy Wilson, His Piano & His Orchestra** (Jazz Unlimited 2068) has ten piano solos from 1938–39 plus a radio transcription date by the Wilson big band.

The 26 concise selections on **Solo Piano** (Storyville 8258), radio transcriptions from 1939–40, were not released until this 1997 CD; a dozen of the songs are obscure Wilson originals. **Associated Transcriptions, 1944** (Storyville 8236) has Wilson's 1944 sextet, which was comprised of trumpeter Emmett Berry, trombonist Benny Morton, clarinetist Edmond Hall (who came into his own during this period), Slam Stewart, and Big Sid Catlett. The set of high-quality swing allows the group to stretch out (some of the songs are almost five minutes long) and shows what Wilson's band of the era sounded like. Also of interest is **Central Avenue Blues** (Vintage Jazz Classics 1013), which includes the pianist's V-disc recordings and some of his work in a sextet with Red Norvo and Charlie Shavers.

Hot Lips Page   An exciting swing trumpeter who was expert at coming up with riffs at jam sessions, and an exuberant blues vocalist, Oran "Hot Lips" Page was a popular figure in the 1940s even if he never quite became a star. Page started playing trumpet in 1920 when he was 12 in his native Dallas. After graduating from high school, he worked behind a variety of blues singers (including Ma Rainey, Bessie Smith, and Ida Cox), and with territory bands. In 1928, he joined Walter Page's Blue Devils in Kansas City and spent 1931–35 playing with the Bennie Moten Orchestra. Page was with the Count Basie Orchestra in 1936 before being discovered and signed by manager Joe Glaser and moving to New York. He led a big band during 1937–38 that did not catch on, led small combos for a few years and was featured with Artie Shaw's Orchestra during 1941–42. Hot Lips was a fixture on 52nd Street and at late-night jam sessions for years.

1938–1940 (Classics 561) has his big band's dozen recordings. Page's orchestra featured tenor saxophonist Benny Waters and clarinetist Ben Smith, and its selections include such swinging tunes as "Jumpin'," "Feelin' High and Happy," and "Skull Duggery," but the band did not last long. This CD also has four small-group sessions with the key sidemen, including Don Byas, Pete Johnson,

and altoist Don Stovall. **1940–1944** (Classics 809) has more combo gems, including "Rockin' at Ryan's," "Uncle Sam Blues," and "Pagin' Mr. Page," with Byas, Lucky Thompson, Earl Bostic, and Vic Dickenson in the supporting cast. **After Hours in Harlem** (High Note 7031) consists of private recordings (captured by Jerry Newman's disc recorder) of Page playing live at jam sessions in New York. Although the recording quality is sometimes shaky, there are some exciting moments by Hot Lips, including interesting trio numbers with pianist Donald Lambert and the hyper tenor of Herbie Fields, and two early appearances by pianist Thelonious Monk.

Frankie Newton and Pete Brown   Trumpeter Frankie Newton and altoist Pete Brown, who both worked with the early John Kirby Sextet in 1937 before being replaced, frequently played together in later years. Newton worked with Lloyd and Cecil Scott (1927), Elmer Snowden, Chick Webb, Charlie Johnson, Sam Wooding, Charlie Johnson (1933–35), Teddy Hill (1936–37), and Lucky Millinder's Blue Rhythm Band (1937–38). Newton had a lyrical style and a soft appealing tone. He led his own groups (usually with Brown on alto) during 1938–44. **1937–1939** (Classics 643) has all of the trumpeter's recordings as a leader, including "The Blues My Baby Gave to Me" (his personal favorite solo), "Please Don't Talk About Me When I'm Gone," "The Brittwood Stomp," a classic rendition of "Rosetta," and "The World Is Waiting for the Sunrise." Among the sidemen in addition to Brown are Edmond Hall, Cecil Scott (on clarinet and tenor), clarinetist Mezz Mezzrow, Dickie Wells, Slim Gaillard as a singer, and pianists James P. Johnson, Albert Ammons, and Ken Kersey.

Pete Brown had a distinctive sound on alto and an eccentric, but somewhat charming staccato jump style. A minor figure during the swing era, Brown often worked with combos on 52nd Street. **1942–1945** (Classics 1029) has most of the studio sessions that Brown led, with trumpeters Joe Thomas and Ed Lewis heard in supporting roles along with several swinging rhythm sections. **1944** (Progressive 7009) consists of nine songs cut during a radio transcription session in a quintet that often finds Jonah Jones stealing the show with his exciting trumpet solos. However, this is really an overly "complete" set, with four false starts, five incomplete attempts at songs, and eight full-length alternate takes, a CD only for true fanatics and completists.

Newton seemed to lose interest in playing after 1944 while Brown's style was soon considered dated. Neither ever advanced much beyond where they were in the early 1940s.

Coleman Hawkins After five years overseas in Europe, Coleman Hawkins moved back to the United States in the summer of 1939, just ahead of World War II. Being in Europe meant that his playing had been little heard by his contemporaries, so his return made many of the up-and-coming tenors curious as to how good Hawkins still was. At a series of jam sessions Hawk showed that, even though Lester Young could be considered an equal, he was still the king of tenors. His tone was as powerful as ever, he had smoothed out any rhythmic awkwardness that was still in his style in the early 1930s, and he had no difficulty keeping up younger players. In fact, he welcomed new innovations for harmonically he remained ahead of most musicians.

1939–1940 (Classics 634) starts out with Hawkins's first American session in five years, three routine numbers with a nonet, and one special feature, "Body and Soul." Barely referring to the melody at the beginning of his improvisation, Hawkins created a three-minute masterpiece that would be his signature song throughout the many years left in his career. Also on this disc are numbers with Benny Carter, an all-star group (resulting in memorable renditions of "When Day Is Done" and "The Sheik of Araby"), and the Coleman Hawkins Big Band. Hawk's orchestra, which only recorded four studio numbers, can be heard at greater length on **The Radio Years—1940** (Jazz Unlimited 201 2075). These broadcasts have spots for trumpeter Joe Guy, trombonist Sandy Williams, pianist Gene Rodgers, and Hawkins, but the best selection is actually a quartet rendition of "I Can't Believe that You're in Love with Me." The Coleman Hawkins Big Band broke up in November 1940 without much fanfare.

The great tenor was barely on records at all during 1941–42, but at the end of 1943 he began a three-year period filled with many significant recordings. ◉ **1943–1944** (Classics 807) has some remarkable music. Four selections match Hawkins in an all-star group arranged by Leonard Feather that includes Cootie Williams, Edmond Hall, Art Tatum, Al Casey, Oscar Pettiford, and Big Sid Catlett. The Hawkins-Tatum matchup was logical since Hawk had been one of the first to discover Tatum in the early 1930s. Hawkins is

also heard on four numbers with Bill Coleman in a septet, two songs with pianist Ellis Larkins in a quartet, and a quintet date with Roy Eldridge and Teddy Wilson. Best of all is the exciting session of December 23, 1943. Joined by Eddie Heywood, Oscar Pettiford, and drummer Shelly Manne, Hawkins follows a very good Heywood solo on "The Man I Love" with one of his greatest improvisations. Also on this date are creative renditions of "Crazy Rhythm" (which really romps), "Get Happy," and "Sweet Lorraine." Concluding this important disc are the three songs from February 16, 1944, the very first full-fledged bebop session.

Rainbow Mist (Delmark 459) contains the latter date plus the other three songs from six days later by a similar group. Hawkins loved to encourage younger musicians, and these sessions were originally supposed to feature trumpeter Dizzy Gillespie and altoist Charlie Parker. Parker could not make it, but with the assistance of Budd Johnson, Hawkins heads a 12-piece group that includes Gillespie, Leo Parker on alto, Don Byas, Budd Johnson on baritone, pianist Clyde Hart, bassist Oscar Pettiford, and drummer Max Roach. In addition to three ballad features for the leader (including "Rainbow Mist," which was based on "Body and Soul") the full group sounds quite beboppish on Dizzy's "Woody'n You," "Budee-daht," and Hawkins's "Disorder at the Border." Also on this CD is a meeting of Hawkins with Ben Webster, Georgie Auld, and Charlie Shavers on a session that includes the earliest version ever of Dizzy's "Salt Peanuts" (though it pales next to Dizzy's rendition), plus four numbers from the 1944 Georgie Auld big band.

◉ **1944** (Classics 842) has the second of Hawkins's early bop sessions, the "Salt Peanuts" date, two quartet sets with Teddy Wilson, and a very interesting date in which Hawkins is teamed with Don Byas, Harry Carney, and altoist Tab Smith in a septet. Best is "On the Sunny Side of the Street," which climaxes with a stunning cadenza by Smith that has him easily taking honors. **1944–1945** (Classics 863) finds Hawkins playing with a variety of top swing stars (including Charlie Shavers, Edmond Hall, Buck Clayton, and Teddy Wilson), but also leading a quartet on October 19, 1944, that was the recording debut for pianist Thelonious Monk.

During an 11-month period (December 1943–October 1944), Coleman Hawkins recorded so many gems that, if this had been his entire career, he would still be remembered today.

Ben Webster   With the premature death of Chu Berry, Ben Webster was Coleman Hawkins's top competitor among tough-toned tenors. Webster was one of the main stars of Duke Ellington's Orchestra during 1940–43 and when he departed (after brief stints with Raymond Scott's CBS Orchestra and the John Kirby Sextet), he led a series of small-groups, often on 52nd Street. Webster led his first record date in 1944 and most of **1944–1946** (Classics 1017) is from that year. Alternating between brash outbursts on uptempo tunes and purring during ballads, Webster teams up with Hot Lips Page in a quintet, leads quartets, and jams with fellow tenor Walter "Foots" Thomas. Highlights include "Teezol," "Horn," "I Surrender Dear," "Tea for Two," "Perdido," and "Honeysuckle Rose."

Don Byas   While Webster was already well known in 1940, Don Byas (three years his junior) was just beginning to gain some attention. As an altoist, Byas worked professionally as early as 1927, having stints with Bennie Moten, Walter Page's Blue Devils, and his own band, called Don Carlos and his Collegiate Ramblers. After switching to tenor in 1933, he played with Bert Johnson's Sharps and Flats, Lionel Hampton, Buck Clayton's Gentlemen of Harlem, Ethel Waters (1936–38), Don Redman, Lucky Millinder, and Andy Kirk (1939–40). Byas had a similar tone to Hawkins's, but was even more advanced harmonically .and able to play stunning double-time runs. He gained some recognition while with Count Basie (1941–43) where he was Lester Young's first permanent replacement. Byas, who loved to jam, often appeared at Minton's Playhouse in the early 1940s and he was caught playing at several jam sessions for **Midnight at Minton's** (High Note 7044). This set is better than most of the privately recorded jams of the period, and has Helen Humes taking fine vocals on "Stardust" and "Exactly Like You," with Byas sounding stunning on the former. In addition, there are four instrumentals with Joe Guy, and the young Thelonious Monk makes some appearances.

An advanced swing stylist, Byas's playing looked toward bop; in fact, he was a member of Dizzy Gillespie's early group on 52nd Street. Byas, who was heard at his best on a pair of duets with Slam Stewart at a Town Hall concert in 1944, has had his first dates as a leader reissued on ◉ **1944–1945** (Classics 882). Byas and Charlie Shavers make a perfect match on two heated sessions,

the tenor plays swing with trumpeter Joe Thomas and Johnny Guarnieri in a 1945 quintet and leads a quartet that, on four of its eight numbers, welcomes the great blues guitarist/singer Big Bill Broonzy. Among the more memorable numbers are "Riffin' and Jivin'," "Don's Idea," the two-part "Savoy Jam Party," "1944 Stomp," and "Jamboree Jump."

Lester Young   When Lester Young emerged with the Count Basie Orchestra, his sound was so different from all the other tenor saxophonists that it sounded as if he were playing a different instrument altogether. Instead of having a hard thick tone like Coleman Hawkins, Young's was very light. Instead of digging into the harmonic complexities of each chord, Young floated over bar lines and seemed to speak directly to listeners in a quiet thoughtful voice, relaxed even at the fastest tempos, cool rather than hot in temperament. Prior to working with Count Basie, Young played trumpet, violin, drums, and alto with his family (in the Young Family Band), settling on alto for a time. He switched to tenor when he worked with Art Bronson's Bostonians (1928–29), was a member of the post–Walter Page Original Blue Devils (1932–33), and had stints with Bennie Moten, King Oliver, and Basie (for the first time in 1934). Hired as Coleman Hawkins's first replacement with the Fletcher Henderson Orchestra, Young only lasted three months (no recordings resulted) because Henderson's sidemen did not care for Lester's radical style. After freelancing, in 1936 he rejoined Basie, this time staying for over four years and being a large part of Basie's great success. Influenced most by Frankie Trumbauer and Jimmy Dorsey, Young emerged fully formed on his first recording date with a quintet from Basie's band called the Jones-Smith Inc., taking a remarkable solo on "Lady Be Good." In addition to his work with Basie, Young played beautifully on many of Billie Holiday's finest recordings; he named her "Lady Day" and she in term called him "Pres."

In December 1940, for unknown reasons (possibly because he did not want to record on Friday the 13th), Young left the Basie band. Despite the recognition he had received, the next two years were mostly uneventful. He co-led a group with his younger brother, drummer Lee Young, worked with Al Sears's combo and made relatively few recordings. In October 1943, Young spontaneously rejoined Basie's orchestra and, although the recording strike kept this reunion from being fully documented, he led some classic dates of his own, can be heard on radio airchecks with the Basie band, and appeared in the Academy Award–winning short film *Jammin' the Blues.*

The Kansas City Sessions (Commodore 402) reissues three complete dates; 13 selections plus nine alternate takes. There are four numbers by the Kansas City Five from March 16, 1938, that are most notable for Eddie Durham's pioneering electric guitar solos, a year before Charlie Christian emerged. The group consists of Buck Clayton, Durham, Freddie Green (on acoustic rhythm guitar), Walter Page, and Jo Jones. Lester Young was added to the band (now known as the Kansas City Six) on September 28, 1938, and, in addition to his tenor solos, Young has a couple of rare spots on clarinet. On "I Want a Little Girl," he sounds eerily like altoist Paul Desmond would, 20 years later! Also on this CD is a different Kansas City Six from March 27, 1944, in which Young is teamed with Bill Coleman, Dickie Wells (at the peak of his powers), pianist Joe Bushkin, bassist John Simmons, and Jo Jones. This group swings hard, particularly on "Three Little Words" and three versions of "I Got Rhythm."

○ The Complete Lester Young on Keynote (Mercury 830920) features Pres at his very best. Half of the CD has him with the Kansas City Seven in 1944, teaming up with Buck Clayton, Dickie Wells, Count Basie, Freddie Green, bassist Rodney Richardson, and Jo Jones; his romp with the rhythm section on "Lester Leaps Again" is a highpoint. However, that fine date is overshadowed by the four numbers (plus four alternate takes) that Young performed with Johnny Guarnieri, Slam Stewart, and Sid Catlett on December 28, 1943. "I Never Knew" and "Afternoon of a Basie-ite" are both exciting jams and "Just You, Just Me" is superb, but it is "Sometimes I'm Happy" that is most memorable. Stewart's charming chorus is matched by an absolutely perfect solo by Pres that would often be quoted by other musicians.

Unfortunately, in the summer of 1944, the sensitive and introverted Lester Young was drafted and experienced a horrific year in the military that would affect his state of mind (although not initially his playing) for the remainder of his life.

Stuff Smith and Eddie South   While the violin never caught on as a major jazz instrument, in the early 1940s it had six major practitioners, all of whom were dealing with the swing era in their own way. Joe Venuti led a low-level big band that only had one record date and

just two significant sidemen (drummer Barrett Deems and the young singer Kay Starr). Stephane Grappelli spent World War II in England and Svend Asmussen remained in his native Denmark, while Ray Nance (also a notable cornetist and singer) had his features with Duke Ellington's Orchestra.

During the second half of the 1930s, Stuff Smith led his most popular band, a sextet with Jonah Jones and Cozy Cole, mostly at the Onyx Club on 52nd Street. In 1940, it broke up and soon both Jones and Cole were members of Cab Calloway's Orchestra. Smith mostly led trios throughout the 1940s, using pianist Jimmy Jones and bassist John Levy for a couple of years. **1939–1944** (Classics 1059) has the final session by his Onyx Club Boys along with rarities by his trio and quartet (with guitarist Mary Osborne added) originally made as radio transcriptions and for the tiny Selmer and Asch labels. Most notable is the original version of Smith's atmospheric "Desert Sands," one of his best-known originals. **1944–1946** (Classics 1081) is Smith's third Classics CD and completes the reissue of all of his dates as a leader prior to the mid-1950s. Most of the numbers are with trios (with Jimmy Jones or Billy Taylor on piano and John Levy or Ted Sturgis on bass), and there are vocals by Billy Daniels, Rosalie Young, and Sarah Vaughan. These rarities were originally put out by Baronet, Selmer, Musicraft, and the Town & Country labels. Best are the three exciting numbers ("Perdido," "Bugle Call Rag," and "Desert Sands" from a famous 1945 Town Hall concert. In addition, this CD has Smith's six recordings with Alphonso Trent's territory band of 1928–30.

Like Stuff Smith, Eddie South would be entering a period of neglect after the swing era ended. **1937–1941** (Classics 737) starts off by completing Smith's Paris recordings of 1937 and then features South in Holland playing with a quintet, performing eight excellent songs in New York in 1940, starring on a date with members of the John Kirby Sextet's frontline plus singer Ginny Sims, and jamming two swinging standards from 1941. South, who would most likely have been a classical violinist were it not for the racism of the times, settled back in Chicago and played in obscurity for years with his small group.

Red Norvo   By 1939, the Red Norvo big band was failing. Other than the xylophonist and his wife, singer Mildred Bailey, there was little to recommend this group, a swinging outfit without a distinctive personality of its own. After 1939, the band only recorded two more songs. **Live at the Blue Gardens** (Music Masters 65090) features the Norvo Orchestra performing live in 1942 when its only "names" were the young trombonist Eddie Bert and guest singer Helen Ward (Bailey is not on this disc). Johnny Thompson's arrangements are excellent and the band shows potential, but it would not survive the year.

However, Norvo kept busy. In 1943, he switched permanently from xylophone to vibes and started leading a series of combos. **Vol. One—The Legendary V-Disc Masters** (Vintage Jazz Classics 1005) has most of Norvo's V-discs of 1943–44, including a few alternate takes. The first 17 cuts feature Norvo leading a septet that also includes trumpeter Dale Pierce, trombonist Dick Taylor, clarinetist Aaron Sachs, Flip Phillips on tenor, pianist Ralph Burns, bassist Clyde Lombardi, and drummer John Blowers, plus Helen Ward and Carol Bruce on vocals. "1-2-3-4 Jump," "Seven Come Eleven," "Flying Home," and "NBC Jump" are highlights. Also on this disc are three numbers by Norvo and Sachs in a sextet. In 1944, Red Norvo joined Benny Goodman's new big band and sextet.

Teddy Bunn   Teddy Bunn was one of the top guitarists of the 1930s. He was self-taught and picked up experience backing up a calypso singer. In 1929, when he was 20, he recorded as a guest with Duke Ellington's Orchestra. Bunn worked with the Washboard Serenaders (1929–31) and was the main soloist with the Spirits of Rhythm during 1932–37 and 1939–41. He had opportunities along the way to record with Jimmie Noone, Johnny Dodds, Trixie Smith, J.C. Higginbotham, Sidney Bechet, Lionel Hampton, and Mezz Mezzrow. **Teddy Bunn (1929–1940)** (RST 1509) has most of his more important recordings. Bunn is heard with Red Allen backing pianist/singer Walter Pichon in 1929, has eight vocal duets with Spencer Williams the following year, and accompanies singers Buck Franklin and Fats Hayden; in addition, there are six alternate takes from his sessions with Mezz Mezzrow in 1938. Most importantly, Bunn is showcased on five unaccompanied guitar solos from 1940 that were cut for Blue Note and were his only real session as a leader. But strangely enough, he did little of significance after 1940, switching to electric guitar and playing anonymously with R&B groups. Despite decades of being active, Teddy Bunn was quickly forgotten by the jazz world.

Herman Chittison   After four years of playing in Europe with Willie Lewis, the impressive stride pianist Herman Chittison, in 1938, left the band, playing in Egypt with the Harlem Rhythmakers before returning home in 1940. He worked with Mildred Bailey in 1941 and then got an interesting job, acting on the radio in the series *Casey-Crime Photographer* during 1942–51. During the same period he led his own trio. **1944–1945** (Classics 1024) features Chittison solo and with a drumless rhythm trio, sounding in prime form on such numbers as "The Song Is Ended," "How High the Moon," and "Triste." Thelma Carpenter helps out with four vocals.

Sammy Price   A fine blues and boogie-woogie pianist who had a long career, Sammy Price got his start playing piano in Dallas in the 1920s. He worked with Alphonso Trent (1927–30), spent periods playing in Kansas City, Chicago, and Detroit, and in 1938 became a house pianist for the Decca label in New York. Price appeared on many records behind blues singers and led a series of blues-oriented sides for Decca during 1940–41. **1929–1941** (Classics 696) has all of his prewar recordings as a leader. There are two early titles ("Blue Rhythm Stomp" by Price's Four Quarters in 1929 and "Nasty but Nice" on which Price accompanies trombonist Bert Johnson). Otherwise this disc features Price's Texas Blusicians, septets, and octets put together especially for his recordings of 1940–41. Price takes several vocals, but these performances are most notable for the playing of altoist Don Stovall, trumpeters Shad Collins and Emmett Berry, and particularly Lester Young (on four songs).

Leonard Feather   Leonard Feather spent most of his career as a jazz critic, in time becoming the most famous jazz journalist in the world. Although he would never be called a major musician, he was a skillful composer and lyricist who led a few record dates. Feather, whose "Evil Gal Blues" became a hit for Dinah Washington in 1943, worked as a record producer and an occasional pianist on sessions that he organized. **1937–1945** (Classics 901) collects six of his diverse sessions; he plays piano or celeste on 11 of the 22 selections. Feather's British Olde English Swynge Band performs swing versions of English folk songs in 1937 and 1938, including "There's a Tavern in the Town," "Colonel Bogey March," and "Drink to Me Only with Thine Eyes." Among the soloists in this British combo are tenor saxophonist Buddy Featherstonhaugh and trumpeter Dave Wilkins. Feather's two All-Star Jam Bands feature Bobby Hackett, Pete Brown, Benny Carter (doubling on alto and trumpet), and clarinetist Joe Marsala on some unusual material, including "Jammin' the Waltz" (Feather was always big on the idea of swinging waltzes). Leo Watson's unusual singing (he enjoyed improvising words) on "For He's a Jolly Good Feather" and "Let's Get Happy" (based on "Happy Birthday") are standouts. This CD also has an all-star group from 1944 with Feather comping adequately behind the likes of Buck Clayton, Edmond Hall, and Coleman Hawkins. The disc concludes with a date on which both Feather and fellow writer Dan Burley both play pianos, mostly on blues.

Cozy Cole   A reliable and colorful yet supportive swing drummer, Cozy Cole already had a long history by the time he began leading sessions of his own in 1944. He was a professional drummer by 1928 and worked with Wilbur Sweatman, Jelly Roll Morton (recording "Load of Cole" in 1930), Blanche Calloway (1931–33), Benny Carter (1933–34), Willie Bryant (1935–36), Stuff Smith (1936–38), and Cab Calloway (1938–42). Cole played regularly on 52nd Street during the next few years. **1944** (Classics 819) has Cole inspiring the solos of Coleman Hawkins, Budd Johnson, Ben Webster, Earl Hines, Trummy Young, Johnny Guarnieri, and trumpeters Joe Thomas and Emmett Berry in a variety of contexts. Unusual for a drummer of the time, Cole contributed five pieces including "Nice and Cozy" and "Concerto for

Cozy." **1944–1945** (Classics 865) has his sessions for Continental, Keynote, and Guild. The two Continental dates are overloaded with star players (including Charlie Shavers, clarinetist Hank D'Amico, Coleman Hawkins, Walter "Foots" Thomas, and/or Don Byas on tenors, Clyde Hart or Johnny Guarnieri on piano, Tiny Grimes, and Slam Stewart) so most of the solos are mere cameos, just eight or sixteen bars apiece. The Keynote and Guild sessions have some excellent Don Byas solos and along the way is the recording debut of 20-year-old trumpeter Shorty Rogers, two extensive drum features ("Stompin" and "Strictly Drums"), and three surprisingly dramatic vocals from June Hawkins.

Jazz Vocalists

In 1939, most jazz-oriented singers were employed by big bands. Other than some instrumentalists (such as Louis Armstrong, Jack Teagarden, and Woody Herman), the only jazz singers who led a regular big band during this period were Cab Calloway, Bob Crosby (who was less important than his sidemen), Ella Fitzgerald (heading the former Chick Webb band), and Billy Eckstine (not till 1944). Such early 1940s greats as Jimmy Rushing (Count Basie), Helen Ward (briefly with Gene Krupa and Harry James), Ivie Anderson (Duke Ellington), Helen Humes (Count Basie), Anita O'Day (Gene Krupa and Stan Kenton), Peggy Lee (Benny Goodman), and Helen Forrest (Artie Shaw, Benny Goodman, and Harry James) were closely identified with certain big bands and rarely had opportunities to lead their own sessions this early in their careers.

TIMELINE 1942

The Musicians Union calls a recording strike that starts August 1. • Glenn Miller breaks up his civilian orchestra in order to enlist in the Army Air Force. • The Bob Crosby and Will Bradley big bands also break up. • Lionel Hampton records "Flying Home." • Django Reinhardt leads and records with an orchestra in France and Brussels despite the war. • Ivie Anderson leaves Duke Ellington after 11 years due to her worsening asthma, settling in Los Angeles, opening up a restaurant and singing locally. • Barney Bigard, having tired of the road, also departs Ellington after 14 years. • Trumpeter Harold "Shorty" Baker, formerly with Andy Kirk's Orchestra, marries Mary Lou Williams and joins Duke Ellington. • Bunny Berigan, Jimmy Blanton, and Charlie Christian all pass away prematurely. • Ben Pollack leads a band that backs comedian/pianist Chico Marx; on drums and occasional vocals is the teenaged Mel Tormé. • The remarkable pianist Dorothy Donegan records her first two numbers, "Piano Boogie" and "Every Day Blues." • Pianist Herman Chittison begins a nine-year period acting on the radio in the series *Casey-Crime Photographer*. • Bunk Johnson makes his first recordings.

However, there were 14 other jazz singers of note (12 of whom were women) who worked as singles for part of the time during 1939–44 and recorded as leaders. And, as the 1940s progressed, more and more vocalists would break away from big bands to have their own careers.

Bing Crosby A solo singer since breaking away from Gus Arnheim's Orchestra in 1931, Bing Crosby was a phenomenal success throughout his career whether on records, radio, live performances, or movies. Originally jazz-influenced, Crosby greatly diversified his repertoire by the mid-1930s and became the most popular and influential pop singer, but he always retained a love for jazz, particularly Dixieland and the music of the 1920s. In fact, his 1941 film *Birth of the Blues* had plenty of trad jazz and a good role for Jack Teagarden. **And Some Jazz Friends** (GRP/Decca 603) features a variety of swinging collaborations from 1934–51, including meetings with Teagarden, Louis Jordan, Connie Boswell, Louis Armstrong (the 1951 hit "Gone Fishin'"), Eddie Condon, Lionel Hampton, Lee Wiley, Woody Herman, and Bing's younger brother Bob Crosby. Highlights include "Your Socks Don't Match," "Pennies from Heaven," "After You've Gone," and "The Waiter and the Porter and the Upstairs Maid."

Cliff Edwards Cliff Edwards (Ukulele Ike), who was possibly the first male jazz singer to record, was at the height of his fame when he sang "Singing in the Rain" in the movie *Hollywood Revue of 1929*. But his gambling and alcoholism ruined his personal life, and his professional career stalled as he became mostly employed as weak comedy relief in low budget "B" movies. Edwards was completely forgotten during the early years of the swing era before he got a big break in 1939 when he was cast as the voice of Jiminy Cricket in the Disney film *Pinocchio*, singing "When You Wish Upon a Star." For a short time it looked like he would make a comeback. **Singing in the Rain** (Audiophile 17) shows that he could still sing pretty well in 1943 (he was 48 at the time), revisiting some of his hits and favorite tunes from the 1920s. Also from the same period is the LP **I Want a Little Girl** (Totem 1014). But Cliff Edwards was not able to make the transition to "modern times" or stop drinking, and he soon slipped away again into complete obscurity.

Billie Holiday For Billie Holiday, 1939 was a bit of a turning point as she began to gradually enter the second phase of her career. During 1935–38 she had had important (but nearly undocumented) stints as a band singer with Count Basie and Artie Shaw, and she was featured on many jazz-oriented records with various swing stars, often in bands led by Teddy Wilson. Her singing was mostly quite happy (even if some of the songs were mere throwaways), and she often functioned as one of the soloists, taking turns with such greats as Lester Young and Buck Clayton.

In 1939, Holiday became one of the stars at the interracial Café Society club in New York. She added the disturbing but effective anti-lynching poem/art song "Strange Fruit" to her repertoire and began to become better known as a dramatic singer. Her records of 1939–42, although usually still jazz-oriented, featured her as the star, with solo space for her sidemen (even at times Lester Young) becoming less significant. And throughout it all, Lady Day's voice became stronger. In fact, at the time that she signed with Decca in 1944, she was at the peak of her powers.

The Complete Billie Holiday on Columbia 1933–1944 (Columbia/Legacy 85470), a ten-CD set that has all of Holiday's recordings from the period (including every alternate take) other than her sessions for Commodore, was reviewed in Chapter 4. The master takes of her Columbia years are also available as nine single CDs. **The Quintessential Billie Holiday, Vol. 7** (Columbia 46180) features (among others) Benny Carter, Roy Eldridge, Hot Lips Page, Tab Smith, and Bobby Hackett with such gems as "More than You Know," "Sugar," "Long Gone Blues," and "Some Other Spring" taking honors. **Vol. 8** (Columbia 47030) has "Falling in Love Again" (with some fine Eldridge trumpet), "Laughing at Life," "Them There Eyes," "Swing, Brother, Swing," "Ghost of Yesterday," "Body and Soul," and "I'm Pulling Through" among the most memorable selections. **Vol. 9** (Columbia/Legacy 47031), which covers the period from October 15, 1940 to February 10, 1942, has Lady Day's first recordings of "God Bless the Child," "I Cover the Waterfront," and "Gloomy Sunday" and her last recordings with Lester Young (including "Let's Do It" and "All of Me"), other than a later television appearance. Depending on one's budget, either the ten-CD box or some of the individual Quintessential volumes are necessities for any serious jazz collection.

When Billie Holiday wanted to record "Strange Fruit" in 1939, the executives at her regular label (Vocalion), fearing controversy, turned her down, but gave her permission to record a session with producer Milt Gabler's new Commodore label. In addition to the still scary "Strange Fruit," she recorded four songs that day, including her trademark blues "Fine and Mellow," which uses some lines that Ida Cox had recorded 15 years earlier. In 1944, shortly before she signed with Decca, Holiday cut a dozen additional songs for Commodore, with the backing of Eddie Heywood's trio and septet. **The Complete Commodore Recordings** (GRP/Commodore 2-401) is a two-CD set that has all 16 of her Commodore numbers (including "Embraceable You," "Billie's Blues," "I Cover the Waterfront," and "On the Sunny Side of the Street"). However, since this two-fer also has 29 alternate takes and there is very little improvising (other than Heywood), most listeners will easily be satisfied with the single disc **Billie Holiday** (Commodore 7001), which leaves out the alternates.

With a new Decca contract in 1944 and her first opportunity to record with strings resulting in "Lover Man" (her biggest seller), Billie Holiday's career certainly looked bright as the year ended.

Ella Fitzgerald   After the long overdue breakup of the Ella Fitzgerald Orchestra, which had become more of a handicap and an obligation than an asset to the singer, Fitzgerald officially began her solo career in the fall of 1941. **1941–1944** (Classics 840) finds Fitzgerald (who was just 24 in 1941) rapidly maturing as a singer. There are three numbers (including "Into Each Life Some Rain Must Fall") with the Ink Spots and a few songs with a less memorable vocal group called the Four Keys, while most of the other selections are just with a rhythm section. Fitzgerald, who was finally being freed from performing juvenile novelties, sounds particularly rewarding on "This Love of Mine," "Somebody Nobody Loves," and "You Don't Know What Love Is." Although she was not seriously scatting yet and the emphasis was on ballads, Fitzgerald already had the ability to outswing most other singers.

Ethel Waters   Ethel Waters was beginning the final phase of her career during 1939–44. **1935–1940** (Classics 755) mostly has her accompanied by Eddie Mallory's orchestra, with six guest spots for Benny Carter. While the majority of the selections are not that famous, Waters still sounds in prime form. Her lone date from 1940 has four songs from the play and upcoming film *Cabin in the Sky*, including the earliest versions of "Taking at Chance on Love" and the title cut. In the 1943 movie *Cabin in the Sky*, Waters dominates the screen (even when sharing scenes with Lena Horne) and is in wonderful form. But although she was still quite active, she made no further recordings during 1941–45 and was beginning to be thought of as primarily an actress rather than just as a singer.

Mildred Bailey   Mildred Bailey continued working with her husband Red Norvo's big band into 1939 before spending a few months as Benny Goodman's singer (before Helen Forrest took her place). As mentioned in Chapter 4, her ten-CD box set **The Complete Columbia Recordings** (Mosaic 10-204), which has most of her recordings from 1932–42, is unfortunately a limited-edition set. The sampler **The Rockin' Chair Lady** (GRP/Decca 644), which has music not on the Mosaic set, includes her 1931 session with the Casa Loma Orchestra, four exciting numbers from 1935 with Bunny Berigan, Johnny Hodges, and Grachan Moncur, performances from 1941–42 with the Delta Rhythm Boys, and her final two studio recordings ("Cry Baby Cry" and "Blue Prelude") from 1950. Those who do not have the Mosaic box may opt for getting the Classics discs, although thus far they only reach up to **1939** (Classics 1187). This CD has particularly intriguing music with Bailey (and sometimes Red Norvo) being joined by the John Kirby Sextet on 16 numbers (including "Begin the Beguine," "Down Hearted Blues," and "The Lamp Is Low"). There are also six other songs in which Waters is accompanied by the rhythm section of the Andy Kirk Orchestra, including Mary Lou Williams and guitarist Floyd Smith.

Bailey was at the height of her career during 1944–45 when she hosted a regular radio series. **The Legendary V-Disc Sessions** (Vintage Jazz Classics 1006) has a complete radio show with her guests the Delta Rhythm Boys, four duets with Teddy Wilson, three selections with Red Norvo's quintet, a few songs with either Paul Baron's studio orchestra or the Ellis Larkins Trio, one number ("There'll Be a Jubilee") with Benny Goodman's big band, and two selections ("Lover, Come Back to Me" and "It's So Peaceful in the Country") from a 1951 radio aircheck that ended up being the last documentation of the singer. **Music, 'Til Midnight** (Mr. Music 7013) has two of Bailey's radio programs. She is joined by Paul Baron's Orchestra, and among her guests are clarinetist Ernie Caceres (featured on "Cherry"), an all-star sextet (Teddy Wilson, Charlie Shavers, Red Norvo, guitarist Remo Palmieri, bassist Billy Taylor, and drummer Specs Powell), Trummy Young (who sings "I'm Living for Today"), Billy Butterfield (showcased on Alec Wilder's "I'm Seeing Her Tonight"), and pianist Hazel Scott (featured on "Soon"). Bailey sounds in happy form on "Someday Sweetheart" and "More than You Know." A special bonus is a five-minute section in which Mildred Bailey reminisces with her former boss, Paul Whiteman. Hopefully someday all 34 of her enjoyable radio programs in this series will be available on CD.

Lee Wiley   Prior to 1939, Lee Wiley was best known as a cabaret singer groomed by composer/bandleader Victor Young who appeared on the radio, mostly singing ballads. However, on November 13, 1939, she recorded the first of four classic songbook albums, full programs dedicated to the work of a single composer. Amazingly enough, this was the first time this was ever done, more than 15 years before Ella Fitzgerald's famous songbooks. Each of Wiley's songbooks was originally released as an eight-song four-78 set; they are now available in full on two CDs.

◉ Lee Wiley Sings the Songs of Ira and George Gershwin and Cole Porter (Audiophile 1) has the music from Wiley's Gershwin and Porter songbooks. The sultry singer (who sang fairly straight, but with a light swing and a great deal of quiet sensuality) is assisted on the Gershwin project by groups led by Joe Bushkin and Max Kaminsky, with fine contributions from Bud Freeman, Pee Wee Russell, and (on four songs) Fats Waller. Highlights include "My One and Only," "I've Got a Crush on You," and "But Not for Me." The Cole Porter songbook has Paul Weston's orchestra on four songs and a quartet headed by Bunny Berigan (during some of his last significant recordings) on the other four numbers, including "Let's Fly Away" and "Let's Do It." **◉ Lee Wiley Sings the Songs of Rodgers & Hart and Harold Arlen** (Audiophile 10) has Bushkin and Kaminsky's pickup bands on the Rodgers and Hart sessions (including "You Took Advantage of Me," "I've Got Five Dollars," and a very haunting "Glad to Be Unhappy"), while the Harold Arlen tribute features Eddie Condon's Dixieland group (with

Billy Butterfield or Bobby Hackett) on particularly classic versions of "Let's Fall in Love" and "Down with Love."

Lee Wiley was famous for breaking men's hearts; she had a torrid affair with the married Bunny Berigan. In 1943, she married Jess Stacy, a relationship that only lasted a few years. She was a favorite of Eddie Condon and often guested with his all-star ensembles, adding a bit of class to the proceedings. But somehow, she never caught on big.

Ida Cox and Alberta Hunter   By 1940, most of the classic jazz singers of the early 1920s were either deceased (Bessie Smith, Clara Smith, and Ma Rainey), retired, or in a few rare cases, able to make the transition to popular music (Ethel Waters). Ida Cox, who had made her last recordings in 1929, continued singing throughout the 1930s although in low-level shows and out of the spotlight. **Vol. 5** (Document 5651) finds her returning to records on October 31, 1939, recording seven numbers plus four alternate takes. Cox (who is most memorable on "One Hour Mama" and "Death Letter Blues") is joined by such swing stars as Hot Lips Page, J.C. Higginbotham, Edmond Hall, Charlie Christian, Artie Bernstein, drummer Lionel Hampton, and James P. Johnson or Fletcher Henderson on piano. She appeared at the December 1939 "From Spirituals to Swing" concert and on December 29, 1940, recorded four numbers (only two of which were released at the time), which are augmented on this disc by four alternate takes. Assisted by Red Allen, Higginbotham, Hall, and a fine rhythm section, Cox tries to sound up to date on "You Got to Swing and Sway" while singing at her best on "Last Mile Blues." But although this session was not quite her "last mile" (there would be a final album in 1961), Ida Cox's comeback largely fizzled away by 1941.

Alberta Hunter had spent most of the 1930s in Europe, working as a cabaret singer and in shows, far away (in both distance and stylistically) from her roots in jazz and blues. However, when she returned to New York in 1939, she showed on her two sessions of 1939–40 that she could sing jazz and blues as well as ever. **Vol. 4** (Document 5425) actually starts off in 1927 with Hunter being accompanied by Fats Waller (on organ and piano) for three duets. She is also heard on two songs from 1929 and two later numbers from 1945. The bulk of this CD is from 1939–40 with Hunter featured on four duets with Eddie Heywood (including "The Castle's Rockin'") and six selections with Charlie Shavers, Buster Bailey, Lil Armstrong, and Wellman Braud, highlighted by "Downhearted Blues," "Fine and Mellow," and "Someday Sweetheart." Hunter spent much of the World War II years touring for the U.S.O., singing for the fighting servicemen.

Maxine Sullivan   Maxine Sullivan's hit version of "Loch Lomond" in 1937 (when she was just 16) launched her career and gave her a reputation for being able to lightly swing ancient folk songs. She appeared briefly in the film *Going Places* with Louis Armstrong, acted in the show *Swinging the Dream*, and married John Kirby in 1938. **1938–1941** (Classics 991) has her joined by a variety of groups including the John Kirby Sextet and the Benny Carter Orchestra, with appearances along the way by Bobby Hackett and Bud Freeman. Included among the folk numbers are "If I Had a Ribbon Bow," "I Dream of Jeanie with the Light Brown Hair," "Drink to Me Only with Thine Eyes," "Turtle Dove," "Molly Malone," and "Barbara Allen" along with more conventional swing tunes such as "It Ain't Necessarily So," "Ill Wind," "The Hour of Parting," and "What a Difference a Day Made." **1941–1946** (Classics 1020) has later selections that are also reissued in definitive fashion by the Tono label (and reviewed in Chapter 6), but is most valuable for the first ten numbers (from 1941–42), which feature Sullivan with the John Kirby Sextet. The Kirby selections include a remake of "Loch Lomond," "St. Louis Blues," and "My Ideal." The later titles have Sullivan joined by strings, the Teddy Wilson Quintet, an orchestra with the prominent harp of Laura Newell, and additional performances with Benny Carter's big band.

Also well worth acquiring by fans of Maxine Sullivan and the John Kirby Sextet are two CDs of radio transcriptions: **Loch Lomond** (Circle 47) and **More 1940–1941** (Circle 125). Although the singer gets first billing, she is actually only on 11 of the 26 numbers on **Loch Lomond** and 6 of the 18 selections on **More**, so these discs are most valuable for adding to the legacy of the unique Kirby group.

By 1943, the Sullivan-Kirby marriage was nearing its end, and the singer was doing well performing at New York clubs as a single.

Blue Lu Barker   Louise "Blue Lu" Barker was a rather unlikely performer, for she had a small voice and was never fond of appearing in public. Her husband, Danny

Barker, was an excellent rhythm banjoist and guitarist who had worked in his native New Orleans and married Blue Lu in 1930. Danny Barker, who worked with a variety of combos and big bands (including Cab Calloway during 1939–46), also recorded with Blue Lu, writing some of her material including her big hit "Don't You Make Me High." **1938–1939** (Classics 704) has all of Blue Lu's early recordings, with backup work from the likes of Charlie Shavers, Red Allen, Benny Carter (on trumpet), Buster Bailey, Chu Berry, Sammy Price, and Lil Armstrong. Despite the strong lineup of musicians, both the music and Blue Lu's voice are pretty limited. Once one gets beyond "Don't You Make Me High" (which also became known as "Don't You Feel My Leg"), there is a sameness to the songs, which include "Never Brag About Your Man," "I Don't Dig You, Jack," and "Jitterbug Blues." Danny Barker's hip jive lyrics are amusing at first, but by the second or third listen, their appeal fades quickly. One can understand why Blue Lu Barker's career never got beyond its early level.

Lena Horne, Dinah Washington, and Kay Starr   In addition to Anita O'Day (who did not lead any solo dates during this era), a list of up-and-coming female jazz singers of the early 1940s would have to include Lena Horne, Dinah Washington, and Kay Starr. Lena Horne spent much of her career on the periphery of jazz, coming much closer to being a jazz singer during 1940–44 than she would later on. A beauty throughout her life, Horne started performing when she was six back in 1923, sang and danced at the Cotton Club (starting in 1934), perfromed with Noble Sissle's Orchestra (1935–36), recorded with Teddy Wilson, was briefly with Charlie Barnet's big band (1940–41), and recorded with Artie Shaw (1941). It was natural that she would be picked to appear in films, and she is wonderful in the short *Boogie Woogie Dream* (with Albert Ammons, Meade Lux Lewis, and Teddy Wilson) and the major black films *Cabin in the Sky* and *Stormy Weather*. Horne was signed to MGM, but was restricted to cameo appearances in a variety of white films, usually just performing a song that could easily be cut out in versions shown to audiences in the segregated South.

Lena Horne, who always defied stereotypes (certainly she did not look like the typical black female who appeared in films of the 1940s) also broke boundaries musically by not being a jazz singer for much of her career, instead becoming associated with middle-of-the-road pop and cabaret music. **Stormy Weather** (Bluebird 9985) has most of her best jazz recordings, including dates with Barnet, Shaw, and Horace Henderson from the 1940s and a few numbers from 1955–58. Best are "You're My Thrill," "Don't Take Your Love from Me," "Stormy Weather," "Ill Wind," "I Didn't Know About You," and "As Long As You Live."

Dinah Washington (born Ruth Jones) was always proud of her ability to sing any style of music, from jazz and blues to R&B, gospel, pop, and even country. She learned to play piano as a child and sang with her church choir. She began working in nightclubs in 1940 when she was 15 and was reportedly renamed Dinah Washington by the manager of the Garrick Stage Bar (although Lionel Hampton later claimed he had done her the service). In 1943, she was hired by Hamp for his big band, but surprisingly she made few recordings with the vibraphonist despite being a major attraction during her three years with his orchestra. In late 1943, she led her first session, performing four songs written by critic Leonard Feather, including her first hit, "Evil Gal Blues."

Kay Starr (born Kathryn Starks) was two years older than Washington, but Dinah in time became her main influence. She performed on the radio in Dallas when she was just nine. In 1937, when she was 15, Starr joined Joe Venuti's orchestra, spending five years touring with his band. As a teenager she recorded with Glenn Miller as a brief fill-in for Marion Hutton, and in 1939 she was briefly with Bob Crosby. Kay Starr spent 1943–45 as a member of Charlie Barnet's Orchestra, which gave her exposure and helped launch her important solo career.

European Jazz During the War Years

While American musicians residing in the United States could avoid thinking too much about World War II prior to Pearl Harbor, the war had a direct effect on European jazz players. The Nazis hated the individualism of jazz, which violated their totalitarian beliefs on several levels, not the least being the many innovative blacks and Jews who were major contributors to the spontaneous music. Jazz musicians who were not fortunate enough to flee were persecuted. Most American players overseas (including Coleman Hawkins, Benny Carter, and Bill Coleman) came home in time, but not trumpeter/singer Valaida Snow. She believed that her popularity overseas would allow her to continue roaming freely. She was mistaken.

Snow was arrested in Denmark in 1941 and spent two horrifying years in a concentration camp before being released in a prisoner exchange. Although she would resume her career eventually in the United States, she never emotionally recovered from the experience nor regained her former prominence in music.

Playing jazz in occupied Europe was dangerous business, but somehow the music continued to exist just beneath the surface. Ironically, by 1943, Nazi Germany had put together its own swing bands from the musicians who had survived, using them on propaganda broadcasts that trumpeted the alleged freedom of the Third Reich.

Django Reinhardt   Django Reinhardt, the most famous jazz musician in Europe, somehow continued to play and even record during the World War II years while mostly avoiding doing any favors or special concerts for the Nazis. He managed to stay one step ahead of the authorities despite being a gypsy, a jazz musician, and not showing much enthusiasm for the "new order."

When World War II broke out, the Quintet of the Hot Club of France was visiting London. Stephane Grappelli elected to stay in England, but Django spontaneously returned to France. **1939–1940** (Classics 813) has the last recordings by the Quintet (including "Melancholy Baby," "Tea for Two," and "Undecided"), a few trio numbers that showcase Django (such as "I'll See You in My Dreams"), and some songs featuring tenor saxophonist Alex Combelle and altoist Andre Ekyan. **1940** (Classics 831) finds Django forming a new Quintet of the Hot Club of France with Hubert Rostaing (on clarinet and tenor) in Grappelli's place and the third guitar dropped in favor of drums. Other combo selections on this rewarding CD of rare material feature tenor saxophonist Noel Chiboust, trumpeter Philippe Brun, and Combelle. **1940–1941** (Classics 852) includes further titles by the new Quintet (expanded to a sextet on some numbers that add Alix Combelle on second reeds) and various all-star groups. Highlights include "Swing '41," "Nuages," "Swing de Paris," "Festival Swing," and several American jazz standards given different names so as to disguise their identity from the Nazis. **1941–1942** (Classics 877) is most notable for including selections that feature Reinhardt at the head of his big band. Improbable as it was to be leading an orchestra in Paris and Brussels in 1942 (including a session with strings), Django was (other than Alvino Rey) virtually the only jazz guitarist in the world to be at the head of his own swing band. **Django's Music** (Hep 1041) duplicates the performances in the Classic series, but has nearly all of Reinhardt's big band work of the 1940–43 period on a single disc. **1942–1943** (Classics 905) features more big band numbers (including "Django Rag," "Belleville," and the haunting "Oubli"), combo sides with both Andre Lluis and Gerard Leveque on clarinets, and a solo guitar workout on the two-part "Improvisation No. 3."

After July 7, 1943, Django Reinhardt was absent from records altogether for 16 months. The intensity of the war during 1943–44 made jazz secondary to even the most dedicated Europeans, who were fighting for their survival. Americans, who had not heard any Reinhardt recordings since 1939, feared that the great guitarist was dead. So after France was liberated in the summer of 1944, it was very happy news in the jazz world when it was discovered that not only was Django alive, but still playing at his best, ready to regain his stature as jazz's top guitarist.

Stephane Grappelli   During 1933–39, the career of Stephane Grappelli was entwined with that of Django Reinhardt. However, when World War II began and Django decided to return to France, Grappelli chose to stay in England. It was the end of the original Quintet of the Hot Club of France and although there would be a few postwar reunions, their musical partnership was over.

With the exception of the last two numbers, **1935–1940** (Classics 708) is comprised of Grappelli-led sessions made while he was regularly collaborating with Reinhardt; in fact, the guitarist is on the great majority of the selections. The first eight numbers (including "St. Louis Blues," "Limehouse Blues," and "I've Found a New Baby") are by the Quintet (released under the violinist's name). There are a few Grappelli-Reinhardt duets, a meeting with violinist Michel Warlop in a quartet, and four unaccompanied solos (three on violin and one on piano) by Grappelli. The last two selections were Grappelli's first with pianist George Shearing, who worked with Grappelli's small groups during 1940–43. **1941–1943** (Classics 779) has Grappelli and Shearing as the main soloists with either a quintet or a sextet. These swing recordings (some of which have Beryl Davis taking vocals) are very obscure, but rewarding, showing that the violinist could excel away

from Django Reinhardt and that, even at this early stage, George Shearing was developing into a major talent.

George Shearing   George Shearing is best known for his work in the United States (starting in 1947), but before then he was a star in Great Britain. Born blind in 1919, Shearing started playing piano when he was three, was trained at the Linden Lodge School for the Blind, and was originally inspired by Teddy Wilson and Fats Waller. As a teenager, Shearing played with Ambrose's orchestra for two years and in 1937 made his recording debut, first recording as a leader in 1939. Shearing, who worked with Stephane Grappelli during the first half of the 1940s, won seven straight *Melody Maker* polls and occasionally doubled on accordion. **The London Years** (Hep 1042) has 25 of the 31 selections that Shearing led during 1939–43. With the exception of two duets with drummer Carlo Krahmer and "Squeezin' the Blues" (which has Shearing on accordion backed by Krahmer and Leonard Feather's piano), all of the music is piano solos. Shearing shows off the influences of Wilson, Waller, Art Tatum, and Earl Hines while improvising in his own sophisticated swing style.

Alix Combelle   An associate of Django Reinhardt and Stephane Grappelli, Alix Combelle was thought of as "the Coleman Hawkins of France." The tenor saxophonist (who doubled on clarinet) was busy during the 1930s, playing with Gregor (1932–33), Arthur Briggs, Michel Warlop, Ray Ventura, and as a leader. He appeared on a famous record date with Coleman Hawkins, Benny Carter, altoist Andre Ekyan, and Django, recorded with both the Quintet of the Hot Club of France and Bill Coleman, and visited the United States twice, turning down a job with Tommy Dorsey in order to return to France. Like Django Reinhardt, Combelle was somehow able to play and record regularly during the war years.

Combelle's most famous dates were as a sideman, but his sessions as a leader during 1935–43 fill up three CDs. **1935–1940** (Classics 714) features Combelle backed by the Quintet of the Hot Club of France, playing in a sextet with Bill Coleman, in a quartet with cornetist Phillippe Brun, and with larger groups filled with French jazz stars. **1940–1941** (Classics 751) mostly features Combelle with his band (Le Jazz de Paris) along with four numbers with the "Trio de Saxophones" (with altoist Christian Wagner, Hubert Rostaing on tenor, and Django). **1942–1943** (Classics 782) has extremely rare material with Combelle heard with both big bands and combos, still playing enthusiastically like Coleman Hawkins. Ironically, after having recorded so much material under such extenuating circumstances, Alix Combelle hardly recorded at all during 1944–53 and became much less prominent on the French jazz scene.

Oscar Aleman, Svend Asmussen, and Svenska Hotkvintetten   Argentinean guitarist Oscar Aleman, who worked in Paris during the 1930s, recorded four titles as a leader in 1939. He left France in 1940 as World War II intensified. Rather than immigrate to the United States where he might have gained some worldwide fame, Aleman chose to move back to Argentina and was not heard from again in Europe (other than a 1959 tour) or the United States. However, he did work and record regularly in Argentina for decades, sticking to the swing music that he loved, recording as late as 1974. ◗ **Swing Guitar Masterpieces** (Acoustic Disc 29), a two-CD set, has Aleman's eight songs from his 1938–39 Paris sessions plus a strong sampling of his Buenos Aires recordings of 1941–47 and 1951–54, featuring the guitarist in a sextet and a nonet. Although in later years he showed more individuality, Aleman always sounded fairly close to the style and sound of Django Reinhardt.

Violinist Svend Asmussen spent the war years in his native Copenhagen, performing and recording despite World War II. Some of the violinist's best recordings from 1941–50 are on ◗ **Phenomenal Fiddler** (Phontastic 9310). Asmussen largely stuck to swing throughout his career (even after the rise of bop), playing small-group jazz in theatres and shows in Denmark. He is heard with a sextet throughout these 1940s recordings, which include spirited versions of such songs as "Ring Dem Bells," "Exactly Like You," "I've Found a New Baby," "When You're Smiling," and other standards along with a few originals. Asmussen could have held his own with American musicians, but resisted offers to come to the United States, deciding to spend his career in his native country and on the European continent.

Even the most fanatical swing collectors might not have heard of Svenska Hotkvintetten (the Swedish Hot Quintet). This little-known Swedish band was comprised of violinist Emil Iwring, three guitarists (including single-string soloist Sven Stiberg and chordal soloist Folke Eriskberg), and a bassist. Formed in 1934, the group made a series of recordings during 1939–41, most of

which are on **Swedish Hot** (Dragon 223). Iwring was nearly Grappelli's equal and, although neither Stiberg or Eriskberg were at Django's level—no one was—they were both excellent soloists. This CD has 27 selections, most of which are so heated that they will be a revelation to fans of the era. Svenska Hotkvintetten broke up in 1941, slipping away into history.

Alice Babs   The top European singer to emerge during the swing era, Alice Babs (born in Sweden as Alice Nilson, but adopting her nickname of Babs as her last name) was only 16 in 1940 when she had a hit with "Swing It Mr. Teacher" ("Swing It Magistern"). She had debuted on records the previous year and combined solid swing singing with occasional yodeling during the period. ◗ **Swing It!** (Phontastic 9302) has some of her finest recordings from the 1939–53 period, with backing from Sweden's top jazz musicians. Most of the singing is in English (including such numbers as "Some of These Days," "You're Driving Me Crazy," "Truckin'," and "I'm Checkin' Out Goo'm Bye"), and Babs's youthful enthusiasm (something she never lost) is difficult to resist. She managed to perform fairly often during the war years in neutral Sweden and has had a long career.

Special All-Star Groups

During the swing era, occasionally all-star groups of musicians who did not normally play together were recorded in special sessions. Both *Metronome* and *Esquire* recorded their pollwinners while Norman Granz began an institution in 1944 with his "Jazz at the Philharmonic."

Metronome All-Stars   During the swing era, there were two main music magazines covering the scene: *Down Beat* (which was founded in 1934) and *Metronome*. *Metronome* had an annual poll during 1939–61 that allowed their readers to pick who they considered to be the top jazz instrumentalists on each instrument for that year. Unlike with most other magazine polls, *Metronome* actually recorded their all-stars (as many winners as possible plus some runners-up) during 1939–42, 1945–50, 1953, and 1956. In most cases, the group recorded two songs and there were short solos (generally one chorus) from practically all of the participants.

◗ **Metronome All-Star Bands** (Bluebird 7636) starts off with two numbers from an unrelated 1937 all-star group that features Bunny Berigan, Tommy Dorsey, Fats Waller, Dick McDonough, and drummer

George Wettling playing "Blues" and a very memorable rendition of "Honeysuckle Rose." In addition, all of the music from the Metronome All-Star Bands of 1939, 1941, 1946, and 1949 (the years that RCA recorded the pollwinners) are here, including the alternate takes. The 1939 group is practically a Benny Goodman reunion band since it includes BG, Berigan, Harry James, Tommy Dorsey, and Jack Teagarden. The 1941 version has such notables as Goodman, James, Cootie Williams, Tommy Dorsey, Benny Carter, Coleman Hawkins, Count Basie, Charlie Christian, and Buddy Rich.

The LP **The Metronome All-Stars** (Tax 8039) has the all-star ensemble's sessions for Columbia dating from 1940, 1941, 1942, 1946, and 1950. The first three sessions are dominated by top swing players, including James, Cootie Williams, Roy Eldridge, Teagarden, Goodman, Benny Carter, Charlie Barnet, Jess Stacy, Count Basie, Charlie Christian, and Gene Krupa, among many others. The solos are brief but usually quite colorful, giving listeners a taste of the many remarkable players who were in their prime during the period.

The later Metronome All-Star Band recordings included on these two sets will be covered in Chapter 6.

Esquire All-Stars In 1943, *Esquire* magazine held their first of three critics' polls, sponsoring a concert featuring many of the winners (those in first or second place). The two-LP set **The First Esquire All-American Jazz Concert** (Radiola 5051) has the one of the greatest jazz events of all time. Held on January 18, 1944, this remarkable concert features many of the who's who of swing. Imagine a version of "I Got Rhythm" by a group comprised of Louis Armstrong, Roy Eldridge, Jack Teagarden, Barney Bigard, Coleman Hawkins, xylophonist Red Norvo, Art Tatum, Al Casey, Oscar Pettiford, and Sid Catlett, with all of the principals getting to solo! In addition, there are individual features and notable appearances by Benny Goodman, Lionel Hampton, Teddy Wilson, Jess Stacy, Billie Holiday, and Mildred Bailey. The recording quality of the performances (some of which were broadcast over the radio) is quite good, and getting to hear Tatum backing Armstrong and Hawkins on "Basin Street Blues" is a unique pleasure that points out the richness of the jazz scene in 1944. It also makes one wonder why this music has not been coherently reissued on CD yet.

Jazz at the Philharmonic On July 2, 1944, 25-year-old producer Norman Granz put together the first "Jazz at the Philharmonic" concert. Granz, who studied at UCLA and served in the army, had assisted with the Academy Award–winning Lester Young short *Jammin' the Blues* earlier in the year. A fighter for integration and civil rights, and a lover of freewheeling modern jam sessions in addition to being a skilled businessman, Granz combined his loves and talents in JATP. The initial event, a fundraiser in Los Angeles, has been fully reissued as **The First Concert** (Verve 314 521 646). The lineup of musicians is trumpeter Shorty Sherock (on the last three numbers), trombonist J.J. Johnson (on the last four selections), Illinois Jacquet and Jack McVea on tenors, Nat King Cole, guitarist Les Paul, Red Callender or Johnny Miller on bass, and drummer Lee Young. The colorful ensemble performs six standards and a blues, with five of the seven jams being over nine minutes long. Most notable are Jacquet's screaming tenor solos, a very funny (and somewhat remarkable) tradeoff between Cole and Paul on "Blues," and the wide variety of styles that are heard interacting including Dixieland (Sherock's solos), swing, early bop, and R&B.

So successful was the concert that Granz (who helped pioneer live recordings with this event) would soon make "Jazz at the Philharmonic" into a lucrative touring all-star jam session.

The Start of Rhythm and Blues

Because rhythm and blues (R&B) has evolved through several different periods since the 1940s and become a very different music than jazz, some may not realize that its origins came out of swing. By the mid-1940s, promoters realized that they could save a lot of money by hiring a two- or three-horn combo rather than a big band. If the musicians riffed a lot, they could emulate a larger orchestra, and if they featured catchy vocals, highly expressive horn solos (particularly saxophonists), and repetition, their sales potential was great. To an extent, R&B began with Illinois Jacquet's "Flying Home" solo with Lionel Hampton and his later honking tenor records, but Louis Jordan was also an early R&B innovator.

Louis Jordan Louis Jordan started on clarinet when he was seven, back in 1915, and he played with his father's group (the Rabbit Foot Minstrels) as a teenager. As an altoist, Jordan worked in 1929 with Jimmy Pryor's

Imperial Serenaders, freelanced in the South and around Philadelphia, and in 1934 arrived in New York, recording with Clarence Williams. After working with LeRoy Smith's Orchestra (1935), he was with Chick Webb (1936–38), but was rarely featured except on three occasions as a ballad vocalist. In August 1938, Jordan put together his own small group. They first recorded in December and the following year became known as the Tympani Five even though they did not feature a timpanist and were almost always at least a sextet. Within a couple of years, Jordan was a fixture on the best-seller charts. His friendly vocals, his hip and humorous personality, the many riff-filled pieces, and the memorable arrangements made Jordan and the Tympani Five among the most popular bands of the 1940s and an influential force on early R&B.

Four CDs have all of Louis Jordan's recordings up to mid-1945. **1934–1940** (Classics 636) includes Jordan's date with Clarence Williams, his forgettable ballad vocals with Webb, his two recordings in 1938 with the "Elks Rendezvous Band," and the first sessions by the Tympani Five. **1940–1941** (Classics 663) consists of 26 jumping but mostly little-known titles. The band had its sound together, but the material was not there yet; "Somebody Done Hoodooed the Hoodoo Man," "The Two Little Squirrels (Nuts to You)," and "De Laff's on You" failed to become hits. But **1941–1943** (Classics 741) finds everything changing as the Tympani Five make such songs as "Knock Me a Kiss," "I'm Gonna Move to the Outskirts of Town," "What's the Use of Getting Sober When You Gonna Get Drunk Again," "Five Guys Named Moe," and "Is You Is or Is You Ain't My Baby" into hits and future

standards. This valuable disc not only includes Jordan's Decca recordings from the period, but also his V-discs. **1943–1945** (Classics 866), which also contains Deccas, V-discs, some originally rejected numbers, and even a radio commercial, is highlighted by "I Like 'Em Fat Like That," "G.I. Jive," and two numbers with Bing Crosby. The fact that Louis Jordan got to record with Crosby as a near-equal is a measure of the great commercial success that he had achieved, becoming one of the most famous black entertainers of the mid-1940s.

The Comeback of New Orleans Jazz and Dixieland

In 1937, swing was the thing, and jazz of the 1920s was considered long passé. After all, some of that music was over ten years old! There were some exceptions, particularly the popular small-group recordings of Fats Waller, Wingy Manone, Louis Prima, and Tommy Dorsey's Clambake Seven, not to mention the Bob Crosby Bobcats and Orchestra, but those were largely overshadowed and considered novelties rather than independent musical movements.

That all began to change in 1938, and by 1944, vintage jazz (which had become widely known as Dixieland) was quickly becoming one of jazz's most popular styles. There were three overlapping movements that fueled the Dixieland revival. There were technically skilled swing players, many of whom were veterans of the late 1920s, who preferred playing in more freewheeling settings than they found in tightly arranged big bands. There were younger revivalists, some of whom were based in San Francisco,

TIMELINE 1943

Glenn Miller forms the Army Air Force band. • Some of the smaller record labels (including Capitol) settle with the Musicians Union and resume recording late in the year. • Duke Ellington debuts "Black, Brown and Beige" at his first Carnegie Hall concert. • Gene Krupa is arrested for marijuana possession (the charges are later dismissed) and is forced to break up his orchestra. • Stan Kenton's Orchestra signs with the Capitol label. • Fats Waller dies. • Dinah Washington joins Lionel Hampton's Orchestra. • Mario Bauza writes "Tanga," considered by some to be the first Afro-Cuban jazz song. • Louie Bellson joins Benny Goodman's Orchestra. • Buck Clayton ends his seven-year period as Count Basie's main trumpet soloist when he is drafted. • Andy Kirk's trumpet section includes both Howard McGhee and Fats Navarro. • Slim & Slam break up when Slim Gaillard is drafted. • Pianist Bud Powell joins the Cootie Williams Orchestra. • Cliff Jackson becomes the house pianist at Café Society Downtown. • The unrecorded Earl Hines's Orchestra features Charlie Parker (on tenor), Dizzy Gillespie, and Sarah Vaughan. • Art Hodes begins editing *The Jazz Record*, an important historical jazz magazine that lasts four years.

who chose to play New Orleans jazz rather than swing. And there were the older players who had stayed in New Orleans rather than relocate north, and who were beginning to be discovered, and in some cases, practically dug up by the more enterprising jazz fans.

While New Orleans jazz traditionally emphasizes ensembles, and the San Francisco variety grew from the foundation of early black Chicago jazz of the 1920s, Dixieland was a bit different. In its most typical form, Dixieland features a group consisting of trumpet, trombone, clarinet, piano, bass (or tuba), drums, and sometimes rhythm guitar (or banjo) and a tenor sax. Although frameworks vary, it is not uncommon for a Dixieland performance to consist of one or two opening ensembles, solos by clarinet, trombone, trumpet, and piano, a couple of closing ensembles, a four-bar drum break, and the ensemble concluding with a four-bar tag. The word "Dixieland" was later associated with a countless number of amateur (and sometimes rather corny) groups in the 1950s when the music's popularity was particularly high (and many people were jumping on the bandwagon). Because creative jazz musicians always hate to be pigeonholed, many players in the idiom prefer other terms such as classic, traditional, or New Orleans jazz. But when hearing the music played at its best, such as by Eddie Condon's many bands, it is obvious that Dixieland is an honorable name that should not be discarded just because of its misuse by some.

Jelly Roll Morton Jelly Roll Morton should have been one of the main beneficiaries of the Dixieland revival movement. He was one of jazz's top pioneers, his piano playing was still in its prime as 1939 began, he was a major composer whose "King Porter Stomp" was being played nightly by swing big bands, and he was showing a desire to sing more often. But there were some major problems. Morton, who should have been prosperous due to his compositions ("Wolverine Blues" and "Milenburg Joys" were also undergoing revivals), was being ripped off by his publisher and barely received any royalty payments. His health was failing due to being stabbed in mid-1938. His abrasive personality had burned many bridges along the way. His bragging about being "the founder of jazz" (which was only a slight exaggeration) did not win him any friends. And 1939 was still a bit early for the classic jazz revival.

Morton had high hopes when he returned to New York in early 1939, having recorded extensively for the Library of Congress the previous year. He returned to commercial records in September 1939, recording two sessions for Victor (his first as a leader since 1930), using Sidney Bechet on one session along with trumpeter Sidney DeParis and clarinetist Albert Nicholas; best are "I Thought I Heard Buddy Bolden Say," "Winin' Boy Blues," and "Don't You Leave Me Here" (each of which include Morton vocals). These dates conclude the five-CD box ◉ **Jelly Roll Morton Centennial: His Complete Victor Recordings** (Bluebird 2361), which was reviewed in Chapter 3. **Last Sessions: The Complete General Recordings** (GRP/Decca 403) contains Morton's final studio recordings. Included are 13 classic piano solos from December 1939, five of which have Jelly Roll's vocals. These versions of "The Crave," "King Porter Stomp," "Winin' Boy Blues," "Buddy Bolden Blues," and "Don't You Leave Me Here" are quite memorable. Also on this CD are three band dates from January 1940. Although Henry "Red" Allen and Albert Nicholas are in the sextet/septet, these dates do not live up to their expectations. Other than a heated version of "Panama," Morton wanted to use the occasion to introduce new songs that could possibly be hits, but his only original to catch on (and it would be years later) was "Sweet Substitute."

Other than an appearance on a July 14, 1940, radio broadcast (performing "Winin' Boy Blues" and "King Porter Stomp"), Jelly Roll Morton would not be documented again. After a frustrating period in New York during which he was unable to gain much work or any recognition, in late 1940 Morton decided to head out to Los Angeles, taking all of his possessions with him. Unfortunately, he found no better luck in L.A., his health quickly declined, and he died on July 10, 1941, at the age of 55. If his health had been a little better and he had lived five more years, Jelly Roll Morton would have enjoyed a great deal of success, for his songs would soon be played nightly again by revivalists.

Johnny Dodds, Jimmie Noone, and Sidney Bechet
The big three of New Orleans clarinet of the 1920s were Johnny Dodds, Jimmie Noone, and Sidney Bechet. All were still alive and active in 1938. Dodds, who had not been on records since 1929, made it through the worst years of the Depression by owning apartment houses in Chicago, working odd jobs, and playing part-time. In 1938, he made his only trip to New York, recording six songs in a sextet that included Lil Armstrong and Charlie

Shavers, sounding pretty strong on "Melancholy" and "Wild Man Blues." Perhaps if he had chosen to remain in New York, he would have worked and recorded more regularly, but Dodds soon returned to Chicago. He suffered a heart attack in May 1939, which kept him inactive until January 1940. Dodds began playing again and on June 5 recorded two songs, but unfortunately the poor playing of cornetist Natty Dominique greatly hurt the music, which is included along with the Shavers date on **1928–1940** (Classics 635). Two months later Johnny Dodds had a second heart attack and this time he did not survive, dying at the age of 48. His brother, Baby Dodds, who had been on the 1940 session, joined Jimmie Noone's band and remained active into the early 1950s. Natty Dominique, who soon had heart trouble of his own, became a part-time player and faded away from the scene.

Jimmie Noone was more active musically than Johnny Dodds in the 1930s, leading annual sessions during 1933–37. No longer leading a trumpetless sextet, Noone excelled in more conventional settings, including eight songs in 1937 made with a septet that included Shavers, Pete Brown, and Teddy Bunn. **1934–1940** (Classics 653) includes that date plus sessions with trumpeter Junie Cobb and pianist Zinky Cohn, and a quartet recording hurt by Ed Thompson's jivey vocals. In addition, Noone recorded on June 5, 1940 (the same day as Dodds), and was also saddled with Natty Dominique, who showed no prejudice by ruining Noone's date too!

Noone did not lead any more studio sessions after 1940, but there is a live quartet date from 1941 that survived. In 1943, he moved to Los Angeles, recorded with the Capital Jazzmen (next to Jack Teagarden and Joe Sullivan), and joined Kid Ory's band. But just when Jimmie Noone looked like he would be participating in the New Orleans revival movement, he died of a heart attack, also (like Johnny Dodds) at the age of 48.

Sidney Bechet, who spent much of 1933–38 in obscurity (often playing with Noble Sissle's orchestra), began to re-emerge during the second half of 1938. He at first teamed up with Tommy Ladnier and Mezz Mezzrow to record four numbers on a session organized by French critic Hugues Panassie that resulted in the memorable "Really the Blues." Bechet and Ladnier had a reunion as the New Orleans Feetwarmers at John Hammond's "From Spirituals to Swing" concert. But Ladnier, who worked a little the next year with Mezzrow, died of a heart attack on June 4, 1939, when he was barely 39.

In 1939, Bechet recorded a lone number for the new Blue Note label and the result was a hit version of "Summertime." He recorded with Jelly Roll Morton later in the year and in February 1940 began cutting a series of exciting sessions for the Bluebird label. ● **The Victor Sessions-Master Takes 1932–43** (Bluebird 2402) is the definitive Sidney Bechet release, a three-CD set that has all of the selections (but unfortunately not the alternate takes) from Bechet's small-group Bluebird dates of 1932–43. The 1932 set with the New Orleans Feetwarmers, the "Really the Blues" session, and the date with Morton are here, along with the music from 16 Bechet-led sessions dating from 1940–41 and 1943. Such stars as Sidney DeParis, Rex Stewart, Red Allen, Charlie Shavers, J.C. Higginbotham, Vic Dickenson, Cliff Jackson, Willie "The Lion" Smith, Earl Hines, and Baby Dodds all make strong contributions, although Bechet is the dominant force. A particular highlight is the historic April 18, 1941, "one-man band" date during which Bechet (via overdubbing) plays clarinet, soprano, tenor, piano, bass, and drums on "The Sheik of Araby" and "Blues of Bechet"; this had never been done before. Other gems on this essential reissue include "Indian Summer," "Old Man Blues," "Nobody Knows the Way I Feels Dis' Mornin'," "Stompy Jones," "Egyptian Fantasy," "The Mooche," and "What Is this Thing Called Love."

Another Bechet CD well worth picking up is **Up a Lazy River** (Good Time Jazz 12064), which is most notable for eight songs matching Bechet in a quartet with Muggsy Spanier, guitarist Carmen Mastren, and Wellman Braud. The pianoless, drumless group is often quite intimate yet heated as Bechet and Spanier play off of each other on such tunes as "China Boy," "That's a Plenty," and "If I Could Be with You." Also included on this disc are Dixieland performances from 1947–49 that team Bechet with such notables as Buster Bailey, James P. Johnson, Albert Nicholas, and (on seven numbers) his protégé Bob Wilber.

Along with Louis Armstrong, Sidney Bechet was the most virtuosic of the early musicians to emerge from New Orleans. He recorded with Satch in a combative date in 1940, worked regularly in New York during the first half of the 1940s, and guested on some of Eddie Condon's Town Hall concerts.

Muggsy Spanier and Wingy Manone Cornetist Muggsy Spanier, after making an impression as part of the Chicago jazz scene of the 1920s, spent the 1929–36 period giving some validity to the band of cornball personality Ted Lewis. He worked with the Ben Pollack Orchestra (1936–38) but became seriously ill and was hospitalized for three months. Fortunately, he made a full recovery and then formed his most significant group.

Spanier's Ragtime Band of 1939 was an octet that recorded 16 Dixieland performances for Bluebird (later dubbed "The Great 16"). ● **The Ragtime Band Sessions** (Bluebird 66550) expands the program with eight alternate takes, so this could be called "The Great 24"! Spanier's group consists of George Brunies, clarinetist Rod Cless, one of three different tenors, and a four-piece rhythm section. Among the most memorable performances are "Big Butter and Egg Man," "I Wish I Could Shimmy Like My Sister Kate" (which has a famous Brunies vocal), "Relaxin' at the Touro" (a blues named after the hospital where Spanier had recovered), "Lonesome Road," and "Mandy Make Up Your Mind." The leader's solid lead and ability to paraphrase a melody in exciting fashion worked very well with the other horn players. These performances became an inspiration for the Dixieland revival movement, but ironically the band could not come up with enough work to survive; it had arrived on the scene a couple of years too early. Spanier reluctantly broke up the group, spent time with Bob Crosby's Orchestra (1940–41), and had a big band of his own during 1941–43 that sounded a lot like Crosby's. **1939–1942** (Classics 709) has "The Great 16" (duplicating the Bluebird set but without the alternate takes) plus the rather scarce eight numbers by Spanier's 1942 big band. By 1944 Spanier had given up his big band and was back to playing with freewheeling Dixieland groups not that different from the band that flopped in 1939. **1944** (Classics 907) has the cornetist jamming happily in septets and octets with Miff Mole, Pee Wee Russell, baritonist Ernie Caceres, tenor saxophonist Boomie Richman, Eddie Condon, and other trad jazz players, digging into such songs as "Angry," "Sugar," "Rosetta," "That's a Plenty," and "Jazz Me Blues."

Because he sang and had built up his reputation with a series of trad jazz recordings that had started in 1934, Wingy Manone was able to continue playing the music he enjoyed throughout the second half of the swing era without worrying about keeping his band together. **1939–1940** (Classics 1023) features Chu Berry on three of the four sessions and there are seven instrumentals,

with Buster Bailey on the first two dates. Highlights of these good-time performances include "Downright Disgusted Blues," "Corrine Corrini," "Royal Garden Blues," "Farewell Blues," "Blue Lou," "When My Sugar Walks Down the Street," and "She's Crying for Me." And while his original competitors Fats Waller (who died in 1943) and Louis Prima (who began leading a big band in 1940) ended their small-group recordings, Manone continued in an unchanged musical direction. **1940–1944** (Classics 1091) features Manone jamming his brand of Dixieland with such players as clarinetists Joe Marsala and Matty Matlock, trombonists George Brunies and Abe Lincoln, pianists Mel Powell and Joe Sullivan, and drummer Zutty Singleton plus many lesser-known names. The best cuts are "Ain't It a Shame About Mame," "Ochi Chornya," "Mama's Gone Good-Bye," a remake of "Isle of Capri," "The Tailgate Ramble" (which has Manone sharing the vocals with its lyricist Johnny Mercer), and the only instrumental, "Memphis Blues." The six-part 16-minute "Jam and Jive" is a disappointment, mostly featuring Manone jiving in unimaginative fashion with the vaudevillian Eddie Marr. Although it is true that a little bit of Wingy Manone goes a long way, it is nice to know that all of his recordings from his prime (most of which are enjoyable) are readily available.

Eddie Condon   In 1938, Eddie Condon and his brand of Dixieland had its first breakthrough. The rhythm guitarist, who rarely soloed and became increasingly inaudible through the years, was a talented bandleader who had a knack for picking perfect tempos, calling out the right tune for the right moment, and managing oversized (and racially integrated) all-star groups in freewheeling ensembles. He was based at Nick's, a top club on 52nd Street, during 1937–44 and began recording frequently in 1938–43 for Milt Gabler's Commodore label, also having dates for Decca in 1939 and 1944. **1938–1940** (Classics 759) has music from six sessions with Condon's all-stars including such major players as Bobby Hackett, Max Kaminsky, Jack Teagarden, Brad Gowans, Pee Wee Russell, Bud Freeman, Jess Stacy, Joe Bushkin, Joe Sullivan, bassist Artie Shapiro, George Wettling, Lionel Hampton on drums, Dave Tough, George Wettling, and Fats Waller. These renditions of "Sunday," "California Here I Come," and "Nobody's Sweetheart" are quite definitive. **1942–1943** (Classics 772) is on the same level, with Kaminsky, Gowans, Russell, Sullivan,

Bushkin, and Wettling joined by such Condon regulars as Yank Lawson, James P. Johnson, Bob Haggart, Tony Sbarbaro, Sid Catlett, Lou McGarity, and pianist Gene Schroeder. "Fidgety Feet," "Rose Room," "Mandy Make Up Your Mind," and "Back in Your Backyard" are standouts. **Eddie Condon and Friends** (Soundies 4118) consists of radio transcriptions from 1943–44 by Condon (with Max Kaminsky, Pee Wee Russell, Bobby Hackett, Billy Butterfield, and Jack Teagarden), Wild Bill Davison (the master takes from his 1943 session with Russell and George Brunies), and Max Kaminsky (a sextet with clarinetist Rod Cless and Willie "The Lion" Smith). The music throughout this rewarding disc is high quality and spirited Dixieland.

During 1944–45, Condon and his groups were featured on a regular basis at a series of Town Hall concerts broadcast on the radio. After decades of only excerpts being available, the Jazzology label has released all of these important and consistently exciting shows on 23 CDs (ten two-CD sets and an 11th volume that has three discs). The performances are of consistent high quality, featuring a core of Condonites, many guests (all of whom are featured liberally), and humorous (and sometimes sarcastic) talking by Condon. Dixieland and Eddie Condon fans will want all 11 of these sets, the first eight of which fit into this period. There are four half-hour programs apiece on each of the Jazzology volumes and every show has quite a few memorable moments. Only the very first program is not all that well recorded; otherwise it is as if one were hearing these performances live on the radio. **Town Hall Concerts, Vol. 1** (Jazzology 1001/1002) is typical of the series in that the lineup of musicians is remarkable, including Billy Butterfield, Bobby Hackett, Max Kaminsky, Hot Lips Page, Rex Stewart, Pee Wee Russell, Edmond Hall, Miff Mole, Benny Morton, trombonist Bill Harris, baritonist Ernie Caceres, James P. Johnson, and Gene Schroeder. Other stars in these special programs include Lee Wiley, Gene Krupa, Muggsy Spanier, Red McKenzie, Jack Teagarden, Jimmy Dorsey, Tommy Dorsey, Wingy Manone, Jonah Jones, Joe Marsala, and Willie "The Lion" Smith. Serious Eddie Condon and Dixieland fans will want to acquire all of these sets, which include ◉ **Vol. 2** (Jazzology 1003/1004), which is a perfect example of this series, **Vol. 3** (Jazzology 1005/1006), **Vol. 4** (Jazzology 1007/1008), **Vol. 5** (Jazzology 1009/1010), **Vol. 6** (Jazzology 1011/1012), **Vol. 7** (Jazzology 1013/1014), and **Vol. 8** (Jazzology 1015/1016).

Wild Bill Davison   One of the main Condonites who did not appear at the Town Hall concerts was Wild Bill Davison, who was in the army at the time. Davison was one of the all-time great Dixieland trumpeters (actually cornetists). A highly expressive player, Wild Bill's vocabulary included growls, shakes, screams in the upper register, and emotions ranging from sentimentality to sarcasm. He was the perfect person to lead ensembles, making most other brassmen seem a bit colorless in comparison.

Born in Defiance, Ohio, Davison worked in the 1920s with the Ohio Lucky Seven, the Chubb-Steinberg Orchestra (with whom he made his recording debut), the Seattle Harmony Kings, and Benny Meroff. He had just opened with his own big band in 1932 in Chicago when he was involved in a car accident that ended the life of Frank Teschemacher. Although blamed by some (due to his reputation as a constant partier and hellraiser), Davison's car had actually been blindsided by a cab. Nevertheless, he went into exile, playing locally in Milwaukee until 1940. In 1941, Davison moved to New York and soon became an important part of the trad jazz scene. In 1943, he recorded some of the most exciting Dixieland ever. ◉ **Commodore Master Takes** (GRP/Commodore 405) has the classic November 27, 1943, session with George Brunies (in superb form), Pee Wee Russell, Gene Schroeder, Eddie Condon, bassist Bob Casey, and George Wettling on four songs, including the best-ever version of "That's a Plenty." Also on this disc are Davison's other Commodore sessions as a leader (from 1944–46). There are 24 titles in all that feature such outstanding players as clarinetists Edmond Hall, Joe Marsala, and Albert Nicholas, trombonist Lou McGarity, pianists Dick Cary and Joe Sullivan, and drummers Danny Alvin and Dave Tough. Additional highlights include "Muskrat Ramble," "At the Jazz Band Ball," "Jazz Me Blues," "Sensation," and "I'm Coming Virginia." If any listener has doubts that Dixieland can be creative and exciting, this disc serves as proof. Also of interest is **Wild Bill Davison and His Jazz Band 1943** (Jazzology 103), which has his original "That's a Plenty" band on December 3, 1943, performing at a radio transcription series (five songs plus five alternate takes including a different version of "That's a Plenty") in addition to three songs and a lot of false starts and alternate versions from a 1955 session with Tony Parenti and Lou McGarity.

Max Kaminsky and Bobby Hackett Eddie Condon used a lot of different trumpeters and cornetists through the years, sometimes two or three on the same recording session. Max Kaminsky was particularly reliable although not as distinctive as Wild Bill Davison. He had been part of the Chicago jazz scene in the 1920s. After moving to New York in 1929, Kaminsky worked with commercial bands, but also recorded with Condon, Benny Carter, and Mezz Mezzrow. He played with Tommy Dorsey (1936), Bud Freeman's Summa Cum Laude Orchestra (1939–40), Tony Pastor (1940–41), and with Artie Shaw on three different occasions (1938, 1942, and in 1943 with Shaw's military orchestra). Kaminsky became a civilian in time to be a major participant on Condon's Town Hall series and he led his first record date in 1944 for Commodore.

Cornetist Bobby Hackett had a mellower tone than most Dixieland-oriented brass players and he rarely tried to hit a high note. A lyrical player, Hackett was originally a guitarist before taking up the cornet. He worked locally in his native Rhode Island and led his own group in 1936. In 1937, he moved to New York, played with Joe Marsala and was dubbed "the new Bix" because of the similarity of his tone to Bix Beiderbecke. He even appeared at Benny Goodman's 1938 Carnegie Hall concert where he recreated Bix's solo on "I'm Coming Virginia," but little of the Beiderbecke influence would remain in his mature style and his real hero was actually Louis Armstrong. Hackett recorded with Eddie Condon in 1938 and his beautiful playing on "Embraceable You" was an inspiration for Miles Davis. During 1939 he led a big band, but it did not last long.

1938–1940 (Classics 890) has the eight numbers by Hackett's big band, a decent outfit that did not have enough time to develop its own sound. Also on this fine CD are some Dixielandish numbers (with George Brunies, Pee Wee Russell, and Eddie Condon helping out) and a few titles sponsored by Horace Heidt; best are "If Dreams Come True," "At the Jazz Band Ball," "Bugle Call Rag," and "Singin' the Blues." After Hackett's big band broke up, he worked with Horace Heidt (an association that helped him repay his debts) and Glenn Miller (1941–42), taking a famous solo with the latter on "String of Pearls." When Miller enlisted, Hackett worked with the Casa Loma Orchestra and then worked in the studios where his pretty tone was in great demand. At night he enjoyed playing in Dixieland groups.

1943–1947 (Classics 1047) has Hackett in various combos, recording for Commodore, Melrose, Brunswick, radio transcriptions, and V-discs. He always sounded so relaxed, no matter what the tempo, and plays beautifully on "But Not for Me," "When a Woman Loves a Man," a remake of "Embraceable You," "When Day Is Done," and "Pennies from Heaven."

George Brunies and Miff Mole The two veteran trombonists of the 1920s both made jazz comebacks during the 1940s. George Brunies, who had been a member of the New Orleans Rhythm Kings during 1922–23, spent 1924–35 with Ted Lewis's Orchestra. A bit of a clown, but a very good ensemble player and a decent soloist, Brunies was with Muggsy Spanier in 1939, worked with Art Hodes and Eddie Condon, and recorded four songs as a leader on November 27, 1943, on the same day and using the same group as Wild Bill Davison's famous "That's a Plenty" Commodore session.

Miff Mole, who had been the most advanced trombonist in jazz during 1926–28, spent many years in the studios in addition to working with Paul Whiteman (1938–40) and Benny Goodman in 1943. His style had become influenced strongly by Jack Teagarden, but he adapted well to Dixieland settings. Mole, who played now and then with Eddie Condon and led his own band at Nick's, used an inventive version of "Peg O' My Heart" as his feature during this period. In 1944, he had his first record date as a leader since 1937 (and only his second since 1930), and he headed a septet for a radio transcription date reissued in full on **World Jam Session Band** (Jazzology 105). Due to the large number of incomplete takes and false starts, this disc is a little hard to listen to, but the accepted versions of the ten songs (which include "Peg O' My Heart," "At the Jazz Band Ball," and "I Would Do Anything for You") are excellent, featuring Mole, Pee Wee Russell, and trumpeter Sterling Bose.

Pee Wee Russell and Edmond Hall Although associated with Eddie Condon and Dixieland throughout much of his life, Pee Wee Russell was not a typical New Orleans-style clarinetist. Never a virtuoso, Russell constantly took chances in his solos, making the oddest-sounding notes fit and playing with a great deal of feeling. Admirers (including Benny Goodman) loved to hear him play to see if he could make it through a chorus without getting too tangled up; he usually made it. In the 1920s, Russell initially sounded a bit like Frank Teschemacher, gaining some attention for his playing with Red Nichols's Five Pennies. But in the 1930s, he became much more original, and after playing and recorded regularly with Louis Prima during 1935–37, he recorded with Condon in 1938, taking a notable spot on "Ja Da." Russell was well featured on Condon's 1944–45 Town Hall concerts, and although sometimes the butt of his jokes (due to his odd facial expressions, highly individual solos, very thin frame, and alcoholism), he was part of Condon's free-wheeling Dixieland settings off and on for 30 years. **Jack Teagarden's Big Eight/Pee Wee Russell's Rhythmakers** (Original Jazz Classics 1708), in addition to a Teagarden small-group date, features Russell in 1938 on his first session as a leader with a group also including such notables as Max Kaminsky, Dickie Wells, and James P. Johnson on "There'll Be Some Changes Made," "I've Found a New Baby," and "Dinah." The programming on **Jazz Original** (Commodore 404) is a bit confusing as it includes some alternate takes whose master versions are on other releases. This sampler has Russell featured on some selections (mostly alternates) with Eddie Condon's all-star groups of 1938–42 and one number apiece (both alternates) with Muggsy Spanier and Wild Bill Davison. Most significant is the inclusion of the four titles he cut in 1941 with "The Three Deuces" (a trio with Joe Sullivan and Zutty Singleton) and all of the performances from 1944 with his "Hot Four" (a quartet with Jess Stacy, Sid Weiss, and George Wettling).

When Pee Wee Russell was not available or was indisposed, Edmond Hall was sometimes called in his place. One of four clarinet-playing brothers (including Herbie Hall) who were the sons of the early clarinetist Edward Hall, Edmond worked in many bands in New Orleans (including Buddy Petit's during 1921–23) before going to New York in 1928 with Alonzo Ross. It took him quite a while to develop his own sound. While with Claude Hopkins's orchestra during 1929–35, Hall doubled on baritone and was not featured all that much. However, during engagements with Lucky Millinder, Zutty Singleton, Joe Sullivan, and Red Allen (1940), Hall's individuality really developed and he was quite recognizable while with Teddy Wilson's sextet (1941–44). Hall, who turned down an opportunity to be Barney Bigard's successor with Duke Ellington in 1942, was already 41 at that time, but just entering his prime. His dirty and cutting tone was instantly recognizable within a note or two, yet he could play with a fluidity approaching Benny

Goodman. He began working with Eddie Condon on an occasional basis in 1944. **1937–1944** (Classics 830) begins with two obscure numbers in which Hall is featured in 1937 with Billy Hicks's Sizzling Six. The four songs from Hall's classic 1941 session with his "Celeste Quartet" not only has Hall, Meade Lux Lewis (on celeste), and bassist Israel Crosby, but Charlie Christian making his only recordings on acoustic guitar. In addition, there is a heated Dixieland session from 1944 with Sidney DeParis and James P. Johnson and more swing-oriented dates with Emmett Berry, Vic Dickenson, Red Norvo, and Teddy Wilson. **1944–1945** (Classics 872) has the master takes from five Hall sessions cut for Blue Note, Commodore, as radio transcriptions, and for Continental. Although there are many alternates that are available on more complete reissues, this CD will suffice for most listeners. It has one gem after another, including versions of "It's Been So Long," "Big City Blues," "Sleepy Time Gal," "I Want to Be Happy," "Ellis Island," and "Lonely Moments." Hall is heard on many numbers in a quartet with Teddy Wilson, leading a 1944–45 sextet with trumpeter Irving "Mouse" Randolph, trombonist Henderson Chambers, and pianist Ellis Larkins, and as part of an unusual trumpetless septet session with Benny Morton and Harry Carney.

Bud Freeman   Unlike many of Eddie Condon's sidemen (including Wild Bill Davison and Pee Wee Russell), Bud Freeman was already pretty well known by 1939. Although the last of the Austin High Gang players to become a talented musician, Freeman had worked steadily in the swing era as a soloist with the big bands of Joe Haymes (1934), Ray Noble (1935), Tommy Dorsey (1936–38), and Benny Goodman (1938). His trio recordings with Jess Stacy and George Wettling in 1938 were among the most exciting performances of the era. In 1939, he formed an octet that he called the Summa Cum Laude Orchestra and featured Russell, Max Kaminsky, Brad Gowans on valve trombone, and Condon himself. As with Muggsy Spanier's Ragtime Band, Freeman's group just lasted a year. ◐ **1939–1940** (Classics 811) has all 24 selections by the Summa Cum Laude Orchestra (which was really a hot Dixieland octet); the group's final session (eight songs) has Jack Teagarden in Gowan's place. This excellent all-star band jams such numbers as "China Boy," Freeman's "The Eel," eight selections from the repertoire of Bix Beiderbecke's Wolverines, and "Jack Hits the Road."

Freeman, who with Eddie Miller (from Bob Crosby's Bobcats), was nearly the only tenor saxophonist to be easily accepted in Dixieland settings, led a short-lived big band, freelanced, and spent 1943–45 in the army.

Joe Sullivan and Art Hodes   Pianist Joe Sullivan, who had recorded with McKenzie-Condon's Chicagoans in 1927, was Bing Crosby's accompanist during 1934–36. He played piano with Bob Crosby's Orchestra for a few months in 1936 and was getting some attention for being featured on his original "Little Rock Getaway." Unfortunately, he had a bout with tuberculosis and had to be hospitalized, so Bob Zurke appeared on Crosby's hit record of that song. Sullivan recovered and in 1938 worked with both Bing and Bob Crosby. After going solo, the pianist led groups on 52nd Street for a few years. ◐ **1933–1941** (Classics 821) has all of his prewar recordings as a leader. There are eight piano solos from 1933–35 including the original themeless version of "Little Rock Getaway" (which sounds a bit odd) and a later rendition that has the famous melody. Sullivan also plays solo on such numbers as "Honeysuckle Rose," "Gin Mill Blues," and "My Little Pride of Joy," is featured on the four "Three Deuces" titles with Pee Wee Russell and Zutty Singleton, and leads a couple of medium-size swing groups with such sidemen as trombonist Benny Morton, Edmond Hall, Danny Polo on clarinet and tenor, and singers Helen Ward and Big Joe Turner.

Art Hodes was always a fighter for traditional jazz, whether through his distinctive piano playing, his writings (which included many articles and liner notes), or his work on radio and educational television. Famed for his blues playing, Hodes was also very effective on uptempo tunes where his on-the-beat chordings from his left hand could be quite exciting. Born in Russia, he came to America with his family when he was six months old and grew up in Chicago. Hodes was part of the Chicago jazz scene of the 1920s, making his recording debut with Wingy Manone in 1928, but spent most of the 1930s in obscurity in Chicago. After moving to New York in 1938, he began to be noticed, playing with Joe Marsala, Mezz Mezzrow, and his own groups (starting in 1941). Hodes went out of his way to promote freewheeling jazz, editing the important jazz magazine *The Jazz Record* during 1943–47, hosting a regular radio show, and starting his own Jazz Record label, one of the first record companies headed by a jazz musician. He also recorded for Solo Art, Commodore, Signature, Decca, Black & White, and quite extensively during 1944–45 for Blue Note.

The Jazz Record Story (Jazzology 82) has all 22 selections that Hodes made for his own label, dating from 1940–47. Oddly enough, the recordings are juggled a bit

TIMELINE 1944

Victor and Columbia finally settle with the Musicians Union, and the recording strike comes to an end in November. • Ten-year-old English drummer Victor Feldman sits in with Glenn Miller's Army Air Force Band. • Lester Young is drafted. • Coleman Hawkins leads the first bebop record date. • Eddie Condon begins broadcasting his Town Hall concert series. • Gene Ammons becomes one of the star soloists with Billy Eckstine's bebop big band, in addition to Charlie Parker and Dizzy Gillespie. • The Bascomb Brothers (Paul and Dud) leave Erskine Hawkins's Orchestra to form their own sextet. • The Candoli Brothers (Pete and Conte) play with Woody Herman as the Herd takes shape. • Buddy Johnson forms his big band and records "Fine Brown Frame." • Louis Metcalf leads the International Band in Montreal. • Les Paul makes his first recordings with his trio. • Singer/pianist Harry "The Hipster" Gibson records "Stop that Dancin' Up There." • Mamie Smith, who had appeared in four black films during 1939–41, retires. • Julia Lee, a fixture in Kansas City, records for the first time since 1929. • Guitarist Johnny Moore, pianist/singer Charles Brown, and bassist Eddie Williams form Johnny Moore's Three Blazers in Los Angeles. • Richard M. Jones leads his last record date. • Red McKenzie makes a comeback after being a beer salesman for five years, performing with Eddie Condon on his Town Hall concerts. • Teenage tenor saxophonist Zoot Sims records with Joe Bushkin. • Pianist Billy Taylor records with Stuff Smith. • Sarah Vaughan makes her recording debut. • Bud Powell plays with the Cootie Williams Big Band. • Harry James has a hit with Duke Ellington's "I'm Beginning to See the Light." • Carmen McRae sings with the Benny Carter Orchestra. • Glenn Miller's plane disappears over the English Channel.

and the exact dates (and which songs match which personnel list) are not given, but all of the music is here. Hodes is heard on six piano solos, four band numbers from 1940 (a quintet with trumpeter Duke DuVal, George Brunies, Rod Cless, and drummer Joe Grauso), eight selections with a 1946 sextet (which includes trumpeter Henry Goodwin, trombonist George Lugg, clarinetist Cecil Scott, Pops Foster, and drummer Kaiser Marshall), and four songs in a trio with Foster and Baby Dodds. The recording quality is a little shaky in the earliest performances, but the joy of the music is very much present on the Dixieland standards, blues, and 1920s tunes, including "You've Got to Give Me Some," "The Mooche," "Too Busy," "Droppin' Shucks," and several Jelly Roll Morton songs. Unfortunately, Hodes's ten Blue Note sessions of 1944–45 (Dixieland dates featuring Max Kaminsky, Wild Bill Davison, Vic Dickenson, Rod Cless, Edmond Hall, Albert Nicholas, Sidney Bechet, and other Condonites) have not been coherently reissued since the five-LP limited-edition box **The Complete Blue Note Art Hodes Sessions** (Mosaic 5-114).

James P. Johnson and Willie "The Lion" Smith In the 1920s, James P. Johnson, Fats Waller, and Willie "The Lion" Smith were competitive pals, playing at rent parties in Harlem. As Fats Waller went on to fame in the 1930s, James P. Johnson spent much of the decade writing "serious" classical works (such as "Harlem Symphony," "Jassamine," "Symphony in Brown," and a blues opera called "De Organizer"), few of which were ever performed and some of which have been permanently lost through the years. He rarely played in public during 1931–37 and practically his only recordings were made with old friend Clarence Williams's groups. In 1938, the great stride pianist recorded with Pee Wee Russell and, after appearing at that year's "From Spirituals to Swing" concert, he began performing regularly again. Despite a minor stroke, he was quite active during the first half of the 1940s, sometimes playing with Eddie Condon including guesting on a few of his Town Hall concerts.

Fortunately, Johnson recorded frequently in the 1940s. **1938–1942** (Classics 711) has band dates from 1939 with Red Allen, J.C. Higginbotham, and singers Anna Robinson (most memorable on "Hungry Blues") and Ruby Smith. There are also some brilliant piano solos (including "If Dreams Come True," "The Mule Walk," and a remake of "Snowy Morning Blues"). **1943–1944** (Classics 824) draws its material from the Folkways label (including two piano solos recorded on July 1943 in violation of the recording strike), Bob Thiele's Signature label, Decca, and Blue Note. The piano solos include "Daintiness Rag," "Backwater Blues," "Caprice Rag," and "Blues for Fats" (along with four Waller songs), while one of the Blue Note sessions is a swing septet date with Sidney DeParis, Vic Dickenson, and Ben Webster. **1944** (Classics 835) has more piano solos, duets with drummer Eddie Dougherty, a scarce Asch/Folkways quintet date with Frankie Newton and Al Casey, and a fine combo session actually released under Sidney DeParis's name. As James P. continued paying tribute to his recently deceased friend, eight Waller tunes join "Hesitation Blues" (which has a very rare Johnson vocal), Scott Joplin's "Euphonic Sounds," and "The Dreams" among the highlights. **1944 Vol. 2** (Classics 856) is most notable for Johnson (who was still at 90 percent of his 1920s strength) remaking some of his best songs ("Snowy Morning Blues," "Carolina Shout," "Keep Off the Grass," "Old Fashioned Love," and "If I Could Be with You") in duets with drummer Dougherty.

While James P. Johnson sounded quite fine revisiting the past, Willie "The Lion" Smith recorded some of his most important work in 1939. Smith, who had barely appeared on records at all in the 1920s, worked in New York clubs during the 1930s. In 1935 and 1937, he led combo sides, mostly dates with The Lion's Cubs (a quartet of Clarence Williams's players including cornetist Ed Allen and Cecil Scott) and the early 1937 version of John Kirby's sextet. In addition, he appeared on no less than 21 numbers with the dated-sounding organ of Milt Herth. Fortunately, that was in the past when he recorded the timeless music reissued on ● **1938–1940** (Classics 692). In February 1939, the Lion recorded eight originals and six standards as piano solos. Although a tough-looking character with his bowler hat, big cigar, and bragging nature, Smith was actually a highly sophisticated, sensitive musician whose originals were impressionistic and picturesque, most notably the haunting "Echoes of Spring," "Passionette," "Rippling Waters," and "Morning Air." He is also heard romping on his "Finger Buster," jamming a couple of slightly earlier numbers with fellow pianists Joe Bushkin and Jess Stacy, playing four originals in February 1940 with an octet that includes Sidney DeParis, and backing the vocals of Big Joe Turner. However, because his songs were so complicated for others to reproduce, none became standards, and by 1944, Smith was often heard playing in rambunctious Dixieland settings, where his sensitivity was de-emphasized.

George Wettling and Dave Tough   While a variety of different bassists (most notably Artie Shapiro and Bob Casey) played background roles in Eddie Condon's band, just walking four-to-the-bar including during their infrequent solos, two of Condon's drummers were standouts. George Wettling worked in Chicago during the 1920s and the early '30s, developing his own style out of that of his idol Baby Dodds. He was flexible enough during the swing era to play with the big bands of Artie Shaw (1936), Bunny Berigan (1937), Red Norvo, Paul Whiteman (1938–40), and Muggsy Spanier, but was at his best in small groups. His alert and colorful playing with the Bud Freeman Trio in 1938 helped make those performances particularly exciting, and he was a master at making every accent and sound count. Although he was a staff musician at ABC for nine years starting in 1943, Wettling played trad jazz nightly, quite often with Eddie Condon. He also appeared at Condon's Town Hall concerts. **1940–1944** (Classics 909) finds him in the rare role of being a leader. Wettling jams Dixieland and swing with such players as Charlie Teagarden, trombonist Floyd O'Brien, Danny Polo, Joe Marsala, Jess Stacy, Billy Butterfield, Wilbur De Paris, Edmond Hall, trumpeter Joe Thomas, Jack Teagarden, and even Mezz Mezzrow (in a trio) and Coleman Hawkins, consistently inspiring the soloists.

With the exception of four numbers from 1946, Dave Tough never led his own record date nor expressed a desire to; he did not even like taking solos. An alcoholic from an early age who was often painfully thin, Tough (a member of the Austin High Gang) spent 1932–35 trying to recover from various illnesses. He was part of the swing era, propelling the big bands of Ray Noble, Tommy Dorsey (1936–37), Red Norvo, Bunny Berigan, Benny Goodman (as Gene Krupa's first replacement in 1938), and Tommy Dorsey again. During 1939–42, he alternated between Dixieland groups (including Bud Freeman's Summa Cum Laude band, Mezz Mezzrow, Joe Marsala, and Eddie Condon) and big bands (Jack Teagarden, Artie Shaw, and Charlie Spivak) before spending part of 1942–44 in the navy where he played with Artie Shaw's Naval Band. After his discharge he was a member of Woody Herman's Herd. Tough was a subtle player who

was felt as much as heard, resulting in him being admired by musicians, but underrated by the jazz public.

Henry "Red" Allen   Henry "Red" Allen began 1939 playing with what was formerly the Luis Russell Orchestra, which Louis Armstrong was using as his backup group. Though Allen occasionally took solos during the band's first set (on songs played before Armstrong took the stage), on records with Satch he was confined to section work. The following year most of the band (including Allen) was laid off, but that ended up being a good thing for the trumpeter. He soon formed a hot sextet that initially included J.C. Higginbotham, Edmond Hall, and Ken Kersey, a band capable of playing Dixieland and swing in an exciting manner, while at times looking forward toward early rhythm and blues. **1937–1941** (Classics 628) has Allen playing and singing eight pop tunes with a pickup group in 1937 that includes Tab Smith, four Dixielandish numbers from 1940 with Lil Armstrong, Edmond Hall, and Benny Morton, and, most significantly, seven selections (including the two-part "Sometimes I'm Happy") with his jubilant 1941 sextet. By 1944, Allen's band had the brilliant young altoist Don Stovall in the frontline with Higginbotham and it was creating great excitement while straddling musical boundaries.

Joe Marsala   One of the most intriguing swing/Dixieland groups of the period was headed by clarinetist Joe Marsala. The older brother of trumpeter Marty Marsala, Joe Marsala played in Chicago in the late 1920s including with Wingy Manone and Ben Pollack. He worked and recorded with Manone during 1935–36 and then became a leader himself, often working at the Hickory House on 52nd Street. He gave Buddy Rich his first important musical job in 1936, and the following year married the great jazz harpist Adele Girard, who worked in most of his groups. Girard was only the second important jazz harpist (following Casper Reardon) and preceded the third, Dorothy Ashby, by 15 years. Although Marsala (who had a tone similar to Benny Goodman's, but an open-minded style of his own) led short-lived big bands in 1939 and 1942, he mostly headed small combos where the clarinet/harp frontline (which was sometimes joined by his brother's trumpet) was quite unique.

◉ **1936–1942** (Classics 763) has Marsala's first 21 selections as a leader. Among the sidemen featured on these six sessions are Marty Marsala, Pee Wee Erwin, Bill Coleman, Max Kaminsky, George Brunies, Pete Brown, violinist Ray Biondi, drummers Buddy Rich and Shelly Manne (both making their recording debuts), and several fine rhythm sections. Adele Girard is a major asset on 11 of the numbers, stealing the show on "Bull's Eye" and "I Know that You Know." Two intriguing LPs add to the legacy of Marsala's bands. **Lower Register** (IAJRC 38) has a variety of sideman appearances by Marsala along with a complete 29-minute radio broadcast from 1939 that has the clarinetist heading an octet also including his brother, his wife, valve trombonist Brad Gowans, and Bud Freeman. The Marsala big band of 1942 is featured during two radio broadcasts that comprise **Featuring Adele Girard** (Aircheck 14), with spots for both Kaminsky and Marty Marsala on trumpets.

Sidney and Wilbur DeParis   Trumpeter Sidney DeParis was a veteran of the 1920s who along the way worked with Charlie Johnson's Paradise Ten (1926–31), Don Redman's big band (1932–36 and 1939), Zutty Singleton (1939–41), Benny Carter (1940–41), and Art Hodes (1941). He made a lot of freelance recordings, including with Jelly Roll Morton (1939) and Sidney Bechet (1940). In 1943, he joined the band of his older brother, Wilbur DeParis, and played on and off with the band for the next 20 years. **Sidney DeParis Story** (EPM 158652) has some of the highlights from the first half of his career including a selection or two with Johnson, Redman, Morton, and Bechet, plus Blue Note dates from 1944 with Hodes, James P. Johnson, and Edmond Hall. Also included are the four Dixieland numbers from DeParis's first date as a leader, a 1944 set that resulted in memorable versions of "Everybody Loves My Baby" and "Who's Sorry Now."

While Sidney DeParis was a highly rated soloist in both Dixieland and swing settings, Wilbur DeParis was mostly thought of as a strong ensemble player although he could take decent solos too. The older DeParis started on alto horn and played C-melody sax with A.J. Piron in 1922 before switching to trombone. DeParis led a band in Philadelphia in 1925 and worked with Leroy Smith, Dave Nelson, Noble Sissle, Edgar Hayes, Teddy Hill (1936–37), the Mills Blue Rhythm Band, and Louis Armstrong (1937–40) without gaining much fame. DeParis began leading an occasional band with his brother in 1943, but it would be eight years before his group caught on.

Bunk Johnson   In 1938, Bunk Johnson was just another forgotten and totally undocumented early New Orleans jazz musician, working at a day job in complete obscurity. Born in 1889 (not 1879 as he later claimed so he could say that he had played with Buddy Bolden), Johnson had been a major player on the New Orleans jazz scene starting around 1910 when he joined the Eagle Band. He was best known for his pretty tone and lyrical style. However, after the early 1930s, he had gone into retirement, unable to play due to his decayed teeth and not owning a decent horn.

In the 1939 book *Jazzmen* (written by Bill Russell and Fred Ramsey), Johnson was favorably profiled. The interest that the book generated led to a collection being taken to get Bunk new teeth and a horn. In 1942, Johnson at last appeared on records, starting on February 2 when he played some unaccompanied trumpet solos and spoke on a record about how someday he hoped to play with his old friend Sidney Bechet again. On June 11, he made his first official record, which has been reissued as **Bunk Johnson & His Superior Jazz Band** (Good Time Jazz 12048). In addition to talking a bit about his life story, Johnson is featured on nine numbers in a septet also including clarinetist George Lewis and trombonist Jim Robinson. The playing is a bit erratic and sometimes out of tune, but Bunk sounds like he has been practicing, and he would steadily improve during the next two years. In 1943, Johnson spent time in San Francisco, playing with the wartime version of the Yerba Buena Jazz Band and various local musicians. **Bunk Johnson in San Francisco** (American Music 16) starts out weak with a May 9, 1943, radio broadcast that has Johnson playing with the Kid Ory band, including trumpeter Mutt Carey. Clarinetist Wade Whaley is way out of tune and overmiked, and dominates the ensembles. It is a pity for, in addition to the rare opportunity to hear Johnson and Carey playing together, this broadcast features the Ory group a year before it caught on. Much better are six rare duets that Johnson has with pianist Bertha Gonsoulin two days before and one day after the concert. The trumpeter's playing on "Sister Kate," "Franklin Street Blues," and "Bolden Medley" ranks with the best of his career. Also on this disc is an oddity, Bunk playing along (and fitting right in both stylistically and volume-wise) with George Lewis's record of "Pacific Street Blues."

In 1944, Johnson was back in New Orleans, using a band consisting of George Lewis, Jim Robinson, banjoist

Lawrence Marrero, bassist Alcide "Slow Drag" Pavageau, and Baby Dodds. Lewis, who was born in 1900, was an early associate of Bunk's and had been playing in New Orleans since 1918, working along the way with the Black Eagle Band, Buddy Petit, the Eureka Brass Band, Chris Kelly, and Kid Rena. Possessor of a charming and original style on clarinet, Lewis was (like Johnson) an erratic player throughout his career, sounding inspired on one song and woefully out of tune on the next, seeming to adjust to whatever level his trumpeter was at. He would become an influential force, and his best performances ranked with the finest New Orleans jazz. Jim Robinson, who had recorded with Sam Morgan in 1927 and Kid Rena in 1940, was a very reliable trombonist and particularly strong in ensembles, saving many a record date with his consistency and enthusiasm. In 1943, when Bunk was in San Francisco, Lewis and Robinson had opportunities to record for the Climax label in a sextet with trumpeter Kid Howard (who was at the peak of his powers), Lawrence Marrero, bassist Chester Zardis, and drummer Edgar Mosley, music that was last available on a five-LP limited-edition box set **The Complete Blue Note George Lewis** (Mosaic 5-132), but not yet on CD.

Bunk Johnson's 1944 band recorded quite a bit with most of the music reissued on four CDs. **The King of the Blues** (American Music 1) has 13 performances (the majority of which are blues) including two vocals by Myrtle Jones, three songs not previously released in the United States, and two numbers ("Weary Blues" and "How Long Blues") being put out for the first time. In general, Bunk plays quite well and the ensemble-oriented music is typically enjoyable and spirited, including "St. Louis Blues," "Royal Garden Blues," and "Tishomingo Blues," which would become one of Lewis's trademark features. **1944** (American Music 3) has 15 selections from four sessions that took place within a five-day period. Once again Bunk sounds fairly strong, and although Lewis is sometimes out of tune, the joy of the ensemble-oriented music overrides the occasional technical deficiencies. Among the better selections are "We Will Walk Through the Streets of the City," a previously unreleased version of "Sister Kate," "There's Yes Yes in Your Eyes," "Panama," and "When the Saints Go Marching In." Some of the same songs are heard in different versions on **1944—2nd Masters** (American Music 8) along with "Darktown Strutters Ball," "Weary Blues," and "Dippermouth Blues." **1944/45** (American Music 12) has three

sessions in July–August 1944 plus two in May 1945, with Bunk generally sounding better than his group (he was improving with practice), and one can understand his impatience with the other players. Lewis is erratic and Dodds's colorful playing is a bit distracting. However, the band's joyful ensembles are appealing and the hotter numbers are "Milenburg Joys," "Shine," "Lady Be Good," "The Sheik of Araby," and "Willie the Weeper."

Bunk Johnson became one of the most controversial jazz musicians of the mid-1940s. His supporters thought that he played "the real jazz" (before it was "commercialized" by swing) and liked to imagine that he sounded like jazz musicians of the early New Orleans era even though in reality he enjoyed performing current pop tunes. Detractors, noting that his intonation could be shaky and that he fell way short of being a virtuoso, thought of Johnson (who tended to exaggerate his role in jazz history) as a fraud. Whether considered a genius or a charlatan, Bunk Johnson would certainly be a colorful figure during the years of his unlikely comeback.

Kid Ory   While Bunk Johnson and George Lewis were the most significant of the formerly undocumented New Orleans jazzmen discovered in the early 1940s, Kid Ory was among the most important of the 1920s New Orleans players to make a comeback. Unlike Jelly Roll Morton and Johnny Dodds, Ory lived long enough to have his second career reach greater heights than his first. Ory had moved to California in the early 1930s and in 1933 dropped out of music altogether, working in the post office and running a chicken farm. His early trumpeter Mutt Carey, who had been on Ory's 1922 record date, was also living near Los Angeles and working outside of music. In 1943, both Ory and Carey became interested in playing music again. Ory started out playing bass with a quartet until his trombone chops were back in prime form. Then he formed a New Orleans jazz band with Carey and frequently clarinetist Wade Whaley, pianist Buster Wilson, guitarist Bud Scott, bassist Ed Garland, and Zutty Singleton.

Ory's big break came in February 1944 when actor Orson Welles decided to add a New Orleans jazz band to his radio show, planning to feature them for one number on each program. Ory was contacted and his group (which now had Jimmie Noone on clarinet) became a very popular attraction on the Welles show. Noone's death in April was a shock; he was replaced initially by

Barney Bigard and then by Omer Simeon and Joe Darensbourg. **Kid Ory's Creole Jazz Band** (Folklyric 9008) is an LP that has a dozen appearances of Ory's group on the Welles show (Noone is on the first five numbers, his final recordings) plus five selections from an unrelated 1945 radio program. The Welles broadcasts revitalized Kid Ory's career and resulted in the veteran trombonist leading one of the top New Orleans jazz bands of the following 15 years.

The First Revivalists: Lu Watters's Yerba Buena Jazz Band　While most of the New Orleans jazz bands of the 1939–44 period featured either swing players turning back toward Dixieland (the Eddie Condon gang) or rediscovered veterans, the musicians in Lu Watters's Yerba Buena Jazz Band were a different breed altogether. These were younger players who made a conscious decision to go back in time musically, playing as if the swing era did not exist and using as their role models King Oliver's Creole Jazz Band, Jelly Roll Morton's Red Hot Peppers, and the Louis Armstrong Hot Five and Seven. Although it is not that uncommon today to decide to play in an earlier style, in the early 1940s this was considered extremely unusual in jazz.

Trumpeter Lu Watters was leading bands as early as 1925 (when he was 13), spent five years with the Carol Lofner Orchestra, and by the late 1930s was in San Francisco leading his own big band. In 1939, he met fellow trumpeter Bob Scobey, trombonist Turk Murphy, and pianist Wally Rose, all of whom were more interested in jazz of the 1920s than in swing. While Watters was 27 at the time, Scobey was 22, Murphy (who had played with the big bands of Mal Hallett and Will Osborne) was 23, and Wally Rose was 25. These were not old men bringing back the music of their youth, but the equivalent of musical archeologists, uncovering gems from the past and writing newer material in the classic jazz style.

Lu Watters's Yerba Buena Jazz Band, which also originally included clarinetist Ellis Horne, both Clancy Hayes and Russ Bennett on banjos, Dick Lammi (succeeded in 1942 by Squire Girsback) on tuba, and drummer Bill Dart, debuted in December 1939 at the Dawn Club. Their first record date was on December 19, 1941. All of the band's studio recordings are available on the four-CD box **The Complete Good Time Jazz Recordings** (Good Time Jazz 4409) and the music is mostly also available individually. **Bunk and Lu** (Good Time Jazz 12024) has

two rather historic sessions. The first eight numbers are the initial recordings by the Yerba Buena Jazz Band and these performances were quite influential, giving momentum to the New Orleans revival movement. Although the group would improve, on such numbers as "Georgia Camp Meeting," "Irish Black Bottom," and "Muskrat Ramble," the band shows that it was not merely a copy of King Oliver's group, but already developing a sound of its own. Wally Rose's feature on "Black & White Rag" helped lead to a minirevival of the long extinct ragtime music. **1942 Series** (Good Time Jazz 12007) has the 14 selections (plus six alternate takes) recorded by the group on March 29, 1942, including "Come Back Sweet Papa," "Sunset Café Stomp," "Cake Walking Babies," and "Tiger Rag."

World War II resulted in Watters and some of his sidemen being drafted, so the original Yerba Buena Jazz Band came to a temporary end. A wartime version of the group initially featured trumpeter Benny Strickler, but the talented Strickler (who can be heard on a radio broadcast from August 1942 included on the Good Time box) was soon struck down by tuberculosis and passed away in 1946. In the spring of 1944, Bunk Johnson was in San Francisco and he recorded one of his finest sessions with some of the members of the group, including Turk Murphy, Ellis Horne, Squire Girsback, and Clancy Hayes (who switched to drums), plus pianist Burt Bales and banjoist Pat Patton. The eight numbers that resulted from this unique collaboration form the second half of **Bunk and Lu**. Bunk sounds so strong on such numbers as "The Girls Go Crazy," "Down by the Riverside," and "Careless Love" that it is a pity that he was not always at this consistently high level. This session should be played for his worst detractors who make the mistake of writing him off.

Even with their promising start, the greatest days of the Yerba Buena Jazz Band would have to wait until the end of World War II.

The Beginnings of Bebop

Most younger players, however, were not looking toward New Orleans jazz for inspiration in the early 1940s. While some admired and emulated such swing stars as Benny Goodman, Harry James, and Teddy Wilson, other musicians wanted to develop their own voices. Some were tired of the way that the swing big bands were relying excessively on simple riffs and copying each other, and they wanted to move the music forward. Of particular concern to younger black musicians was uplifting jazz beyond merely being entertainment and dance music, developing it to a point where it would be considered a serious art form.

The music that by 1945 would be widely called "rebop," "bebop," and finally "bop," differed from swing in a variety of ways that will be outlined in detail in Chapter 6. Basically it relied much more on chordal than melodic improvisation (except for the music of Thelonious Monk), so themes tended to be discarded after the first unison chorus until the conclusion of a song. Chords were more complex than in swing, soloists had a wider choice of what notes to play, since virtually any note could fit in any spot as long as it was later resolved. Drummers were liberated from hitting the bass drum to keep time. The function of the piano changed drastically from how it was utilized by stride players. Tempos no longer kept dancing audiences in mind, and most melodies took several listens before they could be duplicated, unlike pop hits.

Swing fans who were exposed to bop for the first time in 1945 were often quite bewildered because relatively little of the music was documented in its developing forms. This was largely due to the recording strike of 1942–44. Private recordings, radio broadcasts, and some live performances have emerged during the past couple of decades to fill in the gap a bit, but in some ways early bebop is similar to pre-1923 jazz; one can mostly only hear hints of what was to come in the recordings of 1940–44.

Charlie Parker and Jay McShann Following in the wake of Count Basie and Andy Kirk, Jay McShann led an important Kansas City band that briefly made a strong impression in New York. McShann began playing piano when he was 12 in 1928. Born in Muskogee, Oklahoma, he was part of the Kansas City jazz scene by the mid-1930s and formed his big band in 1937. In 1940, McShann brought the orchestra to New York and during 1941–42 they made some recordings for Decca. Unfortunately, the record label wanted McShann to mostly stick to the blues, particularly after "Confessin' the Blues" (which featured Walter Brown's vocal) became a hit, so many of the band's swing charts were not documented. The orchestra lasted until 1944 when the pianist was drafted.

Although McShann was a fine swing pianist who in later years developed into an excellent blues singer, his orchestra is considered most significant for featuring altoist Charlie Parker during 1937–42. Born in Kansas

City, Kansas, in 1920, Parker grew up in Kansas City, Missouri. He started out playing baritone horn, switching to alto when he was ten, and dropping out of school at 14 because he wanted to be a professional musician. However, at that early point, Parker's enthusiasm far outstripped his abilities, and he was humiliated at a few jam sessions when he got lost trying to play double-time runs. After he spent a summer woodshedding to Lester Young records, his early style was together and local musicians began to accept him. He joined McShann's Orchestra in 1937, picked up the lifelong nickname of "Bird" (or "Yardbird"), and also worked with Lawrence Keyes, Harlan Leonard, and Buster Smith, visiting New York for the first time in 1939. While in New York, Parker worked as a dishwasher at a restaurant, but was happy for the experience because Art Tatum was performing at that club every night.

Parker returned to New York in 1940 with McShann's band and appeared on the orchestra's first recordings, taking a few short solos. He met Dizzy Gillespie (they were immediately impressed with each other's playing), participated at jam sessions (often at Monroe's Uptown House, but also at Minton's), and in 1943 joined the Earl Hines Orchestra on tenor. That stint went unrecorded as did his playing with Billy Eckstine's big band in 1944, which followed short stints with Cootie Williams and Andy Kirk. But a small-group date led by Tiny Grimes that year gave listeners their first real hint of what Charlie Parker sounded like.

Nearly all of Bird's few early appearances on records (along with some very rare items) are included on three CDs. Jay McShann's **Blues from Kansas City** (GRP/Decca 614) has all of McShann's recordings from 1941–43, including ten features for small groups and 11 big band cuts. Parker has brief solos on "Swingmatism," "Hootie Blues," "The Jumpin' Blues," and "Sepian Bounce." Unless one was able to catch a radio appearance by McShann's band or see Parker live, these brief glimpses into his playing were all that was heard of Charlie Parker by the average swing fan until 1945. His bluesy playing pushes the music a little bit forward rhythmically while not sounding all that out of place in this setting.

Early Bird (Stash 542) has a great deal of intriguing music. McShann is heard leading a nonet on November 30, 1940 (predating his Decca recordings), on performances not released until the 1970s. The six swing standards and one blues have solid solos from McShann's sideman, but Charlie Parker consistently steals the show, particularly on "Lady Be Good" and "Honeysuckle Rose." His ability to extend the chord changes and come up with fresh new melodies was already very impressive even though he was only 20 at the time. Also on this CD is an example of Parker jamming on "Cherokee" in 1942, eight numbers from McShann's post-Parker 1944 band (featuring Paul Quinichette on tenor), and a radio broadcast by McShann's big band from February 13, 1942. Bird has a few opportunities to really stretch out during the latter, particularly on "I'm Forever Blowing Bubbles." The recording quality is not the greatest (the speed wavers a little in spots), but this aircheck gives one an opportunity

to hear why so many young musicians were impressed by the unknown Parker at the time.

The Complete Birth of the Bebop (Stash 535) fills in more gaps. First off is the earliest recording by Parker, unaccompanied, privately recorded alto solos from May 1940 that have Parker playing "Honeysuckle Rose" and "Body and Soul." Parker is heard in 1942 jamming four standards (including "Cherokee") backed by just guitar and drums. There are selections from 1943 of Bird (on tenor) playing with a variety of small groups, including a remarkable version of "Sweet Georgia Brown" in a trio with Dizzy Gillespie and Oscar Pettiford. Not only is this the first "Diz and Bird" recording, but it is the closest one

41 ESSENTIAL RECORDS OF 1939–1944

Glenn Miller, **The Popular Recordings** (Bluebird 9785), 3 CDs

Glenn Miller, **Glenn Miller Army Air Force Band** (Bluebird 63852), 4 CDs

Duke Ellington, **The Blanton-Webster Band** (Bluebird 5659), 3 CDs

Duke Ellington, **The Carnegie Hall Concerts, January 1943** (Prestige 34004), 2 CDs

Charlie Christian, **The Genius of the Electric Guitar** (Columbia/Legacy 65564)

Artie Shaw, **Self-Portrait** (Bluebird 09026-63808), 5 CDs

Charlie Barnet, **Clap Hands Here Comes Charlie** (Bluebird 6273)

Charlie Barnet, **Drop Me Off in Harlem** (GRP/Decca 612)

Chu Berry, **1937–1941** (Classics 784)

Erskine Hawkins, **The Original Tuxedo Junction** (Bluebird 9682)

Jimmie Lunceford, **Lunceford Special** (Columbia/Legacy 65647)

Tommy Dorsey, **Yes, Indeed** (Bluebird 9987)

Jimmy Dorsey, **Contrasts** (GRP/Decca 626)

Gene Krupa, **Uptown** (Columbia 65448)

Earl Hines, **Piano Man** (Bluebird 6750)

Woody Herman, **Blues on Parade** (GRP/Decca 606)

Claude Thornhill, **Snowfall** (Hep 1058)

Various Artists, **From Spirituals to Swing** (Vanguard 169/71), 3 CDs

Pete Johnson, **1938–1939** (Classics 656)

Jimmy Yancey, **Complete Recorded Works Vol. 1** (Document 5041)

John Kirby Sextet, **1938–1939** (Classics 750)

Nat King Cole Trio, **Jumpin' at Capitol** (Rhino 71009)

Fats Waller, **The Last Years** (Bluebird 9883), 3 CDs

Coleman Hawkins, **1943–1944** (Classics 807)

Coleman Hawkins, **1944** (Classics 842)

Don Byas, **1944–1945** (Classics 882)

Lester Young, **The Complete Lester Young on Keynote** (Mercury 830920)

Lee Wiley, **Lee Wiley Sings the Songs of Ira and George Gershwin and Cole Porter** (Audiophile 1)

Lee Wiley, **Lee Wiley Sings the Songs of Rodgers & Hart and Harold Arlen** (Audiophile 10)

Oscar Aleman, **Swing Guitar Masterpieces** (Acoustic Disc 29), 2 CDs

Svend Asmussen, **Phenomenal Fiddler** (Phontastic 9310)

Alice Babs, **Swing It!** (Phontastic 9302)

Various Artists, **Metronome All-Star Bands** (Bluebird 7636)

Sidney Bechet, **The Victor Sessions-Master Takes 1932–43** (Bluebird 2402), 3 CDs

Muggsy Spanier, **The Ragtime Band Sessions** (Bluebird 66550)

Eddie Condon, **Town Hall Concerts, Vol. 2** (Jazzology 1003/1004), 2 CDs

Wild Bill Davison, **Commodore Master Takes** (GRP/Commodore 405)

Bud Freeman, **1939–1940** (Classics 811)

Joe Sullivan, **1933–1941** (Classics 821)

Willie "The Lion" Smith, **1938–1940** (Classics 692)

Joe Marsala, **1936–1942** (Classics 763)

can get to hearing how they must have sounded with Earl Hines. Concluding this very valuable disc are two numbers taken from a 1945 jam session with Gillespie and Don Byas, and a radio broadcast from December 29, 1945, that has Parker, Gillespie, vibraphonist Milt Jackson, pianist Al Haig, bassist Ray Brown, and drummer Stan Levey (on "Shaw 'Nuff," "Groovin' High," and "Dizzy Atmosphere") showing what bebop became.

Dizzy Gillespie   While Charlie Parker fit well in Jay McShann's band, John Birks "Dizzy" Gillespie was so advanced during his period playing with Cab Calloway (1939–41) that it often sounded as if he were hitting the wrong notes. Since Gillespie was soloing over more advanced chords than the rhythm section was playing, his playing sometimes seemed quite odd, leading Calloway to label it "Chinese music." Born to a poor family as the last of nine children, he started on trombone, switching to trumpet when he was 12 in 1929. Gillespie (who gained the nickname of Dizzy due to his wit and being a bit of a troublemaker) won a scholarship to the Laurinburg Institute in North Carolina, an agriculture school where he studied music. In 1935, he dropped out to try to make it as a musician. Excited and influenced by the trumpet playing of Roy Eldridge (whom he heard on radio broadcasts with Teddy Hill), Gillespie worked with Frankie Fairfax's orchestra in Philadelphia, and in 1937, joined Teddy Hill himself. He made his recording debut with Hill, taking a solo on "King Porter Stomp" that sounded a bit like Eldridge. Soon Dizzy was looking ahead, and getting criticized by other musicians for his chance-taking style.

Gillespie visited Europe with Hill in 1938, freelanced for a year, and then joined Cab Calloway. Despite the singer's reservations about his playing, Dizzy had short solos on many of Cab's records, with "Pickin' the Cabbage" being an early standout. After the Calloway period ended, Gillespie worked for a short time with many big bands, including those of Ella Fitzgerald, Coleman Hawkins, Benny Carter, Charlie Barnet, Fess Williams, Les Hite, Claude Hopkins, Lucky Millinder (where he took a boppish solo on "Little John's Special" in 1942), Calvin Jackson, and Duke Ellington (subbing for four weeks). He also wrote arrangements for Woody Herman ("Down Under" and "Woody'n You"), Benny Carter, and Jimmy Dorsey. Gillespie, who had met Charlie Parker in 1940, teamed up with Bird for the first time in Earl Hines's unrecorded orchestra of 1943, and he wrote "A

Night in Tunisia" during that period. After leaving Hines, Gillespie co-led the first bop combo to play on 52nd Street with Oscar Pettiford. He spent part of 1944 with Billy Eckstine's Orchestra and, unlike Parker (who left first), Dizzy appeared on a few of the Eckstine records, taking solos on "Opus X" and "Blowing the Blues Away." He was also on Coleman Hawkins's two groundbreaking bebop record dates (which included "Woody'n You" and "Disorder at the Border") and at the end of the year was heard on a Sarah Vaughan session.

Vol. 4, 1943–1944 (Masters of Jazz 86), which follows three CDs of Dizzy's earlier solos (mostly with Cab Calloway), has some real rarities. Gillespie is heard jamming "The Dizzy Crawl" at Monroe's Uptown House, the version of "Sweet Georgia Brown" with Parker and Pettiford is here, and the trumpeter is featured on a poorly recorded version of "A Night in Tunisia" with the otherwise undocumented quintet he had with Pettiford. In addition, the selections with Coleman Hawkins, Billy Eckstine, and Sarah Vaughan that have Gillespie solos are included plus a pair of radio broadcasts in which Dizzy is heard as a member of the John Kirby Sextet. It is quite intriguing to hear Gillespie emerge from the tightly arranged, cool-toned ensembles of the Kirby band and play explosive solos that sound a decade ahead of the other musicians. It is a strong hint as to how advanced bebop was becoming compared to swing in 1944.

The Billy Eckstine Orchestra   Billy Eckstine first emerged as a talented ballad singer while with Earl Hines's Orchestra in 1939. His powerful baritone voice became influential (by the mid-1940s quite a few black male singers sounded a bit like him), and he proved to be skilled on romantic ballads ("I Got It Bad"), blues (having a minor hit in "Jelly, Jelly"), and jazz-oriented romps ("The Jitney Man"). If his career had followed the expected path, going from the Hines band to a solo career as a middle-of-the-road pop singer, Eckstine would have been as irrelevant to jazz as Frank Sinatra or Doris Day. But in 1943 he helped persuade Hines to hire such young modern players as Charlie Parker, Dizzy Gillespie, and Sarah Vaughan. The following year he left Hines to form his own big band, which was not only an unusual decision for a singer to make (few vocalists led touring orchestras during the period), but potentially suicidal because he went out of his way to utilize the most advanced young musicians and arrangers, including

Tadd Dameron. In addition to Parker, Gillespie, and Vaughan, Mr. B's 1944 group included tenors Dexter Gordon and Gene Ammons, baritonist Leo Parker, and drummer Art Blakey, with trumpeter Fats Navarro and altoist Sonny Stitt being key soloists in 1945.

1944–1945 (Classics 914) has all of the Eckstine Orchestra's early recordings and shows how schizophrenic the repertoire could be. While "Blowing the Blues Away" (which has a famous tradeoff by Ammons and Gordon), "Opus X," and "I Love the Rhythm in a Riff" are boppish and swing hard, Eckstine's ballad features (including "I Want to Talk About You," "I'll Wait and Pray," "A Cottage for Sale," and "Prisoner of Love") find the band sounding a bit uncomfortable backing the leader's warm, but rather straight vocals. However, Billy Eckstine deserves great credit for keeping his pioneering bebop orchestra going as long as he could.

Some of the Other Bop Musicians Before 1945

Most of the early bop players gained their grounding playing with big bands. Few recorded very much before 1945 and most were quite young. In fact, Dizzy Gillespie—who turned 28 in 1945—was almost considered an elder statesman.

While Gillespie's solos with Cab Calloway and Parker's with Jay McShann inspired younger musicians, much of the groundwork for bebop took place at late night jam sessions during 1940–43 held at Minton's Playhouse, which was managed by retired bandleader Teddy Hill, and Monroe's Uptown House. The house band at Minton's included pianist Thelonious Monk, bassist Nick Fenton, drummer Kenny Clarke, and trumpeter Joe Guy. In addition to Gillespie and Parker, many top swing players also sat in on occasion, including Charlie Christian, Coleman Hawkins, Roy Eldridge, Hot Lips Page, Don Byas, and even Benny Goodman.

Amateur tapes from Minton's show Thelonious Monk sounding a bit like Teddy Wilson in 1941, but by the time he made his recording debut with Coleman Hawkins in 1944, his unique style was quite recognizable. Nick Fenton faded into obscurity after the mid-1940s, while Joe Guy (who was with the 1940 Coleman Hawkins big band) comes across as a Roy Eldridge disciple trying—often awkwardly—to incorporate some of Dizzy Gillespie's ideas into his playing. He was with the Cootie Williams Orchestra in 1942 (soloing on Monk's "Epistrophy"), but

drug use would cut short his career and he never had an opportunity to smooth out his style.

Kenny Clarke, who was three years older than Gillespie, had already had a strong reputation as a swing drummer, working with Roy Eldridge (1935), Edgar Hayes (1937–38), Claude Hopkins, and Teddy Hill (1939–40), in addition to recording with Sidney Bechet. By 1941, he had shifted the timekeeping role of the drums from the bass drum (Gene Krupa) and the hi-hat cymbal (Jo Jones) to the lighter ride cymbal. Clarke used the bass drum to "drop bombs" as irregular accents, which made the drums a more interactive rather than merely supportive instrument. His odd accents resulted in him being given the nickname "Klook-Mop." Clarke would have had a larger role in the key years of bebop except that he was in the military during 1943–46.

Most of the other bop players did not really get started until 1945, but were learning their craft before then. Howard McGhee was featured with Andy Kirk during 1941–43 (including on the recording of "McGhee Special") in addition to playing with Charlie Barnet. Fellow trumpeter Fats Navarro worked with the big bands of Snookum Russell (1941–42) and Kirk (1943–44). Benny Harris was with Boyd Raeburn (1944–45) while Freddie Webster played first trumpet with Earl Hines (1938), Benny Carter, Lucky Millinder, Jimmie Lunceford (1942–43), Cab Calloway, and other swing big bands. Trombonist J.J. Johnson took his first recorded solo with Benny Carter on 1943's "Love for Sale." Altoist Sonny Stitt was in Tiny Bradshaw's orchestra (1943), tenor saxophonist Allan Eager played with Woody Herman's transitional band (1943–44), Lucky Thompson was Count Basie's tenor soloist in 1944, and Stan Getz toured with the big bands of Jack Teagarden (1943) and Stan Kenton (1944–45). Clarinetist Stan Hasselgard spent these years playing swing in his native Sweden.

Bud Powell, who would do so much to change the way that the piano is played in jazz, was with Cootie Williams's big band during 1943–44. Erroll Garner worked with the Slam Stewart Trio (1944–45), Hank Jones was with Hot Lips Page, Clyde Hart often played with Don Byas, and Dodo Marmarosa worked with Charlie Barnet, taking the piano solo on the hit "Skyliner." Oscar Peterson was a sideman in Canada with the Johnnie Holmes Orchestra, while vibraphonist Milt Jackson was in Detroit in 1944 leading the Four Sharps. Oscar Pettiford was one of two bassists (along with

Chubby Jackson) in Charlie Barnet's 1942–43 band, recorded with Coleman Hawkins, Ben Webster, and Earl Hines, and worked with Roy Eldridge before co-leading the first bebop group on 52nd Street with Dizzy Gillespie. Drummer Max Roach, who picked up where Kenny Clarke left off, was a member of the house band at Monroe's Uptown House in 1942, recorded with Hawkins in 1943, and worked with Benny Carter's Orchestra.

All of these musicians would come together with other young players to form a startling new music that would begin to permanently change the jazz world in 1945.

Various Artists: V-Discs, Blue Note, and Black & White

Starting in late 1942 and continuing until after the end of World War II, special V-disc recordings were made specifically for the U.S. military servicemen to enjoy. A good portion of the music (which was supposed to be destroyed, but managed to survive for decades) has been reissued on CD although thus far not complete and in strict chronological order. The two-CD set **The Original V-Disc Collection** (Pickwick 540301) has 40 performances covering a wide range of music including pop, folk music, and the operatic voices of Marian Anderson and Paul Robeson. The majority of the performances are jazz and featured are such notables as Benny Goodman, Louis Armstrong, Hot Lips Page, Muggsy Spanier, Louis Jordan, Red Norvo, Tommy Dorsey, and Art Tatum. **Rare V-Discs Vol. 1—The Combos** (RST 91565) has all-star jams and appearances by Hoagy Carmichael ("Riverboat Shuffle"), the Nat King Cole Trio, Roy Eldridge, and Connie Boswell plus a couple of hilarious Bud Freeman comedy pieces ("For Musicians Only" and "The Latest Thing in Hot Jazz"). **Rare V-Discs Vol. 2—The Big Bands** (RST 91566) has mostly excellent performances from the big bands of Jimmie Lunceford, Louis Prima, Cab Calloway, Jess Stacy (a short-lived outfit), Sam Donahue, Buddy Rich, Stan Kenton, and Jimmy Dorsey. **Rare V-Discs Vol. 3—The Girls** (RST 91567) ranges from jazz to pop with features for singers Martha Tilton, Jo Stafford, Ella Fitzgerald, June Christy, Monica Lewis, Kay Starr, Marie Green, and Dinah Shore.

The Blue Note label was founded by Alfred Lion at the beginning of 1939, and he was soon joined by his partner Francis Wolff. Initially the label (one of the first independent jazz record companies) concentrated on trad and small-group swing dates, all of which have been reissued on Mosaic limited-edition boxes. **The Blue Note Jazzmen** (Blue Note 21262) is an excellent two-CD set with Dixieland sessions from 1944. The four overlapping groups have Edmond Hall, Sidney DeParis, and James P. Johnson as leaders and also spots for Ben Webster and Vic Dickenson. The 29 selections include 12 alternate takes so this reissue is more complete than the equivalent Classics CDs.

Music from the short-lived Black & White label of the mid-1940s (mostly dating from 1944) has been reissued on six various-artists sets. **Black & White & Reeds All Over** (Pickwick 15001) features formerly rare Dixieland sessions by four groups: a quartet with clarinetist Rod Cless, trumpeter Sterling Bose, James P. Johnson, and Pops Foster, a trio headed by Fats Waller protégé Hank Duncan, the George Wettling trio with clarinetist Mezz Mezzrow, and a quartet with Cliff Jackson and Pee Wee Russell. **Dixieland Cajun Style** (Pickwick 15000) unfortunately does not give the full personnel (this is the only disc in this series to leave it out), but it does have fine hot jazz performances from an Eddie Condon all-star group, Matty Matlock leading some Bob Crosby alumni, and Red Nichols with a new version of his Five Pennies. **Greenwich Village Jazz** (Pickwick 15004) has two sessions led by Barney Bigard, one of which features Art Tatum in a rare role as a sideman. Other musicians heard from are both Joe Thomases (on trumpet and tenor) and Georgie Auld. The enjoyable disc also features Cliff Jackson's Village Kats (with the DeParis brothers and Sidney Bechet) and a Willie "The Lion" Smith Dixieland date with Max Kaminsky and Rod Cless. **Greenwich Village Sound** (Pickwick 15005) is more modern overall. Singer Etta Jones (barely 16 at the time) is heard on her recording debut with remakes of four songs associated with Dinah Washington, and Joe Marsala is featured on a pair of his sessions that are also available on a Classics CD (which is covered in Chapter 6), including a classic encounter with Dizzy Gillespie. **Playing the Blacks & Whites** (Pickwick 15002) consists of obscure trio numbers from the short-lived swing pianist Nat Jaffe, a couple of duets by pianist Dick Cary and George Wettling, and piano solos from Cliff Jackson and Art Hodes. **Masters of the Blacks & Whites** (Pickwick 15003) is mostly from 1945, but complementary to the other sets, with trios featuring pianists Erroll Garner, Gene Schroeder (who would work for many years with Eddie Condon), Ray Stokes, and Williams McDaniel (in a group actually led by bassist Red Callender). All six of these Pickwick CDs contain plenty of spontaneous playing that will please trad/swing collectors.

Well worth bidding on if found on auction lists is the incredible 21-LP set **The Complete Keynote Collection** (Polygram/Keynote 18PJ-1051-71), which has all of the music (including alternate takes) recorded by Harry Lim for his Keynote label. Featured are the who's who of swing (plus a little bit of bop), including Lester Young, Roy Eldridge, Coleman Hawkins, the Kansas Seven, Earl Hines, Charlie Shavers, Benny Carter, and countless others. And in the same vein are **The Complete Commodore Jazz Recordings Vols. 1–3** (Mosaic 23-123, 23-128 and 20-134), 66 LPs that have all of the music that Milt Gabler recorded for his Commodore label, mostly from 1938–46, with literally hundreds of Dixieland and small-group swing performances that qualify as timeless gems.

VOICES OF THE FUTURE

Jeanne Lee (vocals), Jan. 29, 1939, New York, NY

Joe Sample (piano), Feb. 1, 1939, Houston, TX

Charles Gayle (tenor), Feb. 28, 1939, Buffalo, NY

Mike Longo (piano), Mar. 19, 1939, Cincinnati, OH

Sonny Fortune (alto, tenor, flute), May 19, 1939, Philadelphia, PA

Marvin Stamm (trumpet), May 23, 1939, Memphis, TN

Bill Watrous (trombone), June 8, 1939, Middletown, CT

Charles McPherson (alto), July 24, 1939, Joplin, MO

Paul Winter (soprano, alto), Aug. 3, 1939, Altoona, PA

Enrico Rava (trumpet), Aug. 20, 1939, Trieste, Italy

Butch Warren (bass), Sept. 8, 1939, Washington, D.C.

Steve Marcus (tenor, soprano), Sept. 18, 1939, New York, NY

Wayne Henderson (trombone), Sept. 24, 1939, Houston, TX

Odeon Pope (tenor), Oct. 24, 1939, Ninety Six, SC

Andy Bey (vocals), Oct. 28, 1939, Newark, NJ

Roger Kellaway (piano), Nov. 1, 1939, Waban, MA

Joe McPhee (tenor, trumpet), Nov. 3, 1939, Miami, FL

Andrew Cyrille (drums), Nov. 10, 1939, Brooklyn, NY

Hubert Laws (flute), Nov. 10, 1939, Houston, TX

Idris Muhammad (drums), Nov. 13, 1939, New Orleans, LA

Bob James (piano, keyboards, arranger), Dec. 25, 1939, Marshall, MO

Astrud Gilberto (vocals), 1940, Bahia, Brazil

Byron Allen (alto), 1940, Omaha, NB

Ronald Shannon Jackson (drums, leader), Jan. 12, 1940, Fort Worth, TX

Don Thompson (bass, piano, vibes), Jan. 18, 1940, Powell River, British Columbia, Canada

Eberhard Weber (bass, composer), Jan. 22, 1940, Stuttgart, Germany

Dave Young (bass), Jan. 29, 1940, Winnipeg, Canada

Paul Rutherford (trombone), Feb. 29, 1940, Liverpool, England

Ralph Towner (guitar), Mar. 1, 1940, Chehalis, WA

Al Jarreau (vocals), Mar. 12, 1940, Milwaukee, WI

Lew Tabackin (tenor, flute), Mar. 26, 1940, Philadelphia, PA

Herbie Hancock (piano, keyboards, composer), Apr. 12, 1940, Chicago, IL

Sal Nistico (tenor), Apr. 12, 1940, Syracuse, NY

George Adams (tenor), Apr. 29, 1940, Covington, GA

Carlos Ward (alto, flute, tenor), May 1, 1940, Ancon, Panama

Arthur Blythe (alto), July 5, 1940, Los Angeles, CA

Ray Draper (tuba), Aug. 3, 1940, New York, NY

Roscoe Mitchell (reeds), Aug. 3, 1940, Chicago, IL

Adam Makowicz (piano), Aug. 18, 1940, Gnojnik, Czechoslovakia

Sonny Sharrock (guitar), Aug. 27, 1940, Ossining, NY

Wilton Felder (tenor, bass), Aug. 31, 1940, Houston, TX

James Dapogny (piano), Sept. 3, 1940, Berwyn, IL

Dave Burrell (piano), Sept. 10, 1940, Middletown, OH

Roy Ayers (vibes), Sept. 10, 1940, Los Angeles, CA

Hamiet Bluiett (baritone), Sept. 16, 1940, Lovejoy, IL

Gary Bartz (alto), Sept. 26, 1940, Baltimore, MD

Steve Swallow (bass), Oct. 4, 1940, New York, NY

Larry Young (organ), Oct. 7, 1940, Newark, NJ

Pharoah Sanders (tenor), Oct. 13, 1940, Little Rock, AR

Eddie Henderson (trumpet), Oct. 26, 1940, New York, NY

Janet Lawson (vocals), Nov. 13 1940, Baltimore, MD

VOICES OF THE FUTURE

Billy Hart (drums), Nov. 29, 1940, Washington, DC.

Chuck Mangione (flugelhorn), Nov. 29, 1940, Rochester, NY

Lonnie Liston Smith (piano, keyboards), Dec. 28, 1940, Richmond, VA

Olu Dara (cornet), Jan. 12, 1941, Louisville, MS

Bobby Hutcherson (vibes, marimba), Jan. 27, 1941, Los Angeles, CA

Eddy Louiss (organ, piano), Mar. 2, 1941, Paris, France

Bobby Shew (trumpet), Mar. 4, 1941, Albuquerque, NM

Peter Brotzmann (tenor, bass sax), Mar. 6, 1941, Remscheid, Germany

Meredith D'Ambrosio (vocals), Mar. 20, 1941, Boston, MA

Don Grusin (keyboards), Apr. 22, 1941, Denver, CO

Stanley Cowell (piano), May 5, 1941, Toledo, OH

Charles Earland (organ), May 24, 1941, Philadelphia, PA

Connie Crothers (piano), June 2, 1941, Palo Alto, CA

Chick Corea (piano, keyboards, composer, leader), June 12, 1941, Chelsea, MA

Jim Pepper (tenor, soprano), June 17, 1941, Portland, OR

Bobby Gordon (clarinet), June 29, 1941, Hartford, CT

Charles Tyler (alto, baritone), July 20, 1941, Cadiz, KY

Airto Moreira (percussion, drums), Aug. 5, 1941, Itaiopolis, Brazil

Lenny Breau (guitar), Aug. 5, 1941, Auburn, ME

Howard Johnson (tuba, baritone, fluegelhorn), Aug. 7, 1941, Montgomery, AL

Milford Graves (drums), Aug. 20, 1941, Queens, NY

Jim Cullum, Jr. (cornet, leader), Sept. 20, 1941, San Antonio, TX

Chucho Valdes (piano, leader), Oct. 9, 1941, Quivican, Cuba

Lester Bowie (trumpet), Oct. 11, 1941, Frederick, MD

Eddie Daniels (clarinet, tenor), Oct. 19, 1941, Brooklyn, NY

Glen Moore (bass), Oct. 28, 1941, Portland, OR

Jay Clayton (vocals), Oct. 28, 1941, Youngstown, OH

P.J. Perry (alto, tenor), Dec. 2, 1941, Calgary, Alberta, Canada

Franco Ambrosetti (flugelhorn, trumpet), Dec. 10, 1941, Lugano, Switzerland

Wadada Leo Smith (trumpet), Dec. 18, 1941, Leland, MS

John Hicks (piano), Dec. 21, 1941, Atlanta, GA

Ronnie Cuber (baritone), Dec. 25, 1941, Brooklyn, NY

John McLaughlin (guitar), Jan. 4, 1942, Yorkshire, England

James Blood Ulmer (guitar), Feb. 2, 1942, St. Matthews, SC

Keith Ingham (piano), Feb. 5, 1942, London, England

Barbara Donald (trumpet), Feb. 9, 1942, Minneapolis, MN

Charles Tolliver (trumpet), Mar. 6, 1942, Jacksonville, FL

Amina Claudine Myers (piano, organ), Mar. 21, 1942, Blackwell, AR

Buster Williams (bass), Apr. 17, 1942, Camden, NJ

Han Bennink (drums), Apr. 17, 1942, Zaandam, Netherlands

David Friesen (bass), May 6, 1942, Tacoma, WA

Flora Purim (vocals), June 3, 1942, Rio de Janeiro, Brazil

Mel Martin (tenor, alto, soprano), June 7, 1942, Sacramento, CA

Joe Chambers (drums), June 25, 1942, Stoneacre, VA

Dr. Lonnie Smith (organ), July 3, 1942, Buffalo, NY

Tomasz Stanko (trumpet), July 11, 1942, Rzeszow, Poland

Carl Saunders (trumpet), Aug. 2, 1942, Indianapolis, IN

Jack DeJohnette (drums, leader, keyboards), Aug. 9, 1942, Chicago, IL

Oliver Lake (alto, soprano, flute), Sept. 14, 1942, Marianna, AK

Jean-Luc Ponty (violin), Sept. 29, 1942, Normandy, France

Donald Ayler (trumpet), Oct. 5, 1942, Cleveland, OH

Cecil Bridgewater (trumpet), Oct. 10, 1942, Urbana, IL

Terumasa Hino (trumpet), Oct. 25, 1942, Tokyo, Japan

Philip Catherine (guitar), Oct. 27, 1942, London, England

Larry Willis (piano), Dec. 20, 1942, New York, NY

Barry Altschul (drums), Jan. 6, 1943, New York, NY

Billy Harper (tenor), Jan. 17, 1943, Houston, TX

Valery Ponomarev (trumpet), Jan. 20, 1943, Moscow, Russia

Michal Urbaniak (violin), Jan. 22, 1943, Warsaw, Poland

Pete Minger (trumpet), Jan. 22, 1943, Orangeburg, SC

Gary Burton (vibes), Jan. 23, 1943, Anderson, IN

George Benson (guitar), Mar. 22, 1943, Pittsburgh, PA

Larry Coryell (guitar), Apr. 2, 1943, Galveston, TX

Bobby Enriquez (piano), May 20, 1943, Bacolod City, Philippines

Kenny Barron (piano), June 9, 1943, Philadelphia, PA

Frank Lowe (tenor), June 24, 1943, Memphis, TN

Jiggs Whigham (trombone), Aug. 20, 1943, Cleveland, OH

VOICES OF THE FUTURE

Urszula Dudziak (vocals), Oct. 22, 1943, Straconka, Poland

Butch Thompson (piano), Nov. 28, 1943, Marine, MN

Grover Washington, Jr. (tenor, soprano, alto, baritone), Dec. 12, 1943, Buffalo, NY

Don Sickler (trumpet, arranger), Jan. 6, 1944, Spokane, WA

Al Foster (drums), Jan. 18, 1944, Richmond, VA

Terry Waldo (piano), Jan. 26, 1944, Ironton, OH

Rufus Reid (bass), Feb. 10, 1944, Atlanta, GA

Henry Threadgill (alto, composer), Feb. 15, 1944, Chicago, IL

Lew Soloff (trumpet), Feb. 20, 1944, New York, NY

Evan Parker (tenor, soprano), Apr. 5, 1944, Bristol, England

Pat LaBarbera (tenor, soprano), Apr. 7, 1944, Warsaw, NY

Billy Cobham (drums), May 16, 1944, Panama

Jack Wilkins (guitar), June 3, 1944, Brooklyn, NY

Monty Alexander (piano), June 6, 1944, Kingston, Jamaica

Butch Miles (drums), July 4, 1944, Ironston, OH

Nana Vasconcelos (percussion), Aug. 2, 1944, Recife, Brazil

Oscar Brashear (trumpet), Aug. 18, 1944, Chicago, IL

Peter Leitch (guitar), Aug. 19, 1944, Ottawa, Ontario, Canada

Terry Clarke (drums), Aug. 20, 1944, Vancouver, British Columbia, Canada

Pat Martino (guitar), Aug. 25, 1944, Philadelphia, PA

John Surman (baritone, soprano, bass clarinet), Aug. 30, 1944, Tavistock, England

George Mraz (bass), Sept. 9, 1944, Pisek, Czechoslovakia

Marlena Shaw (vocals), Sept. 22, 1944, New Rochelle, NY

Eddie Gomez (bass), Oct. 4, 1944, Santurce, Puerto Rico

Willem Breuker (saxophones, leader), Nov. 4, 1944, Amsterdam, Netherlands

George Cables (piano), Nov. 14, 1944, New York, NY

John Abercrombie (guitar), Dec. 16, 1944, Port Chester, NY

Vyacheslav Ganelin (piano), Dec. 17, 1944, Kraskov, Soviet Union

Woody Shaw (trumpet, composer), Dec. 24, 1944, Laurinburg, NC

Don Pullen (piano), Dec. 25, 1944, Roanoke, VA

PASSINGS

Charles Irvis (40), 1939, New York, NY

Herschel Evans (29), Feb. 9, 1939, New York, NY

Tommy Ladnier (39), June 4, 1939, New York, NY

Chick Webb (37), June 16, 1939, Baltimore, MD

Ma Rainey (53), Dec. 22, 1939, Rome, GA

Arthur Whetsol (34), Jan. 5, 1940, New York, NY

Johnny Dodds (48), Aug. 8, 1940, Chicago, IL

Caspar Reardon (33), Mar. 9, 1941, New York, NY

Jelly Roll Morton (55), July 10, 1941, Los Angeles, CA

Chu Berry (31), Oct. 30, 1941, Conneaut, OH

Dick Wilson (30), Nov. 24, 1941, New York, NY

Charlie Christian (25), Mar. 2, 1942, New York, NY

Bunny Berigan (33), June 2, 1942, New York, NY

Jimmy Blanton (23), July 30, 1942, Los Angeles, CA

Tiny Parham (43), Apr. 4, 1943, Milwaukee, WI

Leon Roppolo (41), Oct. 5, 1943, New Orleans, LA

Fats Waller (39), Dec. 14, 1943, Kansas City, MO

Bob Zurke (32), Feb. 16, 1944, Los Angeles, CA

Jimmie Noone (48), Apr. 19, 1944, Los Angeles, CA

O'Neill Spencer (34), July 24, 1944, New York, NY

Glenn Miller (40), Dec. 16, 1944, English Channel

Chapter Six

1945–1949:
Bebop Spoken Here

T he 1945–49 period turned out much different for jazz than one would have predicted in 1944. At that point in time, with World War II finally showing signs of winding down and the ruinous recording strike ending, it was expected that the swing era would continue on as before, with the veteran big bands and plenty of new ones playing for dancing audiences. Glenn Miller may have been lost, but Benny Goodman, Count Basie, Duke Ellington, Harry James, and Tommy Dorsey all had very popular bands, and Artie Shaw had formed yet another orchestra. What was not predicted by anyone in 1944 was that the swing era was about over and that most big bands would be breaking up quite soon.

While there were big band hits in 1945 and at first the return of American servicemen brought back nostalgia for the orchestras, it was only temporary. The former swing audience now was more interested in staying home and raising a family than in going out to dance halls. Small combos, particularly those active in rhythm and blues, were less expensive than big bands and could fill the same need. The top creative jazz soloists and arrangers were more interested in exploring the new bebop music than in revitalizing swing, so the big bands of 1946 (with a few exceptions) tended to lack much originality. The rise in popularity of Dixieland and the dominance of the pop charts by singers (often backed by studio orchestras rather than swing bands) also sliced away a large portion of the audience. By the end of 1946, dozens of big bands were breaking up all over the country, even those led by such big names as Harry James, Benny Goodman, and Artie Shaw. The orchestras that survived had to deal with the rise of bebop and a new Musicians Union recording strike that, although not as effective as the 1942–44 fiasco, kept most groups (particularly orchestras) off records during 1948. In 1949, some big bands joined in the larger record labels' quest to turn bebop into a money-making fad. But once that brief experiment ended in late 1949, most of the remaining big bands (including those of Count Basie, Woody Herman, Charlie Barnet, and Goodman) soon collapsed.

Jazz separated from both pop music and dancing audiences during 1945–47, losing a lot of its mass appeal. But the drop in commercial sales did not mean that the music was losing its way; just that it had changed direction. Bebop, considered a radical new music in 1945, became the mainstream of jazz during

1947–49. The phrases of Charlie Parker, Dizzy Gillespie, and Bud Powell became the language of modern jazz, and the music moved forward quickly. Small combos took over, and most jazz was now performed before sitting-down audiences in nightclubs (even if New York's legendary 52nd Street drastically declined during 1947–48 on its way to extinction) rather than for dancers in large halls. The music was being taken much more seriously as an American-born art form rather than being mere entertainment. While the best swing musicians (such as Coleman Hawkins, Lester Young, and Art Tatum) were greatly respected, the bop players often dismissed the showbiz aspects of early jazz (criticizing Louis Armstrong's crowd pleasing antics) and any compromise of the music.

At the same time, the Dixieland revival continued to gather steam, becoming the most popular style of jazz. The Dixielanders usually took their music seriously too, but they did not mind entertaining audiences or paying tribute to earlier jazz greats. Some of the New Orleans revival's proponents could be a bit strident or silly, particularly those who considered every note of Bunk Johnson's to be precious while thinking of Benny Goodman as a sellout for playing arranged big band swing.

There were a lot of debates during this era over what jazz really was, and a few verbal battles between the beboppers and the moldy figs (a name for the trad lovers who called their music "the real jazz"). Jazz, which had formerly been dominated by swing with occasional variety offered by Dixieland groups, now was not only bebop, swing, and Dixieland, but could be heard as Latin jazz and was an influence in the competing rhythm and blues world. By the end of the 1940s, cool jazz was starting to emerge as both a conservative reaction and an extension to bebop. While moving forward, jazz was splitting up into several different directions at once, all quite exciting musically, even if many of the listeners from the era were usually in one musical camp or another.

There were other changes. While the swing era found the record industry dominated by the big three of Victor, Columbia, and Decca, with the major big bands of the 1930s and early '40s being on the major labels, starting in 1942 (when Capitol was formed) many new companies were born. Bebop emerged on such new small labels as Savoy, Dial, National, and Musicraft. Dixieland was documented by Milt Gabler's Commodore, which became less active after 1947, and Good Time Jazz, founded in 1949. Small-group swing gems appeared on Harry Lim's Keynote, a very busy operation until it was sold to Mercury in 1948.

New innovations in jazz from this point on would rarely be initially recorded by the big companies since they were only interested in the potential revenue and had little real interest in the quality of the music. Victor signed Dizzy Gillespie in 1946 because he was potentially the biggest moneymaker of the beboppers, but Charlie Parker never led a session for Victor, Columbia, Decca, or Capitol. From the mid-1940s on, it would generally be up

TIMELINE 1945

Charlie Parker and Dizzy Gillespie record a series of gems that change the jazz world. • Gillespie's first big band breaks up after an unsuccessful tour. • Bird and Diz travel to Los Angeles. • Seventeen-year-old singer Ernie Andrews (who was still in high school) begins recording for the G&G label, having a regional hit in "Soothe Me." • Sonny Berman joins Woody Herman's Herd. • Erskine Hawkins has a hit in "Tippin' In." • June Christy joins Stan Kenton's Orchestra while Anita O'Day rejoins Gene Krupa's band. • Ray Brown arrives in New York and on his very first day in the city jams with Charlie Parker, Dizzy Gillespie, Bud Powell, and Max Roach. • Ida Cox suffers a heart attack and retires. • Seventeen-year-old trumpeter Art Farmer and his twin brother bassist Addison Farmer move to Los Angeles and play regularly on Central Avenue. • Sippie Wallace records two songs, her first records since 1929, but remains in obscurity and semi-retirement. • Clarinetist/baritonist Peter Schilperoot forms the Dutch Swing College Band, one of the longest running Dixieland/swing bands in the world. • Fletcher Henderson leads his final big band record date. • Urged on by his wife Lee Wiley, Jess Stacy leads a big band. Both the band and the marriage soon break up. • While stationed in Europe, cornetist Jimmy McPartland marries pianist Marian Turner, who becomes much better known as Marian McPartland. • The Coleman Hawkins Sextet features Howard McGhee and visits Los Angeles. • Dave Lambert and Buddy Stewart sing "What's This" with Gene Krupa's orchestra, the earliest bop vocal on record. • Harry James has a big hit with "It's Been a Long Long Time."

to the small labels run by jazz fans (such as Blue Note, which shifted gears from swing and New Orleans jazz toward bebop in 1947) to record the most significant new music. In contrast, the big companies co-opted any radical new movements so as to grab whatever profit it was possible to drain from jazz. An example of this is how bebop first appeared on small record companies, but in 1949 Capitol (which had not shown any interest in bebop previously) jumped on the bandwagon, signing Dizzy Gillespie and recording the bop bands of Benny Goodman and Charlie Barnet. By year-end it had lost interest when sales were not high enough, dumping the bop experiment altogether the following year. Whether the music was worthwhile or not was deemed irrelevant.

Despite the rise and fall of various large record labels' interest in jazz (a phenomenon that has continued up to the present time), jazz continued to flourish artistically. There was so much good jazz being played during the 1945–49 era, whether it was bop, Latin jazz, swing, Dixieland, or the beginnings of cool jazz, that there was almost too much to choose from.

What Is This Thing Called Bop?

Bebop seemed to appear out of nowhere in 1945. Swing fans used to Harry James and Glenn Miller reacted to modernist recordings by Charlie Parker and Dizzy Gillespie (such as " 'Shaw Nuff," "Dizzy Atmosphere," and "Salt Peanuts") not only wondering if the new sounds were jazz, but whether they were even music at all!

How does bebop differ from swing? Most classic bop melodies tend to almost sound like horn solos and few are easily singable after being heard just once or twice (unlike the swing pop hits). Even a humorous song such as "Salt Peanuts" has a bridge that cannot be easily sung without a lot of practice. In most classic bop performances, once the melody is played once or twice (often by the horns in unison), it is totally discarded (except for esoteric references) during the solos until the final chorus of the performance. The horn players' main interaction with each other is trading off phrases rather than improvising together.

While solos in swing settings often kept the melody in mind, in bop the improvisations are based much more on the chord changes as the soloists make up melodies and ideas that fit the chords. It is quite difficult to pick out the melody of "Cherokee" during Charlie Parker's solo on "Ko Ko," or "Just You, Just Me" when Thelonious Monk

played his "Evidence." Because of the complexity of the chord structures (even simple blues often was reharmonized), harmonies became much more advanced, and every possible note could conceivably fit in a certain spot if it was later resolved. Solos were therefore much more unpredictable, leading some observers to ask "Where's the melody?"

Even when using the chord changes of a popular song, the material tended to utilize a completely new melody. The most radical changes, however, were in the function of the rhythm section. Pianists had formerly been a potential one-man band, with the left hand stating the beat either by striding up and down the keyboard (alternating between bass notes and chords) or playing catchy rhythmic patterns (such as boogie-woogie) while the right hand performed variations of the melody. In bebop, the left hand was freed from the timekeeping function and now stated chords in erratic rhythms, commenting on the music rather than functioning as a metronome. The right hand became much more hornlike, with speedy single-note lines and occasional chords. Bud Powell perfected this style (which was a logical progression from Fats Waller to Teddy Wilson to Count Basie), and it became the basis for the playing of most pianists to come after the late 1940s. The timekeeping function fell on the bassist (who became indispensable), while rhythm guitar became a lost art form except for Freddie Green with the Count Basie Orchestra. Drummers also no longer played simple patterns. They still kept time, but now with the ride cymbal, and they were free to "drop bombs" (make odd accents and comment on the playing of the soloists) with the bass drum.

Bebop was a giant step forward for jazz, musically. As far as popularity and accessibility to the general public go, the opposite was true, resulting in a permanent break between jazz and pop music. Although there would be occasional novelty hits through the years that would briefly be popular, no longer would jazz instrumentals be found regularly on the best-seller charts. And while listeners even today generally have heard of Benny Goodman and Count Basie, the name of Charlie Parker would most likely be greeted with a blank stare.

Although by 1947 bebop was grudgingly being accepted in the jazz world as the important new style, and in 1949 the major record labels did their best to make a fad out of bop (hoping that it would catch on like swing), the new style never became popular with the general public for a variety of reasons. The Musicians Union recording strike of 1942–44 kept bop in its earliest stages off records, so when it appeared fully formed in 1945, the public was not ready for it. While swing bands often compromised (adding glamorous female singers, playing some novelties, hiring press agents, and backing nonjazz acts), the bop musicians wanted the audience to come to them rather than the other way around; only Dizzy Gillespie would qualify as an extroverted showman among the early beboppers. Swing was particularly popular because it was seen as dance music. Although bop is also potentially dance music—one can dance at half-speed to the most rapid tempos—the main bop players simply did not want to play for dancers; they preferred attentive audiences. The 30 percent cabaret tax that was imposed on dance halls during World War II (and not eliminated until the late 1940s) was also a major incentive for jazz clubs to eliminate dance floors altogether to save money.

In addition to the difficulty for newcomers in accepting bebop (which sounded to some like a foreign language), there were other nonmusical reasons why bop did not catch on. The swing era was collapsing during 1945–46, partly due to competition from other styles of music, including Dixieland, pop singers, and rhythm and blues. So if Benny Goodman had to break up his band, what chance would Dizzy Gillespie have? While the swing world featured both white and black bands, most of the leading early boppers were black, which in the segregated 1940s made it more difficult for the music to achieve wider recognition.

Making things particularly dicey, the bop musicians had a bad reputation due to their drug use. While musicians from the 1920s on had been susceptible to the excesses of nightlife, with many drinking excessively and some having their lives shortened due to alcohol, and while the swing era had its share of marijuana users, the bebop generation suffered from much more dangerous plague: heroin. Charlie Parker was a heroin addict from the time he was a teenager. Many of Parker's followers (despite his protests about how damaging heroin was) made the mistake of becoming constant users, which led to unreliability, erratic behavior, jail sentences, and many ruined lives. This problem was at its worst from the late 1940s through the '50s.

Despite all of these difficulties, bebop was exciting, many new and significant soloists emerged from bop

during 1945–49, and it became the foundation for all of the jazz styles that have followed since that time.

Charlie Parker and Dizzy Gillespie   As 1945 began, few jazz fans were familiar with altoist Charlie Parker and trumpeter Dizzy Gillespie, but that would change very quickly. Bird and Diz, who had first met in 1940, both gained much of their training playing with big bands—Parker with Jay McShann (1937–42) and Gillespie with Cab Calloway (1939–41). They had teamed together with Earl Hines's unrecorded orchestra in 1943 and with the Billy Eckstine big band of 1944. But it was during 1945, when they co-led a quintet that played regularly on 52nd Street and made their first joint recordings, that Bird and Diz really made their greatest impact.

Charlie Parker had the ability to play remarkably coherent solos at ridiculously fast tempos. If slowed to half speed, his best solos are revealed to have every note fitting. A blues player at heart, Parker developed a musical vocabulary that became so dominant that even his throwaway phrases would be adopted by the next generation and echoed by his contemporaries. Bird packed an awful lot of living into his relatively brief life, which was full of music, excessive drinking and eating, and a heroin addiction that he was never able to kick for long.

Dizzy Gillespie, in contrast, avoided any dangerous habits and was a showman who loved to be able to connect with an audience. The latter was an important quality because Gillespie's trumpet playing was quite esoteric and potentially forbidding. Initially influenced by Roy Eldridge, by 1944 Gillespie's choice of notes were so radical that they seemed wrong. Yet he had the ability to make those notes fit, like putting a triangle in a square, and he was so enthusiastic about teaching his harmonically advanced ideas to other musicians that he was a major force in bebop becoming the foundation of modern jazz.

Due to his outgoing nature, Gillespie became a bigger name in jazz first and also preceded Parker in leading his own record sessions. **1945** (Classics 888) has the trumpeter heard as a sideman on all-star dates headed by Oscar Pettiford, Trummy Young, Clyde Hart, and Tony Scott; Parker is also on the Young and Hart sessions. But the reason to acquire this CD is for the nine selections led by Gillespie. The January 9 session, a sextet set with Trummy Young and Don Byas, introduces Tadd Dameron's "Good Bait" and Dizzy's "Salt Peanuts" and "Bebop," all three of which became standards. Most impressive is Gillespie's reshaping of "I Can't Get Started," which sounds light years more advanced than Bunny Berigan's famous version of eight years before. A date from February 9 with tenor saxophonist Dexter Gordon resulted in the much reissued "Blue 'N' Boogie" and the original (but very rare) version of "Groovin' High," Gillespie's original line written over the chord changes of "Whispering" (a hit for Paul Whiteman in 1920). **1945** concludes with the first real Diz and Bird session, the February 28 meeting that resulted in a better-known version of "Groovin' High," "Dizzy Atmosphere," and "All the Things You Are." While that date used an advanced swing rhythm section (with Clyde Hart, guitarist Remo Palmieri, Slam Stewart, and Cozy Cole), the next encounter with Parker, which is on **1945–1946** (Classics 935), has the duo joined by the boppish pianist Al Haig, bassist Curly Russell, and drummer Big Sid Catlett. They introduce "Shaw 'Nuff" and Tadd Dameron's "Hot House" (based on the chords of "What Is this Thing Called Love") and perform "Lover Man" (with guest singer Sarah Vaughan) and the famous version of "Salt Peanuts." Also on **1945–1946** is "Diggin' Diz" from February 1946 (which also has a spot for Parker), some rare items featuring the trumpeter with Johnny Richards's string orchestra on some standards, Gillespie's set for the Dial label (leading a sextet with tenor saxophonist Lucky Thompson, vibraphonist Milt Jackson, Al Haig, bassist Ray Brown, and drummer Stan Levey), and his initial session for the Victor label, a wonderful combo date that includes Thelonious Monk's "52nd Street Theme," "Anthropology" (based on "I Got Rhythm"), and "A Night in Tunisia."

Dizzy Gillespie and Charlie Parker played together for a few months in 1945, and then Gillespie (who always loved big bands) put together his first orchestra. Unfortunately, his initial bebop big band did not survive a tour through the South—audiences complained that they could not dance to the music—and did not record. In the fall, Diz and Bird traveled to Los Angeles to play at Billy Berg's club in Hollywood. Because of Parker's increasing unreliability (which became worse when he realized that heroin supplies were harder to get in Los Angeles than in New York), Gillespie also hired Lucky Thompson for the group. Since they were largely introducing bebop to the West Coast, the music was considered too radical for the time and, other than the

enthusiastic musicians who attended, the audiences were disappointing. By the spring of 1946, Gillespie and his sidemen were set to fly back to New York, but Parker cashed in his plane ticket and bought drugs instead. Dizzy and the other players left without Bird and, except for occasional reunions (such as a 1947 Carnegie Hall concert), this was the end of their musical partnership.

Charlie Parker led his own record date for the first time on November 26, 1945, just prior to the ill-fated Los Angeles trip. He utilized the 19-year-old trumpeter Miles Davis, pianist Argonne Thornton, bassist Curly Russell, and Max Roach on drums for two classic blues ("Now's the Time" and "Billie's Bounce") and the "I Got Rhythm"–based "Thrivin' from a Riff." For "Ko Ko," a jam on the chord changes of "Cherokee," Davis did not feel comfortable, so Gillespie took a brief trumpet break near its beginning and filled in comping on piano behind Parker's classic solo, an improvisation that by itself would have made Bird considered one of the greats.

In Los Angeles, Parker and Gillespie had a few opportunities to freelance, guesting on a session by Slim Gaillard (that included the rather humorous "Slim's Jam") and performing with "Jazz at the Philharmonic" (Parker took a remarkable two-chorus solo on "Lady Be Good" that would later be given words and recorded by Eddie Jefferson). After Bird missed the plane trip back home, he struggled in the Los Angeles area for a few months. Miles Davis, who had taken a job with Benny Carter's Orchestra so he would have an excuse to rejoin Parker in Los Angeles, recorded with Parker on March 28, 1946, a productive date that resulted in such Parker tunes as "Moose the Mooche," "Yardbird Suite," and "Ornithology" (co-written with trumpeter Benny Harris and based on "How High the Moon"). But as the supply of heroin dried up, Parker tried to overcome his addiction by drinking more and more alcohol, and his behavior became unpredictable. On July 29, he recorded four numbers with a quintet that included Howard McGhee, but Parker was in such bad shape that he was off mike much of the time and stumbling through the rapid "Max Making Wax" and "Bebop." His playing on "Lover Man" and "The Gypsy" is full of emotion, but is barely coherent, and he was unable to finish the session. Later in the day, Parker had a complete mental breakdown, accidentally setting his hotel room on fire. He was committed to the Camarillo State Hospital where he stayed for six months.

When Parker emerged in early 1947, he was in the best health of his life and was temporarily off drugs. Within a short time he was back in New York, leading a quintet consisting of Miles Davis, pianist Duke Jordan, bassist Tommy Potter, and Max Roach. That unit stayed together into December 1948 and was a perfect showcase for Bird's inventive playing.

Although Parker recorded for Savoy during 1945–48, he also made sessions for Ross Russell's Dial label too. After years of being reissued separately, all of the music is now on an eight-CD set, ◉ **The Complete Savoy and Dial Studio Recordings 1944–1948** (Savoy 75679 29112). This magnificent reissue not only has all of Parker's Savoy and Dial sessions as a leader (with all of the valuable alternate takes), but also his 1944 session with Tiny Grimes, the seven Musicraft selections with Dizzy Gillespie from 1945 mentioned above, Bird and Diz's date with Slim Gaillard, and their 1945 set with Red Norvo that contrasts the beboppers' improvisations with the swing playing of Norvo, Teddy Wilson, and Flip Phillips.

Of the selections from Parker's own sessions, the classics include "Ko Ko," "Billie's Bounce," "Now's the Time," "Yardbird Suite," "Ornithology," "This Is Always" (with singer Earl Coleman), "Cool Blues" (with the Erroll Garner Trio), "Relaxin' at Camarillo," "Donna Lee," "Bongo Bop," "Dewey Square," "Embraceable You," "Scrapple from the Apple," "Quasimodo," "Constellation," and "Parker's Mood." The many alternate takes are particularly valuable in this case because Bird was a constant improviser, and each statement of his is spontaneous rather than being worked out in advance.

Because he was such a colorful character and a revolutionary player, Charlie Parker became a bit of a cult figure, with some fans doing what they could to record as many of his live solos as possible, often turning off their disc recorders when the other musicians soloed. Far too many of these poorly recorded live performances have been released on LPs and CDs through the years, and some are quite unlistenable, although one can understand the point of it all. In the recording studios, Parker (like everyone else) was restricted to three-minute performances so his solos were necessarily brief; in clubs he could really stretch out. But far superior to the bootleg recordings is ◉ **The Complete Live Performances on Savoy** (Savoy 17021), an exciting four-CD set that features Parker broadcasting during 1948–49 from the Royal Roost, with Symphony Sid Torin as the announcer.

Parker, who is joined by Miles Davis (succeeded by Kenny Dorham starting in December 1948), Al Haig, Tommy Potter, and Max Roach, is heard throughout at the peak of his powers. The performances are often five minutes long and, in addition to the usual repertoire, there are a few offbeat items including a classic beboppish transformation of "White Christmas." Guests along the way include Lucky Thompson, Milt Jackson, and the vocal team of Dave Lambert and Buddy Stewart. In addition, this box has a decent 1950 club date by Bird in Chicago with local musicians and the five numbers that Parker performed with Dizzy Gillespie at their 1947 Carnegie Hall concert, highlighted by the best-ever version of Bird's "Confirmation."

In 1949, Charlie Parker came the closest he ever did to gaining public recognition during his lifetime. He visited Europe (being quite successful at the Paris Jazz Festival), signed with Norman Granz's Clef label (which later became Verve), and on November 30, 1949, realized a lifelong ambition to record with strings. The "Bird with Strings" sessions were his biggest sellers and although some of the arrangements restrained the altoist, he is quite outstanding on "Just Friends," tearing into that song while still making every note count. Charlie Parker closed off the 1940s by appearing at an all-star bebop Carnegie Hall concert on Christmas Eve, performing five numbers with his quintet (which by then consisted of trumpeter Red Rodney, Al Haig, bassist Tommy Potter, and drummer Roy Haynes), playing remarkably throughout, particularly on "Now's the Time" and "Ko Ko."

Dizzy Gillespie, meanwhile, was far from inactive. When he returned from Los Angeles in the spring of 1946, he formed his second big band. This one lasted over three years and was largely successful. Dizzy was a natural-born leader who loved to joke with the audience and enjoyed singing and dancing. But at the same time, he was a serious musician and he was able to keep his potentially wild sidemen in line. ◉ **1946–1947** (Classics 986) starts off with a sextet date from May 15, 1946, with Sonny Stitt playing alto in Charlie Parker's place. Most of the rest of this CD features the Gillespie big band's Musicraft recordings, including such memorable numbers as Tadd Dameron's "Our Delight," "One Bass Hit" (featuring Ray Brown), "Ray's Idea," and Gil Fuller's futuristic "Things to Come," the most radical chart in the band's repertoire. Among Gillespie's sidemen with his 1946 big band are trumpeter Dave Burns, tenor saxophonist James

Moody, and the future nucleus of the Modern Jazz Quartet: Milt Jackson on vibes, pianist John Lewis, bassist Ray Brown, and drummer Kenny Clarke.

The 1946–47 period concludes with the Gillespie big band's first session for Victor. ⦿ **The Complete Victor Recordings** (Bluebird 66528) is a two-CD set that has Gillespie's initial three recorded solos (cut with Teddy Hill's orchestra in 1937), "Hot Mallets" with Lionel Hampton in 1939, the 1946 septet date that included "A Night in Tunisia," and a session with the 1949 Metronome All-Stars. But most of this two-fer concentrates on the Dizzy Gillespie big band of 1947–49 with such classics as "Manteca," "Two Bass Hit," George Russell's "Cubana Be/Cubana Bop," "Good Bait," "Hey Pete! Le's Eat Mo' Meat," and "Jumpin' with Symphony Sid" along with some Johnny Hartman vocal ballads. In addition to the players already mentioned, Gillespie's big band included such sidemen as tenors Jimmy Heath, Yusef Lateef, and the young John Coltrane, baritonist Cecil Payne and trombonist J.J. Johnson.

As if being one of the founders of bebop and the leader of its top big band was not enough, Dizzy Gillespie was also a major contributor in the beginnings of Afro-Cuban (or Latin) jazz. In early 1947, Gillespie mentioned to Mario Bauza that he would like to add a Latin percussionist to his big band. Bauza was musical director of Machito's orchestra and an associate who had helped Dizzy get the job with Cab Calloway back in 1939. He now introduced Gillespie to Chano Pozo, a Cuban conga player and vocalist who had been in the United States for a year without much success. At first Pozo's role with the bebop orchestra was minor and his rhythms did not mesh in that well with the rhythm section. However, after Al McKibbon became Dizzy's bassist and the other players had gotten used to Pozo, the combination worked on a magical level. On September 29, 1947, the Dizzy Gillespie big band played a set at Carnegie Hall (as did Diz and Bird), and with Pozo on conga and Chiquito on bongos, musical history was made. George Russell's "Afro-Cuban Drum Suite" (soon to be renamed "Cubana Be" and "Cubana Bop") was debuted quite successfully. **Diz 'N Bird at Carnegie Hall** (Roost 57061) has both the Parker/Gillespie set (which has been reissued in the eight-CD Bird box too) and the big band performance. Pozo appeared on just eight studio selections with Gillespie including "Manteca" (which they co-wrote) and "Algo Bueno" (a Latin reworking of "Woody'n You"),

but these made an impact. In 1948, the band with Pozo went on a well-received European tour. **Dizzy Gillespie/ Max Roach in Paris** (Vogue 68213) features the orchestra (including "Two Bass Hit" and Pozo's showcase on the "Afro-Cuban Drum Suite") plus four numbers by the 1949 Max Roach Quintet with Kenny Dorham and James Moody. **Dizzy Gillespie and His Big Band** (GNP/Crescendo 23) adds to the band's legacy by featuring the group's live performance of July 19, 1948, including exciting versions of "Emanon," "Good Bait," and "Manteca."

Tragically the hot-tempered Chano Pozo was killed in a bar on December 2, 1948. And by 1949 the Dizzy Gillespie band was struggling. They switched to the Capitol label in the fall, recorded a few so-so sides (including a number titled "You Stole My Wife, You Horse Thief") and reluctantly broke up early in 1950, having made their place in jazz history.

Bud Powell The piano's role in jazz changed more radically during this era than any other instrument. Bud Powell was largely responsible for the piano moving beyond stride and swing into a completely new area. Powell, who developed his musical talents early in life, left school when he was 15 in 1940 to work as a full-time musician. He sat in at Minton's Playhouse, freelanced at low-level jobs, and was with the Cootie Williams Orchestra during 1943–44, making his recording debut. Shortly after leaving Williams's band, he was beaten on the head by racist police during a fight and, due to that incident, he suffered from mental illness for the rest of his life. The next 20 years would find Powell having a good period followed by erratic behavior, periods in institutions, all kinds of questionable "cures" (including electric shock), and then returning to the jazz scene a little worse off than before. It is miraculous that he played as well as he did at times.

Powell's best musical period took place during 1947–51. ⦿ **The Complete Blue Note and Roost Recordings** (Blue Note 30083) is a four-CD set that has all of his music for those labels from 1947–58, music that is also available as six separate discs including the two mentioned in this paragraph. **The Bud Powell Trio Plays** (Roulette 93902) has Powell's first session as a leader (eight classic trio numbers from 1947) plus a pretty good outing from 1953. **The Amazing Bud Powell, Vol. 1** (Blue Note 81503) lives up to its name.

The first nine numbers are a remarkable quintet set from 1949 with Fats Navarro, the young but already impressive tenor saxophonist Sonny Rollins, Tommy Potter, and Max Roach that includes two of Powell's best originals ("Bouncing with Bud" and "Dance of the Infidels") plus Thelonious Monk's "52nd Street Theme." The second half of this disc, a set with Curly Russell and Max Roach from 1951, features "Parisian Thoroughfare," "A Night in Tunisia," and three stunning versions of "Un Poco Loco."

Powell also recorded extensively for Norman Granz's labels during 1949–56. **The Complete Bud Powell on Verve** (Verve 314 521 669) is a five-CD set, which after a brilliant start in 1949, gets bogged down in indifferent and erratic playing, all outlined in an excess of alternate takes. It is better to acquire the single disc ◉ **Jazz Giant** (Verve 543832), which has Powell's first two Clef/Verve dates. Joined by Max Roach and either Ray Brown or Curly Russell during these sessions from 1949–50, Powell is in superb form on "Tempus Fugit," "Celia," "Cherokee," "I'll Keep Loving You," "So Sorry Please, "Get Happy," and "Sometimes I'm Happy" among others. In fact, if one could only acquire a single disc of Powell (or of bebop piano in general), **Jazz Giant** is the one to get.

Thelonious Monk   While Bud Powell set the standard for other young pianists, Thelonious Monk was too individual as a pianist, composer, and personality to be emulated in the 1940s. An introvert who seemed to go out of his way not to communicate verbally with others (until they had gained his trust), Monk had an image problem that would hinder him for a decade and make his music seem very forbidding, even to the bop musicians.

Thelonious Sphere Monk was born in North Carolina, but moved to New York as a child with his family. He began playing piano when he was six, was inspired early on by James P. Johnson (who was a neighbor) and had his first professional job accompanying an evangelist. Monk worked as a member of the house band at Minton's Playhouse during 1940–43, participating in the jam sessions and developing his unique style. The earliest documentation from the jams find him sounding a little like Teddy Wilson, but he soon pared his style down to the bare essentials. Monk had his own fresh chord voicings, emphasized the value of space and dynamics, and began to compose pieces. The Cootie Williams Orchestra recorded his "Epistrophy" in 1942 and "'Round

Midnight" in 1944. Monk worked for a few months with Lucky Millinder's big band (1942) and in 1944 was a member of Coleman Hawkins's quartet, making his official recording debut with the latter. Already he was quite recognizable and stood apart not only from swing players but from the bop generation.

Of all the bop era musicians, Monk tended to be ridiculed the most, with people commenting as much on his taste in hats as on his playing. Charlie Parker and Dizzy Gillespie thought highly of him and "'Round Midnight" gradually became a standard, but most bop musicians found his music too difficult to play, being too lazy to fully investigate his unique repertoire. Monk's style was fully formed by 1947, but it would take the jazz world almost another decade before they caught up to him.

Fortunately, Alfred Lion and Francis Wolff of the Blue Note label decided to take a chance on Monk. After taking 1946 off to investigate the bop scene (under the guidance of tenor saxophonist Ike Quebec), Lion and Wolff shifted their company away from swing and Dixieland (though they continued to record Sidney Bechet and George Lewis) toward the new bop music. They documented Monk on four occasions during 1947–48, in a sextet, a trio, a quintet, and a quartet, with such players as trumpeter Idrees Sulieman, Art Blakey, altoist Sahib Shihab, and Milt Jackson. All of the music, plus sessions from 1951–52 and 1957–58, have been reissued on ◉ **The Complete Blue Note Recordings** (Blue Note 30363), an essential four-CD set. The 1947–48 sessions include the debut of such Monk songs as "Thelonious," his classic ballad "Ruby My Dear," "Well You Needn't," "Off Minor," "In Walked Bud," "Evidence," and "Misterioso" plus his earliest versions playing "'Round Midnight," "Epistrophy," and "I Mean You." Listeners who only want the 1947 sessions should pick up the single CD **Genius of Modern Music, Vol. 1** (Blue Note 81510).

Although with hindsight it seems obvious that Thelonious Monk was a musical genius, at the time he only worked on an occasional basis, and his individuality was made fun of instead of being treasured.

Other Bop Pianists

Bud Powell was such a dominant force among young modern jazz pianists in the mid-1940s that it was difficult at first for the pianists to develop their own musical personalities. First they had to learn Powell's style so they could play with the bop musicians, and then it was up to them to become individuals. It was a process that generally took some time.

Clyde Hart   Poor Clyde Hart. He could have played an important role in the new music, but instead died at the beginning of the bebop era. Hart had been an active musician since at least 1929 when he played with Gene Coy. His other associations included Jap Allen (1929–31), Blanche Calloway (1931–33), McKinney's Cotton Pickers (1935), Stuff Smith (1936–38), Lucky Millinder, Roy Eldridge, Lester Young, Frankie Newton, John Kirby (1942), Oscar Pettiford, Wilbur DeParis, and Tiny Grimes (1944). Hart was in the process of modernizing his style during 1944–45, a period when he recorded with Coleman Hawkins, Ben Webster, Don Byas, and Lester Young and led three sessions of his own (using such sidemen as Bird and Diz, Budd Johnson, Trummy Young, and singer Rubberlegs Williams). On February 28, 1945, he was on the Dizzy Gillespie session with Charlie Parker that resulted in "Groovin' High" and "Dizzy Atmosphere." But 19 days later, he passed away from tuberculosis at the age of 35.

Al Haig   In 1945, only a few pianists really knew how to play bop. Other than Bud Powell and Thelonious Monk, Al Haig was one of the most highly respected and one of the few whites (along with George Wallington and Dodo Marmarosa) active on the bop scene that early. Haig, who had played music while in the Coast Guard (1942–44), performed with Jerry Wald's orchestra briefly and then worked with Gillespie during 1945–46 (including being in the Bird and Diz group that traveled to Los Angeles). During the next few years he played with Charlie Barnet, Jimmy Dorsey, Ben Webster, Fats Navarro, and Coleman Hawkins, replacing Duke Jordan in the Charlie Parker Quintet (1948–50).

Hank Jones   Hank Jones, who was born in 1918, was the first in a series of major jazz pianists to emerge from Detroit, and he was the oldest of the three musical Jones brothers (preceding cornetist Thad and drummer Elvin). He began playing professionally in 1931 when he was 13, working in territory bands for years. Jones came to New York to play with Hot Lips Page in 1944 and he worked with the John Kirby Sextet, Howard McGhee, Coleman Hawkins, and the big bands of Andy Kirk and Billy Eckstine. Jones, who a half-century later still had the same pleasing swing-to-bop transitional style that he displays on his debut as a leader in 1947, performed with "Jazz at the Philharmonic" and began a five-year period as Ella Fitzgerald's accompanist in 1948. **Urbanity** (Verve 314 537 749) has Jones's six piano solos from 1947 plus four trio numbers with guitarist Johnny Smith and Ray Brown (augmented by multiple alternate takes) from 1953.

Duke Jordan   Duke Jordan is best known for being a member of the Charlie Parker Quintet of 1947–48. He studied classical music from age eight and early on worked with Coleman Hawkins, the Savoy Sultans, and the 1946 Roy Eldridge big band. With Bird, Jordan's gentle playing and lyrical introductions to songs (most memorably "Embraceable You") added a lot to the group even if Miles Davis (for unknown reasons) never liked his playing. After leaving Parker, Jordan worked with Stan Getz's first group (1949).

John Lewis   More to Miles Davis's liking was John Lewis. The "Count Basie of Bebop" in his use of space and ability to make every note count, Lewis was a sophisticated player and lover of classical music who was also quite capable of playing very effective blues. He began taking piano lessons at age seven and attended the University of New Mexico before serving in the army. Lewis first gained recognition for his playing with the Dizzy Gillespie Orchestra (1946–48) for whom he composed "Toccata for Trumpet" and arranged "Two Bass Hit" and "Emanon." He recorded with Charlie Parker on a few sessions during 1947–48 (including taking a famous solo on "Parker's Mood"), worked with Illinois Jacquet (1948–49), and was pianist and one of the arrangers with Miles Davis's "Birth of the Cool" Nonet.

Dodo Marmarosa   Michael "Dodo" Marmarosa should have been one of the major pianists in jazz, but mental problems and personal difficulties kept him from reaching his potential. He gigged locally in his native Pittsburgh and had significant stints playing with the big bands of Gene Krupa (1942–43), Tommy Dorsey (1944), Charlie Barnet, and Artie Shaw (1945). Marmarosa, whose style was boppish by 1944, moved to Los Angeles in 1946 and was house pianist for the Atomic label. He appeared on many records during the next few years, including with Boyd Raeburn, Lester Young, Lucky Thompson, Howard McGhee, Slim Gaillard, Tom Talbert's orchestra, Stan Hasselgard, and Charlie

Parker. He also worked with Artie Shaw's 1949 bebop orchestra, quitting when Shaw answered one too many requests to play "Frenesi" again!

Dodo's Bounce (Fresh Sound 1019) is a generous 30-song CD with music from four of Marmarosa's sessions of 1946–47 plus a date with Lucky Thompson. The pianist is heard on four unaccompanied solos (including his two-part impressionistic "Tone Paintings"), five numbers in a trio with bassist Harry Babasin (who doubles on cello) and drummer Jackie Mills, ten selections with guitarist Barney Kessel and bassist Gene Englund, and six tunes in a quartet with Thompson, bassist Red Callender, and Mills. In addition, there are five alternate takes from the Babasin date. With the exception of four Thompson originals and five standards, all of the music are Dodo's compositions. These concise performances are full of fire and creative ideas. **1945–1950** (Classics 1165), other than duplicating the five numbers from the Babasin session, has entirely different music, including an additional quartet session with Thompson and Dodo's trio set for Savoy from 1950, his last recording in 11 years. Dodo Marmarosa was at his musical peak during 1945–49, but unfortunately he would never regain the power and enthusiasm of those years.

George Shearing   George Shearing, who spent the war years playing with Stephane Grappelli, was a big name in his native England as a swing pianist. In 1947, he first visited the United States, and his nine trio numbers, eight of which were last reissued on the LP **So Rare** (Savoy 1117), find him opening up his style to bop a bit on such numbers as "Bop's Your Uncle" and "Cozy's Bop." In 1949, Shearing moved permanently to the United States. At the urging of his friend Leonard Feather, he put together a quintet comprised of his piano, Marjorie Hyams on vibes, guitarist Chuck Wayne, bassist John Levy, and drummer Denzil Best. The George Shearing Quintet, which featured tight harmony between the piano, vibes, and guitar, recorded eight songs for Discovery on January 31, 1949, which have been reissued (along with four selections from the 1950 Red Norvo Trio) on **Midnight on Cloud 69** (Savoy 208) including "Cherokee," "Four Bars Short," "Bebop's Fables," and "Sorry Wrong Rhumba." The group was a hit from the start and within a couple of weeks had started recording regularly for the MGM label, including such popular numbers as "September in

the Rain," "East of the Sun," Shearing's "Conception," and "Jumpin' with Symphony Sid."

George Wallington   George Wallington, who composed two bebop standards ("Lemon Drop" and "Godchild"), was a bebop pioneer. Born in Sicily, Wallington and his family moved to the United States in 1925. He began playing in New York in the early 1940s and was a member of Dizzy Gillespie's combo of 1943–44, the first bop group to play on 52nd Street. Wallington worked with Joe Marsala during 1945 and then spent the remainder of the 1940s playing with many of the top bop musicians, including Charlie Parker, Serge Chaloff, Allan Eager, Kai Winding, Terry Gibbs, and Brew Moore.

Claude Williamson   Claude Williamson also mastered the Bud Powell style during the mid-to-late 1940s. He started ten years of classical piano lessons when he was seven and studied at the New England Conservatory. Williamson worked with the Charlie Barnet Orchestra (1947), Red Norvo (1948), and back with Barnet, playing with the tenor's bebop big band of 1949 and taking a well-known solo on "Claude Reigns."

Three Major Bebop Trumpeters

While Dizzy Gillespie towered over the other trumpeters of the bebop era due to his technique, very advanced ideas and showmanship, his playing was on such a high level that it was very difficult to closely emulate. Howard McGhee emerged as an important transitional force between swing and bop, influencing the younger Fats Navarro. Navarro and Miles Davis (who made the most out of his more limited technique) ended up spawning many more imitators and followers in the long run than Gillespie.

Howard McGhee   One of the first young trumpeters to emerge playing bebop after Dizzy Gillespie was Howard McGhee, who was born one year after Diz. McGhee started out playing clarinet and tenor and did not switch to trumpet until he was 17 in 1935. He began his career working in territory bands in the Midwest, was with Lionel Hampton (1941), and gained some attention for his work with Andy Kirk (1941–42), being featured on "McGhee Special." He was originally influenced by Roy Eldridge, but always had his own distinctive sound. McGhee jammed at Minton's Playhouse and

Monroe's Uptown House and worked with Charlie Barnet (1942–43), Kirk for a second stint (Fats Navarro was also in the trumpet section at the time), Georgie Auld, and Count Basie. In 1945, he was part of the Coleman Hawkins Quintet, recording with Hawk and traveling to Los Angeles with the great tenor. McGhee stayed around L.A. for a couple of years (helping to introduce bebop to the West Coast), played with "Jazz at the Philharmonic," recorded a couple of sessions with Charlie Parker and worked in Central Avenue clubs. After returning to New York, he recorded an exciting session with Navarro for Blue Note in 1948 and stayed busy for a time.

1945–1946 (Classics 1125) mostly has formerly rare recordings of McGhee, all recorded on the West Coast. There are four selections recorded for Philo in a sextet with tenors Teddy Edwards and James D. King and four full sessions for the Modern label. In addition, there is a big-band outing and three of the selections from Charlie Parker's ill-fated "Lover Man" Dial date (two up-tempo McGhee features and a faltering "Be-Bop") that were originally released under the trumpeter's name. The music on this CD is quite boppish, sometimes a little ragged, but always full of fire and energy, with the highlights including "Stardust," "Mad Hype," the two-part "Around the Clock," a remake of "McGhee Special," and the haunting "Night Mist." **1946–1948** (Classics 1089) has many McGhee originals recorded for the Dial and Savoy labels with such players as Teddy Edwards, Dodo Marmarosa, James Moody, Milt Jackson, Hank Jones, and Jimmy Heath. Most of the songs are obscure, but they serve as viable vehicles for the heated playing of the young boppers. **1948** (Classics 1058) has the remainder of McGhee's Savoy sessions from that year (with Heath, Jackson, and Billy Eckstine on valve trombone) plus two sessions cut in Paris for Vogue and Blue Star (with Heath and tenor saxophonist Jesse Powell). Best is the final session, the meeting with Fats Navarro on Blue Note that resulted in "The Skunk," "Boperation," and the two-part "Double Talk," music also available on Navarro's Blue Note box.

Unfortunately, Howard McGhee's career would become aimless in the 1950s, but his work of 1945–49 put him near the top of his field during the bebop era.

Fats Navarro   Although Dizzy Gillespie was the king of bebop trumpeters, his playing style was so complex that most young trumpeters quickly gave up quickly trying to emulate him. By 1947, they tended to look more toward Fats Navarro and Miles Davis as musical role models. Navarro, who was influenced by Howard McGhee, Roy Eldridge, and Gillespie, was a brilliant player with a fat sound who in turn would influence many later generations of trumpeters.

Navarro played a bit of piano and tenor sax before becoming a trumpeter. He picked up experience working with Snookum Russell's big band (1941–42) and Andy Kirk (1943–44). When Gillespie left the Billy Eckstine Orchestra, Navarro became his replacement (1945–46). During 1946–49, Navarro was on many significant bop sessions in addition to working with Tadd Dameron, Illinois Jacquet (1947–48), Lionel Hampton, and briefly with Benny Goodman (1948).

The four-CD set ◗ **Fats Navarro Story** (Proper 1011), which is fortunately available at a budget price, has virtually every important recording from Navarro's career. Included are Navarro's features with the Billy Eckstine Orchestra, the Bebop Boys (an all-star group with Sonny Stitt, Kenny Dorham, Bud Powell, and Kenny Clarke), Eddie Lockjaw Davis (who is heard at his most excitable), Coleman Hawkins, Tadd Dameron, Illinois Jacquet, Benny Goodman, and Bud Powell plus Fats's own three sessions as a leader. Not only are the studio sides here but also live performances. Among the many highlights are "Epistrophy," "Webb City," "Calling Dr. Jazz," "I Mean You," "Eb Pop," "Goin' to Minton's," "The Chase," "Our Delight," "A Bebop Carol," "Nostalgia," "Half Step Down, Please," "Stealin' Apples" (his one selection with the Benny Goodman Septet), "Boperation," "Move," "Bouncin' with Bud," and "52nd Street Theme."

Other domestic releases mostly duplicate material from the Proper box, but might be preferable to those with a smaller budget. **Goin' to Minton's** (Savoy 92861) has all of the trumpeter's Savoy recordings (as a leader and as a sideman with the Bebop Boys and Lockjaw Davis) other than two vocal numbers and the alternate takes. The two-CD set **Fats Navarro and Tadd Dameron** (Blue Note 33373), in addition to Navarro's recordings with Dameron, has four songs by Tadd's band with Davis in Fats's spot, "Stealin' Apples" with Benny Goodman, and Fats's classic sessions with Howard McGhee and Bud Powell.

But, as with Howard McGhee, Fats Navarro's most important work was completed by the end of 1949. In fact, his days were numbered for his body was weakened by both his heroin addiction and tuberculosis.

Miles Davis While Howard McGhee and Fats Navarro will forever be associated with the 1945–49 period, Miles Davis was just beginning his very important career. He grew up in a middle-class family in East St. Louis, Illinois, and was given his first trumpet for his 13th birthday in 1939. Davis's early trumpet heroes were Bobby Hackett (he was impressed by Hackett's lyrical playing on his 1938 recording of "Embraceable You"), Harry James, and Clark Terry, who at the time was a top local player. Davis played with Eddie Randall's Blue Devils during 1941–43 and had an opportunity to sit next to Dizzy Gillespie and Charlie Parker when the Billy Eckstine Orchestra passed through town in 1944.

Davis's playing differed greatly from that of Gillespie or Navarro in that he had a small range, a quiet sound, less impressive technique, and (at first) a simpler style. However, he was very attracted to the new music and, when he went to New York in September 1944 to study at Julliard, the first thing he did was look for Charlie Parker. Because he spent more time playing at 52nd Street clubs (including with Coleman Hawkins), Davis soon dropped out of school. On April 24, 1945, he made his recording debut with singer/dancer Rubberlegs Williams, but sounded quite nervous. He was in much better form in the fall on a Charlie Parker session that resulted in "Now's the Time" and "Billie's Bounce" although the 19-year-old felt inadequate on "Ko Ko" and had Gillespie fill in for him. After Parker went to Los Angeles with Gillespie, Davis accepted a job with Benny Carter's orchestra because Carter's big band was heading out west. Davis stayed in Los Angeles for a few months and on March 28, 1946, recorded an excellent session with Bird that resulted in "Moose the Mooche," "Yardbird Suite," and "Ornithology." When Parker had a mental breakdown a few months later, Davis returned to New York. He recorded his first session as a leader, leading a sextet that included tenor saxophonist Gene Ammons and featured vocals by Earl Coleman and Ann Baker, but the music was not released until several decades later. **Bopping the Blues** (Black Lion 760102) has four songs and eight alternate takes from this session, but the vocals dominate and the performances are more interesting from a historic rather than musical standpoint.

When Bird was released from Camarillo and came back to New York, he formed a quintet that included Miles Davis. At the time, many bop fans were surprised that Parker would use Davis instead of Gillespie or Navarro. Truth is, Dizzy was tied up with his big band and Fats would be a competitive force. Parker wanted a more complementary player, one whose relaxed solos would contrast with Bird's and whose sound would fit the group well. Miles was with Parker for a year and a half, recording with Parker's group for Savoy and Dial and leading one date (utilizing Bird's quintet, but with Parker switching to tenor) that featured his four compositions "Milestones," "Little Willie Leaps," "Half Nelson," and "Sippin' at Bells." **First Miles** (Savoy 78995) has this session (with the alternate takes), which is easily available on Charlie Parker collections, along with Davis's initial date with Rubberlegs Williams. During 1948, Davis met arranger Gil Evans and formed his "Birth of the Cool" nonet, a project that will be discussed later in this chapter. After leaving Parker's group in December 1948, Davis freelanced, including leading a group at the 1949 Paris Jazz Festival that consisted of James Moody, Tadd Dameron on piano, bassist Barney Spieler, and Kenny Clarke. **In Paris Festival International De Jazz** (Sony 65508) finds Miles defying expectations (which he would do many times in his career) by hitting high notes, sounding a bit like Gillespie, and displaying more technique playing bebop than one would think he had. In addition, he even verbally introduces some of the songs and sounds quite happy. But it would not be long before he moved beyond bop.

The Other Bebop Trumpeters

In addition to Gillespie, McGhee, Navarro, and Miles Davis, the four trumpeters in this section all made their strong contributions to the music, even if they were overshadowed by the bop trumpet giants.

Kenny Dorham Kenny Dorham practically owned the "underrated" tag throughout his career because he was always overshadowed by at least a few other trumpeters. A very good player and a talented composer, Dorham started on piano, switched to trumpet while in high school, and served in the army during 1942–43. After playing briefly with Russell Jacquet (Illinois's older brother), Dorham worked in 1945 with the first Dizzy Gillespie big band and with Billy Eckstine. In 1946, he recorded twice with the Bebop Boys (on one occasion playing opposite Fats Navarro). Dorham had brief stints with Mercer Ellington and Lionel Hampton and became

Miles Davis's replacement with the Charlie Parker Quintet in December 1948, staying a year. **Blues in Bebop** (Savoy 17028) has a sampling of Dorham's sideman sessions for Savoy including with Eckstine ("The Jitney Man"), the eight songs and two alternate takes with the Bebop Boys, three numbers from a broadcast with Parker, a date with vibraphonist Milt Jackson's sextet, and finally four songs from a 1956 Cecil Payne session. Dorham, who had a distinctive tone influenced by Gillespie, would be a very valuable contributor to jazz during the next 15 years.

Benny Harris   Benny Harris was a decent trumpeter and made some important early contributions to bop, but dropped out of music early. Originally a French horn player, he switched to trumpet when he was 18 in 1937. He worked with Tiny Bradshaw (1939) and Earl Hines (1941 and 1943), playing on 52nd Street with Benny Carter, Pete Brown, the John Kirby Sextet, Herbie Fields, Coleman Hawkins, Don Byas, and Thelonious Monk. Harris recorded with Clyde Hart (December 1944) and Don Byas, also working with Boyd Raeburn (1944–45) and the 1949 Dizzy Gillespie big band. However, he was most notable for having written "Ornithology" (co-composed with Charlie Parker), "Crazeology," "Reets and I," and "Wahoo" (derived from "Perdido").

Red Rodney   Red Rodney (born Robert Chudnick) started young, playing at the age of 15 (in 1942–43) with Jerry Wald's Orchestra. Due to the wartime shortage of top section players, Rodney had opportunities to play with the big bands of Jimmy Dorsey, Elliot Lawrence, Georgie Auld, Benny Goodman, and Les Brown. His original idol was Harry James, but by 1945 he had discovered Dizzy Gillespie and was updating his style. He was featured with Gene Krupa's orchestra in 1946, led a session apiece for Mercury and Keynote, and had stints with Buddy Rich, Claude Thornhill, and Woody Herman's Second Herd (1948–49). In 1949, Rodney succeeded Kenny Dorham as the trumpeter with the Charlie Parker Quintet, and sounds particularly brilliant during Bird's Christmas Eve set at Carnegie Hall.

Freddie Webster   Freddie Webster is a mystery figure in jazz history. He was cited by Miles Davis as an important early inspiration, and Dizzy Gillespie said that he had the greatest tone he ever heard on the trumpet, but Webster recorded very little and died young so

his greatness is difficult to ascertain. He began his career mostly playing first trumpet with many swing bands, including Earl Hines (1938), Erskine Tate, Benny Carter, Eddie Durham, Lucky Millinder, Jimmie Lunceford (1942–43), Sabby Lewis, and Cab Calloway, but he took few solos with any of those groups. During 1945–46, Webster recorded with Miss Rhapsody, tenor saxophonist Frankie Socolow, and Sarah Vaughan, and he can be heard fairly well on those sessions. While his atmospheric playing on Vaughan's "If You Could See Me Now" has been praised quite a bit, he actually sounds stronger (and has more space) on her version of "You're Not the Kind." Freddie Webster worked briefly with the John Kirby Sextet and the Dizzy Gillespie big band, but overdosed on heroin on April 1, 1947, passing away at the age of 29 or 30.

Two Great Bop Trombonists

The rapid speed and complexity of bebop could very easily have resulted in the trombone being demoted back to being a minor instrument. However, J.J. Johnson blazed a path that other trombonists were able to follow, de-emphasizing emotional slurs and slides in favor of complete mastery of his horn, including alternate positions. Johnson was such a virtuoso that some who heard his records assumed that he must be playing a valve trombone!

J.J. Johnson   J.J. Johnson (born James Louis Johnson) was born and grew up in Indianapolis. He played with the territory bands of Clarence Love and Snookum Russell during 1941–42 before spending three years (1942–45) with Benny Carter's orchestra. He took his first recorded solo on 1943's "Love for Sale," participated in the initial concert of "Jazz at the Philharmonic," and was a key soloist with Count Basie (1945–46). Johnson recorded with Charlie Parker in 1947 (a classic sextet session also including Miles Davis), toured with Illinois Jacquet (1947–49), was with the 1949 Dizzy Gillespie Orchestra, and recorded with the Miles Davis Nonet and the Metronome All-Stars. ◐ **1946–1949** (Classics 1176) has the master takes from all five of Johnson's bebop era sessions as a leader. The 20 selections match Johnson in quintets with altoist Cecil Payne and Bud Powell, Leo Parker and Hank Jones, Sonny Rollins and John Lewis, and Sonny Stitt and Lewis, plus a sextet session with Kenny Dorham and Rollins. The music is primarily J.J.

originals and shows that he was able to keep up with some of the top young saxophonists around.

Kai Winding   Kai Winding was nearly on J.J. Johnson's level. He moved from his native Denmark to the United States with his family when he was 12. In the early 1940s, he played with the big bands of Shorty Allen, Bobby Say, Alvino Rey, and Sonny Dunham, and was with a service band while serving three years in the Coast Guard. Winding worked with Benny Goodman (1945–46) and then filled a very important role with Stan Kenton (1946–47), bringing the trombone to prominence with Kenton and defining its sound in his band. Winding led two record dates in 1945 (showing that he was one of the first trombonists to really understand bop) and worked with Tadd Dameron during 1948–49, also recording with the Miles Davis Nonet.

The other significant trombonists to emerge during this era were Bill Harris (with Woody Herman) and Bennie Green. But by 1949, most new trombonists who were emerging had to deal first with overcoming the influence of the remarkable J.J. Johnson.

Four Bebop Clarinetists

Because the clarinet was so closely associated with the swing era and Benny Goodman, it greatly declined in importance during the second half of the 1940s and, with a few exceptions, has mostly been heard in Dixieland and swing settings ever since. However, there were four players who tried their best to make the clarinet an important instrument in bebop.

Buddy DeFranco   By all rights, Buddy DeFranco (born Boniface Ferdinand Leonard DeFranco) should have had the fame of Benny Goodman and Artie Shaw, but his timing was off. He started playing clarinet at nine, winning an amateur swing contest sponsored by Tommy Dorsey five years later, in 1937. DeFranco worked with the big bands of Gene Krupa (a couple of occasions during 1941–43), Charlie Barnet (1943–44), Tommy Dorsey (off and on during 1944–48), and Boyd Raeburn (1946). Although sometimes thought of as having a cold tone and of being a technician (since he never seemed to make mistakes), DeFranco constantly took chances and showed that bop could certainly be played on the clarinet. But virtually no one followed him, and he remained obscure to the general public.

Stan Hasselgard   The bop clarinetist with the greatest potential was Stan Hasselgard. Born in Sweden, he was given a clarinet for his 16th birthday. Hasselgard first recorded a year later (1940), and his early influence was Benny Goodman. He worked regularly in Sweden, including with the Royal Swingers, Arthur Osterwall (1944–45), bassist Simon Brehm, and visiting American trombonist Tyree Glenn. In 1947, Hasselgard moved to the United States to study art history at Columbia University. Soon he was playing in New York with Wardell Gray and Dodo Marmarosa. In December 1947, he recorded with Red Norvo and Barney Kessel. In 1948, Hasselgard impressed Benny Goodman so much that he became the only clarinetist ever to perform next to Goodman with BG's small groups, being part of a two-clarinet septet that also included Wardell Gray and Mary Lou Williams. The band did not last long, but radio broadcasts from their engagement at the Click in Philadelphia have since been released on record. After the group broke up, Hasselgard put together a quintet that had Max Roach on drums. By now he was a strong bebop player and he was gaining attention. Tragically on November 23, 1948, Stan Hasselgard died in a car crash at the age of 26.

Hasselgard's earliest recordings have mostly only appeared on LP. **Young Clarinet** (Dragon 163) starts off with 1940's "Ain't She Sweet" and has a lot of rarities from the 1940–44 period plus 1948 V-disc performances of "You Took Advantage of Me" and "Patsy's Idea." **The Jazz Clarinet of Ake "Stan" Hasselgard** (Dragon 25) is mostly from 1945–48 and finds Hasselgard evolving from swing to bop, from a Benny Goodman admirer into his own voice. A highlight is an alternate version of "Patsy's Idea," which starts out with Hasselgard verbally imitating Goodman! **Jammin' at Jubilee** (Dragon 29) mostly has live performances including sessions with the Jackie Mills Quintet, the International All Stars (with Wardell Gray and Dodo Marmarosa), and Arnold Ross's quartet (with Billy Eckstine added on vocals and valve trombone for three numbers).

There are two Stan Hasselgard CDs currently available. **The Permanent Hasselgard** (Phontastic 8802) has highlights from 1945–48 including dates in Sweden with the Kjeld Bonfils Orchestra and Trio, the Royal Swingers, Simon Brehms's sextet, Tyree Glenn, and the Bob Laine-Gosta Torner group. In addition, Hasselgard is heard leading a couple of swing-oriented dates in 1947 (including one in the United States with singer Louise Tobin), playing "Who Sleeps" with Red Norvo, and being featured on four numbers with the Goodman Septet. The latter is duplicated on ● **At Click 1948** (Dragon 183), which contains most of the available radio airchecks of the otherwise lost BG group. This music is often fascinating, and one can contrast the sounds and styles of Goodman and Hasselgard, who are joined by Gray, Teddy Wilson, guitarist Billy Bauer, bassist Arnold Fishkind, and drummer Mel Zelnick.

Tony Scott and John LaPorta   Tony Scott (born Anthony Sciacca) was in some ways the Lester Young of the clarinet, for although harmonically advanced, he floated over bar lines and had a lighter-than-oxygen tone. He studied at Julliard (1940–42), jammed at Minton's Playhouse, and spent three years in the military. In 1946, Scott led a three-song record date that featured Sarah Vaughan and Dizzy Gillespie (under the pseudonym of "B. Bopstein"). He freelanced during the bebop era, playing with Buddy Rich, Ben Webster, Trummy Young, Charlie Ventura, Big Sid Catlett, and the Claude Thornhill Orchestra (1949).

John LaPorta also was significant during this period. He was classically trained, but switched to jazz in 1942 when he played with Bob Chester. LaPorta (who doubled on alto) also worked with Dick Himber, Ray McKinley, and Woody Herman (1944–46) before becoming associated for a time with Lennie Tristano. He had a very advanced style and an unusual sound.

Jamming in L.A.

Although bop first caught on in New York, and Diz and Bird were met with a mostly indifferent reaction when they came out to Los Angeles in late 1945, within two years L.A. had its own strong bop scene developing. In fact, the four top bop-oriented tenors (if one counts Lucky Thompson) were all based in Los Angeles in 1946 and were fixtures on the Central Avenue scene, L.A.'s equivalent of New York's 52nd Street.

Dexter Gordon   A Los Angeles native, Dexter Gordon (nicknamed "Long Tall Dexter" due to his height and laidback personality) played clarinet at 13, alto at 15, and tenor when he turned 17 in 1940. He worked with the Lionel Hampton big band during 1940–43, but due to Illinois Jacquet's presence, he had very little solo space. Gordon took his first recorded solos in a quintet

with Nat King Cole (1943) and worked briefly with Lee Young, Jesse Price, Fletcher Henderson, and the Louis Armstrong big band. He moved to New York in 1944 and was a member of the Billy Eckstine big band, trading phrases with Gene Ammons on Eckstine's famous recording of "Blowin' the Blues Away." Gordon recorded "Blue 'N' Boogie" with Dizzy Gillespie in 1945, began leading record dates of his own for Savoy and spent 1946–49 back in Los Angeles. He participated in many saxophone battles with Wardell Gray and Teddy Edwards, resulting in such exciting recordings as "The Chase" and "The Duel." The four-CD set **Setting the Pace** (Proper 1016), although it skips around chronologically, has all of the master takes of Gordon's 1943–47 sessions plus his main solos as a sideman during this period and six jam sessions with top L.A. players (including Wardell Gray). A single disc with the same title, **Settin' the Pace** (Savoy 17027), has all of Gordon's Savoy recordings except three alternate takes, featuring Argonne Thornton, Bud Powell, Leo Parker, Tadd Dameron, and Fats Navarro in the supporting cast. Included are such originals as "Blow Mr. Dexter," "Dexter's Deck," "Dexter's Cuttin' Out," "Dexter's Minor Mad," "Long Tall Dexter," "Dexter Rides Again," "Dexter Digs In," "Dextrose," and "Dextivity"! **The Chase** (Stash 2513) has Gordon's Dial recordings (including all of the alternate takes), highlighted by "The Chase" (which matches Dexter with Gray), and "The Duel" and "Hornin' In" (the alternate for "The Duel"), which have Gordon battling Teddy Edwards to a draw. In addition, there is a quintet date with trombonist Melba Liston, a few quartet numbers, and a feature for Edwards on "Blues in Teddy's Flat."

Teddy Edwards   Teddy Edwards first worked in public in 1936 when he was 12. Born in Jackson, Mississippi, he was in Detroit by 1942 and, after touring with Ernie Fields's big band, moved permanently to Los Angeles in 1945. Edwards briefly played alto with Roy Milton, then switched to tenor and was a member of Howard McGhee's band, recording often as a sideman and soon leading his own groups. He led two record dates during 1947–48 (quintets with either Benny Bailey or trombonist Herbie Harper), but that music has not been available since coming out on a pair of LPs, **The Foremost** (Onyx 1215) and **Central Avenue Breakdown** (Onyx 1212) in the 1970s.

Wardell Gray   Wardell Gray was the best known of the three young tenors as 1945 began. Like Edwards, he had a softer tone than Gordon, being influenced to an extent by Lester Young. Gray, who was born in Oklahoma City, grew up in Detroit and was featured with the Earl Hines big band during 1943–45. In Los Angeles, he played with Benny Carter, Billy Eckstine, and Tadd Dameron, recorded with Charlie Parker and Dodo Marmarosa, jammed with Dexter and Edwards, and led record dates of his own. Gray was part of the Benny Goodman Septet in 1948 (the group with Stan Hasselgard) and was in Goodman's bebop-oriented big band of 1949. **One for Prez** (Black Lion 60106) is a rather exhaustive reissue of Gray's 1946 quartet date with Dodo Marmarosa, including not just five selections, but also 11 alternate takes. **Wardell Gray Memorial Vol. 1** (Original Jazz Classics 050) has all of the music from two Gray sessions: a quartet from 1949 with Al Haig, Tommy Potter, and Roy Haynes, and a sextet date from 1953 with pianist Sonny Clark, vibraphonist Teddy Charles, and the young altoist Frank Morgan. The earlier session is highlighted by the famous medium-tempo blues "Twisted," which Annie Ross would soon record in a vocalese version (putting words to all of the notes of Gray's solo). This disc actually has four versions of "Twisted" and seven of "Southside," so there is no shortage of repetition; fortunately, Gray is heard throughout in prime form.

Other Bop Tenors

Drawing their initial inspirations from a combination of Coleman Hawkins, Lester Young, and Ben Webster and being inspired by the example of Dexter Gordon, the tenors in this section sought to keep the tenor tone of the swing era while modernizing their musical vocabulary.

Gene Ammons   Gene Ammons, the son of boogie-woogie pianist Albert Ammons, played with King Kolax (1943) and gained some recognition for his work with the Billy Eckstine Orchestra (1944–47), trading fours with Dexter Gordon on "Blowing the Blues Away" and taking quite a few solos along the way. He also played with Woody Herman's Second Herd in 1949, being featured on the recording of "More Moon." Ammons, a fluent tenor saxophonist perfectly home in bebop, also had a huge sound and a very expressive and bluesy style that

TIMELINE 1946

The big bands of Woody Herman, Benny Goodman, Jack Teagarden, and Harry James break up. • Don Byas settles in Europe. • Bop pianist Joe Albany records with Lester Young; he would record just once more during the next 24 years. • The movie *New Orleans*, although flawed, features some good scenes with Louis Armstrong and Billie Holiday. • The Glenn Miller Orchestra is revived, becoming one of the first ghost bands, with Tex Beneke as its original leader. • Charlie Parker suffers a mental breakdown. • Dizzy Gillespie forms a successful big band and signs with Victor. • While studying at Mills College, Dave Brubeck forms an adventurous octet. • The Page Cavanaugh Trio is a popular attraction in the Los Angeles area, recording hit versions of "The Three Bears," "Walkin' My Baby Back Home," and "All of Me." • Oscar Celestin comes out of retirement in New Orleans and forms a new version of the Tuxedo Jazz Orchestra, featuring clarinetist Alphonse Picou. • June Christy and Bob Cooper get married. • At the age of 25, tenor saxophonist Yusef Lateef plays with Lucky Millinder's Orchestra. • Trumpeter Reuben "River" Reeves plays with Harry Dial's Bluesicians. • Nineteen-year-old John Coltrane cuts four privately recorded songs on alto with a navy band, soon joins King Kolax's group. • Mercer Ellington (Duke's son) leads a big band that includes Kenny Dorham and singer Carmen Clarke (later known as Carmen McRae), but the orchestra fails within a year. • Seventeen-year-old altoist Herb Geller plays with Joe Venuti's big band. • Alberta Hunter cuts four songs for the Juke Box label, her only record date of the decade. • Pianist/arranger Sonny Blount (later known as Sun Ra) works with a show band led by Fletcher Henderson. • Ethel Waters has her first recording date since 1940, otherwise working primarily as an actress. • Frankie Trumbauer, who was inactive in music during 1941–45, makes a brief comeback, appears on a few records, and then permanently retires, preferring to work in the aircraft industry. • Trumpeter Pete Daily puts together a strong Dixieland band, Daily's Chicagoans, in Los Angeles. • Don Redman's orchestra tours Europe. • *Really the Blues*, Mezz Mezzrow's colorful memoirs, is published. • Claude Thornhill forms his second orchestra with Gil Evans as his chief arranger.

made it easy for him to cross over to listeners who pre-ferred ballads and R&B-oriented material. He began recording as a leader in 1947 and his EmArcy recordings were last available on the two-LP set **Jug Sessions** (EmArcy 2-400), a reissue that deserves to be duplicated on CD. Ammons is well featured on six four-song ses-sions, including his one recording date with his father, Albert Ammons. How many listeners have noticed that Albert's original "Hiroshima" has the same chord changes as the standard "Nagasaki"? Other highlights include the original version of "Red Top" (which is heard both with and without the later overdubbed vocal), several heated jams, and some warm ballads. Ammons also recorded 24 titles for Chess and its related labels during 1948–51. The CD **Young Jug** (GRP/Chess 801) has 16 of the songs, plus a rare four-song session from 1952 for Decca that had not been reissued previously. Overall Ammons sounds quite lyrical on the ballads and romps with his combos on the jump material, showing that he was very quickly developing into a major tenor saxophonist.

Allan Eager and Don Lanphere　During the bebop era, many young tenor saxophonists, particularly in Woody Herman's "Four Brothers" band, based their cool-toned sound on that of Lester Young. Allan Eager, who was with an earlier version of Herman's orchestra, played as a teenager during World War II in the big bands of Bobby Sherwood, Sonny Dunham, Shorty Sherock, Hal McIntyre, Herman (1943–44), Tommy Dorsey, and Johnny Bothwell. Eager, who led three record dates for Savoy during 1946–47 that are usually reissued as part of samplers (sidemen include Max Roach, Terry Gibbs, and Doug Mettome), was a fixture on 52nd Street during 1945–47. He recorded with Kai Winding and Coleman Hawkins, played with Tadd Dameron in 1948 (next to Fats Navarro), and was among the first to bring the sound of Lester Young into bebop.

Don Lanphere, who also had a cool tone, made his initial impression for a brief period in the late 1940s. He began playing locally in Washington State in 1940 when he was 12, studied at Northwestern University, and at 19 in 1947 moved to New York. Lanphere played with Woody Herman's Second Herd and Artie Shaw's bebop orchestra, leading two record dates including one in which he held his own with Fats Navarro.

James Moody and Sonny Rollins　One of the most advanced of the tenors to emerge during this era, James

Moody served in the Air Force during 1943–46 before joining Dizzy Gillespie's big band (1946–48). Moody mostly played tenor with Gillespie, but also doubled on alto during this period, and he was a forward-looking bebopper from the start. In 1948, Moody began a three-year period living in Europe and in 1949 he cut one of his most famous recordings, playing "I'm in the Mood for Love" on alto. A few years later, it would be given vocalese lyrics by Eddie Jefferson and become a hit for King Pleasure as "Moody's Mood for Love." It is included on **Greatest Hits** (Prestige 24228), a CD also containing some of Moody's European dates of 1950–51 and such up-and-coming Swedish players as baritonist Lars Gullin, altoist Arne Domnerus, and trumpeter Rolf Ericson.

Sonny Rollins was just 19 as 1949 ended, but he was already showing great promise. He had begun on piano, switched to alto and in 1946 settled on the tenor sax. In 1949, Rollins made his recording debut with Babs Gonzales, recorded with J.J. Johnson, and sounded quite mature and fiery on a classic record date with Bud Powell and Fats Navarro.

Lucky Thompson　Lucky Thompson retained the sound of a swing era tenor saxophonist, but his solos had the harmonic complexity of a bop-based improviser. He grew up in Detroit, played locally, moved to New York in 1943, and had stints with Lionel Hampton, Don Redman, Sid Catlett, and Hot Lips Page. In 1944, Thompson spent brief periods with the big bands of Billy Eckstine and Lucky Millinder, and gained attention for his play-ing with Count Basie (1944–45) where he succeeded Don Byas, his main influence. He was hired as "insur-ance" by Dizzy Gillespie for the group that Dizzy took to the West Coast in late 1945, in case Charlie Parker did not show up. Thompson spent much of the next two years around Los Angeles, playing with Boyd Raeburn and the final Louis Armstrong Orchestra in addition to appear-ing on many recordings, including with Parker and Gille-spie. **The Beginning Years** (IAJRC 1001) has some of Thompson's rarer Los Angeles sessions, including outings with Bob Mosley's All-Stars, Estelle Edson, Karl George's Dukes and Duchess, David Allyn, Lyle Griffin, the Basin Street Boys, Ike Carpenter, singer Ernie Andrews, and Mills Blue Rhythm Band plus two songs from his own session in 1945. **1944–1947** (Classics 1113) has all of Thompson's dates as a leader during this era (except for a

Chess session in 1949), including a loose jam session with Erroll Garner and Stuff Smith on "Test Pilots," four songs with fellow Count Basie sidemen, a quartet outing with Dodo Marmarosa, and his notable Victor session of April 22, 1947. The latter, which features Neal Hefti in trumpet, Benny Carter, and Marmarosa, is most notable for the intriguing "From Dixieland to Bop" (which is based on the chord changes of "Tiger Rag") and a magnificent Thompson ballad solo on "Just One More Chance." Later in 1947, Lucky Thompson moved to New York where he was heard with a variety of small groups, playing bop and swing standards.

The Bop Altoists

The younger musicians who played alto sax during the bebop era all had the giant shadow of Charlie Parker hovering above them. Very few were able to escape his dominant influence at the time other than Lee Konitz (with Lennie Tristano), Paul Desmond (playing with the Dave Brubeck Octet), and Art Pepper.

Sonny Criss, Jimmy Heath, Charlie Kennedy, and Art Pepper   Sonny Criss had a heavier sound than Bird and displayed his own brand of fire. Although born in Memphis, Tennessee, he moved with his family to Los Angeles in 1942 when he was 14 and was based in Los Angeles during much of his career. Criss worked with Howard McGhee, Teddy Edwards, Johnny Otis, and Gerald Wilson's Orchestra, appearing fearlessly next to Charlie Parker at a "Jazz at the Philharmonic" concert.

Jimmy Heath, the younger brother of bassist Percy Heath and the older brother of drummer Albert "Tootie" Heath, started playing alto in 1941 when he was 14. He worked in his native Philadelphia with the Calvin Todd-Mel Melvin group (1944) and Nat Towles (1945–46), leading a band of his own in Omaha (1946–47). Heath gained some exposure playing with Howard McGhee (1947–48) and the Dizzy Gillespie big band (1949), but was dubbed "Little Bird" due to the similarity of his sound to Charlie Parker. That title would soon lead to him switching to tenor.

Another impressive Bird-oriented altoist, Charlie Kennedy played with Louis Prima's orchestra in 1943. During 1945–48 while with Gene Krupa, Kennedy became the first bop altoist (other than Parker himself) to be featured regularly with a big band. He led his only record date in 1945 (strangely enough playing tenor on

the five selections) and also had short stints with the orchestras of Charlie Ventura, Chubby Jackson, and Chico O'Farrill.

In Art Pepper's case, it helped that he was initially inspired by Benny Carter before discovering Charlie Parker. Pepper worked early on with the big bands of Gus Arnheim, Carter, and Stan Kenton (1943–44), sitting in with black groups on Los Angeles's Central Avenue before serving in the military (1944–46). Pepper was well featured during his second period with Kenton (1947–48) and displayed the ability to swing and think fast in his own voice no matter how complex the music was.

Sonny Stitt   No one was closer to sounding like Charlie Parker throughout his career than Sonny Stitt, who always claimed that he developed his style before he ever heard Bird. Stitt worked early on in Michigan and Newark, New Jersey. He first met Parker when he was playing with Tiny Bradshaw's big band in 1943, and he gained his earliest recognition while a soloist with Billy Eckstine (1945). In 1946, Stitt filled in for an absent Bird on a Dizzy Gillespie small-group date recorded after the trumpeter returned from Los Angeles. He was with Dizzy's big band for a few months, also recording with the Bebop Boys. Drug problems led to the altoist being only semi-active during 1947–48, but in 1949 Stitt made a strong comeback. By then he was doubling on tenor, where his sound owed more to Lester Young than to Bird, though his solos were pure bebop. ⊙ **Sonny Stitt/Bud Powell/J.J. Johnson** (Original Jazz Classics 009) dates from 1949–50 and has consistently classic music. Stitt (heard exclusively on tenor) stars on two sessions in a quartet also including Bud Powell, Curly Russell, and Max Roach, and is featured in a quintet actually led by J.J. Johnson. Best are "All God's Chillun Got Rhythm," "Fine and Dandy," "Strike Up the Band," and John Lewis's "Afternoon in Paris."

The Bebop Baritonists

The top bebop-oriented baritonist of 1945–49, Serge Chaloff, is covered in this chapter in the section on Woody Herman. There are several more worth noting, though.

Gerry Mulligan, Leo Parker, and Cecil Payne   Gerry Mulligan, who would become the most famous of all baritonists, started to make an impression during this era, but more as a writer than as a soloist. Mulligan's first instruments were piano and clarinet before learning alto and baritone. In 1944 (when he was 17), he wrote arrangements for Johnny Warrington's radio band, followed by work for Tommy Tucker and George Paxton. In 1946, Mulligan moved to New York and became a staff arranger for Gene Krupa; "Disc Jockey Jump" was his best-known chart for the drummer. Occasionally he played alto with Krupa, but mostly stuck to writing, and had a similar position with Claude Thornhill in 1948. Mulligan did play baritone with the Miles Davis Nonet (1948–50), but was considered more significant for contributing five arrangements and three originals ("Jeru," "Rocker," and "Venus De Milo"). In 1949, Mulligan wrote and played with Elliot Lawrence's orchestra. He had not risen above obscurity yet, but he was still just 22 years old.

Leo Parker had a deep tone and a style that could fall between bebop and R&B. He began on alto and appeared on the lighter horn on Coleman Hawkins's debut bop records (1944). Parker switched to baritone when he joined Billy Eckstine (1944–45). He was an asset to the Dizzy Gillespie big band (1946) and Illinois Jacquet's combo (1947–48), also recording with Fats Navarro, J.J. Johnson, Dexter Gordon, and Sir Charles Thompson. **1947–1950** (Classics 1203) has all of the music (except alternate takes and the final two songs) from Parker's first five sessions as a leader. The baritonist welcomes such major players as Howard McGhee, Gene Ammons, Joe Newman, J.J. Johnson, Dexter Gordon, tenor saxophonist Charlie Rouse, Al Haig, and Max Roach to these frequently heated sessions. Highlights include "Wild Leo," "Leapin' Leo," "Wee Dot," "Lion Roars," "Sweet Talkin' Leo," and "Mad Lad Returns."

Cecil Payne also started on alto, taking lessons from Pete Brown. After serving in the military during 1943–46, he recorded on alto with J.J. Johnson, but then switched to baritone. Payne worked briefly with Clarence Briggs and Roy Eldridge and then was the anchor for the Dizzy Gillespie Orchestra (1946–49), being featured on a few numbers, particularly "Ow" and "Stay on It."

The Bebop Vibraphonists

Prior to 1943, there was only one major jazz vibraphonist: Lionel Hampton (Adrian Rollini never made much of an impression on that instrument). In 1943, Red Norvo switched from xylophone to vibes. During 1945–49, the number of significant vibists doubled from two to four thanks to the rise in prominence of Milt Jackson and Terry Gibbs.

Milt Jackson and Terry Gibbs   Milt Jackson started on guitar at seven, played piano at 11, and briefly tried violin and drums in addition to singing gospel with the Evangelist Singers in his native Detroit. Jackson began playing vibes as a teenager, altering his sound by slowing down the speed of the vibraphone's oscillator, getting a warmer and distinctive tone that never sounded like Lionel Hampton. He spent part of 1942–44 in the military and during 1944–45 led the Four Sharps. Jackson made his recording debut with Dinah Washington, was heard in Detroit by Dizzy Gillespie, and soon was playing with Diz and Bird. He recorded with Gillespie's small group in 1946, joined his big band and quickly became in great demand. In addition to playing with Gillespie, Jackson worked with Charlie Parker, Thelonious Monk, Howard McGhee, and (in 1949) Woody Herman's Second Herd. **In the Beginning** (Original Jazz Classics 1771) features Jackson visiting Detroit in 1948 and performing on two sessions, a sextet with Sonny Stitt, trumpeter Russell Jacquet, and pianist Sir Charles Thompson, and an intriguing quintet with John Lewis, Kenny Clarke, bassist Al Jackson, and Chano Pozo on conga. There is also a septet date without Jackson that includes Stitt, Jacquet, and J.J. Johnson. The recording quality is just fair, but the formerly rare music is quite boppish and features many future stars during their early days.

Terry Gibbs (born Julius Gubenko) was always a hard-charging player whose spirit (if not choice of notes) could be reminiscent of Hampton. Gibbs started on xylophone, drums, and tympani. After his military service, he appeared often on 52nd Street, making his recording debut with clarinetist Aaron Sachs and working with Tommy Dorsey (1946), Chubby Jackson (1947–48), and Buddy Rich (1948). He gained fame as a member of Woody Herman's Second Herd (1948–49), taking heated solos, and sometimes joining in on the group's boppish vocals. Jackson succeeded him later in 1949.

Guitarists After Charlie Christian

By all rights, Charlie Christian should have been the leading bebop guitarist, but his death in 1942 meant that he never played with a mature bop rhythm section. It would be over 20 years before the jazz guitar moved far beyond his ideas. In addition to Billy Bauer (who is covered in this chapter under Lennie Tristano), Tiny Grimes (who after using Charlie Parker on a record date in 1944 largely switched to swing and R&B), and Django Reinhardt, the most intriguing bop guitarists were Bill DeArango, Barney Kessel, Mary Osborne, Remo Palmieri, and Chuck Wayne, although only Kessel would make a strong impact in the long run. And with a few exceptions, the electric guitar, although gradually being accepted as a solo instrument, was relatively minor during the bop era.

Bill DeArango   Bill DeArango was the most radical of these players. He had actually started his career playing Dixieland and swing in his native Cleveland. After attending Ohio State University and spending 1942–44 in the army, DeArango moved to New York where he immediately became a member of Ben Webster's group, playing on 52nd Street. He appeared as a sideman on quite a few sessions during 1945–47, including with Webster, Dizzy Gillespie, Sarah Vaughan, Slam Stewart, Charlie Kennedy, Ike Quebec, Eddie "Lockjaw" Davis, and Charlie Ventura. He also had two sessions of his own in 1946 (using Webster, Idrees Sulieman, and Tony Scott) and had a working group that included Terry Gibbs. There were times when DeArango's unusual sound and advanced choice of notes almost made it sound like he was playing his guitar backwards! However, in 1948 when he was 26, he moved home to Cleveland and slipped away into obscurity.

Barney Kessel   Barney Kessel was mostly self-taught on guitar, playing locally in Oklahoma until moving to Los Angeles in 1942 when he was 18. He was with a big band fronted by Chico Marx (1942–43) and actually run by Ben Pollack, and was picked by Norman Granz to be in the Lester Young short film *Jammin' the Blues*. Kessel adjusted his Charlie Christian–influenced style to bop easily and was an important player with Charlie Barnet (1944–45) and Artie Shaw's orchestra and Gramercy Five (1945). Kessel became a busy studio musician in Los Angeles, but always found time to play jazz, recording with Charlie Parker in 1947 and leading a four-song record date of his own in 1945.

Mary Osborne, Remo Palmieri, and Chuck Wayne
Other than Sister Rosetta Tharpe, Mary Osborne was the first female jazz guitarist of any importance. At 15

in her native North Dakota in 1936, she worked with a trio, playing guitar, violin, and bass, in addition to singing and dancing. After hearing Charlie Christian play with Alphonse Trent's band, she switched to electric guitar. During the later part of the swing era, Osborne played with the big bands of Buddy Rogers, Dick Stabile, Terry Shand, Joe Venuti, and Russ Morgan. The bop years found her working with Mary Lou Williams, the Beryl Booker Trio, Coleman Hawkins, and Wynonie Harris among others. She recorded 14 obscure trio numbers as a leader during 1946–48. But despite all of this activity, she never became famous.

Remo Palmieri had a relatively brief career in jazz although he had a fairly long life. In 1942, he became a professional musician, working with pianist Nat Jaffe. Palmieri worked with Coleman Hawkins, Red Norvo, Billie Holiday, and Mildred Bailey, also recording with Charlie Parker and Dizzy Gillespie (their famous "Groovin' High/Dizzy Atmosphere" date), the Esquire All-Stars, Teddy Wilson, and Sarah Vaughan. But in 1945, he joined the staff of CBS and was featured on the Arthur Godfrey radio show for the next 27 years, often playing banjo. He was rarely heard in jazz settings after 1946.

Chuck Wayne was self-taught and started out playing mandolin with a Russian balalaika group. On 52nd Street he was part of the trios of Clarence Profit and Nat Jaffe before serving in the army from 1942–44. After his discharge, the versatile guitarist worked with Joe Marsala (1945–46), Dizzy Gillespie, Red Norvo, Woody Herman's First Herd (1946), Jack Teagarden, Coleman Hawkins, Phil Moore, Bud Powell, Lester Young, the Barbara Carroll Trio, and the original George Shearing Quintet (1949–52). Wayne always cited Lester Young and Charlie Parker as his main influences in addition to Charlie Christian.

Bassists After Jimmy Blanton

As with the guitar, the evolution of the bass was moved forward quickly by one innovator, Jimmy Blanton, who unfortunately died before the bebop era got started. While most bassists of the 1945–49 period (and even into the 1950s) primarily played in a supportive role behind the other musicians, rarely soloing and even then tending to just play four notes to the bar, a few of the bassists sought to extend the ideas of Blanton.

Oscar Pettiford   With Jimmy Blanton's death in 1942, Oscar Pettiford was his main successor, becoming one of the few bassists to consistently get solo space during the second half of the 1940s. One of 11 children, Pettiford started on piano, but soon switched to bass, playing in a family band led by his father, Doc Pettiford. In 1942, he joined Charlie Barnet's orchestra as half of a two-bass team with Chubby Jackson. Pettiford gained recognition for his playing on Coleman Hawkins's 1943 "The Man I Love" record date, also cutting sessions with Ben Webster and Earl Hines. Pettiford worked with Roy Eldridge, co-led the first bop group on 52nd Street with Dizzy Gillespie, and was with the Coleman Hawkins sextet in 1945, visiting Los Angeles. He was a member of the Duke Ellington Orchestra (1945–48) and Woody Herman's Second Herd (1949). After breaking his arm playing baseball, Pettiford had to leave Herman's band to recover, so he spent this downtime learning to play pizzicato solos on the cello. He would soon develop into jazz's second cello soloist; Harry Babasin had preceded him in 1947.

Charles Mingus   A masterful bassist who in time became a very significant bandleader and composer, Charles Mingus grew up in Los Angeles. He had short stints on trombone and cello, but was convinced by Red Callender to switch from the cello to bass while in high school. In 1942, Mingus worked with Barney Bigard (Kid Ory was also in the group, starting his comeback) and toured with Louis Armstrong's big band in 1943. Always interested in the most modern music, while seeing nothing wrong with vintage styles, Mingus defied stereotypes and was a rebel. He worked in Central Avenue clubs for a few years including with drummer Lee Young, the Stars of Swing (1946), and his own combos. During 1947–48, he was part of the Lionel Hampton Orchestra, and Hamp recorded Mingus's futuristic "Mingus Fingers," but the bassist returned to freelancing on the West Coast and remained quite obscure, for the moment.

Charles "Baron" Mingus, West Coast, 1945–49 (Uptown 27.48) is a remarkable CD that collects together all 24 recordings that were led by Mingus during this period for such tiny labels as Excelsior, Four Star, Dolphins of Hollywood, Fentone, and Rex Hollywood. Very few of the performances had even been reissued on LP so this disc fills in a major gap. The music varies widely in styles, from vocal ballads to very advanced instrumentals. Among the performers are the prolific studio tenor Maxwell Davis, drummer Roy Porter, Willie Smith,

Lucky Thompson, Buddy Collette (on alto and clarinet), trombonist Britt Woodman, drummer Cal Tjader, singer Helen Carr (on "Say It Isn't So"), the young altoist Eric Dolphy, and Art Pepper. In some of the selections, one can hear glimpses of what was to come.

Ray Brown, Percy Heath, and Al McKibbon   Ray Brown has always been celebrated for his authoritative tone, impeccable technical skills, and ability to swing at every tempo. He started off playing locally in Pittsburgh with Jimmy Hinsley and Snookum Russell. On the very day in 1945 that he arrived in New York, the 18-year-old jammed with Dizzy Gillespie, Charlie Parker, Bud Powell, and Max Roach! Having survived that encounter, Brown began working with Gillespie and in 1946 he became a member of his big band, being featured on "One Bass Hit" and "Two Bass Hit." In 1947, Brown played with "Jazz at the Philharmonic" and met Ella Fitzgerald. They were married from 1948 to 1952, and for a time the bassist usually worked in Ella's backup group. In 1949, also at JATP, Brown met a young Canadian pianist named Oscar Peterson.

The oldest of the three Heath brothers, Percy Heath started on violin when he was eight, sticking with that instrument until 1946 when he was already 23. Switching to bass, he worked as the house bassist at Philadelphia's Down Beat Club and developed very quickly. In 1947, Percy and younger brother Jimmy moved to New York and the bassist immediately started working with the who's who of bop including Howard McGhee, Charlie Parker, Thelonious Monk, Fats Navarro, and J.J. Johnson.

Al McKibbon studied bass and piano at Cass Technical High School in Detroit and early in his career played locally with Kelly Martin and Teddy Buckner. He moved to New York by 1943, playing with Lucky Millinder, Tab Smith (1945–46), Coleman Hawkins, J.C. Heard, Bud Powell, Thelonious Monk, and, most significantly, the Dizzy Gillespie big band (1948–49) where he was Ray Brown's successor.

Tommy Potter and Curly Russell   Tommy Potter and Curly Russell often had overlapping careers, fulfilling similar roles as supportive, but rarely soloing bassists whose endurance at rapid tempos was impressive if taken for granted. Potter studied piano and guitar, not switching to bass until he was in his early twenties. He worked with pianist John Malachi, Trummy Young, the Billy Eckstine Orchestra (1944–45), tenor saxophonist John

Hardee, and Max Roach, but is most famous for being part of the Charlie Parker Quintet (1947–49). Russell started out as a trombonist before settling on bass. He performed with the big bands of Don Redman (1941) and Benny Carter (1943), and then became involved with bop. Russell worked with Charlie Parker (with whom he recorded in 1945, 1948, and 1950) and Dizzy Gillespie (1945), also playing with Dexter Gordon, Sarah Vaughan, Bud Powell, Tadd Dameron (1947–49), Coleman Hawkins, Fats Navarro, and Miles Davis.

The Bebop Drummers

Playing drums in bebop was much different than playing in a swing big band. The evolution of the instrument had moved quickly beyond Gene Krupa, Buddy Rich, Chick Webb, and Jo Jones, with Kenny Clarke and Max Roach in particular developing a new form of interactive playing.

Kenny Clarke and Max Roach   Kenny Clarke, while jamming nightly at Minton's Playhouse in the early 1940s, shifted the timekeeping role for drummers to the ride cymbal, an innovation soon emulated by most other young drummers. He was much more of an interactive drummer than his predecessors, not only keeping time, but musically commenting on the proceedings, and "dropping bombs" with his bass drum to emphasize unusual accents. Although his drumming drove some conservative horn soloists a little crazy (particularly back in 1939 when he was in Teddy Hill's orchestra), the net result was a gradual liberation of drummers from playing a largely metronomic role, and an opportunity for them to inspire the lead voices.

While Clarke was in the military during 1943–46, Max Roach surpassed his innovations. Although a fiery player, Roach always recognized the value of space and he had an architect's flair for constructing solos. He began playing drums when he was ten and studied at the Manhattan School of Music. Roach was part of the house band at Monroe's Uptown House in 1942 and the following year made his recording debut with Coleman Hawkins. He worked with Benny Carter, sat in with Duke Ellington (1944), was on Hawkins's groundbreaking bop record dates, and often played with Dizzy Gillespie on 52nd Street. Roach was on Charlie Parker's famous "Ko Ko" session in 1945 and worked with Stan Getz, Allen Eager, and Hawkins before becoming a key member of Bird's quintet (1947–49).

By the time he was discharged from the military in 1946, Kenny Clarke found the bebop music that he helped pioneer developing rapidly. He became part of the scene immediately, leading a record date that included Fats Navarro, Kenny Dorham, Sonny Stitt, and Bud Powell. Clarke worked with Tadd Dameron and the Dizzy Gillespie big band (including visiting Europe with Dizzy in 1948). **1946–1948** (Classics 1171) has the all-star session with Navarro and Powell from 1946 (which includes "52nd Street Theme" and a song that Clarke co-wrote with Thelonious Monk, "Epistrophy") and most of his Paris sessions of 1948. Sidemen on the latter include a variety of French players, pianist Raph Schecroun (who would emerge years later as Errol Parker), trumpeter Dick Collins, and altoist Hubert Fol. **1948–1950** (Classics 1214) contains further Paris dates from 1948 and 1950 (with Howard McGhee, Jimmy Heath, and James Moody), a 1949 session in New York (with Kenny Dorham, French horn player Julius Watkins, and Milt Jackson) and sideman dates with Hubert Fol. Although the music throughout is quite worthwhile, Kenny Clarke never did achieve the fame or (after his earliest work) the significance of Max Roach.

Denzil Best   Drummer Denzil Best was also a talented songwriter who co-composed "Bemsha Swing" with Thelonious Monk and wrote "Move," "Allen's Alley," and "Nothing but D. Best." He originally played piano and trumpet, jamming on the latter at Minton's, but a serious lung disease during 1940–41 forced him to give up trumpet. He worked on piano and bass for a few years before switching permanently to drums in 1943 when he was 26. Within a few months he was strong enough to play with the top players, spending nine months in Ben Webster's quartet. Best worked with Coleman Hawkins (1944–45), Illinois Jacquet (1946), Chubby Jackson (1947–48), and as an original member of the George Shearing Quintet (1949–52).

Art Blakey   Few drummers were ever as explosive as Art Blakey. Originally a pianist, Blakey gave up piano after he heard Erroll Garner play. Switching to drums, he played swing with Mary Lou Williams (1942) and the Fletcher Henderson Orchestra (1943–44). But after Blakey joined Billy Eckstine (1944–47), he was persuaded by Dizzy Gillespie to greatly modernize his playing, and he became an inspiring powerhouse drummer. Blakey led a rehearsal group in 1947 called the Seventeen

Messengers, and he recorded five titles with an octet. He visited Africa during much of 1948–49, studying the local music and Islam, returning later in 1949 when he worked with the Lucky Millinder Orchestra. **New Sounds** (Blue Note 84336) has Blakey's 1947 session (his group included Kenny Dorham and pianist Walter Bishop) along with two dates led by James Moody in 1948; Blakey is on drums on one of the latter sessions. The Moody titles have arrangements by Gil Fuller and Gillespie sidemen (including trumpeter Dave Burns, altoist Ernie Henry, Cecil Payne, and Chano Pozo) and include such tunes as "The Fuller Bop Man," "Moody's All Frantic," "Cu-Ba," and "Tin Tin Deo."

Roy Haynes   Roy Haynes was always a subtle but creative drummer, tending to be overshadowed by the flashier players though he was always rated high by his fellow musicians. He worked in the Boston area with Sabby Lewis's big band and Frankie Newton, coming to New York in 1945 where he was a member of the Luis Russell Orchestra (1945–47) and Lester Young's combos (1947–49). Haynes, who sounded quite modern with Russell's commercial outfit and satisfied Young's desire for quiet timekeeping, also played with Kai Winding and recorded with Bud Powell before joining the Charlie Parker Quintet for three years, starting in 1949.

J.C. Heard, Tiny Kahn, and Stan Levey   J.C. Heard (James Charles Heard) was able to play both swing and bop quite effectively. He started his career performing as a dancer in vaudeville. Heard worked locally in Detroit and then had stints with the Teddy Wilson big band and sextet, Coleman Hawkins, Benny Carter, and the Cab Calloway Orchestra (1942–45). He led his own group at Café Society (1946–47), was a member of the Erroll Garner Trio, toured with "Jazz at the Philharmonic," and recorded with many of the top bebop players.

Tiny Kahn (born Norman Kahn and far from tiny in size) was both a fine drummer and an up-and-coming arranger/composer. He began playing drums in 1939 when he was 15 and his main associations during the bebop era were with Georgie Auld (1947), Boyd Raeburn, the Chubby Jackson Big Band, and Charlie Barnet (1949), contributing arrangements to the latter. Among his compositions were "Tiny's Blues," "Father Knickerbopper," and "Leo the Lion."

Stan Levey was one of the earliest bop drummers, and he was comfortable playing with Dizzy Gillespie as

early as 1942 in his native Philadelphia. After moving to New York in 1944, he worked with Charlie Parker, Coleman Hawkins (the quartet with Thelonious Monk), Ben Webster, Woody Herman's Herd (1945), and the Gillespie/Parker quintet that went to Los Angeles. Levey effectively propelled the big bands of Charlie Ventura, Georgie Auld, and Freddie Slack during the remainder of the 1940s.

Roy Porter   For a short time, Roy Porter looked as if he was going to be a very significant force in jazz, before drugs cut short his career. Porter worked with Milt Larkin (1943), served in the military, and then in 1945 settled in Los Angeles. He worked with Howard McGhee (1945–46), recorded with Charlie Parker, and played regularly on Central Avenue. Porter was a sideman on many records recorded in L.A. (especially for the Dial label), including sets with Dexter Gordon, Wardell Gray, and Teddy Edwards. In 1949, Porter formed a very modern big band that included among its sidemen trumpeter Art Farmer, trombonist Jimmy Knepper, and altoist Eric Dolphy. This intriguing orchestra recorded two sessions for Savoy, last reissued on the two-LP multi-artist set **Black California** (Savoy 2215).

The Arrangers of the Bop Years

During the bebop years there was often less of a need for arranger/composers than during the swing era. The classic two-horn quintet usually played originals by band members along with some standards, with the opening and closing ensembles simply being the melody performed in unison. However, some bands, particularly those larger in size, used arranged choruses, and there was a need for writers who understood the new music. Certainly the modern big bands such as Woody Herman, Dizzy Gillespie, and Stan Kenton would have sounded much different if their arrangers had not delved into bebop. Among the arrangers covered later in this chapter are Gil Evans (with Claude Thornhill), George Handy (Boyd Raeburn), Ralph Burns (Woody Herman), and Pete Rugolo (Stan Kenton).

Tadd Dameron   Tadd Dameron was on a different level than most of the other bop era arrangers in that he led his own bands, wrote songs that became standards, and played piano in his groups although he was quite modest about the latter (emphasizing chords rather than Bud Powell–like single-note lines). Among the songs that Dameron contributed to jazz were "Hot House" (which utilized the chords of "What Is this Thing Called Love"), "Good Bait," "Our Delight," "Lady Bird," "Cool Breeze," and the haunting ballad "If You Could See Me Now."

Dameron, who was eight months older than Dizzy Gillespie, had already established himself during the swing era, working with Zack Whyte and Blanche Calloway, and writing for Vido Musso, Harlan Leonard (1940), Jimmie Lunceford, and Count Basie. He gained recognition for his contributions to the books of the Billy Eckstine, Georgie Auld, and Dizzy Gillespie (1945 and 1946–47) big bands. As a pianist, Dameron was a member of Babs Gonzales's Three Bips and a Bop (1947) and led a sextet at the Royal Roost during 1948–49 that at times featured Fats Navarro, Miles Davis, Alan Eager, and Kai Winding. After performing at the 1949 Paris Jazz Festival in a quintet with Miles Davis and James Moody, he stayed in Europe for a few months, writing for Ted Heath. Back in the United States, the busy Dameron wrote some charts for Artie Shaw's short-lived bebop orchestra. **1947–1949** (Classics 1106) has all of Dameron's studio sessions as a leader prior to 1953, music recorded for Blue Note, Savoy, and Capitol that is also easily available elsewhere, often in sets reissued under Fats Navarro's name. Along with the instrumental jams are a few less common vocal numbers for Kay Penton and a 1949 Capitol date with Miles Davis on trumpet.

Gil Fuller   Gil Fuller is best remembered for his work with the Dizzy Gillespie big band. Never a soloist or performer himself, Fuller actually studied engineering in New York University, but developed a talent for writing for large ensembles. In the early 1940s, he wrote in Los Angeles for the big bands of Les Hite and Floyd Ray. After serving in the army (1942–45), he contributed modern charts for the orchestras of Billy Eckstine, Jimmie Lunceford, Woody Herman, Charlie Barnet, Count Basie, Artie Shaw, Machito, and Tito Puente among others. Fuller wrote for Gillespie during 1946–49 with his arrangements including "Manteca," "Oop-Bop-Sh-Bam," "One Bass Hit," "Ray's Idea," and the stunning "Things to Come." But other than a four-song session for Savoy (which found him taking a vocal on "Mean to Me"), Gil Fuller did not lead any sessions of his own other than two albums in 1965.

Neal Hefti, Johnny Mandel, and Nat Pierce   Neal Hefti began to gain a reputation for his arrangements in the 1940s. A decent trumpeter, Hefti first wrote charts in the late 1930s for Nat Towles and a few years later for Earl Hines. He played trumpet with Charlie Barnet, Horace Heidt, and Charlie Spivak (1942–43), touring with Woody Herman's First Herd (1944–46). Hefti, who married Herman's singer Francis Wayne, arranged an updated "Woodchopper's Ball" and "Blowin' Up a Storm" for Herman in addition to composing "The Good Earth" and "Wild Root." His most notable trumpet solo was on "From Dixieland to Bop" during a Lucky Thompson session, but his trumpet playing soon became a rarity as he concentrated on writing. Hefti also wrote during the era for Charlie Ventura (1946) and Harry James (1948–49).

Few probably remember that Johnny Mandel made his main living in the 1940s as a trombonist and trumpeter. He did start playing music professionally quite early, beginning when he was 13 in 1939. Mandel played trumpet in the big bands of Joe Venuti (1943) and trumpeter Billie Rogers, switching to trombone during periods with the orchestras of Boyd Raeburn, Jimmy Dorsey, Buddy Rich, Georgie Auld, Alvino Rey, and most notably Woody Herman's Second Herd (1948) for whom he contributed his classic chart "Not Really the Blues."

Nat Pierce in later years was considered a pianist and arranger whose greatest influence was Count Basie and the style of the Basie band. However, he led a bop-oriented band in Boston during the late 1940s. Pierce studied at the New England Conservatory and by 1943 (when he was 18) was playing piano professionally in the Boston area. He worked with Shorty Sherock and Larry Clinton (1948) before leading his own rehearsal band during 1949–51, an ensemble most notable for including altoist Charlie Mariano and singer Teddi King. **The Boston Bustout** (Hep 13) features Pierce in 1947 with the Ray Borden big band, playing with combos led by Serge Chaloff and Mariano, and on a few numbers with his orchestra during 1949–50, with Teddi King taking three vocals. The collector's LP **Nat Pierce** (Zim 1005) has additional material from the Pierce big band, including the three-part "Red Hills and Green Barns." The soloists (other than Mariano) on this boppish set include trombonist Sonny Truitt and tenor saxophonist Sam Margolis.

George Russell   An important arranger and theorist, George Russell started out as a drummer playing professionally while in high school. At 19 in 1942, he was stricken with tuberculosis, and while recovering, he learned how to arrange from another patient. Russell worked briefly with Benny Carter, but was soon replaced by Max Roach, leading to his decision to focus on composing and arranging. After becoming ill again, he spent 16 months in a Bronx hospital (1945–46). This time he utilized the idle hours developing the ideas for his Lydian concept, a way of improvising jazz based on scales rather than chord changes. After he was released, Russell wrote "Cubana Be" and "Cubana Bop" for the Dizzy Gillespie big band and Chano Pozo, contributed arrangements to the orchestras of Claude Thornhill and Artie Shaw, and composed the remarkable "A Bird in Igor's Yard," which was recorded by Buddy DeFranco. The latter depicted a fictional musical meeting by Charlie Parker and Igor Stravinsky, a collaboration that should have happened.

The Jive Singers

Louis Armstrong, Cab Calloway, and Fats Waller had been among the pioneers of jive singing in the 1920s and '30s, to a small extent developing their own phrases and language before and during the swing era. Slim Gaillard, Harry "the Hipster" Gibson, and Leo Watson took the concept much farther, sometimes into complete absurdity.

Slim Gaillard   Slim Gaillard was always a difficult performer to classify. Was he primarily a Charlie Christian–influenced guitarist, a jive singer, or a somewhat bizarre comedian? Actually, he was a unique combination of all three.

Gaillard gained fame as half of Slim and Slam (with Slam Stewart) during 1938–43. After serving in the military, he settled in Los Angeles and began teaming up with bassist Bam Brown. Their live shows (at Billy Berg's during the same period when Dizzy Gillespie and Charlie Parker were allegedly the main attraction) were often outrageous as they shifted quickly between songs and Gaillard spoke in his own unusual (and frequently hilarious) dialect. **The Legendary McVouty** (Hep 6) shows just how outside Slim and Bam could go on such numbers as "Voutoreene Alias McVouty," "Fried Chicken O'Routee," and the two part "Avocado Seed Soup Symphony." Leo

Watson and Harry "The Hipster" Gibson ("Stop that Dancin' Up There") make guest appearances.

Some of that craziness can also be heard on Gaillard's studio records of the era. **1945** (Classics 864) has Gaillard and Brown in a quartet with Dodo Marmarosa and Zutty Singleton and on some songs utilizing as many as six horns. Most of the songs that Slim performed used the chord changes of either a blues "Flying Home" or "I Got Rhythm." Among the selections on this fun if odd release are "Voot Orenee," "Voot Boogie," "Tutti Frutti," "Laguna," "Dunkin' Bagel," "Ya Ha Ha," "Ding Dong Oreene," and "Buck Dance Rhythm." **1945 Vol. 2** (Classics 911) has Gaillard's famous date with Bird and Diz (best of the four cuts is "Slim's Jam") and such nonsensical items as "Cement Mixer," "Yep-Roc Heresay," "Minuet in Vout," and "Penicillin Boogie."

Although Slim Gaillard's popularity peaked by the end of 1945, and the jive singers were being labeled dangerous and decadent by the conservative media, he continued recording odd classics. **1947–1951** (Classics 1221) has Gaillard (in 1951) overdubbing himself a dozen times on "Genius," including as a vocal group and on trumpet, trombone, tenor, vibes, piano, organ, bass drums, and tap dancing; the last two choruses are remarkably funny. Other selections on this disc include "The Bartender's Just Like a Mother," "Tip Light," "Puerto Vootie," "Serenade to a Poodle," "When Banana Skins Are Falling," "Organ-Oreenie," "Babalu," "Yo Yo Yo," and the classic "Laughing in Rhythm."

Harry "The Hipster" Gibson   Singer/pianist Harry "The Hipster" Gibson just had a brief period in the spotlight. He started out playing on 52nd Street as a stride pianist and in 1944 even performed Bix Beiderbecke's "In a Mist" at an Eddie Condon Town Hall concert. But he soon developed into a demented personality, singer, and pianist who sounded like a rock and roller a decade before that music caught on. His crazy compositions (including "Who Put the Benzedrine in Mrs. Murphy's Ovaltine," "Handsome Harry the Hipster," and "Stop that Dancin' Up There") and frantic singing style gave him an underground reputation. **Boogie Woogie in Blue** (Musicraft 70063) has all 12 of his recordings of 1944 and 1947, including those three songs plus "Get Your Juices at the Deuces," "4F Ferdinand, the Frantic Freak," and "I Stay Brown All Year 'Round." But Gibson's excessive drug use resulted in his quick decline after 1947 and he soon dropped out of the jazz scene.

Leo Watson   Leo Watson's career overlapped with that of Slim Gaillard and Harry "The Hipster" Gibson, both of whom he preceded. A very creative singer, Watson (who had a rather erratic career) loved to make up words and sounds as he went along. In 1929, he was a founding member of the Spirits of Rhythm, singing with the group on and off into 1941 and also playing drums. He recorded along the way with the Washboard Rhythm Kings, Artie Shaw, and Gene Krupa. Watson moved to Los Angeles in the early 1940s and his most remarkable recordings are the four he cut in 1946 on a date with Vic Dickenson, including a rather spaced-out version of "Jingle Bells." **The Original Scat Man** (Indigo 2098) has virtually all of his most important recordings with the Washboard Rhythm Kings, Krupa, Shaw, a Leonard Feather–organized group, and his final date, the 1946 session. Leo Watson, who was later cited by Jon Hendricks as an important influence, never recorded again after the "Jingle Bells" session and was completely forgotten during his last years, working outside of music. He deserved much better.

The Bebop Era Vocalists

With the rise in popularity of the solo (as opposed to band) singer during 1945–46, many of the veteran vocalists from the swing era stuck to standards and drifted toward what would become middle-of-the-road pop, while some of the more creative ones opened their styles a bit toward bebop (such as Ella Fitzgerald, Anita O'Day, and Mel Tormé) without losing their identities. In a different category altogether were the vocalists who emerged during the bebop era.

Earl Coleman and Johnny Hartman   For the newer black male singers, Billy Eckstine's warm baritone voice was often a major influence. Earl Coleman would always be in Eckstine's shadow. An excellent interpreter of ballads, Coleman sang with Ernie Fields, Jay McShann (1943 and 1945), Earl Hines (1944, when he succeeded Eckstine), and King Kolax. In 1947, when Charlie Parker made his first session after his release from Camarillo, he insisted that Coleman get to record a couple of vocals, over producer Ross Russell's objections. Coleman recorded "This Is Always" and "Dark Shadows" with Bird and the Erroll Garner Trio and the former became a

steady seller. But although he recorded some other titles for Dial, Atlantic, Jada, and Savoy in 1948 (the second recording strike was not enforced quite as efficiently as the first) with Fats Navarro being one of his sidemen, Coleman never did have another hit.

Johnny Hartman was also strongly influenced by Eckstine during this period. Hartman had opportunities to sing in the army, he studied music in college, and he worked with Earl Hines during 1947 (making his recording debut). Hartman sang ballads with the Dizzy Gillespie Orchestra during 1948–49, somehow remaining mostly untouched by bebop. **Just You, Just Me** (Savoy 93012) has Hartman's first two sessions as a leader (from December 1947), singing ballads with either a string orchestra or a small group that includes Tyree Glenn on trombone and vibes. While his versions of "I'll Never Smile Again," "Why Was I Born," and the title cut are fine, Hartman was not yet distinctive. He would grow as a singer quite a bit in future years.

Joe "Bebop" Carroll, Babs Gonzales, Pancho Hagood, and Jackie Paris   Earl Coleman and Johnny Hartman were primarily ballad singers who could have emerged in other time periods. However, it would be difficult to imagine Joe "Bebop" Carroll or Babs Gonzales catching on during any other time than the bebop era. Influenced by the craziness of Fats Waller, Leo Watson, and Slim Gaillard, not to mention Dizzy Gillespie (who could be a phenomenal scat singer), Carroll and Gonzales were often zany in their scatting. They both had limited voices, but more than their share of enthusiasm.

Carroll sang with Paul Bascomb's orchestra and in 1949 joined the Dizzy Gillespie big band, singing such numbers as "Hey Pete! Le's Eat Mo' Meat" and Mary Lou Williams bop fable "In the Land of Oo-Bla-Dee." He would be associated with Gillespie for several years.

Babs Gonzales (born Lee Brown) had a knack for self-promotion and developed an odd scatting style that emphasized vowels over consonants. Babs studied piano and drums and had short stints singing with Charlie Barnet and Lionel Hampton. In 1946, he put together the Three Bips and a Bop, a group that featured his vocals and quite a few notable sidemen. **Weird Lullaby** (Blue Note 84464) has all of his 1947–49 recordings (other than an obscure date apiece later put out by Xanadu and Delmark) and features Gonzales when he was at the height of his fame. The sidemen are quite eclectic including Tadd Dameron, Sonny Rollins (in his recording debut), Bennie Green, J.J. Johnson, Julius Watkins on French horn, pianists Linton Garner and Wynton Kelly, Art Pepper, Ray Nance on violin, pioneer jazz flutist Alberto Socarras, and Don Redman on soprano. Babs's jubilant vocals are heard on such numbers as "Oop-Pop-A-Da," "Stompin' at the Savoy," "Babs's Dream," "Weird Lullaby," "Professor Bop," "Prelude to a Nightmare," and "Real Crazy" although he always had the knack of turning everything (even a version of "St. Louis Blues") into a dated novelty. Also on this definitive CD are a pair of selections with organist Jimmy Smith from 1956 and two versions of "Encore" from 1958.

Kenny "Pancho" Hagood never really found a musical niche for himself although for a few years he had some major associations. Hagood had a heavy voice, but was somehow able to sing speedy bebop vocals when it was called upon. He was with Benny Carter's Orchestra in 1943 and is best remembered for his vocalizing with Dizzy Gillespie (1946–48), including duet scat vocals with Gillespie on "Oop-Pop-A-Da" and "Ool-Ya-Koo." He recorded three songs as a leader for Savoy in 1947, cut "I Should Care" with Thelonious Monk the following year, and was the singer with the Miles Davis Nonet, performing "Why Do I Love You" on the group's one live gig in 1948 and "Darn that Dream" in the studio with Miles in 1950.

Jackie Paris has had a long life, but a strangely episodic career. As a guitarist he worked with a trio in the early 1940s. After serving in the army (1944–46), he made his recording debut in 1947 as a singer and had a real feel for bebop. He freelanced for a couple of years (including performing with Charlie Parker), sang with Lionel Hampton (1949–50), and in 1949 recorded the first-ever vocal version of "'Round Midnight." But despite his talents, he never rose above the commercial level of an obscure cult figure.

Dave Lambert and Buddy Stewart   Dave Lambert was a pioneer in singing bop. He started out as a drummer, playing with the Hugh McGuinness Trio during the summers of 1937–39. Lambert served in the army (1940–43) and then sang with Johnny Long's orchestra for a year. As a member of Gene Krupa's big band during 1944–45, he frequently teamed up with fellow singer Buddy Stewart. They collaborated on "What's This," the earliest recorded bop vocal. Lambert and Stewart cut a few selections for the Keynote and Sittin' In labels, and they can be heard with Charlie Parker on a broadcast from the Royal Roost in 1949 that was released by Savoy.

Buddy Stewart was singing in vaudeville by the time he was eight (1930). He formed a vocal trio at 15 and started working in New York in 1940. Stewart sang with the Snowflakes, a vocal group that was briefly with Glenn Miller before becoming part of the Claude Thornhill Orchestra (1940–42). After serving in the army for two years, he worked with Gene Krupa during 1944–46, mostly being featured as a ballad singer in addition to recording "What's This" with Lambert. Stewart also worked with Charlie Ventura (often singing wordless lines in ensembles), Red Rodney, Kai Winding, and Charlie Barnet's bebop orchestra (1949). He would certainly have had a productive career, but Buddy Stewart died in a car accident on February 1, 1950, at the age of 27.

Jackie and Roy   Jackie and Roy (singer Jackie Cain and singer/pianist Roy Kral) sang some crazy boppish vocals with Charlie Ventura in the late 1940s before going out on their own. Roy Kral studied classical piano for eight years, switching to jazz in the mid-1930s. He led his own group during 1939–40, worked with Charlie Agnew, and played in army bands while in the military (1942–46), making his recording debut with Georgie Auld in 1947. Jackie Cain gained her experience singing with obscure bands. Jackie and Roy first met in 1947 and, inspired by the team of Buddy Stewart and Dave Lambert, performed some eccentric bop material. They were important members of Charlie Ventura's "Bop for the People" band in 1948–49, recording such atmospheric pieces as Lou Stein's "East of Suez," "Euphoria," and a nutty version of "I'm Forever Blowing Bubbles." After they married in 1949, they went out on their own, starting a career and a marriage that have both lasted over a half-century.

Sarah Vaughan   During the bebop era, few new female singers emerged who chose to dig into bebop, and only a few of the established names (most notably Ella Fitzgerald and Anita O'Day) updated their styles to include bop. Most of the others instead were happy to follow the lead of Doris Day and Dinah Shore into the more lucrative pop market. Sarah Vaughan was a major exception.

One of the great singers of all time, Sarah Vaughan had a wondrous voice with a wide range and complete control, and she grasped the intricacies of bop early on. She sang in church while quite young and had extensive piano lessons throughout the 1930s. In 1943, she won an Apollo Theatre amateur contest and was hired by Earl Hines as singer and second pianist. Nicknamed Sassy, she was in the perfect place to learn about the emerging bebop music, performing with the band that included Dizzy Gillespie and Charlie Parker. When Billy Eckstine (a close friend of hers for decades) formed his own big band in 1944, Vaughan followed him, gaining additional experience in a bop-oriented atmosphere. She made her recording debut with Eckstine on December 5, 1944, singing "I'll Wait and Pray." But more important was her first session as a leader on December 31, a date organized by Leonard Feather and including classic versions of "East of the Sun" and "Interlude" (a vocal version of Gillespie's "A Night in Tunisia").

During part of 1945–46, Vaughan sang with the John Kirby Sextet, but by the spring of 1946 she had begun her solo career, recording regularly for Musicraft through 1948 and signing with Columbia in 1949. All of Sarah Vaughan's recordings of 1944–50 are available on the superior four-CD set ◉ **Young Sassy** (Proper Box 27). In addition to the numbers already mentioned, Vaughan is heard on four songs with Diz and Bird (including "Lover Man"), four with backing by Kirby's group and on such gems as "If You Could See Me Now," "You're Not the Kind," "Everything I Have Is Yours," "September Song" (which she somehow makes sound believable despite only being 23), "Tenderly" (which she introduced), "I Feel So Smoochie," "It's Magic," and "Black Coffee." The Columbia recordings of 1949–50 sometimes had the singer in commercial settings, but Sassy brings a jazz sensibility to the music. And her two all-star jazz dates of 1950 (with Miles Davis, Bennie Green, Tony Scott, and Budd Johnson) are among the highpoints of her career, particularly her classic versions of "Ain't Misbehavin'" (which has perfect eight-bar solos from each of the horn players), "It Might As Well Be Spring," "Mean to Me," and "Nice Work If You Can Get It." Also quite worthwhile is the two-CD set **Sarah Vaughan/Lester Young: One Night Stand** (Blue Note 32139), which has a 1947 Town Hall concert split evenly between Vaughan and the Lester Young Sextet. Young plays well on his seven numbers even if trumpeter Shorty McConnell was not on Pres's level and the rhythm section (with pianist Argonne Thornton) sounds a bit unsteady. Best are Sassy's eight selections, which

although mostly ballads, have many examples of her taking chances and stretching her voice. Vaughan and Pres meet up on the final selection, "I Cried for You."

By 1950, Sarah Vaughan ranked at the top among female jazz singers, along with Ella Fitzgerald, Billie Holiday, and Dinah Washington.

The Modern Big Bands

With the collapse of so many big bands during 1945–46, it must have seemed foolhardy not only to try to form a new orchestra (or even to keep an older one going), but to lead one that was bebop-oriented. The five bandleaders mentioned in this section led some of the most advanced orchestras of the period (as did Dizzy Gillespie), but none of these ensembles—not even the ones led by the relatively successful Woody Herman and Stan Kenton—survived past 1950.

Billy Eckstine Billy Eckstine, despite the commercial potential of his career as the top black male crooner of the 1940s, was determined to keep his bebop orchestra together as long as possible. **1944–1945** (Classics 914) has all of the band's recordings from those two years, featuring the likes of Dizzy Gillespie, Dexter Gordon, Gene Ammons (who really came into his own with the band), and Fats Navarro along with a lot of Eckstine ballad vocals. Two radio airchecks from 1945, which came out on the LP **The Legendary Big Band of Billy Eckstine** (Spotlite 100), add to the orchestra's musical legacy. The leader takes four vocals and Sarah Vaughan has two, but it is the instrumentals (including "Airmail Special" and "Opus X") that are most memorable. **1946–1947** (Classics 1022) is highlighted by "The Jitney Man," "Second Balcony Jump," "Cool Breeze," "Oo Bop Sh'Bam" and a remake of "Jelly Jelly." Such players as Navarro, Ammons, Kenny Dorham, Sonny Stitt, Art Blakey, Leo Parker, and Miles Davis are in the band and occasionally heard from, and Eckstine's voice sounds strong on his ballads. However, his last two big band recordings add a string section to help their commerciality, and by mid-1947, the Billy Eckstine Orchestra was no more. From that point on, Eckstine pursued a very successful career in middle-of-the-road pop music yet always became wistfully nostalgic when looking back upon his bebop days.

Boyd Raeburn Boyd Raeburn, who played ensemble bass sax in his own big band, but never soloed or wrote any arrangements, led an undistinguished sweet orchestra up until 1944. At that point his band became more swing-oriented and influenced by Count Basie. In 1945, things really changed. George Handy, a rather radical arranger, started working as the band's main writer, and Raeburn's music became boppish, eccentric, and quite dissonant. The ensemble often exploded behind the relatively straight vocals of Ginnie Powell and David Allyn, the instrumentals were sometimes influenced by modern classical music, and there was no possible way that this band stood a chance commercially. Despite that, in 1946 the orchestra actually grew in size, adding French horns and a harp and becoming 20 pieces. Such players as Lucky Thompson, Dodo Marmarosa, Buddy DeFranco, tenor saxophonist Frankie Socolow, and bassist Harry Babasin were among the many who passed through the remarkable band.

George Handy was really the brain behind the new Boyd Raeburn Orchestra. He had studied piano with his mother from age five, attended Juilliard, took lessons with Aaron Copland, and had previously written music for Raymond Scott. Handy's charts helped Raeburn's band make its transition during 1943–44. He left to write for Paramount Studios and then was active with Raeburn during 1945–46, contributing such eccentric numbers as "Tonsillectomy," "Dalvatore Sally," and "Rip Van Winkle" while transforming "Over the Rainbow," "Body and Soul," and "Temptation" in remarkable ways.

Unfortunately, a personality conflict led to Handy quitting Raeburn in August 1946, and although he wrote for other bands, he never again gained a high profile. Johnny Richards quite ably took Handy's place as Raeburn's main arranger and the orchestra struggled to the end of 1947 before breaking up. Although there were other attempts to bring back the Boyd Raeburn Orchestra during 1948–49, they all failed.

Boyd Raeburn's recordings of 1945–47 have not yet been coherently reissued on CD, but for now **Boyd Meets Stravinsky** (Savoy 92984) has 14 of the better studio recordings. "Tonsillectomy" is missing, but such numbers as "Dalvatore Sally," "Over the Rainbow," "March of the Boyds," "Rip Van Winkle," and the title cut give one a strong idea how unique this band was. **Boyd Raeburn and His Orchestra** (Storyville 8313) has the band's top radio appearances of 1945–46, with plenty of arrangements by Handy, Eddie Finckel, a young Johnny Mandel, and (on "A Night in Tunisia") Dizzy Gillespie. Many of the band's best charts are here and there are

TIMELINE 1947

Charlie Parker recovers and forms a quintet with Miles Davis, Duke Jordan, Tommy Potter, and Max Roach. • Chano Pozo joins the Dizzy Gillespie Orchestra. • Louis Armstrong breaks up his big band, forms his All-Stars, and becomes enormously successful. • Guitarist Laurindo Almeida joins Stan Kenton's Orchestra. • Boogie-woogie pianist Albert Ammons has an opportunity to record with his son, tenor saxophonist Gene Ammons. • Nineteen-year-old singer Ernestine Anderson makes her recording debut. • Irving Ashby replaces Oscar Moore as guitarist in the King Cole Trio. • Woody Herman forms his Second Herd, recording "Four Brothers." • Bassist Harry Babasin records the first jazz cello solos on a session with Dodo Marmarosa. • Pianist Graeme Bell's trad jazz band starts recording regularly in Australia, becomes an influential force on the local scene, and tours Europe for much of 1947–48, recording in Czechoslovakia, London, and Paris. • William Correa (later known as Willie Bobo) at 13 works as Machito's band boy, sometimes sitting in on bongos during the last set of the night. • Mutt Carey leaves Kid Ory's band to start his own group. • Trumpeter Joe Guy is busted for possession of drugs, serves time in jail, and fades out of the music scene. • After a decade of retirement, Ruth Etting makes a minor comeback, hosting a regular radio show. • Trombonist Melba Liston records with Dexter Gordon. • John Coltrane switches to tenor sax when he joins Eddie "Cleanhead" Vinson's group. • Sy Oliver forms his own swing big band, no one notices, and the orchestra soon folds. • Tenor saxophonist Charlie Rouse makes his recording debut with Tadd Dameron. • Guitarist Tal Farlow plays with pianist/vibraphonist Dardanelle. • Clark Terry, altoist Bud Shank, and guitarist Joe Pass work with Charlie Barnet's orchestra. • "Little" Johnny Griffin is the tenor soloist with trumpeter Joe Morris's fine jump/R&B band. • Pianist Jimmy Jones becomes Sarah Vaughan's regular accompanist. • Singer Tito Rodriguez forms the Mambo Devils. • Tito Puente becomes the musical director, arranger, and drummer with the Pupi Campo Orchestra. • Thelonious Monk makes his recording debut as a leader. • The Billy Eckstine Orchestra breaks up.

solos from Lucky Thompson, trumpeter Ray Linn, trombonist Britt Woodman, and Dodo Marmarosa. In addition to two appearances from Mel Tormé and the Mel-Tones, there is a version of "Caravan" by the Ray Linn Octet (taken from the orchestra) that features a pioneering flute solo from Harry Klee. The most rewarding all-round CD is ◉ **Jubilee Broadcasts— 1946** (Hep 1), which has some of the same songs in different versions from other radio broadcasts. Best are "Tonsillectomy," bizarre renditions of "Temptation" and "Body and Soul," and a four-part suite. In addition, there is another version of "A Night in Tunisia" (this time with Dizzy Gillespie making a guest appearance), a different rendition of "Caravan" from Linn's septet and two renditions of "Boyd Meets Stravinsky."

Considering how futuristic this music still sounds, it is remarkable that the Boyd Raeburn Orchestra lasted as long as it did.

Tom Talbert   On the West Coast during 1946–49, arranger Tom Talbert had a little-noticed but superior part-time big band. Inspired to write by hearing swing era orchestras on the radio, Talbert played piano and wrote arrangements for groups that he organized while in high school. After serving in the army, he moved to California and put together his bop-influenced orchestra. **Tom Talbert Jazz Orchestra 1946–1949** (Sea Breeze 2069) has 16 selections, the majority of which were unreleased until this CD came out. Talbert's writing is as modern as that heard in the Stan Kenton and even Boyd Raeburn orchestras, but is fresh and original rather than derivative. Among the sidemen who are key soloists are trumpeter Frank Beach, tenors Babe Russin and Jack Montrose, Dodo Marmarosa, Lucky Thompson, Art Pepper, and Claude Williamson. The music, with its cool-toned reeds, powerful brass, advanced harmonies, and solid swing, still sounds fresh and enthusiastic, and the occasional vocals are well done. However, when Stan Kenton reformed his big band in 1950, Talbert broke up his own group and went back to writing full-time, including for Kenton's Innovations Orchestra.

Stan Kenton and June Christy   By 1945, Stan Kenton was recording regularly for the still-new Capitol label, had hit recordings in "Eager Beaver" and Anita O'Day's "And Her Tears Flowed Like Wine," and was growing in popularity. His music, termed "progressive jazz," was

finding a devoted audience and the success of his new singer June Christy's popular recordings (such as "Tampico" and "Across the Alley from the Alamo") was making it possible for Kenton to finance his more ambitious and esoteric projects. The 1945–48 period found Kenton featuring such soloists as Art Pepper, tenors Vido Musso and Bob Cooper, Kai Winding, bassist Ed Safranski, drummer Shelly Manne, and such screaming lead trumpeters as Ray Wetzel and Al Porcino.

The most important new addition to the band (other than possibly Christy) was arranger Pete Rugolo, who for a few years became Kenton's Billy Strayhorn. Rugolo, who had studied with Darius Milhaud at Mills College and served in the army (1942–45), immediately upon his discharge attracted Kenton's attention. His writing could be very much in Kenton's style, but he extended the ideas and came up with fresh innovations of his own. Most of Kenton's most significant recordings of 1945–47 had Rugolo arrangements, some of which were bombastic and a bit classical-oriented. In 1949, Rugolo became the musical director of Capitol Records and, although he occasionally wrote a chart for Kenton, his future work involved writing for singers (including June Christy, Nat King Cole, Peggy Lee, and Billy Eckstine), his own orchestra dates, pop music, and studio work.

Mosaic's limited-edition seven-CD set **The Complete Capitol Studio Recordings of Stan Kenton 1943–1947** (Mosaic 7-163), which also includes previously unreleased performances and alternate takes, is unfortunately out of print. The four-CD set ◉ **Retrospective** (Capitol 97350) is an ideal summary of Kenton's music during 1943–68, with 21 selections from 1943–47, ten songs from 1950–51, and 41 others from 1952–68. It includes all of Kenton's most popular recordings and most of his more notable work, serving as a perfect introduction to his unusual music.

For those collectors who want all of Kenton's recordings of the 1940s, the Classics series should suffice. **1945** (Classics 898) has Anita O'Day's last two vocals with Kenton and June Christy's first recordings (which include "Tampico," "Are You Livin' Old Man," and "Just a Sittin' and a Rockin'") along with "Southern Scandal," "Opus in Pastels," and "Artistry Jumps." **1946** (Classics 949) includes all of Kenton's studio recordings during that busy year including his hit "Intermission Riff," "Artistry in Boogie," "Come Back to Sorrento" (a feature for the thick-toned tenor of Vido Musso), "Artistry in Percussion" (a showcase for

Shelly Manne), "Safranski" (subtitled "Artistry in Bass"), "Artistry in Bolero," the two-part "Concerto to End All Concertos," and "Collaboration." Other orchestras may have been breaking up all over the country, but Stan Kenton had his audience and was able to keep his big band together despite the noncommercial nature of much of the material. **1947** (Classics 1011) balances a few lightweight songs such as "His Feet's Too Big for De Bed" and "Down in Chi-Hua-Hua" (plus the June Christy hit "Across the Alley from the Alamo") with such "serious" and pompous Pete Rugolo pieces as "Monotony," "Elegy for Alto," and "Chorale for Brass, Piano, and Bongo." **1947 Vol. 2** (Classics 1039) wraps up Stan Kenton's "Progressive Jazz" period with Bob Graettinger's very radical (and dense) "Thermopylae," and such forbidding pieces as "Abstraction," "Fugue for Rhythm Section," and "Lament." But it also includes "He Was a Good Man as Good Men Go," "Cuban Carnival," "Harlem Holiday," and the very popular reworking of "The Peanut Vendor," which would be a crowd pleaser for decades.

After making it through 1948 (a year only documented by radio broadcasts due to the recording ban), Stan Kenton was physically exhausted. Even though he had already offered the young Canadian trumpeter Maynard Ferguson a spot in his trumpet section, he decided to break up his orchestra and take a year off. His sidemen scattered, with some of them joining Charlie Barnet's boppish orchestra or settling on the West Coast and getting studio work. Many would rejoin Kenton in 1950, at least temporarily, including June Christy.

June Christy (born Shirley Luster) married tenor saxophonist Bob Cooper while with Kenton, and their marriage would last over 40 years. She sang locally in Chicago, including with an early version of Boyd Raeburn's orchestra. In 1945, she auditioned for Anita O'Day's position with Stan Kenton (her favorite big band) and, because her singing closely resembled O'Day's at that point, the 19-year-old got the position. She soon developed her own style and became Kenton's most popular attraction. Although not blessed with a virtuosic style (and sometimes criticized for singing a little bit flat), Christy managed to balance a "girl next door" persona with a certain amount of sensuality. ● **Tampico** (Memoir 526) consists of 25 of her best recordings with Kenton from 1945–47, nearly her complete output with the band, including "Tampico," "Easy Street," "Shoo Fly Pie and Apple Dan Dandy," "Come Rain or Come Shine," and "I Told You I Love You, Now Get Out." All of this timeless music was recorded before Christy's 22nd birthday. **Day Dreams** (Capitol 32083) has Christy's recordings from 1947–50 made outside of the Kenton orchestra. She is backed by orchestras led by Frank DeVol, Bob Cooper, Pete Rugolo, and Shorty Rogers with highlights including "Get Happy," "If I Should Lose You," "Day Dream," "Do It Again," and Bob Graettinger's very advanced arrangement of "Everything Happens to Me." There are also two previously unreleased songs from her 1955 duet date with Kenton on piano. Although her solo career was still in its earliest stages in 1949, June Christy was already setting the standard for cool-toned female singers.

Woody Herman's First Two Herds In 1945, Woody Herman had the most popular new band in jazz, the Herd. It actually owed very little to his original "Band that Plays the Blues," which had struggled on the second level of big bands during 1937–43. In 1944, with the urging of bassist Chubby Jackson, Herman began to hire one talented young musician after another, and by the summer the personnel of his Herd was already becoming quite impressive.

One of the reasons for the band's success was that Herman was wise enough to use the arrangements of Ralph Burns. Burns started on piano when he was seven, and he studied at the New England Conservatory during 1938–39. Moving to New York, he worked as a pianist/arranger for Nick Jerret, Charlie Barnet, and Red Norvo (1943). Burns joined Herman as a pianist in 1944, but soon gave up the piano chair to work exclusively on arranging and composing. Among his songs for Herman were the exuberant and rather riotous romp "Apple Honey," "Bijou" (a famous feature for trombonist Bill Harris), and the four-part "Summer Sequence."

In addition to Burns, the other main arrangers for Herman's Herd were Neal Hefti and the young trumpeter Shorty Rogers (born Milton Rajonsky). Rogers had worked with Will Bradley and Red Norvo before joining Herman. His main contribution to the Herman book at this early stage was "Backtalk" and "Igor" (the latter recorded by Herman's Woodchoppers).

Trumpeter Sonny Berman was just 19 when he joined Herman's Herd in February 1945. Berman was a fine musician who had picked up experience during the war years playing in the sections of big bands from the time he was 15, including the orchestras of Louis Prima, Sonny Dunham, Tommy Dorsey, Georgie Auld, Harry James, and Benny Goodman. He had a distinctive sound and was open to the influence of bop, sometimes playing brief phrases humorously in a different key than expected. With Herman, he soloed on several recordings, including "Sidewalks of Cuba," "Let It Snow, Let It Snow, Let It Snow," and "Your Father's Mustache," also recording with Herman's Woodchoppers (a small group out of his orchestra), the Metronome All-Stars, Bill Harris (Berman's playing on "Nocturne" is quite eerie), and on a privately recorded jam session released decades later as the LP **Beautiful Jewish Music** (Onyx 211). But unfortunately Sonny Berman used drugs excessively, leading to his death on January 16, 1947, during an all-night jam session; he was just 21.

Several other trumpeters passed through Herman's Herd during 1945–46, including the Candoli Brothers. Pete Candoli was usually used to hit high notes in the ensembles and to play spectacular solos at the conclusions of the group's hottest romps. In fact, at the end of "Apple Honey" he would sometimes play his climatic solo while wearing a Superman costume! Candoli had previously worked with Sonny Dunham (1940–41), Will Bradley, Benny Goodman, Ray McKinley, Tommy Dorsey, Freddie Slack, and Charlie Barnet. After his period with Woody Herman ended, he was in the trumpet section of the Tex Beneke Orchestra (1947–49).

While Pete spent much of his career as a section player, his younger brother Conte Candoli (born Secondo Candoli) developed into a top bop soloist. Conte's first major job was with Herman, playing with his orchestra during summer vacation in 1944 when he was just 16. Conte Candoli was a member of the Herd during January–September 1945 before going into the army. After his discharge he gained recognition as a member of the Chubby Jackson Sextet (1947–48), Stan Kenton's orchestra (1948), and Charlie Ventura's "Bop for the People" band (1949).

The two most popular soloists with Herman's Herd were trombonist Bill Harris and tenor saxophonist Flip Phillips. Harris was nearly the only young trombonist of the era who did not sound like J.J. Johnson. He had an emotional sound that could be either humorous or quite sentimental, almost seeming at times like an opera singer. Harris had started out working locally in Philadelphia in the late 1930s. After two years in the Merchant Marines,

Harris worked during 1942–44 with many big bands, including Buddy Williams, Gene Krupa, Ray McKinley, Bob Chester, Benny Goodman, Charlie Barnet, and Freddie Slack. He joined Herman's Herd in August 1944 and was a prominent force during its entire existence. His dramatic feature on "Bijou" was famous, and he took exuberant solos on the band's uptempo tunes.

Like Harris, Flip Phillips (born Joseph Filipelli) was essentially a swing player. Influenced by Ben Webster, he started on clarinet at age 12 and worked for five years regularly at Schneider's Lobster House in Brooklyn. After playing clarinet with Frankie Newton (1940–41), he switched to the tenor and worked with Larry Bennett, Benny Goodman, Wingy Manone, and Red Norvo. While with Herman (1944–46), Phillips's booting tenor solos and warm playing on ballads made him quite popular. **A Melody from the Sky** (Sony 39419) has four sessions led by Phillips during 1944–45. He mostly uses other Herman sidemen in a variety of settings, sounding mellow on the ballads (such as "Sweet and Lovely") and romping on the more torrid numbers. In 1947, Phillips became a regular with "Jazz at the Philharmonic," holding his own next to Webster, Illinois Jacquet, Coleman Hawkins, Lester Young, and Charlie Parker, becoming greatly in demand with audiences for playing "Perdido."

Bassist Chubby Jackson was the cheerleader for Herman's Herd, not only convincing Herman to hire top young players, but often shouting out encouragement during exciting ensembles and solos. He began playing bass at 16 and was a professional three years later. Jackson worked with the big bands of Raymond Scott, Jan Savitt, Henry Busse, and Charlie Barnet (1941–43) before joining Herman in 1943, staying for three years. The bassist played with Charlie Ventura in 1947 and then organized his own group (which included Conte Candoli, tenor saxophonist Frankie Socolow, Lou Levy, and Terry Gibbs), helping to introduce bop to Scandinavia during an overseas tour. After a few months back with Herman in 1948, Jackson had his own short-lived big band during 1948–49.

Originally, Dave Tough was the drummer for the Herd. He was one of the few Dixielanders to do a credible job playing bop-oriented music and during the era he even participated in a printed debate with Eddie Condon over the merits of bop. Tough was a perfect ensemble drummer and he added a lot of humor to the group.

After leaving Herman in September 1945, he worked in swing and Dixieland settings with Joe Marsala, Condon (1946), Jerry Gray, "Jazz at the Philharmonic," Charlie Ventura, and Muggsy Spanier (1947–48). Unfortunately, his alcoholism and general poor health made his life erratic. In 1948, he died at age 41 from head injuries after falling down on a Newark street.

Don Lamond was Tough's replacement with Herman. An inventive big band drummer, Lamond had previously worked with Sonny Dunham (1943) and Boyd Raeburn, and while with the Herd he played in a similar style as Tough.

Other musicians who made contributions to the music of the Herd included high-note trumpeter Ray Wetzel, vibraphonists Margie Hyams and Red Norvo, guitarists Billy Bauer and Chuck Wayne, pianist Jimmy Rowles and singer Francis Wayne, not to mention Woody Herman himself on clarinet, alto, and an occasional vocal.

The two-CD set ◗ **Blowin' Up a Storm** (Columbia/Legacy 65646) has 26 of the very best recordings by Herman's Herd plus seven alternate takes. Among the many exciting selections are "Apple Honey," "Caldonia," "Happiness Is a Thing Called Joe" (Francis Wayne's main hit), "Bijou," the crazy "Your Father's Mustache," "Blowin' Up a Storm," "Let It Snow, Let It Snow, Let It Snow," "Fan It," and a remake of "Woodchopper's Ball." The band's music, bop-tinged, but really falling into swing, was always full of spirit, an infectious forward momentum, and joy. Also included on this two-fer is the original version of a work that Igor Stravinsky wrote for the band and conducted himself, "Ebony Concerto." Although that historic piece sounds rather awkward rhythmically (and is much more modern classical than jazz), the Herd does a good job with it.

A few other sets add to the musical legacy of this beloved band. **Vol. 2: Live in 1945** (Jass 625) has alternate live versions of such songs as "Northwest Passage," "Goosey Gander," "Bijou," and "Apple Honey." **1946 Broadcasts** (Soundcraft 5006) from September–October 1946 includes two excellent radio appearances plus "Northwest Passage" from a third date and features a few numbers not otherwise recorded by Herman (including Sonny Berman's "They Went That Away"). **At Carnegie Hall, 1946** (Verve 314 559 833) is a two-CD set with all of the surviving music from Herman's Carnegie Hall concert on March 25, 1946. Although a big improvement

over previous releases of this music (and adding six additional numbers), the sound quality is still erratic. However, fans of this group will want this release for the band sounds quite exuberant in spots, with highlights including "Bijou" and longer than usual versions of "Blowin' Up a Storm," "Your Father's Moustache," and "Wildroot."

In late 1946, Woody Herman surprised the jazz world by breaking up the most popular and profitable band he would ever have. Years later it was revealed that he made this decision due to his wife's health and drinking problems. But after a year of freelancing and making occasional record dates in a variety of settings, Herman put together a new band known as the Second Herd; his 1944–46 outfit was thereafter remembered as his First Herd. While the former had fallen between swing and bop, the Second Herd was much more bop-oriented. Shorty Rogers and Don Lamond were the only holdovers from the earlier group although Chubby Jackson and Bill Harris would rejoin Herman later in 1948.

The most unusual aspect of the Second Herd was that, instead of having a sax section comprised of two altos, two tenors, and a baritone, Herman had lead altoist Sam Marowitz joined by three similar-sounding cool-toned tenors (Stan Getz, Zoot Sims, and Herbie Steward) plus baritonist Serge Chaloff. Jimmy Giuffre's "Four Brothers" featured the tenors and Chaloff, becoming a Herman standard and leading to this group also being known as "The Four Brothers Band."

The Second Herd's first important recordings are included on **Blowin' Up a Storm**: Shorty Rogers's "Keen and Peachy" (based on the chord changes of "Fine and Dandy"), Al Cohn's "The Goof and I," "Four Brothers," and the fourth part of Ralph Burns's "Summer Sequence," which includes a brief spot for Stan Getz. The latter would be reborn the following year as "Early Autumn."

Of the tenor players with the Second Herd, Stan Getz was destined for the greatest fame. Possessor of a beautiful tone, Getz had already apprenticed in the big bands of Jack Teagarden (1943 when he was 16), Stan Kenton (1944–45), Jimmy Dorsey, and Benny Goodman (1945–46). His playing on "Early Autumn" in 1948 made him a star, and in early 1949 he left Herman, forming a quartet that featured Al Haig.

Zoot Sims, who (like Getz) looked toward Lester Young for his initial inspiration, had played drums and clarinet as a youth. At 13 (in 1939) he switched to tenor and two years later was working professionally. Sims played with Bobby Sherwood and Benny Goodman (1943), recorded with Joe Bushkin in 1944 and served in the army. After a second stint with Goodman (1946–47), Sims became one of Herman's "Four Brothers." He left the group about the same time as Getz, playing in 1949 with Buddy Rich's short-lived big band and Artie Shaw's bebop orchestra.

The least known of the original "Four Brothers," Herbie Steward had previously had stints with Bob Chester (1942), Freddie Slack, and Artie Shaw (1944–46). He did not stay with Herman that long, departing in 1948, working with Artie Shaw (1949) and often playing alto and flute in later years as a studio musician.

Al Cohn was Steward's replacement, and at the time his tone was nearly identical to both Getz and Sims. Cohn had worked with Joe Marsala (1943), Georgie Auld, Boyd Raeburn (1946), Alvino Rey, and Buddy Rich (1947). He differed from the other tenor players in that he was a very talented writer, and throughout his career his arranging talents would equal his improvising abilities. After leaving Herman in 1949, he too played with Artie Shaw's bebop band.

Serge Chaloff was the top baritone saxophonist of the era. Although he was a rather irresponsible drug addict (Herman's Second Herd had a rampant drug problem), Chaloff was able to play his instrument with the fluency of an altoist. He was with the big bands of Boyd Raeburn (1944–45), Georgie Auld (1945–46), and Jimmy Dorsey (1946–47), leading two record dates (one apiece for Dial and Savoy) before becoming a major part of Herman's sound during 1947–49.

Due to the recording strike, Herman's Second Herd made fewer recordings than one would expect. **The Second Herd 1948** (Storyville 8240) partly fills in the gap, containing three radio appearances from March–May 1948. By that time, Cohn had replaced Steward and other key players included Shorty Rogers (as trumpeter and arranger), trombonist Earl Swope, Don Lamond, and singer Mary Ann McCall. Quite a few of the songs on this CD were not otherwise recorded by the band.

By the time the second recording strike ended in December, Herman's Second Herd had signed with the Capitol label. All of its Capitol recordings are on the single disc ❶ **Keeper of the Flame** (Capitol 98453). The seven selections from December 29–30, 1948, include Ralph Burns's "Early Autumn," Rogers's "Keeper of the

Flame," and the very catchy (and boppish) George Wallington tune "Lemon Drop." At the time, Red Rodney was temporarily Herman's solo trumpeter and Terry Gibbs was back on vibes. However, by May 1949 when the band recorded again, there had been some major changes. Getz, Cohn, and Sims had all departed and now the tenors consisted of Gene Ammons, Buddy Savitt, and Jimmy Giuffre himself. Oscar Pettiford, Shelly Manne, and (near its end) Milt Jackson also spent some time with the band. Highlights of the recordings of the "second Second Herd" include "More Moon" (a Shorty Rogers feature for Ammons), Johnny Mandel's "Not Really the Blues," "Lollipop," and "The Great Lie."

But unlike the First Herd, the Second Herd was a steady money loser, and, at the end of 1949, Woody Herman reluctantly broke up his second classic band in three years.

The Collapse of the Big Band Era

As 1945 began, big bands were everywhere and still considered a dominant force in popular music. By the time 1946 ended, the big bands were breaking up all over the country. Even many of the ones that initially survived did not live much past 1949. Why did it all change so fast?

It seems odd to think that so many large ensembles were flourishing during the Depression years and that, with World War II ending and the economy being relatively healthy, suddenly the big bands were starting to lose money. But there were many reasons why by 1947 people were asking for the first time, "Will big bands ever come back?"

The Musicians Union strike of mid-1942 to late 1944 was disastrous for the swing era because it kept the big bands and the musicians off records during a crucial time in their development. Bands who were signed to Columbia or Victor (including Duke Ellington, Count Basie, and Benny Goodman) went 27 months between record dates, a lifetime in the record industry. In contrast, the singers were free to record (and sometimes did with a cappella groups), and the pause in instrumental recordings allowed the likes of Frank Sinatra, Perry Como, and Dinah Shore to become important solo artists.

Many big bands began to run out of fresh ideas after 1940. Such major bands as Benny Goodman, Glenn Miller, Count Basie, and Jimmie Lunceford had their sounds together before 1940, and the groups that followed (with just a few exceptions such as Stan Kenton) did not depart that much from those models. Much of the new material seemed like rehashes of music of the 1930s with riff-filled blues, basic stomps, soothing ballads, and swinging renditions of classical themes. In addition, World War II made it difficult for new bands to establish themselves, and even the famous ones had difficulty traveling due to wartime restrictions. The draft robbed most orchestras of some of their sidemen, and the quality of musicianship dropped a bit.

Jazz fans were being divided. Where in 1939 swing was everywhere, by 1945 bebop, Dixieland, and rhythm and blues were fragmenting the audience. The more creative younger musicians and arrangers were gravitating toward bebop. The big bands seemed to have two bad choices: either remain the same and be considered stale, or start playing boppish arrangements and be thought of as noncommercial and esoteric.

A cabaret tax that was enacted in 1941 and lingered throughout the 1940s meant that entertainment establishments had to pay 30 percent of their ticket sales in taxes if they permitted dancing. The result was that many dance halls closed, replaced by smaller jazz clubs where dancing was not permitted. Because jazz was beginning to be separated from dancing (partly also due to the attitude of bebop musicians who wanted to play for a listening audience), the audience shrunk dramatically and most big bands became impossible to afford. Another factor was that the more distinctive musicians in 1945 were generally older than the ones in 1940 and wished to be paid more, so the talented white sidemen began to look for more lucrative work in the studios while their black counterparts began to work in rhythm and blues bands.

In addition, big bands were now associated with World War II and the Depression. They were thought of with nostalgia and considered old-fashioned. The established major names were constantly asked to play their hits of the past and were discouraged from moving forward, which resulted in some becoming predictable and others giving up altogether.

And on top of that, by 1949 television was starting to offer free entertainment. The big bands would never come back again—at least not like they had been before.

31 Swing Bands and Their Struggle to Survive the Bebop Years

Despite all of the difficulties with keeping a jazz orchestra together during the second half of the 1940s, many of the big bandleaders (most of whom were alumni of the swing era) struggled on as long as they could. The odds were against them but most of these orchestras recorded some fine music along the way before being forced to call it quits.

Georgie Auld The Georgie Auld Orchestra of 1943–46 bridged the gap between swing and the new emerging bebop music. **Jump, Georgie, Jump** (Hep 27) starts out with recordings from the 1940 Artie Shaw big band shortly after Shaw had fled to Mexico; the 20-year-old Auld was its leader until it broke up. The tenor saxophonist made a strong impression playing with Benny Goodman (particularly his septet of 1941), had a second stint with Shaw (1942), and in 1943 formed a big band of his own. **Jump, Georgie Jump** has a lengthy radio transcription session from 1944 (most notable for the solos of Sonny Berman a year before he joined Woody Herman) and a live date with Auld's orchestra in 1945, a no-name outfit at the time other than the young Serge Chaloff, but a spirited ensemble well worth hearing. During 1945–46, the Auld big band recorded for Musicraft and its recordings have been reissued on a pair of obscure (and probably hard to find) CDs: **In the Middle** (Musicraft 70056) and **Handicap** (Musicraft 70062). On a few of these selections, Auld augmented his band with some stars, including Dizzy Gillespie, Freddie Webster, Billy Butterfield, Trummy Young, and Erroll Garner. His regular lineup at this point included several musicians who would become better known for their association with Woody Herman's Second Herd, including lead trumpeter Al Porcino, Chaloff, and Al Cohn. But because he never became a major name in the commercial world, by the end of 1946 Auld broke up his big band.

Charlie Barnet Starting in 1944, when his band included Dodo Marmarosa and Barney Kessel, and continuing in 1947 when he featured the young trumpeter Clark Terry, Charlie Barnet was open to more modern sounds than swing. During 1948–49, his orchestra became quite bop-oriented, at one point having a screaming trumpet section comprised of Maynard Ferguson, Doc Severinsen, Ray Wetzel, and John Howell (all potential lead players) plus Rolf Ericson, a fine soloist from Sweden. ● **The Capitol Big Band Sessions** (Capitol 21258) has a 1948 version of "Redskin Rhumba" (cut during the recording strike) and four dance band numbers from 1950, but the bulk of the disc is taken up by 17 rather advanced songs from 1949. In addition to the mighty trumpet section, the band at the time featured trombonist Herbie Harper, altoist Vinnie Dean, Dick Hafer on tenor (who had a much cooler tone than Barnet), and pianist Claude Williamson. The arrangements of Manny Albam, Gil Fuller, Pete Rugolo, Dave Matthews, Johnny Richards, Tiny Kahn, and Paul Villepique put the orchestra on the cutting edge of bebop although Barnet played his solos in his usual stomping swing style. Best are "Cu-Ba," two versions of "Charlie's Other Aunt," Matthews's "Portrait of Edward Kennedy Ellington," "Bebop Spoken Here" (which has vocals by Dave Lambert and Buddy Stewart), "Claude Reigns," "Really," and a radical reworking of "All the Things You Are." The latter, a showcase for Maynard Ferguson, was quickly withdrawn due to the protests of Jerome Kern's estate.

But due to lack of business, Charlie Barnet reluctantly broke up his big band late in 1949. He had been a major big band leader for just a decade, but his time in the spotlight was over. For the remainder of his career he would lead nostalgia-oriented swing bands on a part-time basis.

Count Basie   During 1945–49, Count Basie continued to have one of the finest big bands in jazz, an orchestra that virtually defined swing. The influence of bebop was felt in some of the solos of 1947–49 and occasionally in the arrangements, but the sound of the band was basically unchanged. Lester Young and Buck Clayton were permanently gone, but such key players as trumpeters Harry "Sweets" Edison, Emmett Berry, Joe Newman (through 1946), and Clark Terry (starting in 1948), trombonists Dickie Wells and J.J. Johnson (1945–46), tenors Buddy Tate, Paul Gonsalves, and (in the Lester Young chair) Illinois Jacquet (1945–46), singer Jimmy Rushing, and the returning Walter Page and Jo Jones (who rejoined Basie and Freddie Green in the rhythm section) kept the music lively.

Joe Newman would be an important force in Basie's band for years to come. Born in New Orleans and initially influenced by Louis Armstrong and Harry "Sweets"

Edison, Newman played with Lionel Hampton (1941–43) before joining Basie. Another impressive trumpeter, Clark Terry was born and raised in St. Louis, was an early inspiration for Miles Davis, and, after serving in the military (where he played in a navy band), he first gained recognition for his playing with Charlie Barnet (1947–48).

Paul Gonsalves, unlike his predecessors Don Byas, Lucky Thompson, and Illinois Jacquet, was virtually unknown when he was hired by Basie in 1946. But he grew quite a bit as a highly individual soloist during his three years with Count's band.

● **1947: Brand New Wagon** (Bluebird 2292) has 21 of the 40 selections recorded by Basie in 1947, including seven numbers with a small group that stars Berry and Gonsalves. Highlights include Gonsalves on "Sugar" plus big band renditions of "Your Red Wagon," "One o'Clock Boogie," "South," and "Robbins' Nest." **1949: Shouting Blues** (Bluebird 66158) has 17 of the 19 big band selections from 1949 including several boppish arrangements by C.O. Price. Although such tunes as "She's a Wine-O," "Did You See Jackie Robinson Hit that Ball," and "Normania (Blee Bop Blues)" were not destined for immortality, the Basie band was still a mighty swinging outfit. But bad business decisions and a drop-off in business for big bands resulted in Count Basie reluctantly breaking up his orchestra in August 1949, 14 years after it had debuted in Kansas City. After a few months off the scene, Basie returned in early 1950 with what was billed as a sextet (it was actually an octet), and three of the four numbers that it cut on February 6, 1950, are also included on **1949**. Edison, Wells, and tenors Gene Ammons and Georgie Auld are heard from.

Buddy Tate was one of Basie's most reliable sidemen, staying with the band during 1938–48, departing a year before the original Basie band came to an end. **1945–1950** (Classics 1207) has all of his early dates as a leader. The tough-toned Tate is heard as a sideman in 1945 with trumpeter Karl George's swing-to-bop octet (which also included J.J. Johnson), with pianist Skip Hall's combo in 1949 (four instrumentals featuring ex-Basieite Buck Clayton), and on four sessions of his own. Thirteen songs of the latter are from two dates near the end of 1947 and feature some excellent Emmett Berry trumpet, pianist Bill Doggett's arrangements, and a couple of early vocals by Jimmy Witherspoon; Tate comes across effectively in an Illinois Jacquet jump/jazz role. His other two sessions (from 1949–50) are in a similar vein, with Clayton and trombonist Tyree Glenn helping out.

Although quite a few of his former sidemen would have strong careers in the 1950s and Basie's sextet had plenty of potential, many in the jazz world must have been depressed about what seemed like the permanent end of the Count Basie big band.

Tex Beneke   With the death of Glenn Miller, many of his less creative players found themselves playing either swing revivals or working in the studios. Tenor saxophonist and singer Tex Beneke spent 1946–50 at the head of the original Glenn Miller ghost orchestra. He felt restricted by having to constantly recreate the Miller sound and occasionally performed a more boppish piece, but the Glenn Miller estate forbade him from wandering too far from the 1939–42 Miller repertoire. Some worthwhile music was made in the ghost band's early days as can be heard on a pair of releases. **Tex Beneke and His Orchestra** (Nostalgia Arts 301 3026) has live performances from 1946–49 while the two-CD set **Music in the Miller Mood** (Soundies 4130) releases his radio transcriptions for Thesaurus. But Tex Beneke was stuck in a time warp from which he would never escape, leading similar bands for decades and not being creative (or brave) enough to form his own musical niche. Apparently he resigned himself to playing "Chattanooga Choo Choo" forever.

Cab Calloway   With the rise of the bebop era, Cab Calloway (despite his fame) had to cut back to a septet in April 1948, ending his orchestra after 18 years. **1942–1947** (Classics 996) has his final big band recordings, including two selections from 1942 that were originally rejected, a couple of V-disc numbers from 1944, nine songs from 1945, just two from 1946, and a final ten from 1947. There are hints of bop in some of the later arrangements, but in general the swing style of his band remained unchanged. Best are "A Blue Serge Suit with a Belt in the Back," "Don't Falter at the Altar," "Give Me Twenty Nickels for a Dollar," "The Calloway Boogie," "Everybody Eats When They Come to My House," and the bizarre "San Francisco Fan." Jonah Jones and tenors Ike Quebec (1944–46) and Sam "The Man" Taylor (1947) are the solo stars, while Milt Hinton remained Calloway's loyal bassist into the early 1950s. There would be a few recordings in 1949 with his septet (the Cab Jivers) including a hilarious version of "They Beeped

When They Should Have Bopped" (much funnier than the earlier Dizzy Gillespie rendition), but Cab Calloway's prime period was over. Although he would keep on working whenever he liked for the next few decades, he would be forever associated with the swing era and "Minnie the Moocher."

Benny Carter   The rise of bebop caused most of the top swing players to (at least for a short time) reassess their own styles. Altoist Benny Carter, whose band was full of modernists during 1945–46 (including Idrees Sulieman, trombonist Al Grey, Miles Davis, and Dexter Gordon), dealt with Charlie Parker's innovations by modernizing a few of his own ideas and taking from bebop whatever suited him without changing his basic approach or his sound. His big band broke up in 1946 (although he continued leading orchestras on an occasional basis), and Carter spent the next few years primarily writing for the studios. **1943–1946** (Classics 923) has most of the recordings by Carter's Los Angeles big band plus an all-star session from early 1946 with a lineup that includes Shorty Rogers, Trummy Young, Dickie Wells, Tony Scott, Flip Phillips, and Don Byas. **1946–1948** (Classics 1043) features Carter with a quartet, on a final outing from his 1946 big band (including "Be-Bop Boogie"), with the all-star Chocolate Dandies (a 1946 swing group with Buck Clayton, Al Grey, and Ben Webster), on V-discs and playing on a pop-oriented vocal date from 1948. Although the reliable Benny Carter was overshadowed by the beboppers, he had many decades of creativity still ahead of him as the 1940s closed.

Jimmy Dorsey   For Jimmy Dorsey, after the popular successes of his Helen O'Connell-Bob Eberle vocal records of 1941–42, the 1945–49 period found him becoming irrelevant both from the pop and the jazz standpoints. The vocal replacements for O'Connell and Eberle failed to make much of an impression and, although Dorsey had a fine rhythm section during 1946–47 (guitarist Herb Ellis, pianist Lou Carter, and bassist Johnny Frigo), that trio broke away and formed their own group, the Soft Winds. JD was sympathetic toward bebop (using Dizzy Gillespie's arrangement of "Grand Central Getaway" in 1944), and in 1949 he employed Maynard Ferguson for a few months (although no studio recordings existed), but his band was drifting aimlessly. During 1949–50, Dorsey showed a renewed interested in the freewheeling jazz of his youth, forming the Original Dorseyland Jazz Band, a Dixieland group taken out of his big band that featured trumpeter Charlie Teagarden, trombonist Cutty Cutshall, and JD on clarinet.

The Complete Standard Transcriptions (Soundies 4111) shows how the Jimmy Dorsey big band sounded in 1949. These radio transcriptions are particularly valuable because Dorsey made very few studio recordings during this era, only a total of four songs by the orchestra in 1949. Vocals are taken by Claire Hogan and Larry Noble, and there are some strong instrumentals, including "Stop, Look and Listen," "On the Alamo," and "In a Little Spanish Town." The set is rounded off by a rather intriguing half-hour radio interview with Dorsey from 1956. But much of the music was already leaning toward nostalgia, and Dorsey (though only 45) had long since passed his creative peak.

Tommy Dorsey   While Jimmy Dorsey had grudging respect for bebop, his younger brother Tommy Dorsey clearly hated it, blasting it in print a few times. Unfortunately for him, that did not help the fortunes of his suddenly struggling orchestra. In early 1945, Dorsey had a 35-piece orchestra (including 18 strings and a harp) plus solo singers Stuart Foster and Bonnie Lee Williams and the vocal group the Sentimentalists, but his wartime prosperity was near its end. By the fall, the string section was gone and, although still having an impressive orchestra (with the key soloists being Charlie Shavers, Ziggy Elman, and Buddy DeFranco), the band was no longer recording any hits. In late 1946, Dorsey briefly broke up his orchestra and then reorganized a similar unit. Elman and DeFranco were gone, but Boomie Richman took some fine tenor solos and Louie Bellson was on drums. However, the band primarily owed its existence to Tommy Dorsey's legendary name. **The Post War Era** (Bluebird 66156) is a bit ironic in that TD is barely on most of the 22 songs chosen for this reissue of material from 1946–50, other than his feature "Trombonology." Shavers and Richman have some good spots along the way with the arrangements mostly provided by Bill Finegan. But despite some fine playing, the later recordings are generally predictable dance music and lack much enthusiasm. The fire was gone.

Duke Ellington   Duke Ellington had an advantage over his fellow bandleaders in that, being a famous songwriter who had written many standards, he was able to use his royalty payments to keep his band afloat in hard times. He was intrigued and somewhat amused by bebop, but not overly affected by it, evolving independently of the new music. Of his sidemen, clarinetist Jimmy Hamilton was the most boppish although ironically Hamilton's instrument was eclipsed (outside of the Ellington band) by the rise of bop.

Among his other activities, during 1945–46 Duke Ellington and his orchestra appeared regularly on a radio series sponsored by the U.S. Treasury Department that was used to raise money for war bonds. In the 1970s, the Meritt Record Society reissued all of these valuable broadcasts on 44 LPs. In more recent times, Storyville (in their D.E.T.S. series) has been coming out with the shows on a series of two-CD sets (augmented by other live performances from the era). Since the recording quality is flawless, some of the tunes were not otherwise recorded by Duke, and even the more familiar numbers have fresh solos and sometimes altered arrangements, Ellington collectors will want these sets. Available thus far are **The Treasury Shows Vol. 1** (D.E.T.S. 903 9001), **Vol. 2** (D.E.T.S. 903 9002), **Vol. 3** (D.E.T.S. 903 9003), **Vol. 4** (D.E.T.S. 903 9004), and **Vol. 5** (D.E.T.S. 903 9005), which contain the shows from April 7 through June 9, 1945.

As 1945 began, the Duke Ellington Orchestra consisted of Rex Stewart, Taft Jordan, Shelton Hemphill, Cat Anderson and Ray Nance on trumpets or cornets (with Nance doubling on violin); Tricky Sam Nanton, Lawrence Brown, and Claude Jones on trombones; clarinetist Jimmy Hamilton; Johnny Hodges and Otto Hardwick on altos; Al Sears on tenor; baritonist Harry Carney; rhythm guitarist Fred Guy; bassist Junior Raglin; drummer Sonny Greer; with Al Hibbler, Joya Sherrill, Kay Davis, Marie Ellington and Nance taking vocals. By late 1949, only Nance, Brown, Hamilton, Hodges, Carney, Greer, Hibbler, and Davis were still in the band, a turnover of 60 percent, which for Ellington (who had long had very stable personnel) was a huge amount. But, typically, there was no real decline in the quality of his band.

The end of the recording strike in December 1944 found Ellington resuming his series of recordings for Victor. ◉ **Black, Brown and Beige** (Bluebird 86641), a three-CD set, has all of his band's recordings (though just the master takes) through the fall of 1946. Among the songs are "I'm Beginning to See the Light" (which became a hit for Harry James), "I Ain't Got Nothing but the Blues," "I Didn't Know About You," excerpts from "Black, Brown and Beige," the "Perfume Suite," and some inspired remakes of Duke's earlier hits, including a classic rendition of "It Don't Mean a Thing" featuring Al Hibbler and the three female singers.

Duke Ellington continued his important series of Carnegie Hall concerts on January 4, 1946. By then Rex Stewart had departed, Frances Williams was the band's first trumpeter, Oscar Pettiford had taken over for Raglin on bass, and Tricky Sam Nanton was absent. Nanton was recovering from a mild stroke that he had suffered a few months earlier and would return to the band soon, but on July 20, 1946, he died suddenly at the age of 42. The loss of Tricky Sam was a major one for he was an important link to Ellington's "jungle band" of the 1920s. From mid-1946 on, Ellington would employ a series of fine trombonists to emulate Nanton's otherworldly sounds.

The Carnegie Hall Concerts—January 1946 (Prestige 24074) is an excellent two-CD set highlighted by "Caravan," "Air Conditioned Jungle," "I'm Just a Lucky So and So," and the three-part "A Tonal Group" (which includes the catchy "Jam-A-Ditty"). **The Great Chicago Concerts** (Music Masters 65110), also a two-CD set, has a pair of 1946 performances and is most notable for the three-part "Deep South Suite" (which concludes with "Happy-Go-Lucky Local," the future basis for "Night Train") and four numbers in which guest Django Reinhardt (on his only American tour) jams with the rhythm section.

In October 1946, Ellington ended his period with the Victor label and began recording for Musicraft. **1946–1947** (Classics 1051) has all but the first two Musicraft numbers, concluding with Duke's first sessions since 1940 for Columbia. Among the more memorable selections are "Sultry Sunset," a Mary Lou Williams arrangement of "Blue Skies" that is a feature for the trumpet section, Ray Nance's delightful vocal on "Tulip or Turnip," and the second part of "Happy-Go-Lucky Local" with the soon-to-be familiar "Night Train" melody. **1947** (Classics 1086) finds the Ellington band saddled with some erratic material, including "Cowboy Rhumba," "It's Mad, Mad, Mad," "Kitty," and "Singin' in the Rain," but even these have their moments of interest. Particularly intriguing is the tongue-in-cheek "Boogie Bop Blues" and Jimmy Hamilton's feature on "The Air Conditioned Jungle." **1947–1948** (Classics 1119) includes the six-part "Liberian Suite" (one of Ellington's best longer works), the two-part "The Tattooed Bride," and the nearly atonal "Clothed Woman" among its many rewarding performances.

The Carnegie Hall Concerts—December 1947 (Prestige 24075), another two-CD set, was the second best of Duke's famous Carnegie appearances (only dwarfed by his January 1943 concert). In addition to the "Liberian Suite," highlights include "Triple Play," a Johnny Hodges medley, "On a Turquoise Cloud" (a showcase for Kay Davis's wordless vocal), "Cotton Tail," "Trumpets No End" (a renamed "Blue Skies"), and "The Clothed Woman." By now, Tyree Glenn was not only in Tricky Sam Nanton's old spot (doing a fine job of recreating Nanton's sound), but also featured on vibes. Otto Hardwick, who had been with Duke on and off since the beginning, but had been underutilized since the late 1930s, departed after an argument in 1946 and retired from music altogether the following year. His replacement was Russell Procope, John Kirby's former altoist who was used by Ellington now and then on New Orleans style clarinet (where he contrasted with Hamilton's much cooler tone).

Carnegie Hall, November 13, 1948 (Vintage Jazz Classics 1024/25) has Ellington's last major Carnegie Hall concert in his famous series. This two-fer has a rare version of "Lush Life" (sung by its composer Billy Strayhorn), the debut of "The Tattooed Bride," a revival of "Reminiscing in Tempo," and chances for Ben Webster (who was briefly back in the band) to be featured. Al Killian was in the orchestra during this period, playing high note solos, Quentin Jackson (who could also emulate Tricky Sam) joined Lawrence Brown and Tyree Glenn in the trombone section and Wendell Marshall was Duke's new bassist.

In 1949, Al Sears, who had contributed many fine tenor solos during the past five years, left Ellington; he was replaced for a period by Charlie Rouse and Jimmy Forrest. Fred Guy, who with Sonny Greer was the last of the early Washingtonians still in the band, retired. Since Guy had been largely inaudible since the early 1930s when he switched from banjo to guitar, Ellington never bothered to replace him.

Al Hibbler, Duke's main singer since 1943, occasionally recorded dates under his own name during this era. **1946–1949** (Classics 1234) has Hibbler (whose style would become more eccentric in later years) at his prime.

He is accompanied by a variety of Ellington sidemen, the short-lived Mercer Ellington Orchestra and a few outsiders (including tenor saxophonist Jack McVea) on such tunes as "I Got It Bad," his own blues "Fat and Forty," "My Little Brown Book," "Trees," and "It Don't Mean a Thing."

Having survived the bebop years, in the early 1950s Duke Ellington would face the greatest challenge to keeping his orchestra together when three of his major sidemen all defected at once.

Ziggy Elman   Ziggy Elman should have been a big star. He was well featured with the Benny Goodman Orchestra during 1936–40 (although overshadowed a bit by Harry James) and had a hit with "And the Angels Sing." But instead of starting his own orchestra in 1940 when BG temporarily broke up his band, he opted to join Tommy Dorsey instead, playing with TD during 1940–43 and in 1946, after serving in the army. By the time he formed his swing band in 1947, it was much too late. The Ziggy Elman Orchestra (which lasted two years) was a solid band, as can be heard on **The Issued Recordings 1947–1949** (Jazz Band 2154). Among the better selections on this definitive CD are "How High the Moon," "Zaggin' with Ziggy," "Samba with Ziggy," "Bublitchki," "Carolina in the Morning," and a surprisingly effective "Boppin' with Ziggy." But the Ziggy Elman Orchestra was doomed to failure and died before 1949 was over.

Benny Goodman   The King of Swing began 1945 optimistically. He had organized his first regular big band since 1942, and it was a solid unit that included such players as Trummy Young, pianist Charlie Queener, and singer Jane Harvey. In addition he was heading a sextet that featured Red Norvo, Teddy Wilson, and Slam Stewart. While the big band recordings have not yet been covered by the Classics series, the sextet dates are on **Slipped Disc, 1945–1946** (Columbia 44292) including such hot tunes as the classic "Slipped Disc," "Rachel's Dream," "Tiger Rag," "Shine," and "Liza." Listening to these enthusiastic and creative performances, it is difficult to realize that the swing era was rapidly ending.

Goodman's big band underwent a lot of turnover (among the sidemen were singers Liza Morrow and Art Lund, Kai Winding, Stan Getz, Zoot Sims, Joe Bushkin, Barney Kessel, and Louis Bellson plus alumni Chris Griffin, Mel Powell, Bud Freeman, and Lou McGarity) and,

although it sounded like a classic swing orchestra, it broke up near the end of 1946. In 1947, Goodman led a short-lived orchestra in Los Angeles and continued playing and recording with small groups and part-time orchestras.

Having done his best to ignore bebop, in 1948 BG switched courses and organized a bop-oriented septet that also featured Stan Hasselgard on second clarinet, either Teddy Wilson or Mary Lou Williams on piano, and a favorite of his, tenor saxophonist Wardell Gray. The only recording that resulted during that strike-filled year was a boppish rendition of "Stealin' Apples" with Fats Navarro in place of the second clarinet (although broadcasts of the septet have been issued under Hasselgard's name). Under the urging of his new label Capitol, Goodman decided to get "with it" and form a bebop orchestra of his own. **Undercurrent Blues** (Capitol 32086) has all of Goodman's bop recordings, including three numbers from 1947, "Stealin' Apples," and such performances from 1949 as "Undercurrent Blues," "Bop Hop," "Bedlam" and "Blue Lou." With Chico O'Farrill contributing many of the arrangements, and Gray and trumpeter Doug Mettome playing modern solos, Goodman sounded a bit out of place in his own orchestra.

But having failed in his attempt to become the King of Bebop, the King of Swing broke up his bop experiment at the end of the year and permanently returned to the world of swing.

Lionel Hampton   Although a year older than his former boss Benny Goodman, Lionel Hampton was a more flexible player and very open to the sounds of bebop and R&B. His big band was riding high in 1945 due to the success of "Flying Home," and its exciting live shows (which could often be exhibitionistic with honking tenors and screaming trumpets) allowed it to attract an audience as interested in R&B as in jazz.

During the 1945–49 period, such musicians as trumpeters Fats Navarro, Kenny Dorham, Joe Wilder, Snooky Young, Leo "The Whistler" Shepherd, and Benny Bailey, trombonist Al Grey, tenors Arnett Cobb and Johnny Griffin, pianist Milt Buckner, bassist Charles Mingus, the young guitarist Wes Montgomery, and Dinah Washington were among the many who spent time in Hampton's band. The two-CD set ● **Hamp!** (GRP/Decca 652) mostly dates from 1942–50 (with two numbers from 1963) and has the key highpoints of this era for the vibraphonist, including "Flying Home," "Hamp's Boogie Woogie," "Red Cross" (with guest Dizzy Gillespie), Dinah Washington's "Evil Gal Blues," "Blow Top Blues," "Hey! Ba-Ba-Re Bop," "Red Top," the adventurous "Mingus Fingers," "Midnight Sun," and "Rag Mop." In addition, Hampton takes a remarkable double-time solo on a 1947 version of "Stardust" with an all-star group. **Midnight Sun** (GRP/Decca 625) concentrates on the 1946–47 period, duplicating eight selections from Hamp, but adding a dozen more, including a two-part "Air Mail Special," "Cobb's Idea," "Goldwyn Stomp," and "Giddy Up."

Erskine Hawkins Erskine Hawkins, who had the perfect black swing/dance band, kept his orchestra together throughout the 1940s, often playing at the Savoy Ballroom. In 1945, he had his last hit with "Tippin' In," featuring altoist Bobby Smith. Although most of the best-known sidemen gradually left, including Dud and Paul Bascomb and Avery Parrish, the Erskine Hawkins Orchestra remained one of the top swing bands. **1946–1947** (Classics 1008) has 13 vocals (four by Jimmy Mitchelle, one apiece from Ruth Christian and Ace Harris, and seven easy-to-take appearances by Laura Washington), but it is the nine swinging instrumentals (which sometimes have slight hints of bebop) that take honors. The key soloists on this CD are Hawkins and Sammy Lowe on trumpets, trombonist Matthew Gee, Bobby Smith, Julian Dash, and baritonist Haywood Henry, who is often heard on clarinet. **1947–1949** (Classics 1148) has Henry well-featured, occasional vocals by Jimmy Mitchelle, and lots of fine (if sometimes bombastic) trumpet from the leader. Highlights of this program of little-known but enjoyable music includes "Gabriel's Heater," "Rose Room," "Corn Bread," "Texas Hop," and "Fishtail." Erskine Hawkins's audience might have shrunk, but his band was still able to keep New York's dancers satisfied.

Earl Hines The Earl Hines big band was off records altogether from mid-1942 until January 1945. **1945–1947** (Classics 1041) has the final recordings by the orchestra before its breakup. Wardell Gray solos on many of the first 14 numbers and also included are Johnny Hartman's first four recorded vocals. Some of the arrangements are a little boppish, but surprisingly (considering Hines's 1943 bop band) the playing on those numbers sounds a bit awkward. There are also some solid swing instrumentals (along with some forgettable vocals), but this set is of greatest interest due to the rarity of the material rather than the performances being all that essential. In 1948, Hines (who had headed big bands since late 1928) gave up trying to lead his orchestra and joined the Louis Armstrong All-Stars.

International Sweethearts of Rhythm Throughout the swing era there were several "all girl" bands that were popular as much for their novelty and good looks as for their musicianship. Ina Ray Hutton's Melodears (which recorded six songs in 1934) was an excellent orchestra, but most of the other female ensembles (particularly the ones that gained the most publicity) were somewhat forgettable. It was not that women could not play instruments quite well, but that they were discouraged from even starting and were really only accepted as singers and pianists in jazz. There were a few exceptions along the way, such as trumpeters Valaida Snow and Billie Rogers, vibraphonist Marjorie Hyams, and guitarist Mary Osborne, but women (other than pianists) who not only mastered their instruments but had opportunities to record prior to 1960 were few and far between.

Even the greatest of the all-female jazz big bands, the International Sweethearts of Rhythm, only recorded five songs (two for the Guild label in 1945 and three for RCA in 1946). Organized in 1939 at the Piney Woods County Life School in Mississippi, the Sweethearts had fine soloists in tenor saxophonist Viola Burnside and trumpeter Tiny Davis. Headed by singer Anna Mae Winburn (who also played saxophone), the group worked on the East Coast and toured postwar Europe in 1945. They did not neglect the glamorous aspects of their role, but the group did focus on performing excellent music somewhat reminiscent of Count Basie, using the arrangements of Eddie Durham and Jesse Stone. The LP **International Sweethearts of Rhythm** (Rosetta 1312) has four of the five studio sides (the fifth, "Tiny Boogie," is available on a Bluebird sampler CD) and adds to the group's tiny discography by including the band's three appearances on the Jubilee radio series. Producer Rosetta Reitz's extensive and definitive liner notes (plus the many photos) make this an LP well worth searching for.

The International Sweethearts of Rhythm remained a swing band throughout its existence, breaking up in 1949. Unfortunately, none of the sidemen (including

Burnside and Davis) became prominent later on, for there were still very few opportunities for female instrumentalists to make a living in jazz.

Harry James When Harry James's orchestra, the most popular big band in the world, returned to records on November 21, 1944, the first session yielded a hit version of Duke Ellington's "I'm Beginning to See the Light," featuring singer Kitty Kallen. On July 24, 1945, James hit the peak of his popularity with "It's Been a Long Long Time," a song that perfectly symbolized the end of World War II and America's growing euphoria at things getting back to normal. For James, who was leading a 34-piece orchestra (with 18 strings and such soloists as altoist Willie Smith, tenor saxophonist Corky Corcoran, pianist Arnold Ross, and valve trombonist Juan Tizol), it must have seemed as if the hit records would never stop. But with the collapse of the dance band industry and the rise of singers, James's commercial success had hit its peak. In December 1946, with the drop-off in business, he broke up his band.

Being so famous, James soon reorganized and within five months was back again with a similar group. He kept the string section until 1948, became interested for a time in exploring bebop (his solo on a remarkable two-part version of "Tuxedo Junction" could almost pass for Dizzy Gillespie), and remained a popular figure in the music scene. While the Classics reissue of all of his big band recordings has as of this writing not yet reached 1946, ◗ **Snooty Fruity** (Columbia 45447), which has Willie Smith getting co-billing, is a superior sampler of James's jazz-oriented recordings of 1944–55, including the memorable rendition of "Tuxedo Junction," "Moten Swing," "New Two o'Clock Jump," "The Great Lie," and "Stompin' at the Savoy."

Buddy Johnson Pianist/arranger Buddy Johnson led one of the more popular big bands of the post-swing era. Born in South Carolina, he moved to New York in the mid-1930s, freelanced, and headed some small-group dates. **1939–1942** (Classics 884) features Johnson in an octet/nonet with such players as altoist Don Stovall, trumpeter Shad Collins, trombonist Dan Minor, and Kenny Clarke. "Stop Pretending" and "Please, Mister Johnson" were minor hits, and Buddy's sister Ella Johnson has eight vocals; only six of the songs are instrumentals. In 1944, the Buddy Johnson Orchestra was formed and it introduced the bluesy standard "Since I Fell for

You." Swing-oriented at first, Johnson's band leaned more toward R&B by the end of the 1940s. **1942–1947** (Classics 1079) has his final combo dates plus the big band's first recordings. Highlights include "That's the Stuff You Gotta Watch," "Fine Brown Frame," "I Wonder Where Our Love Has Gone," five instrumentals, and the original version of "Since I Fell for You." Ella Johnson is the main vocalist with Arthur Prysock heard twice, and Buddy Johnson sings "Hey Sweet Potato."

Andy Kirk Mary Lou Williams's departure from Andy Kirk's orchestra in 1942 was the beginning of the end for the Twelve Clouds of Joy. There were still some fine players in the organization, including trumpeters Howard McGhee and Fats Navarro and (during 1945–46) both Jimmy Forrest and Eddie "Lockjaw" Davis on tenors, but the band had been fairly obscure for several years by the time it broke up in 1948. **1943–1949** (Classics 1075) has McGhee on the first three numbers, Navarro on four tunes in 1946 (both trumpeters get short spots), and an interesting instrumental in "Hippy-Dippy." However, the vocals of the Jubalaires, Beverly White, Bea Booze, Billy Daniels, and the Four Knights in 1946 are of only minor interest although Joe Williams is heard on two songs (his recording debut). The CD finishes with a pair of R&B-ish numbers from 1949 that have Andy Kirk closing his career by leading an unknown orchestra.

Gene Krupa Gene Krupa was the most famous drummer in the world in 1945, although in jazz his playing sounded old-fashioned compared to Buddy Rich, Big Sid Catlett, Max Roach, and Kenny Clarke. However, he had an open mind toward bebop and encouraged his musicians to play the modern music they enjoyed. Dave Lambert and Buddy Stewart recorded "What's This" (the first bebop vocal) with Krupa as early as January 22, 1945. In addition to the crowd-pleasing tenor Charlie Ventura, Krupa also featured the boppish trumpeter Don Fagerquist in 1945.

1945 (Classics 1143) has eight numbers by the Gene Krupa Trio (with the overly enthusiastic Ventura and pianist George Walters), excellent singing from Anita O'Day (who returned to Krupa's orchestra for much of the year) on such hits as "Opus No. 1," "Boogie Blues," and "Chickery Chick," and some ballad features for Buddy Stewart. **1945–1946** (Classics 1231) has O'Day's last vocals with the band (best is "Tea for Two") and there is lots of singing by Stewart and Carolyn Grey. Only six of the 25 selections are instrumentals, with Gerry Mulligan's early arrangement of "How High the Moon" the most impressive. Red Rodney was Krupa's trumpet soloist during the first half of 1946, but only has a few brief spots, adding a touch of bop to the music. Also heard from is altoist Charlie Kennedy (who emulates Charlie Parker) and a few final statements from Charlie Ventura (including on his showcase "Yesterdays") before he departed. In contrast, Gene Krupa's radio transcriptions of the time, released as an LP called **Transcribed** (IAJRC 10) and as part of a Krupa/Harry James limited-edition box set by Mosaic, is much more open to bop with plenty of solos for Rodney; pity that the Columbia label was not interested in this aspect of Krupa's music.

In 1947, the Gene Krupa Orchestra featured Don Fagerquist back for a second stint, Charlie Kennedy, tenor saxophonist Buddy Wise, and pianist Teddy Napoleon along with too many vocals. The best numbers are Gerry Mulligan's "Disc Jockey Jump" and a song called "Calling Dr. Gillespie." The 1949 version of the Krupa big band had Roy Eldridge returning, Fagerquist and Wise still as key players, and trombonist Frank Rosolino adding a bit of joy to the music (singing on "Lemon Drop"). But that particular orchestra recorded only eight songs and would not survive past 1950.

Jimmie Lunceford   Although it underwent a great deal of turnover during the war years, the Jimmie Lunceford Orchestra emerged in 1945 sounding very similar to how it had in 1940, still featuring tenor saxophonist Joe Thomas and pianist/arranger Edwin Wilcox. Omer Simeon was heard on clarinet and alto, and the band's ensembles were as tight as ever. Unfortunately, the band's string of hits stopped altogether. **Margie** (Savoy 1209) has the band's three sessions of 1946–47. Trummy Young guests on one date (singing on the remake of "Margie") and other highlights include "Cement Maker," "The Jimmies," and "One o'Clock Jump."

On July 3, 1947, in Seaside, Oregon, Jimmie Lunceford died suddenly at the age of 45, allegedly from a heart attack, but some have said that it was actually from food poisoning by a racist restaurant owner who was forced to serve the black musicians. Thomas and Wilcox took over leadership of the orchestra, struggling on for two years. **1948–1949** (Classics 1151) has the ghost band's four record dates and, although the personnel stayed mostly intact, the group does not sound quite as sharp as before and (even with new material) seems stuck in a time warp. There is some fine swing music on this CD (at times hinting at R&B) and, to their credit, there are no remakes, but it all can be summed up with the phrase "Nice try!" Late in 1949, Thomas and Wilcox gave up and broke up the band.

Ray McKinley   Ray McKinley, who had played drums, sang, and been co-leader of the Will Bradley Orchestra (1939–42), briefly had his own big band after splitting with Bradley. After enlisting, he worked with Glenn Miller's Army Air Force Band (1943–45), becoming its leader after Miller's disappearance over the English Channel.

After his discharge, rather than lead a Miller ghost band (as Tex Beneke was doing), McKinley headed an ensemble billed as "The Most Versatile Band in the Land." Although swing-oriented, the group utilized many arrangements by the adventurous Eddie Sauter. **1946–1949** (Jazz Unlimited 2033) has some of the band's best and most eccentric performances, including McKinley's theme "Howdy Friends," "Hangover Square," "Lullaby in Rhythm," "How High the Moon," "Pete's Café," and "Borderline." The 1946 band includes Peanuts Hucko on tenor and guitarist Mundell Lowe. There are some fine short solos along the way, but Sauter's charts are what distinguished this band. As it was, it was not enough, and in 1950 McKinley gave up the orchestra.

Lucky Millinder   Lucky Millinder was able to keep his orchestra together by veering toward R&B and by continuing to play for dancers. **1943–1947** (Classics 1026) starts with four V-discs from 1943 that showcase the singing and guitar playing of Sister Rosetta Tharpe (doing remakes of four of her better numbers) shortly before she decided to switch back to gospel music. Also from that period, "Savoy" has one of Joe Guy's best trumpet solos, and "Shipyard Social Junction" is a superior instrumental. Of the four numbers from 1944, two songs have the recording debut of singer Wynonie Harris, and "Hurry, Hurry" includes a brief trumpet spot from Freddy Webster. There are also two so-so numbers from 1945, six from 1946 (best is Annisteen Allen's singing on "There's Good Blues Tonight" and some spots for the tenor of Sam "The Man" Taylor) and four vocal cuts from the following year. Millinder's band remained a crowd pleaser into the early 1950s.

Louis Prima   Trumpeter/singer Louis Prima formed his big band in 1940, and his combination of swinging instrumentals, novelty vocals, ballad features for singer Lily Ann Carol, and Italian humor served him well during the second half of the 1940s. Although the quality of his recordings declined as the decade progressed, **Play Pretty for the People** (Savoy 4420) sticks to his better selections from 1944–47. Listening to "Robin Hood,"

"Angelina," "I'll Walk Alone," "The Blizzard," and "Brooklyn Boogie," one can understand the timeless popularity of Prima, who (with Carol) is virtually the whole show.

Don Redman   The first great arranger, Don Redman had primarily freelanced since the breakup of his big band in January 1940, contributing charts to Jimmy Dorsey (a hit version of "Deep Purple"), Count Basie,

49 ESSENTIAL RECORDS OF 1945–1949

Charlie Parker, **The Complete Savoy and Dial Studio Recordings 1944–1948** (Savoy 75679 29112), 8 CDs

Charlie Parker, **The Complete Live Performances on Savoy** (Savoy 17021), 4 CDs

Dizzy Gillespie, **1946–1947** (Classics 986)

Dizzy Gillespie, **The Complete Victor Recordings** (Bluebird 66528), 2 CDs

Bud Powell, **The Complete Blue Note and Roost Recordings** (Blue Note 30083), 4 CDs

Bud Powell, **Jazz Giant** (Verve 543832)

Thelonious Monk, **The Complete Blue Note Recordings** (Blue Note 30363), 4 CDs

Fats Navarro, **Fats Navarro Story** (Proper 1011), 4 CDs

J.J. Johnson, **1946–1949** (Classics 1176)

Stan Hasselgard and Benny Goodman, **At Click 1948** (Dragon 183)

Sonny Stitt, **Sonny Stitt/Bud Powell/J.J. Johnson** (Original Jazz Classics 009)

Sarah Vaughan, **Young Sassy** (Proper Box 27), 4 CDs

Boyd Raeburn, **Jubilee Broadcasts, 1946** (Hep 1)

Stan Kenton, **Retrospective** (Capitol 97350), 4 CDs

June Christy, **Tampico** (Memoir 526)

Woody Herman, **Blowin' Up a Storm** (Columbia/Legacy 65646), 2 CDs

Woody Herman, **Keeper of the Flame** (Capitol 98453)

Charlie Barnet, **The Capitol Big Band Sessions** (Capitol 21258)

Count Basie, **1947: Brand New Wagon** (Bluebird 2292)

Duke Ellington, **Black, Brown and Beige** (Bluebird 86641), 3 CDs

Lionel Hampton, **Hamp!** (GRP/Decca 652), 2 CDs

Harry James, **Snooty Fruity** (Columbia 45447)

Ella Fitzgerald, **The War Years** (GRP/Decca 628), 2 CDs

Billie Holiday, **The Complete Decca Recordings** (GRP/Decca 601), 2 CDs

Julia Lee, **Julia Lee and Her Boyfriends** (JSP 3405), 2 CDs

Soft Winds, **Then and Now** (Chiaroscuro 342), 2 CDs

Arnett Cobb, **Arnett Blows for 1300** (Delmark 471)

Illinois Jacquet, **The Black Velvet Band** (Bluebird 6571)

Lester Young, **The Complete Aladdin Sessions** (Blue Note 32787), 2 CDs

Albert Ammons, **1946–1948** (Classics 1100)

Art Tatum, **Piano Starts Here** (Columbia/Legacy 64690)

Erroll Garner, **The Complete Savoy Master Takes** (Savoy 17025/26), 2 CDs

JATP, **The Complete Jazz at the Philharmonic on Verve 1944–1949** (Verve 314 523 8932), 10 CDs

Louis Armstrong, **The 1940's Small-Band Sides** (Bluebird 6378)

Bunk Johnson, **Last Testament** (Delmark 225)

Tony Parenti, **Tony Parenti and His New Orleanians** (Jazzology 1)

This Is Jazz, **Vol. Three** (Jazzology 1029/30), 2 CDs

Henry "Red" Allen, **1944–1947** (Classics 1067)

Lu Watters's Yerba Buena Jazz Band, **The Complete Good Time Jazz Recordings** (Good Time Jazz 4409), 4 CDs

Luckey Roberts and Ralph Sutton, **The Circle Recordings** (Solo Art 10)

Louis Jordan, **The Best of Louis Jordan** (MCA 4079)

Machito, **Mucho Macho** (Pablo 2625-712)

Chano Pozo, **El Tambor De Cuba** (Tumbao 305), 3 CDs

Lennie Tristano and Warne Marsh, **Intuition** (Capital Jazz 52771)

Miles Davis, **The Complete Birth of the Cool** (Blue Note 94550), 2 CDs

Various Artists, **Bebop in Britain** (Esquire 100-4), 4 CDs

Various Artists, **Central Avenue Sounds** (Rhino 75872), 4 CDs

Various Artists, **The Jazz Scene** (Verve 314 521 661), 2 CDs

Various Artists, **Charlie Parker and the Stars of Modern Jazz at Carnegie Hall, Christmas 1949** (Jass 16)

Harry James, and other orchestras. In 1946, he put together an all-star big band that was the first American orchestra to tour Europe after World War II. The band included such notables as Don Byas, trumpeter/singer Peanuts Holland, Quentin Jackson, Tyree Glenn, and pianist Billy Taylor. Both Byas and Holland chose to stay permanently overseas.

The orchestra just recorded four obscure titles, but was captured live on two sets. **For Europeans Only** (Steeplechase 36020) is a poorly recorded but interesting live concert most notable for Byas's playing. Better overall is **Geneva 1946** (TCB 02112), performed six weeks later on a much better recorded radio broadcast. The music is excellent mainstream swing, ignoring the innovations of bebop.

After returning to the United States, Don Redman's creative career was over after a quarter-century. He became Pearl Bailey's musical director and faded into the background.

Buddy Rich Arguably the greatest drummer of all time (certainly technically), Buddy Rich had been a driving force in Tommy Dorsey's band during 1939–45, except during part of 1942–44 when he was in the Marines. In October 1945, he put together his own big band, but it lasted less than a year; the key sidemen included for a time Red Rodney, altoist Aaron Sachs, and trombonist Earl Swope. After touring with "Jazz at the Philharmonic," Rich organized a bop-oriented orchestra in early 1947 that lasted almost two years, featuring along the way Al Cohn, Terry Gibbs, Jimmy Giuffre, and the arrangements of Cohn and George Handy. **The Legendary '47–48 Orchestra** (Hep 12) has live appearances by this potentially exciting big band, which falls between swing and bop, depending on the arrangement. But by the end of 1948, Rich gave up and went back to being a sideman, for the moment.

Luis Russell Pianist/arranger Luis Russell, who had led a major big band on records during 1929–31, played in Louis Armstrong's backup orchestra during 1935–43 in an anonymous role. In 1943, he went out on his own, organizing another big band. Although this ensemble recorded 22 selections (two in 1945 and the remainder in 1946), all of which have been reissued on **1945–1946** (Classics 1066), it never came close to making an impression. All of Russell's later recordings except three songs feature dull vocals (mostly by Lee Richardson),

and the only sideman of any note at all was drummer Roy Haynes, who was 21 at the time. Collectors who explore these later recordings hoping they will be on the level of Russell's earlier gems will be disappointed.

In 1948, Luis Russell retired from full-time playing, becoming a shopkeeper and a music teacher.

Artie Shaw Of all the major swing era big band leaders (other than Woody Herman and Stan Kenton), Artie Shaw had the strongest sympathy toward bebop. As early as his 1945 recording of "Easy to Love," the clarinetist showed that he could improvise a bop solo quite credibly.

After leading an unrecorded service band during 1942–43, Shaw became quite ill, was given a medical discharge in February 1944, and recovered a few months later. He formed his fifth big band later in the year, a fine swing ensemble that looked toward bop. The group featured Roy Eldridge, Dodo Marmarosa, and Barney Kessel, all three of whom were also on Shaw's Gramercy Five recordings of the period. Trombonist Ray Conniff and Eddie Sauter provided some of the group's top arrangements, and this orchestra had a great deal of potential. The definitive five-CD set ● **Self-Portrait** (Bluebird 63808), which sums up the clarinetist's entire career, includes several numbers from the 1945 band, such as "Lady Day," "'S Wonderful," "Summertime," and "Tabu." Unfortunately, by late 1945, Shaw had lost interest and broke up the big band. He did make a series of recordings for Musicraft during 1945–46 with a studio string orchestra, sometimes utilizing Mel Tormé and the Mel-Tones, most prominently on the minor hit "What Is this Thing Called Love."

After being mostly inactive during 1947–48, in 1949 Artie Shaw came out with his sixth and final big band, a bebop-oriented orchestra that featured Don Fagerquist, altoists Herbie Steward and Frankie Socolow, the tenors of Al Cohn (who gets a lot of solo space) and Zoot Sims, and guitarist Jimmy Raney. The band only recorded six songs in the studios for Decca, but **1949** (Music Masters 0234) has a full live set by the orchestra, performing updated versions of swing standards and some originals that look not only toward bebop, but 1950s cool jazz as well. Unfortunately, the public wanted to hear Shaw play his hits (particularly "Begin the Beguine" and "Frenesi") the same way he had in the late 1930s, and this final attempt at a modern orchestra flopped. To fulfill a contract, the clarinetist quickly put together a mundane dance band (one that gained better notices than his bop orchestra) and then soon retired again, disgusted with the music business.

Jack Teagarden It was somewhat miraculous that the Jack Teagarden Big Band lasted for seven years (1939–46), because it never made much of an impression with the general public nor did it have a single hit. **1944–1947** (Classics 1032) wraps up this portion of the great trombonist's life with some obscure orchestra recordings (most of which were V-discs) and two superior small-group dates. The latter includes a 1944 session in which Teagarden leads a sextet that includes Max Kaminsky, clarinetist Ernie Caceres, and Jack's sister, pianist Norma Teagarden, and an intriguing set on March 10, 1947 (with Kaminsky and clarinetist Peanuts Hucko) on which Mr. T. almost hints at bebop in spots (most notably on "Jam Session at Victor"). By then his big band had broken up and he had gone bankrupt after seven years of losing money. But thanks to some assistance from Bing Crosby and his upcoming membership in the Louis Armstrong All-Stars, Jack Teagarden would soon be returning to both solvency and freewheeling jazz.

Charlie Ventura Charlie Ventura, a rambunctious and at times emotionally over-the-top swing tenor saxophonist, became famous during his period with Gene Krupa (1944–46), particularly for his recordings with Krupa's trio, having a hit with "Dark Eyes." He began recording as a leader in 1945 and the following year went out on his own, forming a short-lived big band. In 1947, Ventura had a quintet with Kai Winding, pianist Lou Stein, bassist Bob Carter, drummer Shelly Manne, and Buddy Stewart that fell between swing and bop. Soon he was using the title of "Bop for the People," latching onto bebop, which at least briefly looked like it was going to be the newest fad. In 1949, Ventura had his strongest group, an ensemble consisting of Conte Candoli, trombonist Benny Green, Boots Mussulli on alto and baritone, bassist Kenny O'Brien, drummer Ed Shaughnessy, and the vocal duo of pianist Roy Kral and Jackie Cain (known as Jackie and Roy). The highpoint for the band was their Pasadena Civic Auditorium concert of May 9, 1949. Shortly afterwards, Jackie and Roy got married and departed. A few months later, Ventura switched back to swing, forming a final big band that

lasted less than a year. **Bop for the People** (Proper Box 1041), a four-CD set, has the great majority of Ventura's recordings as a leader from 1945 up to (and including) the Civic Auditorium concert. Among the musicians who are well featured are Howard McGhee, Buck Clayton, Barney Bigard, Red Rodney, Willie Smith, Charlie Kennedy, Charlie Shavers, Bill Harris, Kai Winding, Buddy Stewart, and the band with Jackie and Roy.

Cootie Williams Trumpeter Cootie Williams, who became famous playing with Duke Ellington (1929–40) and who starred with Benny Goodman for a year (1941), formed his big band in 1942, working steadily for five years at the Savoy Ballroom. Although not a modernist himself, Williams featured Bud Powell in 1944, and Charlie Parker had a brief stint with his ensemble, sitting in on "Floogie Boo" in February 1945. With Sam "The Man" Taylor playing spirited tenor solos and Eddie "Cleanhead" Vinson contributing both alto solos and blues vocals, Williams had an underrated band in the mid-1940s. **1945–1946** (Classics 981) has exuberant performances of "House of Joy," "Everything but You," and "That's the Lick" plus a Vinson vocal on "Juice Head Baby" and a feature for the leader on "Echoes of Harlem." Both Taylor and Vinson went out on their own in 1946, but Williams retained a strong and spirited orchestra until he cut back to an octet in 1947. His 1948 combo featured the honking and squealing tenor of Willis Jackson, who was showcased on the two-part "Gator Tail," an R&B favorite of the time. **1946–1949** (Classics 1105), which has the final big band numbers and the combo sessions, alternates ballad singers, a few swing tunes, and romping R&B instrumentals, including "Gator Tail," "Typhoon," and "Slidin' and Glidin'." Overall the music is quite fun even if Cootie Williams was following trends rather than setting them.

Gerald Wilson Trumpeter and arranger with Jimmie Lunceford during 1939–42, Gerald Wilson moved to Los Angeles in 1942, freelanced with the bands of Les Hite, Phil Moore, Willie Smith, and Benny Carter, served in the navy, and in 1944 formed his first big band. Utilizing such players as trumpeters Snooky Young, Emmett Berry, and Hobart Dotson, trombonists Vic Dickenson and Melba Liston, Vernon Slater on tenor, pianists Jimmy Bunn and Gerald Wiggins, and bassist Red Callender at various times, Wilson kept his big band going for three years. **1945–1946** (Classics 976) has the first 20 of their 32 recordings and reveals that Wilson's initial orchestra was quite bop-oriented while having roots in Jimmie Lunceford–type swing. Among the more notable Wilson arrangements are "Synthetic Joe," "Puerto Rican Breakdown," "Groovin' High," "Skip the Gutter," and "Cruisin' with Cab."

Although he achieved a certain amount of regional success, in 1947 Gerald Wilson felt that he needed to study more as a writer, so he broke up his orchestra. During the next two years he freelanced, writing and playing with the big bands of Dizzy Gillespie and Count Basie.

Out of the 31 orchestras covered in this section, only nine survived to the end of 1950: Jimmy Dorsey, Tommy Dorsey, Duke Ellington, Lionel Hampton, Erskine Hawkins, Harry James, Buddy Johnson, Lucky Millinder, and Louis Prima. Never again would big bands dominate popular music.

The Swing Singers as Singles

Most of the jazz-oriented singers who were active during the second half of the 1940s gained at least part of their training singing with big bands. But the collapse of so many orchestras and the rise of the vocalist on pop charts meant that, for a singer to get famous, they had to have a solo career. Few major jazz singers (other than Jimmy Rushing with Count Basie, and June Christy with Stan Kenton) remained with big bands during the post-swing years. Some of the band singers faded quickly (including Helen Forrest, Helen O'Connell, Bob Eberly, the ailing Ivie Anderson, Ray Eberle, Marion Hutton, and Pha Terrell) and were forever associated with the swing era. Others (Frank Sinatra, Doris Day, Dinah Shore, and Dick Haymes among them) followed Bing Crosby in becoming involved in pop music and making films.

The 14 jazz vocalists in this section, all initially based in swing (as opposed to Sarah Vaughan and the more bop-oriented vocalists), had varying amounts of success as solo singers during this era.

Mildred Bailey Mildred Bailey, one of the top singers of the 1930s, was in prime form in the mid-1940s, but her personal life was going through turmoil. She and Red Norvo were divorced in 1945, her lifelong inferiority complex (fueled by her being overweight) led to major mood swings, and respiratory problems started seriously affecting her health in 1947. Her last significant

musical period was during 1944–47, which is covered on **The Blue Angel Years** (Baldwin Street Music 306). Bailey is heard still singing with optimism and in her little girl's voice while accompanied by the Ellis Larkins Trio, Norvo's group, and a jam session band in 1949. "I'll Close My Eyes," "You Started Something," and "More than You Know" are among the highlights. But starting in 1947, Bailey (who was only 40 at the time) sang in public less and less.

Ella Fitzgerald Ella Fitzgerald, who turned 28 in 1945, grew in stature during the next five years. Already a superior ballad interpreter and a natural swinger with a highly appealing (and always in-tune) voice, Ella really learned how to scat during this period, particularly during a tour with the Dizzy Gillespie Orchestra. On such recordings as "Flying Home" (October 4, 1945), "Lady Be Good" (March 19, 1947), and "How High the Moon" (December 20, 1947), she was so inventive in her choice of notes and so joyful in her swinging that it was obvious that no one was on her level. How could anyone swing more than Ella?

Norman Granz became Ella's manager in 1947, she began touring with "Jazz at the Philharmonic," and in 1948 she married bassist Ray Brown, a marriage that lasted only four years. ❍ **The War Years** (GRP/Decca 628) is a two-CD set containing most of Ella's most significant recordings of 1941–47, including "Cow Cow Boogie," "Into Each Life Some Rain Must Fall," "Flying Home" (although strangely enough just the alternate take), "Stone Cold Dead in the Market" (with Louis Jordan), "For Sentimental Reasons," "Lady Be Good," and two takes (both alternates!) of "How High the Moon." Those listeners who just want the master take of everything Ella did during this era will instead opt for **1941–1944** (Classics 840, which is reviewed in the previous chapter), **1945–1947** (Classics 998), and **1947–1948** (Classics 1049). **1945–1947** includes some rare Ella V-discs, while **1947–1948**, which extends beyond **The War Years**, also has such numbers as "Robbins' Nest," "You Turned the Tables on Me," and a couple of songs from 1948 in which Fitzgerald is just backed by a vocal group. Considering that the music on **1949** (Classics 1153) was recorded at the height of the bebop era, the complete absence of bop on these 21 performances is quite surprising. Ballads and bluesy pieces alternate with a few swing-oriented numbers, and the arrangements (for the orchestras of Sy Oliver, Gordon Jenkins, and Sonny

Burke) are often closer to middle-of-the-road pop music than to jazz. Ella is in prime voice as usual on such numbers as "Old Mother Hubbard," "Happy Talk," "Black Coffee," "In the Evening," and "Baby It's Cold Outside" (a charming version with Louis Jordan), imitating Louis Armstrong a bit on "Basin Street Blues."

By the end of 1949, Ella Fitzgerald had come a long way toward becoming America's "First Lady of Song."

Billie Holiday　While the evolution of Ella Fitzgerald's career was logical and smooth, Billie Holiday hit a lot of rough waters during the second half of the 1940s. Things looked bright at first. Lady Day signed a contract with the Decca label in 1944 and immediately recorded her biggest seller, "Lover Man." Her voice was at its peak and she was becoming well known beyond the jazz world. In 1946, she appeared in her only Hollywood film, *New Orleans*. Although she was not happy about having to play a maid (a typical role for a black woman), she was delighted to get to appear opposite Louis Armstrong, one of her early idols.

But by then, Holiday was a heroin addict and her personal life was becoming a mess. In May 1947, Lady Day was busted for possession of heroin and spent a year in jail, which ironically increased her celebrity status. Due to her conviction, she lost her cabaret card and was never permitted to perform in a New York club again, although she was able to sing at concerts, including her comeback appearance at Carnegie Hall. When she was free again, Holiday was in top health and clean for a time. She was arrested again in 1949 for possession, but it turned out that the drugs (opium) were not hers and she got off that time. However, all of this publicity gave Lady Day the image of being a self-destructive martyr, and many in her audience came to see her perform for nonmusical reasons, to view this notorious woman.

The two-CD set ◉ **The Complete Decca Recordings** (GRP/Decca 601) has all of her 1944–50 studio recordings. Holiday's voice rarely sounded better and highlights include definitive versions of such well-known pieces as "Lover Man," "Don't Explain," "Good Morning Heartache," "Easy Living," "My Man," "Tain't Nobody's Business If I Do," "Them There Eyes," "Now or Never," "Crazy He Calls Me," and "God Bless the Child" plus two vocal duets with Louis Armstrong. Although the jazz content is not as strong as on her earlier Columbia recordings (the groups are supportive rather than interactive) and Lester Young was no longer anywhere to be found, Billie Holiday is heard at her very best throughout. If only she could have stayed at this level for another decade.

Lena Horne　Because of her physical beauty and versatile singing style, Lena Horne had moved beyond the jazz world by the late 1940s. She was frustrated by the way Hollywood misused her (casting her in films and then just having her sing one or two songs that could easily be cut out), never giving her a real role in a white film. However, her singing career worked out well. **The Original Black and White Recordings** (Simitar 56782), recorded in 1946, has Horne interpreting 17 jazz standards fairly straight but with a light and happy swing. She interprets the lyrics winningly, and such players as Gerald Wilson, Willie Smith, Tyree Glenn, and Lucky Thompson take solos, making this one of her very few jazz sets. But otherwise, Lena Horne was heading toward a career in middle-of-the-road pop music, so this CD can be viewed as a farewell to her roots in jazz.

Helen Humes　Helen Humes, who sang with the Count Basie Orchestra during 1937–41, had a solid solo career. Her blues-oriented singing and joyful renditions of ballads allowed her to cross over to an R&B audience, and in 1947 she toured with Dizzy Gillespie's big band. **1927–1945** (Classics 892) starts out with the unusual recordings that she made in 1927 as a 13- and 14-year-old. She later claimed that she had no idea what the words in the ten risqué blues meant! Otherwise, Humes is featured during 1941–45 with a sextet that includes Pete Brown and Dizzy Gillespie (unfortunately the trumpeter has no solos), a septet with trumpeter Bobby Stark (the former Fletcher Henderson star's last recordings), and five numbers (including "He May Be Your Man" and "Be-Baba-Laba") with pianist Bill Doggett's octet. **1945–1947** (Classics 1036) finds Humes really entering her prime on such tunes as "See See Rider," "Be Baba Leba Boogie," "If I Could Be with You," "Jet Propelled Papa," and "They Raided the Joint," assisted along the way by Buck Clayton, Willie Smith, and Edmond Hall.

Julia Lee　Julia Lee had previously appeared on record in 1927 and 1929 with her brother George E. Lee's Singing Orchestra in Kansas City, and on two selections of her own in 1929. A strong swing pianist and an appealing singer who became known for her double-entendre songs, she worked regularly as a single in Kansas City. In 1944, she began recording for the Capitol label, an association that continued through 1952. The two-CD set ◉ **Julia Lee and Her Boyfriends** (JSP 3405) has the master takes of all of her recordings from 1944–1947 and shows why she was such a popular entertainer. Lee's vocals are quite enjoyable and particularly cute when she slyly refers to "naughty" activities. Her piano playing is solid, and she features many top Kansas City musicians of the era plus tenor saxophonist Henry Bridges, trumpeter Karl George, Vic Dickenson, Red Norvo (making a rare appearance on xylophone in 1947), Red Nichols, and Benny Carter. Carter, who often denied that he ever recorded on trombone, is clearly heard on that horn (which must have been about his fifth best instrument) trading off with Vic Dickenson on "Crazy World" and soloing on "All I Ever Do Is Worry." Typically, Carter sounds excellent. Other highlights of the two-fer include "Lotus Blossom," "A Porter's Love Song to a Chambermaid," "Snatch and Grab It," "King Size Papa," and "The Spinach Song."

Julia Lee set the standard for female singer/pianists during the era.

Peggy Lee   Peggy Lee (born Norma Egstrom) became well known during her stint with Benny Goodman (1941–43), which culminated in her hit "Why Don't You Do Right." After marrying guitarist Dave Barbour, she retired for a year to be a housewife, but a contract with Capitol (starting in December 1944) and the urging of friends resulted in her returning to singing. Lee, who had a small voice and a cool-toned musical personality, immediately regained her popularity and built upon it. "Mañana" (from November 25, 1947) was a hit, Lee was a constant on the radio, and her records (which were sometimes jazz-oriented) were steady sellers.

Lee's best records of the era were her radio transcriptions for Capitol, which have only been made available on the five-CD limited-edition box set **The Complete Peggy Lee & June Christy Capitol Transcription Sessions** (Mosaic 5-184). Luckily, the single disc **With the Dave Barbour Band** (Laserlight 15 742), which has her singing 14 songs with a combo for MacGregor radio transcriptions, is available at a budget price.

Anita O'Day   Anita O'Day, who was one of the stars of the 1941–43 Gene Krupa Orchestra, sang with Stan Kenton during 1944–45 and had a second stint with Krupa in 1945 (singing "Opus No. 1" and "Boogie Blues"). Because she was much more committed to jazz than many of the former band singers (and she adapted well to bebop), O'Day recorded only for small labels during 1947–50, cutting ten selections for Bob Thiele's Signature label in 1947 (including "What Is this Thing Called Love," "Hi Ho Trailus Boot Whip," and "How High the Moon"). The CD **The Complete Recordings 1949–1950** (Baldwin Street Music 302) has four songs from a 1945 radio show, five radio transcriptions from that year in which O'Day is backed by the King Cole Trio, and all of her studio recordings of 1949–50 (for Gem and London). Best are "Them There Eyes" and "You Took Advantage of Me" although most of the novelties (other than the annoying "Yea Boo") are also reasonably enjoyable. O'Day, who would never have the commercial success of June Christy and Peggy Lee (both of whom she inspired to an extent), was nevertheless rated quite high in jazz circles.

Kay Starr   After leaving Charlie Barnet's orchestra in 1945, Kay Starr signed with Capitol, worked as a single and showed that she was a versatile performer, equally comfortable with swing, pop, and even country music. **The Complete Lamplighter Recordings 1945–1946** (Baldwin Street Music 305) has Starr in jazz settings with Barney Bigard, Vic Dickenson, and Willie Smith. Still in her early twenties, Starr is enthusiastic as she interprets swing standards with class and joy. Also on this valuable CD are her broadcast appearance with Bob Crosby from 1939 ("Memphis Blues"), two songs with Wingy Manone (1944), three with Charlie Barnet, and a couple of outings in 1947 with Barney Kessel's group. The two-CD set **Best of the Standard Transcriptions** (Soundies 4124) has Starr accompanied by orchestras led by either Buzz Adlam or Dave Matthews, or in combos that include her former boss Joe Venuti and Les Paul. Kay Starr is heard throughout in her early prime, uplifting such numbers as "What Can I Say After I Say I'm Sorry," "Honeysuckle Rose," "There's a Lull in My Life," "Them There Eyes," "The Best Things in Life Are Free," and "Down Among the Sheltering Palms."

Maxine Sullivan   No longer closely tied to John Kirby, Maxine Sullivan maintained a successful solo career during the second half of the 1940s although she did not repeat the commercial success of "Loch Lomond."

Ruban Bleu Years: Complete Recordings 1944–1949 (Baldwin Street Music 303) fully covers the period for the gentle and lightly swinging singer, who would be a subtle influence on later generations of vocalists. There are 18 numbers in the studios with string groups, Larry Johnson's Orchestra, or Ellis Larkin's trio. In addition, she is heard as a guest with Teddy Wilson's sextet, Benny Carter's big band, and (on the radio) Jimmie Lunceford's orchestra. Highlights include appealing versions of "Every Time We Say Goodbye," "Mad About the Boy," "Skylark," "Taking My Time," "Legalize My Name," and remakes of "Loch Lomond" and "If I Had a Ribbon Bow."

Mel Tormé   Mel Tormé's career as a singer really got going during the second half of the 1940s even though he had sung in public as early as 1929, when he was four! In 1941–42, Tormé played drums and sang with an orchestra put together by Ben Pollack for Chico Marx. He wrote "The Christmas Song" in 1944; it would be a hit for Nat King Cole two years later. Tormé made his initial impression leading the vocal group the Mel-Tones, recording several numbers with Artie Shaw in 1945, including a catchy rendition of "What Is this Thing Called Love." A swing rather than bop singer who was an expert scatter from near the beginning of his career, Tormé recorded a wide variety of material for Musicraft (1945–47) ranging from swing standards to current pop and Broadway show tunes. **Spotlight on Mel Tormé** (Capitol 89941) has his better Capitol recordings of 1949–51, including a wild "Oh, You Beautiful Doll," "Stompin' at the Savoy," "Blue Moon," a spirited "Sonny Boy," and "You're a Heavenly Thing" (on which Tormé plays piano in a quartet with Mary Osborne).

Big Joe Turner   Big Joe Turner developed his singing style in Kansas City in the 1930s and saw no reason to change his approach through the decades. Fortunately for him, his ability to shout out the blues and his musical personality easily fit into a lot of different idioms. When bebop rose to prominence, he essentially ignored it; his singing fit into the R&B field more naturally anyway. **1946–1947** (Classics 1034) is partly a throwback to Turner's recordings of five years earlier since he is joined on some numbers by Pete Johnson (including the two-part "Around the Clock Blues") or Albert Ammons, and among the 23 selections are remakes of

"Roll 'Em Pete" and "Nobody in Mind." However, the heated riffing combos were very much of the period and Turner's singing is typically timeless. **1947–1948** (Classics 1094) has Turner's recordings for National, Savoy, EmArcy, RPM, and Downbeat, recorded in Chicago (Meade Lux Lewis is on one session) and in Los Angeles including at a spirited "Just Jazz" concert. Big Joe Turner's singing was never out of style.

Dinah Washington   Dinah Washington had surprisingly few chances to record while with Lionel Hampton's Orchestra (1943–46) other than her debut session, which resulted in "Evil Gal Blues." However, she was such a popular attraction with Hamp that, when she went solo in 1946 (at the age of 21), Washington was a hit from the start. **Mellow Mama** (Delmark 451) has her dozen recordings from 1945 for the Apollo label, excellent jazz performances on which she is joined by Lucky Thompson, Karl George, Milt Jackson, and Charles Mingus among others. The music (12 cuts and just 34 minutes of material) is mostly good-humored blues plus "My Voot Is Really Vout" and "No Voot, No Boot."

Signed to Mercury in 1946, Dinah Washington recorded steadily and was a constant on the R&B charts. **The Complete Dinah Washington on Mercury, Vol. 1** (Mercury 832 444), a three-CD set, has all of her recordings from 1946–49. The music ranges from jazz and spirited blues to middle-of-the-road ballads, with plenty of gems and a few duds. Washington is joined by a variety of backup groups, including orchestras led by Gerald Wilson, Tab Smith, Cootie Williams, Chubby Jackson, and Teddy Stewart plus a dozen strong numbers with just a rhythm section. Among the highlights of this perfectly constructed reissue are "Oo Wee Walkie Talkie," "A Slick Chick on the Mellow Side," "I Want to Be Loved," "Mean and Evil Blues," "Record Ban Blues," and "Good Daddy Blues."

Dinah Washington in time became one of the major influences on young black female singers. Although admiring Bessie Smith and Billie Holiday, she sounded quite original from the beginning.

Jimmy Witherspoon   Jimmy Witherspoon, like Big Joe Turner, had a blues-oriented style that fit into many genres through the years. He caught the tail end of the swing era, singing with Jay McShann during 1944–47 and having a hit version of "'Tain't Nobody's Business If I Do" in 1949. Despite getting first billing on **Jimmy**

Witherspoon & Jay McShann (1201 Music 9031), 'Spoon is actually only on 11 of the 24 selections (including two versions of "'Tain't Nobody's Business"). McShann is the real leader of these Los Angeles recordings, and his bands perform swing blues, early R&B, and light touches of bebop. Among the many musicians heard from are the young trumpeter Art Farmer, his twin brother, bassist Addison Farmer, and tenor saxophonist Maxwell Davis. Witherspoon is in excellent form and there are also fine vocals from Lois Booker, Maxine Reed, and Crown Prince Waterford.

Small-Group Swing During the Bebop Era

The rise of bebop forced most of the top swing soloists to at least partly re-evaluate their styles. Musicians such as Roy Eldridge, Coleman Hawkins, and Benny Carter, who had been considered among the most advanced of all improvisers, had to decide whether to update their playing to keep up with the beboppers or stay the same and risk being considered behind the times. Many musicians who had formerly been soloists with big bands now had to either perform with small combos, go into the studios (if they were white and technically skilled), or drop out of music altogether.

The John Kirby Sextet Bassist John Kirby faced a dilemma in 1945. His sextet, which had been so original in 1938, was in serious trouble. Because the arrangements were tricky and depended on a unique blend between trumpeter Charlie Shavers, clarinetist Buster Bailey, and altoist Russell Procope, it was very difficult to find suitable replacements when musicians departed. Shavers was permanently gone, playing with the NBC Orchestra in 1944 and joining Tommy Dorsey's Orchestra in 1945. Emmett Berry, Clarence Berenton, and George Taitt did their best to fill in for Shavers, but none had both his virtuosity and willingness to play muted as part of the ensemble. Procope, after serving in the military and having a reunion with Kirby, joined the Duke Ellington Orchestra in 1946, so he was lost too. Buster Bailey was loyal and Bill Beason was a fine replacement on drums for the late O'Neill Spencer, but pianist Billy Kyle joined Sy Oliver's short-lived big band in 1946.

1945–1946 (Classics 964) has the John Kirby Sextet's final recordings. Altoists George Johnson and

Hilton Jefferson fill in for Procope on some numbers, Budd Johnson makes the group a septet on six songs, Ram Ramirez and Hank Jones are sometimes in Kyle's spot, and there are vocals on four selections by Sarah Vaughan and Shirley Moore on two. Despite the turnover, the group's sound had not changed and there are some colorful arrangements along with a lot of remakes, but the public was no longer interested in the group. In 1947, Kirby's dream dissipated and his sextet passed into history.

The King Cole Trio In 1945, Nat King Cole was best known as a pianist who sang and led a very popular trio that also featured guitarist Oscar Moore and bassist Johnny Miller. During the next six years his musical career would completely change. Before it did, Cole appeared in a variety of jazz settings, including the first "Jazz at the Philharmonic" concert in 1944 and with all-star groups arranged by the Capitol label. **Jazz Encounters** (Capitol 96693) has many of his most interesting dates away from his trio. Cole is heard (mostly as a jazz pianist) with the 1947 Metronome All-Stars, the Capitol International Jazzmen, backing Jo Stafford, collaborating with Nellie Lutcher, singing the bizarre "Mule Train" with Woody Herman, and joyfully sharing "Save the Bones for Henry Jones" with Johnny Mercer.

The King Cole Trio appeared regularly at clubs and on the radio during 1945–48. **Straighten Up and Fly Right** (Vintage Jazz Classics 1044) has a variety of radio appearances (including guest shots on shows hosted by Bing Crosby, Perry Como, and Frank Sinatra), with Sinatra backed by the trio on "I've Found a New Baby" and "Exactly Like You." **Live at the Circle Room** (Capitol 21859) features the trio in top form in September 1946, playing 17 numbers including four instrumentals; these performances were released for the first time in 1999.

In 1947, Oscar Moore left the group (partly due to an argument over money and partly to join his brother Johnny Moore's Three Blazers), replaced by Irving Ashby who had a similar style. **The King Cole Trios: Live 1947–48** (Vintage Jazz Classics 1011) has five of the band's radio shows for NBC during 1947–48. Such guests as singer Clark Dennis, the Dining Sisters, Pearl Bailey, Woody Herman, and Duke Ellington are heard on a song apiece, but otherwise the spotlight is on the trio. The performances are mostly quite brief (sometimes just two minutes) with Cole making every note count.

But things were changing for Nat King Cole. In 1946, his recordings of Bobby Troup's "Route 66," "For Sentimental Reasons," and Mel Tormé's "The Christmas Song" became very popular. In 1947, he recorded "Nature Boy" with an orchestra and, when it was released in 1948, it became a No. 1 hit. Although he still performed regularly with his trio (which by 1949 had Joe Comfort succeeding Johnny Miller on bass and Jack Costanzo added on bongos), his singing was now the main attraction, and the days of the King Cole Trio were numbered.

Page Cavanaugh, Soft Winds, and Charles Brown
The King Cole Trio made the sound of a piano-guitar-bass combo quite popular. In addition to Art Tatum (who often used Tiny Grimes and Slam Stewart during 1944–45), three other similar trios were active during the second half of the 1940s.

Pianist/singer Page Cavanaugh played early on with the Ernie Williamson band (1938–39). While serving in the military he met guitarist Al Viola and bassist Lloyd Pratt. After their discharge, they formed a trio in the Los Angeles area and became quite popular locally. Their musical interplay and whispered group vocals made them a hit for a time, recording best-selling records of "The Three Bears," "Walkin' My Baby Back Home," and "All of Me," and appearing in several movies, including *A Song Is Born* and *Romance on the High Seas*. Unfortunately, the Page Cavanaugh Trio's records (for Victor, ARA, Matt, and Signature) have not been reissued on CD yet. By 1950, Viola had left the group to become a studio musician and eventually work with Frank Sinatra, Pratt had slipped away into obscurity, and Cavanaugh was leading a different quartet in Los Angeles.

In 1946, three members of Jimmy Dorsey's rhythm section (guitarist Herb Ellis, pianist Lou Carter, and bassist Johnny Frigo) broke away to form their own trio, Soft Winds. They recorded 16 titles for Majestic and Mercury in 1947 and 1949 and are credited as co-writers of "Detour Ahead" and "I Told Ya, I Love Ya, Now Get Out" (though Frigo later claimed that he was those songs' only composer). As with the Page Cavanaugh Trio, Soft Winds' recordings have not been reissued, although in 1996 Frigo persuaded producer Hank O'Neal of Chiaroscuro to release 13 of the group's radio

transcriptions from 1947–48, including "Perdido," "Undecided," "All the Things You Are," and "The Way You Look Tonight." The two-CD set, ⬤ **Then and Now** (Chiaroscuro 342) also has a full disc of the Soft Winds' reunion in 1995, with Frigo now on violin (on which he made his mark in later years) and Keter Betts making the group a quartet on bass. A 16-minute "Jazzspeak" in which the three Soft Winds members talk with humor about the group's history wraps up this definitive release.

Another popular piano-guitar-bass trio of the late 1940s was Johnny Moore's Three Blazers. Although guitarist Moore got first billing, the real star of the group was pianist/singer Charles Brown, who was often mistaken for Moore by the public. The band (which also had bassist Eddie Williams) was together during 1943–48 and recorded steadily, particularly after Brown's "Driftin' Blues" in 1946 became a major hit. They also recorded the pianist's popular "Merry Christmas Baby" the following year and were quite popular on the R&B circuit. Charles Brown's **1944–1945** (Classics 894) has the Three Blazers' first recordings and more variety than usual with eight instrumentals, Oscar Moore on second guitar on some numbers, and a couple of guest vocalists including Frankie Laine. The 21st selection on the CD is "Driftin' Blues." **1946** (Classics 971) mostly has songs in the same slow blues ballad vein as "Driftin' Blues" so a certain sameness sets in after awhile. Best are "Rocks in My Bed," "What Do You Know About Love," "You Showed Me the Way," and "More Than You Know." **1946–1947** (Classics 1088) also emphasizes slower tempos and Brown's vocals. Highlights include the original version of "Merry Christmas Baby," "Was I to Blame for Falling in Love with You," "Huggin' Bug," "St. Louis Blues," "Juke Box Lil," and "New Orleans Blues." On **1947–1948** (Classics 1147), Oscar Moore (Johnny Moore's brother) was now a permanent member of the group and the band was varying its tempo a bit more, having given up attempts to duplicate "Driftin' Blues." Brown has vocals on every cut but the instrumental "Scratch Street."

In 1948, Brown finally left the Three Blazers and went out on his own. **1948–1949** (Classics 1210) consists of his first 24 records as a leader, heading a trio with Chuck Norris or Tiny Mitchell on guitar and bassist Eddie Williams. The music (which includes nine previously unreleased performances) was recorded for Aladdin and includes the hits "Trouble Blues" and "Get Yourself Another Fool." Once again, the emphasis is on the same medium-slow tempo, falling as much into the area of laidback blues as jazz. Charles Brown, initially influenced by Nat King Cole, himself became a strong influence on Amos Milburn, Floyd Dixon, and the young Ray Charles, continuing to have hits into the early 1950s.

Buck Clayton   Buck Clayton was one of the stars of the Count Basie big band during 1936–43, appearing on many records (including with Billie Holiday and Teddy Wilson) and contributing arrangements and compositions to the Basie book. He often used a cup mute during his solos and was known for his lyrical style, but Clayton could also hit high notes when he wanted. Drafted in November 1943, Clayton played with service bands while in the military. After he was discharged in 1946, he worked with "Jazz at the Philharmonic" and had his own small groups. **The Classic Swing of Buck Clayton** (Original Jazz Classics 1709) has three different sessions featuring Clayton that were originally recorded by the H.R.S. label. The trumpeter heads an octet with both Trummy Young and Dickie Wells on trombones, leads a pianoless quartet that also includes clarinetist Scoville Brown, Tiny Grimes, and bassist Sid Weiss, and is heard as a sideman (along with Buster Bailey) with Trummy Young's septet. Swing may have been going out of style, but these musicians were all still playing as creatively as ever, showing that the best jazz is always timeless. Besides, most of the musicians were still only in their thirties.

During 1949–50, the trumpeter toured France, where his swing style was still greatly appreciated. **Buck Clayton in Paris** (Vogue 68358) has two sessions from 1949 and one from a later tour in 1953. Clayton is heard in a sextet with Don Byas, a nonet that includes Bill Coleman and Alix Combelle, and a 14-piece group led by Combelle. In addition to his fine trumpet playing, Clayton contributed six originals and the great majority of arrangements to these rare but very rewarding performances.

Roy Eldridge   The highly competitive Roy Eldridge found the bebop years to be a bit difficult. Accustomed to being the winner at jam sessions (although Charlie Shavers and Hot Lips Page gave him stiff competition), he was now consistently topped by the more advanced Dizzy Gillespie. "Little Jazz" was a key soloist with Artie Shaw's orchestra during 1945 (although he found it difficult to deal with the racial discrimination of the outside world), led an unsuccessful big band of his own in

1946, and in 1949 had a second stint with Gene Krupa. **1945–1947** (Classics 983) features Eldridge with his powerful big band, a few pickup groups, and on a radio broadcast with Flip Phillips. But despite some exciting moments (including a fine remake of "Rockin' Chair"), Eldridge's career seemed a bit aimless and uncertain by the late 1940s.

Hot Lips Page   Oran "Hot Lips" Page was a bit more used to leading the freelance life than Eldridge and he worked steadily in small groups during the era. **1946–1950** (Classics 1199) finds Page sticking to his swing/Dixieland/blues style. Other than one cut from 1946, the music is from 1947 and 1949–50. Hot Lips digs into four instrumentals and four vocals with a medium-size group in 1947 (including some previously unreleased numbers from a date for the King label). Page is also heard with other combos, on two numbers ("That Lucky Old Sun" and "I Never See Maggie Alone") with strings and a choir, and featured on a very successful four-song session in which he interacts vocally with Pearl Bailey. Their version of "Baby, It's Cold Outside" is classic. Other highlights along the way include "St. James Infirmary," "Fat Stuff," "Don't Tell a Man About His Woman," "The Hucklebuck," and "Ain't No Flies on Me." It does seem strange that Hot Lips Page's records did not sell better during this era for they are quite fun.

Jump for Joy (Columbia/Legacy 65631) is a more confusing release. Page is heard on 11 selections from 1947–50, seven of which duplicate music on **1946–1950** while the other four are either alternate takes or previously unknown. In addition, there are 11 selections from 1937 and 1939 with Pete Johnson and Big Joe Turner, Chu Berry, Teddy Wilson, and Billie Holiday, three of which were not out before. For completists only.

Rex Stewart   In December 1945, cornetist Rex Stewart ended his 11-year stint with Duke Ellington. After freelancing in New York, he spent October 1947–1950 overseas, recording in Europe and Australia. **1946–1947** (Classics 1016), after a quartet date with Billy Kyle, mostly documents Stewart's playing in Europe where he led a group that included trombonist Sandy Williams. The recording quality is sometimes erratic, and the music is occasionally an uncomfortable mixture of swing and bop although there are interesting moments along the way. **1947–1948** (Classics 1057) continues with Stewart's Paris band, has two numbers ("Night and Day" and

"Confessin'") with Django Reinhardt and also features Stewart jamming with tenor saxophonist Vernon Story and a French rhythm section. **1948–1949** (Classics 1164) also contains plenty of obscure music, featuring Stewart as a leader on dates recorded in Basel, Berlin, Paris, and London. Most of these performances are swing-oriented, although there are hints of bebop here and there along with bits of Dixieland. Stewart is heard with Vernon Story in a combo, featured with the Hot Club of Berlin, showcased in a medium-size group organized by pianist/arranger Claude Bolling, and as the only horn in a quintet, playing with plenty of spirit and wit.

Don Byas   Because the tenor sax was among the most popular of all instruments during the second half of the 1940s and it was expressive enough to be well utilized in rhythm and blues, tenor players who were not exploring bebop had more options than trumpeters and trombonists. In the case of Don Byas, one of the top tenor saxophonists of 1945, he cut short his chances of fame by choosing to move to Europe while on tour in 1946 with Don Redman's Orchestra. Before he left the United States, Byas recorded fairly extensively. **1945** (Classics 910) mostly features Byas in quartets (with Erroll Garner or Johnny Guarnieri on piano) in addition to a quintet with Buck Clayton. **1945 Vol. 2** (Classics 959), which includes "Byas-a-Drink" and "Byas'd Opinion," teams Byas with top-notch swing players (including Guarnieri, Garner, and Emmett Berry), playing with power and melodic invention. **1946** (Classics 1009) has the tenor's final American recordings and his

first date in France, quartet performances that really showcase his improvising. Despite it being the bebop era, Byas (who was harmonically advanced) still played in a swing style.

Because it was a much larger world in those days, once Byas relocated to Europe, he was almost completely forgotten in the United States despite the fact that he worked quite steadily. The recordings on **1947** (Classics 1073), which include such Americans as pianist Billy Taylor, Peanuts Holland, and Tyree Glenn (fellow sidemen with Redman's band) in addition to a variety of French players, alternate between swing standards and some bop tunes (including "Mad Monk," "Billie's Bounce," and "Red Cross"). Unfortunately, those recordings (made for Swing and Blue Star) rarely ever found their way to the United States.

Arnett Cobb   Arnett Cobb's stomping Texas tenor sound fell between swing and R&B. He began his career playing in Texas with Chester Boone (1934–36) and Milt Larkin (1936–42), making a strong impression while with Lionel Hampton (1942–47). Not afraid to step into the recently departed Illinois Jacquet's shoes, Cobb recorded "Flying Home No. 2" (which was the same as "Flying Home") with Hampton, making the song his own. His large tone and robust sound were always accessible, so when he left Hampton, Cobb's recordings were popular from the start. ◐ **Arnett Blows for 1300** (Delmark 471) has all of the tenor's pre-1950 recordings as a leader (except for four songs cut for the Hamp-Tone label). The music is consistently

TIMELINE 1948

A second Musicians Union recording strike makes records very scarce this year. • Ella Fitzgerald and Ray Brown get married. • Betty Carter joins Lionel Hampton's Orchestra for three years. • Bill Coleman permanently returns to Europe after an eight-year absence. • Chano Pozo is killed. • Tenor saxophonist Brew Moore moves to New York and plays with the Claude Thornhill Orchestra. • Darnell Howard joins Muggsy Spanier's Dixieland group for five years. • Tenor saxophonist Hal Singer has an R&B hit with "Cornbread," and its popularity forces him to leave the Duke Ellington Orchestra and go out on his own. • Clarinetist Albert Nicholas is featured with Ralph Sutton's Trio at Jimmy Ryan's. • Wingy Manone's memoirs *Trumpet on the Wing* is published. • A purposely corny version of "Twelfth Street Rag" recorded by trombonist Pee Wee Hunt and clarinetist Rosy McHargue for a Capitol date becomes a major hit, to the surprise of all. • Trombonist Frank Rosolino joins the Gene Krupa Orchestra. • Stan Hasselgard dies in a car crash. • Stan Kenton breaks up his orchestra. • Dizzy Gillespie's big band tours Europe. • "Nature Boy" is a major hit for Nat King Cole. • Cab Calloway, Earl Hines, and Andy Kirk break up their big bands. • Bunk Johnson retires. • The Miles Davis Nonet has its only gig at the Royal Roost.

exciting with Cobb's hot jump sextet including trumpeter David Page and trombonist Booty Wood, with two vocals from his old boss Milt Larkin. Such tunes as "Go, Red, Go," "When I Grow Too Old to Dream," "Cobb's Boogie," and "Still Flying" are among the 15 concise performances.

Arnett Cobb was a potential competitor of Illinois Jacquet's, but bad health (resulting in an operation on his spine) kept him out of action during much of 1948–49. He was able to make a comeback starting in 1950, but some of the initial momentum was gone.

Eddie "Lockjaw" Davis   In his early days, Eddie "Lockjaw" Davis was a honking and screaming tenor saxophonist with a warm if ferocious tone. He worked with the big bands of Cootie Williams (1942–43), Lucky Millinder, Andy Kirk, and Louis Armstrong, but was primarily based with his combo at Minton's Playhouse during 1945–52. **1946–1947** (Classics 1012) has Lockjaw's first 24 selections as a leader and such titles as "Afternoon in a Doghouse," "Hollerin' and Screamin'," "Red Pepper," "Licks-A-Plenty," "Leapin' on Lenox," "Minton's Madhouse," and "Ravin' at the Haven" give one an idea as to the passion of the music. Eight of the songs feature Fats Navarro in the frontline and other sidemen include Argonne Thornton, Bill DeArango, Denzil Best, and Al Haig.

Coleman Hawkins   One thing that Don Byas, Arnett Cobb, Eddie "Lockjaw" Davis, Illinois Jacquet, Ike Quebec, and Ben Webster all had in common was being strongly influenced by Coleman Hawkins's style and especially his tone. During 1944–47, Hawkins was in one of his many prime periods, enjoying the rise of bebop and the challenge of playing with younger musicians. In 1945, he went to Los Angeles with a quintet that included Howard McGhee, Sir Charles Thompson, Oscar Pettiford, and Denzil Best, playing music that fell between swing and bop. While McGhee chose to stay in L.A., Hawkins returned to New York where during the next few years he led record dates that featured such top modernists as Fats Navarro, Miles Davis, J.J. Johnson, Kai Winding, Allen Eager, Milt Jackson, Hank Jones, and Max Roach among others. No other musician from the swing era (with the possible exception of Mary Lou Williams) did more to help the beboppers. In addition, Hawkins toured with "Jazz at the Philharmonic" and in 1948 recorded "Picasso,"

the first unaccompanied tenor sax solo to be released. It had been preceded by 1945's "Hawk Variation," which was not put out for many years.

1945 (Classics 926) has the two-part "Hawk Variation," 15 numbers by Hawkins's group with McGhee (three of the six songs put out by the tiny Asch label and all of their selections for Capitol, including "Rifftide," "Stuffy," and "Bean Soup") and a few selections cut with a pickup band led by Big Sid Catlett. **1946–1947** (Classics 984) has Hawkins leading several all-star groups (with Charlie Shavers, Eager, Navarro, J.J. Johnson, Hank Jones, Milt Jackson, and Miles Davis) with the highlights including "Allen's Alley" (a fine showcase for Allen Eager), the advanced "I Mean You," "Bean and the Boys," and "Bean-A-Re-Bop." In addition, Hawkins is featured with the Esquire All-American Award Winners, with "Blow Me Down" (which has a remarkable Shavers solo) and "Dixieland Stomp" (a satirical jab at Dixieland) being most memorable. **1947–1950** (Classics 1162) includes "Picasso," the complex "Half Step Down, Please" (with Navarro), a small-group date with J.J. Johnson or Benny Green on trombone, a set in Paris, and a relaxed middle-of-the-road quintet session from 1950. For listeners who just want a taste of Hawkins during this era, **Hollywood Stampede** (Capitol 92596) has the tenor's dozen Capitol recordings with McGhee from 1945 plus a septet session from 1947 that has a couple of short solos from Miles Davis.

Being harmonically advanced and open to the innovations of bop resulted in Coleman Hawkins being quite busy during 1945–47, but things began to slow down a bit by the end of the 1940s. The rise in popularity of Lester Young's sound led some to mistakenly believe that Hawkins had somehow become old-fashioned. He would prove them wrong in the future.

Illinois Jacquet   The most popular tenor saxophonist of the 1945–49 period was Illinois Jacquet. His solo on Lionel Hampton's "Flying Home" in 1942 virtually launched R&B. His screaming on "Blues" from the initial 1944 "Jazz at the Philharmonic" concert gained a great deal of attention, and his uptempo romps with Count Basie during 1945–46 (including "Rambo," "The King," and "Mutton Leg") were major crowd pleasers. After leaving Basie, Jacquet formed a medium-size group that was quite popular (sidemen included J.J. Johnson, Leo Parker, and his older brother Russell

Jacquet, Emmett Berry, or Joe Newman on trumpet) and he took time off to occasionally tour with "Jazz at the Philharmonic."

All of Jacquet's recordings as a leader as a leader during 1945–50 were reissued on a four-CD Mosaic box set, which unfortunately is out of print. Some of the music is available (other than the alternate takes) on a pair of Classics discs. **1945–1946** (Classics 948) starts off with a two-part version of "Flying Home" and includes such jumping pieces as "Bottoms Up," "Illinois Stomp," and "Jacquet in the Box." **1946–1947** (Classics 1019) has more jams from Jacquet's group plus a big band session and appearances by Fats Navarro and Miles Davis along with the usual group. Such numbers as "Jumpin' at Apollo," "Blow, Illinois, Blow," and "Riffin' with Jacquet" are as exciting as they sound, and this CD also has the original version of a future standard that Jacquet co-wrote with Sir Charles Thompson, "Robbins' Nest." The next Jacquet Classics CD will undoubtedly include his three remaining Aladdin recordings before moving on to his Victor dates, but listeners may want to forego that release in favor of ◉ **The Black Velvet Band** (Bluebird 6571). The latter reissues all of Jacquet's Victor recordings of 1947–50, 18 colorful numbers that include some warm ballads and such stomps as "Jet Propulsion," "Riffin' at 24th Street," "Mutton Leg," and "Adam's Alley." Wrapping up the release is Jacquet's guest appearance with Lionel Hampton at the 1967 Newport Jazz Festival on "Flying Home."

Jacquet's extroverted playing and creative use of repetition during the climactic moments of performances were an inspiration for a generation of R&B tenors.

Ike Quebec   A warm tenor saxophonist who was particularly rewarding on ballads, Ike Quebec worked with the Barons of Rhythm in 1940 and played in combos during the next few years headed by Frankie Newton, Benny Carter, Coleman Hawkins, Hot Lips Page, and Roy Eldridge. He had a steady job with Cab Calloway (1944–51), in 1944 recorded popular versions of "If I Had You" and "Blue Harlem," and acted as an unofficial talent scout for the Blue Note label, helping to persuade Alfred Lion and Francis Wolff to record bebop and Thelonious Monk. Considering that Quebec stuck to swing throughout his career, it is ironic that he would help lead Blue Note away from recording his style of music.

1944–1946 (Classics 957) has five of Quebec's six record dates as a leader from this era, selections made for Blue Note and Savoy with such sidemen as Tiny Grimes, Jonah Jones, Tyree Glenn, Buck Clayton, and Johnny Guarnieri. In addition to "If I Had You" and "Blue Harlem," Quebec is in superior form on "Tiny's Exercise," "Sweethearts on Parade," "I Found a New Baby," and "Girl of My Dreams."

Ben Webster   A major fixture on 52nd Street during the years after he left Duke Ellington (1943–47), Ben Webster's style was unaffected by bebop even though he was reportedly amazed the first time he heard Charlie Parker. He used Bill DeArango and Al Haig on his lone record date as a leader in 1946 (DeArango was part of his band for a year) and made sideman appearances, but recorded relatively little during this era. After a bit of struggling, Webster rejoined Duke Ellington for a second stint (1948–49) before moving to Los Angeles for a spell. Some of his finest work was just a few years away.

Lester Young   For Lester Young, his period in the army during 1944–45 was the lowpoint of his life. He had been happy and felt somewhat protected while back with Count Basie's band (1943–44), but after he was drafted, he was subject to racism, framed on a drug charge, and spent time in a military prison. Unlike other musicians who were lucky enough to get to play in bands while in the army, Young spent virtually the entire period being harassed because of his race. An introvert who was sensitive to both beauty and ugliness, Young never really recovered emotionally from this experience.

However, those who enjoy simplifying jazz history and have claimed that Young's postwar playing showed an immediate decline due to his experiences are greatly mistaken. The two-CD set ◉ **The Complete Aladdin Sessions** (Blue Note 32787), which concentrates on the 1945–48 period except for a 1942 trio date with Nat King Cole and bassist Red Callender, has some of the greatest playing of Pres's career. On such numbers as "D.B. Blues" (the D.B. was short for "detention barracks"), "New Lester Leaps In," "Sunday," "Jumpin' with Symphony Sid" (the tenor's most famous original), "One o'Clock Jump," "Tea for Two," and "East of the Sun," Young sounds wonderful, still sporting his light tone (although it had darkened a little) and standing out from all of the other tenors. Also quite noteworthy is his 1946 recording for Clef, a trio date with Nat King Cole and Buddy Rich.

By the late 1940s, Lester Young was playing regularly with "Jazz at the Philharmonic" and leading a quintet that included boppish trumpeter Jesse Drakes, pianist Junior Mance, and drummer Roy Haynes. There was a growing sadness to his sound, but he was still in excellent form much of the time when he was not drinking excessively. And, after years of being a nonconformist with a sound of his own, Pres was becoming the idol of a new generation of tenor saxophonists who went out of their way to emulate him, including Stan Getz, Zoot Sims, Al Cohn, Brew Moore, and Allen Eager.

Albert Ammons, Pete Johnson, Meade Lux Lewis, and Jimmy Yancey While the rise of Bud Powell resulted in the great majority of younger pianists being strongly influenced by his new approach to playing piano, most of the veteran players continued improvising in their own timeless styles.

Boogie-woogie had hit its commercial zenith during 1939–42 and was considered passé by many by 1945. But while there were few new practitioners, Albert Ammons, Pete Johnson, Meade Lux Lewis, and Jimmy Yancey continued on without altering their playing. ◉ **1946–1948** (Classics 1100) has the last recordings of Albert Ammons. Most of the selections feature him with his Rhythm Kings, a four-piece boogie-woogie and blues-oriented rhythm section (with bassist Israel Crosby) that had the ability to turn virtually everything into boogie-woogie, including "The Sheik of Araby," "You Are My Sunshine," "Margie," and "When You and I Were Young Maggie." There was one particularly special date when the group was expanded to include Albert's son, the already major tenor saxophonist Gene Ammons.

Albert Ammons played at Harry Truman's inaugural ball in January 1949, but passed away later in the year at the age of 42.

Pete Johnson, who continued working with Big Joe Turner now and then, stayed busy during the second half of the 1940s. **1944–1946** (Classics 933) has eight formerly rare piano solos from 1944, five selections with a hot Kansas City octet that includes Hot Lips Page, Budd Johnson, and two vocals from the young Etta Jones, and eight intriguing numbers in which Johnson is joined by an additional musician on each track. "Page Mr. Trumpet" is an exciting outing for Hot Lips Page and other numbers showcase Albert Nicholas, J.C. Higginbotham, and Ben Webster.

In 1947, Johnson moved to Los Angeles for a couple of years. **1947–1949** (Classics 1110) mostly has the pianist featured with quartets (originally released by the Apollo, Modern, and Jazz Selection labels) plus a sextet (for Down Beat/Swingtime) that includes Maxwell Davis on tenor and altoist Jewell Grant. The music is both spirited and basic with the emphasis being very much on boogie-woogie and sometimes (such as on "Rocket Boogie '88") hinting a little at rock and roll.

Meade Lux Lewis, who primarily worked in Chicago and Los Angeles during this period, was off records altogether after 1944 until 1951 although his four numbers at a 1946 "Jazz at the Philharmonic" concert have been reissued. Jimmy Yancey was also not on records during 1945–49, playing locally on an occasional basis in Chicago and continuing to work as the groundskeeper at the Chicago White Sox's Comiskey Park.

Johnny Guarnieri A bit of a chameleon, Johnny Guarnieri in the mid-1940s often displayed the ability to emulate Teddy Wilson, Count Basie, Art Tatum, and Fats Waller. He had previously had important stints with Benny Goodman (1939–40) and Artie Shaw (twice during 1940–41), in addition to Jimmy Dorsey (1942–43) and Raymond Scott's orchestra at CBS. Guarnieri remained quite busy, working in the studios, appearing on 52nd Street and recording extensively with the who's who of swing (including Lester Young, Coleman Hawkins, Don Byas, Ben Webster, and Roy Eldridge). He led occasional sessions of his own. **1944–1946** (Classics 956) has three trio sets with either Slam Stewart or Bob Haggart on bass and Sammy Weiss or Cozy Cole on drums. The pianist also heads a quartet set with Don Byas and has Lester Young and Billy Butterfield as his sidemen on another occasion. **1946–1947** (Classics 1063) has Guarnieri as the main star in solos, a trio, and a quartet with guitarist Tony Mottola, primarily playing standards and also taking a pair of vocals that purposely sound a bit like Fats Waller.

Perhaps if Guarnieri had chosen to emulate Bud Powell too, he would have had more work in jazz instead of disappearing into the studios.

Eddie Heywood The Eddie Heywood Sextet, which by late 1944 consisted of trumpeter Dick Vance (who had replaced Doc Cheatham), Vic Dickenson, altoist Lem

Davis, bassist Al Lucas, and drummer Keg Purnell, was at the height of its popularity when it signed with Decca. **1944–1946** (Classics 1038) has a remake of their hit "Begin the Beguine," tightly arranged versions of such songs as "Blue Lou," "Please Don't Talk About Me When I'm Gone," and "Just You, Just Me," plus five tunes on which the group accompanies Bing Crosby. By the spring of 1946, Heywood's band (which was now a septet with two trombones) was being billed as his orchestra and the sextet's days in the limelight were over. **1946–1947** (Classics 1219) has six selections by the septet (best is "Temptation") and three songs on which the unit backs up the Andrews Sisters. The rest of this CD, which is from 1947, mostly has Heywood leading a more conventional trio (Peggy Mann has three vocals). Heywood also backs organist Roy Ross on "Jitterbug Waltz," leads a sextet on two songs, and accompanies Bob Eberly (Jimmy Dorsey's former singer) during two ballads.

Shortly after the recording that closes **1946–1947**, Eddie Heywood suffered from a sudden ailment that caused partial paralysis of his hands. He would not be able to play music again for three years.

Jay McShann Jay McShann was in the army for only a few months in 1944, but it was long enough that he had to break up his big band. When he was discharged, he put together a small group and settled in Los Angeles. While most of his sidemen were obscure, McShann was fortunate enough to have Jimmy Witherspoon as his new singer.

1944–1946 (Classics 966) first has McShann recording in Kansas City with some local talent (including Julia Lee on two vocals) and then leading his sextet in Los Angeles. Among the better selections are "Confessin' the Blues," "Hootie Boogie" (a trio feature), "Voodoo Woman," "I Want a Little Girl," and "Have You Ever Loved a Woman." McShann would continue recording in Los Angeles to the end of the decade, performing blues-oriented pieces that extended his brand of Kansas City swing into early R&B. The LP **The Band that Jumps the Blues** (Black Lion 30144) sums up the period well for McShann and deserves to be reissued on CD.

Art Tatum By mid-1945, the Art Tatum Trio (which would have a few reunions) had broken up. Tatum continued his career as a remarkable piano soloist. Although he was aware of Bud Powell and the other contemporary pianists, there was no need for him to "update" his style

because he was still far ahead of everyone! **1945–1947** (Classics 982) has Tatum's piano solos for the ARA and Victor labels plus quite a few V-discs. "Hallelujah," "Lover," "Indiana," and "Cherokee" are among the many standards that are explored.

On April 2, 1949, Tatum was recorded playing at the Shrine Auditorium in Los Angeles. ● **Piano Starts Here** (Columbia/Legacy 64690) features Tatum playing incredible versions of "Yesterdays," "I Know that You Know," and "Humoresque," really tearing into the keyboard. This essential release also has the four songs from his debut studio session from March 21, 1933, including the shocking version of "Tiger Rag" on which Tatum sounds like three pianists.

Also highly recommended is **The Complete Capitol Recordings, Vol. One** (Capitol 92866) and **The Complete Capitol Recordings, Vol. Two** (Capitol 92867). Each disc has ten of Tatum's piano solos for Capitol during 1949 plus four trio numbers with guitarist Everett Barksdale and Slam Stewart from 1952. Highlights include "Willow Weep for Me," "Dardanella," and "Melody in F" from the first disc, and "You Took Advantage of Me," "How High the Moon," and "Indiana" from the second.

Sir Charles Thompson Sir Charles Thompson, a perfect transition pianist between swing and bop, switched from violin to piano as a teenager. He worked early on with Lloyd Hunter's Serenaders (1937), Nat Towles, Floyd Ray, Lionel Hampton (1940), and the Lee and Lester Young band. Thompson appeared often on 52nd Street, wrote arrangements for Count Basie, Lionel Hampton, Fletcher Henderson, and Jimmy Dorsey, composed "Robbins' Nest" with Illinois Jacquet and was part of the Coleman Hawkins Sextet during 1944–45. Thompson also worked with Lucky Millinder (1946) and Jacquet (1947–48).

Takin' Off (Delmark 450) has all of the music from Sir Charles's first three sessions as a leader, all made for the Apollo label during 1945–47. The September 4, 1945, date teams together Charlie Parker, Buck Clayton, and Dexter Gordon on four songs, and there are also a pair of swing-oriented sets from 1947 with Joe Newman, Leo Parker, Taft Jordan, and Pete Brown. Thompson, who was always able to sound like Count Basie whenever he wanted to, shows that he was flexible enough to excel in bop, jump, and swing settings.

Mary Lou Williams Mary Lou Williams fits into several special categories. She was the top female jazz musician prior to 1970 (and possibly of all time), a major swing era arranger, and an underrated composer. In addition, she was just about the only swing era pianist to alter her style so she sounded like a modernist during the bop era; only Duke Ellington is comparable.

After leaving Andy Kirk's Orchestra in 1942, Williams married trumpeter Harold "Shorty" Baker and traveled with Duke Ellington's big band (Baker's new employer), contributing some arrangements including "Blue Skies." Williams's extensive recordings for Asch and Folkways during 1944–45 both looked backward to her stride roots and forward to the innovations of bebop. By then she had befriended both Thelonious Monk and Bud Powell and had become an encouraging force behind the scenes. Williams composed the 12-part "Zodiac Suite," was a member of Benny Goodman's short-lived bebop combo in 1948, and wrote "In the Land of Oo-Bla-Dee" for Dizzy Gillespie's big band.

1944 (Classics 814) features Mary Lou Williams as a piano soloist, heading a sextet with Frankie Newton, Vic Dickenson, and Edmond Hall, playing in a septet with Don Byas, and leading a trio with Bill Coleman and bassist Al Hall. The music is primarily swing with some adventurous moments. **1944–1945** (Classics 1021) has some spots for Coleman, Coleman Hawkins, and folk singer Josh White (on "The Minute Man") before featuring the studio version of "The Zodiac Suite" (seven piano solos, three duets with bassist Al Lucas, and two numbers that add drummer Jack "The Bear" Parker). Each of the latter's themes salute one sign of the zodiac and, although the individual pieces are not overly memorable, the overall effect is haunting and unprecedented for the time.

Town Hall: The Zodiac Suite (Vintage Jazz Classics 1035) features the suite performed by a big band, a symphony orchestra, and Ben Webster at a special concert on December 31, 1945. This version makes for a very interesting contrast with its studio counterpart, and the VJC CD also has a variety of Williams's compositions (including "Lonely Moments," "Roll 'Em," and an extended "Gjon Mill Jam Session") from the concert.

1945–1947 (Classics 1050) is a little more conventional but no less enjoyable. Williams performs nine numbers with an all-female quintet (which includes vibraphonist Marjorie Hyams and Mary Osborne) and

four with a trio (including "Hesitation Boogie" and "Humoresque"), jams with Kenny Dorham in a quartet, and performs "Lonely Moments" and "Whistle Blues" with a big band. Other than a septet date for the King label in 1949, this disc wraps up this period in Mary Lou Williams's lengthy and episodic career.

Teddy Wilson In contrast to Mary Lou Williams, who constantly evolved with the times, Teddy Wilson's swing piano style remained unchanged after 1935. He played with Benny Goodman off and on during 1944–46, worked on CBS radio, and recorded steadily for the Musicraft label during 1945–47. Even when appearing opposite Charlie Parker and Dizzy Gillespie on a classic Red Norvo session, Wilson sounded the same as he always did.

1942–1945 (Classics 908) starts off with the final recordings from Wilson's early 1940s sextet (which included Emmett Berry, Benny Morton, and Edmond Hall), has a V-disc from 1943 (with Hall and trumpeter Joe Thomas), and excellent combo dates with Charlie Shavers, Red Norvo, Buck Clayton, and Ben Webster. **1946** (Classics 997) features Wilson on some sparkling and melodic solos, an octet with Don Byas, and a drumless quartet with Charlie Ventura; Sarah Vaughan has four vocals along the way. **1947–1950** (Classics 1224) includes Wilson's final Musicraft recordings (quartets with Buck Clayton and trio numbers with singer Kay Penton) and a pair of his trio dates from 1950 for the Columbia label. All of Teddy Wilson's recordings are enjoyable enough, but they are so consistent that, by the end of the 1940s, a certain predictability and sameness was apparent. The pianist needed to be inspired, but unfortunately he continued mostly playing with very safe trios.

George Barnes, Tiny Grimes, and Les Paul While Charlie Christian was a major influence on all up-and-coming electric guitarists, inspiring most of them to play bop, the three covered in this section (while all electrified) stuck primarily to swing.

George Barnes was attempting to amplify his guitar as early as 1931. In 1938 when he was only 17, he was hired by NBC in Chicago to be a staff musician and he popped up on a variety of records (mostly by blues artists) during this period. After serving in the army (1942–45), Barnes returned to Chicago and studio work. A fine swing player who specialized in single-note solos, Barnes enjoyed rehearsing with an octet that included four non-improvising reed players who utilized clarinets, bass clarinets, an English horn, an oboe, flutes, and piccolo. This group recorded radio transcriptions and the two-CD set **The Complete Standard Transcriptions** (Soundies 4122) has their 48 performances. The music is witty, a bit off center (like Raymond Scott's work), and an excellent display for Barnes's guitar though it is a pity that the reed players did not get the opportunity to have a single solo.

Tiny Grimes was one of the first guitarists to be influenced by Charlie Christian. As a youth he played drums and worked as a pianist in Washington. In 1938, Grimes switched to electric guitar and in 1940 worked with The Cats and a Fiddle. During 1943–44, Grimes was a member of the Art Tatum Trio, doing his best to keep up with the remarkable pianist. For his first record date (September 15, 1944), Grimes used Charlie Parker in his quintet and the guitarist sang "I'll Always Love You Just the Same" and "Romance Without Finance." He led a session apiece in 1946 and 1947 using tenor saxophonist John Hardee and Trummy Young (on the first date). By 1948, Tiny Grimes was leading an R&B-oriented group, The Rockin' Highlanders, that featured tenor saxophonist Red Prysock.

Les Paul, "the wizard of Waukesha," always had a strong musical curiosity. He loved to improve things and, even if he did not technically invent the electric guitar, he was involved in quite a bit of its development. Paul began playing harmonica at eight, played banjo briefly, and then found his true voice on the guitar. As "Rhubarb Red," he performed in country music groups on the radio and made his recording debut in 1936, while playing jazz as Les Paul. In 1937 he formed a trio that landed a spot on the radio with Fred Waring's Pennsylvanians, an association that lasted until 1941. After a period freelancing, he moved to Hollywood in 1943 and formed a new trio that made some V-discs and radio transcriptions. Paul was part of the first "Jazz at the Philharmonic" concert (trading off with Nat King Cole in witty fashion on "Blues").

Les Paul built his own studio (partly sponsored by Bing Crosby) and recorded with Bing during 1944–45, including a popular version of "It's Been a Long Long Time." During 1944–47, his trio recorded in a variety of settings for Decca, sometimes backing pop singers and at other times being featured as an independent unit.

The Complete Decca Trios Plus (MCA 11708), a two-CD set, has Paul backing blues singer Georgia White, recording as Rhubarb Red, and featured on many swinging selections with his trio, some in back of Crosby, Helen Forrest, and the Andrews Sisters. It is a definitive set of Paul's jazz days.

In 1947, Les Paul experimented and created a version of "Lover" that had him playing eight overdubbed electric guitars, some recorded at different speeds; it was a hit for Capitol in 1948. A bad car accident in January 1948 put him out of action until late 1949 and almost resulted in the guitarist losing his right arm. When he returned, he began working with a country singer/guitarist named Colleen Summers whom he would soon marry and rename Mary Ford.

Django Reinhardt   When France was liberated in the summer of 1944, it was major news in the jazz world that Django Reinhardt was discovered alive and well. He jammed with American servicemen and began to record again. **1944–1946** (Classics 945) has Reinhardt featured with an orchestra, playing with the Glenn Miller All-Stars (which include Mel Powell, trumpeter Bernie Privin, and Peanuts Hucko on tenor), recording with an American big band, leading a new Quintet of the Hot Club of France with Hubert Rostaing, and on eight songs in his first reunion with Stephane Grappelli since 1940; "Liza" from the latter is really blazing. Grappelli, who had been playing in London in a group featuring George Shearing, moved back to France during this period.

Shortly after the Grappelli sessions, Reinhardt switched to electric guitar and made his only trip to the United States, going on tour with Duke Ellington. Unfortunately, it ended up being a disappointment. Ellington did not write anything special to feature Django (who was mostly just featured with the rhythm section), Reinhardt had thought he would be treated as a celebrity and instead most Americans had never heard of him, and he soon became homesick for France, returning at the tour's end after missing a few key concerts.

Back in Europe, Reinhardt struggled to reconcile his playing with bebop and with the electric guitar. **1947** (Classics 1001) has a session with Grappelli, a big band date, and a lot of music with Rostaing in their quintet. There are times during these sessions where Django sounds rhythmically awkward, where he seems to be struggling to find his own voice and to sound comfortable with the boppish arrangements. **1947 Vol. 2** (Classics 1046) shows that the Reinhardt-Rostaing group was quite popular, recording extensively during the era even though its performances are not as timeless or fresh as the Grappelli sessions of a decade earlier.

However, by 1949, Reinhardt had smoothed out his style and seemed to be entering a new prime. During January–February 1949, he had a marathon recording project with Grappelli in Italy with a local rhythm section, recording 65 selections. Twenty of the best are on **Djangology** (Bluebird 9988), which is comprised of swing standards and a few vintage originals, showing that the musical magic was still there. Sadly this would be the last time that Django Reinhardt and Stephane Grappelli recorded together, and the guitarist's days were numbered.

Red Norvo   After breaking up his big band in 1942, Red Norvo switched permanently to vibes from xylophone the following year. He led various combos for a couple of years, worked with Benny Goodman's big band and sextet (1944–45), divorced Mildred Bailey, and was with Woody Herman's First Herd in 1946. **El Rojo** (Definitive 11128) has most of the sessions that Norvo led during 1944–47, utilizing such sidemen as clarinetist Aaron Sachs, Teddy Wilson, Vic Dickenson, Kay Starr, Jimmy Giuffre, Dexter Gordon, Barney Kessel, Benny Carter, and Eddie Miller. The vibraphonist could fit comfortably into swing, trad, and bebop settings as he shows on these performances, which are highlighted by "Seven Come Eleven," "I'll Follow You," "Bop," and "Twelfth Street Rag."

Norvo moved out to Los Angeles in 1947 and by 1949 was putting together a new trio, one that matched his vibes with guitarist Tal Farlow and bassist Charles Mingus.

Big Sid Catlett   Big Sid Catlett, one of the top drummers of the swing era, was certainly one of the most versatile players of the mid-to-late 1940s. A professional since working with Darnell Howard in 1928, Catlett moved to New York in 1930 where he worked with Benny Carter (1932), McKinney's Cotton Pickers (1934–35), Fletcher Henderson, Don Redman, and the Louis Armstrong Orchestra (1938–42), in addition to a short unhappy stint with Benny Goodman (1941). Catlett was renowned for his ability to change patterns behind different soloists, always seeming to bring out

the best in his fellow players. A fixture on 52nd Street after leaving Armstrong, Catlett was quite credible recording with Dizzy Gillespie and Charlie Parker in 1945 and headed some dates of his own. **1944–1946** (Classics 974) has all of the sessions he ever led, including a quartet date with Ben Webster and small group swing sides with Charlie Shavers, Edmond Hall, Illinois Jacquet, Eddie "Lockjaw" Davis, Pete Johnson, and organist Bill Gooden. In 1947, Catlett switched gears altogether and joined the Louis Armstrong All-Stars.

Three New Swing Pianists

In addition to the veteran swing pianists, three new major players emerged in the mid-1940s, each of whom would have long careers playing in their own timeless style. Each was able to adapt to later musical trends while remaining themselves.

Erroll Garner   Bud Powell may have been the most important new pianist of 1945, but his was not the only way to play piano. Erroll Garner was so original that he created his own category. Garner's jubilant style (which often had his left hand strumming chords like a rhythm guitar while his right played a tiny bit behind the beat, giving the music an echo effect) was so accessible that he was a popular attraction throughout his career. He was always quite melodic yet unpredictable, playing such abstract introductions to songs that it was impossible to know what the tune would be, keeping his sidemen guessing. Garner also had the ability to sit at the piano and three hours later emerge with two or three full albums, all flawless first takes.

The younger brother of pianist Linton Garner, Erroll was completely self-taught and never learned to play music. He started playing piano at age three and four years later was appearing on the radio with the Kan-D Kids. Garner was a professional by 1937 (when he was 16), worked locally in Pittsburgh, and moved to New York in 1944. After a period as a member of Slam Stewart's trio (1944–45), he started his solo career, leading a trio and becoming very popular immediately.

Garner recorded many records during his career. During November–December 1944 he was documented extensively by Baron Timme Rosenkrantz practicing and stretching out at the baron's apartment. The music is spontaneous, some of the improvisations are pretty long (sometimes over ten minutes), and the performances (which were first released in the 1950s) were not originally supposed to come out. Garner actually does not quite sound like himself yet and some of his meandering solos are quite impressionistic. **1944** (Classics 802), **1944 Vol. 2** (Classics 818), and **1944 Vol. 3** (Classics 850) are filled with these solos plus **1944 Vol. 2** has Garner's first official studio sides. Oddly enough, the latter were originally solos; bassist John Simmons and drummer Doc West overdubbed their parts a few years later.

The "real" Erroll Garner emerges on **1944–1945** (Classics 873) and **1945–1946** (Classics 924). The former set has the pianist at a jam session with Charlie Shavers and Vic Dickenson that is a bit loose but humorous, along with four piano solos and four trio numbers originally put by the Black & White and Signature labels. **1945–1946** has 21 selections, most of which are from a ten-week period with all but four cuts being solos. This music was originally made for Savoy, Disc, Mercury, and V-discs and it includes Garner's first hit, his version of "Laura." **1946–1947** (Classics 1004), which has songs cut for Mercury, Victor, and Dial, features Garner really in his early prime, being particularly inventive on "Pastel," "Trio," "Erroll's Bounce," "Play, Piano, Play," and "Frankie and Johnny Fantasy."

While **1947–1949** (Classics 1109) starts out with some rarities and concert appearances featuring Wardell Gray, Benny Carter, and Howard McGhee, its second half consists of some of Garner's Savoy recordings. Better to get ❶ **The Complete Savoy Master Takes** (Savoy 17025-26), a two-CD set that has four songs from Garner in 1945, his four numbers with Slam Stewart from that year, and all of his trio performances from 1949 with bassist John Simmons and drummer Alvin Stoller. Despite the title of the release, Garner did not record any alternate takes for Savoy so all of his music for the label is here, including "Laura," "Penthouse Serenade," "Love Walked In," "All of Me," and "A Cottage for Sale."

Erroll Garner records are easy to recommend for he never played an uninspired chorus. He loved to play piano far too much.

Oscar Peterson Oscar Peterson at his prime had such remarkable technique that he was one of the few pianists whose name could be said in the same sentence with Art Tatum. Born in Montreal, Canada, Peterson began taking classical piano lessons when he was six (in 1931), and by the time he was 14 he had won a talent show and was being featured on a weekly radio show. Peterson worked with Johnny Holmes's big band in Canada as a teenager, and during 1945–49 he recorded 32 numbers for the Victor label with his early trio. **The Complete Young Oscar Peterson** (RCA 66609), a two-CD set, has all of those recordings. In piano-bass-drums trios (except one date that has guitar instead of drums), Peterson swings hard. His style was different than it would be, with a liberal number of boogie-woogie numbers plus the strong influence felt of Teddy Wilson and especially Nat King Cole. But his technique and ability to outswing everyone were already in place.

In 1949, producer Norman Granz, who was amazed once he started listening to Peterson (he had originally thought O.P. was just a boogie-woogie player), presented the pianist as a surprise guest at a "Jazz at the Philharmonic" concert, Peterson's American debut. It would not be long before Oscar Peterson would be a household name.

Andre Previn Andre Previn was never a full-time jazz pianist, but he has always been such a skilled musician that he was able to make a strong impression in jazz even while he was involved in other areas of music. Previn was born in Berlin in 1929 and had piano lessons before his family fled the Nazis in 1938. His family settled in Los Angeles where Previn worked as a jazz pianist, an arranger for MGM, and a recording artist for Sunset Records while he was still just 16 and in high school. **Previn at Sunset** (1201 Music 9029), from 1945–46, shows what a talented pianist Previn already was at the beginning of his recording career. A swing soloist, Previn is heard unaccompanied in three different trios and on a couple of jam tunes ("All the Things You Are" and "I Found a New Baby") with a sextet also including either Buddy Childers or Howard McGhee on trumpet, Willie Smith, and Vido Musso on tenor. The teenage pianist keeps up with the other players and really excels in these small group swing settings.

Jazz at the Philharmonic

Producer Norman Granz had such success with his original "Jazz at the Philharmonic" concert in 1944 that he decided to have regular tours, presenting an all-star jam session filled with swing and bop giants, recording the results even though 78s permitted only around three minutes of music per side. It was as if he were getting ready for the LP era. At first, Granz released some of the music split between sections (a 12-minute jam would take both sides of two 78s), leasing the music to other labels. In 1946, he had his own Clef label and, with the rise of LPs a few years later, he was ready.

"Jazz at the Philharmonic" (JATP) was presented at a few concerts later in 1944 and in 1945, soon expanding to annual tours in the spring and fall throughout the United States. Because Granz employed some of the most exciting tenor saxophonists around and they often generated a strong enthusiastic reaction from the audience when they used repetition and honked out notes, JATP was constantly criticized by overly serious jazz critics who felt that the music lacked all subtlety. Their sniping had little effect, for Granz's empire grew quickly and a great deal of rewarding music was presented. In addition, Granz paid his musicians quite well, and his championing of civil rights and integration led to some racial barriers coming down. He hired the best musicians around and treated them the way they deserved.

Among the many stars of JATP during 1945–49 were tenors Flip Phillips (whose solo on "Perdido" became famous), Illinois Jacquet, Coleman Hawkins, and Lester Young; trumpeters Roy Eldridge, Buck Clayton, Dizzy Gillespie, and Howard McGhee; trombonists Bill Harris and Tommy Turk; altoists Charlie Parker and Willie Smith; pianists Hank Jones and Oscar Peterson (who made his American debut at a 1949 concert); a variety of bassists (including Ray Brown); drummers Gene Krupa and Buddy Rich; and vocalists Billie Holiday (who toured with JATP in 1946) and Ella Fitzgerald. The music usually featured jams on fairly basic chord changes, a ballad medley, and some individual features.

The ten-CD set ◎ **The Complete Jazz at the Philharmonic on Verve 1944–1949** (Verve 314 523 8932) is remarkable, both in its quantity (including many previously unreleased performances) and quality. Highlights include "Blues" from the first JATP concert (with its screaming Illinois Jacquet solo), some of Billie Holiday's best live performances, Slim Gaillard's "Opera in Vout," Charlie Parker's perfect two choruses on "Lady Be Good," and "The Closer," with its Roy Eldridge/Jo Jones tradeoff and breathless Bird solo. One only wishes that Verve had come out with a similar set documenting JATP in the 1950s.

A concert that is not covered in the Verve set was first released in 2002 on **Carnegie Hall, 1949** (Pablo 5311).

This is a very different kind of JATP set because it is so boppish, with tricky melody statements and solos from Bird, altoist Sonny Criss, Flip Phillips, Fats Navarro, and Tommy Turk. In addition, there are four songs from a quintet comprised of Coleman Hawkins, Navarro, Hank Jones, Ray Brown, and Shelly Manne. The music is of consistent high quality even if it never quite explodes like the best JATP performances.

Metronome All-Stars While *Esquire*, which held special all-star concerts in 1944 and 1945, discontinued their annual jazz polls after 1946, *Metronome* (and *Down Beat*) continued having popularity polls throughout the 1940s and '50s. *Metronome* recorded the winners (and some runner-ups when the winners were not available) in many of the years during the 1940s.

In addition to the swing sessions covered in Chapter 5, ◎ **Metronome All-Star Bands** (Bluebird 7636) includes a January 1946 session that has a big band overflowing with all-stars who were mostly from the swing era (including Cootie Williams, Harry Edison, Tommy Dorsey, Johnny Hodges, and Teddy Wilson) plus a nucleus taken from Woody Herman's First Herd. The 1949 session is also here, with "Overtime" at one point featuring Dizzy Gillespie, Miles Davis, and Fats Navarro trading off, with all three of the trumpeters sounding like Dizzy. Charlie Parker, Kai Winding, J.J. Johnson, Buddy DeFranco, and Lennie Tristano are among those also heard from, so by 1949 the Metronome All-Stars were quite bop-oriented. **The Metronome All-Stars** (Tax 8039), an LP, has the all-stars' sessions for Columbia including a December 1946 set with Nat King Cole and June Christy singing "Nat Meets June" and an appearance by Frank Sinatra on "Sweet Lorraine." While that group is mostly from swing, the January 10, 1950, date that concludes this LP has Dizzy Gillespie, Kai Winding, Buddy DeFranco, Lee Konitz, Stan Getz, and Lennie Tristano among those playing "Double Date" and "No Figs." The Columbia Metronome All-Star sessions and the one from 1947 that was put out by Capitol ("Leap Here" and "Metronome Riff" with Gillespie, DeFranco, and Phillips joined by the Stan Kenton Orchestra) are long overdue to be made available again.

New Orleans Jazz

Bebop may have been the new thing during the second half of the 1940s, and the breakup of the swing era big bands might have been gaining most of the headlines, but the comeback of pre-swing jazz, known as New Orleans jazz to some and Dixieland to many, was a major movement. The 1920s, the image of which was scorned by many suffering during the Depression in the '30s, were considered nostalgic in the '40s, thought of as "the good old days." Some of the veterans of the era were still quite active, there was a small contingent of talented young musicians who preferred that music over bebop, and many of the big band veterans (who were suddenly "at liberty") saw Dixieland as an opportunity to make a living. It quickly became the most popular jazz style, with fans if not with critics. By 1949, it had largely split away from the mainstream of jazz (which was becoming bebop), developing into an independent world that only occasionally overlapped with the later styles.

Louis Armstrong   During the 1945–49 period, Louis Armstrong's career drastically changed. He had led a big band virtually nonstop since 1935 (and earlier during the 1929–33 period), but throughout the swing era, he was gradually falling behind the times. Armstrong's sidemen were given little chance to be creative and, when his big band's arrangements became a bit more modern during 1944–46, Satch sometimes seemed a little out of touch with his own orchestra's music.

In contrast, at the 1944 Esquire All-American concert, Armstrong was perfectly at home in an all-star combo that included such future sidemen as Jack Teagarden, Barney Bigard, and Big Sid Catlett. After barely recording during 1944–45, in 1946 Satch returned to the Victor label. That year he appeared in the film *New Orleans*, reuniting with his old boss Kid Ory and jamming with some small groups. Although the movie (which was Billie Holiday's only film) was greatly flawed, there were some fine jazz moments along the way. Critic Leonard Feather, who at the time of the Esquire concert felt that his friend Louis Armstrong should return to a small-group format, lobbied Satch although, typically, Armstrong stalled about breaking up his big band because he did not want to put his musicians out of work. However, after a few successful small-group sessions in 1946, it was clear what Armstrong should do.

These dates included the initial recording of "Do You Know What It Means to Miss New Orleans"; a February 8, 1947, Carnegie Hall concert in which the first half (which had Armstrong sitting in with Edmond Hall's sextet) was more successful than the second part (with his big

band); a guest appearance on Rudi Blesh's *This Is Jazz* radio program on April 26; and a May 17 Town Hall concert on which he led a septet with Bobby Hackett, Jack Teagarden, and clarinetist Peanuts Hucko. Finally he was persuaded to break up his big band. After appearing in the movie *A Song Was Born*, he formed the Louis Armstrong All-Stars, a sextet also including Teagarden (who had recently ended his period leading his own orchestra), Bigard, pianist Dick Cary, bassist Arvell Shaw, and Sid Catlett along with singer Velma Middleton.

The Louis Armstrong All-Stars' recorded concert at Symphony Hall on November 30 essentially launched the group. By the following February, with Earl Hines (another former bandleader now without an orchestra) on piano, the band scored a major success in France. From then on, Satchmo would be jazz's top attraction, traveling the world with his All-Stars and spreading the joy of jazz everywhere. Louis Armstrong may not have cared for bebop (he made a few unfortunate public remarks before making peace with the modernists), but he was now considered so timeless and such an icon that most listeners no longer compared him unfavorably with the pacesetters.

New Orleans (Jazz Crusade 3043) has most of the soundtrack from the 1946 film of the same name, including a great deal of rewarding music that did not make it into the movie. **The Complete RCA Victor Recordings** (RCA 68682), a four-disc set, has two CDs covering the 1932–33 period (which are discussed in Chapter 4). The last two discs contain a pair of selections with the Esquire All-Stars (including on "Snafu," an Armstrong solo that hints briefly at bebop, the closest he ever came), the final big band numbers, and such pre–All-Stars combo sides as "Sugar," "Do You Know What It Means to Miss New Orleans," and "Mahogany Hall Stomp." In addition, there are six numbers from the historic Town Hall concert (including the definitive versions of "Ain't Misbehavin'" and "Back O' Town Blues"), the June 10, 1947, session that directly preceded the All-Stars (highlighted by an Armstrong solo on "Jack-Armstrong Blues" that is arguably his finest on records in the 1940s), and the first official All-Stars studio session, along with two unrelated orchestra sides from 1956. Listeners wanting only the combo numbers and not the big band performances are advised to instead pick up the superior single CD ● **The 1940's Small-Band Sides** (Bluebird 6378), which has the 20 key performances from 1946–47.

Satchmo at Symphony Hall (GRP/Decca 661) consists of 15 of the 18 selections originally released on a two-LP set from the important concert including "Royal Garden Blues," "Muskrat Ramble," "On the Sunny Side of the Street," Teagarden's showcase on "Lover," and "High Society." Listening to the joy in this music, one can fully understand why the Louis Armstrong All-Stars became the most popular working band in jazz.

Sidney Bechet and Mezz Mezzrow In 1945, Sidney Bechet decided to try to make his longtime dream of forming an old-time New Orleans jazz band into a reality. He was booked into the Savoy Café in Boston and got his friend Bunk Johnson to play in the quintet along with bassist Pops Foster and a local pianist and drummer. Unfortunately, Bunk proved to be quite erratic in his playing, he hated having to cede the lead in the ensembles to Bechet (there was constant confusion over who should play the melody), and he drank excessively. Within a couple of months Bunk had drunk himself out of the band. His first replacement was 19-year-old cornetist Johnny Windhurst who fared quite well. Bechet, who had not heard of Windhurst previously, had already sent to New Orleans for veteran Peter Bocage (who had been with Armand J. Piron in the 1920s). Bocage, a laidback and gentle player who was a bit rusty, also did not work out, so Windhurst was rehired to finish the engagement before the group broke up. All of the music from this short-lived band (primarily radio broadcasts) was made available in the 1970s on a dozen Fat Cat LPs in their **Jazz Nocturne** series (Fat Cat's Jazz 001-012). More recently, the Jazz Crusade label on the five CDs **Jazz Nocturne 1-5** (Jazz Crusade 3038-3042) reissued all of Bechet's performances with Johnson and Bocage (which are interesting but very streaky), but not the much more rewarding dates with Windhurst.

Mezz Mezzrow, an erratic clarinetist and tenor saxophonist, briefly became a record company executive in 1945. He founded the King Jazz label and mostly featured himself playing the kind of music that he preferred: ensemble-oriented medium-tempo New Orleans blues and near-blues. Sidney Bechet is on most of the recordings, Hot Lips Page appears on several of the dates. Other musicians include Sammy Price (heard in a series of piano solos); blues singer Pleasant Joseph; pianists Fitz Weston and Sox Wilson; rhythm guitarist Danny Barker; bassists Pops Foster and Wellman Braud;

drummers Sid Catlett, Baby Dodds, and Kaiser Marshall (these were his final recordings); and singer Coot Grant. All of the spirited (if somewhat predictable) music, including many alternate takes, has been reissued on the two-CD set **King Jazz Vol. One** (GHB 501/502) and the three disc **King Jazz Vol. Two** (GHB 503/504/505).

The King Jazz label ceased operations after 1947. After appearing at the 1948 Nice Jazz Festival in France, Mezzrow permanently moved to Europe.

Bechet freelanced for the next few years, picking up jobs where he could and at one point deciding to become a jazz music teacher. Although he hoped to have a music school eventually, he attracted only one student, 18-year-old clarinetist Bob Wilber who became his protégé and a promising newcomer to the trad jazz scene. Bechet, who had a couple of opportunities to record with Wilber, in 1949 went to Paris to appear at the Salle Pleyel Jazz Festival. His emotional sound and Dixieland repertoire was such a big hit that he began to entertain thoughts of moving overseas.

1945–1946 (Classics 954) features Bechet on Blue Note in a sextet with Max Kaminsky and Art Hodes, on a few numbers from a studio date with Bunk Johnson (best is "Milenburg Joys"), a quintet set with clarinetist Albert Nicholas, and with Frankie Newton (on one of trumpeter's last recordings). **1947–1949** (Classics 1119) has an additional session with Mezz Mezzrow (plus James P. Johnson) that was released on the Wax rather than King Jazz label, Bechet's exciting set with Bob Wilber's Wildcats (a group of youngsters that includes pianist Dick Wellstood performing "Spreadin' Joy," "I Had It but It's All Gone Now," a remake of "Kansas City Man Blues," and "Polka Dot Stomp"), the beginning of an excellent quintet project with Wild Bill Davison, and eight songs that feature Bechet as the only horn in a quartet. The latter date reaches far beyond Dixieland with the soprano saxophonist performing emotional versions of such pieces as "Song of Songs," "Just One of Those Things," "Love for Sale," and "Laura."

The year 1949 was an especially busy one for Bechet, who recorded enough material as a leader to fill three additional CDs. In contrast to the quartet dates on **1947–1949, 1949** (Classics 1140) is primarily Dixieland with Bechet interacting with Wild Bill Davison, Art Hodes, Buster Bailey, Wilbur DeParis, and (on the final five songs) a group in France. The encounter with Davison is particularly interesting because, instead of the two combative horn players battling each other, Wild Bill is fairly restrained, letting Bechet take the lead when he wants to yet also letting loose an occasional fiery blast to inspire the great soprano player. **1949 Vol. 2** (Classics 1186) features Bechet at the crossroads of his career. After finishing the session in France and appearing at the Paris Jazz Festival, Bechet returned home to the United States where he recorded with Bob Wilber, Dick Wellstood, and a group of veterans. However, by the fall he was back in France and can be heard jamming with clarinetist Claude Luter's orchestra (including a popular version of "Les Oignons") and showcased in a sextet with Bill Coleman (who had preceded Bechet in becoming a permanent expatriate), tenor saxophonist Big Boy Goudie, pianist Charlie Lewis, bassist Pierre Michelot, and the always versatile Kenny Clarke. **1949 Vol. 3** (Classics 1223) has particularly intriguing music for, in addition to two Dixielandish dates with Luter's ensemble, Bechet is heard in London playing six songs with trumpeter Humphrey Lyttelton's band, and stretching out on eight quartet numbers in Paris with pianist Eddie Bernard, Michelot, and Clarke. It is in the latter setting that one can really appreciate how well rounded and powerful a soloist Bechet could be outside of the usual trad band.

Bunk Johnson For Bunk Johnson, the 1945–47 period was quite busy. He was back in New Orleans when he was contacted by Sidney Bechet to join his group in Boston. After a record date with the soprano saxophonist in New York, Bunk joined forces with Bechet until he drank his way out of the group. An alcoholic whose playing was inconsistent when he was drinking, Johnson had soon returned to New Orleans, appearing on records with his local group that featured clarinetist George Lewis, trombonist Jim Robinson, and Baby Dodds. **Bunk's Brass Band and Dance Band 1945** (American Music 8) starts off with the first-ever recording of a New Orleans brass band. Johnson heads a group consisting of two trumpeters (the other is Kid Shots Madison), Jim Robinson, George Lewis on the eerie E flat clarinet, Isidore Barbarin on alto horn, the baritone horn of Adolphe Alexander, Joe Clark on bass horn, Baby Dodds on snare drum, and Lawrence Marrero on bass drum. Unfortunately, the band (particularly Lewis) is so out of tune that it makes the music difficult to listen to. The second half of the disc has

more conventional performances by Bunk, Lewis, and Robinson in a spirited New Orleans jazz sextet, playing numbers such as "Runnin' Wild," "Old Kentucky Home," and "The Sheik of Araby." Much better overall is **Plays Popular Songs** (American Music 15). A dozen tunes feature Johnson's group with Lewis, Robinson, and Dodds, including such offbeat numbers as "I Don't Want to Walk Without You," "The Waltz You Saved for Me," and "You Always Hurt the One You Love." But the reason to acquire this CD is for the June 3, 1946, session that showcases Bunk in a trio with pianist Don Ewell (showing off the strong influence of Jelly Roll Morton) and drummer Alphonse Steele. Among the highlights are "In the Gloaming," "I'll Take You Home Again, Kathleen," "Beautiful Doll," and "Poor Butterfly."

Johnson returned to New York in the fall, taking along the Lewis-Robinson group. **1945–1946** (Document 1001) has the best recordings by this particular unit, collecting together Bunk's sessions for Decca and Victor plus two V-discs and eight alternate takes. Johnson and Lewis never sounded better together. Among the more exciting numbers on this CD are spirited ensemble-oriented renditions of "Maryland, My Maryland," an up-tempo "A Closer Walk with Thee," "When the Saints Go Marching In," and "Darktown Strutters Ball" plus the pair of V-discs ("I Can't Escape from You" and "Snag It"), which were recorded live and exceed five minutes apiece.

However, Bunk Johnson soon became frustrated with the primitive New Orleans players and in early 1946 he sent them back home. At the height of the bebop era, Bunk Johnson was thought of by some of the true believers of New Orleans jazz as a musical god from the past who was suddenly brought back to life playing "true jazz." In reality, Johnson quickly tired of some of his more fanatical fans, particularly since he actually enjoyed current pop tunes and did want to be stuck playing songs from 40 years earlier. In 1947, he went out of his way to play with swing musicians who were sympathetic toward his style. In December he had a group consisting of trombonist Ed Cuffee, clarinetist Garvin Bushell, pianist Don Kirkpatrick, Danny Barker, Wellman Braud (who had temporarily come back from retirement), and drummer Alphonse Steele. ◗ **Last Testament** (Delmark 225) was Johnson's final recording, and his best overall. Bunk is heard performing a wide variety of music, including folk songs, swing standards (such as "Out of Nowhere" and "You're Driving Me Crazy"), and some rags, including a memorable rendition of Scott Joplin's "The Entertainer." Heard at the top of his game, Bunk Johnson throughout this release shows why it was such a good thing that he was dragged out of retirement six years earlier.

In 1948, Johnson returned to his home in New Iberia, New Orleans, and suffered a stroke. He would never play again, passing away the following year. In contrast, George Lewis and Jim Robinson would soon emerge from their exile in New Orleans and gain greater fame than Bunk could have ever imagined.

Kid Ory and Mutt Carey The successful appearances of Kid Ory's band on the Orson Welles radio show in 1944 launched the group and helped make it one of the most consistently popular New Orleans bands of the next 15 years. With veteran trumpeter Mutt Carey, either Omer Simeon, Joe Darensbourg or Darnell Howard on clarinet, pianist Buster Wilson, guitarist Bud Scott, bassist Ed Garland, and drummer Minor Hall, the band recorded for Crescent, Exner, Decca, and the new Good Time Jazz label. **Kid Ory's Creole Jazz Band** (Good Time Jazz 12022) has six selections from 1944–45, including spirited versions of "Blues for Jimmie Noone," "Panama," "Do What Ory Said," "Maryland, My Maryland," "1919 Rag," and "Ory's Creole Trombone." Although Carey was not that strong a trumpeter at that point, the band was typical of the groups that Ory would be leading, featuring a hard-driving rhythm section, excellent horn solos that were in tune, and plenty of ensembles that built as the song progressed. **Legendary 1944–45 Crescent Records** (GHB 10) has the exact same music as the Good Time Jazz release. Ory's group (with Barney Bigard on clarinet) also recorded for Columbia in 1946 and can be heard from a live gig on February 10, 1947 (with Joe Darensbourg) sounding spirited if not flawless on **At the Green Room Vol. 1** (American Music 42) and **Vol. 2** (American Music 43).

Mutt Carey and Lee Collins (American Music 72) gathers together two unrelated sessions cut for the Circle label in 1946 featuring veteran New Orleans trumpeters. Carey is in particularly fine form on a set of blues-oriented duets with pianist/singer Hociel Thomas. Lee Collins, who had been spending his life in obscurity in Chicago, despite playing regularly, accompanies the great blues singer Chippie Hill. Hill, who had recently been rediscovered by the label's head, Rudi Blesh, sounds quite strong in a combo that also includes Lovie Austin (who had not been on records since 1926) and J.H. Shayne on piano, bassist John Lindsay, and Baby Dodds. That portion of the program is highlighted by "Trouble in Mind" (21 years after Hill introduced it), "Careless Love," and "Steady Roll." In addition, this historic and enjoyable CD has a pair of instrumental trio features for Shayne.

Carey also had a couple of opportunities to lead his own record dates for Savoy. In the summer of 1947, he left Ory's band, moved back to Los Angeles, and put together a group of his own. But it never recorded, and Carey died of a heart attack in 1948. Ory meanwhile continued growing in popularity. Andrew Blakeney was his trumpeter during 1947–48 although unfortunately he did not make any commercial recordings with Ory during this period. **Kid Ory at Crystal Pier 1947** (American Music 90), which has Blakeney with the band, is sunk by terrible recording quality and an excess of inaudible vocals by Bud Scott. However, **King of the Tailgate Trombone** (American Music 20) is much better, being decently recorded and featuring Ory's band in 1948 and 1949.

Blakeney (who is on 11 of the 15 numbers) is heard in prime form, Joe Darensbourg has many good spots, and Blakeney's successor Teddy Buckner stars during the last four songs, showing that he was a much better soloist than ensemble player. Romping versions of "Panama," "Mahogany Hall Stomp," "Sugar Foot Stomp," and "High Society" reveal how exciting the Kid Ory band could sound live in concert.

The World of Eddie Condon Eddie Condon was at the peak of his powers during the second half of the 1940s. He ended a seven-year period playing nightly at Nick's in Greenwich Village when he opened his own nightclub, Condon's. His series of Town Hall concerts continued into the spring of 1945 although, due to lack of sponsors, they ended on April 7 after 46 shows. Condon and his all-star groups began recording for the Decca label and his brand of Chicago jazz was rising in popularity. In 1948, his humorous memoirs *We Called It Music* were published, and in 1949 he hosted a pioneering jazz television series that lasted for a few months.

Eddie Condon's sidemen were strong musicians who had high musicianship, were excellent at both solowork and playing in ensembles, and possessed highly individual sounds and musical personalities. Many are considered giants, and they set the standard for Dixieland-oriented players. Among the key Condon players from this period are cornetists/trumpeters Wild Bill Davison (who was a regular at Condon's for quite a few years), Bobby Hackett and Muggsy Spanier, trombonists Miff Mole, Lou McGarity and Brad Gowans (when Jack Teagarden was not available), clarinetists Pee Wee Russell, Edmond Hall and Tony Parenti, tenor saxophonist Bud Freeman, pianists Gene Schroeder (who was with Condon on and off for 20 years), Jess Stacy and Joe Sullivan, a variety of different bassists, and drummers Dave Tough and George Wettling. Many of these musicians had interdependent careers with Condon, getting to lead their own dates and record sessions along the way, but usually being available for Condon's projects.

Eddie Condon's ability to put together all-star groups and somehow manage to feature everyone favorably was very much in evidence on the Town Hall concert broadcasts. **The Town Hall Concerts Vol. Nine** (Jazzology 1017/1018) and **Vol. Ten** (Jazzology 1019/1020) are both two-CD sets containing four of the half-hour shows. Dixieland fans will want all of the releases in this perfectly done series. Tommy Dorsey, Earl Hines, Sidney Bechet, Wild Bill Davison (who was just out of the military), and Woody Herman are among the guests who join Condon's regulars on **Vol. Nine**. The other set has both Tommy and Jimmy Dorsey, Bechet, and Red McKenzie among the featured artists. Wrapping up the series is **Vol. Eleven** (Jazzology 1021/1022/1023), a three-CD set that contains the final five Town Hall concerts plus two brief demo programs for a proposed 15-minute show that was never aired and mostly features Lee Wiley.

1944–1946 (Classics 1033) has two V-disc numbers with Hot Lips Page (including "Uncle Sam's Blues") and Condon's Decca sides with such notables as Bobby Hackett, Wild Bill Davison, Billy Butterfield, Max Kaminsky, Yank Lawson, Jack Teagarden, Lou McGarity, Brad Gowans, Pee Wee Russell, Edmond Hall, Gene Schroeder, Jess Stacy, and Lee Wiley. Hot jazz at its best.

Max Kaminsky and Muggsy Spanier Max Kaminsky was a reliable and consistent soloist who stuck to traditional jazz throughout his career. **Copley Terrace 1945** (Jazzology 15) is a live set teaming Kaminsky with

Pee Wee Russell and valve trombonist Brad Gowans in a sextet. The music is taken from radio broadcasts, with the 16 selections being mostly Dixieland warhorses (including "Love Is Just Around the Corner," "Dippermouth Blues," "Basin Street Blues," and "Honeysuckle Rose") played with plenty of spirit by musicians who really dig into the music.

Muggsy Spanier, who guested with Eddie Condon in the Town Hall series and would play on Rudi Blesh's *This Is Jazz* radio programs of 1947, mostly led his own combos during the period. **1944–1946** (Classics 967) has Spanier's performances for the Commodore, Manhattan, and Disc labels plus some V-discs. Muggsy's style was unchanged since the late 1930s and would remain that way for the rest of his career, essentially swinging melodies with enthusiasm rather than improvising all that much, proving to be an expert ensemble player. He is joined by Lou McGarity, Pee Wee Russell, and various Condon associates on such tunes as "The Lady's in Love with You," "Muskrat Ramble," "You're Lucky to Me," and "China Boy."

Tony Parenti One of the most technically skilled of the clarinetists to emerge from New Orleans, Tony Parenti worked as a studio musician during the first half of the 1930s and then played with the cornball Ted Lewis band during 1939–45. Fortunately, his improvising skills did not decline and he began a long-time association with Eddie Condon in addition to leading his own Dixieland band at Jimmy Ryan's. On November 22, 1947, Parenti recorded six rags in a septet that also included Wild Bill Davison, trombonist Jimmy Archey, pianist Ralph Sutton, banjoist Danny Barker, Cyrus St. Clair (an alumnus of Clarence Williams's bands) on tuba, and Baby Dodds. Since ragtime had been largely dead for 30 years and was very rarely played during that period (other than "Maple Leaf Rag"), this was a rather unusual occasion. The performances (which include "Sunflower Slow Drag," "Grace and Beauty Rag," and "Swipesy Cake Walk") mostly have melodic ensembles and short solos, and work quite well. Surprisingly, the remainder of this CD does not consist of the six similar numbers recorded by the same group in 1949, but ten complimentary selections from April 10, 1966, featuring Parenti with a completely different septet that includes trumpeter Larry Conger, trombonist Charlie Bornemann, and pianist Knocky Parker.

In August 1949, George Buck, a great fan of New Orleans and traditional jazz, realized his dream of producing a hot jazz record. He began the Jazzology label by recording Parenti in a sextet with Wild Bill Davison, Jimmy Archey, Art Hodes, Pops Foster, and drummer Arthur Trappier. It would be a few years before Buck could afford to record a second project, but in time he would become one of the major record producers of classic jazz. All of the music (including alternate takes) from the historic debut session has been reissued as ◉ **Tony Parenti and His New Orleanians** (Jazzology 1). The musicians all play well, with Davison in particularly fiery form. In fact, the four versions of "Bugle Call Rag" are often quite humorous as Wild Bill reacts musically to the other players' mistakes. Other numbers on this exciting set include "Dippermouth Blues," "Sunday," and "Chinatown, My Chinatown."

Bud Freeman   Bud Freeman, who was in the army during 1943–45 and therefore missed participating in the Town Hall concerts, spent the next decade alternating between leading his own groups and playing with Eddie Condon. **1945–1946** (Classics 942) is not as strong as expected because 12 of the 21 selections feature the Five De Marco Sisters, a pleasant but mediocre swing vocal group. Better are four hot numbers in which Freeman is joined in an octet by Yank Lawson, Lou McGarity, and Edmond Hall, "The Atomic Era" (an unprecedented tenor/drums duet with Ray McKinley), and a pair of humorous V-disc numbers ("The Latest Thing in Hot Jazz" and "For Musicians Only") on which Freeman verbally makes fun of jazz critics (including Leonard Feather), beboppers, and "real jazz" purists.

1946 (Classics 975) is more consistent and has all of Freeman's remaining dates as a leader prior to 1953. Most of the music was originally cut for Harry Lim's Keynote label and it features Freeman with various Condon all-stars; the personnel changes from track to track. Among those making appearances are Joe Sullivan, George Wettling, Peanuts Hucko, Wild Bill Davison, Edmond Hall, and Charlie Shavers. There are also rarities that Freeman cut for the Paramount and Gold Seal labels, fine music that falls between swing and Dixieland.

Bob Crosby Alumni: Yank Lawson, Billy Butterfield, and Eddie Miller   After serving in the Marines during 1944–45, Bob Crosby (who had broken up his orchestra in 1942) led another big band during 1945–46, but it failed to make an impression and quietly disbanded. While Crosby attempted a career as a singer/personality, many of his former sidemen kept quite busy in jazz.

Yank Lawson, who primarily worked in the studios during this era in addition to making guest appearances with Eddie Condon, recorded some top-notch Dixieland as a leader during 1943–45. **That's A Plenty** (Doctor Jazz 40064) features no-nonsense playing from Lawson on four complete sessions with such top players as trombonists Brad Gowans, Miff Mole and Lou McGarity; clarinetists Pee Wee Russell, Rod Cless, and Bill Stegmeyer; Joe Marsala on tenor; James P. Johnson; and Yank's longtime friend, bassist Bob Haggart. These performances feature high musicianship, exciting ensembles, and colorful concise solos.

Billy Butterfield was in the military during 1944–45, but was able to make guest appearances at Eddie Condon's Town Hall concerts. After his discharge, he worked with radio orchestras and then during 1946–47 led a big band of his own. Unfortunately, that was not the right era to try to put together a new orchestra and the group flopped commercially despite the excellent musicianship, the fine arrangements of Bill Stegmeyer, and the leader's golden horn. **Pandora's Box 1946–47** (Hep 49) has the Butterfield big band's radio transcriptions, featuring some solid swing, a liberal amount of ballads, and vocals from Pat O'Connor. But by November, Butterfield had broken up the band, was leading a Dixieland group at Nick's, and was soon on the staff of the ABC network.

Tenor saxophonist Eddie Miller, clarinetist/arranger Matty Matlock, guitarist Nappy Lamare, and drummer Ray Bauduc were among the former Bobcats who settled in Los Angeles in the mid-1940s, working in the studios and playing Dixieland in local clubs. The Jump label documented the underrated Los Angeles Dixieland scene quite well during this era although unfortunately the music on many of their LPs has not yet been reissued on CD. One LP well worth searching for is **Eddie Miller/ George Van Eps** (Jump 5), which has trio numbers by Miller with guitarist Van Eps and pianist Stan Wrightsman during 1946 and 1949 along with four numbers that put the focus on the guitarist's beautiful chord voicings.

Rudi Blesh's *This Is Jazz*   Rudi Blesh loved New Orleans jazz and detested both bebop and swing era big bands. In his career he made an impact as a supporter and propagandist for New Orleans jazz and ragtime. After attending Dartmouth College, he worked as a jazz critic for the *San Francisco Chronicle* in the early 1940s and for the *New York Herald Tribune* starting in 1944. His 1946 book *Shining Trumpets* was flawed and biased if well-intentioned, championing the music he loved at the expense of later eras of jazz. Blesh formed the short-lived but valuable Circle label (along with Harriet Janis) to document some classic jazz greats who had been neglected by the larger labels. Among Circle's most notable recordings were Baby Dodds's unaccompanied drum solos, which are included (along with numbers featuring Albert Nicholas, Don Ewell, James P. Johnson, and Danny Barker) on Dodds's **Jazz à La Creole**, recordings by blues singer Bertha "Chippie" Hill (whom Blesh helped bring out of retirement), and the Jelly Roll Morton Library of Congress performances.

In 1947, Blesh hosted the important jazz radio series *This Is Jazz*, which featured top Dixieland players performing on weekly half-hour shows, with "Way Down Yonder in New Orleans" being the program's theme song. Although his narration comes across as a bit wooden and is full of clichés (particularly in the early programs where he sounds overly excited and nervous), it is due to Blesh's diligence that New Orleans jazz artists were featured on the air on a regular basis at the time. After decades of being available only in piecemeal fashion, the *This Is Jazz* programs (like the Condon Town Hall series) are being made available by Jazzology in two-CD sets with four programs per volume. After an audition show on January 18, *This Is Jazz* was broadcast from February 8 until October 4, 1947. The seven sets that have been released thus far have all of the music through August 16.

Vol. One (Jazzology 1025/26) starts with the audition (which has a slightly overcrowded band consisting of Punch Miller, Max Kaminsky, Albert Nicholas, Mezz Mezzrow, George Brunies, Luckey Roberts, Wellman Braud, Cyrus St. Clair, and Baby Dodds). Also on this box are the first three real programs, utilizing Spanier, Brunies, Nicholas, Barker, Cyrus St. Clair (permanently replaced by Pops Foster on March 1), Dodds, and Roberts, Joe Sullivan, or James P. Johnson on piano. Sidney Bechet and the vaudeville team of Coot and Socks make guest appearances. **Vol. Two** (Jazzology 1027/28) has the same lineup of musicians except for the piano slot, which is filled by

Charlie Queener, Joe Sullivan, or Art Hodes; Bechet returns for the March 24 show.

◉ Vol. Three (Jazzology 1029/30) serves as an excellent example of the show. Its first two programs use the same lineup (with Sullivan or Hodes on piano and Dodds unaccountably missing on April 12), but on April 19, Wild Bill Davison takes over for Spanier, adding a great deal of excitement to the performances. The April 26 show is particularly special because Louis Armstrong is the guest and is featured throughout. Listen to how warmly and spontaneously he verbally greets all of the musicians (including such former sidemen as Nicholas, Foster, and Dodds) during the introduction.

Vol. Four (Jazzology 1031/1032), **Vol. Five** (Jazzology 1033/1034), and **Vol. Six** (Jazzology 1035/1036) mostly have the same lineup of musicians except that Jimmy Archey succeeds Brunies starting on June 14 and Ralph Sutton was now the main pianist. Blue Lu Barker and folk singer Leadbelly are guests on **Vol. Five**. **Vol. Six** has pianist Montana Taylor and Sidney Bechet appearing on one show apiece, while Chippie Hill is excellent during her four vocals on two shows. Hill shows that being off the major league scene for 15 years had not resulted in her losing anything. **Vol. Seven** (Jazzology 1037/1038) is a bit of a departure because, after the first two shows (which have Bechet and Hill as guests), *This Is Jazz* went on the road. The August 9 program in Los Angeles features Kid Ory's band (with Andrew Blakeney and Joe Darensbourg in the frontline). The August 16 program from San Francisco showcases Lu Watters's Yerba Buena Jazz Band in its prime. George Buck and the Jazzology label are to be congratulated for doing such a definitive job in reissuing the *This Is Jazz* and Eddie Condon's Town Hall concerts.

After *This Is Jazz* went off the air in October 1947, Rudi Blesh and Harriet Janis began on their next project, interviewing survivors of the ragtime era for their classic 1950 book *They All Played Ragtime*.

Joe Marsala   Clarinetist Joe Marsala led some of the most intriguing sessions of the 1940s even though he is largely forgotten today. **1944–1945** (Classics 902) contains more than its share of remarkable music. First Marsala leads a conventional Dixieland septet with Bobby Hackett and Eddie Condon through two standards and a pair of blues. A sextet date with trumpeter Joe Thomas and singer Linda Keene is most impressive for the playing of Marsala's wife, the great jazz harpist Adele Girard, on "Zero Hour" and "Joe Joe Jump." Keene is also well showcased with Marsala and either Joe Thomas or Marty Marsala on two other dates. But most unusual is the session of January 12, 1945. Joe Marsala, Cliff Jackson, and Dizzy Gillespie on "My Melancholy Baby" take turns being in the spotlight, with the final eight bars being a "battle" between swing clarinet, stride piano, and bop trumpet! This selection really shows the wide variety of jazz styles that were heard nightly in New York in 1945.

Joe Marsala and Adele Girard were based at New York's Hickory House on 52nd Street until 1948 when they gave up playing music full time. Marsala became a successful businessman, but the couple's premature retirement (they played on an occasional basis in later years) resulted in Marsala and Girard being vastly underrated in jazz history books.

Red Nichols and Phil Napoleon   In late 1944, after a period outside music, Red Nichols put together a new version of his Five Pennies. Having played advanced classic jazz in the 1920s, and swing with his unsuccessful big band in the late 1930s, now Nichols began the last phase of his career, as the leader of a solid Dixieland band that, like his 1920s groups, he called the Five Pennies. Based in Los Angeles, Nichols ran through a lot of personnel during 1945–48. In 1949, he added bass saxophonist Joe Rushton (the best on his instrument since Adrian Rollini) and also utilized trombonist King Jackson, several different clarinetists (Ruel Lynch, Matty Matlock, and Rosy McHargue), pianist Bob Hammack, and drummer Rollie Culver with occasional bass players. Nichols remained a distinctive player with a thoughtful solo style that often seemed worked out rather than being overly spontaneous; However, his ideas were consistently quite original.

The Five Pennies recorded for Jump in 1949, but that album (which includes a version of his classic rearrangement of "Battle Hymn of the Republic" in three tempos) has not yet reappeared on CD. Worth picking up are **Red Nichols and His Five Pennies** (Jazzology 90) and **1949—Vol. Two** (Jazzology 290), which consist of radio transcriptions and show the brand of Dixieland that Nichols was making popular.

The veteran trumpeter Phil Napoleon worked with Jimmy Dorsey's band in 1943, but generally stuck to studio work during the 1940s. In 1946, he recorded 16

TIMELINE 1949

The LP is introduced to the general public and, although not making an impact on jazz that year, this signaled the end of the 78 era. • Charlie Parker records with strings. • Ray Anthony's big band signs with Capitol. • British trombonist Chris Barber forms his first band. • The Firehouse Five Plus Two first record for the new Good Time Jazz label. • Sidney Bechet's performance at the Paris Salle Peyel Jazz Festival causes a sensation. • In Australia, bandleader Graeme Bell helps found the Swaggie label. • Cornetist Ruby Braff works in Boston with Edmond Hall. • Dave Brubeck forms a popular trio. • Pianist Joe Bushkin plays and acts in the Broadway play *The Rat Race*. • Cozy Cole replaces Big Sid Catlett as drummer with the Louis Armstrong All-Stars. • The Count Basie Orchestra breaks up. • Pianist Kenny Drew makes his recording debut with Howard McGhee. • Canadian trumpeter Maynard Ferguson moves to the United States and has stints with the big bands of Boyd Raeburn, Jimmy Dorsey, and Charlie Barnet. • Eric Dolphy records with Roy Porter's big band. • Altoist Charlie Mariano works in Boston with Nat Pierce's orchestra. • Eddie Jefferson, the founder of vocalese, performs his lyrics to "Parker's Mood" and "I Cover the Waterfront" (the latter based on Lester Young's solo) on the radio. • Connie Kay is the drummer with Lester Young's quintet. • Former Stan Kenton bassist Howard Rumsey persuades the owner of the Lighthouse, a club in Hermosa Beach (near Los Angeles), to start featuring jazz on a regular basis. • Swedish altoist Arne Domnerus makes his first recordings as a leader in Stockholm. • Pee Wee Erwin leads the Dixieland band at Nick's in Greenwich Village. • Tito Puente begins leading his own Afro-Cuban jazz band. • Trumpeter/bandleader Damaso Perez-Prado's recording of "Mambo No. 5" starts a mambo craze. • The George Shearing Quintet is formed. • James Moody records "I'm in the Mood for Love," which would later be turned into the vocalese classic "Moody's Mood for Love." • Benny Goodman, Charlie Barnet, and Artie Shaw all have bebop bands; none survives the end of the year. • Roy Eldridge rejoins Gene Krupa. • An all-star bebop Carnegie Hall concert on Christmas symbolizes both the height and the end of the bebop era.

selections (mostly Dixieland tunes) with a septet that included Lou McGarity, pianist Frank Signorelli, and Original Dixieland Jazz Band drummer Tony Spargo, but these Mercury recordings have not been reissued in quite a few years. In 1949, Napoleon revived the Memphis Five name and began a long stint playing at Nick's in Greenwich Village. **Live at Nick's, NYC** (Jazzology 39) has radio appearances by Napoleon's band, which at the time was a no-name sextet other than Spargo on drums, kazoo (on which he was talented), and whistling, which is unfortunately off mike. Strangely enough, of the eighteen tracks, all but seven are medleys comprised of two-four songs apiece. The emphasis throughout is on ensembles and nostalgia at danceable tempos, so the reasonably pleasant music is not as heated as one would expect.

Henry "Red" Allen   Veteran trumpeter Henry "Red" Allen really came into his own as a showman during the 1940s. He led an exciting sextet (featuring J.C. Higginbotham and altoist Don Stovall) that by 1944 was performing a brand of jump music that was a mixture of swing, New Orleans jazz, and heated R&B. Allen, who usually counted off tempos with a "Whamp, Whamp" (even ballads) and concluded pieces with a long drawn-out "Niiiiiiiiice," was a bit unusual among jazz musicians. A colorful figure who was quite fun loving, Allen was actually very reliable, showed up on time, was sober, had a longtime and happy marriage, and was always ready to play. Although associated with Dixieland and trad jazz throughout his life, his solos were often much more radical and unpredictable than the settings. ◉ **1944–1947** (Classics 1067) is full of heated romps from his sextet, including such infectious originals as "The Crawl" (which features Stovall at his best), "Ride, Red, Ride," "Get the Mop," "Buzz Me," and "Count Me Out."

While Allen and Higginbotham were old friends dating back to at least their days with Luis Russell in 1929, Don Stovall was one of the great swing/jump alto saxophonists of the 1940s. Stovall worked in St. Louis with Dewey Jackson, Fate Marable, and Eddie Johnson's Crackerjacks (1932–33), moved to New York in 1939 and played with Sammy Price, Snub Mosley, Eddie Durham's Big Band, and the Cootie Williams Orchestra (1941). He sounded perfect with Red Allen's band, but, after 1949, he decided to retire from music at the age of

36, working for the phone company and never playing music again, a major loss to jazz.

Lu Watters's Yerba Buena Jazz Band, Turk Murphy, and Bob Scobey   In 1946, Lu Watters's Yerba Buena Jazz Band (the group that during 1940–42 had helped launch the Dixieland revival) reformed after a four-year absence caused by key members being in the military during World War II. Trumpeters Watters and Bob Scobey, trombonist Turk Murphy, pianist Wally Rose, tuba player Dick Lammi, and drummer Bill Dart were all back, with Bob Helm taking over on clarinet for Ellis Horne, and Harry Mordecai on banjo. All of the band's highly influential studio recordings are available on the four-CD box ◉ **The Complete Good Time Jazz Recordings** (Good Time Jazz 4409) and also individually. The 1946 version of the Yerba Buena Jazz Band was looser than the 1941–42 group, as can be heard on **Dawn Club Favorites** (Good Time Jazz 12001), **Watters's Originals & Ragtime** (Good Time Jazz 12002), and **Stomps, Etc. & The Blues** (Good Time Jazz 12003). While the two-trumpet frontline was a descendant of King Oliver's Creole Jazz Band, the group developed an original sound within the tradition, and such originals as "Big Bear Stomp," "Trombone Rag," "Minstrels of Annie Street," "Sage Hen Strut," and "Emperor Norton's Hunch" became important additions to the repertoire of Dixieland.

Based at the Dawn Club from the band's birth, in 1947 the group switched its home base to Hambone Kelly's in El Cerrito. That year Turk Murphy left to form his own band, and in 1949 Bob Scobey also departed, initially joining Murphy's group before going out on his own. Watters continued being based at Hambone Kelly's, and in late 1949 the Yerba Buenas consisted of his trumpet, trombonist Don Noakes, Bob Helm, Wally Rose, banjoist Pat Patton, Dick Lammi on tuba and bass, drummer Bill Dart, and Clancy Hayes as vocalist and second banjoist. Business was starting to slip, but Watters remained a strong player and a powerful force in classic jazz.

Firehouse Five Plus Two   In 1949, a group of employees (mostly animators) at Walt Disney had fun holding impromptu Dixieland jam sessions. There was so much joy to the sessions that they decided to form a band. The Firehouse Five Plus Two generally wore fireman outfits, employed a liberal amount of humor, and played surprisingly good Dixieland. They were such a hit from the start that a new label, Lester Koenig's Good Time Jazz (a company that soon acquired hot jazz sessions from other tiny labels, including the music of Lu Watters), was founded initially to record the band. The original Firehouse Five's band members were trumpeter Johnny Lucas, trombonist Ward Kimball (who became the group's leader), clarinetist Clarke Mallory, pianist Frank Thomas, banjoist Harper Goff, Ed Penner on bass and tuba, and drummer Jim McDonald. After the May 13, 1949, record date (which resulted in four songs, including "Firehouse Stomp" and "Firemen's Lament"), Lucas (who was unable to travel) and McDonald were replaced by cornetist Danny Alguire (who had formerly been with Bob Wills) and drummer Monte Mountjoy. Tom Sharpsteen became the group's clarinetist by 1952.

The two-CD set **The Firehouse Five Plus Two Story** (Good Time Jazz 22055) has all of the band's recordings from 1949–52. The music is full of spirit and wit, and Alguire's solos and ensemble lead drive the band. The humor could sometimes be slightly corny—although it is fun to hear a siren go off during the final chorus as if the music was so hot that it was setting off a fire!—but this is an enjoyable ensemble that helped add momentum to the Dixieland revival movement.

Trad Jazz a Hit Overseas: Humphrey Lyttelton and Graeme Bell

The rise in popularity of Dixieland was not confined only to the United States. As Sidney Bechet discovered when he visited France and played with Claude Luter in 1949, the music was catching on quickly in France. The same was becoming true in England. While veteran British trumpeter Nat Gonella mostly played variety shows, Humphrey Lyttelton (who can be thought of as a more serious successor to Gonella) was proving himself to be a first-class soloist while with George Webb's Dixielanders in 1947 and in his own groups starting the following year. Lyttelton's late 1940s band, which can be best heard on the LP **Delving Back and Forth with Humph** (Stomp Off 1160), included clarinetist Wally Fawkes, trombonist Harry Brown, and either George Webb or Pat Hawes on piano. On these recordings, Lyttelton mixes together 1920s standards with an offbeat version of "Miss Otis Regrets," "Salty Dog," and his own "Victory House Drag." The second half of the LP dates from 1986 and is an excellent reunion by Lyttelton and Fawkes.

Some of the most creative New Orleans–type jazz being performed during this period was actually being heard in Australia. Pianist Graeme Bell was the center of the Aussie trad jazz movement. He had worked professionally from the late 1930s, but it was after he formed his Australian Jazz Band in 1946 and toured Europe for a full year (including recording in Czechoslovakia, Paris, and London) during 1947–48 that he made a major impact. In 1949, Bell helped found the Swaggie label, a company that on LPs has reissued much of his early music along with that of other local Dixieland groups. Bell's band during this era featured his brother Roger Bell on cornet, the versatile "Lazy" Ade Monsborough on clarinet, valve trombone, and trumpet, clarinetist Don Roberts, and a four-piece rhythm section. Unfortunately, Graeme Bell's recordings have mostly not been reissued on CD yet so one will have to search for these excellent LPs: **Czechoslovak Journey 1947** (Swaggie 1394), **Paris 1948** (Swaggie 1395), **1948–1949** (Swaggie 1396), **Melbourne 1949** (Swaggie 1268), **Graeme Bell and His Australian Jazz Band** (Swaggie 2124), and **1949–52** (Swaggie 1397).

Stride Piano: Past and Future

The death of Fats Waller in 1943 and the dominance of Bud Powell's new piano style among younger players resulted in the decline of stride and swing piano, but not its death. Some of the veterans of the 1920s were still active, and there were a few new major voices who would help keep the two-handed piano style alive for decades to come.

James P. Johnson, Willie "The Lion" Smith, and Luckey Roberts

James P. Johnson was still quite busy in the mid-1940s. He was a guest on Eddie Condon's Town Hall concerts and Rudi Blesh's *This Is Jazz* programs and continued playing his definitive brand of stride piano on a nightly basis for a few years. **1944–1945** (Classics 1027) has a variety of rare material and oddities. First Johnson jams four songs in an all-star group with Sidney DeParis, Vic Dickenson, and Edmond Hall. He accompanies W.C. Handy's daughter Katherine Handy (who had a decent singing voice) on six of her father's more famous songs and plays four numbers with the "Carnival Three" (a trio with Omer Simeon and Pops Foster). Most valuable are the four-part "Yamekraw (A Negro Rhapsody)" and the two-part "Blue Moods," solo piano versions of two of Johnson's better extended pieces. **1945–1947** (Classics 1059) has James P.'s last studio recordings, mostly piano solos except for a quartet date with Albert Nicholas, including "Blues for Jimmy," "Twilight Rag," the two-part "Jazzamine Concerto," "Liza," "Maple Leaf Rag," and "Old Fashioned Love." There was no serious decline in Johnson's playing, and he was just 53 in 1947. The LP **Ain'tcha Got Music** (Pumpkin 117) is filled with valuable recordings. Johnson plays the title cut unaccompanied, is heard as a guest at some Eddie Condon concerts from 1944–47, and (best of all) is featured on five lengthy selections in either solos or duets with drummer Danny Alvin in 1949. This would be the last documentation of the great James P. Johnson, who is still in top form on "Liza" and "Over the Waves."

Willie "The Lion" Smith, who had recorded such sensitive, impressionistic, and sophisticated originals in 1939, was largely confined to not-so-subtle Dixieland settings during the second half of the 1940s. He did get a chance to record a bit as a soloist and in rhythm sections in 1949, but that was in Paris for the Vogue label and those recordings (some of which are remakes of his earlier compositions) are not out yet on CD.

A contemporary of James P. and the Lion, pianist Luckey Roberts amazingly made no recordings until 1946. He had actually predated stride, publishing his "Pork and Beans" and "Junk Man Rag" as early as 1913. Roberts, who participated in some of the Harlem rent party jams in the 1920s, spent most of his career leading society bands and writing for musical comedies. In 1941, his "Ripples of the Nile" was given words, retitled "Moonlight Cocktail" and became a hit for Glenn Miller. ○ **The Circle Recordings** (Solo Art 10), which Roberts shares with Ralph Sutton, has the six songs from his 1946 session. Roberts's virtuosity and total command of the piano are remarkable, and he really tears into his originals, including "Ripples of the Nile" (which has some very fast runs), "Pork and Beans," and "Music Box Rag." Also on this valuable CD are Ralph Sutton's four performances (plus an alternate take) from his debut as a leader in 1949, and his eight exciting duets with George Wettling from 1952.

Ralph Sutton, Dick Wellstood, and Dick Hyman

While James P. Johnson, Willie "The Lion" Smith, and Fats Waller dominated stride piano in the 1920s, during the second half of the 1940s three new names emerged to join Don Ewell (who played with Bunk Johnson and Muggsy Spanier) and Armand Hug (an excellent player based in New Orleans) among the top young stride pianists: Ralph Sutton, Dick Wellstood, and Dick Hyman.

Ralph Sutton drew his inspiration from the piano styles of Waller and Johnson (and later on the Lion), developing into an extremely powerful player. He started off playing with Jack Teagarden's big band (1942) and then, after serving in the army, in 1947 he appeared regularly on the *This Is Jazz* radio show. Sutton's talents were quickly noticed and he became the intermission pianist at Condon's for eight years starting in 1948, often guesting with the main band while developing his own sound.

Dick Wellstood, who recorded five piano solos for the tiny Century and Rampart labels during 1947–49, was also a passionate player, though usually a little more subtle than Sutton and more closely tied (at least early on) to James P. Johnson. He arrived in New York in 1946 as a member of Bob Wilber's Wildcats (with whom he played with Sidney Bechet) and performed with Wilber's group until 1950.

Dick Hyman was at the very beginning of his career in the late 1940s. He had taken lessons from Teddy Wilson, served in the army (1945–46) and studied at Columbia University. During 1949 he played with Tony Scott and Red Norvo and, although he could play bop quite credibly, he was already looking towards earlier styles for inspiration.

Rhythm and Blues

In its early stages, rhythm and blues had a direct connection to swing. R&B bands were essentially small combos that managed to be as exciting as big bands by using repetition, highly expressive saxophonists, and fairly simple chord structures (often the blues or originals based on "Flying Home"). Although the stars were generally singers or saxophonists, quite a few up-and-coming bop players gained experience—or at least a decent salary—playing with R&B outfits, and it was also a potential moneymaker for swing veterans. As time progressed, R&B became its own separate music, but during the second half of the 1940s it often overlapped with jazz. In fact, one could call many of the recordings of Illinois Jacquet, Arnett Cobb, and Lionel Hampton R&B and not be mistaken. The best recordings of the musicians and singers in this section, although not always technically jazz, should be of strong interest to jazz collectors.

Louis Jordan   Although one of the founders of R&B, Louis Jordan's music did not fit that idiom's stereotype. Jordan loved to sing/talk catchy stories and take heated alto solos, and many of his recordings were memorable three-minute gems. It is not surprising that he and his Tympani Five were constantly on the R&B charts. **1945–1946** (Classics 921) features Jordan at the peak of his fame. His Tympani Five at the time included trumpeter Aaron Izenhall, Josh Jackson on tenor, and pianist Wild Bill Davis (who would be succeeded by Bill Doggett). This set has such hits as "Beware," "Don't Let the Sun Catch You Cryin'," "Choo-Choo Ch'Boogie," "Ain't Nobody Here but Us Chickens," and "Let the Good Times Roll." In addition, two duets with Ella Fitzgerald ("Stone Cold Dead in the Market" and "Petootie Pie") are quite fun.

1946–1947 (Classics 1010) includes "Reet, Petite and Gone," "Barnyard Boogie," and "Beans and Corn Bread" along with a lot of lesser-known but enjoyable material. **1947–1949** (Classics 1134) has Jordan's last session from 1947, and the music recorded during his first five recording dates of 1949 including such hits as "Safe, Sane and Single," "School Days," and the two-part "Saturday Night Fish Fry." Other highlights include "Don't Burn the Candle at Both Ends," "Cole Slaw," "Hungry Man," and two vocal duets ("Baby, It's Cold Outside" and "Don't Cry, Cry Baby") with Ella Fitzgerald.

For the general collector, the best all-round Louis Jordan collection (and there are many) is ⊙ **The Best of Louis Jordan** (MCA 4079), which consists of 20 of his top hits from 1941–54, including many of the songs already mentioned. But Jordan's music is such fun that more serious fans will want to investigate his many Classics releases, too.

Amos Milburn and Floyd Dixon   Charles Brown (with Johnny Moore's Three Blazers), was a major influence on the styles of Amos Milburn and Floyd Dixon, both of whom were pianist/singers who at times sounded an awful lot like Brown. Milburn played piano when he was five and was inspired by the boogie-woogie pianists Albert Ammons, Pete Johnson, and Meade Lux Lewis. He lied about his age in 1942 to enlist in the navy when he was barely 15. After his discharge, he worked in his hometown of Houston and also San Antonio before

moving to Los Angeles where he signed with the Aladdin label. During 1946–47, Milburn had hits with "After Midnight," "Hold Me Baby," and especially "Chicken Shack Boogie." Up until 1954, he had many best-selling records, including "Bad Bad Whiskey," "Thinking and Drinking," "Let Me Go Home Whiskey," "One Scotch, One Bourbon, One Beer," and "Good Good Whiskey." The liquor industry must have loved him! A seven-CD limited-edition Mosaic box set has all of his Aladdin recordings, but since that is out of print, **1946–1947** (Classics 5018) gives listeners Milburn's first recordings, while **The Best of Amos Milburn** (EMI 27229) is a 26-song single disc that has the great majority of his most popular recordings.

Floyd Dixon had a similar career. Born in Texas, he moved to Los Angeles when he was 13, and by 1947 when he was 19, he was recording and making a stir. In 1949, Dixon's versions of "Dallas Blues" and "Mississippi Blues" were hits, and these were soon followed by "Sad Journey Blues," "Telephone Blues," "Call Operation 210," "Wine, Wine, Wine," and "Hey Bartender!" The two-fer **His Complete Aladdin Recordings** (Capitol 36293) contains many joyous and jumping performances with Maxwell Davis usually helping out on tenor.

Wynonie Harris   A powerful blues shouter whose music straddled the boundaries between swing, blues, and R&B, Wynonie Harris considered Big Joe Turner (who also had a style that crossed many musical genres) to be his main inspiration. Harris, who was born in Omaha, Nebraska, moved to Los Angeles in 1940, worked on Central Avenue, and as a member of Lucky Millinder's band during 1944–45 became a popular attraction with his records of "Who Threw the Whiskey in the Well" and "Hurry, Hurry." He started his solo career in 1945, toured with Lionel Hampton, and had many hit records during the next nine years.

1944–1945 (Classics 885) has Harris's first 22 recordings including his performances with Lucky Millinder, an exciting session in which he used Illinois Jacquet and a date in which the backup band includes Howard McGhee, Teddy Edwards, and drummer Johnny Otis. Highlights include "Wynonie's Blues," "Somebody Changed the Lock on My Door," "Young Man's Blues," and "Everybody Boogie." **1945–1947** (Classics 1013) consists of five four-song sessions (all quite jazz oriented) that were cut for the Hamp-Tone, Bullet, and Aladdin labels.

Harris sings three numbers (including a two-part "Hey! Ba-Ba-Re-Bop") with a combo taken from the Lionel Hampton big band, performs a date in Nashville that served as Sun Ra's first recording (Ra's piano is well featured throughout, especially on "Dig this Boogie"), and is also heard with a jazz band that includes Joe Newman, Tab Smith, and Allen Eager. In addition, the singer is featured with an obscure backup band and shares the vocal spotlight with Big Joe Turner on three numbers, including a slightly disorganized two-part "Battle of the Blues." **1947–1949** (Classics 1139) traces Harris's career from just before the recording strike of 1948 up until the end of 1949. There are seven sessions that were all originally recorded for King, including such numbers as "Wynonie's Boogie," "Good Morning Mr. Blues," "Crazy Love," "Good Rockin' Tonight" (a major hit), "Grandma Plays the Numbers," "Drinkin' Wine Spo-Dee-O-Dee," and "All She Wants to Do Is Rock." Among the players in the accompanying groups are trumpeters Hot Lips Page, Jesse Drakes, Cat Anderson, and Joe Morris, and tenors Hal Singer, Tom Archia, and Johnny Griffin.

Big Jay McNeely   Cecil "Big Jay" McNeely was the most extreme of all the R&B honking tenor saxophonists. It was not unusual for McNeely to keep on repeating the same note for 20 minutes and to play while lying down on his back. Among the most exhibitionistic and exciting of the honkers, McNeely caused quite a few uproars during his career, particularly in the early days. He was inspired by Illinois Jacquet, played jazz briefly, and then decided that his career was going to be in R&B. McNeely's debut records were for Savoy in 1948, and he had early hits in "The Deacon's Hop" and "Wild Wig." **1948–1950** (Classics 5009) has those two songs plus such rousing performances as "Man Eater," "Blow Big Jay," "Jay's Frantic," "Real Crazy Cool," and "Deacon's Blowout." In Big Jay McNeely's music, good taste, creative improvising, and complex chord changes are largely nonexistent, but no one could scream or honk quite like him.

Johnny Otis   Johnny Otis's roots were in swing, and he loved Count Basie's band. However Otis became best known as one of the top talent scouts in R&B. A drummer who doubled on vibes, Otis worked early on in Los Angeles with Count Otis Matthews, George Morrison, Lloyd Hunter, Harlan Leonard, and Bardu Ali. In 1945, he had his first date as a leader, using a Basie-style big band with Jimmy Rushing taking two vocals, and he introduced "Harlem Nocturne." Otis also recorded as a drummer with Lester Young, Illinois Jacquet, and Johnny Moore's Three Blazers, but his future would be elsewhere. By 1947, he was running a colorful R&B revue that featured up-and-coming talents such as Little Esther Phillips, Linda Hopkins, and Big Mama Thornton. **Rhythm & Blues Caravan** (Savoy 92859) is a three-CD set that has everything that Johnny Otis cut for the Savoy label during 1945–51, including his 15 R&B hits, and it is quite definitive of his career.

Cubop: The Beginnings of Afro-Cuban Jazz

Latin (or more specifically Afro-Cuban) jazz is the combination of Cuban rhythms with jazz improvisation, and it developed into its own style of music during the second half of the 1940s. There had been some earlier mixing of Cuban and American music, but none of those fusions caught on. It was not until the mid-1940s that more than just a token few Cuban musicians were able to fit comfortably into jazz bands, and American jazz musicians were becoming sophisticated enough to understand the clave.

The clave is the basis for all Cuban music. It is an off-beat two-bar rhythmic pattern that can be heard if one claps on the 1-2½-4 beats in the first bar and 2-3 in the second. This infectious rhythm is present (at least beneath the surface) in all Cuban music, and it is quite different than the 4/4 swing rhythm used in most jazz.

There were plenty of examples of Latin and South American rhythms popping up in at least superficial form in American music in earlier years, including classical composer Louis Moreau Gottschalk's pieces in the 1850s, such early standards as "La Paloma" and "Estrellita," the tango rhythm used in Scott Joplin's "Solace" and the "B" theme of W.C. Handy's "St. Louis Blues," and some of Jelly Roll Morton's originals in the 1920s (particularly the "The Crave" and "New Orleans Blues"). In 1930, Don Azpiazu's Havana Casino Orchestra introduced authentic Cuban dance music to the United States and was the first to record "The Peanut Vendor" and "Green Eyes," also recording popular versions of "Mama Inez" and "Marta." Other Latin-flavored songs to become popular during the next 15 years were "La Cucaracha," "Rancho Grande," "Cuando Vuelva a Tu Lado" ("What a Difference a Day Makes"), "Begin the Beguine," and Juan Tizol's "Caravan."

Both Xavier Cugat and Desi Arnaz became national celebrities, but they performed Latin-flavored pop music rather than jazz. Quite a few swing era bands utilized touches of Cuban and Latin music, but primarily as a flavor for variety rather than seriously digging into the music.

In Cuba, the local folk music at first was quite separate from jazz, with the son, rumba, tango (from Argentina), and mambo all being developed as creative danceable rhythms. Their bands of the 1920s and '30s had very different instrumentation than the American swing groups. The septeto consists of trumpet, tres (a nine-string Cuban guitar), bass, maracas, claves, bongo, and at least one singer. The charanga has a flute in the lead along with violins, piano, bass, and timbales. Arsenio Rodriguez in the late 1930s introduced the conjunto, which consists of several trumpets, piano, tres, bass, conga, bongo, and voices.

Somehow, the two different worlds of American and Cuban music met and formed an infectious new style.

Machito and Mario Bauza Machito (Frank Grillo) was born in Florida, but raised in Cuba. His mother gave him the nickname of "Macho" and later a friend suggested he add "ito" to his name à la Tito. A fine singer, Machito started out his career performing with the Miguel Zavalle Sextet in Cuba in the mid-1920s and worked with various bands during the next decade. In 1926, Machito met trumpeter Mario Bauza, who became his brother-in-law four years later when he married Machito's sister.

Bauza was a very skilled musician who started attending Havana's Municipal Academy when he was seven. By the time he was nine, he was playing clarinet with the Havana Philharmonic, becoming a regular member of the orchestra on bass clarinet at 12. He visited New York for the first time in 1926, making his recording debut with Antonio Maria Romeu's Charanga Orchestra. Bauza learned alto sax and bassoon back in Cuba and then moved permanently to the United States in 1930. When singer Antonio Machin offered him a job with his quartet if he could switch to trumpet, the 19-year-old Bauza learned to play trumpet in two weeks! He worked with Machin and other Cuban bands in the 1930s and had stints with Noble Sissle (1931–32), Chick Webb (1933–38), Don Redman (1938–39), and Cab Calloway (1939–40). Along the way he convinced

Webb to hire Ella Fitzgerald and was successful in getting Dizzy Gillespie into Calloway's band.

Machito moved to the United States in 1937 and in 1940 organized an orchestra that was initially a Cuban dance band that he called the Afro-Cubans. After Bauza became the band's musical director and arranger in 1941, he encouraged Machito to hire technically skilled jazz musicians in the horn sections. In 1943, Bauza wrote what many consider to be the first Afro-Cuban jazz song, "Tanga." The orchestra (which by then consisted of three saxophones, two trumpets, piano, bass, bongos, and timbales) recorded for Decca and its records sold fairly well. After the bebop era began, Machito's band grew in stature, and the arrangements of Bauza and pianist Rene Hernandez were often quite jazz-oriented. Stan Kenton was impressed, and on February 13, 1947, he recorded a song called "Machito." When Kenton recorded "The Peanut Vendor" later in the year, he utilized a Latin rhythm section with Machito on maracas, Carlos Vidal on congas, Jose Mangual on timbales, and Jack Costanzo on bongos. The orchestras of Kenton and Machito shared a Town Hall concert on January 24, 1948. When a version of "Tanga" was recorded later that year by Machito and called "Cubop City," the term "Cubop" became popular as a synonym for Afro-Cuban jazz of the era. In December 1948, producer Norman Granz recorded Machito for his Clef label along with Charlie Parker and Flip Phillips.

While Machito's classic recordings with Charlie Parker have usually been reissued under Bird's name, ● **Mucho Macho** (Pablo 2625-712) shows how strong his band was without guests. Recorded during 1948–49, this CD features Machito's band at its best on 24 selections, which include both originals (including the popular "Asia Minor") and Latinized versions of "Jungle Drums," "At Sundown," "Tea for Two," and "St. Louis Blues."

Chano Pozo There were several major Cuban musicians who were instrumental in helping to pioneer Afro-Cuban jazz, including composer Arsenio Rodriguez, bandleader/pianist Noro Morales, Tito Puente (who wrote some important arrangements for Pupi Campo's band in 1947), and Jack Costanzo (who played bongo with Stan Kenton in 1947–48 and the King Cole Trio in 1949–51), not to mention Machito and Mario Bauza. But the one who made the biggest impact was Chano Pozo.

Born in Havana, Cuba, in 1915, Chano Pozo was always a bit wild in his lifestyle, being a street fighter and spending some time in reform school. However, he had a natural musical ability, working in street dance groups, as a choreographer for hotel revues, and as a drummer and singer whose music was rooted in the Cuban Lucumi faith. Although he did not know how to read music, he was talented at composing songs, and some of his tunes (including "Parampampin" and "Arinanara") caught on and were played by other groups. During 1940–43, Pozo co-led El Conjunto Azul and became quite well known in Cuba. In December 1945, when he met Mario Bauza during a visit to Cuba by Machito's orchestra, Bauza encouraged him to come to New York.

Pozo took his advice and arrived in New York in May 1946, but struggled for a year, finding only a little work as a dancer and conga player. He led three little-known record dates for the Coda label during February–March 1947. Around that time, Dizzy Gillespie remarked to Mario Bauza that he would like to add a percussionist to his band, so Bauza introduced the trumpeter to Pozo. Although Pozo did not speak English, the two hit it off quite well, and Gillespie's became the first American jazz band to add a conga to its instrumentation, though Stan Kenton was using Latin percussionists as guests. For a time the music failed to gel, but when Al McKibbon succeeded Ray Brown as Dizzy's bassist, he was able to act as a bridge between Pozo and the American rhythm section and musical magic occurred.

A Carnegie Hall concert on September 29, 1947, gave Gillespie the opportunity to feature Pozo. On December 22, Pozo recorded four songs with Gillespie, "Algo Bueno," "Cool Breeze," and a pair of conga and chanting features composed by George Russell ("Cubana Be" and "Cubana Bop"). On December 30, he recorded four more songs with Dizzy, including "Good Bait" and a number that they co-wrote, "Manteca." In 1948, Pozo toured Europe with Gillespie's big band and they played all over the United States; several concerts were recorded and later released. Pozo also recorded with Milt Jackson, Tadd Dameron ("Jahbero"), and James Moody despite the recording strike, and he co-composed "Tin Tin Deo" and "Guachi Guaro" with Gillespie. However, on December 2, 1948, Pozo was fatally shot in a Harlem bar by a fellow Cuban whom he had beaten up earlier in the day in an argument over being sold weak marijuana. Chano Pozo was a month shy of his 34th birthday.

A remarkable three-CD set, ◉ **El Tambor De Cuba** (Tumbao 305) shows that there was much more to Chano Pozo than his association with Dizzy Gillespie. The first disc has 23 Pozo compositions recorded by other bands during 1939–53, the second CD features Pozo's best recordings prior to joining Gillespie, and the final disc has his studio performances with Gillespie, Jackson, and Moody. Thanks to the talents of Chano Pozo and the musical courage of Dizzy Gillespie, Afro-Cuban jazz became a vital music by the late 1940s, one that overlaps with modern jazz yet has its own traditions and legacy.

Cool Jazz

Even as bebop was maturing in 1947, a new variation on the music was being formed. Throughout jazz history, there have been "cool" reactions to "hot" developments such as Bix Beiderbecke's tone compared to that of Louis Armstrong, swing music in contrast to heated 1920s jazz, and Miles Davis's approach to improvising as opposed to Dizzy Gillespie's. Cool jazz, which employed softer tones, a quiet and smooth rhythm section, a greater emphasis on arranged ensembles, and more interaction between the horn players (rather than always having a string of solos), was in some ways a conservative reaction to the innovations of bebop, a consolidation of the best of bop with swing à la Count Basie. Its predecessors were the John Kirby Sextet, Lester Young, and especially the Claude Thornhill Orchestra.

Lennie Tristano   Pianist Lennie Tristano always followed his own path. Born with weak eyesight, he was totally blind by the age of nine. Tristano threw himself into music, becoming a virtuoso pianist and gaining a degree from the American Conservatory of Music in 1943. He taught music in Chicago before moving to New York in 1946. Tristano made a strong impression from the start, influenced by Bud Powell, but playing very much in his own style. He became the teacher for a group of promising musicians, including Lee Konitz (who played with Claude Thornhill in 1947 and was one of the very few young altoists at the time who did not sound like Charlie Parker), tenor saxophonist Warne Marsh (who was with Buddy Rich in 1948), and guitarist Billy Bauer (with Woody Herman's First Herd during 1944–46). Tristano believed that rhythm sections should serve strictly as a timekeeper behind soloists who play very long melodic lines with unusual accents. He enjoyed reharmonizing songs, sometimes having two or three soloists playing at once, and improvising endlessly over fairly common chord changes. Warm tones and rhythmic excitement were sacrificed in favor of constant melodic creativity.

1946–1947 (Classics 1184) has Tristano's earliest recordings (other than a live solo session), and it puts the emphasis on his piano playing in solos and trios with Bauer and one of several bassists. The tunes (which include "I Can't Get Started," "I Surrender Dear," and "Ghost of a Chance") are mostly standards except for the last session, which has such originals as "Parallel," "Apellation," and "Abstraction." Tristano's powerful attack and constant flow of ideas has a different feel than the usual playing of Bud Powell.

There would be a four-song date with clarinetist John LaPorta added to the trio, a few all-star radio appearances with Charlie Parker and Dizzy Gillespie, and an early 1949 session for Prestige with Lee Konitz in a quintet (that is often issued under the altoist's name). Then in 1949 for Capitol Tristano recorded his most important work. **⦿ Intuition** (Capital Jazz 52771) actually starts off with a dozen selections from an excellent Warne Marsh quintet date (with fellow tenor Ted Brown, pianist Ronnie Ball, bassist George Tucker, and drummer Jeff Morton) from 1956 before dealing with the seven Tristano pieces. In 1949, the pianist had his strongest group, a sextet with Konitz, Marsh, Bauer, bassist Arnold Fishkin, and Harold Granowsky or Denzil Best on drums. The interplay between the horns and the stunning unisons are impressive on "Wow" (which is accurately titled) and "Sax of a Kind." Most intriguing are the first-ever recorded free improvisations in jazz: "Intuition" and "Digression." A decade before avant-garde jazz began to really be heard, Lennie Tristano was already making history.

The Dave Brubeck Octet Dave Brubeck always had an adventurous spirit. The pianist had classical training from his mother, but memorized his lessons and avoided learning to read music, fooling her completely. Even when studying music at the College of the Pacific in 1938–42, his quick ear allowed him to almost get away with becoming a nonreading classical musician until he was finally caught and permitted to graduate anyway; he eventually did learn how to read. The improvising of

jazz always interested Brubeck the most. Even as a youth, he enjoyed playing in two keys at once (exploring polytonality) and utilizing several rhythms simultaneously (polyrhythms) while creating his own fresh chord voicings. After serving in the army during World War II, he studied under classical composer Darius Milhaud at Mills College and formed an unusual octet in 1946 that played infrequently (with very few paid gigs) during the next three years. **Dave Brubeck Octet** (Original Jazz Classics 101) features the pioneering West Coast outfit combining bop with modern classical music. The obscure ensemble was one of the first to explore different time signatures other than 4/4, and its arrangements were quite unpredictable. Its personnel consisted of trumpeter Dick Collins, trombonist Bob Collins, Paul Desmond and Bob Cummings on altos, Bill Smith on clarinet and baritone, tenor saxophonist Dave Van Kreidt, and a rhythm section comprised of Brubeck, bassist Ron Crotty, and drummer Cal Tjader. Although the recording quality is just so-so on their lone disc, the music still sounds a bit futuristic in spots and was certainly ahead of its time.

In 1949, Dave Brubeck decided to put together a more economical group. He formed a trio with Crotty and Tjader that became popular in the San Francisco area and in September began recording for the new Fantasy label.

Claude Thornhill After serving in the military during 1942–45, Claude Thornhill put together his second orchestra. The 1946 band had four trumpets, three trombones, two French horns (which was unprecedented for a jazz big band), six reeds, and a four-piece rhythm section plus two vocalists. Gil Evans was Thornhill's chief arranger by this time and the repertoire included vocal ballads, atmospheric works, and some conventional swing pieces, including a hit version of "A Sunday Kind of Love" that features Fran Warren's cheerful vocal. By 1947, Evans's inventive charts were often quite beboppish, including versions of "Early Autumn," "Anthropology," "Robbins' Nest," "Donna Lee," and "Yardbird Suite." There was one less trumpet in the ensemble, but now the band had a tuba player; later in the year Red Rodney and Lee Konitz joined as key soloists.

While the Hep label has reissued all of the studio recordings by the earlier Thornhill band, it has not yet covered the second orchestra's dates for Columbia. However,

The Transcription Performances 1947 (Hep 60) and **The 1948 Transcription Performances** (Hep 17) are excellent examples of the orchestra's work. The 1947 big band features trumpeters Red Rodney and Ed Zandy, Konitz, clarinetist Danny Polo, and trombonist Tak Takvorian. Best of the Evans charts are "Robbins' Nest," "Polka Dots and Moonbeams," "Anthropology," "Early Autumn," "I Get the Blues When It Rains," "Sorta Kinda," and "Donna Lee." The 1948 edition of the orchestra has trumpeter Gene Roland, Brew Moore, Polo, and Konitz as the key soloists. Some of the same arrangements (with different solos) are heard on both discs with the 1948 set having a few writing contributions from Gerry Mulligan.

By 1949, the Thornhill band had dropped the tuba, the leader was back to doing the majority of the arrangements, and the emphasis was more on ballads, vocals, and remakes of earlier recordings. But by then, the unusual tones of the Claude Thornhill Orchestra were being utilized elsewhere.

The Miles Davis Nonet   In 1948, Miles Davis, who was very impressed by the voicings on Claude Thornhill's records, met arranger Gil Evans. They hit it off from the start and became lifelong best friends. During that year they had many discussions about forming a band that would utilize the best features of Thornhill's orchestra, but with the least number of musicians. They settled on a nonet comprised of Davis's trumpet, altoist Lee Konitz, baritonist Gerry Mulligan, pianist John Lewis, trombone, French horn, tuba, bass, and drums. In addition to Evans, Mulligan and Lewis wrote the bulk of the arrangements. The Miles Davis Nonet landed a gig playing for two weeks at the Royal Roost as the intermission group opposite the Count Basie Orchestra. Davis also interested the Capitol label in recording the group.

⦿ **The Complete Birth of the Cool** (Blue Note 94550) has all of the performances that exist of this classic band. The two-CD set has ten selections that the nonet performed during their radio broadcasts from the Royal Roost, including two songs ("S'il Vous Plait" and a Kenny Hagood vocal on "Why Do I Love You") that were not recorded commercially and several performances that have longer solos than their studio counterparts. The live band consists of Davis, trombonist Mike Zwerin, Junior Collins on French horn, Bill Barber on tuba, Konitz, Mulligan, Lewis, Al McKibbon or Curly Russell on bass, and Roach.

Also on this two-fer are the band's dozen studio performances for Capitol. In addition to Davis, Barber, Konitz, and Mulligan, the trombone is Kai Winding or J.J. Johnson, the French horn slot is filled by Collins, Sandy Siegelstein, or Gunther Schuller, Al Haig fills in for John Lewis on one date, the bassists are Joe Schulman, Nelson Boyd, or Al McKibbon, and the drummers are Roach or Kenny Clarke. Mulligan contributed five arrangements, Lewis did three, Evans wrote two, and there is one apiece from Davis and Johnny Carisi. Among the most memorable performances are "Move," "Godchild," "Boplicity," Carisi's "Israel," and "Moondreams." These subtle yet highly original arrangements are well worth studying closely.

As it turned out, the Royal Roost engagement was the only gig the band had. When the studio performances were grouped together on a ten-inch LP in the early 1950s and a few years later on a standard LP, the music was dubbed "The Birth of the Cool" because of the rise of the West Coast cool jazz style that it influenced. But at the time, the failure of the group to get a second engagement was a disappointment to Miles Davis. And quite typically, by the time his nonet's records were released and they were having their greatest influence, the trumpeter had moved on to other innovative areas.

Various Artists

By the late 1940s, the bebop revolution was being felt in England. The four-CD box set ⦿ **Bebop in Britain** (Esquire 100-4) has many of the top bop English recordings of 1948–53, featuring the Esquire Five (a quintet led by tenor saxophonist Ronnie Scott), the teenage drummer Victor Feldman in a quartet with Johnny Dankworth (heard on clarinet for that date), various groups headed by Ronnie Scott (which include trumpeter Jimmy Deuchar, altoist Spike Robinson, and Victor Feldman on piano) and Dankworth, obscure sessions led by drummer Norman Burns, accordion player Tito Burns and Vic Lewis, and six songs from tenor saxophonist Kenny Graham's Afro-Cubists (featuring two horns and a standard four-piece rhythm section plus conga, bongos, and maracas).

The Blue Note Swingtets (Blue Note 95697) mostly has selections from 1945–46 (with three cuts from 1944) drawn from ten different sessions led by five swing greats. What would have been a definitive two-CD set is, on this single disc, just a decent sampler. The leaders are

Tiny Grimes, tenor saxophonist John Hardee, Ike Quebec (including "If I Had You"), Benny Morton, and Jimmy Hamilton. They are assisted by such sidemen as Trummy Young, Sid Catlett, Jonah Jones, Tyree Glenn, Buck Clayton, Barney Bigard, Ben Webster, Ray Nance, and Harry Carney.

Central Avenue was the center of the black jazz scene in Los Angeles, and it was in its prime from the late 1920s until the early 1950s, outliving New York's 52nd Street. ● **Central Avenue Sounds** (Rhino 75872) is an exciting four-CD box that, although including a few well-known selections, is most valuable for its many obscurities. Starting with Kid Ory's 1922 recording of "Ory's Creole Trombone" and ending with some bop in the mid-1950s, many of the selections fall into the 1945–49 period, including numbers by singer/pianist Hadda Brooks, Johnny Otis, Johnny Moore's Three Blazers, Slim Gaillard, Ernie Andrews, Lester Young, the Gerald Wilson Orchestra, Charlie Parker, Charles Mingus, Lucky Thompson, Howard McGhee, and Roy Porter's big band.

The Continental Sessions Vol. 1 (Storyville 8205) has three transitional bands from 1945 that recorded for the Continental label. Edmond Hall heads the Café Society Orchestra (a sextet) on four songs including the definitive version of Mary Lou Williams's "Lonely Moments." Clyde Hart's lengthy date of January 4, 1945, with Bird and Diz plus Trummy Young and Don Byas, has four vocals apiece by Young and Rubberlegs Williams along with brief spots for Parker and Gillespie. And finally Slam Stewart heads a swing quintet also featuring Red Norvo and Johnny Guarnieri.

Esquire All-American Hot Jazz Sessions (Bluebird 6757) consists of sessions organized by Leonard Feather for the Victor label that were sponsored by or connected to *Esquire*'s prestigious polls. Among the highlights are Charlie Shavers's explosive solos on "The One that Got Away" and "Blow Me Down," Louis Armstrong's advanced improvisation on "Snafu," the beauty of Johnny Hodges's playing on "Gone with the Wind," an Allen Eager feature ("Allen's Alley"), the intriguing "From Dixieland to Bop," and Lucky Thompson's ballad showcase on "Just One More Chance." Also included are a pair of piano solos apiece by Art Tatum and Erroll Garner, Mildred Bailey singing "I Don't Wanna Miss Mississippi," and spots for Buck Clayton, Jack Teagarden, J.J. Johnson, Benny Carter, Don Byas, and Harry Carney.

Clarinetist Bill Reinhardt and his wife Ruth ran Jazz Ltd., Chicago's top Dixieland club, for a couple of decades starting in the mid-1940s. **Jazz Ltd. Vol. 1** (Delmark 226) has performances recorded by the house band plus guests in 1949 and 1951. Among the star players are Sidney Bechet (who romps on three numbers), Muggsy Spanier, Don Ewell, Doc Evans, and Miff Mole. Many of these recordings had been scarce before the release of this CD in 1994.

In 1949, Norman Granz organized and gathered together a series of special works that summed up the jazz world of the time. They were released on a prestigious album of 78s. In 1994, all of the music plus other complementary selections were reissued as the deluxe two-CD set ● **The Jazz Scene** (Verve 314 521 661). Harry Carney is featured on two numbers with strings, Neal Hefti, George Handy, and Ralph Burns contribute some complex arrangements, Lester Young, Charlie Parker, Bud Powell, Machito ("Tanga"), and Willie Smith have features, and Coleman Hawkins is heard playing unaccompanied on "Picasso." The added material includes alternate takes and other selections showcasing Billy Strayhorn, Lester Young, Willie Smith, Coleman Hawkins, Flip Philips, and Ralph Burns.

The Jubilee radio programs constituted one of the hippest jazz-oriented radio series of the 1940s. The announcements and commentary by Ernie "Bubbles" Whitman may have been a touch corny, but the music was often rewarding. Some of the more memorable performances are gathered together on **A Jumpin' Jubilee—The Jam Sessions, 1945–46** (Jazz Unlimited 2054). A lengthy version of "Sonny Boy" has Slim Gaillard introducing the players in an all-star 16-piece orchestra, all of whom get to solo. Peggy Lee sings "You Was Right, Baby," "September in the Rain" features Bobby Hackett and Willie Smith, and there is a mini-set that teams together Buck Clayton, Lester Young, and Coleman Hawkins (with Helen Humes heard on "Don't Blame Me"). In addition, a three-song medley has a feature apiece for altoists Benny Carter, Willie Smith, and Charlie Parker ("Cherokee").

Jumpin' Like Mad (Capitol 52051), which is subtitled "Cool Cats & Hip Chicks Non-Stop Dancin'," is a two-CD set that has one heated performance after another from the prime era of jump jazz. The 51 selections (dating from 1942–56) mix together hits and complete obscurities, late-period swing, melodic blues, and stompin' R&B. This is an infectious sampler of music from the Capitol label's vaults, with numbers from Big Joe Turner, Ella Mae Morse ("Cow Cow Boogie"), Jesse Price, Kay Starr, Cootie Williams, T-Bone Walker, the King Cole Trio, Gene Ammons, Jimmy Liggins, Big Jay McNeely, Louis Jordan, and many others.

The two-CD set **Kansas City Blues 1944–49** (Capitol 52047) puts the focus on Kansas City–type swing and blues from 1949 (there is also a session apiece from 1944 and 1945). At the time, there was a crossover between swinging Kansas City blues and R&B, as can be heard on selections by Jay McShann (some of which feature singer Walter Brown), Julia Lee, Buster Moten (with Ben Webster as a sideman), Tommy Douglas, and Tiny Kennedy. The music is colorful, timeless, and surprisingly obscure.

One of the most attractive reissues (from the packaging standpoint) is the limited-edition seven-CD set **The 1940s Mercury Sessions**, a wonderful collection of music that is housed inside a box that looks like an old radio. Among the valuable recordings that are included are Sippie Wallace's two numbers with Albert Ammons (1945), many sessions by Ammons (1946–49), Helen Humes (1947–48), Jay McShann (1945–47 and 1951), Eddie "Cleanhead" Vinson (1945–47), New Orleans R&B pianist Professor Longhair (1949), Buddy Rich's big band (1946), and Cootie Williams (1947 and 1949) plus a date apiece by Mary Lou Williams (1947), Julia Lee (1945), Myra Taylor (1946), and Rex Stewart (1946). There is also a full disc of previously unreleased alternate takes. The music ranges from jazz-oriented blues and some R&B to bebop and swing. Although some of the dates are also readily available elsewhere, this "radio" is a collector's item.

The 1940s: Small Groups—New Directions (Columbia 44222) features three different groups. Woody Herman's 1946 Woodchoppers has the key players from the First Herd (including Sonny Berman, Bill Harris, Flip Phillips, and Red Norvo) performing ten mostly rousing numbers (including the humorous "Fan It"). The Gene Krupa Trio with Charlie Ventura and pianist Teddy Napoleon romps on the hit "Dark Eyes"

and four previously unreleased cuts. And, as a climax, a sextet led by Harry James performs "Pagan Love Song" and a very boppish "Tuxedo Junction."

Sunset Swing (Black Lion 760171) has 22 selections from 1945 recorded for the Sunset label. Featured in the eight groups are Howard McGhee, Charlie Ventura, Andre Previn, Lucky Thompson, Harry "Sweets" Edison, and Dodo Marmarosa among others. Although the music is technically small-group swing, one can hear how the innovations of bebop were beginning to affect players of the older style.

Titles like **World's Greatest Jazz Concert #1** (Jazzology 301) and **World's Greatest Jazz Concert #2** (Jazzology 302) are a slight exaggeration, but for trad jazz fans they are not too far from the truth. The first CD is from February 22, 1947, and features Wild Bill Davison, Albert Nicholas, George Brunies, Joe Sullivan, Pops Foster, Baby Dodds, Bertha "Chippie" Hill, Muggsy Spanier, Art Hodes, Cecil Scott, Hot Lips Page, and Tony Parenti all in excellent form. **Concert #2**, from April 26, 1947, has Spanier, Brunies, Sidney Bechet, Jack Teagarden, Johnny Windhurst, Dick Wellstood, and Bob Wilber jamming together in different combinations, plus a pair of numbers by the Two Gospel Keys. The recording quality is pretty decent for live performances of that era, and the musicians sound inspired by each other's presence.

Closing off this chapter is ◉ **Charlie Parker and the Stars of Modern Jazz at Carnegie Hall, Christmas 1949** (Jass 16). This CD features the best of bebop, including a septet comprised of Miles Davis, Serge Chaloff, Sonny Stitt, Benny Green, Bud Powell, Curley Russell, and Max Roach, a quintet with Stan Getz and Kai Winding, Sarah Vaughan featured on two songs, Lennie Tristano's sextet with Lee Konitz and Warne Marsh, and the Charlie Parker Quintet. Charlie Parker and his group (with Red Rodney at his best) rip through five songs including a stunning version of "Ko Ko." The concert was recorded just a week before the 1940s ended and perfectly sums up the modern jazz scene of the time.

VOICES OF THE FUTURE

Bob Stewart (tuba), Feb. 3, 1945, Sioux Falls, SD

John Stubblefield (tenor, soprano), Feb. 4, 1945, Little Rock, AR

Ernie Krivda (tenor), Feb. 6, 1945, Cleveland, OH

Pete Christlieb (tenor), Feb. 16, 1945, Los Angeles, CA

Danny D'Imperio (drums), Mar. 14, 1945, Sidney, NY

David Grisman (mandolin), Mar. 23, 1945, Passaic, NJ

Steve Gadd (drums), Apr. 9, 1945, Rochester, NY

Collin Walcott (sitar, tabla), Apr. 24, 1945, New York

Keith Jarrett (piano, leader), May 8, 1945, Allentown, PA

Michael Moore (bass), May 16, 1945, Cincinnati, OH

Anthony Braxton (alto, reeds), June 4, 1945, Chicago, IL

Mick Goodrick (guitar), June 9, 1945, Sharon, PA

Mike Garson (piano), July 1945, Brooklyn, NY

Joe Beck (guitar), July 29, 1945, Philadelphia, PA

David Sanborn (alto), July 30, 1945, Tampa, FL

Peter Ecklund (cornet), Sept. 27, 1945, San Diego, CA

Ernie Watts (tenor, alto), Oct. 23, 1945, Norfolk, CA

Randy Brecker (trumpet), Nov. 29, 1945, Philadelphia, PA

Carter Jefferson (tenor, soprano), Nov. 30, 1945, Washington, D.C.

Johnny Dyani (bass), Nov. 30, 1945, East London, South Africa

Tony Williams (drums), Dec. 12, 1945, Chicago, IL

George Duke (keyboards), Jan. 12, 1946, San Rafael, CA

Pierre Dorge (guitar, leader), Feb. 28, 1946, Copenhagen, Denmark

Vinny Golia (reeds), Mar. 1, 1946, Bronx, NY

Keith Copeland (drums), Apr. 18, 1946, New York, NY

Jack Walrath (trumpet), May 5, 1946, Stuart, FL

Don Moye (drums, percussion), May 23, 1946, Rochester, NY

Niels-Henning Orsted Pedersen (bass), May 27, 1946, Orsted, Denmark

Claudio Roditi (trumpet, flugelhorn), May 28, 1946, Rio de Janeiro, Brazil

Zbigniew Seifert (violin, alto), June 6, 1946, Cracow, Poland

Tom Harrell (trumpet, flugelhorn, composer), June 16, 1946, Urbana, IL

John Klemmer (tenor, electric sax), July 3, 1946, Chicago, IL

Bennie Maupin (tenor, bass clarinet), Aug. 29, 1946, Detroit, MI

Dave Liebman (soprano, tenor, flute), Sept. 4, 1946, Brooklyn, NY

Dave Holland (bass, leader), Oct. 1, 1946, Wolverhampton, England

Bennie Wallace (tenor), Nov. 18, 1946 Chattanooga, TN

Ray Drummond (bass), Nov. 23, 1946, Brookline, MA

Baikida Carroll (trumpet), Jan. 15, 1947, St. Louis, MO

Butch Morris (cornet, conductor), Feb. 10, 1947, Long Beach, CA

Vladimir Chekasin (saxophones), Feb. 24, 1947, Sverdlovsk, Russia

Jan Garbarek (tenor, soprano), Mar. 4, 1947, Mysen, Norway

Paul McCandless (oboe, English horn, bass clarinet), Mar. 24, 1947, Indiana, PA

Marilyn Crispell (piano), Mar. 30, 1947, Philadelphia, PA

Barry Guy (bass, leader), Apr. 22, 1947, London, England

Alan Broadbent (piano), Apr. 23, 1947, Auckland, New Zealand

Steve Khan (guitar), Apr. 28, 1947, Los Angeles, CA

Abdul Wadud (cello), Apr. 30, 1947, Cleveland, OH

Richie Beirach (piano), May 23, 1947, New York, NY

Greg Abate (alto), May 31, 1947, Fall River, MA

Frank Strozier (alto), June 13, 1947, Memphis, TN

Harold Danko (piano), June 13, 1947, Sharon, PA

John Blake (violin), July 3, 1947, Philadelphia, PA

L. Subramaniam (violin), July 23, 1947, Madras, India

Terje Rypdal (guitar), Aug. 23, 1947, Oslo, Norway

Billy Bang (violin), Sept. 20, 1947, Mobile, AL

Don Grolnick (piano), Sept. 23, 1947, Brooklyn, NY

Fred Hopkins (bass), Oct. 11, 1947, Chicago, IL

Jerry Bergonzi (tenor), Oct. 21, 1947, Boston, MA

Banu Gibson (vocals, leader), Oct. 24, 1947, Dayton, OH

Andy LaVerne (piano, keyboards), Dec. 4, 1947, New York, NY

Egberto Gismonti (guitar, piano), Dec. 5, 1947, Carmo, Brazil

Miroslav Vitous (bass), Dec. 6, 1947, Prague, Czechoslovakia

Bob Moses (drums, composer), Jan. 28, 1948, New York, NY

Richie Cole (alto), Feb. 29, 1948, Trenton, NJ

Larry Carlton (guitar), Mar. 2, 1948, Torrance, CA

Jessica Williams (piano), Mar. 17, 1948, Baltimore, MD

VOICES OF THE FUTURE

Jan Hammer (keyboards), Apr. 17, 1948, Prague, Czechoslovakia

Joe Bonner (piano), Apr. 20, 1948, Rocky Mount, NC

Tania Maria (piano, vocals), May 9, 1948, Sao Luis, Brazil

Bill Bruford (drums, leader), May 17, 1948, Sevenoaks, Kent, England

Tom Scott (tenor), May 19, 1948, Los Angeles, CA

Marc Copland (piano), May 27, 1948, Philadelphia, PA

Paquito D'Rivera (alto, clarinet), June 4, 1948, Havana, Cuba

Allan Holdsworth (guitar), Aug. 6, 1948, Bradford, England

Andy Stein (violin), Aug. 31, 1948, New York, NY

Rebecca Kilgore (vocals), Sept. 24, 1948, Waltham, MA

Bill Pierce (tenor, soprano), Sept. 25, 1948, Hampton, VA

Dave Samuels (vibes, marimba), Oct. 9, 1948, Waukegan, IL

Marvin "Hannibal" Peterson (trumpet), Nov. 11, 1948, Smithville, TX

Alphonse Mouzon (drums), Nov. 21, 1948, Charleston, SC

Harvie Swartz (bass), Dec. 6, 1948, Chelsea, MA

Susannah McCorkle (vocals), Jan. 1, 1949, Berkeley, CA

Michael Brecker (tenor), Mar. 29, 1949, Philadelphia, PA

Eric Kloss (tenor, alto), Apr. 3, 1949, Greenville, PA

Jim McNeely (piano, arranger, composer), May 18, 1949, Chicago, IL

Randy Sandke (trumpet), May 23, 1949, Chicago, IL

Jerry Gonzalez (trumpet, conga), June 5, 1949, Bronx, NY

Daryl Sherman (vocals, piano), June 14, 1949, Woonsocket, RI

Chico Freeman (tenor), July 17, 1949, Chicago, IL

Henry Butler (piano, vocals), Sept. 21, 1949, New Orleans, LA

Bill Connors (guitar), Sept. 24, 1949, Los Angeles, CA

Arturo Sandoval (trumpet, piano), Nov. 6, 1949, Artemisa, Havana, Cuba

David S. Ware (tenor), Nov. 7, 1949, Plainfield, NJ

Steve Turre (trombone, conch shells), Dec. 8, 1949, Omaha, NE

Mark Elf (guitar), Dec. 13, 1949, Queens, NY

Lenny White (drums), Dec. 19, 1949, Jamaica, NY

T.S. Monk (drums, leader), Dec. 27, 1949, New York, NY

PASSINGS

Clyde Hart (34), Mar. 19, 1945, New York, NY

Richard M. Jones (53), Dec. 8, 1945, Chicago, IL

Jack Jenney (35), Dec. 16, 1945, Los Angeles, CA

Bobby Stark (38), Dec. 29, 1945, New York, NY

Fred Beckett (29), Jan. 30, 1946, St. Louis, MO

Mamie Smith (63), Oct. 30, 1946, New York, NY

Sonny Berman (21), Jan. 16, 1947, New York, NY

Freddie Webster (30), Apr. 1, 1947, Chicago, IL

Jimmie Lunceford (45), July 13, 1947, Seaside, OR

Red McKenzie (48), Feb. 7, 1948, New York, NY

Chano Pozo (33), Feb. 12, 1948, New York, NY

Tricky Sam Nanton (44), July 20, 1948, San Francisco, CA

Mutt Carey (57), Sept. 3, 1948, Elsinore, CA

Stan Hasselgard (26), Nov. 23, 1948, Decatur, IL

Dave Tough (40), Dec. 6, 1948, Newark, NJ

Irving Fazola (36), Mar. 20, 1949, New Orleans, LA

Bunk Johnson (59), July 7, 1949, New Iberia, LA

Danny Polo (47), July 11, 1949, Chicago, IL

Paul Mares (49), Aug. 18, 1949, Chicago, IL

Albert Ammons (42), Dec. 2, 1949, Chicago, IL

Ivie Anderson (44), Dec. 28, 1949, Los Angeles, CA

Chapter Seven

1950–1955:
West Coast vs. East Coast

The first half of the 1950s found the United States turning conservative in many ways. After 20 years of Democratic rule by Franklin Roosevelt and Harry S. Truman, in 1953 the White House was taken over by the Republicans, led by the relatively moderate Dwight D. Eisenhower. The Cold War had heated up and the Communist witch-hunts were in full swing. The Korean War of 1950–53 made many uneasy (it was the first U.S. conflict that did not result in a decisive victory), and quite a few Americans turned inward, concentrating on their own lives and the struggle to make a living.

Fortunately, the economy was booming overall (particularly compared to the 1930s), and there were a couple of exciting new inventions that were becoming part of most American's lives. Television caught on quickly and by the early 1950s had become the number one form of entertainment. More directly affecting the music world, the long-playing (LP) record, which was introduced to the general public in 1949, replaced 78s, which were completely extinct by the late 1950s. At first, ten-inch LPs were released, containing around 12 minutes of music per side as opposed to the usual 78's three minutes. By the mid-1950s, 12-inch LPs took over, holding 20 minutes or more per side. Due to the 78's time limitations, even live performances during the swing era were often not much longer than three minutes due to the big bands being locked into arrangements. At first, the release of LPs just meant that there were more songs on an album, but by the mid-1950s jazz performances were becoming longer (particularly on live albums), there were lengthier works being written, and jazz soloists were finally having an opportunity to really stretch out beyond private jam sessions. And with such new labels as Pacific Jazz, Contemporary, Prestige, and (by 1955) Riverside, not to mention Blue Note (which had turned its focus to modern jazz) and Norman Granz's Clef and Norgran, there was no shortage of jazz record companies eager to document the music's many styles.

The pop music world was in a strange state during 1946–54. The pop charts were dominated by novelties, ballad singers, and oddities, with the most rewarding hits of the early 1950s often being the overdubbed performances of Les Paul and Mary Ford. Rhythm and blues (which was still connected to jazz but becoming more independent) provided popular dance music for youngsters, since the modern jazz world had largely turned its back on dancers, while nostalgia big bands gave older generations opportunities to reminisce. Rock 'n' roll was just around the corner.

The main debate in the mid-1940s jazz world had been the war between the beboppers and the moldy-figs, even as the swing big bands were breaking up. By the mid-1950s, the atmosphere had changed quite a bit. While Dixieland and Latin jazz flourished as separate worlds, and small-group swing became known as mainstream, bebop had become the modern vocabulary of jazz. There were two new styles that were direct outgrowths of bop: West Coast cool jazz and East Coast hard bop. Neither were radical breaks from bop and they actually mixed in aspects of earlier styles that had been temporarily discarded during the classic bebop era (swing in the case of cool, and the influence of church music in hard bop). Both were viable extensions of the modern jazz scene and made the first half of the 1950s a particularly intriguing period in jazz history.

Gerry Mulligan and Chet Baker   Gerry Mulligan in 1950 had a stronger reputation as an arranger/composer than as a baritone saxophonist. He had written charts for Johnny Warrington's radio band (1944), Tommy Tucker, George Paxton, Gene Krupa (1946), Claude Thornhill (1948), and Elliot Lawrence (1949), playing a little bit of alto and baritone for Krupa and Thornhill. Mulligan was featured on baritone with the Miles Davis Nonet in its 1948 gig and its three record dates of 1949–50. His few other record dates from the era found his tone rougher and darker than it would become.

The "real" Gerry Mulligan first emerged on **Mulligan Plays Mulligan** (Original Jazz Classics 003), recorded in New York shortly before the baritonist relocated to Los Angeles. The tentet date (which has both Mulligan and Max McElroy on baritones plus Allen Eager, trumpeter Nick Travis, and George Wallington) is a hint of things to come. The leader's playing is lighthearted, and his floating tone sometimes makes his baritone seem like a tenor. Mulligan contributed all seven selections, five for the full group and two for a smaller unit, included an extended workout for the baritonist and Eager on "Mulligan's Too." After traveling to Los Angeles, Mulligan wrote some arrangements for Stan Kenton (including "Youngblood," "Swing House," and "Walking Shoes"), worked at the Lighthouse, and then gained a regular

Monday night engagement at the Haig. While rehearsing his group, Mulligan realized that he enjoyed the extra freedom of playing without having a pianist constantly stating the chords. Mulligan's interplay with trumpeter Chet Baker (who was 22 at the time) was often magical.

Baker was born in Oklahoma, moved with his family to California in 1940, and served in the army. In 1952, he impressed Charlie Parker at an audition and became Bird's trumpeter during his visit to Los Angeles; tapes from a concert with Parker are his earliest recordings. Baker, who had a cool and haunting tone, emphasized the middle-register in his thoughtful solos and had a relaxed quality even on uptempo tunes. After Bird headed back East, Baker met Mulligan and they soon began playing at the Haig in their pianoless quartet.

The quartet caught on big, becoming a local and then national sensation. In addition to Mulligan's appealing tone and the atmospheric playing of Baker, it was the ensembles (a form of modern Dixieland at times) that really gave the group its own identity.

Producer Dick Bock started the Pacific Jazz label originally to record the Mulligan quartet, and in a short time it became one of the West Coast's most important labels. The two-CD set ◉ **The Original Quartet with Chet Baker** (Pacific Jazz 94407) has all of the group's recordings for Pacific Jazz (except for a couple of sessions on which Lee Konitz makes the unit a quintet). Mulligan and Baker (joined on most selections by Bob Whitlock or Carson Smith on bass and Chico Hamilton or Larry Bunker on drums) perform classic versions of "Bernie's Tune," "Lullaby of the Leaves," "Nights at the Turntable," "Walkin' Shoes," "Utter Chaos," and a live version of "My Funny Valentine." **Gerry Mulligan Quartet Featuring Chet Baker Plus Chubby Jackson Big Band Featuring Gerry Mulligan** (Original Jazz Classics 711), which has quite a title, includes the eight titles that the Mulligan group made for Fantasy. Among the gems are the quartet's original version of "My Funny Valentine" (which was their biggest hit and became closely associated with Baker), "Line for Lyons," "Bark for Barksdale," and "The Lady Is a Tramp." Also on this disc are eight numbers from an all-star bop orchestra assembled by Chubby Jackson that is full of ex-Woody Herman sidemen plus Howard McGhee, J.J. Johnson, Kai Winding, Charlie Kennedy, Georgie Auld, and Mulligan (who contributed a couple of arrangements). **The Original Gerry Mulligan Tentet and Quartet** (GNP/Crescendo 56) has six more numbers from the quartet plus eight songs (including "Westwood Walk" and "Walkin' Shoes") on which six horns (trumpeter Pete Candoli, valve trombonist Bob Enevoldsen, John Grass on French horn, Ray Siegel on tuba, altoist Bud Shank, and Don Davidson on second baritone) are added.

In the summer of 1953, Mulligan was arrested for possession of heroin and spent quite a few months in prison, resulting in the quartet breaking up. When he was released in the spring of 1954 and tried to get the group back together, he refused to give Baker a raise even though the trumpeter had been working steadily as a leader and had become quite popular, so the original quartet became history. Instead, the baritonist teamed up with valve trombonist Bob Brookmeyer, bassist Red Mitchell, and drummer Frank Isola in a new quartet.

In Paris Vol. 1 (Vogue 68211) and **In Paris Vol. 2** (Vogue 68212) from June 1954 show that Brookmeyer may have actually been a better match for Mulligan than Baker. The two horns often think alike, are equally witty, and delight in creating lines around each other in ensembles. Such tunes as "Walkin' Shoes," "Love Me or Leave Me," and "Five Brothers" from the first disc and "Laura," "Line for Lyons," and "Motel" from the second are among the more memorable selections although every number on these two CDs is well worth hearing. **California Concerts Vol. 1** (EMI/Manhattan 46860), from November 12, 1954, has trumpeter Jon Eardley (whose light tone is similar to Baker's) in Brookmeyer's place and Chico Hamilton back on drums. Mulligan, who also plays a bit of piano, is in top form on a set of standards, blues, and originals, working quite well with Eardley. **California Concerts Vol. 2** (Pacific Jazz 46864) is an unrelated performance from December 14. The first five numbers feature the Mulligan-Eardley-Mitchell-Hamilton quartet, while the final nine have Larry Bunker on drums and add Zoot Sims's tenor and Brookmeyer. The sextet utilized on the second half of the concert (which plays such numbers as Sims's "The Red Door," "There Will Never Be Another You," and "People Will Say We're in Love") was Mulligan's main band during 1955–56.

Chet Baker was far from inactive during this period. After Mulligan's bust, Baker at first performed with the remaining quartet, hiring Stan Getz in Mulligan's place. The interesting and largely successful two-CD set **West Coast Live** (Pacific Jazz 35634) has Getz playing with the quartet in 1953 and with Baker's regular group in 1954. Baker is in top form, but unfortunately, he and Getz never really got along personally and their partnership would be revived on just two occasions in later years.

In July 1953, Chet Baker formed a new quartet, utilizing pianist Russ Freeman and a variety of bassists and drummers. ● **The Chet Baker Quartet with Russ Freeman** (Pacific Jazz 93164), **This Time the Dream's on Me** (Pacific Jazz 25248), and **Out of Nowhere** (Pacific Jazz 27693) document the quartet during 1953–54; the latter two CDs are taken from live performances. The communication between Baker and Freeman is impressive, the rhythm section is quietly supportive, and the trumpeter shows that, even at this early stage, he was a charismatic performer. He takes his earliest recorded vocal on **The Chet Baker Quartet** CD on "I Fall in Love Too Easily," but these are otherwise instrumental sets. **Chet Baker & Strings** (Columbia/Legacy 65562) is an easy-listening affair that has Baker, Zoot Sims, and Bud Shank playing melodic tunes (including Freeman's most famous composition "The Wind") with a string section. **Boston, 1954** (Uptown 27.35), a live set by the quartet (with Freeman, bassist Carson Smith, and drummer Bob Neel), was not released until the early 1990s and features the group playing their standard repertoire including "Isn't It Romantic," "The Wind," "My Funny Valentine," and Mulligan's "Line for Lyons." **Chet Baker Big Band** (Pacific Jazz 81201) is mistitled because only four of the 16 titles (from the fall of 1954) are actually performed by a big band (11 pieces) with a nonet heard on six other titles and a sextet on the remainder. However, the music is consistently excellent and the arrangements (by Jimmy Heath, Jack Montrose, Johnny Mandel, Bill Holman, Christian Chevalier, Pierre Michelot, and Phil Urso) bring out the best in the players.

Gray December (Pacific Jazz 97160) mostly has Baker playing in a septet from 1953 with tenor saxophonist Jack Montrose (who contributed the arrangements), altoist Herb Geller, baritonist Bob Gordon, and Freeman. However, the first four numbers (from 1955) are Baker's first real vocal session. His high-pitched voice (which, like his trumpet playing, was completely untrained) would both puzzle his jazz fans due to its shaky intonation and increase his audience (particularly among women), for his singing always had a vulnerable quality about it.

In mid-1955, Chet Baker seemed poised for stardom, with his movie-star looks and highly accessible style. He was winning jazz polls (which embarrassed him a bit since Dizzy Gillespie was at the peak of his powers) and attracting large audiences. Even Hollywood was interested, and Baker appeared in the low-budget film *Hell's Horizon*, with more major roles promised in the future. But things would not turn out quite as expected.

Baker sailed to Europe in September 1955, staying till the following April. His quartet for the tour started out featuring pianist Richard Twardzik, bassist Jimmy Bond, and drummer Peter Littman. Twardzik was a talented bop-based pianist with a potentially bright future. In 1951, he had played in Boston with Serge Chaloff and appeared on a radio broadcast with Charlie Parker. He worked along the way with Charlie Mariano and Lionel Hampton, and recorded half of a Pacific Jazz album, which he shared with Russ Freeman, **Russ Freeman/Richard Twardzik Trio** (Capitol 46861). That enjoyable bop set contrasts the two complementary Baker-associated pianists, both of whom were making their debuts as leaders.

Chet Baker in Paris Vol. 1 (EmArcy 837 474) has the trumpeter's quartet featured on nine numbers on October 11 and includes some of the best examples of Twardzik on record. It was also his last recordings for, on October 21, the pianist died of an overdose of heroin at the age of 24. One would think that Baker would learn from the tragedy (along with the example of Gerry Mulligan), but unfortunately it had no effect on the decisions he would soon make with his life. The remainder of this CD has four selections with a sextet on October 25, including a song called "In Memory of Dick."

Chet Baker in Paris Vol. 2 (EmArcy 837 475) teams Baker with two mostly French rhythm sections. **Chet Baker in Paris Vol. 3** (EmArcy 837 476) reaches up to March 15, 1956, and has Baker sharing the spotlight with the superb Belgian tenor saxophonist Bobby Jaspar in a quintet, jamming with tenorman Jean-Louis Chautemps and pianist Francy Boland in another group, and concluding his European trip with an excellent octet date. **Chet Baker in Paris Vol. 4** (EmArcy 837 477) is mostly for completists as it consists of alternate takes from four of the sessions. Throughout these discs, Baker is heard at his playing prime (there are no vocals) and he shows why he was rated so high during the period. And with 13 CDs of material recorded as a leader during 1953–early 1956, Baker was (next to Louis Armstrong) clearly the most popular trumpeter in jazz.

West Coast Jazz

What is West Coast (or cool) jazz and how does it differ from bebop?

Cool jazz is in some ways a smoothing down of the rough edges of bop. While classic bop often sounds a bit like a wild jam session, cool employs softer tones, a much quieter and less jarring rhythm section, and greater emphasis on arranged ensembles. In fact, many of the more thoughtful solos almost sound as if they had been arranged ahead of time. Rather than the improvisations giving the impression that they were bursting at the

TIMELINE 1950

Sonny Stitt and Gene Ammons form a two-tenor quintet that lasts two years. • Stan Kenton forms his Innovations Orchestra. • Fats Navarro dies from tuberculosis. • George Girard forms the Basin Street Six in New Orleans. • Steve Brown (bassist with Jean Goldkette during 1924–27) records with Frank Gillis's Dixie Five. • Glen Gray breaks up the Casa Loma Orchestra. • Bertha "Chippie" Hill, who had made a successful comeback since her rediscovery in 1946, is hit by a car in Harlem and dies at the age of 45. • Dodo Marmarosa makes his only studio records of the 1950s, a four-song session for Savoy. • Belgium guitarist Toots Thielemans records his first harmonica solos with the Sphinx Studio Orchestra in Brussels. • The Dukes of Dixieland begin a long engagement at the Famous Door. • Dick Hyman records his first piano solos. • Tex Beneke breaks with the Glenn Miller estate and forms his own orchestra, but it soon becomes another Miller ghost band. • After nearly three years of inactivity, Eddie Heywood recovers from suffering a partial paralysis of his hands, spending much of the rest of his career performing easy-listening music. • High-note trumpeter Al Killian is murdered by a psychotic landlord. • Pete Johnson moves to Buffalo where he plays locally, but in obscurity. • Ray Anthony's big band has hits in "Harlem Nocturne" and "Mr. Anthony's Boogie." • Lu Watters breaks up the Yerba Buena Jazz Band and retires from music. • Stan Getz discovers Horace Silver and adds him to his quartet.

seams, they tend to be emotionally restrained, holding a lot of feeling in check, and are accessible and melodic enough for the average nonjazz listener to enjoy.

During the years since West Coast jazz's heyday, the style has been both harshly criticized and vastly underrated in jazz history books. This has happened for three major reasons. First, West Coast jazz (unlike classic bebop and hard bop) was dominated by whites, so those who specialize in political correctness have written it off as a pale imitation of bebop. Second, much of West Coast jazz was performed in Los Angeles, so New Yorkers who like to feel that their city has been responsible for every innovation in jazz since the late 1920s have gone out of their way to chastise the music. And finally, West Coast jazz was not a radical break from the past or a giant step forward. Like hard bop, it was really a movement within rather than against the world of bop.

The main reason why whites were dominant in the West Coast jazz movement is that in the early-to-mid 1950s many musicians (including from the Stan Kenton and Woody Herman orchestras) settled in Los Angeles to work in the studios. Although jazz has historically been more integrated than American society on a whole, the film and television studios were still largely segregated at the time, even with the pioneering efforts of Benny Carter and multireedist Buddy Collette. The former big band players were all very good readers, and quite a few top jazz arrangers moved to Los Angeles for the studio work. With so many creative talents in one place at one time, the result was the development and evolution of an interesting new jazz style, one that had been born in the 1940s music of Lester Young, the John Kirby Sextet, Lennie Tristano, the Claude Thornhill Orchestra, and the Miles Davis Nonet.

Shorty Rogers Shorty Rogers was one of the most important contributors to West Coast jazz. He was a fine middle-register trumpeter, a talented arranger, an organizer of sessions, and behind the scenes in an uncountable number of ways. He started off his career playing with the big bands of Will Bradley (1942) and Red Norvo (1942–43) before serving in the military (1943–45). Rogers made his mark as a trumpeter and particularly an arranger with Woody Herman's First Herd (1945–46), Second Herd (1947–49), and Stan Kenton's Innovations Orchestra (1950–51). After leaving Kenton, he settled in Los Angeles where he worked

with Howard Rumsey's Lighthouse All-Stars and in 1953 started leading Shorty Rogers and His Giants. That same year, Rogers wrote part of the film score for Marlon Brando's *The Wild One* (at Brando's request), and from that point on, Rogers was very involved in getting jazz music into the Hollywood studios, providing work for dozens of West Coast jazz musicians.

One would naturally assume that, considering his stature in jazz history, Shorty Rogers's records of the 1950s would be easily available on CD, but many require a search. His initial date as a leader, six numbers from October 8, 1951, with a group that (except for substituting tenor for baritone) uses the same instrumentation as the Miles Davis Nonet, are available on ● **The Birth of the Cool Vol. 2** (Capitol 98933). Rogers contributed four of the six numbers (including "Popo," which became his theme song), Jimmy Giuffre (heard on tenor) brought in "Four Mothers," and Art Pepper is showcased on "Over the Rainbow." Also on this disc are the Gerry Mulligan tentet date (that is also available on a GNP/Crescendo CD) and the two songs from the 1951 Metronome All-Stars, which (other than in 1956) was the last time that *Metronome* sponsored a record date. On "Early Spring" and "Local 802 Blues," such major cool jazz players as Miles Davis, Lee Konitz, Stan Getz, Serge Chaloff, and George Shearing are featured.

Shorty Rogers's 1953–54 recordings for Victor are mostly pretty scarce including the LPs **Shorty Rogers and His Giants** (Victor 3137), **Cool and Crazy** (Victor 3138), **Courts the Count** (Victor 1004), and **Collaboration** (RCA 1018). All of the music but **Collaboration** was reissued on the more recent (but still long out of print) double-LP set **Short Stop** (Bluebird 5917). In settings ranging from a nonet to a big band, Rogers utilizes such players as trombonist Milt Bernhart, John Graas on French horn, Art Pepper, the tenors of Jimmy Giuffre and Bob Cooper, pianist Hampton Hawes, drummer Shelly Manne, high-note trumpeter Maynard Ferguson, and bassist Curtis Counce. Such originals as "Powder Puff," "Diablos' Dance," "Coup de Graas," "Infinity Promenade," and "The Sweetheart of Sigmund Freud" helped to define West Coast jazz. Also largely unavailable is the music last out on the limited-edition six-LP set **The Complete Atlantic and EMI Jazz Recordings of Shorty Rogers** (Mosaic 6-125), which has Rogers leading a major quintet in 1955 with Giuffre (on tenor, clarinet, and baritone), either Pete Jolly or Lou Levy on piano, Curtis Counce or

Ralph Pena on bass, and Shelly Manne (including the humorous blues "Martians Go Home"), plus the 1951 Capitol session and various medium-size group dates from 1955–56. These are significant dates that deserve to be widely available and really point out the importance of Shorty Rogers during this period.

Five Major West Coast Jazz Groups

The proliferation of talented young modern jazz musicians on the West Coast (particularly Los Angeles) led to the formation of several regularly working bands. Although underrated on the East Coast, they were among the pacesetters in 1950s jazz.

Howard Rumsey's Lighthouse All-Stars   Howard Rumsey, the original bassist with the Stan Kenton Orchestra (1941–42), settled in Los Angeles in the early 1940s and freelanced in a variety of settings. In 1949, he convinced the owner of the Lighthouse to feature jazz by his pickup group on Sundays. Within a couple of years Rumsey's band (which he named the Lighthouse All-Stars) was playing nightly at the Lighthouse, and the Sunday sessions (which featured a jam session from 2:00 P.M. to 2:00 A.M.) became legendary.

The earliest recordings by the Lighthouse All-Stars were made in 1952 for Skylark and in July for the new Contemporary label. That version of the band had Shorty Rogers, Milt Bernhart, Bob Cooper, and Jimmy Giuffre on tenors, pianist Frank Patchen, Rumsey, and Shelly Manne. Marty Paich took over on piano in 1953, and by the fall Rogers and Giuffre had left. The second important version of the band consisted of trumpeter Rolf Ericson, altoist Herb Geller, Bob Cooper, Bud Shank (on baritone), pianist Claude Williamson, Rumsey and Max Roach, with Bernhart, and bongo player Jack Costanzo as occasional guests. Since there was a large pool of players to choose from, the Lighthouse All-Stars changed their frontline a few times during 1954–55 with such musicians spending time with the group as Stu Williamson (trumpet and valve trombone), Bob Enevoldsen (valve trombone and tenor), Bud Shank (alto, baritone, and flute), Bob Cooper, baritonist Bob Gordon, trumpeter Conte Candoli, and trombonist Frank Rosolino; the rhythm section became Claude Williamson, Rumsey, and drummer Stan Levey. The Lighthouse All-Stars featured many musicians who would excel in bop-oriented settings for the next couple of decades.

The band's Contemporary recordings have all been reissued in the Original Jazz Classics series and each one is rewarding. ❍ **Sunday Jazz à La Lighthouse** (Original Jazz Classics 151) has highlights from a typical marathon Sunday session (February 21, 1953) with Maynard Ferguson and Hampton Hawes joining the usual group of the time; highlights include "Four Brothers," the Latin romp "Viva Zapata," "All the Things You Are," and "Bernie's Tune." **Sunday Jazz à La Lighthouse, Vol. 2** (Original Jazz Classics 973) has the same basic group playing six songs from May 15 plus three previously unreleased numbers from September by a different lineup (with Rolf Ericson and Chet Baker on trumpets, Cooper, and Shank). **Vol. 3** (Original Jazz Classics 266) features three different versions of the group including the band on its first Contemporary date, the Ericson-Geller-Cooper-Shank version of late 1953 (including "Jazz Invention" and "Witch Doctor"), and three numbers from 1956 with Stu Williamson, Rosolino, Shank, and Cooper (including "Mexican Passport" and "The Song Is You").

Oboe/Flute (Original Jazz Classics 154) was quite unusual for the time. For this special project, Bud Shank sticks to flutes and Bob Cooper alternates between oboe and English horn (Coop was among the first jazz improviser on both of those instruments). The quintet date (with Rumsey, Claude Williamson, and Max Roach) is often quite eerie although hard-swinging on "A Night in Tunisia" and "Bags' Groove." The CD reissue also includes four selections from 1956 with Buddy Collette taking Shank's spot on flute and Rumsey joined in the rhythm section by pianist Sonny Clark and Stan Levey. Collette's "Blue Sands" (which would become associated with the Chico Hamilton Quintet) takes honors.

Vol. 6 (Original Jazz Classics 386) is more conventional but particularly strong with Candoli, either Rosolino or Stu Williamson, Shank, Cooper, Williams, and Levey joining Rumsey for three Cooper originals and a variety of songs that hark back to the swing era (including "East of the Sun" and "Dickie's Dream"). The music, however, was quite modern for 1955. Also quite worthwhile is **Lighthouse at Laguna** (Original Jazz Classics 406), which finds the Lighthouse All-Stars on a rare "road trip," performing two hours away from the Lighthouse, at the Irvine Bowl in Laguna Beach. The group was trumpetless at the time, featuring Shank, Cooper, Rosolino, Claude Williamson, Rumsey, and

Levey who are in excellent form on five numbers. In addition, they back Barney Kessel's guitar feature on "'Round Midnight," and the Hampton Hawes Trio (with Red Mitchell and Shelly Manne) is showcased on "Walkin'" and a heated "The Champ."

Shelly Manne's Men   Drummer Shelly Manne was always a beloved figure, a versatile drummer who was so reliable and friendly that he was often underrated, although his fellow musicians always knew how talented he was. Manne was able to swing the complex music of two of Stan Kenton's most significant bands (1946–48 and 1950–51), settling in Los Angeles in December 1951 after leaving Kenton the second time. He first recorded as a leader in 1951 for the Dee Gee label, worked with Howard Rumsey's Lighthouse All-Stars (1952–53) and Shorty Rogers and His Giants (1953–55), became a fixture in the studios, and in 1955 formed the initial version of Shelly Manne and His Men. **The West Coast Sound, Vol. 1** (Original Jazz Classics 152) has four titles from a 1953 septet date with Art Pepper, Bob Cooper, baritonist Jimmy Giuffre, and valve trombonist Bob Enevoldsen, four from a few months later with Bud Shank in Pepper's place, and four other songs from 1955 when Manne headed a septet with altoist Joe Maini and Bill Holman on tenor in addition to Giuffre and Enevoldsen. With arrangements by Marty Paich (who plays piano on the first two dates), Giuffre, Shorty Rogers, Bill Russo, Holman, and Enevoldsen, the music has plenty of variety yet defines the era, ranging from Russo's "Sweets" (a tribute to trumpeter Harry "Sweets" Edison), Giuffre's "Fugue," and the Latin folk tune "La Mucura" to updated charts on older swing tunes.

The Three and the Two (Original Jazz Classics 172) has a pair of very unusual sets from 1954. "The Three" features trumpeter Shorty Rogers, Jimmy Giuffre alternating on clarinet, tenor, and baritone, and Manne on piano or bass. Some of the six performances (particularly the four originals) are quite free, particularly the completely improvised "Abstract No. 1." Although these selections were not influential at all, they rank second in chronological order (behind Lennie Tristano's performances of 1949) among free jazz records. The remainder of the set ("The Two") consists of a series of duets between Russ Freeman and Manne (no bass) and is also quite advanced in spots, swinging but quite unpredictable. As for Shelly

Manne's own regular band, it would start appearing regularly on records in 1956.

The Dave Brubeck Quartet   After he gave up on the Dave Brubeck Octet, which rarely ever appeared in public, Brubeck formed a trio in 1949 with bassist Ron Crotty and Cal Tjader on drums. **24 Classic Original Recordings** (Fantasy 24276) has all of the trio's record sessions, with Tjader also playing a little bit of bongos and vibes. These interpretations of standards are full of surprising moments with Brubeck, even at this early stage, sounding nothing at all like Bud Powell and already being quite recognizable as himself. The group was popular in the San Francisco area, but was forced to break up when Brubeck had a swimming accident that seriously hurt his back and put him out of action for much of a year.

When he had mostly recovered by mid-1951, Brubeck was persuaded by altoist Paul Desmond (who had been in his octet) to form a quartet. Along with the two lead voices, such players as bassists Fred Dutton (who doubled on bassoon), Wyatt Ruther, Ron Crotty, and Bob Bates (who was with the quartet during 1954–55) and drummers Herb Barman, Lloyd Davis, and Joe Dodge (who joined in the fall of 1953) spent time with the band.

Paul Desmond's light, floating, and distinctive tone on alto along with a thoughtful style full of witty song quotes and brilliant melodic improvising seemed to many an odd match with Brubeck's percussive chordings. However, the pair ended up being a perfect contrast for each other, and their occasional improvised counterpoint was quite inspiring. Recording regularly for Fantasy during 1951–53, the Dave Brubeck Quartet acquired a strong following, first in San Francisco, then California, and in time the whole country. Because they were often booked to play on college campuses (which was extremely unusual for a modern jazz band of the time), the quartet built up a large young audience that would remain loyal for many years. By 1954, the band was so popular that Brubeck was signed to the Columbia label and he was featured on the cover of *Time* magazine, which embarrassed him because he felt that Duke Ellington should have been there first.

The Fantasy recordings are available on **Stardust** (Fantasy 24728), **Dave Brubeck/Paul Desmond** (Fantasy 24727), **Jazz at Oberlin** (Original Jazz Classics

046), **Jazz at the College of the Pacific** (Original Jazz Classics 047), and the out-of-print LP **At Wilshire-Ebell** (Fantasy 3249). Each of these sets is easily recommended, but if one had to choose just one, **Jazz at Oberlin** would win. That set from 1953 has Brubeck on "These Foolish Things" playing so percussively and atonal in spots that he sometimes sounds like Cecil Taylor would several years later. Other highpoints of the CD include some miraculous interplay by Brubeck and Desmond on "Perdido" and brilliant renditions of "The Way You Look Tonight," "How High the Moon," and "Stardust."

After signing with Columbia, the Dave Brubeck Quartet became one of the best-known jazz groups in America, never losing its popularity. Their music reached one of its highpoints with ⊙ **Jazz Goes to College** (Columbia 45149), a 1954 concert that has what is arguably Paul Desmond's greatest recorded solo on the lengthy blues "Balcony Rock." His ideas follow so logically from each other, using repetition very creatively to develop his thoughts, that every note is perfectly placed. Brubeck's improvisation on that song builds slowly and almost reaches the heights of Desmond's. Other highlights include "Out of Nowhere," "Take the 'A' Train," "I Want to Be Happy," and "Don't Worry About Me." The other Columbia discs from 1954–55, **Jazz: Red Hot & Cool** (Sony 61468), which introduced Brubeck's "The Duke," and **Brubeck Time** (Columbia 65724), are also quite worthy.

The Dave Pell Octet   A group that really defined the sound of 1950s West Coast jazz with its modern harmonies, restrained ensembles, soft tones, and swing repertoire was the Dave Pell Octet. Pell started out playing tenor as a teenager with the big bands of Tony Pastor, Bob Astor, and Bobby Sherwood, before moving to California in the mid-1940s. Pell was a fixture with the Les Brown Orchestra during 1947–55, and in 1953, he began to lead his own group, mostly drawn from the ranks of the Brown band. The recordings of the Dave Pell Octet (made originally for Trend and Kapp) were popular and fortunately its first four albums have been reissued by the Spanish Fresh Sound label as three CDs. **Plays Irving Berlin** (Fresh Sound 503) has Pell leading his group through a dozen Berlin songs, with arrangements by Shorty Rogers, Jerry Fielding, Wes Hensel, and Ray Sims. The band at the time consisted of

Pell, trumpeter Don Fagerquist (who had been with Gene Krupa in the late 1940s), trombonist Ray Sims (Zoot Sims's brother and a soundalike of Bill Harris), Ronny Lang on baritone, alto, and flute, pianist Jeff Clarkson, guitarist Tony Rizzi, bassist Rolly Bundock, and drummer Jack Sperling. "Change Partners," "Russian Lullaby," and "He Ain't Got Rhythm" are highlights. The colorful yet laidback arrangements, concise solos, and appealing tone colors made the Dave Pell Octet memorable from the start.

Plays Burke & Van Heusen (Fresh Sound 504) features the same group except that Claude Williamson is on piano and Lucy Ann Polk (a delightful singer) helps out on eight of the 16 selections, all compositions by either Johnny Burke or Jimmy Van Heusen. This time around the arrangements are provided by Rogers, Hensel, Bill Holman, Bob Enevoldsen, Jack Montrose, Med Flory, Jim Emerson, and Buddy Bregman. Among the selections are "But Beautiful," "Aren't You Glad You're You," "Imagination," and "Polka Dots and Moonbeams." ⊙ **Plays Rodgers & Hart** (Fresh Sound 505), with Donn Trenner on piano and drummer Bill Richmond, is strictly instrumental and gets the edge due to its particularly classic versions of "Mountain Greenery," "The Blue Room," "I've Got Five Dollars," "The Lady Is a Tramp," and "Spring Is Here."

I Had the Craziest Dream (Capitol 95445) has the first 13 selections that Pell's octet recorded for Capitol (eight songs from 1955 and five from 1957) plus four songs led by Don Fagerquist with a similar band in 1955. The Pell octet utilizes the same lineup of musicians except for having either Bob Gordon or Ronny Lang on baritone, pianist Paul Smith, Sperling back on drums, and Joe Mondragon, Ralph Pena, or Rolly Bundock on bass, performing compositions from a variety of writers (including Shorty Rogers, Pell, and Paich) plus such standards as "Star Eyes," "The Way You Look Tonight," and even "On the Good Ship Lollipop." The Fagerquist miniset utilizes three tenors (Pell, Bill Holman, and Zoot Sims) and arrangements by Paich and Hensel on four familiar tunes. Quintessential West Coast jazz.

The Chico Hamilton Quintet   Chico Hamilton had already been a professional musician for 15 years before he found fame with his own quintet. He had played in the Los Angeles area since high school, recorded with Slim Gaillard, toured with Lionel Hampton, served in the military (1942–46), and worked with Lester Young, Lena Horne (off and on during 1948–55), and the Gerry Mulligan quartet (1952–53). During 1953–54, he led a trio album featuring guitarist Howard Roberts and bassist George Duvivier.

In 1955, Hamilton put together a chamber jazz group featuring the reeds (flute, alto, tenor, and clarinet) of Buddy Collette, guitarist Jim Hall, cellist Fred Katz, and bassist Carson Smith, who was best known for playing bass with Chet Baker. Although Harry Babasin and Oscar Pettiford had previously recorded jazz solos on cello, they were normally bassists while Katz was a classically trained full-time cellist, who also occasionally played piano elsewhere. Collette had worked with Les Hite (1942), led a dance band in the navy during World War II, and gigged in the L.A. area with the Stars of Swing (1946), Louis Jordan, Benny Carter, and the Gerald Wilson Orchestra (1949–50). A pioneer of the flute in jazz and an early teacher of Charles Mingus, Collette was also the first black musician to get a permanent spot in a West Coast studio band starting in 1951.

While the six-CD limited-edition box set **The Complete Pacific Jazz Recordings of the Chico Hamilton Quintet** (Mosaic 6-175) perfectly covers Hamilton's music of 1955–59, unfortunately, most of this material is otherwise unavailable on CD. This is particularly unfortunate for the debut record, **The Chico Hamilton Quintet Featuring Buddy Collette** (Pacific Jazz 1209), which is a classic of its kind, perfectly summing up the group's unusual sound and great potential. Highlights of that magical album (recorded August 4 and 23, 1955) include "A Nice Day," "Blue Sands," and "My Funny Valentine." The band also had a live album later in the year that, alas, is also difficult to obtain outside of the Mosaic box.

Other Top West Coast Players

All of the musicians in this section, as with the previous five groups, are quite underrated due to being classified as West Coast cool players. Truth is, they could hold their own with the better-publicized hard bop musicians, with several of the players being major forces for decades.

Conte Candoli, Jon Eardley, and Jack Sheldon

Conte Candoli was one of the top bop trumpeters based on the West Coast. He gained experience and recognition playing with Woody Herman (1944–45), Chubby Jackson (1947), Stan Kenton (1948), Charlie Ventura (1949), Woody Herman again (1950), and Stan Kenton a second time (1952–54). After Conte moved to Los Angeles, Charlie Parker talked with him about joining Bird's group, but the altoist soon died. Candoli instead became a studio musician and the first call for jazz dates in L.A., including with the Lighthouse All-Stars. **Powerhouse Trumpet** (Bethlehem 75826), a quintet session with tenor saxophonist Bill Holman, Lou Levy, Leroy Vinnegar, and drummer Lawrence Marable, is an excellent example of Candoli's playing in 1955, featuring him digging into "Four," "Groovin' Higher," and "I'm Getting Sentimental Over You."

Jon Eardley had a cool tone similar to Chet Baker's and a swinging boppish style. He played in an Air Force band (1946–49), worked locally in his native Pennsylvania (1950–53), played in New York with Phil Woods (1954), and then was a member of Gerry Mulligan's quartet and sextet for three years, starting in 1954. His first two sessions as a leader are combined together on **From Hollywood to New York** (Original Jazz Classics 1746). Four selections are with a quartet also including pianist Pete Jolly (at the beginning of his career), bassist Red Mitchell, and drummer Larry Bunker while the other four numbers feature Eardley with tenor saxophonist J.R. Monterose, pianist George Syran, bassist Teddy Kotick, and drummer Nick Stabulas. The five originals and three standards serve as perfect examples of cool-toned but inwardly heated bop.

Jack Sheldon has been a popular figure in the Los Angeles area since the early 1950s. He was born in Jacksonville, Florida, started on trumpet when he was 12, moved to Los Angeles in 1947, and played in military bands while in the Air Force (1949–52). Sheldon worked at the Lighthouse and with such players as J.R. Monterose, Art Pepper, Wardell Gray, Dexter Gordon, Jimmy Giuffre, and Herb Geller. He was a strong bop-based player who could play "cool" à la Chet Baker but had more technique. **The Quartet and the Quintet** (Blue Note 93160) not only has the music from Sheldon's first two LPs as a leader, but three additional selections originally put out on samplers. Sheldon is well-featured on three songs in a quintet with altoist Joe Maini, on eight numbers with a quartet that co-stars pianist Walter Norris, and on the remaining eight tunes in a quintet with Zoot Sims and Norris. The straightahead music (standards and basic originals) lets listeners hear how Jack Sheldon sounded at the beginning of his career.

Bob Brookmeyer and Frank Rosolino Bob Brookmeyer emerged as an important musician in the West Coast jazz scene during 1953–54. He had actually started out his career as a pianist in dance bands, but made his mark as both a valve trombonist and an arranger. In 1953, Brookmeyer played with Stan Getz and then was a longtime member (1954–57) of the Gerry Mulligan Quartet where he was in the former Chet Baker role; his interplay with Mulligan was always a joy to hear. Brookmeyer began recording as a leader in 1954. **The Dual Role of Bob Brookmeyer** (Original Jazz Classics 1729) has music from two different combos. Brookmeyer is heard on two songs apiece on valve trombone and piano in 1955 with Jimmy Raney, bassist Teddy Kotick, and Mel Lewis. The second half of the reissue has Brookmeyer on a date actually led by vibraphonist Teddy Charles that also includes Kotick and drummer Ed Shaughnessy; Nancy Overton takes an effective vocal on "Nobody's Heart." Overall the music is effective West Coast–style cool jazz, a solid early effort from Brookmeyer.

Frank Rosolino was an exuberant and technically skilled trombonist who occasionally took a humorous vocal. After serving in the military, Rosolino played with the big bands of Bob Chester, Glen Gray, Gene Krupa (1948–49), Tony Pastor, Herbie Fields, Georgie Auld, and most importantly, Stan Kenton (1952–54), where he gained his initial fame. After leaving Kenton, Rosolino settled in Los Angeles where he became a member of the Lighthouse All-Stars in 1954 and recorded two albums (both unfortunately out of print) for Capital during 1954–55. Whenever there was a call for a trombonist on the West Coast during this period, Frank Rosolino was usually contacted first.

John Graas John Graas was, along with Julius Watkins, the first French horn soloist in jazz. Graas was a member of the Claude Thornhill Orchestra in 1942. A period in the army (1942–45) and stints with the Cleveland Orchestra and Tex Beneke's big band preceded his year with Stan Kenton's Innovations Orchestra (1950–51). Graas settled in Los Angeles in 1951 and primarily worked as a studio musician who was available for jazz dates whenever a French horn was desired. A talented composer, Graas led albums of his own starting in 1953 (including one called **French Horn Jazz**), but these Decca sessions utilizing West Coast all-stars have yet to appear on CD or even LP for many years.

Herb Geller, Art Pepper, and Bud Shank Herb Geller mixed together a lot of Benny Carter in his sound on alto, along with Charlie Parker. Born in Los Angeles, he started out playing with Joe Venuti's Orchestra in 1946. Geller spent 1949–50 with the Claude Thornhill Orchestra, moved back to L.A. in 1951, and married the fine bop pianist Lorraine Walsh. He worked with Billy May (1952), Shorty Rogers, Maynard Ferguson, Bill Holman, Chet Baker, Clifford Brown (on the 1954 jam session records), and with his wife in the Gellers (1954–55). **Herb Geller Plays** (EmArcy 512 252) is one of three projects that Geller recorded for EmArcy during this period. Joined by his wife plus either Curtis Counce or Leroy Vinnegar on bass and Lawrence Marable or Bruz Freeman on drums, the altoist excels on five standards, one of Lorraine's songs and five of his boppish originals.

Art Pepper emerged during his periods with the Stan Kenton Orchestra as one of the most promising of the young alto saxophonists, and one of the few (along with Lee Konitz and Paul Desmond) who did not sound like a cousin of Charlie Parker. He worked with the big bands of Gus Arnheim, Benny Carter (who was an early influence), and Stan Kenton (1943) before spending 1944–46 in the military. Pepper was back with Kenton during 1947–48 and 1950–51, being well-featured and gaining recognition. Unfortunately, he became a heroin addict during the latter period and spent three brief periods in jail during 1951–56. But, as would be true throughout his career, no matter how bad shape he was in physically, Pepper never made an uninspiring record. His earliest recordings as a leader (other than live sets later released on three LPs from the Xanadu label) were three sessions made for Savoy during 1952 and 1954, resulting in 16 selections and 25 alternate takes. **The Discovery Sessions** (Savoy 92846) has the 16 songs plus 6 of the alternates. Pepper, who is featured in a quartet with Hampton Hawes, bassist Joe Mondragon, and drummer Larry Bunker, and in a different quartet with Russ Freeman, bassist Bob Whitlock, and drummer Bobby White, is heard at his best interacting with tenor saxophonist Jack Montrose in a quintet (with Claude Williamson, bassist Monty Budwig, and either Paul Vallerina or Larry Bunker on drums). The two saxophonists constantly echo each other's ideas. Overall, the highlights of these Savoy sessions include "Surf Ride," "Chili Pepper," "Suzy the Poodle," "Tickle Toe," "Deep Purple," "The Way You Look Tonight," and "Straight

Life." There have been other reissues of this material (usually with less music), but other than an earlier two-LP set that included all of the alternates, **The Discovery Sessions** is the best repackaging of this inventive music.

Bud Shank started out his career a bit overshadowed by Pepper, but he gradually built up his own strong reputation, practically symbolizing West Coast jazz with his cool-toned alto and fluid flute. He attended the University of North Carolina (1944–46) and learned all of the reeds, eventually concentrating on alto and flute. Shank played with Charlie Barnet (1947–48) and Stan Kenton (1950–51) and then moved to Los Angeles, working with the Lighthouse All-Stars and leading his own albums starting in 1954. **Jazz in Hollywood** (Original Jazz Classics 1890) has his first date as a leader, six numbers with Shorty Rogers in a quintet that were originally cut for the short-lived Nocturne label. Among the tunes (all Rogers originals) are "Casa de Luz" and "Lotus Bud." Also on this CD are eight boppish selections from a trio date featuring Lou Levy (formerly with Woody Herman and a talented pianist who had just ended a three-year retirement from music), bassist Harry Babasin, and drummer Roy Harte. **Bud Shank and Bill Perkins** (Pacific Jazz 93159) is an interesting hodge-podge collection. Surprisingly, Shank is mostly heard on tenor and baritone while Perkins (best known on tenor) also plays alto and a bit of flute. Shank and Perk are in fine form on a quintet date from 1955 with Hampton Hawes (who has a trio feature on "I Hear Music"), Red Mitchell, and drummer Mel Lewis. There are also four numbers from 1956 that feature Shank, but are actually from a session led by Russ Freeman but never completed and only put out previously on samplers. In addition, there are three later numbers that were leftovers, featuring Perkins and Jimmy Rowles. Although not a classic, this CD has plenty of rewarding music.

Lennie Niehaus   Best known as an arranger, Lennie Niehaus has also been a top-notch cool-toned alto soloist. He graduated from college and occasionally wrote for the Stan Kenton Orchestra during 1951–52 before being drafted, spending two years in the army. After his discharge, Niehaus resumed contributing to Kenton's orchestra, settled in Los Angeles, and led a series of albums for the Contemporary label.

 ◉ **Vol. 1: The Quintets** (Original Jazz Classics 319) has the eight songs from Niehaus's initial dates as a leader

in 1954, a pianoless quintet with Jack Montrose on tenor, baritonist Bob Gordon, bassist Monty Budwig, and Shelly Manne, plus four songs from 1956 with Stu Williamson (doubling on trumpet and valve trombone) in a quintet with Hampton Hawes, Red Mitchell, and Manne. In both cases the concise solos are excellent and Niehaus's arrangements are inspired and colorful. **Zounds** (Original Jazz Classics 1892) has octet sessions from 1954 and 1956 with such notables as Williamson, valve trombonist Bob Enevoldsen, Montrose, and Gordon in the frontline of the earlier set while Frank Rosolino, Vince DeRosa on French horn, Jay McAllister on tuba, Bill Perkins on tenor, and baritonist Pepper Adams join Niehaus on the later date. **Vol. 3: The Octet #2** (Original Jazz Classics 1767) features a similar group (with Williamson, Enevoldsen, Bill Holman on tenor, and baritonist Jimmy Giuffre joining Niehaus, Lou Levy, Budwig, and Manne) playing five of Niehaus's originals, an obscurity, and inventive reworking of six standards. **Vol. 4: The Quintets and Strings** (Original Jazz Classics 1858) is Niehaus's fourth album of material from a nine-month period and showcases his alto well. Five songs have him with Budwig, Manne, three violas, and a cellist. Three songs add Perkins and Gordon, and there are also four unrelated tunes from a quintet set with Williamson, Hawes, Budwig, and Manne.

In reality, all of these Lennie Niehaus CDs (plus a fifth one recorded in 1956) are easily recommended and show that West Coast jazz was far from bloodless despite the comments of its East Coast detractors.

Jimmy Giuffre, Jack Montrose, and Bob Gordon
The composer of "Four Brothers," Jimmy Giuffre played in an army band during World War II, then had stints with the big bands of Boyd Raeburn, Jimmy Dorsey, and Buddy Rich. Two years after Woody Herman recorded "Four Brothers," Giuffre finally joined his band (1949). He moved to Los Angeles the following year where his mellow-toned tenor, clarinet, and baritone were in great demand. Giuffre was an important member of Howard Rumsey's Lighthouse All-Stars (1951–52) and Shorty Rogers and His Giants (1952–56). Unfortunately, his recordings as a leader for Capitol (1954–55) are unavailable.

Jack Montrose was a skilled cool jazz arranger/composer and a fine tenor saxophonist in the 1950s. He graduated from Los Angeles State College in 1953, and then worked with Jerry Gray, Art Pepper (with whom he collaborated on some exciting recordings), and Red Norvo. Montrose, who recorded with Clifford Brown in 1954 (providing the arrangements), can be heard in excellent form on **The Jack Montrose Sextet** (Pacific Jazz 93161). This CD combines two dates: arguably Montrose's finest album as a leader, a 1955 outing with baritonist Bob Gordon, Conte Candoli, pianist Paul Moer, bassist Ralph Pena, and Shelly Manne, plus a quintet set that was actually headed by Gordon, one of only two that the short-lived baritonist led. Montrose contributed five originals plus three reworked standards to his own set and is significant on Gordon's album beyond his playing since he brought in six of his songs. Montrose's arrangements, which are full of unexpected surprises while always swinging and leaving room for plenty of solos, manage to be both restrained and exciting.

Bob Gordon had the potential to be one of jazz's great baritone saxophonists. When he was 18, he worked with Shorty Sherock (1946), following it up with a three-year period with Alvino Rey's Orchestra (1948–51) and a year with Billy May (1952). He worked in the studios and recorded with the likes of Shelly Manne, Maynard Ferguson, Chet Baker, Clifford Brown (1954), Shorty Rogers, Tal Farlow, and Stan Kenton. In addition to his Pacific Jazz sessions (included on the Jack Montrose CD), Gordon's only other date as a leader was **Moods in Jazz** (V.S.O.P. 1415). Once again he is teamed up with Montrose in a quintet, and this is an excellent showcase for his baritone, whose light tone is a little reminiscent of Gerry Mulligan though having his own musical personality. But while on his way to play at a Pete Rugolo concert in San Diego on August 28, 1955, Bob Gordon was killed in a car accident. He was just 27.

Hampton Hawes, Pete Jolly, Gerald Wiggins, and Claude Williamson Pianist Hampton Hawes was one of the few black musicians who were part of the West Coast cool jazz scene of the early 1950s. Born in Los Angeles (unlike many of the West Coast players), Hawes was strongly influenced initially by Bud Powell, carving out his own voice from Powell's conception. He worked on Central Avenue, gigged with Sonny Criss, Dexter Gordon, and Wardell Gray, was part of Howard McGhee's group (1950–51), and played with Shorty Rogers and the Lighthouse All-Stars before spending 1953–54 in the army. An early example of his playing can be heard on

Piano: East/West (Original Jazz Classics 1705), which also has an unrelated session by pianist Freddie Redd from 1955. The Hawes portion has Hampton representing the West Coast in a quartet with vibraphonist Larry Bunker, bassist Clarence Jones, and drummer Lawrence Marable, playing eight straightahead numbers, including a two-minute version of "Move" that lives up to its name. Truth is, there is not that much difference between the West Coast and East Coast versions of bebop piano, but the controversy was a good excuse to introduce Hawes to records. After his release from the military, he led a trio in the Los Angeles area and began recording extensively for Contemporary. **The Trio** (Original Jazz Classics 316) features Hawes, bassist Red Mitchell, and drummer Chuck Thompson on three basic originals and swinging versions of seven standards, revitalizing such tunes as "I Got Rhythm," "What Is this Thing Called Love," and "All the Things You Are." **This Is Hampton Hawes—The Trio Vol. 2** (Original Jazz Classics 318) has the same group digging into such standards as "Stella by Starlight," "Autumn in New York," "'Round Midnight," and "You and the Night and the Music."

A powerful and hard-swinging pianist, Pete Jolly became an important addition to the West Coast jazz scene in the mid-1950s. Jolly had started on accordion when he was three and began piano lessons at eight. In 1946, his family moved to Phoenix and the following year (when he was 15), he joined the Musicians Union and began working regularly in clubs. During a visit to Los Angeles in 1954, Jolly sat in at the Lighthouse and was offered a job with Shorty Rogers and His Giants, playing alongside Rogers and Jimmy Giuffre. He made his recording debut as a leader in 1955, but his early recordings for RCA (mostly trios, but also a rare session on accordion with an all-star sextet) are out of print, as are his important contributions to the LP **The Five** (RCA 1121), a date in a quintet with Conte Candoli and Bill Perkins that is arranged by Rogers.

Gerald Wiggins combined the influences of Erroll Garner and Art Tatum in his piano style to form an original voice of his own. "The Wig" began piano lessons at four, switching from classical music to jazz as a teenager. He worked for a time in the early 1940s as piano accompanist for Stepin Fetchit and played with the big bands of Les Hite, Louis Armstrong, and Benny Carter. While in the military (1944–46), Wiggins often worked in local jazz clubs in Seattle. After his discharge, he settled permanently in the Los Angeles area, often being employed as an accompanist for singers, including Lena Horne (1950–51). In addition, Wiggins has led his own trios since the early 1950s. **1950** (Classics 1218) has his first recordings as a leader, selections cut for the French Vogue and Swing labels. These trio dates have the pianist joined by Pierre Michelot, Buddy Banks, or Jean Boucherty on bass and Kenny Clarke or Chico Hamilton on drums. Wiggins stretches out on such numbers as "The Wig," "Coffee Time," "Limehouse Blues," "Wiggin' with Wig," "All the Things You Are," and a three-part work titled "Ivan Suite," "Wig's Suite," and "Chico's Suite."

The older brother of trumpeter/valve trombonist Stu Williamson, Claude Williamson has long been a fine bop pianist influenced by Bud Powell. He studied classical music for ten years, attended the New England Conservatory, and worked with Charlie Barnet (1947 and 1949) and Red Norvo (1948). Williamson was June Christy's accompanist (1950–51), spent a year in the military, and moved to Los Angeles where he joined the Lighthouse All-Stars for three years starting in 1953. He recorded a pair of trio albums for Capitol during 1954–55, but these are not currently available.

Laurindo Almeida and Barney Kessel   Nine years before Stan Getz and Charlie Byrd teamed together to launch the bossa nova movement in the United States, Brazilian classical guitarist Laurindo Almeida and American alto saxophonist Bud Shank recorded music that hinted strongly at bossa nova. Almeida, who had been a studio guitarist in his native Brazil, played guitar with Stan Kenton (1947–48) and worked in American studios starting in 1950. ● **Brazilliance, Vol. 1** (World Pacific 96339) from April 15–22, 1953, may not have sold a lot of records when it was released, but today it certainly sounds way ahead of its time. Most of the songs are based on Brazilian folk melodies, and the combination of West Coast–type jazz solos with Brazilian rhythms (played by bassist Harry Babasin and drummer Roy Harte) works quite well, making one wonder why this was not a best-seller at the time.

Barney Kessel had made a strong reputation for himself during the bebop era as one of the top Charlie Christian–inspired guitarists. After his stints with Charlie Barnet (1944–45) and Artie Shaw (1945) had ended, he became a busy studio musician in Los Angeles, but always had

time to play jazz dates and to appear on record dates. He spent a year (1952–53) as a member of the Oscar Peterson Trio and then returned to Los Angeles, leading a rewarding series of record dates for Contemporary. **Easy Like** (Original Jazz Classics 153) is Kessel's first full-length album as a leader. He is featured in a pair of quintets, in 1953 with Bud Shank and pianist Arnold Ross, and in 1956 with Buddy Collette and Claude Williamson. Both Shank and Collette double on alto and flute. Highlights include "Easy Like," "Lullaby of Birdland," "North of the Border," and "Salute to Charlie Christian." **Vol. 2: Kessel Plays Standards** (Original Jazz Classics 238) has Kessel interacting with Bob Cooper (mostly on oboe in addition to some tenor), either Claude Williamson or Hampton Hawes, Monty Budwig or Red Mitchell, and Shelly Manne or Chuck Thompson on drums. The colorful frameworks and concise solos uplift a dozen standards, "Barney's Blues," and "64 Bars on Wilshire."

However, the main Barney Kessel CD to get from this era is 1955's ● **Vol. 3: To Swing or Not to Swing** (Original Jazz Classics 317). Bridging the boundaries between bop, cool, and swing, Kessel is heard with a septet that includes Harry "Sweets" Edison, either Georgie Auld or Bill Perkins on tenor, Jimmy Rowles, rhythm guitarist Al Hendrickson, Red Mitchell, and Irv Cottler or Shelly Manne on drums. In addition to four Kessel originals (including "Begin the Blues" and "Wail Street"), such tunes as "Louisiana," "Indiana," and "12th Street Rag" are reinvented in colorful fashion.

Red Mitchell and Stan Levey   One of the major bassists to emerge during the first half of the 1950s, Red Mitchell actually started out as a pianist, doubling on piano occasionally throughout his career. He played with Jackie Paris (1947–48), Mundell Lowe, Chubby Jackson's big band (often on piano), Charlie Ventura (1949), and the Woody Herman Orchestra (1949–51), in addition to being a member of the Red Norvo Trio (1952–54) where he succeeded Charles Mingus. A brilliant soloist (on Oscar Pettiford's level) who was also quite skilled as an accompanist, Mitchell played with the Gerry Mulligan Quartet in 1954 and then settled in Los Angeles where he had the opportunity to work with nearly everyone. **Jam for Your Bread** (Bethlehem 75823) has him leading a quintet that includes Hampton Hawes (with whom he often played regularly during this era), drummer Chuck Thompson, and (on five of the nine songs),

Conte Candoli and the up-and-coming alto and tenor saxophonist Joe Maini. The music is cool-toned bop with the highlights including "East Coast Outpost," "Ornithology," and the uptempo blues "Duff."

Stan Levey had been one of the first drummers to fully understand bebop, touring with the Dizzy Gillespie/Charlie Parker Quintet during its ill-fated trip to Los Angeles in 1945. He was the drummer with the Stan Kenton Orchestra during 1952–54, settled in Los Angeles, worked with the Lighthouse All-Stars, and became a studio musician. Levey's 1955 album **This Time the Drum's on Me** (Bethlehem 76683) emphasizes jazz tunes written since 1945, including George Handy's "Diggin' for Diz," "Tune Up," and Oscar Pettiford's "This Time the Drum's on Me." In addition to Levey, Conte Candoli, Frank Rosolino, Lou Levy, and Leroy Vinnegar, the sextet features Dexter Gordon, who was otherwise almost totally absent from records during 1953–59. Dexter plays quite well on this boppish set, making one regret that he had so many lost years.

Ralph Burns and Pete Rugolo   Ralph Burns's main importance to jazz was being a top arranger for Woody Herman's first two Herds. After the Second Herd broke up, Burns primarily concentrated on becoming a significant composer for films, Broadway shows, and studio work. In 1955, he revisited his jazz roots with **Bijou** (Original Jazz Classics 1917), a unique entry in Burns's discography in that it puts the focus on his piano playing. The music on this CD, originally released on two ten-inch LPs, has Burns playing in a quartet with guitarist Tal Farlow, bassist Clyde Lombardi, and drummer Osie Johnson. Most of the 11 selections are taken at relaxed tempos, featuring harmonically sophisticated chords and light swinging. The first six songs have the word "Spring" or some variation in their titles. Two songs have overdubbed second piano parts, and the highlights overall include "Spring Sequence," Willie "The Lion" Smith's "Echo of Spring," and "Bijou."

Pete Rugolo, who contributed so much to the library of Stan Kenton during 1945–48, has worked primarily in the Hollywood studios in the years since, in addition to writing arrangements for a variety of singers including Nat King Cole, June Christy, and Harry Belafonte. However, during 1954–55 he recorded several notable big band albums for Columbia. **Introducing Pete Rugolo/ Adventures in Rhythm** (Collectables 5893) combines his first two albums on a single CD. The emphasis is on arranged ensembles played by a big band filled with top studio and West Coast jazz players. Among the more memorable selections are "Early Stan" (which does indeed sound like the early Stan Kenton Orchestra), "California Melodies," "360 Special," "Come Back Little Rocket," the humorous "Sidewalks of New York Mambo," "Mañana," "Mixin' the Blues," "Rugolo Meets Shearing," "Jingle Bells Mambo," and "King Porter Stomp." **Rugolomania/New Sounds of Pete Rugolo** (Collectables 6092) has the remainder of Rugolo's Columbia recordings, including the haunting "4:20 A.M.," "Bongo Dance," "Shave and a Haircut," "Manhattan Mambo," and "When You're Smiling." Among the more notable soloists are Doug Mettome, both Julius Watkins ("Hornorama") and John Graas on French horns, Bob Gordon, guitarist Howard Roberts, and John Barber on tuba. Taken as a whole, these two CDs feature the best of Pete Rugolo's post-Kenton work and show how inventive an arranger he was when he explored jazz.

Cool Jazz on the East Coast

Although cool jazz is often considered synonymous with West Coast jazz, the softer and more lyical sounds of cool were also played by some musicians and groups from the East Coast.

Claude Thornhill and John Kirby   Among the main ancestors of cool jazz were the John Kirby Sextet, Claude Thornhill's Orchestra, and Lester Young. Thornhill's big band had its last two record dates in 1950 (best known among his sidemen at that point were altoists Hal McKusick and Herb Geller, and Dick Hafer on tenor) although a project in 1953 featured a specially assembled Thornhill Orchestra recording a full set of Gerry Mulligan arrangements. Unfortunately, those 14 selections (put out as a pair of ten-inch albums by Trend) have not been reissued in decades. Claude Thornhill, who was quite obscure by 1955, led low-level big bands on a part-time basis throughout the 1950s.

John Kirby's sextet broke up in 1946. In 1950, he reassembled as many of the original musicians as he could for a Carnegie Hall concert, but it was poorly attended and his former sidemen soon scattered. Charlie Shavers (Tommy Dorsey) and Russell Procope (Duke Ellington) had regular jobs, Buster Bailey played with Dixieland groups, and Billy Kyle would soon join Louis

Armstrong's All-Stars. But John Kirby, who could have continued working steadily (Benny Carter did his best to help him) had seen his dream vanish. His heart was broken, and he was depressed during the two years before his death in 1952 at the age of 43.

The Modern Jazz Quartet   The Modern Jazz Quartet (MJQ), like the John Kirby Sextet, began with a unique sound and a love for classical music in addition to the mainstream jazz music of the day. Pianist John Lewis, vibraphonist Milt Jackson, bassist Ray Brown, and drummer Kenny Clarke formed the rhythm section of the 1946 Dizzy Gillespie Big Band, having occasional features that gave the horn players a rest. Five years later they recorded as the Milt Jackson Quartet and talked seriously about forming a permanent group. Because Ray Brown was soon traveling the world as a member of the Oscar Peterson Trio, he was not available, so Percy Heath filled the bass slot. Since the group was formed as a co-op (with John Lewis soon becoming its musical director), it was decided to name the ensemble the Modern Jazz Quartet in 1952. Kenny Clarke, feeling restricted by the band's repertoire and Lewis's taste in music, left the group in 1955 and was replaced by Connie Kay. Otherwise, the band's personnel was permanently set.

During an era when jazz was not considered respectable by many, the MJQ was a major contrast. Dressed impeccably, never late for engagements, opening its repertoire to include tastefully swinging versions of classical pieces (without neglecting the blues or standards), and evoking class, the Modern Jazz Quartet broke down racial and musical boundaries. They often performed at prestigious venues formerly closed to jazz and black musicians.

During 1952–55, the MJQ recorded for the Prestige label and all of its studio recordings are available on three CDs. **MJQ** (Original Jazz Classics 125), which has four songs from the band's first session (December 22, 1952), also includes a Milt Jackson quintet session from 1954 with Heath, Clarke, pianist Horace Silver, and trumpeter Henry Boozier. **Django** (Original Jazz Classics 057) has the band's 1953–54 sessions including the original version of John Lewis's title cut (his most famous composition), "One Bass Hit," "Delauney's Dilemma," and the "La Ronde Suite." **Concorde** (Original Jazz Classics 002) from 1955 introduces Connie Kay to the group and is highlighted by a four-song Gershwin medley, "Softly as in a Morning Sunrise," and "I'll Remember April."

Throughout his MJQ years, Milt Jackson would continue recording albums as a leader. **Milt Jackson Quartet** (Original Jazz Classics 001) from 1955 uses the MJQ except with Horace Silver in Lewis's place. Silver's funky piano solos are quite a bit different than Lewis's more genteel statements and the combination works well, but the playing time on this CD is very brief, under 31 minutes. **Opus De Jazz** (Savoy 0109), also from 1955, has the same problem (being under 34 minutes), but the music is more unusual. Jackson, Frank Wess (on flute and tenor), Hank Jones, bassist Eddie Jones, and Kenny Clarke perform two originals, "You Leave Me Breathless" and a definitive 13-minute version of Silver's "Opus De Funk" that has an endless series of solos and tradeoffs.

The Red Norvo Trio   In the late 1940s in Los Angeles, Red Norvo formed an unusual new group consisting of his vibes, guitarist Tal Farlow, and bassist Charles Mingus. Norvo, a flexible swing soloist who was able to adapt well to bop, had no difficulty excelling in the quiet but frequently torrid ensembles, playing speedy unison lines with Farlow while Mingus contributed a driving bass and occasional solos. **The Modern Red Norvo** (Savoy 7113), which starts off with Norvo's 1945 session with Charlie Parker and Dizzy Gillespie, has all of the released takes of the group's 1950–51 recordings and finds the trio playing brilliantly on such numbers as "Swedish Pastry," "Move," "I'll Remember April," "Little White Lies," and "Godchild." In addition, 30 concise radio transcriptions from the band are on **Red Norvo: Vol. Two** (Vintage Jazz Classics 1008).

By 1952, Mingus (who found it very difficult being the only black in a trio and who had his own musical directions to explore) had departed, replaced by Red Mitchell. Jimmy Raney succeeded Farlow in 1953. The trio stayed together into 1955 with Farlow rejoining the group for its final recording session. **Red Norvo Trio** (Original Jazz Classics 641) and **The Red Norvo Trios** (Prestige 24108) have most of the 1953–54 dates by this group (other than three songs bypassed by Fantasy and a few titles cut for Decca). Mitchell proved to be a perfect replacement for Mingus, and these later performances hold their own with the earlier titles. The lack of piano and drums gives this group a very light feel, and the often-rapid tempos make the trio sound as if it were flying, yet completely under control.

Red Norvo also recorded in other settings that further displayed his versatility. Three of his best projects are featured on **Just a Mood** (Bluebird 6278). Four songs are from 1957 with swing all-stars (including Harry "Sweets" Edison and Ben Webster), highlighted by the haunting title cut. In addition, Norvo is heard in a cool jazz group from 1954 with flutist Buddy Collette and Tal Farlow (playing four songs with "Blue" in their title), and in a West Coast unit (also from 1954 with Shorty Rogers, clarinetist Jimmy Giuffre, and Pete Jolly) that plays four "Rose" songs including "Roses of Picardy" and "Rose Room." So whether it was swing (he had occasional reunions with Benny Goodman), bop, or cool jazz, Red Norvo remained near the top of his field.

The George Shearing Quintet   In 1949, the George Shearing Quintet caught on big, and its commercial success continued through the 1950s. Even though it was basically a bebop group, the quintet's trademark sound (with the piano, vibes, and guitar playing close together) and emphasis on strong melodies (along with Shearing's charm) resulted in the group being quite accessible to the wider public. After an initial session for Discovery, Shearing signed with MGM, an association that continued through 1954. The original personnel (in addition to the pianist/leader) was vibraphonist Marjorie Hyams,

guitarist Chuck Wayne, bassist John Levy, and drummer Denzil Best. In 1951, Hyams retired from music and was replaced by Don Elliott. Later in the year, Joe Roland took over on vibes and Al McKibbon was on bass, while in 1952 Dick Garcia became Shearing's guitarist and Marquis Foster (and then Bill Clark) was on drums. The addition of McKibbon allowed the group to play more Latin-oriented pieces, a trend that accelerated in 1953 when vibraphonist Cal Tjader and guitarist Toots Thielemans (who also occasionally played harmonica) joined the quintet and Armanda Peraza became the group's regular guest on conga. George Devins succeeded Tjader in 1954, and in 1955 (when Shearing signed with Capitol), Johnny Rae was on vibes.

102 selections were recorded (including two numbers with Billy Eckstine and four in which they are joined by the Ray Charles Singers) during the George Shearing Quintet's period on MGM, yet only one CD has been released by the classic group from this era. **Verve Jazz Masters 57** (Verve 314 529 900) is an excellent sampler with 16 of their best selections. Although it jumps around chronologically (featuring four versions of the group) it includes classic renditions of "September in the Rain," "East of the Sun," "Mambo Inn," "Jumpin' with Symphony Sid," and "I'll Remember April," plus the original version of Shearing's best-known original, "Lullaby of Birdland." Until all of the Shearing Quintet's recordings are reissued coherently, this is the CD to get.

TIMELINE 1951

The Dave Brubeck Quartet is formed. • Buddy DeFranco leads a quartet that includes Art Blakey. • Earl Bostic's "Flamingo" is a huge hit. • Bob Brookmeyer works with Tex Beneke's Orchestra, on piano. • Johnny Hodges, Lawrence Brown, and Sonny Greer all leave the Duke Ellington Orchestra to join Hodges's new combo. Ellington finds temporary replacements from Harry James's band in Willie Smith, Juan Tizol, and Louie Bellson. • Ray Brown starts working regularly with Oscar Peterson. • Kenny Burrell makes his recording debut with Dizzy Gillespie. • Conte Candoli joins Stan Kenton's Orchestra. • Betty Roche records a classic vocal version of "Take the 'A' Train" with Duke Ellington. • The Four Freshmen, one of the top pop/jazz vocal groups of the 1950s, has its first hit with "It's a Blue World." • In Stockholm, Rolf Ericson and Lars Gullin record with altoist Arne Domnerus's cool jazz group. • James P. Johnson suffers a major stroke that ends his playing career. • The Lawson-Haggart band starts an extensive series of trad recordings for Decca. • John Collins replaces Irving Ashby as the guitarist with Nat King Cole's rhythm section after the King Cole Trio breaks up. • Organist Wild Bill Davis starts recording regularly for Okeh with his trio. • Jackie McLean makes his recording debut. • Illinois Jacquet begins recording for Norman Granz's Clef label. • Peck Kelley, who was famous for not wanting to record, is privately taped on a series of piano solos released decades later. • Joe Williams records "Everyday I Have the Blues" with a pickup group led by trumpeter King Kolax, but no one notices. • Sidney Bechet moves permanently to France where he is recognized as a celebrity and a national hero.

Lennie Tristano and Lee Konitz   Lennie Tristano, who made his most significant recordings in 1949, began to drop out of active playing the following year. He became more interested in teaching than in performing in clubs, and in 1951, founded a school of jazz that lasted for five years. Its faculty included his top students, such as Lee Konitz, Warne Marsh, Billy Bauer, and pianist Sal Mosca, one of the first of many pianists to be so influenced by Tristano that he never really developed his own personality. Tristano recorded very little during 1951–54. The LP **Descent into the Maelstrom** (Inner City 6002) has various odds and ends from 1952–53, 1961, 1965, and 1966. Its title cut from 1953 is completely atonal and has Tristano overdubbing several pianos and creating picturesque and extremely intense music. Nothing like that had been heard in jazz up to that point.

A live quintet set with Konitz and Marsh in 1952 was released on LP by Jazz Records and more recently as the CD **Live in Toronto** (Orchard 7940). The group (with bassist Peter Ind and drummer Al Levitt) explores six common chord changes, five of them given new titles (as was Tristano's habit). In 1955, the pianist recorded an album for Atlantic titled **The Lennie Tristano Quartet** (Atlantic 1224), which unfortunately has only been reissued on CD as part of a limited-edition Mosaic box set. Four of the selections were considered controversial at the time because Tristano overdubbed several pianos and sped up some of the tapes, playing over prerecorded parts by bassist Peter Ind and drummer Jeff Morton. Although the hit pop recordings of Les Paul and Mary Ford had plenty of overdubbing, the procedure was considered unusual in jazz, as was distorting the speed of tapes. The other selections on this album are more conventional, five live numbers with Lee Konitz, bassist Gene Ramey, and drummer Art Taylor. A later double-LP set and the Mosaic set have greatly expanded on the number of selections from this engagement.

Lee Konitz, although always associated with Tristano, has long had a strong solo career of his own. He toured Scandinavia in 1951 where his cool sound was influential. Konitz fit in surprisingly well as a member of Stan Kenton's Orchestra (1952–54), being featured on many charts by Bill Holman and Bill Russo, and has mostly been a leader ever since. **Subconscious-Lee** (Original Jazz Classics 186), from 1949–50, has Konitz's first recordings as a leader (with spots for Marsh, Mosca, and

Bauer), plus two cuts originally released under Tristano's name. The LP **Sax of a Kind** (Dragon 18) features Konitz in Sweden in 1951 (best known among the local sidemen is pianist Bengt Hallberg) plus a version of "Lover Man" from a 1953 concert with Stan Kenton. **Konitz Meets Mulligan** (Pacific Jazz 46847) is an enjoyable CD in which Konitz sits in effectively with the Gerry Mulligan-Chet Baker Quartet, performing standards and two Mulligan pieces. **Lee Konitz at Storyville** (1201 Music 9035) is a particularly fine showcase for the altoist, performing in early 1954 with pianist Ronnie Ball, Percy Heath, and drummer Al Levitt.

The altoist explores a variety of his favorite chord changes (including "Foolin' Myself" and a lengthy exploration of "If I Had You"), some of which were disguised by newer melodies such as "Hi Beck," "Subconscious Lee," and "Sound Lee." **Konitz** (Black Lion 760922) has additional selections by the same group including "Bop Goes the Leesel," "Mean to Me," "I'll Remember April," and "Limehouse Blues," plus six alternate takes. Also quite excellent is **Lee Konitz with Warne Marsh** (Atlantic 75356), which has the two former Tristanoites partly escaping from their teacher's influence, but still playing long melodic lines and improvising over a fairly quiet rhythm section (Mosca, Bauer, Oscar Pettiford, and Kenny Clarke) on "There Will Never Be Another You," "Donna Lee," "Topsy," and the ironically titled "Background Music."

Lester Young   For Lester Young, the 1950–55 period had both its good and bad points. Because of his tie-in with Norman Granz, recording regularly for Clef and Norgran, and going on tours with "Jazz at the Philharmonic," Young was being well paid and documented favorably. He often played brilliantly, with a wider range of emotions than on his prewar recordings. However, his mental state had been permanently shaken by his experiences in the army, and his constant depression led to him drinking excessively (while eating much less than he should), leading to his physical health gradually declining. Also by the early 1950s, Young had become such a major influence on young tenor players that it must have seemed to him as if everyone was imitating his relaxed style, including some who were making much more money than him.

The Complete Lester Young Studio Sessions on Verve (Verve 314 547 087), an eight-CD set, features Pres in a 1946 trio with Nat King Cole and Buddy Rich (an excellent session that would have benefited from the inclusion of a bass) and all of his studio dates of 1950–59. Despite the stereotype that Young's playing greatly declined immediately after his army horrors, in reality he is in excellent form on most of these dates (other than one of the Harry "Sweets" Edison sessions where he is weak, and his final Paris sessions from 1959). Pres is heard at his best on quartet dates with either Hank Jones or John Lewis, and two other albums that are available as individual CDs. ❍ **With the Oscar Peterson Trio** (Verve 314 521 4517) is a classic, featuring Young in 1952 sounding in a happy mood on "Just You, Just Me," "Indiana," and a long series of melodic ballads. A special (if odd) treat is hearing Pres take his only recorded vocal on "It Takes Two to Tango." Also worth picking up is **Pres and Sweets** (Verve 849 391), which has the two former Basie sidemen sharing the bandstand with the Oscar Peterson Trio and Buddy Rich; "Mean to Me," "Pennies from Heaven," and "One o'Clock Jump" are among the standards that are swung in infectious fashion.

Stan Getz   Woody Herman's Second Herd had practically been built on the sound of Lester Young. While Herbie Steward largely faded away, working in the studios (often as an altoist), the other graduates of the "Four Brothers" all had major careers, with Stan Getz becoming the most famous.

Getz's tone was considered so beautiful by the early 1950s that it was known as "The Sound." A masterful player who was not afraid to continue developing and evolving, Getz rarely rested on his laurels, even as he continually achieved commercial success. His playing on "Early Autumn" with Woody Herman led to him being well known before he actually left Herman's band in 1949. **The Brothers** (Original Jazz Classics 008) is most unusual because one of the sessions has Getz, Zoot Sims, Al Cohn, Allan Eager, and Brew Moore all on tenors in 1949; they are impossible to tell apart! However, Getz would soon become a more individual player. Also on that CD is a Sims-Cohn sextet date from 1952 with Kai Winding that is most notable for "Zootcase" and "The Red Door." **Quartets** (Original Jazz Classics 121) has three sessions from 1949–50 featuring Getz with either Al Haig or Tony Aless on piano, playing beautifully on such standards as "There's a Small Hotel," "The Lady in Red," and "Wrap Your Troubles in Dreams" in addition to "Long Island Sound" and "Crazy Chords."

In 1950, Getz discovered pianist Horace Silver while playing with Silver's trio in Hartford, Connecticut, and was so impressed that he used all three of the musicians as members of his quartet for the next year. After touring Sweden in 1951, where he made an impact on local players, Getz formed an exciting quintet that co-starred guitarist Jimmy Raney. Raney's cool tone and quick reactions fit perfectly with Getz and they constantly inspired each other, particularly during a remarkable live performance from Boston's Storyville club on October 28, 1951. The three-CD set ❍ **The Complete Roost Recordings** (Roost 59622) is overflowing with memorable music. Getz is heard on a session with Al Haig and on his two dates with Horace Silver's trio. In addition, his studio sides with Jimmy Raney are here, three guest appearances with the Count Basie Orchestra from 1954, and eight songs actually led by guitarist Johnny Smith (but featuring Getz) including a hit version of "Moonlight in Vermont." But along with such memorable selections as "Sweetie Pie," "Tootsie Roll," "For Stompers Only," and "Split Kick," there are 14 numbers (taking up a full CD) from the Storyville gig. Getz and Raney make for a classic team on "The Song Is You," "Move," "Parker 51" (which is based on "Cherokee"), "Hershey Bar," and "Budo," quietly playing at blazing tempos and never running out of fresh ideas.

Stan Getz Plays (Verve 833 535) has additional studio selections from 1952 (shortly before Raney left the group) plus a quartet date with pianist Jimmy Rowles from 1954. Getz sounds typically beautiful on concise versions of "Time on My Hands," "'Tis Autumn," and "Stars Fell on Alabama." During 1953–54, Bob Brookmeyer often played with Getz's quintet. **Stan Getz at the Shrine** (Verve 314 513 753), recorded at a concert on November 8, 1954, and (in the case of two songs) in the studios the following day, is actually from after Brookmeyer had already departed to join Gerry Mulligan's Quartet. Nevertheless the interplay between Getz and Brookmeyer is quite strong, there are many exciting ensembles, and the better numbers include "Lover Man," "Pernod," "Tasty Pudding," and "It Don't Mean a Thing."

Stan Getz also occasionally appeared in all-star settings. ❍ **Hamp and Getz** (Verve 831 672) must have surprised listeners who thought of the tenor as primarily a superior interpreter of ballads. Getz battles Hampton on uptempo versions of "Cherokee" and "Jumpin' at the Woodside" that are full of blistering tradeoffs and exciting solos. Although there is also a ballad medley and some calmer pieces, it is the two jams (performed with Lou Levy, Leroy Vinnegar, and Shelly Manne) that are unique.

Al Cohn and Zoot Sims   Al Cohn and Zoot Sims had first met when they played with Woody Herman's Second Herd. Though their musical partnership was in the future, they were performing similar music during this era.

Al Cohn went out on his own as a freelance tenor saxophonist/arranger after his stint with Artie Shaw's 1949 bebop orchestra. **The Progressive Al Cohn** (Savoy 0249) has his first two sessions as a leader. Cohn is in excellent form playing with a 1950 quartet (also including George Wallington, Tommy Potter, and drummer Tiny Kahn) and a 1953 quintet with trumpeter Nick Travis, Horace Silver, Curly Russell, and Max Roach. Cohn wrote all but two of the songs, best known of which are "Infinity," "That's What You Think" (heard in two versions), and "Ah-Moore" (named after his wife, singer Marilyn Moore). **Broadway** (Original Jazz Classics 1812) was originally cut for the Progressive label in 1954 and was not released until Prestige put it out in 1970. The music, which features Cohn, Red Mitchell, and three lesser known players (altoist Hal Stein, pianist Harvey Leonard, and drummer Christy Febbo), consists of Mitchell's "Help Keep Your City Clean Blues," a four-song ballad medley, and two versions apiece of "Broadway" and "Suddenly It's Spring." Cohn and Stein (who emphasizes low notes) sound surprisingly similar to each other on this fine straightahead session.

Zoot Sims, who also played with Shaw's band in 1949, worked with Benny Goodman (1950), Chubby Jackson, Elliot Lawrence, Stan Kenton (1953), and Gerry Mulligan's sextet (1954–56). Unlike Stan Getz, Zoot saw no reason to ever change his swinging style, so he sounded virtually the same in 1950 as he would in 1980. Two CDs best show off his early playing. **Zoot Sims in Paris** (Vogue 68207) has Sims on seven songs (plus six alternate takes) in 1950 with Gerald Wiggins, Pierre Michelot, and Kenny Clarke including fine versions of "Night and Day," "I Understand," and "Zoot and Zoot." The second half of the disc jumps to 1953 and a different visit to Paris, teaming Sims with Frank Rosolino and a French rhythm section that includes guitarist Jimmy Gourley. **Zoot Sims Quartets** (Original Jazz Classics 242) has

Sims during 1950–51 in the spotlight in small groups with either John Lewis or Harry Biss on piano, digging into "My Silent Love," "Memories of You," "Zoot Swings the Blues," and "East of the Sun"; only the last two songs exceed three minutes, with "East of the Sun" going on for 11 minutes.

Allen Eager, Don Lanphere, Brew Moore, and Serge Chaloff   While the careers of Stan Getz, Al Cohn, and Zoot Sims moved logically forward, those of Allen Eager, Don Lanphere, and Brew Moore stalled. Allen Eager, who had been among the first of the Lester Young–inspired tenors to emerge, simply lost interest in playing music. He recorded with Gerry Mulligan (1951) and Terry Gibbs (1952), and played with Buddy Rich and his own bands (1953–55) before dropping out of the music scene altogether. Don Lanphere made a strong impression on his two record dates as a leader (including one with Fats Navarro as a sideman) and his stints with Woody Herman's Second Herd and the big bands of Artie Shaw, Claude Thornhill, Charlie Barnet, and Billy May. But he had some drug problems and soon faded into obscurity for many years.

Brew Moore did stay active in jazz; he just did not become famous. He once stated that "Anyone who doesn't play like Lester Young is wrong," and he did not veer from that musical path throughout his career. Moore moved to New York in 1948 and played with Claude Thornhill's Orchestra, Machito, Kai Winding, and Gerry Mulligan. Moore moved to San Francisco in 1954 where he led his own groups and played with Cal Tjader. **Brew Moore Quintet** (Original Jazz Classics 100) has three dates cut in San Francisco with local musicians, none of whom became known nationally. Mixing together standards (such as "Them There Eyes" and "Tea for Two") and originals, Moore is in excellent form throughout this lesser-known program.

One of the great baritone saxophonists, Serge Chaloff was with Woody Herman's Second Herd during its entire existence (1947–49), even while he earned a reputation as an irresponsible drug addict who often ridiculed Herman's playing behind his back. After the band broke up, Chaloff played briefly with the Count Basie octet in 1950 and then returned to his native Boston where he scuffled for a few years. **Boston 1950** (Uptown 27.38) has music released for the first time in 1994. Chaloff is heard on a variety of radio broadcasts including four concise duets from 1946 with pianist Rollins Griffith, and in quartets and quintets from 1950 with Nat Pierce and sometimes trombonists Sonny Truitt or Milt Gold. Chaloff (who at one point is briefly interviewed by a disc jockey) is in excellent form, with the highlights including "The Goof and I," "Four Brothers," "Body and Soul," "Keen and Peachy," and two versions of "Pennies from Heaven." **The Fable of Mabel** (Black Lion 760923) from 1954 features Chaloff on two different Boston sessions. Six selections showcase him in a quintet actually led by altoist Boots Mussulli and also including Russ Freeman on piano; "You Brought a New Kind of Love," "Oh Baby," and "All I Do Is Dream of You" are among the better tunes. The remainder of this CD consists of six titles (and five previously unreleased alternate takes) from a Chaloff nonet date that also includes trumpeter Herb Pomeroy, altoist Charlie Mariano, and Dick Twardzik. The three versions of "The Fable of Mabel" are all rewarding. An LP very much overdue to be reissued on CD, **Boston Blowup** (Capitol 6510) is a superior Chaloff sextet date from 1955 with Pomeroy and Mussulli. Only 31 at the time, Serge Chaloff seemed poised to challenge Gerry Mulligan as jazz's top baritonist, but he only had a little time left.

Paul Quinichette   While the "Four Brothers" tenors were white and looked toward early Lester Young for inspiration, Paul Quinichette was black and sounded like a near-duplicate of Pres in the 1950s. For that reason he was nicknamed "the Vice President." Quinichette had previously worked with Nat Towles, Lloyd Sherock, Ernie Fields, Jay McShann (1942–44), Johnny Otis (1945–47), Louis Jordan, Lucky Millinder (1948–49), Red Allen, and Hot Lips Page. He was a member of the Count Basie Orchestra during 1952–53 and worked with Benny Goodman in 1955. **The Vice Pres** (EmArcy 543750) has Quinichette's sessions for the EmArcy label during 1951–53 plus a version of "Sunday" from 1954. The tenor is heard in a group with both pianist Kenny Drew and organist Bill Doggett, a quintet set with organist Marlowe Morris, and with Count Basie sidemen (both past and present) including Buck Clayton, Dickie Wells, and on seven numbers with Basie himself. It is remarkable how close to Lester Young the Vice Pres sounds.

Jimmy Raney and Johnny Smith   Stan Getz worked with both Jimmy Raney and Johnny Smith. Raney was the definitive cool jazz guitarist, a fluid bop soloist with

a quiet sound who had a great deal of inner fire. After picking up experience gigging in Chicago, he was with Woody Herman (1948), Al Haig, Buddy DeFranco, Artie Shaw, Terry Gibbs, Stan Getz (1951–52), and the Red Norvo Trio (1953–54) where he replaced Tal Farlow. **Visits Paris, Vol. 1** (Vogue 40935) from 1954 features Raney in a quartet with pianist Sonny Clark, Red Mitchell, and drummer Bobby White. The interplay between Raney and Clark is quite impressive, Mitchell sounds a bit ahead of his time (taking the melody on "You Go to My Head"), Clark is showcased on "Once in Awhile," and the group excels on the 11 standards (with "Stella by Starlight" heard in two versions). ○ **A** (Original Jazz Classics 1706) features Jimmy Raney later in 1954 playing with pianist Hall Overton, bassist Teddy Kotick, either Art Mardigan or Nick Stabulas on drums, and occasionally the little-known trumpeter John Wilson. On some numbers, Raney overdubs a second guitar line over the opening and closing ensembles. Best are "Minor," "Double Image," the spirited "On the Square," "Spring Is Here," "You Don't Know What Love Is," and the uptempo "Tomorrow, Fairly Cloudy." Outside of his recordings with Getz, **A** is the best available example of Jimmy Raney's fiery yet subtle and quiet playing.

Johnny Smith was nearly 30 before he led his first record date, but that session in 1952 resulted in a big hit with "Moonlight in Vermont." Self-taught, Smith (who originally played trumpet, violin, and viola) always had impressive technique and a chordal style. He became a studio musician in 1947, and worked steadily both in the studios and in clubs throughout the 1950s. **Moonlight in Vermont** (Roulette 97747) has all of his most important recordings including eight numbers with Stan Getz that are in the tenor's three-CD Roost set plus other dates from 1952–53, some with Zoot Sims or Paul Quinichette. Highlights include "Where or When," "My Funny Valentine," "Tenderly," and "Cherokee."

Sam Most and Herbie Mann   The first jazz flute soloist on records was Alberto Socarras, who recorded with Clarence Williams in 1927. Wayman Carver with Chick Webb's Orchestra was virtually the only flute soloist heard with a swing era big band and his solos were rare, mostly with Chick Webb and his Little Chicks (taken from the orchestra). Although there were a few other examples (Larry Binyon in early 1930s studio bands, Jimmie Lunceford with his big band on "Holiday for

Strings," and Harry Klee with a small group taken out of the Boyd Raeburn Orchestra), the flute was considered at best a novelty in jazz until the early 1950s. Neal Hefti's use of Frank Wess's flute in his arrangements for the Count Basie Orchestra did a great deal to establish the instrument.

Sam Most (the younger brother of swing clarinetist Abe Most) was one of the first great jazz flutists (he is credited with being the first to hum/sing through his flute), a cool-toned tenor, and a fine (if infrequent) clarinetist. He worked early on with the big bands of Tommy Dorsey (1948), Boyd Raeburn, and Don Redman. Most had his first session as a leader (on flute and clarinet) in 1953 and recorded for Prestige, Debut (reissued years later on a Xanadu LP), Vanguard, and Bethlehem during 1953–55, but unfortunately these pioneering sessions have not yet been reissued on CD.

Herbie Mann was destined to become the most famous of all jazz flutists. He started on clarinet when he was nine, soon switching to tenor and flute. After serving in the army, he was with accordion player Mat Mathews's quintet (1953–54) and then began leading his own groups. During 1954–55, he led three boppish albums for Bethlehem.

Herbie Mann Plays (Bethlehem 76681) has his first recordings as a leader (seven cuts from 1954) plus four numbers from 1956 and three alternate takes. Mann (who already sounded distinctive) is heard with either Benny Weeks or Joe Puma on guitar in a pianoless quartet, showing that he knew his bebop. Also well worth searching for is the LP **The Mann with the Most** (Bethlehem 6020), which features both Herbie Mann and Sam Most (arguably the top two in their field at the time) playing in a quintet with Puma.

Charlie Mariano and Hal McKusick   During 1950–55, Charlie Mariano was an altoist who had not yet moved to Los Angeles, but fit very much into the West Coast style. He started out playing in his native Boston with Shorty Sherock (1948), Nat Pierce (1949–50), and his own groups. Mariano worked with the Chubby Jackson-Bill Harris band and spent 1953–55 touring with Stan Kenton. As a leader he recorded two albums for Imperial, two for Prestige, one for Fantasy, and two for Bethlehem during this period. **Boston All-Stars** (Original Jazz Classics 1745) combines the two Prestige dates, recorded in Boston and New York, but mostly featuring Mariano's

Boston associates. Mariano's playing is standard cool-toned bop, but his arrangements (particularly for the earlier octet numbers) are quite advanced. Featured along the way are trumpeters Joe Gordon and Herb Pomeroy, trombonist Sonny Truitt, and the ill-fated but intriguing pianist Dick Twardzik, who is heard mixing together Bud Powell with Lennie Tristano. **Charlie Mariano Plays** (Fresh Sound 115) reissues 16 selections from the altoist's three Bethlehem sessions. Mariano is joined by Claude Williamson, bassist Max Bennett, Stan Levey, and sometimes Frank Rosolino and trumpeter Stu Williamson. The basic group originals and swinging standards inspire some excellent solos. Another Bethlehem album is on **Charlie Mariano Quartet** (Fresh Sound 9). Recorded in 1954, the session features Mariano sounding like a mix between Benny Carter and Charlie Parker. He is supported by a quiet rhythm section comprised of pianist John Williams, Max Bennett, and drummer Mel Lewis. Mariano switches to tenor on four of the dozen selections and is in top form throughout the ten standards, one blues, and his own "Floormat."

Hal McKusick, a fine altoist and an occasional clarinetist, would have fit into the West Coast jazz scene, but he spent most of his career in New York. He worked with the big bands of Les Brown, Woody Herman (1943), Boyd Raeburn (1944–45), Alvino Rey, Buddy Rich, and Claude Thornhill (1948–49). McKusick, who worked in the 1950s with Terry Gibbs and Elliot Lawrence, was a busy studio musician. He recorded an album apiece as a leader during 1955 for Jubilee, Bethlehem, and Victor, but unfortunately all are out of print. The one particularly worth searching for (and will hopefully be reissued soon) is **East Coast Jazz Vol. 7** (Bethlehem 16), an excellent quartet date with guitarist Barry Galbraith, Milt Hinton, and drummer Osie Johnson.

Four Bebop Giants in the Post-Bop Era

Jazz musicians who come to prominence in one era do not suddenly disappear in the next period unless they die prematurely. Charlie Parker, Dizzy Gillespie, Bud Powell, and Thelonious Monk were four of the most significant jazz artists of the 1945–49 period, and they continued to be very important during the first half of the 1950s.

Charlie Parker   Charlie Parker was at the peak of his powers on Christmas Day, 1949, when he performed at

Carnegie Hall with his quintet (featuring Red Rodney and Al Haig). He had recently begun recording for producer Norman Granz's Clef label and had initiated his "Bird with Strings" series, the most popular recordings of his career. He was making good money and was widely recognized as one of the most important innovators in jazz even though the general public was largely unfamiliar with him.

And yet the next five years would find Bird on a gradual decline. His playing mostly remained brilliant, but the years of heroin and alcohol abuse began to be felt. He became more unreliable than earlier, leading to some lost opportunities. His state of mind, which included a growing boredom with his repertoire and bebop in general, became shaky. There were some highpoints including the 1953 Massey Hall concert with Dizzy Gillespie, Bud Powell, Charles Mingus, and Max Roach, but after the death of his baby daughter in 1954, Bird tried to commit suicide twice and spent some time in Bellevue.

● **Bird: Complete on Verve** (Verve 837 141) is a ten-CD set that has all of Parker's studio dates for Granz's labels during 1949–54 plus appearances with "Jazz at the Philharmonic." Included are all of the "Bird with Strings" dates, his Afro-Cuban sessions with Machito's Orchestra (which generally work quite well), a 1950 all-star date with Gillespie, Thelonious Monk, Curly Russell, and Buddy Rich, a Norman Granz jam session with altoists Benny Carter and Johnny Hodges, a few somewhat bizarre encounters with an orchestra and voices (the Dave Lambert Singers), and some small group dates. Highlights include "The Bird," "Just Friends," "Star Eyes," "Au Privave," "K.C. Blues," "My Little Suede Shoes," "Blues for Alice," and "Confirmation." Much of the music is also available in smaller sets. **Bird & Diz** (Verve 831 133) has the 1950 session, all of the altoist's quartet performances are on Charlie Parker (Verve 314 539 757), and **Charlie Parker Big Band** (Verve 314 559 835) has its moments of interest. But to get the full picture, the large Verve box is well worth the money.

There are also many Charlie Parker live performances available. Some are poorly recorded or only include Bird's solos (with the disc recorders being shut off as soon as his solos end) and many of those are largely unlistenable. However, the best live sets feature Parker stretching out and coming up with inventive variations that add a great deal to his legacy. The obscure CD **Inglewood Jam** (Time Is 19801) from 1952 is quite

valuable in that it features Parker on the West Coast on June 10, 1952, playing with Chet Baker (in his recording debut, shortly before he joined Gerry Mulligan), Sonny Criss, Russ Freeman, Harry Babison, and Lawrence Marable on four lengthy numbers. Much of the music on the two-CD set **The Complete Legendary Rockland Palace Concert 1952** (Jazz Classics 5014) had appeared with terrible sound previously on LP, but for this reissue it was greatly cleaned up, the pitch was corrected, and the number of songs expanded from 19 to 31. It finds Parker in excellent shape trying to get beyond his usual repertoire, including performing Gerry Mulligan's "Gold Rush" and "Rocker," plus "Repetition," and "Sly Mongoose." **Boston 1952** (Uptown 27.42) features Parker with a pair of pickup groups, performing seven songs in 1952 (in a quintet with trumpeter Joe Gordon, Dick Twardzik, Charles Mingus, and Roy Haynes) and four numbers in January 1954 with local musicians. Parker seems happy on both occasions and can be heard saying a few words to disc jockey Symphony Sid Torin. Additional material from Parker's Boston visits can be heard on **Bird at the High-Hat** (Blue Note 99787), which features Bird during late 1953–early 1954 in a quintet with trumpeter Herbie Williams, showing that there was still life to be found in such songs as "Ornithology," "Groovin' High," "Cool Blues," and "Now's the Time." **Montreal, 1953** (Uptown 27.36) documents Parker's first of two trips to Canada that year, appearing in concert and on a television special with Canadian musicians including pianist Paul Bley on three songs plus guest tenor Brew Moore on two numbers.

The best of all of the late-period Charlie Parker live sets is ● **Live at Massey Hall** (Original Jazz Classics 044). The remarkable quintet of Bird, Diz, Powell, Mingus, and Roach perform six standards ("Perdido," "Salt Peanuts," "All the Things You Are," "Wee," "Hot House," and "A Night in Tunisia"), and not too surprisingly, plenty of musical magic occurred. Despite some tension before the concert—it was not completely certain that Parker would show up—the resulting music is full of competitive fire. It was also a historic concert, as it is the last joint recording of Charlie Parker and Dizzy Gillespie.

On March 12, 1955, while watching the Dorsey Brothers television show, Charlie Parker died. A doctor examining the body guessed that he was 55 or 60. Bird was only 34.

Dizzy Gillespie   After the breakup of his big band in early 1950, Dizzy Gillespie led a variety of small groups, utilizing both Milt Jackson and the young tenor John Coltrane for a period in 1951. He visited Europe a few times, often using Bill Graham on baritone as his frontline partner and featuring the jubilant singing of Joe "Bebop" Carroll. After co-leading the short-lived record label Dee Gee (the music was later acquired by Savoy) and recording in Europe for Vogue and Blue Star in late 1953, Gillespie signed with Norman Granz's labels and began alternating small-group dates, all-star sessions, and special big band projects. Although he never watered down his style, Dizzy remained the most accessible of beboppers, able to connect immediately with audiences due to his sense of humor and showmanship.

The three-CD set **Odyssey** (Savoy 17109) starts out with familiar music, all of Gillespie's Musicraft recordings (including the classic 1945 encounters with Charlie Parker, the 1946 big band titles, and guest shots with Boyd Raeburn, Ray Brown, and blues singer Albinia Jones), but unfortunately leaving out the early version of "Groovin' High" with Dexter Gordon. The second half of this reissue is from 1950–52 and features Dizzy performing eight intriguing pieces (mostly ballads) with a string orchestra arranged by Johnny Richards, concluding with all of Gillespie's recordings for Dee Gee. The latter includes an early solo from John Coltrane on "We Love to Boogie," spots for J.J. Johnson, Budd Johnson, Milt Jackson, Stuff Smith, and Joe Carroll, a humorous imitation of Louis Armstrong on "The Umbrella Man," some novelties, and the blazing "The Champ."

Dizzy Gillespie in Paris, Vol. 1 (Vogue 68360) from 1953 finds Dizzy's quintet with Bill Graham and Joe Carroll clearly having a good time entertaining a crowd. This version of "The Champ" is a classic and "Good Bait" is definitive, while other pieces include such novelties as "Swing Low...Sweet Cadillac," "Ooh-Shoo-Bee-Doo-Be," and "School Days." **Dizzy Gillespie in Paris, Vol. 2** (Vogue 68361) has the same group (with trombonist Nat Peck in Graham's place) in the studios plus two dates teaming Dizzy with expatriate tenor saxophonist Don Byas. Highlights include some wonderful trumpet playing on "I Cover the Waterfront," "Somebody Loves Me," "She's Funny that Way," and "Wrap Your Troubles in Dreams," all of which were swing (rather than bop) standards.

Soon after signing with Granz, Gillespie recorded **Diz and Getz** (Verve 314 549 749). The 1953 encounter

between the heated trumpeter, the cool-toned tenor, the Oscar Peterson Trio, and Max Roach is quite successful on such tunes as "It Don't Mean a Thing," "Exactly Like You," and "Girl of My Dreams." Even better is ◉ **Dizzy Gillespie with Roy Eldridge** (Verve 314 52 647), which has Dizzy and his original idol battling it out on "I've Found a New Baby" and "Limehouse Blues," sharing the vocals on "Pretty Eyed Baby," and playing a five-song ballad medley with the Oscar Peterson Trio and Louie Bellson. The fireworks between the two trumpeters (Gillespie is more advanced but Eldridge refuses to give up) are quite memorable.

Despite his sadness at the loss of Charlie Parker, Dizzy Gillespie continued to grow in stature and importance throughout the 1950s, and some of his best accomplishments were still in the future.

Bud Powell   Despite his increasingly shaky health, Bud Powell remained the pacesetter among modern jazz pianists during the first half of the 1950s. A couple of discs already reviewed in the previous chapter, ◉ **Jazz Giant** (Verve 543 832), which contains Powell's 1950 trio set with Curly Russell and Max Roach, and **The Amazing Bud Powell Vol. One** (Blue Note 32136), which includes three remarkable versions of the intense "Un Poco Loco" from 1951, are full of essential music. Unfortunately, Powell had a breakdown later in 1951 and was out of action until early 1953. On May 15, 1953, he appeared at the famous Massey Hall concert with Charlie Parker, Dizzy Gillespie, Charles Mingus, and Max Roach. In addition to a set by the quintet, the rhythm trio opened up the concert with a performance of their own. **Jazz at Massey Hall, Vol. 2** (Original Jazz Classics 111) has the trio's numbers from the concert plus a few selections from other venues with Roach being featured on "Drum Conversation." **The Amazing Bud Powell Vol. Two** (Blue Note 32137), a trio outing with bassist George Duvivier and drummer Art Taylor, is (like all of Powell's Blue Note releases) full of explorative and intense music played by the pianist near his prime. Highlights include "Autumn in New York," "I Want to Be Happy," and Powell's "Glass Enclosure." The nine songs are joined by six alternate takes. Otherwise the pianist recorded this era for Norgran/Verve, but his playing was often unfocused and meandering. Considering the treatment he was given during his hospitalizations, which included electric shock, it is surprising that he could play at all, much less lead the field.

Thelonious Monk   While Bud Powell defined bebop piano, his close friend Thelonious Monk was in his own musical world. Due to his unique playing and composing, and his frequently uncommunicative personality, Monk was largely neglected during this era. Although the jazz world generally prizes individuality, the fact that Monk was such a noncomformist both musically and personally hurt him for a few years. ● **The Complete Blue Note Recordings** (Blue Note 30363) is a four-CD set (covered in the last chapter) that, in addition to his sessions from 1947–48, has Monk's final two Blue Note dates, which are also available on the single disc **Genius of Modern Music, Vol. 2** (Blue Note 81511). The 1951 set (a quintet outing with altoist Sahib Shihab, Milt Jackson, Al McKibbon, and Art Blakey) has two of Monk's most difficult pieces ("Four in One" and "Criss Cross") along with more basic music, including the touching ballad "Ask Me Now" and the blues "Straight No Chaser." The session from 1952 (with Kenny Dorham, Lou Donaldson, Lucky Thompson, bassist Nelson Boyd, and Max Roach) introduces "Let's Cool One" and "Skippy" in addition to having intriguing versions of "Carolina Moon" and "I'll Follow You."

Later in 1952, Monk signed with the Prestige label. During the next two years he was featured on three trio dates (highlighted by "Little Rootie Tootie," "Monk's Dream," "Bye-Ya," "Twinkle Tinkle," "Bemsha Swing," "Nutty," and "Blue Monk"), a quintet session with Sonny Rollins and French horn player Julius Watkins ("Let's Call This," "Think of One," and "Friday the 13th"), and a band date with trumpeter Ray Copeland and tenor saxophonist Frank Foster (four titles including "Hackensack" and "We See"). The three-CD set ● **The Complete Prestige Recordings** (Prestige 4428) has all of that music plus Monk's initial studio session as a sideman with Coleman Hawkins in 1944, his guesting on three songs with Sonny Rollins, and a fascinating set from December 24, 1954, led by Miles Davis and also includes Milt Jackson, Percy Heath, and Kenny Clarke. There was a lot of tension between Davis and Monk on that date (the trumpeter did not want Thelonious to accompany his solos), some of which can be heard on the alternate takes. Monk's solo on the master take of "Bags' Groove" is one of his great moments on record, a perfectly constructed and utterly unique take on the blues.

In addition, a trip to Paris in the summer of 1954 resulted in a solo date. The nine songs (which include "'Round Midnight," "Evidence," "Well You Needn't," and "Hackensack") are teamed with 13 solos from the great stride pianist Joe Turner (not to be confused with singer Big Joe Turner) that were cut in 1952; all are included on **Thelonious Monk/Joe Turner in Paris** (Vogue 68210).

But otherwise, Monk did not work much at all during 1950–54, spending much of his time at home practicing the piano. In 1955, Orrin Keepnews of the new Riverside label decided to take a chance on the elusive pianist/composer. To introduce Monk to a new audience and to show that he was not all that forbidding, the first project for Riverside was a set of Duke Ellington songs played by Thelonious in a trio with Oscar Pettiford and Kenny Clarke. It was a logical tribute album because Ellington was one of the main influences on Monk's piano playing. **Plays Duke Ellington** (Original Jazz Classics 024) features Monk's unique take on such Duke tunes as "Mood Indigo," "It Don't Mean a Thing," "Solitude," and "Black and Tan Fantasy." It was a tentative first step toward Thelonious Monk gaining the fame he deserved.

Bebop to Hard Bop

Although the classic bebop era is thought of as 1945–49, bebop did not suddenly become extinct in 1950 (just as swing did not disappear after 1946). The major labels may have lost interest in turning the music into a fad, but bebop not only survived but became the basis for both West Coast cool jazz and East Coast hard bop music.

Hard bop, which began to be heard in 1952 on Miles Davis's records and which grew rapidly as a movement during 1954–55, differed from classic bebop in a few ways. Due to the emergence of the LP, melody statements were longer, rather than just rapid unisons. Bassists started to become freed from just playing a four-to-the-bar role as a metronome, and in some cases a catchy rhythmic bass pattern became the basis of a performance. Rather than just running rapidly through chord changes, there was more of an emphasis placed on soulfulness—developing a powerful tone, bending notes, putting honest feeling into blues, and being open to the influences of church music.

Hard bop, like cool jazz, was an outgrowth (or a subsidiary) of bebop rather than a radical break from the past. And while cool jazz was often based in Los Angeles and dominated by white players, hard bop was at first primarily played by black musicians in New York. In time it would become the new mainstream of jazz.

The Clifford Brown-Max Roach Quintet   In 1950, Fats Navarro, weakened by tuberculosis and his ruinous heroin habit, died at the age of 26. Within three years Clifford Brown, whose main influence was Navarro, was rising to prominence and seemed like the logical replacement for Fats. A brilliant voice on his instrument, Brownie had a complete command of the bebop vocabulary, a warm tone, and limitless potential. He had started on trumpet in 1945 when he was 15 and was working professionally in Philadelphia within three years. Brown was encouraged by Navarro and Dizzy Gillespie, both of whom were impressed early on by his playing. While attending Maryland State University in June 1950, Brown was seriously hurt in a car accident that put him out of action for a year, but fortunately he completely recovered. In 1952, he made his recording debut with Chris Powell's Blue Flames, taking solos on a couple of R&B-oriented numbers.

In 1953, Brownie really began to be noticed. He worked with Tadd Dameron and during August–December was with Lionel Hampton's band, touring Europe and recording overseas in a variety of settings. **Clifford Brown Memorial** (Original Jazz Classics 017) features Brownie with Tadd Dameron (highlighted by "Dial 'B' for Beauty" and "Philly J.J.") and showcases on a date with a Swedish group (including Arne Domnerus, Lars Gullin, pianist Bengt Hallberg, and fellow American Art Farmer) that was made during the Hampton European tour, playing four Quincy Jones arrangements.

For unknown reasons, Lionel Hampton had forbade his sidemen from recording during the European tour, but most of the musicians ignored the "advice," resulting in the breakup of what was arguably Hamp's finest band. Brown was featured on quite a few sessions while overseas, including music that was released as **Clifford Brown Quartet in Paris** (Original Jazz Classics 357), **Clifford Brown Sextet in Paris** (Original Jazz Classics 358), and **Clifford Brown Big Band in Paris** (Original Jazz Classics 359). The date with a quiet French quartet (pianist Henri Renaud, bassist Pierre Michelot, and drummer Benny Bennett) resulted in six songs and six alternate takes (three versions apiece of "I Can Dream, Can't I" and "You're a Lucky Guy"), highlighted by a classic version of "It Might as Well Be Spring." At the age of just 22, Brown

was already a masterful interpreter of ballads. The sextet project teams Brown with altoist Gigi Gryce, guitarist Jimmy Gourley, Renaud, Michelot, and drummer Jean-Louis Viale. Gryce contributed most of the compositions, including "Minority," but it is for Brownie's playing (particularly on "All the Things You Are," "I Cover the Waterfront," and "Minority") that this date is most valuable. The big band session was actually led by Gryce, and although not essential, it does have some excellent trumpet solos from Brown, including on "Keeping Up with Jonesy" and the two takes of "Brownskins."

Because of his consistent brilliance in what would be a tragically short life, every Clifford Brown recording is well worth acquiring. The four-CD set ◉ **The Complete Blue Note and Pacific Jazz Recordings** (Pacific Jazz 34195) has the most significant Brown recordings prior to his work with Max Roach. He is heard during 1953–54 on dates as a sideman with Lou Donaldson and J.J. Johnson, on his first session as a leader, interacting with some of the West Coast's top musicians (playing Jack Montrose arrangements), and on a legendary gig at Birdland with Art Blakey (whose announcements make it sound like he is launching the Jazz Messengers), Lou Donaldson, Horace Silver, and Curly Russell. Among the many highlights of this major reissue are "Brownie Speaks," "De-Dah," "Brownie Eyes," "Cherokee," "Get Happy," "Wee Dot," and early versions of the trumpeter's best-known compositions, "Joy Spring" and "Daahoud."

Max Roach, who left the Charlie Parker Quintet in 1949, was part of Miles Davis's "Birth of the Cool" recordings, worked with Parker on and off during 1951–53, cofounded the Debut label with Charles Mingus in 1952, played with "Jazz at the Philharmonic," and worked with the Lighthouse All-Stars on the West Coast for several months. His first studio date as a leader was **Featuring Hank Mobley** (Original Jazz Classics 202). Hank Mobley, a Sonny Rollins–influenced tenor, is heard on his recording debut, playing five songs as the only horn and four numbers with a septet also including Idrees Sulieman and Gigi Gryce. Nothing essential occurs on this project from 1953, but the music is an interesting transition between bop and hard bop.

In Los Angeles in 1954, Roach and Brown met and decided to co-lead a group. **The Best of Max Roach and Clifford Brown in Concert** (GNP/Crescendo 18) has the earliest documented performances of the Brown-Roach Quintet. On four numbers, the band (which was temporarily on the West Coast) included Teddy Edwards on tenor, pianist Carl Perkins, and bassist George Bledsoe; "All God's Chillun Got Rhythm" and Edwards's "Sunset Eyes" are most memorable. The reissue also has a slightly later set with the more permanent personnel of tenor saxophonist Harold Land, pianist Richie Powell (Bud's younger brother), and bassist George Morrow digging into "Jordu," the trumpeter's feature on "I Can't Get Started," "I Get a Kick Out of You," and "Parisian Thoroughfare."

Although Harold Land, a fine tenor player, had recorded as early as 1949, being with the Clifford Brown-Max Roach Quintet was his first high-profile association. Richie Powell, who was seven years younger than Bud Powell, had played with Johnny Hodges's band during 1952–54 and was a promising bop-oriented pianist and songwriter. George Morrow worked in Los Angeles during 1946–48 (including with Charlie Parker, Sonny Criss, Teddy Edwards, and Hampton Hawes) and in San Francisco during 1948–53 (with Dexter Gordon, Wardell Gray, Billie Holiday, and Sonny Clark among others).

With their lineup set and the group's chemistry growing from month to month, the Clifford Brown-Max Roach Quintet signed a contract with the EmArcy label. The magnificent ten-CD box ◉ **Brownie—The Complete EmArcy Recordings of Clifford Brown** (EmArcy 838 306) is not inexpensive but is a must for all Brownie collectors. Fortunately, most of the music is also available as single discs, including all the ones listed in the next two paragraphs.

While in Los Angeles in the summer of 1954, Brown participated in a couple of jam session recordings. **Best Coast Jazz** (EmArcy 814 647) has the trumpeter in a septet with Roach, altoists Herb Geller and Joe Maini, and tenor saxophonist Walter Benton. The uptempo blues "Coronado" is most notable for the four horns trading off one-bar phrases, while "You Go to My Head" is climaxed by Brown's warm solo. **Jam Session** (EmArcy 36002) has a remarkable lineup of musicians: Brownie, Clark Terry, and Maynard Ferguson all on trumpets, altoist Herb Geller, Harold Land on tenor, Richie Powell or Junior Mance on piano, Keeter Betts or George Morrow on bass, and Max Roach. A ridiculously rapid "Move" and a nearly 15-minute version of "What Is this Thing Called Love" gives one the opportunity to compare the three very different trumpeters. "Darn that Dream" is a vocal feature for Dinah Washington (the remainder of this

intriguing session has been released under her name and in the Brownie box), and a four-song ballad medley includes the trumpeter's classic playing on his second version of "It Might as Well Be Spring."

The Brown-Roach Quintet (with Land, Powell, and Morrow) is featured on **Brown and Roach, Inc.** (EmArcy 814 644), **Clifford Brown and Max Roach** (Verve 314 543 306), and **A Study in Brown** (EmArcy 814 646). **Brown and Roach, Inc.** includes "Stompin' at the Savoy," "I Get a Kick Out of You," and Brownie's ballad feature on "Ghost of a Chance." **Clifford Brown and Max Roach** has such memorable performances as "Daahoud," "Joy Spring," "The Blues Walk" (those three selections are heard in two takes apiece), "Parisian Thoroughfare," and "Jordu." From 1955, **A Study in Brown** includes a brilliant Brown solo on "Cherokee," "Swingin'," and "Sandu." The trumpeter's beautiful tone is showcased on **Clifford Brown with Strings** (EmArcy 814 642) although the mundane string arrangements by Neal Hefti lack any adventure at all. Brown does sound very pretty on such numbers as "Portrait of Jenny," "Memories of You," "Embraceable You," and "Stardust." And his dates with Sarah Vaughan and Helen Merrill (which are both quite memorable) are also included in the EmArcy box.

In late 1955, Harold Land dropped out of the group due to family problems that resulted in his returning to Los Angeles. Sonny Rollins took his place, making the Brown-Roach Quintet into a real super-ensemble, which has been called both the last great bebop band and the first major hard bop group.

Art Blakey and Horace Silver   Art Blakey, after returning from a yearlong stay in Africa in 1949, worked briefly with the Lucky Millinder big band and for two years (1951–53) with Buddy DeFranco. In 1954, he led a quintet at Birdland that was fortunately well-recorded; the group consisted of the drummer, Clifford Brown, Lou Donaldson, Curly Russell and most importantly, Horace Silver. These notable performances are available as **A Night at Birdland Vols. 1–2** (Blue Note 32146 and 32147) and also in the Clifford Brown four-CD Pacific Jazz set.

Horace Silver was discovered by Stan Getz when he was part of a pickup rhythm section backing the tenor at a concert in Hartford, Connecticut. At the time, Silver's playing was quite bop-oriented, most influenced by

Bud Powell. Getz used Silver and the rhythm section for a year, launching the pianist's career. After leaving Getz, Silver worked with Coleman Hawkins, Lester Young, and Oscar Pettiford, recording with Lou Donaldson and Miles Davis. **Horace Silver Vol. 1: Spotlight on Drums** (Blue Note 81520) has his first sessions as a leader, trios with Art Blakey and Gene Ramey, Curly Russell, or Percy Heath on bass. From 1952, Silver was already quite recognizable, playing in a funky style different from any of his contemporaries. His originals "Ecaroh" (Horace backwards) and "Opus de Funk" were introduced on this set. In addition, there are two percussion features: a drum solo by Blakey on "Nothing but Soul" and a duet by Blakey with the percussion and vocals of Sabu Martinez on "Message from Kenya."

Blakey and Silver, who also teamed up on an important Miles Davis session, formed a musical partnership in 1954. Blakey had tired of hearing and performing with jam session–styled pickup groups that played the same old standards in predictable fashion. With Silver, his goal was to feature new material written by band members, and to have a group full of potentially major young players which they agreed to call the Jazz Messengers.

◉ **Horace Silver and the Jazz Messengers** (Blue Note 46140) is a true classic, the first album by the Jazz Messengers. Blakey and Silver are joined by Kenny Dorham, Hank Mobley on tenor, and bassist Doug Watkins. This set includes the original versions of Silver's "The Preacher," and "Doodlin'," funky standards that helped launch hard bop. The two CDs that comprise **Live at Café Bohemia Vols. 1–2** (Blue Note 32148 and 32149) feature the same version of the group on November 11, 1955. The first disc has such numbers as "Soft Winds," "Minor's Holiday," "Alone Together," and Dorham's "Prince Albert," while **Vol. 2** has Mobley's "Sportin' Crowd," "Avila and Tequila," and three standards. Not only did these recordings begin the legacy of the Jazz Messengers, but they helped push the hard bop movement forward by giving that style a major band that showcased top young talent.

Cannonball Adderley and Nat Adderley In June 1955, altoist Cannonball Adderley (who was working as a school band director in Florida) and cornetist Nat Adderley visited New York during Cannonball's summer vacation. Nat, who had played with Lionel Hampton (1954–55), had a bit of big-time experience, but Julian "Cannonball" Adderley (whose original nickname was "Cannibal" due to his large appetite) was a complete unknown. They were persuaded to sit in with Oscar Pettiford's group at the Café Bohemia and their playing (especially Cannonball's) on "I Remember April"

TIMELINE 1952

Gerry Mulligan and Chet Baker team up in a very popular pianoless quartet at the Haig in Los Angeles. • Howard Rumsey's Lighthouse All-Stars make their first recordings. • King Pleasure records "Moody's Mood for Love." • Count Basie successfully forms a new big band. • Jack Teagarden leaves the Louis Armstrong All-Stars and is soon succeeded by Trummy Young. • William Correa plays drums with Mary Lou Williams who renames him Willie Bobo. • Cab Calloway begins a two-year run playing "Sportin' Life" (a character originally based on him) in a New York revival of *Porgy and Bess*. • Don Elliott, the first jazz mellophone player since Dudley Fosdick in the 1920s, leads a record date that also features him on trumpet, vibes, and bongos. • Chubby Jackson co-leads a sextet with Bill Harris. • After a year playing with Benny Goodman, Eddie Safranski becomes a staff musician at NBC, dropping out of the jazz scene. • Singer/pianist Blossom Dearie moves to Paris where she forms and performs with the Blue Stars of France. • Julia Lee records her last titles for Capitol. • After only one record date in 22 years, New Orleans singer Lizzie Miles records again and enjoys a comeback. • The Lucky Millinder Orchestra breaks up. • Benny Harris, after recording with Charlie Parker, retires from music. • San Francisco–based pianist Paul Lingle has his only studio session, cut shortly before he moves to Hawaii. • Fifty-year-old saxophonist and clarinetist Benny Waters moves to Europe. • Bill Holman becomes a key arranger in Stan Kenton's Orchestra. • Jonah Jones leaves Cab Calloway; spends two years playing Dixieland with Earl Hines's group. • Arrangers Eddie Sauter and Bill Finegan form the Sauter-Finegan Orchestra, a big band that has a few hits, but whose novelties and over-arranged works far outweigh its jazz qualities. • At a Bix Beiderbecke tribute at the Dixieland Jubilee in Pasadena, Frankie Trumbauer comes out of retirement to play "Singin' the Blues" one final time.

caused many musicians to immediately take notice. Both Jackie McLean and Phil Woods were in the audience that day and were amazed at the altoist's playing. Within a few days, the Adderleys were making their recording debuts for the Savoy label, and it was not long before Cannonball made the decision to become a full-time musician, putting together a quintet with his younger brother. The two-CD set **Summer of '55** (Savoy 92860) and the single disc **Introducing Nat Adderley** (Verve 314 543 828), both of which are quite boppish and full of youthful enthusiasm, show why Cannonball was being touted as the successor to Bird (Charlie Parker had died just a few months earlier) and why the Adderleys were considered among the most important new discoveries of 1955.

J.J. Johnson and Kai Winding   J.J. Johnson and Kai Winding are among the major trombonists to emerge from the bebop era. In fact, many would argue that Johnson was the best of all time. He was the main influence on the next couple of generations of jazz trombonists who followed. Despite this, after working with Illinois Jacquet (1947–49) and the Dizzy Gillespie Big Band, and recording with Miles Davis and the Metronome All-Stars, he discovered that work was difficult to find. Johnson was mostly outside of music during 1952–54, working as a blueprint inspector! He did lead one very impressive date with Clifford Brown in 1953 (reissued under Brownie's name) and appeared on a four-trombone session with Winding, Bennie Green, and Willie Dennis, but otherwise was little heard from until midway through 1954. In the meantime Kai Winding, who had been an important force with Stan Kenton's Orchestra (1946–47), worked with Tadd Dameron, Charlie Ventura, and Benny Goodman.

In the summer of 1954, Johnson and Winding came together to co-lead a two-trombone quintet that became surprisingly popular for a couple of years. The melodic and witty arrangements, along with the blend of the two similar-sounding trombonists were quite appealing. The band first recorded for Savoy in 1954, music included on **Jay and Kai** (Savoy 0163) such as "Blues for Trombones" and Johnson's "Lament," plus four numbers from earlier unrelated dates. **Kai Winding, Jay Jay Johnson and Bennie Green with Strings** (Original Jazz Classics 1727), in addition to four ballads featuring trombonist Green with a small string section, has eight songs by the Johnson-Winding group, including "How Long

Has This Been Going On," "Dinner for One Please James," and "We'll Be Together Again." The group also recorded during 1954–55 for RCA's X subsidiary and Bethlehem (**Nuf Said**, which is scheduled to be reissued in the near future) before signing with Columbia. Any recording by this band is charming and swinging.

Also worth picking up is **The Eminent Jay Jay Johnson Vol. 2** (Blue Note 81506), which contains two complete sessions from 1954–55 that showcase Johnson without Winding. The first six titles (including "Old Devil Moon" and "Too Marvelous for Words") feature Johnson in a quintet with Wynton Kelly, Charles Mingus, Kenny Clarke, and Sabu Martinez on congas. The other six songs (including "Pennies from Heaven" and "Portrait of Jennie") plus three alternate takes have the trombonist joined by Hank Mobley, Horace Silver, Paul Chambers, and Kenny Clarke. Whether playing with Kai Winding or in his own solo career, few trombonists were on the level of the great J.J. Johnson.

The Oscar Peterson Trio   Discovered by Norman Granz playing in Canada and presented at a 1949 "Jazz at the Philharmonic" concert, Oscar Peterson soon signed with Granz and recorded very prolifically throughout his productive career. The young virtuoso, whose main early influence was Nat King Cole, but who also had technique on the level of an Art Tatum, could swing as hard as any pianist in jazz history.

Peterson was teamed with bassist Ray Brown as a duet during 1950–51, although Major Holley was in Brown's place for an extensive session in 1950. In November 1951, Barney Kessel made the group a trio for one session. Irving Ashby, formerly with the King Cole Trio, was with the group in January 1952 and then Kessel signed up for a year, traveling the world with the increasingly popular group and recording no less than five albums in December. However, Kessel wanted to return to Los Angeles and the lucrative life of being a studio musician, so in mid-1953 he was succeeded by Herb Ellis. The Peterson-Ellis-Brown Trio was one of the great groups, particularly after they were together for a time and worked out complex arrangements, trying constantly to challenge and outdo each other.

1951 (Just a Memory 9501) is unusual for it features Peterson back in Canada performing 20 concise duets with bassist Austin Roberts as radio transcriptions for the Canadian Broadcasting Corporation. Only three songs are over three minutes, and five are under two, so Peterson makes every second count, ripping through such numbers as "Flying Home," "I've Got Rhythm," "Seven Come Eleven," "Air Mail Special," and "Get Happy." The two-CD set **The Oscar Peterson Trio at Zardi's** (Pablo 2620-118) features the trio with Ellis on 31 songs (including three of Peterson's originals) in top form with the pianist in typically miraculous form. Brown's accompaniment is often a bit telepathic while Ellis (whether taking short solos, playing harmonies, or tapping his guitar to make it sound like a conga) proves to be a perfect guitarist for the group. Also quite worthy is **Plays Count Basie** (Verve 314 519 811), the most rewarding of Peterson's early songbooks. With Buddy Rich making the group a quartet, Peterson's arrangements make the nine Basie-associated songs (along with his own "Blues for Basie") all sound fresh and lightly swinging. "Easy Does It," "9:20 Special," "Broadway," and "One o'Clock Jump" are particularly rewarding.

The Ahmad Jamal Trio   Ahmad Jamal was one of the few young pianists of the early 1950s who managed to carve out his own musical personality without sounding like he was closely emulating Bud Powell. He began playing professionally in his native Pittsburgh when he was 11 in 1941. In 1951, Jamal formed the Three Strings, a group with guitarist Ray Crawford and bassist Eddie Calhoun. Due to his use of space, the very close interaction of the trio members (often seeming to think as one), and an inventive use of dynamics, Jamal and his group stood out from the start. **Poinciana** (Portrait 44394) features Jamal in his early trio (with Israel Crosby taking over on bass in 1955), showcasing a style that would be a major influence on Miles Davis's music due to its use of space and dynamics, even in its repertoire. After Jamal recorded "Old Devil Moon," "Will You Still Be Mine," "The Surrey with the Fringe on Top," and "A Gal in Calico," Davis recorded similar versions, and his version of "Billy Boy" inspired a pretty close rendition by the Red Garland Trio. Most intriguing is Jamal's inventive interpretation of "Pavanne," for it has a section very reminiscent of "So What" (which was "composed" by Davis more than two years later) and a melody statement that is exactly the same as John Coltrane's "Impressions."

Miles Davis and His First Classic Quintet   The period from the last of the three record dates by the Miles Davis Nonet's "Birth of the Cool" up until 1955

are generally thought of as the trumpeter's off period. As with too many other jazz musicians of the time, Davis was a heroin addict and he was scuffling. But in early 1954 he used all of his will power and quit heroin cold turkey, successfully breaking his connection with the ruinous drug and then focusing his energy on revitalizing his career.

Despite his messy personal life during this period, Davis led 13 record dates during 1951–54 and all have their moments. In 1950, he was only heard on the final nonet session. In 1951, Davis began a series of records for Prestige that featured him in many settings, all of which have been reissued on the eight-CD box set ◉ **Chronicle—The Complete Prestige Recordings (1951–1956)** (Prestige 012) and are available individually. **And Horns** (Original Jazz Classics 053) has Davis's first session with Sonny Rollins (from 1951) and a 1953 date with Al Cohn (who provided the arrangements) and Zoot Sims. **Dig** (Original Jazz Classics 005) consists of a rewarding sextet session from 1951 with Rollins and altoist Jackie McLean that is highlighted by McLean's "Dig" (based on "Sweet Georgia Brown") and "My Old Flame." **Blue Haze** (Original Jazz Classics 093) features three different pick-up groups from 1953–54. A quartet date with John Lewis, Percy Heath, and Max Roach includes "Tune Up" (a song most likely written by Eddie "Cleanhead" Vinson but claimed by Davis), "Miles Ahead," and Benny Carter's "When Lights Are Low." This disc also has an early hard bop date with Horace Silver, Heath, and Art Blakey that has the initial version of "Four" (which was another song probably penned by Vinson) plus "Old Devil Moon" and "Blue Haze." In addition, there is a quintet version of "I'll Remember April" with altoist Davey Schildkraut. **Collector's Items** (Original Jazz Classics 071) is of particular interest because it includes a 1953 Miles Davis session that has both Sonny Rollins and Charlie Parker on tenors (Bird sounds slightly uncomfortable on his bigger-than-usual sax) plus Davis featured on Dave Brubeck's "In Your Own Sweet Way."

While Miles Davis has long been recognized as one of the founders of cool jazz, his participation in early hard bop dates has often been overlooked. The music on **Dig** from October 5, 1951, with Rollins and McLean certainly sounds like hard bop, as does his three Blue Note sessions of 1952–54. **Vol. One** (Blue Note 81501) has Davis playing six songs and three alternate takes in a 1952 hard bop sextet with J.J. Johnson, Jackie McLean, pianist Gil Coggins, Oscar Pettiford, and Kenny Clarke, including "Dear Old Stockholm," McLean's "Donna," and "Yesterdays." Also on this disc are six songs cut in a quartet on March 6, 1954, with Horace Silver, Percy Heath, and Art Blakey that preceded the birth of the Jazz Messengers. Davis sounds in his early prime on "Take Off," "Well You Needn't," and the ballad "It Never Entered My Mind." The latter has Davis introducing his trademark Harmon mute sound. **Vol. Two** (Blue Note 81502) is from 1953 and features Miles with J.J. Johnson, Jimmy Heath, Gil Coggins, Percy Heath, and Art Blakey, digging into a pair of J.J. songs, "Ray's Idea," Bud Powell's "Tempus Fugit," Jimmy Heath's "C.T.A.," and "I Waited for You"; the set is augmented by five alternates. If proof is needed that Davis was one of the founders of hard bop, these two CDs should suffice.

For Miles Davis, 1954 was an early turning point. Having kicked heroin, he worked on becoming healthy and his playing gradually improved. **Walkin'** (Original Jazz Classics 213), in addition to three songs with Davey Schildkraut in a quintet (including the initial recording version of "Solar"), has jam session versions of "Walkin'" and "Blue 'N' Boogie" with J.J. Johnson and Lucky Thompson that show that Miles Davis was definitely back. **Bags' Groove** (Original Jazz Classics 245) has a brilliant session from June 29, 1954, featuring Davis, Rollins, Silver, Percy Heath, and Clarke on the debut of three of Rollins's most famous originals ("Airegin," "Oleo," and "Doxy") plus two versions of "But Not for Me." In addition, the two lengthy versions of "Bags' Groove" from a Christmas Eve session with Thelonious Monk and Milt Jackson (which is included in full on Monk's three-CD Prestige box) wrap up this CD. **Miles Davis & The Modern Jazz Giants** (Original Jazz Classics 347) has the remainder of the Davis-Monk set (including two versions of "The Man I Love") plus a lesser-known version of "'Round Midnight" played by the Davis quintet with John Coltrane.

One of the great moments of Miles Davis's career occurred at the 1955 Newport Jazz Festival. On July 17, an all-star group made up of Davis, Zoot Sims, Gerry Mulligan, Thelonious Monk, Percy Heath, and Connie Kay jammed on "Hackensack" and "Now's the Time." For "'Round Midnight," Davis was the only horn and his playing was so lyrical and emotional that it garnered headlines and let the critics in the audience know that he

was on his way to becoming a major force in jazz. Quite miraculously, the full 22-minute set (plus a humorous verbal introduction by Duke Ellington) appeared on record for the first time in 1993, on **Miscellaneous Davis, 1955–1957** (Jazz Unlimited 2050); it lives up to one's expectations. Also on the CD are three songs from a European tour in 1956 with a pickup group (Lester Young sits in on "Lady Be Good"), two numbers from a 1957 quintet with tenor saxophonist Bobby Jaspar, and three songs with a European orchestra in 1957.

A month before his Newport triumph, Miles Davis was in the early stages of forming a new group. **The Musings of Miles** (Original Jazz Classics 004) features the quartet of Davis, pianist Red Garland, Oscar Pettiford, and drummer Philly Joe Jones, with Davis sounding quite relaxed and thoughtful on "Will You Still Be Mine," "A Gal in Calico" (from the Ahmad Jamal songbook), and even "A Night in Tunisia." While the hot-tempered Pettiford (who could be rather violent when drinking excessively) did not last long, Miles now had the nucleus of his first classic quintet.

Red Garland had started out playing clarinet and alto, switching to piano when he was 18 in 1941. During 1946–54 he worked steadily on the East Coast including accompanying such players as Charlie Parker, Coleman Hawkins, Lester Young, and Roy Eldridge. But when he joined the Miles Davis Quintet in the summer of 1955 (when he was 32, three years older than the trumpeter), he was still quite obscure. However, Miles liked Ed Garland's chord voicings and urged him to listen more to Ahmad Jamal, and within a year Red Garland was himself becoming an influence on other pianists.

Philly Joe Jones (who added the "Philly" part to his name so he would not be confused with Jo Jones) also made a strong impression on Davis. The same age as Garland, Jones had served in the army, moved to New York in 1947, and had been the house drummer at Café Society, playing with Dizzy Gillespie, Charlie Parker, and Fats Navarro among others. After gigging with Ben Webster, Tiny Grimes, Lionel Hampton, and Tadd Dameron (1953), he joined Davis. His playing was initially criticized by some observers as being too loud, but quickly developed into a streamlined and highly personal approach to timekeeping, giving the trumpeter exactly what he wanted and pushing the soloists.

In the latter part of the summer, Davis added a young bassist to his group, Paul Chambers. Chambers, who at

20 in 1955 was the baby of the group, started on baritone horn and tuba in 1949 before he switched to bass. Although born in Pittsburgh, he was part of the Detroit jazz scene during the first half of the 1950s, playing with Kenny Burrell before leaving town in 1954 for an eight-month stint with Paul Quinichette. After gigging around New York (including with the J.J. Johnson-Kai Winding Quintet and George Wallington), he joined Miles Davis's new quintet. In addition to his fine sound and his work as a very alert timekeeper, Chambers was expert at taking bowed solos, which (aside from Slam Stewart) was considered quite unusual in jazz at the time.

Since Sonny Rollins had temporarily retired from music, Davis hired a young unknown for the tenor spot in his quintet. As 1955 began, there was little in tenor saxophonist John Coltrane's history that hinted at his future greatness. Already 28 (he was four months younger than Davis), Coltrane had begun his career on alto. He played in a navy band and cut some private sides in 1946 that find him sounding a bit like Charlie Parker. Coltrane settled in Philadelphia and worked with King Kolax (1946–47), switching to tenor when he played with Eddie "Cleanhead" Vinson (1947–48). A member of Dizzy Gillespie's big band during 1948–49, Coltrane did not receive any solo space, but was picked to be in the trumpeter's sextet (1950–51). A bootleg LP, **Coltrane 1951** (Oberon 5100), is taken from radio broadcasts of Gillespie's group. Dizzy is in very exciting form (particularly on "Good Bait") while 'Trane shows off the strong influence of Dexter Gordon. However, the next few years were a bit lean as Coltrane worked with the groups of Gay Crosse (1952), Earl Bostic, Johnny Hodges (1953–54), and a few weeks with Jimmy Smith (1955) in addition to lower-level R&B bands. Other than one solo on a Gillespie date cut in 1951 ("We Love to Boogie"), very little was heard from Coltrane on records until mid-1955 when he was asked to join the Miles Davis Quintet. Davis heard something in Coltrane's unusual sound (which, though still touched by Dexter Gordon, was already becoming original) and his eagerness to stretch himself and try out new ideas appealed to Miles.

Other than four songs recorded for Columbia on October 27, 1955 (and not released for a time), the group debuted on **The New Miles Davis Quintet** (Original Jazz Classics 006) from November 16. At that early stage, Coltrane sounds a bit nervous and is fairly insignificant, but the rhythm trio was already quite tight and Davis is in

excellent form, particularly on "There Is No Greater Love," "How Am I to Know," and Benny Golson's "Stablemates."

More would be heard from this group in 1956.

Kenny Dorham, Howard McGhee, and Red Rodney
While Dizzy Gillespie always remained a bebop player, Miles Davis went on to his own musical worlds, and Fats Navarro did not survive 1950, and Kenny Dorham became one of the key bop veterans to make the transition to hard bop. After leaving Charlie Parker's quintet in 1949 (where he was succeeded by Red Rodney), Dorham freelanced in New York and became an original member of the Jazz Messengers (1954–55). **Kenny Dorham Quintet** (Original Jazz Classics 113) from 1953 was the trumpeter's debut as a leader. Originally a ten-inch LP for Debut, it has been expanded with alternate takes and two additional blues. Dorham is featured with Jimmy Heath (on tenor and baritone), pianist Walter Bishop, Percy Heath, and Kenny Clarke on such songs as "Ruby My Dear," "Be My Love," and "An Oscar for Oscar." In 1955, Dorham recorded the first of his many albums for Blue Note, a classic called ◐ **Afro-Cuban** (Blue Note 46815). The first half of the set is Afro-Cuban jazz with Dorham joined by Patato Valdes on conga, J.J. Johnson, Hank Mobley, Cecil Payne, Horace Silver, Oscar Pettiford, and Art Blakey; the final four numbers are without Valdes, Johnson, and Pettiford (who is replaced by Percy Heath) and are more straightahead. This program has the debut versions of three of Dorham's best songs ("Lotus Flower," "Minor Holiday," and "La Villa") and features many fine solos along the way.

One of the top trumpeters of the bebop era, Howard McGhee's career became aimless in the 1950s due to his excessive drug use. He did travel on a USO tour during the Korean War (recording in Guam), made an album for Blue Note in 1953, and led two records for Bethlehem during 1955–56, but otherwise he was only semi-active in this decade. **That Bop Thing** (Affinity 765), McGhee's 1955 Bethlehem recording, is among his best all-around sessions of the era, a quintet outing with baritonist Sahib Shihab (who doubles on alto), Duke Jordan, Percy Heath, and Philly Joe Jones. McGhee's crisp tone and boppish style were virtually changed from the late 1940s, making one wish that he did not waste so many years afterward; he should have still been one of the leaders.

For Red Rodney, who played so brilliantly with Charlie Parker at Carnegie Hall on Christmas 1949, the 1950s would be an on-and-off period, a time when he too was battling heroin addiction. A bust led to him leaving Bird's group, but he made several comebacks on records during the decade. **Red Rodney Quintets** (Original Jazz Classics 24758) combines all of the music originally on his Prestige and Fantasy LPs of 1951 and 1955 that were titled **The New Sounds** and **Modern Music from Chicago**. The former date does not have any "names" among the sidemen (which include altoist Jimmy Ford), but the latter teams Rodney for the first time with the multi-instrumentalist Ira Sullivan (heard on tenor, alto, and second trumpet), pianist Norman Simmons, bassist Victor Sproles, and Roy Haynes. Throughout, Rodney plays quite well (and even takes a decent vocal on "Rhythm in a Riff"), sticks to the classic bebop style, and shows no signs of his hectic personal life.

Donald Byrd In 1955, 22-year-old trumpeter Donald Byrd moved from his native Detroit to New York. An up-and-coming player whose style leaned toward hard bop, Byrd was influenced by Clifford Brown and showed a great deal of promise. Shortly before leaving Detroit, he debuted on records with **First Flight** (Delmark 407), interacting with such fellow Detroiters as Yusef Lateef, Bernard McKinney (who played euphonium), pianist Barry Harris, bassist Alvin Jackson, and drummer Frank Gant. Byrd was not yet distinctive, but he showed promise. Shortly after arriving in New York, he worked with George Wallington's group for a few months, joining the Jazz Messengers in December and recording additional dates for the Savoy, Transition, and Realm labels. His best work was in the future.

Art Farmer Art Farmer (whose twin brother was bassist Addison Farmer) was born in Council Bluffs, Iowa, in 1928. He studied piano, violin, and tuba before settling on trumpet. Farmer moved to Los Angeles in 1945 and became a regular on Central Avenue, playing with Johnny Otis, Jay McShann, Roy Porter (with whom he recorded), Benny Carter, and Gerald Wilson, among others. Farmer worked with Wardell Gray during 1951–52 and in 1953 joined the Lionel Hampton Orchestra, playing next to Clifford Brown and touring Europe. Upon the group's return home, he moved to New York, recording four albums of material as a leader

for Prestige during 1953–55, all of which have been reissued on CD.

Art Farmer Septet (Original Jazz Classics 54) has a pair of four-song sessions from 1953 and 1954. One date has Farmer in a septet arranged by Quincy Jones (who also fills in on piano) and includes trombonist Jimmy Cleveland and the pioneering electric bassist Monk Montgomery. The other set is also with a septet although with Horace Silver and Charlie Rouse, highlighted by "Evening in Paris" and "Elephant Walk." Two other songs from other dates augment this still-brief reissue. **Early Art** (Original Jazz Classics 880) has four numbers by Farmer in a 1954 quintet with Sonny Rollins, Horace Silver, Percy Heath, and Kenny Clarke (including "Soft Shoe" and "I'll Take Romance") and six tunes (including "Autumn Nocturne" and an uptempo "Gone with the Wind") in a quartet with pianist Wynton Kelly, drummer Herbie Lovelle, and Art's brother Addison. The only flaw to the easily enjoyable set is that the songs listed as appearing second through fifth actually appear first through fourth, with "Soft Shoe" being listed first but actually being the fifth song on the CD.

When Farmer Met Gryce (Original Jazz Classics 072), which teams Farmer with altoist Gigi Gryce and two fine rhythm sections, is most notable for the compositions, which include the original version of "Social Call" (one of Gryce's best-known songs), "Capri," "A Night at Tony's," and "Blue Concept." **Featuring Gigi Gryce** (Original Jazz Classics 241) again has Farmer and Gryce sharing the frontline (in a quintet with Duke Jordan, Addison Farmer, and Philly Joe Jones). Other than Jordan's "Forecast," all of the music on this cool-toned hard bop date are Gigi Gryce originals including "Evening in Casablanca" and "Nica's Tempo."

Thad Jones One of the first members of the postwar generation of Detroit jazz musicians to make an impact, Thad Jones (pianist Hank Jones's younger brother) was already 31 when he moved to New York. Jones, who was self-taught on trumpet, started playing professionally in 1939 when he was 16. He served in the military (1943–46), worked in territory bands in the Midwest, and was a member of tenor saxophonist Billy Mitchell's quintet in Detroit during 1950–53. After his arrival in New York, he greatly impressed Charles Mingus (with whom he recorded on a few occasions during 1954–55 for Mingus's Debut label) and became one of the soloists with the Count Basie Orchestra in 1954, taking a famous spot on Basie's hit record "April in Paris." **The Fabulous Thad Jones** (Original Jazz Classics 625) has all of the music from his first two albums as a leader (both cut for Debut). Jones was a harmonically advanced soloist (his choice of notes tended to be unpredictable) with a bright sound and a fertile imagination. With the assistance of Hank Jones or John Dennis on piano, Mingus, Kenny Clarke, or Max Roach on drums, and (on the first date) Frank Wess on tenor and flute, Thad Jones is very much in the spotlight, performing his tricky originals and his inventively reworked renditions of standards.

Eddie Bert   A fine utility trombonist, Eddie Bert has played in a countless number of situations since joining Sam Donahue's Orchestra in 1940, including associations with Red Norvo, Charlie Barnet, Woody Herman, Stan Kenton, and Benny Goodman. A swing player who opened his style to bop, Bert led a series of worthwhile if underrated dates during 1952–55. **Encore** (Savoy 0229) is a good example of his playing, although at 35 minutes this CD is rather brief. Bert is featured with a pianoless quartet that includes guitarist Joe Puma, and with a quintet that includes Hank Jones and J.R. Monterose on tenor. Bert and Puma contributed all of the songs, and this lightly swinging bop date fits very well into the era.

Jimmy Cleveland   Jimmy Cleveland emerged in the mid-1950s as one of the top bebop-oriented trombonists, a very fluent player not overly influenced by J.J. Johnson. After serving in the army and attending Tennessee State University, he was part of the Lionel Hampton Orchestra during 1950–53, recording in Europe. During 1954–60, Cleveland appeared on many record dates including five of his own. **Introducing Jimmy Cleveland** (Verve 314 543 752), the only one to be reissued on CD thus far, has the trombonist in medium-sized groups playing a variety of Quincy Jones arrangements. The band includes trumpeter Ernie Royal, either Lucky Thompson or Jerome Richardson on tenor, baritonist Cecil Payne, Hank Jones, John Williams, or Wade Legge on piano, guitarist Barry Galbraith, Paul Chambers, or Oscar Pettiford on bass, and Max Roach, Osie Johnson, or Joe Harris on drums. Most of the sidemen get some fine spots, but Cleveland generally takes the solo honors, showing that he was one of the major trombonists of the era.

Urbie Green   Urbie Green always had a beautiful tone and he was highly respected by his fellow trombonists, spending much of his career playing in the studios. Green began on trombone when he was 12, and as a teenager during World War II he played with the big bands of Tommy Reynolds, Bob Strong, and Frankie Carle. Green gained recognition for his work with Gene Krupa (1947–50) and Woody Herman's Third Herd. As a leader, Green recorded a date apiece for Blue Note (1953), the X label, and Vanguard, but his Bethlehem album is the only one out on CD thus far. **East Coast Jazz Vol. 6** (Bethlehem 76686) from 1955 has Green's tone well showcased in a septet with Doug Mettome and Al Cohn, performing music that falls between bop, cool jazz, and swing, such as "On Green Dolphin Street," "How About You," "Three Little Words," and "Melody in B Flat."

Sonny Criss   Alto saxophonists of this era were often so touched by Charlie Parker's playing that it was a struggle for many to escape his dominant influence. Sonny Criss's large tone differed from Charlie Parker's though his choice of notes was influenced by Bird, and the intensity that he gave every idea was a large part of his musical personality. Criss, who was not part of the cool jazz scene despite being based in Los Angeles, worked fairly regularly during this period, but mostly in obscurity until he joined Stan Kenton for a tour in 1955. A "Jazz at the Philharmonic" concert from 1951 was discovered decades later and issued under Criss's name as **Intermission Riff** (Original Jazz Classics 961). The lineup of musicians (with trumpeter Joe Newman, trombonist Bennie Green, and tenor saxophonist Eddie "Lockjaw" Davis) is much different from the usual JATP event. Criss's passionate playing on four standards (including "How High the Moon" and "Perdido") and the title cut are the standouts.

Lou Donaldson   Influenced by Charlie Parker, but playing in a soulful style that is more blues-based and a bit simpler, Lou Donaldson carved out a niche for himself. He started out playing clarinet as a teenager, soon switching to the alto. Donaldson attended college, performed in a Navy band while in the military, and moved to New York in 1952 when he was 25. Soon after arriving in town he recorded for Blue Note, an association that would last on and off for decades. The following year he led a session that has usually been reissued under

Clifford Brown's name, and in 1954 he recorded with Art Blakey and Clifford Brown at Birdland. Donaldson has continually led his own groups throughout his long career.

The Lou Donaldson Quartet/Quintet/Sextet (Blue Note 81537) has three of the altoist's first four sessions as a leader (just leaving out the set with Clifford Brown) and is quite beboppish. Donaldson is joined by such players as Horace Silver, trumpeters Blue Mitchell and Kenny Dorham, and pianist Elmo Hope on standards, and a few originals (including Donaldson's "Down Home" and Silver's "Roccus"), showing that he had his own conception from the beginning of his career.

Gigi Gryce Gigi Gryce had a distinctive tone on alto, but was more significant for his writing abilities. He studied at the Boston Conservatory and in Paris before working in New York with Max Roach, Tadd Dameron, and Clifford Brown. Gryce was part of the 1953 Lionel Hampton Orchestra, touring Europe and leading several sessions in France, most of which have been reissued under Brownie's name. He freelanced in 1954, used Thelonious Monk as a sideman on a record date in 1955, worked with Oscar Pettiford, and started teaming up with Donald Byrd in their Jazz Lab quintet. **Nica's Tempo** (Savoy 18057) has the Monk quartet session (which included the pianist's "Shuffle Boil," "Brake's Sake," and "Gallop's Gallop," plus Gryce's "Nica's Tempo") and a date in which Gryce uses a nonet that has the same instrumentation as Miles Davis's "Birth of the Cool" group. Four of the songs ("Kerry Dance" and three of Gryce's originals) are instrumentals, while "Social Call" and "You'll Always Be the One I Love" feature early vocals by Ernestine Anderson.

Jackie McLean An intense player with a tone that is always a little sharp, Jackie McLean sounded quite individual from the beginning of his career. The son of guitarist John McLean (who had played with Tiny Bradshaw), as a teenager McLean knew and was friendly with such neighbors in New York City as Bud Powell, Thelonious Monk, and Sonny Rollins. Well acquainted with the bebop vocabulary, in 1951 the 19-year-old made his recording debut with Miles Davis and also spent time working with George Wallington and Charles Mingus. **The Jackie McLean Quintet** (Fresh Sound 083) is a reissue of McLean's debut as a leader, a 1955 quintet date with Donald Byrd, Mal Waldron,

Doug Watkins, and drummer Roland Tucker that was originally cut for the short-lived Ad-Lib label. Most notable is the original version of McLean's "Little Melonae" and the way that he makes the standards (such as "It's You or No One" and "Lover Man") sound intense and brand new.

Frank Morgan Frank Morgan in 1955 seemed to have a very bright future as one of Charlie Parker's chief musical disciples. Like Jackie McLean, Morgan's father was a guitarist (Stanley Morgan played with the Ink Spots). After taking up clarinet and alto early on, Frank Morgan moved with his family to Los Angeles in 1947. As a youth he won a talent contest, leading to his recording a solo with Freddie Martin's orchestra. Morgan embraced the Los Angeles bop scene of the early 1950s, recorded with Teddy Charles (1953) and Kenny Clarke (1954), and in 1955 led his own album, **Frank Morgan** (GNP/Crescendo 9041). The altoist performs four numbers with Machito's rhythm section and six other songs with a septet that also includes Wardell Gray (heard on his final recordings). Conte Candoli is a strong asset on both of the boppish dates. But tragically, Frank Morgan, whom some were calling "the new Bird," emulated Charlie Parker's drug habits, was soon arrested for the first time, and would have to wait 30 years before he had an opportunity to lead his second record date.

Sonny Stitt During 1950–52, Sonny Stitt (who was now doubling on alto and tenor) co-led a group with Gene Ammons. After that unit broke up, he mostly worked as a single for the remainder of his long career, often with local rhythm sections. Stitt never changed from his original course—playing classic bebop—and he remained a master of the vocabulary. **Prestige First Sessions Vol. 2** (Prestige 24115) has Stitt on tenor for all but two of the 24 selections from 1950–51. He is the lead voice throughout and is typically enthusiastic, whether in trios with Kenny Drew, Duke Jordan, Junior Mance, or Clarence Anderson on piano, or in septets that mostly have Ammons on baritone. **Kaleidoscope** (Original Jazz Classics 060) has selections from 1950–52, including two cuts on which Stitt is heard soloing on baritone, an instrument he used for a few years around this time until he grew weary of lugging it around. Once again Stitt is heard with quartets and septets, digging into such songs as "Stitt's It," "P.S. I Love You," "This Can't Be Love," "Liza," and "Cherokee." **At the Hi-Hat** (Roulette 98582) and **Live at the Hi-Hat Vol. Two** (Roulette 37200) are both from a performance in Boston on February 11, 1954. Stitt utilized a competent local rhythm section (pianist Dean Earl, bassist Bernie Griggs, and drummer Marquis Foster) and is heard jamming his usual standards, 27 numbers in all on the two discs. Most unusual is that Stitt plays all three of his horns (including baritone) on the first set's "Tri-Horn Blues" and **Vol. Two**'s "One o'Clock Jump."

Phil Woods   One of the great bebop altoists, Phil Woods was criticized early in his career for closely emulating Charlie Parker, but in reality he always had his own tone and over time developed an endless stream of fresh ideas within bebop and hard bop. After moving to New York in 1948, Woods studied with Lennie Tristano, at the Manhattan School of Music, and at Juilliard. In 1954, he worked with Charlie Barnet and the following year often played with Jimmy Raney in addition to forming his own group. **Pot Pie** (Original Jazz Classics 1881) was the altoist's debut as a leader, heading a quintet also featuring Jon Eardley and pianist George Syran. This set (seven group originals plus "Mad About the Boy") is full of youthful energy and excitement (Woods was only 22) as the relative youngsters dig into the material. **Woodlore** (Original Jazz Classics 052) is a rather brief 33-minute CD, but also contains plenty of fine playing from November 25, 1955. Woods, pianist John Williams, bassist Teddy Kotick, and drummer Nick Stabulas swing hard on four standards (including "Slow Boat to China" and "Be My Love") plus a pair of Woods's originals. Overall these two CDs serve as a strong start to Phil Woods's career.

Gene Ammons   Tenor saxophonists did not have the same problem as altoists for they had several role models (Coleman Hawkins, Lester Young, Ben Webster, and Illinois Jacquet) to draw upon, not to mention the ideas of Charlie Parker. Gene Ammons, after Woody Herman's Second Herd broke up at the end of 1949, formed a quintet with fellow tenor Sonny Stitt that lasted two years; its most notable recording was "Blues Up and Down." Ammons and Stitt were both competitive players with a great deal of respect for each other. Their collaborations took place on an irregular basis over a quarter-century and usually found them battling to a tie. Ammons's **All-Star Sessions with Sonny Stitt** (Original Jazz Classics 014) has most of the recordings

by the original combo in which the co-leaders both play tenor; they tended to switch to baritone for each other's dates during this era. Highlights are three takes of "Blues Up and Down," two versions of "You Can Depend on Me," and "Stringin' the Jug." In addition, there are two lengthy Ammons jam session numbers from 1955 with Art Farmer and Lou Donaldson. **Young Jug** (Chess 801) has 16 of Ammons's 24 Chess recordings of 1948–51 plus a very obscure Decca session from 1952. Though one wishes that this collection was complete, it does find Ammons in top early form on "Swingin' for Xmas" (during which he has a tenor battle with Tom Archia), a remake of "More Moon," and such ballads as "It's the Talk of the Town," "My Foolish Heart," and "You Go to My Head." **The Gene Ammons Story: The 78 Era** (Prestige 24058) has 26 concise selections that are mostly from 1950–51 and put the focus almost entirely on Ammons's distinctive tone, whether it be boppish romps or ballads.

Gene Ammons began a longtime association with the Prestige label in 1950, which would result in many memorable albums during the next 20 years. Due to his versatility and that enormous tone (one note could immediately capture a crowded room), Ammons would be quite popular throughout his career, in addition to being a jazz giant.

Dexter Gordon   After such a promising start during the second half of the 1940s, the 1950s were largely a waste for Dexter Gordon. Drug problems resulted in him spending much of the time off the scene and some of it in jail. In 1952, Gordon teamed up with Wardell Gray for the last time at a "Just Jazz" concert in Pasadena and on an obscure record date cut for Swingtime. Otherwise, his only significant appearances on record were in 1955 for an album led by Stan Levey and two sets of his own. **Daddy Plays the Horn** (Bethlehem 75991) is a jam session–flavored quartet date with Kenny Drew, Leroy Vinnegar, and Lawrence Marable that finds Gordon in excellent form on four standards and two fairly basic originals. **Dexter Blows Hot and Cool** (Boplicity 6) has Gordon leading a quintet with the obscure trumpeter Jimmy Robinson, pianist Carl Perkins, Leroy Vinnegar, and drummer Chuck Thompson. Dexter really excels on the ballads ("Cry Me a River," "I Should Care," and "Don't Worry 'Bout Me"). But little more would be heard from the classic tenorman until 1960.

Wardell Gray   Admired by beboppers and swing greats like Benny Goodman and Count Basie alike, Wardell Gray's future looked bright in 1950. He played and recorded with the Count Basie septet and on a few special recordings with Basie's big band, including a showcase on "Little Pony." Gray was featured on some Norman Granz jam sessions, recorded with Louie Bellson (1952–53), and his solo on 1949's "Twisted" was turned into a vocalese classic by Annie Ross. But Gray, who was considered an inspiration to some younger musicians in the 1940s for his opposition to drug use, himself became involved in drugs. He died mysteriously in Las Vegas on May 25, 1955, when he was just 34, probably from a drug overdose.

Wardell Gray Memorial, Vol. 2 (Original Jazz Classics 051) features the tenor on nine-minute versions of "Scrapple from the Apple" and "Move" recorded at an L.A. jam session with Clark Terry, Sonny Criss, and (on "Move") Dexter Gordon. Gray is also heard in the studios with a quartet and a sextet that include Art Farmer and Hampton Hawes, with "Jackie" and "Farmer's Market" (two future Annie Ross vocalese pieces) being most memorable. **Live at the Haig** (Fresh Sound 157) is a club date from September 9, 1952, with Farmer, Hawes, Joe Mondragon, and Shelly Manne on nine lengthy numbers, including "Donna Lee," "Pennies from Heaven," and "Get Happy." There would be a final studio date on January 19, 1955 (for Vee Jay), but a little over four months later Wardell Gray was gone.

Bobby Jaspar   A talented flutist and tenor saxophonist, Bobby Jaspar was born in Belgium in 1926. As a teenager he played Dixieland with Toots Thielemans, but was more interested in modern jazz. Jaspar first recorded as a leader in 1951 and often played with touring Americans such as Jimmy Raney and Chet Baker (1953). **Memory of Dick** (EmArcy 837 208), in addition to the title cut tribute to the recently deceased Dick Twardzik, includes such songs as "Milestones," "I'll Remember April," and "A Night in Tunisia." Jaspar, alternating between tenor (where Stan Getz was his main influence) and flute, heads a fine French quintet also featuring pianist Rene Urtreger and guitarist Sacha Distel. Jaspar served as one of many pieces of evidence that jazz in Europe was catching up to the United States very quickly in the 1950s.

Hank Mobley   Hank Mobley was a definitive hard bop tenor saxophonist. He was accurately described by

critic Leonard Feather as "the middleweight champion of the tenor" as his sound was not as light as Lester Young's nor as heavy as that of Sonny Rollins or Coleman Hawkins. Mobley worked with Max Roach on and off during 1951–53 and with Dizzy Gillespie in 1954 before becoming an original member of the Jazz Messengers. **Hank Mobley Quartet** (Blue Note 46816) from March 27, 1955, was the first in a long string of rewarding Mobley Blue Note albums. Joined by Horace Silver, bassist Doug Watkins, and Art Blakey, Mobley is already recognizable on such tunes as "Hank's Pranks," "My Sin," and "Avila and Tequila."

James Moody   James Moody spent 1949–51 in Europe and upon his return to the United States formed a septet that stayed together for five years. In 1952, Babs Gonzales was the group's singer, but a year later Eddie Jefferson succeeded him. The music of Moody's band was boppish, witty, and fairly accessible. **Moody's Mood for Blues** (Original Jazz Classics 1637) has some danceable rhythms and riffing along with many fine solos. Eddie Jefferson sings "Workshop," and "I Got the Blues," while Moody performs two versions of "It Might as Well Be Spring," one on tenor and the other on alto. **Hi-Fi Party** (Original Jazz Classics) has two sessions from 1955 with the septet (which includes trumpeter Dave Burns) performing swinging versions of obscure originals, Benny Golson's "Big Ben," and "There Will Never Be Another You." Jefferson sings his alternate lyrics to Charlie Parker's famous solo on "Lady Be Good," which he renamed "Disappointed." Also from 1955, **Wail, Moody, Wail** (Original Jazz Classics 1791) displays plenty of spirit, highlighted by the 14-minute title cut and "Moody's Blue Again." This was a fun band.

Sonny Rollins   Sonny Rollins, who made a strong impression in 1949, particularly on a session in which he held his own with Bud Powell and Fats Navarro, was considered the top up-and-coming tenor saxophonist of the early 1950s. His hard tone (influenced initially by Coleman Hawkins) became increasingly distinctive, proved constantly that he was a major improviser, and became in great demand. Rollins recorded as a sideman with Miles Davis (starting in 1951) and Thelonious Monk (1953) and started to lead dates for the Prestige label.

● **The Complete Prestige Recordings** (Prestige 4407) is a seven-CD box that features Rollins during

1949–54 and (for the second half of the release) 1956. Rollins is heard as a sideman with J.J. Johnson (1949), Miles Davis (1951, 1953, and 1954), Monk, and Art Farmer, plus on nine of his own albums, three of which are from 1951–54. The material from 1956 will be dealt with in the following chapter. On his sideman dates, Rollins easily keeps up with the better-known players. The Miles Davis session from 1953 is quite unusual for Charlie Parker who is on second tenor, in one of his very few recordings on the larger horn. Strangely enough, Parker sounds more like Rollins on this date than the other way around. A Davis set from 1954 is particularly significant for it introduces three of Rollins's best originals: "Airegin," "Oleo" (based on "I Got Rhythm"), and "Doxy" (which uses the chords of "Ja Da"). Rollins's sessions as a leader in this box are also available individually. **Sonny Rollins with the Modern Jazz Quartet** (Original Jazz Classics 011) has the tenor joined by the members of the MJQ on four numbers in 1953 and the trio of Kenny Drew, Percy Heath, and Art Blakey in 1951 on eight others. There is also a leftover track ("I Know") from a Miles Davis date that has the trumpeter switching to piano so Rollins can be showcased. Even at this early stage, Rollins shows his skill at taking unlikely material, such as "Shadrack," and turning it into creative jazz. **Moving Out** (Original Jazz Classics 058), in addition to a version of "More than You Know" with Thelonious Monk, features Rollins in a hard bop quintet in 1954 with Kenny Dorham, Elmo Hope, Percy Heath, and Art Blakey.

For a time during 1954–55, Sonny Rollins retired from music for the first time. He kicked drugs, improved his health, and practiced constantly. By the time he recorded **Work Time** (Original Jazz Classics 007) on December 2, 1955, he was ready to be jazz's top tenor saxophonist. Backed by pianist Ray Bryant, George Morrow, and Max Roach, Rollins tears into "There's No Business Like Show Business," "Raincheck," and "It's Alright with Me." And with Harold Land leaving the Clifford Brown-Max Roach Quintet, Rollins accepted an offer to join the group.

Lars Gullin During the latter part of the bebop era and the rise of cool, Sweden developed a rather strong jazz scene. Trumpeter Rolf Ericson, altoist Arne Domnerus, and pianist Bengt Hallberg (a major cool bop musician whose dates for the Swedish Metronome label are largely unavailable) were just three of the talented players (preceded by clarinetist Stan Hasselgard) who became world-class players. Probably the greatest of that era's Swedish jazzmen was baritonist Lars Gullin. Gullin, who had previously played clarinet and piano, was working as an altoist in 1949 when at the age of 21 he switched permanently to baritone. His cool and light tone was similar in ways to Gerry Mulligan and Serge Chaloff, but also distinctive, never merely sounding like a copy of the better-known American players. He worked with Arne Domnerus's sextet (1951–53), was in demand for record dates with visiting Americans (including Lee Konitz, James Moody, Clifford Brown, Zoot Sims, and Chet Baker), and played constantly throughout the 1950s.

Gullin's many recordings as a leader (he led 29 dates during 1951–55) are just beginning to become available on CDs. ● **1955/56 Vol. 1** (Dragon 224) has the baritonist starring with four different groups, ranging from a quartet to an octet and featuring Chet Baker on four numbers. Gullin is heard in prime form, stretching out on his most famous original ("Danny's Dream"), featuring the clarinet of Arne Domnerus on "Ma," and holding his own with Baker's quartet. **1953 Vol. 2** (Dragon 234) has Gullin in a variety of mostly obscure performances from 1953, including three songs in which he is teamed with Conte Candoli, Frank Rosolino, Lee Konitz, and Zoot Sims, and appearing on four numbers playing his rarely heard alto. The music is very much in the West Coast jazz style of the time. **1954/55 Vol. 3** (Dragon 244) has seven unusual (and partially successful) numbers in which Gullin and his quartet interact with the 16-voice Moretown Singers. Also featured are a couple of sessions with tenor saxophonist Rolf Billberg and one in which Gullin is heard in a quartet with the up-and-coming German pianist Jutta Hipp.

The Dragon discs are excellent, but it is a pity that a complete reissue of Gullin's 1950s recordings has not taken place yet.

Buddy DeFranco The Charlie Parker of the clarinet, Buddy DeFranco never achieved the fame of Benny Goodman and Artie Shaw simply because his instrument was considered by many to be out-of-place in the modern jazz scene of the 1950s. Nevertheless, he was a brilliant player who did his best to persevere. In 1950, DeFranco was a member of Count Basie's septet, the following year he made an attempt to lead a big band (it soon failed), and in 1952 he formed a quartet comprised of Kenny Drew, Curly Russell, and Art Blakey. DeFranco signed with Norman Granz in 1953 and began recording for Norgran and Verve, appearing in all-star settings in addition to working with his own group. DeFranco's 1954–55 quartet featured Sonny Clark, bassist Eugene Wright, and drummer Bobby White, with Tal Farlow expanding the group for a time in 1955.

While DeFranco's recordings with Clark have appeared on a limited-edition Mosaic box set, his MGM dates of 1951–53 (which include his few big band dates) and his Norgran/Verve combo dates have mostly not been reissued yet. An exception is **Buddy DeFranco and Oscar Peterson Play George Gershwin** (Verve 314 557 099). However, that set, which also includes Herb Ellis, Ray Brown, Bobby White, and a string section arranged by Russ Garcia, is a slight disappointment. The arrangements are decent but nothing special, the tempos are generally on the slower side, and the overall results are a bit sleepy. DeFranco's more significant recordings from this period remain long overdue to be made widely available.

Paul Bley In 1953, a new pianist emerged from Canada. Paul Bley, who was born in Montreal, started on piano when he was eight and studied at Julliard during 1950–52. In 1953, he played with Charlie Parker on a Canadian television show whose soundtrack has survived (talk about starting on top!) and recorded his first album, **Introducing Paul Bley** (Original Jazz Classics 201) when he was 21. Bley is featured in a trio with Charles Mingus and Art Blakey that was originally cut for Mingus's Debut label. The pianist is heard developing his own voice within the bebop tradition, playing stimulating originals, a few standards, Horace Silver's "Split Kick," and an effective version of "Santa Claus Is Coming to Town," a solid beginning to what would be a productive career.

Sonny Clark Sonny Clark emerged in the mid-1950s as one of the top Bud Powell–influenced bop pianists, which is saying a lot as most new jazz pianists sounded a lot like Powell. Clark had played early on with Wardell Gray, Vido Musso, and Oscar Pettiford, making his recording debut with Teddy Charles. He was a member of the Buddy DeFranco Quartet during 1953–56 and worked in Los Angeles with the Lighthouse All-Stars and various top West Coast jazz players. **Oakland, 1955** (Uptown 27.40) gives an early glimpse of the pianist

before he started leading his own record dates. The recording quality of these live sessions is only so-so, but his playing in a trio with bassist Jerry Good and drummer Al Randall is excellent, sounding quite mature on a dozen selections despite only being 23.

Kenny Drew Kenny Drew made his recording debut in 1949 when he was 21, playing with Howard McGhee. In the 1950s, he was a valuable sideman, playing with Charlie Parker, Coleman Hawkins, Lester Young, Milt Jackson, and Buddy DeFranco's quartet (1952–53), among others. As a leader, Drew first recorded for Blue Note in 1953 and had a pair of dates for Norgran the same year. Best among Drew's early records is **Talkin' and Walkin'** (Blue Note 84439), a quartet outing from December 1955 with Joe Maini (on alto and tenor), Leroy Vinnegar, and Lawrence Marable that was recorded in Los Angeles, originally for Pacific Jazz. Maini has a rare opportunity to stretch out on the nine quartet pieces, which include six Drew originals. In addition, the CD reissue adds three selections with the same group under trumpeter Jack Sheldon's leadership (two Drew songs plus "It's Only a Paper Moon") that were originally only available on samplers.

Al Haig One of the first bebop pianists, Al Haig (who worked with Dizzy Gillespie during 1945–46 and the Charlie Parker Quintet in 1948–49) toured with Stan Getz during 1949–51 and then became obscure. He did record a few dates as a leader for Esoteric, Swing, and Period in 1954, but otherwise mostly kept a low profile while still playing quite well. **Trio and Sextet** (Original Jazz Classics 1929) has two lesser-known sessions from 1949 (four songs apiece with either Wardell Gray or Stan Getz) plus a trio set from 1954 with bassist Bill Crow and drummer Lee Abrams. **Al Haig Trio** (Fresh Sound 45) features the latter group on additional titles from the same day (standards and a few bop tunes), while **Al Haig Quartet** (Fresh Sound 12) has Haig joined by guitarist Benny Weeks, bassist Teddy Kotick, and drummer Phil Brown. But despite playing well, Haig primarily worked for years as a single in East Coast clubs and was forgotten by the jazz world.

Elmo Hope A close friend of both Bud Powell and Thelonious Monk, Elmo Hope was nearly on their level as a pianist and composer. He played with trumpeter Joe Morris's R&B band (1948–51) next to tenor saxophonist

Johnny Griffin. In 1953, Hope began to record as a leader and with the likes of Sonny Rollins, Lou Donaldson, and Clifford Brown. But drug problems (which resulted in the loss of his cabaret card) and being overshadowed by other musicians led to him always being underrated. **Trio and Quintet** (Blue Note 84438) has all of the music that Hope recorded for Blue Note and Pacific Jazz, including his first recordings as a leader. His piano playing is perfectly showcased in a 1953 trio date with Percy Heath and Philly Joe Jones. Hope is also heard in a 1954 quintet with tenor saxophonist Frank Foster and on three numbers from 1957 with a West Coast group including Harold Land and Stu Williamson. This CD has 14 rarely played Elmo Hope songs, many of which deserve to be revived. **Meditations** (Original Jazz Classics 1751) includes five more Hope originals played in a trio with bassist John Ore and drummer Willie Jones. **Hope Meets Foster** (Original Jazz Classics 1703) has Hope again meeting up with Frank Foster, in a quartet/quintet with trumpeter Freeman Lee on half of the six songs. All three of these Elmo Hope reissues show how talented a player and composer he was, clearly of the Bud Powell generation, but developed an original voice of his own.

Wynton Kelly   Wynton Kelly got his start in the early 1950s. After growing up in Brooklyn, he played in jazz-oriented R&B bands led by Eddie "Cleanhead" Vinson, Hal Singer, and Eddie "Lockjaw" Davis. Kelly worked with Dizzy Gillespie, Lester Young (1951–52), and after a stint in the military, became Dinah Washington's accompanist in 1955. **Piano Interpretations** (Blue Note 84456) was recorded in 1951 when Kelly was just 19. He performs with Franklin Skeete or Oscar Pettiford on bass and drummer Lee Abrams. Very influenced by Bud Powell at the time (and to a lesser extent Teddy Wilson), Kelly was just starting to work out his own chord voicings and soulful style. Although Wynton Kelly was not quite the pianist that he would become, taken on its own terms this is a superb debut.

Marian McPartland   After marrying Dixieland cornetist Jimmy McPartland, Marian McPartland moved with her husband to the United States in 1946, playing with his bands for a few years even though her style was more modern than his. In 1950, she formed her own trio (which was based at the Embers) and her group played regularly at the Hickory House for eight years, starting in 1952. **Timeless** (Savoy 17117) is a sampling of McPartland's Savoy recordings of 1951–53, a little less than half of the music that she cut for the label. Though the songs on this set are primarily swing standards (such as "Strike Up the Band," "Yesterdays," and "Embraceable You"), McPartland's harmonically sophisticated style and inventive ideas (performed in a trio with Ed Safranski, Max Wayne or Vinnie Burke on bass, and Joe Morello, Don Lamond, or Mel Zelnick on drums) put her far beyond the trad/swing orbit without making her a Bud Powell clone.

Herbie Nichols   Like Thelonious Monk, Herbie Nichols stood apart from his musical generation, both as a pianist and as a composer. After serving in the army (1941–43), he played with a variety of groups, including those led by trumpeter Herman Autrey, Hal Singer, Illinois Jacquet, and John Kirby (1948–49). By the early 1950s, Nichols had developed into an original composer whose songs, which had complex chord changes, set moods rather than featuring catchy melodies. As a pianist, he was accepted in trad jazz and swing settings (where he modified his style a bit), but strangely enough was considered too advanced for bop settings. Few of the "modern" jazz musicians had any interest in performing his compositions, feeling that they were too complex. Nichols recorded four numbers for Savoy in 1952, which are usually reissued as part of samplers. In 1955, he received a break, interesting Alfred Lion and Francis Wolff (who had earlier taken chances on Bud Powell and Thelonious Monk) in recording him for their Blue Note label. There were five trio sessions in all during 1955–56 with Nichols joined by either Al McKibbon or Teddy Kotick on bass and Art Blakey or Max Roach on drums.

⦿ **The Complete Blue Note Recordings** (Blue Note 59352), a three-CD set, has the original 24 titles plus 24 other performances, 18 of which are alternate takes; the music had previously been out on a Mosaic five-LP box set. Other than a version of George Gershwin's "Mine," the music consists solely of Nichols's originals, many of which are orchestral in nature. "Blue Chopsticks," "2300 Skidoo," "Shuffle Montgomery," "The Gig," "House Party Starting," and "Lady Sings the Blues" (which would be recorded by Billie Holiday) are the most memorable of the songs, but none would catch on and the records did not sell well. However, this is subtle and unpredictable music that grows in interest with each listen, hinting at the great musical talents of the neglected Herbie Nichols.

Billy Taylor Billy Taylor, who started out playing swing with Ben Webster and Stuff Smith, worked a bit with Artie Shaw (when Shaw hired his trio as the nucleus for a short-lived Gramercy Five) and in 1951 was the house pianist at Birdland. Taylor led a trio from 1952 on with Earl May on bass and drummer Charlie Smith, who was replaced by Percy Brice in 1954. **Billy Taylor Trio** (Prestige 24154) has two full albums by the Taylor-May-Smith group from 1952–53, showing how the pianist made bebop sound accessible through his good taste, swinging, and subtle creativity. **Cross Section** (Original Jazz Classics 1730) has eight songs by Taylor, May, and Brice from 1954, split between standards and originals, and all dedicated to the disc jockeys of the time. The music falls between swing and bop. In addition, there are four numbers that match Taylor, May, and Charlie Smith (who sticks to conga) with Machito's rhythm section (Jose Mangual on bongos, Uba Nieto playing timbales, and Machito himself on maracas). The four mambos were Taylor's first exploration of Afro-Cuban jazz. In 1954, Taylor added Candido on congas to his group for **Billy Taylor Trio with**

Candido (Original Jazz Classics 015). The matchup works well although this six-song program is quite brief, under 32 minutes. Taylor's "A Live One" has the leader and Candido trading off enthusiastically, and "Mambo Inn" is given a fine workout.

George Wallington George Wallington, one of the earliest of the bop-oriented pianists, freelanced during 1950–52, was part of the Lionel Hampton big band in 1953 that toured Europe, and started leading his own quintets in 1954. **The George Wallington Trios** (Original Jazz Classics 1754), originally a pair of ten-inch LPs, features the pianist with Charles Mingus, Oscar Pettiford or Curly Russell on bass, plus drummer Max Roach. Chuck Wayne sits in on mandola on "Love Beat." Wallington explores ten of his inventive (if obscure) originals plus five standards. He also recorded for Savoy, Vogue, Blue Note, Norgran, and Progressive, with the latter being reissued as **Live! At Café Bohemia** (Original Jazz Classics 1813). Wallington's quintet of the time with Donald Byrd, Jackie McLean, Paul Chambers (who was borrowed from Miles Davis's band), and Art Taylor sounds like they are playing a bebop jam except that most of the songs (other than Oscar Pettiford's "Bohemia After Dark," and "Johnny One Note") are

TIMELINE 1953

Guitarist Laurindo Almeida and altoist Bud Shank team together for Brazilliance, an important set of recordings that hint strongly at bossa nova. • The Lionel Hampton Orchestra (with Clifford Brown) tours Europe. • Tommy and Jimmy Dorsey begin working together again as the Dorsey Brothers Orchestra. • Oscar Celestin's Tuxedo Jazz Orchestra plays a special concert at the White House for President Dwight Eisenhower. • Charles Mingus forms the Jazz Composers Workshop with Teo Macero and Teddy Charles. • Ornette Coleman and Don Cherry meet for the first time in Los Angeles. • Sonny Clark joins Buddy DeFranco's quartet. • With **How Hi the Fi**, the Buck Clayton Jam Session series begins. • Frank Sinatra signs with the Capitol label, has a major comeback, and becomes quite influential with his jazz-tinged collaborations with arranger Nelson Riddle. • Adrian Rollini (now a full-time vibraphonist) makes his first records in over a decade, an obscure album for Mercury. • Valaida Snow records two songs, her final recordings. • John Gilmore joins Sun Ra's Arkestra. • Roy Haynes becomes Sarah Vaughan's drummer for a five-year stint. • British tenor saxophonist Ronnie Scott forms a nonet also featuring trumpeter Jimmy Deuchar, altoist Derek Humble, and Pete King on second tenor. • Jimmy McPartland records an eight-song tribute to Bix Beiderbecke. • Albert Nicholas follows the examples of Sidney Bechet and Mezz Mezzrow and moves to France. • The team of New Orleans singer/pianist Billie Pierce and trumpeter De De Pierce makes their recording debut. • A Rex Stewart session for the Jazztone level features Herbie Nichols on piano. • The Erskine Hawkins big band breaks up. • Buddy Tate begins a 21-year stint playing with his band at Harlem's Celebrity Club. • Gerry Mulligan's bust for drugs breaks up his quartet with Chet Baker. • Chet Baker forms a quartet with Russ Freeman. • Shorty Rogers writes some of the music for the Marlon Brando film *The Wild One*. • Herb Ellis joins the Oscar Peterson Trio, succeeding Barney Kessel.

actually group originals. In addition to Wallington's fine solos, this disc is particularly valuable for its early examples of the playing of Byrd and McLean.

Randy Weston   Randy Weston was 28 when he made his recording debut in 1954. He was initially influenced by Thelonious Monk, calypso music, bebop, and his interest in African folk music. Weston began playing in R&B bands in the late 1940s and worked with Art Blakey (1949), Eddie "Cleanhead" Vinson, Kenny Dorham, and Cecil Payne. In 1954, he began recording for the new Riverside label and worked as a leader from then on. **Solo, Duo & Trio** (Milestone 47085) has the first album (eight Cole Porter songs played as duets with bassist Sam Gill), six songs by Weston, Gill, and Art Blakey, and four piano solos by Weston from 1956. This very impressive debut has plenty of variety and features such numbers as "Get Out of Town," "I Love You," "Zulu," "Pam's Waltz," and "Little Girl Blue." **Get Happy** (Original Jazz Classics 1870), a trio set from 1955 with Gill and drummer G.T. Hogan, has a particularly interesting calypso, "Fire Down Under" which would soon be renamed by Sonny Rollins as "St. Thomas." Also on this fine set are personal versions of such standards as "C Jam Blues," "Summertime," and "Twelfth Street Rag."

Tal Farlow   One of the top bop guitarists of the 1950s, Tal Farlow had huge hands, a very light and fluent touch (he loved to play fast), a constant smile, and a quiet personality. He did not take up the guitar until he was 21 in 1942, but within a year was playing professionally. Farlow was with vibraphonist Marjorie Hyams's band in 1948, recorded with Dardanelle, and became famous as a member of the Red Norvo Trio during 1949–53. After working with Artie Shaw's Gramercy Five for six months, he became a leader himself in 1954. Farlow recorded many fine sets for Verve during 1954–59, but few have thus far been reissued. **Autumn in New York** (Verve 2591) is an exception, a mostly laidback effort recorded in Los Angeles with Gerald Wiggins, Ray Brown, and Chico Hamilton. Only "Cherokee" is uptempo, but all eight numbers (which include "Strike Up the Band," "Little Girl Blue," and "Tal's Blues") are good showcases for Farlow's attractive tone and melodic playing.

Mundell Lowe   Mundell Lowe has always been a reliable cool-toned guitarist, and although he never quite became a household name or poll winner, he was on many sessions through the years. Born in 1922, he played Dixieland in New Orleans and country music in Nashville during 1936–40. Lowe was with Jan Savitt's orchestra (1942), served in the army, and worked with Ray McKinley (1945–47), Mary Lou Williams (1947–49), Red Norvo, Ellis Larkins, the Sauter-Finegan Orchestra (1952–53), and Benny Goodman. Lowe became a staff musician at NBC in 1950, but always found time to play jazz. He led his first date in 1954 and his Riverside album of 1955 has been reissued on CD as **The Mundell Lowe Quartet** (Original Jazz Classics 1773). This straightahead bebop set has Lowe in excellent form, particularly on "Will You Still Be Mine," "I'll Never Be the Same," "All of You," and "Cheek to Cheek." The oddity to the set is Dick Hyman who, in addition to piano and some celeste on "The Night We Called It a Day," mostly plays organ. His tone is dated, thin, and restrained (sounding like he is playing a cheap electric piano), and he was clearly no threat for Jimmy Smith (who was still a year away from becoming known). But Lowe's fine playing makes this a worthwhile acquisition.

Sal Salvador   A fine bop-based guitarist, Sal Salvador developed his own style after being initially influenced by Charlie Christian. He began playing professionally in 1945 and later in the decade worked with Terry Gibbs and Mundell Lowe. Salvador was with Stan Kenton during 1952–53, and unlike his predecessor Laurindo Almeida, he was more of a jazz rather than a Brazilian or classical soloist. His first two albums, which were cut for Blue Note (1953) and Capitol (1954), are available in the single CD **Sal Salvador Quartet/Quintet** (Blue Note 96548). Joined by tenor saxophonist Frankie Socolow and pianist John Williams for the Blue Note session and pianist/vibraphonist Eddie Costa for the Capitol project, Salvador plays concise versions of 18 songs, mostly standards such as "Gone with the Wind," "After You've Gone," "Yesterdays," and "Autumn in New York," plus some originals from Bill Holman and Manny Albam.

Oscar Pettiford   Oscar Pettiford, who played with Woody Herman's Second Herd in 1949, mostly worked as a leader during the 1950s, recording on a regular basis. Although such bassists as Ray Brown, Charles Mingus, and Red Mitchell had emerged, Pettiford still ranked at the top of his instrument (as an accompanist and particularly as a soloist) and on a part-time basis he also proved to be a talented cellist. **The New Oscar Pettiford Sextet**

(Original Jazz Classics 1926) has five numbers in which Pettiford mostly plays cello (with Mingus on bass) in a sextet that included Julius Watkins on French horn and Phil Urso on tenor; Pettiford also wrote four of the songs. In addition, this disc has four numbers in which he plays bass in a background role on a Serge Chaloff octet date arranged by Shorty Rogers in 1949, and two songs from 1959 with a trio in Scandinavia. **First Bass** (IAJRC 1010) has a variety of odds and ends from 1953–60, including four numbers from 1953 in which Pettiford and Harry Babasin (backed by a rhythm section) both play soloing cellos, an unprecedented event. The program also has two numbers with Lionel Hampton in 1956 and otherwise concentrates on Pettiford's European period of 1958–60 (with such guests as guitarist Attila Zoller, Lee Konitz, Zoot Sims, Phineas Newborn, and Kenny Clarke). **Sextet** (Vogue 40945) includes six numbers (plus two alternate takes) from a 1954 session with Al Cohn, Kai Winding, Tal Farlow, pianist Henri Renaud, and Max Roach. Pettiford has occasional bass solos and on "Rhumblues" overdubs on cello. In 1955, the bassist led three albums for Bethlehem, two of which have been reissued thus far. Actually, **Bass by Pettiford/Burke** (Bethlehem 75820) is split between a Pettiford outing with Charlie Rouse and Julius Watkins and a set by bassist Vinnie Burke's quartet (with clarinetist Ronnie Oldrich, Don Burns on accordion, and guitarist Joe Cinderella). The Pettiford portion is notable for including three of his compositions (such as "Tricotism"), for utilizing the Rouse-Watkins front line, and for the leader doubling on cello. The Burke group explores melodic versions of seven standards, plus the bassist's "Time Out." **Another One** (Bethlehem 75910) has Pettiford leading an octet and also including trumpeters Donald Byrd and Ernie Royal, and Bob Brookmeyer, Gigi Gryce, and Jerome Richardson on tenor and clarinet. Best is Pettiford's "Bohemia After Dark," "Oscarlypso," a showcase for his bass on "Stardust," and a feature for his cello on "Minor Seventh Heaven."

Victor Feldman   Victor Feldman started his career very early. He sat in on drums with Glenn Miller's Army Air Force Band in 1944 when he was just ten. In early 1948, he led his first record date and he recorded quite regularly in his native England during 1951–57. Equally talented on drums, piano, and vibes, Feldman mostly concentrates on the latter on the one session from his early period that has been reissued in the United States,

Suite Sixteen (Original Jazz Classics 1768), recorded in 1955 when he was 21. This CD, which also has Feldman playing some piano and drums, serves as a sampler of the modern jazz scene in Great Britain, for it features such notable musicians as trumpeters Jimmy Deuchar and Dizzy Reece, tenors Ronnie Scott and Tubby Hayes, and pianist Tommy Pollard. The music is boppish with some surprises in Feldman's consistently swinging arrangements.

Jimmy Smith and the Beginning of Jazz Organ   The organ was rarely used in jazz until the mid-1950s. Fats Waller had recorded pipe organ solos in the 1920s, and Count Basie once in a great while transferred his sparse piano style to organ. With the rise of R&B, both Bill Doggett and Wild Bill Davis had success in the early 1950s, but it was up to Jimmy Smith to transform the language of bebop into the definitive musical style of the Hammond B-3 organ. Smith began on piano and was well-schooled at the Hamilton and Ornstein Schools of Music. He began practicing on the organ in 1951 when he was 25, working locally in Philadelphia for a few years as he developed his own approach to the instrument. **The Fantastic Jimmy Smith** (Empire 39012) has Smith's first recordings, obscure sessions from 1953–54 with the young organist generally joined by tenor saxophonist Al Cass, an unknown guitarist (possibly Thornel Schwartz), and drummer/singer Don Gardner, who was actually the leader of the combo. Smith displays a heavier touch on these pioneering sides than he would a little later, showing off the influence of Wild Bill Davis and Milt Buckner. The music on this intriguing set was meant for release on 45s and jukeboxes so it is quite concise. In 1955, Jimmy Smith moved to New York, had a very well-received debut at the Café Bohemia, and was quickly signed to the Blue Note label where he made history.

Julius Watkins   The French horn has never been a major solo instrument in jazz, but in the 1950s Julius Watkins did his best to establish the horn. He started playing French horn when he was nine although he worked with the Ernie Fields Orchestra (1943–46) on trumpet. Watkins took some French horn solos in the late 1940s on records by Babs Gonzales and Kenny Clarke. After three years studying at the Manhattan School of Music, he started appearing on more small group dates, including two sessions led by Thelonious

Monk (1953–54). John Graas was the first jazz French horn player to lead his own record date (1953), but Watkins soon surpassed him as a soloist. **Julius Watkins Sextet, Vols. 1–2** (Blue Note 95749) reissues his first two dates as a leader, from 1954–55. Watkins heads sextets that feature either Frank Foster or Hank Mobley on tenor, guitarist Perry Lopez, George Butcher or Duke Jordan on piano, Oscar Pettiford, and Kenny Clarke or Art Blakey on drums. The French horn/tenor front line is an attractive sound, and Watkins plays his horn with the warmth of a trombone and nearly the fluidity of a trumpet. All nine selections on his CD are group originals, with Duke Jordan's "Jordu" being heard in one of its first versions.

The Jazz Vocalists

Billie Holiday   The 1950s should have been a golden age for Billie Holiday. She was world famous, had begun visiting Europe, and although her Decca contract was not renewed after 1950 (she just recorded four numbers for Aladdin the following year), in 1952 she signed with Norman Granz's Clef label. Unfortunately, though, her lifelong inferiority complex and her tendency to make bad decisions in her personal life kept her unhappy much of the time, and heroin and alcohol began to seriously affect her voice after 1952. Although there are times when she became stronger, one can hear a steady decline in her singing throughout the 1950s.

Billie's Blues (Blue Note 48786) mostly features Lady Day at a European concert on January 23, 1954. She is in top form performing before an admiring audience, singing seven standards with her trio and helping out on lengthy jam session versions of "Billie's Blues" and "Lover Come Back to Me" with an all-star group that includes Buddy DeFranco, Red Norvo, and Jimmy Raney. Also on this CD are Holiday's four sides for Aladdin (including "Now or Never" and "Detour Ahead") and her 1942 recording of "Trav'lin' Light" with the Paul Whiteman Orchestra.

The ten-CD set **The Complete Billie Holiday on Verve 1945–1959** (Verve 314 513 860-879) has an enormous amount of music, including Holiday's 1952–57 small-group studio recordings (made for Clef and Verve), her "Jazz at the Philharmonic" concerts of 1945–47, the European concert included on **Billie's Blues**, her comeback Carnegie Hall concert of 1956, lengthy tapes from two informal rehearsals (not worth hearing twice), a weak live performance in 1958, and her final album (1959).

Completists and Holiday's greatest fans will want this box, but most of the best performances are available elsewhere.

Solitude (Verve 519 810) has Holiday's first Clef recordings, two sessions from 1952 with Charlie Shavers, Flip Phillips, Oscar Peterson, Barney Kessel, Ray Brown, and Alvin Stoller or J.C. Heard on drums. The songs are first-rate, Lady Day's voice is still reasonably strong, and the renditions of "East of the Sun," "Blue Moon," "You Go to My Head," and "Love for Sale" are particularly memorable. **Lady Sings the Blues** (Verve 521 429) has a 1955 session with Charlie Shavers, Tony Scott, and Budd Johnson, and a set from 1956 with Paul Quinichette in Johnson's spot. Although Holiday's voice was fading, there are plenty of fine solos and one cannot fault the songs, which include "Say It Isn't So," "I've Got My Love to Keep Me Warm," a touching "Everything Happens to Me," "Strange Fruit," and "Good Morning Heartache." **Music for Torching** (Verve 527 455) consists of two dates from August 23 and 25, 1955, with Harry "Sweets" Edison, Benny Carter, Jimmy Rowles, Barney Kessel, bassist John Simmons, and drummer Larry Bunker. Although Holiday's voice had clearly seen better days, the musicians (who included several old friends) inspire her in spots; best are "When Your Lover Has Gone," "Gone with the Wind," and "Nice Work If You Can Get It." In addition, **Billie Holiday at Storyville** (1201 Music 9001) features the singer in good form performing in 1951 and 1953 live with trios led by pianists Carl Drinkard or Buster Harding; Stan Getz sits in on three songs.

But Lady Day's steady decline would continue.

Ella Fitzgerald   In contrast, Ella Fitzgerald continued to rise in stature throughout the 1950s. Managed by Norman Granz, Ella's performing career (with solo concerts and JATP tours) was really booming, although Granz felt frustrated that she was still bound by a recording contract with Decca. In later years, he would speak in disparaging terms about the singer's output for Decca. There were a few lightweight numbers during the 1950–55 period (such as "M-i-s-s-i-s-s-i-p-p-i," "Santa Claus Got Stuck in My Chimney," "Little Man in a Flying Saucer," and Ella's version of the Rosemary Clooney hit "Come On-A My House"), but there were also many gems along the way. Most notable are Ella's versions of eight George Gershwin tunes in 1950 (her first "songbook") and a dozen standards in 1954, all performed in a duo setting with the tasteful pianist Ellis Larkins and available on **Pure Ella** (GRP/Decca 636). Ella puts plenty of feeling into such songs as "Someone to Watch Over Me," "I've Got a Crush on You," "What Is There to Say," "Imagination," and "You Leave Me Breathless," showing that she was an underrated interpreter of ballads. **The Last Decca Years 1949–1954** (GRP/Decca 668) has some of the other highlights from this period, including "Basin Street Blues" (during which she does a close imitation of Louis Armstrong), her first two vocal duets with Satch ("Dream a Little Dream of Me," and "Can Anyone Explain"), "Mr. Paganini," "Angel Eyes," "Blue Lou," and "Lullaby of Birdland." Despite a few weaker numbers, all of Ella's output during this era (which also includes "Smooth Sailing," "Air Mail Special," "Rough Ridin'," "Takin' a Chance on Love," "Hard Hearted Hannah," and "Ella Hums the Blues") deserves to be reissued in full.

Late in 1955, Norman Granz finally got Ella Fitzgerald out of her contract with Decca. He consolidated his Norgran and Clef labels under the new name of Verve and she became the new label's first artist, recording extensively in 1956.

Sarah Vaughan   Sarah Vaughan also became more famous during the 1950s. The most significant singer to emerge from the bebop era, she was often heard in commercial settings with orchestras during her period with Columbia, which lasted until January 1953, while at the same time performing much more jazz-oriented sets live in concert. **Perdido** (Natasha Imports 4004) mostly features Sassy singing at Birdland in 1953, making such songs as "Tenderly," "I Get a Kick Out of You," and "You're Mine You" sound as if they were written for her. Dizzy Gillespie sits in on a few numbers.

In 1954, Vaughan signed with Mercury, and during the next few years she had an agreement where she recorded jazz dates for their EmArcy subsidiary and more middle-of-the-road pop sessions for the parent Mercury label. Fortunately, her entire output for the two labels has been reissued on a series of very extensive sets. **The Complete Sarah Vaughan on Mercury Vol. 1** (Mercury 826 320), which is six CDs, covers her Mercury and EmArcy recordings from February 1954 through June 1956. In addition to many orchestral sessions, three superb jazz dates are included and are also available individually. **Sarah Vaughan with Clifford Brown** (Verve 543 305) teams Sassy with the great trumpeter Brown in

an all-out jazz date also featuring flutist Herbie Mann and Paul Quinichette. It is difficult to top these versions of "Lullaby of Birdland," "Jim," and "September Song" (though Vaughan was really not old enough yet to interpret the latter); this classic outing is also included in Brownie's EmArcy box. ● **Swingin' Easy** (EmArcy 514 072) has Vaughan accompanied in 1954 and 1957 by her regular trio (with Jimmy Jones or John Malachi on piano) rather than the usual string orchestra, swinging hard on some numbers and singing ballads with intensity. Among the tunes that are uplifted are "Shulie A Bop," "I Cried for You," "Prelude to a Kiss," "Pennies from Heaven," and "Body and Soul." **In the Land of Hi-Fi** (EmArcy 826 454) has Vaughan joined by the swinging Ernie Wilkins Orchestra with the young altoist Cannonball Adderley being well featured. The renditions are quite concise (around three minutes apiece), but Vaughan makes every note count on such songs as "Soon," "Cherokee," "I'll Never Smile Again," and "An Occasional Man."

Dinah Washington   Dinah Washington continued recording steadily for Mercury during this era, and all of her studio recordings are available on a series of three-CD reissues. Not every selection on **The Complete Dinah Washington on Mercury Vol. 2** (Mercury 832 448), **Vol. 3** (Mercury 834 675), and **Vol. 4** (Mercury 834 683), which cover 1950 to April 1956, is a classic, but the quality is generally pretty high. While some of Washington's records were hits on the R&B charts, she was extremely versatile and quite capable of excelling singing swinging jazz, shouting blues, schmaltzy ballads, and novelties with equal skill. On **Vol. 2** she is mostly accompanied by studio orchestras with "I Wanna Be Loved," "Harbor Lights," "Fine Fine Daddy," "Cold Cold Heart," and "Double Dealin' Daddy" being among the 53 selections. **Vol. 3** is the most jazz-oriented overall of the three sets for it includes the music on **Dinah Jams**, has a spontaneous date with Clark Terry and Eddie "Lockjaw" Davis (including uptempo romps on "Bye Bye Blues" and "Blue Skies"), and several notable collaborations with Paul Quinichette, who is to her on some dates what Lester Young was to Billie Holiday. **Vol. 4** alternates between strong swinging jazz with Clark Terry, Paul Quinichette, Wynton Kelly, and Cannonball Adderley, and middle-of-the-road pop performances with studio orchestras. For a single disc, **Dinah Jams** (EmArcy 814 639) cannot be beat. It teams the singer with the likes of Clifford Brown, Clark Terry, Maynard Ferguson, Herb Geller, and Max Roach, but this essential set is also on the Clifford Brown EmArcy box and it is recommended that one acquire the music that way.

Claire Austin   One of the better vocalists of the Dixieland revival movement, Claire Austin had the ability to sing in the style of the early classic blues singers yet could also interpret swing standards of the 1930s and sound quite authentic. Although she had sung a bit in the Midwest, she was already 33 when she debuted with Turk Murphy's band in 1952. ◉ **When Your Lover Has Gone** (Original Jazz Classics 1711) has all of the music from her first two albums as a leader, dating from 1954–55. Austin belts out blues and 1920s classics with a quartet that includes Kid Ory (in a rare sideman appearance) and pianist Don Ewell, and sings 1930s ballads and swing pieces with a quintet that includes Bob Scobey and Barney Kessel. In addition to her work with Murphy, during this era Claire Austin also worked with the bands of Kid Ory (1954) and Bob Scobey (1955–56), but she never became a major name outside of trad circles.

June Christy   June Christy, who went on her own after Stan Kenton broke up his band in 1948, occasionally returned to Kenton's Orchestra (including during part of 1950–51), but by then was considered a star in her own right. Her most famous album, 1953's ◉ **Something Cool** (Capitol 96329) LP, has been expanded from 11 selections to 24 on the CD reissue. As was true during most of Christy's long string of Capitol albums, Pete Rugolo provided the adventurous arrangements for the backing orchestra. The eerie "Something Cool" (which has delusional lyrics by Billy Barnes) is a classic and became Christy's trademark song. Other highlights of the original album ("Midnight Sun," "I Should Care," "The Night We Called It a Day") are joined by such slightly later numbers (mostly released previously as singles) as "Whee Baby," "Love Doesn't Live Here Anymore," and "Pete Kelly's Blues." Also quite rewarding is the underrated **Duet** (Capitol 89285), which features Christy backed by Stan Kenton's piano. Christy's cool sound and careful diction hint at darker feelings than appear on the surface during these ballads, and the results are quite memorable.

Chris Connor   Chris Connor always had a cool-toned smoky voice. She sometimes sounded eerily like Chet Baker, and although best known for ballads, she could swing at medium tempos too. Like June Christy, her original influence was Anita O'Day. While attending the University of Missouri, she sang with a big band led by Bob Brookmeyer. Connor moved to New York in 1947, sang in the early 1950s with Claude Thornhill, and gained fame for her stint with Stan Kenton (1952–53), which included her hit "All About Ronnie."

During 1953–55, Connor recorded three albums for Bethlehem. **Sings Lullaby of Birdland** (Bethlehem 79851) has the singer joined by either Sy Oliver's Orchestra, Ellis Larkins's trio, or a quintet led by bassist Vinnie Burke that includes clarinetist Ronnie Oldrich and Don Burons on accordion. The music also contains plenty of variety with the more memorable selections including "Lullaby of Birdland," "Spring Is Here," "Ask Me," and "A Cottage for Sale." **Chris** (Bethlehem 75988) has four sessions from 1954–55 with the Ellis Larkins trio, Vinnie Burke's quintet, a group with Herbie Mann and guitarist Joe Puma, and an ensemble that has some prominent trombone playing from J.J. Johnson and Kai Winding. The reissue is a bit unusual because, in addition to the original dozen selections (which has her first remake of "All About Ronnie"), the CD also includes an alternate take apiece of each of the songs, so it is really two records in one. **This Is Chris** (Bethlehem 76684) wraps up Connor's Bethlehem period with more titles from the Mann-Puma group and the unit with J.J. Johnson and Kai Winding. Twenty-seven at the time, Connor sounds quite mature on such numbers as "Blame It on My Youth," "It's All Right with Me," "The Thrill Is Gone," and "From this Moment On." The playing time of this ten-song set is brief, but the quality is high. So high in fact that Chris Connor soon signed with the Atlantic label.

Peggy Lee   By 1952, when she signed with the Decca label after recording for a few years for Capitol, Peggy Lee was moving away from jazz toward middle-of-the-road pop music. She always swung lightly and was not shy to look back toward the swing era for repertoire, but she was also interested in recording current pop tunes. **Black Coffee** (MCA/Decca 11122), a two-CD set, has highlights from the singer's 1952–56 period with Decca. Much of the music is outside of jazz and more in the genre of period pop and novelties, but Lee sounds cheerful about the whole thing and does her best. The better titles include "Lover," "You Go to My Head," "Easy Living,"

"Sugar," a duet with Bing Crosby on "Watermelon Weather," and the hit "Black Coffee." This is not an essential set, but it sums up the period for Peggy Lee quite well.

Julie London　Julie London, whose parents were singers and had their own radio show, spent a couple of weeks singing with Matty Malneck's Orchestra back in 1943 when she was 17. However, singing did not interest her all that much. After seven years married to actor Jack Webb, they were divorced and she soon married songwriter/pianist Bobby Troup (who wrote "Route 66," "Daddy," and "Baby, Baby All the Time" among others). In 1955, Troup persuaded London to record four songs on a Bethlehem album with his group and soon she was recording regularly for Liberty. London, who had a limited but sensuous voice and a straightforward delivery, became a surprise hit with her album **Julie Is Her Name** and particularly the song "Cry Me a River." Her LPs became collectors' items due to her sexy poses. Although she became quite active as an actress, London recorded regularly for Liberty until 1966 with a final album in 1969. **Time for Love: The Best of Julie London** (Rhino 70737) has 18 of her best recordings, including "No Moon at All," "You'd Be So Nice to Come Home To," "My Heart Belongs to Daddy," "The Thrill Is Gone," "Daddy," and of course "Cry Me a River." London is sometimes heard accompanied by orchestras, but is at her best when backed by just guitar and bass. However, true music (and photo) collectors will want to search for those LPs.

Carmen McRae　One of the most influential of all jazz singers, Carmen McRae had already been on the scene for quite a few years before she had a chance to record her own album. Born in 1920, she studied piano early on and wrote occasional songs, including "Dream of Life," which was recorded by Billie Holiday in 1939. She sang with Benny Carter's big band in 1944, married and divorced Kenny Clarke in the 1940s, worked briefly with Count Basie and Mercer Ellington (1946–47) as Carmen Clarke, and was the intermission singer and pianist at several clubs. It was not until 1954 (when she was 34) that she led her first record date, **Carmen McRae** (Bethlehem 75990). Her voice was already distinctive (if higher than it would be in later years) and her behind-the-beat phrasing and ironic interpretations of lyrics (influenced a little by Lady Day) made her stand out from the crowd. The debut has McRae joined on four

songs apiece by accordionist Mat Mathews's quintet (which includes Mundell Lowe and Herbie Mann on flute and tenor) and Tony Scott's quartet. Five alternate takes expand the ballad-oriented set, which was a solid (if long overdue) first step for Carmen McRae, who signed with Decca in 1955.

Helen Merrill　Helen Merrill (born Jelena Ana Milcetic) was ten years younger than Carmen McRae, but began her recording career about the same time. An expressive but cool-toned singer, Merrill started singing in public in 1944, was with the Reggie Childs Orchestra (1946–47), married clarinetist Aaron Sachs, and had opportunities to sit in with Charlie Parker, Miles Davis, and Bud Powell. She was with Earl Hines in 1952, recorded two numbers for Roost in 1953, and made notable albums for EmArcy during 1954–58. Merrill, who always took great care in her recordings (they were often special events), recorded four superior ballads with Johnny Richards's Orchestra and then a full album with trumpeter Clifford Brown, which has been reissued in his EmArcy box set and the **Complete Helen Merrill on Mercury** three-CD set reviewed in the next chapter. It is also available individually as **Helen Merrill with Clifford Brown** (EmArcy 534 435) and shows that the singer knew exactly what she wanted and how to get it out of her prized sidemen.

Anita O'Day　The 1950s were the peak of Anita O'Day's career. She began performing as a single in 1946 after leaving Gene Krupa, and while working reasonably steadily, she did not record much for five years. Unlike most former band singers, she was committed to jazz, unwilling to compromise much, and very interested in adding the innovations of bebop to her vocabulary, so it is not surprising that she was not a major commercial success. However, in 1952 O'Day hooked up with Norman Granz, recording for his Clef and Verve labels during the next decade. All of her music from this prime period is on the nine-CD limited-edition set **Complete Anita O'Day Verve/Clef Sessions** (Mosaic 9-188), but only some dates are available individually on CD. Best is **This Is Anita** (Verve 829 261). O'Day is accompanied by an orchestra conducted and arranged by Buddy Bregman, singing memorable renditions of such songs as "You're the Top," "Honeysuckle Rose," an emotional rendition of "A Nightingale Sang in Berkeley Square," and "As Long As I Live."

Kay Starr During the 1950s, Kay Starr moved away from jazz onto the pop charts with a variety of hits including "Wheel of Fortune" and (later in the decade) "The Rock & Roll Waltz." She always had a jazz feeling to her singing even if the settings were sometimes quite commercial, and her tone was strongly influenced by Dinah Washington. **Capitol Collectors Series** (Capitol 94080) is an excellent sampler of this period for Starr. In addition to her hits, such jazz-oriented songs as "I'm the Lonesomest Gal in Town," "You've Got to See Mama Ev'ry Night," "Side by Side," and "When My Dreamboat Comes Home" show that Starr remained at heart a swing singer.

Lee Wiley Lee Wiley's marriage to Jess Stacy ended in 1948, and although still associated with Eddie Condon, she was working less by the late 1940s. However, her very successful Columbia album **Night in Manhattan** (Columbia 75010), which features her backed by cornetist Bobby Hackett and strings, was a strong success. It was followed by the two-piano team of Stan Freeman and Cy Walter accompanying her on sets of the music of Irving Berlin and Vincent Youmans. The two-CD set **Complete Fifties Studio Masters** (Jazz Factory 49811) has those dates, which are highlighted by "A Woman's Intuition," "Sugar," "Anytime, Any Day, Anywhere," "Manhattan," "I've Got a Crush on You," and "More than You Know." There is also a 1952 eight-song rehearsal with trumpeter Johnny Windhurst and pianist George Wein, four songs from 1953 with Carl Prager's orchestra, a 1954 session with Ruby Braff that was formerly out on Black Lion, and six songs from a 1965 demo session with pianist Joe Bushkin. In addition, **Music of Manhattan, 1951** (Uptown 27.48) contains mostly live and rare material dating from 1951–52. The 23 titles on this CD are taken from nine different occasions with three renditions of "Manhattan" and "I've Got a Crush on You," two apiece of "Sugar" and "Street of Dreams," and lone versions of "Oh, Look at Me Now" and "Ghost of a Chance" being among the more memorable numbers. One song has Wiley backed by the Ray Bloch Orchestra, but otherwise she is heard in small trad bands with the likes of Joe Bushkin, Billy Butterfield, Muggsy Spanier, Buck Clayton, and Henry "Red" Allen.

Perhaps because she was too subtle or too tied to jazz, Lee Wiley never did break through to a larger audience as she hoped, remaining mostly a cult figure.

The Beginnings of Vocalese: Eddie Jefferson and King Pleasure Vocalese is the art of writing and performing lyrics to the recorded solos of jazz greats, using the solos as the basis of the song rather than the original melody. In 1929, Bee Palmer's version of "Singin' the Blues" (which was not released until the 1990s) was the earliest example of this technique being used, and singer Marion Harris also did her own vocalese version of "Singin' the Blues" while in England in the mid-1930s. However, neither of those renditions made much of an impression.

Eddie Jefferson is considered the real founder of vocalese. Jefferson, who did not have a great voice, started out working as a tap dancer, but by the late 1940s was singing and writing lyrics. A live session from 1949 (released on Spotlite) finds him pioneering vocalese by singing his lyrics to "Parker's Mood" and Lester Young's solo on "I Cover the Waterfront." However, Jefferson's lyrics to "Moody's Mood for Love" (based on James Moody's alto solo on "I'm in the Mood for Love") was recorded first by King Pleasure in 1952 (who had the hit), and he was overshadowed for a time. However Jefferson was well featured working with James Moody during 1953–57 and he would gain greater fame in the long run.

King Pleasure (born Clarence Beeks) had a better voice than Jefferson, but his life was shrouded in mystery. He recorded on several notable occasions during 1952–62, but otherwise little is known about Beeks. ⦿ **The Bebop Singers** (Prestige 24216) is a definitive reissue of vocalese classics. King Pleasure is featured on seven of the selections, including "Red Top" (based on Gene Ammons's recording and having a cameo appearance by Betty Carter), Lester Young's "Jumpin' with Symphony Sid," Stan Getz's "Don't Get Scared" (with Eddie Jefferson and Jon Hendricks helping out), "Moody's Mood for Love" (Blossom Dearie takes the piano solo as a vocal chorus), and his own lyrics to "Parker's Mood." The latter was his second biggest hit (after "Moody's Mood For Love"). Charlie Parker was not too pleased with its words for it predicted his death! In addition to two appearances on King Pleasure titles, Eddie Jefferson is also heard on six of his early titles including "Disappointed" (Charlie Parker's solo on "Lady Be Good"), there is an out-of-place but enthusiastic session by Joe "Bebop" Carroll in 1952 (when he was appearing regularly with Dizzy Gillespie), Dizzy sings "She's Gone Again," Jon Hendricks is heard on two songs in 1973, and the original version of Annie Ross's three greatest hits are here too. **King Pleasure Sings/Annie Ross Sings** (Original Jazz Classics 217) duplicates six of the Pleasure numbers and expands them to a dozen, and repeats two of the Ross titles while adding two others. The latter set is more comprehensive in reissuing the early dates while **The Bebop Singers** is a better all-around sampler.

Annie Ross, Jon Hendricks, and Dave Lambert
Annie Ross, who was born Annabelle Lynch in England in 1930, moved to the United States with her aunt Ella Logan, a musical performer. At five she appeared in some of the *Our Gang* comedy shorts and at 12 she played Judy Garland's younger sister in the film *Presenting Lily Mars*. Ross spent time back in England singing in night-clubs and in 1952 in New York she recorded four songs for Savoy. On October 9, 1952, she recorded two of her vocalese classics, "Twisted" (based on a Wardell Gray record) and "Farmer's Market," following it up in 1953 with "Jackie." Those three songs are all on **The Bebop Singers**. Ross toured Europe with Lionel Hampton's big band in 1953, and when that ensemble came apart, she stayed in London for several years.

Jon Hendricks grew up in Toledo, Ohio (where he sometimes sang while backed by Art Tatum), served in the military (1942–46), studied law, and played drums before deciding to concentrate on becoming a jazz singer and lyricist. In 1952, his "I Want You to Be My Baby" was recorded by Louis Jordan. In 1955, Hendricks recorded vocalese versions of "Cloudburst" and "Four Brothers" accompanied by the Dave Lambert Singers. Lambert, who had frequently teamed up with the late Buddy Stewart during 1945–49, had long been interested in leading a vocal group. The Dave Lambert Singers accompanied Charlie Parker on a couple of odd records ("In the Still of the Night" and "Old Folks"), but had not found a niche for itself by 1955.

Annie Ross, Jon Hendricks, and Dave Lambert, three complementary but very different singers, would meet up in the near future.

Fred Astaire   The movie actor and dancer Fred Astaire was always jazz-oriented in his singing and dancing. In his 1930s films, he introduced many songs (often written for him) by Irving Berlin, George Gershwin, and Cole Porter that became jazz standards. In 1952, producer Norman Granz persuaded Astaire to record an extended set as a singer (with a few spots for his tap dancing) with an all-star group taken from "Jazz at the Philharmonic": Charlie Shavers, Flip Phillips, Oscar Peterson, Barney Kessel, Ray Brown, and drummer Alvin Stoller. The music, available as a two-CD set ● **The Astaire Story** (Verve 835 649), is typically delightful, with Astaire's good-natured vocals easily interacting with the soloists on 37 songs, including a standard that he wrote himself, "I'm Building Up to an Awful Letdown." Although Fred Astaire would not pursue jazz singing (it did not pay quite as much as being a movie star), he shows on this worthy project that he could have found a niche for himself in that area.

Nat King Cole   Throughout the second half of the 1940s, Nat King Cole's singing began to overshadow his piano playing although he still toured with his popular trio. That situation changed permanently in 1950 when Cole recorded "Mona Lisa" with Les Baxter's Orchestra. The classic pop song established Cole as a crooner, and within a year, most of his greatly expanded audience was not aware that he had been a major jazz pianist. Throughout the 1950s, Nat King Cole would be one of the most beloved American singers, crossing color lines (at least on record) to become a household name. **The Capitol Collector's Series** (Capitol 93590) on one disc has 20 of his hits, starting with 1943's "Straighten Up and Fly Right" and continuing to 1964's "L-O-V-E" and with such songs from 1950–55 as "Mona Lisa," "Too Young," "Unforgettable," and "Answer Me, My Love." Cole only plays piano on the first four selections, but usually still retained a jazz feel and a swinging style even when fronting string orchestras.

Several of Cole's CD reissues are quite intriguing for they feature him during his transition from jazz pianist to ballad crooner. **Lush Life** (Capitol 80595) dates from 1949–52 and has 25 selections in which Cole is joined by an orchestra arranged by Pete Rugolo. His version of "Lush Life" established Billy Strayhorn's song (which was written over a decade earlier) as a hit. Other highlights include "Time Out for Tears," "That's My Girl," "Red Sails in the Sunset," "It's Crazy," and "You Stepped Out of a Dream." **The Billy May Sessions** (Capitol 89545), a two-CD set, has collaborations between Cole and arranger May from 1951, 1953, 1954, 1957, and 1961, including such popular songs as "Walkin' My Baby Back Home," "Angel Eyes," "Papa Loves Mambo," "Send for

Me," "Who's Sorry Now," "The Party's Over," and "When My Sugar Walks Down the Street." Although Cole plays no piano on this two-fer, he is heard taking organ solos on three of the selections from 1961, the only time he ever recorded on that instrument. **Piano Stylings** (Capitol 81203) from 1955 was a bit of an experiment. Cole was famous worldwide by then as a vocalist, but this is an instrumental album in which his piano is backed by an orchestra arranged by Nelson Riddle, with his piano solos taking the place of his voice on a variety of swinging standards. The results are enjoyable although not as stirring as the earlier King Cole Trio performances.

The jazz world mourned the defection of Nat King Cole to commercial music, even as he became one of the first black artists to be a fixture on the pop music charts.

Billy Eckstine and Johnny Hartman   Billy Eckstine was another black singer who left jazz. After his bebop big band broke up in 1947, he signed with MGM and mostly performed ballad vocals that displayed his deep and influential baritone voice. **Everything I Have Is Yours** (Verve 819 442) is a two-CD set that sums up his recordings of 1947–57 quite well. Among the hits included (which usually find Mr. B. backed by string sections) are "Everything I Have Is Yours," "Blue Moon," "Caravan," "My Foolish Heart," and "I Apologize." There are also a few departures along the way. On "Mr. B's Blues," Eckstine plays a rare valve trombone solo, there are dates with Woody Herman and George Shearing, eight numbers on which the singer is accompanied by the Bobby Tucker Quartet, and a pair of superior performances with the 1953 Metronome All-Stars (which includes Roy Eldridge, Terry Gibbs, and both Lester Young and Warne Marsh on tenors), showing that Billy Eckstine could still sing jazz when he wanted to.

Johnny Hartman always specialized in ballads. Initially influenced by Eckstine, Hartman had sung with Dizzy Gillespie's big band (1948–49) and Erroll Garner although he was largely overlooked during the 1950s. 1955's **Songs from the Heart** (Bethlehem 79773) was his debut album as a leader and it features the warm baritone joined by pianist Ralph Sharon's trio and Howard McGhee on a dozen standards plus six alternate takes, mostly taken at ballad tempos, including "What Is There to Say," "They Didn't Believe Me," and "Moonlight in Vermont."

Slim Gaillard   For guitarist/singer/jokester Slim Gaillard, the early 1950s were the end of his prime. He stopped recording for the Norgran label after one final session in 1953 and largely dropped out of sight, having kept his limited but often-hilarious series of jokes going for 15 years. **Slim Gaillard at Birdland 1951** (Hep 21) finds his humor largely unchanged since 1945. Gaillard is assisted by his old partner Slam Stewart, Eddie "Lockjaw" Davis, Art Blakey, Terry Gibbs, Brew Moore, and Billy Taylor among others during these live performances. However, the music (which includes "Flat Foot Floogie," "Cement Maker," "Ya Ha Ha," "Laughin' in Rhythm," and "Serenade in Vout") is secondary to the humor, which though it can wear one out, still comes across as funny and eccentric.

Jimmy Rushing   When Count Basie broke up his big band in 1949, Jimmy Rushing led a septet of Basie veterans, eventually working steadily as a single and popping up with all-star groups. He led some obscure sessions for Gotham, King, and Chess during 1950–53 and then recorded three albums (under John Hammond's guidance) for Vanguard during 1954–57. Unfortunately, the current Vanguard reissue program has mixed together the sessions in somewhat random order, but **Oh Love** (Vanguard 79606) and **Every Day** (Vanguard 79607) contain all of the music from the three former LPs. There are appearances by Buddy Tate, Emmett Berry, Lawrence Brown, Pete Johnson, Vic Dickenson, and Jo Jones among others. Now in his fifties, Rushing could still shout and swing with the best of them as he shows on timeless versions of "Going to Chicago Blues," "Pennies from Heaven," "Gee Baby, Ain't I Good to You," "How Long Blues," and "Dinah" from **Oh Love**, and "Evenin'," "Good Morning Blues," "Sent for You Yesterday," and "My Friend Mr. Blues" from **Every Day**.

Mel Tormé   Mel Tormé recorded a few titles for Capitol during 1950–51 and two albums for Coral during 1953–54, but did not start coming into his own until he hooked up with Bethlehem in 1955. From 1954, **In Hollywood** (GRP/Decca 617), which brings back a live set made for Coral, is an intriguing CD containing 20 performances (seven previously unissued) from one night in his life. Tormé not only sings, but also plays piano with a quartet comprised of clarinetist/pianist Al Pellegrini, bassist James Dupre, and drummer Richard

Shanahan. Tormé is consistently swinging on a well-rounded set highlighted by "That Old Black Magic," "My Shining Hour," "The Christmas Song," "Moonlight in Vermont," "Bernie's Tune," "Mountain Greenery," and "Get Happy." His debut for Bethlehem, **It's a Blue World** (Bethlehem 74378) is mostly ballad-oriented and has Tormé joined by a string orchestra on such numbers as "Till the Clouds Roll By," "Isn't It Romantic," "You Leave Me Breathless," and "Polka Dots and Moonbeams," but this was only a warmup for the great Bethlehem albums to come.

The Dixieland Revival

Dixieland was at the height of its popularity in the early 1950s. The music, which had been largely underground in the 1930s, had begun its comeback in the early 1940s and had really gained steam during the following decade. In the 1950s, however, it was becoming formalized and predictable. Many amateur bands were formed that played the top 20 Dixieland warhorses in predictable fashion (with clichés galore and always concluding their show with "The Saints"), using the same old frameworks and merely copying the masters of the style. Dixieland also began to suffer from an image problem, with club-owners and some fans preferring that the musicians dress in corny old-time outfits (with funny hats, suspenders, and dumb band uniforms). Dixieland became associated with nostalgia for an era that was never was. Although that temporarily helped its commercial appeal, eventually the image became destructive and still hurts the acceptance of the music.

Ragtime also had a mini-revival of sorts. In 1950, Rudi Blesh and Harriet Janis completed their masterful book **They All Played Ragtime**, which for the time was the definitive word on the long-extinct music. However, instead of a full-fledged ragtime revival, some record company owners were more interested in making fast bucks, and a fad called "honky tonk" came into being. Pianists were purposely recorded on out-of-tune pianos (sometimes tacks were put on the inside of the instruments to give them a tinny sound) and they recorded the stereotype "good time" sing-along songs from earlier decades. The results had little to do with ragtime and gave early jazz a bad name for a time.

But despite all of the bad imitations, there was some excellent Dixieland and New Orleans jazz performed during the first half of the 1950s. Eddie Condon performed

nightly with his all-star ensembles at his club. The Louis Armstrong All-Stars were the most popular group in jazz. Dixieland bands in New Orleans became a popular attraction for tourists, resulting in some veterans being rediscovered. George Lewis caught on big, and Los Angeles (a home base for Kid Ory, Red Nichols, Pete Daily, and some of the Bob Crosby alumni) became as significant as San Francisco, which had the Club Hangover and Turk Murphy's band. In addition, trad jazz was growing in popularity in England (which had Humphrey Lyttelton, Chris Barber, and Ken Colyer) and France (Sidney Bechet's new home) and clearly had universal appeal, like the best jazz.

The Louis Armstrong All-Stars   The Louis Armstrong All-Stars underwent a lot of personnel changes during 1950–55, but remained consistent in its music and approach. Sid Catlett's weak heart forced his departure in late 1949 in favor of Cozy Cole, who stayed until 1953, being replaced at first by Kenny Johns and then Barrett Deems. Earl Hines was always frustrated being a sideman and felt restricted with the All-Stars, departing abruptly in 1951; Marty Napoleon and (by 1953) Billy Kyle filled his spot. While Hines's exit was a bit stormy, Jack Teagarden's decision to go out on his own in 1952 did not hurt his friendship with Armstrong; there would be several reunions through the years. His replacement, Trummy Young, would be among the most loyal and valuable of Satch's sidemen. The tireless Arvell Shaw and Velma Middleton stayed on, while Barney Bigard (who sounded increasingly bored as the 1950s progressed) lasted until the fall of 1955 when he was succeeded by Edmond Hall.

Throughout this period, some critics and fans criticized Armstrong's live shows (which were somewhat predictable) because they did not always approve of his clowning. During a time when black jazz musicians were fighting to be accepted in the segregated world, Armstrong's self-effacing showmanship seemed a bit out of step. However, the criticism often did not take into account how brilliantly Armstrong played trumpet (he may have joked around, but his horn playing was serious), his role as a pioneer in breaking down racial boundaries, and the fact that Satch made it through life and became rich and famous without being taken advantage of by whites; quite a feat for that era.

Audience members who were introduced to jazz through Armstrong's music often became lifelong jazz fans. **Live at the Hollywood Empire 1949** (Storyville 8232) and the four-CD set **The California Concerts** (GRP/Decca 4-613), which date from 1951 and 1955, are excellent examples of Satch's live shows and they have dated quite well.

During 1954–55, Louis Armstrong recorded the two finest albums of his All-Stars period. ◗ **Plays W.C. Handy** (Columbia/Legacy 64925) has Satch performing 11 of Handy's best songs, including a definitive version of "St. Louis Blues" (which features a humorous vocal, some roaring Trummy Young trombone, and chorus after chorus of Armstrong's magnificent trumpet), "Loveless Love," "Beale Street Blues," and "Ole Miss Blues." Happily, 80-year-old W.C. Handy (who was blind by then) was on hand for the proceedings. The original LP version of ◗ **Satch Plays Fats** (Columbia/Legacy 64927) had the 1955 All-Stars (with Barney Bigard) playing 11 Fats Waller songs, including joyful versions of "Honeysuckle Rose," "I'm Crazy 'Bout My Baby," and "Ain't Misbehavin'." The CD reissue (Columbia/Legacy 64927) adds four alternate takes plus seven earlier versions of Armstrong playing Waller songs, dating from 1928–32. Both the Handy and Waller projects gave the All-Stars an opportunity to play fresher material than usual and clearly inspired the musicians. However, beware of the initial CD versions of the Handy and Waller classics (not listed here)—the late 1980s compilations inexcusably substituted a lot of alternate takes for the original versions.

In addition to his work with the All-Stars and his continual touring, Armstrong also recorded commercial music with studio bands. **Satchmo Serenades** (Verve 314 543 792) has Satch backed by orchestras often arranged by Sy Oliver or Toots Camarata during 1949–53, introducing his versions of "A Kiss to Build a Dream," "La Vie en Rose," "C'est Si Bon," "Someday You'll Be Sorry" (one of Armstrong's best-known originals), and even "Your Cheatin' Heart." **Satchmo in Style** (Verve 314 549 594), which has Armstrong backed by the Gordon Jenkins Orchestra, is notable for including his hit version of "Blueberry Hill." These recordings may not be that jazz-oriented or have much trumpet playing, but Satch's singing is still a joy.

Throughout the 1950s, Louis Armstrong's fame and popularity continued to grow, and he retained his position as the most famous and beloved jazz musician in the world.

The Basin Street Six, George Girard, and Pete Fountain   A popular band in New Orleans during 1950–54, the Basin Street Six was notable for featuring trumpeter George Girard and the young clarinetist Pete Fountain. Girard, a superior player and a personable singer, became a professional in 1946 when he was 16. He played with Phil Zito before leading the Basin Street Six. After the group broke up, he headed his own bands for a couple of years. Pete Fountain, who (like Girard) turned 20 in 1950, had played with the Junior Dixieland band in 1948 and had also been with Phil Zito. His main influences were Benny Goodman and Irving Fazola and he was a fluent soloist with a warm tone from the start. After the Basin Street Six period ended, Fountain spent 1955 as a member of the Dukes of Dixieland.

The Complete Circle Recordings (GHB 103) has a dozen straightforward Dixieland performances from the Basin Street Six (which also includes trombonist Joe Rotis, pianist Roy Zimmerman, bassist Bunny Franks, and drummer Charlie Duke) that are full of spirit. Girard takes a good-humored vocal on "Margie," while Fountain has a rare spot on tenor on one of the two versions of "That's a Plenty."

Oscar Celestin   One of the most popular bands in New Orleans during the postwar years was led by Oscar "Papa" Celestin. Celestin, who had recorded during 1926–28, went into retirement after the Depression hit. However, in 1946, with the rise in popularity of New Orleans jazz, he put together a new version of his Tuxedo Jazz Orchestra and quickly became a major attraction for tourists visiting New Orleans who wanted to hear "real jazz." **The 1950s Radio Broadcasts** (Arhoolie/Folklyric 7024), despite condescending remarks from the radio announcer (which reminds listeners of how blacks were treated in the South during this period), has plenty of spirited music from the sextet, which consists of trumpeter Celestin, trombonist Bill Matthews, the pioneering clarinetist Alphonse Picou (who was 71 in 1950 and who reprises his famous solo on "High Society" from circa 1905), pianist Octave Crosby, bassist Ricard Alexis (who had played trumpet with Celestin in the 1920s), and drummer Christopher Goldston. The 23 selections (which include some vocals from bandmembers) mostly feature warhorses plus such Celestin specialties as "Eh, La Bas" and "Lil' Liza Jane." ◗ **Marie La Veau** (GHB 106) consists of two former LPs recorded in 1950 and 1954. The earlier date has the same band as heard on the Arhoolie CD, with fine versions of "High Society," "Panama," "Fidgety Feet," and "Sheik of Araby" among the ten selections. The 1954 recording (Celestin's last) has a different version of the group and mostly focuses on the leader's emotional singing on "Down by the Riverside," "Oh Didn't He Ramble," "Marie La Veau," and "The Saints." This CD gives listeners a definitive look at the second part of Oscar Celestin's career.

Oscar Celestin's band was so popular that they had an opportunity to play a special concert at the White House in 1953 for President Eisenhower, a year before the bandleader died at the age of 70.

Christie Brothers Stompers   In 1951, some of the musicians from the Crane River Band and Humphrey Lyttelton Band (two of the top British New Orleans–style jazz groups) joined the Christie Brothers Stompers, an ensemble co-led by trombonist Keith Christie and clarinetist Ian Christie. **Christie Brothers Stompers** (Cadillac 20/1) has all of the band's records (dating from 1951–53), other than some slightly earlier recordings for Esquire and a more modern 1958 session. With Ken Colyer (who is on the first nine of the 23 cuts) or Dickie Hawdon on trumpet and Pat Hawes or Charlie Smith on piano, this was a spirited group with plenty of fine soloists who improvised in the older style. Although the first three numbers are not very well recorded, the technical quality greatly improves with the second session. Among the highlights are "Heebie Jeebies," "Salutation Stomp," "Hiawatha Rag," "Farewell to Storyville," and "Them There Eyes." The Christie Brothers Stompers were most influenced by the Kid Ory and Bunk Johnson groups and set the standard for the British trad jazz bands that followed.

Eddie Condon   Although his short-lived television show did not last beyond 1949, Eddie Condon was still riding high in the 1950s. He performed nightly with his groups at his club, Condon's, recorded for Decca (1950) and Savoy (1951), and in late 1953 began making records regularly for Columbia. Among the musicians performing regularly with Condon during this era were the explosive cornetist Wild Bill Davison, Cutty Cutshall or Lou McGarity on trombone, Peanuts Hucko, Edmond Hall or Pee Wee Russell on clarinet, pianist Gene Schroeder, Bob Casey or Walter Page on bass, and Buzzy Drootin, Cliff Leeman, or George Wettling on drums.

During 1951–52, the *Dr. Jazz* radio series featured live performances from Dixieland bands in New York including, quite frequently, those of Condon. Four CDs have been released from Storyville that showcase Condon's groups. **Dr. Jazz Series, Vol. 11** (Storyville 6051) has the frontline of Davison, Cutshall, and Hall featured on such Dixieland tunes as "Dippermouth Blues," "At the Jazz Band Ball," and "Fidgety Feet." **Dr. Jazz Series, Vol. 5** (Storyville 6045) has the same group from eight different broadcasts playing similar material. **Dr. Jazz Series, Vol. 1** (Storyville 6041) and **Dr. Jazz Series, Vol. 8** (Storyville 6048) put the focus on trumpeter Johnny Windhurst (who holds his own with Cutshall and Hall) and includes some of his best playing on record. The music overall is predictable but filled with plenty of exciting moments.

The limited-edition five-CD set **The Complete CBS Eddie Condon All Stars** (Mosaic 5-152) has all of Condon's dates for Columbia, mostly dating from 1953–57, including two classics, which unfortunately have not been reissued individually yet by Sony. The LP **Jammin' at Condon's** (Columbia 616) from 1954 has Condon's regular group (with Davison, Cutshall, and Hall) more than doubled in size with the additions of Billy Butterfield, Lou McGarity, Peanuts Hucko, Bud Freeman, and Dick Cary (on alto horn). Highlights include "Blues My Naughty Sweetie Gives to Me," "There'll Be Some Changes Made," and "How Come You Do Me Like You Do." **Bixieland** (Columbia 719) is a tribute to the music of Bix Beiderbecke, but not an attempt to recreate Bix's recordings or solos. The ten selections are jams on such tunes as "At the Jazz Band Ball," "I'll Be a Friend with Pleasure," "Fidgety Feet," and "Royal Garden Blues," as played by Wild Bill Davison or Bobby Hackett, Cutty Cutshall, Dick Cary on alto horn, Edmond Hall, and a fine rhythm section.

Wilbur DeParis's New New Orleans Jazz   One of the more inventive Dixieland groups of the 1950s was led by trombonist Wilbur DeParis. A decent soloist who was an inventive ensemble player, DeParis had been playing with major groups since the late 1920s. After working with Duke Ellington (1945–47) and Sidney Bechet (1949–50), he put together a band that played regularly at Ryan's throughout the 1950s, performing what he called "New New Orleans jazz." His brother Sidney DeParis was on trumpet and the clarinet slot was taken by Omer Simeon, who had already made his mark playing with Jelly Roll Morton (1926–28), the Earl Hines big band (1931–37), and Jimmie Lunceford (1942–49) including with the ghost band for a couple of years. The

rhythm section had some turnover, but the frontline stayed constant for quite a while.

DeParis's band not only played some Dixieland standards, but marches, pop tunes, and hymns, all turned

48 ESSENTIAL RECORDS OF 1950–1955

Gerry Mulligan and Chet Baker, **The Original Quartet with Chet Baker** (Pacific Jazz 94407), 2 CDs

Chet Baker, **The Chet Baker Quartet with Russ Freeman** (Pacific Jazz 93164)

Various Artists, **The Birth of the Cool, Vol. 2** (Capitol 98933)

Howard Rumsey's Lighthouse All-Stars, **Sunday Jazz à La Lighthouse** (Original Jazz Classics 151)

Dave Brubeck Quartet, **Jazz Goes to College** (Columbia 45149)

Dave Pell Octet, **Plays Rodgers & Hart** (Fresh Sound 505)

Lennie Niehaus, **Vol. 1: The Quintets** (Original Jazz Classics 319)

Laurindo Almeida and Bud Shank, **Brazilliance, Vol. 1** (World Pacific 96339)

Barney Kessel, **Vol. 3: To Swing or Not to Swing** (Original Jazz Classics 317)

Lester Young, **With the Oscar Peterson Trio** (Verve 314 521 4517)

Stan Getz, **The Complete Roost Recordings** (Roost 59622), 3 CDs

Lionel Hampton and Stan Getz, **Hamp and Getz** (Verve 831 672)

Jimmy Raney, **A** (Original Jazz Classics 1706)

Charlie Parker, **Bird: Complete on Verve** (Verve 837 141), 10 CDs

Charlie Parker and Dizzy Gillespie, **Live at Massey Hall** (Original Jazz Classics 044)

Dizzy Gillespie, **Dizzy Gillespie with Roy Eldridge** (Verve 314 52 647)

Thelonious Monk, **The Complete Prestige Recordings** (Prestige 4428), 3 CDs

Clifford Brown, **The Complete Blue Note and Pacific Jazz Recordings** (Pacific Jazz 34195), 4 CDs

Clifford Brown, **Brownie—The Complete EmArcy Recordings of Clifford Brown** (EmArcy 838 306), 10 CDs

Art Blakey and Horace Silver, **Horace Silver and the Jazz Messengers** (Blue Note 46140)

Miles Davis, **Chronicle—The Complete Prestige Recordings** (Prestige 012), 8 CDs

Kenny Dorham, **Afro-Cuban** (Blue Note 46815)

Sonny Rollins, **The Complete Prestige Recordings** (Prestige 4407), 7 CDs

Lars Gullin, **1955/56 Vol. 1** (Dragon 224)

Herbie Nichols, **The Complete Blue Note Recordings** (Blue Note 59352), 3 CDs

Sarah Vaughan, **Swingin' Easy** (EmArcy 514 072)

Claire Austin, **When Your Lover Has Gone** (Original Jazz Classics 1711)

June Christy, **Something Cool** (Capitol 96329)

Various Artists, **The Bebop Singers** (Prestige 24216)

Fred Astaire, **The Astaire Story** (Verve 835 649), 2 CDs

Louis Armstrong, **Plays W.C. Handy** (Columbia/Legacy 64925)

Louis Armstrong, **Satch Plays Fats** (Columbia/Legacy 64927)

Oscar Celestin, **Marie La Veau** (GHB 106)

George Lewis, **Doctor Jazz** (Good Time Jazz 12062)

Turk Murphy, **Turk Murphy's Jazz Band Favorites** (Good Time Jazz 60-011)

Red Nichols, **Syncopated Chamber Music** (Audiophile 2)

Kid Ory, **The Legendary Kid** (Good Time Jazz 12018)

Ruby Braff, **The Best of Braff** (Avenue Jazz/Bethlehem 75822)

Bobby Hackett, **Coast Concert/Jazz Ultimate** (Collector's Choice Music 165)

Edmond Hall, **Club Hangover 1954** (Storyville 6052)

Jazz at the Philharmonic, **Stockholm '55, The Exciting Battle** (Pablo 2310-713)

Stan Kenton, **The Innovations Orchestra** (Capitol 59965), 2 CDs

Duke Ellington, **Uptown** (Columbia 40836)

Count Basie, **April in Paris** (Verve 314 521 407)

Count Basie, **Count Basie Swings, Joe Williams Sings** (Verve 314 519 852)

Roy Eldridge and Dizzy Gillespie, **Roy & Diz** (Verve 314 521 647)

Erroll Garner, **Concert by the Sea** (Columbia 40859)

Chico O'Farrill, **Cuban Blues** (Verve 314 533 256), 2 CDs

into swinging and spirited jazz. The 1951–52 version of the group is featured on the *Dr. Jazz* radio series on s everal CDs: **Dr. Jazz Series, Vol. 7** (Storyville 6047), **An Evening at Jimmy Ryan's** (Jazz Crusade 3009), **Another Evening at Jimmy Ryan's** (Jazz Crusade 3061), and **One More Evening at Jimmy Ryan's** (Jazz Crusade 3068). The Storyville set gets a slight edge due to slightly better recording quality, but each of these discs should delight fans of the often-rambunctious band.

The group recorded nine albums for Atlantic during 1952–60, all of which have fortunately been reissued by the Collectables label. **Marchin' and Swingin'/At Symphony Hall** (Collectables 6600), a two-CD set, has the group's first album (from 1952) plus their 1956 appearance at Symphony Hall. Typically the band plays a wide variety of material including the leader's colorful "Martinique," "Under the Double Eagle," Rachmaninoff's "Prelude in C Sharp Minor," "Juba Dance," "Wrought Iron Rag," a couple of Jelly Roll Morton tunes, and a version of "When the Saints Go Marching In" that in its second half is taken at a blistering tempo.

The Dukes of Dixieland   In January 1949, trumpeter Frank Assunto (who was 17) and his older brother, trombonist Fred Assunto, formed the Dukes of Dixieland to compete in a Horace Heidt talent contest. After their group won, they toured with Heidt as the Junior Dixie Band. Returning to the Dukes name, the group had a 44-month engagement at the Famous Door in New Orleans that established them as one of the city's top bands. The Dukes recorded for Band Wagon in 1951 and also made records for Imperial and Okeh in 1952. The 1955 version of the group (which had Pete Fountain on clarinet) recorded a very enjoyable LP simply titled **At the Jazz Band Ball** (RCA 2097), but unfortunately none of the Dukes' early recordings have yet been reissued on CD. Later in 1955, the Assunto brothers' father, Jac Assunto, joined on banjo and second trombone, and the Dukes signed with Audio Fidelity.

The Firehouse Five Plus Two   The Firehouse Five Plus Two continued to be a very popular group during the 1950s. By 1954, its personnel consisted of leader/trombonist Ward Kimball, cornetist Danny Alguire, George Probert on clarinet and soprano, pianist Frank Thomas, banjoist Dick Roberts, Ed Penner on tuba and bass, and drummer Monte Mountjoy. Jim Roberts became the group's new drummer in 1955. **Firehouse Five Plus Two**

Goes South (Good Time Jazz 12018) has both straightforward Dixieland and some humor that comes close to being cornball, although the two siren breaks from Kimball are humorous. The ten songs all have something to do with the South, such as "Alabama Jubilee," "Basin Street Blues," "At a Georgia Camp Meeting," etc. **Firehouse Five Plus Two Plays for Lovers** (Good Time Jazz 12014) features a dozen songs having something to do with love; ten have the word "love" in their title, including "Careless Love," "Love Is Just Around the Corner," and "Love Songs of the Nile." However, there are no overly sticky ballads and the music is the Firehouse Five's usual brand of joyful Dixieland.

George Lewis   Clarinetist George Lewis was an unlikely hero. He had gained some recognition from the New Orleans jazz world when he played with Bunk Johnson during 1943–46, but when he returned home to New Orleans, he was still little known to the outside world. Back in New Orleans, Lewis played locally with his own group (which always featured trombonist Jim Robinson), and by 1950 he was gaining some attention. An article that year in *Look* magazine focused attention on the clarinetist and soon he was recording regularly. By 1952, he was touring the United States and soon Europe and Japan. As with Bunk Johnson, Lewis was both overpraised and overcriticized, depending on the listener's outlook. Truth is, he was a primitive player who was not always in the best of health, and unfortunately he was not always in tune. Lewis was a bit of a chameleon at times, rising (or sinking) to the level of his trumpeter. So when Kid Howard, his usual trumpeter, was having an off night (he was frequently drunk), Lewis's playing could be quite erratic. But at his best, Lewis's music was charming, swinging, and a joy to hear.

George Lewis with Red Allen (American Music 71) has the clarinetist performing five numbers with Allen (along with Jim Robinson and a four-piece rhythm section that includes Paul Barbarin) in 1951. These are among the clarinetist's greatest recordings; he rose to Allen's level. Also on this CD are ten excellent selections from the same period on which Alvin Alcorn does a fine job on trumpet.

By 1953, Lewis's band consisted of Kid Howard, Jim Robinson, pianist Alton Purnell, banjoist Lawrence Marrero, bassist Alcide "Slow Drag" Pavageau, and drummer Joe Watkins. Quite a few live sessions have been issued and these are streaky due to an excess of musician vocals, Howard's on and off playing, and Lewis's inconsistency. However, ◉ **Doctor Jazz** (Good Time Jazz 12062), a set formerly put out by Jazzman and Everest, finds the Lewis band sounding inspired, tearing into such tunes as "When the Saints Go Marching In" (one of the top versions of this song ever recorded), "Doctor Jazz," "Ice Cream," and "Panama." This CD reissue adds four fine numbers from a live performance to the original program. More typical of the band is their playing on **The Sounds of New Orleans Vol. 7** (Storyville 6014), which has its charm (including two Lizzie Miles vocals and some good George Lewis solos), but many off moments from Howard and too many vocals from the musicians. The two-CD set **Jass at the Ohio Union 1954** (Storyville 6020/21) is largely sunk by Howard, while **George Lewis and His New Orleans Stompers** (Blue Note 21261), the last Blue Note recording to feature New Orleans jazz, is better if not essential. On the latter CD, the group is at its best on driving ensembles, and the rhythm section is often quite powerful. Even if Lewis slips out of tune occasionally, he is generally in fine form, while Kid Howard is in better shape than on most of the live sets. Highlights include "When You Wore a Tulip," "I Can't Escape from You," "Lord, Lord, Lord, You Sure Been Good to Me," and three versions of "Gettysburg March."

But one has to be careful when buying George Lewis records, for the band's quality was consistently unpredictable from day to day.

Turk Murphy   In 1947, trombonist Turk Murphy left Lu Watters's Yerba Buena Jazz Band to form a group of his own. He had an initial record date that year for Good Time Jazz (four songs in a quintet with Bob Scobey, clarinetist Bob Helm, pianist Burt Bales, and banjoist Harry Mordecai) and another session in 1949 with Dick Lammi added on tuba and bass. Scobey stayed with Murphy until 1950 (when he left to form his own unit). Murphy recorded a few more titles for Good Time Jazz during 1951–52 then got a lucky break and was signed to Columbia where he cut several albums during 1953–56. During this period he often utilized Bob Helm, pianist Wally Rose, and either Don Kinch or Ev Farey (and occasionally tuba player Bob Short) on trumpet. Murphy's approach differed from Watters's in that the trombonist did not care for drums (rarely using

them) and played four-beat rather than two-beat. ◉ **Turk Murphy's Jazz Band Favorites** (Good Time Jazz 60-011) and **Jazz Band Favorites, Vol. 2** (Good Time Jazz 60-026) sum up the Good Time Jazz period quite well. The former CD is highlighted by "When My Sugar Walks Down the Street," "Struttin' with Some Barbecue," Murphy's "Trombone Rag," "Down by the Riverside," and Clare Austin's vocal on "Cakewalkin' Babies from Home." The second volume has the initial Murphy session from 1947 plus "King Porter Stomp," "Grandpa's Spells," "Papa Dip," "Flamin' Mamie," and other hot numbers.

Unfortunately, Murphy's Columbia albums have not been reissued, but a couple of other live releases partly fill the gap. **In Hollywood** (San Francisco Traditional Jazz Foundation 102), recorded in 1950, has 21 of the 28 selections that were released on a pair of Fairmont LPs in the 1970s, music recorded at Hollywood's Cinegrill. Murphy's ensemble (which includes Don Kinch and clarinetist Bill Napier) mostly plays Dixieland standards on this set including "High Society," "Big Butter and Egg Man," "Oh! Didn't He Ramble," and "That's a Plenty." **At the Italian Village 1952–53** (Merry Makers 11) has a historic concert from January 6, 1952, at the Italian Village nightclub that was so successful that the venue became a haven for classic jazz for the next two years. Murphy's band at the time featured Kinch, Bob Helm, and Wally Rose, and this engagement helped introduce Claire Austin, a housewife turned singer. The band performs a dozen hot selections (including four with Austin vocals), and the CD is rounded out by nine numbers from 1953 featuring a trumpetless quintet with Murphy, Helm, and Rose.

Red Nichols's Five Pennies   Red Nichols revived his Five Pennies in late 1944, spending the rest of his life playing his own brand of Dixieland. In 1949, bass saxophonist Joe Rushton joined the Five Pennies, helping to give the Los Angeles–based band its own sound, even when playing warhorses. ◉ **Syncopated Chamber Music** (Audiophile 2) is a particularly intriguing release from 1953, one of the few times when Nichols's later music hinted at the avant-garde arrangements that he often utilized in the late 1920s. The playing time is quite brief on this CD (just a little over 31 minutes), but the quality is high. The music lives up to the title's name, for such songs as "Three Blind Mice," "Candlelights," "I Can't

Believe that You're in Love with Me," "Manhattan Rag," and "Easter Parade" are given unusual and exquisite arrangements. Although the individual solos of Nichols, Matty Matlock, Rushton, and either King Jackson or Ted Vesely on trombone are excellent, it is the unpredictable charts (which have inventive use of space, dynamics, and unusual harmonies) that make this a particularly memorable set.

Kid Ory's Creole Jazz Band   One of the big success stories of the Dixieland revival movement was Kid Ory. Ever since he started his New Orleans jazz band in 1944, the group was quite popular, particularly in Los Angeles. By 1950, the band's lineup consisted of the leader on trombone, the powerful trumpeter Teddy Buckner (who based his style closely on Louis Armstrong), clarinetist Joe Darensbourg, pianist Lloyd Glenn, bassist Ed Garland, and drummer Minor Hall. The group recorded an album that year for Columbia and had a four-song session for Good Time Jazz in 1951. In 1953, when Bob McCracken had taken over on clarinet, Don Ewell was Ory's new pianist, and Morty Cobb was on bass, the band recorded **The Kid's the Greatest** (Good Time Jazz 12045), which also has a few titles from 1954 and 1956. Buckner dominates the ensembles, but Ory's percussive playing and forceful harmonies make it clear who is the band's leader. Among the better tunes are "South Rampart Street Parade," "The Girls Go Crazy," "Bill Bailey," "Milenberg Joys," and "The Bucket's Got a Hole in It."

In 1954, Alvin Alcorn became Ory's trumpeter, and he proved to be a perfect ensemble player, expert at building up ensembles and hitting a perfectly placed note to lead each chorus into the next one, as well as an appealing and subtle soloist. With George Probert on clarinet and Ed Garland back on bass (in the rhythm section with Ewell and Hall), this was arguably Kid Ory's greatest band. Fortunately, the group recorded three wonderful albums during this period. **Kid Ory's Creole Jazz Band 1954** (Good Time Jazz 12004) has memorable versions of "The Saints," "That's a Plenty," "Clarinet Marmalade," "Gettysburg March," and Ory's "Muskrat Ramble." **Kid Ory's Creole Jazz Band** (Good Time Jazz 12008), which has Barney Kessel added to the group on rhythm guitar, includes such favorites as "Savoy Blues," "Royal Garden Blues," and "Indiana." ● **The Legendary Kid** (Good Time Jazz 12018), which is marginally the best of the trio of CDs (although all are quite

rewarding) has Ory, Alcorn, and Hall joined by clarinetist Phil Gomez (an excellent player), pianist Lionel Reason, rhythm guitarist Julian Davidson, and (coming out of retirement) bassist Wellman Braud. The ensembles on such numbers as "There'll Be Some Changes Made," "At the Jazz Band Ball," "Shine," and "Mahogany Stomp" are infectious and show why this was one of the top New Orleans jazz bands of 1955. Ory, at the age of 68, was clearly having the time of his life.

Bob Scobey's Frisco Jazz Band   In 1949, Bob Scobey left Lu Watters's Yerba Buena Jazz Band, at first playing with Turk Murphy and then forming his own Frisco Jazz Band. Like Turk Murphy, Scobey preferred to emphasize four beats to the bar rather than the two-beat style of Watters, but, unlike Murphy, Scobey enjoyed having a forceful rhythm section. **The Scobey Story, Vol. 1** (Good Time Jazz 12032) is a straight reissue of a 35-minute LP and includes Scobey's first studio sessions. Dating from 1950–51, the trumpeter is joined by trombonist Jack Buck, either Darnell Howard, Albert Nicholas, or George Probert on clarinet, Burt Bales or Wally Rose on piano, banjoist Clancy Hayes (who also takes a few vocals), and a few different rhythm sections. Hayes, who was probably the top male jazz singer to be closely associated with the Dixieland revival of the era (not counting Louis Armstrong and Jack Teagarden), would work regularly with Scobey for quite a few years. His versions of "Coney Island Washboard" and "Sailing Down Chesapeake Bay" are highlights of this disc. **The Scobey Story, Vol. 2** (Good Time Jazz 12033) is actually superior to the first disc due to Hayes's vocals on "Silver Dollar," "Ace in the Hole," and the minor hit "Huggin' & A-Chalkin'." The personnel of Scobey's band had stabilized by the time of these 1953 sessions and consisted of the leader, Buck, Probert, Rose, bassist Dick Lammi, and drummer Fred Higuera in addition to Hayes. In 1955, a similar lineup (with Bill Napier on clarinet and Ernie Lewis on piano) recorded **Bob Scobey's Frisco Band** (Good Time Jazz 12006), which includes vocals by Hayes on all but two songs, but is weaker overall than the earlier sets. **Scobey and Clancy** (Good Time Jazz 12009) is an excellent outing that includes "When the Midnight Choo Choo Leaves for Alabam," "At the Devil's Ball," "You Can Depend on Me," and "St. Louis Blues."

Jimmy Archey   Jimmy Archey was a solid if underrated trombonist for decades, who in the early 1950s had an opportunity to lead his own group. Archey first played with jazz bands in the mid-1920s, working with Edgar Hayes (1927), King Oliver (1929–30), and Luis Russell (1931–37), making his recording debut with Oliver. He worked in the big bands of Willie Bryant, Benny Carter (1939), Ella Fitzgerald, Coleman Hawkins, Claude Hopkins (1944–45), and Noble Sissle. Archey first began to be noticed as a soloist on Rudi Blesh's *This Is Jazz* radio series in 1947. He toured France with Mezz Mezzrow in 1948 and became a member of Bob Wilber's group in December. When Wilber departed in April 1950, Archey became the group's leader for the next four years. **Dr. Jazz Series Vol. 4** (Storyville 6044) and **Dr. Jazz Series Vol. 13** (Storyville 6058) are taken from radio broadcasts of 1951–52, featuring Archey's Dixieland band. In addition to the trombonist, such veterans as Benny Waters (heard on clarinet), trumpeter Henry Goodwin, Pops Foster, and drummer Tommy Benford (who was with Jelly Roll Morton in the 1920s) are joined by the great young stride pianist Dick Wellstood. The music (other than their theme song "The Party Is Here at My House") is primarily Dixieland with some of the renditions being a bit riotous, but these discs give one a rare chance to hear Goodwin in this type of freewheeling setting, and they offer important glimpses at how Benny Waters (who was nearing the halfway point of his very long career) sounded in this period. The band lasted until Archey again toured Europe with Mezzrow (November 1954–February 1955). Upon his return, the trombonist joined Earl Hines's San Francisco–based Dixieland band for a seven-year stint.

Paul Barbarin   Paul Barbarin came from a very musical New Orleans family with his father, Isadore Barbarin, three of his brothers, and his uncle Danny Barker all playing music. Paul worked with brass bands in New Orleans, was a fixture in Chicago during 1917–27 (including working with Freddie Keppard, Jimmie Noone, King Oliver, and his own bands) and was with the Luis Russell Orchestra during 1928–32 and 1935–39. By the mid-1940s, he was back in New Orleans where he composed "Bourbon Street Parade" and "The Second Line" and became an important force as a bandleader. His recordings during the 1950s were generally excellent examples of trad jazz. One of his finest albums is **And His New Orleans Jazz** (Atlantic 90977).

Barbarin's 1955 septet consists of trumpeter John Brunious, clarinetist Willie Humphrey, trombonist Bob Thomas, pianist Lester Santiago, banjoist Danny Barker, and guest bassist Milt Hinton. They are all heard in top form, particularly during "Sing On," "Just a Little While to Stay Here," "Bourbon Street Parade," and "Walking Through the Streets of the City."

Chris Barber   Trombonist Chris Barber led his first trad band in 1948 when he was 18. In 1953, he had a group that included trumpeter Ken Colyer, but they had a difference of opinion over the type of music they wished to play. Colyer opted for a more primitive style while Barber was after a cleaner approach. In 1954, Pat Halcox took Colyer's place and Barber's group (a pianoless sextet) also included clarinetist Monty Sunshine, banjoist/guitarist/vocalist Lonnie Donegan, bassist Jim Bray, and drummer Ron Bowden. **The Original Copenhagen Concert** (Storyville 5527) gives a good example of what the band sounded like in its early stages. Sunshine is showcased on "St. Philip Street Breakdown," Donegan sings a pair of folk songs, and both Halcox and Barber take plenty of fine solos. Although influenced at the time to an extent by George Lewis, Chris Barber's band (which was open to blues, folk music, and swing tunes in addition to Dixieland standards) would within a couple of years have its own sound, rising to the top during Britain's trad boom.

Emile Barnes, Albert Burbank, and Raymond Burke   Veteran New Orleans clarinetist Emile Barnes made relatively few recordings in his career, just enough so he could be an inspiration to other trad clarinetists in later decades. He had worked with Buddy Petit and Chris Kelly in the 1920s before being mostly outside of music for the next 15 years. Playing again by the mid-1940s, Barnes made his first recordings in 1946 and popped up on a couple of sessions in 1951–52, released on a pair of Folkways LPs, **Early Recordings Vols. 1–2** (Folkways 2857 and 2858). **Emile Barnes** (American Music 13) has Barnes performing with a sextet/septet in 1951 that includes De De Pierce and/or Lawrence Toca on trumpets, trombonist Harrison Brazley, pianist Billie Pierce (who has seven vocals), bassist Albert Glenny, and drummer Cie Frazier. Barnes's distinctive tone is well featured, and even if the recording quality is not always the greatest, this CD gives listeners a good idea of how he sounded. It is surprising that he did not record much more in future years for he was quite active throughout the 1950s and '60s.

Albert Burbank was a New Orleans clarinetist who had a beautiful tone in his lower register and was a local legend. He was a fixture in New Orleans from the 1920s on, playing along the way with Buddy Petit, Chris Kelly, Punch Miller, Wooden Joe Nicholas, De De Pierce, Herb Morand (1949–50), Paul Barbarin, and others. In 1954, Burbank made a rare venture outside New Orleans, performing in Los Angeles with Kid Ory for a few months before returning back home where he would remain active into the 1970s, only leading one album of his own (in 1969). **Sounds of New Orleans Vol. 3** (Storyville 6010), although released under Burbank's name, actually features the clarinetist with Kid Ory's Creole Jazz Band on radio broadcasts from San Francisco's Club Hangover. Burbank, Ory, Alvin Alcorn, Don Ewell, Ed Garland, and Minor Hall romp through a variety of New Orleans and Dixieland standards (including "Clarinet Marmalade," "Fidgety Feet," "Panama," and "Shine") plus an 11-minute version of "Blues for Jimmie Noone." Burbank fits in so well with Ory that it is a pity he didn't stay up north very long.

Raymond Burke, like Burbank and Barnes, spent nearly his entire career in New Orleans. He worked as a professional starting in 1920, and other than a brief period in Kansas City in the late 1930s, he stayed in his native city. Along the way Burke worked with Sharkey Bonano, Johnny Wiggs, Wooden Joe Nicholas, the Dukes of Dixieland, George Girard, Johnny St. Cyr, Punch Miller, and Kid Thomas Valentine, in addition to his own bands. Although he led a few albums in his career, they were all made for obscure labels. Even the best one, **And His New Orleans Jazz Band** (Southland 209), has not yet been reissued on CD. Two different sessions from November 12, 1953, are included on this LP, which features Burke (in top form) with trombonist Jack Delaney, either Thomas Jefferson (who has two vocals) or Alvin Alcorn on trumpet, and a solid New Orleans rhythm section. Each of the musicians is technically skilled within the style, in tune, and in spirited form on such numbers as "Big Butter and Egg Man," "Over the Waves," and "Who's Sorry Now."

Sidney Bechet Sidney Bechet's big success at the Salle Pleyel Jazz Festival in Paris in 1949 (where he overshadowed Charlie Parker and Miles Davis) led to him moving to France in 1951. Before he departed, he recorded **Live in New York, 1950–51** (Storyville 6039), performances heading a quintet with Vic Dickenson and pianist Ken Kersey, and with a bassless quartet from 1951 that features trombonist Big Chief Russell Moore (who is heard in peak form) and pianist Red Richards. On these dates, Bechet did not have to be concerned with fighting over the lead (there are no trumpets to get in the way), and he happily riffs throughout the enjoyable music, interacting joyfully with the two witty trombonists.

Treated as a national celebrity after his move to France, frequently making headlines and playing at sold-out concerts, Bechet finally gained the fame that he deserved even if he ironically remained unknown to the average American. During his years in France, Bechet recorded regularly for the Vogue label. Often backed by a trad band led by clarinetist Claude Luter, Bechet stuck to the freewheeling music that he loved the most. **Salle Pleyel 31/01/52** (Vogue 655001) is probably most noteworthy for the almost-hysterical reaction of the French audience to the playing of Bechet with Luter's band. The Dixieland music is excellent if overshadowed by the crowd's jubilation. **Jazz at Storyville** (Black Lion 760902), from October 25, 1953, is taken from the soprano's last major visit to the United States. Bechet jams familiar standards with Vic Dickenson and a rhythm section that includes George Wein on piano. **La Legende de Sidney Bechet** (Vogue 600245) is a cross-section of his performances in France from 1949–58, including his popular "Les Oignons," "Petite Fleur," "Summertime," and "Royal Garden Blues." Bechet may not have been blazing any new musical paths, but neither had he declined nor lost his enthusiasm for New Orleans jazz. And it was heartwarming that at least one jazz great was being treated in a way that his talent deserved.

Sharkey Bonano Sharkey Bonano, after recording a series of excellent Dixieland numbers with his Sharks of Rhythm during 1936–37, freelanced in New York, served in the military, and returned to New Orleans. The trumpeter became one of the more popular bandleaders in the Crescent City starting in 1949. Although his studio recordings for Capitol, Southland, and Roulette are mostly unavailable, two CDs taken from live performances in 1952 are in print. **Vol. 8 Sounds**

of New Orleans (Storyville 6015) gets the slight edge due to the appearances of singer Lizzie Miles, who was enjoying a full-fledged comeback. Also heard from on both discs with Bonano are trombonist Jack Delaney, clarinetist Bujie Centobie, pianist Stanley Mendelsohn, bassist Arnold Loyacano, and drummer Abbie Brunies. The music on **Vol. 8** and **Vol. 4 Sounds of New Orleans** (Storyville 6011) is typical of the era, with boisterous versions of such Dixieland warhorses as "High Society," "The Saints," and "Weary Blues" on the first set and "Chinatown My Chinatown," "Royal Garden Blues," and "Tiger Rag" on the second.

Ruby Braff Ruby Braff has always been a world-class musician, but one who is a bit out of place in his own musical generation. A year younger than Miles Davis and John Coltrane, the cornetist was never interested in playing bebop, much preferring the music of Louis Armstrong, Billie Holiday, and Lester Young. Because of the time period in which he came up, Braff had the opportunity to play with a lot of the older swing and Dixieland musicians and was usually the youngest musician on the bandstand. He grew up in Boston, playing with Edmond Hall in 1949 and with Pee Wee Russell when the clarinetist was making a comeback in 1951. Braff moved to New York in 1953 and had a busy decade on records, although he also went through periods when it was difficult to find work. Often grouped with Dixieland bands, he was really more of a swing player, working with Benny Goodman in 1955 and appearing on some of the fabled Buck Clayton jam sessions. A very passionate player who always put a lot of feeling into every note, Braff would develop as an individual voice through the years, but he was pretty distinctive from the start. **Hustlin' and Bustlin'** (Black Lion 760908) has three numbers from 1951 when Braff was playing in a sextet with Edmond Hall and Vic Dickenson, and there is a version of "When It's Sleepy Time Down South" with an octet in 1954. The remainder of the CD has performances from a session in a quintet with tenor saxophonist Sam Margolis, highlighted by "Hustlin' and Bustlin'," "Shoe Shine Boy," and "There's a Small Hotel." In 1955, Braff and the sensitive pianist Ellis Larkins recorded two albums of duets. Although the songs have been shuffled around a bit (one of the original albums was a set of tunes by Rodgers and Hart), they are reissued in full on **Duets Vol. 1** (Vanguard 79609) and

Duets Vol. 2 (Vanguard 79611). The emphasis is on ballads, but there are a few medium-tempo pieces along the way, and the passionate cornet playing keeps the music from ever becoming sleepy.

● **The Best of Braff** (Avenue Jazz/Bethlehem 75822) reissues the album **Adoration of the Melody**, a phrase that perfectly fits Braff's melodic improvising. There are four numbers that showcase Braff in a quartet with Johnny Guarnieri plus eight in which Braff is joined by a full saxophone section. The arrangements (probably by Bob Wilber) perfectly frame Braff's horn and there are many tributes to Billie Holiday, Lester Young, and Louis Armstrong on this memorable set. Highpoints include "When You're Smiling," "You're a Lucky Guy," "Foolin' Myself," and "Mean to Me."

Lee Collins The musical highpoint of Lee Collins's life took place in 1929 when he recorded four hot numbers with the Jones-Collins Astoria Eight. He was based in Chicago in the 1930s and '40s, sometimes recording as a sideman to blues singers but never as a leader. Collins toured Europe with Mezz Mezzrow in 1951, but unfortunately became ill and had to cut the trip short. There are broadcasts from San Francisco's Hangover Club in 1953 that have been reissued as **Lee Collins at Club Hangover Vol. 1** (Jazz Crusade 3056) and **Vol. 2** (Jazz Crusade 3057). On **Vol. 1**, Collins is featured in a group with trombonist Burt Johnson, Pud Brown (clarinet, soprano, and tenor), Ralph Sutton, bassist Dale Jones, and drummer Smokey Stover. There are excellent versions of "Panama," "Indiana," "Johnson Rag" (which was an R&B novelty hit for Brown), and "Muskrat Ramble" along with other Dixieland standards. **Vol. 2** has Don Ewell replacing Sutton after the first four numbers and Bob McCracken is heard on clarinet. It is highlighted by two renditions of "Fidgety Feet" plus "Big Butter and Egg Man" and "After You've Gone."

It is fortunate that these radio appearances exist, for Collins's second European tour with Mezzrow (1954) resulted in him becoming so ill that he had to retire from playing altogether. His last days found him working on his priceless autobiography *Oh Didn't He Ramble*.

Ken Colyer Ken Colyer's early days were the stuff of legend. Self-taught on trumpet and guitar and always a lover of New Orleans jazz, Colyer worked with the Crane River Jazz Band (1949–51) in his native England, also recording with the Christie Brothers Jazz Band. In

1951, he joined the Merchant Marines with one purpose in mind: to jump ship in the United States and head to New Orleans where he would play with the local greats. Colyer did just that, and before he was caught and deported, he had opportunities to admire the music of George Lewis's band and record with a New Orleans group that included Emile Barnes. Unfortunately, the music on **The Complete 1953 Recordings** (504 Records 53) is erratic and poorly recorded, but his adventures in New Orleans made a permanent impression on Colyer.

Back in England, Colyer worked in a group with Chris Barber, but left within a year to pursue his own musical vision. **In the Beginning** (Lake 14) has an excellent record date by the Colyer-Barber group on September 2, 1953, a sextet also featuring clarinetist Monty Sunshine and banjoist Lonnie Donegan. The second half of the disc (from September–October 1954) consists of the first recordings by Colyer's own sextet, and those performances have plenty of spirit although the clarinet playing of Acker Bilk is surprisingly erratic, lowering the quality a bit. Fortunately, Bilk would rapidly improve. In addition to playing cornet, Colyer also enjoyed playing guitar and singing folk songs in a style soon called "skiffle." **The Decca Skiffle Sessions 1954–57** (Lake 7) has Colyer singing à la Leadbelly and sticking to guitar on dates that also sometimes feature Alexis Korner on guitar and mandolin, performing such numbers as "Casey Jones," "Down by the Riverside," "Stack-O-Lee Blues," and "This Train."

Doc Evans   While Ken Colyer helped fuel the trad jazz scene in England, Doc Evans helped keep Dixieland alive in Minneapolis, Minnesota. He led a string of excellent jazz records for the Audiophile label starting in 1949. **Down in Jungle Town** (Jazzology 19) has two of those albums, dating from 1953 and 1955. Other than trombonist Hal Runyon, the personnel is completely different on each date, featuring fine local musicians, including either Lori Helberg or Harry Blons on clarinet. Evans, who played melodically and with both subtlety and fire (sometimes hinting a little at Bix Beiderbecke), is in top form on such numbers as "Riverside Blues," "Down in Jungle Town," "That's a Plenty," and "Bugle Call Rag." He is a cornetist well worth being discovered by Dixieland fans.

Bobby Hackett   In the 1950s, cornetist Bobby Hackett was often utilized by Jackie Gleason for his "mood

music" albums. He worked in the studios, and he guested with Eddie Condon. In addition, Hackett occasionally led his own Dixieland groups. **Dr. Jazz Series Vol. 10** (Storyville 6050) and **Dr. Jazz Series Vol. 2** (Storyville 6042) feature Hackett on radio broadcasts from 1952 teamed up with the very complementary trombonist Vic Dickenson and clarinetist Gene Sedric (formerly with Fats Waller). **Vol. 10** includes such numbers as "Muskrat Ramble," "Sunday," "Perdido," and "Wolverine Blues" while **Vol. 2** has "Struttin' with Some Barbecue," "A Monday Date," and "Rose of Washington Square" among others. Hackett's style was gentler than most cornetists/trumpeters in Dixieland settings, but was no less effective. ◐ **Coast Concert/Jazz Ultimate** (Collector's Choice Music 165) has Hackett's two finest studio albums of the 1950s (recorded in 1955 and 1957) on one CD. Jack Teagarden is on both sets (one of which has Abe Lincoln on second trombone), and the musicians sound quite inspired on such warhorses as "Basin Street Blues," "Fidgety Feet," "Way Down Yonder in New Orleans," and "Oh Baby." The Hackett-Teagarden combination (they are joined by Matty Matlock or Peanuts Hucko on clarinet and baritonist Ernie Caceres on the later date) works extremely well.

Edmond Hall   Edmond Hall spent much of 1950–55 playing in the house band at Condon's before being tapped as Barney Bigard's replacement with the Louis Armstrong All-Stars. His cutting tone and very distinctive sound were at their peak, and it generally only took one or two notes to identify him.

In the summer of 1954, Edmond Hall, Ralph Sutton, Walter Page, and drummer Charlie Lodice had a regular gig at San Francisco's Club Hangover, and a weekly radio broadcast from which this material is drawn. ◐ **Club Hangover 1954** (Storyville 6052) captures him at his most exciting. The Storyville CD has most of the music from two former LPs, including several stirring titles featuring trumpeter Clyde Hurley (whose claim to fame was taking the trumpet solo on Glenn Miller's "In the Mood"). Hall and Sutton are at their most hyper, and Hurley (a hot Dixieland player) never sounded better on records than during this engagement. Highlights include explosive versions of "I Found a New Baby," "Honeysuckle Rose," "St. Louis Blues," "Oh Baby," and "Love Is Just Around the Corner."

Earl Hines   Earl Hines toured with Louis Armstrong's All-Stars during 1948–51, but it was very difficult for the pianist to constantly play second fiddle to Satch after having led his own big band for 18 years. He also found the repertoire to be repetitive and felt frustrated by the way his career was going. After he left Armstrong (not on the best of terms), Hines at first formed a swing-oriented combo which in 1952 featured Jonah Jones, Bennie Green, clarinetist Aaron Sachs, and the vocals of both Helene Merrill and Etta Jones. The following year, Hines moved to San Francisco where in 1954 he led a different swing group. **Esquire All Stars** (Storyville 8223) has music taken from six radio broadcasts, and the repertoire includes swing standards plus a few lesser-known Hines originals ("Sleepwalking," "Jump for Joy," "Hot Soup," and "Low Down Blues"). The personnel of his band is obscure other than Dickie Wells on trombone, with trumpeter Gene Redd, tenor saxophonist Morris Lane, bassist Carl Pruitt, and drummer Eddie Burns all playing well. However, there was no great demand for small-group swing bands in 1954 so Hines soon gave up, forming a Dixieland band in 1955 with Marty Marsala, Jimmy Archey, Darnell Howard, Ed Garland, and drummer Joe Watkins.

Ben Pollack   By 1950, Ben Pollack was regularly playing Dixieland in the Los Angeles area. He led record dates in 1950 and 1952 with either Dick Cathcart or Charlie Teagarden on trumpet, trombonist Moe Schneider, Matty Matlock, and a rhythm section with the talented pianist Ray Sherman. Those sessions for Discovery and Savoy are difficult to locate, but Pollack's combo also recorded 20 selections as radio transcriptions, all of which are included on **And His Pick-A-Rib Boys** (Jazzology 224). The brief performances pack a lot of music into a short period of time, featuring Cathcart on trumpet. The band plays a variety of Dixieland standards, tunes from the 1920s, and a few oddball items, including "San Antonio Shout," "The Third Man Theme," and Matlock's "Echo in the Cavern." This group would be Ben Pollack's last serious attempt at leading a band.

Pee Wee Russell   Pee Wee Russell, who was in and out of Eddie Condon's band during the second half of the 1940s, drank so excessively during the era that in 1951 he almost died from the combination of too much liquor and not enough food. His bad health made headlines in jazz, and he made a near-miraculous comeback during the next couple of years. By 1953, Russell was back to his old form and determined to be more assertive about controlling his career instead of being the butt of Condon's jokes. **We're in the Money** (1201 Music 9032) features the clarinetist in two different settings during 1953–54. Both dates also feature Vic Dickenson and pianist George Wein. On one occasion Russell teams up with Wild Bill Davison, while the other session is one of the few small-group dates of the 1950s to showcase the relatively mellow trumpet of Doc Cheatham, who had thus far spent much of his career playing first trumpet with big bands or with Latin groups. Russell mostly avoids the Dixieland warhorses in favor of such superior swing standards as "Sugar," "Lulu's Back In Town," "She's Funny That Way," and "If I Had You."

Jack Teagarden   After leaving the Louis Armstrong All-Stars in 1952 after nearly five years of appearing next to Satch, Jack Teagarden formed his own Dixieland group. Though the personnel changed now and then, quite often his younger brother Charlie Teagarden was on trumpet, and for a short time his sister Norma Teagarden played piano. **The Club Hangover Broadcasts** (Arbors 19150) is a double CD that contains four half-hour broadcasts by Teagarden's 1954 sextet. The group is excellent and includes trumpeter Jackie Coon, the obscure clarinetist Jay St. John, Norma Teagarden, bassist Kas Malone, and drummer Ray Bauduc. Because of some odd regulations, Mr. T. was not allowed to sing at these engagements (otherwise the music would be classified as "entertainment" and the clubowner would be subject to an additional tax) so the performances are strictly instrumentals. In addition to the band numbers, on each broadcast the intermission pianist had a chance to play one number; Lil Armstrong and Don Ewell are both heard from twice. The music is both predictable and spirited, which would be true of most of Teagarden's later work. **Jazz Great** (Bethlehem 75784) only contains ten of the dozen selections that Teagarden recorded in 1954 for Jazztone (later acquired by Bethlehem), unfortunately leaving out "Blue Funk" and "Milenburg Joys" though there was clearly enough space on the CD for the extra tunes. However, the performances (with either Jimmy McPartland, Fred Greenleaf, or Dick Cary on trumpet and Edmond Hall or Kenny Davern on clarinet) are excellent, alternating strong standards (including "Eccentric," "King Porter Stomp," and "Riverboat Shuffle") with a few offbeat tunes ("Mis'ry and the Blues," "Music to Love By," and "Meet Me Where They Play the Blues").

Lu Watters　In 1950, with the departure of Turk Murphy and Bob Scobey from the Yerba Buena Jazz Band, Lu Watters struggled on. His band still featured Bob Helm, Wally Rose, and Clancy Hayes (who was being heard for the first time on vocals), and with Warren Smith on trombone and the leader as the only trumpeter, Watters still had an excellent band. They played at Hambone Kelly's in El Cerrito during the year, recorded three albums of material for Verve (much of it later reissued on LPs by Homespun), and musically things seemed fine. But business was dropping off by year-end and Watters could foresee the commercialization of the music he loved into more routine Dixieland. Since he had other interests beyond music, he broke up the band and retired from music to become a cook and a geologist.

Jazz at the Philharmonic

Norman Granz's "Jazz at the Philharmonic" was at the height of its popularity during the early 1950s. The traveling all-star jam session had regular tours of the United States and an unbeatable lineup of competitive players. Generally by this time the first half of the show was taken up by the jams while the second half featured major groups. During 1950–55 the roster of musicians included Roy Eldridge, either Charlie Shavers or Dizzy Gillespie, Bill Harris, Flip Phillips, Ben Webster, Oscar Peterson or Hank Jones, Herb Ellis, Ray Brown, Buddy Rich, J.C. Heard or Louie Bellson, and sometimes Benny Carter, Willie Smith, and Coleman Hawkins. There were often also special sets by Ella Fitzgerald, the Gene Krupa Trio, the Oscar Peterson Trio, and Lester Young's quartet.

Unlike the 1944–49 period, which has been completely reissued, the JATP performances from the 1950s have only partly come back on CD. **Frankfurt 1952** (Pablo 5305) has jams on "How High the Moon," "Undecided," and "Dre's Blues" plus a ballad medley, but never really explodes despite some fine spots for Lester Young, Flip Phillips, and Roy Eldridge. **Hartford 1953** (Pablo 2308-240) has a 15-minute version of "Cotton Tail" with Shavers, Eldridge, Harris, Webster, Phillips, Carter, and Smith joined by the Oscar Peterson Trio and Krupa, but surprisingly this is the only all-out jam on the set. Oth-

erwise the Oscar Peterson Quartet (with J.C. Heard) burns on four selections (including "7 Come 11") and Lester Young is fine on three numbers.

Tokyo: Live at the Nichigeki Theatre 1953 (Pablo 2620), a two-CD set, gives one a better picture of what took place during a JATP concert of the era. There are minisets by the Oscar Peterson Trio and Gene Krupa's combo (with Benny Carter and Peterson) plus ten numbers featuring Ella Fitzgerald (who really scats wildly on "Lady Be Good," "How High the Moon" and the climactic "Perdido"). However, the JATP All-Stars (the same seven horn players as on **Hartford 1953**) take honors, playing a seven-song ballad medley and a drum feature, but really stretching out on "Tokyo Blues" and "Cotton Tail." The latter has a trumpet battle on which Shavers just edges out Eldridge. However, ● **Stockholm '55, The Exciting Battle** (Pablo 2310-713) is the best of these four sets. A ballad medley and a drum feature for Louie Bellson are fine, but on the blues "Little David," the statements of Peterson, Phillips, Harris, Dizzy Gillespie, and Ellis are overshadowed by one of the most exciting solos of Roy Eldridge's career, one that brings the performance to a dramatic close.

The popularity of JATP had been fueled by the popularity of R&B and honking saxophonists. By 1955, rock 'n' roll was about ready to take over and the glory days of "Jazz at the Philharmonic" were nearly finished.

The Four Main Big Bands

In 1949, there were still many big bands performing in the United States, including quite a few former swing bands that were open to the influence of bop. But by the end of 1950, the number had drastically shrunk, and when one eliminated all the ensembles that were playing strictly nostalgia (revisiting old hits the same old way), there were barely any full-time jazz orchestras left. By 1955, there were only Duke Ellington, Count Basie (whose new band did not even exist in 1950), Stan Kenton, and Woody Herman, and of those four, only Basie's could be considered to be playing swing.

Stan Kenton　During 1949–50, the big bands of Count Basie, Benny Goodman, Artie Shaw, Woody Herman, Dizzy Gillespie, and Charlie Barnet were among those that broke up. Quite typically, Stan Kenton went in the opposite direction of the current trends. He had been exhausted at the end of 1948 and took a year's vacation.

In 1950, he came back with the most adventurous band he ever had, the Innovations Orchestra.

The Innovations Orchestra differed from Kenton's previous groups in that it had a 16-piece string section along with five trumpets, five trombones, tuba, two French horns, five saxophonists, and a five-piece rhythm section. The 39-piece orchestra went on two major tours during 1950–51, performing music that was highly advanced, difficult, and quite dissonant, along with an occasional swing piece, the latter usually arranged by Shorty Rogers. The two-CD set ◉ **The Innovations Orchestra** (Capitol 59965) has all of the music originally issued as the albums **Innovations in Modern Music** and **Stan Kenton Presents** plus 14 other selections. The key players in the band during this time were trumpeters Maynard Ferguson, Shorty Rogers, and Conte Candoli (1951), altoists Art Pepper and Bud Shank, tenor saxophonist Bob Cooper, guitarist Laurindo Almeida, and drummer Shelly Manne, with the main arrangers being Pete Rugolo, Bill Russo, Shorty Rogers, Chico O'Farrill, and Bob Graettinger. Such forbidding works as "Mirage," "Solitaire," "Art Pepper," "Halls of Brass," "House of Strings," and "Coop's Solo" could not have been played by any other orchestra. For further music by this unique ensemble, **And His Innovations Orchestra** (Laserlight 15 770) has ten live performances and the concert of October 14, 1951, can be heard on **Kenton '51** (Jazz Unlimited 2008).

Of all the musicians in Kenton's orchestra in 1950 (which included a lot of alumni from his previous band), Maynard Ferguson was the most significant new addition. Born in Canada where he led his own big band in Montreal, Ferguson was offered a job with Kenton, but when he arrived in the United States in 1949, Kenton was on a year's hiatus. MF spent the time usefully, gaining experience playing with the big bands of Boyd Raeburn, Jimmy Dorsey, and Charlie Barnet. A phenomenal player, Ferguson hit higher notes than any trumpeter up to that time and was able to "screech" on command, never seeming to miss. He added a great deal to Kenton's ensembles and was a solid bop soloist too. When he left Kenton in 1953, MF moved to Los Angeles where he worked in the studios and led a series of albums for EmArcy, none of which have been reissued yet on CD.

Stan Kenton always believed in opening his orchestra up to his arrangers, who were free to write music as complex as they desired. None were more esoteric than Bob Graettinger, an eccentric who wrote dramatic atonal works that were remarkably dense. Kenton recorded "Thermopylae" in 1947, and during 1950–53 Kenton's bands documented such radical pieces as "House of Strings," the three-movements of "City of Glass," and the six pieces that comprised "This Modern World." **Stan Kenton Plays Bob Graettinger** (Capitol 32084) has the complete Graettinger and shows just how far ahead of his time his writing was—third stream works before the mixture of jazz and classical music had its name.

In 1952, after the Innovations Orchestra broke up, Stan Kenton surprised everyone by leading a more swinging big band, utilizing the arrangements of Bill Holman, Bill Russo, Shorty Rogers, Gerry Mulligan, Lennie Niehaus, Marty Paich, and Johnny Richards. Such top soloists as Conte Candoli, Buddy Childers, Stu Williamson, Frank Rosolino, Carl Fontana, Lee Konitz, Charlie Mariano, Richie Kamuca, Zoot Sims, Bill Perkins, Bob Gordon, Jimmy Giuffre, and Sal Salvador spent time with Kenton. The drummers included Frank Capp, Stan Levey, and Mel Lewis, and Chris Connor (eventually succeeded by Ann Richards) took occasional vocals.

Among the band's main recordings of the time was **New Concepts of Artistry in Rhythm** (Capitol 92865) from 1952, which has a few pompous works, but also such swingers as "Portrait of a Count" (Russo's feature for Conte Candoli), "Young Blood," "Swing House," and "My Lady" (which features Konitz). **Kenton Showcase** (Capitol 25244) has some of the highpoints of the 1953–54 orchestra with the music split between Bill Russo and Bill Holman arrangements. Some of the more memorable selections include "Blues Before and After," "Sweets," "Solo for Buddy," "Fearless Findlay," and several features for Lee Konitz. **Sketches on Standards** (Capitol 34070) mostly has the band playing Russo and Kenton charts on tunes not normally associated with this orchestra, including "Begin the Beguine," "Lover Man," "Over the Rainbow," and "Harlem Nocturne." The interpretations are quite concise (mostly around three minutes apiece), but contain their moments of interest and the overall results are rather surprising.

In addition, there are many live recordings of the Stan Kenton band of this era that have been put out by a variety of collector's labels, including Natasha Imports, Status, Artistry, and Magic.

Duke Ellington   Duke Ellington was one of the very few big band leaders from the 1930s who was able to keep his orchestra together nonstop during the 1945–55 period, but it was not without a struggle. Quite often the royalties from his many songs that became standards kept his orchestra afloat. Other than "Satin Doll," which was first recorded in 1953 and took a few years to catch on, there would be no more hit songs. His orchestra in 1950 only recorded seven songs (including four remakes). However, there was no shortage of major players in the orchestra with Ray Nance, Clark Terry, Willie Cook, Cat Anderson, Lawrence Brown, Quentin Jackson, Tyree Glenn, Jimmy Hamilton, Johnny Hodges, Russell Procope, Paul Gonsalves, Harry Carney, bassist Wendell Marshall, and Sonny Greer all still being present. But in early 1951 Ellington received a shock. Hodges left to form his own combo, and he took Brown and Greer with him. Quickly recovering, Ellington raided Harry James's band, getting the services of Willie Smith, Juan Tizol, and Louie Bellson to fill the slots. In Bellson, Ellington had a major drummer (Greer had become increasingly unreliable) and fine writer who contributed "The Hawk Talks" and the drum feature "Skin Deep" to the band's book.

⦿ **Uptown** (Columbia 40836) is the best recording by this "new" Ellington Orchestra and shows that his big band was still in its prime despite its struggles. This set has many classic moments, including Betty Roche's famous bebop vocal on "Take the 'A' Train," a version of "The Mooche" that contrasts the different clarinet styles of Russell Procope and Jimmy Hamilton, some great Clark Terry trumpet on "Perdido," Louie Bellson's drum solo on "Skin Deep," a definitive version of "Harlem," and the two-part "Controversial Suite," which contrasts New Orleans jazz with futuristic music worthy of Stan Kenton.

However, 1952–54 were lean years for Ellington with his band often playing low-level jobs. By 1953, Smith and Bellson (who married singer Pearl Bailey) had departed, and although the orchestra had just signed a new contract with Capitol, many wondered why Ellington continued to struggle with a big band when he could have restricted himself to special engagements. For Duke there was never really any choice, because he loved to write new music and hear it performed immediately. His band recorded all kinds of material for Capitol (including such throwaways as "Blue Jean Beguine," "Bunny Hop Mambo," and "Twelfth Street Rag Mambo") plus a variety of swing standards and jump pieces. One of the most rewarding

Ellington records of the period was actually a set of trio numbers with Wendell Marshall and either Butch Ballard or Dave Black on drums, **Piano Reflections** (Capitol 92863). Ellington's playing is modern, hints at his roots in stride, and is typically individual, highlighted by "Dancers in Love," "Reflections in D," "Melancholia," and "Kinda Dukish." Live recordings of the band, including the five-CD budget set from 1953–54 **Happy Birthday Duke** (Laserlight 15 965) and the two-CD, **In Hamilton** (Radiex 1000) from 1954 show that the orchestra was still remarkably strong despite its lack of commercial success.

In the summer of 1955, Johnny Hodges gave up trying to be a bandleader and returned to Ellington's big band, which now had 11 major soloists (Terry, Cook, Anderson, Nance, Jackson, trombonist Britt Woodman, Hamilton, Hodges, Gonsalves, Carney, and Ellington), a pair of underutilized players in trombonist John Sanders and altoist Russell Procope, plus a solid rhythm section with bassist Jimmy Woode and drummer Sam Woodyard. Duke Ellington knew that this was too great an orchestra to break up, but he needed a stroke of good luck. He would get it in 1956.

Woody Herman's Third Herd   Near the end of 1949, Woody Herman reluctantly broke up his Second Herd. Unlike his original Herd, the later group was a constant money loser despite the success of "Four Brothers," and "Early Autumn." After the breakup, Herman led a septet (which included trumpeter Neal Hefti and Milt Jackson) that played in Cuba in January 1950. Because there were some contractual obligations that needed to be satisfied, Herman formed a new big band in the spring. Unofficially known as the Third Herd, Herman's orchestra retained some of the repertoire of his first two Herds, but also had a full dance book and generally emphasized slower tempos and more melodic music. Among the key players who were with the Third Herd at least part of the time during 1950–55 were trumpeters Conte Candoli, Don Fagerquist, Doug Mettome, Stu Williamson, Dick Collins, and high-note specialist Al Porcino, trombonists Bill Harris, Urbie Green, and Carl Fontana, tenors Phil Urso, Bill Perkins, Dick Hafer, and Richie Kamuca, pianists Dave McKenna and Nat Pierce, and bassist Chubby Jackson. Herman recorded for Capitol through 1950, MGM (1951–52), the tiny Mars label (1952–54), and Columbia before returning to Capitol in the fall of 1954.

While the band's studio recordings are largely unavailable (other than the Capitol recordings, which are part of a large Mosaic box set), **The Third Herd** (Storyville 8241) has three broadcasts from the band in 1951. "Early Autumn" and "More Moon" are heard, but so are a variety of danceable ballads and vocals by Herman and Dolly Houston. Shorty Rogers, Urbie Green, Phil Urso, and Dave McKenna help boost the jazz content, and the arrangements of Ralph Burns and Neal Hefti are generally excellent. Still, this was not a band that was destined to be remembered.

Count Basie   For Count Basie, 1950 began with him in an unusual situation, at the head of a combo rather than a big band. After he reluctantly broke up his orchestra in August 1949, Basie took a little time off and then put together a small group that he called his sextet even though it was sometimes as large as an octet. Such musicians as Harry "Sweets" Edison, Clark Terry, Gene Ammons, Georgie Auld, Wardell Gray, Charlie Rouse, Buddy DeFranco, Serge Chaloff, and altoist Marshall Royal were among the horn players (Terry, DeFranco,

and Gray are all in the band that filmed television transcriptions in 1951) with Freddie Green, bassist Jimmy Lewis, and drummer Gus Johnson usually completing the rhythm section. But enjoyable as this group was, Basie always preferred a big band. By 1951, he was making tentative moves toward forming a new band, having a record date with an orchestra on April 10 that resulted in four titles, including the classic Wardell Gray feature "Little Pony."

Later in 1951, with altoist Marshall Royal helping him gather together musicians, Count Basie formed his second big band. Basie began recording for Norman Granz's Clef label (later Verve) with the only alumnus from the 1940's band being trumpeter Joe Newman and Freddie Green. The rhythm section's function was the same as in the earlier group, but the arrangements were more ensemble-oriented and less dependent on major soloists. The early recordings of the second Basie orchestra are mostly not available on CD yet, so search for the two-LP sets **Paradise Squat** (Verve 2-2542) and **Sixteen Men Swinging** (Verve 2-2517). During this period, the forceful Eddie "Lockjaw" Davis and the floating Paul Quinichette were

TIMELINE 1954

The Clifford Brown-Max Roach Quintet is formed. • Alvin Alcorn begins the trumpeter with Kid Ory's Creole Jazz Band. • Henry "Red" Allen begins an 11-year stint as leader of the house band at New York's Metropole. • Chris Barber takes over the band that he had co-led during the past year with Ken Colyer; Pat Halcox joins on trumpet for at least a 48-year stay. • Eleven-year-old George Benson records two vocal numbers for a Groove 45. • A historic stint at Birdland by Art Blakey leading a quintet with Clifford Brown, Lou Donaldson, Horace Silver, and Curly Russell is recorded by Blue Note and serves as a direct predecessor of the Jazz Messengers. • Willie Bobo joins Tito Puente's band on bongos. • Dave Brubeck appears on the cover of *Time* magazine. • **Red Callender's Speaks Low** (Crown 5012), which has not been reissued on CD, is the first album to feature the tuba as a major solo voice. • Richie Kamuca works with Woody Herman's Third Herd on tenor. • After three years outside of music (working as an advertising salesman in Minneapolis), pianist Lou Levy returns to jazz, leads his first album, and in 1955 becomes Peggy Lee's accompanist. • Blind and 80 years old, W.C. Handy is present during the recording of the monumental **Louis Armstrong Plays W.C. Handy** album. • An intriguing pop/jazz vocal group, the Hi-Lo's, make their recording debut. • Natty Dominique cuts his final recordings, showing that he had continued to decline since 1940. • Soprano saxophonist Steve Lacy (doubling on clarinet) records modern Dixieland with trumpeter Dick Sutton's group. • George Wein, swing pianist and manager of the Storyville club in Boston, founds the Newport Jazz Festival. • Clarinetist Kenny Davern makes his recording debut with Jack Teagarden. • Stride pianist Dick Wellstood records a set of duets with veteran drummer Tommy Benford for the Riverside label. • Stephane Grappelli records his first full-length album as a leader, on piano. • Milt Hinton becomes a staff musician at CBS where he appears on a countless number of recordings. • Amos Milburn has his last hit with "Good Good Whiskey." • Louis Prima and singer Keely Smith begin teaming up with tenor saxophonist Sam Butera and the Witnesses. • Sun Ra's Arkestra in Chicago features tenor saxophonist John Gilmore, altoist Marshall Allen, and baritonist Pat Patrick. • Big Joe Turner's recording of "Shake, Rattle, and Roll" becomes a major hit.

the two contrasting tenors, with Joe Newman being the key trumpet soloist. By 1954, Newman and Thad Jones were the trumpet stars while Frank Foster (who became an important arranger) and Frank Wess were on tenors, with Wess being a pioneer and highly influential soloist on flute. The most important early arrangers were Ernie Wilkins and Neal Hefti, who often utilized the sound of Wess's flute and contributed many songs to Basie's repertoire. **Class of '54** (Black Lion 7600924) is a pair of live performances by Basie's big band, mostly playing Neal Hefti arrangements, and a nonet taken out of the orchestra that includes Newman, trombonist Henry Coker, Wess, and Foster. **Count Basie, Lester Young, and the Stars of Birdland** (Jass 17), which was recorded in Topeka, Kansas, during a tour, has spots for the Basie band, Lester Young (on three numbers), Joe Williams on five others (including an early version of "Every Day I Have the Blues"), and guests Stan Getz and Sarah Vaughan.

1955 was the breakthrough year for the Count Basie Orchestra. First they had a big hit in organist Wild Bill Davis's arrangement of "April in Paris." The CD ◗ **April in Paris** (Verve 314 521 407) not only has that classic chart (which has Basie shouting out "One more, once!"), but also has the original versions of Frank Foster's "Shiny Stockings" and Freddie Green's "Corner Pocket" (both of which would remain permanent parts of the Basie book), plus seven alternate takes. Also in 1955, Joe Williams became the band's regular singer and he was very popular from the start. ◗ **Count Basie Swings, Joe Williams Sings** (Verve 314 519 852) has famous versions of "Every Day I Have the Blues," "Alright, Okay You Win," "The Comeback," and "In the Evening." After the release of these two albums, the Count Basie Orchestra was never in danger of breaking up again, becoming even more popular than it had been a decade earlier and being recognized as a jazz institution. In fact, while other swing era bandleaders struggled to come to grips with the 1950s music scene, and there were a few attempts to revive bands, Count Basie's was the only new swing orchestra to really catch on.

Swing: 1950–1955

With the rise of cool jazz and hard bop, the acceptance of many of bebop's innovations, the continuing popularity of Dixieland, the evolution of Latin jazz, and the beginnings of the avant-garde, it is easy to forget that the swing era (which by the early 1950s already seemed as if

it were ancient history) had ended less than a decade before. The former sidemen with the big bands who had survived the bebop years had a few options. Since they were generally excellent sight-readers, many (particularly whites in those segregated times) became studio musicians who played jazz now and then for the fun of it. Since small-group swing was pretty scarce, some of the musicians (including Rex Stewart and Buck Clayton) learned the Dixieland repertoire and gained employment playing in trad jazz groups, performing music less modern than they had played in their earlier days. A few of the major names reverted to nostalgic swing, revisiting old hits endlessly, but rarely creating anything new. Other musicians, such as Tab Smith and Paul Bascomb, became involved in rhythm and blues, an idiom that (prior to the rise of rock 'n' roll) often employed former swing musicians. "Jazz at the Philharmonic" gave work to a few of the major soloists while others toiled in obscurity, waiting hopefully for the big bands to come back.

In addition to Norman Granz, who recorded some of the top swing veterans for his Norgran, Clef, and Verve labels as well as using them on his JATP tours, John Hammond (who felt lost during the bebop era) produced many fine swing sessions during 1954–56 for the Vanguard label. Around this period, critic Stanley Dance coined the term "mainstream" to describe the small-group music that the swing veterans often played—not as modern as bebop yet more advanced than Dixieland, falling between the cracks. Swing may not have been thriving as an independent movement, but the greats of the swing era were generally not that old (Benny Goodman turned 46 in 1955) and still had something strong to offer the jazz world.

Swing Big Band Leaders: Past and Present

While it was not economically feasible in 1950 to lead a swing-oriented big band, the low quality of pop music of the era coupled with nostalgia for the 1930s led some of the surviving bandleaders, who still had big names, to try their best to bring back the big bands.

Bob Crosby   After getting out of the Marines in 1945, Bob Crosby worked in Los Angeles with a part-time no-name orchestra for a bit. He had a reunion with a few of the Bobcats on some titles in 1950 cut for the Coral label. During 1951–52, Crosby made an attempt to lead a new Bob Crosby Orchestra; among the sidemen were

Charlie Teagarden, trombonist Warren Smith, Matty Matlock, Eddie Miller, Nappy Lamare, and Nick Fatool. **22 Original Big Band Recordings** (Hindsight 409) and **The Bob Crosby Orchestra** (Hindsight 245) both have radio transcriptions mostly from 1952, with a few vocals by June Christy and Polly Bergen on the latter set. Nothing new is heard (there are a lot of remakes and Dixieland standards), but the band sounds excellent. However, the orchestra did not stand a chance and soon broke up. Bob Crosby instead gained work as a personality and occasional singer on television.

The Dorsey Brothers　Both the Tommy and Jimmy Dorsey Orchestras were starting to struggle in 1950. TD ended his longtime contract with Victor, switching to Decca. With Charlie Shavers, tenor saxophonist Boomie Richman, Johnny Guarnieri, and Louis Bellson among those featured with the orchestra (though Guarnieri and Bellson did not stay long), and Sy Oliver and Bill Finegan contributing arrangements, he still had a strong group even if it was stuck in the swing era. The four-CD set **Complete Standard Transcriptions** (Soundies 4115), which alternates between swing instrumentals and vocal ballads, is an excellent example of how Dorsey's orchestra sounded in the early 1950s. Jimmy Dorsey, meanwhile, featured his Original Dorseyland Jazz Band (a Dixieland group taken from his orchestra) as variety in 1950, but otherwise did little of consequence during 1950–52, making few recordings.

In 1953, the Dorseys got back together, 18 years after their original breakup. JD disbanded and became a featured player with the Tommy Dorsey Orchestra, which was soon known as the Dorsey Brothers Orchestra. The joint venture allowed the brothers to call on the hits of two orchestras and to cut their payroll in half. The music that they played was strictly nostalgia swing, quite unadventurous but pleasing to older listeners who remembered the Dorseys' prime days. In 1954, the Dorseys hosted a summer replacement television program, *Stage Show*, that became a regular weekly series for two years, which made it a bit easier for the brothers to keep their orchestra together.

Benny Goodman　After breaking up his 1949 big band, Benny Goodman reverted permanently back to swing. He toured Europe with a septet that included Roy Eldridge, Zoot Sims, pianist Dick Hyman, and guitarist/harmonica player Toots Thielemans, had a recorded reunion with

Teddy Wilson and Gene Krupa in 1951, and formed a new sextet that featured Wilson and Terry Gibbs. Already at this early stage, the King of Swing was somewhat stuck in a time warp, and although he occasionally used more modern players, they were largely restricted to playing his older charts (when he featured a big band) and performing in a minor role in Goodman's small groups.

The release of the 1938 Carnegie Hall Jazz Concert on LPs in 1951 (Goodman had found the only copy of the concert's tapes sitting in his closet) and the release of other airchecks of the period resulted in interest building in BG putting together an orchestra again. In 1953, Goodman formed a new big band and a tour was set up to feature his orchestra along with Louis Armstrong's All-Stars. If the big bands were going to come back, BG was going to lead the way. His new band featured such fine swing players as Billy Butterfield, Jimmy Maxwell, and Chris Griffin in the trumpet section, trombonists Lou McGarity and Cutty Cutshall, the tenors of Boomie Richman and Al Klink, and Helen Ward coming out of retirement. Four songs were recorded at the February 23, 1953, record date for Columbia (including "I'll Never Say 'Never Again' Again") and one at a second session. Would this be the rebirth of the swing era?

In negotiations, Goodman had insisted that his orchestra follow Armstrong rather than be the opening act. That was a fatal mistake for Satch consistently broke up the show with his exciting set, and then BG's band was considered anticlimactic. Whether it was the pressure or just him wanting to get out of a losing situation is not known, but soon Goodman quit, citing health reasons; Gene Krupa finished the tour in his place. The second swing era never did occur.

In late 1954, Goodman led a sextet with Charlie Shavers and old friend Mel Powell. Due to the success of *The Glenn Miller Story* that year (starring Jimmy Stewart), *The Benny Goodman Story* was filmed in 1955, with Steve Allen in Goodman's role. While BG played the clarinet solos, very little about the moderately entertaining but very musical film was true; however, it did result in more attention being paid to Goodman. Two albums based on the soundtrack were recorded, and in addition, BG led an excellent octet that featured Ruby Braff, Paul Quinichette, and Teddy Wilson.

Sextet (Columbia 40379) has some of the best small-group playing by Goodman from 1950–52, heading a group featuring the exciting vibraphonist Terry Gibbs and

Teddy Wilson. Their explosive version of "Undecided" is a highlight. **B.G. in Hi-Fi** (Capitol 92864) has Goodman performing a dozen selections (mostly Fletcher Henderson arrangements) with a big band filled with sympathetic players in 1954 plus eight other numbers with a pair of smaller units that also feature Mel Powell and either Charlie Shavers or Ruby Braff on trumpets. After his death, the clarinetist willed many private recordings to Yale University, some of which have since been issued. **Yale Recordings, Vol. 2: Live at Basin Street** (Music Masters 5006) features Goodman's 1955 septet in top form. The band (which includes Ruby Braff, Paul Quinichette, and Teddy Wilson) primarily performs swing standards, but the strong solos inspire Goodman to play with a lot of fire and enthusiasm. His music may no longer have offered any real surprises, but Benny Goodman was still at the top of his game much of the time.

Lionel Hampton   Lionel Hampton led big bands on and off during 1950–55. Little Jimmy Scott was with the orchestra in 1950, singing "Everybody's Somebody's Fool" and "I Wish I Knew." Among the sidemen were trumpeter Benny Bailey, trombonists Al Grey and Jimmy Cleveland, altoist Jerome Richardson, tenor saxophonist Johnny Board, and pianist Milt Buckner. Quincy Jones joined as a trumpeter/arranger in 1951 (the year that the band switched from Decca to MGM). Hampton had potentially his greatest band in 1953, an outfit with Quincy Jones, Clifford Brown, Art Farmer, Jimmy Cleveland, Gigi Gryce, tenor saxophonist Clifford Solomon, George Wallington, and Annie Ross. Unfortunately, they never recorded as a unit in the studios, and when Hampton (for unknown reasons) forbade his underpaid musicians from making freelance recordings during a European tour, they soon disobeyed him and it doomed the band. A year later, Hamp had a new big band (including cornetist Nat Adderley and pianist Dwike Mitchell), but he never again led a significant orchestra. His future bands tended to have a very predictable repertoire and their main role was to support the vibraphonist.

Hampton's best recordings after 1950 tended to be in small groups. His encounter with Stan Getz (reviewed earlier in this chapter) is classic, and **Lionel Hampton Quintet** (Verve 589 100) is an exciting matchup with Buddy DeFranco, Oscar Peterson, Ray Brown, and Buddy Rich. Highlights include a 17-minute version of "Flying

Home," "On the Sunny Side of the Street," and a very heated romp on "It's Only a Paper Moon."

Fletcher Henderson   Fletcher Henderson's career came to an end in 1950. He had been leading low-level big bands since the mid-1940s without much success. In December 1950, he played at Café Society Downtown with a sextet that also included trumpeter Dick Vance, clarinetist Eddie Barefield, and Lucky Thompson on tenor. The band broadcast on December 20–21, 1950, and the performances were put out on a budget LP, **Fletcher Henderson's Sextet** (Alamac 2444). The pianist is heard in solid form playing swing standards while Thompson stars among the soloists. But on December 22, Fletcher Henderson suffered a major stroke that put him permanently out of action; he died two years later at the age of 55.

Harry James   It would be very easy to classify Harry James as a has-been in the 1950s since his last real hits were in 1945, though there were a couple of early 1950s collaborations with Doris Day that sold well. His flirtation with bebop during 1947–49 was over, and his music had reverted back to swing. However, the trumpeter still played well and remained a household name. Though he lost Juan Tizol, Willie Smith, and Louie Bellson in early 1951 to Duke Ellington (in what was dubbed "The Great James Robbery"), Herbie Steward was a good replacement on alto, Buddy Rich joined the band in 1953, Corky Corcoran proved to be a fine tenor soloist, and Smith and Tizol eventually returned. But James seemed content to alternate between endlessly replaying his hits, including in the solid selling but overly predictable **In Hi-Fi** album of 1955 and trying to emulate Count Basie, using Neal Hefti as one of his main arrangers. It was becoming clear that Harry James was offering nothing new to the jazz world.

Gene Krupa   The Gene Krupa Orchestra remained together (with less and less success) into 1951. Krupa then formed a trio, not for variety as before but as his main band. At first the group was a reunion with Charlie Ventura and pianist Teddy Napoleon (touring with "Jazz at the Philharmonic"). By 1954, Eddie Shu was in Ventura's place, switching between tenor, alto, clarinet, trumpet, and harmonica. Bobby Scott was on piano, with a variety of different bassists actually making the group a quartet, including John Drew by 1955. Krupa was no longer seriously thought of as jazz's top drummer, but he remained a popular figure, and on drum battle records with Buddy Rich, Rich took it easy to give Krupa a chance.

Billy May   A major arranger from the swing era who gained his early fame with Charlie Barnet (1938–40) and Glenn Miller (1940–42), May spent the postwar years working at NBC studios and Capitol. In 1951, he put together a studio big band that was surprisingly popular and lasted on a part-time basis for three years. **A Band Is Born/Big Band Bash** (Collectors Choice Music 135) is a single CD that has the first two albums by the Billy May big band (1951–52) and displays the sliding sax sound that was his trademark on a variety of swing standards. Such tunes as "All of Me," "Lulu's Back in Town," "When My Sugar Walks Down the Street," "Easy Street," "When I Take My Sugar to Tea," and "Fat Man Boogie" are given colorful arrangements that swing while also sometimes making good-natured fun of themselves.

Artie Shaw   After Artie Shaw's bebop big band of 1949 failed to catch on, he briefly led a thrown-together swing orchestra to fulfill obligations. During 1950–53, he recorded a few isolated titles with big bands, performances that were long forgotten, but are not without interest. In 1953, Shaw put together a new Gramercy Five, consisting of Hank Jones, Tal Farlow (or Joe Puma), Tommy Potter, drummer Irv Kluger, and sometimes vibraphonist Joe Roland. During the next year, Shaw played boppish versions of standards with this outfit and showed that he was still at the top of his game. In fact, when one listens to the many performances by this last Gramercy Five that are included on the definitive five-CD sampler ◉ **Self-Portrait** (Bluebird 63808), it is apparent that Shaw was still getting better with age. Listeners who want more of the classic (if greatly underrated) group are advised to also pick up a pair of two-CD sets, **The Last Recordings** (Music Masters 65071) and **More Last Recordings** (Music Masters 65101), which add to the legacy of this great band. Listen to Shaw's reworking of such songs as "Begin the Beguine," "Stardust," "Summit Ridge Drive," and "Frenesi" into fresh new pieces.

Frustrated by the public's indifference to this group (they wanted to hear him in a big band recreating the past) and having strong interests in other areas (such as writing),

Artie Shaw in 1955 retired permanently from music. He was just 44, and although he continued following the music scene, he has not played clarinet in public since.

Other Swing Soloists

In addition to the former big band leaders, some of the star sidemen continued to play swing in small-group mainstream settings and occasionally in big bands. They may not have been featured on hit records, but their style remained timeless.

Lawrence Brown   Although Lawrence Brown was well known in jazz since the early 1930s, he only led two record dates in his life. Brown, who had played with Paul Howard's Quality Serenaders (1929–30) and Les Hite in Los Angeles, became famous during his 19-year stint with Duke Ellington (1932–51). His strong technique and distinctive sound on trombone were greatly admired by his fellow musicians. Brown played with Johnny Hodges's band during 1951–55 and then became a studio musician. **Slide Trombone** (Verve 314 559 930) features Brown in a quintet with tenor saxophonist Sam "The Man" Taylor and in a nonet with Al Cohn and Hank Jones. As with the style of the Johnny Hodges band, this music sounds very much like a small group taken from the Ellington band even though only Brown and Louis Bellson (who is on the Taylor session) were Duke alumni. Highlights include Brown's longtime feature "Rose of the Rio Grande," "Caravan," "You Took Advantage of Me," and "Blues for Duke."

Don Byas   Though forgotten in the United States after moving away in 1946, tenor saxophonist Don Byas was quite active in Europe during the 1950s, recording frequently for Blue Star and Vogue. **Don Byas on Blue Star** (EmArcy 833 405) repeats six titles from the Classics CD **1947**, but also includes 16 selections from 1950–52 with French and American rhythm sections. Byas shows that being overseas had not resulted in his style being any less powerful, and he really tears into some of the swing standards. But it is a pity that there was no demand for him to return home and tour the United States.

Benny Carter   In the early 1950s, altoist Benny Carter (who was working steadily in the Hollywood studios) went on a few tours with "Jazz at the Philharmonic" and did some recording for Norman Granz's labels. Three CDs (totaling four discs) have reissued all of his work as a leader from 1952–55. **Cosmopolite: The Oscar Peterson Verve Sessions** (Verve 314 521 673) teams Carter with the Oscar Peterson Trio (with Barney Kessel or Herb Ellis and Ray Brown) plus one of three drummers and (on four numbers) trombonist Bill Harris. Carter swings tastefully throughout the 17 standards and four alternate takes. **3, 4, 5—The Verve Small Group Sessions** (Verve 849 395) has Carter playing in a trio with Teddy Wilson and Jo Jones, in a quartet with pianist Don Abney, and performing a few additional numbers with Peterson, Ellis, Brown, and drummer Bobby White. **New Jazz Sounds: The Urbane Sessions** (Verve 314 531 637) is a particularly worthy two-CD set. The first half has Carter's alto backed by strings (Joe Glover and Carter provided all of the surprisingly stimulating arrangements) while the second disc teams Carter in a quintet with Roy Eldridge. There are also four unusual trumpet-drums duets by Eldridge and Alvin Stoller, a leftover track from the Peterson dates, and two jams by a septet with Dizzy Gillespie and Bill Harris. Everything works well.

Buck Clayton   When Buck Clayton returned to the United States in 1950, the trumpeter was at the crossroads of his career. Because swing was out of style and Dixieland had become popular, Clayton hurriedly learned all of the trad jazz standards (particularly while playing with the groups of Joe Bushkin and Tony Parenti) so he would be able to work more. **Dr. Jazz Series Vol. 3** (Storyville 6043), which is taken from the *Dr. Jazz* radio series of 1951–52, features Clayton playing such Dixieland warhorses as "There'll Be Some Changes Made," "Struttin' with Some Barbecue," "Mahogany Hall Stomp," and "Muskrat Ramble" in a sextet with trombonist Herb Flemming, Buster Bailey, and Ken Kersey. Clayton sounds surprisingly comfortable jamming in this setting, playing Kansas City swing solos once the heated ensembles were dispensed with.

Fortunately, Clayton had a champion in producer John Hammond, who recorded Buck in favorable settings for the Vanguard label, some of which are on **The Essential Buck Clayton** (Vanguard 103/4). The three sessions from 1953–54 and 1957 match Clayton on 14 swinging songs (seven of which are his originals) with such players as Edmond Hall, Vic Dickenson, Kenny Burrell, Ruby Braff, Buddy Tate, and Benny Morton. Even better are the series of Buck Clayton Jam sessions that the

trumpeter led for Columbia during 1953–56, all of which were reissued on the limited-edition six-CD box set **Complete CBS Buck Clayton Jam Sessions** (Mosaic 6-144). The lengthy performances (which take advantage of the extra time available on LP) perfectly define mainstream swing. Clayton provided background riffs and frameworks that uplift these jam sessions. Among the notable veterans who took part are trumpeters Joe Newman, Joe Thomas, Ruby Braff, Billy Butterfield, trombonists Trummy Young, Urbie Green, Benny Powell, Henderson Chambers, Bennie Green, Dickie Harris, Tyree Glenn, and J.C. Higginbotham, altoist Lem Davis, tenors Julian Dash, Coleman Hawkins, Buddy Tate, and Al Cohn, baritonist Charles Fowlkes, pianists Sir Charles Thompson, Billy Kyle, Al Waslohn, and Ken Kersey, the rhythm guitars of Freddie Green and Steve Jordan, bassists Walter Page and Milt Hinton, and drummers Jo Jones and Bobby Donaldson. This essential box (which features Buck Clayton at his best) will soon be very difficult to find, and the individual sessions (originally issued as the LPs **How Hi the Fi, Moten Swing/Sentimental Journey, Hucklebuck/Robbins' Nest, All the Cats Join In, Jumpin' at the Woodside**, and **Buck Clayton Jams Benny Goodman Favorites**) are mostly not available individually yet on CD.

Vic Dickenson   Vic Dickenson was a busy freelancer during the first half of the 1950s, mostly playing in Boston and New York. During 1953–54, John Hammond gave the trombonist an opportunity to lead his own sessions for Vanguard. All seven songs from the November 29, 1954, date and two of the five numbers from December 29, 1953, are on **Nice Work** (Vanguard 79610). Dickenson is mostly heard in a septet with trumpeter Shad Collins, Edmond Hall, Sir Charles Thompson, Steve Jordan, Walter Page, and Jo Jones, with Ruby Braff sitting in on two numbers. The earlier session has the same group except that Braff is in Collins's place and Les Erskine is on drums. Highlights of this fine mainstream swing set include "Russian Lullaby," a 12-minute rendition of "Jeepers Creepers," "Old Fashioned Love," and "Everybody Loves My Baby."

Roy Eldridge   In 1950, Roy Eldridge was at a turning point in his career. Formerly proud of his status as the most inventive and advanced trumpeter, "Little Jazz" had seen a new generation of bop-oriented players (led by Dizzy Gillespie) make him sound old-fashioned in comparison. Should he chuck the style he had formed and follow the boppers? Right at that time, he was offered a chance to tour France with Benny Goodman. The trip was so successful that he stayed overseas for a year, felt the acclaim of the French jazz fans, and decided that being modern was not as important as simply being himself.

Roy Eldridge in Paris (Vogue 68209) has the complete output (including seven alternate takes) from two exciting recording sessions. Eldridge heads a quintet with Zoot Sims and pianist Dick Hyman (two songs have vocals from Anita Love), and Roy does a good job of singing the good-humored "Ain't No Flies on Me." While "Wrap Your Troubles in Dreams" (heard in two versions) is the classic of that session, the later date also has Eldridge in top form (particularly on "If I Had You" and "Someone to Watch Over Me") with a quartet comprised of Gerald Wiggins, Pierre Michelot, and Kenny Clarke. Eldridge's other European dates (including an exciting encounter with Don Byas and duets on "Wild Man Blues" and "Fireworks" with pianist Claude Bolling) unfortunately remain scarce.

Upon his return to the United States, Eldridge signed with Norman Granz, began recording for his Clef and Verve labels in very favorable settings, including a couple of albums with the Oscar Peterson Trio, and continued being one of the stars of JATP where he battled Charlie Shavers and Dizzy Gillespie during separate tours. ❍ **Roy & Diz** (Verve 314 521 647) must have been highly satisfying for Eldridge for he matches wits with Dizzy Gillespie (while backed by the Oscar Peterson Trio and Louie Bellson) and holds his own. These versions of "I've Found a New Baby" and "Limehouse Blues" are extremely exciting and feature the two trumpeters at their most competitive. There was no way that Eldridge was going to let "the young upstart" (who was already 37) defeat him, and Dizzy (respect aside) was not going to let a swing stylist (even if it was his idol) make him look bad. A ballad medley and a few slower pieces are also included, but it is the two heated jams that are overflowing with fireworks between these two greats.

Erroll Garner   Erroll Garner's popularity continued to grow during the first half of the 1950s. The pianist's style was naturally very melodic and accessible, so he did not have to alter his playing in the slightest to gain widespread recognition, and both critics and the general public generally applauded his efforts. Garner recorded

quite extensively for Roost, Atlantic, Columbia, and EmArcy/Mercury. The pianist seemed incapable of having an off day, so all of his recordings (particularly the ones that he made quite spontaneously) are worth hearing. **Long Ago and Far Away** (Columbia 40863) from 1950–51 has such romps as "When Johnny Comes Marching Home," "When You're Smiling," and "Lover," while **Body and Soul** (Columbia 47035) continues into 1952 with "The Way You Look Tonight," "Indiana," "Honeysuckle Rose," "Robbins' Nest," and "You're Driving Me Crazy" among many others. But with the joyous Garner style, the tunes mattered less than the pianist's joyful enthusiasm. On July 27, 1954, Garner had a typical recording session. With his regular trio of the period (bassist Wyatt Ruther and drummer Fats Heard) plus Candido guesting on conga, Garner recorded 24 songs (all first takes), 13 of which are reissued on **Contrasts** (EmArcy 558 077), including the earliest recorded version of his best-known composition, "Misty." Other highlights include "I've Got the World on a String," a lengthy "7-11 Jump," "There's a Small Hotel," and "I've Got to Be a Rugcutter." Also easily recommended from 1954–55 by the prolific Garner are **Too Marvelous for Words** (EmArcy 842 419), the two-CD set **Solo Time** (EmArcy 511 821), which was entirely recorded on July 7, 1954, and **Solitaire** (Mercury 518 279).

And yet when one thinks of the definitive Erroll Garner recording, it is of ❍ **Concert by the Sea** (Columbia 40859). Recorded on September 19, 1955, this live set with bassist Eddie Calhoun and drummer Denzil Best is even more inspired than usual and features a wonderful all-around set including "I'll Remember April," "Teach Me Tonight," "It's Alright with Me," "Red Top," and "Where or When." One can debate that some other Erroll Garner sets might be better in some way, but this is the album that made such a strong impression that Garner was considered immortal from then on.

Bennie Green   One of the few trombonists of the 1950s who was not overly influenced by J.J. Johnson, Bennie Green had a witty sound and a full tone that looked back to the swing era yet was open to the influence of R&B. Green worked with the Earl Hines big band during 1942–48 (other than two years in the military), Charlie Ventura (1948–50), and Hines's small group (1951–53) before leading groups of his own. **Bennie Green Blows His Horn** (Original Jazz Classics 1728) has Green in 1955 blending in well with tenor saxophonist Charlie Rouse on standards, blues, and jump tunes, two of which have group vocals. Utilizing a fine rhythm section (pianist Cliff Smalls, Paul Chambers, drummer Osie Johnson, and Candido on congas), Green and his band put on a fun and happy performance filled with swinging music.

Coleman Hawkins For Coleman Hawkins, 1950–55 is considered a bit of an off period. Not that the great tenor played badly or showed any decline, but he was overshadowed in the jazz world by Charlie Parker, Lester Young, and the cool jazz tenors (including Stan Getz), and even by Sonny Rollins, who would be the first to say that he owed his sound to Hawkins. There were fewer opportunities to record than there were earlier and some of the dates were easy-listening in nature. **Body and Soul Revisited** (GRP/Decca 627) has ten selections of melodic "mood" music from 1951–53 in which Hawkins mostly sticks to the melody (an exception is an excellent version of "If I Could Be with You"). The great tenor is also heard in an occasionally exciting session with Cozy Cole's All-Stars, where Rex Stewart sometimes steals the show. In addition, there is a 1955 radio broadcast in which Hawkins plays "Foolin' Around" (based on the chords of "Body and Soul") totally unaccompanied, and roars on "The Man I Love." This interesting CD concludes with three selections (one previously unissued) from a later session led by Tony Scott.

Coleman Hawkins was far from through. He was always proud of being a modern player, and he would soon be taking a few more steps forward.

Johnny Hodges Johnny Hodges was such a reliable soloist for Duke Ellington (who he joined in 1928) that it was a shock in 1951 when the altoist decided to form his own combo, taking Lawrence Brown and Sonny Greer with him. Hodges led a septet that initially also included trumpeter Nelson Williams, pianist Leroy Lovett, bassist Al McKibbon, and former Ellington tenor Al Sears. Emmett Berry soon took over on trumpet and Lloyd Trotman became the bassist. Hodges got lucky by recording a hit version of "Castle Rock," an R&B-ish blues that featured Sears; the altoist is barely even on the record. During the next few years, Hodges's combo worked regularly, but never got away from sounding like a small group taken out of Ellington's band. Other sidemen included drummers Joe Marshall, J.C. Heard, and

Louie Bellson (Greer did not last long), bassists Barney Richmond, Red Callender, and John Williams, pianist Call Cobbs, trumpeter Shorty Baker, and tenors Ben Webster and John Coltrane (who unfortunately did not solo on his one session with the band).

All of the music by Hodges's band was reissued years ago on a six-LP Mosaic box set. Unfortunately, most of the performances are now unavailable other than **Used to Be Duke** (Verve 849394) from 1954, which has the Coltrane date, "On the Sunny Side of the Street," and a seven-song ballad medley. In mid-1955, Hodges gave up trying to be a bandleader and returned to Ellington for another 15-year stint.

Meade Lux Lewis By 1954, both Jimmy Yancey and Albert Ammons were dead and Pete Johnson was living in obscurity in Buffalo. Meade Lux Lewis, however, remained quite active in the Los Angeles area and kept the legacy of boogie-woogie piano alive. **Cat House Piano** (Verve 557 098) has all of the music from Lewis's two Verve LPs of 1954–55. The earlier date is a set of duets with Louie Bellson, while the later session finds Lewis accompanied by Red Callender and drummer Jo Jones. With 76 minutes of playing, the amount of music is generous. The only problem is that there is a definite sameness to the 14 selections (which mostly clock in between four and seven minutes), the majority of which are medium-tempo blues romps. It is advisable to listen to this set in small doses, but the overall momentum of the music is difficult to resist.

Oscar Moore Formerly with the Nat King Cole Trio (1938–47) and his brother Johnny Moore's Three Blazers, guitarist Oscar Moore had three opportunities to lead his own record dates during 1953–55. In addition to four songs cut for Verve (and long out of print), Moore made two albums for the Tampa label with pianist Carl Perkins, bassist Joe Comfort, and drummer George Jenkins (who is believed to be Lee Young) with Mike Pacheco sometimes added on bongos; those two albums are available as the single CD **Oscar Moore Quartet** (V.S.O.P. 34). The results are melodic, easy-listening swing with such songs as "There'll Never Be Another You," "April in Paris," and "The Nearness of You" given pleasing if unadventurous treatment. Unfortunately, the great commercial success of Nat King Cole in the 1950s did not touch his former guitarist at all, and Oscar Moore soon slipped away into complete obscurity.

Hot Lips Page   Although he never became a household name, Hot Lips Page remained popular in jazz circles in the early 1950s. His hot swing trumpet solos and blues vocals were versatile enough to fit comfortably in both swing and Dixieland settings. **Dr. Jazz Series Vol. 6** (Storyville 6046) features him in the latter setting on radio broadcasts from 1951. Page is joined by such stars as drummer George Wettling (who is actually the leader of these groups), Wild Bill Davison, Lou McGarity, Pee Wee Russell, Bob Wilber, Peanuts Hucko, Dick Cary, and Joe Sullivan among others. Hot Lips is in exuberant form whether singing tunes such as "When My Sugar Walks Down the Street" and a riotous "St. Louis Blues" or leading the ensembles. Hot Lips Page recorded a few titles during 1952–54, but died from a heart attack late in 1954 at the age of 46.

Les Paul and Mary Ford   After Les Paul began teaming with country singer Mary Ford (who soon became his wife), utilizing inventive and massive overdubs of his guitar and Ford's voice, the team of Les Paul and Mary Ford became a constant on the pop charts, having one novelty hit after another during 1949–55. Among their best sellers were "How High the Moon," "Tiger Rag," "Nola," "Little Rock Getaway," "The World Is Waiting for the Sunrise," "Whispering," "Carioca," "Smoke Rings," and "Bye Bye Blues." These were all swing standards, but performed in a very different way and are all included in the definitive four-CD box **The Legend & The Legacy** (Capitol 97654). Les Paul may have left his jazz improvising behind, but his inventive pop material should be of interest to jazz listeners.

Flip Phillips   Flip Phillips was a regular star on the "Jazz at the Philharmonic" tours during 1946–57. The tenor also recorded regularly as a leader for Norman Granz's labels during 1949–54. While all of his Verve and Clef performances have been reissued (along with Charlie Ventura's 1950s records) as a limited-edition Mosaic box set, **Flip Wails: The Best of the Verve Years** (Verve 521 645) is a solid single-disc sampler of this period. Its 20 selections cover the entire period, and though the focus is mostly on the stomping tenor, Bill Harris, Howard McGhee and Charlie Shavers also have their spots. The CD, which contains high-quality modern swing music that is influenced by bop, has some fine examples of Phillips's infectious playing.

Mel Powell   By the early 1950s, pianist Mel Powell (formerly with Benny Goodman and the Glenn Miller Army Air Force Band) was shifting his career toward becoming a classical composer. He studied with Paul Hindermith at Yale (1952), but was persuaded by John Hammond to lead a series of six mainstream swing dates for Vanguard during 1953–55. In all, 39 selections were recorded, but the current Vanguard reissue program has just reissued 33, and made it very confusing by shuffling together the numbers from different sessions in random order. **The Best Things in Life** (Vanguard 79602) has music from four of the dates, while **It's Been So Long** (Vanguard 79605) has at least one selection from five. Along the way, Powell is heard with Buck Clayton and Edmund Hall in a septet, in separate trios with either Ruby Braff or Paul Quinichette, heading an octet that includes Boomie Richman on tenor, jamming with Peanuts Hucko in a septet, and matching wits with Ruby Braff and Oscar Pettiford in a quintet. Powell's timeless swing piano style is featured at its prime, but it would be three decades before he would be heard in jazz settings again.

Django Reinhardt   It has been written far too often that Django Reinhardt, having reached his peak with Stephane Grappelli and the Quintet of the Hot Club of France during 1934–39, declined in his postwar years, struggling unsuccessfully both with the electric guitar and bebop. Although his recordings of 1947 do sound a bit awkward, by 1951 Django was actually among the finest electric guitarists in jazz. He had adopted the innovations of bebop into his own musical vocabulary and was playing in peak form again.

Peche à la Mouche (Verve 354 418), a double CD, has his Blue Star recordings of 1947 and 1953. Most of the earlier tracks feature Reinhardt in a later version of the Quintet of the Hot Club of France with clarinetist Hubert Rostaing, and there are two numbers with Rex Stewart. But it is the eight later selections in which he is backed by a standard rhythm section that are particularly interesting, making one realize that he could have held his own against Tal Farlow and Barney Kessel had he ventured to the United States. **Brussels and Paris** (DRG 8473) has a different date with Rostaing in 1947 and features Django with a variety of combos during 1951–53, sounding like he is ready to challenge the world.

Unfortunately, that was not to be. Norman Granz had talked with Django Reinhardt about possibly touring the United States, but the guitarist died on May 16, 1953, from a stroke at the age of 43.

Hazel Scott A fine pianist who often played swing versions of classical themes, Hazel Scott spent much of her career on the periphery of jazz. She was a popular nightclub pianist since she was a teenager in the late 1930s, although she gained the most attention as the wife of the controversial congressman Adam Clayton Powell. In 1955, she recorded her only completely straightforward jazz album, faring pretty well in a trio with Charles Mingus and Max Roach throughout **Relaxed Piano Moods** (Original Jazz Classics 1702), a rather brief six-song date that has been expanded with a seventh song and two alternate takes. Best are "Like Someone in Love," "The Jeep Is Jumpin'," and "A Foggy Day."

Jess Stacy In 1947, Jess Stacy, having broken up his big band and seeing the end of his marriage to Lee Wiley, moved to Los Angeles where he played in relative obscurity for years. Though he made some trio dates for Columbia, Brunswick, and Atlantic, his only band session during the 1950s was **A Tribute to Benny Goodman** (Koch 8506). Stacy (still in excellent form at age 50) leads a reunion of swing veterans (many of whom were Goodman alumni) in a nonet through such songs as "King Porter Stomp," "When Buddha Smiles," "Roll 'Em," "Don't Be that Way," and a surprisingly brief "Sing, Sing, Sing." This set (which has four Stacy trio features) is actually most significant for being the last important session featuring Ziggy Elman, who worked in the studios until his health declined.

Art Tatum Art Tatum continued playing miraculous music throughout the first half of the 1950s, and still sounded ahead stylistically of the other jazz pianists. He befriended Oscar Peterson and was quite aware of Bud Powell, but did not feel any need to alter his style with the passing of years. **20th Century Piano Genius** (Verve 314 531 763) is a two-CD set that features Tatum playing solo at private parties in 1950 and 1955, sounding quite relaxed, stretching out a bit (nine songs exceed four minutes), and effectively throwing in plenty of double-time and even triple-time lines.

In 1953, Norman Granz began recording Tatum prolifically in two different projects: as a soloist and in all-star

combos. The latter will be covered in the next chapter. The piano solos, which have been reissued in the seven-CD set **The Complete Pablo Solo Masterpieces** (Pablo 7PACD-4404), are fine but not as startling as one might expect, for they were recorded in marathon sessions without much planning. Tatum simply ran through one song after another, and a certain sameness of tempo and mood makes this project a slight disappointment, especially compared to the pianist's more exciting Decca solo sessions of the 1930s.

It is a pity that Art Tatum never recorded with "Jazz at the Philharmonic," for one could imagine the mutual inspiration that would have occurred if he had teamed with Dizzy Gillespie or Lester Young.

Sir Charles Thompson A transitional figure whose piano style fell between swing and bop, Sir Charles Thompson was often cast in the role of a surrogate Count Basie in the 1950s, particularly on sessions that he cut (as a leader and sideman) for Vanguard in John Hammond's mainstream swing series. Of the 19 selections that he recorded as a leader for Vanguard during 1953–55, a dozen are on **For the Ears** (Vanguard 79604). Thompson is heard in a sextet with Joe Newman, trombonist Benny Powell, and Pete Brown (who rarely recorded during this era), an octet with Coleman Hawkins, Emmett Berry, Earl Warren, and Benny Morton, and a drumless trio with guitarist Skeeter Best and bassist Aaron Bell. The four songs from a session with the former Count Basie rhythm section of Freddie Green, Walter Page, and Jo Jones are skipped entirely. The swinging Basie-oriented music that has been reissued is excellent, but where is the rest of it?

Ben Webster Ben Webster, after leaving the Duke Ellington Orchestra a second time in 1949, spent some time living in Kansas City before returning to New York and freelancing. After a couple of sessions with EmArcy, in 1953 he signed with Norman Granz and started recording for Verve (in addition to continuing to play with "Jazz at the Philharmonic"). Webster's Verve recordings would be some of the finest of his career, perfectly contrasting the tenor's roars on uptempo tunes with his purrs on ballads. **King of the Tenors** (Verve 314 519 806) has Webster in 1953 playing five songs with the Oscar Peterson Quartet and six with a septet that includes Benny Carter and Harry "Sweets" Edison. Highlights include "Tenderly," "Bounce Blues," "Pennies from Heaven," "Cotton Tail," and "Danny Boy." **Music for Living** (Verve 314 527 774) is a remarkably generous two-CD set that reissues two Webster albums with strings (originally titled **Music for Loving** and **Music with Feeling**) that have Ralph Burns arrangements, five alternate takes, one song from a sampler, four tunes by Webster in a quartet with Teddy Wilson, plus the eight cuts from the unrelated album **Harry Carney with Strings** (one of only two records ever led by the Ellington baritonist). The emphasis throughout is on warm ballads, played by Ben Webster in prime form.

Jimmy Yancey Jimmy Yancey, one of the pioneer boogie-woogie pianists and a very gentle player, died on September 17, 1951, at the age of 57 from diabetes. Two months before, he recorded 14 piano solos that have been reissued as **Chicago Piano, Vol. 1** (Atlantic 82368). Yancey is in surprisingly good form on these introspective and often emotional performances (one gets the impression that he knew that the end was near). Other than Meade Lux Lewis's "Yancey Special" and the traditional "Make Me a Pallet on the Floor," all of the music is comprised of originals by the classic pianist, with his wife Mama Yancey taking five memorable vocals. Although it would be easy to copy Jimmy Yancey's notes, no one has quite recreated his spirit.

Latin Jazz

The combination of bebop with Cuban rhythms (sometimes called Cubop), continued in the early 1950s, particularly in the work of the great arranger Chico O'Farrill and Machito's ensemble. Perez Prado's hit records started a mambo craze, and conga players (including Candido, who moved to the United States in 1952) began to appear on otherwise straightahead jazz dates. Vibraphonist Cal Tjader recorded his earliest Latin jazz records, and in Cuba bassist Cachao (with pianist Bebo Valdes's band) recorded the first "descarga" (Cuban jam session). The "big three" bandleaders of Cuban dance music—which included everything from pop and straight Cuban songs to boppish jazz—were Machito, Tito Puente, and singer Tito Rodriguez. The two Titos had legendary battles at New York's Palladium to see who would be given top billing when they were booked together. Much of their music during this era was vocal-dominated and geared strictly to dancers, but the influence of jazz was felt in the ensembles. And by 1955,

Puente (who mostly played timbales) was joined in his rhythm section by Mongo Santamaria on conga and Willie Bobo on bongos. Add to the mix the continuing support given Afro-Cuban jazz by Dizzy Gillespie, Stan Kenton, and George Shearing, and it is clear that Latin jazz now had to be considered a permanent part of the musical landscape.

Chico O'Farrill One of the great arrangers, Chico O'Farrill was expert at combining Latin rhythms with sophisticated jazz. Born Arturo O'Farrill in Havana, Cuba, he started out as a trumpeter while in military school in Georgia. Back in Cuba, he studied composition and led his own band, giving up the trumpet in 1946 to concentrate on writing. In 1948, O'Farrill moved to New York City where he ghostwrote some charts for Gil Fuller, contributed to Benny Goodman's bebop big band (including "Undercurrent Blues"), and wrote some Afro-Cuban pieces for Stan Kenton (including "Cuban Episode"), Dizzy Gillespie, Miguelito Valdes, and Machito. He was given the nickname of Chico by Goodman. O'Farrill led his own band for a few years in the 1950s and wrote the four-part "Manteca Suite" for Dizzy Gillespie in 1954.

⦿ **Cuban Blues** (Verve 314 533 256) is a two-CD set that has all of Chico O'Farrill's early Norgran and Clef dates as a leader (1950–54), some of the most exciting Afro-Cuban jazz dates ever. Both of O'Farrill's Afro-Cuban Jazz Suites are here, including the initial project, which features Machito's Orchestra with guests Charlie Parker, Flip Phillips, and Buddy Rich. Other musicians taking part along the way include Mario Bauza, Doug Mettome, Roy Eldridge, Harry "Sweets" Edison, Eddie Bert, Bill Harris, Herb Geller, Ray Brown, pianist Rene Hernandez, and percussionists Candido, José Mangual, Luis Marinda, Carlos Vidal, Chino Pozo, and Machito. The lengthy suites and such classic miniatures as "JATP Mambo," "Cuban Blues," "The Peanut Vendor," "Malaguena," "Havana Special," and "Siboney" are all quite memorable, infectious, and exciting.

Cal Tjader One of the most important forces in Afro-Cuban jazz was actually of Swedish descent and born in St. Louis. Cal Tjader started out as a drummer who played with the Dave Brubeck Octet (with whom he made his recording debut) and the Brubeck Trio (1949–51). He dabbled in vibes a bit during that time and had a short stint with Alvino Rey. It was as a vibraphonist that Tjader was a member of the George Shearing Quintet (1953–54), developing a strong interest in Latin music. While his first few sessions as a leader (during 1951–53) were in straight-ahead jazz, on March 2, 1954, Tjader can be heard heading a quintet that includes Armando Peraza on conga. When he left Shearing in April, he soon formed a Latin jazz quintet that included two percussionists. **Los Ritmos Calientes** (Fantasy 24712) dates from 1954–57, contains all of the music from two former LPs, and features Tjader playing an infectious brand of Latin music with flutist Jerome Richardson, pianists Richard Wyands, Eddie Cano, Manuel Duran, and Vince Guaraldi, and quite a few bassists and percussionists; Mongo Santamaria and Willie Bobo are on three songs. Highlights include Ray Bryant's "Cubano Chant," "Mambo Inn," "Bernie's Tune," and "Perdido." **Tjader Plays Mambo** (Original Jazz Classics 274) has the vibraphonist utilizing four trumpets on a quartet of songs from 1954 and an oversized rhythm section on other selections from 1954 and 1956. "Guarachi Guaro" (which would later be retitled "Soul Sauce"), "Fascinating Rhythm," "Mambo Macumba," and "East of the Sun" are among the more memorable selections, all of which clock in around three minutes apiece. **Tjader Plays Tjazz** (Original Jazz Classics 988) is a change of pace, a couple of straightahead sessions from 1954–55 with Tjader (doubling on drums on some songs) jamming such tunes as "How About You," "Brew's Blues," and "Jeepers Creepers" either in a quintet with Brew Moore and Sonny Clark or a pianoless quartet with tenor saxophonist Bob Collins and guitarist Eddie Duran.

Even at this early stage, Cal Tjader was establishing his sound as one of the most appealing in Afro-Cuban jazz.

Rhythm and Blues

During the early 1950s, R&B began to move further away from its roots in swing. Jazz musicians and singers were still able to have R&B hits (including Dinah Washington, Earl Bostic, and Tab Smith), but by the mid-1950s and the beginnings of rock 'n' roll, saxophone solos were being de-emphasized in favor of vocals and guitar. Such perennials as Louis Jordan, Charles Brown, Amos Milburn, and Floyd Dixon were no longer making hit records and the era of screaming sax records based on "Flying Home" had run its course.

Paul Bascomb   The former tenor sax soloist with Erskine Hawkins's big band, Paul Bascomb played with a combo that included his brother trumpeter Dud on 52nd Street in the mid-1940s, and the brothers co-led a big band at the Savoy Ballroom. During 1947–50, Paul Bascomb headed a small group at Small's Paradise before being based at Detroit's El Cino for seven years in the 1950s. In 1952, Bascomb led a series of jump/R&B combo dates for the United label (the first successful black-owned record company), nearly all of which are included on **Bad Bascomb** (Delmark 431). The catchy and often blues-based music is purposely fairly basic and was meant for the jukebox market, but it has many fun moments. Bascomb takes consistently expressive solos although without duplicating the success of Jimmy Forrest's "Night Train" or becoming a honker and screamer. Paul Bascomb essentially played swing solos in more updated settings, and for a time he had some success in this format.

Earl Bostic   A brilliant technician on the alto who had a remarkable range, Earl Bostic was one of the most famous horn players in pop music of the 1950s. He had been a professional since the early 1930s, played early on with Charlie Creath and Fate Marable, and moved to New York in the late '30s. Bostic worked with the big bands of Don Redman, Edgar Hayes, and Lionel Hampton and the small group of Hot Lips Page, becoming a bandleader by 1947. In 1948, he had a hit with "Temptation," and three years later his version of "Flamingo" was a major seller. From then on, Bostic was a constant on the R&B charts, mostly playing melodic versions of swing standards. His alto (with its huge sound) is in the forefront throughout, usually climaxing with a stunning high note. **All His Hits** (King 5010) is a good place to start exploring Bostic's music, for most of these selections (including "Flamingo," "Sleep," the two-part "That's a Groovy Thing," and "Harlem Nocturne") were popular and helped define the Earl Bostic style.

Ruth Brown   Ruth Brown began her career in jazz and would return to it in her later years. However, Brown is best known for her R&B hits of the 1950s, performances that often bordered on both jazz and rock 'n' roll. She began her singing career in 1945 when she ran away from home at age 17 to work with trumpeter Jimmy Brown (her first husband). After a few years of scuffling, in 1949 she was signed to the Atlantic label and recorded the ballad "So Long" with Eddie Condon's band. It was the first in a series of hits that included "Teardrops in My

Eyes," "I'll Wait for You," "I Know," "5-10-15 Hours," "Mama He Treats Your Daughter Mean," "Oh What a Dream," and "Mambo Baby" during 1950–54. All are included on the definitive two-CD set **Miss Rhythm** (Atlantic 82061), which spans 1949–60.

Ray Charles   In 1955, a young blind singer/pianist named Ray Charles began to have hits on the rhythm and blues charts. Charles's initial recordings from 1949–52 found him influenced by Nat King Cole and especially Charles Brown. **The Complete Swing Time and Downbeat Recordings** (Night Train 2001), a two-CD set, shows how Charles sounded at the beginning of his career, crooning on ballads and playing swing-oriented jazz. He formed his own band in 1954, signed with Atlantic, and came up with an innovative way of singing. Charles infused R&B, pop, and swing songs with the emotion of gospel, helping to create soul music. Although never strictly a jazz performer, Charles could play very credible jazz piano and alto sax, and his singing was both an influence and an inspiration to jazz

vocalists. His 1955 hit "I Got a Woman" put him on the map, and he was on his way to becoming an American institution, one whose music crossed many stylistic boundaries.

Jimmy Forrest   An excellent tenor saxophonist, Jimmy Forrest will always be best known for recording "Night Train," a song that he "borrowed" from Duke Ellington. He grew up in St. Louis and while still in high school played with pianist Eddie Johnson, Fate Marable, and the Jeter-Pillars Orchestra. Forrest worked with Don Albert (1938), Jay McShann's Orchestra (1940–42), and Andy Kirk (1942–48) before having a short stint with Duke Ellington in 1949. At his first recording date as a leader on November 27, 1951, Forrest played the last section of Ellington's "Happy Go Lucky Local" as his retitled "original" "Night Train" and had a major hit, establishing the song as an R&B standard. **Night Train** (Delmark 435) has that song and the tenor's other recordings for the Chicago-based United label. Though no other hits emerged, Forrest was a popular performer in the

TIMELINE 1955

Chico Hamilton forms his popular quintet. • Bob Gordon is killed in a car accident. • Thelonious Monk begins recording for the Riverside label. • J.J. Johnson and Kai Winding co-lead a quintet. • Johnny Hodges rejoins Duke Ellington. • Art Blakey and Horace Silver form the Jazz Messengers. • Cannonball Adderley (who is dubbed "the new Bird") and Nat Adderley made a strong impression in New York. • Miles Davis plays "'Round Midnight" at the Newport Jazz Festival with Thelonious Monk and forms his classic quintet with John Coltrane, Red Garland, Paul Chambers, and Philly Joe Jones. • Wardell Gray dies mysteriously in the Las Vegas desert. • Julie London records "Cry Me a River." • Artie Shaw retires. • In New Orleans, Paul Barbarin forms the Onward Brass Band. • Count Basie has big hits in "April in Paris" and (with his new singer Joe Williams) "Everyday I Have the Blues." • Barney Bigard leaves the Louis Armstrong All-Stars after eight years and is replaced by Edmond Hall. • As "Honeyboy Homer," pianist Ray Bryant makes his recording debut, cutting a single for the Gotham label. • Henry Busse, Paul Whiteman's star trumpeter from the early 1920s, dies from a heart attack while playing at the National Undertakers Convention in Memphis, Tennessee. • Detroit trumpeter Donald Byrd moves to New York and plays with George Wallington's group at Café Bohemia. • The Jack Webb film *Pete Kelly's Blues* featured Dick Cathcart ghosting Webb's Dixieland trumpet solos and has appearances by Peggy Lee and Ella Fitzgerald. • Kenny Clarke leaves the Modern Jazz Quartet and is replaced by Connie Kay. • Doris Day stars as the still-active Ruth Etting in the hit movie *Love Me or Leave Me.* • Cleo Laine makes her recording debut as a leader. • Pianist Dwike Mitchell and bassist Willie Ruff form the Mitchell-Ruff Duo. • Israel Crosby becomes the bassist with the Ahmad Jamal Trio. • German bop pianist Jutta Hipp moves to the United States. • Gunther Schuller and John Lewis found the Jazz and Classical Music Society, presenting concerts of the music of both jazz and classical composers. • New Orleans trumpeter Al Hirt makes his first recordings. • In a move that is controversial among British trad followers, Humphrey Lyttelton gradually transforms his band from Dixieland/New Orleans jazz into a mainstream swing group. • Jonah Jones begins leading his quartet at the Embers in New York. The classic Count Basie-Freddie Green-Walter Page-Jo Jones rhythm section reunites on two versions of "Shoe Shine Boy" recorded on a Jo Jones Vanguard date. • Cecil Taylor makes his recording debut.

R&B circuit for several years. The 17 numbers on this CD should be of interest both to early R&B and swing-oriented jazz listeners.

Willis "Gator" Jackson   Willis Jackson first made a name for himself in 1948 at the age of 20 when the young tenor honked and squealed his way throughout the two-part Cootie Williams recording "Gator Tail," which earned him the lifelong nickname of Gator. Jackson, who was always capable of more, rode the wave for a few years, recording a series of honking R&B-ish dates for Apollo in 1950, all of which are on **Call of the Gators** (Delmark 460). Unlike some jazz saxophonists who sounded a bit reluctant in this type of setting, Gator's enthusiasm and variety of highly expressive sounds are full of joy and excitement. He is joined by such players as trombonist Booty Wood, pianist Bill Doggett (shortly before he switched to organ), and drummer Panama Francis on these explosive romps. Gator switched to Atlantic in 1951, but only led a few sides for the label, ten songs in all during 1951–53. However, being married to Ruth Brown resulted in Jackson appearing on many of her popular records.

Louis Jordan   For Louis Jordan, as for many of the early R&B performers, the hits came to an end by the mid-1950s. In fact, for Jordan they largely stopped by 1951, the year that he made the mistake of forming a big band. The orchestra immediately flopped and he returned to the Tympani Five, but despite still singing and playing quite well, the magic was going fast. Jordan's longtime Decca contract ran out in 1953 and his work for Aladdin in 1954, reissued as **One Guy Named Louis** (Blue Note 96804), generated no big sellers. There is nothing wrong with the music, but such songs as "Whiskey Do Your Stuff," "Gal You Need a Whippin'," "Fat Back and Corn Liquor," and "Messy Bessy" (written by Jon Hendricks) were forgotten immediately. Perhaps the song "Time's a Passin'" best summed up Jordan's situation for, at 46 years old, he would not be part of the upcoming rock 'n' roll movement that he had helped inspire.

Big Jay McNeely   The most extreme of the honking saxophonists, Big Jay McNeely continued being a major attraction up until the time that rock 'n' roll took over. **Big "J" in 3-D** (King 650) has the exuberant tenor's dozen recordings for the Federal label from 1952–54, with plenty

of explosive numbers, including "The Goof," "Big Jay Shuffle," "Nervous, Man, Nervous," "Hot Cinders," and "3-D." Next to McNeely, who had a remarkable amount of energy and was known for driving crowds wild, Illinois Jacquet at his most extreme sounds like a moderate!

Hal Singer   In 1948, Hal Singer found himself in a strange situation. He had been playing tenor sax since high school and had gained experience playing with the big bands of Ernie Fields (1938), Lloyd Hunter, Nat Towles, Tommy Douglas, and Jay McShann (1941–42). In New York, Singer freelanced with Hot Lips Page, Roy Eldridge's big band (1944), Earl Bostic, Henry "Red" Allen, Sid Catlett, and Lucky Millinder. In 1948, he realized a lifelong goal by joining the Duke Ellington Orchestra. But shortly before he joined Duke, Singer recorded an R&B record, "Cornbread." It became such a big hit that he was forced to leave Ellington's band. So many fans were coming out specifically to see him that after six months he reluctantly went out on his own.

As it turned out, he never had another hit ("Beef Stew" came close), but Singer did work successfully on the R&B circuit for several years. **Rent Party** (Savoy 0258) has a strong sampling of his R&B records of 1948–56 (including "Cornbread"), with plenty of repetitious honks and highly expressive playing by Singer. The music is simple and fun, predictable overall, but sometimes riotous. One can understand Hal Singer's popularity.

Tab Smith   Tab Smith was an unlikely R&B hero. A major swing altoist who had proven himself with the Count Basie Orchestra (1940–42) and on a 1944 set where he held his own with Coleman Hawkins, Don Byas, and Harry Carney, Smith was a bandleader after spending two years playing with Lucky Millinder (1942–44). He had a low profile during the bebop era (his style was unaffected by bop), but then in 1951 began recording for the United label and had a surprise hit with the ballad "Because of You." Never a honker or screamer, Smith just played the way he normally played, alternating between swinging romps and melodic ballads. Three CDs of his United material, **Jump Time** (Delmark 447), **Ace High** (Delmark 455), and **Top 'N' Bottom** (Delmark 499), cover his 1951–54 recordings including many previously unreleased performances. **Jump Time** gets the edge due to the inclusion of "Because of You" and the fact that the concept was fresher in 1951 than in 1954, but all three discs are enjoyable.

A Few Various Artists Collections

In 1954, bassist Harry Babasin and drummer Roy Harte started a new record label, Nocturne, which during the next couple of years documented some of the top West Coast jazz performers including a few who were overlooked by Contemporary and Pacific Jazz. **The Complete Nocturne Recordings Vol. 1** (Fresh Sound 101) is a three-CD set that has all of the music from the label's first eight albums, all recorded in 1954. Trombonist Herbie Harper heads several sessions (featuring Bob Gordon, Jimmy Rowles, Bud Shank, and guitarist Al Hendrickson) and other leaders include Shank, Babasin, Bob Enevoldsen (on both valve trombone and tenor), baritonist Virgil Gonsalves, Lou Levy, and Jimmy Rowles. This reissue of rare sessions is a must for West Coast jazz collectors.

West Coast Jazz (Contemporary 4425) is a well-conceived four-CD box that draws its music from the Prestige, Debut, Capitol, Contemporary, Pacific Jazz, Fantasy, Norgran, Nocturne, GNP/Crescendo, Jazz West, Pablo, Atlantic, Andex, Specialty, Warner Bros., and Hi Fi Jazz labels. Although there are many cool jazz performances included, there are also examples of bebop, hard bop, the early avant-garde, soul jazz, and swing (Art Tatum) on this interesting set, which programs its 60 selections (dating from 1950–64) in chronological order. There is nothing previously unreleased, but the sampler achieves its purpose of familiarizing listeners with the strong Los Angeles jazz scene of the 1950s and early '60s.

Prestige First Sessions Vol. 3 (Prestige 24116), which dates from 1950–51, has a few R&B-ish titles from Eddie "Lockjaw" Davis, an obscure Dizzy Gillespie combo date, two tunes from Bennie Green, and seven excellent selections from a Red Rodney quintet session—enjoyable music if nothing essential. The same can be said about **New Orleans Styles** (Storyville 6054), which features music from four of the top trad bands: Kid Ory's Creole Jazz Band of 1945 with Mutt Carey, Papa Celestin's Tuxedo Jazz Band co-starring Alphonse Picou, Paul Barbarin's 1954 group with the Humphrey Brothers, and seven songs from Wilbur DeParis's New New Orleans Jazz Band that predate their Atlantic recordings.

Looking Ahead: Hints of the Avant-Garde

Some musicians sought to reach beyond the chordal improvising of bebop and come up with new and freer ways to play jazz. One can hear in the music of Lennie Tristano (who in 1949 recorded two free improvisations), Stan Kenton's Innovations Orchestra, and some of the West Coast jazz sessions a desire to improvise in a different way, utilize instruments not formerly used in jazz, and come up with new and advanced harmonies. Avant-garde jazz did not have a name yet or even a focus, but it was clear to those who paid close attention that jazz would be moving beyond bop in the near future.

Teddy Charles A fine vibraphonist, Teddy Charles was always interested in looking ahead, seeking to fuse aspects of classical music and freer improvisation into bebop. He originally played drums and piano, taking up the vibes in the mid-1940s. He played on 52nd Street and worked with the big bands of Bob Astor (1947), Randy Brooks, Benny Goodman, Chubby Jackson, and Artie Shaw (1950). Charles, who freelanced and led his own groups, recorded with Miles Davis, Wardell Gray, and Charles Mingus, joining with Mingus and Teo Macero in 1953 to form the Jazz Composers Workshop. **New Directions** (Original Jazz Classics 1927) has Charles living up to the album's name during a trio of sessions from 1951–53. Eight selections (all but one are standards) have Charles, guitarist Don Roberts, and bassist Kenny O'Brien deconstructing and reinventing the familiar tunes (which include "Tenderly," "Basin Street Blues," and "The Lady Is a Tramp") in eccentric and atmospheric ways. Four songs with Jimmy Raney, bassist Dick Nivison, and drummer Ed Shaughnessy display some of the advanced harmonies that Charles learned during lessons with Hall Overton and are often as close to classical music as to jazz (particularly "Nocturne"). Most interesting are four Overton originals played by Charles, the composer (on piano), and Shaughnessy in a trio. Some of this music is quite dry, but it certainly breaks away from the typical jazz of the era.

Collaboration: West (Original Jazz Classics 122) from 1952–53 features Charles with three different thought-provoking pianoless quartets/quintets that include the likes of Shorty Rogers, Jimmy Giuffre, Jimmy Raney, Curtis Counce, and Shelly Manne. Although sometimes seeming a bit cold and clinical, there are some swinging sections included in the complex arrangements (which occasionally utilize polytonality). **Evolution** (Original Jazz Classics 1731) has two numbers from 1953 with Rogers, Giuffre, Counce, and Manne (playing an advanced original apiece by Giuffre and Rogers) and a later date in New York with Charles Mingus, tenor saxophonist J.R. Monterose, and drummer Gerry Segal, which is one of the better recorded showcases for Charles's vibes.

Despite all of this activity, Teddy Charles's music has been underrated through the years, and it did not have that much of an impact, being a bit too far ahead of its time.

Charles Mingus   The 1950–55 period was a time when Charles Mingus found his own musical voice. He worked with the Red Norvo Trio during 1950–51 and in 1952 co-founded the Debut label with Max Roach so he could document his own adventurous music and that of others he admired. Most notable was the 1953 Massey Hall concert with Charlie Parker, Dizzy Gillespie, Bud Powell, and Roach. Although an admirer of those musicians, Duke Ellington, and other earlier greats, Mingus wanted to develop a new style of his own that reflected his wide interest in music. During 1952–54, he often experimented with mixing together modern jazz with touches of contemporary classical music, forming the Jazz Composers Workshop, which frequently included clarinetist John LaPorta and tenor saxophonist (and future producer) Teo Macero.

The Complete Debut Recordings (Debut 4402), a 12-CD box, has all of Mingus's sessions for his label (dating from 1951–57) including many adventurous works, duets and trios with pianist Spaulding Givens, the Massey Hall concert, a four-trombone date that would lead to the formation of the J.J. Johnson-Kai Winding Quintet, dates featuring Paul Bley, Thad Jones, and Hazel Scott, an obscure Miles Davis session, and the very significant Café Bohemia recordings, which are discussed in the next paragraph.

The height of Mingus's interest in a classical/jazz fusion can be heard on **Jazz Composers Workshop** (Savoy 92981) from October 31, 1954. The music (played by a sextet with LaPorta, Macero, and pianist Mal Waldron) is advanced but rather cold and overly intellectual, well played but a touch dull. However, the following year Mingus can be heard discovering himself musically at a December 23, 1955, performance released as **Mingus at the Bohemia** (Original Jazz Classics 045) and **Plus Max Roach** (Original Jazz Classics 440). The music on

these quintet sets (with trombonist Eddie Bert, tenor saxophonist George Barrow, Waldron, drummer Willie Jones, and guest Max Roach on the second disc) is also complex, but instead of modern classical music, the emphasis is on soulful and very expressive jazz. Mingus pushes his sidemen to play way above themselves, forcing them to be original under rather intense conditions, with him sometimes shouting out verbally while they played. On such tunes as "Jump Monk," "Work Song" (no relationship to the future Nat Adderley song), "Haitian Fight Song," and "Love Chant," Barrow and Bert are heard at their most fiery. All of the elements of Mingus's future performances—including group improvising, looking both backward and forward musically, and a constant intensity—were now in place.

Cecil Taylor   Cecil Taylor, who turned 26 in 1955, had started piano lessons when he was six and attended the New York College of Music and the New England Conservatory. Although inspired early on by the percussive playing of Duke Ellington, Dave Brubeck, and Thelonious Monk, by the early 1950s he already sounded more advanced and "freer" than just about any other pianist. Taylor had short stints with Johnny Hodges and Hot Lips Page, and in 1955 interested Alfred Lion in recording him for Blue Note.

Jazz Advance (Blue Note 86642) has Cecil Taylor's very first recording session. Already his comping and chord voicings were abstract and his solos were unpredictable, almost atonal in spots even though some of the tunes ("Sweet and Lovely," Monk's "Bemsha Swing," and a solo version of "You'd Be So Nice to Come Home To") were standards and at times hinted at the melody. Four of the songs are trio performances with bassist Buell Neidlinger and drummer Dennis Charles, while two pieces ("Charge 'Em Blues" and "Song") have soprano saxophonist Steve Lacy making the group a quartet. Lacy and Neidlinger had previously played in Dixieland settings, so this was a huge jump stylistically for them. And although little heard by the mainstream jazz public at a time when Ornette Coleman had yet to record, this fascinating recording hints strongly at what was to come in future years when the main debate in jazz would no longer be West Coast vs. East Coast, but straightahead vs. free.

VOICES OF THE FUTURE

Robert Dick (flute), Jan. 4, 1950, New York, NY

Bobby McFerrin (vocals), Mar. 11, 1950, New York, NY

Tiger Okoski (trumpet), Mar. 21, 1950, Ashita, Japan

Bobby Militello (alto, flute), Mar. 25, 1950, Buffalo, NY

Victor Lewis (drums), May 20, 1950, Omaha, NE

Dee Dee Bridgewater (singer), May 27, 1950,
    Memphis, TN

Hal Crook (trombone), July 28, 1950, Providence, RI

Rickey Woodard (tenor), Aug. 5, 1950, Nashville, TN

Charles Fambrough (bass), Aug. 25, 1950,
    Philadelphia, PA

George Garzone (tenor), Sept. 23, 1950, Cambridge, MA

Mark Helias (bass), Oct. 1, 1950, New Brunswick, NJ

Ronnie Laws (tenor), Oct. 3, 1950, Houston, TX

Gil Goldstein (piano, accordion, keyboards), Nov. 6,
    1950, Washington, D.C.

Mark Egan (bass), Jan. 14, 1951, Brockton, MA

Steve Grossman (tenor, soprano), Jan. 18, 1951,
    Brooklyn, NY

Ralph Lalama (tenor), Jan. 30, 1951, Aliquippa, PA

Anthony Davis (piano, composer), Feb. 20, 1951,
    Paterson, NJ

Warren Vache (cornet, fluegelhorn), Feb. 21, 1951,
    Rahway, NJ

Roseanna Vitro (vocals), Feb. 28, 1951, Hot Springs, AR

Eric Allison (tenor), Mar. 7, 1951, South Bend, IN

James Williams (piano), Mar. 8, 1951, Memphis, TN

Bill Frisell (guitar), Mar. 18, 1951, Baltimore, MD

Bob Berg (tenor), Apr. 7, 1951, New York, NY

Marty Krystall (tenor, bass clarinet), Apr. 12, 1951,
    Los Angeles, CA

Stanley Clarke (bass), June 30, 1951, Philadelphia, PA

Bobby Previte (drums, composer), July 16, 1951, Niagara
    Falls, NY

Carla White (vocals), Sept. 15, 1951, Oakland, CA

Poncho Sanchez (conga, leader, vocals), Oct. 30, 1951,
    Laredo, TX

Kenny Werner (piano), Nov. 19, 1951, Brooklyn, NY

Jaco Pastorius (bass), Dec. 1, 1951, Norristown, PA

Robben Ford (guitar), Dec. 16, 1951, Woodlake, CA

John Scofield (guitar), Dec. 26, 1951, Dayton, OH

Rebecca Parris (vocals), Dec. 28, 1951, Needham, MA

William Parker (bass), Jan. 10, 1952, Bronx, NY

Lee Ritenour (guitar), Jan. 11, 1952, Los Angeles, CA

Akira Tana (drums), Mar. 14, 1952, San Jose, CA

Dave Valentin (flute), Apr. 29, 1952, Bronx, NY

Hilton Ruiz (piano), May 29, 1952, New York, NY

George Lewis (trombone, keyboards), July 14, 1952,
    Chicago, IL

John Clayton (bass, arranger), Aug. 4, 1952,
    Los Angeles, CA

Mark Dresser (bass), Sept. 26, 1952, Los Angeles, CA

Ray Anderson (trombone), Oct. 16, 1952, Chicago, IL

Ali Ryerson (flute), Oct. 21, 1952, New York, NY

Judy Carmichael (piano), Nov. 27, 1952, Lynwood, CA

Joe Lovano (tenor, leader), Dec. 29, 1952, Cleveland, OH

Mike Stern (guitar), Jan. 10, 1953, Boston, MA

Bob Mintzer (tenor, soprano, bass clarinet),
    Jan. 27, 1953, New Rochelle, NY

Michele Rosewoman (piano), Mar. 19, 1953,
    Oakland, CA

Danny Gottlieb (drums), Apr. 18, 1953, New York, NY

James Newton (flute), May 1, 1953, Los Angeles, CA

Duffy Jackson (drums), July 3, 1953, Freeport, NY

Jimmy Bruno (guitar), July 22, 1953, Philadelphia, PA

Jon Faddis (trumpet), July 24, 1953, Oakland, CA

Hal Smith (drums), July 30, 1953, Indianapolis, IN

Jeff Hamilton (drums), Aug. 4, 1953, Richmond, IN

Bobby Watson (alto), Aug. 23, 1953, Lawrence, KS

Ron Holloway (tenor), Aug. 24, 1953, Washington, D.C.

John Zorn (alto), Sept. 2, 1953, New York, NY

Craig Harris (trombone), Sept. 10, 1953, Hempstead, NY

Marc Johnson (bass), Oct. 21, 1953, Omaha, NE

Deborah Henson-Conant (harp), Nov. 11, 1953,
    Stockton, CA

Diane Schuur (vocals, piano), Dec. 10, 1953, Tacoma, WA

Jeff Clayton (alto), Feb. 4, 1954, Los Angeles, CA

Ricky Ford (tenor), Mar. 4, 1954, Boston, MA

Judy Niemack (vocals), Mar. 11, 1954, Pasadena, CA

Andy Narell (steel drums), Mar. 18, 1954, New York, NY

Donald Brown (piano), Mar. 28, 1954, Hernando, MI

Michel Camilo (piano), Apr. 4, 1954, Santo Domingo,
    Dominican Republic

Peter Erskine (drums), May 6, 1954, Somers Point, NJ

Lorne Lofsky (guitar), May 10, 1954, Canada

Madeline Eastman (vocals), June 27, 1954,
    San Francisco, CA

Garry Dial (piano), July 2, 1954, Montclair, NJ

Al DiMeola (guitar), July 22, 1954, Jersey City, NJ

Nnenna Freelon (vocals), July 28, 1954, Cambridge, MA

VOICES OF THE FUTURE

Steve Nelson (vibes), Aug. 11, 1954, Pittsburgh, PA

Pat Metheny (guitar, leader), Aug. 12, 1954, Lee's Summit, MO

Tim Hagans (trumpet), Aug. 19, 1954, Dayton, OH

Avery Sharpe (bass), Aug. 23, 1954, Valdosta, GA

Stephanie Nakasian (vocals), Aug. 29, 1954, Washington, D.C.

Scott Hamilton (tenor), Sept. 12, 1954, Providence, RI

Earl Klugh (guitar), Sept. 16, 1954, Detroit, MI

Jay Hoggard (vibes), Sept. 28, 1954, Washington, D.C.

Patrice Rushen (keyboards), Sept. 30, 1954, Los Angeles, CA

Tim Berne (alto), Oct. 16, 1954, Syracuse, NY

Anthony Cox (bass), Oct. 24, 1954, Ardmore, OK

Tom Browne (trumpet), Oct. 30, 1954, Queens, NY

Carmen Lundy (vocals), Nov. 1, 1954, Miami, FL

Ernst Reijsiger (cello), Nov. 13, 1954, Bussum, Netherlands

Jane Ira Bloom (soprano), Jan. 12, 1955, Newton, MA

David Thomas Roberts (piano, composer), Jan. 16, 1955

David Murray (tenor, bass clarinet, leader), Jan. 19, 1955, Oakland, CA

Marty Ehrlich (clarinet, bass clarinet, reeds), May 31, 1955, St. Paul, MN

Joey Baron (drums), June 26, 1955, Richmond, VA

Joshua Breakstone (guitar), July 22, 1955, Elizabeth, NJ

Mulgrew Miller (piano), Aug. 13, 1955, Greenwood, MS

Hiram Bullock (guitar), Sept. 11, 1955, Osaka, Japan

Stacy Rowles (fluegelhorn, vocals), Sept. 11, 1955, Los Angeles, CA

Kenny Kirkland (piano), Sept. 28, 1955, Brooklyn, NY

Fred Hersch (piano), Oct. 21, 1955, Cincinnati, OH

Robin Eubanks (trombone), Oct. 25, 1955, Philadelphia, PA

Kitty Margolis (vocals), Nov. 7, 1955, San Mateo, CA

Neil Swainson (bass), Nov. 15, 1955, Victoria, British Columbia, Canada

Michael Rabinowitz (bassoon), Nov. 27, 1955, New Haven, CT

Adam Nussbaum (drums), Nov. 29, 1955, New York, NY

Cassandra Wilson (vocals), Dec. 4, 1955, Jackson, MS

Dan Barrett (trombone, cornet), Dec. 14, 1955, Pasadena, CA

PASSINGS

Buddy Stewart (27), Feb. 1, 1950, New Mexico

Leo Watson (52), May 2, 1950, Los Angeles, CA

Bertha "Chippie" Hill (45), May 7, 1950, New York, NY

Fats Navarro (26), July 7, 1950, New York, NY

Al Killian (33), Sept. 5, 1950, Los Angeles, CA

Big Sid Catlett (41), Mar. 25, 1951, Chicago, IL

Jimmy Yancey (53), Sept. 17, 1951, Chicago, IL

Charlie Creath (60), Oct. 23, 1951, Chicago, IL

Mildred Bailey (44), Dec. 12, 1951, Poughkeepsie, NY

Vic Berton (55), Dec. 26, 1951, Hollywood, CA

John Kirby (43), June 14, 1952, Hollywood, CA

Fletcher Henderson (54), Dec. 29, 1952, New York, NY

Django Reinhardt (43), May 16, 1953, Fontainebleau, France

Larry Shields (60), Nov. 21, 1953, Los Angeles, CA

Frankie Newton (48), Mar. 11, 1954, New York

Garland Wilson (44), May 31, 1954, Paris, France

Hot Lips Page (46), Nov. 5, 1954, New York, NY

Charlie Parker (34), Mar. 12, 1955, New York, NY

Wardell Gray (34), May 25, 1955, Las Vegas, NV

Bob Gordon (27), Aug. 28, 1955, San Diego, CA

Dick Twardzik (34), Oct. 21, 1955, Paris, France

James P. Johnson (64), Nov. 17, 1955, New York, NY

Chapter Eight

1956–1960:
A Time of Giants

The 1956–60 period was magical in jazz. It might have been a relatively quiet time in American history, the second term of the Dwight Eisenhower administration and an era of uneasy peace, but in jazz there were so many viable styles competing for one's attention and so many major musicians and singers who were in their prime that it is almost mind-boggling. Consider that it was possible in 1957 to go out and see Louis Armstrong, Henry "Red" Allen, Wild Bill Davison, Roy Eldridge, Buck Clayton, Dizzy Gillespie, Miles Davis, Chet Baker, Art Farmer, Donald Byrd, and Lee Morgan, all of whom were in their prime. And that is only a partial list of the major trumpeters!

During this period, jazz continued to develop and evolve quickly. Veterans from the swing era were still around as were the Dixielanders and the bebop survivors. Hard bop grew in popularity while West Coast jazz began to decline. There were attempts at creating "Third Stream" music (a mixture of jazz with classical music), and Latin jazz remained quite vital. In addition, the Ornette Coleman Quartet's debut in New York was the first widely heard example of "free jazz," and it made the once-radical beboppers seem like the conservative guardians of jazz's traditions. The evolution of jazz was moving so quickly that anything over five years old seemed a bit old-fashioned, yet it was possible to hear John Coltrane playing next to Coleman Hawkins, Benny Goodman using Roland Hanna as his pianist, and Dizzy Gillespie playing on the same bill as Louis Armstrong.

The rise of the LP meant that, instead of a group recording four tunes at a session, the goal was a full 40-minute album. No longer confined to cutting three-minute songs, musicians were able to stretch out much more, building up solos rather than having to fit an entire message in 8 or 16 bars. And with all 78s going out of print, there was a great demand for new records by consumers. There were many projects that merely recreated swing hits in "hi-fi," but there was also an enormous amount of new music recorded. Despite complaints at the time from jazz critics who found the deluge a bit difficult to keep up with, the quality overall was high, thanks to such labels as Blue Note, Riverside, Prestige, Contemporary, Pacific Jazz, Savoy, Argo, Atlantic, Bethlehem, Debut, EmArcy/Mercury, Good Time Jazz, Nat Hentoff's short-lived Candid label, and, even at times, Columbia, RCA Victor, and Capitol.

Jazz still had its problems. The heroin epidemic was causing interrupted careers and shortened lives, sometimes punctuated by jail sentences. While the civil rights movement was heating up, the Southern part of the United States was still segregated, and racism remained the law of the land even if mixed-race groups were becoming more common. The rise of Elvis Presley and rock 'n' roll in 1956 was casting a shadow, meaning that the odds were that jazz was never going to dominate the pop charts again. Still, with the many forms of jazz thriving artistically and the rise of the jazz festival (Newport, which started in 1954, was becoming an institution, and the Monterey Jazz Festival began in 1958), the future looked bright.

There were so many major jazz musicians performing during 1956–60 that the music was even able to survive the tragic and premature loss of six household names.

The End for Six Jazz Greats

Every time period in jazz history has its early deaths and regrettable losses of unique musicians and singers. The 1956–60 era was no exception, with the six greats in this section being particularly irreplaceable.

Clifford Brown   Arguably the most tragic loss in jazz history occurred in the early morning hours of June 26, 1956. During a rainstorm in Pennsylvania, a car driven by the near-sighted wife of pianist Richie Powell crashed. In addition to pianist Powell and his wife, 25-year-old trumpeter Clifford Brown (who was in the backseat) died instantly. Brownie's early demise was particularly ironic because he lived a clean life during a period when many of the younger jazz musicians had difficulties with drugs, and was an inspiration to many others; Sonny Rollins had gotten off drugs partly because of Brown's example.

The year 1956 had begun with great promise for the trumpeter. Co-leader of a pacesetting hard bop quintet with Max Roach, Brownie was still improving as a player. With Sonny Rollins now in the band along with Powell and bassist George Morrow, the Brown-Roach group was even stronger than previously. **At Basin Street** (EmArcy 814 648) finds Brownie and Rollins fitting together perfectly on memorable versions of "What Is this Thing Called Love," "I'll Remember April," and a witty arrangement of "Love Is a Many Splendored Thing." ◉ **The Beginning and the End** (Columbia/Legacy 66491) starts off with Brown's two solos from 1952 with the R&B band Chris Powell's Blue Flames. The remainder of the CD features Brown during his very last performance, just a few hours before his death. Performing in Philadelphia before a loving crowd, the 25-year-old is heard playing at his absolute peak. He performs "Walkin'" with a local sextet that includes Billy Root on tenor and pianist Sam Dockery, "A Night in Tunisia" with a quintet, and concludes both his night and his career with a quartet rendition of "Donna Lee" that is simply stunning. It is difficult to believe, even many decades later, that these would be the final notes played by Clifford Brown.

Brown, who acquired his sound and style largely from Fats Navarro, became the main influence on younger trumpeters, including Lee Morgan and in future years Freddie Hubbard and Woody Shaw. His complete control of his horn, his logical ideas, and particularly that beautiful tone have been a model for many other trumpeters ever since.

Art Tatum   Art Tatum was still a miraculous pianist in the mid-1950s. Although his solo piano marathon sessions for Norman Granz were not at the classic level one would expect (they are workmanlike and routine), a series of all-star dates with other greats are much more successful and inspired. All of the latter music has been gathered together on the six-CD box ◉ **The Complete Pablo Group Masterpieces** (Pablo 4401). Tatum is heard in a trio with Benny Carter and Louie Bellson, in separate quartets with a typically combative Roy Eldridge, a somewhat dazzling Buddy DeFranco, and Ben Webster (who wisely emphasizes the beauty of his tone), starring in a regular trio with bassist Red Callender and Jo Jones, jamming with an explosive trio also including Lionel Hampton and Buddy Rich, and leading a sextet with Hampton, Rich, and Harry "Sweets" Edison. Each of these encounters works quite well and brings out the best in the remarkable pianist.

The Ben Webster date was recorded September 11, 1956. Less than two months later, on November 5, Tatum died from uremia at the age of 47. Although many generations of pianists have emerged since then, when it comes to technique, speed, harmonic sophistication, and being so far ahead of his time, Art Tatum still cannot be touched.

Tommy and Jimmy Dorsey   With the success of their *Stage Door* television series (which ironically helped to introduce Elvis Presley to a mass audience), Tommy and

Jimmy Dorsey were able to keep leading a big band in the mid-1950s. The recording **1955** (Jazz Unlimited 2026) is a good example of how the Dorseys sounded near the end, playing jazz-oriented numbers (with concise, but worthy contributions from Charlie Shavers and Louie Bellson plus spots for the brothers) and some vocal cuts featuring Lynn Roberts, Bill Raymond, and Bruce Snyder. The music sounds conservative and there are no surprises, but this brand of nostalgic swing music satisfied older dancers.

On November 26, 1956, Tommy Dorsey (who was just 51) died in his sleep. Jimmy Dorsey temporarily took over the Dorsey Brothers Orchestra, but he was already stricken with cancer. Back on November 11, JD had recorded a version of "So Rare" that was turning into his first hit in over a decade. However, he did not have long to enjoy its success, passing away on June 12, 1957, at the age of 53. Both Dorseys during their final decade seemed like relics from a much earlier time, but their recording careers actually only lasted a little over 30 years.

Lee Castle took over the nucleus of the Dorsey Brothers band (which was renamed the Jimmy Dorsey Orchestra) while trombonist Warren Covington organized and led the Tommy Dorsey big band. Those two ghost bands lasted for decades, grinding out the same old hits the same old way.

Billie Holiday and Lester Young   In 1956, Billie Holiday turned 41 and Lester Young celebrated his 46th birthday. Both should have had bright futures. They were recording under very favorable circumstances for Norman Granz's Verve label, were famous legends, and were making good money. But unfortunately they were both plagued by inner demons, and their time was limited.

Lester Young, who suffered from depression, alternated between playing well and drinking excessively. He started 1956 by recording two superior albums. ● **Jazz Giants '56** (Verve 825 672) has Pres sounding inspired in an all-star group with Roy Eldridge, Vic Dickenson, Teddy Wilson, Freddie Green, bassist Gene Ramey, and Jo Jones. "You Can Depend on Me," and "I Didn't Know What Time It Was" are given wonderful treatment, while "Gigantic Blues" is explosive. The following day, Young recorded ● **Pres and Teddy** (Verve 831 270) in a quartet with Wilson, Ramey, and Jones. The tenorman sounds in classic form, swinging on such numbers as "All of Me," "Love Me or Leave Me," and a touching version

of "Prisoner of Love." Young also showed that he could still play at his best during December 3–9, 1956, when he had an engagement in Washington, D.C., with a local rhythm section. Decades later, five well-recorded CDs from the week were released, **In Washington, D.C., 1956, Vols. 1–5** (Original Jazz Classics 782, 881, 901, 963, and 993). Pres certainly sounds at his prime as he swings through some of his favorite standards and a few basic originals.

Unfortunately, it did not last. Young continued drinking excessively and eating too little; his health became erratic and troublesome. On December 8, 1957, he appeared on the *Sound of Jazz* telecast, but was too ill to play very much. However, he summoned up the strength to join Billie Holiday on "Fine and Mellow," playing a single beautiful chorus that caused tears to come to many people's eyes, including Lady Day's.

Laughin' to Keep from Crying (Verve 543 301) from February 8, 1958, had a lot of difficulties, but the recorded results are excellent. Young was assisted by both Roy Eldridge and Harry "Sweets" Edison along with a rhythm section for two standards, two originals, and the ballad "Gypsy in My Soul." In addition, Pres takes rare clarinet solos on two of the numbers with his emotional statement on "They Can't Take That Away from Me" being quite touching. But this was nearly his last gasp.

In early 1959, Lester Young spent a couple of months in Paris, resulting in his final (and rather weak) record date. Shortly after he returned home, he drank himself to death, passing away on March 15. At Young's funeral, a grieving Billie Holiday told Leonard Feather, "I'm next."

In Lady Day's case, the ravages of heroin, excessive alcohol use, and low self-esteem took its toll. Her voice gradually declined during the 1950s, and, although her very emotional interpretations of lyrics were quite impressive, some of her singing was almost unlistenable. She rallied now and then, and her 1956–57 Verve recordings feature jazz combos that at times include Charlie Shavers, Tony Scott, Paul Quinichette, Harry "Sweets" Edison, Ben Webster, and Jimmy Rowles, but surprisingly never Lester Young. **Songs for Distingué Lovers** (Verve 539 056) has 12 of the 18 songs that she made during January 1957, her last major batch of jazz recordings. Holiday sounds terrible on the record released from the 1957 Newport Jazz Festival (she was disoriented and sometimes lost), but when she appeared on the *Sound of Jazz* telecast, she had temporarily rallied.

The famous clip of "Fine and Mellow" (with Young, Coleman Hawkins, Ben Webster, and Roy Eldridge) is her best-known appearance on film, and she sounds like she had many years ahead of her.

But it was largely over. Recorded in 1958, **Lady in Satin** (Columbia 65144) is the most controversial of all her records. Backed by a string orchestra arranged by Ray Ellis, Holiday sounds like she was 72 rather than 42. At the time she said that this was her personal favorite recording, and some listeners are so attracted to her emotional versions of "You've Changed," "I'm a Fool to Want You," "You Don't Know What Love Is," and "Glad to Be Unhappy" that they consider this to be one of the high points of her career. However, Holiday's voice was almost completely gone, Ellis's arrangements are close to Muzak, and there are parts of this record that are almost unbearable to listen to.

There was a visit in England in early 1959 and an additional record in March, **Last Recordings** (Verve 835 370), which is actually an improvement on **Lady in Satin**. But Lady Day became weaker and weaker. She collapsed, spent a little time in the hospital where she was arrested on her deathbed for possession of heroin

that was probably slipped to her by a "friend," and died on July 17 at the age of 44. Billie Holiday had fulfilled her sad prediction to Leonard Feather.

Ten New Jazz Giants

There were many new jazz greats who were affecting jazz during 1956–60. With the exception of Thelonious Monk, who had been neglected for a decade, the ten in this section would not have been called giants in 1953 even though all (other than Ornette Coleman) were active. But by 1960, each was making a major impact on the music, moving jazz beyond bebop in quite a few different directions.

Miles Davis   Even if he had accomplished nothing except for his work of 1956–60, Miles Davis would be ranked as one of the most important of all jazz musicians. This was certainly a productive period for him. He had formed his first classic quintet the previous summer, a group consisting of his trumpet, tenor saxophonist John Coltrane, pianist Red Garland, bassist Paul Chambers, and drummer Philly Joe Jones. Their first record date (from October 27) was cut for Columbia, but not released until Miles's Prestige contract ran out. Since

TIMELINE 1956

Clifford Brown and Richie Powell die in a car crash. • Horace Silver leaves the Jazz Messengers and forms his own quintet. • Dizzy Gillespie forms a new big band that lasts two years. • Paul Gonsalves's marathon tenor solo on "Diminuendo and Crescendo in Blue" makes Duke Ellington the hit of the Newport Jazz Festival. • The Ramsey Lewis Trio is formed. • The J.J. Johnson-Kai Winding Quintet breaks up. • Kenny Clarke moves to Europe. • Altoist Marshall Allen begins a 37-year period with Sun Ra's Arkestra. • Ernestine Anderson tours Scandinavia with Rolf Ericson. • Chris Barber's band has a hit with Sidney Bechet's "Petit Fleur," featuring clarinetist Monty Sunshine. • Paul Bascomb leads an organ trio at the Esquire in Chicago, beginning a 14-year run. • Glen Gray records **The Casa Loma in Hi-Fi** for Capitol, starting a swing recreation series. • A serious car accident puts Arnett Cobb out of action for two years. • Organist Bill Doggett has a giant R&B hit with "Honky Tonk." • At the age of 61, Alberta Hunter retires from music to become a nurse. • Trombonist Albert Wynn joins Franz Jackson's Dixieland band in Illinois. • Bobby Troup hosts *The Stars of Jazz* television series for two years. • Boyd Raeburn records three big band LPs within a year, but fails to make an impression. • Dannie Richmond becomes Charles Mingus's drummer. • Don Elliott leads three record dates, playing mellophone (as the first significant jazz soloist since Dudley Fosdick in the 1920s), trumpet, vibes, and bongo. • Andy Kirk leads a "reunion" album, but the only alumnus involved is pianist Ken Kersey. • Ray McKinley becomes leader of the Glenn Miller ghost band. • A 21-minute version of "Billie's Bounce" is the highlight of the final recording by the Metronome All-Stars. • Buddy Rich records a set of Johnny Mercer songs, as a vocalist. • Arranger Edgar Sampson leads his only album. • George Van Eps records the near-classic **Mellow Guitar**. • Paul Whiteman celebrates his 50th year in show business with a two-LP set that includes appearances by the Dorsey Brothers, Joe Venuti, Jack Teagarden, Hoagy Carmichael, and Johnny Mercer. • The Miles Davis Quintet with John Coltrane records **'Round About Midnight**.

Columbia had unexpectedly expressed a desire to sign Davis, a deal was worked out with the Prestige label. Miles owed Prestige four albums, so it was decided to have two marathon sessions in which his quintet would play song after song, just as they would in a nightclub. Although the Davis group also recorded an album for Columbia in 1956, that would not be released until the following year.

On May 11 and October 26, 1956, the Miles Davis Quintet recorded 25 selections for Prestige, music that was released as **Cookin'** (Original Jazz Classics 128), **Relaxin'** (Original Jazz Classics 190), **Workin'** (Original Jazz Classics 296), and **Steamin'** (Original Jazz Classics 391). All of these sessions are also reissued in full in the eight-CD set ◉ **Chronicle—The Complete Prestige Recordings (1951–1956)** (Prestige 012). Each of the albums has their classic moments and all are recommended, with highlights including "My Funny Valentine," "It Never Entered My Mind," "If I Were a Bell," "Oleo," "Surrey with the Fringe on Top," and "When I Fall in Love." Davis's ballad playing (utilizing a Harmon mute and putting his horn close to the microphone while playing very softly) became a trademark, but he also jams bebop standards quite well too. Coltrane, who had sounded so hesitant in 1955, grew in confidence and creativity each month in 1956, and he began to reward Davis's faith in him. The rhythm section (with Garland sometimes emulating Ahmad Jamal's use of space, but with his own distinctive chord voicings) was tight and swinging, propelled by Chambers's walking bass and Jones's subtle power.

While the Prestige dates had a jam session feel, the quintet's first full record for Columbia, **'Round About Midnight** (Columbia/Legacy 85201), which is available in the six-CD box ◉ **Miles Davis & John Coltrane— The Complete Columbia Recordings 1955–1961** (Columbia 65833), is a classic. The arrangements and frameworks are inspired, with "'Round Midnight" being given one of its most memorable treatments, Davis's muted trumpet on "Bye Bye Blackbird" turning the trad warhorse into a cool jazz gem, and both "Dear Old Stockholm" and "All of You" becoming jazz standards due to these versions. The single CD also has four additional numbers from other early Columbia dates (including "Two Bass Hit" and "Budo"), but get the larger "complete" box instead.

Due to his signing with Columbia (which garnered him a great deal of publicity) and the release of **'Round About Midnight**, Miles Davis became a celebrity whose taste in clothes became influential, while his stage manner of largely ignoring and sometimes turning his back to the audience became a popular topic. In many ways, Davis was really an antihero—a distant and often unfriendly personality who could switch moods and become angry on a moment's notice. Some of his behavior was inexcusable, particularly his treatment of women in his private life. But during a period when the civil rights movement was gaining in force and blacks were being encouraged not to be subservient (or even particularly friendly) to whites, Davis became a role model of sorts. There was certainly no question about his musical genius, whether it was his skills as a talent scout, as a musical inspiration to his sidemen, or his ability to make his technical deficiencies on the trumpet into an asset.

In early 1957, the Miles Davis Quintet broke up, due partly to Davis's disappointment in John Coltrane's drug use and increasing reliability. While Coltrane permanently kicked heroin a few months later and learned a great deal during his period as a member of Thelonious Monk's quartet, Davis was involved in his first collaboration with Gil Evans since the "Birth of the Cool" days. Evans, who became Davis's best friend, had not been all that active during 1950–55, but he came out of semi-retirement in 1956 to contribute some colorful charts to a Helen Merrill date. Miles always liked his writing from Evans's days with Claude Thornhill and would collaborate with him on four full-scale projects, all of which are reissued on the six-CD set **Miles Davis & Gil Evans—The Complete Columbia Studio Recordings** (Columbia 67397). Since that box has an enormous amount of alternate takes, rehearsal versions, and even studio chatter, it is better to just acquire the individual finished sets. The LP ◉ **Miles Ahead** (Columbia/Legacy 65121), which adds four alternate takes to the original ten songs, has the trumpeter (who switches to the warmer flugelhorn) backed by a 19-piece orchestra and performing such numbers as Dave Brubeck's "The Duke," "My Ship," "Blues for Pablo," J.J. Johnson's "Lament," and the joyful "I Don't Wanna Be Kissed." The ten tunes form a continuous suite, explore many moods, and bring out the very best in Miles Davis.

In the summer of 1957, Davis gigged with a quintet that included Garland, Chambers, drummer Art Taylor, and Sonny Rollins. In the winter he went to France, recording the intriguing soundtrack to **Ascenseur**

Pour L'Echafaud (Lift to the Scaffold), which has been released with additional takes on Fontana 836 305. For that project, Miles is joined by Kenny Clarke, tenor saxophonist Barney Wilen, pianist Rene Urtreger, and the reliable bassist Pierre Michelot.

In 1958, Davis reformed his quintet with Coltrane, Garland, Chambers, and Jones, but also adding altoist Cannonball Adderley. The super sextet was arguably his strongest band, as can be heard on **Milestones** (Columbia/Legacy 85203). This version of "Two Bass Hit" has a heated trade-off by the always serious-sounding Coltrane (who had grown tremendously as a soloist during the past year) and the jubilant Adderley. "Billy Boy" is a feature for Garland (who closely emulates Ahmad Jamal), and "Straight No Chaser" (which is heard in two lengthy versions) has statements from all the soloists. The CD reissue adds three alternate takes to the original six-song program.

By the late spring, Bill Evans and Jimmy Cobb had taken over for Red Garland and Philly Joe Jones. **'58 Sessions** (Columbia/Legacy 47835) has the new sextet featured on versions of "On Green Dolphin Street" and "Stella by Starlight" that helped those songs become jazz standards, plus three of the four lengthy selections ("Straight No Chaser," "My Funny Valentine," and "Oleo") recorded for and also reissued on **Jazz at the Plaza** (Columbia/Legacy 85245); the latter set also has "If I Were a Bell." **At Newport 1958** (Columbia/Legacy 85202) consists of the sextet's 38-minute set at that year's festival, including a remarkably rapid rendition of "Ah-Leu-Cha" and another version of "Straight No Chaser."

The year 1958 also resulted in the Miles Davis/Gil Evans album ◗ **Porgy and Bess** (Columbia/Legacy 65141). This time around, Evans's 18-piece orchestra accompanies Davis on 13 selections from George Gershwin's **Porgy and Bess**. The suite (which is augmented by two alternate takes) has one of the truly great instrumental versions of "Summertime" plus inventive reworkings of such songs as "Bess You Is My Woman Now," "My Man's Gone Now," and "I Loves You Porgy."

The pressure of being the only white in the group plus his desire to lead his own trio led Bill Evans to leave Davis by the end of 1958, being replaced by Wynton Kelly. However, for Davis's next project, he persuaded Evans to play piano on four of the five songs. Many people have cited **Kind of Blue** (Columbia/Legacy 64935) as their favorite jazz recording and one of the most influential of all time. This monumental set, which came together fairly

quickly, features the Miles Davis Sextet often improvising off of scales rather than chord structures. It has the initial (and most famous) versions of "So What" (which only used two chords) and "All Blues," has the scalar approach being utilized on "Flamenco Sketches" (the only song from the session that has an alternate take), includes the haunting "Blue in Green," and features the band (with Kelly) playing the blues on "Freddie Freeloader." Although not as outwardly exciting as some of the group's other recordings (such as their Newport appearance of 1958), the improvising is on a very high level, Davis is heard during one of his prime periods, and for the last time the contrasting styles and moods of Coltrane and Adderley are heard together.

Cannonball Adderley soon departed to form his own successful quintet. Davis had one more major project left in the 1950s, his third album with Gil Evans. ◗ **Sketches of Spain** (Columbia/Legacy 65142), which was recorded in November 1959 and March 1960, is further removed from the jazz tradition than **Miles Ahead** and **Porgy and Bess**. Davis's flugelhorn is heard improvising on two numbers associated with Spanish music (including "Concierto de Aranjuez") and three Evans originals in that style. The CD adds an alternate version of "Concierto" plus the brief "Song of Our Country" to the original program. The music is quite dramatic and often very emotional (particularly "Saeta"), stretching both Davis's inventiveness and the boundaries of jazz.

After all of this activity, 1960 was somewhat anticlimactic for the trumpeter. The Wynton Kelly-Paul Chambers-Jimmy Cobb rhythm section stayed intact, but John Coltrane (who had already recorded "Giant Steps") was itching to go out on his own. Davis did what he could to persuade Coltrane to stay, but after a European tour during March–April, Trane departed. **Live in Stockholm 1960** (Royal Jazz 509) is a four-CD set that features two different versions of the Miles Davis Quintet. The first half is taken from Coltrane's final tour with the band, and finds Trane really stretching out in dynamic fashion; he does not sound like a sideman anymore. Also of interest from the same group is the single disc **Live in Zurich 1960** (Jazz Unlimited 2031) which has lengthy versions of "If I Were a Bell," "So What," and "All Blues." The second half of the Royal Jazz set is taken from Davis's second European tour of the year, dating from September–October By then Sonny Stitt was temporarily Coltrane's replacement and the music sounds much more like a bebop jam session even if the repertoire is not all that different from the Coltrane period. Clearly Stitt was not going to be inspiring Davis to move his music forward, and he was soon replaced by Hank Mobley.

Miles Davis had a very interesting five years, and there were many more accomplishments coming up in the future.

Gil Evans   Prior to 1956, Gil Evans was primarily known for his Claude Thornhill arrangements of 1942 and 1946–47, and for his contributions to the Miles Davis Nonet's "Birth of the Cool." In 1956, he came out of years of obscurity to write some fine charts for a Helen Merrill session, and then in 1957 his collaboration with Miles Davis (**Miles Ahead**) made him immortal. Evans's voicings for brass and his skill at framing Davis's horn were widely respected. The Davis-Evans partnership resulted in two other masterpieces: **Porgy and Bess** (1958) and **Sketches of Spain** (1959–60).

In addition, Evans led some colorful record dates of his own. **Gil Evans and Ten** (Original Jazz Classics 346) from 1957 has his 11-piece band consisting of two trumpets, two trombones, Willie Ruff on French horn, Steve Lacy on soprano, altoist Lee Konitz, a bassoonist, bass, drums, and Evans's sparse piano. The material ranges from Leadbelly to Leonard Bernstein in addition to "Nobody's Heart" and "Just One of those Things." ❍ **New Bottle Old Wine** (Blue Note 46855) has Evans reworking eight jazz classics, including "St. Louis Blues," "Lester Leaps In," and "Struttin' with Some Barbeque" with a band consisting of eight brass (including French horn and tuba), a four-piece rhythm section, and just one reed player, Cannonball Adderley. This version of "King Porter Stomp" (which showcases Adderley) is a classic both for the arrangement and Cannonball's solo, and trumpeter Johnny Coles and guitarist Chuck Wayne get some fine features too. **Great Jazz Standards** (Blue Note 46856) is a follow-up with five more vintage tunes plus "Ballad of the Sad Young Men" and Evans's "Theme." A similar instrumentation is used except this time the reeds are Steve Lacy and Budd Johnson; Coles, Curtis Fuller, Jimmy Cleveland, and guitarist Ray Crawford also get solo space. "Straight No Chaser" is given a particularly inventive arrangement. Also quite worthy is 1960's **Out of the Cool** (MCA/Impulse 5653) which features more obscure and complex material than the other sets, including

"Where Flamingos Fly," George Russell's "Stratusphunk," "La Nevada," and "Sunken Treasure."

Virtually unknown in 1955, by 1960 the formerly reclusive Gil Evans was rated as one of jazz's greatest arrangers.

John Coltrane   In 1955, John Coltrane received the biggest break of his life, becoming the tenor saxophonist with the Miles Davis Quintet despite being a relative unknown. Davis saw something in Coltrane's passionate playing and earnest desire that sparked his interest, and he was soon rewarded as Trane became a major voice on the tenor in 1956. His tone, though born from that of Dexter Gordon, was already quite original. Like Coleman Hawkins, Coltrane developed into a master at dissecting chord structures, and his solos became more and more complex. Rather than concentrating on individual notes, Coltrane's improvisations were waves of passion which writer Ira Gitler termed "sheets of sound." He was used on many jam session style recordings during 1956–58 for the Prestige label and by 1957 was competing with Sonny Rollins as jazz's top tenor.

Due to his drug use, Coltrane was fired by Miles Davis early in 1957. However, within a few months he had discovered religion, quit drugs cold turkey (and permanently), and was growing musically in leaps and bonds. Coltrane spent the summer as a member of the Thelonious Monk Quartet, playing nightly at New York's Five Spot. The publicity greatly benefited Monk's career and the association with Thelonious led to Coltrane's playing becoming even stronger. In 1958, he rejoined Miles Davis's group (which was now a sextet), staying for two years, which included participating on Davis's **Kind of Blue** album and recording regularly for Atlantic (starting in 1959) including his **Giant Steps**. The latter piece could be thought of as the logical end of bebop because it was so overly thick with chords (which sometimes changed every two beats) and was impossible to play coherently without a lot of study. Coltrane would soon be going in the opposite direction.

Although Miles Davis did his best to hold on to Coltrane, by the summer of 1960 Trane was long overdue to go out on his own. He formed a quartet, which initially had pianist Steve Kuhn, bassist Steve Davis, and drummer Pete LaRoca; McCoy Tyner, Reggie Workman, and Elvin Jones soon replaced them. Coltrane began doubling on soprano, creating a piercing and passionate sound much different than any heard on that instrument previously. With the recording of "My Favorite Things" in October 1960 (much of which has Coltrane playing endlessly over a two-chord vamp), he had moved on to his next phase.

All of John Coltrane's work (outside of his dates with Miles Davis) for the Prestige label during 1956–58, both as a leader and as a sideman, are on the magnificent 16-CD box set ● **The Prestige Recordings** (Prestige 4405). One can argue that not every one of these 25 record dates is essential, but, taken as a whole, the consistency is quite impressive. Among the CDs included in the box that are available separately are **Black Pearls** (Original Jazz Classics 352), **Cattin' with Coltrane and Quinichette** (Original Jazz Classics 460), **Tenor Conclave** (Original Jazz Classics 127), **Interplay for 2 Trumpets and 2 Tenors** (Original Jazz Classics 292), **Dakar** (Original Jazz Classics 393), **Bahia** (Original Jazz Classics 415), **Coltrane** (Original Jazz Classics 020), **Lush Life** (Original Jazz Classics 131), **The Last Trane** (Original Jazz Classics 394), **Traneing In** (Original Jazz Classics 189), **Wheelin' and Dealin'** (Original Jazz Classics 672), **The Believer** (Original Jazz Classics 876), **Soultrane** (Original Jazz Classics 021), **Settin' the Pace** (Original Jazz Classics 078), **Standard Coltrane** (Original Jazz Classics 246), and **The Stardust Sessions** (Prestige 24056). In addition, the **Mating Call** (Original Jazz Classics 212) quartet album with Tadd Dameron and Coltrane's one meeting on records with Sonny Rollins (a lengthy "Tenor Madness") are also included. Among the dozens of other highlights are "Soultrane," "Soul Eyes," "While My Lady Sleeps," "Like Someone in Love," "You Leave Me Breathless," "Lush Life," "Black Pearls," and "Stardust." The settings range from a four-tenor septet with Hank Mobley, Al Cohn, and Zoot Sims, various all-star dates, and quartet sessions to two albums led by Gene Ammons that have Coltrane making very rare appearances on alto. If one had to choose just two of the individual CDs to acquire, **Coltrane** and **Lush Life** (which are the most intimate, putting the focus mostly on the tenor) would be recommended first, but serious collectors will want the Prestige box.

In addition to his work with Davis, Monk, and on Prestige, there were some other projects for John Coltrane during this era. Recorded in 1957, ● **Blue Train** (Blue Note 46095) was his only album as a leader for Blue Note (not counting a United Artists date with Cecil Taylor

sometimes reissued under his name on Blue Note), and it is a classic. Cut on September 15, 1957, Coltrane, Lee Morgan, Curtis Fuller, Kenny Drew, Paul Chambers, and Philly Joe Jones perform the lengthy title cut (a memorable blues), one of Trane's greatest compositions ("Moment's Notice"), "I'm Old Fashioned," "Lazy Bird," and "Locomotion." The musicians all sound inspired, with Morgan challenging Coltrane to play his best. In addition, Coltrane recorded some dates for Savoy (under flugelhornist Wilbur Harden's name) and a couple of sessions for Roulette.

During the 28 months that comprised January 1959–May 1961, John Coltrane recorded seven albums as a leader for Atlantic along with being a sideman on a date with Milt Jackson. ● **Heavyweight Champion: The Complete Atlantic Recordings** (Rhino/Atlantic 71984) is a seven-CD set with all of that music plus many alternate takes (including nine of "Giant Steps"). Among the albums reissued in full are **Giant Steps** (Atlantic 1311), **Coltrane Jazz** (Rhino/Atlantic 79891), **The Avant-Garde** (Rhino/Atlantic 79892), **Coltrane Plays the Blues** (Rhino/Atlantic 79966), **Coltrane's Sound** (Rhino/Atlantic 75588), **My Favorite Things** (Rhino/Atlantic 75204), and (from 1961) **Ole Coltrane** (Rhino/Atlantic 79965). While **Giant Steps**, which also debuted Coltrane's haunting ballad "Naima," "Cousin Mary," "Mr. P.C." (for Paul Chambers), and "Countdown," has Coltrane taking chordal improvisation to its extreme, **Coltrane Plays the Blues** is a pretty lyrical date in which he harmonizes beautifully with Don Cherry, particularly on Ornette Coleman's "The Blessing" and Monk's "Bemsha Swing." **My Favorite Things** has Coltrane inventing a completely new way of improvising, one based on emotions and sound explorations much more than chord structure.

As 1960 ended, John Coltrane was poised to be the leader of jazz.

Sonny Rollins   Sonny Rollins's rise to prominence was much less surprising than John Coltrane's. Rollins had already risen through the ranks by 1956, recording as early as 1948, working with Miles Davis in 1951, recording with Thelonious Monk, kicking drugs, and then becoming a major force with the Clifford Brown/Max Roach Quintet in 1956, going out on his own the following year. Still, the level of his accomplishments during 1956–58 was pretty remarkable as he recorded classic after classic.

It is a measure of both his significance and his productivity that three box sets are needed to sum up this era for Rollins. ◉ **The Complete Prestige Recordings** (Prestige 4407), a seven-CD set, covers 1949–54 during its first half and such 1956 recordings as **Plus Four** (Original Jazz Classics 243) that has the group with Brownie and Roach, **Tenor Madness** (Original Jazz Classics 124) that on the title cut has Rollins's only recording with Coltrane, **Saxophone Colossus** (Original Jazz Classics 291), **Plays for Bird** (Original Jazz Classics 214), and **Tour de Force** (Original Jazz Classics 095). Of these individual sets, **Saxophone Colossus** is particularly noteworthy due to its debut of "Blue Seven" (which has a lengthy Rollins solo that was the subject of a scholarly article), "Strode Rode," and "St. Thomas," a latter traditional calypso melody turned into a classic jazz standard. Also on this superb album (a quartet date with Tommy Flanagan, Doug Watkins, and Max Roach) are "You Don't Know What Love Is" and "Moritat," which is a long exploration of "Mack the Knife."

Rollins recorded four albums for Blue Note during December 1956–November 1957. ◉ **The Complete Blue Note Recordings** (Blue Note 21371), a five-CD set, has all of the music from **Vol. 1** (Blue Note 81542), **Vol. 2** (Blue Note 81558), **Newk's Time** (Blue Note 84001), and the very extensive **A Night at the Village Vanguard** (Blue Note 81581). While the first three projects are fairly conventional hard bop (except that Rollins's solos and repertoire are often quite witty), featuring such sidemen as Donald Byrd, Wynton Kelly, J.J. Johnson, Horace Silver, and (on two songs) Thelonious Monk, the Village Vanguard set showcases Rollins in particularly brilliant form. Backed by either Wilbur Ware or Donald Bailey on bass and Elvin Jones or Pete LaRoca on drums (there was no need for a pianist), Rollins stretches out on such songs as "Old Devil Moon," "Softly as in a Morning Sunrise," "Sonnymoon for Two," and "A Night in Tunisia" among others. Other than John Coltrane, no other saxophonist of the era could so dominate a set and never seem to run out of creative ideas.

But that was not all for Sonny Rollins during this era. ◉ **The Complete Riverside & Contemporary Recordings** (Riverside 4427) is a five-CD box that covers Rollins's music for those two labels during 1956–58, including a few sideman appearances. Among the albums reissued in this box is the classic set of Western themes wittily played by Rollins, Ray Brown, and Shelly Manne

called **Way Out West** (Original Jazz Classics 337), **The Sound of Sonny** (Original Jazz Classics 029), the rather impressive **Freedom Suite** (Original Jazz Classics 067), and **Sonny Rollins and the Contemporary Leaders** (Original Jazz Classics 340). Highlights include such songs as "I'm An Old Cowhand," "Come, Gone" (based on "After You've Gone"), an unaccompanied tenor solo on "It Could Happen to You," the unlikely "Toot, Toot, Tootsie," "Someday I'll Find You," the lengthy "Freedom Suite," "I've Found a New Baby," and even "Rock-A-Bye Your Baby with a Dixie Melody." In addition to all of these box sets, the single LP **Brass & Trio** (Verve 8430) has Rollins backed on four numbers by a big band arranged by Ernie Wilkins, jamming on a few pianoless trio selections, and taking "Body and Soul" (in a tribute to his idol Coleman Hawkins) as an unaccompanied tenor solo.

After 14 mostly brilliant albums in less than three years and a European tour in March 1959, Sonny Rollins surprised the jazz world by retiring from active playing for almost three years. Although there were many theories floated about why he dropped out, it turned out that Rollins mostly just wanted to take the time off to practice and relax. But since so few jazz musicians have ever voluntarily retired or even taken an extended vacation, in this area (as in most others) Sonny Rollins proved to be a nonconformist.

Thelonious Monk   Thelonious Monk had his playing and composing style fully formed by 1947 when he made his debut recordings as a leader for Blue Note. But due to his introverted personality, sometimes-eccentric way of communicating, and the fact that he was so advanced and original musically, Monk was considered both a legend and very obscure in the early 1950s. Things began to change in 1955 when he was signed to the new Riverside label and Orrin Keepnews became his regular record producer. First up was a project in which he recorded Duke Ellington tunes, to show that his playing was not all that forbidden and esoteric. In 1956, Monk recorded a trio album of standards with Oscar Pettiford and Art Blakey, **The Unique Thelonious Monk** (Original Jazz Classics 064), including "Liza," "Honeysuckle Rose," and "Tea for Two." Now that the jazz public had become a little more accustomed to Monk, Keepnews had the pianist make an album of his own music, **Brilliant Corners** (Original Jazz Classics 026), a classic set featuring four of his songs (including the catchy but difficult title cut and "Bemsha Swing") plus "I Surrender Dear"; sidemen include Sonny Rollins, Ernie Henry, and Clark Terry.

The year 1957 was Monk's breakthrough year. For a few months in the summer, he appeared nightly at the Half Note leading a quartet also including John Coltrane, Wilbur Ware, and Shadow Wilson. Although Monk's style had not changed in a decade (and never would), he had finally been discovered by the jazz press and public. His image quickly changed from being thought of as some kind of a nut into being crowned a genius. Finally the jazz world was starting to catch up with him.

Thelonious Monk's recordings for Riverside (which continued into 1961) were usually quite inspired, featuring him in a variety of settings. ◉ **The Complete Riverside Recordings** (Riverside 1022), a 15-CD set, has 153 performances in all from 1955–61 and ranks with Monk's earlier output for Blue Note. In addition to the sets already mentioned, such albums as **Thelonious Himself** (Original Jazz Classics 254), **Monk's Music** (Original Jazz Classics 084), **With John Coltrane** (Original Jazz Classics 039), **Thelonious in Action** (Original Jazz Classics 103), **Misterioso** (Original Jazz Classics 206), **At Town Hall** (Original Jazz Classics 135), **5 by Monk by 5** (Original Jazz Classics 362), **Thelonious Alone in San Francisco** (Original Jazz Classics 231), and **At the Blackhawk** (Original Jazz Classics 305) are reissued in full. **Monk's Music** has the pianist leading a notable all-star group that includes John Coltrane, Coleman Hawkins (featured on "Ruby, My Dear"), Gigi Gryce, Ray Copeland, Wilbur Ware, and Art Blakey; their version of "Well You Needn't" is particularly memorable. **With John Coltrane** has the only three studio recordings by the Monk-Coltrane-Ware-Wilson quartet. In the summer of 1958, Johnny Griffin was in Coltrane's spot in Monk's new quartet (a group also including bassist Ahmed Abdul-Malik and Roy Haynes), and he proved to be a perfect fit, really digging into Thelonious's music. Enough music was recorded by this group on August 7, 1958, to fill up **Thelonious in Action** and **Misterioso**.

On February 28, 1959, a special concert took place featuring Monk with a tentet performing Hall Overton arrangements of Monk's tunes, including a remarkable transcription of Monk's original piano solo on "Little Rootie Tootie." The music has been released on **At Town Hall**, and the soloists from this very successful concert

(the first to transfer Monk's music to a larger group) include Donald Byrd, Eddie Bert, Phil Woods, Pepper Adams, and Charlie Rouse. In 1959, Rouse became Monk's regular tenor, staying a decade. **5 by Monk by 5** has Monk's quartet (with Rouse, Sam Jones, and Art Taylor) augmented by Thad Jones on such numbers as "Straight No Chaser," "Jackie-ing," and "Played Twice." **Thelonious Himself** (from 1957) and **Thelonious Alone in San Francisco** are intriguing solo dates from 1957 and 1959, while **At the Blackhawk** has Monk, Rouse, bassist John Ore, and Billy Higgins joined by Harold Land and Joe Gordon on April 29, 1960.

Four decades later, **Discovery, Live at the Five Spot** (Blue Note 99786), a privately recorded session that features John Coltrane with Thelonious Monk's quartet, was released for the first time. Although at first it was believed to have been from 1957, it turns out that it is from the following year, with Coltrane taking Johnny Griffin's place for a night. "Trinkle, Tinkle," "I Mean You," and "In Walked Bud" are among the five selections and Coltrane is really burning with the group.

By then, Thelonious Monk had finally arrived and his fame continued to grow year-by-year.

Charles Mingus In late 1955, Charles Mingus found himself musically. Rather than exploring Third Stream music, he shifted toward a very emotional brand of modern jazz, bringing together his background in bebop, swing, and traditional jazz with the influences of church music, modern harmonies, and sound explorations. He pushed his sidemen very hard (sometimes to the breaking point) and persuaded/inspired/forced them to play above their own potential.

Many of Mingus's finest recordings are from the 1956–60 period, particularly his work for Atlantic, which has been reissued in full on the six-CD set ◉ **Passions of a Man: The Complete Atlantic Recordings** (Rhino/Atlantic 72871) including the albums **Pithecanthropus Erectus** (Atlantic 8809), **The Clown** (Rhino/Atlantic 75590), **Blues & Roots** (Rhino/Atlantic 75205), **Tonight at Noon** (Label M 5723), **Mingus at Antibes** (Rhino/Atlantic 90532), and 1961's **Oh Yeah**, plus a 75-minute interview.

Mingus's Pithecanthropus Erectus was a breakthrough album, with the title cut musically depicting the rise and fall of man. Jackie McLean, tenor saxophonist J.R. Monterose, Mal Waldron, and drummer Willie Jones are all pushed by Mingus on this stirring set, which also includes a humorous rendition of "A Foggy Day." **The Clown** has the classic "Haitian Fight Song," and the famous "Reincarnation of a Lovebird," with fine playing by trombonist Jimmy Knepper and altoist Shafi Hadi. **Blues & Roots** from 1959 has Mingus utilizing a nonet on six diverse and very stimulating originals including "Moanin'" (no relation to Bobby Timmons's song), "Wednesday Night Prayer Meeting," and "Cryin' Blues." **Tonight at Noon** has leftover but worthwhile items from 1957 and 1961, while **Mingus at Antibes** is a stirring 1960 live set in which Mingus, Eric Dolphy (on alto, flute, and bass clarinet), trumpeter Ted Curson, Dannie Richmond (Mingus's drummer since 1956), and tenor saxophonist Booker Ervin romp on such songs as "Wednesday Night Prayer Meeting," "Folk Forms #1," and "Better Git It in Your Soul." Bud Powell sits in on "I'll Remember April."

Charles Mingus also recorded for other labels during this era, and not all of his classics are confined to his Atlantic output. **Tijuana Moods** (Bluebird 63840) is a two-CD set with all of the pieces (and the many alternate takes) from a project inspired by a wild trip to Mexico. Trumpeter Clarence Shaw, Jimmy Knepper, Shafi Hadi, pianist Bill Triglia, and Dannie Richmond all play above their heads on this emotional date that includes "Ysabel's Table Dance," "Tijuana Gift Shop," and a lyrical spot for Shaw on "Flamingo." Mingus's 1957 bands are featured on **East Coasting** (Bethlehem 79807) and **A Modern Jazz Symposium of Music and Poetry** (Bethlehem 76678). Most of the music is obscure, but the latter set includes a memorable narration by Lonnie Elders on "Scenes in the City." **Jazz Portraits** (Blue Note 27325) has Mingus really pushing altoist John Handy and Booker Ervin on four lengthy, advanced hard bop selections, including "Nostalgia in Times Square" and "No Private Income Blues." In 1959, the bassist recorded two albums for Columbia, **Mingus Ah Um** (Columbia/Legacy 65512) and **Mingus Dynasty** (Columbia/Legacy 65513), both of which have been reissued several times, including with alternate takes as the three-CD set **The Complete 1959 Charles Mingus Columbia Sessions** (Columbia/Legacy 65145). In any version, these renditions of "Better Git It in Your Soul," "Goodbye Pork Pie Hat," and "Fables of Faubus" (a protest against a racist governor) on **Mingus Ah Um**, and "Slop," "Song with Orange," and "Far Wells, Mill Valley" from the **Mingus Dynasty** set add to the Mingus legacy.

In 1960, Charles Mingus recorded for Nat Hentoff's Candid label. His quartet of the period was particularly strong and inventive, consisting of Eric Dolphy, trumpeter Ted Curson, and Dannie Richmond. ◉ **Charles Mingus Presents Charles Mingus** (Candid 79005) has that group indulging in remarkable interplay on "What Love" and "Folk Forms Number One." **Mingus** (Candid 79021) has a 19-minute jam session on "MDM" (short for Monk/Duke/Mingus) featuring many of Mingus's favorite sidemen (including Ted Curson, trumpeter Lonnie Hillyer, Jimmy Knepper, Britt Woodman, Eric Dolphy, altoist Charles McPherson, and Booker Ervin), a quartet version of "Stormy Weather," and the brief but rambunctious "Lock 'Em Up."

Art Blakey and the Jazz Messengers   The Jazz Messengers, co-led by Art Blakey and Horace Silver, were one year old as 1956 began. After recording music for **The Jazz Messengers** (Columbia 65265), including such numbers as "Ecaroh," "Hank's Symphony," and the original version of "Nica's Dream," Silver left the group, taking along Donald Byrd (who had recently replaced original member Kenny Dorham), Hank Mobley, and Doug Watkins to start a quintet of his own. Art Blakey became the sole leader of the Jazz Messengers, but was temporarily in a bit of a quandary since he was now the group's only member! He quickly put together a new ensemble though it would be a couple of years before the Jazz Messengers had stable personnel.

The 1957 version of the band, featured on **Second Edition** (Bluebird 66661), has trumpeter Bill Hardman, tenor saxophonist Johnny Griffin, pianist Sam Dockery, bassist Spanky DeBrest, and guest altoist Jackie McLean (who was actually Griffin's predecessor). **Second Edition** reissues an album of Lerner and Lowe show tunes (including "Almost Like Being in Love" and "On the Street Where You Live"), a few obscure alternate takes, and two interesting numbers that have several additional musicians (including the young trumpeter Lee Morgan) added to the Messengers lineup. **Hard Drive** (Avenue Jazz/Bethlehem 75783) is another set by this version of the Jazz Messengers, featuring originals mostly by Griffin, Hardman, and Jimmy Heath. Other projects that Blakey was involved in during this time were a special big band that recorded for Bethlehem with so-so results (most interesting is that John Coltrane was in the lineup) and a pair of albums with percussionists that pay tribute to Blakey's African roots yet also looked ahead toward Afro-Cuban jazz: **Drum Suite** (Sony 480988) and **Orgy in Rhythm Vols. 1–2** (Blue Note 56586). While **Drum Suite** has Blakey joined by fellow drummer Jo Jones, the percussion of Specs Wright, Candido, and Sabu Martinez, pianist Ray Bryant (who brought along "Cubano Chant"), and Oscar Pettiford, the latter has Blakey interacting with drummers Art Taylor, Jo Jones, and Specs Wright (with the latter two doubling on tympani), five percussionists, flutist Herbie Mann, Bryant, and bassist Wendell Marshall. Sabu Martinez leads the chanting and takes three vocals.

Also of strong interest from this period is ◉ **Art Blakey's Jazz Messengers with Thelonious Monk** (Rhino/Atlantic 75598). A perfect matchup, this date (consisting of five of Thelonious Monk's best compositions plus Griffin's "Purple Shades") has Monk playing piano with the Jazz Messengers. Since Blakey was always the perfect drummer for Monk and Johnny Griffin would be joining Thelonious's quartet the following year (he really understood the pianist's complex songs), the session (which also features Bill Hardman and Spanky DeBrest) is a big success.

But even with all of this activity, it was not until 1958 that Art Blakey's Jazz Messengers were on much more solid ground and became poised to become a fixture in the jazz world. By the time the group recorded ◉ **Moanin'** (Blue Note 46516) on October 30, 1958, its lineup consisted of Blakey, 20-year-old trumpeter Lee Morgan, tenor saxophonist Benny Golson, pianist Bobby Timmons, and bassist Jymie Merritt. Morgan's brash and cocky playing added fire to the group as he carved out his own sound from the Clifford Brown tradition. Timmons's funky piano playing (a perfect successor to Horace Silver) and compositional skills (his "Moanin'" became a jazz hit) were major assets while Merritt was steady in support. Golson, in addition to having a tenor style influenced during this era by Lucky Thompson and Don Byas, was also a major composer, contributing "Blues March," "Along Came Betty," "Are You Real," and "The Drum Thunder Suite" to this set; the first two became standards. In addition, he persuaded Blakey to have the band look more professional, helped a great deal with the group's image, and was significant in moving the Jazz Messengers up to a higher level.

With the release of **Moanin'**, the Jazz Messengers became one of the most popular and influential bands in

jazz, the definitive hard bop group. After a European tour, Golson left the band, replaced at first by Hank Mobley. **At the Jazz Corner of the World: Vols. 1 and 2** (Blue Note 28888) is a two-CD set from April 15, 1959, that documents this version of the band as the group performs songs by Thelonious Monk ("Justice"), Ray Bryant, Randy Weston ("Hi-Fly"), Gildo Mahones, the standard "Close Your Eyes," two versions of "The Theme," and three Mobley originals.

A few months later, Wayne Shorter joined the Jazz Messengers as Mobley's successor, with Walter Davis, Jr., temporarily taking Bobby Timmons's place (Timmons for a time joined the new Cannonball Adderley Quintet). **Africaine** (Blue Note 97507) was the first of many gems recorded by the Morgan-Shorter version of the Messengers although this particular set was not released until over 20 years after it was recorded. The high point is Shorter's memorable composition "Lester Left Town" in tribute to the recently deceased Lester Young, and Morgan and Davis also contributed fine originals. In early 1960, Timmons returned to the band and the Morgan-Shorter-Timmons-Merritt-Blakey lineup recorded one memorable album after another. **The Big Beat** (Blue Note 46400) introduced Bobby Timmons's "Dat Dere" (his follow-up to his hit with Adderley, "This Here"), the official version of Shorter's "Lester Left Town," and a colorful arrangement of "It's Only a Paper Moon." **Like Someone in Love** (Blue Note 84245) and **A Night in Tunisia** (Blue Note 84049), both from August 1960, are most notable for classic versions of the title cuts. The Jazz Messengers also made several live albums of which **Lausanne 1960, Part 1** (TCB 02022) and **Lausanne 1960, Part 2** (TCB 02062) are easily recommended, as is every recording by one of the most classic editions of Blakey's band.

The Horace Silver Quintet   In 1956, Horace Silver left the Jazz Messengers, taking three of the four other musicians (Donald Byrd, Hank Mobley, and Doug Watkins) with him. An increasingly distinctive pianist whose witty song quotes, rhythmic phrases, and "funky" playing became quite influential, Silver was always a talented composer and had already written two jazz standards ("Doodlin'" and "The Preacher") that were first recorded with Art Blakey.

Silver's Blue (Columbia 476 521), one of the few early Horace Silver recordings not on Blue Note, launched his new group. The two sessions have Hank Mobley, either Joe Gordon or Donald Byrd on trumpet, Doug Watkins, and Kenny Clarke or Art Taylor on drums. The playing is excellent, but this was just a first step for the group. **Six Pieces of Silver** (Blue Note 25648) is the first major Horace Silver album. The group (Byrd, Mobley, Silver, Watkins, and Louis Hayes) performs a variety of Silver tunes plus "For Heaven's Sake." Best known is "Señor Blues," which is heard in three versions on this reissue including a later vocal rendition by Bill Henderson. **The Stylings of Silver** (Blue Note 1562), not yet out on CD, has the 1957 Silver Quintet (with Art Farmer, Mobley, bassist Teddy Kotick, and Hayes) playing more Silver originals, "My One and Only Love," and his famous "Home Cookin'" which would be turned into vocalese by Lambert, Hendricks, and Ross a few years later. **Further Explorations** (Blue Note 56583), with Clifford Jordan in Mobley's place, has five lesser-known Silver tunes plus "Ill Wind."

◉ **Finger Poppin'** (Blue Note 84008) of February 1, 1959, is notable for being the first recording by the most famous version of the Horace Silver Quintet, an ensemble consisting of the leader, trumpeter Blue Mitchell, tenor saxophonist Junior Cook, bassist Gene Taylor, and drummer Louis Hayes. Other than Roy Brooks becoming the drummer in 1960, this would be the group's personnel into 1963. **Finger Poppin'** is also one of the best albums by Silver, featuring such new tunes by the pianist as "Come on Home," "Juicy Lucy," and "Cookin' at the Continental." **Blowin' the Blues Away** (Blue Note 46526) is notable for Silver's "Sister Sadie" and "Peace" while **Horace-Scope** (Blue Note 84042) introduced "Strollin'" and revived his "Nica's Dream."

In 1960, Horace Silver, with the many songs he had contributed to the jazz repertoire, his pacesetting hard bop quintet, and his influential piano style, was helping to lead the way toward soul jazz.

The Ornette Coleman Quartet Ornette Coleman was the talk of the New York jazz world during 1959–60. A major innovator whose ideas would do a great deal to change jazz in the 1960s, Coleman has remained a controversial figure up to the present time, dividing the jazz audience into those who think he is a giant and others who consider him a bit of a fraud because he never recorded conventional bebop. Coleman's early evolution was not documented (his recording debut did not happen until he was almost 28) so it is difficult to imagine what he really sounded like as a youth. He began playing alto in his native Texas when he was 14 in 1944, adding tenor two years later. Coleman played in R&B bands in the South, including those of Red Connors and Pee Wee Crayton, and his early influence was Charlie Parker, but he met opposition early on whenever he tried to develop his own original style. By 1953, Coleman was in Los Angeles, working as an elevator operator while teaching himself harmony and theory from books. Around that time he began practicing with trumpeter Don Cherry, and during the next few years he also met up with bassist Charlie Haden, drummers Ed Blackwell and Billy Higgins, and trumpeter Bobby Bradford. While those musicians were impressed by Ornette's ideas, he was scorned at local jam sessions by the beboppers who felt that he had no idea what he was playing.

The truth is, it was the inflexible boppers who were confused, for Coleman was in the process of developing his harmelodic theory. The altoist's playing was purposely speechlike, with his sounds and notes often being between the conventional tones. Even more controversial was his desire to dispense with chord changes and harmonies altogether. Although he and Don Cherry played opening and closing melodies together in unison (as the boppers did), their solos were based in abstract form on the original theme or mood of a piece rather than its chords, and Coleman was constantly improvising melodies, expressing himself emotionally. His music had the rhythm section swinging (in its own fashion) in a driving manner, always moving forward, but without setting any chordal patterns to restrict the soloists. Considering that one of the main aspects to bebop is chordal improvisation, Coleman's music was revolutionary and seen as a threat by many of the established jazz players.

In 1958, Ornette Coleman brought Don Cherry along to audition some of his tunes for producer Lester Koenig of Contemporary Records. Koenig surprised Coleman by saying that he liked the songs so much that he would like the altoist to record them himself. **The Music of Ornette Coleman: Something Else!!!** (Original Jazz Classics 163) teams Coleman, Cherry, and Billy Higgins with pianist Walter Norris and bassist Don Payne. While Norris and Payne do their best, they set chordal patterns that restrict the music a bit. However, the two horn players already sound quite mature and are certainly recognizable, and Coleman's nine tunes are strong and original, particularly "The Blessing" and "When Will the Blues Leave."

Don Cherry, who played trumpet and cornet, but was best known for his work on the pocket cornet, was never a virtuoso, but he was certainly an open-minded improviser, and his presence was an invaluable help for Coleman, who recognized his kindred spirit. Cherry's father owned the Cherry Blossom Club in Oklahoma City where Charlie Christian played before joining Benny Goodman in 1939. In 1940, Cherry and his family moved to Los Angeles, and Cherry started on trumpet while in junior high school. As a teenager, he freelanced in the L.A. area, playing bebop with Dexter Gordon, Wardell Gray, and anyone who would let him sit in. When he first met Coleman, he was intrigued by the altoist's method of improvising without using chord changes. They practiced together regularly, and soon Cherry was much less welcome at jam sessions as his playing was now considered too eccentric!

While Ed Blackwell was Ornette Coleman's original drummer, by 1956 he had moved back to his native New Orleans. Billy Higgins, who took his place, would become one of the most recorded of all drummers. A very flexible player who gave Coleman the forward momentum that he wanted without restricting him to a metronomic 4/4 rhythm, Higgins fit very well into the quartet.

The last and most important sideman to join Coleman's quartet was bassist Charlie Haden. In fact, one wonders what the altoist would have done in 1958–59 if Haden had never existed. What other bassist active at that time could have given him such a highly individual voice and a solid pulse without stating chord patterns? Haden had grown up playing and singing country music on a radio show with his family. After moving to Los Angeles in the mid-1950s, he worked with Art Pepper, Hampton Hawes, and pianist Paul Bley. Bley had a long-time gig at the Hillcrest Club in Los Angeles. In 1958, shortly after recording their first album, Coleman and Cherry were invited by Bley to make his trio (which also included Haden and Higgins) into a quintet. Bley knew full well that the presence of the two radical horn players would doom the gig, but he felt it would be worth it for the experience. As expected, Bley was immediately given his two weeks notice by the management. Two albums of material surfaced years later from this gig. **Coleman Classics, Vol. 1** (Improvising Artists 373 852), which was briefly reissued on CD, has extended versions of "When Will the Blues Leave" and "Ramblin'," along with briefer renditions of "Crossroads" and "How Deep Is the

Ocean." **Live at the Hillcrest Club** (Inner City 1007) has unfortunately not reappeared on CD yet. It not only has a different version of "The Blessing" and a well-titled "Free," but also unusual renditions of Charlie Parker's "Klactoveesedstene" and Roy Eldridge's "I Remember Harlem." On both of these historic sets, Bley mostly stays out of the way and clearly benefits from the unique encounters with one of the main pioneers of free jazz. However, this would be the last time that Coleman would be heard with a pianist for many years.

Tomorrow Is the Question (Original Jazz Classics 342), from January–March 1959, has Coleman dropping the piano and interacting with Don Cherry, but using a rhythm section (Percy Heath or Red Mitchell on bass and Shelly Manne on drums) that, although quite sincere and enthusiastically trying their best, was not as loose and free as one would hope. Among the nine Ornette tunes that are debuted are "Tears Inside," "Compassion," and "Turnaround."

In May 1959, Ornette Coleman began recording for the Atlantic label. In the summer (with the assistance of John Lewis and Gunther Schuller, two major supporters of the new free music) Ornette and Don Cherry attended the Lenox School of Jazz. Soon they were booked for an extended stay at New York's Five Spot, an engagement that received a great deal of publicity. Members of the New York jazz establishment were in evidence every night, debating the virtues of the music. The beboppers were in an ironic position for, although they were considered the radicals of 1945, 15 years later they had become conservative traditionalists simply by standing still.

Ornette Coleman's Atlantic recordings (cut during 1959–61), six albums plus two collections not released until years later, were the most significant of his career. ● **Beauty Is a Rare Thing: The Complete Atlantic Recordings** (Rhino/Atlantic 71410) is a six-CD set that has all of the music plus a set (**The Art of Who Keeps a Record**) only out previously in Japan, two songs featuring Coleman on a John Lewis/Gunther Schuller album, and six unreleased selections. Serious collectors will have to get this box.

The individual albums are all worth mentioning. **The Shape of Jazz to Come** (Rhino/Atlantic 19238) has the real recording debut for the Ornette Coleman Quartet (with Cherry, Haden, and Higgins), cut a few months before the group relocated to New York and including such songs as the emotional ballad "Lonely Woman," "Peace," and "Congeniality." **Change of the Century** (Atlantic 81341) from October 1959 includes such intriguing and unpredictable pieces as the swinging "Una Muy Bonita," "Ramblin'," and "Bird Food." **This Is Our Music** (Atlantic 81353), from July–August 1960, has a childlike interpretation of the only non-original recorded by the quartet during the period ("Embraceable You") and the catchy "Blues Connotation" plus five lesser-known Ornette originals (including "Humpty Dumpty" and "Beauty Is a Rare Thing"). This album is most significant for introducing Ed Blackwell (who had relocated to New York) as the new member of the quartet. Blackwell, who had a unique sound that was fairly free yet with roots in New Orleans jazz, was ideal for Coleman's group.

Two other albums of material by the quartet from 1959–61 were not released for many years. **The Art of the Improviser** (Rhino/Atlantic 90978) has quite a few rewarding pieces performed by Coleman, Cherry, Higgins or Blackwell, and Haden, Scott LaFaro, or Jimmy Garrison on bass. Highlights include "The Circle with the Hole in the Middle," "The Fifth of Beethoven," and "The Legend of Bebop." **Twins** (Atlantic 8810), which has not been reissued individually on CD (though its selections have often appeared as "bonus tracks" in the other Coleman sets), has some notable originals (including "Little Symphony" and "Monk and the Nun"), plus "First Take," a shorter 17-minute version of the monumental **Free Jazz**.

"First Take" is logically also included on the reissue of **Free Jazz** (Rhino/Atlantic 75208). Utilizing a double quartet comprised of Freddie Hubbard and Don Cherry on trumpets, Eric Dolphy on bass clarinet, both Charlie Haden and Scott LaFaro on basses, and Ed Blackwell and Billy Higgins on drums plus the leader, this 37-minute work from December 21, 1960, is nearly a complete free improvisation. There is a quick opening melody, a steady pulse generated by the rhythm section, and loose but organized parts between the solos, but otherwise the music is spontaneous. When one player is the main soloist, the other musicians are free to "comment" behind his playing. The ten-minute portion where Ornette is in the lead is stirring, with the altoist coming up with one melodic phrase after another. This set deserves to be heard by all jazz fans, particularly those who may not think that Ornette Coleman swings.

Jazz would never be quite the same again after Ornette Coleman's rise to fame. His innovations affected even later brands of straightahead jazz, giving soloists a wider range of sounds and notes to choose from.

Cecil Taylor   While Ornette Coleman was able to gain a great deal of attention when he debuted in New York in 1959, Cecil Taylor was still being largely ignored. The most advanced of all jazz musicians, Taylor can be heard playing standards a bit on his infrequent recordings of the 1950s although in a percussive and increasingly atonal fashion. The Duke Ellington, Thelonious Monk, and Dave Brubeck influences would be largely gone after 1960 as he played completely free, so his earliest recordings are quite fascinating in retrospect.

During 1955–57, Taylor had a quartet comprised of bassist Buell Neidlinger, drummer Dennis Charles, and Steve Lacy on soprano. Advanced as those musicians were, Taylor was a decade ahead of them. Three songs were recorded at the 1957 Newport Jazz Festival by the group, including a rollicking version of Billy Strayhorn's "Johnny Come Lately" and a medium-tempo (if not too conventional) blues called "Mona's Blues." From 1958, **Lookin' Ahead** (Original Jazz Classics 452) has vibraphonist Earl Griffith in Lacy's place. The sound of the band is more accessible than the originals, which include "Wallering," "Excursion on a Wobbly Rail," and "Of What." Later that year Taylor had an opportunity to lead a quintet for a United Artists record, which was later called **Coltrane Time** (Blue Note 84461) and released under Trane's name. Taylor picked John Coltrane, bassist Chuck Israels, drummer Louis Hayes, and hoped to get trumpeter Ted Curson. Unfortunately, Curson was unavailable so Kenny Dorham was hired in his place. The set, which consists of "Like Someone in Love," "Just Friends," and two blues, is a near-disaster because Dorham openly ridiculed Taylor whose rhythmic clusters behind soloists made Coltrane sound conservative in comparison. The results are fascinating, but quite uneven, with Dorham and Taylor often sounding like they are in two different rooms, doing their best to ignore each other.

In 1959, Cecil Taylor finally had an opportunity to use Curson (and tenor saxophonist Bill Barron) on a few numbers, but the pianist easily earns the solo honors on **Love for Sale** (Blue Note 94107). He plays three rather adventurous interpretations of Cole Porter songs ("Get Out of Town," "I Love Paris," and "Love for Sale") in a trio with Neidlinger and drummer Rudy Collins, using the two horns on three of his radical originals. With 1960's

The World of Cecil Taylor (Candid 79006), one hears the mature Cecil Taylor emerging. While Buell Neidlinger and Dennis Charles are still essentially playing timekeeping roles, Taylor is completely atonal and shows off his remarkable technique. Tenor saxophonist Archie Shepp makes his recording debut on "Air" and "Lazy Afternoon," showing that he was on the same wavelength as Taylor. It was not about melodies or notes anymore, but about emotions and waves of sound. This is where part of the future of jazz was heading.

Bop, Cool Jazz, and Hard Bop

While cool jazz initially developed on the West Coast and hard bop in the East, the formerly separate movements (both of which originated out of bebop) became increasingly entwined as the second half of the 1950s progressed. Hard bop spread to the West, some of the hard bop soloists in the East had cooler sounds than formerly, and racial boundaries began to gradually break apart with blacks being hired more for studio work. By 1960, West Coast cool jazz had faded in importance and hard bop had largely become the modern mainstream jazz of the era. For that reason, the musicians of both styles (along with the classic bebop survivors) are mixed together in this section.

Major Groups of 1956–1960

Although having more turnover than many of the big bands of the 1930s and '40s, some of which were like families, there were quite a few regularly working bands during the second half of the 1950s. The star sidemen often had opportunities to record as leaders, and many were content to draw a regular paycheck while contributing to the music of others during their regular jobs.

Harry Arnold and the Swedish Radio Big Band Harry Arnold, a Swedish arranger who originally played tenor and alto, led the Swedish Radio Big Band during 1956–65, a cool/bop jazz orchestra that made some significant recordings during the second half of the 1950s in Sweden. Among Arnold's sidemen were altoist Arne Domnerus, pianist Bengt Hallberg, trombonist Ake Persson, and American trumpeter Benny Bailey. Stan Getz, Ernestine Anderson, Lucky Thompson, Coleman Hawkins, Toots Thielemans, and Tony Scott all made guest appearances in Sweden with Arnold, and for a period in 1958 the visiting Quincy Jones headed the band, contributing many arrangements.

The Big Band in Concert 1957/58 (Dragon 283), the best available showcase for the orchestra, has music from three concerts and guest spots for Scott, Alice Babs (who sings "Prelude to a Kiss"), and Quincy Jones as arranger/conductor. **Premiari** (Ancha 9501) will be difficult to find since it is from a small Swedish label, but it has excellent radio broadcasts from 1956 and 1960, a lot of swing standards, and Horace Silver's "Sister Sadie" and Ornette Coleman's "Ramblin'." In addition, there are four numbers from a swing sextet headed by clarinetist Putte Wickman. From the same label is **1959** (Ancha 9097), which is on the same level and includes two vocals apiece by Monica Zetterlund and Alice Babs.

The Count Basie Orchestra   The mighty Count Basie Orchestra was riding high in 1956 with its hit recordings of "April in Paris" and "Everyday I Have the Blues." Sporting strong soloists in Thad Jones, Joe Newman, Frank Foster, and Frank Wess, plus an unbeatable rhythm section, the Basie band was recognized worldwide as a swinging machine. It continued recording for Verve until the fall of 1957 when it switched to Roulette. **The Greatest!! Count Basie—Joe Williams** (Verve 833 774) features Williams singing a dozen standards (avoiding blues) with the backing of the Basie band, including "Thou Swell," "A Fine Romance," and "Our Love Is Here to Say." **Count Basie in London** (Verve 833 805), which despite its title was actually recorded live in Sweden, has a fairly typical program by the 1956 band with remakes of "Jumpin' at the Woodside," "Shiny Stockings," "Corner Pocket," and three Joe Williams vocals. Best of the Verve recordings is ● **Count Basie at Newport** (Verve 833 776), which was cut live at the 1957 Newport Jazz Festival. The Basie big band sounds inspired on "Swingin' at Newport" and welcomes Lester Young (during one of his last appearances with Basie) on "Polka Dots and Moonbeams" and "Lester Leaps In." Basie and Pres are joined by Jimmy Rushing for exciting versions of "Sent for You Yesterday and Here You Come Today," "Boogie Woogie," and "Evenin'," which served as a final look back into the 1930s. Five previously unreleased numbers are added to the CD, including four Joe Williams vocals, and the closing "One o'Clock Jump" has solos by Young, Illinois Jacquet, and a screaming Roy Eldridge. Overall it makes for a remarkable night of music.

All of the Count Basie Orchestra's recordings for the Roulette label have been reissued in a pair of magnificent but limited-edition set,s which are respectively ten- and eight-CD boxes: **The Complete Roulette Studio Count Basie** (Mosaic 10-149) and **The Complete Roulette Live Recordings of Count Basie** (Mosaic 8-135). The second Basie big band was at its height during this period (which covers 1957–62). For those listeners who are not able to locate (or afford) these sets, a variety of single CDs are recommended. ◉ **The Complete Atomic Basie** (Roulette 28635) has classic Neal Hefti charts, including "The Kid from Red Bank" (a great feature for Basie's piano), "Flight of the Foo Birds," "Whirlybird," "Splanky," and the famous ballad "Lil' Darlin.'" **One More Time** (Roulette 797271) features Quincy Jones's arrangements for Basie, including "For Lena and Lennie," "I Needs to Be Bee'd With," and "The Midnight Sun Will Never Set." For **Kansas City Suite** (Roulette 794575), Benny Carter had an opportunity to write ten numbers (including "Vine Street Rumble") for the Basie Orchestra although none of his originals caught on. **Breakfast Dance and Barbeque** (Roulette 31791) is an excellent live set from 1959, with charts by Ernie Wilkins, Frank Foster (including "In a Mellotone"), and Thad Jones.

The Dave Brubeck Quartet   Because the Dave Brubeck Quartet was among the most popular bands in jazz by 1956, there was a backlash of criticism from some of the jazz journalists who had formerly been supporters, feeling that if a jazz group catches on, there must be something wrong with the music. Brubeck was often savaged in the press for his "pounding" of unusual chords and for playing in two keys at once, while some writers wondered why Paul Desmond stayed with the group. Brubeck was essentially being criticized for being original and not sounding like Bud Powell, even though individuality is supposed to be one of the main goals of being a jazz musician. But the carping did not matter, for the popularity of the group continued to grow, and their music stayed original and distinctive.

Norman Bates replaced his brother Bob Bates on bass in 1956. The year 1957 found Joe Morello succeeding Joe Dodge on drums and Eugene Wright taking over for Bates at year-end. The Brubeck-Desmond-Wright-Morello version of the quartet would remain intact for a decade. Having an integrated group caused problems even in the late 1950s, and Brubeck cancelled many dates in the South when it was suggested that Eugene Wright be replaced. Although Desmond preferred the laidback approach of the earlier rhythm sections, he eventually accepted the playing of the much more assertive and powerful Joe Morello.

In 1956, **Brubeck Plays Brubeck** (Columbia/Legacy 65722) was the first solo piano album by Brubeck and, in addition to including definitive versions of "The Duke" and "One Moment Worth Years," it introduces one of his most famous originals, "In Your Own Sweet Way." Brubeck's second piano solo album, **Plays and Plays and Plays** (Original Jazz Classics 716), mostly features his fresh renditions of standards. The quartet set **Dave Digs Disney** (Columbia/Legacy 48820) was inspired by a trip to Disneyland by Brubeck's growing family and has jazz versions of eight songs taken from Disney movies (including "Heigh Ho," "When You Wish Upon a Star," and "Someday My Prince Will Come"), most of which were already in the group's repertoire.

In 1958, the Brubeck Quartet played 80 concerts in 14 countries during a three-month period, recording **Jazz Impressions of Eurasia** (Columbia/Legacy 48531) upon their return. The six originals include "Brandenburg Gate" and "Calcutta Blues." From two years later, **Dave Brubeck and Jimmy Rushing** (Columbia/Legacy 65727) has the quartet teaming up with veteran blues/swing singer Jimmy Rushing; they display mutual respect and inspiration on 11 standards. Surprisingly, **Jazz Goes to Junior College** (Columbia 1034) from 1957 (a near-classic), and **Brubeck Plays Bernstein** (Columbia 8257) during which Brubeck and the New York Philharmonic perform his brother Howard Brubeck's "Dialogues for Jazz Combo and Orchestra" plus five Leonard Bernstein songs (four from *West Side Story*), remain out of print.

However, all of those recordings were eclipsed by an album recorded during June–August 1959, ◉ **Time Out** (Columbia/Legacy 65122). Dave Brubeck had had a strong interest in exploring other time signatures beyond 4/4 ever since his octet days in the late 1940s. To the surprise of everyone, "Take Five" (composed by Paul Desmond with a bit of help from Brubeck) became a giant hit, showing that a song in 5/4 time could catch on. Brubeck's "Blue Rondo à la Turk" (which is in 9/4 before resolving into a standard blues) was a close second and "Three to Get Ready" also became well known. If the

Dave Brubeck Quartet had not been famous before, they became immortal with the release of this best-selling album. Brubeck would be performing "Take Five" at virtually every one of his quartet performances from then on. To Dave Brubeck's credit, he would never tire of the song, or his fans of his playing.

The Ray Charles Orchestra   Ray Charles became a household name during the second half of the 1950s. His big band featured such players as altoist Hank Crawford and tenor saxophonist David "Fathead" Newman, and Charles was always a fan of swinging jazz à la Count Basie and Louis Jordan, but he was never strictly a jazz performer. His singing (which epitomized soul music) made such songs as "Hallelujah I Love Her So," "What'd I Say," "Let the Good Times Roll," Lil Hardin Armstrong's "Just for a Thrill," and "Don't Let the Sun Catch You Crying" into big hits.

The three-CD box set **The Birth of Soul** (Atlantic 82310) has Charles's best-sellers of the 1950s. The two-fer **Blues + Jazz** (Rhino 71607) has a few duplicates, but mostly focuses on Brother Ray's more blues- and jazz-oriented work of the period, including his sideman appearances as a pianist on records by Milt Jackson and David Newman. **Soul Brothers/Soul Meeting** (Atlantic 81951), a two-CD set recorded during 1957–58, teams Charles with Milt Jackson and is most notable for both his jazz-oriented piano solos and his rare (and quite effective) alto sax playing. But, as would become quite clear during the early 1960s, Ray Charles was too versatile and accessible a performer to be confined to jazz, and he made his greatest impact in other styles of music.

The Duke Ellington Orchestra   It was one of the magical moments in jazz history. The Duke Ellington Orchestra was playing at the third annual Newport Jazz Festival in 1956. Ellington, a major name for 30 years, had managed to survive some lean years, recently welcomed Johnny Hodges back into his band, and still had his orchestra together despite the odds. After playing the coolly received "Newport Jazz Festival Suite" at Newport, he performed "Diminuendo in Blue" and "Crescendo in Blue," a couple of tunes from the late 1930s that he tied together with a marathon 27-chorus Paul Gonsalves blues tenor solo. After a few choruses of tenor, the quiet crowd began to become excited, people started dancing and a near-riot ensued as Gonsalves's solo went on and on. The performance made headlines

and signaled Duke Ellington's "comeback." There would be no more lean periods for Ellington.

The 1956 Duke Ellington Orchestra consisted of trumpeters Clark Terry, Willie Cook, Cat Anderson, and Ray Nance, trombonists Quentin Jackson, Britt Woodman, and John Sanders, Jimmy Hamilton on clarinet and tenor, altoist Johnny Hodges, Russell Procope on alto and clarinet, Gonsalves, baritonist Harry Carney, bassist Jimmy Woode, and drummer Sam Woodyard. Counting the pianist, there were no less than 12 highly individual soloists in the group—just an average Ellington band! Other than Harold "Shorty" Baker joining on fifth trumpet in 1957 and Willie Cook leaving the group the following year, there were no real changes in the personnel until 1959 at which time Cook had returned and Fats Ford was on sixth trumpet. By 1960, Aaron Bell was on bass, Clark Terry had joined Quincy Jones, and Lawrence Brown had rejoined the band, with Booty Wood taking over for John Sanders. But overall, relatively few changes took place, a sign of Duke Ellington's artistic and commercial success during this period.

Ellington at Newport has been expanded to a two-CD set, showing that the originally released version of "Newport Jazz Festival Suite" was actually a studio version made a couple of days later because the concert rendition was flawed. Also included along with two full-length versions of "Newport Jazz Festival Suite" and the exciting "Diminuendo and Crescendo in Blue" are other selections from the concert previously put out in piecemeal fashion. But many listeners will prefer to get the original single CD version of ◉ **Ellington at Newport** (Columbia/Legacy 40587) instead since the "Newport Jazz Festival Suite" is not that major and the main point of this release is Paul Gonsalves's famous solo.

Among Ellington's other recordings from the period, **Such Sweet Thunder** (Columbia/Legacy 65568), which has been greatly expanded with new takes, is Duke's tribute to William Shakespeare, with some of his key musicians playing the roles of different characters. **Indigos** (Columbia/Legacy 44444) is a mostly easy-listening set of ballads from 1957 that is relaxing if not too exciting. **Black, Brown & Beige** (Columbia 65566) has its moments, but is a bit disappointing overall. This 1958 remake was cut when Johnny Hodges was temporarily ill, so he is missing from "Come Sunday." The suite is only presented in truncated form, and although Mahalia Jackson is impressive on "Come Sunday" and

"The Lord's Prayer," little else memorable occurs. Better to hear the 1943 full-length version.

Blues in Orbit (Columbia/Legacy 44051) mostly emphasizes blues with Ray Nance, Harry Carney, Johnny Hodges, and Jimmy Hamilton being the stars. **Cosmic Scene: Duke Ellington's Spacemen** (Sony France 472083) features a nonet from the orchestra that includes three of the band's most modern soloists (Clark Terry, Jimmy Hamilton, and Paul Gonsalves) showcased on standards. ◉ **Back to Back** (Verve 823 637) is a classic small-group date matching Ellington's piano with Johnny Hodges and Harry "Sweets" Edison in a sextet on a variety of blues-oriented material, played with inspiration. The versions of "Basin Street Blues," "Beale Street Blues," and "Royal Garden Blues" are gems, making one wish that Hodges and Edison had teamed together more often. **Side by Side** (Verve 521 405), which has more Edison and Hodges on "Stompy Jones" and a different Ellington-Hodges group with Ben Webster and Roy Eldridge, is almost as worthy.

Recorded in 1959, **Jazz Party in Stereo** (Columbia 40712) is unusual because Dizzy Gillespie sits in with the band on "Upper Manhattan Medical Group" (his only recording with Ellington), Jimmy Rushing sings "Hello Little Girl," there are two intriguing selections with nine symphonic percussionists, and Hodges and Gonsalves star throughout. Ellington's first chance to score a Hollywood film, **Anatomy of a Murder** (Columbia/Legacy 65569), is interesting, but not essential, with the best known piece being the title cut that is heard before Peggy Lee added lyrics and it became "I'm Gonna Go Fishin'." **Live at the Blue Note** (Roulette 28637) is a superior two-CD set from August 9, 1959, in which the Ellington band stretches out on three full sets. In addition to the usual repertoire, Billy Strayhorn gets to sit in on his "Take the 'A' Train" and a couple of piano duets with Ellington, there are several numbers from the *Anatomy of a Murder* soundtrack, and an 11-minute rendition of "Mood Indigo" works quite well. **Three Suites** (Columbia 46825) has all of the music from three of the finest Ellington-Strayhorn collaborations: Tchaikovsky's "The Nutcracker Suite," Grieg's "Peer Gynt Suites Nos. 1 & 2," and "Suite Thursday" (which was dedicated to author John Steinbeck). "The Nutcracker Suite" in particular is given a delightful treatment.

Although he was no longer writing three-minute standards, Duke Ellington (with the assistance of his mighty orchestra and Billy Strayhorn) was still a vital force in jazz as he entered his early sixties.

The Bill Evans Trio Like Bud Powell, Bill Evans changed the way that the piano is played in jazz. The innovations that he was responsible for were more subtle and less radical than Powell's, but he was the first to really move jazz piano beyond the bebop master's ideas. Evans's chord voicings became highly influential, and his work in his trios found the pianist sharing the spotlight with his bassist and drummer who were nearly equals. Unlike most piano-led groups (such as the Oscar Peterson Trio) where the piano dominates as not only the main soloist, but the one who sets the musical direction, Evans utilized bassists who interacted closely with him in addition to keeping time, often offering ideas that the group followed. His drummers were also free to interact with the lead voices and were often more significant for adding color than for keeping strict time. This approach would be adopted by many piano trios in the future.

Evans attended Southwestern Louisiana University, worked with Mundell Lowe and Red Mitchell, and served in the army. In 1956, when he turned 27, he arrived in New York, playing with Tony Scott. ◉ **The Complete Riverside Recordings** (Riverside 018) is a 12-CD set that has all of Evans's dates as a leader during 1956–63, including each of the sessions that are individually reviewed in this section. **New Jazz Conceptions** (Original Jazz Classics 025) is a reissue of his debut set as a leader. Evans takes three songs solo (including the original version of his most famous original, "Waltz for Debby") and nine others in a trio with bassist Teddy Kotick and drummer Paul Motian, including his future theme song "Five," "Speak Low," and two versions of "No Cover, No Minimum." Already at that early stage, Evans sounded distinctive and nothing at all like Bud Powell.

Evans worked with George Russell, recorded with Charles Mingus, and was part of the remarkable sextet that Miles Davis led in 1958. He greatly impressed Davis with his chord voicings and ideas about scalar improvising, but departed later that year to form his own group, though he did return to record most of the **Kind of Blue** album with the trumpeter (contributing "Blue in Green"). **Everybody Digs Bill Evans** (Original Jazz Classics 068) from December 1958 has Evans, Sam Jones, and Philly Joe Jones interacting on such numbers as "Minority," "Night and Day," and "Oleo," often swinging hard. However, it is Evans's three piano solos (including the haunting and unique "Peace Piece") that are most memorable.

In 1959, Evans formed a classic trio with bassist Scott LaFaro and Paul Motian. LaFaro's emphasis of the upper register of his bass, his fluent solos, and particularly the commentary that he played when the pianist soloed helped lead the way toward the future. **Portraits in Jazz** (Original Jazz Classics 088) from Dec 28, 1959, shows just how intuitive this group could be, particularly on Evans's "Peri's Scope," "Come Rain or Come Shine," "When I Fall in Love," "Someday My Prince Will Come," and especially on two versions of "Autumn Leaves."

The Maynard Ferguson Orchestra   Maynard Ferguson, the high-note trumpet star of Stan Kenton's Orchestra during 1950–53, worked in the studios of Los Angeles for a few years, appearing on some jazz dates along the way. In 1956, he returned to New York and put together the Birdland Dreamband for a tour and a couple of record dates. **The Birdland Dreamband** (Bluebird 6455) has 20 of the band's 25 selections with arrangements from Al Cohn, Bob Brookmeyer, Jimmy Giuffre, Ernie Wilkins, Bill Holman, Marty Paich, Willie Maiden, Johnny Mandel, and Herb Geller. The key soloists include Ferguson, Jimmy Cleveland, Herb Geller, and Al Cohn, and the music is both quite modern and swinging.

The experience gave Ferguson an itch to lead a regular big band of his own and the Maynard Ferguson Orchestra was formed in 1957, catching on fairly quickly and working regularly. Among the musicians who spent time with the MF orchestra during part of 1957–60 are trumpeters Bill Chase and Don Ellis, trombonist/arrangers Slide Hampton and Don Sebesky, altoist Lanny Morgan, tenors Willie Maiden and Joe Farrell, pianists John Bunch, Bobby Timmons, Joe Zawinul, and Jaki Byard (who also contributed arrangements), and drummer Jake Hanna. All of the band's Roulette recordings of 1957–64 (arguably Ferguson's finest records of his career) were reissued on the ten-CD limited-edition box **The Complete Maynard Ferguson on Roulette** (Mosaic 10-156), which is well worth bidding on.

Only a few of the Roulette dates are currently available individually. Fortunately, one of them is **A Message from Newport** (Roulette 93272), an inspired effort

from 1958 that includes such tunes as "Three More Foxes" (which features Ferguson, Slide Hampton, and Don Sebesky battling it out on trombones), "The Fugue," "Slide's Derangement," and "Frame for the Blues." **Maynard '61** (Roulette 93900), which was mostly recorded in December 1960, is also available. "Ole," "Pharoah," and "Blues for Kepp" are among the high points. But it is a pity that the near-classic **Newport Suite** (the LP Roulette 52053) with its trumpet battle between MF, Don Ellis, and Rick Kiefer on "Three More Foxes" and such songs as "Foxy," "Old Man River," and "I Got the Spirit," has not come back yet outside of the Mosaic box.

Few of the big bands that were formed during the second half of the 1950s were able to stay together more than a few months. Maynard Ferguson's worked so regularly that for a time it competed favorably with those of Duke Ellington, Count Basie, Woody Herman, and Stan Kenton.

The Dizzy Gillespie Big Band and Quintets   Dizzy Gillespie turned 39 in 1956 and was still in peak form during this era. **Modern Jazz Sextet** (Verve 1842) from January 12, 1956, was an easy success, teaming Gillespie with Sonny Stitt and a solid rhythm section led by John Lewis on "Tour de Force" (the trumpeter's original based on the chords of "Jeepers Creepers"), "Dizzy Meets Sonny," "Mean to Me," "Blues for Bird," and a ballad medley. Plenty of fireworks fly, and this jam session shows that classic bebop still lived even after the death of Charlie Parker.

In 1956, Gillespie put together a new big band initially to tour overseas. As a goodwill ambassador, Dizzy kept his orchestra together for nearly two years, performing in Europe, the Near East, and South America. The two-CD set ● **Birks' Works—The Verve Big Band Sessions** (Verve 314 527 900) has all of the studio recordings by the highly enjoyable ensemble, which along the way features trumpeters Joe Gordon and Lee Morgan, trombonist Al Grey, altoists Phil Woods and Ernie Henry, tenors Billy Mitchell and Benny Golson, pianists Walter Davis, Jr., and Wynton Kelly, and such arrangers as Quincy Jones, Ernie Wilkins, Melba Liston, and Benny Golson. The two-fer has all of the music from the LPs **Birks' Works**, **Dizzy in Greece**, and **World Statesmen**, plus some unissued material. Highlights of the 42 performances including "Dizzy's Business," "Jessica's

Day," "Dizzy's Blues," "Cool Breeze," "Whisper Not," and "I Remember Clifford." Surprisingly, the music does not contain any real Afro-Cuban jazz (of which Gillespie was a pioneer), but its bebop is of consistently high quality. Two live sets, **Dizzy Gillespie Big Band** (Jazz Hour 1029) and **Live 1957** (Jazz Unlimited 2040), were both recorded June 14, 1957. Despite some repeats in the titles, the music is all completely different from each other and generally rewarding. But the best single disc of the classic band is ● **Dizzy Gillespie at Newport** (Verve 314 513 754), which has very exciting versions of "Cool Breeze" and "Dizzy's Blues" (with blazing solos from Al Grey, Billy Mitchell and Gillespie), a spirited "Manteca," a humorous "Doodlin'," "I Remember Clifford," and two numbers featuring guest Mary Lou Williams (who was coming out of retirement after a few years off the scene).

In December 1957, Gillespie recorded twice with all-star groups. **Duets** (Verve 835 253) has either Sonny Stitt or Sonny Rollins with Dizzy in two different quintets. "Wheatleigh Hall" and the debut of Gillespie's "Con Alma" are highlights. However, a couple of weeks later when ● **Sonny Side Up** (Verve 825 674) was cut, Stitt and Rollins played together with Dizzy in a sextet and the results are classic. "On the Sunny Side of the Street" is sung in memorable fashion by Gillespie (with all three of the horns taking personable solos), "After Hours" gives pianist Ray Bryant a chance to shine, Stitt's "The Eternal Triangle" is romping from start to finish, and on "I Know that You Know," Rollins's stop time solo steals the show.

Unfortunately, the Dizzy Gillespie Big Band broke up in early 1958. For a time Dizzy had a combo comprised of pianist Junior Mance, Les Spann on guitar and flute, bassist Art Davis, and drummer Lex Humphries. In 1959, Leo Wright (on alto and flute) replaced Spann (with Teddy Stewart taking over on drums) as can be heard on **Copenhagen Concert** (Steeple Chase 36024), a fine quintet date highlighted by "I Found a Million Dollar Baby," "Wheatleigh Hall," and "A Night in Tunisia." Later that year, Argentinean pianist/composer Lalo Schifrin became Gillespie's pianist, writing the five-part suite "Gillespiana" (which is reviewed in the next chapter).

Having made the transition from bebop revolutionary to elder statesman/traditionalist in 15 years, Dizzy Gillespie continued to inspire other trumpeters and musicians with his advanced solos, showmanship, and enthusiasm.

The Chico Hamilton Quintet   The last important West Coast cool jazz group to be formed in the 1950s, drummer Hamilton's unit (which consisted of Buddy Collette on flute, tenor, alto, and clarinet, cellist Fred Katz, guitarist Jim Hall, and bassist Carson Smith) had come together in 1955. Although all of its recordings from 1955–58 are on the six-CD limited-edition **The Complete Pacific Jazz Recordings of the Chico Hamilton Quintet** (Mosaic 6-175), virtually none of that music is available individually.

The first Hamilton quintet lasted until the summer of 1956 when, due to its popularity, there was great interest in the group coming east. Because Buddy Collette was a trailblazing black studio musician, he did not want to leave Los Angeles, so he was succeeded by Paul Horn on reeds; guitarist John Pisano soon replaced Jim Hall. This group appeared in the 1957 Burt Lancaster-Tony Curtis movie *Sweet Smell of Success* and made it into 1958 (other than Harold Gaylor becoming the band's bassist).

The third version of the Hamilton Quintet recorded six albums during 1958–59, two of which can be easily acquired. By the spring of 1958, Hamilton, Pisano, and Gaylor were joined by cellist Nate Gershman (who, unlike Katz, did not improvise) and Eric Dolphy on flute, alto sax, and bass clarinet, the latter an instrument on which Dolphy was jazz's first significant soloist. **Gongs East** (Discovery 70831) features Dolphy on quite a few short solos, sounding pretty much like himself, but restricted greatly by the highly arranged music. The highlights of the date include "Beyond the Blue Horizon," "Passion Flower," "Tuesday at Two," and the exotic "Gongs East." A tribute to Duke Ellington called **Ellington Suite** (World Pacific 1258), which has not been reissued individually on CD, features a reunion band with the original Hamilton quintet (with Collette, Katz, Hall, and Smith) expanding to a sextet with Paul Horn added on second reeds. However, in recent times, an earlier version of the program, now titled **The Original Ellington Suite** (Blue Note 24567), has been released. The discarded test pressing was discovered by accident by a jazz collector browsing through a used record store in England who was surprised to realize that this particular recording features the Dolphy version of the group. Apparently producer Richard Bock originally thought that the multireedist's playing was too radical, although Dolphy actually comes across as fairly conservative on most of these pieces, playing some beautiful clarinet on "Day Dream," alto on "Just a-Sittin' and a-Rockin'," and some fine flute and bass clarinet on other selections.

With Eric Dolphy's departure in late 1959 when he started his solo career, Chico Hamilton formed the fourth version of his quintet, with Charles Lloyd on flute and alto (he would switch to tenor a year later), Gershman still on cello, pianist Harry Pope, and bassist Bobby Haynes. A pair of out-of-print Columbia albums resulted, but it was becoming obvious that the West Coast chamber jazz sound that Hamilton had championed was becoming a bit stale and it was time for a change.

The Woody Herman Orchestra   Woody Herman's Third Herd broke up in 1956 after six years. The clarinetist/altoist/vocalist continued leading big bands on a part-time basis along with combos during the next few years. Among the soloists featured in his groups of this period were trumpeter Bill Berry, Bill Harris, tenor saxophonist Jay Migliori, and pianist John Bunch. **Herman's Heat & Puente's Beat** (Evidence 22008) is a special project from 1958. It is of particular interest due to the inclusion of Tito Puente's rhythm section (Puente on timbales, bassist Robert Rodriguez, and Latin percussion from Ray Barretto, Gilbert Lopez, and Raymond Rodriguez) on six of the selections, interacting with studio players and some Herman alumni, including on "Tito Meets Woody," "Carioca," and "Mambo Herd." The remainder of the set is more conventional (with such tunes as "Woodchopper's Ball," "Lullaby of Birdland," and "Midnight Sun"), but nearly as enjoyable.

During part of 1958–59, Herman had a sextet that included cornetist Nat Adderley, Eddie Costa on piano and vibes, and guitarist Charlie Byrd. At the 1959 Monterey Jazz Festival, Herman led a specially assembled big band filled with West Coast–style players (including Conte Candoli, Ray Linn, both Al Porcino and Bill Chase on first trumpets, Urbie Green, Don Lanphere, Zoot Sims, Bill Perkins, Richie Kamuca, Victor Feldman, Charlie Byrd, bassist Monty Budwig, and Mel Lewis) and was one of the hits of the young festival. **Big New Herd at the Monterey Jazz Festival** (Koch 8508) has their main performance from the historic weekend, and 11 different soloists are heard from during an exciting set, which is highlighted by "Four Brothers," "Monterey Apple Tree" (a renamed "Apple Honey"), and an Urbie Green ballad feature on "Skylark."

The success at Monterey resulted in renewed interest in Herman and he soon formed a big band that became known as the Young Thundering Herd. The 1960 version has Rolf Ericson, Don Rader, and Bill Chase in the trumpet section and Don Lanphere and Larry McKenna as the tenor soloists.

The Ahmad Jamal Trio   Ahmad Jamal had gained some attention with his piano-guitar-bass trio, which in 1955 consisted of guitarist Ray Crawford and bassist Israel Crosby. In 1956, he switched to a slightly harder approach, replacing the guitar with drummer Walter Perkins who was soon succeeded by Vernell Fournier. Although he would lead many trios through the years, the Jamal-Crosby-Fournier was the most famous, particularly after recording ❶ **But Not for Me** (MCA/Chess 9108), which is also known as **Ahmad Jamal at the Pershing**. In addition to memorable versions from 1958 of the title cut, "Surrey with the Fringe on Top," and "There Is No Greater Love," the set includes Jamal's catchy hit version of "Poinciana." The close interaction by the musicians (who seem to think as one), the inventive use of dynamics, and the subtle surprises made the Ahmad Jamal Trio influential while remaining unique. **Ahmad's Blues** (GRP/Chess 803) from December 5–6, 1958, reissues the LP **Ahmad Jamal Trio**, plus part of **Portfolio of Ahmad Jamal**. The 16 selections feature the Jamal Trio at its best on such numbers as "It Could Happen to You," "Stompin' at the Savoy," "Squatty Roo," "A Gal in Calico," and "Let's Fall in Love."

All of Ahmad Jamal's recordings from this era (which were cut for the Argo label) are quite worthy, and many of the out-of-print LPs can be found in used record stores. He was at the height of his popularity.

The Jazztet   Trumpeter Art Farmer, tenor saxophonist Benny Golson, and trombonist Curtis Fuller were all familiar with each other's playing. In fact, they had recorded together in several different combinations during 1958–59. In late 1959, they came together as the Jazztet, a sextet also including pianist McCoy Tyner, bassist Addison Farmer, and drummer Lex Humphries. With Golson's writing and the solos of the three horns, this group had to the potential to be one of the great hard bop bands, on a level with Art Blakey's Jazz Messengers and Horace Silver. However, they had the misfortune of opening at the Five Spot opposite the Ornette Coleman Quartet. While the jazz world debated the merits of Coleman's music, the Jazztet sounded conservative in comparison and was overlooked.

The band's first recording, ◉ **Meet the Jazztet** (MCA/Chess 91550) is definitive. In addition to standards, it features three notable Golson originals: "Blues March," "I Remember Clifford," and the original version of "Killer Joe." However, by the time the band recorded again, just seven months later, only Farmer and Golson still remained from the original lineup. Tyner had joined the John Coltrane Quartet, while Fuller was soon to become a member of the Jazz Messengers. **Blues on Down** (Chess 802) should have been a two-CD set reissuing all of the music from the Jazztet's second, third, and fourth releases, but instead it is a so-so sampler that just has seven of the nine selections from 1960's **Big City Sounds** and four of the six numbers from 1962's **Jazztet at Birdhouse**. Despite the personnel changes (which resulted in the Jazztet including trombonist Tom McIntosh, pianist Cedar Walton, bassist Tommy Williams, and drummer Albert "Tootie" Heath), the music is excellent with four Golson originals and such songs as "Hi-Fly," "Con Alma," "Farmer's Market," and a lengthy "'Round Midnight." It is a pity that all of the Jazztet's recordings have not been available in full, but that is typical of how this group was overlooked and underrated.

The Stan Kenton Orchestra　During 1956–60, Stan Kenton continued leading impressive orchestras, emphasizing swinging arrangements much more than prior to 1952, and recording regularly for Capitol. Among the key musicians who were in his big band during the era were trumpeters Sam Noto, Jack Sheldon, Rolf Ericson, Bill Chase, and Steve Huffsteter, trombonist Carl Fontana, altoists Lennie Niehaus, Charlie Mariano, and Gabe Baltazar, tenors Bill Perkins, Lucky Thompson (1956), and Richie Kamuca, baritonist Jack Nimitz, and drummer Mel Lewis, plus singer Ann Richards. Not all of the Capitol dates, some of which emphasize ballads or unlikely standards, have dated that well. **Kenton in Hi-Fi** (Capitol 98451) is a routine remake session of old hits, with Vido Musso temporarily returning to the band on tenor. However, ◉ **Cuban Fire** (Blue Note 96260) is a major work by arranger Johnny Richards and was a high point in his career. The Kenton orchestra was expanded to 27 pieces, adding six percussionists and two French horns, and this stirring work features Thompson, Fontana, Niehaus, Perkins, and Noto. The original six-piece suite

is joined by six other selections that Richards wrote along the way for Kenton.

The Ramsey Lewis Trio　Initially a fine bop-based pianist, Ramsey Lewis always seemed to have the ability to attract a large nonjazz audience through his accessible music. Born in Chicago, Lewis started playing piano when he was six, and in 1956 (when he was 21) he formed a trio with bassist Eldee Young and drummer Red Holt, recording regularly for the Argo label in Chicago. Lewis made records in 1958 with Max Roach and Lem Winchester, but was primarily heard with his trio (which was originally called the Gentlemen of Jazz).

Consider the Source (GRP/Chess 806) has 17 selections taken from three Lewis LPs of 1956–59. Although it is unfortunately not complete (all of the pianist's early records should be reissued), it does give one a good picture of how soulful, bluesy, and swinging his trio sounded from the start. Highlights include "I'll Remember April," a memorable rendition of "Delilah," "Please Send Me Someone to Love," and "On the Street Where You Live." One of the few albums by the early group not made for Argo, 1958's **Down to Earth** (Verve 538 329), has the trio emphasizing folk songs and traditional melodies such as "Dark Eyes," "Come Back to Sorrento," "John Henry," and "Billy Boy." The concise interpretations say a lot in a short period of time—most songs are three minutes or less. Also quite worthy is **Sound of Christmas** (Chess 91566), a pleasing, if rather brief (29 minutes) Christmas jazz album. The trio plays ten Christmas songs (including "Winter Wonderland," "Santa Claus Is Coming to Town," and "Sleigh Ride"), five of which add a string section arranged by Riley Hampton.

The Lighthouse All-Stars　Howard Rumsey's Lighthouse All-Stars' glory days were 1952–57. **In the Solo Spotlight** (Original Jazz Classics 451) has six selections from 1954 and three from 1957. As can be ascertained from its title, each of the numbers puts the focus on one or two improvisers. Among the stars are Stu Williamson, Frank Rosolino, Bud Shank, Bob Cooper, and Claude Williamson in the earlier group and Conte Candoli, Rosolino, altoist Lennie Niehaus, Kamuca, and pianist Dick Shreve in the 1957 edition; Rumsey has a rare feature on "Concerto for Doghouse." **Music for Lighthousekeeping** (Original Jazz Classics 636) from 1956 has some freewheeling playing by Conte Candoli,

Rosolino, Cooper, Sonny Clark, Rumsey, and Stan Levey on such swinging numbers as "Love Me or Levey," "Taxi War Dance," "Mambo Las Vegas," and "Topsy." Although thought of as a symbol of West Coast cool jazz, the music on this CD could also be considered bebop or early hard bop.

The string of Contemporary recordings by the Lighthouse All-Stars came to an end in 1957. There was an album apiece for the Omega (1957) and Philips (1961–62) labels, but by the early 1960s the group had passed into history.

The Mastersounds   Vibraphonist Buddy Montgomery and electric bassist Monk Montgomery came together in 1957 to form the Mastersounds, a quartet also including pianist Richie Crabtree and drummer Benny Barth. The music of the group was essentially melodic and easy-listening bop, similar in its sound to the Modern Jazz Quartet although without John Lewis's classical leanings. During its four years of existence, the group was reasonably popular and kept the same personnel, recording ten records for Pacific Jazz, World Pacific, and Fantasy. Among their eight Pacific Jazz/World Pacific albums (none of which have been released on CD yet) are the music from **Kismet** (which has guitarist Wes Montgomery, the brother of Buddy and Monk, added to

the group) and **The Flower Drum Song**, plus a tribute to Horace Silver. The band's final two recordings (from 1960–61), other than one selection left off because of space, have been reissued as **The Mastersounds** (Fantasy 24770). Highlights include "People Will Say We're in Love," "Golden Earrings," "I Could Write a Book," and Wes's "West Coast Blues."

But due to lack of work, the Mastersounds disbanded in 1961.

The Modern Jazz Quartet   In 1956, the Modern Jazz Quartet (vibraphonist Milt Jackson, pianist John Lewis, bassist Percy Heath, and drummer Connie Kay) began their longtime association with Atlantic Records. **Fontessa** (Atlantic 1231) has a particularly strong all-around program, including Lewis's "Versailles," the rather serious 11-minute title cut, "Bluesology," and "Woody'n You." **No Sun in Venice** (Atlantic 1284) consists of six Lewis compositions used in the French film of the same name. The music is quite complex, somber, and disciplined. **Third Stream Music** (Atlantic 1345) features some unusual performances. Two cuts combine the MJQ with the Jimmy Giuffre Three (Giuffre on clarinet and tenor, guitarist Jim Hall, and bassist Ralph Pena), six classical musicians add color to "Exposure," and a pair of other numbers ("Conversation" and the

---

TIMELINE 1957

The Sound of Jazz television special features timeless performances by Billie Holiday, Lester Young, Henry "Red" Allen, Thelonious Monk, and others. • Miles Davis records **Miles Ahead**. • John Coltrane plays at the Five Spot with Thelonious Monk. • Lester Young and Jimmy Rushing reunite with Count Basie at the Newport Jazz Festival. • The Maynard Ferguson Orchestra debuts. • The Mastersounds are formed. • Lambert, Hendricks, and Ross make their first recordings. • Pete Fountain appears regularly on the *Lawrence Welk Show*. • The first Cannonball Adderley Quintet breaks up. • Francisco Aguabella moves to the United States and is soon working with Tito Puente. • Ray Anthony has a big seller in "The Bunny Hop." • Bing Crosby records a Dixieland-flavored album with Bob Scobey, Matt Matlock, and Ralph Sutton. • Jack Costanzo records **Mr. Bongo** for GNP/Crescendo. • Stephane Grappelli and Stuff Smith record together although the results would not be released for several decades. • Eddie Heywood's "Canadian Sunset" becomes popular. • Chico O'Farrill moves to Mexico City for eight years. • Flute player Moe Koffman's "The Swingin' Shepherd Blues" becomes a surprise hit. • Lou Levy becomes Ella Fitzgerald's accompanist for five years. • Jimmy McPartland records a Dixieland version of songs from "The Music Man." • Ethel Waters, who had not recorded in a decade, records her last nonreligious album before switching exclusively to gospel-oriented themes. • At age 24, Austrian pianist Joe Zawinul records three numbers in a trio. • In Havana the "50 Years of Cuban Music" celebration treats Machito, Mario Bauza, and Tito Puente as national heroes. • Gunther Schuller creates the term "Third Stream" to describe the combination of jazz with classical music. • Rex Stewart leads the Fletcher Henderson All-Stars on a few occasions. • The Newport Jazz Festival features recorded appearances by the Coleman Hawkins-Roy Eldridge Sextet, the Dizzy Gillespie Big Band, Teddy Wilson, Gerry Mulligan, and the Cecil Taylor Quartet.

very successful "Sketch") team the MJQ with the Beaux Arts String Quartet. Even if the music is not quite "Third Stream," there are certainly many interesting moments on this worthy set.

At Music Inn (Atlantic 1299), which has the MJQ performing two Lewis originals, a three-song ballad medley, and "Yardbird Suite," is most notable for Sonny Rollins sitting in with the group on "A Night in Tunisia" and a witty "Bags' Groove." **Pyramid** (Atlantic 1325) includes inventive versions of Lewis's "Vendome," Ray Brown's "Pyramid," Jim Hall's "Romaine," "Django," "How High the Moon," and "It Don't Mean a Thing." **Odds Against Tomorrow** (Blue Note 93415) features the MJQ performing six Lewis compositions that were used in the film of the same name. Best known is "Skating in Central Park," but all of the selections have their memorable moments.

The double CD **Dedicated to Connie** (Atlantic 82763) was first released in the 1990s. This 1960 concert from Slovenia has the MJQ sounding particularly inspired on their usual repertoire plus a 23-minute medley of John Lewis compositions. In contrast, **The Comedy** (Atlantic 1390) is the type of album that led many bop fans to criticize the MJQ and John Lewis in particular for being overly influenced by Western classical music. The seven Lewis compositions are episodic works arranged in a suite that portrays characters from the 16th century Italian Commedia dell'Arte; singer Diahann Carroll guests fairly effectively on "La Cantatrice." The improvisations are not bad, but the music is rather dull. The same could be said of some of the MJQ's collaborations with orchestras.

However, ◉ **European Concert** (Label M 5721) perfectly sums up the MJQ's accomplishments up to 1960. The group performs remakes of 15 of their best songs, including "Django," "Bluesology," "Bags' Groove," "La Ronde," "Odds Against Tomorrow," and "Skating in Central Park" in live and extended versions, and shows their fans that they could out-swing just about anyone when they cut loose.

The Sun Ra Arkestra   A major innovator, Sun Ra (born Herman Sonny Blount) made himself easy to be ridiculed and underrated. His very complex philosophy (which combined beliefs from ancient Egypt, science fiction, and religious texts) was almost impossible to figure out although he was never shy to talk about it.

The members of his Arkestra were encouraged to wear outlandish costumes, his recordings were generally released in haphazard form on his cheapo Saturn label (without recording dates or a list of the personnel), and both his performances and recordings were quite erratic. Sometimes his band sounded 20 years ahead of its time, but at other times it was woefully out of tune.

Born in Birmingham, Alabama (not on Saturn as he often claimed) in 1915, Sun Ra led his first band in 1934. The pianist/arranger freelanced throughout the Midwest, worked with Fletcher Henderson in 1946–47, and made his first recordings on a Wynonie Harris date in the late 1940s. He began leading bands in Chicago in 1953, an ensemble that soon grew to be a large orchestra, which he called his Arkestra. Their first recordings (from around 1956–57) reveal a left-of-center big band, one that swung, but somehow sounded a bit unusual. Early on, Ra experimented with primitive electric keyboards, advanced harmonies, and atonal solos. His key sidemen included tenor saxophonist John Gilmore (an early influence on John Coltrane), altoist Marshall Allen, and baritonist Pat Patrick.

Until recent times, Sun Ra's discography was a real mess and few of his early recordings were available. However, Robert Campbell's book on Ra straightened out most of the record dates, and the Evidence label has reissued many of his sessions. **Sound Sun Pleasure** (Evidence 22016) has 13 selections from 1953–58, including an unusual duet with Stuff Smith on "Deep Purple" and spots for altoist James Spaulding, baritonist Charles Davis, and Bob Northern on flugelhorn. Most of the tunes are standards, but these versions of "'Round Midnight," "Back in Your Own Backyard," and "Don't Blame Me" do not exactly sound conventional. The double CD **The Singles** (Evidence 22164) has totally obscure music released as 45 rpm singles dating from 1954–82, including dates backing mid-1950s doo wop groups and Ra playing such instruments as the Minimoog, harmonium, Wurlitzer electric piano (in 1956), the Gibson Kalamazoo organ, clavinet, and the Rocksichord. **Supersonic Jazz** (Evidence 22015) contains several straightahead blues and good solos from Gilmore, Davis, trumpeter Art Hoyle, and trombonist Julian Priester. However, Ra's advanced piano solos show that he was looking far beyond bop.

Best known among Ra's early records were two albums originally released on Delmark: **Sun Song** (Delmark 411) and **Sound of Joy** (Delmark 414). Dating from 1956–57, the music is mostly advanced hard bop despite some futuristic song titles (including "Call of the Demons," "Street Named Hell," and "Brainville"), ragged ensembles, Jim Herndon's colorful tympani, and Ra's eccentric piano. **Sun Ra Visits Planet Earth/Interstellar Low Ways** (Evidence 22039) is a valuable set, showing Ra's band quickly evolving into its own unusual musical world. The four 1956 titles are highlighted by the baritones of Pat Patrick and Charles Davis battling it out on the boppish "Two Tones." However, the three cuts from 1958 and particularly the seven from 1960 are much more avant-garde, with some group vocals (best is "Rocket Number Nine Take Off for the Planet Venus") setting the stage for Ra's science fiction music. **Angels & Demons at Play/The Nubians of Plutonia** (Evidence 22066) and **We Travel the Spaceways/Bad & Beautiful** (Evidence 22038) also contrast the 1956 and 1960–61 versions of the Arkestra, ranging from a slightly disturbing version of straightahead jazz to freer explorations.

Jazz in Silhouette (Evidence 22012) features Ra's 1958 band, a particularly strong outfit that features trumpeter Hobart Dotson, Julian Priester, James Spaulding, Marshall Allen, Pat Patrick, and Charles Davis. This is one of Ra's most boppish sets with only a few hints of what was to come (particularly "Ancient Alethopia") and with "Blues at Midnight" being a rare uptempo blues. This is the CD to get for listeners who are not sure that Sun Ra ever played bop well. Almost as interesting is **Holiday for Soul Dance** (Evidence 22011), which has Ra's 1960 band playing such numbers as "But Not for Me," "Holiday for Strings," and "Body and Soul" in its own way.

The Max Roach Quintet/Quartet The deaths of Clifford Brown and Richie Powell on June 26, 1956, were a devastating blow to Max Roach. However, he continued on, keeping Sonny Rollins and bassist George Morrow in his group and adding Kenny Dorham and Ray Bryant. Only 32 himself at the time, Roach's playing continued to grow in stature. He led a series of groups during the next few years that were consistently impressive, reaching forward while still tied to hard bop. **The Complete Mercury Max Roach Plus Four Sessions** (Mosaic 7-201) is a seven-CD limited edition set that has the majority of his recordings from 1956–60. Many are also available as single CDs. **Max Roach Plus Four**

(EmArcy 822 673) features the 1956 group with Roach taking plenty of solos and Rollins in typically warm and witty form. **Jazz in 3/4 Time** (Mercury 826 456) was a rarity at the time, an album of jazz waltzes. The quintet (with Billy Wallace on piano) digs into Rollins's "Valse Hot" and waltz versions of "Lover" and "I'll Take Romance," among others. **The Max Roach 4 Plays Charlie Parker** (EmArcy 512 448) from 1957–58 finds the group changed quite a bit, with the piano dropped, Hank Mobley or George Coleman on tenor, and Morrow replaced by Nelson Boyd. But, truth be told, one does miss the piano, and the renditions of six Charlie Parker songs (which in the reissue are augmented by four other tunes) are not all that memorable.

During 1958–59, Roach led a quintet that featured the young trumpeter Booker Little, George Coleman, and bassist Art Davis. Pianist Eddie Baker is on one album while tuba player Ray Draper gives the band an unusual ensemble sound at their recorded 1958 appearance at the Newport Jazz Festival and on **Deeds, Not Words** (Original Jazz Classics 304), which is highlighted by "It's You or No One," "You Stepped Out of a Dream," and Roach's unaccompanied drum piece "Conversation." By the time they recorded the LP **The Many Sides of Max Roach** (Mercury 20911), Draper was gone and the quintet had trombonist Julian Priester in his place. Although that was one of Roach's better groups, by year-end the drummer was leading an almost entirely different unit consisting of Stanley Turrentine on tenor, trumpeter Tommy Turrentine, Priester, and bassist Bob Boswell. Their three Mercury albums of 1960 remain out of print (other than in the Mosaic box).

However, the most important Max Roach recording of this era was quite a bit different than the advanced hard bop he was featuring nightly. Active in the civil rights movement and newly married to the highly expressive singer Abbey Lincoln, Roach recorded ◉ **Freedom Now Suite** (Candid 79002), a topical yet timeless classic. The seven-part suite deals with black history (particularly slavery) and racism. "Driva' Man" has a powerful statement by guest Coleman Hawkins and along the way Booker Little and Julian Priester are heard from, but the performance of Abbey Lincoln is most notable. She is a strong force throughout this intense set, and on "Triptych: Prayer/Protest/Peace" Lincoln is heard in duets with Roach that include wrenching screams of rage. This is a memorable and somewhat scary album, one of the most effective of the jazz protest records.

The George Shearing Quintet   The George Shearing Quintet remained quite popular during the 1956–60 period, fueled by a constant stream of recordings for Capitol. The 1956 version of the band had vibraphonist Emil Richards, Toots Thielemans on guitar and occasional harmonica, bassist Al McKibbon, and drummer Percy Brice with perennial guest Armando Peraza on conga. That lineup stayed constant until late 1958 when Warren Chiasson took over on vibes. By 1960, guitarist Dick Garcia, bassist Herman Wright, and drummer Walter Bolden were in the group, with bassist Ralph Pena and drummer Vernell Fournier taking over by April. But no matter who was playing with Shearing, the quintet's sound and identity remained the same.

There were many special projects for the quintet along the way, including albums with Dakota Staton, Peggy Lee, the Judd Conlan Singers, Billy May's Orchestra, a brass choir (Satin Brass) and a big band, plus such Latin-oriented albums as **Latin Escapade**, **Latin Lace** and **Latin Affair**. Few of these sets are available on CD, but **The Swingin's Mutual** (Capitol 99190) is. Of the dozen selections, six have vocals by a young Nancy Wilson on one of her most jazz-oriented dates. Highlights include Wilson's vocals on "The Nearness of You" and "The Things We Did Last Summer" along with instrumental versions of "Oh! Look at Me Now," "Blue Lou," and Shearing's famous "Lullaby of Birdland." A five-CD limited-edition box, **The Complete Capitol Live Recordings** (Mosaic 5-157) has the best instrumental sets by the Quintet from 1958–63, but the sessions are otherwise difficult to locate.

Bop, Cool Jazz, and Hard Bop Soloists

Unlike in the earlier days when top soloists were closely identified with specific bands, by the mid-1950s many of the top young players were freelancing in the studios, appearing on numerous jam session–oriented dates, and performing new music with pickup groups. There was a remarkable amount of high-quality jazz recordings during this era (particularly compared to five years earlier), and the best jazz musicians were in constant demand in the studios. This was true of the veteran bop performers, the West Coast soloists and the up-and-coming hard boppers.

Trumpeters

The undisputed giants of modern jazz trumpet were Dizzy Gillespie, Miles Davis, Fats Navarro, and Clifford Brown. While Gillespie was an influence for some of his phrases, most trumpeters emulated a combination of Davis and Navarro-Brown, including the many that are included in this section.

Benny Bailey   As is true of many of the releases from the short-lived Candid label, trumpeter Benny Bailey's ◗ **Big Brass** (Candid 9011) is a high point in his career. A veteran of the bebop era, Bailey had worked with Jay McShann, the Dizzy Gillespie Big Band (1947–48), and Lionel Hampton (1948–53) before settling in Europe. While overseas (where he has lived ever since), Bailey worked with the Harry Arnold Orchestra (1957–59) and the touring Quincy Jones Big Band (1959). He briefly returned to the United States in the late fall of 1960, recording **Big Brass**, a superior date with an all-star septet that also includes Phil Woods, Julius Watkins, guitarist/flutist Les Spann, Tommy Flanagan, bassist Buddy Catlett, and Art Taylor. The excellent arrangements (some by Quincy Jones), the individual voices, and the high-quality solos (particularly those of the leader) make this the definitive Benny Bailey set.

Chet Baker   Returning to the United States in the spring of 1956 and not having learned from the examples of Gerry Mulligan, the late Dick Twardzik, and the recently deceased Charlie Parker, Chet Baker soon became a heroin addict. Throughout the remainder of his life, Baker would unapologetically be an addict and, despite all of the turmoil it would cause in his musical and personal lives, he never really quit using drugs, apparently enjoying the feeling too much.

Shortly after his return home, Baker started showing the strong influence of Miles Davis in his playing although he would always deny it. Baker did have his own approach and the influence would fade in later years. He recorded frequently during 1956–59, including **Chet Baker & Crew** (Pacific Jazz 81205), which features his quintet with tenor saxophonist Phil Urso and the young pianist Bobby Timmons, a pretty decent reunion with Russ Freeman called **Quartet** (Pacific Jazz 55453), and two excellent meetings with Art Pepper, **The Route** (Capitol/Pacific Jazz 92931), and **Playboys** (Pacific Jazz 94474), which are surprisingly heated and closer to hard bop than to cool jazz. Listeners who have acquired a taste for Baker's vocals will want **Embrace-able You** (Pacific Jazz 31676) and **It Could Happen to You** (Original Jazz Classics 303), while **Chet Baker in New York** (Original Jazz Classics 207) and **Chet** (Original Jazz Classics 087) are instrumental sessions that find the trumpeter sounding reasonably comfortable playing with, respectively, Johnny Griffin and Pepper Adams.

In 1959, Baker returned to Europe. He recorded a so-so date, **With Fifty Italian Strings** (Original Jazz Classics 492), which has mundane arrangements and five of his vocals. Soon afterward, he was busted for drugs and little would be heard of Chet Baker in the jazz world again until 1962.

Clora Bryant   Clora Bryant was 28 when she recorded **Gal with a Horn** (V.S.O.P. 42). A fine trumpeter, Bryant grew up in Texas, relocated to Los Angeles in the mid-1940s, and worked with such "all-girl" bands as the Darlings of Rhythm (1946), the Four Vees, the Queens of Swing (1948–49), and Jack McVea's female group. She led a quartet during the 1950s and was thought of as a novelty act even though she was an excellent trumpeter. Her V.S.O.P. date (originally recorded for the tiny Mode label), which showcases her in a quartet and sextet, has Bryant stretching out on eight standards (including "Sweet Georgia Brown," "Tea for Two," and "This Can't Be Love"), playing in a style between swing and bop. But although she would be active for another 40 years, this was Clora Bryant's only opportunity to lead her own record date despite her talents. Perhaps the jazz world was just not ready yet for a female trumpeter.

Donald Byrd   During the 1956–60 period, Donald Byrd developed from a promising young trumpeter into a strong player with a hard bop approach of his own. He worked with both Art Blakey and Max Roach in 1956, co-led the Jazz Lab Quintet with altoist Gigi Gryce in 1957, and formed a quintet with Pepper Adams in 1958 that lasted through 1961.

Byrd recorded frequently during this era, participating in many jam session dates for Prestige and having sessions as a leader for Prestige, Columbia, Savoy, Riverside, Polydor, Bethlehem, and (starting in 1958) Blue Note. **Byrd in Paris—Vol. 1** (Polydor 833 394) and **Byrd in Paris—Vol. 2** (Polydor 833 395) are both from October 22, 1958. A single Paris concert resulted in all of this music, featuring Byrd, Bobby Jaspar (on tenor and flute), Walter Davis, Jr., Doug Watkins, and

Art Taylor. The trumpeter was beginning to really find his own sound at the time, and he is heard in excellent form on **Vol. 1**, playing "Dear Old Stockholm," Sonny Rollins's "Paul's Pal," Jaspar's "Flute Blues," "Ray's Idea," and "The Blues Walk." **Vol. 2** sticks to bebop standards (many of which are quite concise) other than two originals. The fairly long versions of "Parisian Thoroughfare" and "52nd Street Theme" are highlights.

Back in the United States, Byrd formed his quintet with Pepper Adams and started recording regularly for Blue Note, the finest work of his career. **Off to the Races** (Blue Note 4007), which has not yet been reissued on CD, and **Byrd in Hand** (Blue Note 84019) are both sextet dates with Adams, either altoist Jackie McLean or Charlie Rouse on tenor, Wynton Kelly or Walter Davis on piano, plus Sam Jones and Art Taylor. Adams is absent from the quintet albums **Fuego** (Blue Note 46534) and **Byrd in Flight** (Blue Note 52435), with the former having McLean in the frontline while the latter features either McLean or Mobley. These are all consistently rewarding sets with originals by the trumpeter alternating with fresh versions of standards. **Motor City Scene** (Avenue Jazz/Bethlehem 75993) has a sextet with Byrd, Adams, Kenny Burrell, Tommy Flanagan, Paul Chambers, and Louis Hayes playing two Adams pieces, Erroll Garner's "Trio," Thad Jones's "Bitty Ditty," and an extended version of "Stardust."

But the Donald Byrd album to get from this period is the two-CD set **At the Half Note Café, Vols. 1 & 2** (Blue Note 57187). Byrd and Adams are joined by pianist Duke Pearson, bassist Laymon Jackson, and drummer Lex Humphries for versions of four originals apiece by Byrd and Pearson plus four standards. Highlights include the definitive jazz version of Henry Mancini's "Theme from Mr. Lucky," plus Pearson's "Jeannine," "My Girl Shirl," "A Portrait of Jenny," and "When Sunny Gets Blue." Throughout, the driving band shows that it was one of the top hard bop groups of the period, with Byrd and Adams offering contrasting but complementary styles.

Conte and Pete Candoli   In 1957, Conte and Pete Candoli started playing together on a fairly regular basis, co-leading a quintet that lasted until 1962; unfortunately, none of this group's recordings are currently available. Pete, always best known for his time with Woody Herman's First Herd (1944–46), mostly worked as a first trumpeter in big bands (including Boyd Raeburn, Tex Beneke, and Jerry Gray) before settling in Los

Angeles to work in the studios, other than touring with Stan Kenton (1954–56). In contrast, Conte Candoli was primarily a bebop soloist, working with the Chubby Jackson Sextet (1947–48), Charlie Ventura, Charlie Barnet, and Kenton (1951–53). In 1954, he moved permanently to Los Angeles, and even with all of the studio work, Candoli was quite active on the local jazz scene for many decades. He worked with the Lighthouse All-Stars and the Terry Gibbs big band in addition to making recordings as a leader. **Conte Candoli Quartet** (V.S.O.P. 43) from 1957 is a rare quartet date with pianist Vince Guaraldi, Monty Budwig, and Stan Levey. In addition to hearing Candoli in his early prime, this set is of interest for its repertoire, which includes originals by both the Candolis, Al Cohn, and Osie Johnson, plus "Flamingo," "Diane," and "No Moon at All."

Kenny Dorham   Kenny Dorham was an original member of the Jazz Messengers (1954–55) and for a brief time led the Jazz Prophets. After Clifford Brown's death, he became his replacement in the Max Roach Quintet (1956–58) and then primarily worked as a bandleader. During the era Dorham recorded as a leader for Blue Note, ABC/Paramount, Riverside, New Jazz, Jaro, and Time (reissued by Bainbridge). Although not a virtuoso or as flashy as Clifford Brown or Lee Morgan, Dorham was one of the top hard bop trumpeters, very valuable both as a sideman and on his own dates. **'Round About Midnight at the Café Bohemia Vols. 1 & 2** (Blue Note 33775) is a double CD that has 17 selections taken from May 31, 1956. Dorham's Jazz Prophets feature J.R. Monterose on tenor, Kenny Burrell, Bobby Timmons, Sam Jones, and drummer Arthur Edgehill. The leader's many originals are excellent, there are fresh renditions of "'Round Midnight," "A Night in Tunisia," and "My Heart Stood Still," and it is intriguing to hear Timmons this early in his career. **Jazz Contrasts** (Original Jazz Classics 028) from 1957 has three songs (including a 12-minute version of "I'll Remember April") with Dorham featured in an all-star quintet with Sonny Rollins, Hank Jones, Oscar Pettiford, and Max Roach. The other three numbers (Rollins is only on "My Old Flame") are a contrast since they add a fine harp player (Betty Glamman) and showcase the trumpeter on ballads. **2 Horns, 2 Rhythm** (Original Jazz Classics 463) has Dorham and altoist Ernie Henry (on his last session) joined by drummer G.T. Hogan and either Eddie Mathias or Wilbur

Ware on bass. Of the four standards and three originals, Dorham's "Lotus Blossom," "I'll Be Seeing You," and a rare version of "Is It True What They Say About Dixie" are most memorable.

This Is the Moment (Original Jazz Classics 812) is particularly interesting as Dorham sings on all ten selections. Although he had sung a blues now and then with Dizzy Gillespie's orchestra in the 1940s, this was his only vocal album. Dorham displays an okay voice that is musical if not a threat to Mel Tormé. However, the arrangements (which team Dorham with Curtis Fuller with both of their horns being muted) are inventive and colorful. Pianist Cedar Walton made his recording debut on this historical curiosity. **Blue Spring** (Original Jazz Classics 134) is a little more conventional, but also has its unusual aspects. All six of the songs have "spring" in their title, the band includes Cannonball Adderley, Cecil Payne, and the French horn of David Amram, and Dorham has many melodic solos. **Quiet Kenny** (Original Jazz Classics 250) puts the emphasis on ballads and the beauty of Dorham's tone. He is featured in a quartet with Tommy Flanagan, Paul Chambers, and Art Taylor on such songs as "Lotus Blossom," "My Ideal," "Alone Together," "Old Folks," and a brief version of "Mack the Knife."

Jazz Contemporary (Bainbridge 1048) from 1960 features excellent playing from Dorham in a quintet with baritonist Charles Davis, pianist Steve Kuhn, either Jimmy Garrison or Butch Warren on bass, and drummer Buddy Enlow. The results are not quite essential, but the musicians all play well on three Dorham originals plus such songs as "In Your Own Sweet Way," "Monk's Mood," and "This Love of Mine." **Showboat** (Bainbridge 1043) is a particularly inspired effort due to the strong material (including "Why Do I Love You," "Nobody Else But Me," "Make Believe," and "Bill"), fine playing from the quintet (which includes Jimmy Heath, Kenny Drew, Jimmy Garrison, and Art Taylor), and inventive frameworks.

Virtually all of the busy Kenny Dorham recordings from this era are easily recommended.

Jon Eardley   Jon Eardley worked with Gerry Mulligan's quartet and sextet off and on during 1954–57 before returning to his native Pennsylvania for a few years. **The Jon Eardley Seven** (Original Jazz Classics 123) finds the cool-toned trumpeter holding his own with Zoot Sims and Phil Woods in a septet also including trombonist Milt Gold, pianist George Syran, bassist

Teddy Kotick, and drummer Nick Stabulas. Five group originals and "There's No You" are swung lightly and with restrained fire. But despite the success of this 1956 session, Jon Eardley would not record again as a leader for 13 years.

Don Ellis One of the most interesting new trumpeters of 1960, Don Ellis was always very curious about other styles of music and was never shy to stretch himself. He graduated from Boston University, played with the big bands of Ray McKinley, Charlie Barnet, and Maynard Ferguson (being featured along with MF and Rick Kiefer on "Three More Foxes"), recorded with Charles Mingus, and played with George Russell's Sextet, with whom he made some of his best early records.

Ellis's first record as a leader, **How Time Passes** (Candid 79004), finds him experimenting a bit with time and tempo. Assisted by Jaki Byard on piano and alto, bassist Ron Carter, and drummer Charlie Persip, Ellis (who already had his own distinctive sound) performs four of his unusual originals, including the 22-minute "Improvisational Suite #1" and Byard's "Waste." The adventurous, but often swinging music is intriguing although it would fail to catch on or have much of an influence.

Don Fagerquist Don Fagerquist was a member of Dave Pell's Octet during 1953–59, becoming a staff musician at Paramount Pictures in 1956. Other than a few titles in 1955, his only date as a leader resulted in **Eight by Eight** (V.S.O.P. 4), a nonet set arranged by pianist Marty Paich that is not all that different from the music that the trumpeter played with Pell. Fagerquist's mellow tone and boppish style are heard in excellent form with a group that also includes Herb Geller and Bob Enevoldsen; highlights include "Aren't You Glad You're You," "The Song Is You," and "Easy Living." By the end of the 1950s, Don Fagerquist was largely lost to jazz, working full time in the studios.

Art Farmer A consistent and reliable trumpeter whose soft appealing tone, impeccable sight-reading abilities, and skill at improvising over any set of chord changes helped make the most esoteric music sound accessible, Farmer was a part of several significant groups during this era. He co-led a quintet with Gigi Gryce (1954–56), was a member of the Horace Silver Quintet (1957–58), and played in the Gerry Mulligan

Quartet (1958–59), all prior to forming the Jazztet with Benny Golson. In addition, he recorded with Gene Ammons, Teddy Charles, Teo Macero, and George Russell, and led several sessions of his own.

Farmer's Market (Original Jazz Classics 398) is a conventional quintet outing with Hank Mobley, Kenny Drew, Addison Farmer, and the young Elvin Jones in 1956 that is perhaps most notable for the two songs ("Reminiscing" and "By Myself") that showcase Farmer with just the rhythm section. **Portrait of Art Farmer** (Original Jazz Classics 166) continues in the same vein with Farmer as the only horn in a quartet comprised of Hank Jones, brother Addison Farmer, and Roy Haynes. The beauty of the leader's tone and his bop improvising skills are well featured on such songs as "Stablemates," "The Very Thought of You," and "Too Late Now." **Modern Art** (Blue Note 9336) teams Farmer with Benny Golson (over a year before the Jazztet was formed) along with Bill Evans, Addison Farmer, and drummer Dave Bailey. The quintet performs two originals apiece from the horn players plus very likable versions of the standards "Darn that Dream," "Like Someone in Love," and "The Touch of Your Lips."

Wilbur Harden Wilbur Harden was on some important recordings in the 1950s before slipping away into history. He began his career playing blues with Roy Brown (1950) and Ivory Joe Hunter. After serving in the navy, Harden moved to Detroit where he played and recorded with Yusef Lateef in 1957. Mostly focusing on flugelhorn, he recorded several sessions with John Coltrane in 1958 including three that he led for Savoy (which have often been reissued under Coltrane's name) and an outing with Tommy Flanagan.

The Complete Savoy Sessions (Savoy 92858) is a two-CD set featuring all of the Harden-Coltrane recordings for Savoy (they also recorded a few dates for Prestige under Trane's name). The 13 selections (and six alternate takes) do not have particularly memorable melodies, but the solos of Harden and Tommy Flanagan (who is on two of the three sessions) are fine and these dates fill in gaps in the career of John Coltrane; Curtis Fuller helps out on one session. **The King and I** (Savoy 0124) has Harden joined by Tommy Flanagan, bassist George Duvivier, and drummer Granville T. Hogan for eight songs from the popular musical and movie; best known among the numbers are "Hello Young Lovers," "Getting to Know

You," and "We Kiss in a Shadow." Nothing that surprising occurs, but the melodic treatment of the show tunes works well.

Unfortunately, an unknown illness forced Wilbur Harden's retirement in 1960 at the age of 35 and he dropped permanently out of sight, becoming a mystery figure in jazz history.

Freddie Hubbard   One of the brightest new voices on the trumpet, Freddie Hubbard came out of the Clifford Brown tradition and was inspired by Lee Morgan. He was born and raised in Indianapolis, Indiana, having a couple of cameo appearances on recordings with Wes Montgomery and the Montgomery Brothers in 1957. In 1958, when he was 20, Hubbard came to New York where he worked with Philly Joe Jones (1958–59), Sonny Rollins, Slide Hampton, J.J. Johnson, and Quincy Jones's big band (1960–61). Sounding a bit nervous on his first sideman records (which include a couple of brief appearances with John Coltrane), Hubbard developed very quickly and by 1960 was already recording for Blue Note as a leader; Miles Davis had recommended him to Alfred Lion. He was picked to appear on **Ornette Coleman's Free Jazz** record and recorded with Eric Dolphy (his roommate) although he was essentially a fiery hard bop player.

Open Sesame (Blue Note 84040) has the 22-year-old making his debut as a leader, holding his own with tenor saxophonist Tina Brooks, McCoy Tyner, Sam Jones, and drummer Clifford Jarvis. The CD reissue adds two alternate takes to the original six-song program. On "But Beautiful," Hubbard displays a beautiful tone, and other high points include a driving "All or Nothing at All" and "One Mint Julep." **Goin' Up** (Blue Note 59380) has the young trumpeter (with Hank Mobley, Tyner, Paul Chambers, and Philly Joe Jones) interpreting two songs apiece by Mobley and Kenny Dorham, the obscure "I Wished I Knew" and his own "Blues for Brenda." Although not yet famous, it was clear in 1960 that Freddie Hubbard was on his way to becoming an important force in jazz.

Thad Jones   In 1954, Thad Jones began a nine-year period playing with the Count Basie Orchestra. Because he was such an inventive soloist within the bebop tradition, he also recorded seven albums as a leader during this period for Blue Note, Period, Prestige, United Artists, and Roulette. **The Complete Blue Note/UA/**

Roulette Recordings of Thad Jones (Mosaic 3-172) is a three-CD set that contains all of the music except for the Period and Prestige dates, but unfortunately it is a limited edition. **The Magnificent Thad Jones** (Blue Note 46814) is one of the trumpeter/cornetist's finest small-group dates. Jones is joined by tenor saxophonist Billy Mitchell, Barry Harris, Percy Heath, Max Roach, and sometimes Kenny Burrell on a couple of his lesser-known, but superior originals, two obscurities, "Something to Remember You By" (a duet with Burrell), "I've Got a Crush on You," and "April in Paris" (which recalls Jones's contribution to Basie's hit version). **After Hours** (Original Jazz Classics 1782) has Jones as the sextet's leader, but pianist Mal Waldron (who contributed all four selections) is the main force behind the music. Jones and Waldron are joined by Frank Wess (tenor and flute), Burrell, Paul Chambers, and Art Taylor on this fine modern mainstream set from 1957.

Booker Little   Among the first trumpeters to emerge after Clifford Brown's death who developed his own sound and moved ahead of the Brownie tradition, Booker Little was a major new voice on the trumpet when he emerged at the age of 20 in 1958. He had a melancholy sound, a thoughtful improvising style, and an approach that was leading him beyond chordal improvisation. Born in Memphis, he started on trumpet when he was 12, spent time in Chicago playing with Johnny Griffin and the MJT + 3 (Modern Jazz Trio plus Three), and attended Chicago Conservatory. In 1958, Little joined the Max Roach Quartet/Quintet for a year before freelancing in New York. **Booker Little 4 and Max Roach** (Blue Note 1041) features the trumpeter on six selections with a quintet also featuring George Coleman, Tommy Flanagan, bassist Art Davis, and Roach, performing three of his originals, two standards, and "Milestones." The remainder of the CD has lengthy versions of "Things Ain't What They Used to Be" and "Blue 'N' Boogie" from a jam session that matches the trumpeter with such fellow Memphisites as Coleman, altoist Frank Strozier, and the masterful pianist Phineas Newborn. Booker Little (Bainbridge 1041) is a quartet outing (with either Wynton Kelly or Tommy Flanagan on piano, Scott LaFaro, and Roy Haynes) that puts the emphasis on relaxed tempos. Little's lyrical style is heard in top form on "Who Can I Turn To" and five of his originals, some of which deserve to be revived.

Both of these Booker Little albums, which comprise half of his total sessions as a leader, are well worth getting, featuring advanced hard bop that was looking toward the future.

Chuck Mangione   Chuck Mangione began his career as a Dizzy Gillespie–inspired bop trumpeter. His father was a big jazz fan who often took Chuck and his brother, pianist Gap Mangione, to concerts as children. In 1960, they formed the Jazz Brothers, a group that recorded three albums during 1960–61. **The Jazz Brothers** (Original Jazz Classics 997) features their sextet, which also includes tenor saxophonist Sal Nistico, altoist Joe Romano, bassist Bill Saunders, and drummer Roy McCurdy, playing straightahead jazz including "Secret Love," "Struttin' with Sandra," and "Girl of My Dreams." The trumpeter, who was studying at the Eastman School at the time, shows strong potential and a good understanding of bebop, while Nistico was already an exciting player.

Blue Mitchell   Richard "Blue" Mitchell had his own sound while playing within the bebop/hard bop tradition. He started on trumpet while in high school and toured with R&B bands in the early 1950s, including the groups of Paul Williams, Earl Bostic, and Chuck Willis. Mitchell, who was from Miami, returned to playing jazz locally until he was discovered by Cannonball Adderley, who recommended him to the Riverside label in 1958. That same year he joined the Horace Silver Quintet where he had a memorable six-year stint.

Producer Orrin Keepnews recorded Mitchell quite frequently during 1958–60, resulting in six albums under his name. **Big Six** (Original Jazz Classics 615) teams the trumpeter with Curtis Fuller, Johnny Griffin, Wynton Kelly, Wilbur Ware, and Philly Joe Jones. The company might have been fast, but Mitchell keeps up with them on some group originals, obscurities, "There Will Never Be Another You," and the earliest recorded version of Benny Golson's "Blues March," predating Art Blakey's famous version. **Out of the Blue** (Original Jazz Classics 667) has Mitchell, Benny Golson, Wynton Kelly or Cedar Walton, Paul Chambers or Sam Jones, and Blakey playing high-quality hard bop, including a surprisingly effective version of "When the Saints Go Marching In," "It Could Happen to You," and "Blues on My Mind." **Blue Soul** (Original Jazz Classics 765) consists of three quartet numbers with Kelly, Sam Jones, and Philly Joe Jones, and

six selections on which Curtis Fuller and altoist Jimmy Heath make the group a sextet. **Blue's Moods** (Original Jazz Classics 138) features Mitchell as the only horn in a quartet with Kelly, Jones, and Roy Brooks, while **Smooth as the Wind** (Original Jazz Classics 671) showcases his horn with brass, strings, and a rhythm section. In reality, all five of these CDs are of equal quality (**Blue Soul** gets a slight edge due to the variety and the strong repertoire) and show that Blue Mitchell was a very consistent and reliable trumpeter from the start.

Lee Morgan   It is often said that most jazz musicians find their own voice by the time they are 30. In Lee Morgan's case, at 18 he was already a very impressive trumpeter and by his 20th birthday he was one of the leaders in his field. Because he emerged right after Clifford Brown's death and Brownie was his main influence, Morgan was thought of as "the new Clifford" initially before his own musical personality made it clear that he had something of his own to offer. Born on July 10, 1938, he was a professional in his native Philadelphia by the time he was 15. Morgan was a member of Dizzy Gillespie's Orchestra during 1956–58 and started recording his own records for Blue Note in November 1956. The four-CD limited-edition **Complete Lee Morgan Fifties Blue Note Sessions** (Mosaic 4-162) has his six Blue Note albums of 1956–58. The first three albums were recorded in less than five months with **Vol. 3** (Blue Note 46817) having five compositions by Golson, who also wrote the arrangements and plays tenor with the sextet (which includes Gigi Gryce, Wynton Kelly, Paul Chambers, and drummer Charlie Persip). Most notable among the songs is the original version of "I Remember Clifford."

Two of Morgan's albums from 1957–58 are classics. **The Cooker** (Blue Note 1568), which is not yet out on CD, teams the 19-year-old with the hard-charging baritone of Pepper Adams, Bobby Timmons, Paul Chambers, and Philly Joe Jones for a particularly strong set that is highlighted by a lengthy and fiery "Night in Tunisia," "Lover Man," and a rapid rendition of "Just One of Those Things." Even better is ❍ **Candy** (Blue Note 46508), Morgan's only quartet date. Joined by Sonny Clark, Doug Watkins, and Art Taylor, Morgan sounds remarkably mature, putting plenty of honest emotion and swing into such songs as "Since I Fell for You," "C.T.A.," "Personality," and "Candy." On the basis of this album alone, it is obvious that he was one of the major trumpeters of the era.

In 1958, Lee Morgan became a member of Art Blakey's Jazz Messengers, staying three years and playing alongside Benny Golson, Hank Mobley, and Wayne Shorter. He recorded a pair of Vee Jay albums in 1960 in quintets with tenor saxophonist Clifford Jordan along with the relatively obscure Blue Note album **Lee-Way** (Blue Note 32089), which matched him on a relatively soulful date with Jackie McLean and Bobby Timmons. Lee Morgan, who also recorded prolifically with Blakey and other Blue Note artists (including being well featured on John Coltrane's **Blue Train**), had accomplished a great deal by the time 1960 ended.

Shorty Rogers West Coast jazz may have been fading in popularity during the second half of the 1950s, but Shorty Rogers remained quite busy, organizing and arranging for record dates, booking musicians for studio work, writing film scores, and leading his Giants in clubs. **Portrait of Shorty** (RCA 51561) from 1957 has a big band with Frank Rosolino, Herb Geller, and both Richie Kamuca and Jack Montrose on tenors playing such oddly titled (but swinging) pieces as "Saturnian Sleigh Ride," "Martian's Lullaby," and "A Geophysical Ear." **Swings** (Bluebird 3012) reissues the Rogers album **Chances Are It Swings** plus five of the eleven numbers from a set titled **The Wizard of Oz & Other Harold Arlen Songs**, skipping all of the *Wizard of Oz* songs. The all-star big bands include Conte Candoli, Don Fagerquist, Bob Enevoldsen, Rosolino, Bud Shank, Bob Cooper, Bill Holman, Kamuca, and clarinetist Jimmy Giuffre among others. Other projects from the era include **Gigi in Jazz**, **The Swinging Nutcracker**, and tunes inspired by Tarzan!

Louis Smith An excellent hard bop trumpeter, Louis Smith had an outburst of activity in the late 1950s before deciding to become an educator. He attended Tennessee State University, playing with the Tennessee State Collegians. Smith also studied at the University of Michigan where he played locally and sat in with musicians passing through town. After serving in the army (1954–55), he recorded with Kenny Burrell in 1956 and the following year led a date for Transition that was later acquired by Blue Note. ◉ **Here Comes Louis Smith** (Blue Note 52438) is a brilliant debut, highlighted by Duke Pearson's "Tribute to Brownie" and a haunting

rendition of "Stardust." Cannonball Adderley (under the pseudonym of Buckshot LaFunke) is also on the date along with Duke Jordan or Tommy Flanagan, Doug Watkins, and Art Taylor. Throughout the set, Smith shows that he was potentially one of the top trumpeters in jazz, displaying a beautiful tone and a fertile imagination.

But after cutting a second album for Blue Note, Louis Smith decided to retire from active playing to teach at the University of Michigan and the nearby Ann Arbor public school system. His next record date would be in 1978.

Ira Sullivan Ira Sullivan was always unusual because he was equally skilled on trumpet and reeds. He was most prominent in the late 1950s when he was based in Chicago, recording fairly often (including with Red Rodney), and he was with Art Blakey's Jazz Messengers for part of 1956. **Nicky's Tune** (Delmark 422) features Sullivan exclusively on trumpet, joined by a Chicago group comprised of the obscure tenor Nicky Hill, pianist Jodie Christian, bassist Victor Sproles, and drummer Wilbur Campbell. The music (two standards and four originals) is straightahead bop and often swings quite hard. **Blue Stroll** (Delmark 402) from 1959 is particularly strong, with Sullivan and the same rhythm section being joined by Johnny Griffin. The 19-minute jam "Bluzinbee" has Sullivan taking solos on trumpet, alto, baritone, and peck horn while Griffin has rare solos on alto and baritone in addition to his usual tenor. Everyone plays throughout the program in prime form and Sullivan's trumpet solos are quite exciting.

Clark Terry During the 1956–60 period, Clark Terry really developed into a very individual soloist, gradually switching from trumpet to the mellower flugelhorn. He worked with Duke Ellington through 1959, leaving to tour Europe with the Quincy Jones Orchestra and in 1960 become a member of the staff at NBC.

Terry had several opportunities to lead his own record dates during this period. **Serenade to a Bus Seat** (Original Jazz Classics 066) has him leading a quintet with Johnny Griffin, Wynton Kelly, Paul Chambers, and Philly Joe Jones. Terry wrote five of the eight songs, which also include "Donna Lee," a pretty version of "Stardust," and a mildly Latinized "That Old Black Magic." Terry and Griffin make for such a lively team that it is a pity that they rarely ever recorded together again. Recorded in 1957, **Duke with a Difference**

(Original Jazz Classics 229) has Terry and some of Ellington's sidemen (including Britt Woodman, Johnny Hodges, Paul Gonsalves, Tyree Glenn on vibes, Jimmy Woode, and Sam Woodyard) performing eight songs associated with Duke, but with fresh arrangements. C.T. and Mercer Ellington provided the charts for the familiar Duke tunes. **In Orbit** (Original Jazz Classics 302) shows just how universal the respect was in jazz for Clark Terry's playing, for it has Thelonious Monk making a very rare appearance as a sideman. The quartet (with Sam Jones and Philly Joe Jones) performs such tunes as "Globetrotter," "One Foot in the Gutter," "Zip Co-Ed," and just one Monk song, "Let's Cool One." **Top and Bottom Brass** (Original Jazz Classics 764) has Terry and tuba player Don Butterfield living up to the album's title, with help from Jimmy Jones's eccentric chord voicings on piano.

● **Color Changes** (Candid 79009) is particularly inspired for it features an octet with arrangements by Yusef Lateef, Budd Johnson, and Al Cohn. The lineup of musicians (C.T., Jimmy Knepper, Julius Watkins, Lateef on tenor, flute, oboe, and English horn, Seldon Powell on tenor and flute, Tommy Flanagan, bassist Joe Benjamin, and drummer Ed Shaughnessy) is well served by the colorful arrangements, and the music (originals by Terry, Lateef, Duke Jordan, and Bob Wilber) is perfectly served by the many meaningful solos. This is one of Clark Terry's best recordings, which is saying a lot considering the high quality of his sessions throughout his career.

Tommy Turrentine   The older brother of tenor saxophonist Stanley Turrentine, Tommy Turrentine was a fine hard bop trumpeter who, due to erratic health, did not accomplish as much as one would expect considering his talent. Early on, he played with Benny Carter (1946), Earl Bostic (1952–55), and Charles Mingus (1956), gaining his greatest recognition while working with Max Roach (1959–60). In addition to recording with Horace Parlan, Jackie McLean, Sonny Clark, Lou Donaldson, and brother Stanley, he led one record date of his own, **Tommy Turrentine** (Bainbridge 1047). Featured are the musicians of Roach's quintet (including Stanley, Julian Priester, bassist Bob Boswell, and Roach) and pianist Horace Parlan. Tommy Turrentine performs five of his songs, plus Parlan's "Blues for J.P." and Bud Powell's "Webb City," sounding in excellent form on the straight-ahead music.

Richard Williams   With his wide range and beautiful tone, it is surprising that Richard Williams (like Tommy Turrentine) led only one record date in his career. He originally played tenor and even gigged on the sax locally in Texas. However, while in the Air Force, he switched to trumpet. Williams toured Europe with Lionel Hampton (1956), played with Gigi Gryce, and was best known for working with Charles Mingus on a few occasions, starting in 1959. **New Horn in Town** (Candid 79003), like so many of the recordings for Nat Hentoff's Candid label, is well planned and definitive of the leader. The date is split between standards (such as "I Can Dream, Can't I" and "I Remember Clifford") and originals with Williams's quintet, which includes altoist Leo Wright, Richard Wyands, Reggie Workman, and drummer Bobby Thomas. It is a pity that this date did not lead to any others.

Trombonists

With the rise of J.J. Johnson in the mid-to-late 1940s, the trombone was saved from possible extinction (unlike the clarinet) in modern jazz. Johnson's influence remained a major factor in the styles of the bop-oriented trombonists who emerged since the 1940s.

Bob Brookmeyer   Bob Brookmeyer played with Gerry Mulligan's quartet through 1957, was part of the most unusual version of the Jimmy Giuffre 3 (a trio with Giuffre's reeds and Jim Hall's guitar), and then by 1960 was playing and writing for Mulligan's Concert Jazz Band. As a leader, Brookmeyer (who doubled on piano and could write both songs and arrangements) was quite busy in the studios, recording during this period for Prestige, Vik, Pacific Jazz, United Artists, Atlantic, Mercury, and Verve. Most of the releases have not yet been reissued on CD and even **Traditionalism Revisited** (Pacific Jazz 94847) might be a little difficult to find. This project is a bit unusual for it features modernized versions of songs from the 1920s and '30s. Brookmeyer is joined by Jimmy Giuffre (switching between clarinet, baritone, and tenor), Jim Hall, either Joe Benjamin or Ralph Pena on bass, and drummer Dave Bailey. The songs receiving respectful updatings include "Louisiana," "Truckin'," "Honeysuckle Rose," and even "Santa Claus Blues." Because the musicians have a respect for the older styles, they extend rather than break the tradition, and this colorful set is much more successful than most.

A particularly interesting session resulted in **The Ivory Hunters** (Blue Note 27324). It was initially planned that Brookmeyer and Bill Evans would perform a couple of numbers together on two pianos before Brookmeyer switched back to valve trombone, but they had so much fun that this ended up being a two-piano quartet date (with Percy Heath and Connie Kay). Brookmeyer brought out the playful side of Evans on the six extended standards, and the two pianists come up with delightful variations on such songs as "Honeysuckle Rose," "As Time Goes By," and "I Got Rhythm."

Curtis Fuller   A major new discovery, Curtis Fuller was one of the top hard bop trombonists to emerge after J.J. Johnson. Although always influenced by Johnson, Fuller had his own ideas and was greatly in demand from 1957 on. In fact, he led six albums of his own that year, one in 1958, four more in 1959, and two in 1960 after he had joined the Jazztet. Of those 13 sets, five are available on CD.

New Trombone (Original Jazz Classics 77) has Fuller blending in well with altoist Sonny Red, Hank Jones, Doug Watkins, and Louis Hayes on four originals (which generally use common chord changes) and two standards. **With Red Garland** (Original Jazz Classics 1862) again has Fuller, Red, and Hayes, but this time with Red Garland and Paul Chambers, playing a pair of originals, two blues, and a couple of ballad features. Garland is outstanding on "Moonlight Becomes You" (one of his finest recordings) while Fuller is excellent on "Stormy Weather." **With French Horns** (Original Jazz Classics 1942) is a particularly interesting set as it has Fuller, altoist Sahib Shihab, Hampton Hawes, Addison Farmer, and drummer Jerry Segal joined by both Julius Watkins and David Amram on French horns. The material (by Amram, Teddy Charles, and Salvatore Zito) utilizes colorful ensembles and an inventive use of the French horns, both in the arrangements and as solo instruments.

Curtis Fuller's four Blue Note albums of 1957–58 (which include matchups with Art Farmer, Slide Hampton, Hank Mobley, and Houston Tate) are currently only available as part of a limited-edition Mosaic box set, **The Complete Blue Note/UA Curtis Fuller Sessions** (Mosaic 3-166). **Blues-ette** (Savoy 78805) from 1959 is a legendary set that became very popular in Japan. Fuller and Benny Golson are well featured along with Tommy Flanagan, bassist Jimmy Garrison, and drummer Al Harewood on two songs apiece by Golson and Fuller (none of which caught on), "Undecided," and "Love, Your Spell Is Everywhere." **Imagination** (Savoy 78996) again has the Fuller-Golson team along with Thad Jones, pianist McCoy Tyner (in his recording debut), Jimmy Garrison, and drummer Dave Bailey. Fuller arranged all five of the songs, four of which are his originals while the lone standard is "Imagination." The catchy chord changes on Fuller's tunes clearly inspire the players, and it is interesting to hear this group sound so close to the as-yet unformed Jazztet.

Bennie Green   Bennie Green tended to be a difficult trombonist to classify. He came up during the bop era and played with the unrecorded Earl Hines big band in 1943 and Charlie Ventura's "Bop for the People" ensemble in the late 1940s. But Green had the tone of a swing player and the rambunctious nature and wit of an early R&B musician, sounding nothing at all like the dominant influence of the era, J.J. Johnson. He led ten record dates of his own during 1956–60, the busiest period of his career. **With Art Farmer** (Original Jazz Classics 1800) finds Green and Farmer at their most competitive, challenging each other on three group originals, "My Blue Heaven," and "Gone with the Wind," with the assistance of pianist Cliff Smalls, Addison Farmer, and Philly Joe Jones. Although not flawless, **Walking Down** (Original Jazz Classics 1752) has plenty of surprises, with "Walkin'" and "The Things We Did Last Summer" being taken at two different tempos along the way, while "It's You or No One" really cooks. Green utilizes four little-known players, including future Basie member tenor saxophonist Eric Dixon. **Soul Stirrin'** (Blue Note 59381) has Green teamed with both Gene Ammons (who uses the pseudonym of Jug for one of his very few appearances on the Blue Note label) and Billy Root on tenors, Sonny Clark, bassist Ike Isaacs, Elvin Jones, and Babs Gonzales on two versions of "Soul Stirrin'." This set's bluesy, witty, and swinging material is typical of a Bennie Green date as are the trombonist's sessions for Time, Bethlehem, and Vee-Jay.

Bill Harris   Bill Harris, who had gone on several tours with "Jazz at the Philharmonic," rejoined Woody Herman now and then during 1956–58, usually just for special recordings or short tours. In 1957, he led two albums of his own. **Bill Harris and Friends** (Original Jazz Classics 083) also features Ben Webster, Jimmy Rowles, Red Mitchell, and Stan Levey. Harris's unique and witty tone is showcased on "It Might as Well Be Spring," he interacts joyfully with Webster on some standards, and he verbally jokes around with the tenor on a funny version of "Just One More Chance." **Bill Harris and the Ex-Hermanites** (V.S.O.P. 108) has the trombonist, Terry Gibbs, Lou Levy, Red Mitchell, and Stan Levey jamming eight songs from the book of Woody Herman's First and Second Herds, including "Apple Honey," "Your Father's Mustache," "Early Autumn," and "Lemon Drop" (which has a guest vocal by Bob Dorough in a wordless duet with Gibbs).

Bill Harris often teamed up with Flip Phillips in the 1950s, and their band became the nucleus of Benny Goodman's combo in 1959. After that association ended, Harris (who was just 43) became semi-retired, moving to Florida.

J.J. Johnson   During 1956–60, J.J. Johnson's career evolved in several areas. His popular two-trombone quintet with Kai Winding broke up in mid-1956 after two years although they would have several reunions. Johnson, who had always written songs (his "Lament" was on its way to becoming a standard), became involved in writing more ambitious and extended Third Stream works that showed off the influence of classical music, including "El Camino Real" and "Perceptions," which showcased Dizzy Gillespie. And Johnson's regular combo featured Belgian tenor and flutist Bobby Jaspar (1956–57), Nat Adderley (1958–59), and Freddie Hubbard (1960).

The Complete J.J. Johnson Columbia Small Group Sessions (Mosaic 7-169), a seven-CD limited edition box, has all of the music from nine Johnson LPs cut during 1956–61, showing that his serious but swinging playing was at its prime during this era. The sampler **Trombone Master** (Columbia 4443) has nine selections highlighted by "Misterioso," "Blue Trombone," and "What Is this Thing Called Love." **J.J. Inc.** (Columbia 65296) features Johnson's 1960 sextet with Hubbard, Clifford Jordan on tenor, Cedar Walton, bassist Arthur Harper, and Albert "Tootle" Heath interpreting seven of Johnson's originals (including "Mohawk," "In Walked Horace," and "Fatback"), plus Dizzy Gillespie's "Blue 'N' Boogie."

The very first release by the new Impulse label (initially run by producer Creed Taylor) was **The Great J.J. and**

Kai (MCA/Impulse 225), the initial recorded reunion of Johnson and Kai Winding. The CD reissue is an exact duplicate of the LP (with liner notes so small as to be unreadable), but the music is still quite fresh, lively, and good-humored. The two trombonists are joined by Bill Evans, either Paul Chambers or Tommy Williams on bass, and Roy Haynes or Art Taylor on drums for such songs as "This Could Be the Start of Something Big," "Blue Monk," "Side by Side," and the "Theme from Picnic."

Julian Priester   A versatile trombonist who was initially influenced by J.J. Johnson, Julian Priester had a wide-ranging career. He started out working in his local Chicago in blues and R&B bands, also gigging with Sun Ra. After moving to New York in 1958, he became a member of Max Roach's group for a few years. **Keep Swingin'** (Original Jazz Classics 1863), one of two albums led by Priester in 1960, is a boppish date comprised of four of the trombonist's originals, one song apiece by Jimmy Heath (whose tenor makes the group a quintet on five of the eight songs) and baritonist Charles Davis, and two standards (including "Once in a While"). The rhythm section (Tommy Flanagan, Sam Jones, and Elvin Jones) is typically supportive and swinging. This album served as a solid start for Julian Priester's career.

Frank Rosolino   Frank Rosolino worked steadily as a fixture with the Lighthouse All-Stars during 1954–60, in the studios, and on a lot of dates as a freelancer. Two of his albums from this era have been reissued on CD. **Frank Rosolino Quartet** (V.S.O.P. 16) has the trombonist and Richie Kamuca making for a potent front line in a quintet with pianist Vince Guaraldi, Monty Budwig, and Stan Levey. The group swings hard on the mixture of standards and originals, showing that not all West Coast jazz was laidback and quiet. **Free for All** (Original Jazz Classics 1763) with Rosolino, Harold Land, pianist Victor Feldman, Leroy Vinnegar, and Levey, falls even more into hard bop than cool and has its exciting moments. But Rosolino's main contributions during this period were as a star sideman where his extroverted solos were always a major asset.

Altoists

Although Charlie Parker died in 1955, his influence remained quite dominant in jazz. Altoists particularly had difficulty escaping being in his shadow, but a few managed to carve out their own voices from the Parker style during 1956–60.

Cannonball Adderley   Considering the fast start that Cannonball and Nat Adderley had after their discovery in 1955, one would have expected the first Cannonball Adderley Quintet to be a big success. The two-CD set ● **Sophisticated Swing: The EmArcy Small-Group Sessions** (Verve 314 528 408) has (with the exception of one hornless trio number) all of the contents from the first Adderley Quintet's four LPs: **To the Ivy League from Nat**, **Sophisticated Swing**, **Cannonball Enroute**, and **Sharpshooters**. It is surprising that this group (with pianist Junior Mance, bassist Sam Jones, and Jimmy Cobb) did not catch on, for their music is a jubilant and exciting brand of bebop, with consistently heated solos from the brothers. But instead, the band struggled for two years as Cannonball found out that his new fame only seemed to reach to the city limits of New York City. By late 1957, the quintet (which made a final album in March 1958) knew that its days were numbered. Cannonball joined Miles Davis, and Nat soon worked with J.J. Johnson and Woody Herman.

Cannonball Adderley and Strings/Jump for Joy (Verve 314 528 699) teams together two unusual dates by the altoist. The first dozen songs have Adderley during October 27–28, 1955 (when he was just 27 and a recent discovery) performing ballads quite melodically with a string section, an effort that was a bit premature (he should have attempted it again in 1965). The second half of the CD has Adderley in 1958 playing ten songs from the Duke Ellington show *Jump for Joy*, mostly obscurities other than "Just Squeeze Me," "I Got It Bad," and the title cut. He is joined by trumpeter Emmett Berry, a string quartet, and a rhythm section (with Bill Evans) arranged by Bill Russo. Although Adderley plays quite well, this CD is not too essential.

Although one can regret the short life of the first Cannonball Adderley Quintet, if it had not broken up, Cannonball would not have been a part of Miles Davis's remarkable sextet of 1958–59 or participated on **Kind of Blue**. And Adderley was also far from inactive as a leader (at least in the recording studios) during this period. **Somethin' Else** (Blue Note 46338) has him leading a quintet that features a very rare sideman appearance by Miles Davis, along with Hank Jones, Sam Jones, and Art Blakey. It is a measure of the trumpeter's

admiration for his altoist that he appeared in this setting although he actually dominates the music, particularly on the near-classic versions of "Autumn Leaves," "Love for Sale," and "One for Daddy-O."

In 1958, Adderley began five years of mostly superb recordings for the Riverside label, sessions that rank with his greatest work. **Portrait of Cannonball** (Original Jazz Classics 361) with trumpeter Blue Mitchell and Bill Evans, and **Alabama Concerto** (Original Jazz Classics 1779), which is an unusual nine-part suite by John Benson Brooks that features Adderley in a pianoless, drumless quartet, contain their share of fine music. However, **Things Are Getting Better** (Original Jazz Classics 032) and ● **Cannonball and Coltrane** (EmArcy 834 588) are on a higher level. **Things Are Getting Better**, which matches Adderley with Milt Jackson, Wynton Kelly, Percy Heath, and Art Blakey, features the altoist at his most joyful, exuberantly digging into such tunes as "Things Are Getting Better," "Just One of Those Things," and "Sidewalks of New York." **Cannonball and Coltrane** is the 1959 Miles Davis Sextet without Davis (Wynton Kelly, Paul Chambers, and Jimmy Cobb form the rhythm section). Adderley is showcased on "Stars Fell on Alabama," and the two saxophone greats battle it out in memorable fashion on "Limehouse Blues."

In October 1959, Cannonball Adderley made a second attempt at leading a quintet, once again featuring his brother cornetist Nat as his "brass section," along with Sam Jones, Louis Hayes, and, most importantly, pianist Bobby Timmons. ● **Cannonball Adderley Quintet in San Francisco** (Original Jazz Classics 035) was a big seller, due in large part to the debut of Timmons's "This Here." That number helped launch Adderley as one of the leaders of hard bop/soul jazz, and its catchy melody made it into a standard. Also featured on this historic live set are memorable versions of "Spontaneous Combustion," "Hi-Fly," "You Got It," "Bohemia After Dark," and "Straight No Chaser." Although the new Adderley group was not all that different from the first one (being a bit more soulful and a touch less boppish), the band caught on big and Adderley was a successful bandleader throughout the rest of his life. The follow-up album, **Them Dirty Blues** (Capitol 95447) from 1960, has the same group (with Timmons and his replacement Barry Harris splitting the piano chair) performing notable versions of "Work Song" (Nat Adderley's most famous composition), Duke Pearson's "Jeannine," Sam Jones's "Del

Sasser," and Timmons's "Dat Dere," all four of which became standards. With such a strong repertoire and the distinctive Cannonball Adderley at the helm, the band was poised to become one of the most popular jazz groups of the 1960s.

Sonny Criss   Sonny Criss spent part of the 1956–60 period playing with Buddy Rich when he was not leading groups of his own. He led three little-known sessions for the R&B Imperial label during 1956, straightahead outings in quartets and quintets featuring Kenny Drew or Sonny Clark on piano, guitarist Barney Kessel or vibraphonist Larry Bunker, and a variety of bassists and drummers. Fortunately, all three albums have been reissued as the double CD **The Complete Imperial Sessions** (Blue Note 24564), featuring the 28-year-old altoist (whose heavy sound made him stand apart from Charlie Parker and his close followers) playing standards (such as "Sunday, "More Than You Know," "How High the Moon," and "The Man I Love"), a few originals and a full set of Cole Porter songs. But being based on the West Coast resulted in Sonny Criss gaining much less recognition than he deserved.

Paul Desmond   Paul Desmond kept busy traveling in the United States and overseas as a member of the Dave Brubeck Quartet during the 1950s. He had three opportunities to lead his own record dates during 1954–59, and as was always true of his sessions, there was no pianist in Brubeck's place. **Featuring Don Elliott** (Original Jazz Classics 712) has a 1956 album matching Desmond with Elliott (who doubles on trumpet and mellophone), with quiet backing by bassist Norman Bates and drummer Joe Dodge. The two witty horn players make for a fine match on such songs as "Line for Lyons," "Look for the Silver Lining," and "5 Acre Blues." Also on this CD are four tunes from 1954 in which Desmond, Barney Kessel, Bates, and Dodge are joined by the Bill Bates Singers (the vocalists, though a frivolity, are not too bad), and a quintet outing with trumpeter Dick Collins, tenor saxophonist Dave Van Kriedt, Bates, and Dodge.

While Desmond's **Featuring Don Elliott** looks back toward cool jazz and the Dave Brubeck Octet (of which Desmond, Collins and Van Kriedt were members), 1959's **East of the Sun** (Discovery 840) is the first in a series of Desmond quartet dates with guitarist Jim Hall. With assistance from Percy Heath and Connie Kay,

Desmond and Hall prove to be a very complementary team on a variety of standards, including "For All We Know," "You Got to My Head," and "East of the Sun." Next to the Brubeck Quartet, this would prove to be Paul Desmond's favorite setting for his lyrical alto.

Eric Dolphy   One of the most unusual jazz improvisers of all time, Eric Dolphy developed a completely unpredictable speechlike style on three different instruments: alto sax, flute, and bass clarinet. Although thought of as avant-garde because his playing was so abstract, he did play (in his own fashion) within chord changes much of the time. He had an often-ecstatic and exuberant style full of wide interval jumps (particularly on alto), following his own unique musical logic. Dolphy was also one of the very first (after Coleman Hawkins) to occasionally play a piece unaccompanied, and he introduced the bass clarinet to jazz as a solo instrument.

Dolphy started his career playing bebop with Roy Porter's Orchestra (1948–50) with whom he made his recording debut. He served in the army, played locally in Los Angeles, and then was a member of the Chico Hamilton Quintet during 1958–59. He moved to New York later in 1959 and spent a year with the Charles Mingus Quartet, playing next to Ted Curson and Dannie Richmond. It was during this time that he began to really be noticed.

During 1960–61, Dolphy recorded quite a few sessions for Prestige and its subsidiary New Jazz, all of which have been reissued on the nine-CD set ❍ **The Complete Prestige Recordings** (Prestige 4418), which will be reviewed in the next chapter. Of the individual albums, four were made in 1960. **Outward Bound** (Original Jazz Classics 022) has Dolphy teamed with Freddie Hubbard, Jaki Byard, bassist George Tucker, and Roy Haynes on April 1, 1960, interpreting particularly strong material. Highlights include Dolphy's tribute to Gerald Wilson ("G.W."), an exciting rendition of "On Green Dolphin Street," a flute feature on "Glad to Be Unhappy," and some jubilant bass clarinet on "Miss Toni." **Out There** (Original Jazz Classics 023) is an intriguing date in which Dolphy (who plays alto, flute, and bass clarinet on two songs apiece) has a rare appearance on clarinet for "Eclipse." He is joined by Ron Carter on cello, bassist George Duvivier, and Roy Haynes on the rather hypnotic and repetitious "Out There" and a variety of originals. **Caribe** (Original Jazz Classics 819) is a somewhat bizarre session in that Dolphy plays as wildly as ever, but is accompanied by Juan Amalbert's Latin Jazz Quintet, a laidback group that not only does not react to his solos, but ignores him completely. It is almost as if Dolphy overdubbed his solos afterward, though apparently the music was recorded live. **Far Cry** (Original Jazz Classics 400), from December 21, 1960, teams Dolphy with Booker Little for the first time in a quintet with Jaki Byard, Ron Carter, and Roy Haynes. Most memorable is the unaccompanied alto feature on "Tenderly" and a very happy rendition of "It's Magic."

Lou Donaldson   Altoist Lou Donaldson was at his most beboppish during the second half of the 1950s. He recorded regularly for Blue Note during 1957–63 and his soulful tone was so popular and accessible that some of his performances were recorded as 45s for jukeboxes. A highly enjoyable but limited-edition Mosaic box set, **The Complete Blue Note Loud Donaldson Sessions 1957–60** (Mosaic 6-215) is well worth bidding on but, as with the other wonderful Mosaic boxes, only stayed in-print a short time. Otherwise only a few of his sessions from this session have appeared on CD thus far. ◯ **Blues Walk** (Blue Note 81593) from 1958 is one of Donaldson's finest sets. Playing with pianist Herman Foster, bassist Peck Morrison, drummer Dave Bailey, and Ray Barretto on conga, Donaldson performs three swinging originals (including "Play Ray" and "Calling All Cats"), a hard-swinging "Move," and a romantic "Autumn Nocturne." Also quite rewarding is **Sunny Side Up** (Blue Note 32098), a quintet outing with Bill Hardman, Horace Parlan, Sam Jones, and drummer Al Harewood that has Donaldson transforming a variety of material (including "Swanee River," "Softly as in a Morning Sunrise," and his own "Goose Grease") into swinging hard bop.

Herb Geller   Herb Geller worked steadily in the Los Angeles area during 1953–58, often using his wife Lorraine Geller on piano. **Stax of Sax** (Fresh Sound 75) features the boppish altoist in 1958 with Victor Feldman (on vibes), Walter Norris, Leroy Vinnegar, and drummer Anthony Vazley. Geller is in top form on three of his originals and two standards ("Change Partners" and "It Might as Well Be Spring"), but little did he know that this recording symbolized the end of an era for him. On October 10, 1958, just a month after her 30th birthday, Lorraine Geller suddenly and unexpectedly

died. Herb Geller was crushed, and though he worked with Benny Goodman on and off during 1958–61, it would be some time before he recovered emotionally.

Gigi Gryce   During 1955–58, Gigi Gryce and Donald Byrd co-led the Jazz Lab Quintet, a group that sought to explore several areas of jazz. The 1957 version is featured on **Gigi Gryce and the Jazz Lab Quintet** (Original Jazz Classics 1774), a fairly conventional but colorful quintet album with pianist Wade Legge, Wendell Marshall, and Art Taylor. "Love for Sale" is taken as a waltz, which was still rather unusual in jazz of the era. Gryce plays his most famous composition, "Minority," "Straight Ahead" is a tricky blues line, and "Zing Went the Strings of My Heart" is swung hard.

Unfortunately, the Jazz Lab Quintet did not last. Instead, during 1959–61 Gryce had a quintet with trumpeter Richard Williams, pianist Richard Wyands, Reggie Workman or Julian Euell on bass, and drummer Mickey Roker. **Sayin' Something** (Original Jazz Classics 1851), **The Rat Race Blues** (Original Jazz Classics 081), and **The Hap'nin's** (Original Jazz Classics 1868), though not as ambitious as some of the Jazz Lab Quintet projects, are excellent examples of high-quality hard bop and include some of the finest playing by Gryce and Williams. But Gigi Gryce, who was becoming involved in independent publishing of musicians' compositions (which was rather controversial in 1960), was starting to feel a great deal of pressure and would soon feel compelled to permanently leave the music business.

John Handy   A major new find on alto, John Handy started playing alto in 1949, worked in his native Dallas, served in the army, and moved to New York in 1958. A fiery player who could hit high notes with ease and whose style was an extension of Charlie Parker's, Handy benefited greatly from his fiery period with Charles Mingus (1958–59). He worked briefly with Randy Weston and then led his own groups. His first two albums, **In the Vernacular** (Roulette 52042) and **No Coast Jazz** (Roulette 52058), have unfortunately not been reissued on CD yet. The former set has Handy in a quintet with Richard Williams, doubling on tenor and showing the influence of John Coltrane in spots. **No Coast Jazz** consists of six Handy originals that are advanced hard bop that sometimes hints at the avant-garde. There is no shortage of passion and exciting playing on either LP.

Ernie Henry   Ernie Henry seemed to live practically his entire musical life in a two-year period. Henry, influenced by Charlie Parker, always had his own sound and displayed a great deal of potential. Early on, he played with Tadd Dameron (1947), Fats Navarro, Charlie Ventura, Max Roach, the Dizzy Gillespie Orchestra (1948–49), and Illinois Jacquet (1950–52). After being off the scene during much of 1953–55, Henry suddenly became prominent in 1956. He recorded the **Brilliant Corners** (Original Jazz Classics 026) album with Thelonious Monk, worked with Charles Mingus, recorded with Kenny Dorham, and was a member of the Dizzy Gillespie Big Band. In addition he led three albums for Riverside. **Presenting Ernie Henry** (Original Jazz Classics 102) teams him with Dorham, Kenny Drew, Wilbur Ware, and Art Taylor on five of his originals, "Gone with the Wind," and "I Should Care"; the music falls between bop and hard bop. **Seven Standards and a Blues** (Original Jazz Classics 1722) showcases the altoist in enthusiastic form in a quartet with Wynton Kelly, Ware, and Philly Joe Jones, interpreting such songs as "I Get a Kick Out of You," "I've Got the World on a String," and "Like Someone in Love." **Last Chorus** (Original Jazz Classics 1906) has four numbers from an incomplete project dating from September 1957 with an octet that also features Lee Morgan, trombonist Melba Liston, Benny Golson, Cecil Payne, Wynton Kelly, Paul Chambers, and Philly Joe Jones (highlighted by "Autumn Leaves," and "All the Things You Are"). In addition, there is an alternate take from a November 13, 1957, session headed by Dorham, two alternates from Henry's previous dates as a leader, and an excerpt from "Ba-Lue Bolivar Ba-Lues-Are" with Monk.

Last Chorus was released posthumously. On December 29, 1957, Ernie Henry died suddenly at the age of 31, ending what should have been a major career.

John Jenkins   John Jenkins (whose style was a mixture of Charlie Parker and Jackie McLean) also had potential although his career ultimately went nowhere. He was born and raised in Chicago, playing locally until 1957 when at the age of 26 he moved to New York. He freelanced (including briefly with Charles Mingus), recording as a sideman with Donald Byrd, Hank Mobley, Paul Quinichette, Clifford Jordan, Sahib Shihab, and Wilbur Ware. Jenkins also led three albums of his own in 1957. **Jenkins, Jordan and Timmons**

(Original Jazz Classics 251) is a quintet set with Clifford Jordan, Bobby Timmons, Wilbur Ware, and Dannie Richmond that is mostly comprised of obscure but swinging originals (along with "Tenderly"). **John Jenkins with Kenny Burrell** (Blue Note 52437) has Jenkins as the only horn in a quintet with Kenny Burrell, Sonny Clark, Paul Chambers, and Dannie Richmond, playing the boppish music in exciting and creative fashion. **Jazz Eyes** (Savoy 6056), a quintet date with Donald Byrd, has not been reissued. But after 1961, John Jenkins dropped out of the jazz scene altogether and rarely played in public during the next two decades.

Lee Konitz   After having an unlikely but successful stint with Stan Kenton's Orchestra (1952–54), Lee Konitz worked primarily as a leader other than his occasional reunions with Lennie Tristano. He recorded fairly often, particularly for Atlantic and Verve. **Inside Hi-Fi** (Koch 8504), a reissue of an Atlantic date, features Konitz with two separate quartets in 1956. With either Billy Bauer or pianist Sal Mosca as the main supporting voices, the music is very much in the Tristano tradition. The most unusual aspect to the set is that on the four selections with Mosca, Konitz switches to tenor, playing quite effectively in his recognizable cool style. **The Real Lee Konitz** (32 Jazz 32157) is in the same vein, a quartet/quintet date with Bauer, bassist Peter Ind, drummer Dick Scott, and sometimes trumpeter Don Ferrara, jamming over common chord changes. Konitz's cliché-free brand of thoughtful freedom always moved his music beyond the predictable and filled it with subtle surprises. **Live at the Half Note** (Verve 521 659) is a two-CD set from 1959 featuring Konitz, Warne Marsh, Bill Evans (who was substituting for Tristano), Jimmy Garrison, and Paul Motian stretching out over familiar tunes. Excerpts from the night (just Marsh's solos) had been put out previously by Revelation, but this two-fer has the performances as they really took place.

Most interesting of all is the two-CD set **Lee Konitz Meets Jimmy Giuffre** (Verve 527 780), which not only has the original LP, but music from three other rare Verve LPs too. Lee Konitz is showcased (originally on the album **An Image**) on a set of adventurous Bill Russo arrangements for an orchestra and strings in 1958 and pops up on half of Ralph Burns's underrated 1951 gem **Free Forms**. He meets up with Jimmy Giuffre, who plays baritone and whose arrangements for five saxes (including Warne Marsh) and a trio with Bill Evans are sometimes equally influenced by classical music and bop. The least interesting date showcases Giuffre's clarinet with a string section on his five-part "Piece for Clarinet and String Orchestra," and the 16 brief movements of "Mobiles." Overall this two-fer, which often falls into the area of Third Stream, contains music that is easier to respect and admire than to love. But Lee Konitz excels in every setting.

Ken McIntyre A fine multi-instrumentalist who played alto, flute, bass clarinet, bassoon, and oboe, Ken McIntyre fell short of being a major improviser, but could hold his own with better-known players. He served in the military and graduated from the Boston Conservatory, arriving in New York in 1960 when he was 28. His debut, **Stone Blues** (Original Jazz Classics 1818), grows more interesting with each listen. On a couple of McIntyre's originals, he slides humorously between notes while the other selections are much more serious. Utilizing obscure sidemen (trombonist John Mancebo Lewis, pianist Dizzy Sal, bassist Paul Morrison, and drummer Bobby Ward), McIntyre (sticking to alto and flute) performs advanced bop influenced a little by the "new thing" music of Ornette Coleman. **Looking Ahead** (Original Jazz Classics 252) shows a great deal of musical courage, for McIntyre is teamed with Eric Dolphy, who not too surprisingly always steals the show. Accompanied by Walter Bishop, Jr., Sam Jones, and Art Taylor, McIntyre mostly keeps up with Dolphy on a variety of originals and "They All Laughed," and the colorful music continually keeps one guessing.

Hal McKusick A busy and versatile studio musician, the cool-toned altoist and clarinetist Hal McKusick led nine albums during 1955–58, only two of which are currently available. **Jazz Workshop** (BMG 91352) features McKusick in four settings, ranging from a pianoless quartet to a quintet and an octet. Among the supporting cast are Art Farmer, guitarist Barry Galbraith, and Jimmy Cleveland. George Russell (who plays drums on one number) contributed three songs, and the other composers are a who's who of the era: Johnny Mandel, Gil Evans (a version of "Blues for Pablo" that predates Miles Davis's version), Jimmy Giuffre, Manny Albam, and Al Cohn. **Triple Exposure** (Original Jazz Classics 1811) teams McKusick (on alto, tenor, and clarinet) with the obscure but talented trombonist

Billy Byers, along with pianist Eddie Costa, Paul Chambers, and Charlie Persip. The two horns get rare opportunities to stretch out on material ranging from "Saturday Night" and an early version of Dizzy Gillespie's "Con Alma" to "I'm Glad There Is You" and three McKusick originals.

After 1958, Hal McKusick faded from the jazz scene, working full time in the studios.

Jackie McLean As one of the top hard bop altoists, Jackie McLean always had a distinctive and passionate sound and an advanced improvising style based initially on Charlie Parker. McLean recorded frequently for the Prestige label during 1956–57, and although years later he would not speak favorably of the sessions (since he was underpaid and most of the dates were thrown together quickly), the music mostly sounds pretty rewarding today if not up to the level of his later Blue Note dates. **Lights Out** (Original Jazz Classics 426) is a fine quintet date with Donald Byrd, Elmo Hope, Doug Watkins, and Art Taylor that has the musicians stretching out on basic chord changes (blues, "I Got Rhythm," "Embraceable You," and "A Foggy Day"), serving as a fine introduction to McLean's sound and style. **4, 5 and 6** (Original Jazz Classics 056) has spots for Byrd and Hank Mobley, but is most notable for McLean's ballad features on "Sentimental Journey," "Why Was I Born," "When I Fall in Love," and Mal Waldron's "Abstraction." **Jackie's Pal** (Original Jazz Classics 1714) features trumpeter Bill Hardman and is very much in the style of Art Blakey's Jazz Messengers. Four originals and two standards (including a showcase for Hardman on "It Could Happen to You") are on this quintet date with Mal Waldron, Paul Chambers, and Philly Joe Jones. **McLean's Scene** (Original Jazz Classics 098) features Hardman, Red Garland, Chambers, and Taylor on half of the selections, while the other three numbers find McLean in top form (particularly on "Our Love Is Here to Stay" and "Old Folks") in a quartet with Waldron, bassist Arthur Phipps, and Taylor.

Jackie McLean and Co. (Original Jazz Classics 074) has McLean, Hardman, Waldron, Watkins, and Taylor joined by tuba player Ray Draper on three of the five numbers, which certainly changes the sound of the ensembles, but without resulting in any major revelations; not too surprisingly the tuba seems out of place. **Strange Blues** (Original Jazz Classics 354) has some interesting and fairly rare material, including "Strange Blues" (with Mal Waldron in a quartet), two additional songs with Ray Draper, and the incomplete "Not So Strange Blues." **Alto Madness** (Original Jazz Classics 1733) is a jam session with McLean and fellow altoist John Jenkins paying tribute to Charlie Parker not so much in the songs ("Bird Feathers" is the only Parker tune), but by emulating his phrases and sound. **A Long Drink of the Blues** (Original Jazz Classics 253) begins with a false start and a verbal argument by the musicians (for two minutes) about the tempo. Then things settle down with a 20-minute jam featuring McLean, Curtis Fuller, trumpeter Webster Young, pianist Gil Coggins, Chambers, and Louis Hayes. The second half of this CD has McLean performing three standard ballads in a quartet with Waldron. **Makin' the Changes** (Original Jazz Classics 197), the ninth record led by McLean for Prestige in 19 months, wraps up this period of the altoist's life with more selections from the two sessions partly covered in **A Long Drink of the Blues.** Highlights include "Bean and the Boys," "I Never Knew," "What's New," and "Chasin' the Bird."

After a year off from leading dates (he played regularly with Art Blakey during 1956–58), McLean was signed to Blue Note where he would make 21 albums as a leader during the next nine years. During 1959–60, he was in a position not that much different from Coleman Hawkins in 1944, a major player from the mainstream style of the time (hard bop) who was open to and supportive of the newer innovations, being quite impressed by aspects of Ornette Coleman's music. McLean's Blue Note albums would increasingly emphasize his adventurous side. **Jackie's Bag** (Blue Note 46142) for the first time shows the influence of Coleman on McLean, not in his sound, but in the improvising approach. Three of the songs match McLean with Byrd, Sonny Clark, Chambers, and Philly Joe Jones, while the other numbers are played with a sextet also including Blue Mitchell, Tina Brooks on tenor, Kenny Drew, Chambers, and Taylor. "Quadrangle," "Fidel" (from a period when Fidel Castro was considered a possible hero), "Appointment in Ghana," and "Melonae's Dance" all look forward while still being tied to hard bop. **New Soil** (Blue Note 84013) from May 1959 has McLean, Byrd, Walter Davis, Jr., Chambers, and Pete LaRoca performing complex and well-rehearsed material: two songs by McLean and four (including "Davis' Cup") from the pianist. **Swing, Swang, Swingin'** (Blue Note 56582) is a bit of a surprise in that all but one song are standards. How-

ever, the passion that McLean gives each note (even on such familiar tunes as "What's New," "I Remember You," and "I Love You") makes each sound coming out of his horn quite intense and highly expressive.

Lennie Niehaus   The fifth and final Lennie Niehaus Contemporary recording, **Vol. 5: The Sextet** (Original Jazz Classics 1944) from 1956, is up to the level of his other sets. Niehaus's group features his alto, Bill Perkins on tenor and flute, baritonist Jimmy Giuffre, Stu Williamson on trumpet and valve trombone, bassist Buddy Clark, and Shelly Manne. Not too surprisingly, the music is vintage West Coast jazz with inventive variations on such songs as "Thou Swell," "As Long as I Live," and "I Wished on the Moon," plus some Niehaus originals. But other than an out-of-print set for EmArcy the following year, this was the end of an era. Niehaus largely put his horn away for decades and became a full-time arranger, primarily working in the studios.

Art Pepper   Considering Art Pepper's erratic lifestyle (spending two periods in jail during 1953–56 due to drug abuse and always seeming to scuffle), the consistency of his 1956–60 recordings is remarkable. His life might have been a mess and he may have been in bad physical shape at times, but Pepper played brilliantly all the time on records. **The Return of Art Pepper Vol. 1** (Blue Note 46863), **Modern Art Vol. 2** (Blue Note 46848), and **The Art of Pepper Vol. 3** (Blue Note 46853) have Pepper's 1956–57 recordings for the Jazz West, Intro, Liberty, Onyx, and Japanese Trio labels. **Vol. 1** features Pepper in a quintet with Jack Sheldon, Russ Freeman, Leroy Vinnegar, and Shelly Manne and on five numbers actually led by drummer Joe Morello that also include Red Norvo, Gerald Wiggins, and bassist Ben Tucker. Pepper is the star throughout, particularly on "Straight Life," "Pepper Steak," "Tenor Blooz" (on which he switches to tenor), "Patricia," and "Art Pepper Returns." **Vol. 2** has him in quartets with either Russ Freeman or Carl Perkins on piano, blowing hard on such tunes as "When You're Smiling," "Stompin' at the Savoy," "Blues In," "Blues Out," and "Webb City." **Vol. 3** is a 1957 quartet set with Carl Perkins; highlights include "Too Close for Comfort," "Fascinating Rhythm," and "Surf Ride."

Good as the Blue Note CDs are, Art Pepper's greatest recordings of the era were for Lester Koenig's Contemporary label, music that has been reissued on six Original Jazz Classics CDs. **The Way It Was** (Original Jazz

Classics 389) actually has the appearance of including leftovers, with four tunes and two alternates from a date with Warne Marsh in a quintet that was never completed plus three songs from other sessions that were originally not released, but the quality is quite high. Pepper and Marsh weave lines around each other so well on "I Can't Believe that You're in Love with Me" and "Tickle Toe" that it is a pity that they did not record together more extensively.

The next two Art Pepper Contemporary sets are considered all-time classics. ● **Meets the Rhythm Section** (Original Jazz Classics 338) has the altoist teamed with Miles Davis's rhythm section (Red Garland, Paul Chambers, and Philly Joe Jones), sounding in peak form on "You'd Be So Nice to Come Home To," "Star Eyes," "Birks' Works," and his original "Straight Life." ● **Art Pepper + Eleven: Modern Jazz Classics** (Original Jazz Classics 341) from 1959 is even better. Marty Paich arranged a dozen jazz standards (including "Move," "Groovin' High," "Four Brothers," "Shaw Nuff," "Anthropology," and "Donna Lee") for a 12-piece group of top West Coast players. Jack Sheldon has a few solos, but this is mostly Pepper's showcase and he sounds quite inspired by the colorful charts, coming up with one memorable solo after another.

In 1960, Pepper recorded **Gettin' Together** (Original Jazz Classics 169), **Smack Up** (Original Jazz Classics 176), and **Intensity** (Original Jazz Classics 387), all of which are on a high level. **Gettin' Together** is a sort of sequel to **Meets the Rhythm Section** for Pepper is again matched with Miles Davis's backing trio, which by this time was Wynton Kelly, Chambers, and Jimmy Cobb; Conte Candoli joins the group on half of the selections. High points include "Bijou the Poodle," "Rhythm-A-Ning," and "Diane." **Smack Up** has Pepper exploring a variety of material (including Ornette Coleman's "Tears Inside" and Buddy Collette's "A Bit of Basie") with Sheldon, Pete Jolly, bassist Jimmy Bond, and drummer Frank Butler. **Intensity**, from November 23–25, 1960, was the altoist's last recording before he began a long prison term for drug abuse. Pepper is quite emotional and passionate during the standards-oriented date, really digging into "I Love You," "Come Rain or Come Shine," and "Gone with the Wind" with the assistance of pianist Dolo Coker, Bond, and Butler, showing that he was one of the major altoists in jazz. But it would be a long time before much would be heard again from Art Pepper.

Bud Shank Bud Shank, a veteran West Coast cool jazz altoist and flutist in the 1950s, recorded regularly for Pacific Jazz and World Pacific during 1956–58 with his quartet, which featured pianist Claude Williamson, bassist Don Prell, and either Chuck Flores or Jimmy Pratt on drums. The five-CD set **Pacific Jazz Bud Shank Studio Sessions** (Mosaic 5-180) is pretty scarce and the dates are not available individually yet. **Live at the Haig** (Bainbridge 6830), club dates from 1956 that were not cut for Pacific Jazz, is the only early Shank quartet CD around at the moment. The music (Williamson's "Ambassador Blues," and such standards as "How About You" and "Out of this World") show how swinging a group this was, and how cool a tone Bud Shank had on alto during an era when he seemed to personify West Coast jazz.

Sonny Stitt Sonny Stitt always kept bebop alive in his playing along with the sound of Charlie Parker on alto. Never under-recorded, during the 1956–60 period he made albums for Roost, which have been reissued on a superb nine-CD Mosaic limited-edition box, **The Complete Roost Sonny Stitt** (Mosaic 9-208), but are not available individually. Stitt also recorded prolifically for Verve and Argo. **Only the Blues** (Verve 537 753) has the very complete results of his October 11, 1957, session with Roy Eldridge, the Oscar Peterson Trio, and Stan Levey. The full group plays three blues and "The String" (which is exactly the same as Stitt's "Eternal Triangle"), and some sparks fly between the two horns. The rest of the set is weaker because Stitt, who is heard on two standards without Eldridge, is also featured on 22 minutes of "I Know that You Know" consisting of three full versions, a false start, five breakdowns, an incomplete version, and seven attempts at a coda. Sometimes more is less!

Much more logical is **Sonny Stitt Sits In with the Oscar Peterson Trio** (Verve 849 396), which combines a complete session that Stitt (doubling on alto and tenor) made with the 1959 Oscar Peterson Trio, and three titles from 1957 with Peterson, Herb Ellis, Ray Brown, and Stan Levey. The music very much has the feel of a jam session, and, other than a themeless blues, all of the songs are veteran standards. Highlights of this fine effort include "I Can't Give You Anything but Love," "The Gypsy," "Scrapple from the Apple," "Easy Does It," and "I Remember You."

Frank Strozier Altoist Frank Strozier was one of many excellent jazz musicians who grew up in Memphis and emerged in the late 1950s. His intense style sometimes recalls Jackie McLean with touches of Charlie Parker. In Chicago he recorded with the MJT + 3, and he led dates for Vee-Jay in 1960, the year he moved to New York. **Fantastic Frank Strozier** (Koch 8550) has the original six selections of the LP plus five previously unreleased performances, only one of which is an alternate take. The altoist's quintet consists of Miles Davis's rhythm section of the time (Wynton Kelly, Paul Chambers, and Jimmy Cobb) along with the great trumpeter Booker Little, whose presence makes the set something special. The advanced hard bop music is mostly comprised of Strozier originals, well played by the quintet. **Cool, Calm and Collected** (Koch 8552) is an excellent Vee-Jay session, also from 1960, that was unreleased until 1994. This time Strozier is featured with a Chicago-based trio comprised of pianist Billy Wallace, bassist Bill Lee, and drummer Vernel Fournier. The music is excellent and at times quite fiery, but due to the many alternate takes (two of the seven pieces are heard three times while four others appear twice), it is probably best not to hear it all in one sitting.

Eddie "Cleanhead" Vinson A very likable performer who sang humorous blues vocals (sometimes making fun of his clean-shaven head) and played alto with a tone similar to Charlie Parker's, Eddie "Cleanhead" Vinson performed music that could fit into blues, 1950s R&B, and jazz. Surprisingly, he did not record much during this era. In fact, **Cleanhead's Back in Town** (Bethlehem 76679) is one of only two recordings that he made as a leader between 1956–66. With arrangements by Ernie Wilkins, Manny Albam, and Harry Tubbs, and his sidemen including several members (past and present) of the Count Basie Orchestra, Vinson performs such numbers as "It Ain't Necessarily So," "Is You Is or Is You Ain't My Baby," and "Caldonia" with his usual enthusiasm and wit.

Phil Woods When it comes to high-powered bebop, few are on Phil Woods's level. Although obviously influenced by Charlie Parker, Woods's sound was further away from Bird's than Sonny Stitt's was, and his individuality grew through the years. In addition to leading his own groups and sometimes teaming up with fellow altoist Gene Quill (as "Phil and Quill"), Woods worked with George Wallington, the Dizzy Gillespie Orchestra, Buddy Rich, and the Quincy Jones Big Band (1959–61). He also recorded frequently during this period as a leader, with sessions for Victor, Mode, Savoy, Epic, and Prestige, some of which are reviewed in the next paragraph.

Pairing Off (Original Jazz Classics 92) gets its title from the fact that it features two altos (Phil Woods and Gene Quill) and two trumpets (Donald Byrd and Kenny Dorham) with the rhythm section of Tommy Flanagan, Doug Watkins, and Philly Joe Jones. The septet stretches out on four lengthy numbers: three Woods originals and the ballad "Suddenly It's Spring." **The Young Bloods** (Original Jazz Classics 1732) is co-led by Woods and Byrd, with the altoist contributing four of the six tunes (including "House of Chan" and "In Walked George") and consistently takes solo honors. Al Haig, bassist Teddy Kotick, and drummer Charlie Persip are in the supporting cast on this fine straightahead set. **Four Altos** (Original Jazz Classics 1734) has Woods, Quill, Sahib Shihab, and Hal Stein all sounding quite similar in a hard-swinging, but not overly memorable jam session with Mal Waldron, Tommy Potter, and Louis Hayes. **Sugan** (Original Jazz Classics 1841) is also essentially a jam. Woods, Ray Copeland, Red Garland, Teddy Kotick, and drummer Nick Stabulas perform three Charlie Parker tunes, and three Woods originals, with the emphasis on heated solos that display the joy and excitement of bebop.

Tenor Saxophonists

There was no shortage of musical role models for tenor-saxophonists of the late 1950s. In addition to the early and still very active giants (Coleman Hawkins, Lester Young, and Ben Webster), such influences as Illinois Jacquet (who was the predecessor for a generation of honking R&B tenors), Stan Getz (the leader of the "cool school"), and Dexter Gordon helped lead to the two young giants: Sonny Rollins and John Coltrane. The tenor fit in nearly every jazz style, from mainstream swing and hard bop to the early avant-garde, and there were dozens of significant players making important contributions during this era.

Gene Ammons Starting in 1956 and continuing into 1960, Gene Ammons led a series of jam session dates for the Prestige label, resulting in ● **The Happy Blues** (Original Jazz Classics 013), **Jammin' in Hi-Fi** (Original

Jazz Classics 129), **Jammin' with Gene** (Original Jazz Classics 211), **Funky** (Original Jazz Classics 244), **The Big Sound** (Original Jazz Classics 651), **Groove Blues** (Original Jazz Classics 723), and **Blue Gene** (Original Jazz Classics 192). **The Happy Blues** is the most successful of these, having classic solos on the title cut by Ammons, Art Farmer, and Jackie McLean, but all of these sets (which feature lengthy explorations of blues and standards, often with horns riffing behind each other's solos) have their memorable moments. There are strong contributions along the way from such musicians as Donald Byrd, Mal Waldron, Idrees Sulieman, Pepper Adams, and (on **The Big Sound** and **Groove Blues**) John Coltrane, who makes some very rare appearances on alto sax. Gene Ammons, whose 1960 recording of "Canadian Sunset," which is included on **Boss Tenor** (Original Jazz Classics 297), is considered a classic ballad statement, also recorded frequently in quartets during this period in addition to occasionally teaming up with Sonny Stitt, and despite some drug problems, which resulted in him being jailed on and off during 1958–60, Ammons was at the peak of his powers during this time.

Tina Brooks   Tina Brooks, an excellent hard bop tenor saxophonist with a warm tone, had recorded as early as 1951 (with Sonny Thompson's rhythm and blues band), and had also worked with Amos Milburn and Lionel Hampton. Brooks led four albums for Blue Note during 1958–61 and appeared as a sideman during his brief prime with Jimmy Smith, Kenny Burrell, Freddie Hubbard, Freddie Redd, Jackie McLean, and Howard McGhee. Unfortunately, his life was ruined by drugs, and he did not record again after June 17, 1961, when he was only 29. All of his dates as a leader were reissued in the out-of-print four-LP box set **The Complete Blue Note Recordings** (Mosaic 4-106), but that valuable box is quite difficult to find now. **True Blue** (Blue Note 28975), a single disc, brings back the only one of his albums to be released during his lifetime, an excellent quintet session with Freddie Hubbard, Duke Jordan, Sam Jones, and Art Taylor. This reissue (from June 25, 1960), which includes two alternate takes left out of the Mosaic "complete" box, is one of Hubbard's earliest recordings and finds Brooks in top form, holding his own with the fiery trumpeter. It is a tragedy that Tina Brooks allowed his lifestyle to short-circuit his promising career.

TIMELINE 1958

Miles Davis forms his sextet with John Coltrane and Cannonball Adderley. • Art Blakey's Jazz Messengers feature Lee Morgan, Benny Golson, and Bobby Timmons. • The Ahmad Jamal Trio records "Poinciana." • Ornette Coleman makes his debut recordings. • The Monterey Jazz Festival is a success. • The Jimmy Giuffre 3 features Bob Brookmeyer and Jim Hall. • Donald Byrd and Pepper Adams begin co-leading a quintet. • Trumpeter Kenny Ball forms a popular trad band in England. • Eubie Blake makes his first recordings in 25 years, other than one song in 1951. • Willie Bobo and Mongo Santamaria become members of Cal Tjader's band. • Veteran swing drummer Cozy Cole has a surprise hit with his recording of "Topsy." • Blue Mitchell and Junior Cook join the Horace Silver Quintet. • Hank Crawford joins Ray Charles for a five-year stay, starting on baritone and switching to alto in 1959. • The third Heath brother, drummer Albert "Tootie" Heath, joins J.J. Johnson's band. • Edmond Hall leaves the Louis Armstrong All-Stars after three years. • Sippie Wallace has her first record date in 13 years (only her second in 29 years). • British tenor saxophonist Ronnie Scott opens the Ronnie Scott's club in London. • Pete Johnson appears at the Newport Jazz Festival, but suffers a stroke a few months later that ends his playing career. • Peggy Lee has a big hit with "Fever." • The Susan Hayward movie *I Want to Live* has a notable jazz soundtrack written by Johnny Mandel. • In Brazil, guitarist/singer Joao Gilberto records a hit record that has his "Bim Bom" and Antonio Carlos Jobim's "Chega de Saudade." • Clarinetist Matty Matlock records the first of his six albums for Warner Bros. with his Paducah Patrol, a Bob Crosby–style Dixieland band playing his colorful arrangements. • Danish trombonist Aren "Papa Bue" Jensen forms his Viking Jazzband. • Pianist Gene Harris, bassist Andy Simpkins, and drummer William Dowdy come together as the soulful Three Sounds, a group that records 11 albums for Blue Note in the next four years. • Sonny Rollins records **The Freedom Suite**.

James Clay James Clay, a fine Texas tenor saxophonist with a big tone and a boppish style, was an early associate of Ornette Coleman in Texas, and he also knew Don Cherry while based in Los Angeles. Clay recorded with drummer Larance Marable in 1956 and led two albums in 1960. **The Sound of the Wide Open Spaces** (Original Jazz Classics 1075) teams him with fellow tenor David "Fathead" Newman, Wynton Kelly, Sam Jones, and Art Taylor. The competitive horns compete closely on the blues "Wide Open Spaces," Clay plays flute on "What's New," and he battles Newman to a tie on the other songs. **A Double Dose of Soul** (Original Jazz Classics 1790) has Clay using members of his producer Cannonball Adderley's group: cornetist Nat Adderley or vibraphonist Victor Feldman, Sam Jones, and Louis Hayes, plus the young Gene Harris on piano. The CD reissue adds two alternate takes to the original LP program and is highlighted by Feldman's "New Delhi," "Come Rain or Come Shine," and the blues "Pockets." However, shortly after recording these two albums, James Clay returned to Texas. He spent a decade working with Ray Charles and recorded with Wes Montgomery, but mostly played in obscurity.

Arnett Cobb Tenor saxophonist Arnett Cobb, after a promising start to his solo career in 1947, had serious health problems resulting in an operation to his spine that put him out of action until 1950. He made a comeback and worked fairly steadily for the next six years. However, in 1956, Cobb was hurt in a major car accident, having both of his legs crushed. By late 1958, he was back on the scene, and although he had to use crutches from then on, his playing was very much intact. During 1959–60, Cobb recorded steadily for the Prestige label, making seven albums (six of which are currently on five CDs). **Blow, Arnett, Blow** (Original Jazz Classics 794) is a rousing meeting with fellow tenor Eddie "Lockjaw" Davis that is filled with heated riff numbers; the Wild Bill Davis Trio helps out. Both Cobb and Davis display robust tones, emotional styles, and an exciting competitiveness. **Smooth Sailing** (Original Jazz Classics 323) features Cobb in top form on three swing-era standards and a variety of blues and riff pieces in a quintet with trombonist Buster Cooper and organist Austin Mitchell. **Party Time** (Original Jazz Classics 219) is pretty definitive of Cobb's playing during this era, featuring him a quintet with Ray Bryant on

such songs as "When My Dreamboat Comes Home," "Lonesome Road," and "Flying Home." **More Party Time** (Original Jazz Classics 979) has a similar format, usually with Tommy Flanagan in the piano slot and highlighted by soulful versions of "Lover Come Back to Me," "Swanee River," and "Down by the Riverside." **Blue and Sentimental** (Prestige 24122) consists of the music from two former LPs that both have Cobb joined by trios led by Red Garland. **Sizzlin'** is well rounded, while the second half (**Ballads**) is rather sleepy.

After all of this activity, Arnett Cobb moved back to his hometown of Houston and mostly played locally for many years, only occasionally reappearing on the national scene and not recording again until 1971.

Al Cohn In 1956, Al Cohn and Zoot Sims began working together on an occasional basis, renewing their friendship from their days with Woody Herman's Second Herd (1948). The two tenors were so complementary that it was often quite difficult to tell them apart. **From A to Z—and Beyond** (Bluebird 6469) was their first joint recording. Joined by Dave McKenna or Hank Jones on piano, Milt Hinton, Osie Johnson, and (on a few numbers) trumpeter Dick Sherman, the tenors mostly play recent originals by Cohn, Sherman, Osie Johnson, Ralph Burns, Manny Albam, Ernie Wilkins, and Milty Gold. In addition, they interpret two standards and Sims's "Tenor for Two Please, Jack" (his answer to the 1930s tune "Dinner for One Please, James"). **Al and Zoot** (MCA/Decca 31372) has Cohn and Sims joined in 1957 by the up-and-coming pianist Mose Allison, bassist Teddy Kotick, and drummer Nick Stabulas. Four standards and five Cohn songs (including "Halley's Comet," which was named after Zoot's middle name) are swung by the fine cool jazz quintet. Recorded in 1960, **You 'N' Me** (Mercury 589318), another Al and Zoot collaboration (with Allison, Johnson, and bassist Major Holley), has the rather unusual "Improvisation for Unaccompanied Saxophones." A short but effective two-tenor workout with a clever arrangement by Cohn, this piece gives one the impression (which is false) that both saxophonists are using circular breathing. Another oddity is "Angel Eyes," which has both Cohn and Sims switching to clarinet while showcasing Holley's singing and bowed bass. Otherwise, the program (which includes "You'd Be So Nice to Come Home To" and "On the Alamo") swings with plenty of spirit.

Bob Cooper   The cool-toned tenor Bob Cooper worked with the Lighthouse All-Stars, his wife June Christy, and in the studios during this era. In addition to an obscure quartet set in Europe, he led a near-classic set for Contemporary, **Coop** (Original Jazz Classics 161). Teamed with Frank Rosolino, vibraphonist Victor Feldman, Lou Levy, bassist Max Bennett, and Mel Lewis, Cooper plays colorful versions of five standards (including "Confirmation," "Easy Living," and "Somebody Loves Me"), plus the 23-minute "Jazz Theme and Four Variations," which adds three trumpeters and one trombonist to the ensembles. Cooper's clever arrangements and appealing tone, plus his ability to swing at every tempo, make this disc a must for West Coast jazz fans.

King Curtis   A top R&B tenor who was in great demand as a session musician starting in 1956, taking the tenor solos on records by the Coasters, and recording many singles under his own name (particularly for Atco/-Atlantic), King Curtis (born Curtis Ousley) made two jazz records for New Jazz and Prestige in 1960. Curtis holds his own with Nat Adderley, Wynton Kelly, either Paul Chambers or Sam Jones on bass, and Oliver Jackson or Belton Evans on drums. All 11 songs from the two dates are reissued on **Soul Meeting** (Prestige 24033). The results are blues-based bop, mixing together seven Curtis originals with four standards and showing that he could have been a major hard bop/soul jazz tenor saxophonist if that had been his main interest.

Eddie "Lockjaw" Davis   The passionate and sometimes ferocious tenor of Eddie "Lockjaw" Davis was featured with the Count Basie Orchestra during 1952–53. He played regularly with organist Shirley Scott during 1955–60 in one of the first successful hard bop/soul jazz organ bands. Davis recorded often during this era as a leader, including for King, Roost, and Roulette with Scott, and for Prestige (and its subsidiaries Moodsville and Jazzland) in a variety of contexts during 1958–60. Many of the latter dates have been reissued in the Original Jazz Classics series. **The Eddie Lockjaw Davis Cookbook** (Original Jazz Classics 652) from June 20, 1958, teams Davis with Shirley Scott, bassist George Duvivier, drummer Arthur Edgehill, and flutist Jerome Richardson, performing three blues at various tempos, "But Beautiful," the boppish "Three Deuces" (which has Richardson switching to tenor), and two originals fitting into the Cookbook idea: "The Chef" and "In the Kitchen." The

same group is heard on **Cookbook Vol. 2** (Original Jazz Classics 653), which has "Stardust," "Willow Weep for Me," "I Surrender Dear," and three Davis-Scott originals (including "Skillet" and "The Broilers") and **Cookbook Vol. 3** (Original Jazz Classics 756), which adds such originals as "Heat 'N' Serve," "The Goose Hangs High," and "Simmerin'" to the repertoire. The Lockjaw-Scott combination is also featured in swinging fashion on **Jaws** (Original Jazz Classics 218), **Jaws in Orbit** (Original Jazz Classics 322), and **Smokin'** (Original Jazz Classics 705), tearing into blues, ballads, and standards with honest, extroverted emotion, swing, and soul.

Gentle Jaws (Prestige 24160) has two sessions originally recorded for Moodsville, Prestige's "background music" label. Lockjaw Davis's dates with the Red Garland Trio (that session was originally put out under the pianist's name) and the Shirley Scott Trio (where Scott switches to piano) are equally sleepy. The tempos are uniformly slow, and the ballad interpretations are purposely laidback and a bit lazy. **Trane Whistle** (Original Jazz Classics 429) has Davis joined by a 13-piece big band arranged by Oliver Nelson. Of greatest interest is the original version of "Stolen Moments" (originally titled "The Stolen Moment"), which preceded the more famous Nelson recording by several months; coincidentally Eric Dolphy (who made a notable statement on the Oliver Nelson recording) is in Davis' backing band, although not getting any solos. There are some spots for trumpeters Richard Williams, Clark Terry, and Bobby Bryant along with Nelson on alto, but Lockjaw is the star throughout. The group performs four Nelson originals, "You Are Too Beautiful," and Davis's "Jaws" with Lockjaw's playing as fiery as usual.

In 1960, Davis and Johnny Griffin (an equally competitive tenorman) started co-leading a high-powered yet unified quintet, one of the more exciting bands of the early 1960s.

Teddy Edwards   A major part of the Los Angeles jazz scene even during the cool jazz era when his harder tone was considered out of style, Teddy Edwards began to record much more regularly starting in 1959. While **It's About Time** (Pacific Jazz 6), a quartet date with the young Les McCann on piano, is long overdue to be reissued on CD, **Sunset Eyes** (Pacific Jazz 94848), and 1960's **Teddy's Ready** (Original Jazz Classics 748) show how strong a player he was during this era. **Sunset**

Eyes (named after Edwards's most famous original) has the tenor joined by either Amos Trice, Joe Castro, or Ronnie Ball on piano, Leroy Vinnegar or Ben Tucker on bass, and Billy Higgins or Al Levitt on drums. Edwards performs six of his originals, a song by Vinnegar, and two standards; three previously unreleased numbers expand the fine set. **Teddy's Ready** is a rewarding quartet outing with Castro, Vinnegar, and Higgins with versions of three jazz standards, three originals ("Higgins' Hideaway" is memorable), and Hampton Hawes's "The Sermon."

Teddy Edwards never made an uninspiring recording, so these two outings are well worth acquiring.

Booker Ervin Booker Ervin was an unusual tenor saxophonist. He had a hard tone like many of his fellow Texans and could play as bluesy as anyone, but his intense style also lent itself well to the music of Charles Mingus and adventurous settings while still being tied to chordal improvising. Ervin started on the trombone, but taught himself tenor while in the Air Force (1950–53). He studied music in Boston for two years, made his recording debut with Ernie Field's R&B band in 1956, and played with Mingus off and on during 1956–62.

Ervin also led his own groups from time to time and began recording as a leader in 1960. **The Book Cooks** (Bethlehem 76691) has Ervin and Zoot Sims playing five originals and "Poor Butterfly" in a sextet with Tommy Turrentine, Tommy Flanagan, bassist George Tucker, and Dannie Richmond. One will certainly not have any trouble telling the two tenors apart. Highlights include Ervin's ballad feature on "Largo," the slow blues "The Blue Book," and the rapid blues "The Book Cooks."

Jimmy Forrest Jimmy Forrest's success with "Night Train" had briefly made him an R&B star, but he was always a swing stylist at heart. After "Night Train" had run its course, he led a straightahead jazz group in St. Louis for a few years and then worked with Harry "Sweet" Edison's combo during 1958–60. As a leader, he recorded enough material for the Delmark label in December 1959 to fill up two albums. His quintet, which included pianist Harold Mabern, bassist Gene Ramey, and Elvin Jones, was particularly notable for featuring guitarist Grant Green in his recording debut. **All the Gin Is Gone** (Delmark 404) has two ballads, "Caravan," and three basic Forrest originals while **Black Forrest** (Delmark 427) has four alternate takes and five

other songs. The music overall is essentially bluesy hard bop that looks toward soul jazz. **Forrest Fire** (Original Jazz Classics 199) continues in that direction. Forrest is matched up with 20-year-old organist Larry Young, guitarist Thornel Schwartz, and drummer Jimmie Smith on a pair of jump tunes ("Dexter's Deck" and Doug Watkins's "Help"), a couple of blues, a swinging version of Irving Berlin's "Remember," and the ballad "When Your Lover Has Gone." This CD shows that Jimmy Forrest (like Willis Jackson) was able to make the transition from R&B to hard bop/soul jazz.

Stan Getz The most popular tenor saxophonist in jazz, Stan Getz almost always played brilliantly even though his personal life could be chaotic. Drug problems plagued him in the mid-1950s, and he was also dissatisfied with being stereotyped as a cool jazz player even though his tone helped define the style. Actually Getz often thrived in competitive situations where he could battle it out with other top musicians, as he showed on Norman Granz's jam session records and encounters with Lionel Hampton and Dizzy Gillespie.

Recorded in 1956 and '57, respectively, **The Steamer** (Verve 547 771) and **Award Winner** (Verve 543 320) both team Getz (in superb form) with the relatively quiet rhythm section of pianist Lou Levy, bassist Leroy Vinnegar, and drummer Stan Levey. The former set has Getz lovingly playing the melodies of "You're Blasé" and "Like Someone in Love," and creating a heated solo on "Blues for Mary Jane," while **Award Winner** ranges from speedy versions of "Smiles" and "This Can't Be Love" to a sensual "But Beautiful." **Stan Getz and the Oscar Peterson Trio** (Verve 827 826) is as exciting as expected. The CD reissue for the first time has all of the music (ten songs plus a five-part ballad medley) from the October 10, 1957, date, and it is obvious that Getz loved playing with Peterson; highlights include "Pennies from Heaven," "I Was Doing All Right," "Three Little Words," and "I Want to Be Happy." Less successful is **Getz Meets Mulligan** (Verve 849 392), for on half of the songs Getz plays Mulligan's baritone, and Mulligan plays Getz's tenor; their tones sound a bit weird. **Stan Meets Chet** (Verve 837 436), a meeting with Chet Baker, also does not come off that well due to the co-leaders' contempt for each other. Listen to how Getz ignores Baker's attempt to state the melody on "I Remember April," and notice how little the two horns actually play together. Much better is **Stan Getz/Cal Tjader Sextet** (Original

Jazz Classics 275), a mostly straightahead outing with the Afro-Cuban jazz vibraphonist, pianist Vince Guaraldi, Scott LaFaro, guitarist Eddie Duran, and Billy Higgins.

The most exciting of all of Getz's collaborations from the 1956–60 period is ● **Stan Getz & J.J. Johnson at the Opera House** (Verve 831 272). Backed by the Oscar Peterson Trio plus drummer Connie Kay (surprisingly there are no solos at all from Peterson or Herb Ellis), Getz and Johnson take heated solos, trade fours, and play exciting ensembles, showing why they were considered at the top of their field. The music on this CD is taken from a pair of "Jazz at the Philharmonic" concerts so there are two versions apiece of "Billie's Bounce," "Crazy Rhythm," "Blues in My Closet," and "My Funny Valentine" (the first three songs really burn in both renditions), plus a pair of ballads. Getz might have had a cool sound, but he is quite heated in these jams with J.J. Johnson.

Stan Getz spent most of 1958–60 in Europe where his tone was influential. He performed with the top European musicians of the era, including guitarist Jimmy Gourley, bassist Pierre Michelot, trombonist Ake Persson, baritonist Lars Gullin, and pianists Martial Solal, Bengt Hallberg, and Bent Axen. When he returned to the United States in early 1961, Getz (who at first seemed a little forgotten by American audiences) would be amazed by just how famous he would become.

Jimmy Giuffre   A fixture in the West Coast Jazz scene and a member of Shorty Rogers and His Giants during 1953–55, Jimmy Giuffre was interested in moving his music beyond cool jazz into freer explorations. Giuffre was a quiet improviser whose tones on tenor, baritone, and clarinet were quite cool, and he soloed thoughtfully, making every note count and utilizing space as a contrast to sound.

The Complete Capitol and Atlantic Recordings of Jimmy Giuffre (Mosaic 6-176) in its six CDs has all of his dates as a leader from 1954–58, but this is a limited-edition box. It actually took Giuffre a little while before he found the format that he preferred. **The Jimmy Giuffre Clarinet** (Collectables 6162) from 1956 has Giuffre sticking exclusively to his clarinet, mostly playing in the lower register. He takes "So Low" unaccompanied, duets with Jimmy Rowles's celeste on "Deep Purple," plays a fairly free "Fascinatin' Rhythm" in a trio, uses three flutes and drums on the atonal "The

Side Papers," interacts with three woodwinds and bassist Ralph Pena on an atmospheric "My Funny Valentine," has a couple of trio numbers (including one with clarinet, alto clarinet, and bass clarinet), and jams a blues with a nonet. Clearly Giuffre was not shy to take chances.

Jimmy Giuffre/Music Man (Collectables 6248) combines together two unrelated sets. The first nine numbers feature the initial version of the Jimmy Giuffre 3, a pianoless and drumless trio with guitarist Jim Hall and bassist Ralph Pena. Best known among these numbers is "The Train and the River," a folk song that the group (with Jim Atlas on bass) would perform on *The Sound of Jazz* television special a year later. The other 11 songs are a real change of pace, tunes from the show *The Music Man*. Quite typically for Giuffre, the score (which includes "Seventy Six Trombones") is played by three trumpets, four reeds, bass, and drums, but no trombones! These renditions (which include "Till There Was You" and "Gary, Indiana") show off the richness of the melodies, and are quite successful even if the leader takes nearly all of the solo space.

In 1958, Giuffre led his most unusual group, a reeds/valve-trombone/guitar trio with Jim Hall and Bob Brookmeyer. The band, which sometimes played free improvisations (but unfortunately did not record any), made three albums for Atlantic. **Trav'lin' Light** (Atlantic 1282), **The Four Brothers Sound** (Atlantic 1295), and **Western Suite** (Atlantic 1330) are all worth searching for, but other than being part of the Mosaic set, these are unavailable domestically on CD yet. The same can be said of Giuffre's 1959–60 recordings, which include more trio dates (with Hall and either Red Mitchell or Ray Brown), and a live quartet set with Hall, bassist Buell Neidlinger, and drummer Billy Osborne. Jimmy Giuffre's music was gradually becoming less melodic and displaying his taste for quiet freedom in an increasingly avant-garde style, which was quite a bit different than the approach utilized by Ornette Coleman.

Benny Golson   Like Gerry Mulligan, Benny Golson first emerged as an arranger-composer before making his name as a soloist. He attended Howard University (1947–50), worked with Bull Moose Jackson's R&B band (1951) next to Tadd Dameron (an early influence on his writing), and played with Dameron (1953), Lionel Hampton (1953–54), Johnny Hodges, and Earl Bostic (1954–56). His "Stablemates" was recorded by Miles

Davis, and he was a member of the Dizzy Gillespie Big Band (1956–58). Golson's tenor playing was influenced by Don Byas and Lucky Thompson, and as a writer he composed such jazz standards as "I Remember Clifford" (for the late Clifford Brown), "Killer Joe," "Whisper Not," "Along Came Betty," and "Blues March." Golson worked with Art Blakey's Jazz Messengers (1958–59), and with Art Farmer in the Jazztet starting in 1959.

Golson began recording as a leader in 1957, making seven albums in two years (including an out-of-print effort for United Artists). **Benny Golson's New York Scene** (Original Jazz Classics 164) includes "Whisper Not" and "Step Lightly" with Golson and Farmer in a quintet and (on three songs) a nonet. **The Modern Touch** (Original Jazz Classics 1797) has three of the more obscure Golson songs, plus two from Gigi Gryce, and the standard "Namely You" played by the tenor, Kenny Dorham, Wynton Kelly, Paul Chambers, and Max Roach. **The Other Side of Benny Golson** (Original Jazz Classics 1750), which matches Golson with Curtis Fuller in a quintet (with Barry Harris, bassist Jymie Merritt, and Philly Joe Jones), gives the tenor a real opportunity to stretch out as a soloist. **Gone with Golson** (Original Jazz Classics 1850), **Groovin' with Golson** (Original Jazz Classics 226), and **Getting' with It** (Original Jazz Classics 1873) are all in a similar vein, with Golson and Fuller teamed up in a variety of quintets, playing standards, some lesser known Golson tunes, and a few ballads.

But Benny Golson's most important work of the era was as a sideman and as a songwriter. He had the knack for writing catchy melodies and outfitting them with complex chord changes. The results were songs that caught on with listeners yet were also adopted by jazz musicians who enjoyed challenges.

Paul Gonsalves   Paul Gonsalves became immortal when his 27-chorus solo on "Diminuendo and Crescendo in Blue" at the 1956 Newport Jazz Festival essentially launched Duke Ellington's comeback. Gonsalves, who had joined Ellington in 1950 and would spend the rest of his days with Duke's band, had a large and distinctive tone, a harmonically advanced style (which found him playing a lot of unusual notes), and the ability to play marathon solos and yet be quite warm on ballads.

Gonsalves led his first session (just four songs for EmArcy) two months after the Newport triumph. Other

than an album for Argo in 1957, his next two records as a leader were in 1960. **Ellingtonia Moods and Blues** (RCA 63562) is a septet set with a Dukish frontline comprised of Ray Nance, trombonist Booty Wood, and Johnny Hodges (hiding under the name of Cue Porter). While that date is predictably excellent, **Getting Together** (Original Jazz Classics 203) has the tenor interacting with Wynton Kelly, Sam Jones, Jimmy Cobb, and (on five songs) Nat Adderley. Essentially this is how Gonsalves would sound if he were in the Cannonball Adderley Quintet in Cannonball's place. Since his style was somewhat boppish anyway, he fits right in, having little trouble with the basic originals and familiar ballads.

Dexter Gordon   For Dexter Gordon, who in the late 1940s was considered the definitive bebop tenor saxophonist, the 1953–59 period was an era of darkness in which drug abuse resulted in prison time and scuffling. He did record three albums (two as a leader) in 1955, but was otherwise not heard from much until 1960. By then, having kicked heroin, he was about ready to start his prime period. **The Resurgence of Dexter Gordon** (Original Jazz Classics 929) served as a good comeback record although it is not as significant as his upcoming Blue Note dates. Gordon is in fine form on six selections, all originals by either him or pianist Dolo Coker. The Los Angeles sextet (which includes trombonist Richard Boone and trumpeter Martin Banks) is solid, but mostly in a supportive role behind the great tenor, whose return to the scene was a major event.

Johnny Griffin   Johnny Griffin became known as "the world's fastest saxophonist" due to his enthusiastic attack, impressive technique, and ability to think very fast. A master of bebop, Griffin had worked with Lionel Hampton (1945–47), trumpeter Joe Morris's underrated R&B group (1947–50), and Arnett Cobb (1951) before serving in the army (1951–53). He was based in Chicago during 1953–60 and began recording as a leader (other than four earlier titles) in 1956 with a set for Argo. During 1957–60, he led three albums for Blue Note and five for Riverside, in addition to playing with the Jazz Messengers (1957) and Thelonious Monk's Quartet (1958). By 1960, Griffin was co-leading a two-tenor quintet with Eddie "Lockjaw" Davis.

Introducing Johnny Griffin (Blue Note 46536), despite its title, was Griffin's second rather than first album, has the tenor really roaring on rapid renditions of "The Way You Look Tonight" and "Cherokee." He also fares well on three originals and two ballads, being assisted by Wynton Kelly, Curly Russell, and Max Roach. ● **A Blowing Session** (Blue Note 81559) has Griffin holding his own with John Coltrane and Hank Mobley on a very fast version of "The Way You Look Tonight," "All the Things You Are," and two basic Griffin tunes. Lee Morgan, Kelly, Paul Chambers, and Art Blakey are also aboard, but it is the three tenors who command most of the attention. There is no one winner of these battles because the saxophonists each had distinctive sounds, and were clearly inspired by the presence of the others. **The Congregation** (Blue Note 89383) has a jubilant title tune (reminiscent of Horace Silver's "The Preacher") and excellent versions of "I'm Glad There Is You," "It's You or No One," and "I Remember You," showcasing Griffin's brilliant playing in a quartet with Sonny Clark, Paul Chambers, and drummer Kenny Dennis.

Signing with Riverside in 1958, Johnny Griffin recorded a series of albums through 1962 that constitute some of the finest work of his career. **Johnny Griffin Sextet** (Original Jazz Classics 1827) teams Griffin with a young all-star group (Donald Byrd, Pepper Adams, Kenny Drew, Wilbur Ware, and Philly Joe Jones) on "What's New," "Woody'n You," and three obscure songs. **Way Out!** (Original Jazz Classics 1855), despite its title, is not avant-garde, but is a typically robust bebop set, highlighted by a roaring version of "Cherokee"; Griffin is featured in a quartet. **The Little Giant** (Original Jazz Classics 136) has lesser-known material (including three songs by Norman Simmons who also contributed the horn arrangements) played by Griffin, Blue Mitchell, Julian Priester, Wynton Kelly, Sam Jones, and Albert "Tootie" Heath. **The Big Soul Band** (Original Jazz Classics 485) also has Norman Simmons arrangements, this time for a ten-piece group that performs several spirituals, including "Wade in the Water," "Nobody Knows The Trouble I've Seen," and "Deep River," plus three complementary Simmons originals. Clark Terry and trombonists Matthew Gee and Julian Priester get some solo space. Finally, there is **Studio Jazz Party** (Original Jazz Classics 1902), a rollicking quintet set with trumpeter Dave Burns, Simmons, bassist Victor Sproles, and drummer Ben Riley that mixes together basic material with a few heated standards (including "Good Bait" and "There Will Never Be Another You").

Although overshadowed a bit by the more innovative John Coltrane and Sonny Rollins, Johnny Griffin showed during this era that he was also one of the truly great tenor soloists.

Jimmy Heath Like Dexter Gordon, Jimmy Heath wrestled with drug problems in the 1950s, but emerged triumphant, and like Johnny Griffin, Heath did some of his finest work for the Riverside label. He cut six superior albums for Riverside during 1959–64, one project a year. **The Thumper** (Original Jazz Classics 1828) finds Heath playing high-quality hard bop in a sextet with Nat Adderley, Curtis Fuller, Wynton Kelly, Paul Chambers, and his younger brother, Albert "Tootie" Heath. The older Heath contributed five of the nine songs (including "For Minors Only") and sounds in superior form on his two ballad features. **Really Big** (Original Jazz Classics 1799) gives Heath an opportunity to solo and to arrange for a ten-piece ensemble that includes Clark Terry, Cannonball, and Nat Adderley, and his brothers Percy and Tootie. "Dat Dere" and "On Green Dolphin Street" are given particularly fresh arrangements, while Heath's "Big P" and "A Picture of Heath" are memorable.

Willis "Gator" Jackson After being a hit on the R&B circuit in the early 1950s and being married to Ruth Brown for eight years (appearing on many of her records), in 1959 tenor saxophonist Willis "Gator" Jackson changed his career. Instead of remaining an R&B squealer and honker, he slightly moderated his expressive qualities and became a soul jazz/hard bop jazz soloist. He recorded steadily for Prestige starting in 1959, and his group of the time featured organist Jack McDuff and guitarist Bill Jennings along with several different drummers and an occasional bassist. **Please Mr. Jackson** (Original Jazz Classics 321) has four group originals, "Come Back to Sorrento," and "Memories of You" all played soulfully. While that release at 34 minutes is a bit brief, **Keep on A Blowin'** (Prestige 24218) has all of the music from two complete albums: 1959's **Keep on A Blowin'** and 1962's **Thunderbird**. Totaling 78 minutes, the earlier set has Gator with McDuff playing blues, ballads, and standards while **Thunderbird** is more commercial and even hints at rock 'n' roll in spots, but still has its moments thanks to the sincere and enthusiastic playing of Jackson and organist Freddie Roach. Best overall of the trio of Jackson releases from this period is **Legends of Acid Jazz** (Prestige 24198), which has all of the music from

Gator's 1959–60 LPs **Blue Gator** and **Cookin' Sherry**. The combination of Jackson, McDuff, and Jennings works very on jump tunes and warm ballads and the music both grooves and swings, showing that Gator had successfully reinvented himself, extending his career for many years in the process.

Bobby Jaspar Belgium tenor saxophonist and flutist Bobby Jaspar moved to New York in 1956, married Blossom Dearie, and worked with J.J. Johnson, Miles Davis (briefly in 1957), and Donald Byrd. **With George Wallington** (Original Jazz Classics 1788) is a fine showcase for Jaspar, featuring him on both of his axes with Wallington, bassist Wilbur Little, Elvin Jones, and (on three numbers) trumpeter Idrees Sulieman. Throughout this excellent introduction to Jaspar's playing, the leader shows how strong a bop improviser he could be. The majority of the tunes (other than "My Old Flame" and "All of You") are originals by group members, straight-ahead tunes with good blowing changes that fit perfectly into the modern mainstream jazz of the period.

Clifford Jordan From the start of his career, Clifford Jordan had his own sound although he would grow quite a bit in the 1960s. Born and raised in Chicago, Jordan played locally with Max Roach and Sonny Stitt in addition to gigging with R&B groups. He moved to New York in 1957 and in his first year led three albums for Blue Note, two of which have been reissued on CD. ● **Blowin' in from Chicago** (Blue Note 28977) is a special date because it teams Jordan with fellow tenor John Gilmore (taking a rare vacation from Sun Ra's band) in a heated jam session. Joined by Horace Silver, Curly Russell, and Art Blakey, the two tenors battle it out mostly on obscurities (other than "Billie's Bounce" and Gigi Gryce's "Blue Lights"), and Gilmore gets the slight edge in their enthusiastic trade-offs. **Cliff Craft** (Blue Note 56584) has three Jordan songs plus "Anthropology," "Confirmation," and "Sophisticated Lady" played by the mutually complementary team of Jordan and Art Farmer in a quintet with Sonny Clark.

Clifford Jordan worked with the Horace Silver Quintet (1957–58) and J.J. Johnson (1959–60). **Spellbound** (Original Jazz Classics 766) features Jordan as an excellent hard bop stylist in a quartet with Cedar Walton, bassist Spanky DeBrest, and Albert "Tootie" Heath. Most memorable is an unusual waltz version of "Lush Life," Jordan's "Toy," and an uptempo "Au Privave."

Richie Kamuca Richie Kamuca found his own voice in the Four Brothers sound influenced by Lester Young. He was a soloist with Stan Kenton (1952–53) and Woody Herman (1954–56), settled in Los Angeles, and worked with Chet Baker, Maynard Ferguson, the Lighthouse All-Stars (1957–58), Shorty Rogers, and Shelly Manne (1959–61). Kamuca led three albums during 1956–59, two of which are available. **Richie Kamuca Quartet** (V.S.O.P. 17) has Kamuca in excellent form in a group with Carl Perkins, Leroy Vinnegar, and Stan Levey, particularly on "Just Friends," "What's New," and "Cherokee." **West Coast Jazz in Hi-Fi** (Original Jazz Classics 1760) is an excellent showcase for Kamuca since he is the main soloist with an octet arranged by Bill Holman (who plays baritone on the date) and with a smaller combo. Also in the band are trumpeters Conte Candoli, and Ed Leddy, Frank Rosolino, Vince Guaraldi, Monty Budwig, and Stan Levey. The music is harder swinging than one might expect, with "Blue Jazz" (a Kamuca blues), "Star Eyes," "Linger Awhile," and "Indiana" being the standouts.

Roland Kirk One of the most amazing musicians of all time, Roland Kirk made the impossible seem logical. He could play three saxophones at once (with two independent lines), functioning as his own horn section. He mastered circular breathing so he could create a 20-minute solo with one breath, and he could play in any style, ranging from bop and early R&B to New Orleans jazz and free form, sometimes all in the same chorus.

Kirk was just at the beginning of his career during 1956–60. Born in 1936, he became blind at the age of two. After briefly playing bugle, trumpet, clarinet, and C-melody sax, he was playing tenor in R&B bands by the time he was 15. Around that time he discovered the manzello (a variant of the soprano sax) and the stritch (a straight alto), and learned to play them in conjunction with the tenor. In 1956, he made his recording debut on **Early Roots** (Bethlehem 76688). Strangely enough, he actually overdubbed two of his three horns on this set, but otherwise he is pretty recognizable, playing blues, ballads, and a touch of R&B with an obscure rhythm section. While that set was largely overlooked, Kirk's second album from four years later, **Introducing Roland Kirk** (MCA/Chess 91551), really launched his career. This time around he actually did play three horns at once, matching wits with Ira Sullivan (heard on tenor and trumpet), and a fine Chicago rhythm section on three of his originals, two obscurities, and "Our Love Is Here to Stay."

Harold Land   In late 1955, Harold Land reluctantly left the Clifford Brown-Max Roach Quintet (which had given him national exposure) to take care of some family problems in Los Angeles. He played locally with Curtis Counce's band (1956–58), recorded for Contemporary, Hi-Fi, World Pacific, Jazzland, and Blue Note (five albums during 1958–60), and led his own groups. **Harold in the Land of Jazz** (Original Jazz Classics 162) is a strong hard bop session with trumpeter Rolf Ericson, Carl Perkins, Leroy Vinnegar, and Frank Butler. At this point in time, Land had a cool and soft tone, different from how he would sound later on. He performs three swinging originals, the original version of Perkins's "Grooveyard," an obscurity by Elmo Hope, and the standards "Speak Low," "You Don't Know What Love Is," and "Promised Land." **The Fox** (Original Jazz Classics 343) is a fine straightahead date with the little-known trumpeter Dupree Bolton, Elmo Hope, bassist Herbie Lewis, and Frank Butler, featuring originals by Land and Hope.

◉ **West Coast Blues** (Original Jazz Classics 146) has Land leading an all-star sextet that includes Wes Montgomery, trumpeter Joe Gordon, Barry Harris, Sam Jones, and Louis Hayes, performing three of Land's originals, "Don't Explain," Charlie Parker's "Klactoveedsedstene," and an early version of Montgomery's "West Coast Blues." Each of the musicians plays up to the high level one would expect, and Wes Montgomery shows that he was already becoming a major force on guitar. **Eastward Ho!** (Original Jazz Classics 493) teams Land with Kenny Dorham and a little-known rhythm section for a solid hard bop outing highlighted by "So in Love," "On a Little Street in Singapore," and Land's "O.K. Blues" (dedicated to producer Orrin Keepnews).

Although the latter album was recorded in New York, Harold Land would stay in Los Angeles throughout his career, being an important contributor to the L.A. music scene for decades.

Yusef Lateef   Yusef Lateef was already 36 in 1957 when he began to record as a leader, but he made an impact pretty fast. A fine tenor saxophonist with a soulful sound and a wide musical vocabulary, Lateef was one of the top flutists in jazz, and he would develop into a stirring soloist on oboe, an occasional bassoonist, and a specialist in such instruments as the argol (a double-reed clarinet that resembles a bassoon), shanai (a type of oboe), and exotic flutes and percussion instruments from other countries. He played "world music" long before it had a name (he never liked to call his music "jazz"), yet could always swing and excel at bebop too.

Lateef was born in Chattanooga, Tennessee, and grew up in Detroit. He played early on with Lucky Millinder (1946), Hot Lips Page, Roy Eldridge, and the Dizzy Gillespie Big Band (1949–50). Returning to Detroit after Gillespie's orchestra broke up, he became an important fixture on the Detroit jazz scene while studying flute at Wayne State University. Lateef began recording as a leader in 1955 for Savoy (and later Riverside and Verve) although he did not move to New York until 1959. He played with Charles Mingus a bit in 1960, but mostly led his own bands.

Many early Yusef Lateef recordings are currently available (though the Savoys are a bit scarce), and all are well worth acquiring for they stand apart from the jazz mainstream of the era, looking toward the Far East for inspiration and ideas. **Before Dawn** (Verve 557 097) from 1957 has Lateef mostly sticking to tenor (with one appearance apiece on flute and the argol) with fellow Detroiters Curtis Fuller, pianist Hugh Lawson, bassist Ernie Farrow, and Louis Hayes. The set is more bop-oriented than normal for a Lateef date, with versions of "Pike's Peak" (based on "What Is this Thing Called Love"), Charlie Parker's "Constellation," and the blues "Chang, Chang, Chang" showing how original Lateef could be even while playing conventional straightahead material. The passionate yet thoughtful ballad "Love Is Eternal" is a high point. **The Sounds of Yusef** (Original Jazz Classics 917) is most notable for Lateef's flute work, some good spots for Wilbur Harden's flugelhorn, and for the Eastern-sounding ensembles that also hint strongly at the avant-garde in spots, utilizing the argol, Turkish finger cymbals, a 7-Up bottle, balloons, a rabat, and an earthboard—very adventurous music for 1957.

Cry! Tender (Original Jazz Classics 482) has Lateef (on tenor, flute, and oboe) leading a quintet also featuring trumpeter Lonnie Hillyer, Hugh Lawson, bassist Herman Wright, and drummer Frank Gant on both straightahead pieces and more atmospheric and exotic works. **The Three Faces of Yusef Lateef** (Original Jazz Classics 759) consists of a few vintage songs (including "Goin' Home," "I'm Just a Lucky So and So," and a lighthearted "Ma, He's

Makin' Eyes at Me") along with some thought-provoking originals played by Lateef, Lawson, cellist Ron Carter, Wright, and drummer Lex Humphries. **The Centaur and the Phoenix** (Original Jazz Classics 721) finds Lateef joined on most selections by five other horns (including a bassoonist) and a rhythm section headed by pianist Joe Zawinul. The music ranges from stomps and ballads to Eastern-influenced explorations with highlights including the title cut, "Jungle Fantasy," "Every Day I Fall in Love," and "Summer Song." Yusef Lateef proves to be quite unpredictable except in his consistent excellence.

Hank Mobley   Hank Mobley worked regularly as a sideman with the Jazz Messengers (1954–56), the Horace Silver Quintet (1956–57), and back with Art Blakey (1959). However, he was most significant for his long string of albums, including 25 for the Blue Note label alone during 1955–70. Not as important in the long run as Sonny Rollins (an influence) and John Coltrane, Mobley nevertheless was just as prolific, and his output is well worth exploring. Most of his recordings do not need much analysis for they are similar, featuring hard bop solos by some of the top young veterans, catchy melodies, and occasional standards. **The Jazz Message of Hank Mobley** (Savoy 133) has two sessions from 1956 with Donald Byrd, Hank Jones or Ronnie Ball on piano, Wendell Marshall or Doug Watkins on bass, Kenny Clarke, and (on three songs) altoist John LaPorta. **Messages** (Prestige 24063) reissues two former LPs (other than one cut left out due to lack of space), quintet outings with either Donald Byrd or Kenny Dorham consisting of five superior bop tunes, two standards, and four of Mobley's originals; Jackie McLean makes a cameo appearance on "Au Privave." **Hank Mobley and His All Stars** (Blue Note 37688) from 1957 teams Mobley with Milt Jackson, Horace Silver, Doug Watkins, and Art Blakey. Mobley contributed five intriguing compositions (best is the lyrical "Mobley's Musings") although the chord changes tend to be more interesting than the individual melodies. **Hank Mobley Quintet** (Blue Note 46816) matches the tenor with Art Farmer, Silver, Watkins, and Blakey playing six more of his originals, including "Funk in Deep Freeze." **Peckin' Time** (Blue Note 81574) has Mobley, Lee Morgan, Wynton Kelly, Paul Chambers, and Charlie Persip in 1958 interpreting

four of the leader's songs (including "High and Flighty" and the 12-minute "Git-Go Blues") plus "Speak Low."

The definitive Hank Mobley set of the era is 1960's ● **Soul Station** (Blue Note 46528), which showcases him in a quartet with Kelly, Chambers, and Blakey. Mobley's four originals are quite strong (particularly "This I Dig of You"), the versions of "If I Should Lose You" and "Remember" are heartfelt, and the musicians communicate very well together. Also worthy is **Roll Call** (Blue Note 46823), which adds Freddie Hubbard to the group. Mobley contributes five more songs (including "My Groove Your Move" and "A Baptist Beat") while the trumpeter often takes solo honors with his explosive solos.

Although he never led any important groups of his own in clubs, Hank Mobley was still becoming more creative and inventive a soloist as the 1960s began.

J.R. Monterose   J.R. Monterose (not to be confused with Jack Montrose) is most famous for playing with Charles Mingus in 1956 even though he personally hated the pressure-packed experience. He grew up in upstate New York, played in territory bands in the Midwest, and moved to New York City in the early 1950s. Monterose worked with Buddy Rich (1952), Claude Thornhill, Mingus, and Kenny Dorham's Jazz Prophets, also recording with Teddy Charles, Jon Eardley, and Eddie Bert. **J.R. Monterose** (Blue Note 29102) from 1956 features him in boppish and passionate form in a quintet with trumpeter Ira Sullivan, Horace Silver, Wilbur Ware, and Philly Joe Jones, performing six obscurities. **Straight Ahead** (Fresh Sound 201) from 1959 is a quartet date with Tommy Flanagan, Jimmy Garrison, and Pete LaRoca that was originally on the Jaro label and at one time was reissued by Xanadu. It features five offbeat yet logical originals and two standard ballads, showing that Monterose was influenced by Sonny Rollins, but also had his own fresh ideas.

After a strong start in his career, J.R. Monterose would never again equal the heights that he had reached with these two fine recordings.

James Moody   James Moody kept his septet together until 1957, learned the flute (which he played along with tenor and alto), and recorded several albums for Argo though most are currently out of print. **Return from Overbrook** (GRP/Chess 810) reissues two of Moody's best albums from the 1956–58 period: **Last Train**

from **Overbook** and **Flute 'N' the Blues.** Moody is heard either backed by ten horns and a four-piece rhythm section or with a septet also featuring trumpeter Johnny Coles. Eddie Jefferson has three vocals along the way, and other highlights include "Last Train from Overbook," "What's New," "Tico-Tico," "The Moody One," and "Easy Living."

Brew Moore   Brew Moore spent much of the 1954–61 period living in San Francisco where he led his own groups, and played now and then with Cal Tjader. The cool-toned tenor recorded two albums' worth of material for Fantasy, but thus far only one has been reissued on CD: **The Brew Moore Quintet** (Original Jazz Classics 100). The three dates on this CD were made with obscure local musicians, including trumpeter Dick Mills and pianist John Marabuto. Marabuto and Mills brought in four originals while the other four songs are familiar standards. Throughout, Brew Moore plays in his usual relaxed Lester Young–inspired cool/swing style.

Oliver Nelson   Oliver Nelson emerged during 1959–60 as not only a distinctive soloist on alto and tenor, but a colorful arranger with his own sound. He became a professional in 1947 when he was 15, picking up experience playing with the Jeter-Pillars Orchestra and in the St. Louis big bands of George Hudson and Nat Towles. In 1951, he worked with Louis Jordan's big band and then served in the navy and attended college. Nelson moved to New York in 1958, working with Erskine Hawkins, Wild Bill Davis, and (on the West Coast) Louie Bellson in addition to the Quincy Jones Big Band (1960–61).

Nelson began leading his own record dates in 1959, and his work for Prestige is of consistently high quality. **Meet Oliver Nelson** (Original Jazz Classics 227) has him holding his own with Kenny Dorham, Ray Bryant, Wendell Marshall, and Art Taylor on four of his originals, "Passion Flower," and "What's New," already sounding quite distinctive on tenor. **Takin' Care of Business** (Original Jazz Classics 1784) features Nelson playing tenor and alto in a quintet with vibraphonist Lem Winchester, organist Johnny "Hammond" Smith, bassist George Tucker, and Roy Haynes. Nelson's unaccompanied spots on "All The Way," and passionate playing on the medium-tempo blues "Groove" are high points. **Screamin' the Blues** (Original Jazz Classics 080) is a rather exciting encounter with Eric Dolphy. Nelson often plays the straight man to the radical multireedist,

but fares quite well and contributes five of the six pieces, including "The Meetin'," "Altoitis," and the title cut; Richard Williams, Richard Wyands, George Duvivier, and Roy Haynes help out. **Nocturne** (Original Jazz Classics 1795), because it was originally recorded for Moodsville, emphasizes slower tempos and more laid-back playing as Nelson, Winchester, Wyands, Duvivier, and Haynes primarily play ballads.

But the next disc is much more exciting. ● **Soul Battle** (Original Jazz Classics 325) teams together the tenors of Nelson, King Curtis, and Jimmy Forrest. With fine backup work from pianist Gene Casey, Duvivier, and Haynes, the tenors battle it out on a set of blues and basic material (including "Perdido") with sparks constantly flying. Overall, it is a three-way tie.

David "Fathead" Newman   A talented and versatile tenor saxophonist, altoist, and flutist, David "Fathead" Newman started his career in his native Texas playing with Buster Smith and Red Connors plus bluesmen Lowell Fulson and T-Bone Walker. He met Ray Charles while with Fulson (Charles was the pianist), and Newman joined Brother Ray's group in 1954, staying for a decade. While much of Ray Charles's music is outside of jazz, Newman's own solo recording career (which began with Atlantic in 1958) was usually jazz-oriented. The two-CD set ● **It's Mister Fathead** (32 Jazz 32053) reissues all of the music from his first four albums as a leader. **Ray Charles Presents David Newman** is highlighted by "Hard Times," "Weird Beard," "Sweet Eyes," and "Mean to Me" as played by Newman in a sextet also including trumpeter Marcus Belgrave, Hank Crawford (who sticks to baritone), and Charles. **Straight Ahead** has Newman showcased with a 1960 quartet also including Wynton Kelly, Paul Chambers, and Charlie Persip, holding his own with the rather heavy company on a date somewhat influenced by John Coltrane. Recorded in 1961, **Fathead Comes On** has Newman and Belgrave in a quintet while 1967's **House of David** is a bit funkier with Newman (who recalls Stanley Turrentine a bit on this date) leading a quartet with organist Kossie Gardner and guitarist Ted Dunbar; "The Holy Land" is a standout.

Bill Perkins   In the 1950s, Bill Perkins was among the "coolest" of the West Coast tenor players. Although best known for his work on that instrument, he also played baritone, alto, soprano, and flute. After serving in the military during World War II, and studying music and engineering, he played in the big bands of Jerry Wald, Woody Herman (1951–53 and 1954), and Stan Kenton (1953–54 and 1955–58). Perk settled in Los Angeles in the mid-1950s and became a busy studio musician, appearing on countless dates, including John Lewis's classic **Grand Encounter** album.

Recorded in 1956, **On Stage** (Pacific Jazz 93163) has Perkins leading an all-star West Coast octet also featuring Bud Shank, baritonist Jack Nimitz, Stu Williamson, Carl Fontana, Russ Freeman, Red Mitchell, and Mel Lewis. The laidback program (which often has Perkins sounding like Lester Young) has five swing-era songs, including "Song of the Islands," "When You're Smiling," and two versions of Harry "Sweets" Edison's "Let Me See" plus three newer pieces. The arrangements of Perkins, Bill Holman, Lennie Niehaus, and Johnny Mandel, plus the quiet rhythm section make this a prime example of West Coast jazz. **Tenors Head On** (Pacific Jazz 97195) has Perkins teamed with the similar-sounding Richie Kamuca on hard-swinging but light-toned renditions of standards. The material is taken from two former LPs, with the tenors backed by trios featuring either Pete Jolly or Hampton Hawes.

Jerome Richardson   A valuable utility man who uplifted other people's sessions, Jerome Richardson (who was equally skilled on tenor, flute, alto, soprano, and baritone) only had a few occasions to lead his own dates. He started playing alto when he was eight, was playing professionally at 14, spent 1942–45 in the military, and worked with the bands of Lionel Hampton (1949–51) and Earl Hines (1952–53) before moving to New York. He played with Lucky Millinder, Cootie Williams, Oscar Pettiford, Chico Hamilton, Gerry Mulligan, and the Quincy Jones Orchestra (1959–60) among many others, in addition to leading his own short-lived bands. **Midnight Oil** (Original Jazz Classics 1815) from 1958 was his debut recording as a leader. He performs three originals, Artie Shaw's "Lyric," and "Caravan" on tenor and flute with Jimmy Cleveland, Hank Jones, Kenny Burrell, bassist Joe Benjamin, and Charlie Persip. **Roamin' with Richardson** (Original Jazz Classics 1849) from 1959 is an excellent showcase for the multireedist with a quartet also featuring Richard Wyands, bassist George Tucker, and Charlie Persip. Richardson plays baritone on three songs, two on tenor,

and one on flute, swinging through three group originals, "I Never Knew," "Poinciana," and a strong version (on baritone) of "Warm Valley."

Charlie Rouse   Charlie Rouse always had his own sound on tenor and could be identified in just a few notes. He was taken for granted during his life, but he always got the job done. Rouse played with Billy Eckstine's orchestra (1944), Dizzy Gillespie's first big band (1945), Tadd Dameron (with whom he made his recording debut in 1947), Duke Ellington (1949–50), Count Basie's Octet (1950), and recorded with Clifford Brown (1953) and Oscar Pettiford (1955). During 1956–59, he co-led the Jazz Modes with Julius Watkins, and then in 1959 he joined Thelonious Monk's quartet for a decade. Not counting the Jazz Modes sessions (discussed under Watkins's entry), Rouse's first two dates as a leader were in 1960. **Takin' Care of Business** (Original Jazz Classics 491) has Rouse in a quintet with Blue Mitchell and Walter Bishop, Jr., playing straightahead material including the tenor's uptempo "Upptankt," "They Didn't Believe Me," and songs by Mitchell, Kenny Drew, and Randy Weston. **Unsung Hero** (Epic 46181) features Rouse playing thoughtful solos with a pair of rhythm sections (either Billy Gardner or Gildo Mahones on piano), sticking mostly to standards that he did not get the chance to play while performing nightly with Monk, such as "Stella by Starlight" and "There Is No Greater Love."

Wayne Shorter   One of the most original tenor saxophonists and composers in jazz history, Wayne Shorter played and wrote quirky and unpredictable lines that were free of clichés and had a logic all their own. He started on the clarinet when he was 16, switched to tenor, and attended New York University (1952–56). A short stint with Horace Silver was interrupted when he was drafted into the army, serving two years. In 1958, Shorter had a brief stint with Maynard Ferguson's big band (where he met Joe Zawinul for the first time). In 1959, Shorter began an important four-year period as tenor and eventually musical director of Art Blakey's Jazz Messengers. At first he sounded a bit like John Coltrane, but he quickly developed his own fresh sound and style.

Wayne Shorter led his first two record dates during 1959–60 for Vee-Jay. **Introducing Wayne Shorter** (Koch 8547) matches Shorter with fellow Jazz Messenger

Lee Morgan, Wynton Kelly, Paul Chambers, and Jimmy Cobb. Together they play five interesting if forgotten Shorter originals plus a surprising version of "Mack the Knife." **Second Genesis** (Collectables 7174) has five more of Shorter's tunes plus the obscure "Ruby & the Pearl" (from a 1950s movie), and a pair of standards ("Getting to Know You" and "I Didn't Know What Time It Was"). The tenor saxophonist is well featured in a quartet with Cedar Walton, Bob Cranshaw, and Art Blakey, tied at the moment to the hard bop tradition, but definitely avoiding the obvious, and searching for new ways to express himself.

Zoot Sims   After leaving the Gerry Mulligan Sextet in 1956, Zoot Sims formed an occasional two-tenor band with Al Cohn (the two horns sounded nearly identical at the time) and worked as a single. Among the most swinging of all jazz musicians in his generation, Sims was extremely consistent throughout his career, not changing his style and sound at all since the early 1950s. His records are all worth hearing, and there are many. A sampling from this period includes **Tonite's Music Today** (Black Lion 6090) and **Morning Fun** (Black Lion 6091), both of which team Sims successfully in a quintet with Bob Brookmeyer, **Zoot!** (Original Jazz Classics 228) which is a quintet date on which Sims switches to alto on two of the seven songs and interacts with trumpeter Nick Travis and pianist George Handy, and **Down Home** (Bethlehem 79853). The latter, which mostly features songs from the swing era, is particularly valuable for giving listeners an early glance at pianist Dave McKenna.

Lucky Thompson   Lucky Thompson had a very episodic career. He led a band regularly at the Savoy in New York during 1951–53, was one of the stars on Miles Davis's **Walkin'** album (1954), toured with Stan Kenton (1956), and then spent five years living and playing in France (1957–62).

Thompson had led just three record dates during 1951–55 (eight songs plus an obscure LP), but during the first half of 1956 he headed no less than 11 albums. Most are not available yet on CD, but fortunately the classic ● **Tricotism** (GRP 135) has come back. Comprised of two memorable sessions, this CD features Thompson (whose style was largely unchanged since 1946) at his very best. One date features the tenor in a trio with guitarist Skeeter Best and Oscar Pettiford (really whizzing through some of the songs) while the other is a quintet with Jimmy Cleveland, Hank Jones or Don Abney on piano, Pettiford, and Osie Johnson. After all of that activity, Thompson only recorded one full album during 1957–62. **Lucky in Paris** (High Note 7045) from 1959 has Thompson doubling on soprano (only Steve Lacy preceded him among bop-oriented soprano soloists), interacting with a high quality French rhythm section that includes pianist Martial Solal and vibraphonist Michel Hauser. In addition to such songs as "How About You," "Pennies from Heaven," "Solitude," and "Tea for Two," there are two unusual tenor percussion duets with Gana M'Bow that come off quite well.

Stanley Turrentine   Stanley Turrentine had such a distinctive and soulful sound, even from the start of his career, that he always sounded good no matter what the setting. If a record was not all that successful musically, it might be the arrangements or the format, but it was never Turrentine's fault. "Mr. T." (a nickname he picked up early as did Jack Teagarden) was born in Pittsburgh in 1934, started his career in the R&B bands of Lowell Fulson (1950–51) and Earl Bostic (1953). After serving in the military, he worked with Max Roach (1959–60) alongside his older brother trumpeter Tommy Turrentine. His debut as a leader, **Stan "The Man" Turrentine** (Bainbridge 1038) from 1959 (with Tommy Turrentine and either Sonny Clark or Tommy Flanagan in a quintet), served as a solid start for his career, highlighted by "Stolen Sweets" and "My Girl Is Just Enough Woman for Me."

The year 1960 was the turning point of Stanley Turrentine's career. He left Max Roach's band, married organist Shirley Scott, and began recording prolifically for the Blue Note label, both as a sideman (including Jimmy Smith's **Back at the Chicken Shack** and **Midnight Special**) and as a leader. **Look Out** (Blue Note 48543) with pianist Horace Parlan, bassist George Tucker, and drummer Al Harewood allows Turrentine to both play bop ("Tiny Capers") and to sound soulful ("Little Sheri"). **Blue Hour** (Blue Note 84057) teams Turrentine with the Three Sounds (pianist Gene Harris, bassist Andy Simpkins, and drummer William Dowdy) on such superior (if typical) soul jazz songs as "Gee Baby Ain't I Good to You," "Since I Fell for You," and "Willow Weep for Me."

Although Stanley Turrentine would never develop into an innovator, his soulful sound, and accessible style would bring many listeners to jazz during the next couple of decades.

Baritone Saxophonists

Prior to 1945, the only major jazz baritone saxophone soloist was Harry Carney. By the mid-1950s, Carney was joined by four other powerful players, all of whom were considered modernists.

Pepper Adams   In 1956, Pepper Adams emerged as a major soloist. His guttural sound and emphasis on the lower register of his horn often made it sound as if he were playing a completely different instrument from Gerry Mulligan (the perennial poll-winner on baritone) yet he had a fluidity that allowed him to play as fast as any other baritonist. Although born in Illinois, Adams spent the 1946–56 period (other than 1951–53 when he was in the army) as part of the very viable Detroit modern jazz scene. In 1956, he began to emerge on a more national level, having stints with Stan Kenton's Orchestra, Maynard Ferguson, and Chet Baker. He made his recording debut as a leader in 1957 with the excellent **Pepper Adams Quintet** (V.S.O.P. 5), and in 1958 co-founded a quintet with Donald Byrd that lasted for four years. The recording **10 to 4 at the 5-Spot** (Original Jazz Classics 031), one of the few by this group that was released under Adams's name, is one of their best. With Bobby Timmons, bassist Doug Watkins, and drummer Elvin Jones completing the group, the music (colorful originals and "You're My Thrill") is high-quality hard bop with Adams and Byrd consistently inspiring each other.

Serge Chaloff   After quite a few years, Serge Chaloff had finally kicked his destructive heroin habit by 1956, and on **Blue Serge** (Capitol 94505) he is heard in brilliant form. This quartet outing with Sonny Clark, Leroy Vinnegar, and Philly Joe Jones is highlighted by "The Goof and I," "I've Got the World on a String," and a beautiful rendition of "Stairway to the Stars." But ironically, having quit drugs, Chaloff contracted spinal paralysis and his health quickly went downhill. At his last recording date, a reunion of the Four Brothers in 1957, he was in a wheelchair. Serge Chaloff passed away in the summer of 1957 when he was just 33.

Lars Gullin   Lars Gullin was at his most active during the 1950s in Sweden. The recording **1959/60 Vol. 4** (Dragon 264) has most of his dates as a leader during this period. Gullin is the main star in settings ranging from an octet to a quartet, he composed 11 of the 14 selections, and wrote all the arrangements. Although

there is some similarity between Gullin's tone and that of Gerry Mulligan, the Swedish baritonist developed along similar lines rather than being a mere copy, and he had a strong musical personality of his own. But strangely enough, he led no record dates at all during 1961–63 and would never again be quite as productive as he was in the 1950s.

Gerry Mulligan   Gerry Mulligan was at the height of his fame during 1956–60, having regrouped successfully after his jail sentence of 1953–54. He had a pianoless quartet with Bob Brookmeyer during part of 1956, recorded along the way with some of his favorite players (including Paul Desmond, Thelonious Monk, Stan Getz, Ben Webster, and Johnny Hodges), had a reunion with Chet Baker, led a new quartet with Art Farmer (1958–59), and in 1960 put together an orchestra that he called his Concert Jazz Band.

Each of these steps was recorded. **At Storyville** (Pacific Jazz 94472) features the magical interplay and wit that always existed between Mulligan and Brookmeyer (who are supported by bassist Bill Crow and drummer Dave Bailey) including on such songs as "Bweebida Bwobbida," "Utter Chaos," and "Bike Up the Strand." **Blues in Time** (Verve 519 850) has Mulligan and Desmond inspiring each other, and there is plenty of humor and swing; highlights include "Battle Hymn of the Republican" (which is really "Tea for Two"), "Line for Lyons," and "Stand Still" ("My Heart Stood Still"). **Mulligan Meets Monk** (Original Jazz Classics 301) has the baritonist meeting Thelonious Monk in the pianist's home court, mostly playing Monk standards and fitting in fairly well. **Reunion** (EMI/Manhattan 46857), one of only two Mulligan-Baker sets after 1953, has its moments even though the old chemistry is largely gone. The two horns players sound fine, but they clearly did not care much for each other anymore. **Gerry Mulligan Meets Ben Webster** (Verve 841661) works a bit better due to the mutual respect that the two hornplayers had for each other. Their set is full of Duke Ellington tunes and rambunctious swing.

What Is There to Say (Sony 52978) is the only studio album by the Mulligan-Farmer pianoless quartet, and fortunately it is a superb one. With backing by Bill Crow and Dave Bailey, the musicians make every note and sound count with memorable renditions of "What Is There to Say," "Just in Time," "Festive Minor," and even

"My Funny Valentine" making one wish that this unit had been more extensively documented.

Mulligan's Concert Jazz Band did make plenty of records (including three in 1960 alone), but Verve has been inexcusably slow in reissuing them. Reissued as an exact replica of the LP, the CD **At the Village Vanguard** (Verve 589 488) has a long and remarkable trade-off by Mulligan and Clark Terry on "Blueport" that is overflowing with spontaneous song quotes. Also in the band at the time were Bob Brookmeyer, Zoot Sims, and drummer Mel Lewis. A two-CD set has the band's concert of November 19, 1960, **The Concert Jazz Band** (RTE 1505). There are many exciting moments among the 14 selections, including "You Took Advantage of Me," "Apple Core," "Moten Swing," and "Body and Soul." Conte Candoli, Brookmeyer, Sims, and Mulligan are the key stars, with the 21-minute medium-tempo blues "Spring Is Sprung" featuring Mulligan soloing on piano.

Pianists

The influence of Bud Powell was the dominant force among post-swing pianists of the second half of the 1950s, many of whom struggled to find their own musical identity. Since Powell had re-defined how to play the piano in jazz, this could be a tough task although the best pianists eventually were able to add something of their own to the music.

Joe Albany   An early bebop pianist who, due to his erratic lifestyle (being a drug addict), only made one recording between 1947–70, Joe Albany should have had a much more significant career. The lone recording from those silent years was actually a rehearsal from the fall of 1957, **The Right Combination** (Original Jazz Classics 1749), which features Albany playing in a trio with Warne Marsh and bassist Bob Whitlock. The fidelity is just okay, but the interplay between the musicians on such songs as Clifford Brown's "Daahoud," "Body and Soul," and "All the Things You Are," and the scarcity of any Joe Albany recordings prior to 1971, make this of strong historic interest.

Bent Axen   A top bop pianist from Denmark, Bent Axen recorded surprisingly little as a leader. **Axen** (Steeple Chase 36003), which consists of three sessions from 1959–61, has the bulk of his jazz dates. He is heard in his working quintet with trumpeter Allan Botschinsky and tenor saxophonist Bent Jaedig on four titles, on

eight songs that add Frank Jensen to the group on second tenor, and, best of all, seven trio numbers that serve as the recording debut of bassist Niels Pedersen, who was just 14 the time. Axen shows off the influence of Bud Powell yet also displays plenty of original ideas within the context of straightahead bop.

Ray Bryant   Ray Bryant, who made his recording debut in 1955, was an unusual pianist for the era because he mixed together bop, swing, blues, boogie-woogie, and gospel in his playing rather than coming out of one specific style. A soulful and bluesy player, Bryant had worked with Tiny Grimes in the late 1940s, was the house pianist at the Blue Note in Philadelphia in 1953, and recorded with Betty Carter in 1956. He accompanied Carmen McRae (1956–57), performed and recorded with Coleman Hawkins and Roy Eldridge at the 1957 Newport Jazz Festival, and played with Jo Jones's Trio (1958), which also included his brother Tommy Bryant on bass. The pianist primarily led trios after 1958. His accessible style made him a popular attraction, his "Cubano Chant" (first recorded in 1956) became a standard, and he had minor hits in "Little Susie" and 1960's "Madison Time."

As a leader, Bryant recorded in his early days for Epic, Prestige/New Jazz, Signature, and Columbia. Though his combo sessions, including 1957's **Ray Bryant Trio** (Original Jazz Classics 793), are all enjoyable, it was his rare unaccompanied solo sets that were particularly special. **Alone with the Blues** (Original Jazz Classics 249) was the first one, a set of five original blues plus "Rockin' Chair" and "Lover Man," featuring Bryant (in his early prime) excelling on the blues at a variety of tempos.

Jaki Byard   Jaki Byard was one of the most versatile and skilled of the jazz pianists to emerge in the late 1950s. He had the ability to play in any jazz style from stride to the avant-garde, to closely emulate Erroll Garner, Dave Brubeck, and Bud Powell, and to sound quite credible playing hard bop. In addition to piano, he had youthful flings on trumpet and trombone, and as an adult occasionally doubled on tenor and alto sax. Byard worked with Earl Bostic (1949–50), the Herb Pomeroy Big Band (1952–55), and around Boston until joining Maynard Ferguson's orchestra in 1959. His debut, ❶ **Blues for Smoke** (Candid 79018), was not released domestically until 1988. Byard is brilliant on this solo piano set, playing originals that look both backward to pre-bop styles and ahead to the avant-garde, including "Pete and Thomas (Tribute to the Ticklers)," "Spanish Tinge No. 1," and "One, Two, Five." The most remarkable selection is "Jaki's Blues Next," which has Byard alternating between James P. Johnson–type stride and free-form à la Cecil Taylor; at its conclusion he plays both styles at the same time!

Sonny Clark   Sonny Clark's musical life shone brightly during his brief existence. After a period on the West Coast, Clark moved to New York in 1956 and was greatly in demand for a few years, playing his own brand of bebop piano. During 1957–60, he recorded enough material as a leader to fill up six CDs for Blue Note and one for Time. **Sonny's Crib** (Blue Note 97367) has been reissued the most due to the inclusion of John Coltrane in the sextet (which also includes Donald Byrd, Curtis Fuller, Paul Chambers, and Art Taylor). The original program of five songs (highlighted by the title cut and "News for Lulu") has been expanded by the inclusion of alternate takes of the other three songs, all standards. **Dial S for Sonny** (Blue Note 56585) is on the same level although a bit cooler in sound since it features Art Farmer, Fuller, Hank Mobley, Wilbur Ware, and Louis Hayes with Clark. The sextet plays four of Clark's underrated originals, including "Sonny's Mood" and two versions of "Bootin' It," plus a couple of standards. **Sonny Clark Trio** (Blue Note 46547), which like **Sonny's Crib** and **Dial S for Sonny** is from 1957, puts the focus on Clark's piano playing in a trio with Paul Chambers and Philly Joe Jones. The music is quite bop-oriented (as opposed to the hard bop combo dates), with Clark romping on "Two Bass Hit," "Be-Bop," and "Tadd's Delight."

⚫ **Cool Struttin'** (Blue Note 46513) is Sonny Clark's most famous album. The quintet (with Art Farmer, Jackie McLean, Chambers, and Jones) is tight, and the original LP consisted of two of the pianist's best compositions ("Cool Struttin'" and "Blue Minor"), plus Miles Davis's "Sippin' at Bells" and "Deep Night." The CD reissue adds a third Clark song ("Royal Flush") and "Lover" without any decrease in its high quality. Much more obscure is the music on **Standards** (Blue Note 21283) and **My Conception** (Blue Note 22674), performances only previously out in Japan or on singles. **Standards** (with Paul Chambers or Jymie Merritt on bass, and drummer Wes Landers) has mostly concise performances of 14 veteran songs, which generally predated the bop era, including "Blues in the Night," "Somebody Loves

Me," "I Cover the Waterfront," and "I Can't Give You Anything but Love." Clark's solos nevertheless are quite boppish, and he makes optimal use of each note. **My Conception** has music from a pair of quintet dates, with Clark joined by either Byrd, Mobley, Chambers, and Art Blakey, or Clifford Jordan, Kenny Burrell, Chambers, and Pete LaRoca. Of particular interest is that all nine songs are Clark originals, most of which are quite obscure, but well worth reviving.

After being so busy on records during 1957–58, Sonny Clark's career began to slow down a bit. In fact, after March 1959 he only recorded two further albums as a leader. **Sonny Clark Trio** (Time 1044) from 1960 has Clark performing eight of his songs with Max Roach and George Duvivier, including "Minor Meeting," "Blues Mambo," and "Junka." Despite an erratic lifestyle caused by drug abuse, Clark was still in prime form on this lesser-known effort, recorded when he was still just 28.

Eddie Costa   Eddie Costa was equally talented on piano and vibes, and became best known for his low-register solos on piano. He played with Joe Venuti in 1948, served in the army, and worked with guitarist Sal Salvador, the Tal Farlow trio, Kai Winding, Don Elliott, and the Woody Herman Orchestra (1958–59). He led combos of his own on an occasional basis starting in the mid-1950s, and of the five albums that he headed, the only one currently available is **Eddie Costa Quintet** (VSOP 7). The excellent set teams Costa (on both of his axes) in a group with Art Farmer, Phil Woods, bassist Teddy Kotick, and Paul Motian, playing hard bop versions of "I Didn't Know What Time It Was," "In Your Own Sweet Way," and some basic originals.

Walter Davis, Jr.   A graduate of the bebop era, Walter Davis, Jr., worked with Babs Gonzales in the late 1940s, Charlie Parker (1952), Max Roach (1952–53), the Dizzy Gillespie Big Band (1956), Donald Byrd, and Art Blakey's Jazz Messengers (1959). Also in 1959, Davis led his first record date, a near-classic titled **Davis Cup** (Blue Note 32098). Donald Byrd, Jackie McLean, Sam Jones, and Art Taylor join Davis on the excellent session, playing six of the pianist's best originals. The musicians all sound quite inspired by each other's presence and the material, and everyone plays even better than expected. But strangely enough, there was no encore for Walter Davis, Jr., and he would not record again as a leader for 18 years.

Kenny Drew   Kenny Drew played and recorded with many of the top jazz musicians during 1956–60, including Dinah Washington, Art Blakey, John Coltrane, Donald Byrd, Johnny Griffin, Buddy Rich, and in his own trios. He also led six record dates during 1956–57 for Riverside, Judson, and Blue Note. **The Kenny Drew Trio** (Original Jazz Classics 065) has Drew, Paul Chambers, and Philly Joe Jones playing six standards and two of the pianist's originals. Most notable is one of the earliest non-Monk versions of "Ruby My Dear." **Plays the Music of Harry Warren and Harold Arlen** (Milestone 47070) combines Drew's two tasteful songbook outings for the Judson label, both of which are duet dates with bassist Wilbur Ware; the music is melodic, tasteful, and swinging. **This Is New** (Original Jazz Classics 483) from 1957 has Drew, Donald Byrd, Ware, and drummer G.T. Hogan joined by Hank Mobley on half of the selections, with the better numbers including "Why Do I Love You," "You're My Thrill," and "It's You or No One." **Pal Joey** (Original Jazz Classics 1809) features Drew interpreting eight Rodgers and Hart tunes, five written for the play *Pal Joey* and three of the writing team's earlier hits that were included in the film version. These fine renditions (which include "Bewitched, Bothered and Bewildered," "I Could Write a Book," and "The Lady Is a Tramp") feature Drew with Ware and Philly Joe Jones.

In 1960, Drew led his lone Blue Note album. **Undercurrent** (Blue Note 84059) is a particularly strong hard bop quintet session with Freddie Hubbard, Hank Mobley, Sam Jones, and Louis Hayes performing six of Drew's originals. But after all of this productive activity, Kenny Drew's next record date as a leader would not take place for another 13 years.

Tommy Flanagan   Born in Detroit in 1930, Tommy Flanagan was part of the local scene during its prime period. A flawless and tasteful player who was influenced early on by Bud Powell but developed his own voice, Flanagan started playing piano at age 11. He played in Detroit (other than during 1951–53 when he was in the army) up until 1956 when he moved to New York. Flanagan immediately became an important part of the New York jazz community and was called for many record dates, working regularly with Oscar Pettiford, J.J. Johnson (1956–58), and Harry "Sweets" Edison (1959–60). He also led an album apiece for New Jazz, Metronome, Savoy, Blue Note, and Moodsville, three of which are currently available.

The Cats (Original Jazz Classics 079) has Flanagan heading the Prestige All-Stars, a hard bop sextet also featuring John Coltrane and trumpeter Idrees Sulieman; the pianist is featured with Doug Watkins and Louis Hayes on "How Long Has This Been Going On." **Overseas** (Original Jazz Classics 1033) is a superior trio outing with bassist Wilbur Little and Elvin Jones that was recorded in Stockholm, originally for the Metronome label. Flanagan shows what he learned from bop and Teddy Wilson while displaying his own approach to straightahead jazz on such tunes as "Relaxin' at Camarillo," "Eclypso," "Verdandi," and "Dalarna." **The Tommy Flanagan Trio** (Original Jazz Classics 182) purposely concentrates on slower tempos since it was originally recorded for the Prestige subsidiary Moodsville although the trio (with Tommy Potter and Roy Haynes) cooks a bit on the pianist's "Jes' Fine." The relaxed and tasteful renditions of "You Go to My Head," "Come Sunday" (taken as a solo piano feature), and "Born to Be Blue" work quite well, but then again so did everything recorded by Flanagan.

Red Garland   Red Garland was a member of the Miles Davis Quintet during 1955–56 and was back with the trumpeter for a few months in 1958 before being succeeded by Bill Evans. He led his own popular trio for the next few years (Garland's chord voicings were original, and he always swung), and recorded very frequently as a leader for Prestige and its Jazzland and Moodsville subsidiaries. Nearly all of his output for those labels is currently on CD, no less than 20 CDs covering 1956–60. The standouts among these sets (most of which feature Garland in a trio) are **High Pressure** (Original Jazz Classics 349), **Soul Junction** (Original Jazz Classics 481), and **Dig It!** (Original Jazz Classics 392), all of which have John Coltrane and Donald Byrd joining Garland in a quintet, **Manteca** (Original Jazz Classics 428) with Ray Barretto in a quartet, **Can't See for Lookin'** (Original Jazz Classics 918), and **Red Garland at the Prelude Vol. 1** (Original Jazz Classics 24132). The other CDs, none of which are throwaways, are **Groovy** (Original Jazz Classics 061), **Red Garland's Piano** (Original Jazz Classics 073), **A Garland of Red** (Original Jazz Classics 126), **All Kinds of Weather** (Original Jazz Classics 193), **All Mornin' Long** (Original Jazz Classics 293),

Red in Bluesville (Original Jazz Classics 295), **With Eddie "Lockjaw" Davis Vol. 1** (Original Jazz Classics 360), **Rediscovered Masters Vol. 1** (Original Jazz Classics 768), **Rediscovered Masters Vol. 2** (Original Jazz Classics 769), **Rojo** (Original Jazz Classics 772), **The P.C. Blues** (Original Jazz Classics 898), **Red Garland Revisited** (Original Jazz Classics 985), **It's a Blue World** (Original Jazz Classics 1028), and **Blues in the Night** (Prestige 24180). All are worth hearing.

Erroll Garner   Although Erroll Garner's piano style was so recognizable as to be a bit predictable by 1956, he never lost his enthusiasm for playing, and his joy at creating music was quite infectious. Few pianists performed in such a happy style, and Garner seemed incapable of playing an indifferent chorus. While Garner's Columbia records of 1956–58 are mostly scarce, two of his other albums (a 1959 trio outing for ABC-Paramount and a 1962 set for Reprise) have been reissued in full on **Dreamstreet & One World Concert** (Telarc 83350). Backed by bassist Eddie Calhoun and drummer Kelly Martin, Garner stretches out in the studios and in concert at the 1962 Seattle World's Fair. Highlights include "Misty," "Dreamstreet," "Mambo Gotham," a medley of songs from the play *Oklahoma*, "Just One of Those Things," "The Way You Look Tonight," and "Mack the Knife."

Vince Guaraldi   Vince Guaraldi had a varied career and proved to be a rather versatile pianist. He was a member of the first Cal Tjader Trio (1951), worked with the Bill Harris/Chubby Jackson band (1953), Georgie Auld (1953), Sonny Criss (1955), Woody Herman (1956–57, 1959), and had a high-profile second association with Tjader (1957–59) when the vibraphonist was leading one of the top Latin jazz bands. Otherwise Guaraldi led his own trios, particularly from 1960 on. He is showcased on a pair of albums from 1956–57, **Vince Guaraldi Trio** (Original Jazz Classics 149) and **A Flower Is a Lovesome Thing** (Original Jazz Classics 235), that team him in a drumless trio with guitarist Eddie Duran and bassist Dean Reilly. Guaraldi plays quite tastefully throughout, swinging lightly and creating music that is as successful as cool jazz as it is as high quality background music.

Barry Harris   Few pianists have sounded as close to Bud Powell as Barry Harris when he wants to. Harris can also credibly emulate Thelonious Monk and loves

the music of Tadd Dameron. He chose to stick to classic bop throughout his career. Harris was playing professionally in his native Detroit as early as 1946, yet was one of the last major jazz musicians to leave Detroit. In the interim he was the house pianist at the Blue Bird club, became an important educator, and played with most of the jazz greats who passed through Detroit. In 1958, Harris led a trio date for Argo, and in 1960 he joined Cannonball Adderley's group for a short time, settling in New York, and recording the first of five albums for Riverside. **At the Jazz Workshop** (Original Jazz Classics 326) was recorded in San Francisco with Sam Jones and Louis Hayes, and has Harris swinging in a boppish fashion on such songs as "Star Eyes," "Moose the Mooche," "Woody'n You," and "Is You Is or Is You Ain't My Baby."

Hampton Hawes   Hampton Hawes, one of the top bop-oriented pianists on the West Coast, recorded prolifically for the Contemporary label during 1955–58, which was a good thing because in 1958 he was busted for heroin possession, was made an example of, and spent five years in prison.

Everybody Loves Hampton Hawes (Original Jazz Classics 421), the third of Hawes's trio dates with Red Mitchell and drummer Chuck Thompson, is on the same high level as the previous two. Hawes introduces his "Coolin' the Blues" and "The Sermon," and swings eight standards, including "Somebody Loves Me," "A Night in Tunisia," and "Billy Boy." **All Night Session Vol. 1** (Original Jazz Classics 638), **All Night Session Vol. 2** (Original Jazz Classics 639), and **All Night Session Vol. 3** (Original Jazz Classics 840) were all recorded the same night (November 12–13, 1956), 17 selections in all performed by Hawes, Jim Hall, Red Mitchell, and drummer Bruz Freeman. **Four** (Original Jazz Classics 165) is just as satisfying, featuring Hawes with Barney Kessel, Red Mitchell, and Shelly Manne in what could be considered the definitive West Coast rhythm section. **For Real** (Original Jazz Classics 713) from March 17, 1958, is a change of pace since it was the pianist's first date as a leader to feature a horn player, Harold Land, who joins Hawes, Scott LaFaro, and Frank Butler on three bop standards and three originals. **The Sermon** (Original Jazz Classics 1067) is even more unusual for it was recorded on November 24–25, 11 days after Hawes's arrest. He chose to record a set of spirituals plus a blues song as he awaited trial. The music, not initially released until 1987, has Hawes (with Leroy Vinnegar, and Stan Levey) performing rich melodies with intense emotion. His renditions of such songs as "Down by the Riverside," "Nobody Knows the Trouble I've Seen," and "When the Roll Is Called Up Yonder" are quite haunting. It is too bad that his judge did not hear this powerful music.

Jutta Hipp   Jutta Hipp could have been a major jazz pianist, but she did not have the desire. Born in Leipzig, Germany, in 1925, she studied painting and played jazz secretly during World War II. Hipp worked as a pianist locally in West Germany, recorded with Hans Koller in 1952, and led a quintet in Frankfurt during 1953–55, recording several albums, including one for Blue Note. She moved to New York in November 1955 and played at the Hickory House for most of the first half of 1956, recording two trio albums for Blue Note. Originally influenced by Lennie Tristano, Hipp was apparently touched a bit by the style of Horace Silver after coming to the United States, and was harshly criticized. However, her studio album from July 1956 in a quintet, **Jutta Hipp with Zoot Sims** (Blue Note 52439), features her playing bop in her own style. Sims dominates the music, which also includes trumpeter Jerry Lloyd (sounding a bit hesitant), bassist Ahmed Abdul-Malik, and Ed Thigpen, but Hipp sounds excellent on a couple of basic originals and a variety of familiar standards.

For mysterious reasons, Jutta Hipp soon dropped out of music, choosing to return to painting, and never again playing in public.

Elmo Hope   Elmo Hope was always a very underrated pianist and composer, overshadowed by his friends Bud Powell and Thelonious Monk. He toured with Chet Baker in 1957, and then settled in Los Angeles for a time, recording with Harold Land and Curtis Counce. **Elmo Hope Trio** (Original Jazz Classics 477) finds him in good form in 1959 playing some of his obscure originals and "Like Someone in Love." Hope's trio with bassist Jimmy Bond and drummer Frank Butler works quite well together. ● **The All Star Sessions** (Milestone 47037) is a single CD reissuing all of the music (except for one alternate take) from the albums **Informal Jazz** and **Homecoming**. The former set is a four-song jam session that has long solos from Donald Byrd, John Coltrane, and Hank Mobley along with Hope; Paul Chambers and Philly Joe Jones give stimulating

support on this 1956 session. **Homecoming** is from 1961 after the pianist had moved back to New York. This time the sextet consists of Blue Mitchell, Jimmy Heath, Frank Foster, Percy Heath, and Philly Joe Jones; there are also four numbers by the trio from the group. All but three selections on these two unrelated sessions are Hope's originals, and many are well worth reviving.

Duke Jordan   Although Duke Jordan's one Blue Note album, 1960's **Flight to Jordan** (Blue Note 46824), is a memorable gem, he never received a second opportunity to lead a date for the label. Jordan (still best known for his membership in the Charlie Parker Quintet of 1947) worked primarily with trios from 1954 on, wrote one jazz standard ("Jor-du"), and played in his unchanged gentle bop style. For his Blue Note session, he utilizes trumpeter Dizzy Reece, Stanley Turrentine, Reggie Workman, and Art Taylor on six of his originals including the title cut, "Split Quick," and "Starbrite." Although none of the tunes became as well known like "Jor-du," they do show that Duke Jordan was an underrated composer. Unfortunately, he would hardly record again until the 1970s.

John Lewis   As pianist and musical director of the Modern Jazz Quartet, John Lewis set the tone for the group, one of sophistication and class, tied to the roots of Bach and bop, classical music and the blues. His own side projects from the era cover a wide range of styles including some orchestral projects, soundtracks (including for the film *Odds Against Tomorrow*), and piano features.

The Grand Encounter (Pacific Jazz 46859) is a classic West Coast jazz–style set featuring tenor saxophonist Bill Perkins at his coolest, in a group with Lewis, Jim Hall, Percy Heath, and Chico Hamilton. "2 Degrees East, 3 Degrees West" is quite atmospheric, and there are individual features for Lewis ("I Can't Get Started") and Hall ("Skylark"). This set has sometimes been issued under Perkins's name (he plays brilliantly while showing great restraint) although Lewis was the brains behind the project. **Improvised Meditations and Excursions** (Atlantic 1104) puts the emphasis on Lewis's piano playing as he performs five standards plus two of his originals ("Delaunay's Dilemma" and "Love Me") in a trio with Connie Kay, and either George Duvivier or Percy Heath on bass. Recorded in 1960, **Wonderful World of Jazz** (Atlantic 90979) is particularly rewarding. Three

90 ESSENTIAL RECORDS OF 1956–1960

Clifford Brown, **The Beginning and the End**
(Columbia/Legacy 66491)

Art Tatum, **The Complete Pablo Group Masterpieces**
(Pablo 4401), 6 CDs

Lester Young, **Jazz Giants '56** (Verve 825 672)

Lester Young, **Pres and Teddy** (Verve 831 270)

Miles Davis and John Coltrane, **Miles Davis & John
Coltrane—The Complete Columbia Recordings
1955–1961** (Columbia 65833), 6 CDs

Miles Davis, **Miles Ahead** (Columbia/Legacy 65121)

Miles Davis, **Porgy and Bess** (Columbia/Legacy 65141)

Miles Davis, **Sketches of Spain** (Columbia/Legacy 65142)

Gil Evans, **New Bottle Old Wine** (Blue Note 46855)

John Coltrane, **The Prestige Recordings** (Prestige 4405),
16 CDs

John Coltrane, **Blue Train** (Blue Note 46095)

John Coltrane, **Heavyweight Champion: The Complete
Atlantic Recordings** (Rhino/Atlantic 71984), 7 CDs

Sonny Rollins, **The Complete Blue Note Recordings** (Blue
Note 21371), 5 CDs

Sonny Rollins, **The Complete Riverside & Contemporary
Recordings** (Riverside 4427), 5 CDs

Thelonious Monk, **The Complete Riverside Recordings**
(Riverside 1022), 15 CDs

Thelonious Monk, **Discovery, Live at the Five Spot**
(Blue Note 99786)

Charles Mingus, **Passions of a Man: The Complete
Atlantic Recordings** (Rhino/Atlantic 72871), 6 CDs

Charles Mingus, **Charles Mingus Presents Charles
Mingus** (Candid 79005)

Art Blakey, **Art Blakey's Jazz Messengers with
Thelonious Monk** (Rhino/Atlantic 75598)

Art Blakey, **Moanin'** (Blue Note 46516)

Horace Silver, **Finger Poppin'** (Blue Note 84008)

Ornette Coleman, **Beauty Is a Rare Thing: The
Complete Atlantic Recordings** (Rhino/Atlantic
71410), 6 CDs

Count Basie, **Count Basie at Newport** (Verve 833 776)

Count Basie, **The Complete Atomic Basie** (Roulette
28635)

Dave Brubeck, **Time Out** (Columbia/Legacy 65122)

Duke Ellington, **Ellington at Newport** (Columbia/
Legacy 40587)

Duke Ellington and Johnny Hodges, **Back to Back**
(Verve 823 637)

Bill Evans, **The Complete Riverside Recordings**
(Riverside 018), 12 CDs

Dizzy Gillespie, **Birks' Works—The Verve Big Band
Sessions** (Verve 314 527 900), 2 CDs

Dizzy Gillespie, **Dizzy Gillespie at Newport**
(Verve 314 513 754)

Dizzy Gillespie, **Sonny Side Up** (Verve 825 674)

Ahmad Jamal, **But Not for Me** (MCA/Chess 9108)

The Jazztet, **Meet The Jazztet** (MCA/Chess 91550)

Stan Kenton, **Cuban Fire** (Blue Note 96260)

Modern Jazz Quartet, **European Concert** (Label M 5721)

Max Roach, **Freedom Now Suite** (Candid 79002)

Benny Bailey, **Big Brass** (Candid 9011)

Lee Morgan, **Candy** (Blue Note 46508)

Louis Smith, **Here Comes Louis Smith**
(Blue Note 52438)

Clark Terry, **Color Changes** (Candid 79009)

Cannonball Adderley, **Sophisticated Swing: The EmArcy
Small-Group Sessions** (Verve 314 528 408), 2 CDs

Cannonball Adderley, **Cannonball and Coltrane**
(EmArcy 834 588)

Cannonball Adderley, **Cannonball Adderley Quintet in
San Francisco** (Original Jazz Classics 035)

Lou Donaldson, **Blues Walk** (Blue Note 81593)

Art Pepper, **Meets the Rhythm Section** (Original Jazz
Classics 338)

Art Pepper, **Art Pepper + Eleven: Modern Jazz Classics**
(Original Jazz Classics 341)

Gene Ammons, **The Happy Blues** (Original Jazz
Classics 013)

Stan Getz, **Stan Getz & J.J. Johnson at the Opera House**
(Verve 831 272)

Johnny Griffin, John Coltrane, and Hank Mobley, **A
Blowing Session** (Blue Note 81559)

Clifford Jordan and John Gilmore, **Blowin' in from
Chicago** (Blue Note 28977)

Harold Land, **West Coast Blues** (Original Jazz
Classics 146)

Hank Mobley, **Soul Station** (Blue Note 46528)

Oliver Nelson, **Soul Battle** (Original Jazz Classics 325)

David "Fathead" Newman, **It's Mister Fathead** (32 Jazz
32053), 2 CDs

Lucky Thompson, **Tricotism** (GRP 135)

Jaki Byard, **Blues for Smoke** (Candid 79018)

Sonny Clark, **Cool Struttin'** (Blue Note 46513)

numbers (including a remake of "2 Degrees East, 3 Degrees West") has Lewis's piano showcased in a quartet with Jim Hall, George Duvivier, and Connie Kay. A 15-minute rendition of "Body and Soul" has one of tenor saxophonist Paul Gonsalves's finest solos, while "Afternoon in Paris" features a diverse cast with trumpeter Herb Pomeroy, Gunther Schuller on French horn, Benny Golson, Jimmy Giuffre (on baritone), and Jim Hall; Eric Dolphy's stunning alto solo cuts everyone.

John Lewis Presents Jazz Abstractions (last out as the LP Atlantic 1365) is a rather unusual date on several levels. Lewis is listed as the leader, but does not actually appear on the record, and only contributed one piece (his famous "Django"). This is really a Gunther Schuller project, for Schuller composed "Abstraction" and was responsible for arranging the adventurous three-part "Variants on a Theme of John Lewis (Django)" and the four-part "Variants on a Theme of Thelonious Monk (Criss-Cross)"; Jim Hall brought

in "Piece for Guitar & Strings." One of the most intriguing Third Stream efforts, this project features Ornette Coleman on "Abstraction" and "Criss Cross" (both of which have been reissued in Coleman's Rhino CD box), and Eric Dolphy is on both of the "Variants." Hall, Bill Evans, Scott LaFaro, and several classical string players are in the eclectic supporting cast of the unique project that hints strongly at the possible future of jazz.

Les McCann   With the rise of Horace Silver, other pianists who emphasized funky rhythms, bluesy chords, and ideas drawn from gospel music started being discovered. Les McCann, always a fine singer, won a talent contest in 1956 while in the navy, resulting in an appearance on *The Ed Sullivan Show* on television. After he was discharged, he formed an instrumental trio in Los Angeles (with drummer Ron Jefferson, and Leroy Vinnegar on bass until he was succeeded by Herbie Lewis in 1960), turning down a chance to join the Cannonball Adderley Quintet so he could work on his own

90 ESSENTIAL RECORDS OF 1956–1960

Phineas Newborn, **Here Is Phineas** (Koch 8505)

Oscar Peterson, **At the Stratford Shakespearean Festival** (Verve 314 513 752)

Billy Taylor, **My Fair Lady Loves Jazz** (GRP/Impulse 141)

Randy Weston, **Uhura Africa/Highlife** (Roulette 94510)

Wes Montgomery, **The Complete Riverside Recordings** (Riverside 4408), 12 CDs

Shelly Manne, **My Fair Lady** (Original Jazz Classics 336)

Steve Lacy, **Reflections** (Original Jazz Classics 63)

Jimmy Smith, **The Sermon** (Blue Note 24541)

Michel Legrand, **Legrand Jazz** (Polygram 830 074)

Thomas Talbert, **Bix Fats Duke** (Sea Breeze 3013)

Lambert, Hendricks, and Ross, **Sing a Song of Basie** (Verve 314 543 827)

Lambert, Hendricks, and Ross, **The Hottest New Group in Jazz** (Columbia/Legacy 64933), 2 CDs

Oscar Brown, Jr., **Sin & Soul…and Then Some** (Columbia/Legacy 64994)

Betty Carter, **I Can't Help It** (GRP/Impulse 114)

Nat King Cole, **The Complete After Midnight Sessions** (Capitol 48328)

Chris Connor, **A Jazz Date with Chris Connor/Criss Craft** (Rhino 71747)

Bob Dorough, **Devil May Care** (Bethlehem 75994)

Ella Fitzgerald, **The Complete Ella in Berlin** (Verve 314 519 584)

Helen Humes, **Songs I Like to Sing** (Original Jazz Classics 171)

Eddie Jefferson, **The Jazz Singer** (Evidence 22062)

Helen Merrill, **The Complete Helen Merrill on Mercury** (Mercury 826 340), 3 CDs

Mel Tormé, **Lulu's Back in Town** (Bethlehem 75732)

Sarah Vaughan, **No Count Sarah** (EmArcy 824 057)

Jimmy Witherspoon, **The 'Spoon Concerts** (Fantasy 24701)

Budd Johnson, **Budd Johnson and the Four Brass Giants** (Original Jazz Classics 1921)

Joe Newman, **The Complete Joe Newman** (RCA 66610), 2 CDs

Louis Prima, **Capitol Collectors Series** (Capitol 94072)

Henry "Red" Allen, **World on a String** (Bluebird 2497)

Barney Bigard, **Barney Bigard—Claude Luter** (Vogue 655003)

Don Ewell, **Free 'N' Easy** (Good Time Jazz 10046)

Bud Freeman, **Chicago/Austin High School Jazz in Hi-Fi** (RCA 13031)

Luckey Roberts and Willie "The Lion" Smith, **Harlem Piano Solos** (Good Time Jazz 10035)

Cal Tjader, **Monterey Concerts** (Prestige 24026)

music. McCann signed with Pacific Jazz, recording his first three albums in 1960 for that label. Strangely enough, **The Truth** (Pacific Jazz 2), which includes "A Little 3/4 for God and Company," **The Shout** (Pacific Jazz 7), and **In San Francisco** (Pacific Jazz 16) have yet to be reissued; they were quite popular at the time and launched Les McCann's career.

Phineas Newborn   Phineas Newborn's arrival on the major league jazz scene in 1956 was considered a major event because of his brilliant technique (which was on the level of Oscar Peterson) and his hard-swinging style. During this period, his potential seemed to be unlimited. Newborn gained early experience playing in Memphis-area R&B bands with his brother (guitarist Calvin Newborn), and he recorded as a sideman with a few of the groups, including with B.B. King in the early 1950s. After playing briefly with Lionel Hampton and Willis Jackson, he served in the military (1952–54), freelanced in the South, and in 1956 moved to New York. Other than short stints with Charles Mingus (1958) and Roy Haynes, Newborn was generally heard leading a trio or quartet.

 ● **Here Is Phineas** (Koch 8505) has Newborn's first full record. At 24, he sounds brilliant, heading a group with Oscar Pettiford, Kenny Clark, and sometimes Calvin Newborn, ripping through such songs as "Barbados," "Celia" (taken at a ridiculously fast tempo), "Daahoud," and "Afternoon in Paris." Some listeners may shake their heads at Newborn's constant outpouring of technically impossible runs; those speedy octaves are remarkable. **Jamaica/Fabulous Phineas** (Collectables 2740) is a single CD that has all of the music from two of the pianist's RCA records, except for leaving off one cut due to space limitations. **Jamaica** is rather unusual because it was the pianist's only album with a medium-size (ten-piece) band. The songs are all taken from the Harold Arlen musical *Jamaica*, a forgotten play that did not generate any hits. Newborn and the musicians (who include trumpeter Ernie Royal, Jimmy Cleveland, Jerome Richardson, and two Latin percussionists) play quite well, even if the material is mostly forgettable. The second half of the CD is on a higher level, a quartet date that puts the focus on the leader's brilliant piano playing. The versions of "Cherokee" and "What's New" are stunning unaccompanied piano solos.

Herbie Nichols   Herbie Nichols recorded for Blue Note during 1955–56, getting rare opportunities to document his own highly original compositions and piano playing. Unfortunately, during a period when Thelonious Monk was just starting to gain recognition after a decade of neglect, there was apparently no room in modern jazz for Nichols. Other than "Lady Sings the Blues" (which was recorded by Billie Holiday), other musicians did not cover his songs. He did continue working in Dixieland-oriented groups where his style was flexible enough to fit in, but the bop world ignored him.

In 1957, Nichols had his last opportunity to record. **Love, Gloom, Cash, Love** (Rhino/Bethlehem 76690) has Nichols (with George Duvivier and Dannie Richmond) playing seven more of his originals plus Denzil Best's obscure "Infatuation Eyes," "All the Way," and "Too Close for Comfort." The music is strikingly original, but once again the record did not sell very well, and Nichols returned to complete obscurity, writing songs that no one had an interest in playing. Despite a few younger musician friends who championed him without any success, Herbie Nichols would not really be discovered until decades after his 1963 death from leukemia.

Horace Parlan   When one considers that Horace Parlan had polio as a childhood that partially crippled his right hand, it seems somewhat illogical that he would end up being a pianist. But Parlan was able to develop his own chord voicings (never trying to play fast single-note lines) and found his place in jazz. He played in his native Pittsburgh during 1952–57 and was a member of Charles Mingus's group during 1957–59, also playing regularly with Booker Ervin (1960–61). As a leader, he recorded seven albums for Blue Note, four in 1960 alone, and all have been reissued on a definitive but limited-edition box set, **The Complete Blue Note Horace Parlan Sessions** (Mosaic 5-197). **Us Three** (Blue Note 56581) is available separately and serves an excellent introduction to his playing. Parlan is featured in a trio with bassist George Tucker and drummer Al Harewood, and his chordal style is heard in fine form on three originals (most notably the catchy "Wadin'"), and four standards, including "I Want to Be Loved" and "The Lady Is a Tramp."

Carl Perkins   Carl Perkins had the potential to be a major figure, but drugs greatly shortened his life, and he died on March 17, 1958, at the age of 29. Perkins, like Parlan, had overcome a slightly crippled hand (due to polio) to become a jazz pianist although in his case it was his left hand that was most affected. Perkins, who was based in Los Angeles during most of his career, played with Tiny Bradshaw, Big Jay McNeely, Oscar Moore's trio (1953–54), and an early version of the Clifford Brown-Max Roach Quintet (1954). Perkins composed one jazz standard ("Grooveyard"), recorded with Chet Baker, Pepper Adams, Dexter Gordon, Jim Hall, Richie Kamuca, Stuff Smith, Leroy Vinnegar, Frank Morgan, and Art Pepper, and was a member of the Curtis Counce Quintet (1956–58). Perkins also led record dates for Savoy (six songs in 1949), Dootone (1956), and Pacific Jazz (1957); unfortunately that music is long out of print. But his premature death robbed Carl Perkins of the opportunity to make a bigger impact on jazz.

Oscar Peterson   During 1956–60, Oscar Peterson led 23 albums, not to mention his dates with "Jazz at the Philharmonic" and as a sideman with Verve's top artists. The Peterson-Herb Ellis-Ray Brown trio reached the height of its power during 1956–58. ● **At the Stratford Shakespearean Festival** (Verve 314 513 752) is quite passionate, utilizes some complex arrangements (often devised by Ellis and Brown to impress the pianist), and contains memorable renditions of "Falling in Love with Love," "How About You," "Swinging on a Star," "How High the Moon," and "52nd Street Theme." Nearly as worthy is 1957's **At the Concertgebouw** (Verve 314 521 649), which includes dazzling renditions of "The Lady Is a Tramp," "Budo," "Daahoud," "Indiana," and "Joy Spring."

In the fall of 1958, Herb Ellis left the group to settle in Los Angeles. After a brief discussion, it was decided to replace the guitarist with a drummer. Gene Gammage filled in briefly, and then Ed Thigpen took over for a seven-year stint. The trio's sound was now quite a bit different with the pianist always being the main voice; no more competition or inspiration from a guitarist.

During 1952–53, the early Peterson Trio had recorded an extensive series of songbooks dedicated to the work of different composers, ten songbooks totaling 113 songs. In 1959, the Peterson-Brown-Thigpen group recorded nine more songbooks (some repeating many of the same tunes as in the earlier project) adding up to 108 more songs. Unfortunately, very little planning went into these projects so it was just a matter of Peterson playing number after number, with nearly everything being first takes. **The Gershwin Songbooks** (Verve

314 529 698) and **Plays the Duke Ellington Songbook** (Verve 314 559 785) both combine two songbooks, one apiece from the guitar and drum trios. The music is pleasing, but not particularly memorable.

Much better is **The Jazz Soul of Oscar Peterson/Affinity** (Verve 314 533 100), a pair of trio albums (from 1959, and 1962) that include "Liza," "Woody'n You," Bill Evans's "Waltz for Debby," "Tangerine," and Ray Brown's most famous song, "Gravy Waltz." A change of pace is provided with **Bursting Out with the All-Star Big Band/Swinging Brass** (Verve 314 529 699), two sets (also from 1959 and 1962) in which Peterson is the lead voice with big bands arranged by Ernie Wilkins and Russ Garcia. James Moody, Cannonball Adderley, and altoist Norris Turney have a few short solos, but the focus is mostly on the pianist on such songs as his "Blues for Big Scotia," "Daahoud," "Tricotism," "Manteca," and "Con Alma." As usual, Oscar Peterson plays with remarkable technique and creative ideas within the style that he preferred.

Bud Powell   Bud Powell declined and became more erratic during the 1956–60 period, but he was still capable of greatness on an occasional basis. **Bud!** (Blue Note 93902), **Time Waits** (Blue Note 46820), and **The Scene Changes** (Blue Note 46529), all of which are included in his four-CD set **Complete Blue Note and Roost Recordings** (Blue Note 30083), each have their strong moments. In general, Powell's best work was done for Blue Note, with his later Verve records being so streaky that they are difficult to sit through. **Bud!** has an unaccompanied solo on "Bud on Bach," four trio numbers with Paul Chambers and Art Taylor, and three bop tunes that have Curtis Fuller making the group a quartet. **Time Waits** (with Sam Jones, and Philly Joe Jones) has several of Powell's originals, including "John's Abbey," "Monopoly," and the title cut, while **The Scene Changes** (with Chambers and Taylor) includes nine more obscure Powell originals. **Strictly Powell** (RCA 51423) and **Swingin' with Bud** (RCA 51507) are okay but uninspiring trio dates with George Duvivier and Art Taylor. **Bud Plays Bird** (Roulette 37137), which was not released for the first time until 1996, has the Powell-Duvivier-Taylor trio playing 15 Charlie Parker songs plus "Salt Peanuts." Even with a few minor errors, this is a worthwhile set, showing that Powell could still find inspiration from bebop on his good days.

Mentally ill, Bud Powell probably had his life extended for a few years when he moved to Paris in 1959. He was treated well, was never short of work, and for a time seemed to be recovering from his various ailments. **The Complete Essen Jazz Festival Concert** (Black Lion 760105) has him sounding exuberant with "The Three Bosses" (the trio he led with Oscar Pettiford and Kenny Clarke) on five boppish numbers, and accompanying Coleman Hawkins for four other tunes (including "All the Things You Are" and "Stuffy").

Andre Previn   The multitalented Andre Previn, who was still just 31 in 1960, had been a major musician for 16 years by then. Whether composing chamber music, writing film scores, or playing jazz piano, he certainly kept busy. He recorded frequently during 1957–60, making nine records as a leader for Contemporary, switching to Columbia in 1960. Previn had incorporated bop quite smoothly into his playing yet usually focused on the composers of the 1930s, keeping the melodies close by. He was the main soloist on Shelly Manne's ● **My Fair Lady** (Original Jazz Classics 336), an album that was so popular that it started a trend of jazz versions of songs from plays and movies. Previn probably felt cheated that the best-seller was released under Manne's name, so he recorded **Gigi** (Original Jazz Classics 407), **West Side Story** (Original Jazz Classics 422), and **Pal Joey** (Original Jazz Classics 637) as the leader of a trio with Manne and Red Mitchell in hopes of duplicating its success. Musically (if not commercially), he succeeded. Among his other projects were **Double Play** (Original Jazz Classics 157), which is a set of two-piano trios with Russ Freeman and Shelly Manne, **Like Previn** (Original Jazz Classics 170), which features his own originals, **King Size** (Original Jazz Classics 691), and a trio of unaccompanied solo albums: **Plays Songs by Vernon Duke** (Original Jazz Classics 1789), **Plays Songs by Jerome Kern** (Original Jazz Classics 1787), and **Plays Songs by Harold Arlen** (Original Jazz Classics 1840). Taken as a whole, these recordings comprise Andre Previn's most significant work in jazz.

Freddie Redd   Freddie Redd was always a fine bop-based pianist and an underrated composer of haunting melodies. After serving in the army (1946–49), he worked with drummer Johnny Mills, Tiny Grimes (with whom he made his recording debut), Cootie Williams, Oscar Pettiford, and the Jive Bombers. He recorded half

an album as a leader for Prestige in 1955, recorded with Gene Ammons and Art Farmer, toured Sweden in 1956 with Ernestine Anderson and Rolf Ericson, and settled in San Francisco. His greatest fame was achieved in 1960 as the composer for *The Connection*, a daring play for the time that dealt with jazz musicians waiting for their drug connection to arrive. The show was filmed and staged in New York, London, and Paris, with Redd appearing in several of the versions.

San Francisco Suite for Jazz Trio (Original Jazz Classics 1748) from 1957 features Redd in a trio with bassist George Tucker and drummer Ali Dreares. The highlight is the 13-minute title piece, a work in five parts that depicts the San Francisco jazz life of the era. **The Music from the Connection** (Blue Note 84027), which strangely enough has not been reissued on CD yet, has seven Redd pieces that feature the pianist in a quartet with Jackie McLean, bassist Michael Mattos, and drummer Larry Ritchie. **Shades of Redd** (Blue Note 21738) reunited the pianist and McLean, who join Tina Brooks, Paul Chambers, and Louis Hayes in a quintet to play seven more original Redd pieces. Although his compositions did not become standards, Freddie Redd's tunes are well worth hearing and still sound fresh today.

Billy Taylor   Always classy and accessible with a style that is boppish but appeals to swing fans too, Billy Taylor has long been one of jazz's most articulate spokesmen. By the late 1950s, he was frequently on television, talking about the importance of jazz. Taylor led several trios during the second half of the 1950s, starting with bassist Earl May and drummer Percy Brice. Ed Thigpen was on drums during 1957–58 with Kenny Dennis succeeding him in 1959. The 1960 version of the Billy Taylor Trio had bassist Henry Grimes and drummer Ray Mosca.

Taylor recorded sets for ABC-Paramount, Atlantic, Argo, and Riverside. ● **My Fair Lady Loves Jazz** (GRP/Impulse 141), which was recorded in 1957 at a time when *My Fair Lady* was a big Broadway hit, is one of the very best jazz interpretations of the classic score. Taylor's trio with May and Thigpen is joined by seven horns arranged by Quincy Jones. There are short solos for trumpeter Ernie Royal, Jimmy Cleveland, altoist Anthony Ortega, and Gerry Mulligan, but Taylor is the main star and sounds quite inspired by the songs, personnel, and arrangements. **Billy Taylor with Four Flutes** (Original Jazz Classics 1830) is an unusual project in that Taylor wrote arrangements for his trio, percussionist Chino Pozo, and the flutes of Frank Wess, Herbie Mann, Jerome Richardson, and Phil Bodner. The music (four Taylor originals, and such tunes as "The Song Is Ended," "St. Thomas," and "How About You") is essentially bebop, but certainly sounds different due to the instrumentation. **Uptown** (Original Jazz Classics 1901) features the 1960 Taylor-Grimes-Mosca trio on a live set. The repertoire is typically wide-ranging, including pieces by Erroll Garner ("La Petite Mambo"), Duke Jordan, and Bobby Timmons (an emotional "Moanin'"), "'S Wonderful," and four of Taylor's originals (highlighted by the boppish "Biddy's Beat").

Bobby Timmons   Bobby Timmons had a similar role to Bunny Berigan in the 1930s, being responsible for his employers having hit records although his own solo career never quite took off. A fine pianist whose use of gospel and funky blues phrases helped form soul jazz of the 1960s, Timmons was initially a Bud Powell–inspired bebop player. He picked up experience playing in his native Philadelphia, moved to New York, and worked with Kenny Dorham (1956), Chet Baker, Sonny Stitt, and the Maynard Ferguson Big Band. As a member of Art Blakey's Jazz Messengers (1958–59), he wrote the classic song "Moanin'," which really helped launch the Jazz Messengers' success. He left Blakey to join the new Cannonball Adderley Quintet for whom his "This Here" and its follow-up "Dat Dere" (which was given lyrics by Oscar Brown, Jr.) became big hits. In 1960, he was persuaded to return to the Jazz Messengers for another year.

In 1960, Timmons led his first two albums. **This Here Is Bobby Timmons** (Original Jazz Classics 104) has the pianist performing an unaccompanied "Lush Life," trio versions (with Sam Jones and Jimmy Cobb) of his three hits, plus his "Joy Ride," and four standards. Of his many albums as a leader, this is the definitive one. **Soul Time** (Original Jazz Classics 820) is almost on the same level, with four more originals (including "So Tired"), and three standards played by Timmons, Jones, Blakey, and Blue Mitchell. But somehow Bobby Timmons never grew beyond where he was in 1960.

Mal Waldron   Mal Waldron, who was influenced by Thelonious Monk's use of space and dissonance, has long had a brooding, rhythmic, and slightly introverted style that features his own chord voicings. He initially played classical piano and jazz alto, switching to jazz piano while studying at Queens College. Waldron began freelancing in New York in the early 1950s, making his recording debut with Ike Quebec, and sometimes playing with R&B groups. He gained recognition when he worked with Charles Mingus (1954–56) and as Billie Holiday's last regular accompanist (1957–59).

Waldron was often hired by the Prestige label to supervise recording sessions and to contribute many arrangements and originals. One of his songs, "Soul Eyes," became a standard. As a leader he recorded fairly frequently for Prestige and New Jazz during 1956–59, and it is his originals (which alternate with arranged versions of standards) and quiet authority that uplift the music beyond being a mere jam session despite the lack of rehearsal time. **Mal 1** (Original Jazz Classics 611) has Waldron heading a quintet featuring trumpeter Idrees Sulieman, and altoist Gigi Gryce, **Mal 2** (Original Jazz Classics 671) has a sextet with Sulieman or Bill Hardman, Jackie McLean or Sahib Shihab (heard on alto and baritone), and John Coltrane (shortly after he left Miles Davis the first time). **Mal 3/Sounds** (Original Jazz Classics 1814) is a little more unusual, for the sextet consists of Art Farmer, flutist Eric Dixon, cellist Calo Scott, Waldron, bassist Julian Euell, Elvin Jones, and Mal's wife, Elaine Waldron, on two vocals. Counting a couple of multi-artist sets not mentioned here, **Mal 4** (Original Jazz Classics 1856) was Waldron's sixth album as a leader, but surprisingly his first trio date (with Addison Farmer and drummer Kenny Dennis), giving him an opportunity to stretch out on such songs as "Like Someone in Love," "Too Close for Comfort," and "By Myself." From 1959, **Impressions** (Original Jazz Classics 132) is also a trio outing (with Farmer and Albert "Tootie" Heath), mixing standards and originals, and showing how highly individual a player Waldron was this early in his career.

Left Alone (Rhino/Bethlehem 79854) was dedicated to Billie Holiday (though it was recorded a few months before her death) and is unusual because only one song ("You Don't Know What Love Is") performed by Waldron's trio (with bassist Julian Euell and drummer Al Dreares) was actually from Lady Day's repertoire. Waldron talks about Holiday in a brief interview, contributes a couple of songs, digs into "Airegin," and has Jackie McLean guest on "Left Alone." Shortly after this album was recorded, Mal Waldron began his long solo career.

George Wallington   One of the first bebop pianists, George Wallington led a series of fine quintets in New York during 1954–60 that usually featured top up-and-coming players. The 1956–57 band consisted of Donald Byrd, Phil Woods, Teddy Kotick, and either Art Taylor or Nick Stabulas on drums, playing music that fell between bop and hard bop. **Jazz for the Carriage Trade** (Original Jazz Classics 1704) has the quintet performing "Our Delight," "Our Love Is Here to Stay," "What's New," Frank Foster's "Foster Dulles," and two Woods songs. The altoist often steals solo honors while Byrd shows potential. **The New York Scene** (Original Jazz Classics 1805) mostly features obscurities (other than "Indian Summer") played with enthusiasm and creativity, and the same group on **Jazz at the Hotchkiss** (Savoy 78994) performs three group originals, "Ow," and Bud Powell's "Dance of the Infidels." While those three sets all feature a promising group, **Knight Music** (Koch 8543) puts the focus on Wallington in a trio (with Teddy Kotick and Nick Stabulas). The pianist shows just how strong a bop player he was on "Godchild," "Will You Still Be Mine," "Billie's Tune," the intense "Up Jumped the Devil," and "It's All Right with Me."

The recordings came to an end after 1957, and in 1960 George Wallington (who was 36) chose to drop out of music to run his family's air conditioning company.

Randy Weston   Randy Weston, like Mal Waldron, learned a bit from Thelonious Monk and showed his influence early in his career. Weston however has a more joyful style than Waldron, and has long also been influenced by Caribbean and African rhythms. He led dates for Riverside during 1954–56 along with albums for Dawn, Jubilee, Metro Jazz, United Artists, and Roulette.

With these Hands (Original Jazz Classics 1883) has Weston in 1956 playing standards (including "The Man I Love," "This Can't Be Love," and "Do Nothing Till You Hear from Me"), plus two originals, highlighted by the debut of his "Little Niles." Weston is joined on this lesser-known set by Cecil Payne, bassist Ahmed Abdul-Malik, and drummer Wilbert Hogan. **Jazz à la Bohemia** (Original Jazz Classics 1747) has the same group (with Al Dreares on drums) playing the calypso "Hold 'Em Joe" (a decade before Sonny Rollins added it to his repertoire), "It's All Right with Me," and Weston's "Chessman's Delight."

Two of Weston's most significant recordings have come back as ◉ **Uhuru Africa/Highlife** (Roulette 94510). Recorded in 1960, **Uhuru Africa** is one of the first and finest examples of African rhythms being combined with advanced jazz. Weston utilizes a 24-piece big band that includes 14 horns, one guitar, two bassists, three drummers, and three percussionists. Martha Flowers and Brock Peters take vocals on "African Lady," the best known of the four movements. Melba Liston was responsible not only for this project's arrangements, but also the ones on the 1963 **Highlife** session (originally released as **Music from the African Nations**), which has Weston showcased in a 12-piece ensemble that also includes Ray Copeland, Julius Watkins, Booker Ervin, and Budd Johnson. The stirring ensembles and solos make these two projects into historic and memorable occasions.

Gerald Wiggins   Unlike Randy Weston, Gerald Wiggins was never that interested in major projects; he just wanted to swing and play good music. In addition to working in the Hollywood studios and coaching actresses to sing (most notably Marilyn Monroe), "the Wig" played in Los Angeles clubs with his combo. **The Gerald Wiggins Trio** (V.S.O.P. 28) has him jamming seven standards and two originals with bassist Joe Comfort and drummer Bill Douglass, including "Love for Sale," "Surrey with the Fringe on Top," and "The Man that Got Away." **Around the World in 80 Days** (Original Jazz Classics 1761) also has solid playing by Wiggins (with Eugene Wright and Douglass), but with the exception of the title cut, the songs from the movie of the same name are quite forgettable and mostly could not be saved.

Reminiscin' with Wig (Fresh Sound 47) from 1957 has Wiggins, Wright, and Douglass playing charming and sly versions of such unlikely material as "Three o'Clock in the Morning," "Oh, You Beautiful Doll," "Ma She's Making Eyes at Me," and "In My Merry Oldsmobile" as Wiggins reminisces musically about music created long before his time. **The King and I** (Fresh Sound 53) has Wiggins, Wright, and Douglass performing eight selections from the show *The King and I*, including "Getting to Know You," "We Kiss in a Shadow," and "Hello Young Lovers." The music is easy-listening and pleasant although overly respectful, and with no real revelations. And although **Wiggin' Out** (Original Jazz Classics 1034) is a bit of a surprise, with Wiggins switching to organ in a trio set with Harold Land and drummer Jackie

Mills, and there is some good playing along the way (particularly on "A Night in Tunisia" and "Without a Song"), one can understand why Gerald Wiggins has long since chosen to stick to the piano where his subtle, witty, and swinging personality come through best.

Guitarists

The shadow of Charlie Christian was felt by all jazz guitarists during the period of 1956–60, even those (such as Laurindo Almeida and Charlie Byrd) who sought to explore Latin music. Christian continued to define not only the sound of the electric guitar but its vocabulary.

With the rise of the LP and the lengthier jazz performances that resulted, guitarists found themselves finally getting a chance to solo regularly alongside the horn players and pianists.

Laurindo Almeida In March 1958, Brazilian guitarist Laurindo Almeida (who mostly worked in the studios during the era) and Bud Shank had a recorded reunion, cutting two albums (**Holiday in Brazil** and **Latin Contrasts**) under Shank's name that have been reissued as **Brazilliance Vol. 2** (World Pacific 96102). With bassist Gary Peacock and drummer Chuck Flores completing the quartet, and altoist Shank doubling on flute, the music combines Brazilian rhythms with cool jazz solos, a few years before the "birth" of bossa nova. Unlike **Vol. 1**, this time around the music was more solo-oriented, and the Brazilian elements are sometimes overridden by the jazz content although the results are once again quite enjoyable.

Billy Bauer Billy Bauer, who gained some fame in the jazz world for his playing with Woody Herman's First Herd (1944–46) and Lennie Tristano (1946–49), became a busy studio player in the 1950s, only appearing in jazz settings on a rare basis. He led just two studio albums in his career, an obscurity for the Ad Lib label, and 1956's **Plectrist** (Verve 314 517 060). The music on the latter CD is mostly gently swinging and lightly boppish. Bauer is teamed with the obscure pianist Arnold Ackers, Milt Hinton, and Osie Johnson on such tunes as "Too Marvelous for Words," "The Way You Look Tonight," "You'd Be So Nice to Come Home To," and several of Bauer's originals. This is excellent music, but it is unfortunate that there never was an encore for the talented Billy Bauer.

Kenny Burrell Kenny Burrell first burst upon the national jazz scene in 1956. Burrell had been part of the fertile Detroit jazz scene since the late 1940s, and, other than a short stint with Dizzy Gillespie in 1951, he primarily played locally until moving to New York in 1955. A superior bop player with a relaxed thoughtful style and a warm sound, Burrell was in great demand shortly after arriving in New York. The double CD **Introducing Kenny Burrell** (Blue Note 24561) has the guitarist's first sessions as a leader other than a single made in Detroit in 1950. Burrell is heard in three different quintets: a combo with Tommy Flanagan, Paul Chambers, Kenny Clarke, and Candido, a group with Frank Foster, Flanagan, Oscar Pettiford, and drummer Shadow Wilson, and a unit with Hank Mobley, Horace Silver, Doug Watkins, and Louis Hayes. Standards, originals, and blues (including Burrell's "Fugue 'N' Blues") all receive favorable and swinging treatment from Burrell and his notable sidemen.

Burrell recorded often during this era (for Prestige, Blue Note, Argo, and Columbia), and among the gems are **All Night Long** (Original Jazz Classics 427), which has him leading a jam session with Donald Byrd, Hank Mobley, and Jerome Richardson, the follow-up **All Day Long** (Original Jazz Classics 456), and **Kenny Burrell with John Coltrane** (Original Jazz Classics 300). **Blue Lights Vols. 1 & 2** (Blue Note 57184), a two-CD set, reissues jam session-flavored music from May 14, 1958. Burrell is teamed with trumpeter Louis Smith (an underrated great), both Junior Cook and Tina Brooks on tenors, either Duke Jordan or Bobby Timmons, Sam Jones, and Art Blakey. The all-star group stretches out on three standards and originals by Burrell, Jordan, and Jones.

Kenny Burrell was one of the first guitarists to perform often with a pianoless trio. **A Night at the Vanguard** (MCA/Chess 9316), from 1959 with Richard Davis and Roy Haynes, was his initial recording in this format, and he sounds quite inventive in a subtle way on such numbers as "Will You Still Be Mine," Erroll Garner's "Trio," "Cheek to Cheek," and "Broadway." Even this early in his career, Kenny Burrell had found his sound.

Charlie Byrd During an era when nearly every jazz guitarist was heavily influenced by Charlie Christian, Charlie Byrd stood apart from the crowd. After serving in the military during the latter part of World War II, the teenager had an opportunity to meet Django Reinhardt.

Back in the United States, Byrd played in the bands of Sol Yaged, Joe Marsala, and Freddie Slack. His career took a different turn in 1950 when he began extensively studying classical music, his main pursuit for the next five years. Byrd developed his own style, playing acoustic guitar. By the time he returned to jazz and made his recording debut in 1957, he had a personal sound and a very different approach than most jazz guitarists, although he too was touched a bit by Charlie Christian.

The rather brief CD **Jazz Recital** (Savoy 192) features Byrd in a trio/quartet with bassist Al Lucas, drummer Bobby Donaldson, and occasionally Tommy Newsom on tenor (sounding a bit like Zoot Sims) and flute. The ten songs include four melodic treatments of Rodgers and Hart songs and four Byrd originals, including the surprising "Homage to Charlie Christian" in which he closely emulates the guitarist. For a few years, Byrd was based in Washington, D.C., recording for the tiny Offbeat label (which was later acquired by Riverside). **Byrd's Word** (Original Jazz Classics 1054) and **The Guitar Artistry of Charlie Byrd** (Original Jazz Classics 945) give listeners an opportunity to hear Byrd before he discovered bossa nova, when his guitar playing was more classical-oriented than it would become. While the latter set features his regular trio with bassist Keter Betts and drummer Buddy Deppenschmidt, **Byrd's Word** has the guitarist with a variety of small groups, including a sextet ("Bobby in Bassoonville" features Kenneth Pasmanick on bassoon), and backing two vocals by his wife, Ginny Byrd. But all of this was just a prelude to Charlie Byrd's upcoming trip to Brazil.

Herb Ellis   As a member of the Oscar Peterson Trio during 1953–58, Herb Ellis stayed quite busy touring the world, playing on all-star dates, and appearing with "Jazz at the Philharmonic." He also led four albums of his own for Verve during 1956–60.

Nothing but the Blues (Verve 521 674) has always been Ellis's favorite personal recording. Teamed up with Roy Eldridge, Stan Getz, Ray Brown, and Stan Levey in a pianoless quintet, Ellis sticks to the blues on eight original tunes, but there is more variety than expected, along with plenty of color and drive. The CD reissue also has four unrelated numbers recorded for a European soundtrack by the JATP stars. Getz, Eldridge, and Coleman Hawkins each have individual features, but Dizzy Gillespie takes honors. The guitarist's other albums

(**Ellis in Wonderland**, **Herb Ellis Meets Jimmy Giuffre**, and **Thank You Charlie Christian**) are each well-conceived, but unfortunately not yet out on CD.

After leaving the Peterson Trio, Ellis spent 1959 playing with Ella Fitzgerald and then became a studio musician on the West Coast.

Tal Farlow   One of the finest bop-oriented guitarists of the decade, Tal Farlow could play quite rapidly, but also had a very light touch along with a fertile imagination. After working with Artie Shaw's Gramercy Five in 1954, Tal Farlow led his own trio, which for a time featured pianist Eddie Costa and bassist Vinnie Burke. He recorded regularly for Norgran and Verve during 1954–59, but unfortunately many of his recordings remain out of print. **The Swinging Guitar of Tal Farlow** (Verve 559 515) and **Tal** (Verve 9227) both feature the Farlow-Costa-Burke group in 1956. The interplay between Farlow and Costa is always exciting, whether they are playing unisons or trading off. The first set is highlighted by "Taking a Chance on Love," "Yardbird Suite," "Like Someone in Love," and Farlow's original "Meteor" (which uses the chord changes of "Confirmation"), while the second CD includes "There Is No Greater Love," "Anything Goes," "Yesterdays," and "Broadway."

Farlow led three other albums for Verve during 1958–59, but by then he was in the process of dropping out of music. The guitarist preferred a more relaxed lifestyle, so he settled in New England and became a sign painter. With the exception of one album, little would be heard from him in jazz during the next 15 years.

Jim Hall   Although initially associated with hard bop, and thought of as a successor to Barney Kessel, Herb Ellis, and Tal Farlow, Jim Hall (who had a more introverted style) was harmonically advanced from the start of his career and always seemed to be looking ahead. He attended the Cleveland Institute of Music, studied classical guitar in Los Angeles, and made a strong impression as an original member of the Chico Hamilton Quintet (1955–56). Hall had a pivotal role with several versions of the Jimmy Giuffre Three (1956–59) and was a member of Ella Fitzgerald's backup quartet during 1960–61.

Hall's debut as a leader, **Jazz Guitar** (Blue Note 46851), was originally a trio set with Carl Perkins and Red Mitchell from 1957 released by Pacific Jazz. However, later versions of the session had drummer Larry

Bunker overdubbed and suffered from an excess of producer Dick Bock's infamous edits. For the CD reissue, Bunker's parts were removed, but unfortunately nothing could be done about the edits (the original master takes had long since disappeared). Although the piano and bass solos were shortened, it is still a worthwhile reissue since Hall plays quite well, and a couple of additional selections from the same date were discovered and added to the CD.

Barney Kessel   One of the most popular jazz guitarists of the 1950s, Barney Kessel's long string of albums for the Contemporary label were among the finest of his career. **Music to Listen to Barney Kessel By** (Original Jazz Classics 746) differs from his usual sessions in that Kessel and his rhythm section (with either Andre Previn, Jimmy Rowles, or Claude Williamson on piano, Buddy Clark or Red Mitchell on bass, and drummer Shelly Manne) are joined by five woodwinds, mostly playing tightly arranged versions of standards, including "Fascinating Rhythm," "I Love You," "Cheerful Little Earful," and "Mountain Greenery." While that CD is very much a West Coast cool jazz project, **Let's Cook** (Original Jazz Classics 1010) is much harder swinging. Kessel, vibraphonist Victor Feldman, Hampton Hawes, Leroy Vinnegar, and Shelly Manne play the extended title cut (which is a blues-with-a-bridge that is over 11 minutes long), "Just in Time," and the ballad "Time Remembered." In addition there are hot and modernized versions of "Tiger Rag" and "Jersey Bounce" played by Kessel with Ben Webster, Frank Rosolino, Jimmie Rowles, Vinnegar, and Manne. It is a pity that the latter group did not record a full album for the combination of Webster, and Rosolino is quite exciting.

Modern Jazz Performances from Bizet's Carmen (Original Jazz Classics 269) has Kessel (who wrote the arrangements) not being shy to swing the themes from *Carmen* while being respectful of the melodies. He is heard in three settings: with Victor Feldman in a quintet, joined by five woodwinds and a rhythm section, and with five jazz horns (including Herb Geller and trumpeter Ray Linn). **Some Like It Hot** (Original Jazz Classics 168) came out after the Marilyn Monroe-Tony Curtis-Jack Lemmon movie became a hit. It served as a good excuse for Kessel to join with Art Pepper (switching between alto, clarinet, and tenor), trumpeter Joe Gordon, Jimmie Rowles, rhythm guitarist Jack Marshall,

Monty Budwig, and Manne to play a variety of vintage numbers from the 1920s, including "I Wanna Be Loved by You," "Runnin' Wild," "Down Among the Sheltering Palms," and "By the Beautiful Sea" with fairly modern arrangements.

Because Kessel, Ray Brown, and Shelly Manne won so many jazz polls conducted by *Down Beat*, *Metronome*, and *Playboy* during this era, they were recorded as the Pollwinners on an annual basis during 1957–60. **The Poll Winners** (Original Jazz Classics 158), **The Poll Winners Ride Again** (Original Jazz Classics 607), **Poll Winners Three** (Original Jazz Classics 692), and **Exploring the Scene** (Original Jazz Classics 969) are each essentially Barney Kessel Trio albums since Brown and Manne are primarily in a supportive role. All four of the sets are equally enjoyable, with 1960's **Exploring the Scene** getting the edge due to a particularly strong repertoire that includes Ray Bryant's "Little Susie," "The Duke," "So What," "This Here," and Ornette Coleman's "The Blessing."

Wes Montgomery   In 1959, Wes Montgomery was considered among jazz's most important new discoveries, even though he was already 34 years old and had been a professional since the mid-1940s. Born in Indianapolis, Indiana, on March 6, 1925, Montgomery (who was inspired by Charlie Christian) taught himself to play guitar, using his thumb instead of a pick so as not to disturb neighbors. He played and toured with Lionel Hampton during 1948–50 (appearing on a few records in a supportive role), but then chose to return to Indianapolis to raise a family. During the 1950s, he somehow worked a day job, played a regular club gig at night, and often appeared at after-hours jam sessions, rarely sleeping very much. Whatever all of this strain eventually did to his heart, it did result in Montgomery developing very quickly into a major guitarist, and one whose fast octave runs became a trademark.

Wes's brothers Buddy Montgomery (vibes and piano) and Monk Montgomery (a pioneering electric bassist) had some success as the Mastersounds, and Wes sometimes played with them, appearing on some of their records. **Fingerpickin'** (Pacific Jazz 37987) has a date originally issued as by the Montgomery Brothers. Recorded in Chicago on December 30, 1957, Wes is showcased on "Finger Pickin'," and the band features the three siblings and local musicians including the 17-year-old trumpet

Freddie Hubbard who was making his recording debut and sounding a bit nervous. In addition, three slightly later numbers that have Wes soloing with the Mastersounds round out the historic CD. **Far Wes** (Pacific Jazz 94775) features Montgomery in two quintets during 1958–59 with his brothers, either Harold Land or altoist Pony Poindexter, and Tony Baxley or Louis Hayes on drums. Wes's sound is quite recognizable on tunes such as "Old Folks," "Montgomery Funk," "Stompin' at the Savoy," and "Falling in Love with Love."

The Pacific Jazz dates were not widely heard, but Montgomery's work for Riverside caused a sensation. **Wes Montgomery Trio** (Original Jazz Classics 034) is an excellent set with organist Mel Rhyne (who was also from Indianapolis) and drummer Paul Parker recorded in October 1959, and highlighted by "Missile Blues," "Jingles," and "'Round Midnight." However, it was 1960's **Incredible Jazz Guitar** (Original Jazz Classics 036) that made the jazz world notice Montgomery. Joined by Tommy Flanagan, Percy Heath, and Albert "Tootie" Heath, Wes introduces "Four on Six" and "West Coast Blues," and swings hard on "Airegin," "In Your Own Sweet Way," and "Gone with the Wind." All of the unique qualities of Wes's playing are on display—the octaves, the rapid single-note lines, his quick imagination, and his mastery of bebop guitar. **Movin' Along** (Original Jazz Classics 089) is almost on the same level, with Montgomery, flutist James Clay (who plays tenor on one song), pianist Victor Feldman, Sam Jones, and Louis Hayes performing four standards (including Clifford Brown's "Sandu" and "Body and Soul"), Jones's "Says You," and two of the guitarist's tunes.

But the Montgomery set to get is the 12-CD box ● **The Complete Riverside Recordings** (Riverside 4408), which has all of his Riverside/Original Jazz Classics recordings of 1959–63, arguably his greatest period. The music on this box shows why Wes Montgomery is still considered one of the greatest jazz guitarists of all time, and why the jazz world of 1960 was so astounded by his playing.

Bassists

Ever so gradually, jazz bassists were starting to grapple with the innovations of Jimmy Blanton and moving their instrument beyond just playing four-to-the-bar walking lines behind soloists and ensembles. Oscar Pettiford expanded upon Blanton's ideas as did Charles Mingus, and with the rise of Scott LaFaro with the Bill Evans Trio, bassists were starting to be a little liberated from their former role as a backup instrument.

Ray Brown   Ray Brown, one of the top bassists to emerge during the bebop era, first came to New York from his native Pittsburgh in 1945. Soon he was a member of the Dizzy Gillespie Big Band, where he was featured on "One Bass Hit" and "Two Bass Hit." He worked with "Jazz at the Philharmonic," married Ella Fitzgerald (their marriage only lasted from 1948 to 1952), was a member of the early Milt Jackson Quartet (which in time became the Modern Jazz Quartet), and officially began his long association with Oscar Peterson in 1951. As a member of the O.P. Trio, Brown appeared on a countless number of recording dates, not only as a separate unit, but as the backing trio/quartet for other top jazz musicians.

Brown, who led his first record date in 1946 (sidemen included Dizzy Gillespie, James Moody, and Milt Jackson), headed his initial album in 1956, **Bass Hit** (Verve 314 559 829). Joined by all-stars based on the West Coast during the era (including Harry "Sweets" Edison, Jimmy Giuffre, Herb Geller, and Jimmy Rowles) and performing Marty Paich arrangements, Brown performs standards ("After You've Gone" is heard in four versions), plus "Blues for Sylvia" and "Blues for Lorraine." This is a fine mainstream bop date, one of several that Brown led during his Oscar Peterson years.

Paul Chambers   Bassist Paul Chambers was 20 when he joined the Miles Davis Quintet in 1955, staying an unprecedented eight years with the trumpeter's groups. Chambers had already played with Paul Quinichette, the J.J. Johnson-Kai Winding Quintet, and George Wallington, and was recognized as one of the top up-and-coming bassists of the era. Not only was he a stimulating accompanist, but Chambers's bowed solos were standouts. During 1956–57, he led four albums of his own for Blue Note, all of which are fine examples of modern hard bop for the era. **Chambers' Music** (Blue Note 844 437) has six numbers with Kenny Drew and Philly Joe Jones, with John Coltrane guesting on four of the songs (including "Dexterity" and "Stablemates"). In addition, there are three tunes from 1955 that have a jam session feel (particularly "Trane's Strain" and "Nixon, Dixon and Yates Blues") and are played by Chambers in a quintet/sextet with Coltrane, Pepper Adams, and Curtis

Fuller. On **Whims of Chambers** (Blue Note 37647), all of the musicians in the all-star sextet (Chambers, John Coltrane, Donald Byrd, Kenny Burrell, Horace Silver, and Philly Joe Jones) have their chances to star. Coltrane's two obscure compositions ("Nita" and "Just for the Love") are well worth reviving, "Tale of the Fingers" features the quintet without Coltrane, the rhythm section stretches out on "Whims of Chambers," and "Tale of the Fingers" is a showcase for Chambers's bowed bass. **Paul Chambers Quintet** (Blue Note 52441) has some modern mainstream music from the period (originals by Chambers, Benny Golson, "Softly as in a Morning Sunrise," and "What's New") played by such young all-stars as Chambers, Donald Byrd, Clifford Jordan, Tommy Flanagan, and Elvin Jones. **Bass on Top** (Blue Note 46533) puts more of a focus on Chambers's playing, in a quartet with Kenny Burrell, Hank Jones, and Art Taylor. Although all four of these Blue Notes are worth picking up, none are quite essential since Chambers was not an important composer, and his playing was just as satisfying on his many sideman dates as it was on the sets that he led.

Chambers also headed three sets for Vee-Jay during 1959–60. All of those have been reissued on a limited-edition box set, **The Complete Vee-Jay Paul Chambers/Wynton Kelly Sessions** (Mosaic 6-205) but are not yet available individually on CD. Best of the Vee-Jay LPs is **Go** (Vee-Jay 1014) as it features Cannonball Adderley and the young trumpeter Freddie Hubbard at the beginning of his career, a matchup that rarely happened again. But surprisingly, despite his prominence, Paul Chambers did not lead any further record dates after 1960.

Curtis Counce   Bassist Curtis Counce worked steadily in Los Angeles during the 1950s. Born in Kansas City, he originally studied violin and tuba in addition to bass. At 16 in 1942, Counce worked with Nat Towles. Three years later, he moved to Los Angeles where he played with Johnny Otis and recorded with Lester Young (1946) and many other jazz greats including Clifford Brown and Shorty Rogers. In 1956, Counce put together a superior hard bop quintet that also included Jack Sheldon, Harold Land, Carl Perkins, and Frank Butler, recording four albums of material for Contemporary during the next two years. **Landslide** (Original Jazz Classics 606) has the standard "Time After Time,"

Gerald Wiggins's "Sonar," and originals by Land (including "Landslide"), Perkins, and Sheldon. **You Get More Bounce with Curtis Counce** (Original Jazz Classics), which has also been titled **Councellation**, has five standards (including "Too Close for Comfort," "Mean to Me," and Charlie Parker's "Big Foot"), and two numbers by Counce. **Carl's Blues** (Original Jazz Classics 423), which has Gerald Wilson in Sheldon's place on some numbers, and Elmo Hope succeeding the late Carl Perkins, includes fine versions of "Love Walked In," Clifford Brown's "Larue," and Frank Butler's "The Butler Did It." **Sonority** (Contemporary 7655) consists of leftover tracks from the other three albums not released until 1989, with the performances from 1956 and 1958 sometimes having Wilson and Hope (who contributed three originals). The music is almost up to the level of the previous releases. The Counce Quintet (with Rolf Ericson succeeding Wilson) recorded one final album in 1958 (**Exploring the Future** for the Dooto label) before breaking up.

Sam Jones   Bassist Sam Jones rarely ever led his own band, but the record dates released under his own name were almost always gems. A supportive player who was expert at making other soloists sound good, Jones played with Tiny Bradshaw (1953–55), Kenny Dorham, Cannonball Adderley (1957), Dizzy Gillespie (1958–59), and Thelonious Monk among many others. He joined the second Adderley Quintet in 1959, staying six years. He was also a fine cello soloist and the composer of "Unit 7" and "Del Sasser."

Jones's debut as a leader, **The Soul Society** (Original Jazz Classics 1789), was the first of his three albums for Riverside. Jones plays four songs apiece on bass and cello. The strong repertoire includes Nat Adderley's "The Old Country," "Just Friends," and Bobby Timmons's "So Tired." The band is colorful, consisting of Adderley or Blue Mitchell on trumpet/cornet, Jimmy Heath, baritonist Charles Davis, Timmons, Keeter Betts on bass for the songs that have Jones playing cello, and drummer Louis Hayes. Although overshadowed by other records, **The Soul Society** was actually one of the better jazz albums of 1960.

Red Mitchell   Red Mitchell stayed busy recording constantly in the Los Angeles area during 1954–68. In 1957, he had an opportunity to record **Presenting Red Mitchell** (Original Jazz Classics 158), and the result is a superior effort featuring James Clay (on tenor and flute), Lorraine Geller, and Billy Higgins. The music is high-quality modern mainstream jazz of the era that includes such songs as "Out of the Blue," "Sandu," "Scrapple from the Apple," and "Cheek to Cheek." Mitchell was one of the most fluent bass soloists of the era, but he was wise not to overly dominate the solo space, and the results are a well-balanced and enjoyable set.

Oscar Pettiford   A major innovator on bass since 1943, Oscar Pettiford should have had many years left, but 1956–60 was his final period. **Deep Passion** (GRP/Impulse 143) combines two former LPs by big bands headed by Pettiford (who doubles on cello) from 1956–57; not too many other bassists had headed jazz orchestras by that point in time. The arrangements by Gigi Gryce, Lucky Thompson, and Benny Golson leave room for a lot of concise solos, an inventive use of the harp (either by Janet Putnam or Betty Glamann), and colorful ensembles. Among the many soloists are Art Farmer, Jimmy Cleveland, Al Grey, Julius Watkins, Thompson, Golson, and Pettiford. The fresh material and many subtle surprises make this a disc well worth searching for.

In 1958, Pettiford moved to Europe where he worked with Bud Powell and Kenny Clarke in a trio, Stan Getz, and local musicians. **Vienna Blues: The Complete Session** (Black Lion 760104) from 1959 is a quartet date with tenor saxophonist Hank Koller, guitarist Attila Zoller, and drummer Jimmy Pratt. On some songs Pettiford switches to cello while Zoller plays bass. Six originals by Pettiford and Zoller alternate with "All the Things You Are," "Stardust," and "There Will Never Be Another You." **Montmartre Blues** (Black Lion 760124) has what would be (except for six selections) Pettiford's final recordings, dating from August 22, 1959–July 6, 1960. The bassist plays with some young and talented Europeans (including trumpeter Allan Botschinsky and pianist Jan Johansson) on five standards, and five of his originals including "Laverne Walk" and his answer to Miles Davis's "So What," "Why Not? That's What."

Just 62 days later, Oscar Pettiford died from a virus, three weeks before his 38th birthday, a major loss to jazz.

Leroy Vinnegar   Famous for his ability to drive ensembles with his walking bass, Leroy Vinnegar was self-taught. He began playing professionally when he was 20 in 1948, working as the house bassist at Chicago's Beehive

in 1952–53. The following year he moved to Los Angeles where he was greatly in demand, working with Shorty Rogers, Chet Baker, Shelly Manne, Teddy Edwards, and many others. In 1957, he had an opportunity to lead his first record date, **Leroy Walks** (Original Jazz Classics 160), which consists of seven songs, six having the word "walk" in their titles including "Would You Like to Take a Walk," "I'll Walk Alone," "Walkin' My Baby Back Home," and the bassist's "Walk On." Vinnegar only solos a little here and there, and instead features his fine sidemen: vibraphonist Victor Feldman, Gerald Wilson on trumpet, Teddy Edwards, Carl Perkins, and drummer Tony Bazley.

Wilbur Ware   An advanced hard bop bassist who could sound comfortable in freer settings too, Wilbur Ware actually played banjo briefly before settling on the bass. He worked with Roy Eldridge and Sonny Stitt in 1946, and was based in his native Chicago for years. Ware recorded with Johnny Griffin (1954), gigged with Sun Ra, was with the Jazz Messengers (1956), played as part of Thelonious Monk's quartet with John Coltrane (1957), and recorded frequently for the Riverside label as a sideman. His one opportunity to lead his own record date resulted in **The Chicago Sound** (Original Jazz Classics 1737), a quintet outing with Griffin, John Jenkins, pianist Junior Mance, and either Wilbur Campbell or Frankie Dunlop on drums. Ware brought in two originals, but generously features his sidemen on such songs as "Body and Soul," Stuff Smith's "Desert Sands," "Lullaby of the Leaves," and "The Man I Love."

Doug Watkins   Doug Watkins was on many record dates during the second half of the 1950s, particularly when Paul Chambers (his cousin by marriage) was not available. He was part of the Detroit jazz scene in the early 1950s, toured with James Moody (1953), played with Barry Harris, and became quite busy after moving to New York in 1954. He was with the original version of the Jazz Messengers (1954–55), spent a year with the Horace Silver Quintet, and worked and recorded with most of the top hard bop players. Watkins led two sessions in his life, one an obscure effort for Transition in 1956, and the other being **Soulnik** (Original Jazz Classics 1848) from 1960. On this set, Watkins doubles on cello (which he had reportedly only begun playing three days earlier) and is joined by Yusef Lateef (heard on tenor, flute, and oboe), pianist Hugh Lawson, bassist Herman Wright, and drummer Lex Humphries, an all-Detroit band. The ensemble performs three standards, the bassist's "Andre's Bag," and a couple of Lateef's tunes. The use of oboe and cello on some numbers makes the date a standout.

Drummers

While Max Roach was the dominant voice among modern drummers, the instrument's evolution was moving ahead. Drummers had more interaction with soloists (commenting musically on their ideas) while still keeping the rhythm and staying supportive.

Ed Blackwell   Drummer Ed Blackwell, a native of New Orleans, spent 1951–53 in Los Angeles where he met his future employer Ornette Coleman, and began to modernize his style beyond the parade rhythms of his hometown. He spent 1953–56 in Texas and then returned to New Orleans until 1960. While in the Crescent City, Blackwell was a member of the American Jazz Quintet, an intriguing group consisting of clarinetist Alvin Batiste, tenor saxophonist Harold Battiste, pianist Ellis Marsalis, and either Richard Payne or Williams Swanson on bass. **In the Beginning** (AFO 91-1028) features the group in 1956 (with one cut from 1958) with all of the musicians being heard on their recording debut. The music is essentially hard bop, a style rarely heard in New Orleans at the time. A high school concert from two years later is on **Boogie Live...1958** (AFO 1228). At that time, the quintet consisted of Blackwell, Batiste, Marsalis, tenor saxophonist Nat Perillat (who was influenced by John Coltrane's sheets of sound), and bassist Otis Deverney. Blackwell, who has several colorful solos, was already distinctive. The group's six originals are generally based on earlier standards, most obviously Batiste's "Fourth Month," which uses the chords of "I Remember April."

In 1960, Ed Blackwell moved to New York, joining the Ornette Coleman Quartet.

Kenny Clarke   During April–May 1956, Kenny Clarke recorded the last of his Savoy records, **Meets the Detroit Jazzmen** (Savoy 243), heading a quintet featuring four major musicians who had recently emigrated from Detroit to New York: Pepper Adams, Tommy Flanagan, Kenny Burrell, and Paul Chambers. The straightahead music includes "Cottontail," "Tricotism," and "Afternoon in Paris." Shortly after this recording was made, Clarke moved permanently to Europe,

settling in France. Other than brief visits, he would spend the remainder of his life on the Continent. Clarke played with Miles Davis during the trumpeter's European visit in 1957, became a member of the Three Bosses (with Bud Powell and Oscar Pettiford), worked in the studios, and in 1960 started co-leading the Kenny Clarke-Francy Boland Orchestra, an all-star big band that lasted 13 years.

Louis Hayes   A fine hard bop drummer who has been mostly in the background as a supportive player, Louis Hayes was part of the Detroit jazz scene during the 1950s, playing with Yusef Lateef (1955–56) shortly before moving to New York. Hayes was a member of the Horace Silver Quintet (1956–59) and in 1959 joined Cannonball Adderley's group. His debut as a leader, **Featuring Yusef Lateef and Nat Adderley** (Vee-Jay 906), which is expanded with the addition of five alternate takes, features the 1960 Adderley Quintet with Lateef in Cannonball's place. The contrast between Nat's exciting (if sometimes erratic) cornet and Lateef's dignified yet soulful tenor make this an above-average session of swinging bop.

Roy Haynes   Roy Haynes was a leading member of the generation of drummers that followed Max Roach and Kenny Clarke. He picked up important experience playing in Massachusetts with the Sabby Lewis big band, Frankie Newton, Luis Russell (1945–47), the Lester Young Quintet (1947–49), Kai Winding, and the Charlie Parker Quintet (1949–52), also recording with Bud Powell, Wardell Gray, and Stan Getz. Haynes was part of Sarah Vaughan's rhythm section during 1953–58, and worked with Thelonious Monk and George Shearing. He first led a few record dates in 1954 while in Europe. **We Three** (Original Jazz Classics 196) from 1958 is really a showcase for Phineas Newborn's brilliant piano playing in a trio with Haynes and Paul Chambers, highlighted by "Our Delight" and "After Hours." In a similar vein is 1960's **Just Us** (Original Jazz Classics 879) in which Haynes accompanies the Red Garland–inspired piano playing of Richard Wyands and bassist Eddie DeHaas. Although Roy Haynes is featured on "Well Now" from the latter album, he seems quite content to inspire the pianist and take a supporting role, a position he would retain throughout his career.

Philly Joe Jones   Miles Davis's favorite drummer of the 1950s, Philly Joe Jones was with the Davis quintet during 1955–57 until his drug use resulted in him being fired. He was back with the trumpeter for a few months in 1958 until the same thing happened. That year he started leading his own bands, recording several albums during 1958–60. **Blues for Dracula** (Original Jazz Classics 230) has Jones doing an amusing but overly long monologue on the title cut (during which he does his best to imitate Bela Lugosi). Otherwise, this is a conventional hard bop date with Nat Adderley, Julian Priester, Johnny Griffin, Tommy Flanagan, and Jimmy Garrison. "Ow" and Cal Massey's "Fiesta" are featured in long versions. **Drums Around the World** (Original Jazz Classics 1792) was supposed to showcase styles from around the world, including Latin America and the Far East, but in general these references are superficial; everything sounds like hard bop. However, Jones takes some fine solos (including on an unaccompanied "The Tribal Message"), and there are some short spots for Lee Morgan, Blue Mitchell, Curtis Fuller, Herbie Mann, Cannonball Adderley, Benny Golson, and Wynton Kelly. **Showcase** (Original Jazz Classics 484) is the most satisfying overall of the three Riverside recordings, with Jones joined by Blue Mitchell, Julian Priester, tenor saxophonist Bill Barron, Jimmy Garrison, and either Dolo Coker or Sonny Clark on piano. Jones is featured on Gil Evans's "Gone" and the unusual "Gwen," an original ballad that has Philly Joe overdubbed on both piano and drums in a trio with Garrison.

But most of Philly Joe Jones's career after leaving Miles Davis the second time was anticlimactic.

Stan Levey   The early bebop drummer Stan Levey was a member of the Lighthouse All-Stars during 1954–58 before becoming a full-time studio musician. He led five record dates during the mid-1950s of which 1957's **Stan Levey 5** (V.S.O.P. 41) was his last. As usual he put together a pretty impressive lineup of West Coast musicians (Conte Candoli, Richie Kamuca, Lou Levy, and Monty Budwig) to perform a variety of swinging material, including the rarely played "Old Man Rebop," "Lover Come Back to Me," and "Stan Still." All of the musicians are in prime form, including the inspired drummer.

Shelly Manne   One of the most popular drummers in jazz, both musically and personally, Shelly Manne kept very busy during 1956–60. He recorded 15 albums as a leader for Contemporary (usually heading his quintet, which was known as Shelly Manne and His Men), worked

constantly in the studios, and in 1960 opened up his club Shelly's Manne-Hole.

Most of Manne's Contemporary releases have been reissued in the Original Jazz Classics series, and they are consistently worthy examples of music that straddles the boundaries between cool West Coast jazz, and hard bop, leaning toward the latter by 1959. **Vol. 4: Swinging Sounds** (Original Jazz Classics 267) has the 1956 version of his group, featuring Stu Williamson, Charlie Mariano, Russ Freeman, and Leroy Vinnegar on the group's theme song "A Gem from Tiffany," various originals, "Doxy," "Bernie's Tune," and "Un Poco Loco." **More Swinging Sounds** (Original Jazz Classics 320) showcases the same group performing some particularly challenging material, including Bill Holman's 15-minute four-part suite "Quartet" and Freeman's "The Wind."

Shelly Manne & His Friends Vol. 1 (Original Jazz Classics 240) has Manne teamed up with Andre Previn and Leroy Vinnegar in a trio that really showcases Previn's playing, mostly on standards and jazz tunes, including "Tangerine," "Stars Fell on Alabama," and Johnny Hodges's "Squatty Roo." The trio's second recording, ● **My Fair Lady** (Original Jazz Classics 336), was a surprise hit that launched a fad of jazz musicians recording music from Broadway shows and movies. This particular album works quite well as the group performs eight themes from the famous show, including "Get Me to the Church on Time," "I've Grown Accustomed to Her Face," and "I Could Have Danced All Night." Less successful saleswise was **Lil' Abner** (last on the LP Contemporary 3533) and **Bells Are Ringing** (Original Jazz Classics 910), the latter with Red Mitchell on bass. The songs were not hits (other than "Just in Time" from **Bells Are Ringing**) although the trio is heard in typically fine form.

Shelly Manne Plays Peter Gunn (Original Jazz Classics 948) is different in that Manne leads his regular quintet from 1959 (Conte Candoli, Herb Geller, Russ Freeman, Monty Budwig, and guest vibraphonist Victor Feldman) rather than a trio, and the music is from a hit television show. The Henry Mancini selections ("Peter Gunn" and "Dreamsville" are best known) work quite well as jazz. A three-day gig from September 22–24, 1959, resulted in no less than five CDs' worth of material from Shelly Manne's Men. Trumpeter Joe Gordon, Richie Kamuca, Victor Feldman (on piano), and Monty Budwig were in the band at that time, and **At the Blackhawk**

Vol. 1 (Original Jazz Classics 656), **Vol. 2** (Original Jazz Classics 657), **Vol. 3** (Original Jazz Classics 658), **Vol. 4** (Original Jazz Classics 659), and **Vol. 5** (Original Jazz Classics 660) certainly document the group quite extensively. Fortunately, this was a strong hard bop band, and they were having a good week.

Art Taylor A major drummer in the 1950s, Art Taylor was on countless hard bop sessions, always inspiring the other musicians and swinging the music. In 1948, when he was 19, he played with Howard McGhee. Other associations included Coleman Hawkins (1950–51), Buddy DeFranco (1952), Bud Powell (1953 and 1955–57), George Wallington (1954–56), Donald Byrd (touring Europe in 1958), Miles Davis, and Thelonious Monk. Taylor also seemed to live in Prestige's recording studios during this time.

The drummer led three dates of his own during 1957–60. **Taylor's Wailers** (Original Jazz Classics 094) has a leftover track (a version of "C.T.A." with a quartet that includes John Coltrane), but otherwise features a young all-star group in 1957 that is comprised of Donald Byrd, Jackie McLean, Charlie Rouse, Ray Bryant, and Wendell Marshall. Highlights include the original version of Bryant's "Cubano Chant" and strong renditions of Thelonious Monk's "Off Minor" and "Well You Needn't." **Taylor's Tenors** (Original Jazz Classics 1852) from 1959 is a jam session–flavored date with both Charlie Rouse and Frank Foster on tenors, along with Walter Davis and Sam Jones. In addition to originals, the quintet plays two of Monk's more jammable songs ("Rhythm-A-Ning" and "Straight No Chaser") and Jackie McLean's "Fidel." From 1960, **Art Taylor's Delight** (Blue Note 84047) has the drummer joined by trumpeter Dave Burns (formerly with the Dizzy Gillespie Big Band in the 1940s), Stanley Turrentine, Wynton Kelly, Paul Chambers, and (on three of the six songs) Patato Valdez on conga. The material is complex at times, but the musicians are certainly up to the challenge and play up to their potential.

Vibraphonists

Although Lionel Hampton and Red Norvo were still quite active, Milt Jackson was the dominant player on the vibes, with his way of interpreting blues, ballads, and standards defining the instrument. Terry Gibbs, who was Bags' equal in ability if not influence, also generated a great deal of excitement.

Teddy Charles One of the pioneers of Third Stream music (although he did not actually work with strings or classical players), vibraphonist Teddy Charles switched his attention more to record producing during the second half of the 1950s, producing more than 40 records. However, he still led his own record dates through 1960, with one of his finest sessions being **The Teddy Charles Tentet** (Atlantic 90983) from 1956. Most of this CD features an advanced group that includes Art Farmer, Gigi Gryce, J.R. Monterose, Mal Waldron, and Jimmy Raney, with the personnel expanding to 12 pieces on two numbers. The arrangements (by George Russell, Gil Evans, Jimmy Giuffre, Mal Waldron, and Charles) uplift the music, leaving room for some swinging spots by the key soloists. Although not as self-consciously classical-oriented as some of Charles's early 1950s work, this underrated gem makes his point that there was important music to be explored beyond bebop.

Victor Feldman The former boy wonder of England, Victor Feldman (who was a professional musician by the time he was seven) was a more mature 22-year-old when he toured with Woody Herman during 1956–57. He moved to Los Angeles in 1957 where he worked with the Lighthouse All-Stars, led some record dates, and became a studio musician, playing vibes, piano, and percussion.

With Mallets a Fore Thought (V.S.O.P. 13) teams Feldman with Carl Perkins, Leroy Vinnegar, Stan Levey, and (on half of the selections) Frank Rosolino, and Harold Land. This fine all-star West Coast date is full of relaxed bop and concise solos from the colorful players. While that album was originally cut for the long-defunct Interlude label, much better known is **The Arrival of Victor Feldman** (Original Jazz Classics 288), a trio session from 1958 with Scott LaFaro (who is in superior form) and Stan Levey. The music is mostly pretty boppish, including "Serpent's Tooth," "There Is No Greater Love," "Bebop," a Chopin waltz, and three diverse Feldman originals. Whether on vibes or piano, Feldman shows that he was capable of becoming a major jazz stylist; it is too bad that the studios ultimately claimed his attention.

Terry Gibbs Terry Gibbs moved to Los Angeles in 1957 where he became a busy studio musician and was a constant in local jazz clubs at night. A project dear to his heart was leading the Terry Gibbs Dream Band, a notable orchestra that was active during 1959–61.

Although its Mercury and Verve recordings remain out of print, decades later tapes of the bands' live performances were released as five sets by the Contemporary label. Three were recorded during 1959–60: **Dream Band, Vol. 1** (Contemporary 7647), **Dream Band, Vol. 2: The Sundown Sessions** (Contemporary 7652), and **Dream Band, Vol. 3: Flying Home** (Contemporary 7654). Although the repertoire is often drawn from the swing era, the arrangements (most by Bill Holman, Bob Brookmeyer, Al Cohn, Marty Paich, and Manny Albam) and soloists fit well into late 1950s bebop and cool jazz. Gibbs's hyper style keeps the music jumping, and along the way such fine players as Stu Williamson, Conte Candoli, Bob Enevoldsen, Bill Holman (on tenor), Bill Perkins, altoists Joe Maini, Charlie Kennedy, and Pete Jolly are heard from. The music swings hard, making this one of the more underrated big bands of the late 1950s.

Milt Jackson   The key soloist with the Modern Jazz Quartet, Milt Jackson toured the world with the MJQ yet also continued recording regularly with all-star groups, leading an extensive series of dates for Atlantic. **Plenty Plenty Soul** (Atlantic 1269) combines two of Jackson's sessions. The vibraphonist is heard with a nine-piece group arranged by Quincy Jones that features Cannonball Adderley in typically exuberant form, Frank Foster, baritonist Sahib Shihab, and Joe Newman, and in a sextet with Newman, Lucky Thompson (the solo star), Horace Silver, Oscar Pettiford, and Connie Kay, performing bluesy material, "Sermonette," and "Heartstrings." **Bean Bags** (Koch 8530) is a successful meeting by Jackson ("Bags") with Coleman Hawkins ("Bean"). The sextet (with Tommy Flanagan, Kenny Burrell, bassist Eddie Jones, and Connie Kay) romps through "Stuffy," "Get Happy," and a pair of Jackson originals while the key players sound quite lyrical on "Don't Take Your Love from Me." **Bags' Opus** (Blue Note 84458) has Jackson joining the future co-leaders of the Jazztet (Art Farmer and Benny Golson) along with Tommy Flanagan, Paul Chambers, and Connie Kay. The high-quality hard bop music includes early versions of two major Golson songs ("Whisper Not" and "I Remember Clifford") plus a Milt Jackson blues and John Lewis's "Afternoon in Paris." **Bags and Trane** (Atlantic 1553) has Jackson and John Coltrane making a surprisingly compatible team on three standards (a cooking "Three Little Words," "The

Night We Called It a Day," and a rapid "Bebop"), and two of Jackson's originals, including "The Late Late Blues." With Hank Jones, Paul Chambers, and Connie Kay helping out, Bags shows that he could keep up with anyone, even the rapidly emerging Coltrane.

Lem Winchester   Lem Winchester had the potential to be one of the top vibraphonists in jazz. Early in his life he played tenor, baritone, and piano before choosing to learn vibes. He worked as a police officer in Wilmington, Delaware, but after making a strong impression at the 1958 Newport Jazz Festival (when he was 30), he became a full-time musician. During 1958–60, he led five record dates. **Lem Winchester and the Ramsey Lewis Trio** (Argo 642) has not been reissued on CD yet, but it is a strong debut, matching Winchester with Lewis's popular group, mostly on bebop standards such as "Jordu," "Sandu," "Joy Spring," and "Easy to Love." **Winchester Special** (Original Jazz Classics 1718) has the vibraphonist (who was strongly influenced by Milt Jackson, but developing his own sound) in 1959 interacting with Benny Golson, Tommy Flanagan, Wendell Marshall, and Art Taylor on a boppish program, keeping up with his better-known sidemen. **Lem's Beat** (Original Jazz Classics 1785) features Winchester heading a sextet with Oliver Nelson, altoist Curtis Peagler, and a solid rhythm section, contributing three of the six songs. **Another Opus** (Original Jazz Classics 1816) puts the focus on Winchester in a quintet with flutist Frank Wess, Hank Jones, Eddie Jones, and Gus Johnson. **Lem Winchester with Feeling** (Original Jazz Classics 1900) is more laidback since it was recorded for the Moodsville subsidiary, and the emphasis is on ballads. However, Winchester's beautiful tone (in a quartet with Richard Wyands, George Duvivier, and Roy Haynes) makes this set worth picking up too.

Tragically, that session from October 7, 1960, would be Lem Winchester's final recording. On January 13, 1961, the 32-year-old was demonstrating a gun trick to a friend, and it was unsuccessful.

Other Instruments

Several jazz soloists emerged on "unusual" instruments during the 1950s including harp, flute, tuba, French horn, soprano sax, organ, and harmonica. The flute, soprano, and organ would soon become standard instruments in jazz although the harp, tuba (outside of Dixieland), French horn, and harmonica remain rarities.

Dorothy Ashby   Jazz harpists have always been very scarce in jazz. A decade after Adele Girard had made her most significant recordings, Dorothy Ashby emerged as jazz's top harpist of the 1950s. She was originally a pianist, studying at Wayne University, switching to harp in 1952. Starting in 1956, Ashby began recording in jazz settings in addition to working as a top studio and session player. Her debut, **The Jazz Harpist** (Savoy 194), teams her with flutist Frank Wess, either Wendell Marshall or Eddie Jones on bass, and drummer Ed Thigpen on three standards (including "Dancing on the Ceiling"), and four of her lightly swinging originals. The best Ashby set available is **In a Minor Groove** (Prestige 24120), which reissues the complete contents of her two 1958 albums **Hip Harp** and **In a Minor Groove**. In both cases, the harpist is joined by Wess, bassist Herman Wright, and either Art Taylor or Roy Haynes on drums. The low-volume bop-oriented sets show that Dorothy Ashby was a top-notch improviser, even if her instrument stood little chance of making much of an impact in jazz.

Buddy Collette   An important pioneer as one of the first black studio musicians, Buddy Collette was a member of the Chico Hamilton Quintet during 1955–56, but left the group because he did not want to travel away from Los Angeles. In 1956, Collette recorded his definitive album, **Man of Many Parts** (Original Jazz Classics 239). The multireedist plays flute (his strongest ax), tenor, alto, and clarinet in addition to contributing nine of the dozen selections. Among his sidemen are trumpeter Gerald Wilson (in one of his best small group dates), Barney Kessel, and Gerald Wiggins. The following year's **Nice Day with Buddy Collette** (Original Jazz Classics 747) also has Collette on his four instruments. Among the five songs that he contributes are "A Nice Day" and "Fall Winds" (which would soon be renamed "Desert Sands"), both of which Collette would shortly record with the Hamilton quintet. The three sessions that comprise this reissue have either Dick Shreve, Don Friedman, or Calvin Jackson on piano. Of lesser interest (due to the very concise treatments of the songs), but not bad is 1958's **Jazz Loves Paris** (Original Jazz Classics 1764), which has Collette performing ten tunes associated with Paris. Red Callender is heard on tuba, and the rest of the band includes Frank Rosolino, Howard Roberts, Red Mitchell, and either Bill

Douglas or Bill Richmond on drums. Highlights include "I Love Paris," "La Vie En Rose," "C'est Si Bon," and "The Song from Moulin Rouge."

Ray Draper   Ray Draper accomplished a great deal at an early age and did his best to make the tuba accepted as a solo instrument in modern jazz; only Red Callender preceded him in leading albums showcasing the tuba as a lead voice. Born August 3, 1940, Draper was only 16 when he played and recorded with Jackie McLean (1956–57) and was still a teenager when he recorded with John Coltrane (1958) and worked with Donald Byrd and Max Roach (1958–59).

Draper led four record dates during 1957–60. **Tuba Jazz** (Original Jazz Classics 1936) has the tuba player heading a sextet with trumpeter Webster Young, Jackie McLean, Mal Waldron, bassist Spanky DeBrest, and drummer Ben Dixon. Draper could be a bit awkward rhythmically (unable to play his tuba with the fluidity of a trumpet), but he fit in well with these players, performing "You're My Thrill" and originals by group members. The best-known Draper date is **Featuring John Coltrane** (Original Jazz Classics 986) although Coltrane's presence (along with pianist Gil Coggins, DeBrest, and drummer Larry Ritchie) completely overshadows Draper. The tuba/tenor front line is an unusual and generally successful sound, heard best on Sonny Rollins's "Paul's Pal" and "Under Paris Skies." Even with Ray Draper a bit out of his league, one does admire his courage. Unfortunately, drugs and an illness eventually cut short his playing career, and by his early twenties Draper was less active in the music scene, but he made an impression in the 1950s.

John Graas   One of three major jazz French horn players of the 1950s (along with Julius Watkins and David Amram), John Graas played with Stan Kenton's Innovations Orchestra (1950–51), became a studio musician in Los Angeles, and recorded fairly regularly as a leader during 1953–58, including such albums as **French Horn Jazz** and **Coup de Graas**. He was a believer in Third Stream music, combining jazz with classical music. Out of the nine albums that he led, only the last one, **International Premiere in Jazz** (V.S.O.P. 65) from 1958, has been reissued. Graas performs his 17-minute three-part "Jazz Chaconne No. 1," and four alternate takes with a nonet that includes Art Pepper, Jack Sheldon, and Buddy Collette. In addition, this CD has

Graas's four-movement "Jazz Symphony No. 1" played by the Rundfunk Symphony Orchestra with guest German musicians. There are enough jazz moments on this disc (particularly in "Jazz Chaconne No. 1") to make this a CD worth checking out.

Steve Lacy   A brilliant soprano saxophonist with a very inquisitive style whose brand of thoughtful freedom was a step beyond Lee Konitz's, Steve Lacy was considered the first "modern" soprano saxophonist when he emerged in the late 1950s. He originally doubled on clarinet, playing Dixieland in New York with Rex Stewart, Cecil Scott, Henry "Red" Allen, and other older musicians during 1952–55. Lacy debuted on record in a modernized Dixieland format with trumpeter Dick Sutton in 1954. It was certainly a major jump stylistically for him when he joined Cecil Taylor's quartet in 1955, skipping over bebop altogether to play avant-garde jazz. After a two-year stint with Taylor (they appeared at the 1957 Newport Jazz Festival), he recorded with Gil Evans, worked a few months with Thelonious Monk in 1960, and freelanced with his own groups.

Lacy led three intriguing albums during 1957–60. **Soprano Sax** (Original Jazz Classics 130) has him with Wynton Kelly, Buell Neidlinger, and Dennis Charles (Neidlinger and Charles were with Lacy in Cecil Taylor's group at the time) exploring some Duke Ellington ("Rockin' in Rhythm" and "Daydream"), Thelonious Monk ("Work"), and standards in a thoughtful and melodic fashion. ● **Reflections** (Original Jazz Classics 63) is Lacy's first of many tributes to Thelonious Monk. Joined by Mal Waldron, Neidlinger, and Elvin Jones, Lacy skips the more typical Monk songs in favor of such tunes as "Skippy," "Four in One," "Bye-Ya," and "Ask Me Now." Lacy really studied Monk's music, and, even this early, he had a real understanding for the complexities and essence of the songs. **The Straight Horn of Steve Lacy** (Candid 79007) has Lacy's soprano contrasting well with Charles Davis's baritone (with backing by bassist John Ore and Roy Haynes) on three of the most difficult Monk tunes ("Introspection," "Played Twice," and "Criss Cross") plus two Cecil Taylor compositions and Charlie Parker's "Donna Lee."

Although Steve Lacy's soprano playing would soon be overshadowed by the towering John Coltrane, he had his own distinctive sound and would continue to explore increasingly freer music in his own thoughtful fashion.

Jimmy Smith   After Jimmy Smith debuted at the Café Bohemia in 1955, he was signed by Blue Note, and the organ for the first time became a major jazz instrument. Smith's ability to transfer the innovations of Charlie Parker to the Hammond B-3 organ, his showmanship and mastery of the blues, and his high-energy performances inspired many pianists to switch to organ. Within a few years, groups comprised of organ, tenor, guitar, and drums had become both common and popular, helping to invigorate what would be called soul jazz. And, as with the best organists, Smith's work on foot pedals made the inclusion of a string bass unnecessary.

During 1956–60, Smith led no less than 25 albums for Blue Note, becoming a very popular attraction. Although a few of these dates are obscure, many of the key ones have been reissued on CD. **A New Sound, A New Star: Jimmy Smith at the Organ, Vols. 1–2** (Blue Note 57191) is a two-CD set that combines Smith's first three LPs along with four previously unreleased cuts. The organist's sound was almost mature at this point in February 1956 (although on "The Way You Look Tonight" he sounds a bit like Wild Bill Davis), and he is quite explosive on the burners, particularly a remarkable version of "The Champ" and "Lady Be Good." Smith's trio at the time consisted of either Ray Perry or Thornel Schwartz on guitar, and drummer Donald Bailey.

A limited-edition Mosaic three-CD set, **The Complete February 1957 Jimmy Smith Sessions** (Mosaic 3-154), reissues his first jam session dates, featuring Donald Byrd, Lou Donaldson, Hank Mobley, Art Blakey, and Kenny Burrell. Recorded during a busy three-day period (February 11–13, 1957), these enjoyable jams are unfortunately not available individually yet. **Jimmy Smith's House Party** (Blue Note 24542) has music from two sessions during 1957–58, featuring Smith with Lee Morgan, Curtis Fuller, George Coleman on alto, Lou Donaldson, Tina Brooks, Kenny Burrell or Eddie McFadden, and Art Blakey or Donald Bailey on various tracks, including "Just Friends," "Au Privave," and "Confirmation." The two-CD set **Groovin' at Small's Paradise** (Blue Note 99777) is a good example of how Smith sounded on a typical night in late 1957 with his regular trio (McFadden and Bailey), romping on "After Hours," "Just Friends," "Indiana," and other swinging and soulful pieces.

● **The Sermon** (Blue Note 24541), which teams Smith with Morgan, Donaldson, Brooks, Burrell, and

Blakey (quite an all-star sextet), is a classic, particularly the 20-minute title cut. **Softly as a Summer Breeze** (Blue Note 97505) is a lesser-known set, featuring Smith with two different trios on ballads, a cooking "Hackensack," and a few numbers backing the vocals of Bill Henderson. **Cool Blues** (Blue Note 84441) expands the original LP of the same name (recorded April 1958) from four to seven selections, featuring Smith with Lou Donaldson, and sometimes Tina Brooks and Art Blakey, playing blues and bop standards. **Home Cookin'** (Blue Note 53360) is an outing with Kenny Burrell, Donald Bailey, and (on four of the seven songs) the obscure but talented tenor saxophonist Percy France. The emphasis is on blues and basic material, including versions of "See See Rider," Ray Charles's "I Got a Woman," and several group originals. **Crazy Baby** (Blue Note 84030) has Smith's regular trio of 1960 (with guitarist Quentin Warren and Donald Bailey) swinging soulfully on such tunes as "When Johnny Comes Marching Home," "Makin' Whoopee," "Sonnymoon for Two," and "Mack the Knife."

Open House/Plain Talk (Blue Note 84269) has the complete contents of two albums, both recorded March 22, 1960. Smith is teamed with Blue Mitchell, Jackie McLean, Ike Quebec, Quentin Warren, and Donald Bailey. Four songs feature the full group, while the remaining ballads are showcases for Quebec ("Old Folks" and "Time After Time"), McLean ("Embraceable You"), and Mitchell ("My One, and Only Love"). A month and a few days later, Smith, Burrell, Bailey, and Stanley Turrentine recorded two more albums in a single session. **Midnight Special** (Blue Note 84078) is highlighted by the title cut, "Jumpin' the Blues," and "One o'Clock Jump," while **Back at the Chicken Shack** (Blue Note 46402) includes "When I Grow Too Old to Dream," "Messy Bessie," and a bonus cut not on the original LP, "On the Sunny Side of the Street."

There is certainly no shortage of Jimmy Smith Blue Note albums, and all can be easily enjoyed by fans of the organist.

Toots Thielemans   The first great jazz harmonica player was Larry Adler, who emerged in the 1930s. Although Adler occasionally recorded in jazz settings (including with the Quintet of the Hot Club of France and the John Kirby Sextet), he was more interested in making the harmonica "legitimate," appearing with

symphony orchestras, and in pop settings. The second great harmonica player, Toots Thielemans, has stuck to jazz throughout his productive career.

Thielemans, who was born in Belgium, started out on accordion when he was three. He began playing harmonica for a lark when he was 17, but was originally best known as a guitarist who was influenced by Django Reinhardt while being open to bop. He visited the United States for the first time in 1947, jammed with Charlie Parker at the Paris Jazz Festival of 1949, and toured Europe on guitar with the Benny Goodman Sextet in 1950. Thielemans moved to the United States in 1951, and during 1953–59 was a member of the George Shearing Quintet, mostly on guitar.

Thielemans had recorded as a leader in Paris back in 1949, and made an album for Columbia in 1955. **Man Bites Harmonica** (Original Jazz Classics 1738) from 1957 is his best early showcase, teaming him with Pepper Adams, Kenny Drew, Wilbur Ware, and Art Taylor. Toots plays harmonica on six of the eight songs (mostly standards), and shows on the straightahead material that he has no peers on his little instrument. The same would still be true 45 years later.

Julius Watkins   The Charlie Parker of the French horn, Julius Watkins co-led the hard bop-oriented group the Jazz Modes with Charlie Rouse in 1956–59. **The Jazz Modes** (Koch 8503) has Watkins and Rouse making for an appealing frontline backed by pianist Gildo Mahones, bassist Martin Rivera, and drummer Ron Jefferson or Jimmy Wormsworth, performing tunes written by either Watkins or Rouse. **The Most Happy Fella** (Koch 8507) is of greater interest for the playing of the group (which is augmented by Chino Pozo on percussion) than for the nine songs from the forgotten play. After five albums, the Jazz Modes failed to create much of a stir, and they broke up, with Rouse soon joining Thelonious Monk's quartet while Julius Watkins became a member of Quincy Jones's big band for two years.

Arrangers

While most of the major arrangers of the 1950s worked primarily in the studios, either writing for large orchestras backing singers or for movies, a few made major contributions to jazz, helping to move the music forward.

Tadd Dameron   Tadd Dameron should have been one of the busiest jazz arrangers of the second half of the 1950s based on his reputation as one of the top writers to emerge from the bebop era. He did freelance a bit and led two notable record dates. **Fontainebleau** (Original Jazz Classics 055) has Dameron performing five of his originals (including the title cut and "The Scene Is Clean") with an octet that includes Kenny Dorham, altoist Sahib Shihab, and Cecil Payne. Although the blues "Bula-Beige" is 11 minutes long, this set is rather brief at just a half-hour although the quality is quite high. **Mating Call** (Original Jazz Classics 212) is also a bit chintzy (at 34 minutes), but it is an unusual set in Dameron's discography for it puts the focus on his piano playing. Always modest about his playing, Dameron is here heard in a quartet in 1958 playing six of his songs (including "Soultrane" and "On a Misty Night") with John Coltrane, bassist John Simmons, and Philly Joe Jones.

Unfortunately, Tadd Dameron had drug problems, resulting in him spending much of 1959–61 in jail (he continued writing arrangements for other bands while behind bars), killing whatever momentum his career might have had.

Bill Holman   As a member of the Stan Kenton Orchestra during 1952–56, Bill Holman played some tenor, but was most significant as one of Kenton's most important arrangers. After leaving Kenton, he settled in Los Angeles, worked in the studios, led an occasional big band, and de-emphasized his playing in favor of his writing.

Holman led five albums during 1957–60, using top West Coast jazz musicians of the era. **The Fabulous Bill Holman** (Sackville 57188) and **Bill Holman's Great Big Band** (Creative World 1053) have not appeared on CD yet, and another set has been reissued under Richie Kamuca's name. **In a Jazz Orbit** (V.S.O.P. 25) from 1958 features a 15-piece band with such soloists as Frank Rosolino, Carl Fontana, Ray Sims (Zoot's trombonist brother), Charles Mariano, Herb Geller, Jack Sheldon, Richie Kamuca, pianist Victor Feldman, and Holman himself on tenor. The leader's arrangements for the five standards and four originals were quite distinctive (although not as complex as they would become), and this big band album still sounds fresh over four decades later. **Jive for Five** (V.S.O.P. 19) has Holman and Mel Lewis co-leading a hard-swinging quintet that also includes trumpeter Lee Katzman, Jimmy Rowles, and bassist Wilford Middlebrook. Rowles contributed "502 Blues Theme," Holman brought in two songs, and the unit also performs the obscure "Mah Lindy Lou" and two originals. Bill Holman's arrangements are a major asset, and his tenor playing (which has rarely been heard since) is excellent.

TIMELINE 1959

The Miles Davis Sextet records **Kind of Blue**. • John Coltrane records **Giant Steps**. • The Dave Brubeck Quartet records "Take Five" and "Blue à la Rondo Turk." • Lester Young and Billie Holiday die. • The Bill Evans Trio with Scott LaFaro and Paul Motian is formed. • Eric Dolphy joins the Chico Hamilton Quintet. • The Ornette Coleman Quartet performs at the Five Spot, creating a major stir in the jazz world. • Bud Powell moves to France. • The Quincy Jones Orchestra tours Europe. • Dinah Washington has a best-seller in "What a Difference a Day Makes." • The Jazztet is formed. • Jimmy Witherspoon is the hit of the 1959 Monterey Jazz Festival. • Louis Armstrong suffers a heart attack but recovers. • Danny Kaye and Louis Armstrong star in the semifictional Red Nichols biography film *The Five Pennies*. • Herbie Mann forms the Afro-Jazz Sextet. • Jean Goldkette supervises an album filled with arrangements from his 1920s band although only one alumnus (Chauncey Morehouse) is in the studio orchestra. • Drummer Ed Thigpen succeeds guitarist Herb Ellis in the Oscar Peterson Trio. • Don Redman makes his last recording, playing soprano on a Dixieland date with his Knights of the Roundtable. • Lalo Schifrin joins the Dizzy Gillespie Quintet. • Zutty Singleton starts a two-year period leading a trio at the Metropole. • Phil Napoleon records the first of three Dixieland albums with his Memphis Five for Capitol. • Flip Phillips moves to Florida where he is semiretired for the next 15 years. • Nick LaRocca (from the ODJB) adds his name to a Southland LP featuring Sharkey Bonano and can be heard speaking on a number called "LaRocca Talks." • Lizzie Miles retires from music to devote herself to religion • Ike Quebec begins a comeback after most of a decade off the scene, recording four singles for Blue Note. • Clarinetist Tony Scott, discouraged with the American jazz scene, becomes a world traveler. • The Cannonball Adderley Quintet catches on, with the success of "This Here."

Quincy Jones   As an arranger, composer, and producer, Quincy Jones would have a multifaceted career, but his early days found him mostly in the jazz world. Born in Chicago, he grew up in Seattle, learned the trumpet, and both played and arranged for the Lionel Hampton Orchestra during 1951–53, starting when he was just 18. Jones sat in the trumpet section next to Clifford Brown and Art Farmer, and learned very quickly that he was not going to be a major soloist. He wisely concentrated on arranging, not only for Hampton, but for his sidemen (including Brown, Farmer, and Gigi Gryce) when they recorded in Europe during a 1953 tour. Back in New York, Jones freelanced as an arranger for the next few years, contributing charts for bands led by Oscar Pettiford, Count Basie, Tommy Dorsey, Cannonball Adderley, and Dinah Washington among others. Jones was the musical director for the Dizzy Gillespie Big Band in 1956, and cut his first full album as a leader that year for ABC-Paramount.

This Is How I Feel About Jazz (GRP 115) reissues that set plus a few additional titles. Jones's arrangements are swinging and inspire the all-star cast (which includes Lucky Thompson, Phil Woods, and Art Farmer) on such songs as "Stockholm Sweetnin'," "Walkin'," and "Sermonette." The remainder of the CD reissues two-thirds of a slightly odd collection led and produced (but not arranged) by Jones that was originally titled **Go West, Man**. The titles show off the talents of West Coast arrangers Jimmy Giuffre, Lennie Niehaus, and Charlie Mariano. Best are three selections by an alto summit with Benny Carter, Art Pepper, Herb Geller, and Charlie Mariano, and there are also some numbers with a more conventional sax section.

Jones worked in Paris during 1957–58 for the Barclay label as an arranger and producer, on a few occasions writing for and even fronting the Harry Arnold Orchestra in Sweden. In 1959, Jones put together an all-star big band to perform for the Harold Arlen show *Free and Easy* in Europe. When the production soon collapsed, Jones managed to keep the orchestra together for a year by touring Europe.

Birth of a Band (EmArcy 822 469) from the first few months of 1959 is one of Jones's best jazz albums. Jones's arrangements feature such top players as Harry "Sweets" Edison, Zoot Sims, Sam "The Man" Taylor, Phil Woods, and Clark Terry on such songs as "The Midnight Sun Will Never Set," "Moanin'," and three Benny Golson tunes

("I Remember Clifford," "Along Came Betty," and "Whisper Not"). The personnel of the orchestra changed quite a bit and solidified during the next few months. **The Great Wide World of Quincy Jones** (EmArcy 822 470) features Jones's big band shortly before they sailed to Europe. Surprisingly, none of the selections are Jones originals, and the arrangements are by Ernie Wilkins, Bill Potts, Al Cohn, and Ralph Burns. Despite Jones's absence musically (he did conduct the group), the music sounds very much like his work, featuring solos from Phil Woods, Budd Johnson, Les Spann on guitar, and flute, Julius Watkins (on "Everybody's Blues"), Art Farmer, and two guest spots for Lee Morgan.

Two CDs have been released featuring Jones's orchestra during its 1960 stay in Europe. **Live in Paris Circa 1960** (Warner Bros. 46190) is from a February 14 concert, featuring Clark Terry, Phil Woods, Budd Johnson, and Jimmy Cleveland on such songs as "Moanin'," "Tickle Toe," and "Stockholm Sweetnin'." Terry had departed (taking an important job on the staff of a studio in New York) by the time the band performed the music released on **Swiss Radio Days Jazz Series Vol. 1** (TCB 2012). Taken from a live concert and radio broadcast recorded June 27, this boppish set features Benny Bailey, Jimmy Cleveland, Phil Woods, Jerome Richardson on tenor, and baritonist Sahib Shihab as the key soloists on arrangements by Jones, Ernie Wilkins, Billy Byers, Melba Liston, Phil Woods, and Al Cohn. But by October the musicians were back in New York, and the Quincy Jones Orchestra was history except for special engagements. It was not quite a major big band, but it produced some fine music along the way.

Michel Legrand   Michel Legrand has made his fame and fortune from writing for films, but on an occasional basis he has done some important work in jazz. In 1958, he took 11 famous jazz compositions and arranged them for three different all-star groups. ● **Legrand Jazz** (Polygram 830 074) is a classic. Ben Webster, Herbie Mann, four trombonists, and a rhythm section perform pieces by Duke Ellington, Earl Hines, Django Reinhardt ("Nuages"), and the Count Basie–associated "Blue and Sentimental." A big band with Art Farmer, Donald Byrd, and Phil Woods plays "Stompin' at the Savoy," "A Night in Tunisia," and Bix Beiderbecke's "In a Mist." The most famous session has Miles Davis, John

Coltrane, Phil Woods, Herbie Mann, and Bill Evans, plus a harpist, vibraphonist, baritone saxophonist, and a rhythm section performing music by Thelonious Monk, John Lewis, Jelly Roll Morton ("Wild Man Blues"), and Fats Waller's "Jitterbug Waltz." The arrangements are colorful and unusual, with plenty of surprises along the way.

George Russell   An important thinker, George Russell's theories helped determine jazz's future. Born in 1923, he started out as a drummer, was hospitalized with tuberculosis when he was 19, and spent his period of inactivity learning to arrange. Russell played with Benny Carter, moved to New York, and then became ill again, spending 16 months in a hospital during 1945–46. Once again he spent his time usefully, formulating the ideas for the Lydian Concept, a way of improvising off of scales rather than chords. After recovering, he wrote "Cubana Be" and "Cubana Bop" for the Dizzy Gillespie Big Band, contributed arrangements for Claude Thornhill and Artie Shaw, and composed "A Bird in Igor's Yard," a rather radical piece recorded by Buddy DeFranco.

In 1953, while working outside of music, Russell published *The Lydian Chromatic Concept of Tonal Organization*, a book that in time would influence Miles Davis, and John Coltrane among others. In 1956, he returned to music, recording **Jazz Workshop** (Koch 7850). The original program (which includes such numbers as "Ye Hypocrite, Ye Beelzebub," "Livingstone I Presume," "Ezz-thetic," and "Knights of the Steamtable") has been joined by alternate second versions of "Ballad of Hix Blewitt" and "Concerto for Billy the Kid." It is difficult to believe that Russell only utilized a sextet for this project (Art Farmer, Hal McKusick, guitarist Barry Galbraith, Bill Evans, one of two bassists, and one of three drummers) because the ensembles are frequently dense, the harmonies are quite original, and there are often several events occurring at the same time. On "Fellow Delegates," Russell plays chromatic drums while joined by Osie Johnson on wood drums; the effect is worthy of Sun Ra.

In 1957, Russell was commissioned by Gunther Schuller to write "All About Rosie" for the Brandeis University Jazz Festival. The following year's **New York, N.Y.** (Impulse 278) has five complex pieces utilizing three different all-star big bands. Most memorable is

"Manhattan" due to Jon Hendricks's catchy narration and John Coltrane's guest tenor solo, but each of the works rewards repeated listenings. Recorded in 1960, **Jazz in the Space Age** (GRP/Decca 826) has two different sessions. Pianists Bill Evans and Paul Bley and a large ensemble perform the three-part suite "Chromatic Universe," which mixes together free improvisation with written passages and "The Lydiot." The other session consists of the mysterious "Waltz from Outer Space" and the fairly free "Dimensions." No one's music in 1960 sounded like George Russell's, and his writing still sounds quite original.

Surprisingly, Russell formed a sextet around this time, playing decent piano in a group that consisted of five of his students from the School of Jazz in Lenox: trumpeter Alan Kiger, trombonist Dave Baker (who would later become a major jazz educator), altoist Dave Young, bassist Chuck Israels, and drummer Joe Hunt. **At the Five Spot** (Verve 112 287) is highlighted by "Sippin' at Bells," Carla Bley's humorous "Dance Class," and John Coltrane's "Moment's Notice." Russell only contributed one song to this date ("Swingdom Come"), but wrote the adventurous arrangements. **Stratusphunk** (Original Jazz Classics 232) was recorded a month later with the same personnel. Once again Russell contributes basic "arranger's piano," but this time he brought in three of the six songs. Carla Bley's "Bent Eagle" is one of the highlights of the intriguing set.

Thomas Talbert   After breaking up his Los Angeles big band in 1950, arranger Thomas Talbert became a freelance arranger/composer, writing for Claude Thornhill, Stan Kenton, Tony Pastor, Johnny Smith, Oscar Pettiford, Don Elliott, and singer Patty McGovern (with whom he recorded the album **Wednesday's Child**). Talbert only recorded one album of his own during this era, but it is a classic, ❶ **Bix Fats Duke** (Sea Breeze 3013). For this project, Talbert recorded three separate sessions devoted to reworkings of tunes by Fats Waller, Bix Beiderbecke, and Duke Ellington; in addition he performed his own "Green Night & Orange Bright." The colorful charts cast new light on such songs as "In a Mist," "Prelude to a Kiss," and "Clothes Line Ballet," featuring such lyrical soloists as Joe Wilder, Eddie Bert, Jimmy Cleveland, and Herb Geller. This was an inspired project, making it a bit of a surprise that there were no follow-up dates.

Jazz Vocalists

The line between jazz and middle-of-the-road pop singers was increasingly blurred during the 1950s. Many of the jazz singers occasionally recorded pop dates while the pop vocalists occasionally performed some jazz standards. This section, with a few exceptions (such as Nat King Cole and Rosemary Clooney), focuses on those singers from the period who were very committed to performing jazz.

Dave Lambert, Jon Hendricks, and Annie Ross   In 1957, Dave Lambert and Jon Hendricks began a project of recreating some of the recordings of the classic Count Basie Orchestra through vocalese. However, a few rehearsals with a group of studio singers proved to be a major struggle, and made them realize that flexible jazz singers were difficult to find. Luckily, Annie Ross was in the ensemble, and it was decided that it would be much easier if the three singers overdubbed their voices a few times for the recording instead of endlessly auditioning other vocalists. The result was the surprise hit ● **Sing a Song of Basie** (Verve 314 543 827), which launched Lambert, Hendricks, and Ross. The finest jazz vocal group since the Boswell Sisters—and arguably of all time—the musical partnership worked very well for four years. Lambert arranged for the voices, Ross added a beautiful sound, and Hendricks wrote the inventive vocalese lyrics. The CD reissue includes such notable vocalese classics as "It's Sand Man," "One o'Clock Jump," a romping "Little Pony," and "Avenue C." In addition there are three earlier efforts from 1955 by Hendricks with the Dave Lambert Singers, including impressive versions of "Four Brothers" and "Cloudburst."

The group was popular from the start, and worked often during 1958–61 including at jazz festivals. Their second project, **Sing Along with Basie** (Roulette 59041), is difficult to find on CD. Rather than just using a rhythm section, this time they had the services of the Count Basie band itself with the more memorable selections being "Jumpin' at the Woodside," "Tickle Toe," "The King," "Swingin' the Blues," and "Li'l Darlin'." Particularly special is a version of "Going to Chicago Blues," which has Joe Williams singing the regular vocal while Lambert, Hendricks, and Ross sing the horn lines around his voice. **The Swingers** (Pacific Jazz 46849) is a little obscure but up to the group's high standards. With assistance from Zoot Sims, Russ Freeman, and Jim Hall, the vocal trio swings on "Airegin," "Jackie" (a feature for Ross), "Swingin' 'Til the Girls Come Home," "Four," and "Now's the Time" among others. ● **The Hottest New Group in Jazz** (Columbia/Legacy 64933) is a two-CD set that has all of the music from the vocal ensemble's three Columbia dates of 1959–62 (**The Hottest New Group in Jazz**, **Sings Ellington**, and **High Flying**) plus four previously unissued and three very obscure selections. Virtually every one of these performances is special. The supporting groups include the Gildo Mahones Trio, Harry "Sweets" Edison, and altoist Pony Poindexter. Among the gems are "Twisted," "Cloudburst," Hendricks's hilarious "Gimme that Wine," "Everybody's Boppin'," "Cotton Tail," "All Too Soon," "Main Stem," "Farmer's Market," "Cookin' at the Continental," "Halloween Spooks," and "Popity Pop."

While **Dave Lambert Sings and Swings Alone** (United Artists 5084), an obscure LP that has never been reissued, was Lambert's only side project during the era, Annie Ross and Jon Hendricks were more active as solo singers. Jon Hendricks, who wrote, produced, and starred in "Evolution of the Blues" at the 1960 Monterey Jazz Festival (which he recorded for a 1960 LP) is heard in superior form on **A Good Git-Together** (World Pacific 1283), a near-classic LP that really should be reissued on CD. This rarity features such major sidemen as Pony Poindexter, Wes Montgomery, and both Nat and Cannonball Adderley. Hendricks sounds in top form on "Everything Started in the House of the Lord," "Social Call," and the jubilant "A Good Git-Together."

Annie Ross's Skylark (DRG 8470) was cut in 1956, a year before she teamed up with Lambert and Hendricks. A fairly straightforward set made in London without any scatting or vocalese, Ross swings on standards while backed by a quartet, showing that she could have had a very viable solo career. From 1958, **Sings a Song of Mulligan** (Pacific Jazz 46852) finds Ross in wonderful form, singing with the inventive backup of Gerry Mulligan, Chet Baker or Art Farmer, either Bill Crow or Henry Grimes on bass, and drummer Dave Bailey. Ross is particularly appealing on "I've Grown Accustomed to Your Face," "Give Me the Simple Life," "How About You," and "The Lady's in Love with You." From 1959, **A Gasser** (Pacific Jazz 46854) is on the same high level. This time Ross is joined by either Zoot Sims or (on two numbers) Bill Perkins on tenor, pianist Russ Freeman, Billy Bean or Jim Hall on guitar, bassist

Monty Budwig, and Mel Lewis or Frank Capp on drums. Ross's renditions of such tunes as "I'm Nobody's Baby," "Invitation to the Blues," "I Didn't Know About You," and "You Took Advantage of Me" are highlights, and there are also five instrumentals from the sessions (featuring Sims and Freeman) originally released on samplers.

Mose Allison   The unique Mose Allison debuted as a leader on records in 1957. After attending college and serving in the army, he began working as a professional in 1950, mostly playing down South until moving to New York in 1956. Allison's background as a pianist was not only in jazz but also country blues, and he always had a distinctive singing voice. Although he worked in instrumental groups with Al Cohn, Zoot Sims, Stan Getz, and Bob Brookmeyer, it would be as a singer/pianist who wrote his own material that Allison would become famous. He recorded six trio albums for Prestige during 1957–59, but these were mostly filled with instrumentals, with Allison averaging just two vocals per album. While the music has been reissued in full on five fine CDs, of which **Back Country Suite** (Original Jazz Classics 075) is most significant, a sampler titled **Greatest Hits** (Original Classics 6004) is the best buy, as it has all of Allison's early vocals plus three instrumentals, including his one recorded trumpet solo, a King Oliver–inspired spot on "Trouble in Mind." The vocals include memorable versions of "The Seventh Son," "Lost Mind," "Parchman Farm," and "Young Man's Blues." It must have seemed clear even at that early time that Allison's future lay in songwriting and singing.

Ernestine Anderson   Ernestine Anderson, a soulful singer who was already a veteran by the time she turned 30 in 1958, had an opportunity to record her first album that year. Back in 1943, she had sung with Russell Jacquet's group, she made her recording debut in 1947, and had stints working with both Johnny Otis (1947–49) and Lionel Hampton (1952–53). After recording with Gigi Gryce in 1955, she toured Scandinavia with Rolf Ericson in 1956, and made a strong impression. Her album for the Swedish Metronome label, **Hot Cargo**, was popular, and back in the United States she signed with the Mercury label. Her albums for Mercury (1958–60) are all scarce except **Ernestine Anderson** (Mercury 314 514 076) from 1958. The playing time is brief on most of the numbers (including a 59-second version of "There Will Never Be Another

You"), but she is in fine form on such songs as Gryce's "Social Call" (which she made her own), "A Sleepin' Bee," and "My Ship."

Oscar Brown, Jr.   Oscar Brown, Jr., a talented lyricist and singer who was also an important social commentator and playwright, made his recording debut in 1960. Brown, who was born in 1926, took a while before he started finding success. He acted on a regular network radio soap opera while in high school, and along the way worked in public relations, real estate, advertising, and politics (running unsuccessfully for office). It was as a songwriter that he initially found his niche, writing "Brown Baby" (recorded by gospel singer Mahalia Jackson) and working with Max Roach on the "Freedom Now Suite." ❍ **Sin & Soul…and Then Some** (Columbia/Legacy 64994) reissues Brown's debut recording (adding five previously unreleased selections) and is a true classic. His lyrics to "Work Song," "Watermelon Man," "Afro-Blue," and particularly "Dat Dere" are famous, "But I Was Cool," and "Signifyin' Money" are humorous, "Bid 'Em In" is a chilling depiction of a slave auction, and "Rags and Old Iron" is quite touching. This is an essential release from a masterful talent who is also a dramatic yet often witty singer.

Hoagy Carmichael   Although he largely left jazz by 1935 when he moved to California, Hoagy Carmichael was always a big fan of the early style. Through the years, many of his songs have been performed a countless number of times by jazz musicians (including "Stardust," "Georgia on My Mind," "Up the Lazy River," "Rockin' Chair," "The Nearness of You," "In the Cool, Cool, Cool of the Evening," "Skylark," and "New Orleans" among others). Carmichael appeared in 14 films during 1935–54, including *Young Man with a Horn*, usually playing a wisecracking pianist who sang. Carmichael recorded on an occasional basis through the years with the last significant project being 1956's **Hoagy Sings Carmichael** (Pacific Jazz 46862). Sticking to vocals, Carmichael performs ten of his compositions and is accompanied by an 11-piece all-star jazz group that includes trumpeters Harry "Sweets" Edison and Don Fagerquist, Art Pepper, and Jimmy Rowles. The matchup works quite well, for Hoagy's songs have long been viable devices for jazz improvising. It is a pity that this was the only time that Carmichael (who felt neglected during his later years) was teamed with modern jazz players.

Betty Carter   Betty Carter (born Lillie Mae Jones) made her first significant recordings in 1956, and, although she was not yet the innovative singer that she would become, she already had an original voice and conception. She studied piano and began working as a singer in 1946 in Detroit. During 1948–51, she was with the Lionel Hampton Orchestra, touring as Lorraine Carter. Due to her boppish scat singing, she was nicknamed "Betty Bebop," a name she disliked; however, she did adopt Betty as her first name. After leaving Hampton, she freelanced around New York, recording "Red Top" with King Pleasure. On **Meet Betty Carter and Ray Bryant** (Columbia/Legacy 64936), Carter is heard on 11 songs either with a big band arranged by Gigi Gryce or with a quartet that includes Ray Bryant and Jerome Richardson on flute. During such numbers as Gryce's "Social Call" (with classic words by Jon Hendricks), "Let's Fall in Love," "Moonlight in Vermont," "I Could Write a Book," and "Tell Him I Said Hello," Carter sings fairly conventionally, but her dark voice and slightly unusual phrasing stand out. The remainder of this CD is comprised of eight instrumentals by the Bryant trio. ◗ **I Can't Help It** (GRP/Impulse 114) has all of the music from Carter's next two albums, recorded in 1958 and 1960. She is heard with a sextet and tentet that include such players as altoist Gryce, Richardson (on tenor, flute, and bass clarinet), Kenny Dorham, and trumpeter Ray Copeland, and with an unidentified orchestra arranged by Richard Wess. The 24 selections are mostly pretty concise, but quite a few are memorable including "I Can't Help It" (which discusses her musical philosophy and need to be individual), "You're Getting to Be a Habit with Me," "You're Driving Me Crazy," "What a Little Moonlight Can Do," "I Don't Want to Set the World on Fire," and "Jazz (Ain't Nothin' but Soul)." However, it would be a couple of decades before Betty Carter began to receive the recognition that she deserved.

June Christy   June Christy, who recorded regularly for Capitol during her prime years, is in excellent shape on **The Misty Miss Christy** (Capitol 98452). Backed by an orchestra filled with West Coast jazz all-stars (with arrangements from Pete Rugolo), the singer is in particularly rewarding form on "I Didn't Know About You," "Day Dream," "Dearly Beloved," "The Wind," and "There's No You." Also well worth picking up from this era are **Gone for the Day** (Capitol 95448), and **The**

Song Is June (Capitol 55455), both of which are really single CD two-fers. **Gone for the Day** not only has the dozen songs from the original LP (which deals with enjoying the weather and having a peaceful life), but all of the music from the complementary album **Fair and Warmer**; both date from 1957. Highlights include "When the Sun Comes Out," "Love Turns Winter to Spring," "Lazy Afternoon," "Imagination," and "When Sunny Gets Blue." **The Song Is June** also includes the full album **Off Beat**, emphasizes ballads, and has memorable versions of "Spring Can Really Hang You Up the Most," "Nobody's Heart," "Night Time Was My Mother," "Out of this World," and "A Sleepin' Bee."

Still only 35 when 1960 ended, June Christy should have had many years of singing ahead of her, but she would soon fade from the scene, losing her interest in performing.

Rosemary Clooney   Not really a jazz singer (any more than Frank Sinatra or Tony Bennett), Rosemary Clooney nevertheless always had a feel for jazz and for swinging lyrics. She first gained recognition along with Betty Clooney as one of the teenaged Clooney Sisters featured with Tony Pastor's big band in the late 1940s. After going out on her own in 1950, she had a variety of pop hits (most notably the novelty "Come On-A My House") and appeared in four movies, including *White Christmas* with Bing Crosby (a friend for decades) and Danny Kaye. In 1956, Clooney surprised many listeners by sounding quite effective singing (via overdub) with the Duke Ellington Orchestra on **Blue Rose** (Columbia/Legacy 65506). Billy Strayhorn, in addition to writing most of the arrangements, coached Clooney, and the results are rewarding, with memorable versions of 11 songs including "I Let a Song Go Out of My Heart," "It Don't Mean a Thing," "Blue Rose" (on which she sings wordlessly), and "I'm Checkin' Out Goombye." Harry Carney, Ray Nance, Johnny Hodges, and Jimmy Hamilton are the key soloists on Rosemary Clooney's most significant jazz session of the 1950s.

Nat King Cole   By 1956, Nat King Cole had been working as a very popular middle-of-the-road pop singer for six years. Some jazz writers called him a sellout since he rarely played piano (except as a novelty) or sang jazz, but Cole never lost his ability to play jazz. ◗ **The Complete After Midnight Sessions** (Capitol 48328) in 1956 features Cole back in a trio format (with guitarist John Collins and bassist Charlie Harris), sort of. Lee Young on drums actually makes the rhythm section four pieces, and each song has one of four added soloists: altoist Willie Smith, trumpeter Harry "Sweets" Edison, valve trombonist Juan Tizol, or violinist Stuff Smith. In addition, the 17 numbers (expanded from a dozen on the original LP) all have vocals by Cole. However, the music is swinging and fun, with the highlights including "Just You, Just Me," "Sweet Lorraine," "It's Only a Paper Moon," "I Know that You Know," "Route 66," and "Candy." Nat King Cole was also frequently heard in jazz-oriented settings during his 1956–57 television show, a breakthrough for a black artist although the lack of sponsors resulted in the historic series being short-lived.

However, the return to jazz was brief, and soon Cole was back to recording ballad-oriented string albums such as **Love Is the Thing** and **The Very Thought of You**. In 1958, Cole did cut a fine set with the Count Basie Orchestra (Gerald Wiggins filled in on piano). Cole shows on the first 12 songs included on **Big Band Cole** (Capitol 96259) that he could have been quite effective as a big band vocalist if he had wanted to stick to more jazz-oriented settings. Also included on this recommended set are five numbers cut with the Stan Kenton Orchestra in 1950 and 1960–61, including two versions of "Orange Colored Sky."

But these brief departures aside, Nat King Cole (who starred as W.C. Handy in the rather abominable 1958 film *St. Louis Blues*) was largely lost to jazz by the late 1950s.

Earl Coleman   Earl Coleman certainly had an episodic career. A warm ballad singer whose baritone voice was strongly influenced by Billy Eckstine, Coleman sang with Ernie Fields, Jay McShann (1943), Earl Hines (1944, when he succeeded Eckstine), King Kolax, and McShann a second time. In 1947, Charlie Parker insisted that Coleman have the opportunity to sing two songs on Bird's comeback date with Erroll Garner: "Dark Shadows" and the hit "This Is Always." After recording 11 songs in 1948 (including five with Fats Navarro), Coleman was largely off records until 1977, other than a few numbers on Sonny Rollins and Elmo Hope records, an obscure album for Atlantic in 1967, and 1956's **Earl Coleman Returns** (Original Jazz Classics 187). Still just 31 at the time, Coleman is heard giving definitive treatment to such songs as Gigi Gryce's "Social Call," "Say It Isn't So," and "It's You or No One." In addition to the original six

numbers (which have him backed by a group featuring Art Farmer, and sometimes Gryce), Coleman is heard on four songs (including a remake of "This Is Always") taken from Gene Ammons sessions from the year before. Earl Coleman is so strong throughout this program that it is strange to think that he would be barely documented during the next 20 years.

Chris Connor   Cool-toned jazz vocalists were at the height of their popularity during the second half of the 1950s. Chris Connor was certainly quite busy, making four records for Atlantic in 1956 alone, and enough music for 14 albums overall during 1956–60. **Chris Connor/He Loves Me, He Loves Me Not** (Collectables 6239) reissues two of her first Atlantics on one CD, but strangely enough replacing two songs on the former LP with unissued versions of "Circus" and "Flying Home." No matter, this set is a particularly good buy. The Chris Connor date has plenty of variety, with Connor accompanied either by a large orchestra arranged by Ralph Burns, a rhythm quartet led by John Lewis, or a six-horn tentet. She shows off her versatility on "Something to Live For," "Get Out of Town," "Almost Like Being in Love," and "Flying Home" while the other set is ballad-oriented and features the Ralph Burns Orchestra in support. Best of the ballads are "Angel Eyes," "Oh You Crazy Moon," and "I Guess I'll Hang My Tears Out to Dry." **I Miss You So/Witchcraft** (Collectables 6814) is a two-CD set reissuing two of the other Atlantics. **I Miss You So** is a so-so date from 1956 that has rather low jazz content (even "My Ideal" and "Speak Low"), and too many current pop tunes, all weighed down by Ray Ellis's arrangements for a string orchestra and distracting background voices. **Witchcraft** is better, with Connor joined by a big band arranged by Richard Wess, and swinging such numbers as Alec Wilder's "The Lady Sings the Blues," "How Little We Know," "Baltimore Oriole," and "Skyscraper Blues."

Chris in Person/Sings George Gershwin (Collectables 6887) has an excellent live appearance from 1959 (recorded at the Village Vanguard with Kenny Burrell) plus ten songs from a Gershwin set. **Sings the George Gershwin Almanac of Song** (Atlantic 601) is a two-CD set that includes the same ten performances plus other Gershwin selections, both from the same sessions and other unrelated dates. Joe Newman, Al Cohn, Herbie Mann, Milt Jackson, and pianist Ralph Sharon are in the backup groups, taking short solos.

⦿ **A Jazz Date with Chris Connor/Criss Craft** (Rhino 71747) is a perfect place to begin in exploring Chris Connor's singing since it reissues two of her finest Atlantic albums on one CD. She is backed by top-notch rhythm sections with either Ralph Sharon or Stan Free as pianist/arranger, and there are occasional horn solos, including Joe Wilder, Sam Most, Al Cohn, Lucky Thompson, and Bobby Jaspar. The 30-year-old singer is heard at her prime on memorable and sometimes haunting versions of "Poor Little Rich Girl," "Lonely Town," "I'm Shooting High," "Moonlight in Vermont," and "Johnny One Note."

Blossom Dearie   Blossom Dearie (her real name) has always been considered a bit unusual because her singing voice sounds like a little girl, which is a strong contrast to the sophisticated lyrics she writes and her fluent piano playing. After graduating from high school, she worked with the Blue Flames (which sometimes performed with Woody Herman) and the Blue Reys, a group that sang with Alvino Rey. Dearie moved to Paris in 1952 and formed the Blue Stars of France (which had a hit in 1954 with a French version of "Lullaby of Birdland"). She appeared in a nightclub act with Annie Ross, took a brief chorus on King Pleasure's "Moody's Mood for Love" and recorded for Barclay (1955–56). Norman Granz signed Dearie to Verve, and she made some of her finest recordings (and her best known albums) for that label during 1956–60. She was also married to Bobby Jaspar during this period.

Blossom Dearie (Verve 837 934) has the singer/pianist joined by Ray Brown and Jo Jones. In addition to the original 14 songs (a couple of French tunes and a variety of swing standards), there are three previously unreleased numbers, including 1959's "Blossom's Blues." **Give Him the Ooh-La-La** (Verve 517 067) has Herb Ellis joining Brown and Jones in the backup group, which includes Dearie's piano. Although this set has a few standards, it is the lesser-known material such as Cy Coleman's "The Riviera," "Bang Goes the Drum," "I Walk a Little Faster," and the title cut that stand out. **Sings Comden and Green** (Verve 589 102) has Dearie interpreting the music of Betty Comden and Adolph Green in successful fashion. Dearie's fragile voice (supported by Brown and Ed Thigpen) is typically restrained yet witty on such numbers as "Just in Time," "The Party's Over," "Lonely Town," "Lucky to Be Me," and especially "Some Other Time."

Bob Dorough   Bob Dorough in some ways was the male Blossom Dearie, although there are differences. A fine jazz pianist and a distinctive singer who writes unusual lyrics full of his dry wit and his slightly skewed view of the world, Dorough started out on piano as a teenager. He played for Sugar Ray Robinson (during a brief period when the boxer was trying to have a second career as an entertainer), lived in Paris during 1954–55 (sometimes working with Blossom Dearie), and then back in the United States he recorded his first album in 1956.

⦿ **Devil May Care** (Bethlehem 75994) is a pretty definitive set. Joined by his longtime bassist Bill Takas, drummer Jerry Segal, and sometimes trumpeter Warren Fitzgerald and vibraphonist Jack Hitchcock, Dorough performs memorable renditions of such songs as "Devil May Care" (which became his greatest hit), "Old Devil Moon," "Yardbird Suite" (which uses his words), "Baltimore Oriole," and "Johnny One Note." But Dorough was never commercial enough to catch on in the pop or jazz worlds, and he would only record infrequently throughout his long career.

Billy Eckstine   Billy Eckstine was rarely heard in jazz settings in the 1950s, but he always retained his love for swinging standards. On 1960's **No Cover, No Minimum** (Roulette 98593), Eckstine takes a few surprisingly effective trumpet solos. He is heard singing 24 songs (13 previously unissued) during one night in Las Vegas, backed by an orchestra arranged by his longtime pianist Bobby Tucker. Eckstine's influential baritone voice was at the peak of its powers around this time, and the music straddles the boundary between middle-of-the-road pop and jazz on such numbers as "I've Grown Accustomed to Her Face," "Without a Song," "Prisoner of Love," "I Apologize," "Alright, Okay, You Win," and "'Deed I Do." But this recording was a rarity, and few of Billy Eckstine's later albums are as jazz-oriented.

Cliff Edwards   Cliff Edwards, as Ukulele Ike, had been one of the first male jazz singers on record in the mid-1920s. He introduced "Singin' in the Rain," became a B-movie actor, drank away his earnings, and had an unexpected comeback in the late 1930s by becoming the voice of Jiminy Cricket in *Pinocchio*, singing "When You Wish Upon a Star." Although he continued working in radio for a time, by the late 1940s he was completely forgotten again. In 1956, the alcoholic Edwards had one last chance to make a comeback, performing on **Ukulele Ike Sings Again** (Disney 60408). He is in surprisingly good form, singing with enthusiasm, and sounding like he was still in his musical prime. Edwards is joined by the Wonderland Jazz Band, a Dixieland group connected with Disney studios, and including trumpeter Don Kinch, clarinetist George Probert, pianist Marvin Ash, bassist Jess Bourgeois, drummer Nick Fatool, and leader George Bruns on trombone and tuba. Edwards mostly sings tunes from the 1920s, including "Singin' in the Rain," "I'll See You in My Dreams," "At Sundown," "Sunday," and "Swingin' Down the Lane," even taking a couple of his trademark scat solos (although he does not play ukulele or kazoo as in the early days). But this happy occasion would be Cliff Edwards's final act in music even though he lived for another 16 years.

Ella Fitzgerald   With Norman Granz initially starting the Verve label specifically to record Ella Fitzgerald (although his other Norgran and Clef artists were soon also recording for Verve), it is not surprising that he recorded Ella prolifically during 1956–60.

The most ambitious project was the Songbook series in which Ella recorded extensive programs of the works of specific composers. **The Complete Ella Fitzgerald Songbooks** (Verve 314 519 832 8487) is a 16-CD box set that features her interpreting the music of Cole Porter, Rodgers and Hart, Duke Ellington, Irving Berlin, George and Ira Gershwin, Harold Arlen, Jerome Kern, and lyricist Johnny Mercer. All of these projects from 1956–64 are also available individually. Ella, who was at her peak during this era, sings beautifully throughout, but many of the projects are fairly straight, with the singer emphasizing the words and melodies rather than improvising much, while being backed by unadventurous orchestras. Because Ella tended to always sound happy, some of the interpretations are less than definitive, but her voice is so appealing that one really does not mind. Both **Sings the Cole Porter Songbook** (Verve 537 257) and **Sings the Rodgers and Hart Songbook** (Verve 537 258) are two-CD sets with Ella joined by an orchestra arranged by Buddy Bregman on 35 performances apiece. **Sings the Duke Ellington Songbook** (Verve 837 035) is much more interesting from a jazz standpoint because the first half is with the Duke Ellington Orchestra while the other cuts feature Ella in a small

group with Stuff Smith, Ben Webster, and Oscar Peterson. **Sings the Irving Berlin Songbook** (Verve 829 533) has Ella joined by a big band arranged by Paul Weston, and it is a two-CD set with 32 songs. Recorded in 1959, **Sings the George and Ira Gershwin Songbook** (Verve 539 759) is the most ambitious of these projects, consisting of 73 songs reissued on four CDs, as Ella sounds quite exuberant while joined by Nelson Riddle's orchestra. **Sings the Harold Arlen Songbook** (Verve 589 108) from 1960 was the last of the songbooks for three years, consisting of 28 songs on two CDs with Billy May's orchestra giving Ella a more jazz-oriented accompaniment than usual.

The combination of Ella Fitzgerald and Louis Armstrong is one of the most beloved of all time. Their mutual love and obvious abilities resulted in three strong projects: **Ella and Louis** (Verve 825 373), **Ella and Louis Again** (Verve 825 374), and **Porgy & Bess** (Verve 827 475). The three-CD set **Complete Ella Fitzgerald & Louis Armstrong on Verve** (Verve 537 284) has all of this music plus two cuts from a 1956 Hollywood Bowl concert. The first two collaborations have the singers joined by the Oscar Peterson Quartet with Satch playing occasional trumpet. The playful interaction between Ella and Louis is delightful. The **Porgy & Bess** set is a bit odd, with Armstrong and Fitzgerald singing all of the parts (even if they do not fit their characters), and the Russ Garcia arrangements for an orchestra are just okay, but once again the vocalists' playfulness makes it all worthwhile.

Ella Fitzgerald also recorded many solo non-songbook albums during this period. **Get Happy** (Verve 314 523 3217), **Like Someone in Love** (Verve 314 511 5247), and **Ella Swings Brightly** (Verve 314 519 3477) are all sets with orchestras. **Get Happy** is a mixture of material, **Like Someone in Love** is with the Frank Devol Orchestra and guest Stan Getz, and **Ella Swings Brightly** is an encounter with Nelson Riddle. None of these dates are classics, but they gave the singer an opportunity to perform songs not covered in the Songbook series.

Ella at the Opera House (Verve 831 2697) is a strong jazz date with the Oscar Peterson Trio that includes similar sets from two separate nights. The pair of nine-song sets have eight repeats but of course different solos. **Ella in Rome: The Birthday Concert** (Verve 835 454) has Fitzgerald celebrating her 40th birthday while joined by pianist Lou Levy, bassist Max Bennett, and drummer Gus Johnson. Ella puts on her usual show of the period, including "St. Louis Blues," "Caravan," "It's All Right with Me," "I Can't Give You Anything but Love" (during which she imitates both Louis Armstrong and pianist/singer Rose Murphy), and a closing "Stompin' at the Savoy" with the Oscar Peterson Trio. But the most memorable of all of these recordings is ◉ **The Complete Ella in Berlin** (Verve 314 519 584). This February 13, 1960, concert became famous because Ella forgot the words to "Mack the Knife" and made up her own hilarious lyrics along the way. Also included are swinging versions of "Gone with the Wind," "The Lady Is a Tramp," and "Too Darn Hot."

In reality, the First Lady of Song could do no wrong, and her performance of "Mack the Knife" by itself would have made her immortal.

Nancy Harrow   Nancy Harrow made a big impression with her first recording, **Wild Women Don't Have the Blues** (Candid 79008), although it would be some time before she was able to make a full-time living as a singer. Harrow had had classical piano lessons from the age of seven and worked a bit as a dancer before becoming a singer. Her Candid set features her singing such older songs as "All Too Soon," "On the Sunny Side of the Street," the seven-minute "Blues for Yesterday," and the title cut (one of classic blues singer Ida Cox's most famous tunes). Harrow was influenced a little by Billie Holiday but was actually a more modern singer than the material she performed at the time. She is assisted by Buck Clayton (who provided the arrangements), Buddy Tate, Dickie Wells, and Dick Wellstood on this spirited, enthusiastic, and memorable outing.

Bill Henderson   Bill Henderson was in some ways the last in a line of male singers who followed in the tradition of Big Joe Turner, Joe Williams, and Ernie Andrews, although he always had his own personality. He began singing professionally in 1952, performed with Ramsey Lewis in his native Chicago, and moved to New York a few years later. Henderson recorded "Señor Blues" with Horace Silver (which was a minor hit), was backed by the Jimmy Smith Trio on four songs released as 45s in 1958, and recorded regularly for the Vee-Jay label during 1959–61. **Complete Vee-Jay Recordings, Vol. 1** (Koch 8548) has Henderson backed by the Ramsey Lewis Trio on seven numbers, accompanied by an all-star sextet (with Booker Little and Yusef Lateef performing arrangements by Benny Golson), and joined by a Count Basie–oriented octet arranged by Frank Wess. He has the assistance of the MJT + 3 on one number and is backed by an orchestra on the final two songs. Among the more memorable performances of this definitive set are "Bye Bye Blackbird," "It Never Entered My Mind," "Moanin'," and "Sleeping Bee."

Helen Humes   The former Count Basie band singer, who had had a successful solo career in the late 1940s, continued working as a single throughout the 1950s. She hardly recorded at all during 1953–58, but then made two of her greatest albums for Contemporary in 1959–60. **'Tain't Nobody's Biz-Ness If I Do** (Original Jazz Classics 453) finds Humes at age 45 at the peak of her powers. Assisted by Benny Carter (on trumpet), Frank Rosolino, Teddy Edwards, Andre Previn, Leroy Vinnegar, and either Shelly Manne or Mel Lewis on drums, Humes is quite appealing throughout this set, singing with great enthusiasm and displaying a wonderful voice. Among the more memorable numbers are "You Can Depend on Me," "When I Grow Too Old to Dream," and the title cut. Even better is ◉ **Songs I Like to Sing** (Original Jazz Classics 171) from 1960. The superior songs, superb backup, and the swinging Marty Paich arrangements make this Humes's definitive set. Her versions of "If I Could Be with You," "You're Driving Me Crazy," and her "Million Dollar Secret" are classic. She is joined by either Ben Webster, a rhythm section, and a string quartet, or a 14-piece band that includes Webster, Teddy Edwards, and Art Pepper. This gem is one of the high points of the veteran singer's career.

Eddie Jefferson   Eddie Jefferson, the founder of vocalese, was initially overshadowed by King Pleasure, who had the hit recordings of Jefferson's "Moody's Mood for Love" and "Parker's Mood." Jefferson worked with James Moody's group during 1955–57 and then freelanced on his own. In 1959, he cut his first full album, ◉ **The Jazz Singer** (Evidence 22062). This CD mostly dates from 1959–61, and has Jefferson backed by several horns (including Howard McGhee and Moody) and sometimes three other vocalists. The many highlights include Jefferson's original classic versions of "Body and Soul" (a tribute to Coleman Hawkins, the "king of the saxophone") and "So What" (based on the already famous Miles Davis recording), a remake of "Moody's

Mood for Love," and vocalese adaptations of a few Lester Young and Charlie Parker solos. There are also some unissued tracks including "Silly Little Cynthia" from 1964 (a duet with pianist Tommy Tucker), and a meeting with guitarist Louisiana Red on 1965's "Red's New Dream." This is the one Eddie Jefferson record to get, although all of his recordings are worth acquiring.

Etta Jones   After a false start, Etta Jones's career really got going in 1960. She had actually made her recording debut on December 29, 1944, when she was 16, recording a few songs associated with Dinah Washington. The recording **1944–1947** (Classics 1065) has Jones's first five sessions as a leader (with such sidemen as Barney Bigard, Georgie Auld, Budd Johnson, and Joe Newman), and guest spots with Pete Johnson, sounding quite credible on "Among My Souvenirs," "I Sold My Heart to the Junkman," "The Richest Guy in the Graveyard," and "Misery Is a Thing Called Moe." But it would be a decade before she led any more sessions. In the interim she worked with J.C. Heard (1948) and Earl Hines, cut an obscure album in 1957 for King, and matured as a singer. In 1960, her version of "Don't Go to Strangers" became her trademark song, and her greatest hit. **Don't Go to Strangers** (Original Jazz Classics 298) finds Jones in superior form on all ten selections, mixing together the dramatic ability of Abbey Lincoln and some of the expressive qualities of late-period Billie Holiday with her own personality. Joined by Frank Wess (on flute and tenor), pianist Richard Wyands, guitarist Skeeter Best, bassist George Duvivier, and Roy Haynes, Jones excels on "Fine and Mellow," "If I Had You," "Bye Bye Blackbird," and of course the title cut. The follow-up album, **Hollar** (Original Jazz Classics 1061), is comparable, with Jones mostly interpreting swing standards with plenty of feeling including "I Got It Bad," "The More I See You," and "Our Love Is Here to Stay," with the assistance of Oliver Nelson, Lem Winchester, and Richard Wyands.

Barbara Lea   Identified with swing and Dixieland, but actually a well-rounded singer who loves older standards, Barbara Lea sang with Detroit-area dance orchestras while in school. She performed with the Crimson Stompers while attending Harvard, cut a record for Riverside in 1955, and made two gems during 1956–57. **Barbara Lea** (Original Jazz Classics 1713) finds her remaining true to the lyrics of such songs as "Nobody

Else but You," "I'm Comin' Virginia," and "Baltimore Oriole," swinging lightly and making the songs her own. While that session has her joined by the sensitive trumpeter Johnny Windhurst, Dick Cary (doubling on piano and alto horn), and a rhythm section, **Lea in Love** (Original Jazz Classics 1742) adds baritonist Ernie Caceres, Garvin Bushell (oboe, and bassoon), Jimmy Raney, and (on "True Love") harpist Adele Girard to a group also featuring Windhurst and Cary. The interpretations are straightforward, heartfelt, and sometimes touching with Lea sounding at her best on "You'd Be So Nice to Come Home To," "Mountain Greenery," and "More than You Know." But despite her talents, Barbara Lea never really caught on with the general public, and it would be 19 years before she led her next record.

Abbey Lincoln   Abbey Lincoln was all set to have a career as a glamorous supper club singer when she took a left turn. She had sung pop standards under a variety of names (including Anna Marie, Gaby Lee, and Gaby Woodridge) before settling on Abbey Lincoln. Her debut recording, **Affair** (Blue Note 81199) from 1956 when she was 26, finds her voice sounding recognizable although many of the ballads are rather lightweight. She is backed by anonymous orchestras arranged by Benny Carter, Jack Montrose, and Marty Paich.

By the time she had made her second recording, **That's Him** (Original Jazz Classics 085) in 1957, she had come under the influence of Max Roach (who would become her husband) and had altered her style to that of a dramatic jazz singer. With Billie Holiday as her main inspiration, Lincoln from then on only interpreted songs that she believed in. She is joined by quite an all-star roster (Sonny Rollins, Kenny Dorham, Wynton Kelly, Paul Chambers, and Roach), and shows that she was already a major jazz singer with a style of her own. Among the numbers are "I Must Have that Man," an emotional "Don't Explain," Oscar Brown, Jr.'s "Strong Man," and an unaccompanied "Tender as a Rose."

It's Magic (Original Jazz Classics 205) includes "I Am in Love," "An Occasional Man," "Out of the Past," and Randy Weston's "Little Niles" in a repertoire that was becoming more challenging all the time. Lincoln is joined by Kenny Dorham or Art Farmer, Curtis Fuller, Benny Golson, Jerome Richardson or Sahib Shihab, Wynton Kelly, Paul Chambers or Sam Jones, and Philly Joe Jones. Recorded in 1959, **Abbey Is Blue** (Original Jazz Classics

069) is particularly emotional and full of chance-taking, highlighted by the first ever vocal version of "Afro Blue," "Come Sunday," "Softly as in a Morning Sunrise," and "Long as You're Living." Dorham is prominent on a few numbers, while Roach's quintet plays on three songs.

Based on the three Riverside recordings (all in the OJC series), Abbey Lincoln was the most potentially significant new female jazz singer of the era, and this was reinforced by her singing on Max Roach's **Freedom Now Suite**. Her next projects would find her growing rapidly in power and importance.

Carmen McRae Carmen McRae recorded steadily for Decca during 1955–58, a period when she began to get fairly well known, partly due to the publicity she received from her champion, writer Ralph Gleason. Several CDs have been released that serve as samplers of this era for her even though a complete reissue of her Decca recordings has not taken place yet. The best of these reissues, **Here to Stay** (GRP/Decca 610), draws its material from the 1955 small group album **By Special Request**, and a 1959 record with the Ernie Wilkins Orchestra (**Something to Swing About**). McRae excels in both settings and could hit high notes that she would not even think of attempting in her later years. An emotional "Supper Time" (which has McRae on piano) and "Something to Live For" (with its composer Billy Strayhorn on piano) are among the more classic performances on this excellent disc. **I'll Be Seeing You** (GRP/Decca 647) is a two-CD set that has some indifferent numbers with orchestras (the arrangements are more middle-of-the-road pop than jazz), but also a fine 1957 set with just a rhythm section and a couple of guest appearances by Ben Webster. Best are "Whatever Lola Wants," "Perdido," "Exactly Like You," "Bye Bye Blackbird," and "Flamingo." **Sings Great American Songwriters** (GRP/Decca 631) has 20 selections taken from ten different sessions with McRae joined by the Mat Mathews Quintet (featuring Herbie Mann), the Ray Bryant Trio, and various orchestras. The tunes are excellent, and McRae's voice was clearly in its early prime.

But perhaps it is time for a true "best of" early Carmen McRae set or, better yet, a large box reissuing all of her recordings from this period.

Helen Merrill Helen Merrill has received the box set that Carmen McRae also deserves. The three-CD set ● **The Complete Helen Merrill on Mercury** (Mercury 826 340) is an unbeatable box. Only two selections for the Roost label in 1953 precede these definitive recordings from 1954–57. Merrill could hold her own with the best jazz musicians of the era, as she shows on her classic encounter with Clifford Brown. Almost as significant is a notable album on which she employed the little-known Gil Evans as arranger, a year before he teamed up with Miles Davis for **Miles Ahead**. His charts perfectly fit her voice and challenge her to improvise at her peak of creativity. Other Mercury dates include work with the Johnny Richards Orchestra, arranger Hal Mooney, Bobby Jaspar, and Bill Evans. Among the many highlights are "Glad to Be Unhappy," "Spring Will Be a Little Late this Year," "Any Place I Hang My Hat Is Home," "Where Flamingos Fly," and "The Things We Did Last Summer." Also quite worthwhile is the single disc **You've Got a Date with the Blues** (Verve 837 936) from 1959. The cool-toned yet inwardly heated singer is heard with an all-star sextet arranged by Quincy Jones and featuring solos by Kenny Dorham and either Frank Wess or Jerome Richardson on flute and tenor. Best are versions of "You Go to My Head" and "Just Squeeze Me" sung in French, Duke Ellington's "The Blues from Black, Brown and Beige," and a haunting rendition of "The Thrill Is Gone."

In 1960, Helen Merrill moved to Italy, which would be her home for the next four years.

Mark Murphy One of the major male jazz singers of the future, Mark Murphy played piano as a child, studied voice and theatre in college, and performed early on in Canada and upstate New York. He recorded a couple of lesser-known albums for Decca (starting in 1956) and three records for Capitol during 1959–60. It was hoped by the record company executives that Murphy would break through to a pop market, and they gave him mostly typical late 1950s tried-and-true tunes to record. **The Best of Mark Murphy** (Capitol 33147) has 17 selections from his Capitol recordings, and these include such songs as "Kansas City," "This Could Be the Start of Something Big," "That Old Black Magic," and "Cheek to Cheek." But even at this early stage, Murphy was too much of an improviser (although much more subtle than he would become) to have much luck capturing a mass audience. He would have better luck when he was able to take complete control over his recording career.

Anita O'Day Anita O'Day reached the peak of her career at the 1958 Newport Jazz Festival, and luckily it was filmed and included in *Jazz on a Summer's Day*. Her versions of "Sweet Georgia Brown" and particularly a scat-filled "Tea for Two" are quite exciting and memorable; everything works during this ten-minute stretch.

Anita O'Day always had the same problem as Mark Murphy, preferring to stick to jazz rather than going for a larger mass audience. Fortunately, she spent most of the 1950s recording for the Verve label, and she was well featured in many settings. A nine-CD limited-edition box set, **The Complete Anita O'Day Verve/Clef Sessions** (Mosaic 9-188), completely covers the era for her. Among the better individual discs are **Pick Yourself Up with Anita O'Day** (Verve 517 329), which teams her with Buddy Bregman's Orchestra, **Anita O'Day Sings the Winners** (Verve 837 939) on which she sings hits associated with other singers and musicians (backed by the Russ Garcia Orchestra), and **Swings Cole Porter with Billy May** (Verve 849 266). **Anita Swings the Most** (Verve 829 577) is the strongest of the lot, teaming O'Day with the Oscar Peterson Quartet (the pianist, Herb Ellis, Ray Brown, and drummer John Poole). There is a "Jazz at the Philharmonic" competitive feel to the date, particularly on the ridiculously fast "Them There Eyes." The ballad renditions of both "We'll Be Together Again" and "Bewitched, Bothered, and Bewildered" are also excellent.

King Pleasure The mysterious Clarence Beeks, known as King Pleasure, who had the best voice of all the vocalese singers, worked on an occasional basis during the second half of the 1950. Other than six isolated titles, his only recording of the period was **Golden Days** (Original Jazz Classics 1772) from 1960. This set is dominated by spirited remakes of past glories including "Moody's Mood for Love," "Don't Get Scared," and "Parker's Mood"; tenors Teddy Edwards and Harold Land, and pianist Gerald Wiggins are strong assets in the backup group. It does seem strange, given the success of Lambert, Hendricks, and Ross, that King Pleasure did not do more during this period.

Betty Roche Betty Roche had a strangely episodic career. She was with the Duke Ellington Orchestra twice, but both stays were brief. In 1943, she had an opportunity to sing the "Blues" section of "Black, Brown and Beige" at Ellington's initial Carnegie Hall concert, and in 1951, she took a classic bebop vocal on "Take the 'A'

Train" that was later adopted by Ray Nance. But otherwise, she spent much of her career in surprising obscurity. Fortunately, Roche did have three opportunities to lead her own record dates, two of which fall into the 1956–60 period. **Take the "A" Train** (Bethlehem 75992) is a fine all-round outing featuring a remake of the title cut, "Something to Live For," "Route 66," and "September in the Rain." Roche, who is joined by Eddie Costa on vibes, Conte Candoli, and pianist Donn Trenner in a quintet, has a definite charm, and she deserved much greater fame. Recorded in 1960, **Singin' & Swingin'** (Original Jazz Classics 1718) matches the singer with Jimmy Forrest, organist Jack McDuff (near the beginning of his career), guitarist Bill Jennings, Wendell Marshall, and Roy Haynes. Roche performs nine famous standards, coming up with fresh variations in her phrasing to such numbers as "Come Rain or Come Shine," "When I Fall in Love," "Blue Moon," and "Billie's Bounce."

Jimmy Rushing The great Basie veteran kept busy in the 1950s. Rushing appeared on *The Sound of Jazz* telecast, sang at the Brussels World's Fair with Benny Goodman (1958), recorded with Duke Ellington and Dave Brubeck, toured with Buck Clayton, and performed with Jon Hendricks's Evolution of the Blues (1960). He also recorded as a leader for Vanguard and Columbia.

Rushing Lullabies/Jimmy Rushing and the Big Brass (Columbia 65118) has the complete contents of two of Rushing's best albums of the 1950s. Singing during 1958–59, Mr. Five by Five is heard on swing-oriented blues, ballads, and jumping standards, with such notable soloists as Buddy Tate, Coleman Hawkins, Buck Clayton, Dickie Wells, organist Sir Charles Thompson, and Ray Bryant. Rushing is in typically exuberant form on "I'm Coming Virginia," "When You're Smiling," "Good Rockin' Tonight," and "Russian Lullaby."

Nina Simone Throughout her career, Nina Simone played many types of music, but never really fit into one single category for long. Much of her work has been outside of jazz although influenced by it, and she also performed folk, R&B, pop, and soul music. Simone had originally planned to become a classical pianist, but had to earn a living while she studied, and caught on as a singer/pianist. Simone's earliest recordings were as jazz-oriented as she ever was. **Little Girl Blue** (Bethlehem 3004) from 1957 was her first recording. Accompanied by bassist Jimmy Bond and Albert "Tootie" Heath, Simone gives a variety of standards some rather emotional treatments, including "Mood Indigo," "Good Bait," "You'll Never Walk Alone" (which is turned into a powerful spiritual), a catchy "My Baby Just Cares for Me," and a hit version of "I Loves You Porgy." The two LPs **The Amazing Nina Simone** (Colpix 407) and **Nina Simone at Town Hall** (Colpix 409) also have their jazz-oriented moments though Simone would move further away from jazz as her career progressed.

Dakota Staton   A soulful and swinging singer with an appealing voice, Dakota Staton first cut a few singles for Capitol during 1954–55. In 1957, she had the one hit of her career with the sexy yet classy "The Late Late Show," leading to a series of albums on Capitol during the next four years. **The Late Late Show** (Collectables 5231), in addition to the memorable title cut, also has fine versions of "Broadway," "A Foggy Day," "What Do You See in Her," and "My Funny Valentine," with backing from a mostly unidentified orchestra arranged by Van Alexander. Also worth exploring (and available on CD) is **More than the Most** (Collectables 5232) with Sid Feller's Orchestra, which includes "Love Walked In," "The Song Is Ended," "East of the Sun," and "September in the Rain."

Maxine Sullivan   **A Tribute to Andy Razaf** (DCC Compact Classics 610) features Maxine Sullivan at age 45 still singing in her timeless and cheerful style. She interprets a dozen songs that have the lyrics of Andy Razaf including "Keeping Out of Mischief Now," "Stompin' at the Savoy," "Honeysuckle Rose," "Memories of You," and "Ain't Misbehavin'." Of particular interest is that the lightly swinging singer is joined by a sextet quite reminiscent of John Kirby's group of 15 years ago, including alumnus Charlie Shavers and Buster Bailey (with altoist Jerome Richardson and pianist Dick Hyman). But shortly after recording this album for Period in 1956, Sullivan made a career change, and (like Alberta Hunter) became a nurse, dropping out of music altogether.

Mel Tormé   From the jazz standpoint, Mel Tormé had two major prime periods, one being during 1956–60, and the other starting in 1983 when he began recording for Concord. He had always been interested in jazz (particularly swing) and had hinted at his interest previously, but it was not until he recorded ❂ **Lulu's Back in Town** (Bethlehem 75732) with the Marty Paich Dek-Tette in

1956 that it became obvious how talented a jazz singer he was. The combination was perfect: Tormé's flexible voice (equally at home scatting à la Ella Fitzgerald and on ballads), Paich's cool jazz arrangements, the West Coast Jazz all-stars that are in the group, and a high-quality and swinging repertoire. The title cut, "Lullaby of Birdland," "The Lady Is a Tramp," and "Fascinating Rhythm" have rarely sounded livelier. Fortunately, the combination was repeated several other times during this period. **Mel Tormé Sings Astaire** (Bethlehem 79847) has such tunes as "Nice Work If You Can Get It," "A Foggy Day," "The Way You Look Tonight," and "Cheek to Cheek," and **Mel Tormé Swings Shubert Alley** (Verve 821 581) from 1960 is highlighted by "Too Close for Comfort," "Too Darn Hot," and "Whatever Lola Wants." Also having Paich arrangements, but quite a bit different is **Back in Town** (Verve 511 512). A rare and final reunion by Tormé with the Mel-Tones, with the more memorable numbers being "It Happened in Monterey," "Hit the Road to Dreamland," and "A Smooth One."

Mel Tormé also recorded in other settings, but his work with Marty Paich remains one of the major high points of his career.

Big Joe Turner   Although a rather unlikely rock 'n' roll star, Big Joe Turner's hit record of "Shake, Rattle and Roll" (1954) made him a popular attraction on a circuit that never heard of Pete Johnson. There are several overlapping collections of his 1950s hits available. **The Very Best of Big Joe Turner** (Rhino/Atlantic 72968) is an excellent single disc having his most popular recordings of 1951–59 including "Chains of Love," "Sweet Sixteen," "Honey Hush," "TV Mama," "Shake, Rattle, and Roll," "Flip Flop and Fly," and "Corrine Corrina."

Boss of the Blues (Atlantic 8812) from 1956 shows that Big Joe was most at home with a blues-oriented jazz band. This set was one of the final times that he teamed up with Pete Johnson. The swinging group also includes Joe Newman, Lawrence Brown, Pete Brown, and Frank Wess. Turner clearly has a good time remaking such early hits as "Cherry Red," "Roll 'Em Pete," and "Wee Baby Blues." **Big Joe Rides Again** (Atlantic 90688) dates from 1959 except for one number ("Pennies from Heaven") left over from the **Boss of the Blues** album. Turner returns to his roots in 1930s blues and standards, belting out "Nobody in Mind," "Rebecca," "Don't You Make Me High," and other tunes from the era. He is assisted by

Coleman Hawkins, Vic Dickenson, and trumpeter Paul Ricard who play arrangements by Ernie Wilkins.

No matter what the setting or the song, Big Joe Turner just sang like he always did, turning everything into the blues.

Sarah Vaughan   Sarah Vaughan's career continued on a steady pace as she gradually grew in stature throughout the 1950s. Through 1959, her more commercial dates were made for Mercury while her more jazz-oriented sessions were on Mercury's subsidiary EmArcy; she switched to the Roulette label in 1960. All of the music from October 1956 through 1959 has been released on the five-CD set **Complete Sarah Vaughan on Mercury Vol. 2** (Mercury 826 327), and the six-CD set **Complete Sarah Vaughan on Mercury Vol. 3** (Mercury 826 333). **Vol. 2** has 13 vocal duets with Billy Eckstine, many dates with orchestras (usually led by Hal Mooney), and just five jazz numbers with her trio though even the least promising songs have their moments of interest due to Sassy's wondrous voice. **Vol. 3** includes two very good jazz dates (available individually as mentioned below), a live set at the London House with Thad Jones and Frank Wess, her first recorded version of "Misty," and some sessions arranged by Quincy Jones.

Listeners who are not completists are advised to instead acquire **At Mister Kelly's** (EmArcy 832 791), and ● **No Count Sarah** (EmArcy 824 057). The former set has Sassy backed by her regular trio of 1957 (Jimmy Jones, Richard Davis, and Roy Haynes), sounding quite relaxed and showing off her remarkable voice on "September in the Rain," "Honeysuckle Rose," "Poor Butterfly," "Sometimes I'm Happy," and other superior standards. **No Count Sarah** teams Vaughan with the Count Basie Orchestra (with Ronnell Bright substituting for Basie) and is quite jazz-oriented, with memorable versions of "Doodlin'," "Darn that Dream," and the wordless "No Count Blues."

Dinah Washington   During 1956–58, Dinah Washington continued singing jazz, ballads, blues, R&B, and commercial music. **The Complete Dinah Washington on Mercury, Vol. 5** (Mercury 832 952) is a three-CD set that has a strong emphasis on jazz, including dates with orchestras led by Quincy Jones, Ernie Wilkins, and Eddie Chamblee. Along the way there are tributes to Fats Waller and Bessie Smith plus Washington's strong performance at the 1958 Newport Jazz Festival.

However, her career changed drastically in 1959 when she had a major pop hit in "What a Difference a Day Makes." From then on, her records found her backed by orchestras given arrangements that would better suit a country singer. **The Complete Dinah Washington on Mercury, Vol. 6** (Mercury 832 956), also a three-CD set, begins with the "Difference" set, and continues until November 1960, featuring the singer on dozens of songs that sought to duplicate the commercial success of her hit. Some came close, but it is difficult to sit through more than a few of these numbers in a row due to the lack of variety and Washington's increasingly predictable delivery. For those who do like what would be Dinah Washington's last period, the single CD **What a Difference a Day Makes** (Mercury 818 815) is available, but jazz listeners will prefer her pre-1959 output.

Lee Wiley   Lee Wiley, who wanted so much to be a popular success, found the late 1950s to be somewhat discouraging. Although rated high by some jazz listeners, she was never able to make the breakthrough to greater stardom. And because so much of her self-esteem was tied into her physical appearance, she was fighting a losing battle as she neared 50. She recorded two excellent albums for Victor during 1956–57, **West of the Moon** and **A Touch of the Blues**. **As Time Goes By** (Bluebird 3138) has ten of the 12 songs from the first album, nine of the 12 from the second, and a rendition of "Stars Fell on Alabama" taken from a sampler album. Other than the latter cut, Wiley is backed by big bands led by either Ralph Burns or Billy Butterfield. She still sounds in prime form on such numbers as "You're a Sweetheart," "Can't Get Out of this Mood," "Ace in the Hole," "Between the Devil and the Deep Blue Sea," and her signature song, "A Hundred Years from Today." Despite that, her career (other than a brief comeback in the 1970s) was essentially over.

Jimmy Witherspoon   After his hits ran out in 1950, Jimmy Witherspoon kept on working although maintaining a lower profile and struggling a little. The smooth yet expressive blues singer made singles for Modern, Federal, Chess, and Checker. In 1956, he recorded a fine album with Wilbur DeParis's band, and the following year had a reunion with old boss Jay McShann for **Goin' to Kansas City Blues** (RCA 51639), mostly singing the type of material featured by McShann in the 1940s.

While that album did not create much of a stir, at the 1959 Monterey Jazz Festival 'Spoon was the surprise hit.

His 25-minute five-song set (which teamed him with Roy Eldridge, Ben Webster, Coleman Hawkins, Woody Herman on clarinet, Earl Hines, bassist Vernon Alley, and Mel Lewis), which includes his trademark "Ain't Nobody's Business If I Do" and "When I Been Drinkin'," was such a sensation that it revitalized his career. ❖ **The 'Spoon Concerts** (Fantasy 24701) has that performance plus Witherspoon romping on ten mostly traditional blues songs two months later in a group with Webster, Gerry Mulligan, Jimmy Rowles, Leroy Vinnegar, and Lewis. Although not as famous, that set is just as exciting as the Monterey performance.

Thanks to the publicity surrounding his Monterey success, Jimmy Witherspoon would never be short of work again.

The End of the JATP Era

With the decline in popularity of honking saxophonists in favor of rock 'n' roll, and the rise of interest in individual acts (particularly Ella Fitzgerald and the Oscar Peterson Trio), the days were numbered for Norman Granz's traveling jam sessions. Although the 1957 "Jazz at the Philharmonic" lineup at various times included Harry Edison, Dizzy Gillespie, J.J. Johnson, Lester Young, Coleman Hawkins, Ben Webster, Illinois Jacquet, Sonny Stitt, Stan Getz, the Oscar Peterson Trio, and Jo Jones, by 1958 JATP was only touring in Europe and even that stopped after 1960. It had been a great 16-year run, resulting in quite a few exciting moments along the way. **Jazz at the Philharmonic in Europe** (Verve 8823) is a double LP with highlights from the 1960 concerts (which add Benny Carter, Cannonball Adderley, and Don Byas to the already overloaded roster) and serves as a rousing close for the JATP story.

Surviving Swing Stars

The swing era had only ended a decade or so earlier and many of its major players were still just in their forties, yet swing was thought of as ancient history. Despite that, the best soloists continued working, quite often in smaller mainstream swing bands. A few record labels were interested in continuing to record the major names and although swing's popularity was minimal, many of these records still sound quite lively and fresh today.

Benny Carter   Benny Carter's career passed the 30-year mark during this period, and he remained in prime form on alto and (on the rare occasions that he played it) trumpet. **Jazz Giant** (Original Jazz Classics 167) teams Carter with Ben Webster and Frank Rosolino in an all-star septet, mostly playing swing standards plus a couple of the altoist's lesser-known originals. **Swingin' the '20s** (Original Jazz Classics 339) is a bit of a disappointment for, although it matches Carter in a quartet with Earl Hines, few sparks fly, and the music lacks any excitement; it is merely lightly swinging and overly tasteful. **Aspects** (Capitol 52677) was Carter's only big-band recording as a playing leader during 1947–86. The song titles are a bit gimmicky, saluting the 12 months of the year, including "June in January," "I'll Remember April," and "June Is Busting Out All Over." But the music (which includes four alternate takes and four Carter originals written to fill in some of the less documented months) is solid, mainstream big-band swing, featuring plenty of solo space from the leader, whose playing style proved to still be quite timeless.

Al Casey   Fats Waller's guitarist during much of 1934–42, Al Casey had a rare chance to lead his own record in 1960, **Buck Jumpin'** (Original Jazz Classics 675). Casey, who had played acoustic guitar during his Waller years, switched to electric by 1944 when he worked with Clarence Profit and had become influenced by Charlie Christian. Casey freelanced for years and played R&B with King Curtis during 1957–61. **Buck Jumpin'** finds him jamming blues and standards back on acoustic guitar in a quintet with Rudy Powell (heard on alto and clarinet) and pianist Herman Foster, including fine versions of "Rosetta," "Ain't Misbehavin'," "Honeysuckle Rose," and the title cut. But although still just 44 years old, Casey was one of the victims of jazz's quick evolution, recording only occasionally and being largely forgotten by much of the jazz world.

Buck Clayton   Buck Clayton, whose swing trumpet fit in with Sidney Bechet (with whom he appeared in concert in 1958), *The Benny Goodman Story*, and Eddie Condon, reverted to Kansas City swing when he put together a Count Basie alumni band for a European tour in 1959. The two-CD set **Copenhagen Concert** (Steeple Chase 36006/7) not only has Clayton in top form, but such Basie veterans as trumpeter Emmett Berry, altoist Earle Warren, Buddy Tate on tenor, trombonist Dickie Wells (who was spelling his first name as Dicky by this time), and a three-piece rhythm section; Jimmy Rushing takes some vocals on the second disc. In addition to a few standards, Clayton contributed three fairly new swing tunes. Highlights include "Outer Drive," "Night Train," "Exactly Like You," and "Sent for You Yesterday," showing that small-group swing (which may have been considered quite passé in the United States) was still very much alive whenever the great veterans got together.

Bill Coleman Bill Coleman, who made a strong impression in Europe during 1935–40, spent the next eight years in the United States playing in many settings, including the Benny Carter Orchestra, Teddy Wilson, Andy Kirk, Mary Lou Williams, and the John Kirby Sextet, recording with Lester Young in the Kansas City Six. However, Coleman, who was always overshadowed in the United States by flashier trumpeters, was unable to find a solid niche for himself (particularly after the rise of bebop), so in December 1948 he returned to France where he lived for the rest of his life. He stayed quite busy on the continent, and, although forgotten in the United States, he was in his prime throughout the 1950s and '60s, playing small-group swing and Dixieland. **The Great Parisian Session** (Polydor 837235) has Coleman teaming up with some top Americans who were temporarily in Paris as part of Quincy Jones's touring orchestra. The septet (with Coleman, Quentin Jackson, Budd Johnson, pianist Patti Bown, bassist Bobby Catlett, drummer Joe Harris, and sometimes guitarist Les Spann) performs five of Coleman's blues-oriented originals including the two-part "From Boogie to Funk," "Colemanology," and "Have Blues, Will Play 'Em."

Benny Goodman Artie Shaw may have chosen to retire, but Benny Goodman's life was his clarinet, and he never seriously considered quitting. He was permanently a household name, and, even though putting together a long-term big band was out of the question economically, he headed orchestras for special occasions and led a combo any time that he desired to play in public. Despite his reputation for being cheap and for being a bit of a space case (only able to think of things from his own perspective), Goodman never had any difficulty attracting younger musicians who wanted to play with the legend.

The King of Swing led a big band successfully at the 1958 Brussels World's Fair, one that featured Taft Jordan, Vernon Brown, Zoot Sims, the young pianist Roland Hanna, and Jimmy Rushing. Otherwise he appeared on television regularly, mostly made predictable studio recordings, and could still sound inspired at certain moments.

His best available recordings from the 1956–60 period are from the private tapes that Goodman donated to Yale. **Yale Recordings, Vol. 4: Big Band Recordings** (Music Masters 5017) has five different sessions with big bands taken from the 1956–64 period. Pepper Adams, Bob Wilber (on tenor), Zoot Sims, and BG's former vocalist Martha Tilton get their spots. Best are a few Eddie Sauter arrangements, but much weaker is a 1964 session that includes "People." **Vol. 8** (Music Masters 65093) has some rather unusual performances. Martha Tilton redoes her hit "Bei Mir Bist Du Schon," Goodman's clarinet is well-featured with a quintet that includes pianist Andre Previn on three tracks, and BG has his last musical encounter with his old friend Mel Powell on a pair of medleys. Most unique are eight selections cut with a nine-piece unit in 1961 that are dominated by songs associated with Hawaii including "On the Beach at Waikiki," "Blue Hawaii," "Sweet Leilani," and "My Little Grass Shack." Thanks to Bill Stegmeyer's creative arrangements and an all-star lineup, this possible dud session is actually surprisingly successful. **Vol. 3: Big Band in Europe** (Music Masters 5007) features Goodman in 1958 playing with his short-lived big band during a week at the Brussels World's Fair in Belgium. Since the originally released recordings from this engagement are long out of print, this CD is quite valuable, and it features Goodman and his big band playing quite a few newer charts for a change.

One of the best bands that Benny Goodman led after his glory years was during 1959–60 when he took over the Flip Phillips-Benny Harris Sextet. **Vol. 7: Florida Sessions** (Music Masters 65058) has some exciting music from this unit, which often features Phillips and Harris riffing and pushing the clarinetist to be at his most competitive and fiery. This is the type of music that Goodman should have played more often, rather than just trotting out the old hits. **Vol. 5** (Music Masters 65040) is a double CD that features two Goodman bands from 1959–60. One is an expanded version of the Phillips-Harris group, which before it broke up was a ten-piece group with Jack Sheldon. In addition, an otherwise unrecorded sextet from 1963 (with Bobby Hackett, bassist Steve Swallow, and the forgotten but talented

Modesto Bresano on tenor and flute) also serves as an excellent setting for the King of Swing.

Tiny Grimes Tiny Grimes led his R&B band the Rocking Highlanders up until 1954. After that, he reverted back to swing, freelancing, and leading three record dates during 1958–59. **Blues Groove** (Original Jazz Classics 817), although a Grimes date, is most notable for the playing of Coleman Hawkins, who takes a lengthy and powerful blues solo on "Marchin' Along." The sextet also includes flutist Musa Kaleen, Ray Bryant, bassist Earl Wormack, and drummer Teagle Fleming performing four blues, "April in Paris," and "A Smooth One." **Callin' the Blues** (Original Jazz Classics 191) has Grimes joined by J.C. Higginbotham, Eddie "Lockjaw" Davis, Bryant, Wendell Marshall, and Osie Johnson, performing three blues and "Airmail Special." Lockjaw is in typically fiery form while Higginbotham (who was past his prime) does his best and causes some sparks to fly. **Tiny in Swingville** (Original Jazz Classics 1796) is the best showcase for Grimes's playing. He is showcased in a group with Jerome Richardson (flute, tenor, and baritone), Bryant, Marshall, and Art Taylor, swinging such tunes as "Annie Laurie," "Frankie and Johnny," and "Ain't Misbehavin'," and showing that his interpretation of Charlie Christian's style was still quite viable.

Coleman Hawkins After being somewhat neglected during 1950–55, Coleman Hawkins was rediscovered in 1957, a very productive year in which he recorded with Thelonious Monk (in a group including John Coltrane), Henry "Red" Allen, Roy Eldridge (including a memorable outing at the Newport Jazz Festival that unfortunately is not on CD yet), and on *The Sound of Jazz* telecast. He made many records as a leader during 1956–60 and was recognized as being eternally modern even though he had played with Mamie Smith in 1921.

Recorded in 1956, **The Hawk in Hi-Fi** (RCA 63842) features Hawkins as the main soloist on eight songs with a string orchestra and four with a big band. Billy Byers provided the functional arrangements to this mostly easy-listening set. Best are "The Bean Stalks Again," and "His Very Own Blues." Nine alternate takes were added to the reissue. **The Hawk in Paris** (Koch 85152) is a happy surprise. Hawkins had always wanted to record with a large string section, and he received his wish on the majority of these 12 romantic melodies, all of which have some association with Paris. The surprise

is that Hawk plays with a great deal of fire (with wondrous double timing on "My Man"), and that Manny Albam's arrangements are creative rather than sounding like Muzak, resulting in a rather memorable album. Recorded in 1957, **The Hawk Flies High** (Original Jazz Classics 027) has the great tenor mostly playing with bop-oriented musicians a couple of decades his junior (including J.J. Johnson and Idrees Sulieman), easily holding his own. The memorable "Sanctity" has a particularly classic Hawkins solo, but all of the six tracks are enjoyable. **Coleman Hawkins Encounters Ben Webster** (Verve 521 427) is not really a tenor battle (Webster would find it difficult to keep up harmonically with his idol Hawkins), but a strong collaboration that includes "Blues for Yolanda," "Tangerine," and "La Rosita." **The Genius of Coleman Hawkins** (Verve 825 673) teams Hawkins with the Oscar Peterson Trio and drummer Alvin Stoller for a relaxed set of standards. **The High and Mighty Hawk** (Verve 820 600) features Hawkins excelling at something he had not really explored that much before, the blues. He really wails on the lengthy "Bird of Prey Blues" with plenty of honking and roars. Buck Clayton and Hank Jones also have their moments on this excellent quintet date.

In general, Coleman Hawkins's work for Prestige during 1958–60 was not as exciting, with too much of an emphasis on slower tempos and show tunes. The sets to get from this period are **Hawk Eyes** (Original Jazz Classics 294) that teams Hawkins with Charlie Shavers, **Bean Stalkin'** (Pablo 2310-933) that has some fiery playing with Roy Eldridge, Don Byas, and Benny Carter in 1960, and **Night Hawk** (Original Jazz Classics 420), an intense and passionate encounter with Eddie "Lockjaw" Davis.

Turning 56 in 1960, Coleman Hawkins was still a very modern and distinctive soloist who remained in peak form after nearly 40 years of recordings.

Johnny Hodges Johnny Hodges rejoined the Duke Ellington Orchestra in 1955, which would once again become his permanent home. He also found time to lead record dates on a regular basis for the Verve label. A six-CD set limited-edition box, **The Complete Verve Johnny Hodges Small Group Sessions 1956–61** (Mosaic 6-200), has all of Hodges's combo dates from this period, only a few of which are available individually. **Blues A-Plenty** (Verve 8358) is an exciting set with

Roy Eldridge, Vic Dickenson, Ben Webster, and Billy Strayhorn from 1958, which in addition to several rollicking blues, has Hodges ballad features on "Gone with the Wind," "I Didn't Know About You," "Satin Doll," and "Don't Take Your Love from Me." Throughout the era, Johnny Hodges continued to have the prettiest tone in jazz, but never lost his ability to sound soulful on blues.

Harry James   In January 1956, Harry James broke up his big band, forming a nonet from the key soloists in his orchestra. That particular outfit did not make any studio recordings, but fortunately two CDs, **Harry James and His New Jazz Band, Vol. 1** (Mr. Music 7010) and **Vol. 2** (Mr. Music 7012), have been released that capture the small group live at the Hollywood Palladium and during a radio transcription session. The ensemble consists of James and Nick Buono on trumpets, tenor saxophonist Herbie Steward (who was subbing for Corky Corcoran), Herb Lorden on clarinet and alto, Willie Smith, Juan Tizol, pianist Larry Kinnamon, bassist Floyd Blanton, and Buddy Rich. Rich and Peggy King take some vocals, and the arrangements are by Neal Hefti. The 40-year-old James was still in top form, jamming on such numbers as "Perdido," "Back Beat Boogie," "Honeysuckle Rose," and "Caxton Hall Swing" on **Vol. 1**, and "Roll 'Em," "Mack the Knife," "Six, Two and Even," and "The Great Lie" on the second set.

By the end of 1956, James was back with a new big band, recording for Capital and MGM (1959–60). His music continued to alternate between nostalgic remakes of his hits, and arrangements by Ernie Wilkins and Neal Hefti in the 1950s Count Basie style, with Ernie Andrews taking occasional vocals. His LPs from the era remain out of print, and most of the music was rather predictable. Despite occasional hot trumpet solos, Harry James was largely coasting. He should have stuck with the nonet and kept his playing open to more modern ideas.

Budd Johnson   An important saxophonist since the mid-1930s, Budd Johnson played with Benny Goodman in 1957, led his own groups, and toured with the Quincy Jones Big Band in 1960. A modern swing player who could easily fit in with bop musicians (he had helped organize Coleman Hawkins's pioneering 1944 bop sessions), Johnson led an album apiece for the Felsted and Stereocraft label, and most importantly in 1960 for Riverside and Swingville. ● **Budd Johnson and the Four Brass Giants** (Original Jazz Classics 1921) is a

gem. Johnson, heard on tenor and clarinet in addition to providing the arrangements, utilizes four distinctive and very different trumpeters: Clark Terry, Harry "Sweets" Edison, Nat Adderley, and Ray Nance (who doubles on violin). With Tommy Flanagan or Jimmy Jones on piano, bassist Joe Benjamin, and drummer Herb Lovelle, the group performs four swing standards and four of Johnson's swinging originals. The colorful brassmen, Budd's versatile solos, and the inventive arrangements make this a particularly memorable set. Also quite worthy is **Let's Swing** (Original Jazz Classics 1720), which is an excellent showcase for Johnson's tenor. He is featured in a quintet with his brother Keg Johnson on trombone, Flanagan, George Duvivier, and drummer Charlie Persip. Johnson has a ballad feature ("Serenade in Blue") and performs three originals (including "Downtown Manhattan" and "Uptown Manhattan") as well as three standards. Rather than sounding like a veteran of the 1930s, Budd Johnson comes across as if he had come of age as one of the "cool school" players.

Lonnie Johnson   After making many appearances in jazz settings during the late 1920s, singer/guitarist Lonnie Johnson carved out a very impressive and prolific career in the blues, having a strong hit in 1948 with "Tomorrow Night" and recording steadily into 1953. But the next six years were pretty lean as Johnson found that his style was considered out of date. Recordings stopped, jobs dried up, and he was working as a janitor at a Philadelphia hotel in 1959 when Elmer Snowden discovered him, and helped get him back on records again. Johnson recorded four albums for Bluesville during 1959–60, two of which were jazz-oriented and feature him in a trio with Wendell Marshall and Snowden (who is heard on acoustic rhythm guitar, making his first recordings since 1934). **Blues and Ballads** (Original Blues Classics 531) has Johnson singing smooth blues and sentimental ballads with equal skill; both guitarists have opportunities to display their complementary but distinctive styles. Recorded the same day, **Blues and Ballads and Swingin' Jazz, Vol. 2** (Original Blues Classics 570) has six instrumentals among the ten songs with the two guitarists sounding quite spontaneous on such tunes as "Lester Leaps In," "C Jam Blues," and "Careless Love." There is also plenty of studio chatter between songs (often allowing one to hear Johnson and

Snowden picking out tunes), which adds to the atmosphere of the superior set.

Jo Jones   The veteran drummer freelanced during the second half of the 1950s, appearing at the 1957 Newport Jazz Festival with both the Count Basie Orchestra and the Coleman Hawkins-Roy Eldridge Sextet. He led sessions for Vanguard and Everest (including a duet album with bassist Milt Hinton), and headed a trio that for a time featured pianist Ray Bryant and his brother bassist Tommy Bryant. **The Essential Jo Jones** (Vanguard 101/2) has all of the music from Jones's Vanguard dates of 1955 and 1958 except for a second take of "Shoe Shine Boy." The latter song is particularly special because Count Basie makes a guest appearance, reuniting with Jones, Walter Page, and Freddy Green. Otherwise, the first half of the CD has Jones in a swing quintet with Emmett Berry, Bennie Green, Lucky Thompson, and pianist Nat Pierce, playing a variety of standards plus "Lincoln Heights." The session from 1958 has the Jones-Bryant-Bryant trio, and, along with a lot of short drum solos, is most notable for its early versions of two of Ray Bryant's best known songs, "Cubano Chant" and "Little Susie."

Jonah Jones   Most swing era musicians by the second half of the 1950s were either scuffling, playing Dixieland, or earning a living playing in the studios. Jonah Jones was a major exception, for he became more famous than he had ever been when swing was king. After leaving Cab Calloway in 1952 after a 12-year run, he worked with Earl Hines (1952–53), played in show bands, visited Europe (where he recorded an exciting session with Sidney Bechet), and in 1955 was hired to lead a quartet at the Embers in New York. Jones was advised to use a mute in the early sets, and he soon hit upon a formula. By utilizing a shuffle rhythm and mixing together current show tunes with older standards, he hit it big playing easy-listening swing. His recordings of "On the Street Where You Live" and "Baubles, Bangles and Beads" became best-sellers, and, after an album for Groove/Vik (1956), he recorded a steady series of records for Capitol during 1957–63.

Strangely enough, only one of these albums has thus far been reissued on CD, **Jumpin' with Jonah** (Capitol 24554). This disc has all of the music from his third Capitol release plus four other songs originally released on other albums, but actually from the same sessions. Jones (who takes three good-humored vocals) is joined by guest pianist Hank Jones—his usual pianists were George Rhodes and (by late 1958) Teddy Brannon—bassist John Brown, and drummer Harold Austin for a mixture of Dixieland and swing standards, newer material, and jump tunes. Highlights include "Bill Bailey," "It's a Good Day," "That's A Plenty," and "Do You Know What It Means to Miss New Orleans." Jones's other albums from the era can often be found in used record stores, and these include **Jonah Jones at the Embers** (Vik 1135), **Muted Jazz** (Capitol 839), **Swingin' on Broadway** (Capitol 963), **Swingin' at the Cinema** (Capitol 1083), **Jonah Jumps Again** (Capitol 1115), **I Dig Chicks** (Capitol 1193), **Swingin' 'Round the World** (Capitol 1237), and **Broadway Swings Again** (Capitol 1641).

Louis Jordan   For Louis Jordan who had so many best-selling records in the 1940s, the hits stopped in 1951. He continued playing throughout the rest of the decade, but his records no longer sold very well, and he had lost the magic touch. **Rock 'N' Roll Call** (Bluebird 66145) from 1955–56 finds Jordan trying to come up with new hits in the music he had helped pioneer while **No Moe!** (Mercury 314 512 523) from 1956–57 is a set of remakes of past successes. Both discs have their moments of interest, but offer no real surprises and do not come up to the level of Jordan's earlier records. Although only 49 in 1957, Louis Jordan was slipping into the role of a has-been despite still being able to play alto and sing quite well. One wonders why he did not make an attempt to switch to jazz and reinvent his career in a similar fashion as Willis Jackson and Jimmy Forrest.

Gene Krupa   Gene Krupa had a reunion of sorts on **Drummer Man** (Verve 827 843). This big band album from 1956 did not have that many of his alumni, but it did give him an opportunity to play with Roy Eldridge and Anita O'Day again, revisiting such songs as "Opus One," "Let Me Off Uptown," "Rockin' Chair," and "Drum Boogie." Although not unpredictable at all nor quite on the level of his 1941–42 recordings, there are some exciting moments along the way, particularly from Eldridge.

Otherwise, Krupa led a quartet during this era, employing either Eddie Shu, Gail Curtis, or Eddie Wasserman on reeds, with Dave McKenna, Teddy Napoleon, or Ronnie Ball on piano, and Wendell Marshall, Mort Herbert, or Jimmy Gannon on bass. He led a big band album of Gerry Mulligan arrangements in 1958, and the following year gave Sal Mineo drum lessons so he could play like Krupa in *The Gene Krupa Story*, a nonsensical but sometimes musical Hollywood movie. There were also occasional television appearances since Gene Krupa remained the most famous drummer in the world even if very few listeners from the jazz world still thought he was even close to being the best.

Joe Newman   Joe Newman, one of the solo stars of the Count Basie Orchestra, led quite a few dates of his own during this era. ● **The Complete Joe Newman** (RCA 66610), a double CD, completely reissues his four RCA albums of 1955–56. The first disc puts the focus on Newman and Al Cohn in a pair of octets with arrangements by Ernie Wilkins, Manny Albam, and Cohn. The second disc starts out with a tribute to Louis Armstrong with a dozen of Satch's songs modernized for a big band; Newman takes a few rare vocals. The final session matches the trumpeter with flutist Frank Wess in a two-guitar septet arranged by Wilkins. The 48 selections are superb examples of Count Basie–style swing.

Newman also led sessions for Storyville (1956), Savoy, Coral, Roulette, and Swingville. **I Feel Like a Newman** (Black Lion 760905) is an excellent set of 1950s swing. Newman is heard either in a quintet with Wess and Sir Charles Thompson or with an octet that includes Frank Foster and Gene Quill, playing veteran standards and newer songs by Ernie Wilkins and Manny Albam. Recorded in 1960, **Jive at Five** (Original Jazz Classics 419) is also in the Count Basie style, which is not too surprising considering that the quintet is comprised of Newman, Wess (on tenor this time), Tommy Flanagan, bassist Eddie Jones, and drummer Oliver Jackson. The quintet plays a few old favorites, including "More than You Know," "Taps Miller," and "Don't Worry 'Bout Me," plus some basic originals.

Red Norvo   After having led successful vibes-guitar-bass trios during 1949–55, Red Norvo mostly headed quintets (with a reed player and a guitarist) for the remainder of the decade. **Music to Listen to Red Norvo By** (Original Jazz Classics 155) has Norvo leading a sextet dominated by clarinetist Bill Smith (formerly with The Dave Brubeck Octet) who contributed the 20-minute classical-oriented four-movement "Divertimento." The five shorter pieces (by Jack Montrose, Barney Kessel, Lennie Niehaus, Duane Tatro, and Norvo) are much more jazz-oriented and inspire Norvo's light-toned sextet,

which also includes flutist Buddy Collette, Barney Kessel, Red Mitchell, and drummer Shelly Manne. While that band was specially assembled, **The Forward Look** (Reference 8) has Norvo's regular group of 1957–58, which includes Jerry Dodgion on alto and flute, guitarist Jimmy Wyble, bassist Red Wooten, and drummer John Markman. Norvo is in excellent form on a set filled with obscurities (including "How's Your Mother-in-Law") plus Quincy Jones's "For Lena and Lennie" and "When You're Smiling."

After 1959, it would be a decade before Red Norvo led another record date, but he continued working as regularly as he wanted, often in Las Vegas.

Louis Prima   By the early 1950s, Louis Prima was at the crossroads of his career. Although he had had a few hits in the 1940s, he was now stuck emphasizing corny novelties that emphasized his Italian heritage. His music was predictable, and there did not seem too much of a future in his approach.

However, things changed. Already married to the fine ballad singer Keely Smith, in 1954 Prima discovered R&B tenor Sam Butera in New Orleans. Within a year, Sam Butera and the Witnesses became part of Louis Prima's group, and a new mixture of styles had occurred. Prima's wild shows in Las Vegas combined his New Orleans trumpet solos, a swing repertoire, Butera's honking tenor, a shuffle rhythm, Smith's ballad singing, Prima's humorous vocals, and a rock 'n' roll sensibility. Decades later it would be the inspiration for retro swing. In the mid-to-late 1950s Prima's shows were so appealing and good-humored that a wide audience enjoyed his antics. Based in Las Vegas, Prima recorded such classic records as "That Old Black Magic" and a pair of medleys, "Just a Gigolo/I Ain't Got Nobody" and "When You're Smiling/The Sheik of Araby."

The Wildest (Capitol 38696) reissues Prima's most famous album, including the aforementioned medleys, "Oh Marie" and "Jump, Jive An' Wail," plus four songs not on the original LP. Surprisingly, many of Prima's other Capitol recordings have not been reissued, but there is one superior sampler. ● **Capitol Collectors Series** (Capitol 94072) has the hits plus most of the musical high points of the 1956–62 period. Prima fans who have access to used record stores will also want to acquire the LPs **The Call of the Wildest** (Capitol 836) and **The Wildest Show at Tahoe** (Capitol 908) as well as a copy of the Louis Prima-Keely Smith movie *Hey Boy! Hey Girl!*.

Paul Quinichette   The year 1959 witnessed both the end for Pres (Lester Young) and the final recording (until the 1970s) by the Vice Pres, Paul Quinichette. Listening to Quinichette is a bit of a guilty pleasure because, on the one hand, his playing is clearly quite derivative, purposely a close copy of Lester Young. On the other hand, the Vice Pres did record one excellent record after another in the 1950s.

The Kid from Denver (Biograph 12066) from 1956 has Quinichette on two numbers with a sextet led by trumpeter Gene Roland, playing two other songs with Roland's septet, and showcased on eight selections with his own ten-piece group (which is filled with Count Basie–associated musicians). Best are two numbers ("Honeysuckle Rose" and "Pennies from Heaven") that feature Quinichette backed by Basie's rhythm section plus pianist Nat Pierce. **On the Sunny Side** (Original Jazz Classics 076) has Quinichette with a more modern group than usual, holding his own with Curtis Fuller, both Sonny Red and John Jenkins on altos, Mal Waldron, Doug Watkins, and Ed Thigpen. They perform three Waldron originals (including the catchy "Cool-Lypso") plus "My Funny Valentine" and "On the Sunny Side of the Street." **Cattin' with Coltrane and Quinichette** (DCC Compact Classics 1085) has four selections (three Mal Waldron originals, plus "Sunday") that match Quinichette with John Coltrane in 1957, and Quinichette holds his own. There are also two rarer numbers without Trane from the same session plus three

previously unknown performances from 1952 with Quinichette in a quintet also including Kenny Drew, Freddie Green, bassist Gene Ramey, and drummer Gus Johnson.

But best of all are two reunion sets. **For Basie** (Original Jazz Classics 978) from October 18, 1957, teams Quinichette with Basie alumnus trumpet Shad Collins (in one of his very best sessions), Nat Pierce, Freddie Green, Jo Jones, and Walter Page in his last session before passing away two months later. The sextet jams on five Basie-associated tunes from the 1930s and '40s: "Rock-A-Bye Basie," "Texas Shuffle," "Out the Window," "Jive at Five," and "Diggin' for Dex." **Basie Reunion** (Original Jazz Classics 1049) from September 25, 1958, has Quinichette, Collins, Pierce, Green, and Jones with Buck Clayton, baritonist Jack Washington (rarely ever heard in such a favorable setting), and bassist Eddie Jones for five more vintage songs from the Basie book, including "Roseland Shuffle" and "John's Idea."

All of the Paul Quinichette recordings are easily recommended. Unfortunately, he chose to retire from music by 1961 when he was just 40.

Al Sears   After being featured on Johnny Hodges's hit "Castle Rock" (which was entirely a tenor solo although Al Sears never received any credit), Sears went out on his own, playing R&B at first before switching back to swing. In 1960, he led two albums for Swingville of which **Swing's the Thing** (Original Jazz Classics 838) has been reissued. Sears is joined by pianist Don Abney, guitarist Wally Richardson, Wendell Marshall, and drummer Joe Marshall on basic originals, blues, and standards,

---

TIMELINE 1960

John Coltrane leaves Miles Davis, forms his own quartet. • Eric Dolphy, Ted Curson, and Dannie Richmond play in the Charles Mingus Quartet. • Archie Shepp makes his recording debut with Cecil Taylor. • Johnny Griffin and Eddie "Lockjaw" Davis co-lead a two-tenor quintet. • Oscar Pettiford dies. • Ed Blackwell replaces Billy Higgins in the Ornette Coleman Quartet. • After nine years off, Lawrence Brown rejoins the Duke Ellington Orchestra. • Vibraphonist Gary Burton makes his recording debut with country/jazz guitarist Hank Garland. • Belgian pianist/arranger Francy Boland and Kenny Clarke form the Clarke-Boland Big Band. • Guitarist Grant Green moves to New York and is signed by Blue Note. • Buddy DeFranco begins teaming up with accordionist Tommy Gumina in a quartet. • McCoy Tyner leaves the Jazztet to join the John Coltrane Quartet. • **The Nutty Squirrels** is a novelty hit album for Don Elliott. • Joao Gilberto records a bossa nova record of Jobim tunes in Brazil that includes versions of "One Note Samba," "Meditation," and "Corcovado." • The Dave Pell Octet records their final album before breaking up. • Ornette Coleman's Double Quartet records the first full-length free improvisation album, **Free Jazz**.

including "In a Mellotone." But shortly after the session, Al Sears semiretired, never recording again despite only being 50.

Buster Smith   Altoist Buster Smith was a lost legend. He played with Walter Page's Blue Devils (1925–33), Bennie Moten (1933–35), and co-led the Barons of Rhythm with Count Basie for whom he is believed to have written "One o'Clock Jump." Unfortunately, he made the mistake of not staying with Basie's band when it moved East in 1936. Instead he led a band in Kansas City that for a time in 1937 also included Charlie Parker, who later said that Smith's sound was an influence. When Smith finally did go to New York later in the decade, he wrote arrangements for several orchestras (including those of Basie, Gene Krupa, and Benny Carter), and played briefly with Don Redman, Hot Lips Page, Eddie Durham, and Snub Mosley, popping up on a few recordings. However, Smith wanted a more relaxed life. He moved back to Kansas City and then settled in his native Texas for the remainder of his life, playing locally. In 1959, he led his only album, **The Legendary Buster Smith** (Koch 8523). This octet outing with local musicians is swing, jump, and blues-oriented (with no real hints of Charlie Parker), including such songs as "Kansas City Riffs," "King Alcohol," and "Organ Grinder's Swing." Buster Smith (who was 54 at the time) plays quite well, but the album remained obscure, and he never left Texas.

Stuff Smith   The great violinist Stuff Smith had not recorded as a leader since 1945 when Norman Granz signed him to Verve in 1956. During the next three years, Smith recorded fairly often for Verve, all of the sessions were reissued on the limited-edition box set **The Complete Verve Stuff Smith Sessions** (Mosaic 4-186), in addition to guesting on Nat King Cole's classic **After Midnight** sessions on Capitol. The two-CD set **Stuff Smith—Dizzy Gillespie—Oscar Peterson** (Verve 521 676) has all of the music from three of Smith's Verve albums of 1957. He is heard on 11 selections with Carl Perkins, either Red Callender or Curtis Counce on bass, and Oscar Bradley or Frank Butler on drums, nine songs with the Oscar Peterson Trio, and five tunes with Dizzy Gillespie. As usual Smith swings his heart out, playing his violin with the intensity of a saxophone, and inspiring both Gillespie and Peterson.

But after the Verve recordings stopped in 1959, Stuff Smith was off records for another five years.

Buddy Tate   Buddy Tate's orchestra had a secure job at the Celebrity Club for 21 years. During the same period he led occasional record dates. **Buddy & Claude** (Prestige 24231) combines a pair of sessions from 1960 on a single CD. One is formerly known as **Yes Indeed**, a rare set by pianist Claude Hopkins with Tate, Emmett Berry, Wendell Marshall, and Osie Johnson that is swing-oriented. The other half of the reissue has Tate's **Tate-A-Tate**, which teams the tenor with Clark Terry, Tommy Flanagan, bassist Larry Gales, and Art Taylor. What the swing and bop dates have in common is Count Basie, and Tate easily fits into both formats, sounding quite distinctive on the wide variety of standards and basic originals. This CD shows that swing was still very much alive in 1960 even if it was increasingly underground.

Ben Webster   Ben Webster continued in prime form throughout the second half of the 1950s, recording for Norman Granz's Verve label. **The Soul of Ben Webster** (Verve 527 475) is an unusual reissue in that this two-CD set actually contains music from an LP apiece led by Webster, Harry "Sweets" Edison, and Johnny Hodges. Webster is on all of the recordings, but really only stars on the first date, a septet outing with Art Farmer and fellow tenor Harold Ashby. Webster is at his best on beautiful versions of "Chelsea Bridge" and "When I Fall in Love." The Edison session is a sextet date with Webster, the Oscar Peterson Trio, and drummer Alvin Stoller, mixing blues, and swing standards; Edison's usually muted trumpet is quite effective. The final set puts the focus on Hodges (who sounds beautiful on "Don't Take Your Love from Me") although the many blues performances also give solo space to Roy Eldridge (whose playing is very explosive on "Honey Hill") and Vic Dickenson. Recorded in 1957, **Soulville** (Verve 833551) has more performances of Webster with the Oscar Peterson Trio (plus drummer Stan Levey) with memorable renditions of "Makin' Whoopee" and "Time on My Hands" being the highlights. An extra bonus (if of limited interest) are three brief examples of Webster playing piano in his primitive stride style. By the time **Ben Webster Meets the Oscar Peterson Trio** (Verve 521 448) was recorded in 1959, Peterson's group consisted of Ray Brown and Ed Thigpen so there was no need for an outside drummer. Webster is at his best on "Sunday," "The Touch of Your Lips," and "Bye Bye Blackbird." Also well worth acquiring is **At the Renaissance** (Original Jazz Classics 360), a live set from 1960 with a quartet that includes Jimmy Rowles and Jim Hall. Whether showing warmth and sentimentality on "Georgia on My Mind" and "Stardust," or growling and roaring on "Caravan" and "Ole Miss Blues," Webster is heard throughout in top form.

But despite all of this activity, Ben Webster was largely taken for granted by the early 1960s, overshadowed by the newer sounds of John Coltrane, Sonny Rollins, and Ornette Coleman.

Cootie Williams   The ex-Ellingtonian Cootie Williams still led a low-level band at the Savoy Ballroom and freelanced in New York during the second half of the 1950s. He only made a few recordings during this time. **The Big Challenge** (Fresh Sound 77) is special, for it teams the trumpeter with Rex Stewart, Lawrence Brown, J.C. Higginbotham, Coleman Hawkins, and Bud Freeman. With Hank Jones, Billy Bauer, Milt Hinton, and Gus Johnson providing solid backup, and Ernie Wilkins sketching out some arrangements, the unique matchups are very successful. This is one of the few times that Hawkins and Freeman (the two top tenors before the rise of Lester Young) recorded together.

Dixieland

Although Dixieland's popularity hit its peak in the early 1950s, it still remained one of jazz's most popular styles during the second half of the decade. Many of the classic greats of the 1920s and '30s were still active and often in prime form. Jazz festivals such as Newport and Monterey usually found a spot to feature some of the surviving pioneers, revivalists, and rediscovered New Orleans greats, sometimes contrasting the "hot" of trad jazz versus the "cool" of modern jazz. In addition, England (which had its own growing trad movement) and France remained hotbeds of New Orleans–style jazz.

Henry "Red" Allen   On a nightly basis starting in 1954 and continuing for quite a few years, trumpeter Henry "Red" Allen led a boisterous Dixieland band at the Metropole, often playing for loud and drunk customers. However, the long hours and the odd atmosphere did not lead to his ideas becoming stale or make him lose enthusiasm for the music. In 1957, Allen was one of the stars of the classic *The Sound of Jazz* telecast, leading an all-star group through dramatic versions of "Wild Man Blues" and "Rosetta." He also recorded what was the finest album of his career that year, reissued as ◉ **World on a String** (Bluebird 2497). With an octet that includes Coleman Hawkins, J.C. Higginbotham, and Buster Bailey, Allen sounds very modern in some of his solos, particularly on "I Cover the Waterfront" and "I've Got the World on a String." He jams happily on "Love Is Just Around the Corner" and "Algier's Bounce," and his sidemen also get plenty of solo space. This is one of those rare recordings where everything works, showing that these veterans (who were mostly in their late forties and early fifties), despite being a few generations behind style-wise (as jazz's evolution raced along), were still quite capable of playing at the peak of their powers.

Louis Armstrong   By the mid-1950s, Louis Armstrong was traveling around the world so much, spreading goodwill everywhere, that he was nicknamed "Ambassador Satch." The CD **Ambassador Satch** (Columbia/Legacy 64926) mostly features the 1955 Louis Armstrong All-Stars (with Edmond Hall on clarinet) wowing European audiences ("Royal Garden Blues," "The Faithful Hussar," and "Muskrat Ramble" are highlights) although this version of "Twelfth Street Rag" (which has a tremendous amount of applause on the record) was actually recorded in the studio with the applause tacked on. In 1956, the legendary newscaster Edward R. Murrow narrated a special feature film that includes some of the highlights from Armstrong's worldwide travels. The CD **Satchmo the Great** (Columbia/Legacy 62170) is a partial soundtrack recording, with some narration by Murrow between songs, a classic interview with Satch, and some fine music, most notably a lengthy "St. Louis Blues" that has the All-Stars playing with Leonard Bernstein and a symphony orchestra. **The Great Chicago Concert—1956** (Columbia/Legacy 65119), a two-CD set, features the All-Stars playing their usual repertoire, but sounding pretty inspired, particularly on a recreation of a New Orleans funeral, a lengthy "West End Blues," "Struttin' with Some Barbeque," "Indiana" (which was usually Satch's opening number), several features for the sidemen, and a new number that had recently become a giant hit for Armstrong, "Mack the Knife."

Although Louis Armstrong had made his peace with the beboppers (he and Dizzy Gillespie became good friends), the rise of the civil rights movement led some in the younger generations to calling the ever-smiling Armstrong an "Uncle Tom." They felt that his old-fashioned music glorified the segregated South, that he was too friendly with whites, they did not care for his clowning on stage, and they believed that he was not doing enough to pave the way toward equal rights. In truth, Armstrong's sunny personality had allowed him to break down many racial boundaries through the years (including traveling with a mixed race band). And although he loved pleasing audiences and was quite sincere in the joy he felt when he was onstage, he always took playing trumpet quite seriously. In addition, he fought for civil rights in his own way behind the scenes, while serving as an example of musical greatness. When President Dwight Eisenhower stalled around about sending troops to Little Rock, Arkansas, to protect black students from angry whites, Armstrong made a public statement blasting the president, something that few other black entertainers dared to do, and he cancelled a goodwill trip to the Soviet Union.

In addition to his work with the All-Stars, Louis Armstrong continued his side projects in different settings. **Louis and the Angels** (Verve 314 549 592) is an unusual but successful set in which Armstrong performs a dozen songs with an orchestra and a "heavenly choir." All of the tunes have "angel" or "heaven" in their title or prominent in the lyrics; Satch's good humor makes this project a delight. **Louis Armstrong Meets Oscar Peterson** (Verve 314 539 060) has Satch completely away from his usual New Orleans/Dixieland setting, singing and playing swing standards in charming fashion with the Oscar Peterson Quartet. He also recorded several albums with Ella Fitzgerald (reviewed under Ella's name). And during 1956–57, on four LPs that have been reissued as the three-CD set **Satchmo: A Musical Autobiography** (Verve 314 543 822), Armstrong revisited his past with revivals of 50 songs that he had mostly recorded in the 1920s and early '30s, adding brief verbal reminiscences about many of the original recordings. While these are the All-Stars' versions rather than strict recreations of the Hot Fives, and there are some inappropriate moments (such as using George Barnes on electric guitar), there are also many inspired spots, with a few of the newer renditions (particularly the songs drawn from the early 1930s) actually topping the originals. Trummy Young and Edmond Hall are in particularly fine form throughout, and Yank Lawson

was always proud that he was picked to play the role of King Oliver on a few numbers.

In 1959, Armstrong recorded a couple of albums with the Dukes of Dixieland. Some of the music has been reissued on **Satchmo and the Dukes of Dixieland** (Leisure 91052). Unfortunately, this CD inexcusably does not bother listing the personnel (which includes trumpeter Frank Assunto, trombonist Fred Assunto, and clarinetist Jerry Fuller), but the music is full of spirit, with Armstrong taking a particularly dramatic spot on "Avalon." This would be one of the last times that the 58-year-old trumpeter would be heard playing with such power because, while on tour in Italy a few months later, he suffered a heart attack that made worldwide headlines. Armstrong recovered, but his range on trumpet began to shrink, and he started taking briefer solos from then on, while still traveling at a dizzying pace.

Sidney Bechet Sidney Bechet was at the height of his fame in the mid-1950s, playing the freewheeling jazz he loved as often as he liked in France. Although he never changed his sound or style, he was more flexible than the Dixieland repertoire that he generally featured in concerts. In fact, in 1957 Bechet recorded sophisticated swing standards with the modern jazz pianist Martial Solal, music that was last available on the LP **When a Soprano Meets a Piano** (Inner City 7008). **Paris Jazz Concert** (RTE 1003), which has previously unreleased music from five different concerts, is more typical, sticking to Dixieland warhorses. Of the three bands heard from, Bechet heads two different French groups, and on "Indiana" and "The Saints" in 1958, he is joined by Buck Clayton, Vic Dickenson, pianist George Wein, Arvell Shaw, and drummer Kansas Fields, sounding very much in command. **Parisian Encounter** (Vogue 600018) from July 4, 1958, has Bechet meeting up with the Louis Armstrong–inspired trumpeter Teddy Buckner at a sextet concert. Although Buckner gets off some hot licks, there is no denying Bechet's supremacy in this setting, and he dominates the music.

The only thing that could stop Sidney Bechet was death, and cancer finally did him in. He passed away in 1959 on his 62nd birthday.

Barney Bigard Barney Bigard will always be known as a distinctive clarinetist who spent much of his life playing in the bands of Duke Ellington (1928–42) and Louis Armstrong (1947–55). He had opportunities to lead dates while with Ellington (utilizing Duke's sidemen on early versions of "Caravan," "Stompy Jones," and "C Jam Blues"), made some small group sessions during 1943–45, and headed an album for Liberty in 1957. The year 1960 resulted in the most exciting album of his life, ◉ **Barney Bigard—Claude Luter** (Vogue 655003). Bigard and fellow clarinetist Claude Luter team up with a fine French rhythm section to romp on two Sidney Bechet tunes, a variety of swing, and Dixieland standards, and the colorfully titled originals "Doo Boo Loo Blues" and "Double Gin Stomp." Bigard and Luter really push each other, and the uptempo tunes are on fire, making this little-known set an unexpected gem and one of the recorded high points of Barney Bigard's career.

Ruby Braff   Cornetist Ruby Braff led eight albums (for Victor, Epic, ABC-Paramount, Verve, Warner Brothers, United Artists, and Stereocraft) during 1956–59, but the only one that is not currently scarce is **This Is My Lucky Day** (Bluebird 6456). This CD has seven of the nine selections that Braff recorded as a tribute to Bunny Berigan, utilizing an octet that includes Benny Morton, Pee Wee Russell, tenor saxophonist Dick Hafer, and Nat Pierce for such songs as "It's Been So Long," "I Can't Get Started," and "Marie." The remainder of the disc has half of a former LP that teams Braff with Roy Eldridge. Surprisingly, there are few fireworks between these two competitive players, but there are some fine musical moments on "Give My Regards to Broadway," "Someday You'll Be Sorry," and "The Song Is Ended." But despite Braff's busy activities in the recording studios, he did not work all that often during this era, particularly with the gradual decline in popularity of trad jazz in the United States. It was in some ways a lonely time for him because he practically stood alone in his musical generation; his contemporaries were more involved in bop and cool jazz.

Abbie and Merritt Brunies   After decades of not being heard on records, Abbie and Merritt Brunies (the brothers of George Brunies) cut an album in 1957 that has been reissued as **The Brunies Brothers** (American Music 77). Cornetist Abbie, who had led the Halfway House Orchestra in the mid-1920s, freelanced in New Orleans for many years, and moved to Biloxi, Mississippi, in 1946 where he ran a café. Merritt, who had played cornet when he led the Friars Inn Orchestra in the 1920s, but switched to valve trombone in his later years, moved to Biloxi in the late 1920s, becoming a

policeman and only playing music on a part-time basis. Their collaboration finds the Brunies siblings in excellent form, playing spontaneous but relaxed New Orleans jazz with a local sextet that includes clarinetist Jules Galle. Among the songs they perform are "Angry" (co-composed by Merritt), "Zero," "Tin Roof Blues" (which brother George had helped make famous), and "Let Me Call You Sweetheart." This would be the last recording for both Abbie and Merritt Brunies, but fortunately it was a joyous occasion.

Teddy Buckner   Teddy Buckner spent his entire career emulating his idol Louis Armstrong, never seeing any reason to grow beyond his influence. Buckner worked on the West Coast in the 1930s, was in Shanghai, China, with Buck Clayton's orchestra in 1934, and was Satch's stand-in in the 1936 movie *Pennies from Heaven*. His most notable associations were with Benny Carter (1945–47), Lionel Hampton (1947–48), and Kid Ory (1949–54). Buckner led his own band from 1955 on (although he traveled to France to play a few concerts with Sidney Bechet in 1958), displaying his strong technique on Dixieland warhorses. He recorded a few albums for GNP/Crescendo and its subsidiary Dixieland Jubilee including **Salute to Louis Armstrong** (GNP/Crescendo 505). Jamming with a sextet that includes trombonist John "Streamline" Ewing and clarinetist Joe Darensbourg, Buckner stretches out on ten songs that Armstrong had recorded in the 1920s and '30s, including "My Monday Date," "Potato Head Blues," "High Society," and "I Want a Big Butter and Egg Man." Buckner is exciting within the Dixieland format, clearly enjoying playing Armstrong's music.

Ken Colyer   During 1955–59, Ken Colyer's British trad band featured trombonist Mac Duncan, clarinetist Ian Wheeler, banjoist John Bastable, bassist Ron Ward, and drummer Colin Bowden. This was his most famous group, and it looked toward Bunk Johnson, George Lewis, Kid Ory, and other New Orleans players for inspiration while developing a sound of its own within the vintage style. Four CDs include some of the band's recordings of the era. Best is **The Decca Years 1955–59** (Lake 1), which serves as a perfect introduction to the group's joyful and heartfelt music. In addition to such New Orleans standards as "Dippermouth Blues" and "Maryland My Maryland," there are several interpretations of rags, including "Heliotrope Bouquet," "The

Entertainer," and Joseph Lamb's "Sensation." **The Classic Years** (Upbeat 149) has the band stretching out on May 31, 1957, pushing themselves on ensemble-oriented versions of "Bogalusa Strut," "Dauphine Street Blues," "Gettysburg March," and "The Old Rugged Cross." **Up Jumped the Devil** (Upbeat 114) sticks to standards recorded during 1957–58, including "Milenburg Joys," "When You Wore a Tulip," and "Doctor Jazz." **Serenading Auntie** (Upbeat 111) has performances taken from radio and television appearances for the BBC during 1955–60, which are more concise but no less exciting. In 1960, Colyer's band changed a bit, with Graham Stewart (soon succeeded by Geoff Cole) taking over on trombone, and the fine young clarinetist Sammy Rimington taking over for Wheeler.

Eddie Condon   Eddie Condon and his all-star Chicago jazz/Dixieland bands continued playing regularly throughout the 1950s, especially at his Condon's club. Unfortunately, his group's recordings from this era are all pretty scarce. The limited-edition five-CD set **The Complete CBS Eddie Condon All Stars** (Mosaic 5-152) has Condon's Columbia recordings of 1953–57, but this box will become increasingly difficult to locate, and the individual sets (which include 1957's **The Roaring Twenties**) are not available on CD yet. Condon's band frequently featured Wild Bill Davison or Billy Butterfield, trombonist Cutty Cutshall, either Peanuts Hucko, Bob Wilber, or Pee Wee Russell on clarinet, pianist Gene Schroeder, Walter Page, Jack Lesberg, or Leonard Gaskin on bass, and George Wettling or Cliff Leeman on drums. When Davison began to become busy with his own projects, Rex Stewart took his place during 1958–59, with Max Kaminsky also filling in. Recordings for MGM, World Pacific, and Dot (one record apiece) in 1958 and a Warner Bros. album in 1959 all remain out of print but worth searching for.

Wild Bill Davison   Known as a hard-charging cornetist who often blew the roof off of Eddie Condon's, Wild Bill Davison had a surprise success in 1956 with **Pretty Wild**, a set in which he played ballads while backed by a string section. That album and its follow-up have been combined on **Pretty Wild/With Strings Attached** (Arbors 19175). While the original project put the focus entirely on Davison, the later date has clarinetist Bob Wilber and Cutty Cutshall helping out. The strings can get a bit sticky in spots, but Davison's highly expres-

sive playing makes the music much more memorable than expected. Among the better selections are "Mandy Make Up Your Mind," "If I Had You," "When Your Lover Has Gone," "Sugar," "Blue and Broken Hearted," and "Moanin' Low." Otherwise Davison continued playing Dixieland, occasionally with Condon but more as a leader after the commercial success of **Pretty Wild**.

Wilbur DeParis's New New Orleans Jazz   Wilbur DeParis's band recorded regularly for Atlantic during 1955–60, and luckily the music of this colorful group has been reissued by the Collectables label. With Sidney DeParis and Omer Simeon in the frontline, and a variety of veterans in the rhythm section (including pianist Sonny White), the DeParis band retained its popularity throughout the 1950s. Due to Sidney DeParis's sometimes streaky health, Doc Cheatham occasionally filled in for him, and there are some recordings that utilize two trumpets. **New Orleans Blues/Plays Cole Porter** (Collectables 6400) from 1957–58 are departures for the band. The first set has the DeParis group accompanying singer Jimmy Witherspoon on such songs as 'Spoon's trademark "'Tain't Nobody's Bizness If I Do," "Trouble in Mind," and "St. Louis Blues" (the musicians get plenty of short solos) while the Cole Porter date has Dixielandish versions of such unusual tunes (for this setting) as "Easy to Love," "I've Got You Under My Skin," and "Begin the Beguine." **Plays Something Old, New, Gay, Blue/That's A Plenty** (Collectables 6601) features the band during 1958–59. Highlights include "Beale Street Blues," "Panama Rag," "That's A Plenty," and "Change O' Key Boogie."

Later in 1959, Omer Simeon died. For the band's final period, Garvin Bushell (who showed his versatility by playing piccolo and bassoon in addition to clarinet, but was not that strong a jazz soloist) took Simeon's place. **The Wild Jazz Age/On the Riviera** (Collectables 6602) date from 1960, and as usual mix together surprising and often-rambunctious versions of Dixieland standards (including "Clarinet Marmalade," "The Charleston," and "Fidgety Feet") with offbeat material ("Tres Moutarde," "Minorca," and "Twelfth Street Rag"). Other than a sampler of leftover tracks from other sessions, these would be the last full albums by Wilbur DeParis's fun band, which successfully revitalized New Orleans jazz.

The Dukes of Dixieland   In 1956, the Dukes of Dixieland began recording for the Audio Fidelity label, cutting

12 LPs during the next four years plus two with Louis Armstrong. Other than a sampling of the latter (reviewed under Armstrong's name), none of the albums have been reissued on CD. The band was pretty strong, with trumpeter/singer Frank Assunto, trombonist Fred Assunto, and the brother's father Jac Assunto on banjo and second trombone. Other musicians who spent time with the Dukes during this era were clarinetists Harold Cooper, Jack Maheu, Eugene Bolen, and Jerry Fuller, pianist Stan Mendelson, either Bill Porter, Barney Mallon, or Lowell Miller on tuba and bass, and drummers John Edwards, Roger Johnson, Paul Ferrara, Tommy Rundell, and Red Hawley. Although some of the albums are a touch gimmicky topic-wise, ranging from circus themes to minstrel songs, the horn solos (particularly those of Frank Assunto) and the general enthusiasm of the band caused it to stand out from the crowd as one of New Orleans's most popular bands of the time.

Don Ewell   A superior stride pianist who could sound like Jelly Roll Morton, Earl Hines, or Fats Waller, Don Ewell also had his own fresh musical personality. He played professionally starting in the mid-1930s and had stints in the 1940s and '50s with Bunk Johnson, Muggsy Spanier, Sidney Bechet, and Kid Ory (1953) before becoming Jack Teagarden's regular pianist in 1957. During 1956–57, Ewell led three of his finest albums for Good Time Jazz. **Music to Listen to Don Ewell By** (Good Time Jazz 12021), **Man Here Plays Fine Piano** (Good Time Jazz 10043), and ◐ **Free 'N' Easy** (Good Time Jazz 10046) each have the pianist joined on half of the programs by veteran clarinetist Darnell Howard and drummer Minor Hall; bassist Pops Foster makes the group a quartet on the latter two discs. There are also a few solo piano numbers on each of the sets, with the emphasis on vintage tunes from the 1920s. All three of the CDs (which are among Howard's finest recordings) will be enjoyed by trad jazz collectors, with **Free 'N' Easy** getting the edge due to the inclusion of four Ewell piano solos from 1946.

Firehouse Five Plus Two   There were no real changes in the Firehouse Five Plus Two's style during the second half of the 1950s when four additional records were cut for the Good Time Jazz label. The frontline of trombonist/leader Ward Kimball (who doubled on siren), cornetist Danny Alguire, and George Probert (on soprano and clarinet) remained intact with pianist Frank Thomas, banjoist Dick Roberts, Ed Penner (on bass and tuba), and drummer Jim McDonald being the rhythm section for the band in 1956. Eddie Forrest took over on drums in 1957, and, after a bit of turnover (Ralph Ball and George Bruns both recorded with the band on tuba and bass), Don Kinch became Penner's permanent replacement in 1958.

Firehouse Five Plus Two Goes to Sea (Good Time Jazz 10028) mostly has songs that have something to do with the sea, including "When My Dreamboat Comes Home," "A Sailboat in the Moonlight," and "She Was Just a Sailor's Sweetheart." **Firehouse Five Plus Two Crashes a Party** (Good Time Jazz 10038) is often quite humorous. The concept is that the Dixieland band is playing for a drunken crowd of partiers, so between songs there are shouts for requests and a variety of odd remarks from the audience. The humor has dated pretty well as have the jubilant versions of "Let's Have a Party," "Ballin' the Jack," "Bill Bailey," and "When the Saints Go Marching In." **Firehouse Five Plus Two Around the World** (Good Time Jazz 10044) has such tunes as "Japanese Sandman," "Panama," "When Irish Eyes Are Smiling," and "It Happened in Monterey." **16 Dixieland Favorites** (Good Time Jazz 60-008) mostly dates from 1958–60 (with a few later selections), reissuing the LP **Dixieland Favorites** plus five additional numbers from other sessions, focusing on warhorses.

Fans of the Firehouse Five Plus Two will enjoy all of their recordings as this was a fun and very consistent trad band.

Pete Fountain   A talented clarinetist whose style was influenced most by Benny Goodman and Irving Fazola, Pete Fountain played with the Dukes of Dixieland in 1955, recorded with Al Hirt in 1956, and then in 1957 had his big break when he was asked to be a featured soloist on *The Lawrence Welk Show*, a television series. His two years with the bubblemeister's shows (where he was featured on occasional Dixieland songs) gave him national attention and made him quite famous. When Fountain left Welk in 1959, he returned to New Orleans, opened his own club, and began recording extensively for Coral.

Unfortunately, Pete Fountain's prime recordings have yet to be coherently reissued on CD, which is surprising considering that he is still quite well known. There is a cheap and poorly constructed sampler titled **The Best of**

Pete Fountain (GRP/Decca 665) that has an erratic sampling of Fountain's Coral recordings. Better to search for his LPs, which show up in used record stores, including **Pete Fountain's New Orleans** (Coral 57282), **Pete Fountain Day** (Coral 57313), **At the Bateau Lounge** (Coral 57419), **Pete Fountain on Tour** (Coral 57337), and **Pete Fountain's French Quarter, New Orleans** (Coral 57359). In each case Fountain is the main voice, interacting with his rhythm section (Stan Wrightsman or Merle Koch on piano, Morty Corb or Don Bagley on bass, drummer Jack Sperling, and sometimes vibraphonist Godfrey Hirsch), playing Dixieland and swing warhorses with a great deal of enthusiasm and warmth.

Bud Freeman   Bud Freeman led a variety of free-wheeling groups during the 1950s and recorded one classic album, ● **Chicago/Austin High School Jazz in Hi Fi** (RCA 13031). Reissued on CD, but most likely difficult to find, this well-conceived project has three overlapping groups that revisit the repertoire of the McKenzie-Condon Chicagoans of 1927 (playing new versions of the four songs originally recorded), and Freeman's 1939–40 Summa Cum Laude Orchestra. The two septets and the octet mostly have Eddie Condon alumni, all of whom were still in their prime in 1957 and sound quite inspired. Such musicians as Freeman, Jimmy McPartland, Billy Butterfield, Tyree Glenn, Jack Teagarden (who also takes some vocals), Pee Wee Russell, Peanuts Hucko, Gene Schroeder, Dick Cary, rhythm guitarist Al Casamenti (surprisingly not Eddie Condon), Milt Hinton, Al Hall or Leonard Gaskin on bass, and George Wettling are featured on heated versions of "Nobody's Sweetheart," "China Boy," "Chicago," "There'll Be Some Changes Made," and "Jack Hits the Road."

George Girard   One of the brightest new stars in New Orleans during the early 1950s, George Girard should have had a long and productive career. After the Basin Street Six broke up, he led his own bands, cutting a few record sessions along the way for Southland (1953), Imperial (1954–55), and Carnival (1955). Sadly, Girard contracted cancer in 1956 and had an operation that put him out of action for four months. He came back, led three songs for a multi-artist collection for Good Time Jazz, and recorded two live albums for the Vik label on June 12, 1956. **Sounds of New Orleans Vol. 6** (Storyville 6013) has valuable performances by Girard. He is heard in 1954 jamming with trombonist Santo

Pecora, Raymond Burke, tenorman Lester Bouchon, pianist Jeff Riddick, bassist Chink Martin, and drummer Monk Hazel; of the four songs, Pecora's "Zero" is the high point. In addition, there are six numbers from July 1 and 15, 1956, on which the trumpeter (who sings on "Sweethearts on Parade" and "Doctor Jazz") still sounds surprisingly viable with a sextet also including trombonist Bob Havens and clarinetist Harry Shields. But the comeback was short-lived. The cancer came back, and on January 18, 1957, George Girard passed away. He was just 26.

Marty Grosz   Born in 1930, it took Marty Grosz a long time to get known, not really coming into his own until the 1980s. The son of a famous German artist, Grosz grew up in New York, attended Columbia University, and in 1951 led a Dixieland band with Dick Wellstood that went unrecorded. Based in Chicago for many years, Grosz did record with pianist/trombonist Dave Remington, Art Hodes, and Albert Nicholas in the 1950s, and he led sessions of his own in 1957 and 1959 for Riverside and Audio Fidelity. A solid rhythm acoustic guitarist who played chordal solos in the tradition of Dick McDonough and Carl Kress (and would later develop into a Fats Waller–inspired singer and a very humorous personality), Grosz's best early record is **Hooray for Bix** (Good Time Jazz 10065). The guitarist performs a dozen songs recorded in the 1920s by Bix Beiderbecke, including "Changes," "Sorry," "Clementine," and "For No Reason at All in C," mostly avoiding the more obvious tunes and the standards.

Grosz, who takes a few vocals and is quite recognizable, heads the Honoris Causa Jazz Band, an octet/nonet with cornetist Carl Halen, and the Pee Wee Russell–influenced clarinetist and baritone saxophonist Frank Chace. Although nothing much came of this early effort and decades of obscurity were to follow, the project still sounds quite enjoyable.

Bobby Hackett   Due to his mellow pretty sound, melodic style, and strong technical skills, Bobby Hackett kept busy in the 1950s. He was a key voice on Jackie Gleason's commercial but jazz-flavored mood music albums, recorded on a few occasions with Eddie Condon and Jack Teagarden, and led his own bands. During 1956–57, the cornetist headed an unusual group that sought to modernize Dixieland (using Dick Cary's arrangements and an offbeat instrumentation), but that band did not catch on. **Off Minor** (Viper's Nest 162) is split between live sessions headed by Hackett in 1957 and Jack Teagarden in 1958. The six Hackett selections are quite intriguing, feature a group consisting of the cornetist, arranger Dick Cary on piano and alto horn, Ernie Caceres doubling on baritone and clarinet, Tom Gwaltney on clarinet and vibes, the tuba of John Dengler, and drummer Buzzy Drootin. In addition to typically rousing versions of "Fidgety Feet" and "Royal Garden Blues," "Caravan" features Cary's peck horn in the lead, Duke Ellington's "Lady of the Lavender Mist," and the pianist's original "Handle with Cary" are much more modern than one would expect. The vibes-piano-tuba-drums rhythm section does a fine job with Thelonious Monk's "Off Minor," although unfortunately Hackett sat out on that song. The remainder of the CD is more conventional, with Teagarden's Dixieland band (featuring trumpeter Dick Oakley, Jerry Fuller, and Don Ewell) running through four Dixieland warhorses with spirit and drive.

Earl Hines   Throughout his career, Earl "Fatha" Hines was always known as a modern pianist. He was the first (as early as 1928) to break up the rhythms of stride piano, and he led a notable big band for 18 years. But after leaving the Louis Armstrong All-Stars in 1951, Hines struggled for the next decade. After trying to lead a small-group swing band without any commercial success, Hines settled in San Francisco in 1955 and put together an old-fashioned Dixieland band. His group featured trumpeters Marty Marsala (1955) or Muggsy Spanier (1956–59), Darnell Howard, trombonist Jimmy Archey, Ed Garland (1955) or Pops Foster on bass, and drummer Joe Watkins. **Earl Hines and his All-Stars** (GNP/Crescendo 9042) and **Live at the Crescendo Club** (GNP/Crescendo 9054) give one an idea what the band sounded like live. Hines plays in a hyper style, but is mostly flashy rather than creative, and he would soon become bored with this format. Nevertheless he kept similar groups going for several years. In contrast, Spanier (whose style never lost its enthusiasm despite becoming quite predictable by the mid-1950s) and Howard both play with plenty of spirit.

On a higher level is **Another Monday Date** (Prestige 24043), which combines together two of Hines's finest recording sessions of the 1950s on one CD. The first project is a tribute to Fats Waller on which Hines (with guitarist Eddie Duran, bassist Dean Reilly, and Earl Watkins) explores such Waller songs as "Jitterbug Waltz," "Honeysuckle Rose," and "I Can't Give You Anything but Love." The other date is Hines's only solo session of the decade, and he mostly features his own compositions, including "Everything Depends on You," "You Can Depend on Me," "Piano Man," and "My Monday Date." Overall this is brilliant music, but because Hines sensed that there was no demand for it at the time, he led Dixieland bands until the early 1960s.

Al Hirt   A trumpet virtuoso, Al Hirt had the technique to be a classical or a modern jazz trumpeter, but he stuck throughout his career to Dixieland and melodic pop music, accomplishing a lot less (while becoming famous) then he could have. Born in 1922, he did not become well known until he was already in his thirties. Hirt studied classical trumpet at the Cincinnati Conservatory (1940–43), and Harry James was his early hero. After serving in the military, he worked with several swing bands (including Jimmy Dorsey, Tommy Dorsey, Horace Heidt, and Ray McKinley), returning to his native New Orleans in the late 1940s. He worked as a studio musician for a local radio station for eight years. Hirt made his recording debut as a leader on **New Orleans All Stars** (Southland 211), but unfortunately that date and his others from this period have not been reissued on CD. The 1957 LP **The Very Best of Al Hirt and Pete Fountain** (MGM 5517) is a classic and does rank with the very best of both Hirt and Fountain. Also worth searching for are the four LPs **Swingin' Dixie Vols. 1–4** (Audio Fidelity 1877, 1878, 1926, and 1927), which have Hirt playing Dixieland standards in a sextet with Bob Havens and clarinetist Harold Cooper. In 1960, the colorful and powerful trumpeter (whose nickname was "Jumbo" due to his weight) signed with RCA, and soon he would have commercial success with a few instrumental pop hits.

Thomas Jefferson   A talented if often overlooked trumpeter/vocalist, Thomas Jefferson was a fixture in New Orleans for several decades. He worked with Oscar Celestin's Tuxedo Orchestra in 1936, and then had gigs locally with Sidney Desvignes, Jump Jackson, Johnny St. Cyr, Santo Pecora, and George Lewis among others. **Thomas Jefferson from New Orleans** (Storyville 131) has Jefferson performing four songs in a 1953 sextet that also includes trombonist Jack Delaney and Raymond

Burke. However, this LP (which is overdue to reappear on CD) is most notable for the eight selections from 1960 that showcase Jefferson's trumpet and vocals in a quintet with pianist Armand Hug and drummer Monk Hazel. Strongly influenced by Louis Armstrong, Jefferson also displays an appealing musical personality of his own on joyful versions of such numbers as "When You're Smiling," "There'll Be Some Changes Made," and "Someday You'll Be Sorry." This was his definitive set.

Peck Kelley, Joseph Lamb, and Donald Lambert
These three legendary pianists almost went unrecorded in their careers. Peck Kelley went out of his way not to be recorded and to play in obscurity. At one time in the 1920s, his group Peck's Bad Boys in Texas featured Jack Teagarden and Pee Wee Russell. Kelly's piano playing was considered quite advanced, and through the years he turned down gigs with the likes of Bing Crosby, Bob Crosby, Tommy Dorsey, Jimmy Dorsey, and Paul Whiteman, preferring to stay home in Houston. The Will Bradley hit "Beat Me Daddy, Eight to the Bar" was a tribute to him although his name was never mentioned. However, in the 1980s after his death, two sets were released that reveal how Kelley sounded later in his career. Private sessions came out as the double LP **Out of Obscurity** (Arcadia 2018). Kelley is heard on a short interview from the early 1970s and on a series of piano solos from 1951 and '53; in addition there are five solos by his friend, fellow pianist Lynn "Son" Harrell. Kelley had evolved through the years from a stride player to one not unaware of the music of Lennie Tristano and Bud Powell. In 1957, Kelley recorded enough music for another double LP that was also released posthumously, a sextet date released as Peck Kelley (Commodore 17017). Along with clarinetist Dick Shannon and guitarist Felix Stagno, Kelley stretches out on 13 standards and a blues, hinting at his roots in 1920s jazz, but often sounding surprisingly modern on such numbers as "Limehouse Blues," "Riverboat Shuffle," "You Took Advantage of Me," and "Tea for Two." Although Peck Kelley would live until 1980, he would never come close to recording again.

Joseph Lamb was 81 when he made his only record, **A Study in Classic Ragtime** (Folkways 3562) in August 1959. Lamb was one of the big three of ragtime composers, and, unlike the long-deceased Scott Joplin and James Scott, he did have this one opportunity to be

documented. In addition to performing ten of his rags (including "Sensation Rag," "Ragtime Nightingale," "American Beauty Rag," and his then-recent "Cottontail Rag"), Lamb is heard talking about four different topics, including remembrances of his first meeting with Scott Joplin and his favorable opinions of the other ragtime composers. This priceless set is also not available on CD yet.

Donald Lambert was considered one of the great stride pianists of the 1920s and '30s, but he preferred to stay in New Jersey, playing in out-of-the-way clubs. The only time that he entered a recording studio was on January 30, 1941, when he cut four stride versions of classical themes for Bluebird. In the 1980s, four privately recorded live sets from 1960–62 were released on low-fi but fascinating LPs: **Giant Strides** (Solo Art 18001), **Meet the Lamb** (IAJRC 23), **Classics in Stride** (Pumpkin 110), and **Harlem Stride Classics** (Pumpkin 104). Even with the erratic sound quality and the out-of-tune pianos, Lambert's brilliant technique and appealing ideas come through, and one can understand why he was held in such high esteem by his contemporaries.

George Lewis's Ragtime Band   The music of clarinetist George Lewis may have been primitive and erratic, but his band continued to grow in popularity during this era, visiting England and Scandinavia. Kid Howard, who was on so many live records with Lewis during 1952–55, departed in 1956, and was replaced by Thomas Jefferson (who was a definite improvement) before returning in 1959. The remainder of the band (Jim Robinson, Alton Purnell, Slow Drag Pavageau, and Joe Watkins) mostly remained intact other than Joe Robichaux taking over on piano in 1957.

In Stockholm 1959 (Dragon 221) is one of the best sessions of Lewis's later years. The first half of the set in particular finds all of the musicians in top form, although Kid Howard's trumpet playing starts getting ragged by the halfway point. Lewis is heard near the peak of his expressive powers on such songs as "Should I," "Burgundy Street Blues," an uptempo "Red Wing," "Runnin' Wild," and "Milenburg Joys," playing before an enthusiastic crowd.

Miff Mole   Miff Mole, who had been among the most advanced trombonists of the mid-1920s, struggled with bad health throughout the 1950s. In 1958, he recorded a pretty good Dixieland album whose dozen selections are reissued as the first half of **The Immortal Miff Mole** (Jazzology 5). Despite being in declining health (he died two years later), Mole sounds fine on this set, which is highlighted by "Fidgety Feet," "For Me and My Gal," "Wolverine Blues," "Who's Sorry Now," and a spontaneous six-minute blues, "Miffology." The group features such veterans as pianist Frank Signorelli, bassist Jack Lesberg, drummer Chauncey Morehouse, either Jack Palmer or Lee Castle on trumpet, and Joe Dixon or Jimmy Lytell on clarinet. Filling out the CD are ten selections taken from Eddie Condon's Town Hall concerts of 1944 that feature Mole along with such notables as Bobby Hackett, Max Kaminsky, Muggsy Spanier, Edmond Hall, and Pee Wee Russell. Although Miff Mole will always be best remembered for his work in the 1920s, if he had had better breaks and much better health, the 1950s could have found him enjoying a renaissance.

Albert Nicholas   Albert Nicholas, who made his permanent home in France in 1953, recorded two albums for Delmark in July 1959 during a rare visit to the United States. **New Orleans-Chicago Connection** (Delmark 207) teams the melodic clarinetist with Art Hodes, bassist Earl Murphy, and drummer Freddy Kohlman, playing a set of standards and blues. The 1997 CD reissue not only has the original 11 selections, but nine alternate takes and a previously unissued "Careless Love" from the same sessions. **All-Star Stompers** (Delmark 209) once again matches Nicholas with Hodes, but this time in a septet also including trumpeter Nappy Trottier, trombonist Floyd O'Brien, and guitarist Marty Grosz. The excellent ensemble plays seven Dixieland standards, "You Gotta See Your Mama Every Night" and "How Long Blues" with plenty of spirit and joy. Both discs are easily enjoyable, making one regret that Albert Nicholas had to live overseas in order to gain the steady work and acclaim that he deserved.

Red Nichols's Five Pennies   Red Nichols recorded several now out-of-print albums for Capitol during 1955–59, mostly playing Dixieland and co-featuring the bass sax of Joe Rushton. In 1959, he recorded the definitive version of "Battle Hymn of the Republic," taking the song at three different tempos in very memorable fashion. That classic was last available on the LP **All Time Hits of Red Nichols** (Pausa 9022).

In 1959, Red Nichols was the subject of the Danny Kaye movie *The Five Pennies*. Although the storyline was mostly fiction, Nichols ghosted the cornet parts for Kaye, Louis Armstrong had a major part, and the film was quite entertaining, one of the best of the jazz movies of the 1950s. It made Nichols into a celebrity again and added momentum to his career during his last years.

Kid Ory's Creole Jazz Band   Kid Ory continued playing regularly during this era, including visiting Europe. His band featured Alvin Alcorn (into 1957), Marty Marsala, Teddy Buckner or Henry "Red" Allen on trumpet, Phil Gomez, Darnell Howard, Caughey Roberts, Cedric Haywood or Bob McCracken on clarinet, and several rhythm sections. **Favorites!** (Good Time Jazz 60-009) has 15 of the 17 selections originally issued on a double LP; the last Ory recordings for Good Time Jazz. Ory, Alcorn, and Gomez make for a very tight but spontaneous frontline, featuring strong melodic solos and exciting ensembles that pay close attention to dynamics, and gradually build up the excitement level. Among the best selections are "Do What Ory Says," "Jazz Me Blues," "Original Dixieland One-Step," "Panama," "Maryland, My Maryland," and "1919 Rag."

Ory's band recorded no less than nine albums for Verve during 1956–60, but these are thus far only available as the limited edition eight-CD box **The Complete Kid Ory Verve Sessions** (Mosaic 8-189). Best are two lengthy sessions with Marty Marsala from 1957 (which are arguably Marsala's most rewarding recordings), and an extended set with Red Allen, who really inspires the group.

Luckey Roberts   After having not been on records at all outside of a very good session in 1946, Luckey Roberts (a contemporary of James P. Johnson) recorded 1½ albums' worth of material in 1958 when he was 70. ● **Harlem Piano Solos** (Good Time Jazz 10035) has Roberts performing six originals. All of them (including "Nothin'," "Inner Space," and "Outer Space") are obscure but worth hearing. The second half of the CD features Willie "The Lion" Smith on six piano solos of his own, including five of his songs (highlighted by "Relaxin'" and "Concentratin'"), and the standard "Between the Devil and the Deep Blue Sea." The other Roberts recording, **Happy Go Lucky** (Period 1929), is not yet out on CD and is a more conventional Dixieland-based quartet date with Garvin Bushell on clarinet and alto. Luckey Roberts, who had ten more years to live, never recorded again.

Pee Wee Russell   Starting in 1957 when he played a blues with fellow clarinetist Jimmy Giuffre on *The Sound of Jazz* telecast, Pee Wee Russell began appearing in more modern settings, which seemed only right since he always had an unusual and advanced style. During 1958–60, he recorded four albums that could be considered modern swing. Two of them are in print and have been reissued together on **Swingin' with Pee Wee** (Prestige 24213). Russell and Buck Clayton make for a very compatible team on a session from 1960 with a relaxed quintet also including Tommy Flanagan, Wendell Marshall, and Osie Johnson. The other date (from 1958) has Nat Pierce's arrangements for a septet also including Ruby Braff, Vic Dickenson, and Bud Freeman. Russell sounds quite comfortable on the medium-tempo material (mostly high quality standards), and he gets to avoid the overly hyper Dixieland warhorses that had helped drive him to drink.

Bob Scobey   Bob Scobey worked steadily throughout the 1950s. The trumpeter was based in Oakland and Los Angeles until 1959 when he opened up his Club Bourbon Street in Chicago. Among his sidemen were trombonists Jack Buck, Jim Beebe, and Ricky Nelson, clarinetist Bill Napier, pianists Jesse Crump, Ralph Sutton, Gene Schroeder, and Art Hodes, and (through 1959) singer/banjoist Clancy Hayes. **Direct from San Francisco** (Good Time Jazz 12023) was the last in a string of excellent sets for Good Time Jazz. This 1956 date features familiar warhorses played with spirit and high musicianship, and includes six excellent Hayes vocals (most memorable are "Curse of an Aching Heart" and "Travelin' Shoes"). Recorded in 1958, **Scobey and Clancy Raid the Juke Box** (Good Time Jazz 12056) was originally recorded for the tiny California label and later acquired by Good Time Jazz. Scobey explores pop tunes, turning them into Dixieland. Some of the tunes (such as "Yellow Dog Blues," "Blueberry Hill," "C.C. Rider," and "Singin' the Blues") were obvious ringers, but these versions of "All Shook Up," "Love Letters in the Sand," "Tammy," and "Bye Bye Love" are certainly unique in their own way.

Bob Scobey also recorded nine albums for Verve, two for Jansco, and one for Ragtime. The Verves are unavailable, but **Bob Scobey Vol. 1** (Jazzology 275) has all of the music from the first Jansco date and six of the ten numbers from the Ragtime LP while **Bob Scobey Vol. 2** (Jazzology 285) has the second Jansco session and the remainder of the Ragtime set. Most notable about the Jansco albums is that Clancy Hayes shares the vocal spotlight with Lizzie Miles.

Unfortunately, Bob Scobey would not record again after 1960. He was soon stricken with cancer and passed away three years later at age 46.

Elmer Snowden   Elmer Snowden must have seemed like a ghost from the distant past in 1960, since he had been the leader of the Washingtonians in 1924, before Duke Ellington had taken over. Snowden had continued playing through the years although he rarely recorded. On December 9, 1960, he had his first opportunity to lead a record date, and it is an excellent one, **Harlem Banjo** (Original Jazz Classics 1756). Assisted by Cliff Jackson, Tommy Bryant, and drummer Jimmy Crawford, Snowden's banjo is the lead voice throughout the dozen standards, all of which date from the 1920s or '30s, including several from the book of Duke Ellington. Single-string banjo playing might have been largely a lost art, but Elmer Snowden still sounds pretty lively on this set.

Jack Teagarden   After leaving the Louis Armstrong All-Stars in 1952, Jack Teagarden led a Dixieland sextet for the rest of his life. He toured Europe in 1957 (using Max Kaminsky, Peanuts Hucko, Earl Hines, bassist Jack Lesberg, and Cozy Cole), and during 1958–59 underwent an extensive tour of Asia; by then his group included Kaminsky, Jerry Fuller, and Don Ewell. Don Goldie succeeded Kaminsky in 1959

The Complete Capitol Fifties Jack Teagarden Sessions (Mosaic 4-168) has Teagarden's six albums for Capitol from 1955–58, but those are not yet available individually; neither are his Roulette albums of 1959–61, which Mosaic also reissued as **The Complete Roulette Jack Teagarden Sessions** (Mosaic 4-218). **Jack Teagarden and His All Stars** (Jazzology 199) is on CD, a live date from 1958 with cornetist Dick Oakley, Jerry Fuller, and Don Ewell. Even on such tunes as "Someday You'll Be Sorry," "High Society," and "When the Saints Go Marching In," Teagarden's group plays with enthusiasm and creativity, coming up with something fresh to say on songs that the musicians had already performed countless times.

Latin Jazz: 1956–1960

Although rising a bit in popularity, there were not that many major changes in the Afro-Cuban/Latin jazz scene during 1956–60. Cal Tjader's band became one of the most popular from the jazz world while the ensembles of Tito Puente, Tito Rodriguez, and Machito continued as the big three from the Cuban side. Herbie Mann in 1959 switched from straightahead to Latin jazz, forming the Afro-Jazz Sextet. Conguero Mongo Santamaria and drummer/timbale player Willie Bobo left Puente's group in 1957 to join Tjader's; Santamaria also began leading his own record dates. Pianist Charlie Palmieri caused a stir in the Latin music world when he formed Charanga Duboney in 1958, bringing back a traditional instrumentation (with flutist Johnny Pacheco and four violins), but with a more modern repertoire.

The two main developments were the gradual acceptance of conga players on otherwise straightahead record dates (Ray Barretto, Candido, Sabu Martinez, and Patato Valdes were important forces in this area) and the closing of Cuba in 1960 after the Castro revolution. With the exception of Cubans who were able to escape and defect, it would not be until the second half of the 1970s before new players from Cuba would start entering the American jazz world again.

Machito   Machito's Orchestra had fewer collaborations with major jazz names in the last half of the 1950s, but 1957's **Kenya** (Roulette 22668) is an exception. The mighty ensemble plays a dozen songs (all originals except "Tin Tin Deo") arranged by either A.K. Salim or the team of Mario Bauza (still Machito's musical director) and pianist Rene Hernandez. Cannonball Adderley and Joe Newman are the featured guests, and the band also includes Doc Cheatham (playing first trumpet), trombonist Eddie Bert, and a seven-piece percussion section with Candido, Jose Mangual, and Patato Valdes. The music is quite infectious and stirring.

Herbie Mann   During 1954–58, flutist Herbie Mann (doubling at times on tenor and bass clarinet) was primarily involved in playing straightahead jazz, recording frequently. Among his more notable sessions were **Flute Soufflé** (Original Jazz Classics 760), which teams him with Bobby Jaspar, the West Coast–flavored **Sultry Serenade** (Original Jazz Classics 927), **Great Ideas of Western Mann** (Original Jazz Classics 1065), which is a quintet date with Jack Sheldon, **Flute Fraternity** (V.S.O.P. 38), which has him sharing the spotlight with Buddy Collette in a quintet, and **Just Wailin'** (Original Jazz Classics 900), a hard bop sextet date with Charlie Rouse, Kenny Burrell, and Mal Waldron.

In 1959, Mann changed direction, forming the Afro-Jazz Sextet, a group comprised of his flute, John Rae on vibes and timbales, bassist Knobby Totah, drummer Santo Miranda, and both Patato Valdes and Jose Mangual on percussion. **Flautista** (Verve 557448) was his first recording in this new format, and he sounds quite at home playing over the Afro-Cuban rhythms on five of his originals (including "Cuban Potato Chips" and "Todos Locos"), "Delilah," and "Caravan." By 1960 his band was expanded (Doc Cheatham was one of the four trumpeters who were added), and Mann took his group to Africa with strong success. But, typical of Herbie Mann, he would not stand still musically for long.

Sabu Martinez   A major conga and bongo player, Sabu Martinez started playing professionally in 1941 when he was only 11. He was Chano Pozo's replacement with Dizzy Gillespie's orchestra in 1948, worked with Benny Goodman's bebop big band in 1949, and freelanced extensively in the 1950s, appearing on dates with Charlie Parker, Duke Ellington, Count Basie, J.J. Johnson, Horace Silver, Thelonious Monk, Charles Mingus, Art Blakey, and many others. In 1957, he put together his own group and recorded **Palo Congo** (Blue Note 22665), a date dominated by percussionists, singers, and Arsenio Rodriguez (who plays the Cuban tres guitar). The lively African-oriented music grows in interest with each listen.

Tito Puente   Tito Puente was one of the main Latin music kings in the 1950s. His percussion section with Mongo Santamaria and Willie Bobo (known with Puente as "Ti-Mon-Bo") during 1955–57 was considered the most exciting. After Santamaria and Bobo left later in 1957 to join Cal Tjader, Puente was able to find perfectly suitable replacements in Ray Barretto and later on Candido and Patato Valdes.

Two of Puente's most interesting jazz-oriented records from the period are **Puente Goes Jazz** (Bluebird 66148) and **Night Beat** (Koch 7847). The first album (from 1956) has Puente leading a big band comprised of studio musicians plus his own rhythm section with Santamaria and Bobo. The music swings, the musicianship of the big band is excellent, and the rhythm section is explosive. **Night Beat** has a similar concept except that it is mostly more straightahead. Trumpeter Doc Severinsen and tenor saxophonist Marty Holmes (who sounds a bit like Paul Quinichette) take excellent solos;

the tunes include an uptempo "Carioca," "Flying Down to Rio," and "Mambo Beat."

Mongo Santamaria   One of the great conga players, Ramon "Mongo" Santamaria came from a very poor family in Cuba. He started on violin, switched to drums, and then had to drop out of school in seventh grade in order to work as a mechanic. He was self-taught on conga, bongos, and timbales, picking up the lifelong nickname of "Mongo" (which means "leader of the tribe"). In 1940 when he was 18, Santamaria became a mailman, playing music at night. It was not until 1948 that he finally became a full-time musician, accompanying dancers in Mexico and New York, permanently settling in the United States in 1950. Santamaria worked with Tito Puente during 1951–57, and, after guesting on an album with Cal Tjader, he left Puente, briefly co-led El Conjunto Manhattan with Willie Bobo, and then became a member of Tjader's band for three years, leading a few of his own sessions for Fantasy.

Afro Roots (Prestige 24018) has Santamaria's first two albums as a leader (**Yambu** and **Mongo**). **Yambu** has six percussionists (including Willie Bobo and Francisco Aguabella), two singers, and bassist Al McKibbon. **Mongo** features six percussionists, three singers, McKibbon, vibraphonist Emil Richards, and flutist Paul Horn. These were among the first largely all-percussion and chant/vocal Afro-Cuban recordings cut in the United States, and a highlight is the debut recording of Santamaria's most famous composition, "Afro Blue." **Our Man in Havana** (Fantasy 24729) has two very different albums from 1960, cut during a visit to Cuba (shortly before the doors closed) by Santamaria and Bobo. While the first set utilizes an unusual instrumentation for a Cuban band (two trumpets, flute, piano, Nino Rivera on tres, bass, timbales, bongos, guiro, conga, and two vocalists) and has its stirring moments, the second date is completely outside of jazz, featuring folk melodies and religious songs performed by a group of singers, with the percussion of Santamaria and Bobo being the only instruments.

Cal Tjader   Leader of the most popular Latin jazz combo of the period, Cal Tjader alternated in his recordings between straightahead jazz and Afro-Cuban music. Among his sidemen were pianists Manuel Duran and Vince Guaraldi, guitarist Eddie Duran, bassists Carlos Duran and Al McKibbon, Luis Miranda on conga, and

Brew Moore. In late 1957, he scored a major coup when Mongo Santamaria and Willie Bobo left Tito Puente to join his band. Paul Horn and Jose "Chombo" Silva spent periods later in the decade as Tjader's reed player. Few other Latin jazz groups could keep up with the increasingly influential Tjader band, both in its productivity and its growing popularity.

Fortunately, Cal Tjader was quite prolific, cutting 18 records for the Fantasy label in five years. **Latin Kick** (Original Jazz Classics 642) has Latinized versions of such songs as "Invitation," "I Love Paris," and "Bye Bye Blues" with Brew Moore being a major asset. **Black Orchid** (Fantasy 24730) contains all of the music from the former LPs **Cal Tjader Quintet** and **Cal Tjader Goes Latin**. The 21 selections (which often feature Horn, Silva, or the Duran brothers) are interpreted with infectious joy. **Cal Tjader's Latin Concert** (Original Jazz Classics 643) from 1958 has the unbeatable quintet of Tjader, Guaraldi, McKibbon, Santamaria, and Bobo performing four of the vibraphonist's tunes (including "Viva Cepeda"), two by Santamaria, "Cubano Chant," and "The Continental." **Black Hawk Nights** (Fantasy 24755) consists of all of the music from the LP **A Night at the Black Hawk** (which has Chombo Silva in prime form sounding like a mixture of Stan Getz and Paul Quinichette), and all but one number from **Live and Direct**, a relatively boppish quartet date (Willie Bobo is on drums) other than the closing "Mambo Terrifico," which adds Santamaria and flutist Rolando Lozano.

One of the high points of Cal Tjader's career was his recorded appearance at a preview concert for the 1959 Monterey Jazz Festival. ● **Monterey Concerts** (Prestige 24026) is a single CD having all of the music from the former two-LP set, alternating boppish standards (such as "Doxy" and "Love Me or Leave Me") with stirring Latin version of "Afro Blue" and "A Night in Tunisia." **Latino** (Fantasy 24732) features Tjader with five different groups from 1960; the music was formerly on the albums **Demasiado Caliente** and **Latino**. The stars include Lozano, Horn, pianist Eddie Cano, McKibbon, Santamaria, and Bobo. In the straightahead area, **Cal Tjader Quartet** (Original Jazz Classics 950) features Tjader playing bebop with the Gerald Wiggins trio, while **Jazz at the Blackhawk** (Original Jazz Classics 436) is a cool bop quartet outing with Vince Guaraldi, highlighted by "I'll Remember April," "Lover Come Back to Me," and Guaraldi's "Thinking of You, MJQ."

Various Artists   Six various artists collections from the 1956–60 period are of interest, covering West Coast jazz, bop, swing, Dixieland, and Third Stream music.

Piano Playhouse (V.S.O.P. 31) has four piano solo performances apiece by Carl Perkins, Jimmy Rowles, Gerald Wiggins, Paul Smith, and Lou Levy, all recorded on September 13, 1957. Originally recorded for the Mode label, the music went unreleased until 1986 because Mode soon went out of business. The musicians display fairly similar and complementary styles, giving listeners a survey of sorts into West Coast jazz piano of the period. Particularly valuable (due to the few recordings he made) are the four solos from Carl Perkins.

Birdland Stars 1956 (Bluebird 66159) has all of the music from two former LPs from 1956 featuring Kenny Dorham, Conte Candoli, Phil Woods, Al Cohn, Hank Jones, bassist John Simmons, and Kenny Clarke. The septet performs six originals apiece by arrangers Manny Albam and Ernie Wilkins. The music is straightahead bebop, showing that there was less difference between East Coast hard bop (Dorham, Woods) and West Coast cool jazz (Candoli, Cohn) than originally thought. The division between the two styles of music would largely come down altogether within a few years.

Swing Trumpet Kings (Verve 314 533 263) is a double CD bringing together the music from three unrelated sessions from 1956–60 featuring swing era trumpeters. One set has Harry "Sweets" Edison and Buck Clayton along with Jimmy Forrest and a supportive rhythm section performing typically tasteful swing. There is not much taste in a rambunctious set featuring Henry "Red" Allen in which he sounds as if he were playing for the drunks at his usual gig at New York's Metropole. The music, which also features Buster Bailey and trombonist Herb Flemming, is certainly full of spirit and adventure even if it is sloppy at times. The oddest of the trio of albums is Roy Eldridge's, for he is heard doing his best to play Dixieland. He plays the melody lines and riffs to Dixieland standards quite well in the ensembles although his own more modern solos do not always fit the music. Pianist Dick Wellstood, trombonist Benny Morton, and clarinetist Eddie Barefield understand the idiom better, and it is intriguing hearing Eldridge playing such unlikely songs as "That's A Plenty," "Royal Garden Blues," "Jazz Me Blues," and "Bugle Call Rag."

Recorded in New Orleans Vol. 1 (Good Time Jazz 12019) and **Vol. 2** (Good Time Jazz 12020) feature four groups that were active in New Orleans during 1956, performing three songs apiece in each CD. **Vol. 1** has hot numbers from Sharkey Bonano's Kings of Dixieland (which includes Pete Fountain), Paul Barbarin, Bill Matthews, and George Girard, while **Vol. 2** features Johnny Wiggs, Eddie Pierson, Santo Pecora's Tailgaters, and Armand Hug's Trio. The musicianship is excellent, the musicians are all in tune, and both the repertoire and the arrangements are inspired.

In the late 1950s, the future of jazz was often being speculated on in print by critics, scholars, and musicians. Many believed in Gunther Schuller's idea of combining the improvisation of jazz with classical music in a new idiom that he called Third Stream. **The Birth of the Third Stream** (Columbia/Legacy 64929) has all of the music from the LP of the same name plus four of the six numbers (leaving out two advanced classical pieces) from **Modern Jazz Concert**. Recorded during 1956–57, the orchestra utilized is essentially a large brass band with plenty of trumpets, trombones, French horns, and baritone horns, but at the most only a few woodwinds and oddly enough no violins, violas, or cellos. Of the eight original works, the most famous of the pieces are two that feature Miles Davis ("Three Little Feelings" and "Poem for Brass") and George Russell's "All About Rosie," which puts the focus on Bill Evans. The other performances are Charles Mingus's "Revelations," and two compositions apiece by Jimmy Giuffre and Gunther Schuller that are somewhat dry.

Was this going to be the future of jazz? Was jazz going to become a music emphasizing sophisticated arrangements as played by symphony orchestras with occasional solos?

John Coltrane, Ornette Coleman, and the up-and-coming avant-garde jazz movement would soon make sure that the answer was not yes.

VOICES OF THE FUTURE

Didier Lockwood (violin), Feb. 11, 1956, Calais, France

Gary Smulyan (baritone), Apr. 4, 1956, Bethpage, NY

Holly Hofmann (flute), Apr. 20, 1956, Painesville, OH

Bruce Forman (guitar), May 14, 1956, Springfield, MA

Uri Caine (piano), June 8, 1956, Philadelphia, PA

Jamaaladeen Tacuma (bass), June 11, 1956, Hempstead, NY

Bill Cunliffe (piano), June 26, 1956, Lawrence, MA

Franklin Kiermyer (drums), July 21, 1956, Montreal, Quebec, Canada

Doug Raney (guitar), Aug. 29, 1956, New York, NY

Brian Lynch (trumpet), Sept. 12, 1956, Champaign, IL

Steve Coleman (alto), Sept. 20, 1956, Chicago, IL

Johnny O'Neal (piano), Oct. 10, 1956, Detroit, MI

Jane Bunnett (flute, soprano), Oct. 22, 1956, Toronto, Canada

Dianne Reeves (vocals), Oct. 23, 1956, Detroit, MI

Bob Belden (arranger, tenor, producer), Oct. 31, 1956, Charleston, SC

Ralph Moore (tenor), Dec. 24, 1956, London, England

Joe Cohn (guitar), Dec. 28, 1956, Flushing, NY

Myra Melford (piano), Jan. 5, 1957, Glencoe, IL

Billy Childs (piano), Mar. 8, 1957, Los Angeles, CA

Thomas Chapin (alto, soprano), Mar. 9, 1957, Manchester, CT

Vanessa Rubin (vocals), Mar. 14, 1957, Cleveland, OH

Geri Allen (piano), June 12, 1957, Pontiac, MI

Tom Varner (French horn), June 17, 1957, Morristown, NJ

Hendrik Meurkens (harmonica, vibes), Aug. 6, 1957, Hamburg, Germany

Emily Remler (guitar), Sept. 18, 1957, New York, NY

Clifton Anderson (trombone), Oct. 5, 1957, New York, NY

Kevin Eubanks (guitar), Nov. 15, 1957, Philadelphia, PA

Eric Marienthal (alto), Dec. 19, 1957, Sacramento, CA

Lori Andrews (harp), Jan. 23, 1958, Philadelphia, PA

Bill Evans (tenor, soprano), Feb. 9, 1958, Clarendon Hills, IL

Leroy Jones (trumpet), Feb. 20, 1958, New Orleans, LA

Jeanie Bryson (vocals), Mar. 10, 1958, New York, NY

Kendra Shank (vocals), Apr. 23, 1958, Woodland, NY

Kenny Washington (drums), May 29, 1958, Brooklyn, NY

Kenny Drew, Jr. (piano), June 14, 1958, New York, NY

Loren Schoenberg (tenor, arranger), July 23, 1958, Fairlawn, NJ

Kevin Mahogany (vocals), July 30, 1958, Kansas City, MO

Howard Alden (guitar), Oct. 17, 1958, Newport Beach, CA

Kent Jordan (flute), Oct. 28, 1958, New Orleans, LA

Don Byron (clarinet), Nov. 8, 1958, New York, NY

Frank Gambale (guitar), Dec. 22, 1958, Canberra, Australia

Lewis Nash (drums), Dec. 30, 1958, Phoenix, AZ

Scott Robinson (tenor, baritone, bass sax), Apr. 27, 1959, Pompton Plains, NJ

Virginia Mayhew (alto, tenor), May 14, 1959, Palo Alto, CA

John Lindberg (bass), May 16, 1959, Royal Oak, MI

Ken Peplowski (clarinet, tenor), May 23, 1959, Garfield Heights, OH

Marcus Miller (bass, bass clarinet), June 14, 1959, New York, NY

Walt Weiskopf (tenor), July 30, 1959, Augusta, GA

Stanley Jordan (guitar), July 31, 1959, Chicago, IL

Ellery Eskelin (tenor), Aug. 16, 1959, Wichita, KS

Michael Mossman (trumpet, trombone), Oct. 12, 1959, Philadelphia, PA

Conrad Herwig (trombone), Nov. 1, 1959, Ft. Sill, OK

Cindy Blackman (drums), Nov. 18, 1959, Yellow Springs, OH

John Patitucci (bass), Dec. 22, 1959, Brooklyn, NY

Ted Nash (tenor), Dec. 28, 1959, Los Angeles, CA

Jeff "Tain" Watts (drums), Jan. 20, 1960, Pittsburgh, PA

Craig Bailey (alto sax), Feb. 3, 1960, Cincinnati, OH

Eliane Elias (piano), Mar. 19, 1960, Sao Paulo, Brazil

John Pizzarelli (guitar, vocals), Apr. 6, 1960, Paterson, NJ

Wallace Roney (trumpet), May 25, 1960, Philadelphia, PA

Arturo O'Farrill (piano), June 22, 1960, Mexico City, Mexico

Donald Harrison (alto), June 23, 1960, New Orleans, LA

Greg Osby (alto), Aug. 3, 1960, St. Louis, MO

Branford Marsalis (tenor, soprano), Aug. 26, 1960, Breaux Bridge, LA

Lonnie Plaxico (bass), Sept. 4, 1960, Chicago, IL

Graham Haynes (cornet), Sept. 16, 1960, Brooklyn, NY

Django Bates (piano), Oct. 2, 1960, Beckenham, England

Kenny Garrett (alto), Oct. 9, 1960, Detroit, MI

Maria Schneider (composer, arranger, piano, leader), Nov. 27, 1960, Windom, MN

Brian Bromberg (bass), Dec. 5, 1960, Tucson, AZ

Matthew Shipp (piano), Dec. 7, 1960, Wilmington, DE

PASSINGS

Adrian Rollini (51), May 15, 1956, Homestead, FL

Valaida Snow (55), May 30, 1956, New York, NY

Frankie Trumbauer (55), June 11, 1956, Kansas City, MO

Clifford Brown (25), June 26, 1956, PA

Isham Jones (62), Oct. 19, 1956, Hollywood, FL

Art Tatum (46), Nov. 5, 1956, Los Angeles, CA

Tommy Dorsey (51), Nov. 26, 1956, Greenwich, CT

George Girard (26), Jan. 18, 1957, New Orleans, LA

Jimmy Dorsey (53), June 12, 1957, New York, NY

Serge Chaloff (33), July 16, 1957, Boston, MA

Walter Page (57), Dec. 20, 1957, New York, NY

Ernie Henry (31), Dec. 29, 1957, New York, NY

Carl Perkins (29), Mar. 17, 1958, Los Angeles, CA

W.C. Handy (84), Mar. 28, 1958, New York, NY

Julia Lee (56), Dec. 8, 1958, Kansas City, MO

Baby Dodds (60), Feb. 14, 1959, Chicago, IL

Lester Young (49), Mar. 15, 1959, New York, NY

Sidney Bechet (62), May 14, 1959, Paris, France

Billie Holiday (44), July 17, 1959, New York, NY

Omer Simeon (57), Sept. 17, 1959, New York, NY

Lee Collins (58), July 3, 1960, Chicago, IL

Joseph Lamb (72), Sept. 3, 1960, Brooklyn, NY

Oscar Pettiford (37), Sept. 8, 1960, Copenhagen, Denmark

Fred Van Eps (71), Nov. 22, 1960, Burbank, CA

Chapter Nine

1961–1967:
The Race Toward Freedom

The music world changed drastically during 1961–67. While rock 'n' roll in 1961 was considered by many to be dance music for teenagers, full of clichés, simplistic rhythms, crooning singers, and heart-throbs who were not half as menacing as many jazz musicians, the rise of the Beatles during 1963–64, the British Invasion, Motown, and rock in general by 1965 took away much of jazz's younger audience. Instead of jazz being seen as the anti-establishment music, rock now assumed that position, while Motown grabbed the attention of a large part of the younger black audience. With many jazz clubs closing and some of the labels struggling, the pressure began to build for jazz musicians to record cover versions of rock hits, even though that repertoire rarely transferred well to jazz. And, although there was a bit of mutual interest between jazz and rock musicians (particularly as rock became more complex and its musicianship rose in quality), during this period the jazz and rock worlds mostly stayed apart from each other.

While the rise of rock would have hurt jazz's commercial potential by itself, jazz's race toward total free-dom also disillusioned and scared away some listeners. In 1960, free jazz was in its early stages, with the Ornette Coleman Quartet being its chief proponent along with Cecil Taylor and Sun Ra (both of whom were largely underground heroes). But within a few years the movement had exploded, John Coltrane had switched to sound explorations, and free (or avant-garde) jazz was the talk of the jazz world, with debates about its validity taking place every month in *Down Beat*. While the more adventurous younger players were happy to eliminate the "straitjacket" of chord changes in favor of more expressive playing, with the emphasis on sounds and emotions rather than notes, this method of improvising proved to be the least popular of all jazz styles, disturbing longtime jazz followers, leading many straightahead musicians to won-der about the musicianship (if not the sanity) of the avant-garde players, and making jazz seem quite for-bidding to newcomers. Looking at the movement from hindsight, its evolution in this direction seems logical, but at the time it must have outraged Dexter Gordon fans to hear Albert Ayler.

Jazz has generally reflected the world at large. In its embrace of civil rights and its occasional use of inte-grated bands onstage in the 1950s, jazz had been ahead of its time on a social level. The same was true in some of the free jazz players' championing of leftist politics and black nationalism during the first half of the 1960s, which seemed to be predicting the future. The United States was becoming a more tumultuous place to live. The optimism of the Kennedy years ended with the murder of the president on November 22, 1963. Although civil rights became the law of the land in 1965, race riots and segregationists' violent opposition to integration in the South led to some of the bad feeling being felt in the jazz world. The escalation of the Vietnam War during 1965–67 (along with the decrease in work for jazz musicians) led to a fair number of players moving to Europe, and some of the music (such as that performed by Archie Shepp) becoming politicized.

However, it is always a mistake to characterize the jazz world purely through the most advanced music of the time. In the 1960s, there were some styles of jazz that were fairly accessible to the general public, particularly bossa nova and soul jazz. The bossa nova music of composer Antonio Carlos Jobim was influenced by West Coast cool jazz, featuring gentle Brazilian rhythms, soothing vocalists, and soft-toned soloists. The Stan Getz-Charlie Byrd recording of "Desafinado" launched bossa nova in the United States in 1962, reaching its height a couple of years later when Getz, Jobim, Joao Gilberto, and Astrud Gilberto recorded "The Girl from Ipanema." Especially compared to free jazz, the bossa nova movement was a much calmer alternative.

Hard bop became the modern mainstream of jazz during the second half of the 1950s, and that continued throughout the 1960s even as the soloists became more advanced and were sometimes touched by the creative possibilities offered by the innovations of the avant-garde. Soul jazz grew out of hard bop, putting a greater emphasis on the influence of church and gospel music, R&B, and blues, with often prominent "funky" playing by pianists influenced by Horace Silver. Soul jazz was eventually mostly associated with the organists who rose to prominence after Jimmy Smith, featuring danceable grooves and (at its best) an inventive use of repetition.

The classic bebop survivors were overshadowed by the newer developments (even Sonny Stitt often played his brand of bebop in soul jazz settings), the West Coast cool jazz veterans were generally employed more in the studios than in clubs, and some of the veteran swing and Dixieland players found work to be scarce, even while the New Orleans revival movement went through

a new phase. The larger record labels (Capitol, Columbia, RCA, and Decca) gradually lost interest in recording anyone but the biggest names in jazz, while Riverside went broke, Savoy switched to gospel music, and Pacific Jazz (which was sold to Liberty in 1965) and Bethlehem died. On the brighter side, Impulse and ESP became major forces in documenting the avant-garde. The most important label of the era, Blue Note, went through its final golden age, releasing dozens of classic hard bop, soul jazz, and even avant-garde releases during 1961–67. Although Alfred Lion sold Blue Note to Liberty in 1966, the label continued as a major force through 1967 before it began its descent into commercialism.

Jazz may have been less popular overall in 1967 than it had been in 1960, but with its many classic recordings, the large number of innovative and highly personal players, and the remarkable diversity of the jazz world in general, the 1961–67 period was a great time for the music, at least artistically. So much happened during those seven years!

John Coltrane   Virtually unknown in the jazz world in 1954, John Coltrane was the most significant jazz musician of 1961–67, a masterful player who towered over the improvised music scene. In 1959, he had recorded "Giant Steps," a monumental work which, with its very complex chord structure, brought bebop and chordal improvisation to its logical extreme and conclusion. In 1960, Trane left the Miles Davis Quintet, formed his own quartet (which originally consisted of pianist Steve Kuhn, bassist Steve Davis, and drummer Pete LaRoca), and took up the soprano sax, which he alternated with his tenor. Within a short time McCoy Tyner (coming over from the Jazztet) was his pianist, and Elvin Jones was on drums, joining Steve Davis in the rhythm section. Coltrane's initial recording of "My Favorite Things" was a milestone, for it featured Trane wailing endlessly on soprano over a two-chord vamp, showing that a great deal could be created with a fairly simple but intense background.

John Coltrane, in addition to his very original sounds on both tenor and soprano, had a searching style, one that found him always pushing himself, often in marathon solos. In 1961, he completed his contract on Atlantic with **Olé** (Rhino/Atlantic 79965), which is also available as part of his **Heavyweight Champion: The Complete Atlantic Recordings** (Rhino/Atlantic 71984) seven-CD set. By then Reggie Workman was his bassist. This intriguing set from May 25 has the Coltrane quartet augmented by Eric Dolphy on alto and flute, trumpeter Freddie Hubbard, and Art Davis on second bass playing the haunting "Olé," "Dahomey Dance" (worthy of becoming a standard)," "Aisha," and "To Her Ladyship." Coltrane's soprano looks toward both the Far and Near East, Dolphy adds his distinctive solo voice to the music, and Hubbard fits in quite well.

Two days earlier, Coltrane had begun his first project for Impulse, his label for the remainder of his life. At Impulse, producer Bob Thiele allowed Coltrane free rein in the studios, resulting in many alternate takes, and a great deal of material that was not released until years later. **The Complete Africa/Brass Sessions** (Impulse 2-168) differs from Coltrane's other work for the label in that he is joined by 14- to 17-piece groups that are essentially an expansion of his quartet. With Eric Dolphy contributing most of the arrangements, and Booker Little's melancholy trumpet sound being a key part of the ensembles, the music is often quite memorable though it is a disappointment that only Coltrane and the members of his quartet have any solo space. This two-CD set has all of the music originally released on the LPs **Africa/Brass, Africa/Brass Sessions Vol. 2,** and **Trane's Modes**. The three versions of "Africa" are high points although the repetition of titles may inspire some listeners to get the single-CD version instead.

During November 1–5, 1961, John Coltrane added Eric Dolphy to his quartet and played a controversial engagement at New York's Village Vanguard that was fully documented by Impulse. Due to the lengthy and often-intense solos, the music of Coltrane and Eric Dolphy was branded "anti-jazz" by some of the New York jazz critics who felt that the improvisations were too lengthy, passionate, and wandering, merely a random barrage of sounds. One can judge for oneself by hearing the four-CD release **The Complete 1961 Village Vanguard Recordings** (Impulse 4-232), which has all 19 surviving performances, including "Chasin' the Trane," "Impressions" (which uses the same two chords as Miles Davis's "So What"), "Greensleeves," "Spiritual," and a swinging "Softly, As in a Morning Sunrise." Coltrane, Dolphy, McCoy Tyner, both Reggie Workman and Jimmy Garrison (who replaced Workman in the quartet in December) on basses, and Elvin Jones perform the remarkable music, which is quite

spiritual and sometimes heart-wrenching. The 1920s veteran Garvin Bushell plays oboe and contrabassoon on "Spiritual" and "India" while Ahmed Abdul-Malik is added on oud for the latter. Since some of the songs are heard in multiple versions, more casual collectors may want to get a smaller "best of" collection, but none of the performances are throwaways.

Even Coltrane's biggest detractors found little to criticize in the three surprisingly conservative special projects that he made during 1961–63. **Ballads** (GRP/Impulse 156) has Trane caressing a variety of pretty melodies with affection, including "What's New," "You Don't Know What Love Is," "All or Nothing at All," and "Say It (Over and Over Again)." If anything, the saxophonist's playing is too respectful of the tunes. **Duke Ellington & John Coltrane** (Impulse 166) has the two masters meeting in a quartet, alternating their two rhythm sections. Although it would have been preferable to hear Coltrane sitting in with Ellington's big band, their encounter generated some memorable music (particularly the definitive version of "In a Sentimental Mood" and Ellington's new piece "Take the Coltrane") and shows the influence that the still-modern and percussive Duke had on the playing of Thelonious Monk and later pianists. ◗ **John Coltrane and Johnny Hartman** (GRP/Impulse 157) is the high point in the career of baritone crooner Johnny Hartman, and it features Coltrane at his most romantic, taking short solos and backing the warm singer. Their versions of both "Lush Life" and "My One and Only Love" have never been topped.

Most of John Coltrane's work during the 1962–64 period was with his increasingly famous quartet of Tyner, Garrison, and Jones. The eight-CD box **The Classic Quartet—Complete Impulse Studio Recordings** (Impulse 8-280) has a large chunk of the band's legacy although it does not include their live performances. Included in this ambitious reissue are all of the music originally issued as **Coltrane, Ballads, Crescent, A Love Supreme,** and **The John Coltrane Quartet Plays,** plus some of the selections put out on **Impressions, Live at Birdland,** and **Kulu Se Mama,** in addition to some numbers from samplers and seven previously unreleased performances (including the alternate take to "Resolution" from **A Love Supreme**). Because of duplication, until there is a complete Coltrane Quartet "live on Impulse" set, all but completists will probably be better off getting reissues of the original individual sets.

Coltrane fans will definitely want **Live Trane** (Pablo 2310-433), a seven-CD box that has his performances from his European concerts of 1961–63. Some of the music was formerly out on such sets as **The Paris Concert** (Original Jazz Classics 781), **Bye Bye Blackbird** (Original Jazz Classics 681), **The European Tour** (Pablo 2308-222), and **Afro Blue Impressions** (Pablo 2620-101). Nineteen of the 37 selections were previously unreleased (except for a few that were on European bootleg LPs), and although the repertoire is a bit predictable (with six versions of "My Favorite Things"), the playing is exciting with the musicians (Coltrane, Tyner, Garrison or Workman, Jones, and Dolphy on three cuts) sounding inspired and really stretching themselves. These selections are taken from concerts organized by producer Norman Granz and do not duplicate any of Trane's Impulse releases.

Recorded in 1962, **Coltrane** (Impulse 215) has the quartet playing a passionate "Out of this World," "The Inch Worm," "Tunji," "Miles' Mode," and a classic version of Mal Waldron's "Soul Eyes." **Newport '63** (GRP/Impulse 128) and ● **Live at Birdland** (Impulse 198) find John Coltrane at one of his creative heights. The former set actually features Roy Haynes on drums for an absent Elvin Jones on three songs recorded at the 1963 Newport Jazz Festival, and one number ("Chasin' Another Trane")

from the 1961 Village Vanguard sessions. The Newport appearance is noteworthy for it has the definitive version of "My Favorite Things" (a song that remained in Coltrane's repertoire no matter how radical his style became), a raging "Impressions," and "I Want to Talk About You." **Live at Birdland** has Coltrane's famous interpretation of Mongo Santamaria's "Afro Blue" (which he stretches out on à la "My Favorite Things") and the best version of "I Want to Talk About You," the only song that featured Coltrane playing a very long cadenza. On the latter, Trane tears into the piece yet never loses sight of the melody or the fact that it is a beautiful ballad. The other three numbers on **Live at Birdland** (including the very somber "Alabama") were actually recorded in the studio. The year 1964 resulted in Coltrane's quartet recording **Crescent** (Impulse 200), which has five originals by the leader, including the title cut, "Lonnie's Lament," and the swinging "Bessie's Blues."

However, 1964 is best remembered in John Coltrane's history for **A Love Supreme** (Impulse 155). Trane's gift to God, this album meant more to him (and to many of his fans) than any of the others. There is the famous chanting of the title, four very different but complete movements, and soloing on a consistently high level, with "Resolution" being the most memorable theme. This is one of the most spiritual of all jazz recordings,

TIMELINE 1961

Duke Ellington records with the Louis Armstrong All-Stars. • Ornette Coleman retires. • Sun Ra's Arkestra moves to New York. • The Jimmy Giuffre 3 features Paul Bley and Steve Swallow. • Freddie Hubbard replaces Lee Morgan with Art Blakey's Jazz Messengers. • Scott LaFaro dies in a car accident. • The Jazz Crusaders make their debut recordings. • Eddie Harris has a hit with "Exodus." • Brew Moore moves to Copenhagen. • Herbie Hancock records "Watermelon Man." • The George Russell Sextet features Eric Dolphy and Don Ellis. • Charlie Byrd visits Brazil and hears bossa nova for the first time. • Ida Cox comes out of retirement to record one final album. • Preservation Hall opens up in New Orleans • Booker Little dies from uremia. • Riverside's "Living Legends" series brings Lovie Austin back to records for the first time since 1926. • Kenny Ball's British trad band has a major hit with "Midnight in Moscow." • Ran Blake and Jeanne Lee make their recording debuts. • Ray Charles and Betty Carter record an album of vocal duets. • At the age of 74, Kid Ory records his last album. • Johnny St. Cyr starts a five-year period leading the ironically named Young Men from New Orleans at Disneyland. • Red Norvo has a serious ear operation and only plays on a part-time basis for the next few years. • Paul Quinichette retires from music at the age of 40. • Howard Rumsey's Lighthouse All-Stars record their final album. • Leon Thomas becomes the new singer with Count Basie's orchestra. • Kenny Drew moves to Paris. • Gigi Gryce permanently drops out of music, becoming a teacher. • The Dave Pell Octet breaks up. • Toots Thielemans first records his "Bluesette." • Eddie Palmieri forms Conjunto La Perfecta, an unusual Afro-Cuban jazz octet featuring a flute and two trombones, performing every Sunday night at New York's Palladium until 1968. • Eric Dolphy plays with John Coltrane's Quartet at the Village Vanguard, but their music is branded "anti-jazz." • Richard Abrams forms the Experimental Band in Chicago.

but without any preaching, just sincere praise from Coltrane in his own searching and adventurous way. The 2002 two-CD set ◉ **A Love Supreme (Deluxe Edition** (Impulse 314 589 945) not only reissues the original version of this classic, but on the second disc includes two alternate takes—a full-length live version from July 1965 and two previously unreleased versions of "Resolution" recorded on a different day with Archie Shepp on second tenor and Art Davis on second bass. The live rendition, which is longer than the studio version, was previously only out on a French LP and is quite stirring.

A Love Supreme essentially closed the book on Coltrane's 1961–64 period, and led the way toward his rather startling music of 1965–67. During 1965, from month to month, one can hear the saxophonist opening up his music to freer and freer improvising, playing with increasingly intense passion. While the influence of Ornette Coleman was felt in Coltrane's 1960–61 music with the de-emphasis of chord structures, in 1965 Coltrane was clearly listening to the furious flights of Albert Ayler and Archie Shepp. Melody statements became quite brief, and Coltrane really drove himself, not only taking marathon solos in performance, but often spending his breaks practicing in a back room. He was searching for a new way of expressing himself, but his increasingly violent playing began to dismay and scare off some of his fans who just could not take the nonstop musical intensity of this ironically soft-spoken man. Even today, many of Coltrane's supporters do not listen to his post-1964 recordings despite their validity.

The John Coltrane Quartet Plays (Impulse 214) has Coltrane's classic quintet in February 1965 tearing into "Chim Chim Cheree" (in a very un-Disney-like fashion), "Nature Boy," and a pair of Trane originals ("Brasilia" and "Song of Praise"). **Transition** (GRP/Impulse 124) from May and June has the quartet displaying a great deal of intensity on a 21-minute "Suite," Coltrane and Jones playing a ferocious duet on the nine-minute "Vigil," and the saxophonist showing that he could still caress a melody when he wanted to, on the warm ballad "Welcome."

On June 28, 1965, John Coltrane permanently crossed the line into atonality with the still-startling "Ascension." The CD reissue **Ascension** (Impulse 314 543 413) has the two versions of this remarkable performance. Utilizing an 11-piece group with trumpeters Freddie Hubbard and Dewey Johnson, altoists Marion Brown and John Tchicai, tenors Pharoah Sanders and Archie Shepp, McCoy Tyner, Elvin Jones, and both Jimmy Garrison and Art Davis on basses, Coltrane provided a little sketch for the ensemble to play at the beginning and between soloists, but otherwise this is completely free-form music. As with Ornette Coleman's **Free Jazz** from five years earlier, each of the musicians gets to solo while the other players "comment" behind the lead voices, and there is a forward momentum to the music. But **Ascension** is much more intense and not melodic at all, instead emphasizing very emotional sounds from the seven horns during the combined 79 minutes of music.

The double-CD set **The Major Works of John Coltrane** (GRP/Impulse 2-113) contains the two versions of "Ascension" plus three other extended pieces from later in the year. "Om" has the quartet joined by Pharoah Sanders, Donald Garrett on bass clarinet and bass, and flutist Joe Brazil. It is a continuous 29-minute performance that is rather spooky in spots (the recitation is quite spacey) with some intense playing by Coltrane and Sanders. Also on this set is "Kulu Se Mama" and "Selflessness," which have Sanders, Garrett, second drummer Frank Butler, and percussionist/vocalist Juno Lewis (a key player on "Kulu Se Mama") joining the quartet.

Another reissue from this period worth mentioning is **Dear Old Stockholm** (GRP/Impulse 120), which features the quartet with Roy Haynes in Elvin Jones's place on two occasions. From 1963, there are memorable versions of "Dear Old Stockholm" and "After the Rain," while the three 1965 selections consist of the beautiful "Dear Lord," and two lengthy and raging performances: fairly rare versions of "One Down, One Up" and "After the Crescent." **New Thing at Newport** (Impulse 314 543 414) features the groups of Coltrane and Archie Shepp at the 1965 Newport Jazz Festival. Coltrane's playing on "One Down, One Up" (which has a quick repetitive theme before becoming quite free) and "My Favorite Things" must have shocked a lot of listeners who were not familiar with his most recent and thus far unreleased recordings of recent months. The Shepp section (with a quartet consisting of vibraphonist Bobby Hutcherson, bassist Barre Phillips, and drummer Joe Chambers) has strong playing on "Gingerbread, Gingerbread Boy," and three other numbers even if Shepp's recitation on the fortunately brief "Scag" is difficult to sit through.

John Coltrane's classic group recorded for the last time as a quartet on **Sun Ship** (Impulse 167) and **First Meditations** (GRP/Impulse 118). For **Sun Ship**, Coltrane used very short themes as jumping off points for explosive improvisations, usually centered around one chord. Jones keeps up with Trane's fire although Tyner seems a bit conservative in comparison. "First Meditations," a five-part suite, was not released at all until 1977 because four of the five movements (which are augmented with an alternate take) were remade later in the year. Coltrane alternates between ferocious playing and more thoughtful and quieter sections.

First Meditations was recorded on September 2, 1965. That month, tenor saxophonist Pharoah Sanders began playing with Coltrane on a regular basis, adding to the fury and intensity of the music. Frequently Coltrane would have an opening solo that evolved from being melodic into pure fire, then Sanders would enter and build up the intensity even more with his shrieks, screams, and howls, starting where Trane left off. Tyner did his best to keep the group grounded, but he was often drowned out while Jones joined in on the overheated ensembles. The two-CD set **Live in Seattle** (GRP-Impulse 146) from September 30 has the group (expanded to a sextet with Donald Garrett added on bass clarinet and second bass) roaring on the nearly free "Cosmos," "Out of this World," "Evolution," and a 34-minute version of "Afro Blue" that is actually incomplete because the tape ran out. Only "Body and Soul" (which also gets intense) and a Garrison feature on "Tapestry in Sound" use space a bit.

The most rewarding of the Coltrane-Sanders collaborations is ◐ **Meditations** (Impulse 199). Recorded November 23, this set is unusual in that (as if the volume were not already loud enough) Rashied Ali is added on second drums, which infuriated Elvin Jones. The five diverse but very intense movements ("The Father and the Son and the Holy Ghost," "Compassion," "Love," "Consequences," and "Serenity") are quite dense, powerful, and emotional, but much more concise and meaningful than some of the endless live jams of the period. In addition to being recommended as a strong example of Coltrane's later work, **Meditations** was the last recording made by the saxophonist with McCoy Tyner and Elvin Jones.

By early 1966, Jones had left in disgust at having to share the bandstand with a second drummer, and Tyner had departed because he felt that he could barely hear

himself. Rashied Ali proved to be a perfect replacement for Jones. He was not the master of polyrhythms that Elvin was, but Ali could give Coltrane a pulse while being quite free, added color to the music, and showed that he could keep up with the frequently screaming saxophonists. On piano, Coltrane had his new wife, Alice Coltrane, formerly a hard bop player (as Alice McLeod) with Terry Gibbs, who had the ability to set a mood and stay static in the same place while Trane and Sanders created otherworldly sounds. Jimmy Garrison, whose style had become quite open (his solo features were essentially drones), stayed with Coltrane until the end.

In 1966, John Coltrane gradually became less active due to health problems, but there was certainly no weakening in either his playing or his desire to push forward into atonality. **Live at the Village Vanguard Again** (Impulse 213) has Trane in fine form on "My Favorite Things" and "Naima," but Sanders largely ruined the latter (which had become a sacred ballad) with his insensitive screeching. **Live in Japan** (GRP/Impulse 4-102) contains two sets of music by the John Coltrane Quintet on July 11 and 22, 1966, and it is fascinating, at least to those with open ears. Coltrane (on tenor, soprano, and his rarely heard alto) and Sanders (featured on tenor, bass clarinet, and alto) perform six very long selections, with the 25-minute "Peace on Earth" being the briefest, and "My Favorite Things" at 57 minutes taking up all of disc four. The music is powerful, mostly well recorded, and gives one a good idea what this band sounded like live. It certainly is not for everyone, but avant-garde jazz fans will want this spirited and often-ecstatic music.

By the beginning of 1967, John Coltrane was suffering from problems with his liver, which may have been liver cancer caused by hepatitis. Although he had given up nearly all of his bad habits in 1957, Trane had driven himself mercilessly and had worn himself out physically by working so hard. Four CDs contain his recordings of 1967. From February 15, **Stellar Regions** (Impulse 169), which was not released until 1995, consists of 11 concise performances (including three alternate takes and "Offering," which was out before) by Trane in a quartet with his wife, Garrison, and Ali. Sticking exclusively to tenor, Coltrane's flights are relatively brief (no song is over nine minutes), but as intense as one would expect, just much more tightly focused than most of the live performances. **Interstellar Space** (Impulse 314 543 415) is a wondrous performance from February 22, a set of explosive but occasionally thoughtful tenor-drums duets by Coltrane and Ali with the original four selections from the 1974 LP ("Mars," "Venus," "Jupiter," and "Saturn") joined in the reissue by "Leo" and "Jupiter Variation." Coltrane shows that he could improvise without any chordal instruments (no great surprise). It is a pity that he never recorded an album or even a full song of unaccompanied solos. **Expression** (GRP/Impulse 131) pales a bit in comparison to **Stellar Regions** and **Interstellar Space**, but has its moments. Recorded on February 15 and March 7, 1967, this would be Coltrane's last studio album, featuring him on tenor (except for a rare spot on flute on "To Be") on five numbers with Alice Coltrane, Jimmy Garrison, and Rashied Ali, with one appearance by Pharoah Sanders (who is on piccolo and flute on "To Be").

On April 23, John Coltrane played at what would be his last performance. **The Olantunji Concert** (Impulse 314 589 120), which was not released until 2001, has marathon versions of "Ogunde" and "My Favorite Things" by Trane and his quintet with Sanders (plus an extra percussionist or two), but unfortunately the recording quality is so bad that the unremittingly intense music is largely unlistenable except by true fanatics. It should have remained legendary and unissued.

There is no hint in the final concert that Trane was seriously ill. To the shock of nearly everyone, on July 17, 1967, John Coltrane's life came to an end; he was just 40. Since then, Coltrane's innovations have become the language of jazz. His sound has been closely emulated and quite a few other saxophonists have spent their entire career just dealing with one of Coltrane's many periods, whether it be his sheets of sound, his classic quartet, or his sound explorations. No other musician who has come to prominence since John Coltrane's passing in 1967 has changed jazz as forcefully and permanently. Although he was certainly not jazz's last giant, Trane has thus far been its last truly dominant force.

The Free Jazz Movement

John Coltrane both led the way in free jazz and was inspired by those in the movement who had either preceded him (Ornette Coleman, Cecil Taylor, and Sun Ra) or were younger and fearless (Albert Ayler, Pharoah Sanders, and Archie Shepp).

One can easily divide free jazz's early evolution into three overlapping periods. The 1958–62 period was dominated by the Ornette Coleman approach of improvising without chord changes and playing in a more speechlike manner, but still retaining a forward momentum (which swings in its own way), and tones that were not that distant from Charlie Parker and the beboppers. The 1963–66 period found the rise of the high-energy saxophonists, of very free jam sessions, and emotional playing that could often be quite violent and dense. Feelings took precedence over individual notes and conventional technique. Expanding the range of instruments was more important than developing melodies, and at times it seemed as if the attitude was anything goes. During 1966–67 in Chicago and isolated pockets (including Europe), a different approach toward freedom began to develop. Since one could now play anything, why not utilize stronger themes, silence, hints of the past, and arrangements using very advanced harmonies (rather than having everything be spontaneously improvised) as part of the radical new music? The Chicago-based AACM (Association for the Advancement of Creative Musicians) is a nonprofit organization that was established in 1965 by pianist Muhal Richard Abrams, pianist Jodie Christian, drummer Steve McCall, and composer Phil Cohran that not only pushed for an open-minded approach to performing music, but came up with ideas to present jazz in other venues beyond the cliché smoky nightclubs.

Because avant-garde (which utilizes some arrangements and planned frameworks) and free jazz are by definition without set rules, not all of the players associated with this movement sound alike or even similar. While John Coltrane is the most famous musician associated with free jazz and has influenced many saxophonists since the 1960s, Archie Shepp looked much more toward the growls of Ben Webster, Albert Ayler was initially influenced by Sonny Rollins, and Ornette Coleman was always in his own musical world. Among trumpeters, Don Cherry's roots were clearly in bebop though he was able to free up his vocabulary and fit in perfectly with Ornette; the same is true of Bobby Bradford. Lester Bowie had the ability to hint at the past while playing fresh new ideas (it is a pity that he never played with Charles Mingus) while Leo Smith's use of space could be startling, and Bill Dixon's work in his lower register was quite original. Dixon deserves special mention because in October 1964 he organized six "October Revolution" concerts in New York that featured 20 avant-garde jazz groups and helped introduce the new music to the New York press.

Among trombonists, the German Albert Mangelsdorff introduced multiphonics (playing more than one note at a time on a single-note instrument), and both Roswell Rudd and Grachan Moncur III worked with Archie Shepp. However, the expressive qualities of the trombone were surprisingly not utilized all that often in the early avant-garde days. While many free jazz groups did not have a piano (not wanting to tie soloists down to following chord changes), both Cecil Taylor and Paul Bley emerged as innovators. Taylor, the most radical of all jazz musicians, became increasingly freer during the early 1960s (no longer playing any standards), and his intense improvisations sometimes resembled a thunderstorm. In contrast, Bley's use of space and occasional melodies preceded by several years the AACM's discovery of the use of silence as part of the music.

While often a bit drowned out by horn players, both bassists and drummers were potentially completely liberated from their former supportive roles. Charlie Haden had freed the bass from following chord changes, Jimmy Garrison showed how his instrument could be utilized as a drone, and David Izenzon (with Ornette Coleman's mid-1960s trio) was a virtuoso who could make a wide variety of unusual sounds, sometimes using a bow. Other free bassists used their instrument to comment on the lead voice's ideas rather than supplying a steady rhythm. The same could be said of some of the drummers, who by 1966 were making even Elvin Jones sound conservative. These pacesetters included Sunny Murray, Rashied Ali, Charles Moffett (with Ornette), and Andrew Cyrille. As far as singers went, other than Jeanne Lee (who recorded with pianist Ran Blake in 1961) and Patty Waters (who was arguably the first avant-garde jazz singer), a place had not been found yet for vocalists in the new music.

For the first time during the second half of the 1960s, Europeans began to create their own fresh brand of jazz music. There had been some major European jazz musicians in earlier times, most notably Django Reinhardt, Stephane Grappelli, George Shearing, Toots Thielemans, Bobby Jaspar, and Martial Solal, but they played within the context of American jazz styles. With the rise of the avant-garde, some Europeans (and South Africans)

came up with their own approach, using native folk music as part of their repertoire and forming their own "schools" of musical thought that ranged from the dry free improvisations of a few British players to the often-hilarious musical rampages by some key Dutchmen. These separate movements would develop much more in the 1970s, but the beginnings could be felt during 1965–67.

Before bebop, some notes were just plain wrong if played over certain chords, except perhaps as quick grace notes leading to another destination. In bebop, any note could by played over any chord (as Dizzy Gillespie showed) if they were resolved. But in free jazz, even when there were chords, any sound could fit anywhere. The way to "evaluate" the music is not through any specific formula or by searching for mistakes, but in simply asking yourself if the music is reaching you. If it sounds colorful, then it is successful; if it is a bore, then it is a dud. Someone's noise may be someone else's abstract beauty. For those with open ears, there is a great deal of unexpected beauty to discover in avant-garde jazz.

Five Avant-Garde Giants

As early as 1960, four of the five giants of the avant-garde covered in this section were already making strong musical contributions (all but Albert Ayler). These five masters (plus John Coltrane) led the way toward avant-garde and free jazz of the late 1960s and '70s, and are still considered major inspirations today.

Ornette Coleman   Ornette Coleman began 1961 with his two final Atlantic recordings. Charlie Haden had gone out on his own by then, and his place as bassist with the quartet was filled briefly by Scott LaFaro and Jimmy Garrison. **Ornette** (last on the LP Atlantic 1378), which is available as part of the six-CD box set **Beauty Is a Rare Thing**, but not yet individually on CD, has Coleman and LaFaro joined by Don Cherry and Ed Blackwell on four pieces that are given abbreviated names (such as "W.R.U." and "R.P.D.D"). Although more of a high-note bassist than Haden, LaFaro works well with Coleman's free jazz quartet even if his regular gig was with Bill Evans. Jimmy Garrison, a year before he joined John Coltrane, is an asset on **Ornette on Tenor** (Rhino/Atlantic 71455), available both individually and on the "Beauty" box. This set is unusual because Coleman returns to the tenor (his original instrument) for the first time in years. His emotional gutbucket sound is not at all accessible, and is actually even more forbidding than his alto playing, particularly on the somewhat startling opener "Cross Breeding."

In mid-1961, Ornette Coleman surprised the jazz world by choosing to retire. He was frustrated with how little money he was being paid to play in clubs and make records, so he decided to withhold his services. Coleman made an exception for a December 21, 1962, performance released as **Town Hall Concert** (ESP 1006). For that special event, he debuted a new trio that featured the remarkable bassist David Izenzon and drummer Charles Moffett, performing "Doughnut," "Sadness," and an extensive 23 ½-minute version of "The Ark." In addition, a string quartet interprets Coleman's "Dedication to Poets and Writers," his first classical piece to be recorded.

In 1965, Coleman changed his mind and returned to active playing, showing that he was as controversial as ever. During the past couple of years he had taken up the trumpet and violin (playing the latter as if it were a drum). He used his new instruments as props on which he could get colors not available on the alto, but he never played either one conventionally or with the same fluency as his main ax. In contrast, on alto Coleman had grown quite a bit as he shows on **The Great London Concert** (last out as the two-LP set Arista/Freedom 1900) and ● **The Golden Circle in Stockholm Vol. 1** (Blue Note 35518) and **Vol. 2** (Blue Note 35519). Teamed with Izenzon and Moffett in his trio, he performed such originals as (from **Vol. 1**) "European Echoes," "Faces and Places," and (on **Vol. 2**) "The Riddle," and "Morning Song." Coleman's alto playing (he only plays violin and trumpet on **Vol. 2**'s "Snowflakes and Sunshine") has rarely sounded better. **The Empty Foxhole** (Blue Note 29982) from 1966 is quite unusual for it is Coleman's first studio album since 1961 and features him in a trio with Charlie Haden and his ten-year-old son Denardo Coleman, who plays surprisingly effective drums. Although it is a pity that Ornette did not leave his trumpet and violin at home (they are featured on half of the six numbers), his alto work is excellent, and it is good to hear Haden interacting with Coleman again.

Ornette Coleman, whose atonal classical works of the era are outside the context of this book, even in 1967 was ahead of most of the younger free jazz and avant-garde players.

Eric Dolphy   One of the most unusual of all jazz improvisers, Eric Dolphy never fit into any particular school and was too unique to be emulated closely by his contemporaries. It would be years before many musicians could figure out what he was doing! On alto, Dolphy's tone was distinctive, his very wide interval jumps were virtuosic, and he could sound quite speechlike. His flute playing was reminiscent at times of birds, while on bass clarinet (where he often leaped into the extreme upper register) he was the first significant solo voice in jazz history. After playing a restrained role with the Chico Hamilton Quintet during 1958–59, he moved to New York, worked with Charles Mingus, and recorded frequently for Prestige during 1960–61.

The nine-CD set ● **The Complete Prestige Recordings** (Prestige 4418) includes four projects from 1960 (covered in the preceding chapter) plus other sets that are also available individually. On July 16, 1961, a night at the Five Spot with trumpeter Booker Little, pianist Mal Waldron, bassist Richard Davis, and drummer Ed Blackwell was extensively recorded, resulting in **Live at the Five Spot Vol. 1** (Original Jazz Classics 0133), **Live at the Five Spot Vol. 2** (Original Jazz Classics 247), and **Memorial Album** (Original Jazz Classics 353). Because of Little's death just three months later, this has long been considered a legendary date despite the out-of-tune piano. The two horns certainly inspire each other although both have sounded more exciting elsewhere. The brief playing time is unfortunate—**Vol. 2** and **Memorial Album** have a combined total under 70 minutes, and the full date should have been reissued as a two-CD set. But the music, which falls between hard bop and the avant-garde, is well worth hearing.

Less known but a better showcase for Dolphy is **Berlin Concerts** (Enja 3007/9), which has him a month later taking "God Bless the Child" as an unaccompanied bass clarinet solo, jamming "When Lights Are Low" and "Hi-Fly" with bass and drums, and playing four songs (including "Hot House") in a quintet with trumpeter Benny Bailey. Dolphy completed his association with Prestige when he recorded three sets (now available as a trio of CDs) while in Copenhagen: **Eric Dolphy in Europe Vols. 1–3**, (Original Jazz Classics 413, 414, and 416). Joined by a Danish rhythm section and guest bassist Chuck Israels, Dolphy is at his best on the first volume, playing a definitive unaccompanied "God Bless the Child," some sensitive flute on "Glad to

Be Unhappy," romping on bass clarinet for "Oleo," and dueting on alto with Israels on "Hi-Fly." Each of the sets has their moments of interest, and the full program is available in the nine-CD Dolphy Prestige box. Also of interest from the same European tour is **Stockholm Sessions** (Enja 3055), which has appearances by trumpeter Idrees Sulieman on similar material plus "Don't Blame Me" and Mal Waldron's "Alone."

Dolphy worked with his friend John Coltrane's group on an occasional basis in 1961 (including the recorded Village Vanguard sessions) although he did not always fit in that comfortably. During 1962–63, he played some Third Stream music with Gunther Schuller and Orchestra USA, and occasionally led his own bands, but did not perform or record all that often considering his abilities. **Vintage Dolphy** (GM 3005), which was released decades later, has some unusual material. Dolphy (switching between alto, bass clarinet, and flute) performs two originals and Jaki Byard's "Ode to Charlie Parker" with trumpeter Edward Armour, Richard Davis, and drummer J.C. Moses in a quartet. He is also heard on three Third Stream avant-garde classical pieces by Gunther Schuller (taking a rare clarinet solo on "Densities"), and jamming on a wild version of "Donna Lee" with an all-star group, including such players as trumpeter Don Ellis, trombonist Jimmy Knepper, Benny Golson, and Jim Hall that gets completely lost during its last two choruses.

In 1963, Dolphy recorded two albums' worth of material for the Douglas label, music that has been reissued several times since. **Conversations** (Fuel 2000 61134) has unusual transformations of Fats Waller's "Jitterbug Waltz" and "Alone Together" (the latter is taken as a lengthy flute-bass duet with Richard Davis) plus an unaccompanied alto solo on "Love Me" and a spirited "Music Matador." Along the way the supporting cast includes altoist Sonny Simmons, flutist Prince Lasha, vibraphonist Bobby Hutcherson, and trumpeter Woody Shaw. **Iron Man** (Restless 72659) utilizes the same musicians, and has three inside/outside Dolphy originals in "Iron Man," "Burning Spear," and "Mandrake." Dolphy also has two additional duets with Davis, on bass clarinet for "Come Sunday" and flute for "Ode to C.P."

The year 1964 should have been one of Eric Dolphy's great years and despite how it turned out, musically it actually was. ● **Out to Lunch** (Blue Note 46524) is a classic, with Dolphy performing five of his most inventive

originals, including the Thelonious Monk tribute "Hat and Beard," "Gazzelloni," and "Straight Up and Down." Utilizing musicians who really understood his conception (Freddie Hubbard, Bobby Hutcherson, Richard Davis, and the young drummer Tony Williams), Dolphy often sounds exuberant and playful even when the music is at its most dissonant. Shortly after this recording, Dolphy visited Europe with the Charles Mingus Sextet (arguably the bassist's greatest touring group) and decided to stay overseas for a bit. **Last Date** (Verve 822 226) was recorded on June 2, 1964. Dolphy is joined by a top European rhythm section comprised of pianist Misha Mengelberg, bassist Jacques Schols, and drummer Han Bennink, performing exciting versions of "Epistrophy," "You Don't Know What Love Is," and four of his originals (best known of which is "Miss Ann"). Nine days later on June 11, Dolphy performed in Paris with a septet that included French musicians plus trumpeter Donald Byrd and tenor saxophonist Nathan Davis. **Naima** (West Wind 2063) and **Unrealized Tapes** (West Wind 016) show that there was no decline in either his playing or his passion.

Just 18 days later, on June 29, Eric Dolphy died from an overdose of insulin given to him by doctors in a Berlin hospital. He was only 36.

Albert Ayler   One of the true giants of free jazz, tenor saxophonist Albert Ayler (like Ornette Coleman) played pure melody in a speechlike emotional style. His huge tone and wide vibrato were a throwback to jazz's prehistory, and he made no pretense of being a virtuoso. He simply played the way he felt without paying attention to the audience's or critics' reactions. As Ayler stated on several occasions, it was about sounds, not notes. He was more concerned with expressing feelings than he was with following chord changes or playing conventionally.

Ayler started off his career working in R&B bands, including with Little Walter. Strangely enough he was briefly nicknamed "Little Bird" because of a similarity in his sound on alto to Charlie Parker. While in the army (1958–61), Ayler played in a service band, switched to tenor, and began exploring much freer sounds. After his discharge, he was unable to find work in the United States because of his style, so he spent time in Sweden and Denmark during 1962–63. He performed a bit with Cecil Taylor, but unfortunately no recordings resulted. Ayler's earliest documented sessions from 1962, which are available as **The First Recordings Vol. 1** (Sonet 604) and **Vol. 2** (DIW 349), have him backed by a bassist and drummer (Torbjorn Hultcrantz and Sune Spanberg) who apparently had no comprehension of what he was attempting to play. The tunes are mostly standards, and, although Ayler at times sounds a little like Sonny Rollins, he is as far ahead of his sidemen as Dizzy Gillespie was over 20 years earlier playing with Cab Calloway's Orchestra. **My Name Is Albert Ayler** (Black Lion 760211) from January 1963 has the same difficulty except that the musicianship of the trio (pianist Niels Bronsted, 16-year-old bassist Niels Pedersen, and drummer Ronnie Gardiner) is on a higher level. Ayler talks for a minute before the music begins (giving listeners a rare chance to hear his voice) and sounds way out of tune on soprano during "Bye Bye Blackbird." Otherwise he sticks to tenor and plays quite well on "Billie's Bounce," "Summertime," "On Green Dolphin Street," and his original "C.T." (for Cecil Taylor), but only on "C.T." does the rhythm section stop playing bop and actually react to Ayler's adventurous flights.

Back in New York in early 1964, Ayler's **Goin' Home** (Black Lion 760197) has him teamed with a much more sympathetic rhythm section (pianist Call Cobbs, bassist Henry Grimes, and drummer Sonny Murray), but the repertoire is certainly offbeat; seven spirituals, including "Ol' Man River," "Down by the Riverside" (a highlight), and even "The Saints." Some of the performances work better than others, and this would make for a splendid record to play at a "blindfold test" for friends.

After those early efforts, the "real" Albert Ayler began to emerge on record in 1964. **Witches and Devils** (1201 Music 9006) has Ayler stretching out on four numbers with either Henry Grimes or Earle Henderson on bass, drummer Sunny Murray, and the unfortunately weak trumpeter Norman Howard (in his only recording). The Ayler pieces, "Holy Holy," "Saints," "Spirits," and "Witches and Devils," are rather scary yet intriguing performances. **Prophecy** (ESP 3030) and **Spiritual Unity** (ESP 1002) both feature Ayler in a trio with bassist Gary Peacock and Murray. The music is quite free and often violent, but there are four versions (two on each album) of Ayler's best known original, the strangely joyful "Ghosts," along with other catchy themes. Unfortunately, both of these CD reissues are quite brief time-wise (as are most of the ESP reissues), but free jazz collectors will consider them essential. **New York Eye and Ear Control** (ESP 1016) is an intriguing if also rather stingy (34 minutes) set, a soundtrack for an experimental film. Ayler, Peacock, and Murray are joined by Don Cherry, trombonist Roswell Rudd, and altoist John Tchicai for two lengthy jams ("Ay" and "Iit") and the very brief "Don's Dawn." Ayler returned to Europe in the fall, but this time with a sympathetic group (Cherry, Peacock, and Murray), recording **Vibrations** (Freedom 41000) and **The Hilversum Session** (Copens 6001). In both cases the simple childlike themes (which can often be hummed) alternate with very passionate improvisations; Ayler's playing makes Don Cherry sound a bit dated and tame in comparison.

Back in the United States in 1965, Albert Ayler formed a new group and went in a slightly different direction. With his younger brother Donald Ayler on trumpet, altoist Charles Tyler, bassist Lewis Worrell, and Sunny Murray, Ayler recorded the one-sided 20-minute LP **Bells** (reissued on ESP-1010 as an extremely brief CD) live at Town Hall on May 1. The military themes look back toward the turn of the century, a hint of what was to come. The music that Ayler created during the next two years could be said to be so far advanced that it came back in at the beginning of jazz. With Donald Ayler sometimes emulating a bugle, the group could sound like an out-of-control marching band circa 1905. Irish jigs, folk melodies, and brass band music were strongly hinted at during the ensembles, and the themes, while the solos were free form and quite expressive. This was the most significant music of Ayler's career, stretching jazz to its breaking point, and fulfilling the "Ancient to the Future" idea that the AACM would use as their motto a few years later.

The Ayler Brothers are joined by Tyler, both Henry Grimes and Gary Peacock on basses, and Sunny Murray for **Spirits Rejoice** (ESP 1020), an exciting set only hurt by the brevity (32 minutes) of the music. **At Slug's Saloon Vols. 1 & 2** (ESP 3031 and 3032) have Albert and Donald Ayler in a quintet with the droning violin of Michel Sampson, bassist Lewis Worrell, and drummer Ronald Shannon Jackson. The playing time is around 40 minutes apiece, and some of Ayler's stronger pieces ("Ghosts," "Truth Is Marching In," and "Our Prayer") receive superior and often-riotous treatment. The recorded high points of this period are ● **Lorrach/Paris 1966** (Hat Art 6039) and the double CD ● **Live in Greenwich Village** (Impulse 2-273), which feature ancient/future concept at its most successful. The Hat Art

CD has the quintet of the Aylers, Sampson, bassist William Folwell, and drummer Beaver Harris, while the Impulse two-fer adds Henry Grimes or Alan Silva on second bass, cellist Joel Freedman, and a few guests. The emotional music is often beyond description, sound explorations that are at times demented, witty, and quite violent.

In 1967, Ayler was signed to the Impulse label, which seemed a logical move since John Coltrane was one of his supporters, and Impulse had become a leader in documenting free jazz. **Love Cry** (GRP/Impulse 108) was the first and best of Ayler's recordings for that label although not quite up to the level of his live performances. Ayler (on tenor and alto) sounds typically emotional, and he is heard for the last time with his brother Donald Ayler, in a group with Alan Silva and drummer Milford Graves. Call Cobbs's four appearances on harpsichord are merely eccentric and a distraction, while the leader's three vocals are not easy to sit through. But overall this is a worthwhile release, filled with concise performances.

Chances are that if Albert Ayler had played his mature music in 1960, he would not have been allowed to appear on a bandstand in the United States. By 1967, the rapid evolution of jazz made it possible for him to be one of its leaders and an influential force in generating headlines for free jazz.

Cecil Taylor   There has been no jazz musician more radical and advanced than Cecil Taylor. After all, how can one create more advanced music than completely free improvisations, particularly when they are played by a virtuosic pianist who emphasizes atonality and dense outbursts of emotion performed during marathon sets?

It is not surprising that Cecil Taylor often found it difficult to gain any work during the 1950s and '60s although fortunately some recordings were made along the way. During 1960–61, Taylor recorded several albums' worth of material for Candid, all of which was collected in a limited edition six-LP Mosaic set, and some of which is available individually. Of the 1961 material, **Jumpin' Punkins** (Candid 79013) has particularly intriguing versions of a pair of Mercer Ellington tunes ("Jumpin' Punkins" and "Things Ain't What They Used to Be") that match Taylor with Clark Terry, Roswell Rudd, Steve Lacy (who was formerly Taylor's sideman), baritonist Charles Davis, Archie Shepp, Buell Neidlinger,

and Billy Higgins. This would be the last time that Taylor would be heard with more conservative soloists playing standards; his jarring comping behind the lead voices is quite intriguing. Also on this CD are a couple of fairly free Taylor originals ("O.P." and "I Forgot") with Neidlinger, drummer Dennis Charles, and (on "I Forgot") Shepp, who made his recording debut on these sessions. **New York City R&B** (Candid 79017), like much of the Candid material, was originally issued under Neidlinger's name. This rather brief CD has two numbers with Taylor, Neidlinger, and Higgins or Charles (with one cut adding Shepp), and an alternate version of "Things Ain't What They Used to Be." **Cell Walk for Celeste** (Candid 79034) consists of similar material, with two additional versions of "Jumpin' Punkins" and more trio/quartet numbers.

Nefertiti, the Beautiful One Has Come (Revenant 202) has the only Cecil Taylor recording (other than two songs on a bootleg LP) from the 1962–65 period. It is also the last time that one can hear any traces of Taylor's early influences (including Duke Ellington) in his playing, and he is heard for the final time on a standard, "What's New." Cut in 1962 at the Café Montmartre in Copenhagen, Taylor is teamed with his new altoist Jimmy Lyons (whose tone occasionally hints at Charlie Parker although his choice of notes is quite original and sympathetic to Taylor's music), and the first truly "free" drummer Sunny Murray; there is no need for a bassist. The atonal music is full of fire and passion, still sounding very futuristic today.

With the rise of the free jazz movement, Alfred Lion of Blue Note decided to stay in the game, recording Ornette Coleman and Cecil Taylor on separate occasions. Taylor's two Blue Note sets gave him an opportunity to utilize larger-than-normal groups. **Unit Structures** (Blue Note 84237) is full of stunning and very intense music, teaming Taylor with Jimmy Lyons, trumpeter Eddie Gale, Ken McIntyre (alternating among alto, oboe, and bass clarinet), both Henry Grimes and Alan Silva on basses, and drummer Andrew Cyrille. **Conquistador** (Blue Note 84260) has the same rhythm section along with Lyons and trumpeter Bill Dixon, consisting of two unremittingly intense pieces (even if Dixon is a comparatively mellow player). Both of the Blue Note albums are decades ahead of their time.

But other than a pair of Paris concerts, Cecil Taylor would be largely off records again until 1973.

Sun Ra   In 1961, Sun Ra and the nucleus of his Arkestra moved from Chicago to New York, starting his most intense and innovative period. Ra, whose earliest music was a bit left-of-center, but still tied (although sometimes in abstract fashion) to the big band tradition, now started emphasizing much freer improvising, sometimes utilizing electric keyboards. As mentioned in the previous chapter, his recordings were in pretty messy shape (almost randomly being released on his Saturn label, usually without date or personnel identification), but in the 1990s the Evidence label reissued a lot of the music much more coherently. Seven Saturn CDs (and two from ESP) cover Ra's 1961–67 period quite well.

Fate in a Pleasant Mood/When Sun Comes Out (Evidence 22068) has two former Saturn LPs reissued on one CD. The **Fate** set was among Ra's last work in Chicago, featuring altoist Marshall Allen, John Gilmore on tenor and clarinet, and several different trumpeters in a sextet/septet, while the remainder of the disc is from 1962–63 with a similar size group and spots for Allen, Gilmore, and baritonist Pat Patrick. These are transitional records as Ra changed his home base and moved his music further to the left toward sound explorations. **Cosmic Tones for Mental Therapy/Art Forms of Dimensions Tomorrow** (Evidence 22036), dating from 1961–63, has two of Ra's rarest albums, and they are both a bit odd. On one session Ra is featured on the Clavioline (an early synthesizer) and the "astro space organ" in a group with as many as three bass clarinets plus alto, baritone, bass, drums, percussion, and log drums, but the excessive use of echo devices makes the music rather forbidding. The **Art Forms** set has a more conventional instrumentation (three reeds, two brass, bass, drums, and Ra on keyboards), but is also free, unsettling, and a bit inconclusive. Despite that, this CD certainly holds one's interest.

When Angels Speak of Love (Evidence 22216) from 1963 hints at other styles (including Miles Davis, Ornette Coleman, and John Coltrane) while still sounding eccentric and original. The key players include Gilmore, altoist Danny Davis, and trumpeter Walter Miller. Highlights include "The Idea of It All," the title cut (a ballad), and the somewhat crazy "Next Stop Mars." **Other Planes of There** (Evidence 22037) has a few throwaway pieces that do little more than set up an atmosphere, but the 22-minute "Other Planes of There" (featuring a Ra ensemble with one trumpet, three trombones, five reeds, piano, bass, and two drums) is quite memorable.

While the Saturn releases were heard by relatively few people (they were mostly sold at Ra's concerts), his two sets for ESP, **Heliocentric Worlds Vol. 1** (ESP 1014) and **Vol. 2** (ESP 1017) from 1965, made more of a stir due to the increased exposure. **Vol. 1** consists of seven relatively brief originals played by an 11-piece band and has its moments although it is often unfocused. **Vol. 2**, recorded seven months later with an octet, features lengthy versions of "The Sun Myth" and "Cosmic Chaos" along with the five-minute "A House of Beauty," and is generally on a higher level, even with Ra spending part of the time playing tuned bongos. **The Magic City** (Evidence 22069) has a somewhat bizarre but quite intriguing tribute to Ra's Birmingham, Alabama, hometown that depicts life in the city as it should have been rather than how it was in 1965; Marshall Allen's piccolo and Ra's keyboards assume major roles. Also on this CD are two brief pieces and the 11-minute "The Shadow World," which at times seems like two or three unrelated selections occurring at once. **Monorails and Satellites** (Evidence 22013) is a change of pace, Ra's first solo piano set. He plays seven originals plus "Easy Street" in an eccentric and sometimes rambling fashion. Ra's unusual piano style is more memorable than the individual cuts. One of the most controversial of Ra's recordings from this period is **Atlantis** (Evidence 22067), particularly the nearly 22-minute title cut that puts the focus on Ra's innovative and unique organ playing, which is much closer to Cecil Taylor than to Jimmy Smith.

One has to take Sun Ra's music of the 1960s on its own terms in order to fully appreciate it, for he stood apart from even the avant-gardists. Despite some throwaway pieces and rambling stretches, at its best Ra's unpredictable music is rewarding.

Other Top Avant-Gardists

From high-energy saxophonists to thoughtful composers, the 1960s avant-garde spanned a wide area of jazz, with the best players carving out their own niche and innovations. Although never achieving much popularity, the influence of these groundbreaking players is still felt today.

Muhal Richard Abrams   On May 8, 1965, the AACM (The Association for the Advancement of Creative

Musicians) was formed in Chicago. Pianist Muhal Richard Abrams had led its predecessor, the Experimental Band (which unfortunately never recorded) since 1961, performing adventurous music open to but not derivative of the free jazz movement then brewing in New York. Abrams, who also played with Eddie Harris, Dexter Gordon, Eddie "Lockjaw" Davis, and other more bop-oriented musicians during the era, became the spiritual father and first president of the AACM. Its basic principles involved self-expression without limitations (not feeling compelled to stick to conventional frameworks), performing original compositions, educating the community about the music, and being as creative in coming up with work as in playing one's instrument. Rather than just playing in smoky nightclubs, AACM members often rented out theatres and lofts where they could perform for attentive and open-minded audiences. Out of the AACM came such important avant-gardists as the members of the Art Ensemble of Chicago, Anthony Braxton, Leo Smith, Henry Threadgill, Leroy Jenkins, and other highly individual players. While the New York free jazz musicians of the period often indulged in blowouts full of high-energy that were consistently intense, their Chicago counterparts used space and silence in unusual ways, and logically mixed together improvisations with complex compositions.

Muhal Richard Abrams's debut as a leader was 1967's **Levels and Degrees of Light** (Delmark 413), and it set the standard for the AACM releases to follow. On this set, Abrams is joined by the young altoist Anthony Braxton (who was already quite recognizable), tenor saxophonist Maurice McIntyre, vibraphonist Gordon Emmanuel, bassist Charles Clark, drummer Thurman Barker, violinist Leroy Jenkins, and bassist Leonard Jones on some of the three originals, with Penelope Taylor taking an eccentric vocal, and David Moore doing a recitation on "The Bird Song." Rather than being a blowout, the music is thoughtful and sometimes hints at the past, but is also very advanced and emotional in the dramatic way that it uses silence.

Rashied Ali   Rashied Ali, one of the earliest free jazz drummers, toured with Sonny Rollins in 1963 and worked in New York with Pharoah Sanders and Albert Ayler. He came to prominence in the fall of 1965 when he was added to the John Coltrane Quartet as the second drummer, playing next to Elvin Jones. Due to the two drummers' different approaches (Jones implied time while Ali often overlooked it), personality conflicts, and the great increase in volume, by early 1966 both Jones and McCoy Tyner left the group. Ali, whose waves of sound inspired Coltrane, remained a member of the new Coltrane Quintet, including recording a duet album with Trane, **Interstellar Space**, until the saxophonist's death in 1967.

Byron Allen   Virtually nothing is known about altoist Byron Allen. He recorded **The Byron Allen Trio** (ESP 1005) on September 25, 1964, with the equally obscure bassist Maceo Gilchrist and drummer Ted Robinson, stretching out on four originals, including "Decision for the Cole-Man" and "Today's Blues Tomorrow." Allen's high-energy and rather free improvisations fit right into the style of music that ESP documented, but there would be no encores. He promptly disappeared for 15 years until he emerged out of nowhere to record a second album, and then slipped away again, apparently permanently.

The Art Ensemble of Chicago   With the formation of the AACM in Chicago in 1965, a new approach developed toward playing avant-garde jazz. While their New York counterparts emphasized high-energy, go-for-broke passionate jams, many of the Chicago players were involved in rediscovering and utilizing silence, dynamics, past styles (though often in distorted or abstract forms), and "little instruments," which were often toys or percussive devices. In August 1966, multireedist Roscoe Mitchell's recording **Sound** helped lead the way to a fascinating new group.

On December 3, 1966, the Roscoe Mitchell Quartet (comprised of Mitchell and Joseph Jarman on reeds, trumpeter Lester Bowie, and bassist Malachi Favors) were first billed at a concert as the Art Ensemble. During 1967–68 they recorded **Old/Quartet**, **Nos. 1 & 2** (under Lester Bowie's name) and **Congliptious** (Nessa 2), intriguing performances full of drama, bits of absurdity, and complete unpredictability. All of that music plus a lot of previously unreleased performances have been made available on the limited edition five-CD set **The Art Ensemble** (Nessa 2500). Although not everything works, and there are periods in which the musicians were clearly searching for inspiration, the performances always hold one's interest. Some of the selections are group improvisations while others have basic ideas that are expanded upon freely. The session from November 25, 1967, is particularly intriguing for Mitchell is heard on two unaccompanied saxophone solos, Favors has one bass feature, and Lester Bowie on "Jazz Death?" performs what may have been the first recorded, full-length unaccompanied trumpet improvisation in jazz history. The Art Ensemble (the "of Chicago" part of their name would come later) was just getting started.

Gato Barbieri   In the late 1960s, Leandro "Gato" Barbieri was a potentially significant avant-garde tenor saxophonist. Born in Argentina, Barbieri took up the clarinet when he was 12, switched to alto the following year, and worked with Lalo Schifrin's Orchestra in the mid-1950s, eventually settling on tenor. He moved to Italy in 1962, and within a year was playing and recording free jazz with Don Cherry. Gato's huge tone was instantly recognizable if often overwhelming, and during this era his solos were quite dissonant. **In Search of the Mystery** (ESP 1049) from 1967 is a good example of Barbieri's avant-garde period. He blows with great intensity on four of his originals, accompanied by cellist Calo Scott, bassist Sirone, and Bobby Kapp on drums.

Paul Bley   Paul Bley started his career as a boppish pianist in his native Canada. He recorded albums for Debut (1953), EmArcy (1954), and GNP (1958) that were essentially bop-oriented. Bley had a long-term gig at the Hillcrest Club in Los Angeles (using Charlie Haden and Billy Higgins in his rhythm section) that was cut short in late 1958 by his decision to add Ornette Coleman and Don Cherry to his group; he was immediately given his two weeks' notice. Bley considered the trade-off to be worth it because he learned a lot playing with Coleman, and his style became much looser and freer.

Moving to New York, Bley worked with Charles Mingus, Don Ellis, and the Jimmy Giuffre 3 (1961–62), becoming one of jazz's first free jazz pianists. In fact, one could say that his most important contribution to jazz was developing an alternative free jazz piano style from the volcanic approach of Cecil Taylor. Bley utilized space and dynamics much more than Taylor, and was a relatively quiet player, not afraid to include melody or a steady rhythm, but also not feeling that he had to be restricted by bebop's structures.

In some ways, Paul Bley's groups could be considered the next logical step in the development of a piano trio after Bill Evans, playing freer than Evans, and having his musicians cooperate as equals. Recorded in 1962, **Footloose** (Savoy 140) features Bley interacting with Steve Swallow and drummer Pete LaRoca on songs by the pianist, his wife Carla Bley, and Ornette Coleman ("When Will the Blues Ever Leave"). Bley, who worked with Sonny Rollins in 1963, recorded fairly frequently as a leader during 1963–67. **Turns** (Savoy 9011), which was not initially released until 1975, has eight performances (including two of Carla Bley's classic "Ida Lupino") from March 9, 1964, that team the pianist, Gary Peacock, and Paul Motian with tenor saxophonist John Gilmore (during a rare vacation from Sun Ra's Arkestra). **Barrage** (ESP 1008) from October 15, 1964, is particularly unusual for Bley because it is a high-powered blowout, the type of music that he usually did not play. This quintet outing features alto saxophonist Marshall Allen (also from Sun Ra's band), trumpeter Dewey Johnson, bassist Eddie Gomez, and drummer Milford Graves, performing Carla Bley tunes. However, the brevity of the CD reissue (under 30 minutes) makes it mostly of historic interest. **Closer** (ESP 1021) has the same fault with only 28 ½ minutes of music, but what is here is quite excellent. Bley and his 1965 trio (with Steve Swallow and Barry Altschul) perform seven Carla Bley songs and one number apiece by the leader, Ornette Coleman ("Crossroads"), and Annette Peacock. **Touching** (Black Lion 760195) has longer performances by the Bley trio (with bassist Kent Carter and Altschul), including a free improvisation on "Pablo," thoughtful interpretations of songs by Carla Bley and Annette Peacock (who after Paul Bley's divorce from Carla became Bley's second wife), and a lengthy performance of "Blood" from a year later with bassist Mark Levinson in Swallow's place.

Listening to these recordings and his others from the period, Paul Bley's approach of freeing up but not completely discarding the structures of 1950s jazz is revealed to be much more influential on pianists from later generations than is often acknowledged.

Dollar Brand   Dollar Brand (who would later change his name to Abdullah Ibrahim) was the first major jazz musician from South Africa. His early music may or may not be considered technically avant-garde, but it was certainly original. His piano playing was always touched by the influences of Duke Ellington and Thelonious Monk along with the folk music of his South African heritage. He began playing piano when he was seven and worked in the 1950s with the Tuxedo Slickers and the Willie Max Big Band. Brand was a key member of the Jazz Epistles, South Africa's first significant jazz band. The sextet (which also included trumpeter Hugh Masekela) made history by recording in 1960.

Due to the worsening racial situation, in 1962 Dollar Brand and singer Bea Benjamin (they would marry in 1965) left South Africa, living for a time in Switzerland. Brand led a trio with bassist Johnny Gertze and drummer Makaya Ntshoko, was heard by Duke Ellington, and made an album for Reprise called **Duke Ellington Presents the Dollar Brand Trio** (Reprise 6111). The pianist performs five originals plus Monk's "Brilliant Corners." His style was not yet that distinctive, but he certainly plays quite well on this stimulating if relatively brief (33 minutes) set.

So impressed was Ellington with Brand's talents that he arranged for the 30-year-old pianist to play at the 1965 Newport Jazz Festival and used him as a substitute for five shows with his own orchestra. In 1966, Brand played with the Elvin Jones Quartet for six months, settled in the United States, and after leaving Jones, formed his own group.

Recorded in 1965, **Anatomy of a South African Village** (Black Lion 6017) features Brand as an avant-garde pianist who was not yet displaying much of his South African heritage in his music. Ibrahim (along with Gertze and Ntshoko) performs the intriguing title cut, brief versions of "Smoke Gets in Your Eyes," and "Mamma," plus a rather hypnotic suite. **Reflections** (Black Lion 760127) is a set of unaccompanied piano solos also from 1965 (other than a version of "Honeysuckle Rose" from 1968). Brand's roots in the music of Ellington and Monk are more apparent on this set than they would be later on. Dollar Brand's interpretations are often introspective, stark (with much use of space), dramatic, dissonant, and occasionally out of tempo and bitonal. The CD reissue is particularly intriguing for those listeners who are mostly familiar with Dollar Brand/Abdullah Ibrahim's later work.

Marion Brown   A lyrical altoist with strong potential, Marion Brown moved to New York from his native

Atlanta in 1965 and was quite active during the next couple of years. Closely associated with the free jazz/avant-garde movement of the period, Brown recorded several albums as a leader, was part of John Coltrane's **Ascension** album, and worked with Archie Shepp and Sun Ra. **Marion Brown Quartet** (ESP 1022) is a typical ESP free-form blowout. The three numbers (two are quite lengthy) are fiery and intense, teaming Brown with either trumpeter Alan Shorter (Wayne's brother) or tenor saxophonist Bennie Maupin, both Ronnie Boykins and Reggie Johnson on basses, and Rashied Ali. **Why Not** (ESP 1040) is an excellent showcase for Brown's abstract flights in a quartet with Stanley Cowell, bassist Norris Jones, and Ali. However, ◉ **Four for Trane** (Impulse 269) is the Marion Brown CD to get. A follow-up of sorts to Archie Shepp's **Four for Trane**, the repertoire is divided between Brown's originals and Shepp's compositions, featuring the adventurous altoist in prime form. Brown is joined by Dave Burrell or Stanley Cowell on piano, Sirone on bass, either Bobby Capp or Beaver Harris on drums, and occasionally trombonist Grachan Moncur III. None of the songs were destined to become standards, but they serve as challenging and very viable devices for Marion Brown's playing.

Don Cherry   As trumpeter with the Ornette Coleman Quartet, Don Cherry may have seemed a little conventional compared to Coleman (his roots in bop were sometimes obvious), but his ideas (usually expressed in a mellow tone) were consistently adventurous, and he blended in perfectly with the altoist. After the last of Coleman's Atlantic recordings in 1961, Ornette became less active for a time, and Cherry went out on his own. He toured with Sonny Rollins in 1963, worked with Steve Lacy, co-led the New York Contemporary Five during 1963–64 (a group also including Archie Shepp and John Tchicai), recorded with Albert Ayler (1964), and relocated to Europe where he often used the up-and-coming Gato Barbieri as his tenor saxophonist.

Don Cherry's trumpet chops were at its best during this era, as heard on his three Blue Note albums. **Complete Communion** (Blue Note 22673) has Cherry, Barbieri, Henry Grimes, and Ed Blackwell performing two four-song suites. Gato's high-register screams contrast with Cherry's more laidback sound, and the interplay between the musicians (the rhythm section is quite active) holds one's interest even if Gato's playing gets a little annoying at times. **Symphony for Improvisers** (Blue Note 28976) is the most interesting of the trio of releases due to the expanded group, which has Cherry's quartet with Barbieri joined by vibraphonist Karl Berger, bassist Jean François Jenny-Clark, and Pharoah Sanders (who doubles on piccolo) on second tenor. The music (eight Cherry originals) is stirring, and the two tenors and two bassists certainly keep the ensembles stimulating, passionate, and explosive. **Where Is Brooklyn** (Blue Note 84311) from 1966 has not been reissued individually yet as a CD. It has the original Cherry quartet except with Sanders in Barbieri's place, and once again would not qualify as peaceful background music!

It seems ironic that the peaceful Cherry teamed up with such fiery saxophonists in the 1960s during his post-Ornette period. A musically curious explorer, Don Cherry would be wandering further from his roots in future years.

Jimmy Giuffre   While a few of the hard bop musicians (such as Jackie McLean and occasionally Lee Morgan) sometimes played in very adventurous settings, Jimmy Giuffre went full force into free jazz, but in his own way. He had performed some free improvisations in West Coast jazz settings, and particularly with his 1958 trio with Bob Brookmeyer and Jim Hall, though none of the latter's free outings were recorded. Giuffre led a trio with Hall and a couple of different bassists during 1959–60, and then in 1961 emerged with an entirely new version of the Jimmy Giuffre 3, featuring mostly his clarinet (with occasional appearances on tenor and baritone) with Paul Bley and bassist Steve Swallow. Though the improvising was mostly taken at a quieter volume than the later high-energy saxophonists, the music was no less radical. The band recorded three studio albums for Verve and Columbia during 1961–62, two of which (**Fusion** and **Thesis**) are on the double CD **1961** (ECM 849 644) along with some previously unreleased material. The three musicians function as equals and perform originals by Giuffre, Bley, and Carla Bley, plus a dramatic version of "Goodbye." **Emphasis, Stuttgart 1961** (Hat Art 6072) and **Flight, Bremen 1961** (Hat Art 6071) have live versions of some of the same material taken from their European tour (when the audience was still expecting Giuffre to play his folk jazz à la "The Train and the River"). The

interpretations are generally more fully developed than the studio renditions, with the musicians making each sound count.

Free Fall (Columbia/Legacy 65446) has nine clarinet solos by Giuffre, three duets with Swallow, and only four numbers by the full trio. Giuffre's playing is often startling, playing between the notes, setting moods on his originals rather than creating any memorable themes. It is intriguing music though it is disappointing how few numbers feature the full trio.

After 1962, the Jimmy Giuffre 3 (which was rarely working) broke up, and Giuffre became an educator. His 1964–65 group with pianist Don Friedman and bassist Barre Phillips did not record, and he did not lead his next record date until 1972.

Milford Graves   Milford Graves was always a very original drummer. He studied Indian and African music, utilizing elements of rhythms from other lands in his fairly free playing. Unlike most other drummers in the free jazz movement, Graves rarely ever played more conventional straightahead jazz so free playing was really his first musical language. After working with Hugh Masekela and Miriam Makeba in the early 1960s, Graves was involved with Bill Dixon in the "October Revolution in Jazz" concert series and played with the Jazz Composers' Orchestra Association. His first album as a leader, **Milford Graves Percussion Ensemble** (ESP 1015), is of limited interest for it features Graves and the obscure Sunny Morgan as a drum duo. The rather brief program (under 35 minutes of music) has titles that fit the meandering music: "Nothing 5–7," "Nothing 11–10," "Nothing 19," "Nothing 13," and "Nothing." Graves, who was better heard as a sideman, also recorded two very obscure albums of duets with pianist Don Pullen in 1966 and worked with Albert Ayler during 1967–68.

Henry Grimes   Henry Grimes, a very versatile bassist, attended Julliard and worked with Arnett Cobb, Willis Jackson, Anita O'Day, Sonny Rollins, and the Gerry Mulligan Quartet (1957–58). Grimes was such a fine bassist that at the 1958 Newport Jazz Festival he played with the very different groups of Benny Goodman, Lee Konitz, Sonny Rollins, and Thelonious Monk. By 1961, Grimes had become part of the free jazz movement, working with Cecil Taylor (off and on during 1961–66), Perry Robinson, Rollins, Albert Ayler (1964–66), and Don Cherry. In 1965, he led his only record date, **The**

Call (ESP 1026). On this trio set with clarinetist Perry Robinson and drummer Tom Price, Grimes performs six group originals and has a generous amount of solo space. But then one day in 1967, Henry Grimes (who was 31) simply disappeared. He would not be heard from again in the jazz world until he was rediscovered in 2002, 35 years later.

Gunter Hampel   Gunter Hampel, who was born in Germany, started on the piano when he was four. While a teenager he played accordion, clarinet, vibes, and various saxophones. After discovering jazz, Hampel became a professional in 1958 when he was 21. By the time he started recording in 1965, he was leading the Heartplants quintet (a group also including trumpeter Manfred Schoof and pianist Alexander Von Schlippenbach), and primarily improvising on vibes, flute, and bass clarinet in a very advanced yet usually accessible manner. **Music from Europe** (ESP 1042) from 1966 gives one a valuable early look at Hampel and Willem Breuker (who is heard on soprano, bass clarinet, tenor, alto, baritone, and clarinet) in a quartet with bassist Piet Veening and drummer Pierre Courbois. The three complex and sometimes eccentric originals are highlighted by the nearly 22-minute "Assemblage." The music overall is an interesting combination of composition and very free improvising, and shows very little debt to Hampel's American counterparts.

Joe Harriott   In some ways, Joe Harriott was the Ornette Coleman of England, blazing an early trail in free jazz that was followed and extended by many other European musicians. Born in Jamaica, Harriott played in his native land (including with trumpeter Dizzy Reece) before moving to England in 1951. He played bop in the United Kingdom during the 1950s, including with trumpeter Pete Pitterson, drummer Tony Kinsey, and Ronnie Scott's big band. Harriott began leading his own record dates in 1953, but his first significant statements were 1960's **Free Form** (Jazzland 49) and 1961's **Abstract** (Columbia 1477). It is unfortunate that none of his recordings (which feature him in a quintet/sextet with trumpeter Shake Keane, pianist Pat Smythe, bassist Coleridge Goode, Phil Seeman or Bobby Orr on drums, and sometimes percussionist Frank Holder) are readily available on CD yet, for they show that Harriott had his own approach to fairly free improvising.

Harriott was also very interested in combining jazz with types of world music and was a pioneer in that area. His **Indo Jazz Suite** (the LP Columbia 6025) from 1965 was groundbreaking in featuring a double quintet comprised of three horns, piano, John Mayer on violin and harpsichord, sitar, bass, drums, tambura, and tabla, as was **Indo Jazz Fusions** (Columbia 6122) that used the same instrumentation the following year. Harriott also did not neglect straightahead jazz, recording some bop standards in 1967.

Joe Harriott faded from the scene by the late 1960s and has never received the recognition he deserves as an important innovator in both free jazz and the fusion of jazz with world music.

Andrew Hill   Andrew Hill is not so much a free jazz improviser as he is an adventurous pianist and composer whose highly original music borders on the avant-garde. He began playing piano when he was 13 in 1950 and was part of the Chicago jazz scene in the 1950s, recording a trio album for Warwick that included bassist Malachi Favors. In 1961, Hill moved to New York and worked as Dinah Washington's accompanist. He was with Rahsaan Roland Kirk in 1962, and since then has primarily led his own groups. Hill's most important recordings, his first eight albums made as a leader for Blue Note, were reissued on the seven-CD limited-edition box set **The Complete Andrew Hill Blue Note Sessions 1963–66** (Mosaic 7-161). The earliest four are also available individually.

Recorded in 1963, **Black Fire** (Blue Note 84151) is a quartet date with Joe Henderson, Richard Davis, and Roy Haynes that shows just how fresh and unpredictable Hill's music was from the start. **Smoke Stack** (Blue Note 32097), which has both Eddie Kahn and Richard Davis on bass along with Haynes, and **Judgment** (Blue Note 28981), a set with Bobby Hutcherson, Richard Davis, and Elvin Jones, are both excellent programs full of intriguing Hill originals and his very personal piano playing, but they are overshadowed by the classic ○ **Point of Departure** (Blue Note 84167). The latter set, from March 21, 1964, has an all-star group with Hill joined by Kenny Dorham, Eric Dolphy (who often steals the show), Joe Henderson, Richard Davis, and Tony Williams. The colorful ensembles and the very individual solo voices uplift a set of strong Hill originals in memorable fashion without compromising Hill's musical vision.

Andrew Hill's four dates of 1965–66 have not been reissued on CD yet outside of the Mosaic box. **Andrew** (Blue Note 84203) teams Hill with Bobby Hutcherson and Sun Ra's tenor star John Gilmore. **One for One** (Blue Note 4489/90) is a double LP that, in addition to a 1965 date with Freddie Hubbard and Joe Henderson, also includes sessions from 1969–70. **Compulsion** (Blue Note 4217) matches Hubbard and Gilmore on four complex originals, while **Involution** (Blue Note 453-H2), a quartet set with tenor saxophonist Sam Rivers, bassist Walter Booker, and drummer J.C. Moses, was originally released in the 1970s as a double LP, coupled with a Rivers date.

Andrew Hill has remained an important voice in jazz up to the present time and virtually every recording he has made is well worth exploring.

Bob James   In 1965, Bob James was a promising 25-year-old pianist who was temporarily exploring the avant-garde. After receiving a master's degree in composition from the University of Michigan in 1962, he recorded a boppish trio LP for Mercury (**Bold Conceptions**). In 1965, James cut **Explosions** (ESP 1009), a rather strange record with bassist Barre Phillips and drummer Robert Pozar. James plays fine, but his use of electronics and distorted tapes are distracting and occasionally unlistenable. The results are high on intellect, but low on emotions, and some of the music sounds more like an experiment than honest expression. However, this project was a one-time thing, for Bob James soon spent three years as Sarah Vaughan's accompanist, and he would never again record anything even remotely avant-garde.

Joseph Jarman   One of the most radical of the reed players of the mid-1960s, Joseph Jarman's abstract playing was always original. Originally a drummer, he switched to reeds in the mid-1950s while in the army. Jarman settled in Chicago in 1958, and worked with Muhal Richard Abrams's Experimental Band during 1961–65 where he met Malachi Favors and Roscoe Mitchell. Jarman joined the AACM in 1965, led his own groups during 1966–68, and became an original member of the Art Ensemble in late 1966. His debut as a leader, 1966's ◉ **Song For** (Delmark 410), is an early avant-garde classic. Jarman, who sticks to alto on this set, is joined by trumpeter William Brimfield, the legendary tenor Fred Anderson, pianist Christopher

Gaddy, bassist Charles Clark, and either Steve McCall or Thurman Barker on drums. The four originals include a Jarman recitation, a dirge, the intense "Little Fox Run" (heard in two versions on the CD reissue), and the title cut, which contrasts sounds and a creative use of silence.

Steve Lacy   For Steve Lacy, the 1961–67 period was one of transition. Having already played Dixieland and as a member of the Cecil Taylor Quartet, Lacy was now on his own. His voice on soprano was quite original, not sounding at all like John Coltrane whom he had actually preceded on the instrument. Lacy led four intriguing small-group albums during 1957–61, including **Evidence** (Original Jazz Classics 1755). Lacy is teamed with Don Cherry, bassist Carl Brown, and Billy Higgins for four Thelonious Monk tunes, Duke Ellington's "The Mystery Song," and Billy Strayhorn's "Something to Live For." It is quite interesting hearing Cherry (who was then with the Ornette Coleman Quartet) playing these standards. Lacy, who had recorded Monk's "Work" back in 1957, was in the process of beginning a lifetime of studying Thelonious's music. In late 1961, he formed a quartet with Roswell Rudd, Henry Grimes, and drummer Dennis Charles whose entire repertoire was of Monk songs. Although the group lasted nearly three years on a part-time basis, only one recording resulted, and that was the tape of a live engagement from March 1963. ◉ **Schooldays** (Hat Art 6140) has the seven existing selections, including two that were made with a trio when Grimes was late for the gig. Highlights from this unique repertory band include "Brilliant Corners," "Monk's Dream," and a trio rendition of "Bye-Ya"; the decently recorded music certainly stands out.

With the breakup of the neglected band, Steve Lacy began to loosen his playing and work in the avant-garde, over time developing a scalar approach to improvising. He had a quartet with Italian trumpeter Enrico Rava that worked in Europe, and then spent much of 1966 in South America. **The Forest and the Zoo** (ESP 1060) was recorded in Buenos Aires with Rava, bassist Johnny Dyani, and drummer Louis Moholo. The two lengthy free improvisations ("Forest" and "Zoo") have their colorful moments along with some overly long wandering stretches. In 1967, Steve Lacy moved to Italy where he played with the top European avant-garde musicians, while never losing his interest in Monk's music.

117 ESSENTIAL RECORDS OF 1961–1967

John Coltrane and Johnny Hartman, **John Coltrane and Johnny Hartman** (Impulse 157)

John Coltrane, **Live at Birdland** (Impulse 198)

John Coltrane, **A Love Supreme: Deluxe Edition** (Impulse 314 589 945), 2 CDs

John Coltrane, **Meditations** (Impulse 199)

Ornette Coleman, **The Golden Circle in Stockholm Vol. 1** (Blue Note 35518)

Eric Dolphy, **The Complete Prestige Recordings** (Prestige 4418), 9 CDs

Eric Dolphy, **Out to Lunch** (Blue Note 46524)

Albert Ayler, **Lorrach/Paris 1966** (Hat Art 6039)

Albert Ayler, **Live in Greenwich Village** (Impulse 2-273), 2 CDs

Marion Brown, **Four for Trane** (Impulse 269)

Andrew Hill, **Point of Departure** (Blue Note 84167)

Joseph Jarman, **Song For** (Delmark 410)

Steve Lacy, **Schooldays** (Hat Art 6140)

Prince Lasha and Sonny Simmons, **Firebirds** (Original Jazz Classics 1822)

Roscoe Mitchell, **Sound** (Delmark 408)

Sam Rivers, **A New Conception** (Blue Note 84249)

The New York Contemporary Five, **The New York Contemporary Five** (Storyville 8209)

Archie Shepp, **Four for Trane** (Impulse 218)

Charles Tyler, **Eastern Man Alone** (ESP 1059)

Miles Davis, **Seven Steps to Heaven** (Columbia/ Legacy 48827)

Miles Davis, **The Complete Concert: 1964** (Columbia/Legacy 48821), 2 CDs

Miles Davis, **Miles Davis Quintet, 1965–68** (Columbia/Legacy 67398), 4 CDs

Cannonball Adderley, **Dizzy's Business** (Milestone 47069)

Cannonball Adderley, **Mercy Mercy Mercy** (Capitol 29915)

Dave Brubeck, **At Carnegie Hall** (Columbia/Legacy 61455), 2 CDs

Bill Evans, **Conversations with Myself** (Verve 521 409)

Bill Evans, **Empathy/A Simple Matter of Conviction** (Verve 837 757)

Charles Lloyd, **Forest Flower** (Rhino 71746)

Charles Mingus, **The Black Saint and the Sinner Lady** (Impulse 174)

Modern Jazz Quartet and Laurindo Almeida, **Collaboration** (Label M 5731)

Thelonious Monk, **Big Band and Quartet in Concert** (Columbia/Legacy 57636), 2 CDs

Oscar Peterson, **Oscar Peterson Trio Plus One** (Verve 818 840)

Horace Silver, **Song for My Father** (Blue Note 84185)

Chet Baker, **The Italian Sessions** (Bluebird 2001)

Ted Curson, **Tears for Dolphy** (Black Lion 760190)

Kenny Dorham, **Una Mas** (Blue Note 46515)

Freddie Hubbard, **Ready for Freddie** (Blue Note 32094)

Blue Mitchell, **The Thing to Do** (Blue Note 84178)

Lee Morgan, **The Sidewinder** (Blue Note 84157)

Lee Morgan, **Cornbread** (Blue Note 84222)

Clark Terry, **The Happy Horns of Clark Terry** (GRP/Impulse 148)

Hank Crawford, **Memphis, Ray, and a Touch of Moody** (32 Jazz 32054), 2 CDs

John Handy, **Live at the Monterey Jazz Festival** (Koch 7820)

Lee Konitz, **The Lee Konitz Duets** (Original Jazz Classics 466)

Jackie McLean, **Let Freedom Ring** (Blue Note 46527)

Jackie McLean, **One Step Beyond** (Blue Note 46821)

Sonny Stitt, **Stitt Plays Bird** (Rhino/Atlantic 1418)

Sonny Stitt and Paul Gonsalves, **Salt and Pepper** (GRP/Impulse 210)

Phil Woods, **The Rights of Swing** (Candid 79016)

Eddie "Lockjaw" Davis and Johnny Griffin, **Blues Up and Down** (Prestige 24084)

Dexter Gordon, **The Complete Blue Note Sixties Sessions** (Blue Note 34200), 6 CDs

Eddie Harris, **Electrifying Eddie Harris/Plug Me In** (Rhino 71516)

Joe Henderson, **Page One** (Blue Note 84140)

Rahsaan Roland Kirk, **The Complete Mercury Recordings of Roland Kirk** (Mercury 846 630), 10 CDs

Yusef Lateef, **Live at Pep's** (Impulse 134)

Oliver Nelson, **The Blues and the Abstract Truth** (Impulse 154)

Sonny Rollins, **The Complete RCA Victor Recordings** (RCA 68675)

117 ESSENTIAL RECORDS OF 1961–1967

Wayne Shorter, **Juju** (Blue Note 46514)

Wayne Shorter, **Speak No Evil** (Blue Note 46509)

Stanley Turrentine and Shirley Scott, **A Chip Off the Old Block** (Blue Note 84129)

Pepper Adams and Thad Jones, **Mean What You Say** (Original Jazz Classics 464)

Vince Guaraldi, **Jazz Impressions of Black Orpheus** (Original Jazz Classics 437)

Herbie Hancock, **Takin' Off** (Blue Note 46506)

Herbie Hancock, **Maiden Voyage** (Blue Note 46339)

Elmo Hope, **The Final Sessions** (Evidence 22147), 2 CDs

Ramsey Lewis, **In Person 1960–1967** (GRP/Chess 814), 2 CDs

Duke Pearson, **Introducing Duke Pearson's Big Band** (Blue Note 94508)

Randy Weston, **Monterey '66** (Verve 314 519 698)

Joe Zawinul, **Rise & Fall of the Third Stream/Money in the Pocket** (Rhino 71675)

Brother Jack McDuff, **Live!** (Prestige 24147)

Shirley Scott, **Queen of the Organ** (Impulse 123)

Jimmy Smith and Wes Montgomery, **The Dynamic Duo** (Verve 521 445)

Larry Young, **Unity** (Blue Note 84221)

George Benson, **The George Benson Cookbook** (Columbia/Legacy 66054)

Kenny Burrell, **Midnight Blue** (Blue Note 46399)

Grant Green, **The Latin Bit** (Blue Note 37645)

Grant Green, **Idle Moments** (Blue Note 84154)

Wes Montgomery, **Impressions: The Verve Jazz Sessions** (Verve 521690), 2 CDs

Joe Pass, **For Django** (BGO 430)

Gabor Szabo, **The Sorceror** (GRP/Impulse 211)

Chico Hamilton, **Man from Two Worlds** (GRP/Impulse 127)

Pete LaRoca, **Basra** (Blue Note 32091)

Max Roach, **Percussion Bitter Suite** (Impulse 122)

Gary Burton, **Duster** (Koch 7846)

Bobby Hutcherson, **Components** (Blue Note 29027)

Tadd Dameron, **The Magic Touch of Tadd Dameron** (Original Jazz Classics 143)

George Russell, **Ezz-thetic** (Original Jazz Classics 70)

Ray Barretto, **Carnaval** (Fantasy 24713)

Mongo Santamaria, **Watermelon Man** (Milestone 47075)

Charlie Byrd, **Latin Byrd** (Milestone 47005)

Stan Getz, **Focus** (Verve 521 419)

Stan Getz, **The Bossa Nova Years** (Verve 823 611), 4 CDs

Stan Getz, **Sweet Rain** (Verve 815 054)

Mose Allison, **I Don't Worry About a Thing** (Rhino/Atlantic 71417)

Mose Allison, **The Sage of Tippo** (32 Jazz 32068), 2 CDs

Al Jarreau, **1965** (Bainbridge 6237)

Sheila Jordan, **Portrait of Sheila** (Blue Note 89002)

Jeanne Lee and Ran Blake, **Legendary Duets** (Bluebird 6461)

Abbey Lincoln, **Straight Ahead** (Candid 79015)

Sarah Vaughan, **Sassy Swings the Tivoli** (Mercury 832 788, 2 CDs)

Joe Williams, **Joe Williams and the Thad Jones-Mel Lewis Orchestra** (Blue Note 30454)

Nancy Wilson and Cannonball Adderley, **Nancy Wilson/Cannonball Adderley** (Capitol 81204)

Duke Ellington, **Duke Ellington Meets Count Basie** (Columbia/Legacy 655471)

Duke Ellington, **Money Jungle** (Blue Note 38227)

Duke Ellington, **The Far East Suite—Special Mix** (Bluebird 6287)

Duke Ellington, **And His Mother Called Him Bill** (Bluebird 6287)

Woody Herman, **Jazz Hoot/Woody's Winners** (Collectables 6678)

Benny Carter, **Further Definitions** (GRP/Impulse 229)

Earl Hines, **Spontaneous Explorations** (Red Baron 57331), 2 CDs

Johnny Hodges, **Everybody Knows Johnny Hodges** (GRP/Impulse 116)

Ben Webster, **See You at the Fair** (GRP/Impulse 2126)

Louis Armstrong & Duke Ellington, **Complete Sessions** (Roulette 93844)

Louis Armstrong, **An American Icon** (Hip-O 40138), 3 CDs

Sweet Emma Barrett, **New Orleans: The Living Legends** (Original Jazz Classics 1832)

Dukes of Dixieland, **The Best of the Dukes of Dixieland** (Sony 13374)

Jack Teagarden, **Think Well of Me** (Verve 557 101)

Jack Teagarden, **A Hundred Years from Today** (Memphis Archives 7010)

Prince Lasha   Eric Dolphy was probably the first avant-garde jazz flutist, but Prince Lasha was close behind. Lasha, who also occasionally played alto and clarinet, was born in Fort Worth, Texas, and jammed with Ornette Coleman when they were both in high school. In 1954, he moved to Los Angeles, but was in obscurity until 1962 when he recorded **The Cry** (Original Jazz Classics 1945) in a quartet with his regular musical partner of the time, altoist Sonny Simmons. The music (which also has bassist Gary Peacock, Mark Proctor on second bass for five of the eight songs, and drummer Gene Stone) is a bit reminiscent of the Ornette Coleman Quartet in its style although Lasha's flute gives the music its own personality, and the originals are not quite so forbidding. A visit to New York in 1965 by Lasha resulted in the LP **Inside Story** (Enja 3073), an obscure but worthy effort that teams Lasha with Herbie Hancock, bassist Cecil McBee, and drummer Jimmy Lovelace. The quartet performs five of Lasha's originals that often swing yet are quite adventurous, with soloing outside of the chord structures.

Lasha, who also recorded as a sideman with Eric Dolphy and the Elvin Jones/Jimmy Garrison Sextet, had a reunion with Simmons on ◉ **Firebirds** (Original Jazz Classics 1822) in 1967. This gem has Lasha (on flute, alto, and alto clarinet) and Simmons (alto and English horn) joined by vibraphonist Bobby Hutcherson, bassist Buster Williams, and Charles Moffett on five stimulating selections. The solos are quite emotional, and although the influence of Ornette Coleman is still felt, this is an underrated classic. Lasha and Simmons make for a very potent team.

Chris McGregor and the Blue Notes   White South African pianist Chris McGregor studied at the Cape Town College of Music and played jazz in his native country, mostly with black musicians, forming the Blue Notes in 1962. Leading an integrated band in South Africa was an increasingly dangerous practice in the early 1960s, and after accepting an invitation to play at the 1964 Antibes Jazz Festival, McGregor and his sidemen (trumpeter Mongezi Feza, tenor saxophonist Nick Moyake, altoist Dudu Pukwana, bassist Johnny Dyani, and drummer Louis Moholo) all moved to Europe, settling in England. The Blue Notes combined avant-garde soloing with South African rhythms and melodies, but did not gain as much work as they hoped. England was

not yet ready for the brand of music offered by these refugees. The Blue Notes only recorded one album, **Very Urgent** (the LP Polydor 184137), and a homesick Moyake soon returned to South Africa while Dyani moved to Scandinavia.

Ken McIntyre   A talented musician who had the courage (or the foolhardiness) to record next to Eric Dolphy (not faring too badly), Ken McIntyre played alto sax, flute, oboe, bass clarinet, and bassoon. He worked primarily as a public school teacher starting in 1961 so did not record all that much in his career. In fact, between 1961–73, his only dates as a leader were two albums that have been reissued (along with eight previously unreleased cuts) on the two-CD set **The Complete United Artists Sessions** (Blue Note 57200). These performances (from 1962–63) are all McIntyre originals except "Laura" and "Speak Low." McIntyre's pieces show the influence of the avant-garde and swing despite often utilizing tricky time signatures. McIntyre is primarily heard on alto along with some flute and oboe. He is showcased with a pianoless rhythm section and a dozen strings on one date, and with a quartet/quintet elsewhere; pianist Jaki Byard and trombonist John Mancebo Lewis are in the supporting cast.

Roscoe Mitchell   Roscoe Mitchell was one of the top saxophonists to come out of Chicago's AACM movement. He began to play reeds as a teenager, served in the army (at one point in Germany he had an opportunity to play with Albert Ayler), and in 1961 at 21 he became an important part of Chicago's modern jazz scene. His style soon became freer, and he worked with Muhal Richard Abrams's Experimental Band during 1962–65, joining the new AACM in '65.

In 1966, Mitchell led the first AACM group to record, resulting in the monumental ◉ **Sound** (Delmark 408). The sextet (with trumpeter Lester Bowie, trombonist Lester Lashley, tenor saxophonist Kalaparusha Maurice McIntyre, bassist Malachi Favors, drummer Alvin Fiedler, and Mitchell on alto and clarinet) performed music that was quite a bit different than the high-energy avant-garde releases coming out of New York and the ESP label. In addition to the use of silence, "little instruments" (including toys and percussion devices) are featured in sections, and the music sometimes hints at earlier styles while also being very advanced. One can hear both the beginnings of the Art Ensemble of Chicago and of freebop (an extension of Ornette Coleman's music) on this important set.

In 1967, the Roscoe Mitchell Art Ensemble consisted of Mitchell, Bowie, Favors, and drummer Phillip Wilson (who would soon leave to join the Butterfield Blues Band). Although little known outside of Chicago, it would soon make its mark on jazz.

Grachan Moncur III   Grachan Moncur III, the son of bassist Grachan Moncur II (who played bass with the Savoy Sultans during 1937–45), was one of the first trombonists to explore free jazz. Grachan III started on trombone when he was 11, toured with Ray Charles (1959–62), was with the Jazztet (1962), and in 1963 started turning toward more advanced jazz, playing with Jackie McLean. Moncur recorded two very impressive Blue Note albums during 1963–64, toured with Sonny Rollins (1964), and worked and recorded with Marion Brown, Joe Henderson, and Archie Shepp.

Recorded in 1963, **Evolution** (Blue Note 84153) has Moncur keeping up with his notable sidemen (Lee Morgan, Jackie McLean, Bobby Hutcherson, bassist Bob Cranshaw, and the teenaged Tony Williams), contributing four originals (including "Monk in Wonderland") and playing very well. Moncur clearly had no fear about indulging in freer explorations. **Some Other Stuff** (Blue Note 32092) from 1964 is even better. Moncur interacts with Wayne Shorter, Herbie Hancock, bassist Cecil McBee, and Williams on four of his challenging originals, including one song ("The Twins") that shows how much can be built from using just one chord. This set is of particular significance because it is one of the first times that Shorter (who had not joined the Miles Davis Quintet yet) recorded with Hancock and Williams.

But while his sidemen on both albums would gain fame in future years, Grachan Moncur III would never get better known than he was in the mid-1960s.

Sunny Murray   Sunny Murray has been described by Paul Bley as the first totally free drummer, one who did not keep time at all, and instead interacted directly with the lead voices of any group he appeared in. Ironically, Murray had begun his career playing trad jazz with Henry "Red" Allen and Willie "The Lion" Smith shortly after moving to New York in 1956, and he also gigged with Jackie McLean and Ted Curson. Murray developed quickly while working with Cecil Taylor (1959–64) and

was perfect for Albert Ayler's band (1964–67), also working with Don Cherry, Ornette Coleman, and John Tchicai.

An obscure album from 1965 has Murray leading a band that has Cherry and Ayler as sidemen. Better known is **Sunny Murray Quintet** (ESP 1032), a fairly typical ESP freeform blowing session. Murray heads a high-powered free jazz quintet also including altoists Byard Lancaster and Jack Graham, trumpeter Jacques Coursil, and bassist Al Silva. The group performs lengthy versions of three Murray originals and one by Graham with coherent but very fiery solos. Throughout this set, Sunny Murray gives momentum to the music while playing totally free.

Dewey Redman   The Fort Worth, Texas, area has not received much due as a major breeding ground for the avant-garde, but when Dewey Redman (who had taken up clarinet when he was 13) played in the high school marching band, the group also included Ornette Coleman, Charles Moffett, and Prince Lasha. Born in 1931, Redman started his playing career fairly late, working instead as a public school teacher during 1956–59 and getting his master's degree in education from North Texas State. However, by 1960 he was freelancing as a musician in San Francisco and opening up his style to freer sounds. In 1966, he made his debut as a leader on the LP **Look for the Black Star** (Freedom 1011), performing five of his expressive originals with pianist Jym Young, bassist Donald Raphael Garrett, and drummer Eddie Moore. He is heard improvising in a style not all that different from Ornette Coleman's (although Redman's Texas tenor sound made his style seem more accessible). In 1967, Dewey Redman began a longtime association with Ornette, joining his quartet.

Sam Rivers   Three years older than John Coltrane and born seven years before Ornette Coleman, Sam Rivers was one of the oldest musicians involved in the 1960s avant-garde, yet he would be fully committed to free jazz for decades. His grandfather had published a book of hymns and black folk songs back in 1882, his mother played piano and taught music, and his father sang with the Fisk Jubilee Singers. As a child, Rivers had piano and violin lessons, spent a period playing trombone, and eventually settled on tenor. He played professionally in Boston starting in 1947 with top local musicians, including Herb Pomeroy, Jaki Byard, Nat

Pierce, and Serge Chaloff. In 1959, Rivers first gigged with drummer Tony Williams, who was 13 at the time. Within a couple of years, Rivers had moved beyond bop to explore much freer music, working with Archie Shepp, Bill Dixon, Paul Bley, and Cecil Taylor. After moving to New York in 1964, Rivers was recommended to Miles Davis by Tony Williams. He was a member of the Davis Quintet (replacing George Coleman and preceding Wayne Shorter), but the association was short-lived because his style was considered too advanced for the group; he does appear on one live record with Miles.

After leaving Davis, Rivers recorded **Life Time** with Tony Williams, and then led four Blue Note albums of his own. **Fuschia Swing Song** (Blue Note 84184) has the tenor exploring his originals with Jaki Byard, Ron Carter, and Williams, displaying a thick tone and a very advanced improvising style. **Contours** (Blue Note 84206), which has Rivers also playing soprano and flute, matches him with Freddie Hubbard, Herbie Hancock, Carter, and drummer Joe Chambers on originals that range from advanced hard bop to nearly free. ⦿ **A New Conception** (Blue Note 84249) is an unusual date in Rivers's discography for he performs standards (with pianist Hal Galper, bassist Herbie Lewis, and drummer Steve Ellington), but turns them inside out and stretches them to the breaking point. His versions of such tunes as "Secret Love," "I'll Never Smile Again," and "That's All," while paying respect to the melodies, are unlike any of the well-known vocal renditions, making this set a perfect introduction to his fresh way of improvising. Recorded in 1967, **Dimensions and Extensions** (Blue Note 84261) was not initially released until the 1970s, and has the most advanced music, with fine playing on the challenging pieces by Rivers, Donald Byrd, altoist James Spaulding, trombonist Julian Priester, Cecil McBee, and Steve Ellington.

Perry Robinson   In the 1960s, clarinetist Perry Robinson tried to do the near-impossible: establish himself as an avant-garde leader on an instrument still closely associated with the swing era. After attending the Lenox School of Jazz in 1959, Robinson worked in New York with such players as Paul Bley, Archie Shepp, and Bill Dixon, recording with Henry Grimes. It is not too surprising that fame eluded Robinson for this was a period when bebopper Buddy DeFranco was himself having difficulty finding jazz jobs. Robinson's only date as a

leader during the time is **Funk Dumpling** (Savoy 255) from 1962, a quartet date with pianist Kenny Barron, Henry Grimes, and Paul Motian. The group plays four of the clarinetist's originals and three by Grimes. The music is warm, lyrical, and thoughtful with Robinson taking some adventurous solos along the way, and showing how original a soloist he already was at that early point.

Roswell Rudd   Like Grachan Moncur III, Roswell Rudd spent time playing with Archie Shepp's band; in fact, for a period both trombonists were with the fiery tenor. Rudd started out on French horn before switching to trombone and originally played Dixieland during 1954–59, including with Eli's Chosen Six, with whom he made his recording debut. Like Steve Lacy, Rudd made the improbable jump from trad jazz to free jazz, bypassing bebop altogether. He recorded with Cecil Taylor in 1960, worked with Herbie Nichols and Bill Dixon, and co-led a quartet with Lacy that exclusively played the music of Thelonious Monk.

During 1964–65, Rudd was in the New York Art Quartet with altoist John Tchicai and a couple of different bassists and drummers. The group recorded three albums; one apiece for ESP, Fontana, and America. The former disc, **New York Art Quartet** (ESP 1004), has Rudd and Tchicai joined by bassist Lewis Worrell and drummer Milford Graves. The four instrumentals are colorful and intriguing although poet Leroi Jones (later renamed Amiri Baraka) is an intrusive force when he is showcased on one endless recitation. The band's later albums have contributions from bassists Reggie Workman and Finn Von Eyben, and drummer Louis Moholo.

After the New York Art Quartet broke up in 1965, Rudd joined Archie Shepp (1965–67). Rudd led an album apiece for America (1965) and Impulse (1966's **Everywhere**), but was mostly a supportive voice during this era, trying (along with Moncur) to find a role for the trombone in the new music.

Pharoah Sanders   Born Ferrell Sanders in Little Rock, Arkansas, Sanders worked and studied in Oakland in 1959, moving to New York three years later. After a period of struggle, the tenor saxophonist had an opportunity to record an album in 1964, **Pharoah's First** (ESP 1003). Joined by trumpeter Stan Foster, pianist Jane Getz, bassist William Bennett, and drummer Marvin Pattillo, Sanders sounds remarkably like

John Coltrane on "Seven by Seven" although he shows some individuality on "Bethera." He soon befriended the saxophonist, who was quite impressed by his increasingly passionate style and energy. By mid-1965, Sanders was regularly sitting in with Coltrane, and later in the year he became an official member of the group, staying until Trane's death in 1967.

Pharoah Sanders had an opportunity to record his debut album for Impulse in 1966, but **Tauhid** (Impulse 129) is a bit of a disappointment. The 16-minute "Upper Egypt and Lower Egypt" takes forever to get going, and Sanders does not really play tenor until 12 minutes into the song. The brief "Japan" mostly focuses on Sanders's off-key singing, and a long medley is most notable for the playing of guitarist Sonny Sharrock. But Pharoah Sanders's best work as a leader would be coming up soon.

Archie Shepp   One of the most important tenor saxophonists of the 1960s free jazz movement, Archie Shepp took his sound largely from Ben Webster, but his choice of notes, growls, roars, and screams were his own. Shepp certainly stood out from the field of Coltrane imitators, not sounding anything like Trane, being politically active and a playwright who occasionally recited an angry poem. He studied dramatic literature at Goddard College and initially played alto in dance bands. However, after he switched to tenor in 1960, Shepp began immediately working in free jazz, making his recording debut with Cecil Taylor (1960–61) and co-leading a group with trumpeter Bill Dixon in 1962 that cut a long-out-of-print album for Savoy. During 1962–64, Shepp worked with the New York Contemporary Five, a group also including Don Cherry, altoist John Tchicai, bassist Don Moore, and drummer J.C. Moses. The band mostly played in Europe and recorded four albums of which two (leaving out one cut) are reissued on the single disc ● **The New York Contemporary Five** (Storyville 8209). Although influenced by the Ornette Coleman Quartet, the inclusion of Tchicai (who did not sound like Ornette) and Shepp gave the band its own sound. They are heard exploring originals by band members Bill Dixon, Ornette Coleman, and Thelonious Monk. Another early Shepp recording, **The House I Live In** (Steeple Chase 36013) from November 21, 1963, is quite intriguing, for he is heard at a Danish concert with the great cool-toned bop baritonist Lars Gullin and a conventional rhythm section that includes pianist Tete Montoliu. The group plays four lengthy standards, including a 19-minute rendition of "You Stepped Out of a Dream." It is particularly interesting to note the reactions of the other musicians to Shepp's rather free flights, and to hear Gullin on a few occasions try to emulate him.

The year 1964 was Archie Shepp's breakthrough year. At the urging of John Coltrane, Shepp was signed to Impulse where he debuted with ● **Four for Trane** (Impulse 218). As the title suggests, Shepp performs four of Trane's compositions ("Naima," "Mr. Syms," "Syeeda's Song Flute," and "Cousin Mary") plus his own "Rufus (Swung His Face at Last to the Wind, then His Neck Snapped)." Shepp plays with a great deal of fire, really pushing the sextet, which also includes flugelhornist Alan Shorter (Wayne Shorter's brother), Roswell Rudd, John Tchicai, Reggie Workman, and Charles Moffett.

With Archie Shepp, the most noteworthy aspect of his style was his emotional and generally raspy sound rather than the notes he played. **Fire Music** (Impulse 158) from 1965 is a bit erratic (particularly a bizarre and overlong exploration of "The Girl from Ipanema"), but there are also some memorable selections, particularly the episodic "Los Olvidaos," a spacey rendition of "Prelude to a Kiss," and a live version of "Hambone." **On this Night** (Impulse 125), which gathers together music from two dates that was formerly scattered, has Shepp leading a quintet also featuring vibraphonist Bobby Hutcherson. The best selections include three very different versions of the explosive "The Chased," a reworking of "In a Sentimental Mood," and "The Original Mr. Sonny Boy Williamson." From 1966, **Live in San Francisco** (Impulse 254) combines two former LPs along with a previously unreleased version of "Things Ain't What They Used to Be." The passionate Shepp is heard with his regular group of the period, a quintet also featuring Roswell Rudd, drummer Beaver Harris, and both Donald Garrett and Lewis Worrell on basses. There are two departures (Shepp's workout on piano on the ballad "Sylvia" and his recitation on "The Wedding") while the quintet sounds particularly strong on Herbie Nichols's "The Lady Sings the Blues" and "Wherever June Bugs Go." Shepp's ballad statement on "In a Sentimental Mood" is both reverential and eccentric. Also on this set is the nearly 33-minute "Three for a Quarter/One for a Dime," a lengthy blowout that was originally released as an album by itself. One can understand why Archie Shepp was rated so highly by fans of the avant-garde and considered a disagreeable musical force by listeners whose ears were not open to the new music.

Also of strong interest are **Mama Too Tight** (Impulse 248) that teams Shepp with five horns, Charlie Haden, and Beaver Harris; **The Magic of Ju-Ju** (Impulse 23036) that showcases Shepp with two horns, Reggie Workman, and five drummers/percussionists; and the LP **Live at the Donaueschingen Music Festival** (MPS 20651). The latter has Shepp in 1967 romping through the continuous 43½-minute "One for the Trane" with both Roswell Rudd and Grachan Moncur on trombones, Jimmy Garrison, and Beaver Harris. The audience at the German music festival seems quite enthusiastic during this mostly free-form music, which surprisingly becomes an eccentric version of "The Shadow of Your Smile" near the end of the performance.

Archie Shepp showed that it was quite possible to explore free jazz on tenor and not sound like John Coltrane.

Sonny Simmons   Born Huey Simmons, young Sonny (who was born in Louisiana) grew up in Oakland and played English horn before taking up the alto when he was 16 in 1949. He worked with the blues bands of Lowell Fulsom and Amos Milburn, and played bop with local bands before he became interested in free jazz. Simmons worked with Charles Mingus a little while in 1961, and the following year started co-leading a group with flutist Prince Lasha that would record two albums. Simmons lived in New York during 1963–65 where he recorded with Elvin Jones and Eric Dolphy before returning to the San Francisco Bay area. He met and married the powerful trumpeter Barbara Donald, and led two albums of his own for ESP during 1966. **Staying on the Watch** (ESP 1030) is a stimulating and somewhat dense blowout with a quintet also including Donald, pianist John Hicks, bassist Teddy Smith, and drummer Marvin Patillo. The four mostly free-form originals give Simmons a strong opportunity to stretch out and show how individual a sound he had. **Music from the Spheres** (ESP 1043) is even more stirring, featuring Simmons and Donald with pianist Michael Cohen, bassist Juney Booth, drummer James Zitro, and on "Dolphy's Days," tenor saxophonist Bert Wilson. Simmons's compositions (which also include "Zarak's Symphony" and "Balladia") are stronger than on the first disc, and the playing is even more intense. Both of

the ESP discs are well worth exploring and show that not all of the top avant-garde improvisers were based in New York and Chicago in the 1960s.

Charles Tyler   A major free jazz baritone and alto saxophonist who tended to be underrated, Charles Tyler had huge tones on both of his instruments and always displayed plenty of fire. He grew up in Indianapolis, and in 1955 when he was 14, Tyler met Albert Ayler. He moved to Cleveland in 1960 where he had some opportunities to jam with Ayler. In 1965, he moved to New York specifically to play with his friend. Tyler was with Ayler's group on and off during 1965–67, and also led two albums of his own, sticking to alto exclusively on the latter. **Charles Tyler Ensemble** (ESP 1029), as with many of the ESP dates, is quite brief (with just 29 minutes of music), but it certainly features a lot of heat on the four Tyler originals. He is joined by Charles Moffett on orchestra vibes, cellist Joel Friedman, Henry Grimes, and drummer Ronald Shannon Jackson. ● **Eastern Man Alone** (ESP 1059) has a lot more playing time (48 minutes), and features the altoist as the lead voice in a quartet comprised of cellist David Baker and both Brent McKesson and Kent Brinkley on basses. The sound explorations are quite colorful and inventive.

Tony Williams   Tony Williams's wide-ranging career made it difficult to classify him under one style for long, but his first two dates as a leader (particularly the second one) certainly fall into the avant-garde. Williams was a bit of a child prodigy, sitting in at clubs on drums by the time he was 11, accompanied by his father, who was a saxophonist. Williams took lessons from Alan Dawson, and as a teenager was a regular in Boston-area clubs, sometimes playing with Sam Rivers. In December 1962 (the month he turned 17), he moved to New York, playing regularly with Jackie McLean. The following year Williams joined the Miles Davis Quintet, where his fresh approach to keeping rhythms without necessarily stating the beat soon became quite influential. In addition to his work with Davis (whom he influenced to keep an open mind toward Ornette Coleman's innovations), Williams appeared on many record dates, often for Blue Note, including Eric Dolphy's **Out to Lunch**.

Life Time (Blue Note 84180) from August 1964 was the drummer's debut as a leader. Holding his own with such sidemen as Sam Rivers, Bobby Hutcherson, Herbie Hancock, and both Richard Davis and Gary Peacock on basses, Williams contributed all four of the pieces and uses a different combination of players on each song, including a lengthy "2 Pieces of One," a feature for Rivers on "Tomorrow Afternoon," and the freely improvised "Memory." The following year Williams led **Spring** (Blue Note 46135), a rather adventurous date with Rivers, Wayne Shorter, Herbie Hancock, and Gary Peacock. Williams's originals are not that memorable, but the playing is of a very high quality, with the highlights including the ten-minute "Tee" and a drum solo on "Echo."

Jimmy Woods   An early participant in the free jazz movement, altoist Jimmy Woods (like Henry Grimes) dropped out of music by his early thirties. Early on he played with Homer Carter's R&B band (1951). After serving in the Air Force (1952–56), Woods spent a few additional years working with R&B bands, including Roy Milton. By 1960, he was playing jazz in the Los Angeles area with pianist Horace Tapscott, and he had opportunities to record with Joe Gordon and play with Chico Hamilton and the Gerald Wilson Orchestra. As a leader he headed two albums during 1962–63. **Awakening** (Original Jazz Classics 1859) has Woods joined by either Joe Gordon or Martin Banks on trumpet, Amos Trice or Dick Whittington on piano, Jimmy Bond or Gary Peacock

on bass, and drummer Milt Turner. Woods proves to easily be the most advanced musician on the date, playing six of his originals, an obscurity, and "Love for Sale." His other set as a leader, **Conflict** (Contemporary 7612), has not been reissued on CD as of this writing. For that project, Woods teams up successfully with the likes of Harold Land, Andrew Hill, and Elvin Jones. His original (Delmark 413) sound and chance-taking style make one regret that his whereabouts since the mid-1960s are largely unknown to the jazz world.

Frank Wright   A fairly obscure name in free jazz, tenor saxophonist Frank Wright deserves much more recognition. He actually started his career playing electric bass with R&B bands in Memphis and Cleveland, meeting Albert Ayler (a key influence) in the latter city. He switched to tenor and moved to New York in the early 1960s, playing along the way with organist Larry Young, Sunny Murray, and briefly John Coltrane and Cecil Taylor. Wright would never be known for making mellow recordings. Recorded in 1965, **Frank Wright Trio** (ESP 1023) has the tenor blowing his guts out on three of his originals in a trio with Henry Grimes and drummer Tom Price. It is a pity, though, that there is only 34 minutes of music on this CD, making the follow-up 1967's

---

TIMELINE 1962

Stan Getz and Charlie Byrd record **Jazz Samba**, highlighted by a hit version of "Desafinado" that launches the bossa nova movement in the United States. • Annie Ross leaves Lambert, Hendricks, and Ross, being replaced by Yolanda Bavan. • Benny Goodman leads a big band on a historic tour of the Soviet Union. • Carl Kress and George Barnes start working regularly as a guitar duo. • Monty Alexander moves to the United States from his native Jamaica. • British trad clarinetist Acker Bilk has a major hit in "Stranger on the Shore." • John Coltrane and Duke Ellington record together. • Albert Ayler makes his recording debut. • The Cecil Taylor Trio features Jimmy Lyons and Sunny Murray. • Don Cherry and Billy Higgins tour as members of the Sonny Rollins Quartet. • Andrew Hill works with Roland Kirk. • The New York Contemporary Five features Archie Shepp, John Tchicai, and Don Cherry. • Yusef Lateef joins the Cannonball Adderley Sextet. • Charles Mingus has a disastrous concert at Town Hall. • The Jazztet breaks up. • Gene Ammons begins a seven-year period in jail. • Dexter Gordon moves to Europe. • Sal Nistico joins Woody Herman's Orchestra. • Sonny Rollins ends his three-year retirement, leading a quartet with Jim Hall. • Red Garland records his 25th album as a leader in six years. • Lennie Tristano records his final album. • Dollar Brand and Bea Benjamin leave South Africa, settling temporarily in Switzerland. • Ray Barretto's hit record of "El Watusi" helps launch the Latin bugalu craze. • Doug Watkins and Eddie Costa die in separate car accidents. • John Lewis records a quartet album in Stockholm with Svend Asmussen. • Shorty Rogers makes his last recording as a player for 21 years. • Herb Geller moves to Berlin. • The Al Grey-Billy Mitchell Sextet features the young vibraphonist Bobby Hutcherson. • Altoist Paul Winter's sextet goes on a well-received State Department tour of Latin America. • Tito Puente first records "Oye Come Va." • Max Roach and Abbey Lincoln are married. • Seventeen-year-old Tony Williams moves to New York to play with Jackie McLean.

Your Prayer (ESP 1053), which has over 50 minutes of music, the better buy. Wright teams up with four little-known players (altoist Arthur Jones, trumpeter Jacques Coursil, bassist Steve Tintweiss, and drummer Muhammad Ali) for passionate explorations of four of his originals plus Jones's "The Lady." This rather intense date features Frank Wright at his best, and displays the spirit and power of high-quality free jazz.

Miles Davis's Second Great Quintet

In mid-1960, John Coltrane finally left the Miles Davis Quintet to form his own quartet. Davis's first replacement on tenor was Sonny Stitt before Hank Mobley joined for a year. With Wynton Kelly, Paul Chambers, and Jimmy Cobb staying intact as the rhythm section, Davis still had a superb band. However, with Coltrane gone, Miles seemed to go through a few years of resting on his laurels. He had accomplished so much during 1954–60 that he could be excused for resting a bit.

In reality, Miles Davis's trumpet chops were in prime form during his so-called "off period" of 1961–63, and he did some of his finest playing in bop and hard bop during this era. **Someday My Prince Will Come** (Columbia/Legacy 65919) has the quintet playing some swinging originals and "I Thought About You." Coltrane makes guest appearances on the title cut and "Teo," his last recordings with the trumpeter. The CD reissue adds an alternate take of "Someday My Prince Will Come" (without Coltrane) and the loose "Blues No. 2," which has Philly Joe Jones having a one-time reunion with his former boss. **In Person: Friday Night at the Blackhawk** (Columbia/Legacy 44257) and **In Person: Saturday Night at the Blackhawk** (Columbia/Legacy 44425) features the Miles Davis Quintet at the popular San Francisco club on April 21 and 22, 1961. The Friday CD gets the edge due to the superior versions of "Walkin'," "Bye Bye Blackbird," and "No Blues" although Saturday has fine renditions of "So What," "Oleo," and "If I Were a Bell." Mobley's solos, which were partly cut out on the original LPs (Davis was dissatisfied with his playing in general), have been mostly restored in the CD reissue. In 2003 all of the music plus quite a few unreleased selections reappeared as the four-CD set **In Person Friday and Saturday Nights at the Blackhawk Complete** (Columbia/Legacy 87106), and despite some repetition in titles, this is the best way to acquire the music. As a straightahead trumpeter, Davis rarely sounded better.

Miles Davis at Carnegie Hall—The Complete Concert (Columbia/Legacy 65027) from May 19, 1961, features Davis with both his quintet (including "So What," "Walkin'," and "No More Blues") and the Gil Evans Orchestra on selections taken from **Miles Ahead** and **Sketches of Spain**. The year 1962 was slower for the trumpeter, for his only significant project, a final official collaboration with Gil Evans, was a bit of a bust. **Quiet Nights** (Columbia/Legacy 65293) was a half-hearted project that was never completed, just six songs totaling 20½ minutes. The music includes "Once Upon a Summertime" and Jobim's "Corcovado," and hints at what Davis might have been able to do with bossa nova if he was really that interested. Also on the original release is a 1963 quintet version of "Summer Night" while the CD adds the lengthy but only moderately interesting "The Time of the Barracudas" from a 1963 project with Evans that never came off. All of this music (other than "Summer Nights") is also available in the six-CD set **Miles Davis & Gil Evans—The Complete Columbia Studio Recordings** (Columbia 67397).

In 1963, after Mobley had departed and the Wynton Kelly Trio became a separate unit, Miles Davis was without a regular band for the first time since 1955. ● **Seven Steps to Heaven** (Columbia/Legacy 48827) features the trumpeter on three songs apiece recorded in Hollywood on April 16 and New York on May 14. The Hollywood quintet has tenor saxophonist George Coleman (a superior hard bop player), pianist Victor Feldman, bassist Ron Carter, and drummer Frank Butler joining Miles on very slow and beautiful ballad versions of "Basin Street Blues," "Baby Won't You Please Come Home," and "I Fall in Love Too Easily." While Coleman and Carter became members of the new Miles Davis Quintet, Feldman turned down the job (preferring the lucrative life of a studio musician), and Davis had other plans for the drum chair. The three songs recorded in New York a month later ("So Near So Far" and ironically two Feldman originals in "Joshua" and the classic "Seven Steps to Heaven") have Davis, Coleman, and Carter joined by pianist Herbie Hancock and 17-year-old drummer Tony Williams, whose breaks on "Seven Steps to Heaven" hint strongly at greatness. The European CD **Cote Blues** (Jazz Music Yesterday 1010) features the band on July 26 really stretching out on five standards (including a 21½-minute version of "Seven Steps to Heaven") and coming together rapidly as a fresh new quintet with its own sound. The following day, the group recorded **Miles Davis in Europe** (Columbia 8983), an excellent set highlighted by "Walkin'," "Autumn Leaves," and "All of You." Strangely enough, that particular set does not seem to have been reissued on CD yet by Columbia, but is available as **Miles Davis at Antibes** (Tristar 36616).

By the time the band recorded music originally out as the two LPs **My Funny Valentine** and **Four & More**, and now available as the double CD ◉ **The Complete Concert: 1964** (Columbia/Legacy 48821), the rhythm section had become much more abstract. Although the repertoire was largely unchanged from the late 1950s (the only new additions were "Joshua" and "Seven Steps to Heaven"), most of the songs were interpreted at a much faster tempo than the original, except for the occasional slow ballads, as if the young band could not wait to get the themes out of the way before jumping right into the group improvisations. Certainly that is true of "All Blues," "So What," "Walkin'," and "Four." This February 12 performance features all of the musicians in top form, including George Coleman whose playing Miles enjoyed, but who was thought of as old-fashioned by the rhythm section, particularly Tony Williams. Williams managed to get Coleman to quit a few months later, and convinced Davis to hire Sam Rivers (the drummer's old mentor) in his place. However, Miles did not care for Rivers's avant-garde style, and the tenor only lasted long enough to take a tour of Japan. **Miles in Tokyo** (Columbia 65335) is a live set that documents the short-lived association. The five lengthy versions of standards (including "So What," "Walkin'," and "All of You") are actually better than expected, but Davis was not happy, so Rivers was soon gone.

Miles Davis had been wanting to get Wayne Shorter in his band since at least 1962 when he used him on three selections (two featuring singer Bob Dorough), but Shorter was committed at the time to Art Blakey's Jazz Messengers. By September 1964 Shorter felt he was ready, and he turned out to be the missing link in the Miles Davis Quintet. Not only did he contribute a very original style on tenor, one that like Miles generally implied more than he stated, but he was a major composer. Davis's quintet may have been sounding new and fresh, but its repertoire was overloaded with songs the trumpeter had been playing since the late 1950s. That would remain true in his live appearances through 1967,

but his studio recordings would soon be featuring Shorter's quirky compositions.

Miles in Berlin (Columbia 62976) from September 25, 1964, is the earliest documentation of Davis's second classic quintet. The group plays long versions of four standards ("Milestones," "Autumn Leaves," "So What," and "Walkin'"), but once the themes are out of the way, the music is quite advanced. Also worth searching for are a pair of live performances released by the European Moon label that feature music from the quintet's October 1 and 8 concerts, put out as **Paris, France** (Moon 021) and **Davisiana** (Moon 033).

All of the studio recordings by the second classic Miles Davis Quintet are available as a four-CD set, ◉ **Miles Davis Quintet, 1965–'68** (Columbia/Legacy 67398), including the music released as **E.S.P.**, **Miles Smiles**, **Sorcerer**, **Nefertiti**, and **Miles in the Sky**, plus the selections by this particular group that were included on **Filles de Kilimanjaro** and **Water Babies**, some alternate takes, and 13 "new" selections. **E.S.P.** (Columbia/Legacy 46863) from January 1965 was a groundbreaking disc for it features the quintet playing seven group originals, including "Eighty-One," "Agitation," and the title cut. Hancock had to find a new role for the piano in the group because the band mostly ignored the chord changes, and soloed in a style not that different from the Ornette Coleman Quartet of 1960. However, the very original voices of Davis, Shorter, and Hancock, the inside/outside bass playing of Carter, and Williams's fiery "accompaniment" made this one of the most stimulating and original bands of 1965, even if it was overshadowed by John Coltrane and the new avant-garde musicians.

Unfortunately, Miles Davis's trumpet chops were erratic during 1965–67, as can be heard on the giant eight-CD box **The Complete Live at the Plugged Nickel** (Columbia/Legacy 66955). Recorded during two nights (December 22–23, 1965) in Chicago, this release has all of the music that exists from seven sets by the quintet, mostly standards plus an occasional song from **E.S.P.** While Davis is not up to his peak level, Shorter is consistently brilliant and creative, while the rhythm section often thinks as one in somewhat miraculous ways.

Of the individual studio albums by the Miles Davis Quintet, **Miles Smiles** (Columbia/Legacy 48849) from October 1966 is the most rewarding. Included are very adventurous versions of Eddie Harris's "Freedom Jazz

Dance," Jimmy Heath's "Gingerbread Boy," and Wayne Shorter's "Footprints," plus three superior obscurities ("Orbits," "Circle," and "Dolores"). The music is unclassifiable, for although it is often quite free, it follows its own logic and is full of surprising twists and turns; nothing is obvious. **Sorcerer** (Columbia/Legacy 52974) from May 1967 has four Shorter originals (including "Masqualero" and "Prince of Darkness"), Hancock's "The Sorcerer," and Williams's "Pee Wee." The music is consistently unpredictable yet quite concise. A vocal number by Bob Dorough ("Nothing Like You") from 1962 is also included on this rather brief set. **Nefertiti** (Columbia/Legacy 46113) from June–July 1967 was the last all-acoustic studio date by the Miles Davis Quintet. Performing compositions by Shorter ("Nefertiti," "Fall," and "Pinocchio"), Hancock ("Madness" and "Riot"), and Williams ("Hand Jive"), the band plays music that is unlike anything else recorded in 1967. As a farewell to this unit before more changes started to take place, search for **No Blues** (Jazz Music Yesterday 1003), a Paris concert from November 6, 1967, that not only has the band performing live versions of "Masqualero" and "Riot," but extensive renditions of "'Round Midnight," "No Blues," "I Fall in Love Too Easily," "Walkin'," and a nearly 17-minute "On Green Dolphin Street" that sound much different from the 1961 or even 1964 band.

Ironically, the Miles Davis Quintet would be much more influential in the 1980s and '90s, when younger musicians had an opportunity to reassess the band's innovations, than they were in the '60s.

12 Major Jazz Groups of 1961–1967

With the hindsight of more than 40 years, the John Coltrane Quartet and the Miles Davis Quintet are today thought of as the two most significant jazz combos of the 1961–67 period. But at the time, there were many other regular bands competing for the attention of the shrinking jazz audience, with the dozen in this section often winning polls and building up their own audience.

Cannonball Adderley Quintet/Sextet Cannonball Adderley's bands during the 1961–66 period were among his most significant. The increasingly influential altoist, whose sound was quite exuberant and seemingly bursting at the seams with joy (as opposed to the much

more serious approach of John Coltrane), was also quite articulate in discussing his music with audiences. That proved to be a major asset when so many jazz musicians gave the impression of completely ignoring their paying customers.

The 1961 Adderley Quintet (with pianist/vibraphonist Victor Feldman, bassist Sam Jones, and drummer Louis Hayes) was an excellent group, as heard at its best (with guest pianist Wynton Kelly) on **Plus** (Original Jazz Classics 306). A special side project was ⦿ **Nancy Wilson & Cannonball Adderley** (Capitol 81204), which featured the up-and-coming singer (whom Adderley had helped discover) on her finest jazz album.

Cannonball's best band was his 1962–63 sextet with Nat Adderley, Jones, Hayes, pianist Joe Zawinul, and Yusef Lateef on tenor, flute, and oboe. Lateef's versatility and openness to world music gave the Adderley Sextet an important new voice, inspiring Cannonball in particular to stretch himself. The group's repertoire at this time included its hits, bebop standards, and ballads, plus atmospheric mood pieces in which Lateef really excelled. Among its recordings are **Jazz Workshop Revisited** (Capital 29441), **In New York** (Original Jazz Classics 142), **Nippon Soul** (Original Jazz Classics 435), and ⦿ **Dizzy's Business** (Milestone 47069). The latter is the most inspired of the four and includes such songs as "Autumn Leaves," Nat Adderley's "Jive Samba," a remake of "This Here," and the atmospheric "Primitivo," although in reality every recording by the Adderley Sextet is well worth acquiring.

In 1964, with the bankruptcy of the Riverside label, Cannonball Adderley signed with Capitol; his new label also gained the right to release some of the earlier unreleased Riverside dates. At first, the basic high-powered soul jazz of the Adderley band was unchanged. Charles Lloyd (straight from the Chico Hamilton group) took Lateef's place for a year, and his best recording with the band was the unexpectedly inspired **Fiddler on the Roof** (last released on the LP Capitol 2216), which finds Cannonball exploring eight songs from the hit play with wit and creativity.

After Lloyd departed to launch his own solo career, the Adderley band reverted to a quintet. In July 1966, the group recorded its finest recording for the Capitol label: ⦿ **Mercy Mercy Mercy** (Capitol 29915). The quintet (which now had a rhythm section comprised of Zawinul, bassist Victor Gaskin, and drummer Roy

McCurdy) performs two songs apiece by each of the Adderley brothers and Zawinul with the highlights being Cannonball's "Sack O' Woe," Nat's "Fun," and "Games." However, it was Zawinul's "Mercy, Mercy, Mercy," which mostly consists of a repeated but catchy melody statement that was played while Cannonball talked to the studio audience, which became an unexpected hit. From that point on, Adderley's direction started going toward funk/soul/pop music, and away from the hard bop/soul jazz style that he had helped to develop.

Art Blakey's Jazz Messengers   In 1961, the Jazz Messengers had a major personnel change when Lee Morgan departed in the summer and was replaced by Freddie Hubbard. Before that happened, earlier in the year the band recorded several Blue Note albums, including, most notably, **The Freedom Rider** (Blue Note 21287), which has a dramatic unaccompanied Blakey drum feature on the title cut plus originals by Morgan, Shorter, and Kenny Dorham. The Jazz Messengers of mid-1961 to 1964 had remarkably stable personnel, expanding to a sextet with the addition of trombonist Curtis Fuller. Hubbard, Shorter, pianist Cedar Walton, Blakey, and bassist Jymie Merritt (who was replaced in 1963 by Reggie Workman) completed the pacesetting hard bop group. Hubbard ended up being the perfect replacement for Morgan, playing in a similar style, but with a personal sound and a fire all his own. Sticking to the hard bop idiom of the late 1950s, but hinting now and then at more advanced styles and performing a repertoire full of new songs by Shorter, Hubbard, Fuller, and Walton, Art Blakey's band recorded one consistently rewarding album after another. **Mosaic** (Blue Note 46253) introduced Hubbard's "Crisis" and Fuller's haunting "Arabia." **Buhaina's Delight** (Blue Note 84104) did not result in any standards, but these versions of "Moon River," "Bu's Delight," and "Backstage Sally" are enjoyable to hear. **Three Blind Mice Vol. 1** (Blue Note 84451) and **Vol. 2** (Blue Note 84452) feature the 1962 Jazz Messengers live at the Renaissance Club (with two cuts from **Vol. 2** being from the previous year at the Village Gate). Highlights include Fuller's reworking of "Three Blind Mice," "Blue Moon," and the earliest two recordings of Hubbard's "Up Jumped Spring" (his best-known original) on **Vol. 1**, and lengthy versions of "It's Only a Paper Moon," Shorter's

"Ping Pong," and Walton's "The Promised Land" on **Vol. 2**.

During 1962–63, the Jazz Messengers also recorded two sets for the Riverside label. **Caravan** (Original Jazz Classics 038) is highlighted by versions of the title cut, "Thermo," and "Skylark," while **Ugetsu** (Original Jazz Classics 090) includes "One by One," "Ping Pong," and Shorter's feature on "I Didn't Know What Time It Was." This well-recorded version of Art Blakey's band concluded in 1964 with **Free for All** (Blue Note 84170), which has lengthy versions of two Shorter pieces, Hubbard's "The Core," and Clare Fischer's "Pensativa" and **Kyoto** (Original Jazz Classics 145), which includes Fuller's "The High Priest," "Never Never Land," and a rare vocal of the leader's son Wellington Blakey on "Wellington's Blues."

In 1964, when Freddie Hubbard left Blakey to form his own group, Lee Morgan returned. Morgan, who had been struggling with drug addiction, had been mostly living in Philadelphia for a couple of years, keeping a low profile. Even though he had a surprise hit with his record "The Sidewinder," he was happy to return to the Jazz Messengers for a year. Unfortunately, Blakey's association with the Blue Note label (which resulted in many classics) came to an end at this time after the group with Morgan recorded **Indestructible** (Blue Note 46429), which typically had five new compositions by band members though none caught on; the closest was Walton's "When Love Is New."

After five years of very stable personnel and recordings, the 1965–71 period was one of constant change for Art Blakey's Jazz Messengers. Many musicians passed through the band, but unfortunately few recordings resulted. **Soulfinger** (a Limelight album not yet reissued on CD) was the group's only recording of 1965 and is primarily of interest due to Hubbard and Morgan splitting the trumpet duties. Pianist John Hicks, altoist Gary Bartz, and bassist Victor Sproles were also in the band at the time. The 1966 version of the Jazz Messengers had two future stars in trumpeter Chuck Mangione and pianist Keith Jarrett (along with Frank Mitchell on tenor and bassist Reggie Johnson), and can be heard on **Get the Message** (Drive 41084). But although he kept up a busy performance schedule, Blakey and his Jazz Messengers barely appeared on record at all during the next five years, being completely undocumented in 1967.

The Dave Brubeck Quartet With "Take Five" becoming such a major hit, the Dave Brubeck Quartet was even more popular during the first half of the 1960s than it had been in the 1950s. **Time Further Out** (Columbia/Legacy 64668) introduced "It's a Raggy Waltz" and the 7/4 "Unsquare Dance," which was the predecessor to Don Ellis's "Pussy Wiggle Stomp" of the late 1960s. Brubeck, Paul Desmond, Eugene Wright, and Joe Morello explore a variety of time signatures (including 5/4 and 9/8), building on the success of their previous **Time Out** record. **Countdown—Time in Outer Space** (Columbia 8575) surprisingly has not been reissued yet on CD. It has more "experiments" in different time signatures, including "Three's a Crowd," "Castilian Drums," and a version of "Someday My Prince Will Come" that is in both 4/4 and 3/4 simultaneously. **Time Changes** (Columbia 8927), also not out on CD, ended this series in 1964 with the quartet performing "Elementals" with an orchestra and five briefer originals, including the 13/4 "World's Fair."

Exploring unusual time signatures was not the only project for the Dave Brubeck Quartet during this era. **The Real Ambassadors** (Columbia/Legacy 57663) documents a show that Brubeck put on at the 1962 Monterey Jazz Festival that was otherwise never performed on stage (at least not until a revised 40th anniversary production was presented in 2002). Utilizing the talents of Louis Armstrong and his All-Stars, Carmen McRae, Lambert, Hendricks, Ross, and his own rhythm section, Brubeck and his wife, lyricist Iola Brubeck, wrote a largely upbeat play full of anti-racism songs and tunes that celebrated human understanding. Although Lambert, Hendricks, and Ross mostly function as background singers, and Armstrong does not play much trumpet, the vocal team of Satch and Carmen McRae is quite potent, and there are many touching and surprising moments.

On February 22, 1963, the Dave Brubeck Quartet performed ◉ **At Carnegie Hall** (Columbia/Legacy 61455). This two-CD set does a superb job of summing up the group's history, with memorable versions of such songs as "St. Louis Blues," "Pennies from Heaven," "Three to Get Ready," and "Blue Rondo à la Turk." The one minus is the rendition of "Take Five." At Joe Morello's urging, Brubeck let him (for the only time) count off the song, and the result was that it was played way too fast; the pianist never made that mistake again!

By 1967, Brubeck felt that his quartet had largely run its course, so he decided to break up the legendary group after 16 years (nine with the exact same personnel). The final album, **The Last Time We Saw Paris** (Columbia 9672), unfortunately has not been reissued since its original release. Taken from the final quartet tour, it includes "Swanee River," a 12-minute version of "These Foolish Things," "Forty Days," "One Moment Worth Years," "La Paloma Azul," and "Three to Get Ready," showing that Brubeck and Desmond were still able to rekindle some of the magic from their concerts of the early 1950s. But everyone was tired of the constant traveling, and by year-end the Dave Brubeck Quartet was no more, for now.

The Bill Evans Trio Bill Evans reached one of the high points of his career in 1961, but it was quickly followed by a tragedy that put him in the depths of despair. His trio with bassist Scott LaFaro and drummer Paul Motian had reached a remarkable level during its two years together, and they were playing with intuition and rapid reactions to every musical thought. LaFaro, one of the most talented soloists of the period, played his instrument with the fluidity of a guitarist, often challenged Evans directly (particularly when he played in his upper register), and although grounded in bebop, even fared well on an album with Ornette Coleman (**Ornette**).

All of Bill Evans's dates for Riverside during 1956–63 (most of which have been reissued individually in the Original Jazz Classics series or on Milestone) are on the 12-CD set ◉ **The Complete Riverside Recordings** (Riverside 018). This includes three albums from 1961 with the LaFaro-Motian Trio. **Explorations** (Original Jazz Classics 037) is the group's second of two studio dates. There are also two records cut at the Village Vanguard on June 25: **Sunday at the Village Vanguard** (Original Jazz Classics 140) and **Waltz for Debby** (Original Jazz Classics 210). Listening to the selections from these dates, one can hear where the modern jazz piano trio originated. Evans acted as the strongest voice in this near-democracy, while LaFaro and Motian commented tastefully on the pianist's ideas while often extending them.

Just ten days after the Village Vanguard recordings, Scott LaFaro was killed in a car crash at the age of 25. Evans immediately dropped out of music, not playing in public for nine months. He returned (reluctantly at first) with four recorded piano solos on April 4, 1962, then later in the month recorded a set of duets with guitarist Jim Hall. **Undercurrent** (Blue Note 38228) shows how much Evans and Hall had in common since both had introspective and harmonically advanced styles with roots in hard bop. Their duets are often exquisite.

With Chuck Israels in LaFaro's place and Paul Motian returning, the Bill Evans Trio soon became active again. Although Israels was not an innovator on LaFaro's level, he was always an excellent bassist, and he handled the difficult role well. **How My Heart Sings** (Original Jazz Classics 369) mostly features uptempo tunes, including such Evans originals as "34 Skidoo" and "Show-Type Tune." **Moonbeams** (Original Jazz Classics 434), from the same two sessions, is primarily ballads with highlights including "Re: Person I Knew" (an anagram of producer Orrin Keepnews's name), "Very Early," and "I Fall in Love Too Easily."

Interplay (Original Jazz Classics 308) gives Evans a rare opportunity to play with an all-star group, a quintet with Freddie Hubbard, Jim Hall, Percy Heath, and Philly Joe Jones. The ensemble plays the title cut and five standards, including "You and the Night and the Music," "You Go to My Head," and "Wrap Your Troubles in Dreams." Hubbard and Evans in particular work well together. **Loose Blues** (Milestone 9200) is more obscure. It was originally shelved and not released until 1982. The musicians (Evans, Zoot Sims, Hall, Ron Carter, and Philly Joe Jones) were not familiar with the difficult material and struggled a bit although that is not obvious in the final results. In addition to such Evans standards as "Time Remembered," "Funkallero," and "My Bells," it is interesting to hear such forgotten songs as "There Came You," "Fun Ride," and "Fudgesickle Built for Four," tunes that could stand to be revived. In January 1963, Evans recorded music not released until decades later as **The Solo Sessions Vol. 1** (Milestone 9170) and **Vol. 2** (Milestone 9200). In need of money at the time due to his drug habit and wanting to fulfill his obligation to Riverside before he signed with the Verve label, Evans recorded the two albums in one day, playing song after song. Although there is not much mood variation, and the results are sometimes dark, Evans is generally creative throughout these thoughtful interpretations of standards. His final Riverside dates were a live sessions from May 30–31, 1963, with Israels and Larry Bunker (who had succeeded Motian): **Time Remembered** (Milestone 47083) and

Bill Evans Trio at Shelly's Manne-Hole (Original Jazz Classics 263). The emphasis is mostly on standards, and the playing is on a high level although offering few surprises. By 1963, Bill Evans had his style very much together, and he would be consistent through his career. Although he continued growing from within, and he never sounded stale, his largely introverted style would not change or evolve that much through the years. Renowned for his ability to dig into lyrical ballads, Evans was also capable of displaying a surprising amount of fire and intensity on uptempo tunes when inspired.

In 1963, Bill Evans signed with Verve, his main label through 1970. **The Complete Bill Evans on Verve** (Verve 527 953) is a remarkably complete 18-CD set that has three titles from 1957 (when the pianist appeared with Don Elliott's band), a featured sideman recording with Gary McFarland, and all of the work by Evans during his Verve years. It should be mentioned that the valuable music is housed inside a rusty steel box, and that it is impossible to open without either cutting oneself or at least getting one's hands filthy! This box would easily win any award for the ugliest and worst-planned packaging, but the music is so enjoyable that Evans fans with a large billfold will still want it.

Fortunately, many of the key dates are also available individually. ◉ **Conversations with Myself** (Verve 521 409) is a rather unusual set because Bill Evans recorded three piano parts via overdubbing. The music on the CD has a surprising amount of spontaneity with Evans constantly reacting to what he had just recorded, and the results are sometimes haunting. Among the more memorable performances are "How About You," "The Love Theme from Spartacus," "Blue Monk," and "Just You Just Me."

Trio '64 (Verve 539 058) features Evans with a short-lived group that has Gary Peacock temporarily in Israels's spot and Paul Motian filling in for Bunker. It is particularly interesting hearing Peacock with this group since he normally played with Paul Bley, who was in some ways the next step beyond Evans. Other than a cartoon theme ("Little Lulu"), the trio sticks to standards although there are a couple of unusual choices in "I'll See You Again," and a swinging version of "Santa Claus Is Coming to Town." **Trio '65** (Verve 519 808) has Evans back with Israels and Bunker, playing creative versions of such songs as "How My Heart Sings," "Who Can I Turn To," and "If You Could See Me Now."

Bill Evans Trio with Symphony Orchestra (Verve 821 983) is of lesser interest with the trio being buried beneath a huge orchestra arranged by Claus Ogerman; the strings greatly weigh down the music, and the charts are unimaginative. **Bill Evans at Town Hall** (Verve 831 271) from February 1966 has the pianist in fine form playing with Chuck Israels (making his last recording in the trio) and drummer Arnold Wise. In addition to such lyrical ballads as "I Should Care," "Who Can I Turn To," and "My Foolish Heart," the most memorable piece is the 13-minute "Solo—In Memory of His Father" that features the pianist unaccompanied and partly uses a theme that would become "Turn Out the Stars." **Intermodulation** (Verve 833 771) is a duet reunion with Jim Hall in 1966. Its only fault is its brevity (just 31 minutes), but otherwise it is the equal of **Undercurrent**, highlighted by memorable versions of "My Man's Gone Now" and "Turn Out the Stars."

⊙ **Empathy/A Simple Matter of Conviction** (Verve 837 757) has two of Evans's better Verve recordings combined on a single CD. Recorded in 1962, **Empathy** (which predates the pianist leaving Riverside) teams him with bassist Monty Budwig and Shelly Manne on some unusual material, including a pair of Irving Berlin obscurities ("The Washington Twist" and "Let's Go Back to the Waltz'") and "Danny Boy" plus three more conventional standards. The **A Simple Matter of Conviction** set, which also has Manne, is notable for bassist Eddie Gomez making his recording debut with Evans; Gomez would be in the Bill Evans Trio for 11 years. The repertoire includes four obscure tunes by the pianist (including "Only Child" and "These Things Called Changes") plus "My Melancholy Baby." **Further Conversations with Myself** (Verve 559 832) is Evans's second record of overdubbed piano solos, but unlike on the first **Conversations**, this time he is only heard on two pianos. The music is less dense, but no less exciting with Evans constantly trading off with and reacting to himself on such songs as "Emily," "Yesterdays," and "The Shadow of Your Smile."

By 1967, the Bill Evans Trio included Eddie Gomez and drummer Philly Joe Jones. Their only recording, a live set from the Village Vanguard called **California Here I Come** (Verve 22545), came out as a two-LP set and as part of the giant Verve box, but unfortunately is not individually on CD yet. Bill Evans had long since proven that his style was strong enough to withstand changes in the music industry and that he could build his own audience without making any compromises. He would continue to be a jazz giant throughout the remainder of his life.

The Dizzy Gillespie Quintet   A former radical whose trumpet solos were still very advanced, Dizzy Gillespie in 1961 was seen at age 43 as being an elder statesman. His regular quintet included Leo Wright on alto and flute, pianist Lalo Schifrin, bassist Bob Cunningham, and drummer Chuck Lampkin. Dizzy was always encouraging Schifrin to write so the pianist came up with the five-movement work "Gillespiana." **Gillespiana/Carnegie Hall Concert** (Verve 314 519 809) combines two complete and related LPs on one CD. The first half is the studio version of "Gillespiana" from November 1960, a work that grows in interest with each listen and features Dizzy with an orchestra. The second half of the disc was recorded at Carnegie Hall the same day that "Gillespiana" was debuted live, but these five pieces are more conventional, including remakes of "Manteca" and "Night in Tunisia" (the latter as "Tunisian Fantasy"). The only weak point is an overly silly version of "Ool Ya Koo" with Gillespie's former vocalist Joe Carroll.

An Electrifying Evening with the Dizzy Gillespie Quintet (Verve 557 544) lives up to its billing thanks to the trumpeter's remarkable break on "A Night in Tunisia," which lasts a half-chorus. The versions of "Kush," "Salt Peanuts," and "The Mooche" are also excellent (and there is a long interview that was added to the CD reissue), but it is the break that sticks in one's mind. In 1962, Gillespie left Verve (since Norman Granz had sold the company) and signed with Philips, staying with that label for two years. Unfortunately, some of its Gillespie albums, including the rewarding **Dizzy on the French Riviera** (Philips 200-048), which features bossa nova the Gillespie way and a rare bass sax from Charlie Ventura, and **New Wave** (Phillips 200-070) with guest guitarists Bola Sete and Elek Bacsik, have not been reissued on CD yet.

By 1963, the Dizzy Gillespie Quintet included James Moody (who was with Gillespie's big band more than 15 years before) on tenor, alto, and flute, pianist Kenny Barron, bassist Chris White, and drummer Rudy Collins. **Something Old, Something New** (Verve 558 079) is at its best during the "Old" section since that includes rapid versions of "Bebop" and "Dizzy Atmosphere," a memorable rendition of "Good Bait," and a definitive medley of "I Can't Get Started," and "'Round Midnight." The "New" part has four pieces (three by Tom McIntosh) of which "Cup Bearers" is best known. **The Cool World/ Dizzy Goes Hollywood** (Verve 531 230) from 1963–64 has two former LPs reissued in full. Gillespie is heard interpreting the score of the obscure film *The Cool World* (composed by Mal Waldron) plus 11 themes from other films. Best are Dizzy's versions of such songs as the "Theme from Exodus," "Moon River," "Days of Wine and Roses," and "Never on Sunday," which he turns into swinging jazz.

In addition to his work with his quintet, Gillespie was also involved in some side projects. **Dizzy Gillespie and the Double Six of Paris** (Verve 830 224) features the Double Six singing vocalese in French to a dozen bebop classics associated with Gillespie. Most songs have the trumpeter with a rhythm section that includes Bud Powell (the last joint recording by the two bebop giants) performing with the singers while two songs feature his regular quintet. Among the tunes explored are "Hot House," "One Bass Hit," "Two Bass Hit," "Anthropology," and "Groovin' High." **With Gil Fuller and the Monterey Jazz Festival Orchestra** (Blue Note 80370) reunites Gillespie with his former big band arranger in 1965. However, this set (which has a specially assembled big band for the Monterey Jazz Festival) is a bit of a disappointment due to the lack of fireworks and the orchestra mostly being in an accompanying role behind Dizzy. The best selections are "The Shadow of Your Smile," "Groovin' High," and "Things Are Here" (the answer to "Things to Come").

Most of the veteran jazz musicians associated with Norman Granz's Verve label in the 1950s found their recordings declining in quality during the next decade. Gillespie was able to stall that trend during his Phillips years, but by late 1964 his recordings started to slip in interest. His Limelight sets of 1964–66 are mostly erratic (1966's **Melody Lingers On** has such pop tunes as "Winchester Cathedral," "Bang Bang!" and "Tequila"), and **Swing Low, Sweet Cadillac** (MCA/Impulse 33121), a live quintet set from 1967, is mostly a waste with an excess of fooling around, only recommended to those dying to hear Gillespie sing "Something in Your Smile" (from the movie *Doctor Doolittle*).

Much better is the challenging music on the two-CD set **Live at the Village Vanguard** (Blue Note 80507), which features the trumpeter on a pair of unusual jam sessions. The first date is particularly eccentric with Gillespie, violinist Ray Nance (who is in adventurous form), Pepper Adams, pianist Chick Corea, bassist Richard Davis, and either Mel Lewis or Elvin Jones on drums stretching out on several lengthy numbers, including a 19-minute "Lover Come Back to Me." It is particularly interesting hearing Gillespie and Corea together, and the unique trumpet-baritone sax-violin frontline. The second date substitutes trombonist Garnett Brown for Nance and is a bit more conventional but still stimulating. Even with some loose and rambling moments, it is enjoyable to hear these all-stars really stretching themselves and Gillespie sounding once again like jazz's leading trumpeter.

The Jazz Crusaders   In Houston in 1954, pianist Joe Sample, tenor saxophonist Wilton Felder, and drummer Stix Hooper, who were going to high school together, formed a group called the Swingsters. They were soon joined by trombonist Wayne Henderson, flutist Hubert Laws, and bassist Henry Wilson, working as the Modern Jazz Sextet. In 1960, Sample, Felder, Hooper, and Henderson moved to Los Angeles, used a variety of different bassists, and settled on the Jazz Crusaders as their new name. In 1961, they were signed by Pacific Jazz and began a series of popular recordings.

Their trombone-tenor frontline became instantly recognizable, and the band staked out its own musical niche between hard bop and soul jazz with an open mind toward R&B and Memphis soul. Unfortunately, out of their dozen Pacific Jazz albums of 1961–67, only two have thus far been reissued on CD. The Jazz Crusaders' debut recording, **Freedom Sound** (Pacific Jazz 96864), has the group already sounding quite mature. With guests Jimmy Bond on bass and guitarist Roy Gaines, the band plays originals by Felder, Henderson, and Sample, plus a cover version of "Theme from Exodus." **Live at the Lighthouse '66** (Pacific Jazz 37988) augments the original seven-song LP program (highlighted by "Blues Up Tight," "Doin' that Thing," and "Milestones") with previously unissued versions of "'Round Midnight" and John Coltrane's "Some Other Blues." With bassist Leroy Vinnegar keeping the music swinging, the Jazz Crusaders are heard in top form on this straightahead but soulful music. But a definitive sampler (or a complete reissue program) of the Jazz Crusaders' early recordings has not yet been released.

The Charles Lloyd Quartet   In 1967, the most popular groups in jazz were the Cannonball Adderley Quintet and the Charles Lloyd Quartet. While Adderley had been a major figure for a decade, Lloyd was a sideman until 1965, and his success was much more unlikely. Born and raised in Memphis, Lloyd played tenor, alto, and flute, often performing with visiting blues and R&B groups or with such up-and-coming local jazz musicians as Booker Little and Phineas Newborn. In the mid-1950s, he moved to Los Angeles to attend USC, working around town with Gerald Wilson's Orchestra. He gained a strong reputation as a member of the Chico Hamilton Orchestra (1961–63), playing tenor in a style touched by John Coltrane (although with a lighter tone), and sounding quite original on flute. After spending a year as a member of the Cannonball Adderley Sextet (1964–65), Lloyd formed his own band.

Prior to going out on his own, Lloyd had recorded **Discovery** (Columbia 2267), a fine straightahead quartet date with pianist Don Friedman that has not yet been reissued. Its best selections are "Little Piece" (dedicated to the late Booker Little), "Days of Wine and Roses," "Sweet Georgia Bright," and the initial recording of "Forest Flower." Also not yet available is 1965's **Of Course, of Course** (Columbia 2412), which teams Lloyd with Gabor Szabo, Ron Carter, and Tony Williams. Lloyd contributed seven of the nine diverse compositions, including "Goin' to Memphis" and "Third Floor Richard," and he takes "The Things We Did Last Summer" as a duet with Szabo.

In 1966, the Charles Lloyd Quartet became a surprise hit. The group featured pianist Keith Jarrett (a highly original soloist who had just finished a year with Art Blakey's Jazz Messengers), the adventurous bassist Cecil McBee (who would be succeeded the following year by Ron McClure), and the up-and-coming drummer Jack DeJohnette. The group managed to balance the adventurous with the melodic, and in a marketing coup, appeared occasionally at rock clubs, including San Francisco's Fillmore West. When jazz's popularity was at its all-time low due to the rock explosion, Lloyd managed to pick up a sizable young audience (as Dave Brubeck had a decade earlier) without compromising his music.

The two-CD set **Just Before Sunrise** (32 Jazz 32117) reissues the first album by the Charles Lloyd Quartet (**Dream Weaver**) and **Love-In** (which was recorded at the Fillmore West) from a year later. It serves as a perfect introduction to the group's music. Among the highlights are "Autumn Leaves" (which is part of an "Autumn Sequence"), "Sombrero Sam," "Memphis Dues Again/Island Blues," and a jazz version of the Beatles' "Here, There and Everywhere." The music somehow hints at both avant-garde jazz and rock at the same time while following its own singular path.

Between those two albums, the Charles Lloyd Quartet was the hit of the 1966 Monterey Jazz Festival, a concert that really launched its fame. ● **Forest Flower** (Rhino 71746) has the music from the resulting album. The band started both their historic Monterey set and the original album by performing the two-part "Forest Flower," which would become Lloyd's most famous original. The music, both tender and fiery just beneath the surface, has an indescribable spiritual feel to it. Two shorter pieces on the album, "Song of Her" and "Sorcery," were actually not recorded at the festival, but in the studios ten days later, and the concluding "East of the Sun" is from the famous set and shows how the band could take a well-known standard and make it their own. Added on to this CD reissue are the four selections from 1968's **Soundtrack**, the quartet's final album. Highlights are remakes of "Sombrero Sam" and a nearly 17-minute "Forest Flower '69." Also well worth acquiring from Lloyd's quartet is **Journey Within/Charles Lloyd in Europe** (Collectables 6236).

Charles Mingus   Charles Mingus's prime period was from late 1955 through 1965. During that decade the fiery bassist/composer/bandleader recorded one classic after another, performing highly original music that combined aspects of the past (Mingus's roots in Duke Ellington, New Orleans jazz, bop, and the church) with freer improvising and consistently fresh ideas. Because he drove his sidemen to play way above their potential, Mingus's bands tended not to last too long, but most of his musicians (before they were driven past the breaking point) performed some of their most vital and exciting music while with the bassist.

As mentioned in the previous chapter, ● **Passions of a Man: The Complete Atlantic Recordings** (Rhino/Atlantic 72871) contains essential music, including Mingus's final Atlantic record, **Oh Yeah** (Rhino 75589) from 1961. Most notable as Mingus's only record with Rahsaan Roland Kirk (who fits right in), the sextet that is featured on such numbers as "Devil Woman" (which has Mingus singing the blues, in his own fashion), "Ecclusiastics," "Peggy's Blue Skylight," "Wham Bam Thank You Ma'am," and "Oh Lord Don't Let 'Em Drop that Atomic Bomb on Me" also includes trombonist Jimmy Knepper, tenor saxophonist Booker Ervin (who cannot help being a bit overshadowed by Kirk), bassist Doug Watkins, drummer Dannie Richmond, and Mingus sticking to piano and occasional vocals.

Less successful was Mingus's infamous Town Hall concert of October 12, 1962. Meant to be the debut of his massive work "Epitaph," it was a disaster. Mingus was simply not ready (writers were actually sitting at their tables copying out parts during the performance), and although tickets were sold, it was essentially an open rehearsal; Mingus advised the confused audience to ask for their money back. Some of the music was released on a rather erratic LP that only made matters more confusing. In more recent times, **The Complete Town Hall Concert** (Blue Note 28353) cleans up the mess as much as possible. The original 36 minutes of playing is joined by over a half-hour of previously unreleased music, and one can hear the full concert as it developed. There are still confusing interludes, inconclusive performances, and songs cut off prematurely, but there are some good moments (such as Eric Dolphy's alto solo on the second version of "Epitaph"), and at least now the music is listenable if still a bit disappointing.

Much more rewarding are Mingus's three Impulse albums of 1963. ◗ **The Black Saint and the Sinner Lady** (Impulse 174) is one of Mingus's finest suites, a six-part work with wild ensembles, many hints of Duke Ellington, and a great deal of variety in moods and colors. Quentin Jackson's wa-wa trombone and Charlie Mariano's passionate alto are quite prominent in the 11-piece group. **Mingus Plays Piano** (Impulse 217) allows listeners the opportunity to hear Mingus musically thinking aloud as he performs a set of solo piano. Although not a virtuoso, he displays enough technique to express his imaginative ideas on a few standards ("Body and Soul," "Memories of You," and "I'm Getting Sentimental Over You") along with some freely improvised originals. **Mingus, Mingus, Mingus, Mingus, Mingus** (Impulse 170) has eight fairly concise selections played by two Mingus units in 1963 with such colorful players as trumpeter Richard Williams, trombonists Quentin Jackson and Britt Woodman, Dick Hafer, and Booker Ervin on tenors, Eric Dolphy and Jerome Richardson on many reeds, Charles

Mariano, and pianist Jaki Byard. All eight numbers are memorable, particularly "Better Get It in Your Sol," "Hora Decubitus" (with its violent Dolphy solo), and "Mood Indigo."

In 1964, Charles Mingus put together what was arguably his finest band for a tour of Europe. Eric Dolphy (on alto sax, bass clarinet, and flute) was heard at the peak of his powers along with tenor saxophonist Clifford Jordan, trumpeter Johnny Coles (who became ill halfway through the tour and had to drop out), Jaki Byard, Dannie Richmond, and Mingus. Although this group made no studio recordings, luckily it was captured live on several occasions during the tour, and even appeared on a European television show. The best performances were last on the three-LP set **The Great Concert of Charles Mingus** (Prestige 34001), which amazingly has not yet been reissued on CD. "Orange Was the Color of Her Dress," a nearly 29-minute "Fables of Faubus," and the passionate "Meditations on Integration" (an utterly fascinating performance) are given definitive treatments. "Parkeriana" (a tribute to Charlie Parker) has some stride piano from Byard (who along the way emulates James P. Johnson, Bud Powell, and Dave Brubeck) and an incredible Dolphy alto solo. While this set inexcusably remains out of print, a few other reissues are available (although some are hard to find) that document other concerts from this historic tour. These include **Town Hall Concert** (Original Jazz Classics 042), **Concertgebouw Amsterdam Vol. 1** (Ulysse Musique 50506), **Concertgebouw Amsterdam Vol. 2** (Ulysse Musique 50507), **Astral Weeks** (Moon 016), **Mingus in Europe** (Enja 79612), and a superior two-CD set put out in recent times by Sue Mingus (Charles's widow), **Revenge** (Revenge 32002). All are worth searching for, and none duplicate each other or the elusive **Great Concert**.

After returning to the United States, Mingus mourned the unexpected death of Eric Dolphy. His next recording, **Right Now: Live at Jazz Workshop** (Original Jazz Classics 207), has excellent and lengthy versions of "Meditations on Integration" and "New Fables" played by a quintet with Jordan, Richmond, pianist Jane Getz, and (on one song) altoist John Handy, but it seems a bit anticlimactic without Dolphy being present. However, Mingus had one more triumph that year: his performance at the 1964 Monterey Jazz Festival. Unfortunately, **Mingus at Monterey** (VDJ 1572) has not been reissued yet for this double LP has Mingus's entire performance, consisting of a lengthy Duke Ellington medley, "Orange Was the Color of Her Dress," and a stunning version of "Meditations on Integration." The 12-piece group includes such alumni as Charles Mc-Pherson, John Handy (sticking to tenor), Lonnie Hillyer, and Jaki Byard. The year 1965 was a struggle for Mingus, and his performance at Monterey was disastrous. Angry that his recordings of the previous year's performance had not arrived in time, that he was playing a matinee instead of in a featured nighttime slot, and at various other things, Mingus had his band storm off before they had finished their set. A week later he performed the music he had planned to feature at Monterey at a UCLA concert, one that is a little chaotic at times; he actually expels a couple of musicians from his group because he felt they had not learned his music well enough. A two-LP set **Music Written for Monterey 1965** (JWS 0013/0014) was put out by his own private label and documents this intriguing set.

And then it all stopped, for a time. Depressed with the way his life and career were going, Charles Mingus stopped performing altogether during much of 1966–69.

The Modern Jazz Quartet   In 1962, the Modern Jazz Quartet (pianist John Lewis, vibraphonist Milt Jackson, bassist Percy Heath, and drummer Connie Kay) celebrated its tenth anniversary. Against all odds, the chamber jazz group was as popular as ever and stood apart from any musical or faddish trends. **Lonely Woman** (Atlantic 90665) is most notable for having the group "cover" Ornette Coleman's ballad as their title cut. Otherwise the music is conventional with the group interpreting six lesser-known John Lewis originals and a song by Gary McFarland in thoughtful and lightly swinging fashion. **In a Crowd** (Knitting Factory Works 3002) features the MJQ from the 1963 Monterey Jazz Festival, playing such tunes as "Bags' Groove," "Mean to Me," and Ray Brown's "Pyramid." Best of their recordings from this era is ● **Collaboration** (Label M 5731), a superb matchup between the MJQ and Brazilian guitarist Laurindo Almeida from 1964. Their version of "One Note Samba," which starts out with Almeida playing unaccompanied, is a classic. The guitarist fits into the four John Lewis compositions quite comfortably, and "Concierto de Aranjuez" is given a lengthy and inventive treatment.

The Thelonious Monk Quartet   One of the most unlikely of all jazz success stories, Thelonious Monk was at the height of his fame during the 1960s. After a long period of neglect, he had had his breakthrough in 1957 when he played all summer at the Five Spot, leading a quartet that featured John Coltrane.

Monk's Riverside recordings of 1955–61 featured the unique pianist/composer in a wide variety of settings. However, by 1961 he was most often heard leading a quartet comprised of tenor saxophonist Charlie Rouse (who had joined him in 1959), bassist John Ore, and drummer Frankie Dunlop. His final recordings for Riverside, **Monk in Italy** (Original Jazz Classics 488) and **Monk in France** (Original Jazz Classics 670), have the quartet playing a variety of Monk standards in concert with spirit and sensitivity although there is an excess of bass and drum solos.

It was a measure of Thelonious Monk's surprising commercial appeal that he was signed to Columbia in 1962, joining a roster that included Miles Davis, Dave Brubeck, and Duke Ellington. Most of Monk's Columbia albums feature his quartet with Rouse; Butch Warren took over on bass in 1963, and both bassist Larry Gales and Ben Riley became longtime members in 1964. Because Monk was not writing many new songs anymore (being content to record new versions of the older ones), these records are often overlooked or unfairly dismissed. Actually Monk was still in prime form throughout the 1960s, and although his style was unchanged from 1947, no one else could play or write like him.

Monk's Columbia recordings have been getting reissued in expanded form, with extra selections being added and edits being taken out, resulting in lengthier performances. **Monk's Dream** (Columbia/Legacy 40786), **Criss-Cross** (Columbia/Legacy 48823), **Tokyo Concerts** (Columbia/Legacy 65480), **Monk at Newport 1963 and 1965** (Columbia/Legacy 63905), **It's Monk's Time** (Columbia/Legacy 468 405), **Monk** (Columbia/Legacy 86564), **Live at the It Club** (Columbia/Legacy 65288), **Solo Monk** (Columbia/Legacy 47854), **Straight No Chaser** (Columbia/Legacy 64886), and **Underground** (Columbia/Legacy 40785) all feature the quartet (except for **Solo Monk**), and although there are not a lot of surprises, the music is consistently excellent. The two-CD set **Newport 1963 and 1965** is a little unusual in that clarinetist Pee Wee Russell sits in for two songs with Monk's quartet in 1963 while the 1965 disc was not released until 2002.

However, the Thelonious Monk Columbia recording that is most essential is the two-CD set ◉ **Big Band and Quartet in Concert** (Columbia/Legacy 57636). This performance from New York's Philharmonic Hall on December 30, 1963, is one of the high points of Monk's career. He takes an unaccompanied piano solo on "Darkness on the Delta," and jams with his quartet on swinging versions of "Played Twice" and a previously unreleased rendition of "Misterioso." The most memorable moments are the six selections performed by a ten-piece group—Monk's quartet plus Thad Jones, trumpeter Nick Travis, Steve Lacy, Phil Woods, baritonist Gene Allen, and trombonist Eddie Bert. Surprisingly, Lacy does not have any solos (although he is prominent in the ensembles), but there is plenty of solo space for Jones and Woods. Most remarkable is "Four in One" which, after one of Monk's happiest improvisations, features the orchestra playing a Hall Overton transcription of a complex and rather exuberant Monk solo taken from the original record.

The Oscar Peterson Trio   During the first half of the 1960s, Oscar Peterson continued touring the world and recording with his trio, which also included bassist Ray Brown and drummer Ed Thigpen. Their recordings range from easy-listening to inspired, and even though this particular trio was rarely as exciting as the one that Peterson had had with Brown and Herb Ellis in the 1950s (there was no competing solo voice to challenge O.P.), and there were few surprises, most of Peterson's work during this era had its moments of interest. The five-CD set **The London House Sessions** (Verve 314 531 766), recorded within a ten-day period in the summer of 1961, has all of the music originally put out as four LPs (**The Trio**, **The Sound of the Trio**, **Put on a Happy Face**, and **Something Warm**) plus 30 previously unreleased selections. There is a lot of repetition of titles, but the playing is on a high level. **Very Tall** (Verve 314 559 830) has the earliest meeting on records by Peterson and Milt Jackson, with the six songs being highlighted by "On Green Dolphin Street," "Work Song," "John Brown's Body," and "Reunion Blues." **Night Train** (Verve 821 724) features the trio playing its usual repertoire, but sounding fairly inspired, particularly on "Bags' Groove," "Easy Does It," "Band Call," and Peterson's "Hymn to Freedom."

◉ **Oscar Peterson Trio Plus One** (Verve 818 840) is a magical session with the trio being joined by flugelhornist Clark Terry. C.T. and O.P. work together remarkably well, and there are many jubilant moments on this 1964 album, including classic versions of "Brotherhood of Man," "Mack the Knife," "They Didn't Believe Me," and "I Want a Little Girl." In addition, Terry introduces his "Mumbles," his hilarious brand of scat singing that would be a trademark for him for decades.

Canadiana Suite (Limelight 818 841) has Peterson and his trio performing eight of his compositions written in tribute to his native Canada; best known are "Hogtown Blues" and "Wheatland." **Eloquence** (Limelight 818 842), from May 1965, is the final recording by the Peterson-Brown-Thigpen trio, highlighted by "Django," "Younger than Springtime," and "Autumn Leaves." Louis Hayes succeeded Thigpen later in 1965, and Ray Brown left the trio (after 15 years) in 1966, with Sam Jones taking his place. **Blues Etude** (Limelight 818 844) has the Peterson-Brown-Hayes trio on five songs, and the Peterson-Jones-Hayes unit on the other numbers. However, because Oscar Peterson was the dominant voice anyway, there was not any significant change in the trio's sound.

The most unusual record of this period for Oscar Peterson has not yet been reissued on CD. **With Respect to Nat** (Limelight 1030) has Peterson paying tribute to the recently deceased Nat King Cole, not just in his piano playing (backed by a big band or playing in a reunion trio with Herb Ellis and Ray Brown), but singing in a voice that was remarkably identical to Cole's. The similarity is the main reason that Oscar Peterson rarely ever sang.

The Horace Silver Quintet   Horace Silver was at the peak of his influence during the 1961–67 period. Recording regularly for Blue Note, Silver's funky piano style and his repertoire were emulated by many followers. During 1960–64, he was fortunate to be able to feature trumpeter Blue Mitchell, tenor saxophonist Junior Cook, bassist Gene Taylor, and drummer Roy Brooks in his quintet.

Doin' the Thing (Blue Note 84076) is a live set from New York's Village Gate that introduces Silver's "Filthy McNasty" along with some lesser-known but worthy songs. **The Tokyo Blues** (Blue Note 53355) has five numbers dedicated to Japan and the Orient although the music is not really all that Asian-oriented, just typical high-quality Horace Silver hard bop. Most famous among the songs (four Silver originals plus "Cherry Blossom") is "Tokyo Blues." **Silver's Serenade** (Blue Note 21288) does not introduce any future standards, but it is notable for being the sixth and final full Silver album with the Mitchell-Cook frontline.

◉ **Song for My Father** (Blue Note 84185) has Mitchell and Cook joining Silver for "Calcutta Cutie," but otherwise the set features an entirely new band with Silver leading a quintet comprised of trumpeter Carmell Jones, tenor saxophonist Joe Henderson, bassist Teddy Smith, and drummer Roger Humphries. Although Henderson is a more advanced soloist than Junior Cook, the quintet's sound is largely unchanged from the former lineup, helping to make the pianist's "Song for My Father" into a jazz standard. Also on this classic album are "Que Pasa," "The Kicker," and a feature for the trio on "Lonely Woman." The LP **Live 1964** (Emerald 1001), released by Silver's own label decades later, has the Jones-Henderson-Smith-Humphries group featured on extended versions of "Filthy McNasty," "Skinney Minnie," "The Tokyo Blues," and "Señor Blues."

By the time Silver recorded **The Cape Verdean Blues** (Blue Note 84220) in 1965, his group (in addition to Henderson and Humphries) featured trumpeter Woody Shaw and bassist Bob Cranshaw. An extra bonus is that J.J. Johnson is added on trombone for three of the six numbers. The set is highlighted by "The Cape Verdean Blues," "Pretty Eyes," and "Mo' Joe." From 1966, **The Jody Grind** (Blue Note 84250) is one of the most advanced albums of Silver's career, since his frontline now consisted of Shaw, tenor saxophonist Tyrone Washington, and (on half of the material) altoist/flutist James Spaulding. Best known among the songs are "The Jody Grind" and "Dimples."

Although Blue Note was just starting to go through major changes, Horace Silver would prove to be its most loyal and reliable artist, staying with the label until its demise.

Hard Bop and Soul Jazz

While free jazz gained most of the headlines, hard bop was the modern mainstream of jazz in the 1960s. A direct descendant of bebop, but with longer melody statements, a more active role for the string bass, and soloists who were not afraid to utilize a stronger blues sensibility, hard bop was at its prime during 1955–68,

fueled by constant releases from the Blue Note label. Soul jazz grew out of hard bop, putting a greater emphasis on the influence of church and gospel music, R&B, and blues. The keyboard was a particularly major element in this music, starting with pianist Horace Silver and other pianists who followed (including Bobby Timmons, Les McCann, and Ramsey Lewis) who utilized bluesy and funky riffs in their playing. With the rise of Jimmy Smith in 1956, many organists became popular playing soul jazz, usually in groups comprised of organ, tenor, guitar, and drums; Shirley Scott, Brother Jack McDuff, Jimmy McGriff, and Groove Holmes were a few of the organists who followed in Smith's footsteps. While hard bop became more complex (often influenced a bit by the avant-garde), soul jazz developed its own repertoire of blues, ballads, and soulful standards, becoming a popular attraction in many neighborhood bars.

Both hard bop and soul jazz declined for various reasons by the late 1960s, but these two overlapping styles were still going very strong in 1967. This section not only deals with some of those idioms' pacesetters (particularly those who recorded as leaders), but features some straight-ahead jazz veterans from bebop and West Coast jazz.

Trumpeters

The hard bop trumpeters tended to use Clifford Brown and Fats Navarro as their role models while being quite aware of Miles Davis. These included such greats as Lee Morgan, Freddie Hubbard, Blue Mitchell, Donald Byrd, and Woody Shaw along with many of the lesser-known players.

Chet Baker Chet Baker spent much of 1959–64 in Italy, part of the time in Italian jails due to his drug problems. Any chances of him becoming a Hollywood movie star were permanently dashed by his destructive habits; he no longer won jazz polls, and he was in danger of being forgotten altogether in the United States. It is therefore a surprise that ◉ **The Italian Sessions** (Bluebird 2001) from 1962 is one of his greatest recordings. Baker sounds quite fiery throughout this exciting set (a sextet date with Bobby Jaspar on tenor and flute and guitarist Rene Thomas), playing superior solos on such tunes as "Well You Needn't," "Barbados," and "Pent-Up House." Forget his association with the West Coast cool jazz school or even the influence of Miles Davis; this is heated hard bop.

Baker returned to the United States in 1964 and recorded several decent albums, including an effective instrumental and vocal tribute to Billie Holiday the following year, **Baker's Holiday** (EmArcy 838 204). By then his trumpet had been stolen, and he was exclusively playing flugelhorn. During August 23–25 and 29, 1965, Baker cut five albums for Prestige in a quintet with tenor saxophonist George Coleman, pianist Kirk Lightsey, bassist Herman Wright, and drummer Roy Brooks that have been reissued as three CDs: **Lonely Star** (Prestige 24172), **Stairway to the Stars** (Prestige 24173), and **On a Misty Night** (Prestige 24174). Baker's playing on this trio of CDs (32 instrumentals in all) is almost as strong as on **The Italian Sessions,** and it gives listeners a last chance to hear him stretch out before some of his bleakest years.

On July 25, 1966, Chet Baker was beaten up by drug dealers and had his teeth seriously damaged. It would be nearly two years before he would be able to play again and quite a few more before he made a serious comeback.

Donald Byrd   Trumpeter Donald Byrd was at the peak of his creative powers during the 1961–67 period. Recording regularly for Blue Note, his music fit securely into hard bop while looking forward, and his playing evolved from being a journeyman in the 1950s into a mature and fairly distinctive voice in the '60s. In 1961, he had a quintet with baritonist Pepper Adams that featured the young Herbie Hancock on piano. While **Chant** (Blue Note 991), **Royal Flush** (Blue Note 4101), and **The Cat Walk** (a strong set with Duke Pearson on piano that was last out as Blue Note 4075) have not been reissued on CD yet outside of a Mosaic limited-edition box set **The Complete Blue Note Donald Byrd/Pepper Adams Studio Sessions** (Mosiac 4-194), **Free Form** (Blue Note 84118) is available. Recorded shortly after the breakup of the quintet with Adams, Byrd is heard with four young and advanced musicians, Wayne Shorter, Herbie Hancock, Butch Warren, and Billy Higgins. The music is not really "free form," but does stretch the limits of hard bop a bit. Byrd plays five of his more adventurous originals, including "Pentecostal Feeling" and the unpredictable "Free Form" plus Hancock's ballad "Night Flower."

After spending 1962–63 studying composition in Europe, Byrd returned to the United States and worked steadily toward becoming an important force in jazz education, eventually teaching at Rutgers, Howard University, and the Hampton Institute. He also sought to create new music. **A New Perspective** (Blue Note 84124) finds him using a gospel choir in a jazz context, teaming a septet that includes Hank Mobley, Kenny Burrell, and Herbie Hancock with an eight-voice choir directed by Coleridge Perkinson. Duke Pearson's arrangements are quite creative, and one song, "Cristo Redentor," became a hit. The follow-up album, **I'm Tryin' to Get Home** (Blue Note 84188), uses a similar concept with a stronger role for the singers and the utilization of a large brass section, but no new hits resulted. During 1966–67, Byrd recorded four fairly conventional, but enjoyable Blue Note albums: **Mustang** (Blue Note 59963), **Blackjack** (Blue Note 21286), **Slow Drag** (Blue Note 35660), and **The Creeper** (only out individually as the LP Blue Note 1096). All team Byrd with altoist Sonny Red along with such players as Hank Mobley, McCoy Tyner, Cedar Walton, Chick Corea, and Pepper Adams (on **The Creeper**). One can sense (with hindsight) while listening to these recordings that Donald Byrd wanted to move forward, but had not yet decided on his future direction. His activities during the next few years would surprise many and dismay quite a few of his jazz fans while finding him an entirely new audience.

Johnny Coles   Johnny Coles was a flexible trumpeter able to fit into both boppish and freer settings. He started off playing with the R&B-oriented bands of Eddie "Cleanhead" Vinson (1948–51), Bull Moose Jackson (1952), and Earl Bostic (1955–56). Coles played with James Moody's septet (1956–58), was featured on some records with Gil Evans, and gained his greatest recognition for his relatively brief period with the 1964 Charles Mingus Sextet during a European tour before an illness forced him to leave. Fortunately, he recovered and stayed active throughout the 1960s, recording with Duke Pearson and Astrud Gilberto. His debut as a leader was 1961's **The Warm Sound** (Koch 7804), a quartet set with either Kenny Drew or Randy Weston on piano, bassist Peck Morrison, and Charlie Persip. Coles is in excellent form on two standards, his blues "Room 3" and four Weston originals, including two versions of "Hi-Fly." **Little Johnny C.** (Blue Note 32129) has pianist Duke Pearson taking a major role, contributing five of the six compositions and all of the arrangements. Coles and Pearson are matched with Leo Wright (alto and flute), Joe Henderson, Bob Cranshaw, and either Walter Perkins or Pete LaRoca on drums. The material is obscure but high quality with a catchy title cut, and Coles and Henderson in particular come up with one creative solo after another.

Ted Curson   Like Johnny Coles, Ted Curson was a flexible trumpeter still best known for his relatively brief association with Charles Mingus. Curson studied at Granoff Musical Conservatory, moved to New York in 1956, and played with Mal Waldron, Red Garland, and Philly Joe Jones, recording with Cecil Taylor in 1961. Curson played next to Eric Dolphy and Dannie Richmond in the classic 1960 Mingus Quartet, and then co-led an excellent post-bop quartet with Bill Barron (1961–65) and worked with Max Roach.

Curson's first date as a leader in April 1961 was for the tiny Old Town label, mostly selections with Bill Barron although Eric Dolphy guests on flute for two songs. Recorded in 1962, **Fire Down Below** (Original Jazz Classics 1744) unfortunately only has 31 minutes of music, but what was recorded is excellent. Curson performs two standards ("Show Me," and "Falling in Love with Love") and four obscurities with pianist Gildo Mahones, bassist George Tucker, Roy Haynes, and (on four numbers) Montego Joe on conga. Curson's appealing and distinctive sound along with his fresh ideas make this an excellent (if brief) set. ◉ **Tears for Dolphy** (Black Lion 760190) is a superior outing by Curson with the pianoless quartet he co-led with tenor saxophonist Bill Barron, which also includes bassist Herb Bushler and drummer Dick Berk. The music falls between hard bop and free jazz, and the nine originals by Curson and Barron are swinging and often a bit witty. The CD reissue has all of the original **Tears for Dolphy** album plus the three songs from the **Flip Top** (Arista 1030) LP recorded the same day; the other three numbers from the latter are unrelated cuts from 1966. Such tunes as "Kassim," "7/4 Funny Time," "Quicksand," and "Searchin' for the Blues" are both explorative and surprisingly accessible, featuring Ted Curson at his best.

Kenny Dorham   One of the main bebop veterans to become involved in hard bop, Kenny Dorham helped define the idiom during 1961–64. He was partly responsible for tenor saxophonist Joe Henderson rising to fame in the jazz world so quickly, using him on his dates, and being a sideman on some of Henderson's sessions.

Dorham recorded often during this period, and his five Blue Note albums are among the high points of his career. **Whistle Stop** (Blue Note 28978) features the trumpeter playing seven of his originals (none of which became standards despite their quality) in a quintet with Hank Mobley, Kenny Drew, Paul Chambers, and Philly Joe Jones. **Matador/Inta Somethin'** (Blue Note 84460) has all of the music from two of Dorham's albums on a single CD. Dorham and the compatible altoist Jackie McLean perform with two different rhythm sections; high points include "Smile," "Beautiful Love," "It Could Happen to You," "Lover Man," and Dorham's "Una Mas." Throughout the two sets, Dorham and McLean stretch the boundaries of hard bop.

◉ **Una Mas** (Blue Note 46515) has Dorham welcoming such musicians as Joe Henderson (in his recording debut), Butch Warren, and (before they played with Miles Davis) Herbie Hancock, and Tony Williams. Together they perform three of the trumpeter's originals (including a version of "Una Mas" that is much longer than its previous recording) and "If Ever I Would Leave You." Dorham sounds at least as young as the other players on this classic set. **Trompeta Tocatta** (Blue Note 84181) from September 4, 1964, has Dorham, Henderson, Tommy Flanagan, Richard Davis, and Albert "Tootie" Heath interpreting three Dorham songs plus the tenor's "Mamacita."

Surprisingly, that was largely it. Dorham was only 40 in 1964, but his health began to fade (he would develop a kidney disease), he became a part-time player, and even spent a period working in the post office. Other than a live set from 1966 not released for decades (eventually on the tiny Raretone label), and two songs from a 1970 concert, Kenny Dorham had made his last recordings.

Art Farmer   Art Farmer, who during this period of time switched from trumpet to the mellow-toned flugelhorn, played with the Jazztet for three years. Recorded in 1962, **Here and Now** (Mercury 558052) was the fifth of the Jazztet's six recordings, and it has the group (Farmer, Benny Golson, Grachan Moncur III, pianist Harold Mabern, bassist Herbie Lewis, and drummer Roy McCurdy) in excellent form on such songs as Ray Bryant's "Tonk," "Whisper Not," "Just in Time," and "Ruby My Dear." It is strange to think that this talented band could not find enough jobs in order to stay together, but before the year was over, the Jazztet had broken up.

Farmer spent much of 1963–64 leading a quartet with Jim Hall. **Live at the Half Note** (Atlantic 9066) has Farmer and Hall joined in late 1963 by bassist Steve Swallow and drummer Walter Perkins. Surprisingly, swing standards are emphasized (other than Miles Davis's "Swing Spring") with Hall taking "I'm Getting Sentimental Over You" as his feature, and the other tunes including "What's New" and "Stompin' at the Savoy." However, the playing is advanced, and the lyrical styles of Farmer and Hall work together very well.

But the group with Hall also did not last, and after a few more recordings (including a couple of quintet sets with Jimmy Heath in 1967 that have not been reissued on CD), a neglected Art Farmer moved to Vienna in 1968.

Joe Gordon An excellent hard bop trumpeter, Joe Gordon started playing professionally in 1947 when he was 19, working along the way with Georgie Auld, Lionel Hampton, Charlie Parker (on a few gigs during 1953–54), Art Blakey (1954 right before the Jazz Messengers were formed), and Don Redman. Gordon was a member of the Dizzy Gillespie big band in 1956, was briefly with the Horace Silver Quintet, and settled in Los Angeles where he worked with most of the top local players, including Barney Kessel, Benny Carter, Harold Land, Shelly Manne, and Dexter Gordon. Gordon was in Shelly Manne's group during 1958–60, recorded with Thelonious Monk, and led two dates of his own. The first album, **Introducing Joe Gordon**, was cut for EmArcy in 1955, and is long out of print. Recorded in 1961, **Lookin' Good** (Original Jazz Classics 1934) has the trumpeter contributing all eight songs and interacting with the adventurous altoist Jimmy Woods, pianist Dick Whittington, bassist Jimmy Bond, and drummer Milt Turner. None of the songs caught on, but the solos are excellent and often full of spirit, hinting at what Joe Gordon might have accomplished had he been luckier. However, on November 4, 1963, he died in a fire at the age of 35.

Freddie Hubbard Freddie Hubbard came of musical age during 1961–67, developing quickly into one of jazz's major trumpeters. His style was influenced by Clifford Brown and Lee Morgan, but he was more advanced harmonically, and he became increasingly individual as the decade progressed. Hubbard had already started recording as a leader for Blue Note in 1960, and then became quite prolific, also cutting sessions for Impulse and Atlantic. Hubbard spent 1961–64 as a member of Art Blakey's Jazz Messengers (both following and preceding stints by Lee Morgan), worked with Max Roach during 1965–66, led a quintet featuring altoist/flutist James Spaulding, and appeared on such important records as Oliver Nelson's **Blues and the Abstract Truth**, Eric Dolphy's **Out to Lunch**, Herbie Hancock's **Maiden Voyage**, John Coltrane's **Ascension**, and Sonny Rollins's **East Broadway Rundown**.

Recorded in 1961, **Hub Cap** (Blue Note 84073) was Hubbard's third album as a leader, a hard bop–oriented sextet date with trombonist Julian Priester, Jimmy Heath, and Cedar Walton. While that set is fine, ● **Ready for Freddie** (Blue Note 32094) has stronger material (including the original versions of Hubbard's "Byrdlike" and "Crisis"), and a particularly superb sextet that consisted of the trumpeter, Bernard McKinney on euphonium, Wayne Shorter, McCoy Tyner, Art Davis, and Elvin Jones. **Hub-Tones** (Blue Note 84115) shows the influence that John Coltrane's modal music was having on the modern mainstream, and this is Hubbard's first meeting on records with James Spaulding; Herbie Hancock is also in the quintet. During the period, Hubbard recorded two relatively conservative but enjoyable sets for Impulse. **The Artistry of Freddie Hubbard** (Impulse 179) has the trumpeter joined by Curtis Fuller, John Gilmore, Tommy Flanagan, Art Davis, and Louis Hayes on three originals, and creative versions of "Summertime" and "Caravan." **The Body and the Soul** (Impulse 183) features lots of variety in three sessions that star Hubbard in a septet with Eric Dolphy and Wayne Shorter backed by a big band and sometimes joined by a string orchestra. High points include "Skylark," "Aries," "Thermo," and the title cut.

Hubbard and Spaulding teamed up in 1964 for **Breaking Point** (Blue Note 84172), performing music that falls between hard bop and the avant-garde with pianist Ronnie Matthews, bassist Eddie Khan, and Joe Chambers. The title cut and "Blue Frenzy" are standouts. **Blue Spirits** (Blue Note 46545) has Hubbard playing challenging music in three different settings with such sidemen as James Spaulding, Joe Henderson, Hank Mobley, Kiane Zawadi on euphonium, Harold Mabern, McCoy Tyner, Herbie Hancock, bassists Larry Ridley, Bob Cranshaw, and Reggie Workman, drummers Clifford Jarvis, Pete LaRoca, and Elvin Jones, Big Black on congas, and (on one song) bassoonist Hosea Taylor. Although none of the seven Hubbard originals became standards, many of the solos are memorable. In contrast, the double CD **The Night of the Cookers Vols. 1 & 2** (Blue Note 28882), which has a rare encounter on records by Hubbard and Lee Morgan, is a definite disappointment. The problem with this live date is that Morgan was having an off night, the individual performances are way too long with lots of meandering, and the recording quality is just so-so, making this a blown opportunity.

In 1966, Freddie Hubbard switched to Atlantic; his first two albums for that label have been reissued by Koch. **Backlash** (Koch 8535) features his working quintet with Spaulding, pianist Albert Dailey, bassist Bob Cunningham, and drummer Otis Ray Appleton. High points include the debut of Hubbard's "Little Sunflower" and an excellent remake of his "Up Jumped Spring." **High Blues Pressure** (Koch 8513), which adds tenor saxophonist Bennie Maupin, Kiane Zawadi on euphonium, and the tuba of Howard Johnson, shows that sometimes more is less. The complex music is not as memorable as on **Backlash** though there are some fine solos along the way from Hubbard, Spaulding, Maupin, and Kenny Barron.

By 1967, Freddie Hubbard's name fit comfortably into the same sentence as those of Lee Morgan, Dizzy Gillespie, and Miles Davis among current trumpeters, and he was still improving year by year.

Carmell Jones Carmell Jones should have been better known, but he moved to Europe just when his career began to get going. Born in Kansas City, Jones served in the military, attended the University of Kansas, and led a band in Kansas City in 1959. In 1960, he moved to Los Angeles where he stayed busy for the next five years, leading three albums for Pacific Jazz and one for Prestige in addition to recording with Bud Shank, Harold Land, Curtis Amy, and Gerald Wilson's Orchestra (1961–63). Jones also toured with the Horace Silver Quintet during 1964–65, recording the original version of "Song for My Father." From 1965, **Jay Hawk Talk** (Original Jazz Classics 1938) is the only one of his own albums to be in print, but it is an excellent one, teaming Jones with Jimmy Heath, Barry Harris, George Tucker, and drummer Roger Humphries. A lengthy version of "What Is this Thing Called Love" is a highlight of the straightforward hard bop date.

However, within a few months, Carmell Jones had moved to Germany, and, although he remained active,

he recorded surprisingly little and was soon forgotten by American jazz fans.

Booker Little For Booker Little, the first important new voice to emerge on the trumpet since the death of Chet Baker, 1961 was both his greatest year on records and the last year of his life. He played in the ensembles of John Coltrane's **Africa/Brass** sessions (where his melancholy tone could easily be heard) and made important appearances on such records as Abbey Lincoln's **Straight Ahead**, Max Roach's **Percussion Bitter Sweet**, and the three albums with Eric Dolphy recorded live at the Five Spot. In addition, he led two records of his own.

Out Front (Candid 79027) is a sextet date with Dolphy, Julian Priester, pianist Don Friedman, Art Davis or Ron Carter on bass, and Max Roach that has seven of Little's obscure (but quite worthy) originals. **Booker Little and Friend** (Bethlehem 79855), which was originally known as **Victory and Sorrow**, features Little leading a similar sextet (with Priester, George Coleman, Friedman, Reggie Workman, and Pete LaRoca) through some harmonically advanced hard bop. Little contributed six originals (best are "Molotone Music" and "Victory and Sorrow") and sounds quite beautiful on the date's one standard, "If I Should Lose You."

But then, just one month after recording **Booker Little and Friend**, the 23-year-old trumpeter died of uremia, a major loss to jazz.

Chuck Mangione Chuck Mangione was a journeyman trumpeter during this period, bop-based and initially influenced by Dizzy Gillespie. He co-led the Jazz Brothers with pianist Gap Mangione during 1960–61, recording **Hey Baby** (Original Jazz Classics 668) and **Spring Fever** (Original Jazz Classics 767) in 1961. With Sal Nistico on tenor (before he joined Woody Herman), bassist Steve Davis (on **Hey Baby**), and drummer Roy McCurdy in the quintet, this was a particularly talented group, particularly for a band based in Rochester, New York. The boppish music should surprise listeners only familiar with Chuck Mangione's later work. In 1962, after the breakup of the band, the trumpeter led his first album under his own name, **Recuerdo** (Original Jazz Classics 495). Mangione is joined by Joe Romano (tenor, flute, and alto), Wynton Kelly, Sam Jones, and Louis Hayes, holding his own with the notable rhythm section. Chuck Mangione at 21 was starting to display his own musical personality and sounds quite at home on the boppish standards and originals.

He picked up important experience playing with the Woody Herman and Maynard Ferguson big bands (both in 1965), and as a member of Art Blakey's Jazz Messengers (1965–67). But considering these associations, Chuck Mangione's future musical direction would be a bit of a surprise.

Howard McGhee   A major trumpeter during the classic bebop era, Howard McGhee only emerged now and then in the 1950s. During 1960–62, he made a comeback on records, leading six sessions, including obscure sessions for Felsted, Bethlehem, Fontana, Winley, and United Artists, but by then his bop-oriented music was considered out of fashion. Best of his albums from this period is **Maggie's Back in Town** (Original Jazz Classics 693), an often-brilliant quartet outing with Phineas Newborn, Leroy Vinnegar, and Shelly Manne. McGhee performs two of Teddy Edwards's originals ("Sunset Eyes" and "Maggie's Back in Town") plus three standards, and the trumpeter's original blues "Demon Chase." McGhee's style proved to be virtually unchanged from the late 1940s. Also quite worthwhile is **Sharp Edge** (Black Lion 760110), which consists of eight selections (plus four previously unreleased alternate takes) by a quintet featuring McGhee, George Coleman, Junior Mance, George Tucker, and Jimmy Cobb. McGhee's inventive arrangements make the band sound like a regularly working group rather than just being a jam session.

But although he continued playing fairly regularly, Howard McGhee only recorded one studio album as a leader during 1963–75, an obscure big band date. He was a victim of his own personal excesses and jazz's rapid evolution.

Blue Mitchell   A fine hard bop trumpeter with his own sweet and soulful sound, Blue Mitchell was a member of the Horace Silver Quintet during 1959–64 before breaking away (taking most of Silver's group with him) to start his own quintet. He recorded regularly as a leader for Riverside through 1962, switching to Blue Note during 1963–69.

A Sure Thing (Original Jazz Classics 837) and **The Cup Bearers** (Original Jazz Classics 797) wrap up Mitchell's Riverside years. **A Sure Thing** has Blue mostly in the spotlight, performing with a nonet arranged by Jimmy Heath; best are "I Can't Get Started," "Hootie's

Blues," and a quintet jam on "Gone with the Wind." **The Cup Bearers** is very much in the Horace Silver tradition, which is not too surprising since Mitchell uses most of Silver's group (including Junior Cook, bassist Gene Taylor, and drummer Roy Brooks) with Cedar Walton in the pianist's place.

Mitchell recorded six albums for Blue Note during 1963–67. All were reissued on **The Complete Blue Note Blue Mitchell Sessions** (Mosaic 4-178), which is a magnificent but limited-edition four-CD box set. Only two of the records are available individually. ◉ **The Thing to Do** (Blue Note 84178) from 1964 is the classic of the series. With Cook and Taylor now regular members of his group, Mitchell is featured in a quintet also including drummer Al Foster and the young but already talented pianist Chick Corea. Best of the five songs is Mitchell's very catchy "Fungii Mama." **Down with It** (Blue Note 54327) has the same band in 1965 digging into such tunes as "Hi-Heel Strangers" and "Samba de Stacy." Blue Mitchell's recordings would decline later in the decade due to the commercialization of Blue Note, but such LPs as **Bring It Home to Me**, **Boss Horn**, and **Heads Up**, which date from 1966–67, are worth searching for.

Lee Morgan   Lee Morgan was in some ways the definitive jazz trumpeter of the 1960s. He was always a solid hard bop improviser, with a brash style of his own that was built out of Clifford Brown's legacy, but he could also play in soul jazz settings and on dates that bordered on the avant-garde. Rather than being an innovator like Miles Davis or Don Cherry, Morgan was a key player in the modern mainstream, pushing jazz ahead while still holding on to his roots.

A member of Art Blakey's Jazz Messengers during 1959–61, Morgan recorded an album shortly after leaving the drummer. **Take Twelve** (Original Jazz Classics 310) has Morgan joined by Clifford Jordan, Barry Harris, Bob Cranshaw, and Louis Hayes for four of his originals, and a song apiece by Jordan and Elmo Hope. Though the individual songs did not become standards, they challenge the musicians to come up with inventive statements. However, Morgan soon moved back to his native Philadelphia, and very little was heard from him again until December 1963.

Although a second stint with Blakey during 1964–65 was mostly uneventful, Morgan led a series of Blue Note recordings during 1963–68 that rank among the finest work of his career. His comeback record, ⊙ **The Side-winder** (Blue Note 84157) from December 1963, is Morgan's best-known recording due to the catchy title cut that became a surprise hit, launching the boogaloo fad of danceable jazz. The trumpeter is joined by Joe Henderson, Barry Harris, Bob Cranshaw, and Billy Higgins for that song plus four other superior originals, including "Totem Pole," and "Gary's Notebook." **Search for the New Land** (Blue Note 84169) is another gem, featuring five challenging Morgan compositions, including "The Joker," "Melancholee," and the title cut. Morgan, Wayne Shorter, guitarist Grant Green, Herbie Hancock, Reggie Workman, and Billy Higgins are in particularly creative form throughout the complex but fairly accessible music. **Tom Cat** (Blue Note 84446), which was not released for the first time until 1980, has more high-quality advanced hard bop music from Morgan along with Jackie McLean, Curtis Fuller, McCoy Tyner, Bob Cranshaw, and Art Blakey.

After **The Sidewinder** became a hit, there were several attempts to duplicate its success. **The Rumproller** (Blue Note 46428) has Morgan reuniting with Henderson and Higgins (along with pianist Ronnie Mathews and bassist Victor Sproles) for the similar-sounding title cut, a ballad tribute to Billie Holiday ("The Lady"), and a few originals, including the memorable bossa nova "Eclipso." **The Gigolo** (Blue Note 84212) from the summer of 1965, recorded at about the time that Morgan began leading his own group, includes such tunes as his memorable blues "Speed Ball," an explorative "You Go to My Head," "Yes I Can, No You Can't," "Trapped," and the lengthy title cut. Morgan, Shorter, Harold Mabern, Cranshaw, and Higgins all play in top form. ⊙ **Corn-bread** (Blue Note 84222) is most notable for introducing Morgan's ballad "Ceora" (which is given an absolutely perfect performance without a misplaced note), but also has strong versions of "Cornbread," "Our Man Higgins," "Most Like Lee," and the standard "Ill Wind." This time around Morgan is joined by McLean, Hank Mobley, Hancock, bassist Larry Ridley, and Higgins.

Although **The Sidewinder**, **The Gigolo**, and **Corn-bread** are the three standouts by Lee Morgan from this era, all of his Blue Notes are well worth acquiring. **Infinity** (Blue Note 97504) from late 1965 has tricky music with complex chord changes (other than the uptempo blues "Zip Code"), well played by Morgan, McLean, Larry Willis, Reggie Workman, and Higgins. **Delightfulee**

(Blue Note 84243) is indeed delightful. Two ballads ("Yesterday" and "Sunrise Sunset") feature a nonet playing Oliver Nelson arrangements behind Morgan's lyrical horn, with assistance from Wayne Shorter and McCoy Tyner. There are also four quintet numbers with Henderson, Tyner, Cranshaw, and Higgins that are highlighted by the very likable "Ca-Lee-So." **Charisma** (Blue Note 59961) has catchy versions of the funky "Hey Chico" and Duke Pearson's "Sweet Honey Bee," as played by Morgan, McLean, Mobley, Cedar Walton, Paul Chambers, and Higgins.

Recorded in 1966, **The Rajah** (Blue Note 84426) is very much in the Jazz Messengers style, with Morgan, Mobley, Walton, Chambers, and Higgins interpreting lesser-known originals and surprising versions of the pop tunes "What Now, My Love" and "Once in My Lifetime." **Standards** (Blue Note 23213) from January 1967 was not released for the first time until 1998, and was probably put aside at the time because it is not quite as modern as Morgan's more modal-oriented explorations. The music is fine, and some of the tunes (which include "This Is the Life," "Somewhere," "If I Were a Carpenter," and "Blue Gardenia") are offbeat. Duke Pearson's arrangements for the septet (which includes James Spaulding, Shorter, Pepper Adams, and Hancock) keep the music colorful and unpredictable. **The Procrastinator** (Blue Note 33579) has four Morgan originals (including "Party Time") and two by Shorter; the two horns are joined by Bobby Hutcherson, Hancock, Ron Carter, and Higgins for a set of stirring post-bop music. **The Sixth Sense** (Blue Note 22467), recorded November 10, 1967, is a lesser-known, but worthy outing by Morgan, McLean, tenor saxophonist Frank Mitchell, Walton, Victor Sproles, and the very busy Billy Higgins. Also worth searching for is the LP **Sonic Boom** (Blue Note 987), which has thus far been left out of the extensive Blue Note reissue series. It features Morgan with David "Fathead" Newman, Walton, Carter, and Higgins on such numbers as the funky "Fathead," the complex "Sneaky Pete," a feature for Morgan's lyricism on "I'll Never Be the Same" and the infectious "Mumbo Jumbo."

Lee Morgan was just 29 as 1967 ended, having already carved out a lifetime of accomplishments in just over 11 years.

Dizzy Reece   Born Alphonso Reece in Kingston, Jamaica, Dizzy began playing trumpet when he was 14 (in 1945), moved to Europe in 1949, and was based in

England during 1954–59. He recorded a bit while in England, met Donald Byrd on a session in 1958, and moved to New York the following year. Although he made a few strong recordings while in the United States, including a pair of long out-of-print Blue Note sets and **Asia Minor**, Reece never became as famous as he should have been. A technically impressive trumpeter who played high-quality hard bop, Reece can be heard at his best on **Asia Minor** (Original Jazz Classics 1806). The sextet date also features baritonist Cecil Payne, Joe Farrell on tenor and flute, Hank Jones, Ron Carter, and Charlie Persip. The solos are concise and meaningful with Reece's three originals clearly inspiring the players. However, despite its artistic success, this record led nowhere, and Dizzy Reece would not lead another record date until 1970 when he was back in Europe.

Woody Shaw   Woody Shaw was a promising young trumpeter during the second half of the 1960s, influenced by Freddie Hubbard's tone, but even more advanced harmonically. He grew up in Newark, New Jersey, starting on trumpet when he was 11. Shaw went on the road with Rufus Jones when he was 18 (1963), played with Willie Bobo's band when Chick Corea was also a member, and recorded with Eric Dolphy. In 1964, Dolphy invited him to join his band in Europe, but by the time Shaw arrived, the altoist had died. Shaw stayed in Paris for a few months (playing with Bud Powell and Johnny Griffin), and then back in the United States became a member of the Horace Silver Quintet (1965–66). He led his first record date in late 1965, released decades later by Muse as **In the Beginning**, and currently part of a two-CD set put out by 32 Jazz and reviewed in the next chapter. Even at his early age, Woody Shaw already had an original message of his own. During the next decade he would develop into one of jazz's most significant trumpeters.

Ira Sullivan   Ira Sullivan was an important part of the Chicago modern jazz scene of the late 1950s. **Bird Lives** (Koch 8553), a reissue that expands the original six-song LP program into a 15-tune double CD, was recorded at a Charlie Parker memorial concert in 1962. Sullivan sticks to trumpet and flugelhorn, playing with the legendary tenor Nicky Hill, pianist Jodie Christian, bassist Donald Garrett, and either Dorrell Anderson or Wilbur Campbell on drums. While most of the performances are of bop standards, it is intriguing to hear

how the innovations of the avant-garde were starting to be felt in this mostly straightahead music. Garrett (who would later play with Coltrane) and Sullivan were particularly open to its influence.

A short time later, Ira Sullivan moved to Florida where he worked as an educator and became a bit of a recluse, mostly just playing locally. His next recording, the 1967 Atlantic LP **Horizons** (Atlantic 1476), has him switching between soprano, tenor, trumpet, and flugelhorn with a quintet of players from Florida, mixing together jazz and pop ("Norwegian Wood"), and keeping his music open to free jazz influences. Unfortunately, Sullivan would not record again for another eight years.

Clark Terry   As a member of the staff of NBC, Clark Terry (who by now was mostly specializing on the fluegelhorn) was an important force in breaking down color lines. A technically brilliant player with his own joyous sound and a lovable personality who was impossible not to both love and admire, Clark Terry was always a joy to be around. Although busy in the studios and as a member of the *Tonight Show*'s big band, C.T. always found time to play and record jazz, including co-leading a witty quintet with Bob Brookmeyer and recording a classic album with the Oscar Peterson Trio.

Mellow Moods (Prestige 24136), which combines two records made for the Moodsville label (**Everything's Mellow** and **All American**), should have been a throwaway but is actually rewarding. The sets were supposed to emphasize quiet ballads, and the second date has songs from a forgotten musical, but Terry overcomes both restrictions. The first session (a quartet outing with Junior Mance) throws in some blues and obscure melodies along with the ballads, while the **All American** date has Oliver Nelson arrangements and good solos from Terry, Budd Johnson, and pianist Eddie Costa.

One of Clark Terry's greatest recordings, **Tread Ye Lightly** (Cameo 1071), has yet to reappear on CD. It matches C.T. with Ray Bryant (who uses the pseudonym Homer Fields), the humming bassist Major Holley, Seldon Powell on reeds, and Buddy Lucas on harmonica among others for definitive renditions of "Georgia on My Mind," "Misty," and "Lillies of the Field." Fortunately, ⦿ **The Happy Horns of Clark Terry** (GRP/Impulse 148) has returned for it has plenty of memorable moments. From 1964, Terry is teamed with Phil Woods (who doubles on clarinet), Ben Webster, Roger Kellaway,

Milt Hinton, and drummer Walter Perkins for a colorful program that includes a rollicking version of "Rockin' in Rhythm," "In a Mist," a Duke Ellington medley, and a flugelhorn-drums duet on "Return to Swahili."

Trombonists

J.J. Johnson was still the pacesetter among trombonists during the 1960s even as he spent more of his time in the studio as a writer. Bennie Green, one of the few trombonists of the 1950s not to sound like Johnson, largely faded away after the early '60s.

Bennie Green   After so much recording activity during the second half of the 1950s, Bennie Green only had one date left as a leader. **Gliding Along** (Original Jazz Classics 1869) is a typically spirited quintet session from 1961 with Johnny Griffin and Junior Mance that is fun and falls between bop and swing. Green remained active, recording with Sonny Stitt in 1964, playing with Duke Ellington for a few months in 1968, and settling in Las Vegas, but he maintained a much lower profile than previously and largely faded from the jazz world.

J.J. Johnson   The perennial poll-winner on trombone, J.J. Johnson occasionally led albums during the 1960s although he was also interested in composing ambitious orchestral works and writing for television and films. He spent part of 1961–62 as a member of Miles Davis's sextet, but otherwise worked mostly as a leader.

Two of the trombonist's projects from this era have been reissued on CD. **Proof Positive** (GRP/Impulse 145) from 1964 mostly has Johnson in a quartet with pianist Harold Mabern, bassist Arthur Harper, and drummer Frank Gant, stretching out on such songs as "Neo," "Minor Blues," and "Blues Waltz." J.J.'s minor-toned explorations are often a bit haunting. In addition, this disc has "Lullaby of Jazzland" (originally from a sampler) with Johnson assisted by guitarist Toots Thielemans, McCoy Tyner, Richard Davis, and Elvin Jones. **Say When** (Bluebird 6277) has most of the music from two of Johnson's big band dates for Victor (leaving out three songs due to lack of space). Not only does J.J. take the trombone solos, but he also contributes nine of the 17 compositions and nearly all of the arranging other than Oliver Nelson's on

TIMELINE 1963

George Coleman, Herbie Hancock, Ron Carter, and Tony Williams join the new Miles Davis Quintet after the Wynton Kelly Trio (with Paul Chambers and Jimmy Cobb) goes out on its own. • Johnny Griffin moves to Europe. • Pat Martino is featured with Willis Jackson. • James Moody joins the Dizzy Gillespie Quintet. • Sonny Clark dies. • Hampton Hawes is pardoned by President Kennedy and released from jail after five years. • Brother Jack McDuff's popular band features Red Holloway and George Benson. • The Riverside label goes bankrupt. • The Chico Hamilton Quintet features Charles Lloyd and Gabor Szabo. • Gary Burton is a member of the George Shearing Quintet. • Mark Murphy, Art Taylor, and Leo Wright move to Europe. • Dinah Washington dies. • Pee Wee Russell sits in with the Thelonious Monk Quartet at the Newport Jazz Festival. • John Coltrane records with Johnny Hartman. • Jack Teagarden has a reunion with his family at Monterey. • Alice Babs records with Duke Ellington. • Bassist Cachao emigrates to the United States from Cuba. • Al Hirt's recordings of "Cotton Candy" and "Java" are quite popular. • Red Nichols cuts his last album with the Five Pennies. • Clarinetist Jim Cullum, Sr.'s, Happy Jazz Band (with his son Jim Cullum, Jr., on cornet) make their first recordings. • Zutty Singleton leads the band at Ryan's. • After 23 years, Ray Nance leaves the Duke Ellington Orchestra. • Seventeen-year-old Danish bassist Niels-Henning Orsted Pedersen has to reluctantly turn down an offer to join the Count Basie Orchestra, becoming the house bassist at the Club Montmartre instead. • Tommy Flanagan begins the first of two long stints as Ella Fitzgerald's accompanist. • Pete Jolly has a minor hit with "Little Bird." • Valve trombonist Rob McConnell records a quintet album with fellow Canadians trumpeter Guido Basso and guitarist Ed Bickert. • Cecil Payne starts a three-year period playing with Machito's Orchestra. • Plas Johnson is heard playing the famous melody of Henry Mancini's "The Pink Panther" throughout the hit film. • Herb Ellis records albums with both Stuff Smith and Charlie Byrd. • Jimmy McGriff has a hit with "I've Got a Woman." • Houston Person joins Johnny Hammond Smith. • The album **Getz/Gilberto** has a major hit in "The Girl from Ipanema" and makes stars out of Antonio Carlos Jobim and Joao and Astrud Gilberto.

a remake of "Stolen Moments." Johnson and Hank Jones are the main soloists with J.J.'s writing on George Russell's "Stratushphunk" and Miles Davis's "Swing Spring" being high points.

Altoists

While in the 1950s, Charlie Parker was the dominant force on alto; by the '60s several other approaches were developing. Hank Crawford and Lou Donaldson helped invigorate soul jazz, Paul Desmond and Lee Konitz had their own cool tones, and the avant-garde (and Ornette Coleman) began to have an effect on some other altoists, including Jackie McLean.

Hank Crawford   Few players have had as soulful a sound as Hank Crawford, who is instantly recognizable on the alto within a couple of notes. Crawford's accessible playing falls between 1950s R&B, bebop, and soul jazz. Born in Memphis, he started on the piano, switched to alto, and learned all of the reeds. Crawford played early on with Ike Turner, B.B. King, Junior Parker, and Bobby "Blue" Bland. In 1958 while attending college, he met Ray Charles who soon hired him for his band on baritone. A year later Crawford was Charles's altoist and musical director, staying until 1963 when he began his solo career.

In 1960, Hank Crawford began a longtime association with the Atlantic label. The two-CD reissue ● **Memphis, Ray, and a Touch of Moody** (32 Jazz 32054) is a rather generous release for it reissues in full four of Crawford's sets from 1960–65, his debut release **More Soul**, his third album **From the Heart**, his fourth **Soul of the Ballad**, and his sixth **Dig These Blues**. On three of the four dates, Crawford is featured in an R&B-ish but swinging septet, performing basic originals and a few standards, including "Sister Sadie," "Dat Dere," "You've Changed," and "Don't Get Around Much Anymore." **The Soul of the Ballad** set is a bit different, for Crawford is backed by a string section arranged by Marty Paich, caressing melodies that are taken at slow tempos. Although the latter date is not too essential (some of the material is rather weak), overall this two-fer gives listeners a definitive look at early Hank Crawford, when he was carving out a fresh new style that fell between musical categories.

Sonny Criss   Sonny Criss lived in Europe during 1962–65 without making much of a stir. Upon his return, the boppish altoist cut seven albums for Prestige during 1966–69, some of the finest work of his career. **This Is Criss** (Original Jazz Classics 430) has Criss joined by Walter Davis, Jr., Paul Chambers, and Alan Dawson on "Sunrise, Sunset," "When Sunny Gets Blue," "Black Coffee," "Days of Wine and Roses," "Skylark," "Love for Sale," and some originals, swinging hard within the bebop idiom. **Portrait of Sonny Criss** (Original Jazz Classics 655) features the same quartet five months later digging into standards (including a fiery "Wee" and an emotional "Smile") plus Davis's gospel-oriented "A Million Times More." **Up, Up and Away** (Original Jazz Classics 982) at first glance may not look that promising because this 1967 set includes the title cut (which actually has more challenging chord changes than expected) and "Sunny." However, the date is actually quite rewarding. It matches the passionate Criss with Tal Farlow (who had briefly come out of retirement) along with Cedar Walton, Bob Cranshaw, and drummer Lenny McBrowne, and includes such numbers as a very soulful "Willow Weep for Me," Horace Tapscott's "This Is for Benny," and an explosive version of "Scrapple from the Apple" which by itself makes this set recommended.

Paul Desmond   Paul Desmond continued playing with the Dave Brubeck Quartet until its breakup in 1967. During 1961–65, he recorded a series of albums for RCA with guitarist Jim Hall that has been reissued on the five-CD set **The Complete RCA Victor Recordings** (RCA 68687). This collection has the complete contents of **Desmond Blue** (which features the two principals joined by a string section arranged by Bob Prince) and the pianoless quartet albums **Take Ten**, **Glad to Be Happy**, **Bossa Antigua**, and **Easy Living**. The subtle interplay between the witty Desmond and the more somber Hall works well, their blend in the ensembles is appealing, and the interplay is sometimes magical. Also well worth acquiring is **Two of a Mind** (RCA 68513), which teams Paul Desmond and Gerry Mulligan in a different sort of pianoless quartet. The songs all utilize common chord changes, including "Blight of the Fumble Bee," and the two saxophonists bring out the best in each other during their playful encounters.

Lou Donaldson   Lou Donaldson's music was primarily bebop in the 1950s. He added a conga player to his group in 1959, and starting in 1961 he frequently used an organist rather than a pianist. His own playing did not change much although his records looked as much toward soul jazz as to hard bop during 1961–63. **Gravy Train** (Blue Note 53357) has Donaldson (who is joined by pianist Herman Foster, bassist Ben Tucker, drummer Dave Bailey, and Alec Dorsey on congas) playing with spirit if sounding predictably soulful on such tunes as "South of the Border," "Polka Dots and Moonbeams," and "Candy." **Good Gracious** (Blue Note 54325) from 1963 ended Donaldson's first 11-year stint on Blue Note with a fine effort in which Grant Green and organist John Patton (along with drummer Ben Dixon) really push the altoist with some heated grooves and trade-offs.

During 1963–67, Donaldson recorded eight generally excellent albums for Argo/Cadet, but none have been reissued on CD. By the time he returned to the Blue Note label in 1967, things had changed drastically. Blue Note was now owned by Liberty and was looking toward the commercial market for hits. Donaldson obliged with **Alligator Boogaloo** (Blue Note 84263), a set with funky grooves, catchy melodies, and fine playing from the leader, cornetist Melvin Lastie, organist Lonnie Smith, George Benson, and Leo Morris (the future Idris Muhammad) on drums. The title cut was a minor hit, and the playing overall is not bad, particularly compared to the follow-up **Mr. Shing-A-Ling** (Blue Note 84271), an attempt at funky jazz that, even with some fine spots for Blue Mitchell, is sunk by the weak material and a certain lack of sincerity. With the exception of occasional projects, the "real" Lou Donaldson would not re-emerge on records again until 1981.

John Handy John Handy was a brilliant altoist who developed his own sound out of the Charlie Parker tradition. He was always able to hit very high notes perfectly in tune, and he really stretched himself in the 1960s. Handy had gained some recognition for his playing with Charles Mingus during 1958–59. He led three albums for Roulette during 1959–62 (including 1962's **Jazz**), but none have been reissued on CD. Handy was part of Mingus's band at the 1964 Monterey Jazz Festival when the group had a very memorable performance.

In 1965, Handy was booked at Monterey as a leader, and he stole the show. Fortunately, the performance was recorded by Columbia and recently has been reissued by Koch as ❶ **Live at the Monterey Jazz Festival** (Koch 7820). The altoist at the time had a quintet comprised of violinist Michael White (the first important new voice

on his instrument in jazz since the swing era), guitarist Jerry Hahn, bassist Don Thompson, and drummer Terry Clarke. The group performed a 27-minute version of "If Only We Knew" (full of brilliant unaccompanied solos) and the 19-minute "Spanish Lady." This fresh new music resulted in Handy being signed to Columbia and recording three additional records. **The Second John Handy Album** (Koch 7812) uses the same group that was at Monterey on five explorative originals, including "Blues for a Highstrung Guitar" and the 5/4 "Theme X." Unfortunately, the Handy quintet broke up in 1966. By the time he recorded **New View** (Koch 7811) the following year, the altoist was using Bobby Hutcherson, the up-and-coming guitarist Pat Martino, bassist Albert Stinson, and drummer Doug Sides. The band performed extensive versions of "Naima," "A Little Quiet," and Handy's emotional and episodic "Tears of Ole Miss (Anatomy of a Riot)," which clocks in at 23:45. The music is fascinating and worthy of several listens. All three of these albums are easily recommended (and sound unlike the music of anyone else from the era), but due to its historic value, get the Monterey CD first.

Eric Kloss A very talented and usually high-powered altoist based in bop but open to funk and the avant-garde, Eric Kloss was one of the most promising new voices on the alto during 1965–67. Born in 1949 and blind since birth, Kloss began playing professionally in Pittsburgh in the early 1960s as a teenager. In 1965, he worked with Pat Martino and made his recording debut at age 16. Kloss would lead ten albums in a little over four years. **About Time** (Prestige 24268) reissues his first two albums (**Introducing Eric Kloss** and **Love and All That Jazz**) on a single CD. Kloss sounds quite brilliant on both alto and tenor. He is heard in quartets with either Don Patterson or Richard "Groove" Holmes on organ, Pat Martino, Vinnie Corrao or Gene Edwards on guitar, and Billy James or Grady Tate on drums, performing two of his originals, one song by Patterson, and ten standards. Highlights include "Close Your Eyes," "All Blues," a cooking version of "Embraceable You," and Miles Davis's "No Blues." Kloss's other somewhat scarce LPs from this era, which include **Grits and Gravy** (Prestige 7486), **First Class Kloss** (Prestige 7520), **Life Force** (Prestige 7535), and **We're Going Up** (Prestige 7565), are well worth searching for. His fiery playing and original style deserve much more recognition.

Lee Konitz   Lee Konitz only recorded two significant albums as a leader during the 1961–67 period. It would be an understatement to say that 1961's **Motion** (Verve 557 107) has been expanded a bit. Konitz recorded the five songs on the original LP with bassist Sonny Dallas and Elvin Jones. When the set came back as a 1990 CD, it had grown to eight songs. But the version from 1998 has three CDs of material, 38 selections in all! The Elvin Jones date was slightly expanded, but the two extra CDs are taken from a couple of earlier sessions with Nick Stabulas on drums along with Konitz and Dallas, adding 28 previously unreleased performances. Fortunately, Konitz was in fine form during this period, and even if no new revelations are heard, he creates plenty of rewarding ideas over the common chord changes.

◉ **The Lee Konitz Duets** (Original Jazz Classics 466) is a classic of its kind. Konitz, whose ears were always open to the avant-garde while retaining his highly personal sound, recorded a series of very diverse duets in 1967. The altoist is matched with valve trombonist Marshall Brown on a delightful version of "Struttin' with Some Barbecue" that concludes with the duo playing a harmonized version of a Louis Armstrong solo. Konitz matches wits with Joe Henderson on a wandering version of "You Don't Know What Love Is," jams "Tickle Toe" on tenor with Richie Kamuca, plays "Checkerboard" with pianist Dick Katz, "Erb" with Jim Hall, and an adventurous and fairly free "Duplexity" with violinist Ray Nance. There are also three different duets on "Alone Together," and a final blowout with most of the players on "Alphanumeric." The range of music is very impressive overall, and this innovative set works quite well.

Jackie McLean   During 1961–67, Jackie McLean led 17 albums for Blue Note which, when coupled with his four Blue Note dates of 1959–60, constitute the finest work of his career. Although he came of musical age during the 1950s and was part of many hard bop sessions, McLean (who always played with a slightly sharp tone and consistent intensity) was very much open to the avant-garde explorations of the younger generation. He played an elder statesman role similar to the one Coleman Hawkins assumed with the 1940s beboppers.

All of McLean's Blue Note recordings are easily recommended, with some being just a little more essential than others. **Bluesnik** (Blue Note 84067) is fairly accessible since it has McLean, Freddie Hubbard, Kenny Drew, Doug Watkins, and Pete LaRoca performing a variety of bluesy tunes that may not fit the exact structure of blues, but are full of the blues feeling and display a variety of tempos, moods, and styles. **A Fickle Sonance** (Blue Note 24544) is also relatively straightahead, with McLean joined by Tommy Turrentine, Sonny Clark, Butch Warren, and Billy Higgins. Recorded in 1962, ◉ **Let Freedom Ring** (Blue Note 46527) is a giant step forward as McLean, pianist Walter Davis, bassist Herbie Lewis, and Higgins play quite emotionally. McLean's style was now including honks, screams, and squeals, going beyond chordal improvisation or even sticking to a steady tempo, and putting the emphasis on emotional outbursts and honest feelings. Although not as radical as Ornette Coleman's music, McLean was clearly touched by Ornette's innovations, expressing adventurous ideas through his own distinctive voice. In contrast, **Tippin' the Scales** (Blue Note 84427) is more boppish, which may be why this recording was not initially released until the 1980s. McLean (joined by Clark, Warren, and Art Taylor) performs two of his originals, three by Clark, and "Cabin in the Sky," pushing at the boundaries of hard bop without really breaking through. **Vertigo** (Blue Note 22669) was also not released for quite a while, not coming out until 1980. The CD has "Formidable" from a 1959 session with Donald Byrd and Walter Davis, and five numbers from a 1963 set with Byrd, Herbie Hancock, Warren, and (on his recording debut) Tony Williams. The music ranges from catchy funk and hard bop to strong hints of the avant-garde.

◉ **One Step Beyond** (Blue Note 46821) and **Destination Out** (Blue Note 32087) are both from 1963 and have McLean in a pianoless quintet with Grachan Moncur III and vibraphonist Bobby Hutcherson really stretching himself. On both sets, the musicians play complex originals by McLean and Moncur, displaying both impressive musicianship and the imagination to make coherent statements on potentially difficult material. **It's Time** (Blue Note 84179) has McLean joined by trumpeter Charles Tolliver, Hancock, Cecil McBee, and Roy Haynes on a repertoire that has some fairly free originals ("Cancellation") along with the funky "Das' Dat." Oddly enough, McLean's intense sound is more advanced than his choice of notes, while Tolliver's Clifford Brown–influenced tone is more conservative than his fiery ideas. From 1965, **Right Now** (Blue Note 84215) is mostly hard charging, intense, and fairly free; McLean is assisted by pianist Larry Willis, Bob Cranshaw, and drummer Clifford Jarvis. **Jacknife** (Blue

Note 40535) consists of two sessions from 1965–66, a hard bop outing with either Lee Morgan or Charles Tolliver on trumpet (they both appear on "Soft Blue"), and a high-quality and freer quartet set with Larry Willis, bassist Don Moore, and Jack DeJohnette. Highlights overall include Tolliver's "On the Nile" and the lengthy "High Frequency."

New and Old Gospel (Blue Note 53356) should have been a classic since this 1967 set teams together Jackie McLean with Ornette Coleman, but unfortunately Ornette sticks exclusively to trumpet, a major mistake. Pianist Lamont Johnson is in top form, and McLean sounds excellent, but Coleman's flawed trumpet playing makes what could have been a major summit meeting into merely a historical curiosity. **'Bout Soul** (Blue Note 59383) is one of McLean's freer albums, a superlative if underrated quintet date with Woody Shaw, Lamont Johnson, bassist Scotty Holt, and drummer Rashied Ali that includes a recitation by poet Barbara Simmons on "Soul" and some passionate playing throughout the date. McLean's final Blue Note album, **Demon's Dance** (Blue Note 84345), made with Shaw, Johnson, Holt, and DeJohnette, is typically intense and stimulating with originals by McLean, Shaw, and Calvin Massey (including "Message from Trane").

In addition, a pair of Steeple Chase sets, **Dr. Jackle** (Steeple Chase 36005) and **Tune Up** (Steeple Chase 36023), feature McLean playing at a December 18, 1966, concert with Johnson, Holt, and Higgins, showing how the altoist sounded in clubs during the time, and adding some fine solos to Lamont Johnson's relatively slim discography. And there are three Jackie McLean Blue Note albums that have not yet been reissued individually on CD. **Hipnosis** (Blue Note 483) is a two-LP set that has a fairly boppish 1962 quintet date with Kenny Dorham and Sonny Clark, and a much more advanced session from 1967 with Grachan Moncur and Lamont Johnson. **Action** (Blue Note 4218) is in a similar vein as **It's Time** with McLean and Tolliver, assisted by Bobby Hutcherson, Cecil McBee, and Billy Higgins, tearing into the free title cut, a pair of Tolliver ballads (including "Plight"), the bluesy "Hootman," and a McLean ballad feature on "I Hear a Rhapsody." From 1965, **Consequences** (Blue Note 994) is fairly straightahead but dynamic with McLean and Lee Morgan inspiring each other, while joined by Harold Mabern, Herbie Lewis, and Higgins; "Bluesanova," "Consequence," and "Tolypso" are high points.

With the artistic decline of Blue Note and the rise of rock, Jackie McLean began to shift his focus in 1967 toward jazz education, becoming a very significant teacher during the next few decades.

Charles McPherson   While Jackie McLean looked toward Ornette Coleman for fresh ideas, Charles McPherson always considered Charlie Parker to be his main musical role model. McPherson was part of the Detroit jazz scene of the 1950s, and Barry Harris was an important teacher in his career. McPherson moved to New York in 1959, and in 1961 joined Charles Mingus's band, playing with the bassist on and off for a decade. He made his first recordings as a leader in 1964, and co-led a quintet with trumpeter Lonnie Hillyer in 1966. **Be-Bop Revisited** (Original Jazz Classics 710) is a rare example of classic bebop being played in 1964. McPherson is joined by Harris, Carmell Jones, bassist Nelson Boyd, and Al "Tootie" Heath on such songs as "Hot House," "Nostalgia," "Wail," and "Si Si." The following year's **Con Alma** (Original Jazz Classics 1875) has the altoist teaming up with Clifford Jordan (who was looking beyond bop), Harris, bassist George Tucker, and drummer Alan Dawson for songs by Thelonious Monk, Duke Ellington, Charlie Parker, Dizzy Gillespie, and Dexter Gordon plus an original blues song, "I Don't Know," that sounds a bit like "Parker's Mood." **Live at the Five Spot** (Prestige 24135) features McPherson and Harris taking honors while Lonnie Hillyer (who stumbles on the rapid "Shaw Nuff"), bassist Ray McKinney, and Billy Higgins do their best on such songs as "Here's that Rainy Day," "Never Let Me Go," and "I Can't Get Started." All three of the CDs are enjoyable, with **Be-Bop Revisited** getting the edge due to its youthful enthusiasm.

Art Pepper   For Art Pepper, the 1960s were largely a waste. After recording **Intensity** (Original Jazz Classics 5387) for Contemporary in 1960, he spent much of the next decade in and out of prison due to his drug problems. Pepper did gig now and then when he was out of jail, but many of his longtime fans were dismayed to realize that he had sacrificed part of his musical individuality in order to be influenced by John Coltrane. **Art Pepper Quartet in San Francisco** (Fresh Sound 1005) from 1964 features the altoist with pianist Frank Strazzeri, bassist Hersh Hamel, and drummer Bill Goodwin, playing a few originals on a television show, being interviewed briefly by Ralph Gleason, and performing two lengthy numbers at the Jazz Workshop in San Francisco. Pepper, who plays with plenty of intensity on these performances and does show off the Coltrane influence, actually sounds pretty good. Although the recording quality is not always the greatest, his followers will find these rare performances quite interesting. But Art Pepper's comeback would not begin in earnest for another 11 years.

Sonny Stitt   Hard bop, soul jazz, and free jazz may have been getting most of the publicity, but Sonny Stitt stuck to his singular path, playing bebop on the alto and tenor. Sometimes he was heard in soulful organ groups, and occasionally in commercial settings, but he was never the most flexible of improvisers and always sounded the same no matter what the surroundings. Never reluctant to record, Stitt led no less than 33 albums during the 1961–67 period for such labels as Verve, Argo, Roost, Jazzland, Atlantic, Black Lion, Pacific Jazz, Impulse, Prestige, Cadet, MPS, Colpix, and Roulette. Three of the discs sum up the era well for Stitt. **Stitt Meets Brother Jack** (Original Jazz Classics 703) from 1962 has the saxophonist playing blues-based originals and a couple of standards with organist Brother Jack McDuff, guitarist Eddie Diehl, Art Taylor, and Ray Barretto. Stitt adjusts well to soul jazz, simply by being himself. ● **Stitt Plays Bird** (Rhino/Atlantic 1418) is a very logical and inspired project with the altoist playing ten Charlie Parker compositions plus Jay McShann's "Hootie Blues" in a quintet with Jim Hall, John Lewis, Richard Davis, and Connie Kay. Stitt both pays tribute to Parker and improvises in his own bebop style on such numbers as "Constellation," "Confirmation," "Ko Ko," and "Yardbird Suite." ● **Salt and Pepper** (GRP/Impulse 210) has all of the music from two former Impulse LPs. The **Salt and Pepper** album teams Stitt and Paul Gonsalves, with the two tenors jamming on the medium-tempo blues "Salt and Pepper," "S'posin'," and a lengthy "Perdido." However, their version of "Stardust" takes honors, with Stitt playing some beautiful alto behind Gonsalves. Also included on this CD is a Sonny Stitt quartet set (**Now**) that has him alternating between alto and tenor, and sounding inspired on such offbeat material as "Estrellita," "Please Don't Talk About Me When I'm Gone," and "My Mother's Eyes."

Phil Woods   Phil Woods, who had recorded extensively as a leader during 1954–60, cut one album in 1961, and then nothing much else as a leader until 1968. Fortunately, the lone record, ● **The Rights of Swing** (Candid 79016), is a classic, as were so many of the releases from Nat Hentoff's short-lived Candid label. Woods's five-part "Rights of Swing" suite has the altoist featured with an all-star octet also including trumpeter Benny Bailey, Curtis Fuller, baritone saxophonist Sahib Shihab, the innovative Julius Watkins (a major factor in this music), Tommy Flanagan, bassist Buddy Catlett, and drummer Osie Johnson. The colorful arrangements use the distinctive horns in inventive fashion, and the music (which leaves room for many concise solos) holds one's interest throughout. This is one of Phil Woods's finest recordings although (due to the quick demise of Candid) it did not lead to an encore.

Tenor Saxophonists

The tenor sax was one of the key instruments in high-energy free jazz, but it also had an important spot in hard bop, soul jazz, and all straightahead jazz styles. In the 1960s, as now, there were a countless number of talented tenors.

Gene Ammons   Far too many jazz musicians of the 1950s were heroin addicts at one time or another, and quite a few spent periods of time in jail. Gene Ammons was one of the unluckiest ones. In addition to some time served during 1958–60, he spent much of 1962–69 behind bars when it was decided to make an example of him. Ammons recorded quite extensively for Prestige during 1961–62, and during his years in jail, the label was able to come out with "new" Ammons releases on a regular basis, using the same strategy that Contemporary had with the similarly incarcerated Art Pepper. Among the better Ammons recordings of the early 1960s are **Jug** (Original Jazz Classics 701), which is a standard quintet date (with Ray Barretto on conga), **Late Hour Special** (Original Jazz Classics 942), which alternates combo numbers with a ten-piece group arranged by Oliver Nelson, an exciting reunion with Sonny Stitt titled **We'll Be Together Again** (Original Jazz Classics 708), and an unusual collection of emotionally played religious hymns, **Preachin'** (Original Jazz Classics 792). **Up Tight** (Prestige 24140) is a particularly rewarding set for it contains two former LPs, and features prime Ammons on such numbers as "The Breeze and I," "I'm Afraid the Masquerade Is Over," and "Lester Leaps In."

But the joy of these recordings (some of which were recorded after the tenor knew that his days of freedom were numbered) was temporary for Gene Ammons would spend much of the 1960s completely off the scene.

Bill Barron A Philadelphia legend for years, tenor saxophonist Bill Barron finally moved to New York in 1958 when he was 31. Although he began recording as a leader in 1961, and for a time co-led a group with Ted Curson, Barron became a music educator, which led to a more stable life, but much less fame than his talent deserved. He recorded five albums as a leader during 1961–63 (three for Savoy and two for Dauntless). **Modern Windows Suite** (Savoy 92878) reissues all of Barron's first record (**The Tenor Stylings of Bill Barron** [Savoy 1184]) plus half of the second (the four-part "Modern Windows Suite"). Curson and Barron's younger brother Kenny Barron (who was on all of his sessions as a leader) are co-stars on this rewarding advanced hard bop set, which demonstrates what an underrated and highly original voice Bill Barron was during this important period.

Tony Coe Tony Coe has long been one of Great Britain's most talented and versatile soloists. He started on clarinet and was self-taught on tenor (where his tone is influenced by Paul Gonsalves). Coe played in an army band during 1953–56, and was a member of Humphrey Lyttelton's mainstream group during 1957–62. He led his own group during 1962–64, and was offered a spot with Count Basie's Orchestra, but immigration difficulties ultimately made that impossible. Coe instead joined Johnny Dankworth's Orchestra in 1966.

Some Other Autumn (Hep 2037) features Coe during 1964–65 after he had just turned 30. Coe is showcased in a straightahead quartet with pianist Brian Lemon, bassist Dave Green, and drummer Phil Seamen, performing swinging group originals plus "Body and Soul," "Perdido," "When Your Lover Has Gone," and "In a Mellow Tone." Even at this early stage, and in this fairly conservative setting, Tony Coe shows a great deal of individuality.

Buddy Collette An important force in integrating the Hollywood studios in the 1950s, Buddy Collette primarily worked as a studio musician and an educator in the 1960s. Other than an obscure album for World

Pacific in 1964, he was largely absent from jazz records during this era. **The Buddy Collette Quintet** (Studio West 104) has previously unissued transcriptions made for the radio show *The Navy Swings* in 1962. As good as the musicians (Collette on flute, clarinet, tenor, and alto, guitarist Al Viola, pianist Jack Wilson, bassist Jimmy Bond, and drummer Bill Goodwin) are on these very concise performances (all clocking in around three minutes or less), it is the six touching vocals by Irene Kral that make this a recommended disc. Her versions of "The Meaning of the Blues," "Nobody Else but Me," and especially "Spring Can Really Hang You Up the Most" are quite haunting.

Eddie "Lockjaw" Davis Eddie "Lockjaw" Davis teamed up with fellow tenor Johnny Griffin in a combative and generally exciting quintet during 1960–62. **Live at Minton's—The First Set** (Prestige 24206) has ten of the 18 selections recorded by the Jaws-Griffin group at the legendary Minton's Playhouse on January 6, 1961, including stimulating versions of "Billie's Bounce," "In Walked Bud," and "Our Delight." **The Tenor Scene** (Original Jazz Classics 940) is also from the same day, adding five more songs. At the time pianist Junior Mance, Larry Gales, and Ben Riley were in the band, jamming on such numbers as "Straight No Chaser" and "I'll Remember April." ● **Blues Up and Down** (Prestige 24084) combines two sessions on a single CD: 1960's **Griff & Lock** and 1961's **Blues Up and Down**. The music is quite competitive (no need for ballads), and includes stirring versions of such numbers as "Good Bait," "Last Train from Overbrook," and "Walkin'." **Afro-Jaws** (Original Jazz Classics 403) from 1961 is a change of pace for Davis is showcased with three trumpeters (including Clark Terry who gets some solos), a rhythm section, and a percussion section led by Ray Barretto. Lockjaw interprets four originals by Gil Lopez (who provided all of the arrangements) plus "Tin Tin Deo," "Star Eyes," and his own "Afro-Jaws," really excelling in the Afro-Cuban jazz setting.

Despite its quality, the Davis-Griffin Quintet did not last beyond 1962. Lockjaw returned to leading an organ group for a time and freelancing. **Goin' to the Meeting** (Prestige 24259) has Davis playing with the Shirley Scott trio in 1960 (on a Moodsville release), and with a quintet featuring pianist Horace Parlan and Willie Bobo on conga from 1962. The music is simple and melodic, with most of the fire coming from the session with Parlan.

Streetlights (Prestige 24150) also has all of the music from two separate albums although in this case both records were recorded on November 15, 1962. Joined by his regular group of the time, with organist Don Patterson, guitarist Paul Weeden, drummer Billy James, and guest bassist George Duvivier, Davis mostly sticks to standards, ripping through such songs as "Day by Day," "The Way You Look Tonight," and "There'll Never Be Another You."

With the rise of the avant-garde, Lockjaw became a bit frustrated. He actually retired during 1963–64 to work as a booking agent, but soon returned to playing, rejoining Count Basie in the mid-1960s, adding his intense tenor to the Basie sound.

Teddy Edwards   After being somewhat neglected during the 1950s (when cool jazz overshadowed bebop on the West Coast), Teddy Edwards found his hard bop–oriented tenor style in greater demand in the 1960s, recording three albums for Contemporary and two for Prestige, all of which have been reissued in the Original Jazz Classics series.

Together Again (Original Jazz Classics 424) has a reunion between Edwards and Howard McGhee, who had played together regularly during 1945–47. With very stimulating playing by Phineas Newborn, Ray Brown, and Ed Thigpen, the quintet interprets three standards and two originals. Most intriguing is the playing of McGhee, who was making a successful if surprisingly brief comeback, still sounding in prime form on the straightahead material. **Good Gravy** (Original Jazz Classics 661) has Edwards (in a quartet with either Newborn or Danny Horton on piano, Leroy Vinnegar, and drummer Milt Turner) playing four of his newer tunes (Edwards has long been an underrated songwriter), and some more familiar songs, including "On Green Dolphin Street," "Stairway to the Stars," and "Just Friends." **Heart and Soul** (Original Jazz Classics 177) has Edwards's group (with Vinnegar and Turner) joined by pianist Gerald Wiggins who sticks exclusively to organ where he is not as individual as on his main instrument. Edwards performs a variety of blues, "No Regrets," and "Secret Love." **Nothin' but the Truth** (Original Jazz Classics 813) from 1966 features Edwards in a quintet with Walter Davis, Jr., and Paul Chambers, sounding at his best on "On the Street Where You Live" and "But Beautiful." **It's All Right** (Original Jazz Classics 944)

shows how the avant-garde was making itself felt on hard bop dates in 1967, particularly in the harmonies and some solos. Edwards (who arranged all but one song), trumpeter Jimmy Owens, trombonist Garnett Brown, Cedar Walton, bassist Ben Tucker, and drummer Lenny McBrowne stretch out on a variety of original material.

But despite these quality releases, Teddy Edwards remained quite underrated because he chose to live in Los Angeles rather than New York.

Booker Ervin   With his hard tone and soulful sound, Booker Ervin probably could have been a commercial success, but his intensity and desire to play in advanced settings made a career in R&B or soul music quite unlikely. Instead he gained respect for his work with Charles Mingus and led a series of impressive albums during 1960–68.

As with most of the artists who recorded for Nat Hentoff's short-lived Candid label, Ervin had one of his best recordings for that label, **That's It** (Candid 79014). Joined by Horace Parlan, bassist George Tucker, and drummer Al Harewood, Ervin performs four of his originals (including "Booker's Blues"), plus "Poinciana" and "Speak Low." Unlike some of the other Candid artists, Ervin never recorded an indifferent or overly laidback record for any other label either. **Exultation** (Original Jazz Classics 835) from 1963 was the first in his series of rewarding recordings for Prestige, teaming the tenor with altoist Frank Strozier, Parlan, Butch Warren, and drummer Walter Perkins for music that is boppish and adventurous.

Among the best work of Ervin's career were his four "books" of 1963–64: **The Freedom Book** (Original Jazz Classics 845), **The Song Book** (Original Jazz Classics 776), **The Blues Book** (Original Jazz Classics 780), and **The Space Book** (Original Jazz Classics 896). **The Freedom Book** and **The Space Book** both match Ervin with the unbeatable rhythm section of Jaki Byard, Richard Davis, and Alan Dawson. **The Song Book** has Tommy Flanagan on piano, and **The Blues Book** is a quintet set with Davis, Dawson, Carmell Jones, and pianist Gildo Mahones. While there are differences in the emphasis of the albums' repertoire (**The Song Book** has standards while **The Blues Book** features blues-oriented material), the playing is unified and not necessarily freer on **The Freedom Book** than on **The Blues**

Book. Ervin just plays the way he plays, and sounds particularly inspired when teamed with Byard. Additional material from these sessions has also been released on **Groovin' High** (Original Jazz Classics 919).

Settin' the Pace (Prestige 24123), which contains two former LPs, is notable for having two marathon tenor battles between Ervin and Dexter Gordon ("Settin' the Pace" and "Dexter's Deck") which clock in between 19 and 22 ½ minutes apiece. Plenty of sparks fly, and due to their different sounds and mutual inspiration, this contest is a draw. In addition, there are two numbers (lengthy versions of "The Trance" and "Speak Low") showcasing Ervin with the rhythm section (Byard, Reggie Workman, and Dawson). **The Trance** (Original Jazz Classics 943) duplicates the latter two selections, adding a third song ("Groovin' at the Jamboree"), but is inferior overall to **Settin' the Pace**.

Recorded in 1966, **Heavy** (Original Jazz Classics 981), a sextet outing with Jimmy Owens, Garnett Brown, and the Byard-Davis-Dawson trio, includes an intense version of "Bei Mir Bist Du Schon," and a fine quartet showcase for Ervin on "You Don't Know What Love Is." **Structurally Sound** (Pacific Jazz 27545) has Ervin sharing the frontline with the very promising trumpeter Charles Tolliver, and their inside/outside approaches work very well together on six standards and two originals. The rhythm section (pianist John Hicks, Red Mitchell, and drummer Lennie McBrowne) keeps the momentum flowing as the two horns play with great intensity while still keeping the themes in mind. **Booker 'N' Brass** (Pacific Jazz 94509) from 1967 is a bit unusual due to the repertoire (which has a variety of material with cities in their titles, including "Do You Know What It Means to Miss New Orleans," "I Left My Heart in San Francisco," and "Harlem Nocturne") and the use of a six-piece horn section behind Ervin; this is the closest he ever came to making a commercial record. But quite typically, Booker Ervin's passion and intensity keep the music from ever being safe or bordering on easy-listening.

Jimmy Forrest   Reborn as a hard-bop/soul jazz tenor saxophonist after his R&B years ran its course, Jimmy Forrest led his own groups during the 1960s, recording several albums for Prestige and New Jazz during 1961–62.

Out of the Forrest (Original Jazz Classics 097) has Forrest joined by a trio with pianist Joe Zawinul reviving his "Bolo Blues," jamming the basic "Crash Program," and soulfully caressing the melodies of several standards. **Sit Down and Relax with Jimmy Forrest** (Original Jazz Classics 895) has three swing era standards, some offbeat material, and "That's All." Forrest plays typically well, and this quintet outing gives guitarist Calvin Newborn (pianist Phineas's brother) a rare opportunity to stretch out. **Most Much** (Original Jazz Classics 350), featuring a group augmented by Ray Barretto on congas, is highlighted by a heated "Annie Laurie," the calypso "Matilda," "My Buddy," "Robbins' Nest," and "Sonny Boy." **Soul Street** (Original Jazz Classics 987) finishes the complete reissue of all of Forrest's recordings of the era, with the tenor heard in several different settings. He teams up with King Curtis and Oliver Nelson on "Soul Street," plays three standards in a combo with pianist Hugh Lawson, is featured on "I Wanna Blow, Blow, Blow" with a nonet, and performs three numbers of lesser interest in an octet arranged by Oliver Nelson.

But strangely enough, considering the rise of soul jazz, Jimmy Forrest was largely off records altogether during 1963–67.

Frank Foster   Frank Foster was one of Count Basie's top tenor soloists during 1953–64 in addition to contributing arrangements and occasional songs (most notably "Shiny Stockings"). When he went out on his own, his style opened up to the influence of John Coltrane, and he sounded much more advanced than one would expect of a former Count Basie sideman, such as Frank Wess or Joe Newman. Recorded in 1965, **Fearless Frank Foster** (Original Jazz Classics 923) has the tenor, trumpeter Virgil Jones, pianist Albert Dailey, bassist Bob Cunningham, and Alan Dawson playing "Jitterbug Waltz" and Foster originals, including the catchy "Raunchy Rita," which would not have sounded out of place if performed by the Horace Silver Quintet. The following year's **Soul Outing** (Original Jazz Classics 984) features a variety of styles including funk, Latin, a bit of gospel, and some straightahead jazz. Foster, Jones, pianist Pat Rebillot, Bob Cunningham or Richard Davis on bass, Dawson, and (on two songs) guitarist Billy Butler play three of the leader's originals and two numbers from the musical *Golden Boy*. Although nothing that memorable occurs (the **Fearless** CD is preferred), Frank Foster deserves credit for growing beyond his roots in Count Basie.

Benny Golson   Benny Golson spent 1959–62 as an important member of the Jazztet. After that band broke up, he freelanced and became much more involved in writing for the studios. **Free** (GRP/Chess 816) from 1962 features Golson for the last time playing tenor in his original Don Byas/Lucky Thompson–influenced style. This 1998 CD reissue brings back the **Free** album plus seven of the ten selections from his **Take a Number from 1 to 10** project of 1960. Since the CD is just 62 minutes long, it is a pity that both sets were not reissued in full. **Free** has Golson in excellent form playing in a quartet also including Tommy Flanagan, Ron Carter, and Art Taylor. The other album has Golson playing unaccompanied on a brief "You're My Thrill" and adding an instrument to each song, with Curtis Fuller making a strong impression on the speedy "Swing It."

But that was all that would be heard from Golson's tenor on record for 15 years. He arranged for a European big band on the swinging and inventive **Stockholm Sojourn** (Original Jazz Classics 1894) while his charts on the gimmicky **Tune In, Turn On to the Hippest Commercials of the 1960s** (Verve 559 793) from 1967 are sometimes witty, but mostly a waste.

By the late 1960s, Benny Golson had become (along with J.J. Johnson, Shorty Rogers, and Benny Carter) one of at least four major jazz musicians who had temporarily given up playing altogether to work as an arranger/composer in the studios.

Dexter Gordon   Having kicked hard drugs by 1960, Dexter Gordon made a full comeback and was very active in the 1960s. Although his decision to move to Europe in 1962 made him less of a presence in the United States than he would have been, Gordon visited the U.S. occasionally during his European years and continued evolving. Having been an important early influence on John Coltrane, it was only right that Gordon would himself become influenced by Trane to an extent while still keeping his own bop-oriented style and distinctive sound.

◉ **The Complete Blue Note Sixties Sessions** (Blue Note 34200), a six-CD set, has all of the music from Gordon's nine Blue Note albums of 1961–65 plus a previously unknown jam session version of "Lady Be Good" with Sonny Stitt, and a few excerpts from a later interview with Gordon. Eight of the nine albums are also available individually. **Doin' Alright** (Blue Note 84077)

is a superior set that teams Dexter with Freddie Hubbard, Horace Parlan, George Tucker, and Al Harewood with highlights including "You've Changed," "Society Red," and "It's You or No One." **Dexter Calling** (Blue Note 46544) showcases Gordon in a quartet with Kenny Drew, Paul Chambers, and Philly Joe Jones mostly playing obscure originals, other than "Smile." **Go** (Blue Note 46094) and **A Swingin' Affair** (Blue Note 84133) were recorded within two days of each other with the same personnel of Sonny Clark, Butch Warren, and Billy Higgins. **Go** is highlighted by "I Guess I'll Hang My Tears Out to Dry" and "Three o'Clock in the Morning," while **A Swingin' Affair** has memorable versions of "You Stepped Out of a Dream," "Until the Real Thing Comes Along," and "Don't Explain."

Dexter Gordon's first album after moving overseas, **Our Man in Paris** (Blue Note 46394), has him teaming up with a trio called the Three Bosses: Bud Powell, bassist Pierre Michelot, and Kenny Clarke. They jam on such standards as "Scrapple from the Apple," "Broadway," and "A Night in Tunisia." **One Flight Up** (Blue Note 84176) has Gordon, Donald Byrd, Drew, Niels Pederson, and Art Taylor digging into four songs, including a lengthy rendition of Byrd's "Tanya" and the tenor's ballad feature on "Darn that Dream." Visiting the United States in 1965, Gordon cut **Clubhouse** (Blue Note 84445) and **Getting Around** (Blue Note 46681). The former, which also has Hubbard, Barry Harris, Bob Cranshaw, and Billy Higgins, was not released until the 1980s, but it holds its own with Gordon's other Blue Notes, particularly the stirring version of "I'm a Fool to Want You." **Getting Around** uses the same group except for vibraphonist Bobby Hutcherson being in Hubbard's place, and features a strong repertoire, including "Manha de Carnaval," "Heartaches," and "Shiny Stockings." The one Gordon Blue Note album not yet on CD, **Landslide** (Blue Note 1051), has music from three sessions in 1961–62, and includes fine versions of "Serenade in Blue" and "Second Balcony Jump."

In addition to the Blue Notes, Gordon was featured on many live records after moving to Europe. Six showcase him on radio broadcasts from the Montmartre (Copenhagen's top jazz club) that were aired every other Thursday during a three-month period in 1964. The quartet (with pianist Tete Montoliu, 18-year-old bassist Niels Pederson, and drummer Alex Riel) proved to be a perfect setting for Dexter, and each of these discs feature the great tenor in excellent form: **Cheesecake** (Steeple Chase 31008), **King Neptune** (Steeple Chase 36102), **I Want More** (Steeple Chase 36015), **Love for Sale** (Steeple Chase 36018), **It's You or No One** (Steeple Chase 36002), and **Billie's Bounce** (Steeple Chase 36028). From later in the year, **After Hours** (Steeple Chase 31224) and **After Midnight** (Steeple Chase 31226) are not as well recorded, but once again find Gordon sounding quite inspired, playing with a Swedish rhythm section and trumpeter Rolf Ericson on rather lengthy performances, including a 26-minute version of Miles Davis's "No Blues."

From 1967, **The Squirrel** (Blue Note 57302) is a live set with Kenny Drew, bassist Bo Stief, and Art Taylor that was not initially released until 1998 (it is not on his Blue Note box), and is highlighted by a 20-minute version of "Cheesecake" and "Sonnymoon for Two." During two days at the Montmartre that year, Gordon recorded a ton of material. The three-CD set **Live at the Montmartre Jazzhus** (Black Lion 7606) has all of the music also available on the single discs **Both Sides of Midnight** (Black Lion 760103), **Body and Soul** (Black Lion 760118), and **Take the "A" Train** (Black Lion 760133). The playing is quite consistent throughout, and Gordon never seems to run out of ideas, particularly on "Doxy," "Sonnymoon for Two," "There Will Never Be Another You," "Blues Walk," and "Love for Sale."

There is certainly no shortage of Dexter Gordon albums from the 1960s, and all of the recordings from the very consistent tenor are quite rewarding.

Johnny Griffin   Johnny Griffin co-led a "tough tenor" quintet with Eddie "Lockjaw" Davis during 1960–62, and then followed Dexter Gordon's lead, moving to Europe in 1963 where he became an important part of the Paris jazz scene and a member of the Kenny Clarke-Francy Boland Orchestra.

Before he left the United States, Griffin continued recording his string of superior albums for Riverside. Most of the sessions that he made with Lockjaw were issued under Davis's name, but there were a few exceptions. **Lookin' at Monk** (Original Jazz Classics 1911) is notable for being one of the earliest examples of a band exploring Thelonious Monk's music for an entire album. Griffin, who had spent the summer of 1958 in Monk's quartet, has no difficulty inspiring Davis on such songs as "In Walked Bud," "Rhythm-A-Ning," and "Well You Needn't." **Tough Tenor Favorites** (Original Jazz Classics 1861) has Griff and Lockjaw battling it out on fiery renditions of "Blue Lou," "Ow," and "From this Moment On."

Of his solo Riverside albums, Griffin's **Change of Pace** (Original Jazz Classics 1922) is quite atmospheric, featuring the tenor in a group with both Bill Lee and Larry Gales on basses, drummer Ben Riley, and (on five of the nine numbers) Julius Watkins on French horn. The music is often haunting with Lee's bowed bass (played over Gales's walking bass lines), and the blend between tenor and French horn being quite unique. **White Gardenia** (Original Jazz Classics 1877) is a Billie Holiday tribute album that was finished on the second anniversary of her death. Griffin is backed by seven brass instruments, a cello-dominated string section, and a four-piece rhythm section, putting plenty of feeling into "Gloomy Sunday," "Good Morning Heartache," and "Don't Explain." The arrangements by Melba Liston and Norman Simmons perfectly fit the music.

The Kerry Dancers and Other Swinging Folk (Original Jazz Classics 1952) has Griffin acknowledging the folk music revival of the early 1960s, jamming such unlikely material as "The Londonderry Air," "Green Grow the Rushes," "The Kerry Dancers," and "Black Is the Color of My True Love's Hair" along with some other unrelated material. Barry Harris, Ron Carter, and Ben Riley help out on this spirited quartet date. **Do Nothing 'Til You Hear from Me** (Original Jazz Classics 1908) is a more conventional but enjoyable set with Buddy Montgomery (on piano and vibes), Monk Montgomery (making a rare appearance on acoustic rather than electric bass), and Art Taylor. The last Griffin Riverside recording, **Grab This** (Original Jazz Classics 1941), is a fine if not overly memorable soul jazz date with organist Paul Bryant, guitarist Joe Pass, bassist Jimmy Bond, and drummer Doug Sides that has Griffin playing in his typical hard-charging style.

After moving to Europe, Griffin recorded less often, but kept busy. **In Copenhagen** (Storyville 8300) from 1964 has the tenor jamming on five standards while assisted by Kenny Drew, Niels Pedersen, and Art Taylor, with lengthy versions of "What Is this Thing Called Love" and "Doctor's Blues" (19 minutes) being highlights. **The Man I Love** (Black Lion 760107) from 1967 was recorded at Copenhagen's Montmartre with Drew, Pederson, and Al "Tootie" Heath, and is comparable to Dexter Gordon's live records of the time, with heated versions of "The Man I Love," "Blues for Harvey," and "The Masquerade Is Over."

Johnny Griffin would wait until the musical and political climate changed in the United States before choosing to return on an occasional basis.

Eddie Harris   When Eddie Harris arrived on the Chicago scene in 1961, he had a distinctive tone, impressive technique, and the ability to hit high notes with ease—not only notes in the alto range, but as high as a soprano. Early on he studied piano, vibes, and clarinet before making the tenor his main ax. Harris worked with Gene Ammons on a few occasions as a pianist, served in the army (having opportunities to play tenor while stationed in France and Germany), and after his discharge he returned to his native Chicago and signed with the Vee-Jay label. His very first recording, **Exodus to Jazz** (Vee-Jay 904), includes a hit version of "Exodus." Harris's effortless solos on "Exodus" and a variety of originals are quite appealing, and he is ably assisted by a Chicago rhythm section that includes pianist Willie Pickens and guitarist Joe Diorio. His follow-up LPs **Mighty Like a Rose** (Vee-Jay 3025) and **Jazz for "Breakfast at Tiffany's"** (Vee-Jay 3027) followed immediately in the same vein. Although neither duplicated the commercial success of "Exodus," these programs (which include such songs as "Spartacus," "My Buddy," and "Moon River") are both enjoyable. **The Lost Album Plus the Better Half** (Collectables 7209) contains an LP's worth of unissued material plus half of an album that was released, dating from 1961–63. Harris is supported on different tracks by trumpeter Ira Sullivan, altoist Bunky Green, organist Mel Rhyne, and Joe Diorio. Harris stretches out on the rhythm changes of "Cuttin' Out," the blues "Shakey Jake" (both are over 15 minutes long), and on some much shorter performances, including a few brief throwaways.

After an album for the Exodus label and two for Columbia, in 1965 Harris began a longtime association with Atlantic. Two of the tenor's best albums have been reissued as **The In Sound/Mean Greens** (Rhino 71515). **The In Sound** is particularly significant for it has the original version of Harris's most famous composition, "Freedom Jazz Dance," along with a memorable rendition of "The Shadow of Your Smile," three standards, and a blues tune. Harris is joined by Cedar Walton, Ron Carter, Billy Higgins, and (on three numbers) trumpeter Roy Codrington. The same personnel is on the first four numbers of **Mean Greens** (the calypso "Yeah Yeah Yeah"

is a high point) while the final three performances have Harris switching to electric piano and jamming with a Latin rhythm section. Among the numbers is the original (and obscure) recording of "Listen Here," a year before the hit version.

In the fall of 1966 for his recording of **The Tender Storm** (Collectables 6358), Eddie Harris began using a Varitone-amplified saxophone for the first time. While it was sometimes utilized as a novelty by other players who might enjoy being able to play octaves, Harris's exploration of the horn was much more extensive, with all kinds of tonal distortions, echoes, and inventive ideas. The breakthrough was on 1967's **Electrifying Eddie Harris**, which has been reissued as half of ◑ **Electrifying Eddie Harris/Plug Me In** (Rhino 71516). Harris utilizes a catchy riff and circular breathing on "Listen Here," and introduces the memorable "Theme in Search of a Movie," while the **Plug Me In** set from 1968 (which has rock and funk rhythms on some numbers) includes "Theme in Search of a T.V. Commercial," "Live Right Now," and "It's Crazy."

Although sometimes considered to be soul jazz or early fusion, in reality Eddie Harris's music was too original during this period to fit into any one category.

Tubby Hayes   Tubby Hayes (born Edward Brian Hayes) was one of England's top jazz musicians of the 1950s and '60s. His main instrument was tenor, but he also occasionally played flute and vibes. Among his associations in the 1950s were Kenny Baker, Ambrose, Vic Lewis, Jack Parnell, and Ronnie Scott (with whom he co-led the Jazz Couriers during 1957–59). Although quite active in Europe during the 1960s, even leading his own big band for a time in London, Hayes also visited the United States on a few occasions during 1961–65.

New York Sessions (Columbia 45446) finds Hayes sounding a bit like Zoot Sims and Al Cohn (with a touch of Johnny Griffin and John Coltrane) on a quartet/quintet date with Horace Parlan, bassist George Duvivier, Dave Bailey, and guests Clark Terry (on four of the ten selections) and vibraphonist Eddie Costa (on three songs). Highlights include an uptempo "Aircgin" and the ballad "You're My Everything." **Night and Day** (Ronnie Scott's Jazz House 013) has one song apiece taken from five different live appearances from 1963–66 with four of the songs being over 13 minutes. Jimmy Deuchar makes one appearance apiece on trumpet and mellophone, while Hayes is mostly heard on tenor, other than doubling on flute on Clark Terry's "The Simple Waltz," and taking "Spring Can Really Hang You Up the Most" as a vibes feature. Pianists Terry Shannon and Mike Pyne also have their spots on this excellent hard bop set, which serves to show how swinging a soloist Tubby Hayes was during his prime.

Jimmy Heath Of Jimmy Heath's six albums for Riverside that really made his reputation as a distinctive tenor saxophonist and a skilled arranger/composer, four were recorded during 1961–64. **The Quota** (Original Jazz Classics 1871) has four Heath songs among the seven tunes and is mostly a blowing date, matching Heath with Freddie Hubbard, Julius Watkins on French horn, Cedar Walton, Percy Heath, and Albert "Tootie" Heath. **Triple Threat** (Original Jazz Classics 1909) from 1962 uses the same personnel for four more of Heath's tunes (best known is "Gemini"), "Goodbye," "Make Someone Happy," and "The More I See You." **Swamp Seed** (Original Jazz Classics 1904) is most notable for Heath's arrangements for Donald Byrd, two French horns, Don Butterfield's tuba, Herbie Hancock, Percy Heath, Connie Kay, and the leader's tenor. Heath's originals from this date did not catch on, but they are excellent, as are his transformations of Thelonious Monk's "Nutty," "Just in Time," and "More than You Know." The final Jimmy Heath Riverside album, **On the Trail** (Original Jazz Classics 1854), is a superior showcase for his tenor, featured with a rhythm section (Wynton Kelly, Kenny Burrell, Paul Chambers, and Albert "Tootie" Heath) on his "Gingerbread Boy" (which would soon be recorded by Miles Davis) and "Project S" plus such standards as "All the Things You Are" and "On the Trail."

After Riverside closed up shop, Jimmy Heath went eight years before leading a record date again. However he did work fairly steadily as both a saxophonist and a writer, including with Art Farmer and Milt Jackson.

Joe Henderson One of the major new tenor saxophonists to emerge during the 1960s, Joe Henderson always had a forceful tone of his own, and the ability to improvise both inside (using chordal improvisation) and outside (freer explorations). He studied at Kentucky State College and Wayne State University, serving in the military (1960–62) before beginning his career. Henderson started out playing briefly with Jack McDuff, and then hooked up with Kenny Dorham, who believed in him, used him on his records, and helped get him signed to Blue Note. Henderson, who was a member of the Horace Silver Quintet during 1964–66, recorded frequently for Blue Note during this period, making five albums as a leader and appearing on many sessions as a sideman. The four-CD box **The Blue Note Years** (Blue Note 89287) is a sampling of his work for the label. Thirty-three of the 36 selections date from 1963–69, and 26 feature him as a sideman. But most of his fans will prefer to get the complete sessions instead.

Henderson's debut as a leader, ● **Page One** (Blue Note 84140), includes the original version of Kenny Dorham's "Blue Bossa" and Henderson's "Recorda Me." This classic quintet set with Dorham, McCoy Tyner, Butch Warren, and Pete LaRoca shows that Henderson, at 26, was already well into his prime. **Our Thing** (Blue Note 25647) has lesser-known material (all written by Henderson or Dorham) interpreted by a quintet with Dorham, Andrew Hill, bassist Eddie Khan, and LaRoca, with the playing up to the level of the previous set. **In 'N' Out** (Blue Note 29156) from 1964 has Dorham providing all the material for the group, which also includes McCoy Tyner, Richard Davis, and Elvin Jones, although once again, none of the tunes caught on. Because of the better songs, **Page One** gets the edge out of these Henderson-Dorham sets, but all three CDs are easily recommended, stretching the boundaries of hard bop.

Inner Urge (Blue Note 84189) is Henderson's first quartet outing (with Tyner, Bob Cranshaw, and Elvin Jones), and it consists of three of the tenor's songs (including "Isotope"), Duke Pearson's You Know I Care," and "Night and Day." The playing is typically brilliant throughout, but one can say that about all of the tenor's Blue Note dates. Henderson's final early Blue Note album as a leader, **Mode for Joe** (Blue Note 84227), features Henderson leading an all-star septet with Lee Morgan, Curtis Fuller, Bobby Hutcherson, Cedar Walton, Ron Carter, and Joe Chambers; best known among the songs are "A Mode for Joe" and "A Shade of Jade."

In 1967, Joe Henderson began an eight-year association with the Milestone label that has been reissued in full on the eight-CD set **The Milestone Years** (Milestone 4413), which is reviewed in the next chapter. Henderson's initial release for the label was **The Kicker** (Original Jazz Classics 465), which is very much a continuation of the type of adventurous music that he had been recording for Blue Note. Joined by trumpeter Mike Lawrence, Grachan Moncur III, Kenny Barron, Ron Carter, and Louis Hayes,

Henderson performs such numbers as "Mamacita," "Chelsea Bridge," "If," "Without a Song," and "Nardis" with fresh ideas and dynamic solos.

Red Holloway   A highly appealing tenor saxophonist who later in his career would double on alto, Red Holloway has a big and joyous tone that fits perfectly well in bop, soul jazz, blues, R&B, and commercial settings. He began his career playing in Chicago with Gene Wright's big band (1943–46), and after serving in the army, he worked with Roosevelt Sykes (1948), Nat Towles (1949–50), and with his own quartet throughout the 1950s, often backing top blues and R&B acts. Holloway gained some fame in the jazz world when he worked with Jack McDuff's band during 1963–65 alongside George Benson.

Holloway led four albums of his own for Prestige during this period, three of which are available. **Legends of Acid Jazz** (Prestige 24199) reissues his first (**The Burner**) and fourth (**Red Soul**) sets on one CD. The earlier session is the more interesting of the two, for in addition to Holloway, there are fine solos from the bluesy guitarist Eric Gale and organist John Patton; "Crib Theme" and "The Burner" are both over ten minutes long. The **Red Soul** album is also excellent, teaming Holloway with Benson and either organist Dr. Lonnie Smith or pianist Norman Simmons for some solid soul jazz. **Brother Red** (Prestige 24141) has the seven songs from **Cookin' Together** with Holloway using the members of the Jack McDuff Quintet, three pieces from a McDuff date in which the lead voices are backed by an orchestra arranged by Benny Golson, and a selection from a sampler. The material varies a bit, but the blues and the uptempo pieces (especially "This Can't Be Love") feature the underrated saxophonist in top form.

Willis "Gator" Jackson   Willis Jackson successfully reinvented himself as a top soul jazz tenor saxophonist in 1959, having previously been known for his honking and squealing R&B records. He recorded an extensive series of recordings for Prestige during 1959–68 that are gradually being reissued.

Gentle Gator (Prestige 24158) is a change of pace for it consists of ballads taken from four of Gator's Prestige and Moodsville albums of 1961–62. Jackson mostly sticks close to the melodies on such songs as "Estrellita," "Girl of My Dreams," "Home," and "They Didn't Believe Me," and although there is a sameness of mood in this restrained set, the music is quite pleasing and warm. **At Large** (Prestige 24243) is a sampling of Jackson's work from 1962–68, digging into such unlikely material as "Arrivederci Roma," "Sometimes I Feel Like a Motherless Child," the boogaloo "Florence of Arabia," "I Left My Heart in San Francisco," and "By the Time I Get to Phoenix."

During 1963–64, Jackson's quintet featured the young guitarist Pat Azzara, who would later become known as Pat Martino. **Gravy** (Prestige 25254) combines the two former LPs **Grease 'N' Gravy** and **The Good Life** with Jackson and Martino joined by organist Carl Wilson, trumpeter Frank Robinson, and drummer Joe Hadrick; occasionally Leonard Gaskin is added on bass. The **Grease** set has quite a few fine grooves, while **The Good Life** is weighed down a bit by the pop standards. Still, the music has plenty of spirit. **Nuter'n Like Thuther'n** (Prestige 24265) reissues a pair of Jackson's LPs (1963's **More Gravy** and 1964's **Boss Shoutin'**) by the same personnel, with Sam Jones or George Tucker added on bass. Among the tunes from this underrated band are "Pool Shark," "Stuffin'," "Fiddlin'," "Shoutin'," and a boogalooish "St. Louis Blues." **With Pat Martino** (Prestige 24181) dates from March 21, 1964, a night when the Willis Jackson quintet recorded no less than four LPs. Two of them are reissued in full on this CD, and although the 19-year-old guitarist gets second billing, Gator is the main star throughout the program of basic material, standards, ballads, and blues.

Willis Jackson's slightly later mid-1960s recordings have not been reissued on CD yet, but most are in a similar vein, featuring Butch Cornell, Carl Wilson or Trudy Pitts on organ, with Vincent Corrao or Bill Jennings on guitar.

Clifford Jordan   Clifford Jordan's tone became increasingly individual as the 1960s progressed. He played regularly with Kenny Dorham (1961–62) and Max Roach (1962–64), was a part of the famous Charles Mingus Sextet that toured Europe in 1964, and worked as a leader after his return home. He led three Jazzland dates in 1961 of which only **Bearcat** (Original Jazz Classics 494) has been reissued on CD. An excellent showcase for the tenor, Jordan is accompanied by Cedar Walton, bassist Teddy Smith, and drummer J.C. Moses on five of his originals, Tom McIntosh's "Malice Toward None," and "How Deep Is the Ocean." From 1965, **These Are My Roots** (Koch 8522) is a rather unusual album, a tribute to folk singer Leadbelly. The results are more successful than one might expect. Jordan performs nine of Leadbelly's originals (including "Goodnight Irene"), turning the music into jazz without lessening the impact of the melodies or their folk roots. He is assisted by trumpeter Roy Burrowes, Julian Priester, Richard Davis, and Albert "Tootie" Heath on most of the selections while the fine young singer Sandra Douglass is excellent on "Take this Hammer" and "Black Girl." This set is certainly a surprise success.

Rahsaan Roland Kirk   An incredible musician, Roland Kirk (he added "Rahsaan" to his name in the mid-1960s) was almost too talented for other players to deal with; a few even wrote him off as gimmicky without listening closely to the miraculous things he could do. Able to play credibly in any style from bop/hard bop (where he showed the influence of Johnny Griffin) to New Orleans jazz (on clarinet), Illinois Jacquet–type jump music, and free jazz à la John Coltrane, able to play three instruments at once, and a master of circular breathing, Kirk was on his own level. He really came into his own during 1961–67 when he recorded some of his finest albums.

Kirk's Work (Original Jazz Classics 459) teams Rahsaan with organist Jack McDuff, bassist Joe Benjamin, and Art Taylor on such songs as "Three for Dizzy," "Makin' Whoopee," a flute feature on "Funk Underneath," and a torrid workout on stritch and manzello on "Skater's Waltz."

Later in 1961, Kirk signed with Mercury, which would be his main label until he spent a year with Limelight (1964–65). All of his recordings for those two labels (and Mercury's subsidiary EmArcy) are on the remarkable ten-CD set ◉ **The Complete Mercury Recordings of Roland Kirk** (Mercury 846 630). In addition to his nine albums plus numerous alternate takes, this box has Kirk's sideman appearances with Quincy Jones, Tubby Hayes, and organist Eddie Baccus. Fortunately, many of Rahsaan's Mercury and Limelight albums are also available individually. **We Free Kings** (Mercury 826 455) has Kirk playing tenor, manzello, stritch, and flute (sometimes as many as three at once) on such numbers as "Three for the Festival," "Moon Song," and "Blues for Alice," and as with many of Rahsaan's Mercury dates, it is mostly straightahead jazz. In its CD reissue, **Domino** (Mercury 534 445), which was originally split

between an excellent quartet date with a trio led by Wynton Kelly and a session that has Kirk's working band (which at the time included Andrew Hill), has been greatly expanded with the addition of many alternate takes and a "new" session with Herbie Hancock. Probably the best buy short of acquiring the ten-CD set of Kirk during this era is **Rip, Rig, and Panic/Now Please Don't You Cry, Beautiful Edith** (EmArcy 832164), which combines two former LPs on one CD. **Rip, Rig and Panic** matches Kirk with Jaki Byard (who shared Rahsaan's knowledge of all jazz styles), Richard Davis, and Elvin Jones, and the result is one of Kirk's greatest sets. "No Tonic Pres," "Once in Awhile," "From Bechet, Byas and Fats," and "Slippery, Hippery, Flippery" are quite memorable. **Now Please Don't You Cry, Beautiful Edith** was originally made for Verve (so it is not on the Mercury box), and it has Kirk with the Lonnie Smith trio (Smith, normally an organist, sticks to piano) on a fine all-around if obscure session that includes "Stompin' Ground," "It's a Grand Night for Swinging," and "Alfie."

Also not on the Mercury box is **I Talk with the Spirits** (Verve 558076), which puts the focus on Kirk's very expressive flute playing (including on "Serenade to a Cuckoo," "My Ship," and "Django"), **Gifts and Messages** (Jazz House 606), which is a live set from the famous Ronnie Scott's club in 1964 (showing how Kirk sounded live in concert during this era), and **Here Comes the Whistleman** (Label M 5720). The latter, cut for Atlantic in 1965, has Rahsaan joined by Jaki Byard or Lonnie Smith on piano, Major Holley on bass, and drummer Charles Crosby; best is a Kirk-Byard duet on "I Wished on the Moon."

Here Comes the Whistleman was a one-shot recorded for Atlantic. In 1967, Kirk officially signed with the label. While his Mercury/EmArcy/Limelight dates usually found him in conventional settings, his Atlantics would be much more eclectic. Kirk's official debut for the label, **The Inflated Tear** (Atlantic/Rhino 75207), is actually fairly straightahead (performed with pianist Ron Burton, bassist Steve Novosel, and drummer Jimmy Hopps), but Kirk expands his cache of instruments to include (in addition to tenor, manzello, stritch, and flute) clarinet, flexaphone, English horn, tonette, whistles, and a siren. "The Black and Crazy Blues," "Creole Love Call," and "A Handful of Fives" are among the highlights of this typically colorful program.

Yusef Lateef   One of the most open-minded of musicians coming out of the bebop era, Yusef Lateef spent 1962–64 as an important member of the Cannonball Adderley Sextet, where his brilliant playing on tenor, flute, and oboe helped make this into Adderley's finest group. Lateef recorded as a leader for several labels in the 1960s, including New Jazz, Impulse, and (starting in 1967) Atlantic. **Eastern Sounds** (Original Jazz Classics 612) has Lateef in 1961 joined by Barry Harris, bassist Ernie Farrow, and drummer Lex Humphries on a wide-ranging set that includes his classic rendition of the "Love Theme from Spartacus" (which is taken on oboe), "Blues for the Orient," and "The Plum Blossom." **Into Something** (Original Jazz Classics 700) features Lateef, Harris, bassist Herman Wright, and Elvin Jones playing some straightahead tunes (including "When You're Smiling" and "You've Changed") and more exotic songs, displaying Lateef's great versatility.

Lateef's Impulse recordings of 1963–66 are among the finest of his career, making it regretful that **Jazz Around the World** (Impulse 56), **1984** (Impulse 84), **A Flat, G Flat and C** (Impulse 9117), and **The Golden Flute** (Impulse 9125) are out of print. ◐ **Live at Pep's** (Impulse 134) features Lateef at his best. He performs with a quintet in 1965 also featuring trumpeter Richard Williams, pianist Mike Nock, bassist Ernie Farrow, and drummer James Black, switching between tenor, oboe, flute, and (on the more exotic pieces), shenai and argol. Whether it be Leonard Feather's "Twelve Tone Blues," "See See Rider" (a perfect feature for the leader's oboe), or the adventurous "The Magnolia Triangle," everything works on this set. **Live at Pep's Vol. 2** (Impulse 547 961) is taken from the same engagement and is of the same quality, highlighted by "I Remember Clifford," a lengthy version of "Delilah," and "Brother John."

In contrast to his earlier work, Lateef's recordings for Atlantic tend to be erratic as he stretched far beyond jazz (a word he detested) to include pop, soul, R&B, spiritual, and world music, some of it more successfully than others. **The Complete Yusef Lateef** from 1967 was his debut for the label and one of his strongest Atlantic albums. Joined by pianist Hugh Lawson, Cecil McBee, and drummer Roy Brooks, Lateef's music ranges from blues ("In the Evening") and boogaloo riffs to New Orleans rhythms and the soulful spiritual "Rosalie." As usual, Lateef displays endless potential, hinting at his many great skills throughout this worthy project.

Hank Mobley   Hank Mobley spent a short and not-too-fulfilling period as a member of the Miles Davis Quintet (1961–62). He was unable to fill the huge shoes of John Coltrane, and his playing made Davis wish he had Sonny Rollins. Fortunately, Mobley's solo career was much more successful, particularly as heard in his long string of high-quality and stimulating Blue Note albums. Alfred Lion appreciated Mobley so he recorded the tenor often, knowing that the results would be consistently exciting hard bop.

Workout (Blue Note 84080) from 1961 is one of Mobley's best-known recordings. An all-star quintet that includes Grant Green, Wynton Kelly, Paul Chambers, and Philly Joe Jones stretches out on four catchy Mobley originals, "The Best Things in Life Are Free" and "Three Coins in the Fountain." The music is played with a great deal of enthusiasm, and these young greats really dig into the music. **No Room for Squares** (Blue Note 24539) from 1963 finds Mobley permanently altering his sound a bit, displaying a darker and harder tone influenced by John Coltrane. Teamed with Lee Morgan, Andrew Hill, bassist John Ore, and Philly Joe Jones, Mobley plays four of his originals and two songs by Morgan plus a pair of alternate takes. Although none of the tunes caught on as standards, the solos are quite colorful and adventurous.

By 1965 when four of the six selections on **The Turnaround** (Blue Note 24540) were recorded (the other two are from 1963), Hank Mobley had developed into a particularly skillful songwriter. Mobley's songs on this set ("Pat 'N' Chat," "Third Time Around," "Hank's Waltz," "The Turnaround," "Straight Ahead," and "My Sin") often utilize unconventional lengths including 44-, 20-, or 50-bar choruses rather than the standard 32. Mobley is joined on this occasion by Freddie Hubbard, Barry Harris, Paul Chambers, and Billy Higgins. **Dippin'** (Blue Note 46511) has Mobley, Lee Morgan, Harold Mabern, bassist Larry Ridley, and Billy Higgins playing four obscure tunes by the tenor, the appealing "Recado Bossa Nova," and "I See Your Face Before Me." **A Caddy for Daddy** (Blue Note 84230) features Mobley, Morgan, Curtis Fuller, McCoy Tyner, Bob Cranshaw, and Higgins interpreting four more Mobley songs plus Wayne Shorter's "Venus di Mildew." **A Slice of the Top** (Blue Note 33582) is unusual for a Hank Mobley session because this 1966 date features an octet playing in the style of Miles Davis's "Birth of the Cool" nonet. Duke

Pearson supplied the arrangements for an ensemble that adds Kiane Zawadi's euphonium and Howard Johnson's tuba to a lineup of musicians that include Morgan, James Spaulding, Tyner, Workman, and Higgins.

The year 1967 was the last great year for Blue Note, and Hank Mobley came through with three more fine albums. **Third Season** (Blue Note 97506) was not originally issued until 1980, which accounts for its obscurity. Mobley, Morgan, Spaulding, Cedar Walton, Walter Booker, and Higgins are joined on some numbers by a wild card, the post-bop Canadian guitarist Sonny Greenwich. The music is mostly hard bop with a gospelish piece ("Give Me that Feeling"), hints of modal music, and three adventurous solos from Greenwich. The most surprising aspect to **Hi Voltage** (Blue Note 84273) is that none of Mobley's originals (which include "Bossa DeLuxe," "Flirty Gerty," and the ballad "No More Goodbye") caught on. Perhaps 1967 was a little too late for the type of catchy hard bop tunes that Mobley wrote to get much exposure and become new standards. Mobley plays as well as usual in a sextet with Blue Mitchell, Jackie McLean, pianist John Hicks, Bob Cranshaw, and the always-busy Higgins. **Far Away Lands** (Blue Note 84425), in addition to a song apiece from Donald Byrd and Jimmy Heath, has such infectious Mobley pieces as "A Dab of This and That," "No Argument," "The Hippity Hop," and "Bossa for Baby." Mobley and Byrd are joined by Walton, Ron Carter, and Higgins for yet another high-quality Hank Mobley Blue Note session, music that throughout the 1960s helped to define the modern mainstream.

Brew Moore   By 1961, Lester Young was dead, Allan Eager and Paul Quinichette were retired, and such Pres-followers as Stan Getz, Zoot Sims, and Al Cohn had developed their own sounds. However, Brew Moore stuck to his musical guns, still closely emulating Young, and seeing no reason to change his style in the slightest. He never found much fame, moving to Copenhagen in 1961. **Svinget 14** (Black Lion 760 164) features Moore in 1962 accompanied by a strong European rhythm section (pianist Bent Axen, the teenaged bassist Niels-Henning Orsted Pedersen, and drummer William Schiopffe) plus (on two songs apiece) altoist Sahib Shihab, the great baritonist Lars Gullin, and vibraphonist Louis Hjulmand. Surprisingly, six of the eight songs are originals by members, but the music is primarily West Coast–style

cool jazz other than some of the playing on "The Monster" by the fiery Shihab.

During his decade in Europe, Brew Moore did not record any studio dates, and all that exists of him after 1962 are four albums' worth of live sessions, two from 1965. **If I Had You** (Steeple Chase 36016) is a quartet date with pianist Atli Bjorn, bassist Benny Nielsen, and drummer William Schiopffe. Moore sounds in prime form on four swing-oriented tunes (including Fats Waller's "Zonky") and a short rendition of "Blue Monk." **I Should Care** (Steeple Chase 36019) is from two weeks later and is slightly more exciting, featuring the same quartet on "Brews Blues," "I Should Care," "Manny's Tune" (based on "Indiana"), and a spirited version of "In a Mellotone."

Oliver Nelson   Oliver Nelson began the year 1961 by recording his greatest album, ❶ **The Blues and the Abstract Truth** (Impulse 154). It would be difficult to top the lineup of musicians: Nelson on tenor and alto, Eric Dolphy doubling on alto and flute, Freddie Hubbard, baritonist George Barrow in the ensembles, Bill Evans, Paul Chambers, and Roy Haynes. The superior Nelson compositions include a song previously recorded by Eddie "Lockjaw" Davis that became a standard ("Stolen Moments") plus the exuberant "Hoe Down" (based on "I Got Rhythm") and "Yearnin'." The arrangements are inventive, and the soloists sound quite inspired, with Dolphy usually taking honors. A classic.

During 1959–61, Nelson recorded a series of small group dates for New Jazz, Prestige, and Moodsville. **Straight Ahead** (Original Jazz Classics 099) finds Nelson showing a lot of musical courage by sharing the frontline of his quintet date with Eric Dolphy. With fine support from pianist Richard Wyands, George Duvivier, and Roy Haynes, Nelson and Dolphy battle it out on five of the leader's originals and Milt Jackson's "Ralph's New Blues." Having rather strong musical abilities himself along with his own sly wit, Nelson proves able to hold his own with the explosive Dolphy, no easy feat. In comparison, **Main Stem** (Original Jazz Classics 1803) is conventional, but it is also fun. This set with Joe Newman (who takes some exciting solos), Hank Jones, Duvivier, Charlie Persip, and Ray Barretto has a jam session feel with the sextet swinging four Nelson tunes, "Main Stem" and "Tangerine."

Afro-American Sketches (Original Jazz Classics 1819) from the fall of 1961 was Nelson's first big band date as a leader. This set pays tribute to the history of blacks in America in a seven-part suite including such movements as "Jungleaire," "Emancipation Blues," "Going Up North," and "Freedom Dance." Nelson, Joe Newman, and flutist Jerry Dodgion are the key soloists.

Although Oliver Nelson was a strong player, he was in greater demand as an arranger. In the 1960s, he wrote for the big band albums of Jimmy Smith, Wes Montgomery, and Billy Taylor among others, and displayed a personal and distinctive writing style. Even his own albums focused more on his writing than his playing. In fact, on his **More Blues and the Abstract Truth** (Impulse 212) from 1964, Nelson does not even play. Nelson contributed three of the eight originals, and all of the arrangements for a group that includes such notables as Thad Jones, Phil Woods, Pepper Adams, pianist Roger Kellaway, and Ben Webster (who is on two songs). The music is excellent, but falls short of its predecessor. **Sound Pieces** (Impulse 103) from 1966 is a bit unusual. Nelson leads a 20-piece big band on three of his interesting (if not overly memorable) compositions, but the reasons to acquire this disc are the five numbers on which Nelson is heard exclusively on soprano sax. Showcased in a quartet with pianist Steve Kuhn, Ron Carter, and Grady Tate, Nelson shows that he was one of the finest players on what was really his third-best instrument.

In 1967, Oliver Nelson recorded a tribute to the late John F. Kennedy, **The Kennedy Dream** (last out on the LP Impulse 9144). Later in the year he moved to Los Angeles where he became a very busy arranger/composer for television and movies.

Sal Nistico   A hard-charging tenor saxophonist with an exciting style, Sal Nistico is best remembered for being the star soloist with Woody Herman's Young Thundering Herd during 1962–65. He started on alto, switching to tenor in 1956 when he was 18, playing with R&B bands for a few years. During 1959–60 he was with the Jazz Brothers, a group co-led by Chuck and Gap Mangione with whom he made his recording debut. **Heavyweights/Comin' On Up** (Milestone 47098) has all of the music from Nistico's first two albums as a leader (except for a version of "Just Friends" that was left out), dating from 1961–62. Nistico is joined by Barry Harris on both quintet sets, with Nat Adderley on **Heavyweights**,

and trumpeter Sal Amico on the other date. The two sets are both quite boppish with Nistico mixing together basic originals with bop standards.

After leaving Woody Herman in 1965, Sal Nistico had a couple of stints with Count Basie (playing well, but not making that strong an impression), returning to Herman's band in 1968.

Bill Perkins   With the decline of the West Coast cool jazz scene, most of the style's top players became studio musicians in Los Angeles. Bill Perkins was a bit different from the other players in that he also doubled as a recording engineer. He only led one significant set during this period, **Quietly There** (Original Jazz Classics 1776). Switching between tenor, baritone, bass clarinet, and flute, Perk stars on one of the first full-length tribute albums to film composer Johnny Mandel. On such classic ballads as "Emily," "A Time for Love," and "The Shadow of Your Smile," plus some of Mandel's lesser-known but worthy medium-tempo tunes, Perk is assisted by pianist Victor Feldman (also heard on vibes and a cheesy-sounding organ), guitarist John Pisano, Red Mitchell, and Larry Bunker.

Sonny Rollins   When Sonny Rollins unexpectedly dropped out of active performing in 1959 at the height of his fame and influence, there was much speculation as to his motives, including theories about health problems, his boredom with jazz, or his difficulty with dealing with the rise of John Coltrane. Actually he dropped out mostly to recharge his batteries, practice more (including late at night on New York's Williamsburg Bridge), and to get his priorities in order. When Rollins returned in early 1962 (leading a pianoless quartet featuring guitarist Jim Hall), many observers were surprised that his playing was at first unchanged from earlier years. However, Rollins's ears were quite open, and soon his improvising had opened up to the point where it sometimes crossed over into the avant-garde. Intrigued by Ornette Coleman's music, Rollins even used Don Cherry and Billy Higgins in his group during part of 1962–63.

During 1962–64, Rollins recorded exclusively for RCA. All of the music has been reissued on the six-CD set ◉ **The Complete RCA Victor Recordings** (RCA 68675). Included are the albums **The Bridge** (Bluebird 68518), **What's New** (Bluebird 66243), **Our Man in Jazz** (RCA 37211), **Sonny Meets Hawk** (RCA 37212),

Now's the Time (RCA 37213), and **The Standard Sonny Rollins** (RCA 68681), plus three selections originally included in the sampler **3 for Jazz**, and 11 alternate takes only previously released on the French album **The Alternative Rollins**. **The Bridge**, Rollins's comeback album, is considered a classic. Rollins, Jim Hall, Bob Cranshaw (who became Sonny's bassist for much of the next 40 years), and drummer Ben Riley play four standards (including "Without a Song" and "God Bless the Child") and two originals with fire and creativity. **What's New** has Rollins augmenting his quartet with Candido on conga, and the calypso "Brownskin Girl" adds an effective vocal ensemble; best is a lengthy version of "If Ever I Would Leave You." **Our Man in Jazz** has Rollins holding his own with Cherry, Higgins, and either Henry Grimes or Bob Cranshaw on bass in 1963. Although the six selections (including "Oleo," "Doxy," and "I Could Write a Book") are veteran standards, Rollins's improvising (which is actually more abstract than Cherry's) shows that he was quite aware of free jazz, and could have been one of the giants of the avant-garde if he had stuck to free-form playing.

The CD reissue **Sonny Meets Hawk** adds three of the numbers with Cherry from **Our Man in Jazz** as "bonus" cuts. The other six selections are from the only session that Rollins shared with his idol Coleman Hawkins, and it is definitely a bizarre encounter. Not wanting to meet Hawkins on the elder tenor's turf, Rollins plays as free as possible on the standards, often indulging in strange sound explorations. Hawkins, who was confused at first, quickly recovers (he had pianist Paul Bley as an ally), and plays in his own timeless style, which was modern in any case. But due to Rollins's eccentric playing, rather than being a classic album, this is mostly just a novelty and a curiosity. **Now's the Time** mostly has Rollins playing rapid, concise, and sometimes incomplete-sounding versions of familiar tunes with Herbie Hancock, Ron Carter, and drummer Roy McCurdy; Thad Jones makes a couple of guest appearances. **The Standard Sonny Rollins** from 1964 has either Hancock or Jim Hall with Rollins, and is in a similar vein. But the best way to acquire this intriguing music is to get the six-CD box and hear the music in chronological order.

During 1965–66, Rollins led four albums for Impulse which in general are more tightly focused than his later RCA sets. That said, **There Will Never Be Another You** (Impulse 120) unfortunately has erratic recording quality. This set features Rollins and his quintet (Tommy Flanagan, Bob Cranshaw, and both Billy Higgins and Mickey Roker on drums) playing at an outdoor concert in the rain. Rollins strolls around and is therefore off-mike much of the time, which is a pity because he was playing quite well, particularly during a 16-minute version of "There Will Never Be Another You." **Sonny Rollins on Impulse** (Impulse 223) has the joyous calypso "Hold 'Em Joe" and four unusual versions of standards (including "Blue Room" and "Three Little Words") in which the rhythms are more important than the actual melodies. Rollins is assisted by Ray Bryant, bassist Walter Booker, and Mickey Roker. **Sonny Rollins Plays Alfie** (Impulse 224) has the tenor playing his themes for the film *Alfie* with a ten-piece band arranged by Oliver Nelson. The music stands by itself without the movie, and Rollins is in exuberant form, particularly during "On Impulse" and "Alfie's Theme."

East Broadway Rundown (Impulse 161) from 1966 has a lengthy and sometimes wandering, but always fascinating title cut with Rollins playing very freely with Freddie Hubbard, Jimmy Garrison, and Elvin Jones. The other two selections, Rollins's memorable original "Blessing in Disguise" and his classic ballad statement on "We Kiss in a Shadow," are by the trio without Hubbard. Just 36 at the time, Sonny Rollins soon decided to retire for the third time, this time for six years. Although he was missed, there were so many other events occurring during the 1966–71 period that Rollins's retirement was not as newsworthy as his 1959–61 disappearance, and he was soon in danger of being forgotten altogether.

Wayne Shorter   As both a tenor saxophonist and a composer, Wayne Shorter has been an innovator from nearly the start of his career. His solos (especially by 1963) are abstract, avoid stating the obvious (often hinting at more than it says), and follow their own logic. The same can be said for his compositions, which are mostly pretty difficult to play and unconventional, but are often quite memorable and haunting. Shorter was one of the first jazz musicians to be impossible to classify accurately. Although he came out of the hard bop tradition, he stood apart from hard bop from the start, yet even at his freest he never seemed to be part of the avant-garde jazz movement either. He was one of the pioneers in what would later be called post-bop, music that is both modern and impossible to neatly pinpoint.

Shorter spent 1959–63 as the musical director of Art Blakey's Jazz Messengers, soloing next to either Lee Morgan or Freddie Hubbard. He led three albums for Vee-Jay during this period of which **Wayning Moments Plus** (Koch 8549) was the last. For this advanced hard bop date with Hubbard, pianist Eddie Higgins, bassist Jymie Merritt, and drummer Marshall Thompson, the original eight songs are augmented by seven alternate takes. Highlights include "Black Orpheus," "Moon of Manakoora," and "All or Nothing at All." The music is excellent, but conservative compared to what was to come.

In 1964, Shorter began recording for Blue Note. He would cut 11 albums for the label as a leader in the next six years, eight during 1964–67. The recordings on a whole are considered his most significant body of work. **Night Dreamer** (Blue Note 84173) is a strong beginning, with Shorter joined by Lee Morgan, McCoy Tyner, Reggie Workman, and Elvin Jones. The quintet performs five of Shorter's originals (including the brooding title cut, the melancholy ballad "Virgo" and "Black Nile"), plus "Oriental Folk Song." ● **Juju** (Blue Note 46514) has the same group without Morgan, and introduces such Shorter songs as "Juju," "House of Jade," "Yes or No," and "Mahjong." Although being joined by John Coltrane's rhythm section (with Jimmy Garrison's predecessor Reggie Workman on bass) may make this seem like a Coltranish date, Shorter's quirky originals, and his more melancholy sound are quite distinctive.

In September 1964, Wayne Shorter joined the Miles Davis Quintet. His playing and his writing ensured that Davis's group permanently moved beyond hard bop; he would be an invaluable asset for the next six years. Meanwhile, he continued recording unique gems for Blue Note. ● **Speak No Evil** (Blue Note 46509) has Shorter joined by two fellow sidemen from Davis's group (Herbie Hancock and Ron Carter) plus Freddie Hubbard and Elvin Jones. The six Shorter originals are all quite memorable with "Infant Eyes," "Fee-Fi-Fo-Fum," and "Speak No Evil" being particularly outstanding. With all of this activity, **The Soothsayer** (Blue Note 84443) was lost in the shuffle, and went unreleased until the late 1970s despite its high quality. Shorter, Hubbard, James Spaulding, Tyner, Carter, and Williams perform five Shorter songs (best known is "Lady Day") and an adaptation of "Valse Triste." **Etcetera** (Blue Note 33581), a quartet outing with Hancock, Cecil McBee, and Joe Chambers, had a similar fate, not coming out until 1980

despite its inventive versions of "Penelope," "Toy Tune," and Gil Evans's "Barracuda."

The All Seeing Eye (Blue Note 24543), Wayne Shorter's sixth Blue Note album as a leader in 18 months, is full of controlled freedom, drama, and dynamic solos from a group consisting of Shorter, Hubbard, Spaulding, Grachan Moncur III, Hancock, Carter, and Chambers, with Wayne's brother trumpeter Alan Shorter guesting on one song. **Adam's Apple** (Blue Note 46403), a quartet set with Hancock, Workman, and Chambers, is most notable for introducing Shorter's most famous original, "Footprints," but it also contains fine moments on the other songs, which include "El Gaucho," "Chief Crazy Horse," and "Adam's Apple." From 1967, **Schizophrenia** (Blue Note 32096) wraps up this period for Shorter, introducing six more originals (including "Tom Thumb" and "Miyako") interpreted by a sextet with Curtis Fuller, Spaulding, Hancock, Ron Carter, and Chambers.

It would be two years before Wayne Shorter's next set as a leader, and the music world would be a different place by then, with him featured on soprano rather than tenor. Shorter had helped to define the post-bop music scene, and although further accomplishments lay ahead, it would be difficult for him to consistently reach the high levels of his classic series of Blue Note recordings.

Lucky Thompson   Although Lucky Thompson (who by the early 1960s was doubling on soprano sax) was playing quite well throughout the '60s, he was largely overlooked by much of the jazz world. He lived in France during 1956–62, and then came back to the United States for a period. Four of his records from 1961–65 are currently available on three CDs. **Lord, Lord, Am I Ever Going to Know** (Candid 79035) from 1961 was originally unissued with the exception of the title cut; the Candid label went under before the album could come out. Thompson is joined by pianist Martial Solal, bassist Peter Trunk, and Kenny Clarke on most selections, which are straightahead originals by Lucky. Most unusual is "Choose Your Own" (which has Thompson playing unaccompanied solos on both tenor and soprano) and an opening spoken monolog from March 20, 1968. The latter has Lucky describing some of his philosophy, and telling the public to ignore hype and decide for themselves what music they like best. Recorded in 1963, **Lucky Strikes** (Original Jazz Classics 194) features Thompson playing four songs apiece on tenor and soprano, interpreting two standards and six originals in a quartet with Hank Jones, Richard Davis, and Connie Kay. **Happy Days** (Prestige 24144) has all of the music from two of Thompson's albums. The earlier set, released originally on Moodsville, emphasizes ballads as Thompson interprets eight Jerome Kern melodies plus his own original "No More." Highlights include "Look for the Silver Lining," "Who," and "They Didn't Believe Me." The second session is a bit offbeat, a six-song tribute to a new singer of the period, Barbra Streisand. "People" is a throwaway, but otherwise most of the songs are veteran standards including a rare medium-tempo rendition of "As Time Goes By."

But Lucky Thompson did not gain much recognition during his six-year stay in the United States, and in 1968 he returned to Europe.

Stanley Turrentine   After leaving the Max Roach Quintet in 1960, Stanley Turrentine married organist Shirley Scott. In addition to working in a group with his wife, Turrentine recorded quite prolifically for Blue Note during 1961–67, cutting 18 albums as a leader, and appearing on a wide variety of sessions as a sideman.

Turrentine (who picked up the nickname of Mr. T.) always sounded distinctive, and he was heard at his best whenever he could stretch out on bluesy material. **Comin' Your Way** (Blue Note 84065), which was not originally released until the 1980s, has Turrentine and his brother Tommy Turrentine (who due to erratic health largely dropped out of the scene a few years later) making for a fine team with the Horace Parlan Trio on such tunes as "My Girl Is Just Enough Woman for Me" and "Then I'll Be Tired of You." The double CD **Up at Minton's** (Blue Note 28885) documents an exciting live set featuring Mr. T. with Grant Green, Parlan, bassist George Tucker, and drummer Al Harewood. On six standards and two blues, Turrentine shows how strong a soloist he already was at this early point in his career. **Z.T.'s Blues** (Blue Note 84424) has Turrentine and Green assisted by Tommy Flanagan, Paul Chambers, and Art Taylor, featuring the tenor caressing such melodies as "More than You Know," "The Lamp Is Low," and "I Wish I Knew." **That's Where It's At** (Blue Note 84096) has Turrentine teaming up with the Les McCann Trio, and the results (as heard on "Soft Pedal Blues," "Light Blue," and "Smile Stacey") are as soulful as one would expect.

Recorded in 1963, **Never Let Me Go** (Blue Note 84129) and ● **A Chip Off the Old Block** (Blue Note 84129) both team Turrentine with his wife Shirley Scott in a quintet. While the former has Ray Barretto helping out on conga, the latter is particularly special because trumpeter Blue Mitchell inspires the other musicians. It also helps that the repertoire includes such stimulating songs as "One o'Clock Jump," "Blues in Hoss' Flat," and "Spring Can Really Hang You Up the Most." While virtually all of Turrentine's Blue Note albums are well worth acquiring, this one is a standout.

Skipping to 1965, **Joyride** (Blue Note 46100) has Turrentine as the star throughout a big band session arranged by Oliver Nelson. "River's Invitation," "Little Sheri," and "A Taste of Honey" are highlights even if the all-star sidemen are restricted to ensembles. **Easy Walker** (Blue Note 29908) mostly features Turrentine, McCoy Tyner, Bob Cranshaw, and Mickey Roker playing some pop tunes (including "What the World Needs Now Is Love") and standards. The CD reissue adds four unrelated numbers from Turrentine and Tyner with bassist Gene Taylor and drummer Billy Cobham. Recorded in 1966, **The Spoiler** (Blue Note 53359) is a decent effort that could have been much more. Considering that the octet includes Tyner, Blue Mitchell, Julian Priester, James Spaulding, and Pepper Adams, arranged by Duke Pearson, one might have expected some challenging music. But instead Turrentine is the only significant soloist. Fortunately, he is in fine form on such songs as "When the Sun Comes Out," "You're Gonna Hear from Me," and even "Sunny," but this set could have been much more essential.

Due to this series of recordings and others that have not yet been reissued on CD, by 1967 Stanley Turrentine was one of the most popular tenor saxophonists in jazz.

Harold Vick   Harold Vick sometimes appeared in similar hard bop and soul jazz settings as Stanley Turrentine, but he was not quite as distinctive or accessible despite being a talented thick-toned tenor. His uncle Prince Robinson (who was most active in the 1920s) gave him a clarinet when he was 13, and three years later Vick switched to tenor. In the 1960s, Vick often played in soul jazz organ groups including with Jack McDuff, Jimmy McGriff, and Big John Patton.

Harold Vick only had one opportunity to lead a date for Blue Note, his 1963 debut **Steppin' Out** (Blue Note

52433). Vick is teamed with Blue Mitchell, Grant Green, Big John Patton, and drummer Ben Dixon on four blues pieces, a tricky original, and "Laura." The music lives up to expectations even if it contains no revelations. It does show that Harold Vick (who was 27 at the time) was a promising young tenor with a swinging style.

Baritonists

No new major baritone saxophonists emerged during the first half of the 1960s. Pepper Adams continued to rise in significance, while Gerry Mulligan's career stalled and Leo Parker had a brief comeback.

Pepper Adams   Baritonist Pepper Adams co-led a quintet with Donald Byrd through 1962, worked with Charles Mingus off and on until 1963, and joined the Thad Jones/Mel Lewis Orchestra in 1965. He recorded two gems during this era as a leader, both with trumpeter Thad Jones. **Plays Charles Mingus** (Fresh Sound 177) has Adams showcased in both a quintet and an octet, playing nine Mingus songs, most of which (such as "Song with Orange," "Portrait," and "Fables of Faubus") are rarely covered by other musicians. ● **Mean What You Say** (Original Jazz Classics 464) is a classic hard bop date with four of Jones's songs, two other originals, "Wives and Lovers," and a tongue-in-cheek version of

"Yes Sir, That's My Baby" being interpreted by a quintet also including Duke Pearson, Ron Carter, and Mel Lewis. The gruff-toned and forceful Adams is in particularly inspired form throughout this informal yet tight session.

Gerry Mulligan   During 1960–63, Gerry Mulligan led the Concert Jazz Band, one of the finest big bands in jazz, boasting a lineup that included Bob Brookmeyer, altoist Gene Quill, and drummer Mel Lewis. Its recordings have been largely neglected by the Verve label, with only its 1960 Village Vanguard appearance thus far being reissued on CD, although an upcoming Mosaic box set will be covering all of those valuable performances. On and off during 1962–64, Mulligan teamed up with Bob Brookmeyer in a new pianoless quartet also including bassist Bill Crow and drummer Gus Johnson (later Dave Bailey). While this group did not enjoy the commercial success of Mulligan's famous unit with Chet Baker or even his 1954 quartet with Brookmeyer, it resulted in some fine music. **Zurich 1962** (TCB 2092) has both Mulligan and Brookmeyer occasionally playing piano, but sounding at their best when they interact with each other on their horns; they had similar senses of humor. **And His Quartet** (RTE 1005) has the same group during the same European tour, this time broadcasting from France. Once again

TIMELINE 1964

The John Coltrane Quartet records **A Love Supreme**. • The "October Revolution" concerts organized by Bill Dixon take place in New York. • The Charles Mingus Sextet tours Europe. • Eric Dolphy dies. • Thelonious Monk is on the cover of *Time* magazine. • Chris McGregor and the Blue Notes flee from South Africa, settling in England. • The New York Art Quartet features Roswell Rudd and John Tchicai. • Charles Mingus is the hit of the 1964 Monterey Jazz Festival. • Lee Morgan's "The Sidewinder" becomes a hit. • Bud Powell returns to the United States. • Wes Montgomery signs with Verve. • Lambert, Hendricks, and Bavan break up. • Earl Hines's three concerts at New York's Little Theater start a major comeback. • Ben Webster moves to Copenhagen. • Louis Armstrong's "Hello Dolly" becomes a No. 1 pop hit. • Eddie Condon tours Japan, Australia, and New Zealand with an all-star group. • Lu Watters records for the first time since 1950, but his comeback is brief. • Chet Baker returns to the United States after a five-year absence. • Carla Bley and Michael Mantler form the Jazz Composers' Guild Orchestra, which a year later became the Jazz Composers' Orchestra. • Clark Terry and Bob Brookmeyer team up to co-lead a quintet. • Gary Burton joins the Stan Getz Quartet. • In Los Angeles, John Carter and Bobby Bradford form the New Art Jazz Ensemble. • Trummy Young leaves the Louis Armstrong All-Stars and moves to Hawaii, being succeeded by Big Chief Russell Moore. • Bobby Hackett's LP **Hello Louis** gives Steve Lacy a very rare chance to be heard in a Dixieland setting. • Pianist/organist/arranger Clare Fischer introduces "Pensativa." • Les Paul and Mary Ford are divorced. • Tony Scott records **Music for Zen Meditation** in Tokyo with a trio also including koto and shakuhachi. • Wayne Shorter joins the Miles Davis Quintet.

Mulligan and Brookmeyer play a lot of piano, and the two horns only interact on "Five Brothers," "Blueport," and a brief "Utter Chaos." But the wit and charm displayed by the lead voices (even on piano), and the heated trade-off on "Blueport" make this set worth acquiring. Recorded in 1963, **Night Lights** (Verve 534 442) has the quartet augmented by Art Farmer and Jim Hall for a rather relaxed program that emphasizes ballads.

This likable but nonessential set really served as the end of an era for Gerry Mulligan. One of the biggest jazz names of the 1950s, Mulligan slowed down after the breakup of the Concert Jazz Band. The evolution of jazz seemed to be passing him by. He recorded a couple of albums of jazzy versions of pop tunes for Mercury and Limelight in 1965 (**If You Can't Beat 'Em Join 'Em** and **Feelin' Good**), but other than a quintet record with Zoot Sims, he became less active for a few years.

Leo Parker   Leo Parker's career followed a path similar to Ike Quebec's. Like Quebec, Parker made a strong impression in the 1940s, wasted much of the '50s due to drug abuse, and made a short-lived comeback at the beginning of the '60s. Originally an altoist (recording with Coleman Hawkins in 1944), Parker switched to baritone to play with Billy Eckstine's big band (1944–46). His deep tone and robust style (which sometimes came close to crossing over to R&B) was featured with Dizzy Gillespie (1946) and Illinois Jacquet (1947–48). He also led sessions of his own for Savoy and Chess (1951–53), but his problems with heroin led to him slipping into obscurity.

In the fall of 1961, Leo Parker had a bit of a comeback, leading two albums for Blue Note. **Let Me Tell You 'Bout It** (Blue Note 84087) has the guttural baritonist joined by obscure players in a sextet, mostly performing a variety of hard swingers plus the gospel-ish funk of the title cut. **Rollin' with Leo** (Blue Note 84095), which was not released until the 1980s, is just as worthy, featuring Parker in a group with trumpeter Dave Burns and pianist Johnny Acea, sounding in prime form on jump tunes, ballads, and some basic blues.

But just like Ike Quebec, Leo Parker was unable to enjoy his comeback for long. Just four months after recording **Rollin' with Leo**, he died from a heart attack at the age of 36.

Pianists

Although the rise of Bill Evans and McCoy Tyner gave jazz pianists two more possible directions to take, in addition to the funky playing of Horace Silver and the free-form flights of Cecil Taylor, Bud Powell was still the dominant influence among modern jazz pianists during this period.

Walter Bishop, Jr.   A fine bop pianist, Walter Bishop, Jr., was the son of a songwriter. He worked early on with Art Blakey (1947–49), Miles Davis, and Charlie Parker's Quintet (off and on during 1951–54). After a period off the scene, Bishop returned in 1959, leading his own trio throughout the 1960s. **Milestones** (Black Lion 760109) from 1961 has the pianist, Jimmy Garrison, and drummer G.T. Hogan performing six standards (along with three alternate takes) in swinging fashion. **The Walter Bishop, Jr., Trio** (Original Jazz Classics 1896) is pretty definitive, for it has Bishop, bassist Butch Warren, and either Hogan or Jimmy Cobb on drums performing concise versions (all under four minutes) of 16 selections (a mixture of obscurities and standards), making every note count. This set gives listeners an excellent sampling of Walter Bishop's bop-oriented playing, along with a lot of fresh material that deserves to be revived.

Jaki Byard   Jaki Byard was a rather unusual pianist in that he could play quite credibly in any style, from stride and ragtime to swing, bop, and the freest explorations. Byard, who played with Maynard Ferguson's big band during 1959–61, gained his greatest recognition while with Charles Mingus on and off during 1962–65. As a leader, Byard recorded regularly for Prestige throughout the 1960s. These were typically eclectic affairs, with the pianist paying tribute to the past while looking ahead and being very aware of the latest musical innovations. Although the sets were never quite definitive "history of jazz" outings (the closest Byard came was on his earlier Candid release), each contains some unique and memorable moments. **Here's Jaki** (Original Jazz Classics 1874), a trio set with Ron Carter and Roy Haynes, features five complex Byard originals (including a 5/4 calypso and a tribute to Erroll Garner called "Garnerin' a Bit"), plus "Giant Steps" and a Gershwin medley. **Hi-Fly** (Original Jazz Classics 1879) has Byard with Carter and Pete LaRoca performing James P. Johnson's "Excerpts from Yamecraw," "Tillie Butterball," and songs by Randy Weston, George Shearing, and Thelonious

Monk. **Out Front** (Original Jazz Classics 1842), which is mostly from 1964, is a quintet set with Richard Williams and Booker Ervin that is more conventional, with the episodic "European Episode" being the most original performance. "When Sunny Gets Blue," which is the lone track from 1961, is a rare outing for Byard on alto sax.

Freedom Together (Original Jazz Classics 1898) not only has Byard on piano, but also celeste, electric piano, vibes, drums, and tenor sax. His tenor playing (best heard on "Just You, Just Me") is particularly excellent, while his piano solos show his usual diversity, hinting at 50 years of jazz styles. Richard Davis (on bass and cello) and Alan Dawson (heard on drums, tympani, and vibes) are major assets, although Junior Parker's two pompous vocals are a slight minus. **Sunshine of Your Soul** (Original Jazz Classics 1946) from 1967 may look like a commercial rock/pop record, but Byard is as adventurous as always, teaming up with David Izenzon and Elvin Jones on six of his diverse originals and "St. Louis Blues." No other pianist from the era had Byard's command of so many different jazz styles.

Sonny Clark   On November 13, 1961, Sonny Clark recorded what would be his final album as a leader, **Leapin' and Lopin'** (Blue Note 84091). A drug addict by this time, the pianist is nevertheless still heard in prime form leading a quintet also including Tommy Turrentine, Charlie Rouse, Butch Warren, and Billy Higgins, with Ike Quebec guesting on "Deep in a Dream." The original LP also included three little-known Clark originals and Butch Warren's "Eric Walks"; the CD reissue adds a fourth Clark song ("Zellmar's Delight") and Turrentine's "Midnight Mambo." Every Clark record is well worth getting, and this fine hard bop set is no exception.

Unfortunately, Sonny Clark never kicked drugs, and he died of a heart attack on January 13, 1963, when he was only 31, a major loss to jazz.

Chick Corea   Chick Corea (born Armando Corea) was one of the most promising young pianists on the scene in the mid-1960s. He began playing piano when he was four, considering Horace Silver and Bud Powell to be his main early influences. However, Corea always sounded original, even in his beginning days when he was exploring jazz's modern mainstream and Afro-Cuban jazz. He worked with Mongo Santamaria, Willie

Bobo (1962–63), Blue Mitchell (1964–66), Herbie Mann, and Stan Getz. Corea's debut as a leader from 1966 resulted in **Inner Space** (Atlantic 305). Actually, this reissue leaves out "This Is New" and "Tones for Joan's Bones" from the original album **Tones for Joan's Bones** (Vortex 2004), but adds four other selections, including two (highlighted by Corea's "Windows") from a Hubert Laws date of the period. Among the key sidemen during these advanced hard bop performances are Woody Shaw, Joe Farrell (on tenor and flute), bassist Steve Swallow, and flutist Laws. This served as a strong start to what would be a very significant career.

Victor Feldman   Victor Feldman was with Cannonball Adderley's quintet for six months during 1960–61, but otherwise spent the 1960s as a busy studio musician. In 1963, he had the opportunity to join Miles Davis's group, but other than making one record date with Davis and contributing the song "Seven Steps to Heaven," he turned down the offer, preferring to have a more lucrative career living in Los Angeles. Feldman recorded on an occasional basis as a leader during 1961–67 for World Pacific, Ava, Vee-Jay, and Pacific Jazz, but only his one Riverside set, **Merry Olde Soul** (Original Jazz Classics 402) has been reissued on CD. For that project, Feldman plays piano on five songs and vibes on four others (three have Hank Jones on piano), interacting with Sam Jones and Louis Hayes. The trio/quartet performs five mostly underplayed standards plus four of Feldman's originals in tasteful and swinging fashion. But for Victor Feldman, who had been playing music professionally since he was a youth in England in the mid-1940s, jazz would only be of secondary concern throughout his career.

Red Garland   Red Garland, who was so prolific on records during 1956–60, started out true to form with six albums cut as a leader for Prestige and Jazzland during 1961–62. **Soul Burnin'** (Original Jazz Classics 921) draws its material from three separate sessions from 1960–61, showcasing the pianist with two trios and a quintet with Oliver Nelson and Richard Williams; best are "Soul Burnin'," "A Little Bit of Basie," and "Green Dolphin Street." **Bright and Breezy** (Original Jazz Classics 265) is an excellent trio set with Sam Jones and drummer Charlie Persip that includes "I Ain't Got Nobody," "Blues in the Closet," and "Lil' Darlin'." **The Nearness of You** (Original Jazz Classics 1003) is a ballad-oriented program that has Garland (with bassist Larry Ridley and drummer Frank Gant) interpreting such tunes as "Why Was I Born," "Don't Worry 'Bout Me," and "All Alone" while **Solar** (Original Jazz Classics 755) has Garland, Jones, Gant, and guitarist Les Spann (who plays flute on one number) digging into "Sophisticated Swing," "This Can't Be Love," and "I Just Can't See for Looking." **Red's Good Groove** (Original Jazz Classics 1064) is a change of pace since it features Garland in a quintet with Blue Mitchell, Pepper Adams, Sam Jones, and Philly Joe Jones.

The end of an era was reached with **When There Are Grey Skies** (Original Jazz Classics 704), a trio outing with Wendell Marshall and Charlie Persip from October 9, 1962, that was Garland's 25th date as a leader in six years; all but an extensive set of piano solos from April 1960 are out on CD. This was also Garland's last recording for nine years as he decided to settle back in his native Texas and only played locally until the 1970s. But there is no shortage of Red Garland recordings from his prime, and all are excellent.

Erroll Garner   The times might have been changing, but there was little reason for Erroll Garner to alter his joyous style that remained quite popular. Usually backed by bassist Eddie Calhoun and drummer Kelly Martin during 1961–64, and other quiet rhythm section mates in later years, Garner continued recording fairly regularly for EmArcy/Mercury and MGM. **Dancing on the Ceiling** (EmArcy 834 935), which is mostly from 1961 other than two cuts from 1964–65, consists of selections not released until the 1990s for unknown reasons. As usual the music is marvelous and sometimes miraculous. **Close Up in Swing/A New Kind of Love** (Telarc 83383) has all of the performances from two former LPs on a single disc. The earlier date is a trio session that is highlighted by a sly version of "My Silent Love," "All of Me," and a joyful "Back in Your Own Backyard." The later date is a bit more unusual, for the pianist improvises on ten themes that were used in the Paul Newman film *A New Kind of Love* while joined by a big band and string orchestra conducted by Leith Stevens. Garner contributed a few original themes to the score and also is heard jamming on "You Brought a New Kind of Love to Me," "Louise," and "Mimi." **Easy to Love** (EmArcy 832 994) has Garner with his trio in 1961 and 1965 uplifting "Somebody Stole My Gal," "Somebody Loves Me,"

"Strike Up the Band," and "A Foggy Day" in his own fashion. **Now Playing: A Night at the Movies/Up in Erroll's Room** (Telarc 83378) is another two-fer, this time having Garner in 1964 romping through 13 songs taken from movies (including "You Made Me Love You," "I Found a Million Dollar Baby," and "It's Only a Paper Moon"), and in 1968 with his trio backed by seven horns arranged by Don Sebesky.

Although none of these four CDs are essential, they are all enjoyable, for Erroll Garner was always consistently inspired; he really loved to play.

Vince Guaraldi   After spending a valuable period with Cal Tjader's Afro-Cuban band (1957–59), Vince Guaraldi resumed working in the San Francisco area with his own combos. In 1962, his classic album ◗ **Jazz Impressions of Black Orpheus** (Original Jazz Classics 437), which mostly featured bossa nova songs played by Guaraldi, bassist Monty Budwig, and drummer Colin Bailey, introduced his most famous composition, the hit "Cast Your Fate to the Wind." Guaraldi recorded some other notable sets for the Fantasy label during the 1960s. **Vince Guaraldi in Person** (Original Jazz Classics 951) alternates between straightahead trio jazz and a bossa nova quintet with guitarist Eddie Duran, **Vince & Bola** (Fantasy 24756) has Guaraldi and acoustic guitarist Bola Sete co-leading a Brazilian-oriented quartet, and **The Latin Side of Vince Guaraldi** (Original Jazz Classics 878) shows how well Guaraldi could alternate between bossa novas and Afro-Cuban jazz. Guaraldi became most famous outside of jazz for **Jazz Impressions of a Boy Named Charlie Brown** (Fantasy 8430), his beloved score for the *Peanuts* animated cartoon series, including "Linus and Lucy."

An accessible and versatile pianist, Vince Guaraldi gained a certain amount of popularity in the 1960s although never quite becoming a major name.

Herbie Hancock   Although he worked primarily as a sideman during 1961–67, Herbie Hancock became a household name in jazz early on due to his classic Blue Note recordings. Initially a strong hard bop pianist influenced by Bill Evans who was not shy to show his soulful side, Hancock studied at Grinnell College, and in 1961 joined the Donald Byrd-Pepper Adams quintet. He first gained fame when he started recording for Blue Note. His initial set as a leader, ◗ **Takin' Off** (Blue Note 46506), is best known for introducing his "Watermelon Man," a song that soon became a hit for Mongo Santamaria. Teamed with Dexter Gordon, Freddie Hubbard, Butch Warren, and Billy Higgins, Hancock already sounds quite original, performing several other notable if obscure originals that are augmented on the CD reissue by three alternate takes (including one of "Watermelon Man").

In May 1963, Hancock joined the Miles Davis Quintet, his musical home for the next five years. While carving out a new role for his piano in the increasingly advanced settings, his own recording career continued on with four additional Blue Note albums. Recorded in 1963, **My Point of View** (Blue Note 84126) did not generate any new standards (the soulful "Blind Man, Blind Man" comes the closest), but has some memorable writing by Hancock for an ensemble consisting of Donald Byrd, Hank Mobley, Chuck Israels, 17-year-old Tony Williams, and sometimes trombonist Grachan Moncur III and Grant Green. **Inventions and Dimensions** (Blue Note 84147) is quite unusual as Hancock plays in a quartet with Paul Chambers, drummer Willie Bobo, and Osvaldo "Chihuahua" Martinez on conga and bongo. Despite the instrumentation, the music is not Latin jazz, but a post-bop effort with a lot of free improvising by Hancock, who often makes up the chords spontaneously as he goes along. **Empyrean Isles** (Blue Note 84175) from 1964 is a quartet outing with Freddie Hubbard, Ron Carter, and Tony Williams that pushes at the boundaries of hard bop, both backward (by adding soul jazz grooves) and forward (adventurous solos). This album introduced "Cantaloupe Island."

● **Maiden Voyage** (Blue Note 46339) is the most significant of Hancock's Blue Note sets, balancing the pianist's lyricism and interest in soul/R&B with his sophisticated improvising abilities. With Freddie Hubbard, George Coleman, Ron Carter, and Tony Williams completing the group, Hancock introduces such memorable pieces as "Dolphin Dance," "The Eye of the Hurricane," and "Maiden Voyage," moving the mainstream of jazz in 1965 forward a couple of steps, and making himself immortal even though he was just 25.

Barry Harris While Herbie Hancock was creating new music in the 1960s, Barry Harris saw himself as the preserver of bebop, teaching younger players (his students included Charles McPherson and Lonnie Hillyer), and keeping the straightahead style alive even while it was being overshadowed by newer developments.

A very consistent performer, Harris recorded four albums for Riverside during 1961–62 and a Prestige date in 1967. **Preminado** (Original Jazz Classics 486), a trio outing with bassist Joe Benjamin and Elvin Jones, includes excellent versions of "My Heart Stood Still," "What Is this Thing Called Love," and "I Should Care." The latter is taken as an unaccompanied solo, as is all the music on **Listen to Barry Harris** (Original Jazz Classics 999). Harris shows that he could be a very effective two-handed pianist (although he really sounds best in trios), alternating originals with standards including an unusual version of "The Londonderry Air" ("Danny Boy"). **Newer than New** (Original Jazz Classics 1082) is a quintet set with McPherson and Hillyer from 1961 that has some classic bebop solos on "Anthropology," "Easy to Love," and Harris's "Mucho Dinero." From 1962, **Chasin' the Bird** (Original Jazz Classics 872) is a high-quality trio date with Bob Cranshaw and drummer Clifford Jarvis that includes the title cut (with Harris playing both countermelodies at the same time), "'Round Midnight," "The Way You Look Tonight," and three excellent and swinging originals. By the time **Luminescence** (Original Jazz Classics 924) was recorded in 1967, bebop sessions were getting rather rare, but Harris shows that there was still plenty of life left in the music. His trumpetless sextet consists of Pepper Adams, Junior Cook, Slide Hampton, Bob Cranshaw, and drummer Lenny McBrowne. The musicians play four of Harris's infectious originals (most of which are based on common chord changes), the ballad "My Ideal," and two Bud Powell tunes, "Dance of the Infidels" and "Webb City," with plenty of spirit and life.

Hampton Hawes In 1958 (a year in which he recorded three albums as a leader), Hampton Hawes was arrested and jailed on drug charges, receiving a long prison sentence. Five years later, he persuaded President John F. Kennedy to pardon him, and he was able to make a return to the jazz scene. Fortunately, Hawes had not lost anything in the interim, and Lester Koenig was ready to resume recording the pianist for his Contemporary label. Recorded in 1964, **The Green Leaves of Summer** (Original Jazz Classics 476) shows that Hawes was just beginning to move beyond bop; he had certainly heard McCoy Tyner and Herbie Hancock a bit. This trio date with bassist Monk Montgomery and drummer Steve Ellington swings quite well, particularly "Vierd

Blues," "St. Thomas," and "Secret Love." **Here and Now** (Original Jazz Classics 178) from the following year has its moments, but some of the tunes (which include "Fly Me to the Moon," "What Kind of Fool Am I," and "People") are largely beyond help in this format, while "The Girl from Ipanema" is stripped of its Brazilian rhythms and taken as bop. **The Seance** (Original Jazz Classics 455) and **I'm All Smiles** (Original Jazz Classics 796) are both taken from the same two live sessions in 1966. Teamed with Red Mitchell and Donald Bailey, Hawes shows the influence of the avant-garde in spots, stretching out his solos while still holding on to his bop roots. **The Seance**, which includes "Oleo," "Easy Street," and "My Romance," gets a slight edge.

Hawes's periods on Contemporary (1955–58 and 1964–66) resulted in the finest recordings of his career. However, he was not through yet by any means.

Elmo Hope   Elmo Hope should have had a major career as a pianist/composer, but drug problems kept him intermittently inactive and shortened his life. The year 1961 was a busy one in the recording studios as Hope led **Homecoming** (Original Jazz Classics 1810), **Hope-full** (Original Jazz Classics 1872), **Here's Hope** (V.S.O.P. 2), and **High Hope** (V.S.O.P. 3). The two V.S.O.P. albums have not been reissued on CD (both are rather brief but enjoyable trio sets that usually feature Hope with Paul Chambers and Philly Joe Jones), while the music on **Homecoming** (except for two alternate takes) is reissued as part of **The All-Star Sessions** (Milestone 47037), a better buy.

Hope-Full is somewhat unusual for Elmo Hope because he is heard on five unaccompanied piano solos, including boppish version of "When Johnny Comes Marching Home" and "Liza." In addition, three songs are colorful piano duets with his young wife, Bertha Hope, who would have a strong career of her own in the 1990s. Unfortunately, Elmo Hope was much less active during 1962–65 (other than making one obscure album). In 1966, he cut enough music during two sessions to fill up the double CD ● **The Final Sessions** (Evidence 22147). Hope's piano is showcased in trios with bassist John Ore and either Clifford Jarvis or Philly Joe Jones on drums. He sounds in inspired form, and 11 of the 14 selections (several of which are well worth reviving) are his originals.

But a year and ten days after the last date, Elmo Hope died at the age of 43.

Roger Kellaway   A virtuoso pianist with a quick imagination who sometimes goes over the top in his playing, Roger Kellaway took classical piano lessons from age seven, but actually started his playing career as a bassist, playing with Ruby Braff and Jimmy McPartland. Switching to piano, he worked with Kai Winding, the Al Cohn/Zoot Sims quartet, Clark Terry/Bob Brookmeyer (1963–65), and Ben Webster. He first recorded as a leader in 1963 on a long-forgotten LP for Regina. Recorded in 1965, **The Roger Kellaway Trio** (Original Jazz Classics 1897) shows how fine a pianist he was when he was just 25. In a trio with bassist Russell George and Dave Bailey, Kellaway shows off a willingness to experiment on such tunes as "Brats" (which uses a prepared piano), the polyrhythmic "Signa: O.N.," the Beatles' "I'll Follow the Sun," and "Ballad of the Sad Young Men."

After moving to Los Angeles in 1966, Roger Kellaway worked with the Don Ellis big band, became Bobby Darin's musical director, and was quite busy as a studio musician.

Wynton Kelly   Wynton Kelly worked with Miles Davis until 1963 when he departed along with the rhythm section (Paul Chambers and Jimmy Cobb) to form the Wynton Kelly Trio. The unit accompanied Wes Montgomery on some notable recordings and worked fairly regularly. Kelly recorded as a leader for Vee-Jay, Verve, and Milestone during this period. **Someday My Prince Will Come** (Collectables 714) has the ten songs from the Kelly-Chambers-Cobb trio's two 1961 sessions, and a few alternate takes although not as many as have been issued on the limited-edition six-CD box **The Complete Vee-Jay Paul Chambers/Wynton Kelly Sessions** (Mosaic 6-205). "Wrinkles" has Lee Morgan and Wayne Shorter dropping by, but they really were not needed for Kelly's trio is a strong unit by itself, swinging its way through "Autumn Leaves," "Surrey with the Fringe on Top," and other appealing numbers.

Kelly's Verve albums have not been reissued yet. By the time he recorded **Full View** (Original Jazz Classics 912) in 1966, the pianist's "personal problems" were beginning to affect his career, along with him being overshadowed by more modern players. Still, Kelly sounds in excellent form during this outing with bassist Ron McClure and Jimmy Cobb. Other than his "Scufflin'" and the recent hit "Walk on By," the set consists of veteran standards, all played in swinging and tasteful fashion.

Ramsey Lewis   The Ramsey Lewis Trio (with bassist Eldee Young and drummer Red Holt) stayed together into early 1966 until commercial success tore it apart. Starting as a melodic bop-oriented group in 1956, the Chicago-based group recorded steadily for Argo/Cadet during this era although most of its pre-hit recordings remain out of print. Things changed permanently in 1965 with the recordings of **The In Crowd** (which has hit versions of the title cut and "Love Theme from Spartacus") and **Hang on Ramsey** (highlighted by "Hang on Sloopy," a catchy version of the Beatles' "A Hard Day's Night," and "High-Heel Sneakers"). Ramsey Lewis became a staple of AM-radio for the next few years. These performances not only have melodic and lightly funky playing, but plenty of interaction with the enthusiastic audience, which is often singing and clapping along. The two-CD set ◉ **In Person 1960–1967** (GRP/Chess 814) does an excellent job of summing up this period, drawing its material from five live sessions (two of which predate "The In Crowd"). The fifth set has bassist Cleveland Eaton and drummer Maurice White replacing Lewis's sidemen who briefly had success with the Young-Holt Unlimited before fading away. Among the many highlights of this definitive two-fer include "Old Devil Moon," "Carmen," "Delilah," "The In Crowd," "Theme from Spartacus," "A Hard Day's Night," "Hang on Sloopy," and a "Black Orpheus Medley."

Junior Mance   A soulful and bluesy pianist whose style developed independently of Horace Silver and who preceded Gene Harris, Mance is often grouped in with the other funky pianists though he is also a fine bop improviser. Mance worked in Chicago with Gene Ammons (1947–49), Lester Young, and the Gene Ammons/Sonny Stitt quintet. After serving in the military, he was the house pianist at Chicago's Bee Hive (1953–54) and had some notable associations, working with Dinah Washington (1954–55), the first Cannonball Adderley Quintet (1956–57), and the Dizzy Gillespie Quintet (1958–60). After leaving Gillespie, Mance was with the Eddie "Lockjaw" Davis-Johnny Griffin group, and has led his own trios ever since.

Mance led his first album in 1959, and he recorded regularly in the 1960s for Jazzland, Riverside, Capitol, and Atlantic. **Junior Mance Trio Live at the Village Vanguard** (Original Jazz Classics 204) from 1961 with bassist Larry Gales and drummer Ben Riley (Thelonious Monk's future rhythm section) is a fine example of his work. In addition to blues and soulful pieces, Mance plays the uptown "Looptown" à la Oscar Peterson and is boppish on "Girl of My Dreams." **Junior's Blues** (Original Jazz Classics 1000) with Bob Cranshaw and drummer Mickey Roker, has a particularly intriguing and successful repertoire that includes "Creole Love Call," "Yancey Special," "Gravy Waltz," and "Jumpin' the Blues." **Happy Time** (Original Jazz Classics 1029) with Ron Carter and Mickey Roker is another fine mixture of blues and bebop including soulful versions of "Jitterbug Waltz," Clark Terry's "The Simple Waltz," and three Mance originals.

Dodo Marmarosa   Dodo Marmarosa, one of the finest bebop pianists of 1945–50, was inactive during much of the 1950s. Suffering from mental illness along with insecurity, Marmarosa re-emerged during 1961–62, recording an LP for Argo (**Dodo's Back!**), and both a trio date and a quartet set with Gene Ammons (**Jug & Dodo**). But those projects did not lead anywhere, and Marmarosa permanently returned to his native Pittsburgh, largely confining his playing to practicing at home.

Les McCann   During 1961–67, Les McCann came into his own as a very popular and influential pianist and (starting in 1964) singer. He recorded often (11 albums for Pacific Jazz during 1961–64), but despite his continuing popularity, few of his records have been reissued on CD, not even **Les McCann Sings** (his 1961 debut as a vocalist), **The Gospel Truth**, **Soul Hits**, or **Spanish Onions**. The same can be said for his Limelight albums of 1964–67. Luckily, **In New York** (Capitol/Pacific Jazz 92929), a date in which McCann's regular trio from 1961 (which has bassist Herbie Lewis and drummer Ron Jefferson) is joined by Blue Mitchell, and both Stanley Turrentine and Frank Haynes on tenors, has been put out on CD. Best are "A Little 3/4 for God & Co." and the previously unissued "Someone Stole My Chitlins." Augmenting this CD are two numbers from 1960 in which vibraphonist Bobby Hutcherson (at the beginning of his career) makes the Les McCann Trio into a quartet. Jumping ahead to 1967, **How's Your Mother** (32 Jazz 32088) is a live set from July that was put out for the first time in 1998. Although McCann was becoming known as a singer by then, this is an instrumental trio date with bassist Leroy Vinnegar and drummer Frank Severino that puts the focus on McCann's piano playing. He is heard in top form on such songs as "Love for Sale," "Sunny," "I Am in Love," and "Goin' Out of My Head."

But when are Les McCann's many trio records from the early 1960s going to finally be reissued?

Phineas Newborn One of the great jazz pianists of the late 1950s, Phineas Newborn started off the 1960s with a couple of fine trio sets. **A World of Piano** (Original Jazz Classics 175) has Newborn with either Paul Chambers or Sam Jones on bass and Philly Joe Jones or Louis Hayes on drums. Actually, Newborn is the main focus throughout, playing quite brilliantly on five jazz standards (including "Manteca," Clifford Brown's "Daahoud," and "Oleo") and three obscurities. His technique was phenomenal (on a level with Oscar Peterson), and he could outswing nearly anyone. **The Great Jazz Piano of Phineas Newborn** (Original Jazz Classics 388) continues at the same high level, with more music from the Jones-Hayes date, and five selections from a 1962 trio with Leroy Vinnegar and drummer Milt Turner. Highlights include "Theme for Basie," "Celia," and "Well You Needn't."

Unfortunately, health problems began to affect Newborn's life at this point, and there was just one recording during the 1963–68 period. Recorded in 1964, **The Newborn Touch** (Original Jazz Classics 270), a trio outing with Vinnegar and drummer Frank Butler, does not reveal any decline or slowing down. Whether it be "The Sermon," "Diane," "Blue Daniel," or "Grooveyard," Phineas Newborn's playing in 1964 was unchanged from five years earlier. But it is a tragedy that he was never able to profit from his masterful piano playing and become as famous as Oscar Peterson or Erroll Garner.

Horace Parlan While Phineas Newborn's technique was limitless, Horace Parlan was a much more limited pianist due to having a crippled right hand from contracting polio as a child. Despite his handicap, Parlan was a member of bands led by Booker Ervin (1960–61), Eddie "Lockjaw" Davis and Johnny Griffin (1962), and Rahsaan Roland Kirk (1963–66). He led seven albums for Blue Note during 1960–63, all of which have been issued on **The Complete Blue Note Horace Parlan Sessions** (Mosaic 5-197), a limited-edition box set. Of the three from 1961–63, which include such sidemen as Booker Ervin, Grant Green, and Johnny Coles, only **On the Spur of the Moment** (Blue Note 21735) is available individually. A quintet date with bassist George

Tucker, drummer Al Harewood, and Tommy and Stanley Turrentine, this set fits very well into the hard bop movement of the early 1960s; the trumpeter is in particularly fine form.

Duke Pearson As a pianist, arranger, composer, and record producer, Duke Pearson was an important force during the last period of the original Blue Note label. Along the way he wrote such songs as "Jeannine," "Cristo Redentor" (made famous by Donald Byrd), and "Sweet Honey Bee." Born Columbus Pearson, Jr., he was nicknamed Duke by his uncle, a fan of Duke Ellington. He gained early experience playing piano in his native Atlanta, moving to New York in 1959 when he was 27. Pearson worked with Donald Byrd, the Jazztet, and Nancy Wilson, and led two obscure albums for Blue Note in 1959. **Dedication** (Original Jazz Classics 1939) from 1961 has Pearson leading a sextet also including Freddie Hubbard, Pepper Adams, trombonist Willie Wilson, bassist Thomas Howard, and Lex Humphries. A straightahead hard bop date with appealing material (including Tommy Flanagan's "Minor Mishap," "The Nearness of You," and some originals), this set has plenty of fine solos from the horn players.

After arranging four numbers for septet and an eight-voice choir for Donald Byrd's popular **A New Perspective Album** in 1963, Pearson began working regularly as a producer for Blue Note. He also led five Blue Note albums of his own during 1964–67. **Wahoo** (Blue Note 84191) has five Pearson originals (including the title cut), and Donald Byrd's "Fly Little Bird Fly" played by a sextet, including Byrd, Joe Henderson, James Spaulding, Bob Cranshaw, and Mickey Roker. The individual solos are fine and a bit explorative, but it is Pearson's arrangements that make this set most memorable. **Sweet Honey Bee** (Blue Note 89792) has seven of Pearson's originals (including the swinging minor-toned "Big Bertha") played by Hubbard, Spaulding, Henderson, Ron Carter, and Mickey Roker. Once again the intelligent frameworks and concise improvisations (which fit each song's themes and moods) make this an enjoyable listen.

The Right Touch (Blue Note 28269) has Pearson writing for an all-star octet (Hubbard, trombonist Garnett Brown, Spaulding, Jerry Dodgion on alto and flute, Stanley Turrentine, bassist Gene Taylor, and drummer Grady Tate) and contributing a full program of colorful originals, although none caught on. Particularly rewarding is

1967's ◉ **Introducing Duke Pearson's Big Band** (Blue Note 94508). It was logical that Pearson would eventually lead a bigger orchestra since his arrangements for smaller groups were so unpredictable and colorful. The original set from December 1967 includes such fine up-and-coming players in the personnel as trumpeters Randy Brecker and Marvin Stamm, trombonist Julian Priester, and tenor saxophonist Lew Tabackin in addition to Frank Foster and Pepper Adams. In addition, six of the nine selections that were originally out on 1968's big band album **Now Hear This** are also included on the CD reissue. Pearson contributed most of the arrangements, and presents a wide variety of music that includes originals, Chick Corea's "Tones for Joan's Bones," and a few standards from the era, including "A Taste of Honey," "Here's that Rainy Day," and "Days of Wine and Roses." Although this big band did not last long (the two albums were its only recordings), the Duke Pearson Orchestra is well worth remembering and enjoying.

Bud Powell   The innovative Bud Powell was on a steep downhill course when he moved to Paris in 1959. The warm welcome and care that he received (under the guidance of his great fan Francois Paudras) helped extend his life. Despite a stay in the hospital during 1962–63, Powell's five years in France were a mostly happy and fairly productive period.

A **Portrait of Thelonious** (Sony 65187) from 1961 is one of Powell's finest European dates. Teamed in a trio with Pierre Michelot and Kenny Clarke, Powell plays four Thelonious Monk tunes, "No Name Blues," and "There Will Never Be Another You," but best are the final two boppish numbers: "I Ain't Foolin'" and "Squatty." The CD adds an alternate and faster version of "Squatty," and reveals that the applause heard throughout the set was added on later; this is really a studio album!

The same group (which was known as the Three Bosses) is heard the following year in fine form on **Round Midnight at the Blue Note** (Dreyfus 36500), playing some of the same songs plus strong versions of "'Shaw 'Nuff" and "A Night in Tunisia." Five CDs titled **At the Golden Circle Vol. 1–5** (Steeple Chase 36001, 36002, 36009, 36014, and 36017) feature Powell on April 19 and 23, 1962, performing at Stockholm's Golden Circle with bassist Torbjorn Hultcrantz and drummer Sune Spangberg. In general, Powell plays quite well, even taking a very rare vocal (on **Vol. 5**) during

"This Is No Laughing atter" although the three and a half hours of music could have fit on three CDs. Also worth acquiring are such excellent trio albums as **Bouncing with Bud** (Delmark 406), **Bud Powell in Paris** (Reprise 45817), **Blues for Bouffemant** (Black Lion 760135), and **Salt Peanuts** (Black Lion 760121); the latter has Johnny Griffin romping with the group on three numbers ("Hot House," "Wee," and "Straight No Chaser"). However, one should skip **Strictly Confidential** (Black Lion 760196), for those private solos performed at Francois Paudras's apartment are quite erratic and poorly recorded.

In 1964, Bud Powell made the fateful decision to return to the United States. He had an engagement at Birdland, recorded two trio albums including the well-titled **Ups 'N' Downs** (Mainstream 724), and then largely disappeared, lost in his own world of inner turmoil and madness. He died on August 1, 1966, at the age of 41.

George Shearing   The George Shearing Quintet, which was formed in 1949, continued being a popular attraction in the 1960s. The group began 1961 featuring vibraphonist Warren Chasen, guitarist Dick Garcia, bassist Ralph Pena, and drummer Vernell Fournier. The recording **George Shearing and the Montgomery Brothers** (Original Jazz Classics 40) was a happy change of pace, matching the pianist with guitarist Wes Montgomery, vibraphonist Buddy, and bassist Monk Montgomery (plus drummer Walter Perkins) for an enjoyable if slightly lightweight outing. The problem is that the performances are a bit too concise, but what is here is delightful and swinging. **Jazz Moments** (Blue Note 32085) from mid-1962 is also a bit different, featuring Shearing in a trio with Ahmad Jamal's former sidemen, bassist Israel Crosby and Vernell Fournier. Crosby is heard in his final recording and receives some rare opportunities to solo. Highlights include "Makin' Whoopee," "Like Someone in Love," "Symphony," and "It Could Happen to You."

One of George Shearing's best recordings of the 1960s, a live set from 1963 with Gary Burton as his vibraphonist, is only currently available as part of a Mosaic limited-edition box set. Most of his other records from the period for Capitol have his quintet joined by strings and/or woodwinds. By the mid-1960s, it was becoming increasingly clear that the Shearing Quintet's formula was running out of gas.

Bobby Timmons   Just 25 as 1961 began, Bobby Timmons had already composed hit songs for Art Blakey ("Moanin'") and Cannonball Adderley ("This Here" and "Dat Dere") in addition to developing his own influential funky piano style. But unfortunately, he was never able to grow musically from that point. Timmons mostly led trios in the 1960s, and recorded fairly frequently for Riverside, Prestige, and Milestone, but seemed to stand still musically, stereotyped as a soul jazz pianist even though he had played credible bop earlier in his career.

Certainly there was nothing wrong with his recordings. **Easy Does It** (Original Jazz Classics 722), **In Person** (Original Jazz Classics 364), **Sweet and Soulful Sounds** (Original Jazz Classics 928), **Born to Be Blue** (Original Jazz Classics 873), and **From the Bottom** (Original Jazz Classics 1032) are each trio sets (dating from 1961–64) in which Timmons (with supportive bassists and drummers) alternates between soulful originals and boppish standards. **From the Bottom** is a bit unusual in that Timmons plays vibes on two songs and organ on one ("Moanin'"), but otherwise it is very much in his style.

Workin' Out (Prestige 24143) is a very different case, for this CD reissues the complete contents of Timmons's two most advanced recordings. There is a date from 1964 with vibraphonist Johnny Lytle, bassist Keter Betts, and drummer William "Peppy" Hinnant that is full of subtle surprises including the pianist's bitonal solo (playing in two keys at once) on "Bags' Groove." The bulk of the CD is from 1966 (originally released as **The Soul Man**), and has Timmons teamed with Wayne Shorter, Ron Carter, and Jimmy Cobb. This very obscure collaboration finds Shorter in top form and introducing his original "Tom Thumb." The modern musicians inspire Timmons to really stretch himself, showing what he could have done with his career if he had taken better care of himself, and managed to escape from the funky soul jazz stereotype.

Lennie Tristano   Lennie Tristano only had one full album left in him, 1962's **The New Tristano** (Atlantic 1357). This LP has thus far only been reissued on CD as part of a limited-edition Mosaic box set. Tristano is heard stretching out on seven piano solos, all of which are his originals (mostly based on common chord changes) other than "You Don't Know What Love Is." The pianist plays with such power and such fresh ideas

that it is quite unfortunate that he had largely withdrawn from active playing by the early 1950s. Other than a few isolated selections from rehearsals and rare concerts (only one selection after 1966) released many years later, Lennie Tristano never appeared on record again even though he continued teaching up until his death in 1978.

McCoy Tyner   McCoy Tyner, who found fame as a key member of the classic John Coltrane Quartet, and Bill Evans moved the mainstream of jazz piano beyond Bud Powell. A very influential pianist, Tyner's chord voicings opened the way to more explorative playing while his spirituality kept his music melodic and meaningful. From virtually the start of his recording career, no one else sounded like him although countless players have since emulated his style.

Tyner was born and grew up in Philadelphia where Bud Powell was a neighbor, and he met John Coltrane while a teenager. He worked locally and was an original member of the Jazztet during 1959–60. However, after six months he left the group to join Coltrane where he would become an increasingly powerful force during the next five years. His open voicings never boxed Coltrane in, and he adopted his style to Trane's explorative flights.

While with Coltrane, Tyner led six albums of his own for the Impulse label. In general these sessions are more conservative and straightahead than the music that the pianist was playing with the saxophonist. **Inception** (Impulse 220) is a trio set with Art Davis and Elvin Jones that introduces Tyner's "Effendi" and "Inception," and has him swinging (in his own fashion) on such songs as "Speak Low" and "There Is No Greater Love." **Reaching Fourth** (Impulse 255) has Tyner, Henry Grimes, and Roy Haynes performing the pianist's "Reaching Fourth" and "Blues Back" plus four standards, including "Have You Met Miss Jones" and "Old Devil Moon." Of these early releases, **Nights of Ballads and Blues** (Impulse 221) must have really surprised listeners only familiar with Tyner's work with Coltrane. Included on this set are easy-listening versions of such songs as "We'll Be Together Again," "Satin Doll," and "Days of Wine and Roses." Still, Tyner's highly original chord voicings let one know that this is an innovator who was applying his fresh ideas to a relaxed setting.

Today and Tomorrow (GRP/Impulse 106) from mid-1963 has more variety than usual. The first three selections feature Tyner leading a sextet comprised of Thad Jones, altoist Frank Strozier, tenor saxophonist John Gilmore, Butch Warren, and Elvin Jones. It is a shame that this group did not record a full album for there are quite a few sparks on these numbers. The rest of the set has Tyner mostly playing standards with Jimmy Garrison and Albert "Tootie" Heath. **Live at Newport** (Impulse 547 980) is an unusual entry in Tyner's discography for it is essentially a jam session. Tyner, Bob Cranshaw, and Mickey Roker are fine on "All of You" and "Monk's Blues," and joined by Clark Terry and altoist Charles Mariano for "Newport Romp," "My Funny Valentine," and "Woody'n You." Although some of these musicians had not played together before, everything works, and Tyner sounds quite happy throughout this unique event. **McCoy Tyner Plays Ellington** (GRP/Impulse 216) is also successful. Tyner, Jimmy Garrison, Elvin Jones, and two Latin percussionists interpret eight Duke Ellington songs and "Caravan." The set gives one a rare opportunity to hear Tyner play such tunes as "Mr. Gentle and Mr. Cool," "It Don't Mean a Thing," and "I Got It Bad."

In late 1965, McCoy Tyner left the John Coltrane Quartet, feeling that with Rashied Ali as a second drummer and Pharoah Sanders joining the band, he simply could no longer hear himself. He struggled for a period, often working as a sideman (including with Ike and Tina Turner). In 1967, he led two albums for Blue Note, and these find Tyner growing in power and starting to really stretch himself. **The Real McCoy** (Blue Note 46502) has Tyner leading a quartet also including Joe Henderson, Ron Carter, and Elvin Jones on five of his originals, including "Passion Dance," "Four by Five," and "Blues on the Corner." **Tender Moments** (Blue Note 84275) features Tyner leading a large group for the first time, a nonet also including Lee Morgan, Julian Priester, James Spaulding, Bennie Maupin on tenor, the french horn of Bob Northern, Howard Johnson on tuba, bassist Herbie Lewis, and Joe Chambers. Although none of Tyner's six originals from this set became standards ("The High Priest" came the closest), the music is quite advanced and colorful. One can hear McCoy Tyner creating music apart from the world of John Coltrane, starting to build on his own legacy.

Mal Waldron Mal Waldron, whose chord voicings and brooding sound were quite original by 1961, utilized Eric Dolphy, Booker Ervin, Ron Carter on cello, bassist Joe Benjamin, and drummer Charlie Persip on his album **The Quest** (Original Jazz Classics 082). This is a fine session of advanced hard bop music often reissued under Dolphy's name and included in the altoist's huge Prestige box set. Waldron, who appeared with Dolphy and Booker Little in their well-documented Five Spot engagement in 1961, and worked a bit with Abbey Lincoln, moved permanently to Europe in 1965, settling in Munich two years later. He wrote the score for the 1967 film *Sweet Love Bitter* (the LP Impulse 9141), which has Dick Gregory playing a character loosely based on Charlie Parker, but that would be his last American recording for many years.

Cedar Walton After attending the University of Denver and serving in the army, Cedar Walton moved to New York where his fluent piano playing soon resulted in him working steadily. He played with Kenny Dorham, J.J. Johnson, and the Jazztet (where he replaced McCoy Tyner) before gaining recognition for his work with Art Blakey's Jazz Messengers (1961–64). Walton accompanied Abbey Lincoln (1965–66) and appeared on many records as a sideman, particularly for the Prestige label starting in 1967. His debut as a leader, **Cedar** (Original Jazz Classics 462), took place on July 10, 1967. This well-planned set features Walton on "My Ship" in a trio with Leroy Vinnegar and Billy Higgins, has the pianist playing with a pair of quartets with either Kenny Dorham or Junior Cook, and also includes two quintet numbers with all of the musicians. The repertoire consists of three standards (including "My Ship" and "Take the 'A' Train") and four Walton originals, serving as a perfect launching pad for Cedar Walton's solo career.

Randy Weston Randy Weston, who visited Nigeria in 1961 and 1963, has always had a strong interest in African culture, and in integrating music from other lands into his own playing. His 1963 project **Music from the African Nations** was reviewed in the last chapter as part of the set **Uhura Africa/Highlife** (Roulette 94510). **Berkshire Blues** (Black Lion 60205) from 1965 features Weston with bassist Bill Wood and drummer Lennie McBrowne on a dissonant version of "Three Blind Mice," a relatively slow "Perdido," and "Purple Gazelle." In addition, the pianist is heard unaccompanied on four of his originals (including "Berkshire Blues" and "Sweet Meat"). This is a fine showcase overall for Weston's playing. ◉ **Monterey '66** (Verve 314 519 698) puts the spotlight on his sextet of 1963–66 during their final concert. The music was not initially released until 1993, but it is wonderful. With trumpeter Ray Copeland, Booker Ervin, Cecil Payne, Wood, McBrowne, and percussionist Big Black, Weston performs seven of his originals, including "Little Niles," "Berkshire Blues," and "African Cookbook." The strong solos and colorful ensembles make this a particularly memorable effort from an often overshadowed but major pianist/composer.

Joe Zawinul   Born in Vienna, Austria, Joe Zawinul has had a very productive career in which he is always looking forward. He started playing accordion in 1938 when he was six, studied classical piano at the Vienna Conservatory, and became interested in jazz after World War II. He worked with saxophonist Hans Koller in 1952 and in his own groups in Europe (recording as early as 1954) before moving to the United States in 1958 after winning a scholarship to the Berklee College of Music. Zawinul was only in school for one week before he left to play with Maynard Ferguson's band for eight months. A short stint with Slide Hampton preceded two years with Dinah Washington (1959–61), a month with Harry "Sweets" Edison, and a nine-year period playing with the Cannonball Adderley Quintet/Sextet. While with Adderley he wrote "Mercy, Mercy, Mercy," began doubling on electric piano (which he played as early as 1966), and developed his own soulful voice.

Other than an obscure quartet date for Strand in 1958, Joe Zawinul's first two albums as a leader (from 1965–67) have been reissued on the single CD ◉ **Rise & Fall of the Third Stream/Money in the Pocket** (Rhino 71675). The **Money in the Pocket** album has Zawinul on acoustic piano in a sextet with Blue Mitchell, Joe Henderson, and Pepper Adams playing high-quality hard bop, including the funky title cut, "If," and "My One, and Only Love." The **In the Pocket** set has a string quartet, trumpeter Jimmy Owens, and the tenor and arrangements of William Fischer. Zawinul doubles on electric piano, and the colorful music hints at fusion. Joe Zawinul was already ahead of his time.

Denny Zeitlin   Denny Zeitlin gained a lot of fame from his unusual double career, being both a top-notch jazz pianist and a psychiatrist. He began playing piano when he was two, studied classical music, and switched to jazz while in high school. He worked locally in his native Chicago while also studying medicine. Zeitlin's playing greatly impressed John Hammond, who recorded him on two occasions in 1964 for Columbia.

Cathexis/Carnival (Collectables 5891) is a single CD that reissues those two albums, except for four numbers from the **Carnival** date. The first session has Zeitlin with bassist Cecil McBee and drummer Freddie Waits, with the emphasis on the pianist's quirky originals plus fresh versions of "Nica's Tempo," "Soon," and "'Round Midnight." The music is boppish yet quite unpredictable and fresh. While Bill Evans was always an influence, Zeitlin's ideas are his own. The **Carnival** set has Zeitlin joined by Charlie Haden and drummer Jerry Granelli, his regular sidemen with his San Francisco trio, and is of the same high quality though one regrets the missing selections.

Due to his work as a psychiatrist, Denny Zeitlin's recording career would be erratic quantity-wise, but despite being a part-time player, the high quality of his output would always be quite impressive.

Organists

After Jimmy Smith exploded on the jazz scene during 1956–57 with his exciting solos on the Hammond B-3 organ, many other up-and-coming pianists made the switch, and began leading organ trio/quartets with guitar, drums, and sometimes tenor sax. Until the rise of Larry Young in the mid-1960s, virtually all organists sounded similar to Jimmy Smith other than the few (Wild Bill Davis, Bill Doggett, and the avant-garde Sun Ra) who had preceded him. The organists swung their soulful way through blues, ballads, veteran standards, and riff-filled originals, adding funky rhythms on top of the straightahead bass lines that they often played with their feet.

Richard "Groove" Holmes   Certainly the influence of Jimmy Smith is obvious in the sound of Richard "Groove' Holmes. After playing locally on the East Coast, in 1960 Holmes was discovered by Les McCann, who helped him secure a recording contract with Pacific Jazz. Holmes led five record dates for Pacific Jazz during 1961–62. **Groove** (Pacific Jazz 94473) from March 1961 was supposed to be a Les McCann vocal album, but the musicians were having such fun during their warmup that it was spontaneously decided to have this be an instrumental set led by the organist. McCann and Holmes blend quite well together, and with Ben Webster and trombonist Tricky Lofton forming the frontline, the results are of stronger than average interest. **Groovin' with Jug** (Pacific Jazz 92930) is an exciting meeting of Holmes and Gene Ammons. Guitarist Gene Edwards and drummer Leroy Henderson give support while the lead voices dig into such songs as "Happy Blues," "Hittin' the Jug," and "Exactly Like You."

After making an album for Warner Bros., Holmes began recording regularly for Prestige in 1965. Around that time, Prestige became one of the most prolific labels in soul jazz, documenting the music of quite a few organists. One of the main incentives was provided by Holmes, who had a hit in 1965 with a medium-tempo version of Erroll Garner's "Misty." In fact, after the release of **Soul Message** (Original Jazz Classics 329), which includes "Misty," Holmes would record seven albums during 1966–67 alone. **Soul Message**, in addition to "Misty," also has a soulful version of Horace Silver's "Song for My Father," the ballad "The Things We Did Last Night," and two originals, performed by Holmes's trio.

Misty (Original Jazz Classics 724) also has the hit version of "Misty" along with medium-tempo romps through ballads in hopes of duplicating the hit, including "The More I See You," "The Shadow of Your Smile," and "Strangers in the Night." More substantial overall is **Blues Groove** (Prestige 24133), which reissues two former LPs in which Holmes is joined by either Teddy Edwards and Pat Martino or Blue Mitchell and Harold Vick. Also worth exploring is 1966's **Spicy** (Prestige 24222), which has both a live set by Holmes's trio (including versions of Gerald Wilson's "Blues for Yna Yna" and "The Girl from Ipanema") and a funky two-guitar outing with Gene Edwards and Boogaloo Joe Jones that is highlighted by "Work Song" and "When Lights Are Low."

Jack McDuff   Although he was born Eugene McDuffy, this organist would become famous as "Brother" Jack McDuff. He actually began his career as a bassist and worked in the 1950s with Denny Zeitlin, Joe Farrell, and Johnny Griffin, among others. Switching to organ and piano in the mid-1950s, McDuff first gained attention working at the end of the decade with Willis Jackson. He signed with Prestige and recorded quite a bit during 1960–66.

Legends of Acid Jazz (Prestige 24220) reissues both McDuff's debut session (a quartet outing with guitarist Bill Jennings, Wendell Marshall, and drummer Alvin Jackson) and a recording from 1961 with Harold Vick, Grant Green, and drummer Joe Dukes. Two dates featuring Jimmy Forrest's tough tenor, **Tough Duff** (Original Jazz Classics 324) and **The Honeydripper** (Original Jazz Classics 222) from 1960–61 show how soulful a swinger McDuff could be. Lem Winchester's vibes are also featured on the former date, while guitarist Grant Green is a strong asset on the latter. **Brother Jack McDuff Meets the Boss** (Original Jazz Classics 326) shows that McDuff had come of age, for it was his chance to jam with Gene Ammons on such numbers as Horace Silver's "Strollin'," "Buzzin' Around," and "Christopher Columbus"; Harold Vick helps out on second tenor. **Screamin'** (Original Jazz Classics 875) is a fine showcase not only for McDuff (with support from Dukes), but also for altoist Leo Wright and Kenny Burrell. "Soulful Drums" (which features drum breaks from Dukes) was a minor hit, and other highlights include such spirited numbers as "He's a Real Gone Guy," "After Hours," and "One o'Clock Jump."

During 1963–65, McDuff led his most famous group, a quartet with Red Holloway, the young George Benson, and Joe Dukes. ● **Live!** (Prestige 24147) has all of the music from two rather exciting sets from 1963, featuring cooking blues, standards, Latin numbers, and originals, all played with drive and inspiration. A few numbers add Harold Vick on second tenor. More music by the same memorable unit is featured on **Legends of Acid Jazz** (Prestige 24184), **Silken Soul** (Prestige 24242), and **The Soulful Drums** (Prestige 24256).

After Holloway and Benson went out on their own, Jack McDuff led other similar groups although they generally did not achieve the same level of excitement and passion as that classic band.

Don Patterson   Sonny Stitt's favorite organist, Don Patterson was a boppish player whose sound was similar (like so many other's) to Jimmy Smith. He studied piano and was initially influenced by Errol Garner, but switched to organ after hearing Smith in 1956. He became a professional organist by 1959, and played with Stitt off and on throughout the 1960s. After recording his debut for Cadet in 1963, Patterson led 14 albums for Prestige during 1964–69. **Legends of Acid Jazz** (Prestige 24178) has all of the music recorded

May 12, 1964 (originally scattered over three albums), matching Patterson with the passionate Booker Ervin and drummer Billy James; altoist Leonard Houston guests on "Hip Cake Walk." Other highlights include "Oleo" and "When Johnny Comes Marching Home," compensating for the inclusion of "People." **Just Friends—Legends of Acid Jazz Vol. 2** (Prestige 24237) is the better buy, for not only does it include a full session with Ervin and James from later in 1964, but a 1967 session in which Patterson is teamed with Houston Person, Pat Martino, and James. The music swings, of course, and includes such tunes as "Sandu," "Red Top," "Last Train from Overbrook," "Rosetta," and "Sentimental Journey."

Big John Patton Big John Patton differed from Mc-Duff, McGriff, and Patterson by being on the Blue Note label rather than Prestige; otherwise his style was quite similar. He began playing piano in 1948, worked with Lloyd Price's R&B band (1954–59), moved to New York, and switched permanently to organ. Patton was to an extent sponsored by Lou Donaldson, who often used him on his records and helped him land a contract with Blue Note. Patton led six albums for Blue Note during 1963–66 (there would be ten in all), three of which are out on CD. His debut, **Along Came John** (Blue Note 31915) has Patton, Grant Green, and drummer Ben Dixon (who together formed one of Blue Note's house rhythm sections) being joined by both Fred Jackson and Harold Vick on tenors on some swinging and groovin' originals. The results overall are not essential, but they fit well into the soul jazz mainstream of 1963. **Blue John** (Blue Note 84143) uses the same rhythm section, but has Tommy Turrentine and George Braith, who plays both soprano sax and stritch, sometimes at the same time. Braith pushes the music at times beyond soul jazz, playing highly expressive solos that are more advanced than that of the other musicians. Recorded in 1965, **Let 'Em Roll** (Blue Note 89795) has Patton, Green, and drummer Otis Finch joined by vibist Bobby Hutcherson who influences the music to become hard bop and even post bop; highlights include "Latona," "The Shadow of Your Smile," and Hank Mobley's "The Turnaround." Strangely enough, it was not until Patton's sixth album (**Got a Good Thing Goin'**, which has not yet been reissued) before he recorded without another lead voice and was able to set the moods for his own records.

Shirley Scott Shirley Scott, who frequently teamed up with Eddie "Lockjaw" Davis in the late 1950s, married Stanley Turrentine and often worked with him in the 1960s. She made many recordings during 1961–67, including 18 as a leader—nine apiece for Prestige and Impulse. She is heard with Turrentine, generally in a quartet, on **Legends of Acid Jazz** (Prestige 24200), **Soul Shoutin'** (Prestige 24142), and **Blue Flames** (Original Jazz Classics 328). The **Acid Jazz** release has all of the music from the former LPs **Hip Soul** and **Hip Twist**, and **Soul Shoutin'** has the performances originally released on **The Soul Is Willing** and **Soul Shoutin'** (highlighted by "Yes Indeed," "Secret Love," "Deep Down Soul," and "The Soul Is Willing"). **Blue Flames** (at 32 minutes) suffers a bit in comparison, but that set (which includes Benny Golson's "Five Spot After Dark" and "Flamingo") also has its fine moments. **Blue Seven** (Original Jazz Classics 1050) is a change of pace since it matches Scott in a quintet with Oliver Nelson (on tenor), Joe Newman, bassist George Tucker, and drummer Roy Brooks; "Blue Seven, "Wagon Wheels," and "Give Me the Simple Life" are high points.

During 1963–64, Scott switched to the Impulse label, and those sessions were split between big band dates (usually with orchestras arranged by Oliver Nelson) and features for her trio. **For Members Only/Great Scott** (MCA/Impulse 33115) has all of the music from two of Scott's better Impulse albums, featuring her in both formats. In general, the trio numbers work better because the big band tracks emphasize current show and movie themes, some of which have slipped into obscurity. **Roll 'Em** (GRP/Impulse 147) has the organist focusing on swing-era tunes, whether playing with a 17-piece big band or in her trio. It is fun to hear an organ performing such numbers as "For Dancers Only," "Little Brown Jug," and "Stompin' at the Savoy." From 1966, **On a Clear Day** (Impulse 9074) is a trio set with Ron Carter and Jimmy Cobb that includes an off-the-wall tune ("What The World Needs Now Is Love"), a couple of basic originals, and songs by Henry Mancini, Antonio Carlos Jobim, and Irving Berlin.

But the Shirley Scott CD to get is ○ **Queen of the Organ** (Impulse 123). It has all of the music from the two-LP set **The Great Live Sessions** except for one number left out due to lack of space. This is a definitive live set featuring Scott with Turrentine, Bob Cranshaw, and drummer Otis "Candy" Finch. Most of the songs are obscurities and originals (other than "Just in Time," "Just Squeeze Me," and a surprisingly effective version of the Beatles' "Can't Buy Me Love"), and everything works, showing why this was one of the top soul jazz combos of the 1960s.

Jimmy Smith   Jimmy Smith made his reputation with his 25 Blue Note albums of 1956–60. He did not record anything in 1961, and just cut one album for the label in 1962, **Jimmy Smith Plays Fats Waller** (Blue Note 4100). Smith's tribute makes no attempt at imitating Waller's organ style, and serves simply as a good excuse to interpret seven jazz standards associated with Fats. Joined by his regular trio (guitarist Quentin Warren and Donald Bailey), Smith adds his brand of soul and swing to such unlikely vintage numbers as "Everybody Loves My Baby," "I've Found a New Baby," "Ain't Misbehavin'," and "Honeysuckle Rose."

In 1962, Smith recorded **Bashin'** (Verve 823308), a set that looked into his future. The first half of the program has the organist joined by a big band (arranged by Oliver Nelson) for the first time, including a popular version of "Walk on the Wild Side." The final three numbers have his trio in the spotlight. Lured by a lucrative contract from Verve, Smith fulfilled his obligations to Blue Note by recording four albums within an eight-day period (January 31–February 8, 1963). Typically for Blue Note, each of the sets has its own personality. **I'm Movin' On** (Blue Note 32750) teams Smith with Grant Green for what would be their only joint recording, with Donald Bailey completing the trio. The repertoire is typical of a Smith session with blues, a couple of standards, and ballads. **Bucket** (Blue Note 24550) has Smith running through "Careless Love," "Just Squeeze Me," "John Brown's Body," "Come Rain or Come Shine," and some originals with Quentin Warren and Bailey. **Rockin' the Boat** (Blue Note 84141) has the same group with Lou Donaldson making the unit a quartet on such fine numbers as "When My Dream Boat Comes Home," "Please Send Me Someone to Love," and "Just a Closer Walk with Thee." Smith's final Blue Note recording is a gem, **Prayer Meeting** (Blue Note 84164). This time Smith's trio is joined by Stanley Turrentine for soulful romps on "Red Top," "Prayer Meeting," and even "When the Saints Go Marching In." Two slightly earlier cuts added to the CD have the same group plus bassist Sam Jones, the only time that Smith used a bassist on all of his Blue Note sets.

Jimmy Smith would record prolifically for Verve for a decade, usually being teamed with big bands. Some of the sets are better than others (since some focused on commercial material and television theme songs). Recorded in 1964, **The Cat** (Verve 810 046) is notable for its colorful Lalo Schifrin arrangements. **Organ Grinder Swing** (Verve 825 675) is a throwback to Smith's Blue Note dates since it showcases the organist in a trio with Kenny Burrell and Grady Tate. **Got My Mojo Workin'/Hoochie Coochie Man** (Verve 533 828) has two former LPs on one CD, and finds Smith doing his best on such songs as the Rolling Stones' "I Can't Get No Satisfaction," "High Heel Sneakers," "Got My Mojo Workin'," "and "Ain't That Just Like a Woman." **Peter and the Wolf** (Verve 8652), which is not out yet on CD, is the most imaginative of Smith's big band albums, featuring Oliver Nelson's arrangements of ten themes from Prokofiev's "Peter and the Wolf" into a swinging suite.

During one week in 1966, Jimmy Smith teamed up with Wes Montgomery. ◉ **The Dynamic Duo** (Verve 521 445) has Smith and Montgomery playing two numbers in a quartet and three memorable cuts with Oliver Nelson's big band, including "Night Train" and "Down by the Riverside," and it makes one wish that they had had further opportunities to work together. **Further Adventures of Jimmy and Wes** (Verve 519 802) has leftovers from the same sessions, mostly quartet cuts other than a big band version of "Milestones."

Jimmy Smith was resting on his laurels by the late 1960s, but since he had virtually founded the modern-day jazz organ, his coasting was excusable.

Johnny "Hammond" Smith   Johnny Smith adopted "Hammond" as his nickname so as to distinguish him from guitarist Johnny Smith and other musicians with similar names. As with most organists of his generation, he started off playing piano. But after hearing Wild Bill Davis, he switched to organ, playing professionally by 1958. He worked briefly for Nancy Wilson, but was primarily a bandleader, recording regularly for Prestige during 1959–70.

Black Coffee (Milestone 47072) has a pair of Smith's early albums (**Black Coffee** and **Mr. Wonderful**) reissued in full, being featured with a quartet that includes tenor saxophonist Seldon Powell, and in a quintet with Houston Person and trumpeter Sonny Williams. The material is primarily straightahead jazz and blues, and the same is true for the two-fer **Open House** (Milestone 47089), which reissues **Open House** and **A Little Taste** (both from 1963). Among the key sidemen are Person, Powell, and either Thad Jones or Virgil Jones on trumpet. Highlights include "I Remember You," "Nica's Dream," and "Why Was I Born."

By 1966, Johnny "Hammond" Smith was recording much more commercial material, but he never lost his ability to groove with the best of the Jimmy Smith–inspired organists.

Larry Young   The one organist from this period who came up after Jimmy Smith and in time broke away from the dominant role model, Larry Young found a place for his instrument in post-bop and avant-garde jazz. Born in 1940, Young studied piano, but had no formal studies on organ. He began to focus on the organ in 1957, playing in his native Newark, New Jersey, in R&B and soul jazz groups. His initial three recordings, **Testifying** (Original Jazz Classics 1793), **Young Blues** (Original Jazz Classics 1831), and **Groove Street** (Original Jazz Classics 1853), dating from 1960–62, are fairly typical organ quartet dates with tenors Joe Holiday and Bill Leslie heard on an album apiece, guitarist Thornell Schwartz and drummer Jimmie Smith being constants, and Wendell Marshall adding his bass to one album. The music is fine in the tradition, but without any real surprises.

That began to change in 1964 when Young started recording regularly for Blue Note. A limited-edition box set on six CDs has all of these albums **The Complete Blue Note Larry Young 1964–67** (Mosaic 6-137) dating from 1964–69, plus three sideman dates with Grant Green. Some of the valuable music is also available individually. **Into Somethin'** (Blue Note 21734) is full of complex music (other than one blues), and features Young holding his own with Sam Rivers, Grant Green, and Elvin Jones. It is obvious, listening to this set, that Young was quite familiar with John Coltrane's music, and he was pushing his music in freer directions.

❍ **Unity** (Blue Note 84221) is considered Larry Young's finest recording. This classic outing with Woody Shaw, Joe Henderson, and Elvin Jones has Young sounding very original on his instrument, digging into three Shaw originals (including "The Moontrane"), Henderson's "If," "Monk's Dream," and "Softly as in a Morning Sunrise." Young's adventurous playing on this date would never be mistaken for Jimmy Smith's. **Of Love and Peace**

(Blue Note 84242) is nearly on the same level, but unfortunately this album has not been reissued on CD yet. Young teams up with trumpeter Eddie Gale (who played with Cecil Taylor during the era), James Spaulding, tenor saxophonist Herbert Morgan, and two drummers (Wilson Moorman III and Jerry Thomas). The music includes two intriguing free improvisations and adventurous versions of "Pavanne" and "Seven Steps to Heaven." From 1967, **Contrasts** (Blue Note 84266), also not out on CD outside of the Mosaic box, has its moments although it is not quite as essential. Young and a variety of mostly lesser-known players from the Newark area (including both Tyrone Washington and Herbert Morgan on tenors) stretch out on four numbers. In addition, the organist's wife, Althea Young, sings a haunting version of "Wild in the Wind," while "Major Affair" is an organ-drums duet.

Although just 27 at the end of 1967, Larry Young's career had already reached its peak.

Guitarists

Even though he had passed away in 1942, Charlie Christian was still the dominant influence on nearly all jazz guitarists during the 1961–67 period, prior to the rise of fusion and rock being taken seriously by jazz musicians. The best jazz guitarists of this era managed to gain their own voice and identity within the Christian style.

George Benson   George Benson was a featured soloist with Jack McDuff's band during 1962–65, the period when Red Holloway was McDuff's saxophonist. In 1965, Benson went out on his own, producer John Hammond signed him to Columbia, and he recorded a few straightahead albums. **It's Uptown** (Columbia/Legacy 66052) and ❍ **The George Benson Cookbook** (Columbia/Legacy 66054) feature Benson's quartet (with organist Lonnie Smith, baritonist Ronnie Cuber, and several different drummers) romping through basic originals, some standards, and a few pieces that show that even at this early stage Benson was not unaware of pop music. He takes three vocals on **It's Uptown**, and belts out "All of Me" on **The George Benson Cookbook** (which has such guests as King Curtis on tenor and trombonist Bennie Green), but the emphasis is primarily on his guitar and the individual solos of Smith and the heated Cuber. At this early stage, George Benson's style was an extension of Charlie Christian and Wes Montgomery, but he was already adding his own musical personality and brand of soul to the largely boppish music.

Kenny Burrell Kenny Burrell, whom Duke Ellington called his favorite guitarist (unfortunately, the two of them never recorded together), stayed busy during the 1960s, leading a pianoless trio, recording frequently, and sometimes teaming up with organist Jimmy Smith. Recorded in 1963, ◉ **Midnight Blue** (Blue Note 46399) is one of Burrell's best-known Blue Note sessions. He is teamed with Stanley Turrentine, Major Holley, drummer Bill English, and Ray Barretto on conga for a blues-oriented date highlighted by "Chitlins Con Carne," "Midnight Blue," "Saturday Night Blues," and the lone standard "Gee Baby Ain't I Good to You." Many listeners have ranked **Guitar Forms** (Verve 314 521 403), a partial collaboration with arranger Gil Evans, as one of Burrell's most significant sessions, but it is a bit overrated. The guitarist certainly plays well enough on the nine selections, but Evans was only involved in five of the tunes, and his arrangements for the 15-piece all-star band find them mostly just setting a melancholy mood behind Burrell. Three other cuts have Burrell in a quintet with Roger Kellaway and conguero Willie Rodriguez, while a tasteful excerpt from Gershwin's "Prelude No. 2" is taken unaccompanied. The music has a fair amount of variety, but surprisingly little occurs that is memorable. It is a pity that there was not much more interaction between Burrell and Evans. The CD reissue adds no less than 11 alternate takes of the three quintet songs, but nothing from the overrated project with Evans. Better to acquire **Blues—The Common Ground** (Verve 314 589 101) on which Burrell is joined by an orchestra arranged by Don Sebesky for such material as "Every Day I Have the Blues," "The Preacher," "Angel Eyes," and "See See Rider." He also excels on a pair of quartet numbers and an unaccompanied version of "Were You There?"

Grant Green During 1960–65, Grant Green was the house guitarist for Blue Note, appearing on quite a few sessions as a sideman and leading 20 albums of his own. Born in St. Louis in 1931, Green was playing guitar professionally at age 13 with a gospel group. He worked throughout the Midwest, including with Jimmy Forrest, but was still largely unknown in 1960 when he moved to New York at the suggestion of Lou Donaldson. He caught on quickly, signed with Blue Note, and was very busy throughout the decade. Green had an unusual

style in that he very rarely played chords, sticking almost exclusively to single-note lines. He was very flexible and could play with adventurous quintets, in a boppish quartet, and in organ groups with equal ease. He was a soulful player yet could hold his own with the likes of McCoy Tyner and Elvin Jones.

All of Green's 1961–65 recordings for Blue Note are recommended, with some really being standouts. **First Session** (Blue Note 27548) from 1960 was not released until the 1990s. Although there are a few hesitant moments, Green plays quite well in a quartet with Wynton Kelly, Paul Chambers, and Philly Joe Jones. There are also two later and previously unknown versions of "Woody'n You" from a session with Sonny Clark. **Grant's First Stand** (Blue Note 21959) was the guitarist's official debut, jamming in a trio with organist Baby Face Willette and drummer Ben Dixon on originals, "Lullaby of the Leaves," and "'T'Ain't Nobody's Business If I Do." **Green Street** (Blue Note 32088) has Green in an unusual setting for him, being joined by just bassist Ben Tucker and Dave Bailey. While Kenny Burrell helped pioneer this pianoless guitar trio format, the fact that Green sticks to single-note playing makes the music sound very sparse although it has its appealing moments. **Sunday Morning** (Blue Note 52434) was recorded with pianist Kenny Drew, Tucker, and Dixon. This hard bop date is highlighted by "So What," "Exodus," and Green's original "Freedom March."

Grantstand (Blue Note 46430) gathers together four musicians who rarely worked together: Green, Yusef Lateef on tenor and flute, organist Brother Jack McDuff, and drummer Al Harewood. Despite their very different musical personalities, this combination works surprisingly well on such songs as the 15-minute "Blues in Maude's Flat," "My Funny Valentine," and "Grantstand." **Standards** (Blue Note 21284) was not released in the United States until 1998; it was previously out in Japan as **Remembering**. Green is heard in fine form in a quiet trio with bassist Wilbur Ware and drummer Al Harewood, performing such songs as "Love Walked In," "I'll Remember April," and "All the Things You Are."

The two-CD set **Complete Quartets with Sonny Clark** (Blue Note 57194) has all of the music from the LPs **Gooden's Corner**, **Nigeria**, and **Oleo** other than one selection that features tenor saxophonist Ike Quebec. With Sam Jones and Louis Hayes or Art Blakey completing the group, the chemistry between Green and

Sonny Clark results in quite a few exciting bebop romps. Unfortunately, due to the pianist's early death, this was a short-lived partnership, but it did result in some lasting music. **Born to Be Blue** (Blue Note 84432) has Clark and Green together again, this time in a quintet with Ike Quebec, Jones, and Hayes. Quebec's presence changes the sound of the group, but keeps the quality high, with his huge swing tone well featured on such numbers as "Back in Your Own Backyard," "Someday My Prince Will Come," and "Born to Be Blue."

● **The Latin Bit** (Blue Note 37645) is an unlikely classic for one would not immediately associate the guitarist with Afro-Cuban jazz. However, for this project, Green and a particularly strong rhythm section (pianist Johnny Acea, bassist Wendell Marshall, drummer Willie Bobo, and percussionists Patato Valdez and Garvin Masseaux) play such melodies as "Mambo Inn," "Besame Mucho," and "Tico Tico" with affection and swing. Three unrelated straightahead tracks from other dates have been added to this essential release.

Goin' West (Blue Note 84310) is one of the few Grant Green Blue Note albums that have not yet been reissued on CD; it is a quartet date with Herbie Hancock that is comprised of jazz interpretations of Western and cowboy themes. **Feelin' the Spirit** (Blue Note 46822) has Green, Herbie Hancock, Butch Warren, Billy Higgins, and Garvin Masseaux on tambourine playing six spirituals, including "Just a Closer Walk with Thee," "Joshua Fit the Battle of Jericho," and "Nobody Knows the Trouble I've Seen," turning them into highly expressive yet reverent jazz. In contrast, **Am I Blue** (Blue Note 35564) is surprisingly weak with just so-so material, a consistent laidback feeling, and plenty of dull stretches (including a 14-minute version of "For All We Know") despite some fiery spots by Joe Henderson.

● **Idle Moments** (Blue Note 84154) from 1963 is widely considered one of the greatest Grant Green recordings. The blend of Green with Joe Henderson, Bobby Hutcherson, Duke Pearson, Bob Cranshaw, and drummer Al Harewood mixes together highly individual yet complementary voices. The music is challenging, has a fair amount of variety, and the musicians all sound quite inspired. Highlights include Pearson's "Idle Moments," "Django," and "Nomad." **Matador** (Blue Note 84442) has Green showing a lot of courage by playing "My Favorite Things" with McCoy Tyner and Elvin

Jones (Bob Cranshaw completes the quartet), displaying plenty of passion and stretching out for over ten minutes. Just as lengthy are a couple of Green's better compositions plus "Wives and Lovers" and Duke Pearson's "Bedouin." **Solid** (Blue Note 33580) has the same rhythm section, with Joe Henderson and altoist James Spaulding making the group a sextet. Green was clearly challenged by the material, which includes George Russell's "Ezz-Thetic" and Henderson's "The Kicker."

Talkin' About (Blue Note 21958) features the unlikely trio of Grant Green, organist Larry Young, and Elvin Jones. The music covers many areas, from soul jazz and hard bop to modal music and more adventurous improvising. Highlights include Young's "Talkin' About J.C.," (for John Coltrane), "I'm an Old Cowhand," and "You Don't Know What Love Is." **Street of Dreams** (Blue Note 21290) has the same trio plus Bobby Hutcherson, stretching out on lengthy versions of four songs, including "I Wish You Love" and "Lazy Afternoon." **I Want to Hold Your Hand** (Blue Note 59962) from March 31, 1965, has to have been one of the very first jazz albums named after a Beatles song. It is also just about the last recording by Grant Green at his musical prime before he switched directions. In a quartet with Hank Mobley, Larry Young, and Elvin Jones, Green turns the Beatles song into worthwhile jazz, and digs creatively into such numbers as "Corcovado," "Speak Low," and "At Long Last Love."

After so much recording activity, Green would just lead two further albums prior to 1969. **His Majesty King Funk** has been coupled with one of the weaker Donald Byrd albums on the single CD **His Majesty King Funk/Up with Donald Byrd** (Verve 527474). Green sounds okay in a quintet with Larry Young and Harold Vick, but the bland material (mostly fairly simple funk tunes) is disappointing. The Donald Byrd set has potential because of the inclusion of Jimmy Heath, Stanley Turrentine, and Herbie Hancock, but the prominence of the three- or four-voice Donald Byrd Singers and mundane arrangements by Claus Ogerman sink the effort. Two years would pass before Green recorded **Iron City** (32 Jazz 32048), a decent trio effort with Big John Patton and Ben Dixon that mostly features bluesy material (plus "Samba de Orfeu") and some uptempo tunes.

When Grant Green re-emerged in 1969, he would still be a fine player, but his musical interests would no longer be in swinging creative jazz.

Barney Kessel   One of the definitive jazz guitarists of the 1950s, Barney Kessel finished off his extensive string of excellent recordings for the Contemporary label in 1961 with **Workin' Out** (Original Jazz Classics 970). The music features a quartet that has three obscure players: pianist Marvin Jenkins (who also plays occasional flute), bassist Jerry Good, and drummer Stan Popper. Although nothing all that unusual happens, Kessel plays well on such songs as "When Johnny Comes Marching Home," Ahmad Jamal's "New Rhumba," and the guitarist's "Pedal Point." But this album was really an end of an era for the guitarist who, other than three somewhat commercial efforts for Reprise, would mostly be off jazz records during this period.

Pat Martino   One of the brightest new guitarists of the mid-1960s, Pat Martino began playing professionally in 1959 when he was 15. He was born and grew up in Philadelphia where he had an opportunity to gain experience playing with soul jazz and hard bop groups led by Willis Jackson, Red Holloway, Don Patterson, Jimmy Smith, Jack McDuff, Richard "Groove" Holmes, and Jimmy McGriff, appearing on quite a few recordings, sometimes under his original name of Pat Azzara. He gigged with John Handy in 1966 and then began leading his own groups. Although grounded in conventional jazz, Martino was one of the first guitarists to have his playing open to the influences of rock, pop, and world music. In 1967, he recorded his first two albums as a leader.

El Hombre (Original Jazz Classics 195) features Martino with a soul jazz group that includes Trudy Pitts on organ, flutist Danny Turner, drummer Mitch Fine, and two percussionists. Although the music (five originals, "Just Friends," and "Once I Loved") is primarily straightahead, the guitar solos are more advanced than the playing of the other musicians. It seems obvious in hindsight that he was not going to be merely a traditionalist in his career. Despite its title, **Strings** (Original Jazz Classics 223) does not feature the guitarist with a string section, but is instead an advanced hard bop date with Joe Farrell (tenor and flute), Cedar Walton, bassist Ben Tucker, and drummer Walter Perkins. "Minority" is given a particularly exciting treatment, while Martino's four originals show that he was looking ahead.

Wes Montgomery   Virtually unknown in jazz in 1957, Wes Montgomery was considered its leading guitarist by 1961. His style was an extension on Charlie Christian's, he could outswing virtually any other guitarist of the era, and his mastery of octaves became his trademark.

Montgomery's recordings for Riverside during 1959–63, which are reissued in full on the 12-CD box ⦿ **The Complete Riverside Recordings** (Riverside 4408), are the most boppish, straightahead, and free-wheeling of his career. Most of the sessions are readily available individually, including **So Much Guitar** (Original Jazz Classics 233), **Full House** (Original Jazz Classics 106), **Fusion!** (Original Jazz Classics 368), **Boss Guitar** (Original Jazz Classics 261), **Portrait of Wes** (Original Jazz Classics 144), and **Guitar on the Go** (Original Jazz Classics 489). **So Much Guitar** is particularly strong, featuring Montgomery in a quintet with Hank Jones that is highlighted by "Cottontail" and "I'm Just a Lucky So and So." **Full House** teams Wes with the always-competitive Johnny Griffin while **Fusion** looks into the future by having Montgomery take brief and melodic guitar solos in a tightly arranged setting with strings. **Boss Guitar**, **Portrait of Wes**, and **Guitar on the Go** (the latter pairs together sessions from 1959 and 1963) all feature Montgomery in a trio with the underrated organist Melvin Rhyne.

Wes Montgomery's recording career can easily be divided into three periods. The second part covers 1964–66 when he was recording regularly for Verve. These collaborations with producer Creed Taylor and arranger Don Sebesky are often quite intriguing, ranging from a few jams similar to his work on Riverside to encounters with big bands and studio orchestras in which Montgomery's solos are purposely kept short. **Movin' Wes** (Verve 521 433) from 1964 has some weak material (such as "People" and "Matchmaker"), and the brass orchestra (arranged by Johnny Pate) is purely in the background, but there are some worthwhile performances, particularly the two-part "Movin' Wes," "Born to Be Blue," and "West Coast Blues." **Bumpin'** (Verve 539 062) is one of Montgomery's better efforts with Don Sebesky, and he gets to stretch out a bit on the title cut and "Here's that Rainy Day."

The two-CD set ⦿ **Impressions: The Verve Jazz Sessions** (Verve 521690) has a full disc of Montgomery in a quartet with Wynton Kelly, Paul Chambers, and Jimmy Cobb, the complete sessions from the **Smokin'** at the Half Note sets, which are Montgomery's finest dates for Verve. Also on this two-fer are most of the better jazz numbers from Wes's other Verve dates. Of lesser interest are Montgomery's rather commercial releases Goin' Out of My Head (Verve 825 676), Tequila (Verve 831 671), and California Dreaming (Verve 827 842). These records not only sold quite well ("Goin' Out of My Head" was a hit), but resulted in Wes Montgomery being heard regularly on AM pop radio of the era. Other than an excellent set with Jimmy Smith (that was issued under the organist's name as two CDs), this trio of bestsellers ended Montgomery's Verve period.

In 1967, Wes followed Creed Taylor to A&M. His three albums for the label were no-nonsense commercial fluff, with the guitarist mostly restricted to melody statements that showed off his pretty octave sound. He primarily performed cover versions of pop hits, and these recordings increased his fame way beyond jazz even while the jazz world felt he was selling out. Although stung a bit by the criticism, Montgomery felt no need to apologize. He had struggled for years to support his oversize family, and now he was finally being well paid. A Day in the Life (A&M 75021 0816) is pleasing as background music with Montgomery backed by Muzak-oriented strings arranged by Don Sebesky on such tunes as a hit version of "Windy," "Watch What Happens," "California Nights," and "Eleanor Rigby." While one can sympathize with his desire to finally make some money, this set (the best of his A&M output) pales in musical significance next to Wes's Riverside and better Verve recordings.

Joe Pass   In the 1960s, four major jazz guitarists emerged whose main influence was Charlie Christian: Grant Green, Wes Montgomery, George Benson, and Joe Pass. Joe Pass, like Wes Montgomery, had a false start in his career before he really got going in the 1960s. Born in 1929, Pass played early on with a few swing bands including those of Tony Pastor and Charlie Barnet (1947). However, after serving in the military, he became a drug addict. The 1950s were largely a waste with some prison time and constant scuffling. Fortunately, Pass was able to recover from his addiction, and in 1962 while at Synanon, he made his first significant record. Settling in Los Angeles, he became a regular with Dick Bock's Pacific Jazz/World Pacific labels, and worked with the Gerald Wilson Big Band, Les McCann, and George Shearing's quintet in addition to his own combos.

During 1963–67, Pass led seven albums, the first four of which have been issued on the limited-edition five-CD box The Complete Pacific Jazz Joe Pass Quartet Sessions (Mosaic 5-207). Unfortunately, The Complete "Catch Me" Sessions (Blue Note 1035) is not currently available individually. Pass, who at 34 was making his debut as a leader on records, was already quite distinctive. For that project, he is well featured in a quartet with pianist Clare Fischer (who doubles on organ), Albert Stinson or Ralph Pena on bass, and Colin Bailey or Larry Bunker on drums, playing such tunes as "Just Friends," "Falling in Love with Love," and "Catch Me."

Joy Spring (Blue Note 35222) has Pass playing live with his quartet (which includes pianist Mike Wofford,

TIMELINE 1965

John Coltrane records **Ascension** and later in the year adds Pharoah Sanders and Rashied Ali to his group, resulting in McCoy Tyner and Elvin Jones soon departing. • Ornette Coleman makes a comeback, leading a trio with David Izenzon and Charles Moffett. • Albert Ayler forms a band with his brother Donald Ayler. • Woody Shaw and Joe Henderson are in the Horace Silver Quintet. • John Handy's Quintet causes a sensation at the Monterey Jazz Festival. • Mal Waldron moves to Europe. • Richard "Groove" Holmes has a hit with a medium-tempo version of "Misty." • John Hammond signs George Benson to Columbia. • Nat King Cole dies. • Ella Fitzgerald records with Duke Ellington. • Maynard Ferguson breaks up his big band. • The Don Ellis Orchestra is formed. • Stuff Smith moves to Copenhagen. • Buster Bailey and Tyree Glenn join the Louis Armstrong All-Stars. • Teddy Buckner begins a 16-year stint playing at Disneyland with his Dixieland band. • Lester Bowie moves to Chicago. • In England, trumpeter Ian Carr leads a jazz quintet that includes the young guitarist John McLaughlin. • Mercer Ellington joins his father's band as a section trumpeter and road manager. • The AACM (Association for the Advancement of Creative Musicians) is formed on May 8, with Muhal Richard Abrams as the organization's first president.

bassist Jim Hughart, and drummer Colin Bailey) in a Los Angeles club in early 1964. The music is straightahead bebop with the group stretching out on five standards (none briefer than six and a half minutes) including "Relaxin' at Camarillo," "There Is No Greater Love," and Clifford Brown's "Joy Spring." As worthy as that set is, the Joe Pass classic of the era is ◐ **For Django** (BGO 430). Pass, who is joined by Hughart, Bailey, and rhythm guitarist John Pisano, performs music that was either composed by Django Reinhardt, was part of his repertoire, or is one of two tributes (John Lewis's "Django" and Pass's "For Django"). Pass was much more influenced by Charlie Christian than by Reinhardt, but he does a superb job of bringing back Django's spirit without losing his own musical personality. Highlights include "Rosetta," "Nuages," and "Limehouse Blues."

Pass's later World Pacific albums pale in comparison although **The Stones Jazz** (the LP World Pacific 1854) is certainly intriguing as he plays ten songs made famous by the Rolling Stones. Few guitarists sounded less like a rock player than Pass, and one almost wishes that this album were much worse than the typically tasteful effort that resulted.

For Joe Pass, his glory period was still a few years in the future.

Gabor Szabo One of the first Europeans to successfully infuse jazz with their own musical heritage, Gabor Szabo always sounded quite original. Born in Budapest, Hungary, he began playing guitar when he was 14, soon discovering jazz. In 1956 when he was 20, he fled his country shortly before its Communist uprising, moving to the United States. Szabo attended the Berklee College of Music (1958–60) and gained fame for his work with the Chico Hamilton Quintet (1961–65), playing alongside Charles Lloyd. After leaving Hamilton, he played and recorded with Gary McFarland and the Charles Lloyd Quartet before starting his solo career in 1966. During 1967–69, his quartet featured the classical guitar of Jimmy Stewart, whose strong bop chops worked quite well with the unique Szabo sound.

Gypsy '66 (Impulse 9099), Szabo's debut as a leader, has such current pop songs as "Yesterday," "If I Fell," and "Walk On By," but Gary McFarland's clever arrangements for the unusual group (two or three guitars, flutist Sadao Watanabe, bass, drums, percussion, and McFarland's marimbas) makes the results more interesting than expected. **Spellbinder** (Impulse 9100) also has a couple of dated pop tunes ("It Was a Very Good Year" and "Bang Bang, My Baby Shot Me Down"), but is actually one of Szabo's better recordings. He is showcased in a sparse quintet with Ron Carter, Chico Hamilton, and both Victor Pantoja and Willie Bobo on Latin percussion. Highlights include "Spellbinder," "Gypsy Queen," and "My Foolish Heart." Best of all the Gabor Szabo albums is ◐ **The Sorcerer** (GRP/Impulse 211), a live concert from 1967 by his quintet with Jimmy Stewart, bassist Louis Kabok, drummer Marty Morrell, and percussionist Hal Gordon. Their version of "What Is this Thing Called Love" effectively contrasts the two very different sounding guitars (though the versatile Stewart could emulate Szabo when called for), and the other songs include "Mizrah," and "Little Beat." The CD also reissues three other selections taken from the same engagement that were previously part of an album called **More Sorcery**.

Unfortunately, Gabor Szabo's other projects from the era are not on the same level, often featuring his sophisticated guitar on weak pop tunes insipidly arranged, including "Light My Fire," "Lucy in the Sky with Diamonds," "To Sir with Love," and "Krishna." His subsequent career would be disappointing considering his great potential and unique sound.

Bassists

Bassists, while still mostly playing in a supportive role, became liberated to a large extent during the 1960s, no longer always being in the background. However, three of the bassists in this section (and to a lesser extent the younger Ray Brown) showed that the former role for the bass could still be played with creativity and color.

Ray Brown Ray Brown, whose large tone and swinging style were definitive of bebop of the 1950s, continued touring and recording with the Oscar Peterson Trio through 1966. Along the way he occasionally collaborated with Milt Jackson, a friend of his since they played together with the Dizzy Gillespie Big Band in the 1940s. The double CD **Much in Common** (Verve 314 533 259) reissues three of their former LPs from 1962–65 (**Ray Brown with the All-Star Big Band**, **Ray Brown-Milt Jackson**, and **Much in Common**). The first two projects are big-band dates with most of the music arranged by either Ernie Wilkins or Oliver Nelson, featuring solos from Brown (who switches to cello on three songs), Jackson, Cannonball Adderley, and Nat Adderley (featured on one of the earliest versions of his hit "Work Song"). **Much in Common** is a bit unusual, a small-group date with either organist Wild Bill Davis or pianist Hank Jones plus the gospel vocals of Marion Williams on a few of the numbers. Overall, the two-fer consists of well-played but fairly conventional music, falling short of being essential while being pleasing to fans of Brown and Jackson.

In 1967, Ray Brown settled in Los Angeles where he worked steadily in the studios and became a major part of the local jazz scene.

Ron Carter A symbol of the new breed of bassists, Ron Carter was classically trained on cello, played bass in Detroit, and attended the Eastman School of Music. He was with Chico Hamilton in 1959, played some classical music, and in New York worked with Eric Dolphy, Don Ellis, Cannonball Adderley, Jaki Byard, Thelonious Monk, Bobby Timmons, and Art Farmer before joining the Miles Davis Quintet in 1963. Carter was always an expert and very versatile accompanist in addition to being a distinctive soloist whose open-minded style made him greatly in demand. His first record date as a leader, 1961's **Where** (Original Jazz Classics 432), which has him doubling on cello, finds Eric Dolphy largely stealing the show. That seemed only right because Carter was such a major voice on Dolphy's **Out There** the previous year. **Where** has been reissued individually and as part of the huge Dolphy Prestige box set.

Sam Jones Sam Jones kept busy in the 1960s, working steadily as a member of the Cannonball Adderley Quintet (1959–65), and then replacing Ray Brown in the Oscar Peterson Trio (1966–70). Although Jones rarely led his own band in public, his occasional dates as a leader on records are consistently rewarding and well planned. **The Chant** (Original Jazz Classics 1839) has Jones on bass and cello for four songs apiece with a group also including Nat Adderley, Blue Mitchell, trombonist Melba Liston, Cannonball Adderley, and Jimmy Heath. Victor Feldman and Heath provide the arrangements to such songs as "Four," "Sonny Boy," "Over the Rainbow," and Jones's "In Walked Ray." Released in 1962, **Down Home** (Original Jazz Classics 1864) also has Jones doubling on bass and cello, this time with an all-star nonet/tentet arranged by Ernie Wilkins, and with a quintet that includes Les Spann or Frank Strozier on

flute. The songs include "Unit Seven," Sam Jones's most famous original.

Leroy Vinnegar Leroy Vinnegar worked in the Los Angeles area with other straightahead players in the 1960s, including Teddy Edwards and pianist Joe Castro. **Leroy Walks Again** (Original Jazz Classics 454), his 1962–63 sequel to 1957's **Leroy Walks**, is on the same level as the earlier date. Vinnegar plays mostly a supportive role behind two overlapping groups that include trumpeter Freddy Hill, Teddy Edwards, Victor Feldman (piano and vibes), drummers Ron Jefferson and Milt Turner, pianist Mike Melvoin, and vibraphonist Roy Ayers. The set mostly features originals (including three by Vinnegar), obscurities, and the one standard "I'll String Along with You." The music falls between cool jazz and hard bop, with Leroy Vinnegar (who was always a supportive player) content to swing and inspire the soloists.

Drummers

Drummers began to assume a much more active role in the 1960s, with Elvin Jones pointing out an alternative way to both accompany and interact with soloists at the same time. A master of polyrhythms, Jones was a step beyond the boppish styles of Max Roach and Kenny Clarke, indirectly inspiring the always inquisitive Roach to continue evolving.

Kenny Clarke Kenny Clarke spent the 1960s being quite busy playing in Europe in his unchanged bebop style, working with Bud Powell, backing visiting Americans, and teaming with top European jazz musicians. In 1960, he joined forces with Belgium pianist Francy Boland to form the Clarke-Boland Big Band (or, as it was sometimes known, the Boland-Clarke Big Band), a group that during the next 13 years featured an all-star lineup of Europeans and expatriate Americans performing Boland's swinging arrangements. Among the personnel along the way who were either members of the band or guests on recordings were trumpeters Benny Bailey, Jimmy Deuchar, Idrees Sulieman, Kenny Wheeler, and Art Farmer, trombonist Ake Persson, saxophonists Zoot Sims, Sahib Shihab, Billy Mitchell, Ronnie Scott, Sal Nistico, Johnny Griffin, Don Menza, Tony Coe, Phil Woods, Stan Getz, and Herb Geller, bassist Jimmy Woode, and Kenny Clare, who played second drums with Kenny Clarke. The ensemble recorded fairly regularly during 1961–71, but its recordings for Atlantic, Columbia, Philips, Saba, Campi, MPS, Polydor, Supraphon, Black Lion, and Verve are almost all quite rare in the United States. **Handle with Care** (Koch 8534) reissues a fine Atlantic album from 1962, with Boland contributing arrangements to the six songs (four of which are his originals). Key soloists include Sulieman, Deuchar, Bailey, Persson, Shihab (on flute), Mitchell, Scott, and altoist Derek Humble on such numbers as "Long Note Blues," "Get Out of Town," and "Speedy Reeds."

Chico Hamilton   Chico Hamilton had gained fame in the 1950s as the leader of a series of reeds-cello-guitar-bass-drums quintets. However, the chamber jazz of his West Coast jazz groups had run its course by 1961, and, at the urging of Charles Lloyd, the cello was dropped in favor of a trombone, giving the band a much different sound. The 1962–63 version of the Chico Hamilton Quintet consisted of Garnett Brown (replaced by George Bohanon by the fall of 1962), Lloyd on tenor and flute, the Hungarian guitarist Gabor Szabo, bassist Albert Stinson, and the leader on drums. The group's music was melodic, but not all that boppish, with Lloyd's tenor-playing recalling John Coltrane (although with a softer sound), and Szabo's guitar sounding completely unique and mysterious. The band could be considered post-bop, looking toward the avant-garde while being soulful in its own way. Its initial recording, **Drumfusion** (Columbia 1807), unfortunately is not yet on CD. **Transfusion** (Studio West 102) has the quintet performing very concise versions of their repertoire (the music is taken from radio broadcasts in 1962), often just featuring one soloist on each cut. Lloyd, Bohanon, and Szabo all fare well on these seven standards and nine Lloyd originals.

 ❍ **Man from Two Worlds** (GRP/Impulse 127) is the definitive CD of this group because this CD has all of the music from Hamilton's **Man from Two Worlds** LP (which is a quartet set without trombone) and four of the six numbers originally on **Passin' Thru**. Among the selections is the original version of "Forest Flower Sunrise/Sunset," which would become famous when played by the later Charles Lloyd Quartet. Just as rewarding is **A Different Journey** (Collectables 6158), a reissue of the band's Reprise LP. The group is featured on several memorable melodies (including "Sun Yen Sen,"

"Voice in the Night," and the closing "Island Blues"), lots of advanced yet logical improvising, and more than its share of variety. The quintet had its own sound although it was quite underrated during its relatively short life; one can understand why Chico Hamilton would later call this his greatest band.

Chico Hamilton's 1965–66 recordings (which include **El Chico**, **The Further Adventures of El Chico**, and **Chic, Chic, Chico**) have their moments of interest even if they are not on the same level as the earlier quintets, and they have not been reissued on CD. However, **The Dealer** (GRP/Impulse 547 958) is available and is significant. The young electric blues/rock guitarist Larry Coryell made his recording debut on this set from 1966, a year before joining Gary Burton. At times Coryell sounds strangely like Chuck Berry (particularly on "The Dealer"), and, due to his appearance, this album is an early missing link to the birth of fusion. Also featured are altoist Arnie Lawrence, bassist Richard Davis, organist Ernie Hayes (on two numbers), and, on his spirited boogaloo "For Mods Only," Archie Shepp on piano.

Roy Haynes   Roy Haynes, who turned 35 in 1961, primarily led his own groups during 1961–65 (when he was not subbing for Elvin Jones with the John Coltrane Quartet) before becoming a member of the Stan Getz Quartet (1965–67) and Gary Burton's band (1967–68). His own recordings tended to put the spotlight on a major player, with earlier sets showcasing Phineas Newborn and Richard Wyands. **Out of the Afternoon** (GRP/Impulse 180) has Haynes, Tommy Flanagan, and Henry Grimes interacting with the remarkable Rahsaan Roland Kirk. Rahsaan takes solos on tenor, manzello, stritch, and flute, with the highlights including rollicking versions of "Fly Me to the Moon," "Moony Ray," "If I Should Lose You," and "Some Other Spring." **Cracklin'** (Original Jazz Classics 818) has Haynes, pianist Ronnie Mathews, and bassist Larry Ridley supporting Booker Ervin. The quartet primarily plays originals (other than "Under Paris Skies"), and Ervin shows how to be very soulful and explorative at the same time.

Elvin Jones   The younger brother of Hank and Thad Jones, Elvin Jones became the most influential drummer of his generation. He spent time in the army (1946–49), and then was part of the exciting Detroit jazz scene during the first half of the 1950s. After moving to New York in 1955, he worked with many top players during the next five years, including Bud Powell, Miles Davis, Sonny Rollins (with whom he recorded at his famous Village Vanguard session), J.J. Johnson (1956–56), Donald Byrd, Tyree Glenn, and Harry "Sweets" Edison. However, he will always be best known for being a member of the John Coltrane Quartet during 1960–65. His ability to imply time without necessarily stating it, to effortlessly play polyrhythms (even on ballads), and to create a constant wave of forward-moving sound permanently altered jazz drumming.

While a member of Coltrane's group, Jones had an opportunity to lead a few albums of his own. Recorded in 1961, **Elvin!** (Original Jazz Classics 259) is different than one would expect because, as with McCoy Tyner's early solo records, Jones's solo dates from the era were more conservative than his work with Coltrane. This is a sextet session that has a strong Count Basie swing feel, featuring his brothers Thad and Hank plus flutist Frank Wess, Frank Foster on tenor, and bassist Art Davis. **Illumination** (Impulse 250) from 1963 is much more advanced. Jones co-led this album with Jimmy Garrison, and, in addition to McCoy Tyner and baritonist Charles Davis, the set features Sonny Simmons (alto and English horn) and Prince Lasha (flute and clarinet), an intriguing pair of avant-gardists. Performing originals by band members, the musicians play music ranging from advanced hard bop to freer sounds that still swing.

Dear John C. (GRP/Impulse 126) from February 1965 may have been dedicated to John Coltrane, but the music is essentially modern hard bop. Altoist Charlie Mariano is the main soloist on this quartet date with Richard Davis and either Roland Hanna or Hank Jones on piano; Davis's inventive solos often take honors.

In late 1965, when Coltrane added Rashied Ali to his band as second drummer, it soon resulted in Jones leaving the group. After going on a European tour with the Duke Ellington Orchestra (no recordings resulted), Jones formed his own band, which for part of 1966 had Dollar Brand on piano. In time, Elvin Jones would become an important bandleader himself.

Pete LaRoca   Born Pete Sims, this drummer went by the name of Pete LaRoca early on so he would seem to be a Latin and could fit in well playing timbales in Latin jazz bands. LaRoca played regularly with Sonny Rollins (1957–59), and in the 1960s worked with Jackie McLean,

John Coltrane (as the original drummer in Trane's quartet before Elvin Jones), Slide Hampton, Marian McPartland, Art Farmer, Freddie Hubbard, Mose Allison, Charles Lloyd (1966), Paul Bley, and others. He led two superior albums during the 1960s. ● **Basra** (Blue Note 32091) from 1965 is a classic. LaRoca contributed three originals (the one-chord "Basra," a blues called "Candu," and the complex "Tears Come from Heaven"), but it is the other three songs that bring out the best in Joe Henderson, pianist Steve Kuhn, and bassist Steve Swallow. "Malaguena" is full of passion, Swallow's "Eiderdown" receives its initial recording, and the ballad "Lazy Afternoon" is given its definitive instrumental treatment. Recorded in 1967, **Bliss** (Muse 99058), which unfortunately has not reappeared on CD yet, is also quite intriguing for it matches La Roca (who contributed all seven numbers) and bassist Walter Booker with tenor saxophonist John Gilmore (on a rare vacation from Sun Ra) and the young up-and-coming pianist Chick Corea.

Shelly Manne   The 1961 version of Shelly Manne and His Men was a quintet consisting of trumpeter Conte Candoli, tenor saxophonist Richie Kamuca, pianist Russ Freeman, bassist Chuck Berghofer, and the drummer/leader. The glory days of West Coast jazz were at an end, but Manne's group was able to survive a few more years playing the music that he loved. One major reason is that he had his own nightclub, Shelly's Manne-Hole, and therefore had a home base. On two CDs (both of which are straight reissues of the original LPs), Shelly Manne and His Men are heard in prime form performing live at their home base. **At the Manne-Hole Vol. 1** (Original Jazz Classics 714) and **Vol. 2** (Original Jazz Classics 715) feature the quintet in March 1961 with Candoli in particular in fine form. Among the better selections are (from **Vol. 1**) Duke Ellington's "How Could It Happen to a Dream" and "The Champ," and (from **Vol. 2**) "On Green Dolphin Street" and "If I Were a Bell."

The recording **2-3-4** (Impulse 11492) is a special project from 1962. There are five numbers from a session teaming Manne with Coleman Hawkins (whom he had recorded with in 1943), Hank Jones, and George Duvivier. "Take the 'A' Train" and "Cherokee" have the quartet playing two tempos at once, showing that they were aware of the latest avant-garde developments. "Me and Some Drums" features Hawkins and Manne in a very effective duet with Hawkins making his only recorded appearance on piano during the song's first half. The CD is rounded off by a pair of trio features for Eddie Costa (with Duvivier and Manne)—one song apiece on vibes and drums. Other recordings during this era for Manne include an unusual duet album with guitarist Jack Marshall (**Sounds Unheard Of**), a set of Jewish melodies (**My Son, the Jazz Drummer**), an interesting if only partly successful revisit to **My Fair Lady** (which has a few vocals from Jack Sheldon and Irene Kral), and Johnny Williams's arrangements of George Gershwin tunes for a big band (**Manne—That's Gershwin**). None of these have been reissued on CD yet.

In 1967, Shelly Manne's Men recorded their last set, **Perk Up** (Concord 401), before undergoing some major changes. The group (Manne, Candoli, altoist/flutist Frank Strozier, pianist Mike Wofford, and bassist Monty Budwig) performs advanced hard bop with Strozier and Wofford sometimes hinting at the avant-garde. The music is swinging while being a bit unpredictable. During the next decade, Shelly Manne would show just how adaptable and versatile a drummer he really was.

Joe Morello   Joe Morello has been rated from the beginning of his career as a brilliant drummer. He picked up experience in the early 1950s working with Johnny Smith, Stan Kenton's Orchestra, Gil Melle, Tal Farlow, Jimmy Raney, and especially the Marian McPartland Trio (1953–56). He became famous as a member of the Dave Brubeck Quartet during 1956–67, and his mastery allowed Brubeck to experiment with unusual time signatures.

Although he has rarely led his own band, Morello did head record dates in 1956 and 1961. The latter set, **Joe Morello** (Bluebird 9784) was originally called **It's About Time** since it featured ten songs with the word "time" in their title. The CD reissue is a bit confusing in that it only includes five of the six quintet numbers (leaving out a John Bunch trio number) that feature Phil Woods and Gary Burton, and just two of the four other songs that have Morello with a big band arranged by Manny Albam. However, this disc does include a totally unreleased and unrelated (but complementary) big band session from the following year, and shows that Joe Morello, in addition to his strong solo abilities, was also a fine accompanist.

Max Roach   Very much involved in the civil rights movement and the career of his soon-to-be wife Abbey Lincoln (they got married in 1962), Max Roach recorded less often during the 1961–67 period than he had during the second half of the 1950s. However, what he did record was at a very high level. ● **Percussion Bitter Suite** (Impulse 122) is one of Roach's finest albums, featuring Booker Little, Julian Priester, Eric Dolphy, Clifford Jordan, Mal Waldron, Art Davis, guest percussionists, and two emotional vocals from Abbey Lincoln. Dolphy's highly expressive alto solo on "Mendacity" is quite memorable as is the melancholy sound of Little's trumpet. In fact, every selection on this set is haunting and very effective.

Recorded in 1962, **It's Time** (Impulse 185) mixes together Roach's sextet (trumpeter Richard Williams, Jordan, Priester, Waldron, and Davis) with a vocal choir conducted by Coleridge Perkinson; Roach contributed all six originals. Although each of the horns has a feature or two, and Abbey Lincoln stars on "Lonesome Lover," there are times when the choir simply gets in the way, lowering the quality of the music overall. **Speak Brother Speak** (Original Jazz Classics 646) is a sort of antidote. Jordan, Waldron, bassist Eddie Khan, and Roach stretch out on two very lengthy tracks (the 25-minute "Speak, Brother, Speak," and a 22 1/2-minute "A Variation") that fall between hard bop and the avant-garde. Clifford Jordan in particular plays quite well.

Featuring the Legendary Hasaan/Drums Unlimited (Collectables 6256) reissues (other than leaving out one number from the former date) the only two albums led by Roach during 1963–67. **Featuring the Legendary Hasaan** is the lone recording made by pianist Hasaan Ibn Ali, who is heard in a trio with Roach and Art Davis. Hasaan was an original player whose style fell somewhere between Thelonious Monk, Herbie Nichols, and Cecil Taylor. His interpretations of his originals are intense, rhythmic, and sometimes quite melodic. **The Drums Unlimited** set has three unaccompanied drum solos that show what an inventive musical architect Roach always was, and three numbers (including "St. Louis Blues") in which Roach leads a quintet/sextet with Freddie Hubbard, James Spaulding, Ronnie Mathews, Jymie Merritt, and sometimes Roland Alexander on soprano. It is a pity that the latter group did not record again under Max Roach's leadership.

Vibraphonists

In 1959, the masters of the vibes were Lionel Hampton, Red Norvo, Milt Jackson, Terry Gibbs, and Cal Tjader. Gary Burton soon joined their ranks, and by 1963 Bobby Hutcherson was also in their company, with Walt Dickerson and Dave Pike being strong contenders.

Gary Burton   One of the two most significant vibraphonists to emerge in the 1960s (along with Bobby Hutcherson), Gary Burton has had a wide-ranging career, most notable for his brilliant four-mallet technique, and his open-minded approach toward other styles of music. He was self-taught on vibes, and developed quickly, making his recording debut in 1960 when he was 17 on a jazz set by country guitarist Hank Garland. In 1961, with **New Vibe Man in Town** (RCA 52420), he was a leader for the first time. Joined by bassist Gene Cherico and Joe Morello, Burton already sounds quite distinctive on "Joy Spring," "You Stepped Out of a Dream," and his original "Our Waltz." The vibist, who recorded as a leader for RCA through 1968, spent 1963 as a member of the George Shearing Quintet, and was a stimulating force with Stan Getz's 1964–66 pianoless quartet. Burton was never all that interested in sticking to bebop, utilizing Mike Gibbs's unusual compositions as early as 1963 and interacting with a variety of Nashville session players on the LP **The Tennessee Firebird** (RCA 3719) in 1966.

After he left Getz, Gary Burton formed what is considered one of the very first fusion groups. Considering that the vibes are not exactly a rockish instrument, and would be rarely utilized in that context, Burton was an unlikely early hero of the as-yet unnamed new style. However, his decision to hire Larry Coryell, at the time an electric blues guitarist whose background was as much in rock as in jazz, helped break down musical boundaries. With Steve Swallow and Roy Haynes, the Gary Burton Quartet debuted on ● **Duster** (Koch 7846). Their music was an alternative to hard bop, soul jazz, and the avant-garde, carving out a fresh new path. On such songs as Michael Gibbs's "Sweet Rain," Swallow's "General Mojo's Well Laid Plan," Coryell's "One, Two, 1-2-3-4," and Carla Bley's "Sing Me Softly of the Blues," Burton's group creates fresh new music that was very difficult to classify, crossing quite a few musical boundaries. The band, with Bob Moses now on drums, also recorded **Lofty Fake Anagram** (One Way 34489)

and the intriguing **A Genuine Tong Funeral** (RCA 66748) in 1967. The former has originals by Burton, Swallow, Carla Bley, and Michael Gibbs plus Duke Ellington's "Fleurette Africaine." **A Genuine Tong Funeral**, a lengthy work by Carla Bley that depicts attitudes toward death in dramatic and occasionally humorous fashion, has the quartet augmented by six top musicians, including Steve Lacy, Gato Barbieri, and Bley on piano and organ. The Bley suite is more notable for setting moods than for stating any significant melodies, but it certainly stands out from the crowd, giving hints as to how the Carla Bley big band would sound in future years. The CD reissue of this work also has five of the nine selections from **Lofty Fake Anagram** added as "bonus" tracks.

Walt Dickerson   A fine vibraphonist whose style was more advanced than the dominant influence Milt Jackson, Dickerson recorded frequently during 1961–65. He graduated from Morgan State College in 1953, served in the army during 1953–55, spent a period of time working in Los Angeles, and moved to New York at the beginning of the 1960s, recording four quartet albums for Prestige during 1961–62. His debut as a leader, **This Is Walt Dickerson** (Original Jazz Classics 1817), has the vibist leading a group that includes pianist Austin Crowe and drummer Andrew Cyrille through six of his moody originals. The music shows the influence of Ornette Coleman, gets away from strictly chordal improvisation, and is quite intriguing. **A Sense of Direction** (Original Jazz Classics 1794) has some additional challenging originals and unpredictable versions of "What's New," "You Go to My Head," and "If I Should Lose You." **Relativity** (Original Jazz Classics 1867) from 1962 also mixes together originals with standards (including "Autumn in New York" and "I Can't Get Started") while **To My Queen** (Original Jazz Classics 1880) is most notable for matching Dickerson with Andrew Hill (before he started recording for Blue Note), bassist George Tucker, and Andrew Cyrille, although the 32-minute playing time is unfortunately rather brief.

It is a pity that two of Dickerson's other albums remain out of print, a set of songs from **Lawrence of Arabia** (Dauntless 4313) and **Impressions of a Patch of Blue** (MGM 4358), which features Sun Ra as a sideman. After 1965, Dickerson retired from active playing for a decade just when his futuristic style (which led the way toward Bobby Hutcherson) could have made its greatest impact.

Terry Gibbs   Terry Gibbs continued leading his well-named Dream Band in the Los Angeles area through 1961. Although its studio recordings remain out of print, six CDs of live material have been released, including two from 1961. **Main Stem Vol. 4** (Contemporary 7656) and **The Big Cat Vol. 5** (Contemporary 7657), both recorded January 20–22, 1961, features such players as Gibbs, Conte Candoli, Frank Rosolino, the tenors of Richie Kamuca and Bill Perkins, and both Charlie Kennedy and Joe Maini on altos. The repertoire is less swing era–oriented than on the previous three volumes, featuring plenty of originals from the arrangers (which include Bill Holman and Al Cohn) and some bop standards.

Although his Dream Band ultimately did not last, Gibbs stayed busy working in the Los Angeles area, sometimes playing with Steve Allen. His 1963 trio featured an intriguing young pianist, Alice McLeod, who would soon meet and marry John Coltrane.

Bobby Hutcherson   Bobby Hutcherson started out with piano lessons, but as a teenager, after hearing a Milt Jackson record, he switched permanently to vibes, studying with Dave Pike. He played locally in his native Los Angeles with altoist Curtis Amy and Charles Lloyd, joining the Al Grey-Billy Mitchell Sextet in 1960. The following year, he settled in New York where he quickly was in demand for dates by both the greats of hard bop and the avant-garde. Hutcherson was at his most advanced during 1962–67, often playing in pianoless groups and recording frequently for Blue Note, both as a sideman and leader. He became the only vibraphonist to record with Jackie McLean, Eric Dolphy, Grant Green, Hank Mobley, Herbie Hancock, and Andrew Hill.

Dialogue (Blue Note 46537), Hutcherson's 1965 debut as a leader, has six adventurous numbers performed by the vibraphonist, Freddie Hubbard, Sam Rivers (tenor, soprano, flute, and bass clarinet), Andrew Hill, Richard Davis, and drummer Joe Chambers. Hill and Chambers supplied the material, complex works that force the musicians to be very alert and to play at their most creative. ◐ **Components** (Blue Note 29027) ranges from hard bop (Hutcherson's "Little B's Poem") to atonal sound explorations ("Air") with four songs apiece by the vibraphonist and Chambers. The sextet also features Hubbard, altoist/flutist James Spaulding, Herbie Hancock, and Ron Carter. One can understand,

listening to this dynamic music, why Bobby Hutcherson was considered the choice vibraphonist of "The New Thing."

Happenings (Blue Note 46530) puts the emphasis on Hutcherson's vibes and marimba in a quartet with Hancock, Bob Cranshaw, and Chambers. Hutcherson performs six of his originals (which again range from hard bop to nearly free) plus a remake of Hancock's "Maiden Voyage." **Stick Up!** (Blue Note 59378) has an unbeatable lineup of young modern musicians (Hutcherson, Joe Henderson, McCoy Tyner, Herbie Lewis, and Billy Higgins) performing five excellent Hutcherson originals plus Ornette Coleman's "Una Muy Bonita." From 1967, **Oblique** (Blue Note 84444) is, like **Happenings**, a quartet set (with Hancock, Albert Stinson, and Chambers), but the tunes are more complex, inspiring the musicians to reach beyond hard bop in their explorative improvisations.

Later in 1967, Bobby Hutcherson moved back to Los Angeles where he formed a post-bop quintet with tenor saxophonist Harold Land.

Milt Jackson   The most influential of all vibraphonists (having surpassed Lionel Hampton as an influence by the late 1940s), Milt Jackson spent the 1960s alternating between tours and recordings with the Modern Jazz Quartet, and leading his own sessions. The latter gave him an opportunity to stretch out away from the strictures of John Lewis's music, playing the bop standards, ballads, and blues that he most loved.

Statements (GRP/Impulse 130) is fairly typical of Jackson's music away from the MJQ. He is heard with Hank Jones in a quartet from 1961, and leading a quintet (with Jimmy Heath and Tommy Flanagan) in 1964. The later recordings originally formed half of the album **Jazz 'N' Samba**. Nothing too unusual occurs, but the results are pleasing. **Bags Meets Wes** (Original Jazz Classics 234) is Jackson's one-time matchup with Wes Montgomery, in a quintet with Wynton Kelly, Sam Jones, and Philly Joe Jones. This fine music (highlighted by "Jingles," "Stairway to the Stars," "Delilah," and "Stablemates") is as successful as one would expect from these major players; the performances are also available on Montgomery's "Complete on Riverside" box set.

Milt Jackson recorded several other sets for Riverside during 1961–62. **Big Bags** (Original Jazz Classics 366) has Jackson backed by a big band playing Ernie Wilkins and Tadd Dameron arrangements. In addition to the vibraphonist, there is solo space for Nat Adderley, Jimmy Cleveland, James Moody, and Jimmy Heath. **Invitation** (Original Jazz Classics 260) has six numbers in which Bags is joined by Kenny Dorham, Jimmy Heath, Tommy Flanagan, Ron Carter, and Connie Kay with two other songs substituting trumpeter Virgil Jones for Heath. The repertoire consists of three standards, a trio of group originals, "Ruby My Dear," and the obscure "Ruby," and not too surprisingly the musicians all swing quite well in the hard bop tradition. **For Someone I Love** (Original Jazz Classics 404) is successful mostly because of Melba Liston's inventive and unpredictable arrangements for a brass orchestra consisting of four or five trumpets, three trombones, three or four French horns, Major Holley's tuba, and a rhythm section. Jackson takes nearly all the solos on a well-conceived set that includes some Duke Ellington ballads, "Days of Wine and Roses" and "Save Your Love for Me." **Live at the Village Gate** (Original Jazz Classics 309), a quintet outing with Jimmy Heath, Hank Jones, Bob Cranshaw, and Albert "Tootie" Heath, features Jackson in typically swinging form on blues, standards, ballads, and Jimmy Heath's "Gemini." The same is true of his slightly later and somewhat scarce releases for Limelight. Milt Jackson's style had long been set, but he never lost enthusiasm for swinging, and nearly all of his many recordings are well worth acquiring.

Dave Pike Influenced by Milt Jackson, but having his own approach to the vibes, Dave Pike is an exciting and at times flamboyant performer, but one who has not gained much fame. He started out on drums before teaching himself the vibes. After moving to Los Angeles in 1954 with his family, Pike became part of the West Coast jazz scene, playing with Curtis Counce, Harold Land, Elmo Hope, Dexter Gordon, Carl Perkins, and Paul Bley among others. He moved to New York in 1960, and was a member of Herbie Mann's popular band during 1961–64.

Dave Pike was always skilled at both straightahead and Latin jazz. His debut as a leader, 1961's **It's Time for Dave Pike** (Original Jazz Classics 1951), is a conventional but enjoyable quartet outing with Barry Harris, Reggie Workman, and Billy Higgins. Pike excels in the boppish format, and highlights include Charlie Parker's "Cheryl," "Hot House," and an unaccompanied vibes solo on "Little Girl Blue."

Pike was a member of Herbie Mann's group by the time he recorded **Carnavals**, and the world music influence shows. **Carnavals** (Prestige 24248) has all of the performances from two former LPs, **Bossa Nova Carnival** and **Limbo Carnival**, both recorded in 1962. The former set focuses on songs by Brazilian composer Joao Donato, with Pike leading a quintet/sextet with Kenny Burrell, bassist Chris White, drummer Rudy Collins, percussionist Jose Paulo, and sometimes Clark Terry. **Limbo Carnival** has more of an emphasis on calypsos, including "St. Thomas," "My Little Suede Shoes," "Mambo Bounce," and "Limbo Rock." Pike is assisted on that project by either pianist Tommy Flanagan or guitarist Jimmy Raney, Ray Barretto, and occasionally altoist Leo Wright.

After leaving Mann, Dave Pike freelanced and showed himself open to trying different things. On 1965's **Jazz for a Jet Set** (Atlantic 73527), he sticks exclusively to the marimba, while Herbie Hancock is heard throughout on organ, an instrument he rarely played again. The septet also includes two trumpeters (most notably Clark Terry who has a few short solos) and a rhythm section with guitarist Billy Butler. The music mixes together standards and obscurities, is open to the influences of the boogaloo and pop rhythms of the day, and high points include Hancock's "Blind Man, Blind Man," "Sunny," and "Devilette."

Arrangers

The five arrangers in this section all made their mark by being highly original. Two (Quincy Jones and Gil Evans) were household names in jazz and two others (Gary McFarland and George Russell) made important contributions, while Tadd Dameron was at the end of his career.

Tadd Dameron One of the major arranger/composers of the bebop era, Tadd Dameron unfortunately picked up a drug habit that resulted in him spending 1959–61 in jail. He did some arranging while behind bars, and after his release he wrote for Sonny Stitt, Blue Mitchell, Milt Jackson, and Benny Goodman in addition to leading one album in 1962. ❂ **The Magic Touch of Tadd Dameron** (Original Jazz Classics 143) is a definitive set that sums up his career. Using up to 14 pieces, Dameron utilized such top players as trumpeters Charlie Shavers, Joe Wilder, and Clark Terry, trombonist Jimmy Cleveland, Julius Watkins on French horn, Bill Evans, and Philly Joe Jones plus singer Barbara Winfield on two songs. In addition to a few newer pieces, Dameron's group performs inventive remakes of a variety of his best songs, including "Our Delight," "Dial 'B' for Beauty," "On a Misty Night," and "If You Could See Me Now."

Unfortunately, Tadd Dameron was soon stricken with cancer, and he passed away in 1965 at the age of 48.

Gil Evans Considering the great success that he had on his three main projects with Miles Davis (**Miles Ahead**, **Porgy and Bess**, and 1960's **Sketches of Spain**), and his own high-quality recordings of the late 1950s, it is surprising that Gil Evans did not record more during 1961–67. In fact, other than more work with Davis (**Quiet Nights** and half of a Carnegie Hall album), writing for a Kenny Burrell project (**Guitar Forms**), and lending his name to the Impulse album **Into the Hot** (which actually features arrangements by Johnny Carisi, and three numbers by Cecil Taylor's septet), all of the arranger's recordings from this era are on **The Individualism of Gil Evans** (Verve 833 804). The personnel varies on the six sessions (which for this CD adds five numbers including two previously unreleased selections) with such major soloists featured as Wayne Shorter, Jimmy Cleveland, Johnny Coles, and Kenny Burrell. Among the high points are "Time of the Barracudas," "The Barbara Song," "Las Vegas Tango," and "Spoonful," making one wish that Evans had been more active as a bandleader during a period when he should have been achieving his greatest recognition.

Quincy Jones After trying his best to keep his big band together in Europe, in October 1960, Quincy Jones broke up the orchestra and came home. He had reunions with the band on a few occasions in 1961, with the final one being at the Newport Jazz Festival. Jones became one of the first Afro-Americans to hold an important executive post at a major record label, working for Mercury as the head of A&R, and becoming a vice president in 1964. Although he continued recording throughout the 1960s, and writing arrangements for singers and big bands, Jones's focus shifted to writing for films and television.

The Quintessence (Impulse 222) from late 1961 is one of Quincy Jones's finest jazz recordings; its extreme brevity is its only bad point. Featured are trumpeters Clark Terry, Thad Jones, and Freddie Hubbard, Julius Watkins on French horn, and most notably Phil Woods in several big-band settings. Highlights include fine versions of "Quintessence" and "For Lena and Lennie." But as the decade progressed, Jones's recordings became less and less interesting from the jazz standpoint, often using the flavor of jazz rather than serious jazz improvising.

Gary McFarland An inventive arranger/composer, Gary McFarland's career did not live up to its great potential, but it had its moments. McFarland briefly played trumpet, trombone, and piano before settling on vibes in 1955 when he was 21. He attended the Berklee College of Music for a semester as a writer, and he was soon in demand as a freelancer, contributing arrangements (and occasionally playing vibes) for Gerry Mulligan, Johnny Hodges, John Lewis, Stan Getz, Bob Brookmeyer, Anita O'Day, and Bill Evans among others.

McFarland began leading his own record dates in late 1961, switching between Verve and Impulse throughout the next few years. Unfortunately, most of his recordings have not been reissued yet, and overall they vary greatly in quality. Best are 1963's **Point of Departure** (Impulse 46), which has an all-star sextet with Richie Kamuca, Jimmy Raney, and trombonist Willie Dennis, and **Profiles** (Impulse 9112), which is a live set of McFarland originals performed by a large band that includes Clark Terry, Bob Brookmeyer, Zoot Sims, Kamuca, Phil Woods, and Gabor Szabo among others. But he also recorded easy-listening sets (**Soft Samba**) and overly concise, radio-friendly jazz (**Tijuana Jazz**) that sold well but confused the jazz audience, and led to him being greatly underrated in the long run.

George Russell George Russell, a very original arranger who utilized fresh theories in his writing, led a sextet during 1960–62 in which he played piano. There were six recordings in all including two in 1960, and a very scarce Decca LP (**George Russell in Kansas City**) the following year. The most renowned of these sets is ● **Ezz-thetic** (Original Jazz Classics 70). Russell's group at that time not only includes trumpeter Don Ellis, trombonist Dave Baker, bassist Steve Swallow, and drummer Joe Hunt, but the remarkable Eric Dolphy on alto and bass clarinet. Among the highlights is a remarkable version of "'Round Midnight" (which has one of Dolphy's greatest solos), "Honesty," "Thoughts," and the title cut. The improvising is at a very high level, and the frameworks (which include free and stop-time sections) really inspire the players. Recorded in 1962, **The Stratus Seekers** (Original Jazz

Classics 365), which has altoist John Pierce in Dolphy's place and Paul Plummer added on tenor, may seem anticlimactic in comparison, but it also has its special moments including "Blues in Orbit" (later recorded by Gil Evans) and "The Stratus Seekers." **The Outer View** (Original Jazz Classics 616), from August 1962, is the last of these combo dates, and has Russell joined by Ellis, trombonist Garnett Brown, Plummer, Swallow, and drummer Pete LaRoca. As usual, the complex material (even a transformation of Charlie Parker's blues "Au Privave") really challenges the musicians. The most famous selection, a very haunting version of "You Are My Sunshine," was singer Sheila Jordan's debut on records. Overall, this series of George Russell records has its own logic and is difficult to classify, deserving much more attention by jazz historians and analysts.

In 1963, George Russell moved to Sweden where he stayed for five years. He fulfilled commissions that allowed him to write for orchestras and recorded an additional combo set in 1965. **At Beethoven Hall** (Polygram 539084) has Russell (who contributes some fairly basic piano) heading a group also including Don Cherry, trumpeter Bertil Lovgren, trombonist Brian Trentham, tenor saxophonist Ray Pitts, bassist Cameron Brown, and Albert "Tootie" Heath. The band explores several lengthy pieces (including a suite dedicated to Russell's Lydian concept that includes abstract versions of "Bags' Groove," "Confirmation," and "'Round Midnight"), and an instrumental remake of "You Are My Sunshine."

Other Instruments

It seems funny to include the clarinet in this category, along with flute, violin, and bagpipes, but the clarinet in the years after the swing era had been demoted to a minor instrument in all jazz styles other than Dixieland and swing. However, there was nothing minor about the talents of Buddy DeFranco and the up-and-coming Eddie Daniels.

Eddie Daniels   By the 1960s, the clarinet was in danger of being a forgotten instrument altogether. Not counting Benny Goodman, the swing survivors, and the use of the clarinet in Dixieland and in the Duke Ellington Orchestra, the instrument was barely heard in jazz. Buddy DeFranco did his best to keep it alive in a bebop context, but Tony Scott had dropped out to become a world traveler, and Jimmy Giuffre became an educator by the middle of the decade. Virtually the only

new modern jazz clarinetists of the period were the avant-gardist Perry Robinson and Eddie Daniels.

Eddie Daniels appeared at the 1957 Newport Jazz Festival as a 15-year-old altoist, playing in Marshall Brown's Youth Band. In 1966, he graduated from Juilliard, and soon began a six-year stint playing tenor and occasional clarinet with the Thad Jones/Mel Lewis Orchestra. His debut album as a leader was also in 1966, **First Prize** (Original Jazz Classics 771). Daniels plays clarinet on three of the eight songs, and tenor on the remainder, already sounding quite original and virtuosic. Daniels is joined on three standards, four originals, and the pop tune "Spanish Flea" by the Thad Jones/Mel Lewis rhythm section of pianist Roland Hanna, bassist Richard Davis, and drummer Mel Lewis. However, it would be 20 years before Eddie Daniels gained the fame that he deserved as one of the greatest of all jazz clarinetists.

Buddy DeFranco   During 1960–64, Buddy DeFranco co-led a swinging quartet/quintet with Tommy Gumina on accordion, recording five albums for Decca, and Mercury that have yet to be reissued. He was also featured on a record (**Blues Bag**) with Art Blakey's Jazz Messengers in which he played bass clarinet. But after the breakup of the group with Gumina, times became tough, and in 1966 he accepted what would be an eight-year stint as the leader of the Glenn Miller ghost band, grinding out the old hits on a nightly basis. It is ironic that a major bebop clarinetist would be stuck leading a tired swing band, but the audience who still enjoyed dancing to "In the Mood" did not notice the irony.

Rufus Harley   Of all of the instruments used throughout jazz history, the one that seems least likely to catch on are bagpipes. Because of its droning sound, and the fact that notes cannot be cut off quickly, the bagpipes never even made an appearance in jazz settings until the rather industrious Rufus Harley gave it a shot in the 1960s. Originally a saxophonist, Harley began playing bagpipes early in the decade, and he led four albums for Atlantic during 1965–69 including **Bagpipe Blues** and **Scotch and Soul**, also playing flute, soprano, and tenor on occasion. **The Pied Piper of Jazz** (Label M 5710) is a sampler with the best selections from those two albums plus guest spots on records with Sonny Stitt and Herbie Mann. "Feeling Good," "Pipin' the Blues," and "Bagpipe Blues" are among the highlights of this unique sampler.

Although Rufus Harley has re-emerged now and then in the decades since, he has generated no potential successors as a jazz bagpiper; one cannot get away from that instrument's sound and lack of dexterity.

Hubert Laws   A technically brilliant flutist, Hubert Laws was a member of the early Jazz Crusaders when they were in Texas (1954–60) and known as the Modern Jazz Sextet. Classically trained, Laws was a virtuoso by the time he led his first record date in 1964. **The Laws of Jazz** (Rhino/Atlantic 71636) is a straightahead set in which Laws is assisted by pianist Armando Corea (before he became known as Chick), Richard Davis, and either Jimmy Cobb or Bobby Thomas on drums. The leader plays piccolo on two of the seven numbers, and in general is in top form on "Miss Thing," "Bessie's Blues," and his own "Bimbe Blue." Laws, who recorded a second (but thus far not reissued) set for Atlantic, worked during this period with Mongo Santamaria, Benny Golson, Jim Hall, James Moody, and Clark Terry among many others, showing a great deal of potential.

Jean-Luc Ponty   The golden age of the violin in jazz was the late 1930s. A decade earlier Joe Venuti had become the first (and some would say the greatest) jazz violinist, playing with a stunning virtuosity, and ranking with the top improvisers of the era on any instrument. The 1930s found such major swing violinists emerging as Stephane Grappelli, Stuff Smith, Eddie South, Svend Asmussen, and (at the end of the decade) Ray Nance. Surprisingly, there were no significant additions to this list of top jazz violinists during the 1940s and '50s, no Charlie Parker of the violin who brought the instrument into the bop era.

It was not until the mid-1960s when Michael White played quite effectively with John Handy's quintet that a new type of post-swing violin style began to emerge. Within a few years, several violinists would emerge from the as-yet-unnamed fusion style, mixing together the sound and power of rock with jazz improvisation. The leading violinist in this field would be Jean-Luc Ponty.

Ponty, who was born in France in 1942, started on violin when he was five and was trained to become a classical violinist. When he was 15, he was accepted into the Paris Conservatoire, and he played with the Concerts Lamoureux Orchestra for three years. However, it was during this period that he discovered jazz and took up the clarinet and tenor for a time, playing jazz on those instruments while sticking to classical music on his violin. In 1962, he took the plunge and began playing jazz on violin, recording two obscure albums during 1963–64 that include some straightahead jazz. A brilliant technician, Ponty soon developed his own sound and was so highly rated that in 1966 he recorded **Violin Summit** (Verve/MPS 821 303), playing alongside Grappelli, Smith, and Asmussen in different combinations, with all four violinists jamming on "It Don't Mean a Thing," and Ponty teaming up with Grappelli on Sonny Rollins's "Pent Up House."

In 1967, Ponty visited the United States for the first time, participating at a workshop at the Monterey Jazz Festival. The LP **Sunday Walk** (Pausa 7033) has the violinist performing in a quartet with pianist Wolfgang Dauner, Niels Pedersen, and drummer Daniel Humair. They play straightahead but advanced music that looks toward John Coltrane with Ponty displaying his fresh approach to playing jazz violin, showing that it could be used to play other styles of jazz beyond swing.

Afro-Cuban Jazz

Afro-Cuban or Latin jazz continued to adapt to new musical trends in the 1960s. While remaining bop-oriented in its solos, the music was open to the influence by soul music and R&B while some musicians also looked back to its roots in Cuba.

Ray Barretto   Ray Barretto helped introduce the conga to jazz in non-Latin settings, recording on small group dates led by Gene Ammons, Red Garland, Lou Donaldson, Cannonball Adderley, Dizzy Gillespie, Sonny Stitt, and others, starting in the mid-1950s. He worked with Tito Puente (1957–59) and Herbie Mann (1961–62), leading his own bands from 1962 on. His hit recording of "El Watusi" helped launch the Latin bugalu craze, which fused together R&B and soul music with Latin jazz. ⦿ **Carnaval** (Fantasy 24713) has Barretto's first two albums as a leader on one CD. One record, **Pachanga with Barretto**, consists of ten compositions by Hector Rivera that were meant to accompany dancers who performed the new Latin dance the Pachanga. This lively set has Barretto joined by flutist Jose Canoura, violinist Mike Stancerone, trumpet, tenor, and an oversized rhythm section. The accompanying **Latino** album is a descarga (a Cuban jam session) with plenty of hot solos, particularly from the underrated Jose "Chombo" Silva on tenor, whose playing is reminiscent at times of Stan Getz.

Willie Bobo Willie Bobo (born William Correa) was one of the most popular figures in Latin jazz. In his career he played drums, congas, bongos, and timbales, working with Mary Lou Williams (1952), Tito Puente (1954–57), Cal Tjader (1958–61), Mongo Santamaria (1961–62), and Herbie Mann (1962–63) before becoming a bandleader himself, though he would always be available to work as a sideman for special projects. **Spanish Grease/Uno Dos Tres** (Verve 314 521 664) is a CD that combines Bobo's two best-known albums, recorded during 1965–66. There are plenty of catchy songs throughout the dates, with the danceable pop-oriented music being in the bugalu vein rather than standard Afro-Cuban jazz. Highlights include "Spanish Grease," "Fried Neck Bones and Some Home Fries," "The Breeze and I," and "I Remember Clifford."

Herbie Mann Originally a cool jazz/bop-oriented flutist and tenor saxophonist, in 1959 Herbie Mann switched whole-heartedly to Afro-Cuban jazz, leading the Afro-Jazz Sextet. Although he quite typically would not stick exclusively to Latin jazz during 1961–67 (recording with Bill Evans, being captivated by the new bossa nova music, and starting to explore more pop-oriented rhythms), Afro-Cuban jazz was the foundation of his music during this time.

Although Mann recorded quite prolifically during 1961–67, relatively few of his popular dates have been reissued on CD yet. **Live at the Village Gate** (Rhino/Atlantic 1380) is an exception. The flutist's version of bassist George Tucker's "Comin' Home Baby" from this set became his first big hit. Also on this relatively brief CD are "Summertime" and a 20-minute version of "It Ain't Necessarily So." Mann is joined by vibraphonist Hagood Hardy, bassist Ahmed Abdul-Malik, drummer Rudy Collins, both Chief Bey and Ray Manilla on percussion, and sometimes Tucker on second bass. Two other LPs cut under similar circumstances (**Monday Night at the Village Gate** and **Returns to the Village Gate**) are also worth searching for.

Nirvana (Koch 5480) is one of Mann's finest jazz dates, an encounter with the Bill Evans Trio (which at the time included Chuck Israels and Paul Motian) shortly after the pianist began playing again after the death of Scotty LaFaro. Included are such songs as "I Love You," "Willow Weep for Me," and Satie's "Gymnopedie," and the flutist fits right into the often-introspective group quite naturally.

After touring Brazil in 1962, Mann occasionally recorded in bossa nova settings including an album apiece with Antonio Carlos Jobim (actually cut in Brazil) and Joao Gilberto. When he appeared at the 1963 Newport Jazz Festival, a set documented by Atlantic, and reissued as **Live at Newport** (Wounded Bird 1413), Mann led a hot Latin jazz group that included Dave Pike, pianist Don Friedman, guitarist Attila Zoller, Ben Tucker, drummer Bob Thomas, and percussionists Willie Bobo and Patato Valdes. However, the most interesting selections are Mann's renditions of three Antonio Carlos Jobim songs: "Samba De Orfeu," a 4/4 non-bossa version of "Desafinado," and a version of "The Girl from Ipanema" performed three months after the famous hit, but before the Stan Getz version was released. Two years later, Mann returned to Newport, recording **Standing Ovation at Newport** (Wounded Bird 1455), this time with a band consisting of Pike, Chick Corea, bassist Earl May, drummer Bruno Carr, Patato Valdes, and two trombonists. The lengthy "Patato," "Stolen Moments," and particularly the encore "Comin' Home Baby" (which has the composer Ben Tucker sitting in) are most memorable. **New Mann at Newport** (Wounded Bird 1471) features Mann at the 1966 festival (except for "All Blues," which is from four months earlier), and has a mostly different group without piano that consists of Mann, two trombones, trumpeter Jimmy Owens, Reggie Workman, Bruno Carr, and Patato Valdes. Highlights include Jimmy Heath's "Project S," Wayne Henderson's "Scratch," and "All Blues."

By 1967, Herbie Mann had moved away from Latin jazz and started collaborating with other backing singers (including Tamiko Jones and Carmen McRae), playing R&B, exploring pop tunes, and recording an unusual album of Middle Eastern–flavored music.

Mongo Santamaria After spending three years with Cal Tjader's group, conguero Mongo Santamaria went out on his own in 1961. At first he had a pachanga band, a variation of a flute and violin charanga, featuring flutist Rolando Lozano, Jose "Chombo" Silva on tenor, and violinist Felix "Pupi" Legarratta plus vocals from Rudy Calzado. In 1962, Herbie Hancock was subbing in the band on piano and played his song "Watermelon Man" for Santamaria. Mongo quickly adopted the song as his own, and it became a major hit the following year. By then, Santamaria's band was more jazz-oriented, featuring Chick Corea and Hubert Laws. In 1964, he signed with the Columbia label where he was a major leader in the Latin bugalu movement for the next few years, performing cover versions of current pop and R&B hits in a Latin style that was very danceable and popular.

Santamaria recorded in each of these musical phases. **Arriba** (Fantasy 24738) has all of the music from his first two albums after leaving Tjader, featuring Lozano, Silva, Legaretta, pianist Joao Donato, and a few too many salsa vocals from Calzado. **At the Blackhawk** (Fantasy 24734), which is also from 1961, has the traditional album **Viva Mongo** (with Silva playing violin) and the more jazz-oriented **Mighty Mongo** with some excellent tenor solos from Chombo. **Sabroso** (Original Jazz Classics 281) is one of Santamaria's best recordings, and it finds him leading a particularly intriguing transitional band. In addition to Silva on both tenor and violin, featured are two obscure but excellent trumpeters (Louis Valizan and Marcus Cabuto), Lozano on flute, pianist Rene Hernandez, bassist Victor Venegas, Willie Bobo, and Pete Escovedo as one of the background singers.

◉ **Watermelon Man** (Milestone 47075) features a variety of concise singles from 1963 (including the original hit version of "Watermelon Man") plus selections from an unissued live performance from the previous year. Highlights include "Funny Money," "The Boogie Cha-Cha Blues," "Yeh-Yeh," "The Peanut Vendor," "I'll Remember April," and Santamaria's most famous composition, "Afro Blue." **Skins** (Milestone 47038) has music from two of Santamaria's strongest groups, a nonet with Pat Patrick (from Sun Ra's band) and Al Abreu on reeds, and Chick Corea, and a ten-piece group with Hubert Laws, trumpeter Marty Sheller, Bobby Capers on alto and baritone, and guest cornetist Nat Adderley. The music is Afro-Cuban jazz, but also looks toward the bugalu/R&B grooves that would be present in Santamaria's music in the near future. **Mongo at the Village Gate** (Original Jazz Classics 490) from September 1963 is an exciting session full of funky pieces influenced by R&B and soul jazz, but still tied to Cuban music. The impressive band includes Sheller, Patrick, Capers, and percussionists Chihuahua Martinez and Julian Cabrera. Highlights include "Fatback," "Mongo's Groove," "Creole," and "Para Ti."

Greatest Hits (Columbia/Legacy 63920) has most of the high points from Mongo Santamaria's period (1965–69) on the Columbia label. The first 11 selections are studio selections that all sold quite well during the era, including a remake of "Watermelon Man," "Fat Back," "Cold Sweat," "Green Onions," and "La Bamba." In addition, there are five numbers added to the CD reissue, including a live version of "Afro Blue." It is obvious, listening to this infectious music, why Mongo Santamaria was one of the most popular performers in Latin jazz of the 1960s.

Cal Tjader   In 1961, Cal Tjader ended his long-time relationship with the Fantasy label (for whom he had first recorded in 1951), signing with Creed Taylor at Verve. While his Fantasy recordings tended to feature his working group, at Verve Tjader was often (like Jimmy Smith) backed by large orchestras. While he received greater exposure due to being with a larger company and had a hit in 1965 with "Soul Sauce," his recordings during this era were less consistent than earlier. **Several Shades of Jade/Breeze from the East** (Verve 537 083) has the music from two rather odd albums from 1963. The former set features Tjader with a huge orchestra arranged by Lalo Schifrin, while **Breeze from the East** has arrangements from Stan Applebaum. In both cases, Tjader's vibes are heard backed by Asian-sounding scales, and much of the time he sounds as if he is lost in a low-level movie soundtrack. There are only slight hints of Afro-Cuban jazz among the corn.

Recorded in 1964, **Soul Sauce** (Verve 314 521 688) is more on the right track, with Tjader joined by Donald Byrd, Jimmy Heath, Kenny Burrell, pianist Lonnie Hewitt, drummer Johnny Rae, and percussionists Armanda Perazo and Willie Bobo among others. "Afro Blue," "Tanya," and "Spring Is Here" are highlights along with the catchy title cut. **Soul Burst** (Verve 314 557 446) is one of Tjader's better big band albums with charts by Oliver Nelson, such players as Chick Corea and guitarist Attila Zoller, and fine versions of Clare Fischer's "Morning," "Manteca," and "My Ship." From 1966, **El Sonido Nuevo: The New Soul Sound** (Verve 519 812) has its moments of interest even if it is not quite up to the level of most of Tjader's Fantasy releases. The vibraphonist is teamed with pianist Eddie Palmieri who provided the arrangements. The CD reissue adds six other songs taken from a pair of

Tjader's Verve albums to the original program. The liner notes have plenty of hype (calling this "a landmark in the history of Latin jazz") that can be written off since much of the music is actually lightweight, but the easy-listening melodies and accessible rhythms hold on to one's interest.

Overall, Cal Tjader's Verve period was not on the level that it should have been, and his recordings tended to be overproduced. However, he remained a major name, and his live shows were always exciting.

The Birth of Bossa Nova

Bossa nova is the combination of light Brazilian rhythms with cool-toned West Coast jazz. Frequently the main bossa nova rhythm, played at doubletime over a two-bar section (which has 16 beats), accents 1, 4, 7, 11, and 14, being played as 3-3-4-3-3. A descendant of the Brazilian samba, the bossa nova may never have been heard outside of Brazil were it not for the fact that there was a genius songwriter by the name of Antonio Carlos Jobim and an American guitarist named Charlie Byrd.

Charlie Byrd   In 1961, guitarist Charlie Byrd toured South America on a U.S. State Department tour, discovering bossa nova while visiting Brazil. Back in the United States, he played bossa nova tapes for Stan Getz, and soon Getz had convinced producer Creed Taylor to let them record a bossa nova record. The resulting album, **Jazz/Samba**, included a hit version of Antonio Carlos Jobim's "Desafinado," launched the bossa nova craze, and made Charlie Byrd well known.

From that point forward, Byrd would be associated with bossa nova although he also played some bop, swing, and classical pieces. **Blues Sonata** (Original Jazz Classics 1063) and **Mr. Guitar** (Original Jazz Classics 998) directly preceded **Jazz/Samba**, and feature Byrd with bassist Keter Betts, either Buddy Deppenschmidt or Bertell Knox on drums, and (on four of the seven numbers of **Blues Sonata**) pianist Barry Harris. ● **Latin Byrd** (Milestone 47005) collects together the music from two former LPs recorded during 1962–63 after the success of **Jazz/Samba**. Byrd plays quite pretty throughout, and his trio is augmented on some numbers by four cellos, a French horn, trumpeter Hal Posey, Tommy Gwaltney on vibes, and some extra percussionists. Surprisingly, only two songs are by Jobim, but the music overall is very much in the bossa nova idiom that Byrd did so much to popularize. In 1964, Charlie Byrd

signed with Columbia, and he would stay with the label through the early 1970s, mostly recording easy listening Latin-tinged music that was often pop.

Stan Getz   Although Charlie Byrd deserves credit for making key people in the United States aware of bossa nova (Herbie Mann, who recorded in Brazil in 1962, was also an important force), it was Stan Getz who was the biggest factor in making the bossa nova a permanent part of the music scene. It seemed only right that Getz would become involved in Brazilian music because his cool tone in the 1950s (along with those of Gerry Mulligan and Chet Baker) had been an influence on the sound of Joao Gilberto and the melodies of Jobim.

Actually Getz's two major projects of 1961 had nothing to do with bossa novas. He had spent 1958–60 living in Scandinavia, and upon his return to the United States he was at the crossroads of his career. John Coltrane and Sonny Rollins were now the main pacesetters on tenor, but Getz had been so popular in the 1950s that luckily he was still remembered. Looking for a musical challenge, he found it by recording ● **Focus** (Verve 521 419) with arranger Eddie Sauter's orchestra. No tenor part was written out for Getz, and the orchestra sounded complete by itself playing Sauter's compositions. It was up to Getz to improvise over the band, and he succeeded admirably, creating beautiful statements that are a logical part of the music. This would always be Stan Getz's personal favorite recording. More conventional, but also enjoyable is **Fall '61** (Verve 549 369), a straightahead quintet date with Bob Brookmeyer and pianist Steve Kuhn that includes three pieces by the valve trombonist, Buck Clayton's "Love Jumped Out," "Nice Work If You Can Get It," and "A Nightingale Sang in Berkeley Square." The interplay between Getz and Brookmeyer (who had worked together in the mid-1950s) recalls their earlier work.

And then Charlie Byrd played his bossa nova tapes for Stan Getz. They immediately interested Creed Taylor of Verve in the project, and the result was **Jazz Samba** (Verve 521 413). With Getz and Byrd joining forces, and backed by rhythm guitarist Gene Byrd, bassist Keeter Betts, and both Buddy Deppenschmidt and Bill Reichenbach on percussion, the band had a major hit in "Desafinado," and introduced such songs as "O Pato," "Baia," and "One Note Samba" to the American public. Although Verve was at first hesitant about releasing the gentle music, it became an immediate best seller and started the bossa nova fad. Within a year, everyone seemed to be recording bossa nova, whether they understood the idiom or not.

Getz's follow-up albums were **Big Band Bossa Nova** (Verve 825 771), which matches him with a big band arranged by Gary McFarland, and **Jazz Samba Encore** (Verve 823 613), which is notable for having Antonio Carlos Jobim and Luiz Bonfa on guitars and helping to introduce "So Danco Samba" and "Insensatez."

But it was the next album that really made the biggest impact. **Getz/Gilberto** (Verve 521 414) matches Getz with Jobim on piano, guitarist/singer Joao Gilberto, and, in a total surprise, Astrud Gilberto (Joao's wife). Astrud was a housewife who sang a bit around the Gilberto household, but had no aspirations to be a singer. While recording "The Girl from Ipanema" with Getz and Jobim, Joao Gilberto's Portuguese singing was exquisite, but his English was simply not understandable enough. It was suggested that Astrud give it a shot, and her simple and straightforward delivery made the song into a major hit. She also shared the vocal with her husband on "Corcovado" ("Quiet Nights of Quiet Stars"), and other songs on this much beloved album include "So Danco Samba," a remake of "Desafinado," and "O Grande Amor." On the basis of this set alone, Antonio Carlos Jobim, Joao Gilberto, and Astrud Gilberto all became famous.

Stan Getz's four-CD box ◉ **The Bossa Nova Years** (Verve 823 611) has all of Getz's classic bossa nova sessions: **Jazz Samba**, **Big Band Bossa Nova**, **Jazz Samba Encore**, **Getz/Gilberto**, and the excellent if overlooked **Stan Getz/Laurindo Almeida** (Verve 823 149). This essential set also has three performances from a 1964 Carnegie Hall Concert, concluding with a remake of "The Girl from Ipanema."

Even as the bossa nova craze hit its peak in 1964, Stan Getz was feeling embarrassed by his commercial success and looking elsewhere. **Stan Getz & Bill Evans** (Verve 833 802) teams the tenor with the increasingly influential Bill Evans, either Richard Davis or Ron Carter on bass, and Elvin Jones. There is no bossa nova to be heard on the swinging and thoughtful versions of "My Heart Stood Still," "Grandfather's Waltz," "Funkallero," and "Night and Day." That year Getz's regular group consisted of vibraphonist Gary Burton, bassist Gene Cherico, and drummer Joe Hunt, the same unit that appeared with Getz and Astrud Gilberto playing "The Girl from Ipanema" in the film *Get Yourself a College Girl*. **Getz au Go Go** (Verve 821 725), Getz's last bossa nova record, is not included in **The Bossa Nova Years**. Half of the set features Astrud Gilberto's soft vocals (including "Corcovado" and "One Note Samba") while the remainder is strictly straightahead with a greater emphasis on Burton's playing.

Rather than continuing to ride on the bossa nova gravy train, by 1965 Getz (other than answering occasional requests for "Desafinado" or "The Girl from Ipanema") had abandoned the music in favor of hard bop. Though some of his recordings from this era are commercial, he did cut one classic in 1967, ◉ **Sweet Rain** (Verve 815 054). Playing with Chick Corea in a quartet with Ron Carter and Grady Tate, Getz sounds beautiful and explorative on such numbers as Corea's "Windows," Dizzy Gillespie's "Con Alma," and (in a final nod to the bossa nova era) "O Grande Amor." Getz and Corea continually push each other, and the results are mutually inspiring.

Antonio Carlos Jobim, Joao Gilberto, and Astrud Gilberto Antonio Carlos Jobim was a fairly basic guitarist, pianist, and vocalist, and his own records tend to sound like a composer demonstrating his own material to song pluggers, but as a songwriter he ranked at the top of his field throughout the 1960s. Jobim started off playing piano in nightclubs and working in recording studios, making his first record in 1954. In 1956, he wrote part of the score for the play *Orfeo do Carnaval*, which a couple of years later became the film *Black Orpheus*. In 1958, singer/guitarist Joao Gilberto recorded some of Jobim's songs, and that was the early first step in launching the bossa nova movement. Gilberto, a quiet crooner whose rhythms on the guitar helped develop bossa nova, made his first recordings during 1958–60, and these include Jobim's "Chega de Saudade" (a regional hit), "One Note Samba," "Meditation," and "Corcovado." Those performances went largely unheard in the United States at first.

With the success of **Jazz/Samba** and particularly **Getz/Gilberto**, Antonio Carlos Jobim became one of the most popular composers of the 1960s. **The Composer of Desafinado Plays** (Verve 521 431) from 1963 (two months after **Getz/Gilberto**) is one of his best releases, featuring Jobim's sincere piano backed by an orchestra arranged by Claus Ogerman. Amazingly enough, all 12 songs on this album became standards, including "Once I Loved," "Corcovado," "One Note Samba," "Meditation," "So Danco Samba" "No More Blues," and the obvious choices "The Girl from Ipanema" and "Desafinado."

Joao Gilberto did not record all that much during the era after his association with Stan Getz ended, becoming somewhat reclusive. The CD to get of his music is **The Legendary Joao Gilberto** (World Pacific 98391), which has no less than 38 (mostly brief) performances from his pre-Getz 1958–61 period—music that helped set the standard for the bossa nova to come.

The success of "The Girl from Ipanema" made Astrud Gilberto into an unexpected singing star, and probably was the cause of the Gilbertos' divorce a few years later. She recorded several charming (if limited) albums for Verve, including **The Astrud Gilberto Album** (Verve 8608), **The Shadow of Your Smile** (Verve 557 184), and **Look to the Rainbow** (Verve 821 556). The latter CD reissues the original album (which has very suitable arrangements by Gil Evans and Al Cohn), and half of a date with organist/arranger Walter Wanderley. Although not really a jazz singer, Astrud Gilberto's simple, sincere, and very heartfelt approach at its best is quite haunting, sensual, and musical.

Bola Sete   *Bola Sete* is Portuguese for the seventh ball on a pool table, the only black one, and guitarist Bola Sete (born Djalma de Andrade) got the name because at one time he was the only black musician in a group. Born in Rio de Janeiro, he played guitar from an early age, starting with folk music before becoming interested in jazz, and was playing professionally by the mid-1940s. He worked throughout Brazil, South America, and Europe before moving to the United States in 1959 when he was 31. Sete became well known in 1962 when he appeared at a bossa nova concert at Carnegie Hall, made some special appearances with Dizzy Gillespie (with whom he recorded), and began recording for Fantasy. Sete worked with Vince Guaraldi during 1963–65.

Tour de Force (Fantasy 24766) reissues the acoustic guitarist's first two Fantasy recordings. One date has him joined by bassist Ben Tucker, drummer Dave Bailey, and two percussionists, while the second session is with bassist Freddy Screiber and drummer John Rae. The music is high-quality bossa novas, mostly avoiding obvious material (other than "Samba de Orpheus"), and focusing on the beauty of Sete's guitar.

Vocalists

There were surprisingly few new jazz vocalists of importance during the 1961–67 period. A major problem that has persisted to the present time is that, with the gradual death of the top songwriters of the 1930s and '40s, there were very few talented songsmiths to take their place who could write future standards that could be sung by a variety of singers. In addition, many of the top young singers opted to make a more lucrative living in pop, soul, or rock music. At the same time, the veteran jazz vocalists found the rise of rock cutting into their opportunities to make records, and it often resulted in them being pressured to "get with it" and make cover versions of pop hits. Particularly after 1964, the climate was just not right for new jazz singers. For every Mose Allison who was able to catch on, there were quite a few Sheila Jordans who recorded one or two impressive albums, and then were not heard from much on record for many years.

Lorez Alexandria   Lorez Alexandria (born Dolorez Turner) was born in Chicago, originally sang religious music, and, after switching to jazz, recorded in her native city for King (1957–59) and Argo (1960–63). She made two of her finest albums for Impulse during 1964. The single CD **The Great Lorez Alexandria, and More of the Great** (MCA/Impulse 33116) has all 20 selections, with the subtle and lightly swinging singer being joined by a couple of different orchestras and (on seven numbers) the Wynton Kelly Trio. But strangely enough, considering how enjoyable this standards set is, Alexandria would not record again (other than a couple of albums for the unknown Pzazz label) for 13 years.

Mose Allison   Mose Allison, who in 1959 was known as a pianist who also sang, developed within a couple of years into an important musical personality, singer, and composer who occupied his own musical niche. During 1959–61, he recorded three albums for the Columbia label, all of which are included in the three-CD box **High Jinks** (Columbia/Epic/Legacy 64275). Considering the success of his Prestige vocals, it is surprising that he only sings on half of the material on these albums, most notably "Baby, Please Don't Go," "Fool's Paradise," and "I Love the Life I Live." The instrumentals (including the eight-part "Transfiguration of Hiram Brown Suite") are fine, but it was not until Allison signed with the Atlantic label that his full musical personality emerged.

Allison's debut for Atlantic, ⦿ **I Don't Worry About a Thing** (Rhino/Atlantic 71417), made him immortal. His homespun vocals on "Your Mind Is on Vacation (but Your Mouth Is Running Overtime)," "I Don't Worry About a Thing," "It Didn't Turn Out that Way," "Meet Me at No Special Place," and "The Song Is Ended" garnered a great deal of attention. He sounded like no one else, with his Southern drawl, world-weary but wise singing, and ironic lyrics. The two-CD set ⦿ **The Sage of Tippo** (32 Jazz 32068) gives listeners a generous amount of prime Mose, for it includes four complete albums (**Swingin' Machine**, **The Word from Mose**, **Wild Man on the Loose**, and **I've Been Doin' Some Thinkin'**) from 1962–68, including performances of "Stop this World," "I Ain't Got Nothing but the Blues," "One of these Days," "Your Red Wagon," "Lost Mind," and a minor-toned transformation of "You Are My Sunshine."

Bea Benjamin   In 1963, Duke Ellington was in Europe scouting for talent to record for the Reprise label. He heard a pair of South African émigrés, pianist Dollar Brand and his wife, singer Sathima Bea Benjamin, and within a week had recorded them both. While Brand's record was released, Benjamin's sat on the shelf and was presumed lost. But miraculously in the mid-1990s, it was discovered that the date's engineer had made a second copy for his own library and still had the tape in perfect condition. The 1997 release of **A Morning in Paris** (Enja 9309) was a major historic event, for it was recorded 16 years before Benjamin's next recording as a leader. Joined by her husband's trio, with guest appearances from violinist Svend Asmussen (who plays his instrument pizzicato like a high-pitched guitar), and pianists Duke Ellington and Billy Strayhorn (on two songs apiece), Benjamin mostly sings ballads and standards, with her voice sounding quite youthful and beautiful.

Oscar Brown, Jr.   One of jazz's great lyricists, whose talents stretch beyond jazz, and a dramatic singer, Oscar Brown, Jr., recorded regularly for Columbia in the 1960s, introducing famous lyrics to such songs as "Jeannine," "When Malindy Sings," and "All Blues." Unfortunately, several of Brown's Columbia albums remain out of print, but 1964's **Mr. Oscar Brown, Jr., Goes to Washington** (Verve 314 557 452) has reappeared on CD. Although the title sounds political, most of Brown's lyrics deal with more universal and timeless topics. Most memorable

among Brown's dozen originals are "Maggie" (a tribute to his young daughter), "Living Double in a World of Trouble" (about having two girlfriends at once), "Forty Acres and a Mule," and "Brother Where Are You."

Betty Carter   In 1961, Betty Carter had the rare opportunity to record an album of vocal duets with Ray Charles, and it must have looked as if she was on the brink of stardom. But Carter was too unusual and eccentric a singer to gain mass market appeal. **'Round Midnight** (Atco 80453) from 1962–63 has her accompanied by orchestras arranged and conducted by either Claus Ogerman or Oliver Nelson, singing such songs as "Heart and Soul," "When I Fall in Love," "The Good Life," and "Everybody's Somebody's Fool," but the album did not become the best seller that the label hoped. **Inside Betty Carter** (Capitol 89702) has the original, brief eight-song LP session from 1964 with a trio, and adds seven previously unreleased numbers from 1965 with a four-piece rhythm section that includes Kenny Burrell. The better selections include "This Is Always," "Spring Can Really Hang You Up the Most," and "You're a Sweetheart." Betty Carter was off records completely during 1966–68 and would emerge as a much more radical vocalist, so **Inside Betty Carter** essentially ended the singer's formative period.

Ray Charles   By the early 1960s, Ray Charles's connection to jazz was becoming more and more distant as he explored country music, Americana (including "Georgia on My Mind," which became his trademark song), and the soul music that he had helped pioneer. However, there were occasional departures. **Genius + Soul = Jazz** (Dunhill Compact Classics 038) reissues an Impulse album that features Charles with the Count Basie Orchestra plus a few all-stars, including Clark Terry. It should have been a classic, particularly since some of the numbers are instrumentals, and Charles sings such standards as "I'm Gonna Move to the Outskirts of Town," "I've Got News for You," and "Birth of the Blues." But for some reason, Charles plays organ instead of piano, and his overly lazy style weighs down the music, making some of the tracks rather sleepy instead of hard swinging. **Ray Charles and Betty Carter** (Dunhill Compact Classics 039) is quite unusual, a dozen vocal duets with the increasingly original singer Betty Carter. This unlikely pairing mostly works well, particularly on a near-classic version of

"Baby, It's Cold Outside," "Takes Two to Tango," and "Side by Side."

But, although Charles and his big band often headlined at jazz festivals in later years, his music became less relevant to jazz as time passed and he became more of an American icon.

Nat King Cole   One of the most famous singers in middle-of-the-road pop music by 1961, Nat King Cole revisited his early hits on **The Nat King Cole Story** (Capitol 95129), which has been reissued as an expanded two-CD set. The 36 selections (mostly pop hits from the 1950s) include remakes of "Straighten Up and Fly Right," "Sweet Lorraine," "It's Only a Paper Moon," "Route 66," and "For Sentimental Reasons" that feature him playing piano in a trio (with John Collins and bassist Charlie Harris) for the last time on records. Also from 1961 is **Nat King Cole Sings, George Shearing Plays** (Capitol 48332), a very popular album that has Cole accompanied tastefully by the George Shearing Quintet and a string section. Best are "September Song," "Pick Yourself Up," and "Serenata."

Nat King Cole continued working quite successfully outside of jazz until December 1964, when he was stricken with lung cancer, passing away two months later at the age of 47.

Ida Cox   The early 1960s was a time of comebacks for some veterans of the 1920s and '30s. The opening of Preservation Hall in New Orleans helped the local players gain some recognition. Conversely, with the rise in interest in country blues singers (fueled by the boom in folk music), some of the surviving classic blues singers returned to records, including Alberta Hunter (who was working full-time as a nurse), Victoria Spivey, Sippie Wallace, and Ida Cox. Cox was the most unlikely choice to make a comeback because she made her last recording in 1940, retired in 1944, and turned 65 in 1961. However, she was coaxed out of retirement and recorded **Blues for Rampart Street** (Original Jazz Classics 1758), a set in which she is joined by Coleman Hawkins, Roy Eldridge, pianist Sammy Price, Milt Hinton, and Jo Jones, all of whom were younger than she. Cox's voice might have been a little rusty, but it was certainly still quite listenable. She still had the feeling, phrasing, and enough tricks to quite ably perform a strong program that includes "Wild Women Don't Have the Blues," "Blues for Rampart Street," "St. Louis Blues," and "Death Letter

Blues." But after this set was recorded, Ida Cox went back into retirement, passing away six years later.

Bob Dorough   Singer/pianist/lyricist Bob Dorough, who combines a homespun rural philosophy with big city sophistication, recorded very little during 1957–75. As a leader there were four numbers in a poetry and jazz date from 1958, and an odd set of tunes from the hit show *Oliver* in 1963. Otherwise, **Just About Everything** (Evidence 22094) is his only significant recording from the era. Joined by guitarist Al Schackman, bassist Ben Tucker, and drummer Percy Brice, Dorough performs haunting versions of "Baltimore Oriole" and "Lazy Afternoon" in addition to memorable interpretations of "I've Got Just About Everything," "Better than Anything," and "'Tis Autumn." But he would not record again as a leader for another decade.

The Double Six of Paris   The success of Lambert, Hendricks, and Ross in 1957 led to some other jazz vocal groups being formed. One of the best was the Double Six of Paris, which was organized in 1959 by Mimi Perrin, who was the ensemble's main arranger. In addition to singing new lyrics to jazz solos, the group was unusual in that its six singers overdubbed a second part so they sound like a dozen voices on their records, and their vocalese is in French. The Double Six at various times included Monique Aldebert-Guerin, Louis Aldebert, Christiane Legrand, Ward Swingle (the future leader of the Swingle Singers), and Roger Guerin among its singers along with Perrin. In addition to a set with Dizzy Gillespie and Bud Powell (released under Dizzy's name), and a 1964 album that paid tribute to Ray Charles, the Double Six recorded two other records which have been reissued in full on **Les Double Six** (RCA 65659). Quite a few of the charts are based on records originally arranged by Quincy Jones for his own band and the orchestras of Count Basie and Harry Arnold, highlighted by "For Lena and Lennie," "Stockholm Sweetnin'," "Doodlin'," and "Meet Benny Bailey." In addition, the Double Six recreates performances recorded by Woody Herman, Shelly Manne, John Coltrane, Gerry Mulligan, J.J. Johnson, Charlie Parker, Miles Davis, and Stan Kenton.

The Double Six of Paris broke up in 1965, and a later attempt to revive the group was unsuccessful.

Ella Fitzgerald   Ella, who turned 44 in 1961, was still in prime voice during this era. Although Norman Granz sold the Verve label that year, she continued recording for Verve through 1966, and Granz still worked as her manager, guiding her increasingly legendary career. **Ella Returns to Berlin** (Verve 837 758) from 1961 may not have any "Mack the Knife" mishaps (this time she remembered the words), but she sounds in superior form on "Take the 'A' Train," "Slow Boat to China," and "Misty." **Clap Hands, Here Comes Charlie** (Verve 835 646) from the same year has Ella with the Lou Levy Quartet performing swing-era songs, including "Jersey Bounce," "Night in Tunisia," "'Round Midnight," and "This Could Be the Start of Something Big" with equal enthusiasm and skill. **Ella Swings Gently** (Verve 314 519 348) has her joined by the anonymous-sounding Nelson Riddle Orchestra, emphasizes medium-tempo versions of ballads, and includes such songs as "The Very Thought of You," "Darn that Dream," "Body and Soul," and a cooking "All of Me."

Actually, the very best Ella Fitzgerald recording from this era is, as of this writing, probably the number one LP overdue to be reissued on CD: **Ella in Hollywood** (Verve 4052). Backed by pianist Lou Levy, Herb Ellis, bassist Wilfred Middlebrooks, and drummer Gus Johnson, Ella is remarkable on "Take the 'A' Train," scatting for nine minutes (her longest vocal ever), building up her long improvisation brilliantly with creative ideas and lots of riffing, showing that no one could ever out-swing her. The rest of the set is also quite jazz-oriented (including "I've Got the World on a String," "You're Driving Me Crazy," and "Air Mail Special"), making one wonder why this album is so obscure.

Ella's Songbook series resumed in 1963, three years after her Harold Arlen set. **Sings the Jerome Kern Songbook** (Verve 825 669) is less ambitious than the previous works, but not without interest. Ella sings 14 Kern songs with the Nelson Riddle Orchestra, including "A Fine Romance," "All the Things You Are," and "Yesterdays." **Ella and Basie** (Verve 821 576) was the first time (other than a couple of songs) that the singer and Count Basie recorded together, but they would cross paths many times during the next 20 years. Quincy Jones's arrangements do not leave much space for solos (other than a few brief spots for Joe Newman, trombonist Urbie Green, and Frank Foster), but Ella sounds quite happy, and there are swinging versions of "Honeysuckle Rose,"

"Them There Eyes," and "Shiny Stockings." From 1963, **These Are the Blues** (Verve 829 536) has Ella stepping a bit out of character as she digs into ten vintage blues from the 1920s and '30s (including "Cherry Red," "Jail House Blues," and "In the Evening"), sounding surprisingly expressive on the ancient material, assisted by Roy Eldridge (who was having a short stint in her backup group) and organist Wild Bill Davis.

In 1964, the final set in Ella's Verve Songbook series was recorded, and it is the only one saluting a lyricist rather than a songwriter. **Sings the Johnny Mercer Songbook** (Verve 539 057), recorded with the Nelson Riddle Orchestra, has particularly fine versions of "Too Marvelous for Words," "Early Autumn," "Laura," "Skylark," and "Midnight Sun." Ella, who by 1965 was regularly accompanied by Tommy Flanagan, bassist Keter Betts, and drummer Gus Johnson, had a few collaborations with Duke Ellington during this period. **Ella at Duke's Place** (Verve 314 529 700) is highlighted by "Something to Live For," "I Like the Sunrise," "Imagine My Frustration," "Duke's Place," and a typically swinging "Cotton Tail." **Stockholm Concert 1966** (Pablo 2308-242) has a live date with Ellington's band, performing similar material. Duke only appears on "Cotton Tail," but Cootie Williams, Johnny Hodges, and Paul Gonsalves all get to interact with the singer and the combination works quite well. Of lesser interest and a hint of things to come is **Whisper Not** (Verve 589 478). Ella, backed by Marty Paich's Orchestra, sings quite a few songs that do not fit her style very well (including "Lover Man," "I've Got Your Number," "Matchmaker, Matchmaker," and "Wives and Lovers"), and points out the dilemma that most jazz singers would soon have. Should they continue performing the warhorses or interpret new material that sounds trivial in jazz settings?

Ella would first try the latter approach, then switch back to the former. In 1967, she left Verve (the label that Norman Granz had formed specifically for her), signing with Capitol. Her first three releases were a religious album, a set of Christmas songs, and a program of quickly forgotten pop songs. When the First Lady of the American Song was having trouble persuading her label to let her record high-quality jazz, what chance did most other jazz singers have?

Johnny Hartman   In 1963, Johnny Hartman recorded one of the most romantic jazz ballad albums of all time,

John Coltrane and Johnny Hartman (Impulse 166), which is reviewed under Coltrane's name. On the success of that album alone, Hartman made his mark in jazz history, helping to define the art of the jazz vocal ballad.

Prior to that recording, Hartman had been a journeyman singer. He had been with the Dizzy Gillespie big band during 1948–49, and recorded two albums for Bethlehem during 1955–56, but the warm-toned baritonist still remained obscure. After the Coltrane collaboration gave him some recognition, Hartman recorded two other excellent records for Impulse. **I Just Dropped By to Say Hello** (Impulse 176) finds him in peak form on 11 pieces, including memorable renditions of "In the Wee Small Hours of the Morning," "Sleepin' Bee," and "Stairway to the Stars." Illinois Jacquet helps out on five songs, and the backup group includes Hank Jones, either Kenny Burrell or Jim Hall on guitar, Milt Hinton, and Elvin Jones. **The Voice That Is** (Impulse 144) is more erratic, with superb versions of "My Ship," "Waltz for Debby," and "It Never Entered My Mind" being weighed down by less interesting movie and show songs, including "Sunrise Sunset" and "Joey Joey Joey." However, Hartman (backed by either Hank Jones's quartet or pianist Bob Hammer's octet) sounds as strong and warm as always.

But as quickly as he found fame, he slipped back into obscurity. Other than an album cut for Japan in 1966, Hartman would not appear on records again until 1972.

Clancy Hayes   In the Dixieland world, quite often a musician from a trad band will be called upon to sing, and most of the time it is obvious that singing is not their forte. However, banjoist Clancy Hayes was a major exception. A performer in San Francisco since 1927, Hayes worked with Lu Watters's Yerba Buena Jazz Band during the 1940s, but did not come into his own as a singer until the following decade when he was frequently featured with Bob Scobey. After Scobey relocated to Chicago, Hayes worked now and then with Turk Murphy and the Firehouse Five Plus Two. He also recorded several albums as a leader including **Oh by Jingo** (Delmark 210) from 1964. Hayes, who displays a strong and likable voice along with a winning personality, is joined by the Salty Dogs, a hot Dixieland septet that features cornetist Lew Green, trombonist Jim Snyder, clarinetist Kim Cusack, and Jim Dapogny (best known as a pianist) on second cornet and valve trombone. Nine songs feature Hayes vocals (including "Oh by Jingo," "Rose of

Washington Square," and "Beale Street Blues"), and these are joined by three instrumentals and six alternate takes. Not only do Clancy Hayes's vocals (in Eddie Condon's phrase) "not hurt anyone," but he shows that he was one of the finest male jazz singers of the period.

Bill Henderson   If Bill Henderson had been born a decade earlier, he might have become much better known as a jazz singer. He did record several very interesting sessions for Vee-Jay during 1959–61, cut a full album with the Oscar Peterson Trio in 1963, and sang with the Count Basie Orchestra in 1965–66. But fame eluded him, and he found himself working more as an actor and less as a singer as the decade progressed. **Complete Vee-Jay Recordings, Vol. 2** (Koch 8572) has swinging tunes and fine versions of ballads. As with **Vol. 1**, the backup groups vary greatly, in this case including string orchestras, the Count Basie orchestra (without Basie), and combos featuring Eddie Harris and Tommy Flanagan. It is a measure of Henderson's talent that **Bill Henderson/Oscar Peterson** (Verve 837 937) was recorded, for Peterson's trio (with Ray Brown and Ed Thigpen) rarely ever backed lesser-known singers, particularly by the 1960s. Henderson rises to the occasion on such songs as "All or Nothing at All," "I've Got a Crush On You," and "The Folks Who Live on the Hill." But after leaving Basie, Bill Henderson did not record again until 1975.

Shirley Horn   Shirley Horn in time became famous as a superior ballad singer and a fluent pianist who used space and silence quite effectively while swinging with subtlety. Born in 1934, she was studying piano from the age of four. After attending Howard University, Horn started leading her own trio in 1954. Miles Davis enjoyed her playing and in the early 1960s insisted that she open for him on a few occasions. She made her recording debut on a few numbers with Stuff Smith that were not released until many years later, and an LP from August 1961, **Live at the Village Vanguard** (Can-Am 6108) features her playing and singing with her trio of the period (bassist John Mixon and drummer Gene Gammage). **Loads of Love/Shirley Horn with Horns** (Mercury 843 454) has her first two "real" albums, but strangely enough Horn does not play piano at all. She sticks exclusively to singing and has less control over the interpretations (some of the songs are taken faster than usual) than she would later on. The big bands backing her were arranged by Jimmy Jones and Quincy Jones, and highlights include "Do It Again," "Wild Is Love," "Wouldn't It Be Loverly," and "In the Wee Small Hours of the Morning." In 1965, Shirley Horn did have a chance to play some piano on **Travelin' Light** (GRP/Impulse 138), and her sidemen include Joe Newman, Frank Wess, Jerome Richardson, and Kenny Burrell. The selections vary in quality, and all are very brief (under three minutes), but Horn's vocals make this a worthwhile set.

With the exception of one obscure record in 1972, Shirley Horn would not record again for 13 years. She chose to stay in her native Washington, D.C., raise a family, and just play locally.

Helen Humes   During 1959–61, Helen Humes recorded three gems for the Contemporary label. The third one, **Swinging with Humes** (Original Jazz Classics 608), has her joined by a sextet that includes trumpeter Joe Gordon, Teddy Edwards, guitarist Al Viola, and Wynton Kelly. On such songs as "When Day Is Done," "Home," "S'posin,'""Pennies from Heaven," and "The Very Thought of You," Humes shows at the age of 48 that she ranked with the top jazz singers in the world, interpreting the music with as much joy and swing as Ella Fitzgerald.

But she would not record again for another dozen years. After freelancing, Humes lived in Australia during 1964–67, returning to the United States in 1967 to take care of her ailing mother, and retired from music for the time being.

Alberta Hunter   In 1956, Alberta Hunter (who had not recorded since 1950, and only waxed eight songs since 1940) quit singing altogether to become a nurse. She was already 61, and lied about her age, saying that she was 44! In 1961, she was persuaded to record twice with veterans of the early days. Hunter is on four songs reissued as **Blues We Taught Your Mother** (Original Blues Classics 520), which is reviewed under the Various Artists section, and has her own album in the **Chicago: The Living Legends** (Original Blues Classics 510) series. The latter CD is particularly noteworthy because of the lineup of musicians, all veterans of the 1920s. In addition to Hunter (who still sounds in prime form on such songs as "St. Louis Blues," "Downhearted Blues," and "Moanin' Low"), the roster includes 74-year-old pianist Lovie Austin (who had been off records since 1926), Jimmy

TIMELINE 1966

The Roscoe Mitchell Quartet is billed for the first time as the Art Ensemble. • Dollar Brand is a member of the Elvin Jones Quartet. • The Jazz Messengers feature Chuck Mangione and Keith Jarrett. • Eddie Gomez joins the Bill Evans Trio. • The Charles Lloyd Quartet is the hit of the Monterey Jazz Festival. • Charlie Barnet leads his final big band. • Charles Mingus drops out of music. • Ray Brown leaves the Oscar Peterson Trio after 15 years. • Blue Note is purchased by Liberty Records. • Chet Baker is beaten up by drug dealers. • Sonny Rollins retires again. • Bud Powell dies. • Joe Zawinul's "Mercy, Mercy, Mercy" is a hit for Cannonball Adderley. • Larry Coryell records with Chico Hamilton. • Buddy DeFranco becomes the leader of the Glenn Miller ghost orchestra. • Dutch saxophonist Willem Breuker makes his recording debut as a leader. • New Zealand pianist Alan Broadbent and Czechoslovakian bassist Miroslav Vitous both move to the United States when they win scholarships to Berklee. • At 61, Doc Cheatham plays regularly with Benny Goodman. • Other than a privately issued LP in 1985, Bob Crosby makes his last recordings. • Kid Ory retires and moves to Hawaii at the age of 79. • Jay McShann records his first album in a decade. • Louis Metcalf (who was with Duke Ellington in 1927) records a surprisingly beboppish LP, **At the Ali Baba**. • Guitarist Sonny Sharrock makes his recording debut with Pharoah Sanders. • Twenty-year-old pianist George Duke records a straightahead quartet album with bass trumpeter David Simons. • Kenny Wheeler begins playing with John Stevens's Spontaneous Music Ensemble. • Pianist Alexander von Schlippenbach forms the Globe Unity Orchestra to perform his "Globe Unity" at the Berlin Jazztage. • Bill Dixon records **Intents and Purposes** for RCA. • The George Benson Quartet features baritonist Ronnie Cuber. • Bud Shank's long series of commercial records for the struggling World Pacific label results in a hit album, **Michelle**. • Both the Thad Jones/Mel Lewis Orchestra and the Buddy Rich big band are formed.

Archey, Darnell Howard, Pops Foster, and drummer Jasper Taylor. There are also three instrumentals.

After the date, Alberta Hunter went back to nursing, and, by the time she recorded again in 1977, all of the sidemen on her **Living Legends** record had passed away.

Al Jarreau   Al Jarreau is associated with a much later era, but he actually made his recording debut and one of his strongest jazz albums in 1965. Already 25 at the time, he had earned a master's degree in psychology and worked as a social worker, but decided instead to sing in jazz clubs. ◉ **1965** (Bainbridge 6237) is a somewhat remarkable set. Jarreau, performing with pianist Cal Bezemer, bassist Gary Allen, and drummer Joe Abodeely, shows what his career could have been like if he had chosen to focus on straightahead jazz instead of going for the money. Although this was recorded a decade before his second album, Jarreau is already quite recognizable, sounding like a superior jazz singer on such numbers as "My Favorite Things," "A Sleeping Bee," and "One Note Samba." But this album was not released at the time, and Al Jarreau would be in obscurity until the mid-1970s.

Eddie Jefferson   Eddie Jefferson's second recording as a leader, **Letter from Home** (Original Jazz Classics 307) from 1961–62, is a very enjoyable effort showing off the vocalese pioneer's singing at its best. Among the more memorable numbers are "I Cover the Waterfront," "A Night in Tunisia," "Body and Soul," and "Parker's Mood" (which has different lyrics than the famous King Pleasure recording). In the strong supporting cast are Johnny Griffin, James Moody (on alto and flute), and either Wynton Kelly or Junior Mance on piano. But despite the success of Lambert, Hendricks, and Ross who built on Jefferson's vocalese innovations, Eddie Jefferson was largely overshadowed during this era, and it would not be until the late 1960s that his talents would finally start to be recognized.

Etta Jones   With the success of "Don't Go to Strangers" in 1960, Etta Jones was able to record quite regularly for Prestige through 1963. Inspired by the phrasing of Billie Holiday (whom she could closely imitate, but usually just used as a slight influence) and Dinah Washington's sound, Jones's voice was at its peak during this era even though she did not sound as individual as she would in later years. **So Warm** (Original Jazz Classics

874) has the singer backed by strings (Oliver Nelson's writing lowers the set's jazz content) on a ballad-oriented set emphasizing soulful melody statements that includes "Unchained Melody," "You Don't Know What Love Is," "You Better Go Now," and "All My Life." **Something Nice** (Original Jazz Classics 221) is a stronger effort overall with plenty of offbeat material (including "My Heart Tells Me," "Through a Long and Sleepless Night," and "Love Is the Thing"), performances with a couple of combos, and guest appearances by Oliver Nelson on tenor and Lem Winchester. **From the Heart** (Original Jazz Classics 1016) has Jones accompanied by a couple of orchestras led by Nelson (including one with strings). The singer's performances are excellent, most notably "You Came a Long Way from St. Louis," "Look for the Silver Lining," "I'm Afraid the Masquerade Is Over," and "Just Friends," but unfortunately the CD has less than a half-hour of music. **Lonely and Blue** (Original Jazz Classics 702) mostly has Jones backed by pianist Patti Bown's trio with assistance from Budd Johnson's tenor and guitarist Wally Richardson. There are also three bonus cuts that are the singer's guest appearances on Gene Ammons dates. Among the songs on the disc are "In the Dark," "My Gentleman Friend," "You Don't Know My Mind," and "Cool Cool Daddy." From 1963, **Love Shout** (Original Jazz Classics 941) has Jones turning both "Hi-Lili, Hi-Lo" and "Some Enchanted Evening" into jazz, performing a rare vocal version of Duke Ellington's "The Gal from Joe's," and uplifting such tunes as "Love Walked In," "Like Someone in Love," and "Old Folks." Jones is joined by either a quintet with organist Larry Young or a larger group that has spots for Jerome Richardson on reeds, and both Kenny Burrell and Bucky Pizzarelli on guitars.

But, as happened to many jazz singers, Etta Jones seemed to fade away as the 1960s progressed, with one album for Roulette in 1965, and then nothing else on records for ten years.

Sheila Jordan   One of the most inventive singers to come out of the 1950s, Sheila Jordan was barely on records at all before the 1970s. She was born in Detroit, spent time living in Pennsylvania, began studying piano at 11, was back in Detroit at the age of 14, and sang vocalese in a vocal group. After moving to New York in the early 1950s, she was married to pianist Duke Jordan for a decade (1952–62), had an opportunity to sing with Charlie Parker, and studied with Lennie Tristano. She believed in bebop yet was able to form her own inventive style and was never merely a revivalist.

In 1962, when she was 33, Sheila Jordan recorded an unusual and atmospheric version of "You Are My Sunshine" with George Russell, and she became one of the very few singers to lead a date for Blue Note during its prime years. ● **Portrait of Sheila** (Blue Note 89002) is a classic. Backed by guitarist Barry Galbraith, bassist Steve Swallow, and the quiet drumming of Denzil Best, Jordan's cool, subtle, and inviting voice is quite adventurous on Oscar Brown, Jr.'s "Hum Drum Blues" and a set of superior standards including "Baltimore Oriole," "Falling in Love with Love," "Am I Blue," and "I'm a Fool to Want You." This is a frequently haunting date, but strangely enough there was no encore. Sheila Jordan would not record again as a leader until 1975, and she spent the 1960s working in an office job.

Irene Kral   Irene Kral, the younger sister of singer/pianist Roy Kral (of Jackie and Roy), developed into a superb ballad singer late in her relatively brief life. She started out singing with the Jay Burkhardt Big Band and freelancing in her native Chicago, including with a vocal group called the Tattle-Tales. Kral worked with Maynard Ferguson's big band for nine months in 1957, made her debut recording on two obscure albums for United Artists (1958–59), got married and settled in Los Angeles, only singing on an occasional basis. In the 1960s, she recorded twice (including a set for Mainstream in 1965). **Better than Anything** (Fresh Sound 69) has Kral accompanied by pianist Junior Mance, bassist Bob Cranshaw, and drummer Mickey Roker. At 31, Kral was a delightful and cheerful singer, heard at her early best on "Better than Anything," "The Meaning of the Blues," "It's a Wonderful World," and "Nobody Else but Me." But Irene Kral's greatest impact would be made during the next decade.

Lambert, Hendricks, and Ross—and Bavan   Lambert, Hendricks, and Ross were easily jazz's most popular vocal group in 1961. However, in the spring of 1962, Annie Ross dropped out, citing health reasons as she moved back to England. She recorded three albums during the remainder of the 1960s, but by 1967 was working primarily as an actress, only singing on a very occasional basis. **Sings a Handful of Songs** (Fresh Sound 61) from 1963 has Ross backed by an orchestra

arranged and conducted by Johnnie Spence. One of the darkest and scariest versions of "Love for Sale" ever recorded is the high point. Surprisingly, Ross does not scat or use vocalese on any of the tunes (which include "All of You," "Nature Boy," and "Limehouse Blues"), instead interpreting the lyrics in a swinging fashion. This was the last real recording of Annie Ross in her prime.

Ross's departure left Dave Lambert and Jon Hendricks in a bit of a fix, trying to come up with a suitable replacement for her difficult role. They settled on Yolanda Bavan, an exotic but more limited singer who was best in ensembles, but took relatively few solos. The group, as Lambert, Hendricks, and Bavan, lasted two years, and recorded three albums. **Live at Newport '63** (RCA 68731) features the ensemble in fine form on "Watermelon Man," "Gimme that Wine," "Walkin'," and a version of "Bye Bye Blackbird" that has Hendricks emulating Miles Davis's 1956 solo. The supporting cast is Coleman Hawkins, Clark Terry, and the Gildo Mahones trio.

In 1964, Dave Lambert tired of the group and quit. Lambert freelanced a bit during the next two years, but was killed in 1966 at the age of 49 when he was hit by a car while changing a tire, meeting the same fate as his earlier musical partner, Buddy Stewart. By then, Yolande Bavan had left jazz altogether, and very little has been heard from her since.

Of the four singers, only Jon Hendricks carried on. As a lyricist and singer, Hendricks has kept the legacy of Lambert, Hendricks, and Ross, and vocalese in general alive for decades, inspiring future jazz singers, and vocal groups.

Jeanne Lee   In 1961, singer Jeanne Lee and pianist Ran Blake recorded an album originally called **The Newest Sound Around** and reissued as ● **Legendary Duets** (Bluebird 6461). Lee, who at the age of 22 already had a beautiful, dark, and very flexible voice, makes the 11 songs on this set her own. She had met the highly individual (and rather dramatic) pianist Ran Blake while attending Bard College where she studied dance. They worked together as a duet for a few years, touring Europe in 1963. Lee, who would become a major singer in the avant-garde, shows that she could sing quite well in the bop tradition too. She moved to California in 1964, and, while in Europe in 1967, started working with vibraphonist Gunter Hampel, but her next record as a leader would not be until 1974. **Legendary Duets**

(which adds bassist George Duvivier to the group on two numbers) has Lee and Blake making every sound count on such songs as "Laura," "Where Flamingos Fly," "Evil Blues," "Sometimes I Feel Like a Motherless Child," and some very slow ballads that are full of tension and suspense.

Abbey Lincoln　Abbey Lincoln, who was quite dramatic on Max Roach's **Freedom Now Suite**, and was becoming involved in both the civil rights movement, and acting, made just one album as a leader during 1961–67, but it is a classic: ❶ **Straight Ahead** (Candid 79015) from 1961. On such memorable performances as "When Malindy Sings," "Blue Monk," Billie Holiday's "Left Alone," and "African Lady," Lincoln is emotional yet perfectly in control, stretching herself while getting her message across. Coleman Hawkins takes a memorable solo on "Blue Monk," Eric Dolphy helps out on flute and alto, Booker Little's melancholy tone on trumpet is very important in the ensembles, and the band also includes Mal Waldron and Max Roach, whom Lincoln married in 1962.

Carmen McRae　Carmen McRae recorded now and then during the 1960s for Columbia, Mainstream, Focus, and Atlantic. Three of her albums are available, and they find her gradually maturing (as her voice became lower) and growing as an interpreter of lyrics. **Sings Lover Man and Other Billie Holiday Classics** (Columbia/Legacy 65115) is a logical tribute since McRae always considered Billie Holiday to be her main influence. Assisted by her regular trio of 1961 (pianist Norman Simmons, bassist Bob Cranshaw, and drummer Walter Perkins) plus guests Nat Adderley, Eddie "Lockjaw" Davis, and guitarist Mundell Lowe, McRae sings a dozen associated with Lady Day. Highlights of the heartfelt tribute are "Them There Eyes," "Miss Brown to You," "I Cried for You," and a coolly restrained version of "Strange Fruit." Two additional songs were added to the CD reissue although "The Christmas Song" is a bit out of place. **Take Five** (Columbia 9116) has McRae backed by the Dave Brubeck Trio (Paul Desmond is absent) for a live set. All 12 songs other than "Take Five" are Brubeck songs, with Iola Brubeck usually contributing the lyrics. McRae's vocal versions of such songs as "In Your Own Sweet Way," "Ode to a Cowboy," "It's a Raggy Waltz," and "Travellin' Blues" are definitive. **Alive** (Columbia/Legacy 57887) has a solid

live set from McRae in 1965 with her trio (Norman Simmons, bassist Paul Breslin, and drummer Frank Severino) plus guitarist Joe Puma, flutist Ray Beckenstein, and Jose Mangual on bongos. The flute and bongos sound a bit dated as do some of the forgettable show tunes, but Carmen McRae is in excellent form on the jazz standards and a few songs associated with Billie Holiday.

Helen Merrill　After recording a series of fine albums for EmArcy during 1954–58, and a few other dates for Atco and Metrojazz, Helen Merrill spent 1959–63 living in Italy. Back in the United States, she recorded a classic in 1967, **The Feeling Is Mutual** (Milestone 9003) which surprisingly has not been reissued on CD in the Original Jazz Classics series yet. This project for Orrin Keepnews's new Milestone label has unpredictable arrangements by pianist Dick Katz, and features Merrill's warm and flexible voice in several different settings. "Here's that Rainy Day" and "Deep in a Dream" are duets with Katz and Jim Hall, "You're My Thrill" is given definitive treatment in a trio with Katz and Ron Carter, and other songs (which include "Baltimore Oriole," "Winter of My Discontent," "It Don't Mean a Thing," and "What Is this Thing Called Love") are given surprising interpretations by Merrill with Thad Jones, Katz, Hall, Carter, and either Pete LaRoca or Arnie Wise on drums. Merrill, like Abbey Lincoln, usually made every recording count, but the audience for her music was much greater overseas than in the United States.

Mark Murphy　Mark Murphy, having not become a commercial hit during his brief period with the Capitol label, recorded two fine jazz albums for Riverside during 1961–62. **Rah** (Original Jazz Classics 141) has him backed by a brass ensemble arranged by Ernie Wilkins, cooking on such numbers as "Angel Eyes," "Milestones," and "Doodlin'," while showing a great deal of sensitivity on "Spring Can Really Hang You Up the Most." **That's How I Love the Blues** (Original Jazz Classics 367) has the word "blues" (or in one case "blue") appearing in the title of 12 of the 13 songs although a few tunes are not technically blues. Al Cohn's charts for two trumpets and a six-piece rhythm section (with both piano and organ) are excellent, and Murphy shows on such songs as "Going to Chicago Blues," "Blues in the Night," and a memorable "Señor Blues" that he was in his early prime.

However, those records did not catch on, and Mark Murphy spent the 1963–72 period overseas, mostly performing in England.

Anita O'Day   During 1961–62, Anita O'Day was still heard in peak form. She recorded four additional Verve albums, all of which are included in her limited edition Mosaic box set. **Trav'lin' Light** (Verve 2651) is a tribute to the recently deceased Billie Holiday with half the selections having O'Day backed by a sextet with Ben Webster and Don Fagerquist, and the remainder being big band selections arranged by Johnny Mandel. Among the selections that she makes her own are "Some Other Spring," "Miss Brown to You," "Crazy He Calls Me," and "Lover Come Back to Me." **All the Sad Young Men** (Verve 517 065) teams the singer with a big band arranged by the 27-year-old Gary McFarland. The charts are colorful and unpredictable, inspiring O'Day (who actually overdubbed her singing on this project) to come up with fresh ideas. Highlights include a remake of "Boogie Blues," "You Came a Long Way from St. Louis," and "The Ballad of the Sad Young Men." Not quite essential but interesting are a project with Cal Tjader, **Time for Two** (Verve 8472) and **Anita O'Day and the Three Sounds** (Verve 8514), neither of which are available individually yet on CD.

For Anita O'Day, her prime period ended in 1962 with the expiration of her Verve contract. Other than a set cut in Japan the following year for a Japanese label, she would not make any other records until 1970. Instead she struggled with a heroin addiction that almost killed her before she made an inspiring comeback.

King Pleasure   In 1962, King Pleasure (Clarence Beeks) had his final recording session though he was only 40 at the time. **Moody's Mood for Love** (Blue Note 84463) has the nine selections from the United Artist LP with Pleasure backed by unidentified personnel (other than tenor saxophonist Seldon Powell). There are some remakes (including a guest appearance by Jon Hendricks on "Don't Get Scared"), a couple of straightforward tunes, and some newer vocalese arrangements, including Lester Young's solo on "Mean to Me." In addition, the CD has two previously unreleased numbers and six selections from very rare singles put out by Aladdin and Jubilee during 1956. When acquired along with the earlier **King Pleasure Sings/Annie Ross Sings** and **Golden Days**, one has every King Pleasure recording.

After his 1962 album, King Pleasure, whose life was shrouded in mystery, permanently slipped away into obscurity, not recording or performing again.

Lou Rawls   In his long career as a soul, R&B, and pop singer, Lou Rawls only recorded one out-and-out jazz album, and it was actually his debut recording, **Stormy Monday** (Blue Note 91441). This memorable effort from 1962 has Rawls singing soulful standards backed by the Les McCann Trio. Although most of the songs were warhorses even at the time, Rawls's enthusiasm and very appealing voice make such tunes as "Stormy Monday," "In the Evening," and "I'd Rather Drink Muddy Water" sound fresh and lively. McCann gets a generous amount of solo space, and virtually everything on this disc works quite well. Rawls occasionally appeared at jazz festivals in later years, but nothing he has recorded since has reached the creative level of this early set, a fact he seemed to recognize when he toured with McCann nearly 40 years later, singing a similar repertoire.

Betty Roche   Betty Roche's third album as a leader, **Lightly and Politely** (Original Jazz Classics 1802), is her strongest overall. Backed by a four-piece rhythm section for this set from January 24, 1961, Roche improvises quite a bit on standards and three Ellington songs, with the highlights including "Someone to Watch Over Me," "Polka Dots and Moonbeams," "Rocks in My Bed," and "I Had the Craziest Dream." But although she was just 43 at the time, Betty Roche soon permanently dropped out of music, never recording again.

Jimmy Rushing   "Mr. Five by Five" was in his sixties during the 1960s, but still remained quite active, singing with Harry James, Benny Goodman, and Eddie Condon (with whom he toured Japan in 1964). **Everyday I Have the Blues** (Polygram 547 697) combines two albums that Jimmy Rushing made for the Bluesway label during 1967–68. Still in prime singing voice, Rushing is joined by such friends as Dickie Wells, Clark Terry, and Buddy Tate. Oliver Nelson arranged the first date for a big band, and there is an electric rhythm section (plus pianist Dave Frishberg) on the second session, but Rushing sings with as much joy as if he were backed by the Basie band 30 years earlier. Among the better selections are "Berkeley Campus Blues," "Blues in the Dark," "I Left My Baby," "Sent for You Yesterday," and the instrumental "We Remember Prez." From 1967,

Who Was It that Sang that Song (New World 80510) has Rushing joined by six veterans: Buck Clayton (on one of his last sessions), Dickie Wells, tenor saxophonist Julian Dash, Sir Charles Thompson, bassist Gene Ramey, and Jo Jones on enthusiastic if predictable versions of swing standards including "Baby Won't You Please Come Home," "'Deed I Do," and "All of Me."

Carol Sloane   Carol Sloane started singing professionally when she was 14. She performed with the Les and Larry Elgart Orchestra (1958–60), and impressed Jon Hendricks at a jazz festival in 1960, getting the chance to sub for Annie Ross with Lambert, Hendricks, and Ross. She made a big stir at the 1961 Newport Jazz Festival, leading to two albums being recorded for Columbia. Her debut, **Out of the Blue** (Koch 7810), shows what the fuss was all about. Although sounding a little like Ella Fitzgerald in spots, Sloane's own winning personality pops through. Most of the songs are ballads (with an occasional swinger), and the arrangements of Bill Finegan and Bob Brookmeyer keep the band in a supportive role, but there are plenty of fine moments on such songs as "Aren't You Glad You're You," "Who Cares," "My Ship," and "Will You Still Be Mine."

Sloane's second Columbia album (which has not been reissued) is lesser-known, and neither set sold well enough for her contract to be renewed. Unable to make a living at singing, Carol Sloane worked as a secretary in North Carolina, and, other than a live date from 1964 with Ben Webster that was released decades later, she would not record again until 1977.

Victoria Spivey   While such classic blues singers as Ida Cox, Alberta Hunter, and Sippie Wallace made brief comebacks during this era, Victoria Spivey (who was in her mid-fifties) made a more permanent return to music. She had retired in 1952, working as a church administrator, but in 1961 returned to records, performing on part of the **Blues We Taught Your Mother** album that also featured Hunter, and cutting a full set of duets with Lonnie Johnson, **Woman Blues** (Original Blues Classics 56). Singing and playing backup piano, Spivey shows that she still had plenty left to offer on the latter set, contributing all ten songs and taking four numbers as unaccompanied features. Always a bit of a hustler, she began her own Spivey label and recorded fairly regularly throughout the 1960s. The results were generally low budget operations with so-so recording quality (unfortunately, none

of the Spivey releases have reappeared yet on CD), but Victoria Spivey's comeback was very successful.

Dakota Staton   Dakota Staton, who had a hit with "The Late Late Show" in 1957, recorded steadily for Capitol through 1961. Her last album for the label was one of her best and has been reissued as **Dakota at Storyville** (Collectables 5233). The soulful singer sounds quite inspired on such numbers as "Is You Is, or Is You Ain't My Baby," "Saturday Night Is the Loneliest Night of the Week," "When I Grow Too Old to Dream" (which spontaneously becomes a crowd sing-along), and "Don't Get Around Much Anymore." The backup group, other than pianist Norman Simmons, is unidentified, but the man on tenor, flute, and (on "Music, Maestro, Please") oboe is obviously Yusef Lateef.

As with too many jazz-oriented singers of the era, Dakota Staton's recording career began to trail off by the mid-1960s. She made three dates for United Artists during 1963–64 and one for London in 1966 before being lost in the crowd for too many years.

Mel Tormé   Mel Tormé, who recorded several classic jazz albums in the late 1950s, found the 1960s to be increasingly tough going. His swinging singing style seemed out of date with the rise of rock, and his records began to decline in quality as some labels tried to push him into other musical directions. **My Kind of Music** (Verve 543 795) was his final recording for Verve, and it has its moments, including versions of "By Myself," "Shine on Your Shoes," "Born to Be Blue," and Tormé's "The Christmas Song." However, the arrangements for the unidentified orchestra are uninspiring, and not on the level of Marty Paich's classic work for the singer a couple of years earlier. Recorded in 1962, **Mel Tormé at the Red Hill** (Atlantic 1234) shows that Tormé was always at his best singing freewheeling jazz such as "Love Is Just Around the Corner," "Mountain Greenery," and "It's DeLovely." Later in 1962, Tormé had a fluke hit with "Comin' Home Baby," a song he grew to hate due to its repetitive nature, and the fact that it led some labels into thinking that he could come up with other similar hit records. Recorded in 1965, **That's All** (Columbia 65165) is disappointing. The 1997 CD reissue has the original LP plus ten songs only previously out as singles and two unreleased titles. Tormé sings quite well, but the arrangements (mostly by Robert Mersey) are unimaginative middle-of-the-road pop utilizing an orchestra, occasional strings, and background singers that greatly weigh down the proceedings. The music (all ballads) is taken at slow tempos, and was clearly geared for radio airplay, clocking in around the three-minute mark, so Tormé was given no opportunities to make the material his own.

Things would get worse for Tormé, who only made two other albums in the next dozen years. But he would survive long enough to enjoy a major comeback.

Big Joe Turner   Big Joe Turner never changed his style yet somehow he managed to fit into nearly every time period. Despite this fact, he barely recorded during 1960–66 (unless one counts a few singles or a 1966 set with Bill Haley's Comets), but in 1967 was one of the stars of John Hammond's "From Spirituals to Swing" concert. His Bluesway album of 1967 was last reissued as an audiophile CD, **Singing the Blues** (Mobile Fidelity 780). Joined by some top studio players of the era (including Buddy Lucas on tenor and harmonica), Turner (56 at the time) still sounds in powerful form, performing "Roll 'Em Pete" and "Cherry Red" along with some forgettable but spirited newer originals.

Sarah Vaughan   During 1960–63, Sarah Vaughan recorded for the Roulette label. Her complete output for the company is scheduled as of this writing to be reissued on a limited-edition Mosaic box set, and quite a few of the sessions are also available individually. **The Singles Sessions** (Roulette 795331) has 14 rather brief performances (totaling just 35 minutes) that were originally meant for the jukebox and singles markets. Sassy's cover versions of "Them There Eyes," "Don't Go to Strangers," "Love," "One Mint Julep," and "Mama He Treats Your Daughter Mean" are fun, but generally not up to the level of the original hit recordings. **Count Basie & Sarah Vaughan** (Roulette 37241) does not have an accurate title since Basie is not actually on this record, but Vaughan sounds fine singing with Basie's band (with Kirk Stuart on piano), particularly on "Perdido," "Mean to Me," and "Until I Met You." Among the three added cuts on the CD reissue are a pair of delightful Vaughan-Joe Williams vocal duets on "Teach Me Tonight" and "If I Were a Bell."

After Hours (Roulette 55468) is a special set for it has Vaughan backed by just guitarist Mundell Lowe and bassist George Duvivier, and she is in the spotlight all the time; Lowe only has one solo. Sassy and her wondrous voice have no difficulty holding one's attention on such

songs as "Ev'ry Time We Say Goodbye," "Easy to Love," and "I'll Wind." **You're Mine, You** (Roulette 57157) features Vaughan joined by an orchestra arranged by Quincy Jones, but the arrangements are more suitable for Frank Sinatra than for a jazz singer. Sassy sounds overly mannered on "The Best Is Yet to Come," "Witchcraft," "The Second Time Around," and much of the rest of the so-so program. **The Benny Carter Sessions** (Roulette 28640) combines together two former albums (**The Explosive Side of Sarah Vaughan** [Roulette 52092] and **The Lonely Hours** [Roulette 52104]) that utilize Carter's arrangements (but not his alto). Vaughan is backed by a big band on the first set (highlighted by "Honeysuckle Rose," "The Lady's in Love with You," and "The Trolley Song") while **The Lonely Hours** is a ballad date with a string orchestra. **Sarah Slightly Classical** (Roulette 95977) is as close as Vaughan came on records to sounding like an opera singer, pouring an excessive amount of emotion into such songs as "Be My Love," "Full Moon and Empty Arms," and "Ah, Sweet Mystery of Life." **Sarah Sings Soulfully** (Roulette 98445) is easier for jazz listeners to get into because Vaughan (who was just 39 when this was recorded in 1963) is wonderful on "Sermonette," "Moanin'," "'Round Midnight," and "Midnight Sun." She is assisted by a sextet that includes Teddy Edwards and Carmell Jones.

In mid-1963, Sarah Vaughan switched back to the Mercury label for the next three and a half years. The six-CD set **Complete Sarah Vaughan on Mercury, Vol. 4** (Mercury 830 774) has all of the music from this period, including such projects as **Vaughan with Voices**, **The Mancini Songbook**, **Sassy Swings Again** (a big band set), and a greatly expanded **Sassy Swings the Tivoli** along with lots of miscellaneous items. Most listeners other than completists will be satisfied acquiring the two-CD set ◉ **Sassy Swings the Tivoli** (Mercury 832 788), a live set from 1963 with her regular trio (pianist Kirk Stuart, bassist Charles Williams, and drummer George Hughes). This freewheeling and spontaneous affair can be considered Sarah Vaughan's best all-around recording of the 1960s, with memorable renditions of "Poor Butterfly," "Misty," "I'll Be Seeing You," and "Black Coffee" being only four of the many high points from the wondrous singer.

Eddie "Cleanhead" Vinson   Other than a set for Bluesway in 1967, Eddie "Cleanhead" Vinson's only recording during this era was a 1961 album produced by Cannonball Adderley, **Cleanhead & Cannonball** (Milestone 9324). On Vinson's five vocal numbers, he is backed by Cannonball Adderley, Nat Adderley, Joe Zawinul, Sam Jones, and drummer Louis Hayes. Unfortunately, on the instrumentals and the one vocal tune ("Kidney Stew") in which he plays, Vinson is the only altoist as Cannonball sits out; it is a missed opportunity that the two very different alto stylists did not have a chance to trade off. But despite that, this is an excellent set highlighted by "Person to Person," "Just a Dream," and the spirited instrumentals; Nat Adderley is in particularly fine form throughout.

Sippie Wallace   Since 1929, Sippie Wallace had recorded two songs in 1945 (with Albert Ammons), six in 1958, and a version of her trademark "I'm a Mighty Tight Woman" for the Spivey label in 1962. Otherwise she was largely inactive in music for decades, but in 1966 she was persuaded to return to active performing by her friend Victoria Spivey. **Woman Be Wise** (Storyville 8024) has Wallace (just a few days shy of her 68th birthday) sounding quite powerful as she shouts out the blues on such songs as "Shorty George Blues," "I'm a Mighty Tight Woman," "You Don't Know My Mind Blues," and "Up the Country Blues." On the latter song, Wallace backs herself on piano; otherwise she is accompanied by either Roosevelt Sykes or Little Brother Montgomery on piano. She also made an LP in 1967, **Jug Band Blues** (Mountain Railroad 52672), with Jim Kweskin's Jug Band and Otis Spann before Sippie Wallace went back into semi-retirement.

Dinah Washington   The success of her 1959 recording "What a Difference a Day Makes" made Dinah Washington into a major success in the pop world. Although she still had the ability to sing anything, her recordings became much more limited and were clearly centered on coming up with other pop hits in a similar vein. **The Complete Dinah Washington on Mercury, Vol. 7** (Mercury 832 969), a three-CD set, has her 1961 recordings for Mercury, and mostly features the singer backed by orchestras on a variety of standards and current pop tunes, all unimaginatively arranged and predictably performed; best known are "Blue Gardenia," "Everybody's Somebody's Fool," and "I Wanna Be Loved." In 1962, Washington switched to the Roulette label, and her output for that company during the next two years has partly

come back on several single CDs. **In Love** (Roulette 97273) and **Dinah '63** (Roulette 94576) both have rather concise interpretations of songs with Washington (who sounds overly mannered in spots) just singing the melody. **Back to the Blues** (Roulette 54334) is the best of these sets due to Miss D. being joined by a swinging big band arranged by Quincy Jones with the tenors of Illinois Jacquet and Eddie Chamblee compensating for the unnecessary strings and background voices.

Unfortunately, it all came to an end on December 14, 1963, when Dinah Washington (who was just 39 and at the height of her fame) died accidentally from a combination of alcohol and diet pills. Even after her death, she was the main influence on most black female singers of the 1960s and '70s, but none of her followers would reach the creative heights or display the versatility of the Queen of the Blues.

Patty Waters   Although preceded by Jeanne Lee (who only recorded once during the period) and the screams of Abbey Lincoln in Max Roach's **Freedom Now Suite**, Patty Waters could be considered the first avant-garde jazz singer. She had started out being influenced by Billie Holiday and Anita O'Day, but shortly after moving to New York in the early 1960s, Waters began appearing in free jazz settings. Albert Ayler heard her perform and recommended her to the ESP label. Her December 1965 album **Patty Waters Sings** (ESP 1025) has seven brief numbers in which she backs herself on piano, but those are easily overshadowed by a remarkable 13 ½-minute version of "Black Is the Color of My True Love's Hair" in which Waters (backed by the Burton Greene Trio) sounds totally possessed, improvising off of the song's title, and taking the song from a whisper to demented screams, shouting out the word "black" in many different ways. Very few other singers would have had the courage to perform something like this in 1965, improvising with the passion of an Archie Shepp or Ayler.

In 1966, on **College Tour** (ESP 1055), Patty Waters (who is backed by a pair of rhythm sections with either Ran Blake or Burton Greene on piano, and occasionally flutist Giuseppe Logan) performs more originals in emotional and highly expressive ways, sounding quite free on much of the music, even the standards "It Never Entered My Mind" and "Wild Is the Wind." But rather than build on these artistic successes, Waters soon dropped out of music altogether. It would be 30 years before she led her third record date, and by then she had become an obscure legend, known only to those who were fortunate enough to own her innovative records.

Joe Williams   In 1961, Joe Williams left the Count Basie Orchestra after seven years, spent a little bit of time collaborating with Harry "Sweets" Edison in a combo, and then became a single. His career would be consistently successful, and there would always be an audience for his joyful blend of blues, standards, and ballads. Recorded in 1962, **A Swingin' Night at Birdland** (Roulette 95335) has Williams teamed with a quintet featuring Edison and Jimmy Forrest, with the highlights including "September in the Rain," "Teach Me Tonight," "Roll 'Em Pete," and "Goin' to Chicago Blues." **At Newport '63** (RCA 63919) has Williams joined on various tracks by Clark Terry, Howard McGhee, Coleman Hawkins, and Zoot Sims. Although it falls short of being classic, Williams sounds quite happy to be in such company; best as usual are "Every Day I Have the Blues" and "In the Evenin'." **Me and the Blues** (RCA 63536) sticks primarily to the blues, with Williams (backed by a nonet including Clark Terry, Thad Jones, Phil Woods, and Ben Webster) putting plenty of feeling into "Rocks in My Bed," "Work Song," and "Hobo Flats."

Best of all is 1966's ● **Joe Williams and the Thad Jones-Mel Lewis Orchestra** (Blue Note 30454), one of his greatest recordings. Although the big band has few solos, Thad Jones's arrangements are inventive, and Williams (who was 47) sounds at his peak on such songs as "Nobody Knows the Way I Feel This Morning," "Hallelujah I Love Her So," and "Night Time Is the Right Time."

Nancy Wilson   Nancy Wilson was one of the most promising new jazz singers of the early 1960s. She had made her recording debut in 1959 after being discovered by Cannonball Adderley and being signed by Capitol. Influenced by Dinah Washington yet having her own soulful sound, Wilson had an accessible style and was able to cross easily between musical boundaries. Her earliest period was her most jazz-oriented years, and she was featured on sessions with the Billy May Orchestra and the George Shearing Quintet; the latter has been reissued as **The Swingin's Mutual** (Capitol 99190). However, the Nancy Wilson CD to get is her classic ● **Nancy Wilson/Cannonball Adderley** (Capitol 81204). Wilson has never sounded better than on her seven vocals, which include memorable versions of "Save Your Love for Me," "Never Will I Marry," "The Masquerade Is Over," and "A Sleepin' Bee." Throughout this date, she shows how great a jazz singer she could have been if she had decided to pursue this musical path, and there are also five fine instrumentals from the Adderley Quintet (including "Unit Seven").

But unfortunately for jazz, Nancy Wilson soon veered permanently toward pop music and R&B, giving up both subtlety and spontaneity. By the time she recorded **Lush Life** (Blue Note 32745) in 1967, Wilson was an overly mannered, middle-of-the-road pop singer who tended to be melodramatic, using preplanned cracks in her voice during ballads. Although she would occasionally appear at jazz festivals in future years, the jazz high point of her career is still her collaboration with Cannonball Adderley.

Jimmy Witherspoon   After his success at the 1959 Monterey Jazz Festival, Jimmy Witherspoon was able to keep quite busy throughout much of the 1960s, straddling the musical boundaries between swinging jazz and blues. His best recordings from this era were generally for Prestige and have been reissued in the Original Blues Classics series; his later Verves were less spontaneous. **Baby, Baby, Baby** (Original Blues Classics 527) has 'Spoon interacting with a pair of medium-size groups on such songs as "Rocks in My Bed," "Bad Bad Whiskey," "It's a Lonesome Old World," and "One Scotch, One Bourbon, One Beer." **Evenin' Blues** (Original Blues Classics 511) features 'Spoon with guitarist T-Bone Walker and tenor saxophonist Clifford Scott on "Don't Let Go," "Evenin'," and "Kansas City." **Blues Around the Clock** (Original Blues Classics 576) would have been better with more stretching out (only "No Rollin' Blues" is over four minutes long), but Witherspoon makes every second count on "I Had a Dream," "Goin' to Chicago Blues," and "Around the Clock." **Some of My Best Friends Are the Blues** (Original Blues Classics 575), despite the title, has Witherspoon in a more jazz-oriented setting, accompanied by a big band arranged by Benny Golson and singing a few non-blues including "Who's Sorry Now" and "And the Angels Sing." **Blues for Easy Lovers** (Original Blues Classics 585) from 1965–66 only has two of the dozen songs being blues, and shows how strong a jazz singer Witherspoon could be. He is joined by trombonist Bill Watrous, Pepper Adams, Roger Kellaway, Richard Davis, and Mel Lewis on such songs as "Lotus Blossom," "P.S. I Love You," "Don't Worry 'Bout Me," "Embraceable You," and "I Got It Bad."

But even Jimmy Witherspoon would have some tough times in the late 1960s when short-sighted record labels began demanding that nearly every jazz/blues singer start recording inferior cover versions of pop hits.

Big Bands

As 1961 began, there were five major big bands in jazz: Duke Ellington, Count Basie, Woody Herman, Stan Kenton, and Maynard Ferguson, along with a nostalgic unit led by Harry James, occasional big bands headed by Benny Goodman, and ghost orchestras dedicated to the music of Tommy Dorsey, Jimmy Dorsey, and Glenn Miller. While Ferguson's band would not survive to 1967, by then there were a few new stimulating large ensembles headed by Gerald Wilson, Buddy Rich, Don Ellis, and the team of Thad Jones and Mel Lewis. Despite the new orchestras, fewer people each year were still asking, "When are the big bands coming back?"

Duke Ellington   Duke Ellington remained a mighty force in jazz during the 1960s. Despite some turnover, his big band still ranked at the top, featuring such key players as trumpeters Ray Nance, Willie Cook, and Cat Anderson, trombonist Lawrence Brown, bassist Aaron Bell, drummer Sam Woodyard, and a saxophone section unchanged since 1955: altoist Johnny Hodges, Russell Procope on alto and clarinet, Jimmy Hamilton on clarinet and tenor, tenor saxophonist Paul Gonsalves, and baritonist Harry Carney.

During this era, Ellington wrote the soundtrack for the movie *Paris Blues*, put together the short-lived 1963 show *My People*, and welcomed such new soloists as trumpeters Bill Berry and Rolf Ericson, and trombonist Buster Cooper. Cootie Williams rejoined Ellington in 1962 after a 22-year "vacation," resulting in Ray Nance (who was suddenly underutilized) departing in 1963 after 23 years with the band.

During 1961–62, Ellington was involved in five special recorded collaborations. He sat in with the Louis Armstrong All-Stars (a set reviewed under Satch's name) and the John Coltrane Quartet (covered under Coltrane's name). ● **Duke Ellington Meets Count Basie** (Columbia/Legacy 655471) is a remarkably successful project in

which the Ellington and Basie orchestras are combined, with 15 major soloists heard from and the leaders playing two pianos. Highlights include unique versions of "Corner Pocket," "Jumpin' at the Woodside," and "Wild Man" plus a classic rendition of "Segue in C." **Duke Ellington Meets Coleman Hawkins** (Impulse 162) has the great Coleman Hawkins featured as part of an all-star octet with Nance, Brown, Hodges, and Carney. Among the most memorable selections are "Mood Indigo," "Self Portrait of the Bean," and a definitive version of "The Jeep Is Jumpin'." ● **Money Jungle** (Blue Note 38227) is a trio project on which Ellington is teamed with Charles Mingus and Max Roach. Although Mingus is heard constantly pushing his former boss (whom he worked for briefly in the early 1950s), Ellington ends up sounding like the most modern player on the date, showing on "Fleurette Africaine," "Caravan," "Wig Wise," and especially "Money Jungle" the influence that he had on Thelonious Monk and Cecil Taylor.

Ellington recorded quite prolifically in the 1960s, using the recording studios as a rehearsal hall and an opportunity to try out new ideas. **Featuring Paul Gonsalves** (Original Jazz Classics 623) from 1962 has Duke showcasing tenor saxophonist Paul Gonsalves as the only soloist on eight numbers including "C Jam Blues," "Take the 'A' Train," and "Jam with Sam"; fortunately Gonsalves was in fine form that day. A constant globetrotter with his orchestra by the early 1960s, Ellington and his right-hand man Billy Strayhorn began to display the influences of their travels in their music. **Afro-Bossa** (Discovery 71002) pays tribute to some of the lands that they were exploring, consisting of "Pyramid" and 11 new selections, which are mostly concise gems. Best known are "Purple Gazelle" and "Eighth Veil." **The Great Paris Concert** (Atlantic 2-304) is one of the best live recordings of Ellington from this period. The two-CD set includes a rousing "Rockin' in Rhythm," "Concerto for Cootie," "Jam with Sam," "Suite Thursday," and "Harlem Suite" among the highlights. **Harlem** (Pablo 2308-245) was recorded in Stockholm and includes "The Opener," "A Happy Reunion," "Blow by Blow," "The Prowling Cat," and various standards. Other superior live dates include **The Great London Concerts** (Music Masters 65106) which mostly has Ellington favorites plus the more recent "Isfahan" and "Single Petal of a Rose," and **New York Concert**. The latter is notable for four thoughtful unaccompanied piano solos, trio features, a guest spot for Willie "The Lion" Smith on "Carolina Shout," and a pair of Ellington-Strayhorn piano duets in addition to more typical work from the big band.

The Symphonic Ellington (Discovery 71003) from 1963 has Duke being given the rare chance to combine his big band with a symphony orchestra for versions of the three-movement "Night Creature," "Harlem Airshaft," "Non-Violent Integration," and "La Scala, She Was Too Pretty to Be Blue." The combination works quite well. **The Pianist** (Original Jazz Classics 717) puts the focus on Ellington's piano playing on sessions from 1966 and 1970 in small groups, including a trio with bassist John Lamb and Sam Woodyard.

Two classic albums attest both to Duke Ellington's continuing creativity and what would eventually be a losing race against mortality. ❍ **The Far East Suite—Special Mix** (Bluebird 6287) was the last classic project that Ellington and Strayhorn worked on together. The nine songs pay tribute to the Asian countries that Ellington's big band visited, not by copying the countries' folk melodies, but by having Ellington's music open to the influences. "Isfahan" (which became a standard), "Ad Lib on Nippon," "Mount Harissa," and "Tourist Point of View" are the standouts.

On May 31, 1967, Billy Strayhorn (a lifelong smoker) died of lung cancer at the age of 51. He had worked closely with Ellington since 1939, and they collaborated on many works through the years, so his death was a major shock to Duke. Ellington considered this a harsh reminder that time would be running out eventually, and he began to drive himself a lot harder, becoming even more prolific than earlier. In tribute to Strayhorn, Duke recorded ❍ **And His Mother Called Him Bill** (Bluebird 6287), an emotional and inspired set that has the orchestra interpreting 15 of Strayhorn's finest songs, including "Blood Count" (his last composition), "Smada," "Rain Check," "Midriff," "Lotus Blossom," and "The Intimacy of the Blues."

Forty years after it had opened at the Cotton Club, the Duke Ellington Orchestra was still going strong in 1967.

Count Basie   The best Basie album of this era was a small-group date, **Count Basie and the Kansas City 7** (Impulse 202). This 1962 set features Count in a septet with Thad Jones, Frank Foster, and Eric Dixon, playing a variety of blues and standards plus two originals apiece by Jones and Frank Wess.

In the fall of 1962, the Count Basie Orchestra ended its association with Roulette and switched back to the Verve label. Unfortunately, the 1960s were an erratic period for Basie, particularly on records. Ironically, even though his band suffered the loss of its main soloists (Thad Jones, Joe Newman, Al Grey, Frank Foster, and Frank Wess), it still sounded quite strong in concerts; the ensemble sound was no longer dependent on individual soloists. And, even with the defections, such players as trumpeter Al Aarons, trombonist Grover Mitchell, and the tenors of Eddie "Lockjaw" Davis and Eric Dixon plus drummer Sonny Payne kept the music stirring.

However, on record, the Basie Orchestra was often used as a prop behind such singers as Frank Sinatra, Tony Bennett, the Mills Brothers, Kay Starr, Teresa Brewer, Arthur Prysock, Jackie Wilson, and Sammy Davis, Jr. In most cases, a studio orchestra would have sufficed. Even some of the instrumental records Basie cut during this era were not too satisfying, including albums of current pop hits and Beatles songs. **This Time by Basie** (Reprise 45162) has the jazz institution wasted on such numbers as "I Left My Heart in San Francisco," "Moon River," "What Kind of Fool Am I," and "Shangri-La." **Frankly Basie** (Verve 314 519 849) is a little better since the Billy Byers arrangements of 14 songs associated with Frank Sinatra are pleasing in spots, but the end results are overly safe and forgettable. The problem was that producer Norman Granz had sold Verve before Basie's return, and his guiding hand was missing. So although revered as a swinging institution, the Count Basie Orchestra often merely functioned as a prop in the 1960s. But better times were coming.

Woody Herman   After leading the Third Herd during 1950–56, Woody Herman headed part-time orchestras and ensembles for a few years before a specially assembled big band was one of the hits of the 1959 Monterey Jazz Festival. Its success led to Herman forming a new orchestra, one often called the Swinging Herd or the Young Thundering Herd, that would last throughout the remainder of his life.

By late 1962, Herman's orchestra featured the high-note trumpeter Bill Chase, trombonist Phil Wilson, pianist/arranger Nat Pierce, drummer Jake Hanna, and the hard-charging tenor of Sal Nistico. Four superior albums were cut for Phillips during 1962–64, and there were also several high-quality sets made for Columbia during 1964–67. One waits with impatience for the **1963** (Phillips 600-065), **Encore** (Phillips 600-071), **1964** (Phillips 600-118), and **Recorded Live at Harrah's Club** (Phillips 600-131) LPs to be reissued on CD, but fortunately ◉ **Jazz Hoot/Woody's Winners** (Collectables 6678) from 1965–66 is available. This single CD brings back two of Herman's best Columbia sets, and is highlighted by "Northwest Passage," "Greasy Sack Blues," and a romping version of Horace Silver's "Opus de Funk." Nistico's playing throughout is among the finest of his career, and he really inspires the band. Other key players include trumpeters Chase, Don Rader, Bobby Shew, and Dusko Gojkovic, and pianist Nat Pierce, plus Herman himself on clarinet and alto. **Woody Live: East and West** (Koch 8592) has dates from 1965 and 1967, and finds the band in transition. In addition to Nistico on the earlier session, the two sets feature such players as trombonist Bill Watrous, tenor saxophonist Steve Marcus, baritonist Joe Temperley, Chase, and Pierce. The excitement of the band and its basic style was largely unchanged during this period as can be heard on such numbers as "The Preacher," "Cousins," and "Four Brothers Revisited," but for Woody Herman, this album signaled the end of an era before he opened his repertoire to pop and rock tunes.

Stan Kenton   Stan Kenton began 1961 with his usual top-notch band, one sporting a full mellophonium section. This unit lasted into 1964 and featured such soloists along the way as altoist Gabe Baltazar, trumpeter Marvin Stamm, tenors Sam Donahue, Charles Mariano, and Don Menza, and trombonist Jiggs Whigham. Most notable of the band's recordings were **West Side Story** (Capitol 29914) and 1964's **Kenton Plays Wagner** (Creative World 2217). Kenton's recordings of Johnny Richards's arrangements of ten of *West Side Story*'s themes was so perfect that the producers of the film were disappointed that they had not thought to ask Kenton to play on the soundtrack. Richards's charts alternate between being dramatic and tender, and are consistently passionate, with solos by Baltazar, Donohue, and Conte Candoli along with plenty of exciting and raging ensembles.

An LP well worth being reissued, **Kenton Plays Wagner** is really the last recording by Stan Kenton's Orchestra (even though it actually utilizes a studio ensemble filled with alumni) before its focus changed. Recorded in 1964, this unlikely success is ultimately logical, for both Kenton and classical composer Richard Wagner were charismatic larger-than-life figures who had right-wing political viewpoints, and a very strong belief in their own musical vision, not being overly concerned if the rest of the world followed. Somehow Kenton turned eight Wagner themes into jazz, capturing the intense emotion, pomposity, and drama with daring ideas.

By 1965, Stan Kenton was involved in organizing a huge classical/jazz orchestra called the Neophonic Orchestra that performed new works at special concerts. He was also heavily involved in running jazz education camps that helped introduce jazz and his music to many teenagers and college students. As far as his own big band went, instead of utilizing musicians who would have major careers and would later think of their period with Kenton to be an important early step, the post-1964 Stan Kenton Orchestra was filled with future academicians and part-time players who would consider their association with Kenton to be the high point of their careers. For example, of the 17 musicians who are on Kenton's 1967 album **The Jazz Compositions of Dee Barton**, only tenor saxophonist Kim Richmond and bassist Don Bagley (an alumnus temporarily back in the band) would have significant solo careers. While Kenton became such an influential force in the college jazz movement that many college big bands sounded like Kenton's orchestra, his own big band (due to utilizing so many young and somewhat faceless players) in turn soon resembled a college stage band.

Maynard Ferguson   During 1961–65, Maynard Ferguson continued leading one of the top big bands in jazz, arguably the finest group he ever had. Among the musicians who spent time in his orchestra during this period were trumpeters Rolf Ericson, Don Rader, and Bill Berry, altoist Lanny Morgan, tenors Don Menza and Willie Maiden, baritonists Frank Hittner and Ronnie Cuber, pianists Jaki Byard and Michael Abene, and drummer Rufus Jones. The orchestra recorded regularly for Roulette through 1964, and all of these valuable recordings have been issued on a limited-edition ten-CD box set, **The Complete Roulette Maynard Feguson** (Mosaic 10-156). Many of the sessions are unfortunately not available individually, but **Si Si!/Maynard '64** (Roulette 95334) reissues two former LPs on one CD. The arrangements (by Ernie Wilkins, Marty Paich, Don Sebesky, Rader, Maiden, Abene, and Menza) take advantage of the band's many strengths, and there are many concise solos along with stratospheric blasts from MF.

By 1965, Ferguson had begun to lose interest in his orchestra, and, since it was becoming economically unfeasible, he cut back to a sextet. In 1967, he appeared at the World's Fair in Montreal, and recorded two CDs of material while in his native land. **Sextet 1967** (Just A Memory 9503) has Ferguson sounding fine although his saxophonists (altoist John Cristie and Brian Barley on tenor) are more avant-garde and sound a bit uncomfortable in the somewhat conservative setting. Ferguson is in excellent form on three ballads and on "Summertime Revisited." **Orchestra 1967** (Just A Memory 9504) has Ferguson leading a band filled with local players put together specifically for the occasion; unfortunately, the individual soloists are not identified. The band is excellent, and Ferguson is the main star, taking quite a few enthusiastic and exciting solos. However, this was the end of an era, and not much would be heard from MF again until 1970.

Gerald Wilson   A trumpeter/arranger with Jimmie Lunceford in the early 1940s, and the leader of his own Los Angeles–based big band during 1944–47, Wilson freelanced as a writer and occasional trumpeter during the 1950s. In 1961, he formed a new big band that soon began recording regularly for Pacific Jazz. Although he had sounded fine as a trumpeter on some combo dates in the 1950s, Wilson soon permanently put away his horn to concentrate on writing.

All of Wilson's albums of 1961–69 are on the limited-edition **The Complete Pacific Jazz Recordings of Gerald Wilson** (Mosaic 5-198); some are also out on individual CDs. Wilson's writing uses dense chord voicings, sometimes reflected his interest in Mexican and Spanish music (and love of bullfighting), and left room for swinging solos. Among the musicians who recorded with Wilson in the 1960s were trumpeters Carmell Jones and Charles Tolliver, tenors Harold Land and Teddy Edwards, altoists Anthony Ortega and Bud Shank, baritonist Jack Nimitz, organist Richard "Groove" Holmes, pianist Jack Wilson, guitarist Joe Pass, and drummer Mel Lewis. Recorded in 1962, **Moment of Truth** (Pacific Jazz 92928) includes the original version of "Viva Tirado" (a catchy number made into a surprise pop hit by El Chicano later in the decade) and a driving rendition of "Milestones." **Portraits** (Pacific Jazz 93414) is notable for its

reworkings of "So What" and "'Round Midnight." Unfortunately, **The Golden Sword** (last out as the LP Discovery 901) has not returned yet outside of the Mosaic box for this is a classic release. Wilson's ten originals pay tribute to different aspects of Mexico with the powerful "Carlos" being a dramatic portrayal of a bullfighter.

The Thad Jones/Mel Lewis Orchestra   A key trumpet soloist with the Count Basie Orchestra during 1954–63, and an increasingly important arranger, Thad Jones worked as a freelancer during 1963–65, co-leading a quintet with Pepper Adams. Near the end of 1965, Jones and Mel Lewis agreed to co-lead a big band. Starting in February 1966, the Thad Jones/Mel Lewis Orchestra began playing regularly on Monday nights at the Village Vanguard, and its fame quickly grew. In the early days, it was very much an all-star group, including such notables as trumpeters Bill Berry and Richard Williams, valve trombonist Bob Brookmeyer, pianist Hank Jones, bassist Richard Davis, and a sax section comprised of Jerome Richardson, Jerry Dodgion, Joe Farrell, Eddie Daniels, and Pepper Adams. Most significant was the writing of Thad Jones, which gave the band its own musical personality and often utilized the soprano of Richardson as a lead voice in the ensembles. With Mel Lewis driving the band, this was one of the most exciting new groups of 1966–67.

All of the Thad Jones/Mel Lewis Orchestra's recordings made during 1966–72 have been reissued on **The Complete Solid State Recordings of the Thad Jones/Mel Lewis Orchestra** (Mosaic 5-151), a limited-edition box set. Unfortunately, its two recordings of 1966–67 have not been made available since they came out as LPs. **Presenting Thad Jones, Mel Lewis and the Jazz Orchestra** (Solid State 17003) includes four Jones originals, "Willow Weep for Me," and Brookmeyer's lengthy "ABC Blues." **Live at the Village Vanguard** (Solid State 18016) has similar personnel (with Snooky Young and Roland Hanna adding more power to the group), and is highlighted by Jones's "Little Pixie," an adaptation of Fats Waller's "Willow Tree," and particularly the catchy "Don't Git Sassy."

The Thad Jones/Mel Lewis Orchestra became the model of future big bands in two ways. It was mostly led by an arranger, and it was always a part-time venture.

Buddy Rich   Buddy Rich was rightfully known as "the world's greatest drummer." When it came to technique, speed, volume, and excitement, he could not be beaten. Rich spent most of the 1962–66 period playing with Harry James's big band. He always had great respect for James, and even if the music was somewhat predictable, it seemed like a logical home for the fiery drummer.

In 1966, Rich, who had been wanting to lead his own big band since the mid-1940s, took the plunge, and put together a high-powered unit that surprised virtually everyone by catching on for a few years. With trumpeter Bobby Shew, altoist Gene Quill, and pianist John Bunch as key players, the group made its recording debut with **Swingin' New Big Band** (Blue Note 35232). The CD reissue has the original LP program plus nine previously unissued performances from the same sessions. The arrangements (mostly by Oliver Nelson, but also with charts by Bill Holman, Phil Wilson, Jay Corre, Don Rader, and others) mostly put the emphasis on the ensembles although there are some fine short solos. Most memorable is Bill Reddie's adaptation of "West Side Story" (long a Rich drum feature) and "Sister Sadie." From 1967, **Big Swing Face** (Blue Note 37989) has mostly different personnel (Rich was difficult to work with!) featuring Shew, altoist Ernie Watts, and tenor saxophonist Jay Corre as the main individual voices in addition to the drummer. This CD reissues the band's second recording and doubles the program with nine new selections from the same dates. The arrangements by Bill Holman, Shorty Rogers, Bob Florence, Bill Potts, and others show off the band quite well, and Rich's teenage daughter Cathy takes a charmingly dated vocal on "The Beat Goes On." **The New One** (Pacific Jazz 94507) is taken from June and November, 1967, which although only five months apart, finds the Rich band undergoing some major turnover; only six of the 15 sidemen are the same. Watts, Corre, and trumpeter Chuck Findley are the main stars among the sidemen, and most of the material (other than "Chicago" and "I Can't Get Started") was new, including "The Rotten Kid," "New Blues," and the complex "Diabolus."

Don Ellis   Don Ellis was always a forward-looking trumpeter with a strong musical curiosity and the desire to try new things. He worked with George Russell's sextet during 1960–62, and led several small group dates during the period. **Out of Nowhere** (Candid 79032) has music from 1961 not initially influenced until 1988. Ellis performs ten standards in a trio with Paul Bley and

Steve Swallow (the Jimmy Giuffre 3 with the trumpeter in Giuffre's place), but the music is never routine or predictable. Ellis takes an unaccompanied trumpet solo on "Just One of those Things," "All the Things You Are" is a trumpet-bass duet, and Ellis interacts with Bley on a moody "My Funny Valentine." The musicians take a lot of chances with time, but virtually everything works, and the results are quite intriguing. **New Ideas** (Original Jazz Classics 431) is a quintet set with vibraphonist Al Francis, Jaki Byard, Ron Carter, and Charlie Persip. Ellis experiments with time, new chord structures, and free improvising with a highlight being his brief unaccompanied workout on the free-form "Solo." The rarest of all Don Ellis records is the 1962 LP **Essence** (Pacific Jazz 55), which teams the trumpeter with Bley, bassist Gary Peacock, and either Nick Martinis or Gene Stone on drums. Ellis continues his experiments with time, tempos, ideas taken from modern classical music, and the use of space while still swinging. Most memorable are fresh versions of Billy Strayhorn's "Johnny Come Lately," "Angel Eyes," "Lover," and Carla Bley's "Wrong Key Donkey," here simply called "Donkey").

In addition to his small-group work, Ellis worked on Third Stream projects (including with Gunther Schuller), avant-garde "jazz happenings," and in 1964 led the Hindustani Jazz Sextet, an early fusion of jazz with world music that unfortunately was not recorded.

But everything in Ellis's career was a prelude to what would be his main focus, leading an unusual series of big bands. In 1965, Ellis organized a 20-piece orchestra that, in addition to five trumpets, three trombones, five reeds, and piano, included three bassists, two drummers, and between one and three percussionists. Even more unique than the instrumentation was Ellis's fondness for performing works in unusual time signatures, including 7/8, 9/8, 31/4, and 11/12. His band became the hit of the 1966 Monterey Jazz Festival and was signed by Columbia in 1967.

Ellis's first three big band albums were made during 1966–67. **Live at Monterey** (Pacific Jazz 94768) has the four numbers played by Ellis's big band at the 1966 festival, including "33 222 1 222," which shows how the band managed to perform in 19/4 time. Other tunes include Hank Levy's "Passacaglia and Fugue," "Concerto for Trumpet" (in 5/4), and "New Nine" in addition to three bonus cuts added to the CD reissue. **Live in 3⅔ /4 Time** (Pacific Jazz 23996) has Ellis's orchestra playing perfectly coherent solos in ridiculous time signatures, including a satirical brand of Dixieland in 5/4 ("Barnum's Revenge"), "Orientation" (which goes back and forth between 7/8 and 9/8), and "Upstart" which is in 11/8 (three and two-thirds beats to the measure). Ellis, Ira Schulman on tenor and clarinet, pianist Dave Mackay, and Tom Scott on saxello are the main soloists. In addition to the original six selections (recorded at the Pacific Jazz Festival in 1966 and at Shelly's Manne-Hole in 1967), there are five additional cuts, including an alternate version of "Freedom Jazz Dance."

Electric Bath (Columbia/Legacy 65522), the Ellis big band's first studio recording, has some remarkable new music. The most memorable selection is "Indian Lady" (accurately described as a "hoedown in 5/4"), which with its many false endings is quite humorous. The other four originals (the trumpeter/leader's feature on "Alone," "Turkish Bath," "Open Beauty," and the 17/4 "New Horizons") are also quite spirited. For the first time Ellis was opening his band to the influence of rock (making liberal use of electronics), and the results lend themselves to some hilarity and lots of often-overlooked innovations.

Swing Survivors

By 1965, the swing era was 20 years in the past. Most of the veterans from that period (unless they were lucky enough to be part of the Duke Ellington or Count Basie orchestras) had either retired, died, gone into the studios, or switched to playing Dixieland, R&B, or bebop. Norman Granz closing down "Jazz at the Philharmonic" and selling Verve in 1961 were major blows that resulted in even many of the better-known swing players having to scuffle a bit. Ironically, most of the swing-era musicians were still not all that ancient (Benny Goodman was only 52 in 1961), and the ones who were given opportunities to record usually showed that they still had a strong contribution left to make to jazz.

Harold "Shorty" Baker   Harold "Shorty" Baker, a lyrical trumpeter with a mellow sound, worked with the big bands of Don Redman (1936–38), Teddy Wilson (1939–40), Andy Kirk (1940–42), and most significantly Duke Ellington (off and on during 1942–62). **Shorty & Doc** (Original Jazz Classics 839) from 1961 was a very rare opportunity for him to be well featured. He co-led the session with Doc Cheatham, a veteran trumpeter from the 1920s who was 53 at the time.

Joined by Walter Bishop, Jr., Wendell Marshall, and J.C. Heard, the two trumpeters perform swing-oriented material, and engage in friendly interplay and harmonizing. This set, originally issued by Swingville, was Baker's second of only two albums as a leader (the other was an obscure session for King in 1958). After leaving Ellington for the last time in 1962, Shorty Baker led a quartet before bad health caused his retirement and premature death in 1966 at the age of 52.

Don Byas   One of the finest American musicians to become an expatriate, tenor saxophonist Don Byas had left the United States in 1946 and would only return home once for a brief visit in 1970. Byas had opportunities overseas to perform with Duke Ellington, Bud Powell, Kenny Clarke, Dizzy Gillespie, Art Blakey, Ben Webster, and "Jazz at the Philharmonic." Two CDs, **Walkin'** (Black Lion 760167) and **A Night in Tunisia** (Black Lion 760136), both feature Byas at Copenhagen's Montmartre Jazzhaus during January 13–14, 1963. Byas, who is joined by pianist Bent Axen, drummer William Schiopffe, and 16-year-old bassist Niels-Henning Orsted Pedersen, really tears into the standards, a dozen familiar bop songs including two versions of "A Night in Tunisia." His exciting playing on such numbers as "I'll Remember April," "Anthropology," "Billie's Bounce," and "All the Things You Are" should have led to Byas being ranked with the top tenors of the period, but few in the United States still remembered him.

Another fine example of late-period Byas can be heard on 1967's **Featuring Sir Charles Thompson** (Storyville 8308). Just 54 (he was 33 when he left the U.S.), Byas sounds as strong as usual on "Autumn Leaves," "But Not for Me," "Gone with the Wind," and "Stella by Starlight," working well with the sparse Basie-ish piano of Charles Thompson in a quartet. The music may have been considered "out of date" in the United States of 1967, but it still sounds quite fresh today.

Benny Carter   Benny Carter was 54 when he recorded ⊙ **Further Definitions** (GRP/Impulse 229) in 1961, but he sounds like the youngest musician on the classic date. Actually, this CD reissues the original **Further Definitions** date plus the entire **Additions to Further Definitions** album from 1966. The earlier set reunites Carter with Coleman Hawkins, and features his arrangements for an octet that also stars altoist Phil Woods and tenor saxophonist Charlie Rouse. "Honeysuckle Rose" and "Crazy Rhythm" recall the 1937 Carter-Hawkins date with Django Reinhardt, while "Cotton Tail" and "Doozy" are comparable romps, and "Body and Soul" gives Hawkins an opportunity to come up with fresh variations. All of the musicians (which include pianist Dick Katz, guitarist John Collins, Jimmy Garrison, and Jo Jones) sound quite inspired. **Further Definitions**, while not quite reaching the same heights, is similar in format and has its moments. Carter and Bud Shank are on altos while the tenor spots are taken by Teddy Edwards and either Buddy Collette or Bill Perkins. This can be considered a West Coast equivalent of the original **Further Definitions**, and it is highlighted by "Fantastic, That's You," "If Dreams Come True," and a remake of "Doozy."

Additions to Further Definitions was Benny Carter's last small group date until 1976. The great altoist put away his horn and concentrated on writing for the studios for the next decade.

Buck Clayton   Buck Clayton began the 1960s still playing at his best. He had a second European tour in 1961, heading an all-star group filled with Basie alumni. Both **Buck Clayton All-Stars 1961** (Storyville 8231) and **Swiss Radio Days Jazz Series, Vol. 7** (TCB 02072) team Clayton with the same frontline that had toured with him in 1959 (Emmett Berry, Dickie Wells, Earl Warren, and Buddy Tate) plus Sir Charles Thompson, bassist Gene Ramey, and drummer Oliver Jackson. Five of the seven songs on the TCB CD are included (in different versions recorded the month before) on the ten-number Storyville set, which has 20 more minutes (75 versus 55) than the TCB. However, both releases are excellent, and feature the mainstream swing musicians still in peak form.

Clayton kept fairly busy during the first half of the 1960s, playing and recording with Buddy Tate and Humphrey Lyttelton, and touring Japan with Eddie Condon. **Baden-Switzerland 1966** (Sackville 2028) features the trumpeter at the age of 54, playing "Good Old Funky Blues" and seven standards from the Basie days, including "I Want a Little Girl," "You Can Depend on Me," and "One o'Clock Jump." Clayton is heard in Switzerland with three Swiss musicians (Michel Pilet on tenor, pianist Henri Chaix, bassist Isla Eckinger), and American expatriate Wallace Bishop on drums.

With any luck, Buck Clayton should have had at least another 15 years of playing ahead of him. But starting in 1967, problems with his health and lips (probably caused by a botched operation), which made it very painful for him to try to play trumpet, virtually ended his playing days. It would be a few years before he would realize that he was a first-class arranger, and that although he could no longer take trumpet solos, he could still make a contribution to jazz through his writing.

Harry "Sweets" Edison   With his distinctive tone and ability to say the most with the fewest notes, trumpeter Harry "Sweets" Edison kept busy in the 1960s, although only infrequently as a leader. He had occasional reunions with Count Basie, and was in demand for studio dates and sessions with big bands in the Los Angeles area. His most significant album of the period is 1962's **Jawbreakers** (Original Jazz Classics 487) because it teams him for the first time on record with tenor saxophonist Eddie "Lockjaw" Davis, a musical partnership that would result in a series of exciting encounters in the 1970s. Joined by pianist Hugh Lawson, bassist Ike Isaacs, and drummer Clarence Johnston, the two highly expressive horns jam on three basic Edison originals plus five swinging standards; "Broadway," "Four," and "A Gal in Calico" are most memorable.

Roy Eldridge   One of the many casualties of Norman Granz selling the Verve label, Roy Eldridge played well in the 1960s, but could not seem to find a role for himself in the jazz world. He was part of Ella Fitzgerald's backup band during 1963–65, but was quite unnecessary and under-featured, and his stint with Count Basie in 1966 found him frustrated by the lack of solo space. His three albums from the era as a leader consisted of a meeting with Bud Freeman on **Saturday Night Fish Fry** (Fontana 88390), a live set with Richie Kamuca that was not released for many years, **Comin' Home Baby** (Pumpkin 107), and a conservative but swinging **The Nifty Cat Strikes West** (Master Jazz 8121); none have been reissued yet on CD.

Benny Goodman   For Benny Goodman, who spent the 1961–67 period alternating between leading nostalgic big bands through his swing era hits and combos that showcased his clarinet, 1962 offered a potentially major opportunity. He was picked to lead a big band on a historic tour of the Soviet Union, one of the first visits by a major jazz artist to Russia since World War II. The 17-piece orchestra, which performed a few newer and more modern charts along with the warhorses, was impressive. Its personnel included trumpeters Joe Newman, Jimmy Maxwell, and Joe Wilder, trombonist Jimmy Knepper, altoist Phil Woods, Zoot Sims as the tenor soloist, pianist John Bunch, drummer Mel Lewis, and (with a small group) Teddy Wilson. A double LP that has not yet been reissued, **Benny Goodman in Moscow** (RCA 6008), shows how strong the big band could be, playing older songs plus "Titter Pipes," "Feathers," "Midgets," and Tadd Dameron's "Fontainebleau."

But unfortunately, Goodman was at his most eccentric during this trip, not wishing to share the spotlight with anyone else and constantly sabotaging soloists who gained too much applause. Horror stories from what should have been a major success became part of the BG legend. The band practically had a mutiny, and, when it later recorded an album, it was under Al Cohn's name. A Benny Goodman broadcast from only a month after the RCA album finds him leading a big band with almost entirely different personnel. That orchestra did not last long either.

A happier event took place in 1963: the first official reunion of the original Benny Goodman Quartet. BG, Teddy Wilson, Lionel Hampton, and Gene Krupa had had informal reunions in the past, but this project resulted in their first full-length recording since Krupa had departed 25 years earlier. **Together Again** (Bluebird 6283) has the musicians performing ten songs that they had not previously documented in this format, including "Seven Come Eleven," "I've Found a New Baby," and "Runnin' Wild." In truth, the band would have sounded better with the addition of a bassist (Krupa's bass drum work was a poor substitute), but the players do sound happy to be jamming together, and there are a few moments where they catch fire.

Otherwise, the best recordings by Goodman during this era can be heard on some of the tapes that he donated to Yale. Eleven CDs were released posthumously. **Yale Archives Vol. 1** (Music Masters 60142) is a sampling of performances dating from 1955–86, including some tunes by the clarinetist's 1959 combo with Flip Phillips and Bill Harris. **Yale Recordings Vol. 10** (Music Masters 65129) has previously unreleased material from the three sessions that resulted in the Benny Goodman Quartet reunion of 1963, including a few

alternates, a rehearsal version of "Four Once More," and quite a few songs not on the original album such as "Love Sends a Little Gift of Roses," "Bernie's Tune," "East of the Sun," and "It's All Right with Me." **Yale Recordings Vol. 6** (Music Masters 5047) includes nine selections from a 1967 septet with Joe Newman, Zoot Sims, and guitarist Attila Zoller, plus six songs from 1966 with a sextet that has both Doc Cheatham and Herbie Hancock (taking time off from Miles Davis to sub for Hank Jones). There are no real surprises in the repertoire or the style, but it is intriguing to hear these musicians adjusting their playing to fit in with the King of Swing.

Lionel Hampton   Lionel Hampton continued leading a big band throughout the 1960s even though it mostly just provided a backdrop for his vibes solos. His best album of the era is **You Better Know It** (GRP/Impulse 140), a sextet date from 1964, featuring Clark Terry, Ben Webster, Hank Jones, Milt Hinton, and Osie Johnson. Hampton sings three numbers (including "Ring Dem Bells") and both Terry and Webster have plenty of strong spots. But this was a departure for Hampton, who continued performing his usual pieces (mostly from 20 years before) with his rather faceless, if spirited, orchestra. Though not minding if his sidemen soloed in a more modern style, Hamp's own playing remained unchanged from the 1940s.

Coleman Hawkins   During 1961–65, it must have seemed as if Coleman Hawkins was ageless. Always proud of how modern a soloist he was, Hawkins continued to evolve. Although his rhythmic attack harked back to an earlier age, his mastery of chords and harmonically advanced style, along with his dignified manner, made him one of the most respected of the 1920s survivors. If someone played for him one of his early sides with Mamie Smith or a slap tongue solo with Fletcher Henderson, Hawkins would claim that it must have been his father or an older brother; it could not possibly be him!

The accomplishments continued to pile up during 1961–65, as did his many recordings, including sets with Duke Ellington and Sonny Rollins. While **The Hawk Relaxes** (Original Jazz Classics 709) and **On Broadway** (Prestige 24189) are disappointing due to an excess of slower tempos and so-so show tunes, **Alive! At the Village Gate** (Verve 829 260) and **Hawkins! Eldridge! Hodges! Alive! At the Village Gate** (Verve 314 513

755) are both quite exciting. Recorded in August 1962, both of the latter sets have Hawkins joined by Tommy Flanagan, bassist Major Holley, and drummer Ed Locke. The first disc has six selections, including long versions of "Joshua Fit the Battle of Jericho" and "Mack the Knife." The second release is highlighted by three explosive jams with Roy Eldridge and Johnny Hodges plus four additional quartet numbers. Both CDs feature Hawkins in enthusiastic and creative form, really tearing into the chord changes with glee.

The last significant recordings by Hawkins were his three albums for Impulse, all of which are out on CD. **Desafinado** (GRP/Impulse 227) has the great tenor exploring bossa novas, sounding quite joyful on "O Pato," "One Note Samba," and "I'm Looking Over a Four Leaf Clover." He is accompanied by two guitars, bass, drums, percussion, and Tommy Flanagan on claves. **Today and Now** (GRP/Impulse 184) is a quartet date that has Hawkins playing plenty of unusual material, including "Go Lil Liza," "Put on Your Old Grey Bonnet," "Swingin' Scotch," and "Don't Sit Under the Apple Tree." From 1965, **Wrapped Tight** (GRP/Impulse 109) has Hawkins showing the subtle influence of the avant-garde (his ears were always open), particularly on "Out of Nowhere." He is also quite creative on "Intermezzo," "Red Roses for a Blue Lady," and "Indian Summer." Forty-four years after Hawkins had debuted on records with Mamie Smith, he still sounded quite contemporary.

Unfortunately, for unknown reasons, Coleman Hawkins went straight downhill from that point on. Whether it was senility, depression, or some other disorder, Hawkins (who had expressed surprise at Lester Young's similar decline in the late 1950s) began drinking excessively, barely ate, and started looking shabby. His breathing became labored and his playing quickly declined during his final four years. He can be heard on a club date from September 1966 on **Supreme** (Enja 9009), and his solos sound aimless and sometimes lost, even on songs that he had been playing for years. His final studio session, **Sirius** (Original Jazz Classics 861) from December 1966, is particularly sad as he sounds so out of breath that he is unable to play long phrases; the ballads in particular are painful to hear.

It was a sad final chapter to the otherwise remarkable Coleman Hawkins story.

Earl Hines   After leaving the Louis Armstrong All-Stars in 1951 and having a short-lived swing combo, Earl Hines put together a hyper but uninspiring Dixieland band, playing regularly in San Francisco for a decade. He was largely overlooked by much of the jazz world during this period, until he played three concerts at New York's Little Theater in 1964, events arranged by writer Stanley Dance. Performing unaccompanied solos and in a quartet with Budd Johnson, Hines's playing greatly impressed the New York jazz press (who were amazed at how modern his playing was) and the concerts launched a comeback that lasted during the remainder of his career.

A Monday Date (Original Jazz Classics 1740) from 1961 is a final Dixieland recording from Hines's San Francisco band, which at the time consisted of trumpeter Eddie Smith, Jimmy Archey, Darnell Howard, Pops Foster, and drummer Earl Watkins. The musicians play well, but the material (which includes "Yes Sir, That's My Baby" and "Bill Bailey") is not too challenging.

Hines did not record at all in 1962 and only made one album in 1963, but he would record prolifically after the Little Theater concerts, which have been released on **The Real Earl Hines** (Focus 335) and **The Legendary Little Theater Concert** (Muse 2001) but not on CD. ◉ **Spontaneous Explorations** (Red Baron 57331), a two-CD set, has a spectacular solo performance from 1964 and a superior trio set from 1966 with bassist Richard Davis and Elvin Jones. Hines sounds more youthful than his modern rhythm section even though he was 62 at the time. **Linger Awhile** (Bluebird 64622) has Hines leading a quintet with Ray Nance and Budd Johnson, **Blues in Thirds** (Black Lion 760 120) is a stunning solo set, and 1967's **Blues & Things** (New World 80465) features Hines's quartet with guest Jimmy Rushing on four of the nine songs.

It is funny how the New York critics thought that Earl Hines was so great in 1965, having neglected him completely in 1963. Fortunately, after 1964, Hines would not be overlooked again.

Johnny Hodges   Although he was regularly employed with Duke Ellington's orchestra, Johnny Hodges also had a busy solo career, especially on records in addition to occasionally leading combos in concerts. While he recorded regularly for Verve as a leader through 1968, most of those sessions have not been reissued on CD yet;

Mosaic has thus far covered Hodges's Verve dates into 1961. However, some of his projects for other labels are currently available. The two-CD set **At the Berlin Sportpalast** (Pablo 2620-102) has Hodges leading an all-star group of Ellington sidemen (including Ray Nance, Lawrence Brown, and Harry Carney) through standards and familiar songs from Duke's repertoire.

○ **Everybody Knows Johnny Hodges** (GRP/I mpulse 116) is a particularly good buy because it has both the original album and Lawrence Brown's **Inspired Abandon**, one of the trombonist's only two sessions as a leader. The overlapping Ellington personnel plays familiar Duke, Strayhorn, and Hodges tunes in inspired fashion. Cat Anderson, Ray Nance, Harold Ashby, and Paul Gonsalves are among those heard from, with exciting versions of "310 Blues," "The Jeep Is Jumpin'," "Stompy Jones," and "Mood Indigo" being among the many highlights.

Frequently in the 1960s, Hodges teamed up with organist Wild Bill Davis. Recorded in 1966, **In a Mellow Tone** (Bluebird 2305) may very well be their best joint recording, with fine solos also taken by Lawrence Brown, the obscure tenor Bob Brown, and guitarist Dickie Thompson. These renditions of "It's Only a Paper Moon," "Taffy," "Good Queen Bess," and the title cut make this a particularly strong effort. **Triple Play** (RCA 68592) from 1967 has Hodges in three different nonets with the likes of Brown, Nance, Anderson, Roy Eldridge, Buster Cooper, Paul Gonsalves, and Jimmy Hamilton, performing basic swinging originals, blues, and ballads with Hodges being the main star. Much more unusual is **Johnny Hodges with Lawrence Welk's Orchestra** (Ranwood 8246). This odd matchup actually works fairly well. Lawrence Welk loved Hodges's tone and showcases him on a dozen standards (mostly ballads), backed by a string section, brass, and a rhythm section. The concise and melodic interpretations are pretty, making this an unusual collector's item.

Jonah Jones Although trumpeter Jonah Jones did not have any more hits like "On the Street Where You Live" and "Baubles, Bangles and Beads" during 1961–67, he remained a popular attraction with his quartet. None of his later Capitol albums, which include **Jumpin' with a Shuffle** (Capitol 1404), **A Touch of Blue** (Capitol 1405), **Greatest Instrumental Hits** (Capitol 1557), **The Unsinkable Molly Brown** (Capitol 1532), **Jonah Jones & Glen Gray** (Capitol 1660), **That Righteous Feeling** (Capitol 1839), **And Now in Person** (Capitol 1948), and **Blowin' Up a Storm** (Capitol 2087), are in print but most are worth searching for. Still using the same formula of Dixieland, show tunes, a shuffle beat, and concise solos with occasional vocals, Jones recorded six additional albums for Decca during 1965–67. But in a world increasingly dominated by rock, his music seemed less and less relevant as time went on, and he was not able to evolve much from the formula that had worked so well in 1957.

Taft Jordan Best known for his associations with Chick Webb (1933–41) and Duke Ellington (1943–47), the fine swing trumpeter Taft Jordan worked in later years with the Lucille Dixon Orchestra (1949–53), Don Redman (1953), and Benny Goodman (1958), in addition to doing some studio work and playing in the pit orchestras of Broadway shows. He only led four record dates in his career (including four numbers in 1935) of which **Mood Indigo** (Prestige 24230) is best known. Jordan is quite lyrical on seven Duke Ellington ballads in a quintet with Kenny Burrell, pianist Richard Wyands, bassist Joe Benjamin, and drummer Charlie Persip. In addition, this generous reissue includes a full album by the Swingville All Stars, a heated sextet session with Al Sears and altoist Hilton Jefferson.

Carl Kress One of the top acoustic guitarists of the late 1920s and '30s, Carl Kress had spent most of the 1930s, '40s, and '50s as a studio musician, teaming up with fellow guitarist Tony Mottola a bit in the 1940s. He recorded a set of unaccompanied guitar solos in 1958, but otherwise was rarely heard on jazz records at all again until 1962. During the next three years, he occasionally performed guitar duets with electric guitar pioneer George Barnes, with Barnes taking the single-note lines and Kress playing complex chords. Two of the albums were reissued on the hard-to-find but well worth discovering CD **Two Guitars (and a Horn)** (Jass 636). The first half of the program has the Kress-Barnes duo, while Bud Freeman makes the group a trio on the remaining numbers, which include his two originals "The Eel's Nephew" and "Disenchanted Trout." The music overall is tasteful, swinging, and full of subtle surprises.

The guitar duo with Barnes was active up until Carl Kress's death in 1965 at age 57 from a heart attack.

Meade Lux Lewis   The last of the early boogie-woogie pianists (Albert Ammons and Jimmy Yancey were dead, and Pete Johnson was retired due to a stroke), Meade Lux Lewis remained active in the early 1960s although he was being forgotten by then. **The Blues Piano Artistry of Meade Lux Lewis** (Original Jazz Classics 1759) from 1961 is an excellent album on which Lewis plays spirited piano (and on three songs, celeste) solos, showing that boogie-woogie could still be an exciting style if played by someone with ample technique and creativity. There would be one further album (an obscure effort for Phillips in 1962) before Meade Lux Lewis died in a car accident in 1964.

Joe Newman   After a nine-year stint (which followed four years in the 1940s), Joe Newman left the Count Basie Orchestra in 1961. He was part of the Benny Goodman big band that toured the Soviet Union in 1962, freelanced around New York, and taught youngsters about jazz through his involvement with Jazz Interactions, becoming its president in 1967. He also recorded two albums for Swingville in 1961 (along with a date for Mercury). One of the Swingville sessions has been combined with a Henry "Red" Allen session; it is reviewed under Various Artists in this chapter. The other set, **Good 'N' Groovy** (Original Jazz Classics 185), is a fine quintet album with Frank Foster, Tommy Flanagan, Eddie Jones, and drummer Billy English that features swinging originals in the tradition of Count Basie, plus Neal Hefti's "Li'l Darlin'" and Duke Ellington's "Just Squeeze Me." Although he had many playing years still left, Joe Newman would always be known as one of the Basieites.

Flip Phillips   After playing with Benny Goodman in 1959, Flip Phillips moved to Florida where he would play on just an occasional basis for the next 15 years. He only made one full album during this period, a set for the tiny Sue label that was reissued by Onyx and on CD by Collectables, **Revisited** (Collectables 5719). Performing with a local rhythm section, Phillips romps on tenor, is warm on the ballads (including on his own "I Remember Lester"), and makes his debut doubling on bass clarinet on "Satin Doll," "The Girl from Ipanema," and "Just Say I Love Her." The music is excellent, but it would be a long time before Flip's next encore.

Louis Prima   After reaching the height of his career during 1955–60, Louis Prima faded quickly in the 1960s. He and Keely Smith were divorced in 1961, and although he stayed active and still utilized Sam Butera and the Witnesses, some of the magic was gone. By 1963, Gia Mione (who would soon become his last wife) was singing in Smith's place, but there were no further hits. Prima did gain some fame for providing the

---

TIMELINE 1967

John Coltrane dies. • Henry Grimes disappears. • Steve Lacy moves to Italy. • Dewey Redman joins the Ornette Coleman Quartet. • The Dave Brubeck Quartet breaks up. • Wes Montgomery records the first of three pop/light jazz albums for A&M that are hugely popular. • The Gary Burton Quartet features Larry Coryell. • Billy Strayhorn dies. • John Hammond produces what is billed as the 30th anniversary of his "From Spirituals to Swing" concert. • Altoist Gary Bartz makes his recording debut as a leader with **Libra**. • Don Ewell and Willie "The Lion" Smith record a set of piano duets. • Joe Venuti, who had been obscure for 30 years, makes a strong impression with his violin solos at Dick Gibson's Colorado Jazz Party. • George Wein's Newport All-Stars, a group with Ruby Braff, Pee Wee Russell, and Bud Freeman, records an album in Mexico. • Billy Taylor's "I Wish I Knew How It Would Feel to Be Free" is a civil rights hit. • Charles Tolliver and Gary Bartz are members of the Max Roach Quartet. • The Three Sounds, led by pianist Gene Harris, records their 20th album since 1958. • Doc Severinsen takes over leadership of Johnny Carson's Tonight Show Band from Skitch Henderson. • Gunter Hampel and Jeanne Lee meet in Europe and begin working together on a regular basis. • On **Greek Cooking**, Phil Woods records songs with a band of Greek musicians, but fails to launch a new musical trend. • In Cuba, pianist Chucho Valdes, altoist Paquito D'Rivera, and trumpeter Arturo Sandoval are among the key musicians involved in playing with the Orquesta Cubana de Musica Moderna (the Cuban Modern Music Orchestra). • Pianist Ellis Marsalis joins Al Hirt's band in New Orleans. Hirt soon gives Marsalis's six-year-old son, Marsalis Wynton, his first trumpet.

speaking and singing voice for King Louie of the apes in Disney's 1967 film *The Jungle Book*. However, he was now thought of as a nostalgia act, which in showbiz was the kiss of death.

Ike Quebec A veteran swing tenor saxophonist who had helped persuade Alfred Lion and Francis Wolff of Blue Note to switch their label toward bebop in 1947, Ike Quebec squandered a promising career by spending most of the 1950s as a scuffling drug addict. By 1959, he was ready to start a comeback and he was successful during the few years he had left. Quebec recorded a dozen songs as singles during 1959–60 and then led six albums for Blue Note during 1961–62, in addition to making some appearances as a sideman.

Heavy Soul (Blue Note 32090) has some warm tenor by Quebec on ballads and medium-tempo pieces, but is weighed down a bit by the dated organ sound of Freddie Roach; best are "Just One More Chance," "The Man I Love," and a duet with bassist Milt Hinton on "Nature Boy." **It Might as Well Be Spring** (Blue Note 21736) has the same group performing such songs as "Ol' Man River," "Willow Weep for Me," and "It Might as Well Be Spring." Again, Quebec largely overcomes Roach's organ sound.

Blue and Sentimental (Blue Note 84098) is the Ike Quebec album to get. The tenor is joined on most cuts by Grant Green, Paul Chambers, and Philly Joe Jones. "Count Every Star" has the tenor assisted by Sonny Clark, Sam Jones, and Louis Hayes. Quebec's soulful playing on "Blue and Sentimental" and "Don't Take Your Love from Me" are quite memorable, alternating with medium-tempo swingers. **Easy Living** (Blue Note 46846) has three additional ballads with the Clark group (including "Easy Living" and "I've Got a Crush on You") plus five tunes from a blues-oriented jam session with Stanley Turrentine, Bennie Green, Sonny Clark, Milt Hinton, and Art Blakey. **With a Song in My Heart** (Blue Note 1052) has not been reissued yet, and it consists of nine concise songs with organist Earl Vandyke in February 1962. **Soul Samba** (Blue Note 52443), made during a period when everyone seemed to have a bossa nova album out, has Quebec backed by a sympathetic rhythm section (Kenny Burrell, Wendell Marshall, drummer Willie Bobo, and Garvin Masseaux on percussion) that adds light bossa rhythms behind his warm long tones.

Just three months later, on January 16, 1963, Ike Quebec was dead at the age of 44 from lung cancer.

Stuff Smith After recording several albums for Verve during 1956–59, Stuff Smith went through a period of neglect. However, when he moved to Copenhagen in 1965, he began working and recording steadily again, finding himself in great demand throughout the Continent. He had not lost a thing in his violin playing, swinging hard, with wit and creativity. **Live at the Montmartre** (Storyville 4142) from 1965 has the music from an exciting concert featuring Smith with Kenny Drew, Niels Pedersen, and drummer Alex Riel, including passionate versions of "Skip It," "Take the 'A' Train," "Bugle Blues," and "Mack the Knife." The LP **Swingin' Stuff** (Storyville 4087), recorded five days later with the same musicians and some of the same tunes, is nearly as stirring. **Hot Violins** (Storyville 4170) features Smith on three different dates, including four memorable collaborations with fellow violinist Svend Asmussen; they both sing on a charming version of "Lady Be Good." In addition, Stuff performs two of his originals in 1967 with the Kenny Drew Trio and matches up with violinist Paul Olsen (who sounds a bit like Stuff) on four numbers, including a riff-filled "One o'Clock Jump." **Late Woman Blues** (Storyville 101 8328) is a Swiss concert from 1965 that was not released initially until 2001. Smith joins with swing pianist Henri Chaix's trio to take a couple of humorous vocals and perform strong versions of "Perdido" (after a rough start), "How High the Moon," and "Body and Soul."

Stuff Smith was quite busy during 1965–66—in fact, probably too busy. He was only semi-active in 1967 before passing away on September 25 at the age of 58.

Willie Smith The year 1967 was particularly bad for swing veterans since quite a few died, including altoist Willie Smith. Having been with Harry James during 1944–51, he returned for a second long stint (1954–63) and then worked now and then for a few years, including recording with Charlie Barnet in late-1966. In 1965, he recorded **The Best of Willie Smith** (GNP/Crescendo 2055), which has not been reissued on CD yet. On his only full-length album as a leader, Smith is heard in top form, performing two basic originals ("Never on Friday" and "Willie's Blues"), a couple of ballads, and a few swing standards. He is featured with two different combos that include such players as Johnny Guarnieri, Tommy

Gumina on accordion, tenor saxophonist Bill Perkins, and Jimmy Rowles. Willie Smith passed away two years later at the age of 56.

Billy Strayhorn Another important swing era veteran who did not make it through 1967 (along with Edmond Hall, Muggsy Spanier, Pete Johnson, Buster Bailey, Henry "Red" Allen, Rex Stewart, and Sidney DeParis) was composer/pianist Billy Strayhorn. Strayhorn, who had a nearly invisible career in which he was an important but often overlooked part of the world of Duke Ellington, recorded his only real album as a leader in 1961 (not counting sets issued under his name but really Ellington and Johnny Hodges dates). **The Peaceful Side of Billy Strayhorn** (Blue Note 52563) is a rather melancholy affair. Strayhorn's piano is in the forefront throughout as he interprets ten of his compositions, including "Lush Life," "Take the 'A' Train," and "Something to Live For." Three numbers have the Paris Blue Notes adding sparse wordless vocals, two other songs add some quiet playing by the Paris String Quartet, and bassist Michel Goudret is on five of the ten selections, including one apiece with the strings and the voices. "Strange Feeling" and "Chelsea Bridge" are taken as unaccompanied piano solos. Of the ten songs, only "Just a-Sittin' and a-Rockin'" seems at least moderately joyful with the other tunes being quite somber and filled with inner tension.

A fascinating posthumous collection not released until 1992, **Lush Life** (Red Baron 52760) is actually Billy Strayhorn's definitive CD. Strayhorn is heard singing "Lush Life" while backed by the Duke Ellington Orchestra in 1964 (his voice is not strong, but his phrasing is quite sincere), jamming on piano with Clark Terry and Bob Wilber in a quintet, backing singer Ozzie Bailey, and taking a pair of piano solos ("Love Came" and "Baby Clementine").

A lifelong cigarette habit resulted in Billy Strayhorn's death in 1967 from lung cancer when he was just 51. His passing was a major shock to Duke Ellington, who saluted his longtime musical collaborator with a particularly strong album, **And His Mother Called Him Bill**.

Buddy Tate Buddy Tate was luckier than most swing-era veterans in that he was able to keep a steady band together throughout the 1960s, having a steady gig at Harlem's Celebrity Club during 1953–74. He maintained

a low profile, but every once in a while would become more visible, recording with Buck Clayton, being one of the stars at John Hammond's 1967 "From Spirituals to Swing" concert, and performing and recording in Paris with organist Milt Buckner. **Groovin' with Tate** (Prestige 24152) has all of the music from two of his albums: **Tate's Date**, a septet session from 1959 that has him interacting with the frontline of his regular band, and **Groovin' with Tate**, a fine set from 1961 showcasing Tate's tenor and clarinet with a four-piece rhythm section. The 1960s might have been lean years for many swing-era players, but Buddy Tate was able to continue growing as a musician and to stay in good shape for the following two busy decades.

Ben Webster The sale of Verve by Norman Granz ended Ben Webster's association with the label. He recorded **Soulmates** (Original Jazz Classics 109) for Riverside in 1963, a quartet/quintet set with Joe Zawinul, either Richard Davis or Sam Jones on bass, Philly Joe Jones, and on some numbers Thad Jones. Webster was clearly still in his prime, and he sounds quite inspired on 1964's ◉ **See You at the Fair** (GRP/ Impulse 2126), a quartet outing with either Hank Jones or Roger Kellaway on piano, Richard Davis, and Osie Johnson. Webster's tone on such tunes as "Our Love Is Here to Stay," "Someone to Watch Over Me," and "Stardust" is often quite touching and filled with emotion. One song originally on a sampler and two numbers featuring Webster with the Oliver Nelson Orchestra have been added to the CD reissue.

Ben Webster was just days short of his 55th birthday when he made the Impulse album, but that would be his final American recording. Before 1964 concluded, Webster moved to Copenhagen, which served as his home base for the next decade. Though he had been neglected in the United States, in Europe Webster was treated as a living legend, and he worked and recorded steadily. During his European period, he tended to stick to a limited repertoire and was mostly featured in quartets, but rarely sounded less than excellent. Well worth picking up are **Stormy Weather** (Black Lion 760108), **Gone with the Wind** (Black Lion 760125), and **There Is No Greater Love** (Black Lion 760151), all of which feature him at the Club Montmartre in Copenhagen in 1965 with Kenny Drew, Niels-Henning Orsted Pedersen, and drummer Alex Riel. **In a Mellow Tone** (Jazz House 007) has Webster visiting England and playing with a local rhythm section at Ronnie Scott's club. **The Jeep Is Jumping** (Black Lion 760147) is a bit unusual, for Webster is heard with a quintet led by trumpeter Arnved Meyer that sounds like a Duke Ellington small group from the 1930s, particularly on "Stompy Jones" and the title cut. Moving to 1967, **Ben Webster Meets Bill Coleman** (Black Lion 760141) teams Webster with fellow expatriate Bill Coleman, who had been living in France since 1948. The two horns work together very well, both still being masterful swing stylists even if they were forgotten in the United States. Another excellent collaboration is **Ben & Buck** (Sackville 2037), which matches Webster with Buck Clayton and the Henri Chaix Quartet in Switzerland. The music was released for the first time in 1994, and it is as swinging and as satisfying as one would hope.

Teddy Wilson   Despite still playing in a timeless style and performing fairly regularly, Teddy Wilson only led one album during 1960–66, an obscure LP with an orchestra for the Cameo-Parkway label. Recorded in London in 1967, **Stompin' at the Savoy** (Black Lion 760 152) shows that the veteran pianist's playing might have been predictable, but he was still capable of sounding inspired. Wilson is joined by clarinetist Dave Shepherd, vibraphonist Ronnie Gleaves, bassist Peter Chapman, and drummer Johnny Richardson for a variety of swing standards, all played with spirit, even the typical warhorses. The younger musicians seem to light a fire under Wilson, who was at his best in this type of setting.

Dixieland and New Orleans Jazz

In general, Dixieland faded in popularity during the 1960s. Unlike in the previous decade, few people went out to clubs to dance to Dixieland anymore (rock 'n' roll took away that audience), many of the veterans from the 1920s were either passing on or declining, and there was not that much new talent being featured. Even relative youths such as Ruby Braff, Bob Wilber, Ralph Sutton, and Dick Wellstood had been active since the late 1940s. The music was no longer considered hip, and sometimes it was associated with conservative politics even though most musicians were apolitical; they just worked for whoever hired them.

However, there were three events that helped keep trad jazz music alive. In 1961, Preservation Hall opened in New Orleans, giving the veteran New Orleans musicians a home base and leading to the formation of the world-touring Preservation Hall Jazz Band. In England, the trad boom hit its peak in the early 1960s and such Dixieland players as Kenny Ball ("Midnight in Moscow"), Chris Barber, and Acker Bilk ("Stranger on the Shore") actually had some of their records become pop hits. And in 1964 for a few weeks, Louis Armstrong had the No. 1 record in the world with "Hello Dolly," temporarily outselling the Beatles.

Henry "Red" Allen   Don Ellis called Henry "Red" Allen "the most creative avant-garde trumpeter heard in New York today." It seemed like an odd pronouncement to be made in the early 1960s about a New Orleans trumpeter, particularly when Don Cherry, Bill Dixon, and Ted Curson were in town, but there was some truth to the statement. Allen's unusual style, although tied to New Orleans jazz and Dixieland, found him constantly playing unusual notes and speechlike sounds that, despite the standards format, could be seen as an abstract ancestor to Ornette Coleman.

From 1961 on, Allen mostly led quartets in the New York area. A good example of the trumpeter's late period work can be heard on **Quartet Live, 1965** (Storyville 8290), which has Allen playing and singing everything from Dixieland standards (such as "Muskrat Ramble" and "Mack the Knife") to current pop tunes ("Hello Dolly" and ""Never on Sunday"). In late 1966, after over 40 years of solid playing, Allen was suffering from pancreatic cancer. However, he had a tour of Great Britain scheduled that served as his last hurrah. While in England, Allen played with Alex Welsh's band. Music from one concert was released for the first time in 2001 as **Henry "Red" Allen with the Alex Welsh Band** (Jazzology 318). Despite Allen's worsening health, he plays and sings quite well on the trad jazz classics and sounds in very good spirits. This would be his final accomplishment for, shortly after he returned home to New York, Red Allen passed away.

Jimmy Archey   Jimmy Archey, a swing trombonist during the 1930s, was reborn the following decade as a fine New Orleans/Dixieland–style soloist. After working during the 1955–62 period in San Francisco with Earl Hines's band, he spent his last years playing with New Orleans veterans. **Reunion** (GHB 310) teams Archey in a sextet with trumpeter Punch Miller and clarinetist

Albert Burbank, romping through such songs as "Put on Your Gray Bonnet," "Shake that Thing," and "The Sheik of Araby." Although Archey is listed as leader of the Crescent City Delegates of Pleasure, this could just as well be considered Miller's date since he takes six vocals. The ensembles may not always be perfectly in tune, but the music certainly has plenty of spirit. Recorded February 26, 1967, this set was cut just nine months before Jimmy Archey's death.

Lil Hardin Armstrong   Lil Hardin Armstrong, who had recorded some excellent swing dates during 1936–40, only appeared on a few obscure selections during the next two decades. However, the pianist remained active, touring Europe in 1952 and appearing regularly at Chicago's Red Arrow during 1952–60. She was part of the television special *Chicago and All that Jazz* in 1961, the year that she made her final recordings. **Chicago: The Living Legends** (Original Jazz Classics 1823) has her leading a rather loose jam session with a band consisting of three trumpets, two trombonists (Preston Jackson and Al Wynn), two clarinetists (Darnell Howard and Franz Jackson), bassist Pops Foster, and drummer Booker T. Washington. The jams (warhorses, blues, and a few basic originals with Armstrong singing on "Clip Joint") are often riotous and overcrowded, fun if not flawless. Armstrong at 63 still sounds like she had more to contribute, but she would not record again after 1961.

Louis Armstrong   Louis Armstrong continued touring the world during the first half of the 1960s. He was a fixture on television variety shows, and although irrelevant when it came to modern jazz, Armstrong was still a major force in popularizing jazz. As his health gradually declined, Satch's trumpet solos became briefer, but he made every note count and never lost his beautiful sound. Strangely enough, Armstrong had only recorded with Duke Ellington once before, a single selection with the Esquire All-Stars back in 1946. In 1961, producer Bob Thiele finally teamed the two masters, having Ellington play piano on his compositions with the Louis Armstrong All-Stars. Although it probably would have been better if Satch had sat in with the Duke Ellington Orchestra (which unfortunately never happened) the music on ● **Complete Sessions** (Roulette 93844) is quite rewarding. Most of the 17 songs performed (which include a vocalized "C Jam Blues" renamed "Duke's Place," "Cotton Tail," "Drop Me Off In Harlem," and "I

Got It Bad") were not in the All-Stars' repertoire, and the results are quite inspired, with Armstrong playing beautifully. In 2000, a double CD **The Complete Sessions** (Roulette 24547/24548) reissued the original session plus a full CD of rehearsal excerpts, but the latter, though interesting, is not worth hearing twice.

The 1961 Louis Armstrong All-Stars consisted of the leader, Trummy Young, Barney Bigard (back for a second stint), Billy Kyle, bassist Mort Herbert, and drummer Danny Barcelona. Velma Middleton's death that year was a major loss to Armstrong (who had used her as an effective comic foil); she was replaced by Jewell Brown. Bigard departed before year-end, with his spot being taken by Joe Darensbourg. The bass spot would be filled by many players during the next few years including a returning Arvell Shaw. The biggest loss was in early 1964 when Trummy Young decided after a dozen years on the road with Satch to retire to Hawaii. But before he left, he was on one final record date, a session that found Armstrong recording a happy pop tune from a show, "Hello Dolly." "Hello Dolly," recorded December 3, 1963, was such a major hit in 1964 that it rose to No. 1 on the charts ahead of the Beatles, and it gave Louis Armstrong a final burst of glory.

The Essential Louis Armstrong (Vanguard 91/92) from a concert performed on June 4, 1965, features Armstrong in his final period, sounding in pretty good form considering his age. Joined by trombonist Tyree Glenn (succeeding Big Chief Russell Moore, who toured with Satch in 1964), clarinetist Eddie Shu, Billy Kyle, bassist Buddy Catlett, Danny Barcelona, and Jewell Brown, Armstrong performs his typical joyous and fun show of the period. An excellent retrospective of Armstrong's later years (1946–68) is the three-CD set ● **An American Icon** (Hip-O 40138), which draws its music from many labels and is highlighted by the original versions of "Mack the Knife" and "Hello Dolly" plus "Baby, It's Cold Outside" (with Velma Middleton), "Gone Fishin'" (with Bing Crosby), and the 1967 version of "What a Wonderful World," a somewhat sappy song that would become famous years after Armstrong's death due to its inclusion in the film *Good Morning Viet Nam*.

Chris Barber   Britain's trad jazz boom helped Chris Barber's band became a major success in England. Barber's hit recording of "Petit Fleur" in 1956 (which featured clarinetist Monty Sunshine and did not even include Barber's trombone) was a major seller. Barber, who sometimes collaborated with blues artists (including Sonny Terry and Brownie McGhee in 1959) and recorded with American Dixieland players (such as Sidney DeParis in 1960), can be heard with his 1961–63 band on **Wireless Days 1961–62** (Upbeat Jazz 148), **In Budapest** (Storyville 408), and **Getting Around** (Storyville 5531). By this time Barber and his reliable trumpeter Pat Halcox were joined by Ian Wheeler on clarinet, alto, and soprano, and blues singer Ottilie Patterson. The versatile band's repertoire ranged from revivals of 1920s tunes, swing, and blues classics to newer pieces that fit into the Barber sound.

Sweet Emma Barrett Sweet Emma Barrett was a popular attraction for a time in New Orleans despite being a rather limited pianist and singer. Born in 1897, she had played with Oscar Celestin in the 1920s and many of the top New Orleans musicians through the years while sticking close to home. Known as "the bell gal" because she wore red garters with bells that sometimes made ringing sounds when she played, Barrett made one excellent album in her career: ◐ **New Orleans: The Living Legends** (Original Jazz Classics 1832). Performing with the future members of the Preservation Hall Jazz Band (trumpeter Percy Humphrey, trombonist Jim Robinson, and clarinetist Willie Humphrey), Barrett and the Humphrey Brothers never sounded better on record, romping through such numbers as "Bill Bailey," "Just a Little While to Stay Here," and "The Saints." Everyone is in tune, the solos are reasonably creative, and the ensembles are frequently exciting. The Preservation Hall Jazz Band would rarely play at this level and neither would Barrett. In fact, after suffering a stroke in 1967, Barrett played piano for her remaining 16 years with just her right hand.

Ruby Braff Ruby Braff, who turned 40 in 1967, had been struggling for work during the past decade. In some ways he was a victim of the rapid evolution of jazz, considered out of date early in his career even though he was a distinctive player because he preferred swing and classic jazz standards to bebop and hard bop. However, in 1967 he began to work with George Wein's Newport All-Stars and his career gradually started an upswing. **Newport All-Stars** (Black Lion 760138) finds him sharing the spotlight with Buddy Tate, playing small-group swing on such numbers as "Mean to Me," "My Monday Date," "Take the 'A' Train," and "The Sheik of Araby." **Hear Me Talkin'** (Black Lion 760161)

is a fun Dixieland/swing date in which Braff in London jams with trumpeter Alex Welsh's octet, a group also featuring trombonist Roy Williams, tenor saxophonist Al Gay, and baritonist Johnny Barnes. Among the better tunes are "No One Else but You," Braff's "Where's Freddie," "Foolin Myself," and "Smart Alex Blues." But it must have been difficult for Braff, as a major small-group swing stylist, to find anyone in his generation to join him in playing the music he loved.

Herman Chittison The great stride pianist Herman Chittison, who acted on the radio series *Casey-Crime Photographer* through 1951, led a trio in near-anonymity during the 1950s and early 1960s, not recording commercially after 1945, and eventually settling in Ohio. **P.S. with Love** (IAJRC 1006) has two solo sets (from 1964 and 1967) that were not been released until 1993. Some of the tunes are weak (such as "Getting to Know You," "People," and "The Sound of Music"), but there are also many swing standards. The final session on this CD was recorded only a couple of months before Chittison's death, yet the stride pianist still played surprisingly well at the end of his life.

Ken Colyer One of the leaders in England's New Orleans jazz movement, trumpeter Ken Colyer did not record all that often during 1961–67. The most easily available CD from this period is 1963's **When I Leave the World Behind** (GHB 152), which features the young and talented clarinetist Sammy Rimington with Colyer in a pianoless sextet that also includes the fine trombonist Geoff Cole. Colyer's clipped phrases sometimes recall Kid Thomas Valentine while Rimington's clarinet solos are strongly reminiscent of George Lewis. Highlights include ensemble-oriented versions of "Dr. Jazz," "Down Home Rag," "After You've Gone," and J.C. Higginbotham's "Give Me Your Telephone Number."

Eddie Condon Although the 1960s found Eddie Condon and his brand of freewheeling jazz past its prime, there were some sparks left. He worked regularly at his club, Condon's, although his health was becoming a bit erratic, not helped by decades of heavy drinking. In 1961, a television special titled *Chicago and All that Jazz* had a few spots for an all-star group of alumni led by Condon, and a record date resulted. The album, **Chicago and All that Jazz** (Verve 8441), has not yet been reissued on CD. Six of the eight original members of the McKenzie-Condon Chicagoans of 1927 (Condon, Bud Freeman, a surprisingly modern sounding Jimmy McPartland, Joe Sullivan, Bob Haggart, and Gene Krupa) are reunited along with Pee Wee Russell (filling in for the long-lost Frankie Teschemacher) and Bob Haggart (taking the spot of the retired Jim Lannigan), with Jack Teagarden (who takes vocals on "Logan Square" and "After You've Gone") being added. In addition, there are two production numbers with vocals by Lil Armstrong, Blossom Seeley, and Teagarden, and a pair of piano solos from Armstrong.

In 1964, Eddie Condon toured Japan, Australia, and New Zealand, leading an all-star group and making his last major recording. **In Japan** (Chiaroscuro 154) has the rhythm guitarist (who does some announcing) heading a band that includes Buck Clayton, Vic Dickenson, Bud Freeman, Pee Wee Russell, Dick Cary (on piano and alto horn), bassist Jack Lesberg, and drummer Cliff Leeman, with Jimmy Rushing taking four vocals. The musicians play the Dixieland and swing standards with the spirit and enthusiasm of the Town Hall concerts of 20 years earlier, with the highlights including "I Can't Believe that You're in Love with Me," "Pee Wee's Blues," "Royal Garden Blues," and Dickenson's charming feature on "Manhattan." But this would be the last time that Russell and Freeman recorded with Condon, and signaled the beginning of the end of the Eddie Condon era.

Wild Bill Davison   Wild Bill Davison still played with Eddie Condon occasionally but mostly freelanced as a leader, visiting Europe (particularly England) on several occasions in the 1960s. **Blowin' Wild** (Jazzology 18) from 1962 has Davison fitting right into British trumpeter Alex Welsh's hot septet (which also features trombonist Roy Crimmins and Johnny Barnes on clarinet and baritone) on such tunes as "Blues My Naughty Sweetie Gives to Me," "'S Wonderful," "Riverboat Shuffle," and "Royal Garden Blues." **'S Wonderful** (Jazzology 181), which was originally put out as the only release by the Davison record label, has 11 typically fiery selections featuring Davison with Vic Dickenson, Buster Bailey, Dick Wellstood, bassist Willie Wayman, and Cliff Leeman in 1962. Davison at 56 was showing no signs of slowing down or altering his Dixieland repertoire. He tosses in high notes in unexpected spots, mixes together sarcasm with sentimentality, and shows on tunes such as "Eccentric" and "Riverside Shuffle" that few could drive

an ensemble like he could. A pair of numbers from the 1972 Manassas Jazz Festival round out this fine reissue. **Rompin' & Stompin'** (Jazzology 14) has Davison teamed with the spirited amateur group the Tailgate Ramblers in 1964 for such songs as "Pagan Love Song," "Hello Dolly," "Angry," and "My Monday Date."

With Freddy Randall (Jazzology 160) features Davison in 1965 playing as part of British trumpeter Freddy Randall's septet. With trombonist George Chisholm, Bruce Turner (on clarinet and alto), and vibraphonist Ronnie Gleaves helping out, this is a strong band. However, Davison easily steals the show on "Memories of You," "Ghost of a Chance," "Struttin' with Some Barbecue," and "Sunday." **Surfside Jazz** (Jazzology 25) is most notable for matching Davison for the first time with cornetist Tom Saunders (who became a lifelong admirer) and a fine no-name Detroit band of Dixielanders. **After Hours** (Jazzology 22) is a bit unusual for it has Davison sitting in with a bassless trio led by drummer George Wettling. Actually, the combination (which includes the up-and-coming clarinetist Kenny Davern and pianist Charlie Queener) works better than expected with Davison's highly expressive playing generating a great deal of excitement on "I Never Knew," "Big Butter and Egg Man," and "You're Lucky to Me."

Sidney and Wilbur DeParis   Wilbur DeParis's New New Orleans Jazz Band made its last recording in 1960, but continued working throughout the 1960s although with a lower profile than earlier. In 1962, trumpeter Sidney DeParis led an unusual album titled **Dixieland Hits Country & Western** (Swingville 2040). DeParis and a fine septet with trombonist Benny Morton and Kenny Davern turn eight country songs (including "Pistol Packin' Mama," "Yellow Rose of Texas," and "Ghost Riders in the Sky") into spirited Dixieland. However, this would be DeParis's last recording. He passed away in 1967 and Wilbur DeParis soon retired.

The Dukes of Dixieland   The Dukes of Dixieland became one of the most popular Dixieland bands in the United States during the second half of the 1950s when they were recording prolifically for Audio Fidelity. In 1961, they signed with Columbia and modernized their rhythm section. In addition to trumpeter/singer Frank Assunto, trombonist Fred Assunto, the brothers' father Jac Assunto on second trombone and banjo, and the talented clarinetist Jerry Fuller, the band had a top-notch rhythm section comprised of guitarist Jim Hall, pianist Gene Schroeder (formerly with Eddie Condon), bassist Jim Atlas, and drummer Charlie Lodice. The following year, Herb Ellis succeeded Hall on guitar.

The Dukes recorded six albums for Columbia during 1961–64, including such exciting sets as **Breakin' It Up on Broadway** (Columbia 1728), **Now Hear This** (Columbia 1793), and **World's Fair** (Columbia 2194). The one record thus far to be reissued on CD is ● **The Best of the Dukes of Dixieland** (Sony 13374), which was formerly known as **The Dukes at Disneyland**. These renditions of "Original Dixieland One Step" (which has a particularly exciting stop-time clarinet solo), "Wolverine Blues," and "Royal Garden Blues" are extended and show just how exciting a Dixieland group the Dukes were in the early 1960s.

Unfortunately, the Dukes of Dixieland's prime ended in 1964. The band switched to the Decca label (where it cut five increasingly commercial LPs with rather brief performances), Fred Assunto was stricken with cancer (dying in 1966), and the band did not record again after '66. Frank Assunto would also contract cancer, passing away in 1974. Later post-Assunto versions of the Dukes (which still work in New Orleans) are not on the same level as the classic group, an ensemble that deserves to be remembered.

The Dutch Swing College Band   Founded in May 1945 by clarinetist/baritonist Peter Schilperoort, the Dutch Swing College Band became one of Europe's top Dixieland and swing bands. The ensemble recorded many albums and along the way recorded with such guests as Sidney Bechet (1951), Jimmy Witherspoon, Billy Butterfield, Joe Venuti, and Teddy Wilson. **Swinging Studio Sessions** (Phillips 824 256) has highlights from seven of the band's dates of 1959–69. The piano-less sextet/septet is in rousing form on "At the Jazz Band Ball," "Fidgety Feet," "Tiger Rag," "Cornet Chop Suey," and "Dippermouth Blues." **Dutch Swing College Band Meets Teddy Wilson** (Timeless 525) partly dates from 1972–73 when Teddy Wilson sat in with the band on six selections (including "Riverboat Shuffle" and "China Boy"), but also has five numbers from 1964–67, with fine spots for Bert De Kort or Ray Kaart on trumpet, trombonist Dick Kaart, and clarinetist Bob Kaper.

The Firehouse Five Plus Two   The Firehouse Five Plus Two continued to play on a part-time basis in the Los Angeles area throughout the 1960s. There were just two recordings made for Good Time Jazz during 1961–67, both utilizing the personnel of trumpeter Danny Alguire, trombonist/leader Ward Kimball, George Probert on clarinet and soprano, pianist Frank Thomas, banjoist Dick Roberts, Don Kinch on tuba and bass, and drummer Eddie Forrest. Recorded in 1962, **At Disneyland** (Good Time Jazz 10049) seems fitting since the band was comprised of Disney employees. Best are rambunctious versions of such crowd pleasers as "Anvil Stomp," "Lassus Trombone," "Coney Island Washboard," and "Tiger Rag." **The Firehouse Five Plus Two Goes to a Fire** (Good Time Jazz 10052) from 1964 has the spirited group playing a dozen songs with titles having something to do with fires, including "Keep the Home Fires Burning," "Hot Lips," "There's Going to Be a Hot Time in the Old Town Tonight," and "I Don't Want to Set the World on Fire." Although sometimes bordering on cornball, the band's enthusiasm and wit still communicate well decades later.

Pete Fountain   The popular clarinetist Pete Fountain kept on recording regularly for the Coral label through 1968 although his record dates dropped in interest after 1965. None of his albums are currently available on CD, but **New Orleans at Midnight** (Coral 57429), **New Orleans Scene** (Coral 573788), **Music from Dixie** (Coral 57401), **Plenty of Pete** (Coral 57429), **South Rampart Street Parade** (Coral 57440), and 1965's **Standing Room Only** (Coral 57474), the latter featuring Fountain in a frontline with trumpeter Charlie Teagarden, trombonist Bob Havens, and Eddie Miller, are worth picking up if found at used record stores. Fountain's best Coral recordings constitute the finest work of his career although his style (displaying the influences of Irving Fazola and Benny Goodman mostly on Dixieland's top 30 warhorses) has not changed in the decades since the 1950s.

Bud Freeman   The veteran tenor saxophonist mostly freelanced as a leader in the 1960s. His top recording of the period is **Something to Remember You By** (Black Lion 760153), recorded in 1962 when he was 55. Well showcased in a quartet with pianist Dave Frishberg, Bob Haggart, and drummer Don Lamond, Freeman performs a dozen of his favorite standards, including "You're a Sweetheart," "Chicago," "It's Only a Paper Moon," and "Somebody Stole My Gal," showing that he was still growing as a player even after 35 years on records.

Edmond Hall   Although he did not really develop his piercing tone until he was 40, Edmond Hall became one of jazz's most distinctive and exciting clarinetists. He toured with the Louis Armstrong All-Stars during 1954–58 and then freelanced, usually as a leader although occasionally guesting with Eddie Condon. **Edmond Hall Quartet in Copenhagen** (Storyville 6022) from 1966 has his final studio sessions, cut just two months before his death. Hall is featured on three hot numbers with Papa Bue's Viking Jazz Band ("Struttin' with Some Barbecue" is quite exciting) and on eleven selections as the only horn with a fine Scandinavian rhythm section. In addition, he takes a brief unaccompanied rendition of "It Ain't Necessarily So."

In January 1967, Edmond Hall played on a few numbers at John Hammond's 30th anniversary "From Spirituals to Swing" concert at Carnegie Hall. **Edmond Hall's Last Concert** (Jazzology 223) was recorded on February 3, featuring Hall playing in Massachusetts as part of a septet that co-stars Bobby Hackett. As usual, Hall solos with a great deal of passion, enthusiastically digging into a set of Dixieland warhorses; he is also heard on three formerly unknown showcases as the only horn in a set from 1964. Just eight days after the February 3 concert, Edmond Hall suffered a fatal heart attack while shoveling snow, dying at the age of 65.

Cap'n John Handy   Cap'n John Handy (no relation to the other altoist John Handy) was quite unusual in the New Orleans revival movement because he played Dixieland alto influenced by R&B and jump music. Handy started out playing clarinet in New Orleans in the 1920s (often with his group the Louisiana Shakers), switching to alto in 1928. Despite his talents, he did not record until 1960 (when he was already 60), not making his second record until 1965. However, Handy made up for lost time during the next few years, playing regularly with trumpeter Kid Sheik Cola's group and the Preservation Hall Jazz Band, touring Europe, and recording for GHB, '77', Jazz Crusade, and RCA (two albums in 1966).

During March–May 1966, Handy recorded over five albums' worth of material, including **John Handy's Quintet** (GHB 261) and **Very Handy** (GHB 325). The first set has Handy showcased with a British quintet that also includes trumpeter Cuff Billett, pianist Pat Hawes,

bassist Dave Green, and drummer Barry Martyn. Handy sounds at his best on "Rose Room," "Indiana," "Dinah," and "Rosetta." For **Very Handy**, he is teamed with trombonist Big Bill Bissonette's Easy Riders band (which includes clarinetist Sammy Rimington and trumpeter Clive Wilson) for some rousing numbers. Best are a blazing version of "Running Wild," "Give Me Your Telephone Number," "Golden Leaf Strut" ("Milenberg Joys"), and an almost out-of-control jam on "Mahogany Hall Stomp." Well worth searching for is the LP **Introducing Cap'n John Handy** (RCA 89503), which has Handy holding his own in a more "modern" setting than usual, playing swing with Doc Cheatham, Benny Morton, and Claude Hopkins. It is a pity, though, that Cap'n John Handy was not discovered in 1940, when he could have made more of an impact, rather than 1960.

Claude Hopkins   Claude Hopkins was barely on records at all from 1941–59 though he remained active playing in swing combos and Dixieland bands, including with Red Allen's group during the second half of the 1950s. To make up for lost time, Hopkins made three albums for Swingville during 1960–63. The second and third sets are reissued as **Swing Time** (Prestige 24215). Rather surprising is that Hopkins hardly strides at all on these dates, sounding much more like Teddy Wilson, and often taking a minor role in the background. One session showcases Buddy Tate and trumpeter Joe Thomas while the other has a frontline of trumpeter Bobby Johnson (formerly with Erskine Hawkins), Vic Dickenson, and Budd Johnson. The music is excellent small-group swing even if Hopkins does much less than expected.

Cliff Jackson   Stride pianist Cliff Jackson, who married singer Maxine Sullivan in the 1960s, had worked steadily in the 1950s despite not appearing on records. He did appear on a few sessions during 1961–62, including **Carolina Shout** (Black Lion 760 194). Actually, this solo set (which features veteran standards and stride classics) promises a great deal, but Jackson sounds rather metronomic (particularly his left hand) and mechanical, keeping such perfect time that life is often missing from these solos.

Franz Jackson   A veteran swing tenor saxophonist, Franz Jackson worked in the Chicago area starting in 1926 and along the way had stints with Carroll Dickerson's Orchestra in the 1930s, Jimmie Noone, Roy

Eldridge, Fletcher Henderson (1937–38), Earl Hines (1940–41), Cootie Williams (1942), Frankie Newton, and Wilbur DeParis (1944–45). In the mid-1950s, he formed his Original Jazz All-Stars, a Dixieland-flavored band that lasted for nearly 20 years. The group (which during 1957–58 included trombonist Albert Wynn) recorded for Riverside, Replica, Phillips, and Jackson's own Pinnacle label. The All-Star's best-known set, **Chicago: The Living Legends** (Original Jazz Classics 1824), has been reissued. This 1961 recording has Jackson exclusively playing clarinet with trumpeter Bob Shoffner (a veteran of the 1920s), trombonist John Thomas, and pianist Rozelle Claxton in a septet. With the exception of his "Blue Thursday," Jackson sticks to tunes from the 1920s, including "Hotter than That," "Sister Kate," and "King Porter Stomp," and the band fares quite well.

Lonnie Johnson   One of the few surviving guitarists from the 1920s, Lonnie Johnson spent most of his life playing blues, but he retained a love for early jazz. He recorded prolifically for decades, but was off records altogether during 1954–59 until being rediscovered. Johnson recorded five albums for Bluesville during 1960–62, music that cemented his comeback. Although Victoria Spivey (who was also making a comeback) gets co-billing on 1961's **Idle Hours** (Original Blues Classics 518), she is only heard on three songs, faring quite well. Most of this set features Johnson backed by pianist Cliff Jackson, and on the mixture of blues and ballads he shows that he still had it, vocally and instrumentally. Also of strong interest is his solo set **Another Night to Cry** (Original Blues Classics 550). Although this CD reissue only has 34 minutes of music, "Blues After Hours" is an instrumental that shows off Johnson's jazz roots, and many of the 11 songs (all originals) have spots for his guitar. Most unusual is **Stompin' at the Penny** (Columbia/Legacy 476720), for this 1965 recording features the 66-year-old Johnson with a Canadian Dixieland band, McHarg's Metro Stompers. In addition to including a few Johnson vocals, he takes credible solos on some trad jazz standards, including "China Boy." Six selections are without Johnson, putting the focus on the trad band, which includes cornetist Charlie Gall and clarinetist Eric Neilson. Other than some solo sessions made for the Smithsonian (and later released by Folkways) in 1967, **Stompin' at the Penny**

was Lonnie Johnson's last recording and serves as a fine ending to his long and very productive career.

George Lewis   Clarinetist George Lewis remained a New Orleans jazz celebrity throughout the 1960s. Although he still worked with the Kid Howard-Jim Robinson frontline on and off into 1963, he was frequently heard in other settings during his final period, whether playing at Preservation Hall in New Orleans or taking tours to Japan and Europe. Among his associates in the 1960s were trumpeters Kid Thomas Valentine and Punch Miller, trombonist Louis Nelson, and pianists Joe Robichaux and Don Ewell.

As usual, Lewis's recordings were erratic as he rose or sank to the level of the other musicians. Recorded in 1964, **George Lewis Plays Hymns** (Milneburg 1) is unusual and quite successful. Lewis, backed by Joe Robichaux and bassist Placide Adams, plays 15 traditional spirituals melodically and with plenty of reverence. Lewis caresses such hymns as "His Eye Is on the Sparrow," "Nearer My God to Thee," "I Shall Not Be Moved," and "Lily of the Valley." A special bonus of the reissue is a seven-minute interview from January 5, 1962, that was conducted before a college audience on which Lewis is charming and humorous in talking about his life. Also excellent is 1966's **Reunion** (Delmark 220), which has Lewis in a trumpetless quartet with Jim Robinson, Don Ewell, and drummer Cie Frazier. Together they play ensemble-oriented versions of such songs as "The Bucket's Got a Hole in It," "There's Yes, Yes in Your Eyes," and "Ole Miss." George Lewis and Jim Robinson had played 22 years of fine music together and although it would end soon (the clarinetist passed away in 1968), the results were generally timeless and still sound joyful today.

Wingy Manone   The Louis Armstrong–inspired trumpeter and jivey singer Wingy Manone had recorded quite regularly during 1927–49 and on an irregular basis during 1950–60. But after 1960, there would just be one further album plus a pair of songs for an Italian label in 1975. The 1966 LP (not yet reissued on CD) **With Papa Bue's Viking Jazzband** (Storyville 4066) is a strong effort, featuring the 62-year-old still sounding in prime form. Manone plays three of his blues and a variety of standards, including "When You're Smiling," "How Come You Do Me Like You Do," and "Sister Kate." Papa Bue's Viking Jazzband (with clarinetist Jorgen Svers and Papa

Bue Jensen on trombone) provides a perfect backing for Manone during his last significant recording.

Papa Bue Jensen   The Danish trombonist known as Papa Bue Jensen formed a sextet called the New Orleans Jazz Band in 1956. In 1958, it changed its name to the Viking Jazz Band, becoming one of Scandinavia's top Dixieland and trad jazz groups, making many records that have been released by the Storyville and Timeless labels, sometimes with American guests including George Lewis, Wingy Manone (a wonderful set from 1967 reviewed under Manone's name), Wild Bill Davison, Edmond Hall, Albert Nicholas, and Art Hodes.

Greatest Hits (Storyville 836) has a dozen songs programmed chronologically that date from 1958–70. The band's style and personnel remained largely the same during the period, featuring Finn Otto Hansen on trumpet and clarinetist Jorgen Svare.

Highlights of the likable set include "1919 March," "The Saints," "Lil' Liza Jane," and "Everybody Loves Saturday Night." **The Hit Singles** (Storyville 5533) has 23 concise selections from 1958–69, including quite a few originals, "Dark Eyes," "Walking with the King," and "Washington Post March." **The Odense Concert 1963** (Storyville 5529) is a good example of how the band sounded live, stretching out on such tunes as "Our Monday Date," "Sibiria," "Hysteric Rag," and "Wolverine Blues." **Everybody Loves Saturday Night** (Storyville 5502) has highlights from 1966–67 and 1969, and even with the inclusion of a couple of lightweight numbers ("Thoroughly Modern Millie" and "She Had to Go Lose It at the Astor"), this is a particularly strong all-around set that features "Jungle Jamboree," "Home," "Stevedore Stomp," "Tar Paper Stomp," and "Bye and Bye."

Tony Parenti   Tony Parenti, who worked regularly at Ryan's during 1963–69 with his own band, only led one and a half albums during the 1950s. However, in the 1960s he was featured on four LPs for the Jazzology label, all of which find him in prime form. A ragtime-oriented date from 1966 has been coupled with a similar session from 1947 and is reviewed in the 1945–49 chapter. Two other Dixieland-oriented dates from 1966–67 with either Ernie Carson or Max Kaminsky on trumpet, have unfortunately not been reissued on CD yet. **Tony Parenti and His Downtown Boys** (Jazzology 11) has four songs (comprising half of an album)

from 1954 with the Armand Hug Trio plus ten rags, blues, and Dixieland standards from 1962 that Parenti made in a trio with pianist Dick Wellstood and drummer Sam Ulanov. Whether it be "Wildcat Blues," "Ballin' the Jack," "At the Jazz Band Ball," or "Eccentric Rag," Parenti shows that he was still one of the top—if one of the most underrated—New Orleans clarinetists, even after 40 years of playing.

Billie and DeDe Pierce   The husband and wife team of pianist/vocalist Billie Pierce and trumpeter DeDe Pierce were married in 1935 and worked together for nearly 40 years. Billie had previously worked with Bessie Smith, Ma Rainey, and Buddy Petit, while DeDe played trumpet with Arnold Dupas's Olympia Band. They generally teamed up as a duet (occasionally using additional musicians) starting in 1935, making their first recordings in 1953. In the mid-1950s, they were both hospitalized with a serious illness. Billie recovered completely, but DeDe was left permanently blind. Billie persuaded him to continue his career, they returned to records in 1959, and were a major part of the Preservation Hall Jazz Band in the 1960s. Two albums from January 27, 1961, **Blues in the Classic Tradition** (Original Blues Classics 534) and **Blues and Tonks from the Delta** (Original Blues Classics 1847), were recorded as part of producer Chris Albertson's valuable "New Orleans: The Living Legends" series. In both cases, the Pierces are joined by drummer Albert Jiles. The former CD gets a slight edge due to the versions of "St. Louis Blues," "Careless Love," "Nobody Knows You When You're Down and Out," and their trademark "Love Song of the Nile." But **Blues and Tonks**, which has 14 of the 23 songs recorded in the one day, has worthy versions of "St. James Infirmary," "Milenberg Joys," "You Tell Me Your Dream," and "Billie's Gumbo Blues" and is almost as rewarding.

The Preservation Hall Jazz Band   With the opening of Preservation Hall in 1961, veteran New Orleans jazz musicians had a home where trad jazz was performed nightly. In addition, the Preservation Hall Jazz Band was formed and toured the world, spreading the joy of the music even if their musicianship was often a bit erratic. The early versions of the band often featured DeDe and Billie Pierce, Louis Nelson, George Lewis, bassist John Joseph, and Abbey Foster or Cie Frazier on drums. The young tuba player Allen Jaffe ran the touring band, which in the 1960s often had banjoist Narvin Kimball and bassist Chester Zardis. Their few recordings from this time period (including one for the Preservation Hall label) are scarce, but the Preservation Hall Jazz Band was successful in helping to popularize New Orleans revival jazz.

Jim Robinson   The most consistent musician in the George Lewis band of the 1950s, Jim Robinson worked with Lewis now and then in the '60s, appeared often at Preservation Hall, and led a few record dates of his own, including two for the "New Orleans: The Living Legends" series. **Jim Robinson's New Orleans Band** (Original Jazz Classics 1844) and **Plays Spirituals and Blues** (Original Jazz Classics 1846), which were recorded during January 24–30, 1961, both have Robinson leading a group also including trumpeter Ernest Cagnolatti, the smooth swing clarinetist Louis Cottrell, banjoist George Guesnon, bassist Slow Drag Pavageau, and drummer Alfred Williams. The music is ensemble-oriented with the first set highlighted by spirited renditions of such tunes as "Ice Cream," "In the Shade of the Old Apple Tree," "Bugle Boy March," and "When You Wore a Tulip." For the other CD, Annie Pavageau takes gospel-oriented vocals on two numbers, and the repertoire consists of either blues or hymns that adapt well to New Orleans jazz, including "Lily of the Valley," "You Pray for Me," "Dippermouth Blues," and "Yearning."

Pee Wee Russell   For Pee Wee Russell, the 1961–67 period found him playing consistently adventurous music, sometimes in surprisingly modern settings. Long associated with Eddie Condon and Dixieland despite having a very distinctive style full of unusual note choices, Russell sought to escape from the hyper Dixieland warhorses. He had recorded small-group swing in the late 1950s and that trend continued on **Jazz Reunion** (Candid 79020). The reunion referred to was between Russell and Coleman Hawkins, who had last recorded one of the songs on the set ("If I Could Be with You") in 1929. Joined by Emmett Berry and Bob Brookmeyer, Pee Wee and Hawk also explore a pair of Duke Ellington songs ("All Too Soon" and "What Am I Here For"), two Russell originals, and the boppish "Tin Tin Deo."

Although Russell participated in an Eddie Condon Chicagoans reunion later in the year, he was heading in the opposite direction. During 1962–65, he was often featured in a pianoless quartet with valve-trombonist Marshall Brown (who doubled on bass trumpet), bassist Russell George, and either Ron Lundberg or Ronnie Bedford on drums. The group was a little reminiscent of Gerry Mulligan's quartets but used a diverse and at times very modern repertoire. Recorded in 1962, **New Groove** (Collectables 6687) has Russell performing such tunes as "Chelsea Bridge," "Moten Swing," Tadd Dameron's "Good Bait," "'Round Midnight," and John Coltrane's "Red Planet" in mostly relaxed fashion. **Ask Me Now** (Impulse 96) from 1965 is long overdue to be reissued on CD, and it is a classic. Russell, Brown, and the quartet perform Ornette Coleman's "Turnaround," Coltrane's "Some Other Blues," two Thelonious Monk tunes ("Ask Me Now" and "Hackensack"), and a few standards. In addition, Russell sat in with the Thelonious Monk Quartet successfully on a couple of numbers at the 1963 Newport Jazz Festival. Somehow, one cannot imagine Eddie Condon, Wild Bill Davison, or George Brunies doing that!

Pee Wee Russell broke with Marshall Brown (who could be a bit dictatorial) by 1966, but still sounds pretty modern in sets with Henry "Red" Allen (**The College Concert**) and the Oliver Nelson big band (**The Spirit of '67**); both are Impulse albums that have not been reissued yet.

The clarinetist, who also proved to be a skilled painter during this era, was having a renaissance, but it ended when his wife died in 1967. Extremely depressed, Russell stopped playing, drank nonstop, and was dead in less than two years at the age of 62.

Willie "The Lion" Smith   James P. Johnson and Fats Waller may have been long dead, but Willie "The Lion" Smith was still active in the 1960s. In fact he wrote his memoirs, *Music on My Mind*, in 1965 when he was 67. **Pork and Beans** (1201 Music 9037) has him paying tribute to some of his contemporaries during a solo set with four numbers by Luckey Roberts, three by Eubie Blake, two apiece from Fats Waller and George Gershwin, and four veteran standards. Smith still sounds in excellent form during this spirited set from 1966. The following year he began occasionally appearing in public with Don Ewell on second piano. **Duets** (Sackville 2004) has Smith and Ewell romping together on a variety of superior swing standards, including "I've Found a New Baby," "I Would Do Anything for

You," "Everybody Loves My Baby," and "You Took Advantage of Me."

Muggsy Spanier After leaving Earl Hines's band in 1959, Muggsy Spanier resumed leading his own Dixieland groups for five years, retiring after appearing at the 1964 Newport Jazz Festival. He died three years later at the age of 60. Spanier's last recording as a leader was a particularly strong effort, **Columbia the Gem of the Ocean** (Mobile Fidelity 857). This CD (which will be difficult to find) features Spanier leading a big band similar to the one he had during 1941–43, a unit inspired by Bob Crosby's. The cornetist and the 15-piece group perform nine Dean Kincaide arrangements from the earlier band's book, of which only "Chicago" had been recorded previously, plus a new chart by Harry Betts of "Midnight in Moscow." Muggsy Spanier is in top form during this final project, sounding joyous in a group also featuring solos by trombonist Moe Schneider, Matty Matlock, and Eddie Miller.

Jack Teagarden Jack Teagarden's Dixieland band in 1961 included trumpeter Don Goldie, clarinetist Henry Cuesta, pianist Don Ewell, bassist Stan Puls, and drummer Barrett Deems. Teagarden's live shows mostly featured his usual warhorses, but in 1962 he recorded an unusual set, ❍ **Think Well of Me** (Verve 557 101), with a string orchestra and Goldie that has him interpreting the intriguing rural compositions of Willard Robison. Robison's songs are nostalgic and wistful, including "Old Folks," "Cottage for Sale," and "'Tain't So, Honey 'Tain't So." Teagarden has vocals on all but one tune, and he puts plenty of restrained feeling into such obscure numbers as "Guess I'll Go Back Home this Summer," "Think Well of Me," and "'Round My Old Deserted Farm" with plenty of exquisite and often touching trombone solos.

At the 1963 Monterey Jazz Festival, Jack Teagarden's life was celebrated as he had a reunion with his brother, trumpeter Charlie Teagarden, his sister, pianist Norma Teagarden, and even his mother, Helen Teagarden, who contributed a couple of ragtime piano solos. ❍ **A Hundred Years from Today** (Memphis Archives 7010) brings back this joyous occasion, which also has spots for Pee Wee Russell, Gerry Mulligan, and Joe Sullivan (in his last significant appearance). Teagarden performed two sets at Monterey and all of the highlights are here, including "A Hundred Years from Today," "Basin

Street Blues," and "St. James Infirmary" along with some heated jams.

Just four months later, Jack Teagarden died from a heart attack at the age of 58.

Lu Watters and Turk Murphy After breaking up the Yerba Buena Jazz Band in 1950, Lu Watters dropped out of music, working in several fields, including as a cook and a geologist. He watched the Dixieland scene from a distance, decrying its commercialization. A dozen years passed in which he rarely ever picked up his trumpet.

In 1963, Watters was alarmed at plans to build a nuclear power plant in Northern California right on an earthquake fault. After thinking it over, he decided that he could be most effective in protesting this decision by temporarily becoming a musician again and raising money to fight the power companies. After much practice, he appeared at three protest rallies playing with Turk Murphy's band (sounding as strong as ever) and recording a record in 1964. **Together Again** (Merry Makers 8), which was released for the first time in 1994, has the music from the second rally and is quite exciting. Watters and Murphy are joined by cornetist Bob Neighbor, clarinetist Bob Helm, either Wally Rose or Pete Clute on piano, banjoist Dave Weirbach, Bob Short on tuba, drummer Thad Vandon, and, on some tracks, bassist Squire Girsback. The performances of Dixieland standards and tunes from the Yerba Buena Jazz Band's repertoire are played with high musicianship, creativity, and plenty of spirit. **Blues Over Bodega** (Good Time Jazz 12066) is a reissue of the studio album, matching Watters with Helm, Rose, and trombonist Bob Mielke in a septet on such tunes as "Some of these Days," "Emperor Norton's Hunch," and his new pieces "San Andreas Fault" and "Blues Over Bodega." Blues singer Barbara Dane helps out a couple of songs. Once again, Watters sounds in prime form.

The nuclear plant was never built, and having achieved his purpose, Lu Watters went back into permanent retirement.

Albert Wynn A fine trombonist from the 1920s, Albert Wynn had recorded with Charlie Creath's Jazz-O-Maniacs (1927) and led six titles of his own during 1926 and 1928. Among his associations through the years were Sam Wooding (with whom he toured Europe), Sidney Bechet (1932), Carroll Dickerson, Jimmie Noone, Richard M. Jones, the Earl Hines Orchestra, Fletcher Henderson (1937–39), Baby Dodds, Lil Armstrong, many groups in the Chicago area, Franz Jackson's Original Jazz All-Stars (1956–60), and the Gold Coast Jazz Band (1960–64).

Wynn returned to records in 1961 as a sideman with Lil Armstrong and for his only LP as a leader, **Albert Wynn and His Gutbucket Seven** (Original Jazz Classics 1826), which was released as part of the "Chicago: The Living Legends" series. This is a particularly exuberant date even if the musicians (who were mostly in their mid-fifties) were thought of as ancient at the time. Wynn is joined by such alumni of the 1920s as Darnell Howard, trumpeter Bill Martin, Bus Moten (Bennie's brother) and Blind John Davis alternating on piano, guitarist Mike McKendrick, bassist Robert Wilson, and drummer Booker T. Washington. The tunes include "Ice Cream," "Someday Sweetheart," "Bourbon Street Parade," and "Nobody's Sweetheart" and show that these underrated veterans still had something special to offer as late as 1961.

Looking Ahead: The Beginnings of Fusion

In 1942, the word "bebop" had not been coined yet, but the style was in its early incubation period. The same can be said for "fusion" in 1967. With the rise of the Beatles during 1963–64 and the dominance of rock in the pop music world during 1965–67, there was an increasing amount of pressure on jazz musicians to play and record pop and rock songs. Short-sighted record labels began to release completely unsuitable projects that sought to capitalize on the popularity of rock by "covering" the hits. Guitarist Joe Pass recorded **The Stones Jazz** even though Pass sounded nothing like a rock guitarist, much less a member of the Rolling Stones. Count Basie came out with **Basie's Beatles Bag**, and Duke Ellington did his version of pop tunes of the day on **Ellington '65** and **Ellington '66**. But except for the repertoire, these musicians did not alter their music at all, and the results sometimes sound a bit ridiculous.

On the rock side of things, some of the more sophisticated musicians were not shy to praise their earlier jazz and blues influences, and they were successful at focusing more attention on the 1950s Chicago blues artists such as Muddy Waters and Howlin' Wolf who had helped inspire them in their younger days.

By 1967, some of the younger jazz musicians were becoming less shy about incorporating aspects of rock in their music, particularly the electric bass, early electric keyboards, and expressive guitarists. The rise of guitarist Larry Coryell, whose roots were in electric blues and rock, helped lead the way; he recorded with Chico Hamilton and became a significant member of the Gary Burton Quartet. An important early pre-fusion record is a self-titled LP by **The Free Spirits** (ABC Paramount 593), a missing link in early fusion that features Coryell in a quintet with tenor saxophonist Jim Pepper and drummer Bob Moses.

But, as in 1945 with bebop, when fusion began to make its mark during 1968–69, it would be quite a surprise to much of the jazz world.

Various Artists

The New Wave in Jazz (GRP/Impulse 137) documents a special concert that took place on March 28, 1965, at the Village Gate. Put on by the Impulse label to show off some of their "New Thing" artists, featured are the John Coltrane Quartet ("Nature Boy"), Archie Shepp's septet ("Hambone"), a quartet comprised of Grachan Moncur III, Bobby Hutcherson, Cecil McBee, and drummer Beaver Harris, and an all-star quintet with trumpeter Charles Tolliver, James Spaulding, Hutcherson, McBee, and Billy Higgins. The music (some of which is also available elsewhere) ranges from quite free to an excellent version of Thelonious Monk's "Brilliant Corners" by Charles Tolliver's group.

On January 3, 1963, German jazz critic and producer Joachim Berendt organized a concert called **Americans in Europe** (GRP/Impulse 150) featuring top American jazzmen who had decided to make their homes in Europe. Originally released as 13 selections on two LPs, this single CD has the eight best numbers. Featured on four songs is the Bud Powell Trio with guests Don Byas and trumpeter Idrees Sulieman. Also heard from is a Kenny Clarke trio with guitarist Jimmy Gourley and organist Lou Bennett, and a quintet with clarinetist Bill Smith, altoist Herb Geller, and Gourley. Best is Byas tearing into "All the Things You Are" and a Sulieman ballad feature on "I Remember Clifford."

From the Newport Jazz Festival—Tribute to Charlie Parker (Bluebird 6457) has two separate sets that both involve veterans playing Charlie Parker–associated tunes. The 1964 Newport Festival performance features Howard McGhee, J.J. Johnson, Sonny Stitt (sticking to tenor), pianist Harold Mabern, bassist Arthur Harper, and Max Roach playing "Buzzy," "Now's the Time," and "Wee." There is also an interesting segment where Father Norman J. O'Connor (the concert's emcee) gets the musicians to say a few words about Bird. In addition, Jackie McLean and his quartet (with pianist Lamont Johnson, bassist Scott Holt, and Billy Higgins) are heard in the studio in 1967 playing intense ballad versions of "Embraceable You" and "Old Folks." It may not have actually been live at Newport, but it holds its own with the opening jam session.

An important historic event but not yet reissued on CD, producer John Hammond presented his third "From Spirituals to Swing" concert in January 1967. Although billed as the **From Spirituals to Swing—30th Anniversary Concert** (Columbia 30776), it really took place 28 years and a month after the initial event. But considering that pianist Pete Johnson, disabled by a stroke from 1958, and clarinetist Edmond Hall would both pass away within months, it is fortunate that the concert took place when it did. There is a wide variety of music on this double LP, including performances by George Benson, spirituals singer Marion Williams, altoist John Handy, R&B vocalist Big Mama Thornton, and the Count Basie Orchestra. Best are "Swingin' the Blues" (featuring a combo that includes Buck Clayton, Buddy Tate, Edmond Hall, and Basie) and an emotional version of "Roll 'Em Pete" on which Joe Turner has a final reunion with Pete Johnson. Johnson plays the right hand of the piano (while Ray Bryant takes the left) in his first public appearance since his stroke nine years earlier; it was also his last performance.

The Hot Trumpets of Joe Newman & Henry "Red" Allen (Prestige 24232) has two separate albums reissued on one CD. Swing trumpeter Joe Newman was still with Count Basie in 1961 when he recorded three originals and four standards in a quartet with Tommy Flanagan, sounding as swinging and solid as usual. The Red Allen date, also with a quartet, is from 1962 and one of his best sets from late in his career, highlighted by "St. Louis Blues," "Biffly Blues," and "Sleepytime Gal."

The Greatest Jazz Concert in the World (Pablo 2625 704) almost lives up to its name. To be accurate, this Norman Granz production from 1967 is actually taken from two concerts. There is a "Jazz at the Philharmonic"–type jam session featuring Clark Terry, Benny Carter, Zoot Sims, Paul Gonsalves, and the Oscar Peterson Trio that includes a few heated standards and a ballad medley. The Peterson trio has a few features, Coleman Hawkins (who was past his prime) struggles on two numbers and joins Benny Carter and Johnny Hodges on "C Jam Blues." In addition, there are a couple of blues from T-Bone Walker, who is joined by the all-stars. But as if that were not enough, the Duke Ellington Orchestra is heard in inspired form, performing some new material and having guest spots for Zoot Sims (who joins fellow tenors Gonsalves and Jimmy Hamilton on "Very Tenor"), Oscar Peterson (who gets to lead the band on "Take the 'A' Train") and Carter. Ella Fitzgerald completes the show with her own miniset (backed by the Jimmy Jones Trio), scatting with the Ellington Orchestra on "Cotton Tail." Maybe calling this "the greatest jazz concert in the world" was not bragging by too much!

VOICES OF THE FUTURE

Ivo Perelman (tenor sax), Jan. 12, 1961, Sao Paulo, Brazil

Makoto Ozone (piano), Mar. 25, 1961, Kobe, Japan

Carl Allen (drums), Apr. 25, 1961, Milwaukee, WI

Gary Thomas (tenor), June 10, 1961, Baltimore, MD

Phil Haynes (drums, composer), June 15, 1961, Hillsboro, OR

Marvin "Smitty" Smith (drums), June 24, 1961, Waukegan, IL

Wynton Marsalis (trumpet, arranger, leader), Oct. 18, 1961, New Orleans, LA

Rick Margitza (tenor), Oct. 24, 1961, Detroit, MI

Terence Blanchard (trumpet), Mar. 13, 1962, New Orleans, LA

Renee Rosnes (piano), Mar. 24, 1962, Regina, Sask., Canada

John Swana (trumpet), Apr. 26, 1962, Norristown, PA

Ralph Peterson (drums, leader), May 20, 1962, Pleasantville, NJ

Winard Harper (drums), June 4, 1962, Baltimore, MD

Charlie Sepulveda (trumpet), July 15, 1962, Bronx, NY

Jim Rotondi (trumpet), Aug. 28, 1962, Butte, MT

Craig Handy (tenor, soprano), Sept. 25, 1962, Oakland, CA

James Morrison (trumpet, trombone, reeds), Nov. 11, 1962, Boorowa, Australia

Michel Petrucciani (piano), Dec. 28, 1962, Orange, France

Rachel Z. (piano, keyboards), Dec. 28, 1962, New York, NY

Cyrus Chestnut (piano), Jan. 17, 1963, Baltimore, MD

Dave Douglas (trumpet), Mar. 24, 1963, East Orange, NJ

Benny Green (piano), Apr. 4, 1963, New York, NY

Ron Miles (trumpet), May 9, 1963, Indianapolis, IN

Gonzalo Rubalcaba (piano), May 27, 1963, Havana, Cuba

Jeff Beal (trumpet, composer), June 20, 1963, Hayward, CA

Marcus Roberts (piano), Aug. 7, 1963, Jacksonville, FL

Sherri Maricle (drums), Sept. 2, 1963, Buffalo, NY

Niels Lan Doky (piano), Oct. 3, 1963, Copenhagen, Denmark

Russell Malone (guitar), Nov. 8, 1963, Albany, GA

Don Braden (tenor), Nov. 20, 1963, Cincinnati, OH

Scott Colley (bass), Nov. 24, 1963, Los Angeles CA

Courtney Pine (tenor, soprano, bass clarinet), Mar. 18, 1964, London, England

Jon-Erik Kellso (cornet), May 8, 1964, Dearborn, MI

Peter Washington (bass), Aug. 28, 1964, Los Angeles, CA

Barbara Dennerlein (organ), Sept. 25, 1964, Munich, Germany

Matt Wilson (drums), Sept. 27, 1964, Knoxville, IL

Bob Hurst (bass), Oct. 4, 1964, Detroit, MI

Diana Krall (vocals, piano), Nov. 16, 1964, Nanaimo, British Columbia, Canada

Vincent Herring (alto, soprano), Nov. 19, 1964, Hopkingsville, KY

Joey Calderazzo (piano), Feb. 27, 1965, New Rochelle, NY

Phillip Harper (trumpet), May 10, 1965, Baltimore, MD

Javon Jackson (tenor), June 16, 1965, Carthage, MO

Scott Wendholt (trumpet), July 21, 1965, Patuxant River, MD

Delfeayo Marsalis (trombone), July 28, 1965, New Orleans, LA

Terri Lyne Carrington (drums), Aug. 4, 1965, Medford, MA

Ravi Coltrane (tenor, soprano), Aug. 6, 1965, Huntington, NY

Leon Parker (drums), Aug. 21, 1965, White Plains, NY

Jesse Davis (alto), Sept. 11, 1965, New Orleans, LA

Mark Turner (tenor), Nov. 10, 1965, Fairborn, OH

Jacky Terrasson (piano), Nov. 27, 1965, Berlin, Germany

Ron Affif (guitar), Dec. 30, 1965, Pittsburgh, PA

Frank Vignola (guitar), Dec. 30, 1965, West Islip, NY

Greg Tardy (tenor), Feb. 3, 1966, New Orleans, LA

Jan Lundgren (piano), Mar. 22, 1966, Kristianstad, Sweden

Michael Cain (piano), Apr. 2, 1966, Los Angeles, CA

Andy Martin (trombone), Aug. 10, 1966, Provo, UT

Bireli Lagrene (guitar), Sept. 4, 1966, Soufflenheim, France

Mark Whitfield (guitar), Oct. 6, 1966, Lindenhurst, NJ

Harry Allen (tenor), Oct. 12, 1966, Washington, D.C.

Bill Charlap (piano), Oct. 15, 1966, New York, NY

Bill Stewart (drums), Oct. 18, 1966, Des Moines, IA

Terell Stafford (trumpet), Nov. 25, 1966, Miami, FL

Danilo Perez (piano, composer), Dec. 29, 1966, Monte Oscruo, Panama

Marcus Printup (trumpet), Jan. 24, 1967, Conyers, GA

D.D. Jackson (piano), Jan. 25, 1967, Ottawa, Ontario, Canada

Junko Onishi (piano), Apr. 16, 1967, Kyoto, Japan

Tommy Smith (tenor), Apr. 27, 1967, Edinburgh, Scotland

Wycliffe Gordon (trombone), May 29, 1967, Waynesboro, GA

Charnett Moffett (bass), June 10, 1967, New York, NY

Darren Barrett (trumpet), June 19, 1967, Manchester, England

Harry Connick, Jr. (piano, vocals), Sept. 11, 1967, New Orleans, LA

Kurt Elling (vocals), Nov. 2, 1967, Chicago, IL

PASSINGS

Lem Winchester (32), Jan. 13, 1961, Indianapolis, IN

Alphonse Picou (82), Feb. 4, 1961, New Orleans, LA

Nick LaRocca (71), Feb. 22, 1961, New Orleans, LA

Miff Mole (63), Apr. 21, 1961, New York, NY

Scott LaFaro (25), July 6, 1961, Geneva NY

Booker Little (23), Oct. 5, 1961, New York, NY

Doug Watkins (27), Feb. 5, 1962, Holbrook, AZ

Leo Parker (36), Feb. 11, 1962, New York, NY

Jean Goldkette (63), Mar. 24, 1962, Santa Barbara, CA

John Graas (37), Apr. 13, 1962, Van Nuys, CA

Eddie South (57), Apr. 25, 1962, Chicago, IL

Donald Lambert (58), May 8, 1962, Princeton, NJ

Eddie Costa (31), July 28, 1962, New York, NY

Israel Crosby (43), Aug. 11, 1962, Chicago, IL

Paul Lingle (59), Oct. 30, 1962, Honolulu, HI

Sonny Clark (31), Jan. 13, 1963, New York, NY

Ike Quebec (44), Jan. 16, 1963, New York, NY

Bobby Jaspar (37), Mar. 4, 1963, New York, NY

Lizzie Miles (67), Mar. 17, 1963, New Orleans, LA

Gene Sedric (55), Apr. 3, 1963, New York, NY

Eddie Edwards (71), Apr. 9, 1963, New York, NY

Herbie Nichols (44), Apr. 12, 1963, New York, NY

Bob Scobey (46), June 12, 1963, Montreal, Quebec, Canada

Curtis Counce (37), July 31, 1963, Los Angeles, CA

Pete Brown (56), Sept. 20, 1963, New York, NY

J. Russell Robinson (71), Sept. 30, 1963, Palmdale, CA

Luis Russell (61), Dec. 11, 1963, New York, NY

Dinah Washington (39), Dec. 14, 1963, Detroit, MI

Jack Teagarden (58), Jan. 15, 1964, Los Angeles, CA

Willie Bryant (55), Feb. 9, 1964, Los Angeles, CA

Joe Maini (34), May 8, 1964, Los Angeles, CA

Meade Lux Lewis (58), June 7, 1964, Minneapolis, MN

Eric Dolphy (36), June 29, 1964, Berlin, Germany

Arthur Schutt (62), Jan. 28, 1965, San Francisco, CA

Nat King Cole (47), Feb. 15, 1965, Santa Monica, CA

Tadd Dameron (48), Mar. 8, 1965, New York, NY

Joe Sanders (70), May 15, 1965, Kansas City, MO

Denzil Best (48), May 24, 1965, New York, NY

Carl Kress (57), June 10, 1965, Reno, NV

Red Nichols (60), June 28, 1965, Las Vegas, NV

Claude Thornhill (55), July 1, 1965, New York, NY

Steve Brown (75), Sept. 15, 1965, Detroit, MI

Earl Bostic (52), Oct. 28, 1965, Rochester, NY

Clarence Williams (72), Nov. 6, 1965, New York, NY

Osie Johnson (43), Feb. 10, 1966, New York, NY

Billy Kyle (51), Feb. 23, 1966, Youngstown, OH

Johnny St. Cyr (76), June 17, 1966, Los Angeles, CA

Jimmy Bertrand (66), Aug. 1966, Chicago, IL

Bud Powell (41), Aug. 1, 1966, New York, NY

Boyd Raeburn (52), Aug. 2, 1966, Lafayette, IN

Darnell Howard (71), Sept. 2, 1966, San Francisco, CA

Lucky Millinder (66), Sept. 28, 1966, New York NY

Dave Lambert (49), Oct. 3, 1966, Westport, CT

Wellman Braud (75), Oct. 29, 1966, Los Angeles, CA

Harold "Shorty" Baker (52), Nov. 8, 1966, New York, NY

Edmond Hall (65), Feb. 11, 1967, Boston, MA

Muggsy Spanier (60), Feb. 12, 1967, Sausalito, CA

Willie Smith (56), Mar. 7, 1967, Los Angeles, CA

Herman Chittison (58), Mar. 8, 1967, Cleveland, OH

Pete Johnson (62), Mar. 23, 1967, Buffalo, NY

Buster Bailey (64), Apr. 12, 1967, New York, NY

Henry "Red" Allen (59), Apr. 17, 1967, New York, NY

Wayman Carver (61), May 6, 1967, Atlanta, GA

Elmo Hope (43), May 19, 1967, New York, NY

Billy Strayhorn (51), May 31, 1967, New York, NY

John Coltrane (40), July 17, 1967, New York, NY

Rex Stewart (60), Sept. 7, 1967, Los Angeles, CA

Sidney DeParis (62), Sept. 13, 1967, New York, NY

Stuff Smith (58), Sept. 25, 1967, Munich, Germany

Ida Cox (71), Nov. 10, 1967, Knoxville, TN

Jimmy Archey (65), Nov. 16, 1967 Amityville, NY

Paul Whiteman (77), Dec. 29, 1967, Doylestown, PA

Chapter Ten

1968–1976:
Fusion and Beyond

The 1968–76 period was a rather tumultuous and event-filled time in American history. In 1968 civil rights leader Martin Luther King, Jr,. and Robert Kennedy (a candidate for president who might very well have won that year's election) were both assassinated. Although the Civil Rights Act had become law, race riots were a common occurrence as segregationists in the South put up a last fruitless stand against integration. The Vietnam War was at its height, and the anti-war movement had spread beyond young radicals to mainstream Americans who could not understand why we were involved in that conflict and what were our ultimate goals. The 1968 Democratic Convention found the Chicago police openly attacking peaceful demonstrators, and a poorly divided Democratic party lost the White House to Richard Nixon. The counterculture was growing in strength, and social commentators in the rock world were speaking for their generation.

By 1976 the mood had changed. The Vietnam War was over, with the United States involvement declining sharply after 1972 and the Communists of the North defeating the South altogether in 1975. Richard Nixon was gone from Washington, destroyed by a variety of law-breaking scandals termed Watergate, and his successor Gerald Ford had doomed his own political future by pardoning Nixon from prosecution, paving the way for Jimmy Carter to win that year's election. On the brighter side, even most of those who were cynical about the U.S. government enjoyed celebrating the country's ideals during 1976's bicentennial celebrations. And year by year, integration and civil rights for all citizens were finally starting to become accepted.

While the United States, despite some inner doubts, seemed stronger and more peaceful in 1976 than it had been in 1968, the future of jazz was a bit less certain, particularly to those who were not following the scene that closely. A new style of music called fusion had divided the audience, both potentially expanding and fragmenting the jazz world.

In 1968 the word "fusion" had not caught on yet, and the concept behind the new style was a theory more than a reality. In contrast, by 1972 fusion seemed to be on its way to making straightahead jazz and the acoustic piano obsolete. But because newer styles do not "replace" older ones (though they may overshadow them for a time), the rise of fusion added to the vocabulary of jazz without invalidating what had come before or the other styles that continued to develop in the 1970s. Its rise, however, did further split the jazz world apart (as did bebop in the mid-1940s and free jazz in the early '60s), making fans of other styles ask what the "con"-fusion was all about.

Fusion (which for a short while was called jazz-rock or rock-jazz) is a word that has often been misused, particularly in more recent times, but essentially it means the mixture of jazz improvisation with the sound and rhythms of rock. By the late 1960s, rock had not only taken over the counterculture, making jazz seem conservative to the general public in comparison, but the music had actually become much more sophisticated. Many of the younger jazz musicians, some of whom grew up on the Beatles, wanted to explore rock in their own way or at least keep their playing open to its influence. The electric piano (which was soon joined by synthesizers and other keyboards) and electric bass, which were rarely utilized in jazz of 1965, by 1969 were competing with the acoustic piano and string bass in importance.

Miles Davis was a major force in fusion catching on because he was a veteran jazz giant with a great deal of credibility as opposed to being a young upstart. He persuaded both Herbie Hancock and Chick Corea to play electric keyboards, utilized unpredictable rock and funk rhythms, and seemed to enjoy having crowded ensembles. By the early 1970s his experimental groups, which

had become a workshop for younger musicians, were being overshadowed by other fusion bands that were rock oriented yet featured virtuosic improvising by musicians whose backgrounds were in more straightahead jazz. That, coupled with the rise of rock (which by the late 1960s was dominating radio, mass media, and record sales) seemed to be pointing toward the death of acoustic jazz. And contributing to some of the pessimism was the decline and imminent death of the Blue Note label, the lack of interest by the major labels (particularly Columbia and RCA) in jazz except as an occasional diversion, and the inevitable passing of some of the older musicians including Louis Armstrong and Duke Ellington.

However, by the mid-1970s, acoustic jazz was looking healthier than it had in years. Such new record labels as Chiaroscuro, Famous Door, Pablo, and Concord were documenting earlier styles of jazz and new young players who enjoyed extending the innovations of the past. Europe had opened up, not only as a haven for some American jazz musicians dissatisfied with the lack of work opportunities in the United States but as the host of major summer festivals, as an incubator of new jazz styles, and as the home of some new significant record labels including ECM and Black Saint/Soul Note. Ragtime had made an unexpected comeback with the use of Scott Joplin's music in the Hollywood film *The Sting*, leading to "The Entertainer" being on the pop charts. And jazz, instead of embracing only the most advanced

TIMELINE 1968

Chick Corea and Dave Holland succeed Herbie Hancock and Ron Carter in the Miles Davis Quintet. • Wes Montgomery dies. • Julius Hemphill helps found the Black Artists Group in St. Louis, Missouri. • Art Pepper plays with the Buddy Rich Orchestra. • Randy Weston moves to Morocco. • Art Farmer moves to Vienna, Italy. • Maxine Sullivan starts her comeback. • Rob McConnell forms the Boss Brass, but it would be eight years before it became a full-fledged jazz band. • Jimmy Hamilton leaves Duke Ellington's Orchestra after 25 years, settling in the Virgin Islands. • Eubie Blake is rediscovered. • Randy Brecker and Billy Cobham join the Horace Silver Quintet. • Dave Brubeck forms a new quartet with Gerry Mulligan, Jack Six, and Alan Dawson. • Don Byas records with Ben Webster. • Dave Frishberg leads his first album, having a surprise hit with "Van Lingle Mungo," a song on which the lyrics are comprised exclusively of baseball players' names. • Slide Hampton moves to Germany while Red Mitchell moves to Stockholm, Sweden. • Paul Horn records flute solos from inside the Taj Mahal. • Czech bassist George Mraz moves to the United States to study at Berklee. • Wynton Kelly makes his last recordings. • Gary McFarland, Gabor Szabo, and Cal Tjader collaborate to form the Skye label, but most of the releases are inferior attempts at commercialism. • Eddie Miller works regularly in New Orleans with Pete Fountain. • Organist Jimmy McGriff has a minor funk/soul jazz hit in "The Worm." • Shirley Scott records for the last time with Stanley Turrentine; they divorce a few years later. • The World's Greatest Jazz Band is formed. • Anthony Braxton makes his recording debut.

musicians, was finally celebrating its classic veterans, many of whom were still playing in their prime.

So, although jazz had gone through some difficult times on a commercial level, it was thriving artistically in the mid-1970s. This chapter attests to the diversity and richness of the scene during this often-misunderstood period.

Miles Davis: 1968–1969

As 1968 began, Miles Davis led the same quintet that he had been heading for the three previous years, a classic unit with tenor saxophonist Wayne Shorter, pianist Herbie Hancock, bassist Ron Carter, and drummer Tony Williams. Their abstract music (which is heard on their earlier records **E.S.P.**, **Miles Smiles**, **The Sorcerer**, and **Nefertiti**) was quite innovative, being unlike that played by any other group of the era. While Davis still played standards during live performances, the highly original compositions of Wayne Shorter and Davis's sidemen were fresh, new, and unpredictable. However, they were not attracting a large audience and were not particularly influential until the 1980s.

Davis, whose trumpet chops had returned to prime form after being erratic during 1965–66, decided to move in a new direction for several reasons. He hoped to attract more young blacks to his music (his audience was largely white), he was curious about rock and intrigued by the music of James Brown, Sly and the Family Stone, and Jimi Hendrix, and he always had a burning desire to move ahead and lead the way. For Davis, 1968 was a transitional year in which he utilized electronics for the first time and his second classic quintet gradually broke up.

Miles in the Sky (Columbia/Legacy 48954) has "Paraphernalia" from January 16, 1968, which adds guitarist George Benson to the quintet with Herbie Hancock playing electric piano. The other three numbers ("Stuff," "Black Comedy," and "Country Son") are extended pieces from May 15–17 by the quintet, with Hancock doubling on acoustic and electric keyboards. There is a slight feel of pop and rock rhythms, but they are quite subtle and largely beneath the surface. All of this music, along with the complete output of the quintet is also on the four-CD set ◉ **Miles Davis Quintet, 1965–'68** (Columbia/Legacy 67398).

Filles de Kilimanjaro (Columbia/Legacy 86555) has the final recordings by the second classic Miles Davis

Quintet and the first by his short-lived third group. "Tout de Suite" (which is heard in two versions), "Petits Machins," and "Filles de Kilimanjaro" were recorded during June 1968 with rock rhythms being heard in the background. Herbie Hancock and Ron Carter (heard on electric bass) soon departed. Hancock left to form his own sextet while Carter (who had been absent a lot during 1967 with Buster Williams often filling in) became a busy freelancer who seemingly spent the 1970s living in the recording studios. "Freelon Brun" and "Mademoiselle Mabry" have Davis, Wayne Shorter, and Williams joined quite capably by Chick Corea on electric keyboards and Dave Holland on acoustic bass. Earlier in the year, Davis had insisted that Hancock play electric piano, and he did the same for Corea, who had formerly been strictly an acoustic player. **Water Babies** (Columbia/Legacy 80877), which was not initially released until the late 1970s, has additional material (all Shorter compositions) performed by both quintets, with the earlier group heard in June 1967 on three songs (including "Capricorn") while the Corea-Holland combination is featured on two early fusion jams ("Two Faced" and "Dual Mr. Tillman Anthony") from November 1968.

The two new musicians fit in quite well with Davis. Chick Corea, who was 27, had already had extensive experience working with Mongo Santamaria, Willie Bobo, Blue Mitchell, Herbie Mann, Stan Getz, and Sarah Vaughan. British-born Dave Holland worked with the who's who of English jazzmen during 1963–68, including Humphrey Lyttelton, John Surman, Evan Parker, Tubby Hayes, Kenny Wheeler, and the Spontaneous Music Ensemble, ranging in style from mainstream swing to the avant-garde. Davis heard Holland at Ronnie Scott's club when Holland was playing with a British group opposite the Bill Evans Trio, and Davis quickly hired him. In early 1969, when Tony Williams decided to leave Davis to form his own trio, Jack DeJohnette, who had been with the Charles Lloyd Quartet during 1966–68, proved to be the perfect replacement.

Unfortunately, this quintet was hardly documented at all. The most rewarding performance is a live date from July 1969 put out by the European Jazz Door label, **It's About that Time** (Jazz Door 1294). The seven-song continuous set from the Montreux Jazz Festival includes two songs that would be recorded for **Bitches Brew** a month later ("Miles Runs the Voodoo Down" and "Sanctuary") and possibly the last versions ever of

688 Chapter Ten 1968–1976: Fusion and Beyond

Davis playing standards—somewhat eccentric renditions of "Milestones" and "'Round About Midnight" plus Wayne Shorter's "Footprints."

Five months earlier, Davis had recorded **In a Silent Way** (Sony 40580), a mostly quiet but revolutionary musical statement. Davis's quintet (with Shorter on soprano, Chick Corea on keyboards, Dave Holland, and Tony Williams, who was still with the band) is joined by keyboardist Herbie Hancock, organist Joe Zawinul (from Cannonball Adderley's band), and guitarist John McLaughlin (who was set to join Tony Williams's Lifetime). The original album consisted of "Shh/Peaceful" and a medley of Zawinul's "In a Silent Way" and "It's About that Time." Other than the surprising sounds made by the three keyboards, the introduction of British guitarist McLaughlin to American listeners, and the unusual song structures, ◐ **In a Silent Way** is most notable for the editing of producer Teo Macero, who utilized the playing on the title cut twice and spliced together the music in unusual ways. From this point on, Davis's studio recordings would no longer be live but would instead be edited versions of jams; the musicians would be continually surprised by the finished results.

The Complete in a Silent Way Sessions (Columbia/Legacy 63362), a three-CD set, has the titles from **Filles de Kilimanjaro** and **Water Babies** that feature Corea and Holland in the quintet, other material from the 1968–69 period (including some unissued tracks), and unedited performances that were partially used in the album along with the released numbers on **In a Silent Way**. The latter is the most rewarding of all of these selections, showing that Macero and Davis did know best.

While the LP **In a Silent Way** created a bit of a stir, ◐ **Bitches Brew** (Columbia/Legacy 65774) from August 1969 and released in 1970 caused major waves. Originally a six-song double LP (the double CD adds a seventh slightly later selection), this was the most important release of the fusion movement, indirectly inspiring the formation of many other fusion bands while bewildering many of the trumpeter's veteran fans who wanted him to continue playing "Walkin'" and "Bye Bye Blackbird." Recorded during a three-day period, Miles, Shorter (sticking to soprano), Corea, Holland, and DeJohnette are joined by the atmospheric bass clarinet of Bennie Maupin (who adds an eerie and slightly menacing feel to the music), the second electric piano of Joe

Zawinul, McLaughlin, the electric bass of Harvey Brooks, and the percussion of Don Alias and Jumma Santos on all of the numbers, with drummer Lenny White on five of the six cuts and Larry Young (playing third electric piano) on two songs. "Miles Runs the Voodoo Down" is the most memorable of these selections, but the other songs (which include "Sanctuary," "Spanish Key," and "Pharoah's Dance") are also innovative and brilliantly played. The four-CD set **The Complete Bitches Brew Sessions** (Columbia/Legacy 65570) has a title that is a bit inaccurate because, rather than having unedited versions of the jams, it adds 15 additional selections (nine previously unreleased) from later sessions, part of which were issued on **Live/Evil** and **Big Fun**. The "new" music is interesting and easily recommended to completists but does not add to one's understanding of the original **Bitches Brew** sessions.

Having shocked the jazz world in 1969, Miles Davis would continue to move ahead during the next six years. In the meantime, many of his alumni also became leaders in fusion.

Fusion: The Sons of Miles

By 1969 it had long been true that when a musician spent a period working with Miles Davis, it increased his chances of developing into a major bandleader and innovator. Among Davis's alumni from earlier times were John Coltrane, Cannonball Adderley, Red Garland, Bill Evans, Wynton Kelly, and George Coleman. While Ron Carter became a busy session player in the 1970s, the other three members of Davis's second classic quintet (Wayne Shorter, Herbie Hancock, and Tony Williams) became significant in the new fusion music. If one adds Chick Corea and such associates as Joe Zawinul, John McLaughlin, Billy Cobham, and Bennie Maupin, it becomes obvious that Miles Davis was, if not the technical founder of fusion, the godfather of the fusion movement. His former sidemen were responsible for the formation of what were arguably the five most significant fusion bands: Weather Report, Return to Forever, Tony Williams's Lifetime, the Mahavishnu Orchestra, and Herbie Hancock's Headhunters.

Weather Report, Joe Zawinul, and Wayne Shorter
In late 1970, Joe Zawinul and Wayne Shorter (who had left Miles Davis earlier in the year) founded Weather Report. Zawinul had gained extensive experience playing

in his native Austria, moving to the United States in 1958 and working with the Maynard Ferguson big band, Dinah Washington (1959–61), and most notably the Cannonball Quintet (1962–70). Just as Bill Evans had been an important inspiration behind Miles Davis's **Kind of Blue**, Zawinul's ideas and melodies (including "In a Silent Way") were a significant part of Davis's early fusion projects. The 1970 album **Zawinul** (Rhino/Atlantic 81375) is a transitional set that slightly predates Weather Report but hints at the group, including Miroslav Vitous on bass and highlighted by a new and complex version of "In a Silent Way." Zawinul and Herbie Hancock are heard on various keyboards, Earl Turbinton is featured on soprano, and trumpeter Woody Shaw fares well in this setting.

Wayne Shorter, whose Bluc Note recordings of 1964–67 constitute the most significant work of his career, cut three additional albums as a leader for the label during 1969–70. **Super Nova** (Blue Note 84332) differs drastically from his previous acoustic dates. The distinctive tenor saxophonist had just begun doubling on soprano, and he was already one of the main voices on that instrument in the post-Coltrane era. On this intriguing set, he plays five of his originals (including "Water Babies") and Antonio Carlos Jobim's "Dindi." Shorter utilized some of the top fusion-oriented players on this set including John McLaughlin and Sonny Sharrock on guitars, Walter Booker (normally a bassist) on classical guitar for "Dindi," Miroslav Vitous, both Jack DeJohnette and Chick Corea on drums, and Airto Moreira on percussion; Maria Booker sings on the expressive version of "Dindi." The music is influenced by Miles Davis's early fusion records but has a personality of its own.

On August 26, 1970, Shorter finished his Blue Note period by recording enough material for two very different albums that are also in the early fusion genre. **Odyssey of Iska** (Blue Note 84363) is the better of the pair and has Shorter utilizing a double rhythm section comprised of vibraphonist Dave Friedman, guitarist Gene Bertoncini, both bassists Ron Carter and Cecil McBee, drummers Billy Hart and Alphonse Mouzon, and percussionist Frank Cuomo. Shorter plays quite well on such melancholy originals as "Wind," "Storm," and "Calm," which are definitely looking forward toward Weather Report (referred to in the liner notes as Weather Forecast). **Moto Grosso Feio** (One Way 17373) is an unusual if wandering record because of the instrumentation. In addition to Shorter on tenor and soprano, Chick Corea plays marimba, drums, and percussion (rather than piano); bassist Ron Carter mostly performs on cello; electric guitarist John McLaughlin sticks to the 12-string acoustic guitar; and bassist Dave Holland also plays guitar, with drummer Michelin Prell rounding out the group. The ensemble interprets four Shorter originals (including "Montezuma") and Milton Nascimento's "Vera Cruz." Shorter's only other solo album from the 1968–76 period is 1974's **Native Dancer** (Columbia/Legacy 46159), an exotic project dominated by Brazilian singer/composer Milton Nascimento, who wrote five of the nine compositions. Herbie Hancock and Airto Moreira also help out on a set whose best-known songs are Shorter's "Ana Maria" and "Beauty and the Beast."

When Zawinul and Shorter came together to found and co-lead Weather Report, they originally headed a quintet including Miroslav Vitous on electric bass, Alphonse Mouzon on drums, and Airto Moreira on percussion. The group's debut album, **Weather Report** (Sony 9658), features that quintet extending Miles Davis's **Bitches Brew** music into different areas. From the start of the group, Zawinul's work on keyboards and synthesizers was a pacesetter although Shorter's soprano playing was initially coequal. The band, which emphasized ensembles rather than individual solos, helped to define fusion of the era even if its music was initially more abstract and esoteric than it would become. Highlights from their debut include "Orange Lady," "Tears," and "Eurydice."

By the time Weather Report recorded ◉ **I Sing the Body Electric** (Columbia 46107) in late 1971–72, both Airto Moreira (who was only with the band briefly) and Alphonse Mouzon had departed, being replaced by drummer Eric Gravatt and percussionist Dom Um Romao. Guitarist Ralph Towner sits in on "The Moore," and three horns and three vocalists are added to "Unknown Soldier." Half of the album was recorded at a concert in Tokyo, and that portion displays the group's drive and individual way of swinging. The studio selections are more tightly arranged and electronic. Overall, Weather Report's first two recordings find the band being a pioneer in mixing advanced jazz with elements from other cultures, blending electronic jazz with world music. Nothing like this group had been heard before. And although Shorter's sound was a key element, Zawinul's musical interests were determining the direction of the group. In fact, one could compare Weather Report to the Modern Jazz Quartet in that way, with Shorter being the star soloist like Milt Jackson, but Zawinul assuming John Lewis's role as the real leader.

From 1973, **Sweetnighter** (Columbia/Legacy 64976) has Shorter being relegated to a more supportive role than earlier, seeming to often be just an extension of Zawinul's keyboards, a part of but not a determining factor in the group's sound. This highly rhythmic and grooving set has Andrew White added on electric bass (with Vitous playing acoustic) or an English horn on five of the six numbers; highlights include "Boogie Woogie Waltz," "125th Street Congress," and "Non-Stop Home."

Mysterious Traveller (Columbia/Legacy 65112) has Alphonso Johnson taking over from Miroslav Vitous on bass and Ishmael Wilburn becoming the band's new drummer. The band's personnel and instrumentation often shift from track to track with "Nubian Sundance" adding several vocalists and "Blackthorn Rose" being a Zawinul-Shorter duet. Although none of these originals would catch on, they do serve as a strong transition between the early experimental explorations of Weather Report and its later emphasis on more of a groove.

Tale Spinnin' (Columbia/Legacy 65110) from 1975 features Weather Report as a quintet consisting of its co-leaders, Alphonso Johnson, drummer James "Ndugu" Chancler, and percussionist Alyrio Lima. The changes in the rhythm section (the group was now using its second bassist, third percussionist, and fourth drummer) were less important than the growing emphasis in Zawinul's music on rhythms and catchier melodies, infused with some wordless vocals and state-of-the-art synthesizer work.

In 1976 **Black Market** (Columbia/Legacy 65169) finds Weather Report at a major transition. Narada Michael Walden and Chester Thompson split the drum duties, Alex Acuna is the percussionist (with Don Alias in his place on "Black Market"), and, most significantly, Alphonso Johnson's spot is gradually taken over by Jaco Pastorius. Johnson remains underrated for defining the bassist's role with Weather Report, which would be greatly expanded by Jaco (as can be heard on "Barbary Coast"). Among the more intriguing selections are "Barbary Coast," "Black Market," and Zawinul's tribute to his recently deceased former boss "Cannonball."

Chick Corea and Return to Forever   Throughout his career, as with Miles Davis, Chick Corea was always open to change. His 1968 trio set ● **Now He Sings, Now He Sobs** (Blue Note 90055) with Miroslav Vitous and Roy Haynes is still considered one of his finest recordings. The CD reissue is greatly expanded from the LP with the original five selections joined by eight others from the same sessions released on the double-LP **Circling In**. Eleven of the songs on this advanced hard bop set are Corea's originals including "Windows," "Matrix," and "Samba Yantra." Other highlights include Monk's "Pannonica," "My One and Only Love," and Corea's tune "Steps—What Was," which hints strongly at his future composition "Spain."

Corea joined the Miles Davis Quintet in late 1968, and at Davis's urging he began playing electric piano. Strangely enough, his two albums as a leader from 1969, **Is** and **Sun Dance**, are acoustic sets that lean toward the avant-garde. All of the music (including the 29-minute "Is") is available on the two-CD set **The Complete "Is" Sessions** (Blue Note 40532) with Corea leading groups that often include trumpeter Woody Shaw, flutist Hubert Laws, and tenor saxophonist Bennie Maupin. The fairly avant-garde music is often rambling (particularly on the second disc) and is not all that memorable, making this mostly a historical curiosity.

After recording **Live at the Fillmore** with Miles Davis in June 1970, Corea went out on his own. Shortly before, Corea had led a trio album, **The Song of Singing** (Blue Note 84353), that looked toward his next phase. Teamed with Dave Holland and drummer Barry Altschul, Corea performs avant-garde music that is influenced by the Art Ensemble of Chicago, including Holland's "Toy Room," "Nefertiti," some spontaneous originals, and Ornette Coleman's "Blues Connotation."

When Corea and Holland left Davis, they formed an avant-garde quartet with Altschul and multireedist Anthony Braxton called Circle. The group lasted for most of a year, and because Corea was fairly well known, they were able to record their forbidding music on several occasions. **Early Circle** (Blue Note 84463) has bass/piano and clarinet/piano duets, two versions of "Chimes," "Percussion Piece," a free ballad, and Braxton's "73 Degrees Kelvin." **A.R.C.** (ECM 833 678) has the trio (without Braxton) in January 1971 playing explorative music (if not as free as that performed by Circle) including four Corea originals, Holland's "Vedana," and Wayne

Shorter's "Nefertiti." The double CD **Paris Concert** (ECM 843 163) is the last and best recording by Circle. The quartet performs a wide variety of fairly free explorations including the playful "Toy Room—Q & A," "73 Degrees Kelvin," and fresh reinterpretations of "There Is No Greater Love" and "Nefertiti."

When Chick Corea left Miles Davis's band, it was because he was interested in playing more adventurous music. But having swung so far in that direction with Circle, he soon tired of the lack of structure and expressed a desire to perform music that would communicate to a larger number of people. In the spring of 1971 Corea left Circle, leading to the group's breakup, with Holland and Altschul joining Braxton's new band. Corea's first solo project after departing Circle was a pair of solo piano albums titled **Piano Improvisations Vol. 1** (ECM 811 979) and **Vol. 2** (ECM 829 190). The first volume has six of Corea's originals including the eight sketches of "Where Are You Now" and the debut of "Sometime Ago" while **Vol. 2** has seven more of the pianist's tunes plus Thelonious Monk's "Trinkle Tinkle" and Wayne Shorter's "Masqualero." In general, the brief sketches are melodic and a bit precious but contain some strong moments and are reasonably enjoyable if not essential.

In late 1971 Chick Corea formed the initial version of Return to Forever, a quintet with Joe Farrell on soprano, flute, and tenor, Stanley Clarke on bass, Airto Moreira on drums/percussion, and Moreira's wife Flora Purim on vocals. This band featured Brazilian fusion, Corea's originals, and a light feel that caused it to stand out from the field in early fusion. Two recordings resulted. **Return to Forever** (ECM 811 978), the group's first album, strangely enough went unreleased until 1975. Most memorable is a long medley of "Sometime Ago" and "La Fiesta." **Light As a Feather** (Polygram 557 145) has been reissued as a double CD, with the original program joined by more than an hour of alternate takes and formerly lost material. This set has the original version of Corea's "Spain" (still his best-known composition), along with memorable renditions of "500 Miles High" and "Captain Marvel." Corea's work on the Fender Rhodes electric piano is distinctive and tasteful, Clarke shows off his virtuosity in places, and this was a well-integrated band, with Purim's vocals featuring some of her best work.

Considering its artistic and commercial success, it is a bit of surprise that this version of Return to Forever only lasted a year before Flora and Airto went out on their own. Having dipped his toes into the world of fusion, Corea now dove in enthusiastically. The second version of Return to Forever was active and recording by 1973 and quite a bit different from its predecessor because it featured Corea and Clarke in an electric quartet with guitarist Bill Connors and drummer Lenny White. The music on ● **Hymn of the Seventh Galaxy** (Polydor 825 336) is quite rock oriented but has the adventure and complex improvising of jazz. "Captain Senor Mouse" and "Hymn of the Seventh Galaxy" are fusion classics and, although Connors would soon leave the group to concentrate mostly on acoustic guitar (tossing away his chance at stardom), he shows that he fit perfectly into this legendary band.

Stanley Clarke was at his best during his years with Return to Forever, and he emerged on **Hymn of the Seventh Galaxy** as the first truly significant electric bassist. Formerly the electric bass was mostly used in jazz as a double, and most acoustic players found it difficult to establish their own personality on the instrument. Clarke had started out playing in R&B and rock bands while in high school in Philadelphia. In the early 1970s he worked briefly with Pharoah Sanders, Gil Evans, Horace Silver, Stan Getz, Dexter Gordon, and Art Blakey before joining Return to Forever. A virtuoso on the acoustic bass, Clarke had no problem becoming a major force on electric bass, and although always interested in funk and rock, he proved that he could play jazz with the best when he had the desire. He recorded a few solo albums during his period with Corea including **Children of Forever** (Polydor 30340), which from 1972 also features Corea, Lenny White, and singer Dee Dee Bridgewater (and is related stylewise to the emerging Return to Forever), **Stanley Clarke** (Epic 36973), and **Journey to Love** (Epic 36974). The latter two albums (from 1974–75), while showcasing Clarke's brilliant playing, show that his main interests were leaning more toward funk than jazz, with keyboardist George Duke playing a major role on **Journey to Love**.

In 1976 Clarke recorded his most famous solo album, **School Days** (Epic 36975). Most notable for the leader's virtuoso playing, this set features the funk side of fusion and is of more interest to rock listeners and fellow bassists than to jazz and even fusion fans. Best is a trio number, "Desert Song," with John McLaughlin and percussionist Milton Holland, but most of the rest of the set lacks any real subtlety, hinting strongly at Clarke's future funk projects.

Like Stanley Clarke, Lenny White was at his most creative when he was a sideman. The versatile White started fast, playing regularly with Jackie McLean in 1968 when he was 19 and participating in Miles Davis's **Bitches Brew** sessions. White freelanced with jazz greats Freddie Hubbard, Joe Henderson, Woody Shaw, Gato Barbieri, Gil Evans, and Stan Getz, among others, before joining Return to Forever.

With the departure of Bill Connors, Chick Corea had to find a replacement fast. Fortunately, he discovered a fiery young guitarist who had not turned 20 yet but already had his style together, Al DiMeola. Return to Forever was DiMeola's first significant playing job, and his passionate and rockish style added to the group's appeal. **Where Have I Known You Before** (Polydor 825 206), DiMeola's debut with the group, is a high energy set from the summer of 1974 that is filled with explosive moments. Brief interludes separate the main pieces: "Vulcan Worlds," "The Shadow of Lo," "Beyond the Seventh Galaxy," "Earth Juice," and the lengthy "Song to the Pharoah Kings." **No Mystery** (Polydor 827 149) has originals by each of the musicians (including the guitarist's "Flight of the Newborn"), but it is obvious that Corea is the band's top composer. His "No Mystery" and the two-part "Celebration Suite" take honors.

By 1975, Return to Forever was so popular that the group could fill rock stadiums. Although Corea enjoyed the music overall, its lack of subtlety and emphasis on complex rockish pieces probably led him to begin looking elsewhere for variety. His recording **The Leprechaun** (Polydor 519 798) is a jazz-oriented effort, featuring Corea with such players as Joe Farrell, trombonist Bill Watrous, and bassist Eddie Gomez, plus Chick's wife Gayle Moran on some vocals. Despite some fine individual moments, the material (mostly Corea's originals) is largely forgettable, and this was only considered a temporary departure from Return to Forever at the time.

In 1976, the most famous version of Return to Forever recorded what would be their final album, **Romantic Warrior** (Columbia/Legacy 65524). One listens in vain to this music for any hints of the group's decline and upcoming breakup. The music at times shows the influence of baroque music, and Corea plays a bit more acoustic piano than normal, but Return to Forever

sounds as strong as ever, continuing to set the standard for fusion bands. However, the group's dissolution was somewhat inevitable because of Al DiMeola's growing popularity, Stanley Clarke's interest in playing funk, and Corea's adventurous spirit. After three years, Return to Forever was no more. There would be a third version of the group in 1977, a nine-piece group with Corea, Clarke, Joe Farrell, and Gayle Moran that lasted for a few months, but things would not be the same.

Al DiMeola had no difficulty finding work when Return to Forever ended. Although he had a reputation for playing an excess of notes (he was as fast as the more versatile John McLaughlin) and for not putting as much feeling into his playing as he should, the criticisms were exaggerated and dealt with over time. **Land of the Midnight Sun** (Columbia 34074) has the 22-year-old guitarist showing his range on such complex pieces as the three-part "Suite-Golden Dawn," an acoustic duet with Corea on "Short Tales of the Black Forest," and a brief Bach violin sonata. DiMeola is assisted along the way by both Jaco Pastorius and Stanley Clarke on basses, Barry Miles on keyboards, and Lenny White and Steve Gadd on drums. **Elegant Gypsy** (Columbia 34461) teams DiMeola with Jan Hammer or Barry Miles, Anthony Jackson, Lenny White or Steve Gadd, and percussionist Mingo Lewis on most of the selections. Although DiMeola was clearly a stronger guitarist than composer, he did put a lot of thought into this music and the care shows. In addition to the passionate fusion pieces, the brief "Lady of Rome, Sister of Brazil" (an acoustic guitar solo) and "Mediterranean Sundance" (an acoustic duet with fellow guitarist Paco de Lucía) hint at DiMeola's growing interest in the acoustic guitar that he would explore in the future.

Later in 1976 for his own first post–Return to Forever solo album, Corea recorded the classic ● **My Spanish Heart** (Polydor 543303). Corea, along with Herbie Hancock and Joe Zawinul, was always one of the most distinctive of all electric keyboardists, having his own sound on electric pianos and synths along with his impish wit. This set puts the emphasis on both his keyboards and his Latin heritage with plenty of fresh new melodies (the last section of "El Bozo" is particularly catchy) and an inventive use of electronic instruments. There are appearances by Gayle Moran, a brass section, drummer Steve Gadd, and percussionist Don Alias, plus cameos from Stanley Clarke and violinist Jean-Luc Ponty, but the focus is almost entirely on Corea and he creates a particularly memorable set.

Counting the final version of Return to Forever, Chick Corea would be involved in one rewarding short-lived project after another for the next decade, not choosing to have a regular band again until 1986.

Herbie Hancock's Sextet and Headhunters For Herbie Hancock, the 1968–75 period was a very busy and episodic period. He concluded his series of Blue Note recordings with two near classics: **Speak Like a Child** (Blue Note 46136) and **The Prisoner** (Blue Note 25649). **Speak Like a Child** has an intriguing front line comprised of flugelhornist Thad Jones, bass trombonist Peter Phillips, and alto flutist Jerry Dodgion, with Hancock, Ron Carter, and Mickey Roker completing the sextet. The haunting tone colors on the four sextet numbers (two are features for the trio) make this a very atmospheric set, one that favorably shows off Hancock's progress on the piano. **The Prisoner** was recorded in 1969 shortly after the keyboardist had left Miles Davis and is a mostly upbeat tribute to the late Martin Luther King, Jr. Hancock utilizes a nonet that includes flugelhornist Johnny Coles, trombonist Garnett Brown, flutist Hubert Laws, and tenor saxophonist Joe Henderson on music that manages to be both challenging and accessible.

In 1969, Hancock formed a very interesting sextet that lasted into 1972. Originally the band consisted of trumpeter Jimmy Owens, Garnett Brown, Joe Henderson, bassist Buster Williams, and either Albert "Tootie" Heath or Bernard Purdie on drums. That unit (with some guests) recorded a set of jazz interpretations of numbers from Bill Cosby's cartoon series *Fat Albert Rotunda*. By 1970 the group consisted of Hancock, Williams, drummer Billy Hart, trumpeter Eddie Henderson, trombonist Julian Priester, and Bennie Maupin on reeds. ❍ **Mwandishi: The Complete Warner Bros. Recordings** (Warner Archives 45732) is a two-CD set that has all of the music from *Fat Albert Rotunda* and the sessions that resulted in **Mwandishi** and **Crossings**. Although hinting at Hancock's interest in the funkier side of jazz, the music is also quite adventurous, electronic (with Patrick Gleeson adding his synthesizer to the **Crossings** album), and unpredictable, bordering at times at both fusion and avant-garde jazz. The Herbie Hancock Sextet recorded one further album, 1972's **Sextant** (Columbia/

Legacy 64983). Once again the music is fascinating, being both funky and explorative, with three lengthy selections that make the most out of the simplest riffs. All of the music by this Hancock ensemble deserves to be heard several times for it is unlike any other group of the period and like few since.

Unfortunately, the Herbie Hancock Sextet was a commercial flop, and Hancock soon became frustrated at its inability to attract an audience. In early 1973 he gave up on the sextet and switched directions, forming the Headhunters. Although Weather Report in its early days was an experimental group that utilized electronics and Return to Forever combined together rock and jazz, the Headhunters mixed jazz with funk and R&B rather than with rock, being inspired more by James Brown than Jimi Hendrix. Comprised of Hancock, Maupin, electric bassist Paul Jackson, drummer Harvey Mason, and percussionist Bill Summers, the band recorded a major seller in ❍ **Headhunters** (Columbia/Legacy 65123), highlighted by its hit version of "Chameleon" and a funky remake of "Watermelon Man." 1974's **Thrust** (Columbia/Legacy 64984), which has Mike Clark taking over on drums, is in a similar vein with four lengthy Hancock tunes, including the ballad "Butterfly," with the emphasis otherwise on funk and the leader's synthesizers. **Secrets** (Sony 65460) from 1976 has Hancock, Maupin, and Jackson assisted by Wah Wah Watson and Ray Parker on guitars, along with drummer James Levi, performing such dance music as "Doin' It," "Swamp Rat," "People Music," and an abstract visit to "Canteloupe Island." Although a bit predictable (certainly much more than Weather Report's music), the Headhunters' brand of danceable funky jazz definitely has its appeal.

On June 29, 1976, George Wein and the Newport Jazz Festival presented a retrospective of Herbie Hancock's career. The performances, put out on the double LP **V.S.O.P.** (Columbia 34688) but surprisingly not on CD yet, feature Hancock with three different bands. His 1969–72 sextet with Henderson, Priester, and Maupin (in their only reunion) are typically explorative on "Toys" and "You'll Know When You Get There," and the Headhunters (performing "Hang Up Your Hang Ups" and "Spider") are heard during what would be their last recording. However, the group that gained all of the attention was a reunion of the Miles Davis Quintet with Freddie Hubbard in Davis's place; Miles turned down the chance to appear. Hancock, Wayne Shorter, Ron Carter, Tony Williams, and Hubbard perform inventive post-bop versions of "Maiden Voyage," "Nefertiti," and "Eye of the Hurricane." Their playing is at such a high level that the group would tour the following year. For many, it signaled the end of fusion and the comeback of acoustic jazz; never mind that Hancock would alternate between electric and acoustic music for many more years to come.

Tony Williams's Lifetime   Tony Williams had helped persuade Miles Davis to open his music to the avant-garde in 1964, helping to push George Coleman out of Davis's sextet and, after unsuccessfully lobbying for Sam Rivers (who was just with the trumpeter for a Japanese tour), happily accepting Wayne Shorter in the band. By 1968, Williams (who turned 23 that year) was into rock, and he was one of the main factors in Davis changing his music and helping to pioneer fusion. In early 1969, Williams left Miles Davis's band and formed Lifetime, a trio with British guitarist John McLaughlin and organist Larry Young. Just three months after **In a Silent Way** was recorded and several months before **Bitches Brew**, Lifetime recorded ◉ **Emergency** (Polygram 539 117). The eight selections (which originally filled two LPs) practically define fusion, with McLaughlin being one of the first guitarists in decades (other than Larry Coryell) not indebted to Charlie Christian for his phrases and ideas and with Larry Young showing just how innovative an organist he could be. The one fault to this intense set is that the recording quality is disappointing, with a great deal of distortion in spots. Released in 1970, **Turn It Over** (Polygram 239 118) has the trio expanding to a quartet with the addition of Jack Bruce on bass, includes a forgettable vocal by Williams, is much more rock oriented, and has overly concise performances, with most of the cuts being shorter than five minutes long. **Ego** (Verve 559 512) is an oddity with more misses than hits. McLaughlin had been succeeded by Ted Dunbar (who is more rockish than expected), Ron Carter is on bass and cello, and there are an excess of vocals by Williams and Bruce.

After a few years of freelancing, in 1975 Tony Williams put together a new version of Lifetime that was reborn as a quartet with guitarist Allan Holdsworth, keyboardist Alan Pasqua, and bassist Tony Newton. Holdsworth, who like McLaughlin was born and raised

in England, did not start on guitar until he was 17 in 1965. He had played with the rock group Tempest prior to joining Williams and, although he had a rockish sound, his conception often allowed him to take the role of a saxophone (his first instrument) or a keyboard. **The Collection** (Columbia/Legacy 47484) has all of the music from this band's existence, consisting of 1975's **Believe It** and the 1976 project **Million Dollar Legs**. The former set is the better of the two, with Holdsworth sometimes hinting at McLaughlin's power and creativity although Newton's occasional vocals are frivolous. Also unnecessary is background brass and strings on some of the numbers on **Million Dollar Legs**. But although a few of the selections are dated, the power of this band and the fire of Williams's drums make this of strong interest to fusion collectors.

John McLaughlin and the Mahavishnu Orchestra Historical revisionists, some black nationalists, and those new to jazz sometimes make the inaccurate statement that all of the jazz innovators have been black Americans. However, it could easily be argued that John McLaughlin, a white British guitarist, was the first innovator on his instrument in jazz since Charlie Christian and Django Reinhardt (another white European). Born in 1942, McLaughlin started on guitar when he was 11 and played both blues and jazz in England with Alexis Korner, Graham Bond, Ginger Baker, and Gunter Hampel in the 1960s. His recording debut as a leader from January 18, 1969, **Extrapolation** (Polygram 841 598), was recorded in London in a quartet with John Surman (on soprano and baritone), featuring ten of the guitarist's early originals. Even at that early stage, McLaughlin (whose control over his guitar was already complete) sounded unlike any of his predecessors.

Shortly after making that recording, McLaughlin moved to New York to join Tony Williams's Lifetime. He had also greatly impressed Miles Davis and was enlisted to be Davis's guitarist on **In a Silent Way** and **Bitches Brew**. In 1970 McLaughlin cut two albums as a leader. **Devotion** (Fuel 2000 61133) is an intriguing transitional recording in which McLaughlin leads a quartet also including Larry Young (from Lifetime), bassist Billy Rich, and drummer Buddy Miles. The jams are closer to rock than jazz (Jimi Hendrix had been on some of the selections next to McLaughlin, but those cuts were not included on the record) and hint at both Lifetime and the music to come. ⬤ **My Goals Beyond** (Knitting Factory Works 3010) is a brilliant set that points to two directions that McLaughlin would take in the future. There are eight unaccompanied acoustic guitar solos (quite a departure for McLaughlin at the time) including several originals ("Follow Your Heart" became a standard), "Goodbye Pork Pie Hat," "Blue in Green," and Chick Corea's "Waltz for Bill Evans." In addition, two longer numbers ("Peace One" and "Peace Two") have McLaughlin exploring Indian rhythms and drones for the first time in a group with Dave Liebman on reeds, Jerry Goodman on violin, Charlie Haden, Billy Cobham, Airto Moreira, Badal Roy on tabla, and Mahalaksmi on tambura.

But McLaughlin's interest in the acoustic guitar and Indian music would have to wait a bit. In 1971 he formed the Mahavishnu Orchestra, the definitive rock-oriented fusion band. Comprised of McLaughlin, Jerry Goodman, keyboardist Jan Hammer, bassist Rick Laird, and Billy Cobham, this was the most powerful of the fusion bands, a true powerhouse that could compete with any rock band in volume and intensity yet was far beyond its competitors in creativity and musicianship. **The Inner Mounting Flame** (Columbia/Legacy 65523) was a startling debut for the band, with fiery solos and ensembles, remarkable unisons, and explosive rhythms. Most jazz listeners were not too interested in the Mahavishnu Orchestra at the time despite its remarkable musicianship, but the band became quite influential on the fusion movement and helped bring some young rockers into jazz. ⬤ **Birds of Fire** (Columbia/Legacy 66081) from 1972 is in a similar vein but has a little more variety and stronger compositions including "One Word" (which has some rapid trades between the players), "Open Country Joy," and "Celestial Terrestrial Commuters." A set originally planned as the group's third album went unreleased until 1999. **The Lost Trident Sessions** (Columbia/Legacy 65959) is explosive with the lengthy "Trilogy" being most memorable. But that album was originally shelved when the group decided to put out the live **Between Nothingness and Eternity** (Columbia/Legacy 32766). Recorded in August 1973 by the same quintet, this album has three lengthy pieces (including another version of "Trilogy") with complex arrangements and lots of speedy playing along with some telepathic interplay. Also of related interest is McLaughlin's 1972 summit meeting with the great Latin rock guitarist Carlos Santana, **Love Devotion Surrender** (Columbia 32034). It was a real stretch for Santana, who holds his own with McLaughlin during an intense spiritual set that includes "A Love Supreme," "Naima," and "Let Us Go into the House of the Lord."

Personality conflicts brought the original Mahavishnu Orchestra to an end later in 1973. McLaughlin put together a new version of the group, featuring violinist Jean-Luc Ponty, singer/keyboardist Gayle Moran (Chick Corea's future wife), bassist Ralphe Armstrong, and drummer Michael Walden. But despite the inclusion of Ponty, this ensemble never really caught on and was much less interesting. **Apocalypse** (Columbia 46111) is a rather dull meeting of the group with the London Symphony Orchestra under the direction of Michael Tilson Thomas and, although **Visions of the Emerald Beyond** (Columbia 46867) is better, the title of "Can't Stand Your Funk" seems to sum up this surprisingly mundane band.

By mid-1975 after just a year, McLaughlin broke up the second version of the Mahavishnu Orchestra and headed in a completely different direction. He formed Shakti, a quintet in which his acoustic guitar was matched with L. Shankar's violin, Ramnad Raghaven's mridangam, T.S. Vinayakaram's ghatan, and Zakir Hussain's tabla. The setting was certainly much different for McLaughlin with pieces influenced by Indian classical music, but his guitar was still full of fire (even if it was now unplugged) and passion, as shown on the group's debut album **Shakti** (Sony 467905). As with Miles Davis, John McLaughlin was more interested in personal growth and evolution than he was with sticking with the same band and concept for too many years.

Other Fusion Groups

By the early 1970s, fusion was dominating jazz in sales, exposure, and its appeal to young musicians and fans. In addition to the pacesetters covered in the last section, many groups and individuals were making strong contributions to the new style.

Gary Burton's Quartet/Quintet   Although Gary Burton's bands of 1968–75 fit more into post-bop than fusion, he is listed here because his group in 1967 featured Larry Coryell (and was therefore groundbreaking) and because his units served as a launching pad for several of the top advanced jazz guitarists of the era.

After a final album with Burton in 1968 (the LP **In Concert**), Coryell left the group, with Jerry Hahn being his successor during most of 1968–69. **Country Roads and Other Places** (Koch 7854) has the Burton-Hahn-Steve Swallow-Roy Haynes quartet exploring melodic and open-minded jazz and incorporating elements of country, rock, pop, and even classical music in a repertoire ranging from "My Foolish Heart" and a "Ravel Prelude" to "Wichita Breakdown." **Gary Burton & Keith Jarrett/Throb** (Rhino 71594) has all of the music from two unrelated Burton dates. **Throb** features the 1969 Burton group (with Bill Goodwin on drums and violinist Richard Greene added), performing obscurities mostly from Swallow and Michael Gibbs that have an unusual avant-country flavor. The date with Keith Jarrett (from 1970 with guitarist Sam Brown who took Hahn's place, Swallow, and Goodwin) has pianist Jarrett and Burton sounding very complementary playing four post-bop originals by the vibraphonist plus Swallow's "Come en Vietnam."

In addition to the Keith Jarrett date, two of Gary Burton's most rewarding sessions from the period were departures from his group projects. On **Paris Encounter** (Label M 5738), Burton, Swallow, and Goodwin team up with violinist Stephane Grappelli for swinging standards (a rarity for the vibraphonist) and newer pieces including Swallow's "Eiderdown." **Alone at Last** (32 Jazz 32115) has three selections in which Burton overdubs vibes with piano, electric piano, and organ, but it is his three unaccompanied vibes showcases from the 1971 Montreux Jazz Festival and one slightly later studio solo that are most memorable. The latter resulted in a remarkable version of "Chega de Saudade (No More Blues)" that has Burton sounding like three vibraphonists at once, one of the high points of his career.

After leaving the Atlantic label, Gary Burton began a longtime association with ECM, starting with his impressive set of acoustic duets with Chick Corea, **Crystal Silence** (ECM 831 331). Burton and Corea (taking a brief vacation from Return to Forever) would always make for a mutually compatible team, as best shown on these versions of "Senor Mouse," "Crystal Silence," and "Children's Song." **The New Quartet** features Burton, guitarist Mick Goodrick, bassist Abraham Laboriel, and drummer Harry Blazer playing numbers by Corea ("Open Your Eyes, You Can Fly"), Keith Jarrett ("Coral"), Gordon Beck, Carla Bley, and Mike Gibbs, plus Burton's

"Brownout." Burton's ECM releases would in general be more introverted and laidback than his earlier RCA sets, and his approach fit in well with that of producer Manfred Eicher, particularly on **Hotel Hello** (ECM 835 586) and **Matchbook** (ECM 835 014), which are quiet duet encounters with Swallow and guitarist Ralph Towner (from the group Oregon). Released in 1974, **Ring** (ECM 829 191) teams Burton's quintet with bassist Eberhard Weber but is most significant for featuring both Mick Goodrick and Pat Metheny on guitars; Metheny would be with Burton's group for the next three years. **Dreams So Real** (ECM 1072), a set of Carla Bley songs from December 1975 (including "Ictus/Syndrome," "Vos Humana," and "Intermission Music"), is a memorable outing from the Burton-Goodrick-Metheny-Swallow-Bob Moses quintet.

For Burton, 1976's **Passengers** (ECM 835 016) was the end of an era. His quartet/quintet had been an important training ground for such guitarists as Larry Coryell, Jerry Hahn, Sam Brown, Mick Goodrick, and Pat Metheny; John Scofield would be with Burton in 1977 (although that version of the group did not record). **Passengers** was the last of the Burton guitar recordings, a quintet outing with Metheny (his lone record with the vibraphonist in which he was the only guitarist), both Steve Swallow and Eberhard Weber on bass, and Danny Gottlieb on drums. The group performs numbers by Metheny, Swallow, Weber, and Chick Corea ("Sea Journey"), giving listeners a strong sampling of how the rapidly emerging Metheny sounded in his early days.

Billy Cobham's Spectrum   Billy Cobham emerged during the late 1960s/early '70s and was quickly recognized as one of fusion's top drummers. Born in Panama, he moved with his family to New York when he was three. Cobham served in the army during 1965–68 (playing in military bands), spent eight months with Horace Silver in 1968, and then became greatly in-demand for sessions, jazz dates, and fusion groups. His powerful drumming can be heard with Miles Davis on **Bitches Brew**, **Live/Evil**, and **Jack Johnson** and on records led during the era by quite a few jazz all-stars including Gene Ammons, George Benson, Kenny Burrell, Larry Coryell, Freddie Hubbard, Milt Jackson, Hubert Laws, and Stanley Turrentine. Cobham gained fame as a member of the Mahavishnu Orchestra during its greatest period (1971–73). In 1973, he formed his own group, Spectrum, and recorded a couple enjoyable dates for Atlantic. The debut recording, **Spectrum** (Rhino/Atlantic 7268), was his best because of some strong tunes (most memorably "Red Baron") and consistently rewarding playing. Cobham is heard in an electric quartet with keyboardist Jan Hammer, guitarist Tommy Bolin, and electric bassist Lee Sklar; two songs match Cobham with Joe Farrell on flute and soprano, Jimmy Owens on trumpet, John Tropea on guitar, Hammer, Ron Carter, and Ray Barretto. This set perfectly balances rockish rhythms with jazz improvising. **Crosswinds** (Rhino/Atlantic 7300), which is almost at the same level, has the four-part "Spanish Moss—A Sound Portrait" and three other pieces, all written by Cobham. The drummer is joined by guitarist John Abercrombie, both trumpeter Randy Brecker and tenor saxophonist Michael Brecker, trombonist Garnett Brown, George Duke, bassist John Williams, and percussionist Lee Pastora for a funky yet sometimes swinging set. **Shabazz** (Wounded Bird 8139) has a similar group (with trombonist Glenn Ferris, Milcho Leviev on keyboards, and John Scofield joining Abercrombie on guitars) performing live. "Red Baron" is heard in a fresh version, and the musicians have opportunities to stretch out on the four numbers. But by 1975 Cobham's band had become much more electronic and funk oriented, and his importance to jazz was beginning to greatly decrease.

Larry Coryell and Eleventh House   With the rise in prominence of John McLaughlin and Al DiMeola, Larry Coryell was overshadowed during the prime fusion years, in a way not dissimilar to how arranger Don Redman was consistently overlooked by the jazz press during the swing era. As with Redman, Coryell had been among the earliest to emerge in his field, leading the way for others to follow.

Coryell had debuted with Chico Hamilton in 1966 and was an important member of the Gary Burton Quartet during 1967–68. After he went out on his own, he recorded with Herbie Mann, was involved in a group called Foreplay in 1969, and recorded regularly in a variety of settings for Vanguard. **Lady Coryell** (Vanguard 6509) from 1968 mostly has Coryell playing both guitar and overdubbed bass in a trio with drummer Bobby Moses, but it is most notable for his duet with drummer Elvin Jones on "Stiff Neck" and a trio version of "Treats Style" with Jones and Jimmy Garrison. **Basics** (Universe

20) from 1968–69 has its moments of interest as Coryell is joined by organist Mike Mandel in a quintet on most cuts, but it is quite brief at just 31 minutes of music. Best of these early efforts is **Spaces** (Vanguard 79345) because two selections match Coryell with John McLaughlin, Miroslav Vitous (doubling on cello), and Billy Cobham. "Rene's Theme" is a guitar duet with McLaughlin; "Gloria's Steps" has Coryell, Vitous, and Cobham jamming as a trio; and Chick Corea sits in on electric piano for "Chris." These intriguing and informal matchups mostly work quite well.

Offering (Universe 28) from 1972 directly preceded the formation of Coryell's Eleventh House. It teams Coryell with Mike Mandel on keyboards, Steve Marcus on soprano, Melvin Bronson on bass, and Harry Wilkinson on drums on six originals. None of the tunes would catch on but some are quite melodic, and the soloists sound inspired. Later in the year Coryell formed Eleventh House, a quintet with Mandel, trumpeter Randy Brecker (who was soon replaced by Mike Lawrence), bassist Danny Trifan, and drummer Alphonse Mouzon (who was eventually considered a co-leader). The band lasted into 1975, recorded several sets, and although it did not catch on to the level of Weather Report, Return to Forever, or the Mahavishnu Orchestra, it did create some worthwhile fusion along the way. **Introducing the Eleventh House** (Vanguard 79342) displays the influence of Miles Davis, Weather Report, and Herbie Hancock, but because of the instrumentation, the distinctive grooves, and the interplay between Coryell and Mandel, the band displays a personality of its own. **At Montreux** (Vanguard 79410) from 1974 is a rather brief 34-minute CD, but the music is excellent. Coryell starts by playing unaccompanied acoustic guitar on a classical piece, and then there are four passionate group originals full of fire before a "The Eleventh House Blues" serves as a strong conclusion. **Planet End** (Vanguard 79367) from 1975 marked the end of both Eleventh House and Coryell's original association with the Vanguard label. Eleventh House is featured on two numbers, Coryell plays all of the instruments on the brief "The Eyes of Love," and two lengthy jams team him with John McLaughlin, Miroslav Vitous, Billy Cobham, and (on "Tyrone") Chick Corea. Once again, the CD is just 34 minutes long, but the high quality of the solos makes this one worth picking up.

By 1976 Coryell, the pioneer of fusion guitar, had become more interested in playing acoustic guitar. He recorded duet guitar albums with Steve Khan, the LP **Two for the Road** (Arista 4156), and Phillip Catherine, **Twin House** (ACT 9202). For these encounters, Coryell performed both originals and occasional standards while turning his back on fusion, at least for the moment.

Gil Evans Orchestra   After being off records during 1964–68, arranger Gil Evans became more active again. In fact, by 1970 he was leading an orchestra on a regular basis in New York clubs, and he recorded five notable albums during 1969–75. One might not think of Evans as leading a fusion band, but his large ensemble by 1969 was among the most successful in blending together acoustic and electric instruments. **Blues in Orbit** (Enja 79611) has several particularly memorable performances including a colorful and witty reworking of George Russell's "Blues in Orbit." The key soloists include Jimmy Cleveland, Howard Johnson on tuba and baritone sax, tenor saxophonist Billy Harper, and guitarist Joe Beck. **Where Flamingos Fly** (A&M 75021-0831) has Evans heading two different but overlapping units ranging from ten to fifteen pieces. He utilizes synthesizers for the first time and there is plenty of solo space for Billy Harper and Howard Johnson, but it is Evans's writing that makes this set a standout. Highlights include "Zee Zee," "Hotel Me," "Where Flamingos Fly," and a 17½-minute version of "El Matador."

Svengali (Koch 8518) ranks with much of Evans's best work. This version of "Blues in Orbit" features the young altoist David Sanborn, and all six selections (including a remake of "Summertime") have their memorable moments. Harper, Johnson, guitarist Ted Dunbar, and bassist Herb Bushler are among the key soloists. Negotiations were underway for Gil Evans to write for a big band on a Jimi Hendrix record when the innovative rock guitarist passed away. In 1974 Evans recorded **Plays the Music of Jimi Hendrix** (Bluebird 25755), exploring Hendrix's compositions with a unique 19-piece unit. The orchestra includes two French horns, the tuba of Howard Johnson, three guitars, two basses, two percussionists, and such soloists as David Sanborn, trumpeter Hannibal Marvin Peterson, Billy Harper, and guitarists Ryo Kawasaki and John Abercrombie. Evans's charts bring some of Hendrix's more blues-oriented tunes back to life, and the result is a rock-oriented but creative set of often-surprising music. The CD reissue of ● **There Comes a Time** (BMG 31392) differs quite a bit from the original LP of the same name, adding three previously unreleased performances, expanding "The Meaning of the Blues" from six to 20 minutes, dropping two numbers, and re-editing four other tracks. The remake of Jelly Roll Morton's "King Porter Stomp" (with David Sanborn in Cannonball Adderley's former spot and an arrangement that hints at the earlier version) is a classic, the expanded version of "The Meaning of the Blues" is memorable, and the music overall is quite rewarding; among the stars are Billy Harper, George Adams on tenors, and Lew Soloff on trumpet. This was one of Gil Evans's last significant recordings.

Pat Metheny   Pat Metheny, who would develop into one of the most significant and distinctive jazz guitarists, was at the beginning of his career during the first half of the 1970s. He started on guitar when he was 13 in 1967 and developed so quickly that he both studied and taught at the University of Miami and Berklee College of Music while still a teenager. In 1974 he made his earliest recording with Jaco Pastorius and Paul Bley on **Jaco** (Improvising Artists 123846), and although his sound was not quite together yet, he would evolve very quickly. Metheny worked with Gary Burton's Quartet/Quintet during 1974–77 and recorded his debut as a leader, **Bright Size Life** (ECM 827 133). This intriguing trio date with Pastorius and drummer Bob Moses has an inventive use of space on ballads that reflect Metheny's upbringing in Missouri, hints of both rock and Wes Montgomery, and an intriguing medley of Ornette Coleman tunes ("Round Trip" and "Broadway Blues"). This CD serves as an impressive beginning for Pat Metheny.

Jaco Pastorius   When the electric bass began to be used on a regular basis in jazz in the late 1960s, most of the players were acoustic bassists who were doubling. Few were able to develop an original personality on electric bass, and virtually all of them would have sounded better on acoustic. The first bassist in jazz to display an individual style on electric bass was Stanley Clarke with Return to Forever although eventually his main interest switched to funk. The second was Jaco Pastorius, who was even more distinctive than Clarke and who played his instrument with the agility and forcefulness of a guitarist.

Pastorius began his career working in Fort Lauderdale, Florida (where he grew up), with local R&B and pop groups. He was born late in 1951, and the electric bass was his main instrument from 1969 on; rarely in his life did he ever play acoustic. On the jazz side, Pastorius gigged with Ira Sullivan, and in 1974 he was in New York playing with Pat Metheny in a group led by Paul Bley. **Jaco** (Improvising Artists 123846) was originally Bley's date, but Pastorius played so well that the keyboardist released it under his name. The quartet (keyboardist Bley, Metheny, Pastorius, and drummer Bruce Ditmas) performs three songs by Bley, five from Carla Bley, and "Blood" by Annette Peacock. The recording quality is shaky and Metheny's tone is very distorted (he did not quite sound like himself yet), but Pastorius was already quite innovative.

The turning point in Jaco's career was 1976. He played and recorded in a trio with German trombonist Albert Mangelsdorff, joined Weather Report (replacing Alphonso Johnson), and recorded the album ❶ **Jaco** (Epic 33949). This set, which had a major impact at the time, starts with Pastorius playing "Donna Lee" as an unaccompanied electric bass solo (other than some background percussion from Don Alias), and then he performs eight of his rather diverse arrangements (plus two bonus tracks on the CD reissue) with such players as Herbie Hancock, Wayne Shorter, Hubert Laws, and the Brecker Brothers among others. Ranging from post-bop

jazz and mood pieces to funky jams, everything works on this inventive and continually intriguing set.

After **Jaco** was released, there was no doubt that the electric bass had found its first major innovator.

Jean-Luc Ponty   The first major jazz violinist to emerge since the swing era, Jean-Luc Ponty started his career (once he switched from classical music) performing advanced jazz, first visiting the United States to participate in a workshop at the 1967 Monterey Jazz Festival. In 1969 while visiting California, he met and played with pianist George Duke and jammed with rock guitarist Frank Zappa. In France he led the Jean-Luc Ponty Experience (1970–72), a fusion group. He spent a period playing with Frank Zappa's Mothers of Invention and was a member of the second version of the Mahavishnu Orchestra (1974–75) before permanently going out on his own.

Live at Donte's (Blue Note 35635) from March 1969 went unreleased for many years, but it is a historic set, featuring Ponty playing with the George Duke Trio about the time that he first met Frank Zappa. The music on this date is relatively straightahead and influenced by the work of the mid-1960s Miles Davis Quintet. Also, it is interesting to hear the future funkster Duke sounding like a mixture of McCoy Tyner and Herbie Hancock. **King Kong** (Blue Note 89539), the violinist's first fusion

TIMELINE 1969

Miles Davis records **In a Silent Way** and **Bitches Brew**. • Herbie Hancock forms a sextet. • Tony Williams leaves Miles Davis's group to form Lifetime with John McLaughlin and Larry Young. • "The Creator Has a Master Plan" is a surprise hit for Pharoah Sanders and Leon Thomas. • Duke Ellington's 70th birthday is celebrated at the White House. • Joanne Brackeen joins the Jazz Messengers. • Charles Mingus returns to active playing after three years off the scene. • The ECM label debuts with a record by Mal Waldron. • Gene Ammons gets out of prison after seven years and makes a comeback. • The Firehouse Five Plus Two records their final album. • Budd Johnson forms the JPJ Quartet. • Many of the key AACM members visit Paris including the Art Ensemble of Chicago, Anthony Braxton, Leo Smith, and Leroy Jenkins. • Arthur Blythe (at the time known as Black Arthur) records in Los Angeles with pianist Horace Tapscott. • Trumpeter Cecil Bridgewater and tenor saxophonist Ron Bridgewater team up in the short-lived Bridgewater Brothers Band. • Alan Broadbent joins Woody Herman's Orchestra as pianist and arranger. • Trumpeter Ian Carr organizes the fusion band Nucleus. • Richie Cole is a member of the Buddy Rich big band. • Jon Eardley moves to Germany. • Stride pianist Cliff Jackson makes his last recordings. • Red Norvo plays with George Wein's Newport All-Stars and makes his first record of the 1960s. • Altoist Norris Turney joins the Duke Ellington Orchestra and becomes his first flute soloist. • Joe Venuti and Stephane Grappelli record together. • Billy Taylor becomes the first black band director for a network television series, the *David Frost Show*. • The Gerald Wilson Orchestra records its final of 11 albums for the Pacific Jazz label. • The Charles Lloyd Quartet breaks up. • Les McCann and Eddie Harris have a successful set at the Montreux Jazz Festival.

project, has Ponty playing six Zappa compositions including the lengthy "Music for Electric Violin and Low Budget Orchestra," "Twenty Small Cigars," and "How Would You Like to Have a Head Like That"; Zappa appears on the latter song. This unusual early fusion album (which is both rockish and avant-garde in spots) also has contributions from Duke, bassist Buell Neidlinger, and saxophonist Ernie Watts in the sextet/septet.

After his period back in France and his tours with Zappa and Mahavishnu ended, Ponty signed with the Atlantic label and began a series of influential fusion albums. Released in 1975, **Upon the Wings of Music** (Atlantic 18138) has Ponty's group with keyboardist Patrice Rushen, Dan Sawyer, or Ray Parker on guitars, bassist Ralphe Armstrong, and drummer Ndugu performing eight of his complex but spirited originals. The same can be said for **Aurora** (Atlantic 19158), which has Rushen, guitarist Darryl Stuermer, electric bassist Tom Fowler, and drummer Norman Fearrington, and **Imaginary Journey** (Atlantic 19136). The latter, which includes a four-part suite titled "Imaginary Voyage," features Ponty, Stuermer, keyboardist Allan Zavod, Fowler, and drummer Mark Craney. There are times when the electrified violin, keyboards, guitar, and even the electric bass all sound very similar tonewise. The high musicianship and the group's spirit (even with the constant change in personnel) make these Atlantic sets a joy for fusion fans to hear.

Miles Davis: 1970–1975

Quite typically, Miles Davis did not stand still after recording **Bitches Brew**. In fact, those of his older fans who write off his post-1969 music as all "sounding the same" were obviously not listening closely because his music continued evolving while carving out a few possible paths for fusion. **Big Fun** (Columbia/Legacy 63973), a double CD, is a mixture of selections from 1969–72, some meandering and a few (such as the quintet numbers "Lonely Fire" and "Go Ahead John") being quite coherent. The original double-LP program has been expanded from four to eight selections and, even if not all of the music is that essential, Davis is joined by several all-star casts. **Live at the Fillmore East** (Columbia/Legacy 85191) has the final performance of Wayne Shorter in Davis's working group. This set (a double CD like all of Davis's recordings of the period other than **Jack Johnson** and **On the Corner**) features Davis's quintet performing nine numbers on March 7, 1970 (including several tunes from **Bitches Brew**); the

lineup teams Davis with Shorter, Chick Corea, Dave Holland, Jack DeJohnette, and guest percussionist Airto Moreira. The young rock audience must have been shocked to hear this unusual music for **Bitches Brew** was still a month away from being released.

Miles Davis, like Charles Lloyd a few years earlier, was occasionally booked at rock palaces during this era, opening for rock groups who the audience had actually come out to see. **Black Beauty** (Columbia/Legacy 65138) from April 10 has Steve Grossman (soprano and tenor) in Shorter's place and the band (captured at the Fillmore West) once again playing some songs from **Bitches Brew** (including "Miles Runs the Voodoo Down," Joe Zawinul's "Directions," and "Spanish Key") although in much more abstract fashion. **Miles Davis at Fillmore** (Columbia/Legacy 65139) from June 17–20 has Keith Jarrett added to the group on electric keyboards (mostly organ) and is generally self-indulgent, with Corea and Jarrett constantly battling each other and sounding like they are doing their best to destroy their keyboards. The lengthy jams (one apiece from four nights) are actually loose medleys, and it is humorous how each night ends with Davis playing the familiar line from "The Theme" as in the old days. But overall, this set is of lesser interest despite a few good trumpet solos.

The studio set ◐ **Live/Evil** (Columbia/Legacy 65135) has some of Davis's best playing of the era with the most rewarding selections ("What I Say" and "Funky Tonk") featuring his late-1970 band comprised of Gary Bartz on soprano and alto, John McLaughlin, Keith Jarrett, the funky electric bassist Michael Henderson, Jack DeJohnette, and Airto Moreira. The tunes themselves are simple, but the ensembles become quite crowded and unpredictable. A few of the other numbers are from the end of the Wayne Shorter period in the band (a medley of "Gemini" and "Double Image") or from Steve Grossman's stint with Davis. **A Tribute to Jack Johnson** (Columbia/Legacy 47036), as with all of Davis's studio recordings of the 1970s, is essentially edited together excerpts from jam sessions. A rather strange soundtrack to a film on the early 20th-century boxer, this music is much better standing apart from the movie because of some particularly strong solos by Davis, Grossman on soprano, Herbie Hancock, and (on "Yesternow") guitarist Sonny Sharrock.

Other than some bootlegs of live recordings, Davis did not record in 1971. The trumpeter's most controversial work was in his next period. When **On the Corner** (Columbia/Legacy 63980) was initially released, it received both rave reviews for its strange uniqueness and slams. One of the few misfires of Davis's career, the music comes across as random excerpts from a not very inspired jam session, with Davis's trumpet (what there is of it) mostly being very distorted electronically. Such major players as Carlos Garnett, Dave Liebman (mostly on soprano), Herbie Hancock, Chick Corea, John McLaughlin, Colin Walcott (on electric sitar), Badal Roy (tabla), and Jack DeJohnette are heard from, but the results are quite messy and the material is quite weak. This is a historical curiosity at best, as is **In Concert: Live at Philharmonic Hall** (Columbia/Legacy 65140), a 1972 concert that includes some similar material from a nonet with Garnett (on soprano and tenor), keyboardist Cedric Lawson, guitarist Reggie Lucas, and electric sitarist Khalil Balakrishna.

After mostly being off records during 1973, Davis emerged in 1974 with an intriguing new band. **Dark Magus** (Columbia/Legacy 65137) has the trumpeter's Carnegie Hall concert of March 30, 1974, when he was heading a group featuring David Liebman (tenor, soprano, and flute), Michael Henderson, drummer Al Foster, Mtume (Jimmy Heath's son) on percussion, and no less than three electric guitarists: Pete Cosey, Reggie Lucas, and Dominique Gaumont. In addition, Azar Lawrence has a spot on tenor on one piece. The music contains its share of magic along with some barren stretches, all of it sounding quite spontaneous. Unlike what fusion would become in its later watered-down form (as it was smoothed to an excess to make it palatable for the pop market), plenty of chances are taken during this stimulating and unpredictable (if noisy) concert.

Get Up with It (Columbia/Legacy 63970) is a grab bag of items from 1970–74 including a 32-minute dirge ("He Loved Him Madly") in tribute to the deceased Duke Ellington, heated jams on "Maiysha" and "Calypso Frelimo," and the very odd "Red China Blues" (with Davis's wah-wah trumpet heard on an R&B blues). Davis actually plays organ nearly half of the time (mostly droning chords), and the oversized rhythm sections generally take honors.

On February 1, 1975, two lengthy sets by Miles Davis's septet were recorded at a concert in Tokyo. The group consists of Sonny Fortune on alto, soprano, and flute, both Cosey and Lucas on guitars, Henderson, Foster,

and Mtume. The first set, **Agharta** (Columbia/Legacy 65348), finds Davis sounding a bit weak (he had been ailing during the past year), but there are some fiery grooves on the extended numbers and Fortune takes some heroic solos over the crowded rhythm section. **Pangaea** (Columbia/Legacy 48115) has the second show, and surprisingly Davis's chops had greatly recovered and his improvisations are quite expressive; in fact, the whole band sounds tighter and more purposeful.

After returning to New York, Davis surprised the jazz world by choosing to drop out of music altogether. In addition to his erratic health, he seemed a bit bored with the direction that his music had taken, and he drifted away into an isolated life full of excessive drug use and hedonism. Despite persistent rumors about him making an imminent comeback, Miles Davis would not perform in public again until 1981, when the music world was a very different place than it was in 1975.

The Beginnings of Pop-Jazz and Crossover

For decades, the boundary lines between jazz and certain aspects of pop music have often been blurred. Whether it was dance bands in the 1920s that incorporated brief jazz solos, otherwise-commercial orchestras during the 1930s that occasionally played an instrumental, middle-of-the-road pop singers in the 1950s who sang some standards, or early R&B bands with their honking saxophonists, there have been times when it was difficult to know whether music was jazz; what really counted was whether it was enjoyable.

With the rise of fusion and the opening of jazz to rock influences (and vice versa), there was a movement to mix some jazz into pop and modern R&B settings, making jazz (a word that some musicians were avoiding by the early 1970s) more commercial and popular, sometimes at the expense of the music. When the results were essentially jazzy pop, the term "crossover" fit although quite often these performances were inaccurately bunched together as fusion. Wes Montgomery playing melodic versions of current pop tunes in the mid-1960s was a hint of what was to come as some musicians sought to capture a bigger audience beyond jazz.

Roy Ayers   Roy Ayers, who would have a rather diverse career, emerged in the late 1960s as a skillful hard bop vibraphonist. The son of a trombonist, Ayers was given a set of vibe mallets by Lionel Hampton when he was five, but he did not start seriously playing vibes until he was 17. Based in Los Angeles, Ayers recorded with Curtis Amy (1962), Jack Wilson, and the Gerald Wilson Orchestra, gaining a strong reputation during a four-year stint (1966–70) with Herbie Mann. He first recorded as a leader in 1963, and 1968's Atlantic release **Stoned Soul Picnic** (32 Jazz 32158) finds him leading a notable septet also including Gary Bartz, Charles Tolliver, Hubert Laws, Herbie Hancock, Ron Carter or Miroslav Vitous, and Grady Tate. The music ranges from fairly straightahead ("Wave") to jazzy versions of current pop tunes including "For Once in My Life" and Laura Nyro's "Stoned Soul Picnic." But after leaving Mann's group in 1970, the vibraphonist formed the Roy Ayers Ubiquity and began recording R&B/funk for Polydor, which, as the 1970s progressed, de-emphasized jazz in favor of dance music and disco. **Live at the Montreux Jazz Festival** (Verve 531 641) from 1972 has some good moments, ranging from lightly funky grooves to a couple lightweight vocals and interesting explorations of "In a Silent Way" and "Raindrops Keep Falling on My Head."

Some of Roy Ayers's groove tunes of the era would be used in later years by acid jazz DJs, but in reality little that he has performed or recorded since the early 1970s has been of much relevance to jazz or even the crossover movement, falling more in the realm of funky pop music.

Randy and Michael Brecker   Twenty-three-year-old trumpeter Randy Brecker recorded his debut as a leader in 1969, **Score** (Blue Note 81202). He had been a member of Blood, Sweat & Tears in 1967, and at the time was playing with Horace Silver. Even with some period trappings, this set (originally cut for Solid State) is mostly straightahead jazz, featuring the trumpeter, his younger brother tenor saxophonist Michael Brecker, Larry Coryell, and Hal Galper on keyboards playing group originals.

Randy Brecker worked with the rock-jazz group Dreams in 1969, played briefly with several big bands and was a member of Larry Coryell's Eleventh House and Billy Cobham's band in the early fusion years. But his main employment during the first half of the 1970s (and during the next decade) was as a studio musician. A fine hard bop-oriented soloist, Brecker was always technically proficient and not adverse to electrifying his horn à la Miles Davis of the era.

Michael Brecker, who is three years younger than Randy, had a similar career in his early days. He started playing with rock and R&B bands, worked with Dreams, was with Horace Silver (1973–74), and performed with Billy Cobham prior to the formation of the Brecker Brothers. And as with Randy, Michael became a busy studio musician because of his versatility and superior musicianship.

In 1975 Randy and Michael came together to co-lead the Brecker Brothers. Rather than being a fusion band, this was an R&B-oriented group with pop sensitivities that utilized up-to-date electronics (which ironically now sound dated), emphasizing funky rhythms over any jazz creativity. It would be one of the more popular groups of the mid-to-late 1970s.

Donald Byrd   For Donald Byrd, the 1968–76 period would completely change his career and his reputation. A highly rated hard bop trumpeter who was becoming a top educator, Byrd had grown tired of playing straight-ahead jazz. In 1969 he recorded **Fancy Free** (Blue Note 89796), a fascinating transition disc that has Byrd utilizing electric keyboards and finding a satisfying balance between jazz improvisation and funky rhythms. The melody of "Fancy Free" is memorable, some of the songs are danceable without being simplistic, and there are some solid solos along the way for Byrd and tenor saxophonist Frank Foster. **Kofi** (Blue Note 31875), which was not initially released until 1995, is in a similar vein with some good spots for Byrd (who sometimes sounds like Miles Davis of the period), Foster, and Lew Tabackin (who plays flute on the title cut). **Electric Byrd** (Blue Note 36195) from 1970 was Byrd's last jazz album during this period. The music combines hard bop with Miles Davis–style fusion, modern Brazilian music, and touches of R&B. Foster and Tabackin have some tenor solos, Pepper Adams has a reunion with Byrd, and both Duke Pearson (on electric piano) and percussionist Airto Moreira make their voices heard.

Unfortunately, instead of exploring this rather intriguing fusion music, Donald Byrd soon went so far into commercialism that he was considered a sellout by most jazz listeners. Released in 1972, **Black Byrd** (Blue Note 84466) finds Byrd playing commercial funk with a group assembled by producer Larry Mizell. The music sounds quite dated today, with popish vocals (including some from Byrd), monotonous dance rhythms, and seven throwaway Mizell originals, yet it was Blue Note's biggest seller and made Donald Byrd a major name in pop/R&B for a time. Byrd soon sponsored and at times played with the Blackbyrds, an R&B group comprised of his students. **Street Lady** (Blue Note 53923) and **Places and Spaces** (Blue Note 54326) followed, with Byrd a minor figure on his own records as he neglected his trumpet playing in favor of singing and letting his producer run the show. The less Donald Byrd actually played, the more famous he became in the R&B/soul world! It would be a long time before he would be heard performing credible jazz again.

Hank Crawford   A soulful altoist whose music fit into soul jazz, Hank Crawford was an inspiration to the young David Sanborn and helped lead the way toward Grover Washington, Jr. In general, Crawford's often-lightweight recordings of this era for Atlantic, Cottillion, and Kudu were not on the same level as his 1960–66 output, but there was one gem: 1972's **We Got a Good Thing Going** (reissued as Columbia 40820). Crawford plays beautifully, the Don Sebesky arrangements for strings and an oversized rhythm section fit the music perfectly, and the songs are consistently strong even while being commercial. Crawford's renditions of "Alone Again (Naturally)," "Imagination," "The Christmas Song," "I'm Just a Lucky So and So," and "Winter Wonderland" dwarf most other versions because of his soulful style and his ability to caress the melodies. If only his other recordings from this era were as memorable.

The Crusaders   The Jazz Crusaders were one of the most popular jazz groups of the 1960s, featuring a soulful brand of hard bop played by trombonist Wayne Henderson, tenor saxophonist Wilton Felder, pianist Joe Sample, drummer Stix Hooper, and a variety of bassists. But by 1970, when the musicians were involved in their own individual projects and no longer wanted to be associated with the word "jazz" (which they thought was very restrictive and noncommercial), the group was renamed the Crusaders.

The band's first record under their new name, ⬤ **I** (MCA 20024), is among their most successful. The reissue of a former two-LP set has the original four members joined by three guitarists (most notably soloist Larry Carlton who for a time became a regular member of the band) and electric bassist Chuck Rainey. "Put It Where You Want It" was a minor hit while their 12-minute

version of Carole King's "So Far Away" is one of the high points of the group's history. **The Second Crusade** (MCA 20025) does not quite reach the heights of **I**, but it has its moments as the group plays 13 originals and mixes together hard bop, soul-jazz, R&B, and funk. **Unsung Heroes** (MCA 31374), **Scratch** (MCA 37072), **Those Southern Knights** (MCA 1649), and **Southern Comfort** (MCA 6016) are in a similar vein, emphasizing groove music, R&Bish originals, and rather safe playing. In 1975 Wayne Henderson went out on his own to work as an independent producer, but the Crusaders carried on with just one horn. The trademark trombone/tenor front line was no more, but on **Free As the Wind** (MCA 37073) the group managed to continue keeping its own identity even if the results are a bit forgettable.

As time went on, the Crusaders gradually became less relevant to the jazz world, so dropping the "Jazz" from its name (although it seemed like a minor insult at the time) ultimately did make sense.

Grant Green   One of the most vital musicians of 1960–65 when he was Blue Note's house guitarist, Grant Green succumbed to the lure of commercialism in the 1970s. He probably felt frustrated when he saw the commercial success of rock guitarists who could not play close to his level, and he also had a strong interest in soul and R&B, so his conversion to funkier music was natural.

Green only recorded one album during 1966–68, and when he returned to Blue Note in 1969 and began to record regularly again, his repertoire was filled with cover versions of pop and soul hits plus funky originals; the standards were gone. **Carryin' On** (Blue Note 31247) has songs made famous by the Meters, Little Anthony and the Imperials, and James Brown in addition to some forgettable originals. Idris Muhammad's drumming works well, but Clarence Palmer's keyboards and the weak material are largely a bore. **Green Is Beautiful** (Blue Note 28265) is better because of some fine solos by Blue Mitchell and Claude Bartee on tenor (particularly on "Ain't It Funky Now"). But three of the five songs are one-chord vamps, and the material overall is pretty inferior. **Alive!** (Blue Note 89793) is another misfire with Green, Bartee, Muhammad, William Bivens on vibraphone, Ronnie Foster or Neal Creque on organ, and Joseph Armstrong on conga indulging in endless jams on four funky but weak numbers including "Sookie, Sookie" and Kool and the Gang's "Let the Music Take Your Mind." One can only imagine what Alfred Lion must have thought of this music.

Live at the Lighthouse (Blue Note 93381), a former double LP now reborn as a single CD, is one of Green's better dates from this period. Performed on April 21, 1972, there is a lot of fat to the six extended jams (three songs are longer than 12 minutes), and the songs (which include Donald Byrd's "Fancy Free" and "Betcha by Golly Wow") are far from classics. It is ironic that Green's attempt to play "contemporary material" resulted in him performing music that now sounds dated as opposed to his much fresher sounding early-1960s recordings. But there are some good moments in this funky material from Green, Bartee (who doubles on soprano), and vibraphonist Gary Coleman despite the simplicity of the music.

Unfortunately, drug problems and the gradual death of Blue Note contributed to Grant Green not making any other recordings during 1972–75. The LP **The Main Attraction** (Kudu 29) from 1976 has the guitarist (who still sounds appealing in spots) playing three rather lengthy, weak, and forgettable pieces. Even the presence of arranger David Matthews, Hubert Laws, and Michael Brecker does not help much. In fact, the musicians are largely on automatic pilot, sounding as if they were counting off the minutes to lunch.

The main result of Grant Green's conversion to funk is that his records (of which there would only be one more) failed to sell and his career became aimless after such a strong start.

Bob James A very capable jazz pianist and arranger, Bob James made the decision by the early 1970s to work in more commercial music. He had started out his recording career recording a boppish trio album in 1962 and a surprisingly avant-garde set for ESP in 1965. After a period working with Sarah Vaughan (1965–68), James became a studio musician and produced some records for CTI. In 1974 with the release of **One** (Tappan Zee 45964), he began to make a name for himself as a crossover solo artist, creating music that defined pop-jazz. Grover Washington, Jr. has two spots on soprano during this album and the brass section includes Jon Faddis, but they are only present for seasoning. Whether it is a pair of classical works, the lightly funky "Feel Like Making Love" or originals that sound

like theme songs for movies, James's music never rises above the level of pleasant background music. But the commercial success of **One** led to a lengthy series of similar projects including **Two** (Tappan Zee 45965), which utilizes strings and vocalists, and 1976's **Three** (Tappan Zee 45966). Throughout, James is heard on electric piano, playing music designed for potential radio airplay and to appeal to pop audiences who desired some light instrumental music. Although sometimes referred to as fusion because of its use of some electric instruments, this crossover music lacked fusion's sense of adventure, creativity, guts, and heart.

John Klemmer A potentially significant tenor saxophonist with very impressive technique and a sound of his own, John Klemmer found surprising commercial success in the mid-1970s. He originally started out as a Coltrane-inspired saxophonist who worked in Chicago, Illinois, and made his recording debut in 1967 when he was a month shy of 21. Klemmer became an important soloist with the Don Ellis Orchestra (1968–70), electrifying his horn and utilizing an echoplex. Unlike most other electric saxists (other than Eddie Harris), Klemmer treated his instrument as more than just a louder acoustic horn and was quite inventive. However, after recording five albums for Cadet during 1966–70, he switched to Impulse where his recordings became increasingly easy listening, climaxing in the 1975 hit album **Touch** (MCA 37152) and the popular **Barefoot Ballet** (MCA 1583). **Mosaic** (GRP 9838) is an excellent sampler that has selections from those two albums plus **Arabesque**, **Lifestyle (Living and Loving)**, **Brazilia**, and 1969's **Blowin' Gold**. Klemmer is joined by oversized rhythm sections sometimes including keyboardist Dave Grusin and Larry Carlton. He is mostly heard caressing melodies, letting his sound tell the story. These recordings, which do not contain much variety, are more useful as romantic backgrounds than for close listening.

Earl Klugh Acoustic guitarist Earl Klugh has always had a pretty sound, and he became a popular success as soon as he went out on his own. Not much of an improviser, Klugh's music tends to be quite predictable, lightly funky, and essentially superior background music that rarely ever gets away from the melody. Klugh, who has said that country guitarist Chet Atkins was his most important influence, recorded with Yusef Lateef when he was 15 (in 1970) and gained some recognition for his playing on George Benson's **White Rabbit** set in 1971. He toured with Benson in 1973, was an odd choice to be Bill Connors's first replacement with Return to Forever in 1974 (he did not stay long), and then began leading his own groups. **Earl Klugh** (EMI 46553) and **Living inside Your Love** (EMI 48385), both from 1976, are quite typical of the music that the guitarist would play throughout his career, pleasant but not at all memorable and completely lacking in surprises.

Ramsey Lewis   A talented pianist, Ramsey Lewis's pop hits of the mid-1960s (including "Hang on Sloopy" and "The In Crowd") led to his trio with bassist Eldee Young and drummer Red Holt disbanding; his sidemen broke away and formed the short-lived Young-Holt Unlimited. At first Lewis's new trio consisted of bassist Cleveland Eaton and drummer Maurice White (who soon left to form the R&B band Earth, Wind & Fire). By 1970 Lewis was doubling on electric piano, and his recordings tended to feature larger ensembles with less of a connection to jazz and spontaneous music. **Maiden Voyage** (Chess 104) has highlights from Lewis's two Argo records of 1968 (**Maiden Voyage** and **Mother Nature's Son**). These pop-oriented sets have Lewis's trio joined by strings, voices (including Minnie Riperton), and sometimes a large orchestra. Both Charles Stepney's arrangements and the repertoire (which is dominated by cover versions of pop songs) are at best period pieces that have not dated well. **Sun Goddess** (Columbia 36194) from 1974 is fairly typical of his mid-'70s output. A strong commercial success, this project has Lewis primarily heard on electric keyboards while joined by overproduced horns and strings, playing mildly funky versions of R&Bish material. It would be quite a few years before Ramsey Lewis's reputation in jazz would begin a comeback, but in the meantime he became well known far beyond jazz.

Chuck Mangione   Chuck Mangione became a celebrity in the pop world in the 1970s. Originally a Dizzy Gillespie–inspired bebopper who played with his older sibling Gap Mangione in the Jazz Brothers and had stints with Woody Herman (1965), Maynard Ferguson, and Art Blakey's Jazz Messengers (1965–67), Mangione switched from trumpet to flugelhorn in 1968, the year he formed a quartet with Gerry Niewood on tenor and soprano. Although his quartet was quite capable of

playing worthwhile jazz, Mangione's projects (starting in 1970) utilizing large orchestras and singer Esther Satterfield were purposely lightweight, essentially being melodic pop music that was both unremittingly upbeat and dull. Such melodies as "Hill Where the Lord Hides," "Land of Make Believe," and "Chase the Clouds Away" made Mangione famous.

It all started with the double LP **Friends and Love** (Mercury 2-800), which has Mangione and several jazz players (including Gerry Niewood and his brother pianist Gap) teamed with the Rochester Philharmonic Orchestra including for the 24-minute title cut and "Hill Where the Lord Hides." A pair of albums by his quartet with Niewood in 1972 are much better, with **Chuck Mangione Quartet** (Mercury 631) including worthwhile versions of "Land of Make Believe," "Little Sunflower," and "Manha de Carnival" and **Alive** (Mercury 824 301) having lengthy and surprisingly fiery versions of "High Heel Sneakers," "Legend of the One-Eyed Sailor," "Sixty-Miles Young," and Sonny Rollins's "St. Thomas." In fact, the latter LP is Chuck Mangione's definitive recording.

However, Mangione's next five orchestral projects, the double LP **Together** (Mercury 2-7501), **Land of Make Believe** (Mercury 822 539), which has also not reappeared yet on CD, **Chase the Clouds Away** (A&M 75021-3115), **Bellavia** (A&M 75021-3172), and **Main Squeeze** (A&M 75021-3220), have little to recommend themselves other than the pretty melodies and the brief glimpses of Mangione's flugelhorn. They have not dated well but indirectly added momentum to the pop-jazz movement that would flourish later in the decade, making Mangione a household name.

Herbie Mann   Having explored bebop, bossa novas, and Afro-Cuban jazz, flutist Herbie Mann turned his attention toward soul, rock, fusion, and pop music during 1968–75, even delving into reggae and disco as he largely left jazz for a time. Mann actually led some of his strongest groups during 1968–72, starting off with a versatile sextet that featured Roy Ayers, tenor saxophonist Steve Marcus, and the avant-garde guitarist Sonny Sharrock. Larry Coryell and Miroslav Vitous also worked with Mann, and for a time in 1972 tenor saxophonist David "Fathead" Newman was part of the Mann band. After 1972, the flutist's music dropped in interest from the jazz standpoint although he remained a famous name.

The 1968 LP **Live at the Whisky-a-Go-Go** (Atlantic 1536) is only a half-hour long, but it has the Mann-Marcus-Ayers-Vitous group with drummer Bruno Carr in fine form on sidelong jams of "Ooh Baby" and "Philly Dog." **Memphis Underground** (Atlantic 1522) has Mann, Ayers, Coryell, and Sharrock going down to Memphis and playing with a top-notch local rhythm section. The music effectively mixes R&B and country rhythms with jazz solos even if the material (which includes "Memphis Underground," "Hold on, I'm Comin'," and "Chain of Fools") is weak. **Push Push** (Embryo 532) has Mann and such players as guitarist Duane Allman and keyboardist Richard Tee performing jazzy R&B, rock, and funk music including appealing versions of "What's Going On," "Never Can Say Goodbye," and "What'd I Say." The most rewarding of Mann's recordings of the 1970s but unfortunately one that has not been reissued yet is **Hold On, I'm Comin'** (Atlantic 1632). Recorded at the 1972 Newport in New York Jazz Festival, this set teams Mann with David Newman, Sonny Sharrock, and a fine backup rhythm section. The high quality and diversity of the solos (Newman is inspired while Sharrock's blasts shocked the audience a bit) and the spirited ensembles on a variety of R&Bish material including "Respect Yourself," "Memphis Underground," and "Hold on, I'm Comin'" make this a memorable outing and certainly far superior to Mann's later pop-oriented Atlantic recordings.

Wes Montgomery   As 1968 began, Wes Montgomery seemed to be on the top of the world. His two A&M albums were unabashedly commercial, with him merely stating the melodies of pop tunes (usually in his trademark octaves) over strings. Those sets were staples of AM radio and made him famous to a wide audience yet he still had respect from his peers because of his live concerts, which were largely unchanged from his earlier days. Finally, after years of struggling, the money was rolling in.

During March–May, Montgomery recorded the music for **Road Song** (A&M 75021-0822), another pop-jazz set with Don Sebesky arrangements for a large orchestra with such songs as "Greensleeves," "Fly Me to the Moon," "Yesterday," and "Scarborough Fair." The music is very safe and pleasing if one does not listen too closely or expect any real adventure.

But then it all ended. On June 15, 1968, Wes Montgomery, who had been overworked for two decades, suffered a fatal heart attack. He was just 43.

Patrice Rushen   Early in her career and later on in her occasional flirtations with jazz, Patrice Rushen showed that if she had desired she could have been a major jazz pianist/keyboardist. As it turned out, the lure of the commercial market and her desire to play dance music greatly influenced her career, and she has accomplished relatively little of importance in jazz despite her talents.

Rushen started on piano when she was three, and as a teenager was impressing many in jazz circles. About the time she turned 20 in 1974, Rushen seemed to be an obvious up-and-comer in jazz. During that era she played with many jazz greats including Gerald Wilson, Benny Golson, Stanley Turrentine, and Sonny Rollins (1976). **Prelusion/Before the Dawn** (Prestige 24207) reissues all of the music from her first two albums except for one song left off because of lack of space. The **Prelusion** date has Rushen with a septet that includes Joe Henderson, trumpeter Oscar Brashear, and trombonist George Bohanon, playing advanced hard bop with hints of fusion. **Before the Dawn** has an R&Bish vocal by Josie James but otherwise is jazz oriented with Bohanon and Brashear helping out again and with appearances by Hubert Laws and Lee Ritenour. But her next LP, 1976's **Shout It Out** (Prestige 10101), was much more R&Bish overall and has Rushen's first vocal, hinting at her future in commercial music.

David Sanborn   Altoist David Sanborn's roots are in R&B although he always considered Hank Crawford to be a strong early influence. Sanborn, who has a distinctive sound full of passion, crying, and squealing high notes and his own brand of soul, in time became one of the most influential of all saxophonists, with many Sanborn soundalikes having records on the pop and jazz charts. He has consistently stated that he does not consider himself a jazz musician and most of Sanborn's records have crossed over into the R&B field, but he has shown now and then that he can play jazz whenever he decides to venture in that direction.

Born in Tampa, Florida, Sanborn grew up in St. Louis, Missouri, where he played with some blues bands, including Albert King, and became aware of avant-garde jazz, admiring Julius Hemphill. Moving to New York, he worked with the Butterfield Blues Band (including at Woodstock), Stevie Wonder, the Brecker Brothers, and on a countless number of studio sessions in pop, rock, and R&B settings. Although he played regularly for Gil Evans a bit in the early 1970s, by the time Sanborn recorded his own albums (starting in 1975), his career was geared toward pop and R&B. **Taking Off** (Warner Brothers 2873) was a major commercial success, a set of commercial but danceable and melodic music; the Brecker Brothers, guitarist Steve Khan, and Howard Johnson on baritone and tuba are important members of the supporting cast. **Sanborn** (Warner Brothers 2957) is best known for the altoist's version of Paul Simon's "I Do It for Your Love" and has some strong playing by Sanborn on "Mamacita" and "7th Avenue" along with funky rhythms and tight grooves. Most of David Sanborn's next dozen records (all of them solid sellers) would be in a similar vein.

Johnny "Hammond" Smith   Of all the soul jazz organists of the 1960s, Johnny "Hammond" Smith (who officially changed his name to Johnny Hammond in 1971) took the most commercial route. **Legends of Acid Jazz** (Prestige 24177) has all of the music from Smith's two 1969 Prestige albums **Soul Talk** and **Black Feeling**. Smith's grooves at the time were somewhat predictable but usually infectious, and he is joined by Rusty Bryant (on alto, tenor, and Varitone sax) or tenor saxophonist Leo Johnson, guitarist Wally Richardson, either Bob Bushnell or Jimmy Lewis on bass, drummer Bernard Purdie, and (on the second date) trumpeter Floyd Jones. **Legends of Acid Jazz Vol. 2** (Prestige 24235) reissues the 1967 album **Soul Flowers** plus **Dirty Grape** from the following year but, despite the presence of Houston Person, the music is mostly funky versions of current pop tunes, well played but ultimately pointless. The same thing can be said for the two sessions combined on **Soulful Blues** (Prestige 24244): **Ebb Tide** and **Nasty**. The music is not bad for what it is, particularly if one likes predictable and unashamedly commercial funk jazz.

The low point musically is 1975's **Gears** (Original Jazz Classics 914). Producers Larry and Fonce Mizell (who made Donald Byrd's most pop-oriented albums) helped persuade Smith to mostly play electric piano and synthesizer. He is in a subsidiary role on some cuts backing the Mizells's horrendous vocalizing, and the music was clearly put together for beginning dancers who needed a strong and obvious beat.

Lonnie Liston Smith   Lonnie Liston Smith started his career as a versatile pianist who played with such notables as Pharoah Sanders, Rahsaan Roland Kirk, Gato Barbieri, Betty Carter, and (briefly) Miles Davis. In 1973 he recorded his first date as a leader and formed the Cosmic Echoes, a group that played high-quality mood music that was a bit mystical and spiritual, building slowly and using repetition expertly; his brother Donald Smith occasionally was heard on vocals.

Smith recorded five albums for Bob Thiele's Flying Dutchman label during 1973–76 including **Expansions** (BMG 85155), **Cosmic Funk** (RCA 50591), and **Visions of a New World** (RCA 51196). The best purchase is **Golden Dreams** (Bluebird 6996), which has all ten selections from **Reflections of a Golden Dream**, plus four of the six cuts from his 1973 debut, **Astral Traveling**. The performances are a bit funky and fusion-oriented while being creative mood music. This CD serves as an excellent introduction to Lonnie Liston Smith's unusual brand of pop-jazz.

Grover Washington, Jr.   A hugely talented saxophonist who had his own voice on soprano, alto, tenor, and even his infrequently played baritone, Grover Washington, Jr., became very popular as a performer of soulful R&B jazz, but he could play effective straightahead, too. The son of a saxophonist, he began playing music when he was ten and was performing in clubs within two years. Washington toured with the Four Clefs (1959–63), freelanced in his native Buffalo for a couple years, and served in the army. After moving to Philadelphia in 1967 (when he was 23), he worked in a variety of organ groups including with Charles Earland and Johnny Hammond Smith, appearing on some records for the Prestige label as a sideman.

Grover Washington, Jr.'s big break took place in 1971 when Hank Crawford could not make it to a record date. He took his place, and ● **Inner City Blues** (Motown 530577) became a hit. Originally released by Creed Taylor's Kudu label, this set has Bob James arrangements, soulful alto and tenor solos from the leader, and memorable versions of "Mercy Mercy Me," "Georgia On My Mind," "I Loves You Porgy," and "Ain't No Sunshine." It was obvious to many listeners that Washington was on his way to becoming a star. He would record an album a year for Kudu through 1976.

Although not quite on the same level, **All the King's Horses** (Motown 5186) also has Bob James arrangements and some excellent versions of "Where Is the Love,"

"Lean on Me," and "Lover Man." **Soul Box** (Motown 5187), which was originally a deluxe two-LP set, has Washington making his recording debut on soprano, which he plays along with tenor and alto. Although one can certainly criticize this project for trying too much, being overproduced, and having far too many musicians (with many strings, brass, and woodwinds), Grover Washington, Jr.'s playing on "You Are the Sunshine of My Life," "Don't Explain," and a medley of "Easy Living" and "Ain't Nobody's Business If I Do" is soulful, emotional, and heartfelt.

Lightning struck with the saxophonist's next release, 1974's ● **Mister Magic** (Motown 5175). A classic of R&Bish jazz, the title cut was a major hit, but all four songs (including Billy Strayhorn's "Passion Flower") are excellent, groove well, and are infectious. Bob James's arrangements and the short solos of guitarist Eric Gale are excellent, but it is the powerful playing of Washington (mostly on tenor and soprano) that makes this set so memorable.

Grover Washington, Jr., whose final two Kudu albums, **Feels So Good** (Motown 5177) and **A Secret Place** (Motown 5165), are pleasing but anticlimactic, spawned many imitators who lacked the originality of his sound, the pacing of his performances (he really knew how to work a crowd), and his roots in soul jazz. He stood, and still stands posthumously, far above nearly all of the R&Bish saxophonists to emerge since 1970.

Free Jazz and the Avant-Garde After Coltrane

The death of John Coltrane in 1967 left avant-garde jazz without its main leader. The music had gained a great deal of attention in the jazz world during the first half of the 1960s (even as it scared away many conservative listeners) and seemed to be making progress commercially with it being documented by Impulse and ESP. The music performed by AACM members in Chicago, Illinois, helped free jazz to grow beyond constant free-form blowouts, and it was a major surprise when Pharoah Sanders and Leon Thomas had a commercial hit with "The Creator Has a Master Plan." But the rise of rock, the passing of Coltrane and Albert Ayler, and the beginnings of fusion resulted in the music going back underground and overseas, with many top avant-gardists spending time in France during 1969–70.

Although avant-garde jazz never caught on commercially (the odds were certainly against that ever happening), it always had an audience just large enough to survive, and many small record companies (along with the new Black Saint/Soul Note labels) documented its many practitioners. Europe became a fertile place both as a market and as an incubator for new talents. The jazz press helped to publicize many of the more advanced musicians, some of whom utilized their New York lofts in the early to mid-1970s as performance spaces when work in clubs became scarce. There were many artistic high points along the way even if record sales remained low.

Air   In 1971, altoist Henry Threadgill was asked to arrange some of Scott Joplin's songs for a production at Chicago's Columbia College. For the show, he teamed up with bassist Fred Hopkins and drummer Steve McCall as a trio called Reflections. In 1975 the same three musicians came together as the co-op group Air. The premise behind the ensemble was for the three players to share an equal role, and although Threadgill on alto, tenor, flute, and his homemade hupkaphone was certainly the most prominent voice, almost as much space was delegated to bass and drum solos. This important avant-garde jazz group's first recording, 1975's **Air Song** (India Navigation 1057), has four lengthy performances but has not yet been reissued on CD. **Live Air** (Black Saint 120034) from 1976 is a strong example of Air's work as the trio stretches out on four Threadgill originals including "Eulogy for Charles Clark" and "Portrait of Leo Smith."

Art Ensemble of Chicago   In 1969, the Art Ensemble of Chicago and Anthony Braxton's Trio left Chicago to relocate for a time in Paris where it was felt that the potential to work was much greater than in the United States. During this period of time, the Art Ensemble of Chicago really developed as a group, recording eight albums. **Tutankhamun** (Black Lion 760199) starts out very weird with a title cut that has bizarre verbal sounds from Malachi Favors. There are also two versions of "Tthinitthedalen," which are rather violent duets by Roscoe Mitchell and Favors. Easily the most interesting selection, "The Ninth Room" points toward the group's future, with advanced solos over Favors's walking bass by Mitchell, Joseph Jarman, and Lester Bowie that hint at the past while being quite inventive. In addition, the drumless quartet utilizes such "little instruments" as bass drum, whistles, sirens, bells, harpsichord, banjo, and toys.

In 1970 Don Moye joined the Art Ensemble of Chicago on drums and percussion, and the band's personnel would be unchanged for the next 23 years. The group moved back to Chicago in 1971 and early the following year recorded the brilliant ● **Live at Mandel Hall** (Delmark 432), a continuous 76½-minute performance that shows how the band typically sounded in concert, exploring the music's outer limits yet also including a humorous drunken march. With all of their instruments, the unique individual voices, the collective improvisations, and a strong sense of both fun and open-mindedness, the Art Ensemble of Chicago gave one the impression that it could go in any musical direction and still sound quite credible and colorful. **Bap-Tizum** (Koch 8500) and **Fanfare of the Warriors** (Atlantic 90046) from 1972–73 conclude the Art Ensemble of Chicago's earliest and most significant period with a great deal of fire, including explosive percussion displays by the full band, sound explorations, relatively straightahead moments, and, amidst all of the intensity, outbursts of outrageous humor. But, despite making a strong impact on the jazz scene, other than a private release on their own AECO label, the Art Ensemble of Chicago would be absent from recordings altogether during 1974–77.

Lester Bowie took time off from the Art Ensemble of Chicago to begin his solo career with a pair of wide-ranging albums for Muse during 1974–75. The contents of both **Fast Last** and **Rope-a-Dope** have been reissued on the two-CD set ● **American Gumbo** (32 Jazz 32139). There is certainly plenty of humor and adventure in these performances with Bowie playing such numbers as "Hello Dolly," "F Troop Rides Again," "Rope-a-Dope" (a sort-of musical re-enactment of a Muhammad Ali fight), and "St. Louis Blues" in witty fashion. Altoist Julius Hemphill and Lester's brother trombonist Joseph Bowie are major assets to the colorful and constantly surprising music.

Albert Ayler   In 1967, Albert Ayler was signed to the Impulse label, a logical move for a major avant-gardist. But unlike Coltrane, Archie Shepp, Pharoah Sanders, and the other adventurous Impulse musicians, Ayler's stay at the company was racked with compromises and even attempts to make him into a crossover artist. Part of it was bad planning, but Ayler's general confusion with where he should go next musically was also partly

to blame. **Love Cry** (Impulse 9165), reviewed in the previous chapter, is easily the best of his four Impulse sets. The other three Ayler projects for the label, **New Grass** (Impulse 9175), **Music Is the Healing Force of the Universe** (Impulse 9191), and **The Last Album** (Impulse 9208) have not yet been reissued on CD, but that is no great loss. By the time **New Grass** was recorded in the fall of 1968, Donald Ayler had returned home to Cleveland and Albert Ayler had broken up his group. This weird set has vocalizing by Ayler and the Soul Singers on nearly every selection, dated arrangements for a horn section, and very trivial material. Ayler's free jazz sax solos sound out of place on his own album. The other two records (both recorded August 26–27, 1969) are also real messes, with blues guitar playing from Canned Heat's Henry Vestine (one song has him battling Ayler's bagpipes!), rotten singing from Ayler and Mary Maria (his girlfriend of the period), and a feeling of aimlessness.

Despite its title, **The Last Album** was not the final word from Ayler. In July 1970 he reappeared back in top form on ● **Fondation Maeght Nights Vol. 1** (Jazz View 004) and **Vol. 2** (Jazz View 005). Although Mary Maria is heard from briefly, the music is mostly quartet performances with pianist Call Cobbs, bassist Steve Tintweiss, and drummer Allen Blairman. Ayler revisits eight of his better themes and shows that he had not lost his passionate style or his sense of adventure.

Three-and-a-half months later, 34-year-old Albert Ayler was discovered drowned in New York's East River. It was never determined if this was suicide (he had been mentally troubled for some time) or murder, but nevertheless it was a major loss to jazz and a further setback to the avant-garde, which was still reeling from the death of John Coltrane.

Carla Bley   Carla Bley already had an interesting and episodic career before she started working as a bandleader. Born Carla Borg, she learned music from her father, a church musician. After moving to New York in 1955, she married Paul Bley and began writing songs for his groups. By 1964 the Bleys had broken up and she was married to trumpeter Michael Mantler. Together they formed the Jazz Composers Guild Orchestra (a year later it was renamed the Jazz Composers' Orchestra). She recorded with Mantler and Steve Lacy in a quintet while in Europe in 1966, formed the Jazz Composers' Orchestra Association (a non-profit distributor of avant-garde jazz records that lasted into the late 1980s), and in 1969 wrote for Charlie Haden's Liberation Music Orchestra. In 1971 Bley completed writing **Escalator over the Hill** (ECM 839 310), which came out as a three-LP set and has been reissued as a two-fer. This massive and episodic work combines many diverse forms of music (avant-garde explorations, satirical cabaret, opera, and rock among them) with only limited success in spots, with the use of voices and the lyrics being quite awkward.

More importantly, in the 1970s Carla Bley began leading a part-time group that would in time grow to become a big band. Bley's music was often both humorous in a wacky way and quite dramatic. Released in 1976, **Dinner Music** (ECM 825815) has such Bley favorites as "Ida Lupino," "Sing Me Softly of the Blues," and "Dreams So Real" performed by a nonet also including Mantler, Roswell Rudd, altoist Carlos Ward, Bob Stewart on tuba, and an oversized rhythm section. It served as an important step in her musical development and one of the early high points in her career.

Paul Bley   Paul Bley's life and music went through a lot of changes during the 1968–75 period. After he married singer/composer Annette Peacock, Bley began playing a primitive prototype of a synthesizer, performing adventurous and spacey music with Peacock, which was often billed as The Paul Bley Synthesizer Show. This phase dominated 1969–71, but much of the music that was recorded (for Polydor, Milestone, America, and Freedom) sounds quite dated today.

In 1972 Bley began his current phase, switching back to acoustic piano although he would play electric piano on an occasional basis into 1974 before discarding it completely. ● **Open to Love** (ECM 827 751) is a superb solo disc that defines Bley's style. Performing songs by Carla Bley (including the definitive version of "Ida Lupino"), Annette Peacock, and himself, the pianist displays his inventive use of space and silence and his ability to make every unpredictable note count.

Starting in 1974 and continuing for three years, Paul Bley and his third wife (the artist Carol Goss) ran the Improvising Artists label. In addition to Bley, such players as Lee Konitz, Jimmy Giuffre, Ran Blake, Sam Rivers, Dave Holland, Lester Bowie, and even Sun Ra (as a piano soloist) recorded for the company. **Alone, Again**

(Improvising Artists 123840), though brief, is a worthy companion to **Open to Love**, adding to Bley's legacy as a solo pianist.

Hamiet Bluiett   Hamiet Bluiett emerged in the 1970s as one of the most original baritone saxophonists in years. His deep tone is a little reminiscent of Harry Carney, but his improvising style is quite advanced and free and he is able to hit high notes in the stratosphere with ease. Born in 1940, Bluiett served in the navy and after his discharge was part of the underrated St. Louis avant-garde jazz scene of the mid-to-late-1960s. After moving to New York in 1972, he worked with Sam Rivers's big band and was with Charles Mingus's group during 1972–75. His first album as a leader, 1976's **Endangered Species** (India Navigation 1025), features Bluiett in a quintet with trumpeter Olu Dara, Jumma Santos on balafon, bassist Juney Booth, and drummer Phillip Wilson, performing lengthy originals that are adventurous, avant-garde, and generally quite colorful.

Anthony Braxton   Anthony Braxton has always been one of the most controversial members of the jazz avant-garde. A true original from the start of his career, Braxton is quite distinctive on his main ax (the alto sax) and the many reed instruments that he plays. These range from the clarinet and sopranino sax to the contrabass sax and contrabass clarinet. Although he has recorded standards in his "in the tradition" projects, Braxton's solos are always quite unpredictable and original, and, as if his writing was not ambitious enough, he has sometimes had his groups play two or three of his compositions at once. Because he often uses mathematical formulas or drawings as names for his originals and because his liner notes for his own albums are nearly impossible to comprehend (using 20 complicated words when three would be preferable), Braxton has sometimes been written off by conservative listeners, but his huge body of work deserves to be studied closely.

After serving in the military, Braxton became a member of the AACM in 1966, making his first recordings two years later, **3 Compositions of New Jazz** (Delmark 415). Braxton, violinist Leroy Jenkins, trumpeter Leo Smith, and (on one of the three selections) pianist Muhal Richard Abrams all play several instruments, utilizing space, dynamics, and a wide variety of sounds in their mostly freeform explorations, building up from spacey stretches to furious interplay. **For Alto**

Saxophone (Delmark 420) is a major avant-garde record, a set of unaccompanied alto solos that find Braxton expanding the sound possibilities of his instrument through dissonant and sometimes violent but ultimately logical explorations.

Braxton spent part of 1969–71 living in Europe, and he played with Chick Corea, Dave Holland, and Barry Altschul in the group Circle. In 1971 he was fortunate enough to be signed to the Arista label, and during the 1970s he recorded often for the label. Unfortunately, most of the records have not yet been reissued on CD (a box set is long overdue), so the albums are scarce. These include **The Complete Braxton** (Arista 1902), which includes everything from an unaccompanied contrabass clarinet performance to pieces featuring five tubas or four overdubbed sopranino saxes); **New York (Fall 1974)** (Arista 4032), which has quartet numbers with Kenny Wheeler, an odd duet with Richard Teitelbaum on moog synthesizer, and a performance by an unaccompanied saxophone quartet (with Julius Hemphill, Oliver Lake, and Hamiet Bluiett) that preceded the World Saxophone Quartet; and **Five Pieces** (1975) (Arista 4064). The latter features the quartet that Braxton had with Wheeler, Dave Holland, and Barry Altschul.

Unintentional humor is heard on **In the Tradition, Vol. 1** (Steeple Chase 31015) and **Vol. 2** (Steeple Chase 31045), which find Braxton extensively exploring standards for the first time. The Tete Montoliu trio essentially ignores the altoist (never reacting to his adventurous flights), similar to the Latin Jazz Quintet's "collaboration" with Eric Dolphy more than a decade earlier. Switching to contrabass clarinet on "Ornithology" from **Vol. 1**, Braxton shows that it is nearly impossible to tell what notes he is hitting when he is in the lower register. These two CDs are mostly of interest from the historical standpoint but are ultimately frustrating because of the lack of communication between the musicians.

Happily, **Town Hall (Trio & Quartet) 1972** (Hat Art 6119) and ◐ **Live** (Bluebird 6626) are much more rewarding and are available on CD. The 1972 concert features Braxton, Dave Holland, and drummer Phillip Wilson on a medley of two Braxton compositions, plus an abstract "All the Things You Are," and it has Braxton (switching between six reeds) playing two numbers with tenor saxophonist John Stubblefield, Holland, Altschul, and singer Jeanne Lee. **Live** serves as the perfect introduction to Anthony Braxton's music for it is more accessible than

most of his recordings. The program is split between two different versions of his quartet: a 1975 set with Kenny Wheeler, Holland, and Altschul and performances from 1976 with trombonist George Lewis in Wheeler's place. In addition to the innovative playing, a lot of wit is displayed on these numbers, particularly the sly encounters with Lewis.

One of the few other Arista projects to re-emerge on CD is **Creative Orchestra Music 1976** (Bluebird 6579). Six of Braxton's compositions are performed by large 15- to 20-piece groups, featuring such soloists as trumpeters Cecil Bridgewater, Leo Smith, Kenny Wheeler, and Jon Faddis, trombonist George Lewis, Roscoe Mitchell on reeds, and Muhal Richard Abrams, plus Braxton himself. There is plenty of variety in the music, which ranges from the forbidding to a humorous Sousa-style march. **Donaueschingen (Duo) 1976** (Hat Art 615) consists of a continuous 41-minute duo by Braxton (heard on alto, sopranino, clarinet, contrabass clarinet, soprano clarinet, flute, and contrabass sax) and George Lewis that is full of adventure and surprises. The biggest surprise is the encore, a relatively straightforward version of Charlie Parker's "Donna Lee!" ◐ **Dortmund (Quartet) 1976** (Hat Art 6075), from eight days later, features Braxton and Lewis in their quartet with Dave Holland and Barry Altschul, the last performance by this particular group. A particularly strong effort, this set features four Braxton originals including one based on a circus march and a hard-swinging original dedicated to Lou Donaldson.

Marion Brown   Avant-garde altoist Marion Brown spent 1967–70 in Europe. **Porto Nova** (Black Lion 760200) was among his most stimulating sessions of the era. Recorded in Holland in a trio with bassist Maarten van Regteben Altena and drummer Han Bennink, Brown stretches out on five of his compositions and is heard at the peak of his creative powers. However, after Brown returned to the United States in 1971, his career became more directionless, work became scarcer, and eventually bad health caused him to become only an occasional player.

Dave Burrell   A fine pianist associated with the avant-garde who has always had an adventurous musical spirit, Dave Burrell, who was born in Ohio, grew up in Hawaii. He attended the University of Hawaii (1958–60) and the Berklee College of Music (graduating in 1965). After moving to New York, he formed the Untraditional Jazz Improvisational Team in New York with Byard Lancaster, Sirone, and drummer Bobby Kapp, also working with Marion Brown and Grachan Moncur. In 1968 he was one of the founders of the 360 Degree Music Experience. Burrell worked and recorded with Pharoah Sanders, Archie Shepp, Sunny Murray, and other avant-garde improvisers. Released in 1968, **High Won-High Two** (Black Lion 760206) displays Burrell's highly original style in a trio set with bassist Sirone and either Bobby Kapp or Sunny Murray on drums; Pharoah Sanders is also heard, on tambourine! The repertoire is quite unusual: an abstract 19-minute "West Side Story" medley, the 15-minute "East Side Colors," five brief originals (four of which are shorter than three minutes), and a "Theme Stream Medley" that has reworkings of those five pieces plus a sixth, "Inside Ouch." Quite typically for Dave Burrell, none of the music is the slightest bit predictable.

John Carter   The clarinet has long been associated with swing and Dixieland, but John Carter moved it into the avant-garde. A scholarly soft-spoken educator who taught in the Fort Worth public school system (1949–61) and Los Angeles (1961–82), Carter had played with Ornette Coleman and Charles Moffett as early as the late 1940s. In Los Angeles in the 1960s, he teamed up with cornetist Bobby Bradford, forming the New Art Jazz Ensemble in 1964; unfortunately, the group was not liberally documented during its early years. Carter at the time also played alto, tenor, and flute, although by 1974

he was exclusively heard on clarinet. In contrast to his personality, Carter's playing was usually very abstract and emotional, with his upper register screeches sometimes being a bit difficult to sit through. 1969's **Seeking** (Hat Art 6085), which was originally put out by the Revelation label, mostly has Carter on his other instruments, only playing clarinet on one of the six pieces, "Sticks and Stones." The music (performed in a quartet with Bradford, bassist Tom Williamson, and drummer Bruz Freeman) is influenced by Ornette Coleman although the horns sound quite individual during the free bop performances. The same group is heard on half of **West Coast Hot** (Novus 3107), a set that they share with pianist Horace Tapscott's group. But in general Carter and Bradford were part of the Los Angeles jazz underground, not gaining much recognition beyond the city limits until the 1980s.

Don Cherry   Don Cherry, who taught at Dartmouth College in 1970, had some reunions with Ornette Coleman and recorded with the Jazz Composers Orchestra (1973), moving to Sweden in the early 1970s. He became a world traveler, not just geographically but musically, taking up the flute, studying Indian and Turkish music, and de-emphasizing his trumpet playing. 1975's **Brown Rice** (A&M 0909) finds Cherry playing keyboards on two of the four cuts, offering verbal recitations on "Degi-Degi" that do not need to be heard twice, and performing some music that is closer to R&B than jazz. Despite some good trumpet on "Malakauns" and a strong contribution by

TIMELINE 1970

Joe Zawinul and Wayne Shorter form Weather Report. • Chick Corea and Dave Holland leave Miles Davis and form the avant-garde quartet Circle with Anthony Braxton and Barry Altschul. • The Jazz Crusaders become the Crusaders. • Don Moye joins the Art Ensemble of Chicago. • Albert Ayler is found drowned in New York's East River. • Steve Lacy moves to France. • Sun Ra's Arkestra settles in Philadelphia. • Hank Mobley records his final of 25 Blue Note albums. • Freddie Hubbard records **Red Clay** and **Straight Life** for CTI. • Betty Carter begins her Bet-Car label. • Johnny Hodges dies. • Barry Guy forms the London Composers Orchestra. • Oregon is formed. • European saxophonist Klaus Doldinger records an album called **Passport** and soon adopts the name Passport for his popular fusion quartet. • British avant-garde soprano saxophonist Lol Coxhill records the unaccompanied set **Ear of Beholder**, his debut as a leader. • Pianist Roland Hanna is knighted by the president of Liberia, becoming Sir Roland Hanna. • Trumpeter Pete Minger joins Count Basie's Orchestra for a ten-year stretch. • Max Roach organizes the all-percussion ensemble M'Boom. • The remarkable British avant-garde tenor and soprano saxophonist Evan Parker makes his first recordings as a leader. • The Ahmad Jamal Trio features bassist Jamil Nasser and drummer Frank Gant. • Charlie Shavers makes his last recordings. • *Radio Free Jazz* is founded by Ira Sabin; it would be renamed *JazzTimes* a decade later and become a close competitor of *Down Beat*.

Charlie Haden's bass, this is a disappointing effort. One applauds Cherry's open-minded approach, but he should have continued working on building his trumpet chops.

Ornette Coleman   In 1968, Ornette Coleman recorded two of his finest albums, **New York Is Now** (Blue Note 84287) and **Love Call** (Blue Note 84356), with a quartet comprised of tenor saxophonist Dewey Redman, Jimmy Garrison (who had played with Coleman back in 1960), and Elvin Jones. Redman's improvising style proved to be very complementary to Ornette's while his Texas tenor sound added an appealing new voice to Coleman's group. **New York Is Now** gets the edge because Coleman plays trumpet on three of the seven numbers on **Love Call** (always a mistake); however, his alto playing is heard very much at its prime.

During 1968–72, Coleman had several reunions with his earlier sidemen, with the LPs **Ornette at 12** (Impulse 9178) and **Crisis** (Impulse 9187) having appearances by Charlie Haden and (on the latter) Don Cherry in addition to Redman and Ornette's son drummer Denardo Coleman. **Friends and Neighbors** (RCA 5159) has the altoist with Redman, Haden, and Ed Blackwell on a variety of lesser tunes including the odd title cut (which has a variety of friends singing along). Best are "Long Time No See" and "Tomorrow," which are typically adventurous and futuristic. The two-CD set **Complete Science Fiction Sessions** (Columbia/Legacy 63569) has all of the music originally on the LPs **Science Fiction** and **Broken Shadows** plus three additional numbers. From 1971–72, Coleman is heard teaming up with virtually all of his living alumni in different combinations including Don Cherry, Dewey Redman, trumpeter Bobby Bradford, Charlie Haden, Billy Higgins, and Ed Blackwell; only David Izenzon and Charles Moffett are missing. It is a sort-of retrospective of Coleman's style up until then (although all of the material was new); there are even two numbers with Jim Hall and Cedar Walton that recall Ornette's guest appearance on a Gunther Schuller album.

After working and recording his avant-classical work **Skies of America** with the London Symphony Orchestra, Ornette Coleman started the second half of his career. He developed a theory called "harmelodics" that emphasized the equal importance of melody, rhythms, and harmony. Coleman sought to form a new and democratic group in which all of the musicians could set the musical direction at any time. By 1975 he had formed Prime Time, a group that in time would grow to be a double quartet consisting of two guitars, two electric bassists, two drummers, and his own alto. The dense, noisy, and often-witty ensembles were typically radical although in reality Coleman's playing was the first among equals. The music could be accurately called "free funk" because it combined loose and unpredictable funk rhythms with Coleman's free improvising.

Dancing in Your Head (A&M 543519) has Coleman jamming in 1973 on a short piece (heard in two takes) with Moroccan musicians and introducing Prime Time on the 27-minute "Theme from a Symphony." At the time, the group included guitarists Bern Nix and Charlie Ellerbee, electric bassist Jamaaladeen Tacuma, and drummer Roland Shannon Jackson. Unfortunately, "Theme from a Symphony" has a rather annoying and repetitious melody, so it is a bit difficult to listen to this piece. **Body Meta** (Verve 531916) has the same quintet in 1976 exploring five of Coleman's originals. The music is quite unusual, and the band's unique sound stands apart from all of the other avant-garde and fusion groups of the era.

Alice Coltrane   The death of John Coltrane greatly shocked and affected the jazz world. Alice Coltrane struggled to bring up a family alone and preserve the legacy of her husband while doing what she could to keep her own musical career alive. **A Monastic Trio** (Impulse 267) has three songs on which Coltrane is joined by Pharoah Sanders (on tenor, flute, or bass clarinet), Jimmy Garrison, and drummer Ben Riley, and it includes two trio sessions with Garrison and Rashied Ali. The music is bluesy and looks a bit toward the Far East in its feel. **Ptah, the El Daoud** (Impulse 201) from 1970 is Alice Coltrane's strongest all-round recording. She is joined by both Pharoah Sanders and Joe Henderson on tenors plus Ron Carter and Ben Riley; Coltrane switches to harp on "Blue Nile" (which has both reeds playing flutes). **Journey in Satchidananda** (Impulse 228) from later in 1970 is an intriguing mixture of adventurous jazz and Indian music. Coltrane (playing piano on three pieces and harp on the other two) is joined by Sanders (who sticks to soprano), Cecil McBee or Charlie Haden, Rashied Ali, and musicians playing the oud, tamboura, and the tambourine. The music is often hypnotic, utilizes both drones and the blues, and holds one's interest.

Coltrane's interest in religions soon began to dominate her life and her music. She moved to Los Angeles in 1972 and three years later founded a center for the study of Eastern religions.

Jimmy Giuffre   Jimmy Giuffre was off records altogether during 1963–71, working as a music educator. He performed now and then (including in a 1964–65 trio with pianist Don Friedman and bassist Barre Phillips) but made no recordings until 1972's **Music for People, Birds, Butterflies & Mosquitoes** (Choice 1001). This LP has Giuffre (on clarinet, tenor, and flute) joined by bassist Kiyoshi Tokunaga and drummer Randy Kaye for a dozen concise originals. The music is moody, fairly spontaneous, and melodic, but it is often wandering and rather insubstantial overall. In 1974 Giuffre recorded **Quiet Song** (Improvising Artists 37.38.39) for Paul Bley's label. On this trio date with Bley and guitarist Bill Connors, Giuffre is typically soft-spoken (on tenor, alto, and clarinet), improvising freely but in a thoughtful fashion. In other words, his style was largely unchanged from 1962, still out of fashion but quite individual.

Charlie Haden   Bassist Charlie Haden, a very important contributor to the Ornette Coleman Quartet during 1959–61, worked in San Francisco with pianist Denny Zeitlin during 1964–66, had several reunions with Coleman, and in 1969 put together his Liberation Music Orchestra. A politically active leftist, Haden blended together a hatred toward fascism with his interest in the Spanish Civil War of the late 1930s, and the result was the intriguing 1970 recording ◉ **Liberation Music Orchestra** (Impulse 188). The band is filled with many of the who's who of the American avant-garde including Don Cherry, Michael Mantler, Gato Barbieri, Dewey Redman, Perry Robinson, Roswell Rudd, Sam Brown (who is well featured), and Carla Bley, who arranged the music. Performing four songs from the Spanish Civil War, three Bley tunes, two by Haden (including his famous "Song for Che"), and Ornette Coleman's "War Orphans," the band is inspired by the unusual material. This is an early example of folk and world music being included as part of jazz and also one of the few overtly political jazz recordings, not only memorializing past battles but being a protest against the Vietnam war and the fascist government that was running Portugal at the time.

In 1976, Haden embarked on a completely different project. On two albums made for John Snyder's Horizon label, he recorded a duet apiece with some of his favorite jazz musicians. **Closeness Duets** (A&M 0808) has the bassist teamed with Keith Jarrett, Ornette Coleman (the memorable "O.C."), harpist Alice Coltrane, and percussionist Paul Motian (on the highly political "For a Free Portugal"). **The Golden Number** (A&M 0825) consists of collaborations with Don Cherry (on trumpet and flutes), Archie Shepp (on the excellent "Shepp's Way"), Hampton Hawes (jamming Ornette Coleman's blues "Turnaround"), and Ornette, who unfortunately just plays trumpet on "The Golden Number." The music in general is quite intriguing with plenty of variety.

Julius Hemphill   As an altoist (where he managed to be both bluish and dissonant at the same time) and a composer, Julius Hemphill was one of the giants of the avant-garde starting in the early 1970s. Born in Fort Worth, Texas, he took clarinet lessons from John Carter, studied music at North Texas State, worked locally, and served in the military. In 1968 when he was 28, Hemphill moved to St. Louis, Missouri, where he formed the Black Artists Group, founded the Mbari label, and recorded **Dogon A.D.** in 1972, a set soon reissued on an LP by Arista Freedom (Arista 1028). Hemphill (on alto and flute), trumpeter Baikida Carroll, cellist Abdul Wadud, and drummer Philip Wilson are in particularly inventive form on three lengthy originals, both as soloists and in ensembles where they react instantly to each other. After moving to New York, Hemphill made records with Anthony Braxton and Lester Bowie in 1974, was part of the loft jazz scene, and in 1975 recorded ◉ **Coon Bid'ness** (Black Lion 760217). This stimulating set includes a 20-minute version of "The Hard Blues" that was taken from the same session as **Dogon A.D.**, with Hamiet Bluiett making the group a quintet. The other four selections are briefer and feature Hemphill, Bluiett, Wadud, Arthur Blythe, Barry Altschul, and Daniel Zebulon on congas. The music is particularly intriguing in its emphasis on building up the improvisations as a logical outgrowth from the advanced compositions.

In 1976 Julius Hemphill became (along with David Murray, Oliver Lake, and Hamiet Bluiett) a founder of the World Saxophone Quartet. Because of his skillful writing, Hemphill would be arguably the most important force in that innovative band for the next 14 years.

Dave Holland   One of the most technically skilled of the avant-garde bassists of the era, Dave Holland was

Ron Carter's replacement with Miles Davis (1968–70), a member of Circle (1970–71), and part of Anthony Braxton's quartet (1972–76) in addition to playing with Paul Bley, Stan Getz, and the trio Gateway (with John Abercrombie and Jack DeJohnette). His 1972 CD set ● **Conference of the Birds** (ECM 1027) is most notable both for his six diverse originals and for being the only joint recording by Braxton and Sam Rivers, who are joined in the quartet by Holland and Barry Altschul. The music is often quite free yet, thanks to the anchor that Holland provides, perfectly under control, quite coherent, and containing plenty of color and variety.

Joseph Jarman A key member of the Art Ensemble of Chicago for decades, Joseph Jarman also occasionally led his own albums. As **If It Were the Seasons** (Delmark 417) was recorded in 1968 just before Jarman joined the Art Ensemble. Jarman is heard on alto, bassoon, soprano, fife, and recorder leading a group with some famous sidemen (Muhal Richard Abrams, tenor saxophonist Fred Anderson, and John Stubblefield) and some obscure players (bassist Charles Clark, drummer Thurman Barker, flutist Joel Brandon, trumpeter John Jackson, and trombonist Lester Lashley). The adventurous Chicago-based musicians perform two lengthy group improvisations (with Sherri Scott's voice added to "Song for Christopher"), contrasting sound with silence, and noise with more conventional playing in fascinating fashion. Released in 1971, **Together Alone** (Delmark 428) has Jarman and Anthony Braxton playing a wide variety of reeds in a set of duets, but the improvisations tend to ramble and the musicians do not seem to communicate all that well, leading to self-indulgence and a bit of tedium. But when taking chances at this level, not every project works equally well.

Steve Lacy In 1967 soprano/saxophone great Steve Lacy moved to Italy, relocating to France three years later. Now a full-fledged member of the avant-garde, Lacy was in some ways the Lee Konitz of free jazz, playing thoughtful and relaxed solos (often built off of scales) rather than completely cutting loose and screaming through his horn. He occasionally still explored Thelonious Monk songs but mostly stuck to originals. Lacy began teaming up with his future wife cellist/singer Irene Aebi in 1970 and by 1972 was heading a quintet with Aebi, altoist Steve Potts, bassist Kent Carter, and drummer Noel McGhie (replaced by Oliver Johnson the following year). Lacy also recorded in a variety of settings ranging from unaccompanied soprano solos to works with larger ensembles.

During this era (starting in 1969 and accelerating by the mid-1970s), Lacy recorded for many small labels including Saravah, BYG, La Compagnie, Futura, Sassetti, America, Emanem, Quark, Vista, L.C.P., FMP, Denon, Alm, Morgue, Japanese Columbia, Red, Ictus, Black Saint, Cramps, and Improvising Artists (the only set made for an American company). Unfortunately, few of these valuable recordings, which include **Moon** (BYG 529352), a set of Thelonious Monk tunes called **Epistrophy** (BYG 529126), **The Crust** (Emanem 304), **Scraps** (Saravah 10 049), **Stabs** (FMP 05), and **Dreams** (Saravah 10058) are out on CD yet, but there are a few exceptions. **Solo** (Emanem 590051) from 1972 was Lacy's first unaccompanied recording, and it is an intriguing and generally thoughtful exploration of his horn's range and potential. Released in 1976, **Trickles** (Black Saint 120008), one of the first releases from the significant Italian Black Saint label, has a reunion between Lacy and Roswell Rudd, with Ken Carter and Beaver Harris completing the quartet. Rather than playing Monk tunes as they had in the early 1960s, the program features lively interplay on five of Lacy's diverse originals including "Robes" and "I Feel a Draught." Less interesting is **Sidelines** (Improvising Artists 123847), a set of duets with the obscure pianist Michael Smith on seven of their originals. The music is thoughtful but quite dry and a bit dull. It is better to pick up **Trickles**.

Oliver Lake One of the most forbidding of the avant-garde altoists of the 1970s, Oliver Lake has also recorded on flute and soprano sax. He grew up in St. Louis, Missouri, playing drums originally until switching to alto when he was 18 in 1960. Lake, who worked for a time as a schoolteacher, was a member of the Black Artists Group (BAG), made his recording debut in 1971, lived and played in Paris during 1972–74, moved to New York in 1975, and the following year became a member of the World Saxophone Quartet.

Unfortunately, Lake's 1971 recording **NTU Point from Which Creation Begins** (Arista/Freedom 1024) has not appeared on CD. Featuring Lake in a ten-piece unit, its avant-garde and loose nature (influenced by the Art Ensemble of Chicago) gives one an idea of the hit-and-miss music that the members of BAG were performing at the time. Among the musicians are trumpeter Baikida E.J. Carroll, trombonist Joseph Bowie, drummer Bobo Shaw, and guest Don Moye (from the Art Ensemble) on congas. Released in 1975, **Heavy Spirits** (Black Lion 760209) is a particularly esoteric set, but repeated listenings will reveal a great deal of beauty for some open-eared listeners. Lake is backed by three violinists on a trio of intense pieces, takes "Lonely Blacks" unaccompanied, and performs "Rocket" in an odd trio with Joseph Bowie and Bobo Shaw. There are also three selections in a regular quintet with trumpeter Olu Dara and pianist Donald Smith, but that music is just as challenging. **Heavy Spirits** effectively shows just how far forward avant-garde jazz had come since the high-energy days of 1965.

George Lewis   No relation to the famous New Orleans clarinetist of the same name who died in 1968, trombonist George Lewis has had dual careers as an avant-garde trombonist and a composer of electronic works. Lewis took up the trombone when he was nine in 1961, attended Yale (where he worked with Anthony Davis's sextet), spent two months with Count Basie in 1976, and then became a member of Anthony Braxton's quartet. His debut as a leader was the adventurous **Solo Trombone Album** (Sackville 3012), which includes plunger work on "Phenomenology," a respectful version of "Lush Life," and his overdubbed bones on "Toneburst: Theme for Three Trombones." This set signaled the start of a rather impressive career.

Frank Lowe   Tenor saxophonist Frank Lowe's roots were in R&B, but he has spent all of his career (especially on record) in the avant-garde field. He started on tenor when he was 12, and after college worked with Sun Ra (1966–68), Alice Coltrane, Rashied Ali, Archie Shepp, and Don Cherry. Lowe's debut as a leader was 1973's **Black Beings** (ESP 3013), an intense blowout with Joseph Jarman (on alto and soprano), violinist Leroy Jenkins (using the pseudonym of "The Wizard"), bassist William Parker, and drummer Rashid Sinan. The three selections (which include the 25-minute "In Trane's Name") sometime wander a bit, but the intense music never gets dull. **Fresh** (Black Lion 760214) is a particularly colorful set, with four of the five numbers (including Thelonious Monk "Epistrophy" and "Misterioso") featuring Lowe with Lester Bowie, Joseph Bowie, cellist Abdul Wadud, and either Steve Reid or Bobo

Shaw on drums. Lowe is also heard with an unknown group of local musicians called The Memphis Four, wailing on "Chu's Blues." Throughout, Lowe is featured at his most expressive, showing off his roots in the blues while still playing pretty outside much of the time. Also quite worthy is **The Flam** (Black Saint 120005), a spirited quintet outing with trumpeter Leo Smith, Joseph Bowie, bassist Alex Blake, and Bobo Shaw. The all-star group performs five originals with plenty of emotion, chance taking, and fire.

Ken McIntyre   Multireedist Ken McIntyre did not record at all during 1964–73, primarily working as a music educator. He emerged to lead a series of albums for Steeple Chase starting in 1974 and showed that both his playing abilities and his open-minded style had not declined through the years. **Hindsight** (Steeple Chase 31014) is his definitive release because McIntyre has separate features on alto, flute, bassoon, oboe, and bass clarinet. McIntyre, who always had a style of his own, was open to the innovations of the avant-garde but not shy to embrace melodies. Joined by Kenny Drew, bassist Bo Stief, and drummer Alex Riel, McIntyre is in consistently brilliant form, with the highlights being "Lush Life" (on bassoon), "Body and Soul" (taken on bass clarinet), "Naima" (for his oboe), and a heated alto workout on "Sonnymoon for Two." **Home** (Steeple Chase 31019) is nearly on the same level. McIntyre once again plays all five reeds, this time assisted by Jaki Byard, Reggie Workman, and drummer Andrew Strobert. The leader's ten originals include a blues, the ballad "Charlotte," a tribute to John Coltrane ("Sea Train"), and freer pieces. Released in 1976, **Introducing the Vibrations** (Steeple Chase 31065) features a short-lived group led by McIntyre that also includes pianist Richie Harper, bassist Alonzo Gardner, drummer Andrei Strobert, and Andy Vega on percussion, with trumpeter Terumasa Hino. McIntyre is heard on alto for two pieces and on one song apiece on flute, bass clarinet, oboe, and bassoon. All six of his songs were written during 1956–62 (only one is from after 1959), but they still sound fairly adventurous.

Roscoe Mitchell   During 1968–75, Roscoe Mitchell was mostly involved with the Art Ensemble of Chicago, but he did record one significant set as a leader, **The Roscoe Mitchell Solo Saxophone Concerts** (Sackville 3006), which has not yet been reissued by the Canadian

Sackville label. Mitchell shows that he is a brilliant architect of sound, frequently building up a simple idea to a very complex and intense level. He is heard on soprano, alto, tenor, and bass saxophones at three different festivals, often seeming to think aloud and coming up with fresh and often startling musical directions.

Charles Moffett   Charles Moffett is best known for being the drummer with the Ornette Coleman Trio of the mid-1960s. He actually started out on trumpet, playing with Jimmy Witherspoon when he was a teenager in the 1940s. After switching to drums while in college. Moffett worked as a high school teacher in Texas (1953–61), playing with jazz and R&B bands on the side. He was with Coleman briefly in 1961 before Ornette went into retirement, worked with Sonny Rollins in 1963, recorded **Four for Trane** with Archie Shepp, and led his own groups that for a time included Pharoah Sanders and Carla Bley. Moffett worked and recorded with Coleman's 1965 group with David Izenzon. His debut as a leader, 1969's **The Gift** (Savoy 217), has Moffett also playing vibes and trumpet in addition to drums. Moffett is joined by tenor saxophonist Paul Jeffrey, bassist Wilbur Ware, and both Dennis O'Toole and Charles's seven-year-old son Codaryl Moffett on drums. Codaryl, the first of Moffett's musical sons (bassist Charnett Moffett, who was born in 1967, would become best known) plays surprisingly well despite his ridiculously young age, and he even supplied two of the five originals. The song title "Avant Garde Got Soul Too" sums up this adventurous and colorful set.

In 1970 Charles Moffett moved to Oakland, California, where he directed a music school and played locally with trombonist Steve Turre and Prince Lasha.

David Murray   One of the most technically skilled saxophonists in the avant-garde, David Murray was one of the leaders of the third generation of free jazz, the passionate players who began to mature in the mid-1970s. Possessor of a distinctive tone on tenor sax who has a wide range (able to scream very high notes) and a fine bass clarinetist, Murray was initially influenced by both Albert Ayler and Paul Gonsalves, but he has had his own approach since near the beginning.

Born in Berkeley, California, in 1955, Murray started on alto when he was nine, switching to tenor a few years later to play with an R&B/soul group. In the Los Angeles

area he had the opportunity to work with Bobby Bradford and Arthur Blythe, moving to New York in 1975. In 1976 he made his recording debut as a leader and helped found the World Saxophone Quartet. **Low Class Conspiracy** (Adelphi 5002) from May–June 1976 has not been reissued yet on CD, which is a pity because it shows that the 21-year-old tenor was already on his way to becoming a giant. His explorations with bassist Fred Hopkins and drummer Phillip Wilson are quite adventurous; Murray takes the opening "Extremininity" as an intense unaccompanied tenor feature, a unique way to begin his prolific recording career. **Flowers for Albert** (India Navigation 2039) from June 16, 1976, fortunately is available and has been greatly expanded into a double CD. Murray joins up with trumpeter Olu Dara, Hopkins, and Wilson for five explorative pieces in addition to duets with Hopkins on "Ballad for a Decomposed Beauty" and Wilson on "Roscoe." The music is often quite free but also takes its time, showing off intense passion in well-chosen spots and helping to launch the career of David Murray.

Don Pullen   An avant-garde pianist who often played dense, dissonant chords, Don Pullen's use of catchy rhythms (even when playing atonally) made his music much more accessible than one would expect. Born in 1941, Pullen played music as a youth, studied with Muhal Richard Abrams in Chicago, and made his recording debut in 1964 with Giuseppi Logan. A versatile player, Pullen recorded duets with Milford Graves, played organ with R&B groups (including with Big Maybelle and Ruth Brown), led his own bands, and worked with Nina Simone (1970–71) and Art Blakey's Jazz Messengers (1974). As a member of Charles Mingus's last great ensemble (1973–75), Pullen gained some recognition. His debut as a leader, **Solo Piano Album** (Sackville 3008) from 1974, is his most rewarding recording from this period. His four originals (which include pieces dedicated to Abrams and Malcolm X) include the infectious "Big Alice" and show off his unique style.

Sun Ra   Sun Ra and his Arkestra had already pioneered in both avant-garde jazz and electronic music years before most of the jazz world noticed. Moving his ensemble's home base to Philadelphia in 1970, Ra continued on his eccentric way, playing concerts all over the world (despite the economic impossibility of supporting such a large orchestra) and making recordings almost haphazardly for his Saturn label and occasionally for larger companies.

Outer Spaceways Incorporated (Black Lion 760191) from 1968 features Ra's band at its most radical, alternating simple vocal chants with very outside playing and dense ensembles. Tenor saxophonist John Gilmore, altoist Marshall Allen, and baritonist Pat Patrick were Ra's veterans, interacting with many obscure (and, in some cases, soon forgotten) players on these outer space originals. **My Brother the Wind Vol. 2** (Evidence 22040) is an intriguing if erratic release of music from 1969–70. Some numbers feature a 15-piece group with eight horns, two drums, and three percussionists and are more melodic than one would expect. But this reissue is hurt by a few tedious cuts that have Ra fooling around on his moog synthesizer and "intergalactic" organ. **Space Is the Place** (GRP 249) from 1972 is one of Ra's most consistent releases from the era, highlighted by such trademark tunes as "Rocket Number Nine," "Discipline 33," and "Space Is the Place"; June Tyson leads the group in some humorous vocalizing. An unrelated album with the same title, **Space Is the Place** (Evidence 22070), is the soundtrack to the film of the same name, with the music being even more fragmented and odd (with bits of dialogue from the film) than usual.

There were many other hard-to-find releases made during this period by Sun Ra, some of which may resurface in the future (including a fine appearance at the 1976 Montreux Jazz Festival). Later in the 1970s, Ra would further confound the jazz world by exploring and distorting standards, hinting at his roots in Fletcher Henderson swing but playing the music his own way.

Dewey Redman   As a member of the Ornette Coleman Quartet during much of 1967–74, Dewey Redman often transferred Ornette's ideas to the tenor but played with his own large Texas tone. Redman's choice of notes was very complementary to Coleman's, and they proved to be a perfect team. After that group broke up, Redman worked with Charlie Haden's Liberation Music Orchestra, with the Keith Jarret Quartet, and with Don Cherry, Charlie Haden, and Ed Blackwell in Old and New Dreams. **Tarik** (Fuel 2000 0161175) from 1969 was originally made for the French BYG label. Joined by the Art Ensemble of Chicago's bassist Malachi Favors and Ed Blackwell, Redman mostly cooks on five originals; in

addition, he plays his droning and atmospheric musette on the title track.

Redman led two records for Impulse during 1973–74. **The Ear of the Beheaver** (Impulse 271) has all of the music from the album of the same name plus four of the seven selections from his **Coincide** record. The music includes some rather adventurous tracks, some free bop, a struttin' blues, and quieter ballads. Strangely enough, Redman plays alto on five of the first six selections, and although he plays quite well, he is not as distinctive as on his main horn. In the supporting cast along the way are trumpeter Ted Daniel, cellist Jane Robertson, bassist Sirone, drummer Eddie Moore, Leroy Jenkins, and percussionist Danny Johnson.

Sam Rivers   Sam Rivers, whose tone on tenor was rare in the avant-garde in that it was not influenced by John Coltrane (who was three years his junior), worked with the Cecil Taylor Unit during much of 1968–73. In 1971 he started a movement in New York by presenting concerts at his loft, Studio Rivbea. Within a few years, other New York avant-gardists who were finding it next to impossible to find work in local clubs also opened up their lofts to live performances. The loft jazz movement lasted into the late 1970s.

Streams (Impulse 39120) has Rivers's continuous 50-minute performance at the 1973 Montreux Jazz Festival. Rivers, who is joined by bassist Cecil McBee and drummer Norman Connors, switches between tenor, flute, piano, and soprano sax, having the most success on the former two during this lengthy free improvisation. **Live** (Impulse 268) has a similar four-part performance ("Hues of Melanin") from later in 1973, but unfortunately Rivers only plays tenor for five of the 44 minutes. This CD also has the two-part "Suite for Molde" (originally a section out of the out-of-print LP **Hues**), which fortunately has an 11-minute stretch featuring Rivers on his main ax. He is joined by either McBee or Arild Anderson on bass and Barry Altschul. Unfortunately, Rivers's radical big-band set **Crystals** (Impulse 9286) has not yet been reissued.

Throughout each of his recordings, Sam Rivers shows that he has never played it safe or felt content to be predictable.

Roswell Rudd   After spending the years 1965–67 playing with Archie Shepp, Roswell Rudd worked with altoist Robin Kenyetta, with Charlie Haden's Liberation

Music Orchestra, with the Jazz Composers' Orchestra, and as a leader. His 1974 album **Flexible Flyer** (Freedom 760215) has Rudd doubling on French horn with a diverse quintet also including bebop pianist Hod O'Brien, bassist Arild Anderson, Barry Altschul, and singer Sheila Jordan. On a repertoire that includes "What Are You Doing the Rest of Your Life," "Maiden Voyage," and a few originals (including a medley of three Rudd tunes), the group is both tight and adventurous. The use of Jordan's voice is a wild card that helps make this unusual date a standout.

Pharoah Sanders Famous (or infamous) for his screaming solos with John Coltrane during 1965–67, Pharoah Sanders showed during the next few years that there was much more to him than ferocious atonal improvisations. In fact, for a short time he proved that avant-garde jazz could actually sell well. After playing a bit with Alice Coltrane and recording an obscure album for Strata East, he teamed up with the yodeling vocalist Leon Thomas for 1969's ○ **Karma** (Impulse 153). Alternating passionate outbursts and surprisingly peaceful, spiritual, and mellow playing (almost as if he had two separate musical personalities), Sanders interacts with Thomas in memorable fashion on the 5 1/2-minute "Colours" and the classic 32-minute "The Creator Has a Master Plan," which was a hit of its kind and is still Sanders's most famous recording.

Jewels of Thought (Impulse 247) uses a similar group (with Leon Thomas, pianist Lonnie Liston Smith, both Richard Davis and Cecil McBee on basses, and drummer Idris Muhammad) on lengthy versions of "Sun in Aquarius" and "Hum-Allah-Hum-Allah-Hum-Allah," demonstrating the amount of passion that can be developed over a two-chord vamp. **Deaf Dumb Blind** (Impulse 265) could have been an important album, particularly because it matches Sanders with Woody Shaw and Gary Bartz, but unfortunately on the two lengthy pieces Sanders is only heard on soprano sax and his tenor is definitely missed. **Thembi** (Impulse 253) from 1971 has its moments with Sanders (on tenor, soprano, alto flute, and percussion) playing mostly concise selections; violinist Michael White's appearances are strong assets. **Black Unity** (Impulse 219) is unfortunately quite self-indulgent, consisting of the 37 1/2-minute title cut. The first ten minutes make sense as the piece builds from a drone up to an intense Sanders tenor solo.

But the final 20 minutes are quite aimless with a lot of wandering playing from the oversized rhythm section (which has two basses and two drums) and nothing of interest occurring.

Through 1973, Pharoah Sanders continued coming out with similar records for Impulse, some more successful than others. Although he did not duplicate the success of "The Creator Has a Master Plan," Sanders would continue being one of the most popular of all avant-gardists, one who punctuated his performances with gut-wrenching screams but could also conjure up peaceful spirits.

Archie Shepp In 1968 Archie Shepp was at the height of his playing abilities and influence. A fiery and at times highly political avant-gardist, Shepp had a distinctive sound on tenor (looking toward Ben Webster's growls rather than John Coltrane) and was adept at creating marathon free-form solos although his studio improvisations were usually more concise. **The Way Ahead** (Impulse 272) mostly has Shepp leading a sextet with trumpeter Jimmy Owens, trombonist Grachan Moncur, Walter Davis, Ron Carter, and either Roy Haynes or Beaver Harris on drums. Fiery versions of Moncur's "Frankenstein" and "Sophisticated Lady" (the latter with Shepp as the only horn) are among the more memorable numbers.

Shepp sent much of 1969–70 in Paris where he recorded several albums for the BYG label. **Yasmina, a Black Woman** (Le Jazz 51) has him meeting up with both past masters and his successors. The 20-minute "Yasmina" features Shepp in a 12-piece group with three members of the Art Ensemble of Chicago (Lester Bowie, Roscoe Mitchell, and Malachi Favors), pianist Dave Burrell, and a trio of drummers: Philly Joe Jones, Sunny Murray, and Art Taylor. Shepp is showcased on "Body and Soul" in a quartet with Burrell, Favors, and Jones and teams up with veteran Hank Mobley on "Sonny's Back." Although the music is not essential overall, it does point out the many generations of jazz musicians who were temporarily based overseas in 1969.

Shepp continued recorded for Impulse in the United States during 1971–72, but those sets (which are long out of print) had less of an impact than his work of five years earlier. Released in 1975, **There's a Trumpet in My Soul** (Freedom 741016) has Shepp (who unfortunately also plays some soprano on this date) as the leader of a group that sometimes grows to 13 pieces, including four brass players, two keyboards, and two percussionists. Two vocals by three singers and a poem recitation weigh down the music a bit, but Shepp generally plays well. **Montreux One** (Freedom 741027) and **Montreux Two** (Freedom 741028) are both excellent discs featuring Shepp at the 1975 Montreux Jazz Festival in a quintet with trombonist Charles Greenlee, Dave Burrell, bassist Cameron Brown, and drummer Beaver Harris. The first set has Shepp adding a lot of emotion to "Lush Life" and digging into his own "U-Jamaa," plus an original apiece by Burrell and Greenlee. **Montreux Two** gets a slight edge because of the superior solos on "Stream," "Blues for Donald Duck," and Benny Golson's "Along Came Betty." 1976's **Steam** (Enja 2076) was the end of an era for Shepp. Starting the following year, he would be spending more time exploring standards although he would never have a conventional style. Shepp (who is also heard a little on piano) explores Duke Ellington's "Solitude," Cal Massey's "A Message from Trane," and his own "Steam" in a trio with Cameron Brown and Beaver Harris. Unlike some of his later, more reverent interpretations, Shepp mostly tears into these tunes with his raspy tone, showing why his style was considered both innovative and a bit scary when he first burst upon the scene in the mid-1960s.

Sonny Simmons   A fixture during this period in the San Francisco Bay Area, altoist Sonny Simmons and his wife, the powerful trumpeter Barbara Donald, played stirring free jazz on a nightly basis for a time. **Manhattan Egos** (Arhoolie 483) from 1969 is a memorable outing, with the pair joined by bassist Juma and drummer Paul Smith for five Simmons originals including "Coltrane in Paradise," "Manhattan Egos," and "Seven Dance of Salami"; the latter has the unique trio of Simmons on English horn with Juma and Voodoo Bembe on congas.

But after recording two long-scarce albums for Contemporary during 1969–70 (**Rumasuma** and **Burning Spirits**), Sonny Simmons drifted away into obscurity, eventually getting divorced from Donald and not recording again for 20 years.

Cecil Taylor   After just working infrequently during much of the 1960s, conditions improved greatly for Cecil Taylor in the following decade. Europe opened up and he appeared frequently at music festivals. He became

an educator, teaching for a time at the University of Wisconsin in Madison, and Antioch College in Ohio, and he was awarded a Guggenheim Fellowship in 1973, which helped his financial situation. None of this resulted in the pianist's music becoming mellow or less relentless; in fact, the opposite was true.

Taylor made few recordings during 1968–72. The three-LP set from 1969 **The Great Concert of Cecil Taylor** (Prestige 34003) has been reissued as three bootleg CDs **Nuits de la Fondation Maeght** (Jazz View 001, 002, and 003). Taylor's quartet, with altoist Jimmy Lyons, Sam Rivers on tenor and soprano, and drummer Andrew Cyrille (with no bass), perform a 90-minute work and a 20-minute encore. The music is intense, thoroughly atonal, extremely passionate, and never lets up.

Indent (Freedom 741038) from 1973 is a solo concert on which Taylor performs three lengthy improvisations while ● **Silent Tongues** (1201 Music 9017) has piano solos from the 1974 Montreux Jazz Festival. The latter features Taylor performing his five-movement work "Silent Tongues" along with a couple of brief encores, and it is a strong example of his forbidding playing.

Dark to Themselves (Enja 79638) from 1976 has a continuous 61-minute performance of "Streams and Chorus of Seed" by a quintet with Lyons, trumpeter Raphe Malik, tenor saxophonist David Ware, and drummer Marc Edwards. Other than a quick theme and a few brief transitions, this is a free improvisation full of great passion and intensity. **Air Above Mountains** (Enja 3005), also from 1976, has Taylor playing solo in Austria for more than 76 minutes with the music never running short of energy.

Taylor essentially played the piano like a drum set, with an emphasis on thunderous sounds, leavened only occasionally by quieter lyrical sections that were also filled with a great deal of tension. No jazz musician was more advanced, then or now.

Hard Bop, Soul-Jazz, and Post-Bop

During 1955–65, hard bop was the modern mainstream of jazz and in its golden age. Soul-jazz was a funkier outgrowth of this music, placing a greater emphasis on bluish solos and funky rhythmic grooves. But with fusion's rise, the growing popularity of electric keyboards at the expense of the Hammond B-3 organ, the influence of the avant-garde on soloists, the decline and eventual death of Blue Note (the top label in documenting this music), and the dominance of the scene by rock and (by the mid-1970s) disco, both hard bop and soul-jazz were in danger of expiring altogether.

After Blue Note quickly declined during 1968–69, there were many fewer hard bop sessions being recorded, and the surviving artists were often heard in more commercial and funkier settings. The subtleties of early soul-jazz were replaced by a more insistent funk beat and throwaway originals in hopes of gaining a larger dancing audience. Many of the veteran organists experimented with electric keyboards, losing much of their musical personality that way. Fans of hard bop and soul-jazz would have to wait until the late 1970s before those styles began to make their comeback.

At the same time, some musicians performed in an open idiom that could be called "post-bop." More advanced than hard bop but not as free as avant-garde jazz, this music featured highly original and unpredictable solos that did not fit securely into any style other than modern jazz. Ranging from Wayne Shorter and McCoy Tyner to Pat Martino and Woody Shaw, the music was based in swinging jazz but always looking forward, being touched by the avant-garde and fusion without really falling into those areas. Although hard bop had specific musical rules that were often bent, post-bop was much more flexible and open to new concepts.

This section charts the activities of a wide variety of modern mainstream hard bop, soul-jazz, and post-bop musicians plus such continually modern veterans as Charles Mingus and Sonny Rollins.

Cannonball and Nat Adderley   After the success of "Mercy, Mercy, Mercy" in 1966, Cannonball Adderley's Capital recordings greatly declined in interest, particularly in jazz content. Although Adderley's band ranked at the top in the late 1960s with the Charles Lloyd Quartet as the most popular group in jazz (during a period when jazz's popularity was at an all-time low), in reality Adderley became quite lazy on his recordings, delegating much of the solo space to his rhythm section, which by 1971 had funk keyboardist George Duke. It is no coincidence that such forgettable efforts as **The Price You Got to Pay to Be Free** (Capitol 636) and **Black Messiah** (Capitol 846) have not been reissued on CD yet.

In 1973 Cannonball Adderley switched to the Fantasy label and his recordings improved a bit. Although **Inside Straight** (Original Jazz Classics 750) and **Pyramid**

(Original Jazz Classics 952), which utilize the rhythm section of keyboardist Hal Galper, bassist Walter Booker, and drummer Roy McCurdy, are far from classics, they at least find Cannonball playing quite well. ❶ **Phenix** (Fantasy 79004) has Cannonball Adderley taking a rare look into the past, reviving such tunes as "Hi-Fly," "Work Song," "Jive Samba," "This Here," and even "The Sidewalks of New York." Cannonball Adderley and his brother and long-time cornetist, Nat Adderley, recapture the spirit of their early days on this superior retrospective, which has excellent playing from keyboardist Mike Wolff, Booker, McCurdy, and such alumni as George Duke, Sam Jones, and Louis Hayes.

Sadly, after recording half of the so-so album **Lovers** (last out on LP as Fantasy 9505), Cannonball Adderley died of a heart attack at the age of just 46, a major loss to jazz.

Nat Adderley, who had recorded occasional albums as a leader since 1955, including **Branching Out** (Original Jazz Classics 255), **Work Song** (Original Jazz Classics 363), and **Much Brass** (Original Jazz Classics 848), plus dates for Atlantic and lightweight orchestra and concept albums for A&M and Capitol, chose to carry on. Originally heavily influenced by Miles Davis (although having a soulful approach of his own), Nat Adderley was heard at his best during the 1958–66 period with his brother's band. His cornet chops began to decline in the late 1960s, along with his range and his endurance. After Cannonball Adderley's death, Nat Adderley led a similar quintet (with various altoists in his brother's place) for the remainder of his life. Although his first record as a leader after his brother's death is titled **Don't Look Back** (Steeple Chase 91059) and this is a fairly adventurous effort with the reeds of Ken McIntyre and John Stubblefield, Adderley would spend the rest of his career in his brother's shadow.

Monty Alexander   Monty Alexander, a talented pianist influenced by Oscar Peterson, Nat Cole, and Gene Harris, came into his own in the 1970s. His band Monty and the Cyclones had been popular in Jamaica during 1958–60. Alexander moved to the United States in 1962, began recording as a leader three years later, and recorded regularly for the European MPS label during 1971–77. **Live at the Montreux Festival** (MPS 817 487) features Alexander (four days past his 32nd birthday) in 1976 leading a trio that also includes bassist John Clayton and drummer Jeff Hamilton, playing his usual repertoire of the period including Ahmad Jamal's "Nite Mist Blues," a lengthy "Work Song," "Battle Hymn of the Republic," and even "Feelings" (which he does his best to uplift).

Kenny Barron   Pianist Kenny Barron, 14 years younger than his brother tenor saxophonist Bill Barron, moved to New York in 1961 when he was 18. After some freelancing, Kenny Barron worked as a member of the Dizzy Gillespie Quintet (1962–66) and the bands of Freddie Hubbard (1966–70) and Yusef Lateef (1970–75). Initially a bop-based pianist, Barron's style was always forward looking, and he developed into a major advanced hard bop/post-bop player. **Soft Spoken Here** (32 Jazz 32023) is a single CD that reissues his first and fifth albums for Muse, recorded in 1973 and 1980. Some of the earlier selections find him sounding a bit unrecognizable on electric piano although his playing is creative, exploring a bit of fusion and funk in addition to straightahead pieces. But it is the later album (a quintet outing with John Stubblefield on tenor and soprano, vibraphonist Steve Nelson, Buster Williams, and Ben Riley) that is of greatest interest. The unit plays four Barron tunes (including "Golden Lotus") plus "Darn that Dream" in a very musical and uncategorizable fashion. Another excellent example of Barron's playing from this period can be heard on 1974's **Peruvian Blue** (32 Jazz 32083), which features the pianist playing solo, in duos, in a trio, and with extra percussionists, assisted by bassist David Williams, guitarist Ted Dunbar, and Albert "Tootie" Heath. An underrated composer, Barron (30 at the time) performs four of his lesser-known originals plus "Blue Monk" and "Here's that Rainy Day."

Gary Bartz   In 1968, 27-year-old Gary Bartz was considered one of the most promising young altoists in jazz. After studying at Juilliard and the Peabody Conservatory, he worked with Max Roach (1964), Art Blakey's Jazz Messengers (1965-66), McCoy Tyner, and Blue Mitchell. Other than one number left off because of lack of space, ● **Libra/Another Earth** (Milestone 47077) reissues his first two albums as a leader, from 1967–68. The **Libra** half has Bartz joined by Jimmy Owens, pianist Albert Dailey, Richard Davis, and Billy Higgins for four originals plus a lyrical "Cabin in the Sky," "Deep River," and Charlie Parker's "Bloomdido." Although that set finds Bartz and his sidemen pushing ahead of the mainstream a bit, **Another Earth** is more

advanced and straddles the avant-garde. Bartz duets with Reggie Workman on "Lost in the Stars," plays three numbers with Workman, pianist Stanley Cowell, and drummer Freddie Waits, and it welcomes Charles Tolliver and Pharoah Sanders (who is more restrained than he usually was during the period) to the 23½-minute, three-part "Another Earth."

Bartz's career was off to a strong start, and it was bolstered by his 1970–71 stint with Miles Davis (which included some excellent solos on **Live/Evil**). In 1972 he formed his Ntu Troop, which at the 1973 Montreux Jazz Festival recorded **I've Known Rivers And Other Bodies**, one of Bartz's finest hours on record and last available as the double LP Prestige 66001 and due at this writing to be reissued on CD. The group (consisting of Bartz who doubles on soprano, keyboardist Hubert Eaves, bassist Stafford James, and drummer Howard King) performs stirring originals and seemed to find an ideal middle ground between hard bop and the avant-garde, hinting at early fusion and funk while sounding quite distinctive.

Unfortunately, from this point on, Bartz's recordings quickly descended into forgettable commercialism. Three LPs, **Singerella/A Ghetto Fairly Tale** (Prestige 10083), **The Shadow Do** (Prestige 10082), and **Music Is My Sanctuary** (Capitol 1647), waste Bartz's potential on low-quality funk productions, forgettable originals, and an emphasis (particularly on the Capitol LP) on dance rhythms. It would be some time before the "real" Gary Bartz appeared on record again on a consistent basis.

Richie Beirach   A subtle pianist with a style of his own, Richie Beirach played with Stan Getz in 1972 and Dave Liebman (off and on starting in 1973). He began to record as a leader in 1974, and **Leaving** (Storyville 4149) from two years later teams Beirach in introspective yet explorative duets with flutist Jeremy Steig. Inspired by both Bill Evans and classical music, Beirach shows at that early point that he can adapt his style to anything from hard bop to free improvisation.

Art Blakey's Jazz Messengers   After having made so many high-quality recordings for Blue Note, Art Blakey's Jazz Messengers were only occasionally documented during the 1968–75 period. **Moanin'** (LaserLight 17127) has the band sounding fairly advanced due to the tenor solos of Billy Harper. This live set from 1968 also features Bill

Hardman (who returned to the Jazz Messengers on a few occasions), Julian Priester, pianist Ronnie Mathews, and bassist Lawrence Evans on such numbers as "Slide's Delight," "You Don't Know What Love Is" (Harper's ballad feature), and a remake of "Moanin.'" The Jazz Messengers only recorded one album during 1969–71, and unfortunately **Jazz from Japan** (Catalyst 7902) has not appeared yet on CD. For that effort, Hardman and Blakey are joined by the adventurous tenor of Carlos Garnett, bassist Jan Arnet, and the only female to ever be a member of the Jazz Messengers, the great pianist Joanne Brackeen.

Two CDs reissue Art Blakey's Prestige recordings of 1973. **Child's Dance** (Prestige 24130) has some unusual personnel for the Messengers (including flutes, Buddy Terry's soprano, guitar, percussionists, and electric piano), new material (some of which is surprisingly funky), and a memorable version of "I Can't Get Started" that puts the spotlight on trumpeter Woody Shaw. **Mission Eternal** (Prestige 24159) features Shaw, tenor saxophonist Carter Jefferson, returning Messenger member Cedar Walton, and bassist Mickey Bass with Blakey plus occasional appearances by trombonist Steve Turre and guitarist Michael Howell; Jon Hendricks drops by to sing "Moanin'" and "Along Came Betty." Other than a European release with Sonny Stitt, the Jazz Messengers were absent from records during 1974–75. Hard bop was considered out of fashion, but Art Blakey did not veer from the music he believed in, continuing to swing hard and inspire younger players.

Joanne Brackeen   Joanne Brackeen already had a lifetime's worth of experiences by 1975 when the 36-year-old pianist recorded her debut as a leader. Self-taught, she worked in Los Angeles during 1958–59 with Teddy Edwards, Harold Land, Dexter Gordon, and other top players. Marrying tenor saxophonist Charles Brackeen (they were divorced years later), the pianist took time off to raise their four children. After moving to New York in 1965, she developed an inventive post-bop style, one with unusual and distinctive chord voicings. Brackeen was the first and only female member of Art Blakey's Jazz Messengers (1969–72) and also had a three-year stint with Joe Henderson (1972–75). About the time that she joined Stan Getz's quartet for two years, Brackeen recorded **Six Ate** (Candid 71009), which was originally titled (in its LP version) **Snooze**. On this trio date with Cecil McBee and Billy Hart, she

performs four of her challenging originals plus Miles Davis's "Circle," Wayne Shorter's "Nefertiti," and two standards, a strong start to Brackeen's solo career. On July 14–15, 1976, she recorded two albums for different labels. **Invitation** (Black Lion 760218) has three of her originals, two obscurities, and the title cut interpreted in a trio also including bassist Clint Houston and Hart. **New True Illusion** (Timeless 103) is a set of duets with Houston, featuring obscurities by McCoy Tyner (Brackeen's main influence) and Chick Corea, two standards, and a pair of Brackeen's quirky originals. The improvisations are quite advanced yet often surprisingly melodic and rhythmic, serving as evidence that Joanne Brackeen was always original and a vital player.

Roy Brooks   Roy Brooks, a fine drummer from Detroit, Michigan, who is still best known for his association with the Horace Silver Quintet (1959–64), led a particularly strong session in 1970, **The Free Slave** (32 Jazz 32070). Brooks is heard heading an all-star group full of young greats: Woody Shaw, George Coleman, pianist Hugh Lawson, and Cecil McBee. The live set is primarily post-bop with some soul-jazz. The four lengthy originals (three by Brooks) are modern for the period, and the leader's unusual percussion (including a device he blows into that can change the pitch of his drums) adds a bit of uniqueness to the music. Shaw in particular is in top form.

Jaki Byard   Pianist Jaki Byard, who had a second stint with Charles Mingus in 1970, started working as an educator in 1969, which was his main job from that point on although he always remained quite active as a performer. During 1968–69 Byard recorded three final gems in his series for Prestige. Two are reissued (except one selection which is left off because of lack of space) on **Solo/Strings** (Prestige 24246). One date is solo piano (typically ranging from stride and hard bop to free jazz, with some unusual combinations of styles) while the **Jaki Byard with Strings** album is unique. Byard does not use a string section but is instead joined by guitarist George Benson, violinist Ray Nance, cellist Ron Carter, and bassist Richard Davis (plus drummer Alan Dawson); Nance and Benson blend together surprisingly well on the mostly swinging material. ● **The Jaki Byard Experience** (Original Jazz Classics 1913) has the dream matchup of Byard with Rahsaan Roland Kirk (plus Richard Davis and Alan Dawson). Byard and

Kirk should have teamed up more often (there was one previous recording) because they were among the few jazz musicians able to play quite credibly in virtually every style. Their duet version of "Memories of You" is a classic while the romps on "Parisian Thoroughfare," "Evidence," and "Teach Me Tonight" are quite exciting.

With the end of his Prestige years in 1969, Jaki Byard's recordings became less frequent, but nearly everything he recorded during the 1960s (his prime period) is currently available.

Stanley Cowell   Stanley Cowell's piano playing was always versatile enough to fit comfortably into both hard bop and avant-garde settings. Art Tatum was an early inspiration. Cowell attended Oberlin College Conservatory and the University of Michigan, played with Rahsaan Roland Kirk while at Oberlin, and moved to New York in 1966 when he was 25. He played with Marion Brown (1966–67), Max Roach (1967–70), the Bobby Hutcherson–Harold Land Quintet (1968–71), and Charles Tolliver. Cowell and Tolliver worked together in the quartet Music Inc. and co-founded the Strata East label in the early 1970s.

In 1969 Cowell recorded two powerful post-bop sets. The LP **Blues for the Viet Cong** (Freedom 41032) showcases Cowell (who switches to electric piano on two numbers) with bassist Steve Novosel and drummer Jimmy Hopps in a trio. Cowell's somber and modal playing is well showcased on seven of his originals, with his stride version of "You Took Advantage of Me" being a tribute to Art Tatum and serving as a welcome change of pace. Fortunately, the LP **Brilliant Circles** (Black Lion 760204) has been reissued because this is one of Cowell's strongest sessions. He leads an all-star sextet that also includes Woody Shaw, Tyrone Washington on tenor, flute, and clarinet, Bobby Hutcherson, Reggie Workman, and Joe Chambers. The musicians interpret a challenging repertoire consisting of an original apiece by Cowell, Washington, Shaw, and Hutcherson, and their playing is consistently inspired and inventive.

King Curtis   King Curtis, one of the last major R&B tenor saxophonists, always had the ability to play jazz as he showed in the early 1960s when he recorded a couple combo dates with Nat Adderley. However, he spent most of his career playing rock 'n' roll, R&B, and soul music, making a name for himself as a greatly in-demand session musician.

At the 1971 Montreux Jazz Festival, Curtis teamed with veteran blues pianist/vocalist Champion Jack Dupree, guitarist Cornell Dupree (in excellent form), bassist Jerry Jemmott, and drummer Oliver Jackson. It is intriguing hearing Curtis adapt his style to Dupree's irregular chorus lengths, often playing a supporting role behind the pianist's witty vocals but getting off a few strong tenor solos. "Junker's Blues" (with Dupree's funny storytelling) is a classic, and virtually everything on **Blues at Montreux** (Collectables 63312) succeeds. But tragically this would be King Curtis's final recording because three months later the 37-year-old was stabbed to death.

Jack DeJohnette   Originally a pianist who studied classical music, Jack DeJohnette switched to drums while a teenager although he continued playing piano and composing music. After moving to New York in 1966, he had an opportunity to sit in with John Coltrane and Jackie McLean before becoming a member of the Charles Lloyd Quartet (1966–68). DeJohnette was next with the Miles Davis Quintet (which evolved into his electric groups) on and off during 1969–72 before emerging as a bandleader himself. A flexible player, DeJohnette could swing in a loose manner à la Tony Williams (who he had replaced with Davis) but was also quite comfortable playing free-form music or in the more introspective settings of the ECM label (for whom he recorded frequently through the years).

His debut as a leader, **The DeJohnette Complex** (Original Jazz Classics 617), has more than its share of variety. Recorded in late 1968, the music ranges from advanced swinging to brief free improvisations and some avant-funk. The drummer is assisted by Bennie Maupin (on tenor and flute), keyboardist Stanley Cowell, bassists Miroslav Vitous and Eddie Gomez, and Roy Haynes. Six different combinations of musicians are utilized on the eight songs, which consist of five DeJohnette originals, John Coltrane's "Miles' Mode," Cowell's "Equipoise," and Vitous' "Mirror Image." In contrast, 1974's **Sorcery** (Original Jazz Classics 1838) is erratic and directionless with an excess of rambling. DeJohnette (doubling on keyboards) plays three fusion pieces in a group with Maupin (heard on bass clarinet this time) and both John Abercrombie and Mick Goodrick on guitars; the attempt at humor on "The Right Time" is a bit of a flop although the nearly 14-minute "Sorcery #1" has its worthwhile moments. The second half of this release, with trios by DeJohnette, bassist Dave Holland, and Michael Fellerman on metaphone and trumpet, is less memorable, and overall this music has not dated well.

Charles Earland   For most organists, the late 1960s was the end of their golden era. Soul-jazz was starting to be overshadowed by fusion by then and soon would be lost in disco while the Hammond B-3 organ was for a time being augmented and even replaced by more portable electric keyboards and synthesizers. An exception to the trend was Charles Earland, who in 1969 was just getting his career started.

Although Jimmy Smith was an influence on Earland (as he was on nearly every organist), Earland quickly developed his own sound out of the hard bop/soul-jazz tradition. He had actually started his career as a saxophonist, working on tenor with Jimmy McGriff's group in Philadelphia for three years. During that period McGriff's playing inspired Earland to the point where he taught himself the organ, switching to that instrument when he went out on his own. Earland worked with Lou Donaldson during 1968–69, signed with Prestige, and recorded the finest albums of his career for that label during 1969–74. **Black Talk** (Original Jazz Classics 335) has the organist heading a sextet also including Houston Person and trumpeter Virgil Jones. Earland effortlessly turns rock and pop songs into hard-swinging and soulful jazz (including "More Today Than Yesterday" and "Aquarius"), and one of the songs, "The Mighty Burner," seems like a perfect title for him. Released in 1970, ◉ **Living Black** (Prestige 24182) is a live set featuring Earland at his most heated. The four original songs, three being quite lengthy, include "Key Club Cookout," "Westbound No. 9," "Killer Joe," and a brief "Milestones"; they are augmented on this reissue by a remake of "More Today Than Yesterday" and "Message from a Black Man." In addition to Earland, the group features guitarist Maynard Parker, trumpeter Gary Chandler, and most notably the young tenor saxophonist Grover Washington, Jr., who was already pretty distinctive.

Intensity (Original Jazz Classics 1021) is most notable for including the final recordings of trumpeter Lee Morgan, just two days before his death. Morgan's blues "Speedball" is one of two bonus cuts on the CD reissue of this 1972 set, which once again has Earland transforming some unpromising pop material (including "Happy 'Cause I'm Going Home" and "Will You Still Love Me Tomorrow") into heated soul-jazz. By the time he recorded 1973's **Leaving This Planet** (Prestige 66002), Earland, like his contemporaries, had added electric keyboards and synthesizers, but this date is more adventurous than expected and has guest spots for the

TIMELINE 1971

Chick Corea forms the first version of Return to Forever. • John McLaughlin forms the Mahavishnu Orchestra. • Anthony Braxton is signed to the Arista label for their "Freedom" series. • Sam Rivers begins presenting concerts in his Studio Rivbea loft. • The Giants of Jazz tour and record. • Louis Armstrong dies. • At a Louis Armstrong tribute concert that took place 52 days after his death, Lil Hardin Armstrong collapses and dies on stage while in the middle of playing "St. Louis Blues." • Carla Bley completes **Escalator over the Hill**. • Trumpeter Oscar Brashear moves to Los Angeles where he becomes an important part of the local scene. • George Duke replaces Joe Zawinul in Cannonball Adderley's quintet. • Ken Colyer breaks up his British traditional band because of his erratic health. • Rolf Ericson settles in Germany as a studio musician. • In the Soviet Union, the avant-garde Ganelin Trio (saxophonist Vladimir Chekasin, pianist Vyacheslav Ganelin, and drummer Vladimir Tarasov) is formed. • Violinist Leroy Jenkins, bassist Sirone, and drummer Frank Clayton (soon replaced by Jerome Cooper) form the avant-garde Revolutionary Ensemble. • Many of the surviving members of the Erskine Hawkins Orchestra (including Hawkins, Dud Bascomb, Bobby Johnson, and Haywood Henry) record a reunion LP **Live at Club Soul Sound** (Chess 9141). • Trumpeter Leo Smith records an LP of unaccompanied solos, **Creative Music** (Kabell 1). • Clarinetist Tony Parenti records his final album, titled **The Final Bar**. • A riot at the Newport Jazz Festival closes the festival and results in it moving to New York the following year. • Grover Washington, Jr., launches his career with **Inner City Blues**.

likes of Freddie Hubbard, Eddie Henderson, and Joe Henderson, highlighted by the title cut and Hubbard's "Red Clay."

Eastern Rebellion   In 1974 the co-op Eastern Rebellion was formed, operating on a part-time basis. Pianist Cedar Walton was the main force behind the group that also originally included bassist Sam Jones, drummer Billy Higgins, and Clifford Jordan on tenor. George Coleman had taken Jordan's place by the time Eastern Rebellion made its initial recording in 1975, ● **Vol. 1** (Timeless 101). This classic set has five noteworthy hard bop performances including the definitive version of Walton's most famous composition "Bolivia," Coleman's tricky "5/4 Thing," and Jones's boppish "Bittersweet." Perhaps hard bop was passé by 1975, but the enthusiastic musicians of Eastern Rebellion certainly did not care.

Booker Ervin   In 1968, 37-year-old Booker Ervin recorded his last two albums as a leader. One of the sets, **Back from the Gig** (which teams Ervin with Woody Shaw), was unissued until the late 1970s when it came out as part of a double LP matched with a Horace Parlan set. **The In Between** (Blue Note 59379) is similar to Ervin's series at Prestige, being an advanced hard bop date that hints at the avant-garde without really crossing the line. Ervin's intense yet soulful tenor is well featured in a quintet with trumpeter Richard Williams, pianist Bobby Few, bassist Cevera Jeffries, and drummer Lennie McBrowne.

But because of a kidney disease, Booker Ervin passed away in 1970, three months short of his 40th birthday.

Bill Evans   While jazz changed during 1968–76, Bill Evans evolved, too, but within himself, growing steadily as an improviser. His trio, which featured bassist Eddie Gomez during 1966–77 and, after stints by Jack DeJohnette and John Dentz in 1968, Marty Morell (1968–75), and Eliot Zigmund (1975–77) on drums, was one of the most popular in jazz. Evans became well known for his interpretations of ballads, for his influential chord voicings, and for his interplay with his sidemen.

Evans recorded regularly for Verve through 1969 and, after a few years of freelancing, signed with Fantasy in 1973. **At the Montreux Jazz Festival** (Verve 539 758) has the Evans-Gomez-DeJohnette Trio performing such songs as "One for Helen," "Quiet Now," "Nardis," and "The Touch of Your Lips." **What's New** (Verve 829 579)

from 1969 was Morell's debut with the group and is actually a quartet date with flutist Jeremy Steig. Most of the tunes on this enjoyable set were played by Miles Davis in earlier years including "So What," "Straight No Chaser," and "Autumn Leaves" although the group also performs Evans's "Time Out for Chris" and the "Spartacus Love Theme." Evans's Verve period ended anticlimactically with **Alone** (Verve 589 319), which originally consisted of five rather rambling solos and has been joined on the reissue by five alternate takes and two additional performances. Evans does not play bad, but nothing memorable occurs.

Jazzhouse (Milestone 9151) and **You're Gonna Hear from Me** (Milestone 9164) are both taken from the same night (November 24, 1969), featuring the Evans Trio at Club Montmartre in Copenhagen. Virtually all of the songs were recorded by the pianist elsewhere, but these versions of "A Sleepin' Bee," "Emily," "Nardis," "Waltz for Debby," and "California Here I Come" hold their own with the previous renditions. In the early 1970s Evans doubled on electric piano occasionally. **The Bill Evans Album** (Columbia/Legacy 64963) has Evans playing both acoustic and electric pianos on seven of his stronger originals including "Funkallero," "The Two Lonely People," "Re: Person I Knew," "T.T.T.," and "Waltz for Debby." Evans's second and final Columbia album, **Living Time** (Sony 65467), has the pianist reuniting with arranger George Russell (with whom he had recorded in the 1950s), but unfortunately the music is not all that interesting. Russell's "Living Time" has eight "events" that feature crowded ensembles played by Evans's trio, two other keyboardists, and 17 additional musicians. Nothing very memorable occurs, making this a disappointing release.

The nine-CD box set, **The Complete Fantasy Recordings** (Fantasy 9-10123), has all of Evans's work for the label during 1973–77. Evans recorded 11 sessions for Fantasy in all, and this box includes all of the issued material plus nine numbers from a previously unreleased 1976 concert and the pianist's appearance on Marian McPartland's "Piano Jazz" radio program, which is a fascinating hour of discussion and music. In addition to the many trio performances, there are duets with Eddie Gomez, a set with singer Tony Bennett, and a couple of quintet albums with Harold Land, Warne Marsh, Lee Konitz, Kenny Burrell, Ray Brown, and Philly Joe Jones as sidemen. Other than the 1976 concert and the McPartland show, the music is also largely available on these individual CDs: **The Tokyo Concert** (Original Jazz Classics 345), **Eloquence** (Original Jazz Classics 814), **Re: Person I Knew** (Original Jazz Classics 749), **Since We Met** (Original Jazz Classics 622), **Intuition** (Original Jazz Classics 470), **The Tony Bennett/Bill Evans Album** (Original Jazz Classics 439), **Montreux III** (Original Jazz Classics 644), **Alone Again** (Original Jazz Classics 795), **Quintessence** (Original Jazz Classics 698), **Cross-Currents** (Original Jazz Classics 718), **I Will Say Goodbye** (Original Jazz Classics 761), and **From the Seventies** (Original Jazz Classics 1069). Although not quite as essential as Bill Evans's earlier Riverside and Verve dates or his work from 1979–80, his underrated Fantasy sessions are well worth exploring.

Leonard Feather   The most famous jazz critic in the world during his 50-plus-year reign (which began in the late 1930s), Leonard Feather was also a songwriter, a rather basic pianist, and an occasional record producer. In 1971 he led all-star groups that he called the Night Blooming Jazzmen, recording a pair of albums for Mainstream. In the early 1990s, the two records were reissued in full on the single CD **Night Blooming** (Mainstream 719). With such notables as Blue Mitchell, either Ernie Watts or Lew Tabackin on reeds, Fred Robinson or Joe Pass on guitar, and Feather himself playing background piano, the music is both boppish and funky. Twelve of the 14 songs were composed by Feather including "Evil Gal Blues" (which has one of two vocals by Kitty Doswell), "I Remember Bird," "Signing Off," "Twelve Tone Blues," and the catchy "Nam M'Yoho Ren' Ge Kyo." This set is well worth searching for and was Feather's last recording even though he still had a couple decades to go in his jazz critic career.

Clare Fischer   Throughout his career, Clare Fischer has excelled in several roles. An excellent pianist, Fischer began doubling on organ early on, became notable as an arranger for both big bands and vocal ensembles, and composed the two standards "Pensativa" and "Morning." Although some of his work has been in straightahead jazz, Fischer has always been a lover of Brazilian and Latin music. After moving to Los Angeles in 1957, Fischer worked as a pianist and arranger for the Hi-Los, arranged for Dizzy Gillespie's 1960 album **A Portrait of Duke Ellington**, and started leading his own record dates in 1962. Most of his sets for Pacific Jazz, Revelation, Columbia, and MPS are scarce today.

Thesaurus (Koch 8540) from 1968 is a strong example of Fischer's big-band writing. With fine solo work from altoist Gary Foster, tenor Warne Marsh, Bill Perkins on baritone, and trumpeters Conte Candoli and Steve Huffsteter, the band performs such songs as "Miles Behind," "Lennie's Pennies," "Upper Manhattan Medical Group," and "In Memoriam" (for the slain Kennedy brothers); the latter has a brief and rare alto solo by the multitalented Fischer.

Tommy Flanagan   One of the top jazz pianists to emerge from Detroit in the 1950s, Tommy Flanagan recorded frequently as a leader and a sideman during the first five years after moving to New York in 1956. However, his two long stints (1963–65 and 1968–78) as Ella Fitzgerald's accompanist led to him being greatly underrated. It is not surprising that Flanagan would be overlooked during this period because he did not have an opportunity to lead an album of his own during 1962–74. However, 1975's **The Tokyo Recital** (Original Jazz Classics 737) shows that all of the years as a supportive player had not dulled his solo abilities. Teamed with bassist Keter Betts and drummer Bobby Durham, Flanagan interprets a full set of Duke Ellington and Billy Strayhorn–associated songs including memorable versions of "UMMG," "Main Stem," "Chelsea Bridge," and "The Intimacy of the Blues."

Frank Foster   After leaving the Count Basie Orchestra, tenor saxophonist Frank Foster modernized his solo style (becoming influenced by John Coltrane), had a stint with Elvin Jones (1970–72), and led a band that he called the Loud Minority (an answer to Richard Nixon's championing of the so-called "silent majority." Released in 1974, **The Loud Minority** (Mainstream 718) has Foster leading a 15-piece band consisting of six horns, a guitarist, two keyboardists (Harold Mabern and Jan Hammer), two bassists (Stanley Clarke and Gene Perla), three drummers (including Elvin Jones), and percussionist Airto Moreira. The music is intriguing in spots but also very much of the period and somewhat dated. Dee Dee Bridgewater speaks and shouts some protest lyrics on the title cut and sings wordlessly on "E.W.—Beautiful People" (which is sunk by Foster's out-of-tune soprano solo). The overcrowded ensembles on the four lengthy numbers have their appeal and there are spots for Hammer, guitarist Earl Dunbar, and trumpeter Marvin Peterson, but this was not a band heading for immortality.

Von and Chico Freeman   A hard bop–oriented improviser, Von Freeman's unusual tone on tenor is an acquired taste and in some ways more advanced than his ideas. He was a Chicago legend long before he made his first recording at age 50. The brother of guitarist George Freeman and drummer Bruz Freeman, he worked with Horace Henderson (1940–41), served in the military (1941–45), was with one of Sun Ra's early bands (1948–49), and played as a member of the house band at the Pershing Hotel in Chicago. He led his own group in the 1950s (sidemen included pianists Ahmad Jamal and Andrew Hill) and in the 1960s worked with some of the AACM musicians. In 1972 Rahsaan Roland Kirk produced his debut recording, **Doin' It Right Now** (Koch 8536). Joined by pianist John Young, Sam Jones, and Jimmy Cobb, Freeman interprets five originals, including a haunting version of "The First Time Ever I Saw Your Face," "Lost in a Fog," and "Sweet and Lovely." Once one gets past the tone, it is obvious that Von Freeman had a strong musical message of his own.

Von Freeman's son, tenor saxophonist Chico Freeman, began to emerge as an important musician himself during 1975–76. He debuted with the obscure LP **Streetdancer Rising** (Dharma 807) in 1975 and then made a strong impression the following year with **Morning Prayer** (India Navigation 1063). This set, unfortunately not yet out on LP, features the 27-year-old Freeman contributing five compositions, playing tenor, soprano, flute, and panpipe, and being joined by Henry Threadgill (on alto, baritone, and flute), Muhal Richard Abrams, Cecil McBee, flutist Douglas Ewart, and both Steve McCall and Ben Montgomery on percussion. The post-bop performances are unpredictable yet logical inside/outside music, showing that Chico Freeman was one of the most promising of the new players of the mid-1970s.

Carlos Garnett   A potentially explosive tenor saxophonist with an intense tone, Carlos Garnett often appeared in hard bop settings where his solos moved the music further ahead than expected. He grew up in Panama, originally playing calypso and Latin music. After moving to New York in 1962, he worked in rock groups and freelanced but became influenced and inspired by some of the free jazz saxophonists. Garnett worked with Freddie Hubbard (1968–69), Art Blakey's Jazz Messengers, Charles Mingus, Miles Davis (1972), Jack McDuff, Andrew Hill, Gary Bartz, and Norman Connors, leading five albums of his own for Muse during 1974–77.

Garnett's Muse recordings are a bit erratic (with explorative pieces joined by attempts at commercialism), but an excellent sampler, **Fire** (32 Jazz 32043), has the six best selections from the five sets. Garnett is heard in a variety of settings including a sextet, with a string section and fronting a big band. This well-conceived sampler gives listeners the best of early Carlos Garnett.

Jim Hall   One of the most harmonically advanced guitarists to come out of the 1950s, Jim Hall played with Sonny Rollins (1961–62) and Art Farmer (1962–64) before leading his own combos; he also worked in the New York studios for a time. Released in 1971, **Where Would I Be** (Original Jazz Classics 649) includes such numbers as Hall's "Simple Samba," "Baubles, Bangles and Beads," an unaccompanied "I Should Care," and Milton Nascimento's "Vera Cruz." Hall is joined by Benny Aronov (on both acoustic and electric piano), bassist Malcolm Cecil, and Airto Moreira on drums and percussion during the modern yet mostly swinging set.

◉ **Alone Together** (Original Jazz Classics 467), a set of guitar/bass duets with Ron Carter, was a revelation to many listeners at the time. The near-telepathic communication between the two players on a quiet and subtle set full of inner tension is quite memorable. Hall and Carter perform six standards (including "St. Thomas," "Autumn Leaves," and "Alone Together") plus an original apiece.

In 1975 Jim Hall recorded his lone album for CTI, **Concierto** (Columbia/Legacy 65132). The guitarist is teamed in a sextet with Chet Baker, Paul Desmond, Roland Hanna, Ron Carter, and drummer Steve Gadd. A 19-minute "Concierto de Aranjuez" is one of the best versions ever of that piece, and other selections include Hall's "The Answer Is Yes," Duke Ellington's "Rock Skippin'," and two versions of "You'd Be So Nice to Come Home To." The combination of Hall, Baker, and Desmond, three cool-toned and very lyrical players, was quite logical and essentially featured 1950s-style cool jazz quite convincingly in a more modern setting. **Commitment** (A&M 0811) from the following year showcases Hall in several different settings. He has separate duets with pianist Don Thompson (Hoagy Carmichael's "One Morning in May"), his wife Jane Hall (who sings "When I Fall in Love"), Tommy Flanagan, and drummer Terry Clarke. Hall also overdubs acoustic and electric guitars on his solo "Down the Line," jams "Indian Summer" and "Walk Soft" in a quintet with Flanagan and Art Farmer, and uses a slightly larger group on "Lament for a Fallen Matador," a Don Sebesky adaptation of a classical piece that has the haunting voice of Joan LaBarbara.

John Handy   John Handy's great success at the 1965 Monterey Jazz Festival led to four excellent albums (counting the Monterey performance) for Columbia. The final one, 1968's **Projections** (Koch 7865), has the altoist leading a quintet comprised of violinist Michael White (from his Monterey group), pianist Mike Nock, bassist Bruce Cale, and drummer Larry Hancock. The band plays eight group originals, and although the performances are much more concise than on the previous Columbia, the music contains plenty of surprising moments and is quite difficult to classify.

Unfortunately, there were no further recordings by Handy until 1975 by which time his Monterey triumph was far in the past. Later that year he collaborated with several Indian musicians (including Ali Akbar Khan on sarod) in performing improvised Indian music. Otherwise, Handy mostly played in the San Francisco Bay Area, teaching at San Francisco State.

The following year Handy did a surprise turn and recorded the LP **Hard Work** (Impulse 9314). The title cut, a catchy R&B tune with a rhythmic Handy vocal, became a surprise hit and was played on the radio quite a bit during the era. The other selections have some strong moments from Handy on both alto and tenor and a backup band that includes keyboardist Hotep Cecil Barnard, guitarist Mike Hoffmann, and three appearances by Zakir Hussain on tabla. Although "Hard Work" would be John Handy's only hit, it kept him working and recording for several years.

Billy Harper   Billy Harper, like Carlos Garnett, is a passionate tenor saxophonist often featured in settings early in his career that were more conservative than his solos. He graduated from North Texas State College and moved to New York in 1966. Harper worked on and off with Gil Evans for a decade, toured with Art Blakey's Jazz Messengers during 1968–70, gigged often with Lee Morgan, worked with Max Roach, and was with the Thad Jones/Mel Lewis Orchestra (taking a memorable solo on their recording of "Fingers").

Harper, who led an album for Charles Tolliver's short-lived Strata East label in 1973, has the distinction of leading the first record put out by the Italian Black Saint label, a project logically titled **Black Saint** (Black Saint 0001). Three lengthy pieces (including the 21-minute "Call of the Wild and Peaceful Heart") give Harper an opportunity to really stretch out with a high-quality post-bop quintet also including trumpeter Virgil Jones and pianist Joe Bonner.

Eddie Harris   Eddie Harris was at the height of his fame during 1968–69. His "Freedom Jazz Dance" had become a standard, and his recording of "Listen Here" was played often on jazz radio stations. The master of the electronic sax, Harris was able to bridge the gap between jazz, rock, funk, and R&B while still sounding like himself. And during a hit performance at the 1969 Montreux Jazz Festival with Les McCann (released as **Swiss Movement** and reviewed under McCann's name), Harris introduced his "Cold Duck Time."

Unfortunately, Harris's Atlantic recordings of 1968–75 are erratic, shooting off in many directions at once with some ideas being more successful than others. **Silver Cycles** (Collectables 6359) jumps around quite a bit, from the funky "Free at Last" and "1974 Blues" to some electronic avant-garde effects on "Smoke Signals" and "Silver Cycles." **Plug Me In** (Atlantic 1506) is more focused but not available on CD and, at 27 minutes, a rather brief program. "Live Right Now," "It's Crazy," and "Theme in Search of a T.V. Commercial" are the standouts. A 1971 reunion album with Les McCann, **Second Movement** (Label M 5708), is quite weak compared to **Swiss Movement**. The out-of-print LP **Instant Death** (Atlantic 1611) has Harris taking what must be the most exciting reed trumpet solo ever on "Instant Death"; it is surprising that the reed trumpet never caught on. "A Little Wes" is also memorable from this excellent all-round set that features guitarist Ronnie Muldrow and keyboardist Richard Abrams.

However, many of Harris's other recordings of the era focused on comedy (**I Need Some Money**, **That Is Why You're Overweight** and **This Is Why I'm Talking S—t**), focused on his unusual vocals, or were largely uninteresting (**Eddie Harris Sings the Blues** and **Eddie Harris in the U.K.**). Though there were certainly nonmusical factors involved, it seems as if Eddie Harris blew his opportunity to create additional gems during an era when he had a major record company behind him.

Hampton Hawes   Hampton Hawes, whose piano style in the 1950s was similar to that of Bud Powell in the early 1970s, disturbed some of his fans by doubling on electric piano. He wanted to stay contemporary and to an extent had tired of the earlier style although he always remained quite capable of returning to bop whenever he desired.

Released in 1968, **Blues for Bud** (Black Lion 760126), a trio set with bassist Jimmy Woode and Art Taylor, is essentially bebop although Hawes shows that he was already familiar with McCoy Tyner's chord voicings, too. **High in the Sky** (Fresh Sound 59) teams Hawes in 1970 with Leroy Vinnegar and drummer Donald Bailey on five of the pianist's originals plus "The Look of Love," sounding like a post-bop pianist who had an open mind toward both more adventurous jazz and pop music. **Trio at Montreux** (Fresh Sound 133) is an unusual set from 1971 because it has Hawes, bassist Henry Franklin, and drummer Mike Carvin playing a 26-minute version of the pianist's "High in the Sky" and a rendition of "This Guy's in Love with You" that lasts more than 31 minutes. Despite their extreme length, both selections hold one's interest, and Hawes is consistently creative throughout these improvisations. **Live at the Montmartre** (Black Lion 760202) and the LP **A Little Copenhagen Night Music** (Freedom 1043) are almost of the same quality and feature the same trio later in the year with Dexter Gordon sitting in on "Long Tall Dexter" from the latter album.

Hawes began to utilize electric keyboards in 1972, but although it was a move meant partly to make him gain a larger audience, ironically none of his four efforts for Prestige have been reissued on CD yet so his switch to keyboards had the opposite effect. He gained some attention when his memoirs, *Get Up Off Me* (which frankly discuss his difficulties with drugs), were published in 1974. In 1976 Hawes was captured live on **Something Special** (Contemporary 14072) performing three originals, "Sunny," "Fly Me to the Moon," and "St. Thomas" in a quartet with guitarist Denny Diaz, Leroy Vinnegar, and drummer Al Williams. He is also heard that year on **At the Piano** (Original Jazz Classics 877). It seemed only right that what would be his final recording was made for the Contemporary label, the scene of so many of his successes in the 1950s. Teamed with Ray Brown and Shelly Manne, Hawes swings on a couple originals, the two pop tunes of "Blue in Green" and "When I Grow Too Old to Dream."

Unfortunately, the latter song title was quite true for Hampton Hawes, who died of a stroke in 1977 at the age of 48.

Louis Hayes   Best known for his associations with the Cannonball Adderley Quintet (1959–65) and the Oscar Peterson Trio (1965–67), drummer Louis Hayes appeared in a variety of groups in the 1970s including co-leading a group with Junior Cook in 1976 that featured the great Woody Shaw. **Ichi-Ban** (Timeless 102) features the sextet, which also includes pianist Ronnie Mathews, bassist Stafford James, and percussionist Guilherme Franco. Highlights of the fiery hard bop date include Shaw's "The Moontrane," Walter Booker's "Book's Bossa," and the title cut. The band did not last long, but the music still sounds fresh today.

Jimmy Heath   After recording quite a few exciting projects for Riverside during 1959–64, Jimmy Heath went eight years before his next record date as a leader. In the meantime, the tenor saxophonist began playing flute and soprano and freelanced as both a player and an arranger. Heath finally had opportunities to lead three albums during 1972–75. **Jimmy** (Muse 5138) has not been reissued on CD, but fortunately **Love and Understanding** (Xanadu 1231) has. Heath plays each of his three reeds on a diverse program (five originals plus Duke Ellington's "In a Sentimental Mood") that not only features hard bop but light funk and R&Bish jazz. Heath and his players (Curtis Fuller, Stanley Cowell, Bob Cranshaw, Billy Higgins, and cellist Bernard Fennell) are particularly inventive during this generally overlooked set.

Picture of Heath (Prevue 2) was originally issued by Xanadu and, as was true of most Xanadu dates, the accent is on bebop. For the enjoyable blowing date, Heath, Barry Harris, Sam Jones, and Billy Higgins romp on five of the leader's better originals (including "For Minor's Only," "C.T.A.," and the title cut) plus "Body and Soul."

In 1975 Jimmy Heath joined together with his brothers Percy Heath (who was suddenly at liberty since the Modern Jazz Quartet had become inactive) and Albert "Tootie" Heath to form the Heath Brothers Band, a group that would last for seven years.

Joe Henderson   The always-distinctive tenor saxophonist Joe Henderson was a perfect example of a musician perfectly comfortable in playing both inside (within chord structures) and outside (freer improvising), often shifting between the two approaches. His Blue Note recordings for the years 1963–66 are consistently rewarding. Other than stints with Herbie Hancock (1969–70) and a short period with Blood, Sweat & Tears, Henderson primarily led his own groups during 1968–75.

Henderson began recording for the Milestone label in 1967, and the eight-CD set ● **The Milestone Years** (Milestone 4413) has all of his recordings for that company as a leader and including sideman appearances with Flora Purim and Nat Adderley plus a duet with Lee Konitz, dating from 1967–76. Although Henderson was somewhat neglected and underrated during this period and a few of these sets hint at fusion and funk, the tenor stylist plays quite well throughout, and the music is generally very rewarding; none of the 82 selections are dull. Among the key sidemen are trumpeters Mike Lawrence, Woody Shaw, and Luis Gasca, trombonist Grachan Moncur III, and keyboardists Kenny Barron, Don Friedman, Joe Zawinul, Herbie Hancock, George Cables, Alice Coltrane, Mark Levine, and George Duke. Of the sets included in this box, 1967's **The Kicker** (Original Jazz Classics 465), **Tetragon** (Original Jazz Classics 844), **In Pursuit of Blackness/Black Is the Color** (Milestone 47080), **Joe Henderson in Japan** (Original Jazz Classics 1040), **Multiple** (Original Jazz Classics 763), **The Elements** (Original Jazz Classics 913), and **Canyon Lady** (Original Jazz Classics 949) are available individually while the LPs **Power to the People** (Milestone 9024), **If You're Not Part of the Solution** (Milestone 9028), **Black Narcissus** (Milestone 9071), and **Black Miracle** (Milestone 9066) are a bit more difficult to locate. If one had to choose just a couple of the CDs, **The Kicker** and **Joe Henderson in Japan** (a particularly strong showcase for the tenor who stretches out on two originals plus "'Round Midnight" and "Blue Bossa") would get the edge although his more devoted fans will want the box. Also quite rewarding (and not on the box) are two CDs, **Four** (Verve 523657) and **Straight No Chaser** (Verve 531561), taken from an April 21, 1968, engagement with Wynton Kelly, Paul Chambers, and Jimmy Cobb on which Henderson stretches out on a variety of jazz standards, some of which (such as "Limehouse Blues," "Four," and "On the Trail") he did not record elsewhere.

Andrew Hill   Andrew Hill, who recorded some of his most significant work for Blue Note during 1963–66, made dates for Blue Note through 1970, became a jazz educator, and during 1974–76 recorded for Steeple Chase, Arista/Freedom, and the Japanese East Wind label. **Grass Roots** (Blue Note 22672) from 1968 teams the pianist/composer with Booker Ervin, Lee Morgan, Ron Carter, and drummer Freddie Waits for five of Hill's originals, which are both complex and surprisingly catchy at times. The CD reissue adds a previously unreleased session by Hill with Woody Shaw, tenor saxophonist Frank Mitchell, guitarist Jimmy Ponder, Reggie Workman, and Idris Muhammad that is just as adventurous and certainly stands out among Blue Note's increasingly commercial releases of 1968. A few months later, Hill recorded **Dance with Death** (Blue Note 1030), but by then Blue Note was less interested in his brand of creative jazz, and this LP was not released until 1980; it features fine playing by Hill, Charles Tolliver, and Joe Farrell. **Lift Every Voice** (Blue Note 27546) from 1969 has Hill's quintet (with Woody Shaw and Carlos Garnett) joined by seven voices, possibly in an attempt by the label to duplicate the commercial success of Donald Byrd's **A New Perspective** (which had yielded "Cristo Redentor"). However, the music was too unsettling to catch on at that level. The reissue adds a previously unreleased session from 1970 that has nine voices interacting with a Hill group that includes Lee Morgan and Bennie Maupin. In both cases the results are intriguing but not all that compelling, with the voices tending to get in the way and lowering the jazz content of the music, signaling an anticlimactic end to Hill's period on Blue Note.

After not recording at all during 1971–73, Andrew Hill made several records during the next few years. **Spiral** (Freedom 741007) is split between quintet numbers with Lee Konitz (who doubles on soprano) and Ted Curson and quartet performances that showcase the somewhat forgotten altoist Robin Kenyatta. In addition, "Invitation," the one song on the set not written by Hill, is taken as a spontaneous duet with Konitz. 1975's **Live at Montreux** (Freedom 741023) is a very good solo piano set in which Hill explores such numbers as a dirge-like "Nefertiti," an abstract "Relativity," and his infectious "Snake Hip Waltz." Throughout all of his recordings, Andrew Hill always sounded like a true original, playing adventurous music that really could not be grouped with that of anyone else.

Richard "Groove" Holmes   Richard "Groove" Holmes's career during 1968–75 was similar to that of most other organists. He started out at the peak of his popularity, but by the mid-1970s with the decline in interest in the Hammond B-3 organ, he was playing other electric keyboards in commercial settings with mixed musical results. His best sets from the period have been combined in **Legends of Acid Jazz** (Prestige 24187), which has all of the music from his two 1968 Prestige albums **The Groover** and **That Healin' Feelin'**. The former set features Holmes grooving in a trio with either George Freeman or Earl Maddox on guitar and drummer Billy Jackson, and the later date has notable playing by Rusty Bryant (on tenor and alto), guitarist Billy Butler, and drummer Herbie Lovelle. Some of the performances are quite bop oriented, and highlights include "Speak Low," "Blue Moon," "Just Friends," and "On a Clear Day."

Bobby Hutcherson   In the mid-1960s, Bobby Hutcherson was the main vibraphonist associated with "the new thing," free jazz. By 1967 when he began co-leading a quintet with Harold Land, Hutcherson was sounding more like an open-minded hard bop stylist than an avant-gardist. Having made his recording debut for Blue Note in 1963, he continued recording for the label through 1976 although his output (along with much of the material released by the label) in general declined in quality after 1969 because of the shift in focus at Blue Note.

   Patterns (Blue Note 33583) has four originals by drummer Joe Chambers plus one apiece from James Spaulding and Stanley Cowell, who join Hutcherson and Reggie Workman in the quintet. Most memorable is Cowell's "Effi" and "Patterns." The soloing is on a consistently high level even if none of the songs ultimately caught on. **Total Eclipse** (Blue Note 84291) was the first Harold Land-Hutcherson recording, a quintet outing with Chick Corea, bassist Reggie Johnson, and Chambers; the adventurous "Pompeian" and Corea's "Matrix" are standouts. **San Francisco** (Blue Note 28268) has the co-leaders assisted by Joe Sample, bassist John Williams, and Mickey Roker. Included are some themes influenced by John Coltrane. In fact, Land, who had a tone in the 1950s that was not that distant from Hank Mobley, by 1970 was quite influenced by Coltrane's sound and would remain so throughout the second half of his career. **Medina/Spiral** (Blue Note 97508) reissues two other albums by this underrated post-bop group on a single CD. The Los Angeles–based band worked much less often after 1971, but Hutcherson and Land would have occasional reunions in later years.

   Bobby Hutcherson's later Blue Note albums are mostly of lesser interest, often being attempts at widening his audience, but **Live at Montreux** (Blue Note 27819) is an exception. Originally only released in Japan and Europe, this superior set did not come out in the United States until 1994. Featuring the vibraphonist with Woody Shaw, pianist Cecil Barnard, bassist Ray Drummond, and drummer Larry Hancock, this set has fiery solos on modal originals with Shaw often taking solo honors. But it is the type of music that the new owners of Blue Note were no longer interested in by 1973.

Chuck Israels   Chuck Israels made his first recording on the 1958 meeting of John Coltrane and Cecil Taylor. He played bass with George Russell's Sextet (1959–61) and the Bill Evans Trio (1961–66). In the 1970s he became an important educator, leading the National Jazz Ensemble (one of the first jazz repertory bands) during 1973–78. They recorded two albums, the highlights of which have been reissued as **National Jazz Ensemble** (Chiaroscuro 140). The range of their repertoire is quite impressive, including tunes from the books of Jelly Roll Morton ("Black Bottom Stomp"), Count Basie ("Every Tub"), Duke Ellington ("Lady of the Lavender Mist"), Charlie Parker ("Confirmation"), Horace Silver ("Room 608"), and Thelonious Monk ("I Mean You") plus a few more modern originals ("Solar Complexes"). Among the key players are trumpeters Jimmy Maxwell and Tom Harrell, trombonist Jimmy Knepper, Sal Nistico, and pianist Ben Aranov with guest appearances by Bill Evans, Lee Konitz, and Israels himself. The repertory idea was a bit ahead of its time in the 1970s (it would become much more common in the 1990s), but this CD shows the validity of the concept.

Keith Jarrett   One of the most important "new" pianists of the 1970s, Keith Jarrett had been playing piano since he was three in 1948. A professional while in grade school, he studied at Berklee in 1962, freelanced in the Boston area, and in 1965 spent four months with Art Blakey's Jazz Messengers. Jarrett became known while a member of the Charles Lloyd Quartet (1966–69), where his unpredictable post-bop playing (which could be quite funky at times in an eccentric way) helped make the group successful. Jarrett was with Miles Davis during 1969–71 playing organ and keyboards including next to Chick Corea for the first year, but this was a temporary departure for him because he soon swore off electric keyboards and fusion to devote himself to the acoustic piano. In 1971 he began to record for ECM and built up his reputation as one of jazz's most significant pianists.

Prior to his association with ECM, Jarrett had recorded three dates as a leader for Vortex/Atlantic. Released in 1968, **Somewhere Before** (Atlantic 8808) has Jarrett (doubling on soprano sax) in a trio with Charlie Haden and Paul Motian performing at Shelly's Manne-Hole. Ranging from Bill Evans–type post-bop to some free jazz, funk, and the originals "Old Rag" and "New Rag," this is an eclectic and intriguing set. **The Mourning of a Star** (Wounded Bird 1596) from 1971 (also with Haden and Motian) has Jarrett nearly sounding distinctive in spots, stretching beyond Evans and Paul Bley to display his own method of playing trio music. **Expectations** (Columbia/Legacy 65900), originally a double LP and now a single CD, was a major step forward. Jarrett is heard at the head of his classic quartet (with Dewey Redman, Haden, and Motian), sometimes adding guitarist Sam Brown and percussionist Airto Moreira to the tight yet loose and spontaneous group. Ranging from avant-garde explorations to gospel-like soul-jazz, this set allows one to hear for the first time the mature Keith Jarrett.

During the first years of his solo career, 1971–76, Keith Jarrett was primarily heard in two different settings, not counting his occasional forays into classical music. As an unaccompanied piano soloist, Jarrett performed concerts that were spontaneously improvised without any preset songs or specific ideas. Using repetition creatively and leading logically from one idea to another, Jarrett's improvisations were sometimes overlong and meandering but much of the time led to inspiring and fresh new music. **Facing You** (ECM 827 132) is a studio set with concise performances that utilize the idea. Most notable are the two-CD set **Solo Concerts** (ECM 827 747), which includes an improvisation lasting more than 64 minutes (along with briefer pieces), the single disc ◉ **The Koln Concert** (ECM 810 067), and the six-CD set **Sun Bear Concerts** (ECM 843 028). Each of these sets has their stirring moments and shows how unique a player Jarrett had become and how he sounded during his live performances of the era; **The**

Koln Concert gets the edge because it is a little tighter focused than the other two worthy sets. Even if Jarrett's occasionally prickly personality (demanding that his audience be completely silent) and habit of singing along with his playing in eccentric fashion could be distracting, most significant was the way he used aspects of the history of jazz to create new music. Also of interest is **Staircase** (ECM 827 337), an introverted, thoughtful, and wistful if somewhat downbeat set of quiet studio piano solos.

The other direction in Jarrett's career during this period was leading the group that he was heard with on **Expectations**. The five-CD set **The Impulse Years 1973–1974** (Impulse 5-237) has all of the music formerly released as the albums **Fort Yawuh**, **Treasure Island**, **Death and the Flower**, and **Backhand** plus quite a bit of previously unreleased material. With Redman, Haden, Motian, and sometimes Guilherme Franco or Danny Johnson on percussion, Jarrett had one of the top jazz groups of the 1970s. The 29 selections (some of which also include Sam Brown) are perfect examples of inside/outside music, hinting at the avant-garde while not discarding the use of melodies and rhythms. Many strong moments are heard along the way with highlights including the 22½-minute "Death and the Flower" and "Inflight." The four-CD set ◉ **Mysteries: The Impulse Years 1975–1976** (Impulse 4-189), which gets the edge, has all of the music recorded at two marathon three-day recording sessions in December 1975 and October 1976 by the same group. During those dates, enough material was documented to fill the four albums **Shades**, **Mysteries**, **Byablue**, and **Bop-Be**. Other than a few brief exotic sound explorations, the music extends the swinging tradition into complex areas and is free bop at its best; "Shades of Jazz" is a special highlight of this continually fascinating reissue. Also from the quartet is **The Survivors Suite** (ECM 827 131), which is a 48-minute two-part work that holds one's interest throughout, and **Eyes of the Heart** (ECM 825 476), a live set with the 33-minute title cut and an 18-minute "Encore." On these and virtually all of the group's recordings, the communication between the musicians is on a very high level, with Jarrett and Redman bringing out the best in each other.

Elvin Jones   After leaving John Coltrane at the end of 1965 and going on a European tour with Duke Ellington, Elvin Jones became an important bandleader, recording regularly and remaining a major influence on other drummers particularly in his mastery of poly-rhythms. In general, Jones's groups featured fiery saxo-phonists influenced by Coltrane and tireless bassists because he rarely utilized a pianist. Released in 1968, **Heavy Sounds** (Impulse 547 959) has Jones, Frank Foster on tenor, pianist Billy Green, and bassist Richard Davis playing such songs as "Shiny Stockings," Foster's funky "Raunchy Rita," and "Elvin's Guitar Blues" (with Jones making his first and only recording on guitar). But the advanced hard bop music is not all that memorable.

All of Jones's Blue Note dates from 1968–73 were reissued on the limited-edition eight-CD box set. **The Complete Blue Note Elvin Jones Sessions** (Mosaic 8-195). Some of the albums are available individually. **Puttin' It Together** (Blue Note 84282) features Joe Far-rell on tenor, soprano, and flute playing with Jones and Jimmy Garrison in a trio. Farrell in particular is in top form on group originals, obscurities, "For Heaven's Sake," and Jimmy Heath's "Gingerbread Boy." From 1969, **Poly-Currents** (Blue Note 84331) mostly features Jones heading a sextet comprised of both George Coleman and Farrell on reeds, baritonist Pepper Adams, bassist Wilbur Little, and Candido on congas; two songs have the quartet of Farrell, Little, Jones, and flutist Fred Tomp-kins. The music is the type of passionate modal hard bop that Jones would be playing for decades.

Jones's 45th birthday (September 9, 1972) was a good excuse to record his group, and the music is currently available as a pair of CDs: **Live at the Lighthouse Vol. 1** and **Vol. 2** (Blue Note 84447 and 84448). An intense blowout featuring the tenor and soprano saxophone work of Dave Liebman and Steve Grossman plus bassist Gene Perla, these are high-powered and sometimes rowdy jams that are occasionally quite lengthy, includ-ing a 28½-minute "Children's Merry-Go-Round." Lieb-man and Grossman sound inspired by Jones and are quite competitive with each other, resulting in some of their most exciting early playing. Other musicians also passing through Elvin Jones's band during this era (and benefiting from the association) were trumpeter Marvin "Hannibal" Peterson, keyboardist Jan Hammer, and tenor saxophonist Pat LaBarbera.

Philly Joe Jones   Unlike Elvin Jones, who has had many productive years after his Coltrane period, Philly Joe Jones's post–Miles Davis career was anticlimactic. He led some groups of his own, lived in London and

Paris during 1967–72 (sometimes working and record-ing with avant-garde players), and back in the United States was a member of the Bill Evans Trio in 1976. From 1968, **Mo' Joe** (Black Lion 760154) is a fine straight-ahead hard bop date on which Jones inspires a group of British musicians including Kenny Wheeler, altoist Peter King, and tenor saxophonist Harold McNair. Best are Jones's "Trailways Express" (a revisit to the Miles Davis arrangement of "Two Bass Hit"), a surprisingly cooking version of "Here's that Rainy Day," and "Gone, Gone, Gone." But it is surprising that Philly Joe Jones did not accomplish more during these years.

Clifford Jordan   The distinctive if underrated tenor saxophonist Clifford Jordan primarily led his own com-bos during 1968–75, including a quartet with Cedar Walton, Sam Jones, and Billy Higgins in 1975 that was sometimes known as the Magic Triangle. That group was well documented on such albums as **Night of the Mark VII** (32 Jazz 32118), **On Stage Vol. 1** (Steeple Chase 31071), **On Stage Vol. 2** (Steeple Chase 31092), **On Stage Vol. 3** (Steeple Chase 31104), **Firm Roots** (Steeple Chase 31033), and **The Highest Mounta in** (Steeple Chase 31047). All are worth picking up with the 32 Jazz CD reissuing an earlier Muse LP. On that set, Jordan performs "Blue Monk," Sam Jones's blues "One for Amos," Walton's appealing "Midnight Waltz," Jordan's title cut, and Bill Lee's "John Coltrane," which hints at part of "A Love Supreme." It may not have been gener-ating headlines, but players such as Clifford Jordan and Cedar Walton were defining the modern mainstream of 1975 jazz.

Rahsaan Roland Kirk   The remarkable Rahsaan Roland Kirk, although never really accepted by the jazz establishment that sometimes painted him as a gim-micky player, was a popular figure in the late 1960s/early '70s. He always had the ability to make the impossible (whether playing three saxes at once, improvising credi-bly in any jazz style, or taking 20-minute one-breath solos) seem like a logical part of his music. Kirk recorded regularly for Atlantic during 1967–75, and although few of his albums quite capture the magic of his live sets, most are worthwhile. **Left and Right** (Collectables 6340) can easily be divided into two. Kirk is heard per-forming his nine-part suite "Expansions" (which covers a lot of moods) while the remainder of the set has him mostly sticking to one horn at a time as he interprets a program of ballads including "I Waited for You" and "A Flower Is a Lovesome Thing." The large backing group includes a string section, harpist Alice Coltrane, Pepper Adams, Julius Watkins, and Roy Haynes among others. **Volunteered Slavery** (Collectables 6346) has Kirk on tenor, manzello, stritch, flute, and gong, performing three melodic originals and two pop tunes ("I Say a Little Prayer" and "My Cherie Amour"), assisted by his regular group plus the Roland Kirk Spirit Choir on background vocals. But the bulk of this set is Kirk's performance (with pianist Ron Burton, bassist Vernon Martin, drummer Jimmy Hopps, and percussionist Joe Texidor) at the 1968 Newport Jazz Festival, highlighted by "Three at the Festival" and a three-song ("Lush Life," "Afro-Blue," and "Bessie's Blues") tribute to John Coltrane during which Kirk closely emulates Trane's sound and style.

Rahsaan/Rahsaan (Collectables 6341) from 1970 has a few typically miraculous moments. At one point Kirk, before a live audience, plays two completely different melodies ("Going Home" and "Sentimental Journey") simultaneously on two different horns, splitting his mouth in two. On the 17-minute "Seeker," Kirk goes through several different musical styles including New Orleans jazz and bebop. And he perfectly harmonizes "Lover" on three of his horns at once. The three-CD set **Dog Years in the Fourth Ring** (32 Jazz 32032) reissues **Natural Black Inventions: Root Strata**, a 1971 set on which Kirk plays tenor, stritch, manzello, clarinets, flutes, black mystery pipes, harmonium, piccolo, a music box, tympani, gong, bells, bird sounds, percussion, and various sound effects. Other than a couple percussionists in a few spots, all of the music was played by Kirk live, and he truly sounds like a virtuoso one-man band. The other two discs, consisting of previously unreleased material taken from private tapes dating from 1963–75, include close impressions of Lester Young ("Lester Leaps In") and Sidney Bechet ("Petite Fleur") and heated versions of "Giant Steps" and "Blues for Alice." **Blacknuss** (Collectables 6345) has Kirk interpreting a variety of R&B/pop hits (including "Ain't No Sunshine," "What's Going On," "Mercy Mercy Me," and "Never Can Say Goodbye"), often to hilarious or at least riotous effect. Kirk often satirizes or tears apart the melodies without losing sight of the themes, and his version of "The Old Rugged Cross" truly redefines sacred music.

The closest that today's listeners can get to experiencing how Rahsaan Roland Kirk performed live (with the exception of some rare videos) is by getting the two-CD set ❶ **Bright Moments** (Rhino 71409). Joined by a four-piece rhythm section at San Francisco's Keystone Korner in 1973, Kirk's colorful monologues between the songs have been left intact, showing how wise he was underneath all of the humor. Kirk plays emotional versions of "Prelude to a Kiss" and "If I Loved You," demonstrates his nose flutes on "Fly Town Nose Blues," shows off his New Orleans clarinet playing on "Dem Red Beans and Rice," and introduces his trademark "Bright Moments." The modestly titled **Prepare Thyself to Deal with a Miracle** (Collectables 6342) has a few relatively brief oddities (including Kirk playing both regular flute and nose flute at the same time on "Seasons") and is highlighted by his 21-minute one-breath solo on "Saxophone Concerto." Unlike many others who indulge in circular breathing, Kirk was not content to just hold one note, and his marathon solo is filled with brilliant ideas and intensity. **The Case of the 3-Sided Dream in Audio Color** (Atlantic 6344) from 1975 originally came out as a double LP with the fourth side blank except for a phone conversation in the middle. One of the few misfires of Kirk's career, this project (now available as a single CD) has him throwing together a lot of interesting ideas but not following through. For example, on "Bye Bye Blackbird," Kirk imitates closely both Miles Davis (on reed trumpet) and John Coltrane, but this piece is unaccountably broken into two parts and only presented as excerpts, destroying the point of it all. The brief and odd dream sequences that are placed between many of the performances hurt the set's continuity and, even with "High Heel Sneakers" and two versions of "The Entertainer," there is not enough meat on this set for it to be recommended.

In 1976 things were looking up for Kirk as he switched to the Warner Bros. label. However, near the end of the year, he suffered a serious stroke that paralyzed one side of his body. Kirk gamely fought back, having a tenor designed that he could play with one hand, making a slight comeback and a final recording. But tragically Rahsaan Roland Kirk died on December 5, 1977 at the age of 41. There will never be a replacement for this musical miracle man.

Eric Kloss   A brilliant young altoist who turned 19 in 1968, Eric Kloss recorded four albums (following his first six) for Prestige during 1968–70. They are available as two CDs. **Sky Shadows/In the Land of the Giants** (Prestige 24217) has Kloss (doubling on tenor) in a quintet with Pat Martino, Jaki Byard, Bob Cranshaw, and Jack DeJohnette and on a set with Booker Ervin, Byard, Richard Davis, and Alan Dawson. Most of the material is comprised of Kloss post-bop originals though he also creates inventive versions of "Summertime," "So What," and "Things Ain't What They Used to Be." **Eric Kloss and the Rhythm Section** (Prestige 24125) reissues all of the music originally on **To Hear Is to See** and **Consciousness**. Kloss is teamed with the Miles Davis rhythm section of the period (Chick Corea, Dave Holland on electric bass, and Jack DeJohnette); the second session also has Pat Martino. Kloss keeps up with his more famous sidemen on the adventurous program, which is comprised of his seven originals and one song apiece by Martino, Joni Mitchell, and Donovan ("Sunshine Superman"). The post-bop music includes aspects of the avant-garde and early fusion.

After a year off, during 1972–76 Kloss stayed busy in the recording studios, making six albums for the Muse label, including collaborations with keyboardist Barry Miles and fellow altoist Richie Cole. **One Two Free** (32 Jazz 32094) has been reissued. Kloss, Martino, keyboardist Ron Thomas, Holland, and drummer Ron Krasinski stretch out on Carole King's "It's Too Late," "Licea," and the three-part "One, Two, Free." Although the Fender Rhodes electric piano sounds a bit dated, the chance taking and fire of this set still communicate well and show how much potential the young Eric Kloss had.

Yusef Lateef   After recording some of his greatest albums for Impulse during 1963–66, multireedist Yusef Lateef switched to the larger Atlantic label where he recorded very diverse (and somewhat eccentric) sets through 1976. Released in 1968, **The Blue Yusef Lateef** (Label M 5724) has some fine tenor and flute from Lateef and spots for altoist Sonny Red and Blue Mitchell, but the background soul vocals of the Sweet Inspirations on two cuts, a frivolous string quartet on "Like It Is," and Lateef's singing/chanting in Tagalog (a dialect from the Philippines) on one number make this quite a mixed bag. **Yusef Lateef's Detroit** (Collectables 6352) has Lateef joined by a brass section and a rhythm section in his salute to his former home, ranging from hints of Motown and the leader's interest in Eastern music to touches of bop. The **Diverse Yusef Lateef/Suite 16**

(Rhino 1552) has all of the music from two of Lateef's Atlantic albums. The music ranges from exotic vamps and some period trappings to the adventurous seven-movement "Symphonic Blues Suite." Earl Klugh's solo guitar rendition of "Michelle" is a bit out of place though pleasant and some of the selections are forgettable, but one certainly could not complain that Lateef was playing it safe. **The Gentle Giant** (Atlantic 1602) has less straightahead swinging than usual, mostly falling into the R&B field other than some exotic pieces and a nine-minute version of "Hey Jude."

Yusef Lateef's Atlantic sets cover quite a bit of ground. Because they are erratic in everything but the quality of his playing, a definitive sampler of this period would be a logical step for his label.

Mel Lewis   In 1966 Mel Lewis became the co-leader of a notable big band with Thad Jones. A decade later he led a rare small-group session, **Mel Lewis and Friends** (A&M 75021-0823). This CD reissue exactly duplicates a former LP from producer John Snyder's Horizon label, so the liner notes are a bit microscopic, but the music still communicates quite well. Freddie Hubbard is in top form during five selections (including "Moose the Mooche" and a quartet feature on "A Child Is Born"), Michael Brecker and Gregory Herbert (mostly on alto) get in their licks, Hank Jones and Ron Carter are typically flawless, and trumpeter Cecil Bridgewater makes a guest appearance on "Sho' Nuff Did." This album gave listeners a rare chance to hear Hubbard play bebop during this period.

Charles Lloyd   In 1968 the Charles Lloyd Quartet (with Keith Jarrett, bassist Ron McClure, and Jack DeJohnette) recorded their final album, **Soundtrack**, which has been reissued as part of ❍ **Forest Flower** (Rhino 71746) and which was covered in the previous chapter. In 1969 when Jarrett left Lloyd's very popular group, the ensemble soon broke up. Lloyd gradually faded out of music, becoming a teacher of transcendental meditation. Once in a while in the 1970s he recorded again, but those sessions tended to emphasize quiet mood music. **Waves** (A&M 75021-0828) is a good example from this period although largely forgettable. Lloyd on tenor and flute mostly plays relaxing and soothing solos, and even the presence on three of the eight numbers of guitarist Gabor Szabo does not help much. The spirituality that one associated with Lloyd is present on this record but little of the passion. Charles Lloyd would be largely retired except for these occasional projects until 1982.

Harold Mabern   An excellent hard bop pianist from Memphis, Tennessee, (following in the wake of Phineas Newborn), Harold Mabern played with the MJT + 3 in the late 1950s and, after moving to New York in 1959, worked with Jimmy Forrest, Lionel Hampton, the Jazztet, Donald Byrd, Miles Davis (1963), J.J. Johnson (1963–65), Sonny Rollins, Freddie Hubbard, Wes Montgomery, Joe Williams (1966–67), Sarah Vaughan, Lee Morgan, and Stanley Cowell's Piano Choir (1972).

Mabern led four albums for Prestige during 1968–70, two of which have been reissued on the single CD **Wailin'** (Prestige 24134). One set has Mabern in a quintet also including trumpeter Virgil Jones, George Coleman, Buster Williams, and Idris Muhammad on four of the pianist's challenging originals and "A Time for Love." The second date is more memorable, matching Mabern, Williams, and Muhammad with Lee Morgan and Hubert Laws (doubling on flute and his rarely heard tenor). Overall, this is excellent advanced hard bop music that hints in spots at fusion.

Pat Martino   Pat Martino, who had gained a lot of experience playing with soul-jazz organ groups, by 1968 was beginning to stretch himself. Open to the influences of both the avant-garde and the emerging fusion music, the guitarist recorded regularly as a leader for Prestige (1967–70), Cobblestone (1972), and Muse (1972–76) before switching to Warner Bros. All of these recordings are of interest, and most are currently available.

East (Original Jazz Classics 248), even with its hints of Eastern mysticism, is essentially a hard bop set by Martino and his quartet (pianist Eddie Green, drummer Lenny McBrowne, and either Ben Tucker or Tyrone Brown) performing two group originals, Benny Golson's "Park Avenue Petite," "Lazy Bird," and "Close Your Eyes." Much more world music–oriented is **Baiyina** (Original Jazz Classics 355), which has Martino assisted by Bobby Rose on second guitar, Gregory Herbert making his recording debut on alto and flute, Richard Davis, Charlie Persip, Reggie Ferguson on tabla, and Balakrishna on tamboura. The use of Indian instruments, drones, and unusual time signatures (including 7/4, 9/4, and 10/8) on Martino's four-part suite (which has sections named

after aspects of the Koran) gives the performance the flavor of early fusion, and some of the effects sound a bit dated although quite sincere. Released in 1970, **Desperado** (Original Jazz Classics 397) is a return to inventive straightahead jazz with Martino often using a 12-string guitar. He and his rhythm section (keyboardist Eddie Green, electric bassist Tyrone Brown, and drummer Sherman Ferguson) perform five of the guitarist's originals plus "Oleo." Eric Kloss makes a guest appearance on soprano during the opening "Blackjack." Martino's Cobblestone release has resurfaced as **Footprints** (32 Jazz 32021). On this tribute to Wes Montgomery, Martino mostly brings back the spirit of Wes rather than his playing style (though he uses octaves a bit more than usual) or his repertoire; only "Road Song" of the six songs was actually recorded by Montgomery. Martino is assisted by Bobby Rose, Richard Davis, and Billy Higgins.

◉ **Head & Heart** (32 Jazz 32050), a double CD, reissues in full the first two of Martino's four recordings for Muse that were originally called **Live!** and **Consciousness**. Martino is heard in 1972 with Tyrone Brown, Sherman Ferguson, and keyboardist Ron Thomas stretching out on three long selections: two originals and the pop song "Sunny." The **Consciousness** half of the set is from 1974 and has the innovative guitarist with Eddie Green, Brown, and Ferguson performing seven numbers that include two versions of "Along Came Betty," "Impressions," a lengthy exploration of Eric Kloss's "Consciousness," and Joni Mitchell's "Both Sides Now." On a whole, these two dates feature Pat Martino at the peak of his powers. Released in 1976, **Exit**, which has been paired with a later set on **Comin' and Goin'** (32 Jazz 32043), and a set of duets with pianist Gil Goldstein titled **We'll Be Together Again** (32 Jazz 32071) that emphasizes lyrical versions of standards, are also well worth acquiring by this consistently inventive guitarist.

Les McCann   Originally finding fame as a pianist but soon developing into a popular vocalist, too, Les McCann had the turning point of his career at the 1969 Montreux Jazz Festival. The year earlier he had recorded **Much Less** (Rhino 71281), an album that matched his trio (which also included bassist Leroy Vinnegar and drummer Donald Dean) with a string section. The program has one vocal number (the minor hit "With These Hands") and such numbers as "Doin' that Thing" and "Love for Sale," plus some moody ballads.

At Montreux the following year, it was decided spontaneously to augment McCann's trio with tenor saxophonist Eddie Harris and trumpeter Benny Bailey. The fireworks that resulted in ● **Swiss Movement** (Rhino 72452) were completely unexpected. The music was a perfect mixture of jazz and funk and is highlighted by McCann's vocal on "Compared to What" and the playing of Harris and the spectacular Bailey on "Cold Duck Time." This set is a highlight of Harris's career as well as the high point of McCann's.

Released in 1971, **Invitation to Openness** (Label M 5713) puts the focus on McCann's keyboards (Yusef Lateef's tenor, flute, and oboe are also prominent) as does **Layers** (Rhino 71280), which finds McCann emulating an orchestra while assisted by bass and percussionists. Neither are essential, but both show that, although the emphasis was shifting in Les McCann's career toward his soulful vocals, he continued to play piano and electric keyboards with creativity.

Jimmy McGriff One of the many organists to gradually rise to prominence in the 1960s, Jimmy McGriff actually started out playing bass, tenor, drums, vibes, and piano first. After serving in the military and working as a policeman in Philadelphia, Pennsylvania, for more than two years, he switched to full-time music. McGriff had lessons from Jimmy Smith, Richard "Groove" Holmes, and Milt Buckner, and his very first recording, 1963's "I Got a Woman," was a hit on the pop charts. McGriff recorded regularly for the Sue label (1963–65) and Solid State (1966–69), cut a few albums for Blue Note, and became a regular for Groove Merchant. By 1975 he was experimenting (with mixed results) with electric keyboards and synthesizers, as were many of his contemporaries. McGriff's best recordings were early in his career and after 1980.

Jackie and Rene McLean Jackie McLean recorded the last in his important string of 21 Blue Note recordings in 1967. He then became involved in jazz education and did not record again until cutting a series of albums for Steeple Chase during 1972–74. **Live at Montmartre** (Steeple Chase 31002) features Jackie McLean really stretching out on two Charlie Parker tunes, "Smile" and his own "Das Dat"; all but the nine-minute "Confirmation" are more than 15 minutes long. Jackie McLean sounds typically intense and passionate on this quartet date with Kenny Drew, bassist Bo Stief, and drummer Alex Riel. In contrast, **Ode to Super** (Steeple Chase 31009), a matchup of Jackie McLean with fellow altoist Gary Bartz, is a disappointment with the solos much stronger than the so-so material. The originals are not at all interesting, and only on a torrid version of Charlie Parker's "Red Cross" do the expected sparks fly.

Released in 1973, **A Ghetto Lullaby** (Steeple Chase 31013) has Jackie McLean, Drew, Niels Pedersen, and Riel at Copenhagen's Montmartre performing stirring solos and inspiring each other. During a two-day period Jackie McLean and his idol Dexter Gordon (with Drew, Pedersen, and Riel) recorded enough material to fill up two sets: **The Meeting** (Steeple Chase 31006) and **The Source** (Steeple Chase 31020). The music is a bit loose and very much a jam session, but there are some strong moments, particularly "On the Trail" and Gordon's 17-minute "All Clean" on the former set and "Another Hair-Do" and "Dexter Digs In" on the latter set. Certainly the spirits are quite high and happy during these sets of bebop. **Antiquity** (Steeple Chase 31028) is quite a bit different because this unusual project matches Jackie McLean (heard on alto, flute, percussion, and a little bit of piano) with drummer/percussionist Michael Carvin in a set of duets. The original music (which grows in interest with each listen) is atmospheric and often haunting, making creative use of space. Some sections meander, but the four-part title piece (which depicts slaves crossing the Atlantic Ocean) certainly holds one's interest.

New York Calling (Steeple Chase 31023) features Jackie McLean's short-lived group the Cosmic Brotherhood during its only recording. The modern hard bop sextet is most notable for introducing Jackie McLean's son, Rene McLean, who is heard on alto, tenor, and soprano. Also heard on the four originals and "Some Other Time" are trumpeter Billy Skinner, pianist Billy Gault, and bassist James Benjamin. Jackie McLean has no real difficulty keeping up with the relative youngsters.

Rene McLean, who was born in 1946, studied alto with his father and Sonny Rollins starting when he was nine. He picked up experience playing baritone and alto with Tito Puente for three years in the early 1970s, and he worked with Sam Rivers, with Lionel Hampton, and with the elder McLean in the Cosmic Brotherhood. To his credit, he mostly avoided sounding like his father and was on his way to developing his own voice in 1975 when he recorded his debut as a leader, **Watch Out** (Steeple Chase 31037). McLean is heard on alto, soprano, tenor, and flute in a hard bop sextet with trumpeter Danny Coleman, pianist Hubert Eaves, and guitarist Nathan Page. The music is reminiscent of Art Blakey's Jazz Messengers while hinting at the avant-garde in spots.

Marian McPartland Marian McPartland was a bit frustrated that she had only one opportunity to record during 1965–68, so in 1969 she started her own Halcyon label. Two of the best Halcyons have since been reissued as CDs by the Jazz Alliance. **Ambiance** (The Jazz Alliance 10029) is an unusual set that finds the veteran pianist playing quite free in spots. Her interplay with bassist Michael Moore and either Jimmy Madison or Billy Hart on drums is very alert, sometimes almost telepathic, and much more adventurous than one might expect. Even such standards as "What Is this Thing Called Love" and "Three Little Words" sound as if they are being performed by lyrical avant-gardists. **Plays the Music of Alec Wilder** (The Jazz Alliance 10016) features McPartland (in five duets with Moore and five trios with bassist Rusty Gilder and drummer Joe Corsello) reviving some of Wilder's best songs, most of which are melancholy and full of little surprises. The two Wilder "hits" are here ("I'll Be Around" and "It's So Peaceful in the Country") plus eight superior obscurities, all tastefully played by the subtle but adventurous pianist.

Charles Mingus Charles Mingus did not play music at all during 1966–68, disheartened by a variety of events (including a disastrous nonappearance at the 1965 Monterey Jazz Festival); however, starting in the summer of 1969, he gradually returned. Although his own playing was a little more conservative than previously (he stated that he was now one of the few bassists around who stuck to playing 4/4), he continued writing music and leading stirring groups. Mingus recorded a couple albums in 1970 for the French America label, heading a sextet with trumpeter Eddie Preston, tenor saxophonist Bobby Jones, alumnus Charles McPherson, Jaki Byard, and Dannie Richmond.

However, Mingus's official comeback record was the LP **Let My Children Hear Music** (Columbia 48910), a favorite album of the bassist. Leading a huge orchestra filled with everyone from Lonnie Hillyer and Jimmy Knepper to Julius Watkins, Hubert Laws, James Moody (featured on "Hobo Ho"), and a large bass section, Mingus performs mostly recent, ambitious, and sprawling works including "The I of Hurricane Sue" (named

after his wife Sue Mingus), "The Chill of Death," and "The Shoes of the Fisherman's Wife Are Some Jive Ass Slippers." As with the best Mingus music, these performances reward repeated listenings, revealing new details each time. **Charles Mingus and Friends in Concert** (Columbia/Legacy 64975) is a loose and sometimes unruly two-CD set that documents a 1972 concert that welcomed Mingus back to the music world. The best moments are on the overcrowded "E's Flat, Ah's Flat Too," which has an outstanding James Moody flute solo, and "Little Royal Suite," which was supposed to be a feature for Roy Eldridge. When the elder trumpeter got ill, 18-year-old Jon Faddis took his place, greatly impressing the crowd. Other notables making appearances along the way include McPherson, Gerry Mulligan, Gene Ammons, Lee Konitz, Randy Weston, and Milt Hinton.

The 1973 Mingus Sextet is heard on **Mingus Moves** (Rhino 71454), a group including the obscure trumpeter Ronald Hampton, tenor saxophonist George Adams, Don Pullen, and Dannie Richmond, who was always a constant. This spirited post-bop date only has three Mingus pieces among the seven songs, and one number ("Moves") features singing from Honi Gordon and Doug Hammond, but the ensembles and fire are pure Mingus. The 1974 Mingus group, with Jack Walrath in Hampton's place, is well showcased on **Changes One** (Rhino 71403) and **Changes Two** (Rhino 71404), the best later sets by the bassist's working bands. **Changes One** has four stimulating Mingus originals (best known are "Devil Blues" and "Duke Ellington's Sound of Love") while **Changes Two** has a vocal version of the latter cut (with singing by Jackie Paris) and a remake of "Orange Was the Color of Her Dress, Then Silk Blue" among the highlights.

◉ **Mingus at Carnegie Hall** (Rhino 1667), recorded at the end of a 1974 concert, has the bassist leading lengthy jam session versions of "C Jam Blues" and "Perdido." The lineup of musicians is somewhat remarkable with Rahsaan Roland Kirk, John Handy, Charles McPherson, George Adams, Hamiet Bluiett, Jon Faddis, Don Pullen, and Dannie Richmond. Of the many highlights, Handy's high-note alto playing on "Perdido," Faddis's mastery of Dizzy Gillespie licks, and Rahsaan's incredible solos (at one point doing a perfect imitation of Adams) make this a memorable set, even if Mingus is actually a minor voice during these jams.

Blue Mitchell　　After Blue Mitchell broke up his quintet in 1969, he worked in the studios, toured with Ray Charles (1969–71), and played regularly with bluesman John Mayall (1971–73). Mitchell eventually settled in Los Angeles, playing with the big bands of Louie Bellson, Bill Holman, and Bill Berry.

As a leader, Blue Mitchell's recordings became increasingly commercial during this era although he always sounded good. His last two Blue Notes have not been reissued yet, and his five Mainstream sets of 1971–74 are mostly pretty scarce. **Graffiti Blues** (Mainstream 709) has Mitchell joined by a soulful and funky rhythm section comprised of either Joe Sample or Walter Bishop, Jr. on keyboards, guitarist Freddie Robinson, electric bassist Darrell Clayborn, and drummer Ray Pounds plus tenor saxophonist Herman Riley. The music is not that challenging, with three straight funky blues (Dave Bailey has a guest spot on harmonica) as well as a couple of basic Sample originals and a Mitchell ballad feature on "Alone Again, Naturally." However, this accessible set does a good job of balancing worthwhile solos with catchy rhythms and has dated surprisingly well.

A 1976 concert not released until 1995, **Live** (Just Jazz 1007) matches Mitchell with four Northern California musicians (tenor saxophonist Mike Morris, pianist Marc Levine, bassist Kenny Jenkins, and drummer Smiley Winters) performing a nearly 17-minute "Pleasure Bent," the warm ballad "Portrait of Jenny," a song called "Sweet Smiley Winters" based on a Coleman Hawkins's "Sweet Georgia Brown" line, Levine's "Something Old, Something Blue," and a brief "Blues Theme." This set lets listeners hear what Blue Mitchell sounded like in performance during his later period, and it shows what a strong hard bop improviser he still was in the 1970s.

Hank Mobley　　A steady and consistent hard bop tenor saxophonist, Hank Mobley's solo career came to an end in the early 1970s. He recorded three final albums for Blue Note during 1968–70, made a date with Cedar Walton in 1972 (when he was still just 42), and then pretty much dropped off the scene, a victim of bad health and his own drug addiction. Recorded in 1968, **Reach Out** (Blue Note 59964) does not live up to its potential because of some weak material and so-so grooves. Mobley, Woody Shaw, pianist Lamont Johnson, George Benson, Bob Cranshaw, and Billy Higgins have all had better days although this soul-jazz offering

has a few good moments along the way. **The Flip** (Blue Note 4329) is Mobley's most obscure Blue Note set and has not been reissued yet on CD; it features the tenor in a sextet with Dizzy Reece and Slide Hampton. **Thinking of Home** (Blue Note 40531) from 1970 was Mobley's final effort as a leader, and fortunately it is a strong date. This time the sextet includes Woody Shaw, guitarist Eddie Diehl, Cedar Walton, bassist Mickey Bass, and drummer Leroy Williams. The musicians perform Mobley's three-part "Suite" and four other group originals in adventurous fashion, with Mobley and Shaw taking many fine solos. Because this date was recorded in 1970 when the Blue Note label had greatly declined, it was not released initially for a decade but was worth the wait. It is only fitting that Hank Mobley, who in his previous 24 Blue Note albums had helped to immortalize the label's sound, would record one of the last worthwhile records by the label before its complete artistic collapse.

Lee Morgan　　Lee Morgan was just 30 years old in 1968 and, despite the changes in the music world, his future seemed bright. He had found his fame playing a soulful variety of hard bop, but he was always flexible enough to play post-bop, was traditional enough to caress ballads, and was open to the influences of funk and early fusion. Recorded in 1968, **Taru** (Blue Note 22670) has two funky boogaloos, a ballad, and three complex group originals; the music was not originally released until 1980. Morgan is quite fiery and explorative, leading a sextet also including Bennie Maupin on tenor, George Benson, John Hicks, Reggie Workman, and Billy Higgins. **Caramba** (Blue Note 56658) has the same group except without Benson and with Cedar Walton in Hicks's place. The music is modal oriented, has a title cut that sounds similar to Eddie Harris's "Listen Here," and includes a catchy melody on "Soulita."

Originally a double LP with four extended performances, **Live at the Lighthouse** (Blue Note 35228) has returned as a three-CD set with a dozen selections. Recorded July 10–12, 1970, Morgan and his regular quintet of the era (with Bennie Maupin on tenor, flute, and bass clarinet, Harold Mabern, Jymie Merritt, and Mickey Roker) perform intense solos that are modal oriented rather than hard bop although there are remakes of "The Sidewinder" and "Speedball." The playing is of a consistent high quality and more advanced in general than Morgan's earlier recordings. It points toward a possible future course for the trumpeter's music in the 1970s.

The Last Session (Blue Note 93401), originally a double LP and now a single CD, is a bit of a disappointment because the modal-oriented numbers ramble on too long and a forgettable debut for Morgan's discovery flutist Bobbi Humphrey on "Croquet Ballet" lets one know that she was not heading for a significant career in creative jazz. The trumpeter's band at the time of these September 17–18, 1971, recordings consisted of Billy Harper, Mabern, either Merritt or Reggie Workman on bass, and drummer Freddie Waits.

Lee Morgan could have gone in several directions in the future. He might have assumed the role that would be filled by Donald Byrd as a crossover pop trumpeter. Or he might have competed with Freddie Hubbard on CTI recordings, explored the avant-garde, or reverted back to hard bop later in the decade. But it was not to be. On February 19, 1972, while at Slug's in New York, he was shot to death by a girlfriend who he had recently dumped for a younger woman. Lee Morgan was 33.

Idris Muhammad   Born in New Orleans in 1939, drummer Idris Muhammad, who was born Leo Morris, starting playing professionally when he was 16, performing R&B and in the studios. He was first noticed by the jazz world during his stint with Lou Donaldson (1965–67). As the house drummer for the Prestige label, he appeared on many sessions during 1970–72 in addition to leading two dates of his own, both of which are reissued in full on the single CD **Legends of Acid Jazz** (Prestige 24170). Trumpeter Virgil Jones and saxophonist Clarence Thomas have their spots and the music is danceable, but this lightweight collection is fairly routine and forgettable. However, 1974's **Power of Soul** (Epic/Legacy 86149), which was originally released on Kudu, is on a higher level. Muhammad leads a septet that includes trumpeter Randy Brecker, guitarist Joe Beck, and most notably Grover Washington, Jr., on tenor and soprano; Washington is in superior form. The tunes often emphasize the groove and Bob James provided the arrangements and keyboard work, but the music is accessible rather than being excessively commercial. This is still Idris Muhammad's finest recording as a leader.

Oliver Nelson   In 1967 Oliver Nelson moved to Los Angeles where he worked constantly in the studios,

writing for television and movies. A fine tenor, alto, and soprano saxophonist, Nelson led big bands on an occasional basis and wrote ambitious works (including lengthy tributes to John F. Kennedy, Martin Luther King, Jr., and a couple suites for Berlin) but did not get to play all that much after he became buried in the studios. **Swiss Suite** (BMG 85158), one of several sets recorded originally for the Flying Dutchman label, has his all-star orchestra's performance from the 1971 Montreux Jazz Festival. Remakes of "Stolen Moments," "Black, Brown & Beautiful," and "Blues and the Abstract Truth" feature solos from Nelson (on alto) and trumpeter Danny Moore. The centerpiece of the performance is the nearly 27-minute "Swiss Suite," which has a couple of lengthy and raging tenor solos from Gato Barbieri. However, a five-minute segment where guest altoist Eddie "Cleanhead" Vinson plays the blues completely steals the show and is one of Vinson's finest instrumental spots on record.

Oliver Nelson recorded a final album on March 6, 1975, sounding fine on the LP **Stolen Moments** (Inner City 6008) with a West Coast nonet. But because of the strain of constant deadlines and nonstop work, he died from a heart attack less than eight months later on October 27 at the age of 43.

Phineas Newborn   The virtuoso pianist Phineas Newborn only recorded six albums after 1964 (when he was 32) because of illnesses that kept him from achieving the stardom he deserved. Two days in 1969 resulted in **Please Send Me Someone to Love** (Original Jazz Classics 947) and **Harlem Blues** (Original Jazz Classics 662), trio performances with Ray Brown and Elvin Jones. The former is a blues and bop set that includes "Rough Ridin'," "He's a Real Gone Guy" and "Little Niles" while the latter is highlighted by "Cookin' at the Continental," "Tenderly," and "Ray's Idea." Newborn plays quite well throughout what would be his only recordings of the 1965–73 period. **Back Home** (Original Jazz Classics 971) also has the pianist with Brown and Jones but in 1976. Despite his health problems, Newborn was never less than superlative on records as he shows on five standards and three of his originals. **Look out…Phineas Is Back** (Original Jazz Classics 866) from later in the year has Newborn performing with Brown and drummer Jimmie Smith. There are no signs of decline either in his playing ability or his enthusiasm on such numbers as

"Abbers Song" (a rapid-paced tune based on "I've Got Rhythm"), "A Night in Tunisia," and an inventive version of Stevie Wonder's "You Are the Sunshine of My Life," making it difficult to believe that this was Phineas Newborn's next-to-last recording.

Don Patterson   A favorite of Sonny Stitt, organist Don Patterson recorded regularly for Prestige as a leader during 1964–69 and made a couple albums for Muse during 1972–73. Unlike most of his fellow organists, Patterson stuck to the Hammond B-3, not switching his focus to other keyboards as the organ's popularity dropped in the 1970s. Recorded in 1968, **Boppin' and Burnin'** (Original Jazz Classics 983) is actually most notable for the exciting playing of Howard McGhee, a trumpeter who did not appear on record much after the early 1960s. McGhee, Charles McPherson, Pat Martino, drummer Billy James, and Patterson make for a formidable quintet on a couple of McGhee's songs (including the haunting "Island Fantasy"), "Epistrophy," "Now's the Time," and "Donna Lee." **Dem New York City Blues** (Prestige 24149) has all of the music from two former LPs dating from 1968–69: **Opus de Don** and **Oh Happy Day**. More soul-jazz oriented in spots than usual, Patterson still sounds quite at home, jamming in a quintet with Blue Mitchell, Junior Cook, and Martino and with a second group featuring Virgil Jones and both George Coleman and Houston Person on tenors.

Genius of the B-3 (Muse 5443) might have been overstating the case, but Patterson is in excellent form on this now hard-to-find 1972 quartet CD with Eddie Daniels (heard on tenor, alto, and soprano but not clarinet), guitarist Ted Dunbar, and drummer Freddie Waits. But drug problems would soon result in Don Patterson being off records altogether during 1974–76 and becoming somewhat forgotten with time.

Art Pepper   After he was sent to prison for drug abuse in early 1961, Art Pepper was nearly absent from the music scene until the early '70s. On a couple occasions between prison terms he would resurface, including showing the strong influence of John Coltrane at some concerts in 1964, playing and recording with Buddy Rich in 1968, and cutting an obscure album with the Mike Vax big band in 1973. Pepper, who spent 1969–71 at Synanon, began his successful comeback in early 1975 with the inspiration and guidance of his wife Laurie. Amazingly enough, considering the many years

that had passed, he was not only in prime form but had continued to evolve and grow. On his three albums of 1975–76, Pepper is a much more expressive player than he had been in the 1950s, not as flawless but much more emotional, intense, and daring, playing each solo as if it might be his last.

I'll Remember April (Storyville 4130) has Pepper performing at a 1975 concert with Tommy Gumina on polychord (an accordion that sounds a bit like an organ), bassist Fred Atwood, and drummer Jimmie Smith, digging into lengthy versions of "Foothill Blues," "I'll Remember April," and "Cherokee" plus a briefer but passionate rendition of "Here's that Rainy Day." **Living Legend** (Original Jazz Classics 408) was the official comeback record as Pepper reunited with producer Lester Koenig at the reactivated Contemporary label. Joined by his old friends Hampton Hawes, Charlie Haden, and Shelly Manne, Pepper's playing is dark, expressive, and adventurous as he introduces five originals and creates another intense version of "Here's that Rainy Day." **The Trip** (Original Jazz Classics 4100) teams Pepper with George Cables (who became his favorite pianist), bassist David Williams, and Elvin Jones on "The Summer Knows" and lesser-known originals (including two versions of "The Trip") plus a song apiece by Woody Shaw ("Sweet Love of Mine") and Joe Gordon.

It would be an unlikely and unexpected comeback, but the 51-year-old Art Pepper, who had lost so many years, was on his way to becoming the top altoist in jazz.

Houston Person   A thick-toned tenor saxophonist whose style is in the tradition of Gene Ammons but who has his own sound, Houston Person is a master of soul-jazz who also can hold his own in hard bop settings. After freelancing and serving in the military, he had an important stint with Johnny Hammond Smith (1963–66) and then became a leader of his own groups that frequently featured organists.

Person recorded regularly for Prestige during the period 1966–72, and considering the increasingly commercial and funk-oriented climate that the soul-jazz/hard bop world was facing, the tenor did not fare too badly. **Goodness** (Original Jazz Classics 332) is a set of funky music that emphasizes boogaloos, danceable rhythms, and repetitive vamps set down by organist Sonny Phillips, guitarist Billy Butler, electric bassist Bob Bushnell, drummer Frankie Jones, and Buddy Caldwell on congas. Person's passionate tenor solos easily take honors even if the music is a bit commercial and not all that essential. **Legends of Acid Jazz—Truth** (Prestige 24767) is in a similar vein reissuing two albums, other than one selection left off because of lack of space. The **Truth** half of the set has the same personnel as **Goodness** while the music originally released as **Soul Dance** has Person in a quartet with organist Billy Gardner, guitarist Boogaloo Joe Jones, and drummer Frankie Jones. Ranging from Sonny Rollins's "Blue 7" and Horace Parlan's "Wadin'" to current R&B tunes, the music is again mostly worthwhile from the jazz standpoint because of Person's heartfelt solos. **Legends of Acid Jazz** (Prestige 24179) has the music from the tenor's 1970–71 releases **Person to Person** and **Houston Express**. These funk-oriented releases include such unlikely songs as the Carpenters's "Close to You," "Young, Gifted and Black," and "Chains of Love," but Person is joined along the way by such strong players as Virgil Jones, Grant Green, Idris Muhammad, and trumpeter Cecil Bridgewater; together they uplift the music.

After leaving Prestige and recording a couple obscure albums for the tiny Eastbound label, in 1976 Person began a longtime relationship with producer Joe Fields and his Muse label, getting to record regularly in soulful hard bop settings.

Sonny Rollins   Unlike his retirement in 1959, when Sonny Rollins dropped out of music in 1966, it was not that widely noticed; so many other events overshadowed his departure. Six years passed before the tenor saxophonist, who now felt he was well rested and hungry to play again, returned. He signed with Milestone in 1972, an association that would last more than 30 years. He showed on **Sonny Rollins' Next Album** (Original Jazz Classics 312) that at 41 he remained a giant. Best is a ten-minute "Skylark" that has a long and thoughtful cadenza. Also excellent are "The Everywhere Calypso" and "Playing in the Yard" although his decision to play soprano on "Poinciana" was a slight mistake. Rollins is backed by George Cables (on both acoustic and electric piano), Bob Cranshaw (who he always wanted to play electric bass), either Jack DeJohnette or David Lee on drums, and sometimes percussionist Arthur Jenkins.

With the release of **Horn Culture** (Original Jazz Classics 314), Rollins began to be criticized for having a fairly anonymous band that was not worthy of him, for

performing some lightweight material, and for his increasingly raspy tone, as if he was never supposed to have evolved from the 1950s. Although the criticisms were partly true, this set does have fine versions of "Good Morning Heartache" and "God Bless the Child," and Rollins continued displaying his ability to build his improvisations off the melodies of the songs rather than just running through the chord changes. **The Cutting Edge** (Original Jazz Classics 468) has Rollins's set from the 1974 Montreux Jazz Festival. Assisted by his regular band (keyboardist Stanley Cowell, guitarist Masuo, Cranshaw, Lee, and percussionist Mtume), Rollins successfully turns "To a Wild Rose" and "A House Is Not a Home" into creative jazz and welcomes Rufus Harley, the world's only jazz bagpipe player, as a guest on "Swing Low, Sweet Chariot." **Nucleus** (Original Jazz Classics 620) is less interesting. George Duke heads a funky rhythm section and neither trombonist Raul DeSouza nor Bennie Maupin on reeds were really needed. The material, other than an updated version of the standard "My Reverie," is generally not up to par. **The Way I Feel** (Original Jazz Classics 666) is only moderately better, with the so-called contemporary playing of keyboardist Patrice Rushen and guitarist Lee Ritenour sounding as dated as the forgettable originals.

But even on the weaker dates (and his recording output would soon be improving again), Sonny Rollins could not help but play extremely well, simply by being himself. And his concert appearances, which most observers considered far superior to his studio sessions, were becoming quite legendary for his endurance and seemingly endless flow of creative ideas.

Woody Shaw   One of the few trumpeters to mature during the 1970s, Woody Shaw worked with Max Roach (1968–69), with Art Blakey's Jazz Messengers (1973), and with Dexter Gordon during the tenor's triumphant homecoming tour in 1976 but otherwise led his own groups. His style continued to evolve even as his tone remained similar to Freddie Hubbard's.

Released in 1970, **Blackstone Legacy** (Contemporary 7627/28) matches Shaw with Gary Bartz, Bennie Maupin (tenor, bass clarinet, and flute), George Cables, both Ron Carter and Clint Houston on basses, and Lenny White. The selections (four by Shaw and two from Cables) are all lengthy (only one is under 10½ minutes), but the high-quality playing and general adventurous nature of the music results in no slow moments. **Song of Songs** (Original Jazz Classics 1893) has four of the trumpeter's originals interpreted by Shaw's 1972 sextet that features Emanuel Boyd on flute and tenor, Cables, bassist Henry Franklin, drummer Woodrow Theus II, and either Ramon Morris or Maupin on tenor. As usual Shaw takes several dynamic solos, and his music is very forward-looking hard bop. **The Moontrane** (32 Jazz 32019) has Shaw at the head of one of his strongest units, a band that includes Azar Lawrence on tenor and soprano, the young trombonist Steve Turre, keyboardist Onaje Allen Gumbs, either Buster Williams or Cecil McBee on bass, drummer Victor Lewis, Tony Waters on congas, and percussionist Guilherme Franco. Best known among the originals on this exciting post-bop date is Shaw's "Moontrane." Also from this era is **Little Red's Fantasy** (32 Jazz 32123), which showcases Shaw in a quintet with Frank Strozier, Ronnie Mathews, bassist Stafford James, and drummer Eddie Moore, performing five more group originals including the trumpeter's "In Case You Haven't Heard."

Although overshadowed by Freddie Hubbard and rarely receiving the recognition he deserved, Woody Shaw was one of the finest trumpeters of the 1970s and virtually every one of his recordings is well worth acquiring.

Horace Silver   The final in Horace Silver's string of classic Blue Note quintet albums is 1968's **Serenade to a Soul Sister** (Blue Note 84277). In addition to Charles Tolliver's contribution, the six songs are split between two different groups with either Stanley Turrentine or Bennie Maupin on tenor, Bob Cranshaw or Johnny Williams on bass, and Mickey Roker or Billy Cobham on drums. With such catchy and funky numbers as "Psychedelic Sally" and "Serenade to a Soul Sister," there is no hint that this is really the end of an era.

Although the Blue Note label quickly declined and dropped most of their jazz artists, Silver would remain with the label until it was completely dead in 1979. The out-of-print LP **You Gotta Take a Little Love** (Blue Note 4309) is a decent quintet effort with Randy Brecker in Tolliver's place. **In Pursuit of the 27th Man** (Blue Note 35758) has Silver joined on three numbers by Randy Brecker, Michael Brecker, Bob Cranshaw, and Mickey Roker plus four unusual quartet pieces with vibraphonist David Friedman, Cranshaw, and Roker. But Silver's other recordings from this era feature his self-help lyrics (he was never as skilled a lyricist as he was a

composer) and the voice of Andy Bey, who was unable to uplift the awkward-sounding words.

During 1975–79, Silver recorded five albums in which his quintet with trumpeter Tom Harrell, tenor saxophonist Bob Berg (during 1975–76), Ron Carter, and drummer Al Foster were joined by a different ensemble each time, mostly pretty successfully. These releases unfortunately have not been reissued yet, including **Silver 'N Brass** (Blue Note 406), **Silver 'N Wood** (Blue Note 581), and **Silver 'N Voices** (Blue Note 708). The five sets (which also have later meetings with percussion and strings) would make for an excellent box set someday, showing that there was some creative hard bop being recorded in Blue Note's dying days.

Dr. Lonnie Smith   Not to be confused with keyboardist Lonnie Liston Smith, organist Dr. Lonnie Smith gained recognition for his playing with the late 1960s group of George Benson and with Lou Donaldson. He led an obscure date for Columbia and then in 1968 recorded **Think** (Blue Note 84290), one of his most rewarding sessions. Heading a group that includes Lee Morgan, David "Fathead" Newman, guitarist Melvin Sparks, drummer Marion Booker, Jr., and three percussionists, Smith mostly plays R&Bish tunes while sticking to infectious soul-jazz; the two horn players add a great deal to this date's appeal.

Smith's recordings for Blue Note became erratic, partly because of the label shifting its focus. **Drives** (Blue Note 31249) was a definite low point with some odd vocals, some distracting verbal sounds, and inferior versions of "Seven Steps to Heaven" and "Spinning Wheel." Much better is 1970's **Live at Club Mozambique** (Blue Note 31880), which has spots for George Benson and baritonist Ronnie Cuber along with some organ solos that show what Smith could do.

Charles Tolliver   Ranking with Woody Shaw as the top young trumpeter of the late 1960s (if one thinks of Freddie Hubbard and Lee Morgan as being in the previous generation), Charles Tolliver made the finest recordings of his career during 1968–76. He started on cornet (soon switching to trumpet) when he was eight and was largely self-taught. Although he majored in pharmacy at Howard University, he chose to become a musician. Tolliver made his recording debut with Jackie McLean in 1964 when he was 22, worked in Los Angeles with Gerald Wilson's Orchestra (1966–67), and played next to Gary Bartz in Max Roach's group (1967–69). He also gained experience during stints with Horace Silver, McCoy Tyner, Sonny Rollins, and Art Blakey's Jazz Messengers.

Tolliver's debut as a leader, **Paper Man** (Black Lion 30117), is not yet available on CD, a pity for this is a near classic featuring the trumpeter with Herbie Hancock, Ron Carter, Joe Chambers, and sometimes Bartz. At the time of this 1968 set, Tolliver already had a fat sound, the ability to play both inside and outside, and a passionate style.

In 1969 Tolliver organized a quartet with pianist Stanley Cowell that they called Music Inc. ❶ **The Ringer** (Black Lion 760174) has the pair joined by bassist Steve Novosel and drummer Jimmy Hopps, performing five of Tolliver's strongest originals including "On the Nile" (which is particularly memorable), "The Ringer," and "Spur." The following year Tolliver and Cowell founded the Strata East label, which became a haven for under-recorded post-bop and avant-garde players. **Live at Slugs Vol. 1 & 2** (Strata East 9016) features the Tolliver-Cowell quartet (with Hopps and Cecil McBee) stretching out on six numbers from May 1, 1970, including the 17-minute "Orientale." **Live at the Loosdrecht Jazz Festival** (Strata East 9032) has Tolliver with John Hicks, Reggie Workman, and drummer Alvin Queen performing five lengthy songs (clocking in between 11–17 minutes) including Neal Hefti's "Repetition" and Cowell's "Prayer for Peace." **Impact** (Strata East 9001) features Tolliver heading a big band with 14 horns and a strong rhythm section on six of his compositions, all of which he arranged. With such top soloists as James Spaulding, Charles McPherson, George Coleman, Harold Vick, Cowell, and the leader, this is a high-quality post-bop set with plenty of stirring moments.

But strangely enough, other than an obscure date in late 1977, Charles Tolliver would not record again until 1988. He maintained a low profile after the mid-1970s, not becoming one of the leaders of jazz despite his great talent.

McCoy Tyner After leaving the John Coltrane Quartet at the end of 1965, McCoy Tyner struggled a bit, working as a sideman in a variety of situations, including playing soul music with Ike and Tina Turner. Fortunately, he signed a contract with Blue Note in 1967, and he led seven albums for the label through 1970.

Time for Tyner (Blue Note 84370) has music from two concerts recorded nearly a year apart but both featuring quartets with Bobby Hutcherson, bassist Herbie Lewis, and Freddie Waits. "I've Grown Accustomed to Your Face" is a piano solo and "Surrey with the Fringe on Top" is by the trio without Hutcherson. Otherwise, the quartet performs three Tyner originals and "I Didn't Know What Time It Was"; Hutcherson and Tyner blend together quite well. **Expansions** (Blue Note 84338) has a particularly strong group with Tyner joined by Woody Shaw, Gary Bartz, Wayne Shorter, Ron Carter (on cello), Lewis, and Waits stretching out on challenging compositions. The advanced hard bop music is often stirring, and the all-star musicians do not disappoint. **Extensions** (Blue Note 37646) also has a particularly interesting lineup of players because it might be the only album to include both Tyner and his successor with John Coltrane, Alice Coltrane, who is heard on harp. Also in the sextet are Bartz, Shorter, Carter (sticking to bass), and Elvin Jones. Performing four of Tyner's modal originals, the musicians play with passion and intensity, particularly Shorter. The last of Tyner's Blue Note albums, **Asante** (Blue Note 93884), puts the emphasis on group interplay rather than individual solos with Tyner joined by altoist Andrew White, guitarist Ted Dunbar, Buster Williams, Billy Hart, and Mtume on congas; singer Songai has two spots.

Although all of Tyner's Blue Note albums contain excellent music, the sets did not sell all that well. After a little more struggle, in 1972 he found a more secure home when he signed with Milestone. With producer Orrin Keepnews helping the pianist to come up with one stimulating project after another (a little reminiscent of Thelonious Monk's treatment at Riverside in the 1950s), Tyner recorded some of his most significant albums for the label during the next nine years, including ten sets during the 1972–76 period.

Sahara (Original Jazz Classics 311) has Tyner showcased in a quartet with Sonny Fortune (heard on alto, soprano, and flute), bassist Calvin Hill, and Alphonse Mouzon. The 23½-minute title cut is most memorable as is Tyner's solo piano feature on "A Prayer for My Family." **Song For My Lady** (Original Jazz Classics 313) has the same group on two numbers (including "The Night Has a Thousand Eyes"), a piano solo version of "A Silent Tear," and two songs in which the quartet is augmented by Charles Tolliver on flugelhorn, violinist Michael

White, and Mtume. ◉ **Echoes of a Friend** (Original Jazz Classics 650) is an obvious classic because it is Tyner's first solo piano tribute to John Coltrane. In addition to three songs associated with Trane ("Naima," "Promise," and "My Favorite Things"), Tyner interprets two originals ("Folks" and the lengthy "The Discovery") that show how much he had grown into a giant since his days with Coltrane. **Song of the New World** (Original Jazz Classics 618) was Tyner's first opportunity to write music for a large group, one that includes brass, flutes, and (on two of the five songs) a string section; the title cut and "Afro Blue" are highlights.

◉ **Enlightenment** (Milestone 55001) is a brilliant group album from 1973 that features the 19-year-old Azar Lawrence on tenor and soprano (it is surprising that he never became famous), bassist Juney Booth, and Mouzon. The three-part "Enlightenment Suite" and the 25-minute "Walk Spirit, Talk Spirit" never lose one's interest and show just how exciting Tyner's modal music could be. **Sama Layuca** (Original Jazz Classics 1071) has Tyner and Lawrence joined by such friends as Bobby Hutcherson, Gary Bartz, John Stubblefield (heard on oboe and flute), Buster Williams, Billy Hart, and both Mtume and Guilherme Franco on percussion. **Atlantis** (Milestone 55002) is on the same level as **Enlightenment**, once again featuring Lawrence and Booth with Tyner plus drummer Wilby Fletcher and Franco. The music is often quite fiery, featuring worthy Tyner originals, "My One and Only Love," and the pianist on a solo version of "In a Sentimental Mood." **Trident** (Original Jazz Classics 720) from 1975 was Tyner's first full-length trio album in 11 years, matching him with Ron Carter and Elvin Jones. Tyner, who also plays a bit of harpsichord and celeste on three of the six pieces, digs into such numbers as "Impressions," "Ruby, My Dear," and Jobim's "Once I Loved." **Fly with the Wind** (Original Jazz Classics 699) gave Tyner a chance to write for piccolo, oboe, harp, six violins, two violas, two cellos, Hubert Laws, Ron Carter, and Billy Cobham. Tyner plays quite well as always on four of his songs plus "You Stepped out of a Dream." The pianist's tenth Milestone album, **Focal Point** (Original Jazz Classics 1009), has Tyner's regular trio of 1976 (with bassist Charles Fambrough and drummer Eric Gravatt) joined by percussionist Franco and three reed players (Gary Bartz, Joe Ford, and Ron Bridgewater). The music is as unpredictable, passionate, and consistent as all ten of these sets.

So, during a four-year period for Milestone, McCoy Tyner was heard with three different quartets, a quintet, a septet, solo, a big band, a trio, a nonet, and a string orchestra, excelling in every setting.

Mal Waldron   Mal Waldron permanently moved to Europe in 1965, settling in Munich, West Germany, two years later. He recorded frequently overseas and retained his brooding piano style even in situations where the music was much more modern than the type he had performed during his earlier years.

Free at Last (ECM 831332) from 1969 is most notable for being the first release by Manfred Eicher's ECM label. Waldron, bassist Isla Eckinger, and drummer Clarence Becton improvise quite freely on five of the pianist's originals plus "Willow Weep for Me." **Black Glory** (Enja 2004) from 1971 was just the fourth release from Matthias Winckelmann's Enja label. Waldron, bassist Jimmy Woode, and drummer Pierre Favre explore five group originals (four by the pianist), and Waldron shows off his mastery of repetition along with his growing knowledge of the avant-garde. The set of nine piano solos, **Blues for Lady Day** (Black Lion 760193), reminds listeners that Waldron was Billie Holiday's last accompanist. The original program included such numbers as "Don't Blame Me," "You're My Thrill," "Strange Fruit," and "Mean to Me" plus Waldron's "Blues for Lady Day." The CD reissue adds two unrelated trio numbers with bassist Henk Haverhoek and drummer Pierre Courbois that, although irrelevant to a Billie Holiday tribute, find Waldron in inventive form.

Released in 1974, **Hard Talk** (Enja 2050) gives the pianist an opportunity to be part of an inventive quintet. The masterful cornetist Manfred Schoof (who often takes solo honors), Steve Lacy (a frequent musical collaborator of Waldron's), Isla Eckinger, and drummer Allen Blairman play four of Waldron's advanced pieces. Plenty of fire is expressed during this post-bop set, which shows how flexible Mal Waldron's percussive style was, fitting comfortably into freer settings.

Cedar Walton   One of the top hard bop pianists, Cedar Walton appeared on quite a few records as a s ideman for the Prestige label during 1967–69 (leading four of his own), co-led a short-lived band with Hank Mobley in the early 1970s, had a return engagement with Art Blakey's Jazz Messengers (1973), often played with Clifford Jordan in a quartet, and organized Eastern

Rebellion. **Spectrum** (Prestige 24145) has all of the music from the LP of the same name plus the performances originally heard on **The Electric Boogaloo Song**. Walton is joined by Blue Mitchell, Clifford Jordan, and a pair of rhythm section, performing six originals (best known is "Ugetsu"), a couple obscurities, and two standards. The music is well played if not overly memorable. **Soul Cycle** (Original Jazz Classics 847) is a lesser effort because of half of the selections being quite commercial, with Walton switching to electric piano where his personality does not come through that well. A couple acoustic trio features with Reggie Workman and Albert "Tootie" Heath and a few appearances by James Moody (on tenor and flute) help a bit, but this is still not too essential.

Walton's ● **Breakthrough** (32 Jazz 32148) from 1972 was Hank Mobley's last significant recording and possibly his final appearance on records altogether. Mobley is in superior form as is the often-overlooked baritonist Charles Davis; the title cut has a memorable tradeoff by the two saxophonists. Walton, who somehow turns the "Theme from Love Story" into jazz, also shows off his skill at accompanying the other soloists, Davis sounds fine on soprano on "Early Morning Stroll," and Mobley is showcased on "Summertime." Although this record (originally cut for Cobblestone) has not had much publicity through the years, it was one of the best jazz recordings of 1972.

Bill Watrous   One of the great trombonists, Bill Watrous (who extended the range of his instrument) has impressive technique and a beautiful tone. Born in 1939, Watrous played in Dixieland bands as a teenager and studied with Herbie Nichols while serving in the military. He began his professional career playing with Billy Butterfield, was part of Kai Winding's four-trombone octet (1962–67), and worked in the New York studios throughout the 1960s. He recorded along the way with Quincy Jones, Maynard Ferguson, Johnny Richards, and Woody Herman, was part of the television band for the *Merv Griffin Show* (1965–68), was on the staff of CBS (1967–69), and played with the jazz-rock group Ten Wheel Drive (1971).

Watrous's debut as a leader, **'Bone Straight Ahead** (Progressive 7115), was made for Harry Lim's Famous Door label during 1972–73. Watrous's sextet features trumpeter Danny Stiles (who takes some brilliant solos),

Al Cohn, Hank Jones, Milt Hinton, and Steve Gadd. "Just Friends," a lengthy "Snafu," and Watrous's "Don't Tell Me What to Do" show just how compatible Watrous and Stiles were.

Bill Watrous led his own big band, the Manhattan Wildlife Refuge, during 1973–77. Their two Columbia albums, **Manhattan Wildlife Refuge** (Columbia 33070) and **Tiger of San Pedro** (Columbia 33701), unfortunately have not been reissued on CD yet. The former has Watrous taking a crazy cadenza on "Fourth Floor Walk-Up" (a piece that received a lot of radio airplay at the time) and superior versions of Chick Corea's "Spain," "Dichotomy," and "Zip City"; key soloists included Watrous, Stiles, guitarist Joe Beck, and Dick Hyman. The follow-up set, **Tiger of San Pedro**, includes "Dirty Dan," "Passion at Three o'Clock," and "Sweet Georgia Upside Down" and features a similar lineup of musicians with Tom Garvin and Derek Smith splitting the keyboard duties.

Randy Weston   During 1968–73 Randy Weston lived, taught, and performed in Morocco where his mastery of the piano and interest in learning about the music of his ancestors made him quite popular. In 1972 on a visit to New York, he recorded his lone CTI album, **Blue Moses** (CTI 6016), which has thus far not been reissued on CD. A unique entry in his discography, it is one of few times that Weston can be heard doubling on electric piano. He receives the CTI treatment including Don Sebesky arrangements and solos from Freddie Hubbard and Grover Washington, Jr. Despite a few commercial touches, the music has the feel of Africa, and Weston plays quite well on four of his pieces including "Ganawa (Blue Moses)" and "Marrakesh Blues."

More to Weston's liking is **Tanyah** (Polygram 527 778), a reunion between the pianist and arranger Melba Liston. The colorful band has such players as 19-year-old Jon Faddis, Al Grey, Billy Harper, and Norris Turney performing seven of Weston's originals including "Hi-Fly," the infectious calypso "Jamaican East," and "Little Niles." The only misstep was the leader's decision to double on electric piano. There is no such reservation about ● **Carnival** (Freedom 741004), which was recorded at the 1974 Montreux Jazz Festival. Weston plays a "Tribute to Duke Ellington" that has him quoting many of the recently deceased Ellington's songs. He is also heard performing the joyous "Carnival" and "Mystery of Love" with Billy Harper, bassist William Allen, drummer Don Moye, and percussionist Steve Berrios. **Blues to Africa** (Freedom 741014) from a month later has Weston playing thought-provoking piano solos of eight of his originals, all of which have some connection to African music, a tribute to his years in Morocco.

The CTI Label

Of all the new labels of the early 1970s, CTI (Creed Taylor Inc.) seemed to best symbolize the era. Producer Creed Taylor, who had worked in important roles at Impulse, Verve, and A&M during the 1960s, had specific goals when he founded CTI in 1970. He believed that

99 ESSENTIAL RECORDS OF 1968–1976

Miles Davis, **In a Silent Way** (Sony 40580)

Miles Davis, **Bitches Brew** (Columbia/Legacy 65774), 2 CDs

Weather Report, **I Sing the Body Electric** (Columbia 46107)

Chick Corea, **Now He Sings, Now He Sobs** (Blue Note 90055)

Return to Forever, **Hymn of the Seventh Galaxy** (Polydor 825 336)

Chick Corea, **My Spanish Heart** (Polydor 543303)

Herbie Hancock, **Mwandishi: the Complete Warner Bros. Recordings** (Warner Archives 45732), 2 CDs

Herbie Hancock, **Headhunters** (Columbia/Legacy 65123)

Tony Williams, **Emergency** (Polygram 539 117)

John McLaughlin, **My Goals Beyond** (Knitting Factory Works 3010)

Mahavishnu Orchestra, **Birds of Fire** (Columbia/Legacy 66081)

Gil Evans, **There Comes a Time** (BMG 31392)

Jaco Pastorius, **Jaco** (Epic 33949)

Miles Davis, **Live/Evil** (Columbia/Legacy 65135), 2 CDs

Crusaders, **I** (MCA 20024)

Grover Washington, Jr., **Inner City Blues** (Motown 530577)

Grover Washington, Jr., **Mister Magic** (Motown 5175)

Art Ensemble of Chicago, **Live at Mandel Hall** (Delmark 432)

Lester Bowie, **American Gumbo** (32 Jazz 32139), 2 CDs

Albert Ayler, **Fondation Maeght Nights Vol. 1** (Jazz View 004)

Paul Bley, **Open to Love** (ECM 827 751)

Anthony Braxton, **Live** (Bluebird 6626)

Anthony Braxton, **Dortmund (Quartet)** 1976 (Hat Art 6075)

Charlie Haden, **Liberation Music Orchestra** (Impulse 188)

Julius Hemphill, **Coon Bid'ness** (Black Lion 760217)

Dave Holland, **Conference of the Birds** (ECM 1027)

Pharoah Sanders, **Karma** (Impulse 153)

Cecil Taylor, **Silent Tongues** (1201 Music 9017)

Cannonball Adderley, **Phenix** (Fantasy 79004)

Gary Bartz, **Libra/Another Earth** (Milestone 47077)

Jaki Byard, **The Jaki Byard Experience** (Original Jazz Classics 1913)

Charles Earland, **Living Black** (Prestige 24182)

Eastern Rebellion, **Vol. 1** (Timeless 101)

Jim Hall and Ron Carter, **Alone Together** (Original Jazz Classics 467)

Joe Henderson, **The Milestone Years** (Milestone 4413), 8 CDs

Keith Jarrett, **The Koln Concert** (ECM 810 067)

Keith Jarrett, **Mysteries: The Impulse Years 1975–1976** (Impulse 4-189), 4 CDs

Rahsaan Roland Kirk, **Bright Moments** (Rhino 71409), 2 CDs

Pat Martino, **Head & Heart** (32 Jazz 32050), 2 CDs

Les McCann and Eddie Harris, **Swiss Movement** (Rhino 72452)

Charles Mingus, **Mingus at Carnegie Hall** (Rhino 1667)

Charles Tolliver, **The Ringer** (Black Lion 760174)

McCoy Tyner, **Echoes of a Friend** (Original Jazz Classics 650)

McCoy Tyner, **Enlightenment** (Milestone 55001)

Cedar Walton, **Breakthrough** (32 Jazz 32148)

Randy Weston, **Carnival** (Freedom 741004)

Freddie Hubbard, **Red Clay** (Epic/Legacy 85216)

Freddie Hubbard, **Straight Life** (Epic/Legacy 65125)

Stanley Turrentine, **Sugar** (Epic/Legacy 85284)

Ray Bryant, **Alone at Montreux** (32 Jazz 32128)

Sonny Criss, **Crisscraft** (32 Jazz 32049)

Eddie "Lockjaw" Davis, **Straight Ahead** (Original Jazz Classics 629)

with proper packaging, publicity, and some accessible arrangements, jazz could sell quite well. He signed a roster of major players (most notably Freddie Hubbard, Stanley Turrentine, Hubert Laws, and George Benson), often utilizing them as sidemen on each other's records and at all-star concerts promoting the label. Some of the CTI releases were stirring small group dates that usually included a few catchy melodies, electric keyboards, and light funk rhythms (along with purely straightahead tracks), and others utilized orchestras (often arranged by Don Sebesky) to back the lead voices. For a few years this formula worked quite well, with the four principal

---

99 ESSENTIAL RECORDS OF 1968–1976

Stan Getz, **Captain Marvel** (Koch 7864)

Stan Getz and Jimmie Rowles, **The Peacocks** (Koch 7867)

Dizzy Gillespie, **Dizzy Gillespie's Big Four** (Original Jazz Classics 443)

Dexter Gordon, **Homecoming: Live at the Village Vanguard** (Columbia 46824), 2 CDs

Modern Jazz Quartet, **The Complete Last Concert** (Atlantic 81976), 2 CDs

Thelonious Monk, **The Complete London Collection** (Black Lion 7601), 3 CDs

Joe Pass, **Virtuoso** (Pablo 2310-708)

Oscar Peterson, **Tracks** (Verve 523 498)

Oscar Peterson and Joe Pass, **A la Salle Pleyel** (Pablo 2625-705), 2 CDs

George Shearing and Stephane Grappelli, **Reunion** (Polygram 821 868)

Zoot Sims and the Gershwin Brothers, **Zoot Sims & the Gershwin Brothers** (Original Jazz Classics 444)

Sonny Stitt, **Endgame Brilliance** (32 Jazz 32009), 2 CDs

Supersax, **Supersax Plays Bird** (Capitol 96264)

Irene Kral, **Where Is Love** (Koch 1012)

Mark Murphy, **Mark Murphy Sings** (Muse 5078)

Maxine Sullivan, **Close As Pages in a Book** (Audiophile 203)

Sarah Vaughan, **Live in Japan** (Mobile Fidelity 844), 2 CDs

Count Basie, **Basie & Zoot** (Original Jazz Classics 822)

Bill Berry L.A. Big Band, **Hello Rev** (Concord Jazz 4027)

Duke Ellington, **Seventieth Birthday Concert** (Blue Note 32746), 2 CDs

Don Ellis, **Autumn** (Tristar 80885)

Thad Jones/Mel Lewis Orchestra, **Consummation** (Blue Note 38226)

Buddy Rich Orchestra, **Mercy, Mercy** (Blue Note 54331)

Ruby Braff and George Barnes, **Live at the New School, the Complete Concert** (Chiaroscuro 126)

John Bunch, **Plays Kurt Weill** (Chiaroscuro 144)

Wild Bill Davison, **Showcase** (Jazzology 083)

Earl Hines, **Four Jazz Giants** (Solo Art 111/112), 2 CDs

Earl Hines, **Live at the New School** (Chiaroscuro 157)

Dick Hyman, **Jelly and James** (Columbia 52552)

Jay McShann and Claude Williams, **Man from Muskogee** (Sackville 3005)

Gunther Schuller and The New England Ragtime Ensemble, **The Art of Scott Joplin** (GM 3030)

Soprano Summit, **Soprano Summit** (Chiaroscuro 148), 2 CDs

Warren Vache, **First Time Out** (Audiophile 196)

Joe Venuti, **Joe & Zoot & More** (Chiaroscuro 128)

Dick Wellstood, **Dick Wellstood and His All Star Orchestra Featuring Kenny Davern/The Big Three** (Chiaroscuro 129)

Mary Lou Williams, **Nite Life/From the Heart** (Chiaroscuro 103), 2 CDs

World's Greatest Jazz Band, **Live at Roosevelt Grill** (Atlantic 90982)

Gato Barbieri, **Latino America** (Impulse 236), 2 CDs

Gato Barbieri, **Chapter Three** (GRP/Impulse 111)

Peter Brotzmann, **Machine Gun** (FMP 024)

Stephane Grappelli, **Live in London** (Black Lion 760139)

Barry Guy, **Ode** (Incus 041)

Albert Mangelsdorff, **Tromboneliness** (Sackville 2011)

Kenny Wheeler, **Gnu High** (ECM 825 591)

Various Artists, **Wildflowers, The New York Loft Jazz Sessions, Complete** (Knitting Factory 3037), 3 CDs

Various Artists, **California Concert** (Columbia 40690)

Various Artists, **Jazz at the Santa Monica Civic** (Pablo 2625-701), 3 CDs

stars recording some of the greatest albums of their careers and music that perfectly balanced the adventurous with the accessible.

Unfortunately, the bubble was bursting by 1975 as financial and distribution problems hurt the company's balance sheet. Even worse, the larger labels, smelling dollar signs, lured away the top CTI players with more lucrative contracts. Quite typically the post-CTI recordings of Hubbard, Turrentine, Laws, and Benson are purely commercial, tossing away Creed Taylor's balancing act in exchange for making a few quick bucks. So although the best CTI albums are still prized today, few collectors are too excited about the Columbia recordings of Hubbard and Laws or the early Fantasy albums of Turrentine.

George Benson   In 1967, guitarist George Benson left Columbia and his early supporter John Hammond to sign with Verve. Under producer Creed Taylor's direction, Benson's music began to become more commercial as can be heard on **Giblet Gravy** (Verve 37542). Although he was still performing standards such as "What's New" and "Billie's Bounce," his repertoire also included such current pop tunes as "Sunny," "Walk on By," and "Along Came Mary." During the next three years, Benson's work for Verve and A&M was streaky and geared toward the marketplace, including **Goodies** and **The Other Side of Abbey Road**. He often seemed as if he were being groomed as Wes Montgomery's successor in performing easy-listening music for AM radio.

However, Benson's recordings for CTI in the early-to-mid-1970s were on a much higher level. These projects were also produced by Creed Taylor but balanced accessible formats with Benson's jazz creativity and resulted in some of his finest albums. **Beyond the Blue Horizon** (CTI 65130) is a superior small group set with Benson showcased in a quartet with organist Clarence Palmer, Ron Carter, and Jack DeJohnette. The CD reissue (highlighted by "So What" and "Ode to a Kudu") augments the original five-song program with three alternate takes. **White Rabbit** (Sony 64768) has Benson joined by a much larger group arranged by Don Sebesky that includes Herbie Hancock's keyboards, Ron Carter, Billy Cobham, Airto Moreira, and 17-year-old acoustic guitarist Earl Klugh. The music is Spanish oriented (Jay Berliner's rhythm guitar adds to the atmosphere) and is highlighted by "California Dreamin'" and "El Mar," which features Klugh.

Also worth exploring from Benson's CTI period is the R&Bish **Body Talk** (Columbia 45222), **Bad Benson** (Columbia 40926), which is highlighted by an excellent version of "Take Five," and **Good King Bad** (Columbia 45226), which has arrangements by David Matthews. Benson's final recording for CTI, actually recorded two months after his first project for Warner Bros, was **Benson & Farrell** (Columbia 44169). This little-known set has Joe Farrell (who mostly sticks to flute) in a co-starring role while accompanied by a large rhythm section and sometimes two other flutists. The group plays four originals by arranger Dave Matthews plus "Old Devil Moon." To many of Benson's jazz fans, his CTI period (which was not without some compromised numbers) and his earlier Columbia releases are the high points of his career, showing how fine a guitarist George Benson could be when inspired.

In 1976 Benson switched to Warner Bros. and immediately recorded **Breezin'** (Warner Bros. 76713). Five of the six songs are conventional and somewhat routine instrumentals in which Benson is backed by an orchestra arranged by Claus Ogerman. The sixth song is the lone vocal, "This Masquerade," which, in addition to having Benson sing the words, features him scatting along with his guitar in what would become his trademark. To the surprise of everyone, this number became a major pop hit, making it to No. 10 on the charts and causing the album to reach No. 1 on the pop charts. Suddenly George Benson was a superstar, and from here on, he would be considered by most listeners a singer first, a guitarist second. The follow-up, **In Flight** (Warner Bros. 2983), has Benson singing on four of the six numbers (including "Nature Boy" and "Everything Must Change").

Most of Benson's recordings for the next decade would be of lesser interest from the jazz standpoint because he emphasized his pop/R&B singing while his guitar took a backseat. One could not blame him for following in the same direction as Nat King Cole in the 1950s because he went from being a struggling (if major league) jazz guitarist to a rich household name, but most in the jazz world mourned his departure from creative music.

Ron Carter   In 1968 Ron Carter left the Miles Davis Quintet. He was in such demand that during his last year with Davis, Carter often had Buster Williams sub in his place. Unlike Wayne Shorter, Herbie Hancock, and Tony Williams, Carter was not a major force in the fusion movement. He was too busy recording constantly, appearing as a sideman on a countless number of situations. The sound of his bass was heard at its best when accompanying strong players, he could always take effective solos, and he was very versatile.

In addition to appearing on many CTI recordings, Carter led five of his own. **Blues Farm** (CTI 60691) finds the bassist taking much of the solo space. Featured in a sextet also including Hubert Laws, either Richard Tee or Bob James on keyboards, and Billy Cobham, Carter is showcased on six numbers including "Django." **Spanish Blue** (Sony 40803) teams Carter in 1974 with Laws and an expanded rhythm section that includes Cobham; best among the four cuts is a fairly lengthy version of "So What." **All Blues** (CTI 6037) is the strongest of Carter's CTI releases, but unfortunately it is not out on CD yet. With Joe Henderson, pianist Roland Hanna (keyboardist Richard Tee sits in on one number), and Cobham also featured in the quartet, they perform a variety of music (including "Will You Still Be Mine?"), all of which is given a blues feeling although several of the tunes are not blues. The quality of the solos is as high as one would expect, and Henderson's presence uplifts the music.

Joe Farrell   Joe Farrell's CTI recordings gave him a bit of fame for a time. He had previously worked with the Maynard Ferguson Big Band (1960–61), Slide Hampton, Charles Mingus, Jaki Byard (1965), the Thad Jones/Mel Lewis big band (1966–69), and Elvin Jones (1967–70). Farrell was best known in the 1960s for his fine hard bop tenor playing. In the 1970s he began playing soprano sax and flute as much as tenor and was a key part of the first version of Chick Corea's Return to Forever during 1971–72.

Farrell recorded six albums for CTI during 1970–74 where he displayed his versatility and warm sound on each of his axes with all-star groups. Best is the 1970 set **Joe Farrell Quartet** (Columbia 40694), a near-classic album. Farrell plays tenor, soprano, flute, and oboe while joined by Chick Corea, John McLaughlin, Dave Holland, and Jack DeJohnette. Most memorable is a famous version of McLaughlin's "Follow Your Heart." Of the five other sets, only **Moon Germs** (Epic/Legacy 61630) has also been reissued on CD. Farrell is heard on the latter

sticking to soprano and flute while assisted by Herbie Hancock, Stanley Clarke, and Jack DeJohnette and this disc is most notable for a memorable version of Chick Corea's "Times Lie" and Clarke's "Bass Folk Song." Of the LP-only releases, **Outback** (CTI 8005) with Corea, Buster Williams, Elvin Jones, and Airta Moreira contains worthy originals while **Penny Arcade** (CTI 6034) matches Farrell with Hancock, guitarist Joe Beck, bassist Herb Bushler, drummer Steve Gadd, and Don Alias on conga. **Upon This Rock** (CTI 6042) is a bit rock oriented in places with Joe Beck being the co-star and the group also including Bushler and drummer Jim Madison; there are guest appearances on "I Won't Be Back" by Hancock, drummer Steve Gadd, and Alias. Farrell's final album for the label, **Canned Funk** (CTI 6053), has lengthy versions of four of his originals and matches the multireedist with Beck, Bushler, Madison, and percussionist Ray Mantilla. On all of these sets the music is melodic, a bit funky, and somewhat explorative in spots yet surprisingly accessible. They are among the most consistently successful of Creed Taylor's projects.

Freddie Hubbard   One of the most exciting trumpeters of the 1960s, Freddie Hubbard developed into the top trumpeter in jazz during the first half of the 1970s. Originally influenced by Clifford Brown and inspired by Lee Morgan, Hubbard became more and more individual as the 1960s developed and, although essentially a hard bop stylist, he was a forward-looking player never shy to take chances.

Hubbard led two interesting albums in 1969. **The Black Angel** (Koch 8538) from 1969 hints at fusion in spots (in some of the rhythms and Kenny Barron's use of electric piano) but is mostly high-quality post-bop (even if none of the originals caught on) with Hubbard for the last time on records leading a combo with altoist James Spaulding. **The Hub of Hubbard** (MPS/Verve 825 956) is a bop-oriented set with Eddie Daniels (who sticks to tenor), Roland Hanna, Richard Davis, and Louis Hayes. Hubbard is in fiery and generally brilliant form on "Without a Song," a ridiculously uptempo version of "Just One of Those Things," his catchy if basic "Blues for Duane," and the ballad "The Things We Did Last Summer."

During 1970–74 Freddie Hubbard was the biggest star of the CTI label, even overshadowing Stanley Turrentine, Hubert Laws, and George Benson. His best CTI albums rank with the greatest work of his career because they are both accessible and quite explorative, with Hubbard (who also appeared of his labelmates' records as a sideman) stretching himself effortlessly.

Hubbard's first three CTI albums are each considered classics in their own way. ● **Red Clay** (Epic/Legacy 85216), his personal favorite recording, was originally four selections but now also includes "Cold Turkey" and a live version of the title cut. Other than the latter number, Hubbard is featured in an unbeatable quintet with Joe Henderson (Stanley Turrentine is on the live "Red Clay"), Herbie Hancock, Ron Carter, and Lenny White, playing a funky variety of hard bop that is filled with fire and excitement. ● **Straight Life** (Epic/Legacy 65125) might even be a better Hubbard set. Joined by Henderson, Hancock, George Benson, Carter, and Jack DeJohnette, the trumpeter is quite astounding on "Straight Life" (with its memorable introduction) and "Mr. Clean," and he duets on flugelhorn (where he has a glorious tone) with Benson on a lyrical version of "Here's that Rainy Day." The biggest seller of Hubbard's CTI recordings, 1971's **First Light** (Epic/Legacy 50562), utilizes the string and woodwind arrangements of Don Sebesky. Hubbard is quite inspired and is particularly rewarding on "First Light" and "Uncle Albert/Admiral Halsey."

Hubbard's other CTI recordings all have their moments even though they do not reach the heights of his first three efforts. **Sky Dive** (Columbia 44171) ranges from Hubbard's "Povo" and "Sky Dive" to the theme from *The Godfather* and Bix Beiderbecke's "In a Mist." The trumpeter is assisted along the way by Benson, Laws, and Keith Jarrett on keyboards. **Keep Your Soul Together** (Columbia 40933) has the trumpeter in excellent form on four of his originals (most memorable is "Spirits of Trane") with a septet consisting of Junior Cook, George Cables, guitarist Aurell Ray, either Kent Brinkley or Ron Carter on bass, drummer Ralph Penland, and Juno Lewis on percussion. Hubbard's sixth and final CTI album, **Polar AC** (CTI 6056), is the only one not yet out on CD. He is backed on four songs (including "People Make the World Go Round" and "Betcha by Golly, Wow") by a string section arranged by either Don Sebesky or Bob James with contributions made by Laws and Benson, and on "Son of Sky Dive" he jams in a sextet with Laws and Cook. Also of strong interest is **In Concert Vols. 1 & 2** (Sony 40688), featuring the CTI

all-stars on March 3, 1973. Including five of the six selections originally out on two LPs, this single CD has Hubbard and Turrentine joined by guitarist Eric Gale, Hancock, Carter, and DeJohnette, stretching out on such tunes as "Povo" and "Gibraltar."

Freddie Hubbard was among the first of Creed Taylor's stars to leave the CTI label, signing with Columbia in 1974. Unfortunately, he made some bad choices, was not given much creative freedom on his own records, and recorded some real junk that was clearly aimed at the commercial market. Although in live performances he ranked at the top of jazz trumpeters, most of his recordings for Columbia during the second half of the decade were obvious sellouts. As it is, the following three LPs have not been reissued on CD. **High Energy** (Columbia 33048) is not as bad as what was to follow as Hubbard's quintet with Cook and Cables is joined by a small orchestra and a string section. The trumpeter does what he can with "Ebony Moonbeams" and Stevie Wonder's "Too High," reviving his piece "Crisis." But **Liquid Love** (Columbia 33556) is pretty dismal; Hubbard would not be performing "Midnight at the Oasis," "Put It in the Pocket," and "Liquid Love" for long. **Windjammer** (Columbia 34166) ranks among Hubbard's worst recordings ever. This funk date has the trumpeter sounding lost on his own album, buried beneath a string section, five vocalists, and an oversized orchestra arranged by Bob James playing turkeys like "Touch Me Baby" and "Feelings." Without Creed Taylor's guiding presence balancing the artistic with the commercial, Hubbard's career went strictly toward the latter for a time, ruining his reputation for years.

Hubert Laws   In the 1970s because of his association with CTI, Hubert Laws became jazz's most popular flutist, even topping Herbie Mann. A technically skilled player who had recorded previously as a leader with Atlantic, Laws cut eight albums for CTI during 1969–75 that, although sometimes a bit commercial and overarranged, included the artistic high points of his career. **Afro-Classic** (CTI/Columbia 44172) made him into celebrity in the jazz world. With Don Sebesky's arrangements being quite supportive of the flutist, Laws's group (which includes a large rhythm section plus bassoon) performs two Bach melodies, one by Mozart, James Taylor's "Fire and Rain," and the theme from *Love Story*. In comparison, **The Rite of Spring** (Epic/Legacy

61628) seems a bit trivial at times as major classical themes by Debussy, Bach, Faure, and Stravinsky are turned into popish jazz. However, Laws plays quite well with his version of "Pavane" being a high point though Stravinsky fans will not be enthralled by the reworking of the title cut. **In the Beginning** (CTI/Columbia 65127), formerly a double LP, has Laws at the peak of his career. Whether performing classical-oriented pieces, straightahead jazz, or 1970s funk, Laws and his rhythm section (Bob James, guitarist Gene Bertoncini, Ron Carter, and Steve Gadd with three strings) play brilliantly. Hubert's brother Ronnie Laws, who would pursue a commercial career in R&B/funk, plays arguably his finest recorded tenor solo ever on John Coltrane's "Moment's Notice." **The San Francisco Concert** from 1975 (CTI/Columbia 40819) looks back toward Laws's best CTI recordings and ahead to his abysmal output for Columbia. Bob James's arrangements are more commercial than Sebesky's and not as good a match with Laws, but the flutist does his best on "Feel Like Making Love" and themes by Bizet and Rimsky-Korsakoff.

Morning Star (CTI 6022), which has Laws with a large string orchestra and sometimes some unnecessary background vocalists on such tunes as "Let Her Go," "Where Is the Love," and "Amazing Grace," and **Carnegie Hall** (CTI 6025) have not been reissued on CD yet. The latter has Laws performing a medley of Chick Corea's "Windows" and "Fire and Rain" plus a 20-minute version of Bach's "Passacaglia in C Minor" in top form. Also not easily available is **The Chicago Theme** (CTI 6058), a lesser effort with Bob James arrangements.

In 1976 Hubert Laws left CTI to sign with Columbia. Most of his releases from then on would be very commercial, using his flute as seasoning or as a prop over funky grooves.

Don Sebesky   Because of his many arrangements for CTI albums during the first half of the 1970s, including dates led by Freddie Hubbard, Hubert Laws, George Benson, and Paul Desmond, Don Sebesky became quite well known. He was originally a trombonist who worked with Kai Winding, Claude Thornhill, the Tommy Dorsey ghost band, Maynard Ferguson (for whom he contributed arrangements), and Stan Kenton. In the early 1960s he gave up playing trombone and was soon working regularly for producer Creed Taylor, arranging

for many albums released by Verve, A&M, and CTI including several records by Wes Montgomery.

After contributing to the success of so many others on the CTI roster, in 1973 Sebesky had the opportunity to lead his own all-star set. **Giant Box** (Sony 40697), originally a deluxe two-LP box that has been reissued as a single CD, has most of the great CTI players making appearances including Hubbard, Benson, Laws, Farrell, Carter, Jack DeJohnette, Billy Cobham, Airto Moreira, Paul Desmond, Milt Jackson, Grover Washington, Jr., (from the subsidiary Kudu), keyboardist Bob James (who was a competing arranger), and Jackie & Roy. The key soloists all have opportunities to stretch out, Sebesky's arrangements (which sometimes blend together classical elements with jazz) are distinctive, and the music works quite well. This is CTI at its best and Creed Taylor at the height of his power.

Stanley Turrentine   Stanley Turrentine, like singer Big Joe Turner, was able to fit into several contexts during his career quite comfortably without changing anything about his sound or style. During 1968–69 the soulful tenor recorded his final five Blue Note albums including **Common Touch** (Blue Note 54719). An easy-listening set that perhaps for the last time teamed together Turrentine with his wife organist Shirley Scott (they would be divorced a few years later), this date has the pair and guitarist Jimmy Ponder uplifting a wide variety of material (all taken at a relaxed pace), even "Blowin' in the Wind."

In 1970 Turrentine signed with Creed Taylor, and his career went in a completely different direction. During the next three years he recorded five albums for CTI as a leader, having the biggest hit of his career with his CTI debut, ◉ **Sugar** (Epic/Legacy 85284). The title cut was perfect for Turrentine's bluesy sound, and the original album also included a hard-swinging version of "Impressions" and organist Butch Cornell's "Sunshine Alley"; the CD reissue adds a second and longer live version of "Sugar" from the following year to the program. Among the key sidemen in the octets are Freddie Hubbard, George Benson, and Ron Carter. Turrentine would be associated with "Sugar" for the remainder of his life.

Salt Song (Sony 65126) has Turrentine joined by a large rhythm section, strings, and background voices for arrangements by Eumir Deodato with the best number being a stirring version of Freddie Hubbard's "Gibraltar."

Cherry (Columbia 40916) finds Turrentine returning to a small group, co-leading a date with Milt Jackson that also has keyboardist Bob James, guitarist Cornell Dupree, Ron Carter, and Billy Cobham. Although not all of the songs are of equal quality, these versions of "I Remember You" and especially "Speedball" are memorable. **Don't Mess with Mr. T.** (Columbia 44173), which is mostly with a large ensemble, is most noteworthy for the title cut and a quintet version of "Two for T." The one Turrentine CTI release not yet out on CD, **The Sugar Man** (CTI 6052), dates from 1971–73 and was not originally released until the mid-1970s. It consists of some big-band numbers, a few sextet tracks, and a variety of leftovers including the initial Turrentine version of "Pieces of Dreams."

In 1974 Turrentine became one of CTI's first big names to leave the label, signing with Fantasy. Unfortunately, many of the tenor's Fantasy releases, particularly the first few, are of lesser interest. Although he always plays well, Turrentine is joined by large orchestras, unimaginative arrangements, and weak material. **Pieces of Dreams** (Original Jazz Classics 831) is only worthy for Turrentine's recording of Michel Legrand's title cut, which is fortunately heard in two versions. However, the other six numbers (plus two alternates) are quite commercial and forgettable as are Gene Page's arrangements for electric keyboards, three guitars, strings, and a few background vocalists. Stanley Turrentine would not be heard in favorable settings on records again until the 1980s.

Bop and Cool Jazz of 1968–1976

Although it is easy to stereotype the 1968–76 period as the fusion era, there was actually a great deal of rewarding bebop recorded during this period. The emergence of fusion did make it tough going for some of the bop and cool jazz veterans at first, but work opportunities often presented themselves in Europe, at jazz festivals, and as teachers at universities where jazz was finally being accepted as more than a stepchild to classical music. Musicians with the bigger names (such as Dizzy Gillespie, Dave Brubeck, and the Modern Jazz Quartet) managed to always keep busy, and by the mid-1970s the climate had greatly improved for most of the other key players. And although most of the younger jazz musicians of the era looked toward fusion and the avant-garde for inspiration, both trumpeter Jon Faddis and altoist Richie Cole showed that bebop was for the young, too.

Joe Albany   A ghost from the past started making an unexpected comeback during 1971–72. Joe Albany, who had performed live with Charlie Parker and recorded with Lester Young in 1946, had let drug abuse largely ruin his life. He was off records altogether during 1947–70 (other than a recorded rehearsal from 1957), and although he played now and then (including with Charles Mingus briefly in the mid-1960s), he was barely remembered when the Spotlite label recorded a solo LP in 1971, **At Home** (Spotlite 1). However, it was soon followed by other albums for Revelation and Steeple Chase, highlighted by a superior duo date of bop standards and ballads with bassist Niels Pedersen, **Two's Company** (Steeple Chase 31019). Remarkably, Albany (after all of those years in obscurity) was playing at his best by the mid-1970s, sticking to the classic bop style that he helped develop 30 years earlier.

Gene Ammons   In October 1969, Gene Ammons was finally released from prison, after serving seven years out of a 15-year sentence for drug possession. Within a short time he was back to playing in clubs again, and although he was now a more emotional player, open to a wider range of expressive sounds (being familiar with the avant-garde players), he still had his distinctive huge sound. **The Boss Is Back** (Prestige 24129), which reissues the first two albums of his comeback period, has an acoustic quintet date with pianist Junior Mance and a session that emphasizes boogaloos with organist Sonny Phillips. Best are the ballads ("Here's that Rainy Day," "Didn't We," and "Feeling Good"), which put the focus on Ammons's tone. Not all of Ammons's later sets are as rewarding, with some being dominated by commercialism and unimaginative pop material. But the Boss was indeed back, and he can be heard in inspired settings, meeting up with Dexter Gordon on **The Chase** (Prestige 24166), Sonny Stitt on the live **God Bless Jug and Sonny** (Prestige 11019) and the LP **Together Again for the Last Time** (Prestige 10100), and having an encounter with Cannonball Adderley and Dexter Gordon on part of 1973's **Gene Ammons and Friends at Montreux** (Original Jazz Classics 1023).

Sadly, the comeback would last fewer than five years. Ammons's final recording date took place in May 1974, and ironically the last song he recorded was "Goodbye." The title cut of **Goodbye** (Original Jazz Classics 1081) is quite emotional and the high point of a septet date with Nat Adderley, Gary Bartz, Kenny Drew, Sam Jones, Louis Hayes, and Ray Barretto. In contrast to some of the commercial studio albums he recorded during the previous couple of years, this set is much more free-wheeling. Ammons sounds in happy form on "It Don't Mean a Thing," "Alone Again (Naturally) ," and "Jean-nine." But soon after the album was completed, he was diagnosed with terminal cancer and in fewer than three months Gene Ammons was gone.

Chet Baker   Chet Baker, who returned to the United States in 1964, showed on his Prestige dates of 1965 that he could still play quite well. Unfortunately, the following year he recorded a series of inferior, strictly-for-the-money, commercial dates for World Pacific, including such turkeys as **A Taste of Tequila**, **Double Shot**, and **In the Mood**, sessions in which he was backed by the Mariachi Brass (a rip-off of the Tijuana Brass) or uninspiring commercial orchestras. Later that year Baker had several of his teeth knocked out during a beating that took place when a drug deal went bad.

After being completely inactive for a couple years, in 1969 Baker returned to records but waxed two of his worst albums: **Albert's House** (a set of inferior Steve Allen tunes in which Baker sounds barely conscious) and **Blood, Chet and Tears**, which is comprised of inferior versions of Blood, Sweat & Tears tunes. He slipped away into obscurity for a few more years.

After being outfitted with new teeth and forcing himself to begin the painful task of regaining his chops, in 1974 Baker returned to the scene, assisted by Dizzy Gillespie who helped him secure some gigs in New York. **She Was Too Good for Me** (Columbia 40804), which was originally on the CTI label, has the trumpeter sounding pretty decent on an outing with strings, Hubert Laws, and Paul Desmond (who is on two songs); highlights include "Autumn Leaves," "Tangerine," and "With a Song in My Heart." Beating the odds, Chet Baker was on his way to becoming one of the few trumpeters in jazz history to make a full comeback.

Dave Brubeck   After Dave Brubeck broke up his quartet in 1967, he took time off to write lengthy religious works including *The Light in the Wilderness*. However, producer George Wein talked Brubeck into playing a jazz concert a few months later, and a new quartet was formed that was comprised of Gerry Mulligan, bassist

Jack Six, and drummer Alan Dawson. The group stayed together on a part-time basis for several years, making a few recordings including the music that resulted in the double-CD set **Live at the Berlin Philharmonic** (Legacy/Columbia 64820). This excellent release (which is greatly expanded from the original LP) is highlighted by "Out of Nowhere," "Things Ain't What They Used to Be," "The Duke," and three encores that were demanded by the enthusiastic audience. The same Brubeck-Mulligan group appeared at the 1971 Newport Jazz Festival (just a short time before a riot shut down the festival), resulting in **Last Set at Newport** (Atlantic 1607), which includes the classic "Blues for Newport," "Open the Gates," and the umpteenth version of "Take Five."

Released in 1972, **We're All Together Again for the First Time** (Atlantic 1641) has the new quartet expanded to a quintet with the addition of Paul Desmond in his first of several recorded reunions with Brubeck. Desmond and Mulligan were old friends, and their interplay is quite delightful throughout this special project. Highlights include Mulligan's "Unfinished Woman," "Rotterdam Blues," "Koto Song," and a definitive 16-minute rendition of "Take Five."

All the Things You Are (Atlantic 1694) is unusual for Brubeck; Six and Dawson are heard in a quartet with Lee Konitz on "Like Someone in Love" and a brief "Don't Get Around Much Anymore," avant-garde giant Anthony Braxton (also on alto) is featured on "In Your Own Sweet Way," and both Konitz and Braxton team up for "All the Things You Are." Although both altoists fit in quite well with Brubeck, in reality the most exciting performance is the Brubeck Trio's 21-minute five-song "Jimmy Van Heusen Medley."

There have been many musical families in jazz history, but few have been as large as Dave Brubeck's. In addition to the pianist and his wife/lyricist Iola, the family has four musical sons: bassist and bass trombonist Chris Brubeck, drummer Danny Brubeck, pianist Darius Brubeck, and the youngest brother, cellist Matthew Brubeck. Recorded in 1973, **Two Generations of Brubeck** (Atlantic 1645) and 1974's **Brother, the Great Spirit Made Us All** (Atlantic 1660) have not been reissued yet, but both are worth finding. In addition to Dave Brubeck and his three older sons (all but Matthew), tenor saxophonist Jerry Bergonzi, clarinetist Perry Robinson, and Madcat Ruth on harmonica help out, giving Brubeck's standards a different and fresh sound. **Brubeck & Desmond: Duets (1975)** (A&M 3290) is another special date, teaming Dave Brubeck and Paul Desmond on a full set of lyrical duets. The old musical friends perform five standards (including "Stardust"), three Brubeck originals (highlighted by "Koto Song" and "Summer Song"), and a remake of "Balcony Rock." 55 years old at the end of 1975, Brubeck was as busy as ever, playing, composing, and recording.

In 1976, the classic Dave Brubeck Quartet (Brubeck, Desmond, Eugene Wright, and Joe Morello) had their only official reunion tour, which was quite successful although it was cut short by Morello's failing eyesight (he would soon be completely blind). The recording **25**th **Anniversary Reunion** (A&M 75021-0806) is highlighted by "St. Louis Blues," a tender "Don't Worry 'Bout Me," "Three to Get Ready," and yet another version of "Take Five." Although it was not obvious at the time, this would be the last time that Paul Desmond and Dave Brubeck would record together. The altoist passed away on May 30, 1977.

Kenny Burrell   Kenny Burrell has always had a great love for the music of Duke Ellington, so in 1975, shortly after Ellington's death, the guitarist put together **Ellington Is Forever, Vol. 1** (Fantasy 79005), a set that features renditions of 15 Ellington and Billy Strayhorn songs. With such all-stars as Jimmy Smith, Thad Jones, Joe Henderson, pianist Jimmy Jones (who takes "Take the 'A' Train" as a solo piece), and singer Ernie Andrews making strong contributions, Burrell's project (which uses a variety of instrumentations) is well conceived and both reverent and a bit explorative.

Ray Bryant   Pianist Ray Bryant had his bluish swing style fully formed by the late 1950s. Because of the success of the danceable "Madison Time" in 1960 and "Little Susie," some of his output in the 1960s were attempts to duplicate his hits (including "Big Susie," "Do that Twist," and "Twist City") although these did not catch on. After his Columbia period ended in 1962, Bryant recorded for the Sue label (1963–65), Cadet (1966–74), and Atlantic (1970 and 1972). There was one classic from this period, 1972's ● **Alone at Montreux** (32 Jazz 32128). The definitive Ray Bryant album, this solo set features him digging into "Gotta Travel On," "Cubana Chant," "Slow Freight," "Little Susie," a variety of other tunes, and a superb version of "After Hours," a song that Bryant has owned ever since.

In 1976 Bryant recorded two excellent albums for the Pablo label. **Here's Ray Bryant** (Original Jazz Classics 826) is a trio set with bassist George Duvivier and drummer Grady Tate. Although there are no actual blues on this date, Bryant infuses such songs as "Girl Talk," "Good Morning Heartache," and "Li'l Darlin'" with plenty of blues feeling. **Solo Flight** (Original Jazz Classics 885) is a superior set of unaccompanied solos that range from old-timey-sounding originals such as "In de Back Room" and "Blues In de Big Brass Bed" to "Moanin'," "Take the 'A' Train," and "What Are You Doing the Rest of Your Life." Although Bryant's combination of swing, blues, gospel, and soul may have been out of style (he never followed musical trends), most of his recordings are quite timeless.

Al Cohn   Al Cohn, one of the Four Brothers from Woody Herman's band (where he had replaced Herbie Steward in 1948), largely de-emphasized his playing during 1963–72 when he primarily wrote for the studios. Fortunately, he became more active as a player again after 1972, leading dates for Muse, Gazell, and most notably Xanadu (1975–80). Most of Cohn's many Xanadu albums (both as a leader and as a sideman) have not been reissued on CD yet (the label went defunct before the CD era began) including **Play It Now** (Xanadu 110) and the particularly memorable **America** (Xanadu 138), both of which are quartet dates with Barry Harris from 1976 that are well worth finding. Cohn's playing style was unchanged from 20 years earlier but he had lost neither his enthusiasm nor his creativity, as he would continually show during the second half of the 1970s.

Dolo Coker   A top-notch bop-based pianist, Dolo Coker played in the 1950s with Sonny Stitt (1955–57), Gene Ammons, Lou Donaldson, Art Pepper (appearing on his album Intensity), Philly Joe Jones, and Dexter Gordon (1960–61). In 1961, Coker moved to Los Angeles where he worked for many years with his trio while being very underrated. In the 1970s Coker reunited with Sonny Stitt and gigged with Herb Ellis, Blue Mitchell, Red Rodney, Lee Konitz, Sonny Criss, and Supersax in addition to some of the artists associated with the Xanadu label. He only had four opportunities to lead his record dates, all albums made for Xanadu during 1976–79. The only set that has thus far reappeared on CD is 1976's **California Hard** (Xanadu

1229), which pays tribute to the underrated hard bop (as opposed to cool jazz) scene that has long existed in California. Coker is joined by Art Pepper (doubling on alto and tenor), Blue Mitchell, Leroy Vinnegar, and Frank Butler. This enjoyable set has originals by Coker, Pepper ("Mr. Yohe"), and Mitchell (a drum feature for Butler on "Roots 4FB") along with a showcase for the trio ("Gone Again") and a vintage standard ("Gone with the Wind"). Throughout, Dolo Coker is heard playing at the peak of his powers.

Richie Cole   In the mid-1970s, it may have appeared to many listeners that bebop was doomed to die, only played by the survivors from 20–30 years ago. However, Richie Cole's arrival on the scene helped launch a generation of younger beboppers while building a new audience for the music. Cole heard jazz from an early age because his father owned a jazz club in New Jersey. He began playing alto sax when he was ten, had lessons from Phil Woods (his biggest influence), attended Berklee College of Music for two years as a teenager, and played with Buddy Rich (1969), Lionel Hampton, and frequently with Eddie Jefferson during 1976–79. In the mid-1970s he formed his Alto Madness band, feeling that any song (no matter how unlikely) could be transformed into bebop and never being shy to infuse the music with his own brand of humor. Twenty-eight years old in 1976, Cole started a string of recordings for Muse (some of which have been reissued by 32 Jazz) that rank with the best work of his career. **New York Afternoon: Alto Madness** (Muse 5119) from 1976 has Cole leading a sextet also featuring guitarist Vic Juris and keyboardist Mickey Tucker. Eddie Jefferson sings two of the seven numbers, and the highlights overall include "Waltz for a Rainy Be-Bop Evening," "New York Afternoon," "Stormy Weather," and "Alto Madness."

Sonny Criss   Altoist Sonny Criss's excellent series of recordings for the Prestige label continued through 1969. **The Beat Goes On** (Original Jazz Classics 1051) has Criss doing his best to make three pop tunes ("Ode to Billie Joe," "Somewhere My Love," and the title cut) into swinging jazz with mixed success. Criss, Cedar Walton, Bob Cranshaw, and Alan Dawson have better luck on the altoist's blues "Calidad," "Yesterdays," and "Georgia Rose." Although most of Criss's sessions as a leader are quartet dates, **Sonny's Dream** (Original Jazz Classics 707) is quite a bit different. Criss is heard in a ten-piece group

arranged by the great Los Angeles–based pianist Horace Tapscott. Criss has most of the solo space, the group includes Conte Candoli, Teddy Edwards, and Tommy Flanagan, and the Tapscott originals challenge the altoist to play in top form. **Rockin' in Rhythm** (Original Jazz Classics 1022) and **I'll Catch the Sun** (Original Jazz Classics 811) are more typical dates from 1968–69. **Rockin' in Rhythm** mostly has Criss, pianist Eddie Green, Cranshaw, and Dawson jamming jazz classics (including "Sonnymoon for Two" and "When the Sun Comes Out") plus "Eleanor Rigby" and a slightly earlier version of "All the Things You Are." The final Prestige album, **I'll Catch the Sun,** has Criss, Hampton Hawes, Monty Budwig, and Shelly Manne alternating jazz and pop songs pretty effectively. A passionate "Cry Me a River" is the most memorable selection.

Because he was mostly based in Los Angeles and playing in a boppish style considered out-of-date, Sonny Criss did not gain the recognition that he deserved. Other than a live set in Italy in 1974 that was put out by the Fresh Sound label, Criss was off records during 1970–74 although still active. However, 1975 ended up being one of Criss's finest years on record as he recorded three superior dates. ◉ **Crisscraft** (32 Jazz 32049) is Criss's definitive session because he sounds quite brilliant on a lengthy and memorable "The Isle of Celia," "Blues in My Heart," the boppish blues "Crisscraft," a slightly later version of "Out of Nowhere," and two other selections. Dolo Coker, bassist Larry Gales, and drummer Jimmy Smith are also in top form. Just a week later, Criss cut **Saturday Morning** (Prevue 7) for Xanadu, a label on which he also made some sideman appearances. On this occasion he is joined by the great bop pianist Barry Harris, Leroy Vinnegar, and drummer Lenny McBrowne, performing four superior standards ("Angel Eyes," "Tin Tin Deo," "My Heart Stood Still," and "Until the Real Thing Comes Along"), his blues "Jeannie's Knees," and one of his better originals, "Saturday Morning." **Out of Nowhere** (32 Jazz 32028) would be the last small-group date of Sonny Criss's career. Back with the team of Coker, Gales, and Smith, Criss (three days short of his 48th birthday) is once again heard at the peak of his powers. His creativity never lets up on two originals, a song by Coker, and four standards including "All the Things You Are" and "My Ideal."

In another time period, Sonny Criss may have become famous in the jazz world for his distinctive sound and fiery solos. But although appreciated by straightahead jazz fans, he was very much overshadowed in the mid-1970s because of the rise of fusion and more advanced styles. In 1976 he recorded two rather commercial projects for the declining Impulse label, neither of which are out on CD: **Warm and Sonny** (Impulse 9312) and **The Joy of Sax** (Impulse 9326). Joined by many other horns, strings, an expanded rhythm section, and (on the latter date) voices, Criss was clearly being recorded with hopes of making a hit record. Otherwise, why document such songs as "The Way We Were," "Memories," "You've Lost that Lovin' Feeling," and "Midnight Mellow"?

It was all for naught because the sales of those projects were as disappointing as the music. Tragically those would be the final recordings of Sonny Criss because in 1977 he was stricken with cancer, reached the point where he could not take the pain anymore, and on November 19 he shot himself. Criss was 50.

Eddie "Lockjaw" Davis   During 1968–75, Eddie "Lockjaw" Davis primarily worked as a single other than making occasional guest appearances with Count Basie. It was a sign of the times that all of his recordings as a leader were made in Europe for European labels during this era; he did not fit into the current musical trends in the United States. There was a recorded reunion with Johnny Griffin, **Tough Tenors Again 'N' Again** (MPS 15283) and one of many matchups with Harry "Sweets" Edison, **Light and Lovely** (Blue & Blue 33121), but those have not been reissued on CD yet. **With Michel Attenoux** (Storyville 5009) from 1975 is available and teams Lockjaw with altoist Attenoux (whose sound looks toward Tab Smith and Johnny Hodges) and his French sextet for a hard-swinging program of standards.

The year 1976 was a particularly busy one for Lockjaw, particularly on recordings. **Jaws Strikes Again** (Black & Blue 233101) has him leading a quartet with organist Wild Bill Davis, romping on such standards as "The Man I Love," "Jumpin' with Symphony Sid," and "After You've Gone." **Swingin' till the Girls Come Home** (Steeple Chase 31058) was recorded in Copenhagen with a Danish trio that includes pianist Thomas Clausen and is highlighted by the title cut, a rapid rendition of "Love for Sale," his original "Locks," and "Indiana." A couple LPs (also cut in Copenhagen) match Lockjaw with Harry "Sweets" Edison along with

trombonist John Darville and the Kenny Drew Trio: **Vol. 1** (Storyville 4004) and **Opus Funk** (Storyville 4025). The best known of Lockjaw's 1976 recordings, ◉ **Straight Ahead** (Original Jazz Classics 629), is pretty definitive of the tough tenor's playing, teaming him with Ella Fitzgerald's rhythm section of the time (Tommy Flanagan, bassist Keeter Betts, and drummer Bobby Durham) on such numbers as "Wave," "On a Clear Day," and "Lover."

His association with the Pablo label (both as a leader and a sideman on many dates) led to Eddie "Lockjaw" Davis finally being widely recognized as the unique stylist he had been since the 1950s.

Buddy DeFranco   Buddy DeFranco had the unfortunate timing of being one of the top jazz clarinetists (some would say the best) during decades when the instrument was considered out of vogue. Instead of being a world-famous celebrity such as Benny Goodman and Artie Shaw, DeFranco was relegated to heading the Glenn Miller ghost orchestra during 1966–74, even though he was never a part of the original band. It must have been difficult for him to be musically satisfied leading the orchestra through the same songs being played the same way night after night.

In 1974, DeFranco got off the treadmill and returned to creative jazz. **Free Sail** (Candid 71008) features him in a quintet with Victor Feldman, guitarist John Chiodini, bassist Victor Sproles, and drummer Joe Cucuzzo. Surprisingly, this is not a bop set and instead includes the clarinetist's lengthy "Threat of Freedom," Feldman's "Free Fall," a couple of standards, and guitarist Jim Gillis's "Free Sail." DeFranco really stretches himself throughout this challenging material. Recorded in 1975, **Boronqin** (Sonet 724) is in a similar vein. DeFranco is joined by Chiodini, pianist Ray Santisi, bassist Mike Richmond, and drummer Randy Jones for three harmonically advanced originals plus "Easy Living" and rapid renditions of "But Not for Me" and "The Song Is You." Buddy DeFranco might have been unknown to the general public, but he still had few competitors among jazz clarinetists.

Paul Desmond   After the Dave Brubeck Quartet broke up in 1967, Paul Desmond only performed now and then. There were a few highlights along the way including some reunions with Brubeck, a 1971 concert with the Modern Jazz Quartet, and collaborations with

Canadian guitarist Ed Bickert that recalled the altoist's earlier work with Jim Hall.

Paul Desmond & the Modern Jazz Quartet (Columbia/Legacy 57337) works quite well because Desmond's cool tone was an excellent fit with the MJQ. Most memorable are "East of the Sun," "Blue Dove," and "You Go to My Head." Desmond, who during 1968–69 led three commercial but not uninteresting sets for producer Creed Taylor at A&M, cut two albums for Taylor at CTI in 1973–74. **Skylark** (Sony 65133) has Desmond featured with a septet that includes Gabor Szabo and Bob James, sounding fine on "Take Ten" and "Indian Summer" although the "contemporary" rhythm section was not ideal for his sound. **Pure Desmond** (Sony 64767) is more successful, the first of four recordings that teamed the lyrical altoist with Bickert in a pianoless quartet. With Ron Carter and Connie Kay helping out, Desmond sounds wonderful on "I'm Old Fashioned," "Till the Clouds Roll By," and "Mean to Be." The other three Desmond-Bickert sets, **Like Someone in Love** (Telearchive 83319), the out-of-print LP **Paul Desmond Quartet** (Artists House 2), and **The Paul Desmond Quartet Live** (A&M 543501) all have bassist Don Thompson and drummer Jerry Fuller completing the group and were recorded live in Toronto in 1975. They are of equal value, are full of subtle interplay between the musicians, and feature Desmond stretching out in relaxed fashion on some of his favorite songs.

After having a final reunion with Dave Brubeck in 1976, Paul Desmond contracted lung cancer (he was a lifelong smoker), passing away the following year at the age of 52.

Lou Donaldson   Lou Donaldson's second period on Blue Note (1967–74) was much less significant than his first despite having a funky hit in 1967 with "Alligator Boogaloo." In fact, that strong seller led to quite a few recordings that hoped to duplicate its commercial success. Donaldson primarily played over funky rhythms during this era, sometimes utilized the Varitone sax (an electric instrument that watered down his sound) and recorded frequently although few of the albums that he churned out featured the "real" Lou Donaldson. **Midnight Creeper** (Blue Note 24549) from 1968 is not bad (Blue Mitchell and Lonnie Smith are assets) but **Hot Dog** (Blue Note 28267), **Everything I Play Is Funky** (Blue Note 31248), **Pretty Things** (Blue Note 89794), and **The Scorpion: Live at the Cadillac**

Club (Blue Note 31876) are just four of the rather weak albums that Donaldson cut during this period. As Blue Note declined, so did Lou Donaldson's music, and it would be quite a few years before he returned to playing the soulful straightahead jazz that suited him best.

Herb Ellis   In the 1960s guitarist Herb Ellis mostly worked as a studio musician on the West Coast in addition to playing occasional jazz dates. When Carl Jefferson formed the Concord label in 1973, Ellis began to record as a leader quite frequently, leading eight sessions (seven for Concord) during the next three years. He also became a member of Great Guitars, interacting with Barney Kessel and Charlie Byrd.

Like Kessel, Ellis needed someone to light a fire under him to keep his sets from being overly relaxed and lazy. He is in excellent form on the Concord label's first three releases. **Jazz/Concord** (Concord Jazz 6001) and **Seven Come Eleven** (Concord Jazz 6002) were both recorded July 29, 1973, and have Ellis, Joe Pass, Ray Brown, and Jake Hanna forming a superior bop-based quartet. Pass would soon surpass Ellis in his own Pablo recordings, but Ellis holds his own on this straightahead material, with **Seven Come Eleven** getting the edge of the two sets because of it including some more fiery solos. **Two for the Road** (Original Jazz Classics 726) from a half-year later is a duo date by Ellis and Pass and works pretty well on such numbers as "Lady Be Good," "I've Found a New Baby," and two versions of "Cherokee."

Soft Shoe (Concord Jazz 6003) and **After You've Gone** (Concord Jazz 6006) were both recorded at the 1974 Concord Jazz Festival, with Ellis leading a group also including pianist George Duke (on two of his very few straightahead sessions), Harry "Sweets" Edison (in fine form), Ray Brown, and Jake Hanna, with tenor saxophonist Plas Johnson added on the latter set. Harry "Sweets" Edison adds fire to the small-group swing dates. Of lesser interest are **Rhythm Willie** (Concord Jazz 6010), which is supposedly a co-led date with rhythm guitarist Freddie Green who never solos, **Hot Tracks** (Concord Jazz 6012), which does not live up to its billing (despite the presence of Edison and Plas Johnson), and the LP **A Pair to Draw To** (Concord Jazz 17), which is a generally dull set of duets with pianist Ross Tompkins.

Jon Faddis   As with Richie Cole, trumpeter Jon Faddis's sudden appearance on the major league scene gave bop fans something to cheer about along with hope for the future. Faddis displayed the ability to sound just like his idol Dizzy Gillespie, except that he had a wider range and could play his solos an octave higher. In the 30 years since Gillespie began making a strong impact, no trumpeter had come that close to emulating him before. In fact, one reason that Fats Navarro and Miles Davis became greater influences on trumpeters is that no one could play with the combination of complexity and virtuosity that Dizzy displayed; that is, no one could until Faddis.

Faddis idolized Gillespie from the time he started playing trumpet at age eight in 1961. In the early 1970s, Faddis (who was still a teenager) moved to New York and played with Lionel Hampton and Charles Mingus (guesting on a recorded concert when Roy Eldridge was ill). He had opportunities to share the bandstand with Gillespie (unfortunately their most exciting collaborations were never recorded), made a duet record with Oscar Peterson, and in 1976 led his first album, **Youngblood** (Pablo 2310-765), which has not been reissued on CD yet. Twenty-two years old at the time, Faddis is heard with a quartet also including Kenny Barron, George Mraz, and Mickey Roker playing a pair of Gillespie songs, "'Round Midnight," "Samba de Orpheus," and an emotional version of Gershwin's "Prelude #2."

After making such a strong impression, Jon Faddis disappeared for a time, playing first trumpet with the Thad Jones/Mel Lewis Orchestra and primarily working as a studio musician for several years.

Tal Farlow   One of the most brilliant jazz guitarists of the 1950s, Tal Farlow dropped out of full-time music in late 1958 to become a sign painter in New England, just playing guitar on a part-time basis locally. He only made one album as a leader during 1960–75, **The Return of Tal Farlow** (Original Jazz Classics 356). Assisted by pianist John Scully, Jack Six, and Alan Dawson on this 1969 quartet date, Farlow performs swinging versions of seven standards including "Straight, No Chaser," "I'll Remember April," and "Crazy, She Calls Me," showing that being semiretired had not dulled either his jazz chops or his enthusiasm for bebop.

In 1976 the 55-year-old Farlow became active again, recording two fine albums for Concord. Although he was not quite as flawless as he had been 20 years earlier, he was still an impressive player. **A Sign of the Times** (Concord Jazz 4026) has Farlow in a drumless trio with Hank Jones and Ray Brown, jamming joyfully on such

songs as "Fascinating Rhythm," "In Your Own Sweet Way," Brown's "Bayside Blues," and "Stompin' at the Savoy." **On Stage** (Concord Jazz 4143) is from the 1976 Concord Jazz Festival and has Farlow, Jones, and Brown joined by drummer Jake Hanna and the guitarist's former employer Red Norvo. Although a bit loose in spots, this set has its memorable moments, particularly Norvo's features on "The One I Love Belongs to Somebody Else" and "Lullaby of Birdland."

Art Farmer   Art Farmer moved to Vienna in 1968 where he was kept busy playing with the Austrian Radio Orchestra, leading his own groups and working with the Kenny Clarke-Francy Boland Big Band. Although the flugelhornist led dates during this time period for Campi, MPS, Mainstream, Sonet, Pye, and East Wind, the only one currently available domestically is a set cut for Contemporary, **On the Road** (Original Jazz Classics 478) from 1976. For the only time, Farmer is heard playing with Art Pepper, and the two veterans sound quite complementary. The group, which also includes Hampton Hawes, Ray Brown, and either Steve Ellington or Shelly Manne on drums, plays four standards and the pianist's "Downwind" while Farmer and Hawes perform an exquisite duet version of "My Funny Valentine." As usual, Art Farmer's cool tone and inner fire make for an appealing style.

Erroll Garner   After so much activity during 1945–67, Erroll Garner's career slowed down and finally stopped. Still quite popular, Garner recorded one album apiece in 1968, 1969, 1971, and 1973, a greatly reduced output compared to his work in the 1950s. All have been paired with an earlier session on a single CD and reissued by Telarc. **Up in Erroll's Room**, a 1968 outing with Don Sebesky arrangements and seven backing horns, has been reissued as half of **Now Playing: A Night at the Movies/Up in Erroll's Room** (Telarc 83378) and was mentioned in the previous chapter. **Campus Concert/Seeing Is Believing** (Telarchive 83390) has a 1962 trio set of veteran standards (including "Indiana," "Stardust," and "Almost Like Being in Love") plus a later quartet date with bassist George Duvivier, Charlie Persip or Joe Cocuzzo on drums, and Jose Mangual on conga. The latter session finds Garner adapting his always joyful style to mostly current pop tunes including "For Once in My Life," "Yesterday," and "The Look of Love." **That's My Kick & Gemini** (Telarchive 83332) has a pair of small group dates from 1966 and 1971 with Jose Mangual's congas adding a Latin flavor to the music. Garner romps through such numbers as "It Ain't Necessarily So," "Autumn Leave," "Blue Moon," "How High the Moon," and "Tea for Two" plus eight of his own compositions. **Magician & Gershwin & Kern** (Telarchive 83337) includes a 1966 set of George Gershwin and Jerome Kern songs, and Garner's final recording, a 1973 outing with Bob Cranshaw, Grady Tate, and Jose Mangual that includes the Carpenters' "Close to You," "Someone to Watch Over Me," "I Only Have Eyes for You," and the pianist's "Mucho Gusto." Throughout these later performances, Garner's style was unchanged from the late 1940s and he showed no decline in his technique, energy, or joyful spirit.

Erroll Garner's health gradually declined during the early 1970s, and in early 1975 he was reluctantly forced to retire, passing away two years later at the age of 55 after a productive life in music.

Stan Getz For Stan Getz, the 1968–75 period was one of diversity, with a few gems recorded along the way. Getz largely abandoned bossa nova (other than occasional requests) by 1965 and was searching for new directions to explore. His group of 1969 consisted of Stanley Cowell, Miroslav Vitous, Jack DeJohnette, and Flora Purim, but it was only captured on a couple broadcasts and did not make it into the studios. In fact, Getz recorded nothing of much value during 1968–70. In 1971 he broke the drought with the double CD **Dynasty** (Polydor 839 117), a successful outing in France with organist Eddy Louiss, guitarist Rene Thomas, and drummer Bernard Lubat. Getz only plays two standards ("I Remember Clifford" and "Invitation"), with most of the music being adventurous group originals. Getz shows that he was aware of the avant-garde players and really stretches himself while retaining his own musical personality and his beautiful tone.

The following year Getz used the nucleus of the first version of Return to Forever (Chick Corea, Stanley Clarke, and Airto on percussion) and Tony Williams on his classic album ❍ **Captain Marvel** (Koch 7864). Performing five Corea compositions (including "Times Lie" and "500 Miles High") plus "Lush Life," Getz shows that he was still one of jazz's great tenors, after 25 years at the top. His version of "La Fiesta" is quite memorable and stirring.

In 1975 Getz had the opportunity to record three albums for Columbia, and each one featured a favorite musician of his. **Best of Two Worlds** (Sony 9655) is a reunion with singer/guitarist Joao Gilberto a dozen years after "The Girl from Ipanema." Although both Getz and Gilberto are in fine form, much of the modern Brazilian material is disappointingly forgettable other than "The Waters of March" and "Double Rainbow." Despite the best efforts of the group (which includes a large percussion section), this set falls short of its goals. **The Master** (Tristar 35245) has Getz playing straightahead jazz in a quartet with pianist Albert Dailey (who is the co-star), bassist Clint Houston, and Billy Hart. They perform four lengthy selections (all between 9–11 minutes long) with "Lover Man" and "Invitation" being the standouts.

The most memorable of the trio of albums is ❍ **The Peacocks** (Koch 7867), a showcase for the underrated but hugely respected pianist Jimmie Rowles. Rowles plays exquisite duets with Getz, is heard solo, and is featured in a quartet with the tenor, Buster Williams, and Elvin Jones. On "The Chess Players," the group is joined by four vocalists including three from Jon Hendricks's family. Highlights include several of Rowles's touching vocals, "Lester Left Town" (a Wayne Shorter tune played in definitive fashion by Getz), and the original version of Rowles's haunting "The Peacocks."

Terry Gibbs Terry Gibbs, based in Los Angeles in the 1960s and '70s, worked in the studios, made local jazz dates, and led the band on the *Steve Allen Show*. His only recording as a leader during 1967–77 is 1974's **Bopstacle Course** (Xanadu 1238). This exciting date matches the hyper vibraphonist with Barry Harris, Sam Jones, and Alan Dawson. The quartet romps through four Gibbs originals, "Body and Soul," "Softly As in a Morning Sunrise," "Manha de Carnaval," and "I'm Getting Sentimental Over You." The combination of Gibbs and Harris works so well on the very boppish set that it is a pity this seems to have been their only joint recording.

Dizzy Gillespie After Dizzy Gillespie's period on Phillips ended in 1964, his recordings became erratic, ranging from some unusual collaborations and some poorly planned live dates to attempts at commercialism, some times using a funky rhythm section. About his only strong session from the 1965–70 period is the little-known LP **Reunion Big Band** (MPS 15207). Heading a very strong big band (which includes Curtis Fuller, altoist Chris Woods, James Moody, both Sahib Shihab, Cecil Payne on baritones, and a screaming trumpet section), Gillespie performs the most exciting version of "Things to Come" ever recorded (topping the original rendition), "One Bass Hit," "Con Alma," and two other originals. Polygram should be alerted to this essential album.

During 1971–72, Dizzy Gillespie went on a few tours with the Giants of Jazz. Although this all-star group with Kai Winding, Sonny Stitt, Thelonious Monk, Al McKibbon, and Art Blakey was supposed to be a co-op, Gillespie was generally thought of as its leader. **In Berlin '71** (EmArcy 834 567) has the unit jamming such standards as "Blue 'N' Boogie," "Tour de Force," and "A Night in Tunisia" although the preferred acquisition, a double LP simply titled **The Giants of Jazz** (Atlantic 2-905), has more inspired playing on a similar program. Stitt's solo on "Everything Happens to Me" takes honors. Gillespie and Monk, who crossed paths through the years on a very infrequent basis, are heard together on these records for the last time.

In 1974 Gillespie began recording regularly for the Pablo label, an association that would last for eight years and mostly featured the trumpeter in favorable settings. Unfortunately, his playing began to slip in the mid-1970s due to his inevitable aging (Dizzy turned 59 in 1976), and although he had a long distance to fall, his later recordings would sometimes be painful to hear, particularly by those familiar with how he sounded in the 1950s. The best of all his Pablo dates and arguably his finest recording of the 1970s is ● **Dizzy Gillespie's Big Four** (Original Jazz Classics 443). Gillespie, Joe Pass, Ray Brown, and Mickey Roker romp through such numbers as "Tanga," "Be Bop," and "Birk's Works," with plenty of sparks flying.

Otherwise, many of Gillespie's Pablo dates as a leader tend to be disappointments because of his gradual decline or some poor planning. A reunion with Machito's Orchestra on **Afro-Cuban Jazz Moods** (Original Jazz Classics 447) is mostly a fizzle because of the use of synthesizers and the influence of rock. **Dizzy Gillespie Big 7** (Original Jazz Classics 739) from the 1975 Montreux Jazz Festival has Gillespie teamed with Milt Jackson, Eddie "Lockjaw" Davis, Johnny Griffin, Tommy Flanagan, Niels Pedersen, and Mickey Rocker for three tunes (including a 16-minute version of "Lover, Come Back to Me"), but not much magic occurs and the players seem to be mostly going through the motions. **Bahiana** (Pablo 2625-708) has Gillespie's regular band of 1975 (including flutist Roger Glenn and both Al Gafa and Mike Howell on guitars), but, other than "Olinga," "Barcelona," and "Carnival," the set is hampered by so-so material. And **Dizzy's Party** (Original Jazz Classics 823) is a throwaway sextet date with Ray Pizzi on reeds and guitarist Rodney Jones, weighed down by such lightweight material as "Harlem Samba" and "Shim-Sham Shimmy on the St. Louis Blues."

Dizzy Gillespie was capable of better, as he would prove now and then in his later years.

Dexter Gordon   Tenor saxophonist Dexter Gordon had such a triumphant return to the United States in the fall of 1976 that it is sometimes forgotten that he had previously visited the United States briefly during 1969–70 and 1972 and that he had already made quite a few of his finest recordings during the first half of the 1970s while still living in Europe.

Gordon's style on tenor stayed virtually unchanged after he became a bit influenced by John Coltrane in the mid-1960s (which was quite fair because he was one of the biggest influences on Trane a decade before). There is no shortage of worthy Dexter albums from the era. Recorded in 1969, **A Day in Copenhagen** (Polygram

TIMELINE 1972

Sonny Rollins ends his six-year retirement. • Donald Byrd's R&B/funk album **Black Byrd** annoys the jazz world. • Lee Morgan is killed. • Supersax is formed. • Phil Woods returns to the United States after four years overseas. • Lee Wiley comes out of retirement to perform a special concert at Carnegie Hall. • Guitarist Robben Ford plays regularly with Jimmy Witherspoon. • Drummer Peter Erskine joins Stan Kenton's Orchestra for a three-year stint. • Jimmy Forrest joins the Count Basie Orchestra. • Eighteen-year old trumpeter Jon Faddis subs for Roy Eldridge and takes an outstanding solo on "Little Royal Suite" at a well-publicized Charles Mingus concert. • Ed Thigpen moves to Copenhagen. • Willie "The Lion" Smith records his last two albums—duet sets with Jo Jones. • The Newport in New York Jazz Festival debuts and is a big success.

821 288) matches Gordon with trombonist Slide Hampton, trumpeter Dizzy Reece, Kenny Drew, Niels Pedersen, and Art Taylor on three Hampton compositions and a trio of standard ballads. Everyone plays well, but Gordon is easily the star. **The Tower of Power** (Original Jazz Classics 299) and **More Power** (Original Jazz Classics 815) are both from April 1969 and have Gordon assisted by Barry Harris, Buster Williams, Albert "Tootie" Heath, and (on a total of three numbers) James Moody. The tenor matchups are slight disappointments (nothing memorable occurs), but Gordon's version of "Those Were the Days" from the former set and his "Fried Bananas" (based on the chords of "It Could Happen to You") on the latter are both standouts. Other albums recorded for Prestige during 1970 and 1972 include **At Montreux** (Prestige 7861), which has Gordon in excellent form playing with the Junior Mance Trio, **The Panther** (Original Jazz Classics 770) , which is highlighted by "Body and Soul" and "The Christmas Song," **The Jumpin' Blues** (Original Jazz Classics 899), with Wynton Kelly's Trio including "Rhythm-a-Ning" and "Star Eyes," **Ca'Purange** (Original Jazz Classics 1005), which is an excellent matchup with Thad Jones, and **Generation** (Original Jazz Classics 836), which is an exciting collaboration with Freddie Hubbard that is highlighted by "We See" and two versions of "Milestones." Also from this era is **Tangerine** (Original Jazz Classics 1041), which is most notable for Gordon's version of the title cut and "Days of Wine and Roses."

However, Dexter Gordon is really heard at the peak of his powers on his Steeple Chase recordings of 1974–76. **The Rainbow People** (Steeple Chase 31521) is a quintet date with trumpeter Benny Bailey that was not initially released until 2002 and has four very extended jams (the briefest track is three seconds short of 12 minutes). **Revelation** (Steeple Chase 31373) has Gordon joined by Bailey and pianist Lars Sjosten's trio with Dexter stealing honors on "Polka Dots and Moonbeams" and "Days of Wine and Roses." **The Apartment** (Steeple Chase 31025) features Gordon, Kenny Drew, Niels Pedersen, and Tootie Heath stretching out on "Wee-Dot," "Old Folks," and "Stablemates." **More Than You Know** (Steeple Chase 31030) has Gordon (best on "Naima" and "More Than You Know") backed by a large orchestra arranged by Palle Mikkelborg. **Stable Mable** (Steeple Chase 31040), a quartet date with Horace Parlan, Pederson, and drummer Tony Inzalaco, is memorable for Gordon happily jamming "Just

Friends," "Red Cross," and "So What" and switching to soprano on "In a Sentimental Mood." **Swiss Nights, Vol. 1**, **Vol. 2**, and **Vol. 3** (Steeple Chase 31050, 31090, and 31110) were recorded August 23–24, 1975, at the Zurich Jazz Festival. Gordon, Drew, Pedersen, and drummer Alex Riel run through some of the tenor's favorite songs, and although few surprises occur (except perhaps on **Vol. 3** where Gordon sings "Jelly Jelly" and Joe Newman sits in on "Days of Wine and Roses"), the music is up to Dexter's high standards of the period. **Something Different** (Steeple Chase 31136) gains its title because Gordon is heard in a pianoless quartet with guitarist Philip Catherine, Pedersen, and Billy Higgins; "Freddie Freeloader," "Invitation," and "Polka Dots and Moonbeams" are highlights.

Bouncin' with Dex (Steeple Chase 31060) has Gordon, Tete Montoliu, Pedersen, and Higgins jamming "Billie's Bounce," "Four," and two versions of "Easy Living." **Strings and Things** (Steeple Chase 31145) was the only miscue for Gordon during this period because the arrangements for a large orchestra sound quite dated, and there are electronic effects that distract from Dexter's playing. Much more rewarding is **Lullaby for a Monster** (Steeple Chase 31156), a trio set with Pederson and Riel that includes "On Green Dolphin Street," "Good Bait," and Donald Byrd's "Tanya." The final Steeple Chase album, **Biting the Apple** (Steeple Chase 31080), was recorded in New York shortly after Gordon returned home, and it is one of his best for the label. With fine playing from Barry Harris, Sam Jones, and Al Foster, Gordon sounds exuberant on "I'll Remember April" and "Skylark."

Gordon had an excellent reason to feel happy for he was receiving an unexpected hero's welcome in the United States. There were lines around the block to see the living legend as he performed at nightclubs across the country. The double CD ◗ **Homecoming: Live at the Village Vanguard** (Columbia 46824) has Gordon joined by Woody Shaw, pianist Ronnie Mathews, bassist Stafford James, and Louis Hayes as he stretches out on "Little Red's Fantasy," "It's You or No One," "Fried Bananas," "Body and Soul," and other favorites for an enthusiastic crowd. It did not matter that Dexter Gordon had sounded like this on a dozen rewarding Steeple Chase records cut the past two years. The American crowds had not yet heard that music and were surprised and thrilled to find the legendary Long Tall Dexter in prime form, helping to keep acoustic jazz and bebop alive.

Great Guitars   In 1973, Barney Kessel, Herb Ellis, and Charlie Byrd came together (with bassist Joe Byrd and drummer John Rae) to form Great Guitars. Occasionally during the next 19 years, the masterful guitarists performed bop and (thanks to Byrd's presence) Brazilian music at special get-togethers. Their initial recording, 1974's **Great Guitars** (Concord Jazz 6004), is a strong example of their playing. Among the highlights are "Undecided," "Charlie's Blues," "Topsy," and "Benny's Bugle." Although Byrd often emerged as the most distinctive soloist, this was an ideal setting for Ellis and Kessel, who tended to sound overly relaxed on their own solo sets of the period. **Great Guitars II** (Concord Jazz 4023) from 1976 is on the same level. With Joe Byrd and drummer Wayne Phillips offering fine support, the trio of guitarists perform four numbers together (best are "Lover" and Ellis's "Outer Drive"), Byrd has two features, Ellis and Kessel duet on "Makin' Whoopee," and a closing medley combines brief versions of "Nuages" and "Goin' Out of My Head" with a heated "Flying Home."

Johnny Griffin   Johnny Griffin moved to Europe in 1963, playing regularly on the Continent and moving to Copenhagen in 1973. **Blues for Harvey** (Steeple Chase 31004), which was recorded at the Montmartre in Copenhagen in 1973 with Kenny Drew, bassist Mads Vinding, and Ed Thigpen, shows that Griffin had lost nothing through the years, ripping into such songs as "That Party Upstairs," "Soft and Furry," and the title cut. Although he no longer competed in American jazz polls and was somewhat forgotten in the United States, Griffin remained one of the top tenor saxophonists in jazz.

Al Haig   One of the earliest of the major bebop pianists, Al Haig was quite active during the classic bebop era but largely neglected during 1955–73, a period when he only made one obscure record. Haig was not inactive during those quiet years, but his out-of-the-way gigs playing on the East Coast in small clubs led to his obscurity. However, things began to change in 1974 when he cut two LPs, **Invitation** (Spotlite 4) and **Special Brew** (Spotlite 8), for the British Spotlite label. Haig is heard playing in top form, and although still quite boppish, his repertoire included more modern jazz songs such as "Dolphin Dance" and "Freedom Jazz Dance"; Haig even plays electric piano (with mixed results) on part of the latter set. Recorded in 1975, **Strings Attached** (the LP Choice 1010) is a particularly rewarding session, a quartet date

with Jimmy Raney, bassist Jamil Nasser, and drummer Frank Gant that includes some of the better tunes that he had already recorded for Spotlite plus an 11-minute version of "Out of Nowhere."

During the remainder of his life, Al Haig would finally be documented the way he should have been all along.

Barry Harris   Bebop may have been considered quite passé by 1968, but Barry Harris ignored musical trends and always went his own way. **Bull's Eye** (Original Jazz Classics 1082) is a brilliant classic bebop date from 1968. Harris's sextet features Kenny Dorham (in one of his last recordings), Charles McPherson (sticking to tenor instead of his usual alto), Pepper Adams, Paul Chambers, and Billy Higgins. Four songs have the full group, and these include the romping title cut (Adams is really in top form) and Harris's "Off Monk." There are also two trio features. **Magnificent** (Original Jazz Classics 1026) is the third of three Prestige albums for Harris, with the pianist showcased in a trio with Ron Carter and drummer Leroy Williams. As usual, Harris is creative within the genre of classic bebop, swinging hard on "Bean and the Boys," "Ah-Leu Cha," and "Dexterity."

After a few years, Harris found a new home with Don Schlitten's Xanadu label, recording frequently as a sideman and leading five albums of his own. The first was 1975's **Barry Harris Plays Tadd Dameron** (Prevue 12). Performing the music of the top bop era composer, Harris (who is joined by bassist Gene Taylor and Leroy Williams) revives such numbers as "Hot House," "The Chase," "Casbah," and "Our Delight." **Tokyo 1976** (Prevue 24) mostly features Harris with Sam Jones and Leroy Williams, including "A Night in Tunisia" and two versions of "Ornithology." Two songs ("Groovin' High" and "Blue 'N' Boogie") add Charles McPherson and Jimmy Raney. As one can tell from the repertoire, the results are pure bebop.

Milt Jackson   Milt Jackson spent the 1968–74 period, as he had the previous 15 years, as a busy member of the Modern Jazz Quartet (MJQ). However, in 1974 he decided that he had tired of not making enough money with the constantly touring group and that he really wanted to play more freewheeling jazz as a solo artist. After a final round of farewell tours, the MJQ broke up, not to get back together again until 1981.

All along, Jackson had led occasional solo albums of his own. During 1972–74 he headed a trio of projects for

CTI. **Sunflower** (Columbia/Legacy 65131) is the most rewarding of the three, featuring fine Don Sebesky string arrangements and excellent solos from Freddie Hubbard (his "Little Sunflower" is a high point) and Herbie Hancock. **Goodbye** (Epic 86148) has four standards (including "Old Devil Moon" and Horace Silver's "Opus de Funk") played by Jackson in a quintet with Hubert Laws, Cedar Walton, Ron Carter, and drummer Steve Gadd while "SKJ" is a leftover track from **Sunflower** that has a large orchestra and Freddie Hubbard. **Olinga** (CTI 44174) from January 1974 features Bags teamed with some of his favorite musicians (Cedar Walton on keyboards, Ron Carter, Mickey Roker, and Jimmy Heath on tenor and soprano) along with an occasional string section. The music is mostly straightahead and includes the ballad "Lost April," Dizzy Gillespie's "Olinga," and three recent songs by Jackson.

After the breakup of the MJQ, Milt Jackson began to record regularly for Norman Granz's Pablo label as both a leader and a sideman. **Montreux '75** (Original Jazz Classics 884) matches Jackson with Oscar Peterson, Niels Pedersen, and Mickey Roker on a variety of exciting performances (Blue Mitchell's "Funji Mama," "Speedball," and "Mack the Knife") and emotional ballad statements ("Everything Must Change" and "Like Someone in Love"). **The Big Three** (Original Jazz Classics 805) has Jackson showcased in a pianoless trio with Joe Pass and Ray Brown. The intriguing repertoire (which includes "The Pink Panther," "Blue Bossa," "Nuages," and "Come Sunday") clearly inspires the masterful musicians. Although those two sets are highly recommended, one should definitely avoid **Feelings** (Original Jazz Classics 448), a rare vocal album that shows Milt Jackson was wise to concentrate on his vibraphone playing throughout his career.

Illinois Jacquet   Tenor saxophonist Illinois Jacquet formed his style by the early 1940s and modified it a bit in the '50s. He made relatively few records in the 1960s (most of them obscure) before leading four superior sets for Prestige during 1968–69. **Bottoms Up** (Original Jazz Classics 417) has Jacquet joined by Barry Harris, bassist Ben Tucker, and Alan Dawson, excelling on both heated numbers ("Bottoms Up," which is similar to "Flying Home," and "Jivin' with Jack the Bellboy") and ballads ("Don't Blame Me" and "You Left Me All Alone"). **The King** (Original Jazz Classics 849), made with a quintet including Joe Newman and pianist Milt Buckner, has some memorable moments (the rousing if brief "The King" and a version of "Caravan" featuring Jacquet's bassoon) but also disappointingly uneventful versions of "How High the Moon" and "I Wish I Knew How It Would Feel to Be Free." **The Soul Explosion** (Original Jazz Classics 674) has the tenor with a ten-piece group, with highlights including Jimmy Mundy's arrangement of "The Soul Explosion," "After Hours," and "Still King." Best of the four sets is **The Blues: That's Me** (Original Jazz Classics 614), a quintet outing with Wynton Kelly, Tiny Grimes, Buster Williams, and drummer Oliver Jackson. A remake of "Still King," "Everyday I Have the Blues," the lengthy title cut, and an atmospheric showcase for Jacquet's bassoon on "'Round Midnight" are particularly noteworthy.

Whether on tenor or bassoon (an instrument he took up in the mid-1960s), Illinois Jacquet played as skillfully as always during this era.

Plas Johnson   A soulful tenor saxophonist who is quite versatile, Plas Johnson's warm tone has been heard in many settings through the years. Part of the New Orleans studio scene of the 1950s before moving to Los Angeles, Johnson is prominent on Henry Mancini's soundtrack of *The Pink Panther* (1963). His own records usually featured brief soulful statements, but during 1975–76 he had a couple rare opportunities to lead jazz dates. **The Blues** (Concord Jazz 4015) teams him with keyboardist Mike Melvoin, Herb Ellis, Ray Brown, Jake Hanna, and Bobbye Hall on congas. Johnson puts plenty of soul and swinging ideas into such songs as "Georgia on My Mind," "Please Send Me Someone to Love," and "Parking Lot Blues." **Positively** (Concord Jazz 4024) has the same group (Jimmie Smith is on drums for some of the songs) with Plas Johnson in particularly expressive form on such ballads as "Lover Man," "My Foolish Heart," and "Careless Love."

Quincy Jones   Quincy Jones did not lead a regularly working orchestra after 1961, but his last two real jazz projects were both with specially assembled big bands. On **Walking in Space** (A&M 543499) and **Gula Matari** (A&M 75021 0820) from 1969–70, Jones used a variety of unique jazz voices in inspired fashion, almost as a painter picks out unusual colors to add emphasis to different parts of a picture. The former set has spots for Freddie Hubbard, Rahsaan Roland Kirk, Hubert Laws,

J.J. Johnson, and Kai Winding in the huge cast, with Benny Golson's "Killer Joe" and the lengthy "Walking in Space" being most memorable. **Gula Matari** has surprising renditions of "Walkin'" and "Hummin'" as Jones utilizes Milt Jackson, Herbie Hancock, Hubert Laws, and the singing and bowing bassist Major Holley (in top form), compensating for an R&Bish "Bridge over Troubled Water." But soon Quincy Jones would leave jazz altogether to become a pop producer, and, despite taking bows for the past three decades, Q's relevance to jazz largely stopped after 1970.

Duke Jordan   After having a low profile for nearly a decade, in 1973 bebop veteran Duke Jordan began a longtime association with the Danish Steeple Chase label, starting with **Flight to Denmark** (Steeple Chase 31011). On this trio set with bassist Mads Vinding and Ed Thigpen, Jordan plays five of his originals (including "No Problem," "Flight to Denmark," and his famous "Jordu") and four standards in a boppish style virtually unchanged since 1947. Other excellent Jordan albums from 1973–76 include **Two Loves** (Steeple Chase 31011), **Truth** (Steeple Chase 31175), **Misty Thursday** (Steeple Chase 31053), **Duke's Delight** (Steeple Chase 31046), which differs from the others in being a quintet album with trumpeter Richard Williams and Charlie Rouse, **Lover Man** (Steeple Chase 31127), **Live in Japan Vol. 1** (Steeple Chase 31063), **Live in Japan Vol. 2**, (Steeple Chase 31064) and **Flight to Japan** (Steeple Chase 31088). Although little publicized in the United States, Duke Jordan was one of the finest bop-based pianists of the 1970s, three decades after he had made his initial impact.

Barney Kessel   Barney Kessel toured with George Wein's Newport All-Stars in 1968, lived in London during 1969–70 (working with Stephane Grappelli), and in 1973 became a member of the Great Guitars with Herb Ellis and Charlie Byrd. Recorded in 1968, **Autumn Leaves** (Black Lion 760112) is a decent but unremarkable trio session with bassist Kenny Nepper and drummer John Marshall that also includes three numbers with a big band. In 1969 Kessel returned to the Contemporary label (where in the 1950s he recorded his finest string of recordings) for one effort, **Feeling Free** (Original Jazz Classics 1043). Matched in a quartet with Bobby Hutcherson, bassist Chuck Domanico, and Elvin Jones, Kessel is heard at his most advanced, contributing

some fairly free originals including "Blues, Up, Down & All Around" and "Two Note Samba," showing the slight influence of the avant-garde. Coming from the other direction, **Limehouse Blues** (Black Lion 760158) matches Kessel in a pianoless quintet with Grappelli for such swing standards as heated versions of "It Don't Mean a Thing," "How High the Moon," and "Undecided"; it is an exciting and joyful set.

In 1975, the Poll Winners trio of Kessel, Ray Brown, and Shelly Manne had a reunion and made their first recording since 1960: **Straight Ahead** (Original Jazz Classics 409). The music is predictably excellent with the musicians contributing one song apiece and playing three standards, showing how they had grown in the past 15 years. Also in 1975, Kessel began recording regularly for the Concord label. In general, his Concord sets are a bit disappointing, being overly lazy affairs with not much heat generated. **Barney Kessel & Friends** (Concord 6009) has Kessel, Herbie Steward (one of Woody Herman's Four Brothers who is heard on alto, soprano, and flute), vibraphonist Victor Feldman, and Jimmy Rowles in a septet playing nine of Kessel's obscure originals, but nothing that remarkable occurs. **Soaring** (Concord Jazz 6033) features Kessel interpreting six ballads at faster than usual tempos plus two originals in a trio with bassist Monty Budwig and Jake Hanna. **Poor Butterfly** (Concord Jazz 4034) has Kessel sharing the spotlight with Herb Ellis in a quartet with Budwig and Hanna, playing standards, obscurities, and originals tastefully but with rather predictable and dull results.

By this point in his career, Barney Kessel needed someone to light a fire under him, but outside of the competitiveness of the Great Guitars group, that would rarely happen in the guitarist's later years.

Lee Konitz   Lee Konitz, who recorded relatively little during 1961–67, appeared on records much more during the next nine years. Always a musically curious improviser, Konitz sometimes revisited his roots in Lennie Tristano, occasionally played quite free, and by the mid-1970s was leading an impressive nonet. Recorded in 1969, **Peacemeal** (Milestone 9025) is long overdue to be reissued on CD because it is one of Konitz's most successful recordings of the era. Featured in a quintet with valve trombonist Marshall Brown, Dick Katz, Eddie Gomez, and Jack DeJohnette, Konitz performs jazz adaptations of three Bela Bartok piano compositions, a trio of Dick Katz originals, two of his own pieces, and versions of "Lester Leaps In" and "Body and Soul" that include transcriptions of recorded solos by Lester Young and Roy Eldridge. **Spirits** (Original Jazz Classics) from 1971 is much more intimate with Konitz playing four duets with pianist Sal Mosca (who sounds a lot like Tristano) and five quartet numbers with Mosca, Ron Carter, and drummer Mousie Alexander. The music (tunes by Konitz, Tristano, or Warne Marsh) is all based on the chord changes of standards, featuring the altoist stretching out on some of his favorite songs even if the melodies are different. **Jazz a Juan** (Steeple Chase 31072) features Konitz in adventurous form playing unpredictable and sometimes eccentric versions of five standards and his original "Antibes" in a quartet with Martial Solal, Niels Pedersen, and drummer Daniel Humair.

I Concentrate on You (Steeple Chase 31018) is a duet set with bassist Red Mitchell (who switches to piano on "Night and Day"). Konitz has nowhere to hide on the 11 Cole Porter songs, but does not need to take cover because he improvises in his typically thoughtful and unhurried style. **Lone-Lee** (Steeple Chase 31035) is even more extreme in that way because Konitz is heard playing completely unaccompanied. His 38-minute version of "The Song Is You" and a 17-minute rendition of "Cherokee" are fairly free, relaxed, and swinging without ever being overly predictable. **Satori** (Original Jazz Classics 958) is a reunion with Solar in a quartet with Dave Holland and Jack DeJohnette. Konitz plays a few standards (including "Just Friends" and "What's New") and some advanced pieces, coming up with many fresh statements while playing fairly quietly. **Oleo** (Sonet 690) has eight familiar tunes interpreted by Konitz, Dick Katz, and bassist Wilbur Little (their interplay is consistently outstanding) while **Figure and Spirit** (Progressive 7003) gives Konitz (heard doubling on soprano) an opportunity to jam with tenor saxophonist Ted Brown (who recalls Warne Marsh in spots), pianist Albert Dailey, Rufus Reid, and Joe Chambers on spontaneous and often exciting renditions of six familiar sets of chord changes.

All seven of these releases and a few others that are out of print are easily recommended. As with **Peacemeal**, **The Lee Konitz Nonet** (Roulette 5006) was last out on LP. Konitz's nonet was formed at the height of the fusion era, struggled for a few years, and broke up. Its debut recording from 1976 (which includes trumpeter

Burt Collins, Jimmy Knepper, and keyboardist Andy Laverne among the personnel) ranges from swing classics such as "If Dreams Come True" and "A Pretty Girl Is Like a Melody" to "Nefertiti" and Chick Corea's "Matrix" (which in Sy Johnson's arrangement has an orchestration of six choruses from Corea's piano solo). The Lee Konitz Nonet was one of the most underrated bands of the 1970s.

L.A. Four   In 1954 Bud Shank (on alto and flute) and acoustic guitarist Laurindo Almeida had recorded Brazilian music that hinted at bossa nova years before the music actually came together. In 1974 Shank and Almeida, along with Ray Brown and Shelly Manne, formed the L.A. Four. Their mixture of cool jazz and Brazilian music was quite appealing and is well displayed on their string of records for the Concord label. **The L.A. Four Scores** (Concord Jazz 6008), was recorded at the 1974 Concord Jazz Festival. Their debut album ranges from the bossa nova of "Manha de Carnaval" to Almeida's classical-oriented originals and some swinging pieces. **Concierto de Aranjuez** (Concord Jazz 4018) is just as enjoyable, being highlighted by the 13-minute title cut, "Dindi," "Manteca," and "St. Thomas." The L.A. Four helped introduce Laurindo Almeida to a wider jazz audience and brought Bud Shank (who had been mostly working in the studios since the early 1960s) back to jazz on a more regular basis.

Michel Legrand   A film composer best known for "What Are You Doing the Rest of Your Life" and "Watch What Happens," pianist Michel Legrand occasionally recorded jazz through the years. In 1968 he recorded something that was unusual for him, a trio set. **At Shelly's Manne-Hole** (Verve 834827) has Legrand as the lead voice in a group with Ray Brown and Shelly Manne. There are four fairly free improvisations ("Los Gatos" is most adventurous), a few swinging numbers (including "Ray's Riff" and "Another Blues"), and an odd vocal by Legrand on "My Funny Valentine." This is an intriguing set by a composer who should have recorded in this type of informal setting more often.

Shelly Manne   Shelly Manne, who ran the popular Los Angeles jazz club Shelly's Manne-Hole during 1960-74, began to open his music up to freer explorations during 1968-69 after his quintet had evolved from cool jazz to hard bop in the early 1960s. His new quintet consisted of trumpeter Gary Barone, tenor saxophonist John Gross, pianist Pete Robinson, and bassist Juney Booth. By 1970 Mike Wofford had returned but was often on electric piano, playing alongside Barone, Gross, guitarist John Morell, and bassist Roland Haynes. **Alive in London** (Original Jazz Classics 773) from 1970 features Manne swinging as much as usual while his group indulges in much freer improvising than his earlier bands. The music actually sounds a bit uncomfortable, and by 1972 Manne had reverted to hard bop. He would continue leading groups in the 1970s (although none made the impact that his 1950s bands had) and work with the L.A. Four.

Warne Marsh   After moving to Los Angeles in 1966, Warne Marsh worked in the studios, taught, and was a member of Supersax (1972–77). His 1969 album **Ne Plus Ultra** (Hat Art 6063) was his first as a leader since 1960. Marsh, who stuck to his roots in Lennie Tristano's music throughout his career, on this occasion teamed up with altoist Gary Foster (most influenced by Lee Konitz), bassist Dave Parlato, and drummer John Tirabasso, running through such tunes as "Lennie's Pennies," "Subconscious-Lee," and "You Stepped Out of a Dream." In addition, there is a fairly free group improvisation (the 15-minute "Touch and Go") and a brief rendition of Bach's "Two-Part Inventions #13."

A December 1975 tour of Europe with Lee Konitz resulted in five excellent CDs, **Warne Marsh-Lee Konitz Quintet Vol. 1, Vol. 2, and Vol. 3** (Storyville 8201, 8202, and 8203) plus a couple discs without Konitz, both subtitled "Unissued Copenhagen Recordings": **Warne Marsh Quartet** (Storyville 8259) and **Warne Marsh Trio** (Storyville 8278). Throughout the first three sets, which show the growth of Marsh and Konitz during the 25 years since they worked with Tristano, the two saxophonists show how complementary their styles still were as they dig into familiar chord changes with both affection and a sense of adventure. Although Konitz was much better known in the jazz world, Marsh's continual evolution reveal him to be a master, too, and he sounds in prime form throughout each of these albums.

Charles McPherson   Bebop may have been considered out of style during 1968–75, but Charles McPherson managed to work and record fairly often, with Charles Mingus on and off through 1972 and as a

bandleader himself. He recorded six albums for Prestige during 1964–69, three of them after 1967. **From This Moment On** (Original Jazz Classics 1899) has some songs utilizing boogaloo and pop rhythms. Although not one of McPherson's most essential releases (the music includes a couple okay originals, a few standards, and the show tune "Once in a Lifetime"), nevertheless there is plenty of fine playing from McPherson, Cedar Walton, Pat Martino, bassist Peck Morrison, and drummer Lennie McBrowne. **Horizons** (Original Jazz Classics 1912) has McPherson, Walton, Martino, Walter Booker, Billy Higgins, and (on three of the six songs) vibraphonist Nasir Hafiz playing four of the altoist's originals and a standard. In addition, there is a fine alto guitar duet on "Lush Life." Best of the trio of releases is **McPherson's Mood** (Original Jazz Classics 1947), which teams the altoist with Barry Harris, Buster Williams and drummer Roy Brooks for a very boppish date. Even Stevie Wonder's "My Cherie Amour" sounds like straightahead jazz in this setting.

After recording a pair of moderately successful albums for Mainstream, McPherson became a mainstay of the Xanadu label for a few years. Recorded in 1975, **Beautiful** (Xanadu 1230) has McPherson, Duke Jordan, Sam Jones, and Leroy Williams playing such songs as "They Say It's Wonderful," "It Could Happen to You," and "This Can't Be Love." There is also a feature for the rhythm section on "All God's Chillun Got Rhythm." An LP worth searching for, **Live in Tokyo** (Xanadu 131) has McPherson, Harris, Jones, and Williams sounding quite inspired on "East of the Sun," "Bouncing with Bud," and other superior jam tunes.

Modern Jazz Quartet   Formed in 1952 and somewhat taken for granted by the late 1960s as a constant on the jazz scene that would always be there, the Modern Jazz Quartet (MJQ) surprised the jazz world by breaking up in 1974. Milt Jackson had tired of the restrictive music of John Lewis and also was frustrated that the individual musicians had not made more money after their artistic successes. The group would not come back together again until 1981 after a seven-year "vacation."

The MJQ made two albums for the Beatles's Apple label during 1967–69 and then returned to Atlantic. **Plastic Dreams** (Collectables 6185) is a bit streaky with an overly repetitious "Variations on a Christmas Theme" and with "England's Carol" being a bit forgettable. Much better are "Walkin' Stomp," the tango "Plastic Dreams," and "Trav'lin." Two selections add a five-piece brass section to the classic group. Recorded in 1973, **Blues on Bach** (Atlantic 1652) alternates four original blues with five adaptations of melodies from classical works by Bach. Because John Lewis and the MJQ have long been expert in both areas, this concept works quite well.

When the MJQ announced they were breaking up in 1974, a final tour was arranged and the group played for a series of sold-out crowds. The two-CD set ● **The Complete Last Concert** (Atlantic 81976) finds Milt Jackson, John Lewis, Percy Heath, and Connie Kay in inspired and sometimes emotional form, performing their most popular numbers (including "Softly As in a Morning Sunrise," "Bag's Groove," "Skating in Central Park," and of course "Django") for what many thought would be the last time. Although one can understand why the Modern Jazz Quartet, after 22 years, called it quits, the jazz world seemed like an emptier place in 1975 without this group's presence.

Thelonious Monk   A year before the Modern Jazz Quartet broke up, Thelonious Monk retired. Five years earlier in 1968, the pianist/composer recorded his final album for Columbia, the rather odd **Monk's Blues** (Columbia 53581). For this project, the Thelonious Monk Quartet (with the reliable tenor saxophonist Charlie Rouse) is joined by 11 additional horns, guitar, and percussion for a set arranged by Oliver Nelson. The trouble is that Nelson's charts do not fit Monk's style that well although there are moments when Monk was obviously challenged by the unusual setting. In addition to remakes of a variety of Thelonious tunes, there are a pair of forgettable Teo Macero songs and a piano solo version of "'Round Midnight." Overall, this is one of the least essential of Monk's recordings.

In 1970 Rouse left the Thelonious Monk Quartet, being replaced by tenor saxophonist Paul Jeffreys. The pianist went on a couple tours with the all-star sextet the Giants of Jazz during 1971–72, which gave him an opportunity to play next to Dizzy Gillespie, Sonny Stitt, Kai Winding, Al McKibbon, and Art Blakey although he was somewhat underutilized, mostly consigned to jamming bebop warhorses. However, one good thing came out of the association. On November 15, 1971, Monk made his last recordings as a leader, three CDs worth of material reissued separately and in a box called ● **The**

Complete London Collection (Black Lion 7601). Heard in trios with McKibbon and Blakey and (best of all) on a series of unaccompanied solos, Monk is in brilliant and surprisingly exuberant form, still very much at the peak of his powers. Among the many highlights of the 29 performances are "Little Rootie Tootie," "Meet Me Tonight in Dreamland," "Blue Sphere," "Criss Cross," "The Man I Love," and "Evidence."

But after the Giants of Jazz tours ended, Thelonious Monk simply stopped playing. Other than a couple later appearances at special concerts, his musical career was over as he succumbed to mental illness and lived his last years in isolation.

James Moody   After leaving the Dizzy Gillespie Quintet in 1968, James Moody freelanced a bit and then settled in Las Vegas where he played with show bands during much of the 1970s. He started the period with a pair of worthwhile albums, one apiece for Milestone and Prestige. **Don't Look Away Now** (Original Jazz Classics 965) has a remake of "Last Train from Overbrook," "Easy Living," and an Eddie Jefferson vocal on "Hey Herb! Where's Alpert?" **The Blues and Other Colors** (Original Jazz Classics 954) is unusual because Moody (best known for his tenor and alto playing) is heard exclusively on soprano (which he rarely ever played) and flute. Trombonist Tom McIntosh contributed a tune and arranged all eight pieces (which include four Moody originals). Five of the numbers feature Moody in a nonet, including an emotional "Old Folks" while the other three selections have Moody's flute joined by trombone, French horn, three strings, a rhythm section, and Linda November's wordless vocalizing. "Gone Are the Days" is rather eccentric, being turned into a protest piece with quite a few quotes from other songs.

Released in 1971, **Never Again** (Muse 5001) is actually Moody's best all-round recording from this period, but it has not yet appeared on CD. Moody, who swore "never again" to play alto, sticks here to tenor and is in top form, swinging hard on "Secret Love," "St. Thomas," and an adventurous version of "Freedom Jazz Dance." He is assisted by organist Mickey Tucker, electric bassist Roland Wilson, and drummer Eddie Gladden. Recorded in 1972, **Feelin' It Together** (32 Jazz 32045) has returned, with Moody on tenor, alto (so much for his pledge!), and flute with a quartet comprised of Kenny Barron (who in addition to piano plays some surprisingly distinctive electric piano and electric harpsichord), bassist Larry Ridley, and drummer Freddie Waits. Moody's music on this occasion ranges from bebop ("Anthropology" and "Autumn Leaves") and spacey ballads to the eccentric "Kriss Kross."

Brew Moore   The cool-toned tenor saxophonist Brew Moore, who moved to Copenhagen in 1961, was back in the United States during 1967–70 but failed to make an impression or any recordings. He eventually returned to Denmark where he spent his last years. On the night of February 25, 1971, Moore recorded two albums of material with a Scandinavian rhythm section. Although **Brew's Stockholm Dew** (Sonet 624) has not been reissued on CD yet, **No More Brew** (Storyville 8275) is out. The latter has seven- to nine-minute versions of "It Could Happen to You," "Manny's Tune," "No More Brew," and "Blue Monk." Moore, at 46, was still in peak form. But two years later Brew Moore died suddenly from a fall down the stairs.

Gerry Mulligan   Other than touring now and then as a member of the Dave Brubeck Quartet (1968–72), Gerry Mulligan was only semiactive musically during the first part of this period. **The Age of Steam** (A&M 75021-0804) from 1971 was the baritonist's only significant record as a leader from the 1967–73 period. For this set, Mulligan heads a 14-piece band that features solos by the leader (who was also doubling on soprano), Tom Scott on tenor and soprano, Bud Shank on alto and flute, Bob Brookmeyer, and Harry "Sweets" Edison. The group plays eight of Mulligan's recent originals (none were destined to become standards), and the old Mulligan spirit was still present.

In 1974 for the first and only time since 1957, Gerry Mulligan and Chet Baker had a reunion, performing at Carnegie Hall. Unfortunately, the former magic was only hinted at (Mulligan and Baker had disliked each other for years), and, rather than use a pianoless quartet for old time's sake, they were joined by a fairly contemporary rhythm section consisting of Bob James on keyboards, vibraphonist Dave Samuels, Ron Carter, drummer Harvey Mason, and, on one of his first recordings, guitarist John Scofield. **Carnegie Hall Concert** (Epic 450554) has all of the music formerly on two LPs. Best are "Line for Lyons," "My Funny Valentine," and "Bernie's Tune," but this set does not live up to expectations.

From 1976 **Idol Gossip** (Chiaroscuro 155) is a solid showcase for Mulligan, who is joined by Samuels, pianist Tom Fay, guitarist Mike Santiago, bassist George Duvivier, and drummer Bobby Rosengarden. Mulligan performs such originals as "Walk on the Water," "Idol Gossip," and "Strayhorn 2" (a reworking of his "Song for Strayhorn"). But although playing well and being a perennial poll winner (Pepper Adams always seemed to finish second on baritone no matter what he did), Gerry Mulligan's career was a bit directionless in the mid-1970s.

Joe Pass   Guitarist Joe Pass, who had lost the 1950s to drug addiction, made several impressive group albums in the 1960s and worked fairly regularly. However, it was 1973 when he had a real breakthrough, signing with Norman Granz's Pablo label. A bop-based guitarist who was most influenced by Charlie Christian, Pass differed from his contemporaries by emerging as a brilliant solo guitarist who could play unaccompanied on any standard (including uptempo romps), filling in the melody, harmony, and bass lines simultaneously. Granz recorded him regularly as a soloist, with groups and as a sideman (including with Oscar Peterson) throughout the remainder of the 1970s.

◉ **Virtuoso** (Pablo 2310-708) made Joe Pass famous and for good reason. Pass performs such songs as "Cherokee," "How High the Moon," and "The Song Is You" unaccompanied, and he sounds like a one-man band while using conventional technique. This album amazed his fellow guitarists and led to him being considered one of the giants of his instrument. **Virtuoso #2** (Pablo 2310-788), which includes an unaccompanied "Giant Steps," **Virtuoso #3** (Original Jazz Classics 684) from 1977, and **Virtuoso #4** (Pablo 2640-102) are on the same level. A two-CD set, **Virtuoso #4** was actually recorded a month before the original **Virtuoso** (it was not released until years later) and is particularly unusual because Pass is heard exclusively playing acoustic guitar. Two other solo recitals, **At the Montreux Jazz Festival 1975** (Original Jazz Classics 934) and **At Akron University** (Pablo 2308-249) feature Pass performing his magic live in concert.

Of Pass's group albums from this era, **Portraits of Duke Ellington** (Pablo 2310-716), recorded just a month after Duke Ellington's death, has the guitarist, Ray Brown, and drummer Bobby Durham swinging on nine of Duke's most famous songs. **Live at Donte's**

(Pablo 2620-114) is also excellent, featuring Pass with electric bassist Jim Hughart and drummer Frank Severino, playing both recent songs and vintage standards.

Joe Pass, like Oscar Peterson, would record excessively for Norman Granz, but virtually all of his recordings are quite enjoyable.

Oscar Peterson   In 1968, the Oscar Peterson Trio featured bassist Sam Jones and drummer Bobby Durham. In 1970, bassist George Mraz and drummer Ray Price took their spots but, with the founding of Norman Granz's Pablo label in 1972, Peterson was thereafter often showcased as a soloist and with Joe Pass and Niels Pedersen. Never under-recorded during any period of his career, Peterson had kept busy in the 1960s and his recording activity accelerated even more during the next decade. Freed from leading the same trio all the time, Peterson tended to get particularly inspired when either playing unaccompanied solos or teamed with fellow all-stars.

Strangely enough considering all of the recordings he made during 1945–67, Peterson had never been heard on a full-length solo piano date until cutting **My Favourite Instrument** (Verve 821 843) in 1968. Peterson stretches out on nine familiar standards, some of which he tears into including "Perdido," "Bye Bye Blackbird," and "Lulu's Back in Town." That date is also included in the four-CD set **Exclusively for My Friends** (Verve 314 513 830), along with a variety of trio sets that Peterson cut for the MPS label during 1963–68. ◉ **Tracks** (Verve 523 498) from 1970 actually tops **My Favourite Instrument** because this solo set has memorable versions of "Give Me the Simple Life," "Honeysuckle Rose," and the brilliant "A Little Jazz Exercise," showing that no pianist could swing harder than Oscar Peterson.

Peterson recorded so often for Pablo during 1972–76 and the output was generally of such high quality that virtually every one of his CDs is easily recommended to his fans. The two-CD set **History of an Artist** (Pablo 2625-702) has Peterson summing up his previous 22 years; it includes a couple duets with Ray Brown plus trio numbers with Brown and Irving Ashby (who came briefly out of retirement for the occasion), Brown and Barney Kessel, Brown and Herb Ellis, and such recent sidemen as Sam Jones, George Mraz, Louis Hayes, and Bobby Durham in addition to Joe Pass and Niels Pederson. Each combination works quite well.

The Trio (Original Jazz Classics 992) has some astounding playing by Peterson in a group with Pass and Pederson, including on "Blues Etude" (which has Peterson playing some stride and boogie-woogie), "Secret Love," and "Easy Listening Blues." **The Good Life** (Original Jazz Classics 627) has additional numbers from the same sessions and is nearly at the same level. The two-CD set **Oscar Peterson in Russia** (Pablo 2625-711) consists of music that is much less exotic than the location. However, this is a well-rounded set with Peterson taking five unaccompanied solos, duets with Pedersen, and trio numbers with Pedersen and Jake Hanna.

◉ **A La Salle Pleyel** (Pablo 2625-705), a double CD from 1975, has some incredible playing from Peterson who is heard solo on a Duke Ellington medley and seven numbers (including remarkably rapid renditions of "Indiana" and "Sweet Georgia Brown"), five Joe Pass guitar solo features, and six piano/guitar duets (including "Honeysuckle Rose" and "Blues for Bise") that are unspeakably brilliant.

Never one for moderation, during 1974–75 Norman Granz teamed Peterson on five duet albums with different trumpeters. Each of the sets, **Oscar Peterson and Dizzy Gillespie** (Pablo 2310-740), **Oscar Peterson and Roy Eldridge** (Original Jazz Classics 727), **Oscar Peterson and Harry Edison** (Original Jazz Classics 738), **Oscar Peterson and Clark Terry** (Original Jazz Classics 806), and **Oscar Peterson and Jon Faddis** (Original Jazz Classics 1036), has its exciting moments. Dizzy Gillespie (who was just beginning to fade) fares quite well, Roy Eldridge is as competitive as ever, Edison is friendly and easy going, Clark Terry's date is both playful and a bit fiery, and Jon Faddis (22 at the time) overcomes his awe of Peterson to show off his impressive range and Gillespie licks.

In the mid-1970s, Oscar Peterson still had to be rated as one of the greatest jazz pianists on the scene.

Jimmy Raney   Guitarist Jimmy Raney was mostly outside of music during 1965–73, living in Louisville, Kentucky, until he began to make a comeback. He recorded a set for MPS in 1974 and then signed with Xanadu where he led three albums during 1975–76, still playing in prime form. **The Influence** (Prevue 23) is a trio set with Sam Jones and Billy Higgins that is highlighted by "I Love You," "It Could Happen to You," and "There Will Never Be Another You." Most unusual is a free-form "Suzanne" that has Raney (via overdubbing) heard on two guitars. **Live in Tokyo** (Prevue 14) is similar and even a touch better, with Raney, Jones, and Leroy Williams jamming in boppish fashion on such numbers as "Anthropology" and "Cherokee"; Raney plays exquisitely on an unaccompanied "Stella by Starlight." **Solo** (Prevue 8) is not quite accurate in its title because Raney is heard in a set of overdubbed guitar duets with himself, building upon the "Suzanne" experiment. The thoughtful music ranges from being nearly free to preplanned classical-type numbers and some swinging tunes.

Jimmy Raney would remain active in jazz (sometimes playing duets with his son guitarist Doug Raney) for the remainder of his life.

Red Rodney   After successfully battling heroin addiction, veteran bebop trumpeter Red Rodney spent a long period playing for shows in Las Vegas. When he moved to New York in 1972 and started playing jazz again, it took him awhile to get his trumpet chops up to its former form. Recorded in 1973, **Bird Lives** (Muse 5371), which was reissued on CD in 1989 but is difficult to find (as are all of the Muse CDs), was Rodney's first date as a leader since 1959. Rodney teams up with Charles McPherson, Barry Harris, Sam Jones, and drummer Roy Brooks for a tribute to Charlie Parker. Rodney was just beginning to regain his form, but he is certainly helped by the presence of Harris and McPherson, who are excellent on such songs as "I'll Remember April," "Donna Lee," and "'Round Midnight." It is a real pity that the following year's **Superbop** (Muse 5046) has not come back yet because it teams Rodney and fellow trumpeter Sam Noto on some heated numbers including the title cut, which has a transcription of Clifford Brown's solo on "Daahoud." Also not available are 1975's **The Red Tornado** (Muse 5088) with Bill Watrous and Roland Hanna and the following year's **Red, White and Blues** (Muse 5111) with Richie Cole.

Throughout these sessions, Red Rodney was cast as a bebop survivor who was helping to keep the music alive. Rodney was actually uncomfortable in this role, wanting to play more modern music. In 1980 when he began teaming up with Ira Sullivan and pianist Garry Dial, he would get his wish.

George Shearing   George Shearing recorded regularly for Capitol during 1955–69, heading a popular piano/vibes/guitar/bass/drums quintet. After parting ways with Capitol, Shearing began his own Sheba label and phased out the quintet, opting instead to feature his piano playing in a trio and solo. The seven Sheba albums had been out of print for many years until Koch recently began to reissue them. **Out of This World** (Koch 51001) is a solo set filled with pretty and melancholy interpretations of a dozen songs including an impressionistic version of the title cut, a throwaway rendition of "Hey Jude," "Serenade in Blue," and "You're My Everything." **The George Shearing Quartet** (Koch 51004) is just a so-so set from Shearing, bassist Andy Simpkins, drummer Harvey Mason, and organist Don Heitler, sunk by funky rhythms and too much popish material. **The George Shearing Trio** (Koch 51003) by the same group without Heitler has better songs (mostly sticking to jazz standards) and shows what a swinging pianist Shearing could be.

But the most rewarding George Shearing set from the era is ◉ **Reunion** (Polygram 821 868). Shearing had played in violinist Stephane Grappelli's group during the early 1940s but they had not worked together in 30 years when they recorded this exciting date. With Simpkins and drummer Rusty Jones giving support, Shearing and Grappelli romp joyfully on such numbers as "I'm Coming Virginia," "Too Marvelous for Words," and "After You've Gone," some of their hottest playing of the 1970s.

Zoot Sims   The consistently swinging tenor saxophonist Zoot Sims was in his prime in the 1970s when he began doubling now and then on soprano. He recorded very little during 1967–72 but then starting popping on records much more often. Recorded in 1973, **Zoot at Ease** (Progressive 7110) brings back a set cut for the Famous Door label. Zoot is joined by Hank Jones, Milt Hinton, and either Louie Bellson or Grady Tate on drums. In addition to a few standards, Sims plays such obscurities as "Alabamy Home," "In the Middle of a Kiss," and the theme of *Rosemary's Baby*, turning everything into swinging jazz.

In 1975, Sims began recording regularly for the Pablo label, including a stunning meeting with Count Basie (issued under the pianist's name). ◉ **Zoot Sims & the Gershwin Brothers** (Original Jazz Classics 444) is on the same level. Along with Oscar Peterson, Joe Pass, bassist George Mraz, and Grady Tate, Zoot digs into ten songs written by George and Ira Gershwin including

"The Man I Love," "Lady Be Good," "I Got Rhythm," "I've Got a Crush on You," and "Embraceable You." These exciting renditions rank with the top instrumental versions of these much-played songs.

Hawthorne Nights (Original Jazz Classics 830) has Sims joined by a nine-piece group that includes six horns, performing Bill Holman's inventive and challenging arrangements in swinging style. Also worth acquiring but not yet out on CD is **Zoot Plays Soprano** (Pablo 2310-770), which has Sims interacting exclusively on soprano with Ray Bryant, Mraz, and Tate in delightful fashion.

Sonny Stitt   Always a bebopper, whether playing alto or tenor, Sonny Stitt during 1968–69 often utilized an electronic Varitone sax, which allowed him to play octaves. But unlike Eddie Harris and John Klemmer, Stitt was not an innovator on the electric horn. He just played like he always did, and because the Varitone resulted in his sound being watered down, he discarded it in 1971. **Legends of Acid Jazz Vol. 2** (Prestige 24210) reissues the music from the albums **Funk You** and **Soul Electricity**. The former set teams Stitt with Charles McPherson, Pat Martino, Don Patterson, and drummer Billy James on a fine bop-oriented date that includes "Airegin," "It's You or No One," and a better than expected "Funk in 3/4." The **Soul Electricity** session has Stitt using the Varitone on some numbers in a quartet with Patterson, James, and guitarist Billy Butler that are worthwhile but not up to the level they would have been had Stitt played acoustically. **Legends of Acid Jazz** (Prestige 24169), which dates from 1971, has a couple of Stitt's lesser dates. The first part (originally called **Turn It On**) has the dreaded Varitone and a chugging rhythm section with organist Leon Spencer, and although the second half (**Black Vibrations**) is a little better and has Stitt playing acoustically with Patterson, very little memorable occurs because of the weak material.

All of that activity is greatly overshadowed by a pair of Stitt's sessions for Cobblestone in 1972 that have been reissued as the double CD ◐ **Endgame Brilliance** (32 Jazz 32009). Stitt is heard in the best possible setting on these sets (originally released as **Tune-Up** and **Constellation**), playing in quartets with Barry Harris (the top classic bop pianist of the 1970s), bassist Sam Jones, and either Roy Brooks or Alan Dawson on drums. Stitt, who had recorded so much during the past 25 years, is quite

inspired and never sounded better than he does on such tunes as "Constellation," "Webb City," "It's Magic," "Tune Up," "Groovin' High," and a lengthy "I Got Rhythm" (which has him taking exciting solos on both tenor and alto). He certainly shows that bebop was alive and well (if sometimes overlooked) in the 1970s. The recording **12!** (32 Jazz 32176) from later in 1972 is almost on the same level, a rematch with Harris and Jones (with Louis Hayes on drums) highlighted by "I Got It Bad," "Every Tub," and "Our Delight."

Stitt, who toured with the Giants of Jazz during parts of 1971–72, kept busy during this period, having a few final reunions with Gene Ammons and recording as a leader for Solid State, Prestige, Cadet, Muse, Sonet, Flying Dutchman, and Catalyst, including an exciting LP with Red Holloway, **Forecast Sonny & Red** (Catalyst 7608).

Supersax   The idea of harmonizing Charlie Parker's remarkable solos for a saxophone section had first been attempted as early as 1947 in Woody Herman's version of "I've Got News for You," which has a passage taken from Bird's solo on "Dark Shadows." Saxophonist Med Flory had long been interested in forming a band around that concept, and after a couple false starts, in 1972 he teamed up with bassist Buddy Clark to form Supersax. The idea was for the five saxophonists (joined by a rhythm section and usually a trumpeter) not to play the melodies of songs but to use Parker's solos as the theme. Although in concert the band also featured individual sax solos, on records the only solos were by the trumpeter (or trombonist) and pianist, with the saxophonists restricted to the complex arrangements.

Their first album, ◐ **Supersax Plays Bird** (Capitol 96264), caused quite a stir when it was released in 1973. Conte Candoli, pianist Ronnell Bright, Clark, and Jake Hanna were in the group, but the main focus was on the saxes (Flory, Joe Lopes, Warne Marsh, Jay Migliori, and Jack Nimitz). Highlights of the memorable set include "Just Friends," "Parker's Mood," "Lady Be Good," "Hot House," and the remarkable "Ko-Ko." Unfortunately, the follow-up albums, **Salt Peanuts** (Capitol 11271) and **Supersax Plays Bird with Strings** (Capitol 11371), although quite worthy, have not been reissued on CD yet and even the original set will be difficult to locate.

Supersax remained active in the Los Angeles area on a part-time basis into the 1990s.

Clark Terry On an occasional basis during 1970–76, Clark "C.T." Terry led a part-time big band. Terry, whose joyful style was unchanged from the 1950s and whose "Mumbles" routine of incoherent scat singing was now part of his act, was in prime form throughout the decade. **Live at the Wichita Jazz Festival** (Vanguard 79355) has his 18-piece orchestra playing charts by Ernie Wilkins, Phil Woods, Jimmy Heath, and Allan Foust, with the key soloists being C.T., Woods, Heath, and Duke Jordan. The music is quite boppish but also includes "Una Mas" and "Nefertiti." The other two recordings by this fine swinging orchestra, **Big Bad Band** (Etoile 1A) and **Big B-A-D Band Live at Buddy's Place** (Vanguard 79373), have not come out yet on CD.

Lucky Thompson An excellent tenor saxophonist who started doubling on soprano in the late 1950s, Lucky Thompson never achieved the recognition that he deserved although he had periods of time when he recorded a great deal. Thompson lived in France during 1968–71 and taught at Dartmouth (1973–74). The 1970 LP **Body and Soul** (Nessa 70) features Thompson playing in Barcelona, Spain, with the Tete Montoliu trio, digging into basic originals and such standards as "I Got It Bad," "Blue 'N' Boogie," and "When Sunny Gets Blue." During 1972–73, Thompson made two albums, **Goodbye Yesterday** (the LP Groove Merchant 508) and **I Offer You** (Simitar 1205). The latter set has the saxophonist performing six of his originals and "Cherokee" with Cedar Walton, Sam Jones, and Louis Hayes. Thompson's new songs would not catch on, but the 49-year-old saxophonist was clearly still in his playing prime.

After 1974, Lucky Thompson, who was apparently quite sick of the music business, voluntarily disappeared. Despite some sightings now and then, he never played music in public again and became a mysterious figure.

Phil Woods Frustrated with the jazz scene in the United States for his kind of music, Phil Woods (who had not led a record date since 1960) moved to France in 1968. During the next few years he had the most advanced group he ever led, a quartet with pianist George Gruntz called the European Rhythm Machine. Unfortunately, their records are hard to find, but they are worth the search. The LP **At Montreux Jazz Festival** (Verve 8797) from 1969 has Woods, Gruntz, bassist Henri Texier, and drummer Daniel Humair exploring lengthy renditions of compositions by Gruntz, Carla

Bley, Herbie Hancock ("Riot"), and Leonard Feather (an emotional "I Remember Bird"). Recorded in 1970, **At the Frankfurt Jazz Festival** (Atlantic 790531) borders on the avant-garde at times and features the quartet playing two originals, Victor Feldman's "Joshua" and "Freedom Jazz Dance." All of the performances are at least 11 minutes long, and some of the improvising is surprisingly free.

Woods returned to the United States in 1972. For a few months he had an avant-garde group with keyboardist Pete Robinson (formerly with Don Ellis) and then he returned to straightahead hard bop. **Musique Du Bois** (32 Jazz 32016) is a fairly challenging meeting on records with Jaki Byard, Richard Davis, and Alan Dawson that includes Wayne Shorter's "Nefertiti," "Airegin," and two versions of the title cut; Byard keeps the music from ever being predictable.

In 1976 Woods decided that, instead of freelancing and being stuck playing the same bebop standards all of the time with pickup groups, he wanted to have a regularly working combo. **Live from the Showboat** (Novus 3104) is the first recording by a unit that would soon become the Phil Woods Quartet. Originally released as a two-LP set, the CD reissue unfortunately leaves out four performances including a 21½-minute "Brazilian Affair," but what remains on this single CD is excellent. Woods is joined by guitarist Harry Leahey, pianist Mike Melillo, bassist Steve Gilmore, drummer Bill Goodwin, and percussionist Alyrio Lima, playing such numbers as "A Sleepin' Bee," "Bye Bye Baby," and a lengthy "Cheek to Cheek." Lima would soon depart and Leahey lasted for only one more record, but Melillo stayed with Woods into 1980, and Gilmore and Goodwin would play with the altoist for more than 25 years, keeping the legacy of hard bop alive for decades to come.

Vocalists

The 1968–76 period was an odd time for jazz vocalists in general. There was little room in most fusion bands for singers, and Flora Purim was one of the few to emerge from the fusion movement. There were some singers exploring avant-garde jazz, but quite often sound explorations from vocalists are much more difficult to listen to than that from saxophonists. Leon Thomas found a certain amount of fame when he sang "The Creator Has a Master Plan" on a Pharoah Sanders record, and his idea of yodeling at climactic moments was in time adopted by many other singers as an option to use in their improvisations, but he failed to build upon that success.

Jazz singers for decades had taken a large part of their repertoire from current popular songs, movie musicals, and Broadway show tunes, but those sources had largely dried up. The pop charts were now dominated by originals from singer/songwriters that were not easily translated into a jazz idiom (cover versions never sounded as good as the hit record), and rock numbers generally seemed dumb when interpreted by a jazz singer. Veterans such as Ella Fitzgerald, Sarah Vaughan, Carmen McRae, and Joe Williams sounded at their worst when trying to get "with it" by adopting songs from the pop and rock worlds. But, commercial pressures from labels aside, one could not blame the jazz singers of the period for wanting fresh material because how many more decades could they sing the same old Cole Porter and Gershwin warhorses?

Some singers fared better than others. Mel Tormé went nearly unrecorded during 1968–76 because he wanted to avoid performing inferior material, and Betty Carter had to start her own Bet-Car label in order to be documented. But Mark Murphy had a good association with the new

Muse label, Helen Humes and Maxine Sullivan made successful comebacks, and by the mid-1970s Ella Fitzgerald was recording strong jazz sets for Norman Granz at Pablo. Looking toward the future via the past, the young swing singer Susannah McCorkle and the new vocal group Manhattan Transfer both found that there was an audience for vintage standards performed in a creative way.

Mose Allison   Considering his status as a unique and highly personal lyricist/composer, singer, and pianist, it is surprising that Mose Allison only made one record during the 1973–81 period. That set, 1976's **Your Mind Is on Vacation** (Koch 8537), shows that Allison was still very much his own man musically; in fact, his piano playing had become more eccentric through the years. On such songs as "Your Mind Is on Vacation," "One of these Days," "I Can't See for Looking," "Your Molecular Structure," and "What Do You Do After You Ruin Your Life," Allison is as ironically philosophical and witty as ever. His trio is joined on some cuts by altoist David Sanborn, Joe Farrell or Al Cohn on tenor, and trumpeter Al Porcino.

Ernestine Anderson   Ernestine Anderson first recorded back in 1947 when she was touring with Johnny Otis as a promising 18-year-old blues singer. In

TIMELINE 1973

Return to Forever is reborn as a fusion quartet with Chick Corea, Stanley Clarke, Lenny White, and Bill Connors. • Herbie Hancock breaks up his sextet and forms the Headhunters. • The original Mahavishnu Orchestra breaks up. • Cecil Taylor is awarded a Guggenheim Fellowship. • Chuck Israels leads the National Jazz Ensemble. • Woody Shaw plays with Art Blakey's Jazz Messengers. • The Concord label makes its first recordings. • Great Guitars is formed. • Thelonious Monk retires. • Helen Humes begins a comeback. • The Toshiko-Akiyoshi Big Band is formed. • Maynard Ferguson returns to the United States after leading a big band in England for three years. • Louis Jordan records his final album. • The Kenny Clarke-Francy Boland big band breaks up. • George Adams joins Charles Mingus's group. • Rashied Ali starts recording for his own Survival label. • Ruby Braff and George Barnes co-lead a popular swing quartet. • Michael Brecker and Tom Harrell play with the Horace Silver Quintet. • Blossom Dearie begins recording for her own Daffodil label. • Irakere is formed in Cuba, featuring pianist Chucho Valdes, altoist Paquito D'Rivera, and trumpeter Arturo Sandoval. • Altoist Earl Warren organizes the Count's Men, a group that includes some fellow Count Basie alumni. • Pianist Alexander Von Schlippenbach's Globe Unity Orchestra, which at the time includes Manfred Schoof, Kenny Wheeler, Paul Rutherford, Evan Parker, Peter Brotzmann, and drummer Paul Lovens, makes its first recording. • Roger Kellaway's Cello Quartet (with cellist Edgar Lustgarten) is popular for a time. • Horace Parlan moves to Copenhagen. • Abbey Lincoln records **People in Me**, her only album as a leader during 1962–79. • Drummer Barry Martyn's Legends of Jazz with trumpeter Andy Blakeney, trombonist Louis Nelson, clarinetist Joe Darensbourg, pianist Alton Purnell, and 88-year-old bassist Ed Garland (who played with Buddy Bolden in 1904) records its first of two albums. • Tom Scott makes his first recording with the L.A. Express, a well-known pop-jazz group that includes Joe Sample, Larry Carlton (later Robben Ford), bassist Max Bennett, and drummer John Guerin. • Jimmy Smith records his final album for Verve. • Joe Pass's solo guitar records and concerts make him famous.

the 1950s she switched to jazz and made a strong impression during her 1956 tour of Scandinavia with Rolf Ericson, recording for the Mercury label during 1958–60. However, after that, she faded from the jazz scene, moving to England in 1965.

In 1975 Ray Brown (an underrated talent scout) heard Anderson sing at the Turnwater Festival in Canada, became her manager, and gained her an important appearance at the 1976 Concord Jazz Festival. That success led to her signing with Concord and becoming a regular fixture in U.S. jazz clubs. **Live from Concord to London** (Concord Jazz 4054) has 17 minutes (five songs) from the historic Concord performance, and one can hear the excitement that the audience felt while discovering the forgotten singer. The London half of the CD, from a year later, has a long Duke Ellington medley and a funky version of "Love for Sale," but it is the Concord set that is most memorable. **Hello Like Before** (Concord Jazz 4031), from two months after the Concord performance, was Anderson's official debut for the label, and she sounds quite exuberant and soulful on such numbers as "Yes Sir, That's My Baby," "Tain't Nobody's Bizness," "It Don't Mean a Thing," and even "Send in the Clowns," while being joined by Hank Jones, Ray Brown, and drummer Jimmie Smith.

Claire Austin Singer Claire Austin, who had caused a stir in traditional jazz circles in the 1950s with her two recordings and her work with Turk Murphy, Kid Ory, and Bob Scobey, only led one album during the 1956–74 period. In 1975 she re-emerged with an obscure set for Jazzology. **Memories of You** (Audiophile 143), also from 1975, was released for the first time in 1993 and features Austin (then 56) singing 1930s standards while backed by pianist Don Ewell. Her voice was still in fine form, as she shows on such tunes as "Ghost of a Chance," "I Got It Bad," and "You Took Advantage of Me," but Austin chose not to return to music full-time and has since been largely forgotten except by veteran traditional jazz collectors.

Betty Carter After being off records for three years, in 1969 Betty Carter recorded **Finally** (Roulette 7953332) and **'Round Midnight** (Roulette 95999) at the same concert. For the first time the singer was heard in her mature form, singing unusual medleys on **Finally**, taking ballads at a very slow pace and romps extremely fast, and quickly tossing away the melodies in order to improvise fairly freely. She certainly keeps the rhythm section (pianist Norman Simmons, bassist Lisle Atkinson, and drummer Al Harewood) constantly guessing. At age 39, Betty Carter had found her own sound, but the jazz world would overlook her for many years to come.

In 1970 Carter began her own Bet-Car label, recording four albums during the next dozen years, three of which would be reissued eventually by Verve. **Live at the Village Vanguard** (Verve 835 681) features her altering and swinging such numbers as "I Didn't Know What Time It Was," "I Could Write a Book," and Randy Weston's "Berkshire Blues." **The Betty Carter Album** (Verve 835 682), from 1972–73, has Carter assisted by either Daniel Mixon or Onaje Allen Gumbs on piano, bassist Buster Williams, and Chip Lyles or Louis Hayes on drums. Carter sings six of her originals (including a radical remake of "I Can't Help It") plus four standards. The 1976 LP **It's My Turn** (Roulette 5005) has yet to be reissued on CD. Carter (with pianist John Hicks, bassist Walter Booker, and an unidentified drummer) tears into and reinvents such unlikely numbers as "Music Maestro Please," "Wagon Wheels," and "Most Gentlemen Don't Like Love." But because she was so far ahead of the other vocalists of the era and could not be easily categorized, Carter recorded only two albums during 1977–87 and would remain an underground legend for years.

Ella Fitzgerald Ella Fitzgerald, who turned 51 in 1968, was still one of the most famous and beloved singers in the world despite the rise of rock. However, her recording career was going through some tough times. She had left Verve, the label that Norman Granz created for her, in 1966. Her Capitol recordings of 1967–68 were not too inspiring, consisting of a set of spirituals, a Christmas album, a record of current pop tunes, and a program of medleys. Recorded in 1969, **Sunshine of Your Love** (Verve 314 533 102) was a low point as Ella attempted to swing such songs as "Hey Jude," "This Girl's in Love with You," and "Sunshine of Your Love" although her versions of "Give Me the Simple Life," "Don't Cha Go 'Way Mad," and "Alright, Okay, You Win" were on a higher level. Ella was having the same difficulty as most jazz singers of the time in that there was very little worthwhile new material being written that she could interpret. This is a problem that has persisted up to the current day for swinging jazz vocalists.

However, Ella did have the advantage of having a famous name and a busy concert schedule. Recorded in 1971, **Ella a Nice** (Original Jazz Classics 442) is a decent live set with the Tommy Flanagan Trio that includes medleys focusing on bossa novas, Cole Porter, Duke Ellington and ballads, plus a few pop tunes ("Put a Little Love in Your Heart" is a mistake) and a fine "Night and Day." But Ella was capable of doing better if guided properly.

Fortunately, Norman Granz came back into the picture. Actually he had been Ella's manager since the late 1940s and continued through the '60s, but in 1972 he became even more significant when he organized the Pablo label. It became Ella's home for the remainder of her career. Gone were the attempts at hit records, and instead the singer had the opportunity to interact with jazz all-stars and to scat her heart out. The label was unofficially launched with a June 2, 1972, all-star concert at the Santa Monica Civic that was capped by a remarkable version of "C Jam Blues" featuring Ella scatting in inspired fashion; that set is covered in the "Various Artists" section of this chapter.

The one exception to Ella's stay at Pablo was a special concert at the 1973 Newport Jazz Festival that was released as **Newport Jazz Festival/Live at Carnegie Hall** (Columbia/Legacy 66809). This double CD is a retrospective of Ella's career up to that point. She is heard performing with a Chick Webb reunion band (a set that should have lasted much longer) and dueting with pianist Ellis Larkins. There are a few instrumentals from a JATP group with Roy Eldridge, Eddie "Lockjaw" Davis, and Al Grey before Ella performs some duets with Joe Pass and has a mini-set with her regular trio.

Ella Fitzgerald was never under-recorded by Norman Granz. Her Pablo years officially began with **Take Love Easy** (Pablo 2310-702), a full set of duets with Joe Pass. Not all of the ballads (such as "Lush Life" and "I Want to Talk About You") really fit her happy swinging style, but there are some touching moments along the way and "A Foggy Day" and "Don't Be that Way" work quite well. **Fine and Mellow** (Pablo 2310-829) has her being inspired by such players as Clark Terry, Harry "Sweets" Edison, Zoot Sims, and Eddie "Lockjaw" Davis, jamming a variety of standards. **Ella in London** (Original Jazz Classics 974) with Flanagan, Pass, bassist Keeter Betts, and drummer Bobby Durham, is an improvement on **Ella a Nice** despite the inclusion of "You've Got a Friend"; that pop tune is easily overshadowed by "The

Man I Love," "It Don't Mean a Thing," and a scat-filled "Lemon Drop."

By 1975 when Ella was 58, her voice was just beginning to lose its edge and faultless intonation. Although her phrasing, ideas, and sense of swing were as impeccable as ever, age was starting to take its toll, gradually, year by year. Ella still sounds in mostly excellent shape on her three recordings of 1975–76. **Ella and Oscar** (Pablo 2310-759) is a set of duets/trios with Oscar Peterson and sometimes Ray Brown (her husband of 25 years earlier) including "Mean to Me," "More Than You Know," and "Midnight Sun." **At the Montreux Jazz Festival 1975** (Original Jazz Classics 789) is a jazz-oriented performance with Flanagan, Betts, and Durham that includes "Caravan," "It's All Right with Me," and "How High the Moon." And although not quite as strong as **Take Love Easy**, **Fitzgerald & Pass...Again** (Pablo 2310-772) has 14 concise versions of standards including "I Ain't Got Nothin' But the Blues," a wordless "Rain," "You Took Advantage of Me," and "Tennessee Waltz."

Even a few years later when her voice was clearly declining, Ella Fitzgerald was still "the First Lady of Song."

Johnny Hartman Though much beloved years later for his recording with John Coltrane, Johnny Hartman actually made relatively few records during his life, particularly after his third Impulse album in 1964. Not counting a couple commercial albums of current pop tunes for the Perception label in 1972–73, the warm baritone's only recordings of this period were a pair of dates cut in Japan in 1972: **Hartman Meets Hino** and **Hartman Sings Trane's Favorites**. **For Trane** (Blue Note 35346) has all eight songs from the former date (which teams Hartman with trumpeter Terumasa Hino and a Japanese rhythm section) and three of the seven songs from the latter. The reissue title is inaccurate, but the music is excellent, alternating between ballads ("Violets for Your Furs" and "The Nearness of You" are high points) and swinging pieces, showcasing Hartman's voice at its best.

Helen Humes Helen Humes had been off records since 1961 and retired since 1967 (taking care of her ill mother) when she re-emerged in 1973. The LP **Let the Good Times Roll** (Black & Blue 33050) let the jazz world know that not only was she back, but at 60 she was still a top-notch swing and blues singer. This classic album, which regrettably has not been reissued on CD yet, mostly has Humes doing remakes, some of which top her earlier versions. Among the high points from what was the definitive recording from her later years are memorable and spirited versions of Louis Jordan's "They Raided the Joint," "That Old Feeling," "Ooo Baba Leba," "He May Be Your Man," and the Humes classic "A Million Dollar Secret." The backup group includes Arnett Cobb, guitarists Al Casey and Clarence "Gatemouth" Brown, Jay McShann, and organist Milt Buckner.

On the Sunny Side of the Street (Black Lion 760185), recorded at the 1974 Montreux Jazz Festival, has Humes sticking to standards and blues (including "If I Could Be with You" and "I Got It Bad") while accompanied by either Earl Hines or Jay McShann on piano, Buddy Tate, bassist Jimmy Woode, and Ed Thigpen. The singer's lone major label release, **Talk of the Town** (Columbia 33488), is not out yet on CD and is a bit tame though still enjoyable. Humes is assisted by Tate, George Benson, Ellis Larkins, Major Holley, and drummer Oliver Jackson on such standbys in her repertoire as "He May Be Your Man," "If I Could Be with You," and "Deed I Do."

Eddie Jefferson   After struggling a bit during the first half of the 1960s, Eddie Jefferson worked regularly with James Moody (1968–73), co-led the Artistic Truth with drummer Roy Brooks (1974–75), and then hooked up with the young bebop altoist Richie Cole. Recorded in 1968, **Body and Soul** (Original Jazz Classics 396) has Jefferson joined by Moody, trumpeter Dave Burns, and the Barry Harris trio for vocalese versions of "Body and Soul," "So What," "Now's the Time," "Mercy, Mercy, Mercy," and Horace Silver's "Filthy McNasty." Come Along with Me (Original Jazz Classics 613) includes such gems as Jefferson's lyrics to "The Preacher," "Yardbird Suite," "Dexter Digs In," and "Baby Girl" (based on "These Foolish Things") with assistance from trumpeter Bill Hardman, Charles McPherson, and Barry Harris. By the time he recorded **Things Are Getting Better** (Muse 5043) in 1974, Jefferson was doing his best to apply his vocalese technique to such difficult material as Miles Davis's "Bitches Brew" and "Freedom Jazz Dance" in addition to "A Night in Tunisia" and James Moody's solo on "I Cover the Waterfront" (which he renamed "I Just Got Back in Town"). Recorded in 1976, **Godfather of Vocalese** (Muse 6013) is a reissue of an album originally titled **Still on the Planet**. With assistance from Richie Cole and trumpeter Wayman

Reed, Jefferson is quite enthusiastic on "I Got the Blues," "Ornithology," and Herbie Hancock's "Chameleon," showing that in 1976 vocalese was still alive and well.

Irene Kral   A ballad singer of the highest order, Irene Kral made her most significant recordings near the end of her short life. The younger sister of singer/pianist Roy Kral (of Jackie & Roy), Kral sang with the Jay Burkhardt Big Band, a vocal group in Chicago called the Tattle-Tales, and the big bands of Maynard Ferguson (1957) and Herb Pomeroy. She recorded albums for United Artists (1958–59), Ava (1963), and Mainstream (1965) but got married and spent a long period outside of music.

In 1974 when she was 42, Kral returned with the classic ● **Where Is Love** (Koch 1012). On this set of ballads she is accompanied very sympathetically by pianist Alan Broadbent and the tempos are quite slow, but the emotional yet cool intensity given by Kral and Broadbent results in no slow moments. Among the songs given definitive and memorable treatment are Blossom Dearie's "I Like You, You're Nice," Bob Dorough's "Love Came on Stealthy Fingers," and "Never Let Me Go." Her haunting version of "Spring Can Really Hang You up the Most" has never been topped. This is one of the finest sets of ballads ever recorded, and it would be followed in 1977 with two other gems before Irene Kral's death from cancer the following year.

Barbara Lea   Not much had been heard from singer Barbara Lea since her 1956–57 recordings for Prestige. She spent much of the 1960s as a stage actress and a teacher, but it was not until the 1970s that she finally returned to singing the vintage standards that she enjoyed, often performing with trumpeters Dick Sudhalter and Ed Polcer.

Upon her return, Lea recorded two very good albums. **The Devil Is Afraid of Music** (Audiophile 119) features Lea interpreting a set of tunes by the underrated songwriter Willard Robison. Robison's wistful melodies, unexpected chord changes, and nostalgic lyrics were always charming, and Lea very ably revives many of his best songs. Most of the selections feature her with a rhythm section headed by pianist Loonis McGlohon from 1976 although five tunes from 1992 with pianist Dick Cary were added to fill up the CD. Lea performs such numbers as "Think Well of Me," "Guess I'll Go Back Home," "Deep Elm," "A Woman Alone with the Blues," and Robison's best-known songs: "A Cottage for Sale," "'Tain't So, Honey, 'Tain't So," and "Old Folks." **Remember Lee Wiley** (Audiophile 125), recorded shortly after Lee Wiley's death, is a logical and heartfelt tribute to the singer who was always Lea's greatest influence. The original 14 songs from 1976–77 have been joined by eight numbers from 1995 (which have Randy Reinhart doubling on trumpet and trombone), and together they form a full portrait of Lee Wiley's musical legacy. Lea sounds quite natural singing such songs associated with Wiley as "I Left My Sugar Standing in the Rain," "Time on My Hands," "Down to Steamboat Tennessee," "Sugar," and "Wherever There's Love."

Manhattan Transfer   In 1976 Manhattan Transfer burst upon the scene as the most significant jazz-oriented vocal group since Lambert, Hendricks, and Ross 15 years earlier. The band had a false start in the late 1960s when they were more satirical and corny. The only member of that group to continue on, Tim Hauser, met Janis Siegel and Laurel Masse in 1972 when he was driving a cab and they were his customers. With the addition of Alan Paul shortly after, Manhattan Transfer was reformed. In the summer of 1975 they were featured on a summer replacement television series, and the following year they signed with Atlantic, recording **Manhattan Transfer** (Rhino 18133). Never strictly a jazz group, the vocal ensemble's debut does include such numbers as "You Can Depend on Me" (featuring a Zoot Sims tenor solo), "Java Jive," "Tuxedo Junction," "The Cat Is High," and "Candy" in addition to a pop/gospel hit in "Operator." Their next couple of projects would have less of a jazz content, but whenever they tackled vocalese or jazz standards, the Manhattan Transfer consistently showed that they were at the top of their field.

Susannah McCorkle   Most singers who were performing vintage standards in the 1970s were veterans from earlier periods. But during an era when fresh new talent was in short supply, Susannah McCorkle gave youthful energy and life to decades-old songs. McCorkle had originally planned to be an interpreter, and she spent time in Europe learning languages, but while in Italy she discovered the music of Billie Holiday. In 1971 when she moved to England, her goal was to become a jazz singer, and she had opportunities to work with Dick Sudhalter, Bobby Hackett, Ben Webster, and Dexter Gordon, using pianist Keith Ingham as her accompanist. The music on **The**

Beginning 1975 (A Records 73233) was not released for the first time until 2002, and most of the 22 selections were originally made as a demo. Although she was not yet as distinctive as she would become, McCorkle was already growing away from her Lady Day influence; highlights include "I Won't Dance," "A Lady Must Live," "The Trouble with Me Is You," and "By Myself."

Virtually all of McCorkle's records since then have been reissued on CD, except for her initial set, **The Music of Harry Warren** (Inner City 1141). Well worth searching for, this delightful record has McCorkle interpreting 17 of Harry Warren's best songs, and at this early stage the singer's ability to bring out the beauty and hidden meanings in lyrics was quite impressive. Joined by Ingham, Bruce Turner on alto and clarinet, bassist Len Skeat, and drummer Johnny Richardson, McCorkle joyfully sings such numbers as "Lullaby of Birdland," "About a Quarter to Nine," and "With Plenty of Money and You." It was obvious from this record that the 30-year-old singer had a potentially great future.

Carmen McRae   The change in musical styles that took place during the 1960s did not help Carmen McRae's career. A superior singer when performing top-notch material, McRae was never able to uplift really terrible songs, and most of her recordings from 1968–76, including such turkeys as **Just a Little Lovin'** (Atlantic 1568), **I Am Music** (Blue Note 462), and **Can't Hide Love** (Blue Note 89540), the first two of which have not been reissued, are not worthy of her. **The Great American Songbook** (Atlantic 2904) is a rare exception from this period. Joined by pianist Jimmy Rowles, Joe Pass, bassist Chuck Domanico, and drummer Chuck Flores, McRae interprets songs by Duke Ellington, Cole Porter, Michel Legrand, Warren & Dubin, Henry Mancini, and Jimmy Van Heusen among others, but it is Jimmy Rowles's humorous novelty "The Ballad of Thelonious Monk" that steals the show. Other highlights include "At Long Last Love," "I Only Have Eyes for You," "Sunday," "I Cried for You," and "I Thought About You."

Still in her prime while in her early fifties, Carmen McRae would have to wait quite a few more years before getting the opportunity to record under such favorable circumstances again.

Helen Merrill   Helen Merrill spent 1959–63 living in Italy. While in New York during 1967–68, she recorded two albums for Milestone including **The Feeling Is**

Mutual, which was reviewed in the previous chapter. **A Shade of Difference** (last out as the LP Landmark 1308) is a particularly strong set that has arrangements by pianist Dick Katz for an adventurous yet sympathetic group that includes Thad Jones, Hubert Laws, Katz, Jim Hall, either Ron Carter or Richard Davis on bass, Elvin Jones, and (just on Ornette Coleman's "Lonely Woman") Gary Bartz. Merrill, who like Abbey Lincoln made every one of her relatively rare recordings into an event, is heard in top form on a wide repertoire that includes plenty of surprises (including a fairly free-form duet with Ron Carter on "My Funny Valentine"). But after moving to Japan in the late 1960s, Merrill would be largely forgotten in the United States for another decade.

Mark Murphy   After recording for Capital and Riverside during 1959–62, Mark Murphy moved to England, living in Europe until 1972. Although he worked steadily including on television and radio, when he moved back to the United States, he pretty much had to start from the beginning. Murphy was a much different singer by the early 1970s than he had been a decade earlier because he was now a full-fledged jazz vocalist who took many chances in his solos, was not afraid to improvise words, and had developed an adventurous and increasingly eccentric scatting style. Murphy began recording regularly for the Muse label in 1972, and his third album for the label (which was briefly available on CD) is one of his very best, ❍ **Mark Murphy Sings** (Muse 5078). His versions of Freddie Hubbard's "Red Clay" (renamed "On the Red Clay"), "Body and Soul," and "Cantaloupe Island" are particularly memorable. Murphy is joined by a rhythm section led by keyboardist Don Grolnick, and there are occasional spots for David Sanborn, Michael Brecker, and Randy Brecker.

With his Muse recordings, Mark Murphy became Betty Carter's male equivalent, ranking with Carter as the most important "new" jazz singer after 1970.

Anita O'Day   One of the top jazz singers of the 1950s, Anita O'Day's career went straight downhill after her period recording for Verve ended in 1962. Her heroin addiction almost led to her death, and she struggled through a long and difficult comeback. Other than a Japanese album in 1963 and a few privately issued live dates, she only made one LP after leaving Verve until 1975. **Live at the Berlin Jazz Festival** (MPS 27050)

from 1970 finds O'Day still possessing a fine voice at the age of 50. Backed by pianist George Arvanitas's trio, O'Day is in excellent form on "Honeysuckle Rose," "Street of Dreams," and a medley of the Beatles's "Yesterday" and "Yesterdays." Although some of the more recent material is of lesser interest, this set is quite successful. It was just a temporary break in the silence though, and O'Day would not record again for five years.

Her next project, **I Get a Kick Out of You** (Evidence 22054) from 1975, was recorded live in Japan. O'Day stretches out on nine numbers, choosing a tune or two from each of six decades (from the 1920s to the '70s) with "What Are You Doing the Rest of Your Life," Leon Russell's "A Song for You," "Undecided," "I Get a Kick Out of You," and "Opus One" being most memorable. Anita O'Day's comeback had officially begun, and soon she was working on her very frank memoirs.

Flora Purim   Flora Purim was one of the few singers who could fit comfortably into fusion, performing her own Brazilian brand of jazz-rock music. Born in Rio de Janeiro, Brazil, and married early on to percussionist/drummer Airto Moreira, she moved with Airto to the United States in the late 1960s when she was in her mid-twenties. Her appealing voice was heard with Stan Getz, Duke Pearson, and most notably the original version of Chick Corea's Return to Forever (1972), an association that made her famous. Purim's versions of "500 Miles High," "Light as a Feather," and "Spain" gave her recognition in the jazz world.

Signed to Orrin Keepnews's Milestone label, Purim recorded steadily for the company through 1978. **Butterfly Dreams** (Original Jazz Classics 315) was an impressive start with the singer holding her own with Joe Henderson, George Duke, Stanley Clarke, and Airto. Among the numbers interpreted are the two-part "Dr. Jive," Jobim's "Dindi," "Summer Night," "Moon Dreams," and a remake of "Light as a Feather." **Stories to Tell** (Original Jazz Classics 619) is most notable for Purim's versions of "Vera Cruz," "Insensatez," and McCoy Tyner's "Search for Peace" while **500 Miles High** (Original Jazz Classics 1018) is a fine example of Purim's live show of 1974. The title cut gets a rousing treatment and the band (which includes keyboardist Pat Rebillot, guitarist David Amaro, and Airto) gets to stretch out quite a bit; Milton Nascimento has a guest appearance. **Open Your Eyes You Can Fly** (Original Jazz Classics 1042) from 1976 has the singer digging into three Chick Corea songs (including "Times Lie" and "Sometime Ago") and a variety of inventive obscurities. Possibly the best all-round jazz set of Flora Purim's Milestones is **Encounter** (Original Jazz Classics 798). Purim sings two songs ("Above the Rainbow" and "Tomara") with McCoy Tyner, teams up with Joe Henderson on "Black Narcissus" and Chick Corea's "Windows," and features such players as trombonist Raul de Souza, keyboardists Hermeto Pascoal and George Duke, singer Urszula Dudziak (heard on "Encounter"), and Airto.

Although Flora Purim would never really exceed the heights of her work from the first half of the 1970s, she had made a permanent mark on jazz, showing that a vocalist could be utilized quite effectively in Brazilian fusion.

Jimmy Rushing   Veteran jazz, blues, and swing singer Jimmy Rushing may have been 68 when he recorded **The You and Me that Used to Be** (Bluebird 6460) in 1971, but he still had plenty of energy and power left. On ten swing standards and one blues ("Fine and Mellow"), Rushing is joined by pianist Dave Frishberg (who wrote the arrangements), Milt Hinton, and Mel Lewis, plus either Zoot Sims and Ray Nance (cornet and violin) or Budd Johnson (on soprano) and Al Cohn. On expressive and wistful renditions of "I Surrender Dear" and "More Than You Know," Rushing is backed by just Frishberg's piano, putting a lot of feeling into his interpretations.

Less than a year later "Mr. Five by Five" passed away, having ended his recording career on top.

Maxine Sullivan   A popular singer since her debut in 1937 whose lightly swinging style would become more influential as time passed, Maxine Sullivan had dropped out of music after 1956, becoming a nurse. In 1968 the 57-year-old began having a successful comeback, performing at festivals and clubs, and even playing a bit of valve trombone and flugelhorn now and then. Married to pianist Cliff Jackson, Sullivan performed in an unchanged and timeless style. ◐ **Close as Pages in a Book** (Audiophile 203) from 1969 was her comeback record, originally made for the Monmouth-Evergreen label. Sullivan shares the spotlight with Bob Wilber (heard on clarinet and soprano in addition to providing the arrangements), with fine backup work provided by pianist Bernie Leighton, bassist George Duvivier, and drummer Gus Johnson. Sullivan sings ten high-quality

swing tunes including "As Long As I Live," "Darn that Dream," the title cut, and a remake of "Loch Lomond."

In contrast, 1971's **Sullivan, Shakespeare, Hyman** (Audiophile 250) is of limited interest. Pianist Dick Hyman wrote the music for a dozen sonnets by William Shakespeare, some of which had originally appeared in Shakespeare's comedies. Because of the antiquated lyrics, Sullivan's vocals are difficult to take, and it does not help that none of Hyman's melodies are all that memorable. To augment the original brief vocals, Hyman in more recent times recorded additional solo renditions to most of the selections, but this set never gets lifted above the level of a historical curiosity. But fortunately there are many other superior and currently available Maxine Sullivan records from her later period, including **Close as Pages in a Book**.

Big Joe Turner   Big Joe Turner was fortunate throughout his career. Although his blues-oriented singing style was virtually unchanged from the late 1930s, it was accessible enough to fit into a variety of contemporary settings, whether it was Kansas City blues, early rhythm and blues, rock 'n' roll, and jazz jam sessions. By 1972 when he was 61, his career could logically be thought of as being about over, except that Turner was experiencing yet another renaissance and was signed by Norman Granz to his Pablo label. The previous year's **Texas Style** (Evidence 26013) had Turner joined by pianist Milt Buckner, Slam Stewart, and Jo Jones for a spirited bluish swing date that includes such standbys as "Cherry Red" and "'Tain't Nobody's Bizness If I Do" along with some basic originals. Turner's debut for Pablo, 1972's **Flip, Flop & Fly** (Original Jazz Classics 1053), was not initially released until 1989. Its music is taken from two concerts that Turner performed while accompanied by the Count Basie Orchestra, an unusual setting for him. Among the soloists are Eddie "Lockjaw" Davis, Jimmy Forrest, trumpeter Pete Minger, altoist Curtis Peagler, Al Grey, and Count Basie himself. **The Bosses** (Original Jazz Classics 821) was Turner's first official Pablo release. He is in top form on such songs as "Night Time Is the Right Time," "Wee Baby Blues," and "Roll 'Em Pete," assisted by Basie and an all-star band that includes Harry "Sweets" Edison, J.J. Johnson, Eddie "Lockjaw" Davis, and Zoot Sims.

Most of Big Joe Turner's Pablo records are loose jam sessions in which he sings his usual stanzas (even if the tune itself is allegedly a recent original) while joined by a mixture of all-stars and Los Angeles blues players. **Life Ain't Easy** (Original Jazz Classics 809) matches Turner with such notables as Roy Eldridge, Al Grey, tenor saxophonist Lee Allen, Ray Brown, and drummer Earl Palmer, performing Woody Guthrie's "So Long" and five tossed-together pieces. The competitive solos of Eldridge and Grey make it all worthwhile. **The Trumpet Kings Meet Joe Turner** (Original Jazz Classics 497) is certainly a bit unusual. Turner and his usual rhythm section of the era (with guitarist Pee Wee Crayton) are joined by Dizzy Gillespie, Roy Eldridge, Harry "Sweets" Edison, and Clark Terry. Unfortunately, the material, three blues (including the 15-minute "I Know You Love Me Baby") and "Tain't Nobody's Bizness If I Do," is not too imaginative or inspiring although each of the trumpeters gets in their solos.

Everyday I Have the Blues (Original Jazz Classics 634) from 1975 is better organized. This time around Sonny Stitt guests on tenor and alto while Turner digs into "Stormy Monday," "Piney Brown," and "Shake, Rattle and Roll." **Nobody in Mind** (Original Jazz Classics 729) has Turner assisted by Roy Eldridge (whose determination makes up for his occasional misses) and Milt Jackson; the most unusual song is "Red Sails in the Sunset," which Turner somehow turns into a blues. **In the Evening** (Original Jazz Classics 852) has Big Joe using his working band of the era without any guests; altoist Bob Smith (who sounds like a mixture of Tab Smith and Johnny Hodges) and Pee Wee Crayton are excellent. Turner turns everything into blues, including "Sweet Lorraine" and "Pennies from Heaven." **The Midnight Special** (Pablo 2310-822) is similar, with Turner's four-piece rhythm section joined by trumpeter Jake Porter, Roy Brewster on baritone horn, and Curtis Kirk on harmonica. One would never think of "I Left My Heart in San Francisco," "I'm Gonna Sit Right Down and Write Myself a Letter," "I Can't Give You Anything but Love," or "You're Driving Me Crazy" as blues, at least not until hearing Big Joe Turner's intriguing versions.

Sarah Vaughan   Considering how famous she was by 1968, one would think that Sarah Vaughan would have recorded regularly during this period despite the changes in the music world. However, after her Mercury contract ended that year, Sassy was off records altogether during 1969–70, and her only recordings from the 1971–74 period were six albums for the tiny Mainstream

label. And, other than a live set for a Polish label, she was also unrecorded during 1975–76.

Unfortunately, most of the Mainstream recordings are rather weak, not because of Vaughan's singing but because of the commercial material that included songs such as "Imagine," "Rainy Days and Mondays," "Just a Little Lovin,'" "Love Doesn't Live Here Anymore," and "Send in the Clowns" (a tune that Vaughan unaccountably loved). However, as with Carmen McRae, there was one set that featured the singer at her best, the two-CD set ● **Live in Japan** (Mobile Fidelity 844), which has also been released as two separate CDs. From a Tokyo concert on September 24, 1973, the 49-year-old singer is heard at the height of her powers, really digging into the standards and making magic out of such numbers as "Poor Butterfly," "Misty," "'Round Midnight," "Willow Weep for Me," "My Funny Valentine," "Summertime," and "Bye Bye Blackbird." With supportive backing by pianist Carl Schroeder, bassist John Gianelli, and Jimmy Cobb, Sassy's voice is often in miraculous form on this definitive set.

Lee Wiley   By the late 1950s, Lee Wiley was quite disappointed with her career. Her 1957 RCA album **A Touch of the Blues** came out fine but was not a big seller, and she failed to become known beyond a small and loyal jazz audience. Depressed by her inevitable aging, she gradually retired.

In 1971, Wiley was persuaded into recording a final album, **Back Home Again** (Audiophile 300). She does a good job on "Indiana" and "I'm Coming Virginia," and the backup band features hot solos from clarinetist Johnny Mince, trombonist Buddy Morrow, Dick Hyman, and particularly trumpeter Rusty Dedrick. But because Wiley's voice was no longer in its prime, this set is a slight disappointment although not without interest. The reissue CD adds some interesting historic tracks from a 1965 demo session with pianist Joe Bushkin that were never released previously.

There was one final act in the Lee Wiley story. After recording her final record, she was booked to perform at the first Newport in New York Festival in 1972. **The Carnegie Hall Concert** (Audiophile 170), in addition to the main event, has ten previously unreleased songs from a 1952 rehearsal with George Wein on piano, bassist John Field, drummer Marquis Foster, and a trumpeter listed as Johnny Windhurst but who sounds very much like Bobby Hackett. This informal rehearsal adds an interesting set to the slim discography of Wiley. But the main reason to acquire this CD is for the 1972 concert. Accompanied by Hackett, Teddy Wilson, Bucky Pizzarelli, George Duvivier, and Don Lamond, Wiley sounds in surprisingly good form. Before a loving crowd that was clearly quite delighted at the rare chance to see her, Wiley sings 11 songs. Best are "Indiana," "You're Lucky to Me," an emotional "Come Sunday," and "Sugar." Even with her forgetting the words at one point to "Manhattan" (a surprise request from Wein), Lee Wiley does very well, exiting her career in memorable fashion. She passed away in 1975.

Joe Williams   Joe Williams's solo career after leaving Count Basie in 1961 was consistently successful. Surprisingly, though, he only made four albums as a leader during 1968–73 and none during 1974–78 despite his continuing popularity. Easily the best of the lot is **Joe Williams Live** (Original Jazz Classics 438). For this set he is joined by Cannonball Adderley's band (with Cannonball and Nat Adderley, George Duke on keyboards, bassist Walter Booker, and drummer Roy McCurdy), which is augmented by electric bassist Carol Kaye and percussionist King Errisson for the occasion. Although the band is often funky and there are some solos for the two horns, Williams is the main star. Best is a passionate version of "Goin' to Chicago Blues," "Who She Do," and Duke Ellington's "Heritage."

Big Bands

With the rise of jazz education, which was partly fostered by Stan Kenton's summer jazz camps, many colleges began to have student stage bands, playing music in the style of Kenton, Woody Herman, and occasionally Count Basie. In addition, there was an increase during this period of "kicks" bands; part-time local orchestras that ran through charts and occasionally played special concerts and local gigs.

However, there were relatively few full-time professional big bands left other than ghost bands (such as those performing the music of Glenn Miller and Tommy Dorsey). Count Basie still toured the world as did Duke Ellington until his death. Harry James kept his swing ensemble together while Woody Herman and Stan Kenton mostly performed modern music. Of the newer bands, Toshiko Akiyoshi/Lew Tabackin, and Don Ellis

were based in Los Angeles, and Thad Jones/Mel Lewis mostly stayed close to their weekly home base in New York; the sidemen in all three groups also had other musical jobs. The big bands of Buddy Rich and the increasingly commercial Maynard Ferguson were among the few new orchestras that joined the swing veterans in ongoing extensive tours. The big bands were clearly not coming back, but at least they were not totally extinct.

The Toshiko Akiyoshi–Lew Tabackin Orchestra   Pianist Toshiko Akiyoshi, who was born in China but moved to Japan with her family when she was 17 in 1946, was one of the top musicians based in Japan during the 1950s. Her Bud Powell–inspired piano playing impressed many listeners including Norman Granz who in 1953 recorded her with Oscar Peterson's rhythm section (Barney Kessel and Ray Brown) and drummer J.C. Heard in a quartet. She studied at Berklee College of Music in 1956, was married to altoist Charlie Mariano during 1959–65 (co-leading a quartet), worked in both New York and Japan, and by the late 1960s had married Lew Tabackin.

Tabackin was a flute major at the Philadelphia Conservatory (1958–62), served in the army, and worked in New York during 1965–71 including with Maynard Ferguson, the Thad Jones-Mel Lewis Orchestra, Joe Henderson, Elvin Jones, and the Tonight Show Band in addition to being the main soloist with the Danish Radio Orchestra during 1968–69. Although his hard-charging tenor playing recalls Sonny Rollins and Don Byas, on flute Tabackin is very influenced by Asian music.

In 1972 the couple moved to Los Angeles, and the following year they formed a big band that was a showcase for Akiyoshi's inventive arrangements and Tabackin's exciting solos. The orchestra began recording for RCA in 1974, making **Kogun** (RCA 6246), **Long Yellow Road** (RCA 1350), **Tales of a Courtesan** (RCA 10723), **Road Time** (RCA 2242), and **Insights** (RCA 2678); unfortunately, none of these sets has been reissued on CD yet. In addition to the co-leaders, the arrangements feature solos by trumpeters Don Rader and Bobby Shew and altoist Gary Foster. Most interesting is how Akiyoshi excels at writing both boppish charts and pieces that reflect her Asian heritage.

Clearly a box set of Toshiko Akiyoshi's RCA recordings is long overdue.

Count Basie In 1968 Count Basie was no longer on the Verve label, and his recording career continued being quite erratic, backing indifferent singers on ill-suited projects one day and then playing an exciting concert the next. **Afrique** (BMG 37508) was possibly the most unusual Basie album, featuring arrangements by Oliver Nelson of mostly modern songs including Albert Ayler's "Love Flower" and Pharoah Sanders'"Japan," not normal repertoire for a swing band! This was a successful experiment but unfortunately was never repeated.

By 1972, Basie had a particularly strong orchestra, his third great band. Among the soloists were Pete Minger and Waymon Reed on trumpets, trombonist Al Grey, altoist Bobby Plater, Jimmy Forrest on tenor, and Eric Dixon doubling on flute and tenor; three years later drummer Butch Miles was driving the rhythm section, which always included Freddie Green's rhythm guitar. Fortunately for Basie, in 1972 Norman Granz returned to the record business, starting the Pablo label. One of his first acts was signing Basie and staging a concert at the Santa Monica Civic on June 2 featuring Basie, Ella Fitzgerald, and some of his favorite all-stars (which is reviewed later in this chapter). During the next 11 years, Basie recorded extensively for Granz and Pablo, with his big band, in all-star groups, and with vocalists.

Of Basie's combo dates from this era, **Basie Jam** (Pablo 2310-718), which features Harry Edison, J.J. Johnson, Eddie "Lockjaw" Davis, and Zoot Sims, is a bit of a disappointment because of the mundane material, one blues after another. **At the Montreux Jazz Festival 1975** (Original Jazz Classics 933) has Basie leading an exciting sextet that includes Roy Eldridge, Johnny Griffin, and Milt Jackson. **Basie Jam #2** (Original Jazz Classics 632) with Benny Carter, Lockjaw Davis, Clark Terry, and Al Grey, is a big improvement over its predecessor while **Basie Jam #3** (from the same day with the same musicians) is even better because of its four strong standards that include "Bye Bye Blues" and "Song of the Islands."

But the best Basie combo date on Pablo, and perhaps his best ever, is ● **Basie & Zoot** (Original Jazz Classics 822). This quartet session with Zoot Sims, bassist John Heard, and Louie Bellson is full of unexpected fireworks and heat. Basie and Sims both sound inspired and dig into such tunes as "I Never Knew," "It's Only a Paper Moon," and "Honeysuckle Rose" with joy and exuberance. Basie both lights a fire under Zoot and sounds quite exuberant himself.

Norman Granz always loved Count Basie's piano playing, so he featured him in a trio with Ray Brown and Louie Bellson on **For the First Time** (Pablo 2310-712) and **For the Second Time** (Original Jazz Classics 600), performances that (predictably) are full of space, sly wit, and perfect placement of every note. Granz also teamed Basie in a two-piano quartet with Oscar Peterson, a matchup that is successful (Basie and Peterson had much more in common than expected) but was probably recorded excessively, with five CDs resulting. **Satch and Josh** (Original Jazz Classics 959) is their best collaboration.

Granz had less enthusiasm for the Basie orchestra than he did for Basie's piano playing (he wished that Basie would eventually just tour with a combo), so it was some time before he started extensively recording the band. **Fun Time** (Pablo 2310-945) is a spirited live set from the 1975 Montreux Jazz Festival that is worth picking up. In contrast, **The Basie Big Band** (Pablo 2310-756) is a decent but ultimately lightweight program of Sammy Nestico arrangements, a studio project that would be topped by Basie's upcoming recordings. The orchestra sounds much more dynamic performing Bill Holman's challenging charts on **I Told You So** (Original Jazz Classics 824).

Bill Berry Bill Berry, who was always proud of having played trumpet with the Duke Ellington Orchestra during 1961–63, led the L.A. Big Band, one of the finest jazz orchestra of the mid-to-late-1970s. The all-star unit recorded far too little, just one album for Berry's Beez label and ● **Hello Rev** (Concord Jazz 4027). The latter was cut at the 1976 Concord Jazz Festival and has solos by trumpeters Berry, Jack Sheldon (who also sings "Tulip or Turnip"), Blue Mitchell, and Cat Anderson (whose section work on "Cotton Tail" is remarkable); trombonists Tricky Lofton, Jimmy Cleveland, and Britt Woodman; tenor saxophonists Richie Kamuca and Don Menza; and pianist Dave Frishberg. Quite a band.

Capp-Pierce Juggernaut In 1976, veterans Frank Capp and Nat Pierce joined forces to form the Capp-Pierce Juggernaut. Pianist Pierce took care of most of the arrangements while drummer Capp kept the band afloat and well organized. The Juggernaut was from the start a soundalike of Count Basie's big band, a West Coast equivalent featuring many of the top players based in Los Angeles. Their debut recording, **Juggernaut** (Concord Jazz 4040), features such soloists as trombonist Buster Cooper, tenors Richie Kamuca and Plas Johnson, trumpeter Blue Mitchell, altoist Marshal Royal (formerly with Basie), and Pierce (who consistently sounds like Basie) along with Ernie Andrews who sings three numbers. Highlights of this hard-swinging affair include "Avenue 'C'," "Moten Swing," and "Dickie's Dream."

Duke Ellington   The death of Billy Strayhorn in 1967 was a reminder to Duke Ellington of his own mortality. Typically, Ellington threw himself into his work and increased his already mind-boggling productivity. He wrote the music for his second and third sacred concerts, composed a few new suites, had his 70th birthday celebrated at the White House, toured the world constantly, continued leading his still-mighty orchestra, and recorded on a regular basis. It was a mad race against time, and for a time Ellington seemed to remain quite ageless.

Yale Concert (Original Jazz Classics 664) has the Duke Ellington Orchestra very much intact in 1968 and, other than a Johnny Hodges medley and "Take the 'A' Train," all of the music was recent. There are showcases along the way for Cootie Williams, Harry Carney, Paul Gonsalves, Cat Anderson, and Russell Procope's New Orleans–style clarinet. A few months later Jimmy Hamilton left Ellington after 25 years to retire to the Virgin Islands. Harold Ashby took his place on tenor sax with Procope now being the group's only clarinetist. A tour of South America resulted in **The Latin American Suite** (Original Jazz Classics 469), a seven-part work celebrating the atmosphere and rhythms of the countries visited by the band.

The White House celebration took place in 1969 and later in the year Ellington recorded the two-CD set
● **Seventieth Birthday Concert** (Blue Note 32746) while touring England. There are many inspired moments during this concert including superb versions of "Rockin' in Rhythm," "Take the 'A' Train" (with Cootie Williams), and "Perdido" (featuring trumpeter Rolf Ericson), a nine-song 16½-minute "hits medley," and an incredible high-note chorus on "Satin Doll" by Cat Anderson that serves as proof that he was the most remarkable of all high-note trumpeters. At the time of the concert, Ellington boasted major soloists in Williams, Anderson, Ericson, Lawrence Brown, Johnny Hodges, new member Norris Turney on alto and flute, Russell

Procope, Paul Gonsalves, Harold Ashby, and Harry Carney plus guest organist Wild Bill Davis. Unfortunately, though, it would not last much longer.

New Orleans Suite (Atlantic 1580) is a reasonably enjoyable but minor work most notable for having Johnny Hodges's last appearance on records. It had been planned that he would take his first soprano solo on records in nearly 30 years on "Portrait of Sidney Bechet," but he suffered a fatal heart attack while visiting his dentist; Gonsalves took a tenor solo instead. There are other tributes to Ellington's early bassist Wellman Braud, Louis Armstrong (a feature for Cootie Williams), and Mahalia Jackson, but nothing that essential takes place. By the time the Duke Ellington Orchestra recorded **The Afro-Eurasian Eclipse** (Original Jazz Classics 645) in February 1971, both Cat Anderson and Lawrence Brown had departed, with the latter soon retiring. Most interesting about this eight-part suite, which looks toward African folk music and also more advanced areas of jazz, is that "Acht o'Clock Rock" hints at rock.

"Togo Brava Suite" is now available in two versions, an early studio album (Storyville 8323) and a concert album (Blue Note 30082), both simply called **Togo Brava Suite**. The full-length version is on the Storyville set (which was not released until the late 1990s), and although rough in spots, it is enjoyable to hear what Ellington had in mind. The Blue Note CD just has excerpts from the suite along with shorter pieces that feature Cootie Williams (whose solos became more dramatic and heroic in his later years), Norris Turney (his tribute to Hodges called "The Checkered Hat"), trombonist Booty Wood, Gonsalves, and Ashby.

As Ellington's orchestra became weaker with the aging and in some cases retirement of his veterans, the leader assumed more and more of the solo work. His percussive piano playing remained quite modern and stimulating. Two of Ellington's main albums of 1972–73 feature him in small groups. **This One's for Blanton** (Original Jazz Classics 810) is a set of duets with Ray Brown consisting of five standards (including "Pitter Panther Patter") and the four-part "Fragmented Suite for Piano and Bass"; all of it is reminiscent of Ellington's duets with Jimmy Blanton. **Duke's Big Four** (Pablo 2310-703) has Ellington at the age of 73 keeping up with Joe Pass, Ray Brown, and Louie Bellson in a quartet, jamming such songs as "Cotton Tail," "Love You Madly," and "The Hawk Talks."

The last recording by the Duke Ellington Orchestra, the LP **Eastbourne Performance** (RCA 1023), almost sounds like a transitional album as Ellington welcomes such new and potentially significant players as tenor saxophonist Percy Marion and trumpeters Barry Lee Hall (whose mastery of the plunger mute was in the tradition of Bubber Miley, Cootie Williams, and Ray Nance), Johnny Coles, and Money Johnson. Recorded in December 1973, the set also features Russell Procope, Harold "Geezil" Minerve on alto, Harold Ashby, and singer Anita Moore. Although still with the band, Paul Gonsalves and Cootie Williams were absent that day. Ellington gets solo honors with his playing on "The Piano Player" and a touching version of "Meditation," which closes the album.

Within a short time after this recording, Duke Ellington was diagnosed with cancer and curtailed his activities although he kept on writing music until the end. He spent his 75th birthday in the hospital and passed away on May 24, 1974. His son, Mercer Ellington, who had been playing section trumpet with the band for several years (in addition to being its road manager) became its new leader so as to fulfill contractual obligations. **Continuum** (Fantasy 24765) was the band's last album before becoming just a part-time orchestra. Paul Gonsalves had died shortly before Ellington. Harry Carney is on two numbers (taking a solo on "Drop Me Off in Harlem") but passed away before the second session. His place was taken by Joe Temperley who is in the spotlight on the tribute "Carney." Cootie Williams is featured in spots during his last significant appearance on records, and there are also solos from Ricky Ford on tenor, Barry Lee Hall, Harold Minerve, and trombonist Art Baron. But there was no way that this orchestra could survive the deaths and retirement of so many of its players or the passing of the remarkable Duke Ellington.

Don Ellis   Don Ellis led a series of big bands during 1966–74 that were among the funnest, most humorous, and most colorful of the era. They featured unusual instrumentation, an intriguing utilization of electronic devices (particularly by 1970), and originals written in crazy-time signatures that made the music seem more radical than it actually was. For example, the band's trademark song, "Pussy Wiggle Stomp," is in 7/4 time (the audience would request it by clapping on beats two, four, six, and seven) but has a melody based on a child's song ("My Dad's Better Than Your Dad") that the band built on in often-hilarious fashion.

In 1967 the Don Ellis Orchestra signed with Columbia. Unfortunately, most of its music for the label has not been reissued on CD although 1968's **Shock Treatment** (Koch 8590) recently returned. At the time, the band consisted of five trumpets, three trombones, five reeds, keyboardist Mike Lang, three bassists, and four drummer/percussionists. Although not quite an essential release, this CD does include such selections as the Indian-influenced "The Tihai," "Beat Me Daddy, Seven to the Bar," "Homecoming," and "Mercy, Maybe Mercy." The band's greatest all-round album, ● **Autumn** (Tristar 80885), will be difficult to locate although Tristar reissued it on CD; it could become more widely available in the near future. Recorded in the summer of 1968, this set features such notables as first trumpeter Glenn Stuart, trombonist Glenn Ferris, the altos of Frank Strozier and Ira Schulman, both John Klemmer and Sam Falzone on tenors, and keyboardist Pete Robinson. Strozier plays beautifully on a relatively straightforward version of Charlie Parker's "K.C. Blues," the original version of "Pussy Wiggle Stomp" has its riotous moments (and a lot of false endings), "Scratt and Fluggs" is a brief bit of silliness, and the 19½-minute six-part "Variations for Trumpet" is an impressive showcase for Ellis. But it is the 17½-minute remake of "Indian Lady" that is most memorable because the band really goes crazy in spots. Ellis, Ferris, and Robinson play humorous solos followed by a nutty tenor tradeoff by Klemmer and Falzone. Who says modern jazz cannot be fun?

The New Don Ellis Big Band Goes Underground (Columbia 9889), an LP from early 1969, is a bit of a disappointment because the dozen songs are overly concise and overarranged. The brief solos, so-so vocals of Patti Allen, and the melodies (other than the very complex "Bulgarian Bulge" and "Eli's Coming") fail to be at all memorable. However, the opposite is true of the double-LP **Live at Fillmore** (Columbia 66261). When this set came out in 1970, it seemed to signal a new era for jazz big bands although its influence ended up being much less than expected. The 20-piece Ellis orchestra, consisting of five trumpets, three trombones, one tuba, five saxes, keyboards, one guitar, one bass, and three drummer/percussionists (not counting Ellis who had also begun doubling on drums) often sounds quite crazy during its performance from the Fillmore West. The band had begun using some electronic devices (including ring modulators) to distort their sounds, and Glenn Ferris and John Klemmer (showcased on "Excursion II") were playing at their most extroverted. This sometimes bizarre but always very colorful set includes "Final Analysis" (which has a countless number of false endings, satirizing the typical end of a symphony), a particularly strange version of "Hey Jude," and a remarkable remake of "Pussy Wiggle Stomp" that is filled with jokes.

By 1971 the Don Ellis Orchestra had changed a bit, consisting of an eight-piece brass section (four trumpets, one trombone, one bass trombone, one French horn, and one tuba), a four-piece woodwind section, a string quartet, Milcho Leviev (to whom odd-time signatures were second nature) on keyboards, bass, two drums (not counting Ellis), and congas. Unfortunately, its one release, **Tears of Joy** (Columbia 30927), has not been reissued since it came out as a double LP. The potential of the band was enormous (later Ellis would also add a vocal quartet), as particularly shown on the 17½-minute "Strawberry Soup." Other highlights include "5/4 Getaway" (a reworking of Joe Sullivan's "Little Rock Getaway"), a remake of "Bulgarian Bulge," and the 11/4 "Blues in Elf." As it turned out, this was Don Ellis's last significant album. The remaining three Ellis recordings from the period have not been reissued on CD yet. **Connection** (Columbia 31766) has the big band in 1972 playing Ellis's award-winning theme to the film *The French Connection* and otherwise mostly a variety of pop tunes. Although "Put It Where You Want It," "Alone Again (Naturally)," and "Chain Reaction" are worthwhile, most of the other performances are brief and forgettable. **Haiku** (MPS 25341) has Ellis's trumpet in the lead while backed by a large string section on ten moody and picturesque originals. Recorded in 1974, **Soaring** (MPS 25123) includes some good moments from Ellis's orchestra, particularly "Invincible," which is an outstanding feature for altoist Vince Denham. But despite the inclusion of an original called "The Devil Made Me Write This Piece," some of the former craziness of the earlier groups is missing on this generally enjoyable outing.

Don Ellis, who drove himself relentlessly whether playing trumpet, jumping to drums, or conducting his orchestra, suffered a heart attack in the mid-1970s and was forced out of action for a couple years. He would never regain his former prominence.

Maynard Ferguson   After Maynard Ferguson broke up his big band in the mid-1960s, he had a few freelance projects during 1966–67 and then drifted away from jazz for a time, spending time living in India. By 1970 he was itching to get going again, and Ferguson, who at the time was living in England, put together a new orchestra. Unlike his boppish Roulette band, this ensemble was open to the influences and repertoire of pop music while still including some straightahead pieces. The band's three Columbia records, **M.F. Horn** (Columbia 30566), **M.F. Horn 2** (Columbia 31709), and **M.F. Horn 3** (Columbia 32403), are not available on CD yet, but they were popular at the time. Pianist Pete Robinson, drummer Randy Jones, altoist Pete King (on the first album), and baritonist Bruce Johnstone (on the third) are the best known of the sidemen although Ferguson's high-note flights consistently take honors. "MacArthur Park" from **M.F. Horn** was a hit, **M.F. Horn 2** includes surprisingly successful versions of "Theme from Shaft," "Spinning Wheel," and "Hey Jude," and **M.F. Horn 3**, with "Awright, Awright," "'Round Midnight," and "Nice 'n Juicy" as the high points, is the best of the trio.

In 1973 Maynard Ferguson returned to the United States and reorganized his band, keeping a few of the sidemen but mostly filling the slots with Americans. **M.F. Horn 4 & 5: Live at Jimmy's** (Columbia 32732) is a double LP that has Ferguson's most jazz-oriented session for Columbia. With such songs as "I'm Getting Sentimental Over You," "Two for Otis," "Stay Loose with Bruce," "The Fox Hunt," and "Got the Spirit," this is a strong straightahead date, a departure for Ferguson in the 1970s. There are fine solos from Ferguson, altoist Andy MacIntosh, Ferdinand Povel on tenor, Bruce Johnstone, and Pete Jackson, with first trumpeter Lin Biviano leading the brass section.

However, the Columbia label had other plans for Maynard Ferguson, and so did the trumpeter. Recorded in 1974, **Chameleon** (Columbia/Legacy 46112), which has been reissued, is quite streaky. Ferguson's version of Herbie Hancock's hit "Chameleon" is enjoyable, and he does a fine job with Chick Corea's "La Fiesta," "I Can't Get Started," and "Superbone Meets the Bad Man" (which also features Johnstone). But the renditions of "The Way We Were," Paul McCartney's "Jet," and "Livin' for the City" are forgettable and difficult to sit through. Recorded in 1975, **Primal Scream** (Columbia 33953), which has fortunately not returned, is worse, utilizing disco and funk rhythms along with Ferguson's stratospheric blasts, tasteless arrangements (even "Pagliacci" and "Invitation" are turned into disco), a studio orchestra, strings, vocalists, and a remarkable number of unnecessary guests.

Ironically as Maynard Ferguson's records declined in quality, he became better and better known to a generation of high school and college players who were astonished by his high-note prowess.

Woody Herman   Throughout his career, Woody Herman kept his band and his music young by encouraging his sidemen to bring in fresh material and by not being shy to try new things. Originally leading a swing band, Herman embraced bebop with his first two Herds, had the cool-toned Third Herd in the 1950s, and during the first half of the '60s featured hard-swinging numbers including some Horace Silver songs. With rock making such a big impact by 1968, he opened up his repertoire to include some tunes from the rock world. He hoped to increase his band's audience (so the orchestra could keep on working) while performing music that would be considered both topical and relevant to younger listeners. It was a nice try.

The flaw to the idea was that if someone wanted to hear songs such as "Light My Fire," "I Say a Little Prayer," "Hey Jude," and "Aquarius," Woody Herman's Orchestra is not the first place they would look. By playing rock pieces that were generally unsuitable for a big band, the results tended to be instantly dated, and that was true of Herman's Cadet recordings of 1968–70. Some of the "highlights" from his three albums of the period can be heard on **Keep on Keepin' On** (GRP/Chess 818). Although Herman was still a masterful talent scout, with his sidemen including such up-and-coming players as pianist John Hicks, guitarists Phil Upchurch and Mick Goodrick, trumpeter Tom Harrell, and tenor saxophonist Frank Tiberi, his recordings from these years can be safely passed by.

In 1971 Woody Herman began recording for Fantasy, and his records returned to more straightahead jazz although he remained open to including more modern tunes in his repertoire. **Brand New** (Original Jazz Classics 1044) has Herman welcoming electric blues/rock guitarist Michael Bloomfield as a guest on four numbers. Some of the performances are better than others with the highlights being "After Hours" (which has a Nat

TIMELINE 1974

Al DiMeola joins Return to Forever. • Pat Metheny joins Gary Burton. • The Modern Jazz Quartet breaks up. • Paul Bley forms the Improvising Artists label. • Lucky Thompson retires. • Duke Ellington dies at the age of 75. • Eastern Rebellion is formed. • Buddy DeFranco ends his eight-year period of leading the Glenn Miller Orchestra. • Gerry Mulligan and Chet Baker reunite for a Carnegie Hall concert. • Scott Joplin's "The Entertainer" appears on the pop charts. • The L.A. Four is formed. • Guitarist John Abercrombie records **Timeless** (ECM 1047). • Arthur Blythe joins Chico Hamilton's group. • Willem Breuker forms the Willem Breuker Kollektief, an often-hilarious avant-garde Dutch band. • Dee Dee Bridgewater, who had formerly sung with the Thad Jones/Mel Lewis Orchestra, acts in the Broadway musical *The Wiz*. • Trumpeter Bill Chase, on tour with a reorganized version of his pop-jazz group Chase, dies along with three of his musicians in a plane crash. • Polish violinist Michal Urbaniak and his wife, singer Urszula Dudziak, move to the United States. • Eddie Durham leads his first record date since 1940. • Clarinetist Jim Cullum, Sr.'s death leads to his son cornetist Jim Cullum, Jr. taking over the Happy Jazz Band of San Antonio, Texas. • Pianist Connie Crothers records her first album. • Altoist Sonny Fortune plays with Miles Davis. • Jon Faddis performs regularly with his idol Dizzy Gillespie. • Harry "the Hipster" Gibson records a somewhat demented Christmas jazz album. • Rufus Harley plays bagpipes on a Sonny Rollins record. • Paul Quinichette, who had retired in 1960, makes a brief comeback. • Paul Rutherford records **Gentle Harm of the Bourgeoisie** (Emanem 4019), a set of unaccompanied trombone solos. • Roland Hanna and Frank Wess form the New York Jazz Quartet. • Guitarist James "Blood" Ulmer joins Ornette Coleman's Prime Time. • Dave Liebman forms Lookout Farm with Richie Beirach. • Red Norvo records for Harry Lim's Famous Door label. • Pianist Butch Thompson becomes a regular on Garrison Keillor's popular radio series "A Prairie Home Companion." • The Sacramento Jazz Jubilee, a huge Dixieland-oriented festival held over Memorial Day weekend, debuts.

Pierce arrangement) and "I Almost Lost My Mind." In addition to playing alto and clarinet, Herman takes two vocals and is heard for the first time on soprano. **The Raven Speaks** (Original Jazz Classics 663) is the most rewarding of Herman's Fantasy albums, particularly a memorable jam on "Reunion at Newport," "Watermelon Man," and "Alone Again (Naturally)." The soloists along the way include Herman, pianist Harold Danko, trumpeter Bill Stapleton, and both Frank Tiberi and Gregory Herbert on tenors. **Giant Steps** (Original Jazz Classics 344) has mostly fairly recent and modern (within the past 15 years) jazz tunes including Chick Corea's "La Fiesta," "Freedom Jazz Dance," "A Child Is Born," and "Giant Steps." One could not imagine such Herman contemporaries as Benny Goodman or Tommy Dorsey tackling this type of material. **Feelin' So Blue** (Original Jazz Classics 953) has a variety of tunes taken from three different sessions from 1973–75 including "Brotherhood of Man" and "Sombrero Sam." **The Thundering Herd** (Original Jazz Classics 841) features arrangements by Alan Broadbent (who was a strong contributor to Herman's book at the time), Tony Klatka, and Bill Stapleton and solos from Tiberi, Herbert, Stapleton, trumpeter Klatka, and keyboardist Andy Laverne on material ranging from Coltrane's "Lazy Bird" and "Naima" to Frank Zappa's "America Drinks and Goes Home" and "Evergreen." **Herd at Montreux** (Original Jazz Classics 991) mostly consists of odd material that did not stay in the Herman repertoire for long, but it does include Aaron Copland's "Fanfare for the Common Man" while **King Cobra** (Original Jazz Classics 1065) has excellent versions of "Spain" and "Come Rain or Come Shine."

On November 20, 1976, Woody Herman had a Carnegie Hall concert that celebrated a personal milestone: his fortieth year as a bandleader. **Featuring Stan Getz** (Bluebird 68702) has highlights from what was originally a two-LP set. The concert starred both the current version of Herman's orchestra and many of his alumni. Not everything came off well ("Four Brothers" is just okay, and "Caldonia" is taken much too fast), and Herman's habit of introducing soloists over the music is sometimes distracting. The single CD only has two cuts by the 1976 Herman big band ("Fanfare for the Common Man" and a lengthy "Blues in the Night"), both of which have solos from tenor saxophonist Joe Lovano. Stan Getz fares best among the alumni, being showcased on "Blue Serge," "Early Autumn," and "Blue Getz." Otherwise, there are appearances from

Flip Phillips, Jimmy Giuffre, Al Cohn, Zoot Sims, Ralph Burns, and Jimmy Rowles. Although not without its bright moments, this concert fell short of being the classic it should have been.

Harry James   Harry James, who turned 60 in 1976, led unadventurous and rather predictable swing orchestras since he discarded bop in 1950, but he could still impress listeners with his trumpet playing when he was inspired. Recorded in 1972, **Mr. Trumpet** (Hindsight 702) starts strong with a Dixielandish version of "The Sheik of Araby." Unfortunately, the disc is quite brief (just 29 minutes), and there are some muzaky strings on the ballads. However, James is in excellent form, whether on a relaxed rendition of "Indiana," a re-creation of Benny Goodman's version of "Don't Be that Way," or a swinging "Hot Lips," making one wish that much more music was produced from this project. There were three final big-band albums for the swing era hero (in 1976 and 1979 for Sheffield Lab), but those are forgettable and much less inspired than **Mr. Trumpet**. Harry James would remain a famous name up until his death in 1983.

Thad Jones/Mel Lewis Orchestra   The Thad Jones/Mel Lewis Orchestra, founded in early 1966, played every Monday night at the Village Vanguard for years. Although a part-time orchestra, it was one of jazz's major big bands of the era because of Thad Jones's arrangements, the all-star personnel, and a strong group sound. All of the band's 1966–70 recordings for Solid State have been reissued on a five-CD limited-edition box set by Mosaic. Most of the individual dates are otherwise out of print but fortunately not the band's finest recording, 1970's ● **Consummation** (Blue Note 38226). The original version of Jones's best-known composition "A Child Is Born," the sly "Tiptoe," and the lengthy and exciting "Fingers" make this set a classic. Among the key players are Jones on flugelhorn, drummer Mel Lewis, trumpeter Marvin Stamm, trombonist Jimmy Knepper, Billy Harper (who takes a heated tenor solo on "Fingers"), Jerome Richardson, Jerry Dodgion, and Eddie Daniels on reeds, pianist Roland Hanna, and bassist Richard Davis. **Basle 1969** (TCB 2042), a broadcast over Swiss radio, has additional material from the great band including "Second Race," "The Waltz You Swang for Me," "Don't Get Sassy," and "Groove Merchant."

The Thad Jones/Mel Lewis Orchestra underwent a lot of turnover during the first half of the 1970s and although its recordings (mostly for Horizon) became infrequent and less significant, it remained a powerful and influential force among modern big bands.

Stan Kenton   Prior to the mid-1960s, Stan Kenton's orchestra featured many top future all-stars who graduated from his big band to have significant careers of their own. But after 1965, few of his sidemen became important improvisers, and most regarded their association with Kenton to be a high point in their playing career before they settled down to be educators or have other day jobs. The only significant graduates from the big band during 1968–75 were trumpeters Mike Vax, Tom Harrell and Tim Hagans, tenor saxophonist Tony Campise, bassist Dave Stone, and drummers Peter Erskine and John Von Ohlen. Kenton's main interest by that time was mostly in jazz education, and his orchestra was used as a house band at many clinics, seminars, and jazz camps. Because of its youth and lack of individuality, the Kenton big band by the late 1960s often sounded like a college stage band itself.

In 1968 Stan Kenton recorded his final selections for Capitol (his record company for the past 25 years). Two years later he formed his own Creative World label, reissuing some of his earlier recordings and making some new sessions. Although his newer projects were rarely memorable, the musicianship of the band remained high as did its spirit. **Live at Redlands University** (Creative World 1015), **Live at Brigham Young University** (Creative World 1039), **Live at Butler University** (Creative World 1058), and **Birthday in Britain** (Creative World 1065) show how the somewhat faceless band sounded in concert during 1971–73 with the arrangements (particularly those of Hank Levy) being challenging but none of the solos really standing out. **7.5 on the Richter Scale** (Creative World 1070) unfortunately does not live up to its name and has the band performing such weak material as "Live and Let Die," the "Love Theme from the Godfather," and "It's Not Easy Bein' Green," the latter with a glee club group vocal. Other forgettable efforts include **Stan Kenton Plays Chicago** (Creative World 1072), **Fire, Fury and Fun** (Creative World 1073), **Kenton '76** (Creative World 1076), and the bandleader's final studio album, **Journey into Capricorn** (Creative World 1077), all of which can be enjoyed by fans of college bands but none of which contain anything too memorable. Stan Kenton turned 65 late in 1976, and the legendary bandleader's career was gradually nearing its end.

Buddy Rich   The Buddy Rich Big Band, which was formed by the temperamental drummer in 1966, cut its finest record in 1968, ● **Mercy, Mercy** (Blue Note 54331). Most notable is the original classic version of "Channel One Suite," which has tenor saxophonist Don Menza's memorable solo (one on which he utilizes both his dazzling technique and circular breathing) plus a couple of brilliant spots for Rich. Other highlights include Phil Wilson's colorful arrangement of "Mercy, Mercy, Mercy" and a version of "Alfie" that is a melodic feature for altoist Art Pepper. For the CD reissue, three additional selections were released for the first time including a showcase for Pepper on "Chelsea Bridge." Pepper plays well, but this was just a brief and unsuccessful comeback for him, seven years before he more forcefully returned to the jazz scene.

The next album, **Buddy & Soul** (Blue Note 23998), does not reach quite the same heights but features fine spots for Richie Cole, tenor saxophonist Pat LaBarbera, and guitarist David Dana in addition to Rich. Although a pair of tunes by the Doors are throwaways in this context, there are excellent versions of Don Sebesky's "Soul Lady," Bill Holman's "Ruth," and "The Meaning of the Blues." As with most of these big-band CD reissues, the program has been expanded a bit. **Keep the Customers Satisfied** (Blue Note 23999) has an 11-minute four-song "Midnight Cowboy Medley" and the catchy Paul Simon title cut but is otherwise not particularly commercial, with arrangements and some originals by Bill Holman, Don Piestrup, and Roger Neumann; LaBarbera and Cole are again the star soloists. Buddy Rich was doing what he could with rock (which he generally disliked), taking some current tunes but swinging them in his own fashion, and he was battling the constant pressure to become more commercial.

Time Being (Bluebird 6459) is a sampler having some of the best selections from the Rich big band's 1971–72 LPs **A Different Drummer**, **Rich in London** (the most rewarding of the trio), and **Stick It**. The performances on the CD are enjoyable, and one gets to hear Pat LaBarbera on tenor and soprano, trombonist Bruce Paulson, and altoists Jimmy Mosher and Joe Romano well featured. Although the Buddy Rich big band recorded for World Pacific/Liberty (1966–69) and RCA (1971–72) during its prime years, it was clearly struggling a bit by 1973 when it began making records for Groove Merchant, not helped by Rich often firing his sidemen. However, **The Roar of '74** (Simitar 1284) has its heated moments and plenty of solos from LaBarbera. Highlights include "Nuttville," "Senator Sam," and Menza's "Time Check."

Buddy Rich, who always gave the maximum effort in his playing (and was still "the world's greatest drummer"), continued driving his big band hard for the next decade.

Dixieland, New Orleans Jazz, Ragtime, and Mainstream Swing

With the passing of time, more and more of the great Dixieland, New Orleans, and swing masters passed away. Although the top players were always irreplaceable, none of those styles died and each continued flourishing at a lower level.

There were a few favorable trends in traditional jazz during this period. Ragtime unexpectedly made a major comeback in 1974 when Marvin Hamlisch used the music of Scott Joplin prominently in the film *The Sting*. Joplin, who died in 1917, would have been surprised to know that his rag "The Entertainer" made it onto the pop charts in the mid-1970s. The public briefly became aware of ragtime before switching to other fads, but ragtime's audience in general increased quite a bit, leading to the proliferation of ragtime festivals, the writing of new rags, and increased work for the one surviving ragtime composer of the classic era, the ageless Eubie Blake.

Dixieland and New Orleans jazz gradually grew in popularity again while essentially remaining underground music that occasionally came above ground during large festivals, most notably the Sacramento Jazz Jubilee that began in 1974. Several new mainstream swing/traditional bands were active in the early 1970s including the Ruby Braff/George Barnes Quartet, Soprano Summit, and the World's Greatest Jazz Band. A jazz repertory movement in which orchestras and ensembles were organized specifically to re-create and/or revive earlier music was in its beginning stages, often featuring Dick Hyman. Veteran trumpeter Doc Cheatham (who turned 70 in 1975) emerged as a hot new swing soloist. Although not documented that thoroughly yet, Europe was becoming the home for many classic jazz bands bringing back the music of the 1920s. And a pair of young world-class soloists, Warren Vache and Scott Hamilton, were just beginning to emerge and show the jazz world that there was no reason why small-group swing could not be played with enthusiasm, fire, and creativity.

Louis Armstrong   By 1968, Louis Armstrong was having serious health problems. He played some brief but effective trumpet solos on the LPs **Disney Songs the Satchmo Way** (Walt Disney Records 609207) and **Louis Armstrong's Greatest Hits Live** (Brunswick 81008) but was soon advised by doctors to put down his horn and stick exclusively to singing. Satch made a final film appearance, singing one chorus of "Hello Dolly" with Barbara Streisand in the film of the same name (typically stealing the show) but was inactive during much of 1969. There was an outburst of activity in 1970 when what was believed to have been Armstrong's 70th birthday was celebrated both in Los Angeles (the three-CD set **Hello Louis** on GHB 421/422/423 reissues the entire all-star concert including a couple vocals from the star) and the Newport Jazz Festival. And there were a few final attempts to play gigs with the All-Stars but Armstrong's health was quite shaky.

On July 6, 1971, two days after what was thought to have been his 71st birthday (but actually a month before his 70th), Louis Armstrong passed away. Even three decades after his death, he remains the most famous and beloved of all jazz musicians.

Paul and Emile Barnes   A couple of New Orleans clarinetists who were brothers share **Paul Barnes Quartet/Emile Barnes Quartet** (American Music 94). Emile Barnes was not in the best of health in 1961 (when he was 69) but works well with trumpeter Eddie Richardson, pianist Joe James, and drummer Sammy Penn on eight numbers. Paul Barnes was 67 at the time of his 1969 set; he had recorded in the 1920s with Oscar Celestin and played along the way with King Oliver, Jelly Roll Morton, Kid Howard, Celestin a second time (1946–51), Paul Barbarin, and many New Orleans musicians in the 1960s. Paul Barnes (doubling on alto) sounds fine on his quartet set with the smooth Louis Cottrell (clarinet and tenor), pianist Jeanette Kimball, and guitarist Emanuel Sayles. In fact, even with the so-so recording quality, this CD has some of the best playing by both of the Barnes brothers; it is pity that they did not record together at some point.

Barney Bigard   Dixieland may have been out of style in the mainstream jazz world in 1968, but it still flourished in isolated pockets, and rewarding dates were being recorded out of the spotlight. **Bucket's Got a Hole in It** (Delmark 211) matches clarinetist Barney Bigard with Art Hodes in a quartet also including bassist Rail Wilson and drummer Barrett Deems for seven swinging numbers. The six other cuts are more Dixieland-oriented, adding trumpeter Nappy Trottier and veteran trombonist George Brunies to the group. The music is happy and swinging with Bigard and Hodes still in prime form. The clarinetist (who had left Louis Armstrong's All-Stars seven years earlier) was only playing on a part-time basis by then, but his sound remained quite distinctive. He worked with the Legends of Jazz in 1974 and two years later recorded his final album, **Barney Bigard & The Pelican Trio** (Jazzology 228), a safe but pleasing swing set with pianist Duke Burrell and drummer Barry Martyn that is actually more notable for the name of the group and the cover drawing (of three pelicans playing jazz) than it is for the music.

Eubie Blake   One of the happier events of 1968 was the rediscovery of ragtime pioneer Eubie Blake. An important early ragtime pianist and composer for shows (in collaboration with his partner Noble Sissle), Blake had written such songs as "Memories of You," "I'm Just Wild About Harry," and "You're Lucky to Me." **The 86 Years of Eubie Blake** (Columbia 22223) is a two-LP set that surprisingly has not yet been reissued on CD. A perfect retrospective of Blake's career, this two-fer (which has the pianist playing solos and backing his own singing) includes Blake's hits, his "Charleston Rag" (written 69 years earlier), "Troublesome Ivories," a medley from "Shuffle Along," and a wonderful rendition of the "Stars and Stripes Forever." He is also reunited with Sissle on record for the first time since the 1920s.

Eubie Blake became a familiar figure on the jazz scene after the release of his Columbia record, starting his own Eubie Blake Music label in 1971 (unfortunately those releases have also not been reissued on CD), charming audiences with his singing, playing and storytelling, and appearing often on television. He was the last survivor of the pre-jazz era and, as he entered his nineties, he showed no signs of slowing down.

Ruby Braff   In the 1970s, Ruby Braff was gradually recognized as one of jazz's greats, after a long period of neglect. **The Grand Reunion** (Chiaroscuro 117) from 1972 teams the cornetist with pianist Ellis Larkins for a set of duets, their first since 1955. Larkins, a superb ballad player, has long been considered the perfect accompanist. With Braff displaying plenty of fire and feeling on the 14 swing standards, the music (mostly taken at slower tempos) is full of subtlety and quiet swing.

In 1973 Braff formed a quartet that he co-led with guitarist George Barnes that also included Wayne Wright on rhythm guitar and bassist Michael Moore. The group recorded five albums (for Chiaroscuro, Concord, and RCA) before it broke up in 1975 when the fiery co-leaders decided that they could not get along. Although the Concord sets (which have the quartet playing the music of George Gershwin and Rodgers & Hart) and the RCA album (an LP that salutes Fred Astaire) are out of print, one of the Chiaroscuros, **⦿ Live at the New School–The Complete Concert** (Chiaroscuro 126), is available and definitive. Doubled in volume from ten to 20 songs in the CD reissue, the 1974 performance displays the musical magic that flowed between Braff and Barnes and the sly wit that was always part of their performances. It is a pity that the group did not last longer, but it did lead to Ruby Braff finally becoming known as a superb swing stylist.

John Bunch   During the early part of his career, pianist John Bunch was such a fine accompanist that he was often taken for granted. Essentially a swing player who was inspired by Teddy Wilson, Bunch worked with Woody Herman (1956–57), Benny Goodman, Maynard Ferguson, Buddy Rich, the Al Cohn-Zoot Sims Quintet, Gene Krupa (1961–64), and Tony Bennett (1966–72). Starting in 1975 (when he was already 54), Bunch began leading his own record dates. **⦿ John Bunch Plays Kurt Weill** (Chiaroscuro 144) originally consisted of a dozen Weill compositions, including "The Alabama Song," "My Ship," "This Is New," and "Speak Low." For the CD reissue, Bunch recorded five additional Weill songs in 1991. Mixing together standards with complete obscurities, Bunch's solo recital is quite memorable and one of the finest recordings of his career.

Benny Carter   Benny Carter officially returned to jazz in 1976 after a decade spent mostly writing for the studios. His alto playing was as strong as ever (he turned 70 in 1977), and his recordings were as consistent as they had formerly been. At first Carter recorded for Norman Granz's Pablo label in a variety of settings. **The King** (Original Jazz Classics 883) matches him with the Pablo All-Stars (including Milt Jackson, Joe Pass, and Tommy Flanagan) on eight of his originals including "Easy Money" and "Blue Star." **Carter, Gillespie, Inc.** (Original Jazz Classics 682), which teams him with Dizzy Gillespie, is decent but Dizzy was just starting to be past his prime, and the collaboration (though it has its pleasing moments) falls short of being classic. **Wonderland** (Original Jazz Classics 967) has the feel of a jam session although five of the songs are actually obscurities by Carter. The ageless altoist, who showed no signs of decline, is in top form with Eddie "Lockjaw" Davis, Harry "Sweets" Edison, Ray Bryant, Milt Hinton, and Grady Tate.

Dick Cary   Throughout his long career, Dick Cary was known in traditional and swing circles as a top-notch utility player, making contributions behind the scenes. A pianist, a trumpeter, and a soloist on alto horn, Cary first recorded with Joe Marsala in 1942, worked at Nick's during 1942–43, and had short stints with the Casa Loma Orchestra and Brad Gowans. He was in the army during 1944–46 (but was somehow able to keep on recording during this period), was the pianist with the original version of the Louis Armstrong All-Stars in 1947, both played and wrote arrangements for Jimmy Dorsey's Orchestra (1949–50), and worked on and off with Eddie Condon and his associates during the 1950s as a writer, organizer, second trumpeter, and alto horn player. In 1959 he settled in Los Angeles where he continued working as a freelance musician. **The Amazing Dick Cary/California Doings** (Progressive 7125) reissues dates that he led for Riff and Famous Door during 1975 and 1981. Cary only actually plays piano on two of the dozen songs, but he contributed the arrangements and is well featured on trumpet and alto horn. Whether jamming in a septet with trombonist Bob Havens, tenors Dick Hafer and Tommy Newsom, and pianist Ross Tompkins or joining in with Ted Easton's Dutch traditional band (with guests Bob Wilber and Ralph Sutton), these performances have some of Cary's best showcases as a player, performing music that falls between swing and West Coast cool jazz.

Doc Cheatham   Doc Cheatham had one of the most unusual careers of any jazz musician. Self-taught, he was playing trumpet in the early 1920s in the South,

accompanying many top blues singers (including Bessie Smith) in pit bands. He moved to Chicago in 1925, recorded with Ma Rainey (on soprano sax), worked with many show bands, and spent time in Philadelphia, Pennsylvania (playing with Wilbur DeParis during 1927–28), and New York (including with Chick Webb's band). Cheatham toured Europe with Sam Wooding during 1928–30 and worked with Marion Hardy's Alabamians in New York. In 1932 he became a member of Cab Calloway's Orchestra, but because he was first trumpeter, he did not receive any solo space. Cheatham stayed with Calloway for seven years and also had stints with the Teddy Wilson big band, Benny Carter, Fletcher Henderson, Don Redman, Billie Holiday, and the Eddie Heywood Sextet (1943–45). After the swing era ended, Cheatham freelanced for the next 25 years, playing with Latin bands (including Machito and in the late 1950s Herbie Mann), Dixieland groups (Wilbur DeParis's New New Orleans Jazz Band and Eddie Condon), Benny Goodman (1965–66), and his own combos.

Most trumpeters start fading once they hit their sixties, but Cheatham's career was really just beginning as the 1970s began. He developed and smoothed out his phrasing, became a major soloist, displayed an impressive range, and started taking charming vocals. Other than an obscure date in 1950, Cheatham made his recording debut as a leader in 1973 when he was already 68. The double CD **Duets & Solos** (Sackville 5002) has all of the music from a pair of duet albums with veteran pianist Sammy Price recorded in 1976 and 1979 plus a separate solo set by Price (who was 70 himself by the time of the later date). Already in his seventies, Cheatham sounds quite relaxed yet joyful throughout, acting like it was no big deal that he played so well at his age, digging into a variety of standards, and coming up with fresh melodic variations during the delightful program while hitting high notes with ease. Doc Cheatham had a long way to go.

Buck Clayton   Buck Clayton's playing career virtually ended in 1967 because of serious problems with his lips that made it too painful for him to play trumpet. Clayton was depressed for a time, but he gradually returned to jazz as an arranger/composer. His most notable projects during this period were three annual jam session records made for Chiaroscuro during 1974–76, the first two of which have been reissued on CD as **A Buck Clayton Jam**

Session (Chiaroscuro 132) and **A Buck Clayton Jam Session–1975** (Chiaroscuro 143). Although Clayton's trumpet is missed, he contributed four swinging originals to each date, and there are quite a few all-stars featured like in the old days although only Joe Newman, Urbie Green, Buddy Tate and Milt Hinton had been on the sessions of two decades earlier. The 1974 date has Newman, Doc Cheatham, Green, Earl Warren, Zoot Sims, Budd Johnson on tenor, baritonist Joe Temperley, Earl Hines, Hinton, and drummer Gus Johnson. The 1975 set features Newman, trumpeter Money Johnson, trombonists Vic Dickenson and George Masso, Lee Konitz, Warren, Budd Johnson, Tate, Sal Nistico, Tommy Flanagan, Hinton, and Mel Lewis. Although some of the musicians are a bit modern for these swing jams (particularly Konitz, Nistico, and the ageless Earl Hines), they prove to be quite flexible and both dates are successful and often joyous.

George "Kid Sheik" Colar　One of the veterans of the New Orleans revival, trumpeter George "Kid Sheik" Colar was a fixture in the Crescent City for many years. He led his first band in 1925, playing around the city until joining the army in 1943. After he was discharged in 1945, he returned to New Orleans where he worked with George Lewis, various brass bands, and his own groups. Colar first recorded in 1961 (when he was 52), and he was a spirited if erratic trumpeter. He gigged with Captain John Handy, toured England with Barry Martyn (1963), and was based in later years at Preservation Hall. Recorded in 1971, **New Orleans Stompers** (GHB 76) is a set that Colar co-led with veteran trombonist Jim Robinson. They are joined by four members of Big Bill Bissonnette's Easy Riders Jazz Band: Sammy Rimington on clarinet and alto, banjoist Dick Griffith, bassist Dick McCarthy, and trombonist Bissonnette, who switches to drums for the date. Rimington, who sounds close to George Lewis on clarinet and emulates Capt. John Handy on alto, fits in well with the much older veterans. Colar is in pretty good form (even if not always perfectly in tune), and Robinson shows once again that he was one of the great New Orleans ensemble players.

Bill Coleman　The 1973 Montreux Jazz Festival resulted in a recording of trumpeter Bill Coleman (69 at the time) that was a bit unusual because, unlike his other later dates, it was made available in the United States. Coleman, who had moved permanently to France in 1948, still sounds quite fine on **Bill Coleman Meets Guy Lafitte** (Black Lion 760182), jamming swing standards such as "Blue Lou," "Idaho," and "I Know That You Know" in a quintet with tenor saxophonist Guy Lafitte and pianist Marc Hemmeler. Living in Europe turned out be good for Coleman, who was able to work steadily, feel appreciated by audiences, and have a long life, making it to 77.

Eddie Condon and Gene Krupa　After decades of exciting music, the freewheeling world of Eddie Condon gradually came to an end. By 1968 the decades of hard drinking were taking its toll, and Condon only made infrequent public appearances and even fewer recordings. He appeared with pickup groups at the Manassas Jazz Festival for a few years but otherwise mostly just played occasionally in his club Condon's. The 1970 LP **Eddie Condon Jam Session** (Jazzology 100) was probably the rhythm guitarist's final studio session. Wild Bill Davison is the main star, inspiring a septet also including trombonist Ed Hubble, clarinetist Johnny Mince, and pianist Dill Jones. The music is typically freewheeling Dixieland even if two of the five songs ("Time After Time" and "Crazy Rhythm") have arrangements.

Eddie Condon and Gene Krupa made their recording debuts together in 1927, and 45 years later the 1972 recording **Live at the New School** (Chiaroscuro 110) features them closing their careers together. Krupa, whose health had been increasingly erratic since the mid-1960s, made the most significant appearances of his last few years at occasional reunions with Benny Goodman's quartet. For this final recording, Condon and Krupa play with a quintet also including Wild Bill Davison, Kenny Davern on soprano, and Dick Wellstood on piano; Wellstood's left hand makes up for the lack of a bass. The CD reissue adds two songs and some talking by the musicians to the original release. Highlights include "China Boy," "I Want to Be Happy," "That Da Da Strain," and "I Can't Believe That You're in Love with Me." The musicians sound in happy and spirited form.

Sixteen months later, on August 4, 1973, Eddie Condon died at the age of 67 after a very full life. Gene Krupa, who was 64, passed away 73 days later on October 16.

Wild Bill Davison　While many of his contemporaries in the world of Eddie Condon either passed away, declined, or became semiretired in the 1970s, Wild Bill Davison (who turned 70 in 1976) continued to work steadily. His range gradually shrunk during the decade (particularly after the mid-1970s), but his sound never declined, and Davison never tired of adding fire and excitement to Dixieland warhorses. It is estimated that during 1965–75, Davison played with more than 100 bands all over the world, making dozens of records.

In 1968 Davison led **The Jazz Giants** (Sackville 3002), a sextet with trombonist Benny Morton, clarinetist Herbie Hall (the brother of the late Edmond Hall), pianist Claude Hopkins, bassist Arvell Shaw, and drummer Buzzy Drootin. Hall in particular is in fine form on the band's lone record, with highlights including "Struttin' with Some Barbeque," "I Would Do Anything for You," and "I Found a New Baby."

In 1970 Davison appeared at a concert sponsored by the Atlanta Jazz Society that has been released as **Jazz on a Sunday Evening Vol. 1** (Jazzology 37) and **Vol. 2** (Jazzology 38). Wild Bill is heard performing with fine local players including trombonist Wray Thomas, clarinetist Herman Foretich, and cornetist Ernie Carson who is heard sticking to piano on the first set (other than on "Royal Garden Blues"), but making the group a two-cornet ensemble on most of the second volume. Highlights of the Dixieland date include "Avalon," "You Took Advantage of Me," "Jazz Me Blues," and "Fidgety Feet." **Lady of the Evening** (Jazzology 141) is a ballad-oriented set on which Davison plays melodically while backed by a tasteful swing rhythm section that includes pianist John Eaton. Recorded in 1973, **Just a Gig** (Jazzology 191) is a loose jam session from the 1973 Manassas Jazz Festival, with a couple good-time vocals from concert producer "Fat Cat" Johnson McRee and some heated solos by Davison and clarinetist Tom Gwaltney on the usual Dixieland tunes.

Davison recorded often in Europe during 1974–77, particularly during his annual visits to Copenhagen. **But Beautiful** (Storyville 8233) mostly has the cornetist playing ballads, but some are taken at faster than usual tempos. Davison is showcased with either a rhythm section or a medium-sized group with a sax section, sounding particularly warm on "You Took Advantage of Me," "But Beautiful," "I'm Confessin'," and "Blue Turning Gray Over You." Some of Wild Bill's most exciting playing from the era was when he sat in with Papa Bue Jensen's Viking Jazz Band. **Wild Bill in Denmark Vol. 1** (Storyville 5523) and **Vol. 2** (Storyville 5524) have Davison supported by a stimulating four-piece rhythm section,

clarinetist Joren Svare, trombonist Jensen (who sometimes recalls Kid Ory), and guest tenor Bent Jaedig. Both of these sets are full of stirring moments with **Vol. 1** highlighted by a lengthy "Christopher Columbus," "Runnin' Wild," a dramatic "When It's Sleepy Time Down South," and an emotional version of "Memories of You" while **Vol. 2** has "Our Monday Date," "Fidgety Feet," and "White Cliffs of Dover" among the gems.

But the Wild Bill Davison CD to get first from this era is ◗ **Showcase** (Jazzology 083). Actually this disc has two unrelated but rewarding sessions, starting with a fine 1947 ballad set by Wild Bill with trombonist Jimmy Archey, Garvin Bushell on clarinet and (on "Yesterdays") bassoon, Ralph Sutton, bassist Sid Weiss, and drummer Morey Feld. The bulk of the CD is Davison's 1976 matchup with the Classic Jazz Collegium Orchestra, a high-quality ten-member Czechoslovakian group. Because the arrangements (including a classic version of "Sunday") make the band sound like it is from the 1920s, this set allows one to hear how Davison might have sounded if he had been in his prime during that decade instead of five decades later.

Harry "Sweets" Edison   Unlike many of the swing era veterans, trumpeter Harry "Sweets" Edison was rarely out of work even during the 1960s. His distinctive and witty sound kept him busy in the studios, on jazz dates, and in guest appearances with Count Basie. By the mid-1970s, Edison was often teaming up with Eddie "Lockjaw" Davis, another Basie veteran who could be identified in two notes. Recorded in 1976, **Edison's Lights** (Original Jazz Classics 804) is a particularly strong collaboration. Edison contributed four of the eight selections (the songs are familiar), but the competitive Lockjaw gets in his fiery licks and is far from overshadowed. While Dolo Coker is on half of the program, Count Basie drops by to sit in on the other four songs. **Harry "Sweets" Edison and Eddie "Lockjaw" Davis Vol. 1** (Storyville 4004) and **Vol. 2** (Storyville 4025) both contain plenty of fireworks. Joined by Kenny Drew, bassist Hugo Rasmussen, and drummer Svend Erik Norregaard (with guest spots for trombonist John Darville), Sweets and Lockjaw perform such exciting jams as (from **Vol. 1**) "Lullaby for Dancers," "Lester Leaps In," "Spotlite," "Blues Walk," and (on **Vol. 2**) "Robbins' Nest," "Candy," and "There Is No Greater Love."

Roy Eldridge   Roy Eldridge only led one record date during 1967–74, **The Nifty Cat** (New World 349). The trumpeter is teamed with such mainstream veterans as Budd Johnson (tenor and soprano), trombonist Benny Morton, Nat Pierce, bassist Tommy Bryant, and drummer Oliver Jackson. Eldridge contributed all six jump tunes and sounds in fine form.

He spent most of the 1970s leading the house band at Nick's and recording both as a leader and a sideman for Norman Granz's Pablo label. Eldridge's range had shrunk and his sound was a bit shaky at time, but he never lost his determination or competitive spirit. In 1975 Eldridge led three record dates for Pablo. **Little Jazz & the Jimmy Ryan All-Stars** (Original Jazz Classics 1058) has Eldridge playing with his club band of the period, a sextet with Joe Muranyi on clarinet and soprano, trombonist Bobby Pratt, pianist Dick Katz, bassist Major Holley, and drummer Eddie Locke. The music falls between swing and Dixieland, with Eldridge performing such numbers as "Between the Devil and the Deep Blue Sea," "All of Me," "Beale Street Blues," and "Bourbon Street Parade." Eldridge is quite joyful and exuberant throughout the fun date. In contrast, **Jazz Maturity** (Original Jazz Classics 807) is a disappointment. The combination of Eldridge and Dizzy Gillespie should have resulted in classic music (like their encounter 21 years earlier) but both trumpeters were fading by 1975, and Oscar Peterson easily takes solo honors.

It is better to get **Happy Time** (Original Jazz Classics 628). Eldridge actually spends as much time singing as playing during the ten standards, but his concise solos have their explosive moments. Roy is assisted by Peterson, Joe Pass, Ray Brown, and Eddie Locke on such songs as "Sweethearts on Parade," "Makin' Whoopee," "I Want a Little Girl," and a remake of "Let Me Off Uptown." 1976's **What It's All About** (Original Jazz Classics 853) features the trumpeter still pushing himself on three originals and two obscurities. The lineup of veteran greats is particularly strong with altoist Norris Turney, Budd Johnson on tenor, and (on half of the set) Milt Jackson.

Don Ewell   One of the top surviving stride pianists of the 1970s, Don Ewell had opportunities to record during this period with Chiaroscuro (three high-quality LPs), Jazzology, and Fat Cat Jazz. Few of his dates from the era have been reissued on CD, but **Live at the 100 Club** (Solo Art 89) is available. Recorded from February 24, 1971, and mostly originally put out by the British 77 label, this program has Ewell mixing together elements of Jelly

Roll Morton, Fats Waller, and Joe Sullivan in his own style. His set of piano solos includes spirited versions of such numbers as "If Dreams Come True," "Handful of Keys," "Aunt Hagar's Blues," and "Old Fashioned Love."

Firehouse Five Plus Two   In 1969 both the Firehouse Five Plus Two and the Good Time Jazz label celebrated their twentieth anniversary. But as it turned out, that was the final active year for both. **Twenty Years Later** (Good Time Jazz 10054) is the last recording by the Firehouse Five. There are two numbers from 1966 ("Mame" and "Winchester Cathedral") along with the later performances. Rather than emphasizing Dixieland warhorses, the group mostly plays more recent offbeat material, including such pop/jazz hits as "Mame," "Hello Dolly," "Midnight in Moscow," and "Stranger on the Shore." For the only time, the front line had two trumpets (Danny Alguire and the band's former tuba player Don Kinch) in addition to leader Ward Kimball on trombone and George Probert on soprano, but the band's cheerful and witty sound was unchanged from 1949.

Bud Freeman   Veteran tenor saxophonist was a member of the World's Greatest Jazz Band during 1968–71, a perfect setting for his playing. He only led one album during 1968–73, a gem called **The Complete Bud Freeman** (Monmouth-Evergreen 7022) that is long overdue to be reissued on CD. For the set, Freeman is teamed with the World's Greatest Jazz Band's rhythm section (Ralph Sutton, Bob Haggart, and Gus Johnson) with Bob Wilber making the group a quintet on half of the swinging selections. Another high-quality LP is 1974's **The Joy of Sax** (Chiaroscuro 135), a wonderful trio date with Jess Stacy and drummer Cliff Leeman. Fortunately, **Superbud** (Jazzology 185) is available to show how strong Freeman was still sounding in 1974 when he was 68. The bulk of the CD is a reissue of an LP put out by the British 77 label featuring Freeman with pianist Keith Ingham, bassist Pete Chapman, and drummer Johnny Armitage. Highlights include "Please," "'S Wonderful," "You Took Advantage of Me," and "Tea for Two." Although a piano solo by Ingham has been left off the release, he recorded six additional solos in 1992 of rarely performed Freeman compositions (including "After Awhile," "Crazeology," and "Tillie's Downtown Now"), and those add to the value of this enjoyable set.

Paul Gonsalves   One of Duke Ellington's most loyal sidemen, Paul Gonsalves played with Ellington for 24 years, from 1950 up until virtually the end in 1974. During his last few years, the hard-charging tenor saxophonist had several opportunities to lead his own record dates away from Ellington. **Encuentro** (Fresh Sound 72) from 1968 reissues an LP from the long-deceased Catalyst label, one of Gonsalves's best albums as a leader. Recorded in Argentina with a local rhythm section led by pianist Enrique Villegas and trumpeter Willie Cook, this superior mainstream swing set include a lengthy "Perdido," "St. Louis Blues," and "Just Friends." **Just a-Sittin' and a-Rockin'** (Black Lion 760148) emphasizes slower tempos and relaxed material although it also includes a few romps, including "Stompy Jones." Gonsalves is joined by former Ellington member Ray Nance (on trumpet, violin, and vocals) and, for half of the CD, by altoist Norris Turney. **Paul Gonsalves Meets Earl Hines** (Black Lion 760177) is mostly from 1970 with Gonsalves teamed with Earl Hines, bassist Al Hall, and Jo Jones. The quartet plays five standards including three by Ellington, and plenty of fireworks occur between Gonsalves and the unpredictable pianist. Also on this set is a 1972 solo piano version of "Blue Sands" from Hines. **Mexican Bandit Meets Pittsburgh Pirate** (Original Jazz Classics 751) from 1973 has Gonsalves and Roy Eldridge co-leading a quintet (with pianist Cliff Smalls, Sam Jones, and Eddie Locke), but Gonsalves sounds streaky in spots and a bit past his prime. The always-combative Eldridge is in pretty good shape for this period, particularly on "5400 North" and "C Jam Blues."

Paul Gonsalves was active only on an occasional basis in 1973, and his health had declined. He passed away ten days before Duke Ellington, on May 14, 1974, at the age of 53.

Benny Goodman   Even though the swing era was now more than 20 years in the past, Benny Goodman remained a household name and one of the most famous figures in jazz. He only worked when he wanted to, and although he often used younger players, there were no attempts by BG to modernize either his playing or his repertoire.

Goodman, who did not record at all in 1968, made only a few worthwhile recordings during this era. The double LP **Benny Goodman Today** (London 21) from 1970, which was recorded with a British big band (plus Bucky Pizzarelli) in Stockholm, Sweden, shows that Goodman was still playing his same old hits from the 1930s. **On Stage** (London 44172/73), another double LP that has not been reissued, is much better because it features Goodman happily jamming in a sextet with Zoot Sims, vibraphonist Peter Appleyard, and Pizzarelli, showing that he could still be inspired by strong musicians.

In 1975 Benny Goodman was featured on a television special that paid tribute to producer John Hammond. The high point of the show was when George Benson sat in with Goodman on "Seven Come Eleven," and it was a matter of lightning striking twice. Just as Charlie Christian had amazed BG back in 1939 when they jammed "Rose Room," Benson's choruses brought out the best in the clarinetist. The LP **Seven Come Eleven** (Columbia 38265) has three numbers (including the title cut) by the Goodman septet with Benson. In addition, the 66-year-old clarinetist performs four songs (including unfortunately "Send in the Clowns") with a quintet that includes Bucky Pizzarelli, adds trombonist Al Grey to a similar group for "Sweet Lorraine," and reunites him with Joe Venuti (who he had last recorded with in 1933) for spirited versions of "Slipped Disc" and "Limehouse Blues." This album is one of many that are sitting neglected in Sony/Columbia's vaults.

Bobby Hackett   Cornetist Bobby Hackett's last period was most notable for the quintet that he co-led with trombonist Vic Dickenson. Hackett and Dickenson had very complementary styles. They were able to harmonize quickly and spontaneously with each other, sounded relaxed and quiet even when playing rapid lines, and always displayed sly senses of humor along with distinctive sounds. Fortunately, they were well documented during 1968–70. Currently available are the three CDs **Live at the Roosevelt Grill Vols. 1–3** (Chiaroscuro 105, 138 and 161), which have the two horns joined by Dave McKenna, bassist Jack Lesberg, and drummer Cliff Leeman. The music consists mostly of swing and traditional standards (**Vol. 3** has fresh versions of Dixieland warhorses). Each of the sets is easily recommended for Hackett and Dickenson brought out the best in each other. Also worth searching for are the Hackett-Dickenson LPs **This Is My Bag** (Project 3 5034), **Melody Is a Must** (Phontastic 7571), **Live at**

the Roosevelt Grill Vol. 2 (Phontastic 7572), and **Live from Manassas** (Jazzology 76).

After the group with Dickenson ended, Hackett continued freelancing and making guest appearances. Recorded in 1973, **What a Wonderful World** (Sony 40234) has four vocals by pop singer Teresa Brewer (producer/husband Bob Thiele was trying to groom her to be a jazz singer, with mixed results) but fine spots for Hackett, Dickenson, and clarinetist Johnny Mince with three different units ranging from seven to 15 pieces. Other than a couple slightly later bootleg albums, Bobby Hackett's last recording as a leader was **Strike up the Band** (Flying Dutchman 0829), a 1974 LP that served as a perfect closer to his career. Featured in a sextet with Zoot Sims and Buck Pizzarelli, Hackett plays a variety of favorite songs, a few basic originals, an uptempo "Strike up the Band," and a revisit to "Embraceable You," 34 years after recording his famous solo on that standard. Despite his declining health, Bobby Hackett plays as beautifully as always.

Captain John Handy   During 1968–70 Capt. John Handy (who was in his late sixties) was quite active, consistently demonstrating how well his jump style alto fit in New Orleans jazz settings. **Television Airshots** (Jazz Crusade 3008) contains the soundtracks from two television appearances dating from 1968 and 1970; sadly, the films are presumed lost. Handy shows throughout these dates that he could easily outswing the competition. The first seven selections showcase him in a septet with trumpeter Punch Miller (who was obviously past his prime by then) and Dick Wellstood. The band really rocks on "Joe Avery's Piece," "Capt's Boogie Woogie," and "Exactly Like You." The second group is weakened a bit by trumpeter Kid Sheik Cola, whose sincere but out-of-tune whinnying tone is a liability, but the rhythm section really pushes the band hard in exciting fashion.

Six months after the second broadcast, Capt. John Handy passed away at the age of 70.

Jake Hanna   Jake Hanna has always been a valuable drummer, and although his main interest is in mainstream swing, he fares quite well in more modern settings and with big bands, too. Hanna played locally in his native Boston before having stints with Toshiko Akiyoshi (1957), Maynard Ferguson (1958), Marian McPartland (1959–61), and the Woody Herman Orchestra (1962–64).

Hanna worked as a studio musician and appeared in a countless number of settings in the 1960s and '70s. In 1975 he co-led a group with trombonist Carl Fontana at the Concord Jazz Festival (the Hanna/Fontana Band). **Live at Concord** (Concord Jazz 4011) has their all-star septet, which also includes Bill Berry, Plas Johnson, Dave McKenna, Herb Ellis, and bassist Herb Mickman. The group mostly plays swing era standards, and highlights include Johnson's ballad feature on "Old Folks," "Take the 'A' Train," and Hanna's classic brushwork on "I Found a New Baby."

In 1976 Hanna recorded a pair of out-of-print LPs at the head of two other small groups. **Kansas City Express** (Concord Jazz 22) features a quintet with Berry, Richie Kamuca, Nat Pierce, and Monty Budwig. In addition to such instrumentals as "Robbins' Nest," "It's Sand, Man," and "Castle Rock," there are four rare late-period vocals by the still viable Mary Ann McCall, who had sung with Woody Herman's orchestra more than 30 years earlier. **Jake Takes Manhattan** (Concord Jazz 35) teams the drummer with trumpeter Danny Stiles, Carmen Leggio on alto and tenor, John Bunch, and bassist Michael Moore. They perform nine swing standards including "Northwest Passage," "Lester Leaps In," "Sultry Serenade," and "Them There Eyes."

This trio of Jake Hanna releases shows that small-group swing was still very much alive (if largely overlooked) in the mid-1970s.

Coleman Hawkins   Coleman Hawkins was in his playing prime during 1923–65 when he virtually introduced the tenor sax to jazz, became its first major voice, and continually modernized his style. No other musician recorded with both Mamie Smith and Abbey Lincoln, not to mention Fletcher Henderson, Fats Navarro, Thelonious Monk, and Eric Dolphy. But for unknown reasons, Hawkins's mental health began to decline in the summer of 1965, and from then on it was a steep downward descent. Just like Lester Young during the second half of the 1950s, during his last few years Hawkins drank too much, ate very little, and had an increasingly shabby appearance. In general, his playing is not worth hearing after mid-1965, with the following year's Pablo album **Sirius** being a particular low point; one can hear him constantly gasping for air. Surprisingly Hawkins rallied for a "Jazz at the Philharmonic" reunion concert in March 1969, but he passed away two months later at the age of 64.

Earl Hines After Earl Hines made a major impact with his two concerts at New York's Little Theatre in 1964, his career underwent a renaissance. Still a modern soloist (particularly rhythmically where he took wild chances by often suspending time), Hines continued to delight audiences on a nightly basis in his classic but unpredictable style. He recorded prolifically during 1968–76 with 15 albums in 1974 alone. He can be heard on releases put out by MCA, Black & Blue, Master Jazz, Delmark, Prestige, EPM, Chiaroscuro, MPS, America, Black Lion, Audiophile, Quicksilver, Denon, Swaggie, Carosello, Fairmont, French RCA, Halcyon, Sonet, and Improv. Not bad for a pianist who turned 73 in 1976!

Based in San Francisco, Earl Hines by the mid-1970s performed regularly with a quartet also including Rudy Rutherford on reeds and singer Marva Josie. The highlights of his live performances were when he played unaccompanied solos, challenging himself constantly to come up with fresh ideas. He had outlived most of his contemporaries and, most importantly, was still playing with great creativity within his timeless style.

With so much to choose from, here are a few of the choicest items, all of them solo albums: **Earl Hines at Home** (Delmark 212) has Hines performing four of his lesser-known compositions ("Love at Night Is out of Sight," "Minor Nothing," "Moon Mare," and "The Cannery Walk") plus two standards and a vocal version of "It Happens to Be Me." **The Quintessential Recording Session** (Chiaroscuro 101) is an LP long overdue to be reissued on CD, featuring Hines performing new versions of the eight solo numbers that he had recorded at the beginning of his career 42 years earlier, including "My Monday Date," "Chimes in Blue," and "Chicago High Life." The double CD ◉ **Four Jazz Giants** (Solo Art 111/112) has all of the music recorded by Hines during a two-day period in 1971 when he recorded full-length solo tributes to W.C. Handy, Hoagy Carmichael, and Louis Armstrong (who had passed away two weeks earlier). These three albums were each gems, so it is a delight to have them all available together. The inventive performances include a ten-minute version of "Stardust," "Ole Buttermilk Sky," "Struttin' with Some Barbecue," "Someday You'll Be Sorry," "St. Louis Blues," "Ole Miss," and "Beale Street Blues." Also in the tribute category are four former LPs that have been released as the double-CD **Earl Hines Plays Duke Ellington** (New World 361) and the disc **Earl Hines Plays Duke Ellington**

Vol. 2 (New World 80532). In addition to the expected standards, Hines explores some of Duke Ellington's superior obscurities and consistently comes up with fresh ideas.

Even with all of these major recordings ◉ **Live at the New School** (Chiaroscuro 157) may be the most exciting of Hines's later recordings. Heard at the absolute peak of his powers, Hines is quite daring throughout this performance with his version of "I've Got the World on a String" being somewhat breathtaking and a six-song Fats Waller medley also standing out. Although he may not have been winning critics polls, Earl Hines in the mid-1970s was still one of jazz's greatest pianists, as he had been a half-century earlier.

Art Hodes The veteran pianist, who turned 64 in 1968, founds himself in increasingly greater demand in the 1970s. Art Hodes (who was based in Chicago) mostly continued sticking to the blues, vintage jazz standards, and Dixieland music that he enjoyed most. Recorded in 1968, **Hodes' Art** (Delmark 213) has three numbers with a trio, a version of "Struttin' with Some Barbeque" that features clarinetist Volly De Faut (who had not recorded much since the 1920s), "When My Sugar Walks Down the Street" (with DeFaut, George Brunies, and trumpeter Nappy Trottier), and six relaxed selections in a trio with clarinetist Raymond Burke (in excellent form) and veteran bassist Pops Foster. Recorded in 1972, **Up in Volly's Room** (Delmark 217) has particularly strong playing by DeFaut on seven numbers with Hodes, bassist Truck Parham, and Barrett Deems. There are also four Hodes-Parham duets and versions of "Ja Da" and "Panama Rag" that add Trottier and Brunies to the full group. Hodes, who is really rollicking on the more uptempo material, adds a strong blues sensibility to each of the songs. Also quite enjoyable is the 1970 LP **Selections from the Gutter** (Storyville 4057), which has Hodes playing unaccompanied solos and duets with bassist Jens Solund.

Dick Hyman A brilliant pianist who is capable of playing credibly in just about any jazz style, Dick Hyman largely settled on early jazz when he began to really emerge as a significant soloist in 1973. He recorded as a piano soloist as early as 1950, worked with Red Norvo (1949–50) and Benny Goodman (1950), and spent much of the 1950s and '60s as a studio musician. Along the way, he appeared on film with Charlie

Parker and Dizzy Gillespie (1952's *Hot House*), made honky tonk piano albums under pseudonyms, recorded on organ and early synthesizers, was Arthur Godfrey's music director (1959–62), and even performed some rock and free jazz. In the 1970s Hyman came into his own, working with the New York Jazz Repertory Company (recording a well-conceived Louis Armstrong tribute album for Atlantic in 1974, **Satchmo Remembered**), forming the Perfect Jazz Repertory Quintet in 1976, and writing soundtracks for Woody Allen films.

⊙ Jelly and James (Columbia 52552) has all of the music (except one song) from Dick Hyman's Jelly Roll Morton and James P. Johnson tribute albums. Dating from 1973 and 1975, these performances constantly vary the instrumentation, ranging from a piano solo and duets to a big band. Hyman utilizes such musicians on the Morton date as Kenny Davern, Joe Venuti, trumpeter Pee Wee Erwin, and Vic Dickenson while the James P. Johnson project (which on various tracks uses a theater orchestra or a jazz band) is highlighted by three Hyman duets (one on pipe organ) with Ruby Braff. Among the songs that are revived on these classic revivals are "Fingerbuster," "King Porter Stomp," "Black Bottom Stomp," "Carolina Shout," and "You've Got to Be Modernistic." All of the musicians involved really understand early jazz, and the results are sensitive, swinging, and loving.

Budd Johnson Tenor saxophonist Budd Johnson (who had also mastered the soprano) participated in occasional reunions with Earl Hines starting in 1964. In 1969 he put together the JPJ Quartet. **The JPJ Quartet** (Storyville 8235) features Johnson, pianist Dill Jones, bassist Bill Pemberton, and drummer Oliver Jackson on six numbers from 1969 plus their performance (formerly on a Master Jazz LP) from the 1971 Montreux Jazz Festival. The musicians play small-group swing with melodic creativity. Highlights include Johnson's "Tag Along," "Honeysuckle Rose" (a feature for the pianist), "Lester Leaps In," and an exciting rendition of "The Best Things in Life Are Free." But despite recording a couple additional albums for Master Jazz, the JPJ Quartet was both ahead (predating the comeback of mainstream swing) and behind (stylistically) the times, breaking up in 1975.

Jo Jones Jo Jones turned 65 in 1976, but he never mellowed with age, offering sharp opinions on many aspects of the jazz world. He only worked on a part-time basis in the 1970s but did record an LP of unaccompanied solos called **The Drums** (Jazz Odyssey 008) for a French label in 1973 and in 1976 led **The Main Man** (Original Jazz Classics 869). For the latter, Jones jams on four swing standards and a couple of basic originals with Harry "Sweets" Edison, Roy Eldridge, Vic Dickenson, Eddie "Lockjaw" Davis, Tommy Flanagan, Freddie Green, and Sam Jones. The music is very much in the Count Basie style, with concise but meaningful solos by all of the principals. The veteran musicians were all sounding older, but they still had a lot to offer listeners.

Jonah Jones Jonah Jones continued with his popular quartet format even after his string of Capitol recordings ended in 1963. He made similar sessions for Decca during 1965–68 and then recorded a couple sets of current pop tunes for Motown during 1968–69. By then his formula had run its course, but the trumpeter still was well known enough to work as often as he liked. In 1972 he recorded the last album from his prime, **Back on the Street** (Chiaroscuro 118), a sextet set with Earl Hines and Buddy Tate. Although one can hear a bit of slickness in Jones's playing (which could be overly mannered), the presence of Tate and particularly the adventurous Hines inspires the trumpeter to come up with creative swing solos. The music falls between Dixieland and swing with an emphasis on familiar standards including "Rose Room," "Pennies from Heaven," and "Bill Bailey."

Louis Jordan Louis Jordan's series of hits had stopped altogether by the mid-1950s, but he continued playing, often as a nostalgia act. In 1973 he made his final recording, **I Believe in Music** (Evidence 26006), 15 months before his death. Jordan still played and sang quite well as he shows on a few remakes of past hits (such as "Caldonia," "Is You Is or Is You Ain't My Baby," "Saturday Night Fish Fry," and "I'm Gonna Move to the Outskirts of Town") and some newer jump material. The altoist is teamed with tenor man Irv Cox and a rhythm section led by pianist Duke Burrell for a spirited effort that concluded Louis Jordan's legendary career on a high level.

Dave McKenna Although the swing/Dixieland world of the early 1970s was dominated by aging veterans in their final years, there were a few younger players who were helping to keep the music alive. Pianist Dave McKenna, who turned 46 in 1976, was not exactly a beginner, but he was just beginning to be noticed. He had worked decades earlier with Boots Mussulli (1947), Charlie Ventura (1949), and Woody Herman's Third Herd (1950–51) before spending two years in the military. After his discharge, McKenna had a second stint with Ventura (1953–54), played as a soloist at piano bars in Massachusetts, and performed with such mainstream players as Gene Krupa, Stan Getz, Zoot Sims, Al Cohn, Eddie Condon, and Bobby Hackett. His hard-driving bass lines became a trademark, as did his vast repertoire of songs from the 1920s, '30s, and '40s.

McKenna led record dates for ABC-Paramount (1956), Epic (1958), Bethlehem (a two-piano date shared with Hall Overton in 1960), and Realm (1963), but these gained little attention. There was also an obscure set for Marian McPartland's Halcyon label in 1973; however, it was McKenna's two albums for Hank O'Neal's Chiaroscuro label in 1973–74 that gained him some long overdue recognition. **Solo Piano** (Chiaroscuro 119), other than a couple of attempts at uplifting current material ("Norwegian Wood" and "My Cherie Amour"), is a superior effort with McKenna displaying his infectious swing style on a variety of veteran tunes including a three-part "Have You Met Miss Jones Sequence." **Featuring Zoot Sims** (Chiaroscuro 136) features McKenna, bassist Major Holley, drummer Ray Mosca, and the great Zoot Sims, who is heard on tenor and soprano. Four previously unreleased numbers join the original nine songs, and plenty of sparks fly. Highlights include "Limehouse Blues," "Deed I Do," "Linger Awhile," and two versions of "I Cover the Waterfront."

Jimmy McPartland   Jimmy McPartland, who would turn 70 in 1977, was still active now and then during the first half of the 1970s. Among his last significant recordings were a pair of sets recorded with his wife, the much more modern pianist Marian McPartland, for her Halcyon label during 1972–73. **A Sentimental Journey** (The Jazz Alliance 10025) reissues 12 of the 14 selections. Joined by front lines that feature either Vic Dickenson and Buddy Tate or trombonist Hank Berger and clarinetist Jack Maheu, Jimmy McPartland (nearly 50 years after succeeding Bix Beiderbecke with the Wolverines) performs Dixieland and swing standards with enthusiasm and power, taking an occasional vocal and clearly having a great time. Marian McPartland adjusts her style a little to fit in securely on such numbers as "Royal Garden Blues," "Dinah," and "Wolverine Blues."

Jay McShann and Claude Williams   A fixture in Kansas City, Missouri, for decades, Jay McShann did not appear on records at all during 1952–65 with the exception of a handful of numbers cut for Vee-Jay in 1955–56. In 1966 he recorded an album for Capitol that for the first time had him taking a few vocals. In 1969

TIMELINE 1975

Miles Davis drops out of music. • The Brecker Brothers are formed. • Wayne Henderson leaves the Crusaders. • Ornette Coleman begins leading his electric free funk group, Prime Time. • Cannonball Adderley dies. • Jimmy, Percy and Tootie Heath form the Heath Brothers Band. • Art Pepper begins his successful comeback. • Benny Goodman and George Benson play an exciting version of "Seven Come Eleven" together on a John Hammond television tribute. • Muhal Richard Abrams begins recording regularly for the Black Saint label, an association that would last for more than 20 years. • Pianist Claude Bolling and classical flutist Jean-Pierre Rampal team up for the popular recording **Suite for Flute and Jazz Piano Trio**. • The Monty Alexander Trio features bassist John Clayton and drummer Jeff Hamilton. • Avant-garde pianist Borah Bergman records his first solo album. • The Dirty Dozen Brass Band is formed in New Orleans, Louisiana. • Poncho Sanchez joins Cal Tjader's band. • Sheila Jordan records her second album as a leader, 13 years after her first. • Pianist Lyle Mays is a member of Woody Herman's Orchestra. • British swing era trumpeter/vocalist Nat Gonella records three albums, his final recordings. • The jazz/R&B band Pieces of a Dream is formed in Philadelphia by a group of teenage musicians. • Singer Al Jarreau records his second album, **We Got By**, a decade after his first. • Butch Miles becomes the drummer with the Count Basie Orchestra. • Flip Phillips returns to full time music after being semiretired for 15 years. • The Swiss avant-garde Hat Hut jazz label is started, initially to document the music of the adventurous Joe McPhee. • John Klemmer has a hit with "Touch." • Air is formed.

McShann was finally officially rediscovered, and although often primarily known as Charlie Parker's former boss, he proved to still be a viable blues-swing pianist and an effective blues vocalist in his own right. McShann recorded a couple LPs for the French Black & Blue label in 1969 and in 1972 came out with **Going to Kansas City** (New World 358). Heard in prime form, McShann teams up with a couple of major swing tenors (Buddy Tate, who doubles on clarinet, and Julian Dash), bassist Gene Ramey, and drummer Gus Johnson. McShann plays a few forgotten numbers from his 1940s big band (including "Say Forward, I'll March" and "Four Day Rider"), takes two vocals, and swings a few originals and tunes associated with Count Basie.

Claude Williams, who was born in 1908, has had a long career. In fact, in 2002 after Lionel Hampton's death, Williams was the last active jazz musician left who had recorded before 1930. A violinist who doubled on guitar in his earlier years, Williams was with Andy Kirk's 12 Clouds of Joys (with whom he recorded in 1929–30), settled in Kansas City, Missouri, and played rhythm guitar and occasional violin with the Count Basie Orchestra in 1936, appearing on the Basie band's first recordings. Unfortunately, producer John Hammond never cared for jazz violinists and that led to Williams being replaced by Freddie Green. After returning to Kansas City, Williams worked in obscurity for decades. In 1972 he began working occasionally with Jay McShann, and at 64 he finally began to be considered one of the top surviving swing violinists. Recorded in 1976, **Call for the Fiddler** (Steeple Chase 31051), which has him jamming such songs as "How High the Moon," "Get Happy," and "Honeysuckle Rose" with Horace Parlan in a quartet, is an excellent example of the talents of Claude Williams.

Williams and McShann team up on the pianist's ● **Man from Muskogee** (Sackville 3005) from 1972. The quartet date with bassist Don Thompson and drummer Paul Gunther has four McShann vocals and spirited versions of such songs as "After You've Gone," "Yardbird Suite," "Hootie Blues," and "Jumpin' at the Woodside." Also worth exploring is **Vine Street Boogie** (Black Lion 760187), McShann's excellent solo performance from the 1974 Montreux Jazz Festival on which he explores six mostly blues-based originals and a couple Duke Ellington songs.

Albert Nicholas   A resident of France since 1953, New Orleans clarinetist Albert Nicholas was in excellent form up until shortly before his 1973 death. **Baden 1969** (Sackville 2045), which was released for the first time in 1997, features Nicholas as the only horn in a quartet with pianist Henri Chaix at a Swiss concert. Nicholas, who always had his own sound, shows that he still had fresh statements to make on such warhorses as "Rosetta," "Please Don't Talk About Me When I'm Gone," "Rose Room," and "I Found a New Baby."

Bucky Pizzarelli   Long considered one of the most tasteful of guitarists, Bucky Pizzarelli is a throwback to the days of Carl Kress and Dick McDonough without being a copy of either. A master of the seven-string guitar who was largely self-taught, Pizzarelli had a couple stints with Vaughan Monroe's orchestra in the 1940s before and after his military service. He spent most of the 1950s and 1960s working in the studios and also played with Benny Goodman now and then. He began to emerge much more in the jazz world in the 1970s when he co-led a duo with George Barnes and played with Zoot Sims, Bud Freeman, and Stephane Grappelli.

During 1972–73 Pizz (who had only previously led an obscure date for Savoy in 1960) recorded two albums as a leader, both LPs for the soon-defunct Monmouth Evergreen label. **Green Guitar Blues** (Monmouth Evergreen 7047) is a trio set with bassist George Duvivier and drummer Don Lamond. Pizzarelli performs swing standards, two originals, a few medleys, and a couple of classical numbers in lightly swinging and melodic fashion. In addition, there is a version of the Dick McDonough-Carl Kress piece "Chicken a la Swing" that Bucky plays as a guitar duet with his 14-year-old daughter Mary Pizzarelli. **Plays Bix Beiderbecke Arrangements by Bill Challis** (Monmouth Evergreen 7066) is a near classic long overdue to be reissued on CD. Pizzarelli and fellow guitarists Artie Ryerson, Barry Galbraith, Allen Hanlon, and Howie Collins (with Tony Mottola subbing on a few numbers) perform Bill Challis's arrangements of Bix Beiderbecke's "Davenport Blues," "Candlelights," "Flashes," "In the Dark," and "In a Mist." Challis, who wrote for Jean Goldkette and Paul Whiteman in the 1920s, was the perfect person for the job, and his exquisite arrangements show off the beauty of the guitarists' tones. The remainder of this memorable LP has Pizzarelli and his daughter Mary (who was now 16) performing guitar duets of obscure 1930s pieces by either Carl Kress (including the three-part "After Thoughts") or the team of Kress and Dick McDonough. Mary Pizzarelli never pursued music as a career, but her younger brother John Pizzarelli was already starting to learn guitar and be inspired by his father.

Gunther Schuller   Gunther Schuller has certainly had a diverse career. In addition to being an educator, a composer, and an author, Schuller played French horn on the 1950 session of Miles Davis's "Birth of the Cool" Nonet, founded the Jazz and Classical Music Society with John Lewis in 1955, came up with the term "Third Stream" in 1957 to describe a mixture of jazz with classical music, and in 1967 became the president of the New England Conservatory of Music where he soon established a jazz department. Schuller also founded the New England Ragtime Ensemble, performing ragtime a few years before *The Sting* brought the nearly extinct back.

❶ **The Art of Scott Joplin** (GM 3030) features Schuller conducting the New England Ragtime Ensemble through a dozen Scott Joplin pieces that had been orchestrated 70 years earlier for the legendary Red Back Book. With a group consisting of trumpet, trombone, flute/piccolo, clarinet, tuba, piano, bass, drums, and a string quartet with occasional guests on oboe, clarinet, bassoon, and French horn, Schuller presents colorful versions of such numbers as "Elite Syncopations," "Wall Street Rag," "Solace," "Euphonic Sounds," and "Gladiolus Rag," showing that ragtime was not just solo piano music.

Soprano Summit   Among the most exciting swing/Dixieland/classic jazz bands to be formed in the early 1970s was Soprano Summit. At Dick Gibson's annual Colorado Jazz Party in 1972, Bob Wilber and Kenny Davern were teamed together, and they enjoyed the music they created so much that they formed a group that featured them on both soprano sax and clarinet. The original version of the group, which also had Dick Hyman, Buck Pizzarelli, George Duvivier, and drummer Bobby Rosengarden, made two excellent LPs for World Jazz simply titled **Soprano Summit I** (World Jazz 5) and **Soprano Summit II** (World Jazz 13). The first set is full of hot swing and competitive reed solos and has a few numbers associated with Sidney Bechet while **Soprano Summit II** is more ragtime oriented but just as worthy.

By 1976, the group consisted of Wilber, Davern, acoustic guitarist/vocalist Marty Grosz (who was a major asset to the band), and a variety of different bassists and drummers. **In Concert** (Concord Jazz 4029), recorded at the 1976 Concord Jazz Festival, is a delight as the band (with Ray Brown and Jake Hanna) swings hard on exciting renditions of "Stompy Jones," "Doin' the New Lowdown," and "Swing that Music." **Soprano Summit** (Storyville 8254) is a European concert not initially released until 1996, containing 11 songs that include "How Can You Face Me," "Meet Me Tonight in Dreamland," and Wilber's "Grenadilla Stomp."

The best buy of all is the two-CD set ❶ **Soprano Summit** (Chiaroscuro 148), which includes two complete LPs from 1976–77 (highlighted by "Ole Miss," "When Day Is Done," "Crazy Rhythm," and two versions of "Nagasaki"), five previously unreleased selections from a live performance, and a 13-minute "Jazzspeak" during which Marty Grosz talks (with humor) about the history of this important group.

Jess Stacy   In 1974 pianist Jess Stacy, who had only been semiactive since the early 1960s, recorded his first album (other than an obscure record for Hanover) since 1956. He had just performed at Carnegie Hall and sounds in fine form on **Stacy Still Swings** (Chiaroscuro 133). Most of the tempos are quite relaxed, with Stacy playing in a style unchanged since the late-1930s and really sparkling on "Riverboat Shuffle." A typically definitive and fascinating essay by Whitney Balliett perfectly sums up Jess Stacy's life.

Ralph Sutton   The great stride pianist Ralph Sutton often performed at his wife's Colorado club, Sunnie's in the late 1960s. No less than nine CDs have thus far come out that were made at that establishment during 1968–69: **With Ruby Braff Vol. 1** (Storyville 8243), **With Ruby Braff Vol. 2** (Storyville 8246), **With Ruby Braff Vol. 3** (Storyville 8301), **With Ruby Braff Vol. 4** (Storyville 8312), **Ralph Sutton Trio Vol. 1** (Storyville 8286), **Ralph Sutton Trio Vol. 2** (Storyville 8294), **With Bob Wilbur Vol. 1** (Storyville 8280), **With Bob Wilbur Vol. 2** (Storyville 8281), and **With Bob Wilber Vol. 3** (Storyville 8305). Suffice it to say that Sutton is typically inspired throughout, pushing Ruby Braff and Bob Wilber to play at their most inspired. Some standards are repeated on various sessions, but the musicians continually come up with fresh statements; Sutton's passionate striding does not let the other players ever get complacent. However, with his powerful left hand, Ralph Sutton really did not need any other players in order to form a complete band. Recorded in 1976, **Alligator Crawl** (Solo Art 92) has Sutton playing unaccompanied versions of a variety of vintage tunes including quite a few from Fats Waller, "Honky Tonk Train Blues," "I've Found a New Baby," "Dinah," and Willie "The Lion" Smith's "Echo of Spring."

Buddy Tate   Buddy Tate was fortunate enough to have a practically unprecedented 21-year gig (1953–74) leading his band at Harlem's Celebrity Club. He also made occasional recordings during those years. **Buddy Tate and His Buddies** (Chiaroscuro 123) from 1973 is a jam session record that is most notable for having Mary Lou Williams as one of the key soloists. Also featured are Tate, Illinois Jacquet, and an aging but still exciting Roy Eldridge with the rhythm section of rhythm guitarist Steve Jordan, Milt Hinton, and drummer Gus Johnson. The all-star swing group sounds fine on a trio of group originals, Buck Clayton's "Rockaway," and "Sunday."

After the Celebrity Club ended, Tate began to record quite prolifically. At 61 in 1974, he was still in prime form. **Swingin' Scorpio** (Black Lion 760165) teams Tate with trumpeter Humphrey Lyttelton, playing a set of tunes by Buck Clayton, who was retired from playing but not writing. The co-leaders (who both double on clarinet) are joined by several British jazz musicians including altoist Bruce Turner, Kathleen Stobart (on tenor and baritone), and pianist Mick Pyne. **The Texas Twister** (New World 352) is very much in the Count Basie style. Tate not only plays tenor and clarinet but takes a few rare vocals à la Jimmy Rushing. Paul Quinichette, who had retired in 1960, is heard in one of his few later recordings along with pianist Cliff Smalls, Major Holley, and drummer Jackie Williams. Most of the music is from the vintage Basie book including "Chicago," "Boogie Woogie," and "Topsy." **Jive at Five** (Storyville 5010) has a particularly interesting group of swing greats heard fairly late in their careers. Tate, Vic Dickenson, and trumpeter Doc Cheatham (who was 70 at the time and just beginning to emerge as a soloist) make for a potent front line, Johnny Guarnieri shows that he was still a brilliant player, and George Duvivier and Oliver Jackson are tasteful in support. There are four spirited group jams and features for Dickenson (who sings and plays his own "Constantly"), Cheatham ("I've Got a Right to Sing the Blues"), and Tate ("There Goes My Heart").

Warren Vache and Scott Hamilton   Although some history books call trumpeter Wynton Marsalis the leader of the "Young Lions," meaning that he headed a movement in the 1980s in which younger musicians played creatively within an older style, he was actually preceded by cornetist Warren Vache and tenor saxophonist Scott Hamilton. Vache (who is three years older than Hamilton) emerged first. The son of bassist Warren Vache, Sr. and the brother of clarinetist Allen Vache, Vache studied music with Pee Wee Erwin. In the early 1970s he had opportunities to play with Benny Goodman, Vic Dickenson, and Bob Wilber. Vache first recorded as a leader on a privately issued album from New Year's Eve 1976 titled **Jersey Jazz at Midnight** (New Jersey Jazz Society 1002). Vache's first official release is from November–December 1976, **○ First Time Out** (Audiophile 196). This impressive set has the 25-year-old cornetist showcased on five numbers backed only by guitarist Bucky Pizzarelli, and he displays both a lovely tone and a creative imagination within the boundaries of small group swing. Four other songs are more Dixieland oriented and have Vache joined by soprano saxophonist Kenny Davern, both Pizzarelli and Wayne Wright on guitars, bassist Michael Moore, and Connie Kay. In addition, for the CD reissue, six other selections were recorded in 1993. Overall, this is a superior release by Vache with "Oh Baby" and "All of Me" in particular getting heated treatment.

Scott Hamilton would not begin recording until 1977, but he was already creating a stir the previous year. Hamilton did not start playing the tenor sax until he was 16, developing quickly. Rather than looking toward John Coltrane, Wayne Shorter, or Michael Brecker as his role models, Hamilton was much more interested in the sounds and styles of Ben Webster, Zoot Sims, and Illinois Jacquet. When he moved to New York, it greatly surprised jazz fans and critics to hear a young world-class soloist who chose to play mainstream swing.

It was a time for a change in the old beliefs that new was automatically better than old, that every time a new style came up it "replaced" what came before, and that young creative musicians had to play in the most advanced style in order to be relevant. Warren Vache and Scott Hamilton proved otherwise, at the beginning of their careers and in the decades to follow. In addition, their arrival on the scene gradually led to the development of a strong small-group swing movement.

Joe Venuti   Although he was musically active much of the time, for violinist Joe Venuti the 1936–66 period was the Dark Ages as he became an alcoholic and mostly played low-level jobs. That all began to change in 1967, the year he turned 64. Venuti was featured at Dick Gibson's Colorado Jazz Party, playing enthusiastically in a style unchanged since the 1930s. Work began to come in, he went on several tours of Italy and Europe, he began to record again, and Venuti ended up being quite busy in the 11 years he had left.

Three of Venuti's finest late-period recordings were made with Zoot Sims (heard on tenor and soprano). Although coming from different musical generations, the co-leaders were always hard swingers, and they proved to be quite compatible. ❍ **Joe & Zoot & More** (Chiaroscuro 128) from 1973–74 is consistently exciting. The violinist is heard on the original nine-song LP program with Sims, Dick Wellstood, George Duvivier, and drummer Cliff Leeman plus eight of the dozen selections that he cut in 1974 for the album **Joe Venuti Blue Fours** (Chiaroscuro 134). The numbers from the latter are three duets with Bucky Pizzarelli, some songs in a trio with Milt Hinton and Leeman, and a few tunes with a hot quartet consisting of bass saxophonist Spencer Clark, pianist Dill Jones, and Pizzarelli. Among the high points of this highly enjoyable reissue are "I Found a New Baby," "The Wild Cat," "Lady Be Good," "Dinah," and "The Blue Room." From 1975, **Joe Venuti and Zoot Sims** (Chiaroscuro 142), which has the other four **Blue Fours** numbers, is at the same level, with a variety of standards (including "Shine," "My Honey's Lovin' Arms," and "Avalon") being played by Venuti, Sims, John Bunch, Milt Hinton, and Bobby Rosengarden. "Don't Take Your Love from Me" has a guest appearance by 73-year-old trombonist Spiegel Willcox, who had played with Jean Goldkette's Orchestra next to Venuti 49 years earlier.

Venuti also recorded three albums for Concord during 1975–77. **Gems** (Concord Jazz 6014) teams Venuti with veteran guitarist George Barnes (plus rhythm guitarist Bob Gibbons, bassist Herb Mickman, and Jake Hanna) for a superior swing date that includes "I Want to Be Happy," "Oh Baby," "Hindustan," and "Lady Be Good." Venuti and Barnes are also heard together on the LP **Live at the Concord Summer Festival** (Concord Jazz 30) along with Ross Tompkins, Ray Brown, and Hanna, but **Gems** is the better of the two releases and the one that is currently available. **Hot Sonatas** (Chiaroscuro 145) is an unusual and frequently exciting album of encounters between Venuti and Earl Hines, two veteran greats who had never played together before. The violin/piano duets are consistently unpredictable and display strong communication on a variety of vintage tunes and three songs written by Hines decades earlier.

The comeback of Joe Venuti was one of the happiest events in jazz of the 1970s.

Eddie "Cleanhead" Vinson   Possessor of a timeless blues singing style and an underrated boppish altoist (whose tone could sound similar to Charlie Parker's), Eddie "Cleanhead" Vinson began to work more frequently in both blues and jazz settings in the late 1960s after a period of relative neglect. **Old Kidney Stew Is Fine** (Delmark 631), which was originally released by the French Black & Blue label, teams him with Jay McShann, blues guitarist T-Bone Walker, and tenor saxophonist Hal Singer in a sextet. Highlights include "Old Maid Boogie," "Somebody's Gotta Go," "Just a Dream," and "Juice Head Baby." **Jamming the Blues** (Black Lion 760188) has Vinson in fine form at the 1974 Montreux Jazz Festival. Joined by Singer and a rhythm section, Cleanhead plays and sings a few of his familiar numbers ("Just a Dream," "Person to Person," and "Hold It Right There"), "Laura," and some instrumental blues. His other recordings from this era are in a similar vein, and Vinson (who stole the show at the 1971 Montreux Jazz Festival while sitting in with Oliver Nelson's Orchestra on "Swiss Suite"), although rarely including any surprises in his shows, remained a crowd pleaser and an entertaining performer.

Ben Webster   Based in Copenhagen during his final nine years (1964–73), Ben Webster continued playing in his timeless swing style, often sticking to a fairly basic repertoire and alternating romps with ballads. Webster recorded frequently during his last five years for such labels as Storyville, Saba, Affinity, Spotlite, RST, Cat, Hot House, and Steeple Chase. **Master of Jazz Vol. 5** (Storyville 4105) gives a well-rounded picture of Webster during his last period. The great tenor is joined by trios led by pianists Kenny Drew and Teddy Wilson, plays with a piano/bass duo and a Scandinavian quartet, romps with the Danish Radio Big Band on two numbers, and is accompanied on "Goin' Home" and "Come Sunday" by a string orchestra. **Live at the Haarlemse Jazz Club** (Cat 1104) features Webster in Holland with a group of Europeans (including Tete Montoliu) playing such swinging standbys as "Sunday," "How Long Has This Been Going On," and "Perdido." **My Man** (Steeple Chase 31008) was recorded in January 1973 just months before Webster's death. Even with an occasional shortness of breath, Webster never really declined musically. The six selections (five standards and his "Set Call") are all familiar, but Webster (who is assisted by pianist Ole Kock Hansen, bassist Bo Stief, and drummer Alex Riel) still sounds quite enthusiastic. His warm ballad renditions and hard-driving romps are quite enjoyable to hear, but he had only eight months left before his death at age 64.

George Wein and the Newport All-Stars   The founder of the Newport Jazz Festival and an organizer and booker for many festivals, George Wein has also been a fine swing pianist on a part-time basis since the late 1940s. Occasionally since the late 1950s, he has led the Newport All-Stars, an ensemble of top swing and Dixieland players. **George Wein's Newport All-Stars** (Collectables 6194) from 1969 features Wein with Ruby Braff (the star of the set), Red Norvo, both Tal Farlow and Barney Kessel on guitars, bassist Larry Ridley, and drummer Don Lamond. Among the most memorable performances are "In a Little Spanish Town," "Ja-Da," "My Melancholy Baby," "Exactly Like You," and an effective reworking of "Sunny." Their association with the Newport All-Stars led to Red Norvo's comeback and much greater recognition being given to Ruby Braff.

Dick Wellstood   One of the great stride pianists (along with Ralph Sutton and Dick Hyman) to emerge after World War II, Dick Wellstood only recorded relatively few selections as a leader prior to 1971, but then things became much busier. **Dick Wellstood Alone** (Solo Art 73) is a solo set that ranges from tunes by Fats Waller, James P. Johnson, and Scott Joplin ("Fig Leaf") to Zez Confrey's obscure "Poor Buttermilk," "Russian Rag," and two originals. ◉ **And His All Star Orchestra Featuring Kenny Davern/The Big Three** (Chiaroscuro 129) reissues two of Wellstood's finest albums on a single CD. Eight numbers from 1973 are duets with Kenny Davern (who sticks to soprano) while the final nine songs have a trio comprised of Wellstood, Davern (this time on clarinet), and drummer Bobby Rosengarden. The music is wonderful and swinging, whether creative versions of Dixieland standards (including "Original Dixieland One Step," "Tiger Rag,"

and "Indiana") or lesser-known songs such as "Oh Peter" and the original "Fast as a Bastard."

This Is the One…Dig (Solo Art 119) was Wellstood's personal favorite record, and he sounds quite inspired throughout the solo set. Along the way he performs surprising stride versions of Stevie Wonder's "You Are the Sunshine of My Life" and John Coltrane's "Giant Steps" in addition to some swing standards and such classics as "Snowy Morning Blues," "If Dreams Come True," and "Rosetta." But it is difficult to call any one Dick Wellstood record the best of his career because he was quite consistent and never recorded an indifferent album.

Mary Lou Williams   By 1975, pianist Mary Lou Williams was virtually the only survivor of the 1920s to still be playing modern jazz. Her concerts tended to feature her going through her version of the history of jazz (much of which she had seen), from ragtime and stride to swing, bop, modal music, and sometimes even a free improvisation (though she never explored fusion). Williams played all of those styles quite credibly.

After her conversion to the Catholic religion in the mid-1950s, Williams performed relatively little for years though she did write and record several masses. By the beginning of the 1970s she was ready to play jazz again. The double CD ◉ **Nite Life/From the Heart** (Chiaroscuro 103) has the 11 solo piano numbers from her LP **From the Heart** and nine additional performances, some of which are rather different alternate takes. Williams at 61 was at the peak of her powers as one can hear on a remake of her stride classic "Nite Life," "What's Your Story Morning Glory," and "Little Joe from Chicago" plus some more modern and impressionistic pieces. Also on this valuable two-fer is a fascinating 32-minute monologue by Williams in which she talks about her life story up to the late 1930s. In addition, there is her unusual performance at a Scott Joplin tribute concert. Disturbed by the very straight performances of the classically trained ragtime pianists who preceded her, she improvises wildly on three Joplin pieces, adding stride, swing, and the blues while probably disturbing some in the audience.

The more modern side of Mary Lou Williams is featured on the next two releases. **Zoning** (Smithsonian/Folkways 40811) has duos and trios with Bob Cranshaw and Mickey Roker, Williams uses Zita Carno on second piano during a couple of the more avant-garde pieces, and she also plays some trio numbers with bassist Milton Suggs and Tony Waters on congas. On this set and on **Free Spirits** (Steeple Chase 31043), an explorative trio date with Buster Williams and Mickey Roker, Williams sounds like a follower of McCoy Tyner and Herbie Hancock rather than a veteran of the 1920s, quite a feat. Also well worth picking up is **Live at the Cookery** (Chiaroscuro 146), which has Williams doing her history of jazz show in 1975. With assistance from bassist Brian Torff, she shows the music evolving from a hymn, a blues and stride up to "All Blues," and "A Grand Night for Swinging."

Teddy Wilson   Teddy Wilson recorded prolifically during 1968–76 for such labels as Black Lion, Metronome, Storyville, Sonet, Halcyon, Trio, Chiaroscuro, and Black & Blue. His style had been quite predictable for decades and was largely unchanged since 1935, but once in awhile Wilson would get inspired. **With Billie in Mind** (Chiaroscuro 111) features the veteran swing great playing piano solo versions of 20 songs associated with Billie Holiday during the period in the 1930s when they often recorded together. He clearly enjoyed playing several tunes that he had not performed in years and is heard at the top of his game. **Runnin' Wild** (Black Lion 760184) is easily the most exciting of Wilson's many Black Lion CDs. Recorded at the 1973 Montreux Jazz Festival, Wilson plays some surprisingly extroverted solos, some of which include torrid boogie-woogie and many of which are taken at faster than usual tempos. Bassist Kenny Baldok, drummer Johnny Richardson, and (on four of the nine numbers) clarinetist Dave Shepherd prove to be strong assets on one of Wilson's most spirited recordings. In contrast, **Teddy Wilson and His All-Stars** (Chiaroscuro 150) falls short of expectations. Wilson, who almost always played with his trio by the time of this 1976 session, is teamed in a sextet with Harry "Sweets" Edison, Vic Dickenson, Bob Wilber on clarinet and soprano, Major Holley, and Oliver Jackson. Unfortunately, instead of jamming on the set of standards and obscurities, the musicians mostly play Bob Wilber's conservative dance band arrangements, which result in the rather concise (usually three minutes apiece) music sounding quite conservative. But as usual Wilson sounds tasteful and flawless.

World's Greatest Jazz Band   It was clearly an outrageous name for a band, but the title that concert promoter Dick Gibson gave the all-star group in 1968 at his sixth annual jazz party in Colorado somehow fit the musicians, at least in the musical world they inhabited. Trumpeter Yank Lawson and bassist Bob Haggart had played together with Bob Crosby in the 1930s and co-led the Lawson-Haggart band (a recording group) in the 1950s. They became the co-leaders of the WGJB, a band that after a little shuffling of personnel also included trumpeter Billy Butterfield, both Carl Fontana and Lou McGarity on trombones, Bob Wilber on clarinet and soprano, tenor saxophonist Bud Freeman, pianist Ralph Sutton, banjoist Clancy Hayes (who dropped out after 1969), and drummer Morey Feld (replaced by Gus Johnson in 1969). With the decline of Eddie Condon by the late 1960s, maybe this was the world's greatest jazz band!

Originally the idea behind the band was to alternate veteran standards with Dixiefied versions of current pop tunes. The group's two 1968 albums for Project 3 (which have not come out on CD) include such unlikely tunes as "Up Up and Away," "Sunny," "Ode to Billy Joe," "Mrs. Robinson," "Love Is Blue," "Alfie," and "Wichita Lineman." Fortunately, the idea was discarded by 1969, and the band reverted to the high-quality standards that it excelled at interpreting.

Released in 1970, ◐ **Live at Roosevelt Grill** (Atlantic 90982) is the WGJB's finest recording. With Vic Dickenson taking over for Fontana, the band was a mighty force with seven major soloists. The many high points include an explosive version of "That's a-Plenty," "Five Point Blues," a spirited "My Honey's Lovin' Arms," the heated trumpet solos on "Come Back Sweet Papa," and Dickenson's feature on "Constantly." The follow-up album, **What's New** (Atlantic 1582), unfortunately has not been reissued on CD. With Ed Hubble succeeding McGarity, the band is in fine form on "The Eel," "What's New," "Bourbon Street Parade," and a duet by the co-leaders on "Smile."

After being dropped by Atlantic, the group recorded regularly for the tiny World Jazz label starting in 1972, cutting ten albums during the next five years. Jazzology has since acquired the catalog and is gradually reissuing these dates although the music is not as fiery or as special as the two Atlantic albums; some of the magic and spontaneity is missing. A Christmas album, **Hark the Herald Angels Swing** (World Jazz 2) is probably the best of these LPs.

By 1975 the WGJB's personnel had changed quite a bit, with Lawson, Sutton, Haggart, and Johnson being joined by trumpeter Johnny Best, trombonists George Masso and Carl Fontana, clarinetist Peanuts Hucko, and Tommy Newsom or Al Klink on tenor. Though Butterfield would rejoin the band later in the year, the WGJB had dropped in importance although still performing fairly regularly until its breakup in 1978. But the World's Greatest Jazz Band had successfully defied the dominant musical trends and for a time lived up to its name.

A Smaller World

The world was a much larger place in the 1930s when major names such as Coleman Hawkins and Benny Carter seemed to totally disappear during their long stays in Europe even though they were very active. Although visits to Europe by jazz musicians became more common in the 1950s and '60s, the same phenomenon occurred. Don Byas was totally forgotten in the United States after relocating to Europe in 1946, Ben Webster was little heard of after the mid-1960s, and Dexter Gordon's return to the United States in 1976 was treated as a major comeback, as if he had not been recording classics for the Danish Steeple Chase label. This situation was finally beginning to change a bit during the first half of the 1970s because of the increased availability of records from Europe although the jazz press mostly stayed focused on events in the United States.

In constantly proclaiming that jazz was American music (and sometimes stating inaccurately that it could be properly created only by American blacks), many in the American jazz world missed out on one of the biggest trends occurring in the music during 1968–76: the proliferation of important new jazz musicians in Europe, Latin/South America, and Canada. Ever since the European visits of the Original Dixieland Jazz Band and Sidney Bechet during 1919, jazz had not been confined strictly to the borders of the United States. It is true that many of the early Europeans and South Americans who played jazz sounded influenced by their American counterparts and there were only a handful of original voices overseas prior to 1950, but the name of Django Reinhardt should be enough to convince any listener that non-Americans could play creative jazz, too.

Starting in the early 1960s with Joe Harriott in England and continuing with such adventurous players as Derek Bailey, Peter Brotzmann, and Jan Garbarek to name just three, there were many original and creative jazz musicians to be found in countries other than the United States. In addition to developing their own brand of avant-garde jazz (ranging from the intensity of German jazz to the hilarity featured by some Dutch groups), some European players combined their own folk heritage with advanced jazz to create something new. This had already occurred earlier with Afro-Cuban jazz, and Gato Barbieri from Argentina continued the idea by rediscovering his own musical heritage in the late 1960s, changing from a passionate but derivative avant-gardist into a true original.

This section discusses some of the key European, Canadian, and South American musicians who cover a wide range of styles from free to traditional. In addition, some of the Americans who spent much of this time overseas and a few of those at home whose music was heavily touched by other cultures (such as Cal Tjader's Latin jazz band and Oregon) are discussed. By 1976 there could be little doubt that jazz had truly become a world music.

Derek Bailey One of the most radical and unusual of all musicians is guitarist Derek Bailey, a leader of the British avant-garde. An explorer of atonal sounds rather than notes, Bailey has not bothered with playing melodies, chords, or conventional harmonies since his earliest days. A spontaneous player who reacts instantly to his surroundings and the ideas of other musicians, Bailey's music is quite forbidding yet logical to those who make the major effort to study his approach to improvisation.

Bailey actually played more conventional jazz until he worked in a trio called Joseph Holbrooke during 1963–66 that also included bassist Gavin Bryars and drummer Tony Oxley. During its last period, this group played totally free. In 1966 the guitarist moved to London where he worked with the Spontaneous Music Ensemble (led by drummer John Stevens) off and on during 1968–74, recording alongside such major British avant-gardists as saxophonist Evan Parker, trumpeter Kenny Wheeler, bassist Dave Holland, and altoist Trevor Watts. **Karyobin** (Chronoscope 2001) from 1968 actually has Bailey mostly in the background as the quintet (with Stevens, Wheeler, Parker, and Holland) stretches out on the six-part "Karyobin," playing quite freely in an idiom influenced a bit by American contemporaries but already on its way to becoming a more European style.

Bailey also played with drummer Tony Oxley's sextet (1968–73) and (starting in 1970) the trio Iskra with trombonist Paul Rutherford and bassist Barry Guy. Bailey, Oxley, and Evan Parker in 1970 founded the Incus label. The guitarist, who had recorded a duo set with drummer Han Bennink for the Dutch ICP label in 1969, began recording for Incus in 1971 and also led albums for ECM (duets with Dave Holland), Emanem, Nondo, Quark, and Cramps during the period. Recorded in 1971, **Solo Guitar** (Incus 10) has ten improvisations and three abstract renditions of avant-garde pieces. It is as good a place as any to start exploring Bailey's unique and often-disturbing barrage of sound explorations.

In 1976 the guitarist formed Company, a free improvisation ensemble that had continually shifting personnel. In the first year alone Bailey recorded four LPs under that name: **Company 1** (Incus 21) with Evan Parker in a quartet, **Company 2** (Incus 23), which features a trio with Anthony Braxton and Parker, **Company 3** (Incus 25) with Han Bennink, and **Company 4** (Incus 26) with Steve Lacy. Quite typically this music is extremely adventurous, focusing on sound explorations and abstract communication between the very alert musicians.

Gato Barbieri   Gato Barbieri, an explosive tenor saxophonist from Argentina with a passionate tone, discovered himself musically during this era by looking back into his own past. He had made his initial impression as an avantgardist, but around 1969 Barbieri started digging into his roots in Argentinean folk melodies, adding some of the traditional songs to his repertoire and playing them with a great deal of passion while making his style much more melodic. **The Third World** (BMG 25758), **Fenix** (BMG 85148), and **El Pampero** (BMG 31314) all have Barbieri joined by a rhythm section that includes Lonnie Liston Smith (who had played a similar role with Pharoah Sanders), with the tenor alternating between screaming interludes and embracing romantic melodies. In 1972 Barbieri was prominently featured in the soundtrack of *Last Tango in Paris* and then during 1973–75 he made his most significant recordings, which were simply titled **Chapter One**, **Chapter Two**, **Chapter Three**, and **Chapter Four**. ◉ **Latino America** (Impulse 236) is a two-CD set that has all of the music from the first two chapters plus five previously unreleased selections. Recorded in both Buenos Aires, Argentina, and Los Angeles, California, Barbieri is mostly joined by South American musicians who perform the highly rhythmic music (which contains many lengthy vamps) with a jubilant spirit. Gato's tenor had found its

perfect showcase. ◉ **Chapter Three** (GRP/Impulse 111) has Barbieri joined by a big band arranged by Chico O'Farrill and is also a gem, consisting of four of Barbieri's better originals, "Milonga Triste," and "What a Difference a Day Makes." Unfortunately, **Chapter Four**, a live set with multi-instrumentalist Howard Johnson and a strong rhythm section, has not yet been reissued on CD but it is also worth finding.

Karl Berger   German vibraphonist Karl Berger started out on the piano, accompanied visiting Americans in Germany, switched his main instrument to vibes in the early 1960s, and gained a degree in musicology. In 1965 Berger joined Don Cherry's group, moving to the United States with the cornetist the following year. Influenced by Ornette Coleman, Berger recorded his own album for ESP and appeared on Cherry's **Symphony for Improvisers**. In 1972 he founded the Creative Music Studio in Woodstock, keeping the important school (which emphasized self-expression and adventurous improvising) going until the mid-1980s. Berger has not recorded all that often in his career, but **All Kinds of Time** (Sackville 3010), a set of duets with Dave Holland, is an excellent showcase (if occasionally a little dry) with Berger heard on vibes, piano, and the balafon (an African marimba) on a set of his originals.

Peter Brotzmann   One of the most ferocious of all saxophonists and one whose intense playing could make Albert Ayler and Archie Shepp at their prime sound a bit tame in comparison, Peter Brotzmann improvises with a consistently scary passion. The power of his tenor and baritone sax playing is impossible to ignore, and he dominates every group with which he performs. A self-taught musician who was born in Remscheid, Germany, Brotzmann ironically began his career in 1959 playing with Dixieland bands. Within five years he had evolved to free jazz. He worked with a group headed by Michael Mantler and Carla Bley and was part of the Globe Unity Orchestra. Brotzmann made his recording debut with 1967's **For Adolphe Sax** (the LP FMP 080), a furious blowout in a trio with bassist Peter Kowald and drummer Sven Ake Johansson. Recorded in 1968, ◉ **Machine Gun** (FMP 024) is certainly not for the faint-hearted because it is an explosive octet date in which Brotzmann is joined by Willem Breuker on tenor and bass clarinet, Evan Parker (also on tenor), Fred Van Hove on piano, both Peter Kowald and Buschi Niebergall on basses, and Sven Ake Johansson and Han Bennink on drums. This is one of the few Brotzmann sets that he does not dominate because Breuker and Parker play with as much intensity and volume. This is the equivalent of an ESP freeform jam played with triple the intensity.

In 1969 Peter Brotzmann was one of the founders of the FMP (Free Music Productions) label, and he would record many fiery sets for the company through the years and reissue his earlier sessions. He has never lost his intensity or enthusiasm at playing completely free.

Kenny Clarke-Francy Boland Big Band Few recordings of the Kenny Clarke-Francy Boland Orchestra (which was considered among the top big bands based in Europe in the 1960s) have ever been widely available in the United States. In 1992 a two-CD set of the band's live concert from October 29, 1969, **Clarke/Boland Big Band** (RTE 1501), was released. With the soloists including trumpeters Benny Bailey, Art Farmer, and Idrees Sulieman, trombonist Ake Persson, both Johnny Griffin and Tony Coe on tenors, pianist/arranger Francy Boland, and drummer Kenny Clarke, this was a mighty band as shown on such numbers as "Pentonville," "Now Hear My Meaning," "Volcano," "Box 702," "The Jamfs Are Coming," and a 19-minute version of "Sax No End." The music is conventional but swings hard, and the orchestra clearly had its own personality within the modern jazz mainstream.

After 13 years, the Clarke-Boland big band broke up in 1973.

Ken Colyer Ken Colyer's British traditional band, featuring trombonist Geoff Cole and clarinetist Tony Puke, broke up in 1971 because the leader/cornetist's shaky health. However, Colyer continued playing on a part-time basis, and he made a few fine recordings and broadcasts in 1972. **Boston Church Service** (GHB 351) was performed before a live audience. The music is primarily hymns, but the interpretations are jazz oriented and full of spirit with plenty of stomps and ensemble-oriented jams. There are strong contributions from clarinetist Sammy Remington, trombonist Barry Palser, and pianist Ray Smith as the band romps through such songs as "Just a Little While to Stay Here," "Sing On," "Bye and Bye," and "Walking with the King."

Arne Domnerus Arne Domnerus, who plays alto and clarinet with equal skill, has been a major jazz musician from Sweden since the mid-1940s. His style falls between swing and bop, with Johnny Hodges and Lee Konitz both being influences. Domnerus led his first group in 1942 when he was 17, made his debut recordings in 1945, and was leading record dates by 1949. Because he has spent his life in Sweden, most of his recordings have been made for Swedish labels.

During two days in December 1976, Domnerus, pianist Bengt Hallbert, vibraphonist Lars Erstrand, bassist Georg Riedel, and drummer Egil Johansen were extensively recorded playing live at the Pawnshop Jazz Club in Stockholm. The four CDs **Jazz at the Pawnshop Vol. 1, Vol. 2, Vol. 3, Vol. 4** (Proprius 7778, 9044, 9058, and 9144) fully document this engagement. In general, swing standards are emphasized with the music sometimes recalling the small groups of Benny Goodman. **Vol. 1** includes a heated "Limehouse Blues," the African folk song "High Life," "Lady Be Good," and Coleman Hawkins' "Stuffy." **Vol. 2**, which is without Erstrand, has such songs as a lengthy "In a Mellow Tone," "Poor Butterfly," and "Things Ain't What They Used to Be." In contrast, Estrand gets top billing on **Vol. 3** and is well showcased during a program that includes "Now's the Time," "Take the 'A' Train," and "Struttin' with Some Barbeque." The final volume is strictly for completists because it only consists of the first selection of the engagement ("Mood Indigo") and the final song played ("Jeep's Blues"), just 19 minutes in all. Small group swing collectors will want all four discs.

Dutch Swing College Band The Dutch Swing College Band was founded in 1948 by Peter Schilperoort who started out mostly as a clarinetist before switching his focus to baritone sax. At the time that the group recorded **Dutch Swing College Band Live** (Timeless 73080) in 1974, it had been together for 26 years. This CD (one of the few available of the band) has all of the music from a 1974 concert LP plus seven previously unreleased tracks from the same performance. The septet features Schilperoort, cornetist Bert de Kort, trombonist Dick Kaart, and Bob Kaper on clarinet and alto romping through some Dixieland standards, two obscurities ("Charleston Hound" and Jack Pettis's "Bag O'Blues"), and a surprisingly hot rendition of Frank Foster's "Shiny Stockings."

Jim Galloway A fine swing/Dixieland player, Jim Galloway is best known for his work on soprano but also plays tenor and clarinet. Born in Scotland in 1936, he moved to Canada in 1965 where three years later he began leading the Metro Stompers. Galloway's tone on soprano is much lighter than Sidney Bechet's as can be heard on his debut album as a leader, 1973's **Three Is Company** (Sackville 2007). Teamed with Dick Wellstood and drummer Pete Magadini for a live set, Galloway jams such numbers as Fats Waller's "Minor Drag," "After You've Gone," and "Everything I've Got."

Jan Garbarek   Although he was not on ECM's initial release, Norwegian tenor saxophonist Jan Garbarek practically defined that label's distinctive sound from the start. His icy tone, emphasis on space and long tones, and ability to build up his atmospheric solos slowly made him an increasingly popular figure in the European jazz scene. Although sometimes grouped with the avant-garde movements, Garbarek was worlds apart from the high energy of the first wave of New York free jazzers, both geographically and musically. A professional from the time he turned 15 in 1962, Garbarek had an opportunity to work with George Russell for four years later in the decade. **The Esoteric Circle** (Freedom 741031) has Garbarek matched in 1969 with future ECM mates guitarist Terje Rypdal, bassist Arild Anderson, and drummer Jon Christensen for an album originally released by Bob Thiele's Flying Dutchman label. In fact, the same quartet in 1970 recorded Garbarek's debut for ECM, **Afric Pepperbird** (ECM 843475).

During this period, Jan Garbarek became most famous for his association with Keith Jarrett's European Quartet, a group also including Anderson and Christensen that would several notable albums after 1976. Throughout the 1970s, Garbarek would come to symbolize the growing individuality of European jazz musicians.

Egberto Gismonti   Born in Brazil, Egberto Gismonti is equally skilled on guitar and piano. In the 1970s he became symbolic of the impossible-to-classify music featured on the ECM label. He was originally a classical-trained pianist until he discovered funk and jazz in the late '60s. By then Gismonti was also playing a six-stringed classical guitar. He became a studio musician in Brazil, and in November 1976 made his third recording as a leader and his debut for the ECM label, **Danca Das Cabecas** (ECM 1089). A set of duets with the exotic and imaginative percussionist Nana Vascencelos, this set blurs the boundary lines between improvised jazz and world music. Gismonti, who in addition to guitar and piano is heard on flute, joins with Vascencelos to perform subtle music that is quite sophisticated and full of unusual melodies and surprises.

Stephane Grappelli   During the 1950s and '60s, violinist Stephane Grappelli mostly worked in his native France and only recorded on an occasional basis. However, he began to record more often starting in 1969 and in the early '70s became a world traveler, visiting the United States on a regular basis. Fans were happily surprised to realize that Grappelli, best known for his association with Django Reinhardt in the 1930s, had improved through the years and was now a hard-swinging and delightful violinist, an open-minded swing stylist who was not afraid to play with younger musicians.

Stephane Grappelli Meets Barney Kessel (Black Lion 760150) and **Limehouse Blues** (Black Lion 760180) were both recorded in Paris during June 23–24, 1969, with a quintet that includes Barney Kessel. Although the guitarist contributed three originals apiece to each disc, the emphasis is on swing standards and heated playing including exciting versions of "Honeysuckle Rose" (a Grappelli-Kessel duet), "I Found a New Baby," "It Don't Mean a Thing," and "Tea for Two."

On October 22, 1969, a very special collaboration took place. **Venupelli Blues** (Le Jazz 18) is the only joint recording by Grappelli and Joe Venuti (who had just begun his comeback). With a four-piece rhythm section that includes Kessel and pianist George Wein, the two great violinists romp on such tunes as "I Can't Give You Anything but Love," "After You've Gone," and "Undecided," making one wish that they had crossed paths much more during their lengthy careers.

Grappelli recorded in a variety of settings during the first half of the 1970s. **Just One of Those Things** (Black Lion 760180) is an enjoyable set during which Grappelli swings hard with a European trio, **Parisian Thoroughfare** (Black Lion 760132) with Roland Hanna, George Mraz, and Mel Lewis shows that Grappelli could play more modern material, and there were also several recorded collaborations with classical violinist Yehudi Menuhin during this era.

However, the best setting for the violinist was one that he resisted for many years because of the comparison to Django Reinhardt before he finally relented: a string group. ❍ **Live in London** (Black Lion 760139) has

Grappelli playing with the Hot Club of London, a unit led by guitarist Diz Disley that includes rhythm guitarist Denny Wright and bassist Len Skeat. This Black Lion CD contains the entire contents of a former two-LP set plus a previously unreleased version of "Them There Eyes." Grappelli sounds particularly inspired playing with this group, and sparks fly on such numbers as "This Can't Be Love," "Honeysuckle Rose," and "After You've Gone." Grappelli also constructs a fine four-song Gershwin medley and pays tribute to Django on "Nuages."

For the next 23 years, Stephane Grappelli became world famous performing concerts with similar groups and keeping the legacy of swing violin alive.

Lars Gullin   One of jazz's greatest baritone saxophonists, Lars Gullin was off records during 1961–63 and 1965–68, only recording infrequently during his later years. Gullin had let excessive drug use affect his health, but he still sounds in fine form on the 1975 LP **Featuring Bernt Rosengren** (Storyville 432). Gullin leads a quintet with Bernt Rosengren (tenor and flute) that stretches out on two originals, "I Love You," and "Just Friends"; Rosengren is showcased on "'Round Midnight." For Lars Gullin, this set was practically a last gasp (there would be only one further recording) because he had less than a year left to live before his death in 1976 at the age of 48.

Barry Guy   A major bassist from England, Barry Guy had extensive classical training and developed parallel careers in both avant-garde jazz and contemporary classical music. During 1967–70 he was a member of the Spontaneous Music Ensemble along with saxophonist Trevor Watts and drummer John Stevens. In 1970 he formed the London Jazz Composers Orchestra, an innovative 21-piece group that mixes free improvising with some tightly organized ensembles. Its first recording, 1972's ❍ **Ode** (Incus 041), has been reissued as a double CD. The seven-part "Ode" (the final part was not released until this CD) is an atonal work featuring such players as Watts, trumpeter Harry Beckett, trombonist Paul Rutherford, pianist Howard Riley, Derek Bailey, and Evan Parker on tenor and soprano among the key payers. The music is quite dense, unpredictable, and exciting; it is a classic in big-band jazz, European music, and the jazz avant-garde.

Abdullah Ibrahim   In 1968 pianist Dollar Brand converted to Islam and changed his name to Abdullah Ibrahim. Although associated with the avant-garde a bit in his early days (while always eager to pay his musical debt to Duke Ellington and Thelonious Monk), Ibrahim began in the late 1960s to infuse his music with folk melodies influenced by his memories of his native land, South Africa. Recorded in 1969, **African Piano** (ECM 835020), which was issued under the name of Dollar Brand, is a continuous live performance on which Ibrahim explores eight of his originals. Although he had not quite found his own sound yet, the use of repetition and vamps is quite inventive.

By February 18, 1973, when he recorded enough music for two piano solo CDs in one day, Ibrahim's style was much more distinctive. **Ancient Africa** (Sackville 3049) and **Fats, Duke & the Monk** (Sackville 3048) have all of the music from the albums **Sangoma** and **Africa Portraits** although they shuffle the order of the songs a bit. **Ancient Africa** is the better of the two, with spiritual, picturesque, and lengthy improvisations that clock in between 13–21 minutes apiece. **Fats, Duke & the Monk** has three lengthy medleys: "Salaam Peace," "African Portraits," and "Fats, Duke & the Monk." On the latter there is not much of Waller (just a brief "Honeysuckle Rose"), but Ibrahim pays his respect to Ellington and Monk. The solos are passionate, episodic, and consistently fascinating.

Abdullah Ibrahim returned home to South Africa where he spent much of 1974–76, but the racial situation with apartheid became so perilous that he reluctantly left in 1976, moving to the United States and vowing not to return to his native land until apartheid was abolished. His first record back after he arrived back in the States was **The Banyanas: Children of Africa** (Enja 79619). On a trio set with Cecil McBee and Roy Brooks, Ibrahim performs six folkish melodies that pay tribute to his South African heritage, singing and playing soprano sax on "Ishmael." Ibrahim's music sometimes becomes quite intense, but eventually his flights return to earth and end optimistically. Despite everything, Abdullah Ibrahim was hopeful about the future of South Africa.

Papa Bue Jensen's Viking Jazz Band   One of the top Dixieland groups in Europe since it changed its name to the Viking Jazz Band in 1958, trombonist Papa Bue Jensen's ensemble recorded fairly regularly during

1968–75. **Live at Mosebacke, Stockholm** (Storyville 5532) is a live date from 1970. Trumpeter Finn Otto Hansen is particularly impressive while clarinetist Jorgen Svare is also quite talented. Other than "The Entertainer" (played a few years before it became hugely popular), "Now's the Hour" (their theme), and four Duke Ellington songs, all of the music consists of Dixieland standards including such rousers as "Dippermouth Blues," "Panama," and "Tiger Rag." **Down by the Riverside** (Storyville 5503), which is subtitled "The Complete Original Recordings, Vol. 2," has all of Jensen's studio recordings from December 1969–November 1971. The spirited New Orleans–style band is heard in top form and joined on some numbers by singer Bjarne "Liller" Petersen and guest clarinetist Albert Nicholas. Highlights include "Tailgate Ramble," "Bill Bailey," "Doctor Jazz," and "I've Found a New Baby." Also well worth picking up is **Live in Dresden 1971** (Storyville 5530), which has a typical concert by the band including "Weary Blues," a medley of early Duke Ellington tunes, and "Savoy Blues."

Fraser MacPherson   Canadian tenor saxophonist Fraser MacPherson was already 47 in 1975 when he recorded his first album to find its way south of the border. A swinging

player in the tradition of Zoot Sims and Woody Herman's Four Brothers, MacPherson had played professionally since 1951, mostly working in studios and dance bands. He led several record dates in Canada starting in 1962, but it was a 1975 session for the tiny West End label (which four years later was released in the United States by Concord) that gave him his first recognition in the United States. Unfortunately, **Live at the Planetarium** (Concord Jazz 92) has not been reissued on CD yet. Recorded in a trio with guitarist Oliver Gannon and bassist Wyatt Ruther, MacPherson alternately romps and caresses seven standards including "Tangerine," "I'm Getting Sentimental Over You," and "Li'l Darlin'."

Albert Mangelsdorff   Trombonist Albert Mangelsdorff was a pioneer in multiphonics, playing chords on the trombone (partly by humming through the horn). Although he first recorded as a leader back in 1954, it was not until the late 1960s that he began to make a strong impact. Born in Frankfurt, Germany, Mangelsdorff's first instrument was the violin, and he worked as a jazz guitarist before switching to trombone in 1948. He was primarily a bop player in the 1950s, visiting the United States in 1958 (when he was 29) to play with Marshall Brown's International Youth Band at the

---

TIMELINE 1976

Jaco Pastorius records his album **Jaco** and joins Weather Report. • Return to Forever breaks up. • The success of a Carnegie Hall concert inspires Herbie Hancock to return to acoustic jazz with VSOP. • The World Saxophone Quartet is formed. • John Handy has a hit with "Hard Work." • Rahsaan Roland Kirk suffers a serious stroke. • George Benson has a major bestseller with "This Masquerade" from his album **Breezin'**. • The Dave Brubeck Quartet has a reunion. • Lou Stein recreates a dozen Art Tatum piano solos on the LP **Tribute to Tatum** (Chiaroscuro 149). • Dexter Gordon enjoys a triumphant homecoming when he returns to the United States, playing before enthusiastic capacity crowds. • Ernestine Anderson is rediscovered at the Concord Jazz Festival. • Eddie Jefferson works with Richie Cole. • Manhattan Transfer releases their first record. • The Juggernaut is formed. • Tom Harrell leads his first record date. • Woody Herman celebrates his fortieth anniversary as a bandleader by playing at Carnegie Hall. • At the age of 68, Benny Carter returns to active playing. • Derek Bailey forms Company. • The acoustic guitar duo of Larry Coryell and Philip Catherine are a hit at the Berlin Jazz Festival. • Old and New Dreams is formed. • Baritonist Ronnie Cuber leads his first record date. • James Dapogny records a solo set of Jelly Roll Morton tunes for the Smithsonian label. • Polish singer Urszula Dudziak's Arista LP **Urszula** is her stunning American debut, featuring electronic distortions, fairly free improvising, and wild scatting. • Swing pianist Johnny Guarnieri records an LP titled **Breakthrough in 5/4** that features him striding his way through a variety of swing standards in 5/4 time. • Alto saxophonist Jay Beckenstein records the debut album of his new group, **Spyro Gyra** (Amherst 8002). • Max Roach documents a set of drums/tenor duets with Archie Shepp for the French Uniteledis label. • Bob Rusch founds *Cadence*, a monthly that has been one of jazz's top magazines ever since. • Eubie Blake turns 91.

Newport Jazz Festival but soon returning to Germany. After recording an album with John Lewis in 1962, Mangelsdorff soon switched to exploring avant-garde jazz. A rare LP of duets with the likes of Don Cherry, Lee Konitz, and Elvin Jones, **Albert Mangelsdorff and His Friends** (MPS 15210) was cut in 1968. Three years later he was caught **Live in Tokyo** (Enja 2006), leading a quartet with tenor saxophonist Heinz Sauer, bassist Gunter Lenz, and drummer Ralf Huber but better known is ○ **Tromboneliness** (Sackville 2011), a set of unaccompanied trombone solos. Because of his use of multiphonics and his inventive utilization of a plunger mute in spots, Mangelsdorff always holds one's interest. In addition to his originals, his version of "Creole Love Call" is a classic.

Rob McConnell   Rob McConnell emerged as a top valve trombone soloist and arranger in Canada during the late 1950s, but it would be some time before he made an impact in jazz. McConnell worked in the studios and in local jazz settings, recording in a quintet with trumpeter Guido Basso and guitarist Ed Bickert as early as 1963. McConnell, who played with Nimmons 'N' Nine plus Six during 1965–69, in 1968 formed the Boss Brass. Originally the group consisted of four trumpets, five trombones, three French horns, vibes, two guitars, bass, and drums, emphasizing pop music recorded for the radio. By 1971 the French horns were replaced by saxophones, but it was not until 1976 before the Boss Brass became a jazz-oriented swing band.

The Jazz Album (Sea Breeze 2080) reissues the ensemble's first real jazz date. The 21-piece big band, which includes such notables as trumpeters Basso and Sam Noto, trombonist Ian McDougall, the reeds of Moe Koffman and Rick Wilkins, Bickert, bassist Don Thompson, and drummer Terry Clarke, performs three of McConnell's originals plus features for Basso ("Portrait of Jenny") and Bickert ("Body and Soul"). Although never more than a part-time orchestra, Rob McConnell's Boss Brass would soon be recognized as one of jazz's finest big bands.

Chris McGregor   By the late 1960s, South African pianist Chris McGregor had reluctantly broken up the Blue Notes but was engaged in a new project, the Brotherhood of Breath. This avant-garde big band was quite adventurous and included some of the top British players (including at times trumpeter Harry Beckett and

tenor saxophonist Evan Parker) plus Blue Noters Dudu Pukwana, Mongezi Feza, and Louis Moholo. Although the orchestra (which combined free solos with African-influenced folk melodies) never became a commercial success, a few recordings resulted, including two live sets from their 1973 tour of the European continent. **Travelling Somewhere** (Cuneiform 152) has the 12-piece ensemble filling nine group originals with free improvisation while **Live at Willisau** (Ogun 001) has lots of spots for Parker, Beckett, trombonist Radu Malfatti, altoist Pukwana, trumpeter Feza, drummer Moholo, and the leader on piano. It is a pity that this unique band (which in some ways was a European/South African equivalent of Sun Ra's Arkestra) could not have lasted longer, but at least it made it onto records, including three scarce studio albums.

Tete Montoliu   A virtuoso pianist from Spain who was born blind, Tete Montoliu would have been much better known in the United States if he had visited the U.S. more often. Montoliu started on piano when he was seven, always had dazzling technique, and could swing hard in a boppish style. He recorded with Lionel Hampton in 1956, led his first record date in 1958, and went on a European tour with Roland Kirk in 1963. Montoliu worked at various times with such Americans as Kenny Dorham, Dexter Gordon, Ben Webster, Lucky Thompson, and Anthony Braxton. His recordings for Steeple Chase (a pair in 1971 and then quite a few during 1974–82) are among his finest work. **That's All** (Steeple Chase 31199), which includes eight familiar standards (including "You Go to My Head," "A Child Is Born," and "Giant Steps"), and **Lush Life** (Steeple Chase 31216), which has six standards plus an original and Perry Robinson's "Margareta," both feature Montoliu on unaccompanied solos. On these 1971 recordings, Montoliu mixes together aspects of Bud Powell, McCoy Tyner, and Bill Evans quite effectively. For a good sampling of Montoliu's trio work, try **Tete** (Steeple Chase 31029), which teams him with Niels Pedersen and Albert "Tootie" Heath on such songs as "Body and Soul," "Solar," and "Hot House."

Airto Moreira   The husband of singer Flora Purim, Airto Moreira (often known simply as Airto) is a masterful percussionist who helped make percussion an essential part of many modern jazz groups. He started on guitar and piano before studying more than 120 different percussion instruments in his native Brazil. After moving to the United States with Purim in 1968, he worked with Miles Davis (1969–70), Lee Morgan, Weather Report (appearing on that group's first record), the initial version of Return to Forever (1972), and Stan Getz. By 1973 he was leading his own band and often recording with his wife.

Airto led three albums for CTI during 1972–74 of which **Free** (Columbia 40927) is the most famous. The tunes include "Return to Forever," "Flora's Song," and "Free" (which has a vocal from Purim). Airto is joined on two numbers by a brass section arranged by Don Sebesky and is assisted along the way by Chick Corea, Hubert Laws, Joe Farrell, Keith Jarrett, and George Benson. The music could be classified as jazz, fusion, Brazilian music, or funk and still be accurately described.

Oregon   A very unusual group, the members of Oregon (Ralph Towner on guitar, Paul McCandless on oboe, English horn, and bass clarinet, Glen Moore on bass, and Collin Walcott on tabla and sitar) first came together as members of the Paul Winter Consort before breaking away in 1970 to form their own band. Their music mixes together folk music from all over the world with jazz improvisation, and they partly achieve their unusual sound by avoiding blue notes. No other jazz group sounded like Oregon when they first recorded in 1970, and they still stand apart from all other ensembles.

It seemed only right that Oregon's early days were documented by Vanguard, a label best known for its folk and blues records. **Music of Another Present Era** (Vanguard 79326), **Distant Hills** (Vanguard 79341), and **Winter Light** (Vanguard 79350) are each excellent examples of this band's unique style that has always been open to the influence of Indian, African, Latin, and even American music.

Cal Tjader   Still retaining his great popularity as leader of one of the top Afro-Cuban jazz bands, vibraphonist Cal Tjader ended his association with the Verve label in 1967, recording a few so-so commercial dates for Skye during 1968–69 and more rewarding efforts during his second period with Fantasy (1970–76).

Descarga (Fantasy 24737) has the music from two former albums (**Agua Dulce** and **Live at the Funky Quarters**) dating from 1971–72. Tjader is featured with a 14-piece big band of mostly San Francisco–based players (including trumpeter Luis Gasca, Bill Perkins, and percussionists Pete and Coke Escovedo) and in a quintet

with electric keyboardist Al Zulaica. Recorded in 1973, **Primo** (Original Jazz Classics 762) has Tjader in excellent form with four horns, keyboardist Charlie Palmieri, electric bass, and six percussionists. The infectious arrangements are provided by Palmieri and Tito Puente, who sits in on timbales on Mario Bauza's "Tanga," a highlight along with "Vibe Mambo," and "El Watusi." **Tambu** (Original Jazz Classics 891) is mostly a clash between Tjader's Afro-Cuban jazz and Charlie Byrd's Brazilian music. There are some sparks, but Mike Wolff's electric piano sounds dated and often the different styles do not fit very smoothly together. **Amazonas** (Original Jazz Classics 840) matches Tjader with such modern Brazilian players as pianist Egberto Gismonti, flutist Hermeto Pascoal, and guitarist David Amaro. It has its moments even if George Duke's funky arrangements are a bit of a departure for Tjader.

The Grace Cathedral Concert (Fantasy 7677) is more comfortable as Tjader and his regular band perform "Bluesology," "Body and Soul," a medley from "Black Orpheus," and the vibraphonist's original "I Showed Them." The group consists of Tjader, Lonnie Hewitt on keyboards, bassist Rob Fisher, drummer Pete Riso, and, making his recording debut, Poncho Sanchez on congas.

Sadao Watanabe   Japanese alto saxophonist Sadao Watanabe started his career playing with Toshiko Akiyoshi's group in Tokyo during 1953–56. When Akiyoshi moved to the United States, Watanabe took over the combo. He ventured to the United States himself when he attended Berklee College of Music (1962–65) and had stints playing with Gary McFarland, Chico Hamilton, and Gabor Szabo. But by 1966 he was back in Japan, alternating between playing bop, Brazilian music, and crossover pop.

Round Trip (Vanguard 79344) is a notable session from 1970 on which Watanabe holds his own with Chick Corea, Miroslav Vitous, and Jack DeJohnette, highlighted by the 20-minute title cut. Most unusual about this post-bop set is that Watanabe plays sopranino sax and flute rather than his usual alto. Although most of Watanabe's recordings in the 1970s that were aimed at the U.S. market tended to be popish with the saxophonist sounding like a weak version of Grover Washington, Jr., **I'm Old Fashioned** (Polygram 4008) was a rare standout. With the assistance of Hank Jones, Ron

Carter, and Tony Williams, Watanabe emphasizes bebop on three of his originals, two Billy Strayhorn songs, "Confirmation," "I Concentrate On You," and the title cut. This set shows just how creative an alto soloist Sadao Watanabe could be when he had the desire.

Kenny Wheeler   A versatile and technically skilled trumpeter fully capable of playing hard bop but mostly interested in performing more advanced music, Kenny Wheeler took his time before he found his own voice. Born in Toronto, Canada, in 1930, he began on cornet when he was 12 and studied at the Toronto Conservatory. In 1952 he moved permanently to England where he quickly became part of the local jazz scene. Wheeler worked with various big bands including John Dankworth (1959–65) and mastered bebop. But in 1966 he discovered free jazz while playing with John Stevens's Spontaneous Music Ensemble, and he changed his direction to avant-garde music. Wheeler worked with Tony Oxley, the Mike Gibbs Orchestra, the Globe University Orchestra, the Anthony Braxton Quartet (1975), and Azimuth (starting in 1976).

Although he recorded sets for Fontana (1969) and Incus (1973), it was Kenny Wheeler's 1975 debut for ECM, ◗ **Gnu High** (ECM 825 591), that gained him attention worldwide. Already 45, Wheeler performs three of his originals (including the 21-minute "Heyoke") in a quartet with Keith Jarrett, Dave Holland, and Jack DeJohnette. Wheeler's wide range (hitting some surprising high notes), beautiful tone, and explorative style work well with Jarrett's bluesy and rhythmic piano. The recording **1976** (Just A Memory 9506) has performances that Wheeler had recorded for the Canadian Broadcasting Corp. and had forgotten about for more than 20 years. The music, comprised of six group originals, is much more straightahead than expected (almost similar to Freddie Hubbard's music of a few years earlier), and it is unusual to hear Wheeler joined by an electric pianist (Gary Williamson); the band also includes tenor saxophonist Art Ellefson, bassist Dave Young, and drummer Marty Morell.

Paul Winter   Paul Winter's later career bore little resemblance to his earlier music. Originally a cool-toned altoist, Winter first recorded with Charlie Byrd in 1959. He won a collegiate jazz festival in 1961, which led to him being signed to Columbia by producer John Hammond and leading six albums for the label. A tour of Latin America in 1962 piqued his interest in Brazilian music

(recording albums with Sergio Mendes and Luiz Bonfa), and then in 1967 he widened his scope even more by forming an unusual world jazz group called the Paul Winter Consort. Winter became interested in exploring folk music from Africa, South America, and Asia, often utilizing instruments that were unusual for jazz.

Released in 1969, **Road** (A&M 0826) has Winter on soprano and alto leading a group that includes cellist David Darling, guitarist Ralph Towner, Paul McCandless (on oboe and English horn), bassist Glen Moore, and Colin Walcott on tabla and percussion. The music is superior folk jazz and was quite unique for the period.

It therefore must have been quite a blow to Winter when in 1970 Towner, McCandless, Moore, and Walcott broke away to form their own band, Oregon. He continued leading similar groups for a few years with less success before shifting his focus to mood music that would later develop into new age.

Various Artists

The music on ◗ **Wildflowers—The New York Loft Jazz Sessions—Complete** (Knitting Factory 3037) was originally out as five LPs and is now available as a three-CD set. Recorded at Sam River's Studio Rivbea loft in June 1976, these 22 performances showcase many of the who's who of avant-garde jazz of the time in inventive and inspired settings. Featured along the way are such notables as tenor saxophonist Kalaparusha Maurice McIntyre, the unrelated Ken McIntyre, Sunny Murray, altoist Byard Lancaster, Air, Anthony Braxton, Marion Brown, Leo Smith, Oliver Lake, Anthony Davis, Randy Weston (a bit out of place but faring quite well), Dave Burrell, trumpeter Ahmed Abdullah, Andrew Cyrille, Hamiet Bluiett, Julius Hemphill, Jimmy Lyons, Oliver Lake, David Murray, Roscoe Mitchell, and Rivers himself.

◗ **California Concert** (Columbia 40690) was originally a five-song double LP and is now available with four of the songs (all but "Leaving Wes") as a single CD. At a concert held at the Hollywood Palladium in 1971, Creed Taylor presented the top stars of the CTI label. The lengthy renditions of "Fire and Rain," "Red Clay," "Sugar," and "Blues West" feature Freddie Hubbard, Stanley Turrentine, Hank Crawford, Hubert Laws, George Benson, keyboardist Johnny Hammond, Ron Carter, Billy Cobham, and Airto Moreira in inspired form, showing why CTI was such a significant label at the time.

After a riot in 1971 killed the Newport Jazz Festival, producer George Wein relocated the festival the following year to New York. A series of jam sessions held at the 1972 festival at Radio City Music Hall were released as two double LPs and a pair of single albums by Cobblestone, but they have not been reissued on CD yet. These all-stars jams (particularly the music on the two-fers) have many great moments as a wide variety of top jazz musicians (many of whom did not play together often) interact and jam standards. **Newport in New York '72: The Jam Sessions Vols. 1 & 2** (Cobblestone 9025) has three standards and a blues explored in 16- to 23-minute versions by two different groups. One band features trumpeters Cat Anderson (who screams over the ensembles), Jimmy Owens, Charles McPherson, Buddy Tate, organist Milt Buckner, Roland Hanna, Charles Mingus, and drummer Alan Dawson while the second group consists of Dizzy Gillespie, trombonist Benny Green, Stan Getz, Milt Jackson, violinist John Blair, Kenny Burrell, Mary Lou Williams, Percy Heath, Max Roach, and Big Black on congas. **Newport in New York '72: The Jam Sessions Vols. 3 & 4** (Cobblestone 9026) has some extraordinary music. Joe Newman, Nat Adderley, Illinois Jacquet, Budd Johnson, trombonist Tyree Glenn, Gerry Mulligan, Jaki Byard, bassist Chubby Jackson, and Elvin Jones stretch out on three numbers with "Perdido" being particularly memorable. "Blue 'N' Boogie," which is more than 28 minutes long, features Clark Terry, Howard McGhee, Sonny Stitt, Dexter Gordon, Gary Burton, Jimmy Smith, pianist George Duke, bassist Al McKibbon, and Art Blakey. However, the top solo of the two-fer is by Rahsaan Roland Kirk on "So What," stealing the show by playing tenor, stritch, manzello, and a whistle. Considering that the band also includes Harry "Sweets" Edison, Kai Winding, guitarist Chuck Wayne, Herbie Hancock, bassist Larry Ridley, Tony Williams, and the tenors of James Moody, Flip Phillips, Dexter Gordon, and Zoot Sims, taking solo honors was really an accomplishment.

The Jam Sessions Vol. 5 (Cobblestone 9027), recorded at Yankee Stadium, has a worthwhile version of "Blue 'N' Boogie" and a five-song ballad medley most notable for including bluesman B.B. King in the lineup along with Jimmy Smith, Joe Newman, Clark Terry, Illinois Jacquet, Zoot Sims, Kenny Burrell, and Roy Haynes. **The Jam Sessions Vol. 6** (Cobblestone 9028) is a bit weak, mostly focusing on R&B. Best is Billy Eckstine

singing two numbers, assisted by Dizzy Gillespie and Sonny Stitt on "Jelly Jelly." But otherwise the program has so-so features for Curtis Mayfield, B.B. King, Les McCann (singing "The Price You Got to Pay to Be Free"), Herbie Mann, and Roberta Flack (who is heard twice).

◉ Jazz at the Santa Monica Civic (Pablo 2625-701) is a three-CD reissue that has the 1972 concert that launched the Pablo label. The night was originally supposed to only feature the Count Basie Orchestra and Ella Fitzgerald, but Norman Granz surprised everyone by inviting along Roy Eldridge, Harry "Sweets" Edison, Stan Getz, Eddie "Lockjaw" Davis, Oscar Peterson, and Ray Brown. With Basie's trombone soloist Al Grey added, they form the Jazz at the Philharmonic All-Stars and play with plenty of spirit on three jams and a ballad medley. In addition, there are five selections from Basie's band (featuring tenor saxophonist Jimmy Forrest, trumpeter Pete Minger, and altoist Curtis Peagler), a full set from Fitzgerald and a Peterson-Brown duet on "You Are My Sunshine." But everything is overshadowed by the final number, a classic version of "C Jam Blues" that has Ella trading off in spontaneous and sometimes hilarious fashion with Grey, Getz, Sweets, Lockjaw, and Eldridge. Virtually everything works on this essential release.

Trumpet Kings at Montreux (Original Jazz Classics 445) has Dizzy Gillespie, Roy Eldridge, Clark Terry, Oscar Peterson, Niels Pedersen, and Louie Bellson jamming in 1975 on such numbers as "There Is No Greater Love," "On the Alamo," and "Indiana." The competitive trumpeters inspire each other, but the remarkable Peterson does not exactly get lost in the shuffle either.

Duke Ellington: 1969 All-Star White House Tribute (Blue Note 35249) in 2002 finally made available the music performed during Duke Ellington's 70th birthday celebration at Richard Nixon's White House. The extended program of Ellington songs, some of which were played in medleys, features Clark Terry, Bill Berry, Urbie Green, J.J. Johnson, Paul Desmond, Gerry Mulligan, Hank Jones, Jim Hall, Milt Hinton, and Louie Bellson with appearances by Dave Brubeck, Earl Hines, Billy Taylor, Joe Williams, and singer Mary Mayo. Ellington himself is just heard on the final piece, a freely improvised solo piano number, "Pat." The good spirits and the bit of planning that went into these organized jams make the results quite coherent and enjoyable.

And closing with vintage piano stylists, **Jazz Piano Masters** (Chiaroscuro 170) has selections from a 1972 concert featuring mini-sets by Teddy Wilson, Claude Hopkins (one of his last recordings), the underrated but talented Welsh swing player Dill Jones and 89-year-old Eubie Blake, who steals the show. Blake, who had seen jazz develop since the 1890s, shows on such songs as "Charleston Rag" (which he wrote in 1899), "Troublesome Ivories," and "Memories of You" that the best jazz truly is timeless.

Jazz Beyond 1976

As stated previously, jazz of 1917–76 was a constant race to freedom, from the group improvising of New Orleans bands who sought to infuse marches and pop tunes with blues, from Louis Armstrong creating swinging solos, and from bebop musicians coming up with virtuoso statements to the innovators of free jazz who added a wider range of expressiveness to jazz and to fusion musicians who found a way to turn rock into jazz. Since 1976, jazz has no longer had a dominant new style but instead has headed in a countless number of directions at once. The race to complete freedom was reached by the mid-1960s; after all, how can one play freer than Cecil Taylor?

Instead of necessarily breaking down new boundaries, the goal for jazz musicians and singers after 1976 was to develop their own individual sound and musical personality, being creative in whatever idiom they chose. The rise of new approaches does not invalidate or replace older styles and, as Scott Hamilton and Warren Vache began to show in the mid-1970s and many other musicians have demonstrated since, no jazz style has been completely exhausted of all creative possibilities.

Newcomers to the music such as film maker Ken Burns, whose 2001 documentary managed to be overrun by errors, oversights, and fanciful commentary, have sometimes claimed that not much was going on in jazz in the 1970s. This chapter should prove the error of that statement and should result in further study by these so-called experts, many of whom have distorted jazz history in hopes of proving some dubious points.

Some of the lazier observers of the current jazz scene have complained that jazz has lost its direction since the 1970s and that the music has run out of fresh ideas. The truth is that jazz is in a golden age that started in the mid-1890s, accelerated around 1920, and has not stopped since. The music on a whole has never had an

artistic off period, and it continues with brilliant performances and recordings up to the current time.

Although this book covers jazz through 1976, the following is a very condensed list of some of the musicians and singers who have made major contributions to jazz since 1976, not counting the famous veterans whose earlier accomplishments are recounted in this book and emphasizing artists who were unknown in the mid-1970s but have since added their talents to jazz's legacy. This list should convince any detractor that jazz is still very much alive and well today.

Pianists

Geri Allen, Lynne Arriale, Borah Bergman, Joanne Brackeen, Uri Caine, Michel Camilo, Judy Carmichael, Bill Charlap, Cyrus Chestnut, Marilyn Crispell, Connie Crothers, Bill Cunliffe, James Dapogny, Garry Dial, Neville Dickie, Niels Lan Doky, Kenny Drew, Jr., Eliane Elias, Dave Frishberg, Mike Garson, Gil Goldstein, Benny Green, Fred Hersch, Keith Ingham, D.D. Jackson, Jon Jang, Oliver Jones, Geoff Keezer, Kenny Kirkland, Jan Lundgren, Adam Makowicz, Lyle Mays, Jim McNeely, Brad Mehldau, Myra Melford, Jason Moran, Amina Claudine Myers, Hod O'Brien, Johnny O'Neal, Makoto Ozone, Danilo Perez, Michel Petrucciani, Paul Plimley, Eric Reed, David Thomas Roberts, Marcus Roberts, Reginald Robinson, Michele Rosewoman, Renee Rosnes, Gonzalo Rubalcaba, Hilton Ruiz, Matthew Shipp, Jacky Terrasson, Chucho Valdes, Kenny Werner, Jessica Williams, and Rachel Z.

Reeds

Eric Alexander, Fred Anderson, Harry Allen, Tim Berne, Jane Ira Bloom, Peter Brotzmann, Rob Brown, Jane Bunnett, Don Byron, James Carter, Thomas Chapin, Pete Christlieb, Steve Coleman, Ravi Coltrane, Lol Coxhill, Jesse Davis, Paquito D'Rivera, Marty Ehrlich, Ellery Eskelin, Ricky Ford, Kenny Garrett, George Garzone, Charles Gayle, Vinny Golia, Lin Halliday, Donald Harrison, Antonio Hart, Vincent Herring, Sherman Irby, Javon Jackson, Marty Krystall, Ralph Lalama, Joe Lovano, Joe Maneri, Rick Margitza, Branford Marsalis, Virginia Mayhew, Mike Murley, Greg Osby, Ken Peplowski, Odeon Pope, Chris Potter, Joshua Redman, Scott Robinson, Dave Sanchez, Loren Schoenberg, Gary Smulyan, John Surman, Joe Temperley, Gary Thomas, Mark Turner, David Ware, Bobby Watson, Steve Wilson, and John Zorn.

Trumpeters

Dave Douglas, Peter Ecklund, Russell Gunn, Tim Hagans, Roy Hargrove, Phillip Harper, Tom Harrell, Ingrid Jensen, Jon-Erik Kellso, Ryan Kisor, Brian Lynch, Wynton Marsalis, James Morrison, Nicholas Payton, Valery Ponomarev, Marcus Printup, Hugh Ragin, Wallace Roney, Randy Sandke, Arturo Sandoval, Carl Saunders, Lew Soloff, and Terell Stafford.

Trombonists

Ray Anderson, Dan Barrett, Robin Eubanks, Wycliffe Gordon, Craig Harris, Conrad Herwig, Frank Lacy, Delfeayo Marsalis, Andy Martin, and Steve Turre.

Guitarists

Howard Alden, Jimmy Bruno, Hiram Bullock, Pierre Dorge, Mark Elf, Kevin Eubanks, Bill Frisell, Frank Gambale, Marty Grosz, Scott Henderson, Charlie Hunter, Stanley Jordan, Steve Khan, Bireli Lagrene, Peter Leitch, Russell Malone, Pat Metheny, John Pizzarelli, Kurt Rosenwinkel, John Scofield, Frank Vignola, and Anthony Wilson.

Bassists

Brian Bromberg, John Clayton, Scott Colley, Anthony Cox, Mark Dresser, Mark Egan, Matthew Garrison, Barry Guy, Mark Helias, Robert Hurst III, Marc Johnson, John Lindberg, Christian McBride, Marcus Miller, Charnett Moffett, William Parker, John Patitucci, Jamaaladeen Tacuma, and Victor Wooten.

Drummers/Percussionists

Brian Blade, Dennis Chambers, Hamid Drake, Peter Erskine, Jerry Gonzalez, Danny Gottlieb, Jeff Hamilton, Winard Harper, Gerry Hemingway, Matt Wilson, Leon Parker, Ralph Peterson, Hal Smith, and Bill Stewart.

Singers

Claudia Acuna, Karrin Allyson, Peter Cincotti, Dee Dee Bridgewater, Harry Connick, Jr., Meredith D'Ambrosio, Ann Dyer, Madeline Eastman, Kurt Elling, Nnenna Freelon, Banu Gibson, Rebecca Kilgore, Nancy King, Diana Krall, Janet Lawson, Ranee Lee, Carmen Lundy, Kitty Margolis, Tania Maria, Claire Martin, Tina May, Bobby McFerrin, Jane Monheit, Stephanie Nakasian, Dianne Reeves, Diane Schuur, Daryl Sherman, Luciana Souza, Roseanna Vitro, Carla White, Wesla Whitfield, and Cassandra Wilson.

Organists

Joey DeFrancesco, Barbara Dennerlein, and Larry Goldings.

Vibraphonists

Stefan Harris, Jay Hoggard, and Steve Nelson.

Flutists

Robert Dick, Kent Jordan, James Newton, and Ali Ryerson.

Violinists

Billy Bang, Regina Carter, Mark Feldman, Johnny Frigo, Didier Lockwood, and Mat Maneri.

And not to mention banjoist Bela Fleck; mandolist David Grisman; arrangers Bob Florence, George Gruntz, Dave Grusin, and Maria Schneider; plus such groups as the Ganelin Trio, Medeski, Martin and Wood, the Mingus Big Band, Rova, and the Yellowjackets.

Because the previous list could be two to three times as long, it is not an understatement to say that jazz music is still in its prime, and, artistically at least, its future remains very bright.

PASSINGS

Luckey Roberts (80), Feb. 5, 1968, New York, NY
George Wettling (60), June 6, 1968, New York, NY
Wes Montgomery (43), June 15, 1968, Indianapolis, IN
Ziggy Elman (54), June 26, 1968, Los Angeles, CA
Cutty Cutshall (56), Aug. 16, 1968, Toronto, Ontario, Canada
Johnny Richards (56), Oct. 7, 1968, New York, NY
George Lewis (68), Dec. 31, 1968, New Orleans, LA
Paul Chambers (33), Jan. 4, 1969, New York, NY
Pee Wee Russell (62), Feb. 15, 1969, Alexandria, VA
Paul Barbarin (69), Feb. 17, 1969, New Orleans, LA
Coleman Hawkins (64), May 19, 1969, New York, NY
Wynonie Harris (53), June 14, 1969, Los Angeles, CA
Pops Foster (77), Oct. 30, 1969, San Francisco, CA
Tony Spargo (72), Oct. 30, 1969, New York, NY
Emile Barnes (78), Mar. 2, 1970, New Orleans, LA
Johnny Hodges (63), May 11, 1970, New York, NY
Cliff Jackson (67), May 24, 1970, New York, NY
Lonnie Johnson (81), June 16, 1970, Toronto, Ontario, Canada
Otto Hardwicke (66), Aug. 5, 1970, Washington, D.C.
Booker Ervin (39), Aug. 31, 1970, New York, NY
Albert Ayler (34), Nov. 5, 1970, New York, NY
Ernie Caceres (59), Jan. 10, 1971, San Antonio, TX
Capt. John Handy (70), Jan. 12, 1971, Pass Christian, MS
Harry Arnold (50), Feb. 11, 1971, Stockholm, Sweden
Wynton Kelly (39), Apr. 12, 1971, Toronto, Ontario, Canada
Ben Pollack (67), June 7, 1971, Palm Springs, CA
Ambrose (74), June 12, 1971, Leeds, England
Louis Armstrong (69), July 6, 1971, New York, NY
Charlie Shavers (53), July 8, 1971, New York, NY
Cliff Edwards (76), July 17, 1971, Hollywood, CA
King Curtis (37), Aug. 13, 1971, New York, NY
Tab Smith (62), Aug. 17, 1971, St. Louis, MO
Lil Harden Armstrong (73), Aug. 27, 1971, Chicago, IL
Lou McGarity (54), Aug. 28, 1971, Alexandria, VA
Joe Sullivan (64), Oct. 13, 1971, San Francisco, CA
Gary McFarland (38), Nov. 3, 1971, New York, NY
Punch Miller (77), Dec. 2, 1971, New Orleans, LA
Lee Morgan (33), Feb. 19, 1972, New York, NY
Clancy Hayes (63), Mar. 13, 1972, San Francisco, CA
Sharkey Bonano (69), Mar. 27, 1972, New Orleans, LA
Tony Parenti (71), Apr. 17, 1972, New York, NY
George Mitchell (73), May 22, 1972, Chicago, IL
Jimmy Rushing (68), June 8, 1972, New York, NY
Lovie Austin (84), July 10, 1972, Chicago, IL
Mezz Mezzrow (72), Aug. 5, 1972, Paris, France
Don Byas (59), Aug. 24, 1972, Amsterdam, Netherlands
Jimmy Lytell (67), Nov. 28, 1972, Kings Point, NY
Kenny Dorham (48), Dec. 5, 1972, New York, NY

Dud Bascomb (56), Dec. 25, 1972, New York, NY
Joe Harriott (44), Jan. 2, 1973, London, England
Wilbur DeParis (72), Jan. 3, 1973, New York, NY
Edgar Sampson (65), Jan. 16, 1973, Englewood, NJ
Kid Ory (86), Jan. 23, 1973, Honolulu, HI
Merritt Brunies (77), Feb. 5, 1973, Biloxi, MS
Willie "The Lion" Smith (85), Apr. 18, 1973, New York, NY
Albert Wynn (65), May 1973, Chicago, IL
Elmer Snowden (72), May 14, 1973, Philadelphia, PA
J.C. Higginbotham (67), May 26, 1973, New York, NY
Tubby Hayes (38), June 8, 1973, London, England
Eddie Condon (67), Aug. 4, 1973, New York, NY
Brew Moore (49), Aug. 19, 1973, Copenhagen, Denmark
Bill Harris (56), Aug. 21, 1973, Hallandale, FL
Albert Nichols (73), Sept. 3, 1973, Basel, Switzerland
Ben Webster (64), Sept. 20, 1973, Amsterdam, Netherlands
Gene Krupa (64), Oct. 16, 1973, Yonkers, NY
De De Pierce (69), Nov. 23, 1973, New Orleans, LA
Don Fagerquist (46), Jan. 24, 1974, Los Angeles, CA
Bobby Timmons (38), Mar. 1, 1974, New York, NY
Paul Gonsalves (53), May 15, 1974, London, England
Tyree Glenn (61), May 18, 1974, Englewood, NJ
Duke Ellington (75), May 24, 1974, New York NY
Gene Ammons (49), Aug. 6, 1974, Chicago, IL
Bill Chase (39), Aug. 9, 1974, Jackson, MN
Billie Pierce (67), Sept. 29, 1974, New Orleans, LA
Harry Carney (74), Oct. 8, 1974, New York, NY
George Brunies (72), Nov. 19, 1974, Chicago, IL
Louis Jordan (66), Feb. 4, 1975, Los Angeles, CA
Benny Harris (55), Feb. 11, 1975, San Francisco, CA
Marty Marsala (66), Apr. 27, 1975, Chicago, IL
Zutty Singleton (77), July 14, 1975, New York, NY
Cannonball Adderley (46), Aug. 8, 1975, Gary, IN
Reuben Reeves (69), September 1975, New York, NY
Oliver Nelson (43), Oct. 28, 1975, Los Angeles, CA
Frank Signorelli (74), Dec. 9, 1975, New York, NY
Lee Wiley (60), Dec. 11, 1975, New York, NY
Noble Sissle (86), Dec. 17, 1975, Tampa, FL
Ray Nance (62), Jan. 28, 1976, New York, NY
Vince Guaraldi (47), Feb. 6, 1976, Menlo Park, CA
Jimmy Garrison (42), Apr. 7, 1976, New York, NY
Jim Robinson (83), May 4, 1976, New Orleans, LA
Lars Gullin (48), May 17, 1976, Vissefjarda, Sweden
Bobby Hackett (61), June 7, 1976, Chatham, MA
Johnny Mercer (66), June 25, 1976, Los Angeles, CA
Albert Burbank (74), Aug. 15, 1976, New Orleans, LA
Quentin Jackson (67), Oct. 2, 1976, New York, NY
Victoria Spivey (69), Oct. 3, 1976, New York, NY
Connie Boswell (68), Oct. 11, 1976, New York, NY

About the Author

S cott Yanow has been a self-described jazz fanatic since 1970 and a jazz journalist since 1975. Jazz editor of *Record Review* (1976–84), he has written for *Down Beat, JazzTimes, Jazziz, Jazz Forum, Coda, Jazz News, Jazz Now, Mississippi Rag,* and *Strictly Jazz* magazines. Yanow currently is a regular contributor to *Cadence, The L.A. Jazz Scene, Jazz Improv, Jazz Report,* and *Planet Jazz.* He has penned over 300 album liner notes and is estimated to have written more jazz record reviews than anyone in history. Editor of the *All Music Guide to Jazz, 3rd Edition* and author of *Duke Ellington,* Yanow also wrote *Trumpet Kings, Classic Jazz, Swing, Bebop,* and *Afro-Cuban Jazz*—all published by Backbeat Books. He is proud of having written five full-length reference books on jazz in 22 months. It is his goal to collect every good jazz record ever made and have time to listen to them!

Bibliography

Bruyninckx, Walter. *Seventy Years of Recorded Jazz 1917–1987*. Belgium: self published, updated in the 1990s.

Chilton, John. *Who's Who of Jazz*. Radnor, PA: Chilton Book Co., 1978.

Feather, Leonard and Ira Gitler, ed. *The Biographical Encyclopedia of Jazz*. New York: Oxford University Press, 1999.

Bogdanov, Vladimir, Michael Erlewine, Chris Woodstra, and Scott Yanow, ed. *All Music Guide to Jazz*, 3d ed. San Francisco: Backbeat Books, 1998.

Index